CONGRESS
AND THE
NATION

VOLUME III

1969-1972

A Review of Government and Politics

Published by

CONGRESSIONAL QUARTERLY SERVICE
1735 K Street, N.W.   Washington, D.C., 20006

CQ

"By providing a link between the local newspaper and Capitol Hill we hope Congressional Quarterly can help to make public opinion the only effective pressure group in the country. Since many citizens other than editors are also interested in Congress, we hope that they too will find Congressional Quarterly an aid to a better understanding of their government.

"Congressional Quarterly presents the facts in as complete, concise and unbiased form as we know how. The editorial comment on the acts and votes of Congress, we leave to our subscribers." Foreword, Congressional Quarterly, Vol. I, 1945—Henrietta and Nelson Poynter.

Introduction

"The greatest honor history can bestow is the title of peacemaker.... After a period of confrontation we are entering an era of negotiation. Let all nations know that during this administration our lines of communication will be open to the exchange of goods and people, a world in which no people great or small, will live in angry isolation."

—President Richard M. Nixon
Inaugural Address, January 20, 1969

In these broad terms, the 37th President of the United States outlined the primary objectives of his first administration—reconciliation with Communist China, detente with the Soviet Union and the extrication of the United States from the longest and most frustrating war in its history.

Elsewhere in that address the new President set forth two other themes which would mark his administration. His government did not confront a "material" crisis such as had faced Franklin Roosevelt in 1933 when the "nation (was) ravaged by depression." Rather, said Nixon, Americans in 1969 found themselves "rich in goods, but ragged in spirit.... To a crisis of the spirit," he offered "an answer of the spirit."

'Era of Negotiation'

The President's accomplishments as statesman and peacemaker during his first term are difficult to overstate. And it is equally remarkable to trace the distance Mr. Nixon, who had earned a reputation in the 1950s for uncompromising toughness on communism, had traveled by the year 1972.

In 1952, he had accused the Truman administration of "toleration and defense of communism in high places." In 1959, in the famous "kitchen debate" he had stood up to Soviet communist boss Nikita Khrushchev. And in his 1960 campaign televised debates with John F. Kennedy, he asserted that the Chinese Communists "don't want just Formosa. They want the world."

Twelve years later, in 1972, Richard Nixon became the first President in American history to visit Communist China and the Soviet Union. The journey to Peking overturned a policy considered axiomatic by four preceding administrations whereby the proper posture for Washington to assume toward Communist China was military containment and diplomatic isolation. The voyage to Moscow resulted in the signing, and subsequent congressional approval, of two agreements, which placed controls on nuclear arms competition between the two nations.

With these two historic diplomatic initiatives, the President had laid to rest two of the most recurrent nightmares of the Cold War—first, the distinct possibility of a direct U.S.-Soviet nuclear confrontation; and second, the spectre which haunted Dean Rusk and the Johnson administration, that a "billion Chinese Communists" armed with nuclear weapons were poised for military aggression.

In Southeast Asia, the President fulfilled his campaign promises of 1968. While many critics charged that he had prolonged U.S. involvement in the Vietnam war unnecessarily, there was no denying that four years after his first inaugural, on January 27, 1973, a ceasefire agreement had been signed. And although U.S. bombing of Cambodia continued into the summer of 1973, it was clear that Mr. Nixon had terminated the extensive U.S. involvement in a war on the Asian mainland. More significantly, and taking the longer view, the "Nixon Doctrine" appeared to turn an important page in America's military and diplomatic history—ending a 25-year period during which it had been the U.S. role to stem the tide of communism throughout the world.

By the end of the President's first term, his first inaugural appeal that we "lower our voices" had softened the more alarming rhetoric of the Cold War. There was considerably less talk than one had heard in the 1950s and 1960s about "massive retaliation," "first strike capability" and "overkill." And it no longer seemed to matter if a military coup in some remote corner of the globe was a victory or defeat for the "Free World." Indeed, the very term "Free World" and its corollary "Sino-Soviet bloc" had become muted anachronisms by the end of 1972.

'Limits of Government'

Candidate Nixon had told a cheering Republican National Convention in 1968 his would not be an administration which would launch new and costly social programs. He charged that the anti-poverty programs of Lyndon Johnson's Great Society had "reaped...an ugly harvest of frustration, violence and failure across the land." In his inaugural address, he maintained that "We are approaching the limits of what government alone can do."

Consistent with these views, the general thrust of his domestic policies was to cut back many of the social programs developed in the 1960s, amid a rhetoric which appealed to the "self-reliance" of individual Americans.

Repeatedly, this policy set him at odds with the Democratic-controlled Congress on spending priorities over a broad range of domestic programs. By the end of the first term, he had reached the brink of a constitutional crisis with Congress over his asserted power to refuse to spend funds appropriated by the legislative branch.

But supremely confident on the eve of his near record landslide victory, he calmly contemplated (in an interview with the *Washington Star)* the further dismantling in his second term of what he regarded as excess government bureaucracies and programs. He prided himself on a re-election campaign that had not presented the American people "with a whole bag of goodies."

For the second term, he promised "leaner (government) institutions so that this new spirit of independence, self-reliance, pride that I sense in the American people can be nurtured."

An Assessment. One thoughtful effort to assess and capture the direction of Nixon's first term accomplishments in domestic and foreign policy came from Walter Lippmann. In an interview published in March 25, 1973, in *The Washington Post,* the 83-year old grey eminence of American journalism gave this description of Nixon's performance:

> His role...has been that of a man who had to liquidate, defuse, deflate the exaggerations of the romantic period of American imperialism and American inflation. Inflation of promises, inflation of hopes, the Great Society, American supremacy—all that had to be deflated because it was all beyond our power.... His role has been to do that. I think on the whole he's done pretty well at it.

'Crisis of the Spirit'

From the vantage point of January 1973, the President's first term had ended on a note of triumph. In 1972, he had achieved a series of remarkable successes—the diplomatic spectaculars in China and the Soviet Union, the historic landslide re-election and the prospect of "peace with honor" in Vietnam.

There was a single blemish marring the administration's record in 1972; that blemish was Watergate—the June 17, 1972 break-in and attempted bugging of the headquarters of the Democratic Party. But at the time of Nixon's second inauguration, the circle of those implicated in the crime included no one higher than an attorney in the Committee for the Re-election of the President and a former White House consultant.

Few observers could have predicted in January 1973—with the President riding a crest of popularity—that six months later his status in public opinion polls would drop to an all time low and that his administration would be waging a fight for survival amid calls by some for his resignation and with impeachment mentioned as a possibility. The flood of revelations in the spring of 1973 of political sabotage and espionage surrounding Watergate had presented a completely new perspective from which to assess the President's first term.

The irony of Watergate is that Nixon had pitched his 1968 campaign and his first term to a call for "law and order," moral rectitude and a "war against crime." He told the 1968 Republican Convention that Johnson administration Attorney General Ramsey Clark was "leading an official retreat" in the face of rising crime. "If we are going to restore order and respect for law in this country, there's one place we're going to begin; we're going to have a new Attorney General of the United States." Two years later, in 1970, in what was the high water year for Nixon anti-crime legislation, four major pieces of legislation drafted by Attorney General John N. Mitchell's Justice Department cleared Congress.

Mitchell left the Justice Department in February 1972 to manage the President's re-election campaign. And he resigned from the campaign to return to private practice on July 1, two weeks after the Watergate break-in.

Less than one year later, in May 1973, Mitchell and former Secretary of Commerce, Maurice H. Stans, who served as finance chief of the Nixon re-election committee, stood indicted by a federal grand jury in New York on charges of conspiring to defraud the United States and to obstruct justice in connection with the alleged concealment of a $200,000 contribution to the Nixon campaign by financier Robert L. Vesco, a fugitive from U.S. justice residing in Costa Rica.

Mitchell's indictment was but one aspect of an unprecedented scandal which by mid-July had led to the resignation of one cabinet officer, the acting director of the Federal Bureau of Investigation, three top White House aides, and the admission by several former administration officials and campaign aides to criminal acts. Even a conservative inventory of the possible crimes committed in the Watergate affair included burglary, wiretapping, perjury, bribery, theft, forgery, conspiracy, tampering with witnesses, misrepresentation of facts material to an investigation, destruction of official records, obstruction of justice and misconduct in public office.

The President's role in the scandal was unclear. He acknowledged White House attempts to cover up the scandal, but denied any personal involvement in the affair. He said he had no plans to resign.

Speculation centered on whether his ability to govern had been irrevocably impaired by the continuing disclosures of misconduct by his former aides. One thing was clear: Watergate had raised the deepest questions concerning the public's confidence in its leaders. The "crisis of the spirit" to which the President had alluded in his first inaugural was an enduring phenomenon in mid-1973.

About this Book

Congress and the Nation, Vol. III, is a comprehensive summary of presidential, legislative and political developments during the four-year period, 1969 through 1972. The volume continues a series launched by Congressional Quarterly in 1965, with the publication of *Congress and the Nation, Vol. I*, a 2,000-page reference volume covering government and politics from 1945 through 1964. *Congress and the Nation, Vol. II*, published in 1969 covered the years 1965-68.

With publication of this volume, librarians, historians, political scientists and journalists now have three volumes containing references for the entire scope of public policy spanning 28 years. Greater detail on specific points will, of course, be found in the appropriate Congressional Quarterly *Almanacs* published for each of the years.

News Research

This book is news research in a refined form. It is designed to make editorial and political comment more reliable and less burdensome. Without it, the writer, teacher or politician would be less informed or their time would be largely consumed with pursuit of basic facts, leaving less opportunity for creative reflection. Also, the deeper, harder-to-get data—full election returns, for example, or complete roll-call voting—might never even be sought except by those committed to a historical task.

News research lies somewhere between spot newspaper reporting and scholarly pursuit. It must produce lasting, useful and recognizable facts—originally organized if not original in themselves—without burying its reader in complexity and esoteric technique. These facts must be arranged so they are quickly found; careful indexing is therefore an important part of this technique.

News research, to be useful, must be pertinent. It must not only ride with the breaking news but, whenever possible, anticipate it. Nothing is more satisfying in this field than to watch a great news event unfold and know that there is available a report or assembled facts which make that event more meaningful, which help the harried reporter or editor cover the event with greater finesse and greater speed, accurately and completely.

As an exercise in news research, *Congress and the Nation, Vol. III*, attempts to meet these standards.

How to Use This Book

Briefly study the *Summary* of the *Table of Contents* which follows this introduction. It indicates the organization of *Congress and the Nation, Vol. III*.

A detailed Table of Contents follows the Summary, showing the outline and content of each chapter.

Note the organization of each legislative chapter —economic policy, national security, etc. Each usually contains a summary, a program discussion when necessary, and then a *chronology* of legislative action from 1969 through 1972. Often, related programs or legislative actions are discussed separately in a section.

The first chapter, Politics, constitutes a history of the kind of Congress each was and the resultant election issues that developed, Congress by Congress and election by election, from 1969 through 1972. This chapter forms a framework for the legislative chapters which follow.

The Appendix, which can be reached at the first thumb tab, contains material which will be used with all of the chapters of the book—biographical data on the members; committee chairmen since 1947; Senate and House Key Votes 1969-1972, with each member's vote given; the Presidents and their Cabinets; Controversial Nominations; Presidential Vetoes; the full texts of Nixon's first inaugural address and his three State of the Union messages. Pages in the Appendix are numbered: 1a, 2a, 3a, etc.

The detailed *Index* to this book begins at the second thumb tab.

Credits

A list of those staffers who had a direct role in the production of this book appears on p. viii. Such a list in a project of this dimension is necessarily incomplete, for it neglects those many dedicated former staffers of Congressional Quarterly and Editorial Research Reports whose original research and reporting became the raw material for much of what appears between the covers of this book.

Congressional Quarterly Managing Editor Wayne Kelley and Research Director Robert E. Cuthriell provided key staff and research support without which this volume would not have been possible.

Special mention must be made of the role of William B. Dickinson Jr., Editor of Congressional Quarterly and Editorial Research Reports. As supervisory editor of *Congress and the Nation, Vol. II*, Mr. Dickinson set the high standards we have sought to emulate in this volume.

ROBERT A. DIAMOND
Book Service Editor

Washington, D.C.
July 31, 1973

The Contributors to Congress and the Nation, Vol. III

The work of many dedicated people went into the writing, editing and production of this volume. Special mention must be made of the contributions of the following six writers:

Carolyn S. Mathiasen   **Bonita Siverd**

James G. Phillips   **Michael D. Wormser**

Patricia Ann O'Connor   **Elder Witt**

Writers and the chapters for which they were responsible include:

Chapter I, Politics: Mercer Cross
   Political Charts: Janice L. Goldstein, Robert E. Healy, Andrea W. Loewenstein

Chapter II, Economic Policy:
   Introduction: Carolyn S. Mathiasen
   Budget Policy: James G. Phillips
   Tax Policy: James G. Phillips
   Revenue Sharing: Patrick McMahon
   International
    Economic Policy: Carolyn S. Mathiasen
   Stabilization: James G. Phillips
   Banking Policy: Carolyn S. Mathiasen
   Transportation: David M. Maxfield
   Miscellaneous
    Economic Policy: Carolyn S. Mathiasen

Chapter III, National Security: James G. Phillips

Chapter IV, Crime Legislation: Barry Polsky

Chapter V, Federal Judiciary: Elder Witt

Chapter VI, Agriculture: Robert A. Barnes, Buel W. Patch

Chapter VII, Congress and Government:
   Congressional Affairs: Michael D. Wormser
   Legislative Reorganization: Michael D. Wormser
   Congressional Ethics: Michael D. Wormser
   Campaign Spending: Michael D. Wormser
   Financial Disclosures: Michael D. Wormser, Prudence Crewdson
   Postal and Federal Pay: David M. Maxfield
   District of Columbia: Martha V. Gottron
   Lobbies: Robert A. Barnes, Jack Nease, Prudence Crewdson

Chapter VIII, Civil Liberties: Barry Polsky
   Civil Rights: Elder Witt

Chapter IX, Space: Janice L. Goldstein, Margaret Thompson

Chapter X, Veterans: Carol Moore, Buel W. Patch

Chapter XI, Health, Education, Welfare:
   Health: Carolyn S. Mathiasen
   Education: Elder Witt
   Welfare: Carolyn S. Mathiasen
   Housing: Patrick McMahon
   Consumers: Martha V. Gottron

Chapter XII, Labor and Manpower:
    Carol Moore, Mary Cohn

Chapter XIII, Environmental Policy:
   Introduction: Donald Smith
   Environment Legislation: Bonita Siverd
   Parks and Recreation: Andrew Hamilton
   Water and Power: Bonita Siverd
   Energy Policy: Bonita Siverd

Chapter XIV, Foreign Policy and Vietnam: Patricia Ann O'Connor, Thomas J. Arrandale

Chapter XI, The Presidency
   Nixon's First Term: Carolyn S. Mathiasen
   White House and Cabinet   Oliver W. Cromwell, Andrea
    Biographies: W. Loewenstein, Herbert Trix, Jane Wales
   Watergate: Mercer Cross, Margaret Thompson
   Press Relations: Barry Polsky

Chapter XVI, Election Laws and Procedures: Mercer Cross, Oliver W. Cromwell, Warden Moxley, Margaret Thompson

Appendix: Janice L. Goldstein, Robert E. Healy, James W. Lawrence, Wayne Walker

Index: William Gerber

Graphics and Dust Jacket: Howard Chapman

Proofreaders: Susan A. Bischoff, Bill F. Chamberlin, Robert E. Healy, Diane Huffman, Robin Meszoly

The following persons were responsible for editing and production of Congress and the Nation, Vol. III:

Supervisory Editor: Robert A. Diamond

Copy Editors: Mary Cohn, Buel W. Patch, Margaret Thompson, Jack Nease, Marlyn Aycock

Editorial Assistant: Janice L. Goldstein

Production Supervisor: Richard C. Young

Assistant Production Supervisor: Richard Butler

Summary of Table of Contents

TABLE OF CONTENTS

Chapter 1 — Politics and National Issues

Chapter 2 — Economic Policy

Chapter 3 — National Security Policy

Chapter 4 — Crime Legislation

Chapter 5 — Federal Judiciary

Chapter 6 — Agriculture Policy

Chapter 7 — Congress and Government

Chapter 8 — Civil Liberties and Civil Rights

Chapter 9 — Space Activities

Chapter 10 — Veterans' Affairs

Chapter 11 — Health, Education and Welfare

Chapter 12 — Labor and Manpower

Chapter 13 — Environmental Programs

Chapter 14 — Foreign Policy

Chapter 15 — The Presidency

Chapter 16 — Election Laws and Procedures

Appendix

GLOSSARY OF CONGRESSIONAL TERMS

Act—The term for legislation which has passed both houses of Congress and has been signed by the President or passed over his veto, thus becoming law.

Also used technically for a bill that has been passed by one house and engrossed.

Adjournment sine die—Adjournment without definitely fixing a day for reconvening; literally "adjournment without a day." A session can continue until noon, Jan. 3, of the following year, when a new session usually begins.

Adjournment to a Day Certain—Adjournment under a motion or resolution which fixes the next time of meeting. Neither house can adjourn for more than three days without the concurrence of the other. A session of Congress is not ended by adjournment to a day certain.

Amendment—Proposal of a Congressman to alter the language or stipulations in a bill or act. It is usually printed, debated, and voted upon in the same manner as a bill.

Appeal—A Congressman's challenge of a ruling or decision made by the presiding officer of the Senate or House. The Congressman appeals to Members of the chamber to override the decision. If carried by a majority vote, the appeal nullifies the chair's ruling.

Appropriation Bill—Grants the actual monies approved by authorization bills, but not necessarily to the total permissible under the authorization bill. Normally an appropriation bill originates in the House, and is not acted on until its authorization measure is enacted. Regular appropriations are supposed to be passed before the start of the fiscal year to which they apply, but in recent years this has rarely happened. (*See Continuing Appropriations.*) In addition to general appropriation bills, there are two specialized types. (*See Deficiency and Supplemental.*)

Authorization Bill—Authorizes a program, specifies its general aim and conduct, and unless "open-ended," puts a ceiling on monies that can be used to finance it. Usually enacted before appropriation bill is passed. (*See Contract Authorization.*)

Bills—Most legislative proposals before Congress are in the form of bills, and are designated as HR (House of Representatives) or S (Senate) according to the house in which they originate and by a number assigned in the order in which they were introduced, from the beginning of each two-year Congressional term. "Public bills" deal with general questions, and become Public Laws if approved by Congress and signed by the President. "Private bills" deal with individual matters such as claims against the Government, immigration and naturalization cases, land titles, etc., and become Private Laws if approved and signed.

The introduction of a bill, and its referral to an appropriate committee for action, follows the process given in "How A Bill Becomes Law." (*See also Concurrent Resolution, Joint Resolution, Resolution, in this Glossary.*)

Bills Introduced—In the Senate, any number of Senators may join in introducing a single bill. In the House, until 1967, only one Member's name could appear on a single bill. But the House April 25, 1967, voted to allow cosponsorship of bills, setting a limit of 25 cosponsors on any one bill.

Many bills in reality are committee bills and are introduced under the name of the chairman of the committee or subcommittee as a formality. All appropriation bills fall into this category, as do many other bills, particularly those dealing with complicated, technical subjects. A committee frequently holds hearings on a number of related bills, and may agree on one of them or on an entirely new bill. (*See Clean Bill and By Request.*)

Bills Referred—When introduced, a bill is referred to the committee which has jurisdiction over the subject with which the bill is concerned. The appropriate reference for bills is spelled out in the Legislative Reorganization Act of 1946. Bills are referred by the Speaker in the House and the Presiding Officer in the Senate. Appeals may be made from their decisions.

Budget—The document sent to Congress by the President in January of each year estimating Government revenue and expenditures for the ensuing fiscal year and recommending appropriations in detail. The President's Budget Message forms the basis for Congressional hearings and legislation on the year's appropriations.

By Request—A phrase used when a Senator or Representative introduces a bill at the request of an executive agency or private organization but does not necessarily endorse the legislation.

Calendar—An agenda or list of pending business before committees or either chamber. The House uses five legislative calendars. (*See Consent, Discharge, House, Private and Union Calendar.*)

In the Senate, all legislative matters reported from committee go on a single calendar. They are listed there in order, but may be called up irregularly by the Majority Leader either by a motion to do so, or by obtaining the unanimous consent of the Senate. Frequently the Minority Leader is consulted to assure unanimous consent. Only cloture can limit debate on bills thus called up. (*See Call of the Calendar.*)

The Senate also uses one non-legislative calendar, for treaties, etc. (*See Executive Calendar.*)

Calendar Wednesday—In the House on Wednesdays, committees may be called in the order in which they appear in Rule X of the House Manual, for the purpose of bringing up any of their bills from the House or the Union Calendars, except bills which are privileged. General debate is limited to two hours. Bills called up from the Union Calendar are considered in Committee of the Whole. Calendar Wednesday is not observed during the last two weeks of a session, and may be dispensed with at other times -- by a two-thirds vote. It usually is dispensed with.

Call of the Calendar—Senate bills which are not brought up for debate by a motion or a unanimous consent agreement are brought before the Senate for action when the calendar listing them in order is "called." Bills considered in this fashion are usually noncontroversial, and debate is limited to five minutes for each Senator on a bill or on amendments to it.

Chamber—Meeting place for the total membership of either the House or the Senate, as distinguished from the respective committee rooms.

Clean Bill—Frequently after a committee has finished a major revision of a bill, one of the committee members, usually the chairman, will assemble the changes plus what is left of the original bill into a new measure and introduce it as a "clean bill." The new measure, which carries a new number, is then sent to the floor for consideration. This often is a timesaver, as committee-recommended changes do not have to be considered one at a time by the chamber.

Clerk of the House—Chief administrative officer of the House of Representatives with duties corresponding to those of the Secretary of the Senate. *(See Secretary of the Senate.)*

Cloture—The process by which debate can be limited in the Senate, other than by unanimous consent. A motion for cloture can apply to any measure before the Senate, including a proposal to change the chamber's rules. It requires 16 Senators' signatures for introduction and the votes of two-thirds of the Senators present and voting. It is put to a roll-call vote one hour after the Senate meets on the second day following introduction of the motion. If voted, cloture limits each Senator to one hour of debate.

Committee—A subdivision of the House or Senate which prepares legislation for action by the parent chamber, or makes investigations as directed by the parent chamber. There are several types of committees. *(See Standing, and Select or Special.)* Most standing committees are divided into subcommittees, which study legislation, hold hearings, and report their recommendations to the full committee. Only the full committee can report legislation for action by the House or Senate.

Committee of the Whole—The working title of what is formally "The Committee of the Whole House (of Representatives) on the State of the Union." Unlike other committees, it has no fixed membership. It is comprised of any 100 or more House Members who participate —on the floor of the chamber—in debating or altering legislation before the body. Such measures, however, must first have passed through the regular committees and be on the calendar.

Technically, the Committee of the Whole considers only bills directly or indirectly appropriating money, authorizing appropriations, or involving taxes or charges on the public. Actually, the Committee of the Whole often considers other types of legislation. Because the Committee of the Whole need number only 100 Representatives, a quorum is more readily attained, and business is expedited. Prior to 1971, Members' positions were not individually recorded on any votes taken in Committee of the Whole. *(See Teller Vote.)*

When the full House resolves itself into the Committee of the Whole, it supplants the Speaker with a "chairman." The measure is debated or amended, with non-roll-call votes as needed. When the Committee completes its action on the measure, it dissolves itself by "rising." The Speaker returns, and the full House hears the erstwhile chairman of the Committee report that group's recommendations. The full House then acts upon them.

At this time Members may demand a roll-call vote on any amendment *adopted* in the Committee of the Whole.

Concurrent Resolution—A concurrent resolution, designated H Con Res or S Con Res, must be passed by both houses but does not require the signature of the President and does not have the force of law. Concurrent resolutions generally are used to make or amend rules applicable to both houses or to express the sentiment of the two houses. A concurrent resolution, for example, is used to fix the time for adjournment of a Congress. It might also be used to convey the congratulations of Congress to another country on the anniversary of its independence.

Conference—A meeting between the representatives of the House and Senate to reconcile differences between the two houses over provisions of a bill. Members of the conference committee are appointed by the Speaker and the President of the Senate and are called "managers" for their respective chambers. A majority of the managers for each house must reach agreement on the provisions of the bill (often a compromise between the versions of the two chambers) before it can be sent up for floor action in the form of a "conference report." There it cannot be amended, and if not approved by both chambers, the bill goes back to conference. Elaborate rules govern the conduct of the conferences. All bills which are passed by House and Senate in slightly different form need not be sent to conference; either chamber may "concur" in the other's amendments. *(See Custody of the Papers.)*

Congressional Record—The daily, printed account of proceedings in both House and Senate chambers, with debate, statements, and the like reported verbatim. Committee activities are not covered, excepting their reports to the parent body. Highlights of legislative and committee action are embodied in a Digest section of the Record, and Congressmen are entitled to have their extraneous remarks printed in an appendix. They may edit and revise remarks made on the floor, and frequently do, so that quotations reported by the press are not always found in the Record.

Congressional Terms of Office—Begin on Jan. 3 of the year following the general election.

Consent Calendar—Members of the House may place on this calendar any bill on the Union or House Calendar which is considered to be noncontroversial. Bills on the Consent Calendar are normally called on the first and third Mondays of each month. On the first occasion when a bill is called in this manner, consideration may be blocked by the objection of any Member. On the second time, if there are three objections, the bill is stricken from the Consent Calendar; if less than three Members object, the bill is given immediate consideration.

A bill on the Consent Calendar may be postponed in another way. A Member may ask that the measure be passed over "without prejudice." In that case, no objection is recorded against the bill, and its status on the Consent Calendar remains unchanged.

A bill stricken from the Consent Calendar remains on the Union or House Calendar.

Continuing Appropriations—When a fiscal year begins and Congress has not yet enacted all the regular appropriation bills for that year, it passes a joint resolution "continuing appropriations" for Government agencies at rates generally based on their previous year's appropriations.

Contract Authorizations—Found in both authorization and appropriation bills, these authorizations are stop-gap provisions which permit the Federal Government to let contracts or obligate itself for future payments from funds not yet appropriated. The assumption is that funds will be available for payment when contracted debts come due.

Correcting the Record—Rules prohibit Members from changing their votes after the result has been announced. But frequently, hours, days, or months after a vote has been taken, a Member announces that he was "incorrectly recorded" and requests -- and almost always receives -- unanimous consent to have the vote corrected in the permanent edition of the Congressional Record. This occurs more frequently in the House than in the Senate. Errors in the text of the Record may be corrected in the same manner.

Custody of the Papers—To reconcile differences on a bill between the House and Senate, a conference may be arranged. The chamber with "custody of the papers" -- the engrossed bill, engrossed amendments, messages of transmittal -- is the only body empowered to request the conference. That body then has the advantage of acting last on the conference report when it is submitted.

Deficiency Appropriation—An appropriation to cover the difference between an agency's regular appropriation and the amount deemed necessary for it to operate for the full fiscal year. In recent years deficiency bills have usually been called supplemental appropriations.

Dilatory Motion—A motion, usually made upon a technical point, for the purpose of killing time and preventing action on a bill. The rules outlaw dilatory motions, but enforcement is largely within the discretion of the presiding officer.

Discharge a Committee—Relieve a committee from jurisdiction over a measure before it. This is rarely a successful procedure, attempted more often in the House than in the Senate.

In the House, if a committee does not report a bill within 30 days after the bill was referred to it, any Member may file a discharge motion. This motion, treated as a petition, needs the signatures of 218 Members (a majority of the House). After the required signatures have been obtained, there is a delay of seven days. Then, on the second and fourth Monday of each month, except during the last six days of a session, any Member who has signed the petition may be recognized to move that the committee be discharged. Debate on the motion to discharge is limited to 20 minutes, and, if the motion is carried, consideration of the bill becomes a matter of high privilege.

If a resolution to consider a bill (*See Rule*) is held up in the Rules Committee for more than seven legislative days, any Member may enter a motion to discharge the Committee. The motion is handled like any other discharge petition in the House.

Occasionally, to expedite noncontroversial legislative business, a committee is discharged upon unanimous consent of the House, and a petition is not required. *(For Senate procedure, see Discharge Resolution.)*

Discharge Calendar—The House calendar to which motions to discharge committees are referred when they have the necessary 218 signatures and are awaiting action.

Discharge Petition—In the House, a motion to discharge a committee from considering a bill. The motion, or petition, requires signatures of 218 House Members.

Discharge Resolution—In the Senate, a special motion any Senator may introduce to relieve a committee from consideration of a bill before it. The resolution can be called up on motion for approval or disapproval, in the same manner as other matters of Senate business. *(For House procedure, see Discharge a Committee.)*

Division Vote—Same as Standing Vote. *(See below.)*

Enacting Clause—Key phrase in bills saying, "Be it enacted by the Senate and House of Representatives..." A successful motion to strike it from legislation kills the measure.

Engrossed Bill—The final copy of a bill as passed by one chamber, with the text as amended by floor action and certified to by the Clerk of the House or the Secretary of the Senate.

Enrolled Bill—The final copy of a bill which has been passed in identical form by both chambers. It is certified to by an officer of the house of origin (House Clerk or Senate Secretary) and then sent on for signatures of the House Speaker, the Senate President, and the U.S. President. An enrolled bill is printed on parchment.

Executive Calendar—This is an additional, non-legislative calendar, in the Senate, on which Presidential documents such as treaties and nominations are listed.

Executive Document—A document, usually a treaty, sent to the Senate by the President for considera tion or ratification. These are identified for each session of Congress as Executive A, 90th Congress, 1st Session; Executive B, etc. They are referred to committee in the same manner as other measures. Unlike legislative documents, however, treaties do not die at the end of a Congress, but remain "live" proposals until acted on by the Senate or withdrawn by the President.

Executive Session—Meeting of a Senate or a House committee (or, very rarely, of the entire chamber) which only the group's members are privileged to attend. Frequently witnesses appear before committees meeting in executive session, and other Congressmen may be invited, but the public and press are not allowed.

Expenditures—The actual spending of money as distinguished from the appropriation of it. Expenditures are made by the disbursing officers of the Administration; appropriations are made only by Congress. The two are rarely identical in any fiscal year; expenditures may represent money appropriated one, two or more years previously.

Filibuster—A time-delaying tactic used by a minority in an effort to prevent a vote on a bill which probably would pass if brought to a vote. The most common method is to take advantage of the Senate's rules permitting unlimited debate, but other forms of parliamentary maneuvering may be used. The stricter rules in the House make filibusters more difficult, but they are attempted from time to time through devices such as repeated demands for quorum calls.

Fiscal Year—Financial operations of the Government are carried out in a 12-month fiscal year, beginning on July 1 and ending on June 30. The fiscal year carries the date of the calendar year in which it ends.

Floor Manager—A Member, usually representing sponsors of a bill, who attempts to steer it through debate and revision to a final vote in the chamber. Floor managers are frequently chairmen or ranking members of the committee that reported the bill. Managers are responsible for apportioning the time granted supporters of the bill for debating it. The Minority Leader or the ranking minority member of the committee often apportions time for the opposition.

Frank—A Congressman's facsimile signature on envelopes, used in lieu of stamps for his official outgoing mail, thus postage-free. Also the privilege of sending mail postage-free.

Germane—Pertaining to the subject matter of the measure at hand. All House amendments must be germane to the bill. The Senate requires that amendments be germane only when they are proposed to general appropriation bills, bills being considered under cloture, or often when proceeding under an agreement to limit debate.

Grants-in-Aid—Payments by the Federal Government which aid the recipient state, local government or individual in administering specified programs, services or activities.

Hearings—Committee sessions for hearing witnesses. At hearings on legislation, witnesses usually include specialists, government officials and spokesmen for persons affected by the bills under study. Hearings related to special investigations bring forth a variety of witnesses. Committees sometimes use their subpoena power to summon reluctant witnesses. The public and press may attend "open" hearings, but are barred from "closed" or "executive" hearings.

The committee announces its hearings, from one day to many weeks in advance, and may invite certain persons to testify. Persons who request time to testify may be turned down by the committee but most requests are honored.

Hopper—Box on House Clerk's desk where bills are deposited on introduction.

House—The House of Representatives, as distinct from the Senate, although each body is a "house" of Congress.

House Calendar—Listing for action by the House of Representatives of public bills which do not directly or indirectly appropriate money or raise revenue.

Immunity—Constitutional privilege of Congressmen to make verbal statements on the floor and in committee for which they cannot be sued or arrested for slander or libel. Also, freedom from arrest while traveling to or from sessions of Congress or on official business. Congressmen in this status may be arrested only for treason, felonies or a breach of the peace, as defined by Congressional manuals.

Joint Committee—A committee composed of a specified number of Members of both House and Senate. Usually a joint committee is investigative in nature. There are a few standing joint committees, such as the Joint Committee on Atomic Energy and the Joint Economic Committee.

Joint Resolution—A joint resolution, designated H J Res or S J Res, requires the approval of both houses and the signature of the President, just as a bill does, and has the force of law if approved. There is no real difference between a bill and a joint resolution. The latter is generally used in dealing with limited matters, such as a single appropriation for a specific purpose.

Joint resolutions also are used to propose amendments to the Constitution. These do not require Presidential signature, but become a part of the Constitution when three-fourths of the states have ratified them.

Journal—The official record of the proceedings of the House and Senate. The Journal records the actions taken in each chamber, but unlike the Congressional Record, it does not include the verbatim report of speeches, debate, etc.

Law—An Act of Congress which has been signed by the President, or passed over his veto by the Congress. Laws are listed numerically by Congress; for example, the Civil Rights Act of 1964 (HR 7152) became Public Law 88-352 during the 88th Congress.

Legislative Day—The "day" extending from the time either house meets after an adjournment until the time it next adjourns. Because the House normally adjourns from day to day, legislative days and calendar days usually coincide. But in the Senate, a legislative day may, and frequently does, extend over several calendar days. *(See Recess.)*

Lobby—A group seeking to influence the passage or defeat of legislation. Originally the term referred to persons frequenting the lobbies or corridors of legislative chambers in order to speak to lawmakers.

The exact definition of a lobby and the activity of lobbying is a matter of opinion. By some definitions, lobbying is limited to attempts at direct influence by personal interview and persuasion. Under other definitions, lobbying includes attempts at indirect influence, such as stirring members of a group to write or visit Congressmen, or attempting to create a climate of opinion favorable to a desired legislative action.

The right to attempt to influence legislation is based on the 1st Amendment to the Constitution, which says Congress shall make no law abridging the right of the people "to petition the Government for a redress of grievances."

Majority Leader—Chief strategist and floor spokesman for the party in nominal control in either chamber. He is elected by his party colleagues and is virtually program director for his chamber, since he usually speaks for its majority.

Majority Whip—In effect, the assistant majority leader, in House or Senate. His job is to help marshal majority forces in support of party strategy.

Manual—The official handbook in each house prescribing its organization, procedures and operations in detail. The Senate Manual contains standing rules, orders, laws and resolutions affecting Senate business; the House Manual is the equivalent for that chamber. Both volumes contain previous codes under which Congress functioned and from which it continues to derive precedents. Committee powers are outlined. The rules set forth in the Manuals may be changed by elaborate chamber actions also specified by the Manuals.

Marking Up a Bill—Going through a measure, usually in committee, taking it section by section, revising language, penciling in new phrases, etc. If the bill is extensively revised, the new version may be introduced as a separate bill, with a new number. *(See Clean Bill.)*

Memorial—A request for Congressional opposition or an objection from an organization or citizens' group to particular legislation or government practice under the purview of Congress. All communications, both supporting and opposing legislation, from state legislatures are embodied in memorials. They are referred to appropriate committees unless the legislation dealt with in the memorial has been reported to the Senate, in which case the memorial is placed on the table. It can be called up for consideration at the time the bill is read for amendments. *(See Petition.)*

Minority Leader—Floor leader for the minority party. *(See Majority Leader.)*

Minority Whip—Performs duties of whip for the minority party. *(See Majority Whip.)*

Morning Hour—The time set aside at the beginning of each legislative day for the consideration of regular routine business. The "hour" is of indefinite duration in the House, where it is rarely used. In the Senate it is the first two hours of a session following an adjournment, as distinguished from a recess. The morning hour can be terminated earlier if the morning business has been completed. This business includes such matters as messages from the President, communications from the heads of departments, messages from the House, the presentation of petitions and memorials, reports of standing and select committees, and the introduction of bills and resolutions.

During the first hour of the morning hour in the Senate, no motion to proceed to the consideration of any bill on the calendar is in order except by unanimous consent. During the second hour, motions can be made but must be decided without debate. Senate committees may meet while the Senate is in the morning hour.

Motion—Request by a Congressman for any one of a wide array of parliamentary actions. He "moves" for a certain procedure, or the consideration of a measure or a vote, etc. The precedence of motions, and whether they are debatable, is set forth in the House and Senate Manuals.

Nominations—Appointments to office by the Executive Branch of the Government, subject to Senate confirmation. Although most nominations win quick Senate approval, some are controversial and become the topic of hearings and debate. Sometimes Senators object to appointees for patronage reasons—for example, when a nomination to a local federal job is made without consulting the Senators of the state concerned. Then a Senator may use the stock objection that the nominee is "personally obnoxious" to him. Usually other Senators join in blocking such an appointment out of courtesy to their colleague.

One Minute Speeches—Addresses by House Members at the beginning of a legislative day. The speeches may cover any subject, but are limited strictly to one minute's duration.

Override a Veto—If the President disapproves a bill and sends it back to Congress with his objections, Congress may override his veto by a two-thirds vote in each chamber. The Constitution requires a yea-and-nay roll call. The question put to each house is: "Shall the bill pass, the objections of the President to the contrary notwithstanding?" *(See also Pocket Veto and Veto.)*

Pair—A "gentlemen's agreement" between two lawmakers on opposite sides to withhold their votes on roll calls so their absence from Congress will not affect the outcome of record voting. If passage of the measure requires a two-thirds majority, a pair would require two Members favoring the action to one opposed to it.

Two kinds of pairs—special and general—are used; neither is counted in vote totals. The names of lawmakers pairing on a given vote and their stands, if known, are printed in the Congressional Record.

The special pair applies to one or a series of roll-call votes on the same subject. On special pairs, lawmakers usually specify how they would have voted.

A general pair in the Senate, now rarely used in the chamber, applies to all votes on which the Members pairing are on opposite sides, and it lasts for the length of time pairing Senators agree on. It usually does not specify a Senator's stand on a given vote.

The general pair in the House differs from the other pairs. No agreement is involved and the pair does not tie up votes. A Representative expecting to be absent may notify the House Clerk he wishes to make a "general" pair. His name then is paired arbitrarily with that of another Member desiring a general pair, and the list is printed in the Congressional Record. He may or may not be paired with a Member taking the opposite position. General pairs in the House give no indication of how a Congressman would have voted. *(See Record Vote and Stand.)*

Petition—A request or plea sent to one or both chambers from an organization or private-citizens group asking support of particular legislation or favorable consideration of a matter not yet receiving Congressional attention. They are referred to appropriate committees and considered or not, according to committee decision. *(See Memorial.)*

Pocket Veto—The act of the President in withholding his approval of a bill after Congress has adjourned—either for the year or for a specified period. When Congress is in session, a bill becomes law without the President's signature if he does not act upon it within 10 days, excluding Sundays, from the time he gets it. But if Congress adjourns within that 10-day period, the bill is killed without the President's formal veto.

Point of Order—An objection raised by a Congressman that the chamber is departing from rules governing its conduct of business. The objector cites the rule violated, the chair sustaining his objection if correctly made. Order is restored by the chair's suspending proceedings of the chamber until it conforms to the prescribed "order of business." Members sometimes raise a "point of no order"—when there is noise and disorderly conduct in the chamber.

President of the Senate—Presiding officer of the upper chamber, normally the Vice President of the United States. In his absence, a President pro tempore (President for the time being) presides.

President pro tempore—The chief officer of the Senate in the absence of the Vice President. He is elected by his fellow Senators. The recent practice has been to elect to the office the Senator of the majority party with longest continuous service.

Previous Question—In this sense, a "question" is an "issue" before the House for a vote and the issue is "previous" when some other topic has superseded it in the attention of the chamber. A motion for the previous question, when carried, has the effect of cutting off all debate and forcing a vote on the subject originally at hand. If, however, the previous question is moved and carried before there has been any debate on the subject at hand and the subject is debatable, then 40 minutes of debate is allowed before the vote. The previous question is sometimes moved in order to prevent amendments. The motion for the previous question is a debate-limiting device and is not in order in the Senate.

Private Calendar—Private House bills dealing with individual matters such as claims against the Government, immigration, land titles, etc., are put on this calendar. When it is before the chamber, two Members may block a private bill, which then is recommitted to committee.

Backers of a private bill thus recommitted have another recourse. The measure can be put into an "omnibus claims bill"—several private bills rolled into one. As with any bill, no part of an omnibus claims bill may be deleted without a vote. When a private bill goes back to the floor in this form, it can be defeated only by a majority of those present. The Private Calendar can be called on the first and third Tuesdays of each month.

Privilege—Privilege relates to the rights of Congressmen and to the relative priority of the motions and actions they may make in their respective chambers. The two are distinct. "Privileged questions" concern legislative business. "Questions of privilege" concern legislators themselves. *(See below.)*

Privileged Questions—The order in which bills, motions and other legislative measures may be considered by Congress is governed by strict priorities. A motion to table, for instance, is more privileged than a motion to recommit. Thus, a motion to recommit can be superseded by a motion to table, and a vote would be forced on the latter motion only. A motion to adjourn, however, would take precedence over this one, and is thus considered of the "highest privilege."

Pro Forma Amendment—*See Strike Out the Last Word.*

Questions of Privilege—These are matters affecting Members of Congress individually or collectively.

Questions affecting the rights, safety, dignity and integrity of proceedings of the House or Senate as a whole are questions of privilege of the House or Senate, as the case may be.

Congressmen singly involve questions of "personal privilege." A Member's rising to a question of personal privilege is given precedence over almost all other proceedings. An annotation in the House Rules points out that the privilege of the Member rests primarily on the Constitution, which gives him a conditional immunity from arrest and an unconditional freedom to speak in the House.

Quorum—The number of Members whose presence is necessary for the transaction of business. In the Senate and House, it is a majority of the membership (when there are no vacancies, this is 51 in the Senate and 218 in the House). A quorum is 100 in the Committee of the Whole House. If a point of order is made that a quorum is not present, the only business in order is either a motion to adjourn or a motion to direct the Sergeant-at-Arms to request the attendance of absentees.

Readings of Bills—Traditional parliamentary law required bills to be read three times before they were passed. This custom is of little modern significance except in rare instances. Normally the bill is considered to have its first reading when it is introduced and printed, by title, in the Congressional Record. Its second reading comes when floor consideration begins. (This is the most likely point at which there is an actual reading of the bill, if there is any.) The third reading (usually by title) takes place when action has been completed on amendments.

Recess—Distinguished from adjournment in that a recess does not end a legislative day and therefore does not interfere with unfinished business. The rules in each house set forth certain matters to be taken up and disposed of at the beginning of each legislative day. The House, which operates under much stricter rules than the Senate, usually adjourns from day to day. The Senate often recesses.

Recommit to Committee—A simple motion, made on the floor after deliberation on a bill, to return it to the committee which reported it. If approved, recommittal usually is considered a death blow to the bill. In the House a motion to recommit can be made only by a Member opposed to the bill, and in recognizing a Member to make the motion, the Speaker gives the minority party preference over the majority.

A motion to recommit may include instructions to the committee to report the bill again with specific amendments or by a certain date. Or the instructions may be to make a particular study, with no definite deadline for final action.

Reconsider a Vote—A motion to reconsider the vote by which an action was taken has, until it is disposed of, the effect of suspending the action. In the Senate the motion can be made only by a Member who voted on the prevailing side of the original question, or by a Member who did not vote at all. In the House it can be made only by a Member on the prevailing side.

A common practice after close votes in the Senate is a motion to reconsider, followed by a motion to table the motion to reconsider. On this motion to table, Senators vote as they voted on the original question, to enable the motion to table to prevail. The matter is then finally closed and further motions to reconsider are not entertained. In the House, as a routine precaution, a motion to reconsider usually is made every time a measure is passed. Such a motion almost always is tabled immediately, thus shutting off the possibility of future reconsideration except by unanimous consent.

Motions to reconsider must be entered in the Senate within the next two days of actual session after the original vote has been taken. In the House they must be entered either on the same day or on the next succeeding day the House is in session.

Record Vote—This is a roll call of the entire chamber membership, to which each Member on the floor must answer "yea," "nay," or, if he does not wish to vote, "present." The Constitution requires yea-and-nay votes on the question of overriding a veto. In other cases, they can be obtained by the demand of one-fifth of the Members present. In the House, the yeas and nays are required automatically whenever a Member objects to a non-record vote taken when a quorum was not present, if the question is one which requires a quorum. The yeas and nays are not taken in the Committee of the Whole. *(See also Teller Vote.)*

Report—Both a verb and a noun, as a Congressional term. A committee which has been examining a bill referred to it by the parent chamber "reports" its finding and recommendations to the chamber when the committee returns the measure. The process is called "reporting" a bill.

A "report" is the document setting forth the committee's explanation of its action. House and Senate reports are numbered separately and are designated S Rept or H Rept. Conference reports are numbered and designated in the same way as regular House reports.

Most reports favor a bill's passage. Adverse reports are occasionally submitted, but more often, when a committee disapproves a bill, it simply fails to report it at all. When a committee report is not unanimous, the dissenting committeemen may file a statement of their views, called Minority Views and referred to as a Minority Report. Sometimes a bill is reported without recommendation.

Recision—An item in an appropriation bill rescinding, or cancelling, funds previously appropriated but not spent.

Resolution—A simple resolution, designated H Res or S Res, deals with matters entirely within the prerogatives of one house or the other. It requires neither passage by the other chamber nor approval by the President, and does not have the force of law. Most resolutions deal with the rules of one house. They also are used to express the sentiments of a single house, as condolences to the family of a deceased Member or to give "advice" on foreign policy or other executive business. *(Also see Concurrent and Joint Resolutions.)*

Rider—A provision, usually not germane, tacked on to a bill which its sponsor hopes to get through more easily by including in other legislation. Riders become law if the bills embodying them do. Riders providing for legislation in appropriations bills are outstanding examples, though technically they are banned.

Rule—The term has two specific Congressional meanings. A rule may be a standing order governing the conduct of House or Senate business and listed in the chamber's book of rules. The rules deal with duties of officers, order of business, admission to the floor, voting procedures, etc.

In the House, a rule also may be a decision made by its Rules Committee about the handling of a particular bill on the floor. The Committee may determine under which standing rule a bill shall be considered, or it may provide a "special rule" in the form of a resolution. If the resolution is adopted by the House, the temporary rule becomes as valid as any standing rule, and lapses only after action has been completed on the measure to which it pertains.

A special rule sets the time limit on general debate. It may also waive points of order against provisions of the bill in question or against specified amendments intended to be proposed to the bill. It may even forbid all amendments or all amendments except, in some cases, those proposed by the legislative committee which handled the bill. In this instance it is known as a "closed" or "gag" rule as opposed to an "open" rule which puts no limitation on floor action, thus leaving the bill open to alteration. *(See Suspend the Rules.)*

Secretary of the Senate—Chief administrative officer of the Senate, responsible for direction of duties of Senate employees, education of pages, administration of oaths, receipt of registration of lobbyists and other activities necessary for the continuing operation of the Senate.

Select or Special Committee—A committee set up for a special purpose and a limited time by resolution of either House or Senate. Most special committees are investigative in nature.

Senatorial Courtesy—Sometimes referred to as "the courtesy of the Senate," it is a general practice without written rule applied to consideration of executive nominations. In practice, generally it means nominations from a state are not to be confirmed unless they have been approved by the Senators of the President's party of that state, with other Senators following their lead in the attitude they take toward such nominations.

Sine Die—See Adjournment sine die.

Slip Laws—The first official publication of a bill that has been enacted into law. Each is published separately in unbound single-sheet or pamphlet form. It usually takes two to three days from the date of Presidential approval to the time when slip laws become available.

Speaker—The presiding officer of the House of Representatives, elected by its Members.

Special Session—A session of Congress after it has adjourned sine die, completing its regular session. Special sessions are convened by the President of the United States under his constitutional powers.

Stand—A lawmaker's position, for or against, on a given issue or vote. He can make known his stand on a roll-call vote by answering "yea" or "nay," by "pairing" for or against, or by "announcing" his position to the House or Senate. Members also may go on record by answering the Congressional Quarterly Poll of unrecorded Congressmen on roll calls. *(See Pair, and Record Vote, above. See also Teller Vote, below.)*

Standing Committee—A group permanently provided for by House or Senate rules. The standing committees at present are specified by the Legislative Reorganization Act of 1946, which broadly defines their respective jurisdictions.

Standing Vote—A non-record vote used in both House and Senate. A standing vote, also called a division vote, is taken as follows: Members in favor of a proposal stand and are counted by the presiding officer; then Members opposed stand and are counted. There is no record of how individual Members voted. In the House, the presiding officer announces the number of and against. In the Senate, usually only the result is announced.

Statutes-at-Large—A chronological arrangement of the laws enacted in each session of Congress. Though indexed, the laws are not arranged by subject matter nor is there an indication of how they affect previous law. *(See U.S. Code.)*

Strike from the Record—Remarks made on the House floor may offend some Member, who moves that the offending words be "taken down" for the Speaker's cognizance, and then expunged from the verbatim report to be carried in the Congressional Record.

Strike Out the Last Word—A move whereby House Members are entitled to speak for a fixed time on a measure then being debated by the chamber. A Member gains recognition from the chair by moving to strike out the last word of the amendment or section of the bill then under consideration. The motion is pro forma, and customarily requires no vote.

Substitute—A motion, an amendment, or an entire bill introduced in place of pending business. Passage of a substitute measure kills the original measure by supplanting it. A substitute may be amended.

Supplemental Appropriations—Normally are passed after the regular appropriation, but supposedly before the fiscal year to which they apply. Deficiencies are passed in the same fiscal year to which they apply but in recent practice have been called supplementals.

Suspend the Rules—Often a time-saving procedure for passing bills in the House. The wording of the motion, which may be made by any Member recognized by the Speaker, is: "I move to suspend the rules and pass the bill...." A favorable vote by two-thirds of those present is required for passage. Debate is limited to 40 minutes and no amendments from the floor are permitted. If a two-thirds favorable vote is not attained, the bill may be considered later under regular procedures.

Table a Bill—The motion to "lay on the table" is not debatable in either house, and is usually a method of making a final, adverse disposition of a matter. In the Senate, however, different language is sometimes used. The motion is worded to let a bill "lie on the table," perhaps for subsequent "picking up." This motion is more flexible, merely keeping the bill pending for later action, if desired.

Teller Vote—In the House, Members file past tellers and are counted as for or against a measure, but they are not recorded individually. The teller vote is not used in the Senate. In the House, tellers are ordered upon demand of one-fifth of a quorum. This is 44 in the House, 20 in Committee of the Whole.

The House also has a recorded teller vote procedure under which the individual votes of Members are made public just as they would be on a yea-nay vote. This procedure, introduced in 1971, has forced Members to take a public position on amendments to key bills considered in Committee of the Whole. An electronic voting system was to be introduced in 1973.

Treaties—Executive proposals which must be submitted to the Senate for approval by two-thirds of the Senators present. Before they act on such foreign policy matters, Senators usually send them to committee for scrutiny. Treaties are read three times and debated in the chamber much as are legislative proposals, but are rarely amended. After approval by the Senate, they are ratified by the President.

Unanimous Consent—Synonymous with Without Objection. *(See below.)*

Union Calendar—Bills which directly or indirectly appropriate money or raise revenue are placed on this House calendar according to the date reported from committee.

U.S. Code—A consolidation and codification of the general and permanent laws of the United States ar-ranged by subject under 50 Titles, the first six dealing with general or political subjects, and the other 44 alphabetically arranged from Agriculture to War and National Defense. The Code is now revised every six years and a supplement is published after each session of Congress.

Veto—Disapproval by the President of a bill or joint resolution, other than one proposing an amendment to the Constitution. When Congress is in session, the President must veto a bill within 10 days, excluding Sundays, after he has received it; otherwise it becomes law with or without his signature. When the President vetoes a bill, he returns it to the house of its origin with a message stating his objections. The veto then becomes a question of high privilege. *(See Override a Veto.)*

When Congress has adjourned, the President may pocket veto a bill by failing to sign it. *(See Pocket Veto.)*

Voice Vote—In either House or Senate, Members answer "aye" or "no" in chorus and the presiding officer decides the result. The term also is used loosely to indicate action by unanimous consent or without objection.

Whip—See Majority Whip.

Without Objection—Used in lieu of a vote on non-controversial motions, amendments or bills, which may be passed in either the House or the Senate if no Member voices an objection.

HOW A BILL BECOMES LAW

The following explanation of how a bill becomes law incorporates the changes made in the legislative process by the Legislative Reorganization Act of 1970. The Act, which cleared Congress Oct. 8, 1970, was designed to improve the operations of Congress in committee and on the floor, to provide Congress with better means of evaluating the Federal Budget and with improved resources for research and information. Parliamentary terms used below are defined in the Glossary.

INTRODUCTION OF BILLS

A House Member (including the Resident Commissioner of Puerto Rico and, starting in 1971, a nonvoting delegate of the District of Columbia) may introduce any one of several types of bills and resolutions by handing it to the Clerk of the House or placing it in a box called the hopper. A Senator first gains recognition of the presiding officer to announce the introduction of a bill. If objection is offered by any Senator the introduction of the bill is postponed until the following day.

As the next step in either the House or Senate, the bill is numbered, referred to the appropriate committee, labeled with the sponsor's name, and sent to the Government Printing Office so that copies can be made for subsequent study and action. Senate bills may be jointly sponsored and carry several Senators' names. In the House, until 1967, each bill carried the name of one sponsor only; however, the House April 25, 1967, voted to allow cosponsorship of bills, setting a limit of 25 cosponsors on any one bill. Bills written in the Executive Branch and proposed as Administration measures usually are intro-duced by the chairmen of the Congressional committees that have jurisdiction over the subjects involved.

Types of Congressional measures:

Bills—Prefixed with "HR" in the House, "S" in the Senate, followed by a number. Used as the form for most legislation, whether general or special, public or private.

Joint Resolutions—Designated H J Res or S J Res. Subject to the same procedure as bills, with the exception of a joint resolution proposing an amendment to the Constitution. The latter must be approved by two-thirds of both houses and is thereupon sent directly to the Administrator of General Services for submission to the states for ratification rather than being presented to the President for his approval.

Concurrent Resolutions—Designated H Con Res or S Con Res. Used for matters affecting the operations of both houses. These resolutions do not become law.

Resolutions—Designated H Res or S Res. Used for a matter concerning the operation of either house alone and adopted only by the chamber in which it originates.

COMMITTEE ACTION

A bill is referred to the appropriate committee by the House parliamentarian on the Speaker's order, or by the Senate President. Sponsors may indicate their preferences for referral, although custom and chamber rule generally govern. An exception is the referral of private bills, which are sent to whatever group is designated by their sponsors. Bills are technically considered "read for the first time" when referred to House committees.

When a bill reaches a committee it is placed upon the group's calendar. At that time it comes under the sharpest Congressional focus. Its chances for passage are quickly determined—and the great majority of bills fall by the legislative roadside. Failure of a committee to act on a bill is equivalent to killing it; the measure can be withdrawn from the group's purview only by a discharge petition signed by a majority of the House membership on House bills, or by adoption of a special resolution in the Senate. Discharge attempts rarely succeed.

The first committee action taken on a bill usually is a request for comment on it by interested agencies of the Government. The committee chairman may assign the bill to a subcommittee for study and hearings, or it may be considered by the full committee. Hearings may be public, closed (executive session), or both. A subcommittee, after considering a bill, reports to the full committee its recommendations for action and any proposed amendments.

The full committee then votes on its recommendation to the House or Senate. This procedure is called "ordering a bill reported." Occasionally a committee may order a bill reported unfavorably; most of the time a report, submitted by the chairman of the committee to the House or Senate, calls for favorable action on the measure since the committee can effectively "kill" a bill by simply failing to take any action.

When a committee sends a bill to the chamber floor, it explains its reasons in a written statement, called a report, which accompanies the bill. Often committee members opposing a measure issue a dissenting minority report.

Frequently, the committee proposes amendments to the bill. If they are substantial and the measure is complicated, the committee may order a "clean bill" introduced, which will embody the proposed amendments. The original bill then is put aside and the "clean bill," with a new number, is reported to the floor.

The chamber must approve, alter, or reject the committee amendments before the bill itself can be put to a vote.

FLOOR ACTION

After a bill is reported back to the house where it originated, it is placed on the calendar.

There are five legislative calendars in the House, issued in one cumulative calendar titled Calendars of the United States House of Representatives and History of Legislation. The House Calendars are:

The Union Calendar to which are referred bills raising revenues, general appropriation bills and any measures directly or indirectly appropriating money or property. It is the Calendar of the Committee of the Whole House on the State of the Union.

The House Calendar to which are referred all bills of a public character not raising revenue or appropriating money or property.

The Consent Calendar to which are referred bills of a noncontroversial nature that are passed without debate when the Consent Calendar is called on the first and third Mondays of each month.

The Private Calendar to which are referred bills for relief in the nature of claims against the United States or private immigration bills that are passed without de-

bate when the Private Calendar is called the first and third Tuesdays of each month.

The Discharge Calendar to which are referred motions to discharge committees when the necessary signatures are signed to a discharge petition.

There is only one legislative calendar in the Senate and one "executive calendar" for treaties and nominations presented to the Senate. When the Senate Calendar is called, each Senator is limited to five minutes' debate on each bill.

DEBATE. A bill is brought to debate by varying procedures. If a routine measure, it may await the call of the calendar. If it is urgent or important, it can be taken up in the Senate either by unanimous consent or by a majority vote. The Policy Committee of the majority party in the Senate schedules the bills that it wants taken up for debate.

In the House, precedence is granted if a special rule is obtained from the Rules Committee. A request for a special rule is usually made by the chairman of the committee that favorably reported the bill, supported by the bill's sponsor and other committee members. The request, considered by the Rules Committee in the same fashion that other committees consider legislative measures, is in the form of a resolution providing for immediate consideration of the bill. The Rules Committee reports the resolution to the House where it is debated and voted upon in the same fashion as regular bills. If the Rules Committee should fail to report a rule requested by a committee, there are several ways to bring the bill to the House floor—under suspension of the rules, on Calendar Wednesday or by a discharge motion.

The resolutions providing special rules are important because they specify how long the bill may be debated and whether it may be amended from the floor. If floor amendment is banned, the bill is considered under a "closed rule" which permits only members of the committee that first reported the measure to the House to alter its language, subject to chamber acceptance.

When a bill is debated under an "open rule," amendments may be offered from the floor. Committee amendments are always taken up first, but may be changed, as may all amendments up to the second degree, i.e., an amendment to an amendment to an amendment is not in order.

Duration of debate in the House depends on whether the bill is under discussion by the House proper or before the House when it is sitting as the Committee of the Whole on the State of the Union. In the former, the amount of time for debate is determined either by special rule or is allocated with an hour for each Member if the measure is under consideration without a rule. In the Committee of the Whole the amount of time agreed on for general debate is equally divided between proponents and opponents. At the end of general discussion, the bill is read section by section for amendment. Debate on an amendment is limited to five minutes for supporters and five minutes for opponents.

Senate debate is usually unlimited. It can be halted only by unanimous consent or by "cloture," which requires a two-thirds vote.

The House sits as the Committee of the Whole on the State of the Union when it first considers any tax measure or bill dealing with public appropriations. It can also resolve itself into the Committee of the Whole if a Mem-

HOW A BILL BECOMES LAW

THIS GRAPHIC SHOWS THE MOST TYPICAL WAY IN WHICH PROPOSED LEGISLATION IS ENACTED INTO LAW. THERE ARE MORE COMPLICATED, AS WELL AS SIMPLER, ROUTES, AND MOST BILLS FALL BY THE WAYSIDE AND NEVER BECOME LAW.

INTRODUCTION   **COMMITTEE ACTION**   **FLOOR ACTION**   **ENACTMENT INTO LAW**

INTRODUCED IN HOUSE

REFERRED TO HOUSE COMMITTEE

COMMITTEE HOLDS HEARINGS, RECOMMENDS PASSAGE

HOUSE DEBATES AND PASSES

INTRODUCED IN SENATE

REFERRED TO SENATE COMMITTEE

COMMITTEE HOLDS HEARINGS, RECOMMENDS PASSAGE

SENATE DEBATES AND PASSES

HOUSE AND SENATE MEMBERS CONFER, REACH COMPROMISE

HOUSE AND SENATE APPROVE COMPROMISE

PRESIDENT SIGNS INTO LAW

MOST LEGISLATION BEGINS AS SIMILAR PROPOSALS IN BOTH HOUSES

ALL BILLS MUST GO THROUGH BOTH HOUSE AND SENATE BEFORE REACHING PRESIDENT

ber moves to do so and the motion is carried. The Speaker appoints a Member to serve as the chairman. The rules of the House permit the Committee of the Whole to meet with any 100 Members on the floor, and to amend and act on bills with a quorum of the 100, within the time limitations mentioned previously. When the Committee of the Whole has acted, it "rises," the Speaker returns as the presiding officer of the House and the Member appointed chairman of the Committee of the Whole reports the action of the Committee and its recommendations.

VOTES. Voting on bills may occur repeatedly before they are finally approved or rejected. The House votes on the rule for the bill and on various amendments to the bill. Voting on amendments often is a more illuminating test of a bill's support than is the final tally. Sometimes Members approve final passage of bills after vigorously supporting amendments which, if adopted, would have scuttled the legislation.

The House and Senate vote both on untabulated voice votes and on a recorded roll call of their names, to which they answer "yea" or "nay." The House also uses a standing vote, called a division, and a teller vote, when Members file up the center aisle past counters. The Senate also has a division, or standing vote. It does not employ the teller vote. Division vote totals are announced in the House but not in the Senate. Under the Legislative Reorganization Act of 1970, the positions of Members voting on teller votes in the House may be recorded upon request of one-fifth of a quorum; previously only vote totals were recorded on teller votes, and a roll-call vote was the sole means by which Members' positions could be individually recorded.

After amendments to a bill have been voted upon, a vote may be taken on a motion to recommit the bill to committee. If carried, this vote removes the bill from the chamber's calendar. If the motion is unsuccessful, the bill then is "read for the third time." An actual reading usually is dispensed with. Until 1965, an opponent of a bill could delay this move by objecting and asking for a full reading of an engrossed (certified in final form) copy of the bill. After the "third reading," the vote on final passage is taken.

The final vote may be followed by a motion to reconsider, and this motion itself may be followed by a move to lay the motion on the table. Usually, those voting for the bill's passage vote for the tabling motion, thus safeguarding the final passage action. With that, the bill has been formally passed by the chamber. While a motion to reconsider a Senate vote is pending on a bill, the measure cannot be sent to the House. Once a bill has been passed by either chamber, it becomes, officially, an "act," though it continues generally to be referred to as a bill.

ACTION IN SECOND HOUSE

After a bill is passed it is sent to the other chamber. This body may then take one of several steps. It may pass the bill as is—accepting the other chamber's language. It may send the bill to committee for scrutiny or alteration, or reject the entire bill, advising the other house of its actions. Or it may simply ignore the bill submitted while it continues work on its own version of the proposed legislation. Frequently, one chamber may approve a version of a bill that is greatly at variance with the version already passed by the other house, and then substitute its amendments for the language of the other, retaining only the latter's bill designation.

A provision of the Legislative Reorganization Act of 1970 permits a separate House vote on any nongermane amendment added by the Senate to a House-passed bill and requires a majority vote to approve the amendment. Previously the House was forced to act on the bill as a whole; the only way to defeat the nongermane amendment was to reject the entire bill.

Often the second chamber makes only minor changes. If these are readily agreed to by the other house, the bill then is routed to the White House for signing. However, if the opposite chamber basically alters the bill submitted to it, the measure usually is "sent to conference." The chamber that has possession of the "papers" (engrossed bill, engrossed amendments, messages of transmittal) requests a conference and the other chamber agrees to it.

Conference. A conference undertakes to harmonize conflicting House and Senate versions of a legislative bill. The conference is staffed by interested senior Members, appointed by the presiding officers of the two houses, from the committees which managed the bills. Under this arrangement the Members of one house who are most familiar with the bill have the duty of trying to maintain their chamber's position in the face of amending actions by the conferees (or "managers") of the other house.

The number of conferees from each chamber may vary, the range usually being from three to nine Members in each group, depending upon the length or complexity of the bill involved. There may be five Representatives and three Senators on the conference committee, or the reverse. But a majority vote controls the action of each group so that a larger representation does not give one chamber a voting advantage over the other chamber's conferees.

Theoretically, conferees are not allowed to write new legislation in reconciling the two versions before them, but this curb sometimes is bypassed. Many bills have been put into acceptable compromise form only after new language was provided by the conferees. The 1970 Reorganization Act attempted to tighten restrictions on conferees by forbidding them to introduce any language on a topic that neither chamber sent to conference or to modify any topic beyond the scope of the different House and Senate versions.

Frequently the ironing out of difficulties takes days or even weeks. Conferences on involved appropriation bills sometimes are particularly drawn out.

As a conference proceeds, conferees reconcile their differences, but generally they grant concessions only insofar as they remain sure that the chamber they represent will accept the compromises. Occasionally, uncertainty over how either house will react, or the positive refusal of a chamber to back down on a disputed amendment, results in an impasse, and the bills die in conference even though each was approved by its sponsoring chamber.

Conferees sometimes go back to their respective chambers for further instructions, when they report certain portions in disagreement. Then the chamber concerned can either "recede and concur" in the amendment of the other house, or "insist on its amendment."

When the conferees have reached agreement, they prepare a conference report embodying their recommendations. The reports, in document form, must be submitted to each house. The Legislative Reorganization Act of 1970 provides that Senate and House conferees must jointly prepare an explanatory statement for every conference report and that all conference reports and accompanying statements must be printed in both houses. Previously conference reports were printed in the House with an explanatory statement prepared by the House conferees only; in the Senate an explanation was often made orally by one of the conferees.

The conference report must be approved by each house. Consequently, approval of the report is approval of the compromise bill. In the order of voting on conference reports, the chamber which asked for a conference yields to the other chamber the opportunity to vote first.

Final Steps. After a bill has been passed by both the House and Senate, all of the original papers are sent to the enrolling clerk of the chamber in which the bill originated. He then prepares an enrolled bill which is printed on parchment paper. When this bill has been **certified as correct by the Secretary of the Senate or** the Clerk of the House, depending on which chamber originated the bill, it is signed first (no matter whether it originated in the Senate or House) by the Speaker of the House and then by the President of the Senate. It is next sent to the White House to await action.

If the President approves the bill he signs it, dates it and usually writes the word "approved" on the document. If he does not sign it within 10 days (Sundays excepted) and Congress is in session, the bill becomes law without his signature.

However, should Congress adjourn before the 10 days expire, and the President has failed to sign the measure, it does not become law. This procedure is called the pocket veto. Occasionally a President vetoes a bill by refusing to sign it and returning it to the Congress with a message stating his reasons. The message is sent to the chamber which originated the bill. If no action is taken there on the message, the bill dies. Sometimes, however, Congress attempts to override the President's veto and enact the bill, "the objections of the President to the contrary notwithstanding." Overriding of a veto requires a two-thirds vote of those present, who must number a quorum and vote by roll call.

Debate can precede this vote, with motions permitted to lay the message on the table, postpone action on it, or refer it to committee. If the President's veto is overridden by a two-thirds vote in both houses, the bill becomes law. Otherwise it is dead, and can be revived only by reintroduction and routing through the process all bills undergo.

When bills are passed finally and signed, or passed over a veto, they are given law numbers in numerical order as they become law. There are two series of numbers, one for public and one for private laws, starting at the number "1" for each two-year term of Congress. They are then identified by law number and by Congress—i.e., Private Law 21, 90th Congress; Public Law 250, 90th Congress (or PL 90-250).

Chapter 1—Politics and National Issues

Politics and National Issues

Eight years of Democratic rule came to an end on Jan. 20, 1969, with the inauguration of Richard M. Nixon as 37th President of the United States. It was the climax of one of the great comeback stories of American political history for the Republican whose career had seemed to lie in ruins on the California coast only a dozen years earlier.

International peace and national unity were the themes of Nixon's inaugural address. He asked for a lowering of voices. "No people has ever been so close to the achievement of a just and abundant society, or so possessed of the will to achieve it," he said. But, he warned, "We cannot learn from one another until we stop shouting at one another—until we speak quietly enough so that our words can be heard as well as our voices."

Despite Nixon's appeal for a deflation in rhetoric, his first term was characterized by considerable conflict. He was the first newly elected President in more than a century to be confronted by a Congress controlled by the opposition party. He had been narrowly elected in a three-way contest by a minority of the popular vote. He was assuming the leadership of a nation deeply divided by its most unpopular war. His party, however, had emerged from the 1968 campaign well-organized and well-heeled. The Democrats, by contrast, were splintered and disorganized, with a $9.3-million debt.

But, by the end of Nixon's first four years, much of the dissent had disappeared. This was attributable in large part to his gradual turnover of the Vietnam war by the Americans to the South Vietnamese, and to the apparent assurance of a truce or cease-fire as 1972 neared an end. Nixon carried 49 of the 50 states that November in a second-term triumph of historic dimensions.

1969. Sizable Democratic majorities in both houses of Congress prevented Nixon from realizing many of his goals. The White House and Capitol Hill fought to a standoff on several issues in the President's first year. Administration victory on approval of an anti-ballistic missile system was tempered by Senate defeat of two Supreme Court nominees (one late in 1969, the other early in 1970).

In the fall of 1969, anti-war demonstrators produced the largest crowd, some quarter of a million, in the history of the capital. But Nixon took much of the momentum out of the peace movement by his November announcement of gradual American troop withdrawals.

Besides the war, the country's other most important problem was the economy. "Gradualism" was the administration's initial response. It was less than effective.

1970. Vietnam and the economy continued to preoccupy Congress and the administration in 1970. The President spelled out the "Nixon Doctrine" of foreign policy—economic and military assistance, without direct U.S. involvement, to countries requesting American help.

The war continued, expanding into Laos and Cambodia, and the pitch of the demonstrations became higher. But American troop withdrawals continued as the process of "Vietnamization" went on. Debates on the war tied up the Senate for months.

Four deaths on one college campus and two on another resulted during the quelling of student demonstrations after the U.S. invasion of Cambodia. A presidential commission that studied the problem called for "moral leadership" from Nixon in its report. Vice President Spiro T. Agnew, the administration's alliterative hatchet man, denounced the report as "more pablum for permissiveness."

The economy continued to limp along in what some of its critics described as a combination of inflation, unemployment and recession.

The Democratic-controlled 91st Congress was limping along, too, charged one of its Republican critics, who said it "dawdled, postured, delayed," leading to "confusion and loss of confidence in government." Nixon and Agnew tried to do something about that in the off-year elections, campaigning extensively for Republican House, Senate and gubernatorial candidates. The payoff was limited: A Republican gain of two in the Senate but a loss of nine in the House and 11 in the statehouses.

1971. Nixon's third year was marked by innovation and change. His boldest innovations were in foreign policy; he scheduled trips to China and the Soviet Union in 1972. To dampen inflation, he instituted wage and price controls (the New Economic Policy) that he had rejected when the Democratic Congress gave him the authority to use them in 1970.

Troop withdrawals continued—and so did congressional demands for scheduling a withdrawal deadline for all remaining troops. Three times the Senate passed bills setting a deadline. Twice the House passed weakened versions of the bills. But the President made clear that he did not consider the legislation binding.

References

Discussion of political developments in the United States from 1945-64 may be found in *Congress and the Nation Vol. I*, p. 1-87; for the years 1965-68, *Congress and the Nation Vol. II*, p. 1-45.

1972. In 1971, Nixon had outlined the "six great goals" of his administration: welfare reform, revenue sharing, health insurance reform, environmental initiatives, government reorganization and full employment. In 1972, only one of the six goals was achieved when a bill for general revenue sharing with state and local governments was enacted.

The administration's limited success with domestic legislation was more than balanced by its achievements in foreign policy. A Vietnam cease-fire was within reach at year's end. Nixon had opened a new era of accommodation with China and had become the first American President to visit China and the Soviet Union. The United States and the U.S.S.R. had signed an arms limitation agreement.

Nixon's economic policies in 1972 paid off with additional stability and a growing gross national product, although unemployment remained high. The President vetoed as inflationary a $24.7-billion water pollution control bill, but Congress overrode the veto. Congress refused to give Nixon the $250-billion spending ceiling he asked for.

It all came together for Richard Nixon on Nov. 7, when he was elected to a second term with more than 60 per cent of the popular vote, defeating Sen. George McGovern of South Dakota, the Democratic nominee. Nixon's campaign was a well-financed model of low-profile efficiency. His public appearances were few, and he relied chiefly on surrogates from his administration to wage the campaign. McGovern never recovered from the bitter intraparty dissension that drove many traditional Democrats to vote for the Republican ticket.

Even with his historic landslide, however, Nixon again failed to carry many other candidates with him. The Republicans gained only 13 seats in the House in the 93rd Congress, far short of a majority. The Democrats won two new Senate seats and one governorship. If Nixon's much-touted "new American majority" was approaching reality, it was not reflected in Congress.

Congress in 1969

The first session of the 91st Congress, the sixth longest in history, adjourned on Dec. 23, 1969, with the lowest legislative output in 36 years. Congress cleared 190 bills during the session, all of which were signed by the President. The total number of public laws enacted was the lowest since 1933, when the first session of the 73rd Congress enacted 93 bills into law. Congress was in session for 100 days in 1933, compared with 355 days in 1969. *(Public Laws p. 17)*

Despite the slow pace of the first session—two fiscal 1970 appropriations bills were still pending at adjournment—Congress took major initiatives both in international and domestic areas. The session:

• Passed the most sweeping revision of the tax code in the history of the tax program.

• Expressed a renewed interest in controlling and subjecting to close examination foreign and defense policy, as formulated in the executive branch.

• Shifted priorities proposed by the administration by appropriating $1-billion more for education and half a billion more for pollution control and $5.6-billion less for defense than requested by President Nixon.

The slow pace, which quickened only in November and December as adjournment approached, meant that most government agencies and departments did not receive their appropriations for fiscal 1970 until late in 1969. At the end of session, action was still incomplete on appropriations for foreign aid and Labor-Health, Education and Welfare.

A number of reasons were cited to explain the low legislative yield, which left a large volume of business for the second session:

• The Nixon administration's relatively slow speed in sending its program up to Capitol Hill. Most administration proposals did not emerge until summer.

• A two-month debate in the Senate on deployment of the administration-backed anti-ballistic missile system (ABM).

• The Democratic-controlled Congress' unwillingness to act on Republican Nixon's proposals with the same speed as it had on those of former President Johnson, a Democrat.

• The death of long-time Minority Leader Everett McKinley Dirksen (R Ill.). Dirksen's parliamentary expertise had facilitated White House-congressional liaison.

The low-keyed administration took a strong stand on few issues; the result was that there were few direct confrontations with Congress and few clear-cut victories or defeats.

The administration counted among its victories:

• The Senate's razor-thin defeat by a 50-50 vote of a proposal to kill the ABM program.

• Congress' approval of the draft lottery system, which Nixon termed a top-priority item.

• Congress' retention, in a key House vote, of the administration's plan (the so-called "Philadelphia Plan") to ensure minority hiring by contractors on federal construction projects.

The administration also achieved a defusing of the bitter national and congressional debate on the Vietnam war which had characterized the last two years of the Johnson administration.

The major defeat suffered by the administration came on the Senate's rejection of the nomination of Judge Clement F. Haynsworth Jr. to the Supreme Court. The Senate rejected the nomination by a 45-55 vote Nov. 21 after a three-month-long administration effort to secure confirmation.

LEGISLATIVE ACTION

These were the major domestic and foreign policy developments of the first session of the 91st Congress:

DOMESTIC POLICY. The major piece of legislation passed during the session was the tax reform bill, the most comprehensive revision of the tax code since the income tax was established in 1913. The bill, which required seven months to complete in the House Ways and Means Committee, cleared Congress Dec. 22 with overwhelming majorities in both chambers approving the Senate-House conference report. It was estimated that the bill, when in full effect, would combine annually $9.1-billion in tax cuts and $4.4-billion in Social Security increases with $6.6-billion (net revenue) in long-run tax reform.

A key issue in the year-long debate on tax reform was Nixon's request for extension of the income tax surcharge past its June 30, 1969, expiration date. The President March 26 requested extension of the 10 per cent surtax through June 30, 1970. On April 21, however, he offered his tax reform plan and called for extension of the surtax at 10 per cent through Dec. 31, 1969, and at 5 per cent through June 30, 1970. The House June 30, by a 210-205 vote, approved the President's request for an extension of the surtax. The bulk of the opposition came from liberals who had insisted on meaningful tax reform as a price for the one-year surtax extension and from conservatives who were opposed to increased federal spending implied by higher taxes.

The Senate initially permitted only a six-month extension of the surtax at 10 per cent through Dec. 31, 1969. Senate action came July 31 on a 51-48 vote approving the extension. The House then added the 5 per cent extension to the Tax Reform Act, which it passed Aug. 7; the Senate retained this extension in the tax bill, which it passed Dec. 11.

In another key vote during the debate on tax reform, Senate liberals Dec. 1 won a sizable victory over a traditional target as they defeated by a 30-62 vote an attempt to retain for tax purposes the 27.5 per cent depletion allowance for oil and gas companies. A subsequent vote to reduce the allowance to the 20 per cent voted by the House was defeated 38-52. The final version reduced the figure to 22 per cent, although the President favored retention of the 27.5 per cent allowance.

Congress cleared the administration's draft reform bill, instituting the first draft lottery in 27 years. Nixon Oct. 13 described draft reform as his top-priority legislative request of the session.

Civil Rights. An administration plan to obtain more construction jobs for Negroes on federal projects, the so-called "Philadelphia Plan," was saved Dec. 22 when the House by a 156-208 vote defeated a motion to agree to a Senate rider to the fiscal 1970 supplemental appropriations bill which would have killed the plan.

Education, Welfare. Congress completed action on one education measure, clearing Oct. 16 a bill raising to 10 per cent the ceiling on interest rates on government-insured student loans.

Congress Dec. 20 cleared a bill, requested by the President, extending the antipoverty program through fiscal 1971. This action came after a strong effort in the House, led by Republicans and southern Democrats, attempted to turn the federal program over to the states.

Congress Nov. 6 cleared a bill increasing the fiscal 1970 authorization for the food stamp program from $340-million to $610-million, the figure requested by the President.

Social Security benefits for the 25 million Americans covered were increased by 15 per cent effective Jan. 1, 1970. The increase, incorporated in the tax reform bill which cleared Congress Dec. 22, was 5 per cent more than requested by the President.

The $4.8-billion Housing and Urban Development Act of 1969, passed by Congress Dec. 12, extended major programs under the 1968 Housing and Urban Development Act through fiscal 1971. The act required for the first time that a new low-income dwelling be built for each one razed as part of an urban renewal project.

The Senate Dec. 20 and the House Dec. 22 approved a conference report on the National Environmental Policy Act, aimed at dealing with environmental problems

Historical Comparisons

Richard M. Nixon was the first President elected for a first term failing to obtain control of either chamber of Congress since Zachary Taylor in 1848.

He was the third President elected to either a first or second term since the Civil War failing to carry control of the House of Representatives along with his own election victory. The other three were: Rutherford B. Hayes (R) in 1876, Woodrow Wilson (D) in 1916 and Dwight D. Eisenhower (R) in 1956.

Wilson, elected to his second term in 1916, failed to obtain a Democratic majority in the House. But House Democrats with the support of third party members were able to retain control of the House.

When the presidency changes from control of one party to another, the President-elect's party usually —but not always—gains seats in the House. Since the Civil War, this has happened in six of the 10 elections where the opposition party won the presidency. In four of the elections, however, the party winning the presidency lost seats in the House. This was because the party had made large gains in the off-year election preceding the presidential election year.

The six Presidents whose party gained House seats were:

Harrison (R), 1888—plus 22 seats
Wilson (D), 1912—plus 62 seats
Harding (R), 1920—plus 63 seats
Roosevelt (D), 1932—plus 97 seats
Eisenhower (R), 1952—plus 22 seats
Nixon (R), 1968—plus 4 seats

The Presidents whose party lost seats in the House, despite winning the White House from the opposite party, were:

Cleveland (D), 1884 and 1892—lost 18 and 11 seats
McKinley (R), 1896—lost 40 seats
Kennedy (D), 1960—lost 20 seats

on a preventive basis, setting up a Council on Environmental Quality and establishing a national policy on the environment.

Mine Safety. Congress approved a comprehensive coal mine health and safety act providing compensation for victims of black lung disease and setting standards to prevent coal mine disasters.

FOREIGN, DEFENSE POLICY. Foreign economic and military assistance continued on a downward trend as Congress Dec. 19 passed a bill authorizing the lowest amount in the history of the foreign assistance program, $1.6-billion for economic assistance and $350-million in military assistance. The $1.97-billion total was below the administration's $2.6-billion request, also the lowest request in the program's history.

Foreign aid legislation was incomplete as the session ended. The Senate voted Dec. 20 to table the conference report on the foreign aid appropriations bill, objecting to a House-voted $54.5-million for jet aircraft for Nationalist China. The Senate vote delayed final action on other related foreign aid programs contained in the aid appropriations bill, including funds for a new Overseas Private

Investment Corporation, for the Peace Corps and for the U.S. contribution to the International Development Association.

Congressional debate on the administration's Vietnam policy was muted throughout most of the year. In the aftermath of the nationwide "moratorium" anti-war demonstrations and mass rally in Washington, the House Dec. 15 passed by a 334-55 vote a resolution supporting the President's efforts to achieve "peace with honor" in Vietnam. While Nixon regarded the vote as manifesting approval of his Vietnam policy, House doves voting for the resolution said it should not be interpreted as support for the administration's policy in Vietnam.

In a major effort to reassert congressional prerogatives in foreign policy, the Senate June 25 passed by a 70-16 vote a "national commitments resolution" designed to place the executive branch on notice that the Senate regarded the commitment of U.S. forces to the defense of a foreign country as requiring congressional approval. The resolution did not have the force of law, however.

In a more specific effort to limit the use of U.S. troops abroad, the Senate Dec. 15 by a 73-17 vote added a provision to the defense appropriations bill prohibiting the use of U.S. ground combat troops in Laos or Thailand.

In other major foreign policy actions:

● The Senate March 13 ratified the treaty banning the spread of nuclear arms to non-nuclear nations.

● Congress Dec. 23 cleared a two-year extension of the Export Control Act.

A major development during the session was the critical scrutiny that Congress, particularly the Senate, focused on defense spending. The main result of this attention was passage Dec. 18 of a defense appropriations bill totaling $69.6-billion, $8-billion under the outgoing Johnson administration's estimate of $77.7-billion and $5.6-billion under the revised Nixon administration estimate.

A two-month debate in the Senate took place over the administration's plan (Safeguard) to deploy ABM missiles to defend U.S. retaliatory missile sites against a first-strike attack. The administration won a narrow victory Aug. 6 as two key votes defeated efforts to block Safeguard. A 50-50 vote defeated a proposal to block any work on the Safeguard system, and a 49-51 vote defeated a proposal to limit work on Safeguard to research.

INTERNAL CONGRESSIONAL MATTERS

The House was struck a smarting blow in June when the Supreme Court held, by a 7-1 vote, that Rep. Adam C. Powell (D N.Y.) had been unconstitutionally excluded from the House March 1, 1967. The House Jan. 3, 1969, had voted to fine Powell $25,000, purportedly for at least partial recovery of about $40,000 in congressional funds he allegedly misused, and to strip him of his 22-year seniority. It then permitted him to take the oath of office.

In the Senate, there were signs of renewed liberal vigor on both sides of the aisle. The Democratic leadership Jan. 3 voted 31-26 to make Sen. Edward M. Kennedy (Mass.) its majority whip (assistant majority leader). The vote, by secret ballot, was a major upset for Sen. Russell B. Long (D La.), who had held the job since 1965.

Republican senators became increasingly vocal in their criticism of their conservative fellow members. At the core of their unrest early in the year was Minority Leader Everett McKinley Dirksen (Ill. 1951-69). Before his death Sept. 7, Dirksen was a central figure in the fight against the effort by Secretary of Health, Education and Welfare Robert H. Finch to nominate Dr. John Knowles as his chief aide on health matters. Opposed because of his views on public medicine, Knowles met with resistance from elements of the American Medical Association and from Dirksen. Dirksen told an April news conference he would prevent confirmation if the nomination went to the Senate.

Dirksen also was credited with blocking the nomination of Dr. Franklin Long to head the National Science Foundation. Long was an opponent of the antiballistic missile proposals, and Dirksen favored the ABM system.

Senate Republicans Sept. 24 elected Hugh Scott (Pa.), a moderate, over conservative Howard H. Baker Jr. (Tenn.) to succeed Dirksen as minority leader. Appointed to serve the remainder of Dirksen's Senate term, which expired in 1971, was Ralph T. Smith (R).

Presidential Record, 1969

President Nixon ended his first year in office confronted with the two overriding problems he had faced when he was sworn in Jan. 20—the war in Vietnam and the inflationary growth of the economy.

Against this backdrop, Nixon during 1969 was faced with the difficulties inherent in turning campaign slogans and promises into real policies, programs and proposals. He had to restaff the top echelons of the government while ensuring that the huge federal bureaucracy kept moving. He had to give direction to the Republican Party and make peace with the Democratic-controlled Congress. And he had to perform the duties and make the decisions that American citizens and the rest of the world expect from a President of the United States.

As 1969 drew to a close, the news media and other White House watchers attempted to assess Nixon's first year in the presidency. Throughout their comments, there seemed to run two recurrent thoughts: the President increasingly was trying to isolate his critics by broad appeals to "middle America"—to the "silent majority" which he conceived of as his real constituency; the President had miscalculated the level of opposition to his policies in Congress and had failed to listen either seriously or regularly to the views of members of Congress.

Critics acknowledged that Nixon in 1969 faced some unusual problems and some largely uncontrollable problems—he was the first President in more than a century to face a Congress dominated by the opposition party in his first term, and he entered office with the burdens of an unpopular war affecting every facet of domestic life.

Nixon's first year brought him both a reassuring victory and a stunning defeat on Capitol Hill. His foremost victory came with congressional approval of the controversial Safeguard (ABM). His worst defeat was the Senate's refusal to confirm his nomination of Haynsworth to the United States Supreme Court.

1969 Elections

Two governorships, seven vacant U.S. House seats and the mayoralties of several major cities were at stake in the 1969 elections. These contests were closely watched as an indication of voter acceptance of the Nixon administration and of what could be expected in the 1970 elections.

Voters in New Jersey and Virginia elected new governors and the lower houses of their state legislatures, while voters in Kentucky elected a new general assembly. About 850 cities held municipal elections.

(Most major mayoral elections are held in odd-numbered years. This timing prevents conflict between these elections and most state and federal elections held in even-numbered years.)

GOVERNORS

The success of Republican gubernatorial candidates Linwood Holton in Virginia and Rep. William T. Cahill in New Jersey gave President Nixon a big political boost in a year when Democrats won five of the seven special elections for the House.

Holton's victory gave Virginia Republicans their first governor in 100 years. Holton, a Roanoke attorney and staunch supporter of Nixon, defeated William C. Battle (D), a former ambassador to Australia. Incumbent Mills E. Godwin Jr. (D) was ineligible to succeed himself to a second four-year term.

Cahill, a member of the House since 1959, defeated former Democratic Gov. Robert B. Meyner (1954-62) by 500,902 votes—the largest margin ever recorded in a race for governor in New Jersey. The Republicans had not held the statehouse in 16 years. Incumbent Gov. Richard J. Hughes (D) was ineligible to succeed himself to a third four-year term.

HOUSE

Of the seven House seats filled by special elections in 1969, two of the vacancies resulted from the deaths of Rep. Robert A. Everett (D Tenn. 1958-69) and Rep. William H. Bates (R Mass. 1950-69). A third resulted from an appointment made by Gov. Ronald Reagan (R Calif.). A fourth resulted from the resignation of Rep. Charles S. Joelson (D N.J. 1961-69) to accept a state judgeship. The other three vacancies resulted from appointments made by Nixon. Democrats captured five of the seven seats.

One vacant House seat remained at the end of the year. Illinois Gov. Richard B. Ogilvie (R) decided against calling a special election to fill the vacancy created by the Aug. 13 death of Rep. Daniel J. Ronan (D Ill. 1956-69), and the seat remained vacant until the regular 1970 election.

These were the results of the seven elections:

California. Voters in California's 27th Congressional District (North Central Los Angeles County—parts of Burbank, Sherman Oaks) April 29 elected Barry Goldwater Jr. (R), 30, a Los Angeles stockbroker, to fill the vacancy caused by the resignation of Edwin Reinecke (R 1965-69). Reinecke resigned, at Gov. Reagan's request, to become lieutenant governor of California. Goldwater, son of Sen. Barry Goldwater (R Ariz.), the 1964 Republican nominee for President, defeated John K. Van de Kamp (D), 33, a former attorney for the Department of Justice.

Montana. Voters in Montana's 2nd Congressional District (East—Great Falls, Billings) June 24 elected John Melcher (D) to fill the vacancy caused by the Feb. 27 resignation of James F. Battin (R 1961-69). Battin was appointed by Nixon to a federal district court judgeship. Melcher defeated State Rep. William S. Mather (R).

Tennessee. Voters in Tennessee's 8th Congressional District (Northeast—Memphis suburbs, Dyersburg) March 25 chose Edward Jones (D), 56, a former state commissioner of agriculture, to fill the vacancy created by the death of Everett. Jones led a field of 10 candidates.

Wisconsin. Voters in Wisconsin's 7th Congressional District (Central—Wausau) April 1 chose State Assemblyman David R. Obey (D), 30, to fill the seat vacated by Melvin R. Laird (R 1953-69), who resigned as representative in January to become secretary of defense. Obey defeated State Sen. Walter J. Chilsen (R), 45.

Massachusetts. Voters in Massachusetts' 6th Congressional District (Northeast) Sept. 30 elected State Rep. Michael J. Harrington (D), 33, an opponent of administration Vietnam policies, to fill the vacancy created by the death of Bates. Harrington scored a narrow victory over State Sen. William L. Saltonstall (R), 42.

New Jersey. Voters in New Jersey's 8th Congressional District (Passaic County) Nov. 4 chose Robert A. Roe (D), 45, state commissioner of conservation and economic development, to fill the vacancy created by the Sept. 4 resignation of Joelson, who resigned to become a state superior court judge. Roe defeated Eugene Boyle Jr. (R), 49, a restaurant owner.

Illinois. Voters in Illinois' 13th Congressional District (Cook County—north and northwest suburbs) Nov. 25 elected Philip M. Crane (R), 39, to fill the seat vacated by Donald Rumsfeld (R 1963-69), who resigned as representative May 26 to become director of the Office of Economic Opportunity.

MAYORALTIES

Mayoral contests in early 1969 underscored the concern of white voters over law and order. Observers at the time thought that these contests would set the theme for the 1970 elections. But by the end of the year, although law and order was a consideration, it was not generally the determining factor in the Nov. 4 municipal election results. In most of the major cities, candidates who took the strongest law-and-order positions were defeated. Following are summaries of some of the key contests.

Los Angeles. Mayor Sam Yorty May 27 won election to a third term, defeating City Councilman Thomas Bradley, who sought to become Los Angeles' first black mayor.

Minneapolis. Police Lt. Charles Stenvig June 10 was elected mayor of Minneapolis in voting that appeared to reflect the concern of middle- and lower-income white residents with law and order. Stenvig, 41, as an independent Democrat, easily defeated Republican City Council President Dan Cohen, 32, in the nonpartisan runoff election.

Atlanta. Vice Mayor Sam Massell, a liberal Democrat backed by a new coalition of Negroes and white liberals, Oct. 21 won a runoff election for mayor of Atlanta. Massell, 42, defeated Alderman Rodney Cook, 45, a moderate Republican who had the backing of Atlanta's white business community.

New York. Mayor John V. Lindsay climaxed an uphill fight for a second four-year term Nov. 4 with a victory over candidates of the major parties in New

York City. Lindsay's win, as the Liberal Party Nominee, over Democrat Mario A. Procaccino and Republican-Conservative John J. Marchi affirmed on axiom of New York City politics: the most liberal candidate will be elected. He outran two men who campaigned heavily on law-and-order issues and appeals to the so-called "forgotten American" of the white middle class. Lindsay demonstrated that a candidacy built on "the poor, the young and the black" could have electoral potency. His comeback, after he lost to Marchi in the Republican primary, was forged through support from those groups, received much of its initial momentum from dissident and reform Democrats and was confirmed by the mayor's determined attention to the Jewish voters who gave him the winning margin.

Detroit. Wayne County Sheriff Roman S. Gribbs won election Nov. 4 as mayor of Detroit, surviving a late surge in voter appeal by County Auditor Richard H. Austin, a black. The winning margin was the narrowest in city history. The underlying issues of the campaign were crime and race, though both candidates ran low-key campaigns. Gribbs, while emphasizing crime and his ability as a professional to deal with it, tried at the same time to cast a moderate image.

Cleveland. Cleveland's Carl B. Stokes (D), the first black mayor of a major American city, won a second term Nov. 4, defeating Republican Ralph J. Perk, the Cuyahoga County auditor, and a third candidate.

Pittsburgh. Peter F. Flaherty (D), running without full support of the city's traditionally powerful Democratic machine, easily defeated John K. Tabor (R), a moderate.

Buffalo. Mayor Frank A. Sedita (D) was elected to his second consecutive term over Alfreda W. Slominski (R), a conservative whose campaign stressed law and order. A liberal Negro candidate, running as an independent, ran third.

Louisville. Former Rep. Frank W. Burke (D 1959-63) defeated Republican John P. Sawyer and two minor-party candidates for mayor, returning Democratic rule to the city after an eight-year Republican reign.

Congress in 1970

The second session of the 91st Congress, which did not adjourn until Jan. 2, 1971, compiled a substantial record of domestic accomplishments despite drawn-out disputes with President Nixon over foreign policy and spending. The session finally ended less than 24 hours before the constitutional adjournment deadline of noon on Jan. 3.

In the final rush, Congress cleared a series of bills dealing with foreign aid and foreign military sales, including a repeal of the 1964 Tonkin Gulf resolution, and agreed to interim funding for the controversial supersonic transport (SST) plane. Bills which died at the session's end were a Social Security increase, the President's welfare reform plan, import restrictions and aid for school districts in the process of desegregating.

The Senate in the 91st Congress made the first substantial attempt since World War II to challenge the President's authority on foreign policy and military involvement. Although the House generally agreed to uphold Nixon's requests to finance new weapons systems

and to send money and troops into Southeast Asia, the Senate engaged in numerous long debates on those issues.

At the end of 1970, during debates on foreign aid authorizations and appropriations, the Senate challenged Nixon's policy in Cambodia. Congress finally cleared the legislation but included a modified restriction on the use of ground troops in that nation.

It was in the field of domestic legislation, however, that Congress compiled its most substantial record of accomplishment. This included establishment of a government-owned postal corporation, major air and water pollution control measures, a $25-billion education authorization, a farm bill including a limit on subsidy payments, an airport-airway trust fund, a package extending the 1965 Voting Rights Act and allowing 18-year-olds to vote in national elections, the first national occupational safety bill, extension of unemployment compensation and four major crime bills.

Clashing Views. Apparently anticipating more partisan skirmishes in the first session of the 92nd Congress—scheduled to convene on Jan. 21, 1971, only 19 days after adjournment of the 91st—leaders of both parties had conflicting assessments of the 91st Congress' record.

"The nation was the loser" in the prolonged legislative battles, said the Republican President in a statement assessing the 91st Congress. The Democratic House majority leader, Carl Albert (Okla.), retorted that he was dismayed at Nixon's comments, in view of Congress' "major accomplishments" in the face of administration shortcomings.

The President reserved his strongest criticism for the Senate. "In the final month and weeks of 1970," he said, "the nation was presented with the spectacle of a legislative body that had seemingly lost the capacity to decide and the will to act. When the path was finally cleared, vital days had been lost, and major failures insured.

"In probably no month in recent memory did the reputation of the whole Congress suffer more in the eyes of the American people than in the month of December 1970," Nixon said. "In these times when the need to build confidence in government is so apparent, that was good neither for the Congress nor the country. Let us hope that it never takes place again."

Albert, who was to be elected House Speaker at the beginning of the 92nd Congress, said, "It is difficult to understand the President's most recent attack on Congress. In light of the major accomplishments of the 91st Congress in the fields of health, pollution control, human rights and crime control, among others, the condemnation voiced by the President is amazing. Not Congress but the administration will surely be remembered for what it failed to do—for its failure to halt inflation, for its failure to stop rising unemployment and for its failure to gain and hold the confidence of the country," Albert said in a prepared statement.

Nixon listed legislative areas in which he charged Congress did not take needed action during the final session, and he emphasized three reform measures. These were consolidation of federal grant-in-aid programs, a proposal to share federal revenues with states and local governments, and the Family Assistance Plan, a welfare reform bill.

Albert said the House passed nearly every measure mentioned by the President in his statement. He did not mention Nixon's vetoes of nine measures that cleared the 91st Congress. *(Vetoes, Appendix p. 101a)*

Legislative proposals, Mr. Nixon said, which were neglected included emergency funds to help school districts desegregate, new methods of dealing with national emergency strikes, increases in Social Security benefits, assistance to American Indians and a tax on airline tickets to pay for protection against hijackings.

The President also called for revision of the "turn-of-the-century" work schedules and procedures that are used in Congress. "While there are many excuses for congressional inaction, there are no good reasons," he said.

Disputes with President. Congress in 1970 quarreled with the President over spending priorities. It sliced funds from his military, foreign aid and space requests and added money to numerous domestic programs, notably education, health, manpower training and pollution control. Congress enacted a spending ceiling for fiscal 1971, the third year in a row it had done so.

In addition to disputes over spending, Nixon and the Congress disagreed several times over the form of domestic programs. Among the bills vetoed by the President were two health measures—authorizing hospital construction and setting up a program to encourage family doctors. He sought unsuccessfully to get Congress to consolidate elementary and secondary education programs and a variety of housing programs. He pressed without success for a revenue-sharing proposal in which a portion of federal tax revenues would be turned back to the states. All these moves, he said, would help simplify the proliferation of related federal programs and would give states a greater role in establishing programs within their borders.

In response, Congress continued to fund these programs separately and in some cases added new federal programs rather than consolidating old ones.

Just before the November elections, Nixon vetoed a bill to reduce campaign spending for radio and television advertising. He said it discriminated against broadcasters, helped incumbents and did not provide needed over-all reform. Despite complaints during the 1970 congressional elections of record spending on broadcast advertising, the veto was sustained in a post-election vote. Sponsors promised to consider a stronger campaign spending measure before the 1972 presidential election.

LEGISLATIVE ACTION

These were the major domestic and foreign policy developments of the second session of the 91st Congress:

DOMESTIC. Congress and the administration worked in greater harmony to establish new federal agencies to handle special duties. Foremost among these was the government-owned postal corporation to replace the Post Office Department. Congress also agreed to the President's reorganization plans to set up an independent Environmental Protection Agency and a National Atmospheric and Oceanic Administration in the Commerce Department. The 1970 housing bill established a corporation to help finance new communities.

In the transportation field, Congress enacted legislation establishing an airport-airways development trust fund and a semi-public corporation to operate a nationwide rail passenger service.

Economic Policy and Welfare. Congress imposed ceilings on federal spending—$200.8-billion plus $4.5-billion in uncontrollables for fiscal 1971. And it insisted on giving the President authority to set wage and price controls—although Nixon said he did not want such authority.

In the final days of the 1970 session, Congress completed action on a bill extending the food stamp program which, for the first time, provided free food stamps for the poorest families. Included was a requirement that recipients must register for and accept employment as a condition for receiving the stamps. Earlier in the year, Congress enacted an extension of the subsidized lunch program for school children.

The administration's Family Assistance Plan would have provided welfare families with a minimum federal benefit of $1,600 a year, with reduced benefits for families with limited incomes. It would have increased benefits for the blind, disabled and elderly poor and reduced state costs for welfare programs. The House approved the plan early in 1970, but the Senate Finance Committee approved only a trial run rather than full implementation. In the last days of the 1970 session, the Senate balked at even a welfare test, and the legislation died at adjournment.

Environment, Consumers, Labor. Congress cleared two far-reaching pollution abatement measures. The Clean Air Amendments of 1970 established specific deadlines for a 90 per cent reduction of certain pollutants from new automobiles. The bill contained new research programs, establishment of national air quality standards, fuel limitations and standards for new stationary sources of pollution. Earlier in the second session, Congress completed action on the Water Quality Improvement Act, which set liability for cleanup costs of oil spills and established controls on acid mine drainage.

Concern for child protection moved the 91st Congress to enact two major consumer protection bills. A toy safety bill was designed to protect children from toys which contained thermal, electrical or mechanical hazards. A Safe Packaging Act required manufacturers to market dangerous substances in safety containers to reduce the accidental poisonings of children from cleansers, polishes, medicines and other potentially hazardous household goods.

Congress cleared an industrial safety and health bill authorizing the secretary of labor to establish work standards and setting up a special commission to enforce regulations. In December 1970, President Nixon vetoed a $9.5-billion manpower training authorization which would have reorganized manpower programs and established a public service job program. Nixon said that the bill failed to link public jobs with training or other employment opportunities. The Senate sustained the veto by a 48-35 vote—eight short of the two-thirds majority needed to override.

Civil Rights. In 1970, Congress enacted an organized crime bill extending federal jurisdiction over gambling and authorizing the use of civil antitrust remedies against businesses infiltrated by racketeers. Another approved package was the District of Columbia crime bill, which authorized pre-trial or preventive detention, allowed police officers to enter the premises of a suspect under certain conditions without announcing themselves (the "no-knock" provision), revamped the city's court system and revised the juvenile code.

Over initial administration opposition, Congress cleared the Voting Rights Act of 1970 extending the 1965 voting rights law for another five years. The new law lowered the voting age to 18 for presidential and congressional elections, suspended literacy tests and limited residence requirements for presidential elections to 30 days.

Housing, Education, Welfare. In mid-December 1970, Congress finished action on a housing bill including a new program of federal crime insurance and creating a Community Development Corporation to carry out loan and grant programs for development of new communities.

The major education legislation of the 91st Congress was a three-year, $25-billion authorization for elementary and secondary education programs. The bill, cleared in early 1970, raised the income ceiling for determining the number of poor children in the existing program of aid to school districts with concentrations of underprivileged children.

Congress overrode President Nixon's veto to enact a three-year authorization of the Hill-Burton hospital construction program. The bill provided $2.79-billion for grants and loans to construct and modernize hospitals and health facilities. The President had recommended establishing a system of direct loans and grants rather than categorical grants.

Congressional, Federal Operations. Congress enacted the first substantial legislative reform bill in 24 years, the Legislative Reorganization Act of 1970. The bill revised committee procedures in the House and Senate, required that House teller votes be recorded by name, made committee votes public and reorganized the legislative reference service.

In another 1970 law, Congress authorized a nonvoting delegate in the House to represent the District of Columbia. The city scheduled a delegate election for early 1971.

In 1970, Congress set up an independent government-owned corporation to take over mail service. The bill gave federal employees, including postal employees, pay raises and eliminated political patronage in the appointment of postmasters.

Court Nominees. The Senate rejected a second Nixon nominee to the Supreme Court. G. Harrold Carswell was rejected by a 45-51 vote in April 1970. In May 1970, the Senate approved the nomination of Harry A. Blackmun.

Supersonic Transport. Final adjournment was held up because of disagreement over continued funding for the SST, included in the fiscal 1971 Transportation Department appropriations bill. The House approved $290-million for further development of the plane; the Senate voted to drop the funds altogether. Conferees settled on $210-million, which the House approved. But the Senate got tied up in a filibuster over the funds, and eventually agreed to a temporary funding measure extending only through March 30, 1971, with the understanding that SST funds for the rest of fiscal 1971 would be voted on separately from other transportation funds.

FOREIGN, DEFENSE POLICY. In 1970, the President sought to add six additional sites to the Safeguard ABM network, but Congress approved only one.

Congress engaged in debates over the Indochina war in attempts to limit deployment of troops and additional funding. The Senate voted twice to repeal the Tonkin Gulf resolution, and the House eventually agreed to enact one repeal into law.

Major Senate anti-war debates centered on the foreign aid and defense money bills. In November 1970, Nixon asked for a supplemental foreign aid allotment of $1.035-billion—including $500-million for military credit sales to Israel, $255-million for aid to Cambodia, and additional funds for Vietnam and Korea. Congress approved this in a supplemental appropriations bill.

Presidential Record, 1970

At the end of his second year in office, President Nixon had been credited by many Americans with devising a workable formula for disengaging the United States from what continued to be a frustrating war in Southeast Asia. His troop withdrawals from Vietnam and the turning over of combat responsibilities to the South Vietnamese were widely regarded as an acceptable beginning.

In addition, the President had set forth in February 1970 a new policy—termed the Nixon Doctrine—which had as its goal avoiding direct U.S. military involvement in remote corners of the globe. Washington would continue and possibly increase its economic and military assistance to enable foreign nations to defend themselves without recourse to direct U.S. involvement.

Despite Nixon's efforts in Vietnam, the apparent extension of the Vietnam war to neighboring Laos and Cambodia gave rise to the fear that the United States might still be bogged down in Southeast Asia. Nixon's April decision to send U.S. troops into Cambodia triggered widespread opposition demonstrations.

The war was not a prominent issue in the 1970 elections. The administration's troop withdrawal policy had effectively nullified the war as a campaign issue.

Members of Congress from both political parties praised the President for his Oct. 7, 1970, speech calling for an Indochina cease-fire, widened peace talks and the release of war and political prisoners.

The war re-emerged as an issue after the election as a result of the President's decisions in November ordering an attempted helicopter rescue mission of U.S. prisoners of war near Hanoi and renewed bombing missions in North Vietnam and his decision to seek funds from Congress for military assistance to Cambodia.

The American economy, which had reached the trillion-dollar level in its annual output of goods and services on Dec. 15, continued to be plagued with deeply rooted inflation. The Nixon administration, critics charged, had achieved recession, unemployment and inflation simultaneously.

In early 1970, the emphasis of the President's economic policies shifted to recovery from the slowdown, although efforts continued to control inflation. The administration took some comfort publicly that unemployment remained below 6 per cent of the labor force until December, that the rate of price increases slowed modestly and that the economy would have registered substantial gains if output had not fallen in the fourth quarter because of a General Motors strike.

But as Mr. Nixon began his third year as President, the nation was still experiencing rising unemployment, falling output and profits of a recession, and had gained little relief from the escalating prices of inflation. As 1970 ended, critical demands increased that the administration adopt more effective policies both to stimulate a rapid recovery and to control inflation.

1970 Elections

Despite the unprecedented off-year campaign efforts of President Nixon and Vice President Agnew, most observers felt the Republicans suffered a net loss in the congressional and gubernatorial elections of Nov. 3, 1970.

In 35 Senate contests, Republicans made a net gain of two seats. But they fell five short of their goal of seven, the minimum needed to take numerical control. The Senate in the 92nd Congress was divided between 55 Democrats and 45 Republicans.

Democratic gains in the nation's governorships were the most impressive since 1938. The net improvement for the Democrats in the 45 gubernatorial contests was 11, reversing control of the statehouses from 32 Republican and 18 Democratic to 29 Democratic and 21 Republican.

In the 435 House elections, Democrats strengthened their existing majority by a net gain of nine seats, giving them a 255-180 advantage over the Republicans in the 92nd Congress. Republicans could claim success in limiting Democratic gains to far less than the 38-seat average improvement shown by the party out of power in non-presidential election years. Fifty-six newcomers were seated in the new House convening in January 1971—33 Democrats and 23 Republicans.

Two aspects of the 1970 campaigns were of particular interest:

● The influence of television and "image-making" made the congressional campaigns the most expensive in history up to that time. Some estimates of expenditures ranged as high as $125-million for total costs of production and air time for political broadcasts, and for other normal costs of primary and general election campaigns. Skyrocketing campaign costs spawned new demands for reducing political spending and more stringent laws regarding reporting of campaign contributions.

● Two dominant issues of the 1960s—the Vietnam war and the struggle for equal civil rights—were subdued in 1970. Chief concerns in most campaigns were economic matters, particularly unemployment and inflation. Another issue was the repeated call for "law and order" by many candidates.

These issues gave voters a chance to express their views on the performance of the Nixon administration, but the verdict was ambiguous. A Congressional Quarterly survey indicated that the 1970 Senate campaigns produced no clear trends on national issues. The survey showed conservatives receiving a slight boost in the Senate, with the House taking a slight turn to the left.

In a statement Nov. 4, 1970, at the Western White House, Nixon emphasized what he regarded as an ideological shift in his party's favor. "We have increased our majority now to a working majority," he said. "We have a working majority in both the House and the Senate for national defense and also for foreign policy, a working majority of four in the Senate, which means that in terms of the President's ability to conduct foreign policy, to make decisions that he considers and that his administration considers are important to the future of the country

Results of 1970 Elections

SENATE

	Old Lineup	Gains/ Losses	New Line-up
Democrats	57	— 2	55*
Republicans	43	+ 2	45*

GOVERNORS

Democrats	18	+11	29
Republicans	32	—11	21

HOUSE

Democrats	247	+ 9	255
Republicans	188	— 9	180

* *Harry F. Byrd Jr. (Va.), elected as an independent, caucused with the Democrats; James L. Buckley (N.Y.), elected as a Conservative, caucused with the Republicans.*

and to the cause of peace generally, that he can speak with a much stronger voice in the world than was previously the case."

Lawrence F. O'Brien, the Democratic national chairman, made no mention of ideology but claimed a "resounding defeat" for the Republicans, particularly in their losses of governorships. "The presidency was won and lost—in 1968 in precisely those areas where the Democrats scored their most impressive victories on Tuesday: in the South, the Midwest, the Southwest and the Far West," said O'Brien. The Democrats, he said, had "recaptured the electoral base that is vital to winning the White House in 1972."

Administration Campaigning. O'Brien also took a slap at the activist role played by Nixon and Agnew during the campaign. "It need not have been a national referendum and would not have been one had the administration not insisted on calling it one, and now President Nixon must live with the results," said the Democratic leader.

Those results amounted to only a limited success. In their drive to improve the Republican position in Congress and in state capitals, the President campaigned for candidates in 23 states during the weeks preceding the election, and the Vice President, who began traveling early in September, visited 29 states.

Although the impact of a presidential appearance for a candidate was unclear, Nixon and Agnew could point to victories in several states where they campaigned: Senate victories in Maryland, Connecticut, Ohio and Tennessee, for example, and gubernatorial victories in Connecticut, Tennessee, California, Arizona, Iowa, Vermont and Wyoming.

But administration efforts failed to pay off in other states on the Republican target list. Democratic candidates were elected to the Senate in Utah, New Mexico, Wyoming, Nevada, North Dakota and Indiana, despite the high-level administration campaigning. And Nixon or

Agnew visits failed to persuade voters to elect Republican senators in California, Texas, Illinois or Florida. Republicans lost governorships in 11 states visited by the President or Vice President: Nevada, New Mexico, Minnesota, Nebraska, Ohio, Oklahoma, Wisconsin, South Dakota, Arkansas, Florida and Pennsylvania.

Third-Party Candidates. A total of 274 independent or minor-party candidates were on the ballots in 40 states. Most were conservatives; at least 85 candidates in 22 states ran for Congress or governorships on the remnants of the 1968 American Independent Party (AIP) organization of George C. Wallace.

The most spectacular third-party victory of the year was that of James L. Buckley of New York, a Conservative who was elected to the Senate with a minority of the votes. Buckley's election was made possible by a division of the votes for the Republican-Liberal incumbent, Charles E. Goodell, and the Democratic candidate, Rep. Richard L. Ottinger. Buckley said he was a registered Republican who would caucus with Senate Republicans.

Another third-party success belonged to Sen. Harry F. Byrd Jr. of Virginia. In March 1970, veteran Democrat Byrd announced that he would not run as a Democrat because of a party "loyalty oath" that he claimed would force him to committee himself to the Democratic presidential candidate in 1972.

Instead, Byrd ran as an independent. He easily defeated the Democratic and Republican candidates. He continued caucusing with the majority Democrats in the 92nd Congress.

Although neither Buckley nor Byrd had the Republican endorsement, both were unusual cases in that they had the tacit endorsement of the White House. Without endorsing Buckley directly, Agnew assailed Republican Sen. Goodell as a "radical-liberal" who should be replaced. And the White House pointedly refused to endorse Byrd's conservative Republican opponent, Ray L. Garland.

A second incumbent Democratic senator who ran as an independent was Thomas J. Dodd of Connecticut. Dodd had been censured by the Senate in 1967 for diverting testimonial funds to his personal use. He was regarded as unlikely to win the Senate nomination in a Democratic primary. His independent candidacy divided the Democratic vote and helped elect a Republican to his seat.

Other minor-party candidates did even less well. No others were elected to Congress or governorships, although several candidates of the predominantly black National Democratic Party of Alabama made respectable showings. The party's gubernatorial candidate, Dr. John Cashin, received 15 per cent of the vote in a three-way race.

The Alabama elections were not without irony. Wallace, the AIP presidential candidate in 1968, was returned by a large majority in 1970, as a Democrat, to the governorship he had held from 1963 to 1967. But in other states, most AIP candidates received less than 3 per cent of the vote.

SENATE

Of the 35 Senate seats contested in 1970, 11 were won by Republicans, 22 by Democrats, one by a Conserva-

tive Party candidate (who caucused with the Republicans) and one by an independent (who caucused with the Democrats). Democrats had held 25 of the seats and Republicans, 10.

Republicans who captured Democratic seats were:
- Rep. Lowell P. Weicker Jr. (R Conn. 1969-71), who beat Democrat Joseph D. Duffey and incumbent Thomas J. Dodd, a Democrat running as an independent.
- Rep. J. Glenn Beall Jr. (R Md. 1969-71), who upset Sen. Joseph D. Tydings (D 1965-71) by a narrow margin.
- Rep. Robert Taft Jr. (R Ohio 1963-65, 1967-71), who resisted a strong challenge by Democrat Howard Metzenbaum for the Senate seat being vacated by retiring Stephen M. Young (D 1959-71).
- Rep. Bill Brock (R Tenn. 1963-71), who defeated incumbent Albert Gore (D 1953-71) in a bitter contest.

But Democratic candidates won seats from Republicans in two key states, California and Illinois. Winners were:
- Rep. John V. Tunney (D Calif. 1965-71), who defeated Sen. George Murphy (R 1965-71).
- Adlai E. Stevenson III, son of the late Democratic presidential candidate, who defeated appointee Ralph T. Smith (R 1969-70).

Incumbents were re-elected in all but four other states. The four, in which the incumbent Senators were retiring or were defeated in primaries, were:
- **Delaware.** Rep. William V. Roth Jr. (R 1967-71) easily won election over Jacob W. Zimmerman (D) to the seat vacated by retiring Sen. John J. Williams (R 1947-71).
- **Florida.** State Sen. Lawton Chiles (D) defeated Rep. William C. Cramer (R 1955-71) by a sizable margin for the seat held by retiring Spessard L. Holland (D 1946-71).
- **Minnesota.** Hubert H. Humphrey (D) won back a seat in the Senate, where he served from 1949 to 1965, the year he became vice president. He defeated Rep. Clark MacGregor (R 1961-71) for retiring Democrat Eugene J. McCarthy's seat (1959-71).
- **Texas.** Former Rep. Lloyd M. Bentsen Jr. (D 1948-55) defeated Rep. George Bush (R 1967-71) for the seat held by Ralph W. Yarborough (D 1957-71), defeated in the May 2 primary.

GOVERNORS

Democrats in 1970 took 13 governorships from Republican control, while losing only two—in Tennessee and Connecticut.

The state-level gains were doubly significant in 1970. Democratic control of a majority of the states furnished vital power bases for the 1972 presidential elections. Newly elected Democratic governors immediately emerged as potential national leaders. Among them were:
- Dale Bumpers, the relatively unknown country lawyer who defeated Republican Winthrop Rockefeller's bid for a third term as governor of Arkansas.
- Reubin Askew, the state senator who unseated Florida's eccentric incumbent Republican, Claude R. Kirk Jr.
- John J. Gilligan, a former representative (1965-67) who took the Ohio statehouse from Republican hands by defeating State Auditor Roger Cloud (R).

• Millionaire industrialist Milton J. Shapp, who won Pennsylvania's Democratic primary without his party's endorsement and went on to win the governorship.

• Wendell R. Anderson, a young former all-American hockey player, who won the Minnesota governorship.

The Democratic gubernatorial gains in 1970 held implications for the make-up of future Congresses. Before the 1972 elections, state legislatures had the task of redrawing congressional district lines to match the changes in population distribution indicated by the 1970 census figures. Every governor but one—in North Carolina—had the power to veto redistricting plans.

Democrats won governorships in Ohio and Pennsylvania and held Texas. These are three of the nation's seven most populous states. Republicans continued to hold four others in 1970—New York, California, Michigan and Illinois.

Democrats also wrested from Republican control the governorships of Alaska, Florida, Arkansas, Oklahoma, Idaho, Minnesota, Nebraska, Nevada, New Mexico, South Dakota and Wisconsin.

Democrats in the 1970 elections retained control of the governorships in Alabama, Georgia, Maryland, South Carolina, Texas, Kansas, Maine, Rhode Island and Hawaii. Republican governors continued to hold Arizona, Colorado, Iowa, Massachusetts, New Hampshire, Oregon, Vermont and Wyoming.

Democrats won 22 of the 35 governorships at stake in 1970. These victories combined with the seven Democratic holdovers (in Louisiana, Mississippi, Missouri, Montana, North Carolina, North Dakota and Utah) to give the Democrats control of 29 states. Thus the Democrats resumed control of a majority of the nation's states, which they lost in 1967 after holding it since 1954.

(In 1967, Kentucky's election of Republican Louie B. Nunn as governor tipped the balance 24-26 in favor of the Republicans. In 1968, Republicans chalked up a net gain of four more statehouses and added two more in 1969, bringing the balance before the 1970 elections to 32 Republican governors and 18 Democratic governors.)

Republicans won 13 of the 35 gubernatorial elections in 1970, and these, with their eight holdovers (Delaware, Illinois, Indiana, Kentucky, New Jersey, Virginia, Washington and West Virginia), gave the party control of 21 states.

HOUSE

The Democratic Party showed renewed strength in the Great Plains and the Far West in the 1970 elections as it gained nine House seats to open up a 255-180* margin for the 92nd Congress.

Republicans claimed success in holding the off-year Democratic gains below the average for the non-presidential party. Democrats said their gains were significant because President Nixon's 1968 victory carried in few of the marginal candidates who are normally easy prey to the party out of power in off-year contests.

Eighteen of the 33 Democratic newcomers in the 92nd Congress and nine of the 23 Republicans took over seats previously held by the opposite party. Twenty-nine others replaced members of their own party who died, retired or lost in primaries.

---

* *The death Dec. 28, 1970, of L. Mendel Rivers (D S.C.) reduced the Democratic majority to 254.*

The 56 newcomers were a larger House freshman class than the 39 elected in 1968, but still smaller than the average of about 70 that prevailed in elections between 1950 and 1966. In most cases, local factors rather than a clear national trend appeared to be responsible for the party switches that occurred.

Farm Dissatisfaction. The major regional impact came in the Midwest, chiefly from farm communities dissatisfied with Nixon administration agricultural policy.

South Dakota, which had elected only one Democrat to the House in the quarter century since World War II, chose Democratic candidates, Frank E. Denholm and James Abourezk, to fill both its House seats in 1970.

Another heavily rural district, Minnesota's 7th, selected Democrat Bob Bergland over six-term Republican incumbent Odin Langen.

Farm problems also may have been decisive in North Dakota's 2nd District, where Democrat Arthur A. Link defeated Republican Robert P. McCarney for the House seat being vacated by unsuccessful Republican Senate candidate Tom Kleppe.

In several other rural districts in the Midwest, the same effect was present but was less obvious, because the seats did not change hands. Four of five Republican representatives in both Iowa and Wisconsin were re-elected by smaller pluralities than in 1968. Democrat David R. Obey, narrowly elected in a special 1969 election in Wisconsin's rural 7th District, won a full term by a margin of about 2-1 in 1970.

But this reaction had its exceptions. Nebraska, one of the most rural of the midwestern states, re-elected one Republican representative and chose Republicans to fill the two seats that did not have incumbent candidates. Michigan's 12 Republican representatives, most of whom were from rural constituencies, all won re-election with little difficulty.

Economic Factors. Throughout the country, the effects of recession and rising unemployment played a modified but detectable role in determining results of House elections.

Wisconsin's 1st District provided perhaps the most graphic example. Always a hotly contested district, heavily dependent on the automobile industry, it had elected conservative Republican Henry C. Schadeberg in four of the five previous elections. In 1970, with unemployment up to about 6 per cent in the district's largest cities of Racine and Kenosha, voters gave more than 60 per cent of the vote to liberal Democrat Les Aspin. It was the largest plurality any candidate had received in the district since World War II.

Other districts in which recession and unemployment appeared to be significant factors were Washington's 4th, Connecticut's 6th, Utah's 2nd and New Mexico's 2nd. All had been designated by the Labor Department as areas with more than 5 per cent unemployment.

The Connecticut 6th included New Britain, a 19th-century industrial town whose hardware and machinery industries were depressed in 1970. The Washington 4th was largely agricultural, but there was a significant lumber industry that was hit hard by a slowdown in housing starts. Republican incumbent Catherine May was upset by Democrat Mike McCormack in the Washington district, and Democrat Ella T. Grasso won her first term in the Connecticut district.

But in several other districts, Republican incumbents were able to achieve re-election despite economic problems that made them vulnerable.

Republican Hastings Keith won a narrow re-election victory in Massachusetts' 12th District, where the city of New Bedford had experienced substantial and persistent unemployment. In Oregon's 4th District, where a decline in the demand for lumber had sent unemployment past 10 per cent in some counties, Republican John R. Dellenback had little trouble disposing of his Democratic challenger. And in the suburbs of Detroit, seriously affected by a General Motors strike, Republicans William S. Broomfield and Jack McDonald of the 18th and 19th Districts were re-elected with relative ease.

Most of the districts with substantial unemployment already were represented by Democrats, and several of these men were re-elected by margins far greater than in the past. They included Kenneth J. Gray of Illinois' 21st, John Brademas of Indiana's 3rd and Henry Helstoski of New Jersey's 9th. All saw their districts lifted from the marginal column because they won with pluralities of more than 55 per cent.

Black Members. Five blacks were elected to the House for the first time in 1970, bringing Negro membership in the 92nd Congress to 13, the highest number in history.

The five newcomers, all Democrats, included Charles B. Rangel (N.Y. 18th), who conquered Adam C. Powell (1945-71) in a Democratic primary; Ronald V. Dellums (Calif. 7th), a self-described militant elected from a largely white district around the University of California at Berkeley; Ralph Metcalfe (Ill. 1st), a former Olympic sprint champion and protege of Chicago Mayor Richard J. Daley; Parren J. Mitchell (Md. 7th), who narrowly defeated Samuel N. Friedel (D 1953-71) in a primary campaign that mirrored the district's change from heavily Jewish to heavily Negro, and George W. Collins (Ill. 6th), whose district included not only black neighborhoods on Chicago's West Side but the white working-class suburbs of Cicero and Berwyn.

Another new member of the 92nd House was Puerto Rico-born Democrat Herman Badillo (N.Y. 21st), the first of his nationality ever to serve in Congress. Badillo was elected from a New York City district that took in parts of three boroughs and included much of the city's Puerto Rican community.

Other freshman members of the House who attracted special interest included:

• Bella S. Abzug (D N.Y.), a militant crusader for peace and women's liberation.

• John G. Dow (D N.Y.), a former House member (1965-69) and early opponent of the Vietnam war, he completed a successful comeback after it was announced his Republican opponent was being investigated for possible income-tax evasion.

• Pierre S. (Pete) du Pont (R Del.), scion of the famous chemical family, he won an easy victory on a platform of moderate Republicanism and anti-pollution.

• Louise Day Hicks (D Mass.). Elected to replace retiring House Speaker John W. McCormack (D 1928-71), she was a hard-liner who nearly won the Boston mayoralty in 1967 on a platform of opposition to busing and open-housing laws.

• Jack F. Kemp (R N.Y.), former quarterback of the Buffalo Bills professional football team.

Number of Black Members 1947-73

Forty-two blacks have served in Congress through the start of the 93rd Congress in 1973—39 in the House and three in the Senate. (An additional one was elected to the House during Reconstruction but was not seated.) Listed below are the number of black members of Congress since the 80th Congress. Figures do not include the non-voting delegate from the District of Columbia.

Congress	Senate	House
93rd	1	15
92nd	1	12
91st	1	9
90th	1	5
89th		6
88th		5
87th		4
86th		4
85th		4
84th		3
83rd		2
82nd		2
81st		2
80th		2

• Teno Roncalio (D Wyo.). This colorful mountain populist narrowly won back the seat he relinquished in 1966 to make an unsuccessful race for the Senate.

• J. Edward Roush (D Ind.). Defeated in 1968 after 10 years in the House, he came back in 1970 with a whirlwind campaign that ousted the man who toppled him two years before, Republican E. Ross Adair.

• William R. Roy Sr. (D Kan.). Roy, who was both a lawyer and a physician, pulled perhaps the year's most stunning upset by defeating Republican incumbent Chester L. Mize (1965-71).

Departed Veterans. Also notable as the House convened in January 1971 were the absences of several veterans who had served for more than a generation. Death claimed Michael J. Kirwan (D Ohio 1937-70) and William L. Dawson (D Ill. 1943-70).

Several older big-city Democrats were defeated in primaries, deprived of their electoral base by the collapse of the organizations that had renominated them with little opposition year after year. Among them were George H. Fallon (Md. 1945-71), Michael A. Feighan (Ohio 1943-71), Samuel N. Friedel (Md. 1953-71) and Philip J. Philbin (Mass. 1943-71). All four were beaten by younger liberals who built their own political base.

Congress in 1971

Foreign policy dominated the concerns of the House and Senate in 1971 as Congress took little action toward achieving the domestic "New American Revolution" President Nixon envisioned in January in his State of the Union address.

Vietnam debate centered on the "Mansfield amendment," a proposal for troop withdrawals. Passed three times by the Senate, it was watered down twice in conference committees and was lodged in conference a third time for almost a month until rejected by the House Dec. 16.

Late in October the Senate stunned itself, the President and the nation by rejecting the foreign aid bill. But it came back with an amended version that split the aid into military and economic components.

New Economic Policy. On the domestic front, Congress extended the President's authority to regulate the economy and passed a major tax bill, cutting personal and business taxes by nearly $16-billion over three years. Both measures were requested by the President as part of his New Economic Policy.

Congress also voted a new military draft bill, a $250-million loan to the ailing Lockheed Aircraft Corporation and an end to supersonic transport subsidy.

All these developments overshadowed traditional social service issues. But Congress did clear a bill appropriating more than $1-billion to fight cancer and another establishing day care centers for children of working parents. Nixon vetoed the day care bill. There were two other presidential vetoes during the session.

LEGISLATIVE ACTION

These were the major foreign and domestic policy developments of the first session of the 92nd Congress:

FOREIGN, DEFENSE POLICY. Much of the 1971 conflict between Nixon and the Democrats revolved around foreign policy. Many Democrats sought to scale down defense spending and foreign commitments, and the President sought to hold the line. The President generally won.

The most recurrent legislative proposal with which congressional doves challenged the President was the Mansfield amendment, setting a date for the withdrawal of American troops from Indochina. Passed twice by the Senate, the amendment was weakened in conference both times, only to appear a third time as a rider to a foreign aid bill.

The Mansfield amendment passed the Senate for the first time as part of the military draft extension in June. Introduced by Majority Leader Mike Mansfield (D Mont.), it called for withdrawal of all American troops within nine months of enactment. A conference committee then removed the deadline and simply declared it to be the sense of Congress that troops would be withdrawn at the earliest practicable date.

The amendment was passed by the Senate again in September, this time as part of a defense procurement authorization bill. The second version called for withdrawal within six months of enactment, provided U.S. prisoners of war had been released. But a conference committee again deleted the deadline, leaving only the declaration that it was the policy of the United States to accomplish withdrawal by a date to be announced by the President. The President said in signing the bill that the amendment was "without binding force" and that he would ignore it.

The original amendment reappeared in October in the Senate foreign aid bill, but died when the entire bill was defeated on the Senate floor Oct. 29. It was resurrected as a part of the revised Senate foreign aid bill in November. Its inclusion in the foreign aid bill led to

another deadlock in conference from Nov. 18 until Dec. 16, when the House voted 130-101 against instructing its conferees to agree to the amendment. Thus the President survived a year of repeated congressional challenges to his Indochina policy without having to accept more than a symbolic statement against it.

Troops in Europe. Earlier in the year, another Mansfield amendment had provoked the President. This amendment, offered by Mansfield as part of the draft bill, would have reduced the number of American troops in Europe to 150,000 from 300,000. After a week of debate, the amendment failed May 19 by a 36-61 roll-call vote. In November, the Senate Appropriations Committee added to the defense appropriations bill a provision reducing the American troop strength in Europe to 250,000 from 300,000. It was deleted on the Senate floor Nov. 23.

Foreign Aid. The foreign aid issue itself provided another test of strength between the administration and Congress, one in which the President won no clearcut victory but averted a major defeat.

The Senate Oct. 29 voted 41-27 to kill the $2.9-billion foreign aid program proposed for fiscal 1972. The defeat was engineered by an unusual coalition—conservatives who saw the program as a giant giveaway and liberals who felt it placed too much emphasis on military aid. Nixon called the rejection of the program an irresponsible and dangerous action.

But by the end of the session, it was clear that foreign aid was not as dead as it appeared to be Oct. 29. The Senate divided the foreign aid into an economic assistance bill and a military assistance bill, then passed both by wide margins. The House repassed its version of the earlier foreign aid bill and took it to conference with the two new Senate bills. When conferees bogged down in disagreement over the Mansfield anti-war amendment, both houses passed continuing resolutions extending the existing aid into early 1972. A compromise authorization bill was agreed upon, and the Senate passed it before adjourning. The House delayed action until 1972.

Draft Law. Extended debate and threats of filibuster in the Senate prevented final action on the draft law until after the authority for the draft system had expired—the first such expiration of draft authority since World War II. But by September, when Congress finally cleared the draft bill for the President's signature, President Nixon had most of the things he wanted. Among them were a two-year extension of the draft authority and pay increases for servicemen estimated to cost $2.4-billion after the first year of the law's enactment.

Lockheed Loan. One of the closest decisions of the year—and probably the President's narrowest victory in his dealings with Congress—involved a loan guarantee for the Lockheed Aircraft Corporation. Lockheed, the nation's largest defense contractor, was near bankruptcy.

The Nixon administration sought a guarantee of $250-million in bank loans to keep the company from collapsing. Proponents said national security would be endangered by the collapse of Lockheed. Critics argued that granting the $250-million loan would reward the firm for inefficiency and bad management.

The administration suffered defections not only from liberals but from conservatives who were reluctant to endorse government interference in free market processes. But the bill squeaked by, 192-189 in the House and 49-48 in the Senate.

DOMESTIC POLICY. The Economic Stabilization Act of 1970, giving the President authority to impose wage-price controls, passed in the 91st Congress over the active objections of the administration. In March 1971, the 92nd Congress approved a one-year extension of the act to April 1972. This time the administration did not oppose the measure; neither did it actively support it. On Aug. 15, Nixon announced his New Economic Policy and imposed a wage-price freeze.

On Dec. 14, at the request of the President, Congress cleared Nixon's Economic Stabilization Act extending the presidential wage-price-rent control powers through April 1973. The bill also granted the President standby power to control dividends and interest rates, and permitted consumers to sue price violators for willful overcharging. The bill ordered a pay increase for federal workers to take effect Jan. 1, 1972, rather than six months later, as the President had preferred.

Congress also cleared the President's tax bill, cutting taxes by almost $16-billion over three years in an effort to stimulate the economy. Among its major provisions, the bill repealed the 7 per cent auto excise tax, gave business a 7 per cent investment tax credit and raised the personal income tax exemption from $650 in 1970 to $675 in 1971 and $750 in 1972. Nixon signed the bill Dec. 10 after conferees had removed a provision establishing federal financing for the 1972 presidential campaign. He had threatened a veto if the campaign provision were not deleted.

Supersonic Transport. The aircraft industry also figured in the administration's most prominent defeat of the year, the issue of the supersonic transport plane. The question was on federal funding for development of the plane, a commercial airliner designed to carry 300 passengers at speeds up to 1,800 miles an hour.

The White House and the Department of Transportation mounted an intensive lobbying campaign on behalf of the plane, but it went down to defeat in March. A later attempt to revive the appropriation succeeded in the House but failed to pass the Senate.

Day Care. A battle developed in the closing days of the session over the day care centers for children of working parents. On Dec. 9, the President vetoed a $6.3-billion bill for the Office of Economic Opportunity because of day care and child development provisions he said were irresponsible and unworkable. The next day, supporters of the child care provisions sought to override the veto on the Senate floor, but the 51 votes in favor of overriding it were seven short of the two-thirds majority needed.

Consumer Bill. The House passed a bill establishing an independent agency to represent consumers in federal proceedings. Liberals wanted to strengthen it to allow the agency to intervene in a larger number of cases. Conservatives sought to weaken the agency. The final passage rejecting both attempts left the bill closer to President Nixon's choice than it would have been if it had been amended either way.

Cancer Research. In the field of health, the President had only limited success in dealing with Congress over the expansion of efforts to find a cure for cancer. In his state of the union address, Nixon touched on the matter by calling for an additional $100-million for cancer research.

The major discussion in Congress, however, was about the organization of the task, not its funding. Congress finally appropriated $1.59-billion for cancer research over a three-year period. The Senate voted to use the money to establish and finance an independent cancer research agency. The House chose to expand existing efforts by the National Institutes of Health. The House won.

Youth Vote. A constitutional amendment was passed to grant the vote to 18- to 21-year-olds in all federal, state and local elections. A 1970 law had granted them this right by statute, but the Supreme Court had ruled that Congress had the power to make the change only for federal elections, nullifying the statute for state and local contests. Congress again took up the original legislation in 1971 as a constitutional amendment, requiring approval by two-thirds of each house and by three-fourths of the states but eliminating legal problems. The amendment cleared Congress March 23, and the states, eager to avoid the complication of separating teen-age and older voters in the 1972 election, ratified it quickly. On June 30 it became law.

Campaign Spending. The campaign spending issue played an important role in congressional debate during the last month of the session, as Senate Democrats attached to the President's tax bill a rider earmarking up to $20-million in tax funds for financing the 1972 presidential campaign. Under the plan, taxpayers were allowed to indicate on their federal tax forms whether they wished $1 of their payment to be used for campaign finance. Democrats, with their party more than $9-million in debt as the campaign began, hoped to enact the plan against the President's wishes by linking it to the tax bill he regarded as crucial.

Nixon responded, however, by threatening to veto the entire bill if it contained the campaign funding provision. Democrats knew that they did not have enough votes to override a veto, and conferees ultimately gave in to the President by enacting the provision but delaying the effective date until after the 1972 election. Nixon accepted this change and signed the bill Dec. 10.

Efforts to limit the amount of money spent on political campaigns achieved some success in 1971, as the Senate in August and the House in November passed a bill placing a ceiling on such spending and tightening requirements for reporting and disclosure of contributions. Under the bill as it emerged from conference, candidates for federal offices were allowed to spend on communications media either $50,000 or 10 cents per voting constituent, whichever was greater.

Nominations. The President drew some criticism in Congress over two of his appointments, those of William H. Rehnquist for the Supreme Court and Earl L. Butz for secretary of agriculture. But both men were confirmed.

Rehnquist and Lewis F. Powell Jr. were nominated to the court by the President Oct. 21 to fill the seats previously held by Hugo L. Black and John M. Harlan. Powell, a Richmond lawyer, drew little opposition from the legal profession and was confirmed Dec. 6 by an 89-1 vote.

But Rehnquist had a more difficult time. As an assistant attorney general, he was involved in the Justice Department's handling of May 1971 protest demonstrations in Washington, D.C., and liberals feared he was insensitive to the rights of dissenters.

Opponents won a preliminary victory on the floor Dec. 10 when they defeated a cloture vote that would have shut off debate. But a few hours later, Birch Bayh

(D Ind.) lost on a motion to delay the decision until the following month, and the Senate took a final vote the same day and confirmed Rehnquist by a surprisingly easy 68-26 margin.

The margin was closer Dec. 2, as the Senate approved the nomination of Butz on a 51-44 vote. Chosen by the President to replace retiring Agriculture Secretary Clifford M. Hardin, Butz found he was caught in the economic discontent gripping farmers and their representatives in a lean year for agriculture. His close ties to corporate farming interests made many members fear he would be unwilling to use government policy to protect the small family farmer in time of need.

CONGRESSIONAL LEADERSHIP CHANGES

Democrats in both houses of Congress elected some new leaders in 1971. Republican dissidents challenged their leaders in both houses but failed to replace any of them.

House Democrats. The principal change was in the House speakership. Rep. John W. McCormack (D Mass. 1928-71) retired from the House. He had been speaker since 1962, when he replaced the late Sam Rayburn (D Texas 1913-61). With only token opposition, Rep. Carl Albert (Okla.) was chosen by the Democratic caucus to replace McCormack. The vote was 220-20. The opposition votes went to Rep. John Conyers Jr. (Mich.).

The election of Albert to be the 54th speaker of the House created a series of vacancies in the House Democratic leadership. Albert had been majority leader since 1962. Hale Boggs (La.) had to overcome strong liberal opposition within the party to move up from assistant majority leader, or whip, to the majority leadership. In other moves, Rep. Thomas P. O'Neill Jr. (Mass.) succeeded Boggs as whip, and Olin E. Teague (Texas) defeated incumbent Dan Rostenkowski (Ill.) as Democratic caucus chairman.

Senate Democrats. In the Senate, the Democratic caucus elected Robert C. Byrd (W.Va.) as majority whip over incumbent Edward M. Kennedy (Mass.) by a vote of 31 to 24. Byrd's surprise victory resulted from Byrd's covert but assiduous campaign for the job. He had been caucus secretary for four years. His defeat of the more liberal Kennedy eliminated Kennedy from a leadership position he had held only two years and cast doubt on his standing as a possible presidential contender in 1972.

Another Senate change was caused by the death Jan. 21 of Richard B. Russell (Ga.), 73, who had been a member since 1933 and was the Senate's senior Democrat. He was succeeded by Allen J. Ellender (D La.), 80, a senator since 1937, in two positions: president pro tempore—which goes automatically to the ranking majority member—and chairman of the Appropriations Committee.

Republicans. At their organizational caucus, House Republicans elected Rep. John B. Anderson (Ill.) to a second term as conference (caucus) chairman by a vote of 89 to 81 over the more conservative Samuel L. Devine of Ohio. Senate Republican Leader Hugh Scott (Pa.) survived a challenge by Howard H. Baker Jr. (Tenn.), whom he had defeated two years earlier; his 1971 margin was 24 to 20.

CONGRESSIONAL ETHICS

Corruption tarnished the record of both houses of Congress in 1971. A Democratic representative and a Republican administrative aide in the Senate were convicted of felonies in separate cases.

Dowdy. The representative, John Dowdy of Texas, was convicted Dec. 30 of charges arising from acceptance of a bribe, conspiracy and perjury. The verdict followed a 27-day trial in U.S. District Court in Baltimore. At the trial, Dowdy claimed that he had not received a $25,000 payoff to thwart a federal investigation of a Maryland home improvement company in 1965.

In February 1972, Dowdy was sentenced to 18 months in prison and a $25,000 fine. The Texan, who was serving his 10th term in the House, was the first member of Congress since 1956 to be convicted of a felony while still in office. The last had been Rep. Thomas J. Lane (D Mass. 1941-62), who pleaded guilty to willful evasion of income taxes. *(Congress and the Nation Vol. I, p. 1420)*

Carson. The Senate staffer was Robert T. Carson, suspended administrative assistant to Sen. Hiram L. Fong (R Hawaii). Carson was a former president of the Honolulu Stock Exchange and former Hawaii state Republican chairman. He was found guilty Nov. 20 of conspiring to accept and offer bribes to help quash stock fraud indictments and of perjuring himself before a federal grand jury. He was sentenced on Jan. 4, 1972, in U.S. District Court in New York City to 18 months in prison and a fine of $5,000.

Presidential Record, 1971

The third year of the Nixon presidency was highlighted by a series of actions that marked reversals of positions Nixon had taken earlier in his political life:

● The administration started a diplomatic revolution in U.S. policy toward Communist China and the Soviet Union by scheduling presidential trips to Peking and Moscow in 1972—efforts by a President who made his early political reputation as a strong anti-Communist.

● Wage and price controls were imposed on an ailing economy by a Republican President who had objected to such controls and who had actively opposed the congressional authority granted him in 1970 to impose them.

● Nixon Dec. 14 announced plans to devalue the U.S. dollar after earlier resisting moves that would have increased the price of gold in relation to the dollar.

● A new international trade policy imposing a 10 per cent surcharge on most imports hurt the nation's relations with Canada, Japan, Western Europe, Latin America and the underdeveloped countries of Asia and Africa. The thrust of Nixon's earlier actions had been to improve U.S. relations with foreign countries.

1971 Elections

Seers examining the election returns of Nov. 2, 1971, for clues to 1972 politics found few clear hints of things to come.

Democrat Wendell Ford won the governorship of Kentucky and called it the first step in a "dump-Nixon" campaign. But Republican H. John Heinz III was elected to the House from suburban Pittsburgh after a campaign in which he defended the President's economic policies.

Those hoping for a dramatic demonstration of black political power were disappointed by the defeat of Arnold Pinkney for mayor of Cleveland and by the poor showing of Charles Evers for the Mississippi governorship. But Richard Hatcher won a second four-year term as mayor of Gary, Ind., piling up a more than two-to-one margin over his white Republican opponent.

Law-and-order proponents won a point with the election of former Police Commissioner Frank L. Rizzo as mayor of Philadelphia. But they were disappointed by the crushing defeat of Rep. Louise Day Hicks (D) by incumbent Kevin H. White for Boston's mayoralty.

Conflicting Claims. As is traditional in off-year elections, each party produced spokesmen who claimed that the results were a major triumph for the party cause. "Yesterday's election returns from Boston to San Francisco show impressive Democratic gains," said Sen. Hubert H. Humphrey (D Minn.) Nov. 3. "I believe the results foreshadow a Democratic trend that will carry through to November 1972."

The Republican national chairman, Sen. Robert Dole (R Kan.), had the opposite view. "There is no question but what the results of yesterday's elections are a plus for the Republican Party," he said. "Over-all, I believe that it is clear that Republicans are continuing to build strength toward the 1972 presidential elections...."

Deaths left two Senate seats vacant in 1971. Voters elected two governors and a lieutenant governor. Elections were held for five House seats vacated by resignations or deaths. A non-voting delegate to the House was elected for the first time in a century. And several big-city mayoralties were filled. The results:

SENATE

Georgia. Sen. Russell of Georgia died on Jan. 21. The Democratic governor of Georgia appointed another Democrat, Atlanta attorney David H. Gambrell, to serve the remaining two years of Russell's term.

Vermont. Sen. Winston L. Prouty (R Vt.), who had been elected to a third term in 1970, died Sept. 10 at age 65. Appointed to succeed him was Robert T. Stafford, a Republican governor from 1959 to 1961 and a U.S. representative since 1961. In a special election Jan. 7, 1972, Stafford was elected to serve the last five years of Prouty's term.

GOVERNORS

Kentucky. The return of Democrat Ford to Kentucky's governorship brought the party an office it had held for 20 straight years after World War II but had lost in 1967 to Louie B. Nunn. Nunn was ineligible for a second term in 1971, and his attempt to bequeath the job to fellow Republican Thomas Emberton fell short by more than 50,000 votes, Former Gov. A. B. (Happy) Chandler (D 1955-59), seeking a comeback at age 73 as an independent, drew less than 5 per cent. Ford's election climaxed a Democratic resurgence in Kentucky that had brought back the Louisville mayoralty in 1969 and a congressional seat in 1970.

Mississippi. Charles Evers, the black mayor of Fayette, Miss., failed to run a close race against white Democrat William Waller in their contest for Governor. Returns showed Evers, running as an independent, with less than a quarter of the vote cast, as an unusually high turnout of white voters boosted Waller's margin. But Evers' supporters saw evidence of a symbolic victory, as the moderate Waller declined to play upon racial feelings in the campaign and promised to appoint qualified blacks to posts in his administration.

LIEUTENANT GOVERNOR

Lt. Gov. J. Sargeant Reynolds (D Va.) died June 23. He was replaced in a special election Nov. 2 by State Sen. Henry E. Howell (D) of Norfolk, who ran as an independent against Republican and Democratic nominees. Howell, an unsuccessful candidate for the Democratic gubernatorial nomination in 1969, frankly said that he was running for lieutenant governor to position himself for another run at the governorship in 1973.

HOUSE

South Carolina. Voters in South Carolina's 1st District (South—Charleston) April 27 elected Mendel J. Davis (D) to fill the House vacancy created Dec. 28, 1970, by the death of Rep. L. Mendel Rivers (D 1941-70) at age 65. Davis' election at age 28 made him the youngest member of Congress at that time. Rivers had been chairman of the House Armed Services Committee.

Maryland. Incumbent Rogers C. B. Morton (R), who had represented Maryland's 1st District (Eastern and Western Shores—Annapolis, Salisbury) since 1963, resigned Jan. 29 to accept an appointment as secretary of the interior. The House vacancy was filled by William O. Mills (R) in a special election May 25.

Pennsylvania. Rep. Robert J. Corbett (R Pa. 1939-41, 1945-71) died April 25. Republican Heinz was elected his successor in the 18th District (Pittsburgh—north suburbs) in a special election Nov. 2. Republican Heinz, an executive in his family's food-canning business, won an unexpectedly easy victory over a Democrat thought to be less liberal than he.

Kentucky. In Kentucky's 6th District (North central —Lexington), voters elected State Rep. William P. Curlin (D) to fill the House vacancy created by the death Sept. 24 of Rep. John C. Watts (D 1951-71), 69.

Vermont. Republican Richard W. Mallary succeeded Sen. Stafford in Vermont's at-large House seat in the Jan. 7, 1972, election.

District of Columbia. Democrat Walter E. Fauntroy was elected as the capital city's delegate to the House by a heavy margin March 23. Fauntroy's election was made possible by legislation passed in 1970.

Like the other non-voting delegate, from Puerto Rico, Fauntroy, a black Baptist minister, was barred from participating in House roll calls. But he had all the other privileges and duties of full members and was paid the same salary and staff allowances.

MAYORALTIES

The law-and-order issue, a factor in American municipal politics since 1967, was tested twice in 1971, in Philadelphia and Boston. It was less important in the year's other major mayoral contests. All but Chicago's were on Nov. 2.

Philadelphia. Democrat Rizzo won with a combination of his "tough cop" image, his Italian ancestry and an overwhelming Democratic registration advantage. Despite charges that Rizzo lacked sufficient concern for civil liberties and some allegations that he was a racist, he won by nearly 50,000 votes over Princeton-educated Thacher Longstreth, a liberal and civil-rights-minded Republican.

Boston. Mayor Kevin H. White won a second term by a lopsided margin over Rep. Louise Day Hicks, who made law and order and opposition to busing famous when she opposed White in 1967. That year, White's plurality was 12,429 votes; in 1971, it was more than 40,000. Politicians interpreted the change not as a retreat from law and order but as a reflection of the fact that White campaigned efficiently and pursued ethnic groups with specific programs, while Rep. Hicks made only an informal bid for votes and produced few ideas beyond her 1967 theme, "You know where I stand."

Chicago. The year's first important mayoral election was April 6 in Chicago, where Richard J. Daley (D) won an unprecedented fifth four-year term by a 3-to-1 margin over Republican Richard E. Friedman. Friedman, a former Democrat who ran with Republican organizational support, had attempted to build a coalition of independents, Republicans and dissident Democrats to upset Daley.

Cleveland. Cleveland's mayoralty was more of a test for incumbent black Democrat Carl Stokes, who was not running, than for his designee, Arnold Pinkney, who was. Stokes persuaded most black voters to back white candidate James Carney in September's Democratic primary. Then he switched from Carney to black independent candidate Pinkney in the general election. The idea was to demonstrate the power of the machine Stokes had built in Cleveland's black neighborhoods. But blacks divided their votes between Carney and Pinkney, assuring an easy win for Republican Ralph J. Perk, the county auditor and a specialist in the white ethnic vote. He had narrowly lost to Stokes two years earlier.

San Francisco. Despite his indictment in March on fee-splitting charges (he was exonerated the next year), Mayor Joseph L. Alioto (D) won a second four-year term in a nominally nonpartisan election. Alioto defeated 10 other candidates, winning with less than 40 per cent of the vote.

Congress in 1972

Under the shadow of election year politics, the second session of the 92nd Congress spurted to final adjournment in the evening hours of Oct. 18, 1972, after two last-minute, acrimonious encounters with the Nixon White House.

As those lawmakers who had not already gone home streamed into the House and Senate chambers for the last roll calls, the leaders of both parties rendered their predictably partisan assessments of the 92nd. It was, said the Democrats, an independent Congress trying to determine its own priorities to meet the nation's needs. For the Republicans, it was a Congress that had learned to add and multiply, but rarely subtract.

With that, the leadership retired to the White House to sip coffee with the President, and their fellow legislators left the cold, drizzly capital for home, preparing to explain to their constituents their final votes on two crucial and intertwined issues—an unprecedented spending ceiling bill and a massive water pollution control measure.

By lopsided margins, both the House (247-23) and Senate (52-12) had overridden a Nixon veto of the Democratic-inspired water bill, which authorized the spending of $24.7-billion in the next three years to clean the nation's waterways. And House acquiescence to a Senate vote rejecting a $250-billion ceiling on federal spending in fiscal 1973 killed the President's proposal that Congress grant him the authority to slash whatever he wanted from any congressional appropriations.

But whatever the White House had suffered from the two legislative defeats, it hoped to make up as the President took his case to the voters in the final days before the Nov. 7 election. After observing from the galleries the Senate's rejection of the spending ceiling, presidential aide John D. Ehrlichman returned to the White House to release the Nixon veto message on the water bill.

To the President, the issue was spending and taxes, and votes to override his midnight veto of the "staggering, budget-wrecking" anti-pollution measure were votes for "higher prices and higher taxes." In his veto message, the President noted: "I have nailed my colors to the mast on this issue; the political winds may blow where they may."

Record Evaluated. To conclude that it was a "do-nothing" Congress would be incorrect. The 92nd compiled a respectable record of accomplishments. And if more of the administration's "great goals" were not enacted, the blame would have to rest on the White House as well as Capitol Hill.

The fact was that the White House did not work very hard for some of its proposals (government reorganization), and was unwilling to accept congressional substitutes for others (environmental legislation).

In general, the administration received what it wanted in foreign affairs and national security, while the Democratic-controlled Congress was successful in bolstering some domestic social welfare programs. In a sense, then it was a standoff.

Nixon Goals. When the 92nd Congress convened in January 1971, the President pledged a domestic "New American Revolution" by introducing "six great goals" toward which he and the Congress would work together—revenue sharing, welfare reform, environmental initiatives, government reorganization, health insurance reforms and full employment.

Public Laws

In 1972, a total of 483 bills became public laws. Following is a list of the number of public laws enacted since 1963:

Congress	Public Laws	Congress	Public Laws
1972	483	1967	249
1971	224	1966	461
1970	505	1965	349
1969	190	1964	409
1968	391	1963	257

When the 92nd finally adjourned, only one of the Nixon programs had been enacted—general revenue sharing. Beyond his great goals, the President also was unable to persuade Congress to pass his proposals for the spending ceiling, continued development of a supersonic transport (SST) aircraft or for a moratorium on school busing.

Victories. But the administration also garnered some significant victories. Congress approved the Nixon strategic arms limitation agreements and other treaties with the Soviet Union. It granted him the authority to freeze wages, prices and rents seven months before he decided to use it. But when he requested an extension of such authority, Congress readily complied, and then cleared an administration bill cutting taxes by almost $16-billion over three years to stimulate the bearish economy. It also passed measures authorizing the devaluation of the U.S. dollar and permitting four increases in the federal debt ceiling.

Congress also granted the President's requests for a new draft law, a military pay raise as a step toward an all-volunteer army, a new space shuttle program, a cancer research program, an expanded federal attack against drug abuse and for a federal guarantee of $250-million in bank loans for the nearly bankrupt Lockheed Aircraft Corporation.

Spending. The water bill-spending ceiling battle in October was like an exclamation point at the end of a Congress in which the issue of how-much-to-spend-on-what was its recurrent theme.

Generally, the President had wanted to spend more than Congress for the military and for foreign aid. Congress had pushed to spend more than Nixon proposed for public works jobs (to ease unemployment), day care facilities, health care, environmental protection, education and Social Security benefits (which were boosted by a total of 30 per cent during both sessions).

The refusal of Congress to enact the Nixon spending ceiling proposal at the end of the 92nd Congress reflected the view of many Democrats and some Republicans that what influence they had exerted during 1971 and 1972 in establishing the nation's priorities would be lost.

Accomplishments. Aside from the victories and defeats of the President's own legislative program, however, the 92nd Congress could claim some accomplishments of its own.

It approved two proposed constitutional amendments (the 18-year-old vote and women's rights), a rural development measure and flood control and disaster relief bills; it reformed campaign spending procedures; it increased benefits for veterans' education, victims of black lung disease, and added funds to the school lunch program and for heart and lung research; it established a consumer product safety agency and standards for automobile bumpers; it extended the import quota system for sugar and the poverty programs under the Office of Economic Opportunity; and it granted court-enforcement powers to the Equal Employment Opportunity Commission and federal lands, payments and mineral royalties to Alaskan natives.

In the area of environmental protection alone—aside from the clean water bill—it cleared legislation dealing with coastal zone management, ocean dumping, protection of marine mammals, noise pollution, regulation of toxic chemicals and the protection of wildlife.

Leftovers and Defeats. But a number of significant bills also either were defeated by or died with the 92nd Congress. These included a number of end-the-war amendments, tax reform, a measure establishing a consumer protection agency, legislation raising the federal minimum wage, a highway-mass transit bill, an omnibus housing bill, no-fault insurance and a school prayer amendment.

LEGISLATIVE ACTION

These were the major domestic and foreign policy developments of the second session of the 92nd Congress:

DOMESTIC POLICY. Approving one of the "six great goals" first proposed by Nixon in 1971, Congress cleared a bill establishing a five-year program of general revenue sharing to distribute $30,236,400,000 in federal revenues to state and local governments. The law appropriated federal revenues to a trust fund for distribution among the state and local governments at an initial annual level of $5.3-billion. The program, made retroactive to Jan. 1, 1972, was approved for five years (through 1976).

Federal Debt, Dollar Devaluation. Congress approved three temporary increases in the federal debt ceiling in 1972, the last only after a bitter fight over Nixon's request for unprecedented authority to cut federal spending in fiscal 1973 to $250-billion. After raising the temporary debt limit to $450-billion from $430-billion on March 15, Congress extended the ceiling from June 30 to Oct. 31 and finally through June 30.

Congress in March approved the President's request for legislation authorizing the secretary of the treasury to implement the dollar devaluation agreed to in December 1971 by increasing the official price of gold to $38 from $35 an ounce.

Social Security, Welfare. Congress increased Social Security benefits by 20 per cent across the board in June and provided for an automatic increase in benefits whenever the cost of living rose more than 3 per cent in a calendar year.

In October, Congress raised widows' and widowers' benefits to 100 per cent from 82.5 per cent of a deceased spouse's benefits, increased to $2,100 from $1,680 the amount that a Social Security beneficiary under age 72 could earn and still receive full benefits, and provided a minimum monthly benefit of $170 for persons who worked in Social Security-covered employment for at least 30 years.

To pay the costs of the expanded benefits, Congress increased the maximum Social Security tax paid by an employee and matched by an employer to $632 each in 1973 (5.85 per cent on a $10,800 wage base) and to $702 each in 1974 (5.85 per cent on a $12,000 wage base) from the existing level of $468 each (5.2 per cent on a $9,000 wage base).

Congress authorized federal takeover of the federal-state welfare system for the aged, blind and disabled effective Jan. 1, 1974. The measure guaranteed such persons who had no income a minimum federal benefit of $130 a month ($195 for a couple).

Congress approved a program of federal grants to states for the establishment of programs to provide nutritionally sound meals to the low-income elderly.

Environment. Congress Oct. 18 overrode President Nixon's veto of the Federal Water Pollution Control Act Amendments of 1972, a $24.7-billion measure aimed at cleaning up the nation's waters by 1985. The final bill set a national goal of eliminating all pollutant discharges into the nation's waters by 1985 and making the waters safe for fish, shellfish, wildlife and recreation by 1983. It included more than $18-billion in federal grants to states for construction of waste treatment plants.

A bill to establish a national program for the management, use, protection and development of U.S. coastal zones and estuaries was cleared by Congress Oct. 12. The bill also encouraged states to develop such programs.

Congress also completed action on a bill to regulate the dumping of material in the oceans and coastal waters. The bill, the Marine Protection, Research and Sanctuaries Act of 1973, was passed by both houses in the fall of 1971 but was tied up in a conference committee for nearly a year. The measure provided for a continuing program of research into the effects of pollution on ocean ecosystems.

On the last day of the session, Congress cleared a bill establishing the first comprehensive federal regulatory program to control noise. The bill set federal noise standards for commercial products and gave the Environmental Protection Agency authority to set restrictions on aircraft noise, subject to a veto by the Federal Aviation Administration.

Congress completed action on the Federal Environmental Pesticide Control Act, making the first major changes in federal pesticide regulation in 25 years. But the final version was widely criticized by environmentalists as weak from an environmental viewpoint—specifically that it favored the pesticide industry. The bill contained a controversial indemnity clause to compensate manufacturers if their products were declared unsafe and removed from the market.

Rural Development. Congress cleared for the President a bill to provide a comprehensive program to improve job opportunity, income and the quality of life in rural America. The law authorized about $500-million annually in federal grants and loans for rural programs.

Civil Rights. President Nixon March 24 signed a bill that provided court-enforcement powers for the Equal Employment Opportunity Commission (EEOC). The measure authorized the EEOC to institute suits in federal court to enforce U.S. laws against job discrimination.

Forty-nine years after it was introduced, Congress completed action March 22 on a proposed constitutional amendment guaranteeing equal rights for women. The amendment then went to the states, where approval of 38 state legislatures was required for ratification.

Federal Election Campaign Act. Congress Jan. 19 cleared for the President the Federal Election Campaign Act, a political spending law that plugged many loopholes through which candidates had evaded earlier political spending regulations. The law strengthened requirements for reporting contributions and campaign costs, regulated media spending, defined more strictly the roles unions and corporations could play in political campaigns and limited the amount a candidate or his family could contribute to his own campaign.

Consumer Product Safety Agency. Congress cleared a bill creating an independent agency to protect consumers against hazardous products. The final version was weaker than that approved by the Senate, which would also have transferred the Food and Drug Administration out of the Department of Health, Education and Welfare into the new agency.

FOREIGN, DEFENSE POLICY. Congress cut $5.2-billion from the administration's requests for the Defense Department, but the $74.4-billion it provided in defense appropriations for fiscal 1973 still constituted the largest single appropriation in the nation's history.

In addition to the $74.4-billion defense appropriations bill, Congress appropriated $2.3-billion for military construction and military family housing for fiscal 1973 in separate legislation.

SALT Agreements. Congress cleared a joint resolution authorizing the President to give final approval to a five-year U.S.-Soviet agreement limiting the deployment of all offensive nuclear weapons. The Senate earlier in the session had approved ratification of a companion treaty limiting each nation to two anti-ballistic missile sites.

Both agreements had been signed by President Nixon and Soviet Communist Party General Secretary Leonid I. Brezhnev during the President's visit to Moscow in May. Approval of the interim agreement was delayed six weeks by debate over an amendment to the resolution offered by Sen. Henry M. Jackson (D Wash.).

The Jackson amendment, which prompted a bitter debate by its opponents, led by Foreign Relations Committee Chairman J. W. Fulbright (D Ark.), specified that any future treaty on offensive arms must assure each country rough numerical equality in intercontinental strategic forces. The amendment was adopted by a 56-35 vote after the Senate had voted cloture to end a filibuster.

Foreign Aid. Unable to pass a regular appropriations bill because of House-Senate differences over policy amendments to the military aid authorization bill, Congress before adjourning approved a continuing funding resolution providing emergency financing for the foreign aid program until Feb. 28, 1973. The continuing resolution allowed interim spending for economic and military aid programs at an annual level of $3.65-billion.

Executive Agreements. Approving one of several attempts to assert greater powers over foreign policy, Congress completed action on a bill requiring the executive branch to submit to both houses the texts of all international agreements. The measure, drafted by the Senate Foreign Relations Committee under the sponsorship of Clifford P. Case (R N.J.), was in reaction to disclosures that some executive agreements with other nations had been kept secret.

Seabed Treaty. The Senate gave unanimous approval to ratification of a 1971 treaty prohibiting deployment of nuclear weapons on the ocean floor. The treaty pledged the United States and 85 other signatory nations (including nuclear powers Great Britain and the Soviet Union but not France and Communist China) not to place nuclear weapons or other weapons of mass destruction on the seabed outside a 12-mile territorial limit recognized by most nations.

MEMBERSHIP CHANGES

Ellender. There was one change in the top leadership of the two chambers of Congress in 1972—the death of Allen J. Ellender (D La.), president pro tempore of the Senate. He was replaced by Sen. James O. Eastland (D Miss.).

Ellender, 81, a veteran of 36 years' service in the Senate, died of a heart attack July 27 while campaigning for his seventh successive term. His death resulted in changes in two committee chairmanships. Sen. John L. McClellan (D Ark.) replaced Ellender as chairman of the Appropriations Committee, and Sen. Sam J. Ervin Jr. (D N.C.) replaced McClellan as chairman of the Government Operations Committee.

House Majority Leader Hale Boggs (D La.) disappeared in a light plane while campaigning for freshman Rep. Nick Begich (D Alaska) on Oct. 16. Begich and two other men were lost with Boggs. Boggs' loss did not affect the 92nd Congress, which was about to adjourn at the time. A new majority leader was elected at the start of the 93rd Congress in January 1973.

Reid. Rep. Ogden R. Reid, who had represented New York's 26th District as a Republican since 1963, became a Democrat on March 22. He said he "could not support the re-election of President Nixon" and that the Republican Party was "no longer in the mainstream of American life."

Presidential Record, 1972

For Richard Nixon, 1972 was the year to put it all together—to accelerate the economy, slow down inflation, seek an "honorable peace" in Vietnam, open up a dialogue with Communist China and cool off the arms race with the Russians.

Finally, it was the year to face the voters in his fifth national campaign, to seek a "new American majority" that would grant him four more years in the White House. The Nixon sweep of every state except Massachusetts and the District of Columbia—achieved by a politician who never before had commanded the trust or affection of the American electorate—was clear evidence of the President's political skill, his keen sense of timing and his mastery of events.

In the year when it counted most, he looked his best. He had eased tensions abroad and brought some semblance of stability to the nation. In a pre-election analysis, television commentator David Brinkley sought to put the 1972 campaign in some perspective by listing all the traumatic events the nation had endured since the end of the Korean war. "No other democratic country has put up with so much," he concluded. "A people with that history must hunger for some calm and order. How that translated into votes everyone can decide for himself. But seeing the election as a sequel to all that might help explain whatever happens" on election day.

What seemed important to the voters in 1972 was the prospect of peace in Vietnam, an upsurge in the economy, a leveling off of unemployment and a slowdown of inflation. It appeared that the President's hard line on the war, his diplomatic initiatives with the largest communist nations and his continuance of economic controls all were decisions that contributed to his lopsided victory in the polls.

In a sense, then, his fourth year in office marked the grand finale of a four-year campaign for re-election, which with only one exception went without a hitch.

Results of 1972 Elections

SENATE

	Old Lineup	Gains/ Losses	New Lineup
Democrats	55	+ 2	57
Republicans	45	— 2	43

GOVERNORS

	Old Lineup	Gains/ Losses	New Lineup
Democrats	30	+ 1	31
Republicans	20	— 1	19

HOUSE

	Old Lineup	Gains/ Losses	New Lineup
Democrats	256	—13	243
Republicans	179*	+13	192

* Includes switch of Rep. Ogden R. Reid (N.Y.) from Republican to Democrat in March 1972.

The exception was the Watergate incident. Although the President maintained a lofty, presidential demeanor throughout the campaign, revelations of political dirty work being conducted by his lieutenants cast a pall over the White House, conjuring up for many the apparition of the old "Tricky Dick." While reports that the Republicans had conducted an unprecedented espionage and sabotage operation against the Democrats inflicted only limited damage on the Republican campaign, most observers felt its repercussions would be evident well into the second Nixon administration. *(Box p. 21)*

1972 Elections

Richard M. Nixon was elected to a second term in the White House on Nov. 7, 1972, by one of the greatest landslides in history. But at the same time he was obliterating his Democratic opponent, Sen. George McGovern of South Dakota, his Republican Party lost two Senate seats and one governorship and made a modest gain of 13 seats in the House of Representatives.

Nixon's victory, predicted by nearly all political observers, gave him 520 electoral votes, the third highest total ever and nearly twice the 270 required for election. His popular vote total of more than 47 million gave him a plurality of nearly 18 million over McGovern, or 60.7 per cent—second only to the drubbing Lyndon B. Johnson handed Barry Goldwater in 1964. Nixon carried 49 states, losing only the 14 electoral votes of Massachusetts, the three of the District of Columbia—and one cast in Virginia for the Libertarian Party by a Republican elector.

Nixon Campaign. It was a remarkable mandate for the 59-year-old former Vice President, who 10 years earlier, to the day, had held his famous "last press conference" after his defeat in the 1962 California gubernatorial race and had been all but written off as a force in American politics. He won his second term with a minimum of personal campaigning, relying instead on the appearances of his Vice President, Spiro T. Agnew, and a troupe of "surrogate" campaigners—cabinet officers and other prestigious Republicans. The campaign was probably without parallel in the efficiency and completeness of its organization and in the money it spent. Some estimates were in the vicinity of $50-million, which, if accurate, would have been an all-time high for one campaign.

In a televised statement from the White House shortly before midnight on election night, the President said, "A huge landslide margin means nothing at all unless it is a victory for America. It will be a victory for America, if in these next four years we, all of us, can work together to achieve our common great goals of peace at home and peace for all nations in the world and for that new progress and prosperity which all America deserves."

Soon after the election, Nixon gave a few clues to the direction his administration would take in its second four years. He announced on Nov. 8 that the first order of business for his second term would be "a significant reorganization" of the White House staff and executive departments. He took the unusual step of having his press secretary publicly remind presidential employees to submit their resignations—a customary procedure at such a time, but not with so much fanfare.

In an exclusive interview with *The Washington Star-News*, conducted Nov. 5 and published Nov. 9, Nixon emphasized his desire to hold the line on domestic programs and to avoid a tax increase. "The reforms that we are instituting are ones which will diffuse the power throughout the country and which will make government leaner, but in a sense will make it stronger," he said.

McGovern Campaign. From almost every standpoint, the Democratic campaign contrasted sharply with that of the Republicans. McGovern and his running mate, Sargent Shriver, first director of the Peace Corps and then of the Office of Economic Opportunity, and later the U.S. ambassador to France, were on the road incessantly from Labor Day until election day.

McGovern tried in vain to draw Nixon into debate. His initial tax and welfare reform proposals attracted widespread criticism and helped alienate several traditional sources of Democratic strength, such as ethnic groups and blue-collar workers. When he substituted Shriver for Sen. Thomas F. Eagleton of Missouri, his original running mate, after disclosures of Eagleton's earlier psychiatric problems, he was attacked for poor judgment and vacillation. His chief issue, administration conduct of the Vietnam war, lost whatever remaining impact it might have had when an administration-negotiated peace appeared to be in sight during the last days of the campaign.

The McGovern-Shriver campaign depended, to a much larger extent than did the Republicans, on small contributions from many Americans, solicited in mass mailings. Reports indicated the amount collected was far smaller than the amount in the Republican treasury, but it was adequate to wage a presidential campaign.

McGovern's organization, too, suffered by comparison with the Committee to Re-elect the President. In addition to the delay caused by the replacing of Eagleton, the machinery of the South Dakotan's campaign was slowed further by squabbling and disorganization in the top echelons.

Instead of moving into the offensive against the administration, McGovern was kept on the defensive throughout the campaign, constantly forced to explain

(Continued on p. 22)

The Watergate Affair

Five men, wearing surgical gloves and carrying electronic surveillance equipment, were arrested early in the morning of June 17, 1972, in the Democratic national headquarters in the Watergate office building in Washington, D.C.

The bungled break-in turned out to be only one incident in a well-financed conspiracy against the Democrats. It led to allegations of sabotage and espionage involving officials of President Nixon's re-election committee and the White House staff. It was paid for with hundreds of thousands of dollars in unreported campaign funds.

By the end of the year, the incident had grown into one of the largest campaign scandals in the history of presidential politics. Seven men were charged with conspiracy, burglary and wiretapping; they were convicted early in 1973 by a federal court jury in Washington. Three civil suits were pending in early 1973 as Democratic and Republican officials filed charges and countercharges. In the 93rd Congress that convened in January 1973, a select committee of the Senate was appointed to investigate the matter in detail. *(Later developments, presidential chapter)*

Seven Defendants. The five men arrested in the Watergate were:

• James W. McCord Jr., a former FBI and CIA agent and, until he was fired June 19, security coordinator of the Committee for the Re-election of the President.

• Four men from Miami, Fla.: Bernard L. Barker, Virgilio R. Gonzalez, Eugenio R. Martinez and Frank A. Sturgis. All but Gonzalez were said to have CIA connections, and all had been active in the movement against the Castro government in Cuba.

Also indicted with the five men by a federal grand jury in Washington Sept. 15 were:

• E. Howard Hunt Jr., a former CIA agent, a writer of spy novels and a former White House consultant.

• G. Gordon Liddy, counsel to the President's re-election finance committee at the time of the break-in—he was fired nine days later—and former FBI agent.

Expensive Intelligence. After the break-in, various investigations disclosed meetings, phone calls, financial transactions and other related events that occurred months before the actual incident. News reports Oct. 10 said that a widespread Republican intelligence operation had been financed with a secret re-election committee fund containing several hundred thousand dollars.

Alfred C. Baldwin, a former FBI agent, became a key witness in the case in return for immunity from prosecution. He described in detail on Oct. 4 how he had wiretapped Democratic phones and given his findings to Republican officials. His charges were denied.

Later reports said that *agents provocateurs* had been recruited by a man with White House contacts to undermine Democratic presidential campaign operations.

earlier positions and rebut Republican charges. One issue that was potentially damaging to Nixon was the break-in a Democratic headquarters in Washington in June and ensuing disclosures of the alleged involvement of administration officials in espionage and sabotage directed against the Democrats. McGovern linked this issue with other charges of Republican favoritism toward big business, calling it "the most corrupt administration in history." The charge failed to excite the voters enough to head off the Nixon sweep.

Yet another factor working for Nixon and against McGovern was the absence of Democratic Gov. George C. Wallace of Alabama from the ballot as a third-party candidate. Every one of the 13 states of the formerly solidly Democratic South supported Nixon by a sizable margin. In that region, and among blue-collar workers in other parts of the country, it was clear that Wallace would have won votes that went to Nixon. Wallace's strong showing in several presidential primary states, especially Florida and Michigan, was evidence of his potential strength in a three-way general election contest in 1972; four years earlier, as the candidate of the American Independent Party, he carried five southern states with 13.5 per cent of the popular vote and 46 electoral votes. Any presidential plans he might have had in 1972 were gunned out of sight in May by an assassination attempt that left him permanently crippled and nearly cost him his life.

McGovern, who spent election night in Sioux Falls, S.D., said in his concession statement, "There can be no question at all that we have pushed this country in the direction of peace, and I think each one of us loves the title of peacemaker more than any office in the land."

With McGovern's candidacy had come a new Democratic national chairman, Jean Westwood, and a reorganized national committee. McGovern had been chairman of a party reform commission that had opened up the national convention and its procedures to unprecedented numbers of youths, women and members of minority groups. The reforms brought deep resentments from some of the traditional elements of the party, including organized labor, which thought they had been cast aside.

Short Coattails. As the campaign failed to develop a discussion between the two standard-bearers on substantive issues, the chief issue became personalities. The electorate demonstrated resoundingly that it liked Richard Nixon better than George McGovern. But public opinion pollsters found that affection for Nixon ran quite shallow. And support for him did not transfer to many contests for lower offices. On election night, Sen. Robert Dole of Kansas, the Republican national chairman, called the President's re-election victory "a personal triumph for Mr. Nixon but not a party triumph."

The 1972 election marked the first time in the nation's history that a party had carried 60 per cent or more of the presidential vote but failed to add seats in both the House and Senate. And it was the first time in such a runaway election that the party taking the presidency failed to win both chambers of Congress.

In a drastic break with tradition, Democratic control of the Senate was widened to 57-43 in the 93rd Congress, a gain of two Democratic seats from the 55-45 in the 92nd. Republican gains in the House narrowed the gap to 243-192 in the Democrats' favor, a net gain of 13 Republican seats from the previous line-up of 255 Democrats, 177 Republicans and three vacancies (one Democratic and two Republicans, making the breakdown of seats 256-179). And the Democrats increased their already strong hold on statehouses, adding one governorship for a total of 31 to the Republicans' 19.

One reason for the relatively poor showing of the Republicans in these contests was the almost total concentration on re-electing the President by Republicans at the national level. Nixon campaigned for only a few senatorial and gubernatorial candidates, several of whom won. Some Republicans felt their party's cause would have been helped in those races by more assistance from the President and his committee.

Another element of the Republicans' failure to take control of either house of Congress—they needed 39 new seats in the House and five in the Senate—was their low starting point. In the three previous instances when presidential candidates won by more than 60 per cent—Harding in 1920, Roosevelt in 1936 and Johnson in 1964—their parties already held majorities in both chambers.

Voter Turnout. The total votes cast for presidential candidates in the election—nearly 78 million—continued an unbroken trend, begun in 1936, of increasing vote totals in each successive presidential election year. But for the third straight election, the percentage of eligible voters who actually voted dropped off. Fewer than 55 per cent of eligible voters voted, the lowest percentage since 1948. The percentage was 62.1 in 1964 and 60.7 in 1968.

PRESIDENCY

Richard M. Nixon, a man who once had the image of a political loser, swept back into the White House Nov. 7 with a devastating landslide victory over Sen. George McGovern (D S.D.).

Nixon, who barely lost and then barely won in his two previous bids for the presidency, carried a record of 49 states for 521 electoral votes. (A "faithless elector" in Virginia voted for a third-party candidate and reduced the total to 520 when the electors met in December.) Only Massachusetts and the District of Columbia went for McGovern, for a meager total of 17 electoral votes.

The margin of Nixon's electoral vote victory was the third largest in the nation's history, eclipsed only by the elections of 1820, when James Monroe rolled up 231 electoral votes to one for John Quincy Adams, and 1936, when

---

Votes Cast for President, 1920-1972

(Rounded off to nearest thousand)

1920	26,769,000	**1948**	48,794,000
1924	29,095,000	**1952**	61,551,000
1928	36,806,000	**1956**	62,027,000
1932	39,759,000	**1960**	68,838,000
1936	45,655,000	**1964**	70,645,000
1940	49,900,000	**1968**	73,211,000
1944	47,977,000	**1972**	77,734,000

SOURCES: Census Bureau and CQ

Franklin D. Roosevelt outdistanced Alfred M. Landon by 523 to 8.

Nixon's popular vote totaled 60.7 per cent, slightly behind the 61.1 per cent recorded by Lyndon B. Johnson in his 1964 landslide over Barry Goldwater. (McGovern received 37.5 per cent of the vote, with 1.8 per cent going to American Independent Party candidate John G. Schmitz and several other minor-party candidates. Only two other presidential candidates besides Johnson and Nixon have taken 60 per cent or more of the popular vote: Warren G. Harding in 1920 (60.3 per cent) and Franklin D. Roosevelt in 1936 (60.8 per cent).

Another feature of the Nixon landslide was the first Republican sweep since Reconstruction of the once solidly Democratic South. (And it was the first time since 1944 that the South had gone solidly for anybody.) By runaway margins, Nixon took all 11 states of the old Confederacy, plus all the border states. His victory in Arkansas marked the first presidential race since 1872 in which the state had gone Republican.

The outcome of the race appeared so certain after a few sample returns that television networks projected Nixon the winner before the polls even closed in a number of western states. NBC projected the outcome at 8:30 p.m. (EST), 20 minutes before CBS' announcement. But the timing of these projections was behind that of the 1964 election, when NBC projected Johnson the winner at 6:44 p.m.

Components of Victory. A key ingredient of McGovern's defeat was the crumbling of the old Roosevelt coalition of blacks, Jews and Catholic voters. A survey taken by CBS on election day showed Nixon taking the Catholic vote by 60 to 33 per cent, in contrast to the 55 to 70 per cent of that vote that Democrats had carried in previous elections. The CBS poll, compiled from a random sample of 15,000 voters as they left the polls, also revealed other surprises: Nixon taking 59 per cent of the blue-collar vote, 47 per cent of the vote of unemployed persons and 48 per cent of the youth vote—three categories of voters that McGovern strategists had considered solidly in their column.

According to NBC, which sampled 1,500 strategically located precincts, Nixon corralled 39 per cent of the Jewish vote, compared with 17 per cent in 1968. The NBC poll also showed Nixon winning 58 per cent of the vote in the nation's cities—another traditional bastion of Democratic strength.

The final days of campaigning were marked by vigorous efforts by McGovern to provoke Nixon into partisan rhetoric—something that had proved damaging to Nixon in previous campaigns. To the end, McGovern discounted reports that Nixon's peace efforts were on the verge of success. He said they were a "cynical effort" to win the election. "Peace is not at hand," McGovern said Nov. 5. "It is not even in sight."

Nixon countered that a vote for him was a "message to those with whom we are negotiating and to the leaders of the world that you back the President of the United States as he insists that we seek peace with honor and never peace with surrender."

SENATE

Despite the avalanche of votes for Nixon, the Democrats scored a net gain of two seats in the Senate, there-by increasing their majority to 57-43 in the 93rd Congress. Of the 33 seats contested, the Democrats won 16 and the Republicans won 17. Nineteen of those seats had been controlled by the Republicans in the 92nd Congress, 14 by the Democrats.

The most significant—and surprising—element of the Democratic gain was the upset of four seemingly well-entrenched Republican incumbents—Gordon Allott of Colorado, J. Caleb Boggs of Delaware, Jack Miller of Iowa and Margaret Chase Smith of Maine. If it had not been for Republican victories in four southern states (Virginia, North Carolina, Oklahoma and Texas), the Democratic majority in the Senate would have been much larger.

Ideological Shift. But what might have been more important than the change in party labels in the Senate was the apparent shift in the Senate's ideological orientation. If anything, it would be more liberal.

When the new Congress convened Jan. 3, 1973, there would be 13 new faces among the 100 men (no women) sworn into the Senate. Eight of the 13 would be Democrats and five would be Republicans.

Half of those new Democrats were considered significantly more liberal than the incumbent Republicans they upset. In this category were Floyd D. Haskell, who beat Allott in Colorado; Joseph R. Biden Jr., who defeated Boggs in Delaware; Dick Clark, who retired Miller in Iowa, and Rep. William D. Hathaway, who upset Smith in Maine. A fifth Democrat, Rep. James Abourezk, defeated Republican Robert W. Hirsch in South Dakota to take the seat of retiring Republican incumbent Karl E. Mundt. Abourezk was considered far more liberal than the conservative Mundt.

Two more new Democrats were conservatives who would replace conservatives. Sam Nunn of Georgia and J. Bennett Johnston Jr. of Louisiana defeated Republican opponents to fill the seats of Democratic incumbents David H. Gambrell (Ga.) and the late Allen J. Ellender (La.). The remaining Democrat, Walter (Dee) Huddleston, defied the southern election trend by winning his race against Republican Louie B. Nunn in Kentucky for the seat of retiring Republican John Sherman Cooper. Both the incumbent and his successor were moderates.

Of the five new Republicans winning Senate seats, only one—Rep. William Lloyd Scott of Virginia—defeated an incumbent Democrat. Scott upset moderate William B. Spong Jr. in what was seen as a gain for conservative forces in the Senate. Another conservative gain came in Oklahoma, where Republican Dewey F. Bartlett defeated Rep. Ed Edmondson (D) for the seat of retiring incumbent Fred R. Harris (D), an outspoken liberal.

Two more Republicans, Jesse A. Helms in North Carolina and Rep. James A. McClure in Idaho, defeated

Vote Breakdown

	Popular Votes	Per Cent	Electoral Votes
Nixon	47,169,905	60.7	520
McGovern	29,170,303	37.5	17
Minor Parties	1,394,042	1.8	1

(Official returns compiled by CQ from secretaries of state and election boards.)

Democratic opponents to win the seats of the Senate's two Jordans—B. Everett Jordan (D N.C.), who was upset in a primary, and Len B. Jordan (R Idaho), who retired. The incumbent Jordans both compiled conservative voting records. Helms, an arch-conservative, beat Rep. Nick Galifianakis (D); McClure, also a conservative, defeated William E. (Bud) Davis (D).

In New Mexico, moderately conservative Republican Peter V. Domenici defeated Democrat Jack Daniels for the seat of retiring incumbent Clinton P. Anderson (D), a moderate.

On balance, then, the conservatives probably lost some ground in the Senate elections. Of the 13 incumbents leaving office, nine could be considered conservative, three moderate and one liberal. Of their 13 replacements, four were considered liberal, two moderate and seven conservative.

Such ideological labels can be misleading. But trends were apparent in 1972. While the South was leaning toward Republican conservatives, other states long considered conservative bastions no longer could be taken for granted.

Incumbents Re-Elected. Aside from the 13 new members, 20 incumbents were returned to the Senate by the voters. The 12 Republican incumbents re-elected were Ted Stevens (Alaska), Charles H. Percy (Ill.), James B. Pearson (Kan.), Edward W. Brooke (Mass.), Robert P. Griffin (Mich.), Carl T. Curtis (Neb.), Clifford P. Case (N.J.), Mark O. Hatfield (Ore.), Strom Thurmond (S.C.), Howard H. Baker Jr. (Tenn.), John G. Tower (Texas) and Clifford P. Hansen (Wyo.).

The eight returning Democrats were John Sparkman (Ala.), John L. McClellan (Ark.), Walter F. Mondale (Minn.), James O. Eastland (Miss.), Lee Metcalf (Mont.), Thomas J. McIntyre (N.H.), Claiborne Pell (R.I.) and Jennings Randolph (W.Va.).

HOUSE

The House of Representatives in the 93rd Congress would look quite a bit different from the 1972 version, but the reasons were chiefly redistricting and retirement, not election defeats. The new count was 243 Democrats and 192 Republicans.

Republicans gained 13 House seats in the 1972 elections, far short of the 39 they needed to win control of the House. The 13-seat pickup was slightly more than the four House seats gained when President Nixon first was elected in 1968, but it was far less than the winning party usually gains in a presidential landslide.

A close look at the House figures showed that the President not only lacked coattails, but appeared to have little if any perceptible effect on House races.

The 1972 election was the first to take place after the reapportionment and redistricting that followed the 1970 census. More than a dozen entirely new districts were created, and others had major changes in their boundary lines. Most of these changes tended to favor the Republicans, because many new districts were placed in fast-growing Republican suburbs and because legislatures in several key states drew the lines to partisan Republican advantage. With redistricting and reapportionment eliminated, the 1972 House elections would have been a virtual standoff.

Redistricting also played a significant part in the defeat of House incumbents. Thirteen incumbents, eight Democrats and five Republicans, were defeated. For nine of these incumbents, seven of them Democrats, redistricting was the dominant factor in their defeat. Three lost because redistricting forced them to run against other incumbents.

Retirement, primary defeat and candidacy for higher office produced far more personnel changes for the 93rd Congress than did the results of the Nov. 7 election. Before the balloting even took place, 57 incumbent representatives were assured of replacement in January. The list did not include Rep. Hale Boggs (D La.) and Rep. Nick Begich (D Alaska), whose airplane disappeared in Alaska Oct. 16. Both were re-elected. Another plane crash, on Dec. 8 at Chicago, claimed the life of Rep. George W. Collins (D Ill.). Special elections to fill the three vacancies were scheduled early in 1973.

South. The only semblance of coattail effects was in the South, where Republicans took seven House seats out of Democratic hands.

For several states, the election of Republican representatives meant drastic breaks with tradition. Louisiana's 3rd District elected David C. Treen as the first Republican House member from the state since Reconstruction. Mississippi chose Republicans Thad Cochran and Trent Lott, who broke into what had been an entirely Democratic delegation. Neither district had been represented by a Republican in this century. Like Treen in Louisiana, both men took advantage of the retirements of popular Democratic incumbents to win against lesser-known Democratic rivals.

Other Republican breakthroughs were made in South Carolina, where former State Rep. Edward L. Young beat Democrat John W. Jenrette Jr., the primary election conqueror of veteran Democratic Rep. John L. McMillan; in Tennessee, where Robin L. Beard Jr. (R) ousted controversial Rep. William R. Anderson (D), former submarine commander and friend of the Berrigan brothers, two Catholic priests jailed for their anti-war activities; and in Virginia, where the seat of retiring Rep. Watkins M. Abbitt (D) went to Republican Robert W. Daniel Jr.

Texas and Florida were the big southern beneficiaries of reapportionment. Population growth entitled Florida to three new districts, and the results matched the prediction that one would go Democratic, one would be Republican and one would be a tossup. State Sen. William D. Gunter Jr. settled the tossup issue by winning his race in the 5th District against Republican Jack P. Insco. The other two went as expected.

The Texas Legislature created two new districts, and both followed the plan by going Democratic. State Sen. Barbara C. Jordan won in the 18th, in downtown Houston, and thereby became the first black to represent Texas in Congress in this century. Weather forecaster Dale Milford won the other new district, the 24th. In the 5th, Democratic Rep. Earle Cabell lost to a youthful challenger, Alan Steelman.

The Texas redistricting produced one bitter contest between incumbents, as Rep. Robert Price (R) and Democratic incumbent Graham Purcell fought it out in the 13th along the Oklahoma border. Price won by a comfortable margin.

Southern bright spots for Democrats came in Oklahoma, where James R. Jones, a former aide to President

Johnson, took the 1st District seat being vacated by Rep. Page Belcher (R), and in Georgia, where Andrew Young won the seat in Atlanta that Republican Fletcher Thompson left to run for the Senate. Like Jordan in Texas, Young was the first black to represent his state in this century.

East. Most of the attention in the East was focused on New York and its 39 House seats. As in the past, the Republican legislature designed the new district lines for Republican benefit. But, as in the past, there was none. Although the new boundaries made half a dozen New York Democratic representatives vulnerable, only one was defeated—three-term incumbent John G. Dow. When the results were all in, Republicans had 17 seats in the New York delegation, the same number they had after the 1970 election. But Democrats lost three in reapportionment.

The New Jersey returns told a similar story. Prospects of a Nixon landslide appeared to endanger three marginal Democratic incumbents—Henry Helstoski, James J. Howard and Frank Thompson Jr. But all three won. Connecticut, also seen as a focal point for Republican gains, did produce one. It was in the 5th, where six-term Rep. John M. Monagan (D) lost to Republican Ronald A. Sarasin.

There were three new faces in the Massachusetts delegation. One was John J. Moakley, a Democrat who ran in the 9th District as an independent and defeated the more conservative Rep. Louise Day Hicks (D). Moakley caucused with the Democrats in the 93rd Congress. Republican Paul W. Cronin won a come-from-behind victory over anti-war leader John F. Kerry in the 5th, keeping the party's grip on a seat previously held by Republican F. Bradford Morse, Cronin's former employer, who had been appointed under secretary to the United Nations. And in the 12th, Democrat Gerry E. Studds won a victory that had barely eluded him two years before as he defeated Republican William D. Weeks to capture the seat held by retiring Rep. Hastings Keith (R).

Republicans were pleased with the results from Maine and Maryland. In Maine, Bangor Mayor William Cohen reversed what had been a Democratic trend by winning the seat Democrat William D. Hathaway left to run successfully for the Senate. In Maryland, Republican Marjorie S. Holt, the Anne Arundel County clerk, won an easy victory over German-born Democratic candidate Werner H. Fornos.

Midwest. Illinois was the best Republican state in the Midwest, as Republicans realized a two-seat profit from a redistricting plan they favored in the legislature. The best-known Democratic casualty was liberal Rep. Abner J. Mikva (D), who was forced to run in a suburban district after the mapmakers eliminated his old constituency on Chicago's south side. Mikva lost narrowly to Republican Samuel H. Young. Rep. Frank Annunzio (D), also forced to move by redistricting, was able to survive. And another incumbent Democrat, down-stater George E. Shipley, won his eighth term in a Republican district experts said couldn't possibly go Democratic.

In Indiana, Republican William L. Hudnut III defeated Rep. Andrew Jacobs Jr. (D) in an Indianapolis district drawn especially so that Jacobs could not win. Rep. J. Edward Roush (D), faced with a similar situation in the Fort Wayne area, managed to pull out a close victory.

Women Members, 1947-72*

Starting with the first woman member of Congress, Rep. Jeannette Rankin (R Mont. 1917-19, 1941-43), 86 women had been elected or appointed to congressional seats through the 1972 elections—10 in the Senate only, 75 in the House only and one—Margaret Chase Smith (R Maine)—in both chambers. Listed below are the number of women members since the 80th Congress.

Congress	Senate	House
93rd	0	14
92nd	2	13
91st	1	10
90th	1	11
89th	2	10
88th	2	11
87th	2	17
86th	1	16
85th	1	15
84th	1	16
83rd	3	12
82nd	1	10
81st	1	9
80th	1	7

* Figures include not only those elected in the general election, but also those chosen in special elections and appointed to the office. Members who were elected after Congress had adjourned and, therefore, did not actually serve are included in the count.

Democrats gained a seat in Iowa. Two years earlier, Democrat Edward L. Mezvinsky challenged Rep. Fred Schwengel (R) and came within 765 votes of winning. In 1972, Mezvinsky tried again and won.

The only other district to change hands in the Midwest was in South Dakota, where former Lt. Gov. James Abdnor (R) took the seat that Democrat James Abourezk left to run for the Senate.

There were two battles between incumbents in the Midwest, both won by Democrats. Neal Smith had little trouble defeating Republican John H. Kyl in Iowa's 4th District, while David Obey trounced 30-year-veteran Alvin E. O'Konski (R) in Wisconsin's 7th.

West. Returns from the West were dominated by California, with its rich prize of five new House seats. Neither party had the votes to pass a partisan redistricting bill, so they settled on a compromise that divided the five new seats this way: two Democratic, two Republican, one tossup. That was the way it worked out. Rep. Paul N. McCloskey Jr. (R), who led an anti-war crusade against President Nixon in the 1972 presidential primaries, moved into one of the Republican districts and won it. The other Republican district went to a popular state senator, Republican Clair M. Burgener. The two Democratic districts went to Yvonne Brathwaite Burke, a black state representative, and to former U.S. Rep. George E. Brown Jr. (D 1963-71). The tossup district went narrowly to State Rep. William M. Ketchum (R).

Colorado's new suburban district went Republican, as expected, for State Sen. William L. Armstrong. But two Colorado seats switched parties. In Denver, Democrat

Patricia Schroeder won an upset victory over freshman Rep. James D. (Mike) McKevitt (R). And Republican James T. Johnson won the seat held by veteran Rep. Wayne N. Aspinall (D), who was defeated in a primary by law professor Alan Merson.

GOVERNORS

Chalking up a net gain of one, the Democrats in 1972 retained the wide margin of statehouse control they won in 1970, holding 31 governorships to the Republicans' 19. Of the 18 seats up for election in 1972, Democrats won 11 and Republicans seven. Despite upsets in several states, the net result was only a minimal change in party power.

Republicans lost governorships in Illinois, Delaware and Vermont, while ousting Democrats in North Carolina and Missouri. Close races in New Hampshire, West Virginia, North Carolina and Washington were won by Republicans, who also upset a favored Democratic candidate in Indiana. As expected, they won gubernatorial contests in Missouri and Iowa.

Incumbent or favored Republicans were upset by Democrats in Illinois, Rhode Island, North Dakota and Vermont, while Democratic incumbents were re-elected in Arkansas, Kansas, South Dakota and Utah. In Montana and Texas, Democrats were elected to succeed retiring Democratic governors. As expected, the Democratic challenger unseated Delaware's Republican incumbent by capitalizing on the issue of taxes.

Money and Taxes. In West Virginia's gubernatorial race, which drew national attention, Republican Gov. Arch A. Moore put together his general popularity and campaigning ability with Nixon's strong showing in the state—and the obvious incongruity of a millionaire populist candidate running in one of the nation's poorest states—to defeat Democratic challenger John D. (Jay) Rockefeller IV, the secretary of state. The loss was expected to slow Rockefeller's rise in national Democratic politics.

If money played a role in the West Virginia outcome, money and taxes were particularly crucial issues in three other races in which Republican governors had strong challenges. Only one of the Republicans, Daniel J. Evans of Washington, was able to surmount charges of excessive government spending and taxing raised by his opponent, former Gov. Albert D. Rosellini (D 1957-65). Evans reminded the state's voters that both spending and taxes had increased during Rosellini's administrations.

Gov. Russell W. Peterson (R Del.) was not successful in overcoming the tax issue and went down to defeat before Sherman W. Tribbitt (D). Taxes were also a major factor in the loss of Illinois Gov. Richard B. Ogilvie (R) to Democratic challenger Daniel Walker.

Close Races, New Faces. Despite little over-all shift in party power, there were a number of surprises in the gubernatorial races, resulting in several new faces. Some of the newcomers, besides Walker and Tribbitt, were:

● Indiana's Otis T. Bowen (R), who overwhelmed his favored opponent, former Gov. Matthew E. Welsh (D 1961-65).

● Missouri's Christopher (Kit) Bond (R), at age 33 the youngest governor-elect in 1972.

Governor Party Control, 1946-72

Following elections of	Democrats	Republicans
1946	23	25
1948	30	18
1950	23	25
1952	18	30
1954	27	21
1956	28	20
1958	35	14
1960	34	16
1962	34	16
1964	33	17
1966	25	25
1968 [1]	19	31
1970	29	21
1972	31	19

1 *The Republican total includes Gov. Agnew of Maryland, who was elected Vice President. Following his resignation, a Democrat was elected by the state legislature to succeed him, making the new lineup Democrats 20, Republicans 30.*

● James E. Holshouser, elected North Carolina's first Republican governor since 1901.

● Texan Dolph Briscoe, the Democratic challenger who defeated incumbent Preston Smith in the Democratic primary and came from behind in the early returns to defeat Republican Henry C. Grover Jr. despite a strong Nixon vote in the state.

● Lt. Gov. Thomas L. Judge, elected the new Democratic governor of Montana.

● Meldrim Thomson Jr., a conservative Republican elected governor of New Hampshire.

● Democratic Rep. Arthur A. Link, who pulled ahead to defeat his favored opponent, Lt. Gov. Richard Larsen (R) for the governorship of North Dakota.

● Democrat Philip W. Noel, who upset favored Republican Herbert F. DeSimone in Rhode Island.

● Thomas P. Salmon (D), who defeated Luther F. Hackett (R), chosen by retiring Gov. Deane C. Davis (R) to succeed him as governor of Vermont.

Successful Incumbents. All but two of the nine incumbent governors running for re-election in the November election were re-elected. Defeated were two Republicans—Peterson of Delaware and Ogilvie of Illinois. Successful incumbent gubernatorial candidates were:

● Democrat Dale Bumpers, who won his second term in Arkansas with more than 3-1 support from the voters.

● Republican Robert Ray, Iowa.

● Democrat Robert Docking, who won an unprecedented fourth two-year term as governor of Kansas.

● Democrat Richard F. Kneip, South Dakota.

● Democrat Calvin L. Rampton, Utah.

● Republican Daniel J. Evans, Washington.

● Republican Arch A. Moore, West Virginia.

Of the nine incumbent governors who were not candidates in the November elections, three were ineligible to succeed themselves, four were retiring and two—Republican Walter R. Peterson of New Hampshire and Democrat Preston Smith of Texas—were defeated in primary elections.

Political Charts

Results of Presidential Elections, 1860-1972

YEAR	NO. OF STATES	CANDIDATES		ELECTORAL VOTE		POPULAR VOTE	
		DEM.	GOP	DEM.	GOP	DEM.	GOP
1860 (a.	33	Stephen A. Douglas Herschel V. Johnson	Abraham Lincoln Hannibal Hamlin	12 4%	180 59%	1,379,434 29.4%	1,867,198 39.8%
1864 (b)	36	George B. McClellan George H. Pendelton	Abraham Lincoln Andrew Johnson	21 9%	212 91%	1,805,063 44.9%	2,219,362 55.1%
1868 (c)	37	Horatio Seymour Francis P. Blair Jr.	Ulysses S. Grant Schuyler Colfax	80 27%	214 73%	2,703,933 47.3%	3,013,313 52.7%
1872 (d)	37	Horace Greeley Benjamin Gratz Brown	Ulysses S. Grant Henry Wilson	(e)	286 82%	2,833,711 43.8%	3,597,375 55.6%
1876	38	Samuel J. Tilden Thomas A. Hendricks	Rutherford B. Hayes William A. Wheeler	184 50%	185 50%	4,287,670 50.9%	4,035,924 47.9%
1880	38	Winfield S. Hancock William H. English	James A. Garfield Chester A. Arthur	155 42%	214 58%	4,444,976 48.2%	4,454,433 48.3%
1884	38	Grover Cleveland Thomas A. Hendricks	James G. Blaine John A. Logan	219 55%	182 45%	4,875,971 48.5%	4,852,234 48.3%
1888	38	Grover Cleveland Allen G. Thurman	Benjamin Harrison Levi P. Morton	168 42%	233 58%	5,540,365 48.6%	5,445,269 47.8%
1892 (e)	44	Grover Cleveland Adlai E. Stevenson	Benjamin Harrison Whitelaw Reid	277 62%	145 33%	5,556,982 46.0%	5,191,466 43.0%
1896	45	William J. Bryan Arthur Sewall	William McKinley Garret A. Hobart	176 39%	271 61%	6,516,722 46.7%	7,113,734 51.0%
1900	45	William J. Bryan Adlai E. Stevenson	William McKinley Theodore Roosevelt	155 35%	292 65%	6,358,160 45.5%	7,219,828 51.7%
1904	45	Alton B. Parker Henry G. Davis	Theodore Roosevelt Charles W. Fairbanks	140 29%	336 71%	5,084,533 37.6%	7,628,831 56.4%
1908	46	William J. Bryan John W. Kern	William H. Taft James S. Sherman	162 34%	321 66%	6,410,665 43.1%	7,679,114 51.6%
1912 (f)	48	Woodrow Wilson Thomas R. Marshall	William H. Taft James S. Sherman	435 82%	8 1%	6,301,254 41.9%	3,485,831 23.2%
1916	48	Woodrow Wilson Thomas R. Marshall	Charles E. Hughes Charles W. Fairbanks	277 52%	254 48%	9,131,511 49.3%	8,548,935 46.1%
1920	48	James M. Cox Franklin D. Roosevelt	Warren G. Harding Calvin Coolidge	127 24%	404 76%	9,133,092 34.1%	16,153,115 60.3%
1924 (g)	48	John W. Davis Charles W. Bryan	Calvin Coolidge Charles G. Dawes	136 26%	382 71%	8,386,704 28.8%	15,719,921 54.0%
1928	48	Alfred E. Smith Joseph T. Robinson	Herbert C. Hoover Charles Curtis	87 16%	444 84%	15,007,698 40.8%	21,437,277 58.2%
1932	48	Franklin D. Roosevelt John N. Garner	Herbert C. Hoover Charles Curtis	472 89%	59 11%	22,829,501 57.4%	15,760,684 39.6%
1936	48	Franklin D. Roosevelt John N. Garner	Alfred M. Landon Frank Knox	523 98%	8 2%	27,757,333 60.8%	16,684,231 36.5%
1940	48	Franklin D. Roosevelt Henry A. Wallace	Wendell L. Willkie Charles L. McNary	449 85%	82 15%	27,313,041 54.7%	22,348,480 44.8%
1944	48	Franklin D. Roosevelt Harry S Truman	Thomas E. Dewey John W. Bricker	432 81%	99 19%	25,612,610 53.4%	22,017,617 45.9%
1948 (h	48	Harry S Truman Alben W. Barkley	Thomas E. Dewey Earl Warren	303 57%	189 36%	24,179,345 49.6%	21,991,291 45.1%
1952	48	Adlai E. Stevenson John J. Sparkman	Dwight D. Eisenhower Richard M. Nixon	89 16%	442 83%	27,314,992 44.4%	33,936,234 55.1%
1956	48	Adlai E. Stevenson Estes Kefauver	Dwight D. Eisenhower Richard M. Nixon	74 14%	457 86%	26,022,752 42.0%	35,590,472 57.4%
1960	50	John F. Kennedy Lyndon B. Johnson	Richard M. Nixon Henry Cabot Lodge	303 62%	219 36%	34,220,984 49.5%	34,108,157 49.3%
1964	50*	Lyndon B. Johnson Hubert H. Humphrey	Barry Goldwater William E. Miller	486 90%	52 10%	43,129,484 61.1%	27,178,188 38.5%
1968 (j)	50*	Hubert H. Humphrey Edmund S. Muskie	Richard M. Nixon Spiro T. Agnew	191 36%	301 56%	31,275,165 42.7%	31,785,480 43.4%
1972	50*	George McGovern Sargent Shriver	Richard M. Nixon Spiro T. Agnew	520 97%	17 3%	29,170,583 38%	47,169,905 61%

*50 states plus District of Columbia.

(a) 1860: John C. Breckinridge, southern Democratic nominee, polled 72 electoral votes. John Bell, Constitutional Union, polled 39 electoral votes.

(b) 1864: 81 electoral votes were not cast.

(c) 1868: 23 electoral votes were not cast.

(d) 1872: Horace Greeley died after election; 63 Democratic electoral votes were scattered. 17 were not voted.

(e) 1892: James B. Weaver, People's Party, polled 22 electoral votes.

(f) 1912: Theodore Roosevelt, Progressive, polled 88 electoral votes.

(g) 1924: Robert M. LaFollette, Progressive, polled 13 electoral votes.

(h) 1948: J. Strom Thurmond, States' Rights, polled 39 electoral votes.

(i) 1960: 15 electoral votes cast for Sen. Harry Flood Byrd (D Va.).

(j) 1968: 46 electoral votes cast for George C. Wallace.

Election Results, Congress and Presidency, 1854-1972

Election Year	Congress Elected	HOUSE					SENATE					PRESIDENCY	
		Members Elected			Gains/Losses		Members Elected			Gains/Losses		Elected	Popular Vote Plurality
		Dem.	Rep.	Misc.	Dem.	Rep.	Dem.	Rep.	Misc.	Dem.	Rep.		
1854	34th	83	108	43			42	15	5			Pierce (D)	
1856	35th	131	92	14	+ 48	— 16	39	20	5	— 3	+ 5	Buchanan (D)	498,209
1858	36th	101	113	23	— 30	+ 21	38	26	2	— 1	+ 6		
1860	37th	42	106	28	— 59	— 7	11	31	7	—27	+ 5	Lincoln (R)	487,764
1862	38th	80	103		+ 38	— 3	12	39		+ 1	+ 8		
1864	39th	46	145		— 34	+ 42	10	42		— 2	+ 3	Lincoln (R)	414,299
1866	40th	49	143		+ 3	— 2	11	42		+ 1	0	Johnson (R)	
1868	41st	73	170		+ 24	+ 27	11	61		0	+ 19	Grant (R)	309,380
1870	42nd	104	139		+ 31	— 31	17	57		+ 6	— 4		
1872	43rd	88	203		— 16	+ 64	19	54		+ 2	— 3	Grant (R)	763,664
1874	44th	181	107	3	+ 93	— 96	29	46		+ 10	— 8		
1876	45th	156	137		— 25	+ 30	36	39	1	+ 7	— 7	Hayes (R)	—251,746
1878	46th	150	128	14	— 6	— 9	43	33		+ 7	— 6		
1880	47th	130	152	11	— 20	+ 24	37	37	2	— 6	+ 4	Garfield (R)	9,457
1882	48th	200	119	6	+ 70	— 33	36	40		— 1	+ 3	Arthur (R)	
1884	49th	182	140	2	— 18	+ 21	34	41		— 2	+ 2	Cleveland (D)	23,737
1886	50th	170	151	4	— 12	+ 11	37	39		+ 3	— 2		
1888	51st	156	173	1	— 14	+ 22	37	47		0	+ 8	Harrison (R)	—95,096
1890	52nd	231	88	14	+ 75	— 85	39	47	2	+ 2	0		
1892	53rd	220	126	8	— 11	+ 38	44	38	3	+ 5	— 9	Cleveland (D)	365,516
1894	54th	104	246	7	—116	+ 120	30	44	5	— 5	+ 6		
1896	55th	134	206	16	+ 30	— 40	34	46	10	— 5	+ 2	McKinley (R)	597,012
1898	56th	163	185	9	+ 29	— 21	26	53	11	— 8	+ 7		
1900	57th	153	198	5	— 10	+ 13	29	56	3	+ 3	+ 3	McKinley (R)	861,668
1902	58th	178	207		+ 25	+ 9	32	58		+ 3	+ 2	Roosevelt (R)	
1904	59th	136	250		— 42	+ 43	32	58		0	0	Roosevelt (R)	2,544,298
1906	60th	164	222		+ 28	— 28	29	61		— 3	— 3		
1908	61st	172	219		+ 8	— 3	32	59		+ 3	— 2	Taft (R)	1,268,449
1910	62nd	228	162	1	+ 56	— 57	42	49		+ 10	—10		
1912	63rd	290	127	18	+ 62	— 35	51	44	1	+ 9	— 5	Wilson (D)	2,173,466
1914	64th	231	193	8	— 59	+ 66	56	39	1	+ 5	— 5		
1916	65th	210	216	9	— 21	+ 23	53	42	1	— 3	+ 3	Wilson (D)	582,576
1918	66th	191	237	7	— 19	+ 21	47	48	1	— 6	+ 6		
1920	67th	132	300	1	— 59	+ 63	37	59		—10	+ 11	Harding (R)	7,020,023
1922	68th	207	225	3	+ 75	— 75	43	51	2	+ 6	— 8	Coolidge (R)	
1924	69th	183	247	5	— 24	+ 22	40	54	1	— 3	+ 3	Coolidge (R)	333,217
1926	70th	195	237	3	+ 12	— 10	47	48	1	+ 7	— 6		
1928	71st	163	267	1	— 32	+ 30	39	56	1	— 8	+ 8	Hoover (R)	6,429,579
1930	72nd	216	218	1	+ 53	— 49	47	48	1	+ 8	— 8		
1932	73rd	313	117	5	+ 97	—101	59	36	1	+ 12	—12	Roosevelt (D)	7,068,817
1934	74th	322	103	10	+ 9	— 14	69	25	2	+ 10	—11		
1936	75th	333	89	13	+ 11	— 14	75	17	4	+ 6	— 8	Roosevelt (D)	11,073,102
1938	76th	262	169	4	— 71	+ 80	69	23	4	— 6	+ 6		
1940	77th	267	162	6	+ 5	— 7	66	28	2	— 3	+ 5	Roosevelt (D)	4,964,561
1942	78th	222	209	4	— 45	+ 47	57	38	1	— 9	+ 10		
1944	79th	243	190	2	+ 21	— 19	57	38	1	0	0	Roosevelt (D)	3,594,993
1946	80th	188	246	1	— 55	+ 56	45	51		—12	+ 13	Truman	
1948	81st	263	171	1	+ 75	— 75	54	42		+ 9	— 9	Truman (D)	2,188,054
1950	82nd	234	199	2	— 29	+ 28	48	47		— 6	+ 5		
1952	83rd	213	221	1	— 21	+ 22	47	48	1	— 1	+ 1	Eisenhower (R)	6,621,242
1954	84th	232	203		+ 19	— 18	48	47	1	+ 1	— 1		
1956	85th	234	201		+ 2	— 2	49	47		+ 1	0	Eisenhower (R)	9,567,720
1958	86th	283	154		+ 49	— 47	66	34		+ 17	—13		
1960	87th	263	174		— 20	+ 20	64	36		— 2	+ 2	Kennedy (D)	118,574*
1962	88th	258	176	1**	— 4	+ 2	68	32		+ 4	— 4		
1964	89th	295	140		+ 38	— 38	67	33		+ 2	— 2	Johnson (D)	15,951,296
1966	90th	248	187		— 47	+ 47	64	36		— 3	+ 3		
1968	91st	243	192		— 4	+ 4	58	42		— 5	+ 5	Nixon (R)	510,314
1970	92nd	255	180		+ 12	— 12	55	45		— 4	+ 2		
1972	93rd	244†	191†		— 12	+ 12	57	43		+ 2	— 2	Nixon (R)	17,999,222

*Includes divided Alabama elector slate votes.

**Vacancy—Rep. Clem Miller (D Calif. 1959-62) died Oct. 6, 1962, but his name remained on the ballot and he received a plurality.

†The House lineup as of Nov. 6, 1972, was 255 Democrats, 177 Republicans and three vacancies.

State-by-State Presidential Election Returns, 1900-1972

State	Victorious Party in Presidential Races, 1900-1972																			No. of Times Parties Won		
	1900	1904	1908	1912	1916	1920	1924	1928	1932	1936	1940	1944	1948	1952	1956	1960	1964	1968	1972	Dem.	Rep.	Other
Alabama	D	D	D	D	D	D	D	D	D	D	D	D	SR	D	D[5]	D[6]	R	AI	R	15	2	2
Alaska																R	D	R	R	1	3	0
Arizona			D	D	R	R	R	R	D	D	D	D	D	R	R	R	R	R	R	7	9	0
Arkansas	D	D	D	D	D	D	D	D	D	D	D	D	D	D	D	D	D	AI	R	17	1	1
California	R	R	R	PR	D	R	R	R	D	D	D	D	D	R	R	R	D	R	R	7	11	1
Colorado	D	R	D	D	D	R	R	R	D	D	R	R	D	R	R	R	D	R	R	8	11	0
Connecticut	R	R	R	D	R	R	R	R	D	D	D	D	D	R	R	D	D	D	R	12	7	0
Delaware	R	R	R	D	R	R	R	R	D	D	D	D	D	R	R	D	D	R	R	13	6	0
District of Columbia																	D	D	D	3		
Florida	D	D	D	D	D	D	D	R	D	D	D	D	D	R	R	R	D	R	R	13	6	0
Georgia	D	D	D	D	D	D	D	D	D	D	D	D	D	D	D	D	R	AI	R	16	2	1
Hawaii																D	D	D	R	3	1	0
Idaho	D	R	R	D	D	R	R	R	D	D	D	D	D	R	R	R	D	R	R	9	10	0
Illinois	R	R	R	D	R	R	R	R	D	D	D	D	D	R	R	D	D	R	R	11	8	0
Indiana	R	R	R	D	R	R	R	R	D	D	R	R	R	R	R	R	D	R	R	4	15	0
Iowa	R	R	R	D	R	R	R	R	D	D	R	R	D	R	R	R	D	R	R	5	14	0
Kansas	R	R	R	D	D	R	R	R	D	D	R	R	R	R	R	R	D	R	R	6	14	0
Kentucky	D	D	D	D	D	D	R	R	D	D	D	D	D	R	R	D	D	R	R	13	6	0
Louisiana	D	D	D	D	D	D	D	D	D	D	D	D	SR	D	R	D	R	AI	R	14		0
Maine	R	R	R	D	R	R	R	R	R	R	R	R	R	R	R	R	D	D	R	3	16	0
Maryland	R	D[1]	D[2]	D	D	R	R	R	D	D	D	D	R	R	R	D	D	D	R	11	8	0
Massachusetts	R	R	R	D	R	R	R	D	D	D	D	D	D	R	R	D	D	D	D	11	8	0
Michigan	R	R	R	PR	R	R	R	R	D	D	D	D	R	R	R	D	D	D	R	6	12	1
Minnesota	R	R	R	PR	R	R	R	R	D	D	D	D	D	R	R	D	D	D	R	8	10	1
Mississippi	D	D	D	D	D	D	D	D	D	D	D	D	SR	D	D	[7]	R	AI	R	14	2	2
Missouri	D	R	R	D	D	R	R	R	D	D	D	D	D	R	R	D	D	D	R	11	8	0
Montana	D	R	R	D	D	R	R	R	D	D	D	D	D	R	R	R	D	R	R	9	10	0
Nebraska	R	R	D	D	D	R	R	R	D	D	R	R	R	R	R	R	D	R	R	6	13	0
Nevada	D	R	D	D	D	R	R	R	D	D	D	D	D	R	R	D	D	R	R	11	8	0
New Hampshire	R	R	R	D	D	R	R	R	R	D	D	D	D	R	R	R	D	R	R	7	12	0
New Jersey	R	R	R	D	R	R	R	R	D	D	D	D	R	R	R	D	D	R	R	7	12	0
New Mexico				D	D	R	R	R	D	D	D	D	D	R	R	D	D	R	R	9	7	0
New York	R	R	R	D	R	R	R	R	D	D	D	D	R	R	R	D	D	D	R	8	11	0
North Carolina	D	D	D	D	D	D	D	R	D	D	D	D	D	D	D	D	D	R[9]	R	16	3	0
North Dakota	R	R	R	D	D	R	R	R	D	D	R	R	R	R	R	R	D	R	R	5	14	0
Ohio	R	R	R	D	D	R	R	R	D	D	D	D	D	R	R	R	D	R	R	8	11	0
Oklahoma			D	D	D	R	D	R	D	D	D	D	D	R	R	R	D	R	R	10	7	0
Oregon	R	R	R	D	R	R	R	R	D	D	D	D	R	R	R[8]	R	D	R	R	6	13	0
Pennsylvania	R	R	R	PR	R	R	R	R	R	D	D	D	R	R	R	D	D	D	R	6	12	1
Rhode Island	R	R	R	D	R	R	R	D	D	D	D	D	D	R	R	D	D	D	R	10	9	0
South Carolina	D	D	D	D	D	D	D	D	D	D	D	D	SR	D	D	D	R	R	R	15	3	1
South Dakota	R	R	R	PR	R	R	R	R	D	D	R	R	R	R	R	R	D	R	R	3	15	1
Tennessee	D	D	D	D	D	R	D	R	D	D	D	D[4]	D	R	R	R	D	R	R	12	7	0
Texas	D	D	D	D	D	D	D	R	D	D	D	D	D	R	R	D	D	D	R	15	4	0
Utah	R	R	R	R	D	R	R	R	D	D	D	D	D	R	R	R	D	R	R	7	12	0
Vermont	R	R	R	R	R	R	R	R	R	R	R	R	R	R	R	R	D	R	R	1	18	0
Virginia	D	D	D	D	D	D	D	R	D	D	D	D	D	R	R	R	D	R	R	13	6	0
Washington	R	R	R	PR	D	R	R	R	D	D	D	D	D	R	R	R	D	D	R	8	10	1
West Virginia	R	R	R	D	R[3]	R	R	R	D	D	D	D	D	R	R	D	D	D	R	10	9	0
Wisconsin	R	R	R	D	R	R	PR	R	D	D	D	R	D	R	R	R	D	R	R	6	12	1
Wyoming	R	R	R	D	D	R	R	R	D	D	D	D	R	R	R	R	D	R	R	7	12	0
Winning Party	R	R	R	D	D	R	R	R	D	D	D	D	D	R	R	D	D	R	R	9	10	0

1 Seven electors voted Democratic; one Republican.
2 Six electors voted Democratic; two Republican.
3 Seven electors voted Republican; one Democratic.
4 Eleven electors voted Democratic; one States' Rights.
5 One elector voted for Walter Jones.
6 Six of 11 electors were not pledged to support national ticket and voted for Sen. Harry F. Byrd (D Va.).
7 Eight independent electors voted for Byrd.
8 One vote cast for Byrd.

9 Twelve electors voted Republican; one American Independent.
   With the exception of the District of Columbia, blanks indicate states not yet admitted to the Union. The District of Columbia received the presidential vote upon ratification of the 23rd Amendment to the Constitution in 1961.
AI - American Independent Party
D - Democratic Party
PR - Progressive (Bullmoose) Party
R - Republican Party
SR - States' Rights Party

Final 1968 Presidential Election Results

(For 1948-60 results, see Congress and the Nation, Vol. I,
p. 64-65. For 1964 results see Vol. II, p. 28.)

Based on complete vote totals reported to Congressional Quarterly
by the Governmental Affairs Institute

Total popular vote cast: 73,211,562

STATE	TOTAL POPULAR VOTE				ELECTORAL VOTE				PERCENTAGES		
	NIXON (R)	HUMPHREY (D)	WALLACE (AIP)	ALL OTHERS	NIXON	HUMPHREY	WALLACE	PLURALITY	NIXON	HUMPHREY	WALLACE
ALABAMA†	146,923	196,579	691,425	14,982			10	494,846 AIP	14.0	18.7	65.9
ALASKA	37,600	35,411	10,024	——	3			2,189 R	45.3	42.6	12.1
ARIZONA	266,721	170,514	46,573	3,128	5			96,207 R	54.8	35.0	9.6
ARKANSAS #	190,759	188,228	240,982	——			6	50,223 AIP	30.8	30.4	38.9
CALIFORNIA	3,467,664	3,244,318	487,270	52,335	40			223,346 R	47.8	44.7	6.7
COLORADO	409,345	335,174	60,813	5,867	6			74,171 R	50.5	41.3	7.5
CONNECTICUT	556,721	621,561	76,650	1,300		8		64,840 D	44.3	49.5	6.1
DELAWARE	96,714	89,194	28,459	——	3			7,520 R	45.1	41.6	13.3
FLORIDA	886,804	676,794	624,207	——	14			210,010 R	40.5	30.9	28.5
GEORGIA	380,111	334,439	535,550	——			12	155,439 AIP	30.4	26.8	42.8
HAWAII	91,425	141,324	3,469	——		4		49,899 D	38.7	59.8	1.5
IDAHO	165,369	89,273	36,541	——	4			76,096 R	56.8	30.7	12.5
ILLINOIS	2,174,774	2,039,814	390,958	14,203	26			134,960 R	47.1	44.2	8.5
INDIANA	1,067,885	806,659	243,108	5,945	13			261,226 R	50.3	38.0	11.4
IOWA	619,106	476,699	66,422	5,454	9			142,407 R	53.0	40.8	5.7
KANSAS	478,674	302,996	88,921	2,192	7			175,678 R	54.8	34.7	10.2
KENTUCKY	462,411	397,541	193,098	2,843	9			64,870 R	43.8	37.6	18.3
LOUISIANA	257,535	309,615	530,300	——			10	220,685 AIP	23.5	28.2	48.3
MAINE	169,254	217,312	6,370	——		4		48,058 D	43.1	55.3	1.6
MARYLAND	517,995	538,310	178,734	——		10		20,315 D	41.9	43.6	14.5
MASSACHUSETTS	766,844	1,469,218	87,088	8,602		14		702,374 D	32.9	63.0	3.7
MICHIGAN	1,370,665	1,593,082	331,968	10,535		21		222,417 D	41.5	48.2	10.0
MINNESOTA	658,643	857,738	68,931	3,198		10		199,095 D	41.5	54.0	4.3
MISSISSIPPI	88,516	150,644	415,349	——			7	264,705 AIP	13.5	23.0	63.5
MISSOURI	811,932	791,444	206,126	——	12			20,488 R	44.9	43.7	11.4
MONTANA	138,835	114,117	20,015	1,437	4			24,718 R	50.6	41.6	7.3
NEBRASKA	321,163	170,784	44,904	——	5			150,379 R	59.8	31.8	8.4
NEVADA	73,188	60,598	20,432	——	3			12,590 R	47.5	39.3	13.2
NEW HAMPSHIRE	154,903	130,589	11,173	633	4			24,314 R	52.1	43.9	3.8
NEW JERSEY	1,325,467	1,264,206	262,187	23,535	17			61,261 R	46.1	44.0	9.1
NEW MEXICO	169,692	130,081	25,737	1,828	4			39,611 R	51.8	39.7	7.9
NEW YORK *	3,007,932	3,378,470	358,864	46,421		43		370,538 D	44.3	49.7	5.3
NORTH CAROLINA	627,192	464,113	496,188	——	12		1•	131,004 R	39.5	29.2	31.3
NORTH DAKOTA	138,669	94,769	14,244	200	4			43,900 R	55.9	38.2	5.7
OHIO	1,791,014	1,700,586	467,495	603	26			90,428 R	45.2	42.9	11.8
OKLAHOMA	449,697	301,658	191,731	——	8			148,039 R	47.7	32.0	20.3
OREGON	408,433	358,866	49,683	2,640	6			49,567 R	49.8	43.8	6.1
PENNSYLVANIA	2,090,017	2,259,405	378,582	19,924		29		169,388 D	44.0	47.6	8.0
RHODE ISLAND	122,359	246,518	15,678	383		4		124,159 D	31.8	64.0	4.1
SOUTH CAROLINA	254,062	197,486	215,430	——	8			38,632 R	38.1	29.6	32.3
SOUTH DAKOTA	149,841	118,023	13,400	——	4			31,818 R	53.3	42.0	4.8
TENNESSEE	472,592	351,233	424,792	——	11			47,800 R	37.8	28.1	34.0
TEXAS	1,227,844	1,266,804	584,269	489		25		38,960 D	39.8	41.1	19.0
UTAH	238,728	156,665	26,906	269	4			82,063 R	56.5	37.1	6.3
VERMONT	85,142	70,255	5,104	902	3			14,887 R	52.8	43.5	3.2
VIRGINIA @	590,319	442,387	321,833	6,950	12			147,932 R	43.4	32.5	23.6
WASHINGTON	588,510	616,037	96,990	2,744		9		27,527 D	45.1	47.2	7.4
WEST VIRGINIA	307,555	374,091	72,560	——		7		66,536 D	40.8	49.6	9.6
WISCONSIN	809,997	748,804	127,835	4,902	12			61,193 R	47.9	44.3	7.6
WYOMING	70,927	45,173	11,105	——	3			25,754 R	55.8	35.5	8.7
DIST. OF COL.	31,012	139,566	——	——		3		108,554 D	18.2	81.8	——
TOTALS	31,785,480	31,275,165	9,906,473	244,444	301	191	46	510,315 R‡	43.4	42.7	13.5

Arkansas—Nixon, Humphrey, and Wallace vote each increased by amendment to early canvass in Jefferson County.

@ Virginia—Wallace vote increased by 1,561 over state canvass for vote in Shanandoah County omitted in original report.

• One North Carolina Republican elector cast his vote for Wallace.

† Alabama—Humphrey total is a combination of National Democratic (54,144) and Independent Democratic (142,435) votes; the AIP Wallace vote was cast as Democratic in this state.

* New York—Humphrey total includes 311,622 votes as Liberal candidate.

‡ Because of Humphrey's third-place finish in the South, plurality column does not add up to national total.

Final 1972 Presidential Election Results

Based on complete vote totals reported to Congressional Quarterly by the Secretaries of State

Total popular vote cast: 77,734,330

STATE	TOTAL POPULAR VOTE NIXON (R)	McGOVERN (D)	SCHMITZ (AIP)	ELECTORAL VOTE NIXON	McGOVERN	PLURALITY	PERCENTAGES NIXON	McGOVERN	SCHMITZ
ALABAMA	728,701	256,923	11,918	9		471,778 R	72.4	25.5	1.2
ALASKA	55,349	32,967	6,903	3		22,382 R	58.1	34.6	7.3
ARIZONA	402,812	198,540	21,208	6		204,272 R	61.6	30.4	3.3
ARKANSAS	448,541	199,892	2,887	6		248,649 R	68.9	30.7	0.4
CALIFORNIA	4,602,096	3,475,847	232,554	45		1,126,249 R	55.0	41.5	2.8
COLORADO	597,189	329,980	17,269	7		267,209 R	62.6	34.6	1.8
CONNECTICUT	810,763	555,498	17,239	8		255,265 R	58.6	40.1	1.3
DELAWARE	140,357	92,283	2,638	3		48,074 R	59.6	39.2	1.1
DIST. OF COL.	35,226	127,627	——		3	92,401 D	21.6	78.1	
FLORIDA	1,857,759	718,117	——	17		1,139,642 R	71.9	27.8	
GEORGIA	881,490	289,529	——	12		591,961 R	75.3	24.7	
HAWAII	168,865	101,409	——	4		67,456 R	62.5	37.5	
IDAHO	199,384	80,826	28,869	4		118,558 R	64.2	26.1	9.3
ILLINOIS	2,788,179	1,913,472	2,471*	26		874,707 R	59.0	40.5	0.1
INDIANA	1,405,154	708,568	——	13		696,586 R	66.1	33.3	
IOWA	706,207	496,206	22,056	8		210,001 R	57.6	40.5	1.8
KANSAS	619,812	270,287	21,808	7		349,529 R	67.6	29.5	2.4
KENTUCKY	676,446	371,159	17,627	9		305,287 R	63.4	34.8	1.6
LOUISIANA	686,852	298,142	52,099	10		388,710 R	65.3	28.3	5.0
MAINE	256,458	160,584	——	4		95,874 R	61.5	38.5	
MARYLAND	829,305	505,781	18,726	10		323,524 R	61.2	37.4	1.4
MASSACHUSETTS	1,112,078	1,332,540	2,877		14	220,462 D	45.2	54.2	0.1
MICHIGAN	1,961,721	1,459,435	63,321	21		502,286 R	56.2	41.8	1.8
MINNESOTA	898,269	802,346	31,407	10		95,923 R	51.6	46.1	1.7
MISSISSIPPI	505,125	126,782	11,598	7		378,343 R	78.2	19.6	1.8
MISSOURI	1,153,852	697,147	——	12		456,705 R	62.3	37.7	
MONTANA	183,976	120,197	13,430	4		63,779 R	57.9	37.9	4.2
NEBRASKA	406,298	169,991	——	5		236,307 R	70.5	29.5	
NEVADA	115,750	66,016	——	3		49,734 R	63.7	36.3	
NEW HAMPSHIRE	213,724	116,435	3,386	4		97,289 R	64.0	34.9	1.0
NEW JERSEY	1,845,502	1,102,211	34,378	17		743,291 R	61.6	36.8	1.1
NEW MEXICO	235,606	141,084	8,767	4		95,522 R	61.0	36.6	2.3
NEW YORK	4,192,778	2,951,084	——	41		1,241,694 R	58.5	41.2	
NORTH CAROLINA	1,054,889	438,705	25,018	13		616,184 R	69.5	28.9	1.6
NORTH DAKOTA	174,109	100,384	5,646	3		73,725 R	62.1	35.8	2.0
OHIO	2,441,827	1,558,889	80,067	25		882,938 R	59.6	38.1	1.9
OKLAHOMA	759,025	247,147	23,728	8		511,878 R	73.7	24.0	2.3
OREGON	486,686	392,760	46,211	6		93,926 R	52.4	42.3	5.0
PENNSYLVANIA	2,714,521	1,796,951	70,593	27		917,570 R	59.1	39.1	1.5
RHODE ISLAND	220,383	194,645		4		25,738 R	53.0	46.8	—
SOUTH CAROLINA	477,044	186,824	10,075	8		290,220 R	70.8	27.7	1.5
SOUTH DAKOTA	166,476	139,945	——	4		26,531 R	54.2	45.5	
TENNESSEE	813,147	357,293	30,373	10		455,854 R	67.7	29.7	2.6
TEXAS	2,298,896	1,154,289	6,039*	26		1,144,607 R	66.2	33.3	0.2
UTAH	323,643	126,284	28,549	4		197,359 R	67.6	26.4	6.0
VERMONT	117,149	68,174	——	3		48,975 R	62.8	36.5	
VIRGINIA	988,493	438,887	19,721	11†		549,606 R	67.8	30.1	1.4
WASHINGTON	837,135	568,334	58,906	9		268,801 R	56.9	38.6	4.0
WEST VIRGINIA	484,964	277,435	——	6		207,529 R	63.6	36.4	
WISCONSIN	989,430	810,174	47,525	11		179,256 R	53.4	43.7	2.6
WYOMING	100,464	44,358	748*	3		56,106 R	69.0	30.5	0.5
TOTAL	47,169,905	29,170,383	1,098,635	520	17	17,999,522	(60.7)	(37.5)	(1.4)

* Schmitz was not on ballot. Votes listed for him were write-in votes.
† One Virginia Republican elector pledged to Nixon voted for Libertarian Party candidates John Hospers and Theodora Nathan.

Democratic Convention Voting, 1948-1972

1948—Philadelphia

- For President:

Harry S. Truman, Mo.	947 ½
Richard B. Russell, Ga.	263
Paul McNutt, Ind.	½

- For Vice President: Alben W. Barkley, Ky., nominated by acclamation on the first ballot.

1952—Chicago

- For President: Adlai E. Stevenson, Ill. (ballots as follows):

	1st*	2nd**	3rd***
Kefauver, Tenn.	300 ½	362 ½	279 ½
Russell, Ga.	267 ½	294	260
Stevenson, Ill.	248 ½	324 ½	613
Harriman, N.Y.	126	121	
Kerr, Okla.	69	5 ½	67 ½
Barkley, Ky.	49 ½	78 ½	67 ½
Williams, Mich.	40 ½	—	—
Dever, Mass.	37 ½	30 ½	½
Humphrey, Minn.	26	—	—
Fulbright, Ark.	22	—	—
McMahon, Conn.	16	—	—
Murray, Mont.	12	—	—
Truman, Mo.	6	6	—
Ewing, N.Y.	4	1	3
Douglas, P., Ill.	3	3	3
Douglas, W.O., Wash.	½	—	

- For Vice President: John J. Sparkman, Ala., by acclamation.

*After several delegations switched their vote, the final result was: Stevenson 273, Kefauver 340, Russell 268, Harriman 123½, Barkley 48½, Kerr 65, with other candidates holding the same total.

**This is the final result of the ballot. Before the final result was announced, changes were as follows: Harriman, one additional vote; Barkley, 5 additional votes; Stevenson, 5 less votes.

***The ballot ended as carried in this column, with Stevenson 2½ votes short of the nomination. Utah which had balloted 7½ of its 12 votes for Stevenson, gave him the remaining 4½. A motion by Minnesota to make the nomination unanimous then was agreed to by voice vote.

1956—Chicago

- For President: Adlai E. Stevenson, Ill. (balloting as follows):

	1st*		1st*
Stevenson	905 ½	Chandler, Ky.	36 ½
Harriman, N.Y.	210	Davis, Ga.	33
Johnson, Texas	80	Battle, Va.	32 ½
Symington, Mo.	45 ½	Timmerman, S.C.	23 ½
		Lausche, Ohio	5 ½

- For Vice President: Estes Kefauver, Tenn. (balloting as follows):

	1st	2nd**
Kefauver, Tenn.	483 ½	551 ½
Kennedy, Mass.	304	618
Gore, Tenn.	178	110 ½
Wagner, N.Y.	162 ½	9 ½
Humphrey, Minn.	134 ½	74
Hodges, N.C.	40	½
Maner, Ala.	33	—
Anderson, N.M.	16	—
Clement, Tenn.	13 ½	½
Brown, Calif.	1	½
Collins, Fla.	1 ½	—
Symington, Mo.	1	—
Johnson, Texas	½	—

*The nomination was made unanimous when the first ballot ended.

**After switches the totals were: Kefauver 750, Kennedy, 593, Gore 11½, Wagner 6, Humphrey 5½, Clement ½. Following the roll call, the nomination was made unanimous.

***The ballot ended as carried in this column, with Stevenson 2½ votes short of the nomination. Utah which had balloted 7½ of its 12 votes for Stevenson, gave him the remaining 4½. A motion by Minnesota to make the nomination unanimous then was agreed to by voice vote.

1960—Los Angeles

- For President: John F. Kennedy, Mass. (balloting as follows):

	1st*		1st*
Kennedy	801	Smathers, Fla.	30
Johnson, Texas	409	Barnett, Miss.	23
Symington, Mo.	86	Loveless, Iowa	1 ½
Stevenson, Ill.	79 ½	Faubus, Ark.	½
Meyner, N.J.	43	Brown, Calif.	½
Humphrey, Minn.	41 ½	Rosellini, Wash.	½

- For Vice President: Lyndon B. Johnson, Texas, nominated by acclamation on the first ballot.

*The nomination was made unanimous when the first ballot ended.

1964—Atlantic City

- For President: Lyndon B. Johnson, Texas, by acclamation.
- For Vice President: Hubert H. Humphrey, Minn., by acclamation.

1968—Chicago

- For President: Hubert H. Humphrey, Minn. (balloting as follows):

	1st*		1st*
Humphrey	1,760-1/4	Kennedy, Mass.	12-3/4
McCarthy, Minn.	601	Bryant, Ala.	1 ½
McGovern, S.D.	146 ½	Wallace, Ala.	½
Phillips, D.C.	67 ½	Gray, Ga.	½
Moore, N.C.	17 ½		

*The nomination was made unanimous when the first ballot ended.

- For Vice President: Edmund S. Muskie, Maine (balloting as follows):

	1st*		1st*
Muskie	1,944 ½	McNair, S.C.	1 ½
Bond, Ga.	48 ½	Tate, Pa.	1 ½
Hoeh, N.H.	4	Sanford, N.C.	1
Kennedy, Mass.	3	Shriver, Ill. and Md.	1
McCarthy, Minn.	3	Lowenstein, N.Y.	1
Ribicoff, Conn.	2	Reuss, Wis.	1
McGovern, S.D.	2	O'Dwyer, N.Y.	1
Edwards, Calif.	2	Ryan, N.Y.	3/4
Daley, Ill.	1 ½		

*Muskie was later declared nominee by acclamation before conclusion of first ballot.

1972—Miami Beach

- For President: George McGovern, South Dakota (balloting as follows):

	1st*		
McGovern	1,715 ½	Humphrey	66 ½
Jackson	534	Mills	33 ½
Wallace	385 ½	Muskie	24 ½
Chisholm	152	Kennedy	12 ½
Sanford	77 ½	Others	9

*Before switches.

- For Vice President: Thomas Eagleton, Missouri* (balloting as follows):

	1st
Eagleton	1,735
Others	1,038
Abstentions	13.5
Absent	1.6

* Eagleton withdrew July 31 and was replaced by Sargent Shriver Aug. 8.

Republican Convention Voting, 1948-1972

1948—Philadelphia

• For President: Thomas E. Dewey, N.Y. (ballots as follows):

	1st	2nd	3rd
Dewey, N.Y.	434	515	All
Taft, Ohio	224	274	———
Stassen, Minn.	157	149	——
Vandenberg, Mich.	62	62	——
Warren, Calif.	59	57	——
Martin, Mass.	18	10	——
MacArthur, Wis.	11	7	——

• For Vice President: Earl Warren, Calif., nominated by acclamation on the first ballot.

1952—Chicago

• For President: Dwight D. Eisenhower, Kan. (ballots as follows):

	1st*
Eisenhower, Kan.	595
Taft, Ohio	500
Warren, Calif.	81
Stassen, Minn.	20
MacArthur, N.Y.	10

• For Vice President: Richard M. Nixon, Calif., by acclamation.

After switches the totals were: Eisenhower 841, MacArthur 4, Taft 284, Warren 77. A motion to make the nomination unanimous then was agreed to by voice vote.

1956—San Francisco

• For President: Dwight D. Eisenhower, Kan., unanimously nominated on first ballot.

• For Vice President: Richard M. Nixon, Calif., unanimously nominated on first ballot.

1960—Chicago

• For President: Richard M. Nixon Calif. (ballots as follows):

	1st*
Nixon	1,321
Goldwater, Ariz.	10

• For Vice President: Henry Cabot Lodge Jr., Mass., unanimously nominated on the first ballot.

The nomination was made unanimous when the first ballot ended.

1964—San Francisco

• For President: Barry Goldwater, Ariz. (ballots as follows):

	1st
Goldwater	883
Scranton	214
Rockefeller	114
Smith	27
Fong	5
Judd	22
Romney	41
Lodge	2

• For Vice President: William E. Miller, New York, nominated by acclamation on the first ballot.

1968—Miami Beach

• For President: Richard M. Nixon, N.Y. (ballots as follows):

	1st *
Nixon	692
Rockefeller, N.Y.	277
Reagan, Calif.	182
Rhodes, Ohio	55
Romney, Mich.	50
Case, N.J.	22
Carlson, Kan.	20
Rockefeller, Ark.	18
Fong, Hawaii	14
Stassen, Pa.	2
Lindsay, N.Y.	1

Before switches. Because of parliamentary confusion, Nixon never was declared the unanimous choice.

• For Vice President: Spiro T. Agnew, Md. (ballots as follows):

	1st*
Agnew	1,119
Romney, Mich.	186
Lindsay, N.Y.	10
Brooke, Mass.	1
Rhodes, Ohio	1

The nomination was made unanimous when the first ballot ended.

1972—Miami Beach

• For President: Richard M. Nixon, N.Y. (ballots as follows):

	1st
Nixon	1,347
McCloskey	1

• For Vice President: Spiro T. Agnew, Md. (ballots as follows):

	1st
Agnew	1,345
David Brinkley (newscaster)	1
Abstentions	2

DISTRIBUTION OF HOUSE SEATS AND ELECTORAL VOTES

Based on Censuses of 1940, 1950, 1960 and 1970

	U.S. HOUSE SEATS							ELECTORAL VOTES Presidential Elections of			
	1943-1953	1950 Census Changes	1953-1963	1960 Census Changes	1963-1973	1970 Census Changes	1973-1983	1944, 1948	1952, 1956, 1960	1964, 1968	1972
Alabama	9	—	9	—1	8	—1	7	11	11	10	9
Alaska			1	—	1	—	1		3	3	3
Arizona	2	—	2	+1	3	+1	4	4	4	5	6
Arkansas	7	—1	6	—2	4	—	4	9	8	6	6
California	23	+7	30	+8	38	+5	43	25	32	40	45
Colorado	4	—	4	—	4	+1	5	6	6	6	7
Connecticut	6	—	6	—	6	—	6	8	8	8	8
Delaware	1	—	1	—	1	—	1	3	3	3	3
District of Columbia							—	—	—	3	3
Florida	6	+2	8	+4	12	+3	15	8	10	14	17
Georiga	10	—	10	—	10	—	10	12	12	12	12
Hawaii			1	+1	2	—	2		3	4	4
Idaho	2	—	2	—	2	—	2	4	4	4	4
Illinois	26	—1	25	—1	24	—	24	28	27	26	26
Indiana	11	—	11	—	11	—	11	13	13	13	13
Iowa	8	—	8	—1	7	—1	6	10	10	9	8
Kansas	6	—	6	—1	5	—	5	8	8	7	7
Kentucky	9	—1	8	—1	7	—	7	11	10	9	9
Louisiana	8	—	8	—	8	—	8	10	10	10	10
Maine	3	—	3	—1	2	—	2	5	5	4	4
Maryland	6	+1	7	+1	8	—	8	8	9	10	10
Massachusetts	14	—	14	—2	12	—	12	16	16	14	14
Michigan	17	+1	18	+1	19	—	19	19	20	21	21
Minnesota	9	—	9	—1	8	—	8	11	11	10	10
Mississippi	7	—1	6	—1	5	—	5	9	8	7	7
Missouri	13	—2	11	—1	10	—	10	15	13	12	12
Montana	2	—	2	—	2	—	2	4	4	4	4
Nebraska	4	—	4	—1	3	—	3	6	6	5	5
Nevada	1	—	1	—	1	—	1	3	3	3	3
New Hampshire	2	—	2	—	2	—	2	4	4	4	4
New Jersey	14	—	14	+1	15	—	15	16	16	17	17
New Mexico	2	—	2	—	2	—	2	4	4	4	4
New York	45	—2	43	—2	41	—2	39	47	45	43	41
North Carolina	12	—	12	—1	11	—	11	14	14	13	13
North Dakota	2	—	2	—	2	—1	1	4	4	4	3
Ohio	23	—	23	+1	24	—1	23	25	25	26	25
Oklahoma	8	—2	6	—	6	—	6	10	8	8	8
Oregon	4	—	4	—	4	—	4	6	6	6	6
Pennsylvania	33	—3	30	—3	27	—2	25	35	32	29	27
Rhode Island	2	—	2	—	2	—	2	4	4	4	4
South Carolina	6	—	6	—	6	—	6	8	8	8	8
South Dakota	2	—	2	—	2	—	2	4	4	4	4
Tennessee	10	—1	9	—	9	—1	8	12	11	11	10
Texas	21	+1	22	+1	23	+1	24	23	24	25	26
Utah	2	—	2	—	2	—	2	4	4	4	4
Vermont	1	—	1	—	1	—	1	3	3	3	3
Virginia	9	+1	10	—	10	—	10	11	12	12	12
Washington	6	+1	7	—	7	—	7	8	9	9	9
West Virginia	6	—	6	—1	5	—1	4	8	8	7	6
Wisconsin	10	—	10	—	10	—1	9	12	12	12	11
Wyoming	1	—	1	—	1	—	1	3	3	3	3

Results of Elections in House of Representatives, 1950-1972

	50	52	54	56	58	60	62	64	66	68	70	72
NATIONAL TOTALS												
Democrats	235	213	232	234	283	262	259	295	248	243	255	243
Republicans	199	221	203	201	153	175	176	140	187	192	180	192
ALABAMA												
Democrats	9	9	9	9	9	9	8	3	5	5	5	4
Republicans	0	0	0	0	0	0	0	5	3	3	3	3[2]
ALASKA												
Democrats	—	—	—	—	1	1	1	1	0	0	1	1
Republicans	—	—	—	—	0	0	0	0	1	1	0	0
ARIZONA												
Democrats	2	1	1	1	1	1	2	2	1	1	1	1
Republicans	0	1	1	1	1	1	1	1	2	2	2	3[1]
ARKANSAS												
Democrats	7	6	6	6	6	6	4	4	3	3	3	3
Republicans	0	0	0	0	0	0	0	0	1	1	1	1
CALIFORNIA												
Democrats	10	11	11	13	16	16	25	23*	21	21	20	23[1]
Republicans	13	19	19	17	14	14	13	15*	17	17	18	20
COLORADO												
Democrats	2	2	2	2	3	2	2	4	3	3	2	2
Republicans	2	2	2	2	1	2	2	0	1	1	2	3[1]
CONNECTICUT												
Democrats	2	1	1	0	6	4	5	6	5	4	4	3
Republicans	4	5	5	6	0	2	1	0	1	2	2	3
DELAWARE												
Democrats	0	0	1	0	1	1	1	1	0	0	0	0
Republicans	1	1	0	1	0	0	0	0	1	1	1	1
FLORIDA												
Democrats	6	8	7	7	7	7	10	10	9	9	9	11[1]
Republicans	0	0	1	1	1	1	2	2	3	3	3	4
GEORGIA												
Democrats	10	10	10	10	10	10	10	9	8	8	8	9
Republicans	0	0	0	0	0	0	0	1	2	2	2	1
HAWAII												
Democrats	—	—	—	—	—	1	2	2	2	2	2	2
Republicans	—	—	—	—	—	0	0	0	0	0	0	0
IDAHO												
Democrats	0	1	1	1	1	2	2	1	0	0	0	0
Republicans	2	1	1	1	1	0	0	1	2	2	2	2
ILLINOIS												
Democrats	8	9	12	11	14	14	12	13	12	12	12	10
Republicans	18	16	13	14	11	11	12	11	12	12	12	14
INDIANA												
Democrats	2	1	2	2	8	3	4	6	5	4	5	4
Republicans	9	10	9	9	3	8	7	5	6	7	6	7
IOWA												
Democrats	0	0	0	1	4	2	1	6	2	2	2	3
Republicans	8	8	8	7	4	6	6	1	5	5	5	3[2]
KANSAS												
Democrats	0	1	0	1	3	1	0	0	0	0	1	1
Republicans	6	5	6	5	3	5	5	5	5	5	4	4
KENTUCKY												
Democrats	7	6	6	6	7	7	5	6	4	4	5	5
Republicans	2	2	2	2	1	1	2	1	3	3	2	2
LOUISIANA												
Democrats	8	8	8	8	8	8	8	8	8	8	8	7
Republicans	0	0	0	0	0	0	0	0	0	0	0	1
MAINE												
Democrats	0	0	0	1	2	0	0	1	2	2	2	1
Republicans	3	3	3	2	1	3	2	1	0	0	0	1
MARYLAND												
Democrats	3	3	4	4	7	6	6	6	5	4	5	4
Republicans	3	4	3	3	0	1	2	2	3	4	3	4
MASSACHUSETTS												
Democrats	6	6	7	7	8	7	7	7	7	7	8	9
Republicans	8	8	7	7	6	6	5	5	5	5	4	3
MICHIGAN												
Democrats	5	5	7	6	7	7	8	12	7	7	7	7
Republicans	12	13	11	12	11	11	11	7	12	12	12	12
MINNESOTA												
Democrats	4	4	5	5	4	3	4	4	3	3	4	4
Republicans	5	5	4	4	5	6	4	4	5	5	4	4
MISSISSIPPI												
Democrats	7	6	6	6	6	6	5	4	5	5	5	3
Republicans	0	0	0	0	0	0	0	1	0	0	0	2

	50	52	54	56	58	60	62	64	66	68	70	72
MISSOURI												
Democrats	10	7	9	10	10	9	8	8	8	9	9	9
Republicans	3	4	2	1	1	2	2	2	2	1	1	1
MONTANA												
Democrats	1	1	1	2	2	1	1	1	1	1	1	1
Republicans	1	1	1	0	0	1	1	1	1	1	1	1
NEBRASKA												
Democrats	0	0	0	0	2	0	0	1	0	0	0	0
Republicans	4	4	4	4	2	4	3	2	3	3	3	3
NEVADA												
Democrats	1	0	0	1	1	1	1	1	1	1	1	0
Republicans	0	1	1	0	0	0	0	0	0	0	0	1
NEW HAMPSHIRE												
Democrats	0	0	0	0	0	0	0	1	0	0	0	0
Republicans	2	2	2	2	2	2	2	1	2	2	2	2
NEW JERSEY												
Democrats	5	5	6	4	5	6	7	11	9	9	9	8
Republicans	9	9	8	10	9	8	8	4	6	6	6	7
NEW MEXICO												
Democrats	2	2	2	2	2	2	2	2	2	0	1	1
Republicans	0	0	0	0	0	0	0	0	0	0	1	1
NEW YORK												
Democrats	23	16	17	17	19	22	20	27	26	26	24	22[2]
Republicans	22	27	26	26	24	21	21	14	15	15	17	17
NORTH CAROLINA												
Democrats	12	11	11	11	11	11	9	9	8	7	7	7
Republicans	0	1	1	1	1	1	2	2	3	4	4	4
NORTH DAKOTA												
Democrats	0	0	0	0	1	0	0	1	0	0	1	0[2]
Republicans	2	2	2	2	1	2	2	1	2	2	1	1
OHIO												
Democrats	7	6	6	6	9	7	6	10	5	6	7	7
Republicans	15	16	17	17	14	16	18	14	19	18	17	16[2]
OKLAHOMA												
Democrats	6	5	5	5	5	5	5	5	4	4	4	5
Republicans	2	1	1	1	1	1	1	1	2	2	2	1
OREGON												
Democrats	0	0	1	3	3	2	3	3	2	2	2	2
Republicans	4	4	3	1	1	2	1	1	2	2	2	2
PENNSYLVANIA												
Democrats	13	11	14	13	16	14	13	15	14	14	14	13[2]
Republicans	20	19	16	17	14	16	14	12	13	13	13	12
RHODE ISLAND												
Democrats	2	2	2	2	2	2	2	2	2	2	2	2
Republicans	0	0	0	0	0	0	0	0	0	0	0	0
SOUTH CAROLINA												
Democrats	6	6	6	6	6	6	6	6*	5	5	5	4
Republicans	0	0	0	0	0	0	0	0*	1	1	1	2
SOUTH DAKOTA												
Democrats	0	0	0	1	1	0	0	0	0	0	2	1
Republicans	2	2	2	1	1	2	2	2	2	2	0	1
TENNESSEE												
Democrats	8	7	7	7	7	7	6	6	5	5	5	3[2]
Republicans	2	2	2	2	2	2	3	4	4	4	4	5
TEXAS												
Democrats	21	21	21	21	21	21	21	23	21†	20	20	20[1]
Republicans	0	0	1	1	1	1	2	0	2†	3	3	4
UTAH												
Democrats	2	0	0	0	1	2	0	1	0	0	1	2
Republicans	0	2	2	2	1	0	2	1	2	2	1	0
VERMONT												
Democrats	0	0	0	0	1	0	0	0	0	0	0	0
Republicans	1	1	1	1	0	1	1	1	1	1	1	1
VIRGINIA												
Democrats	9	7	8	8	8	8	8	8	6	6	4	3
Republicans	0	3	2	2	2	2	2	2	4	4	6	7
WASHINGTON												
Democrats	2	1	1	1	1	2	1	5	5	5	6	7
Republicans	4	6	6	6	6	5	6	2	2	2	1	0
WEST VIRGINIA												
Democrats	6	5	4	4	5	5	4	4	4	5	5	4[2]
Republicans	0	1	2	2	1	1	1	1	1	0	0	0
WISCONSIN												
Democrats	1	1	3	3	5	4	5	3	3*	5	5	5
Republicans	9	9	7	7	5	6	5	7	7*	5	5	4[2]
WYOMING												
Democrats	0	0	0	0	0	0	0	1	0	0	1	1
Republicans	1	1	1	1	1	1	1	0	1	1	0	0

*Shifted since 1964 election. South Carolina became 5D, 1 R in 1965; California became 24D, 14R in June 1966.

†Shifted since 1966 election. Texas became 20D, 3R in August 1968.

•Shifted since 1968 election. Wisconsin became 4D, 6R in April 1969.

1 New seats created by reapportionment.

2 Lost seats through reapportionment.

Senate Elections, 1968

(For results of elections from 1946-62, see Congress and the Nation, Vol. I, p. 72-78. For 1964-66 results see Vol. II, p. 34-35.)

State	Winner	Winner's %	Winner's Plurality	Loser
Alabama	James B. Allen (D)	70.0	437,547	Perry O. Hooper (R)
Alaska	Mike Gravel (D)	45.1	6,241	Elmer E. Rasmuson (R)
Arizona	Barry Goldwater (R)	57.2	69,269	Roy L. Elson (D)
Arkansas	*J. W. Fulbright (D)	59.1	108,226	Charles T. Bernard (R)
California	Alan Cranston (D)	51.8	351,204	Max Rafferty (R)
Colorado	*Peter H. Dominick (R)	58.6	134,368	Stephen L.R. McNichols (D)
Connecticut	*Abraham A. Ribicoff (D)	54.3	103,588	Edwin H. May Jr. (R)
Florida	Edward J. Gurney (R)	55.9	238,862	LeRoy Collins (D)
Georgia	*Herman E. Talmadge (D)	77.5	628,297	E. Earl Patton Jr. (R)
Hawaii	*Daniel K. Inouye (D)	83.4	155,240	Wayne C. Thiessen (R)
Idaho	*Frank Church (D)	60.3	59,088	George V. Hansen (R)
Illinois	*Everett M. Dirksen (R)	53.0	285,705	William G. Clark (D)
Indiana	*Birch Bayh (D)	51.7	71,885	William D. Ruckelshaus (R)
Iowa	Harold E. Hughes (D)	50.2	6,415	David M. Stanley (R)
Kansas	Robert Dole (R)	60.1	175,000	William I. Robinson (D)
Kentucky	Marlow W. Cook (R)	51.4	35,300	Katherine Peden (D)
Louisiana	*Russel B. Long (D)	X	518,586	
Maryland	Charles McC. Mathias Jr. (R)	47.8	98,526	*Daniel B. Brewster (D)
Missouri	Thomas F. Eagleton (D)	51.1	36,870	Thomas B. Curtis (R)
Nevada	*Alan Bible (D)	54.8	14,554	Ed Fike (R)
New Hampshire	*Norris Cotton (R)	59.3	53,347	John W. King (D)
New York	*Jacob K. Javits (R)	49.7	1,119,077	Paul O'Dwyer (D)
North Carolina	*Sam J. Ervin (D)	60.6	303,472	Robert Vance Somers (R)
North Dakota	*Milton R Young (R)	64.8	74,153	Herschel Lashkowitz (D)
Ohio	William B. Saxbe (R)	51.5	114,812	John J. Gilligan (D)
Oklahoma	Henry Bellmon (R)	51.7	50,462	*A.S. Mike Monroney (D)
Oregon	Robert W. Packwood (R)	50.2	3,293	*Wayne Morse (D)
Pennsylvania	Richard S. Schweiker (R)	51.9	282,100	*Joseph S. Clark (D)
South Carolina	*Ernest F. Hollings (D)	61.9	155,280	Marshall Parker (R)
South Dakota	*George McGovern (D)	56.8	38,010	Archie Gubbrud (R)
Utah	*Wallace F. Bennett (R)	53.7	32,907	Milton L. Weilenmann (D)
Vermont	*George D. Aiken (R)	X	157,154	
Washington	*Warren Magnuson (D)	64.4	360,289	Jack Metcalf (R)
Wisconsin	*Gaylord Nelson (D)	61.7	387,021	Jerris Leonard (R)

*Incumbent
X - Unopposed

Incumbent Senators Defeated for Renomination

ALASKA	Ernest Gruening (D)
CALIFORNIA	Thomas H. Kuchel (R)
MISSOURI	Edward V. Long (D)
OHIO	Frank J. Lausche (D)

Senate Elections, 1970

State	Winner	Winner's%	Winner's Plurality	Loser
Alaska	*Theodore R. Stevens (R)	60.0	12,563	Wendell P. Kay (D)
Arizona	*Paul J. Fannin (R)	55.9	46,620	Sam Grossman (D)
California	John V. Tunney (D)	53.7	598,092	*George Murphy (R)
Connecticut	Lowell P. Weicker Jr. (R)	41.7	82,914	Joseph D. Duffey (D) *Thomas J. Dodd (Ind.)
Delaware	William V. Roth Jr. (R)	58.6	30,186	Jacob W. Zimmerman (D)
Florida	Lawton Chiles (D)	54.0	130,084	William C. Cramer (R)
Hawaii	*Hiram L. Fong (R)	51.5	7,295	Cecil Heftel (D)
Illinois	Adlai E. Stevenson III (D)	56.4	451,954	*Ralph T. Smith (R)
Indiana	*Vance Hartke (D)	50.1	3,698	Richard L. Roudebush (R)
Maine	*Edmund S. Muskie (D)	61.7	73,820	Neil S. Bishop (R)
Maryland	J. Glenn Beall Jr. (R)	51.0	29,752	*Joseph D. Tydings (D)
Massachusetts	*Edward M. Kennedy (D)	62.6	463,986	Josiah A. Spaulding (R)
Michigan	*Philip A. Hart (D)	64.4	633,456	Lenore Romney (R)
Minnesota	Hubert H. Humphrey (D)	58.0	204,613	Clark MacGregor (R)
Mississippi	*John C. Stennis (D)	88.3	240,994	William Richard Thompson (Ind.)
Missouri	*Stuart Symington (D)	51.1	37,473	John C. Danforth (R)
Montana	*Mike Mansfield (D)	61.1	48,076	Harold E. Wallace (R)
Nebraska	*Roman L. Hruska (R)	52.3	19,656	Frank B. Morrison (D)
Nevada	*Howard W. Cannon (D)	57.8	22,530	William J. Raggio (R)
New Jersey	*Harrison A. Williams Jr. (D)	54.5	242,837	Nelson Gross (R)
New Mexico	*Joseph M. Montoya (D)	51.9	14,377	Anderson Carter (R)
New York	James L. Buckley (Cons.)	38.8	131,018	Richard L. Ottinger (D) *Charles E. Goodell (R-L)
North Dakota	*Quentin N. Burdick (D)	62.4	46,942	Thomas S. Kleppe (R)
Ohio	Robert Taft Jr. (R)	50.1	70,226	Howard Metzenbaum (D)
Pennsylvania	*Hugh Scott (R)	51.7	222,267	William G. Sesler (D)
Rhode Island	*John O. Pastore (D)	67.7	119,986	John McLaughlin (R)
Tennessee	Bill Brock (R)	51.6	46,229	*Albert Gore (D)
Texas	Lloyd Bentsen (D)	53.4	148,298	George Bush (R)
Utah	*Frank E. Moss (D)	56.1	50,204	Laurence J. Burton (R)
Vermont	*Winston L. Prouty (R)	59.0	28,765	Philip H. Hoff (D)
Virginia	*Harry F. Byrd Jr. (Ind.)	53.5	210,843	George C. Rawlings (D) Ray L. Garland (R)
Washington	*Henry M. Jackson (D)	83.9	641,291	Charles W. Elicker (R)
West Virginia	*Robert C. Byrd (D)	77.5	244,103	Elmer H. Dodson (R)
Wisconsin	*William Proxmire (D)	71.2	580,575	John E. Erickson (R)
Wyoming	*Gale W. McGee (D)	55.7	13,773	John S. Wold (R)

*Incumbent.
Candidates who received less than 10 percent of the vote are not included.

Incumbent Senators Defeated For Renomination

TEXAS   Ralph W. Yarborough (D)

Senate Elections, 1972

State	Winner	Winner's %	Winner's Plurality	Loser
Alabama	*John Sparkman (D)	62.3	306,968	Winton Blount (R)
Alaska	*Ted Stevens (R)	77.3	52,425	Gene Guess (D)
Arkansas	*John L. McClellan (D)	60.9	138,425	Wayne H. Babbitt (R)
Colorado	Floyd K. Haskell (D)	49.4	9,588	*Gordon Allott (R)
Delaware	Joe Biden (D)	50.5	3,162	J. Caleb Boggs (R)
Georgia	Sam Nunn (D)	54.0	93,639	Fletcher Thompson (R)
Idaho	James A. McClure (R)	52.3	20,981	William E. Davis (D)
Illinois	*Charles H. Percy (R)	62.2	1,146,047	Roman C. Pucinski (D)
Iowa	Dick Clark (D)	55.1	132,112	*Jack Miller (R)
Kansas	*James B. Pearson (R)	71.4	421,827	Arch O. Tetzlaff (D)
Kentucky	Walter (Dee) Huddleston (D)	50.9	34,213	Louie B. Nunn (R)
Louisiana	J. Bennett Johnson Jr. (D)	55.2	392,141	John J. McKeiten (Ind.)
Maine	William D. Hathaway (D)	53.2	27,230	*Margaret Chase Smith (R)
Massachusetts	*Edward W. Brooke (R)	63.5	682,654	John J. Droney (D)
Michigan	*Robert P. Griffin (R)	52.3	203,887	Frank J. Kelley (D)
Minnesota	*Walter F. Mondale (D)	56.7	239,199	Philip Hansen (R)
Mississippi	*James O. Eastland (D)	58.1	125,303	Gil Carmichael (R)
Montana	*Lee Metcalf (D)	52.0	12,293	Henry S. Hubbard (R)
Nebraska	*Carl T. Curtis (R)	53.2	35,919	Terry M. Carpenter (D)
New Hampshire	*Thomas J. McIntyre (D)	56.9	44,643	Wesley Powell (R)
New Jersey	*Clifford P. Case (R)	62.5	780,281	Paul J. Krebs (D)
New Mexico	Pete V. Domenici (R)	54.0	30,438	Jack Daniels (D)
North Carolina	Jesse A. Helms (R)	54.0	117,955	Nick Galifianakis (D)
Oklahoma	Dewey F. Bartlett (R)	51.4	38,722	Ed Edmondson (D)
Oregon	*Mark O. Hatfield (R)	53.7	69,635	Wayne L. Morse (D)
Rhode Island	*Claiborne Pell (D)	53.7	32,952	John H. Chaffee (R)
South Carolina	*Strom Thurmond (R)	63.3	174,750	Eugene N. Zeigler (D)
South Dakota	James Abourezk (D)	57.0	43,160	Robert Hirsch (R)
Tennessee	*Howard H. Baker Jr. (R)	61.5	275,940	Ray Blanton (D)
Texas	*John G. Tower (R)	53.4	310,892	Barefoot Sanders (D)
Virginia	William Lloyd Scott (R)	51.5	74,374	*William B. Spong (D)
West Virginia	*Jennings Randolph	66.5	240,779	Louise Leonard (R)
Wyoming	*Clifford P. Hansen (R)	71.3	60,561	Mike M. Vinich (D)

* Incumbent

Incumbent Senators Defeated for Renomination

Georgia	David H. Gambrell (D)
North Carolina	B. Everett Jordan (D)

GOVERNORS OF THE STATES SINCE 1944

Alabama

Four-Year Term

1943-1947	Chauncey M. Sparks (D)
1947-1951	James Elisha Folsom (D)
1951-1955	Gordon Persons (D)
1955-1959	James Elisha Folsom (D)
1959-1963	John Patterson (D)
1963-1967	George C. Wallace (D)
1967-1971	Lurleen Wallace (D)*
1968-1971	Albert Brewer (D)
1971-1975	George C. Wallace (D)

Wallace died May 7, 1968 and was replaced by Lt. Gov. Brewer who was sworn in on May 7, 1968.

Alaska

Four-Year Term

1959-1963	William A. Egan (D)
1963-1967	Egan
1967-1971	Walter J. Hickel (R)*
1969-1971	Keith Miller (R)
1971-1975	William A. Egan (D)

Hickel resigned Jan. 20, 1969 to become Secretary of Interior. He was replaced by Secretary of State Keith Miller.

Arizona

Two-Year Term

1941-1942	Sidney P. Osborn (D)
1943-1944	Osborn
1945-1946	Osborn
1947-1948	Osborn*
1948	Dan E. Garvey (D)**
1949-1950	Garvey
1951-1952	J. Howard Pyle (R)
1953-1954	Pyle
1955-1956	Ernest W. McFarland (D)
1957-1958	McFarland
1959-1960	Paul Fannin (R)
1961-1962	Fannin
1963-1964	Fannin
1965-1966	Sam Goddard (D)
1967-1968	Jack Williams (R)
1969-1970	Williams
1971-1975	Williams (4-year term)

Osborn died in office, May 23, 1948.
**Garvey served as Acting Gov. from July 25, 1948 to Nov. 2, when elected Governor.*

Arkansas

Two-Year Term

1941-1943	Homer M. Adkins (D)
1943-1945	Adkins
1945-1947	Benjamin T. Laney (D)
1947-1949	Laney
1949-1951	Sidney S. McMath (D)
1951-1953	McMath
1953-1955	Francis Cherry (D)

1955-1957	Orval E. Faubus (D)
1957-1959	Faubus
1959-1961	Faubus
1961-1963	Faubus
1963-1965	Faubus
1965-1967	Faubus
1967-1969	Winthrop Rockefeller (R)
1969-1971	Rockefeller
1971-1973	Dale Bumpers (D)

California

Four-Year Term

1943-1947	Earl Warren (R)
1947-1951	Warren
1951-1953	Warren*
1953-1955	Goodwin J. Knight (R)
1955-1959	Knight
1959-1963	Edmund G. Brown (D)
1963-1967	Brown
1967-1971	Ronald Reagan (R)
1971-1975	Reagan

Warren resigned office on Oct. 5, 1953 to become Chief Justice of the United States; Knight, as Lt. Governor, sworn in as Governor on Oct. 5, 1953.

Colorado

Two-Year Term

1943-1945	John C. Vivian (R)
1945-1947	Vivian
1947-1949	William Lee Knous (D)
1949-1950	Knous*
1950-1951	Walter Warren Johnson (D)
1951-1953	Dan Thornton (R)
1953-1955	Thornton
1955-1957	Edwin C. Johnson (D)
1957-1959	Stephen L.R. McNichols (D)

Four-Year Term

1959-1963	McNichols
1963-1967	John A. Love (R)
1967-1971	Love
1971-1975	Love

Knous resigned March 1, 1950; Johnson sworn in March 1, 1950 for the remainder of the term.

Connecticut

Two-Year Term

1943-1945	Raymond Earl Baldwin (R)
1945-1946	Baldwin*
1946-1947	Charles Wilbert Snow (D)
1947-1948	James Lukens McConaughy (R)**
1948-1949	James Coughlin Shannon (R)
1949-1951	Chester Bowles (D)

Baldwin resigned Dec. 26, 1946 to enter the U.S. Senate; Snow sworn in Dec. 26th, 1946 and served until Jan. 8, 1947.
**McConaughy died March 7, 1948 and was replaced by Shannon who was sworn in on March 8, 1948.*

Four-Year Term

1951-1955	John Davis Lodge (R)
1955-1959	Abraham A. Ribicoff (D)
1959-1961	Ribicoff***
1961-1963	John N. Dempsey (D)
1963-1967	Dempsey
1967-1971	Dempsey
1971-1975	Thomas J. Meskill (R)

***Ribicoff resigned Jan. 21, 1961 to become Secretary of Health, Education and Welfare. He was replaced by Lt. Gov. Dempsey who was sworn in on Jan. 21, 1961.*

Delaware
Four-Year Term

1941-1945	Walter W. Bacon (R)
1945-1949	Bacon
1949-1953	Elbert N. Carvel (D)
1953-1957	J. Caleb Boggs (R)
1957-1961	Boggs
1961-1965	Elbert N. Carvel (D)
1965-1969	Charles L. Terry Jr. (D)
1969-1973	Russell W. Peterson (R)
1973-1977	Sherman W. Tribbit (D)

Florida
Four-Year Term

1941-1945	Spessard Lindsey Holland (D)
1945-1949	Millard Fillmore Caldwell (D)
1949-1953	Fuller Warren (D)
1953	Dan E. McCarty (D)*
1953-1955	Charley E. Johns (D)
1955-1957	LeRoy Collins (D)
1957-1961	Collins
1961-1965	C. Farris Bryant (D)
1965-1967	Haydon Burns (D)**
1967-1971	Claude R. Kirk Jr. (R)
1971-1975	Reubin Askew (D)

McCarty died Sept. 28, 1953; Charley E. Johns sworn in Sept. 29, 1953 to serve until the 1954 elections.
**Burns served a two-year term necessitated by a changeover from electing Governors in Presidential election years to electing them in non-Presidential election years.*

Georgia
Two-Year Term

1943-1945	Ellis Gibbs Arnall (D)
1945-1947	Arnall

Four-Year Term

1947-1948	Melvin E. Thompson (D)*
1948-1951	Herman E. Talmadge (D)**
1951-1955	Talmadge
1955-1959	S. Marvin Griffin (D)
1959-1963	Ernest Vandiver (D)
1963-1967	Carl E. Sanders (D)
1967-1971	Lester G. Maddox (D)
1971-1975	Jimmy Carter (D)

Melvin E. Thompson was sworn in as acting Governor on Jan. 20, 1947 and was declared legal Governor on March 19, 1947. Eugene Talmadge (D) had been elected in 1946 for a four-year term but died Dec. 21, 1946, prior to inauguration date.
**Herman E. Talmadge was elected Governor in a special election Sept. 8, 1948, and was sworn in as Governor on Nov. 17, 1948.*

Hawaii
Four-Year Term

1959-1963	William F. Quinn (R)
1963-1967	John A. Burns (D)
1967-1971	Burns
1971-1975	Burns

Idaho
Two-Year Term

1943-1945	C.A. Bottolfsen (R)
1945	Charles C. Gossett (D)*
1945-1947	Arnold Williams (D)

Four-Year Term

1947-1951	Charles A. Robins (R)
1951-1955	Leonard B. Jordan (R)
1955-1959	Robert E. Smylie (R)
1959-1963	Smylie
1963-1967	Smylie
1967-1971	Don Samuelson (R)
1971-1975	Cecil D. Andrus (D)

Gossett resigned Nov. 17, 1945 and was succeeded the same day by Lt. Gov. Williams who then appointed Gossett to the U.S. Senate to succeed John Thomas who died Nov. 10, 1945.

Illinois
Four-Year Term

1941-1945	Dwight H. Green (R)
1945-1949	Green
1949-1953	Adlai E. Stevenson (D)
1953-1957	William G. Stratton (R)
1957-1961	Stratton
1961-1965	Otto Kerner (D)
1965-1968	Kerner*
1968-1969	Samuel H. Shapiro (D)
1969-1973	Richard B. Ogilvie (R)
1973-1977	Daniel Walker (D)

Kerner resigned May 20, 1968 to become a judge of the United States Court of Appeals in Chicago. He was replaced by Lt. Gov. Shapiro who was sworn in on May 21, 1968.

Indiana
Four-Year Term

1941-1945	Henry F. Schricker (D)
1945-1949	Ralph F. Gates (R)
1949-1953	Henry F. Schricker (D)
1953-1957	George N. Craig (R)
1957-1961	Harold W. Handley (R)
1961-1965	Matthew E. Welsh (D)
1965-1969	Roger D. Branigin (D)
1969-1973	Edgar D. Whitcomb (R)
1973-1977	Otis R. Bowen (R)

Iowa
Two-Year Term

1943-1945	Bourke B. Hickenlooper (R)
1945-1947	Robert D. Blue (R)

1947-1949	Blue
1949-1951	William S. Beardsley (R)*
1951-1953	Beardsley
1953-1954	Beardsley
1954-1955	Leo Elthon (R)
1955-1957	Leo A. Hoegh (R)
1957-1959	Herschel C. Loveless (D)
1959-1961	Loveless
1961-1963	Norman A. Erbe (R)
1963-1965	Harold E. Hughes (D)
1965-1967	Hughes
1967-1969	Hughes
1969-1971	Robert Ray (R)
1971-1973	Ray

Beardsley died Nov. 21, 1954; Leo Elthon was sworn in as acting Governor on Nov. 22, 1954 to serve the remainder of the term.

Kansas
Two-Year Term

1943-1945	Andrew F. Schoeppel (R)
1945-1947	Schoeppel
1947-1949	Frank Carlson (R)
1949-1951	Carlson
1951-1953	Edward F. Arn (R)
1953-1955	Arn
1955-1957	Fred Hall (R)
1957-1959	George Docking (D)
1959-1961	Docking
1961-1963	John Anderson Jr. (R)
1963-1965	Anderson
1965-1967	William H. Avery (R)
1967-1969	Robert Docking (D)
1969-1971	Docking
1971-1973	Docking

Kentucky
Four-Year Term

1943-1947	Simeon S. Willis (R)
1947-1950	Earle C. Clements (D)*
1950-1951	Lawrence W. Wetherby (D)
1951-1955	Wetherby
1955-1959	Albert B. Chandler (D)
1959-1963	Bert C. Combs (D)
1963-1967	Edward T. Breathitt (D)
1967-1971	Louie B. Nunn
1971-1975	Wendell Ford (D)

Clements resigned office to become Senator on Nov. 27, 1950; Wetherby sworn in as acting Governor Nov. 27, 1950 for the remainder of the term.

Louisiana
Four-Year Term

1944-1948	Jimmie H. Davis (D)
1948-1952	Earl Kemp Long (D)
1952-1956	Robert F. Kennon (D)
1956-1960	Earl Kemp Long (D)
1960-1964	Jimmie H. Davis (D)
1964-1968	John J. McKeithen (D)
1968-1972	McKeithen
1972-1976	Edwin W. Edwards (D)

Maine
Two-Year Term

1941-1943	Sumner Sewall (R)
1943-1945	Sewall
1945-1947	Horace A. Hildreth (R)
1947-1949	Hildreth
1949-1951	Frederick G. Payne (R)
1951-1952	Payne *
1952-1953	Burton M. Cross (R)*
1953-1955	Cross
1955-1957	Edmund S. Muskie (D)
1957-1959	Muskie
1959	Clinton A. Clauson (D)**
1960-1961	John H. Reed (R)**
1961-1963	Reed

Four-Year Term

1963-1967	Reed
1967-1971	Kenneth M. Curtis (D)
1971-1975	Curtis

Payne resigned Dec. 16, 1952 effective Dec. 25, 1952; Cross became acting Governor on Dec. 26, 1952.
**Clauson died Dec. 31, 1959; Reed sworn in Jan. 1, 1960.*

Maryland
Four-Year Term

1939-1943	Herbert R. O'Conor (D)
1943-1947	O'Conor
1947-1951	William Preston Lane Jr. (D)
1951-1955	Theodore R. McKeldin (R)
1955-1959	McKeldin
1959-1963	J. Millard Tawes (D)
1963-1967	Tawes
1967-1971	Spiro T. Agnew (R)*
1969-1971	Marvin Mandel (D)
1971-1975	Mandel

Agnew resigned Jan. 7, 1969 to become Vice President of the United States. Mandel was elected Governor Jan. 7, 1969 by the State Legislature.

Massachusetts
Two-Year Term

1939-1941	Leverett Saltonstall (R)
1941-1943	Saltonstall
1943-1945	Saltonstall
1945-1947	Maurice J. Tobin (D)
1947-1949	Robert F. Bradford (R)
1949-1951	Paul A. Dever (D)
1951-1953	Dever
1953-1955	Christian A. Herter (R)
1955-1957	Herter
1957-1959	Foster Furcolo (D)
1959-1961	Furcolo
1961-1963	John A. Volpe (R)
1963-1965	Endicott Peabody (D)
1965-1967	John A. Volpe (R)

Four-Year Term

1967-1971	Volpe*
1969-1971	Francis W. Sargent (R)
1971-1975	Sargent

Volpe resigned Jan. 20, 1969, to become Secretary of Transportation. He was replaced by Lt. Gov. Sargent who was sworn in on Jan. 20, 1969.

Michigan

Two-Year Term

1943-1945	Harry F. Kelly (R)
1945-1947	Kelly
1947-1949	Kim Sigler (R)
1949-1951	G. Mennen Williams (D)
1951-1953	Williams
1953-1955	Williams
1955-1957	Williams
1957-1959	Williams
1959-1961	Williams
1961-1963	John B. Swainson (D)
1963-1965	George W. Romney (R)
1965-1967	Romney

Four-Year Term

1967-1971	Romney*
1969-1971	William G. Milliken (R)
1971-1975	Milliken

*Romney resigned Jan. 20, 1969, to become Secretary of Housing and Urban Development. He was replaced by Lt. Gov. Milliken who was sworn in on Jan. 20, 1969.

Minnesota

Two-Year Term

1943-1945	Edward J. Thye (R)
1945-1947	Thye
1947-1949	Luther W. Youngdahl (R)*
1949-1951	Youngdahl
1951	C. Elmer Anderson (R)
1951-1953	Anderson
1953-1955	Anderson
1955-1957	Orville L. Freeman (D Farmer-Labor)
1957-1959	Freeman
1959-1961	Freeman
1961-1963	Elmer L. Andersen (R)

Four-Year Term

1963-1967	Karl F. Rolvaag (D)
1967-1971	Harold E. LeVander (R)
1971-1975	Wendell R. Anderson (D)

*Youngdahl resigned Sept. 27, 1951, to accept appointment as judge of the United States District Court for the District of Columbia. Anderson sworn in Sept. 27, 1951, for remainder of the term.

Mississippi

Four-Year Term

1944-1946	Thomas L. Bailey (D)*
1946-1948	Fielding L. Wright (D)**
1948-1952	Wright
1952-1956	Hugh L. White (D)
1956-1960	James Plemon Coleman (D)
1960-1964	Ross R. Barnett (D)
1964-1968	Paul B. Johnson (D)
1968-1972	John B. Williams (D)
1972-1976	William Walker (D)

*Bailey died Nov. 2, 1946.
**Wright sworn in as Governor Nov. 2, 1946.

Missouri

Four-Year Term

1941-1945	Forrest C. Donnell (R)
1945-1949	Phil M. Donnelly (D)
1949-1953	Forrest Smith (D)
1953-1957	Phil M. Donnelly (D)
1957-1961	James T. Blair Jr. (D)
1961-1965	John M. Dalton (D)
1965-1969	Warren E. Hearnes (D)
1969-1973	Hearnes
1973-1977	Christopher (Kit) Bond (R)

Montana

Four-Year Term

1941-1945	Sam C. Ford (R)
1945-1949	Ford
1949-1953	John W. Bonner (D)
1953-1957	J. Hugo Aronson (R)
1957-1961	Aronson
1961-1962	Donald G. Nutter (R)*
1962-1965	Tim M. Babcock (R)**
1965-1969	Babcock
1969-1973	Forrest H. Anderson (D)
1973-1977	Thomas L. Judge (D)

*Nutter died Jan. 26, 1962.
**Babcock sworn in as Governor Jan. 26, 1962.

Nebraska

Two-Year Term

1941-1943	Dwight P. Griswold (R)
1943-1945	Griswold
1945-1947	Griswold
1947-1949	Val Peterson (R)
1949-1951	Peterson
1951-1953	Peterson
1953-1955	Robert B. Crosby (R)
1955-1957	Victor E. Anderson (R)
1957-1959	Anderson
1959-1961	Ralph G. Brooks (D)
1961-1963	Frank B. Morrison (D)
1963-1965	Morrison
1965-1967	Morrison

Four-Year Term

1967-1971	Norbert T. Tiemann (R)
1971-1975	J. J. Exon (D)

Nevada

Four-Year Term

1939-1943	Edward P. Carville (D)*
1943-1945	Carville
1945-1947	Vail Pittman (D)**

*Carville resigned from office July 24, 1945.
**Pittman succeeded Carville on July 24, 1945 and then appointed Carville to the U.S. Senate the same day.

1947-1951	Pittman
1951-1955	Charles H. Russell (R)
1955-1959	Russell
1959-1963	Grant Sawyer (D)
1963-1967	Sawyer
1967-1971	Paul Laxalt (R)
1971-1975	Mike O'Callaghan (D)

New Hampshire

Two-Year Term

1939-1941	Robert O. Blood (R)
1941-1943	Blood
1943-1945	Blood
1945-1947	Charles M. Dale (R)
1947-1949	Dale
1949-1951	Sherman Adams (R)
1951-1953	Adams
1953-1955	Hugh Gregg (R)
1955-1957	Lane Dwinell (R)
1957-1959	Dwinell
1959-1961	Wesley Powell (R)
1961-1963	Powell
1963-1965	John W. King (D)
1965-1967	King
1967-1969	King
1969-1971	Walter R. Peterson Jr. (R)
1971-1973	Peterson
1973-1975	Meldrim Thomson Jr. (R)

New Jersey

Three-Year Term

1941-1944	Charles Edison (D)
1944-1947	Walter E. Edge (R)
1947-1950	Alfred E. Driscoll (R)

Four-Year Term

1950-1954	Driscoll
1954-1958	Robert B. Meyner (D)
1958-1962	Meyner
1962-1966	Richard J. Hughes (D)
1966-1970	Hughes
1970-1974	William T. Cahill (R)

New Mexico

Two-Year Term

1943-1945	John J. Dempsey (D)
1945-1947	Dempsey
1947-1949	Thomas J. Mabry (D)
1949-1951	Mabry
1951-1953	Edwin L. Mechem (R)
1953-1955	Mechem
1955-1957	John Field Simms (D)
1957-1959	Edwin L. Mechem (R)
1959-1961	John Burroughs (D)
1961-1963	Edwin L. Mechem (R)
1963-1965	Jack M. Campbell (D)
1965-1967	Campbell
1967-1969	David F. Cargo (R)
1969-1971	Cargo
1971-1973	Bruce King (D)

New York

Four-Year Term

1943-1947	Thomas E. Dewey (R)
1947-1951	Dewey
1951-1955	Dewey
1955-1959	Averell Harriman (D)
1959-1963	Nelson A. Rockefeller (R)
1963-1967	Rockefeller
1967-1971	Rockefeller
1971-1975	Rockefeller

North Carolina

Four-Year Term

1941-1945	Melville Broughton (D)
1945-1949	R. Gregg Cherry (D)
1949-1953	William Kerr Scott (D)
1953-1954	William B. Umstead (D)*
1954-1957	Luther H. Hodges (D)**
1957-1961	Hodges
1961-1965	Terry Sanford (D)
1965-1969	Dan K. Moore (D)
1969-1973	Robert W. Scott (D)
1973-1977	James A. Holshouser (R)

*Umstead died November 7, 1954.
**Hodges sworn in Nov. 9, 1954, to fill remainder of term.

North Dakota

Two-Year Term

1939-1941	John Moses (D)
1941-1943	Moses
1943-1945	Moses
1945-1947	Fred G. Aandahl (R)
1947-1949	Aandahl
1949-1951	Aandahl
1951-1953	C. Norman Brunsdale (R)
1953-1955	Brunsdale
1955-1957	Brunsdale
1957-1959	John E. Davis (R)
1959-1961	Davis
1961-1963	William L. Guy (D)
1963-1965	Guy

Four-Year Term

1965-1969	Guy
1969-1973	Guy
1973-1977	Arthur A. Link (D)

Ohio

Two-Year Term

1939-1941	John W. Bricker (R)
1941-1943	Bricker
1943-1945	Bricker
1945-1947	Frank J. Lausche (D)
1947-1949	Thomas J. Herbert (R)

1949-1951	Frank J. Lausche (D)
1951-1953	Lausche
1953-1955	Lausche
1955-1957	Lausche
1957-1959	C. William O'Neill (R)

Four-Year Term

1959-1963	Michael V. DiSalle (D)
1963-1967	James A. Rhodes (R)
1967-1971	Rhodes
1971-1975	John J. Gilligan (D)

Oklahoma

Four-Year Term

1943-1947	Robert S. Kerr (D)
1947-1951	Roy J. Turner (D)
1951-1955	Johnston Murray (D)
1955-1959	Raymond Gary (D)
1959-1963	J. Howard Edmondson (D)
1963-1967	Henry Bellmon (R)
1967-1971	Dewey F. Bartlett (R)
1971-1975	David Hall (D)

Oregon

Four-Year Term

1943-1947	Earl Snell (R)*
1947	Snell
1947-1949	John H. Hall (R)**
1949-1951	Douglas McKay (R)***
1951-1952	McKay
1952-1955	Paul L. Patterson (R)****
1955-1956	Patterson
1956-1957	Elmo E. Smith (R)*****
1957-1959	Robert D. Holmes (D)
1959-1963	Mark O. Hatfield (R)
1963-1967	Hatfield
1967-1971	Tom McCall (R)
1971-1975	McCall

*Snell died in office beginning his second term Oct. 28, 1947.
**John H. Hall sworn in Oct. 28, 1947, but was defeated by Douglas McKay in 1948 primary.
***McKay elected for remainder of four-year term on Nov. 2, 1948, re-elected for four-year term Nov. 7, 1950, resigned to become Secretary of Interior, Dec. 11, 1952.
****Patterson sworn in as Governor Dec. 11, 1952, re-elected for a four-year term in 1954 but died in office Jan. 31, 1956.
*****Elmo Smith sworn in Jan. 31, but lost to Robert D. Holmes in 1956 election.

Pennsylvania

Four-Year Term

1943-1947	Edward Martin (R)
1947-1951	James H. Duff (R)
1951-1955	John S. Fine (R)
1955-1959	George M. Leader (D)
1959-1963	David L. Lawrence (D)
1963-1967	William W. Scranton (R)
1967-1971	Raymond P. Shafer (R)
1971-1975	Milton J. Shapp (D)

Rhode Island

Two-Year Term

1941-1943	J. Howard McGrath (D)
1943-1945	McGrath*
1945-1947	John O. Pastore (D)
1947-1949	Pastore
1949-1951	Pastore
1951-1953	Dennis J. Roberts (D)
1953-1955	Roberts
1955-1957	Roberts
1957-1959	Roberts
1959-1961	Christopher Del Sesto (R)
1961-1963	John A. Notte Jr. (D)
1963-1965	John H. Chafee (R)
1965-1967	Chafee
1967-1969	Chafee
1969-1971	Frank Licht (D)
1971-1973	Phillip W. Noel (D)

*McGrath resigned Oct. 4, 1945 to become Solicitor General of the U.S.; Pastore sworn in as Governor Oct. 6, 1945.

South Carolina

Four-Year Term

1943-1945	Olin Dewitt Talmadge Johnston (D)*
1945-1947	Ransome Judson Williams (D)
1947-1951	J. Strom Thurmond (D)
1951-1955	James F. Byrnes (D)
1955-1959	George Bell Timmerman Jr. (D)
1959-1963	Ernest F. Hollings (D)
1963-1965	Donald S. Russell (D)**
1965-1967	Robert E. McNair (D)
1967-1971	McNair
1971-1975	John C. West (D)

*Johnston, who was previously Governor from 1935-1939, resigned from office to enter the U.S. Senate on Jan. 2, 1945; Williams was sworn in on Jan. 2, 1945 for the remainder of the term.
**Russell resigned April 21, 1965, to accept appointment to U.S. Senate; McNair sworn in as Governor on April 22, 1965.

South Dakota

Two-Year Term

1943-1945	M.Q. Sharpe (R)
1945-1947	Sharpe
1947-1949	George T. Michelson (R)
1949-1951	Mickelson
1951-1953	Sigurd Anderson (R)
1953-1955	Anderson
1955-1957	Joe Foss (R)
1957-1959	Foss
1959-1961	Ralph Herseth (D)
1961-1963	Archie M. Gubbrud (R)
1963-1965	Gubbrud
1965-1967	Nils Boe (R)
1967-1969	Boe
1969-1971	Frank Farrar (R)
1971-1973	Richard F. Kneip (D)

Tennessee

Two-Year Term

1939-1941	Prentice Cooper (D)
1941-1943	Cooper
1943-1945	Cooper
1945-1947	Jim Nance McCord (D)
1947-1949	McCord
1949-1951	Gordon Browning (D)
1951-1953	Browning
1953-1955	Frank G. Clement (D)

Four-Year Term

1955-1959	Clement
1959-1963	Buford Ellington (D)
1963-1967	Frank G. Clement (D)
1967-1971	Buford Ellington (D)
1971-1975	Winfield Dunn (R)

Texas

Two-Year Term

1941-1943	Coke R. Stevenson (D)
1943-1945	Stevenson
1945-1947	Stevenson
1947-1949	Beauford H. Jester (D)*
1949-1951	Allan Shivers (D)
1951-1953	Shivers
1953-1955	Shivers
1955-1957	Shivers
1957-1959	Price Daniel (D)
1959-1961	Daniel
1961-1963	Daniel
1963-1965	John B. Connally (D)
1965-1967	Connally
1967-1969	Connally
1969-1971	Preston Smith (D)
1971-1973	Dolph Briscoe (D)

Jester died in office July 11, 1949; Shivers sworn in as Governor July 16, 1949.

Utah

Four-Year Term

1941-1945	Herbert B. Maw (D)
1945-1949	Maw
1949-1953	J. Bracken Lee (R)
1953-1957	Lee
1957-1961	George Dewey Clyde (R)
1961-1965	Clyde
1965-1969	Calvin L. Rampton (D)
1969-1973	Rampton

Vermont

Two-Year Term

1941-1943	William H. Wills (R)
1943-1945	Wills

1945-1947	Mortimer R. Proctor (R)
1947-1949	Ernest W. Gibson (R)
1949-1950	Gibson*
1950-1951	Harold J. Arthur (R)
1951-1953	Lee E. Emerson (R)
1953-1955	Emerson
1955-1957	Joseph Blaine Johnson (R)
1957-1959	Johnson
1959-1961	Robert T. Stafford (R)
1961-1963	F. Ray Keyser (R)
1963-1965	Philip H. Hoff (D)
1965-1967	Hoff
1967-1969	Hoff
1969-1971	Deane C. Davis (R)
1971-1973	Thomas P. Salmon (D)

Gibson resigned Jan. 3, 1950 effective Jan. 15, 1950; Arthur sworn in on Jan 15, 1950 for the remainder of the term.

Virginia

Four-Year Term

1942-1946	Colgate W. Darden Jr. (D)
1946-1950	William Munford Tuck (D)
1950-1954	John Stewart Battle (D)
1954-1958	Thomas B. Stanley (D)
1958-1962	J. Lindsay Almond Jr. (D)
1962-1966	Albertis S. Harrison (D)
1966-1970	Mills E. Godwin Jr. (D)
1970-1974	Linwood Holton (R)

Washington

Four-Year Term

1941-1945	Arthur B. Langlie (R)
1945-1949	Monrad Charles Wallgren (D)
1949-1953	Arthur B. Langlie (R)
1953-1957	Langlie
1957-1961	Albert D. Rosellini (D)
1961-1965	Rosellini
1965-1969	Daniel J. Evans (R)
1969-1973	Evans
1973-1977	Evans

West Virginia

Four-Year Term

1941-1945	Matthew Mansfield Neely (D)
1945-1949	Clarence W. Meadows (D)
1949-1953	Okey L. Patteson (D)
1953-1957	William C. Marland (D)
1957-1961	Cecil H. Underwood (R)
1961-1965	W.W. Barron (D)
1965-1969	Hulett C. Smith (D)
1969-1973	Arch A. Moore (R)
1973-1977	Moore

Wisconsin

Two-Year Term

1943-1945	Walter S. Goodland (R)
1945-1947	Goodland
1947	Goodland*
1947-1949	Oscar A. Rennebohm (R)
1949-1951	Rennebohm
1951-1953	Walter J. Kohler Jr. (R)
1953-1955	Kohler
1955-1957	Kohler
1957-1959	Vernon W. Thomson (R)
1959-1961	Gaylord A. Nelson (D)
1961-1963	Nelson
1963-1965	John W. Reynolds (D)
1965-1967	Warren P. Knowles (R)
1967-1969	Knowles
1969-1971	Knowles
1971-1975	Patrick J. Lucey (D)

*Goodland died in office March 12, 1947; Rennebohm was sworn in on March 13, 1947 for the remainder of the term.

Wyoming

Four-Year Term

1943-1947	Lester C. Hunt (D)
1947-1949	Hunt*
1949-1951	Arthur G. Crane (R)
1951-1953	Frank A. Barrett (R)**
1953-1955	Clifford J. Rogers (R)
1955-1959	Milward L. Simpson (R)
1959-1961	J.J. Hickey (D)***
1961-1963	Jack Gage (D)
1963-1967	Clifford P. Hansen (R)
1967-1971	Stanley K. Hathaway (R)
1971-1975	Hathaway

*Hunt resigned as Governor to become U.S. Senator on Jan. 3, 1949; Arthur G. Crane became Acting Governor on Jan. 3, 1949.

**Barrett resigned as Governor to become U.S. Senator on Jan. 3, 1953; C.J. Rogers became Acting Governor on Jan. 3, 1953.

***Hickey resigned as Governor to become U.S. Senator on Jan. 3, 1961; Gage became acting Governor on Jan. 3, 1961.

1972 ELECTORAL VOTES BY STATES

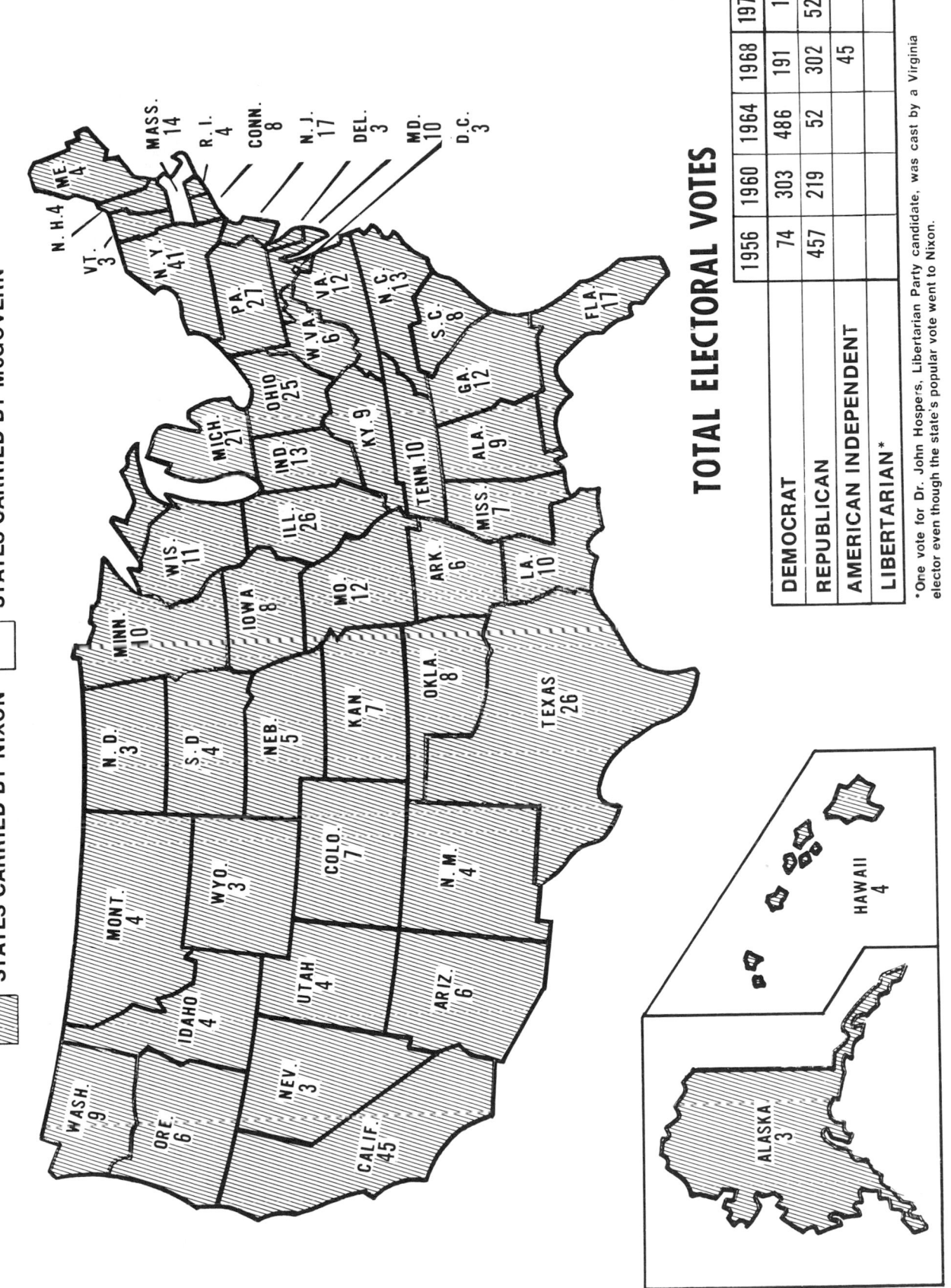

STATES CARRIED BY NIXON

STATES CARRIED BY McGOVERN

ME. 4
N. H. 4
VT. 3
N.Y. 41
MASS. 14
R.I. 4
CONN. 8
N.J. 17
DEL. 3
MD. 10
D.C. 3
PA. 27
OHIO 25
W.VA. 6
VA. 12
N.C. 13
S.C. 8
GA. 12
FLA. 17
MICH. 21
IND. 13
KY. 9
TENN. 10
ALA. 9
MISS. 7
ILL. 26
WIS. 11
IOWA 8
MO. 12
ARK. 6
LA. 10
MINN. 10
N.D. 3
S.D. 4
NEB. 5
KAN. 7
OKLA. 8
TEXAS 26
MONT. 4
WYO. 3
COLO. 7
N.M. 4
IDAHO 4
UTAH 4
ARIZ. 6
WASH. 9
ORE. 6
NEV. 3
CALIF. 45
HAWAII 4
ALASKA 3

TOTAL ELECTORAL VOTES

	1956	1960	1964	1968	1972
DEMOCRAT	74	303	486	191	17
REPUBLICAN	457	219	52	302	520
AMERICAN INDEPENDENT				45	
LIBERTARIAN*					1

*One vote for Dr. John Hospers, Libertarian Party candidate, was cast by a Virginia elector even though the state's popular vote went to Nixon.

49

Chapter 2—Economic Policy

Key Votes

In this chapter, key roll-call votes are shown in bold-face type. The party breakdown on each of these votes and the position taken by each member of Congress may be found in the key vote charts which appear in the appendix to this book.

Economic Policy

There were great variations in economic policy during the first Nixon administration. The management of the economy was at one time one of the President's greatest political liabilities and at another an outstanding political asset. The most popular policies were in effect during the 12 months prior to the 1972 election and were part of the explanation for the President's smashing reelection victory.

Nixon inherited a war economy plagued by inflation, and for a while it was to be one of his most serious problems. He first followed a cautious road in line with his conservative predilections—non-intervention coupled with restrictive monetary and fiscal policies. This helped to deepen inflation, increase unemployment and bring about a brief recession.

After the handling of the economy had become a major political issue, the President in mid-1971 made a surprise switch to a policy of strong economic controls. The widely-praised new program involved a "Phase One" freeze on wages, prices and rents which was succeeded by a "Phase Two" program of strict controls.

Phase Two lasted until January 1973 when it was succeeded by a voluntary "Phase Three" program which apparently reflected the President's basic economic leanings. Widely criticized from the beginning, "Phase Three" kicked off a new round of price increases which resulted in the highest rate of inflation in 22 years. The President June 13 acknowledged that it had not worked and announced a new price freeze to be followed by an as yet undetermined "Phase Four."

When President Nixon took office the economy had been expanding for nine years, and deeply rooted inflation begun by Vietnam war spending had been underway for more than three. The President, then considered a fiscal and monetary policies to reduce inflation.

Before the end of 1969 a recession had begun, the end of 1969 a recession had begun, the stock market was slikding and unemployment began what was to be a long unbroken rise. Yet inflation also continued to increase.

Monetary policy was eased beginning in 1970 and late that year the President endorsed what was in effect deficit budget spending to combat the recession. The economy began to pull out of the recession in 1971, but at mid-year unemployment and the inflation rate were higher than ever. A serious rise in the U.S. balance of payments deficit added to the troubled economic picture. The polls indicated widespread public dissatisfaction with administration economic policies, and Democratic presidential hopefuls began to savor the prospect of running against an incumbent who was apparently unable to control either unemployment or inflation.

Then, on Aug. 15, 1971, the President in a surprise announcement established some of the most comprehensive economic controls in the nation's history. The program involved a 90-day freeze of wages, prices and rents followed by a Phase Two program featuring a Pay Board and Price Commission. At the same time, the President announced a temporary import surcharge and suspension of the convertibility of the dollar into gold—steps which led to international monetary negotiations and, in December, the first devaluation of the dollar since 1934. The President called the devaluation agreement, made at a Smithsonian Institution meeting, "the most significant monetary agreement in the history of the world."

The new policies were widely approved. Inflation decreased substantially, unemployment dropped a bit and 1972 was a good year for the economy. Despite the fact that food, clothing and other consumer prices were substantially higher than when Nixon took office, handling of the economy was hardly an issue in the 1972 presidential campaign, and the President's willingness to take decisive action on economic policy was considered a real plus for his candidacy.

ECONOMIC CHAPTER ORGANIZATION. The economic policy chapter of this book is subdivided into the following subchapter: budget, p. 63; tax, p. 77; economic stabilization, p. 105; international, p. 119; banking, p. 135; transportation, p. 147; and miscellaneous economic legislation, p. 177. Revenue sharing is discussed following tax policy, p. 97. (*Economic policy 1945-64, Congress and the Nation Vol. I, p. 337-562; 1965-68, Vol. II, p. 119-305*)

Following in this introduction is a brief chronological summary of the major developments discussed in detail in the subchapters. Budget, tax, international and economic stabilization policy are discussed for the four-year period are discussed first. Then follows summaries of banking transportation and revenue sharing.

Budget, Tax and Stabilization Policy

1969

Three months after taking office, President Nixon sent Congress a general message on his domestic legislative program. The President said that one priority which had emerged "clearly and compellingly" since he took office was to halt the inflationary surge, then in its fourth year.

Changes in GNP, Real GNP, and Price Deflator

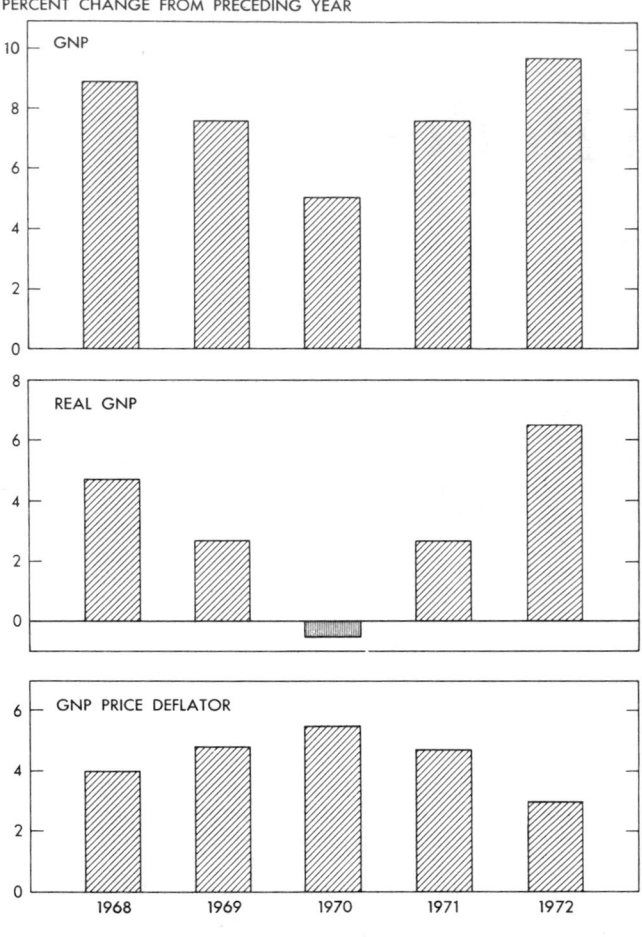

PERCENT CHANGE FROM PRECEDING YEAR

SOURCE: DEPARTMENT OF COMMERCE.

To combat inflation, the President, unlike his Democratic predecessors, chose at first to maintain an official hands-off policy on wage-price increases. Instead, in 1969 he looked to restrictive fiscal and monetary policies.

The President's fiscal policies to bring inflation under control were, first, restriction of federal expenditures to keep the government increment of total spending low and, second, maintenance of federal revenues to divert funds from private spending and to hold down government borrowing in the money market.

In pursuit of the first goal, the President in April proposed successive cuts in the fiscal 1970 budget that President Johnson had sent to Congress in the final days of his administration. The cuts totaled $8 billion; the revised budget was to bring in a surplus of $5.8 billion.

By the end of the fiscal year, the surplus had vanished. Congress' failure to enact presidential requests on items such as postal rate increases, coupled with increases in uncontrollable spending such as Social Security payments, helped throw the budget into deficit instead.

The budget deficit finally totalled $2.8 billion. This was caused only in part because Congress did not go along with restriction of federal expenditures. The other part of the President's fiscal policy—maintenance of the current level of federal revenues—also did not work. The President had asked Congress to help continue the level of federal revenues by extending a 10 per cent income tax surcharge enacted in 1968. Congress agreed, but did so only as part of an unusual congressionally-initiated tax reform bill which carried a substantial net revenue loss. On top of this, federal revenues were lower than expected because of the recession which set in November 1969. Profits were down, and government tax receipts were therefore lower than had been anticipated.

In the area of monetary policy, the Federal Reserve Board in 1969 continued the policy of tight money and high credit it had begun late in the Johnson administration. It held the money supply almost constant through 1969 despite warnings by some economists that inadequate monetary expansion was likely to cause a recession. Investment capital—particularly mortgage money for housing—grew scarce, and interest rates climbed to the highest level in 100 years.

Gross National Product (GNP)—total output of goods and services—rose at an annual rate of $66 billion in 1969 (to $897.6 billion), measured in current prices. But as measured by economists in constant (1958) prices, GNP increased by less than one-third that amount. The rest were price increases. The average inflation of consumer prices was 5.4 percent. Thus, at the end of his first year, President Nixon had had no success at all in meeting his number one domestic goal—control of inflation.

1970

In his first State of the Union address, delivered in January 1970, President Nixon said, "When I speak of actions which would be beneficial to the American people, I can think of none more important than for Congress to join this administration in the battle to stop the rise in the cost of living." He specifically avoided blaming either business or labor, but said U.S. deficit spending in the 1960s was the primary cause of inflation: "Millions of Americans are forced to go into debt today because the federal government decided to go into debt yesterday."

To fight inflation, the President again called for the restrictive fiscal policies he had supported in 1969—a budget in surplus with federal spending held down. The Federal Reserve Board, however, moved to a more expansive monetary policy.

As proposed, the President's fiscal 1971 budget called for a surplus of $1.3 billion. When the fiscal year came to an end, however, he had a deficit of $23 billion instead. There were a number of reasons for this. Tax revenues were $13.7 billion lower than projected because of the continuing recession. The economy had begun to pick up slowly in mid-1970, but was thrown back again by a two-month General Motors strike. In addition, late in the year the President indicated that he was converted to the theory that deficit spending was a valuable tool for countering recession, and the administration made less of an attempt to hold the lid on spending.

There was, however, as in 1969, a continuing struggle between the President and Congress over federal spending priorities. The President vetoed five bills on economy grounds and two of the vetoes were overriden. There was no major request or action on taxes in 1970. Congress did

(Continued on p. 56)

Economic Trends, Events of Nixon's First Term

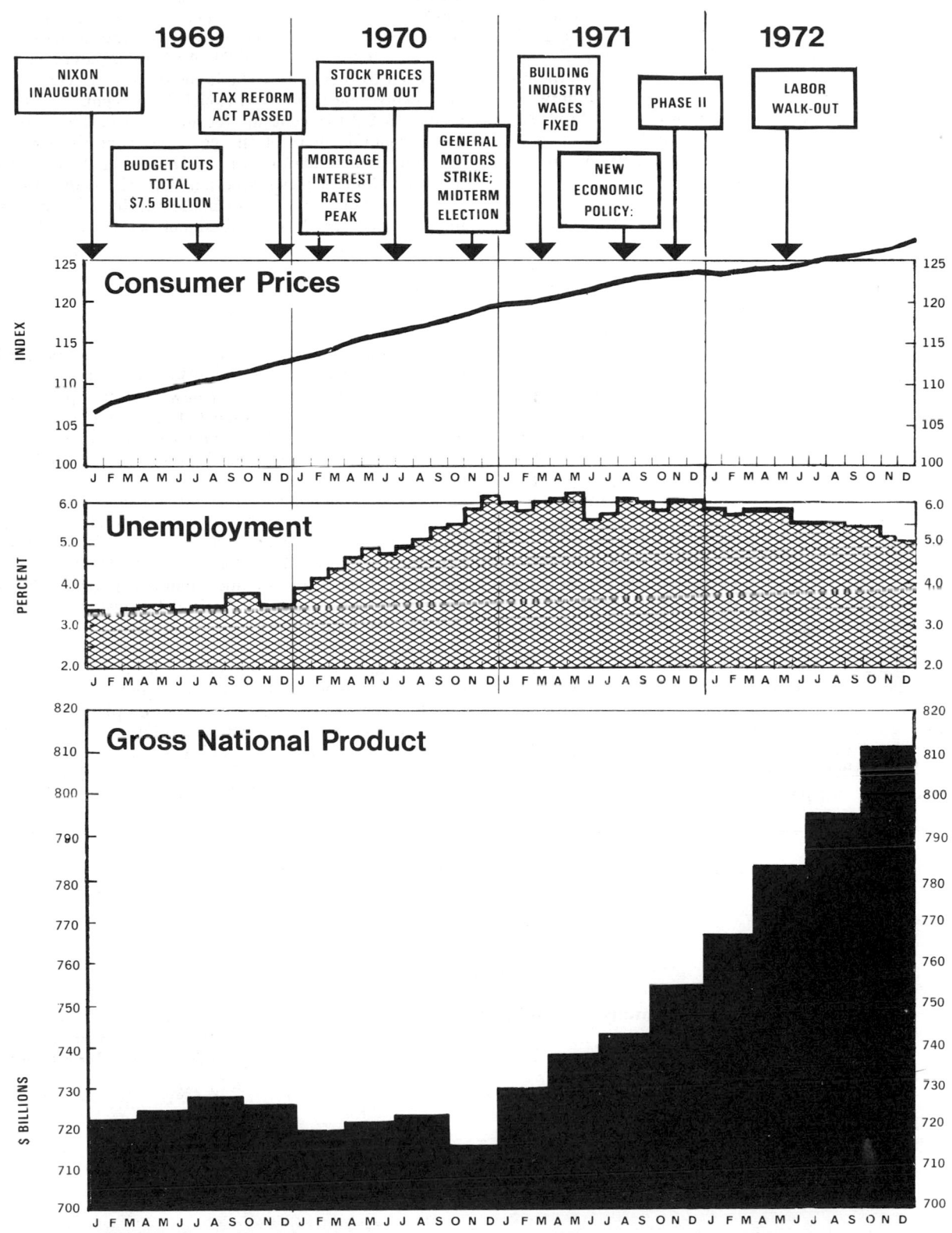

1969   **1970**   **1971**   **1972**

NIXON INAUGURATION

BUDGET CUTS TOTAL $7.5 BILLION

TAX REFORM ACT PASSED

MORTGAGE INTEREST RATES PEAK

STOCK PRICES BOTTOM OUT

GENERAL MOTORS STRIKE; MIDTERM ELECTION

BUILDING INDUSTRY WAGES FIXED

NEW ECONOMIC POLICY:

PHASE II

LABOR WALK-OUT

Consumer Prices

INDEX

J F M A M J J A S O N D J F M A M J J A S O N D J F M A M J J A S O N D J F M A M J J A S O N D

Unemployment

PERCENT

J F M A M J J A S O N D J F M A M J J A S O N D J F M A M J J A S O N D J F M A M J J A S O N D

Gross National Product

$ BILLIONS

J F M A M J J A S O N D J F M A M J J A S O N D J F M A M J J A S O N D J F M A M J J A S O N D

Gross National Product: Annual rates of output, by quarters, in billions of constant (1958) dollars.

Unemployment: Percent of labor force, adjusted for seasonal fluctuations.

Consumer Price Index: Average of 1967 prices equals 100.

Sources: U.S. Labor Dept., Commerce Dept.

pass an administration bill extending excise taxes and speeding up collection of gift and estate taxes.

Monetary policy in 1970 was quite different from the restrictive tight money policy of 1969. The Federal Reserve Board permitted the money supply to expand at a relatively high average of about 5.5 per cent during the year. Both the discount rate at which the Federal Reserve System lends money to member banks and the prime rate—the interest rate banks charge their best customers—underwent successive reductions. Mortgage interest rates stabilized, and other interest rates fell sharply. The Federal Reserve Board continued this kind of expansionary monetary policy for the rest of Nixon's first term.

During the year as the recession and inflation continued and unemployment began to climb, a number of critics urged the President to adopt some sort of system of wage-price controls. The new Federal Reserve Board Chairman Arthur F. Burns publicly supported adoption of an "incomes policy," a term which came into fashionable use. It referred to a broad range of activities, from guideposts to wage and price controls. It connoted an effort to influence incomes through wages and prices parallel to other policy efforts to influence the money supply through fiscal and monetary policy.

On June 17 in a televised address to the nation, the President declared: "I will not take this nation down the road of wage and price controls, however politically expedient they may seem...Wage and price controls only postpone a day of reckoning, and in so doing they rob every American of an important part of his freedom."

In August, the Democratic-controlled Congress added to a Defense Production Act extension an amendment empowering the President to freeze salaries, rents and prices. The President opposed the amendment and said he would not use it.

However, during 1970 the President did change his economic policies somewhat. He moved toward "jawboning" (administration persuasion of business and labor to hold price and wage lines) with the issuance of two "inflation alerts" to publicize excessive wage and price increases. In December, he announced measures to offset oil price increases and plans to intervene in wage negoti-

ations in the construction industry if strikes and rising costs were not abated.

At year's end, the economic figures for 1970 were dreary. GNP for the year reached $974.1 billion but in constant prices totaled 0.5 per cent less than in 1969. Consumer price increases above 1969 levels averaged 5.9 per cent, more than in 1969. And unemployment, which had been 3.5 percent of the labor force in December 1969, skyrocketed past the traditional 4 per cent "full employment" to 6.2 per cent in December 1970. The only really good economic news of the year was that the stock market slide which had begun in December 1968 bottomed in June. General dissatisfaction with the economic situation was reflected in the mediocre Republican showing in the November 1970 congressional elections.

1971

President Nixon in 1971 switched the economic issue from the foremost of his liabilities into a potential asset. This occurred when the major new economic policy of controls was announced in August. Before that the President attempted to silence critics and end the recession with a switch to expansionary fiscal policy in the budget proposed in January.

The President began his third year in office with the new fiscal policy and a new secretary of the treasury. The new secretary was John B. Connally, Democratic Governor of Texas from 1962 to 1968. He had long and varied experience in law and business, particularly in the oil and gas industries, but limited background in banking and finance. During the year Connally, a highly persuasive man, became the administration's chief economic spokesman, and was responsible for development of the new incomes policy announced in August.

The new fiscal policy was a "full-employment budget," which meant that the budget, with large deficits projected for both fiscal years 1971 and 1972, would have been in balance if the economy had been at full output and employment. The actual deficits represented the loss of

Total Private Domestic Economy

(Nonfarm and Farm)

Average Annual Rate of Change

	Output per Man-Hour [1]	Compensation Per Man-Hour [2]	Labor Cost Per Unit of Output	Non-Labor Cost Per Unit of Output	Consumer Price Index	Real Compensation Per Man-Hour
1968	4.8%	7.6%	4.6%	2.1%	4.7%	3.3%
1969	2.8	7.6	7.1	1.4	6.1	1.5
1970	5.0	7.6	6.5	2.9	5.5	1.2
1971	3.0	7.1	3.4	5.8	3.4	2.7
1972 (Est.)	7.0	6.2	1.9	3.0	3.4	2.8

1 *Output refers to gross national product in constant (1958) dollars.*
2 *Wages, salaries, fringe benefits, labor compensation of self-employed.*
SOURCE: Department of Labor, Bureau of Labor Statistics

Selected Economic Data, 1968-72

	1968	1969	1970	1971	1972 [1]
Average annual percent changes in:					
Gross national product, 1958 dollars	5.0%	2.7%	—.5%	2.7%	6.5%
GNP deflator	3.8	4.8	5.5	4.7	3.0
Consumer price index	4.2	6.1	5.5	3.4	3.4
Wholesale price index	2.5	4.8	2.2	4.0	6.5
Disposable personal income, billions of 1958 dollars	$499.0	$513.6	$533.2	$554.7	$578.7
Corporate profits after taxes, billions of dollars	$ 47.8	1,499.5	$ 40.2	$45.9	$ 52.6
Money Supply (demand deposits plus currency), billions of dollars	$197.4	$203.7	$214.8	$228.2	$246.9
Housing starts, thousands of units	1,545.4	1,499.5	1,469.0	2,084.5	2,377.7
Industrial production index, 1967 (100)	105.7	110.7	106.6	106.8	114.3
Average unemployment rate, percent	3.6%	3.5%	4.9%	5.9%	5.6%
Nonwhite workers	6.7	6.4	8.2	9.9	10.0
White workers	3.2	3.1	4.5	5.4	5.0

1 Preliminary

SOURCE: Annual report of the Council of Economic Advisers, 1973

federal revenues caused by economic performance below potential. In essence, the concept was the same as the deficit federal spending used by Presidents Kennedy and Johnson to stimulate the economy; President Nixon avoided that term because it was anathema to some Republicans. However, he did admit that he had been converted to new economic attitudes. To those economic conservatives who thought they had elected a proponent of fiscal orthodoxy, the President had a quick reply. He told an interviewer in January 1971: "I am now a Keynesian in economics."

The projected deficit for fiscal 1972 was $18.6 billion (the actual deficit when fiscal 1972 ended was $23 billion). The need for a large deficit was widely accepted in Congress but there was substantial Democratic criticism of the President's handling of the economy, because unemployment and the cost of living continued to rise. The consumer price index rose in May at an annual rate of 6 per cent and in June at a rate of 7.2 per cent. The nation's balance-of-payments deficit hit a record high at mid-year. The Harris Survey reported that, in a sampling taken in June, only 26 per cent of the persons questioned thought Mr. Nixon was doing a good job in economic matters while 70 per cent did not.

During the year the President was urged with increasing frequency by Democrats and Republicans to adopt some sort of incomes policy which would include use of wage and price controls. For the first seven months of the year Nixon continued to publicly oppose controls, although he did invoke the unwanted power Congress had given him in 1970 to impose controls on the construction industry in March. Congress in May extended the authority for controls until April 1972. The administration at that time said it did not intend to use it again, but the act eventually provided the authority under which Nixon imposed a price-wage freeze Aug. 15.

The sweeping program announced in August came largely as a surprise. To combat inflation, it called for a 90-day wage-price and rent freeze to be followed by a

"Phase Two" program of controls. To bring the U.S. balance of payments under control, the President suspended convertibility of the dollar to gold and announced a temporary 10 per cent surtax on imports. This led to a series of major foreign currency negotiations with other countries and culminated in what the President described as a "historic" December international agreement, signed at the Smithsonian Institution in Washington, in which the surtax was dropped and the dollar in effect devalued 8.57 per cent in return for concessions by foreign countries.

The Aug. 15 program also called for a number of cuts in federal expenditures. But to get the economy growing more rapidly, the President asked for a tax cut for business and individuals and for reinstatement of a form of the business investment tax credit which had been used intermittently since 1962. Congress agreed to both requests. The 1971 Revenue Act cut taxes by an average of $8.6-billion a year over the 1971-73 period and the restoration of the tax credit amounted to a tax cut of an estimated $2.4-billion in fiscal 1972, rising to $4-billion by 1974.

The Phase Two program which replaced the wage price freeze was announced Oct. 7. It involved establishment of a Pay Board and a Price Commission with authority to set guidelines for wage and price increases, issue orders and hear cases. The largest businesses and unions were to be controlled most stringently and required prior approval for pay and price increases. The Pay Board set a general guideline of 5.5 per cent per year for wage increases and 2.5 per cent for price increases.

At year's end it was too early to tell how well the new policy would work. The rate of unemployment hovered at around 6 per cent all year, but the economy was clearly out of the 1970 recession. GNP expanded vigorously in the fourth quarter of the year, bringing the total to $1,065-billion—an increase of approximately 9.5 per cent over the 1971 total. About $60-billion of the increase was in actual gain or output. The remainder represented price increases. The cost of living increase was 4.6 per cent for the year. It had begun to level off in July.

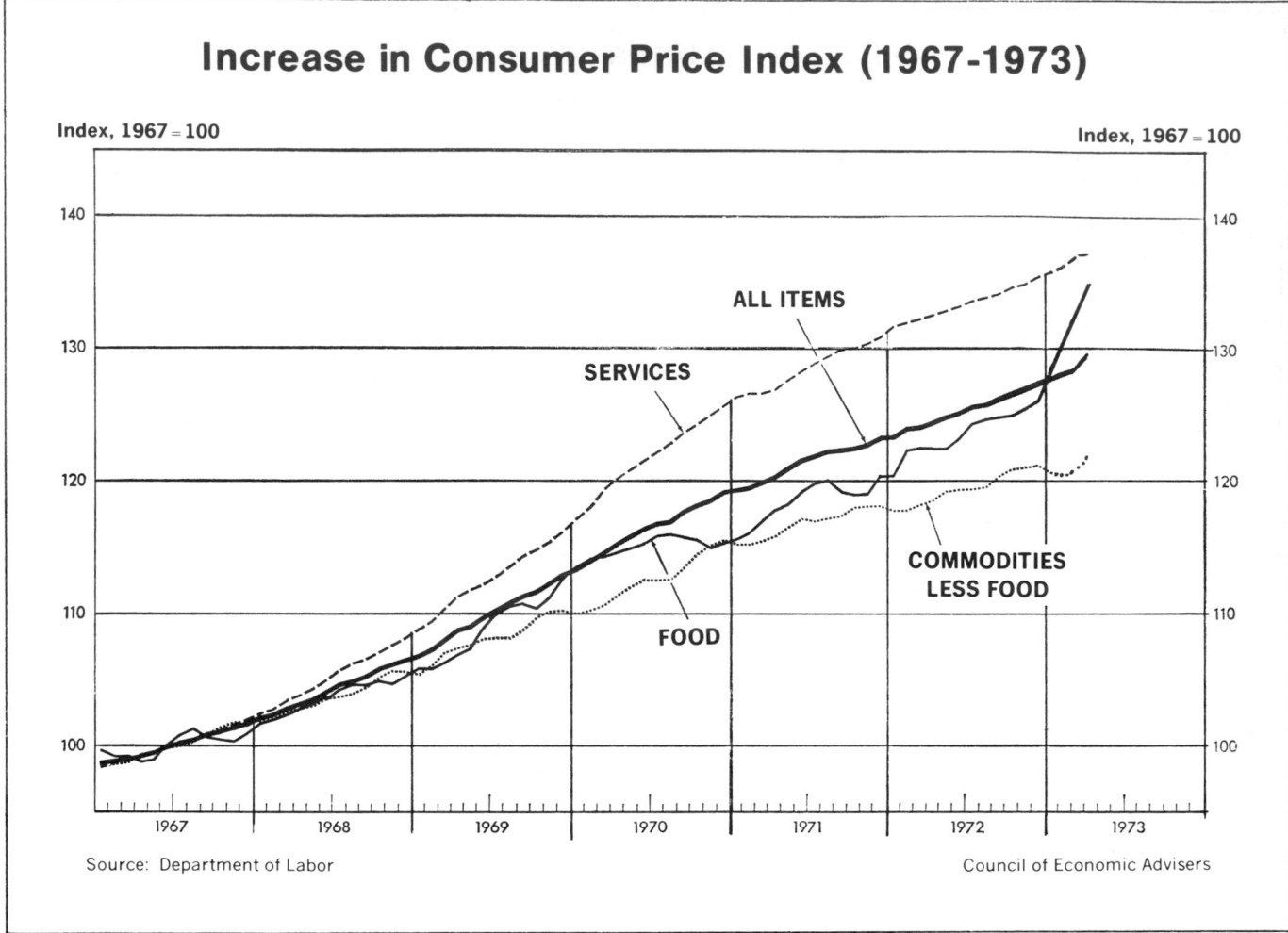

Increase in Consumer Price Index (1967-1973)

Index, 1967 = 100

ALL ITEMS

SERVICES

COMMODITIES LESS FOOD

FOOD

Source: Department of Labor   Council of Economic Advisers

1972

Administration economic policy in 1972 continued along the lines established in 1971. The President submitted another "full employment" expansionary budget and the Phase Two controls continued throughout the year. The rate of inflation was reduced substantially and unemployment dropped a little. The economy expanded rapidly, earning approval for the wisdom of the President's domestic economic policies.

On the international side, however, the devaluation had not improved the balance of payments situation as much as had been hoped. On an official settlements basis, the deficit was $10.1 billion, the second largest in the nation's history (after 1971). A major contributor to this was a tripling (from $2.7 billion to $6.9 billion.) in the deficit in the U.S. balance of trade (the excess of imports over exports). The administration, divided by conflicting trade philosophies, did not develop an over-all coordinated trade policy and submitted no major trade proposals to Congress during its first term.

The budget submitted in January 1972 called for a $25.5-billion deficit to stimulate the economy. But the President emphasized in his State of the Union message that the deficit was not "irresponsible" and would disappear under full employment conditions. He asked Congress to "resist the temptation to overspend" and for the rest of the year he battled with Congress on the spending issue. By mid-year Congress had added almost $7-billion to the budget and was considering programs which could add billions more. This led the President to threaten a tax increase and to ask Congress to fix a federal spending limit of $250-billion. The request was turned down in the final floor fight of the session.

Congress and the President also confronted each other over presidential impoundment of money. At session's end, the veto of an expensive water pollution bill was overridden, but the President said he would not spend spend that other unwanted money. The battles over economic priorities left considerable bitterness between the President and Congress as the first Nixon administration ended. (*Impoundment controversy p. 74.*)

But if Congress had quarrels with the administration over fiscal policy, the general public seemed satisfied with economic policy as a whole. It was not an issue in the November 1972 elections, and approval of the President's decisive 1971 policies was undoubtedly a factor in his huge reelection victory. Former President Eisenhower's 1968 prediction was proven very wrong. During the 1968 campaign he said: "I think Dick's going to be elected President, but I think he's going to be a one-term President. I think he's really going to fight inflation, and that will kill him politically."

The year-end figures for 1972 showed that GNP for the year averaged $1,152.1-billion—9.7 per cent over 1971. Real growth averaged 6.5 per cent and inflation just over 3 per cent. The growth figure was slightly higher and the inflation rate slightly lower than the 6.0 and 3.25 per cent targets that the administration set for itself in January. The unemployment rate was considered less satisfactory, but fell to 5.2 per cent from 6 per cent the year before. There were also certain other remaining problems hidden in the figures. In December, the wholesale price index rose at a seasonally adjusted annual rate of 19.2 per cent with a continuing jump, in food prices a major factor in the gain.

Phase Three. Just before the end of his first term in office, on Jan. 11, 1973, the President made the surprise announcement that he had ended most of the mandatory wage-price controls of Phase Two. The system was to be replaced by Phase Three—voluntary guidelines backed by the threat that the government would intervene to roll back wage and price increases it considered inflationary. Controls were left in force only for three "particularly troublesome" areas: processed agricultural products, health costs and the construction industry.

While dropping most mandatory controls, the President said that he was returning to fiscal and monetary policies as the principal weapons to continue to attack inflation. He set an over-all inflation rate of 2.5 per cent as his goal for 1973 and said its attainment would depend on federal budgetary restraint. He called on Congress to cooperate in holding federal spending down to avoid the inflationary impetus of a large government deficit.

According to the *New York Times*, the end of Phase Two was largely the product of consultation between AFL-CIO President George Meany and Treasury Secretary George P. Shultz. Labor in 1972 had walked off the Pay Board established under Phase Two, forcing its reorganization. Shultz had succeeded Connally as treasury secretary in May 1972. Formerly secretary of labor and then director of the Office of Management and Budget in the first Nixon administration, Shultz, like Connally, came to be a powerful economic spokesman for the President.

Phase Three was widely criticized from the beginning as being too weak, especially in Europe. This lead to unexpectedly strong pressure on the dollar abroad, and the administration Feb. 12 announced the second devaluation of the dollar in 14 months. The dollar was officially devalued 10 per cent, but as pressure continued it was allowed to float in relation to other currencies, bringing the effective rate lower.

At home prices began to climb quickly, especially in the supermarkets. The President March 29 ordered

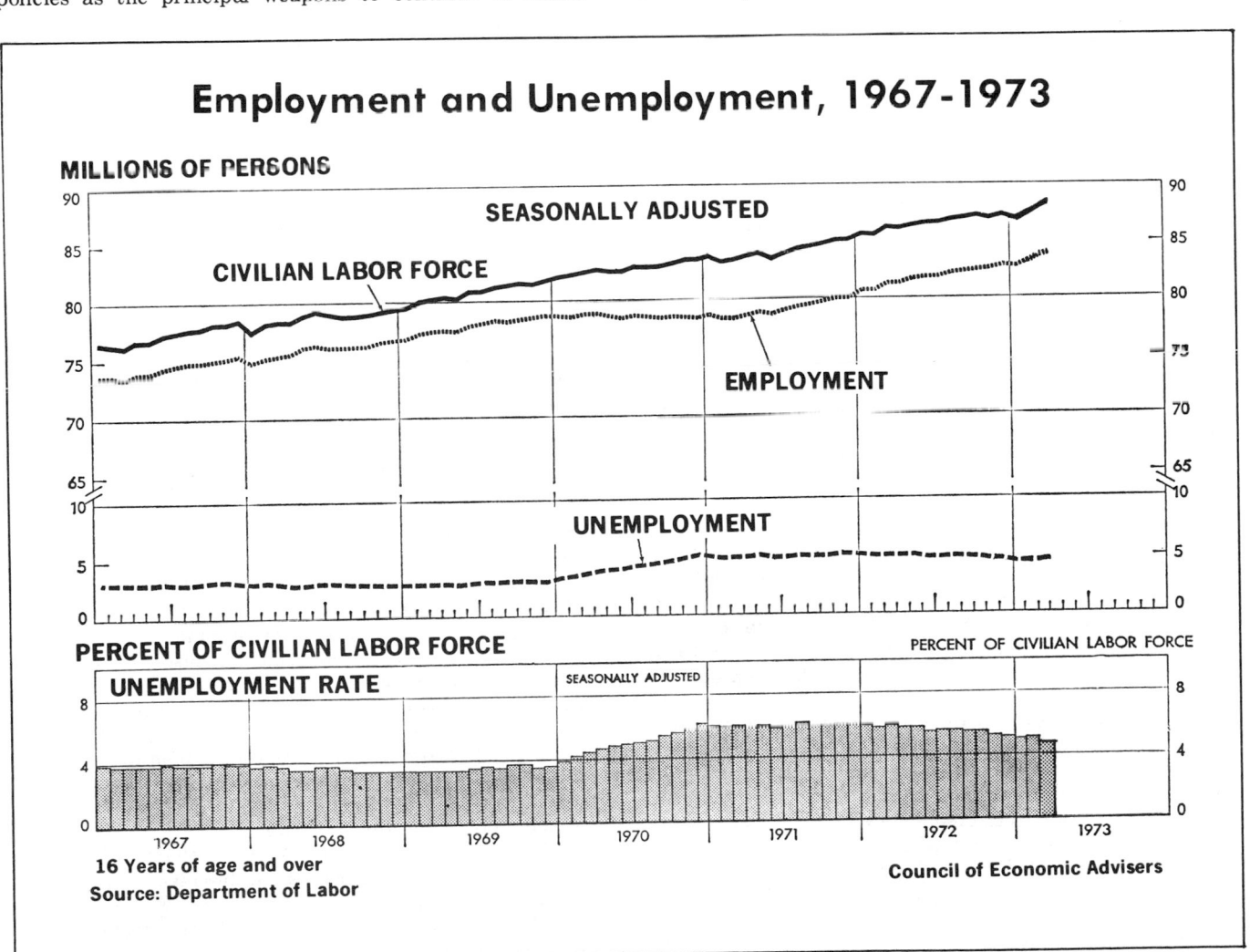

Employment and Unemployment, 1967-1973

MILLIONS OF PERSONS

SEASONALLY ADJUSTED

CIVILIAN LABOR FORCE

EMPLOYMENT

UNEMPLOYMENT

PERCENT OF CIVILIAN LABOR FORCE   PERCENT OF CIVILIAN LABOR FORCE

UNEMPLOYMENT RATE   SEASONALLY ADJUSTED

1967   1968   1969   1970   1971   1972   1973

16 Years of age and over   **Council of Economic Advisers**
Source: Department of Labor

imposition of price ceilings on beef, lamb and pork, but refused to yield to public pressure for additional economic controls.

After that the economic news was almost all bad. Interest rates climbed quickly. Retail prices, which rose at an annual rate of 3.6 per cent during Phase II, rose at a 9.2 per cent pace in the three months from February through April.

Shultz June 13 acknowledged that Phase III had not worked, and the President went on television to announce a 60-day freeze on all prices except those of raw agricultural products. He said it would be followed by Phase IV, as yet undecided, that would involve strong new wage and price controls.

Banking, Securities Policy

Congressional action in the areas of securities and banking was influenced by the stock market slump of 1969-70. A number of committees held hearings on a range of securities issues and in 1970, Congress finally passed a controversial bill, long under consideration, which made the first substantial changes in the regulation of mutual funds in 30 years. The Securities Investor Protection bill, also passed in 1970, established an insurance fund to protect customers from losses when brokers become insolvent. A dramatic growth of the securities industry during the 1960s, followed by the market decline, had led to brokerage failures and concern about management of funds and outdated methods of operation in the industry.

Congress also considered a number of bills dealing with banks. The most important was a hard-fought measure which extended federal regulation to holding companies controlling a single bank. Multi-bank holding companies had been regulated since 1956, but a special exemption had been made for one-bank companies in order to aid small rural banks. Increasingly, large banks had taken advantage of this loophole, and Congress in 1970 finally ended it.

Transportation Policy

As in the Johnson years, many members of Congress and the administration agreed on the need to develop a coordinated federal transportation policy, but were unable to come up with one.

As road congestion increased, there was a growing feeling that federal aid for transportation had been mistakenly biased toward highway construction. The President in 1972 endorsed a Senate plan to divert some highway trust fund revenues to mass transportation. The amendment was dropped in conference from a multi-billion highway bill and then the bill itself died when the House failed to obtain a quorum in the final hours of the session.

Congress in 1970 passed two important bills to help move the country away from dependence on the automobile. One authorized a new long-range program for expansion and improvement of the U.S. airport and airways systems. The other created AMTRAK, a semi-public corporation to operate a nationwide rail passenger service. The bill enabled railroads, if they wished, to transfer all of their inter-city passenger operations to the corporation in exchange for a sum of money, equipment or services.

Interest Rates

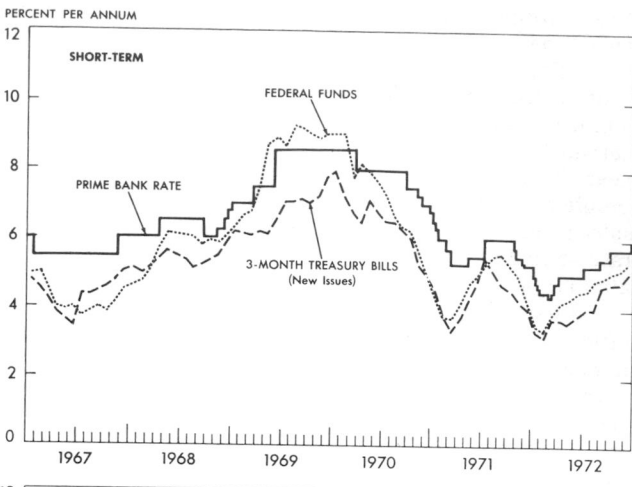

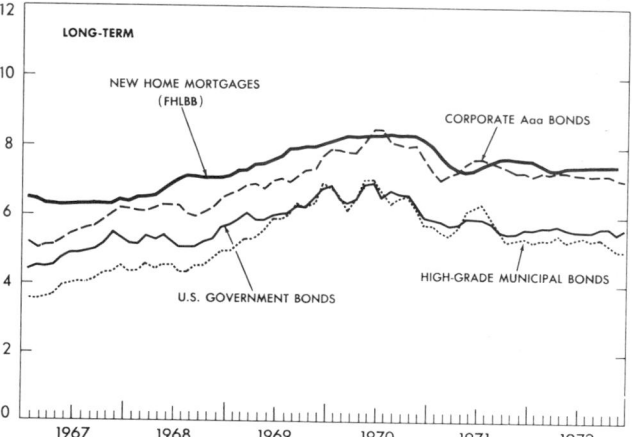

SOURCES: TREASURY DEPARTMENT, BOARD OF GOVERNORS OF THE FEDERAL RESERVE SYSTEM, FEDERAL HOME LOAN BANK BOARD, MOODY'S INVESTORS SERVICE, AND STANDARD & POOR'S CORPORATION.

In other transportation developments, Congress in 1971 gave the administration a major legislative setback when it refused to vote funds to continue development of a U.S. supersonic transport aircraft (SST).

Revenue Sharing

In 1972, Congress cleared legislation to share federal government revenues with state and local governments. The idea was developed by Kennedy and Johnson administration economists at a time when it appeared that the booming economy might begin to produce a substantial excess of revenues. It was not endorsed by President Johnson because Vietnam war spending changed the economic outlook, but was adopted by President Nixon as part of his program to decentralize the U.S. government.

In 1969, Nixon initially proposed a plan to make $500-million in federal revenues available for fiscal 1971. The annual total would rise to $5-billion by fiscal 1976. Congress did not act on this proposal.

In 1971, the President's state of the union message included a revenue sharing plan broader in scope than his earlier proposal.

He called for $5-billion annually in general revenue for distribution to states, local communities and the

CORPORATE PROFITS, 1966-1972

Because of the investment tax credit, the 1971-72 percentage rise in profits after taxes exceeded the rise before taxes. Most of the after-tax rise showed up in undistributed profits. Cash flow was up $14.5-billion.

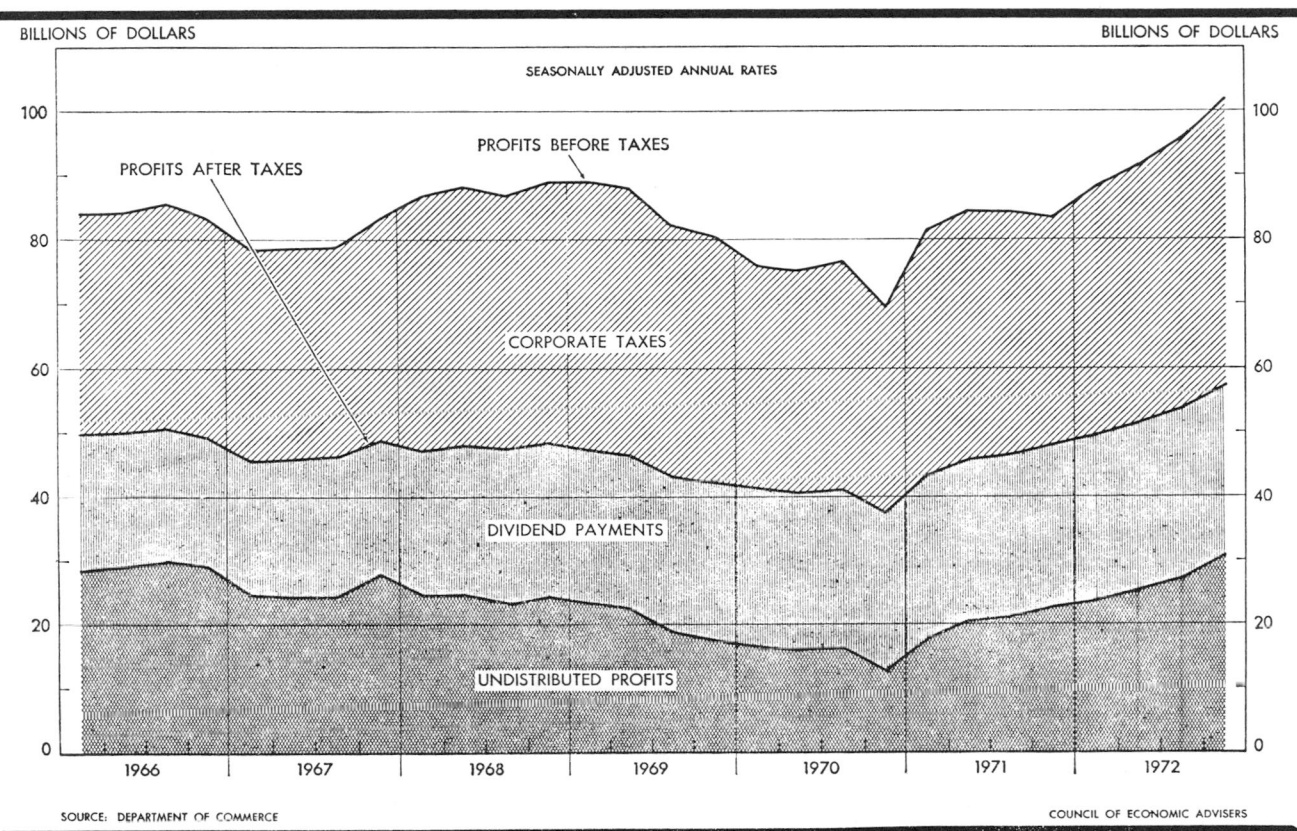

District of Columbia and for $11-billion in special revenue sharing.

The five-year program finally enacted called for sharing $30,236,400,000 from January 1972 through 1976. The funds were appropriated to a special trust fund for distribution to the states by the higher of two revenue-sharing allotments: the House formula, which favored more populous and industrialized states, or the Senate formula, which provided more money to smaller, more rural states.

Spending priorities for revenue sharing funds listed in the bill were capital expenditures and ordinary op-erating expenses on public safety, environmental protection, public transportation, health, recreation, libraries, social services for the poor and aged and financial administration.

Congress did not approve the President's proposal for $11 billion for six special revenue sharing programs which would have been created by consolidating about 105 existing federal aid programs into six broad purposes with fewer federal specifications. The six areas were law enforcement, manpower training, urban community development, rural community development, transportation and education.

The Federal Budget

The highlight of federal budget policy during the 1969-72 period was an abrupt shift by President Nixon at midpoint in his term of office from a restrictive to an expansionary fiscal strategy. Faced with stubborn inflation in the economy, the President proposed budgetary surpluses in each of his first two years in office (although neither materialized). But after recession as well as inflation took hold in 1970, the President put ideology aside and called for massive deficit spending in an attempt to restore full production and employment to the economy.

The President's new expansionary policy—which he called his "full employment" budget (to avoid the term "deficit financing," which was anathema to Republicans) —prevented further tailspins in the economy, although it did not immediately produce the desired effect of full economic recovery. The rate of unemployment, which had skyrocketed from 3.6 percent of the labor force at the end of 1969 to 5.8 percent at the close of 1970, hovered around the six percent mark throughout 1971. Interest rates fell sharply in late 1970 and in early 1971, but increased in late 1971, although not back to their mid-1970 levels. By mid-1972, however, the program appeared to be taking hold, although its results were scarcely dramatic. Unemployment for June was down to 5.5 percent, as compared to six percent a year before. And interest rates showed little upward movement through the first eight months of the year.

As the Vietnam war wound down, the Nixon budgets showed a shift in priorities from defense to domestic spending, a development that the President announced with considerable fanfare. In his fiscal 1971 budget, Nixon outlined a "strategy for the seventies" in which spending for education, health, manpower and other domestic programs (called "human resource" programs by the administration) would claim a larger percentage of the budget than would defense programs. Under the fiscal 1971 budget, 41 percent was allocated for human resource programs and 37 percent for defense. This pattern continued in the fiscal 1972 budget, when the figures were 42 and 34 percent, respectively, and in fiscal 1973, when they were 45 and 32 per cent *(Peace dividend, p. 199)*

Despite the dramatic shift in these allocations, however, few new domestic programs were started during the period, existing programs were seldom enlarged, and defense spending was actually reduced from the previous year's level in only two of the four years—fiscal 1971, when it was cut by $1-billion, and fiscal 1972, when $2.6-billion was cut. Rather, most of the shift was attributable to large built-in increases in payments for Social Security, welfare, and other income security programs, which were beyond control of Congress and the administration. Spending for these programs increased from $37.7-billion in fiscal 1969 to an estimated $69.7-billion in fiscal 1973. The 1973 spending figure for this category exceeded the entire defense budget for fiscal 1966 ($56.8-billion), the year U.S. escalation of the Vietnam war began.

Throughout the four-year period, President Nixon met with little success in his budget projections, primarily because of overly optimistic revenue forecasts which failed to materialize because of the sluggish economy. In fiscal 1972, for instance, the President projected revenues of $217.6-billion, but actual collections came to only $208.6-billion. To a lesser extent, the projections were upset by Congress, which added on funds for environmental and other programs while refusing to eliminate certain agricultural programs and other low-priority activities that the President sought to scrap.

But on another important front, Nixon fared better with Congress. The President met little opposition in pushing through bills to increase the national debt limit —an item that produced several cliff-hanging votes in the House during the Kennedy and Johnson administrations. House Republicans, who fought every new debt limit proposed during the Kennedy and Johnson years, voted overwhelmingly with President Nixon on his proposed new debt ceilings. During the Nixon term, the permanent debt ceiling was raised in stages from $358-billion to $400-billion and the temporary ceiling from $365-billion to $465-billion. *(1972 spending ceiling controversy p. 73)*

In another development, the President streamlined the budget process by restructuring the Bureau of the Budget—the most extensive reorganization of the Bureau since its creation in 1921. The new office, called the Office of Management and Budget, was given sweeping authority to coordinate the execution of government programs as well as the Budget Bureau's old role of advising the President on agency funding requests. Until this 1970 reorganization, budget functions had remained much the same since 1939, when the bureau was shifted from the Treasury Department to the Executive Office of the President.

References

Discussion of federal budget policy for the years 1945-64 may be found in *Congress and the Nation Vol. I,* p. 387-395; for the years 1965-68, *Congress and the Nation Vol. II,* p. 127-140.

Chronology Of Action On the Budget 1969

As one of his last acts in office, President Lyndon B. Johnson sent Congress a fiscal 1970 budget calling for a relatively small increase in overall defense spending, modest growth in urban aid and education programs and a sharp increase in spending for public health and welfare. Johnson's budget was designed to produce a $3.4-billion surplus, which the President said would "contain" the inflationary pressures that had been building up in the economy since 1965.

After a three-month study, however, Nixon administration economists decided that even greater surpluses would be necessary to stem the tide of inflation. On April 15, Nixon sent Congress a revised budget calling for cuts in both the domestic and defense spending projections laid out by President Johnson in January. The result was expected to be a $5.8-billion surplus—fourth largest in the nation's history. If attained, it would be the second surplus in a row after eight consecutive years of deficits, culminating in a deficit of $25.2-billion in fiscal 1968—the largest deficit since fiscal 1945. (The Johnson budget for fiscal 1969 produced a surplus of $3.2-billion—$800-million more than President Johnson had predicted and $2-billion above Mr. Nixon's estimates.)

But as fiscal 1970 wore on, actions and inactions by Congress, coupled with increases in uncontrollable spending such as Social Security payments and interest on the national debt, cast doubt on the likelihood of such a large surplus by the end of fiscal 1970. Moves by Congress to increase Social Security benefits by 15 percent and to reduce tax revenues in conjunction with the 1969 Tax Reform Act helped throw the Nixon budget out of alignment. *(1969 tax act, 78)*

Congress did cut $5.8-billion from budget requests for defense spending; but it added unrequested funds for a wide range of domestic programs, such as $600-million for pollution control. Failure to enact presidential requests on items like postal rate increases and adjustment of credit programs of the Veterans Administration and Farmers Home Administration also reduced the new revenues that the President had figured into his budget estimates. Worse still, revenues from existing taxes fell below expectations because of the recession that hit in early 1970. By the end of the fiscal year, the projected surplus of almost $6-billion had become a deficit of $2.8-billion.

Debt Ceiling

Congress in 1969 approved a $7-billion increase in the permanent national debt limit, to $365-billion. The legislation (HR 8508—PL 91-8) also raised the temporary ceiling, which would have expired June 30, from $365-billion to $377-billion. The temporary lid was to remain in effect from the date of enactment, April 7, through June 30, 1970, the end of fiscal 1970.

Although the higher limits were a victory of sorts for President Nixon, Congress dealt the President a defeat by rejecting his request to redefine the debt limit concept by excluding federal trust fund investments in government securities and reducing the permanent ceiling to $300-billion. The effect would have been comparable to a ceiling of $382-billion.

The permanent statutory debt limit was set at $285-billion in 1959. Temporary increases were approved by Congress in the following years as government borrowing pushed up the national debt. Congress in 1967 enacted a law (PL 90-39) which raised the permanent debt ceiling to $358-billion from $285-billion. PL 90-39 also provided for a temporary debt ceiling of $365-billion, to be in effect every day of the year except June 30, the last day of the fiscal year. The fluctuating temporary limit was designed to hold government spending in line and yet allow the Treasury to overcome "timing" problems in the mesh between spending and the collection of tax revenues. *(Background on debt limit, Congress and the Nation Vol. II, p. 139)*

Although only about 45 percent of revenues were collected in the first half of the fiscal year, spending was spread out rather evenly over the entire year. This temporary lag created the timing problem, usually forcing the Treasury to borrow in the first half of the fiscal year, even where there was a budget surplus over the full year.

A matter of even greater concern to the administration in 1969 was a legal requirement that the surpluses of federal trust funds be invested in U.S. government securities. Although this purchasing technically added to the public debt, it did not reflect increased competition for money-market funds. Thus, administration economists argued that the trust fund purchases should be excluded from the public debt subject to the ceiling. The request was rejected by the House Ways and Means Committee, whose position was sustained throughout further consideration of the bill.

Debate on HR 8508 took a sharp turn from a pattern that had developed during the Kennedy and Johnson administrations, when Southern Democrats and Republicans used the occasions as a forum for attacks on administration fiscal policy. House passage of the bill, by a 313-93 roll-call vote (R 140-41; D 173-52) marked the first time since 1958 that a majority of Republicans in that chamber supported an increase in the debt limit. Senate passage of the measure came on an equally easy, 67-18 roll call (R 31-4; D 36-14), with many Republican members who traditionally voted against increases voting for the new limits. (A majority of Senate Republicans had last favored a debt limit increase in 1966.) Some liberal senators who normally voted for higher ceilings voted against HR 8508 to protest what they saw as excessive levels of defense spending.

Spending Limit

In its own move to cool down inflation, Congress in 1969 approved legislation establishing a ceiling on expenditures of $191.9-billion for fiscal 1970. The spending limit, attached to a $4.3-billion supplemental appropriations bill for fiscal 1969 (PL 91-47), appeared to have the effect of ordering a $1-billion reduction in spending because it was $1-billion below the Nixon administration's projections for the year. In reality, however, the ceiling

Federal Finances Compared With Gross National Product

(in billions of dollars)

| Fiscal year | Gross national product | Budget receipts | | Budget outlays (expenditures and net lending) | | | |
| | | | | Total | | Budget expenditures (excludes net lending) | |
		Amount	Percent of GNP	Amount	Percent of GNP	Amount	Percent of GNP
1954	362.1	69.7	19.3	70.9	19.6	*(1)*	*(1)*
1955	378.6	65.5	17.3	68.5	18.1	*(1)*	*(1)*
1956	409.4	74.5	18.2	70.5	17.2	*(1)*	*(1)*
1957	431.3	80.0	18.5	76.7	17.8	*(1)*	*(1)*
1958	440.3	79.6	18.1	82.6	18.8	81.0	18.4
1959	469.1	79.2	16.9	92.1	19.6	89.4	19.1
1960	495.2	92.5	18.7	92.2	18.6	90.3	18.2
1961	506.5	94.4	18.6	97.8	19.3	96.6	19.1
1962	542.1	99.7	18.4	106.8	19.7	104.5	19.3
1963	573.4	106.6	18.6	111.3	19.4	111.5	19.4
1964	612.2	112.7	18.4	118.6	19.4	118.0	19.3
1965	654.2	116.8	17.9	118.4	18.1	117.2	17.9
1966	721.2	130.9	18.1	134.7	18.7	130.8	18.1
1967	769.8	149.6	19.4	158.3	20.6	153.2	19.9
1968	826.1	153.7	18.6	170.0	21.8	172.8	20.9
1969	897.6	187.8	20.9	184.5	20.6	183.1	20.4
1970	953.2	193.7	20.3	196.6	20.6	194.5	20.4
1971	1,008.2	188.4	18.7	211.4	21.0	210.3	20.9
1972	1,089.5	197.8	18.2	236.6	21.7	235.6	21.6

1 Not available.

SOURCE: Office of Management and Budget

was adjustable because it could be increased or lowered by any congressional action affecting the budget (such as add-ons for unrequested items) and could be increased by as much as $2-billion by the President to reflect the increased costs for uncontrollable items such as Social Security payments.

As it developed, even the $2-billion cushion for uncontrollables was not enough to cover the sharp increase in spending for these requirements. In a second supplemental appropriations bill (HR 17399—PL 91-305), passed in mid-1970, Congress increased the fiscal 1970 ceiling to $197.9-billion, plus another $2-billion cushion for uncontrollables. Actual spending for the fiscal year came to $196.6-billion, $3.3-billion less than the revised legal ceiling.

1970

President Nixon in the fiscal 1971 federal budget, the first budget fully under his own influence, sought to continue the policy of fiscal restraint that he had outlined in his budget amendments the year before. The new budget, prepared on the assumption that inflation would continue during fiscal 1970 though at a reduced rate, called for a slight spending increase of $2.9-billion and a surplus of $1.3-billion.

By late winter, however, inflation was still rampant and new problems had appeared: creeping recession, growing unemployment (reaching six percent by the end of the year), declining stock prices, a rising budget deficit and a dissatisifed public. The Nixon administration, critics charged, had achieved recession, unemployment and inflation simultaneously.

Critics faulted Nixon's original stringent fiscal and monetary policies for the strains they placed on the economy, including the unemployment and rising interest rates. Allocation of credit and controls on wages and prices would have restrained rising prices without the loss of employment and output which the administration's program produced, some argued. Democratic leaders in Congress issued a new call for controls on Dec. 3. Congress had passed legislation authorizing controls in

(Continued on p. 67)

Budget Receipts and Outlays, 1789-1973

(in millions of dollars)

Fiscal Year	Receipts	Outlays	Surplus or Deficit	Fiscal Year	Receipts	Outlays	Surplus or Deficit
ADMINISTRATIVE BUDGET †				**ADMINISTRATIVE BUDGET—Cont.**			
1789-1849	1,160	1,090	+70	1939	4,979	8,841	—3,862
1850-1900	14,462	15,453	—991				
				CONSOLIDATED CASH STATEMENT †			
1901	588	525	+63				
1902	562	485	+77	1940	6,879	9,589	—2,710
1903	562	517	+45				
1904	541	584	—43	1941	9,202	13,980	—4,778
1905	544	567	—23	1942	15,104	34,500	—19,396
				1943	25,097	78,909	—53,812
1906	595	570	+25	1944	47,818	93,956	—46,138
1907	666	579	+87	1945	50,162	95,184	—45,022
1908	602	659	—57				
1909	604	694	—89	1946	43,537	61,738	—18,201
1910	676	694	—18	1947	43,531	36,931	+6,600
				1948	45,357	36,493	+8,864
1911	702	691	+11	1949	41,576	40,570	+1,006
1912	693	690	+3	1950	40,940	43,147	—2,207
1913	714	715	—*				
1914	725	726	—*	1951	53,390	45,797	+7,593
1915	683	746	—63	1952	68,011	67,962	+49
				1953	71,495	76,769	—5,274
1916	761	713	+48				
1917	1,101	1,954	—853	**UNIFIED BUDGET** †			
1918	3,645	12,677	—9,032				
1919	5,130	18,493	—13,363	1954	69,719	70,890	—1,170
1920	6,649	6,358	+291	1955	65,469	68,509	—3,041
1921	5,571	5,062	+509	1956	74,547	70,460	+4,087
1922	4,026	3,289	+736	1957	79,990	76,741	+3,249
1923	3,853	3,140	+713	1958	79,636	82,757	—2,939
1924	3,871	2,908	+963	1959	79,249	92,104	—12,855
1925	3,641	2,924	+717	1960	92,492	92,223	+269
1926	3,795	2,930	+865	1961	94,389	97,795	—3,406
1927	4,031	2,857	+1,155	1962	99,676	106,813	—7,137
1928	3,900	2,961	+939	1963	106,560	111,311	—4751
1929	3,862	3,127	+734	1964	112,662	118,584	—5,922
1930	4,058	3,320	+738	1965	116,833	118,430	—1,596
1931	3,116	3,577	—462	1966	130,856	134,652	—3,796
1932	1,924	4,659	—2,735	1967	149,552	158,254	—8,702
1933	1,997	4,598	—2,602	1968	153,671	178,833	—25,161
1934	3,015	6,645	—3,630	1969	187,784	184,548	+3,236
1935	3,706	6,497	—2,791	1970	193,743	196,588	—2,845
1936	3,997	8,422	—4,425	1971	**188,392**	**211,425**	—23,033
1937	4,956	7,733	—2,777	1972	**208,649**	**231,876**	**—23,227**
1938	5,588	6,765	—1,177	1973 est.	220,765	246,327	**—25,472**

Notes.—Certain interfund transactions are excluded from receipts and outlays starting in 1932. For years prior to 1932 the amounts of such transactions are not significant.

Refunds of receipts are excluded from receipts and outlays starting in 1913; comparable data are not available for prior years.

*Less than $500,000.

† **Administrative budget:** *all federal fiscal operations except federally administered trust funds, such as Social Security and highway program funds;* **consolidated cash statement:** *included the elements of the administrative budget plus trust fund transactions on a cash basis (i.e., as payments and receipts were made);* **unified budget** *included the elements of both the other budget concepts but entered receipts and expenditures on an accrual basis (i.e., as they became due). Congress and the Nation Vol. II, p. 137.*

SOURCE: Office of Management and Budget

(Continued from p. 65)

December 1969 (PL 91-151) and a wage-price freeze on Aug. 13, 1970 (PL 91-379) over the President's opposition.

Nixon remained opposed to the wage-price controls —commonly known as an "incomes policy"—throughout the year, despite pressure from Federal Reserve Board Chairman Arthur F. Burns that he move in that direction. But by year's end, the President had announced a marked shift in his monetary and fiscal strategy. In a major economic speech Dec. 4, the President stressed the obligation of the government to move the economy toward full employment. That would require greater ease in monetary policy, he indicated. And on the fiscal front, the President indicated he would use deficit spending to stimulate economic growth. He said he was planning the new budget "on the basis that it would be balanced if we were at full employment and the economy were producing full revenues." Under impact of the President's new policy, coupled with sluggish revenues, the planned $1.3-billion surplus plummeted to a $23.0-billion deficit by the end of the fiscal year.

In other developments, Congress again disputed the President over spending priorities. For the third consecutive year, it enacted a spending ceiling. Congress sliced funds from Nixon's military, foreign aid and space requests, and added money to numerous domestic programs, notably education, health, manpower, training and pollution control. The President responded with vetoes to ward off some of the unwanted spending, but this was not always successful. Of five vetoes cast over budget matters, two were overridden by Congress.

Spending Limit

The limit on spending for fiscal 1971 was embodied in a second supplemental appropriations bill for fiscal 1970 (PL 91-305), the same bill that had placed a limit of $197.9-billion plus a $2-billion cushion for uncontrollable items on the fiscal 1970 budget. The limits for fiscal 1971 were to be $200.8-billion, plus a $4.8-billion allowance for uncontrollables, and an unlimited ceiling for congressional add-ons. The basic $200.8-billion ceiling was the amount projected by the President in his fiscal 1971 budget.

The only dispute over the spending limit focused on the amount of leeway to be given the administration to handle the controllables. The House voted a $3-billion allotment, and the Senate $6-billion. "In view of the history of increases on uncontrollable items, the committee believed it prudent" to double the cushion, the Senate Appropriations Committee said in its report on the bill. House and Senate conferees compromised on a cushion of $4.5-billion. Congress later approved a series of add-ons to the President's budget, resulting in actual spending of $211.4-billion for the year.

Debt Ceiling

Congress in 1970 increased the temporary limit in the national debt for fiscal 1971 by $18-billion, to a level of $395-billion, and the permanent ceiling by $15-billion, to $380-billion. President Nixon requested the $18-billion increase in May (for both temporary and permanent ceilings) after it became apparent that the budget would be in deficit instead of in mild surplus as he had predicted in January.

Budget Terminology

The federal budget is a plan of expected receipts and expenditures, a statement of priorities, an accounting of how funds have been and will be spent and a request for authority to spend public money.

The federal expenditures reported are most frequently outlays: amounts spent, obligated or committed during the year. Examples are funds spent to buy equipment or property, to meet the government's liability under a contract or to pay the salary of an employee. Outlays also include net lending—the difference between disbursements and repayments under government lending programs.

The administration's request to Congress, presented in the form of the budget, is for authority to obligate or lend funds: New Obligational Authority (abbreviated NOA) and Loan Authority (LA).

Budget authority determines the scope of operations of the government. Congress confers budget authority on a federal agency generally in the form of appropriations.

Appropriations may be for a single year, a specified period of years, or an indefinite number of years, according to the restrictions Congress wishes to place on spending for particular purposes.

Congress also restricts itself in the appropriation process by requiring that an appropriation be preceded by an authorization to appropriate a certain or an indefinite amount of money for a certain purpose over a period of time. These authorizations, which in practice are often larger than the actual appropriations, are self-imposed limits on Congress, distinct from budget authority.

Usually an authorization establishes the scope of a particular program, and Congress appropriates funds within the limits it has previously approved. In the case of authority to enter contract obligations, however, Congress authorizes the administration to make firm commitments for which funds must be appropriated later. Congress occasionally includes mandatory spending requirements, designed to ensure spending at a certain level.

Budget authority, either NOA or LA, often differs from actual outlays. This is because, in practice, funds actually spent or obligated during a year are drawn partly from the budget authority conferred in the year in question and partly from budget authority conferred in previous years.

Similarly, part of the budget authority granted for the current year will not be spent or obligated until succeeding years. Delays, first in appropriating and then in making expenditures under federal programs, produce the lag. Consequently, a change in budget authority is not necessarily reflected immediately in a change of the same amount in outlays.

Without the new temporary ceiling, the debt limit— set at $377-billion for fiscal 1970—would have dropped to the existing permanent ceiling level of $365-billion on June 30, the end of the fiscal year. It was estimated that the public debt would total $372-billion on July 1. While, according to the Senate Finance Committee, there would have been no question about the legality of the existing debt, no new debt instruments could have been issued and consequently no existing debt could have been refinanced. Without authority to refinance short-term Treasury bills becoming due in July, the Treasury Department would have exhausted its cash balances on July 9, according to the committee. More than $3-billion in Treasury bills was scheduled to mature on that date. Without cash on hand, the government would have been unable to meet its payrolls and make payments under federal programs.

Presidential Vetoes

President Nixon's disputes with Congress over spending priorities led to presidential vetoes of five bills during the 1970 session of Congress (four other bills were vetoed but not primarily because of spending disputes). The bills vetoed over budgeting controversies included HR 13111, appropriating $19.7-billion for the Departments of Labor and Health, Education and Welfare (HEW) and the Office of Economic Opportunity for fiscal 1970 (the first veto Nixon cast since becoming President); HR 11102, authorizing $2.79-billion through fiscal 1973 for the Hill-Burton hospital construction programs; HR 16916, appropriating $4.4-billion for fiscal 1971 programs administered by the Office of Education in HEW; HR 17548, appropriating $18-billion for the Department of Housing and Urban Development and other agencies for fiscal 1971; and S 3867, authorizing $9.5-billion in fiscal 1971-74 for federal manpower training and public service employment programs. The hospital construction and Office of Education vetoes were overridden and the other vetoes sustained (including the four bills vetoed over non-spending issues). When the hospital construction bill became law on June 30, it marked the first occasion in 10 years in which Congress had passed a bill over a President's veto. In 1960 Congress overrode President Eisenhower's veto of a federal employees' pay raise bill (HR 9883—PL 86-568).

Program Terminations

An effort by President Nixon to reduce, restructure or terminate a number of low-priority government programs was blocked by Congress in 1970. Among the President's budget-cutting proposals, designed to save $2.1-billion a year, were the disposal of $750-million in material from the nation's stockpile of strategic and critical materials, reductions in the federal impact-areas school assistance program, and termination of the Agriculture Department's special milk program and agricultural conservation program. Congress June 29 did approve legislation (in 17 separate bills) authorizing the sale of $150-million worth of materials from the nation's stockpile. But action was never taken on the other requests in the President's package. An effort to cut $1.4-billion from such programs had failed the year before.

Budget Bureau Reorganization

In another key budget development, Congress in 1970 approved a reorganization plan submitted by President Nixon to establish an Office of Management and Budget (OMB), to be built around the nucleus of the Bureau of the Budget, which would be abolished. The changes came in Reorganization Plan No. 2, one of four

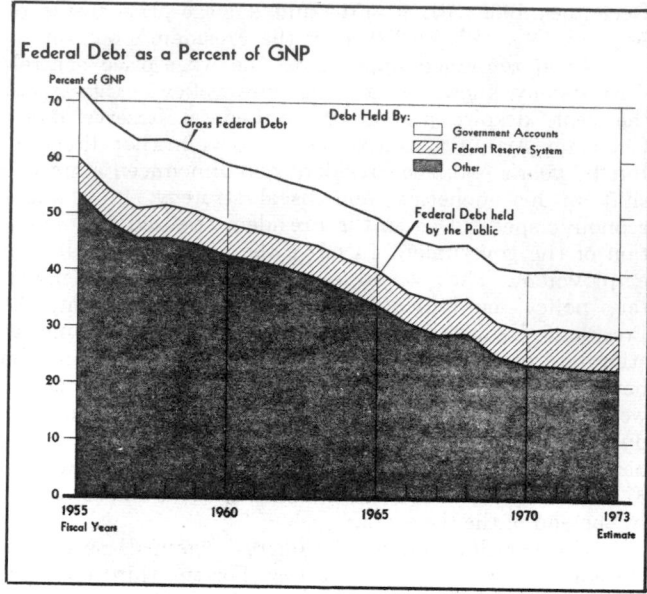

reorganization plans proposed by the President and accepted by Congress during the year. (Plan No. 2 also set up a Domestic Council, which would advise the President on programs and policies outside the military and foreign affairs areas.) *(History of Budget Bureau, p. 73)*

Nixon's decision to establish OMB was the first rearrangement of a President's traditional relationship with his cabinet officers and his budget officials in 31 years. The plan, in effect, won congressional approval May 16, after Congress failed to disapprove the proposal within the 60-day period required by the Reorganization Act of 1949. The plan took effect July 1.

The new office did not downgrade the budgeting function but amplified it. The existing responsibilities of the Bureau of the Budget were extended and greater use made of organization and management systems, development of executive talent and a broader career staff, better dissemination of information and appropriate use of modern techniques and equipment. The rationale for these changes was to provide greater executive capability for analyzing, coordinating, evaluating and improving the efficiency of government programs. Major new roles of the office would be:

• Assistance in implementing major legislation, such as recent legislation for preservation of the environment, under which several agencies would share responsibility for action;

• Coordination of the complex system of federal grants, which often involved not only more than one federal agency in a particular area but also various agencies and government entities at the state and local levels.

• Evaluation of cost effectiveness of particular programs and the relative priority of needs they were designed to meet. This was to be the Nixon administration's version of the Planning-Programming-Budgeting (PPB) System developed by former Defense Secretary Robert S. McNamara and used by other federal agencies during the Johnson administration.

Some observers thought that another rationale for OMB was a strengthening of the budget planners' hand in questioning the expenditure requests of the Department of Defense—a function that had fallen into virtual disuse during the Kennedy and Johnson administrations. This contention was never confirmed by the Nixon administration, however, despite hefty cuts by OMB in the budget requested by the Defense Department for fiscal 1972.

Approval of the reorganization plan came three days after a House resolution disapproving the proposal was rejected by a 164-193 roll-call vote. No resolution of disapproval was submitted in the Senate.

The effort to shoot down the plan in the House originated in the Government Operations Committee, which reported a resolution on May 8 (H Res 960—H Rept 91-1066) disapproving the proposal. The committee, which approved the resolution by a 20-9 vote, objected primarily to features of the reorganization plan which would transfer all existing statutory authority of the Bureau of the Budget to the President himself. The committee report said this provision would give the President in the future "almost unlimited power to restructure the administration of those functions...without any action or review by Congress."

The committee's plan had been to report a bill (HR 17376), introduced by John A. Blatnik (D Minn.) and Chet Holifield (D Calif.), to approve part of the reorganization plan by means of specific legislation. The bill, among other provisions, would have blocked the President's authority to make unlimited changes in the Budget Bureau's statutory authority. House Republicans outflanked proponents of this strategy by holding their own ranks firmly in the floor vote May 13 on the disapproval resolution (only six voted for it) and persuading 38 Democrats (mostly southerners) to join them.

Creation of OMB and the Domestic Council was the first recommendation of the President's Advisory Council on Executive Reorganization, appointed by Nixon April 5, 1969. (Roy L. Ash, president of Litton Industries Inc., served as chairman.) The Ash commission, as it was called, argued that creation of these offices would largely eliminate the need for such advisory groups as the commission itself and the task forces used by Presidents in modern times to develop ideas and propose solutions to problems. Such special-purpose bodies would now be institutionalized within the Executive Office of the President. Named as first director of OMB was George P. Shultz, who had served as secretary of labor from the outset of the Nixon administration.

1971

In his state of the union message on Jan. 22, 1971, President Nixon outlined a new economic strategy which was the guiding principle of the budget for fiscal year 1972. Nixon called his new fiscal plan a "full-employment" budget, which meant that the budget, with large deficits projected for both fiscal years 1971 and 1972, would have been in balance if the economy had been at full output and employment. The projected deficits, totaling $18.6-billion and $11.6-billion, respectively, represented the loss of federal revenues caused by economic performance below potential. (Actual deficits came to $23-billion for both fiscal 1971 and fiscal 1972.)

The purpose of the new plan was to stimulate a faster recovery from the recession. "By operating as if we were at full employment," the President said, "we will help to bring about that full employment." Chief among

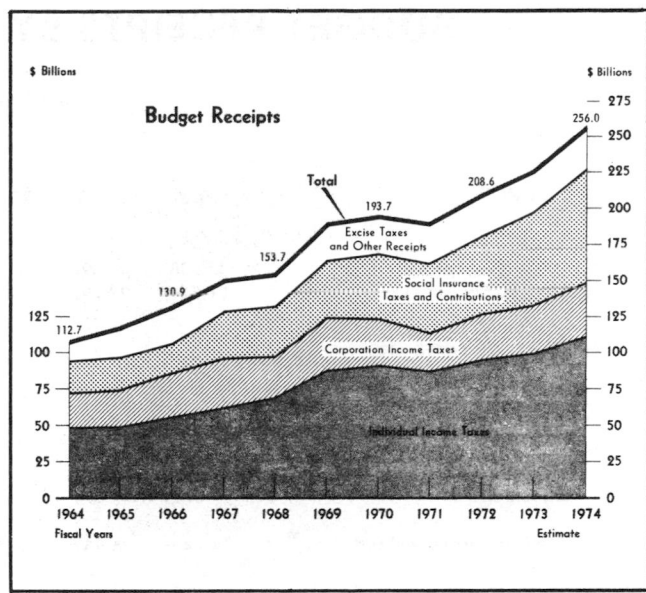

the assumptions underlying the budget was a total output of the economy (gross national product) of $1,065-billion in calendar year 1971. This was approximately $20-billion higher than the consensus of estimates by economists outside the government and about $18-billion more than the economy actually achieved.

As in 1970, Mr. Nixon was urged with increasing frequency during the year to adopt an incomes policy, under which the government would influence or intervene in wage and price decisions in the private economy to curb inflation. Nixon maintained an unremitting hostility toward wage and price controls well into the year. Then in a surprise move Aug. 15, the President froze wages and prices and ordered a series of other tough actions, including a 5 per cent reduction in federal employment, six months' deferral of a federal pay raise scheduled for early 1972 and postponement of the starting dates for his welfare reform and revenue-sharing program, neither of which was expected to be enacted soon. Nixon's decisive effort to cope with the nation's worsening economic problems gained him the initiative and some relief from criticism—at least until announcement later in the year of Phase Two—the post-freeze period of the new policy. *(Details of the President's stabilization program, p. 105)*

In another development, the Senate Feb. 8 confirmed the President's nomination of a Democrat, former Gov. John Connally of Texas (1963-69), as treasury secretary to succeed David M. Kennedy. Connally soon became the President's most influential economic adviser. He was regarded as the principal architect of the new economic policy.

Debt Ceiling

Congress in 1971 increased the temporary national debt ceiling for fiscal 1972 to $430-billion from $395-billion and the permanent ceiling to $400-billion from $380-billion. The debt limit bill (HR 4690—PL 92-5) also provided for the sale by the Treasury Department of $10-billion in long-term bonds (maturing after seven years) without regard to the existing 4.25 per cent interest ceiling

(Continued on p. 71)

BUDGET RECEIPTS BY SOURCE, FISCAL 1963-72

(in millions of dollars)

SOURCE	1963	1964	1965	1966	1967	1968	1969	1970	1971	1972
INDIVIDUAL INCOME TAXES	$ 47,588	$ 48,697	$ 48,792	$ 55,446	$ 61,526	$ 68,726	$ 87,249	$ 90,412	$ 86,230	$ 94,737
CORPORATION INCOME TAXES	21,579	23,493	25,461	30,073	33,971	28,665	36,678	32,829	26,785	32,166
SOCIAL INSURANCE TAXES AND CONTRIBUTIONS (TRUST FUNDS):										
Employment taxes and contributions:										
Old-age and survivors insurance	13,117	15,242	15,567	17,556	22,197	22,265	25,484	29,396	31,354	35,132
Disability insurance	1,058	1,124	1,156	1,530	2,204	2,651	3,469	4,063	4,490	4,775
Hospital insurance	—	—	—	893	2,645	3,493	4,398	4,755	4,874	5,205
Railroad retirement	572	593	636	683	776	814	885	919	980	1,008
Total employment taxes and contributions	14,746	16,959	17,359	20,662	27,823	29,224	34,236	39,133	41,699	46,120
Unemployment insurance	4,112	4,045	3,819	3,777	3,659	3,346	3,328	3,464	3,674	4,357
Contributions for other insurance and retirement:										
Supplementary medical insurance	—	—	—	—	647	698	903	936	1,253	1,340
Employees' retirement—employee contributions	932	993	1,065	1,111	1,201	1,334	1,426	1,735	1,916	2,058
Other retirement contributions	13	15	16	18	19	20	24	29	37	39
Total contributions for other insurance and retirement	946	1,008	1,081	1,129	1,867	2,052	2,353	2,701	3,205	3,437
Sub-total social insurance taxes and contributions	19,804	22,012	22,258	25,567	33,349	34,622	39,918	45,298	48,578	53,914
EXCISE TAXES:										
Federal funds:										
Alcohol	3,366	3,499	3,689	3,720	3,980	4,189	4,482	4,610	4,696	5,004
Tobacco	2,075	2,048	2,142	2,066	2,077	2,121	2,136	2,093	2,205	2,205
Other	4,474	4,664	5,081	3,358	3,221	3,390	3,967	3,649	3,609	2,297
Total federal excise taxes	9,915	10,211	10,911	9,145	9,278	9,700	10,585	10,352	10,510	9,506
TRUST FUNDS:										
Highway	3,279	3,519	3,659	3,917	4,441	4,379	4,637	5,354	5,542	5,322
Airport and airway	—	—	—	—	—	—	—	—	563	649
Total trust taxes	3,279	3,519	3,659	3,917	4,441	4,379	4,637	5,354	6,105	5,971
Sub-total trust and excise taxes	13,194	13,731	14,570	13,062	13,719	14,079	15,222	15,705	16,614	15,477
ESTATE AND GIFT TAXES	2,167	2,394	2,716	3,066	2,978	3,051	3,491	3,644	3,735	5,436
CUSTOMS DUTIES	1,205	1,252	1,442	1,767	1,901	2,038	2,319	2,430	2,591	3,287
MISCELLANEOUS RECEIPTS:										
Deposit of earnings by Federal Reserve System	828	947	1,372	1,713	1,805	2,091	2,662	3,266	3,533	3,252
Other miscellaneous receipts [1]	194	138	222	162	303	400	247	158	325	381
Sub-total miscellaneous receipts	1,023	1,084	1,594	1,875	2,108	2,491	2,908	3,424	3,858	3,635
GRAND TOTAL BUDGET RECEIPTS	$106,560	$112,662	$116,833	$130,856	$149,552	$153,671	$187,784	$193,743	$188,392	$208,652

1 Includes both federal funds and trust funds.

SOURCE: Office of Management and Budget

BUDGET OUTLAYS BY FUNCTION, FISCAL 1963-1972

(in millions of dollars)

FISCAL YEAR	1963	1964	1965	1966	1967	1968	1969	1970	1971	1972
National Defense	$ 52,257	$ 53,591	$ 49,578	$ 56,785	$ 70,081	$ 80,517	$ 81,232	$ 80,295	$ 77,661	$ 78,336
International Affairs and Finance	4,115	4,117	4,340	4,490	4,547	4,619	3,785	3,570	3,095	3,726
Space Research and Technology	2,522	4,170	5,091	5,933	5,423	4,721	4,247	3,749	3,381	3,422
Agriculture and Rural Development	5,138	5,184	4,805	3,676	4,373	5,940	6,218	6,201	5,096	7,063
Natural Resources and Environment	1,498	1,966	2,056	2,036	1,878	1,722	2,169	2,568	2,716	3,761
Commerce and Transportation	5,765	6,511	7,399	7,171	7,594	8,094	7,921	9,310	11,310	11,201
Community Development and Housing	—880	—185	288	2,644	2,616	4,076	1,961	2,965	3,357	4,282
Education and Manpower	1,502	1,751	2,284	4,258	5,853	6,739	6,525	7,289	8,654	9,751
Health	1,379	1,716	1,704	2,509	6,667	9,608	11,611	12,907	14,463	17,112
Income Security	24,084	25,110	25,702	29,016	31,164	34,108	37,699	43,790	55,712	64,876
Veterans Benefits and Services	5,520	5,681	5,722	5,920	6,897	6,882	7,640	8,677	9,766	10,731
Interest	9,215	9,810	10,357	11,285	11,588	13,744	15,791	18,312	19,609	20,582
General Government	1,810	2,040	2,210	2,292	2,510	2,561	2,866	3,336	3,970	4,891
Undistributed Intergovernmental Transactions:										
Employer share, employee retirement	—1,159	—1,256	—1,329	—1,447	—1,661	—1,825	—2,018	—2,444	—2,611	—2,768
Interest received by trust funds	—1,485	—1,621	—1,780	—1,917	—2,275	—2,674	—3,099	—3,936	—4,765	—5,089
TOTAL	$111,311	$118,584	$118,430	$134,652	$158,254	$179,823	$184,540	$196,588	$211,425	$231,876

SOURCE: Office of Management and Budget

(Continued from p. 69)

that had been in effect for 53 years; closed a tax loophole under which it was possible to use government notes and bonds at their face value to pay federal taxes even if the bond's current market price was lower than the face value; and provided a 10-percent across-the-board increase in Social Security benefits, together with provisions to finance the benefits.

In House debate on the bill, an amendment which would have deleted the $10-billion bond program was defeated by a vote of 181-212, in the first recorded teller vote in the history of the House of Representatives. The amendment was offered by Banking and Currency Committee Chairman Wright Patman (D Texas), a longtime critic of high interest rates. The recorded teller vote was authorized by the Legislative Reorganization Act of 1970 (PL 91-510), which went into effect at the opening of the 92nd Congress.

In appearances before the House Ways and Means Committee, the administration had requested a $40-billion increase in the debt ceiling and elimination of the 4.25-percent ceiling on interest paid on the Treasury bonds. The $10-billion limitation originated in the Ways and Means Committee, whose chairman, Wilbur D. Mills (D Ark.), termed it a "limited experiment." The Senate added the Social Security and tax-loophole closing amendments.

Fiscal Year Change

The Joint Committee on Congressional Operations held hearings in 1971 on proposals to change the federal fiscal year to coincide with the calendar year and on Nov. 5 filed a report (H Rept 92-614) advising Congress against establishment of such a budget cycle.

Support for proposals to change the federal fiscal year (July 1-June 30 since 1842) had grown in Congress since 1969, spurred by lengthy delays in congressional actions on appropriation bills. At the time of the committee's report, Congress had not completed action by July 1 on all appropriation bills for the upcoming fiscal year since the end of World War II. None was enacted prior to the start of the fiscal year in 1969 or 1970, although in 1971 Congress had cleared 9 of 14 fiscal 1972 appropriation bills before the August 6 recess.

Vietnam War Costs

Acting on the request of the Senate Foreign Relations Committee, the Congressional Research Service of the Library of Congress compiled a study of Indochina war costs and announced July 11 that total budgeted outlays for the war from fiscal 1965 through 1971 were about $120-billion. In addition, it said, U.S. assistance to South Vietnam, Laos and Cambodia prior to 1965 totaled $1.1-billion in budget expenses. Not included in the total cost estimates was the expense of veterans' benefits, which the report said could raise total war costs by as much as 50 percent over the next 100 years. (The report also measured costs of the war in terms of lives, injuries and economic devastation).

Presidential Vetoes

President Nixon vetoed three bills during the 1971 session, each time largely because of budgetary issues. The measures were S 575, a $5.7-billion public works acceleration and regional development bill; HR 2600, a bill increasing retirement benefits for certain District of Columbia policemen and firemen, U.S. park policemen and members of the Executive Protection Service and the U.S. Secret Service; and S 2007, a $6.3-billion, two-year OEO extension and child development bill. All three vetoes were sustained.

Program Terminations

The Nixon administration again called unsuccessfully for reductions and terminations in what it saw as nonessential federal programs. Nixon in his fiscal 1972 budget proposed $2.9-billion in cuts ($3.7-billion on a one-time, nonrecurring basis), including termination of the Agriculture Department's special milk program, sale of $635-million in materials from the national stockpile and cuts and termination of many other programs. As in 1970, the program was only partially approved by Congress.

1972

For the second consecutive year, President Nixon submitted a "full employment" budget in 1972, calling for extensive deficit spending to take up the slack in the economy. The President's economic plan for fiscal 1973 embodied a record quarter-trillion-dollar budget with a $25.5-billion deficit. By mid-year, however, indications were that congressional add-ons to the budget could increase the deficit by $10-billion or more. The President responded with veto threats and hints that higher taxes might be necessary to fund the growing deficit.

The economy had been able to absorb the planned budget deficit for fiscal 1972, the President said in his budget message, even though that deficit had swollen to more than three times his January 1971 projections. An expected shortfall of almost $20-billion in tax revenues from the January 1971 projections, combined with $7.4-billion in increased spending above 1971 estimates, would produce an expected deficit of $38.8-billion, which would translate into a full employment deficit of $8.1-billion. (The actual fiscal 1972 deficit came to $23-billion and the full employment deficit to $3.6-billion.) "While our economy can absorb such a deficit for a time, the experience of the late 1960s provides ample warning of the danger of continued, and rising, full-employment deficits. The lesson of 1966-68, when such deficits led to an intolerable inflation, is too clear and too close to permit any relaxation of control of government spending," the President said.

Statutory Debt Limitations, Fiscal Years 1941-1973

(In billions)

FISCAL YEAR	Statutory debt limitation		
	Permanent	Temporary additional	Total
1941 through Feb. 18	$ 49	—	$ 49
1941: Feb. 19 through June 30	65	—	65
1942 through Mar. 27	65	—	65
1942: Mar. 28 through June 30	125	—	125
1943 through Apr. 10	125	—	125
1943: Apr. 11 through June 30	210	—	210
1944 through June 8	210	—	210
1944: June 9 through June 30	260	—	260
1945 through Apr. 2	260	—	260
1945: Apr. 3 through June 30	300	—	300
1946 through June 25	300	—	300
1946: June 26 through June 30	275	—	275
1947-54	275	—	275
1955 through Aug. 27, 1954	275	—	275
1955: Aug. 28 through June 30	275	$ 6	281
1956	275	6	281
1957	275	3	278
1958 through Feb. 25	275	—	275
1958: Feb. 26 through June 30	275	5	280
1959 through Sept. 1, 1958	275	5	280
1959: Sept. 2 through June 29	283	5	288
1959: June 30	285	5	290
1960	285	10	295
1961	285	8	293
1962 through Mar. 12	285	13	298
1962: Mar. 13 through June 30	285	15	300
1963 through Mar. 31	285	23	308
1963: Apr. 1 through May 28	285	20	305
1963: May 29 through June 30	285	22	307
1964 through Nov. 30, 1963	285	24	309
1964: Dec. 1 through June 28	285	30	315
1964: June 29 and 30	285	39	324
1965	285	39	324
1966	285	43	328
1967 through Mar. 1	285	45	330
1967: Mar. 2 through June 30	285	51	336
1968	358	7	365
1969 through Apr. 6	358	7	365
1969: Apr. 7 through June 30	365	12	377
1972	365	12	377
1971	380	15	395
1972 through Mar. 15	400	30	430
1972: Mar. 15-June 30	400	50	450
1973 through Oct. 31, 1972	400	50	450
1973: Nov. 1 through June 30	400	65	465

Holding the year's increase in outlays to $9.7-billion in fiscal 1973 while receipts were expected to rise by $23-billion was designed to reduce the actual deficit in the 1973 budget and keep it just above balance on a full-employment basis. The spending plan also provided less stimulation during fiscal 1973, when the administration forecast that the economy would be expanding vigorously.

Debt Ceiling

Although it took three hard-fought bills to do so, Congress in 1972 increased the temporary federal debt limit by $35-billion, to $465-billion, and extended that new limit through the end of fiscal 1973. *(Box, p. 72)*

The first of the three debt ceiling bills (HR 12910—PL 92-250) authorized a temporary $20-billion rise in the debt ceiling from March 15 to June 30, 1972. The second bill (HR 15390—PL 92-336) extended the $20-billion increase through Oct. 31, while the third bill (HR 16810—PL 92-599) increased the ceiling by another $15-billion through the end of fiscal 1973. None of the bills changed the permanent debt limit of $400-billion, set in 1971.

First Extension. HR 12910, first of the year's three debt limit measures, became necessary when Treasury officials concluded early in 1972 that they had overestimated fiscal 1972 tax receipts by more than $25-billion. (As it developed, however, the actual overestimation of revenues came to $9-billion.) Consequently, the administration called for a $50-billion hike in the ceiling (to $480-billion), which they said would meet government borrowing needs until February 1973. When opposition to the huge increase surfaced in the House Ways and Means Committee, however, the administration revealed it would settle for a $20-billion increase, which it said would meet borrowing needs through June 30, 1972.

During consideration of the bill, the Senate added a provision imposing a $246.3-billion limit on federal spending through fiscal 1973, excluding uncontrollable expenditures, but the ceiling was dropped in conference as Congress rushed to clear an increase in the debt limit before the Treasury exceeded the temporary ceiling of $430-billion. On March 15, the day the bill was cleared and signed into law, Ways and Means Chairman Mills told the House that the debt that morning stood at $429-billion, perilously close to the limit.

Second Extension. Congress June 30 cleared HR 15390, the second debt limit bill, which coupled a four-month extension of the limit with a presidentially opposed 20-percent across-the-board increase in Social Security benefits. During consideration of the bill, House liberals moved for adoption of a new package of tax reforms, but consideration of their proposals was foreclosed by House adoption of a closed rule prohibiting floor amendments.

Third Extension. At the eve of adjournment, Congress cleared a bill (HR 16810) increasing the temporary debt limit to $465-billion through June 30, 1973. The increase was cleared without controversy in either the House or Senate; however, a related provision to clamp a lid on government spending touched off a heated dispute between Nixon (its architect) and Senate Democrats. *(Below)*

Spending Limits

In the final floor battle of the session, Congress dealt the President a scathing defeat by denying authority he had requested to fix a spending limit of $250-billion on federal spending for fiscal 1973. The administration proposal, considered as a rider to the debt limit bill, was accepted intact by the House but was rewritten by the

(Continued on p. 75)

History of Budget Bureau

Prior to 1921, no system existed in the executive branch for unified consideraton or control of fiscal policy. The secretary of the treasury did no more than compile the estimates of the various departments before forwarding them to Congress.

With passage of the Budget and Accounting Act of 1921, Congress ended the right of federal agencies to decide for themselves what appropriations levels to ask of Congress. The act set up the Bureau of the Budget, which was to serve under the President's direction as a central clearinghouse for administration budget requests. Another important part of the budget reform was a change of House rules in 1920 that reduced from eight to one the number of committees authorized to act on appropriations. The Senate followed suit in 1922.

Budget Circular 49, approved by President Harding on Dec. 19, 1921, required that all agency proposals for appropriations be submitted to the President prior to presentation to Congress. Agency proposals were to be studied for their relationship to "the President's financial program" and were to be sent on to Capitol Hill only if approved by the President. The Bureau, though placed in the Treasury, was kept under the supervision of the President.

In 1935, President Roosevelt broadened the clearance function to include other legislation as well as the appropriation requests. As his rationale for that action, Roosevelt told the National Emergency Council that he had been "quite horrified—not once but a dozen times—by reading in the paper that some department or agency was after this, that or the other without my knowledge." The new function, vested at first in the Secretariat of the National Emergency Council, was transferred to the Budget Bureau on Dec. 21, 1935.

According to political scientist Richard E. Neustadt, writing in the *American Political Science Review* for September 1954, Roosevelt's new clearance system was not a mere extension of the budget process. "On the contrary...this was Roosevelt's creation, intended to protect not just his budget, but his prerogatives, his freedom of action, and his choice of policies in an era of fast-growing government and of determined presidential leadership."

Roosevelt in 1939 issued, and Congress approved, Reorganization Plan No. 1, creating the Executive Office of the President and transferring the Budget Bureau from the Treasury to the new office. By presidential directive, Roosevelt also broadened the Bureau's clearance function by making it responsible for coordination of department views on all measures sent to the White House for the President's signature or veto. That responsibility had been limited previously to views on appropriations bills. Any recommendation that the President withhold his approval of a bill was required to have to be accompanied by a draft veto message or, in the case of a pocket veto, a memorandum of disapproval. These procedures were further strengthened by later Presidents.

Nixon Sought New Authority to Control Spending in 1972

Congress, which in 1972 came under political pressure from President Nixon on the issue of government spending, responded by laying the groundwork for reforming the way it handles the federal government budget.

The issue, raised during the 1972 presidential election campaign, was how Congress could keep federal spending under control—and whether the President could or should do it himself.

The immediate stakes included the size of the fiscal 1973 budget deficit—threatening to reach $35-billion—and the political blame for tax increases that might be needed to restore the budget to better balance.

At stake in the long run was the ability of Congress to manage the government's fiscal affairs without turning over to the executive branch much of its power of the purse.

If congressional procedures for controlling federal spending are not strengthened, "the inevitable result will be a growing loss of congressional influence on decisions about national priorities," Paul W. Mc-Cracken, former chairman of the Council of Economic Advisers, warned in an Oct. 20 article in *The Wall Street Journal.*

Spending Ceiling. In what Democrats conceded was a masterful political stroke, President Nixon in July 1972 asked Congress for authority to trim federal spending as he saw fit to meet a $250-billion ceiling on fiscal 1973 outlays. If such power were denied, the President warned, Congress would be responsible for tax increases in 1973.

In its final second-session battle, the 92nd Congress denied the request. Adamant Senate opposition to conceding the power to the President led to deletion of a spending ceiling provision from a bill authorizing a temporary increase in the national debt. *(p. 73)*

In passing the debt-limit legislation, however, Congress acknowledged that its powers over the federal budget were not working. One amendment to the bill created a special joint committee to study the congressional appropriations process. Another provision required the President to report on funds authorized by Congress which he had not spent. This was a tacit acceptance by Congress that the President could overrule congressional decisions by refusing to spend money previously appropriated.

Vetoes and Impounding. His request for a spending ceiling denied, the President turned to other methods of holding outlays down to keep total spending at $250-billion. Using a power expressly granted by the Constitution, Nixon pocket vetoed 12 measures he said would "breach the budget," including a second veto of a bill appropriating funds for the Departments of Labor and Health, Education and Welfare. *(Presidential vetoes, appendix p. 101a)*

Using another power claimed by several Presidents but disputed by many members of Congress, Nixon ordered appropriated funds impounded—deferring their expenditures to keep total spending down in fiscal 1973.

Citing authority claimed by several Presidents, George P. Shultz said Nixon would withhold funds from spending.

In passing the debt ceiling bill, Shultz said Oct. 26, Congress "at least backhandedly" recognized that an impounding power existed by requiring the President to report on funds he had previously withheld.

Although members had frequently complained about the impounding of funds, Congress never acted to halt the practice. And federal courts never had ruled definitely on whether the President had such power.

The Office of Management and Budget (OMB) in January 1972 informed the House and Senate Appropriations Committees that the administration had impounded or reserved $12.3-billion in funds otherwise made available by Congress for fiscal 1972.

OMB officials drew a distinction between impounded funds and reserved funds. Impounded funds were defined as money withheld to reduce total spending to the budgeted level to keep the national debt below its statutory limit or for other economic objectives. Reserved funds were defined as money routinely withheld to be used more efficiently at a later date to fit construction schedules or other factors.

Of the $12.3-billion withheld in fiscal 1972 at that point, OMB classified $1.7-billion as impounded and $10.6-billion as reserved.

Members of Congress attacked the practice of impounding funds as an informal line item veto of congressional appropriations—with no chance for Congress to override the President.

The administration found an unlikely ally in Sen. William Proxmire (D Wis.), the chairman of the Joint Economic Committee and critic of many Nixon economic policies. Asking that fiscal 1973 spending be limited to $245-billion, Proxmire Oct. 21 urged Nixon "to use the long-standing and traditional power of your office and set a spending ceiling now."

The President had the power to set a spending ceiling, Proxmire told his Senate colleagues during an Oct. 16 debate on the spending ceiling request, because congressional appropriations in any given year and federal government spending in that year "are only remotely connected."

"When Congress appropriates money for military procurement, construction of public works, funds for housing and urban renewal, or foreign aid, those funds may not be spent for several years in the future. Within certain limitations, the President controls the rate or timing of that spending. Congress does not."

Proxmire pointed out that only $126.8-billion out of $246.3-billion in federal spending projected by the President's fiscal 1973 budget would be made "available through current action by Congress"—subject to congressional appropriations for fiscal 1973.

(Continued from p. 73)
Senate to place strict limits on the nature and size of any proposed cutbacks. Yielding to Senate pressures against broad presidential authority, House-Senate conferees dropped the ceiling altogether.

Deletion of the spending ceiling, which Nixon said was necessary to avoid the need for a tax increase, was the climax of a dramatic series of maneuvers between Congress and the President. In the first of these ploys, the President had withheld his approval of a water pollution control bill (S 2770) awaiting the outcome of the spending controversy. Shortly after the Senate balked on the spending ceiling, Nixon vetoed the water bill; but Congress overrode his action the following day.

At the last minute, the White House had sought to compromise the issue by backing a conference bill that would have circumscribed the President's authority to dictate spending cuts, although not as severely as under the Senate bill. The Senate rejected the conference report by a 27-39 roll-call vote, leaving the administration with the choice of a spending limit with the Senate's tight restrictions, or no ceiling at all. The President took the latter route.

Throughout the debate on the proposed ceiling, the central issue was the scope of authority to be given the President. Most members of both chambers agreed that some curb was needed on federal outlays, projected to reach $256-billion in fiscal 1973. But key senators objected to Nixon's demand of unlimited discretion to choose the areas where spending would be trimmed. *(Additional detail p. 74)*

Powerful political considerations fueled the debate, which developed into the liveliest sparring match between the White House and Congress in 1972. Nixon had made clear his intention to hold Congress responsible in the upcoming elections for continued inflation and any future tax increases made necessary by unfettered federal spending. Democrats hotly disputed that contention, arguing that the President was equally responsible for the high spending level of the past four years, since he could have vetoed any spending he considered inflationary.

Nixon Vetoes

Reiterating his theme of economy in government, Nixon vetoed 16 bills during the 1972 session, including a mammoth $30.5-billion appropriation for the Departments of Labor and Health, Education and Welfare (HEW).

Nine of the 16 vetoes, among them the Labor-HEW measure (HR 16654) came by pocket veto Oct. 27—nine days after Congress had adjourned. Nixon's post-adjournment rejection of the Labor-HEW money bill marked his second veto of those agencies' appropriations in 1972. An earlier Labor-HEW bill (HR 15417) had been vetoed Aug. 16. Among the other bills vetoed by the pocket route Oct. 27 were the Public Works and Economic Development Act of 1972 (HR 16071), the Flood Control Act of 1972 (S 4018), the Rehabilitation Act of 1972 (HR 8395) and the Veterans' Health Care Expansion Act of 1972 (HR 10880).

In a combined veto message, Nixon said: "If I were to sign these measures into law, I would, in effect, be making promises that could not be kept since the funds required to finance the promised services are not available and would not be available without the higher taxes I have promised to resist."

Nixon said that the bills would have pushed spending over the fiscal 1973 budget by $750-million and over the fiscal 1974 budget by almost $2-billion.

After the House sustained the first Labor-HEW bill veto Aug. 16, Congress cleared a second bill appropriating the same amount of money $30,538,919,500—but permitting the President to impound up to $1.2-billion. If he impounded the maximum, the bill would still have been $532-million more than he requested. Thus the President remained opposed to the bill.

In the wake of the Nixon veto, Labor-HEW programs for fiscal 1973 were funded under a continuing appropriations resolution (H J Res 1331), good through Feb. 28, 1973. The resolution continued spending at the lower of the fiscal 1972 appropriations or the fiscal 1973 budget request, except for funds to aid victims of black lung disease, which were increased by $1-billion.

Tax Policy

Tax policy, like other tools for manipulating the economy, underwent marked change during the first four Nixon years. At the outset of his administration, Nixon sought and won continuation of the 1968 income tax surcharge as a means of curbing economic activity that was contributing to runaway inflation. But by 1971, when Nixon's concern over recession overshadowed his worries over inflation, the President turned to tax cuts to get the economy moving again. By mid-1972, the administration's priorities had shifted once more: the President decided that stimulation of the economy had gone far enough and that funds added to his budget by Congress were threatening a new inflationary spiral. The term ended with the President warning Congress that further hikes in government spending would necessitate a tax increase.

Nixon's shift to expansionary fiscal policy—a surprise to most observers because of his long-standing reputation as a conservative on economic issues—left him responsible for three of the four largest budget deficits recorded since World War II. Shortfalls in projected revenues—caused by lags in business activity, Nixon's tax cuts and refusal by Congress to enact all of the President's revenue proposals—led to successive budget deficits of $23-billion in fiscal 1971, $23-billion in fiscal 1972 and an estimated $25.5-billion in fiscal 1973. The only comparable deficit in the post-war period was one of $25.2-billion in fiscal 1968, when Congress denied President Johnson a requested tax increase.

Prospects for continuing deficits led the President to probe for new sources of revenue as he neared the end of his first term. Chief among them was a value added tax (VAT)—a form of federal sales tax on goods and services which was widely used in Europe. The VAT—whose proceeds would be used primarily to finance education—was still under study at the end of 1972.

Tax Reform. Perhaps the most heated battle over a tax issue during the Nixon presidency came in 1969 over the demands by congressional liberals for comprehensive tax reform. Early in Nixon's term, liberal Democrats threatened to block action on the President's surcharge request unless the surcharge was considered together with tax reform. What resulted was the most massive overhaul of the nation's tax statutes since the founding of the republic. Even so, the bill did not eliminate every existing tax loophole. By the end of 1972, there was talk of further reform. Among the leading proposals was one by Rep. Wilbur D. Mills (D Ark.), chairman of the tax-writing House Ways and Means Committee. Mills suggested repealing the entire tax code, thus making continuation of all existing tax deductions and exemptions contingent on congressional approval.

1971 Revenue Act. In addition to the 1969 Tax Reform Act, Congress enacted one other major tax bill during the 1969-72 period, the 1971 Revenue Act, cutting individual and business taxes by an average of $8.6-billion a year over the 1971-73 period (and indeterminate amounts for later years, depending upon the performance of the economy). In addition to its tax provisions, the bill contained a controversial rider (non-germane amendment) authorizing taxpayers to allot $1 of their annual taxes for use by the party of their choice in presidential election campaigns. The rider, favored by Democrats and opposed by Republicans, aroused the threat of a presidential veto of the tax bill. Congress then amended the measure to put off the effective date of the campaign fund until after the 1972 election—a provision satisfactory to President Nixon.

Investment Tax Credit. As a means of fine-tuning the economy, the President asked and received repeal of the 7 per cent investment tax credit in 1969 and restoration of it in 1971. The credit, which had also been suspended and restored during the Johnson administration, was the most readily available implement on hand for Nixon's surgery on the economy. Repeal of the tax in 1969 was designed to produce $2.5-billion in additional revenues in fiscal 1971. Restoration of the credit in 1971 amounted to a tax cut of an estimated $2.4-billion in fiscal 1972, rising to $4.0-billion by fiscal 1974.

Other Taxes. Other tax measures approved by Congress included periodic extensions of excise taxes at levels established in 1966, extension of the Interest Equalization Tax on the purchase by Americans of foreign securities, increases in Social Security taxes, and new and increased user charges to pay for modernization and expansion of the nation's airports. Congress denied the President's proposals for increased highway user charges. (*Revenue effects of all tax legislation, 1969-72, box p. 94*)

References

Discussion of tax policy for the years 1945-64 may be found in *Congress and the Nation* Vol. I, pp. 397-442; for the years 1965-68, *Congress and the Nation Vol. II*, pp. 141-182.

Chronology Of Legislation On Tax Policy

1969

To cool down inflation and bring the budget into balance, President Johnson requested a series of tax measures designed to produce $11.9-billion in new revenues for fiscal 1970. The President's package included a **one-year extension of the 10 per cent income tax surcharge** enacted in 1968, a year's suspension of reductions in federal excise taxes scheduled for Jan. 1, 1970, an increase in the tax rate and taxable wage base for Social Security, adoption of user charges for special government services which benefit specific individuals or groups, and acceleration of the collection of federal unemployment insurance taxes from an annual to a quarterly basis. In his budget message, Johnson also urged that Congress "give serious consideration" to granting the President discretionary authority to lower or remove the surtax if such action was warranted by economic developments. "For the longer run," the President said, "consideration should be given to establishing...an element of flexibility" in the federal income tax system, under which the President might alter tax rates "within specific limits—such as **5 per cent in either direction**," subject to congressional veto. *(Background, Congress and the Nation Vol. II, p. 171)*

These same proposals (except for the discretionary authority to adjust taxes) were endorsed by President Nixon in his first amendments to the Johnson budget, submitted on April 15. On April 21, however, Nixon **modified his request to continue the surcharge at the 10 per** cent level only through the end of calendar 1969 and at 5 percent for the first six months of 1970, after which it would be abolished. As a further hedge against inflation, **the President called for repeal of the 7 per cent tax credit** on business investment—an incentive first passed in 1962, suspended in 1966 and restored in 1967. The President also proposed a postal rate increase and extension of the Interest Equalization Tax on purchases by Americans of foreign securities.

After considerable debate, Congress approved the President's surcharge requests, although it did so in phases—one bill extending the tax through the end of August and another the following January providing the final extension through June. Approval of the excise tax, investment tax credit, Interest Equalization Tax and unemployment tax proposals came easily. To Nixon's consternation, however, Congress approved a sweeping tax reform, tax relief and Social Security bill which was to cost the Treasury an estimated net loss of $2.5-billion a year when fully effective in 1979. And in another blow to the President, Congress took no action on his user charge, postal rate and Social Security tax rate and tax base increase proposals.

First Surtax Extension

Following intense infighting in Congress and a strong lobbying effort by the Nixon administration, Congress Aug. 4 approved compromise legislation to extend for six months (through Dec. 31, 1969) the 10 per cent surcharge on personal and corporate income taxes. The administration had sought a year's extension.

Final action came when the House accepted a Senate amendment, containing the surtax, to a House-passed bill (HR 9951) to put the collection of federal unemployment taxes on a quarterly basis.

Total revenue from the surtax extension was estimated at $5.6-billion for fiscal 1970.

From the outset, the tax bill ran into trouble from congressional liberals who sought to link the surcharge extension with tax reform. Responding to opponents of the surtax extension, the administration June 12 agreed to add tax relief for the poor to the surtax bill and to speed up its own timetable for other tax reform proposals. House Democratic leaders, too, said they would speed up consideration of the tax reform bill.

Despite these efforts, a surtax extension bill (HR 12290) squeaked through the House, by a **210-205 key roll-call vote,** and the controversy then continued in the Senate. There, liberals, including Majority Leader Mike Mansfield (D Mont.), were even more adamant about holding up the surtax extension until floor consideration of tax reform was assured.

Against the announced wishes of Chairman Russell B. Long (D La.), the Senate Finance Committee July 17 reported out HR 12290 by the margin of a single vote. Two Democrats joined all seven Republicans in voting to report the bill. Long said he favored the extension but had given his word that some tax reform provisions would be considered along with the surtax.

The Democratic Policy Committee, however, which schedules legislation for Senate floor action, stuck by its June 24 statement coupling the surtax to tax reform.

The deadlock was broken July 30 when Senate Democratic and Republican leaders reached a compromise by agreeing to a six-month extension of the surtax with a promise by the Democrats to take up the rest of the tax package contained in the House-passed bill after they had acted on tax reform. The Senate Finance Committee pledged to send a tax reform measure to the floor by Oct. 31. The House Ways and Means Committee, meanwhile, had attached the rest of President Nixon's tax package to the committee's tax reform bill (HR 13270).

The Senate voted 70-30 the next day to approve the surtax extension. Approval came after a key vote on an amendment providing for extension to be attached to a routine House bill (HR 9951). The amendment, offered by Long, was accepted by a **51-48 roll-call vote** amid **Republican criticism of the leadership compromise.**

PROVISIONS

As enacted, PL 91-53:

• **Extended the surtax at 10 per cent through Dec. 31,** 1969.

• Required that federal unemployment taxes be paid quarterly rather than annually.

• Provided for a three-year transition period for the unemployment taxes.

• Exempted an employer from the quarterly requirement if his cumulative tax liability was $100 or less.

• Made certain other changes to ensure that the accelerated revenues collected could be used for state and federal administrative purposes.

Excise Tax Extension—Almost An Annual Ritual Since 1941

The extension of excise taxes (special taxes levied on such items as tobacco, liquor and the like) had been an almost annual event in Congress since the outset of World War II.

In 1932, a number of World War I excise taxes were reimposed to compensate for lagging income tax revenues.

The Revenue Act of 1941 made most of the earlier excises permanent and imposed many others to support the military buildup for World War II. Other wartime excises were imposed during 1942 and 1944.

The Revenue Act of 1950 was conceived as a measure to cut the annual $7.5-billion excise tax intake by about $1-billion, but the outbreak of the Korean War in June 1950 forced an extension of the old taxes and imposition of new ones. Faced by expanding defense expenditures, Congress in 1951 increased excise taxes by $1.2-billion. In 1954, a number of World War II excises were slashed; however, all of the 1951 rate increases were extended for one year. These included cigarettes (8 cents a pack), liquor ($10.50 a gallon), beer ($9 a barrel), wines (varying rates), automobiles (10 per cent of the manufacturer's price), gasoline (2 cents a gallon), auto parts and accessories (8 percent of the manufacturer's price). After 1954, the emergency rate increases of 1951 were re-extended for one-year periods in every session of Congress through 1964. Various taxes imposed in 1951 were made subject to annual extension in 1959. The major changes in the excise tax structure after 1954 were the 1956 levy on highway vehicles weighing more than 26,000 pounds and the 1962 reduction or repeal of various excises on passenger transportation.

Extension of excise taxes met strong opposition in Congress beginning about 1960. Early in 1964, White House intervention averted excise-cutting amendments to the 1964 income tax cut in the Senate Finance Committee and on the Senate floor. Legislation to repeal numerous excise taxes and to reduce others barely missed congressional approval later in 1964. *(Action in 1964 and earlier, Congress and the Nation Vol. I, p. 397)*

In 1965, Congress repealed a variety of excise taxes. The law (PL 89-44) called for a staged reduction in excise levies that would terminate Jan. 1, 1969. As the Vietnam war grew in scale, however, President Johnson asked for and received extensions on excise items already scheduled for repeal.

The Revenue and Expenditure Control Act of 1968 (PL 90-364) provided for continuation of telephone service and automobile excise taxes at current rates, followed by staged reductions and elimination of both levies by Jan. 1, 1973. Under provisions of the act, excise taxes on both items would have been reduced to 5 per cent during calendar 1970, to 3 per cent during calendar 1971 and to 1 per cent during 1972, the final year of the tax. *(Action during the 1965-68 period, Congress and the Nation Vol. II, pp. 145-47, 153, 173)*

President Nixon in 1969 asked and Congress provided for extension through calendar 1970 of the 7 per cent excise tax on automobiles and the 10 per cent tax on telephone service. (The automobile levy had been at the 7 per cent level since 1966, the telephone tax at 10 per cent since 1954, except for parts of 1965 and 1966.) And the President proposed another year's extension in his fiscal 1971 budget. Congress in a bill approved at the close of the 1970 session (PL 91-614) authorized a two-year extension, through Jan. 1, 1973, and a phased reduction culminating in termination of the levies on Jan. 1, 1982. At President Nixon's request, the 7 per cent automobile tax was repealed in 1971 (PL 92-178).

Tax Reform, Second Surtax Extension

In a move initiated on Capitol Hill instead of by the President, Congress in 1969 passed legislation providing the most comprehensive reform of the nation's tax statutes in history and the largest tax cut since the Revenue Act of 1964. The Tax Reform Act of 1969 (HR 13270—PL 91-172), passed over the threat of a presidential veto, coupled tax reforms worth $6.6-billion a year when fully effective with cuts of $9.1-billion—an annual loss to the Treasury of $2.5-billion.

Although far-reaching, the bill left untouched a number of tax avoidance loopholes in existing law; and many of the original tax reform proposals were diluted during congressional action on the legislation.

The bill, cleared by both houses of Congress Dec. 22 and signed by the President Dec. 30 despite some major reservations, also provided a 15 per cent increase in basic Social Security benefits, which were to cost an estimated $4.4-billion a year. The increases were, for the time being, to be financed out of surplus balances in the Social Security Trust Fund and did not require an immediate increase in Social Security taxes. (Because of the financing from their own trust fund, the increased Social Security benefits were not included in the above estimates for the bill's revenue effects.)

Impetus for tax revision came just before President Nixon took office Jan. 20, when retiring Treasury Secretary Joseph W. Barr warned Congress of an emerging "taxpayer's revolt" spurred on by increased public awareness of existing tax inequities. While middle-income persons were bearing the brunt of taxation, Barr said, some millionaires were able to avoid taxes altogether through investment in tax-exempt securities and use of other tax shelters. Tax reform became a major issue almost overnight, and on Feb. 18 the House Ways and Means Committee opened the most extensive hearings on the subject in a decade. Finally, in mid-April, the Nixon administration introduced its own tax proposals; but, as it developed, Congress wrote almost the entire bill.

Nixon Administration Proposals. President Nixon April 21 sent Congress his tax reform package in which he proposed immediate repeal of the 7 per cent tax credit for business investment and extension of the surtax—at the existing 10 per cent rate until Dec. 31, 1969, and at 5 per cent from Jan. 1 to June 30, 1970.

The President also called for tax reforms to remove from the tax rolls 2 million families with incomes below officially designated poverty levels and to reduce the tax preferences available to the wealthy.

In immediate revenue effect, the investment credit repeal was to partly offset the loss from reduction of the surtax. In the long term, at $3.3-billion, it was the only major revenue gainer. The reforms would have granted $665-million in relief to the poor in the long term and reduced tax preferences of the wealthy by $580-million. Other reforms would have produced a net revenue gain of $550-million.

In his message, Mr. Nixon said that "repeal of the investment tax credit will permit relief to every taxpayer through relaxation of the surcharge earlier than I had contemplated." Treasury officials later made it clear that further extension of the surtax would depend on the demands of the Vietnam war.

HOUSE ACTION

COMMITTEE. The House Ways and Means Committee Aug. 2 reported a clean bill (HR 13270) coupling rate reductions for taxpayers in almost all categories of income with a six-month extension of the tax surcharge through June 30, 1970, as requested by the administration. As reported originally by the committee, the bill balanced $6.81-billion of tax relief with $6.86-billion of tax increases. An amendment adopted by the committee Aug. 5, however, added another $2.44-billion of tax relief to the measure, extending rate reductions to all categories of income.

The committee bill also included a provision reducing the controversial 27.5 per cent depletion allowance on oil and gas to 20 per cent and cutting allowances on many other minerals in proportion to the cutback on oil and gas allowances. The panel approved the reduction by an 18-7 vote despite heavy lobbying by the oil industry for retaining the full allowance.

FLOOR ACTION. The House Aug. 7 by a 394-30 roll-call vote passed HR 13270 and sent the measure to the Senate. A motion to recommit (kill) the bill was rejected by a 78-345 roll call.

At the outset of a two-day debate on the bill, House Ways and Means Committee Chairman Wilbur D. Mills (D Ark.) told House members that if they were concerned over the provisions of the bill they could "go back to their constituents," and tell them that if they have been getting preferential treatment "this legislation will help put them on a level with the less fortunate citizens in the community."

He said that they could also tell the "less fortunate taxpayers that they are going to get tax relief."

The ranking minority member of the Ways and Means Committee, John W. Byrnes (R Wis.), praised the tax bill but said it was not a panacea.

"Certainly we'll find loopholes that we'll have to caulk up as soon as we find them," he said, "but they won't be the same ones we have now."

SENATE ACTION

COMMITTEE. Treasury Secretary David M. Kennedy presented changes the administration proposed in the House-passed bill to the Senate Finance Committee Sept. 4. He told the committee that the $2.4-billion tax revenue loss provided in the House bill would "represent a significant decision with respect to national priorities." He advocated trimming the revenue loss to $1.3-billion, stressing "due consideration for other national needs."

Kennedy criticized the equity of tax reduction provided in HR 13270, noting unequal tax breaks for some income groups.

Proposed cutbacks in individual tax relief drew some fire from both Republicans and Democrats on the committee. Vance Hartke (D Ind.) said, "You're taking $1.7-billion from the average forgotten American and giving it to the corporations."

But Kennedy and Edwin S. Cohen, assistant secretary of the treasury for tax policy, argued that extensive individual tax reductions and corporate tax increases in the House bill overloaded the legislation in favor of the consumer—a potential future inflationary threat.

The administration changes proposed to increase taxes for individuals with incomes of more than $100,000 a year and lower them for persons earning less. The changes would have been less generous than the House bill to low- and middle-income taxpayers.

Committee Report. The Finance Committee Nov. 21 reported a heavily amended version of HR 13270 combining an annual $9-billion in estimated tax relief when fully effective in 1972 with tax reforms estimated at almost $5-billion in 1972 and $6.6-billion in 1979.

Many of the bill's reforms were modified to make them less stringent than those approved by the House. Some, such as those dealing with foreign income, particularly from oil, were deleted. The oil depletion allowance, which had been cut by the House from 27.5 to 20 per cent, was raised to 23 per cent. In general, the Senate committee diluted the effect of reforms by amounts ranging from $235-million in 1971 to $435-million in 1979, but offset the loss to the Treasury, except in 1971, with reductions in tax relief ranging from $200-million in 1970 to $305-million in 1972 and subsequent years. In 1971, adjustments in tax relief measures aimed to cut total House-approved relief by $1.4-billion, yielding a revenue loss almost $1-billion smaller for that year than provided in the House bill.

Major Provisions of 1969 Tax Act

Following are the major provisions of HR 13270, as signed into law Dec. 30, 1969:

• Increased the personal income tax exemption for each taxpayer and his dependents in stages from $600 to $750. The exemption would be raised to $650 on July 1, 1970, $700 on Jan. 1, 1972, and $750 a year later.

• Increased basic Social Security benefits by 15 per cent, effective Jan. 1, 1970.

• Extended the income tax surcharge, currently 10 per cent, at a rate of 5 per cent from Jan. 1, 1970, through June 30, 1970.

• Repealed the existing 7 per cent investment tax credit for machinery and equipment purchases, effective retroactively to April 19, 1969.

• Postponed scheduled reductions in excise taxes on telephone service and new automobile purchases.

• Reduced the 27.5 per cent depletion allowance on gas and oil to 22 per cent. Also applied a one-point reduction to most other minerals, receiving 23 and 15 per cent under existing law but increased the allowance on one mineral, molybdenum, from 15 to 22 per cent.

• Lowered tax rates for single persons so they would not, in any instance, be required to pay rates more than 20 per cent higher than those for married taxpayers with the same income. Effective in 1971.

• Increased in stages the maximum standard deduction for taxpayers who do not itemize from the present 10 per cent of income with a $1,000 ceiling to 15 per cent with a $2,000 ceiling, to be fully effective in 1973.

• Provided a minimum standard deduction designed to remove 5.5 million low-income taxpayers from paying any tax at all. The deduction was set at $1,100 for 1970 but was to be reduced to $1,050 in 1971 and $1,000 in 1972 as the personal exemption increased.

• Provided a minimum 10 per cent tax on most kinds of "tax preference" (tax-free) income in excess of $30,000, except that a taxpayer could continue to get tax-free treatment on an amount of excess income equal to his normal tax liabilities.

• Placed a $50,000 ceiling on the amount of individual capital gains eligible for the "alternative," or lower, capital gains tax rate of 25 per cent. Raised capital gains taxes from 25 to 30 per cent for corporations and to a maximum of 35 per cent for individuals on their excess above $50,000.

• Levied a 4 per cent audit tax on the investment income of private foundations. Also provided restrictions on attempts by private foundations to influence legislation and elections.

• Provided numerous other measures to reduce taxes of certain taxpayers and to tighten existing tax "loopholes."

One major area of concentration during last-minute action on the bill was taxation of private foundations. The committee loosened some of the restrictions voted by the House. But in a new proposal it established a 40-year lifespan for them, adopted a tax on their assets in place of the House tax on their investment income, agreed to strictures on their holdings and activities, and concurred with modifications in House requirements for disclosure of information.

SENATE FLOOR. The Senate Dec. 11 passed HR 13270 by a 69-22 roll-call vote and sent the measure to conference with the House.

Prior to passing the bill, the Senate adopted major floor amendments (1) increasing basic Social Security benefits by 15 per cent, (2) increasing the personal income tax exemption for each taxpayer and his dependents in stages from $600 to $800, (3) granting authority to the President to impose restrictions on imported goods, and (4) opening new "loopholes" for certain categories of taxpayers and broadening some existing ones.

As passed by the Senate, HR 13270 provided an estimated net revenue gain of $2.9-billion in fiscal 1970, a $4.7-billion loss in fiscal 1971, and a long-term annual loss of $5.4-billion. The revenue estimates did not include the cost of the increased Social Security benefits ($5.7-billion in 1970 and $6.4-billion in subsequent years), which were to be financed out of surpluses in the Social Security Trust Fund and through subsequent increases in Social Security taxes. Beginning in 1973, the bill increased the base of personal income on which Social Security taxes were paid from $7,800 to $12,000.

At the latter stages of a 13-day floor debate on HR 13270, the bill became known as a "Christmas tree," with senators from each party blaming those of the other for loading the bill with its "ornaments." In the vote on final passage, 51 Democrats—all but two of those voting —supported the bill; Republicans were virtually split, with 18 voting for it and 20 against. The lone Democrats opposing the measure were Spessard L. Holland (Fla.) and Richard B. Russell (Ga.).

Shortly before the final vote, the Senate rejected a GOP-sponsored recommittal motion to send the bill back to the Finance Committee with instructions to strip it of a number of its revenue-losing amendments. The motion, introduced by John J. Williams (R Del.), failed on a 31-60 roll-call vote, largely along party lines. The Democratic breakdown was virtually the same as on final passage, with 48 members opposing the motion and only Holland and Russell favoring it. Two Louisiana Democrats, Russell B. Long, chairman of the Finance Committee and floor manager of the bill, and Allen J. Ellender, were paired for recommittal. Republicans supported the motion, 29-12.

The Nixon administration reportedly lobbied hard against both the Social Security increase (the President had asked for 10 per cent) and the higher personal exemptions. Asked at a Dec. 8 news conference if he would sign the bill if it contained the two provisions, the President replied, "No."

AMENDMENTS

Personal Exemption. After what turned out to be the most heated floor fight on the bill, the Senate Dec. 3 adopted an amendment by Albert Gore (D Tenn.) to substitute an increase in the personal exemption, together with a new minimum standard deduction, for the relief provisions approved by the Finance Committee.

Depletion Allowances: Longtime Target of Liberals

Throughout the period since World War II, few issues evoked as much criticism by congressional liberals as did the percentage depletion allowances against taxable income from mineral properties and timber lands.

The allowances, ranging from 27.5 per cent (of gross income) for oil and gas to 5 per cent for clay, were designed as an offset for the exhaustion of natural resources. Consequently, they were originally limited to the recovery of costs, like depreciation. But percentage depletion, introduced in 1926, bore no relation to cost and permitted tax-free recovery vastly in excess of investment costs in many cases. Criticism focused on the oil and gas allowance because it conferred the greatest benefit and its chief beneficiaries were conspicuously identified as "oil millionaires."

Truman Era. President Truman opened the attack in 1950: no tax loophole, he said, was "so inequitable" as the "excessive" oil depletion allowance. Truman cited what he called the "shocking example" of one beneficiary who had built up a tax-free income of almost $5-million. The President proposed cutting the allowance of 15 per cent for oil and gas and lesser amounts for other minerals. Congress not only ignored his request, however, but enlarged the loophole (in the Revenue Act of 1950) by authorizing producers of depletable assets to deduct certain transportation costs in computing net income and depletion allowances.

· Truman repeated his request in 1951 and was again rebuffed; an amendment to cut the oil and gas allowance to 15 percent, introduced by Sen. Hubert H. Humphrey (D Minn.), was rejected 9-71. The Revenue Act of 1951, while raising taxes generally, extended depletion allowances to a new group of minerals ranging from aplite to wollastonite.

Eisenhower. President Eisenhower ignored the issue, but it was kept alive in the Senate by Paul H. Douglas (D Ill.), John J. Williams (R Del.) and William Proxmire (D Wis.). Douglas pressed an amendment to reduce the oil and gas allowance on incomes over $1-million, while Williams continued support for the Truman proposal. The Senate rejected both amendments by voice vote in 1954 and again in 1957. In 1958, the Williams amendment was defeated, 26-63, and the Douglas amendment, offered by Proxmire, 31-58.

1960s. Offered again in 1960, the Douglas amendment was rejected, 30-56. In 1962, Williams altered his amendment to cut the allowance to 20 per cent; it was tabled 57-30, while the Douglas amendment was defeated, 23-50. In 1964, Williams' amendment was defeated 33-61 and Douglas', 35-57.

The 1964 test was the first in which the man who had been the most powerful Senate proponent of the allowance during the 1950s was not on hand for the fray: Sen. Robert S. Kerr (D Okla.), often known as the "Uncrowned King of the Senate" because of his powerful behind-the-scenes maneuvering, had died in 1963. Kerr, as second-ranking Democrat on the Senate Finance Committee, always kept an eye out for his state's oil interests.

In 1966, Senators encountered vigorous lobbying efforts by groups desiring higher percentage depletion on mineral ores and other materials. Their efforts paid off. Congress in the foreign investors' tax bill—which came to be known as the "Christmas Tree" bill because of an extensive number of special-interest riders—increased the allowance for clam or oyster shells used for cement or lime from 5 to 15 per cent, the allowance for alumina-bearing clay from 15 per cent to 23 per cent, the clay and shale used in sewer pipe and brick from 5 per cent to 7½ per cent, and the clay, shale and slate used as a light-weight aggregate, from 5 to 7½ per cent.

The next test for the oil and gas depletion allowance came in 1967, during consideration of a bill to restore the 7 per cent investment tax credit. Proxmire proposed reducing the allowance to 15 per cent, but was defeated by voice vote.

1969 Act. It was not until 1969 and the public's "revolt" over tax inequities that enough pressure was brought to bear on Congress to scale down the controversial tax benefit. The 1969 Tax Reform Act cut the oil and gas depletion allowance to 20 per cent and reduced the benefit on all other minerals except gold, silver, copper, iron ore and oil shale by approximately 25 per cent.

Proceeds. The value of depletion allowances, although small relative to total income, has not been inconsiderable. The amount claimed on active corporation returns increased from $2.1-billion in 1951-52 to $3.5-billion in 1961-62 and $2.9-billion in 1968-69. Reflecting the reduction in rates provided by the 1969 act, the amount claimed for 1970-71 was down to $2.0-billion.

Gore's amendment, adopted by a 58-37 roll-call vote, increased the personal exemption in stages from $600 to $800, substituted a minimum standard deduction of $1,000 for the $1,100 low-income allowance recommended by the administration and the Finance Committee, and retained, effective in 1971, a provision from the committee bill limiting taxes on single persons to 20 per cent of taxes on married couples with the same income (they currently paid about one-third more.) The Treasury estimated that the amendment would mean about $2.25-billion in lost revenues in calendar 1970.

Social Security. Inclusion of the increase in Social Security benefits came Dec. 5 when the Senate approved the proposal in a floor amendment by Long. As approved, by a 73-14 roll-call vote, the amendment raised basic benefits under the program by 15 per cent effective Jan. 1, 1969. Long's plan increased minimum payments for single persons to $100 and for married couples to $150 and ensured that some 3 million handicapped persons would also receive larger payments.

Inclusion of increased Social Security benefits in the bill was the largest single revenue-loser, although the President had himself asked for increased benefits which would have increased government outlays. Mr. Nixon on Sept. 25 proposed a 10 per cent increase in benefits to take effect March 1, 1970. The House Ways and Means Committee, deciding that 10 per cent was less than the inflation of prices that had occurred since benefits were last raised, on Dec. 5 reported HR 15095 incorporating a 15 per cent increase in benefits.

Depletion Allowances. Senate liberals won a major victory Dec. 1 when an attempt to restore the oil and gas depletion allowance to its 43-year level of 27.5 per cent was defeated by a 30-62 roll-call vote. Allen J. Ellender (D La.) offered the amendment after the committee cut the allowance to 23 per cent.

But the liberals' fortunes shifted almost immediately when they, in turn, lost by a 38-52 roll-call vote in an attempt by John J. Williams (R Del.) to reduce the allowance further to the 20 per cent level approved by the House. Long led the successful resistance to the amendment, arguing that further depletion cuts would make unprofitable the necessary exploration for oil to maintain adequate reserve supplies.

Other Amendments. The Senate accepted a total of 70 other amendments, including major proposals by Vance Hartke (D Ind.) to exempt a business' first $20,000 of investment from the repeal of the investment tax credit, and by Abraham Ribicoff (D Conn.) to provide a tax credit of up to $325 per student for college tuition expenses.

CONFERENCE ACTION

Just before adjournment, conferees Dec. 19 worked out a bill compromising the House and Senate differences. Major conference compromises included:

• An increase in the personal exemption in stages from $600 to $750 by 1973 instead of the Senate's increase to $800 in 1971. Saving from the change was estimated at approximately $2.5-billion in 1970, $4.8-billion in 1971 and $3.1-billion in 1972.

• Reduction of new minimum Social Security benefits of $100 per month for a single person and $150 for a couple, as voted by the Senate, to $64 and $96 respectively. This saved roughly $2-billion.

• Elimination of a Senate amendment modifying repeal of the 7 per cent tax credit for business investment by maintaining it in force for investments up to $20,000. This raised revenues by $700-million, to a total of $2.5-billion for the investment credit in calendar 1970 and a long-run total of $3.3 billion.

• Elimination of another Senate amendment making expenses for higher education deductible, which would have cost $1.8-billion a year beginning in 1972.

Final Action. The House and Senate Dec. 22 adopted the conference report on HR 13270, clearing the measure for the President's signature. Senate passage was by a roll-call vote, 71-6. In the House, action came on a 391-2 roll call. The eight negative votes were all by Republicans: John J. Williams (Del.), William B. Saxbe (Ohio), Henry Bellmon (Okla.), Carl T. Curtis (Neb.), Charles E. Goodell (N.Y.) and Jacob K. Javits (N.Y.) in the Senate; John M. Ashbrook (Ohio) and Earl F. Landgrebe (Ind.) in the House.

Nixon Signature. President Nixon Dec. 30 signed the Tax Reform Act of 1969 (PL 91-172) into law, bringing to a conclusion the year-long effort to reform the tax system.

In signing the measure, the President called it "an unbalanced bill that is both good and bad." He said the tax reforms were good but the effect of the bill on the budget and the cost of living was bad. "But I sign it because I believe that, on balance, it is a necessary beginning in the process of making our tax system fair to the taxpayer."

PROVISIONS OF 1969 TAX ACT

As signed by the President, HR 13270, the Tax Reform Act of 1969, contained the following major provisions:

Private Foundations

• Levied an audit tax of 4 per cent on net annual investment income.

• Required foundations to distribute annually for charitable, educational, or other exempt purposes their total income, but not less than 6 per cent of their total assets.

• Limited combined stock holdings of a foundation and its contributors and officers to 50 per cent of any single business and the foundation itself to 25 per cent, requiring

---

Fiscal Effect of HR 13270

(By Fiscal Years, in Billions of Dollars)

Provision	Fiscal Year 1970	1971
Tax reform provisions		
Corporations	+$0.2	+$0.9
Individual	*	+.2
Total, tax reform provisions	+.2	+1.1
Tax relief provisions		
Individual	—.3	—3.1
Other provisions		
Repeal of investment credit:		
Corporation	+.9	+1.9
Individual	+.4	+.6
Total, repeal of investment credit	+1.3	+2.5
Extension of tax surcharge:		
Corporation	+.3	+.7
Individual	+1.7	+.4
Total, surcharge extension	+2.0	+1.1
Extension of excise taxes	+.5	+1.1
Total, other provisions	+3.8	+4.7
Subtotal	+3.7	+2.7
Social Security increase	—1.8**	—4.3
GRAND TOTAL	**+$1.9**	**—$1.6**

* Less than $50-million.
** Took effect January 1970—second half of fiscal year.

SOURCE: Joint Committee on Internal Revenue Taxation, 1969

---

divestiture of excess holdings generally within 10 years, with exceptions for certain conditions.

• Prohibited use of foundation funds to finance attempts to influence legislation or the outcome of specific elections.

• Provided three levels of sanctions: moderate taxes on the amounts involved in violations; confiscatory taxes on the amounts involved in uncorrected violations; and loss of tax-exemption and assessment of taxes equivalent to the aggregate tax benefits previously enjoyed, plus interest, as under the change of status provisions.

• Increased the allowable deduction for charitable contributions from 30 per cent of income to 50 per cent.

Farm Income

• Restricted paper farm losses which could be offset against nonfarm income where losses exceeded $25,000 and nonfarm income exceeded $50,000.

• Disallowed deduction of losses from farm operations not engaged in for profit.

Corporate Reforms

• Limited multiple corporations to a single surtax exemption and a single tax credit for accumulated earnings rather than credits and deductions for each subsidiary.

• Disallowed deductions for interest on convertible bonds issued by a corporation to acquire assets of another corporation.

• Authorized the Treasury to issue guidelines for distinguishing between debt and equity for tax purposes.

Financial Institutions

• Reduced allowable deductions for bad-debt reserves for commercial banks, mutual savings banks, savings and loan associations, and cooperative banks.

• Allowed new small business investment corporations to base their allowable bad-debt reserves on the industry average during their first 10 years.

• Required banks to treat their gains and losses from corporate and government bonds as ordinary income.

Oil and Other Minerals

• Reduced the percentage depletion allowance on oil and gas from 27.5 per cent to 22 per cent for both foreign and domestic production.

• Reduced percentage depletion on minerals receiving 23 per cent to 22 per cent, raised molybdenum from 15 to 22 per cent, and reduced minerals receiving 15 per cent to 14 per cent except for silver, gold, copper, oil shale and iron ore.

Capital Gains and Losses

• Retained the "alternative" (maximum) 25 per cent capital gains tax rate for individuals (not including surtax) on gains up to $50,000 and raised the rate on gains above that figure in stages to 35 per cent.

• Increased the alternative capital gains rate for corporations from 25 per cent to 30 per cent (without surtax).

• Limited individual capital losses which could be offset against ordinary income to 50 per cent, up to the existing $1,000 limit.

Real Estate Depreciation

• Limited double-declining-balance and sum-of-the-years-digits accelerated depreciation to new residential housing from which at least 80 per cent of income was rental.

• Allowed 150 per cent accelerated depreciation on new commercial and industrial real estate.

• Allowed 125 per cent depreciation of used residential rental property with an expected lifespan of 20 years or more.

• Provided a special five-year amortization deduction for expenses of rehabilitating used residential housing for rental to low- and moderate-income families.

Municipal Bonds

• Preserved the nontaxability of income from municipal and state bonds except those issued for arbitrage.

• Made income taxable from municipal and state arbitrage bonds—those issued in order to acquire other higher-yielding securities.

Investment Credit Repeal

• Repealed the 7 per cent tax credit for business investment, effective April 19, 1969 (two days before the President's April 21 proposal for repeal), with provisions maintaining it in force where there were binding contracts for facilities entered into before the effective date.

• Allowed five-year amortization deductions for pollution-control facilities installed in existing plants and placed in service before 1975.

Individual Tax Reform

• Established a 10 per cent minimum tax on otherwise tax-free income (except that from municipal and state bonds) and on income offset by certain major deductions, to the extent that the income exceeded $30,000 plus normal tax liability on taxable income, applicable to individuals, personal holding companies, and "Subchapter S" corporations (those with 10 or fewer stockholders, each owning 5 per cent or more of the stock and all taxed more or less as partners).

Individual Tax Relief

• Increased the personal income tax exemption from $600 to $750 in $50-dollar increments taking effect in mid-1970, 1971 and 1972.

• Replaced the minimum standard deduction with a low-income allowance of $1,100 per taxpayer in 1970, which was reduced to $1,050 for 1971 and $1,000 in 1972.

• Set new rates to reduce taxes paid by single persons to 20 per cent more than the amount couples filing joint returns on the same income would pay, and provided new head-of-household rates midway between the two.

• Lowered the amount by which an individual's income must have increased—from 33 1/3 per cent of income to 20 per cent—in order for him to average his income for taxes.

- Liberalized deductions for moving expenses to include additional expenses up to a total of $2,500.
- Increased the standard deduction to 15 per cent of income with a $2,000 ceiling, in three stages with full effect in 1973.
- Established a maximum tax rate on earned income at 50 per cent, except that earned income equivalent to the amount by which tax preferences exceeded $30,000 would be subject to higher existing rates.

Withholding

- Allowed employers to use more flexible procedures in withholding taxes from employees' wages in order to withhold the correct amount of tax for the year.
- Liberalized requirements for claiming additional exemptions to reduce withholding in order to reflect excess itemized deductions.

Surtax and Excises

- Extended the income tax surcharge (which was originally 10 per cent but which expired Dec. 31, 1969) at 5 per cent from Jan. 1 to June 30, 1970.
- Extended the 10 per cent excise tax on local and toll telephone service (which was to have been reduced to 5 per cent during 1970) and the 7 per cent excise on passenger automobiles (which was to have dropped to 5 per cent on Jan. 1) until Jan. 1, 1971, and postponed scheduled reductions and ultimate repeal of both by one year.

Social Security

- Increased Social Security retirement, disability and dependents' benefits by 15 per cent across the board beginning in January 1970.
- Guaranteed every recipient of both public assistance and Social Security a minimum increase of $4 per month in benefits until July 1970 by limiting state readjustments of public assistance following the Social Security increase; prohibited state reduction of public assistance benefits to offset the Social Security benefit increase to be paid in April for previous months of the year.

Postal Rates

The House Postal Rates Subcommittee held hearings during 1969 on HR 10877, the administration's proposal for increases in postal rates of first, second and third class mail. No further action was taken in the House in 1969, and the Senate took no action.

The rate increases proposed by the President included one-cent increases starting July 1, 1969, for first-class letters and post cards (to seven cents and six cents each, respectively) and for third-class single piece rates, to seven cents. Air mail rates were to remain at 10 cents per ounce, but rates for second-class mail (chiefly publications) were to go up 12 per cent and third-class bulk rates by 16 per cent. The increases were designed to provide annual revenue increases of $621.5-million for the rest of fiscal 1970 and $663-million in later years.

Interest Equalization Tax

Congress in 1969 passed a bill (HR 12829—PL 91-128) extending the Interest Equalization Tax on foreign securi-

---

Bank Taxation Background

Since 1926, federal law had permitted levying certain state taxes—in general, those levied on state banks—on national banks. Courts had held, however, that only those taxes specifically enumerated under the law could be levied.

Subsequent court decisions had denied state power to levy sales taxes and other taxes on national banks which were less common or not in use in 1926.

A. U.S. Supreme Court decision June 17, 1968, prevented Massachusetts from imposing sales and use taxes on the sale to national banks of tangible personal property for their own use. *(First Agricultural National Bank of Berkshire County v. Massachusetts State Tax Commissioner, 1968)* The high court on Jan. 29, 1969, held that a bank did not have to pay Florida documentary stamp taxes. *(Dickinson v. First National Bank of Homestead, 1969)* Impetus for passage of the 1969 act came from lobbying by local authorities and the leadership of House Banking and Currency Committee Chairman Wright Patman (D Texas), a foe of special privileges for banks.

---

ties from September 30, 1969, to March 31, 1971. The tax, more of a balance-of-payments remedy than a revenue raiser, was requested by President Nixon. *(Details, see chapter on International Economic Policy, p. 119)*

State Taxation of National Banks

Congress broke new ground Dec. 12 when it completed action on a bill (HR 7491—PL 91-156) broadening state taxing authority over national banks. The new law for the first time permitted a state to tax national banks headquartered in the state in almost the same way as state-chartered banks, thus providing equality of taxation by state legislatures of state-chartered and nationally chartered banks.

Under the bill, national banks were not required to pay intangible personal property taxes until Jan. 1, 1972. After that date, states could also tax branches of national banks headquartered in other states.

The new state taxing authority was to be tentative until 1972, when it was to become permanent unless the Federal Reserve Board found after a study that changes were needed.

New taxes permitted under the bill included sales and use taxes. A House Banking and Currency Committee spokesman said the law would raise about $50-million annually in new taxes for the states.

As passed by the House, HR 7491 focused only on state taxes of national banks located within the state. The bill was broadened by the Senate to include coverage of branches and other arms of national banks headquartered in other states and intangible personal property, such as loan paper, bonds and stocks—the form in which financial institutions held most of their assets. Conferees accepted the Senate provisions.

Provisions. As signed into law, HR 7491 contained the following major provisions:

- Amended the National Bank Act to grant states authority to levy the same taxes on national banks, including branches of national banks headquartered in other states, as they did on state banks. The provision was to take effect Jan. 1, 1972.

• Provided that until the above provision took effect a state or political subdivision thereof could impose any tax which was imposed generally on a nondiscriminatory basis (other than a tax on intangible personal property).

• Prohibited a state from levying a tax on a bank, except sales, use, documentary, and real and tangible personal property taxes, unless either the tax was applicable before enactment of HR 7491 or the state legislature authorized its imposition by positive action taken after enactment of the bill. The provision was effective only to Jan. 1, 1972.

• Provided that until Jan. 1, 1972, states could levy only sales, use, real property, tangible personal property, documentary stamp and license or excise taxes on branches of banks headquartered in other states.

• Required a study by the Federal Reserve Board to determine the probable impact on the banking systems as well as other economic effects of changes made by the new legislation. The study was to be completed no later than Dec. 31, 1970.

Interstate Taxation

For the fourth consecutive year, Congress considered but failed to complete action on legislation to establish uniform limitations on the power of states to tax small, out-of-state firms doing business within their borders. A bill (HR 7906) providing such uniform standards was passed by the House but did not receive action in the Senate.

The uniform tax procedures, long opposed by state revenue commissioners, had been approved by the House Judiciary Committee in 1966 and 1967 and were finally passed by the House in 1968. The 1968 bill died at the close of the 90th Congress but was revived by the committee in 1969 and passed in identical form by the House (HR 7906) June 25. Over the entire four-year period, the measure never was reported in the Senate. HR 7906 cleared the House overwhelmingly, by a 311-87 roll-call vote.

Legislative History. The Supreme Court, in a series of 1959 cases dealing with state powers to tax interstate commerce, ruled that a state could tax that portion of an out-of-state company's income earned within its borders.

Later in 1959, Congress passed a law (PL 86-272) prohibiting a state from levying a tax on the net income of an out-of-state business if the business' only activity within the state was the solicitation of out-of-state orders. PL 86-272 also called for a congressional study of income taxes imposed on business in interstate commerce, the study to be the basis for further legislation.

The PL 86-272 study, completed in June 1965, was conducted by the Judiciary Committee's Special Subcommittee on State Taxation of Interstate Commerce, which released its findings and legislative recommendations in a special report (H Rept 952) published Sept. 2, 1965.

The subcommittee found the existing system of state taxation of interstate commerce characterized by "a conflict between the diversity and multiplicity" of state laws and the "limited extent" to which such a system

could be complied with or enforced. The subcommittee called for a program of rigid federal standards for state taxation of interstate business activity.

Provisions. As passed by the House June 25, 1969, HR 7906 contained the following major provisions:

• Established a uniform federal standard for determining circumstances under which a company might be subjected to tax on its interstate business. No state was permitted to impose a corporate net income tax, capital stock tax or gross receipts tax on a business earning less than $1-million average federal net taxable income unless that business (1) owned or leased realty within the state; (2) had at least one employee whose service was performed entirely within the state (except for incidental out-of-state service) and whose duties were more than taking orders; or (3) regularly maintained in the state an inventory for sale in its "ordinary course of...business." Sales or use taxes by states were prohibited unless a business met one of the above three criteria for the income tax or unless it made regular house deliveries within the state.

• Provided specific exemptions from the business locations formula (thus allowing continuation of existing taxation procedures) with regard to transportation companies, insurance firms, banks and other financial institutions, utilities, companies receiving income in the form of dividends, interest or certain royalties, certain foreign and domestic holding companies, and firms of any kind whose average annual income for federal taxation purposes was in excess of $1-million.

• Broadened the PL 86-272 provision prohibiting imposition of a net income tax on persons soliciting orders for acceptance and filing out-of-state to provide the same prohibition on imposition of capital stock, sales, use, and gross receipts taxes.

• Gave businesses liable for state income or capital stock taxes and earning less than $1-million average federal net taxable income the option of computing state income or capital stock tax liability (1) in accordance with a federal formula based on two factors, payroll and property; or (2) in accordance with the various existing state formulas based on three factors: payroll, property and sales. No business, however, could be obligated to pay a tax greater than that calculated under the two-factor federal formula.

Other Provisions. Also prohibited states from: (1) requiring any covered business or taxpayer to pay costs of a state audit on interstate business operations; (2) imposing discriminatory sales or gross receipts taxes against out-of-state sellers; (3) charging a back liability for companies which would not be liable for state taxes subsequent to enactment of the bill and (4) taxing income earned outside the state or by a person not domiciled within the state, unless the source of the income was within the state.

1970

In the wake of the massive changes made in the U.S. tax code by the Tax Reform Act of 1969, only minor tax revisions were considered by Congress in 1970. In his January budget message for fiscal 1971, President Nixon again proposed user charges for special government services, an increase in the maximum taxable wage base for Social Security and another year's extension of automobile and telephone excise taxes at their current rates. Later in the year he proposed higher postal rates, a speedup in collection of estate and gift taxes and another user charge—a tax on lead additives used in gasoline. Congress passed the excise tax measure and a bill establishing user charges for the airways system. But it balked at the remainder of the Nixon tax program.

An even greater blow for the President came, however, when tax revenues fell far short of projections because of the unexpected business recession that developed during the year. For fiscal 1970, revenues were $5-billion short of the $198.7-billion Nixon had forecast in his budget message of January 1969. And for fiscal 1971, they were $13.7-billion less than the $202.1-billion he had projected in January 1970. Nixon did not attempt to offset the deficits by a general tax increase. Instead, he sought to stimulate the lagging economy through even greater deficit spending.

Excise, Gift Taxes

Two days before adjournment, Congress sent the President a bill (HR 16199—PL 91-614) which was expected to produce an estimated $4-billion in tax revenues over the two-year period of fiscal 1971 and 1972.

The bill, cleared Dec. 31, extended excise taxes on telephone service and automobiles, speeded up collection of estate and gift taxes and established a working capital fund for the Treasury Department.

The bill also opened a new tax loophole for certain persons and businesses that in previous years had legally avoided most or all federal income tax liability but were made subject to taxation in 1970 by the minimum income tax provision in the Tax Reform Act of 1969. The loophole amendment, sponsored by Sen. Jack Miller (R Iowa), enabled some persons and businesses again to avoid tax liability.

The House Ways and Means Committee first reported the bill Nov. 30 as HR 19868. It was passed by the House Dec. 11. The Senate Finance Committee then attached the provisions of HR 19868 to another bill (HR 16199), which the House had passed May 19, establishing a $1-million working capital fund for the Treasury Department. The Senate Committee reported the combined bill as HR 16199.

Final action came when the Senate by voice vote accepted a House amendment to the loophole provision. Earlier on the same day, the House, with the one further amendment, had agreed to the Senate's amendments. Acceptance of each chamber's amendments by the other body, eliminating the need for a conference on differing versions of the bill, made enactment possible before the end of the session.

The bill's excise taxes were expected to produce $630-million in additional revenue in fiscal 1971 and $1.9 billion in fiscal 1972. The collection speedup was expected to produce $100-million in fiscal 1971 and $1.5-billion the next fiscal year. These revenues would be reduced by $100-million a year, however, by the loophole-opening amendment modifying the "minimum tax" provision of the 1969 Tax Reform Act. President Nixon had requested the excise extension in his January budget message and the accelerated estate and gift tax payments in a separate statement on April 2. (Existing law required

Excise Tax Timetable

The following table compares the schedule for excise tax rate reductions under HR 16199 with the existing schedule of reductions provided under the Tax Reform Act of 1969 (PL 91-172):

EXISTING LAW

Effective Date	Telephone	Automobile
Current rate	10%	7%
Jan. 1, 1971	5	5
Jan. 1, 1972	3	3
Jan. 1, 1973	1	1
Jan. 1, 1974	0	0

HR 16199

Effective Date	Telephone	Automobile
Current rate	10%	7%
Jan. 1, 1973	9	6
Jan. 1, 1974	8	5
Jan. 1, 1975	7	5
Jan. 1, 1976	6	5
Jan. 1, 1977	5	5
Jan. 1, 1978	4	4
Jan. 1, 1979	3	3
Jan. 1, 1980	2	2
Jan. 1, 1981	1	1
Jan. 1, 1982	0	0

Note: Automobile excise was repealed in subsequent legislation, the Revenue Act of 1971 (PL 92-178), effective Aug. 16, 1971.

filing an estate tax return and paying the tax due 15 months after the date of death. And existing law required filing a return and paying the tax due on a gift by April 15 of the year after the gift was given. The bill cut the filing period for estate taxes to nine months and required payment of gift taxes on a quarterly basis.)

Provisions. As signed into law, HR 16199 contained the following major provisions:

Excise Taxes

• Postponed reductions in automobile and telephone service excise taxes, which were to have gone into effect Jan. 1, 1971, for two years.

• Phased out both taxes over a 10-year period beginning Jan. 1, 1973, and repealed both as of Jan. 1, 1982.

Estate and Gift Taxes

• Required filing of estate tax returns and payment of such tax nine months after death.

• Provided for discharge of executors and fiduciaries from liability for a decedent's taxes.

• Permitted extensions up to 12 months (instead of the six months allowed by existing law) for filing estate tax returns in cases of hardship.

• Required donors to file quarterly (instead of annual) gift tax returns and pay gift taxes on the same basis—returns and payments to be due in the middle of the quarter after the quarter in which gifts were given.

Estimated Aviation User Tax Revenues of PL 91-258
(millions of dollars)

	1971	1972	1973	1974	1979	1980
As approved by Congress:						
Passenger ticket tax, 8 per cent	526.2	584.4	653.5	731.7	1,293.2	1,444.2
Waybill tax, 5 per cent [1]	37.4	42.7	49.0	55.3	117.6	138.1
Fuel tax, 7 cents a gallon [2]	47.2	50.9	55.1	59.2	81.0	85.4
International tax, $3	28.4	31.2	35.0	39.6	68.4	74.5
Aircraft use tax [3]	23.6	25.6	27.9	29.8	40.4	42.6
Taxes on tires and tubes	3.0	3.2	3.3	3.5	5.0	5.3
Total	665.8	738.0	823.8	919.1	1,605.6	1,790.1

1 *Revised. Exempts charges for portion of flights to or from Alaska and Hawaii not over U.S. territory, excess baggage, and imported freight.*
2 *General aviation aircraft.*
3 *Annual use tax of $25 for all aircraft plus 2 cents a pound for piston-engine aircraft of more than 2,500 pounds "maximum certificated takeoff weight" and 3½ cents a pound for turbine-engine aircraft.*

SOURCE: Department of Transportation, Federal Aviation Administration, Office of Aviation Economics

• Retained the structure of existing law concerning gifts, including the $3,000 maximum annual exemption per person and the $30,000 maximum lifetime exemption.

• Exempted fully deductible charitable gifts from the requirement.

Working Capital Fund

• Established a $1-million working capital fund in the Office of the Secretary of the Treasury.

• Authorized the Office of the Secretary to furnish, on a reimbursable basis, various centralized services, such as printing, procurement and telecommunications services, to Treasury Department bureaus financed under separate appropriations.

Minimum Income Tax

• Allowed a seven-year carryover of normal income taxes in excess of tax preferences over $30,000 to offset income in future years that would be subject to the 10-per cent minimum income tax (established by the Tax Reform Act of 1969—PL 91-172).

Aircraft User Tax

• Extended the 1970 Airport and Airway Development Act's exemption for piston-powered aircraft of less than 2,500 pounds to the first 2,500 pounds of weight of all piston-powered aircraft. *(For tax aspects of airways act, see below.)*

Aviation User Charges

At the President's request, Congress in 1970 passed a massive new aid program for the nation's airports and airways and provided new user charges to pay for the program. The Airport and Airway Development Act of 1970 (HR 14465—PL 91-258) was intended to alleviate severe inadequacies in the nation's aviation system by providing for major new investments in modernized air-

ports and federal air navigation facilities. The program was to be funded by a new Airport and Airway Trust Fund in the U.S. Treasury similar to the existing Highway Trust Fund. The fund would be financed mainly from a series of new and increased airport and airway user charges. In its major provisions affecting the trust fund, the bill:

• Increased the user tax on gasoline used by general aviation from 2 cents to 7 cents a gallon and imposed a new tax of 7 cents per gallon on general aviation jet fuel. (President Nixon requested a 9-cent tax on both types of fuel.)

• Increased the passenger ticket tax on all domestic flights from 5 to 8 per cent and imposed a new "head tax" of $3 on passengers on international commercial flights originating in the United States after June 30, 1970, and until June 30, 1980. (Request: same.)

• Imposed a new tax of 5 per cent on air freight waybills after June 30, 1970, and before July 1, 1980. (Request: same.)

• Provided that revenues from the fuel, ticket, freight and registration taxes be placed in an "Airport and Airway Trust Fund." (Request: same.)

• Provided that receipts from taxes on tires and tubes used for aircraft be transferred from the Highway Trust Fund to the Airport and Airway Trust Fund and that any general revenues necessary to supplement the air user taxes also be paid into the trust fund. (Request: same.)

• Imposed an annual aircraft registration tax of $25 plus 2 cents a pound for piston-powered aircraft with a maximum weight of more than 2,500 pounds and 3.5 cents a pound for all turbine-powered aircraft. (Request: none.)

• Provided that the aviation user taxes and the Airport and Airway Trust Fund terminate June 30, 1980. (Request: open-ended.)

Armed Guards. In response to a wave of aircraft hijackings, the House Sept. 30 passed a bill requested by President Nixon authorizing use of funds for the newly created Airport and Airway Trust Fund to cover expenses of placing armed guards on U.S. commercial aircraft and providing for an increase in air travel taxes to replenish the fund. The bill (HR 19444) was not considered by the Senate. The full request of $28-million was later provided, however, in a continuing resolution (H J Res 1421—PL 91-645), permitting the Department of Transportation and related agencies to spend funds through March 30, 1971, at the level agreed to in the House-Senate conference report on the fiscal 1971 appropriation bill (HR 17755) for those agencies. Further extension of the spending authority, through June 30, 1971, was provided in a second continuing resolution (H J Res 468—PL 92-7), approved in 1971.

Highway User Charges. Congress took no action on proposals by the President for an increase from 4 to 6 cents per gallon in the diesel fuel tax charged truck operators, a change in the fixed use tax on heavy trucks to a graduated tax based on weight and a tax on lead additives in gasoline. The latter tax, designed to yield $1.1-billion in fiscal 1971, was proposed May 19, after President Nixon announced that his budget, for which he had predicted a surplus of $1.3-billion, would be in deficit by that amount, largely because of a decrease in revenues due to a slowdown of the economy.

Social Security

Another round of Social Security benefit increases for the nation's elderly, together with higher tax rates and a broader taxable wage base to pay for them, barely missed congressional approval in 1970. Although both houses passed bills, they died at the end of the session because of a Senate filibuster over non-germane amendments involving import quotas and welfare reform.

President Nixon had not requested the higher benefits—an increase of 10 per cent under the Senate bill and 5 per cent under the House measure—but he later supported the House figure. The President in his fiscal 1971 budget had asked for an increase in the annual wage base on which Social Security taxes were computed from $7,800 to $9,000, effective Jan. 1, 1971. Both bills included that provision. In addition, both measures increased Social Security taxes in stages from the present 4.2 per cent to 5.5 per cent by 1980.

Postal Rate Increase

No action was taken in 1970 on President Nixon's postal rate increase requests. Nixon April 3 asked for an increase in first class mail from 6 to 10 cents per ounce and various increases for other classes. On April 16 he changed his proposal on the first class rate to 8 cents but increased the rate request for second and third class mail. The combined revenue effects of the proposals for fiscal 1971 were estimated at an additional $2.5-billion a year. The House Post Office and Civil Service Committee held hearings on postal rates in 1970, but legislation containing the President's requests was not introduced in either house.

Transportation Property Taxes

Although passed by the Senate early in 1970, the House did not take action on a bill (S 2289) barring states from taxing transportation property at higher rates than other property. Impetus for the bill came when Senate Commerce Committee hearings held in 1969 determined that states deliberately assessed transportation property —particularly railroad property—at higher valuations than other property and applied a higher tax rate to it. In reporting the bill, the commerce panel said that "in the last nine years, the railroads alone have been assessed more than $900-million in discriminatory taxes." The bill was supported by the transportation industry but opposed by state tax officials. The Nixon administration endorsed but did not work actively for the bill.

City Income Tax Withholding

The House Aug. 3, by a 145-184 roll-call vote, rejected a bill (HR 2076) authorizing the withholding of income taxes imposed by certain cities on the compensation of federal employees. A two-thirds majority (220 in this case) would have been required for passage of the bill under suspension of the House rules.

During debate on the bill, members voiced concern over possible costs to the federal government of collecting the tax and over the possibility that the bill would open the door for commuter taxes by the city of Washington, D.C., and other cities. Supporters of the measure argued that the bill would be a reciprocal move on the part of the federal government to municipal governments which had long withheld federal income taxes.

1971

Despite the government's growing budgetary deficit, tax cuts to stimulate the economy were the centerpiece of Nixon's fiscal policy in 1971. Early in the year, the President used his administrative authority to give businesses a tax break worth more than $3-billion a year by allowing them an accelerated tax writeoff of their depreciation costs. (The program was known as ADR for "asset depreciation range.") And in his Aug. 15 announcement of his new economic program, the President called for additional tax cuts averaging $5.7-billion a year over the next three years and indeterminate amounts after that. Congress modified the ADR program, wrote it into law, and provided a tax cut of $8.6-billion a year, including the ADR benefits. In doing so, Congress provided more tax relief than the President had requested for individuals and less than he had sought for businesses.

The President's tax proposals were coupled with a program to fight inflation and strengthen the nation's balance-of-payments position on one hand and to move the country out of recession on the other. By early 1972, it appeared that the program was making headway on each of these fronts.

The President's original budget for fiscal 1972, submitted in January, gave little indication of the bold tax moves that were in store for late summer. If there was a hint of what was to come, it was in the President's January announcement that he would move by administrative order to institute the ADR program in hopes of stimulating business investment. Otherwise, the President asked for relatively routine tax measures: a two-year extension of the Interest Equalization Tax, an increase in the taxable wage base for Social Security, airline user charges to pay the costs of air marshals to guard against aircraft

Tax Reduction Under HR 10947 By Calendar Years

(in billions of dollars)

	NIXON PROGRAM			FINAL BILL		
	1971	1972	1973	1971	1972	1973
INDIVIDUAL TAXES						
Personal Exemption, Standard Deduction and Low-Income Allowance	0	2.2	0	1.4	3.2	1.1
Other Individual Taxes	0	0	0	0	0.2	0.1
Subtotal Individual Taxes	0	2.2	0	1.4	3.4	1.2
BUSINESS TAXES						
Investment Credit	1.5	4.8	2.8	1.6	3.6	3.9
DISC	0	.3	.6	0	.1	.2
ADR	2.8	3.4	3.9	.7	1.7	2.4
Subtotal Business Taxes	4.3	8.5	7.3	2.3	5.4	6.5
AUTOMOBILE EXCISE	.8	2.2	2.0	.8	2.6	2.3
GRAND TOTAL	$5.1	$12.9	$9.3	$4.5	$11.4	$10.0

Note: Application of personal exemption increases to 1971 and 1972 and application of standard deduction increase to 1972 were non-recurring tax cuts. Other cuts continued to provide benefits in subsequent years.

hijackings, higher user charges on automotive diesel fuel and a change in the present fixed-rate use tax on heavy trucks to a graduated scale based on weight. Congress provided the broader Social Security tax and the Interest Equalization Tax extension but again turned down the user charge proposals. (A postal rate increase went into effect during the year, but this did not affect the budget. Under the 1970 Postal Reorganization Act, the Post Office Department became the U.S. Postal Service, with independent rate-making authority.)

Omnibus Tax Bill

Congress Dec. 9 cleared for the President's signature a bill, the Revenue Act of 1971 (HR 10947—PL 92-178), cutting tax liabilities by $25.9-billion over a three-year period (and indeterminate amounts in later years) in order to stimulate the economy.

The bill, requested by President Nixon to implement his new economic policy, announced Aug. 15, was the first major tax legislation passed by Congress since the Tax Reform Act of 1969 (PL 91-172). *(Basis for presidential authority, p. 91)*

Campaign Fund. The measure passed the House Oct. 6 by voice vote after limited debate but became the subject of extensive partisan conflict in the Senate where numerous attempts were made to amend the bill. In the Senate, a major point of contention became an amendment to establish a special fund, financed by $1 contributions by individual taxpayers, to pay the costs of presidential campaigns. Democrats, whose party was deeply in debt and traditionally received less campaign financing than the Republican organization, sponsored and defended the move. They argued that such a financing plan would remove politics from the influence of

large contributors. Republicans decried the move as a brazen political act and succeeded in conference under the threat of a Nixon veto to put off the effective date of the fund until after the 1972 election.

Tax Cuts. What remained after conference was a bill which reduced individual and business taxes by an average of $8.6-billion a year over the next three years ($4.5-billion in 1971, $11.4-billion in 1972, and $10-billion in 1973; there would be ongoing savings in subsequent years, but projections were not available at the time). The bill reinstated the 7 per cent investment tax credit, eliminated by the 1969 Tax Reform Act; repealed the federal excise tax on automobiles; made the ADR program statutory in a modifed form; created tax incentives for exports; and accelerated a scheduled increase in the personal income tax exemption and in the standard deduction. Each of these provisions except the personal exemption and standard deduction would provide ongoing benefits past 1973.

Inclusion of all these features of the bill was requested in identical or similar form by President Nixon. In that sense, they were a victory for Nixon but in another they were a defeat: Congress put more emphasis on individual tax cuts than it did on tax breaks for business. The final bill provided $3.8-billion more in individual tax relief than the President had requested over the 1971-73 period, while providing $5.9-billion less for business than he had sought. (Most of the restoration of business taxes came in Congress' modification of the ADR program. The bill provided $4.8-billion in business tax relief through ADR over the 1971-73 period, compared with $10.1-billion in benefits under the program as originally approved by the President. As modified, ADR would be worth $700-million in 1971, $1.7-billion in 1972 and $2.4-billion in 1973.)

Nixon's Authority: Congressional Action Needed on Taxes

While major parts of President Nixon's economic initiatives announced Aug. 15, 1971, were based on authority previously granted the President, the key tax relief proposals required approval by Congress.

Congressional Action Required

Taxes. Congress had to consider these tax proposals:

• A 10 per cent investment tax credit for business, retroactive to Aug. 15, to be reduced to 5 per cent after one year. In the Tax Reform Act of 1969 (PL 91-172), Congress repealed a 7 per cent tax credit for business investment enacted in 1962 at the request of President Kennedy. President Nixon supported repeal of the credit in 1969. (Outcome: restoration at flat 7 per cent level.)

• Repeal of the 7 per cent excise tax on automobiles. The auto excise tax, which had been scheduled to drop to 5 per cent on Jan. 1, 1971, was extended at the 7 per cent level for two more years when Congress enacted HR 16199 (PL 91-614) on Dec. 31, 1970. (Outcome: as requested.)

• Acceleration of scheduled increases in the personal income tax exemption to $750 per person and in the standard deduction to 15 per cent.

Under the 1969 tax reform measure, the personal exemption was scheduled to rise to $700 in 1972 and $750 in 1973. The standard deduction was scheduled to rise to 14 per cent with a maximum of $2,000 in 1972 and 15 per cent with a maximum of $2,000 in 1973. The President requested that the increases scheduled for Jan. 1, 1973, be advanced to Jan. 1, 1972. (Outcome: as requested.)

• One other step recommended by the President—tax deferrals for earnings from export sales by any business qualifying as a Domestic International Sales Corporation (DISC)—was approved by the House in 1970 as part of the foreign trade bill that died in the Senate at the end of the 91st Congress.

The President Aug. 15 recommended that his 1970 proposal be changed to take full effect on Jan. 1, 1972, and to permit use of DISC export earnings to finance industrial economic adjustments such as worker retraining, relocation and adjustment assistance without loss of the deferral benefit. (Outcome: as requested, with some modifications.)

Existing Presidential Authority

Controls. Congress May 5 cleared a bill (HR 4246) extending through April 30, 1972, the President's discretionary authority to impose controls on wages, prices, salaries and rents. The President's authority under the 1970 Defense Production Act (PL 91-379) would have expired on June 1, 1971. The authority was subsequently extended through April 30, 1973.

The administration opposed authorization of the controls in 1970, but Treasury Secretary John Connally Feb. 23, 1971, told the House Banking and Currency Committee that the administration accepted extension of power to impose controls under HR 4246.

As signed by the President on May 18, 1971, HR 4246 (PL 92-15) also extended the authority of federal banking agencies to set ceilings on interest rates paid by financial institutions on time and savings deposits through March 31, 1973.

The administration rejected controls on interest rates in announcing the policy changes but urged bankers not to raise rates.

Import Surcharge. Mr. Nixon used powers granted in the Trade Expansion Act of 1962 to impose a 10 per cent surcharge on imports.

The Act, which gave the President wide powers to reduce or eliminate tariffs, also authorized restrictions on imports if they threatened the national security and an increase in tariffs in case of injury to domestic workers or businesses through earlier or subsequent tariff cuts. The surcharge was removed after an international monetary agreement in December 1971.

Suspension of Gold Sale. There was no legal requirement that the United States exchange gold for dollars, the Treasury Department said. The Gold Reserve Act of 1934 empowered the secretary of the treasury to buy or sell gold on terms he deemed to be in the public interest.

Employment Reduction. The President ordered the 5 per cent reduction in employment of federal personnel under his authority as head of the executive branch granted by the Constitution.

Pay Raise Delay. The Federal Pay Comparability Act of 1970 (HR 13000—PL 91-656) authorized the President to adjust federal pay rates for 1971 and 1972, effective Jan. 1, based on Bureau of Labor Statistics surveys of pay in private industry.

The act also required the President to submit an alternative plan to Congress before Sept. 1 if he determined that national emergency or economic conditions made the proposed pay adjustment inappropriate.

If either house of Congress rejected the alternative plan within 30 days after the date of transmittal, the original pay plan would take effect.

Legislative History. President Nixon Aug. 15 announced his new economic program on a suddenly scheduled telecast after a weekend of intensive planning with advisers at Camp David, Md., the presidential retreat. The program included a broad range of actions, some of which would be accomplished by executive order and others by legislation. *(See box above.)*

Acting on his own authority, the President, among other actions, ordered a 90-day freeze on all wages, prices and rents, freed the dollar from its historic $35-an-ounce gold price, imposed a temporary 10 per cent surcharge on most imports, ordered a 10 per cent cut in foreign economic aid, and ordered a five per cent reduction in federal executive branch employment. The President asked Congress to provide: a 10 per cent investment tax credit for business machinery (dubbed "job development" credit by the President instead of its traditional title) retroactive to Aug. 15, to be reduced to five per cent after one year; repeal of the 7 per cent excise tax on automobiles; tax incentives for U.S. firms engaged primarily in the export business; and an advance to Jan. 1, 1972, of the income tax cuts already scheduled to become effective Jan. 1, 1973, through an increase in the personal income tax exemption and the standard deduction. (Under the Tax Reform Act of 1969, the personal exemption was scheduled to rise to $700 in 1972 and $750 in 1973. The existing 13 per cent standard deduction with a maximum of $1,500 was scheduled to rise to 14 per cent with a maximum of $2,000 in 1972 and 15 per cent with a maximum of $2,000 in 1973.)

House Action. The House Ways and Means Committee Sept. 29 reported HR 10947, a clean bill incorporating the President's tax proposals for implementing his new economic policy. In its major changes in the President's Aug. 15 proposals, the committee:

• Reinstated the investment tax credit at its traditional 7 per cent level instead of the President's request of 10 per cent for the first year and 5 per cent for subsequent years.

• Eliminated a provision of the asset depreciation range (ADR) program—promulgated by the Treasury June 22—allowing increased tax advantages on property during the first year after purchase.

• Eliminated a scheduled 1972 reduction in the low-income allowance (minimum standard deduction) from $1,050 to $1,000 and increased the level for 1972 and subsequent years to $1,300.

• Increased the individual tax exemption from $650 to $675 for 1971.

The House Oct. 6 approved HR 10947 by voice vote. Considering the measure under a closed rule prohibiting floor amendments, the House approved the version of the bill reported out by the Ways and Means Committee.

Senate Action. The Senate Finance Committee Nov. 9 reported HR 10947 with amendments. Major committee changes in the House bill included authority for the President to impose selective or general import quotas and to impose an import surcharge of up to 15 per cent during a balance-of-payments emergency. Committee approval of the bill came on a 12-2 vote, with Gaylord Nelson (D Wis.) and Fred R. Harris (D Okla.) dissenting.

The Senate Nov. 22 passed a heavily amended version of HR 10947 by a 64-30 roll-call vote.

Debate on the bill took on a partisan political tone when Democrats succeeded in attaching a rider authorizing the use of federal funds to finance presidential election campaigns.

The campaign financing plan, proposed as a floor amendment by John O. Pastore (D R.I.), was adopted by a key 52-47 roll-call vote, largely along party lines. The amendment gave each taxpayer the option of designating $1 of his annual federal income tax payment for use by the candidate of the party of his choice in presidential election campaigns. It was estimated that about $20.4-million would be made available to each of the major party candidates in the 1972 presidential election and

---

1966 Campaign Fund Plan

Congress in 1966 approved a plan setting up a presidential election campaign fund to be divided evenly between the Republican and Democratic parties with provision for a share of the funds to be given to minor parties that won more than 5 million votes in the preceding presidential election.

The fund was to be financed by allowing taxpayers to check a box on their tax forms if they wished to designate $1 of their tax payments to a general presidential campaign fund. No choice of parties was permitted.

Senate opponents of the plan, including most Republicans, renewed their efforts in 1967 to repeal the fund provision. In a compromise solution offered by Majority Leader Mike Mansfield (D Mont.), Congress attached to a bill restoring the suspended investment tax credit and certain accelerated depreciation practices an amendment suspending the campaign financing system until Congress adopted guidelines for distributing money from the fund.

Congress did not adopt guidelines prior to passage of HR 10947. The new bill did not require congressional guidelines. (*Congress and the Nation Vol. II, p. 160*)

---

about $6.3-million for Gov. George C. Wallace (D Ala.) if he ran for President as a third-party candidate.

Democrats, whose party was $9-million in debt, said the voluntary tax check-off for campaign contributions was needed to free presidential candidates from obligation to wealthy contributors. But Republicans, whose party treasury was well stocked, charged that the Pastore amendment was a plan to rescue the Democratic party from financial difficulty and assure a Wallace candidacy in 1972 that would lessen Nixon's re-election chances.

Pastore accepted an amendment by Charles McC. Mathias Jr. (R Md.) allowing each taxpayer to designate which party he wanted to donate his $1 to. The Mathias amendment was adopted by a 72-27 roll-call vote.

The Pastore amendment, which became law, divided the total amount designated for contributions among major party candidates according to a formula based on the number of Americans 18 years old or over; for minor party candidates, according to a formula based on the number of votes received by the party in the preceding presidential election.

After acceptance of the Mathias amendment, Mathias and Clifford P. Case (R N.J.) joined 50 Democrats in voting for adoption of the Pastore amendment.

Four Democrats—James O. Eastland (Miss.), Sam J. Ervin Jr. (N.C.), John L. McClellan (Ark.) and John C. Stennis (Miss.)—joined 42 Republicans and Harry F. Byrd Jr. (Ind Va.) in voting against it.

By margins of one and two votes, the Senate rejected amendments by Birch Bayh (D Ind.) to increase business taxes while granting further individual tax cuts. The Bayh amendments proposed to couple repeal or reduction of the ADR system with an additional $25 personal tax credit ($50 for a married couple), effective only for 1971.

Investment Tax Credit: Mechanism to Fine-Tune the Economy

Throughout the 1960s and early 1970s, no other aspect of fiscal policy was called on so often as a measure to fine-tune the economy as was the 7 per cent tax credit on specified types of new and used business equipment.

Enacted in 1962, the credit was suspended in 1966, restored in 1967, suspended again in 1969 and restored again in 1971. Each time, the actions were requested by the White House as a means to either dampen inflationary pressures or to pump more investment into a lagging economy, whichever was the case at the time.

Background. The investment credit—which permits an investor to subtract from his tax bill 7 per cent of eligible investment up to certain limits—was originally proposed by President Kennedy in 1961.

The credit, which was the centerpiece of the President's first major tax proposals, grew out of the belief of both Kennedy and his top economic advisers that the nation's production facilities in many areas were inadequate and outdated. The credit was designed to stimulate the nation's economic growth and lessen the chances for recession such as the new administration found upon taking office in January 1961.

As proposed, the credit amounted to 15 per cent on all new plant and equipment investment in excess of current depreciation allowances, and 6 per cent of such investment below that level but in excess of one-half of current depreciation allowances. In place of these proposals, Congress in the 1962 Revenue Act (PL 87-834) provided a credit of 7 per cent of the costs of assets with useful lives of eight years or more (3 percent in the case of regulated utilities). Among other specific limitations, credit in any one year could not exceed $25,000 plus 25 per cent of any tax liability above that amount. Unused credits could be carried forward five years or carried back three years.

1966. As part of the Johnson administration's program to stem the rising inflation caused by increased Vietnam war spending, Congress in 1966 enacted legislation (PL 89-800) suspending the tax from Oct. 10, 1966, through Dec. 31, 1967.

Throughout 1966, the President's Council of Economic Advisers (CEA) had urged the suspension but this had been opposed by the Treasury Department. The CEA had contended that monetary policy alone was not sufficient to diminish inflationary pressures, while the Treasury asserted that permanent tax measures such as investment credit should not be altered to influence economic trends of a temporary nature.

President Johnson, who had accepted the Treasury arguments until late summer, sought the suspension Sept. 8 after it became apparent that business was making record investments despite the tight money and high interest rates that prevailed at the time. One

survey, conducted jointly by the Securities and Exchange Commission and the Commerce Department, estimated planned business investment in plant and equipment at $60.8-billion for the year—an increase of 17 per cent over 1965. The Commerce Department early in 1967 announced that businesses had cut back their investment plans by an estimated $300-million in the last quarter of 1966 as a result of the investment credit suspension.

1967. Pressures for early restoration of the tax credit built up in the first few months of 1967, when key members of Congress began talking of an "air pocket" toward the end of the year in which business orders for new equipment might virtually disappear while businessmen waited for the Jan. 1, 1968, restoration of the tax credit. At the Johnson administration's request, Congress May 31 cleared a bill (PL 90-26) accelerating restoration retroactively to March 9, 1967. Termination of the suspension automatically put into effect provisions of the 1966 suspension law which broadened the credit by permitting the taxpayer a maximum credit of $25,000 plus 50 per cent (instead of 25 per cent) of the tax liability above $25,000 and allowing unused credits to be carried forward for seven years (instead of five).

1969. As part of the 1969 Tax Reform Act (PL 91-172), Congress approved a Nixon administration request to repeal the investment credit, effective April 19 (two days before the President's request for repeal), with provisions maintaining it in force where there were binding contracts for equipment entered into before the effective date. "This subsidy to business investment," the President said, "no longer has priority over other pressing national needs." Nixon noted that U.S. businesses had invested almost $400-billion in new plant and equipment since institution of the credit in 1962. Repeal of the credit would be a substitute for the inflation-dampening 10 per cent income tax surcharge, which the President asked to be continued at only a 5 per cent rate for the first six months of 1970 and then abolished.

1971. With the country mired in recession, Nixon asked Congress in 1971 to restore the credit at a 10 per cent level, retroactive to Aug. 15, to be reduced to 5 per cent after one year. "The investment credit can create hundreds of thousands of jobs," said Nixon's Treasury Secretary, John Connally, in a hearing before the House Ways and Means Committee. Congress in the 1971 Revenue Act (PL 92-178) restored the credit indefinitely at its original 7 per cent level and laid down specific provisions and limits on application of the credit to certain types of property, uses and other conditions.

The first Bayh amendment, defeated Nov. 12 by a 35-37 roll call, would have eliminated ADR completely. The second Bayh amendment, rejected Nov. 15 by a 39-40 roll-call vote, would have reduced to 5 per cent from 20 per cent the shortening of the life of plant and

equipment assets which could be depreciated under the ADR system.

In addition to the campaign financing amendment, the Senate made the following major changes in the committee version:

• Provided up to 26 weeks of additional unemployment compensation in states where unemployment rates exceeded 6 per cent.

• Increased the personal income tax exemption to $800 from $750 in 1972.

• Provided a tax credit of up to $325 for expenses of sending a child to college or other higher education institution.

• Advanced the effective date of the House's 1972 increase in the low-income allowance (minimum standard deduction) to 1971.

• Increased the investment credit to 10 percent from 7 per cent for investments creating new jobs in rural areas or in central cities with unemployment rates of 6 per cent or more.

Conference Action. A House-Senate conference committee Dec. 4 filed a report reconciling the differences between House and Senate versions of HR 10947. Calendar year revenue losses under the bill as proposed by the administration, passed by the House, passed by the Senate and approved in conference were:

(in billions of dollars)

	1971	1972	1973
Administration	$5.1	$12.9	$ 9.3
Senate	5.7	16.8	15.6
House	4.5	11.2	9.9
Conference	4.5	11.4	10.0

(The figures above all treat the parts of the Treasury-instituted Asset Depreciation Range system (ADR) sanctioned by the bill as a new provision of law, making the revenue reductions greater than if ADR had been treated as existing law.)

Faced with the threat of a presidential veto, the conference committee amended the Senate provision setting up a federal fund to finance presidential election campaigns to make it effective only after the 1972 presidential election.

The conferees also agreed to require that Congress appropriate payments into the fund, thus making distribution of the contributions designated for presidential campaigns by federal taxpayers subject to further congressional action and the risk of a veto.

Conferees in other major actions dropped the Senate provisions authorizing emergency unemployment benefits, emergency import quotas and surcharge, a 3 per cent additional investment tax credit (for a total of 10 per cent) for investments in high-unemployment rural or central city areas, a $325 tax credit for college expenses, a 1971 (instead of 1972) effective date for the increase in the low-income allowance (minimum standard deduction), and an additional $50 increase (to $800) in the personal income tax exemption for 1972.

Adoption of the conference report, clearing the bill for the President's signature, came routinely Dec. 9 with little discussion in either chamber. The House adopted the conference report by a 321-75 roll-call vote and the Senate acquiesced on a 71-6 roll call.

Provisions. As signed into law, HR 10947 contained the following major provisions:

• Increased the personal exemption per taxpayer and dependent to $675, from $650, for 1971; moved up the scheduled increase to $750 from 1973 to 1972.

┌───┐

Revenue Effects: Tax Legislation 1969-72

The column on the left below indicates what tax revenues *would have been* for fiscal 1970-73 if no new legislation had cleared Congress from 1969-70. The column on the right shows *actual revenues* from fiscal 1970-73.

(in millions of dollars)

Year		
1970	$182.8	$193.7
1971	183.7	188.4
1972	208.4	208.6
1973	230.1	224.8 [1]

1 Estimated totals in the Budget of the United States Government for fiscal year 1974.

SOURCE: Joint Committee on Internal Revenue Taxation

└───┘

• Moved up to 1972, from 1973, the effective date of an increase in the standard deduction to 15 per cent of income with a maximum of $2,000.

• Raised the minimum income levels at which taxpayers must file tax returns to correspond to increases in the personal exemption and low-income allowance.

• Eliminated a scheduled 1972 reduction in the low-income allowance from $1,050 to $1,000; increased the allowance for 1972 and subsequent years to $1,300.

• Revised withholding rates and schedules to prevent underwithholding, effective Jan. 15, 1972.

• Raised the minimum level of total income not withheld and the tax levels at which declarations of estimated tax were required; waived penalties for failure to declare estimated taxes for some taxpayers for 1971.

• Allowed increased deductions for care of disabled children and other children up to age 15, in or outside the home, beginning in 1972, up to $400 per month, for single parents, parents treated as single and couples of whom one was disabled, and for working couples with combined incomes after the deduction of $18,000 or less; included a 50 per cent phase-out of the deductions for incomes over $18,000 and required that the deductions be itemized.

Excise Tax Repeal

• Repealed the 7 per cent excise tax on foreign and domestic automobiles and light trailers effective Aug. 16, 1971.

• Authorized refunding of excise tax on vehicles sold between Aug. 15 and the date of enactment of the bill (Dec. 10, 1971), including floor stocks of vehicles sold but not delivered by Aug. 15.

Investment Credit

• Reinstated the 7 per cent tax credit for business investment (repealed in 1969) applicable generally to tangible property integrally involved in the functioning of a business (not real estate) and effective for property ordered on or after April 1, 1971, or acquired after Aug. 15, 1971.

• Denied the credit for foreign-produced property for the duration of the 10 per cent import surcharge imposed by the President on Aug. 15, 1971, but allowed the credit for foreign property ordered between April 1 and Aug. 16, 1971.

- Authorized the President to continue to deny the credit to foreign property under certain conditions after termination of the surcharge.
- Allowed the President by executive order to permit the credit retroactively for up to two years to any date after Aug. 15, 1971, for foreign property otherwise denied the credit.
- Established specific provisions and limits on application of the credit to certain types of property, businesses, conditions and situations, including the useful life of the property, carryover of unused credits, public utilities, anti-pollution equipment, transmission facilities and equipment, storage facilities, used property, amortized property, leased property, livestock, recapture, depreciation and accounting.
- Modified effective Jan. 1, 1972, the first-year depreciation allowed for property under the asset depreciation range (ADR) system put into effect in 1971 by the Treasury Department.
- Established a tax credit of 20 per cent of the wages paid by a business to persons employed for two years or more under the Work Incentive Program (WIN) administered by the Department of Labor.

Exports and Imports

- Exempted from taxation the profits of businesses engaged primarily in exporting which qualified (under the criteria below) as Domestic International Sales Corporations (DISC) and provided for taxation of half the profits of such businesses when distributed to shareholders, effective for a period of five years beginning in 1972.
- Required that, for a business to qualify as a DISC, 95 per cent of its gross receipts must arise from export sales, leases, investments and related activities and that 95 per cent of its assets must be export-related.

Political Contributions

- Established, effective in 1973, a tax credit of $12.50 for an individual ($25 for a married couple filing a joint return) and as an alternative a deduction of $50 for an individual ($100 for a married couple) for contributions to candidates for federal, state or local political office in general, primary or special elections.
- Authorized taxpayers starting in 1973 to designate on their tax returns that $1 ($2 for a couple) be paid into a public campaign fund for the presidential and vice presidential candidates of a qualified major or minor party or alternatively into a general public campaign fund to be distributed among qualified candidates.

Miscellaneous

- Increased to $1-million from $250,000 the limit on spending from private sources for unanticipated expenses allowed on any project financed by tax-exempt bonds. Under existing law, a municipality was allowed to issue up to $5-million in tax-exempt bonds to build a plant or other facility provided that total expenditures on the project did not exceed the value of the bonds, plus

Social Security Taxes

Year	Taxable earnings	Employer-employee tax rate	Maximum each pays	Self-employed tax rate
1937-49	$ 3,000	1.0%	$ 30.00	——
1950	3,000	1.5	45.00	——
1951-53	3,600	1.5	54.00	2.25 %
1951	3,600	2.0	72.00	3.0
1955-56	4,200	2.0	84.00	3.0
1957-58	4,200	2.25	94.50	3.375
1959	4,800	2.5	120.00	3.75
1960-61	4,800	3.0	144.00	4.5
1962	4,800	3.125	150.00	4.7
1963-65	4,800	3.625	174.00	5.4
1966	6,600	4.2	277.20	6.15
1967	6,600	4.4	290.40	6.4
1968	7,800	4.4	343.20	6.4
1969-70	7,800	4.8	374.40	6.9
1971	7,800	5.2	405.60	7.5
1972	9,000	5.2	468.00	7.5
1973	10,800	5.85	594.00	8.0
1974	12,000	5.85	660.00	8.0

SOURCE: Social Security Administration

$250,000 for unanticipated expenses required by inaccurate estimates or similar problems.

Social Security Tax

In a bill increasing the federal debt ceiling (HR 4690 —PL 92-5), Congress in 1971 raised the taxable wage base for Social Security levies from $7,800 to $9,000 but did not make the higher taxes effective until January 1972. (President Nixon had sought a January 1971 effective date.) The bill also increased Social Security benefits by 10 per cent and increased the Social Security tax rates on employees and employers to 5.15 per cent from 5 per cent beginning in 1976. (Under existing law, the tax rate was scheduled to remain at 4.6 per cent through 1972 and to increase to 5 per cent in 1973.) The President had requested a 6 per cent increase in Social Security benefits; he had not requested the higher 1976 tax rates.

Interest Equalization Tax

For the second time in his administration, President Nixon sought and won congressional approval of an extension of the Interest Equalization Tax on purchase by U.S. citizens of the securities of foreign countries. Congress March 30 cleared for the President's signature a bill (HR 5432—PL 92-9) extending the levy for two more years, through March 31, 1973.

1972

Nixon fiscal strategy shifted in 1972 from stimulation of the economy to an all-out effort to hold the budget in line and avoid an excessive deficit. The President repeatedly fought the Democratic-controlled Congress over increases for domestic social programs such as health and education, and he cautioned that a tax increase might be necessary unless Congress towed the mark of his spending proposals.

The administration considered but did not propose a value added tax—a kind of federal sales tax—as a new source of revenue that could be earmarked for education and as a relief to property owners.

Two tax proposals were offered in the President's January budget message: an increase in the taxable earnings base for Social Security and repetition of the request—which had become an annual ritual—for a 2-cent increase in the diesel fuel tax and the change to a graduated-scale use tax on heavy trucks based on weight. Congress provided the broader Social Security wage base but snubbed the President on the highway user charges for the fourth straight year (the eighth straight including four unsucessful tries by President Johnson).

Social Security Tax

In June, Congress cleared a bill (HR 15390—PL 92-336) granting a 20 per cent increase in Social Security benefits. The cost of the increased benefits would be financed in part by an increase in the taxable wage base and in part by an increase in the Social Security tax rate. The increase in the taxable wage base would rise to $10,800 from $9,000 beginning Jan. 1, 1973, and would rise to $12,000 beginning Jan. 1, 1974. The Social Security tax rate would rise to 5.8 per cent from 5.2 per cent, effective Jan. 1, 1973. The bill also authorized an automatic increase in the taxable wage base whenever the cost of living rose more than three per cent in any calendar year, beginning with calendar year 1975. *(Details of benefits in HR 15390, welfare chapter)*

Revenue Sharing (1972)

NEW CONCEPT IN AID-TO-STATES, COMMUNITIES LAUNCHED

"The time has come to reverse the flow of power and resources from the states and communities to Washington, and start power and resources flowing back from Washington to the states and communities and, more important, to the people, all across America."

—President Nixon Jan. 22, 1971, State of the Union address

During the early years of President Johnson's administration, it appeared that by the late 1960s there would be large surpluses of federal revenue in the Treasury. One proposal advanced was a program of payments to aid state and local governments with no strings attached—revenue sharing.

The concept was never publicly accepted by President Johnson who by the end of his term faced mounting budget deficits brought on by U.S. involvement in the Vietnam war.

By the late 1960's, a system of sharing tax revenues with the states was firmly part of the Republican program and adopted by President Nixon when he took office. It fell neatly among other Nixon proposals to shift many government responsibilities to the state and local level and drew wide support from governors and mayors. Revenue sharing was a major departure from federal aid programs of the past. It meant more federal dollars with no strings attached, with no narrow-purpose guidelines and promised no red tape.

Nixon's Proposals. President Nixon in 1969 first proposed a revenue-sharing plan that would have made $500-million in federal revenues available to state and local governments in fiscal 1971, with the total rising to $5-billion by fiscal 1976. Congress did not act on it.

In his 1971 state of the union address, the President unveiled a second revenue-sharing plan that exceeded the scope of previous proposals, including his own.

The second proposal included two elements:

● $5-billion annually for allocation to the states, counties, municipalities and the District of Columbia.

● $11-billion annually for "special revenue-sharing" programs created by consolidating about 105 existing federal aid programs into six broad purposes with fewer federal specifications.

Under the general revenue-sharing proposal, 90 per cent of the $5-billion would be allocated according to each state's percentage of total U.S. population, with adjustments reflecting a state's tax effort.

The remaining 10 per cent would be available to states that had negotiated a formula for sharing federal funds with local governments.

Of the total share of each state, about 50 per cent would be passed on to local governments, with school districts and other special purpose government units excluded. The local shares would be distributed according to the ratio of local revenues to state revenues—at least until a negotiated local sharing formula had been adopted.

House Ways and Means Committee Chairman Wilbur D. Mills (D Ark.), supported by the panel's ranking Republican, John W. Byrnes (R Wis.), fought the general revenue-sharing plan. Because it involved sharing a proportion of federal tax revenues, the bill was referred to Mills' committee. The special revenue-sharing proposals were referred to the various committees with jurisdiction over the six areas of activity involved.

The Ways and Means Committee held extensive hearings in June 1971 on the administration's bill. But Mills announced that their purpose was to expose the dangers and weaknesses of the revenue-sharing concept and to kill the bill.

But midway through the hearings Mills announced that he favored a revenue-sharing plan that would give most of its benefits to urban areas.

On Nov. 30, 1971, Mills and nine other members of the Ways and Means Committee introduced HR 11950, a $5.3-billion revenue-sharing bill which provided two-thirds of its funds for local governments and one-third for states.

Mills' endorsement of the revenue-sharing concept set legislative wheels turning and one year later, Oct. 20, 1972, President Nixon signed the State and Local Fiscal Assistance Act of 1972 (PL 92-512) in a ceremony at Independence Hall in Philadelphia.

The five-year program to share $30.2-billion in federal revenues with states and local governments became a realization, but the President's program for special revenue sharing which would have combined categorical grant programs into large block grants for education, urban community development and several other purposes were not enacted in 1972 and died at the end of the 92nd Congress.

House Committee Action

The House Ways and Means Committee April 26, 1972, reported a clean bill, the State and Local Fiscal Assistance Act of 1972 (HR 14370—H Rept 92-1018), establishing general revenue sharing with state and local governments at a first-year rate of $5.3-billion.

The committee April 17 voted 18-7 to report the bill. HR 14370 was written by the committee based on Chairman Mills' earlier bill, HR 11950.

The bill appropriated $3.5-billion per year for local governments for five years, beginning with calendar 1972. It appropriated funds for state governments at an initial annual rate of $1.8-billion (for the first six-month period ending June 30, 1972) and increased that rate by $150-million for the following year and $300-million for each succeeding year for the rest of the five-year period.

(Continued on p. 99)

Evolution in Aid: Categorical Grants to Revenue Sharing

The enactment of general revenue sharing by Congress in 1972 marked a significant transformation in the way federal money was disbursed to states, cities and counties.

Since the 1930s when the federal government moved in a major way to aid state and local governments, money had moved in relatively small amounts for specific purposes with requirements for grant applications, regulations and reports. Revenue sharing, while not supplanting the earlier grant approach, provided large amounts of additional federal dollars for states and local governments for a wide range of activities with few guidelines and no application and approval process. The Treasury Department simply mailed checks periodically to states and cities in an amount determined by formula.

Background

While the general concept of revenue-sharing had been offered as early as 1958, it was first studied in detail in 1964 when a presidential task force was appointed to study the idea. While it was reported in late 1964 that President Johnson was close to urging its enactment, his support for the plan never came. *(Congress and the Nation Vol. II, p. 164)*

Congressional Republicans during the Johnson years supported plans to share tax revenues with the states and local governments, but they were never successful. They did have some sucess in adapting the approach to many of the narrow-purpose grant-in-aid bills considered by Congress in the 1960's, by urging some consolidation of many programs for health, education, law enforcement and manpower into larger package of funds. By giving local governments and sponsoring agencies more leeway in how they spent federal dollars, many Republicans saw a way to reduce the size and proliferation of federal programs.

In 1971, President Nixon proposed a $25-billion, five-year program of general revenue sharing which formed the basis for the program as enacted and a plan to consolidate 105 existing grant programs into six "special revenue sharing" programs for education, community development, transportation, rural development, law enforcement and manpower training. While the 92nd Congress approved the new program to share federal revenues, it either did not consider or it rejected each of the six Nixon plans to rearrange and regroup existing grant programs.

Glossary of Terms

By late 1972, there were 1,054 federal domestic assistance programs conducted by 60 federal agencies, offering grants and loans to states, local governments, colleges, non-profit groups and individuals. As the programs differed in approach and funding, whole sets of terms emerged to distinguish the various kinds of federal aid.

Of the several hundred federal aid programs for states and local governments, most are targeted for specifically designated activities. These programs are called **Categorical Grant** programs. Hospital construction, school aid for disadvantaged children and mass transit construction funds are all categorical aid. Categorical aid programs generally require applications and approvals to obtain funds from the federal agency running the programs.

Categorical grants are often either **Formula Grants**—funds disbursed according to a formula established by law or agency regulation or **Discretionary Grants**—money allocated for projects and activities the program administrator, at his discretion, chooses to support. Aid to disadvantaged children was disbursed, for example, according to a formula providing funds for all school districts with certain concentrations of such children. Model Cities grants by contrast, are disbursed among some but not all of those cities that apply for them, resulting in intense competition for the grants.

Block Grants, which Congress enacted in a few cases, are intended to give recipient states and local governments wider latitude as to how it uses grant funds within a broad area. For example, law enforcement block grants could be used for police equipment, prison reform or any other recognized law enforcement activity. State governments first had to submit a plan on how they intended to use the funds to the Justice Department's Law Enforcement Assistance Administration. Local governments then applied to the states for part of that money.

Revenue Sharing, or **General Revenue Sharing** as it came to be known in order to distinguish it from the **Special Revenue Sharing** programs, would in theory and as first proposed by President Nixon, guarantee a fixed amount of federal revenues which would be shared with states and local government as supplements to their own revenues. to use as they saw fit. It would give states and cities a claim to a proportion of revenues, rather than a share of funds expended under a federal aid program.

As enacted by Congress, revenue sharing created a general aid program for states with no restrictions at all as to the purposes for which the funds would be spent. For cities it limited expenditures to public safety, capital expenditures, health, transportation, libraries, social services and other "priority expenditures," while excluding education and welfare. Congress did not set aside any proportion of federal revenues for the states, but authorized and appropriated $30.2-billion for a five-year program.

Special Revenue Sharing is similar to the block grant in that it would fund a great number of activities within a specific area such as transportation or education. Under the special revenue sharing approach, however, there would be no federal approval of state and local plans and no other provisions such as requiring states to match certain federal funds or to distribute the money according to a certain formula.

None of President Nixon's six special revenue sharing proposals were enacted in the 92nd Congress, and several were reintroduced in the 93rd Congress.

(Continued from p. 97)

By appropriating the funds—rather than authorizing the funds, the bill obviated the need for an annual appropriation measure for each fiscal year. House Appropriations Committee Chairman George Mahon (D Texas) objected vigorously to the revenue sharing concept. *(Box p. 101)*

Since the government operates on a fiscal year, the committee bill appropriated half of the initial allocation for the period Jan. 1 to June 30, 1972, the remainder of fiscal year 1972. It appropriated funds for the four succeeding fiscal years and a final half-year allocation. The appropriations were (in billions of dollars):

Year	State	Local	Total
FY 1972 *(half-year)*	.9	1.75	2.65
FY 1973	1.95	3.5	5.45
FY 1974	2.25	3.5	5.75
FY 1975	2.55	3.5	6.05
FY 1976	2.85	3.5	6.35
FY 1977 *(half-year)*	1.575	1.75	3.325
TOTALS	12.075	17.5	29.575

The appropriation for the final half-year was at an annual rate of $6.65-billion.

Committee Views. The committee justified the larger proportion of funds to local governments as follows:

"In considering the financial problems of local governments, your committee came to the conclusion that many localities face most severe financial crises. In part, this stems from the increasing demand for public services resulting from the substantial increase in urbanization occurring in recent years.

"Closely related to this is the problem arising from the limited jurisdictions of many local governments: they often are called upon to provide many services for persons who do not live in their taxing jurisdictions. At the same time, those within their taxing jurisdictions often are poor and unable to pay for their share of the services demanded. This financial problem for local governments has been significantly worsened by the twin problems of rising costs resulting from inflation and the lower than normal increase in revenues because of the stagnant condition of the economy."

The committee noted that state and local expenditures rose from $33.7-billion in fiscal year 1955 to $131.3-billion in fiscal 1970. In the period 1946-70 (fiscal years), state and local revenues, excluding federal aid, rose at an average rate of almost 10 per cent per year.

The committee found that many states did not make effective use of their revenue sources, either by not using certain taxes (individual and corporate income taxes and general sales taxes) or by keeping rates too low.

The heavy reliance of state and local governments on property and sales taxes, the committee said, made it harder for them to increase their revenues because those taxes did not respond rapidly to increases in income.

In aggregate, the committee said, local governments accounted for about two-thirds of total state-local expenditures and states the remaining one-third. This was the approximate division of revenue sharing incorporated in the bill.

Federal Finances. The committee noted a federal deficit of almost $39-billion was forecast for fiscal year

Revenue Sharing in 1837

During the 1830s Treasury accounts showed a series of exceptionally large surpluses, due chiefly to sales of public lands in connection with a boom in land speculation. After the Revolutionary War the federal government came into possession of an enormous domain through the cession of claims to western lands by eastern states. Between 1810 and 1830 the annual proceeds from the sale of these lands ranged between $1-million and $2-million, but beginning in 1830 there was a considerable increase until in 1834 the receipts were nearly $5-million. In 1835 they were $14,757,600 and in 1836, $24,877,179. In the latter year revenue from this source exceeded revenue from customs for the first and last time in the history of the country.

By 1835 virtually the entire public debt had been paid off through the purchase of government securities in the open market at a premium, and the problem of what to do with the Treasury surpluses thereafter became acute. Thomas Jefferson had foreseen that a policy of economy, coupled with national prosperity, might lead to an overflowing Treasury. In his second inaugural address he advocated a constitutional amendment clearly authorizing the use of government funds for internal improvements, arts, manufactures and education. It was later proposed that a part of the recurring surpluses be distributed among the states to aid in education and internal improvements.

Henry Clay offered a bill in 1835 to distribute 90 per cent of the proceeds of land sales to the states. Other proposals called for reductions in customs duties to cut the government's revenues, but this course was strongly opposed by protectionists. Finally, on June 23, 1836, Congress approved a bill which provided that all money in the Treasury on January 1, 1837, reserving the sum of $5-million, should be "deposited" with the states in proportion to their representation in the House and Senate.

The amount available for distribution on Jan. 1, 1837, was about $37-million. Of this sum more than $28-million was paid out in three quarterly installments. By May 1837, however, speculation in Western lands had collapsed and a bank panic plunged the country into deep depression. A dozen years of surpluses came to an end with a large deficit, and the fourth installment was never paid to the states.

1972 and a deficit of $25.5-billion in fiscal 1973. The cost of revenue sharing was included in calculating the deficits.

To postpone revenue sharing in order to cut the deficit, the report said, would be to assign a lower priority to state and local financial problems than to other needs.

Restrictions on Use of Funds. The bill tied more "strings" to the revenues shared with local governments than did the administration's proposal. Funds allocated to local governments were limited in use to "generally recognized...national high-priority objectives," which the committee defined as operational and maintenance expenses for public safety, environmental protection and public transportation.

The committee justified exclusion of such major local expenses as education and welfare on various grounds. It noted the great diversity of state and local responsibilities in those areas. It also noted that the House had passed a welfare reform bill (HR 1), which, among other purposes, was designed to provide greater federal welfare assistance, and that the federal government operated a number of major programs of aid for education. *(Welfare chapter)*

The bill required states to maintain at least the level of aid to their local governments prevailing before revenue sharing. It prohibited use of revenue-sharing funds for matching federal funds for other purposes.

Federal Tax Collection. The bill required that the Internal Revenue Service at states' requests administer and collect state income taxes in the process of its collection of federal tax returns, when certain circumstances were met.

The purpose of combining the state and federal tax collection effort was to enable states to establish and use a state income tax with minimum administrative effort, to reduce duplication of effort, to simplify taxpayer recordkeeping, to establish uniform treatment for individual taxpayers at both the state and local levels, and to free state courts from individual tax controversies.

Dissenting Views. Seven committee members, after voting against reporting the bill, filed dissenting views.

The dissenters first objected to the fact that states were to be unrestricted in their use of funds while local governments were restricted to uses given high priority by the committee majority. "The 'priorities' were plucked out of thin air," they said, "for the sole purpose of distinguishing the committee bill from the administration's 'no-strings-attached' revenue sharing proposal which had been consistently denounced by some members of the committee."

The dissent incorporated a long list of provisions and effects which the seven found objectionable, including:

• Divorce of tax-raising responsibility from spending authority.

• Restructuring of federal-state-local relationships.

• Lack of surplus revenues to share.

• Failure of the bill to deal with the existing weaknesses of state and local government.

• Lack of any rationale for the amounts of money or relationship of the amounts to state or local needs.

• Lack of a rationale for the various formulas.

• Failure of the bill to take account of federal aid programs or state aids to local governments.

• Lack of effective accountability requirements.

House Floor Action

The House June 22, by a **key 275-122 roll-call vote,** passed HR 14370 without amendment.

Passage of the bill was virtually assured June 21, the first of two days of debate on HR 14370, when proponents of the revenue-sharing plan prevailed in a key procedural vote. By a roll-call vote of 223-185, the House called for the previous question (closing off debate and precluding the opportunity of offering amendments) on a controversial closed rule (H Res 996) under which the bill was taken up.

Republicans supported the rule by 113-57; Democrats opposed it, 110-128 (northern Democrats, 89-69, southern Democrats, 21-59). The rule then was approved by voice vote.

The closed rule provided for eight hours of debate on HR 14370 but prohibited floor amendments and waived points of order against the bill. The rule permitted amendments offered by the Ways and Means Committee, which reported the bill April 26, but the committee offered none.

Thus the rule limited action on the House floor to the alternatives of passing the bill, killing it or returning it to the Ways and Means Committee. With governors, mayors and their organizations and other state and local officials lobbying vigorously for the bill with strong support from taxpayers, the bill commanded an impressive majority when it came to a vote.

Opponents had little hope of defeating the new aid program for hard-pressed state and local governments on a direct vote, but they hoped to make changes in the bill by raising a point of order against it or by amending it if they could defeat the rule. Ways and Means Committee revenue bills customarily were granted closed rules on grounds that they were too complicated to amend on the floor and that open rules would open the entire Internal Revenue Code to amendment. The privilege had been granted to other Ways and Means non-revenue-raising legislation on grounds of complexity; thus welfare reform (HR 1) was passed by the House under a modified closed rule permitting only one amendment.

Mills, Mahon Conflict. The bill pitted two leaders of the House, Chairman Wilbur D. Mills (D Ark.) of Ways and Means and Chairman George Mahon (D Texas) of the Appropriations Committee. *(Box p. 101)* Mills, originally a vociferous critic of revenue sharing, changed his mind in 1971 and drafted the bill on which his committee's bill was based. Mahon fought the bill on two grounds: that it spent money the government did not have (the latest official estimate of the federal deficit for fiscal year 1972 was $26-billion and for fiscal 1973, $27-billion), and that it appropriated funds in a legislative bill.

The bill established the revenue-sharing program and also appropriated the necessary funds, though it was never referred to Mahon's committee. (House rules prohibit appropriations in a legislative bill, hence the waiver of points of order in the rule.) Customarily a program is established and funds authorized in one bill handled by the committee responsible for the particular area of activity; funds are appropriated in a separate bill handled by the Appropriations Committee.

Mahon hoped to delete the bill's provisions appropriating funds and to require funding of the program with annual appropriations as in the case of most other aid programs. But proponents objected to subjecting revenue sharing to the annual appropriations process.

Had the bill been opened to amendment, attempts were contemplated to change the complicated formula for distribution of the funds, to add tax reform to the bill and to make other changes in tax statutes. As with other legislation in similar circumstances, Mills announced before the bill was taken up that he was under instructions from his committee to withdraw the bill from floor consideration if it was opened to amendment. The Rules Committee on May 23 had voted 8-7 to approve the closed rule.

Following committee adoption of the rule, floor action was postponed twice while the bill's proponents sought to build up the lobbying muscle necessary to push the measure through.

Senate Committee Action

The Senate Finance Committee held hearings June 29, July 26 and July 27 on HR 14370 and on Aug. 16 reported it amended to the Senate floor (S Rept 92-1050).

The revenue-sharing bill which was passed by the House June 22 was substantially revised by the Senate committee.

The committee bill provided the same total amount for revenue sharing as the House bill but, in addition, authorized supplementary social service grants at a level of $1-billion per calendar years 1973-1976. It reduced the revenue shares for more urbanized states but increased shares for urbanized areas as well as less urban states.

The bill provided trust fund financing for revenue sharing to avoid the congressional appropriations process. It eliminated the restrictions placed on local government use of funds provided by the Houe bill.

Appropriations Dispute. The Senate bill initially was ordered reported Aug. 9 as a thoroughly amended version of the House bill. However, when the Senate Appropriations Committee tried to assert jurisdiction over the bill, the Finance Committee reconsidered its action Aug. 11. (The appropriations panel had voted Aug. 10 to demand an opportunity to consider the bill before it went to the floor.) To keep the program out of the normal appropriations process, within which it could have been subject to annual appropriations, the Finance Committee revised the bill's financing provisions to provide a "permanent" appropriation of 7 per cent of personal income tax receipts to a special revenue-sharing trust fund for the five-year life of the legislation. From the trust fund the secretary of the treasury was directed to pay out to the state and local governments the amounts to which they were entitled under the aid formulas adopted by the committees. The trust fund was expected to provide substantially more than the amounts mandated by the bill, which began retroactively at an annual level of $5.3-billion for the latter half of fiscal 1973 (Jan. 1 to June 30, 1972).

The Treasury was authorized to pay the supplementary social service grants out of sums remaining from revenue sharing in the trust fund. Any remaining amounts were to be added to the general funds of the Treasury.

The committee report noted that other trust-funded programs, such as Social Security, were financed under permanent appropriations and did not require annual or periodic action by the appropriations bodies of the two houses. If the Appropriations Committee was successful in asserting jurisdiction, it could require annual appropriations which would be subject to pressures both from recipients and from conflicting claims of other federal programs.

The decision to report the bill Aug. 16 came after unsuccessful efforts to reach an accommodation with the Appropriations Committee. The action reflected the confidence of Chairman Russell B. Long (D La.) of the Finance Committee that, as amended, the bill had sufficient support to block any effort by the Appropriations Committee on the floor to take control of it.

Mahon Comments

By far the most vigorous House opponent of the revenue-sharing bill was House Appropriations Committee Chairman George Mahon (D Texas) who charged the measure would actually appropriate the funds without further congressional review, and thus subvert the legislative-appropriations process.

On June 7, Mahon printed his objections in the *Congressional Record*:

"Next week there is also scheduled to be before the House a $30-billion appropriation bill out of the Ways and Means Committee.

"Mr. Speaker, this Ways and Means Committee bill does not raise one penny of revenue. It is an authorization bill and it is an appropriation bill for 5 years. It bypasses the established authorization process involving a number of major legislative committees, and it bypasses the established appropriations process which we have known for the last 52 years.

"Not in the history of Congress that I can find has an appropriation bill come to the floor under a closed rule, which is now proposed for this Ways and Means Committee bill. (The House Rules Committee May 23 approved a closed rule, allowing eight hours of general debate but prohibiting amendments from the floor. The House must approve the rule before the bill itself can be considered.)

"I say it is indefensible that the appropriation bill of $30-billion should come before the House next week under a closed rule. Members should have the right to make points of order and offer amendments. I propose to do what I can to open up the rule so the House can work its will on that appropriation bill, just as it does on other appropriation bills."

Mahon's opposition resulted in two postponements of floor consideration of the bill—a ploy by the measure's proponents to gain more time in which to mobilize a lobby campaign of state and local officials and other groups in behalf of HR 14370. In effect, Mahon lost the battle June 21 when the House, by a 223-185 roll-call vote, agreed to a procedural motion that paved the way for consideration of the revenue sharing bill under a procedure barring floor amendments.

Many observers regarded the Appropriations Committee's effort as an initial assertion of authority by John L. McClellan (D Ark.), who succeeded to the committee chairmanship on the death of Allen J. Ellender (D La.) July 27. The move scuttled the chance for Senate passage before the Aug. 18 recess for the Republican national convention. A move similar to McClellan's by Mahon failed when the bill was considered in the House. *(Above)*

Although amounts allocated to individual states and to their local governments differed substantially from the House bill's distribution, the Senate committee bill provided nearly identical total amounts for the states and local governments, starting at an annual level of $5.3-billion. By fiscal years, the amounts provided were, in billions of dollars:

Fiscal Year	Revenue Sharing	Supplementary Grants	Total	State	Local
		(in billions)			
1972	$2.650*	$0.000	$ 2.650	$ .870	$ 1.78
1973	5.450	.500*	5.950	1.980	3.97
1974	5.750	1.000	6.750	2.250	4.50
1975	6.050	1.000	7.050	2.350	4.70
1976	6.350	1.000	7.350	2.450	4.90
1977	3.325*	.500*	3.825	1.275	2.55
TOTALS	$29.575	$ 4.000	$33.575	$11.175	$22.4

* Indicates half-year funding

The committee voted 12-4 to report the bill. The dissenters were Fred R. Harris (D Okla.), Harry F. Byrd Jr. (Ind. Va.), Carl T. Curtis (R Neb.) and Len B. Jordan (R Idaho).

Senate Floor Action

The Senate Sept. 12 by a **key 64-20 roll-call vote** passed HR 14370 establishing a five-year program to share $29,583,560,000 in federal revenues with state and local governments and $4-billion over four years for social services.

During floor action on HR 14370, the Senate upheld the major revisions in the House-passed bill recommended by the Senate Finance Committee. The Senate version increased the amounts provided the smaller states, at the expense of the more populous urban states.

As passed, HR 14370 reflected the greater representation in the Senate of states with smaller populations and fewer cities. The votes against passage of HR 14370 were cast by fiscal conservatives opposed to the extent of the appropriations in the bill and by large-state senators opposed to the reduced shares it gave their states.

In an effort to offset reductions in shared revenues to urban states, the Senate added $1-billion for each of 1973-76, not provided by the House, for a separate program of grants for social services based on each state's urban population. At the same time, however, the Senate limited total federal spending on such programs to $1.6-billion: $1-billion for programs funded by the bill and $600-million for child-care and family-planning services to be funded under existing matching grant programs.

In debate on the bill, Long said the House formula for distributions to local governments "would distribute relatively large amounts of aid to well-to-do suburbs, reducing the amounts available for distribution to the cities and low-income rural areas."

"The committee bill, by emphasizing both low-income levels and tax effort, channels more of the revenue-sharing funds both to the cities and to the poorer rural areas," Long added.

Conceding that the Senate committee had reduced revenue-sharing allocations to the most populous states, Long argued that the committee's bill provided offsetting aid to urban states through the $1-billion supplemental grant program for social services.

"The committee bill is more effective than the House bill in putting the money where the needs are," Long contended. The committee version's single formula for distributing funds to states and to political divisions within states "has the advantage of providing consistent treatment in allocating funds to state and local governments," he added.

The dispute between the Finance Committee and the Appropriations Committee over control of revenue sharing arose again on the Senate floor in an amendment by McClellan.

McClellan's amendment, an attempt to assert Appropriations Committee jurisdiction over revenue-sharing funds, would have required the committee's approval of amounts distributed to the states during fiscal years 1974-76. The Finance Committee bill provided a permanent annual appropriation of 7 per cent of personal income tax revenue to a special revenue-sharing trust fund and authorized the secretary of the treasury to distribute the money in fiscal 1972-76 according to amounts authorized by the bill.

By a **key 34-49 roll-call vote**, the Senate rejected McClellan's amendment eliminating from the committee version authority to appropriate revenue-sharing funds for the last three years (fiscal 1974-76) covered under the bill.

Of 34 votes for McClellan's amendment, 21 were cast by members of the Appropriations Committee.

Conference Report

House and Senate conferees Sept. 25 filed a conference report on the bill (HR 14370—S Rept 92-1229), and the House on Oct. 12 and the Senate on Oct. 13 agreed to the conference agreement, clearing the bill for the President.

In an unusual compromise, the conference agreement allowed each state the larger of the revenue-sharing allocations its state and local governments would receive under conflicting House- and Senate-approved distribution formulas.

The House formula, based on five factors, provided larger amounts to more populous, urbanized states. The Senate formula, based on three factors, favored less populous, rural states.

While allowing a choice between two methods of determining how much federal revenue would go to all governments within a state, the conferees adopted the Senate bill's provisions for determining how the state total would be allocated among the state government and various local government units.

(Continued on p. 104)

Top Ten City Recipients

The following ten cities received the most dollars under general revenue sharing for the first half of calendar 1972 under PL 92-512.

New York, N.Y.	$100,847,538
Chicago, Ill.	31,185,549
Philadelphia, Pa.	21,981,080
Detroit, Mich.	18,302,265
Los Angeles, Calif.	15,781,264
Washington, D.C.	11,834,502
Baltimore, Md.	11,831,968
Boston, Mass.	8,904,129
San Francisco, Calif.	8,833,517
New Orleans, La.	8,448,471

State, Local Government Funds For Calendar 1972

Following are the amounts of revenue-sharing funds distributed to each state for calendar 1972 as announced by the Treasury Department Dec. 8, 1972. Some governments received substantially more or less than the amounts that were indicated by estimates provided with the conference report on the revenue-sharing bill (HR 14370—PL 92-512) approved by Congress Oct. 13. The conference figures were based on 1967 data, which were later updated in preparing the first installments.

State	State Governments (33.3%)	Local Governments (66.7%)	Total	Change From Conference Figure
Alabama	$29,892,174	$59,702,596	$89,594,770	—22.0%
Alaska	2,186,606	3,760,436	5,947,042	+ 4.7
Arizona	16,574,260	31,278,524	47,852,784	+ 0.1
Arkansas	19,420,754	34,485,030	53,905,784	— 0.8
California	184,887,118	369,425,992	554,313,110	+ 0.7
Colorado	17,991,384	35,888,394	53,879,778	— 0.2
Connecticut	22,183,052	44,359,974	66,543,026	+ 1.6
Delaware	6,294,918	9,583,860	15,878,778	+ 1.7
District of Columbia		23,669,004	23,669,004	+ 1.1
Florida	48,413,376	96,791,718	145,205,094	+ 0.5
Georgia	36,184,678	72,280,724	108,465,402	— 0.3
Hawaii	7,821,572	15,643,142	23,464,714	— 0.3
Idaho	7,024,126	13,927,316	20,951,442	+ 7.2
Illinois	90,422,816	179,941,610	270,364,426	— 0.3
Indiana	37,550,956	74,787,292	112,338,248	+ 3.1
Iowa	24,915,572	49,791,114	74,706,686	— 2.0
Kansas	17,307,542	34,282,792	51,590,334	— 0.8
Kentucky	34,374,286	51,637,088	86,011,374	— 0.4
Louisiana	40,820,042	80,426,774	121,246,816	+ 7.8
Maine	10,245,108	20,328,990	30,574,098	— 0.3
Maryland	35,343,536	70,668,832	106,012,368	+ 0.1
Massachusetts	54,487,270	108,948,210	163,435,480	+ 1.3
Michigan	74,066,310	147,725,244	221,791,554	+ 1.1
Minnesota	35,121,224	69,671,432	104,792,656	+ 2.4
Mississippi	29,493,530	58,025,804	87,519,334	— 2.5
Missouri	32,433,860	64,454,446	96,888,306	— 0.8
Montana	6,763,820	12,931,220	19,695,040	— 0.4
Nebraska	12,827,234	25,484,672	38,311,906	— 9.3
Nevada	3,799,940	7,536,048	11,335,988	+ 3.4
New Hampshire	5,474,734	10,860,736	16,335,470	+ 9.0
New Jersey	54,992,636	109,960,094	164,961,530	+ 1.9
New Mexico	11,361,804	19,675,978	31,037,782	— 0.8
New York	194,354,250	388,208,452	582,562,702	— 0.4
North Carolina	44,884,258	89,574,598	134,458,856	+ 0.4
North Dakota	7,318,376	14,093,744	21,412,120	+ 12.4
Ohio	70,600,794	140,746,498	211,347,292	+ 3.3
Oklahoma	19,447,124	38,757,866	58,204,990	— 0.8
Oregon	17,495,564	34,894,766	52,390,330	— 5.7
Pennsylvania	91,725,062	182,719,272	274,444,334	+ 1.5
Rhode Island	7,973,318	15,946,674	23,919,992	+ 2.5
South Carolina	24,330,682	47,008,088	71,338,770	—11.5
South Dakota	7,962,912	15,337,234	23,300,146	— 3.9
Tennessee	32,621,442	65,211,590	97,833,032	+ 0.5
Texas	81,916,606	163,445,306	245,361,912	+ 1.4
Utah	10,095,346	19,985,760	30,081,106	— 2.6
Vermont	4,857,782	9,518,666	14,376,448	— 0.9
Virginia	35,092,142	70,165,112	105,257,254	+ 1.0
Washington	25,729,412	51,167,182	76,896,594	— 7.3
West Virginia	23,007,114	28,372,000	51,379,114	— 0.7
Wisconsin	43,975,094	87,497,614	131,472,708	— 0.5
Wyoming	3,289,728	6,470,792	9,760,520	+ 2.8
TOTALS	$1,757,353,244	$3,477,065,100	$5,234,418,380	

Accepting a principle followed by the House bill, the conference committee agreed to a modified provision placing restrictions on how local governments could use federally shared revenues.

The conferees also agreed to drop a Senate provision providing $4-billion over four years for supplementary social services grants and to propose a substitute limiting existing federal matching grants for state and local social service programs to $2.5-billion a year for specified purposes.

Under the conference agreement, the federal government would distribute $5,303,900,000 to state and local governments in 1972. The effective date of revenue sharing was retroactive to Jan. 1.

In subsequent years, the amount of federal revenues shared with other governments would rise by $150-million a year, reaching $6,350,000,000 for the last full fiscal year (1976) of the program. On a fiscal year basis, the conference agreement provided for sharing federal revenues in the last half of fiscal 1972, fiscal 1973-76 and the first half of fiscal 1977. On a calendar year basis, the program would run from Jan. 1, 1972, to Dec. 31, 1976.

PROVISIONS. As signed by the President on Oct. 20, HR 14370 (PL 92-512):

• Created a State and Local Government Fiscal Assistance Trust Fund, to remain available without fiscal year limitation.

• Appropriated $30,212,500,000 to the trust fund from federal income tax revenues in the following amounts:

1) $2,390,000 for Jan. 1-June 30, 1972
2) $2,390,000 for July 1-Dec. 31, 1972.
3) $2,390,000 for Jan. 1-June 30, 1973.
4) $4,780,000 for fiscal 1974.
5) $4,780,000 for fiscal 1975.
6) $4,780,000 for fiscal 1976.
7) $2,390,000 for July 1-Dec. 31, 1976.

• Appropriated to the trust fund $23,900,000 from income tax collections for adjustments in allocations to non-contiguous states (Alaska and Hawaii) in the following amounts:

1) $2,650,000,000 for the period Jan. 1-June 30, 1972.
2) $2,650,000,000 for July 1—Dec. 31, 1972.
3) $2,987,500,000 for Jan. 1-June 30, 1973.
4) $6,050,000,000 for fiscal 1974.
5) $6,200,000,000 for fiscal 1975.
6) $6,350,000,000 for fiscal 1976.
7) $3,325,000,000 for the period July 1-Dec. 31, 1976.

• Allocated to each state for each period the greater of two amounts computed by the following methods:

1) A three-factor formula allocating to each state an amount in the same ratio to $5.3-billion (the initial annual rate) as the figure produced by the state's population multiplied by its state and local government tax effort multiplied by its relative income was to the figure produced by the same factors for the nation as a whole.

2) A five-factor formula allocating (at an initial annual level of $5.3-billion) $3.5-billion among the states according to population (one-third), urbanized population (one-third) and population weighted by per capita income (one-third) and the remaining $1.8-billion according to individual income tax collections by state governments (one-half) and the general tax effort of state and local governments (one-half).

• Allocated one-third of each state's entitlement to the state government and the remaining two-thirds to local governments within the state. The local governments' two-thirds would be divided as follows:

1) Allocated to each county within a state an amount computed on the basis of population, tax effort and relative income.

2) Allocated to each county government an amount determined by the ratio of its tax collections to total tax collections by all governments in the county.

3) Allocated among all township governments within a county a total amount determined by their combined share of tax collections, with each township's amount determined by population, tax effort and relative income.

4) Allocated the remainder of the county's share among municipal governments according to population, tax effort and relative income.

5) Allocated part of a county area's allotment to the governing bodies of local Indian tribes or Alaskan native villages on the basis of population.

• Permitted states to legislate optional formulas for distributing local government funds by population and tax effort or by population and relative income, or both.

• Increased revenue-sharing entitlements for Alaska and Hawaii by the same percentage as cost-of-living adjustments given federal employees in those non-contiguous states.

• Required that a state government's revenue-sharing entitlement be reduced if it reduced transfers of state funds to local governments. (The penalty could be reduced or offset if the state had assumed responsibility for expenditures previously made by local governments or had conferred new taxing authority on local governments to provide the funds.)

• Required each government receiving revenue-sharing funds to submit to the secretary of the treasury and publish in local newspapers reports on the planned and actual uses of shared revenues.

• Prohibited discrimination by race, color, national origin or sex in any activity or program funded in whole or in part with revenue-sharing money.

• Required local governments to use revenue-sharing funds only for "priority expenditures": capital expenditures authorized by law or maintenance and operating expenditures on public safety (including law enforcement, fire protection and building code enforcement), environmental protection (including sewage disposal, sanitation and pollution abatement), public transportation (including transit systems and streets and roads), health, recreation, libraries, social services for the poor and aged, and financial administration.

• Provided for collection by the federal government's Internal Revenue Service of state income taxes.

• Placed a $2.5-billion ceiling on annual, federal 75-per cent matching grants to state and local governments for social services, with each state limited to the same percentage of $2.5-billion as the percentage of its population to total U.S. population.

• Required that not more than 10 per cent of each State's federal matching grants be used for assistance to persons not receiving welfare. Programs for child care, family planning, the mentally retarded, drug addicts and alcoholics and foster homes for children would be exempted from the 10 per cent limit.

Economic Stabilization Policy

By far the most significant economic development of Nixon's first term was the President's adoption of wage and price controls as a last-ditch measure to curb inflation. With dramatic suddenness, the President on Aug. 15, 1971, ordered the most comprehensive system of government economic controls ever imposed during a peacetime period. Before the heart of the program—a 90-day freeze on wages, prices, salaries and rents—could expire, the President announced Phase Two, a long-range system of controls designed to keep inflation under control while his program of fiscal stimulus (tax cuts and deficit spending) worked to move the country out of recession.

Like his conversion to expansionary fiscal strategy, the President's shift to government intervention in the market place (known as an "incomes policy"), was slow in coming. Since late 1969 the President's counselor (later chairman of the Federal Reserve Board), Arthur F. Burns, had pressured Nixon for an incomes policy. But Burns made little headway until late 1970, when Nixon made limited use of "jawboning," that is, urging industries to avoid inflationary price increases and wage settlements. (The term was coined during the Johnson administration when the White House used wage and price guideposts and other voluntary measures to persuade industries to curb inflation.) In early 1971, Nixon followed up by imposing a stabilization program on the construction industry, where wage and price increases had been particularly inflationary. Still, the nation was taken by surprise by the sweep of Nixon's Aug. 15 program.

Approval of Nixon's incomes policy came after torrid in-fighting in the President's cabinet and among the inner circle of his economic advisers. Pitted against controls were Paul W. McCracken, chairman of the Council of Economic Advisers, and George P. Shultz, director of the Office of Management and Budget (OMB). In favor were Burns, who became chairman of the independent Federal Reserve Board in Febuary 1970, and Treasury Secretary John Connally, a powerfully persuasive man who had been designated (June 29) as the administration's chief economic spokesman. It was reported that what finally tipped the balance was advice by Connally that a tough program of controls could be a political plus instead of a liability.

Congressional Pressure. From the outset of the Nixon administration, leading Democrats in Congress, particularly those on its Joint Economic Committee, urged adoption of an incomes policy to break the back of inflation. Over the President's opposition, Congress in 1969 passed legislation authorizing the President to impose controls on consumer credit. The next year, over even stronger White House opposition, Congress approved a bill authorizing the President to place a freeze on wages, prices, rents and salaries. (It was this authority that the President used for his 1971 controls on the construction industry and, subsequently, for Phases One and Two.) The President acquiesced in three more extensions of the authority in 1970 and early 1971, and requested another extension himself before 1971 was over. The last of the three extensions, approved in December 1971, continued the authority for controls through April 30, 1973.

Scope of Program. In addition to its anti-inflationary features, the President's new economic policy contained provisions aimed at stimulating the economy to faster growth and at righting the adverse balance of international payments which was draining away billions of dollars to foreign countries. Highlights of the Aug. 15 program included cuts in federal spending, tax reductions for individuals and businesses, freeing the dollar from its traditional $35-per-ounce gold price, and imposition of a 10 per cent surtax on imports. (The import tax was dropped in December 1971 following adoption of a new international monetary agreement.) *(International monetary developments, p. 119)*

To implement Phase Two, the President named three quasi-governmental review boards, a Pay Board and Price Commission, supervised by a Cost of Living Council, to rule on wage and price decisions. By early 1972, the program had incurred the wrath of organized labor which thought that it discriminated in favor of business interests. *(Pay Board and Price Commission, p. 112, 113)*

By and large, however, the program was well received by the general public. In May 1972, the Harris Survey reported that 48 per cent of persons questioned thought Nixon was doing a good job on economic matters, while 34 per cent gave him a negative rating. This contrasted with figures of 32 and 40 per cent, respectively, in a similar Harris poll taken on the same question the previous May, prior to the imposition of the Phase I program. *(January 1973 Phase III, announcement p. 117)*

Performance. After its first year of operation, indications were that Nixon's program had worked well to curb inflation. From August 1971 to August 1972, the consumer price index increased by 2.7 per cent, compared with 3.8 per cent for the first eight months of 1971, 5.5 per cent for 1970 and 6.1 per cent for 1969.

By late 1972, the Cost of Living Council director, Donald Rumsfeld, conceded that inflation might have slowed anyway as a natural reaction to two years of excess capacity in the economy. But without the controls, he argued, the President would not have been able to apply his program of fiscal stimulus to the lagging economy without risking a new wave of inflation.

Phase Three. President Nixon Jan. 11, 1973, provided another surprise in the war against inflation by abruptly ending the Phase Two system of controls. He replaced them with Phase Three, a system of voluntary guidelines backed by the threat that the government would intervene to roll back wage and price increases it considered inflationary. Mandatory controls were left in effect for only three industries—processed foods, health costs and construction.

The President's action was hailed by labor leaders as "a step in the right direction," but a number of congressmen, economists and editorials insisted that controls had been taken off too soon, and that inflation would surge forward. The administration responded that Phase Three was being misinterpreted and emphasized that the program "kept a club in the closet."

Chronology

Of Action

On Economic Stabilization

1969

Congress laid the first, modest step in its groundwork for an incomes policy at the close of the 1969 session when it approved legislation (S 2577—PL 91-151) empowering the President to place controls on consumer credit, or, as an alternative, to reinstate a system of Korean War-era controls in which he could urge the credit industry to work out the restraints voluntarily. Both provisions were opposed by the administration and were not used in 1969 or 1970. In 1971, however, as part of his new economic policy, Nixon did urge banks not to raise interest rates. But he did not formally invoke a voluntary controls program.

Impetus for the bill came from the failure of Nixon's policy of fiscal restraint to make inroads in the pace of inflation during the President's first 10 months in office. Democrats saw the credit controls as a mild step which, if taken quickly, might stave off the need for wage, price and rent controls at a later date. Republicans opposed the controls as an affront to Nixon's economic program.

S 2577 cleared the Senate Nov. 13 on a 69-14 roll-call vote after a GOP-sponsored amendment to delete the voluntary controls section was rejected by a party line vote of 30-49 (R: 30-5; D: 0-44). House passage came Dec. 17 by a 260-136 roll call (R: 47-128; D 213-8). In a surprise development, conferees accepted both the Senate's voluntary controls provision and a House provision authorizing the President to impose the mandatory credit restrictions. The House had dropped the voluntary controls in favor of the stiffer restriction.

As enacted, the bill in its major provisions authorized the President to instruct the Federal Reserve Board (FRB) to regulate the terms, amounts and interest rates of all forms of credit when he deemed it necessary to combat inflation; permitted the establishment of the voluntary controls by repealing a prohibition in the Defense Production Act against reactivating the voluntary restraints, and restoring the President's authority to do so; raised maximum insurance protection on deposits in federally chartered banks and savings and loan institutions from $15,000 to $20,000; extended through March 22, 1971, the existing authority for federal regulatory agencies to set different limits on the interest rates that banks and other financial institutions could pay on different types and amounts of fixed maturity (time) deposits *(box p. 107)*; and increased the supply of home mortgage money by increasing the Federal Home Loan Bank Board's authority to borrow from the Treasury by $3-billion, from $1-billion to $4-billion. (The Home Loan Bank Board was the source of about half the home loan funds disbursed by savings and loan institutions, which made most home loans.) Despite his opposition to the credit controls, President Nixon signed the bill Dec. 23 because of its other banking provisions.

1970

President Nixon's gradual shift from a hands-off approach to private wage and price decisions to one of strong government intervention in those decisions took shape during 1970. Throughout the year, pressure for an incomes policy came from Democrats in Congress and, perhaps more importantly, from the President's longtime friend and former adviser, Arthur F. Burns, who became chairman of the Federal Reserve Board (Fed) Feb. 1. Nixon's initial reaction was to completely reject Burns' reasoning. By the end of the year, however, the President had shown signs of wavering.

The ambivalence of Nixon's approach to tougher controls was illustrated by three contrasting economic developments that occurred during the year:

• Congress passed legislation authorizing the President to freeze wages, prices, rents and salaries at existing or higher levels. The President signed the bill but opposed the freeze provisions and said emphatically that he would not use them.

• By contrast, the President took a step toward "jawboning" by directing his Council of Economic Advisers (CEA) to prepare periodic "inflation alerts" to publicize excessive wage and price increases. (Two alerts were published during the year, on Aug. 7 and Dec. 1.)

• In another step toward jawboning, Nixon in a major economic speech on Dec. 4 announced measures to offset oil price increases and plans for intervention in wage negotiations in the construction industry if strikes and rising costs were not abated. (In 1970, average hourly earnings in that industry increased by 9.2 per cent, which exceeded increases in all other industries.)

For his part, Burns fared better in his efforts to counter recession than he did in his attempts to persuade the President to adopt an incomes policy. The Fed under its new chairman sought to spur economic activity by permitting the money supply to expand by a relatively high average of 5.5 percent during the year. Both the discount

1966 Act: Flexible Authority on Interest Rate Controls

An extremely tight policy of credit restraint maintained by the Federal Reserve Board induced Congress in 1966 to enact legislation (HR 14026—PL 89-597) giving flexible authority to bank regulatory agencies to set different limits on the interest rates that banks and other financial institutions may pay on different types and amounts of fixed maturity (time) deposits.

The purpose of the bill was to protect savings and loan institutions (S&Ls), traditional source of financing for home loans, from the competition of high-interest certificates of deposit (CDs) issued by commercial banks. (The CDs were issued by the banks as a receipt for funds deposited for a specific length of time and bearing a specific rate of interest; the instruments were often negotiable; if they were, they could be bought and sold like an IOU.)

Despite the Federal Reserve Board's policy to reduce inflationary pressures by limited availability of loan funds and increasing loan interest rates, a high demand for loans prevailed throughout 1966. Consequently, banks and savings and loan institutions began competing vigorously for the savings dollar—a major source of loan money.

The banks, in order to acquire funds to meet a high demand for industrial and consumer loans, had begun to offer the certificates in amounts far smaller than in the past and at interest rates higher than S&Ls could afford to pay. The result was that persons with relatively small amounts of money to invest (such as, for instance, a family attempting to put aside some money for future use or for an emergency) were taking funds out of S&Ls (or not going there in the first place) and instead buying small denomination CDs from banks. This in turn limited the funds available to S&Ls and dried up the major source of home financing; a sharp downturn in housing industry activity was one of the most prominent imbalances in the economy during 1966.

The "rate war" for savings arose because existing law required federal authorities to set a single general limit on time deposits, with variations permitted only with respect to differing maturities and other related factors. Thus, when banks began offering CDs in low denominations, authorities could make them less attractive only by lowering the rates on time deposits across the board. Because this would have included large-denomination CDs, an obligation bought in substantial quantities by major corporations, it would have cut into a major source of funds available to banks for lending.

Although the authority provided by the bill applied only to the rates on deposits left with financial institutions, and not on loans by the institutions, some backers of the measure contended it would result in reduction of loan rates as well. If banks were required to reduce rates on deposits, they reasoned, their lower costs in obtaining money would be reflected in lower rates on loans. This contention was disputed by financial experts, however, who feared the lower rates on time deposits might drive funds into higher-yield securities or bonds. This, they said, would keep loan rates high and force banks to curtail lending.

The discretionary rate controls authorized by PL 89-597 were to expire one year after the bill's enactment. (However, they were extended in stages through March 31, 1973.) Agencies given the new powers were the Federal Reserve Board (Fed), the Federal Deposit Insurance Corp. (FDIC), and the Federal Home Loan Bank Board (FHLBB). Together, these three agencies regulated all banks and savings and loan institutions insured by the federal government.

Other major provisions of the 1966 act gave the FHLBB authority for the first time directly to establish interest and dividend rates which S&Ls could pay their depositors, increased the reserves which the Fed could require member banks to hold against time deposits and enlarged the types of government securities that the Fed could buy and sell. The reserves provision (not subsequently implemented) was designed to crimp CD operations by banks even further, while the authority to deal in a broadened portfolio of securities was designed to enlarge the Fed's role in economic management by moving funds in and out of sensitive areas of the economy. Like the discretionary rate controls, these provisions were subject to annual renewal. The FHLBB authority was extended in stages through March 31, 1973, and the other two provisions were made permanent in 1968. (For additional detail on 1968 act, see *Congress and the Nation Vol. II,* p. 260; for extensions of authority, *Vol. II,* pp. 271, 276.)

---

rate at which the Federal Reserve system lends money to member banks and the prime rate—the interest rate that banks charge their best customers—underwent successive reductions. Mortgage interest rates stabilized and other interest rates fell sharply.

Other actions served to expand the economy despite President Nixon's reliance on a tight budget policy. These included the first impact of the Tax Reform Act of 1969 and pay raises for postal and other federal employees. The impact of these developments was blunted somewhat, however, by effects of a 67-day strike of the General Motors Corp. by the United Auto Workers. The strike, which idled 400,000 General Motors employees and another 100,000 workers at parts plants, cost the nation at least $14-billion in gross national product, according to estimates by the President's Council of Economic Advisers. And the liberal terms under which the strike was settled threatened to spur more inflation in the years ahead.

Wage-Price Controls

In a strategic ploy, the Democratic Congress avoided a veto of the wage-price controls by attaching them to a bill (S 3302—PL 91-379) extending the Defense Production Act of 1950 (PL 81-774) to June 30, 1972.

The controls, called the Economic Stabilization Act of 1970 (a separate title of S 3302), gave the President discretionary authority through Feb. 28, 1971, to freeze wages, prices, rents and salaries at levels not lower than those prevailing on May 25, 1970. And they backed up the President's authority by authorizing use of injunctions to carry out the provision and a $5,000 fine for violations. The controls section was added to the Senate bill by the House Banking and Currency Committee, which said in reporting the measure: "...If the Congress, in its wisdom, enacts this legislation, the President will have all of the necessary weapons needed to control inflation." Republicans charged that the controls were an election-year gimmick by Democrats to place the onus on President Nixon for either imposing or not imposing the controls—whichever seemed the greatest political liability.

Some of the stiffest GOP criticism of the controls came in minority views to the House committee report, signed by all Republican members of the Banking and Currency panel. The statement said that the committee's "Cost of Living Amendment" (the controls) should be renamed the "Election Year Squeezeplay" or "Devious Democratic Demagoguery." In the key test for the controls, a House vote on the conference report on S 3302, Republicans opposed the measure, 23-144. Democrats favored it, 194-9. (Republicans favored the bill on House passage, 90-16 because of its extension of the Defense Production Act, which the President had requested. They voted against the conference report in hopes that a new conference would drop the controls.)

President Nixon issued a blistering attack on the bill when he signed it into law Aug. 15. Nixon said that if it were not for some important provisions in the Defense Production Act, he would have vetoed the measure. Primarily, the President said, he had no intention of using the authority to freeze wages and prices because such action "simply does not fit the economic conditions which exist today." He added that if Congress felt that wage-price controls should be mandatory it should "face up to its responsibilities and make such controls mandatory."

Extension of Controls

At the insistence of the House Banking and Currency Committee, Congress at the end of the session approved a rider to a bill affecting the Small Business Administration (S 4536—PL 91-558) which extended the President's wage-price control authority for another month, through March 31, 1971. Purpose of the brief extension was to give Congress more time to act on a longer extension after the 92nd Congress convened in January 1971. The bill, cleared Dec. 10, was signed by the President Dec. 17 despite his continued opposition to controls.

1971

President Nixon, with decisive action, switched the economic issue in 1971 from the foremost of his political liabilities to a potential asset. After months of deliberation, the President Aug. 15 displayed full conversion to an incomes policy by ordering a 90-day freeze on wages, prices, salaries and rents (to be followed, the President decided later, by Phase Two, a period

of continued presidential intervention in private wage and price decisions). The Aug. 15 program, whose decisiveness came as a surprise to both Congress and the public, coupled the freeze with far-reaching measures to stimulate the economy and bring the nation's adverse balance of international payments under control: tax cuts for individuals and businesses, imposition of a **10 per cent surtax on imports and a move to free the** dollar from the $35-per-ounce gold price that had prevailed for almost 40 years. By year's end, there was no doubt that, at least temporarily, the President had seized the economic issue from his opponents in a fashion that won broad support from the nation and left the Democratic Congress in some degree of disarray.

Construction Industry Controls

The President's first step of the year toward an incomes policy came in late winter when he intervened in the collective bargaining of the construction industry. Wage and price increases in the industry had been exceeding those in other areas of the economy by a substantial margin. Nixon had tried but failed to get the industry to adopt a program of voluntary restraint.

On Feb. 23, Nixon moved to counter further inflation in the industry by implementing his authority to suspend the Davis-Bacon Act of 1931, which required contractors on government-financed construction to pay prevailing (union) wage scales. *(Congress and the Nation, Vol. I, p. 634)* A month later, on March 29, he invoked power to control wages and prices which Congress had given him the previous year and imposed a wage-price stabilization system on the industry. This was the first use of the authority granted him by the Stabilization Act of 1970, a new title added to the Defense Production Act.

Nixon vs. Congress

Congress opened the year in the same role it had played since Nixon took office—that of critic of his economic policies. Until Aug. 15, the majority Democrats, joined on occasion by Republicans, peppered the President with economic advice.

Phase Two brought promises that Congress would restrict the President's authority to control the economy and carefully oversee his stabilization program. But the major thrust at the President was a Senate effort to capitalize on his request for tax reduction by piggybacking the tax bill with a plan to finance the 1972—and subsequent—presidential election campaigns with public funds. Democrats wanted the campaign financing chiefly because they faced 1972 with a large deficit and limited fund-raising potential. Republicans, with full party coffers, generally opposed the plan.

Both efforts collapsed under presidential pressure. Congress extended the President's economic stabilization authority for a year—until April 30, 1973—before anyone knew whether the Phase Two program would work effectively and fairly and more than four months before the existing legislation was to expire. Nixon's power to control the economy was not significantly altered.

Under Nixon's threat to veto the tax bill if the campaign financing provision was included, Congress abandoned the effort for 1972 by making the plan effec-

History of Economic Controls: Promises and Pitfalls

Considerable precedent existed for the sweeping program of economic controls that President Nixon imposed on Aug. 15, 1971. Stiff controls were in effect during World Wars I and II and during the Korean War. And a peacetime precedent stemmed from the years between World War II and Korea, when controls were imposed on rents and consumer credit.

In each case, the controls worked well although they produced considerable public grumbling (with the exception of World War II, when they were better accepted). Removal of the controls was always followed by inflation, except at the end of the Korean War.

World War I. In August 1917, four and a half months after the United States declared war on Germany, President Wilson ordered price controls on the sale of wheat and coal under authority derived from acts of Congress and from his war powers as commander-in-chief. From then until the end of the war the price controls were gradually extended to a wide range of commodities. These controls were lifted soon after the Nov. 11, 1918, armistice and prices rose rapidly during the following winter and spring.

World War II. Increased demand, coupled with a scarcity of commodities, forced the consumer price index up nearly 10 points during 1941. This prompted Congress to pass the Price Control Act on Jan. 30, 1942, which provided the legal foundation for a network of price controls.

As for wages, an executive order issued by President Roosevelt on Oct. 3, 1942, under the Price Stabilization Act, signed the previous day, instructed the War Labor Board not "to approve any increases in wage rates prevailing on Sept. 15, 1942, unless such increase is necessary to correct maladjustment or inequities...or to aid in the effective prosecution of the war."

Controls over consumer credit (minimum down payments, maximum maturities) were established by Roosevelt under an executive order in 1941 and were administered by the Federal Reserve Board (Fed) throughout the war. On Dec. 1, 1946, the Fed lifted controls on everything except a dozen consumer durables, including automobiles.

The controls were highly effective. The consumer price index rose a total of only five points between April 1943 and June 1946, when most of the controls ended. Prices then shot up until, in December 1948, the consumer price index was 70 per cent higher than its level in the 1935-40 period.

Post-World War II. Because of an acute shortage of housing, President Truman asked and received authority to extend the World War II-era rent controls to Feb. 28, 1948. At the President's request, the controls were subsequently extended in stages through the outbreak of the Korean War, after which they became a part of the new structure of controls established during the war period.

On June 12, 1947, President Truman asked for specific legislative authority to impose credit controls, saying that without such authority he would rescind the 1941 executive order on that subject. Congress responded by passing a bill declaring that all existing credit controls should end Nov. 1, 1947, and could not be reimposed by the President except in a future state of war or emergency. But in 1948, Congress passed legislation authorizing the Federal Reserve Board to impose controls at its discretion. (The Fed imposed restrictions in 1948 but eased them in March and April 1949, before they expired on June 30 of that year.)

Korean War. President Truman asked Congress on July 19, 1950, for authority to freeze wages and prices and to impose a variety of other controls designed to ease adjustment from civilian to military production. The Defense Production Act (PL 81-774), signed into law Sept. 8, 1950, authorized the President to assign priorities, allocate materials and facilities, and requisition property for defense production; to regulate consumer credit and to impose selective or general wage and price controls.

Controls on consumer installment credit were ordered on Sept. 18, and in mid-December, the President's Economic Stabilization Agency ordered a rollback in auto price increases and a freeze in auto wages. Further controls were ordered in 1951. And rent control authority, scheduled to expire in early 1951, was lumped together with the remainder of the stabilization program under an extension of the Defense Production Act. Rent control in non-critical defense areas was repealed as of July 31, 1953, while authority to control consumer credit was repealed as of June 30, 1952.

Under full impact of the controls, the cost of living rose 4 per cent in the last 11 months of 1951—a mark that was less than one-third the annual rate in the last half of 1950. In 1952, it rose less than one per cent. By the end of March 1953, the Eisenhower administration had removed all price and wage controls, and the legal authority behind them lapsed April 30. The general price level remained stable through 1955.

tive in 1973. The President clearly won both battles. *(Details of tax bill, tax chapter, p. 77)*

Among the more persistent congressional critics of the President's economic policy was the Joint Economic Committee. In its March 29 report on the Economic Report of the President (which accompanied the budget submitted in January), the committee found "serious deficiencies" in the administration's economic programs and judged the administration's goals unlikely to be achieved.

The committee urged the President to adopt a clear-cut and comprehensive wage-price policy. It further recommended adoption of interim and long-term goals for inflation and unemployment and establishment of guidelines for the economy to meet the goals.

The committee recommended a speed-up in the effective dates, to 1971 from 1973, of individual tax reduction scheduled by the Tax Reform Act of 1969. A number of individual Senators and Representatives, in addition to committee members, endorsed this recommendation. Another proposal which gained congressional support was re-enactment of the tax credit for business investment, which had been repealed by the 1969 Act.

Both proposals were advanced as means of stimulating the economy to faster growth in order to reduce unemployment. Similar provisions were subsequently included in the President's tax bill.

Near midyear Congress passed a bill (S 31—PL 92-54) providing $2.25-billion for emergency employment in public service jobs at the state and local levels. President Nixon praised this bill, but he vetoed another congressional initiative—a $5.7-billion emergency public works bill (S 575) also designed to provide jobs.

Both bills reflected congressional concern over unemployment, which reached 6.2 per cent of the work force in May, and mixed indications on the strength of the recovery from the recession.

Wage-Price Controls Extensions

Despite the President's use of his Stabilization Act powers to curb inflation in the construction industry, the administration was lukewarm toward extension of that authority in early 1971. Treasury Secretary John Connally, testifying before the House Banking and Currency Committee on Feb. 23, 1971, said the administration accepted the legislation but still did not plan to use it. Congress May 5 passed an extension of the act (HR 4246—PL 92-15) until April 30, 1972. While studying that extension, Congress March 29 had cleared a bill (S J Res 55—PL 92-8) temporarily extending the authority to June 1, 1971. Without that extension, the authority would have expired on March 31.

Final action on a second extension bill came when the House by voice vote concurred in Senate amendments which had the effect of extending the President's authority six months longer than that provided by the House version. As passed by the House March 10 by a 382-19 roll-call vote, HR 4246 extended the standby controls until March 31, 1973. However, a provision of the House-passed bill stipulated that if the President imposed such controls, his authority would expire after six months unless renewed by Congress. Because the President imposed controls on the construction industry March 29, his authority under the House version of the bill would have expired Sept. 29, 1971.

Provisions. As signed into law May 18, HR 4246:

• Extended the President's authority to impose controls on wages, prices, salaries and rents from June 1, 1971, through April 30, 1972.

• Prohibited the President from applying wage and price controls to a single industry unless he determined that wages or prices in that industry had increased in a grossly disproportionate rate compared to the economy as a whole. (This was repealed later in the year. *See p. 114*)

• Extended the authority of federal banking agencies to establish different ceilings on interest rates paid by financial institutions on different types and amounts of time and savings deposits through March 31, 1973.

• Granted permanent authority to the President to initiate a program of voluntary credit controls which would be implemented by the Federal Reserve Board.

New Economic Policy

Genesis of Aug. 15 Program. Despite mounting congressional criticism, administration spokesmen in the pre-Aug. 15 period downplayed the need for an incomes policy and singled out favorable indications as proof that the economy was progressing. They minimized other indications which were less favorable. In March the Labor Department had discontinued its monthly press briefings on the unemployment rate, apparently in disapproval of interpretations of the figures by career-service economists who supervised their preparation. The Joint Economic Committee began a series of monthly hearings on the unemployment rates to take the place of the briefings.

Treasury Secretary Connally said repeatedly that President Nixon was convinced that the economy was progressing and that further action was not necessary. But the administration was well aware that further action was needed, for various offices were already at work secretly devising the outlines and the justification for the new economic policy, which was to be revealed six weeks later. Connally had general responsibility for this effort.

Appearing on a television interview program, Connally on July 25 dropped a hint of what was afoot. He said international monetary problems, inflationary wage settlements and high interest rates might influence the President to impose wage and price controls.

On Aug. 4 a group of 14 Republican senators publicly urged the President to adopt wage and price restraints to bring inflation under control. Twelve of the group said they planned to introduce a bill creating a wage-price board.

On July 28 the administration had announced that the budget for the fiscal year just ended—fiscal 1971—had resulted in a deficit of $23.2-billion—nearly $5-billion more than had been estimated at the beginning of the year. It was the next-largest deficit since World War II, exceeded only by President Johnson's 1968 red-ink figure.

The nation's balance-of-payments deficit in the second quarter of the year was at annual rates of almost $23-billion on both the broad bases used to calculate the over-all position: net liquidity and official reserve transactions. These were record deficits, although they were subsequently exceeded by the third quarter figures.

Commerce Secretary Maurice H. Stans forecast on July 27 that the United States in 1971 faced the probability of a deficit in its export-import trade, which would be the nation's first in the 20th century.

Meanwhile the consumer price index had risen in May at an annual rate of 6 per cent and in June at a rate of 7.2 per cent. The Harris Survey reported that, in a sampling taken in June, only 26 per cent of the persons questioned thought Mr. Nixon was doing a goob job in economic matters while 70 per cent gave him a negative rating.

In another important development, the Gallup Poll found in July that 49 per cent of persons surveyed believed unemployment would be higher in six months while only 25 per cent believed the rate would be lower. The Gallup organization found Republican support among business and professional persons at an all-time low—only 31 per cent identified themselves with the Republican Party while 34 per cent said they supported the Democratic Party. Surveying in August on the question of which party was best able to maintain prosperity, the Gallup Poll found that 46 per cent of those questioned thought the Democratic Party was better in this regard and only 23 per cent had faith in the Republican Party.

In a survey taken in late June, the Gallup organization found that 50 per cent of the persons questioned favored wage and price controls.

What the indicators and public opinion surveys showed was that the old game plan was not stabilizing prices or fostering economic recovery fast enough to make an acceptable showing in 1972 and that the public did not approve of the results the administration was getting.

Policy Announced. Amid this setting, President Nixon announced his new economic policy on Aug. 15, imposing a 90-day wage-price freeze and 10 per cent surtax on imports without warning to the public other than hints dropped in late July and early August. In addition to the freeze and surtax, Nixon:

• Freed the U.S. dollar from its historic $35-an-ounce gold price, in effect establishing a "floating" dollar in world markets.

• Ordered a 10 per cent cut in foreign economic aid.

• Acted to cut $4.7-billion from the federal budget in fiscal 1971-72 by:

—Ordering a 5 per cent reduction in federal employment, "largely by attrition," by summer 1972.

—Deferring for six months a federal pay increase scheduled for Jan. 1, 1972.

—Postponing the proposed starting dates for general revenue sharing—for three months—and for welfare law changes—for one year. Both proposals were before Congress.

• Asked Congress as its first priority after the summer recess to consider a Job Development Act of 1971, provisions of which would include an accelerated investment tax credit of 10 per cent for one year and a 5 per cent permanent rapid write-off after that. The purpose was to stimulate business growth.

• Asked Congress to repeal the 7 per cent federal excise taxes on automobiles, which would result in an average price reduction of about $200 per car and thus presumably spur automobile sales.

• Recommended that Congress advance to Jan. 1, 1972, income tax cuts already scheduled to become effective Jan. 1, 1973, through an increase in the personal tax exemption and the standard deduction.

• Asked corporations to freeze dividends for 90 days.

• Appointed a Cost of Living Council headed by Connally, "to work with leaders of labor and business to set up the proper mechanism for achieving continued price and wage stability after the 90-day freeze is over."

Exports. As part of the new program, Nixon proposed to submit to Congress legislation establishing tax incentives for U.S. export sales. The bill would provide tax deferral for earnings from export sales by firms qualifying as a Domestic International Sales Corporation (DISC)—a firm engaged primarily in the export business. It was estimated that this would increase export sales by about $1.5-billion annually.

Monetary. The United States notified the International Monetary Fund that it would no longer freely buy and sell gold for the settlement of international transactions. The administration asked the Federal Reserve to suspend the virtually automatic use of its "swap network" to convert dollars into other currencies.

Return to 1956. The President said the changes he proposed, coupled with improvements in the domestic economy during the first half of 1971, "will move us strongly toward a goal this nation has not reached since 1956—prosperity with full employment in peacetime." The year he cited—1956—was during the Eisenhower administration when Nixon was Vice President.

Temporary Freezes. Nixon stressed two factors in connection with the freezes: that they were temporary and he intended to avoid permanent, mandatory wage and price controls in peacetime.

"To put the strong, vigorous American economy into a permanent straitjacket would lock in unfairness and stifle the expansion of our free enterprise system," Nixon said. He added that "while the wage-price freeze will be backed by government sanctions if necessary, it will not be accompanied by the establishment of a huge price-control bureaucracy. I am relying on the voluntary cooperation of all American—workers, employers, consumers—to make this freeze work."

Phase Two. President Nixon addressed the nation Oct. 7 and outlined Phase Two of his stabilization program. He had previously—in a Sept. 9 address to Congress—said that the freeze would not extend beyond the original term of 90 days which he had ordered.

The President asked Congress to speed passage of his tax bill and to extend his economic stabilization authority for a year. He established a Pay Board and a Price Commission with authority to set guidelines for wage and price increases, issue orders and hear cases.

The administration announced that, for stabilization purposes, the economy was to be divided into three sectors: the largest businesses and unions, which would be controlled most stringently and which would require prior approval for pay and price increases; less critical units, which would be required to report their wage and price actions, and the remainder, which would be controlled only through spot-checks and case investigations.

The control structure and distribution of authority showed that the administration had not made the basic decisions on wages and prices but had left them to the Price Commission, composed of seven members representing the public, and the Pay Board, composed of five members each from labor, business and the public. The President won organized labor's participation in the Pay Board with a pledge that it would be autonomous—that the Cost of Living Council would not oversee either the board or the commission. *(Box p. 112-113)*

The Pay Board's general guideline of 5.5 per cent per year for wage increases and its policy against retroactive payment of scheduled wage increases deferred by the freeze were adopted over labor's objections. The labor members considered terminating their relationship with

Nixon Created Elaborate Machinery to Operate His...

Machinery to implement Phase Two—the indefinite, long-range phase of President Nixon's new economic policy—was vested in four main bodies—a Cost of Living Council (COLC), responsible for overall coordination of the program; and a Pay Board, Price Commission and Committee on Interest and Dividends, responsible for detailed decisionmaking.

The COLC was to determine coverage and establish appropriate exemptions for the Phase Two program. (The avowed goal of the program was to reduce the annual rate of price inflation to a range of 2 to 3 per cent by the end of 1972.) The Pay Board and Price Commission were to establish guidelines and regulations for meeting the stabilization goal, while the Interest and Dividends Committee was to set up a program for obtaining voluntary restraints on interest rates and dividends. Maximum regulation was to be applied to the leading businesses which, being less subject to competition, were most likely to contribute to inflation.

Nixon established all four groups under authority granted him by the Economic Stabilization Act of 1970 (PL 91-379), which Congress extended in phases through April 30, 1973. The COLC, established during Phase One, was extended and the other bodies created by executive order of the President on Oct. 15, 1971 (Executive Order 11627).

Cost of Living Council

The COLC, in consultation with the President, was to establish the government's basic approach to wage and price controls and monitor the entire stabilization system. But it could not overrule case decisions or specific standards or criteria adopted by the Pay Board and Price Commission.

On Nov. 10, 1971, the council defined the categories of businesses and labor organizations that would be regulated intensively under Phase Two. Businesses and unions with $100-million or more in sales or with 5,000 or more workers were to be the most closely controlled. They were required to seek advance approval of wage and price increases. There were 1,666 units in this category by council estimate. The next group—1,555 units with $50-million to $100-million in revenues or 1,000 to 5,000 workers—were required to report increases after they were made. A third group, some eight million units with less than $50-million in revenues or fewer than 1,000 workers, was subject to

all stabilization regulations but was not required to report. This group was to be monitored by the Internal Revenue Service (IRS). On May 1, 1972, the COLC exempted from controls about 5 million businesses with 60 or fewer employees. The exemption did not apply, however, to construction firms or to health service concerns, such as hospitals.

Under the President's Oct. 15 executive order, the COLC was to get a full-time director, to be appointed by the President. Named as the first director was Donald Rumsfeld, a former U.S. representative (R Ill. 1963-69) and former director of the Office of Economic Opportunity. Rumsfeld succeeded Treasury Secretary John Connally, who served as chairman of the body throughout Phase One, as head of COLC. Under the executive order, other permanent members of the council were to be the secretaries of the treasury, agriculture, commerce, labor, housing and urban development; the directors of the Office of Management and Budget and the Office of Emergency Preparedness; the chairman of the Council of Economic Advisers (CEA) and the President's special assistant for consumer affairs.

Pay Board

Authority to review and act on pay increases was vested in the Pay Board, originally a 15-member body consisting of five members each from labor, management and the public (citizens representing neither labor, business nor the government).

After a dispute with labor members in early 1972, membership was curtailed to seven members, all representing the public. Under both membership schemes, one public member, to be designated by the President, would serve as full-time chairman. (Senate confirmation of the appointment was required by legislation (PL 92-210) extending the Economic Stabilization Act.) First chairman of the board was George H. Boldt, a former U.S. district judge in the state of Washington.

In its first key decision, the Pay Board on Nov. 8, 1971, in a 10-5 vote (with labor representatives the dissenters) set 5.5 per cent a year as the general guideline for wage and other benefit increases. The board's actions also made increases due under contracts negotiated before the wage-price freeze subject to review. Congress, in extending the Economic Stabilization Act in December, however, limited the board's authority

the program but subsequently prevailed on Congress to provide for payment of the lost increases in most cases.

The Price Commission established an over-all annual guideline of 2.5 per cent for price increases. The difference between the two guidelines was approximately equal to the long-term trend of increase in productivity. Phase Two began Nov. 14 in an aura of uncertainty heightened by the Pay Board's early approval of large wage increases greatly exceeding its guidelines.

Devaluation

President Nixon met Dec. 14 with President Georges Pompidou of France and subsequently, in a joint announcement, approved devaluation of the dollar as part of a general realignment of currencies. This concession by the United States broke an impasse in the international monetary arena which had prevailed since Aug. 15. It

...'Phase Two' Program of Economic Stabilization

over existing contracts. The bill required retroactive payment of deferred pay raises and payment of scheduled increases which were not reasonably inconsistent with the guidelines or which were financed or offset by price and tax increases or productivity increases.

The board in its early days appeared unable to hold the line against major union contract settlements. The group in late 1971 permitted a large scheduled pay increase for coal miners to go into effect and approved increases for railroaders well in excess of its 5.5 per cent guideline for average annual raises. But in early 1972, the board rolled back large increases won by aerospace workers and West Coast longshoremen. Labor representatives dissented furiously on the latter issues, culminating in the resignation of four labor members.

Price Commission

The Price Commission Nov. 11, 1971, the President said in creating that body, would be "empowered to restrain price and rent increases to the necessary minimum and to prevent windfall profits."

The commission was to be made up of seven members—all public—one of whom would serve as full-time chairman. As the first chairman, the President named and the Senate confirmed C. Jackson Grayson Jr., a former dean of the School of Business Administration at Southern Methodist University.

The commission was granted authority to consider cases of price increases and to disapprove them if they exceeded the commission guidelines. Nixon provided the commission no control over profits, however, other than "windfalls," which he described as "exorbitant profits" generated from a system where wages and other costs were held down while prices remained stable.

The price commission Nov. 11, 1971, laid down guidelines limiting aggregate price increases to a rate of 2.5 per cent per year. Many individual prices would exceed that rate and many others would have to be less to achieve that mean.

To achieve the general goal, the commission allowed price increases only to the extent of allowable cost increases offset by productivity gains. The commission established a limit on profits by providing that price increases could not increase profit margins (expressed as a percentage of sales) during a base period

of the preceding fiscal years. (The lack of any stiffer controls over profits was a frequent criticism of the program, particularly by organized labor. The administration argued that tougher profit controls would dampen economic activity.)

The commission established detailed regulations for controlling rents, health care charges and insurance premiums. Generally, it allowed utility rate increases that were approved by state and local regulatory agencies.

A number of goods and services were exempted from control. These included used products, life insurance, most real estate, securities, some rentals, most restaurants and unprocessed agricultural products and seafoods. (In June 1972, however, the controls were extended to cover unprocessed agricultural products and seafood, except for the first sale (the farmer's and fishermen's sale). The controls were extended by the President under Executive Order No. 11640.)

Committee on Interest and Dividends

To administer a voluntary program of credit restraint, the President named a Committee on Interest and Dividends, to be headed by the chairman of the Federal Reserve Board (Fed). The committee would formulate and execute the program, subject to Cost of Living Council review. In addition to the Fed chairman, its members would be the secretaries of the treasury, commerce and housing and urban development; and the chairmen of the Federal Deposit Insurance Corp. and of the Federal Home Loan Bank Board.

On Nov. 2, 1971, the committee announced a guideline of 4 per cent per year for increases in dividends after Jan. 1, 1972. Dividends for the rest of 1971 remained subject to the President's request that they stay at or below pre-freeze levels. The same pertained to interest rates.

Other Bodies

The President in his Oct. 15 executive order also established a Committee on the Health Services Industry and a Committee on State and Local Government Cooperation. Both panels were to advise the Pay Board and Price Commission on stabilization in their respective areas.

would have been virtually impossible politically for other countries to give up a major advantage in world trade by raising the value of their currencies if the United States had not agreed to devalue. The dollar was to be devalued 8.57 per cent by raising the price of gold to $38-from $35-per-ounce. Under the new currency alignment, the United States rescinded the import surcharge immediately. *(Details of currency agreement, chapter on international economic developments, p. 119)*

1971 Revenue Act

Congress Dec. 9 cleared for the President's tax bill, cutting taxes by $25.9-billion over the next three fiscal years and by indeterminate amounts in subsequent years. The bill included a 7 per cent investment tax credit (instead of the 10 per cent the President had requested for the first year, to be followed by a 5 per cent credit), repeal of the automobile excise tax, the requested tax incentives for exports, and the accelerated schedule of increases in the income tax exemption and in the standard deduction. *(Details, chapter on tax policy, p. 77)*

Wage-Price Controls—Third Extension

In a move consistent with his "New Economic Policy," President Nixon asked and received a year's extension, through April 30, 1973, of the Economic Stabilization Act—statutory authority for his Phase II program. The extension measure (S 2891—PL 92-210) also broadened the President's stabilization powers to cover interest rates and corporate dividends.

The President proposed the extension (and the authority to control interest rates and dividends) on Oct. 19—four days after he had issued Executive Order 11627 establishing the Pay Board, Price Commission and the remaining structure for administering his follow-on program for economic stabilization. In the House, liberal Democrats sought to amend the bill to require payment of wage raises—including retroactive payment where appropriate—agreed to in labor contracts signed before Nixon embarked on his new economic policy Aug. 15. But in a victory for Nixon, the House accepted instead, on a key teller vote of 209-151 (R 141-13; D 68-138) an amendment by Robert G. Stephens (D Ga.) requiring payment of such raises only if they were already financed by price or tax increases or offset by productivity increases. The House went on to pass the bill by a 326-33 roll-call vote.

Debate in the Senate centered on the advisability of extending the act before the Phase Two program could be evaluated fully. The attack on extension was led by William Proxmire (D Wis.), who criticized Phase Two as unworkable, unenforceable and inequitable. Proxmire failed in his effort to hold up extension but did win approval of an amendment to require Senate confirmation of the chairmen of the Pay Board and Price Commission. (The provision was retained by House and Senate conferees.) Senate passage of the measure came on a key 86-4 roll-call vote, with Proxmire, Barry Goldwater (R Ariz.), J. W. Fulbright (D Ark.) and Fred R. Harris (D Okla.) the lone dissenters.

Provisions. As signed into law Dec. 22, (PL 92-210), S 2891 contained the following major provisions:

- Extended the President's authority to control wages, salaries, prices and rents through April 30, 1973.
- Expanded the President's authority to include control of interest rates and finance charges, corporate dividends and similar transfers, for the same time period.
- Required the President to stabilize interest rates and finance charges whenever he used his authority to control wages and prices, unless he determined that the action was unnecessary to stabilize the economy.
- Required the President to issue stabilization standards and guidelines which were to be fair and equitable, to reflect changes in productivity and the cost of living, to require price reductions when warranted by conditions

and to provide for general exceptions to foster economic growth and prevent inequities and disruptions.

- Permitted reduction of prices below the levels prevailing on May 25, 1970, when necessary to stabilize the economy (the original act established wage and price levels prevailing on May 25, 1970, as the minimum level for stabilization).
- Eliminated a provision of the existing act prohibiting application of controls to a single industry or segment of the economy.
- Exempted from control earnings below the minimum wage and those below officially designated poverty levels.
- Required retroactive payment of deferred pay raises and payment of scheduled increases which were not unreasonably inconsistent with the guidelines or which were financed or offset by price and tax increases, appropriations or other provisions for funds or increases in productivity.
- Required unregulated mass transportation systems to obtain prior approval for fare increases.
- Subjected rents under state and local controls to federal stabilization.
- Clarified the President's power to delegate his economic control authority to the stabilization boards, commissions and committees he created.
- Required Senate confirmation of the chairmen of the Pay Board and Price Commission, the members of those bodies appointed in the future and any member raised to the chairmanship; permitted current chairmen to serve 60 days on an interim basis.
- Vested legal authority in the full-time members of the stabilization bodies (the chairmen) but required majority rule in the decisions of those bodies.
- Exempted the stabilization program from some provisions of the Administrative Procedures Act but required public notice, public hearings and publication of decisions in rulemaking proceedings in matters having a significant impact on the economy.
- Prohibited disclosure of trade secrets and other confidential information by the stabilization bodies.
- Added a civil penalty of $2,500 for each offense to the criminal fine of $5,000 in the existing act.
- Authorized consumers to sue violators of price and rent regulations and orders for damages ranging from $100 to the greater of three times the amount of the overcharge and $1,000, plus court costs and legal fees, but, where violations resulted from errors, limited damages to the actual overcharges and to those cases in which the violators refused to make restitution.
- Established a temporary emergency court of appeals, composed of three or more federal judges to be designated by the chief justice, with exclusive jurisdiction over appeals from the district courts and challenges on constitutional grounds.
- Required the National Commission on Productivity to promote productivity increases by encouraging establishment of local, plant-level, regional and industry-wide productivity councils embracing labor, management and the public, and by other action.
- Required a federal pay raise of not more than 5.5 **per cent (the Pay Board's general pay-increase guide**line) to take effect with the first government pay period beginning after Jan. 1, 1972.

```
┌────────────────────────────────────────────────────────────────────────────┐
│                                                                              │
│            A Comparison of Two Wage-Price Control Programs                    │
│                                                                              │
│                   Phase II (October 1971)              Phase III (January 1973)│
│                                                                              │
│  Administration      • Mandatory government approval of    • Voluntary        │
│                        individual actions                  • Self-administered │
│                                                            • CLC monitoring    │
│                                                                              │
│  Price Standard      • Detailed cost justification plus    • Cost justification subject to 1.5% average price │
│                      • Profit margin limitation              limits or profit margin limitation │
│                                                                              │
│  Pay Standard        • 5.5 per cent with adjustments       • Interim 5.5 per cent │
│                                                            • Labor-management committee review │
│                                                                              │
│  Notification Reporting  • Prenotification: $100-million in sales and │
│                            5,000 employees                                   │
│                          • Reporting: $50-million to $100-million in  • Reporting: $250-million in sales and 5,000 │
│                            sales and 1,000 to 5,000 employees          employees │
│                          • Recordkeeping                   • Recordkeeping: $50-million to $250-million in sales │
│                                                              and 1,000 to 5,000 employees │
│                                                                              │
│  Enforcement Criterion   • Technical compliance            • Voluntary until special rule established │
│  Treatment of Food       • Same as others                  • Continued controls │
│                                                            • Special policy attention │
│                                                                              │
│  Treatment of Health     • Special rules                   • Continued controls │
│                                                            • Special policy attention │
│                                                                              │
│                              Source: White House                             │
└────────────────────────────────────────────────────────────────────────────┘
```

1972

Controversy over implementation of Nixon's Phase Two program dominated developments on the economic stabilization scene in 1972. The hottest dispute was between organized labor and the Pay Board, which reversed its 1971 trend and began taking a tough stance against wage and benefit settlements that exceeded board guidelines. The board's actions culminated in the resignation of four of its five labor members, including AFL-CIO president George Meany.

Widespread public criticism focused on the Price Commission because of sharp increases in food prices, which the Council had exempted from controls. By midyear, the public outcry had prompted President Nixon to order decisive action to bring food prices under control. The President moved by executive order to extend controls to unprocessed agricultural products and seafood. And in an effort to stem meat price increases, he ordered all import quotas on meat imports lifted for the remainder of 1972.

Labor—Pay Board Dispute

The issue over which organized labor split from the Pay Board was a decision by the board's public and business representatives to scale down a 20.6 per cent increase won by the International Longshoremen's and Warehousemen's Union after a long strike. The Pay Board March 16, over labor's objections, cut the increase to 14.9 per cent, a figure that still far exceeded the board's general 5.5 per cent guideline for pay raises. (The board's majority had already incurred labor's enmity by

a Jan. 5 decision to scale back a 12 per cent aerospace industry settlement to 8.3 per cent.)

But labor's disaffection went back to the beginning of the Phase Two program. As a condition for serving on the Pay Board, Meany and other labor leaders insisted that it be a tripartite, independent body. But since the board's earliest votes, the labor movement charged that it was neither tripartite nor independent—that the White House dominated the public and business members, who outvoted the labor members.

Labor members added a second charge against the entire stabilization program—that it was ineffective in holding down prices, so that only wages, in fact, were stabilized. An AFL-CIO statement March 22, announcing the resignations of the three AFL-CIO members on the board, described the program:

"In the guise of an anti-inflation policy, the American people are being gouged at the supermarket and squeezed in the paycheck.... While the administration permits (a) rising tide of price increases, its pay board persists in holding down workers' wages. Yet prices are free to rise, without even the pretense of controls."

Resignation of the three AFL-CIO members on March 22 was followed the next day by that of Leonard Woodcock, president of the independent United Auto Workers. The only labor member who did not resign was Frank Fitzsimmons, president of the International Brotherhood of Teamsters, another independent union.

President Nixon's response to the labor walkout was to reorganize the Pay Board and declare that it would go on functioning. The new board was to have seven members, all representing the public. They were the five original public members plus Fitzsimmons and one of the five business representatives, Rocco C. Siciliano, former under secretary of labor in the Nixon administration. Nixon's move was interpreted as a tough counter-maneuver in the battle with labor over his stabilization program.

Price Commission Controversies

The exemption of food prices from Phase Two controls brought outspoken criticism to the stabilization program in February, when grocery prices rose 2 per cent, the largest monthly increase in 14 years. The grumbling grew louder in March when Agriculture Secretary Earl L. Butz expressed approval to farmers and ranchers over soaring meat prices.

Both President Nixon and the Price Commission chairman, C. Jackson Grayson Jr., promised action if the food prices did not recede. Treasury Secretary John Connally conferred with the heads of 12 large retail food chains in March. Afterward, the increases slowed down, but not enough to satisfy President Nixon. On June 29 he issued an executive order (No. 11640) extending price controls to unprocessed agricultural products and seafood (except for the first sale—the farmer's and fisherman's sale). Three days earlier the President removed all quota

restrictions on meat imports for the rest of 1972 in an attempt to help stem meat price increases.

Other Issues. Rents also brought the Price Commission a share of criticism. Although many rents were regulated, widespread abuses were reported at hearings in March. A common theme in the complaints was that tenants facing large increases—and frequently the threat of eviction if they did not pay—were unable to get help from the Internal Revenue Service. Sen. Clifford P. Case (R N.J.) said IRS officials had acknowledged that they were unable to cope with the flood of complaints about rents.

Still another issue was the allowance of the customary mark-up on increased costs. Critics said the commission's regulations permitted businesses to increase their profits unjustifiably. A member of the commission, Dean Robert F. Lanzillotti of the University of Florida College of Business Administration, expressed support for a dollar-for-dollar pass-through of increased costs which would not permit additional profits.

Grayson, in testimony April 18, reported that the commission had approved 2,400 individual price-increase applications (some covering more than one price), reduced 425 and denied 140. An additional 1,070 had been with-

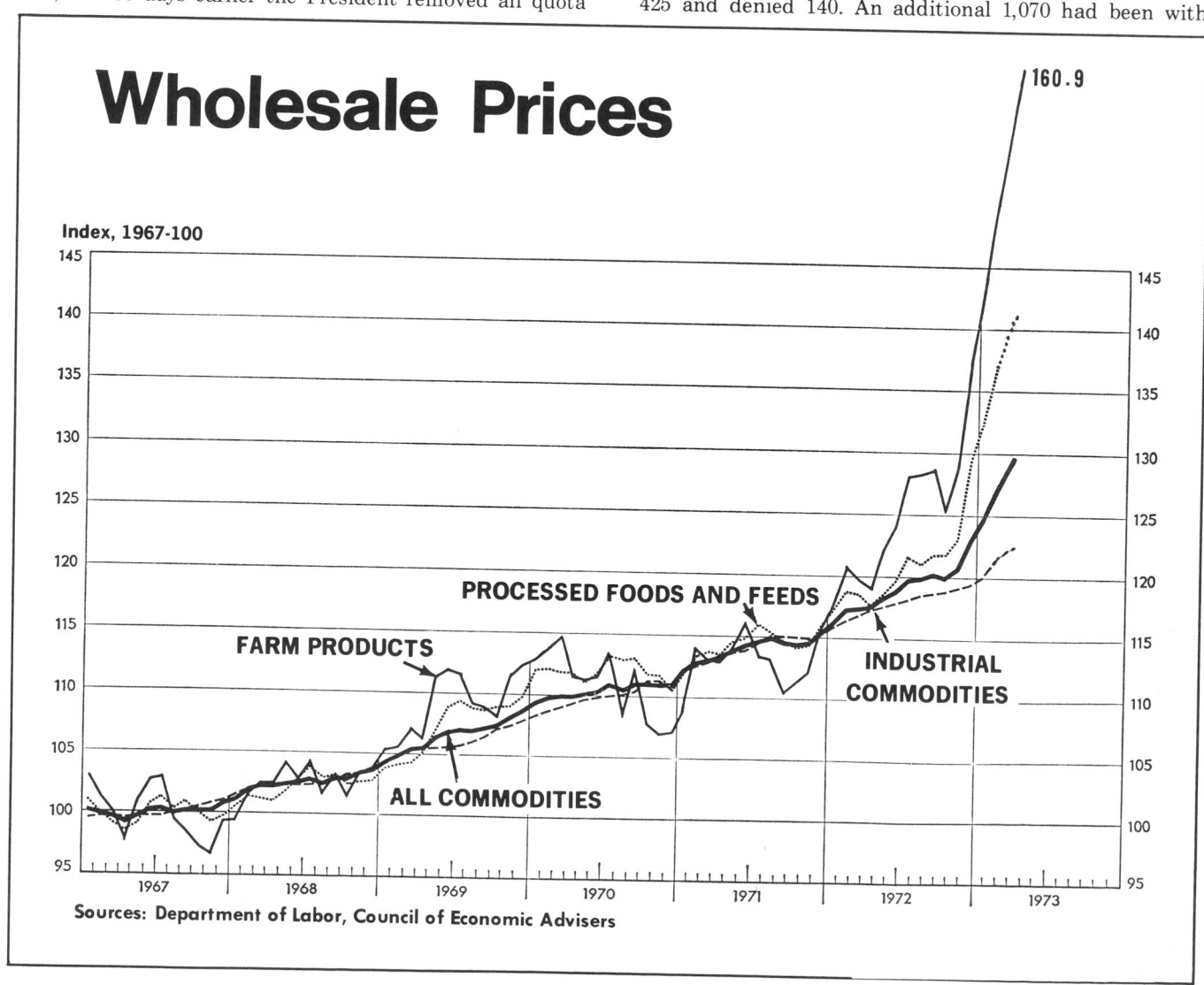

Wholesale Prices

160.9

Index, 1967-100

FARM PRODUCTS

PROCESSED FOODS AND FEEDS

INDUSTRIAL COMMODITIES

ALL COMMODITIES

Sources: Department of Labor, Council of Economic Advisers

drawn, he said, and 1,450 were pending. The average increase granted was 1.6 per cent of total revenues of the firms involved, Grayson said, and 3.2 per cent of affected product-line sales.

To reduce the number of individual price increases, the commission negotiated 162 term-limit pricing agreements that permitted average price increases of 2 per cent for all products of the participating companies. On March 15, the commission reduced the ceiling on term-limit prices to 1.8 per cent per year and placed a ceiling of 8 per cent on increases for any single product line.

Phase Three

In an announcement nearly as unexpected as the 1971 wage-price freeze, President Nixon Jan. 11, 1973, terminated most mandatory wage and price controls. He announced the beginning of Phase Three, a system of voluntary restraints backed by the threat of government action if it felt wage and price increases were inflationary. He called on Congress for a fourth extension for one year (through April 30, 1974) of the Economic Stabilization Act.

The President abolished Phase Two's Pay Board and Price Commission, transferring their functions to the Cost of Living Council (CLC). The CLC and the Internal Revenue Service were to monitor wage and price performance by reviewing reports filed by companies, auditing records and analyzing government and trade data. If the CLC determined that an action that had been taken or was about to be taken would violate the stabilization program's goal of 2.5 per cent annual inflation, it could issue a temporary order setting interim price and wage levels. It could then issue an order setting a legally binding level.

As a general rule for Phase Three, the White House said, price increases above levels authorized in Phase Two should not exceed cost increases. As under Price Commission regulations for Phase II, price increases were subjected to a profit-margin limit. A firm was allowed to make price increases regardless of its profit margin if the firm's average price increase on all products did not exceed 1.5 per cent in one year.

For Phase Three wage standards, the President retained at least temporarily the Pay Board's Phase Two general standard limiting wage increases to 5.5 per cent. He created a 10-member Labor-Management Advisory Committee to advise the CLC on whether the standard should be modified. The panel included George Meany, who had quit the Pay Board the year before.

The President continued mandatory controls for three "particularly troublesome" industries—health costs, processed food prices and construction costs. He indicated that food price increases had been especially serious and said controls would be continued "with special vigor for firms involved in food processing and food retailing." As under Phase Two, raw agricultural product prices were exempt from controls.

Inflationary Spiral. By early spring 1973 it was apparent that the switch to a voluntary system of controls was not controlling galloping inflation.

The Senate March 20 extended the President's authority under the 1971 Economic Stabilization Act through April 30, 1974. But demonstrating its lack of confidence in Phase III's effectiveness, it adopted 50-38 an amendment re-imposing mandatory federal rent controls.

The Senate defeated amendments to restore Phase II controls on major companies and unions, to slap an across-the-board six-month freeze on most of the economy to freeze retail food prices for 90 days and to set interest rates at March 16 levels.

Meat Ceiling. President Nixon March 29 in a televised address to the nation ordered imposition of price ceilings on beef, lamb, and pork for an indefinite period. His announcement came against a background of meat boycotts by shoppers against record high prices for those products.

Confidence in the administration's anti-inflation policies was diminished April 5 when the government reported wholesale prices during March. For all commodities the Labor Department reported the wholesale price index rose 2.2 per cent during March. At an annual rate of 26.4 per cent, the March increases were the highest monthly rise since 1951. *(Chart, p. 116)*

The House April 16 passed a simple one-year extension of the 1971 Economic Stabilization Act after it had rejected an amendment to roll back prices and interest rates to their March 16, 1973, levels.

On April 30, the last day to extend the President's control authority, both houses accepted the conference report on this legislation, and the President signed the bill.

International Economic Policy

A serious rise in the U.S. balance of payments deficit was responsible for the major congressional and executive actions affecting international economic policy between 1969 and 1972. Attempts to control the deficit led ultimately to the first devaluation of the dollar since 1934. Before the devaluation was announced in late 1971 concern about the balance of payments had led to passage of several bills designed to control the outflow of dollars and a presidential order suspending the convertibility of dollars into gold.

The balance of payments position was also an important factor in the rather confused actions on international trade during this period. For the first time, the United States began to import more than it exported, and this contributed to the worsening balance of payments. An administration trade bill designed to increase exports died in 1970 after being saddled with protectionist amendments. However, Congress reversed a trend of the mid-60s and passed bills permitting expansion of U.S. exports to communist countries.

1971 Devaluation. Events leading to devaluation began Aug. 15, 1971, when President Nixon announced a broad new economic policy designed to stop inflation, create new jobs and protect the dollar. To achieve the latter goal he suspended the convertibility of the dollar into gold. This repudiated the 26-year old U.S. commitment to maintain the external value of the dollar by buying and selling gold at $35 an ounce. It allowed the value of the dollar to float on demand in international markets.

To put pressure on other countries for more permanent changes in the international monetary system, the President also announced a temporary 10 percent surcharge on all imports into the United States. This was a primary bargaining weapon for the United States when finance ministers of the industrial countries met throughout the fall to negotiate a new pattern of exchange rates. The United States during the bargaining pressured such countries as West Germany and Japan to revalue their undervalued currencies upward to eliminate what it felt was an unfair trade advantage. Those countries insisted that the United States must first devalue.

Agreement was reached and the import surcharge rescinded Dec. 18 at an historic meeting of finance ministers at the Smithsonian Institution in Washington, D.C. The United States agreed to devalue the dollar by 8.5 per cent by raising the price of gold to $38 from the $35-an-ounce price in effect since 1934. The effect was to make the value of the dollar less but to make the price of American products more competitive. At the same time

several other nations revalued their currency upward. The total resulting devaluation was placed at 12 per cent.

The devaluation decision won general acceptance among congressional leaders, who were resigned to a reappraisal of the dollar's role in the world economy. In early 1972 Congress gave formal approval to the devaluation, passing the authorization with one dissent in the Senate and by a 342-43 roll call in the House.

In September 1972 the Nixon administration, through Treasury Secretary George P. Shultz, put forth proposals for a complete overhaul of the international currency system. The proposals continued the administration's efforts to diminish the importance of gold and replace the dollar as the standard measure of world monetary relationships. Shultz acknowledged that the proposals were "difficult, complicated and controversial" and would take some time to negotiate. Once negotiated, the new system would have to be approved by national legislatures, including the U.S. Congress.

1973 Devaluation. President Nixon in December 1971 had called the Smithsonian Agreement "the most significant monetary agreement in the history of the world." But little more than a year later, at the end of the President's first term, it was clear that it had been little more than a stop on the way to a further devaluation. The over-all improvement in the balance of payments deficit in 1972 was disappointing, largely because of a sharp increase in the U.S. trade deficit which forms part of the over-all balance. The trade deficit rose from $2.7 billion in 1971 to $6.9 billion in 1972, and early in 1973 the dollar began to run into trouble in foreign money markets. On Feb. 12, 1973, the administration announced that Nixon would ask Congress to authorize a 10 per cent dollar devaluation. *(p. 133)*

Trade Policy. Administration signals on a trade policy were conflicting during the period 1969-72. This was apparently a result of disagreement among high administration officials. In addition, the President, who had supported freer trade during his election campaign, was indebted to southern protectionists for substantial help during that campaign.

Mr. Nixon sent Congress late in 1969 a "modest" omnibus bill which would have permitted him to reduce tariffs and increase assistance to U.S. businesses harmed by imports. During long and complicated action on that bill in 1970 conservatives succeeded in amending it to create strong protectionist legislation. Senate liberals managed a successful filibuster against the measure at the session's end and it died at the finish of the 91st Congress. It was unclear whether the President would have vetoed the bill if it had reached his desk. He did not resubmit a trade bill to the 92nd Congress, but Treasury Secretary Shultz, in his September 1972 speech on international monetary reform, called for a system with built-in incentives for trade liberalization.

Although Congress and the administration could not decide on omnibus trade legislation, Congress passed several other bills designed to improve the U.S. balance of trade by increasing exports. In 1969 it replaced the Export Control Act, which had hindered the sale of U.S. goods to communist countries, with a less restrictive measure. The new bill, the Export Administration Act, was extended and liberalized in 1972. Congress also raised the limit on Export-Import Bank loans and removed some restrictions on its operations in order to increase U.S. trade.

Other Actions. Other congressional actions during the four-year period affecting international economic policy included tow extensions of the interest equalization tax, a measure to protect the balance of payments first enacted in 1964. The bill had originally been controversial, but was generally accepted as a necessity by the late 1960s.

Congress also authorized additional U.S. support for several international banks—the International Bank for Reconstruction and Development (World Bank), the International Monetary Fund, the Inter-American Development Bank, the International Development Association and the Asian Development Bank. Controversy over authorizations for "soft" (long-term, low-interest) loans by some of the banks occurred in the 91st Congress but seemed to have died down in the 92nd.

Congress also voted two extensions of U.S. membership in the International Coffee Agreement. There was some controversy about the agreement's effect on high coffee prices and Congress temporarily permitted U.S. membership to lapse in 1971.

Chronology of International Economic Legislation 1969

The most important congressional action in the area of international economics in 1969 was passage of a new Export Administration Act (HR 4293). The act replaced the 1949 Export Control Act, a restrictive measure affecting U.S. trade with communist countries, with a new law which had the effect of encouraging East-West trade.

Congress also extended the Interest Equalization Tax, a measure designed to lessen the outflow of dollars for investment capital overseas. In another action affecting the balance of payments the administration, despite a continued high dollar outflow, announced a relaxation of strict controls on U.S. investment abroad.

Export Administration

Congress replaced existing legislation governing U.S. trade with communist countries with a less restrictive measure. The new act (HR 4293—PL 91-184), the Export

Administration Act of 1969, succeeded the expiring Export Control Act of 1949. The chief difference between the two bills was a provision enabling the United States easily to sell items to communist countries if they were freely available from such areas as Western Europe and Japan. HR 4293 also recognized that "the unwarranted restrictions of exports from the United States has a serious adverse effect on our balance of payments."

The new act was not requested by the President; instead he had asked for a simple four-year extension of the 1949 act. That act in effect set up a system under which licenses were required for shipment of certain items to communist countries. As of December 1968, 1,200 items were controlled by the system. All but 200 of those could be obtained by the communist countries from West European allies of the United States. (*Details on the Export Control Act, Congress and the Nation Vol. I, p. 206*)

The House in 1969 agreed to the President's request for extension of the expiring act. The Senate however substituted for the text of the House bill the new measure, the Export Administration Act, eliminating the requirement of export licenses for non-military goods which communist countries could readily obtain elsewhere. Like the Export Control Act, the bill permitted the President to prohibit all trade for reasons of national security, but it required him to explain in detail reasons for restricting trade in non-military goods and items which could be obtained from other nations. It included a declaration that it was U.S. policy to promote trade with all nations.

During debate on the Senate bill, supporters argued that cold war hostilities had eased, and that the main effect of the controls in the old act was to deny U.S. exporters a growing East European market.

Senate-House conferees first filed a conference report including most of the provisions of the Senate bill, effective until June 30, 1971. When the report came before the House, a number of members objected to the provision requiring the President to make a detailed report of reasons for restricting trade in non-military goods. The report was returned to conference. Conferees then agreed on a compromise provision requiring the President to explain decisions to restrict imports "to the extent permitted by national security considerations." This language was accepted by both houses and the bill was cleared for the President.

PROVISIONS. As signed into law, HR 4293:

● Replaced the Export Control Act of 1949 with the "Export Administration Act of 1969" which would terminate on June 30, 1971.

● Declared that the "unrestricted export of materials, information and technology without regard to whether they make a significant contribution to the military potential of any other nation...may adversely affect the national security of the United States."

● Declared that "the unwarranted restrictions of exports from the United States has a serious adverse effect on our balance of payments."

● Declared that "the uncertainty of policy toward certain categories of exports has curtailed the efforts of American business...to the detriment of the overall attempt to improve the trade balance of the United States."

● Declared it to be U.S. policy to encourage trade with "all countries with which we have diplomatic or trading relations, except those countries with which such trade has been determined by the President to be against the national interest; and to restrict export of goods and technology which would make a significant contribution to the military potential of any other nation...which would prove detrimental to the national security of the United States."

• Declared it to be U.S. policy to control exports where factors of short supply, foreign policy or national security were concerned.

• Declared it to be U.S. policy to formulate and apply controls in cooperation with all nations with which the United States had defense treaty commitments.

• Directed the secretary of commerce to make such changes in the office of export control as were necessary to facilitate the policies set forth in the act.

• Required the secretary of commerce to review the export control list, with a view to making changes, and instructed him to report actions taken to Congress.

• Directed the secretary of commerce to keep the business sector informed of changes in export control policy.

• Authorized the President to prohibit or curtail exports of goods, including technical data, to any nations threatening U.S. national security, if he determined that such export would harm national security, regardless of the availability of the goods from other free-world sources. However, if he so determined, he was required to report to Congress the reasons for his decision to the extent that national security and foreign policy permitted.

• Provided that violations of the act were punishable by a fine of not more than $10,000 or imprisonment for not more than one year, with a $20,000 fine for subsequent offenses.

• Required that exporters be fully informed of the reasons for denial of licenses, and be given an opportunity to present evidence related to issuance of an export license.

Interest Equalization Tax

At President Nixon's request, Congress extended the Interest Equalization Tax for 20 months. The legislation (HR 12829—PL 91-128) continued for the third time a tax that was first imposed in 1963 to help relieve the balance of payments deficit by making it more expensive for foreigners to borrow from U.S. sources. *(See box)*

HR 12829 extended the tax from Sept. 30, 1969, until March 31, 1971. It also gave the President authority to reduce the tax on new foreign securities without reducing the tax on outstanding securities and made other minor changes in the law.

The bill also contained a controversial non-germane Senate amendment repealing the provision of the 1968 Gun Control Act requiring sellers of shotgun and rifle ammunition to register purchasers. The amendment left in force the registration requirement for handgun cartridges and ammunition, mainly .22 caliber rimfire, that is interchangeable between rifles and handguns. Controversy over the amendment held up action on the bill until late in the session. As the existing law expired July 31, 1969, two temporary extensions were necessary to keep the act in effect until HR 12829 was passed.

In testimony on the bill administration witnesses said the tax was still necessary because of a continued decline in the U.S. balance of trade and that it provided "the minimum insurance necessary to guard against the risk of potentially large portfolio outflows." In reporting the bill, the House Ways and Means Committee said that

Interest Equalization Background

The Interest Equalization Tax was enacted in 1964 (PL 88-563). It was part of a package of measures proposed by President Kennedy to reduce the U.S. balance of payments deficit. The original bill made the tax retroactive to July 18, 1963, and extended it through 1965. Subsequent acts (PL 89-243, PL 90-59) extended it through July 1967 and then July 1968. *(Details, Congress and the Nation Vol. II, p. 144, 162)*

The tax was originally intended as a temporary measure to increase the cost to foreigners of obtaining long-term investment capital in the United States. The tax worked this way: Americans would pay the tax, at rates provided in the bill, when they acquired a foreign security which would mature in more than three years. And a foreign borrower would pay the tax if he borrowed U.S. dollars to purchase a foreign security. With these tax increases, the cost of obtaining capital in the United States was expected to be at a level comparable with European markets, where generally higher interest rates had prevailed.

In 1965 a combination of executive and congressional actions revised the effect of the act to make the tax also applicable to securities with a maturity period of one to three years. In the course of extending the act once again in 1967 Congress further amended it to give the President authority to eliminate the tax or set it at any level up to 50 per cent above the amount of the levy.

The 1964 act had set the tax at 15 per cent of actual value (equivalent to 1 per cent annual interest) on U.S. purchases of foreign stocks and bonds which had a maturity of 28½ years or longer. A lower graduated rate was set for bonds with an earlier maturity. In extending the act in July 1967, Congress increased the tax from 1 per cent annual effective interest equivalent to 1.5 per cent. In August 1967 President Johnson used his discretionary power to vary the rate and lowered it to 18.75 per cent or an annual interest equivalent of 1.25 per cent. As U.S. interest rates rose to more nearly the level of interest rates abroad, President Nixon again used this authority on April 4, 1969, to lower the tax rate to 11.25 per cent or 0.75 per cent equivalent annual interest.

without the tax progress made in moderating capital outflow and other balance-of-payments programs would be jeopardized. It said the tax had reduced the outflow of private capital but had not eliminated it.

The bill was passed by both houses with only minor Republican opposition. Republicans had strongly opposed enactment of the tax in 1964.

PROVISIONS. As signed into law (PL 91-128) Nov. 26, HR 12829:

• Extended the Interest Equalization Tax until March 31, 1971.

• Gave the President authority to reduce the tax on new foreign securities without reducing the tax on outstanding securities.

(Continued on p. 123)

Gold as Monetary Standard: A Short History

The use of gold coins as money goes back to antiquity, but only in the 19th century did gold assume the role of the standard by which the values of various nation's currencies were fixed.

The practice of setting the relative values of all moneys in relation to standard gold coin was a product of the 19th century and Britain's economic supremacy.

An international gold standard actually was in effect only about 40 years, roughly the Victorian Age of British economic and political supremacy.

During that period, most major countries tied their money to gold at substantially fixed ratios and allowed the unrestricted import and export of gold.

The monetary authorities of a nation on the gold standard kept the monetary unit equal to a certain quantity of gold in market value by buying and selling unlimited amounts of gold at the same fixed price.

The international gold standard, along with Great Britain's economic predominance, came to an end in the disruptions caused by World War I.

United States Policy

Britain had led the way onto the full gold standard in 1821, but the United States followed only gradually from a bimetallic system adopted when the nation was formed. The Coinage Act of 1792 defined gold and silver dollars. The silver dollar was 15 times as heavy.

The United States in effect went on an unofficial gold standard with the Coinage Acts of 1834 and 1837. The de facto gold standard was interrupted, however, when the government issued inconvertible paper "greenbacks" to help finance the Civil War.

Congress in 1873 omitted the silver dollar from coins to be minted, ending the bimetallic standard, and in 1879 the government resumed the redemption of paper money in gold.

Before the gold standard was made official, however, demands for coinage of silver became a political issue. The populist movement of the 1890s, supported by a political alliance of silver-mine interests and farmers seeking inflation of the money supply to ease their debt burdens, campaigned for unlimited coinage of silver at a 16-1 ratio to gold.

"...you shall not crucify mankind upon a cross of gold," William Jennings Bryan said in his famous speech to the 1896 Democratic National Convention that nominated him for President. But Bryan's defeat by William McKinley helped pave the way for an official gold standard.

The Gold Standard Act of 1900 formally adopted the gold standard by requiring the Secretary of the Treasury to keep all forms of money issued by the United States at parity with gold. The same act set the price of gold at $20.67 an ounce.

The New Deal changed the monetary standard as it did other areas of American economic life. The United States had stayed on the gold standard while weakened European nations struggled to resurrect a stable monetary system in the wake of World War I. At best, Europe restored the facade of a gold standard and maintained it only through extreme measures to economize on gold. The precarious system fell apart in the worldwide financial and economic crises of the Great Depression.

Bank Holiday

When Franklin D. Roosevelt took office as President on March 4, 1933, the U.S. banking system was near collapse.

After summoning Congress into special session, Roosevelt March 6 proclaimed a bank holiday and forbade banks to pay out gold. The Emergency Banking Act that Congress passed March 9 reaffirmed the President's authority to regulate transactions in foreign exchange and the export or hoarding of gold.

The President April 5, by executive order, prohibited private holding and circulation of gold and required all holders, including banks, to turn their gold over to Federal Reserve banks.

Congress June 5 adopted a joint resolution abrogating the clauses in public and private contracts requiring payment in dollars of the original gold value or the equivalent in gold content. The resolution declared that all outstanding obligations to pay in gold coin could be paid instead in any legal tender.

Congress May 12, 1933, gave the President authority to reduce the gold content of the dollar by as much as 50 per cent. The authority was granted by a nongermane amendment to the Agricultural Adjustment Act.

In the latter part of 1933, the administration manipulated the price of gold upward by directing the Reconstruction Finance Corporation to buy gold from American mines and on foreign markets.

In a special monetary message Jan. 15, 1934, Mr. Roosevelt asked Congress for authority to devalue the dollar as much as 60 per cent. He also proposed that the government take title to all monetary gold held by Federal Reserve banks, including gold previously turned in by the public.

Gold Reserve Act

Despite opposition from Federal Reserve officials and private bankers, Congress responded Jan. 30, 1934, by passing the Gold Reserve Act. The House approved Roosevelt's recommendations, 370-40, and the Senate passed the bill 66-23.

Roosevelt Jan. 31 devalued the dollar by raising the price of gold to $35 an ounce, from $20.67, reducing the dollar to 59.06 per cent of its previous gold content.

Roosevelt's policy put the United States on a limited gold standard. The Treasury bought gold at $35 an ounce and sold it at the same price to foreign central banks.

The full gold standard had been abolished, however, because Americans no longer were permitted to hold gold or to convert paper currency into gold.

(Continued from 121)
- Granted exemption from the tax to certain financing transactions in connection with U.S. exports.
- Exempted certain leases having substantially the same effect as sales in connection with U.S. exports.
- Repealed the registration requirement of the 1968 Gun Control Act as it applied to shotgun and most rifle ammunition.
- Made the provisions effective as of Sept. 30, 1969.

Foreign Investment Controls

President Nixon April 4 announced a three-point relaxation of strict controls on U.S. foreign investment of dollars which had been established by the Johnson administration effective Jan. 1, 1968. The mandatory controls, imposed for the first time in the United States, had been prompted by a serious deterioration of the U.S. balance of payments position in 1967. They had prohibited any individual from making new net private investment above $100,000 in Western Europe and limited investment levels elsewhere. A certain percentage of foreign earnings was required to be repatriated and short-term financial assets abroad not held as direct investments were to be reduced. *(Congress and the Nation Vol. II, p. 176.)*

President Nixon's April 4 administrative action raised the maximum investment quota free of controls to $1-million and relaxed regulations for international airlines and extractive industries. In related actions affecting the balance of payments, the same day the President announced that the Federal Reserve would revise its credit restraints on banks to permit them to be more flexible in financing U.S. exports and making foreign loans. He signed an executive order reducing the interest equalization tax on purchases of foreign stocks and bonds. *(Interest equalization. 121)*

Paul A. Volcker, under secretary of the treasury, said the balance of payments measures could cause a dollar outflow of $800-million. He said the administration was "under no delusions" that the U.S. balance of payments was in a satisfactory condition but that it was making the moves to signal that it intended to pursue a liberal trade policy. In a message announcing the changes, the President said that the causes rather than the symptoms of the balance of payments problem had to be treated. He said "fundamental economics" called for rebuilding the U.S. trade surplus and the "ultimate dismantling of the network of direct controls which may seem useful in the short run but are self-defeating in the long run."

Before the President's action the House Foreign Affairs Subcommittee on Foreign Economic Policy had begun hearings on resolutions to terminate the mandatory controls. Most of the testimony was from businesses which said the short-term improvement in the balance of payments resulting from the controls was obtained at the expense of a future loss in export sales, dividends and royalties, and at the risk of loss of markets to foreign competitors. No congressional action was taken on the resolutions after President Nixon announced relaxation of the controls.

1970

Congressional concern with economic matters in 1970 was directed largely at the domestic economy, where deep-rooted inflation was becoming steadily more serious.

The only international economic issue on which Congress spent much time was the President's trade bill. By the end of the session the Trade Act had been altered almost unrecognizably into a protectionist measure. But, before the President had to make up his mind about whether to sign the bill, Senate liberals succeeded in having it recommitted.

Congress also increased U.S. financial subscriptions to the World Bank, International Monetary Fund and Inter-American Development Bank, but balked at providing most of the funds requested for "soft" loans. For the third time, it continued U.S. membership in the controversial International Coffee Agreement.

Congress attempted to control use of secret foreign bank accounts by instituting new reporting requirements on money sent overseas.

Trade Legislation

Congress invested a major effort in a controversial foreign trade bill, but an impasse developed at the session's end and the bill was not enacted.

Action began with consideration of the President's trade proposals, which permitted the President to reduce U.S. tariffs and liberalize existing law aiding industries harmed by imports. The bill did not include import quotas; the President had placed himself on record against them although he was pressured to limit textile imports by southerners who had given him crucial help in his election campaign.

As it emerged from the Ways and Means Committee and passed the House, the Trade Act (HR 18970) contained a number of changes including the textile quotas and other controversial provisions such as shoe and oil import quotas and a trigger system instituting quotas on other products when they increased their share of the U.S. market.

The House-passed bill was bitterly attacked by liberals; the *New York Times* called it "the worst piece of trade legislation in 40 years." Representatives of farm, aircraft and electronics groups lobbied against it. They felt it would invite retaliation against their products. Nevertheless the bill, when reported by the Senate Finance Committee, contained basically the same protectionist amendments. Senate backers sought to ensure passage of the controversial measure by attaching it to a widely popular bill (HR 17550) increasing Social Security benefits. The strategy failed when a filibuster forced trade bill proponents to strip it from the Social Security bill and send it back to the Finance Committee, where it died at the end of the session.

Nixon's Trade Bill. President Nixon Nov. 18, 1969, had sent Congress a bill containing trade proposals which he said were "modest in scope" but "significant in impact." The measure liberalized certain provisions of the comprehensive Trade Expansion Act of 1962 and restored a provision of that act which had expired two years earlier. *(Congress and the Nation, Vol. I, p. 203)*

The President's bill (HR 14870) had these major provisions:
- Restore expired presidential authority to make minor adjustments in U.S. tariffs.
- Eliminate the American Selling Price (ASP) system of calculating duties on imports. (The ASP primarily affected benzenoid chemicals and rubber-soled footwear.

It based duty on the prices of equivalent U.S. goods rather than the prices of the goods to be imported.)

• Liberalize the 1962 Trade Act's escape clause provisions for relief to industries adversely affected by imports. The President said the 1962 provisions were "so rigid, so technical" that in not a single case has the Tariff Commission been able to justify a recommendation for relief.

• Liberalize the 1962 Trade Act's adjustment assistance provisions to allow individual firms and workers to receive loans, technical aid, tax relief, relocation and training when increased imports were found to be a "substantial" rather than primary cause of actual or potential serious injury.

• Strengthen the President's authority to retaliate against unfair trade practices by other nations. Existing authority to retaliate against unfair practices in agricultural trade would be extended to all products.

House Action. The House Ways and Means Committee held extensive hearings between May 11 and June 16, 1970, on HR 14870 and on a number of other bills relating to trade. Among these was a bill (HR 16920) sponsored by Ways and Means Committee Chairman Wilbur D. Mills (D Ark.) establishing quotas on imports of textiles and footwear. During the course of hearings on the bills negotiations with Japan and other textile-producing nations on voluntary restrictions broke down. This led the President to "reluctantly" support the textile quotas in the Mills bill. He opposed the footwear quotas.

The Ways and Means Committee reported a clean bill (HR 18970) Aug. 21. The bill contained provisions establishing mandatory import quotas on shoes and textiles as proposed by Mills; it was estimated the provisions would cut back textile imports by 40 per cent.

Another highly controversial provision of the new bill had been proposed by ranking minority member John W. Byrnes (R Wis.). This established a "trigger" system which would impose quotas on other products whenever imports exceeded a certain share of the U.S. market.

The bill also included another provision, not recommended by the administration, fixing the oil import quota system in legislation. The system had been established by presidential proclamation in 1959 and could be rescinded through presidential proclamation. The provision in effect barred the President from adopting the majority recommendation of a presidential task force which had earlier in 1970 recommended replacing the oil import quota system with a tariff system.

In addition to these protectionist provisions, the Committee measure also contained most of the provisions of the administration bill. However, it rejected the administration request to eliminate the American Selling Price system of fixing import duties.

HR 18970 was passed by the House Nov. 19 by a 215-165 roll-call vote. A motion to kill the bill by sending it back to Committee had earlier been rejected by 172-207 roll call.

Opponents of the bill attacked it as inflationary during a time when rising prices were already a serious problem in the United States. The mandatory oil import quota was attacked as costing consumers $5- to $7-billion annually. Representatives of districts with a heavy aircraft and electronics industry and representatives of farm areas opposed the trigger quota provision because of possible retaliation against those products.

In presenting a detailed defense of the bill, floor manager Mills said that the bill was not a retreat into protectionism, but rather a warning to competing countries that certain U.S. industries had critical problems. "If this legislation is not passed now," he said, "I shudder to think of the legislation that the Congress might well pass two years from now, when I suspect you will have a very high percentage of the people of the United States unemployed."

Senate Action. The Senate Finance Committee Dec. 11 reported a House-passed bill (HR 17550) raising Social Security benefits. In an attempt to secure passage of the by then highly controversial trade bill, the Committee attached to the Social Security bill a modified version of the House-passed Trade Act. The Senate added some new trade provisions and made some other changes in the House bill. However, the most controversial provisions— oil, textile and shoe quotas and the system that would trigger quotas—were basically unchanged. Like the House, the Senate Committee turned down the President's request for elimination of the American Selling Price system.

HR 17550 was brought to the Senate floor Dec. 16. An attempt by the managers of the bill to get a unanimous consent motion to limit debate was thwarted by the bill's opponents, led by Jacob K. Javits (R N.Y.) and Walter F. Mondale (D Minn.). Opponents then began a filibuster against the trade provisions which ended Dec. 28 when bill manager Russell B. Long (D La.) moved that HR 17550 be returned to Committee for deletion of the trade section. A supporter of the trade provisions, Long said he thought there were enough votes in the Senate to pass the trade bill, but there was not time remaining in the 91st Congress to break the filibuster. Long's recommittal motion was adopted by a 49-21 roll-call vote and killed the Trade Act.

International Banks

Congress enacted a bill (HR 18306—PL 91-599) authorizing a total $2.7-billion increase in U.S. subscriptions to three international financial institutions—the International Bank for Reconstruction and Development (World Bank), the International Monetary Fund and the Inter-American Development Bank.

HR 18306 authorized U.S. support of a $3-billion increase in the total authorized capital stock of the World Bank and, if the increase became effective, a U.S. purchase of 2,461 additional shares of the stock (at a cost of $246,100,000). It authorized an increase of $1,540,000,-000 (to $6.7-billion) in the U.S. contribution to the International Monetary Fund. For the Inter-American Development Bank, it authorized support of an increase in the bank's capital stock and authorized the United States to subscribe to 82,352 shares at $10,000 par value each. The bill also authorized one U.S. installment of $100-million for the Inter-American Bank's fund for soft-loan (long-term, low-interest) operations.

In other provisions, the administration-backed bill required the National Advisory Council on International Monetary and Financial Policy to include in its annual report to Congress a list of loans approved by the three banks, an evaluation of each loan and a statement on steps taken by the member nations of the Inter-American Development Bank to restrain their military expenditures and preserve free and democratic institutions.

As passed by the House, HR 18306 had also included a $100-million authorization for soft loan operations of the Asian Development Bank and $1-billion requested by the administration for Inter-American Development Bank soft loans. Those funds were cut sharply on the Senate floor after a filibuster led by Albert Gore (D Tenn.). Gore and other opponents of soft-loan funding objected to financing foreign projects when domestic programs were being curtailed or wiped out. As cleared by Congress, only $100-million for the Inter-American Bank's soft loans was authorized. Congress in 1968 had also failed to enact an administration bill to contribute funds for Asian Development Bank soft loans. *(Congress and the Nation Vol. II, p. 114)*

Export-Import Bank

Congress failed to complete action on a bill (S 4268) that would have excluded disbursements and receipts of the Export-Import Bank from the U.S. budget and exempted the bank's operations from a net expenditure limit of $4,082,096,000 imposed by the fiscal 1971 budget. Supporters of the bill said it would have permitted substantial expansion of the bank's activities and would improve the U.S. balance of payments. The Export-Import Bank is a U.S. government agency established in 1945 to promote American exports with short-term credits to foreign businessmen.

S 4268 was passed by the Senate late in the session. It died when the House by a 161-102 vote failed to pass the bill under suspension of the rules requiring a two-thirds majority vote. Opponents objected that it was being considered too hastily in the last days of the session.

International Coffee Agreement

Congress voted to continue U.S. membership in the International Coffee Agreement until June 30, 1971. The bill (HR 19567—PL 91-694) continued the President's authority to restrict entry into the United States of coffee imported from countries not participants of the agreement and to prohibit entry of coffee shipments from participating members that were not accompanied by certificates of origin or re-export.

In passing the bill, Congress turned down the President's request to continue participation through June 30, 1973. The House Ways and Means Committee said this was because Brazil had been discriminating in favor of exports of processed coffee, as compared to exports of green coffee, and that this was in violation of the agreement.

The Coffee Agreement was signed in 1962 by 32 coffee-exporting nations and 22 importing nations. It was designed to stop a continuing downward trend in coffee prices and to stabilize production by setting minimum world prices at the 1962 level. Congress did not ratify U.S. membership in the agreement until 1965 because of controversy over a rise in the price of coffee. In 1968 the President signed a new International Coffee Agreement which extended the earlier agreement, with more flexible provisions for adjusting export quotas, for five years—through Sept. 30, 1973. Congress the same year authorized continued U.S. participation in the agreement, but for only two years. It said it had not provided for five-year participation at that time because it wished to allow for an interim review of the agreement. *(Congress and the Nation Vol. II, p. 61, 113)*

Foreign Bank Accounts

Congress passed an administration-backed bill (HR 15073—PL 91-508) designed to curb violations of U.S. laws and avoidance of taxes through use of secret foreign bank accounts and foreign financial transactions.

Bank secrecy laws of numerous countries, including Switzerland, Panama, Liechtenstein, the Bahamas, Luxembourg and West Germany, had made possible in recent years the increasing use of foreign bank accounts to avoid payment of U.S. taxes, screen illegal operations and "sanitize" money made in illegal operations. U.S. law could not affect those bank secrecy laws, but HR 15073 attempted to control illegal use of the banks by U.S. citizens by requiring U.S. banks and businesses to keep records and file reports on transactions involving the import and export of $5,000 or more.

In addition to a variety of reporting and record-keeping requirements, the final version of HR 15073 also included the texts of two other non-germane bills added on the Senate floor. These prohibited the issuance of unsolicited credit cards and regulated credit information reporting and use.

PROVISIONS. As signed into law, the provisions of HR 15073 designed to curb use of foreign bank accounts:

● Expressed a congressional finding that maintenance of adequate records by banks and other financial institutions had "a high degree of usefulness in criminal, tax and regulatory investigations and proceedings" and required keeping of "appropriate types of records."

● Authorized the secretary of the treasury, when he determined that the information to be provided had the high degree of usefulness cited above, to issue regulations requiring banks and other institutions to maintain records of (1) account holders and persons with access to accounts, (2) checks drawn and paid, (3) checks received for deposit and collection, (4) currency transactions for which reporting was required by the provision immediately below and (5) such other transactions as he considered necessary to accomplish the purposes of the bill.

● Required reporting of individual transactions involving export or import of $5,000 or more in currency or other monetary instruments, including travelers' checks and negotiable securities.

● Directed the secretary to require U.S. citizens, residents and businesses involved in transactions or relationships with foreign financial agencies to keep records or submit reports, or both, of (1) the parties involved, (2) their legal capacities, (3) the real parties at interest and (4) the nature of the transactions or relationships, including amounts of money, credit and property involved.

● Extended applicability of the Federal Reserve Board's margin requirements to borrowers who were U.S. citizens, residents or businesses or foreign businesses controlled by U.S. interests.

● Established civil and criminal penalties and authorized the secretary to seek injunctions to stop or prevent violations.

1971

As the balance of payments deficit hit an all-time high, President Nixon's Aug. 15 suspension of convertibility of the dollar into gold and the subsequent Dec.

(Continued on p. 128)

International Monetary System 1945-71: Pre-Eminent...

Following is a description of the international monetary system which prevailed through the postwar period until Aug. 15, 1971, and of the United States' balance of payments deterioration which led to abolition of that system.

Bretton Woods System

The United States emerged from World War II as the dominant economic power in the world. Consequently the dollar assumed pre-eminence in monetary relations. Monetary authorities of the western nations assigned it the central role in restructuring the international monetary system after the war.

IMF. The postwar international monetary system was shaped by the representatives of 44 nations at a 1944 conference in Bretton Woods, N.H. The conference produced agreement to set up the International Monetary Fund and a new system which was to foster stability without restoring an international gold standard or impinging on national monetary and fiscal independence.

Going into operation in 1947, the IMF provided international drawing rights to help member nations overcome temporary exchange deficits. A member nation's right to draw on the fund was determined by its quota—its contribution to the fund. As a general rule, each nation contributed 25 per cent of its quota in gold or U.S. dollars and the rest in its own currency.

Each IMF member was required to declare a par value of its currency in relation to the gold content of the U.S. dollar in 1944. Transactions between the fund and a member nation were based on the official par value; each member also pledged that transactions within its territory involving currencies of member nations would be allowed only at exchange rates not more than 1 per cent above or below parity.

Thus the IMF gave form to an international agreement to set fixed exchange rates in both government and private transactions. A member nation was allowed to propose a change in its currency's par value only as needed to correct a "fundamental disequilibrium" in its balance of payments.

Dollar's Role. As the currency most widely used in international transactions, the dollar provided a convenient base on which to set international exchange rates.

In a 1949 letter to the IMF managing director, Treasury Secretary John W. Snyder committed the United States to maintain the international value of the dollar by buying and selling gold at the established price of $35 an ounce.

Other countries pledged to maintain their currencies' external values by buying or selling dollars on international exchange markets. In effect, the dollar's value was pegged to gold, and other currencies were pegged to the dollar.

Under these arrangements, the dollar was used by other nations as an intervention currency and, with gold, as a reserve for their own currencies.

In 1968, the IMF created Special Drawing Rights (SDRs) to supplement gold and dollars as currency reserves. Popularly, SDRs have been referred to as "paper gold."

U.S. Balance of Payments

The Bretton Woods system functioned well in the immediate postwar period but ran into difficulty as economic realities changed. Dependent on the dollar, the Bretton Woods arrangements were strained when the dollar's strength waned.

American dollars, like American influence, spread over much of the world through foreign aid, defense spending, overseas investment, trade and foreign travel.

For two decades, the outflow of dollars has not been matched by dollars returning from abroad, producing persistent deficits in the U.S. balance of payments.

Over the years the government has made many efforts to reduce the deficits. But as the deficits have occurred, the United States has had either to absorb them itself or to prevail upon other countries to absorb them.

As other nations have presented surplus dollars for redemption, the U.S. gold stock has dwindled. In 1949 the American gold supply totalled $23.4-billion. By late 1971 it had fallen to $10.1-billion.

Foreign Holdings. Foreign governments and central banks held substantial amounts of dollars as reserves; further amounts were held both officially and in private hands for trade and exchange purposes. These needs absorbed some of the surplus dollars sent abroad as a result of payments deficits.

Beyond these amounts, however, the United States in recent years financed its deficits by requiring foreign countries and persons involved in financial transactions abroad to hold dollars which were surplus to their needs. By making it clear to foreign governments that it would not welcome attempts to exchange surplus dollars, the United States to a great extent made a fiction of its commitment to buy and sell gold at the request of IMF members. The fiction was necessary to keep the system functioning.

Surplus dollars held abroad greatly exceeded U.S. reserves. In 1971 foreign governments and international organizations held $29-billion in U.S. monetary liabilities; private citizens held about $17-billion. In addition, there was a $47-billion market of Eurodollars—dollars held by private citizens, including Americans, in foreign business transactions.

Volatile, unconvertible dollars held abroad contributed significantly to instability in the international monetary system.

Countermeasures. Beginning in the late 1950s, the federal government adopted a variety of measures to control the balance-of-payments deficit. As listed by the Joint Economic Subcommittee on International Exchange and Payments, they included:

• Tying foreign aid to purchases of goods and services in the United States.

...Role of U.S. Dollar and the Growing Payments Crisis

• Reduction of the duty-free allowance permitted Americans returning from travel abroad.

• Reduction of government agency spending abroad.

• Imposition of an interest equalization tax to discourage sale of foreign stocks and bonds in the United States.

• Sale of notes and bonds to foreign monetary authorities to absorb dollar balances.

• Negotiated prepayment of foreign debts.

• Advance payments by foreign countries for military purchases in the United States.

• Voluntary and later mandatory controls on investment abroad by U.S. corporations.

• Lower Federal Reserve ceilings on bank lending to foreigners.

• Export-Import Bank and Treasury borrowing in Europe to hold down foreign central banks' dollar reserves.

• Creation of a gold pool with the central banks of other industrial nations to intervene in the London gold market in order to keep the price of gold substantially equal to the official price.

Gold Cover Removal

Despite such measures, Congress twice during the Johnson administration was called upon to respond to gold crises by enacting major changes in the U.S. monetary structure.

In an action taken to free gold to meet claims for redemption of dollars from abroad, Congress in 1965 passed legislation (PL 89-3) eliminating a requirement of the Federal Reserve Act of 1913 that each Federal Reserve bank keep a reserve of gold certificates worth not less than 25 per cent of its holdings in commercial bank deposits. *(Congress and the Nation Vol. II, p. 253)*

Repeal of this requirement freed about $4.9-billion in gold held by the Treasury as backing for the gold certificates. President Johnson requested the measure after the U.S. gold supply in excess of required currency reserves fell to $1.4-billion, leaving only that amount available to meet potential international claims of $28.9-billion.

Congress was called on to meet another gold crisis in 1968 by freeing more of the gold supply from currency reserves.

A rush of gold buying that year forced the seven major industrial nations to abandon efforts to maintain the market price of gold at $35 an ounce.

Under the gold pool formed in 1961, the major nations made available for sale through the Bank of England enough gold to meet private demands. This arrangement generally kept speculators from driving up the market price of gold, until the effort was terminated.

The United States nevertheless agreed to continue selling gold to other governments at $35 an ounce, creating a two-tier price system: the market price of gold was allowed to fluctuate freely but the official price for government transactions between governments was kept at $35 an ounce.

Gold Backing. In another effort to ease the 1968 gold crisis, Congress adopted legislation removing the remaining gold backing from the dollar.

The bill (PL 90-269) eliminated the requirement that each Federal Reserve bank maintain reserves in gold certificates of not less than 25 per cent of its Federal Reserve notes (currency) in circulation.

At the time, the gold supply was about $12-billion, with $10.7-billion earmarked to meet the 25 per cent backing requirement. *(Congress and the Nation Vol. II, p. 272)*

Dollar Overvaluation. These measures bought time, but the deficit grew. According to one measure—current and longterm capital account—the deficit rose from a yearly average of $1-billion (1960 to 1966) to an annual average of $2.6-billion for 1967-70.

In 1971, despite slow recovery from a recession that should have reduced imports, the United States faced its first trade deficit since 1893 and a payments deficit (again in current and longterm capital account) of $4-billion to $5-billion. The U.S. government used a different measure from that used generally in other countries for its trade balance; on a comparable basis the United States has been running a trade deficit since the mid-1960s.

In the words of a report by the Joint Economic Subcommittee on International Exchange and Payments, the failure of previous efforts to improve the balance of payments "leads to one inescapable conclusion—the dollar is overvalued. It is not really worth as much in international transactions as exchange rates imply, and its foreign currency value is thus overstated."

Paul W. McCracken, chairman of the Council of Economic Advisers, attributed the overvaluation of the dollar to its central role in the world monetary system.

Over the years, he said, other nations tended to devalue their currencies against the standard of value the dollar.

"Thus the exchange rate of the dollar was slowly appreciated by the actions of others," McCracken said, "and this—plus our own inflation after 1965—finally overvalued the dollar to the point of producing a basic imbalance in our external trade and competitive position."

The overvaluation of the dollar "impedes sales of U.S. exports abroad, stimulates purchases of imports here, encourages American firms to invest abroad, and retards foreign investment in the United States," the subcommittee report said.

The IMF was founded, in part, to help member nations deal with disequilibrium in their payments balances. But it failed to assume responsiblity for recommending exchange rate changes by the dollar's overvaluation, the subcommittee said.

Because of the dollar's international role, however, the United States could not take action to correct its overvaluation without upsetting the world monetary system. Until Aug. 15, 1971, the United States was unwilling to do so.

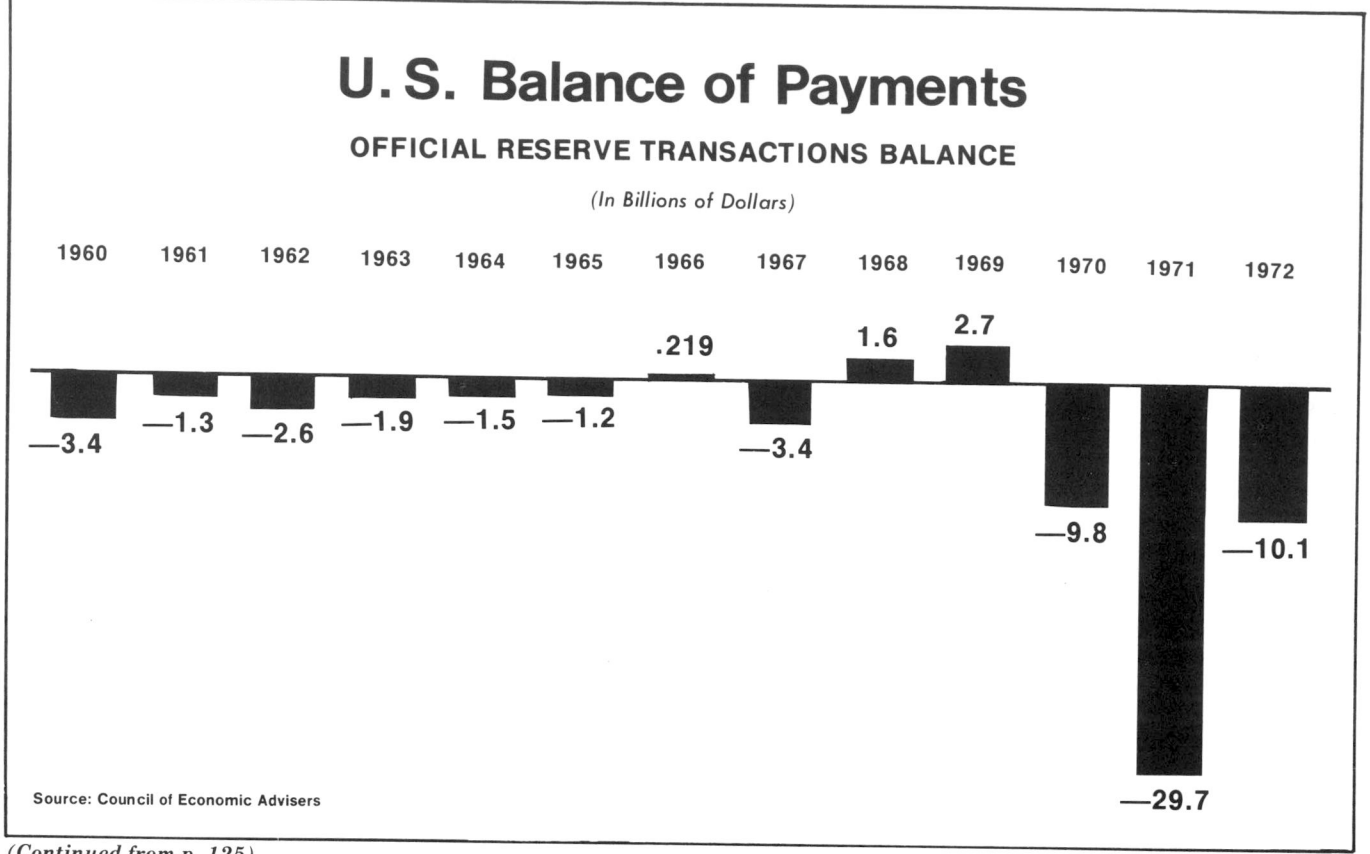

U. S. Balance of Payments
OFFICIAL RESERVE TRANSACTIONS BALANCE
(In Billions of Dollars)

| 1960 | 1961 | 1962 | 1963 | 1964 | 1965 | 1966 | 1967 | 1968 | 1969 | 1970 | 1971 | 1972 |

—3.4 —1.3 —2.6 —1.9 —1.5 —1.2 .219 —3.4 1.6 2.7 —9.8 —29.7 —10.1

Source: Council of Economic Advisers

(Continued from p. 125)

18 devaluation of the dollar were certainly the most important U.S. government actions affecting international monetary matters in 1971.

Beyond those landmark measures, which were generally approved by members of Congress, came passage of several bills designed to help strengthen the U.S. balance of payments position. The interest equalization tax on capital sent abroad was extended for the fourth time. The ceiling on Export-Import Bank loans was lifted and restrictions on Eximbank credits that hindered U.S. trade were lifted. The Export Administration Act was given a routine extension pending more thoughtful consideration in 1972.

Legal Authority for Devaluation. President Nixon drew upon existing authority for the two important international monetary moves in his Aug. 15 program.

Powers granted to the President by the 1962 Trade Expansion Act enabled him to impose the 10 per cent surcharge on imports. The act authorized restrictions on imports if they threatened the national security, and an increase in tariffs in case of injury to domestic workers or businesses through earlier or subsequent tariff cuts.

The President could suspend gold sales because there was no legal requirement that the United States exchange gold for dollars. The Gold Reserve Act of 1934 empowered the secretary of the treasury to buy or sell gold on terms he deemed to be in the public interest.

Devaluation

President Nixon Aug. 15 cut the dollar loose from the $35-per-ounce gold price which had prevailed for almost 40 years. He suspended convertibility of the dollar

into gold and announced a temporary 10 per cent surcharge on all imports. The actions constituted the international aspects of the decisive new economic policy announced the same day. *(The President's domestic program, chapter on economic stabilization, p 105)*

The President's action came at a time when the nation's balance-of-payments deficit had reached almost $23-billion on the three bases used to calculate the overall position—an all-time record. Moreover, a deficit in the U.S. export-import trade was forecast for the first time. *(Explanation of the balance-of-payments situation chart, p. 129)*

Removing the gold backing from the dollar allowed the dollar to float according to demand on international markets and had the effect of devaluing the overvalued dollar and thus reducing the growing U.S. disadvantage in foreign trade. In testimony on the President's new economic policy before congressional committees, administration witnesses made clear that suspension of convertibility and the import surcharge were only temporary measures. Paul A. Volcker, under secretary of the treasury for monetary affairs, said the two actions provided "temporary support to our external financial and trading position while durable arrangements to cope with the difficult problems of international payments are developed." He said such strong actions had been necessary to create "a common understanding of the magnitude of the adjustment required if the United States balance of payments is to be secure and of the implications of that adjustment."

During the four months following the Aug. 15 announcement finance ministers of major developed countries met at frequent intervals to attempt to devise a new

U.S. OVERALL BALANCES ON INTERNATIONAL TRANSACTIONS

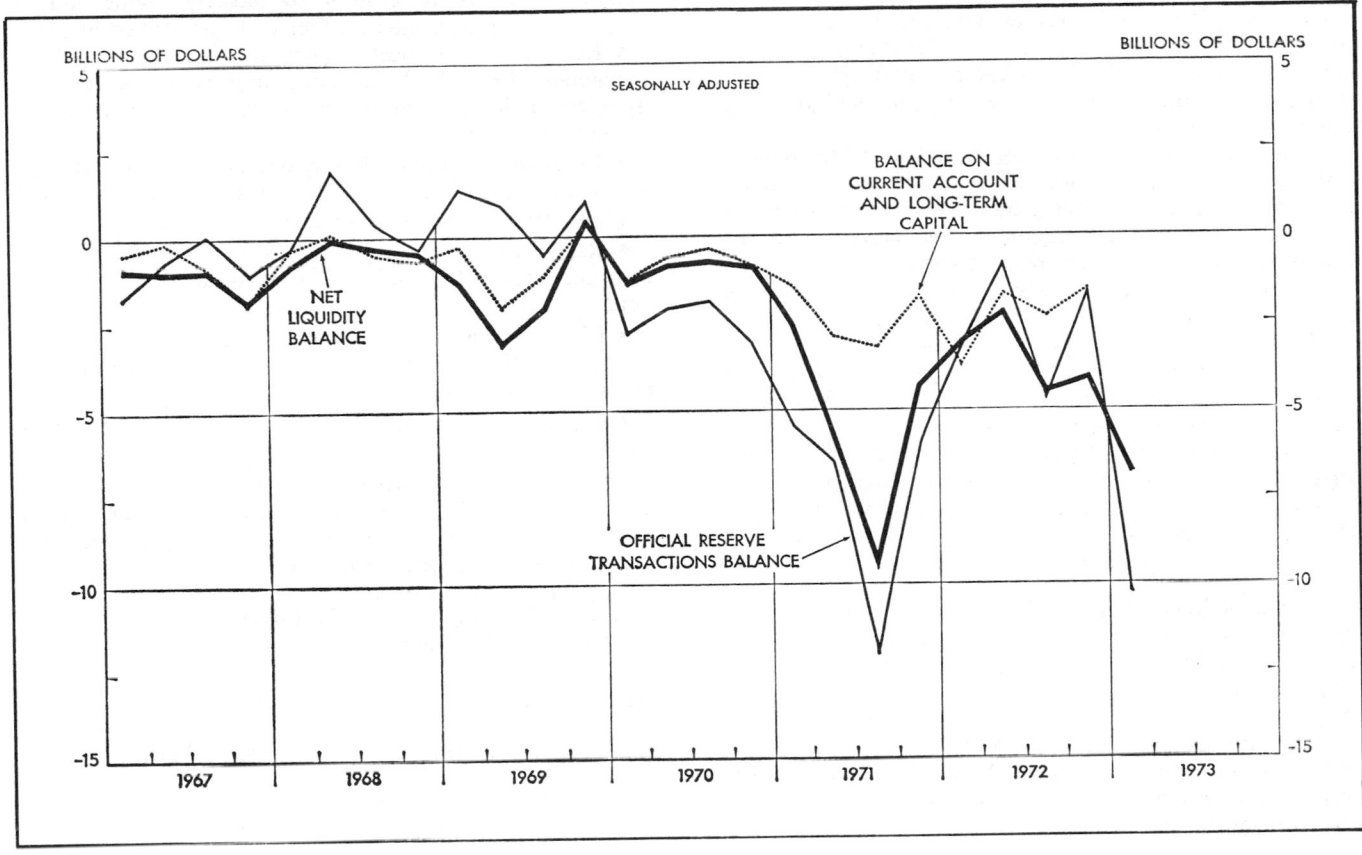

There are now three measures of the U.S. balance of payments which the U.S. government uses. This results from controversy among experts as to what statistical measure most correctly represents the "true" balance of payments deficit.

The **"balance on current account and long-term capital"** measures U.S. transactions with the world in terms of exports and imports, military transactions (U.S. military expenditures overseas offset by sales of military equipment), net income from U.S. investments overseas, travel and transportation expenditures (including tourism), long-term capital investments and similar payments and receipts. This "basic balance" changes relatively slowly and reflects such longer term international economic relationships as the rate of inflation in the U.S. compared with that of major trading partners and relative growth rates of the U.S. and other economies.

The **"net liquidity balance"** adds the influences of non-liquid short-term capital transactions, the effects of receiving allocations of Special Drawing Rights (so-called "paper gold") from the International Monetary Fund and errors and omissions (transactions which slip through the usual reporting net).

The third measure, **"official reserve transactions balance,"** includes the influences of liquid private capital flows. It also indicates the official reserve transactions between the U.S. and the official monetary authorities of other countries.

Both the net liquidity balance and the official reserve transactions balance take into account flows of money which respond relatively to changes in interest rates and to speculation about changes in exchange rates.

set of exchange rates and bring order to the system again. The 10 per cent import surcharge was the United States' prime bargaining weapon in its effort to win a revaluation favorable to the U.S. balance of payments. The United States took the position that it could remove the surcharge when Western European countries and Japan raised the value of their currencies and reduced trade barriers which discriminated against U.S. products. Those countries took the position that realignment of currencies would not take place until the surtax was removed and then must include formal devaluation of the dollar as well as revaluation of other currencies.

Devaluation Announcement. President Nixon met Dec. 14 with President Georges Pompidou of France and subsequently, in a joint announcement, approved devaluation of the dollar as part of a general realignment of currencies. This concession by the United States broke the impasse in the international monetary arena which had prevailed since Aug. 15. It would have been virtually impossible politically for other countries to give up a major advantage in world trade by raising the value of their currencies if the United States had not agreed to devalue.

Moving with unforeseen speed, the major industrial nations, known as the Group of Ten, reached agreement on realignment at a Washington meeting at the Smithsonian Institution Dec. 18. The dollar was to be devalued 8.57 per cent by raising the price of gold to $38—from $35—per ounce. The West German mark and Japanese yen were to be raised the most through revaluation; the British pound, French franc and Canadian dollar were not revalued at all and the new values of other leading countries fell in between.

But the effect was that all were valued in relation to the dollar. The currencies of West Germany and Japan, with which the United States had the greatest deficits in trade and international payments, effectively were revalued by 13 and 17 per cent respectively.

Under the agreement the United States rescinded the import surcharge immediately. The monetary crisis which the new economic policy had deliberately precipitated was effectively resolved, and the way was cleared for negotiation leading toward attainment of the remaining U.S. international economic goals.

The International Monetary Fund placed the new currency values in effect on a temporary basis on Dec. 19. President Nixon, meeting in Bermuda Dec. 20 with Prime Minister Edward Heath of Great Britain, announced termination of the surcharge.

Congressional Action. While the devaluation took effect immediately, legally only Congress could officially change the gold value of the dollar. Administration officials made it clear that such legislation would be requested early in 1972 as soon as there were clear indications that other countries would begin dismantling trade barriers that discouraged American products. Key congressional leaders from both parties expressed willingness to authorize the devaluation.

Export-Import Bank

Congress extended the life of the Export-Import Bank, raised the ceiling on loans and excluded Bank receipts and disbursements from the U.S. budget. The bill (S 581—PL 92-126) also deleted controversial language in existing law that prohibited Export-Import Bank credits to nations giving aid to another country in armed conflict with the United States. The intent of the bill was to increase U.S. trade at a time when the U.S. balance of payments was seriously deteriorating.

The Export-Import Bank was established in 1934 as a banking corporation and in 1945 was made an independent agency of the U.S. Government. Its purpose was to provide financial aid to promote U.S. exports. It provides credits, credit guarantees and insurance to foreign businessmen desiring to purchase American exports.

The prohibition on Eximbank credits to nations aiding countries at war with the United States had been voted in 1968 when Congress refused to go along with Johnson administration proposals to expand trade with Eastern European Communist nations. There was still some sentiment for the prohibition in 1971, but the Nixon administration favored repeal and a number of congressmen argued that it was necessary to pursue every possible means of expanding U.S. trade during the current period of high unemployment and a worsening balance of payments. *(Background, Congress and the Nation Vol. II, p. 110; action on the Eximbank in the 91st Congress, p. 125)*

PROVISIONS. As signed into law, S 581:

• Deleted language in existing law that prohibited Export-Import Bank credits to nations giving aid to another country in armed conflict with the United States.

• Removed the Export-Import Bank's receipts and disbursements from the U.S. budget and exempted the bank from any federal expenditure and net lending limits imposed by the budget.

• Extended the bank's life by one year, to June 30, 1974, and made clear that the bank had authority to sell obligations with maturities beyond its statutory life.

• Raised the ceiling on all loans, credit guarantees and insurance issued by the bank to $20-billion from $13.5-billion.

• Directed the bank to provide terms competitive with government-backed credit available to nations whose exporters competed with U.S. exporters.

• Eliminated Federal Reserve System restraints on export credit.

• Required the President to submit to Congress an annual budget for the bank, including the estimated annual net borrowing from the Treasury, and an annual report on the amount of net lending by the bank, including any net lending created by borrowing from the Treasury that previously would have been included in the federal budget.

• Directed the bank to offer equal opportunities for credit to export agents and managers, independent export firms and small commercial banks.

Interest Equalization Tax

Congress passed a bill (HR 5432—PL 92-9) providing another two-year extension of the interest equalization tax, through March 31, 1973. The tax applied to purchases of foreign securities by Americans and to loans by American banks to foreign customers. Its purpose was to help the U.S. balance of payments by reducing the flow of capital abroad. *(Details p. 121, 123)*

In addition to providing a two-year extension, HR 5432 also included a provision giving the President discretionary authority to apply the tax to loans and securities with a maturity of less than one year. The previous law applied only to maturities of one year or longer. The bill also removed an existing exemption from the tax for new investment made by certain mutual funds.

International Coffee Agreement

Congress failed to complete action on a bill (HR 8293) extending the President's authority to carry out the provisions of the International Coffee Agreement of 1968. Authority to participate in the agreement, last extended in 1970, expired June 30.

HR 8293 was passed by the House Nov. 5. During debate, opponents charged that the agreement made coffee unnecessarily expensive for the American consumer and constituted an unnecessary form of foreign aid to Latin America. In defense of the agreement, Wilbur D. Mills (D Ark.), chairman of the Ways and Means Committee, said coffee prices had been relatively stable during the years of the agreement and that its end would bring chaos to the industry and threaten the American supply in the long run. The Senate took no action on HR 8293 in 1971.

Export Administration Act

Congress twice voted temporary extensions of the Export Administration Act of 1969 which gave the President authority to regulate exports to Communist countries. The act was scheduled to expire June 30, but was extended first until Oct. 31 and then until May 1, 1972. The temporary extensions permitted postponement until 1972 of hearings and full-scale congressional action on the legislation.

Sugar Act

Congress passed a bill (HR 8866—PL 92-138) extending the Sugar Act of 1948 through Dec. 31, 1974, and adjusting production quotas for foreign and domestic producers. The Sugar Act is designed primarily to protect the domestic sugar industry by guaranteeing domestic sugar growers a large share of the U.S. market. It assigns the remainder of the market to various favored foreign countries. The latter are anxious to obtain quotas because the protected U.S. sugar price is normally higher than the world price.

HR 8866 increased quotas for domestic producers while the relative shares of several of the largest foreign suppliers were reduced.

1972

In 1972 Congress quickly gave its approval to the 1971 devaluation with very little dissent. The balance of payments deficit began to decline during 1972. In September, the adminstration proposed much broader changes in the international monetary system in an important speech by Treasury Secretary George P. Shultz.

Shultz proposed a diminishing role for gold as the international reserve asset and a growing role for the new Special Drawing Rights (SDRs) or "paper gold."

Under the administration proposal, SDRs would replace the dollar as the standard measure of money relationships between different currencies. However, holdings of dollars and other currencies as reserves by other countries could continue, and the United States would return to exchanging other countries' surplus dollars for gold or some other monetary reserve if the new system was worked out.

Under the proposed system, each currency would have a central exchange rate. However, the currency would be allowed to fluctuate by as much as 4.5 per cent on either side of the central rate.

Countries which failed to control balance of payments surpluses or deficits would be subject to strict penalties. Surplus countries would face import surcharges against their goods. Deficit countries could lose their Special Drawing Rights if they failed to take corrective actions.

In other official actions relating to international economic matters in 1972, Congress extended and liberalized the 1969 Export Administration Act to ease controls on East-West trade. It passed three bills providing for U.S. contributions to international development banks, and authorized a further extension of the International Coffee Agreement.

Gold Price Increase

Congress early in the year passed a bill (S 3160—PL 92-268) giving formal approval to the dollar devaluation put into effect in December 1971.

The bill directed the secretary of the treasury to communicate to the International Monetary Fund a new par value for the dollar of one thirty-eighth of an ounce of gold. The previous par value, in effect since 1934, was one thirty-fifth of an ounce of gold. The result was an 8.57 per cent devaluation of the dollar and an increase in the official price of gold to $38 from $35 an ounce.

S 3160 also authorized the Secretary of the Treasury to maintain the pre-devaluation value of U.S. dollar holdings in the International Monetary Fund, World Bank, International Development Association, Inter-American Development Bank and the Asian Development Bank. It authorized the appropriation of such funds as necessary to maintain the value of the U.S. pledges to those institutions.

S 3160 also authorized the secretary of the treasury and by the House by a 342-43 roll-call vote. Both supporters and opponents of the bill agreed that devaluation could not by itself solve international and U.S. economic problems. Supporters termed the bill an important first step, however, while opponents contended that more fundamental reforms were required.

During consideration of S 3160 both Senate and House committees rejected related bills which would have permitted American citizens to own gold privately, a practice made illegal in 1933 except for industrial and artistic purposes.

Export Administration Act

Congress continued its policy of relaxing restraints on East-West trade. It passed a bill (S 3726—PL 92-412) requiring prompt removal of unilateral export controls except where it was determined that such action would be detrimental to the national security. S 3726 also extended until June 30, 1974 the President's authority to control exports under the Export Administration Act of 1969; when enacted, the Export Administration Act had replaced a more restrictive measure governing East-West trade. *(Background and provisios of the act, p. 120)*

There was little controversy in Congress over removal of export controls or extension of the Export Administration Act. The Senate Banking, Housing and Urban Affairs Committee summed up the general view in its report: "Title I is needed because the United States is handicapping itself by continuing to control the export of many items which are not of strategic value and are not controlled by our foreign competitors....Excessive restrictions result in a worsened balance of payments situation, fewer export sales for American industries and fewer jobs for American workers."

S 3726 also contained two more controversial sections. One, which constituted Title II, gave statutory authority to the Council on International Economic Policy in the Executive Office of the President and authorized funds for its operations in fiscal 1973 and 1974. The council was to coordinate all federal activities affecting international economic policy. It had been established by executive order in January 1971.

During consideration of the bill a number of members objected to the cost of the council, questioned its effectiveness and suggested that its job could be better handled through expansion of the Council of Economic Advisers. During House consideration of the bill the title authorizing the council was deleted by voice vote. However, the title was restored by the conferees and the House adopted the conference report.

The other controversial provision of S 3726 required the secretary of commerce to obtain the approval of the secretary of agriculture before placing export restrictions on any agricultural commodity. The provision stipulated that any order restricting such exports, issued after July 1, 1972, would cease to be effective upon enactment of the legislation. The provision was aimed directly at an order issued July 15 by the Commerce Department limiting export levels of cattle hides to 1971 export levels. The order was issued after the Department of Commerce projected a shortage of hides in 1972 and determined that it would have an inflationary effect on the domestic shoe and leather industries. Supporters of the amendment said the export restriction would hurt cattle producers by lowering the price of hides without reducing shoe prices. Opponents argued that the amendment would send up the price of shoes and eliminate jobs for shoe and leather workers.

PROVISIONS. As signed into law, S 3726:

Title I

• Required prompt removal of unilateral export controls except where it was determined that such action would be detrimental to the national security.

• Extended the President's authority under the Export Administration Act to June 30, 1974.

• Made provisions of Title I effective Aug. 1, 1972.

• Required the secretary of commerce to obtain approval from the secretary of agriculture before placing any restrictions on the export of agricultural commodities and provided that any order restricting such exports issued after July 1, 1972, would cease to be effective upon enactment of S 3726.

Title II

• Established within the Executive Office of the President a Council on International Economic Policy to coordinate all federal activities affecting international economic policy.

• Authorized appropriations of $1,400,000 for the council in fiscal 1973.

• Required the executive director of the council (who would be appointed by the President without Senate confirmation) to keep the appropriate committees of Congress fully and currently informed of the council's activities.

• Required the President to transmit to Congress an annual report on international economic policy prepared with the council's assistance.

• Provided that Title II would expire June 30, 1973, unless extended by Congress.

International Banks

Congress passed three bills authorizing continued U.S. financial support for three international banks. S 2010 (PL 92-247) authorized $960 million as the U.S. contribution to the third replenishment of the International Development Association. S 748 (PL 92-246) authorized $900 million to the Inter-American Development Bank's special funds, and S 749 (PL 92-245) authorized $100-million to the Asian Development Bank's special funds.

The money authorized for the Inter-American Development Bank and Asian Development Bank was to be used for special soft-loan (long-term, low-interest) operations. In the 1970 authorizations for international bank funding, Congress had severely cut administration requests for funds for Inter-American Bank soft loan funds. *(p. 124)*

All three bills contained House amendments requiring the U.S. representative to each of the banks to oppose loans to nations that had expropriated U.S. property without just compensation or refused to crack down on the international drug traffic.

International Coffee Agreement

Congress completed action on a bill (HR 8293—PL 92-262) extending U.S. membership in the International Coffee Agreement until the agreement expired Sept. 30, 1973. U.S. participation had expired in 1971 when Congress failed to complete action on HR 8293.

The House had passed HR 8293 in 1971. Final action came in March when the Senate passed the House bill without amendment. The Senate Finance Committee report on the bill noted that the agreement "appears to have achieved reasonable stability in the coffee market." However, it said the committee staff was undertaking a special study of the agreement as a result of "reports of monopolistic practices and inequities in the coffee trade."

 **1973 Devaluation**

1971 SMITHSONIAN AGREEMENT BROKE DOWN IN 14 MONTHS

In a late night news conference on Feb. 12, 1973, Treasury Secretary George P. Shultz announced that President Nixon would ask Congress to authorize a formal 10 per cent reduction in the dollar's par value—its official value as recorded with the International Monetary Fund (IMF)—raising the price of gold to $42.22 an ounce from the $38 price in effect since the dollar was devalued in December 1971.

The 1971 devaluation, announced as part of a general currency exchange rate realignment negotiated at the Smithsonian Institution, had been the first change in the official gold price since it was set at $34 an ounce in 1934.

The February 1973 devaluation of the dollar's value was announced after hurried discussions by Paul A. Volcker, under secretary of the treasury for monetary affairs, with the finance ministers of Japan, West Germany, France, Italy and Great Britain.

The discussions produced agreement that the dollar would be devalued, that the Japanese yen would be allowed to float upward in value on monetary exchange markets, and that the West German mark and the French franc would stay at the par values assigned by the Smithsonian Agreement. The British pound had been floating since June 1972.

In announcing devaluation, Shultz also said President Nixon had decided to send to Congress "proposals for comprehensive trade legislation" providing presidential authority both to lower tariff and non-tariff barriers or to raise tariffs if required to protect U.S. interests.

(On April 10, 1973, the President sent Congress a message requesting broad authority to raise, lower or eliminate tariff barriers to strengthen the bargaining position of U.S. representatives at international negotiations scheduled to open in the fall.)

In a third international economic move, Shultz announced that the administration would phase out by the end of 1974 existing U.S. controls on the flow of capital abroad.

Failure of Smithsonian

Devaluation ended, for the time being at least, a wave of currency speculation that had created pressure to change exchange rate alignments put into effect by the 1971 Smithsonian Agreement.

The immediate cause of the early February monetary crisis was the speculative selling of dollars for West German marks and Japanese yen by individuals, bankers, Middle Eastern nations and large corporations who expected an upward revaluation of those currencies against the dollar.

The underlying cause was overvaluation of the dollar, meaning that the dollar's par value as set by the Smithsonian Agreement was greater than its actual worth as determined by the strength of the U.S. economy and judged by international markets. Conversely, the mark and the yen were undervalued.

At the root of the international markets' lack of confidence in the dollar's strength were continuing deficits in the U.S. balance of international payments and trade balance.

Although the Smithsonian Agreement had been expected to improve U.S. performance in both the payments and trade accounts, 1972 brought a rise in the trade deficit and only disappointing improvement in the over-all payments deficit.

Another factor—although disputed by the Nixon administration—was doubt overseas about the effectiveness of the Phase III voluntary wage and price controls in keeping U.S. inflation under control. *(p. 117)*

In the face of upward pressure on their currencies, both West Germany and Japan resisted revaluation for domestic economic and political reasons. Undervalued currencies gave their export industries substantial advantages in competing in U.S. markets.

In the Feb. 12 agreement, West Germany accepted an effective 10 per cent increase in the mark's value against the dollar by pledging not to match the U.S. devaluation.

Terminology

Devaluation—Reduction of a currency's value in relation to other nations' currencies, accomplished by raising the official price of gold. By increasing the official gold price to $42.22 an ounce from $38 an ounce, the United States reduced the dollar's gold worth to 1/42.22 ounce from 1/38 ounce.

Par value—A currency's official value, measured in gold, as recorded with the International Monetary Fund. By international agreement, most nations pledged to keep the actual market value including not only trade but also transfers of capital, defense spending, foreign aid and transfers of monetary reserve assets such as gold.

Float—The practice of allowing a currency's market value to reach whatever level is dictated by supply and demand, without central bank intervention to keep the market value within certain limits around the official par value.

Balance of trade—The relationship between a nation's total exports and imports of goods and services, with an excess of exports producing a trade surplus and an excess of imports a trade deficit.

Balance of payments—The relationship between total flows of assets into or out of a nation, including not only trade but also transfers of capital, defense spending, foreign aid and transfers of monetary reserve assets such as gold.

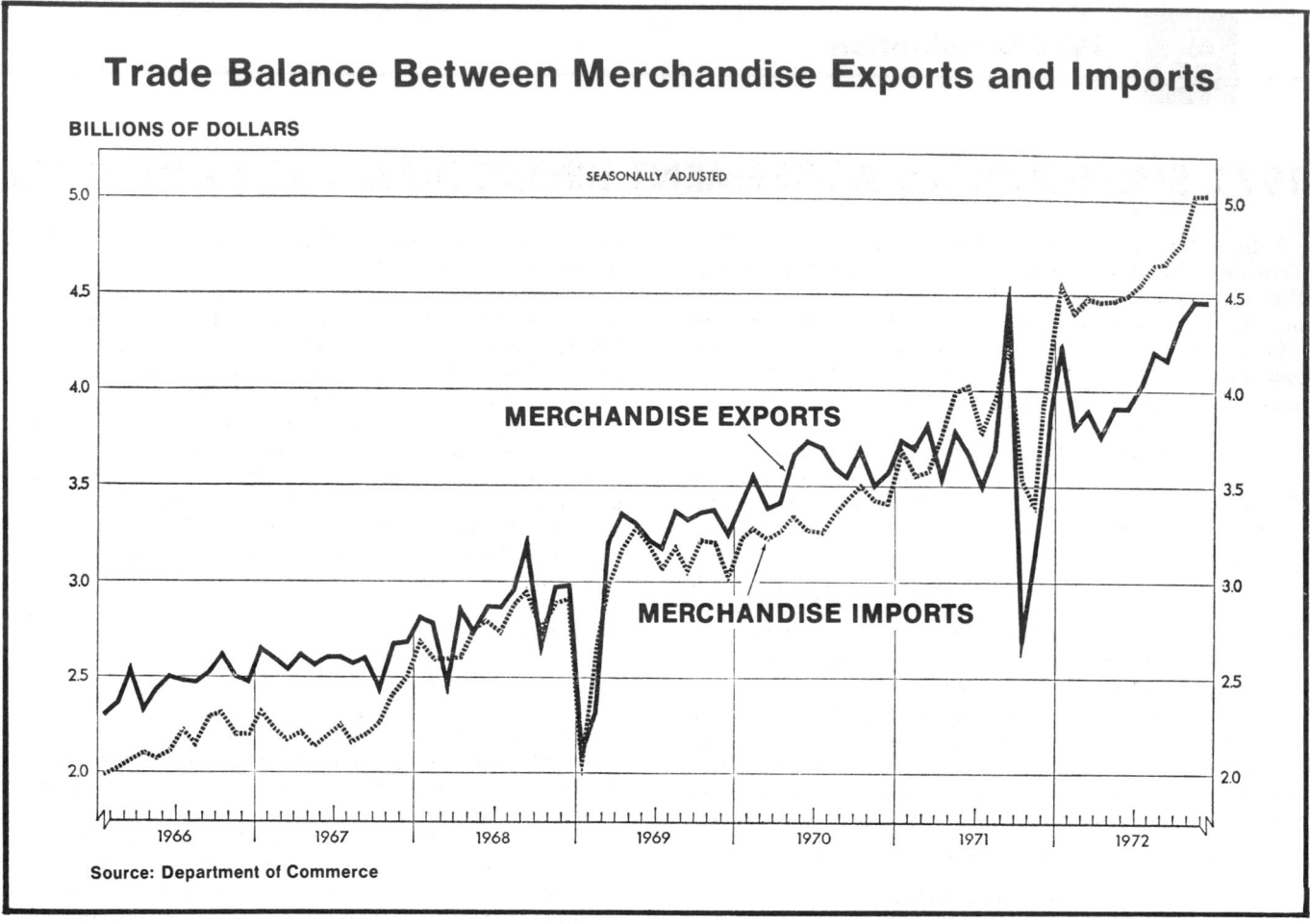

Trade Balance Between Merchandise Exports and Imports

BILLIONS OF DOLLARS

SEASONALLY ADJUSTED

MERCHANDISE EXPORTS

MERCHANDISE IMPORTS

1966   1967   1968   1969   1970   1971   1972

Source: Department of Commerce

Japan accepted a larger increase in the yen's value against the dollar through a combination of the 10-per cent dollar devaluation and upward movement of the yen's par value as determined by market forces.

Shultz acknowledged that the devaluation and trade package primarily was aimed at Japan, which in 1972 enjoyed a $4.2-billion surplus in trade with the United States.

The revised currency alignments "are designed, together with appropriate trade liberalization, to correct the major payments imbalance between Japan and the United States which has persisted in the past year," Shultz said.

Reform Proposals

While only a stop-gap measure, the 1973 dollar devaluation and negotiations that preceded it perhaps pointed the way toward more basic reform.

As a result of the crisis, Rep. Henry S. Reuss (D Wis.), chairman of the Joint Economic Subcommittee on International Economics, said Feb. 13, "the Group of Twenty, charged with working out a fundamental reform along the lines laid out at the IMF (International Monetary Fund) meeting in September 1972, has been told to get moving."

The directions in which the United States would like to see negotiations move were outlined by Shultz in a Sept. 26, 1972, speech to the IMF annual meeting in Washington, D.C. A central feature of the U.S. proposals would be the requirement that nations enjoying balance-of-payments surpluses share with deficit nations the burdens of maintaining over-all payments equilibrium.

Using increases or decreases in a nation's monetary reserve supply as warning signals that an imbalance existed, the U.S. proposals would obligate a nation whose reserves were increasing unduly as the result of a payments surplus to take steps to reduce that surplus. At present, a surplus was viewed as desirable by most nations, putting the burden of resolving payments imbalances on nations—such as the United States—that are saddled with troublesome deficits.

If a nation refused to act against a fundamental payments surplus or deficit, the IMF could apply international sanctions. In the case of a nation refusing to adjust a substantial surplus, for instance, the IMF could authorize other nations to impose general import surcharges against the surplus nation.

Other features of the U.S. proposals include greater exchange rate flexibility, and more reliance on Special Drawing Rights (paper gold) rather than the dollar and gold as the primary measure of monetary reserves. The dollar's role as a reserve for other nations' currencies would be reduced.

The Feb. 12 agreement, in which a deficit nation (the United States) devalued and a surplus nation (Japan) allowed its currency to float upward, indicated some acceptance of the principle of joint responsibility for resolving payments imbalances.

Banking Policy

Action on banking and monetary legislation by the 91st and 92nd Congresses was focused on the changing securities industry. Two major bills for increased securities regulation were passed in 1970. In other years, Congress held extended hearings on the stock market and considered other legislation.

In the area of banking, Congress, also in 1970, passed a major bill to control bank holding companies. There was also a substantial amount of lesser banking legislation enacted or considered between 1969 and 1972; much of it related to a continuing high level of interest rates in the United States.

Securities Legislation. The average daily volume of trading on the New York Stock Exchange more than tripled in the four years ending December 1968. That month, the stock market began a decline which continued until mid-1970. The increased volume put the industry in a situation in which it was difficult to fill orders promptly and correctly. There was general concern about the manner in which customers' cash and securities were handled by brokers. In addition, the market decline precipitated the failure of several small brokerage hours.

This was the situation in the securities industry when the 91st Congress convened. Several committees in 1969 held investigations into the problems revealed by the heavy volume of trading and the market decline. In 1970 congressional concern about protection of investors led to passage of two major pieces of securities legislation—a controversial bill for increased regulation of mutual funds and a bill establishing an insurance fund to protect customers from losses when brokerage houses.

Another bill passed in 1970 was designed to protect stockholders during corporate takeover attempts, chiefly by broadening reporting requirements governing efforts to acquire significant portions of a company's stock.

The 92nd Congress also looked into the problems of the securities industry. Senate and House committees held general investigations in 1971 and 1972. Late in the 1972 session both houses passed a bill strengthening federal regulation of the processing of securities transactions. The bill, which grew out of the hearings, directed the Securities and Exchange Commission (SEC) to move toward an integrated national system for clearing stock transactions with the goal of eliminating the physical transfer of stock certificates. There was no time for a House-Senate conference to work out relatively small differences between the two versions of the bill. A move to get the Senate to accept the House bill with a modification failed, and the measure died with adjournment.

Mutual Funds. The 1970 bill increasing controls over the mutual funds industry had been under congressional consideration since 1967. The original proposal, drafted by the SEC, had been a very tough bill setting ceilings on mutual fund charges and banning altogether certain kinds of funds (known as front-end loads—where an investor paid a disproportionate portion of the amount he would owe in the first year for shares purchased on the installment plan). The bill was strongly opposed by the industry, which lobbied vigorously to kill it. The final bill was a compromise unenthusiastically accepted by the industry. It prohibited "excessive" sales charges and limited sales charges by front-end loads.

Protection of Investors. The other major securities legislation passed in 1970 was largely noncontroversial. It set up an insurance fund to insure investors against losses of up to $50,000 in cash and securities left on deposit and lost when brokerage houses failed. The final bill did not include Senate floor amendments requiring brokers to segregate customers' securities and establish reserves to insure customers' cash balances. Similar provisions were strongly supported by the SEC and opposed by the industry in subsequent years. No further action was taken.

Banking Legislation. Congress in 1970 passed a major piece of banking legislation, a controversial bill extending federal regulation to holding companies controlling a single bank. During the other three years of the first Nixon administration it acted on a number of lesser banking bills. Continuing high interest rates were of concern. Congress held hearings on interest rates, gave the President a bill he did not request empowering him to limit credit and twice raised the interest on U.S. Savings Bonds to make them more competitive with other savings plans. Other banking bills ranged from establishment of an insurance system for credit unions to a bill ending an old discrimination against state taxation of national bank branches.

References

Discussion of banking legislation for the years 1945-64 may be found in *Congress and the Nation, Vol. I,* p. 337-386, 448-450; for the years 1965-68, *Congress and the Nation, Vol. II,* p. 253-279.

One Bank Holding Companies. The complex and controversial banking bill passed in 1970 removed a major exemption from the 1956 Bank Holding Company Act. That act had been intended to halt the growth of banking monopolies by preventing the concentration of control over banks in the hands of holding companies. However, to avoid hardship to small banks away from urban centers, the 1956 bill had exempted from regulation holding companies which controlled only one bank. The result of the exemption had been a trend toward formation of or entrance into one-bank holding companies by major banks.

Congress since 1965 had considered bills to remove the one-bank exemption. There was strong and continuous opposition from the banking lobby, but the House in 1969 passed a stringent bill. The Senate passed a much more lenient version in 1970. The final bill represented a compromise between the two versions. During final action on the conference report there was disagreement as to whether the effect of the final bill was closer to that of the Senate or House measure.

Other Bills. In other action on banking legislation by the 91st Congress, Congress in 1969 changed the law on state taxation of banks, raised the interest on savings bonds, voted to permit more federal controls over interest rates and included a number of provisions affecting banking in the omnibus tax bill. In 1970 it established a federal insurance system for credit unions; previously most credit union funds had been uninsured. It also raised savings bond interest a second time and clarified ambiguities in bankruptcy law.

There was less action on banking legislation by the 92nd Congress. In 1971 the credit union insurance system set up the previous year was changed to give more credit unions a chance to qualify. In 1972 the Senate passed a bill establishing a Federal Financing Bank to coordinate government borrowing. The bill was reported to the House late in the session but did not come up for a vote.

Chronology

Of Banking

Legislation

1969

Credit Controls

In an effort to control continuing inflation, Congress passed a bill empowering the President to set limits on credit or, as an alternative, to reactivate voluntary credit controls in the Defense Production Act which were used in the Korean War. President Nixon opposed the provisions and did not invoke them; but Dec. 23 he signed the bill (S 2577—PL 91-151) because he favored its other banking provisions. *(1970, 1972 extensions of Defense Production Act, national security chapter p. 209, 221)*

The other banking provisions of S 2577: raised maximum insurance protection on deposits in federally chartered banks from $15,000 to $20,000; extended to March 22, 1971, the authority of federal regulatory agencies to set flexible ceiling on rates paid by financial institutions on time and savings deposits, increased the supply of home mortgage money by increasing the Federal Home Loan Bank Board's authority to borrow from the Treasury from $1 billion to $4 billion, and authorized the Federal Reserve Board to establish reserve requirements of up to 22 per cent on funds borrowed by U.S. banks from foreign-owned banks. *(Additional details on S 2577, economic stabilization chapter, p. 106)*

Financial Institutions

Among the multitude of provisions in the omnibus Tax Reform Act of 1969 (HR 13270—PL 91-172) were the following noncontroversial provisions affecting financial institutions. *(Additional details on the tax bill, p. 79)*

In its provisions on financial institutions, HR 13270:

• Reduced allowable deductions for bad-debt reserves for commercial banks, mutual savings banks, savings and loan associations, and cooperative banks.

• Allowed new small business investment corporations to base their allowable bad-debt reserves on the industry average during their first 10 years.

• Required banks to treat their gains and losses from corporate and government bonds as ordinary income.

• Clarified existing law regarding restoration of bad-debt reserve funds to income in mergers of savings and loan associations.

• Provided that until after 1975 bank deposits of nonresident aliens and foreign corporations in American banks would continue to be regarded as non-U.S. property (and interest on them as non-U.S. income) unless effectively connected with the conduct of business in the United States.

• Permitted special banks for cooperatives a 10-year loss carryback for net operating losses.

• Treated periodic payment mutual fund plans as if the stock shares held by a custodian were owned directly by the investors.

State Taxation of Banks

Congress Dec. 12 cleared legislation allowing states to levy the same taxes on national banks located in a state that they levy on state banks. The bill (HR 7491—PL 91-156) amended the National Bank Act of 1864. That act imposed state income and real property taxes on national banks located in the state, but exempted them from paying sales, use and intangible property taxes. The old exemptions had been designed to deliberately discriminate against state banks at a time when "wildcat" state banks were being formed which issued bank notes against little security.

HR 7491 applied to branches of national banks headquartered in another state as well as headquarters offices. The Treasury Department and American Bankers Association had proposed that the bill subject national banks only to taxes imposed by states in which the bank's principal offices were located.

The provisions of HR 7491 did not take effect until Jan. 1, 1972, to give state legislatures time to make necessary changes which took account of the new law. The bill authorized the Federal Reserve Board to conduct a study of the probable impact of the new law, to be completed by Dec. 31, 1970.

Saving Bond Interest

Congress Nov. 26 cleared a bill raising the interest rate on series E and H savings bonds from 4.25 per cent to 5 per cent. The bill (HR 14020—PL 91-130) made the new ceiling retroactive to June 1, 1969, and applied it to both new and outstanding bonds.

The bill was requested by the administration to make the bonds competitive with other investment and savings plans; long-term interest rates had risen substantially in recent years. In testimony on the legislation the Treasury Department said in June 1969 savings bonds redemptions had been $483-million while sales were $383 million—the seventh successive month redemptions had exceeded sales.

The administration initially requested that interest rates be raised on all U.S. Savings Bonds. Critics, however, objected to raising the rates on all bonds at a time when the administration was trying to hold down spending.

The administration then agreed to drop its request for a general raise if Congress would increase the rate for series E and H bonds.

One Bank Holding Companies

The House in November passed a complex bill (HR 6778) placing holding companies which control a single bank under the regulatory authority of the Federal Reserve Board and requiring them to divest themselves of most nonbanking business. The bill extended the Bank Holding Company Act of 1956, which provided for regulation of holding companies controlling more than one bank, to the one-bank companies. House passage was a major victory for the Fed, which had long sought the extension of coverage.

The Senate took no action on HR 6778 in 1969. In 1970 it was to pass a much weaker bill. A compromise between the two versions was worked out and the bill became law at session's end. *(Details of both 1969 and 1970 action, 1970 chronology below).*

Mutual Funds

For the third year in a row Congress worked on controversial major legislation to provide increased regulation of the $50-billion mutual fund industry. The Senate in May passed a bill (S 2224), similar to one it had passed in 1968 but slightly more palatable to the industry. The House Interstate and Foreign Commerce Committee held hearings on S 2224 but deferred action until 1970. *(1968 action, Congress and the Nation II, p. 278; details on action in 1969 and 1970, 1970 chronology below)*

Investigations

Several Subcommittees held hearings in 1969 on issues relating to the securities and banking industries. A proposal for another investigation—on the banking lobby—was rejected.

Securities Hearings. The House Interstate and Foreign Commerce Subcommittee on Commerce and Finance and the Senate Banking and Currency Subcommittee on Securities held hearings in late February and early March to examine a wide range of issues relating to the securities industry. Witnesses from government and the securities business agreed that there were a number of problems confronting the industry, including the strong trend toward more speculative issues on the part of investors, the deluge of paper work caused by a tripling of the daily volume of trading in the previous four years, the growth of conglomerate mergers which were "pumping a lot of water" into the stock market and the possibility of an organized crime role in securities thefts from overloaded brokerage houses.

High Interest Rates. Spiraling interest rates were the focus of lengthy hearings by the Banking and Currency Committees of both chambers. The Senate committee looked into the issue in general; the House committee investigated the June increase in the prime commercial bank rate from 7.5 to 8.5 per cent. There was wide disagreement between the administration, members of Congress and representatives of the banking and housing industries on the causes and effects of the high rates and the hearings did not result in legislative proposals from either Congress or the administration.

Bank Lobby. The House Banking and Currency Committee blocked an investigation of charges of improper influence by the banking lobby. The investigation had been assigned to the Subcommittee on Domestic Finance by Committee and Subcommittee Chairman Wright Patman (D Texas). It was stopped when the full Committee voted 19-13 Sept. 24 in closed session to adopt a motion by Rep. Robert G. Stephens Jr. (D Ga.) to stipulate that the Banking Committee was not the proper forum for the investigation and that Patman should take up his charges with the House Rules Committee if he wished to pursue the issue.

New financial disclosure rules passed by the House in 1968 required members to make public bank holdings valued at more than $5,000 or from which income of $1,000 or more was derived. Nine members of the 35-member House Banking and Currency Committee reported such holdings in 1969.

Patman, a longtime critic of big banks, called the action "simply a backdoor means of killing the investigation." He said that the banking lobby was "the single most potent lobby that operates year-round in Washington" and objected particularly to its tactics in attempting to block legislation regulating one-bank holding companies.

1970

Mutual Funds

Congress Dec. 1 cleared a bill (S 2224—PL 91-547) making the first substantial changes in the regulation of mutual funds in 30 years. The legislation, based on a 1966 Securities and Exchange Commission (SEC)

Mutual Funds: How They Operate; How They Have Grown

A mutual fund is an investment company in which a number of persons invest money and which re-invests these funds in stocks or other assets. There are other types of investment companies, but mutual funds outnumber all the others and greatly exceed their assets.

The primary attraction of mutual funds is that they offer the advantages of diversified investment in a single company. Shareholders receive the benefits of growth or income, or both, from all the assets in a fund's portfolio of investments in different companies or activities. Ordinarily, the breadth of the portfolio protects them from severe loss resulting from a drop in value or income of any single investment.

Mutual funds are not limited to specific issues of their stock; for practical purposes they are open to unlimited investment by purchasers of shares, and they are obligated to redeem their shares when shareholders want to sell back their holdings. To offset continual liquidations by shareholders who need cash or want to invest their money in other activities, mutual funds actively sell their shares through underwriters and sales organizations.

1940 Legislation. The two federal laws under which mutual funds were regulated were passed when the industry was in its infancy and had not been amended substantially through 1969. When the Investment Company Act and Investment Advisers Act were passed in 1940, total assets of all investment companies were approximately $2 billion and mutual fund assets were less than $450 million.

In 1970 the Investment Company Institute (ICI), the principal organization of mutual funds, claiming 93 per cent of the industry, listed 339 mutual funds. Their total assets were $45 billion, reflecting current market values (mutual fund assets had reached $48 billion at the end of 1969). ICI counted 10.5 million shareholder accounts with approximately 5.5 million owners—individuals, couples and families. Approximately one of every six of the 31 million Americans owning stock in 1970 held mutual fund shares.

Nearly all funds charge purchasers a sales fee. For most funds the amount is 8.5 per cent of the amount paid, or 9.3 per cent of the amount actually invested.

The best-known type of fund merchandising is the contractual plan. About 50 companies offer plans under which the buyer agrees to pay a fixed amount monthly for a period of years.

Most contractual plans involve a practice known as the front-end load. To provide monetary incentive to salesmen and sales organizations, front-end-load contracts provide for allocation of up to 50 per cent of the first year's payments to the sales charge. The remainder of the fee is spaced out over the life of the contract.

The buyer is not obligated to make the payments called for under the contract and can take longer than the prescribed time period to complete his payments. But he cannot alter the allocation of the sales charge, and if he sells his shares he forfeits the amount of the sales charge he has paid. Most plans provide two exceptions to those terms: A buyer may cancel his contract within 60 days of purchase and receive a refund of all the money he has paid in; and during the first year a buyer who meets certain hardship conditions can be refunded 90 per cent of his payments.

As an example of how the front-end load system worked, suppose an investor agreed to buy $3,000 worth of shares in a mutual fund over a period of 10 years in monthly installments of $25. The commission, at 8.5 per cent, would amount to $255. But from the investor's $300 payment in the first 12 months, $150 could be deducted against the total sales charge of $255. The remainder of the sales charge would be evenly distributed over the following nine years. Thus, if the investor decided to pull out of the fund after one year, 50 per cent of his payment would have gone to sales charges.

Contractual plans were popular because they were within the financial reach of small investors. According to the Association of Mutual Fund Plan Sponsors, the major organization of companies offering contractual plans, there were more than one million shareholders under contractual plans holding more than $7 billion in shares in 1969. More than two million such contracts had been sold since 1940, the organization estimated.

study, had been under consideration for four years. The final version represented a compromise between the SEC and the mutual fund industry, which had strongly opposed the original proposals. It established broad regulatory authority over mutual funds, limited their sales charges and performance fees, and restricted creation and operation of mutual fund holding companies. *(Full discussion of the original SEC proposals, Congress and the Nation II, p. 268, 278; For explanation of terms, box above)*

Background 1967-69. Of the many provisions of the original SEC proposal submitted to Congress in 1967, the SEC cited three as particularly important, and these points became the most controversial: (1) Fees paid by the mutual funds to their management and advisory

organizations must be "reasonable" and would be subject to court review; (2) a 5 per cent ceiling should be placed on the charges levied on investors when they purchase shares in a mutual fund; (3) there should be a ban on "front-end loads," in which an investor paid in the first year a disproportionately large portion of the amount he would owe over a period of years for shares purchased on the installment plan.

During 1967 hearings on the SEC proposals, these provisions received strong opposition from the principal mutual fund organizations—the Investment Company Institute (ICI) and the Association of Mutual Fund Plan Sponsors (AMFPS). They argued that sales charges and advisers' fees as they stood were necessary to provide incentives to sales forces to merchandise the funds actively. They said the plan to abolish front-end loads would wipe out an industry "which has produced large profits for many hundreds of thousands of small investors since the 1940 act was enacted by Congress, with virtually no complaints from the public since then." *(1940 legislation, box p. 138)*

In defense of its proposals, the SEC said high sales charges largely nullified the benefits of diversified investment available through mutual funds. It said that only a little more than a quarter of all front-end load contractual plans sold were completed and that the sales charges to investors who did not complete plans amounted to 20 to 50 per cent of total payments. Thus many investors in front-load plans lost money despite rising stock prices.

Congress took no action on the SEC proposals in 1967 beyond holding hearings. However, members of the congressional committees with jurisdiction over the proposals began urging the SEC and the industry to compromise their differences.

The Senate in 1968 passed a version of the SEC draft bill containing most of the SEC proposals, including modified but still stiff provisions on sales commissions and front-end loads. That bill died at the end of the 90th Congress when the House Interstate and Foreign Commerce Committee voted not to consider it. House members had been receiving heavy mail from brokers and salesmen opposing the legislation.

The Senate in 1969 again passed a version of the SEC bill (S 2224). Although the bill was somewhat less restrictive than the 1968 measure, the funds industry agreed to it only reluctantly, and when the measure went to the House some of the industry opposition resurfaced.

1970 Action. The House Sept. 23 passed its version of S 2224 by voice vote. The bill was similar to the Senate version and about as stiff in the amount of regulation it authorized. Comments on the floor consisted mostly of praise for the bill—a sharp contrast to the four years of committee infighting which preceded passage.

The final version of the bill resolved the three major issues as follows:

- On the issue of adviser's fees, the adviser was given a legal obligation (known as a fiduciary duty) to the shareholders of the fund. Both the SEC and shareholders were empowered to seek redress in the courts for dereliction of this duty. The ICI said it agreed to the compromise "without enthusiasm" but did not oppose the provision. Special fees for performance, which the SEC had originally wanted abolished, were permitted but only in relation to an appropriate index so that both declines and advances could be measured and fees adjusted accordingly.

- On the issue of sales charges, the bill prohibited "excessive" charges and gave the National Association of Securities Dealers responsibility for preventing them. The SEC was authorized to change and supplement NASD regulations.

- Front-end load plans were given the alternative of limiting sales charges to 20 per cent of the amount paid in any year or charging up to 50 per cent with the under-sales charges exceeding 15 per cent if a shareholder wished to cash in his shares during the first 18 months of a plan.

Provisions. As cleared by Congress, S 2224:

- Prohibited excessive mutual fund sales charges and gave the National Association of Securities Dealers (NASD) initial responsibility for preventing excessive charges.

- Authorized the SEC to amend or add to NASD regulations on sales charges.

- Required the SEC to establish regulations for securities dealers not subject to NASD regulation, and gave such dealers the choice of being governed by SEC or NASD regulations.

- Limited front-end loads to 20 per cent of total payments in any one year and an average of 16 per cent during the first four years of a contractual plan. *(Explanation of terms, box p. 138)*

- As an alternative, permitted front-end loads of up to 50 per cent of total payments, but required that a shareholder who wished to cash in his shares during the first 18 months of a plan be paid the current value of his account and be refunded all sales charges exceeding 15 per cent of his total payments.

- Required that a shareholder under a contractual plan be informed of the total amount of sales charges he was contracting for and that he be refunded his total payments if he wished to discontinue the plan within 45 days after being so informed.

- In plans promising to pay a fixed amount on maturity (face-amount certificates), required spreading front-end loads over five years.

- Established a fiduciary duty to shareholders on the part of investment advisers and managers.

- Empowered a shareholder or the SEC to sue fund advisers and managers for breach of fiduciary duty.

- Permitted fees for management based on performance provided that fees were adjusted according to a comparison of the growth or decline in the value of investments with an established index.

- Codified administrative treatment of banks' collective trust funds and insurance companies' separate accounts for corporate pension plans and those of self-employed persons.

- Restricted creation and operation of mutual fund holding companies.

- Eliminated a number of exemptions from regulation of investment advisers in existing law and gave the SEC broader authority to administer the Investment Advisers Act.

One Bank Holding Companies

Congress in 1970 completed action on a bill to extend federal regulation to holding companies controlling a single bank. This removed a major exemption from the 1956 Bank Holding Company Act. The bill (HR 6778—PL 91-607) became law Dec. 31.

Background. The 1956 Bank Holding Company Act (PL 84-511) was designed to halt the growth of potential banking monopolies by regulating holding companies which control more than one bank and by prohibiting such companies from managing or controlling both banks and nonbanking businesses. The prohibition did not apply to holding companies which controlled only one bank. The exemption was made primarily to accommodate the 117 small companies controlling a single bank which were in operation in 1955; they were located chiefly in small communities with limited market areas.

In late 1967 a trend became apparent toward formation of or entry into one-bank holding companies by major banks. As they decided to expand into or acquire activities not permitted to them as banks, many large banks availed themselves of the exemption for one-bank holding companies by forming or joining such companies. The Federal Reserve Board in 1970 estimated that the total number of one-bank holding companies had grown from 117 in 1955 to 1,100. It estimated that deposits in banks controlled by these unregulated companies had increased tenfold in the period 1965-70.

During 1966 action on a bill (PL 89-485) closing other loopholes in the 1956 act, the House voted to repeal the one-bank holding company exemption. The Johnson administration took no position on the proposal and it was eliminated by the Senate. *(Congress and the Nation, Vol. II, p. 941)*

Shortly after he took office, President Nixon proposed a bill regulating single-bank holding companies. The House Nov. 5, 1969, passed HR 6778, amended. The bill, generally considered a stong regulatory measure, required holding companies formed since enactment of the 1956 legislation to divest themselves of nonbanking activities. Moreover, all but the smaller companies were required to dispose of nonbanking activities acquired before 1956. Holding companies were specifically prohibited from engaging in certain businesses, including securities, insurance, travel arrangements and accounting. The Federal Reserve Board was authorized to permit activities that were "functionally related" to banking if they could be expected to "produce benefits to the public."

1970 Action. The Senate Sept. 16, 1970, passed a much more lenient version of HR 6778. The bill authorized suspension of nonbanking activities begun after June 30, 1968 (instead of 1956). It did not specifically prohibit holding companies from engaging in certain activities. The Senate exempted altogether from regulation small companies and modern conglomerates controlling a bank (the latter exemption was defined as being for cases where the bank's net worth was $50 million or less and was less than 25 per cent of the net worth of the entire company).

The conference report on HR 6778 was approved three months after Senate passage. During the interval there was intensive lobbying by the American Bankers Association to obtain conferees' acceptance of the Senate provisions of the bill. The final form of the bill, however, represented a compromise between the two versions. During floor debate in both chambers members argued inconclusively about whether it essentially had the same effect as the Senate bill. The final provisions kept the June 1968 date set by the Senate for the divestiture of non-banking activities but required termination of activities acquired before that date if they did not meet standards set by the Federal Reserve Board. The final bill did not include provisions specifically outlawing certain activities, and dropped Senate language on exemptions from regulation for small companies and conglomerates. Instead it contained new language permitting the Federal Reserve Board to grant exemptions under certain conditions. The final bill also contained a non-germane Senate amendment

authorizing minting of commemorative part-silver dollars bearing the likeness of the late President Dwight D. Eisenhower.

PROVISIONS

As cleared by Congress, HR 6778:

● Placed one-bank holding companies under regulation by the Federal Reserve Board.

● Defined such companies as those controlling 25 per cent or more of a bank or the election of a majority of its governing body or those found formally by the Federal Reserve Board to have controlling influence over a bank.

Bank-Related Activities

● Required the Federal Reserve Board to determine which activities were bank-related and permissible for bank holding companies to engage in; authorized the board to make its determinations in specific cases or general rules.

● Required the board in reaching a determination that an activity was bank-related to find that it was "so closely related to banking or managing or controlling banks as to be a proper incident thereto" (language similar to that of the 1956 act).

● Further required the board to determine that engaging in an activity would result in public benefits, such as greater convenience, increased competition or gains in efficiency, which would outweigh possible adverse effects, such as undue concentration, decreased or unfair competition, conflicts of interest or unsound banking practices.

Effective Date: June 30, 1968

● Authorized a one-bank holding company to retain or continue nonbanking activities acquired or begun on or before June 30, 1968, and continuously engaged in since then, provided that the Federal Reserve Board determined that retention or continuation of the activities would not result in undue concentration, decreased or unfair competition, conflicts of interest or unsound banking practices, and subject to such conditions as the board might impose to ensure avoidance of those situations.

● Required the board to deny exemption under the June 30, 1968, clause if it found the established standards would not be met; authorized the board to terminate exemption at any time for failure to maintain the standards.

● Required termination if a one-bank holding company established a new nonbanking activity or acquired a going concern engaged in such an activity.

● Required the board to determine within two years after enactment whether to grant exemption under the grandfather clause for all companies with bank assets of $60 million or more.

● Allowed 10 years for divestiture of nonbanking activities where exemption was not allowed.

Exemptions

● Authorized the board to grant terminable exemption from the provisions of the act in cases involving activities begun or acquired on or before June 30, 1968, where it found the banking activities involved were so small in relation to the market as to minimize the influence of their credit power or where it found that divestiture would result in forced sales or disruption of long-standing business relationships.

- Granted specific exemptions, in some cases requiring determination by the board, for: labor, agricultural and horticultural organizations; banks in which the same family had owned an 85 per cent controlling interest since June 30, 1968; mutual savings banks controlling another bank under specific authorization of state law; any bank not making commercial loans; a bank operating solely in foreign commerce; any company doing most of its business outside the United States, and any bank with restricted operations wholly owned by thrift institutions.

- Terminated the 1956 act's exemption for partnerships; extended regulation in cases of control through assets held in trust or as security; maintained the 1956 act's exemption of banks controlled by individuals.

Competition

- Prohibited any condition that made providing credit, property or service contingent on obtaining from or providing to a bank or its holding company any additional credit, property or service, except for transactions exclusively involving loans, discounts, deposits or trust services.

- Prohibited any condition that made providing credit, property or service contingent on agreement not to obtain other credit, property or service from a competitor.

- Granted legal standing to competitors and other interested parties in cases before the Federal Reserve Board and the courts.

Coinage

- Authorized minting of $150 million in 40 per cent silver Eisenhower dollar coins for uncirculated commemoratives and proof sets, minting of clad-copper (cupro-nickel) Kennedy half-dollars and Eisenhower dollars for circulation, transfer of $3 million in rare (collector's item) silver dollars from the Treasury to the General Services Administration for public sale and transfer of silver from government stockpiles for the Eisenhower dollars, which would phase out the silver-sale operations of the Treasury.

Protection of Investors

Congress Dec. 22 cleared the Securities Investor Protection Act to insure customers against losses occurring when brokers become insolvent. The bill (HR 19333—PL 91-598) established a private nonprofit Securities Investor Protection Corporation (SIPC) and an insurance fund financed through a combination of existing stock exchange trust funds, assessments and lines of bank credit. Stockholders were insured against losses of up to $50,000 in cash and securities left on deposit and lost when brokerage houses failed.

The major provisions of HR 19333 were worked out by the Securities and Exchange Commission and representatives of the securities industry. The bill was prompted by a series of failures of brokerage houses during the 1969 stock market decline. The stock exchanges did have special trust funds to cover customer losses from brokerage failures, but they were considered potentially inadequate. They applied only to cus-

tomers of firms which were exchange members and did not have the force of law behind them.

The final version of HR 19333 was very close to the version passed almost unanimously by the House Dec. 1. It did not include floor amendments to the bill passed by the Senate Dec. 10 requiring brokers to segregate customers' securities, to establish reserves to insure customers' cash balances left on deposit with the brokerage firm and to require SIPC to impose financial standards on brokerage firms formed in future. During debate on the conference report several members objected that the final bill therefore insured the industry without requiring reform of unsound practices in return. They said the SEC should have asked for legislation to prohibit the common practice of using customers' securities for lending and as security and customers' cash balances, left on deposit, for operating capital. Supporters of the conference report pointed out that the final bill did require the SEC to study unsound practices of brokers and recommend legislation to end them. *(Box p. 142)*

PROVISIONS

As cleared by Congress, HR 19333:

SIPC

- Created a Securities Investor Protection Corporation (SIPC) as a private nonprofit corporation to provide financial protection for customers against loss due to brokerage insolvencies.

- Required all broker-dealers to be members of the SIPC except those confining their activities to sale of mutual fund shares, variable annuities and insurance or professional advice to mutual funds and insurance companies.

- Vested control of the SIPC in a seven-member board of directors, five of whom would be appointed by the President—three representing the securities industry and two representing the general public—and one each appointed by the Secretary of the Treasury from the Treasury Department and by the Federal Reserve Board from its officials and employees.

Insurance Fund

- Established an insurance fund to insure each customer account with an SIPC member against loss due to broker insolvency; insured cash on deposit with a member firm up to $20,000 and cash and securities together to a maximum of $50,000, in addition to fully paid-for securities traced and claimed.

- Required that the fund contain $75 million within 120 days of enactment, of which $65 million was to be in the form of a line of credit from banks and $10 million was to be cash—$3 million from existing stock exchange trust funds and $7 million from an initial assessment of members of one-eighth of 1 percent of gross revenues.

- Required the SIPC to increase the fund to $150 million by assessments; required lines of credit to be retired and a minimum balance of $100 million to be kept in the fund unless the SEC required a larger amount or authorized a smaller amount.

- Established a maximum assessment on brokerages of 1 percent of gross revenues; prohibited assessments of more than 0.5 per cent unless the SIPC determined that a larger assessment would not adversely affect the financial condition of its members.

● Authorized the SIPC, through the Securities and Exchange Commission (SEC), to borrow up to $1 billion from the U.S. Treasury.

● Authorized the SEC to impose a transactions fee on securities purchases of more than $5,000 to ensure prompt repayment of a loan from the Treasury.

● Exempted from assessment revenues from sale of real estate and oil, gas and other mineral rights except those required by law to be registered with the SEC.

● Exempted from assessment revenues from the insurance business, distribution of mutual fund shares and investment advisory services.

Regulation

● Authorized the SEC to examine and oversee the SIPC and to require periodic reports on its activities.

● Authorized the SEC to require the SIPC to adopt new rules or change existing rules.

● Authorized the SIPC to require periodic reports of its members' activities, to be made through members' self-regulatory organizations recognized by the SEC.

● Authorized the SEC to require the self-regulatory organizations to adopt or amend rules governing examination of and reporting on the financial condition of members.

● Required the SEC to establish regulations governing financial responsibility and related practices of brokers, specifically including handling of customers' cash and securities and establishment of reserve requirements for cash on deposit.

Liquidation

● Authorized the SIPC to initiate court proceedings by asking for appointment of a trustee to liquidate a broker-dealer considered to be in danger of failing to meet its financial obligations to its customers.

● Provided for liquidation proceedings under bankruptcy law.

● Required appointed trustees to distribute paid-for securities and securities held for customers' accounts and to complete open contractual commitments of brokers in liquidation; authorized the SIPC to advance funds to meet such commitments.

● Required the SIPC to advance money from the insurance fund to meet customer claims.

Miscellaneous

● Required the SEC to study unsound practices of brokers and report to Congress within a year on steps taken to correct those practices and legislation needed to end them.

● Required public access to information about the operations of the SIPC except to the extent that the SIPC or the SEC determined that disclosure would not be in the public interest.

Credit Union Insurance

Congress Oct. 5 cleared legislation establishing a federal insurance system for state and federally chartered credit unions. The bill (S 3822—PL 91-468) required federally chartered credit unions to insure

---

Brokers Hold Money

Stockbrokers and securities dealers, in addition to carrying out the purchasing and selling mandates of their customers, have responsibility for safeguarding billions of dollars of their customers' money and securities.

When customers accrue dividends or funds from the sale of securities, they frequently leave these credit balances on deposit with their broker-dealers. Although the customers may withdraw their balances on demand, the funds are left with the brokers largely as a convenience, in anticipation of future purchases.

Brokers are free to use these funds in the conduct of their businesses for most types of transactions requiring financing. The practice is somewhat comparable to banks' use of customers' deposits.

When customers buy securities, they frequently leave them with brokers for safekeeping. Those held on margin—not fully paid-for—may be loaned to other brokers or used for collateral on loans. These securities are freely transferable, enabling brokers to fulfill customers' orders promptly and easily but also creating the risk of incorrect transfer. Further, such securities may be attached by creditors of a firm in difficulty.

Fully paid-for securities are required to be segregated, and customers have the right to demand delivery. But segregation and identification of securities in high-volume conditions are difficult to maintain.

Federal laws and regulations require broker-dealers to register with the Securities and Exchange Commission, maintain records and report to each customer concerning transactions in his account. Conditions are prescribed in which brokers may lend customers' securities. Brokers are required to meet certain capital requirements continuously, including maintenance of a prescribed minimum ratio of debt to net capital. They are further limited by state law and by the regulations of the stock exchanges.

---

their accounts (up to $20,000 per depositor) and allowed state groups to join the program.

The insurance system would be financed by a Treasury Department revolving fund which was funded by annual premiums of one-twelfth of 1 per cent of total accounts. To qualify for insurance, a credit union was required to maintain certain reserves; if it failed to qualify within one year its charter would be revoked or suspended.

Committee reports on S 3822 said that most credit union funds were uninsured. They noted that credit unions were the only federally chartered financial institutions that did not have a federal insurance program, although 22 million Americans had almost $14 billion saved in more than 24,000 credit unions.

S 3822 was passed first by the Senate and then, without amendment, by the House. The House committee report noted that it had not amended the bill because it was late in the session and said the program could be changed in later years. *(Later legislation, 1971 chronology below.)*

Provisions. As cleared by Congress, S 3822:

● Required that the administrator of the National Credit Union Administration insure the accounts of all Federally chartered credit unions, and authorized him to insure state-chartered credit unions which apply for coverage and which maintain the same reserves as Federally chartered credit unions. All Federally chartered credit unions would be given one year in which to qualify for insurance; after that time, the charters of noncomplying credit unions would be revoked or suspended.

● Set annual premiums at one-twelfth of 1 percent of total accounts. When the fund reached its normal operating level of 1 per cent of member accounts, the administrator could reduce the premiums. If expenditures exceeded the fund's income for a year, the administrator could raise the premium for that year up to one-sixth of 1 per cent.

● Allowed credit unions serving predominantly low-income members (as defined by the administrator) to accept funds from nonmembers.

● Established a revolving fund in the Treasury for administering and operating the program.

Other Legislation

'TAKEOVER' REPORTING REQUIREMENTS. Congress Dec. 10 cleared a bill (S 3431—PL 91-567) broadening reporting requirements governing efforts to acquire a significant proportion of a company's stock.

Amendments in 1968 (PL 90-439) to the 1934 Securities and Exchange Act had required reporting any acquisition that resulted in holding more than 10 per cent of the stock of a business with $1 million or more in assets. S 3431 applied the reporting requirements to acquisitions of more than 5 per cent. In supporting the bill, the SEC said acquisitions of 5 to 10 per cent of a company's stock could have a significant impact on the public market for that stock. The SEC also found that companies intent on 'takeovers' had limited open-market purchases to 8 or 9 per cent to avoid the reporting requirement.

SERIES E SAVINGS BONDS. In a non-germane rider to a tariff bill Congress Aug. 12 cleared a bill (HR 14956—PL 91-388) raising the interest rate on Series E bonds held to full 10-year maturity from 5 to 5.5 per cent. The ceiling had been raised from 4.5 per cent in 1969.

BANKRUPTCY LAW. Congress Oct. 5 cleared a bill (S 4247—PL 91-467) to clarify federal bankruptcy law. S 4247 gave federal bankruptcy courts exclusive and final jurisidiction to determine whether a debt had been discharged. It enjoined creditors against commencing or continuing actions to collect debts for which bankruptcy courts had discharged a debtor of personal liability.

Before passage of S 4247 state courts—not federal bankruptcy courts—could dtermine whether a specific debt was discharged after a federal court had granted an over-all discharge from debts. According to the Senate Judiciary Committee report, state jurisdiction had given rise to abuses by creditors. Debtors adjudged bankrupt and discharged of their debts had still been harassed for payment of debts for which they were not legally liable.

1971

Credit Union Insurance

Congress provided temporary insurance for two years for certain federally chartered credit unions. The bill (HR 9961—PL 92-221), which cleared Dec. 13, was designed to give credit unions which could not meet cash requirements for insurance a chance to build up reserves.

HR 9961 amended a law, enacted in 1970 (PL 91-468), which established a mandatory federal insurance system for credit unions. PL 91-468 provided that credit unions which failed to have high enough reserves to qualify for insurance after one year would have their charters revoked. HR 9961 gave them two more years to build up reserves before facing liquidation. By late 1971, 11,000 credit unions had been certified for insurance under the 1971 law by the National Credit Union Administration. Some 1,400 had been rejected. *(PL 91-468, p. 142)*

Securities Hearings

House and Senate subcommittees each held general investigations into the problems of the securities industry. A Senate subcommittee also looked into the role of organized crime in the rising number of securities thefts.

General Investigations. General hearings on the stock market were held by the House Interstate and Foreign Commerce Committee Subcommittee on Commerce and Finance, August through October, and by the Senate Banking, Housing and Urban Affairs Subcommittee on Securities in September and October

During the House hearings, witnesses from the Securities and Exchange Commission testified on the need for changes in the securities industry. Much of the testimony centered on the need to change the current methods of processing and handling stock certificates. SEC witnesses proposed that industry problems coping with the increasing bookkeeping and paperwork volume could be eased by elimination of stock certificates or development of a national securities depository. Many industry witnesses agreed on the need to move in that direction.

SEC witnesses also criticized the lack of restrictions on the use by brokers of customers' credit balances (cash from dividends or sales of securities which customers allowed to accumulate in their accounts). Some industry representatives supported curtailment of the use of customer credits; others said the loss of opportunity to use customers' cash as working capital would be a major hardship for brokerage firms and, ultimately, for the public.

The Senate hearings were also concerned with these issues and, in addition, heard testimony on whether the current system of fixed commission rates should be substituted for a system of competitive rates negotiated by the broker and customer. The SEC in April 1971 had ordered that rates on orders above $500,000 be subject to negotiation. Before that date, commission rates on all transactions were fixed by the stock exchange. Competitive rates were opposed by some stock exchange representatives and supported by representatives of a number of companies.

Securities Thefts. The Senate Government Operations Subcommittee on Permanent Investigations held hearings on thefts of securities, which had exceeded $400 million in 1969 and 1970. Government witnesses said that the pressure of the unprecedented volume of business in the stock exchanges had resulted in an almost casual handling of securities. They proposed that the need for the physical movement of securities be reduced by replacing certificates with a central system of debits and credits to accounts. The subcommittee also heard testimony that important racketeers had been involved in securities thefts at brokerage houses and from mail bags at airports.

Banking Hearings

The House Banking and Currency Committee held hearings in April and May on proposals for greater federal control over the banking industry.

The major bill under consideration was HR 5700, sponsored by Committee Chairman Wright Patman (D Texas) to limit interlocking controlling interests in banking. The bill prohibited interlocking directorates among financial institutions and between banks and corporations which maintained substantial loan relationships. Patman said the bill was prompted in part by the collapse of the Penn Central Transportation Company. He said 16 of Penn Central's 23 directors were officers or directors of large commercial banks. *(Penn Central story, transportation chapter, p. 147)*

"The general purpose of HR 5700" was supported by the Justice Department, which said it was preparing legislation to deal with the kinds of abuses against which the bill was directed. The chairman of the Federal Deposit Insurance Corporation supported increased control over interlocking directorates but preferred that it be accomplished by strengthening existing anti-trust law. The Federal Reserve Board favored a less restrictive version of the legislation.

The American Bankers Association said the prohibition of interlocking management "would decimate commercial bank boards of directors." It endorsed prohibition of certain types of interlocks between banks and competing institutions. Representatives of a number of banks opposed the bill. They said that bank directors were not involved in allocation of credit and that the bill would interfere with the ability of banks to discharge their obligations and to obtain the best judgment and advice at the board-of-directors level.

1972

Federal Financing Bank

The Senate passed a bill June 22 establishing a Federal Financing Bank to coordinate federal and federally assisted borrowing from the public. The bill (S 3001) was reported with amendments by the House Ways and Means Committee late in the session, but the House did not act.

S 3001 would have coordinated the activities of the many federal agencies (such as the Federal Home Loan Bank Board, Federal National Mortgage Assn., Export-Import Bank) which finance operations through the sale of bonds on the open market. The bill was designed to reduce the cost of borrowing and ensure that federal borrowing was financed in the manner least disruptive to private financial markets.

As passed by the Senate, the bill established a Federal Financing Bank through which the marketing of federal and federally assisted borrowing activities would be centralized. The bill required advance submission of financing to the Secretary of the Treasury for his approval of the methods and sources of financing. The secretary was required to explain to Congress if he withheld financing for more than 120 days.

In reporting S 3001, the House Ways and Means Committee eliminated a provision making the bank's bonds subject to state and local taxation. It also eliminated a provision requiring federal agencies to submit budget programs for federally guaranteed obligations to the President, who would have power to limit them. Obligations sold by the Tennessee Valley Authority (TVA) were exempted from the bill's requirement of advance approval by the Secretary of the Treasury.

Committee reports said the bill was "urgently needed because the increase in federal credit program activity in recent years has greatly expanded the total federal impact on credit markets."

Securities Transactions

Congress failed to complete action on a bill to strengthen federal regulation of the processing of securities transactions. The bill (S 3876) would have given the Securities and Exchange Commission enlarged responsibility for dealing with the operational problems encountered by the securities industry as a result of the growing volume of stock transactions. It was drafted by the Senate Banking Committee's Securities Subcommittee and was in part a result of extensive congressional hearings on problems of the securities industry.

S 3876 was passed by voice votes of the Senate and House in slightly different forms near the end of the session. The major difference between the two versions was that the Senate bill gave bank regulatory agencies rule-making authority over securities handled by banks; the House gave this authority to the SEC. With Congress moving toward adjournment, the committees with jurisdiction over the bill worked out an informal compromise giving the SEC authority over banks in certain areas. No formal conference action was taken, but the committees agreed to try to get the Senate and the House to accept the House bill with the compromise amendment. The strategy failed in the final days of the session when Sen. Paul J. Fannin (R Ariz.) blocked consideration by objecting to a unanimous consent agreement to take up the bill in the Senate.

Other than the division of responsibility between the SEC and bank regulatory agencies, the only major difference between the House and Senate versions was a Senate provision creating a 14-member National Commission on Uniform Securities Laws to assist states in updating their laws governing securities transactions.

In addition to enlarging and clarifying the SEC's authority over all steps in the sale and transfer of securities, the bills would have directed the commission to move toward an integrated national system for clearing and handling stock transactions. One specific goal was elimination of the physical transfer of stock certificates in securities transactions.

The bills would have clarified the SEC's power to regulate the way stock brokers or dealers handled securities settlements, payments, deliveries and the closing of accounts. It would have extended SEC rule-making jurisdiction to securities-clearing agencies (intermediaries in payments and deliveries), depositories (persons or institutions who held securities which could be traded or loaned without actual physical delivery of the certificates) and transfer agents (persons who recorded, monitored and exchanged securities).

Other Action

BANK ACCOUNT PRIVACY. The Senate Banking, Currency and Urban Affairs Subcommittee on Financial Institutions held hearings in August on bills designed to protect the privacy of bank accounts. The proposals permitted a financial institution to disclose financial records only if authorized by the account holder or by court order. No further action was taken.

The bills would have amended the Bank Secrecy Act of 1970 (PL 91-508) to overrule Treasury Department regulations for implementing the act's requirements. PL 91-508 was designed to curb violation of U.S. laws and federal tax evasion by use of secret foreign bank accounts and foreign financial transactions. It authorized the Secretary of the Treasury to issue regulations requiring financial institutions to keep records of account holders, checks drawn and deposits made, and to report individual transactions involving export or import of $5,000 or more. *(Foreign bank accounts, international economic policy chapter, p. 119)*

The American Civil Liberties Union and California Bankers Association in 1972 challenged the 1970 act in a lawsuit filed in federal courts. The suit, still underway at the end of 1972, contended that the act violated constitutional guarantees against unreasonable search and seizure, posed an unnecessary burden on interstate commerce and threatened the private fiduciary relationship between a bank and its customers.

During the congressional hearings; the bills to amend PL 91-508 were supported by the ACLU and representatives of banker's associations. They were opposed by representatives of the Treasury and Justice Departments. They said the bills would seriously impair criminal, tax and regulatory investigations and proceedings.

BANK TAX BILL. The Senate Banking, Housing and Urban Affairs Committee voted 10-4 to table a bill (S 3652) restricting state taxation of nationally chartered banks.

S 3652 was drafted by the American Bankers Association (ABA). It was based on the recommendations of a Federal Reserve Board study authorized by a 1969 law (PL 91-156) broadening state authority to tax nationally chartered banks. *(p. 136)*

The 1969 act allowed some restrictions on state taxation of banks to expire Dec. 31, 1972. It provided that after Jan. 1, 1973, states could impose sales, use and intangible property taxes on any branch of a nationally chartered bank in a state.

The ABA bill would have prohibited state taxes on intangible property (principally securities) held by either state or nationally chartered banks. It also would have established standards for state taxation of interstate operations of national banks, limiting application of income taxes to branches operating within a state, and prohibited special bank taxes unless they were applied to other financial institutions.

SECURITIES HEARINGS. Senate and House subcommittees continued hearings begun in 1971 on the problems of the securities industry. *(1971 testimony, p. 143)*

As in 1971, much of the testimony centered on the issue of whether commission rates on stock transactions should be set by the stock exchange or negotiated by the broker and customer ("competitive rates"). The Securities and Exchange Commission in February 1972 ordered that commission rates on securities orders in excess of $300,000 should be set competitively; previously the floor for competitive rates had been $500,000. During the hearings there was some support for proposed legislation prohibiting fixed commission rates on transactions above $100,000. The bill was opposed by stock exchange representatives and by the SEC. The SEC supported slow administrative changes to competitive rates because "the stakes in making a satisfactory adjustment to competitive rates are such that the public interest calls for... careful measurement of the impact at each step."

INTERSTATE HIGHWAY SYSTEM MILEAGE, SEPT. 30, 1972

State	Preliminary Status or Not Yet in Progress	Work In Progress			Open to Traffic				Total Designated System Mileage
		Engineering or Right-of-Way	Under Construction	Total Underway	Toll Facilities	Improved to Standards Adequate For Present Traffic	Completed to Full or Acceptable Standards	Total Open To Traffic	
Alabama	18.70	139.60	95.10	234.70	—	51.10	593.90	645.00	898.40
Arizona	1.00	98.52	149.58	248.10	—	168.43	755.06	923.49	1,172.59
Arkansas	—	11.57	21.58	33.15	—	4.30	488.89	493.19	526.34
California	4.70	174.60	164.80	339.40	10.20	220.70	1,712.80	1,943.70	2,287.80
Colorado	66.19	95.60	53.73	149.33	—	56.43	704.50	760.93	976.45
Connecticut	40.21	24.78	6.19	30.97	12.31	48.46	215.03	275.80	346.98
Delaware	—	—	11.47	11.47	14.30	—	14.84	29.14	40.61
Florida	182.61	194.11	137.25	331.36	56.45	—	828.83	885.28	1,399.25
Georgia	38.70	165.95	138.69	304.64	—	2.32	804.03	806.35	1,149.69
Hawaii	—	19.91	10.57	30.48	—	2.24	19.53	21.77	52.25
Idaho	—	52.39	46.58	98.97	—	125.75	387.35	513.10	612.07
Illinois	17.70	184.14	168.62	352.76	154.92	98.22	1,104.01	1,357.15	1,727.61
Indiana	14.30	34.79	96.03	130.82	156.90	—	827.40	984.30	1,129.42
Iowa	47.92	34.18	85.13	119.31	3.17	—	610.56	613.73	780.96
Kansas	—	34.55	51.40	85.95	187.70	2.45	545.60	735.75	821.70
Kentucky	—	57.74	93.60	151.34	39.20	15.42	530.49	585.11	736.45
Louisiana	40.91	31.99	227.70	259.69	—	0.86	416.58	417.44	718.04
Maine	—	24.12	9.94	34.06	54.48	103.41	119.86	277.75	311.81
Maryland	26.56	3.46	0.24	3.70	53.04	74.55	199.96	327.55	357.81
Massachusetts	21.57	21.33	10.66	31.99	134.41	22.29	259.99	416.69	470.25
Michigan	41.00	68.92	98.12	167.04	5.39	42.96	918.29	966.64	1,174.68
Minnesota	21.32	119.26	135.46	254.72	—	61.48	576.61	638.09	914.13
Mississippi	—	33.90	110.40	144.30	—	4.10	534.80	538.90	683.20
Missouri	—	124.20	68.00	192.20	0.30	120.10	833.50	953.90	1,146.10
Montana	—	204.92	176.48	381.40	—	268.66	538.59	807.25	1,188.65
Nebraska	—	16.75	30.96	47.72	0.22	12.88	419.77	432.87	480.59
Nevada	—	77.84	18.94	96.78	—	4.92	432.86	437.78	534.56
New Hampshire	—	21.32	9.63	30.95	21.02	15.02	147.29	183.33	214.28
New Jersey	18.90	65.50	84.20	149.70	45.70	18.40	151.70	215.80	384.40
New Mexico	32.16	51.33	37.19	88.52	—	55.88	822.37	878.25	998.93
New York	117.72	37.04	27.93	64.97	490.38	56.12	618.16	1,164.66	1,347.35
North Carolina	52.86	120.12	81.71	201.83	—	10.62	576.34	586.96	841.65
North Dakota	—	22.20	55.17	77.37	—	51.49	442.47	493.96	571.33
Ohio	8.80	81.45	76.40	157.85	206.20	57.63	1,103.49	1,367.32	1,533.97
Oklahoma	—	8.07	58.24	66.31	174.04	17.11	551.88	743.03	809.34
Oregon	21.07	11.18	47.96	59.14	—	86.43	567.53	653.96	734.17
Pennsylvania	34.53	65.31	70.58	135.89	360.18	8.35	1,035.45	1,403.98	1,574.40
Rhode Island	26.59	0.40	6.49	6.89	—	8.44	58.36	66.80	100.28
South Carolina	60.77	0.64	125.08	125.72	—	8.17	563.45	571.62	758.11
South Dakota	—	83.26	67.84	151.10	—	49.28	478.58	527.86	678.96
Tennessee	—	96.60	159.45	256.05	—	78.10	711.25	789.35	1,045.40
Texas	115.04	288.89	203.35	492.24	—	216.98	2,336.31	2,553.29	3,160.57
Utah	—	263.98	122.09	386.07	—	67.56	483.74	551.30	937.37
Vermont	—	37.23	51.19	88.42	—	—	231.96	231.96	320.38
Virginia	10.82	161.75	56.94	218.69	37.60	41.65	764.12	843.37	1,072.88
Washington	69.85	61.80	37.81	99.61	—	154.13	439.31	593.44	762.90
West Virginia	17.33	44.06	127.28	171.34	86.51	2.70	233.90	323.11	511.78
Wisconsin	110.50	0.67	1.73	2.40	—	0.79	455.18	455.97	568.87
Wyoming	49.27	52.65	14.71	67.36	—	13.82	783.14	796.96	913.59
District of Columbia	9.36	7.62	1.81	9.43	—	2.92	7.84	10.76	29.55
Totals	1,338.96	3,632.19	3,742.01	7,374.20	2,304.62	2,533.62	28,957.45	33,795.69	42,508.85

SOURCE: Department of Transportation

Transportation Policy

By the late 1960s, the nation's enchantment with the automobile clearly had waned. Nowhere was this more true than in urban areas where the expense of owning a car and the effects of its use—traffic congestion and air pollution—often outweighed the automobile's convenience.

In 1971, at a time when 82 cents of every dollar spent on transportation in the United States was related to highway travel, a Department of Transportation report concluded: "There is a need to rethink the way this nation should go about developing a transportation system...for the next three decades, all indicators point to more people, more affluence, more urbanization and a rapidly escalating intolerance for undesirable environmental side effects (of automobiles). In the face of this, the practices and policies of the past will almost certainly be inadequate for the future.

Proposals for a "balanced transportation system"— a phrase that generally meant less federal spending on roads, more on mass transit—had long circulated among environmentalists, city planners, members of Congress and the executive branch.

But the search for an integrated program intended to promote a diversified transportation system was complicated by a long-standing political struggle affecting all phases of the transportation industry. Each of the different modes of transportation had some vested interest in existing policy, regulations and legislation. They tended to oppose any change which would alter their advantages.

Chief among these groups was the automobile industry and its related interests: road builders, oil companies, real estate developers, and construction unions. In 1971 alone, the federal government spent $5.5-billion for road construction compared to $1.6-billion for air transportation, $440-million for waterways and $65-million for railroads. (It was estimated that between 1921 and 1971, all levels of government spent $326-billion for highways, $25-billion for air transportation, $15-billion for waterways and $200-million for railroads.)

An indication of public awareness that automobile transportation had begun to create as many problems as it solved was congressional enactment in 1970 of major programs which could be considered initial steps toward a more balanced transportation system.

That year Congress passed the Airport and Airways Development Act, authorizing about $600-million annually for five years to improve airports and air traffic control systems; approved the Urban Mass Transportation Assistance Act, committing the nation to a 12-year, $10-billion, program to upgrade public transit systems;

enacted the Rail Passenger Service Act (Amtrak), preserving train service across the nation, and established a 10-year subsidy program to revitalize the U.S. Merchant Marine.

The same year, Congress completed action on the most comprehensive air pollution control bill in U.S. history, setting specific deadlines for the reduction of certain hazardous automobile emissions.

Despite the strenuous lobbying effort by automobile manufacturers, Congress adopted a provision which required that model year 1975 cars must emit 90 per cent less carbon monoxide and hydrocarbons than did model 1970 cars. The bill also specified that nitrogen oxides in 1976 models must be reduced by 90 per cent compared with 1971 levels. (*Environment chapter*)

In 1972, the Nixon administration endorsed a controversial plan—one strongly opposed by highway interests—to divert a portion of Highway Trust Fund revenues for developing mass transportation systems in urban areas.

While the federal government began to initiate new transportation programs during the 1969-72 period, state and local governments generally favored a continuation of highway building. A 1972 Department of Transportation study reported that state governments had estimated $670-billion worth of transportation needs through 1990. Eighty-five per cent ($560-billion) was projected for highways. Following is a summary of key action on transportation issues during the years 1969-72 on highways, air transportation, the supersonic transport, railroads, maritime shipping and mass transit.

Interstate Highway System

The Interstate Highway System, a standardized freeway network approved by Congress in 1956, was designed to improve transportation between the nation's agricultural and industrial centers. Few federal programs enacted during the post-World War II period proved more popular: the public viewed the interstate as a remedy for increasing congestion on antiquated, two-lane roads, and the farming and business communities anticipated the system's economic benefits. Originally planned as a

References

Discussion of transportation policies for the years 1945-64 may be found in *Congress and the Nation, Vol. I*, p. 517-561; for the years 1965-68, *Congress and the Nation, Vol. II*, p. 227-251.

41,000-mile, $41-billion network, the interstate was hailed by President Eisenhower as "the greatest public works program in history."

By 1972, however—the year the interstate was scheduled to be completed—cost estimates had risen to $76.3-billion (for a 42,500-mile system) and 1980 was considered a possible date for finishing the project. Moreover, the entire undertaking, while still popular with many, was racked by controversy.

Intense criticism of highway construction centered in metropolitan areas where new roads either had (or were scheduled to) cut wide swaths across residential areas and business districts, lowering tax bases, raising air pollution levels and disrupting community life.

By the late 1960s, environmentalists and urban residents began to turn their attention—and anger—to the Highway Trust Fund, an earmarked-federal account specifically set up to pay for the interstate as well as other federal-aid roads with tax revenues collected on gasoline and other motor products.

They argued that the fund assured continued road construction at the expense of a balanced transportation system. In 1970, Congress included a provision in that year's federal-aid highway bill allowing states to use some of the trust fund monies for exclusive bus lane construction to reduce traffic congestion. The concession to mass transit advocates aroused the suspicion of highway builders that the precedent would lead to additional demand on trust fund revenues.

In 1972, a coalition of environmentalists and urban groups persuaded the Senate to open the fund for financing bus purchases by local communities. The Senate also —in an action strongly opposed by road building interests—opened the fund for rail and subway construction. The House balked however, and the issue, coupled with a plan to subsidize transit systems in poor financial condition, killed the 1972 bill, postponing resolution of both controversies until 1973.

Air Transportation

While the federal government spent billions of dollars on highway construction during the 1960s, the nation's airport system, funded at a $75-million level, experienced major congestion and safety problems caused by increasing numbers of Americans traveling by air.

In 1969, as several major air terminals reached the passenger saturation point, appropriations for airport development dropped to the $30-million level. That year, the Nixon administration proposed a 10-year, $5-billion program to relieve the "years of neglect (that) have permitted the problems of air transportation to stack up like aircraft circling a congested airport."

In 1970, Congress approved legislation that followed administration recommendations, authorizing $280-million a year for airport construction in addition to $250-million annually to improve air navigation facilities. The programs were to be financed by new taxes on users of the aviation system with the revenues funneled into a federal account similar to the Highway Trust Fund.

Supersonic Transport

By halting federal participation in the construction of a supersonic transport plane, Congress in 1971 resolved an issue that had become increasingly controversial since 1964. The cutoff in federal funds prompted the Boeing Company, General Electric Company and other contractors to terminate the project.

The congressional decision was a serious rebuff to the Nixon administration and the aviation industry, which viewed the SST as necessary to maintain U.S. superiority in aerospace technology and eventually to help reverse the nation's balance-of-payments deficit.

Environmentalists, however, argued that the SST could contaminate the atmosphere, that its principal beneficiaries would be wealthy travelers and that federal funding should be directed instead toward more activities of more general benefit to the public as a whole.

Between fiscal 1962 and fiscal 1971, Congress appropriated about $1-billion for the SST, including $91.3-million to terminate the project. It was estimated that the total federal contribution—had the project been continued—would amount to $1.3-billion by 1972 for completing two prototype planes, the first phase of the SST program.

Railroads

As automobile and airline travel increased dramatically during the 1950s and 60s, railroad passenger service rapidly declined. Mounting deficits caused railroads to discontinue hundreds of trains, and poor service often prevailed on existing lines.

Reacting to reports that passenger service would not survive without a major change in federal and rail industry policy, Congress in 1970 enacted the Rail Passenger Service Act, creating a semi-public corporation to operate a nationwide train system (Amtrak). A $50-million federal grant, $100-million in loan guarantees, payments by the railroads choosing to transfer their operations to the corporation, plus Amtrak's ticket revenues, were intended to finance the new system.

But less than six months after the start of Amtrak service, the corporation estimated that it would run into debt by the end of fiscal 1972. Congress subsequently appropriated an additional $170-million and authorized another $100-million in loan guarantees that were intended to keep the system in operation until July 1, 1973, when Amtrak by law could discontinue any routes it found unprofitable.

Maritime Program

As subsidies for the U.S. Merchant Marine continued to rise during the 1960s, the maritime industry steadily declined, both in the number of ships and amount of cargo transported.

By 1970, only 5 per cent of U.S. imports and exports were transported on American lines compared with 10.5 per cent in 1960 and 23.5 per cent in 1955. Foreign fleets, especially that of the Soviet Union, continued to expand and to handle more and more of America's foreign commerce.

In addition, higher costs and less efficient production methods were blamed for the fact that it cost 50 to 55 per cent more to build a ship in the United States than in a foreign nation.

In 1969, President Nixon proposed a new 10-year subsidy program for the construction of 300 merchant marine vessels. Congress enacted the program the following year to revitalize the maritime industry, but it required that funds be authorized annually.

Mass Transit

Congress in 1970 enacted a five-year, $3.1-billion program to finance mass transit projects in urban areas. Proposed by President Nixon in 1969 "to make public transportation an attractive alternative to private car use," the plan called for spending $10-billion on mass transit within 12 years.

The proposal was based in part on the conviction that federal aid for transportation had been mistakenly biased toward highway construction at the expense of the urban environment and persons without cars.

The Department of Transportation reported that more than $5-billion was spent in 1969 for new highway construction, with federal aid from the Highway Trust Fund financing up to 90 per cent of the cost. In comparison, total federal expenditures on mass transit from 1964-70 were less than federal expenditures on urban highways in a single six-month period since 1964.

Chronology

Of Legislation

On Transportation

1969

Congress in 1969 moved toward enactment of far-reaching transportation legislation, laying the ground-work for passage of a half-dozen major programs in 1970. The Nixon administration introduced bills to aid airport and airway development, mass transportation and the ever-declining merchant marine. Congress on its own initiative prepared bills to set federal standards for railroad safety and to keep alive intercity passenger train service.

At the end of the first session of the 91st Congress, administration-backed legislation to increase the safety and capacity of airports and airways was close to final approval, with the Senate Finance Committee left to give its approval to tax measures in the bill.

Administration proposals to provide long-term financing for mass transit ran into opposition from those who said the plan would not assure the funds promised; the conflict, however, was resolved late in the session.

Preliminary hearings were held in 1969 on another administration proposal to overhaul the U.S. Merchant Marine, and House and Senate committees considered plans to subsidize passenger train service. The supersonic transport (SST) project was given a go-ahead over objections within both the administration and Congress.

Mass Transit Crisis

In spite of population growth and increasing urbanization, the use of public transportation in American cities declined steadily, giving way to the expensive but convenient automobile. But planners and policymakers were increasingly critical of the private car and skeptical of public policy which they said fostered continued reliance on automobile transportation to the virtual exclusion of buses, subways and technologically advanced systems for mass transportation.

The key problem facing most mass transportation systems was the decline in the number of passengers. Since most of the decline occurred in off-peak hours while rush-hour travel remained almost constant, the financial problems of the transit industry were greater than the decline in patronage would suggest. The drop in usage did not bring a proportionate decline in industry man-hours, and it made scarcely any difference in overhead costs.

Meanwhile, the number of automobiles in the United States increased from 25.8 million in 1945 to 80 million in 1967. In the same period the annual number of passengers riding buses, subways and elevated local trains decreased from 23 billion to 7.7 billion, according to the American Transit Association. The number of railroad commuter passengers decreased from 323 million to 204 million.

Federal Programs. By the 1960s, many persons were convinced that improved mass transportation systems offered a practical solution to metropolitan congestion. The first major federal program for mass transit was enacted by Congress as part of the 1961 Housing Act (PL 87-70). Under the 1961 act, Congress authorized and appropriated $25 million for grants and $50 million for loans.

The program was expanded with the Urban Mass Transportation Act of 1964 (PL 88-365) and continued and expanded again with the extension of the act in 1966 (Pl 89-562). Assistance to mass transportation was incorporated in the Housing and Urban Development Act of 1968 (PL 90-448). *(Congress and the Nation, Vol. I, p. 558; Vol. II, p. 241)*

Until mid-1968, urban mass transportation programs were administered by the Office of Metropolitan Development in the Department of Housing and Urban Development (HUD). President Johnson's Reorganization Plan No. 2 of 1968 transferred them to the Department of Transportation.

Proposals for increased federal aid to mass transportation were made in part on the conviction that federal aid for transportation had been mistakenly biased toward highway construction at the expense of the urban environment and persons without cars. The Department of Transportation noted that more than $5 billion was spent in 1969 for new highway construction, with federal aid from the highway trust fund financing up to 90 percent of the cost. The Department said total federal expenditures on mass transit since 1964 were less than federal expenditures on urban highways in a six-month period.

Highway Aid

Congress completed no action on highway bills in 1969, although each house did approve one measure. The Senate approved a bill (S 1442) authorizing some funds for pilot highway beautification programs to remove billboards from the highways. The House approved a catch-all highway bill (HR 14741) which included a new formula for allocation of highway safety funds to state governments.

Final action on these programs was incorporated in 1970 federal-aid-for-highways legislation. *(1970 chronology p. 152)*

Billboard Control. The Senate Nov. 6 passed and sent to the House S 1442 authorizing $15 million for pilot programs to remove billboards along federal-aid highways. The Highway Beautification Act of 1965 (PL 89-285) required that signs near federal-aid highways be limited to directional, official and on-premise signs and that sign companies be compensated for the removal of signs which did not fit those categories. The federal government was to pay 75 percent of the cost of compensation.

The Committee on Public Works, which reported (S Rept 91-520) S 1422 Nov. 5, said most of the $1.9 million spent on billboard removal since 1965 had gone for a sign inventory.

The committee said the time lag between passage of the Highway Beautification Act and funding of the billboard-removal program had prevented sign companies from either financing their ongoing operations or liquidating their investment. The committee claimed that private businesses were being forced to subsidize a federal program. The Department of Transportation estimated in 1967 that removal of all nonconforming billboards sign by sign would cost more than $500-million.

Frank E. Moss (D Utah) said passage of S 1442 would allow experiments with a plan under which the states would acquire by contract all of a company's nonconforming signs at the same time. He said this plan would cost between a third and a half as much as removal sign by sign. He also said the plan would be more efficient since companies themselves would be responsible for taking down their signs.

Highway Amendments. The House Nov. 25 passed a catch-all bill (HR 14741) containing assorted amendments to existing federal highway law.

Among the bill's provisions was a three-month extension of the due date for a revised estimate of the cost of completing the Interstate Highway System and a minimal authorization for highway beautification programs. HR 14741 also established a new formula for allocation of highway safety funds and authorized a demonstration project to eliminate grade crossing on the highspeed rail line between Washington, D.C. and Boston, Mass.

Merchant Marine Proposal

President Nixon Oct. 23, proposed a new maritime program intended "to restore this country to a proud position in the shipping lanes of the world."

Both houses held brief hearings on the proposal within days after Nixon's announcement; but because the proposals (S 3287, HR 15424) were not actually in-

---

Highway Trust Fund

Prior to 1956, authorizations for federal-aid highway programs were made from general revenues of the Treasury. Although there were no clear congressional guidelines, authorizations were usually made in amounts equal to the revenues collected by the Treasury from certain highway user taxes, such as those on motor fuels, tires and truck weights.

The Federal-Aid Highway Act of 1956 established a Highway Trust Fund into which certain specific highway user taxes were to be channeled and from which funds were to be apportioned to finance the federal share of major highway programs. *(Congress and the Nation, Vol. I, p. 524, 526, 531; Vol. II, p. 229, 237, 245)*

The law provided that the Highway Trust Fund could not operate at a deficit at any time and stipulated that if the secretary of the treasury determined that payment of the full amounts apportioned to the states would create a deficit, the secretary of commerce was to reduce apportionments so that obligations could be paid as they came due.

Two key programs were financed from the Highway Trust Fund. The first was a 41,000-mile Interstate Highway System authorized by Congress in 1956 for completion by 1972. Originally, the cost of this program was estimated at nearly $41-billion, with the federal government putting up 90 percent of the construction funds and the states the remaining 10 per cent. Periodically, revised cost estimates were submitted to Congress, and congressional approval of these estimates was required before funds could be apportioned. By 1972, the estimated cost of the system had risen to $76.3-billion for a 42,500-mile system scheduled for completion in 1980.

The second program financed from the Highway Trust Fund was construction of federal-aid primary, secondary and urban roads. These roads were financed on a 70-30 matching basis with the states. Congress authorized appropriations for the roads on a regular, biennial basis.

Construction of strictly federal roads, such as forest highways and public land highways, was funded from general revenues.

---

troduced until late in December, no action was taken on them in 1969. Final action was completed on HR 15424 in 1970. *(p. 154)*

In his Oct. 23 message, the President warned that a strong Merchant Marine was necessary for international trade and wartime mobility but that the U.S. Merchant Marine was rapidly approaching obsolescence. About three-quarters of American trading vessels were more than 20 years old, he said, and in the next four years much of the fleet would be scrapped.

The President proposed to triple annual cargo ship construction to 30 ships a year while providing incentives to the shipping industry to reduce costs and increase efficiency.

Higher labor costs and less efficient production methods were blamed for the fact that it cost from 50 to

55 percent more to build a ship in an American shipyard than in the yards of a foreign shipbuilding nation such as Japan. In order to maintain the U.S. shipbuilding industry, the government made up the difference between foreign and domestic construction and operating costs. The subsidy program was authorized first under the Merchant Marine Act of 1936, which Congress has repeatedly extended. *(Congress and the Nation Vol. I, p. 545)*

Maritime Bills

Subsidies and Ceilings. President Nixon Oct. 10 signed into law HR 4152 (PL 91-85), authorizing $367 million for construction and operating differential subsidies in fiscal 1970, $130 million more than was requested by the administration.

Congress June 26 completed action on HR 265 (PL 91-40) extending through fiscal 1970 ceilings on construction-differential subsidies paid on vessels built or reconditioned in U.S. shipyards.

HR 265 extended for one year authorization of government payment of 55 percent of the difference in the cost of building a cargo ship in an American shipyard and in the lowest cost foreign yards. It also extended the 60 percent ceiling on payments for reconstruction or reconditioning of passenger vessels. The 55 and 60 percent ceilings were to have expired June 30, 1969, and revert to a permanent 50 percent limit authorized under the Merchant Marine Act of 1936.

Passenger Ships. Congress cleared Dec. 12 a bill (HR 210—PL 91-154) repealing the requirement, enacted in 1966, that steamship companies disclose their compliance with safety standards in advertising and in booking passengers.

The requirement, enacted after several ocean cruise ship fires in 1965-66, became superfluous by the enforcement of uniform safety standards that applied to all ships sailing from American ports.

Cruise Ships. The House approved a bill (HR 12605) eliminating several restrictions on the operation of cruise ships. The Senate did not act on the measure in 1969, but the bill was enacted in 1970. *(p. 155)*

HR 12605 allowed a cruise to begin and end on a U.S. seacoast other than the one from which the cruise operator regularly sailed. It also allowed a vessel to carry one-way passengers between ports on another operator's routes if that operator consented. And it permitted cruise ships to embark passengers at one domestic port and disembark them at another domestic port.

Fishing Fleet. The House in 1969 approved, but the Senate did not act upon a measure (HR 4813) to extend for two years, until June 30, 1971, the provisions of the U.S. Fishing Fleet Improvement Act (PL 86-516), the law authorizing the federal program of subsidies for construction of fishing vessels. The failure of Congress to complete action upon HR 4813 before June 30, 1969, allowed the act to expire on that date.

Airport Development Plan

Both the House and Senate in 1969 took action on legislation to expand and improve the U.S. airport and airway system, but final action on the proposals was not completed.

The House passed a bill (HR 14465) similar to the administration proposal recommending a 10-year, $5-

Air Controllers "Sick-Out"

Post-war growth of air traffic outstripped the growth of facilities to handle it, and the problem was expected to grow worse with the introduction of more and bigger planes. The summer of 1968 was marked by massive congestion at major airports, aggravated by a "slowdown" by air traffic controllers, who were regularly working long overtime hours because of the congestion and personnel shortages. Major legislation to deal with air traffic congestion was proposed in 1968 but was not acted on by Congress. *(Congress and the Nation, Vol. II, p. 249)*

Although the Federal Aviation Administration (FAA) in 1969 imposed air traffic quotas, effective May 31, for the nation's five most congested airports, almost 500 controllers called in "sick" instead of reporting to work June 18-20, 1969, and an epidemic of airport traffic jams spread from Denver, Colo., to New York and through the country. Without enough controllers on the job, particularly in the key New York area, take-offs were delayed as much as four hours and airlines were forced into wholesale cancellations.

Although brief, the June tieup was reminiscent of the summer of 1968, when air traffic slowed down after the then newly-formed Professional Air Traffic Controllers' Organization (PATCO) recommended that controllers be certain to space airplanes at a safe distance from each other.

PATCO, which represented about 7,500 of 14,000 controllers, disclaimed responsibility for the June 1969 "sick-out," calling it a "spontaneous" expression of disappointment with the administration airport bill. But John F. Maher, PATCO's national coordinator, said, "We are telling our people that if there is any indication that physically or mentally they aren't able to do topnotch jobs, they shouldn't go to work, (but should) call in sick, have everything they need taken care of."

The controllers were back at work on June 20, but FAA Administrator John H. Shaffer announced the FAA would cancel a dues check-off agreement with PATCO and would issue reprimands, suspensions or dismissals to individual controllers it found had called in sick without justification.

PATCO in turn announced it was stockpiling controllers' resignations and had 4,000 ready to turn in if the FAA took action against controllers.

PATCO never carried out its threat, although the FAA stopped deducting PATCO dues from controllers' paychecks and issued suspension notices for three to five days to more than 80 controllers.

Maher announced Aug. 18 that the threat of mass resignations had become a dead issue, because the FAA was beginning to take encouraging steps toward meeting controller complaints.

billion airport-airway development program, while the Senate Commerce Committee reported a similar measure (S 3108) late in the session. Final action was completed on HR 14465 in 1970. *(p. 156)*

President Nixon June 16 proposed a $5 billion development program for the nation's airports and airways control systems over the next 10 years. The program would be financed through user taxes.

Mr. Nixon said problems of air transportation had been allowed "to stack up like aircraft circling a congested airport...we simply do not have the capacity in our airways and airports ample to our present needs or reflective of the future."

The Federal Aviation Administration (FAA) forecasted a doubling of air passenger miles by 1975 and a tripling by 1980.

The legislation, as sent to Congress, proposed to:

• Increase federal aid for airways facilities and equipment from $93 million to $250 million annually, beginning in fiscal 1970. Airways facilities and equipment include air traffic control systems, navigation aids, landing devices and the like.

• Double funds for research in air traffic systems to $60 million a year.

• Increase grants for airport construction and improvement from $65 million to $180 million in fiscal 1970. The grants, matched on a 50-50 basis by local and state governments, would be increased each year for a 10-year total of $2.5 billion.

Taxes to be imposed on users of air transportation were to be placed in a special fund—similar to the highway trust fund—to be used only for the airport and airways program. The taxes proposed:

• Increase from 5 percent to 8 percent on domestic airline tickets.

• A new levy of 5 percent on air freight.

• Increase from 2 cents to 9 cents a gallon on general aviation (but not airlines) fuels.

• Three dollars per passenger for most international flights originating in the United States.

Urban Mass Transit

The Senate Banking and Currency Committee in 1969 reported a bill (S 3154) to provide long-term financing for urban public transportation programs. *(Mass transit problems, box p. 149)*

The measure was a compromise between the administration proposal (S 2821) authorizing $3.1 billion in contract authority for the five-year period beginning in fiscal 1971 and a bill (S 1032) introduced by Sen. Harrison A. Williams Jr. (D N.J.) to create a mass transit trust fund to be financed by revenue from the existing automobile excise tax. Mass transit supporters complained that the administration measure would not assure cities of the funds it would authorize.

S 3154 resolved the financing issue by providing that $3.1 billion be authorized for an expanded mass transit program but that the funds would only be obligated and released in small increments.

The House took no action on separate mass transit legislation in 1969, but in 1970, Congress completed action on S 3154, retaining the financing compromise. *(p. 156)*

1969 Proposals. President Nixon Aug. 7 proposed a $10 billion, 12-year program to "make public transportation an attractive alternative to private car use."

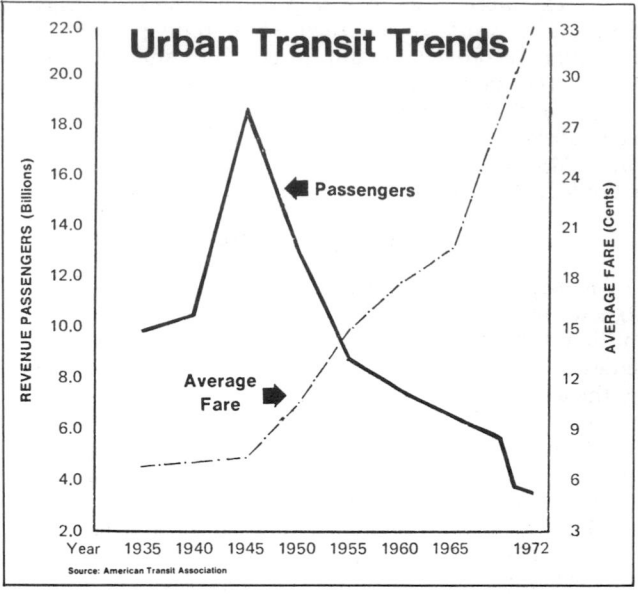

The administration said its proposal would assure enough federal funds to make public transit an attractive alternative to the automobile. Transportation Secretary John A. Volpe said that a 1961 study by the Institute of Public Administration, updated by HUD in 1966, showed that during a 10-year period almost $12 billion (adjusted to 1969 values) could be effectively invested in rail rapid transit and in buses.

The administration bill (S 2821, HR 13422) proposed a declaration of congressional intent that $10 billion be invested over a 12-year period to upgrade local mass transit. Funds for the program would be appropriated from general revenues. Contract authorization totaling $3.1 billion would be provided for the first five years of the program, starting with a first-year authorization of $300 million in fiscal 1971 and increasing to $1 billion annually by fiscal 1975. Contract authorization would be renewed every two years so that there would always be three years of outstanding contract authority.

Funding Issue. President Nixon's mass transit proposal met immediate opposition on grounds that "contract authority" provided no certainty that the program would receive appropriations at the level proposed by the administration. Sen. Harrison A. Williams Jr. (D N.J.), a member of the Banking and Currency Committee and author of a proposal (S 1032) for a mass transit trust fund, called the administration proposal "a paper promise."

S 1032 would create a mass transit trust fund similar to the Highway Trust Fund. The fund would be financed by earmarking part of the existing 7-percent automobile excise tax. Unlike other highway-related taxes, revenues from the excise tax go into the general fund of the Treasury, instead of into the Highway Trust Fund.

But the administration said that the only difference between contract authority and a trust fund was that, under contract authority, appropriations would be made from general Treasury receipts. As under the highway program, the Department of Transportation said, the full amounts authorized by Congress would become available for obligation in contracts binding on the federal government at the beginning of each fiscal year, without awaiting congressional appropriations. Congress later would have to appropriate the funds necessary to liquidate the government's debts. The department said this method, combined with authorization for two years at a time, would provide adequate assurance to city governments, public agencies and private companies that federal commitments to projects would be met.

Supersonic Transport

Congress in 1969 appropriated $85-million for continued development of the controversial supersonic transport (SST) project first funded in fiscal 1962. Attempts in the Senate and House to delete the SST funds from a fiscal 1970 Department of Transportation bill (HR 14794) were rejected, although SST opponents had argued that the plane was uneconomical, noisy and should not be funded when social programs were being cut back.

President Nixon decided to go ahead with federal funding for the aircraft despite the recommendation of an interdepartmental committee to withdraw the program. *(Box p. 159)*

1970

In a burst of legislative activity intended to modernize the nation's transportation system, Congress in 1970 cleared a half-dozen major bills involving federal-aid highways, the merchant marine, airports and airways, mass transit systems, passenger trains, the bankrupt Penn Central Railroad and rail safety. Congress, however, postponed an ultimate decision on the fate of the controversial SST, delaying a vote on the project until 1971.

In May, Congress cleared legislation authorizing a new long-range program for expansion and improvement of the U.S. airport and airway system. The following October, Congress created a corporation to operate a nationwide passenger rail service; approved a 10-year subsidy program for construction of 300 merchant marine vessels and passed a bill authorizing $3.1 billion in grants for mass transit projects.

In December, Congress authorized the federal government to guarantee loans for up to $125 million for the bankrupt Penn Central. The same month, legislation was approved extending the federal aid highway program through 1977 and authorizing $9.8 billion for continued construction of the interstate highway system.

Congress also averted a nationwide rail strike in 1970 by drafting a settlement between the railroads and shopcraft unions involved.

Highway Aid

Congress Dec. 19 cleared for the President a bill (HR 19504—PL 91-605) to amend the Federal-Aid Highway Act of 1968 by extending authorizations for the Interstate Highway System through fiscal 1976, authorizing funds for other highway programs and establishing new highway-related activities.

The bill authorized $9,775,000,000 from the Highway Trust Fund for continued construction of the interstate

highway system in fiscal years 1974-1976. The total included an additional $1,775,000,000 for fiscal 1974 and $4-billion each for fiscal years 1975 and 1976. By June 1970, the interstate system, designed to connect the nation's metropolitan areas and industrial centers, was 70 percent complete.

The bill authorized an additional $4,712,960,000 for other federal-aid highway programs; extended the Highway Trust Fund for an additional five years, through fiscal 1977, and increased the federal share of most federal-aid highway programs, not including the interstate system, to 70 percent from 50 percent, beginning with fiscal 1974.

The bill also required the District of Columbia and the Department of Transportation to restudy projects for the construction of certain interstate highway segments in the District and to make a report to Congress on recommendations, including alternative routes and plans.

During Senate debate on the conference report, Jennings Randolph (D W.Va.), chairman of the Public Works Committee, said the most controversial sections of the Senate-passed and House-passed bills were those pertaining to the construction of interstate highways in Washington, D.C. The House had required that the roads be constructed; the Senate deleted the construction order entirely.

"The conference decision," he said, "was the only one we could reach to avoid an impasse that would have imperiled the national highway program. It is a reasonable compromise...there is no mandating of freeway construction in the city."

The final version authorized $200 million for fiscal years 1972 and 1973 for a new urban highway system and stipulated that the new system's routes could not be the same as routes of any other federal-aid highway program. In addition, up to 50 percent of each state's appropriation for primary- and secondary-road urban extensions and Urban Areas Traffic Operations Improvement Programs (TOPICS) could be used in the new urban system.

The bill also authorized states to use urban area highway funds to build exclusive or preferential bus lanes and other traffic-reducing projects.

Major Provisions. As signed into law, HR 19504:

● Extended authority for construction of the interstate highway system for two years, through fiscal 1976.

● Required the Secretary of Transportation to provide Congress with revised cost estimates for the interstate system in January 1972 for fiscal years 1974 and 1975 and in January 1974 for fiscal 1976.

● Established a new federal-aid urban system in each urbanized area to serve major centers of activity and highest traffic volume corridors; prohibited urban system routes to be the same as any other federal-aid route; determined that routes would be selected and project specifications would be made by state highway departments and appropriate local road officials working together; permitted up to half of the amounts appropriated to each state for urban extensions to primary and secondary highways and up to half of the amounts for the TOPICS program to be used for the new urban system; set the level of federal funding at 50 percent.

● Prohibited the impounding of appropriated highway funds by the executive branch for such reasons as to control inflation; prohibited the use of trust funds by any federal agency except the Federal Highway Administration and for any use except highways.

• Increased the share of federal funding of any federal-aid highway program, except the interstate system, to 70 percent from 50 percent for fiscal 1974 and all subsequent fiscal years.

• Authorized funds appropriated to states for urban extensions of primary and secondary highways, interstate highways and urban system highways to be used for the construction of exclusive or preferential bus lanes and other traffic-reducing projects including fringe-parking facilities.

• Directed the Secretary to include in his report on highway needs, which was to be submitted to Congress in January 1972, his recommendations for a continuing federal-aid highway program between 1976 and 1990; the recommendations were to deal with the construction costs of a continuing new urban system.

• Established a Commission on Highway Beautification to review existing law, policies and practices on outdoor advertising and junk yard control and to submit a report to Congress within one year of enactment; authorized $200,000 for the commission. The commission would be composed of four members each from the Senate and House Public Works Committees and three members of the public appointed by the President; it would cease to exist six months after its final report was issued.

• Set a deadline of July 1, 1973, after which any interstate segments for which the respective states had not established a construction schedule would be removed by the Secretary of Transportation from designation as part of the interstate system; set a deadline of July 1, 1975, for states to submit plans, estimates and specifications for interstate segments, after which time the segments would be removed from the system if states did not comply.

• Clarified the application of the TOPICS program to include urban areas of 5,000 to 50,000 population as well as larger urban areas.

• Authorized the secretary to conduct demonstration projects for the elimination of all ground-level railroad-highway crossings along the route of the Metroliner—the federal rail demonstration project between Washington, D.C., and New York City—and for the elimination or protection of such crossings in the vicinity of Greenwood, S.C.; set the federal share at 90 percent and the railroad's at 10 percent, except on non-federal-aid highways where the federal share would be 80 percent, the railroad's share 10 percent and the state's share 10 percent.

Merchant Marine

Congress Oct. 7 enacted legislation (HR 15424—PL 91-469) amending the Merchant Marine Act of 1936 (PL 74-835) to establish a 10-year subsidy program for the construction of 300 merchant marine vessels.

President Nixon Oct. 23, 1969, keeping a campaign pledge, had proposed a program to triple U.S. cargo vessel construction to 30 ships a year. About three-quarters of the American merchant marine fleet was more than 20 years old, the President said, and in the next four years much of the fleet would be scrapped.

Highway Authorizations

Following is the breakdown by program of authorizations contained in HR 19504 to be appropriated from general Treasury funds, except where the source is the Highway Trust Fund, indicated by (TF):

Interstate Highway System	$9,775,000,000 (TF)	(1974-76)
Primary, secondary highways and their urban extensions	2,200,000,000 (TF)	(1972-73)
Primary, secondary highways, exclusive of their urban extensions	250,000,000 (TF)	(1972-73)
New urban system highways	200,000,000 (TF)	(1972-73)
Urban Areas Traffic Operations Improvement Programs (TOPICS)	200,000,000 (TF)	(1972-73)
Forest and public lands highways	98,000,000 (TF)	(1972-73)
Forest and public lands development (roads and trails), park roads and trails, parkways, Indian reservation roads and bridges	485,000,000	(1972-73)
For states with less than .05 percent of total interstate appropriation	110,000,000	(1972-73)
Highway beautification, administration	17,500,000	(1971-73)
Outdoor advertising control	97,500,000	(1971-73)
Junkyards control	11,000,000	(1971-73)
Highway beautification commission	200,000 *	
Territories (Virgin Islands, Guam, American Samoa) highway development	13,500,000	(1971-73)
Darien Gap Highway	100,000,000*	
Bridges on Federal dams	3,760,000*	
Economic growth center highways	100,000,000 (TF)	(1972-73)
Alaskan assistance	40,000,000 (TF)	(1972-73)
Urban transportation planning	500,000*	
Baltimore-Washington Parkway	65,000,000 (TF)*	
Research and development, highway safety programs by the Federal Highway Administration and National Highway Traffic Safety Administration	440,000,000 (TF)**	(1972-73)
Bridge replacement	250,000,000 (TF)**	(1972-73)
Rail crossing demonstration projects	31,000,000 (TF)**	
TOTAL	$14,487,960,000	

* Total authorized and available until expended.
** Funds split between trust fund (TF) and general Treasury.

PROVISIONS. As cleared by Congress, HR 15424:

• Authorized the Secretary of Commerce to subsidize construction of 300 merchant ships over a 10-year period beginning in fiscal 1971 (the fiscal 1971 appropriation provided for 19 ships; the annual average was to be raised to 30 ships by fiscal 1973; the existing average was 10 ships per year) and extended subsidized construction to bulk cargo carriers. (Such subsidy had been limited to scheduled carriers under existing legislation.)

• Required funds to be authorized annually. *(Box next page)*

• Broadened the definition of qualified applicants for construction subsidies, previously limited to shipowners, to include shipbuilders; provided that construction subsidies were to be paid directly to builders; and required the secretary to give preference to applicants promoting standardization and cost reduction.

• Required the secretary to compute the costs of construction in foreign shipyards annually; but allowed the maximum subsidy on U.S. ship construction to fall to 50 percent (from 55 percent) as of July 1, 1970, and established goals of a 45-percent maximum for fiscal 1971 and a reduction of 2 percent per year thereafter to a permanent level of 35 percent.

• Required the secretary to obtain competitive bids for each ship to be built under subsidy and to contract with the low bidder if the bid was below the subsidy goal limit; and authorized the secretary to negotiate with bidders to reduce costs if bids were above the goal.

• Retained the original 1936 act's requirement that all materials under construction subsidy be of U.S. origin, but allowed the secretary to waive the requirement if the delivery date of a vessel was threatened.

• Repealed the existing requirement for recapture of profits exceeding 10 percent from subsidized shipbuilders.

• Liberalized the definition of obsolete vessels; extended the secretary's authority and broadened his discretion to determine the appropriate age under subsidy programs for retirement of vessels for trade-in, unsubsidized service and transfer to the reserve fleet.

• Extended subsidies for operation of merchant ships (previously limited to scheduled carriers) to bulk cargo carriers and adjusted the terms of subsidies.

• Provided that operating subsidies "shall equal" the difference between U.S. and foreign operating expenses, principally wages and benefits contained in collective bargaining agreements; permitted less than full subsidies upon agreement of the parties.

• Established a seven-member, presidentially appointed Commission on American Shipbuilding to review industry status toward achieving the goal of decreasing subsidy levels.

• Established a new position of Assistant Secretary of Commerce for maritime affairs and required that it be combined with the position of Maritime Administrator.

• Provided that government agencies must administer their various programs under an existing provision of the Maritime Act requiring at least one-half of certain government-generated cargoes to be carried by U.S. vessels and in accordance with regulations promulgated by the Secretary of Commerce.

• Authorized the secretary to promulgate regulations under existing "foreign trade" or "foreign commerce" definitions to include carriage between foreign ports.

• Granted to the St. Lawrence Seaway Corporation forgiveness of accrued and unpaid interest ($22.4 million by mid-1970) and future interest to prevent a future increase in seaway tolls.

• Extended to most shipping companies the authority previously granted to subsidized carriers to defer taxes on income paid into a capital fund to replace old or add new ships.

• Refined the scope for operating-subsidy participation by:

1. Limiting continued foreign-flag holdings during a 20-year period to bulk cargo vessels rather than all vessels.

2. Determining that the 20-year period for divestiture of foreign holdings for subsidy participation would begin April 15, 1970.

3. Determining that mere broker or agent activities in dual-flag operation (not involving ownership) could not continue beyond April 15, 1972, for subsidy participants.

Maritime Subsidies

The following table shows the amounts appropriated by Congress for maritime construction subsidies and operating subsidies for fiscal years 1970-73: (*Fiscal 1966-69, Congress and the Nation Vol. II, p. 248*)

	Construction Subsidies	Operating Subsidies
Fiscal 1970	$ 15,900,000	194,400,000
Fiscal 1971	187,500,000	273,000,000
Fiscal 1972	229,687,000	239,145,000
Fiscal 1973	455,000,000	232,000,000

4. Requiring that shipowners who wished to qualify under the 20-year gradual divestiture plan must have filed with the Secretary of Commerce a complete statement of foreign-flag activities and affiliations within 90 days of enactment of the legislation. (In addition, the Secretary was required to report to Congress annually about such foreign-flag operations by U.S. subsidized owners and recommend any legislation he deemed necessary.)

• Added Great Lakes commerce to the trade qualifying under the subsidy and other provisions.

• Increased the allowable amount of outstanding federal mortgage insurance on ships to $3 billion from $1 billion and extended the Secretary's authority to grant war risk insurance.

• Required the secretary to develop a long-range plan to create an adequate merchant marine.

1971 Authorization. Congress May 11 cleared for the President a bill (HR 15945—PL 91-247) authorizing $429.4 million to subsidize construction and operation of merchant marine vessels in fiscal year 1971. The bill included authorizations of $199.5 million for construction of 19 sips during the first year of the new merchant marine program (*above*) and $193 million for ship operation subsidies.

Cruise Ships. The Senate April 30 completed action on a bill (HR 12605—PL 91-250) to eliminate several restrictions on the operation of American cruise ships. (*1969 House action, p. 154*)

As cleared by Congress, HR 12605:

• Eliminated the requirement that a cruise begin and end at ports on the same seacoast of the United States from which the operator conducted his regular service.

• Permitted a cruise ship to carry one-way passengers between ports on another operator's routes if the other operator consented.

• Allowed a cruise operator to disembark at one domestic port passengers who were embarked at another, if this did not compete with another American ship operator or if the other operator consented.

• Allowed passenger ships engaged in regular foreign service to carry passengers between domestic ports without losing operating subsidies or having to repay part of their construction subsidies, provided the secretary of Commerce found the service would not deviate substantially from the regular route or harm the service. Ship operators regularly serving the route would also have to consent.

Urban Mass Transit

Congress Oct. 5 cleared for the President a bill (S 3154—PL 91-453) authorizing $3.1-billion in grants and loans for state and local governments for mass transportation projects. The program was similar to the plan proposed by the Nixon administration in 1969. *(p. 152)* S 3154 had been reported by the Senate Banking and Currency Committee in 1969.

The administration bill (S 2821) had authorized $3.1 billion in contract authority for mass transit for a five-year period beginning with fiscal 1971. Mass transit backers had complained the administration bill would not assure cities of the funds it authorized. They preferred S 1032, introduced by Sen. Harrison A. Williams Jr. (D N.J.), which would create a mass transit trust fund deriving its revenues from the existing automobile excise tax.

S 3154 resolved the financing issue by making $3.1 billion available to the Secretary of Transportation for obligation through contracts for transportation projects but authorizing appropriation of the funds to meet the obligations incurred in smaller annual increments.

S 3154 expressed the finding of Congress that at least $10 billion in federal funds would be needed over the 12-year period, beginning in fiscal 1971, for urban mass transit programs.

Background. The Urban Mass Transportation Act of 1964 (PL 88-365), as amended in 1966, 1967 and 1968, established grant and loan programs for research, development, demonstration projects and direct assistance to state and local governments for construction and improvement of urban mass transportation systems. Grants of up to two-thirds of the net cost of specific projects were authorized.

Authorizations for the programs reached $190 million in fiscal year 1970 (which ended June 30, 1970). The Transportation Department appropriation bill for fiscal year 1970 (HR 14794—PL 91-168)—cleared by Congress Dec. 19, 1969—appropriated $214 million for the programs in advance for fiscal year 1971.

Provisions. As cleared by Congress, S 3154:

• Expressed the finding of Congress that at least $10 billion in federal funds would be needed over the 12-year period, beginning with fiscal 1971, for urban mass transportation.

• Authorized $3.1 billion for grants to state and local governments to meet up to two-thirds of the net costs of construction and improvement of mass transit systems and other programs funded under the bill; authorized aggregate totals of $80 million in fiscal year 1971, $310 million in fiscal 1972, $710 million in fiscal 1973, $1.26 billion in fiscal 1974, $1.86 billion in fiscal 1975 and $3.1 billion thereafter.

• Required further authorization requests to meet the $10-billion federal commitment to be submitted at two-year intervals.

• Authorized 10-year loans for acquisition of land needed for mass transit purposes.

• Required the Secretary of Transportation to determine that a project was the best alternative in terms of protecting the environment.

• Required state and local governments seeking grants or loans to hold public hearings on projects that substantially affected communities or their mass transit systems.

Mass Transit Funds

The following table shows the amounts appropriated by Congress for urban mass transit grants for fiscal years 1971-73. Appropriations were to liquidate contract obligations authorized by the Urban Mass Transit Act of 1970. (An additional $241-million in federal grants was appropriated in fiscal 1971. *(Fiscal 1966-69, Congress and the Nation, Vol. II, p. 251)*

Fiscal 1971	$ 7.5 million
Fiscal 1972	150.0 million
Fiscal 1973	232.0 million

• Changed the $12.5-million discretionary fund established in the 1964 act to fund consisting of 15 percent of the aggregate amount authorized, to be used in states where two-thirds of the maximum amounts had been committed.

• Limited the amount any single state, including its local governments, could receive to 12 1/2 percent of the aggregate total authorized and permitted the secretary to use discretionary funds without regard to the limit.

• Authorized the secretary to conduct a one-year study of the feasibility of providing federal subsidies for operating costs of mass transit systems.

• Authorized private transit systems to meet all of the one-third state and local share of net project costs without regard to the financial capabilities of the state and local governments involved.

Airport Development

Congress May 13 cleared for the President a bill (HR 14465—PL 91-258), the Airport and Airway Development Act.

HR 14465 repealed the Federal Airport Act of 1946 (PL 79-377), the basic legislation providing federal aid for aviation facilities, and authorized a new long-range program for expansion and improvement of the U.S. airport and airways system. The program was to be financed in major part by new taxes on users of the aviation system. Revenues from the user charges would be paid into a trust fund in the U.S. Treasury similar to the existing Highway Trust Fund.

The new program was intended to alleviate severe inadequacies in the nation's aviation system by providing for major new investments in modernized airports and federal air navigational facilities. Air traffic had increased at an unexpectedly high rate after World War II while expenditures on airports and airways failed to keep pace.

In a 1969 message to Congress proposing the act, President Nixon noted that "Years of neglect have permitted the problems of air transportation in America to stack up like aircraft circling a congested airport."

Background. Federal aid to airports, made from general revenues, averaged about $75 million a year under the existing airport aid program. In fiscal 1969, appropriations reached a low point of $30 million, while requests for federal grants reached an all-time high of $455.2 million.

Several major airports had reached the saturation point by 1969. The Federal Aviation Administration (FAA) imposed air traffic quotas for the nation's five most congested airports, where delays caused backups in traffic throughout the system.

In 1970, the first jumbo jets, carrying about 400 passengers each, began service. Pan American inaugurated flights on the Boeing 747 in January. While the jumbos were more economical for the airlines, they greatly added to the urgency of solving airway safety problems.

The burden of moving traffic safely and efficiently rested on an air traffic control system plagued by obsolete equipment and personnel shortages. The FAA said in a 1969 summary of long-range planning assumptions that if age and the state of technology were used as criteria for obsolescence then most equipment in commissioned facilities was obsolete, though not unsafe.

Air traffic controllers, whose job was to keep planes separated on take-off, landing and between airports, found their work increasingly difficult. A shortage of trained controllers because of a hiring hiatus in the 1950s aggravated the situation, forcing controllers at high-density airports to work abnormally long hours at their taxing jobs. *(Box p. 151)*

In 1969, the administration proposed a 10-year $5 billion program of airport and airway expansion, to be financed in major part by new taxes on airway users. HR 14465, passed by the House in 1969. *(See p. 151)* was in close accord with the original administration request (HR 12374). The Senate completed work on the bill in 1970.

PROVISIONS. As cleared by Congress, HR 14465:

Declaration of Policy

• Declared that the amount available for obligation for improvement of the airways system should be no less than $250 million annually between Jan. 1, 1970, and June 30, 1980.

• Declared that the total amount available for obligation for airport assistance between Jan. 1, 1970, and June 30, 1980, should be $2.5 billion.

National Airport System Plan

• Directed the Secretary of Transportation to formulate, within two years, a national airport system plan after consultation with other federal agencies.

• Established a nine-member Aviation Advisory Commission, composed of private citizens appointed by the President, to formulate recommendations for land uses surrounding airports, for ground access to airports and for airways and airports; directed the commission to make its final report by Jan. 1, 1972.

Planning Grants

• Authorized a maximum of $75 million for five years for grants for planning the location and development of airports, at a rate of not more than $15 million per year. No more than 7.5 percent of the funds made available in a given year could be allocated for projects in a single state.

Airport and Airway Development Program

• Authorized the Secretary of Transportation to make grants of $250 million in each of fiscal years 1971 through 1975 for construction and modernization of air-

---

Federal Airport Funds

The following table shows the amounts appropriated by Congress from the Airport Trust Fund to meet airport development obligations (fiscal years 1971-73) authorized by the Airport and Airway Development Act of 1970. *(Fiscal 1966-70 appropriations, Congress and the Nation Vol. II, p. 250)*

Fiscal 1971	$ 60,000,000
Fiscal 1972	92,000,000
Fiscal 1973	100,000,000

---

ports served by the certificated airlines and other airports needed to relieve air traffic congestion.

• Authorized $30 million a year from fiscal 1971 through fiscal 1975 specifically for grants to develop reliever airports (those serving general aviation—private and business planes).

• Authorized the Secretary of Transportation to incur obligations for not more than $840 million in contracts for airport projects before June 30, 1973. Obligations could not extend for more than three fiscal years or beyond June 30, 1975. No more than one obligation could be incurred for any single project.

• Authorized not less than $250 million a year from fiscal 1970 through fiscal 1975 for air navigation facilities.

• Required that unallocated revenues in the trust fund be used for administrative, operating and research expenses, provided that the first $50 million appropriated from general revenues be allocated to research and development.

(Obligational authority differs from regular grant authority in that a congressional appropriation is not needed prior to commitment of the funds in contracts. Ordinarily Congress must first authorize funds and then appropriate them before contracts may be made.)

Distribution of Funds

• Provided that one-third of airline and reliever airport development funds be distributed to states and territories according to area and population, one-third according to the number of passengers enplaned at each airport and one-third at the discretion of the Secretary of Transportation.

• Provided that 75 percent of the funds authorized for grants specifically to general aviation airports be distributed according to area and population and 25 percent at the discretion of the Secretary of Transportation.

United States Share of Costs

• Established as a general rule that the Federal share of an approved airport development project should not exceed 50 percent, but provided that in the case of elements of a project related to navigation needs, such as land needed for approach lighting, the U.S. share could be as large as 82 percent. In the Virgin Islands, and in cases where states contained unappropriated and unreserved public lands and nontaxable Indian lands exceeding 5 percent of the total land used, the U.S. share should not exceed 75 percent.

Approval of Projects

• Required federal certification of air carrier airports to ensure that they met minimum safety standards.

● Required that opportunity be given for public hearings on proposed airport locations and their consistency with local urban planning.

● Required that an airport location, runway location or runway extension be approved only if there was reasonable assurance from a state's governor that the project would be located, designed and constructed so as to comply with applicable air and water quality standards.

User Taxes and Trust Fund

● Imposed a user charge tax of 7 cents a gallon on all general aviation fuel.

● Increased the passenger ticket tax on all domestic flights from 5 to 8 percent and imposed a new "head tax" of $3 on passengers on international commercial flights originating in the United States after June 30, 1970, and until June 30, 1980.

● Imposed a new tax of 5 percent on air freight waybills after June 30, 1970, and before July 1, 1980.

● Provided that revenues from the fuel, ticket, freight and registration taxes be placed in an "Airport and Airway Trust Fund."

● Provided that receipts from taxes on tires and tubes used for aircraft be transferred from the Highway Trust Fund to the Airport and Airway Trust Fund and that any general revenues necessary to supplement the air user taxes also be paid into the latter trust fund.

● Imposed an annual aircraft registration tax of $25 plus 2 cents a pound for piston-powered aircraft with a maximum weight of more than 2,500 pounds and 3.5 cents a pound for all turbine-powered aircraft.

● Provided that the new airway user charges be effective July 1, 1970.

● Provided that the aviation user taxes and the Airport and Airway Trust Fund terminate June 30, 1980.

Supersonic Transport

Congress Jan. 2 cleared a continuing resolution (H J Res 1421—PL 91-645), permitting the Department of Transportation and related agencies to spend funds through March 30, 1971, at the level agreed to in the House-Senate conference report on the fiscal 1971 appropriations bill (HR 17755).

Passage of the continuing appropriations bill represented a compromise reached by the House and Senate to end a two-week Senate filibuster over funds for the supersonic transport (SST). Conferees on the Department of Transportation appropriation bill (HR 17755) had provided $210 million for the SST after the Senate had deleted all funds for development of the controversial aircraft. The House had appropriated the full $290 million requested by the administration for development of two prototype planes.

Under the terms of the continuing resolution, all agencies covered by the bill were to be funded through March 30 at the level of the appropriations in the conference report. Senate opponents of the SST were assured that there would be a separate vote on the SST funds when further fiscal 1971 appropriations for the Department of Transportation were considered during the 1st session of the 92nd Congress. In March 1971, Congress terminated the project *(p. 167)*.

SST Background

The Federal Aviation Administration (FAA) began to consider development of an SST as early as 1959. In 1961, Congress appropriated the first money for the project—$11-million for an FAA feasibility study.

The idea was given impetus in November 1962 when the British and French governments announced a joint program to develop an SST called the Concorde. And when Pan American World Airways ordered six Concordes June 4, 1963, President Kennedy responded the next day by announcing a federal commitment to help private industry develop an American SST.

Under the plan, the government would pay 75 per cent of the development costs, estimated at $1 billion. "In no event," Kennedy wrote Congress, "will the government investment be permitted to exceed $750 million. Moreover, the government does not intend to pay any production, purchase, or operating subsidies to manufacturers or airlines."

From 1962-70, the federal government had invested between $700 million and $800 million in the SST program and the House May 27 appropriated an additional $290 million for fiscal 1971 to continue development of the controversial 1,800-mile-an-hour plane. Over-all government development investment was expected to reach at least $1.3 billion.

Opposition. In 1964, opposition appeared on the floor of the House. Rep. Henry S. Reuss (D Wis.) offered an amendment to cut $24.7 million earmarked for the SST from the National Aeronautics and Space Administration authorization. It was rejected on a 26-109 standing vote. No funds were appropriated for the plane in fiscal 1965 or fiscal 1969. *(Congress and the Nation Vol. II, p. 228, 232, 244, 250)*

Senate opposition surfaced in 1966. William Proxmire (D Wis.) offered an amendment to cut the SST appropriation to $80 million from $280 million, but it was rejected on a 31-55 roll call.

Contracts were awarded the Boeing Company and Lockheed Aircraft Corporation to design the SST airframe and to the General Electric Company and Pratt & Whitney Inc. to design the engines. The government paid 94.5 percent of the costs. The work went slowly; the contracts were extended 18 months. At the end of 1966, the FAA announced that Boeing and General Electric had been chosen to build an SST prototype.

The government agreed to pay 90 percent of the costs and 75 percent on every plane sold starting with the 101st. The government's investment would be repaid by sale of 300 planes.

Boeing's design incorporated an idea its engineers had studied for years: a wing that extended out straight for maximum lift on takeoff and landing, but swung back close to the fuselage to cut air resistance at high speeds.

But Boeing was forced to abandon the concept in October 1968, and in January of the following year, it submitted a conventional delta wing design similar to the rejected Lockheed design, the Concorde and the Russian SST.

President Kennedy had hoped SST would be flying before the end of the 1960s. By 1968 it was plain the project was almost a decade behind schedule. *(1969 action p. 53, Nixon views p. 159)*

Nixon on the SST: Two Reports and Final Approval in 1969

When Richard M. Nixon moved into the White House in January 1969, he was faced with the decision of whether or not to continue work on the SST. On Feb. 19, he appointed an ad hoc committee of high officials from 12 departments and agencies to review the program. The committee was divided into four working panels:

• Balance of payments and international relations: representatives from the Treasury, Commerce and State Departments.

• Technological fallout: representatives from the Office of Science and Technology, the National Aeronautics and Space Administration (NASA) and the Defense Department.

• Environmental and sociological impact: representatives from the Departments of Health, Education and Welfare and Interior and from the Office of Science and Technology.

• Economics: representatives from the Council of Economic Advisers and from the Departments of Labor and Commerce.

First Report

A month later the panels' reports were given to Under Secretary of Transportation James Beggs, who wrote a summary of them for submission to the President. When committee members saw the summary, they said it distorted their positions, which were generally critical. They could not agree on a final position, so their reports, Beggs' summary, and their responses to it all were forwarded to the President. None of the material was made public at the time.

Lee A. DuBridge, the President's Science Adviser, wrote Beggs: "On the whole, I come out negative on the desirability for further government subsidy for the development of the plane.... Any technological benefits which would accrue from its further development, either for civilian or military purposes, would seem to be minimal.

"Granted that this is an exciting technological development, it still seems best to me to avoid the serious environmental and nuisance problems and the government should not be subsidizing a device which has neither commercial attractiveness nor public acceptance."

DuBridge's views reflected the over-all tone of the ad hoc committee report.

Second Report

The President then apparently asked DuBridge for another report. A panel of scientists was set up, headed by Dr. Richard L. Garwin, a Columbia University physicist, former member of the President's Science Advisory Committee, and consultant to the Defense Department.

The panel's report to the President remained secret, but Rep. Henry S. Reuss (D Wis.) claimed that it concluded the SST was "economically wasteful and environmentally harmful."

The White House refused to release the report. Questioned by Congressional Quarterly, Garwin refused to comment. But in public testimony before Congress May 7, 1970, he opposed building the SST. Garwin said the SST "has not fulfilled its contract requirements; it is too heavy, too noisy...."

Nixon Go-Ahead

Nevertheless, Mr. Nixon announced Sept. 23, 1969, that he had decided to proceed with the program in order to preserve American aviation leadership. At his side was a delegation from the state of Washington, home of Boeing: Gov. Daniel J. Evans (R), Sen. Henry M. Jackson (D); Sen. Warren G. Magnuson's (D) chief aide; and the state's two Republican Representatives, Catherine May and Thomas M. Pelly.

When the House took up the 1970 transportation appropriation bill in November 1969, Rep. Sidney R. Yates (D Ill.) offered an amendment to delete the entire $96 million for the SST. It was defeated on a 64-126 standing vote.

Yates said the federal government would not recoup its investment in the SST since the prospective cost of the U.S. plane was twice as high as that of the British and French supersonic Concorde.

The Senate took up the appropriations bill in December 1969. Sen. William Proxmire (D Wis.) said he had concluded that "there are just two strong persuasive arguments for the SST. One of them is the distinguished senior Senator from Washington and the other is the distinguished junior Senator from Washington." Proxmire offered an amendment to delete the SST funds. It was cosponsored by Senators Harry F. Byrd Jr. (D Va.), J. W. Fulbright (D Ark.), Charles E. Goodell (R N.Y.) and Stephen M. Young (D Ohio). The Senate rejected it, 22-58.

During the debates in both Senate and House, most of the arguments for and against the plane were heard. Opponents leaned heavily on the ad hoc review committee's report, made public by Reuss, who had pried it out of the Department of Transportation after accusing Secretary Volpe of violating a Presidential agreement on the release of Executive Department documents to Congress.

The Department called the report "the least definitive and most outdated of the documents furnished Volpe." It said the committee "tended to rely on past findings and that the progress made on the Concorde (the Anglo-French SST) invalidated much of the report."

(After the Senate rejected appropriations for the SST on Dec. 3, 1970, Nixon called the action "a devastating mistake both because of its immediate impact and because it will have profound long-range consequences for this country." Nixon added that halting work on the SST would be a "mortal blow for our aerospace industry for years to come.")

ARGUMENTS IN FAVOR

Prestige and Jobs. The basic argument for the SST was that it was necessary if the U.S. was to maintain international leadership in commercial aviation.

The prestige argument seemed to convince many members of Congress. "I suspect...that national prestige is the real reason for President Nixon's decision to request funds for SST development," Proxmire said during the fiscal 1970 appropriations debate in December 1969.

Other members disagreed. Rep. John V. Tunney (D Calif.) said when the House debated the SST 1970 appropriation, that prestige had become "a device for avoiding careful analysis."

The administration said the main reason for building the SST was to preserve the aircraft industry. Transportation Secretary John A. Volpe said March 31 that "the aviation industry is essential to our nation."

SST opponents replied that the government and Boeing might well lose money on the plane, and that Boeing might go bankrupt as a result.

Reuss asked during the 1969 debate, "Why in the name of common sense do we not put Boeing to work making a mass transit vehicle, and GE to work producing a pollution-free engine for it?"

Balance of Payments. The administration contended that the sale of American SSTs to foreign countries would improve the nation's balance of payments. It said the United States could lose $16 billion by 1990 if the SST were not built.

The President's ad hoc review committee disputed this view. While it said the Commerce Department thought an American SST would help the balance of payments, the Treasury and State Departments believed that the increased travel by Americans that the SST presumably would generate actually would have a harmful effect on the balance of payments. *(Box p. 159)*

Technological Advances. Supporters of the SST said technological knowledge would be advanced by the plane's development and that some of these advances could be applied in other areas. The ad hoc committee acknowledged that this would happen, but said the possibilities appeared to be small. It concluded that technological advances would not be important enough in themselves to justify building the plane.

Speed. SST supporters argued that the speed of the plane represented progress, and as one aviation trade magazine put it, "Progress is what this country is all about."

Opponents asked whether speed necessarily represented progress. They wondered whether progress might not also include making air travel cheaper or planes quieter.

Opponents also pointed out that there were ways to cut travel time other than increasing the speed of the plane. "Of what value is it to me," asked Rep. Bertram L. Podell (D N.Y.) during the 1969 debate, "to go from Kennedy (Airport) to London in two hours when it sometimes takes me two hours to go from my home to Kennedy Airport? Of what value is it to arrive at Kennedy Airport in two hours flight time and then circle the airport for two additional hours because there is an utter lack of airport facilities?"

ARGUMENTS AGAINST

Sonic Boom. A major argument against the SST was that the sonic boom it would produce would be annoying and dangerous. The entire time an airplane flies faster than the speed of sound (about 760 miles per hour at sea level) it produces a shock wave, or sonic boom, about 50 miles wide on the ground under its path.

The SST's boom would be louder than those produced by existing military planes because it was bigger.

The Department of Transportation announced April 16 that it would prohibit the SST from flying over the United States at supersonic speeds. Reuss questioned whether the regulation would be effective in the long run.

If the plane ever flew over the United States, critics said, it would do millions of dollars worth of damage to buildings every day, disturb peace of mind, and startle people engaged in delicate or dangerous work.

Noise. The other major complaint was that it would be more than twice as noisy on the ground as existing craft. It would make as much noise as the simultaneous takeoff of 50 subsonic planes, opponents said.

The ad hoc committee said it expected that "significant numbers of people will file complaints and resort to legal action, and that a very high percentage of the exposed population will find the noise intolerable and the apparent cause of a wide variety of adverse effects."

The plane's backers conceded that airport noise was a problem, but said that landing noise would be no worse than that of a Boeing 707 and that takeoff noise would be less—once the SST reached one nautical mile from the end of the runway. It would be quieter past that point because it would have climbed higher and could cut its power more than a conventional plane.

Other Environmental Problems. Reuss called the SST "an environmental outrage." Russell E. Train, chairman of the President's Council on Environmental Quality, said Feb. 5 that "the environmental problems posed by the SST are exceedingly serious and have not been solved yet." The ad hoc committee said it considered "the environment disadvantages to be of extreme significance.... The program should not be pursued in the absence of overwhelming evidence of positive advantages."

The environmentalists complained of air pollution, possible weather changes and the sonic boom's effect on animals. They claimed the plane would produce a heavy discharge of pollutants into the air at subsonic speeds. The ad hoc committee warned it would release tons of water vapor into the upper atmosphere, possibly affecting the weather.

LEGISLATIVE ACTION

The House May 27 passed HR 17755, appropriating funds for the Department of Transportation—including the SST—after the House on a **key 176-162 roll call** agreed to vote on a motion to recommit the bill to committee.

By agreeing on the roll call to order a vote immediately on the recommittal motion—a procedure that cuts off floor debate—the House prevented a parliamentary maneuver to recommit the bill with instructions to delete almost $290 million for construction of the SST. The motion to recommit then was defeated by voice vote.

Senate. After several weeks of intense lobbying on both sides of the SST issue, the Senate Dec. 3 on a **key 52-41 roll call** adopted an amendment offered by Proxmire to delete the entire $290 million in funds for two prototype supersonic transports. The Senate then passed HR 17755 by voice vote.

But the House Dec. 8, in a victory for SST supporters, refused by a 213-175 roll call to instruct its conferees to agree to the Senate's action.

Conference Report. The House Dec. 16 agreed to a conference report on HR 17755 after SST opponents failed to recommit the bill to conference committee. Senate and House conferees had reduced the SST appropriation by $80 million, prompting Sidney Yates (D Ill.), a leading SST opponent, to call the agreement a "strange sleight-of-hand compromise."

After a two-week filibuster in the Senate on the conference report (two attempts to invoke cloture failed) the Senate Dec. 29 adopted a motion to table the report and return to a conference with the House.

Senate Majority Leader Mike Mansfield (D Mont.) then named two additional conferees—Proxmire and Norris Cotton (R N.H.), the latter who favored the original $290-million SST appropriation.

House-Senate conferees subsequently agreed on a compromise whereby the Transportation Department and the SST program would continue to be funded at the level of appropriations in the original conference report—but only through March 30, 1971. SST opponents were assured that there would be a separate vote on SST funds when further 1971 appropriations were considered in the 1st session of the 92nd Congress. *(p. 167)*

Final Action. The House Dec. 31 by an 180-37 roll-call vote passed H J Res 1421 providing a continuing appropriation through March 31, 1971.

The Senate Jan. 2 by voice vote passed the resolution, clearing the bill for the President. Before passage, Proxmire said he was prepared to continue filibustering the SST appropriation unless he received assurances "on the record" that the SST would be given a separate vote in March. He said SST supporters had refused to permit a House vote on the merits of the SST.

John Stennis (D Miss.), one of the Senate's conferees, told Proxmire that if the House and Senate disagreed again in March on further funds for the SST, he (Stennis) would join the Senate opponents in conference in not accepting the conference report, thereby tipping the balance against the SST among the Senate conferees.

The Senate conferees, appointed Dec. 3, after passage of HR 17755, and their votes on the amendment to delete the $290 million for the SST were as follows (a "yea" was a vote against the SST.): John Stennis (D Miss.), nay; Warren G. Magnuson (D Wash.), nay; John O. Pastore (D R.I.), yea; Alan Bible (D Nev.), nay; Clifford P. Case (R N.J.), yea; Margaret Chase Smith (R Maine), yea; Gordon Allott (R Colo.), nay.

Rail Passenger Corporation

Congress Oct. 14 completed action on a bill (HR 17849—PL 91-518), the Rail Passenger Service Act of 1970, creating a semipublic corporation to operate a nationwide railroad passenger system beginning May 1, 1971.

The corporation, which would seek to make a profit, was considered semipublic since federal funds were authorized to launch and back the corporation and some of its directors were to be appointed by the President. The financial arrangement was similar to the Communications Satellite Corporation (COMSAT). *Congress and the Nation Vol. II p. 536)*

The bill enabled railroads, if they wished, to transfer all their intercity passenger operations—except commuter services—to the new corporation. For being relieved of passenger responsibilities, a railroad would pay the corporation a fixed amount during each of three years in either money, equipment or services. In return the railroad would receive either common stock in the corporation or a tax deduction, but not both, equal to the value of the funds, goods or services given the corporation. It was uncertain whether most railroads would prefer the stock or the tax deduction.

The size of a railroad's payment for each of the three years in money, equipment or services would be determined by one of three formulas based on 1969 passenger operating expenses.

Railroads were allowed to purchase stock in the corporation but were forbidden to hold such stock for a period of three years after the last payment to the corporation if they claimed a tax deduction for the payments. A railroad therefore could have to wait up to nearly six years to acquire stock in the new corporation. Stock could not be redeemed for five years after enactment of the legislation, until Oct. 31, 1975.

No railroad could hold more than 33.3 percent of the corporation's common stock; railroads could not hold preferred stock.

Railroads choosing not to transfer their passenger operations to the corporation during the periods provided in the bill were prohibited from discontinuing any passenger trains for five years, until Jan. 1, 1975. The bill exempted all parties from antitrust laws and outlawed competition with the corporation along any routes it regularly served. One estimate held that 80 percent of the nation's 1970 intercity passenger services would be maintained under provisions of the bill.

The corporation would operate intercity rail passenger service over a nationwide "basic system," which would be designated by the Secretary of Transportation after he considered recommendations of interested parties. Most services were expected to be provided through contracts between the corporation and the railroads, although the corporation could own and operate its own equipment.

Senate Bill. The Senate Commerce Committee April 9 reported S 3706, which authorized government subsidies to reimburse railroads for their losses on passenger trains. The committee bill did not set up a national corporation.

The administration opposed the bill. It had promised Congress a rail passenger bill by January 1970, but the Department of Transportation's proposal for a semipublic corporation, called Railpax (later Amtrak), was rejected by the White House for budgetary reasons, and an administration bill never emerged.

By the end of April, however, the administration was faced with a Senate Commerce Committee ready to go to the floor with a politically popular bill. The committee, in turn, was faced with a potential presidential veto.

The committee and the administration compromised on a bill similar to Railpax when the committee accepted the corporation idea.

The legislation also was supported by the railroads, unions and rail passenger associations.

House Bill. The House Interstate and Foreign Commerce Committee Oct. 7 reported HR 17849. The House Transportation and Aeronautics Subcommittee had amended S 3706 and reported it to the full committee where a tax provision authored by the House Ways and Means Committee was added. The bill then was given a House number because tax legislation must originate in the House.

The tax provision gave participating railroads a choice between accepting common stock in the corporation and claiming a tax deduction, in exchange for payments to the corporation for being relieved of passenger obligations. Railroads could not accept both.

The House Oct. 14 by voice vote passed HR 17849 and the Senate the same day approved the bill as passed by the House, thus completing congressional action.

BACKGROUND

In the century's early years, passenger trains dominated intercity transportation, rolling between cavernous Roman- and Greek-styled stations.

But by the end of the 1920s, the public's use of the railroads began to decline. The automobile already accounted for 79.8 percent of intercity passenger miles, trains only 15.5 percent, though there were still about 20,000 intercity passenger trains running.

Railroad passenger-miles halved in the depression years. In 1939, the automobile's share of intercity passenger-miles rose to 88.82 percent. Airlines had two-tenths of one percent, and buses claimed 2.93 percent.

It was World War II that halted the downturn. No automobiles were built from February 1942 to July 1945, and gasoline and tires were rationed.

In 1944, the automobile's share of intercity passenger-miles plummeted to 58.38 percent. Trains carried 595.3 million passengers an unprecedented 90.2 billion miles—31.51 percent of intercity passenger-miles.

After the war most travelers reverted to prewar travel habits, though there were only about one-half as many intercity passenger trains as there had been before the depression. Automobile and railroad shares of intercity passenger-miles were down slightly, but the airlines' share was up to 1.98 percent from .22 percent.

The railroads claimed they spent $1 billion in the postwar decade to modernize their passenger fleets. But the Association of American Railroads (AAR) stated in a report on passenger traffic that its members were neglecting to advertise passenger service. It said that they spent "insignificant sums" in 1946 for advertising—25 times less than the airlines, in relation to revenues.

In the 1950s, airplanes overtook trains, doubling their percentage of intercity passenger-miles while trains halved theirs. The same thing happened in the 1960s.

Federal Action. Heeding the railroads' financial condition, Congress in 1958 passed a law (PL 85-625, the Transportation Act of 1958) that made it easier for the railroads to discontinue passenger trains. *(Congress and the Nation Vol. I p. 555)*

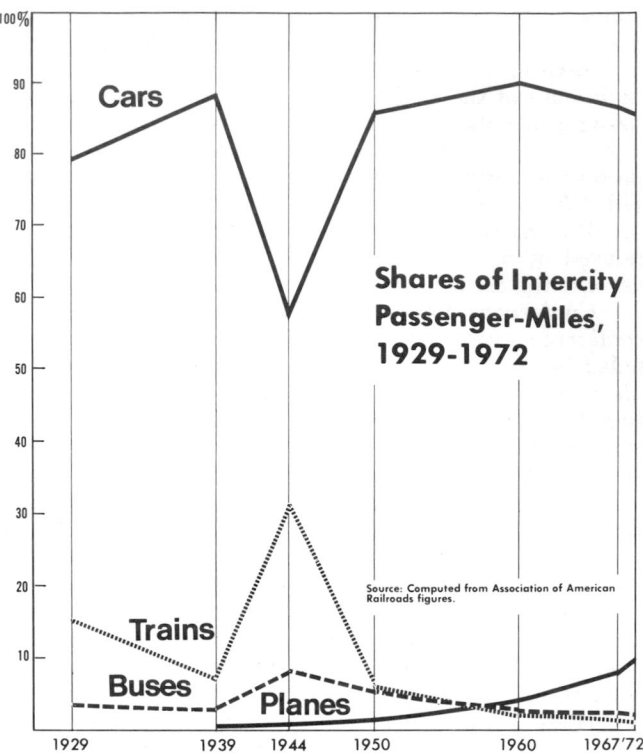

Graph shows rail travel decline since 1929.

It amended the Interstate Commerce Act to allow the ICC to grant train discontinuances regardless of state laws, if the Commission found the service would "unduly burden" interstate commerce (meaning, in practice, the railroad) and was not "required by public convenience and necessity." (Previously, one state could prevent a discontinuance on an interstate run.) The amendment was designated Section 13a.

Under the 13a provision, the railroads discontinued hundreds of passenger trains. In August 1958, there were 1,448 intercity passenger trains. A decade later there were 590. Slightly less than half of the 858 discontinued trains were dropped under the 1958 provision; the rest died by state action. Thirteen railroads had abandoned all intercity passenger service. Passenger traffic had decreased 40 percent, and Pullman and parlor car passengers 70 percent. Investment in passenger equipment had almost ceased.

In 1956, Pullman-Standard built its last sleeping car and dismantled its production facilities. (It still was building freight and mass-transit cars in 1970.)

In 1962, several proposals were made to aid rail passenger services, but no action was taken. President Kennedy assigned an interagency task force to study transportation problems in the Northeast and it discovered major gaps in information about how people and goods moved and about the demand for high quality intercity rail service. It concluded that a systematic study should be made. Sen. Claiborne Pell (D R.I.) proposed legislation creating an eight-state public authority to provide high-speed intercity rail service in the Northeast Corridor. And the ICC proposed subsidies for passenger trains.

The same year, Congress repealed a 10 percent excise tax on passenger fares which the railroads had long complained hurt their business. Most carriers—including the Pennsylvania, the New York Central and the Baltimore and Ohio—then raised passenger fares by 10 percent.

Deficit. The railroads complained of a crushing passenger deficit that damaged their freight operations, but critics disputed their accounting methods. Called the ICC full deficit, it subtracted expenses solely related to passenger service and those common costs apportioned to passenger service, such as track maintenance, from passenger revenues. Under this formula, passenger service lost money every year since World War II.

But the ICC, in a July 16, 1969, report, said: "All attempts to portray the passenger burden in terms of that data should...be wholly disregarded.... A more adequate method...lies in the application of avoidable costing."

Avoidable costs were those that would be saved if passenger operations ceased. An ICC study of eight intercity rail passenger systems computed their avoidable costs in 1968 at $118 million, as compared to an ICC full deficit of $214 million.

A simpler method of determining the passenger burden disregarded common costs apportioned to passenger service because most of these costs could not be saved even if passenger services ceased.

Using this "solely related" costs method, passenger service actually showed a profit in 1961 and 1962 for American railroads as a whole, and the Eastern District roads made money from 1958 to 1966.

But the passenger deficit in 1968 was real, no matter how it was computed. The ICC full deficit was $485 million; the solely related deficit, $255 million. The railroads' 1968 net income was $569 million.

An ICC report issued June 25, 1968, warned that "significant segments" of the remaining intercity rail passenger service would not "survive the next few years without a major change in federal and carrier policies." It said a comprehensive government review of the need for intercity rail service should be undertaken "at once."

MAJOR PROVISIONS

As cleared by Congress HR 17849:
• Directed the Secretary of Transportation to submit recommendations for a basic national rail passenger system to Congress and the Interstate Commerce Commission (ICC) within 30 days after enactment and to provide a final report within 90 days which could not be reviewed in court.
• Created a National Railroad Passenger Corporation to provide intercity rail passenger service (excluding commuter service). It was to be a semipublic corporation run at a profit, somewhat similar to the Communications Satellite Corporation.
• Authorized the corporation to own, manage, operate or contract for the operation of intercity passenger trains, and to carry mail and express packages.
• Authorized to be appropriated $40 million in federal grants to help establish the corporation and improve its equipment and facilities.
• Authorized to be appropriated $100 million to guarantee loans made to the corporation.

• Directed the corporation to use operating crews from the existing railroads to run its passenger trains.
• Authorized the corporation to take over any railroad's entire passenger corporation, with the railroad's consent, on or before March 1, 1971, or during the period from March 1, 1973, to Jan. 1, 1975. In return for being relieved of its obligation to provide passenger service, the railroad was to give the corporation, over a period of three years, either equipment, services or a sum of money *(see below)*. It would receive common stock in the corporation or a tax deduction—but not both—equal to the value of the goods or services given the corporation.
• Provided that, as an alternative to receipt of stock, a railroad could claim a tax deduction on its payment to the corporation.
• Authorized the corporation to operate trains outside the basic system and to operate trains requested by any state, regional or local agency if such agency agreed to pay the corporation at least two-thirds of the deficit solely related to the service.
• Required the corporation to provide continuous service until July 1, 1973, and forbade any railroad not turning over its operations to the corporation from discontinuing any trains before Jan. 1, 1975.
• Prohibited anyone, without consent of the corporation, to provide intercity passenger service over routes served regularly by the corporation.
• Provided that if at any time after July 1, 1973, the corporation determined that any train in the basic system was not required by the public convenience and necessity or would impair the ability of the corporation to adequately provide other services, the train could be discontinued under the normal procedures of the Interstate Commerce Act. However, train service would have to be continued if any state, local, or regional agency agreed to pay at least two-thirds of the deficit solely related to such service.
• Authorized the corporation to issue stock: common at $10 a share to be sold initially to railroads only, and preferred at $100 a share to be sold to the public and to pay dividends of at least 6 percent. No railroad was allowed to hold more than 33.3 percent of the common stock; railroads could not hold preferred stock.
• Authorized the corporation to issue nonvoting securities, bonds, debentures and other certificates of indebtedness.
• Created a board of 15 directors.

Penn Central Loan

President Nixon Jan. 8, 1971, signed into law a bill (HR 19953—PL 91-663), the Emergency Rail Services Act of 1970, authorizing up to $125 million in federal loan guarantees for the bankrupt Penn Central Railroad.

Passage of HR 19953 ended a six-month debate over federal aid to the bankrupt Penn Central, or any other railroad which had declared bankruptcy.

The Nixon administration had sought legislation (S 4011) which would have authorized the Secretary of Transportation to guarantee up to $750 million in loans to rail carriers. The Penn Central was to receive $200 million in loan guarantees from the total authorized in S 4011.

But the administration in June was forced to abandon that bill because of overwhelming congressional opposition, and the Penn Central June 22 filed for reorganization under the Bankruptcy Act.

Provisions. As cleared by Congress, HR 19953:

● Authorized the secretary, after consultation with the Interstate Commerce Commission, to guarantee certificates of up to $125 million to any railroad undergoing reorganization under Section 77 of the Bankruptcy Act.

● Provided that the secretary could guarantee the certificates if he found that:

1) Cessation of essential transportation services by a railroad would endanger the public welfare;

2) Cessation of such services was imminent;

3) Issuance of the certificates was the only practicable means of obtaining funds to meet payroll and other expenses needed to continue rail service;

4) Such certificates could not be sold without a guarantee;

5) The railroad could reasonably be expected to become self-sustaining;

6) Probable value of the assets of the railroad in the event of liquidation would provide reasonable protection to the government.

● Authorized the secretary to require that proceeds of the sale of the certificates be used solely for meeting payroll and other expenses needed to keep rail service going.

● Prohibited the secretary from guaranteeing any certificate unless the certificate was treated as an administrative expense and received the highest lien on the railroad's property and priority in payment under the Bankruptcy Act.

Ground Transportation

Congress Sept. 30 cleared for the President a bill (S 3730—PL 91-444) extending for one year, through June 30, 1972, the High Speed Ground Transportation Act of 1965 and authorizing $21.7 million for fiscal 1971 for research and development.

Under amendments passed in 1968 (PL 90-423), the 1965 act was extended for two years, to June 30, 1971, and appropriations were authorized of $16.2 million for fiscal year 1969 and $21.2 million for fiscal 1970. No funds had been authorized for fiscal 1971. (*Congress and the Nation Vol. II, p. 249*)

Programs which had been instituted under the Act included: a Transportation Department research and development program involving various ground and air transportation systems; a demonstration project which included the Metroliner high-speed rail service between Washington, D.C., and New York City, and the Turbo-Train operating one daily round trip between New York City and Boston; and a five-year report released in April 1970 by the Transportation Department on the Northeastern Corridor project. The report was intended to promote better planning for a balanced transportation system for the Northeast and throughout the country.

Extension of the act was expected to enable a number of completed research projects to be utilized for regular transportation needs.

Rail Experiment. To determine whether the public would use improved rail service in a densely populated corridor, the Department of Transportation and the Penn Central Railroad initiated a demonstration project, called

Metroliner, under the provisions of the High Speed Ground Transportation Act of 1965.

The six-car Metroliner electric train began operations Jan. 16, 1969. It cut time on its route between Washington, D.C., and New York City to two hours and 59 minutes from three hours and 35 minutes. Nonstop runs sliced off another half-hour, occasionally making the trip faster than the air shuttle between the two cities.

Penn Central had spent about $60 million to buy cars and improve track and the Transportation Department had spent about $2 million to upgrade stations and train crews. The department planned to spend up to $12 million over the two-year demonstration period which began officially in October 1970.

In the Metroliner's first nine months, rail travel between Washington and New York jumped 72 percent over the previous year. An ICC source said the train was making money.

Rail-Labor Disputes

Congress in the spring of 1970 averted a nationwide railway strike first by postponing the strike for more than one month and then, five weeks later, by enacting legislation that imposed a settlement in the 17-month dispute between the railroads and four shopcraft unions.

Under the Nixon administration, the federal government generally had followed a policy of "nonintervention" in labor disputes. Labor Secretary George P. Shultz's strategy had been to allow the process of collective bargaining to settle disputes without governmental interference. "I feel we should extend a helping hand, but not use the strong arm," Shultz said Feb. 4.

But the railroad-labor dispute forced the administration to abandon that policy.

Postponement. Congress temporarily put off a politically touchy decision on how to settle the threatened nationwide rail strike by passing a resolution (S J Res 180) March 4 banning a strike for 37 days. It rejected President Nixon's proposal to make binding the tentative agreement union and railroad negotiators reached Dec. 4, 1969, that was voted down by the members of one of the four unions involved.

The President signed the strike ban law (PL 91-203) only a few hours before 48,000 shopcraft workers were to walk off their jobs at 12:01 a.m. March 5.

Congress traditionally was reluctant to get involved in labor disputes. The changes in the Railway Labor Act and the 1947 Taft-Hartley Act, which Mr. Nixon proposed in a message to Congress Feb. 27, would impose a settlement on the parties if no agreement could be reached in disputes involving the national welfare.

Few were happy with the 37-day strike-lockout ban. Both union and management negotiators favored the President's proposal, though the union that voted down the Dec. 4 agreement—the Sheet Metal Workers—opposed it. So did the AFL-CIO.

Settlement. President Nixon April 8 signed into law a bill (S J Res 190) proposed by the administration to impose a settlement on the parties in the dispute.

The resolution was intended to force a settlement in the 17-month dispute over a contract between the na-

Penn Central: Bankruptcy Filed After First Loan Bill Fails

Penn Central Company, the nation's sixth largest corporation, June 22, 1970, filed a bankruptcy petition covering its subsidiary, the Penn Central Transportation Company, the nation's largest railroad. The petition was filed after the Nixon administration backed down on a promised $200 million loan guarantee.

The administration reportedly switched signals on the promise because it seemed certain Congress would refuse to pass legislation providing $750 million in emergency loans for railroads. Without the legislation, the loan guarantee was considered only a postponement of bankruptcy proceedings.

The pledge to guarantee up to $200 million in bank loans for the financially troubled Penn Central was made through the Navy Department under the Defense Production Act. The act was designed to assure an adequate supply of defense resources.

Congressional opposition to the guarantee was led by Wright Patman (D Texas), chairman of the House Banking and Currency Committee, which had jurisdiction over the Defense Production Act. Other opponents included Armed Services Committees chairmen Sen. John Stennis (D Miss.), Rep. L. Mendel Rivers (D S.C.) and Rep. George H. Mahon, Appropriations Committee chairman.

Defense Department Rejection. On June 19, the Defense Department announced it would not back the loan. The Department said the decision to guarantee bank loans to Penn Central had been predicated on prompt passage of legislation to transfer the guarantee to the Department of Transportation.

In a speech on the House floor June 22, Patman listed the reasons for his opposition to government aid:

• Unlawful use of the Defense Production Act, which he said was designed to help small and medium-sized defense contractors perform specific contracts.

• Involvement of the government in bailing out private investors and lenders who took risks.

• Misplaced priorities in allocating $200 million when other needs were more urgent.

• Establishing the precedent of bailing out huge corporations which made management mistakes.

With cancellation of the Defense Department guarantee, the House Banking and Currency Committee postponed indefinitely hearings on the emergency railroad financing bill.

The bankruptcy petition was filed to protect the railroad from having to meet short-term obligations coming due in June. Federal District Court Judge John P. Fullam in Philadelphia signed the petition, which provided for reorganization of the company and continuance of its operations, not for liquidation.

The Pennsylvania and New York Central railroads had merged in 1968 after years of ICC and court hearings. The merger, intended to improve efficiency, was widely regarded as having accomplished the opposite. The company's 1969 annual report listed $182.3 million in losses on passenger and freight service provided through its transportation subsidiary. Other subsidiaries of the conglomerate reported a profit of $61 million.

ICC Report. A 1969 ICC report on the operations of five railroads that were part of diversified corporations concluded that assets from the rail carriers were being used to finance nontransportation companies in the conglomerates. The report warned that such "dissipation" was "detrimental to the carriers and hence to the national transportation needs of the public and national defense." The report was not released, but was made available to the House and Senate Commerce Committees.

On July 2, the ICC announced it would begin a thorough investigation of the Penn Central Transportation Company, the railroad subsidiary of the Penn Central Company. Sen. Warren G. Magnuson (D Wash.), chairman of the Senate Commerce Committee, and Sen. Vance Hartke (D Ind.), chairman of the committee's Subcommittee on Surface Transportation, joined in praising the inquiry.

The Association of American Railroads June 30 proposed a broad revamping of federal involvement in the railroad industry. The association called for a single transportation fund and a single regulatory agency for all transportation modes, greater rate-making freedom for railroads, elimination of state and local taxes on railroad property and federal assistance for railroad operating costs and equipment.

Train Suspensions. The Penn Central July 21 asked the ICC for immediate suspension of 24 trains among 34 the railroad in March had asked to be dropped. The deficit from the 10 it would run until Oct. 1, according to the previous agreement with the ICC, would result in a deficit of only $3.4 million instead of $16 million if all 34 ran until Oct. 1.

Its cash position, the Penn Central said, was "so low" that without cutting expenses it "soon may be unable to meet its current payrolls," $20 million weekly.

Securities and Exchange Commission reports indicated that at least 15 Penn Central executives disposed Penn Central stock in 1969 and early 1970 at a saving to themselves of more than $1 million.

tion's railroads and four shopcraft unions, covering the period from Jan. 1, 1969, to Dec. 31, 1970.

As enacted, S J Res 190 (PL 91-226) imposed a settlement based on the memorandum of understanding reached Dec. 4, 1969, between representatives of the railroads and the four unions involved—the machinists, boilermakers, electricians and sheet metal workers.

Rail Strike. On Dec. 10, Congress attempted to avert another nationwide rail strike by enacting an 81-day strike moratorium, but the action came too late to stop a midnight walkout by four railroad operating unions.

Meeting until about 1 a.m. on the 10th, Congress agreed to a compromise bill (H J Res 1413-PL 91-541) to delay the strike until March 1, 1971. The bill also provided a 13 1/2-percent retroactive pay raise for the combined 400,000 membership of the unions.

But the unions had begun setting up picket lines shortly before the midnight Dec. 9 deadline for the expiration of a previous 60-day strike moratorium. The President had appointed an Emergency Board in September when the unions and railroads failed to reach agreement on a new contract. The President's action halted a possible strike at that time.

The strike was the third nationwide walkout affecting the rail system since World War II.

Signing the bill at 2:10 a.m., President Nixon chided Congress for not acting on his Feb. 27 proposal for a new law to stop national transportation strikes. Congress had not held a single day of hearings on his recommendation, he said *(Nixon proposal, box this page)*

"With the results of this neglect again apparent," Mr. Nixon said, "I again urge the Congress to make the reforms so badly needed."

The President objected to Congress' going beyond his request for a 45-day moratorium to impose a pay settlement as well. By "increasing wages sharply without increasing productivity," Mr. Nixon said, Congress voted to "speed up the rise in costs and prices."

The strike ended minutes after 6 p.m. Dec. 10 when a federal judge ordered $200,000-a-day fines if the strike continued after midnight Dec. 10.

Congress April 8 had imposed a settlement in a different dispute between the railroads and four shopcraft unions *(above)*.

Railroad Safety

President Nixon Oct. 16 signed into law a bill (S 1933—PL 91-458), the Federal Railroad Safety Act of 1970, standardizing federal railroad safety standards in an attempt to reduce railroad-related accidents, especially involving the shipment of hazardous materials.

The railroads were the only transportation industry not subject to comprehensive federal safety regulation, and existing federal laws were 50 to 75 years old.

By 1970, accidents involving trains had increased for 12 consecutive years, and the total of 8,543 accidents in 1969 was 60 percent more than the 1964 figure. Additionally, 178 rail employees were killed in such accidents in 1969, with 16,758 injured. Including all classes of persons (not just employees) in 1969, there were 2,299 killed and 23,356 injured in train accidents.

As cleared by Congress, S 1933 gave the Secretary of Transportation power to prescribe safety regulations and conduct research and development in all areas of rail safety.

The bill permitted the states under most circumstances to set railroad safety standards wherever federal regulations did not apply and to set more stringent standards than existing federal regulations. The states were permitted to participate in investigative and surveillance activities in areas already covered by federal regulation.

The bill represented a compromise between interests which sought direct safety enforcement by the states and those wanting no state enforcement at all. The Senate version of S 1933, which passed Dec. 19, 1969, had provided that states could enforce Federal safety regulations in state courts.

Such state authority was opposed by officials of the Association of American Railroads. But spokesmen for organizations such as the National Association of Regula-

---

Nixon Anti-Strike Proposal

President Nixon asked Congress Feb. 27, 1970, for a new law to stop national transportation strikes. He said that such strikes "are more likely to imperil the national health or safety" than strikes in other industries.

Mr. Nixon said his proposal would protect both the nation and collective bargaining.

The proposed new law sought to discontinue the emergency strike provisions of the Railway Labor Act of 1926 and amend the Taft-Hartley Act of 1947 as it applied to transportation industries. The new legislation would give the President three options to deal with strike threats.

The Railway Labor Act, which applied to railroads and airlines, allowed the President to postpone a strike for 60 days by appointing an emergency board to recommend a settlement. The President said that this procedure forced each side to make extreme demands because they expected the emergency board to recommend a compromise of the two positions.

The Taft-Hartley Act, on the other hand, allowed the President to block a strike for 80 days by appointing a board of inquiry and requesting a federal court injunction. But the board could not propose a settlement, and at the end of the 80-day cooling-off period the President was forced to ask Congress to step in or let the strike begin.

Mr. Nixon asked that in transportation disputes he be granted three new options under Taft-Hartley, of which he could choose only one:

● Extend the cooling-off period for up to 30 days if a settlement appeared near.

● Require partial operation of the industry up to six months. The major part of the strike or lockout could continue, but "essential segments" would operate to protect the national health and safety.

● Appoint a neutral three-member group to choose between the "final offers" of each side. Each party would have three days to submit one or two such offers. If they could not settle within five days, they would appoint the three-man group; or if they could not agree on the three, the President would name them. They would hold formal hearings and choose one of the offers in its exact form.

If the Taft-Hartley changes worked well, Congress could later apply them to other industries. The final offer selection proposal was the most controversial of the three options. Railroad management said it would emasculate the Railway Labor Act, which they claimed had generally worked well. The AFL-CIO called it "a novel form of compulsory arbitration," which it opposed.

The President also proposed:

● Creation of a National Special Industries Commission to make a two-year study of national strikes.

● Abolition of the National Railroad Adjustment Board.

● Transfer to the Federal Mediation and Conciliation Service from the National Mediation Board of the Board's mediation functions.

tory Utility Commissioners claimed the railroads were trying to "emasculate" state regulatory authority, a charge the railroads called "absurd."

The House bill enabled states to seek relief in federal courts to restrain violations of federal safety regulations.

Conferees rejected the provision for state enforcement of federal regulations in state courts, but allowed states to seek relief in federal courts and petition the courts to assess civil penalties of up to $2,500 for violations of federal safety regulations if the Transportation Secretary failed to do so within 90 days of the violation.

Administration Position. The administration had proposed repeal of all existing rail safety laws and adoption of them as federal safety regulations.

The administration had recommended that only interstate lines be subject to federal regulation. S 1933 applied to both intrastate and interstate operations.

In general, S 1933 was in substantial accord with the administration bill (HR 14417) based on the recommendations of the rail safety task force.

1971

Congress in 1971—after a year marked by passage of major transportation programs—turned to a controversial issue left unresolved in 1970: the question of continued of federal funding for the supersonic transport (SST).

In March, cabinet members, government agency heads, labor union officials and aerospace executives and scientists, as well as the President and his aides, told members of Congress during an intensive lobby campaign to save the SST that the aircraft was essential to the economic interests of the nation. But Congress bowed to the project's opponents, who argued that the SST was an environmental threat, a potential economic disaster and that government should stay out of the aircraft business and allow private enterprise to finance the plane.

After a two-day nationwide rail strike in May 1971, Congress began hearings on legislation to resolve future transportation disputes. The Nixon administration offered a plan to head off strikes by allowing a neutral panel to pick one of the "final offers" submitted by rail management and by unions as the terms of a binding contract settlement. Labor, however, strongly opposed the proposal, branding it a "novel form" of compulsory arbitration. No bills were reported.

Merchant Marine Authorization

Congress June 29 cleared a bill (HR 4724—PL 92-53) authorizing $507,820,000 for maritime programs in fiscal 1972, including subsidies for continuation of a 10-year ship construction program.

The Merchant Marine Act of 1970 (PL 91-469) authorized a 10-year, government-financed program to revitalize the U.S.-Flag Merchant Marine (See above). The act provided for construction of approximately 300 ships during the period (22 in 1972) and established a subsidy rate of 45 percent in fiscal 1971 to be reduced by 2 per-

---

Railway Labor Act

The Railway Labor Act of 1926 was one of two general laws that dealt with strikes that represented a potential national emergency. The other was the Taft-Hartley Act of 1947 which was not applicable to industries covered by the Railway Act—railroads, airlines and certain subsidiary undertakings such as bridges, tunnels and ferries. By 1970, the Railway Labor Act had been used well over 100 times in disputes since the end of World War II. (Congress and the Nation Vol. II p. 620)

---

cent thereafter to a permanent level of 35 percent reached in 1976. Funds for the program were required to be authorized annually.

As cleared by Congress, HR 4724 authorized $507,-820,000 in fiscal 1972 for the following:

- $229.7-million for construction and renovation of cargo vessels (contract awards for 22 ships were anticipated in fiscal 1972).
- $239.1-million for ship operating-differential subsidies.
- $25-million for research and development activities.
- $4.3-million for reserve fleet expenses.
- $7.3-million for maritime training at the Merchant Marine Academy, Kings Point, N.Y.
- $2,370,000 for assistance to state marine schools.

Supplemental. Congress May 18, cleared for the President a bill (HR 5332—PL 92-21) authorizing $80-million in fiscal 1971 supplemental appropriations for the following maritime programs:

- $39.7-million to implement a new subsidy payment schedule provided by the Merchant Marine Act of 1970.
- $40.3-million to liquidate accrued but unpaid subsidies for fiscal 1969 and prior years.

Edward A. Garmatz (D Md.), chairman of the House Merchant Marine and Fisheries Committee, said $39.7-million in supplemental authorizations were required to implement the new subsidy payment schedule. In the past, shipping companies were reimbursed for operating subsidies three months after the expense was incurred. Under the new procedure, payments were to be made as currently as possible; the payment of two months' additional subsidy was required in fiscal 1971.

Regarding the $40.3-million in the bill for liquidation of accrued but unpaid subsidies in prior years, Thomas M. Pelly (R Wash.) said the backlog of subsidies had not been settled because of a difference of opinion between the ship operators and the Maritime Administration as to what the rate of subsidy should be.

Supersonic Transport

Congress in 1971 dramatically handed the administration and the U.S. aviation industry a serious rebuff by halting federal government participation in the construction of a supersonic transport plane (SST).

The action took place in the House on March 18 and in the Senate March 24. The two chambers on those dates voted to delete $134-million in SST funds contained in a resolution (H J Res 468) providing appropriations for the Department of Transportation (DOT) for the last quarter of fiscal 1971. The rest of the DOT funds in H J Res 468 were approved routinely (PL 92-7).

The House vote was a **key 217-204 recorded teller vote** which caught many observers by surprise. The Senate made the decision final on a **key 51-46 roll call vote** which climaxed weeks of intense lobbying by both sides of the controversy.

After the Senate vote, President Nixon, in a statement released by Press Secretary Ronald Ziegler, said the outcome was "distressing and disappointing...a severe blow not only to the tens of thousands of workers affected but also to the United States' continued leadership in the aerospace industry."

The congressional termination of federal funds for the project had the effect of ending the U.S. SST operation for the foreseeable future since private financing of the aircraft seemed improbable. It brought to a close an aerospace industry program which had its origins in 1959 with a goal of creating a fleet of giant supersonic passenger planes to whisk riders across the globe at speeds previously unequalled by commercial carriers. European and Soviet SST aircraft began flight tests in 1971.

Normally, Congress appropriated financing for agencies and programs for a full fiscal year. However, on Jan. 2, 1971—the last day of the second session of the 91st Congress—Congress provided funds for the Department and the SST only for the first three quarters of fiscal 1971 in order to break a Senate filibuster in opposition to the full SST funding in the fiscal 1971 DOT appropriations bill (HR 17755). In a compromise Congress then agreed to pass a resolution (H J Res 1421—PL 91-645) allowing DOT programs, including the SST, to be financed until March 30, 1971 *(1970 chronology p. 158)*. By that time, Congress was to decide whether to continue funding the project.

In preparation for that 1971 action, both sides of the controversy unleashed a massive lobbying campaign. In favor of the SST a strong coalition of administration, aviation industry, labor and regional interests was mobilized. Its backers argued that continuation of the giant high-speed airliner was necessary to maintain U.S. superiority in aerospace technology and marketing, to sustain a sound U.S. balance of payments position in the future and to avoid massive unemployment and deterioration in the aerospace industry.

The environmental attacks were a main pillar of the opposition case. Charges were levied that the fleet of SSTs could contaminate the atmosphere, generate harmful noise and even trigger a cancer-producing fallout. It was also argued that no market existed for the aircraft, that its only beneficiaries would be wealthy travellers and that federal funding should be directed instead toward more generally beneficial activities.

The congressional action, by halting federal participation in the government-industry project, in effect terminated the program and forced an estimated 7,000 layoffs at the Seattle plant of the Boeing Company, the main contractor. By 1971, the U.S. government had contributed about $840-million into the project and Boeing $125-million. The firm was working on two prototype aircraft to compete with proposed Anglo-French (Concorde) and Soviet (TU-144) entries in the SST aircraft market.

SST Appropriations

Fiscal 1962	$ 11,000,000
Fiscal 1963	20,000,000
Fiscal 1964	60,000,000
Fiscal 1965	None
Fiscal 1966	140,000,000
Fiscal 1967	280,000,000
Fiscal 1968	142,375,000
Fiscal 1969	None*
Fiscal 1970	85,000,000
Fiscal 1971	307,500,000†

* $30,000,000 previous appropriation rescinded.
† Included $97.3-million for termination cost.

A surprise effort to reverse the congressional cancellation of the SST program surfaced in May when supporters of the plane suddenly gained House backing to continue the U.S. funding of the project. The action came when Congress considered the second fiscal 1971 appropriations bill (HR 8190—PL 92-18), which contained $97.3-million to terminate the SST operation. In a turnabout from its negative vote in March, the House May 12 voted 201-195 to use the termination funds to continue the program. The Senate, however, later refused to go along and the SST's resurrection was doomed when it became clear that it would cost more to resume work on the plane than to end it.

Rail Strike

A nationwide two-day strike ended late May 18 when President Nixon signed a hurriedly passed congressional resolution (S J Res 100—PL 92-17) directing railmen to return to work.

The law gave the Brotherhood of Railway Signalmen a 13 1/2-percent wage increase, prohibited a further rail strike through Oct. 1, 1971, and directed that contract negotiations continue through Oct. 1, 1971. Rail and union negotiators reached agreement to settle the dispute before the expiration of the legislation Oct. 1.

The walkout was called for 6 a.m. May 17 by the signalmen, a relatively small union with 13,000 members. More than 500,000 other rail workers refused to cross the picket lines, shutting down all trains except a few kept running by supervisory personnel.

The same day, President Nixon sent a message to Congress calling for immediate emergency legislation requiring the signalmen to return to work and extending the negotiating period to July 1.

Senate. The Senate passed S J Res 100, by voice vote, after agreeing to an amendment offered by Robert P. Griffin (R Mich.) that reduced the proposed salary increase from 17.5 percent, as approved by the Senate Labor and Public Welfare Committee, to 13.5 percent.

House. The House by voice vote passed H J Res 642, which had been reported by the Interstate and Foreign Commerce Committee and granted the signalmen a 13.5 percent increase. Before approving the resolution, the House agreed to substitute the Senate's Oct. 1 no-strike extension date for the July 20 date favored by the

House committee. An amendment to forbid retaliatory nationwide lockouts was rejected.

The House then passed the identical Senate resolution by voice vote. J. J. Pickle (D Texas), who voted against the legislation, said that temporary railroad settlements would not work.

Although the administration proposed a no-strike, no-lockout negotiation extension to July 1 and did not offer any pay increase, President Nixon signed the congressional resolution at 10:40 p.m. May 18. He said the strike, if continued, would "sharply curtail the current upturn in the nation's economy" and that action was necessary to get the trains moving again.

The striking signalmen, who install and operate complex electrical equipment, earned an average of $3.78 an hour. When wage talks originally broke down in February, the union was demanding an increase of $2.40 an hour over a three-year period, a 54-percent increase.

The union called a strike for March 5, but it was postponed March 4 when President Nixon, under the authority of the Railway Labor Act, established an emergency board to study the case and recommend a settlement. The signalmen subsequently reduced their demand to an increase of $1.99 per hour over a three-year period. This was 34 cents more than the railroad's best offer of a $1.65-an-hour raise.

The last time Mr. Nixon had sought—and received— congressional action on a rail strike was in December 1970, when Congress ended a one-day walkout by four major unions, not including signalmen.

President Nixon had asked Congress in 1970 for a new law to stop national transportation strikes. At the time, he said that such strikes "are more likely to imperil the national health or safety" than strikes in other industries. The President's proposal—first introduced in the Senate on Feb. 28, 1970—attracted little attention *(p. 166)*. Reintroduced in the 92nd Congress, the measure (S 560, HR 3596) had drawn little congressional support but had generated several alternative proposals. These included:

● **Labor-backed Proposal.** A bill (S 832) introduced in the Senate by Harrison A. Williams Jr (D N.J.), chairman of the Labor and Public Welfare Committee, and a companion measure (HR 3595) offered in the House by Rep. Harley O. Staggers (D W.Va.), head of the House Commerce Committee, would amend the Railway Labor Act to authorize selective rail strikes. The proposals would prohibit the railroads from starting a nationwide lockout to retaliate against a selective strike. The Williams-Staggers legislation was introduced to allow a union to call a selective strike as long as it did not strike more than three carriers in any one of the nation's eastern, western or southeastern regions.

● **Javits' Bill.** The legislation introduced by Sen. Jacob Javits (R N.Y.) to settle transportation disputes went beyond either the administration's proposal or the Democratic plan. Javits' bill (S 594) applied to all industries, dealt with both regional and national disputes and gave the President authority to invoke any of the traditional options used to resolve labor disputes: fact-finding, mediation and arbitration. The bill provided for "final offer" settlements.

● **Management Plan.** The Association of American Railroads, the Air Transport Association and the National Railway Labor Conference drafted a proposal (not introduced in Congress) that would preserve but amend the Railway Labor Act for settlement of transportation disputes.

The proposal provided that when the regular procedures of the Railway Labor Act fail to produce a settlement and a strike seems likely, the Secretaries of Labor, Commerce and Transportation would select one of the following alternatives: (1) The government would do nothing, leaving the parties to a test of economic strength. (2) The dispute would be assigned to a panel, which would find the facts, make them public and make non-binding recommendations. (3) A panel would be created to make a choice between the final offers of the parties; the choice would be binding. (4) The dispute would be referred to a panel for binding arbitration.

Hearings. Both the Senate Labor and Public Welfare Committee and the House Interstate and Foreign Commerce Committee studied the various proposals in 1971 but took no further action. In 1972, President Nixon withdrew his strike plan.

Penn Central Report

The House Banking and Currency Committee in 1971 issued a staff report (The Penn Central Failure and the Role of Financial Institutions) charging that officials of the Penn Central Transportation Corporation "manipulated" the company's investment program" for the benefit of themselves and their friends." *(Penn Central bankruptcy, above)*

Committee Chairman Wright Patman (D Texas) underscored the charges in a letter accompanying the report which focused on Penphil Company, an investment club established in 1962, whose members consisted mainly of Penn Central officials and their associates. The situation, according to Patman, "constitutes a classic example of the use of corporate power for personal benefit."

The staff report asserted that Penphil investments, which on occasion paralleled those of Penn Central, raised "serious issues concerning the use of inside information to benefit the members of Penphil."

In 1963, the investment group purchased 10,000 shares of Great Southwest Corporation stock for $165,000. Seventeen months after the Penn Central gained control of Great Southwest, Penphil sold its shares at a net profit of $212,500, according to the report.

Patman charged that David C. Bevan, former chief financial officer of the Penn Central, and Charles J. Hodge, former chief investment adviser of the railroad, "manipulated the financial resources, the assets and the credit" of the corporation for the benefit of Penphil.

"The ultimate goal of Bevan and Hodge was to create a large conglomerate operating and holding company while orchestrating Penn Central investments.... to serve the interests of Penphil," Patman wrote.

The staff report charged that Bevan and Hodge used the $300-million Penn Central Supplemental Pension Plan and the $11-million Penn Central Contingent Compensation Fund to enhance Penphil investments.

In addition to manipulation of investments, the key factor which made the growth of Penphil possible, Patman wrote, was the "unrestricted line of credit provided Penphil by the Chemical Bank New York Trust Company—a line of credit that was based primarily on the large loan and deposit accounts maintained in the bank by Penn Central...."

Patman said that the Chemical bank loans were made on such favorable terms that they enabled Penphil members to claim a profit of $83,500 on a cash investment of $16,500.

The staff report accused Bevan and Hodge of conflicts-of-interest. Besides serving as the chief financial officer of Penn Central, Bevan was chairman of the management committee of the Penn Central Contingent Compensation Fund and served on the board of some of the corporations in which Penphil and Penn Central invested, the report stated.

Among the corporations in which Penphil had invested were: Kaneb Pipe Line Company; Tropical Gas Company Inc.; Continental Mortgage Investors; Great Southwest Corporation; First Bank & Trust Company of Boca Raton, Fla., and National Homes Corporation.

Patman concluded that the investigation had illustrated an "undeniable need" for new legislation.

The report also stated the investing public was "kept in the dark" while nine banks and investing firms "unloaded" 1.8 million shares of Penn Central stock.

The stock sales occurred between April 1 and June 21, 1970, when the Penn Central Transportation Corporation declared bankruptcy.

Patman accused President Nixon, the Securities and Exchange Commission and the Interstate Commerce Commission of failing to alert the investing public and criticized the press "...(which) might have given the public some indication of the grave nature of Penn Central's financial problems...."

Amtrak

An 11th-hour attempt by Majority Leader Mike Mansfield (D Mont.) and Lee Metcalf (D Mont.) to postpone operation of the new Amtrak rail passenger service for seven months, to Dec. 1, 1971, so that additional routes could be considered was blocked April 30.

To delay the May 1 start of the new Amtrak system, Mansfield and Metcalf had offered a nongermane amendment to a bill (S 699) requiring radio-telephones on certain vessels. The amendment was never considered because of the lack of a quorum.

The Amtrak system began operation at 12:01 a.m. May 1. On May 3, with the amendment to S 699 still pending in the Senate, Mansfield said that "voting now on this amendment would...be a gesture of blatant futility." He said the issue was moot.

But concern voiced by leaders of Congress over routes and service provided by the National Railroad Passenger Corporation (Amtrak) prompted decisions to expand the basic system in operation after May 1, 1971.

In October 1971, the administration requested $170-million through fiscal 1973 to help resolve Amtrak's financial problems. By July, Amtrak had spent a $40-million start-up grant provided by the Rail Passenger Service Act of 1970. *(Above).* Both the House and Senate held hearings on the request, but took no further action in 1971. In 1972, additional funds were authorized *(See p. 174)*

Other Legislation

Wider Buses. The House in 1971 passed a bill (HR 4354) permitting wider buses to operate on the nation's interstate highway system. The Senate held a one-day hearing on the bill.

Passage came after the House, by a 213-178 roll-call vote, rejected a motion by Fred Schwengel (R Iowa) recommitting the bill to the Public Works Committee. Schwengel said HR 4354 was "the first step" toward allowing wider trucks on interstate highways.

The bill would permit buses 102 inches wide, instead of the existing 96 inches, to operate on interstate highways beginning July 1, 1973, unless the Secretary of Transportation found the wider buses created a safety hazard.

Although critics said passage would lead to legislation permitting wider and heavier trucks on interstate roads, sponsors said they had but one purpose—making bus travel more comfortable and convenient for commuters so they will leave their cars at home.

(There were about 22,000 102-inch wide buses operating in large cities and on non-interstate highways in 1971.)

Freight Transportation. The Senate Commerce Surface Transportation Subcommittee held hearings in 1971 on legislation to benefit railway, trucking and barge freight transportation industries.

Legislation submitted by the Nixon administration in November 1971 proposed to reduce government regulation of railroads and other surface transportation, primarily the trucking industry, and provide direct financial assistance to the railroad industry.

The package of proposals (S 2841, Transportation Assistance Act; S 2842, Transportation Regulatory Modernization Act) was submitted several months after the railroad, barge and trucking industries joined forces, drafted legislation and appealed to Sen. Vance Hartke (D Ind.) to introduce their plan (S 2362, Surface Transportation Act), which was a moderate approach to freight industry reform compared to the administration's bills.

The alliance of freight industries objected to the administration plan, particularly a provision that would allow truckers, railroads and barge lines to raise or lower freight rates without Interstate Commerce Commission approval, but within a "zone of reasonableness."

The Senate Commerce Committee reported a modified version of S 2362 in 1972.

Passenger Ships. The House in 1971 passed a bill (HR 11589) authorizing the sale of five U.S.-flag passenger vessels to foreign interests.

The legislation also required the Secretary of Commerce to purchase the *SS United States* for inclusion in the National Defense Reserve Fleet.

Because the ships were built with $60-million in federal subsidies, which required that they remain under the U.S. flag for 25 years, specific statutory authority was needed for the sale.

Senate action was taken on the bill in 1972.

Supporters of the bill said U.S. owners could not afford to operate the ships and that layup expenses were amounting to about $4.5-million a year; opponents argued that if other American investors could be found to buy the vessels, they could provide thousands of jobs for American workers and help reverse the U.S. balance of payments deficit by competing for the vacation trade dollar, particularly in the Caribbean.

Funds recovered from the sale of the ships—about $18-million—would be reinvested in the construction of new cargo ships.

The measure was supported by the Maritime Administration and by U.S. ship owners (Moore-McCormack Lines, Inc., Export-Isbrandtsen Lines, Inc., and Prudential-Grace Lines, Inc.), but it was opposed by the AFL-CIO Maritime Committee, the AFL-CIO Industrial Unions Department and the National Maritime Union.

Airport Fund. Congress in 1971 enacted a bill (HR 7072—PL 92-174) clarifying the intent of Congress regarding expenditure authorized by the Airport and Airway Development Act of 1970 (PL 91-258).

As cleared, the bill specified that aviation user taxes were to be retained in the Airport and Airway Trust Fund until used for purposes specifically authorized by Congress in 1971: airport construction ($280-million annually) and air traffic control systems ($250-million annually). The intent of the bill was to prohibit diversion of trust fund revenues to finance general aviation administration expenses.

1972

Congress in 1972, after disposing of the SST the previous year, turned to another controversial transportation issue—a proposal to allow the Highway Trust Fund to be used for financing mass transit systems in urban areas.

Congress, however, failed to approve a compromise on the matter worked out during the final hours of the 92nd Congress, leaving the issue for the 93rd Congress.

The Nixon administration July 20 acknowledged that it had withdrawn support for legislation to prevent strikes in the transportation industry, a plan it had strongly backed the previous two years but one that was opposed by organized labor.

In other 1972 action: Congress authorized $225-million for Amtrak to continue operations through July 1, 1973, when it could discontinue unprofitable passenger trains, and ended a West Coast dock strike which had begun July 1, 1971. On Feb. 21, during his visit to the People's Republic of China, President Nixon signed the legislation, although dock workers were voluntarily returning to work.

President Nixon in 1972 also pocket vetoed a bill prohibiting local taxes on airline tickets and increasing the federal share of airport construction costs.

Highway Aid

Federal-aid highway legislation that authorized road-building funds for fiscal 1974 and contained $400-million in operating subsidies for failing mass transit systems died at the close of the 92nd Congress when the House failed to obtain a quorum to approve a compromise bill (S 3939) agreed to by House-Senate conferees in the final hours of the session.

(It was believed, though never acknowledged, that the Nixon administration had directed House Republicans to refuse to answer the quorum call—a tactic devised to kill the highway bill—because of White House opposition to the transit subsidy provision.)

Previously, conferees had been unable to reach agreement on another issue that had deeply divided

Congress in 1972—the Senate's insistence that $800-million in each of fiscal years 1974 and 1975 be appropriated from the Highway Trust Fund for urban bus and subway projects. The plan had been backed by environmental groups, including the Highway Action Coalition, Friends of the Earth and the Sierra Club, but strongly opposed by highway interests and members of Congress from rural areas. On Oct. 18 (adjournment day), the Senate conferees agreed to drop the provision in exchange for House agreement to delete a new 10,000-mile freeway program and to settle for a one-year extension of highway programs rather than the traditional two-year authorization. (The one-year extension gave mass transit forces an opportunity to revive their "trust busting" battle in 1973 while ensuring that road-building funds were available in fiscal 1974.)

Senate Action. On Sept. 19, the Senate, by a 77-0 vote, passed S 3939 extending the Federal-Aid Highway Act of 1970 and authorizing $14.2-billion for federally supported highway programs for fiscal years 1974-75.

For the first time since the highway trust fund was created in 1956 to finance construction of the Interstate Highway System, the bill as passed by the Senate, allowed revenues from the fund—supplied by taxes on gasoline and other motor products—to be spent on rail rapid transit systems.

The provision opening up the trust fund was introduced as a floor amendment by Edmund S. Muskie (D Maine) and John Sherman Cooper (R Ky.). It gave states the option of using up to $800-million annually for road construction, bus purchases, fringe parking facilities or rail transit.

Backed by the Department of Transportation and various environmental groups, the Muskie-Cooper amendment drew bipartisan support and was adopted 48-26. Twenty-four Democrats and 24 Republicans voted for the amendment; 18 Democrats including 10 southerners, and 8 Republicans opposed it.

Jennings Randolph (D W.Va.), chairman of the Public Works Committee, and Birch Bayh (D Ind.), former chairman of the Roads Subcommittee, voted against the amendment, while Harrison A. Williams Jr. (D N.J.), chairman of the Banking, Housing and Urban Affairs Committee which has jurisdiction over mass transit legislation, supported it.

During debate, Bayh said that under federal law disbursements from the trust fund could be made only for expenses "which are attributable to federal-aid highways"—a position endorsed by highway interest groups that opposed diversion of trust fund monies to mass transit programs.

Randolph said he would be "willing to accept the amendment but for the fact that the law by which the highway trust funds are collected will not allow it"; nevertheless, he told the Senate he would accept a decision of the House Ways and Means Committee and the Senate Finance Committee, which have jurisdiction over the fund, regarding the financing of mass transit projects from the trust fund.

Muskie and Cooper maintained that the federal-aid highway program had created severe urban problems—suburban sprawl, congestion, pollution—and that the states should be allowed to determine how funds allocated for urban areas should be spent. They might choose to spend it all on roads, Cooper said, but that decision should be left to the people most directly concerned with the needs of the cities.

Earlier, the Senate, by an 18-60 roll-call vote, rejected a broader version of the amendment, offered by Edward M. Kennedy (D Mass.) and Lowell P. Weicker Jr. (R Conn.), that would have permitted the use of about $2.3-billion in non-interstate highways funds for rail transit. Weicker said the amendment would "not force cities or states to build mass transit facilities" but would give local areas the discretion to use trust fund revenues according to their transportation needs.

House Action. The House Oct. 5, by a 263-30 roll-call vote, passed HR 16656 authorizing $16.5-billion for federal-aid highway programs over fiscal years 1974-75.

Despite efforts by the Nixon administration, environmental groups and urban House members to allow Highway Trust Fund revenues to be used for bus and rail transit programs, the House never voted on the issue.

Two amendments introduced by Glenn M. Anderson (D Calif.), which would have given urban officials the option to use up to $700-million from the trust fund for either roads or public transportation facilities, were ruled out of order because they were not germane to the highway legislation.

Previously, the House had voted by a 200-168 roll call to adopt the rule for HR 16656. That action killed a last-minute effort by pro-mass transit members to alter the rule so the Anderson amendments would be in order.

The mass transit effort was opposed by the House leadership and by House Roads Subcommittee Chairman John C. Kluczynski (D Ill.) and Public Works Committee Chairman John A. Blatnik (D Minn.).

Minority Leader Gerald R. Ford (R Mich.) argued that if highway trust fund revenues were diverted for mass transit "you are going to have the floodgates opened." He added: "Once the precedent has been established in the highway trust fund diversion...the Airport Trust Fund is in jeopardy."

But Anderson said his amendments were not a "raid" on the trust fund. "...(They) do not require mass transit; they merely permit local officials the option of using their share of the trust fund for mass transportation."

Conference. House-Senate conferees Oct. 18 filed a conference report on S 3939 (H Rept 92-1619). The Senate approved the report by voice vote, but the House failed to vote on the report, killing the federal-aid highway bill.

Major differences were resolved as follows: Conferees agreed to delete a Senate provision authorizing the use of $800-million for each of fiscal 1974 and 1975 from the Highway Trust Fund for mass transit projects in urban areas. In return, House conferees agreed to settle for a one-year extension of highway programs.

Conferees also agreed to delete a House provision prohibiting judicial review of administrative actions relating to the construction of the Three Sisters Bridge across the Potomac River between Virginia and Washington, D.C. *(Chapter on District of Columbia)*

Conferees dropped a House provision authorizing $300-million for each of fiscal 1974 and 1975 to construct a new 10,000-mile highway system connecting with interstate roads. However, conferees required the secretary of transportation and state highway departments to

---

Federal-Aid Highway Funds

In the annual Department of Transportation appropriation bills, Congress approved appropriations from the Highway Trust Fund to meet previous federal-aid highway construction obligations. The fund, into which certain highway user taxes were channeled, was used to finance the federal share of major highway programs. Following are the appropriations from the Highway Trust Fund for fiscal years 1970-73:

Fiscal 1970	$ 4,419,279,000
Fiscal 1971	4,626,365,000
Fiscal 1972	4,662,093,000
Fiscal 1973	4,891,990,000

---

report to Congress by June 30, 1973, on possible routes for a new highway system.

Conferees also deleted all fiscal 1975 authorizations for the Interstate Highway System and other federal-aid highways.

Conferees authorized $400-million through fiscal 1974, as provided by the Senate, to aid debt-ridden mass transit systems.

Other Highway Bills

Flooded Roads. Congress July 25 cleared for the President a bill (HR 15950—PL 92-361) authorizing $200-million in appropriations for fiscal 1973 for repairing highways damaged by natural disasters.

The $200-million authorization was requested by President Nixon July 17 as an addition to $1.6-billion in supplemental appropriations for loans and other relief to victims of tropical storm Agnes during June 1972.

The bill also authorized $100-million in successive years for repairing damaged roads. Under existing law, $50-million a year was authorized, but highway damage caused by tropical storm Agnes, as well as floods in West Virginia and South Dakota, prompted Congress to increase the funding levels.

Wider Buses. The Senate Public Works Roads Subcommittee held a hearing Feb. 14 on a bill (HR 4354) permitting buses 102 inches wide to operate on the Interstate Highway System. The House had passed the bill in 1971 *(Above)*.

The legislation allowed "over-size" buses to operate only on sections of the interstate that have 12-foot lanes. In addition, the measure was not to be binding on any state and would not take effect if the secretary of transportation reported before July 1, 1973, that such operations were unsafe.

Opponents claimed HR 4354, if enacted, would lead to use of wider trucks on interstate roads.

The bill was not reported to the Senate.

Maritime Legislation

Merchant Marine Authorization. Congress Aug. 11 cleared for the President a bill (HR 13324—PL 92-402) authorizing $555,860,000 for Maritime Administration programs in fiscal 1973, including subsidies for construction of new cargo ships.

As cleared, the bill authorized $250-million for the construction of 17 cargo ships and $30-million to purchase 10 existing transport vessels for lay-up in the National Reserve Fleet.

The funds for ship construction were part of a 10-year government program to revitalize the U.S. merchant fleet. The Merchant Marine Act of 1970 (PL 91-469) established a plan for construction of 300 new cargo ships but required Congress to authorize construction subsidies on an annual basis.

The bill also authorized $232-million for operating subsidies for four passenger liners, 196 cargo ships and 20 bulk carriers.

Supplemental. President Nixon Oct. 21 signed into law a bill (HR 16987—PL 92-523) authorizing $175-million in supplemental funds for fiscal 1973 for subsidizing construction of eight additional merchant ships.

In his January 1972 budget message, President Nixon requested $250-million to finance shipbuilding in fiscal 1973; Congress Aug. 14 cleared a bill (HR 13324—PL 92-402) authorizing those funds. But the President's budget message also noted a possible need for additional funds in fiscal 1973.

Subsequently, the administration requested $175-million in supplemental appropriations to permit the construction of eight more ships in addition to the 16 financed by PL 92-402.

The House Interstate and Foreign Commerce Committee, which reported HR 16987 (H Rept 92-1569) Oct. 11, said that "without these funds, confidence in the government could falter to the detriment of the entire maritime program."

The committee noted that while "it was impossible to forecast accurately the increase in shipbuilding activity ...as early as last spring, the possible need for additional funds for construction subsidy purposes was foreseen."

Cruise Ships. Congress June 21 cleared for the President's signature a bill (HR 9552—PL 92-323) permitting U.S. passenger ships to engage in year-round cruise operations.

The bill provided that passenger ships which received government subsidies could operate permanently as cruise ships if they were not needed on normal routes.

Under existing law (PL 90-358), owners of passenger ships could place them on the cruise trade for a maximum of seven months a year.

The legislation applied to four operating passenger ships still under the U.S. flag. They were the *SS Mariposa, SS Monterey, SS President Cleveland* and *SS President Wilson,* all of which were operating out of West Coast ports.

Passenger Ship Sale. Congress May 2 cleared for the President's signature a bill (HR 11589—PL 92-296) authorizing the foreign sale of five U.S.-flag passenger vessels to foreign investors.

Final action came when the Senate by voice vote passed the bill without amendment. The House had approved the measure Dec. 1, 1971.

The bill also permitted the secretary of commerce to purchase the *SS United States* for inclusion in the National Defense Reserve Fleet.

Because the ships were built in the 1950s with federal subsidies under a law which required that they remain under the U.S. flag for 25 years, specific statutory authority was needed for the sale.

Proceeds recovered by owners from the sale of the ships—about $29.3-million—were required to be reinvested in the construction of new cargo ships. The Maritime Administration estimated that as many as seven modern cargo vessels could be constructed with these funds.

The passenger vessels authorized to be sold—*SS Brazil, SS Argentina, SS Constitution, SS Santa Paula* and *SS Santa Rosa*—had been out of service for varying lengths of time, ranging from 16 months to four years, and they required $5-million annually in lay-up costs.

Sponsors of the bill said the ships were making no contribution to commerce or the balance of payments and were not providing seagoing jobs. "These funds are completely wasted and unproductive," said Russell B. Long (D La.), chairman of the Finance Committee.

Opponents said other nations were making a profit on cruise ships, particularly on Caribbean runs. Ernest F. Hollings (D S.C.), pointing out that U.S. taxpayers had put some $388-million into construction of the five ships, said "one last effort should be made to preserve the vessels for the U.S. flag."

HR 11589 was supported by the Maritime Administration and by U.S. shipowners (Moore-McCormack Lines, Inc., Export-Isbrandtsen Lines, Inc., and Prudential-Grace Lines, Inc.) but opposed by the AFL-CIO Maritime Committee, the AFL-CIO Industrial Unions Department and the National Maritime Union.

Airport Assistance

President Nixon in 1972 vetoed a bill (S 3755) increasing federal assistance for airport development and banning imposition of boarding taxes on airline passengers by local governments. By 1972, an increasing number of cities had boarding taxes of $1 to $3.

In his October veto message, the President said: "This bill would increase federal expenditures and raise percentage participation in categorical grant programs.... I believe this would be inconsistent with sound fiscal policy. Airport development funds have been almost quadrupled since 1970 under this administration."

As cleared by Congress, the bill closely followed the Senate version of S 3755. Senate-House conferees had accepted the Senate's ban on local taxation rather than a House provision providing an 18-month moratorium on those taxes, pending a study by the Civil Aeronautics Board. The bill also increased federal assistance for airport development, as provided by the Senate, from 50 to 75 percent, except at the nation's largest airports.

Court Action. Pressure on Congress to ban boarding taxes mounted after the Supreme Court April 19 upheld departure fees levied by Evansville, Ind., and the state of New Hampshire. Justice William J. Brennan Jr., delivering the opinion of the court, wrote: "The commercial airlines argue...that a proliferation of these taxes in airports over the country will eventually follow in the wake of a decision sustaining the validity of the Indiana and New Hampshire fees.... But there is no suggestion that... the charges do not in fact advance the constitutionally permissible objective of having interstate commerce bear a fair share of the costs to the states of airport (construction and maintenance)...." After the court decision, 15 states imposed local taxes on departing passengers, confirming the airlines' fears and prompting members of the House and Senate to introduce a bill that would ban the taxes but increase federal airport aid.

Other Air Legislation

Air Traffic Controllers. President Nixon May 16 signed into law a bill (HR 8083—PL 92-297) providing new career training opportunities and early retirement benefits for air traffic controllers.

The purpose of HR 8083 was to ensure high standards in air traffic safety by requiring the Federal Aviation Administration to maintain a proficient controller work force to handle physically and mentally taxing jobs at airport towers and regional radar control centers.

Provisions. As cleared by Congress, HR 8083:

• Authorized new career training at government expense for air traffic controllers with at least five years experience if the secretary of transportation determined that a controller had to be dismissed from his duties for medical reasons or inability to maintain technical proficiency.

• Authorized the secretary of transportation to dismiss an employee in the interest of aviation safety; established appeal procedures.

• Authorized early retirement benefits for any controller voluntarily or involuntarily separated from government service provided he had completed 25 years of service or had reached age 50 and completed 20 years of service.

• Provided for mandatory retirement of a controller at age 56 or at age 61 in special cases.

Loan Guarantees. President Nixon Oct. 25 signed into law a bill (S 2741—PL 92-556) increasing federal guarantees on loans to local service airlines.

The bill extended the Aircraft Loan Guarantee Program of 1957 (which expired Sept. 7, 1972) until January 1977 and increased from $10-million to $30-million the maximum amount of loans an air carrier could borrow with a federal guarantee.

The purpose of the program was to help local service air carriers and metropolitan helicopter service programs obtain funds for new aircraft where commercial loans were not available without a federal guarantee.

Dock Strike

Congress Feb. 9 cleared for the President's signature a bill (S J Res 197—92-235) to end a West Coast dock strike by establishing a three-member board to settle all issues in the dispute by compulsory arbitration.

The House completed action on the bill late in the evening of the 9th after having approved a similar House version (H J Res 1025) by a 214-139 roll-call vote. The Senate bill was then passed by voice vote to avoid a House-Senate conference on the legislation. Final House action was in doubt until the rule for consideration of H J Res 1025, which was opposed by the Democratic leadership, was adopted by a mere 33-vote margin, 203-170.

H J Res 1025 had been brought to the House floor by the Rules Committee in an unusual procedure that bypassed the Education and Labor Committee, which previously had rejected the measure.

The Senate had passed S J Res 197 on Feb. 8 by a 79-3 roll call.

Although negotiators for the International Longshoremen's and Warehousemen's Union (ILWU) and the Pacific Maritime Association (PMA), representing the shipping industry, had reached tentative agreement on a new contract Feb. 8, Congress completed action on S J Res 197 to assure that the strike would be halted if the contract was not ratified by members of the ILWU.

S J Res 197 contained a provision voiding the legislation in its entirety if a voluntary agreement was reached between the ILWU and PMA.

The bill provided for an immediate end to the strike and the submission of all issues to a three-member panel which would be required to establish a new contract within 40 days. The congressionally mandated agreement would be in force at least 18 months; no strike or lockout would be permitted during that time.

Final action on S J Res 197 followed three weeks of legislative maneuvering on the measure in Congress. The strike on the West Coast began July 1, 1971, and the dispute involved wages, fringe benefits, retroactive pay and payments for handling cargo containers.

Striking members of the ILWU Feb. 19 ratified the tentative settlement that had been reached by negotiators Feb. 8. The longshoremen were returning to work at West Coast ports on Feb. 21 when President Nixon signed S J Res 197 in Peking during his visit to China. Their action therefore nullified the legislation.

Anti-strike legislation. The Nixon administration acknowledged July 20 that it had withdrawn support of legislation first introduced in 1970, then again in 1971, to prevent strikes in the transportation industry, a proposal strongly opposed by organized labor *(1970-71 chronologies, p. 166, 169)*

Sen. Robert W. Packwood (R Ore.) had been preparing to offer his version of the anti-strike plan as an amendment to the minimum wage bill passed by the Senate July 20. But on July 17, Packwood said, Under Secretary of Labor Laurence H. Silberman told him the administration would not support that move.

Although Packwood had counted 47 senators in favor of the measure, 45 opposed and seven uncommitted, White House Press Secretary Ronald L. Ziegler said July 20 that support for the bill was withdrawn because it "has no chance of passage this year." Ziegler said "we will take the opportunity to review it with organized labor."

Secretary of Labor James D. Hodgson told newsmen July 21 that the administration had notified the International Brotherhood of Teamsters of the decision on the bill during the weekend of July 15-16.

On July 17, the Teamsters endorsed President Nixon for re-election. On July 19, the AFL-CIO executive council announced it would take no position on the 1972 presidential contest.

Amtrak

Congress June 13 cleared for the President's signature a bill (HR 11417—PL 92-316) authorizing $225-million in appropriations for the National Railroad Passenger Corporation (Amtrak) through June 30, 1973.

The amount agreed to by House-Senate conferees was $55-million more than that authorized by the House but $60-million less than the Senate-passed figure. In addition to the $225-million authorized, $2-million was provided to establish passenger services to Mexico and Canada.

The additional federal subsidy was needed to continue rail passenger service until July 1, 1973, as required by the Rail Passenger Service Act of 1970 (PL 91-518). In 1971, Amtrak had requested $170-million.

House-Senate conferees also increased Amtrak's loan guarantee authority by $100-million, to $200-million, but placed a limit of $150-million on the total amount of loans which could be outstanding through June 30, 1973, and a ceiling of $200-million thereafter. The Senate had increased the loan guarantee authority by $250-million, including $100-million for use in urban corridor improvements; the House had not altered the loan guarantee authority of the original act.

Conferees also deleted $50-million in loans, authorized in the Senate version, for capital improvements to rail facilities along urban corridors.

The corporation began service May 1, 1971, with a $40-million federal grant plus payments from participating railroads totaling $197-million over 36 months. Although it had been estimated that these funds, in addition to the $100-million loan, would be sufficient for Amtrak to provide rail service until July 1973, the corporation reported in October 1971 that it would run a deficit of $152.3-million in fiscal 1972 and $123.8-million in fiscal 1973.

After the Senate April 26 authorized $285-million in additional funds, plus $50-million in loans and $250-million extra in loan guarantee authority, Amtrak President Roger Lewis said $170-million was all the corporation could "sensibly commit" during fiscal 1973.

Included was a provision reducing Lewis' salary to $60,000 annually from $125,000.

Other Rail Legislation

Railroad Repairs. President Nixon Oct. 27 signed a bill (S 3843—PL 92-591) authorizing $58-million in federal loans to repair railroad equipment and facilities damaged by floods during the summer of 1972.

Five financially troubled railroads—Penn Central, Lehigh Valley Railroad, Reading Co., Erie-Lackawanna and the Central Railroad of New Jersey—had claimed their survival could be in jeopardy if they did not receive federal loans to repair flood-damaged facilities.

According to Interstate Commerce Commission information, 11 railroads suffered $47.6-million in flood damages to property and equipment.

The bill authorized $48-million in loans to railroads which met certain financial conditions, and an additional $10-million to state and local governments.

Rail Crossings. The Senate Commerce Committee Aug. 3 reported a bill (S 3879—S Rept. 92-1001) requiring states to spend at least 5 percent of their federal highway aid for improving rail-highway crossings. The bill was then referred to the Public Works Committee. Existing federal law permitted states to spend up to 10 percent of highway funds for rail crossing safety; but because the funds could be used only for improvements on federal aid highways, few crossings on state and local roads—where most accidents occur—had been reconstructed.

Between 1920 and 1970, according to a Department of Transportation report on railroad-highway safety, 86,000 people were killed and 230,000 injured at grade crossings. The report concluded the grade crossing problem "is a substantial one requiring remedial action at the federal level."

High-Speed Transportation. Congress June 30 cleared for the President a bill (S 979—PL 92-348) authorizing $135.9-million over fiscal years 1973-75 for research and development projects authorized under the High-Speed Ground Transportation Act.

S 979 provided annual funds for high-speed ground transportation projects, including the Washington-New York Metroliner, the Boston-New York Turbo Train and the Tracked Air Cushion Research Vehicle (TACRV).

Areas with high unemployment were to be given special consideration for ground transportation development contracts.

As cleared, the bill followed the House-passed version, with conferees agreeing to provisions authorizing the General Accounting Office to audit any railroad having a federal guaranteed loan, extending the repayment period on federal guaranteed loans and authorizing research on "door-to-door" (mini-bus) type ground transportation.

To prevent bankruptcies in the railroad industry, the bill extended the repayment time for federally guaranteed loans from 15 to 25 years.

The Senate version merely eliminated the existing termination date (June 30, 1972) of the High-Speed Ground Transportation Act of 1965, as amended in 1968 and 1970, and authorized open-ended appropriations. The Senate had passed S 979 by voice vote June 15, 1971.

Freight Cars. The Senate Aug. 4, by an 81-0 rollcall vote, passed a bill (S 1729) to alleviate railroad freight car shortages. There was no House action.

As passed by the Senate, the bill authorized $2-billion in guaranteed loans for acquisition of freight cars, cabooses and locomotives by railroads. An additional $1-billion was to be available in 1975. The bill also authorized $35-million to establish a computer tracking system to monitor boxcar movements and locations.

The Senate Commerce Committee, which reported the bill (S Rept 92-982) July 24, concluded legislative action was necessary for the following reasons; (1) the number of freight cars had been declining for many years; (2) the weak financial condition of a sizable portion of the rail industry hampered its ability to acquire rolling stock; (3) utilization of existing freight cars was "woefully low"; (4) procedures needed to be developed to coordinate the operations of individual railroads, and (5) government action must focus upon the needs of the rail industry as a system rather than upon the interests of individual companies.

Although another bill (S 2362)—the Surface Transportation Act of 1972—originally provided financial assistance for acquisition of freight cars, the Commerce Committee later deleted reference to boxcars because the subject was treated in S 1729.

Surface Transportation. The Senate Commerce Committee Sept. 15 reported the Surface Transportation Act (S 2362—S Rept 92-1155), authorizing $3-billion in federally-guaranteed loans to railroads, truck companies and barge lines. No further action was taken on the bill in 1972.

The loans were designed to aid regulated surface transportation industries unable, without federal backing to obtain credit at reasonable rates from private sources. Guaranteed loans would be restricted to $450-million over

15 years for any one carrier and could be used for capital expenditures but not to cover operating costs or to purchase freight cars.

The bill also authorized $50-million in federal grants to assist states in subsidizing branch rail lines otherwise abandoned.

Not included in the bill were administration proposals to permit transportation companies to charge shipping rates within a "zone of reasonableness" without Interstate Commerce Commission approval and to liberalize entry control over motor and barge lines seeking to compete in interstate trade.

Although the Department of Transportation had maintained that "revision and modernization of complex and increasingly outdated economic regulatory laws" would stimulate more competitive prices in interstate commerce, the railroads, truckers and barge industries opposed such action on the basis that it would lead to destructive competition between them. In 1971, they drafted and proposed, instead, the Surface Transportation Act, which the Commerce Committee reported with major modifications.

State Taxes. The Senate Commerce Committee Sept. 1 reported a bill (S 3945—S Rept 92-1085) to eliminate discriminatory state taxes on transportation property. No further action was taken in 1972.

(The bill was initially considered by the committee as a section of the Surface Transportation Act (S 2362) but was reported separately to expedite Senate action.)

The committee said that regulated interstate carriers, especially railroads, were "easy prey" for state and local tax assessors because transportation companies were non-voting, often non-resident targets for local taxation and could not remove their rights-of-way and terminals when tax burdens became too heavy.

The committee estimated that in 1970 discriminatory taxes cost transportation companies about $54-million.

Tax discrimination, the committee said, arose in two ways: transportation property might be assessed at a higher proportion of its true market value than comparable non-transportation property and transportation property might be assessed at a higher tax rate than comparable non-transportation property.

The Department of Transportation and the Interstate Commerce Commission supported the bill.

Transpo '72

Congress March 8 completed action on a bill (S 3244—PL 92-252) authorizing a $2-million increase in appropriations for a transportation exhibition.

The bill increased to $5-million from $3-million the authorization for Transpo '72, an international aeronautical and transportation exposition which opened at Dulles International Airport (just outside Washington, D.C.) May 27 and ran through June 4.

The Senate March 1 by voice vote passed S 3244. The House March 8 passed and sent to the President the Senate bill by voice vote after passing an identical House bill (HR 11624) by a 278-109 roll call.

As originally proposed, the exposition was to include only aircraft. In 1969, an amendment to the Military Construction Authorization Act of 1970 (PL 91-142), authorized $750,000 for the exposition.

In 1970, the Transportation Department requested that the authorization be increased to $3-million and Congress in PL 91-511 granted the increase.

H. R. Gross (R Iowa), a persistent critic of increases in government spending, led House opposition against additional funds in 1971 and 1972.

When S 3244 was brought to the House floor, Gross debated the bill with F. Edward Hebert (D La.), chairman of the Armed Services Committee.

Gross: "So you started out by asking for $750,000 for this deal, did you not? The $750,000 was the camel's nose under the tent....Now it has ballooned into $5-million."

Hebert: "I would not call it a balloon but perhaps a little popsicle. But it is well worth the taste for the size of the popsicle because we are going to get our money back."

Gross: "That $750,000 was the all-day sucker that was handed to Congress?"

Transpo Attendance. Department of Transportation figures released July 17 by Sen. William Proxmire (D Wis.)—a persistent critic of Transpo '72—revealed that attendance at the exposition was about half the 1.5-million estimated by the agency at the close of the transportation show. According to the figures, only 438,-603 persons paid to see Transpo.

Miscellaneous Economic Legislation

The 91st and 92nd Congresses gave broad support for continuing two of the earliest Johnson administration social welfare programs. The programs were in the Appalachian Redevelopment Act and the Public Works and Economic Development Act. First enacted in 1965, various titles of the two acts were scheduled to expire at different times in succeeding years. When titles of both measures came up for extension in the same year between 1969 and 1972, Congress extended them in a single bill. Laws passed in 1969, 1970 and 1971 extended parts of both measures.

The extensions received general bipartisan support, and authorizations under the programs were increased from their early levels. Both programs provided for federal-state commissions to coordinate planning and action. During debate on the extensions, a number of members of Congress praised the federal-state operations under the program as being well coordinated and fruitful.

In the last extension of the two programs, a 1971 omnibus bill, Congress attempted also to extend another program—the 1962 Public Works Acceleration Act. It voted $2 billion for construction of basic public works facilities in areas of substantial unemployment. President Nixon vetoed this bill, objecting that the accelerated public works concept had proven too slow to be an effective anti-unemployment device. Congress could not find the votes to override the veto. It quickly passed a new bill, extending only the two 1965 acts, which the President supported. In 1972, Nixon, after the 92nd Congress adjourned at the end of the second session, pocket vetoed a bill which would have transformed the 1965 Economic Development Act into a program to attack the existing high rate of unemployment.

Congress was also in general agreement as it moved to consolidate and increase federal disaster aid. In 1970, it pulled most of the existing disaster relief programs into one bill and added several new programs. During lengthy hearings that year a number of philosophical questions were raised about the quality and obligations of disaster relief. Some of the new programs grew out of these. One question was whether the relief effort should merely restore a disaster area to its original state or use the disaster as an opportunity to construct a more attractive and useful community. Congress opted for the latter, setting minimum standards for construction of the new buildings which replaced those that had been destroyed. The 1970 bill also tried to make federal disaster programs less discriminatory against minorities, the aged and the poor.

The devastation caused by 1972 tropical storm Agnes led Congress that year to make substantial changes in special disaster loan programs. The interest rate under Small Business Administration and Farmers Home Administration disaster loans was reduced (to 1 per cent for 1972 disasters) and the amount of a loan repayment which could be cancelled was increased.

In 1967 Congress had established the Corporation for Public Broadcasting (CPB) to provide a mechanism for financing noncommercial broadcasting. A permanent source of funds for the CPB, however, was not decided on, and Congress was forced to finance it through the politically sensitive annual appropriations process. A promise by the Johnson administration to propose a long-range source of funding free of congressional politics was not fulfilled.

The Nixon administration between 1969 and 1971 also continued to promise a new financing proposal for CPB but failed to submit one. Congress therefore went on financing the CPB through increasingly large annual appropriations. In 1972 the President, instead of promising different financing, said "serious questions" about the CPB would have to be resolved before long-range financing was decided on. He vetoed a two-year CPB authorization on the ground that the corporation was becoming a power center rather than a service organization for local stations. After the veto Congress passed a one-year authorization, which the President signed.

There were other questions raised about public broadcasting operations, such as the justification for high salaries and whether foundations were influencing programming. But in general Congress during the years 1969-72 gave public broadcasting wide support, passing increasingly large authorizations for both the CPB and construction of broadcast facilities.

In 1970, Congress cleared the Newspaper Preservation Act, which exempted from anti-trust laws agreements pooling certain operations of competing newspapers. The agreements permitted pooling of printing and business operations if one paper was in danger of failing.

Legislation to aid failing newspapers had been under consideration since the Justice Department challenged one newspaper pooling agreement in 1967. It was supported by the Nixon administration and the Commerce Department because of a rising number of failures of independent newspapers. The Justice Department opposed it on the ground that it would stifle competition.

Several pieces of legislation affecting small business were passed between 1969-72. In 1972, Congress gave a legal basis for a special program of support to limited small business investment companies (SBICs) which aided businesses owned by the disadvantaged. The same bill also liberalized the Small Business Administration's regular SBIC program. Legislation enacted in

1970, 1971 and 1972 steadily increased the ceiling on the SBA's business loan and investment fund (from $1.9 billion to $4.3 billion). The disaster aid legislation enacted in 1972 *(above)* related largely to liberalizations of the SBA disaster relief program.

Chronology

Of

Legislation

(NOTE: The following chronology is organized by subject matter. When action occurred in different years, it is reported entirely within the story about the subject.)

Appalachia, Economic Development

The 91st and 92nd Congresses voted several extensions of two important Johnson administration 'Great Society' programs. The original laws were the Appalachian Regional Development Act of 1965 (PL 89-4) and the Public Works and Economic Development Act of 1965 (PL 89-136), aimed at helping other economically depressed areas. Parts of PL 89-4 had already been extended in 1967.

A 1969 act (PL 91-123) extended most programs under the Appalachian Development Act as well as the programs authorized under the two expiring titles of the Public Works and Economic Development Act. In 1970 Congress voted a routine one-year extension of titles one through four of PL 89-136, pending a re-evaluation of the program. Congress in 1971 passed an omnibus bill (PL 92-65) extending titles of both the Public Works Act and the Appalachian Development Act for varying periods. Similar provisions had also been included in an earlier bill (S 575) vetoed by President Nixon because he objected to an additional title which provided $2 billion for accelerated public works. Passage of the second 1971 bill, while not opposed by the administration, was in lieu of action on the President's 1971 proposal to combine federal rural development programs in a new rural revenue sharing plan. A congressionally-initiated bill, substantially expanding the programs to try and attack rising unemployment, was vetoed by the President in 1972.

Appalachian Act Background. The Appalachian Regional Development Act (PL 89-4), enacted in 1965, was the Johnson administration's first major effort to deal with rural poverty. The legislation provided funds for highway development and public works projects related generally to health, education and industrial development in the 13-state Appalachian region. It created a federal-state commission to coordinate regional planning and action on which all Appalachian states were represented.

PL 89-4 authorized a total of $1,092,400,000 for development programs, of which the bulk ($840 million) was allocated for building highways and local access roads. The highway money was authorized through fiscal 1971. The remaining $252.4 million was authorized for fiscal 1966-67 for public facilities such as health facilities and vocational schools needed by the areas as a basis for economic expansion.

In 1967 Congress added another state (Mississippi) to the region covered by the act and authorized an additional $175 million for highways for fiscal 1968-71 and $170 million for nonhighway programs for fiscal 1968-69 (PL 90-103). The 1967 bill ran into an economy drive in the House, and the final version authorized $93 million less than the administration had requested. *(Congress and the Nation II p. 286, 288)*

Economic Development Act Background. Passage of the Appalachian bill in 1965 brought pressure for aid to other economically depressed regions of the country. This led to drafting of the Public Works and Economic Development Act by the administration and its congressional supporters. The final bill (PL 89-136) contained five titles: Title I provided $500 million a year in fiscal years 1966-69 for matching grants to local public agencies and non-profit groups for construction of public works facilities that would foster the economic growth of depressed areas; Title II provided $170 million a year in fiscal years 1966-70 for federal loans for the above purpose and for loans for acquisition of land, buildings and equipment for commercial use in depressed areas; Title III provided $25 million a year in fiscal 1966-70 for federal technical assistance to depressed areas; Title IV provided $50 million a year in fiscal 1967-70 in grants and loans to towns which had a potential for economic growth which would aid nearby depressed areas; and Title V encouraged the states to set up multi-state regional commissions to plan and foster economic development programs in depressed regions, and provided $15 million a year in fiscal 1966-70 in federal aid to the commissions. *(Congress and the Nation II p. 291)*

Following enactment of PL 89-136 five economic development commissions were established under the provisions of Title V. *(Box p. 179)*

The 1967 Appalachian Act amendments *(above)* provided $75 million for fiscal 1968-69 for the commissions. The funds were to be used for a supplemental grant program similar to the program established by the 1965 Appalachian legislation for that area.

1969 DEVELOPMENT, APPALACHIAN LEGISLATION

Congress in 1969 passed a bill further extending the programs first authorized by the Appalachian Regional Development Act of 1965 and the expiring programs authorized under Titles I and V of the Public Works and Economic Development Act of 1965 (PL 89-136). Other provisions of PL 89-136 did not expire in 1969.

The bill (S 1072—PL 91-123) provided a simple one year extension of the grant program authorized under Title I of the Economic Development Act, thereby meeting an administration request to bring the expiration date in line with that of Titles II-IV of the legislation. It extended Title V for two years, through fiscal 1971, and authorized $255 million for grant programs

Economic Development Regions

Region	Number of Counties	Number of Congressional Districts in Region	Population (in millions)	Per Capita Income (1966)
New England	67	25	10.5	$3,270
Maine	16			
Vermont	14			
New Hampshire	10			
Massachusetts	14			
Connecticut	8			
Rhode Island	5			
Upper Great Lakes	119	10	2.7	2,340
Michigan	45			
Minnesota	38			
Wisconsin	36			
Ozarks	134	13	2.5	2,130
Arkansas	44			
Kansas	9			
Missouri	44			
Oklahoma	37			
Coastal Plains	159	16	5.3	1,960
North Carolina	45			
South Carolina	28			
Georgia	86			
Four Corners	92	8	1.8	2,240
Arizona	9			
Colorado	40			
New Mexico	22			
Utah	1			
Appalachia	419	59	17.7	2,320
Alabama	35			
Georgia	35			
North Carolina	29			
Virginia	21			
Kentucky	49			
Tennessee	49			
Maryland	3			
Pennsylvania	52			
West Virginia	55			
Ohio	28			
South Carolina	28			
New York	14			
Mississippi	20			

*U.S. per capita income, 1966: $2,980.
(Department of Commerce)

operated by the five regional commissions authorized by that title. This was a sharp increase (from $75 million) over the previous two-year funding for the commissions; it represented an effort to bring aid to other depressed areas closer to the level of aid to Appalachia.

In its provisions affecting the Appalachian area, S 1072 extended the Appalachian highway program for two years, through fiscal 1973, and authorized an additional $150 million for the program. It authorized $268.5 million for fiscal 1970-71 for the non-highway Appalachian programs.

S 1072 moved through the legislative process with little controversy. Most floor debate consisted of praise

for the programs. Congressmen from the regions affected lauded the federal-state cooperation in the programs and listed economic progress in their districts.

Provisions—As signed into law Nov. 25, S 1072—PL 91-123:

● Extended the Appalachian highway program for two years through fiscal 1973 and authorized an additional $150 million for the program.

● Authorized $268.5 million for nonhighway Appalachian programs for fiscal 1970-71.

● Stipulated that Appalachian Regional Commission funds could be used in conjunction with other federal grant funds to raise to 100 percent the federal share of Appalachian child health and nutrition programs.

● Converted the Appalachian highway program from annual appropriations to contract authority which allowed highway funds to be obligated in advance of appriations.

● Authorized the Secretary of Housing and Urban Development to assist nonprofit organizations in Appalachia to construct, rehabilitate and operate housing units.

● Authorized $255 million for the programs of five other regional commissions for fiscal 1970-71 and $20 million for a study of regional transportation systems by the five commissions and the Secretary of Transportation.

● Authorized the Secretary of Commerce to use up to 10 per cent of the $255 million for technical assistance for the commissions and directed him to allocate the remaining amount of the $255 million to the commissions in such a way that no commission received less than 10 percent nor more than 25 percent.

● Allowed the commissions to use the funds allocated to them to supplement federal grant-in-aid funds to raise the federal share to 80 percent.

● Authorized $500,000 for fiscal 1970-71 for the Alaska Federal Field Committee for planning programs and projects in Alaska.

● Extended Title I of the Public Works and Economic Development Act for one year through fiscal 1970 and continued the $500 million authorization under Title I for grants to depressed areas for public facilities.

● Increased from $25 million to $50 million the fiscal 1970 funds under Title III of the Public Works and Economic Development Act for demonstration grants and technical assistance.

● Amended Title IV by authorizing the Secretary of Commerce to designate as redevelopment areas eligible for Title III assistance the "special impact areas" created under the Economic Development Act of 1964 in low-income urban and rural areas.

● Required the federal cochairmen of the Title V commissions to maintain their offices in Washington, D.C.

1970, 1971 EXTENSIONS

Congress June 29, 1970 cleared a straight one-year extension (PL 91-304) of the existing authorized annual amounts for Titles I through IV of the 1965 Economic Development Act. The administration had requested the simple extension pending completion of a thorough Commerce Department review of the program, and Congress agreed without controversy.

ECONOMIC DEVELOPMENT REGIONS

Congress July 30, 1971 cleared a bill (S 2317—PL 92-65) extending most of the Economic Development Act for two years, extending nonhighway Appalachian provisions for four years and extending the Appalachian highway program through fiscal 1978.

Enactment of PL 92-65 followed the veto of an earlier bill (S 575) in 1971. S 575 had contained identical provisions for Appalachia. Its provisions extending the Economic Development Act were similar to that of the bill finally enacted, except that the final bill provided $250 million more per year ($800 million instead of $550 million) for development grants.

The administration had accepted the Appalachian and Economic Development provisions of S 575, which comprised Titles II and III of that bill. The veto was caused by objection to Title I of S 575, an extension of the 1962 Public Works Acceleration Act. Title I had authorized $2 billion for grants for construction of basic public works in localities of substantial unemployment and in areas of high unemployment among veterans of the Vietnam war. In vetoing S 575 because he objected to Title I, the President said the program would not become effective for 18 months at which time it would be unnecessary and inflationary, and that it would have little effect in reducing unemployment where it was most serious. In floor debate on the bill, Republicans had objected that the Title I provisions amounted to an

attempt to apply a weak anti-unemployment device of the early 1960s to the different problems of the 1970s.

Following the President's veto of S 575 an attempt to override the veto in the Senate failed by five votes. The Senate voted July 14 in a **key vote 57-36** to override, thus failing to reach the necessary two-thirds majority. Voting to override were 51 Democrats and six Republicans; 35 Republicans and one Democrat voted to uphold the veto.

A week after the veto was sustained, the Senate passed the new bill (S 2317), containing most of the provisions of Titles II and III, by an 88-2 roll call. The House passed the bill with a minor amendment by a 376-27 roll-call vote July 28 and the Senate cleared that bill for the President two days later. No one spoke against the bill during floor debate.

Besides the omission of the accelerated public works program, the only major difference between S 2317 and the vetoed bill was that the new bill authorized up to $800 million annually for grants to public works facilities whereas the earlier bill had provided $550 million. The new bill authorized a total of $4,161,-000,000 for extension of programs under the two acts—$1,815,500,000 for Appalachian regional development and $2,345,500,000 for programs under the Economic Development Act. The bill continued the programs along the lines set forth in the original authorizations. New provisions included a four-year $40 million airport safety program and a mine drainage pollution control program, both in the Appalachian region.

Provisions—As signed into law Aug. 5, PL 92-65:

Title I—Public Works and Economic Development Act Amendments of 1971:

- Authorized direct grants of up to $800 million annually through fiscal 1973 for public works and development facilities, and provided that unused authorizations for which funds were not appropriated in fiscal 1972 could be carried over to fiscal 1973.
- Extended through fiscal 1973 authorizations of $170 million annually for business development loans in redevelopment areas.
- Extended through fiscal 1973 authorizations of $50 million annually for technical planning and operational assistance for redevelopment regions.
- Defined "redevelopment area" as:

Having a median family income of 50 per cent or less of the national median;

Including special impact regions with large concentrations of low-income persons; rural areas with substantial out-migration, areas with severe economic distress due to substantial unemployment and areas where per capita employment had declined significantly during the preceding 10-year period.

Having an actual or threatened abrupt rise of unemployment due to the closing or curtailment of a major source of employment.

- Provided that localities designated "redevelopment areas" coul d not have such designation terminated in less than three years from the date of designation.
- Provided up to 80 per cent federal matching funds for special impact area projects, with up to 100 per cent matching funds when state or local government resources were exhausted.
- Authorized a total of $305 million through fiscal 1972 to continue the work of regional development commissions.
- Authorized a total of $500,000 through fiscal 1972 for the Federal Field Committee for Development Planning in Alaska.
- Provided that no area designated as a redevelopment area would have its designation modified before June 1, 1972.

Title II—Appalachian Regional Development Act Amendments of 1971:

- Authorized for administrative expenses a total of $2,700,000 for fiscal years 1972 and 1973 and a total of $3,300,000 for fiscal years 1974 and 1975.
- Authorized through fiscal 1978 an additional $925 million for Appalachian highway systems and local access roads.
- Authorized the following appropriations for the Appalachian regional development program through fiscal 1975: $268,500,000 for the two-fiscal-year period ending June 30, 1971, $282 million for fiscal years 1972 and 1973 and $294 million for 1974 and 1975.
- Added a 4-year, $40-million Appalachian airport safety improvements program to increase the safety of airports in the Appalachian region.
- Permitted Appalachian funds to be used with other federal funds in child-care programs.

- Authorized mine drainage pollution control projects relating to mine area restoration, and extended the 75-25 federal-state cost-sharing ratio for such restoration projects.
- Provided additional assistance in making low- and moderate-income housing available by subsidizing site development costs through grants and loans to non-profit, limited dividend or cooperative organizations.
- Provided financial assistance for area-wide demonstration projects at the level of existing vocational and technical education demonstration projects.

1972 PUBLIC WORKS VETO

Congress in 1972 made another effort to transform the 1965 Public Works and Economic Development Act from a program for long-term rural development into a measure to attack the current high rate of unemployment. As in 1971 the President objected, and the bill was pocket-vetoed after Congress had adjourned.

The bill (HR 10671) extended PL 89-136 for one year, through June 30, 1974. Its estimated cost was more than $3 billion, of which some $2.2 billion was for fiscal 1974 and the balance was new authorizations for fiscal 1973.

HR 10671 amended the 1965 act to broaden the definition of economic development districts so that assistance under the bill in effect would be available to all areas of "substantial" unemployment. It authorized $250 million annually in fiscal 1973 and 1974 for special public works impact program grants, and $550 million for other development grants in both years. Authorizations for the regional commissions were set at $100 million annually. The bill also added a new title to the 1965 act which provided federal assistance (unemployment compensation, mortgage or rental payments, re-employment aid and some moving expenses) to workers who lost jobs as a result of federal environmental improvement laws.

HR 16071 was passed by the House Aug. 16 by a 285-92 roll-call vote and by the Senate Oct. 12 by a 65-16 roll call.

The President's Oct. 27 veto message objected to the public works funding in HR 16071 for the same reasons he had objected to the public works acceleration extension vetoed in 1971: public works projects were ineffective in creating jobs and have notoriously long lead times" so that by the time spending was effective the need for it has passed. The President also opposed the new title to assist workers affected by federal environmental actions as "highly inequitable and almost impossible to administer."

Emergency Public Works Bill Rejected. Before it passed HR 10671 the House had rejected a more expensive bill which had some of the same purposes.

The bill (HR 13853) amended Title VII of the Housing and Urban Development Act of 1965 to authorize $5 billion in grants to state and local governments for construction of basic public works and community facilities. Priority was to be given to communities designated as redevelopment areas, communities defined as areas of substantial unemployment and communities designated as areas with a large concentration of low-income persons or substantial out-migration.

HR 13853 was rejected by the House July 19 by a 189-206 roll-call vote. According to supporters of the bill, most of whom were Democrats, the funds were intended primarily for building water and sewer systems. They said the bill was vital to help reduce water pollution, create jobs for construction workers and combat unemployment.

Opponents of the bill, mostly Republicans and southern Democrats, argued that HR 13853 was inflationary, duplicative and politically inspired. They said a pending water pollution control bill (S 2770) would provide sufficient funds for construction and pollution abatement, and called HR 13853 part of an election year tactic to force President Nixon to veto a popular bill. *(Water pollution, environment chapter)*

Disaster Relief

Two of the worst storms ever to hit North America prompted Congress to consolidate and strengthen federal disaster aid legislation during President Nixon's first term.

Hurricane Camille, which caused $1.5 billion in damage to the southern states in August 1969, led to enactment a year later of the Disaster Relief Act of 1970 (S 3619—PL 91-606). The bill consolidated the three major existing federal disaster measures and established several new programs. It grew from criticism by Congress and charitable organizations that the government relief effort had been slow, uncoordinated and discriminatory.

Tropical storm Agnes caused four days of flooding in June 1972 and some $1.7 billion in property damage. Congress cleared a bill (HR 15692—PL 92-385) Aug. 14 permitting lower interest rates and larger cancellation of loan repayments under the Small Business Administration and Farmers Home Administration disaster loan programs. It directed the President by 1973 to submit further legislative proposals to standardize benefits, eliminate bureaucracy and prevent misuse of benefits.

BACKGROUND. Federal disaster relief financing came largely from the President's Disaster Relief Fund and from special revolving funds in the Small Business Administration and Farmers Home Administration. Before 1970, the programs financed by these funds were authorized in scattered legislation written in 1950, 1966 and 1969.

The basic 1950 disaster relief law directed most federal aid to the public sector—restoring highways, water systems, federal buildings and communications systems. The 1966 law sought to provide relief for individual victims of disasters as well. It allowed the government to alter the terms of loans made by certain agencies to victims. It also provided housing mortgage insurance for disaster victims, aid to rural areas and to colleges and universities and provisions for rebuilding public facilities. *(Congress and the Nation II p. 967)*

1969 LEGISLATION

Legislation enacted in 1969 (HR 6508—PL 91-79), which cleared Congress Sept. 18, included provisions for larger federal loan adjustments, repair and reconstruction of non-federal highways, temporary shelter, unemployment aid, food relief and removal of debris from private land. It required the President to designate a coordinating officer for major disaster areas and stressed formulation of state plans for aiding individuals.

The Senate Public Works Committee in January 1970 issued a report of its Special Subcommittee on Disaster Relief which had investigated the operation of federal disaster relief programs following Hurricane Camille. The report found that federal efforts lacked coordination, were slow to respond while victims suffered and in the South discriminated against blacks in dispensing aid.

A report issued by the American Friends Service Committee and the Southern Regional Council agreed with this assessment. It also said the existing federal programs were "cruel" to the poor who did not have collateral to back a loan. It concluded that "the general theory which guides the federal government in its disbursement of disaster aid is that no one should have, even temporarily, better living standards than they had before, even if they were poverty-stricken.... Though certainly a reasonable sounding approach, the net result—coupled with no minimum standard and a graduated level of care—is inequality and inadequacy for many."

1970 LEGISLATION

Congress Dec. 18 cleared a major bill (S 3619—PL 91-606) consolidating existing federal disaster laws and authorizing several new programs. Some of the new programs were designed to meet criticisms of federal relief operations. They included legal aid for the poor; prohibition of discrimination in providing relief; minimum standards for construction of new buildings to replace destroyed ones; aid to communities which had suffered a substantial loss of property tax revenues as a result of a disaster; and aid to firms and industries which were major sources of employment.

The final version of S 3619 was close to the bill drawn up by the Public Works Committee and passed by the Senate 54-0. The House later passed a much narrower bill by voice vote, but the Senate approach and most of its major provisions prevailed in conference.

Provisions—As signed into law, S 3619:

• Made provisions of the act applicable when the President declared that a major disaster had occurred.

• Required the President to appoint for the disaster area a Federal coordinating officer to operate under the Office of Emergency Preparedness (OEP) to determine what types of relief were needed, to establish field offices, to coordinate distribution of relief and to supervise activities concerning aid.

• Authorized federal agencies to aid disaster areas in several ways: lending Federal personnel, facilities, supplies, equipment and other resources (except extension of credit), with or without compensation, to state and local governments; distributing medicine, food and supplies; rendering emergency services; donating or lending federal surplus equipment and supplies; performing emergency work such as debris removal and repairing damaged state and local government facilities; providing emergency shelter, and contributing funds to state or local governments to perform any of these functions. The federal share of emergency repair of government facilities must not exceed the net cost of restoring the facilities to their pre-disaster capacity and to a minimum safe, usable condition. Funds appropriated under the act could be used to reimburse agencies for their services. The federal government would not be liable for damages based on the performance or failure to perform any action in carrying out emergency aid. Temporary employees could be hired, and special groups could be established to provide aid.

● Required that preference should be given to residents and local businesses in spending funds for debris clearance, distribution of supplies, reconstruction and other activities.

● Provided that states must formulate comprehensive plans for handling disasters; authorized grants up to $250-000 for each state for drawing up the plans and up to $25,000 annually to update them.

● Authorized the director of OEP to make agreements with relief or disaster assistance organizations (such as the American National Red Cross, the Salvation Army and the Mennonite Disaster Service) to help distribute food, clothing, medicine and other supplies and restore community services and facilities.

● Provided that no person or business could receive aid from more than one source for the same damage. No person or business could receive government aid for any loss or portion of loss covered by insurance. Any person or business receiving duplicate aid could be required to reimburse the federal government for that amount.

● Prohibited discrimination by race, color, age, sex, nationality, religion or economic status in providing disaster relief supplies and services by the government or any organization participating in relief distribution.

● Required the President to provide warnings to governments and citizens of imminent natural disasters, and allowed him to provide aid to cope with such disasters.

● Authorized the director of OEP to establish temporary emergency communications and public transportation in disaster areas.

● Authorized the use of federal agencies to remove debris and wreckage from public and private lands and waters, and authorized grants to states for that purpose. The federal government would not be liable for claims resulting from debris removal.

● Authorized grants for firefighting in public or private forests or grasslands.

● Authorized the OEP director to provide temporary housing or emergency shelter, including mobile homes, for disaster victims. No rent would be charged during the first 12 months of occupancy; after that period, rents would be set according to market value and the tenant's ability to pay. Emergency shelter could also be sold to the occupants at fair market prices. (This provision was made retroactive to Aug. 1, 1969, to cover victims of Hurricane Camille, which struck the Gulf Coast states in 1969.)

● Allowed the OEP to provide temporary mortgage or rental assistance or re-employment assistance services to disaster victims.

● Allowed the Small Business Administration (SBA) or the Farmers Home Administration (FaHA) to make loans for the repair or replacement of property damaged by a disaster, up to the amount of actual damage involved. (This section allows the SBA administrator or the Secretary of Agriculture as well as the President to determine whether a disaster area exists.) The principal of any loan exceeding $500 could be cancelled, up to a total of $2,500, in the case of disasters declared by the President. Mort-

gages or liens held against homes or businesses which suffered major damage or total destruction could be refinanced up to the amount of the physical loss sustained. (The provisions concerning SBA and FHA loans were made retroactive to April 1, 1970.)

● Allowed the Veterans Administration (VA) to modify loan requirements on residential property affected by disasters, effective April 1, 1970. The VA would provide counseling and services, as well as information about other forms of aid available to victims.

● Authorized the Secretary of the Treasury to set actual interest rates for SBA and FHA loans. Rates could be up to 2 per cent lower than the prevailing market level. A ceiling of 6 per cent was set on interest rates.

● Prohibited discrimination on account of age in making disaster loans.

● Authorized the secretary of agriculture to adjust the schedule of payments of interest and principal on Rural Electrification Administration (REA) loans, and to extend the maturity of the loans for up to 40 years where damage has occurred on account of disaster.

● Authorized the SBA or FHA to make loans to businesses and industries which provided substantial employment in disaster areas and which were no longer in operation, effective Aug. 1, 1969. Loans could exceed the maximum amounts otherwise applicable. Interest rates would be 2 per cent lower than the market level, and payments could be deferred up to three years.

● Authorized distribution of food stamps and surplus commodities to poor families who could not afford food.

● Authorized the OEP to arrange for needed legal services to poor people.

● Authorized unemployment assistance for people unemployed as a result of a disaster.

● Authorized federal grants to local governments which had suffered substantial property or income tax revenue losses because of a disaster. The localities would be eligible for aid only in the year of the disaster and the following two years. Grants would be allocated on the average tax revenue base of the locality immediately preceding the disaster. (Provision was made retroactive to Aug. 1, 1969.)

● Authorized the OEP to make grants for removing damaged timber from privately owned land.

● Required that minimum standards of safety, decency and sanitation, set according to current building codes, be applied to rebuilding or repair of any housing carried out with aid loans or grants from relief organizations.

● Authorized restoration of federal facilities. If the restoration was so urgent it could not be delayed, work could begin even if sufficient funds had not yet been appropriated.

● Authorized the federal government to pay all costs of repairing or rebuilding state and local government facilities (or up to 50 per cent of facilities under construction), effective Aug. 1, 1969. Recreation facilities were excluded from this type of aid.

● Allowed the President to proclaim a six-month period in which priority in processing applications would be given to housing programs operated by public agencies

● Authorized relocation payments under the urban renewal program in certain cases to people displaced by a major disaster. (Provision was made retroactive to Aug. 1, 1969.)

● Repealed disaster relief acts of 1950, 1966 and 1969.

1972 LEGISLATION

Congress after tropical storm Agnes in 1972 rapidly moved to liberalize certain provisions of the 1970 bill.

On June 30 Congress cleared a bill (H J Res 1238—PL 92-337) making supplemental appropriations of $200-million for areas devastated by Agnes and other natural disasters. President Nixon had requested the legislation June 27 in the immediate aftermath of Agnes.

A more comprehensive bill (HR 15692—PL 92-385) was passed almost unanimously and signed into law Aug. 16. The major provisions of HR 15692 related to the most widely used disaster relief program—the low-interest disaster loans under the Small Business Administration and Farmers Home Administration. The loans permit businesses to borrow up to $500,000 for real property and individuals to borrow up to $55,000 for property and personal effects. The 1970 law had provided that these loans would have an interest rate of 2 per cent lower than the prevailing level (set by the Treasury Department) and that up to $2,500 could be cancelled.

HR 15692 provided for cancellation of up to $5,000 of an SBA loan for a disaster occurring between Jan. 1, 1972 and July 1, 1973 and set the interest at 1 per cent. It set the interest on SBA loans for disasters which occurred in 1971 at 3 per cent. It provided that Farmers Home Administration loans were to be repaid at the same interest as SBA loans, and that up to 50 per cent of a loan for a disaster since June 30, 1971, could be cancelled, not exceeding $5,000.

In other provisions affecting the SBA, the bill provided civil penalties of one and one-half times the original principal of the loan for violators of loan regulations. It gave the SBA administrator authority to suspend principal payments and interest charges for five years and authorized disaster loans for working capital as well as repair and refinancing costs. SBA loans were authorized to small businesses adversely affected by any international agreements limiting the development or installation of strategic arms facilities.

HR 15692 also authorized the President to make grants to private non-profit educational institutions damaged by hurricane Agnes, provided that the grants not be used for religious facilities.

Congressmen said it was impossible to estimate the cost of the bill. In a supplemental appropriations bill for fiscal 1973 which cleared Aug. 16 (HR 16254—PL 92-353), Congress provided $1.3 billion for SBA disaster loans and $200 million for the President's disaster relief fund.

Public Broadcasting Funds

The 91st and 92nd Congresses voted by substantial margins to provide steadily increasing assistance to noncommercial broadcasting. However, the administration failed to come up with the plan for permanent, long-range financing independent of Congress which had been promised for the Corporation for Public Broadcasting ever since it was set up in 1967.

As a result, Congress was forced to continue voting annual authorizations. In 1969 it voted $20 million for the CPB in fiscal 1970; in 1970 it provided $30 million annually for both fiscal years 1971 and 1972. In 1972 it

voted $45 million for fiscal 1973 after President Nixon had vetoed a bill providing a larger two-year authorization. In his veto message, the President objected that the CPB was becoming a "center of power" over local stations instead of serving them, and said the administration would not present a permanent financing plan for the CPB until "serious questions" were resolved.

In addition to providing funds for the CPB, Congress also voted funds to continue a 1962 program of federal grants for construction of educational television broadcasting facilities. In 1969 it authorized $15 million for that program in each of fiscal years 1971-73 and in 1972 it increased the fiscal 1973 funds by $10 million.

Background. Congressional support of noncommercial broadcasting began in 1962 when Congress cleared a bill (PL 87-447) authorizing a $32 million, five-year program of matching grants to the states for construction of noncommercial broadcasting facilities. That program was extended in 1967 with a $38 million, three-year authorization. The 1967 extension (PL 90-129) also established a framework for assisting educational broadcasting. This was the Corporation for Public Broadcasting, a nonprofit, nongovernmental corporation with a 15-member board of directors. The corporation was to make payments to local noncommercial stations to help produce local programs and meet operating costs, and to provide grants to groups for production of educational programs (such as the Children's Television Workshop, which produced Sesame Street).

PL 90-129, an administration bill, endeavored to insulate the CPB from political pressure in all areas except financing. For financing, it provided that the corporation would initially be funded through annual authorizations and appropriations; President Johnson said he would make further proposals for the corporation's long-term financing in 1968. Experts objected that the corporation should have a source of funding free of political influence from the beginning. Without permanent financing, they said, educational broadcasters would hesitate to present controversial subjects for fear of losing their financial support in Congress the following year. Many congressmen echoed this view of succeeding years, but a long-term plan was not proposed. *(1967 legislation, Congress and the Nation II p. 297.)*

1969 Action. Congress gave the administration more than it wanted for public broadcasting in 1969. The authorizing legislation (S 1242—PL 91-97), which cleared Oct. 14, provided $15 million in each of fiscal 1971, 1972, and 1973 for the program of federal matching grants for construction of noncommercial radio and television stations. It authorized $20 million in fiscal 1970 to finance the Corporation for Public Broadcasting.

The administration in testimony on S 1242 had supported the $15 million annual construction authorization but had recommended that the authorization for CPB funds be reduced to $10 million. It said that $10 million would represent a doubling of fiscal 1969 support and would be consistent with the corporation's stage of development. It said that the satisfactory long-range financing plan for the CPB, promised in 1967, had not yet been worked out.

Congress refused to go along with the administration on the $10 million reduction; a motion to that effect was defeated in the House on a 131-190 roll-call vote. The House indicated strong support for public broadcasting by passing S 1242 by a 279-21 roll call. The Senate passed the bill by voice vote and without debate.

1970 Action. Again in 1970 the administration failed to come forth with the long-term financing plan independent of congressional approval for the Corporation for Public Broadcasting. Because there was no permanent financing proposal, Congress instead Sept. 29 cleared a two-year, $30 million annual authorization for the CPB. The authorizing legislation (S 3558—PL 91-437) also provided an additional $5 million in both fiscal years 1971 and 1972 to match funds from non-federal sources for the CPB.

As initially passed by the Senate and supported by the administration, S 3558 had provided an open-ended three-year authorization for the CPB. In order to put pressure on the corporation to come up with a permanent financing plan, the House reduced the authorization to one year and conferees eventually agreed on two.

1972 Action. President Nixon June 30, 1972, unexpectedly vetoed the first bill (HR 13918) authorizing funds for the Corporation for Public Broadcasting. HR 13918 had authorized $155 million for the CPB for fiscal years 1973-74. In vetoing the bill, Mr. Nixon asked Congress to replace it with a one-year $45 million authorization for the CPB. Congress did not attempt an override; it cleared Aug. 16 a bill (S 3824—PL 92-411) which authorized the $45 million (of which $5 million was to be matched from non-federal sources) plus $10 million for grants for broadcast station facilities and equipment in fiscal 1973. The $10 million was in addition to $15 million for broadcast facilities in fiscal 1973 already authorized in 1969 by PL 91-97.

In vetoing the first authorization, Nixon said that the CPB, "originally intended only to serve local stations, is becoming instead the center of power and the focal point of control of the entire public broadcasting system." Rather than promising a long-range financing proposal, as the administration had done in earlier years, the President said serious questions remained which "must be resolved before any long-range public broadcasting financing can be soundly devised and before the statutory framework for public broadcasting is changed."

At issue in the 1972 dispute was what the Nixon administration called "communications federalism"— the relationship between national and local broadcasting organizations. The controversy had been launched in October 1971 by Clay T. Whitehead, director, White House Office of Telecommunications Policy. In a speech before the National Association of Educational Broadcasters, Whitehead said CPB was becoming a fourth national network, had placed too much emphasis on public affairs programming and was over-centralized. Whitehead further spelled out the administration position in testimony before the House Interstate and Foreign Commerce Committee on the original 1972 administration CPB proposal. That plan would have provided $45 million in fiscal 1963 with $15 million to go directly to local stations. Whitehead said the administration's concerns about public broadcasting were that:

• "The independence of the local stations has suffered because CPB has not devoted sufficient funds to station-support grants and grants for purely local program production.

• "Local station autonomy has been undercut by the CPB and PBS (Public Broadcasting Service) use of interconnection facilities to establish a fixed-schedule, real-time network....

• "Program diversity has not been enhanced, since national programs are produced or acquired in effect by CPB's inhouse production entities, which are also local broadcast stations.

• "Not enough attention is devoted to achieving two important balances: the balance between local and national programming, and the broad balance among cultural, entertainment, news, public affairs, educational and instructional programs."

Lengthy House debate on HR 13918 reflected other concerns about the CPB. The high salaries of two news commentators ($85,000 and $65,000) drew repeated attention. An attempt to limit CPB salaries to $42,500 failed after proponents learned it would not affect the most controversial employees because they were paid by affiliates of the corporation. There was also substantial debate on whether private foundations, which provided some of the funding for the CPB, had undue influence over programming.

Conservatives also expressed concern that public broadcasting had placed too much emphasis on public affairs and cultural programming at the expense of educational shows and that news programs were biased with a liberal slant, rather than balanced and objective as required by 1967 legislation that set up the corporation.

In spite of these questions, the margins for passage of HR 13918 were high. The House passed it by a 256-69 roll-call vote and the Senate passed it 82-1. Moves to reduce the authorization to one year had failed in the House by a 166-183 teller vote and in the Senate on a 26-58 roll call. The latter House vote led congressional leaders to feel they did not have the votes to override President Nixon's veto and they did not try. Instead, the second bill, S 3824, was passed quickly and almost unanimously.

Newspaper Mergers

Congress on July 15, 1970, cleared the Newspaper Preservation Act, which exempted certain operating agreements between newspapers from the antitrust laws. The bill (S 1520—PL 91-353) allowed competing newspapers in the same city to pool their printing and business operations if one of them was in danger of failing. It had the effect of legalizing existing agreements which covered 44 newspapers in 22 cities. In addition, the bill permitted similar agreements in the future if the attorney general approved.

Background. Arrangements by which newspapers in financial difficulty entered into joint operating agreements with stronger newspapers date back to 1933. By 1966 the number of such arrangements had grown to 22. In 1967 the Justice Department for the first time challenged one such agreement. It brought an antitrust suit to block the merger of two Tucson, Ariz. newspapers, the *Tucson Citizen* and the *Arizona Daily Star*. The papers had been operating under a joint agreement since 1940, and the government held that the agreement violated the Sherman Antitrust Act and a merger violated both the Sherman and Clayton Antitrust Acts.

The Supreme Court March 10, 1969, ruled the 29-year-old joint operating agreement violated the antitrust laws "beyond peradventure of doubt." It said the basic elements that made the compact run afoul of the laws were: (1) price-fixing, (2) profit-pooling and (3) market control.

Congress in 1967-68 held extensive hearings on a bill to exempt certain pooled newspaper operations from the antitrust laws but no action was taken. *(Congress and the Nation, Vol. II, p. 293)*

Interest revived after the Supreme Court decision. Committees of both houses held hearings on such proposals in 1969 and the Newspaper Preservation Act (S 1520) was reported to the Senate. In reporting the bill, the Senate Judiciary Committee found that with newspaper costs rising and advertising revenues being lost to television the situation warranted bypassing the antitrust laws.

The hearings on S 1520 revealed an unusual public conflict of views within the administration. The Justice Department and the Federal Trade Commission opposed S 1520 as unnecessary and stifling to competition. The Department of Commerce, speaking for the administration, recommended its passage. It expressed concern with a continuing trend to fewer independent newspapers and said, "S 1520 would appear to provide a means whereby that trend may be countered by permitting separate newspapers to continue in operation when a given economic situation is such that not more than one could be expected to survive in full commercial competition."

1970 Action. S 1520 was passed by the Senate by a 64-13 roll-call vote and by the House on a 292-87 roll call. The opposition, while relatively small, was vocal. Opponents charged that the bill represented a sweeping repudiation of competition in the communications industry and objected to lobbying tactics used by supporters of the bill. Chief lobbyists in favor of the bill had been the American Newspaper Publishers' Association (ANPA) and several news chains. Opponents included most newspaper labor unions and the National Newspaper Association, an organization of owners of some 7,000 small daily and weekly newspapers.

Provisions—As signed into law, S 1520:

• Declared it the public policy of the United States to preserve "a newspaper press editorially and reportorially independent and competitive" where a joint operating agreement had been or would be entered into because of the economic distress of one newspaper.

• Defined "joint newspaper operating agreement" as valid only if it included the establishment and operation of joint production facilities.

• Specified that such arrangements could not include any merger, combination, or amalgamation of editorial or reportorial staffs and that editorial policies be independently determined.

• Defined "newspaper publication" to exclude magazines and advertising circulars.

• Defined "failing newspaper" as a publication which, regardless of its ownership or affiliation, was in probable danger of financial failure.

• Exempted from prosecution under antitrust laws any joint newspaper operating agreement begun prior to the effective date of S 1520 if, when the agreement was

made, only one of the newspapers involved was likely to remain or become a financially sound publication.

• Barred interpretation of the provisions of S 1520 to exempt any predatory pricing or other predatory or monopolistic practices from prosecution under the antitrust laws.

• Required any joint newspaper operating agreement not already in effect to be approved by the attorney general before taking effect.

• Provided that any previous judgment declaring joint newspaper operating agreements illegal under antitrust laws be revised to allow reinstatement of the agreement to the extent consistent with the other provisions of the bill.

• Provided that the provisions of the bill should apply to any pending action against a joint operating agreement.

Small Business Investment Companies

Congress Oct. 12, 1972, cleared amendments to a 1958 program under which the Small Business Administration chartered and made loans to small business investment companies (SBICs). SBICs were companies which were organized to provide equity capital and long-term loans to small businesses. They received the money from private sources and from the SBA. SBA aid came in the form of long-term loans and SBA purchase of SBIC subordinated debentures. The last legislative changes in the SBIC program were made in 1967. *(Congress and the Nation, Vol. II, p. 295)*

The 1972 bill (S 3337—PL 92-595) contained many of the provisions requested by President Nixon in a special message on small business in October 1971. Its major provisions gave legislative authority to a program operated by the SBA since 1969. The program permitted federal funding for limited small business investment companies which provided capital and long-term loans to businesses owned by poor people. The special companies had been known as MESBICs (Minority Enterprise Small Business Investment Companies). The House Banking and Currency Committee, in its report on the bill, recommended elimination of the term MESBIC because it implied that only members of minority groups were eligible for this assistance; in fact the companies were to aid "persons whose participation in the free enterprise system is hampered because of social or economic disadvantages."

S 3337 provided that the SBA could subsidize the interest rate charged on the debentures issued by the limited SBICs. It also authorized the SBA to purchase preferred stock in those SBICs (preferred stock had no set repayment rate). These provisions were designed to reduced high debt-management costs which had so far hindered the program.

The bill also set up another special program. This was an SBA program of loans to handicapped persons or organizations which helped the handicapped to acquire or operate a small business. Under this program the SBA loan guarantees could be 100 per cent with repayment spread over 15 years. The SBA share of any loan would be limited to $350,000.

S 3337 also included several provisions affecting regular SBICs. It reduced to $500,000 from $1 million the level of private capital required for regular SBICs to qualify for three to one government financing. It raised to $20 million from $10 million the limit on SBA funding to a regular SBIC specializing in high risk ventures and raised from $7.5 million to $15 million the limit of SBA financing to other regular SBICs. For the first time, SBICs were allowed to invest in unincorporated businesses.

S 3337 was passed without controversy. Some of its provisions were the same as those of a broader bill (S 4316) passed by the Senate but not the House in 1970.

Small Business Loans

Congress raised the ceiling on the Small Business Administration's business loan and investment fund three times between 1969 and 1972. The over-all increase was from $1.9 billion to $4.3 billion. The fund provided money for five SBA programs—regular business loans, displaced business loans, prime contract authority, and the loan programs under the Trade Expansion Act of 1962 and Title IV of the Economic Opportunity Act of 1964. Disaster loans were financed under a separate fund.

The first increase was made in 1970 (PL 91-558) and raised the fund ceiling from $1.9 billion to $2.2 billion. In 1971 the ceiling was increased to $3.1 billion (PL 92-16), and in 1972 it was raised to $4.3 billion (PL 92-418). The increases were all requested by the Small Business Administration because of unanticipated growth in the loan program and a decline in loan repayments. They were passed without controversy.

Copyright Laws

Congress Oct. 6, 1971 cleared a bill establishing a limited copyright to prevent unauthorized duplication and piracy of sound recordings. The bill (S 646—PL 92-140) provided legal protection to producers of phonograph records and tapes. At the time of passage, it was estimated that the retail value of unauthorized reproduction of phonograph records had passed $100 million a year.

Passage of S 646 marked the first recognition in U.S. copyright law of sound recordings. Congress had begun consideration of such legislation in 1965 as part of a general revision of copyright law. The House in 1967 had passed a general bill, but controversy over some provisions, especially the question of who paid royalty fees for works used on cable television, was strong enough to prevent the Senate from acting. The cable television controversy continued during 1969-72; and Congress, therefore, continued to pass one-year extensions of the outmoded 1909 copyright law instead of a new general bill. *(Background, Congress and the Nation Vol. II, p. 282)*

Chapter 3—National Security Policy

Key Votes

In this chapter, key roll-call votes are shown in bold-face type. The party breakdown on each of these votes and the position taken by each member of Congress may be found in the key vote charts which appear in the appendix to this book.

National Security Policy

Weapons cost overruns, poor morale in the ranks, army spying on civilians and the My Lai massacre—all these problems and more made the first term of the Nixon administration a nightmare for the American military services.

Never in the nation's history—with the possible exception of the period between the First and Second World Wars—had the prestige of the men in uniform slipped so low. Both the public and press, tired of the Vietnam war and of the inflation wreaked by expanding defense budgets, took aim at the Pentagon. It was a far cry from the "Cold War" days when the military could do no wrong.

The public's discontent was manifested in Congress, which became the battleground for an annual fight over defense spending. In the end, the Pentagon was able to ride out most of the attacks by the congressional rank and file, although the public mood did lead to some self-imposed budget cutting by President Nixon and some largely cosmetic cuts by friendly congressional committees. But the cost of victory came high. The Pentagon pulled out all the stops to win—often relying more on arguments such as a possible Soviet threat and the specter of unemployment in the defense industry than it did on specific justifications for new weapons proposals.

Cost Overruns

The Defense Department's biggest problems over the first four Nixon years were the rising costs of weapon systems and weapons performance problems. Some critics of defense spending also saw many new weapons projects as militarily unnecessary, but the Pentagon always countered by pointing to a mounting Soviet threat.

Massive cost overruns—which the Pentagon preferred to call "cost growth"—were in prospect by the early 1970s on virtually every new weapons project, many of which were experiencing serious performance shortcomings. Nixon's defense planners attributed both these problems mainly to inefficient procurement practices used by the Johnson administration or, when it came to projects that the Nixon administration had initiated, to the "unknowns" of tackling new weapons concepts. But to the Pentagon's critics, the explanation hardly mattered. As they saw it, the overruns, performance fiascos and questionable justifications meant waste. And to most of these critics, they meant an unconscionable diversion of the nation's resources away from pressing domestic needs.

Even some of the military's oldest friends in Congress parted ways with the Pentagon over the weapons procurement issue. Chief among them was Sen. Stuart Symington

(D Mo.), a former secretary of the Air Force in the Truman administration and longtime Pentagon ally on the Senate Armed Services Committee. As Symington saw it, the burgeoning defense budget, which increased from $49.6-billion in fiscal 1965 to $76.4-billion in fiscal 1973, was having serious effects on the economy. "The next great struggle will be an economic war," Symington wrote in *The New York Times*, Dec. 28, 1972. "Every American should consider that, as of now, we are just as unprepared to wage an economic war as we were unprepared militarily the day before Pearl Harbor." Earlier, in a 1971 Senate floor speech, he had asserted: "One of the chief reasons why we are heading toward further financial trouble...is the fact that we are already purchasing, or planning to purchase, many weapons systems which are not necessary to our national security."

The Pentagon sought to remedy the cost problems by overhauling its procurement practices in a way that discouraged premature deployment decisions. Nixon's first-term secretary of defense, Melvin R. Laird, instituted a "fly before buy" procurement policy, under which competing contractors would build working prototypes of proposed new weapons before development contracts were awarded. But Laird's approach, defined and administered by Deputy Defense Secretary David Packard, did not seem to solve the problem. Most weapons contracts initiated by Packard, notably the S-3A Navy anti-submarine aircraft and DD-963 destroyer, encountered cost problems rivaling those of the programs Packard inherited.

Nonetheless, the Pentagon maintained enough allies in Congress to steer its budgets through in good shape. Opponents' strength crested in an August 1969 Senate showdown over the antiballistic missile (ABM) system, which critics saw as unworkable and provocative. After a long and acrimonious debate, the Senate, by a cliff-hanging 50-51 vote (with Vice President Agnew voting), upheld Nixon's request to begin deploying the $11-billion system. Equally bitter battles over other weapons followed during

References

Discussion of national security policy for the years 1945-64 may be found in *Congress and the Nation, Vol. I*, p. 237-251; for the years 1965-68 see *Congress and the Nation, Vol. II*, p. 827-890.

Vietnam developments, 1969-72, except as they affected the defense budget and weapons acquisition, will be found in the foreign policy chapter of this volume, p. 899.

the next three years, but the Pentagon never lost a major system on a floor vote. Among other weapons that critics sought in vain to scuttle were the C-5A transport aircraft, the CVN-70 nuclear-powered aircraft carrier, B-1 bomber, F-14 fighter, multiple-warhead (MIRV) missile and Trident missile-firing submarine.

Costly Weapons

An issue that constantly plagued the Defense Department in the 1969-72 period was weapons cost overruns—that is, cost growth over initial planning estimates for the weapons. On July 17, 1972, the General Accounting Office (GAO) forecast overruns at completion of $28.7-billion on major weapons projects —an increase of $7.8-billion since a similar report was issued by the GAO in December 1969. Some of the worst and projected overruns:

F-111. Original estimates for the program included the purchase of 1,726 of the supersonic swing-wing aircraft for $5.8-billion, or $3.4-million a plane. Due to steep cost increases, performance problems and cancellation of the Navy version of the plane (F 111B), the Pentagon purchased only 543 of the craft for $8.2-billion, or about $15-million a plane. The overrun was $2.4-billion for 1,183 fewer planes.

C-5A. Except for the World War II blimp, a helium filled dirigible, the Air Force had never purchased a larger flying machine than the C-5A Galaxy, a jet cargo aircraft. Original estimates for the program called for the purchase of 120 aircraft at $28.4-million per plane ($3.4-billion program cost). The GAO's 1972 estimates of program costs were $4.9-billion; the total order was reduced to 81 aircraft at a cost of $59-million per plane. Cost overruns were kept below $2-billion by reducing the number of aircraft purchased by the Air Force.

F-14. Original estimates for the F-14—the Navy's sucessor to the ill-fated F-111B, were $6.2-billion for 710 aircraft, or $8.3-million per plane. The GAO's 1972 estimates were $5.4-billion for 313 planes, or $16.8-million per plane.

A whopping overrun also occurred in the F-14's Phoenix missile component—a complex missile for fleet air defense. The original estimate for the Phoenix system was $370.8-million, the 1972 estimate $1.3-billion.

Mark-48 Torpedo. The GAO's mid-1972 figures showed a tripling of cost estimates for a new generation of Navy torpedoes, the Mark 48. Original planning estimates for the project were $720.5-million. The 1972 estimate was $2.3-billion.

Army. For the most part, Army overruns were not as bad as those of the Navy and Air Force, because most Army weapons were not as complex. Some Army missile programs showed massive overruns, however, and the worst of these were the Chapparal/Vulcan and Improved Hawk (Homing All the Way Killer) anti-aircraft missiles. Original estimates for Vulcan were $58.2-million and those for Hawk were $335.5-million. The 1972 estimates were up to $741.1 million and $846.8-million, respectively.

Contractor Bailouts. A corollary to the cost overrun issue was the question of strict enforcement of defense contracts in cases where government payment of the overruns was specifically prohibited by contract. Was the rigid enforcement of a contract worth sending a leading defense contractor reeling into bankruptcy and thus losing him as a future defense supplier and throwing thousands of employees out of work?

Congress thought not. In a 1971 fight as intense as the 1969 ABM battle, a Nixon-backed bill providing a $250-million loan guarantee for the financially troubled Lockheed Aircraft Corporation survived the Senate by a one-vote margin and the House by three votes. (Lockheed had been forced earlier that year to accept a $200-million loss, out of an expected total overrun of more than $2-billion, on the C-5A transport aircraft contract. It threatened bankruptcy unless it got the government guarantee to cover private bank loans for its L-1011, a commercial aircraft project.)

During the Lockheed debate, the bill's critics argued that the measure would establish a principle for "breadline" type handouts to giant defense contractors. By the end of 1972, it appeared that the apprehensions had been well founded. Two other leading defense suppliers—the Grumman Aerospace Corporation and Litton Industries Inc.—were pressuring Congress for bailouts on major defense contracts. Grumman had experienced overruns on the F-14 Navy fighter aircraft program, while Litton had encountered cost problems with the DD-963 and other ship contracts. *(Lockheed chapter p. 233)*

Morale and Discipline

For the U.S. armed forces, the war in Vietnam meant frustration, turmoil, and change. The military was ordered to fight an unpopular and confusing war against an elusive enemy employing unfamiliar tactics. It found that the world's most sophisticated military machine could not master the highly motivated forces of what President Johnson once called "a two-bit country."

The frustrations of Vietnam affected the armed forces in a number of ways throughout the world: rising rates of desertion and absence without leave (AWOL), drug abuse, racial tension, low morale, refusal to obey orders, and disturbing incidents of fragging—attempts by soldiers to murder each other, usually with fragmentation grenades.

Vietnam did not cause all these problems. But it made all of them worse, leaving the armed services with a badly tarnished image among the young people it depended on to fill its ranks.

One reason for morale problems was the large number of draftees sent to Vietnam. At the end of 1968, draftees accounted for 38 per cent of all American troops stationed in Vietnam. In the Army, the figure was much higher.

More than 12 per cent of the draftees were college graduates, and officers sometimes found that these educated soldiers questioned the wisdom of assignments that risked their lives. The Army also lowered induction standards, bringing in more men with disciplinary problems and resentments against authority.

Studies of the morale problem indicated that some of it was caused by simple boredom with the tasks to which troops were assigned. This became more serious after 1969, when the majority of U.S. combat troops were with-

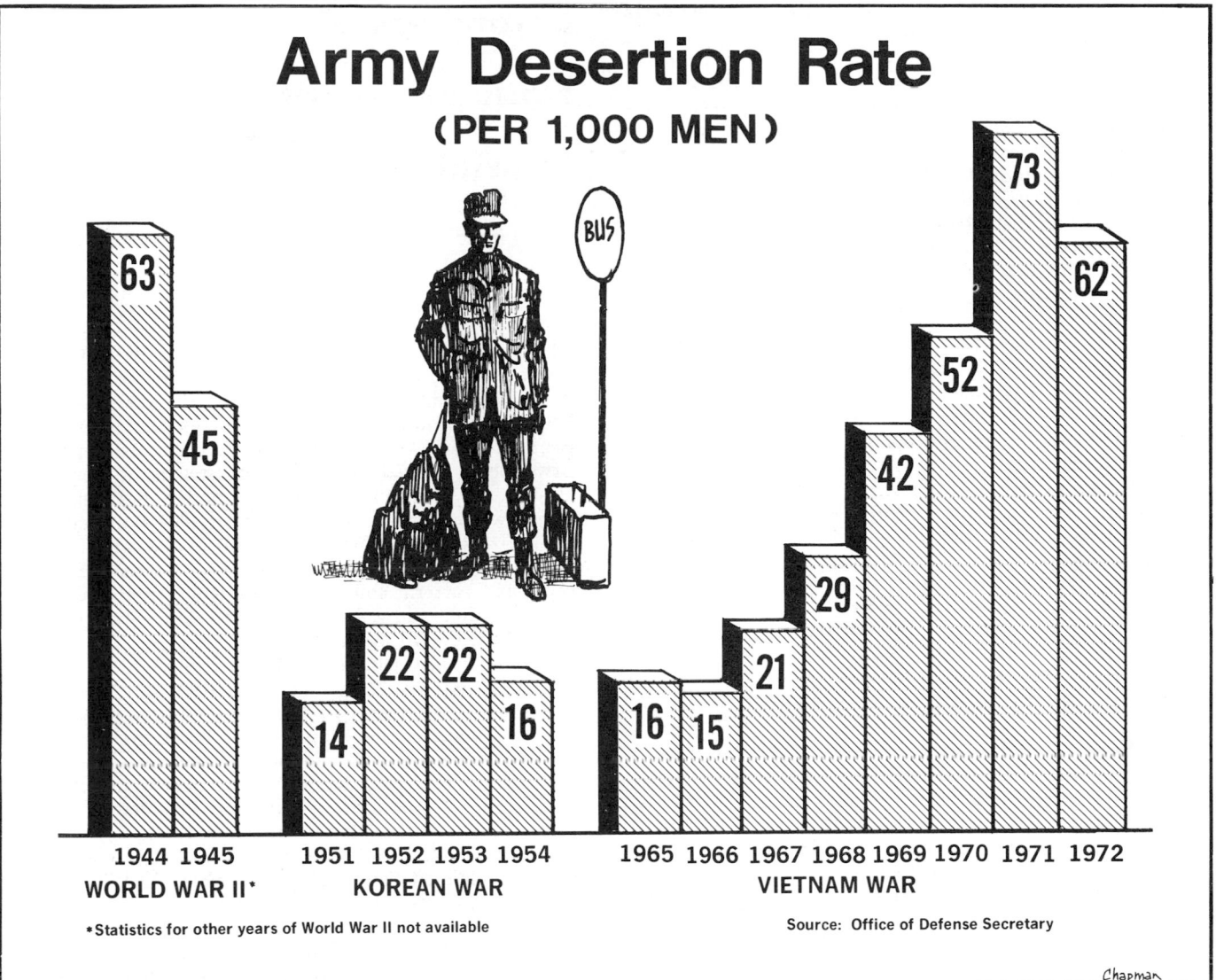

Army Desertion Rate
(PER 1,000 MEN)

| 1944 1945 | 1951 1952 1953 1954 | 1965 1966 1967 1968 1969 1970 1971 1972 |
| WORLD WAR II* | KOREAN WAR | VIETNAM WAR |

*Statistics for other years of World War II not available

Source: Office of Defense Secretary

Chapman

drawn from Vietnam and many of those remaining felt they had no particular mission to perform.

My Lai. The most serious blow to military morale during the war was the trial of Lt. William Calley, accused of murdering South Vietnamese civilians at the hamlet of My Lai in the spring of 1968. Americans at first refused to believe the massacre had taken place, then grew angry after Calley was convicted and sentenced to life imprisonment in 1971—later reduced to 20 years at hard labor. Many felt Calley was being used as a scapegoat for senior officers involved in My Lai and other incidents like it.

Evaders and Deserters. The military had an increasingly hard time coping with unauthorized absences within its ranks, and draft evasion among those it sought to induct. For many young men, particularly the college-educated, draft evasion became a way of life. They piled deferment upon deferment, schemed to obtain permanent medical exemptions, or hired attorneys specialized in selective service law to keep them out.

Some who could not win deferments fled to Canada, while others simply refused to take the one step forward that meant official induction. They went to jail. By the end of the war, it was estimated that as many as 70,000 draft evaders and deserters were living in Canada. This unhappy experience was reportedly a leading factor in a decison by President Nixon, announced in January 1973, to drop the draft in mid-1973 in favor of a highly-paid all-volunteer military force.

Drug Abuse. Drug and alcohol dependence was a problem that remained with many members of the armed forces even after their tours of duty ended. A 1971 report classified 5 per cent of all those serving in the armed forces as alcoholics. A series of reports issued by congressional committees in 1971 found that drug abuse was a problem of almost epidemic proportions in Vietnam. According to the reports, between 10 and 30 per cent of the military personnel stationed in Vietnam used drugs.

Most of the heavy users were first-term enlistees, turning to alcohol and then to drugs to relieve the stress of the combat situation. By 1972, reports indicated that the problem was declining in Vietnam as more and more troops left the war zone. But there also were reports that it was becoming worse among those stationed in other parts of the world, especially Europe.

The rehabilitative approach was thought to be losing steam in the military. The commander of the 7th Army in Germany Jan. 19, 1973, announced a return to strict discipline as the principal weapon against growing drug abuse among troops in Europe.

Racial Tension. The frustrations of black members of the armed forces came to public attention in late 1972, following racial disturbances aboard two Navy aircraft carriers. In mid-1972, blacks made up 11 per cent of the U.S. armed services, but less than 4 per cent of its officer corps in any service.

The Navy pioneered in liberalizing its rules, under the direction of Adm. Elmo R. Zumwalt Jr., chief of naval operations. But black naval officers argued that the reforms had not kept pace with the rising expectations of black enlistees enticed by a recruiting program that stressed the excitement and opportunity for advancement in a naval career.

A House subcommittee charged in January 1973 that the Navy's liberal rules had contributed to a climate of permissiveness and a breakdown of discipline that caused the two incidents. Zumwalt denied it.

Army Spying. For much of the public, one of the most shocking revelations of the first Nixon term was the 1970 disclosure of widespread Army surveillance of peace groups, politicians and other civilians who differed with the Pentagon. The spying, which the Army admitted to, aroused the enmity of another of the Pentagon's oldest and staunchest friends, Sen. Sam J. Ervin Jr. (D N.C.), whose Senate Judiciary subcommittee held lengthy hearings on the issue. In the wake of Ervin's hearings, Defense Secretary Laird ordered the spying stopped. And in a followup move, he combined all Defense Department security investigative activities in a central agency that reported directly to him instead of to the separate services for whom the investigators had worked under the previous setup.

Other Issues

The new-found respectability—and even popularity—of criticizing the military led inevitably to other unpleasant disclosures. A Senate subcommittee uncovered a massive scandal in the post exchange (PX) system in Vietnam and in other overseas areas. The same Senate panel also implicated several high-ranking military officers in an extensive black market ring and found alleged irregularities in the Pentagon's surplus equipment disposal system. And a Joint Economic subcommittee under Sen. William Proxmire (D Wis.) had a field day criticizing the administration for firing A. Ernest Fitzgerald, a high-ranking Air Force civilian, after he testified to Congress on the $2-billion cost overrun in the C-5A program.

By the end of Nixon's first term in office, a growing minority in the Senate and House were resisting the temptation to push through complicated military bills without at least a cursory examination on the floor of the implications. The longstanding, generally harmonious relationship between the Pentagon and a majority in Congress also had been shaken by foreign policy matters—the discovery of military operations in Laos about which Congress had no knowledge and the numerous bitter debates over the Indochina war.

Chronology of National Security Legislation 1969

In an abrupt break with the past, Pentagon policies in 1969 became the focus of a searching review in Congress and the target of widespread criticism on the part of the press and public. Alleged waste in the defense budget became the dominant issue in Congress and tied up the Senate for more than two months during the summer. The news media poured forth a steady stream of stories disclosing cost overruns and performance problems with major weapon systems. And revelations of atrocities by U.S. troops in Vietnam touched off a new wave of anti-war sentiment. By year's end the term "military-industrial complex"—a term coined by President Eisenhower in his 1961 farewell address and then all but forgotten—had entered the everyday vocabulary.

The defense debate had far-reaching effects, both on Congress and the Nixon administration. For one thing, Nixon and his defense planners decided on a re-examination and modification of the anti-ballistic missile (ABM) system, moving missile sites away from big cities, where there was considerable opposition to nearby missile sites. Nixon himself pared $3-billion from President Johnson's proposed fiscal 1970 defense budget, and Congress cut $5.9-billion more. "Military spending is no longer out of control," proclaimed Sen. William Proxmire (D Wis.), one of the most vigorous of the Pentagon's critics.

Despite the deep over-all cut in its budget, the Pentagon won the most significant fight of the session over a single weapons program. After a month's debate over the ABM system, the Senate rejected by a close **key 50-50 roll-call vote** an amendment to the defense procurement authorization bill which would have blocked ABM deployment. The outcome was never in question in the House, where ABM proponents won overwhelmingly. Opponents of the ABM tried again to block the system during consideration of the defense appropriations bill, but again they were unsuccessful.

The debate in Congress was decidedly bipartisan, dividing members more along conservative or liberal ideological lines than around party affiliations. Liberals argued that it was unconscionable to channel scarce resources into weapon systems that they saw as unworkable or unnecessary at a time that they thought crucial domestic social programs were underfunded. Conservative backers of Pentagon policy admitted that inefficiency and waste existed but warned against hastily thought out cuts in military spending which might wealen the nation's defense posture.

President Nixon stepped into the defense debate June 4 with a strongly worded speech at the U.S. Air Force Academy. In his address, Nixon castigated some critics of defense policy as "isolationists" and advocates of "unilateral disarmament." He defended patriotism and military strength and promised that the United States would never become a garrison or police state as some critics were charging.

But, for the most part, Nixon was a master politician on the issue, avoiding provocative statements. In addition to his cuts in Johnson's budget and his reconfiguration of the ABM system—both politically popular developments—Nixon ordered other actions that produced political mileage. He entered into arms control talks with the Soviet Union—a move that had been considered during the Johnson years but dropped after the Soviets' 1968 invasion of Czechosolvakia. And he told the Defense Department to plan for the destruction of stockpiled biological weapons and reaffirmed U.S. renunciation of the first use of lethal or incapacitating chemical weapons. These moves helped Nixon defuse the defense issue and fend off public pressures for greater budget cuts.

In another major development, the outline for administration defense policy over the next decade began to emerge in 1969 when Nixon announced his views on the respective roles of the United States and its allies in the free world defense posture.

The new policy, first outlined in a July 29 speech at Guam, then expanded on in a Nov. 3 speech on Vietnam and in a 1970 foreign policy message to Congress, stressed more self-help on the part of countries threatened by Communist aggression. As explained by the President Nov. 3, the three cornerstones of his policy—which he dubbed the "Nixon doctrine"—were:

● "The United States will keep all of its treaty commitments."

● "We shall provide a shield if a nuclear power threatens the freedom of a nation allied with us or of a nation whose survival we consider vital to our security."

● "In cases involving other types of aggression, we shall furnish military and economic assistance when requested in accordance with our treaty commitments. But we shall look to the nation directly threatened to assume the primary responsibility of providing the manpower for its defense."

Defense Budget

President Johnson's defense budget for fiscal 1970, submitted Jan. 15, 1969, estimated that the Defense Department would spend $78.5-billion in the coming fiscal year and would need new obligational authority (appropriations) of $80.2-billion. (Both the spending and appropriations figures were exclusive of military assistance, activities of the Atomic Energy Commission and defense-related functions of other agencies; the budget for these additional activities forecast $3.1-billion in spending and $2.7-billion in appropriations.)

In his budget message, the outgoing President recounted the increases in U.S. force levels and innovations in weaponry that had occurred during the past eight years of Democratic control of the White House, beginning with the Kennedy administration in 1961 and continuing through his own five years in office. The Democrats' defense program, Johnson said, had produced increases of 185 per cent in the number of nuclear weapons in the strategic alert force, 140 per cent in the payload capability of all U.S. fighter and attack aircraft, 66 per cent in combat-ready Army and Marine divisions, 326 per cent in the

(Continued on p. 198)

MIRV Controversy

Although its opponents never put the issue to a vote in 1969, one of the most heatedly debated defense topics of the year was development and testing of the multiple independently targeted re-entry vehicle (MIRV)—an innovation that would vastly improve the striking power of each U.S. strategic missile. (There were votes in 1970 in the House and in both chambers in 1971 on amendments to the defense procurement authorization bills to slow MIRV development, but the proposals were overwhelmingly defeated.)

MIRV was challenged for a variety of reasons: international relations, arms control and cost overruns. Opponents argued that once refined by testing or deployed, MIRVs—to be placed on the new Poseidon and Minuteman III missiles—would render the policing of any arms control pact impossible.

The Soviet Union had steadfastly refused onsite inspection and the United States might also, it was argued. Only onsite inspection, it was argued, could detect the number of warheads on each missile. Each Poseidon and Minuteman III, as well as the Soviet SS 9 missiles, could carry anywhere from three to 10 MIRV warheads.

In a major nuclear strategy speech April 24, Sen. Edward W. Brooke (R Mass.) called the MIRV concept "the most disturbing breakthrough in strategic weapons since the advent of intercontinental ballistic missiles" because it could create "insurmountable" inspection problems.

The MIRV deployment was seen as a new escalation in the international arms race which critics regarded as inimical to U.S. security.

Also under attack was the primary U.S. rationale for development of the MIRV—its use in penetrating a potential Soviet anti-ballistic missile system.

Another argument revolved around the possibility MIRVs might be intended for a U.S. first strike or preemptive attack against the USSR retaliatory missiles.

The MIRV program had its cost problems as well. In 1967 the Poseidon and Minuteman III MIRV programs were expected to cost a total of $3.7-billion, according to early planning estimates. The estimate released by the Pentagon June 13, 1969, forecast costs of $10-billion for the two projects.

A small group in both chambers, led by Republican members, repeatedly attacked the MIRV program and urged a U.S.-Soviet moratorium on MIRV tests. But the group, though vocal in its opposition, could never assemble enough strength in 1969 to make it worth challenging MIRV funds in a House or Senate floor vote. And its call for a MIRV moratorium went unheeded by both the U.S. and Soviet governments. MIRV deployment did become an issue at the Strategic Arms Limitation Talks (SALT), which opened Nov. 17 at Helsinki, Finland, and continued through early 1972. But although an agreement finally was reached which limited future increases in offensive nuclear weapons, it did not outlaw the MIRVs that were deployed or under construction.

Nixon's Controversial 'Safeguard' ABM System...

By far the most controversial defense issue of the 1969 session was President Nixon's plan for deployment of a "thin" anti-ballistic missile (ABM) system—dubbed "Safeguard"—to protect the nation against a Communist Chinese missile attack and U.S. offensive missiles from a Soviet nuclear assault.

No issue was debated more in Congress during the session and no other major defense program came as close to being curtailed or eliminated as did the Safeguard program. After a month's debate in the Senate during consideration of the annual defense procurement authorization bill, the Senate narrowly upheld the Safeguard plan by a **50-50 roll-call vote.** In later years, the project survived numerous other cost-cutting amendments. But it was finally cut back at the administration's own volition in 1972 as part of the U.S.-Soviet arms control agreement.

Opposition to the Safeguard system was based on contentions by some prominent scientists that the system would not work as advertised and could be easily overwhelmed by an all-out Soviet missile attack. Other critics argued that the system would merely add fuel to the arms race, because the Soviets would respond to its deployment by beefing up their offensive missile force. Administration officials contended that the system would be effective against the types of attack it was designed against, and that—at any rate—it was a valuable "bargaining chip" at the Strategic Arms Limitation Talks (SALT), that got underway with the Soviet Union late in the year.

Background

Throughout his years in office, Defense Secretary Robert S. McNamara (1961-68) vigorously opposed ABM deployment as too costly, possibly ineffective and a measure sure to provoke escalation of the arms race. But under White House orders, McNamara announced late in 1967 that the nation would deploy a limited ABM net—called "Sentinel"—which might defend effectively against the threat of a relatively unsophisticated Chinese missile attack. McNamara showed no enthusiasm for the decision, noting that it had been made on only "marginal" grounds.

Doubts over the efficacy of the system and pressures to divert more arms spending to meet pressing domestic needs combined in 1968 to spark a year-long Senate ABM debate. Although the Johnson administration won all the ABM money it sought, opponents lost one of the Senate tests by only three votes—a surprising show of strength against an administration position on a matter the White House considered vital to national security. (The issue was not as closely fought in the House, where ABM funds sailed through.) By the end of the year, widespread opposition from citizens in some of the areas where the system was to be installed had given the ABM opposition group in the Senate hope that it might be able to defeat the additional funds that would be requested for the system in 1969. *(Congress and the Nation, Vol. II, p. 869)*

1969 Developments

A bipartisan group of Senators in a series of floor speeches on Feb. 4 urged the Nixon administration to reconsider Johnson's decision to deploy the Sentinel and warned they would renew the effort to block funds for further deployment during the 1969 session. The bipartisan group secured from Sen. John C. Stennis (D Miss.) the assurance that his Armed Services Committee would closely scrutinize the Sentinel question and receive testimony from opponents of the program.

The anti-ABM forces were led by John Sherman Cooper (R Ky.), who had been in the forefront of the 1968 fight. Others siding with him were Sens. J.W. Fulbright (D Ark.), chairman of the Foreign Relations Committee, Stuart Symington (D Mo.), Edward W. Brooke (R Mass.) Jacob K. Javits (R N.Y.), George McGovern (D S.D.), Majority Leader Mike Mansfield (D Mont.), Mark O. Hatfield (R Ore.), Gaylord Nelson (D Wis.), Harrison A. Williams Jr. (D N.J.) and Claiborne Pell (D R.I.).

Nixon Safeguard Plan. President Nixon March 14 ordered the deployment of a "substantially modified" version of the controversial Sentinel anti-ballistic missile (ABM) system.

The new system, called "Safeguard," differed from Sentinel primarily in that its missile sites would be moved away from major cities and placed nearer to U.S. offensive missile bases. Nixon said the ABM net would be effective in shielding U.S. offensive missiles from a surprise Soviet attack and would thus ensure a U.S. retaliatory capability in that event. Like Sentinel, the new system would also provide an "area" defense of the entire country against a Chinese missile attack. This would be accomplished with the long-range Spartan missile, which, it was thought, would provide an effective screen against the small missile force the Chinese were expected to have in their arsenal by the mid- and late 1970s.

Nixon also said that construction of the system—to total 12 to 14 sites if fully deployed—would be in separate phases which would be dependent on the offensive threat of other countries and would be reviewed periodically. The changes in plans, he said, would create a system costing $6-billion to $7-billion, compared to an estimated $5-billion for Johnson's Sentinel plan. (Later in the year the Defense Department upped the Safeguard estimate to $11-billion.) But Nixon added that the request of $1.8-billion originally sought by Johnson for fiscal 1970 could be cut by more than half because of the modification and program stretchout. Nixon asked for deployment funds for only two Safeguard sites in fiscal 1970—around U.S. offensive missile bases at Great Falls, Mont., and Grand Forks, N.D.

Hearings. Defense Secretary Melvin R. Laird, backed by a team of Pentagon technical experts, testified extensively on the ABM system before two Sen-

...Was Sustained in 1969 on Dramatic Senate Tie Vote

ate committees in 1969—the basically friendly Armed Services Committee and the decidedly hostile Committee on Foreign Relations.

In a nationally televised hearing March 21 before the Foreign Relations Subcommittee on International Organization and Disarmament Affairs, Laird was pressed hard for answers to numerous critical questions about the new ABM net. Laird argued repeatedly that the ABM was needed as a "bargaining chip" against the Soviets in the SALT negotiations and that, failing an agreement, it would be needed to counter the growing inventories of giant Soviet SS-9 missiles— a missile Laird had cast as a "first-strike" weapon instead of a retaliatory one. "With the large tonnage the Soviets have, they are going for our missiles, and they are going for a first-strike capability," Laird said. "There is no question about that."

Senate Floor Action. From July 8 through Aug. 6, the Senate debated the administration's request for a $759.1-million authorization to begin deployment and continue research on the Safeguard system. With the outcome uncertain until the last votes were counted, the Senate Aug. 6 narrowly upheld Nixon's controversial plan.

On dramatic 50-51 and 49-51 roll-call votes, a coalition of mostly Republicans and Southern Democrats rebuffed vigorous attempts to delay or block the Safeguard proposal. The ABM votes came on an amendment by Sen. Margaret Chase Smith (R Maine) to prohibit all research and development on the Safeguard ABM system and an amendment by John Sherman Cooper (R Ky.) and Philip A. Hart (D Mich.) to allow only research on, and not deployment of, the Safeguard network.

(The 50-51 vote was explained by Vice President Agnew's "nay" vote to break the tie. However, since Senate rules provided that an amendment needed a clear majority to carry, Agnew's vote was not necessary to defeat the amendment.)

Prior to the two close votes on the issue, the Senate by an 11-89 roll call had rejected an amendment by Smith that appeared to forbid any work at all on components of Safeguard even if they related to advanced ABM systems. A last-ditch attempt to curtail the program also failed by a 27-70 vote Aug. 7.

The drama had mounted during the final week of debate on the amendments, when only four Senators had not announced how they planned to vote. They were Clinton P. Anderson (D N.M.), Warren G. Magnuson (D Wash.), Mike Gravel (D Alaska) and John J. Williams (R Del.). During the last days before the showdown, both Magnuson and Gravel declared their opposition to the Safeguard plan. Newspaper reports indicated their announcement had tipped the vote to 50 against, 48 for the plan, and two undecided.

But on the final day of discussion, the limelight shifted to Sen. Smith, the Senate's only woman member. As an avowed opponent of the Johnson and Nixon administrations' ABM deployment plans, she had been counted on to support the Cooper-Hart amendment— considered the most realistic of the attempts to curtail the ABM. But at the last minute, she denounced that proposal as a "foot-in-the-door" authorization for eventual Safeguard deployment because of the authority it provided for continued Safeguard R&D. Smith then introduced the amendment to block all work on Safeguard, which ABM proponents interpreted, despite her denials, as a move to drop all further ABM research.

After the amendment, which she said clarified her original intentions had been defeated, Smith joined the pro-ABM forces in voting against the Cooper-Hart amendment, tipping the count to 49-51. She was the only member to shift position on the two crucial votes.

House Action. ABM proponents had a far easier time in the House, defeating proposed cuts in the Safeguard program by votes of better than two to one. The main anti-ABM proposal the House considered was an amendment by Charles H. Wilson (D Calif.) to eliminate the $345.5-million for procurement of the Safeguard network. It was rejected by a 105-219 teller vote. Just before the bill was approved, the House sustained that action by rejecting, on a 93-270 roll-call, a motion to delete funds for both procurement and research on the ABM program. Consideration of the motion, introduced by Alvin E. O'Konski (R Wis.), an ABM supporter, was protested by ABM opponents, who claimed that such a proposal to cut research funds did not represent the position of most ABM critics and was merely designed to ensure a substantial vote in favor of the President's ABM proposal. House Minority Leader Gerald R. Ford (R Mich.) virtually admitted that this was the intent of the move.

Appropriations. In action later in the year on the annual defense appropriations bill, ABM opponents again sought to knock out funds for the Safeguard system but were overwhelmed by Safeguard backers. A Senate amendment by Mrs. Smith to delete all funds for the system was rejected by a 36-49 roll-call vote. And a move in the House by Sidney R. Yates (D Ill.) to knock out about half the Safeguard money was defeated by a 25-78 standing vote.

1972 ABM Treaty

The defensive missile treaty signed between the United States and Soviet Union in May 1972 limited the U.S. ABM deployment to just two sites—the one already constructed at Grand Forks, N.D., and one to be constructed in Washington, D.C. (The other ABM site already under construction—at Great Falls, Mont., was to be dismantled.) However, Congress in the fiscal 1973 defense procurement bill prohibited work on the Washington site pending development of a comprehensive site plan.

During the first Nixon term (fiscal 1970 through 1973), Congress appropriated $3.6-billion for the Safeguard net, and the Pentagon spent $2.4-billion.

Navy's fleet of nuclear-powered warships, and 900 per cent in the capability of helicopters to deploy land forces.

To continue the "momentum" of the Kennedy-Johnson defense program, Johnson's new budget emphasized deployment of the ABM system, conversion of Polaris missile-firing submarines to accommodate the new Poseidon ballistic missile and stepped-up work on modification of land-based missile forces. The budget estimated spending of $53.1-billion for activities not related to the war and $25.4-billion for Vietnam operations. The budget revealed that war costs for fiscal 1969 had increased by $3-billion over the previous January's estimate, largely due to unexpected expenses associated with repelling the Viet Cong's 1968 Tet offensive and higher personnel costs attributable to military and civilian pay increases.

In a move that reflected the impact of the country's growing defense debate, President Nixon April 15 sent Congress proposed modifications to the Johnson budget that would cut defense spending by $1.1-billion and appropriations by $3-billion for the upcoming fiscal year. Major cuts in the appropriations levels (some of which would translate into spending cuts in fiscal 1970 and some in later years) included reductions of $990-million for Vietnam military operations related to lower projected ammunition requirements and almost $1-billion in funds for ABM deployment—more than half the amount Johnson had sought. The cut in ABM money was related to Nixon's March 14 decision to modify the ABM network and stretch out its deployment schedule. Nixon did not reduce an additional $175-million that Johnson sought for advanced ABM development work.

AUTHORIZATION

The annual defense procurement authorization, which must precede the year's appropriations bill and is usually subject to only perfunctory floor debate, became the focal point in 1969 for one of the most intense legislative battles of recent years. (Prior authorization was first required in 1961 for major procurement and research items; other portions of the defense budget, such as procurement of small arms and ammunition, personnel costs and operation and maintenance money, could still be appropriated without prior authorization.)

During a two-month discussion in the Senate and a three-day battle in the House, most of the major programs in the fiscal 1970 authorization measure (S 2546—PL 91-121) were roundly criticized. Despite some close votes, however, critics were able to gain approval only for meager money cuts and non-budget-cutting amendments such as restrictions on chemical-biological warfare and studies on defense industry profits.

ABM Debate. By far the most controversial item in the bill was the ABM money—a matter that took up almost a month of Senate debate. After a bitter floor battle, the Senate Aug. 6 narrowly voted to uphold the President's ABM deployment scheme by a **key 50-50** and then a 49-51 roll-call vote. The actions left intact the entire $759.1-million request for research and the early stages of deployment on the "safeguard" ABM network— the name Nixon chose for the "thin" ABM network which Johnson had dubbed "Sentinel." *(Box p. 196)*

The tie vote came on an amendment by Margaret Chase Smith (R Maine) to prohibit all research and procurement on the Safeguard deployment but to permit con-

Defense Budgets

FISCAL YEARS 1950-1973

(in thousands)

Fiscal Year	Budget Estimates	Appropriation
1973	$79,594,184	$74,372,976
1972	73,543,829	70,518,463
1971	68,745,666	66,595,937
1970	75,278,200 [1]	69,640,568
1969	77,074,000	71,869,828
1968	71,584,000	69,936,620
1967	57,664,353	58,067,472
1966	45,248,844	46,887,163
1965	47,471,000	46,752,051
1964	49,014,237	47,220,010
1963	47,907,000	48,136,247
1962	42,942,345	46,662,556
1961	39,335,000	39,996,608
1960	39,248,200	39,228,239
1959	38,196,947	39,602,827
1958	36,128,000	33,759,850
1957	34,147,850	34,656,727
1956	32,232,815	31,882,815
1955	29,887,055	28,800,125
1954	40,719,931	34,371,541
1953	51,390,709	46,610,938
1952	57,679,625	56,939,568
1951	13,078,675	13,294,299
1950	13,248,960	12,949,562

[1] *Original Johnson request was $2.5-billion higher.*

Note: Above amounts do not include any supplemental estimates or appropriations not considered or made in the regular annual Defense Appropriation Acts.

SOURCE: House Appropriations Committee (1960-1973), Congressional Quarterly (1950-1959)

tinued work on advanced ABM systems. (The final, recorded vote on the amendment was 50-51, with Vice President Agnew joining the dissenters. His vote was anticlimatic, however, because a clear majority is needed for a proposal to carry under Senate rules.)

The 49-51 vote came later in the day on an amendment by John Sherman Cooper (R Ky.) and Philip A. Hart (D Mich.) to allow only research on, and not deployment of, the Safeguard system. Both votes were victories for the conservative coalition of Republicans and Southern Democrats. The breakdown on the Smith amendment was R: 14-29; D 36-21 (ND 31-7; SD 5-14). On the Cooper-Hart amendment it was R: 13-30; D 36-21 (ND 31-7; SD 5-14).

Other Weapons. After lengthy debate, the Senate overwhelmingly rejected amendments to cut funds for development of the Army's Main Battle Tank, procurement of the C-5A aircraft, procurement of a nuclear-powered aircraft carrier, and development of the B-1 bomber. Similar budget-cutting efforts were rejected in the House. However, the Senate did approve, and a House-Senate conference sustained, a number of non-budget-cutting amendments, including major ones setting requirements limiting chemical and biological warfare, authorizing the General Accounting Office (GAO) to conduct a study of defense contractor profits, authorizing a congressional study of the need for nuclear-powered air-

(Continued on p. 200)

Post-Vietnam War Budget Cuts Proved Illusory

In mid-1968, a new phrase—"peace dividend"—whetted the interest of members of Congress, economists, governors and mayors.

That phrase—also expressed as "peace and growth dividend"—was later termed "fiscal dividend" and "budgetary gap," but all referred to the same thing: the vision of huge federal revenues that could accumulate from cuts in military spending after the war in Vietnam was ended.

But by 1972, the vision had proved illusory. Despite a cut in U.S. troop strength in Southeast Asia from 549,500 in January 1969 to 28,000 at the end of 1972, the fiscal 1973 defense budget called for $83.4-billion in total obligational authority—$1.6-billion more than was requested in fiscal 1969. The reason: higher military pay and other benefits and funding requirements for a whole range of new weapons systems approved by the White House, including a new manned bomber, new fighters for both the Air Force and the Navy, new strategic missile systems and other weapons.

The peace dividend concept was officially laid to rest on Jan. 23, 1973—the day President Nixon announced agreement on a Vietnam peace settlement. "We are already spending the peace dividend," said presidential assistant John D. Ehrlichman. Ehrlichman said the Pentagon budget as a percentage of overall federal outlays would fall to 35 per cent in the fiscal 1974 budget. This compared to 41 per cent in fiscal 1970, the first full fiscal year of the Nixon administration.

The peace dividend had become a watchword among urban and state leaders and social planners who hoped to siphon off a cut of a fiscal windfall that had been variously estimated from $8-billion to $40-billion a year. The top figure mentioned by any U.S. government official was given by Murray L. Weidenbaum, assistant secretary of the treasury, when he wrote in August 1969, "It is easy enough to conjure up visions of so-called fiscal dividends and peace dividends totaling more than $40-billion in the year after peace is achieved."

Several analysts reviewed postwar spending after dividend hopes were spawned by a task force working for Vice President Hubert H. Humphrey during the 1968 presidential campaign, and their reports both nurtured and negated the prospects for such a bonus.

Conflicting Views. On Aug. 25, 1969, a series of conflicting reports about post-Vietnam spending emanated from the California White House. Daniel P. Moynihan, executive secretary of the Council on Urban Affairs and special assistant to the President, said existing claims on the budget would consume any defense savings.

"I think the peace dividends turned out to be evanescent, like the morning clouds around San Clemente," Moynihan told a news conference Aug. 25.

Some economists in the administration said Moynihan appeared to have used a bit of poetic license. Arthur Burns, the President's chief economic adviser, appearing at the National Governors' Conference Sept. 1, countered such pessimism by saying there had been a "little misunderstanding" of Moynihan's remarks. Burns added that if the war ended immediately, as much as $8-billion would be available for "civilian" programs.

The same day, however, President Nixon told the nation's governors, "Dreams of unlimited billions of dollars being released once the war in Vietnam ends are just that—dreams."

New Defense Costs. Many members of Congress said new military programs would soak up most of any money made available should peace come. That suspicion was reinforced when the fiscal 1970 military procurement debate ended with passage of the $20-billion defense spending authorization. Almost every item in the measure was approved, including the $11-billion Safeguard antiballistic missile system.

As it developed, Safeguard was curtailed as a result of an ABM-limitation treaty arrived at with the Soviet Union in 1972. But in the meantime, the military pushed successfully to catch up on spending for a whole series of new weapons delayed by Vietnam's priorities on the defense budget.

Despite the increases in military spending and the accompanying inflation, expenditures for civilian programs increased by a larger amount than did the military budget. One Treasury official said that "simultaneously with the $30-billion rise in defense spending due to the Vietnam war, civilian agencies of the government have increased their expenditures by $35-billion since the war began."

John C. Stennis (D Miss.), chairman of the Senate Armed Services Committee, said Aug. 1 that at least $10-billion could be cut from the defense budget "as soon as the shooting stops."

One representative disagreed; William S. Moorhead (D Pa.), spoke in March 1969 of the "defense expenditure ratchet," which he described as "a set of inertial forces that prevent defense spending from falling back to its initial level once the original rationalization for increased spending is no longer valid."

Overcoming the inertia of the defense budget depended upon whether Congress could persuade U.S. industry of convert to peacetime production instead of pressing for increased defense contracts. Through 1972, such efforts were not successful.

Nonetheless, discussion of a peace dividend continued during fiscal 1970 and 1971 when token savings of $1-billion and $2.6-billion were pared from the previous years' defense spending. But the talk died down with submission of the 1973 budget, which called for a $6.3-billion increase in the Pentagon's total obligational authority despite a further winddown of the war. The outlook in early 1973 was for even greater military spending unless Congress cut military manpower (which cost $21-billion more than in fiscal 1964) or cancelled some of the more expensive weapon systems that were moving from the drawing board to production and deployment. Neither course was deemed likely by seasoned observers of the Pentagon and Capitol Hill.

craft carriers and requiring former military officers and civilians presently involved in defense procurement matters to make financial disclosure statements.

In what was probably the major issue decided by House-Senate conferees, the two houses compromised on a House add-on of almost $1-billion to accelerate the Navy's shipbuilding program. Conferees agreed to an increase of $351.8-million above the administration request, bringing the total allotment for shipbuilding to $2.9-billion. As cleared by Congress Nov. 6, the bill authorized $20,710,502,000 for military procurement and research in fiscal 1970. The total was $1,240,458,000 less than President Nixon had sought and $915,248,000 less than the amount authorized in the 1968 session for fiscal 1969.

APPROPRIATION

Congress completed action Dec. 18 on the fiscal 1970 defense appropriations bill (HR 15090—PL 91-171) carrying $69,640,568,000, a cut of $5,637,632,000 from administration requests and $2,229,260,000 from the fiscal 1969 appropriation. The cut was the largest in a military money bill since the end of the Korean War, when Congress pared $6.3-billion from the fiscal 1954 appropriation. Together with cuts in the military construction money bill, the reductions brought the total amount slashed by Congress from Nixon's fiscal 1970 requests to $5,994,476,000.

The most significant cuts in HR 15090 were initiated by the administration itself and the House and Senate Appropriations Committees, acting in response to public grumbling over the extent of defense spending and to a government-wide anti-inflation drive. Among the major changes made by the administration were the cancellation of the Air Force's Manned Orbiting Laboratory (MOL) project (a space station in earth orbit) and the production (though not research) contract for the Army's Cheyenne helicopter. (The entire Cheyenne project was finally canceled in 1972.) Cuts for the MOL and Cheyenne—which came to about $1-billion—were in addition to the $3-billion that Nixon had sliced from the Johnson budget earlier in the year. The major cuts initiated by the appropriations committees included $2.8-billion in weapons research and procurement and $1.7-billion in personnel and operations accounts.

The main impetus for the cuts came from House Appropriations Committee Chairman George H. Mahon (D Texas), who warned the Pentagon Aug. 13 that he intended to cut the fiscal 1970 defense budget by at least $5-billion. On the day Mahon announced his budget-cutting plans, the Gallup Poll showed that 52 per cent of persons interviewed in a nationwide survey thought that the country was spending too much on defense. Mahon reportedly was influenced by this public sentiment and, as his committee's report showed later, concern over "inefficient management practices" in the Pentagon and a "great need" to cut the bill in order "to halt the erosion of the economy by inflation."

In the weeks that followed Mahon's Aug. 13 announcement, Defense Secretary Melvin R. Laird reportedly met frequently with the chairman to show him where the Defense Department could best afford the cuts. As the bill emerged from Congress Dec. 18, most of the Pentagon's new generation of weapon systems—including the Safeguard ABM, the B-1 bomber, the Air Force's F-15

fighter and the Navy's F-14 fighter-interceptor—were funded at or near the requested levels. The measure appropriated $23.2-billion for the war in Vietnam.

Military Bases Funds

Congress Nov. 21 cleared a bill (HR 13018—PL 91-142) authorizing $1,650,597,000 for military construction and family housing in fiscal 1970. Appropriations of $1,647,074,000 were made for these purposes in the fiscal 1970 military construction appropriations bill (HR 14751—PL 91-170), cleared Dec. 19. The sum appropriated was $356,844,000 less than administration requests and $153,077,000 less than the amount appropriated for the same purposes in fiscal 1969.

The appropriations bill carried the full $16.6-million the administration sought in ABM construction funds, including $14.1-million for construction, planning, operation and maintenance at the Kwajalein missile range in the Pacific and $2.5-million for improvement of the North American Air Defense Command complex at Cheyenne Mountain, Colorado, to link up with the ABM system. In its report on the bill, the House Appropriations Committee observed that an additional $279-million in carryover funds appropriated for fiscal 1969 for the old Sentinel system would be available for construction of the new Safeguard ABM deployment.

Draft Lottery

At the request of President Nixon, Congress Nov. 19 approved legislation (HR 14001—PL 91-124) giving the President the authority to institute a draft lottery system aimed at inducting 19-year-olds before older persons. The legislation, widely acclaimed by youth groups and other critics of the existing draft system, culminated a three-year battle in Congress over draft reform. On Nov. 26, the same day he signed the bill into law, Nixon issued an executive order implementing the new lottery system.

The bill had been approved overwhelmingly in Congress. It moved through the Senate by voice vote and through the House by a **key 382-12 roll-call vote.** As passed, HR 14001 overturned a section of the 1967 draft law (PL 90-40) which specifically prohibited the President from instituting a lottery system. Under the new lottery plan, the period of prime draft eligibility was reduced from seven years to one year. A registrant's period of maximum eligibility would begin on his 19th birthday and end on his 20th. Men not drafted during those 12 months would be assigned a lower priority and would be called up only in case of an emergency. *(1967 draft law, Congress and the Nation, Vol. II, p. 879)*

Mechanically, the lottery would work by scrambling all the dates of the year and then drawing them at random. The order of drafting the 19-year-olds would be established by matching their birthdays with the dates drawn. If a young man were granted a deferment at age 19 or 20 he would re-enter the prime eligibility pool when the deferment expired, taking the same place in the order of sequence as he was originally assigned. The draft still would be made by local boards acting under a quota system, but the boards would induct registrants in the order of call established by the lottery.

In a ceremony Dec. 1 at Selective Service headquarters in Washington, D.C., the first draft lottery in 27 years was held. The first birth date selected was Sept. 14. In a related development Oct. 10, the Nixon administration announced the retirement of Lt. Gen. Lewis B. Hershey, a longtime opponent of the lottery system and a combatant in may bruising battles with draft reform advocates, as chief of the Selective Service System. Hershey stepped down on Feb. 16, 1970, and was replaced by Curtis W. Tarr.

Nuclear Non-Proliferation Treaty

After four days of debate, the Senate March 13, by a **key 83-15 roll-call vote,** consented to the ratification of the Nuclear Nonproliferation Treaty (Exec H, 90th Congress, 2nd Session)—a landmark pact to ban the spread of nuclear weapons. Although the treaty had been submitted to Congress by his predecessor, Lyndon Johnson, President Nixon March 14 said he was "delighted" over the Senate's action.

The Nonproliferation Treaty consisted of a preamble and 11 articles, the most important of which were those banning the spread of nuclear weapons, providing for safeguard arrangements and ensuring nondiscriminatory access to peaceful uses of nuclear energy. The treaty, proposed June 12, 1968, by the United Nations General Assembly, was signed July 1 of that year by the United States, the Soviet Union and 60 other nations.

During the Senate Foreign Relations Committee's 1968 hearings on the treaty, several reservations had been raised. Some members contended that safeguards against proliferation would be inadequate, but administration witnesses replied that inspection would be carried out effectively under the treaty by the International Atomic Energy Agency (IAEA). Another feature which caused some concern was that the treaty had not been signed by a number of the world's leading countries, including France and Communist China—which already possessed nuclear weapons—and other potential nuclear powers, including West Germany, India, Israel and Japan. The Johnson administration contended that the nuclear "haves" among the signatories would be duty-bound not to assist the non-signing "have nots." And it expressed doubt that the French and Chinese had the desire or capability to spur proliferation of nuclear weapons.

In Senate floor debate on the treaty, discussion centered on an amendment by Sen. Sam J. Ervin Jr. (D N.C.) expressing the reservation that the United States did not obligate itself by signing the treaty to defend nonnuclear states against aggression. His proposal was rejected by a 61-30 roll-call vote.

Chemical-Biological Warfare

Concern over chemical-biological warfare (CBW) reached new heights in 1969, culminating in a Nov. 25 announcement by President Nixon that he had ordered the Army to dispose of its stockpiles of biological weapons and that he would submit to the Senate a 1925 Geneva Protocol banning first use in war of "asphyxiating poisonous or other gases and of bacteriological methods of warfare." The 1925 treaty had never been ratified by the Senate, although every previous administration had accepted its provisions as binding. *(1970 action on the treaty, p. 209)*

SALT Talks

In a move of historic importance, U.S. and Soviet negotiators opened talks in Helsinki, Finland, aimed at reaching an agreement on strategic arms limitation. The SALT talks, which began Nov. 17, 1969, were an outgrowth of years of nuclear arms escalation and international attempts to arrange some limitation to the arms race. Their immediate impetus came from a provision of the Nonproliferation Treaty (Article VI) pledging the nuclear states to pursue at an early date talks aimed at halting the arms race and eventual complete disarmament. The talks ultimately led in 1972 to the signing of two agreements— a treaty limiting each nation to two anti-ballistic missile sites and a five-year agreement placing limits on U.S. and Soviet deployment of offensive nuclear weapons. *(1972 action, p. 217)*

Several well-publicized incidents preceded the President's announcement:

• Accidental death of 6,400 sheep in Utah during March 1968. The death of the sheep was widely attributed to the testing of a deadly nerve gas agent known as VX at the Army's nearby Dugway testing facility.

• A May 7 disclosure that the Army planned to ship 27,000 tons of obsolete chemical warfare agents by train from Rocky Mountain Arsenal near Denver, Colo., and Edgwood Arsenal near Baltimore, Md., to the Naval Mountain Depot at Earle, N.J., for dumping into the Atlantic Ocean.

• A July 18 revelation that CBW agents were being transported and stored outside the United States.

That disclosure came after word leaked out that 23 U.S. servicemen on Okinawa had been treated for effects of nerve gas poisoning after an accident July 8.

Congress in action on the defense procurement authorization bill laid down a range of restraints and reviews on the development, testing, storage and shipment of chemical-biological warfare agents. But in a House-Senate conference on the bill, conferees dropped the most far-reaching proposal considered during action on the measure—a Senate amendment banning procurement of missiles or other delivery systems for lethal chemical or biological warfare agents.

Congressional opposition to the CBW program was led by Rep. Richard D. McCarthy (D N.Y.), who claimed that the United States was spending between $300-million and $500-million on CBW each year. The total cost of the program remained classified, however. It had been hidden and spread throughout the defense budget for years.

My Lai Massacre

Reports of an alleged massacre of more than 100 Vietnamese civilians by a U.S. Army unit in South Vietnam precipitated public indignation and triggered a congressional investigation late in 1969.

Reports of the alleged massacre, first disclosed by journalist Seymour M. Hersh of Dispatch News Service, painted a grim picture of slaughter of women and children at My Lai Village, Quang Ngai Province, South Vietnam, on March 16, 1968. Following Hersh's report, the House

Background of Geneva Protocol on Chemical-Biological Warfare

The Senate first ratified a ban on "the use in war of asphyxiating, poisonous or other gases" in the aftermath of the First World War. That language was contained in Art. 5 of the 1922 Washington Treaty, which never came into effect because France rejected it. The same language was then incorporated in the Geneva Protocol of 1925 which also banned "the use of bacteriological methods of warfare." The Senate Foreign Relations Committee approved the treaty, and it was debated on the Senate floor for one day in December 1926, but no vote was taken.

The protocol was returned to the Foreign Relations Committee, where it remained until 1947 when it was sent back to the State Department along with several other old treaties, as part of a committee "housecleaning."

On Sept. 3, 1959, Rep. Robert W. Kastenmeier (D Wis.) introduced a resolution (H Con Res 433) calling for reaffirmation of "the longstanding policy of the United States that in the event of war the United States shall under no circumstances resort to the use of biological weapons or the use of poisonous or noxious gases unless they are first used by our enemies." No action was taken, however, and the Departments of Defense and State opposed the resolution.

The issue was not revived until 1969, when Congressional criticism of U.S. chemical-biological warfare (CBW) programs intensified. In April, J. W. Fulbright (D Ark.), chairman of the Senate Foreign Relations Committee, urged President Nixon to resubmit the treaty.

The protocol, which came into force on Feb. 8, 1928, had been ratified by 84 nations (including the Soviet Union). Several signatories added reservations that they did not consider themselves bound to apply the provisions to nonsignatory countries. Among the major powers, only the United States and Japan had not ratified the pact.

The production and use of CBW agents had been the subject of controversy in recent years, much of which resulted from the U.S. use of tear gas and herbicides in Vietnam. U.S. officials insisted that the use of such non-lethal agents did not violate the 1925 Geneva Protocol which although not ratified by the United States had been accepted as binding by prior administrations.

Nixon Statement. Shortly after entering office, President Nixon ordered the National Security Council to conduct a thorough review of CBW activities.

The result of this White House study was an announcement by Mr. Nixon Nov. 25, 1969, repeating the vow that the United States would never be the first to use chemical weapons and renouncing the use in any form of biological weapons. He said that in the future U.S. activities would be restricted to defensive operations. And he asked for the Senate's approval of the 1925 Geneva treaty. On the treaty, he said he had asked congressional leaders "to expedite" action.

Another portion of the statement expressed U.S. support for a pending British proposal at the Geneva disarmament conference for a ban on biological weaponry.

Despite the President's attempt to clarify the U.S. policy, his decision left some questions unanswered and stimulated some controversy.

First, related statements by another White House official at a background briefing indicated the administration was holding fast to its belief that tear gas and defoliants, which U.S. forces were using in Vietnam, were not prohibited by the treaty. This interpretation brought instant comments from Capitol Hill. Senate Foreign Relations Committee Chairman Fulbright said the issue needed to be "clarified." Rep. Richard D. McCarthy (D N.Y.), who had crusaded against U.S. CBW policies, observed that most signatories to the 1925 treaty felt it covered tear gas and defoliants.

In December 1969, the United Nations General Assembly adopted a resolution by an 80-3 vote, with 36 abstentions, stating that the Geneva Protocol prohibited all chemical agents, a move aimed directly at the U.S. activities in Vietnam. Voting in opposition were the United States, Australia and Portugal.

Another issue the President did not immediately resolve was whether his ban on biological agents involved toxin weapons. Toxins are the dead but poisonous by-products of bacteria, which can produce such diseases as botulism, diphtheria, food poisoning and typhoid.

Mr. Nixon did clear up that controversy Feb. 14, 1970, when he renounced operations in the offensive use of toxins and confined U.S. activities on toxins to defensive research. And he cleared up the tear gas and defoliant controversy Aug. 19, 1970, by asking the Senate to add a reservation to the treaty stating that its provisions did not cover the two chemicals. That reservation proved controversial, however, and the treaty consequently remained pigeonholed in the Senate Foreign Relations Committee through the end of 1972.

and Senate Armed Services Committees held closed hearings Nov. 26 on the incident and a House Armed Services special investigating subcommittee continued hearings Dec. 9-10.

The hearings were suddenly canceled Dec. 11 by Committee Chairman L. Mendel Rivers (D S.C.), who expressed doubts as to the authenticity of reports of the massacre. But Rivers promised further hearings in 1970 and set up a special panel to continue the probe.

The first press report of the massacre came Nov. 13, when Hersh wrote that the Army had drawn up six specifications of murder against 1st Lt. William L. Calley Jr., whose unit had conducted the My Lai raid. (Calley was a platoon leader in C Company, 1st Battalion, 11th Infantry Brigade, of the Army's American Division.) Hersh cited eyewitness accounts of Calley's subordinates testifying that the massacre could have been avoided despite Calley's professed belief that the village harbored hard-core Viet Cong and orders he had received to kill "every living thing" in the village.

President Nixon Dec. 8 denounced the alleged massacre but argued that the incident should not reflect on the conduct of the majority of Americans stationed in Vietnam. "What appears was certainly a massacre," he told a White House news conference. "Under no circumstances was it justified.... I believe that it is an isolated incident. Certainly...we are doing everything possible to find out whether it was isolated and so far our investigation indicates that it was."

Fitzgerald Firing

Another heated controversy of 1969 was the Pentagon's firing of A. Ernest Fitzgerald, deputy for management systems in the office of the assistant secretary of the air force, following Fitzgerald's testimony to Congress in 1968 on cost overruns in the C-5A transport aircraft program. *(Congress and the Nation, Vol. II, p. 856)*

On Nov. 4—almost a year after his testimony—the Defense Department disclosed that Fitzgerald's post was being abolished as a budgetary move. On the same day, the Air Force hired as a consultant a partner in an accounting firm that had held contracts with the manufacturer of the C-5A, the Lockheed Aircraft Corporation, and assigned him duties once held by Fitzgerald. After vigorous criticism from Sen. William Proxmire (D Wis.) and Rep. William S. Moorhead (D Pa.), the Air Force Nov. 7 announced that the $107-a-day consultant, John J. Dyment, would not be hired after all.

Fitzgerald was first catapulted into prominence Nov. 13, 1968, when he confirmed Proxmire's estimate of a $2-billion cost overrun in the C-5A program. Shortly after he testified, Fitzgerald was told that a notification he had received a few weeks earlier stating his job was protected by Civil Service regulations was a "computer error" and that his job was not protected. Later, Proxmire obtained a report to the air force secretary by a top subordinate listing ways to force Fitzgerald from his Pentagon job.

Nonappropriated Funds

Nonappropriated funds were self-generating supplies of money used by the military to supplement appropriated funds in financing major recreational and consumer programs within the armed forces. Two of the largest revenue-generating programs for the military's nonappropriated fund activities had been the post exchange (PX) system and open messes (restaurants and bars).

The armed forces exchange system ranked as the third largest American department store with gross sales of $3.3-billion for the year ending Jan. 25, 1972. Only Sears, Roebuck and Company with $10.9-billion in gross sales and J.C. Penney with $4.8-billion in gross sales were larger than the PX system.

Military clubs and open mess facilities, which provided the services of a bar and grill plus entertainment, had gross sales of $625-million in calendar year 1971.

SOURCE: Defense Department; Sears, Roebuck and Company, and J.C. Penney Company.

Fitzgerald's firing touched off a wave of press criticism and a stormy two-day hearing before the Joint Economic Subcommittee on Economy in Government. Amid the Fitzgerald controversy, the Air Force Nov. 15 announced a decision to buy only 81 instead of the 120 C-5As it had originally planned to purchase. The service cited "budget constraints" as the reason for its change in plans.

Service Clubs Scandal

Senate hearings on alleged improprieties and profiteering in the operation of servicemen's clubs around the world and on alleged black market currency operations in Vietnam also drew headlines in 1969.

The probe, conducted by the Senate Government Operations Committee's Permanent Subcommittee on Investigations, with Sen. Abraham A. Ribicoff (D Conn.) serving as acting chairman, lasted for eight weeks from late September through late November. During that time, witness after witness unveiled a spectacular picture of misuse of Army non-appropriated funds by high-ranking officers and non-commissioned officers associated with service clubs and a complicated and often bizarre currency racket in Vietnam that was reported to have involved more than $150-million a year.

The fireworks began before the probe officially opened, following a secret five-month investigation by the subcommittee staff. On Sept. 4, retired Maj. Gen. Carl C. Turner, former provost marshal of the Army, resigned from the post of chief of the United States marshals to which he had just been appointed by President Nixon. His resignation was unofficially attributed to inaction in the face of charges of improprieties while he was the Army's chief law enforcement officer. A day later the Defense Department withdrew a Distinguished Service Medal it had awarded to Sgt. Major William O. Wooldridge, who had been named in 1966 to the post of sergeant major of the Army—the services' top enlisted post. It was reported that the action had some connection with the probe of service clubs.

Both Turner and Wooldridge were implicated during the Senate hearings. There was testimony that Turner allegedly had halted an inquiry into Wooldridge's activities and also that he allegedly had obtained without charge in the United States about 700 police-confiscated weapons by signing receipts saying the guns were for U.S. Army use. He then admittedly sold some of them to a dealer for his own profit. (A federal court in 1971 convicted Turner of income tax evasion and violation of the Federal Firearms Act; it sentenced him to a year's imprisonment and a $25,000 fine; with the trial of Wooldridge still pending in a federal court, the army Feb. 1, 1972 allowed him to retire with full pension.)

In hearings on the service clubs issue, Ribicoff and the staff's eight-month probe indicated that small groups had gained control of the servicemen's clubs in some areas and had become involved in improprieties, corruption and kickbacks. He noted that these clubs were major unregulated economic enterprises involving millions of dollars each week all over the world.

Ranking minority member Karl E. Mundt (R S.D.) added that the corruption had been so brazenly conducted with no official action against it that "the situation certainly suggests a coverup at high military levels."

Other Developments

Joint Economic Committee Probe. The Joint Economic Subcommittee on Economy in Government Dec. 23 climaxed a year of aggressive inquiry into alleged waste and inefficiency in military procurement with recommendations which included a $10-billion reduction in defense spending.

The panel's report, "The Military Budget and National Economic Priorities," drew its conclusions from hearings throughout the year that were conducted by Sen. William Proxmire (D Wis.), the subcommittee chairman. These conclusions and recommendations were rejected in part, however, by the four Republican members of the panel in supplementary views accompanying the report. In addition, Rep. Wright Patman (D Texas), chairman of the full committee, stated he did not wish to take a position on the issues.

The report stated that the testimony it had gathered disclosed substantial "fat" in a defense budget characterized by lack of controls or fiscal restraints and by over-optimism in forecasts and cost estimates for major weapon systems.

Procurement Commission. Congress Nov. 13 completed action on legislation (HR 474—PL 91-129) creating a commission to study the federal government's procurement policies and practices. The bill established a 12-member panel, composed of the U.S. comptroller general; six members selected by the President of the Senate and Speaker of the House (including one member from each party in each chamber and two from outside government), and five members selected by the President (two from the executive branch and three from outside the government). The commission was charged with making a two-year investigation of government procurement with a view toward reforming regulations, eliminating waste, duplication, and inefficiency and cutting costs. The commission was granted subpoena power and an open-ended authorization for as much money as was needed for staff and investigations. It received an extension of time and was expected to release a final report in 1973.

Wheeler Reappointment. Congress May 19 cleared the way for reappointment of Gen. Earle G. Wheeler as chairman of the Joint Chiefs of Staff. The legislation (S J Res 104—PL 91-19) amended a law (PL 81-216) restricting the chairman to two two-year terms except during a congressionally declared war. President Nixon had requested the legislation in order to reappoint Wheeler to an additional year—his sixth. A similar waiver, providing for Wheeler's reappointment for a fifth year, was approved in 1968. Both bills applied only to Wheeler. *(Congress and the Nation, Vol. II, p. 858)*

1970

As in 1969, the issue of waste in the defense budget dominated the year's debate over national security policy. And the outcome, after another session of congressional in-fighting, was much the same as it was in 1969—a few anxious moments for Pentagon planners in fending off attacks on their new weapon systems, followed by a large measure of success for them when the showdown finally came.

As it had the year before, the Nixon administration stole much of the critics' thunder by imposing defense cuts of its own—in areas where it could best afford them. The Defense Department's fiscal 1971 budget called for appropriations of $70.8-billion—almost $10-billion less than President Johnson had sought for the previous fiscal year, and $7-billion less than Nixon himself had sought; Defense Secretary Melvin R. Laird repeatedly characterized his spending plan as a "rock-bottom budget," and he used that term effectively to dissuade Congress from voting any further significant budget cuts.

The one major victory for Pentagon critics came when Congress adopted an amendment to deny a presidential request to start work on a nationwide "area" ABM defense, aligned against Communist China, and to limit the present deployment to a Soviet-oriented defense of Minuteman offensive missile sites. Although the move entailed a cut of only $10-million (only site survey money had been requested for the "area" defense), the amendment did put the administration on notice that it faced hard bargaining with Congress before it could expect any future expansion of the controversial ABM net.

As a further elaboration of the 1969 Nixon Doctrine, the President said in a Feb. 18 foreign policy message to Congress that he was abandoning the Johnson administration's planning concept of programming the armed forces to fight "two and a half wars" simultaneously. Nixon reduced the plan to a "one-and-a-half war" strategy —a strategy "for simultaneously meeting a major Communist attack in either Europe or Asia, assisting allies against non-Chinese threats in Asia, and contending with a contingency elsewhere." Johnson had sought to prepare the military to fight major wars simultaneously in Europe and Asia and to be ready for a contingency somewhere else. Nixon said Johnson had never attained the force levels necessary to make such a strategy work.

In other defense developments, a House Armed Services subcommittee resumed its investigation of the My Lai massacre, culminating in a report charging a division-level "cover-up" of events surrounding the 1968 raid. The Pentagon also was embarrassed by revelations that the Army had conducted massive surveillance of civilians whom they considered potential—if not actual—participants in political protest movements.

President Nixon sought further reform of the draft system in 1970, but Congress put off action until 1971. The President did achieve a measure of reform, however, when he moved by executive order to end occupational and parental deferments for draft-eligible youth.

In other action, a Senate investigating subcommittee conducted a much-publicized investigation of the F-111 (formerly TFX) aircraft program, but the outcome was little more than an expression of the subcommittee's discontent with the procurement policies of former Secretary of Defense Robert S. McNamara, architect of the F-111 program. Despite periodic groundings by the Air Force, procurement of the controversial plane went on through fiscal 1973, when the buy was completed.

Defense Budget

As part of the first federal budget prepared fully under his direction, President Nixon Feb. 2 outlined a defense program for fiscal 1971 calling for $71.2-billion in spending and $70.8-billion in appropriations.

The requests represented cuts of $5.8-billion in spending and $500-million in appropriations from the actual fiscal 1970 levels. The reductions were seen both as a ploy to discourage congressionally initiated cuts and as part of an effort to reduce over-all government spending in order to dampen inflationary pressures in the economy.

The new budget, the President said, would provide for procurement "of carefully selected weapons systems and for a prudent research and development program designed to assure our future military strength." Nixon said the cuts could be made because of plans to retire "ineffective" and "expensive" older weapon systems such as the SAGE anti-bomber system and to reduce manpower in line with efforts to wind down the war in Vietnam. (The budget did not break down expected war costs, but news leaks put the figure at $17-billion.)

Indications that the days of reduced defense budgets would be short-lived, however, came in Defense Secretary Laird's annual defense posture statement to Congress, which characterized the 1971 program as an "austere" and "transitional" program. The Soviet Union, in not making corresponding cuts, he said, was "pulling abreast of us in many major areas of military strength and ahead of us in others." If the Soviet build-up continued, he added, "we will need additional costly steps to preserve an efficient deterrent."

AUTHORIZATION

For the second year in a row, the annual defense procurement and research authorization bill (HR 17123—PL 91-144) became the year's main focal point for floor fights over Nixon's defense budget.

In addition to moves to cut weapon systems, attempts were made to restrict U.S. and allied operations in Southeast Asia and to cut off funds for the Vietnam war altogether. All these amendments were rejected, most of them overwhelmingly. However, Senate critics of the war made a respectable showing when they lost by a **39-55 key roll-call vote** on an amendment by George McGovern (D S.D.) and Mark O. Hatfield (R Ore.) to set a deadline of Dec. 31, 1971, for the complete withdrawal of U.S. troops from Southeast Asia. *(Vietnam policy chapter)*

As it emerged from Congress, the only significant changes in the bill were initiated by the House and Senate Armed Services Committees. These included authorization of an additional $435-million over administration requests for Navy shipbuilding, written into the bill by the House committee, and a cutback in the President's program for expansion of the ABM system, initiated by the Senate panel.

The restriction on ABM expansion was one of the more significant military policy moves made by Congress in recent years. The Senate committee dropped $10-million requested for site surveys at five sites to be used in a nationwide "area" defense and approved work on only two additional batteries—at Sedalia, Mo., and Cheyenne, Wyo., for protection of U.S. offensive missiles.

But despite the curtailment of the system, ABM opponents in the Senate failed narrowly for the third straight year to delete the ABM authorization. An amendment by John Sherman Cooper (R Ky.) and Philip A. Hart (D Mich.) to block ABM expansion was rejected by a **47-52 key roll-call vote.** *(Vote changes, box this page)*

Vote Changes on ABM

Six Senators changed their stance on the ABM issue between 1969 and 1970, as reflected by their votes on the Hart-Cooper amendments in both years.

On Aug. 6, 1969, the Senate voted on an amendment by the two Senators to provide funds only for research and development of an antiballistic missile system other than Safeguard and to bar deployment funds for Safeguard. That amendment was rejected 49-51. Other Hart-Cooper proposals against the Johnson Administration's Sentinel system in 1968 had been rejected by 28-31 and 34-52 roll calls.

The following Senators changed their position on the Hart-Cooper amendment in the 1970, 47-52, vote:

From Opposition to Support
Republican Margaret Chase Smith (Maine) and Democrat John O. Pastore (R.I.)

From Support to Opposition
Republicans Marlow W. Cook (Ky.) and James B. Pearson (Kan.)

Democrats Howard W. Cannon (Nev.) and Thomas J. McIntyre (N.H.)

Republican Karl E. Mundt (S.D.), who opposed the amendment in 1969, did not vote in 1970 because of illness.

As cleared, HR 17123 authorized appropriations of $19,929,089,000 for defense procurement and research and development in fiscal 1971, including $1.9-billion in ABM money. The total approved in the bill was $646,400,000 less than administration requests and $781,413,000 less than the amount authorized for the same purposes in fiscal 1970.

APPROPRIATION

Congress Dec. 29 cleared for the President a bill (HR 19590—PL 91-668) appropriating $66,595,937,000 for the Defense Department in fiscal 1971—the smallest amount voted for defense since fiscal 1967.

The bill's lower price tag reflected Nixon's self-imposed defense cuts more than it reflected paring by Congress. Nixon himself had asked for $7-billion less than he had sought for fiscal 1970. Congressional cuts in the bill came to $2,149,729,000—less than half the $5.6-billion Congress had cut from the fiscal 1970 measure. The final amount appropriated was $3,044,631,000 less than the total provided in the defense appropriations bill for the year before.

Major controversies on the bill included a dispute between House and Senate conferees over restrictions on troop deployments in Cambodia, a House controversy over the F-111 aircraft program and a Senate hassle over Pentagon public relations programs. House debate also featured an outburst of animosity—rarely seen in public between the powerful chairmen of the Armed Services and Appropriations Committees, L. Mendel Rivers (D S.C.) and George H. Mahon (D Texas).

The dispute over the Cambodia provision delayed congressional adjournment for two weeks and was resolved only when conferees took the unusual step of writing a second conference report. The House had adopted the first report Dec. 16, but liberal Senators had blocked a vote on it because of a House-added provision which they thought would nullify language in the supplemental foreign aid appropriations bill prohibiting the entry of U.S. troops into Cambodia. Finally, the Senate tabled the first report on Dec. 28, and a second conference was hastily devised for the following day. Agreement on a report dropping the House proviso was reached on the first day of the new conference, and both houses ratified the conference actions.

The House debate on the F-111 centered on an amendment by William E. Minshall (R Ohio) to knock out $548-million in procurement money for the controversial aircraft. Minshall and other opponents of the program pointed out that another F-111 had crashed the previous day (Oct. 7) and that most of the planes had been grounded. The Minshall amendment was rejected by a 28-89 standing vote after House Armed Services Committee Chairman Rivers and several members of the Texas delegation (the plane was built in Ft. Worth) argued that the F-111 had a better safety record than most other aircraft at a comparable stage of development.

But the highlight of House debate on the bill was an abrupt and heated exchange between Rivers and Mahon over defense policy. Rivers criticized Mahon's strong statements alleging Pentagon mismanagement. And he urged the Appropriations chairman to retract some of his comments. The record of the Rivers-Mahon colloquy was expunged from that day's *Congressional Record*.

In the Senate, most of the debate on HR 19590 focused on an amendment by J. W. Fulbright (D Ark.) to place a limit of $20-million on funds for publicity and public relations activities by the Defense Department. The amendment, to reduce the limit from the committee-proposed level of $30.4-million, was rejected by a 44-46 roll-call vote.

Fulbright, author of a book on the subject, *The Pentagon Propaganda Machine* (1970), said that funds for publicity had increased fifteenfold. Opponents of his amendment countered that spending for such purposes had been scaled down from a $44.1-million level in fiscal 1969 and that the Appropriations Committee had put the Pentagon on notice that the next fiscal year's funds would be slashed to $28-million.

Major items funded in HR 19590 as the bill cleared Congress included more than $1-billion for the Safeguard antiballistic missile system; $932-million for the Navy's F-14 fighter; $921-million for the Navy's Poseidon missile program, $898.5-million for the Air Force Minuteman missile system; $622-million for the Air Force C-5A transport plane and $562.7-million for the F-111 aircraft. Funds for Vietnam operations included $358.5-million for President Nixon's Vietnamization program. During House floor debate, Mahon said that the exact cost of the war for fiscal 1971 was classified by the Pentagon. But estimates emerging from Capitol Hill and the Pentagon placed the figure at between $15-billion and $20-billion annually.

Military Bases Funds

Congress Oct. 14 cleared the annual military construction authorization bill (HR 17604—PL 91-511), authorizing $1,667,154,000 for base construction and mili-

tary family housing for fiscal 1971. In the fiscal 1971 military construction appropriations bill (HR 17970—PL 91-544), approved Nov. 25, Congress voted $2,037,814,000 for the same activities. The amount appropriated was larger than that authorized because some items in the appropriations bill did not require prior authorization. These included funds for access roads, planning, minor construction projects and programs which had been authorized under earlier bills.

The largest items funded under the appropriations measure were $357-million for construction of additional Safeguard ABM sites; $716-million for military family housing and $25-million for construction in Vietnam. Together with ABM money in the defense appropriations bill (HR 19590), the construction allotment brought total Safeguard appropriations for the year to about $1.4-billion.

Fitzhugh Commission Report

A wide range of organizational and management changes were recommended to the Pentagon by a blue ribbon panel of defense experts in 1970, but its key recommendation was ignored. The panel, commissioned by the White House and headed by insurance executive Gilbert Fitzhugh, sent shock waves through the offices of the Pentagon's top brass by recommending that the Joint Chiefs of Staff be relieved of day-to-day military operations in favor of a new staff headed by a single military officer. Over the next several years, however, the Pentagon did implement several panel recommendations calling for less controversial changes, such as addition of a second deputy secretary of defense.

Draft Developments

A presidential commission Feb. 21 recommended institution of an all-volunteer army and elimination of the draft before expiration of the existing Selective Service law on June 30, 1971.

The commission, headed by former Defense Secretary Thomas S. Gates Jr. (1959-61) proposed pay increases, increased recruiting efforts and improvement of the management of the armed services in order to make a successful transition to an all-volunteer force.

But while Nixon had advocated the all-volunteer concept in his 1968 election campaign, he declined to push for implementation of the Gates recommendations in 1970. During consideration of the annual defense procurement authorization bill (HR 17123), an effort was made in the Senate to implement the Gates proposals, but the move failed when the President withheld his support. The amendment, introduced by Barry Goldwater (R Ariz.) and Mark O. Hatfield (R Ore.), was rejected Aug. 25 by a **key 35-52 roll-call vote.**

In another development, President Nixon April 23 called for far-reaching draft reform, including proposals to restore the President's authority (withdrawn by Congress in 1967) to suspend deferments for students seeking undergraduate degrees, to establish a direct national draft call which would replace the existing local board quota system (under which youths with lower lottery numbers in high-quota areas were sometimes drafted ahead of youths with higher numbers in lower quota areas), and to provide a 20-per-cent pay increase for enlisted men with less than two years of service, effective Jan. 1, 1971. Congress deferred action on Nixon's entire package until 1971. But in a move that did not require prior approval by Congress, Nixon issued an executive order April 23 that ended all occupational deferments and most paternity deferments. The only exception for paternity would be cases of "extreme hardship," as determined by local draft boards.

My Lai Investigation

After a seven-month probe, a special investigating subcommittee of the House Armed Services Committee charged July 15 that a massive and planned "cover-up" by responsible Army officers had suppressed information about the My Lai massacre of 1968.

The four-man subcommittee, under Rep. F. Edward Hebert (D La.), also criticized the Department of the Army for what it called a lack of cooperation during the investigation. And it questioned the sanity of U.S. servicemen involved in the My Lai raid, which resulted in the deaths of more than 100 Vietnamese civilians. Concerning the alleged killings, the panel observed that the incident was "so wrong and so foreign to the normal character and actions of our military forces as to immediately raise a question as to the legal sanity at that time of those men involved."

The panel in its 53-page report placed the blame for the cover-up on officers of the Americal Division (parent unit of Lt. William L. Calley's platoon) and on U.S. civilian and military advisers to the South Vietnamese forces. The report found that numerous officers of the division, including its commanding general and chief of staff, had received reports of the alleged massacre but had failed to pass them on to the Military Assistance Command Vietnam (MACV), the highest U.S. command in the war zone. And it found that the matter had been reported to U.S. district and province advisers, who also had squelched the reports.

"To keep the My Lai matter bottled up within the American Division and the district and province advisory teams", the report said, "required the concerted action or inaction on the part of so many individuals that it would be unreasonable to conclude that this dereliction of duty was without plan or direction."

The My Lai investigation led to a heated dispute between the subcommittee and the Department of the Army, which claimed that the probe could prejudice future courts-martial in the My Lai case. The panel resisted alleged Pentagon pressure that it withhold its report, but it did agree to keep the hearing transcript secret.

During 1970, court-martial proceedings were instituted against three servicemen involved in the My Lai raid. Charged and brought to trial in 1970 were platoon leader Calley, Staff Sgt. David M. Mitchell and Sgt. Charles E. Hutto. Sgts. Mitchell and Hutto were acquitted of the charges of assault with intent to commit murder, but the trial of Lt. Calley was not completed until 1971.

To deal with similar situations in the future, the subcommittee in its report recommended that a test of sanity be required in military capital offenses, that dissemination of pre-court martial publicity be prohibited,

Drugs At My Lai

Shortly after testifying before the Senate Juvenile Delinquency Subcommittee investigating drug abuse by U.S. soldiers in Vietnam, a former serviceman whose letters to 30 government officials in the spring of 1969 sparked the Army's investigation of the alleged My Lai massacre accused the subcommittee of "stacking the evidence" to show that the My Lai incident was caused by marijuana.

Ronald Ridenhour told reporters he thought the Senate subcommittee, chaired by Thomas J. Dodd (D Conn.), "didn't want anyone to disagree with the impression they were trying to make" that many of the soldiers involved in the alleged massacre were high on marijuana.

As Ridenhour was testifying, the Pentagon issued a statement claiming that, although drug abuse had become a serious problem in South Vietnam, there was no indication that marijuana had any connection with the alleged massacre. The statement said the Army's investigation "developed no evidence that any unit engaged in the Song My operation was under the influence of marijuana or other narcotics."

Ridenhour agreed with the Army's conclusion, and added that "many, many Americans are looking for any reason other than a command decision" for the alleged massacre. Dodd's subcommittee, he said, was looking for that excuse.

He said he wanted to disagree with previous testimony heard by the subcommittee that drugs could have influenced the actions of soldiers involved in the My Lai incident, but that Sen. Dodd avoided asking him any direct questions on My Lai. "It would have been out of order to bring it up," Ridenhour said.

The night before he testified, he talked to subcommittee staff members, who assured him there would be no attempt to make a connection between drugs and My Lai. "They knew I disagreed with the thrust" of what the subcommittee was trying to accomplish, he said.

The Vietnam veteran pointed out that the attack on My Lai began about 7:40 a.m., almost eight hours after some of the troops were said to have smoked marijuana, and that "it took about three hours to kill all those people." The subcommittee was told the previous day that the effects of the Vietnamese marijuana could take from three to four hours to wear off.

Ridenhour said he talked to a number of My Lai veterans after the attack. "Nobody mentioned drugs at My Lai after it happened," he said, "and they would have been looking for any excuse."

Marijuana was in "no way a significant factor" in the events that occurred there, he added.

that the military to be permitted to prosecute former servicemen for military offenses and that independent investigations (that is, ones emanating from outside the command involved) be required in cases involving atrocity charges. The report was endorsed by all four members of the subcommittee: Hebert, Samuel S. Stratton

(D N.Y.), Charles S. Gubser (R Calif.) and William L. Dickinson (R Ala.).

TFX Probe

After a seven-year interval, an investigation into the F-111 (TFX) aircraft program was resumed in 1970 by the Permanent Subcommittee on Investigations of the Senate Government Operations Committee. But unlike the 1963 hearings—which focused on alleged contract irregularities—the 1970 hearings became a forum for criticizing the procurement policies of former Defense Secretary Robert S. McNamara, the man who ordered development of the controversial craft. *(1963 hearings, Congress and the Nation, Vol. 1, p. 1766; subsequent developments, Congress and the Nation, Vol. II, p. 875)*

The impetus for the 1970 hearings was the continuation of a range of technical difficulties and mounting cost overruns that had plagued the plane's development almost from its inception. In 1968, the Navy version of the craft, the F-111B, was abandoned, largely because it was deemed too heavy to perform aircraft carrier duty. In addition, the Air Force bomber version (FB-111) was curtailed, and the fighter version experienced repeated flight problems and was gounded periodically for new tests and modifications.

The subcommittee's probe included months of investigations by staffers and eight days of hearings in March and April on the contract and performance of the troubled craft. Witnesses included top Pentagon military and civilian officials and subcommittee investigators. Among the panel's conclusions, contained in a Dec. 18 report:

• The TFX program had been "a blunder of the greatest magnitude" and its failure had a "serious impact" on national security and undermined "public confidence in our defense establishment."

• Costs of the program had ballooned from $5.8-billion for 1,726 planes to $7.9-billion for only 538 planes. This meant average per plane costs had increased from $3.4-million to $14.7-million. (The total F-111 buy, which came to 543 planes, including 24 for Australia was completed in fiscal 1973. Program costs came to $8.2 billion. In addition, $29-million was requested in the fiscal 1974 budget for modifications of the planes.)

• Defense Secretary McNamara made repeated management errors and made deliberate attempts to conceal the results of those errors from Congress, the press and the American people.

• Roswell L. Gilpatric, deputy secretary of defense under McNamara (1961-64), was guilty of "a flagrant conflict of interest in the TFX award" to General Dynamics. He was a "top level policy counselor to General Dynamics for 2 1/2 years before his appointment" and "should have disqualified himself from any part in the decision."

• Fred J. Korth, secretary of the navy at the time the development contract was let (1962-63), was guilty of "at best an impropriety" by not disqualifying himself from participating in the contract decision. Korth had been president of the Continental National Bank of Fort Worth, Texas (a creditor of General Dynamics) before coming to the Navy Department. He had practiced law in Fort Worth, home of General Dynamics.

• General Dynamics knew early in the plane's development that serious problems existed with the aircraft's aerodynamics and weight. But the company "apparently made a corporate decision at about that time to deny the former and conceal the latter."

Mismanagement Errors. The report cited "at least five major management errors" by McNamara and his top civilian assistants during the course of the program:

• An original decision by McNamara to overrule service recommendations and proceed with the development of a single, multimission aircraft to meet the differing requirements of the Air Force and Navy.

• Selection of General Dynamics Corporation rather than Boeing Company as prime contractor for the TFX, despite higher evaluations of the less costly Boeing design by military evaluation panels.

• Failure to heed warnings in 1964 of technical difficulties with the Navy version and allow redesign of the F-111B.

• Assumption of personal management of the foundering program in 1966 by the secretary of defense's office.

• Continuing production of F-111As in 1967 before many technical design problems had been solved. This resulted in production funds being wasted prior to the emergence of an adequate aircraft, the F-111F.

McNamara, president of the World Bank, declined comment on the report. Gilpatric, a senior partner in the New York law firm of Cravath, Swaine & Moore, told reporters in New York that he did not agree with the general criticism of the F-111 program. He said that the Justice Department had studied the matter in 1963 and concluded that he had not violated any conflict-of-interest statutes.

Korth, who was cleared by the Justice Department in 1963, did not comment. General Dynamics issued a statement that characterized the report as making "no suggestion of wrong-doing by General Dynamics or any of its employees."

Aircraft Carrier Study

A joint Senate-House Armed Services subcommittee studying the cost and effectiveness of Navy nuclear aircraft carriers April 22 recommended that Congress approve the start on construction of a third modern carrier.

The study grew out of a 1969 debate on the need for additional carriers. After the Senate beat back attempts led by Senators Clifford P. Case (R N.J.) and Walter F. Mondale (D Minn.) to delete funds in the fiscal 1970 defense procurement authorization bill (S 2546—PL 91-121), it approved a study on the value of carriers.

The critics had charged that carriers were too costly and vulnerable and would tend to encourage foreign involvements. They added that other nations were cool to the carrier concept and that the 15-carrier task forces the Navy viewed as necessary were based on an arbitrary decision made in 1921.

Report Findings. In a brief, five-page report, the joint subcommittee, co-chaired by Sen. John C. Stennis (D Miss.) and Rep. Charles E. Bennett (D Fla.), "strongly" recommended that Congress approve funds for the long leadtime items for the third Nimitz-type carrier known as CVAN-70.

The report observed that President Nixon in his fiscal 1971 budget had requested $152 million for the project but had also stated that the funds would not be obligated until the completion of studies by the National Security Council on carriers. The report took note of a request by Defense Secretary Melvin R. Laird for approval of the CVAN-70 as the final ship in a three-vessel program begun in fiscal 1967.

No agreement was reached within the Defense Department or the subcommittee, the report said, on the number of carriers needed or the cost advantages or disadvantages of carriers. The report stated there was a division among the Joint Chiefs of Staff over the numbers needed in the future. The panel was also "unable to resolve the question" of how many carriers should be provided in the 1975-1980 period. It said modernization of ships and future foreign policy decisions would affect the answer.

Military Spying

Alleged Army spying on private citizens, including peace groups, politicians and newspaper reporters, touched off a furor on Capital Hill in 1970. No legislation resulted, but Defense Secretary Melvin R. Laird ordered the Army to drop such activities and to destroy files it had accumulated in the program.

The controversy was sparked by an article in the January issue of *Washington Monthly* magazine, which described an intelligence network of "nearly 1,000 plainclothes investigators, working out of some 200 offices from coast to coast" who wrote reports on "political protests of all kinds." The article, written by a former Army intelligence officer, Christopher H. Pyle, went on to describe a nationwide teletype network which provided information on political protests for every major troop command in the nation, and an elaborate domestic intelligence operation that stored and disseminated data on both groups and individuals who "might cause trouble for the Army."

The groups Pyle said the Army spied on included the American Civil Liberties Union, the Southern Christian Leadership Conference, the John Birch Society, the National Association for the Advancement of Colored People, the Women Strike for Peace, the Center for the Study of Democratic Institutions, and the Clergy and Laymen United Against the War in Vietnam.

The scope of the controversy broadened in December when Sen. Sam J. Ervin Jr. (D N.C.), chairman of the Senate Judiciary Subcommittee on Constitutional Rights, told the Senate he had been informed that the Army had conducted "surveillance" of more than 800 Illinois citizens, including politicians, newspaper reporters, religious figures and political contributors. Among those named by Ervin as targets of the surveillance were Sen. Adlai E. Stevenson III (D Ill.), Rep. Abner J. Mikva (D Ill.) and U.S. Circuit Court Judge Otto Kerner.

The reason for the snooping, said Ervin, was "so that the Army could determine the political proclivities of the individuals involved.... It was enough that they opposed or did not actively support the government's policy in Vietnam or that they disagreed with domestic policies of the administration, or that they were in contact with or sympathetic to people with such views. Apparently, anyone who in the Army's definition was 'left of center' was a prospective candidate for political surveillance."

CBW Developments

After months of wrangling between his defense and foreign policy advisers, President Nixon Aug. 19 made good on his Nov. 25, 1969, promise to submit a 1925 international treaty against chemical and biological warfare to the Senate for ratification. But Senate consideration was not forthcoming during the 1970 session because of a controversy over Nixon's interpretation of the treaty.

What touched off the dispute among Nixon's advisers was the issue of the legality of tear gas and defoliants, which were deployed extensively in Vietnam. The Defense Department insisted that the treaty be submitted with an accompanying reservation giving the interpretation that its provisions did not cover tear gas and defoliants. But the State Department argued that these two chemicals should be included in the ban.

In the end the Pentagon won. In submitting the treaty Aug. 19, the administration gave its interpretation that tear gas and defoliants were not covered by the pact. The Senate also was asked to approve a reservation preserving the nation's right to retaliate with chemical weapons in response to a chemical attack on the United States. (Many other nations, in approving the pact years before, had reserved the right to retaliate.)

Nixon's two reservations sparked considerable controversy. Congressional sources indicated that there was not enough time left to debate them during the 1970 session, particularly in view of preoccupation by the Senate Foreign Relations Committee with other pressing matters. (The committee held hearings on the treaty in executive session in 1971, but did not take further action through the end of 1972.)

In another CBW development, the Defense Department in 1970 found itself in a quandary over how to dispose of unneeded stockpiles of chemical weapons. Under pressure from local citizens, the Pentagon decided to move a stockpile of nerve and mustard gas in Okinawa to the United States. But its plans to dispose of the gas—first in Oregon and then in Alaska—were blocked by political pressure. Finally, the gas was disposed of at Johnston Island in the Pacific. In another controversy, the Army ran into opposition to plans to dispose of 66 tons of obsolete nerve gas weapons. But despite citizen pressure, the plan was carried out Aug. 10 to move the shipment by rail to a military sea terminal in North Carolina, from where it was eventually dumped 282 miles at sea.

Defense Production Act

Congress Aug. 13 cleared for the President's signature a bill (S 3302—PL 91-379) extending the Defense Production Act of 1950 (PL 81-774) to June 30, 1972, setting up a board to create uniform cost-accounting standards for the defense industry and granting the President authority to freeze wages and prices throughout the economy.

The wage-price controls—which Nixon opposed—became a major point of controversy during the bill's consideration. In signing the bill Aug. 15, Nixon said he would have vetoed the measure if it had not been for the bill's defense provisions. *(Wage-price controls p. 107)*

During consideration of the bill—a Korean War statute designed to assure a sufficient supply of national resources for defense needs—a provision authorizing the guarantee of loans to defense firms became another source of controversy. This arose when it was proposed by the administration that a $200-million loan for the financially troubled Penn Central Railroad also be guaranteed through the bill. A provision restricting such loans was later incorporated in S 3302.

In addition, the nature of the board created by the bill to set up standards for accounting for the defense industry was widely debated. The Senate Banking and Currency Committee had added a provision exempting contractors whose government business amounted to less than $25-million the previous year. An amendment to drop the provision, offered by Sen. William Proxmire (D Wis.), was adopted on the floor by an overwhelming 51-22 roll-call vote. But the Senate by voice vote later adopted an amendment to exempt contracts of $100,-000 or less from the accounting requirements. These Senate actions were sustained by the House.

Provisions. As cleared by Congress, S 3302:

• Extended to June 30, 1972, the provisions of the 1950 Defense Production Act to assure defense production in case of emergency and to guarantee loans to contractors; added aerospace-related firms to the list of industries covered by the act.

• Authorized the establishment of a five-member board headed and selected by the comptroller general, with two members of the accounting profession, including one familiar with small business problems, and one representative each from industry and the executive branch of the government, to serve for a four-year period.

• Directed the board to promulgate uniform cost-accounting standards for negotiated defense, atomic energy, space and other stockpiling or military assistance contracts.

• Exempted from the uniform cost-accounting standards provision contracts under $100,000, those where costs were fixed or regulated by the government, those covering commercial items, or those where the board deemed exemption necessary.

• Gave the board authority to examine contractors' books, authorized appropriations as might be necessary and required the board to make an annual report beginning two years after the bill's enactment.

• Placed a limit of $20-million per contractor on the amount of loans guaranteed by the government, except by congressional approval, and prohibited guarantees primarily to prevent bankruptcy or insolvency of any company unless the President certified such a prohibition would adversely affect defense production to a substantial degree.

• Authorized the President, as he saw fit, until Feb. 28, 1971, to freeze prices, rents, wages and salaries at levels not lower than those prevailing on May 25, 1970; authorized the use of injunctions to carry out the provision and provided for a $5,000 penalty for violators.

Black Marketeering

Allegations that black marketeering in Vietnam had spread to Laos was the focus of a one-day hearing, March 4, before the Senate Government Operations Subcommittee on Executive Reorganization and Government Research. (*1969 hearings, p. 203*)

The new disclosure came from Subcommittee Chairman Abraham A. Ribicoff (D Conn.), who revealed that as much as $400,000 in black market money was being smuggled out of Saigon each week by American civilian pilots to Bangkok, Thailand, and then on to the Bank of Indochina in Laos. "The Bank of Indochina sends an average of two bundles of currency and checks weekly to New York by air," Ribicoff said. "In 1969, a total of $19.7-million of funds were received by the bank. Of this, $9.3-million were greenbacks and $10.4-million were checks."

Ribicoff also reported that a foreign aid program for Laos, funded by the United States, Great Britain, France, Japan and Australia, had deposited some of its funds in a known black market account at the Manufacturers Hanover Trust Bank in New York. In 1967, he said, at least $45,000 was deposited in the account, which he said was code-named "Prysumeen." The total funding for the project was $19,400,000 in 1968, Ribicoff reported, of which the United States paid 70 per cent.

In a related development, the Army March 9, 1970, charged Master Sgt. William E. Higdon with larceny, bribery and graft in connection with alleged thefts and embezzlements of funds from enlisted men's clubs in South Vietnam from 1966 through 1968. Higdon was the first serviceman formally accused in the case. His role had emerged during the subcommittee's 1969 hearings on black marketeering.

Security of Documents

Although it passed the House, the Senate did not take action in 1970 on a bill (HR 14864) amending the Internal Security Act of 1950 to institute measures to protect defense production and classified information against subversion.

The bill would have added a new title to the act, to provide a legislative base for three existing national security programs: protection of industrial facilities involved in defense production, protection of classified data related to contractors, and protection of vessels and waterfront activities.

In two decisions, the U.S. Supreme Court had struck down the first and last of these programs. It first declared unconstitutional a provision of the 1950 act which forbade members of Communist-action organizations to work in a defense facility (*U.S. v. Robel*, 1967). The court then declared that Congress had not authorized the program used to screen personnel for access to merchant vessels and waterfront activities (*Schneider v. Smith*, 1968).

In a related move, the House Internal Security Committee reported a bill (HR 959) to amend the Internal Security Act to add a new section prohibiting international misconduct that obstructed the military forces of the United States. But the bill received no further action. The measure would have provided heavy fines and prison sentences for persons aiding countries with which the United States was at armed conflict, and for persons who intentionally, forcibly or illegally obstructed the movement of military personnel or supplies when the United States was at war.

Military Drug Abuse

News stories concerning widespread use of drugs by U.S. troops in Vietnam led to congressional hearings in 1970 on the use of narcotics and dangerous drugs by U.S. servicemen in Vietnam and elsewhere.

The Senate Judiciary Subcommittee on Drug Abuse held hearings in March and August, while subcommittees of the House Armed Services Committee and Senate Labor and Public Welfare Committee probed the issue in November. During the Senate Judiciary hearings, Subcommittee Chairman Thomas J. Dodd (D Conn.) said he had learned that in Vietnam, "marijuana, dangerous drugs and even heroin are almost as available as candy bars." Estimates of drug abuse among U.S. troops in the war zone ran as high as 80 per cent, he said, compared to 50 per cent among youth in the United States. Dodd also hinted that use of marijuana among U.S. troops at My Lai "might have had something to do with the disaster there." *(Box, p. 207)*

Other Developments

Moorer Appointment. The Senate June 17, by a 78-2 roll-call vote, confirmed the nomination of Adm. Thomas H. Moorer to be the chairman of the Joint Chiefs of Staff. The nomination had been submitted by President Nixon on April 15.

Moorer, chief of Naval Operations since 1967, replaced Gen. Earle G. Wheeler, who had been chairman since 1964. The appointment was for a two-year term, beginning July 1, 1970.

Servicemen's Life Insurance. President Nixon June 25 signed into law a bill (S 1479—PL 91-291) increasing to $15,000 from $10,000 the maximum coverage under servicemen's group life insurance. The bill continued the price of the insurance to the serviceman at $1 per month for each $5,000 worth of insurance.

Stockpile Disposal. Congress June 29 cleared for the President's signature 17 bills authorizing the sale of various commodities from the government's stockpile of strategic resources. The bills, requested by the administration, were expected to produce an additional $150-million in annual revenue.

1971

Two issues—a proposed government "bailout" for the financially troubled Lockheed Aircraft Corporation and extension of the draft as an interim step toward building an all-volunteer army—highlighted congressional action on defense policy in 1971. A third defense controversy—the question of the right of the news media to publish a classified Pentagon history of the Vietnam war (the so-called "Pentagon Papers") got equal or greater public attention but did not involve Congress in a substantial way. Congress handed President Nixon victories in the Lockheed and draft hassles, but the Supreme Court ruled against the White House in the Pentagon Papers case. *(Supreme Court chapter p. 319)*

The Lockheed issue touched off a long and acrimonious debate over whether the company—the nation's leading defense contractor—should be expected to "sink or swim" like any ordinary firm or whether it should be treated as a special national asset which could not be allowed to go bankrupt. (The company's financial problems sprang from cost overruns on the L-1011 commercial aircraft program and from various military contracts, including the C-5A transport craft.) After cliffhanging votes in the House and Senate, Lockheed won a government loan guarantee of up to $250-million to pull it through its current crisis. *(Lockheed Loan Chapter p. 233)*

In passing the draft bill, Congress gave Nixon the three major draft reforms he had proposed in 1970 and continued to press for in 1971: restoration of presidential authority to suspend undergraduate deferments, substitution of a direct national draft call to replace the existing local board quota system, and higher pay for draftees and first-term enlistees. The bill became a vehicle for Senate amendments, opposed by the administration, to cut U.S. troop strength in Europe and to require a withdrawal from Vietnam within nine months of the bill's passage. The Senate rejected the European troop cuts, however, and a tough Senate "end-the-war" amendment was watered down in conference into a mere resolution urging—but not ordering—the President to withdraw as soon as practicable. *(Draft bill chapter p. 225)*

Although Nixon asked for a massive increase in defense spending *(below)*, there were only half-hearted efforts, none successful, to curtail major weapons systems. The one program that encountered trouble was military intelligence activities, whose budget was cut $250-million at the behest of the Appropriations Committees. But when non-committee members in the Senate sought to take the matter a step further and legislate an annual ceiling on intelligence spending, their amendment was overwhelmed by administration supporters.

Defense Budget

President Nixon's fiscal 1972 defense budget, sent to Congress Jan. 29, 1971, called for spending of $75-billion and appropriations of $77.7-billion, increases of $500-million and $9.1-billion, respectively, over the previous year's levels. The bulk of the appropriations increase ($3.8-billion) was for civilian and military pay hikes, which would be only slightly reflected in the year's spending figures. Other big increases in appropriations were $2.2-billion for military procurement and $500-million for research and development.

In his annual defense posture statement, submitted March 9 to the House Armed Services Committee, Defense Secretary Melvin R. Laird explained that the hefty increases were part of a new "Strategy of Realistic Deterrence," designed to prevent future wars by deterring "armed conflict at all levels." The new posture signaled little change on the strategic front, where the ABM and other missile programs continued at previous levels, but it meant sharp increases for some general purpose force programs, particularly Navy ship construction. Total obligational authority (i.e., new and unspent old appropriations) for shipbuilding was to be $3.3-billion in the fiscal 1972 budget, about $1.5-billion above the average programs over the years 1964 through 1969.

Unlike the transitional budget of fiscal 1971, the new budget outlined a five-year defense program which forecast ever-increasing budget needs over the next four years of the cycle. (Five-year budget forecasts had been submitted during the McNamara and Clifford regimes, but one had not been provided by Laird in 1970.) Key to the "realistic deterrence" strategy that the budget supported, Laird said, was the Defense Department's "sober and clear view of the multiple threats to peace which exist in today's world. (The policy) neither exaggerates nor underestimates those threats." The policy was genuinely new, Laird added, and not "a mere continuation of past policies in new packaging." "Past policy was responsive and reactive," he said. "Our new strategy is positive and active. Past policy focused on containment and accommodation. The new strategy emphasizes measured, meaningful involvement and vigorous negotiation from a position of strength."

Laird further elaborated on the realistic deterrence strategy in his fiscal 1973 defense posture statement, outlining the responsibilities of the United States and its allies under various scenarios of war. The guidelines, which were a refinement of the 1969 Nixon Doctrine, included:

- "In deterring strategic nuclear warfare, primary reliance will continue to be placed on U.S. strategic deterrence forces.
- "In deterring theater nuclear warfare, the U.S. also has primary responsibility, but certain of our allies are able to share this responsibility by virtue of their own nuclear capabilities.
- "In deterring theater conventional warfare—for example, a major war in Europe—U.S. and allied forces share responsibility.
- "In deterring subtheater or localized warfare, the country or ally which is threatened bears the primary burden, particularly for providing manpower, but when U.S. interests or obligations are at stake we must be prepared to provide help as appropriate."

AUTHORIZATION

Floor fights over the Navy's Project Sanguine communications system, military pay increases and a forced U.S. withdrawal from Vietnam highlighted debate on the fiscal 1972 defense procurement authorization bill (HR 8687—PL 92-156), cleared by Congress Nov. 11. *(Details, Vietnam chapter)*

The pay increase issue arose in the Senate where Gordon Allott (R Colo.) fought for an additional $381,-100,000 for the men in uniform above an already scheduled increase of $2.4-billion. Allott's amendment, aimed primarily at further increasing salaries for lower ranking personnel, was supported by the President as part of an earlier agreement with the Coloradan to secure his support of the draft extension bill (HR 6531). *(p. 225)*

But House conferees, armed with a Pentagon position paper showing that the $2.4-billion increase was sufficient, stood fast on the issue, and the Allott amendment was dropped in conference.

Heated debate in the Senate developed over the Sanguine program—a long-range, low-frequency transmitting network to communicate with submerged submarines—which critics said would cause severe environmental damage in the 6,400-square-mile area of Wis-

(Continued on p. 213)

'Sanguine' Sparked Controversy

The Navy, in an effort to develop new ways of communicating with submerged submarines around the world, sought development in the late 1960s of a low-frequency transmitter system. As envisioned by Navy planners, the Project Sanguine system would involve burying six feet below the ground 1,000 miles of cable in a grid pattern. The area to be covered by the giant grid would total about 6,400 square miles and was originally to be located in northern Wisconsin. In 1972, however, the Pentagon decided it would place the system in Texas if deployment proved feasible. The decision on an actual deployment go-ahead was expected by 1976.

During consideration at the fiscal 1972 defense procurement bill, Sen. Gaylord Nelson (D Wis.) offered an amendment which would have withheld all of Project Sanguine's $5,557,000 authorization except $450,000 for studying the ecological effects of the program. The purpose of the amendment was to withhold expenditure of funds until the Navy filed an environmental impact statement, as required by the National Environmental Policy Act, and until the entire project was subjected to a feasibility review by the National Academy of Sciences and the National Academy of Engineering.

Nelson said that not only had the Navy failed to file an impact statement, but that "there is a serious question whether the technology proposed by the Navy for communicating via Project Sanguine will even work."

The amendment was rejected Sept. 22 by a 35-45 roll-call vote.

In debate on the same bill, a second amendment dealing with Project Sanguine was brought to the floor by Nelson Sept. 29. In it, Nelson requested that the $5,557,000 authorization in fiscal 1972 research funds on the project be reduced to $3,492,000, of which $450,000 would be used for environmental studies.

Nelson explained that Project Sanguine included two experimental parts—the grid pattern communications system buried six feet below the ground and a deep drilling project where cables were to be sunk thousands of feet into the ground. Nelson said the Navy had hand-delivered a letter to his office Sept. 10 informing him that the deep drilling portion of the program had been abandoned. The Navy then took the $2,065,000, which was to be used for the deep drilling experiment, and transferred the money to grid pattern research.

"In effect, the Navy has substantially increased the research and development effort for the shallow Sanguine system without bothering to present Congress with any justification whatsoever for it," Nelson said.

The second Nelson amendment was adopted Sept. 29 by a 44-42 roll-call vote. A measure of victory was preserved for Nelson when House conferees compromised on a cut in the program to $4,492,000, a reduction of $1,065,000 from the House amount.

consin where it was to be installed *(box, p. 212)*. When Gaylord Nelson (D Wis.) introduced an amendment to withhold all of Sanguine's $5,557,000 authorization except $450,000 for an ecological study, his amendment was rejected by a 35-45 roll-call vote. However, a second Nelson amendment, to cut the authorization to $3,492,000, was accepted by a 44-42 roll call. Conferees compromised on an allotment of $4,492,000, restoring about half the Senate cut.

Unlike the debate in the three previous years, discussion of the Safeguard ABM system was neither heated nor prolonged. Amendments to cut funds for the system were turned back easily in both the House and Senate. However, a dispute over the pace of ABM deployment did develop between the Armed Services Committees of the two chambers. The Senate committee limited deployment of ABM missiles and radars to two of the four authorized sites—Grand Forks, N.D., and Great Falls, Mont. The House panel provided for full deployment at all four previously authorized sites and for advanced deployment at a possible fifth ABM site located in the Washington, D.C., area. Conferees agreed to the Senate restrictions.

As cleared, HR 8687 authorized appropriations of $21,316,870,000 in fiscal 1972 for military research and procurement. The final figure represented a cut of $1,-253,567,000 from administration requests but an increase of $1,387,791,000 over the amount authorized for the previous year's program.

APPROPRIATIONS

Military intelligence operations were the focus of controversy during consideration of a $70.5-billion defense appropriations bill (HR 11731—PL 92-204) for fiscal 1972, cleared Dec. 15.

The House Appropriations Committee, noting that "intelligence operations of the Department of Defense have grown beyond the actual needs of the department," pared $181-million from the administration request for intelligence activities. (The request level itself was classified.) On the Senate floor, Stuart Symington (D Mo.), a former secretary of the air force, offered an amendment to place a $4-billion ceiling on intelligence activities for the entire U.S. intelligence community (including the Central Intelligence Agency, National Security Agency, Defense Intelligence Agency and the military services' intelligence apparatus), but his amendment failed by a 31-56 roll-call vote. Although the Senate bill did not provide any reduction, Senate conferees agreed with their House counterparts to a $250-million cut for intelligence activities. *(Intelligence reorganization, p. 216)*

The appropriations bill also became the vehicle for an attempt in the Senate to reduce U.S. troop strength in Europe—an issue that had been raised periodically before but had never been put to a vote. In a scare for the White House and Pentagon, the Senate Appropriations Committee approved an amendment calling for a 250,000-man ceiling on U.S. forces in Europe (about a 50,000 reduction), effective June 15, 1972. But the committee provision failed to win confirmation on the Senate floor by a **39-54 key roll-call vote**. *(Other action on troop cuts, box, p. 214)*

In other action, Congress canceled the Army's trouble-plagued main battle tank (MBT-70) program and provided $40-million as the first step of a new tank prototype program. Congress also limited to two years the availability of unexpended research and development money—a category of appropriations where there previously was no time limit on spending. (For research and development on shipbuilding, however, the limit was set at five years.) If the funds were not spent within these years, they would revert back to the general funds of the Treasury.

As sent to the White House, the bill appropriated $70,518,463,000 for the Defense Department in fiscal 1972—a defense bill surpassed in dollar value only by the fiscal 1969 appropriations measure, which carried $71,-869,828,000. The final amount was $3,025,366,000 less than administration requests but $3,922,526,000 more than the total appropriated for fiscal 1971. Major appropriations included $1,189,070,000 for the Safeguard ABM, $801,600,000 for the Navy's F-14 fighter, $579,900,000 for continued development and procurement of the Navy's carrier-based S-3A anti-submarine warfare aircraft, and $321,500,000 for the Air Force's C-5A super cargo transport plane. The bill included $7-billion for costs related to the war in Vietnam.

MILITARY BASES FUNDS

In the annual military construction authorization measure (HR 9844—PL 92-127), cleared Oct. 21, Congress voted $1,986,323,000 for base construction and military family housing in fiscal 1972. As in 1970, a greater total than this was actually appropriated, because of activities funded under the appropriations bill that did not require prior authorization. The defense construction money bill (HR 11418—PL 92-160), cleared Nov. 15, appropriated $2,037,097,000, a reduction of $92,708,000 from administration requests, and $717,000 from the amount appropriated for the same purposes in fiscal 1971.

Draft Extension

After almost six months of debate, which ranged over basic military and foreign policy issues, Congress Sept. 21 cleared for the President a bill (HR 6531—PL 92-129) extending the draft for two more years and raising military pay.

HR 6531, signed by Nixon Sept. 28, provided all these major draft reforms that the President had sought: a nationalized selection process that eliminated the local board draft quota system, discretionary authority for the President to suspend educational deferments and higher pay for lower-ranking personnel. The bill provided a $2.4-billion military pay increase, weighted toward first-term enlistees and draftees and low-ranking officers. Also included in the bill was a non-binding provision putting Congress on record as backing an early end to the Vietnam war. (The Senate had adopted tougher language directing a conclusion to the war within nine months of the bill's enactment, but the provision was watered down in conference.)

In other action, the Senate rejected an amendment to cut U.S. troop strength in Europe by a 36-61 roll-call vote. *(Special chapter on draft, p. 225; box on European troop cuts, p. 214)*

NATO Commitment: Two Attempts, Both Unsuccessful...

Twice during 1971 the Senate considered proposals which sought to force reductions in the number of U.S. troops stationed in Europe. On both occasions, after heavy White House lobbying, the measures were defeated.

Although the House did not confront the issue of U.S. troops stationed in Europe in direct floor votes, the House Armed Services and Appropriations Committees both used strong language to urge that other North Atlantic Treaty Organization (NATO) countries, besides the United States, assume a greater financial burden in behalf of their own defense efforts.

The first debate in the Senate, which lasted nine days, came to a head May 19 with a series of roll-call votes ending just before midnight. The proposal, which was an amendment to the military draft extension bill (HR 6531—PL 92-129), was rejected in a final 36-61 roll-call vote.

The second attempt to force a reduction of U.S. troops in Europe came as a committee amendment to the defense appropriations bill (HR 11731—PL 92-204). The Senate Appropriations Committee's provision requiring a reduction of U.S. troops garrisoned in Europe was rejected on the floor Nov. 23 by a **key 39-54 roll-call vote**.

U.S. Deployment. According to the Pentagon, the United States as of Sept. 30, 1970, had approximately 300,000 troops with 250,000 dependents stationed in Europe.

Of the 300,000 troops, 215,000 were stationed in West Germany; 20,000 in the United Kingdom; 10,000 in Italy; 10,000 in Spain; 8,000 in Turkey; 3,000 in Greece, and 1,700 in Morocco.

In addition to the troops actually stationed in Europe, the United States maintained a 188,000-man force in the Atlantic Fleet, the spokesman said.

The Pentagon estimate as of Jan. 1, 1972, was that 310,000 U.S. troops were stationed in Europe with an estimated 218,000 dependents. *(Previous proposals, Congress and the Nation, Vol. II, p. 106.)*

First Reduction Vote

The initial proposal, introduced May 11 by Senate Majority Leader Mike Mansfield (D Mont.), which sought to impose a limit of 150,000 U.S. troops stationed in Europe (a 50-percent reduction) as of Dec. 31, 1971, was defeated by a 36-61 roll-call vote which came just before midnight May 19.

The intent of the Mansfield proposal was to reduce the U.S. balance-of-payments deficit and ease pressure on the dollar by authorizing funds for deployment in Europe of no more than 150,000 U.S. troops.

It would have forced the NATO allies to assume a greater portion of the economic burden for defending Central Europe.

During the nine days the Mansfield amendment was considered by the Senate, it drew severe criticism from the White House, the Senate Republican leadership and John C. Stennis (D Miss.), chairman of the

Armed Services Committee and floor manager of the draft bill. The White House mounted an intensive lobbying campaign to defeat the proposal.

President Nixon had announced he would accept no amendments to the draft bill which dealt in any way with U.S. military commitments to Europe. Minority Leader Hugh Scott (R Pa.) said the President would veto the draft bill if the Mansfield amendment passed.

In the Senate, the proposal aroused intense interest which was reflected by the five other amendments introduced after Mansfield's initiative. The other amendments, which sought to soften the Mansfield proposal, were introduced as compromise measures. They were all defeated by a coalition of Mansfield supporters, who wanted a record vote on the strongest possible version, and administration supporters, who felt the Mansfield amendment would be more difficult to defeat with the addition of more moderate language.

The Soviet Union watched the progress of the Mansfield amendment with interest. In a May 18 editorial in the defense ministry's official newspaper *Red Star*, the Soviets accused President Nixon of opposing the amendment for fear it would "encourage antimilitarist moods among the United States' European allies."

One of the major reasons cited in the defeat of the proposals to limit U.S. troop strength in Europe was the Soviet offer to negotiate a multilateral reduction in Central Europe of Warsaw Pact and NATO forces. The Mansfield amendment sought to force a unilateral reduction by the United States regardless of the Soviet position.

"Excess, waste or obsolescence in the U.S. troop commitments under NATO," said Mansfield, "are not bargaining chips in negotiations. They are as an albatross around the neck of the nation's basic policies."

Stennis and Scott argued that the current troop levels in Europe were not excessive but were vital minimal forces needed to defend Europe and the United States against possible Soviet aggression and to maintain the balance of power in the Middle East.

White House Lobbying. The Nixon administration rolled out the heaviest artillery available in its effort to beat back the Mansfield proposal.

Included on the list of those publicly supporting the administration's proposal were two Democratic former Presidents—Lyndon B. Johnson and Harry S Truman—and two dozen high-ranking officials from past administrations, most of whom were Democrats.

Two former secretaries of state—Dean Rusk, who served under Presidents Kennedy and Johnson, and Dean Acheson, who served in the Truman administration—were on the list. Acheson, who was one of the first former administration officials to throw the weight of his name behind Nixon's lobbying effort, was assigned May 13 to the job of collecting signatures of support for the President's position.

The morning of May 12, Henry A. Kissinger, the President's adviser on national security, met to discuss plans for defeating the amendment with the

...To Legislate Reductions of U.S. Forces in Europe

two ranking Republicans in the Senate—Minority Leader Scott and Minority Whip Robert P. Griffin (Mich.).

With Mansfield's consent, the final vote on the troop cut amendment was delayed for one week (to May 19). Mansfield refused to withdraw his amendment or to replace it with a sense-of-the-Congress resolution which would not have been binding. Such proposals were included by other senators in their substitutes for the Mansfield amendment.

Throughout the day, statements condemning Mansfield's resolution were issued from the White House.

By May 13, the White House had developed a hard line on the Mansfield amendment. No amendments and no resolutions dealing in any way with U.S. foreign policy and U.S. NATO commitments would be acceptable to the President, said White House Press Secretary Ronald L. Ziegler. Scott told reporters that he was "as sure as a man can be" that the President would veto the draft bill if it required a cutback of U.S. troops stationed in Europe.

At the White House, the President convened the first of several stragegy sessions. Included in the meeting were Acheson; Cyrus T. Vance, former deputy defense secretary; George Ball, former under secretary of state; and Gen. Andrew Goodpaster, supreme allied commander of NATO forces, and Robert Ellsworth (R Kan. 1961-67), U.S. ambassador to NATO, both of whom had arrived that morning from Europe. Ball assisted Acheson while working as a lobbyist on select members of the Senate. Secretary of State William P. Rogers also was meeting with a number of senators individually.

Through Ziegler, the President announced May 15 that his opposition to Mansfield's amendment was supported by 24 high-ranking officials of past administrations.

The list included Acheson and Rusk; three former Defense Secretaries, Robert Lovett, Neil McElroy and Thomas Gates; former Under Secretaries of State James Webb, Robert Murphy, Livingston Merchant, C. Douglas Dillon, Ball and Nicholas Katzenbach; former Deputy Defense Secretaries Vance and Roswell Gilpatric; former supreme allied commanders in Europe Matthew Ridgway, Alfred Gruenther, Lauris Norstad and Lyman Lemnitzer; former NATO ambassadors Charles Spofford, W. Randolph Burgess, Thomas Finletter and Harlan Cleveland, and former military governors or high commissioners for Germany Lucius Clay, John McCloy and James Conant.

Later on May 15, former Presidents Johnson and Truman issued statements of opposition to Mansfield's proposal. Johnson, who was succeeded as majority leader of the Senate by Mansfield, said the amendment "would endanger what we have achieved in the past and shatter our hopes for the future."

According to Ziegler, only two of the persons who were asked to support the President's position declined to do so. They were Clark M. Clifford, defense secretary under Johnson, and James Douglas, Truman's deputy defense secretary.

Former Defense Secretary Robert P. McNamara, who served during the Kennedy and Johnson Administrations, was included on the list with a footnote by his name which read: "Former Secretary McNamara declines to comment because of his position as head of an international institution (World Bank). He does not want this abstention to be interpreted as non-support of the statement (Nixon's position)."

Mansfield, who remained unyielding to requests for a compromise, was asked to comment on the President's array of supporters. "It looks to me like the resurrection of the Old Guard," he said. "It took me back 20 or 25 years when the NATO treaty was written."

Second Reduction Attempt

The Senate Appropriations Committee, in marking up the fiscal 1972 defense appropriations bill (HR 11731—PL 92-204), added a provision which limited the number of U.S. troops stationed in Europe to 250,000 men.

The provision called for all funds supporting troops in excess of the 250,000-man ceiling to be cut off June 15, 1972.

When the Senate took up the committee's version of the defense appropriations bill, debate on the provision placing a ceiling on U.S. troop strength was limited to 80 minutes on the afternoon of Nov. 23.

Armed Services Committee Chairman Stennis, an adamant foe of legislating U.S. troop reductions in Europe, produced a letter from President Nixon, dated Nov. 22, which said: "This week the Senate will once again consider a proposal to make a substantial unilateral reduction in United States armed forces maintained in Europe for the common defense. I believe passage of such a measure would be a great mistake.

"Passage of the proposed troop cut," the letter continued, "would with one stroke diminish Western military capability in Europe and signal to friend and adversary alike a disarray and weakness of purpose in the American government."

Mansfield argued that the United States had garrisoned troops in Europe since the end of World War II and it was time for the countries of the North Atlantic Treaty Organization to assume a greater role in defending themselves.

Opponents of the committee provision countered that any withdrawal on the part of the United States would substantially weaken politically and militarily—the position of America's Western European allies. They also said that negotiations between the United States and the Soviet Union to mutually reduce troop strengths in Europe would be worthless if the United States acted first.

In a vote asking for confirmation of the committee's amendment, the Senate Nov. 23 rejected the provision by a 39-54 roll-call vote.

Lockheed Loan Guarantee

At the request of the White House, Congress in 1971 approved legislation (HR 8432—PL 92-70) authorizing a federal loan guarantee of $250-million in commercial bank loans for the financially troubled Lockheed Aircraft Corporation, the nation's largest defense contractor.

After long and bitter debate, which centered on the issues of the guarantee's violation of free enterprise principles and on the unemployment that a Lockheed bankruptcy would create, both the House and Senate passed the loan measure on narrow roll-call votes. Senate approval came on a **key vote of 49-48**—House approval by a **key vote 192-189.** Despite the loan money, designed to keep Lockheed afloat during production of its L-1011 commercial airliner project, indications were in late 1972 that the giant defense contractor might be headed for another financial crisis. *(Lockheed chapter, p. 233)*

Other Developments

Intelligence Reorganization. In a move to trim costs and improve the output of the U.S. global intelligence system, President Nixon Nov. 5, 1971, disclosed details of a reorganization plan he had ordered for the nation's intelligence program. The plan contained the following changes:

• It gave authority to Richard Helms, Director of Central Intelligence, to review the budgets of the CIA, the FBI, units within the Defense and State Departments and the Atomic Energy Commission. It was believed $1-billion could be cut from the $5-billion to $6-billion the U.S. spent yearly to ascertain Soviet and Chinese Communist military developments.

• It created a new intelligence subcommittee under the National Security Council to tailor the results of the nation's vast overseas intelligence network closer to the needs of the President and his top staff.

• It created a "net assessment group" inside the National Security Council to compare over-all U.S.S.R. forces and capabilities with those of the U.S.

• It created an Intelligence Resources Advisory Committee headed by Helms to advise on the preparation of a consolidated program budget. This would permit Helms to see the Department of Defense intelligence budget—estimated to be 80 per cent of everything the U.S. spent for intelligence—and advise on it before its submission to Congress.

In a related move, Defense Secretary Melvin R. Laird Nov. 3 ordered a reorganization of Pentagon intelligence activities. Laird abolished the position of assistant secretary of defense for administration and replaced it with an assistant secretary for intelligence to oversee the department's intelligence activities.

My Lai Conviction. Army Lt. William L. Calley Jr., was convicted March 29 for the premeditated murder of at least 22 Vietnamese civilians in connection with the 1968 raid at My Lai. An Army court sentenced him to life imprisonment, but personal intervention by the President left the outcome in doubt. Following an outpouring of letters, telegrams and phone calls to Nixon in Calley's favor, White House aides said April 3 that the President would personally review the case after other routes of appeal had been exhausted. In the meantime, Nixon

---

CIA Oversight

The following exchange was excerpted from the Nov. 23, 1971, Senate debate over an amendment to the defense appropriations bill placing a flat $4-billion annual ceiling on U.S. intelligence activities.

Allen J. Ellender (D La.), then chairman of the Appropriations Committee and head of its five-man Intelligence Operations Subcommittee, discussed his knowledge of CIA-run operations in Laos with J.W. Fulbright (D Ark.) and Alan Cranston (D Calif.).

Fulbright: "Would the Senator (Ellender) say that before the creation of the army in Laos they (the CIA) came before the committee and the committee knew of it and approved it?"

Ellender: "Probably so."

Fulbright: "Did the Senator approve it?"

Ellender: "It was not—I did not know anything about it."

Fulbright: "So the whole idea of Congress declaring war is really circumvented by such a procedure, is it not?"...

Ellender: "No, I do not think so."

Fulbright: "Well, if you can create an army and support it through the CIA, without anyone knowing about it, I do not know why it is not..."

Ellender: "I wish to say that I do not know. I never asked, to begin with, whether or not there were any funds to carry on the war in this sum the CIA asked for. It never dawned on me to ask about it. I did see it publicized in the newspapers...."

Cranston: "...the chairman stated that he never would have thought of even asking about CIA funds being used to conduct the war in Laos....I would like to ask the Senator if, since then, he has inquired and now knows whether that is being done?"

Ellender: "I have not inquired."

Cranston: "You do not know in fact?"

Ellender: "No."

Cranston: "As you are one of the five men privy to this information, in fact you are the number-one man of the five men who would know, then who would know what happened to this money? The fact is, not even the five men know the facts in the situation."

Ellender: "Probably not."

---

ordered that Calley be removed from imprisonment in the Ft. Benning, Ga., stockade and placed under house arrest in his apartment on the base.

In the midst of the public reaction, Capt. Aubrey M. Daniel III, the Army's prosecutor in the Calley trial, wrote a letter to Nixon, made public April 6, in which he protested the White House intervention. Daniel told Nixon that the "greatest tragedy of all will be if political expediency dictates the compromise of such a fundamental moral principle as the inherent unlawfulness of the murder of innocent persons."

Servicemen's Life Insurance. Congress Dec. 4 cleared for the President a bill (HR 9097—PL 92-184) defining the terms "widow," "widower," "child" and "parent" for servicemen's group life insurance purposes. Existing law did not define those terms, thus leaving the definitions to state laws; this resulted in a lack of uniformity in the disbursement of federal funds. The Senate passed the bill Dec. 4 by voice vote; the House had passed it Nov. 15 by voice vote.

1972

A major step towards limiting the nuclear arms race was taken in 1972 with the conclusion of two U.S.-Soviet agreements limiting both offensive and defensive nuclear weapons. The two accords were products of the Strategic Arms Limitation Talks (SALT) which had opened in Helsinki, Finland, on Nov. 17, 1969. One of the agreements was a treaty limiting each nation to two anti-ballistic missile sites; the second was a five-year accord limiting the deployment of all offensive nuclear weapons.

Both agreements had been signed by President Nixon and Soviet Communist Party General Secretary Leonid I. Brezhnev during the President's visit to Moscow in May 1972. Nixon submitted the two agreements to Congress for ratification on June 13, urging approval "without delay." The permanent ABM treaty was overwhelmingly approved 88-2 by the Senate Aug. 3. No House action was required for ratification of a treaty. On Sept. 25, Congress cleared the bill (H J Res 1227—PL 92-448) authorizing the President's approval of the five-year interim agreement on offensive nuclear weapons, after adopting several amendments to the resolution. The measure passed the House by a 329-7 roll-call vote and the Senate by 88-2. *(Background p. 181; additional details, foreign policy chapter)*

Shortcomings of the U.S. command structure in Vietnam got more attention on Capitol Hill in 1972 than did any other defense issue. Two congressional committees launched major investigations after word leaked out that the U.S. air commander in the war zone had ordered a series of unauthorized bombing raids over North Vietnam during late 1971 and early 1972. One panel tended to sanction the raids while the other criticized them. The upshot of the controversy was the firing and demotion (in retirement rank) for the man who ordered the raids—Gen. John D. Lavelle—and a directive by Defense Secretary Melvin R. Laird that the military services tighten up their command and control systems.

For the first time since 1968, military procurement and research programs met little resistance on the floor. Nonetheless, $5.6-billion was cut from President Nixon's defense budget requests, with the vast bulk of the reduction initiated by the Armed Services and Appropriations Committees. But even after the cuts, the fiscal 1973 defense appropriations bill, carrying $74.4-billion, became the largest single money bill ever passed by Congress.

The other major defense issue of the year was a contention that an easing of Navy discipline by Adm. Elmo R. Zumwalt Jr., the chief of naval operations, was responsible for a wave of shipboard racial riots. An investigating panel of the House Armed Services Committee made that statement but it was vigorously denied by Zumwalt, who said the Navy's minority affairs officers had been "effectively hamstrung" by commanders in their efforts to promote racial understanding.

Combat Readiness Report

The General Accounting Office (GAO) May 8, 1972, issued a report on the readiness capabilities of the Strategic Army Forces—general purpose forces relied upon for military actions short of nuclear war.

"It would be difficult for STRAF (Strategic Army Forces) units to deploy quickly at full strength because many units are not combat ready," the GAO report stated. More than one-third of the essential equipment for combat and combat-support operations was not functional.

The GAO report also found that:

• "About 83 percent of the M-60 tanks available to units of two divisions had deficiencies which seriously impaired their ability to perform effectively."

• Fifty-five percent of the tracked vehicles inspected were unable to perform their primary mission.

• In three of the divisions studied no stock was available for about 25 per cent of the repair parts authorized for stockage.

• "No follow up actions were being taken on unfilled requisitions."

The GAO report concluded: "The high turnover of personnel, lack of qualified personnel and funding restrictions which were beyond the direct control of the divisions, prevented them from achieving and maintaining a high state of readiness. The two divisions were being manned almost entirely with Vietnam returnees who had only a few months of service remaining..."

The only portion of the GAO report which was released to the public was a four-page summary of the classified report.

Defense Budget

Nixon's fiscal 1973 defense budget, reflecting pressure from military manpower cost increases, outlined a defense program calling for $81.6-billion in new budget authority and $75.9-billion in spending—increases of $7.7-billion and $800-million, respectively, over the fiscal 1972 program. More than half the increase in budget authority—$4.1-billion—was for military and civilian pay increases, including rises in retirement pay. Other major increases in budget authority included $1.2-billion for strategic nuclear forces, $1-billion for research and development, $600-million for a buildup of National Guard and Reserve forces and $500-million for ship construction.

The areas in which Nixon broke new ground in his fiscal 1973 program were the augmentations of strategic forces and the guard and reserve. (Increases in the other programs, particularly personnel costs, got under way in fiscal 1972.) In his defense posture statement, Laird told Congress that the $1.2-billion expansion of strategic forces was "a major new strategic initiative" designed to offset growing Soviet nuclear might. The reserve forces buildup, Laird said in the posture statement, was necessary because of deep cuts in active duty manpower over recent years. By the end of fiscal 1973, he announced, total military manpower was to be cut to 2.3-million, a reduction of 1.2 million from the Vietnam war peak of fiscal 1968 and 300,000 from the pre-Vietnam days of fiscal 1964.

Malfunctions, Rising Costs Plagued F-14 Program

Production slippage, cost increases, test malfunctions, and the manufacturer's request that the original contract be renegotiated plagued development of the F-14 fighter—a weapon designed to be the Navy's premier fleet defense aircraft for the 1970s.

The F-14, conceived as a replacement for the illfated F-111B (TFX), canceled by Congress in 1968, encountered problems from the beginning. When the House Appropriations Committee reviewed the first year's development of the aircraft Dec. 3, 1969, it said: "It is the considered judgment of the committee that the Navy is moving too fast into production on the F-14 aircraft. The committee does not share the optimism of Navy officials that the F-14 aircraft development represents a low-risk program."

During the aircraft's second test flight Dec. 31, 1970, the test plane crashed and was destroyed after its hydraulic systems failed.

For two years, 1969 and 1970, said a House Appropriations Committee report late in 1971, the Navy "virtually ignored" growing production problems of the F-14 and did not disclose any of the difficulties or rising costs to Congress. Yet officials of the plane's contractor, Grumman Aerospace Corporation, when questioned on the Navy's optimistic reports, documented several instances where they had told the Navy of production problems which would be passed on in higher costs.

The estimated costs for each F-14 more than doubled, from an $8.3-million planning estimate in 1968 to a $16.8-million estimate in mid-1972. Over that period the size at the projected purchase was reduced from 710 to 313 aircraft, but total program costs were reduced only $900-million, from $6.2-billion to $5.3-billion.

The original contract, signed in February 1969, provided for the production of up to 469 aircraft (although the Navy indicated it would put in a second order to bring the total to 710). But by March 1, 1972, the Navy order for F-14s had been reduced to 313 aircraft.

Another problem with the F-14 was revealed when the second phase of the program was about to go into production. The Navy was originally scheduled during fiscal 1972 to purchase 28 F-14A aircraft and 20 of the advanced F-14B planes. The difference in the two models, according to the House Appropriations Committee, "was almost as great as the performance differences between the F-4 Phantom jet fighter and the F-14A," the plane scheduled to replace the Phantom as the Navy's top jet fighter. The fiscal 1972 program was revised, however, to include only the purchase of the F-14A model. The F-14B aircraft development program slipped almost a full year behind schedule.

The Navy was advised by Grumman in a March 31, 1971, letter "that present data demonstrates that performance of (the F-14)...contract is commercially impracticable under the existing terms and conditions." Under pressure from Congress and the Navy, Grumman backed down from its initial request for a new contract on the F-14 program during fiscal 1972. Further production during fiscal 1973, however, appeared unlikely without a renegotiated contract, according to staff sources on the Senate Armed Services Committee.

The Armed Services and Appropriations Committees of the House and Senate conceded the need for an aircraft to succeed the Navy's F-4 Phantom jet fighter. Although all four committees expressed reservations about the F-14 program, they authorized and appropriated the necessary funds (through fiscal 1973) for continued development and production—despite rising costs—for fewer aircraft.

The F-14 controversy escalated late in 1972 when Grumman refused to honor its existing contract to provide 48 more F-14s without an increase in price. On Dec. 11, the Defense Department announced that it would hold the company to terms of the contract. Grumman said it had lost $85-million on the program already and would lose $105-million more if it built the additional fighters without a price hike.

In similar contract disputes, the Pentagon had usually given in to the contractor, either rewriting the contract completely or ordering system modifications that increased the contract price.

But in this instance, Congress itself ordered in the fiscal 1973 defense appropriations bill that the purchase of the 48 additional planes be made at the existing contract price.

The dispute threatened to spill over into Congress. By late 1972, a move was under way on Capitol Hill to provide Grumman a "bailout" similar to the one the Lockheed Aircraft Corporation received in 1971 *(p. 223)*

New York's senators, Jacob K. Javits (R) and James L. Buckley (Cons.-R), announced Dec. 13 they would propose legislation in the 1973 session to permit the Bethpage, N.Y., aerospace firm a higher price for the F-14s. Similar action was promised on the House side by four New York Republicans—Representatives James R. Grover Jr., Norman F. Lent and John W. Wydler and Rep.-elect Angelo D. Roncallo.

The four told President Nixon Dec. 13 that enforcement of the existing contract would "destroy" Grumman.

AUTHORIZATION

Aside from lengthy maneuvering over another end-the-war amendment, controversy during consideration of the fiscal 1973 defense procurement authorization (HR 15495—PL 92-436) swirled around continued deployment of the Safeguard ABM system and proposed increases in military retirement pay.

The House, in passing the bill, had included the full $800.5-million the administration sought, including funds for an ABM site around Washington, D.C. But the Senate Armed Services Committee prohibited work on the Washington site and reduced the ABM allotment by $239-million to reflect its action. "Until more definitive data is developed," the committee said, "further committee action regarding the (Washington) site cannot be taken." House conferees went along with the Senate action.

The $561.5-million authorization for the ABM in the final bill provided for continued research on the system and for continued deployment at just one site—Grand Forks, N.D. Prior to agreement on a defensive missile treaty with the Soviets in May, the administration had sought $1.5-billion for four antimissile sites. But under terms of the ABM treaty, only a two-site antimissile system was permitted. After the agreement was worked out, the administration cut its request to $800.5-million, to be spent on the Grand Forks and Washington sites.

The retirement pay issue developed in the Senate where Vance Hartke (D Ind.), at the request of veteran groups, offered a floor amendment providing for a one-time recomputation of retirement pay to base the payment levels on Jan. 1, 1972, active-duty pay scales. (The plan did not provide for recomputation of retired pay in the future to keep up with subsequent active duty pay increases.) Despite the opposition of Senate Armed Services Committee Chairman John C. Stennis (D Miss.), the amendment won easy approval, 82-4. But House conferees stood steadfast against the proposal and it was dropped in conference.

In other action on the bill, both houses rejected a flurry of amendments to cut or cancel various new weapon systems. Among the amendments rejected in the Senate were moves to slice funds from the CVN-70 nuclear aircraft carrier, Trident submarine, and SAM-D Army missile programs. The House shot down efforts to cut funds for the DD-963 destroyer, CVN-70 carrier and F-111 fighter. And for the second year in a row, the Senate rejected an amendment to speed expiration of the draft law (to Dec. 31, 1972, instead of Jan. 1, 1973, as provided in the 1971 draft extension bill). As sent to the White House the bill authorized $20,943,847,000—$2,-329,124,000 less than administration requests and $373,-023,000 less than the amount authorized by Congress for the previous fiscal year.

APPROPRIATION

Congress Oct. 13 cleared a fiscal 1973 appropriations bill (HR 16593—PL 92-570) carrying $74.4-billion for the Defense Department—the largest appropriation of any kind ever passed by Congress. The bill included $6.2-billion for costs associated with the Vietnam war.

The sum appropriated by HR 16593 was about $500-million more than the previous record high—a $71.9-billion appropriation voted in fiscal 1969, the peak year of the Vietnam war. Although a total defense appropriation of $86.4-billion was passed in fiscal 1944, it came in two separate bills: one for the combined Army and Army Air Corps and the other for the Navy.

Debate on the bill skirted the familiar procurement issues and centered on a plan by the Pentagon to phase out military kitchen police (KP) duties at all but basic training bases and replace KP details with hired civilian help. The Senate had provided the full administration request of $123.2-million for this activity, but the House had provided only $63.3-million and ordered the military services to absorb the difference from other appropriations if they wished to carry out the KP plan. House-Senate conferees approved $118.2-million—all but $5-million of the Senate figure.

In other key actions, conferees dropped a Senate amendment instructing the President to seek a withdrawal of U.S. troops from Vietnam at the earliest practicable date and agreed to House provisions terminating popular new programs to liberalize import allowances for servicemen returning from abroad.

As passed, HR 16593 carried appropriations of $74,-372,976,000—$5,221,208,000 less than the administration request but $3,854,513,000 more than the amount appropriated in fiscal 1972. Largest single appropriations in the bill included $958-million for the Air Force's new F-15 fighter aircraft; $839.9-million for the Navy's Trident missile-launching submarine; $732.7-million for the Navy's F-14 fighter; $638.5-million for the Safeguard ABM system, and $445.1-million for the Air Force's B-1 bomber.

Military Bases Funds

A House-Senate dispute over the location of a base for the Navy's Trident submarine fleet dominated action on the fiscal 1973 defense construction authorization bill (HR 15641—PL 92-545), cleared Oct. 12.

The House had approved the Navy's full request of $14.3-million to begin construction of the base, which was to cost an estimated $886-million. But the Senate, piqued over the Navy's refusal to identify a site for the proposed facility, knocked out the entire amount. The action was initiated by the Senate Armed Services Committee, which said in its report: "The committee is unable to comprehend how the Navy can foretell with any accuracy their needs for the coming fiscal years until a site has been selected." House-Senate conferees agreed on a compromise authorization of $3.5-million to begin work.

As approved by Congress, the authorization bill provided $2,557,972,000 for military construction and military family housing in fiscal 1973. On Oct. 12, the same day the authorization was approved, Congress cleared the annual defense construction appropriation bill (HR 16754—PL 92-547), carrying $2,323,403,000. The amount appropriated was $337,981,000 less than administration requests and $287,638,000 more than the amount Congress had voted for the previous fiscal year.

Lavelle Controversy

Unauthorized bombing of North Vietnam by a maverick Air Force general led to hearings by both the House and Senate Armed Services Committees in 1972. The House panel generally favored the general's action, while the Senate group was against it.

The controversy surfaced in late winter when word leaked out that Gen. John D. Lavelle had ordered 28 air strikes in violation of Pentagon "protective reaction" bombing rules between Nov. 7, 1971, and March 9, 1972. Lavelle was summarily dismissed from his job and retired from the Air Force with a demotion to major general.

The Senate probe came during a confirmation hearing on the nomination of Gen. Creighton W. Abrams for the post of Army chief of staff. After a four-month hearing, the committee reported that Abrams, over-all U.S. commander in Vietnam at the time of the unauthorized air raids, should be absolved of any blame for Lavelle's ac-

(Continued on p. 221)

Defense Department Lost Struggle for Second Pentagon in 1972

Since 1968 the Defense Department had been pushing for a second giant office building on the banks of the Potomac River. The first was the Pentagon—the largest office building in the world. The second, or at least what the Defense Department hoped would be the second, had been dubbed the "little Pentagon" or in military jargon, the DOB (Defense Office Building).

The Armed Services Committees of the Senate and House consistently supported construction of the DOB, but the Appropriations Committees stood in the way. During hearings on the fiscal 1973 defense budget, however, the House Appropriations Military Construction Subcommittee offered the armed forces a deal—one military office building in exchange for a Defense Department commitment to increase the number of military employees being relocated outside the Washington, D.C., area.

In the end the deal fell through, without explanation. Both House and Senate Appropriations committees denied the administration's $19.4-million request for the down payment on construction in fiscal 1973.

Defense planners, appearing before the House Appropriations Committee envisioned a 1,107-acre military complex along three miles of Potomac River shoreline, the center of which would be the new $170-million DOB—designed so that it would resemble a three-armed pinwheel from the air. With the DOB as its center, the development would include 2,000 new units of family housing, bachelor living quarters, other administrative and intelligence office buildings, plus a small industrial and technological area for military purposes.

The area earmarked for the new military complex was land occupied by Bolling Air Force Base and the Anacostia Naval Station, adjoining tracts of land in Southeast Washington, D.C., across the Potomac River and slightly downstream from the Pentagon.

Several points of controversy surrounded the military's first major step toward developing the complex:

• Despite Defense Department claims that the project had full community support, many local groups—including the District of Columbia government until 1971—had lobbied for years to gain local control over the valuable Bolling-Anacostia tract of land. Local groups hoped to convert the 1,107 acres into low- and moderate-income housing projects with an adjoining industrial park, thus breathing new life into the depressed Anacostia section of the District of Columbia. The city's most recent squabble over the project had been focused on the military's plan to build 2,000 units of family housing in the area instead of utilizing local housing the city claims is already in existence in the surrounding area.

• The Defense Department, with full support of Defense Secretary Melvin R. Laird, had been conducting a campaign to relocate various military missions outside of the capital region. The push to build a new defense office building in Washington, D.C., struck some members of Congress as contrary to proclaimed policy.

• Memories of the last time the Defense Department built an office building on the banks of the Potomac River still lingered in the minds of some members of Congress; the Pentagon cost twice as much as planners said it would and ended up providing substantially less office space than had been promised. When the Pentagon was built in 1941-42, defense planners said only part of its office space would be needed for the military when World War II ended.

Defense Department witnesses told an executive session of the House Appropriations Committee in 1972 that plans were underway to reduce the number of military employees in the District of Columbia region by 30 percent over a 15-year period beginning in 1969. This would be accomplished by attrition and by relocation. Ten percent of the reduction had already been accomplished, witnesses said, by reducing capital area military manpower from 188,900 persons in mid-1969 to 166,800 by mid-1971.

The Deal. Rep. Elford A. Cederberg (R Mich.) asked the Pentagon witnesses: "You are asking for 1.5-million net square feet in the new Defense Office Building. So that and the 2 million (square feet) to be relocated is 3.5 million square feet. You have 4 million (square feet) that is substandard. Why, instead of moving 2 million (square feet), could you not move out 2.5 million?.... You are planning to move out 2 million anyway. Why not move out 2.6 million? Then you would have all of your substandard space eliminated and have your new office building?"

Rep. Robert L.F. Sikes (D Fla.), chairman of the Military Construction Subcommittee, added: "You better buy that. That is the best deal I have heard offered.... All we want is a yes or no answer on this."

David O. Cooke, deputy assistant defense secretary, answered: "Yes." The subcommittee then proceeded to other business.

Earlier in the subcommittee session, Chairman Sikes told the Pentagon witnesses what he thought about their plan to relocate 2 million square feet of office space. Sikes asked: "You are using 62 million square feet and you propose to move only 2 million?

Lt. Cmdr. A. P. Booth, a Navy engineering expert, said: "Two million."

Sikes: "That is not much decentralization. That is ...only one-thirtieth."

Booth: "Yes, sir."

Sikes: "That is not very impressive. That would indicate at best you are only going to leave things as they are. You are not going to move very much out of Washington. Is that correct?

Booth: "Yes, sir."

Deal Dies. In reporting the fiscal 1973 military construction appropriations bill, the House Appropriations Committee deleted all funds requested for the new DOB. The panel in its report said: "The committee has had serious doubts about approving this building in view of its high cost, the over-concentration of the Department of Defense in the Washington, D.C., area and its relative priority in comparison to other types of military construction and family housing projects." The Senate Appropriations Committee sustained the action of its House counterpart without comment, killing the project for another Congress.

(Continued from p. 219)
tions. The committee roundly criticized Lavelle and endorsed the Pentagon's decision to give a two-rank demotion in retirement.

By contrast, the House committee said the air strikes ordered by Lavelle were "not only proper but essential" for the protection of Lavelle's men. The panel said the strikes were aimed at wiping out anti-aircraft missiles and new radar networks which posed a threat to the normal operations of Lavelle's 7th Air Force. But, on the other hand, the report criticized Lavelle for filing false reports on the bombing to hide his actions from his superiors.

In the wake of the Lavelle controversy, Defense Secretary Melvin R. Laird wrote Armed Services Committee Chairman John C. Stennis (D Miss.) that he was beefing up the military's inspector general system in order to prevent unauthorized actions by commanders in the future. Noting that "the existing inspector general system is military service-oriented in both organization and purview," Laird directed that the inspector generals of all the services report to the civilian secretaries of their departments in the future, in addition to their existing job of reporting to the service chief of staff. Laird also directed unified commands (such as the over-all U.S. command in Vietnam) to set up their own inspector general systems to check on operations of the service commands (such as 7th Air Force) attached to them. "Had there been on the staff of the unified and sub-unified commands in 1971 and 1972 an inspector general who had the responsibility to inspect service component commands as to military operational matters," Laird wrote Stennis, "it is probable that any deviations from operating authorities by the service component command, 7th Air Force, could have been detected by the inspector general of the Military Advisory Command Vietnam (MACV)."

Defense Production Act

Congress June 28 cleared for the President's signature a bill (S 3715—PL 92-325) extending the provisions of the Defense Production Act for two years, until June 30, 1974.

Also extended—until June 30, 1985—was the time period in which the government could purchase and dispose of materials in the Defense Production Act inventory which included various metals needed for defense and space production programs. The bill did not provide any further extension of the presidential controls over wages and prices that had been authorized under the 1970 extension of the act. In separate legislation, the wage-price controls had been extended through April 30, 1973. *(p. 114)*

As cleared by Congress, S 3715:

• Extended to June 30, 1974, the provisions of the 1950 Defense Production Act to assure defense production in case of emergency and to guarantee loans to contractors in defense and aerospace-related industries.

• Authorized the establishment of a reserve of trained executives to fill government positions in a time of mobilization.

• Exempted from uniform cost-accounting standards regulations contracts under $100,000, those where costs were fixed or regulated by the government, those covering commercial items or those where the board deemed exemption necessary.

• Extended the authority of the five-member board established by the act to examine contractors' books, authorized appropriations as might be necessary and required the board to make an annual report.

• Extended to June 30, 1985, the authority to enter into commitments to purchase materials essential to defense production, to stockpile those materials and to sell materials already contained in the inventory.

Military Surplus Disposal

The Pentagon's surplus disposal system came under the eye of Senate investigators during the 1972 congressional session.

The highlight of the Senate probe, conducted by the Government Operations Permanent Investigating Subcommittee, was a report by two agents of the army's criminal investigations division (CID) on six cases of improprieties in the European disposal operation. The agents told the panel that "Excess property operations generally were poorly managed. Property disposal yards kept no reliable inventories of material...(and) functioned separately from one another, each operating independently, largely as if the others did not exist."

The agents said that in one instance a depot sold arms to a known gun merchant on the condition that the gun merchant promise to demilitarize the arms after he purchased them. "Simple common sense should indicate that a merchant in the gun business wants to buy guns not for scrap but because he intends to sell the property as guns."

The prevailing attitude among U.S. servicemen who worked in the disposal yards was "hear no evil, see no evil, speak no evil," according to the CID agents. "Contractors were stealing from and cheating the property disposal depots. Rarely was anything done to protect American interests. Rarely was a crooked contractor barred from future sales. Rarely were compromised (German) employees fired. Property disposal operations in Western Europe were inefficient, wasteful and corrupt."

In other testimony, J. Fred Buzhardt, general counsel for the Defense Department, told the committee that the armed forces had been concerned about property disposal operations for several years and that programs to correct the situation were already underway.

He said that the military departments and the Defense Supply Agency had been directed to develop a better system for identifying and controlling the disposal of militarily sensitive items but that "due to the volume of different items in the supply systems, this may be a difficult and long-range effort."

Other Developments

Additional Deputy Secretary. After two years of consideration, Congress on the eve of adjournment cleared administration-proposed legislation authorizing an additional deputy secretary of defense (for a total of two). Authority for the new post was attached as a rider to a bill (HR 14911—PL 92-596) removing limits on the amount of military leave that a U.S. serviceman may accumulate while he is a prisoner of war. The Senate Armed Services Committee had deferred action on the deputy secretary proposal in 1971 because of the Pentagon's failure to spell out the duties for each of the two deputies. But

(Continued on p. 223)

Chronology of Action Involving Drug Abuse in the Military

Despite numerous reports documenting widespread drug abuse among soldiers in Vietnam during the late 1960s, very little progress was made in Congress or the Defense Department toward solving the drug problem by 1972. A chronology of action follows:

1969

July 14—President Nixon's message to Congress on drug abuse prevention. No mention of military.

October—Army establishes the military's first amnesty program for drug abusers providing rehabilitation and limited protection from prosecution.

1970

March, August and November—Hearings related to the drug problem in the military conducted by Special Subcommittee of the House Armed Services Committee, the Senate Labor and Public Welfare Special Subcommittee on Alcoholism and Narcotics and the Senate Judiciary Subcommittee on Drug Abuse.

October—Defense Department recommended that amnesty program for drug abusers be adopted by all branches of the military.

October—Congress cleared the Comprehensive Drug Abuse Prevention and Control Act (PL 91-513) which contained no mention of the Defense Department or the Veterans Administration.

1971

March 8—Air Force started amnesty program.

April 20—Senate Armed Services Special Subcommittee on Alcoholism and Drug Abuse, chaired by Harold E. Hughes (D Iowa), issued staff report on drug abuse in military jointly with Labor and Public Welfare Committee.

April 23—The House Armed Services Special Subcommittee to Investigate Alleged Drug Abuse in the Armed Services issued a report concluding that "there is a serious drug problem in the military," estimating that as many as 10 per cent of the men stationed in Vietnam were heroin users.

May 27—The House Foreign Affairs special study mission on the world heroin problem issued a report estimating that from 10 to 15 per cent of U.S. troops stationed in Vietnam were using heroin; "in some units heroin addiction might be as high as 25 per cent."

May 30—Navy started amnesty program.

June 1—President Nixon gave first indication that the drug problem in the military is a major one; announced that his program would include holding addicts in military for treatment although their term of service may have expired.

June 4—Defense Secretary Melving R. Laird announced that he was not completely satisfied that the government of South Vietnam was doing all it could to stem the flow of heroin into the country.

June 9—Senate adopted an amendment authorizing drug control and rehabilitation programs in military.

June 15.—Sen. Alan Cranston (D Calif.) announced that the Veterans Administration treating a total of 219 drug patients at just five centers.

June 17—President Nixon announced the establishment of a special action office within the Executive Office to "develop over-all federal strategy for drug abuse programs"; requested $14-million increase in the Veterans Administration budget for rehabilitation efforts of veterans and appointed Dr. Jerome H. Jaffe as consultant to the President on narcotics.

June 22—Veterans Administration announced it would open 27 new drug treatment centers by Oct. 1 bringing to 32 the number of treatment centers.

June 30—Pentagon submitted to Congress a supplemental budget request for fiscal 1972 of $34,225,000 for drug abuse prevention and rehabilitation programs.

July 7—Pentagon announced that any serviceman who volunteered for drug treatment could not be disciplined under the Uniform Code of Military Justice or discharged under dishonorable conditions.

Sept. 21—Brig. Gen. John K. Singlaub named to fill the new position of deputy assistant defense secretary for drug and alcohol abuse.

Sept. 28—President Nixon signs the military draft extension bill (HR 6531—PL 92-129) which authorized the Defense Secretary to "utilize all practical available methods" to identify, treat and rehabilitate military personnel who were drug or alcohol dependents.

Oct. 24—Rep. Seymour Halpern (R N.Y.) issued a report on his special study mission of the heroin problem and estimated that from 20 per cent to 30 per cent of the servicemen in Vietnam were using heroin.

Dec. 16—The Army sent 132 enlisted men and officers to Yale University, New Haven, Conn., for the Army's first two-week intensive training program at the University's Drug Dependence Institute.

Dec. 26—Rep. G. V. (Sonny) Montgomery (D Miss.) told newsmen after his tour of Vietnam that the military's drug program "hasn't reduced the problem percentage-wise that much but it's under control and it doesn't affect the over-all efficiency."

1972

Jan. 7—Dr. Richard S. Wilbur, Assistant Defense Secretary, announced that the military had "reversed a heroin epidemic in Vietnam" and that the percentage of drug abusers in Vietnam has been reduced to 4.5 per cent of the men checked in unannounced tests.

April 17—The House Armed Services Committee reported a bill (HR 12846) aimed at dealing with the military's drug problem. "The Defense Department is making encouraging advances in attacking the drug problem," the committee report stated. "However, this advance is modest and much remains to be done."

June 12—The House passed HR 12846 without amendments by a roll-call vote of 322-1. The bill then went to the Senate Armed Services Committee.

The Senate committee failed to report the bill before the adjournment of the 92nd Congress.

(Continued from p. 221)

the committee did an about-face in 1972 when Defense Secretary Melvin R. Laird assured the panel that he planned to make "an allocation of primary responsibilities and tasks" among himself and the two deputy secretaries.

Servicemen's Survivor Benefits. Congress Sept. 12 cleared for the President a bill (HR 10670—PL 92-425) establishing a new survivor benefits program for retired members of the armed forces.

HR 10670 would enable a serviceman to provide benefits to his survivors of up to 55 per cent of his retirement income. For such coverage, the retiree would pay 2.5 per cent of the first $3,600 of his annual retirement income plus 10 per cent of the remaining amount of his pension. Benefits provided upon his death would depend upon the amount of his income at retirement.

The measure was intended to provide a program of survivor benefits comparable to that offered by the federal government for civil service personnel. Unless the cause of death was service-connected, survivors of retired military personnel were not automatically entitled under existing law to any part of the deceased serviceman's pension.

Hostile Fire Areas Duty. President Nixon Oct. 9 signed a bill (HR 14537—PL 92-481) extending authority to grant special 30-day leave for members of the uniformed services who voluntarily extend their tour of duty in hostile fire areas. Final action came when the Senate passed HR 14537 by voice vote Sept. 30. The bill had been reported in the Senate by the Armed Services Committee (S Rept 92-1233) Sept. 28. It had been reported in the House (H Rept 92-1159) June 21 by the House Armed Services Committee and passed the House July 17.

Military Incentive Pay. Congress Oct. 3 cleared for the President a bill (HR 14909—PL 92-482) providing authority to continue incentive pay for hazardous duty to members of the armed forces following return from missing status.

The bill permitted continued payment during the period of hospitalization and rehabilitation even when requirements for performance of hazardous duty were not met.

Final action came Oct. 3 when the House by voice vote agreed to a Senate amendment. The House originally had passed HR 14909 July 17, the Senate Sept. 30.

Members of the military who received incentive pay for hazardous duty prior to becoming missing had continued to be entitled to that pay while missing. However, entitlement ceased upon termination of the missing status. HR 14909 was proposed by the Defense Department to extend payment during a one-year rehabilitation period.

Military Drug Treatment. The House June 12 passed a bill (HR 12846) authorizing drug treatment for drug dependent persons in the military. The measure, requested by the Nixon administration, died when Congress adjourned without the Senate Armed Services Committee reporting the bill.

As reported by the House Armed Services Committee April 17 and passed by the House June 12, HR 12846 with minor exceptions was the same as HR 9503, introduced on behalf of the administration by F. Edward Hebert (D La.), committee chairman. Included in the bill were provisions for treatment and rehabilitation services for drug-dependent persons in the armed forces and a required urinalysis testing of all armed forces personnel for traces of narcotic drugs.

Abrams Confirmation. Following its Armed Services Committee's probe of the Lavelle issue, the Senate Oct. 12 confirmed President Nixon's nomination of Gen. Creighton Abrams for Army Chief of Staff. Confirmation came on an 84-2 roll-call vote, with Frank Church (D Idaho) and William Proxmire (D Wis.) the lone dissenters.

Navy Racial Strife. A series of race-related incidents plagued the Navy in 1972, including a fight aboard the aircraft carrier *Kitty Hawk* in October which left 46 sailors injured. Other serious disturbances took place aboard the carrier *Constellation* and the oiler *Hassayampa*. The incidents triggered a congressional investigation which sought to link the racial trouble to a relaxation of Navy regulations under its new chief of naval operations, Adm. Elmo R. Zumwalt Jr.

The investigation was conducted by a special subcommittee of the House Armed Services Committee, headed by Rep. Floyd V. Hicks (D Wash.), who said in opening the hearings that "we cannot overlook the possibility that there may exist at this time an environment of—for lack of a better word—'permissiveness'—wherein all that is needed is a catalyst. Perhaps perceptions of racial relations in these cases provided that spark." The panel issued a report on Jan. 23, 1973, that blamed lax discipline rather than discrimination for the racial problems.

In an outspoken defense of his overhaul of the Navy's rule book, Zumwalt Nov. 20 denied that his reforms had led to the racial strife. "The Navy will maintain order and discipline," he told newsmen during a break in one of the Hicks hearings. "I have absolutely no problem about the statement of whether or not there is permissiveness in the Navy."

Zumwalt's reforms (published in communiques called Z-Grams), which ranged from a loosening of dress regulations to a wider role for women personnel, touched off considerable animosity among the Navy's traditionalists, who saw them as a threat to good discipline. Speculation thus developed that the Hicks hearings were engineered by "old guard" naval officers who hoped to put Zumwalt and his program in a bad light. Confronted with that suggestion by newsmen, however, Zumwalt said that he "would certainly not think that admirals who are of the quality we have in the U.S. Navy would be up to anything like that."

Prior to the hearings, Zumwalt moved to head off any further racial disturbances. In a statement to naval commanders Nov. 10, he called for an expanded effort by the Navy's shipboard and unit-level minority affairs assistants, who he said had been "effectively hamstrung in all too many cases." Among other moves, Zumwalt ordered that racial relations training get the same priority in the Navy as job training currently receives.

Other racial incidents had occurred sporadically at Marine bases and in Army compounds in Germany and Japan in the late 1960s and early 1970s. But they paled to insignificance compared with the Navy's 1972 shipboard riots.

Selective Service

1971 DRAFT LAW: INTERIM STEP TOWARD VOLUNTEER ARMY

It was the end of January 1971 when Richard Nixon sent Congress a military draft bill conceived as an interim step toward his 1968 campaign goal of building an all-volunteer military force. Nixon wanted a two-year extension of conscription and a substantial pay increase for the men in uniform. The President got what he asked for, and more.

The draft bill (HR 6531—PL 92-129), which was cleared for Nixon's signature Sept. 21, 1971, after eight stormy months of debate, extended the draft two years—through June 30, 1973—and increased military pay and other benefits by $2.4-billion annually. The bill when passed was a ploy by the administration and its congressional supporters to undercut pending draft repeal bills with the promise that a volunteer force was in the works, while assuring opponents of the all-volunteer concept that no rash moves were contemplated.

But on Jan. 27, 1973, the Defense Department announced that it was dropping plans to draft 5,000 more young men in the first half of 1973 and would not seek renewal of the draft after it expired June 30. The end of the draft placed the armed forces on an all-volunteer basis for the first time since 1948. *(Box p. 230; background on draft and volunteer force, Congress and the Nation Vol. II, p. 879)*

In both the House and Senate, the greatest threat to extending the draft in the manner requested by the White House came on votes aimed at renewing induction authority for just one year. In the House, a one-year extension amendment was rejected by just two votes. A similar proposal in the Senate lost by a six-vote margin.

Final Action. HR 6531 cleared Congress Sept. 21 when Nixon's forces in the Senate broke the back of an emerging filibuster by draft opponents on a 61-30 cloture vote and then passed the bill, 55-30.

The House had adopted the conference report on the measure Aug. 4, but the Senate delayed action until after a congressional summer recess despite heavy White House and Pentagon lobbying for earlier action.

The delay in Senate approval of the final bill resulted in almost a three-month interruption of the process of inducting young men into the armed services, the first time the draft had not been in effect since 1948. During the debate, Selective Service Director Curtis W. Tarr had assured Congress that the nation could go for several months without inductions and without harm to its defense posture. Regular inductions began again in November 1971.

In most instances, the final bill paralleled the views of the Nixon administration, which was happy to get the two-year draft extension and reluctantly gave in to the bigger pay hike. The only major setback presented Nixon in the bill was a rider urging, but not ordering, the President to withdraw troops from Vietnam at the earliest practicable date. The Senate had passed a far tougher provision, but Nixon backers succeeded in watering it down in conference.

Changes in the Law. The end product of Congress' eight-month work on the bill was a substantial change in who would serve in the military services, how he would be chosen, who would sit on his draft board and what his rights were in dealing with that board.

The age group vulnerable to induction was unchanged (18-26). But within the framework of existing law fewer young men were able to escape draft eligibility. Student deferments were abolished for 1971 college freshmen, although the sophomores, juniors and seniors maintained their deferments.

A new set of procedural rights for the draft registrant was part of the draft law, including the right to present witnesses to the draft board, the right to appear in person, a requirement that the board have a quorum present when the registrant appeared in person and the stipulation that if the registrant so requested the board must

---

1971 Draft Bill Highlights

In its final form, the draft extension bill (HR 6531—PL 92-129) provided for:

- A two-year extension of the draft to June 30, 1973.
- A sense of Congress resolution urging the President to negotiate for a Vietnam cease-fire and for the President to withdraw U.S. troops from Indochina at the earliest practicable date pending the release of all U.S. prisoners of war.
- An increase in pay and other types of compensation for servicemen estimated to cost a total of $2.4-billion a year over present compensation.
- A nationalized lottery call eliminating the local board quota system of selecting draftees.
- The return to the President of authority—withdrawn in 1967—to draft college students who entered school after the spring of 1971.
- Expansion of the procedural rights of the draft registrant.
- Interim steps for setting up programs to treat, identify and rehabilitate drug addicts and alcoholics in the military.
- A 2.5-million-man ceiling on the armed forces' active duty strength and a 130,000-man ceiling on the number of men who could be drafted during fiscal 1972.
- An extension of the statute of limitations making a person who failed to register for the draft eligible for prosecution until age 31.

provide him a written statement if it ruled against his claim for a particular draft status.

Despite several attempts to revise the definition of a conscientious objector on the floor of the Senate and House, there was no change in existing law. The House-passed version of the bill extended an objector's term of alternate service to three years from two years. The extra year of service was removed from the bill in the House-Senate conference. The final version of the bill stipulated that a CO was subject to recall to his alternate service in case of a declared national emergency.

Background: The Volunteer Force

The idea of replacing the draft with an all-volunteer system first was placed in the Republican platform during the 1964 presidential campaign. In 1968, stronger language was used. "When military manpower needs can be appreciably reduced, we will place the Selective Service System on standby and substitute a voluntary force obtained through adequate pay and career incentives," the platform stated.

Democrats also seized on the issue. The presidential platform of the Democratic party included a phrase about the all-volunteer concept in 1968.

Two months after Nixon moved into the White House, he appointed a 15-man presidential commission to work out plans for conversion of the armed forces into an all-volunteer service. The commission, headed by former Defense Secretary Thomas S. Gates Jr., reported its recommendations to the President Feb. 21, 1970.

The commission recommended implementation of an all-volunteer force by July 1, 1971. To obtain an all-volunteer force of 2.5 million men, the commission estimated additional costs of $2.7-billion for wages and total new costs of $3.2-billion. About 75,000 additional volunteers would have to be found.

After the Gates commission recommended that an all-volunteer military should be instituted by mid-1971, Sen. Mark O. Hatfield (R Ore.) cosponsored with Sen. Barry Goldwater (R Ariz.) an amendment to the fiscal 1971 military procurement authorization bill calling for implementation of the Gates commission's recommendations.

Although the Hatfield proposal picked up 26 more votes than did a similar effort by Hatfield in 1967, the margin was still insufficient to gain passage. The amendment was rejected Aug. 25, 1970, by a **key 35-52 roll-call vote.** The amendment did not have Nixon's backing.

Support for improvements in the soldier's life (i.e. pay increases), whether the improvements led to an all-volunteer military or not, was the unanimous position of witnesses appearing before the Armed Services Committees in 1971. The Nixon administration, anticipating the need for improvements, began modifying some of the stricter military regulations in January in an effort to make service more appealing.

Nixon Message. In a Jan. 28, 1971, message to Congress, the President said, "We should begin moving toward the end of the draft and its replacement with an all-volunteer force." Nixon added the caveat, however, that "no one knows precisely when we can end conscription." He said that "even the most optimistic observers agree that we would not be able to end the draft in the next year or so without seriously weakening our military forces."

Two alternatives for the length of a draft extension were proposed. The administration bill (S 427, HR 2476) requested a two-year extension and the Hatfield joint resolution, S J Res 20, identical to H J Res 345, sponsored in the House by Rep. Bella S. Abzug (D N.Y.), proposed repeal of the draft by Dec. 31, which would be the same as a six-month extension. Another alternative, which required no formal proposal, was for Congress to allow the President's induction authority to simply expire June 30.

Administration Proposals. Three bills included in the administration's two-year draft extension and volunteer force package were designed to improve conditions in the military in anticipation of the day when draft calls no longer would be needed. The cost of the three bills totaled $1.5-billion.

The administration bill (S 496, HR 3496) to increase pay was estimated to cost an additional $908-million in fiscal year 1972. The proposal requested that a recruit's pay be increased by 50 per cent or from $134 to $201 per month.

An estimated $79-million increase in quarters allowances for low-grade enlisted men (E-1 through E-4) with dependents was requested in the bill. During fiscal 1971, cash expenditures for quarters allowances were $1.48-billion, according to the Pentagon.

An enlistment bonus for combat soldiers was requested in the second administration bill (S 495, HR 3498). Although the bonus specified in the proposal was a maximum of $6,000 for a three-year enlistment, Assistant Defense Secretary Roger T. Kelley told the Senate Armed Services Committee that a $3,000 bonus would be used initially.

The third bill in the package (HR 3497, S 494) requested a 71 per cent increase in the military recruiting budget for fiscal 1972. The proposal was designed to allow the recruiting officer a larger expense account when out in the field. The military recruiting budget in fiscal 1971 was $156-million. The proposed budget for fiscal 1972 was $267-million or an increase of $111-million.

Included in the $1.5-billion total for the three bills was $100-million to be held in a contingency fund.

House Committee Action

The portion of the House Armed Services Committee bill (HR 6531), reported March 25, that dealt with the all-volunteer force went further than the administration bill did in allotting pay raises ($1.87-billion), but did not include any type of incentive for enlistment in combat units. Chairman F. Edward Hebert (D La.), who repeatedly voiced skepticism about the possibility of attaining the voluntary force, told reporters March 22 that the committee bill put no obstacles in the way of attaining the all-volunteer force. Assistant Defense Secretary Kelley told a press briefing the same day that without the enlistment bonus, "it will be very, very difficult" to achieve the voluntary force by mid-1973.

The committee bill authorized twice as much money for pay increases as did the administration proposal. The $1.87-billion provided by the committee for wage hikes would increase a recruit's pay from $134 to $268 per month.

(Continued on p. 228)

All-Volunteer Force or the Draft: The Issues

At issue in the 1971 draft-volunteer force debate were matters of morality, of economy, class inequities and control of foreign policy.

Mercenary Force. Some of those who opposed the volunteer force said that such a force would be a band of "professional killers" with little in common with civilian society. Those supporting the measure discounted such arguments by telling critics that the military was largely an all-volunteer force already.

Rep. Paul N. McCloskey Jr. (R Calif.) told the Armed Services Committee: "There are men who love to kill, but it seems to me the nation is far safer when its army is made up of reluctant citizen-soldiers than by men who take pride in being professional killers."

Dr. Harry Marmion, representing the American Veterans Committee, testified before the House committee: "There is the danger that an isolated military establishment will be a potential political force in American life that must not be underestimated. Instead of the present picture of a mammoth military-industrial complex dominating our society, we can expect an even greater establishment which will have little stake in civilian society, and will seek a larger budget and more wars to perpetuate itself."

Army of Poor. Opponents of the all-volunteer force claimed that military enlistments would be predominantly from lower socio-economic backgrounds than the men touched by the draft. Why should the poor fight this country's wars?, the critics asked. Supporters relied on the Gates commission projections when answering the question. The commission's findings, they said, predicted only a slight increase in blacks and underprivileged would be noticed if the program were implemented.

Sen. Edward F. Kennedy (D Mass.) told the Senate Armed Services Committee: "I would support a volunteer army in peacetime. But when American men are dying in Vietnam, Cambodia and perhaps Laos, I believe a volunteer army is both unwise and inequitable. I frankly do not want to insulate middle- and upper-class Americans from the horrors of war."

Assistant Defense Secretary Roger T. Kelley: "The alleged pitfalls of the voluntary military organization—that it will be dominated by mercenaries or be all black—are gratuitous and false claims. They should be knocked down hard lest the American public be misled by them."

Control War-Making. If there had not been a draft, Vietnam never would have happened, argued some opponents of draft extension. They said the draft provided the President with an unlimited supply of manpower which tended to perpetuate American "adventurism" abroad, and that the draft was eroding the power of Congress to control the nation's destiny. Supporters of draft extension called the claims "sheer speculation" and urged a two-year extension. Supporters of the draft said draftees were crucial in permitting a withdrawal from Vietnam.

Rep. Bella S. Abzug (D N.Y.) before the House committee testified: "The draft has made possible the escalation and continuation of the war in Indochina. As an important step toward ending the wretched war, the President's power to induct men into the armed forces must not be extended beyond June 30."

Sanford Gottlieb, director of an anti-war group known as SANE, told both the House and Senate committees: "To suggest that we need draftees to generate anti-war pressures is to suggest that the burden of halting the war should be placed upon the men who are being shot at rather than exercised by the elected representatives of the American people."

Kennedy took an opposite view: "There are some who argue that we never would have become involved in a large-scale war in Indochina if there had been no draft. This is sheer speculation. Some suggest that if the draft were ended, American involvement in Indochina would have to come to a grinding halt. This is also speculation. In any event, if the Congress wishes to end the war, it can do so by legislation aimed directly at that goal."

Money-Saver. Critics and supporters of the all-volunteer force agreed that in the long run, such a force probably would be more economical. Opponents argued, however, that the country could ill-afford the initial expense of launching the program.

Testifying in support of the all-volunteer force, Kelley said such a force would be more efficient because it would be functioning in "a free environment" and would be more effective and economical because it would consist of fewer people than its conscripted counterpart.

Kennedy said: "In wartime, a society can least afford the extra cost of trying to achieve a volunteer army. When compared to pressing domestic needs, the extra costs of a volunteer army become highly questionable."

American Way. The draft was unfair, argued opponents of extension, because it interrupted a young man's life, forced him to fight in unjust wars and went against the tradition of volunteerism in the United States. Supporters of the extension asked: Who would volunteer if the draft is eliminated?

Sen. Barry Goldwater (R Ariz.) told the Senate committee, "I believe that the most precious and fundamental right of a man is his right to live his own life. When force is used to tell a young man how he shall spend several years of his life, I consider this to invade his...personal liberty." Sen. Mark O. Hatfield (R Ore.) called the draft "involuntary servitude that is contrary to every value and tradition that has made our country strong."

Director Curtis W. Tarr of Selective Service said: "I've talked with countless numbers of young people who would have gained a great deal personally by interrupting their college work so they might understand better their motivations for study and how better they might orient their lives." He said the draft might provide just such an interruption.

For quarters allowances, the committee approved 10 times more money than the administration bill carried. Where the administration requested $79-million, HR 6531 provided $830-million for increases in quarters allowances. The administration bill emphasized enlisted men with dependents while the committee bill spread additional compensation through all ranks of military personnel. The total committee allotment for wage increases and quarters allowances was $2.7-billion.

House Floor Action

The House April 1, after three days of debate, by a 293-99 roll-call vote approved a two-year extension of the military draft. Only five amendments were adopted during the entire debate. One amendment reversed a committee action which had abolished the deferment for divinity students. The bill also was amended to require draft boards, clerks and records to be established in each county; to include private non-public hospitals, in addition to public institutions, as places where conscientious objectors (COs) could meet their alternate service requirements; and to exempt from induction all male members of an immediate family in which one member either had been killed or totally disabled or was a prisoner of war or missing in action.

During the House debate, new attitudes by a significant number of House members toward the draft and U.S. military involvement in Vietnam became evident.

Although HR 6531 dealt specifically with manpower needs of the military for 1971-73, the three days of debate March 30-April 1 comprised the most extensive review of U.S. policy in Indochina ever allowed by the House leadership. A new element in the debate was the March 29 conviction of Lt. William L. Calley Jr. *(p. 193)*

Support for the concept of an all-volunteer military service was expressed throughout the debate. Differences of opinion were expressed, however, as to when the volunteer force could begin replacing draftees and draft-motivated volunteers, who were supplying about 48 per cent of the manpower for the Army.

Four attempts were made on the floor to reduce the period of the draft extension to less than the two years recommended in the committee bill.

Not since passage in 1951 of the Universal Military Training and Service Act, which reinstated the draft as a part of the American way of life, had the House spent more than one day debating the draft.

The 1971 extension was opposed by 99 members. This was the largest protest vote against the draft in the House since before World War II. Nine House members voted against the 1967 draft extension.

Senate Committee Action

The Senate Armed Services Committee May 5 unanimously reported a heavily amended version of the House bill, HR 6531.

As reported, the only major provision in HR 6531 that was identical to the House version was the administration's requested two-year extension, to June 30, 1973, of the President's induction authority.

Although both the House and Senate committee versions eliminated deferments for undergraduate students, the Senate-reported bill denied the President

Draft Extensions

Before 1971, the draft had been extended four times since 1951. Each extension had been for four years. The closest margin on House passage of any military draft bill since World War II was in 1951 when the House first approved legislation establishing the current authority to induct men into the armed forces. The vote that year was 372-44.

In the Senate, no more than five votes were ever cast against a draft bill during the period 1951-1967.

1971 (two-year extension)

House—Passed by 293-99 roll-call vote; three days of debate; 23 amendments offered, 5 adopted.

Senate—Passed by 72-16 roll-call vote; over a month of debate; 60 amendments offered, 24 adopted.

1967 (four-year extension)

House—Passed by 362-9 roll-call vote; one day of debate; 13 amendments offered, 3 adopted.

Senate—Passed by 70-2 roll-call vote; one day of debate; 7 amendments offered, none adopted.

1963 (four-year extension)

House—Passed by 388-3 roll-call vote; one day of debate; 3 amendments offered, none adopted.

Senate—Passed by voice vote; one day of debate; no amendments offered.

1959 (four-year extension)

House—Passed by 381-20 roll-call vote; one day of debate; three amendments offered, none adopted.

Senate—Passed by 90-1 roll-call vote; one day of debate; two amendments offered, none adopted.

1955 (four-year extension)

House—Passed by 394-4 roll-call vote; one day of debate; 5 amendments offered, 2 adopted.

Senate—Passed by voice vote; one day of debate; one amendment offered, one adopted.

1951 Universal Military Training and Service Act

House—Passed by 372-44 roll-call vote; four days of debate; 34 amendments offered, 16 adopted.

Senate—Passed by 79-5 roll-call vote; seven days of debate; 17 amendments offered, 3 adopted.

discretion to remove student deferments retroactive to April 23, 1970. The administration had previously announced its intention to abolish student deferments as of April 23, 1970, if such authority was enacted.

The committee restored the conscientious objector requirement in existing law of two years' alternate service. The House-passed bill set a three-year obligation.

Increased compensation (pay, quarters allowances, subsistence pay, recruiting expenses for members of the armed services) provided by the Senate committee totaled $1-billion, which was $1.7-billion less than that in the House-passed version. The major committee cuts were in pay hikes and quarters allowances for enlisted men and their dependents. The Senate committee's bill, unlike the House version, included an enlistment bonus program designed to increase voluntary enlistments in combat units.

The reported bill also included a 150,000-man annual ceiling on the draft and a 2.55-million manpower ceiling on total military personnel for each of fiscal 1972 and 1973.

Senate Floor Action

The Senate by a 72-16 roll-call vote June 24 passed HR 6531 and sent the bill to conference.

The measure as passed by the Senate also contained a controversial amendment by Senate Majority Leader Mike Mansfield (D Mont.) setting a national policy of withdrawing troops from Indochina nine months after the bill's enactment. During consideration of the bill the Senate acted on 60 amendments. Major proposals rejected by the chamber were a bid by Mansfield to reduce by one-half the number of U.S. troops in Europe, attempts to eliminate or shorten the draft authorization and a 1971 version of a 1970 McGovern-Hatfield "end the war" amendment. *(Foreign Policy chapter)*

The Senate considered the bill from May 6 to June 24 during which time it was the subject of vigorous debate and lobbying. And passage of the bill came only after the Senate had voted to end the debate on a 65-27 cloture vote.

Mike Gravel (D Alaska) announced during the first day of debate that he intended to talk the draft to death if proposed amendments to do the same were rejected. Gravel, the first senator on the floor, said that the President's "induction power...will expire June 30." He asked for support to filibuster the bill, but none was forthcoming.

John C. Stennis (D Miss.), chairman of the Armed Services Committee, was the first to rise in opposition to Gravel's tactic. "I believe that failure to renew this induction authority, whether by vote or by the inaction resulting from extended debate, would be calamitous," he said.

Conference Action

House Rejected Vietnam Amendment. Following Senate passage June 24 of the draft extension bill, the House June 28 refused to instruct House conferees to accept the Senate-passed Mansfield amendment declaring it U.S. policy to withdraw troops from Indochina within 9 months.

The motion to instruct conferees was proposed by Charles W. Whalen Jr. (R Ohio), cosponsor of an earlier "end-the-war" measure that had been rejected by the House on a 158-255 vote June 17. The House June 28 killed the Whalen motion by adopting, by a 219-175 roll-call vote, a motion by Armed Services Committee Chairman Hebert to table the motion.

The 175 members voting for the Whalen motion constituted the largest anti-Vietnam war vote in the House up to that time; the 43-vote margin was also the closest of any such vote. The number of representatives voting for such a measure had steadily increased through early 1971.

One Month Deadlock. The bill was sent to conference June 28. Two days later the chief House conferee, Hebert, announced that only one provision of the bill remained in contention—the troop withdrawal amendment. But it took a month to resolve that issue.

CONFERENCE REPORT

When the conferees finally reached agreement on July 30, the compromise conference report contained the following major actions.

Vietnam Withdrawal. On the critical Vietnam issue, conferees softened the Senate amendment, declaring it the sense of Congress that the United States terminate military operations in Indochina "at the earliest practicable date." The Senate bill had ordered a U.S. withdrawal within nine months, pending release of U.S. prisoners. The conference report urged the President to begin negotiations for an immediate cease-fire and for establishing a definite withdrawal deadline along with the release of prisoners.

Induction Ceiling. Conferees adopted the Senate version, providing draft ceilings of 130,000 and 140,000 men for fiscal years 1972 and 1973 respectively and providing that the ceilings could be exceeded only with the approval of Congress. The House version had no similar provision.

Troop Strength. Conferees adopted the Senate authorized strength of 2,553,409 men but made it clear that the ceiling would in no way inhibit the President from calling up the reserves to cope with civil disturbances and other national emergencies. The House had authorized a manpower level of 2,609,409.

Conscientious Objector. Conferees dropped all language requiring a third year of service for COs and providing authority for the induction of a CO who did not perform his civilian job satisfactorily. The House had provided the third year plus a provision for immediate induction in the event the CO did not perform well in his civilian job. The Senate required the third year only when the reserves were called up because of a national emergency.

High School Students. Conferees adopted a Senate measure providing that a high school senior who reached the age of 20 during his senior year would be permitted to graduate before induction.

Student Induction. The Senate version provided that a college student could finish the semester or term or, in the case of a senior, the academic year, after receiving his induction notice. The House version was similar, but the Senate language was adopted.

Pay Increases. The over-all compensation package (pay increases, quarters allowances, subsistence allowances) which was adopted by the conference committee totaled less than either the House or Senate versions. The largest item was for basic pay increases for which conferees adopted the House provision which called for $1.8-billion.

Conferees compromised on the amounts passed by the House for quarters allowances and dependents' allowances, but the conference version was still substantially greater than approved by the Senate. In the allowances sections, the compensation tended to be spread through all levels of the military, not just the low-ranking personnel at which the pay increases were aimed. The House had failed to adopt a provision providing for an enlistment bonus, while the Senate had established a $6,000 enlistment bonus ceiling. Conferees settled on a $3,000 bonus maximum.

The following were amounts for each type of compensation increases provided for in the bill:

After July 1, 1973, For the First Time in a Quarter . . .

On Jan. 27, 1973—the day the Vietnam peace agreements were signed—Defense Secretary Melvin R. Laird surprised many of the nation's young men with an announcement that the Nixon administration would not seek renewal of the military draft after the existing draft authority expired on June 30.

Laird also revealed that the Pentagon was dropping plans to draft another 5,000 youths in the period from March through June 1973. No draft had been scheduled for January and February.

Expiration of the general drafting authority on June 30 would be the first time the nation was without the draft since 1948, except for a three-month interval in 1971 when Congress was debating the draft law.

In making the announcement, Laird made public a memorandum to top Pentagon officials stating: "With the signing of the peace agreement in Paris today, and after receiving a report from the secretary of the army that he forsees no need for further inductions, I wish to inform you that the armed forces henceforth will rely exclusively on volunteer soldiers, sailors and airmen and marines. Use of the draft has ended."

In Jan. 8 testimony before the House Armed Services Committee, however, Laird indicated that the Pentagon might want to retain draft boards and other machinery of the Selective Service System in the event the draft has to be reinstituted. "Certainly," he said, "it is prudent that we maintain a standby draft mechanism to provide authority to register and classify military eligibles and thus reduce the time needed to mobilize them if necessary." He added that drafting of men for reserve units might be needed unless Congress acted on the administration's Uniform Services Special Pay Act. The House passed the bill in 1972, but it died when the Senate took no action.

Laird said Jan. 27 that he wanted to hold the door open for possible drafting of doctors and dentists unless enough of them were attracted to the all-volunteer force. The medical draft and a draft for the reserves, which were 56,000 below strength in early 1973, would take new legislation. The standby draft mechanism would not. The only portion of the existing draft law due to expire was a section authorizing the President to draft men into the military.

Congressional sources told Congressional Quarterly that they expected little problem in attaining an all-volunteer force at the level programmed by the Pentagon for fiscal 1973—a total force of 2.3 million. But if the force had to be increased suddenly and substantially, they said, there could be serious problems—both in terms of cost and in finding sufficient numbers of volunteers.

"If you had to build the force up 200,000 or 300,000 men at a time, you'd have one hell of a problem," said Derek Vanderschaaf, a professional member of the House Defense Appropriations Subcommittee staff. Added Rep. Otis G. Pike (D N.Y.), a member of the House Armed Services Committee and a longtime critic of the all-volunteer concept: "The volunteer force is a fiction. You can always get all the men you need in peacetime. But you won't be able to get them in wartime when the need is really there."

Background

The nation's first peacetime selective service law was the Selective Training and Service Act of 1940. Most characteristics of that and the other draft laws enacted through the draft extension of 1971, however, had been established in the Selective Service Act of 1917, enacted to meet U.S. commitments in World War I.

During World War II, the Selective Service System registered about 50 million men. Problems of deferments during the war produced several instances of conflict between the System and Congress. In 1942, for example, Congress provided for a conditional exemption of agricultural workers. On Dec. 5, 1942, President Roosevelt by executive order placed the system under the War Manpower Commission, but Congress amended the law on Dec. 5, 1943, to make the System an independent agency.

Congress did not extend the 1940 act when it expired March 31, 1947, and the nation was without a conscription law until enactment of the Selective Service Act of 1948 on June 24, 1948. The Universal Military Training and Service Act of 1951, enacted during the Korean War, extended the draft until 1955. The

	House	Senate	Conference
(in millions)			
Basic pay	$1,825.4	$2,667	$1,825.4
Dependents' allowance	184.1	79	105.9
Quarters allowance	640.1	0	409.8
Subsistence allowance	37.8	0	0
Enlistment bonus	0	40	20.0
Recruiter expenses	2.9	2.9	2.9
Optometrists special pay	.5	.6	.6
Dependents' allowance for reservists	20.0	0	20.0
Annual Total	$2,710.8	$2,789.5	$2,384.6

Student Deferments. Conferees accepted the Senate version, stating that all students who had entered

college before the summer of 1971 would be able to maintain their deferment until graduation or to age 24. The House had given the President blanket authority to rule on the deferments.

Sole Surviving Son. Conferees adopted a Senate provision with minor changes which provided that no person could be inducted who had lost a member of his immediate family through service in the armed forces or through subsequent death as a result of injuries or disease incurred in the line of duty.

Divinity Students. Conferees adopted the Senate version declaring that divinity students would be provided a statutory deferment from the draft, not an exemption, and that divinity students would be eligible for the draft until age 35. If they should either drop out

. . . Century the Military to Operate Without a Draft

1951 act was extended by Congress five more times, until July 1, 1973. The first four extensions were for four-year periods, the last for two years. The biggest change in the draft over this period came in 1969 when President Nixon by executive order set up a lottery to establish the order of the draft call.

Registration and Deferments. The draft law provided for the registration of all males as they became 18 years of age. While the law provided for a few specific exemptions and deferments, those affecting the largest number of registrants were left to the discretion of the President, who in turn was authorized to delegate authority in draft matters to the director of the Selective Service System.

Deferments generally were granted in the areas of industry, agriculture, education and dependency. (In 1971, however, Nixon by executive order eliminated all occupational and most parental deferments.) Draft boards based occupational deferments on a List of Essential Activities and Critical Occupations drawn up by a committee comprising officials of the Departments of Commerce and Labor. The Commerce Department identified essential activities and the Labor Department determined critical occupations. There also were deferments for persons physically, mentally or morally unacceptable for military service, with standards in those categories set by the secretary of defense and not by the Selective Service System. By adjusting standards and changing regulations on deferments, the President could expand or contract inductions to meet changing needs of the armed services.

Selective Service System. The system was administered by the director and his staff, located in the District of Columbia, and about 4,000 local boards in the states. The local draft boards were under the supervision of a state director. Draft calls originated with a request from the Department of Defense for a given number of men, based on projected enlistments and needs. The system then determined which states would provide the men, basing its decision on a credit-debit procedure reflecting the number of men from each state already in the military. Each state then was assigned a quota of inductees, and the state director proceeded to provide the men through the state's local draft boards. The local board quota system was abolished by Congress at Nixon's request, in 1971; inductees were to be chosen on a nationwide basis related to their draft lottery numbers, instead of making induction dependent on both the lottery number and the quotas of their local boards. (Under the old system, persons with lower lottery numbers in high-quota areas were sometimes drafted ahead of persons with higher numbers elsewhere.)

The entire system operated under regulations drawn at the national level, but these left local boards with considerable latitude in selecting men for service. Some draft boards, for example, imposed more stringent requirements on student deferments in the liberal arts field than on such deferments in the sciences or medical arts, having determined at the local level that the training of doctors and scientists, for example, was more important to the national interest than was the training of lawyers or English professors.

After institution of the draft lottery in 1969, local boards retained their authority over deferments. But the 1971 law expanded the rights of young men facing induction and broadened representation of local draft boards. Among its other features, the 1971 act provided that members of a local draft board could not serve for more than 20 years and directed that the President, in making future appointments to local boards, should see "to the maximum extent possible" that the boards reflected proportionately the racial and religious breakdowns of the community in which the board served.

Hershey. Pressures to drop or reform the draft came over the Vietnam years from youths who opposed the war altogether or considered it unfair for college students to receive deferments while less privileged youths were drafted and sent off to war. The center of the controversy—which reached its height in the late 1960s—was Lt. Gen. Lewis B. Hershey (USA ret.), the longtime director of the Selective Service, who staunchly opposed reforms. After many bruising battles with his critics, Hershey retired on Feb. 16, 1970, and was replaced by Curtis W. Tarr, an assistant secretary of the Air Force.

of divinity school or fail to become an ordained minister they would be subject to induction. The House bill had no similar provision.

Procedural Rights. Conferees accepted Senate provisions, not in the House bill, making four basic changes in existing law: 1) granting the right to appear in person before any local or appeal board; 2) granting the right to present witnesses before a local board; 3) requiring attendance of a quorum of any local or appeal board during a registrant's personal appearance; and 4) requiring that a written report, upon request, be provided to the registrant by the local or appeal board when the board ruled against the registrant. Conferees dropped a fifth Senate provision, granting the right to be accompanied and advised by private counsel at a personal appearance before a local or appeal board.

Draft Board Regulations. Three provisions affecting the function of the local draft boards were decided in the Senate's favor. First, conferees limited to 20 years, the Senate-passed ceiling, the service of local draft board members. Existing law limited service to 25 years; the House had set a ceiling of 15 years.

Second, conferees accepted the Senate version providing that in making future appointments to local boards, the President should see to the "maximum extent possible" that the boards reflected proportionately the racial and religious breakdowns of the community they served. The House had adopted a stricter provision specifying that all boards should reflect the community they served, and the changes were to be made on all boards, not just in cases where appointments were made to fill vacancies.

The third Senate provision accepted by conferees permitted joint headquarters and consolidation of local draft boards within states when the governor of the state consented. The House bill had prohibited such actions outright.

Enlistment After Induction. Conferees adopted Senate language providing that no person could enlist after an induction order had been issued for him. The House had no similar provision.

Standby Draft. House conferees accepted a provision contained in the Senate version which provided that the Selective Service System would remain as an active standby organization if manpower needs were being met by volunteers instead of draftees.

FINAL ACTION

HOUSE. The House Aug. 4, two days before a month-long congressional recess, by a 298-108 roll-call vote, adopted the conference report.

With adoption of the report, the House went on record for the first time in support of the withdrawal of all U.S. troops from Indochina at the earliest practical date.

After the House had voted, attention focused on the possibility of a Senate filibuster attempt against the bill because of the conferees' modification of the Mansfield amendment.

SENATE. The Senate Sept. 21, by a 55-30 roll-call vote, adopted the conference report on HR 6531, clearing it for the President's signature.

Adoption of the report occurred minutes after the Senate, by a roll-call vote of 61-30, the exact two-thirds majority required to invoke cloture and limit debate, blocked a filibuster attempt on the measure.

With only Senate approval needed before the bill could be sent to the President for his signature, the Senate Aug. 5 was unable to take a vote on the conference report because several of its members objected to a time limit on the debate. The Senate agreed to again consider the report Sept. 13, but without a time limit on debate.

In contention were two points of the conference agreement: the pay increase provisions which conferees altered substantially from the Senate-passed version, and the Vietnam troop withdrawal proposal offered by Mansfield in which the nine-month withdrawal deadline provision had been deleted by the conferees.

During the Aug. 5 deliberation, Stennis, leader of the Senate conferees, read a letter from President Nixon intended to prod the Senate into quick action on the bill.

The letter said the conference version of the draft bill "represents responsible compromise between differing viewpoints and remains consistent with the objectives sought by the administration in Southeast Asia." The President wrote: "I am hopeful that the Senate can quickly adopt the report so that I may sign it before the Congress takes its month-long summer vacation."

The President had been opposed to the Mansfield amendment when it was adopted by the Senate, but he was willing to accept the softened version of the withdrawal proposal drafted by conferees.

The Senate Sept. 17, by a 36-47 roll-call vote, had rejected an attempt to send the military draft extension bill back to a House-Senate conference for a second round of negotiations with House conferees.

Both the White House and the Pentagon had been heavily lobbying senators the day before the vote. It appeared likely that opponents of the House-Senate compromise would succeed until Gordon Allott (R Colo.), who opposed the pay raise provisions of the compromise version and had led the effort on the Republican side to table, announced to the Senate late on the afternoon of Sept. 16 that he would support the compromise.

Administration Lobbying. The Nixon administration stepped up its campaign of pressure Sept. 15. Every senator received a letter signed by the civilian heads of the three military services warning that further delay "might jeopardize beyond redemption the prospects of achieving an all-volunteer force by July 1, 1973 (the Nixon administration's target date)." The letter was signed by Navy Secretary John H. Chafee, Air Force Secretary Robert C. Seamans and Army Secretary Robert F. Froehlke.

Then in rapid succession Sept. 21, the Senate voted to limit debate and adopted the conference report.

On final passage of the bill, which came just minutes after the cloture vote although each senator was technically allowed one hour apiece for debate after adoption of cloture, Democrats split evenly (23-23). As on initial Senate passage in June, southern Democrats overwhelmingly supported passage (15-1) and northern Democrats opposed it 8-22. Republicans supported the President's position by a 32-7 margin.

Lockheed Loan Guarantee (1971)

CONGRESS BAILED OUT GIANT DEFENSE CONTRACTOR

Should the nation's leading defense contractors be treated as part of the free enterprise system, i.e., absorb their losses like any other private firm, even to the point of bankruptcy? Or should the government treat these contractors as national assets who deserve special government assistance when their financial position becomes shaky? After long debate, Congress took the latter option in a bruising 1971 legislative struggle.

By a narrow **key 49-48 roll-call vote,** the Senate Aug. 2, 1971, cleared for the President's signature a bill (HR 8432—PL 92-70) authorizing a federal guarantee of up to $250-million in bank loans for the Lockheed Aircraft Corporation, the nation's largest defense contractor. The House had passed a bill in identical form by an equally close **key roll call, 192-189,** on July 30. President Nixon signed the bill Aug. 9.

The main purpose of the measure was to prevent a Lockheed bankruptcy. The company's problems developed soon after Rolls-Royce Ltd., the British manufacturer of engines for Lockheed's L-1011 (Tristar) commercial airliner, declared bankruptcy Feb. 4, 1971. Reeling from large penalties assessed by the Defense Department for cost overruns on the C-5A transport aircraft and other defense contracts, Lockheed needed additional credit to go into production with its Tristar. And the company needed the Tristar to stay in business.

The administration, which requested the loan guarantee, argued that the free enterprise issue should be cast aside in Lockheed's case because of the unique nature of the problem. Although the government did not need the Tristar, the argument went, it did need to take measures to maintain Lockheed's defense production capability. Another argument that scored points for loan proponents was that Lockheed bankrupty would worsen the nation's already serious unemployment problem. Critics of the loan guarantee, led by Sen. William Proxmire (D Wis.), countered that since the government already owned much of Lockheed's production facilities, another company could simply step in and take over Lockheed's defense work. The only persons who would lose their jobs, the critics said, were Lockheed's top executives.

The Problem

The possibility of a government loan guarantee for Lockheed had been considered briefly in 1970 by leaders among a group of 24 banks which eventually agreed to lend the company $400-million, without a guarantee, to complete development of the Tristar. The idea was raised again, soon after Rolls-Royce went bankrupt, when the banks indicated they would not extend further credit to Lockheed.

Cautious support and determined opposition met the legislation the Nixon administration sent to Congress May 13 to guarantee $250-million in bank loans to the beleaguered company.

Treasury Secretary John Connally sent the draft bill to Congress. Connally, who became the guarantee's most ardent proponent, said: "The failure of major business enterprises can have serious national and regional consequences, including the causing of substantial unemployment, as well as other business failures. To provide for credit to avoid such consequences, government guarantees may be warranted."

Drafted in general terms, the bill did not mention Lockheed by name. If Congress increased the dollar total of guarantees permitted, the bill would have authorized the same kind of assistance to other major companies.

The Defense Department announced May 7 that it would start making progress payments to Lockheed from a $200-million contingency fund established in the fiscal 1971 federal budget to enable the company to meet its financing needs while continuing to produce the C-5A.

The employment aspect of the Lockheed loan guarantee made the administration's proposal difficult for many members of Congress to oppose. Yet a number hedged their support. Some posed conditions: that Lockheed be required to use American engines on the Tristar; that the legislation be broadened so that it would apply to future cases involving other companies; or that Lockheed's management be required to resign.

The position of organized labor was crucial to many members. George Meany, president of the AFL-CIO, publicly announced support for the loan guarantee. But some influential labor spokesmen regarded Lockheed as a "runaway" because of its contract with foreign-based Rolls-Royce.

President Nixon at San Clemente, Calif., May 5 told a news conference the major factor, in his view, was the unemployment that would be caused by a Lockheed bankruptcy and consequent abandonment of the L-1011 program. "Lockheed is one of the nation's great companies," Nixon said. "It provides an enormous employment lift to this part of the country, and I am going to be heavily influenced by the need to see to it that Southern California, after taking the disappointment of not getting the SST, which would, of course, have brought many, many jobs to this part of the country—that California does not have the additional jolt of losing Lockheed."

Connally said Lockheed had employed 17,000 persons in the airbus program, of whom some 7,000 had been laid off because of financial difficulties and the uncertainty of the project. The payroll for the 17,000, he said, was $5-million per week. In addition, the secretary said, 14,000 persons were employed by the principal suppliers for the L-1011. Lockheed had 35,000 subcontracting companies, according to Connally, most of which were small businesses. If Lockheed went bankrupt, the secretary said, the $1.4-billion invested in the L-1011 would be written off

(Continued on p. 235)

History of C-5A Controversy, Lockheed Involvement

In October 1965, the Pentagon drafted one of the most sophisticated "total package procurement" contracts ever awarded to a defense contractor. The contract, won by the Lockheed Aircraft Corporation, called for the development and construction of 120 giant transport aircraft—the C-5A Galaxy. The plane was to be nearly as long as a football field.

By setting a fixed-price on the project, the Pentagon hoped to eliminate the expensive cost overruns that had for so long inflated the defense budget. Yet, written into the fine print of the agreement was a web of complex mutual assurances designed to protect both parties from extraordinary financial penalties.

A Defense Department spokesman who had been involved over the years with negotiations between the Pentagon and Lockheed told Congressional Quarterly the total package procurement contract for the C-5A was "the most sophisticated we've ever done. We've never tied anything up like this one before." It was designed so "neither of us would lose our shirts."

Fitzgerald Testimony. The C-5A program remained in relative obscurity until the fall of 1968. The Air Force had given little indication that the program was already running far above original cost estimates.

On Nov. 13, 1968, the Joint Congressional Economic Committee heard testimony from a civilian accountant, A.E. Fitzgerald, who was deputy for management systems in the Office of the Assistant Secretary of the Air Force. In response to a question by Sen. William Proxmire (D Wis.) as to whether the C-5A program was running $2-billion above initial cost estimates, Fitzgerald replied that Proxmire's figure was "approximately right." Fitzgerald was later dismissed from his Pentagon position and became a consultant with the Joint Economic Committee.

New Contract. During 1969, the pressure exerted by the Joint Economic Committee and broad national publicity on the estimated cost overruns caused the Air Force to modify its contract with Lockheed in an effort to bring costs down. In June, the Pentagon announced that the number of aircraft initially requested was being reduced from 120 to 81.

New cost estimates for Lockheed's share of total expenditures for producing the reduced number of aircraft were put at from $4-billion to $4.5-billion. Lockheed and Deputy Secretary of Defense David Packard negotiated throughout 1969 and 1970 on the question of who was going to absorb the losses on the program. After 17 months of negotiation, Lockheed agreed Feb. 1, 1971, to take a $200-million fixed-loss on the C-5A contract. The Defense Department was to pick up the tab for all additional cost overruns.

Losing an Engine. Within minutes after the Senate Oct. 6, 1971, passed the $21-billion defense procurement bill (HR 8687)—which authorized funds for such weapon systems as the ABM, the F-14 jet fighter and the C-5A—the Air Force announced that on Sept. 29 a jet engine on one of the giant C-5A transport planes had dropped off onto a runway at Altus Air Force Base, Okla., while the pilot was making routine checks before takeoff.

Pentagon spokesman Jerry W. Friedheim apologized to reporters for the delay in disclosing the incident and denied charges that the information had been released with an eye to the Senate's action.

When the announcement about the engine was first made at the Pentagon Oct. 6, seven of the 47 operational C-5As were already grounded. The following day, 15 more were grounded pending safety tests, and on Oct. 12 the entire fleet was prohibited from flying.

Two weeks before the Sept. 29 incident, the Air Force announced that a crack in the wing of another C-5A had been detected.

GAO Report on Lockheed. Investigators for the General Accounting Office filed a partial report with the Joint Economic Committee in March 1972, which documented charges that the Air Force knowingly made overpayments amounting to $1.1-billion to Lockheed Aircraft Corp. The report was released March 27.

According to the report, the money was turned over to Lockheed as progress payments on the C-5A jet transport, manufactured primarily at the Lockheed plant in Marietta, Ga.

(The report was not considered complete, according to Comptroller General Elmer B. Staats, head of the GAO, because it had not been reviewed by the Air Force or Lockheed for comment prior to release by the Joint Economic Committee.)

Report On C-5A. Proxmire April 6, 1972, read into the *Congressional Record* the full text of the GAO report on the C-5A. The GAO report stated that:

● During one six-month period in 1971 there were 3,327 reported failures in C-5A landing gear.

● "The wing continues to be one of the major problem areas on the C-5A," and wing fatigue tests were not scheduled for completion until September 1974—two and one-half years behind schedule.

● Final delivery of the 81 aircraft was scheduled for May 1973 which was a 13-month delay from the original schedule. Initially, 120 aircraft were to be delivered by April 1972.

● Of 15 aircraft that were accepted by the Air Force during eight months of 1971, each plane showed an average of 257 deficiencies in Air Force specifications.

In a related development, Air Force Secretary Robert C. Seamans Jr. told the House Appropriations Defense Subcommittee Jan. 25 that training flights of the C-5A had been restricted to make the fleet last longer.

"Yes, I am disappointed in the airplane," Semans said. "Not from the standpoint of its performance measured in terms of range, speed and the requirements for landing. But from the standpoint of the structure itself. It was designed too close to the margin."

Seamans' testimony was released April 6 after censoring by the Defense Department.

(Continued from p. 233)

"as best it can be" by the investors, with a substantial loss in revenues to the government, and an important defense capability would be lost.

House Committee Action

STUDY. The House Banking and Currency Committee held hearings on HR 8432 in July. The committee July 8 received in executive session a staff report recommending rejection of the proposed Lockheed loan guarantee bill (HR 8432). The result of two months' work by the majority staff, the study concluded:

• There was substantial risk of default and loss to the government in the proposed guarantee.

• There would be great pressure to give Lockheed preferential treatment in defense contracts.

• There was doubt that lack of the guarantee would force Lockheed into reorganization under bankruptcy law and that severe unemployment would result.

• The guarantee would be fundamentally inconsistent with a free-enterprise system, would involve government favoritism toward Lockheed in relation to its competitors and might lead to similar guarantees for other aerospace firms.

• The request for the guarantee might rest on information not made available to Congress or might involve "a game of chicken" or a bluff.

The staff material included a year-old Defense Department study, previously classified, which said Lockheed would have to sell about 370 of its Tristars to break even. Lockheed's cost estimates had placed the break-even point more recently at 255 to 265 aircraft. At 252 aircraft sales, according to the study, the firm would lose at least $359-million. Lockheed predicted July 8 it would sell at least 400 of its airbuses. (But by the end of 1972, the company had only 117 firm orders and options for 67 more.)

REPORT. The House Banking and Currency Committee by 23-11 vote July 26 reported the bill (HR 8432) authorizing the federal government to guarantee loans of up to $250-million to individual businesses, to a total of $2-billion in outstanding guarantees at any one time.

Prospects for passage of the bill in the House improved dramatically July 15 when Chairman Wright Patman (D Texas) of the committee changed his position from opposition to support for a bill limited to a guarantee for Lockheed. Patman had announced his opposition the bill May 4.

A source close to Patman said the chairman had decided reluctantly to support the limited bill. Patman was said to believe the bill should be brought to a vote in the House because the administration regarded the Lockheed situation as an emergency.

House Floor Action

The House by a **key roll-call vote of 192-189** July 30 passed HR 8432 after accepting amendments whittling down its provisions to provide only a $250-million loan guarantee for the Lockheed Corporation, as originally proposed by the administration, instead of the broader bill reported by the House Banking and Currency Committee.

Under an agreement among the majority and minority committee leadership, Chairman Patman and ranking minority member William B. Widnall (R N.J.), four amendments were offered by Rep. Thomas L. Ashley (D Ohio) to return the bill to a form similar to that of the original administration bill. The amendments were accepted as a package by a voice vote.

Ashley's amendments limited the loan guarantee authority to $250-million, the amount requested by Lockheed, and substituted the chairman of the Securities and Exchange Commission on the three-member Emergency Loan Guarantee Board for the president of the Federal Reserve bank of the district in which a firm applying for a guarantee was located.

The amendments required the board to limit interest rates on guaranteed loans to reflect the reduced risk to the lender and to charge a guarantee fee to the borrower that was at least equal to the difference between the interest cost of a guaranteed loan and prevailing interest costs. The amendments further struck out a provision for congressional review of proposed loan guarantees.

John D. Dingell (D Mich.) offered an amendment requiring the General Accounting Office to make a detailed audit of each applicant for a guarantee and report the results to the loan guarantee board and to Congress. The House accepted the amendment by a teller vote, 163-76.

The House rejected an amendment by Chairman William M. Colmer (D Miss.) of the Rules Committee to limit the government guarantee to 90 per cent of the loans involved. The amendment failed by a recorded teller vote, 176-205.

A second Dingell amendment was rejected by a voice vote. This would have given the government the highest lien on the borrower's property and first priority for payment under bankruptcy law. An amendment to Dingell's amendment, offered by Sam Gibbons (D Fla.), previously was approved by voice vote. Gibbons' amendment explicitly preserved the priority of employees for their wages, which Dingell's amendment brought into question.

H. R. Gross (R Iowa) was unsuccessful in an attempt to kill the bill with an amendment to strike the enacting clause. Pointing out that the hour was late, Gross said, "By adopting the motion, we can settle this issue the way it ought to be settled—by killing this monstrosity—and go home promptly." His move failed by a voice vote.

Senate Committee Action

The Senate Banking, Housing and Urban Affairs Committee July 19 reported a bill (S 2308), authorizing the federal government to guarantee loans up to $250-million for individual businesses, up to a total of $2-billion in outstanding guarantees at any one time.

Proxmire Views. In a long dissenting statement, Proxmire charged that S 2308 was simply the original Lockheed guarantee bill in disguise. "It is apparent that the proposed Lockheed guarantee has practically no benefit and serious disadvantages," he said. "It is a big-business giveaway of the worst sort and should be rejected by the Congress."

Senate Floor Action

The Senate by a **key 49-48 roll call** Aug. 2 cleared HR 8432 for the President's signature.

Final action came after nearly two full weeks of debate on the Senate floor and after the Senate dropped

(Continued on p. 238)

Study on C-5A Overruns Demonstrated Congressional...

The massive cost overruns experienced by Lockheed Aircraft Corp. in producing the C-5A jet transport illustrated some of the difficulties Congress faced in trying to check rising defense costs. The following study of one phase in this cost overrun problem also highlighted some of the limitations of the General Accounting Office (GAO) in its role as Congress' investigative arm and watchdog agency.

Cost increases of more than $1-billion for procurement of 81 Air Force C-5A jet transports prompted the Joint Economic Committee in 1970 to request an investigation by the GAO of financially troubled Lockheed, developer of the C-5A. The committee asked for a thorough audit of the contractor's "cash-flow" statement (an account of expenditures and receipts for both defense and commercial programs).

Without a thorough congressionally initiated audit of the company's books, said Senators William Proxmire (D Wis.) and Richard S. Schweiker (R Pa.) and Rep. William S. Moorhead (D Pa.), Congress would not have sufficient knowledge about Lockheed's shaky financial situation to make an evaluation on appropriating additional money for the project.

Proxmire said Lockheed could go bankrupt whether additional funds were provided or not. He also charged that some of the money appropriated for the C-5A had been transferred into the company's commercial airliner project—the L-1011 Tristar—and, consequently, that costs on the C-5A had gone up (from an estimated $31.8-million per plane in 1965 to $66-million in February 1971).

The GAO never conducted the thorough audit requested by members of the Joint Economic Committee. The Defense Department refused to allow it despite contentions by Proxmire and Schweiker that such an audit was within the statutory authority of the GAO.

Instead of a detailed audit, Comptroller General Elmer B. Staats, head of the GAO, announced Dec. 3, 1970, that the Pentagon was allowing only a "review" of the crucial cash-flow statement. Proxmire said that limitations on the "review" were so severe that the value of even bothering with the study was questionable.

According to the agreement reached with the Defense Department, GAO staff members were allowed to look at Lockheed's books, but they could not write down any figures, remove the material from the Pentagon or release to Congress any of the figures they saw concerning Lockheed's commercial problems.

The Pentagon restricted the GAO to an evaluation of whether or not Lockheed would be able to complete C-5A production if additional money were appropriated. No facts or figures about the interrelated commercial ventures of Lockheed accompanied the GAO report.

When Congress had to vote on the Lockheed loan guarantee six months later, it had no independent analysis of Lockheed's over-all financial situation upon which to base its decision.

What Went Wrong. A detailed Congressional Quarterly study of a series of letters exchanged between the Defense Department, the GAO and the Joint

Economic Committee, plus a review of various key statutes, showed several factors which contributed to the GAO's inability to conduct a full audit:

• Congress initially failed to demand a thorough GAO study—one which would have disclosed the full scope of Lockheed's dilemma. Long after it was known that the C-5A program had incurred cost overruns in excess of $1-billion, the Senate rejected a Proxmire-Schweiker amendment to the defense procurement authorization bill (HR 17123—PL 91-441) which, among other things, would have required a thorough GAO study. The amendment was rejected Aug. 26, 1970, by a 30-to-48 roll-call vote.

• The GAO failed to offer, over the years, an interpretation of the law, thereby permitting the Pentagon to renegotiate the Lockheed contract without regard to normal contract procedures. The responsibility of interpreting contract laws affecting any government agency rests with the GAO.

• With regard to conducting an audit of Lockheed's cash-flow statement, the GAO failed initially to exert its statutory authority until pressed by the Joint Economic Committee. (Proxmire and Schweiker still questioned whether the GAO flexed its statutory muscles to the fullest.)

• The Defense Department refused to accommodate requests of the Joint Economic Committee and did not allow the GAO to gather detailed information for presentation to Congress.

Accounting Office

The Joint Economic Committee was the most aggressive group in Congress in seeking explanations for the C-5A cost overruns. But as Richard F. Kaufman, the committee's staff economist, told Congressional Quarterly, "There's a limit to the number of times we can hold hearings on this one subject." Instead of more hearings, the committee, in the spring of 1970, sought the aid of the GAO.

As an arm of the legislative branch, one of the GAO functions was to respond to congressional requests for investigative and evaluative audits of government agencies and programs.

The Joint Economic Committee (regarded as a study committee) did not have the authority to subpoena records such as those held by the Defense Department on the C-5A. Only legislative and investigative committees (the Armed Services Committees, for example) had this authority, and none of these committees used the power to investigate C-5A cost overruns.

Proxmire, who was chairman of the Joint Economic Subcommittee on Economy in Government during the 91st Congress, first requested that the GAO obtain information on Lockheed's financial status in a March 10, 1970, letter to the Comptroller General. In response to the request, Comptroller General Staats sent to the Joint Economic Committee Lockheed's annual report and certain financial statements provided by the Air Force concerning expenditures on defense projects. On May 12, Staats wrote Proxmire, saying that "we

...Ignorance of Crucial Financial Data on Lockheed

have been informed by Defense on April 27, that Lockheed's legal staff had reservations about release of certain financial data which the company considers extremely sensitive."

Senators Proxmire and Schweiker signed the following letter, dated Sept. 14, to the Comptroller General:

"Lockheed Aircraft Corp. has refused to make public the fundamental facts about its financial position. We have only their word that they are in grave financial difficulties.... There is, in fact, an appalling lack of specific knowledge as to Lockheed's real financial condition and its causes."

Proxmire and Schweiker then requested the GAO to find out what the firm's financial capabilities were "to complete and deliver the 81 aircraft...and what is the total amount which would have to be expended to insure the complete delivery of the 81 planes."

In a Nov. 19, 1970, letter to Proxmire, the Comptroller General said: "We have been unable to conduct a study of Lockheed's financial capability to deliver C-5A aircraft because we have not been able to gain access to the necessary data."

Confidential Relationship. As an alternative to a full audit, the GAO suggested that it merely examine the data in the hands of the Defense Department without removing it from their offices. After examination the GAO would then furnish Congress "only with our opinion as to whether Lockheed has the financial capability to deliver C-5A aircraft." A spokesman for the Office of the Secretary of Defense refused the alternative, saying "it would constitute a violation of the confidential relationship existing between the department and the contractor."

When Proxmire received word that the GAO was not going to conduct an audit, he wrote Staats Nov. 20 saying that not only was he "deeply disturbed" by the Defense Department's actions, but also "by GAO's passive refusal to assert the statutory authority that clearly gives it access to the information desired."

Proxmire referred to the U.S. Code, Title 31, Section 54, which states: "All departments and establishments shall furnish to the Comptroller General such information regarding the powers, duties, activities, organization, financial transactions and methods of business of their respective offices...and the Comptroller General...shall, for the purpose of securing such information, have access to and the right to examine any books, documents, papers or records of any such department or establishment."

Proxmire then charged that the Defense Department was "in direct violation of the law" and asked Staats what the GAO planned to do about it.

Limited Review. Fourteen days after Proxmire's letter to the Comptroller General, Staats informed the Joint Economic Committee that the secretary of defense had changed his position. After further communication with Staats, the Defense Department decided to allow a GAO "review" of Lockheed's cash-flow statement.

A GAO representative would be allowed to look at the material but could "not copy or otherwise repeat data" about what he found. The GAO was not permitted "to disclose the reasons" for its opinion as a condition of the agreement with the Defense Department.

James H. Hammond, head of the GAO team that worked on Lockheed's cash-flow statement, said that if Congress wanted the confidential information on Lockheed's commercial difficulties, a subpoena would probably be necessary. Since neither the GAO nor the Joint Economic Committee had the authority to subpoena records, legislative committees would have to take the initiative.

The Senate and House Armed Services Committees and Appropriations Committees would probably be where such a subpoena would logically originate, Hammond said. As pointed out by a Joint Committee staff member, however, these four legislative committees had been "traditionally friendly" to the military services on these matters.

The Comptroller General subsequently issued a statement defending the GAO's position in the dispute with the Joint Economic Committee. He said that the GAO "has a proper concern" for the Defense Department's negotiations with Lockheed. He explained that the GAO had "no legal authority to demand from the contractors their records relating to commercial—that is, non-government—transactions. The fact that Lockheed's ability to make delivery is dependent upon its over-all financial situation has, therefore, complicated our ability to develop the data needed to reach such an opinion."

Interpretation of Contract Law

In dealing with another phase of the C-5A dispute, Comptroller General Staats turned back all queries concerning the legality of the Defense Department's authority to renegotiate the Lockheed contract, by citing a 1958 law (PL 85-804) that was broadly interpreted by the Pentagon.

PL 85-804 authorized department heads to modify defense contracts when it was determined that such action was necessary to "facilitate the national defense" in times of emergency. The Defense Department interpretation was used to renegotiate the C-5A contract in 1971 to set a fixed-loss of $200-million on Lockheed.

Prior to the C-5A controversy, the department had renegotiated a total of only $60-million in cost overruns between 1958 and 1969 under provisions of PL 85-804.

In lieu of any other interpretation of PL 85-804, the Defense Department was within legal boundaries in renegotiating the C-5A project. However, one of the GAO's important functions was to interpret statutes involving contracts with government agencies. Any GAO legal opinion, with certain exceptions, had the force of law and was binding on all government agencies unless decided otherwise in the federal courts.

No alternative interpretation of PL 85-804 was offered by the GAO, despite the latitude such a law gave the Department of Defense.

its own bill (S 2308), which authorized emergency loan guarantees up to $2-billion to major business enterprises, in favor of the House bill for Lockheed alone.

The Senate debated its measure July 21-24 and 26-31, including Saturday sessions July 24 and 31. Proxmire and his allies sought principally to delay passage until Congress recessed Aug. 6. Supporters tried to shut off debate so the bill could be enacted before the recess.

The House, which initially had tried to stay in step with the Senate in order to avoid a conference or an impasse on differing versions of the bill, ultimately anticipated the Senate with passage of the limited version.

DEBATE HIGHLIGHTS

July 21. Proxmire moved to send the bill back to committee for further hearings, with instructions that the measure was to be reported back to the Senate not later than July 29. Banking Committee Chairman John Sparkman (D Ala.) moved to table Proxmire's motion. Proxmire urged delay in voting on the Sparkman motion, arguing that the printed record of hearings on the bill was not yet available and could not have been studied by senators who did not attend them. Sparkman's motion carried by a roll-call vote, 56-36.

July 22. Majority Whip Robert C. Byrd (D W.Va.) announced that a motion would be entered July 23 to invoke cloture on debate on the bill. Proxmire said the bill deserved four to five weeks of discussion. Wallace F. Bennett (R Utah) and Bill Brock (R Tenn.) argued that Lockheed would be in bankruptcy by the time the bill passed if debate continued that long.

July 23. Byrd announced that the first vote on cloture would be held July 26.

Proxmire displayed a half-page advertisement from *The Milwaukee Journal* in the form of an open letter attacking him for his opposition to the bill and threatening a boycott of Wisconsin products. The letter was signed by the National Group for the Preservation of the Aviation Industry, Marietta, Ga., which described itself as an organization representing aerospace workers.

July 24. John G. Tower (R Texas) read President Nixon's and Defense Secretary Melvin R. Laird's statements issued earlier the same day in support of the bill. Lowell P. Weicker Jr. (R Conn.) read Laird's July 23 statement in which the secretary conceded that there was disagreement on the bill within the administration.

July 26. The Senate rejected the first cloture motion by a roll-call vote, 42-47. A second motion was filed, and the vote was scheduled for July 28.

Adlai E. Stevenson III (D Ill.) argued that the bill, though broadened, was still designed primarily to accommodate Lockheed. He urged support for his amendment to eliminate a provision that would have exempted a Lockheed guarantee from congressional review and veto. By a roll-call vote, 38-45, a motion by Tower to table Stevenson's amendment was rejected.

July 27. Stevenson continued his case against the Lockheed exemption. Proxmire accused Tower of delaying a vote on Stevenson's amendment by offering the July 26 tabling motion.

July 28. The Senate refused for the second time, by a 59-39 roll-call vote, to impose cloture and end debate on S 2308.

The cloture motion required a majority of two-thirds of those present and voting—66 votes—for adoption. Supporters of the bill thus fell seven votes short of thwarting the effort of opponents to debate the legislation until Congress began its summer recess Aug. 6. Proponents immediately filed a motion for a third attempt to close off debate. The vote was scheduled for July 30.

July 29. George McGovern (D S.D.) offered an amendment to double the loan guarantee authority of the bill (S 2308) by adding $2-billion for guaranteed loans for farmers and small businessmen. Congress could not justify assistance for major businesses, McGovern said, unless it provided similar help for others. The Senate rejected the amendment by a roll-call vote of 18-75.

Proxmire cited studies by the Transportation Department, the National Aeronautics and Space Administration and an unnamed group of executives and engineers employed by "a number of highly reputable aerospace firms," all of which, he said, showed that the airline market would not support both Lockheed and the McDonnell-Douglas Corporation, maker of the DC-10 airliner. Tower disputed Proxmire's conclusions. He referred to a study by McDonnell-Douglas and one by the Federal Aviation Administration (part of the Transportation Department), both of which showed the market was adequate, he said.

July 30. The third attempt to invoke cloture failed by a roll-call vote of 53-37. A majority of two-thirds of those present and voting, or 60, was necessary to close off debate. A fourth cloture vote was scheduled for Aug. 2.

July 31. By unanimous consent the Senate agreed to take up the House bill (HR 8432) on Aug. 2 and limit debate to two hours plus 20 minutes for any amendment or motion. The order for the fourth cloture vote was withdrawn.

Proxmire argued that the loan guarantee was not necessary and that there would be more jobs in the aerospace industry if Lockheed left the commercial field. He said either American banks that had already loaned $400-million to Lockheed or British banks with a stake in Rolls-Royce were likely to lend Lockheed additional funds without the guarantee. Even if Lockheed went bankrupt, he said, the firm would continue at least the 85 per cent of its work which was under defense contracts, though under new management.

Aug. 2. Ted Stevens (R Alaska) offered an amendment to create a $200-million emergency loan guarantee fund for small business. Stevens said he did not intend to have his amendment called up for a vote. After he was assured by Sparkman that hearings would be held on small business problems, he withdrew it.

Hubert H. Humphrey (D Minn.) offered an amendment to extend the existing unemployment compensation program by 26 weeks and provide federal financing. On Tower's point of order the chair ruled that Humphrey's amendment was not germane and thus was not in order.

Alan Cranston (D Calif.) said the government bore substantial responsibility for Lockheed's problems under defense contracts.

In the final roll call, the Senate passed the House bill without amendment, 49-48, thus clearing it for the President.

Aftermath

New problems for Lockheed emerged during hearings Dec. 18-21, 1972, on weapons acquisition by a Joint Economic subcommittee.

The revelations came from Comptroller General Elmer B. Staats, who told the Subcommittee on Priorities and Economy in Government Dec. 18 that Lockheed's orders for the L-1011 were running far below the company's break-even point on the multi-million dollar aircraft project. At present, Staats said, Lockheed had only 117 firm orders for the plane and options for 67 more—far below the firm's own projected break-even point of 275 aircraft. Unless the company got a "substantial number" of additional orders. Staats said, losses on the L-1011 program could "impair the financial condition of the company."

Already, Staats said, Lockheed had made plans to draw a greater portion of the government guaranteed loan authorization than the company originally had contemplated. When the loan guarantee program passed Congress in 1971, Lockheed said it would need only $150-million of the $250-million maximum, but current pro-jections had increased to a level of between $195-million and $220-million, according to Staats. Staats also revealed that Lockheed would be unable to meet its self-imposed timetable of paying back the guaranteed loan by the end of 1974. The timetable would probably slip by three to six months, he said, but this would still be within Lockheed's legal obligation to repay the loan by Dec. 31, 1975.

Staats complained that the General Accounting Office's auditors had encountered resistance from the Emergency Loan Guarantee Board—the federal agency that administers the Lockheed loan guarantee—in their efforts to audit the loan operation. The 1971 bailout law did not require the GAO to audit the board's activities.

Staats said such a review was "clearly authorized" under general authority granted the GAO by Congress to review the records of the agencies of the executive branch of the government. But until Congress clarified the situation, Staats said, the GAO would be unable to take corrective action—such as cutting off loan funds—because the loan money was disbursed by banks and not by the federal government.

Congressional Defense Committees

ADVOCATES OR OVERSEERS OF THE MILITARY ESTABLISHMENT

"I must confess that I have not really exerted myself as much as I might have in an effort to control the military. Actually, I have been under the feeling that it was useless and utterly futile, that nothing could be done, for example, to cut an appropriation for the Defense Department no matter what I did.... The Congress simply does not review or investigate or exercise control over defense spending."

—Sen. J. W. Fulbright (D Ark.), quoted in *The Military Establishment*, Harper and Row, 1971, p. 53.

In the days since World War II, no other department or agency of the executive branch of the government enjoyed such comparative autonomy from congressional scrutiny and supervision as did the Department of Defense.

Congress, which so readily wielded the paring knife on other agencies' budgets, made cost control secondary to the objective of maintaining a strong national defense. With few exceptions, Congress approved all the major programs the Pentagon asked for. And in the days of economy-minded Defense Secretary Robert S. McNamara (1961-68), the legislators usually provided more.

Since the end of World War II, Congress has appropriated $1.2-trillion for the Pentagon to spend on national defense. The $83.4-billion requested for defense spending in fiscal 1973 was by far the largest single item in the federal budget.

The key to the Pentagon's success has been the close relationship it attained with the powerful military committees on Capitol Hill—the Armed Services Committees and Defense Appropriations Subcommittees. It was a relationship based both on common ideological ties and on the "pork barrel"—the immense political clout that went with Pentagon decisions on where to locate military bases and assign lucrative defense contracts. Defense Department spending was especially high in states and congressional districts which were represented by members of the Senate and House Armed Services Committees. *(Box p. 242)*

But despite what appeared to critics as collusion, members of the military committees saw the Pentagon-congressional relationship in a much different light. Members were quick to point out that they stood ready to "slap the Pentagon's hands" whenever it got out of line, such as the House Armed Services Committee did in investigating and roundly criticizing the military for the alleged My Lai massacre of 1969. Thus the committees, they said, were an overseer as well as an advocate of the military. What follows is an examination of the relative emphasis that both these roles received during the first four Nixon years. (The quotations from members of Congress were made in interviews conducted by Congressional Quarterly in 1972.)

Armed Services Committees

Rep. Otis G. Pike (D N.Y.) told Congressional Quarterly: "The House Armed Services Committee doesn't control the Pentagon; the Pentagon controls the House Armed Services Committee."

Rep. F. Edward Hebert (D La.), chairman of the committee, replied in a separate interview: "Now that is the type of irresponsible statements that are made without being documented. That statement is so foolish it answers itself."

"I'd like to see somebody document that," Hebert challenged. "Why, I'm the last man in the world the military wants to get into a fight with. They don't want any confrontation with me, believe me. That accusation is absolutely wrong."

Hebert went on to say: "I intend to build the strongest military we can get. Money is no question. The yardstick should be necessity, not money.

The divergent views expressed by Pike and Hebert represented what many, both in and out of Congress, felt about the roles of the House and Senate Armed Services Committees in the early 1970s in overseeing Defense Department spending for weapons and research and development.

Though the committees chopped money from the Pentagon's requests each year, critics—including one member of Congress who once worked at the Pentagon—contend that the military budget was padded in anticipation of the cuts.

And once the committee had finished working on the annual procurement authorization bill—a $20.9-billion measure in fiscal 1973—it was a rare phenomenon when the dollar value of the bill was changed by amendment on the floor.

Only three times in the 11 years that the committee had this type of authorizing power did the Senate override opposition by the Armed Services Committee chairman and change the dollar total of the bill reported from committee. On one other occasion, the Senate changed the total with the agreement of the committee chairman.

The House Armed Services Committee had what might be regarded as a perfect record. Not once in 11 years had the dollar value of the procurement authorization bill been altered on the House floor over the objections of the committee chairman.

"That's right," said Chairman Hebert. "The power is awesome."

BACKGROUND: BUILDING POWER

The Armed Services Committees were formed as a consolidation of the Military Affairs and Naval Affairs Committees by the Legislative Reorganization Act of 1946. As a result of the act, the number of standing committees in the Senate was reduced from 33 to 16 and duties of the 48 standing committees in the House were consolidated in 18 committees.

In some cases the committee reorganizations resulted in a substantial consolidation of power. For the newly formed Armed Services Committees, however, the power to enforce committee decisions was limited. The Appropriations Committees were responsible for scrutinizing the "line items" in the military budget, not the Armed Services Committees. Not until late in the 1950s did the Armed Services Committees make a bid to exercise more authority.

Where the Armed Services Committees then exercised power was in military organization, policy and the authorization and procurement of manpower through the draft. The committees reviewed plans for developing new weapon systems, but it was the Appropriations Committees which both authorized and appropriated funds for specific military programs. The Appropriations Committees were sensitive to recommendations by the Armed Services Committees, but acceptance of them was not guaranteed by law.

Housing and Construction. Through military housing construction authorizations—a matter long under their jurisdiction—the Armed Services Committees began in the late 1950s to authorize limits for appropriations.

The committees in 1959 attached to their military construction authorization bill a rider which greatly expanded the committees' role in overseeing military spending. The rider required the Armed Services Committees to authorize limits on appropriations used to purchase aircraft, missiles and ships. This was a major breakthrough for the committees, giving them the power to authorize appropriations for approximately 15 per cent of the Defense Department's annual expenditures. Prior to this time the committee authorized funds for procurement, not by specific programs, but as bulk figures.

In 1959, as the Armed Services Committees moved to acquire greater power, Richard B. Russell (D Ga. 1933-1971) was chairman of the Senate Armed Services Committee and Lyndon B. Johnson (D Texas Senate 1949-1961) was the third-ranking Democrat. Rep. Carl Vinson (D Ga. 1914-1965) was chairman of the House Armed Services Committee and L. Mendel Rivers (D S.C. 1941-1970), who succeeded Vinson as chairman, was the fourth-ranking Democrat.

The 1959 rider to PL 86-149 went into effect during consideration of the fiscal 1962 budget request. In calendar year 1962 the committees again expanded their authorizing function of appropriations. In PL 87-436 the Armed Services Committees were given the power to authorize limits on appropriations for research, development, testing and evaluation (RDT&E) associated with aircraft, missiles and ships. The following year, 1963, the committees took over the authorizing function for all RDT&E conducted by the Defense Department (PL 88-174).

In subsequent years the Armed Services Committees assumed an increasingly active role in examining the Pentagon's budget request. Of the $76.7-billion appropriated in fiscal 1973 for the Defense Department, 31 per cent ($23.5-billion) received prior authorization from bills originating in the Armed Services Committees.

By the end of 1972, the Armed Services Committees were originating legislation which authorized appropria-

---

Spending and Districts

The Department of Defense spent three times as much money as any other federal agency in fiscal 1971 and 1972.

In 21 states (42 percent), Pentagon spending ranked above outlays from any other federal source in fiscal 1971. In 18 states the Department of Health, Education and Welfare ranked as the top federal agency in spending. In the other 11 states, top federal agency spenders were the Agriculture Department and the Atomic Energy Commission.

Armed Services Committees. Sixty-nine per cent (11 of 16) of the members serving on the Senate Armed Services Committee and 64 per cent (25 of 39) of those serving on the House committee were from states or districts for which the number one source of federal outlays was the Defense Department.

Appropriations Subcommittees. Forty-four per cent (7 of 16) of the members serving on the Senate Appropriations Defense Subcommittee (including the three ex officio members) represented states for which Pentagon spending was the top source of federal income during fiscal 1971. This percentage was only *slightly above* the average for the Senate.

Thirty-six percent (4 of 11) of the House Appropriations Defense Subcommittee membership represented districts for which Defense Department outlays ranked as the top source of federal expenditures in fiscal 1971. This percentage was *slightly below* the average for the House.

Sen. Allen J. Ellender (D), who at the time of his death in 1972 was serving as chairman of the Senate Appropriations Committee and its Defense Subcommittee, represented Louisiana. Despite the fact that Louisiana had been well represented on key defense committees—for example, by Chairman F. Edward Hebert (D) of the House Armed Services Committee—the state showed no drastic jumps in its share of defense outlays or in prime defense contracts since Ellender and Hebert became chairmen in 1971.

Rep. George Mahon (D), chairman of the House Appropriations Committee and its Defense Subcommittee, represented a district in Texas. Although Texas had moved from the seventh to the third largest recipient of defense prime contracts in the last decade, the state population and general growth of industry paralleled the increase in defense dollars.

---

tions for all RDT&E, for the procurement of all weapons and weapon systems, tracked vehicles and torpedoes, for active duty personnel salaries and almost all construction.

Until authorizing measures from the Armed Services Committees were passed by Congress and signed by the President, no Defense Department appropriation bill could be adopted by the House or Senate. And once the authorizing measure had been signed into law, its limits could not be exceeded by the appropriations bill.

In addition to authorizing appropriations for the Pentagon, the Armed Services Committees set manpower limits and salaries.

The Armed Services Committees did not authorize annual funds for operation and maintenance of the armed forces ($21.1-billion in fiscal 1973), for retired military personnel benefits and pensions ($4.4-billion in fiscal 1973) or for active duty military personnel benefits and salaries ($23.1-billion in fiscal 1973). The three categories of spending were carried annually only in the appropriations bill.

BALANCED COMMITTEE

"The problem as I see it," said Pike, "lies in the fact that none of the committees in Congress is representative of Congress. I think that Congress is representative of the American people, but none of the committees is representative of Congress.

"Take the Judiciary Committee, for example. It's just loaded with guys who are lawyers bucking to be judges. And so the law, the judges and judiciary system can do no wrong in the eyes of the Judiciary Committee."

Rep. Les Aspin (D Wis.), a youthful (33) Armed Services Committee member and one of its most severe critics, cited examples of how amendments he had offered in committee got 10 per cent support from the 39 members. "But on the floor, that same amendment will get 25 or 30 per cent," he said.

Hebert's response to criticism about the committee's makeup was: "All I can say is look at the record. You can't beat the vote, can you?"

The record showed the House had supported the recommendations of the Armed Services Committee on all issues. On controversial issues, however, the voting margin had been closer on the floor than in committee.

The Senate Armed Services Committee, according to two of its more critical members, was undergoing a change during the years 1969-72.

Stuart Symington (D Mo.), ranking Democrat next to John C. Stennis (D Miss.) on the Senate committee, said that an increasing number of senators were "feeling their way into a group that says we have to have a better concept of priorities incident to our increasingly limited resources."

"More than ever before in the years that I've been around here," Symington said, "people—liberals and conservatives—are apprehensive about the future viability of the economy and the soundness of the currency." This kind of apprehension, he said, is having a direct effect on the way the Senate Armed Services Committee and the Senate in general look at the defense budget.

Asked why he thought the House committee generally reported larger defense authorization bills than did the Senate Armed Services Committee, Symington said: "The only reason there could be for it would be that the House committee was more amenable to the wishes of the Pentagon." (The House committee had averaged $464-million more in authorization bills than the Senate committee.)

PLUMS FOR DISTRICTS

"It's a natural thing when people come to Congress," Aspin said, "they want to get on a committee that can help the district they represent."

In 1972, 25 of 39 members of the House Armed Services Committee represented districts for which Defense Department outlays ranked as the top source of federal spending in fiscal 1971. On the Senate committee 11 of 16 members came from states for which Pentagon spending ranked as the top federal source of income.

Symington, in an *Atlantic* magazine interview with Flora Lewis, told of visits he made to the home state of the late Mendel Rivers, former House Armed Services Committee chairman. "You go down to Charleston, South Carolina, and you can't turn around without seeing a Mendel this and Mendel Rivers that....

"They (members of Congress) can go to the source of authority and make a trade," Symington continued. "But I'm not saying Mendel ever voted for something he didn't think was right for our security.... He was sincere about it. If I had come up that way in the Congress and not gone through the Pentagon, I might have felt exactly the same way he did." (Symington became the first secretary of the Air Force in 1947.)

Hebert, Rivers' successor, said: "I told them (defense industry and Pentagon) as soon as I took office (as chairman), 'don't you put anything in there because I'm chairman.'

"It is wrong if those installations are put in because those members are on the committee," Hebert said. "Realistically, and without indicating anybody does this, you've got to take our system of government into play and look at the reality of it. A man is elected from a district by a majority of the people. And if he does not give the majority of the people what they want, he is not going back. I don't believe that philosophy, but it is a fact of life.

"And why pick on the Armed Services Committee?" asked Hebert. "You take the areas where they have the so-called social problems—welfare and food stamps—well, those members go back and give them the welfare and give them food stamps and give them all the things the majority wanted for nothing and they vote for him. So why pick on our committee?"

Sen. John C. Stennis (D Miss.), chairman of the Senate Armed Services Committee, told Congressional Quarterly that his chairmanship had "had very little effect" on Mississippi's growing defense industry. "I want to help (Mississippi) in a legitimate way, of course," he said. The state has been undergoing a general industrialization process, he said, and part of that has been defense industry.

The record shows that Stennis' state, whatever the impetus was, received substantial increases in its share of the prime defense contract dollar during his years as chairman (beginning in 1969) and his earlier years as an influential committee member. From fiscal 1972, when Mississippi ranked as the 34th largest recipient of defense contract money, the state moved up to the 17th position in fiscal 1971. Mississippi ranked 29th in population by the 1970 census.

Louisiana, home state of Hebert, remained at about the same position during the years 1962-1971. In fiscal 1971, Louisiana ranked as the 26th largest recipient of contract money. The state was the 20th largest in population.

Virginia, which has one senator and two members of the House serving on Armed Services Committees, had a dramatic rise in defense contract dollars. In fiscal 1962, Virginia ranked as the 17th largest recipient of prime contract money and in fiscal 1971 the state had moved to the number four position. Virginia was the 14th largest state in population according to the 1970 census.

Georgia, which at one time had chairmen of both the House and Senate Armed Services Committees, increased its share of prime contract dollars over the decade during which both men—Sen. Richard B. Russell (D) and Rep. Carl Vinson (D)—served as committee chairmen. From fiscal 1962 to 1970, the state climbed from the 19th to 9th largest prime contract recipient. It was the 15th largest state by population.

Old Pentagon Hands. Aspin, who once served as an economic adviser to former Defense Secretary Robert S. McNamara, said: "We used to think of the House Armed Services Committee as the ones we could count on to carry water for us." The Senate committee, Aspin said, generally caused the Pentagon more problems than did the House.

Symington said that part of the game at the Pentagon was vying for funds with the other branches of the military. One of Symington's first jobs as Air Force secretary was "to get as much of the pie as I could for the Air Force because I believe in air power....Everybody fights for their own team; you can't blame them for trying."

"The Armed Services Committees were the jury before which you had to make your case," Symington said.

One member of Congress who asked not to be named told Congressional Quarterly that he once sat in on sessions with leading military budget planners in which they were trying to estimate how much extra they should add to their budget request in anticipation of Congress' annual trimming.

ROLE OF CHAIRMAN

Both Stennis and Hebert were praised by committee members for the way they ran their committees, but they were accused of being tied too closely to military interests.

Because the House had been less able to amend bills which originated in his committee, Hebert operated from the stronger power base. Moreover, Hebert had a larger proportion of supporting committee votes than did Stennis.

The Senate demonstrated increasing interest in scrutinizing the work of its committee and in the years 1967-71 did hold up key legislation. There was little support for a parallel movement in the House.

"It's really hard to object to anything Hebert does on procedural grounds," said Aspin. "He's very fair. Of course he can afford to be because he's got the votes. Only five of us oppose him on most things in committee." They are Aspin, Pike, Michael J. Harrington (D Mass.), Lucien N. Nedzi (D Mich.) and Robert L. Leggett (D Calif.).

"Nobody on that committee can say they have any favoritism," Hebert said. "I frankly think without modesty which is not one of my virtues—modesty is definitely not one of my virtues. I think that committee is conducted with full decorum, in a high level. We have a couple of laughs, but hell, you've got to have a laugh sometimes."

"Stennis is always facing a problem that Hebert never faces—the possibility that there are amendments that could take something out of his bill," Aspin said. "I can't remember the last time in the House that Hebert lost an amendment."

Even Hebert admitted that Stennis faced a tougher fight in the Senate than he did in the House. "I think Stennis has got a much tougher job than I have. Now why's that so? You'll have to ask somebody else."

Hebert continued: "Now John's a gentleman. I've told John many times. 'Now John, I wish you weren't such a gentleman. I'd rather you were a no-good son-of-a-bitch. Then I could do business with you much better.' But you know how courtly he is and how nice he is."

Defense Appropriations Subcommittees

From 1947, when Congress consolidated the War and Navy Departments (administering the Army, Navy and Air Force) into the Department of Defense, until 1966, the House Appropriations Committee consistently cut the Pentagon's budget requests although the cuts were seldom deep ones. Usually, the House cuts were greater than the Senate cuts.

But traditional patterns had given way by the early 1970s to new roles for the committees, reflecting changing attitudes about national defense in Congress.

• Beginning in 1967, the Senate Appropriations Committee took over the role as the leading defense budget cutter.

• The House committee increasingly engaged in defense policy-making, a role normally left to the legislative committee responsible for defense matters—the Armed Services Committee.

Key to the changing trends were the Appropriations Defense Subcommittees of the House and Senate. These subcommittees operated with a high degree of autonomy (more so in the House) and rarely did either the full committees of the House and Senate alter the subcommittees' recommendations on defense appropriations.

For example, George Mahon (D Texas), who had been chairman of the House Defense Subcommittee since it was created in 1947, had not lost a floor fight on a defense appropriations bill since 1958. In other words, the House adopted the position Mahon took on all amendments.

The record for Mahon's counterpart in the Senate (four men have held the position) was unblemished for 20 years until Allen J. Ellender (D La.) became subcommittee chairman early in 1971. Ellender, often an outspoken critic of high defense spending, lost three floor battles his first year. In each case he was opposing amendments which sought to add funds to the bill his subcommittee had reported. The next chairman, John L. McClellan (D Ark.), who took over when Ellender died in 1972, did not lose on the floor in his first year as chairman.

The changing roles of the Appropriations Committees in reviewing defense budgets reflected in part a growing dissatisfaction in Congress with the rising cost of buying weapons and with long-range administration defense planning. An additional irritant had been discontent with the war in Indochina.

The impact of these issues was felt more in the Senate than in the House, according to Congressional Quarterly interviews.

"The Senate as a body tends to be more closely in tune with the American electorate," said Donald W. Riegle Jr. (R Mich.), a member of the House Appropriations Committee.

"Senators are more visible and more closely reported," Riegle continued. "They tend to reflect more fully the very dramatic shift in national priorities that has taken place with respect to the electorate."

It had been the House Appropriations Defense Subcommittee which first reviewed the Pentagon's massive budget requests, the House committee which went further in analyzing the budget request and the House committee that first reported a version of the defense appropriations bill to Congress.

Until 1967, the Senate committee would wait until the House committee had finished with the defense appropriations bill before they even began hearings. But under the leadership of Richard B. Russell (D Ga. 1933-1971), the Senate subcommittee began holding simultaneous hearings on the defense appropriations bill. One Senate staff member said the subcommittee also began independently digging into more of the specific programs covered by the bill. In years before 1967, the Senate subcommittee relied heavily upon the work of its House counterpart.

Gordon Allott (R Colo.), a member of the Senate Defense Subcommittee, said that "in a true sense, as a matter of practice on most appropriations bills, the Senate has become sort of an appeal committee."

STRUCTURE AND POWERS

To coordinate efforts in Congress to cut spending, the House in 1865 and the Senate in 1867 reorganized their committee systems. The task of reviewing appropriation requests was centralized in two groups—the newly formed Committees on Appropriations.

Jealousy concerning the new committee's autonomy in making decisions was the primary motivating factor which led the House to emasculate systematically the committee's original role. Between 1877 and 1885, the House stripped the Appropriations Committee of its jurisdiction in eight of the 14 appropriations areas—this included loss of control over appropriations for the Army, Navy and consular and diplomatic affairs.

Full authority to review appropriations requests and to recommend funding levels for all government agencies was returned to the House committee June 1, 1920. The House had anticipated an executive branch reorganization which centralized the federal government's budgetary process—the Budget and Accounting Act of 1921.

Both the House and Senate Appropriations Committees had over the years reorganized their subcommittee structures to conform to changes in the executive branch.

When in 1947 the Departments of the Army and Navy were put under the broad control of the Defense Department and the Air Force was made a co-equal of the other two services, the Appropriations Committee adjusted its subcommittee structure accordingly. The Defense Subcommittees were formed to handle the appropriations requests of the consolidated department.

The House Defense Subcommittee, however, maintained three separate panels within the subcommittee itself to review independently the funding requests for the Army, Navy and Air Force.

Clarence Cannon (D Mo. 1923-1964), who was chairman of the House committee for more than 20 years, abolished the three-panel Defense Subcommittee structure in 1956 because he found that inter-service rivalries for funds were rubbing off on the respective subcommittee panels.

Since 1956 both the House and Senate Defense Subcommittees had remained structurally constant. The units had been responsible each year for reviewing appropriations requests for the Defense Department and for recommending spending levels to the full committee and the House and Senate.

Authorizing and Appropriating. Prior to 1960 the Defense Subcommittees appropriated funds for weapon systems with little interference from other committees. The Armed Services Committees made lump-sum authorizations which did not specify amounts for particular programs. This left the Appropriations Committees free to divide these authorized subtotals in any way they saw fit within the limits of budget requests by the Defense Department.

But since the early 1960s the House and Senate Armed Services Committees had gained substantial powers. The two committees were empowered to authorize appropriation levels in the elastic spending areas of weapons research, development and purchasing and to set limits for spending on individual weapons programs. The Appropriations Committees were required to fund the systems within those limits.

Two-thirds of the Pentagon's annual budget request did not require authorization by the Armed Services Committees, however. Most of these funds which came before the Defense Subcommittee were fairly stable amounts which did not receive the kind of attention that had been commonly directed toward the weapons programs.

COMMITTEES AT WORK

In both the House and Senate, the membership of the Appropriations Committees tended to be more conservative than the norm for their respective chambers.

Rarely did members find themselves assigned to the prestigious Appropriations Committees during their first few years on Capitol Hill.

Even after his assignment to the committee, however, a member usually served an apprenticeship period on the less important appropriations subcommittees before being assigned to the Defense Subcommittee.

Riegle, a member of the House committee and its Foreign Operations Subcommittee, said: "There's a long-term tendency to put the more progressive and liberal members on the authorizing committee where they can sort of vent their fury, but then to maintain an armlock on the final expenditure of money by putting the more conservative members on the Appropriations Committee."

Riegle said he got his assignment to the committee before the Republican leadership knew what his ideas were. Once on the committee, Riegle spoke out against the war in Indochina and against high levels of defense spending. He rated his chances of ever being assigned to the Defense Subcommittee as extremely poor.

In the House, the committee chairman and ranking minority member made the subcommittee assignments. On the Senate committee, members chose subcommittees on the basis of their seniority on the full committee.

The role of the full Appropriations Committee in passing judgment on the recommendations of the Defense Subcommittees had been minimal. All persons interviewed by Congressional Quarterly were quick to say that all the subcommittee's work had to pass the scrutiny of the full committee before a bill was reported to the floor, *(Continued on p. 247)*

Service Clubs: Committee Report on 'Corruption'

Following two years of investigations, the Senate Government Operations Subcommittee on Executive Reorganization and Government Research released Nov. 2, 1971, a 300-page report documenting "corruption, criminality and moral compromise" at all military levels in connection with nonappropriated fund activities.

"Military personnel—both uniformed and civilian —stole, received kickbacks and gratuities and otherwise profited dishonestly from their association with clubs and exchanges," the report stated. "Too often dishonest practices were considered the normal and customary means of operation."

Investigators pieced together two major examples of corruption which took place over a decade. One involved a group of sergeants whose influence extended to the joint chiefs of staff. The second example involved a powerful merchant who illegally sold goods and services to U.S. military facilities.

The Sergeants. The report identified the owners of the Maredem Co., which sold goods to NCO (non-commissioned officers) clubs in Vietnam, as being the same Army sergeants who controlled the NCO clubs' purchasing systems.

The five sergeants who were shareholders in the Maredem Co. were Sgt. Maj. William O. Wooldridge, Sgts. Narvaez Hatcher, William Higdon, Seymour Lazar and Theodore Bass. Two non-shareholders cited as friends of the enterprise were Sgts. William Bagby and John Nelson.

The sergeants had been first investigated in 1963 following disclosures by another sergeant that money was being cleared from military club slot machines in Germany in an irregular manner. The man raising the issue, Sgt. Maj. Kenneth Parrent, also found that $50,000 from a club acount had been paid to a non-existent construction company.

Parrent testified to the subcommittee that he had reported the irregularities to superiors but that a probe had been blocked by Wooldridge, who was then the service's highest ranking enlisted officer.

Wooldridge's name turned up in several investigations involving the illegal transportation of liquor from Vietnam to Ft. Benning, Georgia, and then to Washington where Wooldridge was serving.

Three months after Wooldridge had been assigned to Vietnam in 1965 he helped Sgt. Lazar become the custodian in charge of the 1st Infantry Division's mess system. Lazar was succeeded in his position by sergeants Hatcher and Nelson. All three had served together in Germany and had been involved in several investigations for their handling of open mess and service club funds.

It was during November 1967 that Wooldridge, Lazar, Hatcher and Higdon formed the Maredem Co., which soon became one of the major supply brokers for the open mess system in Vietnam. Capital for the new company was acquired by selling the Army a walk-in freezer, for $13,000, that it already owned.

Soon after the company was formed, Lazar retired from the Army to become Maredem's chief salesman— selling primarily to his successor at 1st Division's mess, Sgt. Hatcher. At the time, Hatcher was a full partner in Maredem.

During Maredem's first year in business, the company sold more than $1-million in goods to clubs in Vietnam. Eighty per cent of the sales were to clubs run by Higdon, Hatcher and Bagby.

Wooldridge, Bass, Lazar and Higdon were convicted by a federal district court in 1972 of fraud, but sentencing was postponed pending the completion of their testimony before Senate investigators. The men had pleaded the fifth amendment before a Senate committee on numerous occasions but agreed to testify in May of 1973.

Asian Merchant. The second major part of the subcommittee investigation concentrated on the business activities of William John Crum, who was, according to the subcommittee report, the "most successful businessman in Vietnam."

In the early 1960s Crum had switched his base of operations from Korea to South Vietnam where American military presence was increasing. Through a company called Sarl Electronics, Crum managed to become a major supplier of electronic slot machines, pinball games, textiles and liquor to the military.

In its report the Senate subcommittee said that Crum provided a villa, which he decorated and staffed, to five military officers arriving in Vietnam in late 1965. The officers were assigned to Vietnam to process a changeover in the military's mess operations. While the five were living in Crum's villa and paying marginal rent of $100 per month, Sarl Electronics was awarded a $1-million contract with the military.

In the years that followed, Crum built a massive business empire in Vietnam with the help of Brig. Gen. Earl F. Cole, who had administrative control over the service club system and the Army's intelligence division in Vietnam (CID).

Crum used Cole's friendship to import merchandise into Vietnam duty-free, to store goods in military warehouses and to transfer surplus military supplies to the black market. When various branches of the Army tried to investigate Crum, Cole intervened, blocking their efforts and transferring troublesome CID agents from Vietnam.

Following the disclosures by the Senate investigating committee, Gen. Cole was relieved of his command Sept. 7, 1969, and allowed to retire July 30, 1970, with the rank of colonel. He never faced a court martial, but was later convicted of making false statements to the Army in connection with another investigation. Crum was barred by the Pentagon from doing future business with the U.S. military.

(Continued from p. 245)
but no one in either committee could recall the last time that the full committee did anything to a defense appropriations bill once it left the subcommittee.

HOUSE SUBCOMMITTEE

The House Appropriations Committee functioned as one of the most autonomous groups in the House. Most of the members had only the one committee assignment.

The Defense Subcommittee also had great freedom to operate without interference or much oversight by the full committee. Most members had just one other subcommittee assignment which left them free to devote much more time to subcommittee work than their Senate counterparts.

Sen. Allott said the autonomy of the House Appropriations Committee was "characteristic of all committees in the House. They are just much more of a solid unit (than Senate committees) and the House structure tends to give the chairmen an opportunity—and they do use it—to control their committees much more than is done in the Senate in any of the committees."

Unlike the Senate group, the House Defense Subcommittee had few dealings with the Armed Services Committee. Subcommittee members did not generally read the hearings or reports produced by the Armed Services Committee, admitted one representative. Staff members, he said, did read some of the other committee's material.

The top three Democrats on the Defense Subcommittee were the same men who sat on the subcommittee when it was established in 1947. They were Chairman Mahon, Robert L. F. Sikes (Fla.) and Jamie L. Whitten (Miss.).

"The House subcommittee is strikingly interested in policy-making contrary to traditional impressions of what their role is supposed to be," said Kerry Jones, Indiana State University professor of political science.

Jones said he found that the House subcommittee "is interested in shaping a strong national defense policy. They've developed a new role—guardians of the national security rather than guardians of the treasury."

Rep. Joseph P. Addabbo (D N.Y.), a member of the subcommittee, said: "In our case the only real place where the subcommittee has gone into it (policy-making role) in any real degree has been in the case of the Navy. There are many who believe that our Navy has become almost second rate and I'm one of them.

"The administration plays games in submitting their budget," Addabbo said. To keep a low budget total for defense, he said, the administration purposely undercuts an area which the subcommittee feels is essential—such as the Navy—"knowing there will be ample justification presented to almost force us to increase areas where they have not made requests."

Both chairmen of the Defense Subcommittees in the House and Senate also served as chairmen of the full Appropriations Committees.

Unlike his counterpart in the Senate, Mahon had long experience as the top man on the Defense Subcommittee—more than 25 years—and had built a reputation as a tough budget trimmer in all appropriations matters. Mahon's critics contended that he sometimes leaned more heavily on social programs than on defense requests when pushing for budget cuts.

"Mahon has a good sense of what the House is feeling at any given time," Addabbo said. "He has mellowed

to a certain extent since the days of Cannon (Mahon's predecessor as committee chairman). He still has his own ways of operating, but has liberalized things in certain ways. He tries to give junior members a little more chance to operate—to chair the subcommittee."

Riegle, often a critic of the war and military spending levels, said: "I've found that Mahon rules much more by persuasion and reason than he does by an arbitrary use of power."

SENATE SUBCOMMITTEE

The Senate Appropriations Defense Subcommittee, as its House counterpart, also tended to have a membership slightly more conservative than the norm.

The subcommittee operated quite differently from the House subcommittee. Because there were fewer senators than representatives, members of the Senate were required to sit on at least two full committees. Seventy-five per cent of the Defense Subcommittee members, however, served on at least three full committees and had as many as 20 subcommittee assignments.

According to staff sources on the subcommittee, the members had time only to delve into about 20 or 25 areas of major controversy or concern each year when they considered the defense appropriations bill. Ninety per cent of the subcommittee's focus, staff sources said, was directed toward the weapons procurement and research and development portions of the budget.

The Senate Defense Subcommittee had extensive interplay with the Armed Services Committee. The chairman of the Armed Services Committee, John C. Stennis (D Miss.), and the ranking minority member, Margaret Chase Smith (R Maine), had both been members of this appropriations subcommittee for more than a decade.

In addition to Stennis and Smith, the Defense Subcommittee had three ex officio members from the Armed Services Committee. Each appropriations subcommittee had ex officio members from the pertinent authorizing committee.

The ex officio members had full voting rights in the subcommittee—no votes at the full committee level—and one ex officio member sat with the conference committee when the Senate and House were ironing out differences in their versions of appropriation bills.

The three ex officio members of the Defense Subcommittee were chosen by Stennis, chairman of the Armed Services Committee. Stennis also named the one ex officio member who sat with the conference committee.

Ex officio members of the subcommittee during 1972 were Stuart Symington (D Mo.), Henry M. Jackson (D Wash.) and Strom Thurmond (R S.C.).

One senator on the subcommittee told Congressional Quarterly that these members participated too much. Sen. Allott said: "The subcommittee members who are ex officio do consume in my opinion an inordinate amount of time to the point of where they actually restrict the time that should be available to the (regular) committee members."

Conclusion

Armed Services Committees. Critics and supporters of the Armed Services Committees agreed that the committees acted as both advocate and overseer of the armed forces. They differed on the degree that advocacy and oversight had been exercised.

"L. Mendel Rivers (former Armed Services Committee chairman), and to a lesser extent Eddie Hebert, saw the function of the Armed Services Committee as being that of the only advocate which the military has in Congress," Pike said. "They have tended in my opinion, and this is much less true in the case of Eddie, to defend the military against all critics."

Samuel S. Stratton (D N.Y.), sixth-ranking member of the 39-man House Armed Services Committee, said: "I think the Armed Services Committee is an advocate for the military in the sense that most of us recognize that the military is an important part of any free society.

"As Mr. Rivers used to say, 'If you don't have a friend on this committee, you don't have a friend anywhere.' I think we want to keep the armed services strong," Stratton remarked.

Les Aspin added: "The Armed Services Committee looks on its role as the protector of the uniformed military officer. The committee thinks its role is to find out what the military wants and then try to get it for them.

"The majority of the committee," Aspin said, "are constantly looking for things that the services want and the civilians (in the Pentagon and the administration) have rejected. And then we go and put it back in the budget."

The committee should be an advocate of the budget on which it finally decides, Aspin conceded, but the committee must first vigorously scrutinize that budget. "Take it another way," he said. "If the Armed Services Committee isn't looking out for the taxpayer, then who the hell is? Nobody on the floor of the House is going to be able to push through an amendment to an Armed Services Committee bill and God knows, we've tried."

Sen. Richard S. Schweiker (R Pa.), who had served on both the House and Senate Armed Services Committees, observed that the Senate committee had too often acted as an advocate for the military.

"The Senate Armed Services Committee, however, is less of an advocate for the military than the House committee is," Schweiker said. "That's a small differentiation, but there is some difference."

Stennis, the committee chairman, conceded that his panel could do a better job of riding herd on the military. "One way to improve the military is to put them on their mettle and make them justify what they are doing," he said. "We put that budget through a fine-toothed comb. Every weapon system ought to justify itself on the facts."

Appropriations Subcommittees. Most of those Congressional Quarterly interviewed said the Defense subcommittees were more overseers than advocates for the Defense Department. But none provided strong documentation to back that assertion up.

One committee member, Rep. Riegle, said the question was academic. "What happens is the enormity of the federal bureaucracy is such—particularly in the Defense Department which is the biggest of the big ones—that decades ago we lost any real control over monitoring their activity.

"We go through the motions of saying we do it, but as a practical matter, it's just not physically possible for us to keep up the way we're staffed," he declared.

Addabbo said: "As long as we're limited on staff (the Defense Subcommittee has five professional staff members) and we have to face this tremendous mass of the Pentagon machine," it is all the subcommittee can do just to keep up.

Why the Support? Why do the recommendations of the military committees and subcommittees carry such weight in Congress? Chairman Hebert said it was because of the respect that other members have for the expertise of the committee members. "It is the job of the committee to know what's going on in the military and the House knows that."

Aspin cited several factors: "The weapon systems are complicated, people don't like to vote against defense measures, and there's always that lurking fear that there's some secret classified document which shows that this thing is really necessary and not just the pet project of some general."

The military's ability "through sheer resources to get their point of view out" also has aided the committee in collecting support among members of Congress, Aspin said. "You can't pick up a newspaper without reading that some admiral said that the Soviet Navy is threatening us in some way."

"I'll tell you why they support us," Hebert said. "We're about at parity with the Russians now. If we stop now where we are, we will lose parity and become inferior.... In war they don't pay off for second place. There's no exacta or daily double. There's one bet and you've got to have the winner."

 **Defense Secretary Laird**

PENDULUM OF POWER SHIFTED FROM CIVILIANS TO MILITARY

Of all President Nixon's first-term cabinet appointees, probably none had as much impact on his department—for better or worse—as did his choice for secretary of defense, Melvin R. Laird.

Laird, who resigned Jan. 30, 1973, to return to private life, overhauled his mammoth department from top to bottom during his four years on the job. His policies represented as far-reaching a departure from those of his immediate predecessors, Robert S. McNamara (1961-68) and Clark M. Clifford (1968-69), as did those that McNamara instituted at the outset of the Kennedy administration after an eight-year Republican regime. *(McNamara profile, Congress and the Nation, Vol. II, p. 863)*

Laird, the first professional politician ever named defense secretary, took the reins of power away from Pentagon civilians and put them back in the military's hands. Nowhere was this more evident than in weapons procurement—a job that military planners insisted they could do better than the civilian architects of the F-111 (TFX) aircraft program and other procurement fiascos of the McNamara era.

In other notable developments during his tenure, Laird became the leading proponent of an all-volunteer army and "Vietnamization" of the Vietnam war. A strategic arms limitation treaty with the Soviet Union was negotiated in 1972, and some observers attributed the treaty to Laird's efforts to convince the Soviets that the United States meant business about expanding its nuclear forces in the event the agreement fell through.

Because of his intimate knowledge of Congress, achieved during 16 years in the House, Laird was able to restore a close working relationship between the Pentagon and the powerful congressional committees that act on the military budget—a relationship that McNamara had left frayed and that Clifford had little time to repair. Assessments of Laird's performance differed according to the various interpretations that were put on the many controversial issues on which he took a stand.

In announcing that he had accepted Laird's resignation, President Nixon said Nov. 28, 1972, that he had a "profound sense of pride" over Laird's stewardship at the Pentagon. But in naming former Health, Education and Welfare Secretary Elliot L. Richardson as Laird's successor, Nixon was believed to be opting for a shift back to tougher civilian management of the far-flung defense establishment. Richardson, in more than two years in the HEW post, had earned the reputation of a hard-driving, no-nonsense administrator who had vastly improved the efficiency of one of the government's most unwieldy departments.

Laird Political Background. Republican Laird, 50, won his first elective office in 1946 when he was elected to the Wisconsin Senate, succeeding his father who had died. He continued as a state senator until his election to the U.S. House in 1952.

During his eight terms in the House, Laird was a constant, methodical analyst and critic of Democratic administrations. He was an outspoken opponent of former Defense Secretary McNamara's concept of "parity" in strategic weaponry between the United States and the Soviet Union. As a member of the powerful House Defense Appropriations Subcommittee, Laird called for a nuclear navy, strengthened anti-submarine forces, more Polaris missile submarines and stepped-up research and development for defense. At the time he was named defense secretary, he held the enormously influential post of chairman of the Republican Conference, the party's caucus in the House.

Much of Laird's prestige and power were acquired because of his participation in Republican national convention platform committees from 1952 through 1968. As vice chairman of the committee in 1960, he assumed a crucial role in guiding through a controversial platform accord between candidates Richard Nixon and Nelson Rockefeller, which had threatened to disrupt the Republican convention. As full chairman of the 1964 platform committee, he was instrumental in the writing of a platform acceptable to presidential candidate Barry Goldwater in the face of stiff resistance from the party's liberal wing.

Laird also emerged as a top party spokesman and ideologist through his service as chairman of a joint House-Senate committee which in 1962 drafted a 2,500-word declaration of Republican principles and policy to dispel the party's "negative" image, and as editor of

---

Biography

Melvin Robert Laird was born Sept. 1, 1922, in Omaha, Neb.

Education: Carleton College, Northfield, Minn., B.A.

Military: U.S. Navy, 1942-46, served in 3rd Fleet, Pacific theater, received Purple Heart, Asiatic-Pacific, Philippine Liberation, American Theater, Japanese Occupation medals.

Family: Married Barbara Masters, Oct. 15, 1945; three children: John Osborne (1948), Alison (1951), David Malcolm (1954).

Religion: Presbyterian.

Career Highlights: Wisconsin State Senate, 1946-1952; U.S. House of Representatives, 1953-1969; served on House Agriculture Committee, 1955-57, and House Appropriations Committee (Defense and Labor and Health, Education and Welfare subcommittees); chairman, Joint House-Senate Committee on Republican Policy, 1960; chairman, House Republican Conference, 1965-69; secretary of defense, 1969-72.

two books, *The Conservative Papers* (1964) and *Republican Papers* (1968).

Laird also wrote *A House Divided: America's Strategy Gap* (1962), in which he advocated the controversial position, which he later retracted, that the United States should move to a "first strike" nuclear capability vis-a-vis the Soviet Union and that nuclear war was not unthinkable.

Vietnam Policy

As secretary of defense, Laird was credited with successfully urging Nixon to wind down U.S. troop involvement in the Vietnam war and to shift the ground combat role to the South Vietnamese, aided by U.S. weaponry and air support.

Despite the May 1970 incursion into Cambodia, which he reportedly opposed, Laird consistently maintained that his program of "Vietnamization" was progressing at the planned rate. As of Nov. 23, 1972, the U.S. troop level in Indochina stood at 28,000—a cut of 515,400 since troop levels peaked at 543,400 on April 30, 1969.

Laird's Vietnamization policy represented an abrupt shift in position for a man who was once known as a leading congressional "hawk." As late as Jan. 31, 1968, he had criticized a Johnson administration pledge to withdraw American troops from Vietnam six months after the shooting there had ended. This "would ensure a communist takeover of South Vietnam," Laird said, "and would give rise to the very serious question of whether the American sacrifice and bloodshed of the past three years had been justified."

Weapons Acquisition

Upon taking office, Laird moved quickly to return much of the weapons acquisition process to the military, who had held a subordinate role to civilian "whiz kids" during the McNamara regime. Laird called his new management policy "participatory decision-making, defined decentralization and delegation of authority under specific guidance."

In the first step of his new policy, Laird all but dismantled the department's powerful systems analysis office—which had reputedly held life or death authority over military weapons proposals during the McNamara days. Laird cut back sharply on the office's manpower and curtailed most of its functions. This move effectively eliminated an independent civilian review of the military's weapons proposals. Under the new policy, Laird would tell the services how much they could expect to spend, and then let them decide how to spend it. In the McNamara and Clifford years, the secretaries would ask the military what they wanted and then decide themselves what they would get, often on the basis of recommendations by systems analysis.

Laird sought to eliminate weapons cost overruns—which he re-named "cost growths" by instituting a "fly-before-buy" policy—developing working models of major weapon systems before making the final decision to buy them. By contrast, his two immediate predecessors relied on a "total package procurement" approach, under which a single company would contract early in the game for both research and initial procurement.

In what was probably the major failure of Laird's term, however, his policy appeared to have no more effect on holding down weapons costs than had the McNamara policies. Major weapons contracted for during the Laird years—particularly the DD-963 destroyer and S-3A anti-submarine warfare aircraft—were showing cost growths similar to the procurement disasters that plagued his Pentagon predecessors.

Handling of Congress

Public and congressional anti-military sentiment, caused in large part by the seemingly endless Vietnam war and alleged waste in weapons procurement, led to vigorous debates in Congress and fights with the press and television networks throughout the Laird years.

Critics of Laird's budget directed particularly heated barbs at the huge sums committed to badly overrun weapon systems, such as the C-5A transport aircraft, antiballistic missile (ABM) system, nuclear aircraft carriers and the B-1 "advanced manned" bomber where no more than a shaky Pentagon consensus existed that the weapons really were needed.

By far the major congressional battle of the Laird years was a 1969 fight over deployment of the ABM—a controversy that erupted within days after Laird assumed office. In defending the ABM, Laird cited alleged Soviet attempts to move to a "first strike" strategy which he said could be deterred only if the Soviets feared that the strike could be blunted long enough for U.S. missiles to go into action. Critics contended that U.S. intelligence reports on Soviet missile construction were inaccurate and that the ABM would not be effective in the face of an all-out Soviet missile attack. In the showdown over the issue, the Senate Aug. 6, 1969, by a cliff-hanging **50-50 roll-call vote,** rejected an amendment to block President Nixon from deploying "Safeguard," his recently announced version of the system. The strength of opponents crested with that vote and they never again mounted serious threat against the ABM.

Over-all, Laird handled Congress masterfully, never losing a battle over a major weapons system. Playing on his intimate knowledge of constituent pressures on legislators, Laird defused the defense spending issue by reminding recalcitrant members of Congress of the unemployment they could expect in their districts in the event of deep cuts in the defense budget. His former colleagues on Capitol Hill were far more comfortable with Laird, one of their own, than they were with the aloof and professorial McNamara, who miffed more than one congressional committee with his complex computer analyses on weapons procurement. Among the congressional observations of Laird, as expressed during interviews with Congressional Quarterly:

● F. Edward Hebert (D La.), chairman of the House Armed Services Committee, said Laird "will go down as one of the greatest secretaries of defense." Hebert, a bitter critic of McNamara, characterized Laird as a "very warm man," well-liked, always available and particularly good with congressional committees. Laird had "never failed" before his committee, he said, and the committee had been gratified because Laird had always "talked it over" with committee members before announcing a major decision. Hebert added that Laird knew and allowed for the "shortcomings and foibles" of Congress and that he was a man the committee knew would never spring "the double-play" on them.

• William E. Minshall (R Ohio), ranking Republican on the House Defense Appropriations Subcommittee, also applauded Laird for being "street wise" in the ways of Congress. He professed a "tremendous admiration" for Laird, who he said has "no weak points (as secretary) as far as I'm concerned." With regard to Laird's procurement policies, Minshall said that Laird's techniques were "working not as well as they should" but that more time would be needed before they could be put to thorough evaluation.

• Rep. Les Aspin (D Wis.), a member of the Armed Services Committee, a former Pentagon systems analyst and an outspoken critic of the level of defense spending, said that Laird's "greatest asset has been to restore relations with Congress." "The thing I don't know," Aspin continued, "is just how well he's run the department. I think it has been more of the arbiter role than the initiator role." Aspin added that there had been problems at the Pentagon when Laird took over and that "I don't see that Laird has done anything about them." Aspin cited "gold plating" of weapon systems with expensive and unnecessary extras and "enormous waste" in support forces, particularly in the Army.

Deterrence Strategy

On the strategic front, Laird in his 1971 defense posture statement to Congress introduced a "strategy of realistic deterrence," which was an elaboration of a policy of "nuclear sufficiency" that had been enunciated by President Nixon in 1969. The cornerstone of the new posture was that the United States must maintain "technical superiority" in both offensive and defensive weapons over the Soviets. Laird said his strategy "emphasizes measured, meaningful involvement and vigorous negotiation from a position of strength." It was a full break from McNamara and the days of nuclear "parity."

Laird told Congress that his new strategy was "realistic" for three reasons:

"First, it is based on a sober and clear view of the multiple threats to peace which exist in today's world. It neither exaggerates nor underestimates those threats. Second, it provides for the maintenance of a strong free world military capability as the essential foundation of deterrence. It rejects the view that peace is well served if our military power is unilaterally weakened. Third, it takes account of the strategic, fiscal, manpower and political realities while steering a prudent middle course between two policy extremes—world policeman or new isolationism."

SALT Agreement. As it developed, Laird's "realistic deterrence" strategy was used as a "bargaining chip" to achieve a strategic arms limitation agreement with the Soviet Union. After three years of hard bargaining, in what became known as the SALT agreement (for Strategic Arms Limitation Talks), the two countries agreed in 1972 to an historic arms limitation agreement. Advocates of a "hard line" in the talks contended that the agreement could not have been worked out without Laird's insistence on U.S. technical superiority in the absence of such an agreement.

Defense Costs

To pay for the strategy of realistic deterrence, and for the nation's continued capability to fight conventionally if necessary, the Pentagon asked for $83.4-billion for fiscal 1973—the largest dollar amount ever requested for defense.

Laird said the 1973 budget request was the "absolute minimum amount necessary to safeguard our national security. We are moving in orderly transition into our peacetime or Nixon Doctrine base-line deterrent forces. This Nixon Doctrine posture, together with our increased emphasis on technological superiority, total force planning and weapons modernization, will provide for our nation's defense needs at the lowest possible cost while taking into account the strategic manpower, political and fiscal realities, including the huge pay increase which Congress has approved for military and civilian personnel of the department."

During the 1968 presidential campaign, candidate Nixon had promised to increase defense spending, to close what he called a "security gap" between U.S. and Soviet forces. In a move to mollify the Pentagon's critics, Nixon actually cut defense spending for fiscal 1971, the first budget over which he had total control, but began carrying out his campaign promise to hike the Pentagon budget beginning the next fiscal year. While the fiscal 1973 request of $83.4-billion initiated several new weapons projects, Nixon and Laird outflanked their critics by repeatedly emphasizing that spending for human resources in the over-all federal budget would exceed spending for defense. While defense spending was 31.8 per cent of the total budget, they said, spending for human resources was 45 per cent of the total.

Pentagon Reorganization

In Pentagon reorganizational moves, Laird abolished the department's assistant secretary of administration in favor of an assistant secretary of intelligence to oversee the department's intelligence activities. At Nixon's directive, the department established a Defense Investigative Service to centralize control of all personnel security investigations. The intelligence activity overhauls were in large part spurred by the *Pueblo* incident of 1968 and charges in 1970 that Army investigators were conducting surveillance of anti-war protestors.

Laird pressed Congress successfully to authorize the addition of a second deputy secretary for his office the recommendation of a blue ribbon advisory panel, headed by Gilbert Fitzhugh, chairman of the board of the Metropolitan Life Insurance Co., which reported to Nixon in 1970. But the secretary ignored the more controversial panel recommendations, including a proposal to relieve the Joint Chiefs of Staff from day-to-day military operations in favor of a new staff headed by a single military officer. In doing so, he responded to reportedly stiff pressure from the Pentagon's top military brass.

Volunteer Army

In consonance with Nixon's 1968 campaign pledge to create an all-volunteer military force, Laird moved steadily toward abolishing the military draft.

Calls for 1972 were not to exceed 50,000 men, the lowest draft call since 1949. At the same time, the department set up incentives for volunteer military service and national guard and reserve forces. Congress increased military pay and fringe benefits in anticipation of the all-volunteer army. On Jan. 27, 1973, Laird announced that the administration would not seek renewal of the draft after its expiration June 30, and would henceforth rely on an all-volunteer force. *(p. 225)*

Role in 1972 Election

During the 1972 presidential election, Laird played what was widely regarded as the most partisan political role on record for a defense secretary in a presidential campaign. Although Laird stopped short of becoming an official "surrogate" for Nixon, he was as outspoken a critic of Democratic presidential candidate George McGovern as were any of the surrogates, which included other cabinet members and top Republican politicians.

Traditionally, the Department of Defense and its top civilian leader have stayed out of the center political ring during presidential election years. The tradition suffered its first major erosion during the 1964 campaign when McNamara struck back at Republican candidate Barry Goldwater's allegations that President Johnson had cut back the nation's nuclear arsenal to the danger point.

Paul C. Warnke, who served as assistant defense secretary with McNamara and as an aide to McGovern during the 1968 campaign, blasted Laird's role in the campaign at an Aug. 16, 1972, news conference. Warnke charged that Laird's "political attacks" were inconsistent with the responsibilities of high office and asked Laird to cease his attacks on McGovern or resign.

Before McGovern had even won the crucial California primary, which made him the strongest contender for the Democratic nomination, Laird was publicly denouncing the Democrat's proposal to reduce the Pentagon budget to $55-billion by 1975. "I would say that the thing to do if you go the $30-billion (reduction) route is to direct the Defense Department to spend at least a billion dollars in white flags so they could run them up all over because it means surrender," Laird said June 5 before the Senate Appropriations Committee.

The key to Laird's criticism of McGovern was the legwork done for the defense secretary by the Pentagon's budget division. Between May 31 and Aug. 10,

Laird released three critical analyses of McGovern's proposals prepared by Defense Department comptroller Robert Moot. The third report—a 193-page book, prepared at the government's expense—defended the Pentagon's level of spending and attacked the ideas advanced by McGovern. "Those who suggest," the report stated, "that we can solve our public spending problem by peeling some easy billions off the defense budget are arguing not only with the Pentagon, but with reality."

Assessment

Traditionally, the job of managing the Pentagon was viewed as the toughest in the government next to the Presidency. Secretaries had been sharply criticized both while they held the office and after they left. The job had been viewed as a graveyard for any secretary with future political ambitions.

But most observers believed that Laird would leave the job relatively unscathed. A consummate politician, he avoided the bitter fights with Congress and the military that marked the terms of his predecessors. But it would be several years before Laird's management of the Pentagon could be fully assessed. While McNamara was widely hailed as possibly the greatest of all secretaries of defense at the time he left office, he later encountered criticism from earlier admirers after cost overruns and performance problems with weapons began to surface.

Some observers thought the assessment of Laird would hinge on his procurement policies and whether the downgrading of the systems analysis function would create an atmosphere of permissiveness for defense contractors in which cost overruns and faulty weapons performance became greater problems than ever. On July 17, 1972, the General Accounting Office reported cost overruns of $28.7-billion on major weapons systems—an increase of $7.8-billion since a similar GAO report was released in December 1969. By this standard, unless the record changed, the Laird regime might reasonably be considered a failure.

But other observers felt that Laird would attain a niche in history for his role in persuading President Nixon to wind down the war in Vietnam and for pressuring the Russians into the SALT agreement. These observers saw these moves as solid achievements that far transcended the cost growth issue.

Chapter 4—Crime Legislation

Key Votes

In this chapter, key roll-call votes are shown in bold-face type. The party breakdown on each of these votes and the position taken by each member of Congress may be found in the key vote charts which appear in the appendix to this book.

Crime Legislation

Soaring crime rates, and the anxiety they aroused, led to a stiffening of attitudes toward crime during the 1960s. Widespread willingness to consider crime as a symptom of deeper social and economic problems gave way to demands for quick decisive action against criminals. This shift in public opinion was echoed in the evolving political slogans of the sixties—from the Johnson administration's war on poverty to the Nixon administration's war on crime.

Throughout his 1968 campaign to oust the Democrats from the White House, Richard M. Nixon emphasized the nation's rising crime rate and the need for "law and order" to reverse the trend. Nixon in 1968 said the Johnson administration and then Attorney General Ramsey Clark were "leading an official retreat" in the face of rising crime.

Nixon pledged to reduce crime by strengthening the "peace forces" and refusing to coddle criminals. "The truth is," he said, "that we will reduce crime and violence when we enforce our laws—when we make it less profitable, and a lot more risky, to break our laws."

Upon assuming office in 1969, the Nixon administration took the position that it had a mandate to deal vigorously with crime. The contrast between administrations was sharp. President Johnson rarely mentioned crime without tracing it to the social and economic problems of poverty. To Johnson, the war on crime could not be separated from the war on poverty. His Great Society programs were geared to reduce the crime rate by improving the quality of life and diminishing the reasons for crime.

President Nixon, however, spoke of crime as primarily a law enforcement problem. A few days after his inauguration, he addressed himself to the crime problem in Washington, D.C. "I recognize...that in the long run crime itself also requires much more far-reaching and subtle approaches," he said. "But the rapidly mounting urgency of the crime crisis...marks immediate, direct anticrime measures as the first-priority task."

By 1972, he was pointing to FBI crime statistics as evidence that his administration had made "truly significant progress" in its efforts to curb crime. "We have dramatically increased federal assistance for state and local authorities," Nixon said. "Where the federal government has direct enforcement authority, such as in organized crime, drug trafficking, and in the District of Columbia, we have both strengthened the laws and poured more men and money into enforcement. Through court appointments, conferences on the judiciary and on corrections and other administration actions, law enforcement has been given additional vigor."

Nixon's claims of progress did not go unchallenged, however. Sen. George McGovern (S.D.), his unsuccessful Democratic opponent in the 1972 election, charged that the Nixon administration was "perpetrating a cruel hoax on the American people." McGovern said the administration had been "long on tough talk (and) short on performance" in the fight against crime.

Statistics

Federal Bureau of Investigation statistics showed the rate of crime (the number of crimes per 100,000 persons) rose only seven per cent in 1971, the lowest annual increase in six years, and the rate was one per cent in the first half of 1972, the lowest percentage increase in 12 years. Preliminary statistics for 1972, released in March 1973, showed an over-all three per cent drop in crime as compared with 1971.

The same FBI statistics, however, showed over-all crime had soared 30 per cent in the 1969-71 period, with violent crimes up 50 per cent and property crimes up 45 per cent.

As a result of the 1971 statistics, the administration boasted that "the forces of crime in America have begun to yield to an all-out counterattack by the forces of law and order."

While the advocates of a "hard line" against criminals could argue with proponents of the "soft line" over who could do more to cut crime, the American people faced the problem with increasing impatience and frustration.

Public Opinion. A Gallup Poll taken late in 1972 found 51 per cent of those interviewed thought crime had increased, versus 35 per cent a year before. More startling were these findings:

• Residents of the nation's largest cities said crime was their top concern (22 per cent named crime, versus 4 per cent in 1949), four persons in 10 nationally were afraid to walk alone at night in their own neighborhoods and one out of six did not feel safe in his own home at night.

References

Discussion of crime policy in the 1945-64 period may be found in *Congress and the Nation, Vol. I* p. 1671-1675. For the years 1965-68, see *Congress and the Nation, Vol. II*, p. 309-334.

• Increased use of drugs and allegedly lenient courts were cited most often by respondents as the reasons for increased crime. Asked specifically about courts in their area, 74 per cent replied that they were not dealing harshly enough with criminals, an increase of 26 percentage points since a similar survey in 1965.

• The poll also found that 21 per cent of those surveyed above age 18 had suffered one or more of the following crimes in the previous year: breaking and entering, mugging, assault, robbery, burglary, vandalism or auto theft.

Civil Disturbances

The years 1969-72 did see the virtual elimination of two types of massive social eruptions which had plagued the country: urban riots and campus disorders.

The riots, which paralyzed cities large and small in the mid-1960s, seemed to die out in the early 1970s. No one really could explain why the cities became quiet, but the end of campus disorders was traced to the killing of four Kent State University students by Ohio National Guardsmen during an anti-war demonstration in May 1970 and a reduction in the draft of young people for the war.

Hijacking and Drugs

Replacing city and campus disorders in the public's awareness were two new activities: drugs and airplane hijackings. The Federal Aviation Administration reported in November 1972 that there had been 159 skyjackings since 1961, almost all of them after 1967. Of the 218 persons taking part in them, 124 still were at large and most were believed to be in Cuba or Algeria. The motives of the skyjackers were political or monetary—some extorted hundreds of thousands of dollars from airlines on threats of destroying the planes and passengers.

The drug problem was not a new one—but a new awareness of it developed as more and more people from white middle-class began using narcotics, becoming addicted or dying of overdoses. There were an estimated 600,000 heroin addicts in the country in 1972, a tenfold

CRIME AND POPULATION
1966 - 1971
PERCENT CHANGE OVER 1966

CRIME = CRIME INDEX OFFENSES
CRIME RATE = NUMBER OF OFFENSES PER 100,000 INHABITANTS

CRIME UP 83%
CRIME RATE UP 74%
POPULATION UP 5%

FBI CHART

increase from 1960. Law enforcement officials said 50 to 60 per cent of all street crimes and burglaries were drug-connected.

Nixon Policy

The first Nixon administration attacked the crime problem on three major fronts: money, legislation and judicial appointments.

It spent about $1.5-billion on crime control and prevention in its last three years. The money was funneled to the states through the Law Enforcement Assistance Administration (LEAA) in the form of block grants.

LEAA was a politically popular program with Congress, which gave President Nixon almost all the funds he requested for it. But by 1972 there was much criticism that the money was being spent on fancy hardware instead of crime control. *(LEAA funding, p. 258)*

The election year of 1970 was the high-water mark for Nixon anticrime legislation; four major administration bills were approved by Congress. These were an extension of the 1968 Safe Streets Act, which created the LEAA; a drug control act which revised federal statutes and expanded federal support for drug treatment and prevention; an organized crime act designed to curb large-scale professional criminal operations, and a District of Columbia crime bill which was to be a model for national legislation. *(1970 legislation, p. 266)*

The President made good on his pledge to appoint to the Supreme Court and other courts men who were, in his view, "strict constructionists" of the Constitution. His four Supreme Court appointees in particular were billed as men who would reverse the "liberal" trend of the Warren court which in many peoples' minds interpreted the Constitution to the benefit of criminals. *(Chapter on Supreme Court, p. 287)*

In other actions, the administration beefed up the Justice Department's criminal division with manpower and funds so it could concentrate on crime syndicates. Although division chief Henry E. Petersen said there was

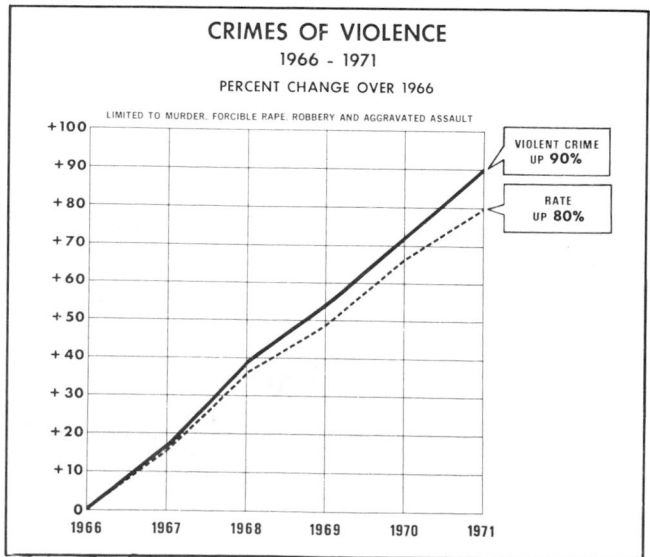

CRIMES OF VIOLENCE
1966 - 1971
PERCENT CHANGE OVER 1966

LIMITED TO MURDER, FORCIBLE RAPE, ROBBERY AND AGGRAVATED ASSAULT

VIOLENT CRIME UP 90%
RATE UP 80%

FBI CHART

a 50 per cent increase in indictments and convictions of organized crime figures between 1969 and 1972, he conceded there were no reliable statistics to show the syndicate was less powerful than earlier.

The federal government vastly increased the use of electronic eavesdropping (wiretaps and bugs) on criminal suspects under President Nixon. Official figures of the Administrative Office of the U.S. Courts showed federal surveillances rose from 30 in 1969 to 180 in 1970 and 281 in 1971. The figures did not include eavesdrops placed without court approval, a practice which the Supreme Court ruled unconstitutional in 1972. *(Table on federal and state eavesdropping, internal security chapter p. 491)*

Gun Control. Throughout the four-year period, critics of the administration's crime policy called for tough gun control legislation as an effective method of controlling violent crimes; but the administration proposed no gun control legislation during its first term, and Congress was equally reluctant to take the initiative. In 1969, Congress in fact relaxed controls over access to ammunition by clearing a bill repealing a record keeping requirement contained in the 1968 Gun Control Act for the sales of certain types of ammunition. In 1972, despite the attempted assassination of Alabama Governor George C. Wallace (D), a bill to outlaw the sale of cheap handguns passed the Senate in August but did not reach the House floor. The President had said in June he would sign the measure if Congress passed it.

Chronology

Of Legislation

On Crime

1969

As campaign oratory urging law and order and deploring crime died away and the nation's crime continued to climb, Congress' answer was vastly increased anticrime funding but no new programs for crime control.

Part of the responsibility lay with the President, whose long-promised anticrime program did not reach Capitol Hill until late in the spring. Most of it was still pending at the session's end.

The administration anticrime program was directed toward four main objectives:
• Increasing funds available for local, state and federal law enforcement agencies. *(Box on LEAA, p. 258)*
• Curbing organized crime's growth, infiltration into legitimate businesses and corruption of local officials.
• Halting the expansion in drug and narcotics traffic.
• Slowing the flow of obscene material into homes. *(Civil Liberties chapter, p. 483)*

Later proposals which the Nixon administration made for federal anticrime legislation were foreshadowed in a "model anticrime package" for the District of Columbia, which Nixon sent to Congress in July.

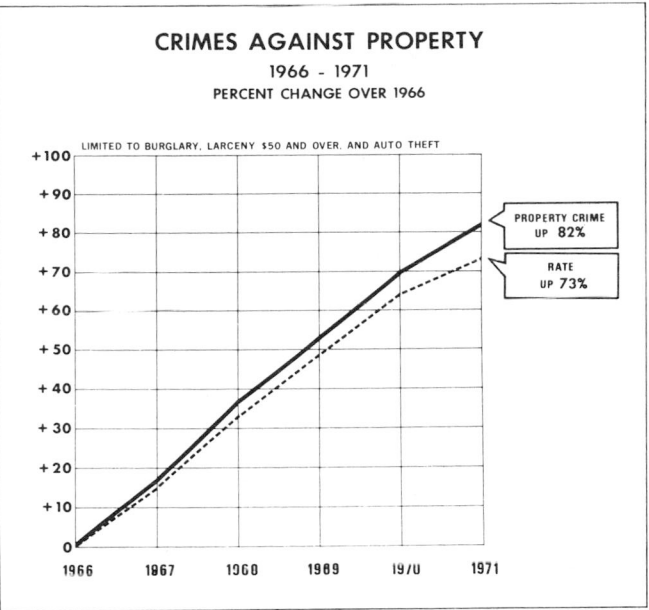

CRIMES AGAINST PROPERTY
1966 - 1971
PERCENT CHANGE OVER 1966

LIMITED TO BURGLARY, LARCENY $50 AND OVER, AND AUTO THEFT

PROPERTY CRIME UP 82%

RATE UP 73%

FBI CHART

To combat crime in the nation's capital, which he had described during the 1968 campaign as the "crime capital of the world," Nixon proposed a program including bail reform, court reorganization, "no-knock" searches and preventive detention.

As part of the administration's campaign against organized crime, Nixon, within days of assuming office, ordered use of wiretapping and bugging as authorized by Title III of the Omnibus Crime Control and Safe Streets Act of 1968. Attorney General John N. Mitchell said July 14 that the use of electronic eavesdropping against organized criminal elements had proved effective.

Congress approved bills restricting the use of some higher education funds by students taking part in campus disorders and removing record-keeping requirements for some types of rifle and shotgun ammunition. Congress also held hearings on crime in general and on juvenile penal institutions.

The National Commission on the Causes and Prevention of Violence issued its final report Dec. 12, urging a reordering of national priorities and increased investment of resources to ensure justice and domestic peace.

Organized Crime

The Senate Judiciary Subcommittee on Criminal Laws and Procedures reported a bill (S 30) introduced by Chairman John L. McClellan (D Ark.), but later revamped to include many administration requests. The measure was not acted on by the full Senate until 1970, when Congress passed the bill. *(Final provisions, p. 274)*

The administration's proposals for combating organized crime were contained in the President's message to Congress of April 23. In the message he stressed the problem of organized crime, requested an increase of about $25-million over the amount asked by the Johnson administration for organized crime control in fiscal 1970 and proposed new legislation.

Legislative proposals included new statutes on witness immunity, making bribery and corruption of police

LEAA Funds

The Law Enforcement Assistance Administration (LEAA), which channeled federal crime-fighting funds to the states in the form of block grants, was one of the most popular programs with Congress. It obtained practically all the money requested for it from its creation in 1968, but criticism was evident by 1972.

With crime on the upswing, and voters demanding solutions, it was felt that massive funding to improve law enforcement would be the answer. Following are the budget requests and appropriations voted by Congress, in millions of dollars:

Fiscal Year	1969	1970	1971	1972	1973
Request	98.6	296.5	480.0	698.9	850.5
Appropriation	63.0	268.0	480.0	698.9	850.5

The LEAA was created in 1968 by the Omnibus Crime Control and Safe Streets Act (PL 90-351). The block grant approach was adopted on the theory that the funds were needed rapidly and there would be less red tape in sending money to the states for distribution to each city than with direct grants to the cities. Also, congressional Republicans were fearful that direct grants would enhance the power of Democratic-controlled cities at the expense of Republican-dominated state legislatures. *(Creation of LEAA, Congress and the Nation, Vol. II, p. 323)*

The law required states to set up planning agencies to develop state-wide crime-fighting plans. The grants were to be spent to carry out the plan as approved by the LEAA. Funds were allocated to the states according to population and 75 per cent of a state's allotment was reserved for local law enforcement. With its block grant approach, LEAA was generally regarded as a forerunner of revenue sharing.

The first congressional attacks on LEAA began in 1972. Rep. James V. Stanton (D Ohio) offered an amendment to the fiscal 1973 appropriation bill for the Justice Department that would have cut all LEAA funding. It was rejected on a 4-82 standing vote.

The House Government Operations Committee in May split virtually along party lines in issuing a report, based on a six-month study by its Legal and Monetary Affairs Subcommittee, condemning the LEAA, as wasteful, inefficient and ineffective.

It said the LEAA grant programs "have had no visible impact on the incidence of crime in the United States." The committee cited such reasons as diversion of funds for political purposes and social action, waste of funds on high consultants' fees and military-type equipment, and underutilization of funds.

Committee Republicans said the majority's conclusions were erroneous and based on biased witnesses and the study of only a small portion of LEAA's activities. They pointed out that the administration was relatively new and said it should be given more time to work out its deficiencies.

or other local officials a federal offense and redefining the elements that make local gambling a federal crime in order to give the Justice Department more leeway in assisting local authorities.

In his message, Nixon described the Cosa Nostra as "a totalitarian and closed society operating within an open and democratic one" and said that an apathetic public, which contributes to the problem by such things as buying numbers bets and football cards, "has permitted most organized criminals to escape prosecution by corrupting officials, by intimidating witnesses and by terrorizing victims into silence."

The subcommittee held six days of hearings on S 30 and several other anticrime bills.

Chairman McClellan said organized crime received income of $7-billion annually from illegal gambling and $350-million each from narcotics and loan-sharking. Corruption of local officials, he said, represented organized crime's greatest threat.

Administration witnesses from the Justice Department and other agencies supported S 30 generally, but said their own recommendations would improve the final bill.

Will R. Wilson, assistant attorney general in charge of the criminal division, said that the Justice Department favored the grand jury reforms in S 30, but opposed provisions requiring each federal district court to convene a grand jury every 18 months and allowing grand juries to ask the attorney general to replace a federal agent or attorney whose performance seemed unsatisfactory to the grand jury. Wilson opposed a bill written by Sen. Joseph D. Tydings (D Md.) creating a new position of assistant attorney general for organized crime. He said splitting the organized crime operation away from the criminal division might create more problems than solutions.

Eugene T. Rossides, assistant secretary of the treasury, supported an amendment by Roman L. Hruska (R Neb.) to the wagering tax laws that would remedy the situation caused by two Supreme Court decisions, *Marchetti v. U.S.* and *Grosso v. U.S.* Those rulings effectively barred prosecution for non-compliance with the gambling tax laws by holding that assertion of the privilege against self-incrimination, guaranteed by the Fifth Amendment to the Constitution, was a complete defense to such prosecution.

Liberal opponents of S 30 and the other proposals testified that they were not limited to organized crime. Lawrence Speiser, director of the Washington office of the American Civil Liberties Union (ACLU), said the proposals provided opportunities for abuse of government and law enforcement powers at the expense of individual constitutional rights. He criticized proposals which would authorize grand juries to issue reports, provide witness immunity in order to allow the government to compel testimony, codify procedures to detain recalcitrant witnesses, allow the admission of co-conspirators' statements in evidence and provide for increased sentences for special offenders.

Witness Immunity

House Judiciary Subcommittee No. 3 held a hearing on a bill (HR 11157), the Federal Immunity of Witnesses Act. The bill was based on a proposal by the National Commission on Reform of Federal Criminal Laws and had the support of the Nixon administration. A revised witness immunity statute later was included in the Organized Crime Control Act of 1970.

The commission recommended a new and broader witness immunity law covering all violations of federal statutes. It specifically proposed that a new law provide that a witness could not be prosecuted on the basis of his testimony, but would not be immune from prosecution on other evidence against him.

Proponents of the bill said it would correct a pro-criminal bias in existing laws which provided blanket immunity for everything relating to a witness' testimony. Opponents said the bill would undermine the Fifth Amendment guarantee against self-incrimination.

Preventive Detention

House Judiciary Subcommittee No. 4 held hearings on an administration-sponsored bill (HR 12806) amending the Bail Reform Act of 1966 (PL 89-465) by permitting detention of defendants believed likely to commit offenses if released from custody while awaiting trial.

The bill would allow consideration of danger to the community in setting conditions of release and authorize pre-trial detention of up to 60 days for dangerous persons. (A similar bill became law in 1970 as part of the District of Columbia Crime Control Act.)

The basic federal law on bail was established by the Judiciary Act of 1789, which provided for mandatory release on bail in all federal criminal cases except those requiring death as the punishment. The first significant change was the Bail Reform Act of 1966, which set up new procedures for release of persons charged with non-capital offenses. In passing the act, Congress specifically postponed consideration of issues relating to crimes committed by persons awaiting trial. *(Box, p. 270)*

Eleven days after taking office, Nixon recommended pre-trial detention. "Increasing numbers of crimes are being committed by persons already indicted for earlier crimes, but free on pre-trial release," he said in a Jan. 31 statement on crime in the District of Columbia. "Many are now being arrested two, three, even seven times for new offenses while awaiting trials. This requires that a new provision be made in the law, whereby dangerous, hard-core recidivists could be held in temporary pre-trial detention when they have been charged with crimes and when their continued pre-trial release presents a clear danger to the community."

The House held hearings on HR 12806 in late 1969. Sen. Sam J. Ervin Jr. (D N.C.), chairman of the Senate Judiciary Subcommittee on Constitutional Rights and father of the Bail Reform Act, criticized the administration bill as an unconstitutional infringement on guarantees of reasonable bail (the Eighth Amendment), due process (Fifth Amendment), right to counsel (Sixth Amendment) and the opportunity to participate in preparing a defense.

"Preventive detention legislation convicts individuals of 'probable' guilt and 'dangerousness' and sentences them to 60 days', in prisonment without trial and conviction of a crime. Such flagrant violation of due process smacks of a police state," Ervin said.

The bill was supported by Rep. Gilbert Gude (R Md.), who said a carefully drawn bill would not violate constitutional rights, and by Rep. William M. McCulloch (R Ohio), the ranking minority member of the House Ju-

Justice Department Strike Forces

In November 1966, Henry Petersen, chief of the Justice Department's Organized Crime and Racketeering Section, put together a mixed team of investigators and lawyers for a many-pronged attack on a Buffalo-based Mafia operation allegedly headed by Stefano Magaddino. The team consisted of agents from the Justice Department, the Internal Revenue Service, the Bureau of Customs, the Secret Service, the Department of Labor, the Bureau of Narcotics and Dangerous Drugs, and the Royal Canadian Mounted Police. New York state and city police later contributed to this first strike force.

The tactics worked so well in the Buffalo area that similar strike forces were set up with headquarters in Brooklyn, Newark, Philadelphia, Boston, Chicago, Detroit and Miami. These strike forces had chalked up more than 321 indictments, with some 60 convictions, by mid-1969.

The eight strike forces were given permanent status in 1969 and the Justice Department established 10 more in other cities by 1973.

diciary Committee, who said the Bail Reform Act was a "noble experiment" but a failure.

Attorney General John N. Mitchell, in testifying for the bill, said pre-trial release of potentially dangerous defendants was one of the major factors in increasing street crime. He urged that detention not be limited only to persons charged with capital offenses.

Judge Tim Murphy of the District of Columbia Court of General Sessions and D.C. Police Chief Jerry V. Wilson both supported the bill. Representatives of the American Civil Liberties Union and the National Association of Defense Attorneys opposed it.

Hearings earlier in the year on the Bail Reform Act, held by Senator Ervin's subcommittee, elicited testimony from several D.C. judges that the act was adequate, but that it had been imperfectly administered. They called for more judges and prosecutors in order to be cut down on trial delays. D.C. street crimes were covered by the act, although elsewhere nationally it applied only to federal crimes.

Drug Control

Congress investigated a variety of problems involving drugs, but did not clear any major legislation dealing with the matter.

Congressional action was complicated by a jurisdictional question of whether to consider drug abuse a health problem or a law enforcement issue and whether the Justice Department or the Health, Education and Welfare Department (HEW) should have primary responsibility for control of drug abuse. Various congressional committees—Judiciary, Education and Labor, Crime, and Labor and Public Welfare—held hearings in the area.

A bill (S 3246) revising the federal narcotics laws administered by the Justice Department was reported in the Senate, while a measure (HR 14252) authorizing an expanded drug abuse education program to be administered by HEW was passed by the House. (*Story on HR 14252, health chapter*)

The administration sent Congress a comprehensive bill (S 2637) to revise and modernize the system for control of dangerous drugs (some of the proposals later were incorporated into S 3246) and began action to stop the flow of illegal drugs from Mexico into the United States. (*box p. 261*)

The Senate Judiciary Committee reported S 3246 (the Controlled Dangerous Substances Act of 1969), a clean bill, Dec. 16. It combined the provisions of the administration's bill with those of S 1895, introduced by Thomas J. Dodd (D Conn.).

The most important change it would have made in existing law was to eliminate mandatory minimum sentences for all drug offenses, except those committed by professional criminals. The new penalty structure, originally contained in S 1895, allowed a judge to use his discretion and impose serious punishment on violators such as traffickers in heroin, while imposing lesser sentences on offenders merely possessing marijuana or other drugs.

The bill also provided for search warrants which allowed entry without notice ("no-knock") to premises for the purpose of seizing evidence that might otherwise be destroyed.

Other provisions vested authority for control of dangerous substances with the attorney general and classified drugs into four schedules based on their degree of abuse potential, known effect, harmfulness and level of medical use. Heroin and marijuana were classed under Schedule I, for example, while amphetamines and barbiturates were classed under Schedule III.

The "no-knock" provision was attacked by Sam J. Ervin Jr. (D N.C.) and Philip A. Hart (D Mich.) as permitting an unconstitutional search and seizure, but the full committee said it would help law enforcement officials obtain vital evidence necessary for drug prosecutions.

A month of testimony on the bills was highlighted by the Nixon administration's reversal of its position on drug

Witness Immunity

Witness immunity laws were designed to give prosecutors a means of getting the testimony of a witness who claimed his privilege of remaining silent on grounds that his testimony would tend to incriminate him. The Fifth Amendment guarantees that no person shall be compelled to be a witness against himself in a criminal case.

The first immunity law was an 1893 statute which required a subpoenaed witness to testify before the Interstate Commerce Commission on penalty of fine and imprisonment, but protected him from prosecution "on account of any transaction, matter or thing concerning which he may testify or produce evidence" except for perjury in testifying or contempt for failure to testify. Subsequent statutes extended the immunity to other specific types of investigatings including antitrust prosecutions, using similar language.

penalties. The administration softened its original proposal after criticism of provisions that retained mandatory minimum sentences for possession of drugs and treated possession and use of marijuana and hallucinogenic drugs as felonies.

John E. Ingersoll, director of the Bureau of Narcotics and Dangerous Drugs, presented the revised administration position in testimony Oct. 20. The alternate proposals, he said, would provide a more flexible penalty structure, distinguish marijuana offenses from those involving hard drugs and distinguish between persons who possessed marijuana for their own use and those who distributed it.

Critics of the administration's penalty provisions included two of its top health officials, Dr. Stanley F. Yolles, director of the National Institute of Mental Health, and Dr. Sidney Cohen, director of the institute's narcotics division. Mandatory minimum penalties for all types of drug abuse should be removed, Dr. Yolles told the committee.

D.C. Crime Proposals

The Nixon administration in 1969 made numerous proposals aimed at curbing crime in the District of Columbia, but Congress failed to complete action on any of the requests. The Senate approved four of the five major D.C. crime bills, but the House took no action beyond hearings.

The administration July 11 sent Congress a "model anticrime program" for the District. The program assumed additional significance because some observers felt that the proposals, if successfully implemented, could be the basis for future changes in federal law enforcement.

The package included proposals to:

• Amend the Bail Reform Act of 1966 to permit a judge to set strict conditions of release or to detain a criminal suspect in non-capital cases—the preventive detention provision (S 2600).

• Reorganize the court system of the District, consolidating into a single Superior Court the Court of General Sessions, the Juvenile Court and the District Tax Court (S 2601).

• Convert the Legal Aid Agency of the District into a Public Defender Service (S 2602).

S 2601 included amendments in criminal procedure to allow nighttime searches by officials with warrants and to allow them to enter the premises to be searched without first announcing themselves. The last amendment was known as a "no knocking" provision. The bill also included an amendment to give District law enforcement officials the same wiretapping and electronic eavesdropping powers which were granted to state authorities by the Crime Control and Safe Streets Act of 1968 (PL 90-351).

Most of the proposed revisions in criminal procedure were deleted from S 2601 by the Senate committee, which considered them in a separate bill, S 2869.

Nixon, later in 1969, proposed revision of the District of Columbia juvenile code. His proposals were introduced as S 2981 by Joseph D. Tydings (D Md.), chairman of the Senate District of Columbia Committee.

The Senate approved S 2601, S 2602, S 2869 and S 2981 but ignored S 2600, chiefly because of criticism that preventive detention was unconstitutional.

S 2601—Court Reorganization. The Senate Sept. 18 passed by voice vote and without debate the bill reorganizing the District of Columbia court system. It included a "no-knock" provision. The bill, an amended version of that introduced by the administration, was reported by the District of Columbia Committee Sept. 16.

The committee said S 2601 had been amended with the cooperation of the Justice Department chiefly to remove provisions which "fell outside the scope of court reorganization." The deleted provisions were incorporated into another bill (S 2869) to revise the District's criminal law and procedure. *(Below)*

As reported by the committee, the bill created a District of Columbia Superior Court; a unified and expanded trial bench incorporating the existing court of General Sessions, Juvenile Court and D.C. Tax Court, with eventual jurisdiction over all civil and criminal matters of a purely local nature.

The bill also authorized police executing a search warrant not to give notice of their identity and authority before entering the premises to be searched—if they had probable cause to believe that should notice be given, the evidence sought would be destroyed or the safety of an officer endangered.

S 2602—Public Defender Service. The Senate Nov. 26 passed by voice vote and without debate the District of Columbia Public Defender Act of 1969. The bill renamed the District Legal Aid Agency the D.C. Public Defender Service, authorized the service to represent up to 60 per cent of persons unable to obtain adequate representation who were involved in a variety of offenses, and authorized the service to aid private attorneys in representing the remaining 40 per cent of defendants.

S 2869—Criminal Law Revision. The Senate Dec. 5 passed by voice vote the bill revising the District of Columbia criminal code. Included in the bill were two provisions recommended by the Nixon administration in S 2601. These allowed the execution of search warrants at night and established a comprehensive wiretapping law modeled after Title III of the Omnibus Crime Control Act of 1968. *(Congress and the Nation, Vol. II, p. 323)*

The bill also authorized "no-knock" search warrants and imposition of a sentence "for an indeterminate number of years up to life" for persons convicted three times of a felony and found "demonstrably incorrigible."

S 2869 was reported by the District of Columbia Committee Nov. 18. Hearings on the bill in September disclosed opposition to many of the criminal law changes by District officials. Acting Public Safety Director Charles T. Duncan and District City Council Chairman Gilbert Hahn Jr. told the committee the District's major requirement in the fight against crime was more judges, prosecutors, court personnel and policemen.

S 2981—Juvenile Code Revision. The Senate Dec. 22 passed by voice vote and without debate the bill revising juvenile court procedures in the District of Columbia. As reported by the District Committee and passed by the Senate, the bill provided that children age 16 and older charged with violent crimes should be excluded from juvenile court jurisdiction and tried as adults only if they had received prior treatment since age 15 as a juvenile delinquent. The administration had proposed that all persons age 16 and older charged with certain violent crimes be tried as adults.

Drug Operation 'Intercept'

The Nixon Administration's "Operation Intercept" went into effect at 2:30 p.m. PDT Sept. 21 as land, air and sea surveillance was imposed upon the 2500-mile Mexican-American border to halt the flow of drugs from Mexico into the United States.

A search of all cars, persons and aircraft crossing the border from 2:30 PDT until midnight Sept. 21 failed to uncover any drug smuggling. Federal inspectors were reported to have searched 418,161 persons, 106,563 cars and 100 aircraft at 31 landpoints and 27 airports. The car-by-car search resulted in massive traffic tie-ups, dwindling trade for merchants in border cities, and many irritated tourists.

U.S. and Mexican officials, meeting in Washington Oct. 7-10, agreed to replace "Operation Intercept" with "Operation Cooperation." The three-week attempt to curb narcotics traffic was strongly criticized by the Mexican government and members of Congress from border districts as causing economic turmoil and ill-will between the two countries. Under the new program, the United States would "adjust" border inspection procedures "to eliminate unnecessary inconvenience, delay and irritation." In return, the Mexican government gave assurances that it would increase its efforts to eliminate production and smuggling of marijuana and other narcotics.

The bill also set time limits for juvenile court proceedings and provided that no child could be detained in a juvenile facility without undergoing a thorough screening prior to detention.

Gun Control

An amendment to the 1968 Gun Control Act (PL 90-618), repealing record-keeping requirements for sales of rifle and shotgun ammunition except the .22 caliber rimfire variety, was approved by Congress Nov. 20. The repealer was contained in a bill (HR 12829—PL 91-128) extending the interest equalization tax, a balance of payments measure, to March 31, 1971. *(HR 12829, Economy chapter; 1968 act, Congress and the Nation, Vol. II, p. 328)*

The amendment, as introduced by Sen. Wallace F. Bennett (R Utah) and as adopted by the Finance Committee, also exempted .22 caliber rimfire ammunition from the record-keeping requirements of the 1968 act. Bennett later modified his own amendment on the floor by dropping the .22 caliber rimfire exclusion.

Acceptance of the amendment by the Senate and House left in force the registration of purchasers requirement for handgun cartridges and ammunition, mainly .22 caliber rimfire, that was interchangeable between rifles and handguns.

In other gun legislation, the Senate Nov. 19 passed a bill (S 849) authorizing separate additional prison terms for persons using or carrying a gun in committing a federal crime. The bill would have imposed 1-10 year sentences for initial convictions and 2-25 year sentences for repeaters. The House failed to act on the measure.

Campus Disorders

Widespread and violent campus disorders early in the year brought on strong reaction from Congress and the administration during 1969.

President Nixon said student disorders endangered academic freedom and that school officials should "have the backbone to stand up against" campus violence. Attorney General John N. Mitchell warned that "the time has come for an end to patience."

Congress included in three enacted pieces of legislation provisions aimed at cutting off federal aid to college students participating in campus disruptions.

However, a bipartisan band of liberals, most of them members of the House Education and Labor Committee, joined forces to block action on three other bills aimed at disruptive college students.

The first instance came in June and July, when liberals on the committee, led by John Brademas (D Ind.) and Ogden R. Reid (R N.Y.), for four weeks used a variety of parliamentary tactics to prevent a campus disorders bill (HR 11941) from being reported to the full House.

On July 31, the same members were the leaders in a floor fight on a student unrest provision included in the appropriations bill (HR 13111) for the Departments of Labor and Health, Education and Welfare (HEW). Again using parliamentary strategy, they knocked out the section of the bill, although the House added another amendment, generally considered to be weaker.

And in mid-August, committee liberals agreed to report an emergency college student loan bill (HR 13194) only on the condition that no floor amendments such as an antistudent riot amendment could be added by the full House.

Provisions to cut off federal aid to students who participated in campus disturbances were included in other bills, including the appropriations bill for the Departments of State, Justice and Commerce (HR 12964—PL 91-153) and the authorization bills for the National Aeronautics and Space Administration (HR 11271—PL 91-119) and the National Science Foundation (S 1857—PL 91-120).

Other congressional action in this area centered on investigations by the Senate Government Operations Committee's Permanent Investigations Subcommittee and the House Internal Security Committee into activities of militant student groups such as the Students for a Democratic Society (SDS).

Twenty-two House Republicans made a private tour of college campuses in May. They later told President Nixon that "repressive" laws would not resolve campus disorders.

Throughout the session House members were more concerned with taking action against students engaged in campus disruptions than were senators. For instance, House action on the student loan bill was held up for a month over a dispute about adding student rioting amendments, while in the Senate the issue never arose.

Smaller disputes centered about the Reserve Officers Training Corps (ROTC) and military recruitment on campus after antimilitary demonstrations occurred on several campuses in the spring.

The NASA authorization bill (HR 11271) contained a provision which barred funds to any school which prohibited the recruiting of military personnel. The House version of the defense procurement bill (HR 14000) contained a provision requiring annual reports to Congress on how universities cooperated with military recruitment and ROTC programs as a prerequisite for getting funds under the bill. The provision was dropped in conference.

Another antistudent provision was included in the House version of the appropriations bill for certain independent offices and the Department of Housing and Urban Development (HR 12307). That provision was also dropped by House and Senate conferees.

Death Penalty

The House and Senate in December approved by voice votes amendments to the Atomic Energy Act of 1954 that ended the death penalty for violations of the act. *(1954 act, Congress and the Nation, Vol. I, p. 281)*

The amendments (S 3169—PL 91-161), in addition to dropping the death penalty, increased the maximum penalty for unauthorized diversion of special nuclear material to 10 years from 5 and retained the existing $10,000 fine. They also deleted the requirement that a jury had to recommend life imprisonment for violations of the act before it could be imposed.

According to committee reports on the bill, the deletion of the death penalty and the requirement for jury recommendation of life imprisonment were in keeping with existing legal philosophies and Supreme Court decisions.

Other Action

JUVENILE INSTITUTIONS. The Senate Judiciary Subcommittee on Juvenile Delinquency, chaired by Thomas J. Dodd (D Conn.), held hearings in March and July on juvenile institutions and prisons. Dodd said a subcommittee investigation of how more than 100,000 juveniles were detained or confined annually showed that "rather than performing correction, our institutions release more dangerous, more hostile and more embittered human beings than they received. It is imperative that we make the public understand the vital necessity of large-scale prison reform and improvement." Testimony at the hearings brought criticism of juvenile institutions as overcrowded and understaffed, and included tales of drug abuse, homosexual rape and racial tension.

SMALL BUSINESS CRIME. The Senate Select Committee on Small Business, chaired by Alan Bible (D Nev.), held hearings in May and July on the impact of crime on small businesses (defined as having annual receipts of less than $1-million). Witnesses said 68 per cent of the $3-billion annual loss to all businesses from crime hit small businesses, and that most small businessmen lacked sound crime insurance and protection programs. Cargo thefts at airports were cited as one of the top loss leaders for small businesses.

CRIME. The House Select Committee on Crime, which was established May 1, held hearings in Washington and in several other cities on various aspects of the national crime problem and the adequacy of the national response. The committee chairman was Claude Pepper (D Fla.). *(Committee's creation, Congress chapter p. 353)*

1970

Spurred by election-year considerations and the Nixon administration's declared "war on crime," the 91st Congress in 1970 compiled an impressive record in the passage of four crime control measures.

Over the vigorous, but futile, opposition of certain members alarmed by the constitutional questions which certain anticrime provisions raise, Congress completed action in 1970 on four major anticrime bills:

• The Comprehensive Drug Abuse Prevention and Control Act of 1970 (PL 91-513) which revised federal narcotics and dangerous drug laws and the penalties for violations and which expanded federal support for programs of drug abuse rehabilitation, treatment and education.

• The Omnibus Crime Control Act of 1970 (PL 91-644) which authorized $3.55-billion in federal aid to state and local law enforcement agencies in fiscal 1971-1973.

• The "model anticrime package" for the District of Columbia—which had in the 1968 campaign been labeled the nation's "crime capital"—the District of Columbia Court Reorganization and Criminal Procedure Act of 1970 (PL 91-358). The new law authorized controversial law enforcement measures such as preventive detention—before trial—of certain dangerous defendants and "no-knock" search warrants allowing police to enter homes without announcement.

• The massive Organized Crime Control Act of 1970 (PL 91-452) which was designed to facilitate the task of gathering and presenting evidence against large-scale professional criminal operations.

The new administration and the 91st Congress moved slowly in 1969 to fulfill campaign promises to crack down on street crime and on large-scale organized crime.

President Nixon did not send his anticrime proposals to Congress until late spring. By the end of that first year, Congress had provided greatly increased funds for federal law enforcement grants, but had completed action on no new crime control programs.

But election year 1970 saw the enactment of most of the anticrime measures proposed or endorsed by the administration.

The D.C. crime bill cleared in midsummer; the drug control and organized crime control measures in October just before the election recess; and the omnibus crime bill just before Christmas.

Drug Abuse

Congress Oct. 14 cleared for the President the Comprehensive Drug Abuse Prevention and Control Act of 1970 (HR 18583—PL 91-513), to provide expanded programs of rehabilitation, treatment and drug abuse education, to unify and revise federal narcotics laws, to revise the entire penalty structure for violations of those laws and to provide new tools for enforcement.

Final action on the massive drug control bill came Oct. 14 when the House and Senate by voice votes adopted the conference report on HR 18583. The Senate had approved the bill Oct. 7 by a 54-0 roll-call vote; the House had passed it Sept. 24 by a 341-6 roll-call vote.

Enactment of HR 18583 climaxed a concerted effort by the administration and congressional leaders during the 91st Congress to reform the heterogeneous body of federal narcotics legislation and to make more uniform the penalty structure for violations of drug laws.

Background. Federal legislation controlling narcotic drugs and other dangerous substances, such as stimulant and depressant drugs, developed from the early 20th century in patchwork fashion. The resulting body of laws lacked consistency, unity and, at times, logic.

The federal anti-narcotics effort began in 1909 with the Opium Exclusion Act, barring the import of opium except for medicinal purposes. Subsequent laws enacted prior to World War II made it illegal to import or export narcotics in any form, or to make, sell, buy or transport narcotics unless for medicinal or scientific purposes and under approval of the Treasury Department's Narcotics Bureau. Under most of these laws, merely possessing a narcotic without being registered with the Treasury Department was considered evidence that some illegal act had been committed to obtain it.

The Bureau of Narcotics was created in the Treasury Department in 1930 to enforce these narcotics laws, most of which were based upon the power of Congress to impose taxes.

In the postwar period a number of new drug laws were passed, each one stiffening the penalties for violations of federal drug regulations. Mandatory minimum sentences were set for most narcotics offenses in 1951 (PL 82-255), and five years later another law (PL 84-728) increased the penalties and allowed the death sentence to be imposed upon someone convicted of selling heroin to a minor.

Drug legislation in the 1960s began to move in new directions, with the expansion of federal control over depressant, stimulant and hallucinogenic drugs (including barbiturates, "pep pills" and LSD) in 1965 (PL 89-74) and passage of the Narcotics Rehabilitation Act (PL 89-793) the following year to provide that addicts convicted of drug offenses not be sent to prison, but instead be committed to medical institutions for treatment. In 1968 Congress amended the 1965 law to set penalties for the illegal possession of stimulant, depressant or hallucinogenic drugs (PL 90-639).

An initial move toward coordination of the enforcement of all these various drug laws was the reorganization in 1968 of the federal agencies responsible for their enforcement. President Johnson, through an executive reorganization plan, combined the Bureau of Narcotics in the Department of the Treasury with the Bureau of Drug Abuse Control from the Department of Health, Education and Welfare (HEW), creating a Bureau of Narcotics and Dangerous Drugs in the Department of Justice. (*Congress and the Nation, Vol. II, p. 315, 673, 702*)

Legislative History. President Nixon July 14, 1969, asked Congress to enact legislation to combat the increasingly serious problem of drug abuse. Hearings on narcotics and drug abuse were held in both chambers by various committees. The administration July 16, 1969, proposed a law enforcement-oriented bill, the Controlled Dangerous Substances Act of 1969 (S 2637), which was criticized for retaining mandatory minimum sentences for possession of drugs and continuing to treat possession and use of marijuana as a felony. Later, the administration revised its proposals to provide for a more flexible penalty structure, and to distinguish between the possession and sale of marijuana.

The Senate Jan. 28, 1970, unanimously approved the Controlled Dangerous Substances Act (S 3246), a bill substantially different from the original S 2637, but still supported by the administration. The Senate bill was essentially a law enforcement measure, unifying and revising federal drug and narcotics laws and rationalizing the penalty structure.

During debate on S 3246, the Senate rejected an amendment by Sam J. Ervin Jr. (D N.C.) that would have deleted an amendment by Robert P. Griffin (R Mich.) which added a controversial "no-knock" provision to the bill. The provision authorized law enforcement officers to enter a place to be searched without first giving notice of their presence and intention.

The Ervin Amendment was rejected on a **key roll-call vote of 35-50,** with a majority of southern Democrats lining up with Republicans to defeat it.

Because of a jurisdictional dispute arising from the way in which drug and narcotics control legislation was handled, both the House Interstate and Foreign Commerce and Ways and Means Committees held hearings on the administration's drug bill in 1970.

The two House committees cooperated in reporting a new bill (HR 18583) which was a much broader attack on the drug problem. It included a title dealing with treatment and rehabilitation of drug abusers and narcotics addicts and with drug abuse prevention and education, as well as with drug laws and their enforcement.

During Senate consideration of HR 18583, a new, even broader title was substituted for the House-approved title concerning rehabilitation, drug abuse education and treatment. The conferees, however, subsequently eliminated this title and restored the House-passed version.

PROVISIONS

As cleared by Congress, HR 18583, the Comprehensive Drug Abuse Prevention and Control Act of 1970:

Title I: Rehabilitation

• Authorized the Department of Health, Education and Welfare (HEW) to increase its programs of rehabilitation, treatment and prevention of drug abuse by:

Amending the Community Mental Health Centers Act (Title II of PL 88-164) to increase authorizations for funds for community facilities for treatment of narcotics addicts and drug dependent persons by $75-million for fiscal 1971, 1972 and 1973 (to $40-million from $30-million for 1971; to $60-million from $35-million for 1972; to $80-million from $40-million for 1973).

Amending PL 88-164 to authorize $29-million for drug abuse education projects for fiscal 1971, 1972 and 1973 ($3-million for 1971; $12-million for 1972, and $14-million for 1973).

Amending PL 88-164 to authorize $85-million for grants in fiscal 1971, 1972 and 1973 for special projects in the treatment and rehabilitation of addicts and drug dependent persons ($20-million for 1971; $30-million for 1972, $35-million for 1973).

Amending the Public Health Service Act (PL 78-410) to expand the direct patient care authority of the Department of HEW to include drug dependent persons as well as addicts, to grant the secretary of HEW new authority to protect the privacy of drug research subjects and to define "drug dependent person."

• Authorized the secretary of HEW, after consultation with the attorney general and professional organizations, to report to Congress on appropriate and legal methods of professional practice in the medical treatment of narcotics addicts.

Title II: Control Enforcement

• Authorized the Bureau of Narcotics and Dangerous Drugs in fiscal 1971 to add at least 300 agents to its existing enforcement staff, and authorized an annual appropriation of $6-million for that purpose, beginning in fiscal 1971.

• Vested authority for the control of the dangerous substances specified in the title in the attorney general, empowered him to add, remove or transfer substances to, from or between categories (schedules), but required him to seek, and be bound by, the advice of the secretary of HEW before placing a substance under control or removing it from control.

• Classified drugs to be controlled into five schedules to be updated regularly. The schedules were based on the degree of abuse potential, the known effect or harmfulness and level of accepted medical use. Heroin, marijuana, LSD (lysergic acid diethylamide), mescaline and peyote were classified under Schedule I, which included substances with a high potential for abuse and no accepted medical use in the United States. Methadone, used in drug treatment programs as a substitute for heroin, and liquid injectable methamphetamine ("speed") were classified under Schedule II, which included substances with a high potential for abuse and a restricted medical use. Most other amphetamines and barbiturates were classified under Schedule III, which included substances with currently accepted medical uses and lower physical dependence than the drugs in Schedules I and II (although high potential psychological dependence).

• Authorized the attorney general to adopt rules for the registration and control of the manufacture, distribution and dispensing of substances classified as controlled, and to set production quotas for the amount of substances in Schedules I and II to be produced each year.

• Revised the entire penalty structure for unlawful manufacture, distribution, dispensing or possession or the intent to manufacture, distribute or dispense a controlled substance or counterfeit. All mandatory minimum sentences were eliminated except for professional criminals.

• Provided that possession of a controlled substance by a first offender, for his own use, be treated as a misdemeanor punishable by up to one year in prison and a fine of up to $5,000 or both.

• Provided that anyone 18 or older who distributed a controlled substance to someone under 21 should receive twice the authorized penalty for that offense.

• Provided that any professional criminal trafficking in drugs should receive a mandatory minimum sentence of 10 years and a maximum fine of $100,000 for a first offense and a minimum term of 20 years and a maximum fine of $200,000 for a second.

• Provided that the penalty for distributing a small amount of marijuana for no remuneration be the same as that for mere possession.

• Authorized special sentencing procedures under which special dangerous drug offenders could be given more severe sentences—up to 25 years and not disproportionate in severity to the usual prescribed penalty for their offense. Defendants who might be found—in a special postconviction hearing—to fall into this category included a person convicted of a third serious drug offense, or an organized crime figure.

• Authorized the attorney general to carry out educational and research programs directly related to the enforcement of drug laws.

• Provided for search warrants which specifically allowed enforcement officers to enter without notice ("no knock") premises to be searched—if there was probable cause to believe that the property sought would be destroyed or someone's life or safety endangered if notice were given.

• Created a Commission on Marijuana and Drug Abuse to report to Congress, within one year, on marijuana, and, within two years, on the causes of drug abuse.

• Authorized $60-million for the Justice Department in fiscal 1972, $70-million in 1973 and $90-million in 1974 to carry out the provisions of Title II.

Title III: Import and Export

• Established a unified system of controls over the importation and exportation of dangerous substances listed in the act. No Schedule I or II substance or any narcotic drug in Schedules III, IV or V could be imported without the special consent of the attorney general. No narcotic drug in Schedules I, II, III or IV, or other controlled substance in Schedules I or II could be exported without a permit from the attorney general.

• Provided stricter supervision over the importation and exportation of depressant and stiumlant drugs.

• Revised the penalty structure for violations of these control laws, eliminating mandatory minimum sentences.

Title IV: Advisory Councils Report

• Directed the secretary of HEW to report annually—to the Senate Committee on Labor and Public Welfare and the House Committee on Interstate and Foreign Commerce—on activities of all advisory councils set up by the Public Health Service Act (PL 78-410) or the Mental Retardation Facilities and Community Mental Health Centers Construction Act of 1963 (PL 88-164).

Omnibus Crime Control

The 91st Congress on Dec. 17 cleared the way for massive federal aid to state and local programs designed to strength the system of criminal justice.

Congress, in the Omnibus Crime Control Act of 1970 (HR 17825—PL 91-644), authorized appropriations of $3.55-billion for the Law Enforcement Assistance Administration (LEAA) in fiscal 1971, 1972 and 1973.

The LEAA, created by Title I of the Omnibus Crime Control and Safe Streets Act of 1968 (PL 90-351) channeled these federal funds in block grants to states, which allocated them among state and local programs. The amount authorized by PL 91-644 was more than 10 times the total funding of LEAA in its first two years of operation.

PL 91-644 also amended the 1968 law to facilitate the administration of the LEAA, by erasing the requirement that its three-man head be unanimous in its decisions. Despite pressure from the nation's mayors, however, the 1970 law did not change the block-grant approach through which at least 85 per cent of LEAA grants went first to states.

Instead the new law seemed to weaken the cities' claim on LEAA funds even further by allowing LEAA to waive the requirement that states pass on at least 40 per cent of all planning grants and 75 per cent of all action grants to local units. It did, however, require that all states must allocate "an adequate share" of aid to areas with high crime rates or much law enforcement activity.

PL 91-644 set up a new program of grants to improve correctional programs and facilities, with particular emphasis upon the development of community-based corrections. Under this program up to 50 per cent of the funds could go directly to cities or other local units. The law also earmarked $120-million for this purpose in fiscal 1971, and provided that at least 20 per cent of the amount used for law enforcement programs in future years be used in this program.

The 1970 act increased from 60 to 75 per cent the portion of the total cost of a project which the LEAA funds could cover, reducing the amount which states or local units must provide to match the federal grant. But it provided that, as of fiscal 1973, the states themselves must provide at least 25 per cent of the total matching funds for LEAA programs. *(Additional LEAA background, 1969 summary, p. 258)*

The Senate added to the bill several extraneous titles which provided for stricter sentences when a person committing a federal crime carried a gun, authorized the federal government to appeal more adverse decisions in criminal cases, and increased the legal protection of members of Congress and the President.

The bill was non-controversial. The House and Senate approved the conference report on the bill Dec. 17 by voice votes without debate. The House had approved its version June 30 by a roll-call vote of 342-2. The Senate's version was passed on a 59-0 roll call Oct. 8. Separate amendments by Philip A. Hart (D Mich.) to allow one-third instead of 15 per cent of LEAA discretionary funds to be granted directly to local agencies, and increasing LEAA authorizations, were beaten by identical 18-42 roll-call votes.

PROVISIONS

As cleared by Congress, HR 17825, the Omnibus Crime Control Act of 1970:

Title I—Law Enforcement Funds

Amended the 1968 Crime Control and Safe Streets Act (PL 90-351) to:

• Authorize appropriations of $650-million for fiscal 1971—of which $120-million was to be used for correctional programs and facilities; $1.15-billion for fiscal 1972 and $1.75-billion for fiscal 1973—of which no less than 20 per cent of the amount used for law enforcement grants was to be used for corrections.

● Retain the "troika" (administrator and two associate administrators) leadership of LEAA, but designate the administrator as executive head of LEAA with full administrative powers, and exercising all substantive powers with the concurrence of one or both associate anministrators.

● Establish a new grant program to improve correctional facilities, with emphasis on community-based corrections; under the program, grants might be for up to 75 per cent of the cost of any particular project, and up to 50 per cent of the funds for such grants might be given directly to local or city agencies.

● Require that all state plans allocate an adequate share of law enforcement aid to areas with high crime rates and high law enforcement activity.

● Increase to 75 per cent (from 60 per cent) the federal share of the cost of certain law enforcement programs.

● Provide that LEAA might waive matching requirements—thus increasing the federal share of programs to as much as 100 per cent—in the case of grants to Indian and other aboriginal groups.

● Make clear that the limitation (to one-third of any grant) on funds for salaries applied only to salaries of regular law enforcement personnel and applied the same limitation to discretionary grants.

● Require that at least 40 per cent of the non-federal matching funds for LEAA-grant programs be included in appropriations specifically for this purpose from state or local units, effective July 1, 1972.

● Revise the requirement that each state transfer 75 per cent of its block-grant action funds to local units by requiring, effective July 1, 1972, that each state pass on at least that part of the federal grant which corresponded to the part of total statewide law enforcement expenditures for the preceding year funded and spent by local units.

● Authorize LEAA to waive the requirement that state planning agencies make at least 40 per cent of federal planning grant funds available to local units.

● Require states to provide at least 25 per cent of the aggregate matching funds for law enforcement programs, effective July 1, 1972.

● Limit to 75 per cent (except in the case of Indians and aborigines) the share of program costs which might be paid with LEAA discretionary funds.

● Authorize LEAA grants to universities to allow students to serve internships with law enforcement agencies.

● Direct the attorney general to submit to the President and to Congress, within 90 days of the end of each fiscal year, a report on federal law enforcement and criminal justice activities.

Title II—Stricter Sentences

Amended the Gun Control Act of 1968 (PL 90-618) to make it a crime to carry a gun while committing another federal crime and to provide that anyone convicted of carrying a gun at such a time should be sentenced to an additional non-concurrent term of from one

to 10 years for a first offense and from two to 25 years for a second offense.

Title III—Criminal Appeals

Authorized the federal government to appeal any decision dismissing an indictment in a criminal case unless such an appeal would place a defendant in double jeopardy, and to appeal orders suppressing evidence.

Provided that this title not apply to any case begun in any federal court before its effective date.

Title IV—Protection of Members

Made it a federal crime to kidnap, assault or kill— or endeavor or conspire to do so—a member or member-elect of Congress.

Title V—Protection of the President

Prohibited unauthorized entry into the building or grounds of any temporary residence or office of the President.

Title VI—Wiretap Commission

Re-established the National Commission for Review of Federal and State Laws Relating to Wiretapping and Electronic Surveillance (established by Title III of PL 90-351 and abolished by the Organized Crime Control Act of 1970 (PL 91-452)) and granted the commission power to issue subpoenas, to hold hearings and to grant witnesses immunity.

D.C. Crime Control

President Nixon July 29 signed into law a bill (S 2601—PL 91-358), the District of Columbia Court Reform and Criminal Procedure Act of 1970, commonly known as the D.C. crime bill.

Final action on the massive anticrime program for the District of Columbia—proposed in mid-1969 by the administration as a "model anticrime package" but attacked as unconstitutional by its critics—came when the Senate July 23, by a 54-33 roll-call vote, adopted the conference report on the bill.

Senate approval overrrode the determined opposition of many senators concerned about some of the bill's more drastic crime-control provisions. The House adopted the conference report July 15 by a 332-64 roll-call vote.

The massive bill was the first administration crime-control measure enacted. It was acclaimed by Attorney General John N. Mitchell as a model anticrime package and attacked by Sam J. Ervin Jr. (D N.C.) as a "blueprint for a police state."

President Nixon in a statement Jan. 31, 1969, promised legislation to curb crime in the District. Bills incorporating his proposals were sent to Congress in July 1969.

The Senate by 1970 had approved, with amendments, all of Mr. Nixon's District of Columbia crime proposals— except one, the preventive detention measure (S 2600). *(1969 chronology)*

The House moved more slowly. The House District of Columbia Committee stitched together all of the ad-

Two Views on D.C. Crime Act

"This model anticrime program will point the way for the entire nation at a time when crime and fear of crime are forcing us, a free people, to alter the pattern of our lives."

Attorney General John N. Mitchell, July 11, 1969

"This...is as full of unconstitutional, unjust, and unwise provisions as a mangy hound dog is full of fleas...a garbage pail of some of the most repressive, nearsighted, intolerant, unfair and vindictive legislation that the Senate has ever been presented...an affront to constitutional principles and to the intelligence of the people of the United States.

Sen. Sam J. Ervin Jr. (D N.C.), March 23, 1970

ministration crime measures for the District into an omnibus bill, adding a number of its own original provisions as well. This massive bill (HR 16196)—differing in more than 170 items from the Senate-approved bills and including provisions never considered by the Senate—was approved by the House March 19, 1970, on a 294-47 roll-call vote.

The Senate March 24 combined its bills into one measure and the two versions of the bill went to conference April 9. The conference version emerged July 14.

LEGISLATIVE ISSUES

Ervin called the omnibus bill "a blueprint for a police state," and criticized the Department of Justice for trying "to put a fast one over on the Senate and the American people."

Not only did the House version of the District crime bill contain authorization for pretrial detention "hidden under false colors," within its pages, Ervin said, but it also held numerous drastic and double-edged provisions "squirreled away" in its recesses.

Under its provisions:

- Policemen—in a variety of circumstances—could enter homes or other buildings without knocking or announcing themselves—the "no-knock" provision.
- Law enforcement officers were granted broad wiretapping powers to obtain evidence of abortion, arson, blackmail, bribery, burglary, destruction of property, gambling, grand larceny, kidnapping, manslaughter, murder, obstruction of justice, receiving stolen property and robbery. Such surveillance was not forbidden to intrude upon traditionally privileged conversations such as those between doctor and patient, lawyer and client, priest and penitent.
- Policemen could conduct chemical, scientific and medical tests upon anyone found where a search warrant was being served.
- During a search, policemen could seize any property—even that not specifically described in the warrant—if they believed it stolen, illegal, used in a crime or to identify a crime or criminal.
- There was no justifiable reason for forcibly resisting arrest—even an unlawful arrest.
- Any judgment in a wrongful arrest suit, whether for or against the police officer sued, had to include payment of his lawyer's fees.

- Juveniles had no right to trial by jury.
- Juveniles could be found delinquent on the basis of a "preponderance of the evidence."
- Juveniles 15 years old charged with certain crimes could—upon motion of the prosecutor—be tried in adult court.
- Once a juvenile had been tried in adult court, even if he was acquitted, he could never again be tried as a juvenile.
- A man convicted for the third time of a violent crime—which, under the bill's definition, could be purse-snatching—received a mandatory life sentence with no parole, probation or suspended sentence for 20 years.
- Any person convicted of an "armed crime of violence"—even if the weapon was a toy gun not used or even in sight during the crime—received a mandatory minimum sentence of three years.

Constitutionality? Critics of the omnibus bill questioned the constitutionality and the effectiveness of many of its provisions. One of its provisions—that allowing juveniles to be found delinquent by a "preponderance of the evidence"—was invalidated within days of House passage by a Supreme Court decision March 31, 1970. *(Decision, p. 269)*

The Fourth Amendment guaranteed the right of citizens to be "secure in their persons, houses, papers and effects, against unreasonable searches and seizures." It also provided that search warrants must contain particular descriptions of the place to be searched and the persons or things to be seized.

Opponents said the "no-knock," wiretapping and search warrant provisions of the District crime bill came perilously close to violating this amendment.

Police were authorized to enter homes without knocking whenever they believed that knocking would endanger their lives or allow destruction of evidence.

Outspoken black leaders had advised citizens to resist such entry into their homes by "appropriate action"—which might include shooting any "no-knock" entrant. Rep. Abner J. Mikva (D Ill.) pointed out that "the reaction of the average citizen to an unexpected attempt to break into his home is to fight like hell."

The Justice Department defended the "no-knock" provision, assuring Congress that it would not expand police authority but would merely place on the books guidelines for the practice aready allowed by court decisions.

The broad wiretapping powers which the bill granted constituted, critics said, an unnecessary invastion into the privacy of District citizens and an impractical way of fighting crime. No proof had been presented that wiretapping would be of aid in solving many of the crimes for which it was authorized.

Three dissenting members of the House District Committee warned that the wiretap provisions "falsely assume that crime will be reduced by wiretaps, yet it will in fact result in more police officers being taken off the streets and put on phone taps and will thus likely lead to continuation in the rising crime rate."

Furthermore, the effect of some of the changes in the criminal code might be the reverse of that intended, a Senate subcommittee aide said.

Provisions facilitating the transfer for trial of certain juveniles as adults appeared severe, he said. But youthful offenders appearing in adult court—no matter the

Major Supreme Court Decisions...

Following is a list of major criminal law decisions announced by the Supreme Court from 1967 until 1972:

Self-Incrimination

Haynes v. U.S. (1968)—The court unanimously held that the federal government could not require the possessor of an illegal firearm to register that weapon without violating the Fifth Amendment which guarantees that no one shall be required to incriminate himself.

Marchetti v. U.S. (1968)—By a 7-1 vote, the court held that the federal government could not require gamblers to register and pay a wagering tax without violating the Fifth Amendment guarantee that no one shall be required to incriminate himself.

Minor v. U.S., Buie v. U.S. (1969)—By a 6-2 vote, the court held that the government could-without violating the Fifth Amendment guarantee against self-incrimination—require persons who sold heroin and marijuana to use a prescribed order blank.

Harris v. New York (1971)—By a 5-4 vote, the court limited the application of its 1966 decision in *Miranda v. Arizona,* holding that voluntary statements made by a defendant who had not properly been warned of his rights by the police could be used to impeach his credibility if he testified and contradicted the earlier statement.

Kastigar v. U.S. (1972)—By a 5-3 vote, the court held that the government did not violate the constitutional guarantee against self-incrimination by granting only limited immunity from prosecution to witnesses compelled to testify.

Search and Seizure

Katz v. U.S. (1967)—By a 7-1 vote, the court held electronic eavesdropping to be "search and seizure" within the Fourth Amendment protection against unreasonable searches and that evidence obtained by such means was inadmissible at trial unless obtained with a court warrant.

Terry v. Ohio (1968)—By an 8-1 vote, the court held that a police officer could stop a citizen briefly on the street and search him for dangerous weapons.

Alderman v. U.S. (1969)—By a 5-3 vote, the court held that the government must allow a defendant against whom material obtained by illegal electronic surveillance might be used to examine all material obtained in this way before the trial.

Chimel v. California (1969)—By a 6-2 vote, the court held that the Constitution allowed police, without a warrant and incident to an arrest, to search only the area within which the arrested person might obtain a weapon or destroy evidence.

U.S. v. White (1971)—By a 6-3 vote, the court held that it was permissible for someone, without a warrant, to carry an eavesdropping device and use it to monitor his conversations with another person.

Bivens v. Six Unknown Federal Agents (1971)—By a 6-3 vote, the court held that a person whose constitutional guarantee against unreasonable searches has been violated by a federal agent acting officially can sue the government for damages.

U.S. v. U.S. District Court, Eastern Michigan (1972)—By a 6-2 vote, the court held that the executive branch could not, without court authorization, use electronic surveillance to monitor the communications of allegedly subversive domestic groups and individuals.

---

charge—were likely to receive more sympathetic treatment. To avoid sending a young offender to an adult prison, or to minimize his time there, a jury and a judge might lean toward acquittal, or a light or suspended sentence, he added.

Mandatory sentences—severely restricting a court's discretion—also could boomerang, critics said. If a judge and jury were aware that a guilty verdict carried with it a mandatory sentence, they were likely to be swayed from that verdict by any possible doubt of guilt.

No Real Solution. Ervin and Assistant Senate Majority Leader Edward M. Kennedy (D Mass.) May 13 asked all senators to join them in opposition to the "repressive" features of the District crime bill.

Enactment of the bill, they said, would discredit the Congress: The legislation offered a great threat to individual rights but no real solution to the problem of crime. Former Attorney General Ramsey Clark (1967-69) blasted those who had drafted the bill: "They fail to demon-

strate how their proposals will protect the public, or what they will cost in wasted effort, violence and public confidence."

But an administration spokesman already had told Congress late in 1969 that the proposed measures for the District—if enacted and proved successful—would be proposed for application nationwide.

PRE-TRIAL DETENTION

Pre-trial, or preventive, detention of "dangerous" suspects was the most hotly debated of the Nixon administration's crime control proposals.

Ramsey Clark May 21 told the Senate Judiciary Subcommittee on Constitutional Rights that enactment of pre-trial detention legislation would be "a tragic step backward."

The next day Deputy Attorney General Richard G. Kleindienst told the subcommittee that it was "un-

...on Criminal Law and Procedure, 1967-1972

Trial by Jury

Duncan v. Louisiana (1968)—By a 7-2 vote, the court held that the Sixth Amendment right to a jury trial applied to the states in all cases in which it applied to the federal courts.

Williams v. Florida (1970)—By a 7-1 vote, the court held that the Constitution does not require a jury in a noncapital case to be composed of 12 persons.

Baldwin v. New York (1970)—By a 5-3 vote, the court held that states must provide jury trials for all persons charged with offenses punishable by more than six months in prison.

McKeiver v. Pennsylvania (1971)—By a 5-3 vote, the court held that juveniles do not have a constitutional right to trial by jury.

Johnson v. Louisiana, Apodaca v. Oregon (1972) —By a 5-4 vote, the court held that the right to be acquitted unless found guilty beyond a reasonable doubt did not preclude states from permitting guilty verdicts to be handed down by less-than-unanimous juries.

Death Penalty

Witherspoon v. Illinois (1968)—By a 6-3 vote, the court held that a death penalty was invalid if imposed by a jury from which persons opposed to the death penalty had been excluded.

Brady v. U.S., Parker v. North Carolina (1970— By a 5-3 vote, the court held constitutional the practice of plea bargaining—in which defendants agree to plead guilty to capital crimes in return for a pledge that they will not receive the death penalty.

Furman v. Georgia (1972)—By a 5-4 vote, the court held the death penalty as presently imposed (giving too much latitude to the discretion of judges and juries) to be unconstitutional.

Right to Counsel

Coleman v. Alabama (1970)—By a 6-2 vote, the court held that defendants are entitled to counsel at every "critical" stage in a criminal proceeding.

Kirby v. Illinois (1972)—By a 5-4 vote, the court held that the right to counsel did not apply to proceedings before indictment, such as line-ups.

Argersinger v. Hamlin (1972)—The court unanimously held that the right to counsel applied to all cases involving any risk of imprisonment.

Miscellaneous

Powell v. Texas (1968)—By a 5-4 vote, the court held that chronic alcoholism was not a complete defense to a charge of public drunkenness.

Benton v. Maryland (1969)—By a 6-2 vote, the court held that the constitutional guarantee against double jeopardy applied to the states.

Davis v. Mississippi (1969)—By a 6-2 vote, the court held that police must obtain a warrant in order to fingerprint an unarrested suspect.

Illinois v. Allen (1970)—By an 8-0 vote, the court held that a judge could have an unruly defendant removed from the courtroom if necessary to conduct an orderly trial.

In Re Winship (1970)—By a 5-3 vote, the court held that juveniles, like adults, must be found guilty "beyond a reasonable doubt," not merely by "a preponderance of the evidence."

Williams v. Illinois (1970)—By an 8-0 vote, the court held that a poor person could not be kept in prison longer than the maximum term for his offense simply because he could not pay a fine.

Tate v. Short (1971)—The court held unanimously that a $30-or-30-days sentence unconstitutionally discriminated against poorer persons unable to pay the fine and thus compelled to go to jail.

---

conscionable" for Congress to refuse to authorize preventive detention.

Under existing federal law, a person charged with a non-capital offense could be released on bail unless it appeared likely that he would not appear for trial. In setting conditions of release, courts were not authorized to consider the danger a defendant on bail could pose to the community. Nor could courts unconditionally deny release—although this frequently was effected by a high money bond.

But within 11 days of taking office, President Nixon proposed that Congress authorize federal courts to detain before trial "dangerous hard-core recidivists" whose release would pose "a clear danger to the community."

Administration Bill. Six months after the President voiced his support for pre-trial detention, the administration bill (S 2600, HR 12806) reached Capitol Hill. It authorized federal judges to consider danger to the community in setting non-financial conditions of release.

The proposed law affected defendants charged with:

• A dangerous crime (robbery or attempted robbery; burglary or attempted burglary; arson or attempted arson; rape; unlawful sale or distribution of drugs, if the offense was punishable by more than one year's sentence).

• A violent crime (murder, rape, mayhem, kidnapping, robbery, burglary, voluntary manslaughter, extortion or blackmail with threats of violence, arson, assault with intent to commit any of these offenses, assault with a dangerous weapon, or the attempt or conspiracy to commit any of those offenses, if punishable by more than one year's sentence) committed by a person free on bail, probation or parole, or a person convicted of a violent crime within the previous 10 years.

• Attempting to harm or threaten a prospective juror or witness.

(The list of crimes in these categories included many capital offenses. Defendants in capital cases had

Bail Reform Act of 1966

The first significant change in bail law came in the Bail Reform Act of 1966 (PL 89-465), which established new procedures for the release of federal prisoners charged with non-capital offenses. The purpose as stated in the act was "to revise the practices relating to bail to assure that all persons, regardless of their financial status, shall not needlessly be detained pending their appearance to answer charges, to testify, or pending appeal, when detention serves neither the ends of justice nor the public interest."

The act provided generally for the release of persons charged with non-capital federal offenses unless it appeared they were unlikely to return for trial. It was generally accepted that congressional supporters intended the act to serve as a prototype for the states, within which the main burden of criminal law enforcement fell.

In passing the act, Congress specifically postponed consideration of issues relating to crimes committed by persons released while awaiting trial. The House Judiciary Committee in its report on the bill said a solution to the problem of preventive detention "involves many difficult and complex problems which require deep study and analysis."

no right to bail and could, under existing law, be detained before trial.)

If a judge found convincing evidence that a defendant was dangerous and that no conditions of release could reasonably assure the community's safety from him, he could order that person detained for 60 days before his trial.

Attorney General Mitchell told the House Judiciary Committee late in 1969 that crime committed by persons free on bail was "a major factor in the rising crime rate," and that existing law had to be amended to cope with that problem.

In answer to criticism that this bill would require judges to be prophets, Mitchell said that judges always have had to make certain predictions—whether of likelihood of flight or of rehabilitation.

Opposition. Pre-trial detention, its critics said, was unjustified, ineffective and unconstitutional.

The Justice Department—after sending its proposed bill to Congress—commissioned a study of the rearrest rate of persons free on bail.

But before the results of the study were released, a pre-trial detention provision was inserted into the District of Columbia crime bill and approved by the House. Opponents cited this maneuver as evidence of the flimsy case for pre-trial detention.

The study, released April 7, showed that of all persons charged (during four weeks in 1968 in the District of Columbia) with felonies or misdemeanors 11 per cent were rearrested while awaiting trial.

The basic premise of the bill was that persons arrested for violent or dangerous crimes were likely to be rearrested for similar offenses while free on bail awaiting trial. The study found one of every 20 persons so charged was rearrested for a similar crime while out on bail.

The study also found that two of every three persons charged with serious crimes and rearrested pending trial were rearrested for minor offenses.

In a Senate speech May 18, Ervin pointed out that on the basis of the study's findings preventive detention would mean that the Justice Department would detain 19 non-dangerous persons in order to hold one dangerous defendant.

Furthermore, he said, detention for 60 days would not reduce crime committed by persons awaiting trial, because it would detain them at the wrong time.

Very few persons free on bail were rearrested within the first two months after release, Ervin said. The longer the period of time before trial, the more frequent and serious a second crime.

If pre-trial detention was to be effective, Ervin said, it either had to cover the entire time between arrest and trial or it had to begin, not immediately after arrest but two or three months later. He urged speedy trials instead.

Rep. Mikva summarized this attack on preventive detention: It won't work—"it won't reduce crime, it will clog our already overburdened courts, and will further delay justice which is already too long delayed. For a group which likes to style itself 'pragmatic,' I find this an incredibly impractical approach."

Presumed Innocent. A fundamental tradition of the American system of justice held a man innocent until proven guilty. The Sixth Amendment assured that "the accused (in all criminal cases) shall enjoy the right to a speedy and public trial." The Eighth Amendment prohibited excessive bail. Preventive detention was attacked as a reversal and violation of all three. Pretrial detention presumed arrest a sufficient indication of guilt to warrant consideration of detention; it added another layer of judicial procedure to the already clogged court dockets; and it denied bail.

Ramsey Clark criticized Nixon administration spokesmen for describing the presumption of innocence as a "mere role of procedural evidence."

PROVISIONS

As cleared by Congress, S 2601 (PL 91-358), the District of Columbia Court Reform and Criminal Procedure Act of 1970:

Title I: Court Reorganization

• Authorized the modernization of the court system for the District of Columbia, which would, in a three-year, three-step transfer, receive from federal courts all jurisdiction over local matters. A Superior Court would incorporate the existing General Sessions, Tax and Juvenile Courts. The District of Columbia Court of Appeals would function as a state supreme court.

• Authorized 17 additional judges for the new Superior Court.

• Created a joint commission to supervise removal of judges for disability or misconduct.

• Authorized an executive officer to manage court operations.

Title I: Juvenile Code

• Provided that a juvenile 16 or older would be tried as an adult if charged with murder, forcible rape, first-degree burglary, armed robbery or assault with the intent to commit any of those offenses.

• Lowered from 16 to 15 the age at which a juvenile charged with a felony could be transferred from the juvenile court for criminal prosecution as an adult.

• Required "proof beyond a reasonable doubt" to find a juvenile guilty of delinquency, but only proof by "a preponderance of the evidence" to find him neglected or in need of supervision.

• Provided that a juvenile was entitled to counsel at all critical stages of proceedings against him, and provided that although he might be excluded from his hearing under certain circumstances, his counsel could not.

• Specified that a neglected child could not be placed in a detention home for delinquents.

Title I: Witness Credibility

• Broadened admissibility of evidence of a witness' prior conviction (of a felony or of an offense involving dishonesty) to impeach his credibility.

Title II: Criminal Law

• Authorized imposition of a sentence of life imprisonment for a third felony conviction and of up to three times the maximum penalty (for a first offense) for a third offense.

• Set a three-year maximum prison sentence for robbery of a vending machine, parking meter or coin telephone.

• Set a mandatory minimum additional sentence of five years for a second armed crime of violence.

• Stated that there was no justifiable or excusable reason for forcibly resisting arrest, even if the arrest was unlawful.

• Declared it a crime to possess, make or use a molotov cocktail or other incendiary device in the District of Columbia.

Title II: Criminal Procedures

• Allowed the government or the District of Columbia to appeal an order suppressing evidence against a defendant.

• Provided for a nighttime search warrant when there was "probable cause to believe" that it could not be executed in daylight, the property sought was likely to be removed or destroyed if not seized immediately or the property was not likely to be found except at certain times and in certain circumstances.

• Provided for "no-knock" search and arrest warrants (allowing policemen to enter premises without notice) if the officer had "probable cause to believe" that notice was likely to result in destruction of evidence sought, danger to the life or safety of the policeman or another person, escape of the party to be arrested or where such notice would be a useless gesture.

• Provided for "no-knock" entries by officers without such authorization in the warrant if they found the

---

"No-Flush" Amendment

In offering an amendment March 19 to HR 16196 to make it a crime to own a building in the District of Columbia with indoor plumbing, Rep. Cornelius E. Gallagher (D N.J.) made the following statement:

"Mr. Chairman, I know the hour is late. I feel, however, that the hour is even later for liberty.

"As I sat here through the debate, it struck me how terrible it was that the invention of indoor plumbing has become the apparatus to cause the Fourth Amendment to disappear.

"The rationale for the no-knock provision is that if the policeman knocks before he enters a home, evidence of narcotic or other violations could be flushed down the drain. There just has to be a viable alternative to putting a match to the Fourth Amendment. Ridiculous as my proposal may sound, I would rather opt for liberty than indoor plumbing, if there really is no other option....

"The amendment I have just introduced will make it a crime, punishable by a $5,000 fine, for any dwelling in the District to have indoor plumbing. I propose to substitute a "no-flush" law for a "no-knock" law....

"Next, of course, we will want to confiscate all the matches in the District to prevent the evidence from being burned. Further, what we must eventually do, to be wholly consistent with the thrust of the provisions of this legislation and others offered recently, would be to require all doors and houses of dwellings in the District to be made of glass...."

Gallagher's amendment was defeated by voice vote.

---

specified circumstances after obtaining the warrant. If the circumstances were known at the time of the application for warrant, the "no-knock" provision must be included in it.

• Authorized District of Columbia law enforcement agents to use wiretapping and electronic surveillance—under conditions in accordance with Title III of the 1968 Omnibus Crime Control and Safe Streets Act (PL 90-351)—in investigating arson, blackmail, bribery, burglary, destruction of property valued at more than $200, gambling, grand larceny, kidnapping, murder, obstruction of justice, receiving stolen property valued at more than $100 and robbery.

• Provided penalties for illegal wiretapping and electronic surveillance.

• Provided that a special need (connection with organized crime) must be shown for any interception of communication from the facilities of a doctor, clergyman or attorney.

• Authorized pre-trial detention for up to 60 days of: (1) a person charged with a dangerous crime (forcible taking of property, unlawful entry, arson, forcible rape, or unlawful sale or distribution of drugs) when a court found that there was no combination of release conditions which would assure the community's safety from him; (2) a person charged with a crime of violence (murder, forcible rape, certain sex crimes, mayhem, kidnaping, robbery, burglary, voluntary manslaughter, extortion or blackmail with threats of violence, arson, assault) who was a drug addict, who had been convicted of a violent crime within the previous 10 years or who allegedly committeed the crime while free on bail, on probation or parole; or (3) a person charged with threatening a prospective witness or juror.

● Barred detention of any defendant charged with a non-capital crime solely on the basis of the nature and circumstances of the alleged crime.

● Guaranteed that the 60-day detention period could not be extended by the filing of timely motions by the defendant—other than through motions by the defendant for postponement of the trial.

● Provided for expedited trials within the 60-day period, specifying that cases of persons detained should be placed on an expedited calendar.

Title III: Public Defender Service

● Renamed the District Legal Aid Agency the District Public Defender Service.

● Authorized the Public Defender Service to represent up to 60 per cent of the persons unable to obtain adequate representation and to work to find private counsel for the remaining 40 per cent.

Title IV: Interstate Compact

● Authorized the District of Columbia to enter into the Interstate Compact on Juveniles for cooperation in the return of runaway juveniles.

Title V: Police Counsel

● Provided that the corporation counsel of the District of Columbia would represent any police officer sued for wrongful arrest or would pay the officer's attorney's fees.

Title VI: Commission Abolition

● Abolished the Commission on Revision of the Criminal Laws of the District of Columbia.

Title VII: Federal Payment

● Authorized federal payment of $5-million in fiscal 1971 to the District: $3,010,000 for reorganizing the courts and the Legal Aid Agency; $580,000 for facilities for the additional court personnel; $350,000 for expansion of the Bail Agency; plus $1,060,000 for other purposes of the act.

Title VIII: Kite-Flying

● Repealed the law prohibiting kite-flying in the District of Columbia.

Organized Crime Control

Congress Oct. 12 cleared for the White House the Organized Crime Control Act of 1970 (S 30—PL 91-452), the most comprehensive federal law ever enacted to combat organized crime.

Proposed first by John L. McClellan (D Ark.), S 30 was eagerly adopted by the Nixon administration which added several of its own proposals to the final version.

President Nixon April 23, 1969, asked Congress to enact S 30, to provide the federal government with new tools to use against sophisticated, nationwide criminal operations.

Saxbe-Ervin Dispute

District of Columbia police officer Ronald R. Watson was critically wounded June 18 by a robbery suspect who had twice been arrested for armed robbery and released on bond. After being wounded, Watson shot and killed the suspect, Franklin E. Moyler.

Sen. William B. Saxbe (R Ohio), in a Senate speech June 19, charged that Watson would not have been wounded if preventive detention had been in effect. He noted that Moyler, twice convicted of assault, had been arrested for armed robbery on Jan. 23, 1970—and released on bail prior to trial— then again had been arrested for robbery June 1—and again released on bail.

Sen. Sam J. Ervin Jr. (D N.C.) chairman of the subcommittee holding hearings on pre-trial detention, replied to Saxbe's speech, pointing out that Moyler would have been free on June 1 even had he been detained for 60 days after Jan. 23—as the administration bill prescribed.

Had his trial taken place speedily—between January and June—Ervin's office said, the second arrest and the shooting of Officer Watson might have been prevented.

The bill moved easily through the Senate, where it passed Jan. 23, 1970, with only one dissenting vote. But House Judiciary Committee Chairman Emanuel Celler (D N.Y.) considered many of the provisions of the Senate version of the bill unconstitutional, and did not move to speed its passage in the House.

Criticism of the bill's provisions—and opposition to its enactment—swelled during the first half of 1970. House hearings began late in May, just after the New York City Bar Association released a study of the bill which called for its complete revision, and warned that it contained "the seeds of official repression."

Double Standard? The major objection leveled at S 30 as a whole argued that—although use of its provisions against organized crime was presented as justification for its passage—its changes in criminal laws and procedures were not limited to that use.

"Organized crime," the bill's advocates replied, is a functional concept like "street crime" or "white-collar crime," not susceptible to hard definition in legal terms. Besides, at the outset of an investigation, the involvement of organized crime in a matter is not always clear. To find such an involvement may be the purpose of the inquiry.

McClellan pointed out that this objection implied a double standard of constitutional rights: one applicable to persons involved in organized crime and one applicable to the rest of the nation.

S 30, McClellan said, "must stand or fall on the constitutional question without regard to the degree to which it is limited to organized crime cases." If it violated the rights of those engaged in organized crime, then it should not be approved, he said. If it did not, then it did not violate the rights of persons not engaged in such crime. *(Criticisms S 30, p. 274-5)*

Celler continued to hold hearings on S 30 into early August. But when Congress returned in September from its recess, election)year pressure for House action on S 30 was intense. The Judiciary Committee, under threat of a discharge petition reported S 30 in late September with a few amendments, claiming to have eliminated many of its worst flaws.

The House approved the bill Oct. 7 on a 341-26 roll call. The Senate within days agreed to the version passed by the House, and President Nixon signed S 30 into law Oct. 15, turning then to Attorney General John N. Mitchell and Federal Bureau of Investigation Director J. Edgar Hoover to say, "I give you the tools. You do the job."

Background. Only sporadically during recent decades had Congress turned its attention to the activities of organized crime.

In 1950 and 1951 hearings before the Special Senate Crime Investigating Committee led by Estes Kefauver (D Tenn. 1949-1963) drew national attention to nationwide criminal operations. Again in 1957, 1958, and 1959, the investigations of McClellan and his Senate Select Committee on Improper Activities in the Labor or Management Field spotlighted organized crime.

But Congress did not bestir itself to enact any major legislation to combat the menace of criminal syndicates.

During the Kennedy administration federal concern about organized crime was renewed. Robert F. Kennedy came to the post of attorney general in 1961, fresh from his experience as chief counsel for the McClellan committee.

A stepped-up federal effort against organized crime became a priority program during his years as attorney general.

An organized crime and racketeering section had been created in the Justice Department in 1954, but it was composed of only 17 attorneys in 1960. Under Kennedy, the section was expanded to 63 attorneys by 1964, spending 1,364 man-days in court, in contrast to 61 man-days in 1960.

Despite the increased federal effort, between 1960 and March 1969, of 5,000 known or suspected organized crime figures, only 257 were indicted.

Crime Commission. In 1965, President Johnson created the President's Commission on Law Enforcement and the Administration of Justice (Crime Commission), headed by then Attorney General Nicholas deB. Katzenbach and authorized it not only to study the causes of crime and to analyze the federal failure to cope with organized crime but also to suggest cures.

Published in February 1967, the Commission's comprehensive final report contained more than 200 recommendations for action to reduce crime. Twenty-two of these recommendations were directed specifically toward dealing with organized crime. This report was the source of many of the provisions of S 30.

PROVISIONS

As cleared by Congress, S 30, the Organized Crime Control Act of 1970:

- Authorized special grand juries to sit in heavily populated areas or where designated by the attorney general for periods up to 36 months, subject to the control of the federal district courts, to return indictments, and to submit to the court reports concerning non-criminal misconduct by an appointed public official involving organized criminal activity, or organized crime conditions in the area. When such a report did name an individual official, he would be notified and given an opportunity to be heard by the grand jury and to present witnesses, and the chance to file a rebuttal to the report which was included in the full report (Title I).

- Repealed all previous witness-immunity laws and authorized federal legislative, administrative and judicial bodies to grant witnesses immunity from prosecution using their testimony, but not from all prosecution for any act mentioned in their testimony. This comprehensive new law provided "use-immunity," a narrower grant than the "transaction-immunity" authorized by most previous laws. "Transaction-immunity" protected the witness from prosecution for any offense mentioned in or related to his testimony, regardless of independent evidence against him. This was sometimes referred to as an "immunity bath." "Use-immunity" protected him from prosecution directly or indirectly using his testimony or anything directly derived from it against him (Title II).

- Authorized detention of recalcitrant witnesses until they complied with the orders of the court, but for no longer than 18 months (Title III). This title did not change existing law, but codified civil contempt procedures which had evolved in case-by-case decisions.

- Authorized a conviction for perjury based on obviously contradictory statements made under oath—eliminating the rules that there must be direct proof that a statement was false and that there must be testimony from two witnesses (Title IV).

- Authorized the attorney general to protect and maintain federal or state witnesses (and their families) in organized crime cases (Title V).

- Authorized use of depositions in criminal cases subject to constitutional guarantees and certification by the attorney general that the case involved organized crime (Title V). (Depositions preserve evidence in form usable at trial if the evidence becomes otherwise unavailable through the illness, death, disappearance or bribery of the witness.)

- Limited to five years the period within which government action to obtain evidence could be challenged as illegal; required court review of government records to ascertain their possible relevance prior to their disclosure to a defendant who established that their origin was illegal; restricted effect of this title to federal proceedings and to surveillance occurring before June 19, 1968 (Title VII). (PL 90-351 authorizing federal electronic surveillance was signed June 20, 1968. Title VII limited the disclosure of government records required by a 1969 Supreme Court decision. (*Alderman v. U.S.*, p. 269)

- Declared it a federal crime to plot to obstruct state law, particularly through corruption of government officials, in order to facilitate an "illegal gambling business," defined as one which violated a state or local law, involved five or more persons, and operated for more than 30 days or had a gross income of $2,000 in one day (Title VIII).

- Declared it a crime to use income from organized crime to acquire, establish, or operate a business engaged in interstate commerce, and prescribed use of forfeiture,

(Continued on p. 276)

Organized Crime Act: "The Seeds of Official Repression"...

Criticism of the Organized Crime Control Act mounted steadily between Senate passage in January—with only one dissenting vote—and the beginning of House hearings in May. This opposition to S 30 as the Senate had approved it was led by Emanuel Celler (D N.Y.), chairman of the House Judiciary Committee, armed with an analysis of the bill by the New York City Bar Association committee on Federal legislation.

Celler labeled the bill "repressive."

The Bar Association report warned that S 30 contained "the seeds of official repression." It warned against the attitude reflected in the bill "that the innocent do not need such rights and the guilty do not deserve them." These constitutional rights, it pointed out, protect all citizens; infringement of them threatens the innocent as well as the guilty.

Other critics warned that the bill did not contain safeguards to assure that the extraordinary powers it granted would be used only to fight organized crime. The threat of organized crime provided the justification for the bill and they reasoned that the provisions of the bill should specify that they applied only to cases involving such offenses.

But the opposition to the bill tended to obscure the source of many of its provisions—the 1967 report of the President's Crime Commission—their complexity and the safeguards which they contained.

Special Grand Juries

"As an instrument of discovery against organized crime," John L. McClellan (D Ark.), the Senate sponsor of S 30, had said, "The grand jury has no counterpart."

Title I, in line with recommendations of the Crime Commission, reinforced and expanded the investigatory powers of the grand jury.

Most of the criticism of Title I concerned the grand jury's power to file reports on the misconduct of a public official. (In 1970, 22 states allowed grand juries to make similar reports.)

The non-adversary nature of grand jury proceedings, critics said, made it nearly impossible for an official to defend or vindicate himself because there was no indictment and no trial.

Sen. McClellan explained that an official so criticized under S 30 had the right to appear before the grand jury to present his witnesses and to file a rebuttal to the report, which then was included in the report.

The court would study the report and rebuttal to ascertain that the report was supported by a preponderance of the evidence and that each person named was given a chance to testify.

Only if both of these requirements were met would the court release the report, with the rebuttal, for publication.

Publication would be further delayed, if the order of the court releasing the report were appealed. The report would be not published until there had been a final decision on its validity.

Witnesses

Witnesses are essential to a prosecutor's case. Titles II-VI of S 30 revised criminal investigatory procedures to facilitate securing reliable testimony from witnesses.

Immunity. The Fifth Amendment guarantees that "no person shall be compelled in any criminal case to be a witness against himself." Witness after witness in organized crime investigations "takes the Fifth" refusing to testify. To overcome this objection and compel testimony, Congress had enacted a multiplicity of witness-immunity laws.

Title II replaced all existing witness-immunity laws with one comprehensive law, ensuring all witnesses compelled to testify before congressional, judicial or administrative bodies that neither their testimony, nor any evidence obtained by exploiting their testimony, would be used against them. The Crime Commission recommended enactment of a general immunity law.

Recalcitrant Witnesses. If an immunized witness still refused to testify, Title II provided that the court could order him confined, in contempt of court, until he testified or until the investigation ended.

The Crime Commission said that once a witness was immunized, he must testify or face jail for contempt.

Perjury. To encourage a witness to give truthful testimony, the Crime Commission, as had the American Bar Association (ABA) in 1952, recommended that Congress abolish the two-witness and direct-evidence rules for perjury prosecutions. Title IV did just that.

Title IV defined perjury as a knowingly false statement made under oath and permitted a witness to be charged with perjury if he made contradictory statements under oath and did not correct them of his own volition.

Further, Title IV provided that a statement was false if it was proved, beyond a reasonable doubt, to be one of two manifestly contradictory statements which the same person made under oath. Proof need no longer be made by any particular number of witnesses or by any particular type of evidence.

Protection. Title V of S 30 authorized protection of witnesses; Title VI authorized protection of evidence.

The Crime Commission recommended that the federal government set up residential facilities for the protection of witnesses from reprisals. Under Title V, the attorney general could provide such security for witnesses, potential witnesses and their families.

When there is substantial risk that a witness might die, hide, flee, become ill, be killed, injured, kidnapped or bribed, Title VI allowed, upon court order and certification that the case involved organized crime, the recording of his testimony in a deposition, a sworn statement, which either side could take of its own witnesses. Taken under full guarantees of counsel and cross-examination, depositions preserve evidence in a form usable at trial.

... or New Weapon in War Against Organized Crime?

Use of Evidence

The use of evidence, once obtained, frequently is challenged by a defendant who claims that his constitutional rights were violated by the way in which it was obtained and who asserts that it should not be used against him.

Because of legal uncertainty and policy conflicts, evidence obtained by electronic surveillance is particularly vulnerable to such challenge. The Supreme Court in March 1969 held that all government records from a surveillance device must be disclosed to a defendant who claims that evidence against him is the result of that surveillance and who proves that his rights have been invaded. If the government does not disclose its records, the case can be dismissed.

McClellan said that this decision encouraged a defendant who at any time had been unlawfully surveyed to challenge evidence in any case against him—however unrelated—since he knew that he could thus win disclosure of confidential files or, if disclosure would be too harmful to the government, dismissal of the charges against him.

Several times since this decision wholesale turnover of wiretap logs to defendants had resulted in the publication of material irrelevant to the case, but harmful and embarrassing to third persons who were not involved in the case against the defendant.

Title VII narrowed the time span within which challenges could be made to evidence alleged to have been indirectly derived from an illegal wiretap and allowed a judge to screen government records before turning them over to a defendant. It provided that no challenge to evidence which was the indirect product of an unlawful act could be considered if that act occurred more than five years before the event to be proved.

Disclosure of surveillance records would be limited to that part of such records which a judge found "may be relevant" and "in the interest of justice."

Critics of S 30 expressed alarm that Title VII diluted a citizen's protections against illegal acts by law enforcement agents. The ABA Criminal Law Council, however, approved the five-year limit. McClellan stated that the five-year limit did not affect challenges to evidence directly produced by an unlawful government act. The law continued to bar the use of such directly produced evidence as the transcript of an illegal wiretap. It limited challenges to evidence obtained by the exploitation of such an unlawful act—by the use of that transcript.

A staff member of the Senate Criminal Laws and Procedures Subcommittee pointed out that—under previously existing law—as soon as a criminal realized that he had inadvertently been "caught" on a surveillance device which could not be disclosed, he had virtually "a license to kill."

If brought to trial for any crime he could challenge the evidence against him as indirectly related to the undisclosable surveillance and—because the government could not disclose the fact of the surveillance or the records—the case against him had to be dismissed.

Under Title VII, a judge would see—from the government records—that the surveillance had no possible relevance to the pending case, and there would be no disclosure. If more than five years had elapsed between the time the defendant was recorded on the device and the time of the crime with which he was charged, no challenge to the evidence would even be considered.

Illegal Gambling

Gambling produced billions of dollars annually for the operations of organized crime. Title VIII extended federal jurisdiction over all major illicit gambling operations.

This title contained most of the provisions of S 2022, an administration bill to give the attorney general latitude to assist local and state governments in cracking down on illegal gambling."

Corrupted Business

Title IX, derived from S 1861 introduced April 18, 1969, by McClellan, contained the most innovative of S 30's provisions. To cope with the infiltration of organized crime into legitimate business and labor, Title IX declared it a crime to use organized crime profits or methods to establish, acquire or operate any legitimate business.

Title IX provided both criminal and civil sanctions to remove organized crime from legitimate organizations. Under this section, courts could order crime syndicates to divest themselves of certain holdings, never to re-enter a certain type of business and to dissolve infiltrated enterprises.

Special Sentences

The Crime Commission recommended that extended sentences be authorized for organized crime figures convicted of a felony. The ABA, American Law Institute, and the National Council on Crime and Delinquency recommended similar measures. Title X authorized sentences of up to 25 years for persons convicted of a felony—if they were found to be dangerous and found to be "habitual" offenders, a "professional" criminal, or an "organized crime figure."

A defendant would be found to fall into one of these categories only after a special pre-sentencing hearing at which he had the right to counsel and cross-examination. After the decision, both the defendant and the government had the right to appeal.

A Senate staff study for the Judiciary Subcommittee on Criminal Laws and Procedures found that of all organized crime figures sentenced in federal court from 1960 to 1969, two-thirds faced maximum jail terms of five years or less and fewer than one-fourth received a maximum sentence.

antitrust devices, special investigative procedures and damage suits against such crimes (Title IX).

- Authorized increased sentences (up to 25 years) for dangerous adult special offenders. Defendants found, during a special post-conviction hearing, to fall into this category might include a person convicted of a third felony, a professional criminal convicted of a felony or an organized crime figure (Title X).

- Established a system of federal controls over the interstate and foreign commerce of explosives through licensing and permits; prohibited distribution of explosives to certain categories of persons; strengthened and expanded the scope of federal law with regard to the illegal use, transportation or possession of explosives to damage or destroy federal property or that of institutions or organizations receiving federal aid (Title XI).

- Established effective Jan. 1, 1972, a National Commission on Individual Rights to review certain federal laws and practices which might infringe upon individual rights (including the special grand jury and special offender sentencing provisions of S 30, wiretapping and electronic surveillance, bail reform and preventive detention, no-knock search warrants and data banks) and to make a final report to the President and Congress by Jan. 1, 1978 (Title XII).

Other Legislation

AIRCRAFT HIJACKINGS. The hijackings of four international airliners in September by Palestinian terrorists and the detention for several days of more than 50 passengers, many of them Americans, caused widespread alarm in Congress and the executive branch.

The President responded Sept. 12 by ordering armed guards on selected international and domestic commercial flights. The personnel were drawn initially from the armed forces and Secret Service.

On Sept. 14 the President asked for and received an additional $28-million in the fiscal 1971 Department of Transportation appropriations bill (HR 17755—PL 91-645) to finance recruitment and training of 2,500 security guards to protect commercial flights.

Congress also responded by holding hearings on measures urging the administration to negotiate international agreements providing for the mandatory extradition of aircraft hijackers and authorizing the temporary use of the Airport and Airway Trust Fund to pay for the air guards. A bill (HR 19444) containing such an authorization was passed by the House Sept. 30 but was not considered by the Senate.

Congress did pass a bill (S 2176—PL 91-449) clarifying the jurisdiction of the 1963 Tokyo Convention to assure the application of U.S. laws regarding acts endangering air safety aboard all U.S.-registered aircraft.

A Supplementary Extradition Convention with France, ratified by the Senate Sept. 21, added aircraft hijacking to the list of crimes for which extradition would be granted by each country.

EXECUTIVE BRANCH POLICE. The President March 19 signed a bill (HR 14944—PL 91-217) authorizing an increase in the White House police force. The measure changed the name of the force to the Executive Protective Service, increased its personnel to 850 from 250, and required it to protect foreign diplomatic missions in Washington and elsewhere in addition to the White House and

---

Explosives Control

A rash of bombings in early 1970 aroused congressional concern. President Nixon March 25 sent to Congress a bill (HR 1699, S 3650) to strengthen federal laws and stiffen penalties for violations. He asked that the death penalty be authorized for persons convicted of a bombing which resulted in death.

Hearings were held in both chambers during 1970 and explosive control sections were added to S 30 (by the House committee) and to HR 17825, the 1970 Omnibus Crime Control Act amendments (by the Senate). The explosives control section was dropped from HR 17825 in conference. *(Omnibus Crime Control Act amendments of 1970, p. 265)*

Existing federal law prohibited transportation of explosives in interstate commerce for criminal purposes and the possession or use of explosives to damage equipment or facilities used in commerce. Federal law prohibited falsely reporting bombs aboard planes, motor vehicles, railroads or vessels.

The National Firearms Act, while prohibiting making, transferring and possessing destructive devices without registration, failed to include dynamite and other explosives unless the explosive was possessed with other components of destructive devices.

Several government agencies and departments controlled various aspects of the bomb problem—the Bureau of Mines in the Department of Interior, Department of Justice, Department of the Treasury, Department of Transportation, Department of Agriculture and the Department of Commerce.

---

its grounds. The bill was passed by the Senate Feb. 24 on an 84-1 roll-call vote. Stephen M. Young (D Ohio) opposed the bill. The House had approved the bill Dec. 18, 1969, on a 394-7 roll-call vote.

PUBLIC DEFENDER SYSTEM. Congress Oct. 7 cleared a bill (S 1461—PL 91-447) amending the Criminal Justice Act of 1964 (PL 88-455) to expand its coverage and authorize creation of federal and community defender systems. Final action came when the Senate by voice vote approved the House version of S 1461. The Senate originally passed its version April 30 by voice vote and without debate, but the House amended it slightly and passed its own version Oct. 5 by a 277-21 roll-call vote.

The final bill expanded the coverage of the 1964 act to authorize appointment and compensation of counsel for persons (including juvenile delinquents) charged with a crime, financially unable to secure counsel and (1) charged with violating probation; (2) under arrest and for whom counsel was required by law; (3) subject to revocation of parole; (4) who were material witnesses in custody, or (5) who sought collateral relief.

The bill also increased the hourly rate of payment for court-appointed counsel to $30 for hours in court and $20 for hours out of court and barred a federal public defender or any attorney appointed by him from engaging in the private practice of law.

GUN CONTROL. Congress failed to complete action on a bill (HR 14233) exempting .22 caliber rimfire ammunition from the record-keeping requirements of the Gun Control Act of 1968 (PL 90-618). The bill was passed by the House Dec. 21 on a 246-59 roll-call vote, but the Senate did not act on it. Congress, in a 1969 extension of the Interest Equalization Tax (PL 91-128), had repealed most of the record-keeping requirements for rifle and shotgun ammuniton, but not for the .22 caliber rimfire variety. Proponents of HR 14233 said the record-keeping requirements were burdensome to ammunition dealers.

ASSAULTS ON POLICE. The Senate Judiciary Subcommittee on Internal Security held hearings in October on several bills dealing with assaults on police, but none was reported. More than 1,200 policemen from around the country rallied at the Capitol steps Oct. 14 to urge stiffer penalties against "revolutionaries" who attacked police. Sixty-one policemen were killed in 1970 and about 20 were victims of unprovoked attacks, according to rally sponsors. Some of the bills introduced would have made it a federal crime to assault or injure a state or local policeman or required the FBI to join in the hunt for a policeman's killer after 24 hours had elapsed from the time of the crime.

1971

There was no major crime or law enforcement legislative request from President Nixon in 1971, and Congress did little beyond holding hearings on a wide variety of bills in those areas. Congress did clear a non-controversial extension of the Juvenile Delinquency Prevention and Control Act of 1968.

Hearings were held on cargo thefts, prison reform and gun control. The Senate approved an international convention against airplane hijackings, and the House defeated an attempt to create an institute to study juvenile delinquency.

Outside the legislative field, the Federal Bureau of Investigation and its long-time director, J. Edgar Hoover, were subjected to harsh criticism over bureau practices. *(Box, p. 278)*

GUN CONTROL. House consideration of a bill (HR 3599) to exempt .22 caliber rimfire ammunition from the record-keeping requirements of the 1968 Gun Control Act was postponed Nov. 15 when its sponsor, Al Ullman (D Ore.), pulled the bill off the floor agenda for fear it would be defeated. The bill was not rescheduled for a vote in 1971.

Ullman explained later that the members were irritated with the Ways and Means Committee, from which the bill had been reported, and would probably have defeated the bill by "voting their emotions" against the committee rather than voting on the bill's merits.

The Senate Judiciary Subcommittee on Juvenile Delinquency held four days of hearings on a bill (S 2507) outlawing the sale of cheap handguns. The bill, sponsored by Subcommittee Chairman Birch Bayh (D Ind.), was aimed at so-called "Saturday night specials" which sold for under $25.

Edmund G. Brown, chairman of the National Commission on Reform of Federal Criminal Laws, and Lloyd N. Cutler, former executive director of the National Commission on Causes and Prevention of Violence, supported the bill. It was opposed by the administration, sportsmen and the National Rifle Association. The Senate passed the bill in 1972. *(1972 action, p. 282)*

CARGO THEFTS. The Senate Sept. 8 passed a bill (S 942) establishing a commission to study the causes and prevention of cargo thefts. Congress failed to complete action on the bill. The problem of cargo thefts gained prominence in 1971 after hearings in June and July by the Senate Government Operations Subcommittee on Permanent Investigations revealed that a ring of thieves had systematically stolen an estimated $100-million in stocks, bonds, jewelry, cash and furs from numerous airport freight terminals throughout the country.

JUVENILE DELINQUENCY. Congress June 21 cleared a bill (S 1732—PL 92-31) amending and extending for one year the Juvenile Delinquency Prevention and Control Act of 1968 (PL 90-445). House and Senate passage of the noncontroversial measure came on voice votes.

The bill extended the 1968 act through fiscal 1972, authorized $75-million to carry it out and created an Interdepartmental Council on Juvenile Delinquency to coordinate all federal delinquency programs. The bill also authorized the secretary of health, education and welfare to make grants of up to 75 per cent of the cost of rehabilitation projects and programs for delinquents, an increase of 15 per cent over the authorizations in the 1968 act.

Creation of the interdepartmental council stemmed from testimony at hearings on the bill that there was little coordination among the federal departments and agencies—Justice, Health, Education and Welfare, and Housing and Urban Development, among others—that had responsibility for delinquency programs.

In other delinquency legislation, the House Dec. 6 failed to suspend the rules and pass a bill (HR 45) creating an Institute for the Continuing Studies of Juvenile Delinquency. The roll call vote was 240-135, 10 votes shy of the two-thirds necessary to pass the bill under the suspension procedure.

The institute would have gathered and disseminated information on juvenile justice and trained criminal justice personnel in the area of juvenile crime and delinquency. The administration objected to the bill as duplicative of existing programs.

Proponents of the bill said administration programs had failed while juvenile crime grew. They pointed to FBI statistics showing 52 per cent of all persons arrested in 1970 were under age 25, and 25 per cent of those arrested were under age 18. Opponents charged the bill would be a waste of money and effort.

HOUSE CRIME COMMITTEE. The House March 9 by voice vote approved a resolution (H Res 115) extending the life of the House Select Committee on Crime through the 92nd Congress and increasing its membership to 11 from seven. The committee was set up in 1969 to study "all aspects of crime affecting the United States." Questions were raised by members over whether the committee's work justified the $900,000 that already had been appropriated for it, but Chairman Claude Pepper (D Fla.) outlined its efforts and said there was a "compelling need" for the House to have an investigating committee that could probe the full range of criminal activity

AIRCRAFT HIJACKING. The Senate Sept. 8, by a 53-0 roll-call vote, adopted a resolution (Exec. A, 92nd Congress, First Session) ratifying an international convention to prevent aircraft hijackings. The United States was among 50 nations that in December 1970 signed the treaty, formally called the Convention for the Suppression of Unlawful Seizure of Aircraft, at the Hague. International aircraft hijackings had grown rapidly in 1970. Cuba, where most hijacked U.S. aircraft landed, did not participate in the Hague convention. The treaty required signatory nations to prosecute hijackers in their custody or extradite them.

PRISON REFORM. The House Select Committee on Crime held hearings Nov. 29-Dec. 3 on the Attica, N.Y., and Raiford, Fla., prison riots. Thirty-two inmates and 11 hostages were killed Sept. 9-13 at Attica, most of them on Sept. 13 by state troopers who stormed the prison to end the riot. At Raiford Prison, 20 inmates were wounded and 23 injured Feb. 12 when guards fired on about 600 prisoners taking part in a one-day hunger strike.

Vincent R. Mancusi, Attica warden, blamed the riot on an inmate conspiracy, but Russell G. Oswald, commissioner of the New York Department of Correctional Services, disputed this. He said the root cause of the riot was an obsolete prison starved of funds by the legislature.

A guard and former inmate at Raiford testified that guards were taught to hate prisoners. Other correctional experts who testified said more money was needed to improve prison conditions and to train and pay guards.

The Senate Judiciary Subcommittee on Penitentiaries held hearings May 18-20 on a bill (S 662) providing for a series of demonstration correctional programs to serve as models for prison improvement. The purpose of the bill won general support from witnesses, but the administration urged that the programs be integrated into the Law Enforcement Assistance Administration.

1972

Congress in 1972 enacted little major anticrime legislation, perhaps taking its cue from the President, who requested very little. The administration appeared to believe that money for local law enforcement was the answer to swelling crime statistics, and Congress agreed by increasing the Law Enforcement Assistance Administration's budget to a record high of $850-million.

Congress did clear two bills of limited significance: a two-year extension of the 1968 juvenile delinquency act with direct grants to localities and another that set severe penalties for harming or kidnapping foreign officials or guests.

Three important bills failed to gain congressional approval. One, an anti-hijacking bill supported in part by the administration, came close to clearance, but conferees could not agree on a final version. The bill would have implemented an international convention against airplane hijackings by providing stiff penalties for air pirates—as the administration wanted—but it also called for an air transport security force at U.S. airports—which the Transportation Department opposed.

FBI Under Attack

The FBI and its director, J. Edgar Hoover, came under some of the most intense criticism from Congress in 1971 that either had ever experienced. The assault coincided with the general dissatisfaction felt for many years by civil rights and anti-war groups against the bureau and Hoover.

House Majority Leader Hale Boggs (D La.) charged April 5 that the FBI had tapped his telephone, although he never conclusively proved his charge. Senate Majority Leader Mike Mansfield (D Mont.) said the bureau had acted improperly in its electronic surveillance of Rep. John Dowdy (D Texas) during a bribery investigation, and called for a congressional review of its activities. (*Dowdy case, chapter on Congress*)

Sen. Edmund S. Muskie (D Maine) charged April 14 that the FBI conducted surveillance at Earth Day rallies in 1970, including one where he spoke. "Is there any political activity in the country which the FBI doesn't consider a legitimate subject for watching?," he asked.

Rep. Henry Reuss (D Wis.) said the bureau had listed his daughter as a former member of the leftist Students for a Democratic Society (SDS), and Sen. George McGovern (D S.D.) charged April 19 that Hoover tried unsuccessfully to sabotage the career of a Trans World Airlines pilot who had criticized FBI attempts to prevent an aircraft hijacking.

Hoover and the bureau were staunchly defended by other members of Congress and the administration. But his age (77), his years as director (47), embarrassment over the theft of files from the FBI's Media, Pa., office, high administrative shakeups and seemingly endless surveillance practices all combined to increase the tempo of attack on the previously immune director and bureau.

A Senate-approved bill providing aid to innocent victims of crime and injured police and firemen, plus survivors' benefits for families of public safety officers killed in the line of duty, was not acted on by the House. Another Senate-passed measure, outlawing the sale and distribution of cheap handguns, also failed to gain House action before adjournment.

Congressional activity in the federal law enforcement field was highlighted by a non-legislative request from the President—the nomination of Richard G. Kleindienst as attorney general. For nearly four months the Senate Judiciary Committee tangled with itself and witnesses with failing memories over allegations that the Justice Department allowed a settlement of an antitrust case against the International Telephone and Telegraph Corporation (ITT) in exchange for an ITT contribution to the Republican convention. But in the end the Senate easily confirmed Kleindienst. (*Box, p. 284*)

The death of J. Edgar Hoover May 2, after 47 years as the sole director of the FBI, and his replacement as acting director by a Nixon friend, brought a sigh of relief from opponents of Hoover and the bureau and set the stage for a fight over his permanent successor in 1973. *(Box, p. 280)*

Juvenile Delinquency

Congress in 1972 departed from precedent on juvenile delinquency legislation in two respects: by authorizing direct grants to local agencies and preventive services separate from law enforcement authorities.

These departures were contained in a bill (HR 15635—PL 92-381) amending and extending the Juvenile Delinquency Prevention and Control Act of 1968 (PL 90-445) for two years, to June 30, 1974.

HR 15635 authorized $75-million for each of fiscal 1973-74 and provided for direct grants for youth service programs to state, county, municipal and other public and non-profit private agencies.

The primary focus of the amendments was to develop community-based preventive services separate from those of law enforcement agencies (police and courts) to aid delinquents or persons in danger of becoming delinquents and their families. The services were to be linked to the school system whenever possible.

The major difference between the 1968 act and the 1972 amendments was the direct grants provided in HR 15635. The 1968 act, which was extended for one year in 1971, provided block grants to states for prevention and rehabilitation programs. Congress in 1968 had rejected a Senate bill which would have allowed direct grants much as did HR 15635.

The Juvenile Delinquency Prevention and Control Act of 1968 was designed to provide a broad program of support to state and local governments for rehabilitative and prevention projects, comprehensive planning, personnel training and the development of improved practices and techniques in dealing with juvenile delinquents.

The act was scheduled to expire June 30, 1971, but Congress passed a bill (PL 92-31) extending it for one year and adding several minor provisions to improve its administration. The extension expired June 30, 1972. Authority under provisions of the act was extended temporarily by a continuing resolution (H J Res 1234).

The total authorization under the 1968 legislation for 1969-71 was $150-million, but only $30-million was actually appropriated by Congress during that period.

The House passed HR 15635 July 17 by a 337-12 roll-call vote. The Senate initially passed a similar bill (S 3443), but later took up the House-passed bill and approved it by voice vote July 31.

Provisions. As cleared by Congress, HR 15635:
• Extended the Juvenile Delinquency Prevention and Control Act of 1968 for two years, to June 30, 1974.
• Authorized direct grants to state, county, municipal and other public and non-profit private agencies for planning and executing preventive services.
• Required that the focus of any juvenile delinquency program granted federal money or contracts under the act be on prevention of delinquency and that efforts under the act be tied closely to the school system wherever possible.
• Required that funds made available by Congress be concentrated in areas which had the highest rates of youth crime, youth unemployment and school dropouts.
• Retained authority under the 1968 act for grants to be made for construction of community-based special pur-

pose or innovative types of facilities, but limited the amount to 10 per cent of the available funds.
• Decreased the percentage of the total appropriation which could be made to any one state to 12 per cent from 15 per cent.
• Stated that nothing in the act would infringe upon "the moral and legal rights of parents" of children participating in programs funded under the act.
• Repealed the authority under the 1968 act to fund improved techniques and practices in dealing with juvenile delinquency and the authority to fund rehabilitative programs and state planning, but retained the authority to provide technical assistance and information services.
• Authorized funding under the act at $75-million annually for two years (fiscal 1973-74).

Hijacking Penalties

Increasing congressional concern over international aircraft hijackings was reflected in House and Senate passage of similar bills imposing stiff penalties on skyjackers, but the two chambers could not agree on an identical version before adjournment Oct. 18.

Air hijackings rose steadily in the 1960s, and by 1972 appeared to be almost weekly occurrences, particularly in Europe, the Middle East and the United States. Most hijacked U.S. aircraft were diverted to Cuba. Pilots staged an international strike June 12 to protest inadequate enforcement of anti-hijacking treaties.

A bill (S 2280), passed by both chambers, would have implemented the 1971 Hague Convention for the Suppression of Unlawful Seizures of Aircraft and would have provided harsh penalties for hijackers. The bill also would have authorized the President to impose airline boycotts on nations that violated the Hague convention or aided air pirates.

Two Senate provisions not in the House version of S 2280 were the main roadblocks to conference agreement. One required the screening by metal detectors of all passengers and carry-on luggage at U.S. airports. The other created a consolidated air transportation security force under the Federal Aviation Administration (FAA) to guard U.S. airports against hijackers.

Background. A bill (S 2176—PL 91-449) providing criminal penalties for persons who committed air piracy or other offenses aboard aircraft under U.S. jurisdiction was cleared by Congress Oct. 5, 1970. The measure fulfilled U.S. obligations under the 1963 Tokyo convention on hijacking, which the United States ratified in 1969.

In an effort to strengthen prosecution of hijackers under the Tokyo convention, representatives of 77 nations met at the Hague in December 1970 to consider a treaty drafted by the International Civil Aviation Organization. The convention which resulted obligated signatories to establish jurisdiction over hijackings and to agree to prosecute or extradite offenders in their custody. It was signed Dec. 16 by 50 nations, including the United States and Soviet bloc countries.

The treaty was ratified by the Senate Sept. 8, 1971. S 2280 was submitted by the Transportation Department to fulfill U.S. obligations under the Hague convention.

(Continued on p. 282)

J. Edgar Hoover, 1895-1972: First...

The death of FBI director J. Edgar Hoover May 2, 1972 brought a eulogy from President Nixon and expressions of grief from both friends and critics. It also set the stage for a political fight over his successor and congressional debate on the philosophy of law enforcement and civil liberties.

Hoover, 77, so dominated the bureau during his 47 years as its sole director that the man and the institution merged as one in the public eye. It was difficult to conceive of another person heading it—and therein lay the problem.

Hoover's successor would have to be tough on law and order to satisfy conservatives, yet sensitive to civil liberties issues to gain the support of liberals. A nominee unacceptable to either of the two ideologies would face a Senate confirmation fight that could rival anything ever encountered by a Supreme Court or cabinet appointee.

Controversy over Successor

President Nixon moved immediately to get politics out of the successor issue—at least temporarily—by announcing May 3 that he would not nominate Hoover's replacement until after the Nov. 7 presidential election. At the same time, he ordered the appointment of L. (Louis) Patrick Gray III, a close friend, as acting director.

Gray, 55, was assistant attorney general in charge of the civil division and had been nominated for deputy attorney general. He had not been confirmed for that post, however, because his nomination had been tied to that of Richard G. Kleindienst as attorney general. Kliendienst's confirmation hearings had just ended before the Senate Judiciary Committee April 27. Nixon said he would send the Senate another nomination for deputy attorney general. *(Kleindienst story, p. 284)*

Gray was a career naval officer who retired in 1960 with the rank of captain to help Nixon's first presidential campaign. He practiced law in Connecticut during the 1960s and in 1969 joined the administration as executive assistant to Robert Finch, secretary of health, education and welfare.

Early in 1973, Nixon nominated Gray as FBI director, but the nomination was withdrawn April 5 and Gray resigned as acting director April 26, following press reports that he had destroyed documents relating to the Watergate investigation. William D. Ruckelshaus, administrator of the Environmental Protection Agency, was named to succeed him temporarily as acting director.

Until 1968 the President could have picked the FBI director without Senate confirmation. But Republicans that year were worried that President Johnson would be re-elected and might have a chance to name Hoover's successor, so they succeeded in tacking on a provision to the Omnibus Crime Control and Safe Streets Act calling for Senate confirmation of future directors.

Flood of Tributes

Hoover's death was attributed to "hypertensive cardiovascular disease" by the District of Columbia coroner, Dr. James L. Luke. He said Hoover had been suffering from a heart condition and that death could have been caused by heart failure associated with high blood pressure. No autopsy was performed.

Congress immediately passed a joint resolution ordering that his body lie in state in the Capitol rotunda, an honor usually reserved for presidents, military heroes and members of Congress. He was buried May 4 in Washington, the city of his birth.

Tributes flowed in from friends and critics at the word of his death. President Nixon called him a "legend in his own lifetime" and the "symbol and embodiment of the values he cherished most: courage, patriotism, dedication to his country and a granite-like honesty and integrity."

Former Attorney General Ramsey Clark, who was cool to Hoover and whom the director once called a "jellyfish," said he was saddened to hear of his death. Chief Justice Warren F. Burger said Hoover built the FBI "without impinging on the liberties guaranteed by the Constitution and our traditions."

Recent critics of Hoover and the bureau were generous in their reaction to the news of his death. House Majority Leader Hale Boggs (D La.), who in 1971 accused the FBI of tapping congressmen's telephones, and called for Hoover's retirement, said, "No man served his nation with greater dedication or productivity. He leaves a great name."

Sen. George McGovern (D S.C.), who carried on a running feud with Hoover and the bureau for the prior two years, said, "I am sad at his passing." Sen. Edmund S. Muskie (D Maine), who had accused the FBI of spying on Earth Day rallies in 1970, said, "No one could question his dedication and loyalty to his country."

But not everyone could forget his animosity toward Hoover, especially those who had been prosecuted by the Justice Department after FBI investigations. Dr. Benjamin Spock, who was acquitted of aiding draft resisters, said of Hoover's death, "It's a great relief, especially if his replacement is a man who better understands democratic institutions and the American process."

Rep. Cornelius E. Gallagher (D N.J.), indicted April 7 by the federal government for tax evasion and perjury, said a civilian review board was necessary to "cleanse and purify" the FBI's files, which he said had been used "for political and publicity purposes."

Hoover's Achievements

Hoover was appointed director of the Bureau of Investigation (the FBI's predecessor) Dec. 10, 1924. He served eight presidents of both parties, beginning with Calvin Coolidge, and 16 attorneys general.

His extraordinary length of tenure as director of the bureau enabled him to achieve enormous in-

Director of Federal Bureau of Investigation

fluence and power for himself and the bureau, but there was never a hint of scandal involving either.

He changed the old bureau's image from one of scandal and corruption to a model investigative arm of the federal government. He applied the techniques of science to police work by establishing a modern crime laboratory, a fingerprint file of criminals and the FBI Academy for the training of local policemen.

While Hoover was criticized in later years for his seemingly harsh views on civil liberties, be was one of the few high officials who opposed incarcerating Japanese-Americans during World War II.

Under Hoover, the bureau grew to 19,857 fulltime employees: 8,631 agents and 11,226 clerks. Yet the director resisted suggestions to turn the bureau into a national police force.

Nominally, the bureau was a part of the Justice Department, but Hoover's prestige and skill in handling people enabled him to run the FBI as an autonomous unit. No President and no attorney general dared criticize him publicly.

Part of his power lay in friends on Capitol Hill, whom he could always count on at critical moments to rush to his defense. Rep. John J. Rooney (D N.Y.), whose appropriations subcommittee handled the FBI's budget, never cut the bureau's request.

Critics and Discontent

But it was this enormous power base that seemed to erode his near unanimous support as years went by. Civil rights workers criticized the bureau in the early 1960s for ignoring their complaints about southern law enforcement officials. Civil liberties and anti-war activists accused the bureau of unwarranted spying and electronic eavesdropping.

In addition to the Ramsey Clark "jellyfish" remark, Hoover was criticized for calling the late Rev. Martin Luther King Jr. a "notorious liar" and having his agents release tape recordings and other material on the civil rights leader's alleged sexual indiscretions.

The last few years of his life saw further embarrassments for Hoover, although he weathered them all. In 1970, a newspaper was the first to discover Supreme Court nominee G. Harold Carswell's racist speeach of 1948. FBI files stolen from its Media, Pa., office in 1971 gave details on the bureau's network of informers and its plans to infiltrate black organizations. A hung jury in Harrisburg, Pa., failed to convict seven anti-war activists of cospiring to kidnap presidential aide Henry Kissinger, although Hoover had told Congress of the plot in 1970 before indictments were even sought.

The New York Times reported May 4 that an administration source said President Nixon's chief policy advisers had urged him three times in 1971 to dismiss Hoover. The President reportedly refused each time.

Some thought Hoover might retire in 1974, after 50 years as director and the same year the new FBI building was scheduled to be completed on Pennsylvania Avenue. But Hoover never confirmed this. He said he was happy in his job and would continue as long as his health held out. Nixon directed May 5 that the building be named for him.

Hoover Career Highlights

1895: Born Jan. 1, in Washington, D.C.

1916: Received law degree from George Washington University (took night courses while working as a Library of Congress clerk).

1917: Received L.L.M. from George Washington University; joined Justice Department July 26 as a clerk.

1919: After bombing attempts on the home of the attorney general in June, appointed to head new intelligence division to study subversive activities.

1919-21: Served as special assistant to the attorney general: appointed assistant director of the Bureau of Investigation Aug. 22, 1921.

1924: Appointed acting director May 10 (modern FBI considered born on this date); became director Dec. 10; FBI identification division established.

1932: FBI crime laboratory established: March 1 kidnaping of flyer Charles Lindbergh's son led to enactment June 22 of the Federal Kidnaping Statute giving federal government jurisdiction in kidnaping cases; legislation marked turning point in FBI history.

1932-34: Series of laws enacted to broaden FBI power; agents granted power of arrest and right to bear firearms. During early 1930s numerous FBI arrests or killings of notorious criminals (including John Dillinger July 22, 1934) earned Hoover and bureau popular acclaim.

1935: Bureau's name formally changed to Federal Bureau of Investigation; FBI academy founded.

1936: Hoover personally led May 1 raid that captured gangster Alvin "Old Creepy" Karpis.

1939: President Roosevelt in September gave FBI "primary responsibility for the protection of the internal security of the United States."

1941: FBI captured 33 German agents during weekend of June 28; bureau concentrated on Nazi, fifth column activities during war years.

1946: Atomic Energy Act specified that violations should be investigated by the FBI; emphasis of bureau shifted to Communist activity during 1940s and 1950s.

1958: Received President's award for distinguished service.

1964: House unanimously adopted resolution honoring Hoover on completion of 40 years as FBI director; controversy over eavesdropping led to clash between Hoover and Rev. Martin Luther King Jr.

1965: President Johnson praised Hoover and FBI role in civil rights, crackdown on Ku Klux Klan; Congress enacted law giving FBI responsibility for investigating crimes against a President or vice president; Johnson waived mandatory retirement age of 70 for Hoover.

The bill as introduced would have amended the Federal Aviation Act of 1958 (PL 85-726) to include under U.S. jurisdiction offenses committed by foreign nationals during international flights when the hijackers were later found in the United States. It would have provided a penalty of at least 20 years in prison for persons convicted of such offenses. The new criminal provisions would not have applied to U.S. domestic hijackings or those that occurred within a foreign country; such seizures were not offenses covered by the Hague convention. *(1958 act, Congress and the Nation, Vol. I, p. 541; 1970, 1971 action, p. 276, 278)*

Congressional Action. The Senate passed an amended version of S 2280 Sept. 21 by a 75-1 roll-call vote. As amended by the Senate, the bill not only implemented the Hague convention, but also required the screening by metal detectors of all passengers and carry-on luggage at U.S. airports, created an air transportation security force to guard U.S. airports against hijackers, allowed the President to suspend service to nations that harbored terrorists who hijacked airplanes, allowed reduced fares for certain classes of citizens and called for penalties ranging from 20 years in prison to death for convicted hijackers.

Harold E. Hughes (D Iowa), saying he objected to the death penalty, cast the lone Senate vote against S 2280. The administration opposed the airport security force and the presidential sanctions against nations that harbored terrorists.

During Senate debate on the bill, Howard W. Cannon (D Nev.), chairman of the Commerce Subcommittee on Aviation, dismissed State Department objections to the sanctions.

The simple threat of a U.S. boycott "should have a salutary effect" on nations that did not abide by the Hague convention, he said. Warren G. Magnuson (D Wash.), seconded Cannon's view, singling out France as one of the nations that was "dilly-dallying about coming to some agreement" on halting international air piracy.

A Cannon amendment setting up the electronic screening requirement and the airport security force was approved by voice vote. Another amendment, introduced by Jacob J. Javits (R N.Y.) and John V. Tunney (D Calif.), allowing the President to cut off service to countries harboring groups that seized aircraft to further their aims, was approved by voice vote.

The Javits-Tunney amendment was aimed at Middle East countries which were used as training grounds and havens by Arab terrorists opposed to Israel.

The House approved its somewhat narrower bill (HR 16191) Oct. 2 by a 354-2 recorded teller vote. Philip Burton (D Calif.) and John Conyers (D Mich.), who objected to the death penalty for hijackers, voted against it.

Conferees reported the bill in disagreement Oct. 13.

Other Action. The Senate Sept. 21 passed an administration-requested bill (S 2567) making it unlawful to threaten to destroy or hijack an aircraft with the apparent determination to carry out the threat. The purpose of the bill was to facilitate prosecution of air piracy or threatened air piracy and other crimes committed aboard aircraft.

The Judiciary Committee, in its report on the bill, said actual attempts to hijack aircraft were punishable under existing laws, but threats to do so were not.

The bill made such threats punishable by fines of up to $5,000, five years in prison, or both.

The bill also set the same penalties for persons who took part in hijack hoaxes. The House did not act on the measure.

Omnibus Crime Victims Bill

Congress failed to complete action on a five-part bill (HR 8389) that would have provided aid for crime victims. As passed by the House in 1971, HR 8389 provided for narcotics treatment programs in state and local prisons and jails. The Senate, in passing HR 8389 on Sept. 18, 1972, added to it four separate Senate-passed bills relating to crime victims. The measure was never sent to conference and died at the end of the 92nd Congress.

As passed by the Senate, the omnibus bill consisted of:

• S 750—Compensating innocent victims of violent crime, or their survivors, and those who intervened to prevent such crime. The Senate passed S 750 Sept. 18.

• S 33—Authorizing the U.S. attorney general to provide a group life insurance program for state and local public safety officers. Passed Sept. 18.

• S 2087—Providing cash benefits to survivors of public safety officers killed in the line of duty or to the officer himself if he was dismembered. Passed Sept. 5.

• S 16—Strengthening the civil remedies for victims of racketeering. Passed Sept. 5.

• HR 8389, plus amendments, providing for drug treatment programs at state and local prisons. This bill had been passed separately by the House in 1971. *(Health chapter)*

The Senate version of HR 8389 also made it a federal crime to assault or kill a state or local public safety officer, and extended the Omnibus Crime Control and Safe Streets Act of 1968 (PL 90-351) for one year, to June 30, 1974. All the bills except S 16 amended the 1968 act.

Although there was no further congressional action on the omnibus bill, the House did pass on Oct. 11 an amended version of S 2087. That bill also died when the House failed to act on the conference report, which was filed Oct. 17.

Gun Control

The attempted assassination of Alabama Gov. George C. Wallace in mid-May gave new impetus to the movement for controlling the manufacture, sale and distribution of guns.

The assassinations of Sen. Robert F. Kennedy (D N.Y.) and civil rights leader Rev. Martin Luther King Jr. in 1968 aided in passing two gun control bills that year, but subsequent attempts to strengthen or weaken those acts were unsuccessful. *(1970-71 chronology)*

The Senate Aug. 9, after three days of debate on 14 amendments, approved, 68-25, a bill (S 2507) outlawing the sale of cheap, domestically produced handguns commonly called "Saturday night specials."

Amendments aimed at seriously weakening or strengthening the bill as it was reported from the Judiciary Committee were beaten.

Although passage of the bill was a defeat for the gun lobby, it did manage to attach two amendments it had sought since passage of the Gun Control Act of 1968 (PL 90-618). Each weakened the 1968 act, one by eliminating record-keeping requirements for .22-caliber rimfire ammunition; the other by allowing family members in different states to transfer long guns among themselves without going through licensed gun dealers.

Hearings were held in the House on gun control but no bill was reported. President Nixon said June 29 he would sign a bill outlawing cheap handguns.

Background. S 2507 was introduced by Birch Bayh (D Ind.), chairman of the Subcommittee on Juvenile Delinquency. It was designed to plug a loophole in the 1968 act, which banned the importation of cheap handguns, but not of their parts, thus allowing domestic arms manufacturers to import the parts and assemble the guns in the United States.

The 1968 act reduced imports of such weapons from 1,239,930 in 1968 to 279,536 in 1970. But domestically produced, cheap handguns were estimated at 1 million in 1970 versus 60,000 in 1968.

And, increasingly, handguns were becoming the major weapon in criminal offenses. According to FBI statistics, handguns were used in 52 per cent of murders committed in 1970, an increase from 44 per cent in 1966. Of 126 policemen killed in 1971, 94 were struck down by bullets from handguns.

The subcommittee found a unanimity of opinion that such cheap handguns, unsuited for any sporting purpose, should be banned, although there was disagreement on what standards should be used to define these weapons. Gun lobby and administration witnesses preferred standards of safety and reliability, while others spoke for the "sporting purposes" test contained in the 1968 act.

That test, created by an advisory panel appointed by the secretary of the treasury, involved a point system based on criteria of size, frame construction, weight, caliber, safety features and miscellaneous equipment. A weapon's failure to pass the test indicated it was not suitable for sporting purposes, and was, therefore, banned from importation.

Senate Action. Bill Brock (R Tenn.) offered the amendment, adopted 71-21, deleting the record-keeping requirements for .22 caliber rimfire ammunition contained in the 1968 Gun Control Act. The amendment had been sought by ammunition dealers and users since 1968. The act required dealers to keep records of the name, age and address of purchasers of the specific ammunition along with the date of sale and name of manufacturer. Brock termed the requirements "burdensome, time-consuming and costly."

The amendment allowing family members to transfer sporting shotguns and rifles interstate among themselves, introduced by Peter H. Dominick (R Colo.), was adopted 89-4. The 1968 act required such transfers to be handled by a licensed gun dealer.

Amendments offered by Philip A. Hart (D Mich.), Edward M. Kennedy (D Mass.) and Adlai E. Stevenson III (D Ill.), to strengthen the bill by outlawing possession of handguns or requiring owners to register them, were overwhelmingly defeated.

An amendment offered by Ted Stevens (R Alaska), which would have substituted standards of safety and reliability for sporting purpose as the tests of whether a gun was a Saturday night special, was defeated, 35-57. It generally was considered a weakening amendment.

House Hearings. House Judiciary Subcommittee No. 5 held hearings in June on a bill (HR 8828) regulating the manufacture, distribution and possession of firearms.

Mayors, governors and police officials supported strong gun control measures, particularly for handguns. Maryland Gov. Marvin Mandel, whose state had a gun control law, said federal controls were needed because states were not empowered to inspect the mails or interfere with interstate commerce.

Administration spokesmen opposed federal legislation, saying gun control was a state responsibility because what was appropriate for one area of the country might not be good for another. The National Rifle Association testified that stiffer penalties for people who used guns in crime would help more than stronger gun control laws.

Other Legislation

DEATH PENALTY. House Judiciary Subcommittee No. 3 held hearings in March and May on capital punishment. There were seven bills before the subcommittee: four would have abolished the death penalty for 13 federal crimes which permitted it, while three would have allowed a two-year moratorium on executions in federal and state prison systems so Congress could consider whether to abolish capital punishment.

As the hearings were being held, almost 600 persons were under the death sentence in the United States, two of them in the federal system. Nine states had outlawed capital punishment and five had limited it to a few crimes. The last execution took place in 1967. Meanwhile, states waited to see what the Supreme Court would do with several capital punishment cases working their way to it.

The court ruled June 29, in a 5-4 decision, that capital punishment as imposed in the United States was unconstitutional. The California Supreme Court Feb. 18 outlawed the state's death penalty, ruling that executions were cruel and unusual punishment in violation of the state's constitution. *(Supreme Court decision, Supreme Court chapter)*

Opponents of the death penalty testified that it was imposed in a racially discriminatory manner. Jack Greenberg, director-counsel of the Legal Defense and Educational Fund of the National Association for the Advancement of Colored People (NAACP), said statistics showed that of the 455 persons executed for rape since 1930, 405 were black. Of the 77 men on death rows in 10 southern states, 66 were black, Greenberg said.

Other capital punishment opponents, including lawyers and criminologists, charged that it was no deterrent to crime and possibly unconstitutional.

The administration and law enforcement representatives opposed the bills before the committee. Henry E. Peterson, assistant attorney general, said the death penalty was a deterrent in some situations, such as premeditated murder. "It is the department's position that if the threat of the death penalty deters the killing of innocent victims even to a limited extent, its retention is justified," Peterson said.

(Continued on p. 286)

Dispute Over ITT Contribution to Republicans Failed...

President Nixon's 1972 nomination of Richard G. Kleindienst as attorney general appeared set for easy sailing through the Senate until a storm of controversy broke over the nominee's role in the Justice Department's 1971 settlement of an antitrust case against International Telephone and Telegraph Corporation (ITT).

The Senate finally confirmed the nomination June 8, on a **64-19 key roll-call vote**, following what were described as "the longest confirmation hearings" in the history of the Senate. Over Republican protests, Democratic senators prolonged the hearings in an unsuccessful effort to substantiate charges, first aired by syndicated columnist Jack Anderson, that Kleindienst had lied in disclaiming any role in the case and that the settlement had been influenced by an ITT pledge to contribute to the 1972 Republican convention.

Kleindienst's tenure as attorney general was brief. He resigned April 30, 1973, citing "close personal and professional associations" with persons who were implicated in the unfolding Watergate scandal.

ITT Settlement

The Justice Department in 1969 attempted to force ITT to divest itself of the Canteen Corporation (vending machines), Grinnell Corporation (manufacturing) and the Hartford Fire Insurance Corporation through an antitrust lawsuit. If successful, it would have been the biggest divestiture in antitrust history.

In July 1971, however, the department announced it had reached an out-of-court settlement with ITT whereby the huge conglomerate would voluntarily give up Grinnell and Canteen and other smaller acquisitions in exchange for keeping Hartford.

The department gave up one of its prime reasons for the suit: to get a Supreme Court ruling on the applicability of the Clayton Antitrust Act to conglomerate-type mergers.

In December 1971, it was reported that an ITT subsidiary, the Sheraton Corporation of America, had pledged $400,000 to help support costs of the 1972 Republican national convention, then scheduled to be held in San Diego, Calif. The convention ultimately was transferred to Miami.

Anderson Charges

Anderson, in a March 1 column, said Kleindienst had written Lawrence O'Brien, Democratic national chairman, Dec. 13, 1971, saying the ITT settlement had been "handled and negotiated exclusively" by Richard W. McLaren, then head of Justice's antitrust division.

Kleindienst said in the letter that the only role he had played was to approve McLaren's settlement with ITT lawyers.

It was on the basis of those statements in the letter to O'Brien that Anderson charged Kleindienst with lying. Anderson said the nominee "held roughly half a dozen secret meetings" on the case with a director of ITT before settlement.

The ITT director was identified by Anderson as Felix Rohatyn, a New York financier.

Anderson also charged that former Attorney General John Mitchell helped arrange the settlement with Dita Beard, ITT's Washington lobbyist.

According to Anderson, Beard met with Mitchell during the 1971 Kentucky Derby festivities at the governor's mansion in Louisville, where they arranged the settlement in exchange for a promise of a $400,000 contribution to the Republican convention.

Anderson based his charges on a purported June 25, 1971 memorandum from Beard to W.R. Merriam, ITT's Washington manager, in which she urged that the convention deal be kept secret. "John Mitchell has certainly kept it on the higher level only, we should be able to do the same," the memo said.

Elsewhere it said:

"I am convinced, because of several conversations with Louie (identified by Anderson as former Kentucky Gov. Louie Nunn) re Mitchell, that our noble commitment has gone a long way toward our negotiations on the mergers eventually coming out as Hal (Harold Geneen, ITT president) wants them. Certainly the President has told Mitchell to see that things are worked out fairly. It is still only antitrust chief McLaren's mickeymouse we are suffering.

"If it gets too much publicity, you can believe our negotiations with Justice will wind up shot down. Mitchell is definitely helping us, but cannot let it be known. Please destroy this, huh?"

The memo also left the impression that White House aide H.R. Haldeman, Lt. Gov. Edward Reinecke of California and President Nixon were knowledgeable about the alleged deal, although it was not explicit on that point.

Kleindienst Hearings

Prior to publication of the Anderson charges, Kleindienst—who had served as deputy attorney general since 1969 and had a reputation as an ideological conservative—had appeared virtually assured of confirmation. President Nixon nominated him Feb. 15 to succeed Mitchell, who was resigning to head Nixon's re-election campaign. Following two days of hearings, the Senate Judiciary Committee unanimously reported the nomination Feb. 29. Kleindienst became acting attorney general upon Mitchell's resignation March 1.

However, the Judiciary Committee reopened its hearings March 2 at Kleindienst's request, to give him an opportunity to explain his role in the ITT settlement.

The lengthy hearings that followed brought little clarification. Witnesses' testimony was marked by frequent contradictions, inconsistencies and lapses of memory. The committee voted unanimously on June 27 to refer the hearing record to the Justice Department to determine whether any witness had committed perjury.

The authenticity of the Beard memorandum published by Anderson remained in dispute. ITT represen-

...to Block Kleindienst Confirmation as Attorney General

tatives branded it a fraud. Brit Hume, an associate of Anderson, said Beard told him she wrote the memo.

Beard, according to Hume, said ITT security people came down from New York and used a document shredder to destroy other papers in the Washington office to keep them from being subpoenaed. ITT denied that the document shredding was an attempt to frustrate the committee investigation.

Beard, who dropped out of sight when the controversy erupted, was found and interviewed by a special subcommittee in a Denver osteopathic hospital where she was undergoing treatment for a heart ailment. She denied having written portions of the memo linking the ITT settlement with the convention pledge. She said she had written a memo on the convention offer at Merriam's request. Her testimony conflicted with that of Merriam, who said he never received such a memo. Beard's testimony was cut short by her doctor when she suffered an apparent heart seizure.

Earlier in the hearings, another of Beard's doctors, Victor L. Liszka, said she was suffering from periodic "distorted and irrational" behavior when she wrote the memo published by Anderson. Anderson charged that ITT was trying to discredit Beard by painting her "as a crackpot and a drunk."

Mitchell said he had repulsed Beard's efforts to discuss the ITT case with him, a point upon which he was supported by Nunn. Mitchell denied that he had taken any part in the case or that he knew about the Sheraton pledge, but both denials were challenged.

Kleindienst denied any substantive role in the negotiations that led to the ITT settlement, but he acknowledged that he had brought together ITT director Felix Rohatyn and McLaren, the official who negotiated the settlement. Their meeting set in motion the sequence of events that led to the settlement. Kleindienst also acknowledged that he had had a number of conversations about the case with ITT representatives and administration officials.

McLaren, who resigned from the Justice Department Feb. 2 to accept an appointment as a federal district judge, acknowledged that he had asked White House aide Peter M. Flanigan to obtain the services of Richard J. Ramsden, a New York financial consultant, who made an assessment of the economic effects of the antitrust suit. McLaren, who had a reputation as a vigorous trust-buster, had initiated the suit in 1969. He defended the out-of-court settlement on grounds that "we obtained a very substantial divestiture" and "success was far from certain" in the courts.

Harold S. Geneen, ITT president, said ITT had offered a $200,000, not $400,000, guarantee for the convention. He described the pledge as a "normal promotional expense" tied to the opening of a new Sheraton hotel in San Diego. It had no connection with the antitrust settlement, he said.

The White House first invoked the claim of executive privilege to keep Flanigan from testifying. Flanigan finally agreed to appear but limited his testimony to narrow areas of questioning. He said he had acted as a "conduit" for the Justice Department in obtaining Ramsden's services but had not attempted to influence Ramsden's report. Ramsden said Flanigan gave him a report prepared by ITT on the effects of the suit but did not try to influence his views. Ramsden's report, which McLaren said he found "persuasive," supported ITT's arguments.

Nomination Approved

After 22 days of hearings, the Judiciary Committee voted 11-4 on April 27 to reconfirm its prior recommendation of Kleindienst. The majority found the nominee innocent of illegal or improper action in the ITT settlement and found no connection between the settlement and the convention pledge.

The Senate confirmed Kleindienst's nomination June 8, by a **64-19 key roll-call vote**. All dissenting votes were cast by Democrats.

The action followed seven days of desultory debate, in which Republicans charged that the Democrats had prolonged the hearings in an attempt to embarrass the administration. Democrats countered that the Senate had not had a chance to examine all the relevant facts because the administration barred certain documents from the committee and prevented testimony from some White House aides.

Kleindienst Resignation

Kleindienst submitted his resignation to President Nixon on April 30, 1973. He was apparently an innocent victim of the Watergate scandal which implicated, as he noted in his letter of resignation, many persons with whom he had been closely associated.

"Fair and impartial enforcement of the law requires," wrote Kleindienst to Nixon, "that a person who has not had such intimate relationships be the attorney general." Kleindienst, national director of field operations for the 1968 Nixon campaign, had worked then and later with John N. Mitchell, campaign manager; John D. Ehrlichman, campaign "tour director," and H. R. Haldeman, Nixon's personal chief of staff. Kleindienst, after the election, had served under Mitchell as deputy attorney general from early 1969 until Mitchell's resignation to head the 1972 campaign early in 1972. Also at the Justice Department, Kleindienst had worked with John W. Dean III, who spent a year and a half as one of Kleindienst's associates before moving over to the post of White House counsel.

Post-election rumors in 1972 pointed to Kleindienst as one of the first cabinet members whose resignation would be accepted. The basis for the supposition was the feeling that the Nixon administration had been badly embarrassed by the airing of the ITT charges. But intervention by Kleindienst's old friend and patron, Sen. Barry Goldwater (R Ariz.), apparently saved Kleindienst his post—for a time. It was expected, nevertheless, that Kleindienst would resign during 1973.

JUVENILE JUSTICE. The House April 18 passed a bill (HR 45) creating an Institute for the Continuing Studies of Juvenile Justice to collect data and train personnel in the juvenile justice area. The same bill had been defeated in the House on Dec. 6, 1971. The Senate Judiciary Subcommittee on Juvenile Delinquency held hearings on a similar bill (S 1428), but took no further action. The administration opposed the bills.

The Senate July 31 passed a bill (S 2829) authorizing the Department of Health, Education and Welfare to assist local groups in giving shelter and care to runaway youngsters. The bill, which authorized $30-million for fiscal 1973-75, would have required that participating shelters provide medical and psychological care and counseling in addition to living quarters for runaways. The House did not act on the bill.

FOREIGN OFFICIALS. Congress Oct. 11 cleared a bill (HR 15883—PL 92-539) making murder, manslaughter or kidnaping of foreign officials and their families, or official foreign guests, punishable under federal law, with life imprisonment for first-degree murder.

The bill was designed to deter increasing harassment of and violence against foreign officials, particularly those from the Soviet Union and Middle East nations. The House and Senate overwhelmingly approved the bill.

In addition to making the federal kidnaping law apply specifically to foreign officials, the bill formally abolished the death penalty for kidnaping as permitted under the U.S. Code. The latter was a formality, because the Supreme Court effectively overturned the death penalty for kidnaping in a 1968 case.

The bill also made it a federal offense to willfully damage property in the United States owned by foreign governments and made it unlawful to demonstrate within 100 feet of a foreign government's building located outside the District of Columbia. D.C. law already had a 500-foot demonstration limit.

A Senate provision establishing a grievance procedure for State Department personnel was dropped from the bill during Senate debate under pressure from the Nixon administration. The administration approved the criminal sanctions in the bill.

PAROLE. House Judiciary Subcommittee No. 3 and the Senate Judiciary Subcommittee on National Penitentiaries held hearings on parole reform. Members of the U.S. parole board testified that it was overworked and understaffed. Critics charged that the board reached decisions on parole applications after only a 10- or 15-minute interview with prisoners and that the applicants were not represented by counsel or told why parole was denied. Administration witnesses opposed a bill that would have established an independent federal parole board and created minimum standards for state and local parole processes.

PENAL REFORM. The Senate Judiciary Subcommittee on National Penitentiaries held hearings in June and July on prison reform. Norman A. Carlson, director of the Federal Bureau of Prisons, testified that the "most critical" problems with prisons were their age (many close to 75 years) and overcrowding. James R. Hoffa, former Teamster Union president who recently had been released from the Lewisburg (Pa.) federal penitentiary, presented a list of 26 suggestions for prison improvement, ranging from limits on inmate population to liberalized dress and haircut regulations.

CRIMINAL CODE. The Senate Judiciary Subcommittee on Criminal Laws held hearings in May on a proposed new federal code. Witnesses urged stiffer penalties for white-collar criminals, opposed proposed espionage laws, urged experiments in legalizing heroin and said police brutality should be made a crime.

POSTAL MONEY ORDERS. Congress overwhelmingly approved legislation (HR 9222—PL 92-430) making it a crime to use or possess stolen postal money orders and money order imprinting machines. The Senate report on the bill said more than 78,000 postal money orders were stolen in fiscal 1970, and that 4,868 eventually were fraudulently cashed at a total value of $450,000.

Chapter 5—Federal Judiciary

Key Votes

In this chapter, key roll-call votes are shown in bold-face type. The party breakdown on each of these votes and the position taken by each member of Congress may be found in the key vote charts which appear in the appendix to this book.

Federal Judiciary

The Supreme Court in 1972 looked quite different from the Supreme Court of early 1969. Gone was Chief Justice Earl Warren, the towering figure who had led the court longer than any other man in the century, whose name had become a synonym for the rulings affirming the rights of black citizens, the right of each citizen to an equal vote, and the rights of suspected criminals. In that center seat on the bench sat a new white-maned chief justice, Warren Earl Burger, a conservative appeals court judge selected by President Nixon to lead the court back to "interpreting...not making law."

Departed also from the bench as it was in 1969 were the articulate Abe Fortas, and two veteran justices—Hugo L. Black, fierce champion of First Amendment rights, and John M. Harlan, the court's conservative conscience. Now closer to the center of the redesigned bench as senior justices sat William O. Douglas, placed there by Roosevelt; Eisenhower nominees William J. Brennan Jr. and Potter Stewart; Kennedy choice Byron R. White, and Johnson nominee Thurgood Marshall.

Toward the ends of the now-curving bench (remodeled in the summer of 1972) sat the bespectacled Harry A. Blackmun, the quiet appeals court judge finally approved by the Senate to fill the Fortas seat; Virginia lawyer and former American Bar Association president Lewis F. Powell Jr. filling the "southern" seat held for 34 years by Black; and, in the Harlan seat, William H. Rehnquist, youngest and most conservative of the justices.

In June 1968 Warren had informed Johnson of his desire to retire as soon as a successor could be confirmed. But his departure was delayed for a year when the Senate, reacting to charges of "cronyism" and questionable extra-judicial activities, some of which involved the generally unpopular outgoing administration, refused to confirm Fortas, whom Johnson had chosen to promote to chief justice.

By a wry twist of fate Fortas left the court before Warren, the first justice in history to resign under charges of misconduct. *Life* magazine early in May 1969 published reports that Fortas, during his first year on the court, had received the first of what were to be annual fees of $20,000 from the family foundation of a wealthy industrialist convicted of violating federal securities laws. Demands for Fortas' resignation followed immediately, coming most loudly from the conservative wing of Congress.

Denying any wrongdoing and stating that the fee in question had been returned and the arrangement terminated, Fortas resigned on May 14, hoping to quiet the controversy and enable the court to "proceed with its work without the harassment of debate concerning one of its members." But his seat remained vacant for more than a year: the legacy of bitterness remaining created a difficult atmosphere for the nomination of any possible successor.

As the court labored through Burger's first term—October 1969 to June 1970—with only eight members, its image was further dimmed during two painful and unsuccessful confirmation fights.

Soft-spoken Clement F. Haynsworth, a wealthy South Carolinian serving as chief judge of the court of appeals, 4th circuit, was named as Nixon's nominee for the Fortas seat in mid-August 1969. Still stinging from the criticism which had forced Fortas to resign, liberal members of the Senate attacked Haynsworth as "lacking in ethical sensitivity," questioning his participation in certain decisions involving parties in which he had some indirect financial interest. In November the Senate denied him confirmation, the first time in nearly 40 years that a Supreme Court nominee had been rejected by the Senate.

In January 1970 the second nominee for the Fortas seat was named, G. Harrold Carswell, a Floridian sitting as a judge on the court of appeals, 5th circuit. Criticism of his views as segregationist and of his ability as "mediocre," led to a Senate vote in April refusing him confirmation. Not since 1894 had a President had two Supreme Court nominees rejected outright.

A few days after the rejection of Carswell, Nixon named Blackmun to the empty seat. A respected member of the court of appeals, 8th circuit, a long-time friend of Burger, a fellow Minnesotan, and a specialist in medical law, Blackmun won quick approval from the Senate.

But a cycle of reaction appeared to be in motion: conservatives in Congress retaliated to the rejection of Carswell by calling for the impeachment of Douglas, who had apparently offended as many people by his liberal lifestyle as by his liberal views. But like an earlier removal effort, the 1970 impeachment move died young.

Just before the opening of its 1971-1972 term, predictions that age and illness would bring further changes in the court came true: Black, 85, resigned in mid-September and died within days; Harlan, 72, resigned a few days after Black and died at the end of the year.

To fill the gaping holes left by the departure of these two—whose total service on the court amounted to more than half a century—Nixon in October nominated Powell and Rehnquist. Never in doubt, Powell's confirmation was delayed by being linked to the more controversial Rehnquist nomination. But despite criticism of Rehnquist's personal views and those he had expressed as the administration's advocate to Congress during his years as assistant attorney general, both men were confirmed in December 1971.

Supreme Court Personnel

Following is a summary of changes in Supreme Court membership during the years 1969-72, with details on resignations, nominations and controversies over Senate confirmation.

Burger: A New Chief Justice

A judicial epoch of unprecedented impact upon the life of the average American ended on the morning of June 23, 1969. Behind the high Supreme Court bench, with President Richard Nixon watching, retiring Chief Justice Earl Warren administered the oath of his office to Warren Earl Burger, who became the nation's fifteenth chief justice. Warren had just adjourned the court's 1968 term, the sixteenth over which he had presided.

With the retirement of Warren, the California governor-turned-jurist who led the court longer than any other man in the century, an era ended. Led by Warren, the court had issued a series of landmark rulings beginning with its 1954 decision that it was unconstitutional for states to require that black and white children attend separate schools.

"Impeach Earl Warren" became a conservative by-word, emblazoned on billboards and bumpers, signaling a citizen's resentment of the decisions which outlawed school segregation or barred official school prayers or spelled out the rights of persons accused of crimes or laid down the rules of "one man, one vote" for drawing legislative district lines. *(Box on decisions, p. 291)*

Among the critics of the court's rulings was Richard Nixon, who made an unprecedented presidential visit to the Supreme Court on June 23 for the inauguration of his nominee as chief justice. During his 1968 campaign he had accused the Warren court of hamstringing law enforcement officials by its decisions safeguarding the rights of accused persons. He had promised to change the court's direction by any appointments he might make to fill its vacancies.

Yet on Warren's retirement Nixon praised Warren the man as an "example of humanity," symbolizing in his person the integrity, fairness and dignity of the nation's highest court. "His example," said Nixon, "as the chief law official of this country, has helped to keep America on the path of continuity and change, which is so essential for our progress."

Burger Record. In accord with his campaign statements describing the qualifications of the men he would appoint to the Supreme Court, Nixon named as the new chief justice a man known in legal circles for his conservative views on questions of criminal law. Burger, 61, and since 1956 a judge on the court of appeals for the District of Columbia circuit, had also criticized Warren court rulings: "This seeming anxiety of judges to protect every accused person from every consequence of his voluntary utterances is giving rise to myriad rules, subrules, variations, and exceptions which even the most alert and sophisticated lawyers and judges are taxed to follow. Each time judges add nuances to these 'rules' we make it less likely that any police officer will be able to follow the guidelines we lay down."

A native of Minnesota, Burger had worked his way through school and then practiced law for 22 years. First involved in national politics as a supporter of Minnesota Gov. Harold E. Stassen's 1948 bid for the Republican presidential nomination, Burger came to Washington to serve as assistant attorney general, civil division, in 1953. President Eisenhower appointed him from that post to the court of appeals in 1956.

More than a year before the Burger swearing-in, Chief Justice Warren had informed President Johnson that he would retire whenever his successor was confirmed. Johnson had quickly nominated his longtime friend and adviser, Associate Justice Abe Fortas, as Warren's successor. But the Senate, led by Republicans and conservative Democrats, filibustered the nomination, taking the opportunity to attack the decisions of the Warren court and to launch charges of 'cronyism' at the nomination. The Senate failed to invoke cloture to end debate on the nomination; Fortas asked the President to withdraw the nomination to avoid further attack on the court, and the President did so early in October 1968. In May of 1969 Fortas resigned from the court amid controversy over his off-the-bench activities. *(Story p. 292)*

A week after the Fortas resignation, President Nixon announced his nomination of Burger, then little-known outside of judicial and legal circles, on May 21. During the controversy surrounding the Fortas resignation various senators pledged that all future court nominations would be carefully scrutinized. But the Senate Judiciary Committee unanimously reported the Burger nomination on June 3 and the full Senate confirmed the nomination on June 9. The confirmation vote was 74-3; the three dissenters were Eugene McCarthy (D Minn.), Stephen Young (D Ohio) and Gaylord Nelson (D Wis.).

Burger Views. Excerpts from Burger's opinions written before his move to the Supreme Court added another dimension to the description of "strict constructionist"—the label selected by Nixon to depict his choice for what he termed "the most important nomination that a President...makes."

Burger was at times blunt, reserving some of his most severe criticism for members of the legal profession. Solidly committed to the constitutional concept of three coequal branches of government, he was anxious to guard against what he deemed judicial excess in any forum, including lower courts.

His statements included the following:

Court Conduct. "The government may prosecute vigorously, zealously with hard blows if the facts warrant, for a criminal trial is not a minuet. Nevertheless, there are standards which a government counsel should meet to uphold the dignity of the government. The language of the prosecutor here was hardly in keeping with what the courts and the public expect of its representatives." *(Taylor v. U.S., 1969)*

Rights of Accused Persons. "Each time judges add nuances to these 'rules' we make it less likely that any police officer will be able to follow the guidelines we lay down. We are approaching the predicament of the centipede on the fly paper—each time one leg is placed to give support for relief of a leg already 'stuck,' another becomes captive and soon all are securely immobilized. Like the hapless centipede on the flypaper, our efforts to extricate ourselves from this self-imposed dilemma will, if we keep it up, soon have all of us immobilized." *(Frazier v. U.S., 1969)*

The Warren Court Record: Activism and Controversy

Under the leadership of Earl Warren, the Supreme Court was more activist and more controversial than at any other time in the nation's history.

Liberalism and a willingness to deal with questions previously untouched by the high court and traditionally the domain only of Congress or the presidency made the Warren Court a target of unrelenting criticism.

The court ventured into the touchy areas of racial discrimination, religion, rights of accused persons and political redistricting. As such, it became a catalyst for social and political change.

The first year Earl Warren was chief justice of the United States, the court handed down its unanimous landmark decision *(Brown v. Board of Education of Topeka, 1954)* reversing the long-held "separate but equal" doctrine and declaring that racially segregated schools were unconstitutional and "inherently unequal." This was followed in 1955 by the second *Brown* decision which advised local school officials to proceed "with all deliberate speed" to end segregated school systems.

School segregation was only the first of a series of civil rights controversies with which the court dealt.

In several voting rights cases, the court declared unconstitutional the drawing of political districts along racial lines *(Gomillion v. Lightfoot, 1960)*, the requirement that a candidate's race be noted on a ballot *(Anderson v. Martin, 1964)* and the collection of poll taxes in state elections *(Harper v. Virginia State Board of Elections, 1966)*.

The court in 1967 struck down state antimiscegenation laws *(Loving v. Virginia)* and in 1968 held that a century-old Civil Rights Act (1866) banned all racial discrimination, public or private, in the sale or rental of property *(Jones v. Mayer)*.

Criminal Due Process. The Warren Court spelled out in a series of rulings the rights of persons accused or suspected of crimes, restricting law enforcement officers to what it determined to be constitutional methods of obtaining evidence against an accused.

The court declared that states must supply indigent defendants with counsel *(Gideon v. Wainwright, 1963)*, that juvenile offenders had the same basic constitutional rights as adult defendants *(In Re Gault, 1967)* and that the right of jury trial extended to trials in state courts *(Duncan v. Louisiana, 1968)*.

The court reversed the rule allowing evidence obtained by state officers in an illegal search to be admitted in federal court, holding that no evidence obtained by illegal search was admissible *(Elkins v. U.S., 1960)*.

The court in 1967 overturned a rule which had stood since 1928 and held that electronic eavesdropping or wiretapping, even that involving no physical trespass, constituted "search and seizure" and was unconstitutional and thereby inadmissible as evidence unless authorized by a warrant *(Katz v. U.S.)*.

In 1969 the court held that, if illegal surveillance had occurred, defendants with standing to object must be allowed to examine the entire record of such surveillance without any preliminary screening of that record *(Alderman and Alderisio v. U.S.; Butenko v. U.S.; Ivanov v. U.S., 1969)*.

Perhaps the court's most widely controversial criminal law decisions were those *(Escobedo v. Illinois, 1964* and *Miranda v. Arizona, 1966)* holding that police must—before interrogating a suspect—advise him that any statement he made might be used against him, that he had a right to have legal counsel and that he had the right to remain silent.

President Nixon criticized these decisions as "seriously hamstringing the peace forces in our society and strengthening the criminal forces." These controversial decisions were made by a closely divided court.

Prayers and Votes. The sensitive areas of political districting and religion also came under the purview of the Warren Court, in both instances engendering strong reaction from Congress and the public.

The court *(Baker v. Carr)* in 1962 reversed a statement by the court two decades earlier—that legislative apportionment was of "a peculiarly political nature and therefore not meet for judicial determination"—and ruled that federal courts could review that question.

A number of important decisions followed *Baker v. Carr*: the rule of "one man, one vote" was set forth *(Gray v. Sanders, 1963)* and applied to congressional *(Wesberry v. Sanders, 1964; Kirkpatrick v. Preisler* and *Wells v. Rockefeller, 1969)* and state legislative *(Reynolds v. Sims, 1964)* districts.

In the case of *Engel v. Vitale* (1962) the court declared that state officials could not require that an official prayer be recited in public schools.

This ruling was amplified the following year by the court's decision *(Abington Township School District v. Schempp, 1963)* that the state could not order recitation of the Lord's Prayer or Bible reading in public schools without violating the "establishment of religion" clause of the First Amendment, which was extended to the states by the Fourteenth Amendment.

Police and Arrests. "We need not blindfold the police, nor ask them to abandon their experience when they encounter situations which call for...effective intervention.... The test of probable cause (for arrest) is not what reaction victims—or judges—might have but what the totality of the circumstances means to police officers." *(Davis v. U.S., Sams v. U.S., 1969)*

Rule-making by the Supreme Court. Over these past dozen years...the Supreme Court has been revising the code of criminal procedure and evidence 'piecemeal' on a case-by-case basis, on inadequate records and incomplete factual data rather than by the orderly process of statutory rule-making.... I suggest to you that a large measure of responsibility for some of the bitterness in

American life today over the administration of criminal justice can fairly be laid to the method which the Supreme Court elected to use for this comprehensive—this enormous—task.... To put this in simple terms, the Supreme Court helped make the problems we have because it did not 'go by the book' and use the tested... process of rule-making through use of the advisory committee mechanism provided by Congress.... I question... not the court or the last decade's holdings...but its methodology and the loose ends, confusion and bitterness that methodology has left in its wake." (Address to the Ohio Judicial Conference at Columbus, Ohio, Sept. 4, 1968)

Fortas' Resignation

Abe Fortas became the first Supreme Court justice to step down under threat of impeachment when he resigned on May 14, 1969.

The resignation followed by less than eight months a successful Senate filibuster against President Johnson's nomination of Fortas to be chief justice. His departure from the court climaxed a furor brought on by the disclosure early in May that Fortas had received and held for 11 months a $20,000 fee from the family foundation of a man later imprisoned for illegal stock manipulation. The resignation was accepted May 15 by President Nixon. Fortas, a prominent Washington attorney, had been named an associate justice in 1965 by President Johnson.

According to an article in *Life* magazine, Fortas in January 1966 accepted a $20,000 check from a foundation established by multimillionaire industrialist, Louis E. Wolfson. In September 1966, Wolfson was indicted for selling unregistered securities. In December 1966, according to the article, Fortas returned the $20,000.

Wolfson was convicted in September 1967 and sentenced to one year in prison and fined $100,000. His appeal for review of the conviction was denied on April 1, 1969, by the Supreme Court, with Fortas taking no part in consideration of the case. His former law firm had on occasion represented Wolfson.

Fortas May 4 issued a statement saying that he did not feel that the fee in question implied any inducement for him to try to influence Wolfson's case. But that statement did nothing to quiet the rising furor.

Critics noted that the canons of judicial ethics state that "A judge should avoid giving ground for any reasonable suspicion that he is utilizing the power or prestige of his office to persuade or coerce others to patronize or contribute, either to the success of private business or to charitable enterprises." After Fortas resigned, the American Bar Association released an informal opinion from its committee on professional ethics which found Fortas' conduct "clearly contrary" to the canons.

Attorney General John N. Mitchell met May 7 with Chief Justice Warren; on May 8 it was reported that the Justice Department was investigating the Fortas-Wolfson relationship to determine possible violations of federal law.

A flurry of bills were introduced in Congress requiring financial disclosure by federal judges and Supreme Court justices. Rep. H. R. Gross (R Iowa) announced May 11 that he would present to the House articles of impeachment against Fortas if Fortas did not resign within a reasonable time. The articles accused Fortas of malfeasance, misconduct and impropriety, Gross said. That

same day Sen. Walter F. Mondale (D Minn.) became the first Democratic senator to call for Fortas' resignation.

On May 14 the resignation came. In a letter of that date to Warren, Fortas said that he was guilty of no wrongdoing, but that he was resigning in order that the court not continue to be "subjected to extraneous stress" which might adversely affect its performance.

Fortas detailed his acquaintance with Wolfson and his relationship to the Wolfson Family Foundation. When that relationship began late in 1965, he said, he saw no conflict between the nature of that work and his judicial duties and he thought his court duties would leave him time for such nonjudicial activities. He explained that the foundation paid him a $20,000 annual fee for his continuing services, and that the agreement provided for this fee to be paid to his wife, in the event of his death.

Fortas explained that in June 1966 he decided to terminate his role with the foundation due to the heavy demand on his time by the court's workload and to the fact that he learned that the Justice Department was considering prosecution of Wolfson for securities law violations. He terminated his role late in June via letter, he said, and returned the $20,000 fee in December.

Fortas concluded his letter: "There has been no wrongdoing on my part. There has been no default in the performance of my judicial duties in accordance with the high standards of the office I hold. So far as I am concerned the welfare and maximum effectiveness of the court to perform its critical role in our system of government are factors that are paramount to all others. It is this consideration that prompts my resignation which, I hope, by terminating the public controversy, will permit the court to proceed with its work without the harassment of debate concerning one of its members."

Haynsworth Rejected

In his effort to replace Abe Fortas with a southern conservative, Richard Nixon suffered his first major congressional defeat when the Senate in November 1969 rejected his nomination of Clement F. Haynsworth Jr. to the Supreme Court.

Haynsworth, a wealthy South Carolinian and chief judge of the court of appeals, 4th circuit, was named by Nixon Aug. 18 to fill the seat left vacant by the resignation of Fortas in May. A graduate of Harvard Law School, Haynsworth, 56 at the time of his nomination, had headed a Greenville, S.C., law firm which his father and grandfather had also led. In 1952 and 1956 a Democrat for Eisenhower, he became a Republican in 1964. Eisenhower appointed him to the appeals court in 1957. His record there became the target of his critics.

Opponents of the nomination, led by Birch Bayh (D Ind.), said repeatedly that they did not question Haynsworth's honesty or integrity. They did question his sensitivity to the appearance of ethical impropriety and his judgment regarding participation in cases where his financial interests could be said to be involved, even indirectly. Haynsworth was also opposed by labor and civil rights leaders.

Demands for President Nixon to withdraw the nomination merely stiffened the President's determination to stand behind his nominee and to reassert his confidence in him. Considerable political pressure preceded the final vote, brought to bear on individual senators by both opponents and advocates of the nomination.

The key to Haynsworth's defeat was the defection of liberal Republicans who voted with northern Democrats to deny confirmation Nov. 21, on a **key roll-call vote of 45-55.** All three top Republican leaders in the Senate voted against confirmation.

Haynsworth was the 23rd man denied confirmation to the Supreme Court, the first to be formally rejected since 1930 when John J. Parker of North Carolina lost confirmation by one vote, 39-41.

Controversies. Overshadowing complaints about Haynsworth's record on labor and civil rights issues was the argument—reinforced by the recent Fortas charges—that Haynsworth was not sensitive enough to the need to avoid even the appearance of impropriety. His critics charged that he had participated in decisions indirectly affecting the welfare of companies in which he had a monetary interest.

The primary cases scrutinized during Senate Judiciary Committee hearings on the nomination in September were those growing out of a lengthy dispute between a textile mill—which was a subsidiary of Deering Milliken Inc.—and the Textile Workers Union. (*Deering Milliken Inc. v. Johnston, Darlington Manufacturing Co. and Deering Milliken v. NLRB*)

Critics of the nomination argued that Haynsworth should not have taken part in the decisions involving Deering Milliken, because he owned a one-seventh interest in a company, Carolina Vend-A-Matic Company, which held a contract to supply vending services to some Deering Milliken plants. The value of Haynsworth's share, at the time the company was sold to a larger operation, was about $450,000.

William Pollock, president of the union, said that Haynsworth should have disqualified himself from the case. But William H. Rehnquist, assistant attorney general in charge of the office of legal counsel, concluded that Haynsworth "was under a duty to take part in that decision." Rehnquist said that the question raised was "whether a judge, who owns stock in one corporation, which in turn does business with a second corporation, should disqualify himself when the second corporation is a party litigant in his court." For Rehnquist and the Justice Department, the answer was no.

Joseph L. Rauh Jr., vice chairman of Americans for Democratic Action, said that Haynsworth's action was "far worse than that of Justice Fortas; he decided an important case for a litigant with which a company partially owned by him did substantial business and sought more. Whereas Justice Fortas had a potential conflict of interest in his outside activities, Judge Haynsworth had an actual conflict of interest in a case before him at the bench."

Haynsworth said that at the time of his participation in the controversial decision, he had no conscious awareness of the business relationship between the vending company and affiliates of Deering Milliken. He said that had he known of the relationship, he would not have viewed it as a conflict of interest for him to take part in the decision. He said that the vending company was in no way affected by the outcome of the labor case. Haynsworth said he had disqualified himself from participation "in all cases in which (his) former law firm or any of its

Resigning Justices

Abe Fortas was the 41st Supreme Court justice to resign or retire from the court; he was the first to quit under charges of extra-judicial misconduct.

Justices quit for several reasons. Most resigning justices retired in advanced age and after lengthy service. Some 47 died while still serving. Some resigned for reasons of conscience, some to do other work, some because they were too ill to carry on. Three who quit died before their resignations became effective.

Benjamin R. Curtis resigned in 1857 after disagreements with Chief Justice Roger B. Taney over the Dred Scott decision. Curtis, whose brother had argued the case for Dred Scott, advocated freedom for slaves once they were on free territory.

John Campbell from Georgia resigned in April 1861 to return to the South, although he opposed secession and had freed all of his own slaves.

Tom Clark resigned in 1967 to avoid conflict of interest when his son, Ramsey Clark, was appointed U.S. attorney general.

John Jay left the court in 1795 to serve as governor of New York. He was reappointed to the court as chief justice in 1800, but declined. Jay felt the Supreme Court then lacked "the energy, weight and dignity which are essential to its affording due support to the national government."

Charles Evans Hughes resigned in 1916 to run for President.

Arthur Goldberg resigned in 1965 to serve as U.S. ambassador to the United Nations.

The only Supreme Court justice to be impeached was Samuel Chase. In 1804 the House charged him with "misconduct in trials impairing the confidence and respect for the courts," but he was acquitted by the Senate.

members were counsel, cases in which certain relatives were counsel, and all cases in which I had a stock interest in a party or in one which would be directly affected by the outcome of the litigation."

During the hearings, Haynsworth told the committee that the gross amount of business done by the vending company in 1963, the year of the decision, with plants controlled by Deering Milliken was $100,000—three per cent of the vending company's total gross for that year. The total after-tax profit which the company realized in 1963 from its business with the Deering Milliken subsidiaries was $2,730, of which his share was $390.

But, Haynsworth said, the Senate should decide the case for his nomination on the merits of the facts presented: "If there is substantial doubt about the propriety of what I did, I hope the Senate will resolve the doubts against me.... While I am concerned about my reputation, I am much more concerned about my country and the Supreme Court as an institution."

Among those speaking in behalf of Haynsworth, particularly in regard to the charges that he had ignored a conflict of interest in the Deering Milliken case, were John P. Frank of Phoenix, Ariz., an expert on the subject of judicial disqualification; Lawrence E. Walsh, chairman of the American Bar Association committee on the federal judiciary; and Judge Harrison L. Winter, a colleague from the court of appeals.

Among those leading the opposition testimony were George Meany, president of the AFL-CIO; Clarence Mitchell, director of the Washington bureau of the National Association for the Advancement of Colored People; Rauh, also representing the Leadership Conference on Civil Rights; and Pollock.

Committee Action. The Senate Judiciary Committee Oct. 9 voted 10-7 to report the nomination of Haynsworth favorably to the full Senate; the report was filed Nov. 12.

The majority set forth, in a 22-page report, its conclusion that Haynsworth was "extraordinarily well qualified" to fill the seat of an associate justice of the Supreme Court. It supported that conclusion with a point-by-point analysis and rebuttal of the ethical and philosophical charges against him.

Noting the high recommendation given Haynsworth by the American Bar Association and by his colleagues on the 4th circuit court of appeals, the majority described the nominee as a man of "outstanding judicial temperament" who approached controversial and complex legal matters in a balanced manner. The majority concluded that attacks on his ethical sensitivity were not substantiated and that "nothing in his judicial conduct...would in any way justify recommending against his confirmation."

The majority refuted the position which some opponents of the nomination had adopted—that even if ethical attacks could not be substantiated, the very fact that they were made constituted reason to deny confirmation. Such a position, the majority said, was contrary both to "traditional notions of fair play and to the lessons of history."

"To accede to such a view," the report stated, "would be to place a nominee's fate, not in the hands of those charged with advising and consenting to his nomination, but in the hands of his accusers. The most basic concept of fairness demands vindication where a charge is found to be unsubstantiated, just as surely as it demands condemnation where the objection is found to have merit."

The committee majority said that for Haynsworth to disqualify himself in the Deering Milliken case would have been contrary to all precedents for judicial disqualification. It said that judges had never been required to disqualify themselves simply because they owned stock in a parent corporation which controlled a litigant.

Those committee members voting against reporting the Haynsworth nomination favorably were Birch Bayh (D Ind.), who had spearheaded the Senate opposition, Philip A. Hart (D Mich.), Edward M. Kennedy (D Mass.), Quentin N. Burdick (D N.D.), Joseph D. Tydings (D Md.), Robert P. Griffin (R Mich.) and Charles McC. Mathias Jr. (R Md.).

Stating his views again, Bayh emphasized that the Senate must look at its action in confirming a Supreme Court nominee as one which should "shore up public confidence" in the judiciary. Bayh agreed that Haynsworth was an honest man, but he said that his record was nevertheless "blemished by a pattern of insensitivity to the appearance of impropriety."

Republican Defections. The loss of the votes of more than a third of the Republicans in the Senate was the key factor in the defeat of Haynsworth's nomination. The first indication of a crack in the Republican bloc came Oct. 1 —more than six weeks before the final vote—when Edward W. Brooke (R Mass.) wrote Nixon to request that the nomination be withdrawn. On the day before the vote in the Judiciary Committee, Assistant Senate Minority Leader Griffin and Margaret Chase Smith (R Maine), chairman of the Republican Conference, announced that they would oppose the nomination. Griffin, leader of the earlier fight against the Fortas nomination as chief justice, said that "legitimate and substantial doubt" had been raised about Haynsworth's ethical sensitivity. And Smith said that after opposing Fortas, she could not apply a double standard and support Haynsworth.

Ernest F. Hollings (D S.C.), Haynsworth's primary sponsor in the Senate, criticized the White House Oct. 9 for failing to rally Republican leadership behind the nomination. He said that Nixon had just sent the name to the Senate and left it there "hanging on the clothesline."

Floor Action. White House pressure mounted steadily during the weeks between the vote of the committee and that of the full Senate, alienating perhaps as many senators as it persuaded. Few issues had generated more pressure on his office, said Len B. Jordan (R Idaho), who voted against the nomination: "Support of the President is urged as if it were a personal matter rather than an issue of grave constitutional importance."

When the tense ten-minute roll call began Nov. 21 on the motion to confirm the nomination, there were only a dozen senators who had not made their positions known. When the vote ended—short by five of the 50 needed for confirmation (Vice President Agnew would have cast the deciding vote in favor of the nominee if the Senate had tied)—11 of the 12 had voted against the nomination. Of the 45 votes for Clement F. Haynsworth Jr., 26 were Republican and 19 Democrat—all but three from the South. Of the 55 votes against him 17 were Republican and 38 Democrats—only five of whom were from the South.

Republican opponents ranged from conservatives such as John J. Williams (Del.) and Jordan to liberals such as Charles H. Percy (Ill.) and Mark O. Hatfield (Ore.). The top Republican leaders in the Senate—Hugh Scott (Pa.), the minority leader; Griffin, the party whip; Smith, chairman of the Senate Republican Conference; and John J. William (Del.), chairman of the GOP Committee on Committees—all voted against Haynsworth.

Hollings told reporters after the vote, "We weren't in the ball park the last six weeks. You can't win if you can't get your leadership." Hollings said he told White House officials as long as two weeks before the vote that Haynsworth could not be confirmed.

Hatfield told Congressional Quarterly that lack of active support by the Senate's Republican leaders was one of the main factors leading to the Haynsworth defeat.

In a statement after the Senate vote, Nixon expressed regret that the Senate had failed to confirm "this distinguished man" and he deplored the attacks on Haynsworth, whose integrity he described as unimpeachable and whose ability, he said, was unquestioned. Referring to his campaign promises, he pledged to nominate another man selected by the same criteria as Hayns-

Supreme Court Membership, 1968-1972

Name	State	Date of Birth	Nominated By	To Replace	Date of Appointment	Date Confirmed	Date Resigned
Hugo L. Black	Ala.	2/27/1886	Roosevelt	Van Devanter	8/12/37	8/17/37	9/17/71
William O. Douglas	Conn.	10/16/1898	Roosevelt	Brandeis	3/20/39	4/4/39	
Earl Warren*	Calif.	3/19/1891	Eisenhower	Vinson	9/30/53	3/1/54	6/23/69
John M. Harlan	N.Y.	5/20/1899	Eisenhower	Jackson	1/10/55	3/16/55	9/23/71
William J. Brennan Jr.	N.J.	4/25/1906	Eisenhower	Minton	10/16/56	3/19/57	
Potter Stewart	Ohio	1/23/1915	Eisenhower	Burton	1/17/59	5/5/59	
Byron R. White	Colo.	6/8/1917	Kennedy	Whittaker	4/3/62	4/11/62	
Abe Fortas	Tenn.	6/19/1910	Johnson	Goldberg	7/28/65	8/11/65	5/14/69
Thurgood Marshall	N.Y.	6/2/1908	Johnson	Clark	6/13/67	8/30/67	
Warren E. Burger*	D.C.	9/17/1907	Nixon	Warren	5/21/69	6/9/69	
Harry A. Blackmun	Minn.	11/12/1908	Nixon	Fortas	4/14/70	5/12/70	
Lewis F. Powell Jr.	Va.	9/19/1907	Nixon	Black	10/21/71	12/6/71	
William H. Rehnquist	Ariz.	10/1/1924	Nixon	Harlan	10/21/71	12/10/71	

* Chief Justice

Supreme Court appointments, 1789-1964, *Congress and the Nation Vol. I,* **p. 1452**
Supreme Court membership, 1965-1968, *Congress and the Nation Vol. II,* **p. 340**

worth had been: "The Supreme Court needs men of his legal philosophy to restore the proper balance to that great institution."

Carswell Rejected

The Senate dealt President Nixon a second stinging defeat in April 1970 when it rejected his second nominee to the Fortas seat on the Supreme Court, G. Harrold Carswell of Florida.

The rejection came two and a half months after Nixon had announced his selection Jan. 19 of Carswell, 50, a judge on the court of appeals, 5th circuit, as an associate justice. The Senate's action, on a **key roll-call vote of 45-51**, took place on April 8, less than five months after its rejection of Clement F. Haynsworth Jr., whom Nixon had first chosen to fill the court vacancy.

Not since 1894, during the second Cleveland administration, had a President had two Supreme Court nominees rejected outright by the Senate. Carswell was the 24th man denied confirmation to a seat on the court.

Thirty-eight Democrats and 13 Republicans voted against Carswell, compared to 38 Democrats and 17 Republicans who voted against Haynsworth. Despite statements by administration spokesmen that the defeats of both Haynsworth and Carswell were partisan attempts to embarrass the President, only 23 of the 43 Republican senators voted for or announced their support of both nominees.

Whereas all four Republican leaders voted against Haynsworth—Minority Leader Hugh Scott (Pa.), Assistant Minority Leader Robert P. Griffin (Mich.), Margaret Chase Smith (Maine), chairman of the Republican Conference, and John J. Williams, chairman of the GOP committee on committees—only Smith voted against Carswell.

Background. Carswell, a native of Georgia, graduated from Duke University, served in the Navy during World War II and graduated from a small Georgia law school in 1948. He ran unsuccessfully for the Georgia legislature soon after his graduation from law school.

Moving to Tallahassee, Fla., in 1949, Carswell practiced law first with a firm in which LeRoy Collins, later governor of Florida, was a partner, and then with his own firm. Initially a Democrat, Carswell supported Eisenhower for President in 1952 and 1956, and changed his registration to Republican. In 1953 Eisenhower named Carswell federal attorney for northern Florida; five years later he nominated him as federal district judge for the same area—at 38, Carswell was the nation's youngest federal judge. In May 1969, less than a year before the Senate rejection of his Supreme Court nomination, Nixon elevated Carswell to the court of appeals. Within a month the Senate confirmed that nomination by voice vote and without opposition.

Early Opposition. Although the White House stated that Carswell had been thoroughly cleared, in advance of his nomination, of any of the financial conflict-of-interest and ethical impropriety charges that brought on the Haynsworth defeat, the news media disclosed Jan. 21 that during an unsuccessful campaign for a seat in the Georgia legislature in 1948 Carswell had made a speech supporting white supremacy. Carswell immediately repudiated any continuing belief in white supremacy, but civil rights groups charged that he was still a segregationist and that his record as a judge since 1948 had not reflected any change in his views or philosophy. Labor joined the opposition Jan. 26 when AFL CIO President George Meany announced AFL-CIO opposition to the nomination and called it "a slap in the face to the nation's Negro citizens." Thus early opponents of the nomination included many of the same civil rights organizations and labor unions that had fought the Haynsworth nomination—the latter despite the fact that, unlike Haynsworth, Carswell was not accused of being anti-labor. In addition, the anti-Carswell forces later were joined by a substantial number of law school deans and professors

CONGRESS AND THE NATION, VOL. III

from across the nation and by lawyers who objected to Carswell as mediocre, undistinguished and hostile to civil rights causes.

Opposition in the Senate to the nomination was slow to arise, largely because of a disposition by senators to avoid another bitter confirmation struggle. It was only with the persistent opposition of Edward W. Brooke (R Mass.) and the conviction, only belatedly held, of other senators that Carswell's record was such that he had to be opposed, that a concerted effort was mounted against him. As with Haynsworth, the Democratic opposition to Carswell was led by Birch Bayh (Ind.).

Controversies. Civil rights criticism of Carswell was much more strident than that of Haynsworth. The various points on which Carswell was attacked included the 1948 speech, his 1956 participation in the conversion of a municipal golf course to private ownership to avoid desegregation, his 1966 sale of a lot with a restrictive covenant, and his reported hostility to civil rights workers and lawyers appearing in his courtroom.

During Senate Judiciary Committee hearings on the nomination, which continued for five days in late January and early February, Carswell rejected charges that he was a racist. After the disclosure of the 1948 speech, Nixon said that he was not concerned by its contents, although he had not known of it previously. He instead pointed to Carswell's record of federal service since 1953, a record he described as "impeccable...without a taint of racism: a record of strict constructionism as far as interpretation of the Constitution and the role of the court, which I think the court needs."

But groups including the National Association for the Advancement of Colored People, the AFL-CIO, civil rights attorneys who had appeared before Carswell, and the National Organization of Women disagreed with this assessment. In the words of Joseph L. Rauh Jr., chairman of the Leadership Conference on Civil Rights, they felt that "Judge Carswell is Judge Haynsworth with a cutting edge, with a bitterness and a meanness that Judge Haynsworth never had."

The most telling element in the opposition which rose against the Carswell nomination was the criticism leveled at him from within the ranks of his own profession. Although the American Bar Association committee on the federal judiciary found him qualified for appointment to the court, many practicing lawyers and judges and legal scholars publicly challenged this assessment. By voicing their concern about his ability and competence as a jurist, they aroused concern in the minds of men undisturbed by the charges from civil rights and labor groups.

The liberal Republican Ripon Society characterized the nomination as "exceptionally inadequate." Derek Bok, dean of Harvard Law School, and 24 other faculty members said that Carswell lacked "minimum qualifications" for the court seat. More than 200 men who had served as law clerks to Supreme Court justices agreed that Carswell was only of "mediocre ability. His performance on the lower courts...reflects the absence of the qualities which, we believe, all Supreme Court nominees should possess." Faculty members from more than 35 other law schools across the country expressed their concern about Carswell's lack of qualifications for the legal profession's highest post.

Roman L. Hruska (R Neb.), ranking minority member of the Senate Judiciary Committee and leader of the fight for the Carswell nomination, attempted to respond to such charges in March when he said that "even if he was mediocre, there are a lot of mediocre judges and people and lawyers. They are entitled to a little representation, aren't they, and a little chance? We can't have all Brandeises, and Cardozos and Frankfurters and stuff like that there." Hruska aides later said that the remarks were made in jest, but they were repeated many times by Carswell critics.

Committee Action. After committee members twice delayed a vote on the Carswell nomination, the committee Feb. 16 approved it by a vote of 13-4. Voting against the nomination were Bayh, Philip A. Hart (D Mich.), Edward M. Kennedy (D Mass.) and Joseph D. Tydings (D Md.). The report was filed Feb. 27.

The majority of the committee found Carswell "thoroughly qualified" to serve on the court, noting that they felt he no longer held the "notions...expressed in his 1948 speech." The other charges of bias, they said, were insubstantial and unproved.

Bayh, Hart, Kennedy and Tydings found Carswell presenting "credentials too meager to justify confirmation."

Floor Action. A civil rights measure to amend the 1965 Voting Rights Act had long been set for consideration by the full Senate beginning March 1. Senate Majority Leader Mike Mansfield (D Mont.) said Feb. 17 that the Senate would complete action on that bill before considering the Carswell nomination. Those who opposed the Carswell nomination saw this delay, extended by southern opposition to the passage of the civil rights bill, as working to the advantage of the forces seeking to reject the nomination. *(Story p. 498)*

Debate on the nomination finally began March 13, but it was not until three weeks later that the Senate took its first vote on the matter. On April 6 the Senate rejected, 44-52, a motion to send the nomination back to the Judiciary Committee.

First conceived as a way of killing the nomination by burying it in committee, the motion had, by the time of the vote, become instead a diversionary tactic, a preliminary skirmish won by the administration. The vote was defective as a clear test of the strength of the opposition to Carswell because some senators oppose any recommittal motion in principle, and because others voted against the motion in order to bring the nomination to an up-or-down vote on the Senate floor. Seven senators who had voted against recommittal then voted against the nomination as well.

After rejecting recommittal, the Senate April 8 refused, **45-51**, to confirm the nomination of Carswell to the Supreme Court. Of the 13 Republicans voting "nay," 10 had also voted against the Haynsworth nomination. One of the most surprising negative votes was cast by Marlow W. Cook (R Ky.), leader of the pro-Haynsworth forces. His vote, which brought a gasp from the packed Senate galleries, came early in the roll call and signaled the nomination's probable defeat.

Cook described his "nay" vote as the most politically dangerous of his career. He said he would like to see a southern conservative sit on the Supreme Court, but that he should be an outstanding southerner: "Haynsworth satisfied my standard of excellence. Carswell did not."

Also voting against the nomination were four southern Democrats—J. W. Fulbright (Ark.), William B. Spong Jr. (Va.), Albert Gore (Tenn.) and Ralph W. Yarborough (Texas). This vote by Gore and Yarborough was considered a significant factor in the primary defeats both suffered later in 1970.

In a speech before the final vote, Carswell supporter Robert Dole (R Kan.) virtually admitted defeat, and suggested that Nixon wait until after the November 1970 election to send up another nomination for the vacant court seat. "It may be easier," said Dole, "to change the Senate than the Supreme Court."

Expressing agreement with this sentiment, Nixon April 9 said that he felt the Senate "as presently constituted" would not confirm a southern court nominee "who believes as I do in the strict construction of the Constitution."

"As long as the Senate is constituted the way it is today, I will not nominate another southerner and let him be subjected to the kind of malicious character assassination accorded both Judges Haynsworth and Carswell," Nixon promised. He said, however, that "the day will come when men like Judges Carswell and Haynsworth can and will sit on the High Court."

(Haynsworth continued his work as chief judge of the court of appeals, 4th circuit. Carswell, only a few months after his Senate rejection, resigned his seat on the court of appeals, 5th circuit, to run unsuccessfully in 1970 for one of the Florida seats in the Senate.)

Blackmun Approved

Ending one of the longest court vacancies in history, the Senate May 12, 1970, confirmed Harry A. Blackmun of Minnesota as an associate justice of the Supreme Court. Blackmun filled the seat left vacant on May 14, 1969, by the resignation of Abe Fortas. The Senate vote on confirmation was 94-0 and came only a month after the nomination was announced. Blackmun formally took his seat on the court June 9, 1970.

Only six times had a Supreme Court seat remained vacant for as long as a year; the last such vacancy had occurred during the Civil War.

Background. Within a week after the Senate's rejection of the Carswell nomination, Nixon named Blackmun, a judge on the court of appeals, 8th circuit, to fill the empty seat. Like Haynsworth and Carswell, Blackmun suited the President's image of a strict constructionist, and came to the court from experience on one of the federal appeals courts.

Blackmun, a Phi Beta Kappa graduate of Harvard College and an honors graduate of Harvard Law School, was considered an expert in taxation matters, estate management and medical law. From 1950 to 1959, he was resident legal counsel for the Mayo Clinic in Rochester, Minn.

Blackmun was a member of the Interim Advisory Committee on Judicial Activities, established by Chief Justice Burger late in 1969 to render opinions concerning the extrajudicial activities of federal judges until a new set of guidelines for such activities was formulated and adopted.

Describing himself as a "nominal Republican," Blackmun said April 14 that he had never taken an active political role. His nomination, even before the White

Executive Prerogative

President Nixon April 1 declared that rejection of the Carswell nomination would impair the constitutional relationship of the President to Congress.

"What is centrally at issue in this nomination," Nixon said, "is the constitutional responsibility of the President to appoint members of the court—and whether this responsibility can be frustrated by those who wish to substitute their own philosophy or their own subjective judgment for that of the one person entrusted by the Constitution with the power of appointment. The question arises whether I, as President of the United States, shall be accorded the same right of choice in naming Supreme Court Justices which has been freely accorded to my predecessors of both parties."

President Nixon said he respected the right of any senator to differ with his selection. But, he continued, "the fact remains under the Constitution, it is the duty of the President to appoint and of the Senate to advise and consent. But if the Senate attempts to substitute its judgment as to who should be appointed the traditional constitutional balance is in jeopardy and the duty of the President under the Constitution impaired."

Senate Majority Leader Mike Mansfield (D Mont.) April 2 rejected Mr. Nixon's contentions concerning impairment of constitutional duty and relationships and said that the Senate, in advising and consenting, shared the appointive power with the President.

House announcement, was endorsed by former Vice President (and former Minnesota senator, 1948-1964) Hubert H. Humphrey. Humphrey said that Blackmun was "the kind of man I'd like to see on the court...completely devoid of any racial bias...(a man) of a moderate political persuasion."

Deputy Attorney General Richard G. Kleindienst April 15 sent to Judiciary Committee Chairman James O. Eastland (D Miss.) a letter detailing Blackmun's background, qualifications, major rulings and three cases in which he had ruled although he owned stock in one of the litigants.

According to the letter, Blackmun held approximately $75,000 in stocks, bonds and bank accounts and approximately $50,000 in equity in his house in Minnesota.

The letter, at Blackmun's request—in light of the controversy concerning Haynsworth's participation in cases involving litigants in which he had an interest—explained three instances in which Blackmun had participated in a case involving a company in which he held stock:

• *Hanson v. Ford Motor Co.* (1960)—Judge Blackmun in October 1957 bought 50 shares of stock in Ford Motor Co. for slightly more than $2,500. He later participated in this case, after discussing whether or not he should do so with the chief judge and deciding that his interest was too small to require disqualification. He wrote the opinion, reinstating a verdict against the Ford Motor Co.

• In 1964 Judge Blackmun was part of a court of appeals panel which decided the case of *Kotula v. Ford*
(Continued p. 299)

Douglas: House Committee Finds No Basis for Impeachment

The controversies over Fortas, Haynsworth and Carswell kindled many enmities and a renewed concern for the off-bench activities of federal judges and Supreme Court justices. One product of this concern was a second serious attempt, in 1970, to impeach Supreme Court Justice William O. Douglas.

Appointed to the court in 1939 by Franklin D. Roosevelt, Douglas quickly became one of the most controversial justices in history. His staunchly liberal views, his outspoken opinions, and his several marriages, two to women in their twenties, made him the target of continuing criticism. The first attempt to impeach him came in 1953 after he had stayed the execution of convicted spies Julius and Ethel Rosenberg.

The second was sparked in great part by frustration among supporters of the nomination of G. Harrold Carswell to the court. Even before the vote rejecting Carswell's nomination, Sen. Robert C. Byrd (D W.Va.) said that the House should begin impeachment proceedings against Douglas if Carswell were rejected.

The Charges

In an April 15 speech on the House floor a week after the rejection of the Carswell nomination, Republican Leader Gerald R. Ford (Mich.) began such a move. Ford made five major charges against Douglas:

• In 1966, Douglas dissented in a 5 to 4 decision that upheld the obscenity conviction of Ralph Ginzburg, publisher of *Eros*.

Sen. Barry Goldwater (R Ariz.) won a libel suit against *Fact*, another Ginzburg publication. On Jan. 26, 1970, the Supreme Court, with Justices Douglas and Black dissenting, affirmed the award of punitive damages against Ginzburg and *Fact*. In March 1969, *Avant Garde*, also published by Ginzburg, paid Douglas $350 for an article entitled "Appeal of Folk Singing: A Landmark Opinion." Douglas' failure to disqualify himself in the Ginzburg cases, according to Ford, amounted to a "gross impropriety."

• *Points of Rebellion*, a book written by Douglas and published by Random House Inc., presented the thesis that violence could be justified and perhaps only revolutionary overthrow of "the establishment" could save the country, Ford said. He charged the book violated the standard of good behavior.

• "Redress in Revolution," an article by Douglas in *Evergreen Review*, April 1970, appeared in the same issue with nude photographs.

• Associations by Douglas with Albert Parvin and the Albert Parvin Foundation resulted in his practicing law in violation of federal law.

Ford said Douglas assisted in the organization of the Albert Parvin Foundation, established in November 1960, and gave legal advice to the foundation in dealing with an investigation by the Internal Revenue Service. Douglas voluntarily ended his association with the foundation in May 1969.

• The Center for the Study of Democratic Institutions in Santa Barbara, Calif., Ford said, was a "left-ish" organization. He said Douglas was a consultant at the same time the center was recipient of Parvin Foundation funds.

In his speech, Ford urged creation of a special House committee to investigate the behavior of Douglas. But instead, the impeachment resolution was referred, as is usual, to the House Judiciary Committee.

The Report

A special House Judiciary subcommittee created to investigate these charges voted 3-1 Dec. 3 that it had found no grounds for impeachment. The report containing its conclusions and findings was released Dec. 16. It was endorsed by the five-member subcommittee's Democratic majority—Reps. Emanuel Celler (N.Y.), Byron G. Rogers (Colo.) and Jack Brooks (Texas). Rep. Edward Hutchinson (R Mich.) filed a two-page dissent and Rep. William M. McCulloch (R Ohio) abstained.

In his dissent, Hutchinson said the subcommittee could not consider its work complete without testimony and cross-examination of Douglas and other principals.

The subcommittee reported that:

• Douglas did not violate the Canons of Judicial Ethics in submitting and receiving payment for the article on folk singing which appeared in *Avant Garde*. The Ginzburg case was not before the Supreme Court at the time Douglas submitted the article.

• Douglas did not violate federal law in failing to disqualify himself from participation in the Supreme Court decision on a petition by Ginzburg to overturn the libel verdict. The law requires disqualification only if there is a substantial interest in a case.

• Douglas was not guilty of practicing law on behalf of the Parvin Foundation. Another attorney assumed responsibility for authorship of the articles incorporating the foundation. The foundation retained outside tax counsel.

The subcommittee considered charges made against Douglas on the basis of his relationship to Parvin and the Parvin Foundation, but found them "difficult to analyze because of the extreme tenuousness of the circumstantial evidence."

• It was neither illegal nor unethical for Douglas to accept an annual salary of $12,000 plus traveling expenses from the Parvin Foundation.

• Douglas' participation in a program sponsored by the Center for the Study of Democratic Institutions did not constitute a violation of the Logan Act which makes it unlawful for private citizens, without the authority of the U.S. government, to communicate with foreign governments with the intent to influence government relations.

• Charges that Douglas published statements encouraging violence in his book, *Points of Rebellion*, were based on a misinterpretation of the book.

• Douglas had no control over publication by *Evergreen Review* of excerpts from his book. Douglas' publisher, Random House, made the arrangements with the magazine without informing Douglas.

(Continued from p. 297)

Motor Co. The court of appeals upheld a lower court's action setting aside a verdict against Ford.

• *Mahoney v. Northwestern Bell Telephone Co.* (1967) —Judge Blackmun in 1963-1964 acquired 22 shares of American Telephone and Telegraph Co. stock at a total cost of about $1,350. He later participated in this decision which dismissed Mahoney's complaint for lack of the required jurisdiction.

The American Bar Association's committee on the federal judiciary April 28 endorsed Blackmun as a man with "high standards of professional competence, temperament and integrity." Blackmun's fellow judges notified the Judiciary Committee April 26 that they enthusiastically supported his nomination.

Committee Action. The Senate Judiciary Committee held one day of hearings April 29 on Blackmun's nomination. On May 5 it unanimously voted to report the nomination favorably, recommending confirmation. The committee report, filed May 9, described Blackmun as "thoroughly qualified" for the post of associate justice.

Noting that Blackmun had "answered every inquiry intelligently, cooperatively and frankly," the committee report said that the judge had impressed the committee as a "man of learning and humility."

Birch Bayh (D Ind.), Robert P. Griffin (R Mich.), Philip A. Hart (D Mich.), Edward M. Kennedy (D Mass.) and Joseph D. Tydings (D Md.) included a more detailed description of Blackmun's procedures in regard to cases involving companies in which he held stock. The five senators also added a statement describing Blackmun as "fully devoted to the statutory and constitutional precepts which control in federal courts," and as "sensitive to the problems and challenges facing not only the courts, but the entire nation today."

Bayh, leader of the opposition to Haynsworth and Carswell, joined the committee views, stating that his study of Blackmun's conduct on ethical matters led him to conclude that Blackmun's record showed a high standard of integrity, "fully consistent with service on the High Court."

Robert C. Byrd (D W.Va.) stated that he supported Blackmun's nomination because of the judicial restraint evident in the nominee's "deference for the legislative branch of the government in legislative matters," and "his recognition of the nice delineation of powers between the legislative and judicial branches."

Floor Action. The Senate approved the Blackmun nomination May 12 by a 94-0 roll-call vote.

After several hours of uneventful debate May 11 and 12, the Senate unanimously approved the nomination. The six senators not voting were Bayh, Barry Goldwater (R Ariz.), Albert Gore (D Tenn.), Karl E. Mundt (R S.D.), Richard B. Russell (D Ga.) and John G. Tower (R Texas).

John L. McClellan (D Ark.), during debate May 11, expressed the hope that confirmation of Blackmun would close the unpleasant chapter in the court's history which began with the Fortas resignation and begin "restoring the Supreme Court to its rightful place of respect and reverence."

Black, Harlan Depart

The Supreme Court suffered a sudden and significant loss in September 1971, with the resignations of Hugo L. Black and John Marshall Harlan.

Black, 85, resigned Sept. 17, 1971; Harlan, 72, resigned Sept. 23. Both gave failing health as the reason. Black died Sept. 25; Harlan, Dec. 29.

BLACK: KINDLY COLOSSUS

The resignation of Hugo Lafayette Black from his seat as associate justice of the Supreme Court removed from that bench one of the most influential men ever to sit there.

The White House, announcing the resignation of the man who had served more than 34 years—longer than all but two other men in history, said that the President had accepted it with deep regret. Chief Justice Warren E. Burger called Black's retirement "a great loss to the court." Burger said that "no disagreement on legal issues has ever affected the warm friendship that he and I developed."

Hugo L. Black was born in rural Alabama in 1886, less than 20 years after the end of the Civil War. He graduated with honors from the University of Alabama law school in 1906, despite the fact that he had never gone to college.

For a time a country lawyer, Birmingham police court judge, county prosecutor and, by 1925, respected attorney specializing in labor union and personal injury cases, Black decided to go into politics.

In early 1927, Sen. Hugo L. Black (D Ala.), 41, arrived in Washington. Soon linked with the liberal forces in the Senate, Black was later one of the staunchest backers of the New Deal legislation.

On August 12, 1937, the President nominated Black to the Supreme Court to succeed Willis Van Devanter, who had resigned. The Senate confirmed the nomination, Roosevelt's first, Aug. 17, 1937, by a 53-16 vote.

Before he took his seat, a newspaper series pointed out that Black had been a member of the Ku Klux Klan early in the 1920s. The storm of criticism subsided when Black stated that he no longer had any ties with the KKK. Black took his seat on the bench Oct. 4, 1937.

Black left an indelible imprint upon constitutional law and the history of the Supreme Court. He sat on that bench with one-fourth of all the justices in history—and with one-third of all the chief justices. He participated in more than one of every four decisions ever announced by the court.

His fierce independence and absolute belief in the letter, as well as the spirit, of the Constitution were expressed in concise and vivid language. His most enduring legacy may well be the series of rulings by the court during the 1950s and 1960s which held that the 14th Amendment made the Bill of Rights binding upon the states, not just the federal government.

Among his other outstanding opinions are those which invalidated the seizure of the steel mills by President Truman during the Korean War, which barred the use of any officially prescribed prayer in public schools, which declared the right of an indigent defendant in a state court to have counsel and which upheld the action of Congress in granting the vote to 18-year-old citizens.

HARLAN: CONSERVATIVE CONSCIENCE

John Marshall Harlan, namesake of the fourth chief justice and of a grandfather who served on the Supreme Court for 34 years (1877-1911), had served almost 17 years. Chief Justice Burger expressed regret at his resignation and said that "the quality of his penetrating, incisive mind and the grace of his spirit have made him a unique figure and he will rank with the great justices of this court."

John Marshall Harlan was born in Chicago in 1899; his grandfather was at that time sitting on the Supreme Court bench.

Harlan graduated from Princeton in 1920 and spent three years at Oxford as a Rhodes Scholar. Beginning his study of law at Oxford, he completed those studies at New York Law School in 1924 and began his practice on Wall Street. Most of Harlan's life for the next 30 years centered on his New York practice. He became one of the city's leading trial lawyers.

After serving for two years as chief counsel for the New York State Crime Commission during its investigation of the ties between organized crime and the state government, Harlan was named to the court of appeals, 2nd circuit, in early 1954. He had served there only a matter of months when President Eisenhower on Nov. 8 nominated him to succeed Robert H. Jackson on the Supreme Court. He took his seat March 28, 1955.

A conservative member of the Supreme Court during one of its most innovative periods, Harlan often served, one biographer noted, as the "conservative conscience" of the court. Often in dissent and frequently in a separate or concurring opinion, Harlan's scholarly writings provided a balance for the majority position, expressing his devotion to the concept of judicial restraint.

In 1965, he wrote a dissenting opinion when the majority of the court ruled that a federal court could intervene to halt proceedings in a criminal trial in a state court (*Dombrowski v. Pfister*). Six years later, the court issued a series of opinions agreeing with Harlan's view and severely limiting the circumstances under which such intervention could occur.

Harlan registered dissents to two of the Warren court's most controversial decisions. In 1964, the court held in *Reynolds v. Sims* that the standard for the reapportionment of legislative districts was "one man, one vote." Harlan disagreed: the court should not have ventured into this political thicket, he said.

Two years later, in the case of *Miranda v. Arizona*, the court held that police could not constitutionally interrogate a prisoner suspect unless he had been advised of his constitutional rights. Harlan dissented vigorously, saying that the decision created unnecessary problems for the police.

Powell, Rehnquist Confirmed

The Senate in December 1971 confirmed the nominations of Lewis F. Powell Jr. and William H. Rehnquist as associate justices of the Supreme Court, the third and fourth men placed on that bench by Richard Nixon. Not since Warren G. Harding had one President in his first term had the opportunity to appoint so many members of the Supreme Court.

Powell, 64, of Virginia, succeeded to the southern seat left vacant by the resignation of the late Hugo L. Black, and Rehnquist, 47, took the seat vacated by the resignation of ailing John Marshall Harlan.

President Nixon named Powell and Rehnquist to the court Oct. 21. Powell was confirmed by the Senate Dec.

6; Rehnquist—whose nomination aroused more controversy—was confirmed Dec. 10.

Powell, a former president of the American Bar Association (ABA), was nationally recognized as a leader in the legal profession. Rehnquist, since 1969 serving as the President's lawyer's lawyer in his role as assistant attorney general, office of legal counsel, was less well-known.

In a nationally televised announcement of the nominations, Mr. Nixon said Oct. 21 his two criteria for nominees were professional excellence and a judicial philosophy that judges should "interpret...not twist or bend the Constitution in order to perpetuate (their) personal political or social views."

Rehnquist had testified frequently before Congress in behalf of administration programs. He had offered legal opinions on presidential authority to conduct the war in Vietnam, government use of mass-arrest techniques against demonstrators, equal rights for women and other topics that could come before the court.

Powell, of Richmond, Va., was a senior partner in the law firm of Hunton, Williams, Gay, Powell & Gibson. He was a past president of the American Bar Association and was a member of President Johnson's Commission on Law Enforcement and the Administration of Justice.

Neither nominee had served before as a judge. Both had highly regarded academic backgrounds. Both were elected to Phi Beta Kappa in college, finished first in their law school classes and went on to earn masters' degrees from Harvard University. Rehnquist served as a law clerk to the late Supreme Court Justice Robert H. Jackson in 1952-53.

Congressional reaction the night of the announcement and the next day was almost uniformly favorable or guarded—with no immediate expressions of opposition.

Sen. Birch Bayh (D Ind.), who led opposition in the Senate to Nixon's previous Haynsworth and Carswell nominations, said Rehnquist and Powell "appear to be significantly better qualified than some of the other names leaked to the public." Senate Minority Leader Hugh Scott (R Pa.) said the two men "appear to be well qualified."

Judiciary Committee Chairman James O. Eastland (D Miss.) told reporters he did not know Powell but that Rehnquist was a "lawyer's lawyer" and would make an "outstanding justice."

Criticism of the two nominees was voiced Oct. 22 by George Meany, president of the AFL-CIO: "These appointments seem to be part and parcel of the administration's effort to pack the court with ultraconservatives who subscribe to the President's narrow views on human rights and civil rights."

During the week of Oct. 25, some opposition to Rehnquist's nomination was announced by groups that disagreed with his civil rights and civil liberties views. In an effort to defuse such opposition, the Justice Department Oct. 29 released three documents in which Rehnquist had taken positions in opposition to many civil rights advocates.

Two of the documents, written in 1964, expressed his opposition to a public accommodations law proposed —and enacted—for his home town of Phoenix, Ariz. Rehnquist argued that the ordinance would destroy "a measure of our traditional freedom."

Three years later, Rehnquist argued for the neighborhood school concept. "We are no more dedicated to an 'integrated' society, than we are to a 'segregated' society" he said. "We are instead dedicated to a free society in which each man is accorded the maximum amount of freedom of choice in his individual activities."

The only possible hitch in confirmation of Powell appeared to be the question of the manner in which he would deal with his investments while he sat on the court. Data provided to the Senate Judiciary Committee showed that Powell, his wife and son held stocks and other investments worth about $1.5-million. (A similar listing for Rehnquist and his immediate family placed their holdings' worth at about $77,000.) Powell had said earlier that he would make any arrangement necessary to insulate himself from holdings which might create conflicts of interest.

Hearings. The Senate Judiciary Committee held hearings on the nominations Nov. 3-4, and 8-10.

Opening the hearings, Eastland reported that the FBI investigations of the nominees had uncovered no flaw in either man's background or character. The American Bar Association committee on the federal judiciary had also found both men qualified for the nominations, Eastland said.

The ABA committee unanimously recommended Powell as meeting, to an exceptional degree, high standards of professional competence, judicial temperament and integrity. "He is one of the best qualified lawyers available," the report concluded. Rehnquist received a similar highly favorable endorsement from nine members of the ABA committee, but three members—while not opposing his nomination did not give him such a high rating.

Appearing Nov. 3-4 before the committee, Rehnquist was questioned closely as committee members attempted with relatively little success to uncover his personal philosophy. He did agree with conservative members that the Constitution should not be interpreted in order to achieve socially desirable ends, and that previous Supreme Court decisions should be given great weight in present and future rulings.

He promised to dissociate his personal philosophy "to the greatest extent possible" from his role on the court, but said too that he would not hesitate, as a justice, to adopt a position different from one he had advocated during his days in the Nixon administration. He said that those positions were not necessarily in accord with his personal feelings, but that he would have resigned his post, had those views been obnoxious to him.

Rehnquist disclaimed his 1964 writings on the public accommodations issue, saying that he no longer opposed such laws and that he had "come to realize the strong concern of minorities for the recognition of these rights." But he said he still opposed the use of busing for racial balance in school systems which had not formerly been dual segregated systems.

Declining to expound his personal views on various controversial matters on which the administration had taken a position, Rehnquist said that "it is a generally applicable principle in a lawyer-client relationship that the lawyer does not express personal views as to the merits of the client's case.... It would be disadvantageous to the government's position if I did disagree with it after having acted as an advocate for it)." His clients, he said, were the attorney general and the President.

Bayh, interested in probing Rehnquist's views further, wrote Nixon and Attorney General John N. Mitchell asking them to waive this lawyer-client privilege. Mitchell responded that this would be inappropriate because it would expose to the public confidential policy discussions within the executive branch.

"There is a limit beyond which no nominee can go in expressing an opinion at this particular juncture," said Roman L. Hruska (R Neb.). "Since Franklin Roosevelt, philosophy has played a part in the selection of court nominees. And...they have, since that time, all been of liberal views. It's about time for some balance."

Appearing before the committee Nov. 8, Powell told them that he would disqualify himself from any case involving a party in which he had any interest. He said that he would move promptly to limit his holdings but that he would retain certain investments in which sale of the stock would not remove his interest, such as those in companies which were clients of his firm.

The device of a "blind trust"—used to insulate a public official from knowledge of the holdings he has—accomplished little, Powell said. A judge needed to know what he owned in order to avoid inadvertent participation in cases in which he did have an interest, he said.

Powell said his concept of the role of the Supreme Court was based upon these tenets:

"I believe in the doctrine of the separation of powers...and that the court should not encroach upon the responsibility of the executive or the legislature; I believe in the federal system...; I believe in the importance of judicial restraint...that the court should avoid making a decision on constitutional grounds when other grounds are present; I believe in the power of precedent and a strong presumption in favor of upholding precedent; I believe that cases should be decided on the basis of the Constitution, the law and the facts before the court, putting aside one's own political and economic views and, to the extent possible, what one brings with him from his own background and experience. The court is the final authority and has great responsibility to uphold the rule of law...and to protect and safeguard the rights and liberties...of all our people."

Rehnquist Opposition. A number of witnesses appeared Nov. 9-10 to express opposition to the Rehnquist nomination. Among them were:

• Joseph L. Rauh, vice chairman, Americans for Democratic Action (ADA), who criticized Rehnquist for lacking respect for the rights of minorities and for the Bill of Rights. "This nominee," said Rauh, "is probably further to the right than any Supreme Court justice of this century."

• Clarence Mitchell, director, Washington bureau, National Association for the Advancement of Colored People (NAACP), and legislative chairman, Leadership Conference on Civil Rights, warned against this "self-proclaimed segregationist." "The Rehnquist nomination," he said, "raises a grim warning. Through that nomination the foot of racism is placed in the door of the temple of Justice. The Rehnquist record tells us that the hand of the oppressor will be given a chance to write opinions that will seek to turn back the clock of progress."

• Andrew J. Biemiller, AFL-CIO, described Rehnquist as a "right wing zealot" nominated to the court because he had demonstrated his "complete fealty to the administration's programs." "It is precisely because he is the administration's man," said Biemiller, "rather than his own that he should not sit on the high court."

Committee Action. After a delay of almost two weeks, the committee Nov. 23 voted unanimously to report favorably the Powell nomination and voted 12-4 to report favorably the Rehnquist nomination. The reports were filed Nov. 30.

Powell. The committee found Powell "thoroughly qualified" for the post of associate justice. It noted that supporting statements had come from black and white Virginians of different views, all "attesting to their respect for Mr. Powell's competence and fairness."

The committee said that in examining Powell's role in public education after the Supreme Court's 1954 school desegregation decision, it found that his predominant interest was in preserving and obtaining quality education for all Virginians, white and black. "He is remembered by those involved in the controversies of those years," wrote the committee, "as a moderating influence, seeking always to avoid hasty or extreme solutions and at the same time striving to obey the law of the land." The committee said it was entirely satisfied that Powell was dedicated to the concept of equal justice under law for all Americans.

Bayh, Philip A. Hart (D Mich.), Edward M. Kennedy (D Mass.) and John V. Tunney (D Calif.) supported the nomination, explaining their decision in light of some of the questions raised during the hearings about Powell's stand on questions of civil liberties and civil rights.

Questions about Powell's civil rights views—raised primarily in regard to his role in Virginia education—were resolved, the four senators said, by the record of his courageous efforts to keep the public schools open in the face of the massive resistance efforts to close, rather than desegregate, the schools.

"What his critics all too often have failed to realize," wrote the four senators, "is that it would be unfair to judge his individual specific actions without reference to the political context. We are convinced that...Powell was bucking the tide of opposition to change, pushing slowly but steadily toward the time when all the schools could be integrated."

Rehnquist. The committee found Rehnquist "thoroughly qualified" for the post of associate justice.

The committee felt that Rehnquist was "as responsive as he could be (in testimony before the committee) in view of his position in the government (as adviser to the President and the attorney general) and in view of the possibility that some of the questions he was asked might ultimately come before the Supreme Court."

The committee found the charges of Rehnquist's insensitivity on questions of civil rights to be "totally unfounded."

In a general observation, the committee majority pointed out that a judge and an advocate have essentially different roles: "The former must carefully weigh the strengths of competing arguments and public policy considerations while the latter owes a duty to his client to argue vigorously in support of his client's case.... Thus to draw sweeping generalizations from the positions an advocate has taken as a means of determining his fitness to be a judge is...mistaken."

The committee found that Rehnquist fully understood and believed in the guarantees of individual freedom embodied in the Bill of Rights: "He sees both sides of the difficult questions in this area, which require working out the delicate balance established by the Constitution between the rights of individuals and the duty of government to enforce the laws." His views, the committee concluded, "reflect a deep and unwavering commitment to the Constitution and represent advocacy in the best tradition of our legal system."

Bayh, Hart, Kennedy and Tunney included a lengthy memorandum outlining their reasons for opposing the Rehnquist nomination.

The Senate's role in confirmation of Supreme Court nominees, they said, went beyond rejecting those who were "obviously flawed by impropriety or incompetence." The Senate should weigh "the nominee's attitude toward the fundamental values of our constitutional system: limits on government power, individual liberty, human equality. A man takes what he is and believes to the bench," they said.

Rehnquist's record presented no problems of integrity or excellence, they said, but it raised serious questions about his commitment to those fundamental values.

Rather than reflecting a strict constructionist's point of view, said the committee minority, Rehnquist's statements mirrored a "strangely elastic approach to constitutional interpretation: The Bill of Rights and decisions upholding them...are read as narrowly as possible.... But provisions and precedents conferring executive power and declaring the general purposes of government are read loosely and expansively to justify the most intrusive kinds of official interference with those rights."

Furthermore, the four Democrats said, Rehnquist's record was "one of persistent indifference to the evils of discrimination and an almost hostile unwillingness to accept the use of law to overcome racial injustice in America."

Floor Action. The Senate Dec. 6, after three days of discussion, confirmed Powell by a vote of 89-1. The dissenting vote was cast by Fred R. Harris (D Okla.), who found Powell an elitist lacking compassion for "the little people."

Not a single critical word was directed at the nomination during debate. Paul J. Fannin (R Ariz.) pointed out that "debate is not very exciting when—as in this case—there is nothing to debate. After the first round of wonderful praise for Mr. Powell, all else is repetition."

William B. Spong Jr. (D Va.) remembered that "in the bitter aftermath of the Senate's rejection of the nomination of Judge Harrold Carswell, it was believed by many that a southerner could never be confirmed to a seat on the Supreme Court. I contested that view. I have always believed that a qualified southerner should be nominated, and, if nominated, could be confirmed, and if confirmed would serve the court and the nation with great distinction...Lewis F. Powell Jr...is such a man."

After the vote to confirm Powell, debate began on the more controversial Rehnquist nomination. Supporters complained that opponents of the nomination were filibustering, but the Senate, after four days of debate, refused Dec. 10 to limit debate. That day a cloture motion was rejected 52-42; a two-thirds majority—63 in this case—was needed for approval.

Bayh, leader of the opposition, then moved that the Senate put off the Rehnquist vote until Jan. 18, 1972. The Senate soundly rejected this motion, 22-70, and then voted, on a **key roll-call vote of 68-26**, to confirm Rehnquist. Opposing the nomination on the final vote were three Republicans—Edward W. Brooke (Mass.), Clifford P. Case (N.J.) and Jacob K. Javits (N.Y.)—and 23 Democrats.

Chronology Of Legislation On the Courts, 1969-1972

FEDERAL JUDGESHIPS. During his first term Nixon named almost as many federal judges and Supreme Court justices as had any President. Franklin D. Roosevelt held the existing record at 194 during his more than 12 years as President, but Nixon's 177 showed him certain to break that record during his second term. Nixon's achievement in this area was given substantial help by the Democratic Congress, which in 1970 approved legislation creating 58 additional permanent federal judgeships and three temporary ones.

1969. The Senate June 23 by voice vote and without debate passed and sent to the House a bill (S 952) creating 67 new permanent district judgeships and three temporary judgeships, most of which had been recommended by the U.S. Judicial Conference in 1968. The House Judiciary Committee held one day of hearings in October but took no further action.

The Senate Oct. 29, by a vote of 61-25, passed and sent to the House another bill (S 1508) which would allow federal judges to retire after 20 years on the federal bench, regardless of their age. The House failed to pass the bill. Under existing law, a federal judge could retire at age 65 after 15 years of service or at 70 after 10 years.

1970. Congress May 20 cleared S 952 for the White House. As finally approved, the bill created 58 new permanent federal district judgeships and three temporary posts. As signed by the President, the bill (PL 91-272):

• Authorized new permanent district judgeships for Alabama (2), Arizona (1), California (8), Colorado (1), Florida (3), Georgia (4), Illinois (2), Kentucky (2), Louisiana (3), Maryland (2), Michigan (2), Missouri (1), Nebraska (1), New Jersey (1), New Mexico (1), New York (4), Ohio (2), Pennsylvania (8), Puerto Rico (1), South Carolina (1), Tennessee (1), Texas (4), Virginia (1), Virgin Islands (1), West Virginia (1).

• Made permanent temporary judgeships in Kansas, Pennsylvania and Wisconsin.

• Authorized temporary judgeships in New Jersey, Pennsylvania and North Carolina.

The House Judiciary Committee had cut the number of judgeships in the bill by 13; the House had approved the amended bill March 18, 366-18. Conferees had compromised by adding to the House bill four more judgeships, one each in Maryland, Florida, Nebraska and West Virginia. The House adopted the conference report, 333-20, May 19; the Senate by voice vote the following day. The last judgeships bill cleared by Congress before 1970 was in 1966.

1971. The House Judiciary Committee Nov. 18 reported a bill (HR 11394) creating a new judicial district in Louisiana, and providing additional federal judgeships for Indiana, Florida, Texas and Missouri.

1972. The House Feb. 2 approved by voice vote HR 11394, providing five new federal district judgeships, one each in Indiana, Florida, Texas, Missouri and Wisconsin. The Senate took no action on the bill.

During floor consideration, the provisions creating a new judicial district for Louisiana were deleted without opposition; the same provisions had been attached to a private bill (HR 3749—PL 92-208) signed into law Dec. 18, 1971.

Congress July 31 cleared a bill (HR 6745—PL 92-376) altering the boundaries of the judicial district for the state of South Dakota. The state is one district made up of four divisions served by two district judges. The House passed the bill Feb. 7; the Senate July 31.

JUDICIAL SALARIES. A pay raise for Supreme Court justices and federal appeals and district judges went into effect Feb. 14, 1969, after Congress failed to veto the proposed increases. The pay raises increased the salary of the chief justice to $62,500 from $40,000, of associate justices to $60,000 from $39,500, of appeals court judges to $42,500 from $33,000, and of district judges to $40,000 from $30,000. The last judicial pay raise had been in 1964.

1972. Congress Aug. 9 cleared a bill (S 2854—PL 92-397) increasing the annuities paid to widows of Supreme Court justices to $10,000 each year from $5,000, and creating a contributory annuity system for retired and active justices. The Senate approved the bill June 30; the House approved a revised version Aug. 7; the Senate accepted the House version Aug. 9.

COURT PERSONNEL. Responding to the interest of Chief Justice Warren E. Burger in more efficient administration of the federal courts, Congress in 1970 cleared a bill (HR 17901—PL 91-647) providing for an executive to handle administrative duties for each of the 11 federal court circuits.

As signed into law, PL 91-647:

• Authorized the judicial council of each circuit to appoint a court executive and to delegate to him whatever administrative duties it considered advisable to delegate, subject to the general supervision of the circuit's chief judge.

• Established a five-member board of certification to set standards for and to certify qualified court executives.

• Authorized the Judicial Conference of the United States to set each executive's salary.

The court executive would, it was hoped, free the circuit's chief judge from many day-to-day administrative tasks; the concept was backed by the Justice Department, the Administrative Office of the U.S. Courts, and the American Bar Association (ABA). With ABA backing, an institute was established to train these executives.

The House approved the bill by voice vote under suspension of rules Oct. 5. The Senate approved the bill without change Dec. 22.

National Court of Appeals

Creation of a new high federal court to decide what cases the Supreme Court should consider was formally proposed Dec. 19, 1972, by a study group appointed by Chief Justice Warren E. Burger.

Headed by Harvard law professor Paul A. Freund, the study group was assembled under the aegis of the Federal Judicial Center. After a year's study, the group recommended:

- Creation, by law, of a National Court of Appeals to screen all requests for review of cases that now go to the Supreme Court and to decide certain cases in which courts within two judicial circuits have issued conflicting rulings.
- Elimination, by statute, of three-judge federal district courts (most often convened to hear constitutional questions) and elimination of the provision for direct review by the Supreme Court of three-judge court decisions, and of decisions in Interstate Commerce Commission (ICC) and antitrust cases.
- Establishment, by law, of a nonjudicial body to investigate and report on the complaints of prisoners.
- Increased staff support for the justices.

The new court was not to have a permanent set of its own judges, but would instead be composed of seven judges, drawn from the judges sitting on federal courts of appeals, to sit for staggered three-year terms.

All cases (except, it is assumed, those which go to the court under its own special original jurisdiction) which are now filed in the Supreme Court would go to this National Court of Appeals. There, they would be screened and denied or referred to the Supreme Court.

The study group's recommendations were expected to go to Congress and to the newly established federal Commission on Revision of the Federal Court Appellate System.

1971. The House approved a bill (HR 8699) on July 13, by a 263-139 vote, providing the Chief Justice with an administrative assistant similar to that provided by PL 91-647 for the chief judges of the federal circuits. The Senate took no action.

1972. Congress Feb. 18 cleared HR 8699 (PL 92-238) authorizing the Chief Justice to appoint himself an administrative aide, to assign certain duties to him and to pay him a salary of up to $40,000. Final action came with Senate passage, by voice vote, of the bill as approved by the House.

JUDICIAL REFORM. Two Senate Judiciary subcommittees held hearings in 1969 on legislation dealing with judicial reform in the aftermath of the resignation of Associate Justice Abe Fortas, but Congress left the matter of setting limits on the extrajudicial activities of federal judges to the federal judiciary.

1969. The Senate Dec. 9 approved by voice vote a bill (S 2624) to modernize the customs courts.

1970. Congress May 19 cleared S 2624 (PL 91-271) which:

- Provided a single, continuous procedure for deciding all issues in any entry of merchandise.

- Increased the length of time for importers to file requests for administrative and judicial review.
- Eliminated automatic referrals to the Customs Court by the bureau of denials of appeals, and set a two-year limit on the period the bureau had to dispose of an appeal.
- Provided that normally all customs cases before the Customs Court should be tried by a single judge (instead of by a three-judge panel as previously required).

The House approved an amended bill May 18 by a 310-0 roll-call vote; the Senate concurred May 19.

1972. Congress Oct. 4 cleared HR 7378 (PL 92-489) establishing a Commission on Revision of the Federal Court Appellate System of the United States to study and recommend changes in the geographic boundaries of the circuit courts and the structure and procedure of all federal appeals courts.

The House approved one version of the bill May 15, by a 317-25 roll-call vote, only authorizing the study of the geographic boundaries of the appeals courts circuits. The Senate approved an amended bill by voice vote June 30, expanding the time and scope of the mandate, and authorizing the commission to look into all facets of the problems of the appellate courts.

Conferees, reporting Sept. 28, gave the 16-member commission six months to study and recommend changes in the boundaries of the circuits, and 15 months to study and recommend more structural and procedural changes. The 16 members were to be appointed, four each by the chief justice, Senate, House and President. The Senate adopted the conference report by voice vote Sept. 29, the House Oct. 4.

MAGISTRATES. Congress in 1972 cleared two bills concerning U.S. magistrates, the judicial officers of federal district courts. Their functions include issuing search and arrest warrants, fixing bail, holding preliminary hearings and conducting trials for minor offenses.

On Feb. 18 the Senate by voice vote approved and cleared HR 9180 (PL 92-239), which authorized temporary assignment of magistrates outside their regular jurisdictions during emergencies. The bill, backed by the Justice Department, was an amendment to the Federal Magistrates Act of 1968. The House had approved HR 9180 by a 344-10 roll-call vote Nov. 1, 1971.

Congress Sept. 12 cleared a bill (HR 7375—PL 92-428) increasing the statutory ceiling for magistrates' salaries to $30,000 annually from $22,500. The ceiling for part-time magistrates was increased to $15,000 from $11,000. The House approved the bill by voice vote May 16; the Senate approved an amended version by voice vote Aug. 18. The House agreed to the Senate changes Sept. 12.

CLAIMS AND JURIES. Congress in 1972 cleared a bill (HR 12979—PL 92-375) providing for the temporary recall of retired senior commissioners of the U.S. Court of Claims when the court needed them. The commissioners hold hearings to determine facts and make recommendations and determinations which are reviewed by the court. The House approved the bill by voice vote April 17; the Senate by voice vote July 31.

Congress in 1972 also cleared a bill (S 1975—PL 92-269) lowering the required age for federal jury service to 18 from 21. The Senate had approved the bill Dec. 1, 1971, by voice vote; the House approved an amended bill March 6 by voice vote; the Senate cleared the bill by accepting the House changes March 24.

Supreme Court Decisions, 1969-1972

"We need a court which looks upon its function as being that of interpretation rather than of breaking through into new areas," declared candidate Richard Nixon in 1968. He promised to rebalance the court with men who realized that some Warren court decisions had "tended to weaken the peace forces as against the criminal forces."

Between 1969 and 1972 Nixon placed a new chief justice and three new associate justices on the court, more in a four-year period than any president since Harding. But by 1972 it was apparent that Nixon's reshaping of the court had not had quite the result he envisioned: over administration protest the court had outlawed the death penalty, refused to halt publication of the Pentagon Papers articles in *The New York Times* and *The Washington Post,* approved the use of busing to desegregate public schools, and rejected the administration's claim that it did not have to get court approval of wiretaps on domestic groups suspected of subversion.

No Warren court ruling had been overturned: the very decisions decried by Nixon had hardened quickly into precedent requiring respect from the new conservative justices. The court chipped away at the scope of some of these rulings, such as the *Miranda* decision, announced in 1966 by a 5-4 court. In that ruling the court had barred use as evidence of any statements made by a defendant whom police had not properly informed of his constitutional rights. Joined by Blackmun and Burger, the three *Miranda* dissenters who remained—Harlan, Stewart and White—formed a new majority by 1971 in ruling that such statements, if voluntary, could be used under certain circumstances to impeach a defendant's credibility.

Another way in which the force of some earlier rulings was limited was by holdings condoning certain violations of rights as merely harmless error, given other facts in a particular case. Rehnquist, in the first majority opinion he wrote, applied this approach to violation of the right to face one's accusers.

Criminal Law. Because of Supreme Court rulings in criminal law during this post-Warren period, by 1972 *(Criminal law decisions, p. 306):*

- The death penalty as it had been imposed in the United States was outlawed.

- If a defendant had been overheard on an illegal wiretap, the government had to chose between disclosing to him all material obtained from the wiretap and dropping the case against him.

- The government had to go to court to get approval for electronic surveillance of domestic groups suspected to be subversive.

- State juries of fewer than 12 persons could try persons charged with non-capital offenses; but states had to provide jury trials for all persons charged with offenses entailing possible sentences of more than six months.

- State juries could find a person guilty by a less than unanimous vote.

- Judges could order disruptive defendants bound, gagged and removed from the courtroom if necessary to proceed with the trial; but if the judge charged a defendant with contempt for behavior during the trial, another judge would preside over the contempt trial.

- Juveniles had the right to be found guilty—or delinquent—beyond a reasonable doubt, but did not have a constitutional right to trial by jury.

- The right to legal counsel applied to all persons charged with any offense involving possible imprisonment, and to persons at certain preliminary stages of the criminal proceedings, but not to persons in pre-indictment line-ups.

- States could not make the private possession of obscene material or the distribution of contraceptives to unmarried persons a crime.

- Judges could no longer sentence a guilty man to "$30 or 30 days"; nor could poor prisoners be held in jail beyond their maximum sentence to "work off" fines they could not pay.

Civil Rights. All court-ordered efforts to erase the effects of legal school segregation continued to win Supreme Court backing. In other civil rights cases, the court held that community swim clubs could not exclude black residents from membership when all white residents were accepted, but that federal civil rights law did not reach a private club with a state liquor license and a discriminatory guest policy.

A city, held the court, could close all its municipal swimming pools rather than desegregate them; states could condition all construction of low-income housing projects on approval by local referendum. But employers could not impose job requirements on applicants if those criteria were unrelated to job performance and disqualified more black job applicants than whites.

Congress could, by law—not just by constitutional amendment—lower the voting age to 18 for federal elections, held the court, at the same time disapproving congressional enactment of the lower voting age for state and local elections. State residency requirements of more than 30 days for voters were invalidated. And the court insisted on strict mathematical equality of population between congressional districts within a state.

First Amendment Rights. Watching over the separation of church and state, the court in 1970 backed property tax exemptions for church-owned lands used for religious purposes; but the next year it invalidated state laws allowing state reimbursement of private schools for certain educational costs. In 1972 it approved the exemption of Amish children from compulsory public school attendance laws.

The fairness doctrine for broadcasters was upheld and libel protection for newspapers was reinforced. In a historic confrontation, the court sided with the press in denying the government's plea to halt publication of newspaper articles based on the once-classified Pentagon Papers. A year later, the court held that the First Amendment did not protect newsmen from grand jury efforts to obtain information, even confidential information. And it narrowed congressional immunity by holding that a senator could be prosecuted for accepting a bribe to cast a certain vote.

New Horizons. Despite Nixon's desire that the Supreme Court stick to interpreting the law and not break through into new areas, the court by 1972 was dealing with the problems of sex discrimination, the rights of consumers, of tenants and of welfare recipients, and the growing concern over man's effect on his environment. The court's docket reflected the new concern of the nation it served, and the court in 1972 evidenced its traditional caution but no reluctance in grasping those issues and blazing—carefully—new legal trails.

Crime and Constitutional Rights

Spinelli v. U.S., decided by a 5-3 vote, Jan. 27, 1969. Harlan wrote the opinion; Marshall did not participate; Black, Fortas and Stewart dissented.

Just a report of a reliable informer's tip containing some specific details is not sufficient cause for issuing search warrant, even though tip was corroborated by other sworn charges resulting from independent investigation and by reputation of suspect.

Davis v. Mississippi, decided by a 6-2 vote, April 22, 1969. Brennan wrote the opinion; Fortas did not participate; Black and Stewart dissented.

John Davis, a young black Mississippian, was convicted of rape after his fingerprints, obtained by the police during his warrantless detention as part of a police dragnet, matched those found at the scene of the crime. The court reversed his conviction, finding that this taking of his fingerprints violated the Fourth Amendment guarantee against unreasonable search and seizure. The fingerprints so obtained could thus not be used as evidence against him, held the court, directing that henceforth, such "investigatory arrests" must be authorized by warrants if the evidence obtained during them was to be used in court.

"Nothing is more clear," stated the majority, "than that the Fourth Amendment was meant to prevent wholesale intrusions upon the personal security of our citizenry, whether these intrusions be termed 'arrests' or 'investigatory detentions'." In dissent, Justice Black lamented the decision as "one more in an ever-expanding list of cases in which this court has been so widely blowing up the Fourth Amendment's scope that its original authors would be hard put to recognize their creation."

Chimel v. California, decided by a 6-2 vote, June 23, 1969, Stewart wrote the opinion; Black and White dissented.

Over complaints from Justices Black and White that the court was imposing unreasonable restrictions upon police action, the court overruled a 20-year-old decision (*U.S. v. Rabinowitz, 1950*) to narrow the area which could be searched, without a warrant, incident to an lawful arrest. If police wished to search further than the immediate area from which the arrested person could reach to obtain a weapon or destroy evidence, they must obtain a search warrant, held the court. A person's entire dwelling could not be subjected to a warrantless search simply because he was arrested there.

Colonnade Catering Corp. v. U.S. decided by a 5-3 vote, Feb. 25, 1970. Opinion by Douglas; Burger, Black and Stewart dissented.

Congress has not authorized federal tax agents, forcibly and without a warrant, to enter the premises owned or operated by a liquor dealer. Congress has instead made it an offense for a dealer to refuse to admit the inspecting agent.

Vale v. Louisiana, decided by a 6-2 vote, June 22, 1970. Stewart wrote the opinion; Blackmun did not participate; Burger and Black dissented.

Police without a warrant cannot constitutionally search a suspect's house incident to his arrest just outside. Burger and Black criticized the majority for failing to appreciate the problem faced by a police officer who had now to leave the premises—and possible evidence—to obtain a search warrant. The ruling, they said, made "unnecessarily difficult the conviction of those who prey upon society."

Whiteley v. Warden, decided by a 6-3 vote, March 29, 1971. Harlan wrote the opinion; Black, Burger and Blackmun dissented.

Police cannot constitutionally arrest someone on the basis of information broadcast over police radio when that information had been considered insufficient for issuing an arrest warrant. Black complained that this decision was "a gross and wholly indefensible miscarriage of justice," a decision "calculated to make many good people believe our court actually enjoys frustrating justice by unnecessarily turning professional criminals loose to prey upon society with impunity."

Williams v. U.S., Hill v. California, decided by a 6-2 vote, April 5, 1971. White wrote the opinions; Douglas did not participate; Harlan and Marshall dissented in part.

The court refused to make its *Chimel* decision retroactive, applying it only to searches occurring after that ruling. The court in *Hill* refused to invalidate the warrantless, pre-*Chimel* search of the entire apartment of a defendant incident to the mistaken warrantless arrest there of a person resembling the defendant.

Coolidge v. New Hampshire, decided by a 5-4 vote, June 21, 1971. Stewart wrote the opinion; Burger, Black, Blackmun and White dissented in part.

Evidence cannot be used at trial if it was seized, held the court, by officers acting with a search warrant issued by an official actively involved in prosecuting the particular case: warrants must be authorized by "neutral and detached magistrates" in order to be constitutionally valid. Evidence obtained by police from a defendant's home without a warrant but with his wife's permission is admissible at trial, but not evidence obtained from his car by a warrantless search.

Search and Seizure

The right of the people to be secure in their persons, houses, papers and effects, against unreasonable searches and seizures, shall not be violated, and no warrants shall issue, but upon probable cause, supported by oath or affirmation and particularly describing the place to be searched, and the persons or things to be seized.

Fourth Amendment, U.S. Constitution

Bivens v. Six Unknown Federal Agents, decided by a 6-3 vote, June 21, 1971. Brennan wrote the opinion; Burger, Black and Blackmun dissented.

A person whose dwelling was searched illegally by federal agents who arrested him may sue those agents for damages for violation of his constitutional right against unreasonable search and seizure. Chief Justice Burger dissented, arguing that Congress alone could create this remedy—of a damage suit—against the federal government.

U.S. v. Harris, decided by a 5-4 vote, June 28, 1971. Burger wrote the opinion; Harlan, Douglas, Brennan and Marshall dissented.

The court upheld as probable cause for a search of a suspected moonshiner's premises an affidavit based on an informer's tip and the suspect's reputation.

U.S. v. Biswell, decided by an 8-1 vote, May 15, 1972. White wrote the opinion; Douglas dissented.

A warrantless inspection of a gun dealer's storeroom during business hours was not an unreasonable search if necessary for effective enforcement of federal firearms law.

Adams v. Williams, decided by a 6-3 vote, June 12, 1972. Rehnquist wrote the opinion; dissenting were Douglas, Brennan and Marshall.

Police, with informer's tip but without search warrant, can properly and reasonably stop a person and search him for an illegally possessed weapon.

WIRETAPPING

Alderman v. U.S., Butenko v. U.S., Ivanov v. U.S., decided by a 5-3 vote, March 10, 1969. White wrote the opinion; Marshall did not participate; Black, Harlan and Fortas dissented.

The court, to the dismay of the Justice Department, ruled that the federal government must turn over for examination all material obtained by illegal electronic surveillance to a defendant whose rights were violated by the surveillance and against whom they might be used, even if the surveillance involved the national security. The court also held that such material, although unusable as evidence against anyone whose constitutional rights against unreasonable search and seizure had been violated in the surveillance, might be usable as evidence against another defendant whose rights had not been so violated.

Justice White, in his opinion, made clear the "search and seizure" aspect of electronic surveillance; "the right to be secure in one's house against unauthorized intrusion is not limited to protection against a policeman viewing or seizing tangible property." This right is "as clearly invaded when the police enter and install a listening device in his house as they are when the entry is made to undertake a warrantless search for tangible property.... Like physical evidence which might be seized overheard conversations are fruits of an illegal entry and are inadmissible in evidence," against the owner, whether or not he was present or participating in the conversations.

The court rejected the government's argument that a judge should first determine, through inspection in his chambers the "arguably relevant" information in the illegally obtained material and then turn over to the defendant only such relevant matter:

"The task is too complex, and the margin for error too great, to rely wholly on the...judgment of the trial court to identify those records which might have contributed to the government's case."

Desist v. U.S., decided by a 5-3 vote, March 24, 1969. Stewart wrote the opinion; Marshall did not participate; dissenting were Harlan, Fortas and Douglas.

The court refused to apply its landmark 1968 decision on wiretapping in the case of *Katz v. U.S.* retroactively. In *Katz* the court had reversed a 40-year-old decision *(Olmstead v. U.S. 1928)* to hold that whether or not actual physical trespass occurs (as in the installation of an electronic device), any electronic surveillance which is not approved ahead of time by a court is unconstitutional as an unreasonable search and seizure. Stewart said that the court felt the decision should only apply to cases occurring after it because it was a "clear break" with the 1928 holding.

U.S. v. White, decided by a 6-3 vote, April 5, 1971. White wrote the opinion; Douglas, Harlan and Marshall dissented.

Opening a loophole in its wall of disapproval of warrantless electronic surveillance, the court held that it was not unconstitutional for an electronic device to be voluntarily carried by an informer, without a warrant, to overhear conversations between the informer and another person. In his dissent, Douglas argued that such monitoring of conversations stifled free speech: "Free discourse...may be frivolous or serious, humble or defiant, reactionary or revolutionary, profane or in good taste; but it is not free if there is surveillance.... Must everyone live in fear that every word he speaks may be transmitted or recorded and later repeated to the entire world? I can imagine nothing that has a more chilling effect on people speaking their minds and expressing their views on important matters."

U.S. v. U.S. District Court, Eastern Michigan, decided by a 6-2 vote, June 19, 1972. Powell wrote the opinion; Rehnquist did not participate; Burger and White dissented.

The court rejected the Justice Department's claim that it did not have to get court approval for the use of electronic surveillance of persons or domestic groups suspected to be subversive. Powell wrote: "The price of lawful public dissent must not be a dread of subjection to an unchecked surveillance power. Nor must the fear of unauthorized official eavesdropping deter vigorous citizen dissent and discussion of government action in private conversation. For private dissent, no less than open public discourse, is essential to our free society."

"Unreviewed executive discretion," warned Powell, "may yield too readily to pressures to obtain incriminating evidence and overlook potential invasions of privacy and protected speech.... We cannot accept the government's argument that internal security matters are too subtle and complex for judicial evaluation.... If the threat is too subtle or complex for our senior law enforcement officers to convey its significance to a court, one may question whether there is probable cause for surveillance."

CONGRESS AND THE NATION, VOL. III

Gelbard v. U.S., U.S. v. Egan, decided by a 5-4 vote, June 26, 1972. Brennan wrote the opinion; Burger, Blackmun, Powell and Rehnquist dissented.

A grand jury witness may refuse to testify—without risking contempt charges—until the government proves that the evidence on which he was called to appear was not obtained by illegal electronic surveillance. The Nixon nominees, in dissent, complained that the majority had "stood on its head both the language and the legislative history" of the law to reach this result; neither the 1968 Omnibus Crime Control and Safe Streets Act nor the 1970 Organized Crime Control Act supported such "expansive and novel claims" as those upheld by the majority. *(Story p. 265; Congress and the Nation Vol. II p. 323)*

DOUBLE JEOPARDY

Benton v. Maryland, decided by a 6-2 vote, June 23, 1969. Marshall wrote the opinion; Harlan and Stewart dissented.

In the last announced decision of the Warren Court, the court overruled its 32-year-old holding in *Palko v. Connecticut (1937)* to apply the constitutional guarantee against double jeopardy to the states. The double jeopardy clause was thus the last of the provisions of the Bill of Rights to be found to apply to the states through the Fourteenth Amendment guarantee of due process. In an earlier decision the majority had held that if a right guaranteed by the Bill of Rights is "fundamental to the American scheme of justice," it must also apply to the states. The double jeopardy clause was certainly fundamental, ruled the court.

North Carolina v. Pearce, Simpson v. Rice, decided by a 6-2 vote, June 23, 1969. Stewart wrote the opinion; Black and Harlan dissented in part.

The double jeopardy clause requires that a judge credit punishment already exacted when resentencing a defendant who has been retried for an offense for which he has already once been convicted and sentenced. If a more severe sentence is imposed after the retrial, the judge must place in the record affirmative reasons for the heavier penalty, based objectively on the conduct of the defendant since his original sentencing.

Ashe v. Swenson, decided by a 7-1 vote, April 6, 1970. Stewart wrote the opinion; Burger dissented.

After a jury has acquitted a man on charges of robbing one victim of a multi-victim single robbery, that same man cannot be retried on charges of robbing another of the victims. The majority held that the doctrine of collateral estoppel was part of the double jeopardy guarantee: "when an issue of ultimate fact once has been determined by a valid and final judgment, that issue cannot again be litigated between the same parties in any future lawsuit."

Waller v. Florida, decided by a 8-0 vote, April 6, 1970. Burger wrote the opinion.

State cannot try person on charge arising from same action for which he has already been tried and convicted by municipal court.

Double Jeopardy

"...Nor shall any person be subject for the same offense to be twice put in jeopardy of life or limb; nor shall be compelled in any criminal case to be a witness against himself, nor be deprived of life, liberty, or property, without due process of law...."

Fifth Amendment, U.S. Constitution

Price v. Georgia, decided by an 8-0 vote, June 15, 1970. Burger wrote the opinion; Blackmun did not participate.

Once a man has been tried on murder charges, convicted only of manslaughter, and had that conviction overturned, he cannot be retried by the state on any more serious charge than manslaughter. A guilty verdict on a lesser included offense, such as manslaughter, is an "implicit acquittal" on a greater charge, such as murder.

SELF-INCRIMINATION

Orozco v. Texas, decided by a 6-2 vote, March 25, 1969. Black wrote the opinion; Fortas did not participate; White and Stewart dissented.

The court's landmark ruling in *Miranda v. Arizona* —that a suspect, before interrogation by police, must be advised of his constitutional right to remain silent and to have legal counsel—applied to questioning of a suspect in custody outside as well as inside a police station, even in bed in his own home. White complained that the court was tightening the constitutional straitjacket into which *Miranda* had laced law enforcement officials. *(Congress and the Nation Vol. II p. 323)*

Leary v. U.S., decided by an 8-0 vote, May 19, 1969. Harlan wrote the opinion.

Reversing the conviction of former Harvard psychologist Timothy F. Leary for failing to pay a federal tax on marijuana transfers, the court found the law imposing the tax unconstitutional as a violation of the right not to incriminate oneself. Anyone complying with the federal law would provide evidence which would incriminate him under state laws forbidding the possession of marijuana.

Minor v. U.S., Buie v. U.S., decided by a 6-2 vote, Dec. 8, 1969. White wrote the opinion; Douglas and Black dissented.

Refusing to reverse convictions of men for selling heroin and marijuana without the federal order forms required by law, the court held that the law requiring use of those forms did not violate the privilege against self-incrimination. Drug dealers were not forced to incriminate themselves by selling without the required forms; they did have the alternative of not selling the drugs at all.

Turner v. U.S., decided by a 6-2 vote, Jan. 20, 1970. White wrote the opinion; Black and Douglas dissented.

The court upheld a federal law presuming that a person possessing heroin—not stamped with federal tax stamps—knows that it is illegally produced, purchased, possessed and distributed—because heroin is not produced in the United States or legally imported. But the court invalidated a similar law concerning possession of unstamped cocaine, because some cocaine is produced in the United States, and some is legally imported.

Brady v. U.S., decided by an 8-0 vote, ***Parker v. North Carolina,*** decided by a 5-3 vote, May 4, 1970. White wrote the opinions; Douglas, Brennan and Marshall dissented in the second case.

A guilty plea entered in a capital case to avoid a possible death sentence is not an involuntary guilty plea in violation of the right against self-incrimination.

McMann v. Richardson, decided by a 5-3 vote, May 4, 1970. White wrote the opinion; Douglas, Brennan and Marshall dissented.

Prisoner's claim that his guilty plea, entered with advice of counsel, was induced by an earlier coerced confession does not win him a federal *habeas corpus* hearing on the voluntariness of the plea.

North Carolina v. Alford, decided by a 6-3 vote, Nov. 23, 1970. White wrote the opinion; Douglas, Brennan and Marshall dissented.

A murder defendant's claim to innocence did not foreclose court acceptance of his plea of guilty to second-degree murder when the plea was made with the advice of counsel, supported by substantial evidence and motivated by the desire to avoid the death penalty.

Harris v. New York, decided by a 5-4 vote, Feb. 24, 1971. Burger wrote the opinion; Black, Douglas, Brennan and Marshall dissented.

Modifying its ban imposed in *Miranda v. Arizona (1966)* on any in-court use of statements made by defendants not properly advised of their rights, the court held that these statements, so long as they were voluntary, could be used to impeach a defendant's credibility if he contradicted them in testifying in his own behalf. Burger wrote that "every criminal defendant is privileged to testify in his own defense or to refuse to do so. But that privilege cannot be construed to include the right to commit perjury.... The shield provided by *Miranda* cannot be perverted into a license to use perjury by way of a defense, free from the risk of confrontation with prior inconsistent utterances." In dissent, Brennan warned that the court was undoing much of the progress made by the Warren court in requiring police methods to remain within constitutional bounds.

U.S. v. Freed, decided by a 9-0 vote, April 5, 1971. Douglas wrote the opinion.

As revised in 1968, the existing federal gun control law, requiring registration of firearms only by transferor and forbidding use of information provided by registration for prosecution, does not violate the privilege against self-incrimination. *(Congress and the Nation Vol. II p. 328)*

California v. Byers, decided by a 5-4 vote, May 17, 1971. Burger wrote the opinion; Black, Douglas, Brennan and Marshall dissented.

The five-man majority declined to overthrow, as a violation of the Fifth Amendment right not to incriminate

---

Fair Trial

In all criminal prosecutions, the accused shall enjoy the right to a speedy and public trial, by an impartial jury of the state and district wherein the crime shall have been committed,...and to be informed of the nature and cause of the accusation; to be confronted with the witnesses against him; to have compulsory process for obtaining witnesses in his favor, and to have the assistance of counsel for his defense.

—Sixth Amendment, U.S. Constitution

---

oneself, state laws requiring motorists involved in accidents to stop and identify themselves even though no restriction is imposed on prosecutorial use of that information.

Lego v. Twomey, decided by a 4-3 vote, Jan. 12, 1972. White wrote the opinion; Douglas, Brennan and Marshall dissented.

A confession could be used as evidence, held a bare majority, if it was proved voluntary by a preponderance of the evidence (not beyond a reasonable doubt). Brennan, writing for the dissenters, argued that "it is...critical to our system of criminal justice that when a person's words are used against him, no reasonable doubt remains that he spoke of his own free will."

Kastigar v. U.S., decided by a 5-2 vote, May 22, 1972. Powell wrote the opinion; Rehnquist and Brennan did not participate; Douglas and Marshall dissented.

The court upheld the narrowed witness immunity provisions of the 1970 Organized Crime Control Act, approving—as no infringement of the Fifth Amendment—a limited grant of immunity from prosecution to a witness compelled to testify. The court did specify however that in any subsequent prosecution of the witness, the prosecution must show that the evidence against the witness was derived from sources independent of his own testimony. *(Story, p. 265)*

Brooks v. Tennessee, decided by a 6-3 vote, June 7, 1972. Brennan wrote the opinion; Burger, Blackmun and Rehnquist dissented.

A defendant's Fifth Amendment right against self-incrimination is violated by a state law which requires him to testify first in his defense presentation or not at all.

FAIR TRIAL

Illinois v. Allen, decided by an 8-0 vote, March 31, 1970. Black wrote the opinion.

The right to be present at one's own trial is not absolute, ruled the court. A defendant can lose his right to be present if, after being warned that he will be removed from the courtroom if he continues to disrupt the trial, he continues to act in such a way that the trial cannot continue while he is present. Black noted that it would also be constitutionally permissible, if necessary, for a judge to have an obstreperous defendant bound and gagged.

Dickey v. Florida, decided by an 8-0 vote, May 25, 1970. Burger wrote the opinion.

The right to a speedy trial is denied by a seven-year-delay between arrest and trial, even if the defendant is, for that period, in federal prison in another state.

Williams v. Florida, decided by a 7-1 vote, June 22, 1970. White wrote the opinion; Blackmun did not participate; Marshall dissented.

In non-capital cases a six-member jury can try a defendant just as constitutionally as a 12-member panel. The number 12 as applied to jury composition was merely an "historical accident"; the number had significance only to mystics; the jury could perform its role just as well with six as with 12 members.

On a secondary question, the court ruled, 6-2, that a defendant's rights are not violated by a state requirement that he inform the prosecution of his alibi defense and the related witnesses ahead of time. Black and Douglas dissented.

Baldwin v. New York, decided by a 5-3 vote, June 22, 1970. White wrote the opinion; Blackmun did not participate; Burger, Harlan and Stewart dissented.

States must provide trial by jury for all persons charged with offenses punishable by more than six months imprisonment.

Coleman v. Alabama, decided by a 6-2 vote, June 22, 1970. Brennan wrote the opinion; Blackmun did not participate; Burger and Stewart dissented.

The right to counsel applies at a preliminary hearing which is a critical stage in a state's criminal proceedings.

California v. Green, decided by a 7-1 vote, June 22, 1970. White wrote the opinion; Blackmun did not participate; Brennan dissented.

A sworn pre-trial statement made by a witness may be used as evidence at trial if the witness at the trial contradicts the earlier statement; it may also be used as evidence even if the witness is not present at the trial so long as the defense had opportunity to cross-examine at pretrial hearing.

Dutton v. Evans, decided by a 5-4 vote, Dec. 14, 1970. Stewart wrote the opinion; Black, Douglas, Brennan and Marshall dissented.

The right to confront witnesses testifying against oneself is not violated by Georgia's law allowing, as an exception to the rule against hearsay evidence, the use, as evidence, of a statement made by a non-testifying co-conspirator, during a conspiracy's "concealment" phase.

Mayberry v. Pennsylvania, decided by a 9-0 vote, Jan. 20, 1971. Douglas wrote the opinion.

Criminal defendant charged with contempt for insulting the trial judge while disrupting trial proceedings is entitled to a public trial by another judge on the contempt charges.

Groppi v. Wisconsin, decided by an 8-1 vote, Jan. 25, 1971. Stewart wrote the opinion; Black dissented.

State law barring change of place of trial for any misdemeanor case deprives defendant—who could be sentenced to one year in prison—of his right to trial by an impartial jury.

Nelson v. O'Neil, decided by a 6-3 vote, June 1, 1971. Stewart wrote the opinion; Douglas, Brennan and Marshall dissented.

The right to confront witnesses testifying against oneself was not denied the defendant whose jointly-tried co-defendant came to the witness stand after his statement implicating the defendant was admitted into evidence, denied making the statement and testified favorably to the defendant.

McKeiver v. Pennsylvania, decided by a 6-3 vote, and *In Re Burrus*, decided by a 5-4 vote, June 21, 1971. Blackmun wrote the opinion; Douglas, Black and Marshall dissented in both, joined by Brennan in the second case.

The Sixth Amendment does not establish a right to trial by jury for a juvenile delinquent.

U.S. v. Marion, decided by a 7-0 vote, Dec. 20, 1971. White wrote the opinion.

The right to a speedy trial does not require dismissal of an indictment returned three years after the alleged crime became known to the government; that right concerns the interval between arrest or charges and the trial. The right to due process may bar excessive and unjustified delay in seeking the indictment, but harm from the delay must be shown before the indictment can be dismissed on that basis.

Adams v. Illinois, decided by a 5-2 vote, March 6, 1972. Brennan wrote the decision; Powell and Rehnquist did not participate; Douglas and Marshall dissented.

The court held that its 1970 decision in *Coleman v. Alabama*—requiring that counsel be provided at preliminary hearings—was not retroactive and applied only to hearings held after the date of its announcement.

Schneble v. Florida, decided by a 6-3 vote, March 21, 1972. Rehnquist wrote the opinion; Douglas, Marshall and Brennan dissented.

The right to confront witnesses against oneself was not violated by use, as evidence against murder defendant, of out-of-court statement by non-testifying jointly-tried co-defendant which contradicted an initial out-of-court statement of innocence by defendant and corroborated a later confession. If this use of evidence violated the court's 1968 decision *(Bruton v. U.S.)* guaranteeing this right of confrontation, it was only a harmless error. The dissenters said that the court had emasculated the 1968 decision.

Johnson v. Louisiana, Apodaca v. Oregon, decided by a 5-4 vote, May 22, 1972. White wrote the opinion; Douglas, Brennan, Stewart, and Marshall dissented.

The constitutional guarantee of a jury trial, as applied to states, does not require the jury to be unanimous in its verdict; lack of unanimity on the question of guilt does not itself indicate reasonable doubt of guilt. Douglas found the decision "a radical departure from American tradition." He and the other dissenters warned that this would allow nine jurors to ignore the views of their fellow jurors who were of a different race or class. And Marshall viewed this as cutting the heart out of the right to a jury trial and the right to be found guilty beyond a reasonable doubt.

Kirby v. Illinois, decided by a 5-4 vote, June 7, 1972. Stewart wrote the opinion; Douglas, Brennan, Marshall and White dissented.

Before indictment, the right to counsel does not apply at post-arrest investigatory confrontations, like line-ups.

Argersinger v. Hamlin, decided by a 9-0 vote, June 12, 1972. Douglas wrote the opinion.

The right to counsel applies to all offenses, state or federal, which involve any potential incarceration.

Barker v. Wingo, decided by a 9-0 vote, June 22, 1972. Powell wrote the opinion.

When defining the precise meaning of the constitutional right to a speedy trial, the court "cannot definitely say how long is too long in a system where justice is supposed to be swift but deliberate." No inflexible rule can be set, but a balancing test must be applied in which the conduct of both the prosecution and the defense are considered. Among the factors which should be considered also are: length of delay, reason for delay, defendant's assertion of his right to a speedy trial and the harm to the defendant resulting from the delay.

CAPITAL PUNISHMENT

Furman v. Georgia, Jackson v. Georgia, Branch v. Texas, decided by a 5-4 vote, June 29, 1972. Unsigned opinion with separate opinions filed by Douglas, Brennan, Stewart, White and Marshall in the majority; Burger, Blackmun, Powell and Rehnquist each in dissent.

"The court holds that the imposition and carrying out of the death penalty in these cases constitutes cruel and unusual punishment in violation of the Eighth and Fourteenth Amendments." And so the death penalty, as it was at that time imposed in each of the 50 states, was declared unconstitutional.

Brennan and Marshall held executions *per se* "cruel and unusual punishment." "The calculated killing of a human being by the state," wrote Brennan, "involves, by its very nature, a denial of the executed person's humanity."

Continuing, Brennan wrote: "The punishment of death is inconsistent with...four principles: Death is an unusually severe and degrading punishment; there is a strong probability that it is inflicted arbitrarily; its rejection by contemporary society is virtually total, and there is no reason to believe it serves any penal purpose more effectively than the less severe punishment of imprisonment. The function of these principles is to enable a court to determine whether a punishment comports with human dignity: Death, quite simply, does not."

Douglas found that the laws allowing imposition of the death penalty at the discretion of judge or jury provided the opportunity, which was often taken, he said,

---

Due Process, Equal Protection

"...Nor shall any state deprive any person of life, liberty, or property, without due process of law; nor deny to any person within its jurisdiction the equal protection of the laws."
Fourteenth Amendment, U.S. Constitution

---

for discrimination, for imposing that sentence on the "poor and despised...lacking political clout...a member of a suspect or unpopular minority."

Stewart and White found that the present system of imposing the death penalty under which "this unique penalty...(is) so wantonly and freakishly imposed" was clearly unconstitutional.

Stewart wrote that these death sentences were "cruel and unusual in the same way, that being struck by lightning is cruel and unusual. For of all the people convicted of rapes and murders in 1967 and 1968...the petitioners are among a capriciously selected random handful upon whom the sentence of death has been imposed."

In dissent, Chief Justice Burger was quick to point out that the opinions of White and Stewart implied that states might enact a constitutional capital punishment law: "Since the two pivotal concurring opinions turn on the assumption that the punishment of death is now meted out in a random and unpredictable manner, legislative bodies may seek to bring their laws into compliance with the court's ruling by providing standards for juries and judges to follow in determining the sentences in capital cases or by more narrowly defining the crimes for which the penalty is to be imposed."

DUE PROCESS

Foster v. California, decided by an 8-1 vote, April 1, 1969. Fortas wrote the opinion; Black dissented.

Use at trial of victim's identification of suspect without legal counsel after a suggestive line-up, an individual confrontation, and a second line-up (in which no other participants in the first were present) violates due process. Judged by the "totality of the circumstances," the identification procedures were conducted in such a suggestive way that they constituted a denial of due process, held the court.

In Re Winship, decided by a 5-3 vote, March 31, 1970. Brennan wrote the opinion; Burger, Black and Stewart dissented.

Due process requires that the guilt of juveniles like that of adults be found "beyond a reasonable doubt," not just "by a preponderance of the evidence." This decision, complained Burger and Stewart, further strait-jacketed "an already overly restricted (juvenile court) system.... I cannot regard it as...progress to transform juvenile courts into criminal courts."

McGautha v. California, Crampton v. Ohio, decided by a 6-3 vote, May 3, 1971. Harlan wrote the opinion; Douglas, Brennan and Marshall dissented.

States do not violate due process by giving juries complete discretion in deciding in what capital cases to impose a death sentence; states do not violate the privilege against self-incrimination by allowing one jury simultaneously to determine guilt and punishment.

Loper v. Beto, decided by a 5-4 vote, March 22, 1972. Stewart wrote the opinion; Burger, Powell, Blackmun and Rehnquist dissented.

Prior invalid convictions cannot be used to impeach the credibility of a defendant—if their use influences the outcome of his case.

McNeil v. Director, Patuxent Institution, decided by a 9-0 vote, June 19, 1972. Marshall wrote the opinion.

Defendant convicted, sentenced to five years' imprisonment, and referred as possible defective delinquent to institution for psychiatric examination, cannot be held in that institution longer than five years, without violation of his constitutional rights.

Morrissey v. Brewer, decided by an 8-1 vote, June 29, 1972. Burger wrote the opinion; Douglas dissented in part.

Parole revocation proceedings must adhere to certain standards and procedural safeguards to protect the liberty of the paroled person and to ensure that revocation is based on verified facts.

EQUAL PROTECTION

Williams v. Illinois, decided by an 8-0 vote, June 29, 1970. Burger wrote the opinion; Blackmun did not take part.

Equal protection of the laws requires that the maximum imprisonment for any offense be the same for all defendants, rich and poor. Therefore, states cannot hold poor people in prison beyond the maximum sentence merely to work off a fine they cannot pay. (Forty-seven of the 50 states allowed such further imprisonment.)

Tate v. Short, decided by a 9-0 vote, March 2, 1971. Brennan wrote the opinion.

The "$30 or 30 days" sentence was an unconstitutional denial of equal protection; that guarantee barred any state or municipality from limiting punishment for an offense to a fine for those who could pay, but expanding punishment for the same offense to imprisonment for those who could not pay the fine.

Younger v. Gilmore, decided by a 7-0 vote, Nov. 8, 1971. Unsigned opinion.

States must provide poor prisoners with sufficient legal research materials to ensure that they have equal access to advice and courts as do wealthier prisoners.

Mayer v. Chicago, decided by a 7-0 vote, Dec. 13, 1971. Brennan wrote the opinion.

States must supply a free trial transcript to every poor person appealing a misdemeanor conviction.

Schilb v. Kuebel, decided by a 4-3 vote, Dec. 20, 1971. Blackmun wrote the opinion; Douglas, Brennan and Stewart dissented.

States do not violate equal protection or due process when they impose a bail administration fee on persons released on bail when they have deposited only ten per cent of the bail amount, but impose no fee on those who deposit the full amount of bail.

Eisenstadt v. Baird, decided by a 6-1 vote, March 22, 1972. Brennan wrote the opinion; Powell and Rehnquist did not participate; Burger dissented.

States cannot, without violating the equal protection guarantee, ban distribution of contraceptives to unmarried individuals.

Alexander v. Louisiana, decided by a 7-0 vote, April 3, 1972. White wrote the opinion; Powell and Rehnquist did not participate.

A black man indicted for rape by all-white state grand jury selected from class which was partially black by an all-white jury commission was denied equal protection of the laws by obvious racial discrimination in jury selection.

Jackson v. Indiana, decided by a 7-0 vote, June 7, 1972. Blackmun wrote the opinion; Powell and Rehnquist did not participate.

Equal protection and due process guarantees require state, after a reasonable period, to release or civilly commit defendant who was found incompetent to stand trial and confined as criminally insane, since law makes release more difficult in criminal than in civil cases.

Peters v. Kiff, decided by a 6-3 vote, June 22, 1972. Marshall wrote the opinion; dissenting were Burger, Rehnquist and Blackmun.

White defendant indicted and convicted by juries from which blacks had been systematically excluded was by that discrimination denied his rights to equal protection and due process.

Civil Rights

SCHOOL DESEGREGATION

U.S. v. Montgomery County Board of Education, decided by an 8-0 vote, June 2, 1969. Black wrote the opinion.

Federal district judge may order Alabama school board to desegregate faculty and staff of schools according to specific mathematical ratio.

Alexander v. Holmes County Board of Education, decided by an 8-0 vote, Oct. 29, 1969. Unsigned opinion.

In the first decision of Chief Justice Warren E. Burger's first term, the court rebuffed the Nixon administration's request for further delay in desegregation of 33 Mississippi school systems. The court held that continued segregation of public schools was no longer constitutionally permissible and that the schools must desegregate immediately.

Northcross v. Memphis Board of Education, decided by a 7-0 vote, March 9, 1970. Unsigned opinion; Marshall did not participate.

Memphis school system must eliminate dual schools during current school year. In a concurring opinion, Burger said that the full court should consider some of the basic problems of school desegregation, such as whether a particular racial balance must be achieved and whether busing must be or may be used. The court, he said, had defined a unitary school system as one "from which no person is to be effectively excluded from any school because of race or color."

Swann v. Charlotte-Mecklenburg County Board of Education, decided by a 9-0 vote, April 20, 1971. Burger wrote the opinion.

Busing, racial balance ratios, and gerrymandered school districts are all permissible interim methods of eliminating the vestiges of state-imposed segregation from southern schools.

The court said remedies which might be authorized under this decision and previous decisions might be "administratively awkward, inconvenient and even bizarre in some situations and may impose burdens on some; but all awkwardness and inconvenience cannot be avoided in the interim period when the remedial adjustments are being made to eliminate the dual school systems."

There were limits to the remedies which might be used to eliminate the vestiges of segregation, the court said, but no fixed guidelines setting such limits could be established.

The court pointed out that federal courts entered the desegregation process only when local school authorities did not fulfill their obligation to eliminate the dual school system. If school authorities do default as the lower federal court found that the school board of Charlotte, North Carolina, had in the case before the court—then the federal judge has wide discretion in selecting the means of desegregating the school system.

The court did not deal with *de facto* segregation resulting from factors other than state law. It specifically said that it did not reach the question of the action which would be taken concerning schools which are segregated as a result of "other types of state action, without any discriminatory action by the school authorities."

Limited use of mathematical racial ratios—as a starting point for the remedial process—is within the discretion of the federal court. But "if we were to read the holding of the district court to require, as a matter of substantive constitutional right, any particular degree of racial balance or mixing, that approach would be disapproved and we would be obliged to reverse. The constitutional command to desegregate schools does not mean that every school in every community must always reflect the racial composition of the school system as a whole."

The existence of a few schools within a system, which are attended almost completely by children of one race, is not in itself a mark of a still-segregated system, but school authorities will have to prove to courts that such schools are not the result of present or past discriminatory action on their part.

As "an interim corrective measure" courts may order drastically gerrymandered school districts and attendance zones, and pairing, grouping or clustering of schools. Without a constitutional violation there would be no basis for court orders directing the assignment of pupils on a racial basis.

Bus transportation of students has been an "integral part of the public education system for years" and is a permissible remedial technique when ordered by a court to implement desegregation. "Desegregation plans cannot be limited to the walk-in school."

There may be some valid objections to busing when so much time or distance is involved as to risk the children's health or to impinge significantly on the educational process. "Limits on time of travel will vary with many factors but probably with none more than the age of the students."

The court concluded its opinion with the statement— in apparent reference to the resegregation which might follow the achievement of a unitary school system: "Neither school authorities nor district courts are constitutionally required to make year-by-year adjustments of the racial composition of student bodies once the affirmative duty to desegregate has been accomplished and racial discrimination through official action is eliminated from the system.

"This does not mean that federal courts are without power to deal with future problems; but in the absence of a showing that either the school authorities or some other agency of the state has deliberately attempted to fix or alter demographic patterns to affect the racial composition of the schools, further intervention by a district court should not be necessary."

U.S. v. Scotland Neck Board of Education, decided by a 9-0 vote, *Wright v. Emporia City Council,* decided by a 5-4 vote, June 22, 1972. Stewart wrote the opinions; Burger, Blackmun, Powell and Rehnquist dissented in the second case.

Federal court can halt state or local action creating new school district with the effect of impeding school desegregation.

HOUSING, JOBS, JURIES, PARKS, CLUBS

Hunter v. Erickson, decided by an 8-1 decision, Jan. 20, 1969. White wrote the opinion; Black dissented.

A city cannot constitutionally require that any local fair housing ordinance be subject to approval by referendum; such a requirement is a real, substantial and invidious denial of equal protection. Official action cannot any more disadvantage any particular group by making it difficult to enact legislation in its behalf than it can dilute any person's vote.

Daniel v. Paul, decided by a 7-1 vote, June 2, 1969. Brennan wrote the opinion; Black dissented.

Civil Rights Act of 1964 prohibits privately owned recreational club, which serves some interstate travelers and qualifies as place of public accommodation, from excluding persons on the basis of race.

Sullivan v. Little Hunting Park Inc., decided by a 5-3 vote, Dec. 15, 1969. Douglas wrote the opinion; Burger, Harlan and White dissented.

Civil Rights Act of 1866—which expressly protects the right to lease property—prohibits a community recreational club from refusing membership to a black man who received a club share as part of his lease of a home in the neighborhood.

Carter v. Jury Commission of Greene County, decided by a 7-1 vote, Jan. 19, 1970. Stewart wrote the opinion; Douglas dissented.

State law providing for jury selection is not unconstitutional, despite abuse of discretion under law to exclude blacks systematically from jury service.

Turner v. Fouche, decided by an 8-0 vote, Jan. 19, 1970. Stewart wrote the opinion.

State law governing selection of jurors and school board members is not unconstitutional, despite systematic exclusion of blacks from juries and school boards; exclusion must cease; property requirement for membership on school board is unconstitutional violation of equal protection.

Evans v. Abney, decided by a 5-2 vote, Jan. 26, 1970. Black wrote the opinion; Marshall did not participate; Brennan and Douglas dissented.

Termination of a trust, and reversion of property to heirs, is not unconstitutional when purpose of trust —to create a park for use by white people only—has failed. Individual action was the cause for termination of the trust; state law had only allowed inclusion of such racial restrictions in bequests. Termination of the trust followed a neutral application of state law; both races shared the loss of the park.

Adickes v. Kress and Co., decided by a 5-2 vote, June 1, 1970. Harlan wrote the opinion; Marshall did not participate; Brennan and Douglas dissented.

Civil Rights Act of 1871 allows person to recover damages from restaurant owners for refusing service on the basis of race only if discrimination was based on state-enforced custom of segregation.

Griggs v. Duke Power Co., decided by an 8-0 vote; March 8, 1971. Burger wrote the opinion; Brennan did not participate.

Civil Rights Act of 1964 bars employer requirement of high school diploma or score on general intelligence test—as condition for employment or promotion—so long as neither is related to job skills and so long as both tend to disqualify more black than white applicants.

James v. Valtierra, decided by a 5-3 vote, April 26, 1971. Black wrote the opinion; Douglas did not participate; Brennan, Blackmun and Marshall dissented.

Equal protection guarantee not violated by language in state constitution forbidding construction of any low-income housing projects not expressly approved by a referendum in affected area.

Griffin v. Breckenridge, decided by a 9-0 vote, June 7, 1971. Stewart wrote the opinion.

Federal civil rights law barring conspiracy to deprive persons of equal protection reaches private conspiracies.

Palmer v. Thompson, decided by a 5-4 vote June 14, 1971. Black wrote the opinion; White, Douglas, Brennan and Marshall dissented.

Constitution does not bar city from closing public swimming pools which had been directed by a court to cease segregated operation, but which could not be operated safely and economically in integrated fashion.

Moose Lodge 107 v. Irvis, decided by a 6-3 vote, June 12, 1972. Rehnquist wrote the opinion; Douglas, Brennan and Marshall dissented.

Private club's possession of state liquor license does not render club's discriminatory guest policy state action within the reach of the equal protection guarantee.

SEX DISCRIMINATION

Phillips v. Martin Marietta Corp., decided by a 9-0 vote, Jan. 25, 1971. Unsigned opinion.

1964 Civil Rights Act bars job discrimination on basis of sex against mother of pre-school children and, in absence of *bona fide* occupational qualification, requires one hiring policy for men and women. "The existence of such conflicting family obligations, if demonstrably more relevant to job performance for a woman than for a man could arguably be a basis for distinction."

Reed v. Reed, decided by a 7-0 vote, Nov. 22, 1971. Burger wrote the opinion.

Guarantee of equal protection invalidates state law which automatically prefers father over mother as executor of son's estate: "To give a mandatory preference to members of either sex over members of the other...is to make the very kind of arbitrary legislative choice forbidden by the equal protection clause."

Stanley v. Illinois, decided by a 5-2 vote, April 2, 1972. White wrote the opinion; Powell and Rehnquist did not participate; Burger and Blackmun dissented.

Guarantee of equal protection invalidates state law which presumes that unwed father is unfit custodian of child while allowing all other parents, whose custody of child is challenged, including the unwed mother, a hearing to determine their fitness as a parent.

Election Laws

Oregon v. Mitchell, Texas v. Mitchell, U.S. v. Idaho, U.S. v. Arizona, decided by a 5-4 vote on the lower voting age, by an 8-1 vote on residency requirements, and by a 9-0 vote on literacy test ban, Dec. 21, 1970. Black wrote the opinion; Stewart, Burger, Harlan and Blackmun dissented on the question of age; Harlan dissented alone on the residency issue.

Congress has the power to lower the voting age to 18 for federal elections, but not for state and local elections; Congress has the power to restrict state residency requirements to 30 days for persons wishing to vote in presidential elections; Congress has the power to ban the use of literacy tests as voter qualification devices in any national, state or local election.

Black wrote the majority opinion and cast the pivotal vote: his position—that Congress had the power to lower the voting age in federal, but not state or local, elections—prevailed, although the was the only justice holding that view in its entirety.

Four justices—Brennan, Douglas, Marshall and White—considered the 18-year-old vote provision fully constitutional for federal and state elections. Four others—Burger, Blackmun, Harlan and Stewart—believed it was unconstitutional as to both state and federal elections. None agreed completely with Black's position.

"I believe that Congress has the final authority over federal elections," Black said but added, "I would hold that Congress has exceeded its powers in attempting to lower the voting age in state and local elections."

In a concurring opinion, Douglas wrote: "It is said, why draw the line at 18? Why not 17? Congress can draw lines and I see no reason why it cannot conclude that 18-year-olds have that degree of maturity which entitles them to the franchise.... It is a reasoned judgment that those who have such a large 'stake' in modern elections as 18-year-olds, whether in times of war or peace, should have political equality."

Stewart in dissent emphasized that the Supreme Court was not attempting to determine the value of lowering the voting age. "Our single duty as judges is to determine whether the legislation before us was within the constitutional power of Congress to enact.... A casual reader could easily get the impression that what we are being asked in these cases is whether or not we think allowing people 18 years old to vote is a good idea. Nothing could be wider of the mark."

Stewart, joined by Burger and Blackmun, argued that state laws that deny the vote to persons under 21 "do not invidiously discriminate against any discrete and insular minority." They concluded that the laws do not violate the Fourteenth Amendment's antidiscrimination ban and thus Congress was in error when it passed the law to combat the "discrimination" against youths.

Dun v. Blumstein, decided by a 6-1 vote, March 21, 1972. Marshall wrote the opinion; Powell and Rehnquist did not participate; Burger dissented.

State cannot constitutionally restrict franchise to persons who have lived in state at least one year and in county at least three months.

Allen v. State Board of Elections, decided by an 8-1 vote; ***Bunton v. Patterson*** and ***Whitley v. Williams,*** decided by an 8-1 vote; ***Fairley v. Patterson,*** decided by a 7-2 vote, March 3, 1969. Warren wrote the opinions; Black dissented in each case, joined by Harlan in *Fairley.*

Enactments by certain states—which are covered by the Voting Rights Act of 1965—changing from district to at-large election of county officials, changing from elective to appointive selection of a county official, imposing stricter requirements for the inclusion of independent candidates upon a ballot, and changing write-in procedures—are "standard(s), practice(s) or procedure(s) with respect to voting" within the meaning of Section 5 of the Act and must, therefore, be submitted to the Attorney General before they can be enforced. *(Congress and the Nation Vol. II, p. 356)*

Hadnott v. Amos decided by a 6-2 vote, March 25, 1969. Douglas wrote the opinion; White and Stewart dissented; Black did not take part.

Unequal application of state laws which had the effect of disqualifying candidates, usually Negroes, from place on the ballot violated Fifteenth Amendment; new election law requiring independent candidates to file declaration of intent at same time as primary candidates is "standard practice or procedure with respect to voting" which, without approval required by the Voting Rights Act of 1965, cannot be enforced.

Gaston County v. U.S. decided by a 7-1 vote, June 2, 1969. Harlan wrote the opinion; Black dissented.

Previous maintenance of segregated land and unequal school systems in county required denial of county's request under the Voting Rights Act of 1965 for judicial reinstatement of literacy test because such test, in conjunction with previous deprivation of equal educational opportunity for black residents now of voting age, had the effect of abridging the right to vote on account of race. Because of such past discrimination, the court held that " 'impartial' administration of the literacy test today would serve only to perpetuate these (past) inequities in a different form."

Perkins v. Matthews, decided by a 7-2 vote, Jan. 14, 1971. Brennan wrote the opinion; Harlan and Black dissented.

Towns and cities covered by the 1965 Voting Rights Act cannot annex territory or relocate polling places without federal approval.

NEW DISTRICTS

Kirkpatrick v. Preisler, decided by a 6-3 vote, April 7, 1969. Brennan wrote the opinion; Harlan, Stewart and White dissented.

Missouri redistricting statute producing congressional districts with a maximum population variance of 3.1 per cent from perfect mathematical equality was unconstitutional without justification or proof that such variation was unavoidable.

Brennan held that states must strive to create congressional districts of precisely equal population. Any variance in population, "no matter how small," must be justified by the state or shown to result despite a "good-faith effort." There is no fixed population variance small enough to be considered negligible. "Equal representation for equal numbers of people is a principle designed to prevent debasement of voting power and diminution of access to elected representatives. Toleration of even small deviations detracts from these purposes."

Fortas, concurring in the rejection of the Missouri plan, disagreed with the standard of mathematical precision announced in the court's opinion. Fortas said he would accept districts with "small disparities" in population: "The majority's pursuit of precision is a search for a will-o'-the-wisp." Legislatures implementing the standard "might have to ignore the boundaries of common sense, running the...district line down the middle of the corridor of an apartment house or even dividing the residents of a single-family house between two districts."

Harlan complained that the court had transformed "a political slogan into a constitutional absolute." He said: "Strait indeed is the path of the righteous legislator. Slide rule in hand, he must avoid all thought of county lines, local traditions, politics, history and economics, so as to achieve the magic formula: one man, one vote."

Wells v. Rockefeller, decided by a 6-3 vote, April 7, 1969. Brennan wrote the opinion; White, Harlan and Stewart dissented.

New York redistricting statute not producing congressional districts of equal population is unconstitutional, although the statute did produce districts of nearly equal population within the regions in the state.

Population must be equal in all the districts of a state, not just in "defined substates." The court noted that "New York...does not claim that the legislature made a good-faith effort to achieve precise mathematical equality among its 41 congressional districts."

Whitcomb v. Chavis, decided by a 5-4 vote, June 7, 1971. White wrote the opinion; Douglas, Stewart, Brennan and Marshall dissented.

Without actual proof that black residents' votes are diluted by the creation of multi-member legislative districts, the court cannot find multi-member districts in themselves unconstitutional.

ELECTIONS

Williams v. Rhodes, decided by a 6-3 vote; ***Socialist Labor Party v. Rhodes,*** decided by an 8-1 vote, Oct. 15, 1968. Opinion by Black.

State's imposition of substantially greater burden upon small or newly organized political parties than upon the Democratic or Republican party for obtaining a place on the ballot violated the equal protection of the law guaranteed by the Fourteenth Amendment. (The *Williams* case was initiated by presidential candidate George C. Wallace's American Independent party in Ohio and resulted in Wallace's name appearing on the ballot in Ohio in the Nov. 5, 1968, elections.)

Moore v. Ogilvie, decided by a 7-2 vote, May 5, 1969. Douglas wrote the opinion; Stewart and Harlan dissented.

State requirement that nominating petitions for independent presidential electors must include at least 200 signatures from each of 50 counties among the required 25,000 signatures violates the "one-man, one vote" principle guaranteed under the equal protection clause of the Fourteenth Amendment by discriminating against voters residing in populous counties.

In 1948 the Supreme Court upheld this particular requirement as constitutional and not denying equal protection *(MacDougall v. Green).* *(Congress and the Nation Vol. I, p. 116a)*

The court in 1969 overruled *MacDougall v. Green* as out of line with the court's more recent decisions on apportionment.

Kramer v. Union Free School District No. 15, decided by a 5-3 vote, June 16, 1969. Opinion by Warren; Stewart, Black and Harlan dissented.

State cannot bar from voting in school district elections persons who are neither owners or lessees of real estate within the district nor parents or guardians of children attending the public schools without violating the constitutional guarantee of equal protection.

Cipriano v. City of Houma, decided by an 8-0 vote, June 16, 1969. Unsigned opinion.

Louisiana law providing that only "property taxpayers" might vote in elections to approve the issuance of municipal utility revenue bonds violates the guarantee of equal protection.

Hadley v. Junior College District of Metropolitan Kansas City, Mo., decided by a 5-3 vote, Feb. 25, 1970. Black wrote the opinion; Harlan, Burger and Stewart dissented.

The "one-man, one-vote" rule must be applied to any election—state or local—of persons to perform governmental functions.

There was no valid reason, the court held, for courts to try to apply the "one-man, one-vote" rule selectively, distinguishing between types of elections or between types of elected officials: "If one person's vote is given less weight through unequal apportionment, his right to equal voting participation is impaired just as much when he votes for a school board member as when he votes for a state legislator.... The crucial consideration is the right of each qualified voter to participate on an equal footing in the election process.

"We therefore hold today that as a general rule, whenever a state or local government decides to select persons by popular election to perform governmental functions, the equal protection clause of the Fourteenth Amendment requires that each qualified voter must be given an equal opportunity to participate in that election, and when members of an elected body are chosen from separate districts, each district must be established on a basis which will insure, as far as is practicable, that equal numbers of voters can vote for proportionally equal numbers of officials."

Phoenix v. Kolodziejski, decided by a 5-3 vote, June 23, 1970. White wrote the opinion; Blackmun did not participate; Burger, Stewart and Harlan dissented.

Equal protection guarantee bars states from excluding nonproperty owners from voting in elections to approve the issuance of general obligation bonds.

Evans v. Cornman, decided by an 8-0 vote, June 15, 1970. Marshall wrote the opinion; Blackmun did not participate.

State may not deny the right to vote to persons living within federal enclave in state and otherwise treated as state residents.

Gordon v. Lance, decided by a 7-2 vote, June 7, 1971. Burger wrote the opinion; dissenting were Brennan and Marshall.

Equal protection guarantee is not violated by requirement that a political subdivision cannot exceed constitutionally set limits of bonded indebtedness or tax rates without an affirmative vote of 60 per cent in a referendum.

Roudebush v. Hartke, decided by a 5-2 vote, Feb. 22, 1972. Stewart wrote the opinion; Powell and Rehnquist did not participate; Douglas and Brennan dissented.

State vote recount procedures are part of its electoral process and do not usurp the Senate's power to act as exclusive judge of its members' qualifications.

Bullock v. Carter, decided by a 7-0 vote, Feb. 24, 1972. Burger wrote the opinion.

State filing fee, the amount of which is based on the estimated total cost of the election, is an unconstitutional discrimination against the political candidate who cannot pay such a large fee.

Church and State

Epperson v. Arkansas, decided by a 9-0 vote, Nov. 12, 1968. Fortas wrote the opinion.

State "monkey law" forbidding public school teaching of the Darwinian theory of evolution violates First Amendment ban on establishment of religion and its guarantee of freedom of religion: "The First Amendment mandates governmental neutrality between religion and religion and between religion and nonreligion."

Walz v. Tax Commission of the City of New York, decided by a 7-1 vote, May 4, 1970. Burger wrote the opinion; Douglas dissented.

Property tax exemption for church-owned land used solely for religious purposes does not violate First Amendment guarantee against establishment of religion as applied to the states by the Fourteenth Amendment. Such exemptions were only evidence of the state's "benevolent neutrality" toward religion, held the court:

"There is no genuine nexus between tax exemption and establishment of religion... The exemption creates only a minimal and remote involvement between church and state and far less than taxation of churches. It restricts the fiscal relationship between church and state, and tends to complement and reinforce the desired separation insulating each from the other."

Tilton v. Richardson, decided by a 5-4 vote, June 28, 1971. Burger wrote the opinion; Douglas, Black, Marshall and Brennan dissented.

Higher Education Facilities Act of 1963—under which federal grants are provided for construction of buildings by colleges and universities, regardless of religious affiliation, so long as buildings are used exclusively for secular educational purposes—does not violate First Amendment; First Amendment does invalidate provision of law limiting to 20 years the restriction of use of facility to secular educational purposes.

Lemon v. Kurtzman, decided by an 8-0 vote, June 28, 1971. Burger wrote the opinion; Marshall did not participate.

First Amendment invalidates state law authorizing state reimbursement of nonpublic school for costs of teachers' salaries, textbooks and instructional materials in secular subjects; First Amendment invalidates state law authorizing supplementary salary grants to nonpublic school teachers of secular subjects while barring such grants to teachers in schools that spend more per pupil on secular education than do public schools; such laws foster excessive entanglement between government and religion.

Religion, Speech, and Press

Congress shall make no law respecting an establishment of religion, or prohibiting the free exercise thereof; or abridging the freedom of speech, or of the press; or the right of the people peaceably to assembly, and to petition the Government for a redress of grievances.

—First Amendment, U.S. Constitution

Wisconsin v. Yoder, decided by a 6-1 vote, May 15, 1972. Burger wrote the opinion; Powell and Rehnquist did not participate; Douglas dissented.

First Amendment guarantee of freedom of religion prohibits the application of state's compulsory education law requiring school attendance until a child is 16 to members of the Amish sect, "whose long-established, self-sufficient agrarian lifestyle is essential to their religious faith" and is threatened by the exposure of their children to modern educational influences.

Free Speech

Tinker v. Des Moines Independent Community School District, decided by a 7-2 vote, Feb. 24, 1969. Fortas wrote the opinion; Harlan and Black dissented.

Students have the right to engage in peaceful non-disruptive protest. The wearing of black armbands to protest the Vietnam war was "closely akin" to the "pure speech" protected by the First Amendment, and therefore a public school ban on this form of protest, which did not disrupt the school's work or offend the rights of others, violated these students' rights. "In the absence of a specific showing of constitutionally valid reasons to regulate their speech, students are entitled to freedom of expression of their views."

Street v. New York, decided by a 5-4 vote, April 21, 1969. Harlan wrote the opinion; Warren, Fortas, White and Black dissented.

State law making it a crime to "cast contempt" upon American flag by words or acts is unconstitutional in allowing persons to be punished merely for speaking derogatory words about the flag.

Harlan concluded that "disrespect for our flag is to be deplored no less in these vexed times than in calmer periods of our history.... Nevertheless, we are unable to sustain a conviction that may have rested on a form of expression, however distasteful, which the Constitution tolerates and protects."

Brandenburg v. Ohio, decided by an 8-0 vote, June 9, 1969. Unsigned opinion.

State law making a crime of advocating violence or terrorism as a mode of reform and of meeting with any group formed to advocate such ideas is unconstitutional violation of the freedoms of speech and association.

Any law, the court held, which did not make the distinction between "mere abstract teaching" of the need for the use of force and violence and the actual preparation of a group for such violent action, impermissibly intruded upon individual freedom and condemned constitutionally protected speech.

Bachellar v. Maryland, decided by an 8-0 vote, April 20, 1970. Opinion by Brennan.

Disorderly conduct conviction of antiwar protesters must be overturned because it may have rested upon the unconstitutional grounds—suggested by the judge—that their views were offensive to bystanders.

Schacht v. U.S., decided by an 8-0 vote, May 25, 1970. Black wrote the opinion.

Actors, as well as other citizens, have the right openly to criticize the government, ruled the court, invalidating a law which made it a crime for an actor to wear an official military uniform in a production which was unfavorable to the armed forces.

Organization for a Better Austin v. Keefe, decided by an 8-1 vote, May 17, 1971. Burger wrote the opinion; Harlan dissented.

State court cannot constitutionally order community group to cease peacefully distributing leaflets charging real estate broker with "blockbusting" or to cease picketing in the broker's community.

Coates v. Cincinnati, decided by a 6-3 vote, June 1, 1971. Stewart wrote the opinion; White, Burger and Blackmun dissented.

City ordinance is unconstitutionally broad and vague in barring any assembly of three or more persons on sidewalk to annoy passers-by.

Lloyd Corporation v. Tanner, decided by a 5-4 vote, June 22, 1972. Powell wrote the opinion; Douglas, Brennan, Marshall and Stewart dissented.

First Amendment is not violated by ban imposed by privately owned and operated shopping mall on distribution of handbills by peaceful group without any grievance against the merchants in the mall.

Laird v. Tatum, decided by a 5-4 vote, June 26, 1972. Burger wrote the opinion; Douglas, Brennan, Stewart and Marshall dissented.

Persons who cannot claim that their own activities have been affected by military surveillance of legal civilian political activity cannot bring a court challenge to the constitutionality of that surveillance.

Kleindienst v. Mandel, decided by a 6-3 vote, June 29, 1972. Blackmun wrote the opinion; Douglas, Brennan and Marshall dissented.

Congress has properly delegated to the executive branch the power to exclude aliens or prescribe the conditions for their entry into the United States; when the Attorney General decides for a good reason not to waive the statutory exclusion of an alien, that decision will not be scrutinized by the courts or weighed against the free speech rights of persons wishing to speak with the excluded alien.

Obscenity

Stanley v. Georgia, decided by a 9-0 vote, April 7, 1969. Marshall wrote the opinion.

The First Amendment guarantee of freedom of expression bars states from making it a crime to privately possess obscene material: "The Constitution protects the right to receive information and ideas.... Also fundamental is the right to be free, except in very limited circumstances, from unwanted governmental intrusions into one's privacy.... Whatever may be the justifications for other statutes regulating obscenity, we do not think they reach into the privacy of one's own home.... If the First Amendment means anything, it means that the

Shift to Restraint

A signal of the Supreme Court's return to a less activist position was sounded on Feb. 23, 1971. In a series of decisions, the court sharply curtailed the application of a 1965 decision which allowed federal courts to halt state criminal proceedings, when the law involved was challenged as unconstitutional by the defendant.

Before the 1965 decision, federal courts observed the doctrine of judicial abstention, refraining from intervention in any ongoing state court proceedings. In 1965, the Supreme Court ruled, 5-2, that this doctrine did not apply in cases involving laws which defendants challenged as unconstitutional infringements of their freedom of expression *(Dombrowski v. Pfister).*

Defendants prosecuted under state laws subject to such challenge did not hesitate to take full advantage of this ruling. A wave of petitions in federal courts produced an increasing number of injunctions halting state trials.

In the 1971 decisions, Justice Black—with only Justice Douglas dissenting—wrote that "the normal thing to do when federal courts are asked to enjoin pending proceedings in state courts is not to issue such injunctions."

However, as Justices Stewart and Harlan pointed out in a concurring opinion, there were certain limited circumstances in which a federal court could intervene in pending state proceedings. Such circumstances existed when there was a great and immediate threat of irreparable injury, when a state law was flagrantly unconstitutional on its face, or when there had been official lawlessness.

The principle of federal restraint, wrote Black, was based on "a proper respect for state functions ...and a continuance of the belief that the national government will fare best if the states and their institutions are left free to perform their separate functions in their separate ways." With this pronouncement, the court, by varying votes, disapproved the actions of federal courts:

• Halting prosecution of a movie exhibitor for showing the allegedly obscene movie "I Am Curious (Yellow)" *(Byrne v. Karalexis).*

• Suppressing allegedly obscene materials during an obscenity trial *(Perez v. Ledesma).*

• Halting prosecution under the California criminal syndicalism law *(Younger v. Harris).*

• Considering the constitutionality of the New York criminal anarchy law *(Samuels v. Mackell, Fernandez v. Mackell).*

• Declaring a Texas obscenity law unconstitutional and halting the prosecution of a newspaper publisher under that law *(Dyson v. Stein).*

But a year later, in a decision announced by a unanimous seven-man court on June 19, 1972, the court held that federal courts could halt state court proceedings when citizens whose constitutional rights were threatened by actions under authority of state law requested federal courts to halt that threat *(Mitchum v. Foster).*

state has no business telling a man, sitting alone in his own house, what books he may read or what films he may watch."

Rowan v. U.S. Post Office Dept., decided by 8-0 vote, May 4, 1970. Burger wrote the opinion.

Neither freedom of the press nor freedom of speech is violated by the 1967 law authorizing individuals to request the Postmaster General to order a company to cease sending that individual obscene material. The right of privacy was paramount in this case, held the court: "To hold less would tend to license a form of trespass and would make hardly more sense than to say that a radio or television viewer may not twist the dial to cut off an offensive or boring communication." *(1967 Almanac p. 593)*

Blount v. Rizzi, U.S. v. The Book Bin, decided by a 9-0 vote, Jan. 14, 1971. Brennan wrote the opinion.

The court invalidated two laws—one enacted in 1950 and the other in 1960—which allowed the Post Office to stop mail to businesses under investigation for or found to sell pornographic material. The laws did not contain sufficient safeguards against unconstitutional curtailment of free speech, according to the court. *(Congress and the Nation Vol. I, p. 1671, 1672)*

U.S. v. Reidel, decided by a 7-2 vote, May 3, 1971. White wrote the opinion; Black and Douglas dissented.

The court upheld a law which forbade use of the mails to deliver obscene material, even if the material was being distributed to willing adult recipients.

U.S. v. 37 Photographs, decided by a 6-3 vote, May 3, 1971. White wrote the opinion; Black, Douglas and Marshall dissented.

Federal laws authorizing customs officials to seize imported obscene material do not violate First Amendment, nor does seizure of obscene matter privately possessed at port of entry by person who intends it for commercial distribution.

Cohen v. California, decided by a 5-4 vote, June 7, 1971. Harlan wrote the opinion; Burger, Black, White and Blackmun dissented.

The court invalidated the conviction—under a state disturbing-the-peace law which forbade offensive conduct—of a demonstrator who wore a jacket inscribed "Fuck the Draft" into a courthouse.

Free Press

Red Lion Broadcasting Co. v. Federal Communications Commission and *U.S. v. Radio Television News Directors Assn.,* decided by a 7-0 vote, June 9, 1969. White wrote the opinion; Douglas did not take part.

The court held that the general public's right to fair treatment of all aspects of important issues by news media required broadcasters to comply with the fairness doctrine set forth by the Federal Communications Commission. Therefore, the court ruled, broadcasters must continue to provide free time for persons to reply to broadcasts of political editorials or endorsements.

The right of broadcasters to free speech must be balanced with the right of the people as a whole to free speech and their "collective right to have the medium function consistently with the ends and purposes of the First Amendment." This right—of viewers and listeners—the Court held paramount.

"It is the purpose of the First Amendment to preserve an uninhibited marketplace of ideas in which truth will ultimately prevail, rather than to countenance monopolization of that market, whether it be by the government itself, or a private licensee."

Greenbelt Cooperative Publishing Assn. v. Bresler, decided by an 8-0 vote, May 18, 1970. Stewart wrote the opinion.

First Amendment guarantee of free press protects newspaper against libel suit for accurate reporting of charges made against a public figure. The fundamental meaning of a free press would be subverted if newspapers could be punished for publishing accurate, truthful reports of matters of public importance.

Monitor Patriot Co. v. Roy, Ocala Star-Banner Co. v. Damron, decided by 7-2 votes, Feb. 24, 1971. Stewart wrote the opinions; Black and Douglas dissented in part.

Any allegation of criminal activity, no matter how remote, is relevant to the fitness of a candidate for office; therefore—unless such allegation is printed with knowledge that it is false or with actual malice, no libel judgment can be entered against the publication printing the charge.

Time Inc. v. Pape, decided by a 8-1 vote, Feb. 24, 1971. Stewart wrote the opinion; Harlan dissented.

Mere omission of the word 'alleged' from an article reporting a charge of police brutality does not show malice nor provide grounds for a libel judgment against the publisher of the article.

Rosenbloom v. Metromedia Inc., decided by a 5-3 vote, June 7, 1971. Brennan wrote the opinion; Douglas did not participate; Harlan, Stewart and Marshall dissented.

Rule of *New York Times v. Sullivan* (1964)—that defamatory falsehood concerning public official is libel only if it is proven to have been uttered with knowledge of its falsity or in reckless disregard of its truth or falsity—applies to libel action brought by private individual for falsehood used by radio news program about individual's arrest.

New York Times Co. v. U.S., U.S. v. The Washington Post, decided by a 6-3 vote, June 30, 1971. Unsigned opinion; each justice wrote a separate opinion expressing his views. Dissenting were Burger, Blackmun and Harlan.

The government failed to show sufficient justification for its request for court orders barring publication—by *The New York Times* and *The Washington Post*—of articles based on classified documents, a multi-volume history of U.S. involvement in Indochina, popularly known as the Pentagon Papers.

Black, joined by Douglas, wrote: "I believe that every moment's continuance of the injunctions against these newspapers amounts to a flagrant, indefensible, and continuing violation of the First Amendment.... In my view, it is unfortunate that some of my brethren are apparently willing to hold that the publication of news may sometimes be enjoined. Such a holding would make a shambles of the First Amendment."

"The press was to serve the governed, not the governors. The government's power to censor the press was abolished so that the press would remain forever free to censure the government."

Marshall wrote: "The issue is whether this court or the Congress has the power to make law.... It would...be utterly inconsistent with the concept of separation of power for this court to use its power of contempt to prevent behavior that Congress has specifically declined to prohibit.... The Constitution provides that Congress shall make laws, the President execute laws and courts interpret law.... It did not provide for government by injunction in which the courts and the executive can 'make law' without regard to the action of Congress."

White, joined by Stewart, wrote: "I concur...but only because of the concededly extraordinary protection against prior restraints enjoyed by the press under our constitutional system. I do not say that in no circumstances would the First Amendment permit an injunction against publishing information about government plans or operations.... But...the United States has not satisfied the very heavy burden which it must meet to warrant an injunction against publication in these cases."

And Stewart, joined by White, said: "The only effective restraint upon executive policy and power in the areas of national defense and international affairs may lie in an enlightened citizenry.... Without an informed and free press there cannot be an enlightened people."

Brennan wrote: "The error which has pervaded these cases from the outset was the granting of any injunctive relief whatsoever, interim or otherwise.... The First Amendment tolerates absolutely no prior judicial restraints of the press predicated upon surmise or conjecture that untoward consequences may result."

Douglas, joined by Black, wrote: "The dominant purpose of the First Amendment was to prohibit the widespread practice of government suppression of embarrassing information.... The First Amendment was adopted against the widespread use of the common law of seditious libel to punish the dissemination of material that is embarrassing to the powers-that-be.... The present cases will, I think, go down in history as the most dramatic example of that principle.... Secrecy in government is fundamentally anti-democratic, perpetuating bureaucratic errors."

In dissent, Harlan, joined by Burger and Blackmun, declared: "The Court has been almost irresponsibly feverish in dealing with these cases.... The scope of the judicial function in passing upon the activities of the executive branch of the government in the field of foreign affairs is very narrowly restricted."

Blackmun dissented: "The First Amendment, after all, is only one part of an entire Constitution. Article II... vests in the executive branch primary power over the conduct of foreign affairs....

"Each provision...is important and I cannot subscribe to a doctrine of unlimited absolutism for the First Amendment at the cost of downgrading other provisions."

Burger dissented: "To me it is hardly believable that a newspaper long regarded as a great institution in American life would fail to perform one of the basic and simple duties of every citizen with respect to the discovery or possession of stolen property or secret government documents. That duty, I had thought—perhaps naively—was to report forthwith, to responsible public officers. This duty rests on taxi drivers, justices and *The New York Times*."

Branzburg v. Hayes, In re Pappas, U.S. v. Caldwell, decided by a 5-4 vote, June 29, 1972. White wrote the opinion; dissenting were Douglas, Brennan, Stewart and Marshall.

The constitutional freedom of the press does not privilege newsmen to refuse—without risking contempt charges—to provide information to grand juries concerning a crime or the sources of evidence concerning a crime. White wrote that the majority saw no basis "for holding that the public interest in law enforcement and in ensuring effective grand jury proceedings is insufficient to override the consequential but uncertain burden on newsgathering which is said to result from insisting that reporters, like other citizens, respond to relevant questions put to them in the course of a valid grand jury investigation or criminal trial." Stewart in dissent complained about the court's "crabbed view of the First Amendment." He saw the right to gather news as a corollary of the right to publish.

Freedom of Association

In Re Stolar, Baird v. State Bar of Arizona, decided by 5-4 votes, Feb. 23, 1971. Black wrote the opinion; Burger, Blackmun, Harlan and White dissented.

First Amendment bars state from excluding applicant for admission to bar solely because he or she refused to state whether he had belonged to any organization advocating violent overthrow of the government.

Law Students Civil Rights Research Council v. Wadmond, decided by a 5-4 vote, Feb. 23, 1971. Stewart wrote the opinion; Black, Douglas, Marshall and Brennan dissented.

Constitutional rights are not infringed by state requirements that applicants for state bar be of good moral character and loyal to the Constitution (even if latter is interpreted to require sworn support for state and federal constitution and statement concerning any membership in organization advocating violent overthrow of government).

Connell v. Higginbotham, decided by an 8-1 vote, June 7, 1971. Unsigned opinion; Stewart dissented in part.

State requirement that teachers swear to support state and federal constitutions is constitutional, but due process bars dismissal of teacher—without hearing— for failure to swear that he or she does not believe in the overthrow of the government by force.

Cole v. Richardson, decided by a 4-3 vote, April 18, 1972. Burger wrote the opinion; Douglas, Brennan and Marshall dissented.

First Amendment is not violated by a state requirement that all employees take oath to "oppose the overthrow of the government by force, violence or by any illegal or unconstitutional method."

Healy v. James, decided by a 9-0 vote, June 26, 1972. Powell wrote the opinion.

University's denial of recognition to student group—in this case a local chapter of Students for a Democratic Society—is an unconstitutional infringement of the freedom of association; nonrecognition could be justified by showing that group's activities would be disruptive influence on campus.

Rights of Individuals

Sniadach v. Family Finance Corp., decided by a 7-1 vote, June 9, 1969. Douglas wrote the opinion; Black dissented.

State cannot constitutionally allow garnishment of wages to pay debts before allowing notice and hearings for debtor.

Perez v. U.S., decided by an 8-1 vote, April 26, 1971. Opinion by Douglas; Stewart dissented.

Consumer Protection Act of 1968 is proper exercise of Congressional authority under the commerce power to bar loansharking; no explicit connection need be provided between loan shark and interstate commerce to convict loan shark of illicit activities.

Lynch v. Household Finance Corp., decided by a 4-3 vote, March 23, 1972. Stewart wrote the opinion; Burger, Blackmun and White dissented.

Federal courts have power to halt state court proceedings in cases involving impairment of property rights as well as in cases involving impairment of personal liberties: "The dichotomy between personal liberties and property rights is a false one. Property does not have rights. People have rights. The right to enjoy property without unlawful deprivation, no less than the right to speak or the right to travel, is in truth a 'personal' right, whether the 'property' in question be a welfare check, a home or a savings account. In fact, a fundamental interdependence exists between the personal right to liberty and the personal right in property. Neither could have meaning without the other. That rights in property are basic civil rights has long been recognized." *(p. 318)*

Fuentes v. Shevin, decided by a 4-3 vote, June 12, 1972. Stewart wrote the opinion; Burger, Blackmun and White dissented.

Due process invalidates state laws which allow summary seizure of goods from installment purchasers without prior notice or hearing, upon application of creditor.

Thorpe v. Durham Housing Authority, decided by a 9-0 vote, Jan. 13, 1969. Warren wrote the opinion.

Tenants of public housing projects cannot be evicted without being given reasons for any notice to vacate and an opportunity to reply to those reasons, as directed in 1967 regulations by the Department of Housing and Urban Development.

Lindsey v. Normet, decided by a 5-2 vote, Feb. 22, 1972. White wrote the opinion; Rehnquist and Powell did not participate; Douglas and Brennan dissented.

Equal protection does not invalidate state law which requires trial for nonpayment of rent within six days of service of a formal complaint of nonpayment and which bars a tenant from using, as a defense to the complaint, the fact that the landlord had failed to maintain or repair the rented premises.

Labine v. Vincent, decided by a 5-4 vote, March 29, 1971. Black wrote the opinion; Douglas, Brennan, White and Marshall dissented.

Neither due process nor equal protection bars state from denying illegitimate children an equal right of inheritance from father with legitimate children.

Weber v. Aetna Casualty and Surety Co., decided by an 8-1 vote, April 24, 1972. Powell wrote the opinion; Rehnquist dissented.

Equal protection invalidates workmen's compensation laws which prefer acknowledged illegitimate children to unacknowledged illegitimate children in allocating benefits of deceased father. "Imposing disabilities on the illegitimate child is contrary to the basic concept of our system that legal burdens should bear some relationship to individual responsibility or wrongdoing.... Courts are powerless to prevent the social opprobrium suffered by these hapless children, but the equal protection clause does enable us to strike down discriminatory laws relating to status of birth where—as in this case—the classification is justified by no legitimate state interest."

Shapiro v. Thompson, Washington v. Legrant, Reynolds v. Smith, decided by a 6-3 vote, April 21, 1969. Brennan wrote the opinion; dissenting were Warren, Black, Harlan.

State or federal requirement that person must reside within a certain jurisdiction for one year before becoming eligible for welfare assistance violates individual rights to due process and equal protection of the laws; no compelling government interest has been presented to justify this infringement of the right to travel.

Wheeler v. Montgomery, Goldberg v. Kelly, decided by 5-3 votes, March 23, 1970. Brennan wrote the opinion; Burger, Black and Stewart dissented.

Due process requires state to give welfare recipient opportunity for full hearing before terminating his or her welfare payments. The crucial factor in the situation, noted the court, was that "termination of aid pending resolution of a controversy over eligibility may deprive an eligible recipient of the very means by which to live."

Dandridge v. Williams, decided by a 5-3 vote, April 6, 1970. Stewart wrote the opinion; Douglas, Brennan and Marshall dissented.

States do not violate federal law or the equal protection guarantee by limiting the amount of welfare aid which one family may receive.

Rosado v. Wyman, decided by a 6-2 vote, April 6, 1970. Harlan wrote the opinion; Burger and Black dissented.

New York revision of welfare program to reduce benefits does not comply with requirements of 1967 Social Security Amendments that states readjust the standard of need in welfare programs in order to reflect the increased cost-of-living.

Lewis v. Martin, decided by a 6-2 vote, April 20, 1970. Douglas wrote the opinion; Burger and Black dissented.

State cannot reduce welfare aid to children because there is a man living in the same house unless he actually contributes to the support of the children. (This followed up a 1968 ruling in the case of *King v. Smith* in which the court had invalidated a state regulation which terminated all welfare aid to children if a man was living in the same house.)

Wyman v. James. decided by an 8-1 vote, Jan. 12, 1971. Blackmun wrote the opinion; Douglas dissented.

Constitutional protection against unreasonable searches does not invalidate state law conditioning receipt of aid to dependent children on periodic, warrantless visits to home by caseworker.

California Department of Human Resources v. Java, decided by a 9-0 vote, April 26, 1971. Burger wrote the opinion.

Federal law forbids state withholding unemployment compensation payments pending outcome of employer's appeal of initial valid determination of recipient's eligibility.

Graham v. Richardson, decided by a 9-0 vote, June 14, 1971. Blackmun wrote the opinion.

Equal protection guarantee violated by state laws denying welfare benefits to aliens who have lived in the United States less than 15 years or denying benefits to all resident aliens.

Richardson v. Belcher, decided by a 4-3 vote, Nov. 22, 1971. Stewart wrote the opinion; Douglas, Brennan and Marshall dissented.

Federal law allowing reduction in disability payments to reflect workman's compensation payments, but not other payments, is not in violation of due process.

Jefferson v. Hackney, decided by a 5-4 decision, May 30, 1972. Rehnquist wrote the opinion; Douglas, Brennan, Stewart and Marshall dissented.

Neither federal law nor equal protection guarantees are violated by state reducing its aid to dependent children by a larger percentage than it reduced its aid to aged and disabled persons.

Carleson v. Remillard, decided by a 9-0 vote June 7, 1972. Douglas wrote the opinion.

State cannot deny aid to dependent children of servicemen absent without leave from duty.

Boddie v. Connecticut, decided by an 8-1 vote, March 2, 1971. Harlan wrote the opinion; Black dissented.

Due process bars states from denying persons divorces simply because the applicants are too poor to pay the court fees.

Wisconsin v. Constantineau, decided by a 6-3 vote, Jan. 19, 1971. Douglas wrote the opinion; Burger, Black and Blackmun dissented.

Due process bars states from posting the names of excessive drinkers in liquor stores without giving individuals named notice and opportunity for hearing on listing.

Rogers v. Bellei, decided by a 5-4 vote, April 5, 1971. Blackmun wrote the opinion; Douglas, Black, Brennan and Marshall dissented.

Foreign-born child of alien and American parents is not citizen within Fourteenth Amendment protection of due process and loses citizenship if he or she fails to live in United States for a period of five years between the ages of 14 and 28. Black complained that the court was overruling a 1967 decision that Congress had no power to strip anyone of citizenship not voluntarily renounced (*Afroyim v. Rusk*).

U.S. v. Vuitch, decided by a 5-4 vote, April 21, 1971. Black wrote the opinion; Douglas, Brennan, Marshall and Stewart dissented.

Law barring all abortions except those performed to save the life or health of the mother is not void as over-vague, since "health" has been interpreted to include mental well-being; law can be constitutionally applied because it requires prosecution to prove that abortion was unnecessary in order to convict physician.

Bell v. Burson, decided by a 9-0 vote, May 24, 1971. Brennan wrote the opinion.

State cannot constitutionally suspend, without hearing, car registration and driver's license of uninsured motorist after accident unless he posts security for damages, while exempting from this suspension motorists who are released by victim from liability or who are found non-liable by court.

Military Law

Oestereich v. Selective Service System Board, decided by a 6-3 vote, Dec. 16, 1968. Douglas wrote the opinion; Stewart, Brennan and White dissented.

Draft board did not have authority to withdraw divinity student's draft exemption because of his participation in anti-war protest.

McKart v. U.S., decided by an 8-0 vote, May 26, 1969. Marshall wrote the opinion.

Draft exemption of sole surviving son continues even after the death of all family members except son.

Gutknecht v. U.S., decided by an 8-0 vote, Jan. 19, 1970. Douglas wrote the opinion.

Selective service system is not authorized to accelerate induction of man found delinquent for turning in his draft card in anti-war protest. The court held that the law allowed the system to prosecute such delinquents, but not to punish them through accelerated induction.

Breen v. Selective Service System Local Board, decided by a 6-2 vote, Jan. 26, 1970. Black wrote the opinion; Stewart and Burger dissented.

Selective Service System is not authorized to reclassify person holding valid student deferment as punishment for turning in his draft card as protest against war; person so reclassified may challenge legality of his induction prior to actual induction.

Toussie v. U.S., decided by a 5-3 vote, March 2, 1970. Black wrote the opinion; Burger, Harlan and White dissented.

A man who failed to register for the draft at the time of his 18th birthday cannot—under the statute of limitations—be prosecuted after his 23rd birthday.

Welsh v. U.S., decided by a 5-3 vote, June 15, 1970. Black wrote the opinion; Blackmun did not take part; White, Burger and Stewart dissented.

Persons objecting to war because of deeply held moral or ethical beliefs are entitled to conscientious objector exemption even if any religious basis for their belief is expressly disavowed.

"What is necessary," Black said, "for a registrant's conscientious objection to all war to be 'religious'...is that this opposition to war stem from...(his) moral, ethical or religious beliefs about what is right and wrong and that these beliefs be held with the strength of traditional religious convictions."

All persons "whose consciences, spurred by deeply held moral, ethical, or religious beliefs, would give them no rest or peace if they allowed themselves to become part of an instrument of war" are entitled to exemption as conscientious objectors.

Mulloy v. U.S., decided by an 8-0 vote, June 15, 1970. Stewart wrote the opinion; Blackmun did not participate.

A draft board must—when presented with a registrant's nonfrivolous request for reclassification—reopen his case, and decide again on his classification, so that he may have the right to appeal an adverse decision.

Gillette v. U.S., Negre v. Larsen, decided by an 8-1 vote, March 8, 1971. Marshall wrote the opinion; Douglas dissented.

Neither First Amendment nor federal law are violated by selective service system's denial of conscientious objector exemption and discharge to persons objecting only to participation in a particular war.

Ehlert v. U.S., decided by a 6-3 vote, April 21, 1971. Stewart wrote the opinion; Douglas, Brennan and Marshall dissented.

Individual's right not to be involuntarily subject to combatant training or service is not violated by policy that conscientious objector applicant—whose antiwar beliefs crystallized after receipt of his induction notice—will receive hearing and, until decision, be employed in duties involving minimum conflict with beliefs.

Clay v. U.S., decided by an 8-0 vote, June 28, 1971. Unsigned opinion; Marshall did not participate.

Conviction of Cassius Clay for refusing induction must be reversed because appeals board, in refusing his conscientious objector claim, failed to specify the reasons for its disapproval, two of which—as suggested by the Justice Department—were incorrect.

Parisi v. Davidson, decided by a 7-0 vote, Feb. 23, 1972. Stewart wrote the opinion; Powell and Rehnquist did not participate.

Federal district court can move on *habeas corpus* petition alleging wrongful denial by army of conscientious objector discharge, even though military man filing petition is presently being court-martialed for refusal to board plane for Vietnam.

O'Callahan v. Parker, decided by a 5-3 vote, June 2, 1969. Douglas wrote the opinion; Harlan, Stewart and White dissented.

A serviceman is entitled to trial by civilian court, not court-martial, for non-service-connected crimes committed during peacetime while off post, on leave and out of uniform.

Only service-connected crimes came under military jurisdiction. Otherwise, the court said, military jurisdiction might be expanded to deny all members of the armed services in all cases the benefits of an indictment by grand jury and a trial by jury.

Relford v. Commandant, decided by a 9-0 vote, Feb. 24, 1971. Blackmun wrote the opinion.

Court-martial had jurisdiction to try soldier charged with on-base kidnaping and rape, since on-post offenses are "service-connected."

Congressional Powers, Immunities

Powell v. McCormack, decided by a 7-1 vote, June 16, 1969. Warren wrote the opinion; Stewart dissented.

The House of Representatives does not have the authority to exclude from membership a duly elected Representative who meets the constitutional qualifications of age, residence and citizenship.

Background. Adam Clayton Powell Jr. (D N.Y.) was in 1966 elected for his 12th term as Representative from New York's 18th Congressional District (Harlem).

On the first day of the 90th Congress, Jan. 10, 1967, the House (H Res 1) decided that Powell's eligibility to be sworn in and seated as a Member should be determined by a select committee.

The committee, Feb. 23, 1967, concluded that Powell had claimed an unwarranted immunity from the New York courts, submitted false expense reports to the Committee on House Administration and misused House funds. The House March 1, 1967, voted 307-116 to exclude Powell from the 90th Congress.

Powell and a number of his constituents March 8 filed suit in federal district court for the District of Columbia against House Speaker John W. McCormack (D Mass.) and other House leaders and officials.

The suit requested a declaratory judgment that the exclusion of Powell by the House was unconstitutional, a permanent order forbidding McCormack to refuse to administer the oath to Powell, the Clerk to refuse to perform duties due a Representative, the Sergeant-at-Arms to refuse to pay Powell his salary, and the Doorkeeper to threaten not to admit him to the House Chamber.

The federal district court dismissed the suit because, it said, it did not have jurisdiction over its subject matter. The court of appeals, District of Columbia circuit, Feb. 28, 1968, affirmed the action of the lower court in dismissing the suit. The court of appeals held that the lower court did have jurisdiction over the subject matter but that the case involved a political question, which if decided, would constitute a violation of the separation of powers and produce an embarrassing confrontation between Congress and the courts. Judge Warren E. Burger wrote the court of appeals opinion.

While *Powell v. McCormack* was pending on the Court's docket, the 90th Congress ended. Powell was elected again to represent New York's 18th District in the House. He was seated in January 1969 by the 91st Congress and fined $25,000.

Opinion. Chief Justice Warren, for the court, ruled that the House had improperly excluded Powell, a duly elected Representative who met all constitutional qualifications.

Warren then proceeded to the question whether the speech or debate clause of the Constitution (Article I, Section 6) protected those named by Powell in his suit from judicial review of their actions.

Freedom of legislative activity, the objective of the constitutional clause, was protected, the court held, so long as legislators were not forced to defend themselves for their legislative actions. Therefore, the action against McCormack and the other members was dismissed. The court, however, allowed Powell to maintain the suit against the House employees.

The Constitution, the court ruled, in giving to the House the power to "be the Judge of the...Qualifications of its own Members," (Article I, Section 5, clause 1) left the House without the authority to exclude any duly elected Representative who met the requirements for membership expressly stated in the Constitution.

The court did not deny the unquestionable interest of the Congress in maintaining its own integrity. In most cases, however, the court felt that that interest could be properly safeguarded by the use of each House's power to punish or expel its Members. "The Constitution does not vest in the Congress a discretionary power, to deny membership by a majority vote."

The court dismissed the argument that the case presented a "political question" which, if decided by the court, could produce an explosive confrontation between the legislative and judicial branches. Determination of Powell's right to his seat in the 90th Congress, the court held, required only the interpretation of the Constitution, the traditional function of the court.

The Supreme Court sent the case back to the court of appeals with instructions to enter a declaratory judgment stating that the House action was unconstitutional and to conduct further proceedings on the unresolved issues of seniority, back pay and the $25,000 fine.

Stewart dissented, holding that the end of the 90th Congress and the seating of Powell in the 91st Congress rendered the case moot. *(Details, see chapter on Congress)*

U.S. v. Brewster, decided by a 6-3 vote, June 29, 1972. Burger wrote the opinion; Brennan, Douglas and White dissented.

The constitutional immunity conferred on members of Congress does not protect them from prosecution for accepting a bribe in order to vote a certain way on a legislative matter.

Background. Former Sen. Daniel B. Brewster (D Md. 1963-1969) was indicted in 1969 on charges of accepting $24,000 in bribes between 1966 and 1968 from the mail order firm of Spiegel Inc. During that time, Brewster was a member of the Senate Post Office and Civil Service Committee, which was considering proposed changes in postal rates. The indictment alleged that he was influenced in his action on these proposals by the bribes.

In November 1970, a federal district judge in the District of Columbia, George L. Hart, dismissed the charges against Brewster, stating that the immunity granted members of Congress by the Constitution shielded him from prosecution for bribery related to performance of a legislative act. The Justice Department immediately asked the Supreme Court to review this decision.

Opinion. Chief Justice Burger, for the court, reversed the lower court ruling and held that Brewster could indeed be prosecuted on the bribery charges. The constitutional protection granting members of Congress freedom from prosecution "in any other place" for "any speech or debate in either House" did not protect members' illegal actions in accepting bribes, even if the bribe was directed at a legislative act, such as a committee vote. Taking a bribe is illegal, is no part of the legislative process, and is therefore subject to prosecution and punishment in the nation's courts, held the court. *(Details, see chapter on Congress)*

In dissent, the justices argued that the majority was weakening the independence of Congress and should leave the disciplining of Brewster to Congress itself: "The speech or debate clause does not immunize corrupt congressmen. It reserves the power to discipline (them) in the houses of Congress."

Gravel v. U.S., U.S. v. Gravel, decided by a 5-4 vote, June 29, 1972. White wrote the opinion; Douglas, Stewart, Brennan and Marshall dissented.

The constitutional immunity of members of Congress extends also to their aides, if the conduct in question would be a protected legislative act if performed by the member himself; immunity does not shield an aide or member from testifying to a grand jury about acts unconnected with the legislative process.

Background. At the peak of the controversy over publication of the Pentagon Papers in 1971, Sen. Mike Gravel (D Alaska) called a nocturnal meeting of the public works subcommittee of which he was chairman. Before an audience composed of members of the press and general public, Gravel read, hour after hour, from the classified documents. Later he arranged for the Beacon Press to publish the record of these hearings, known as the Gravel version of the Pentagon Papers.

In August 1971 a grand jury investigating the release of the papers called Leonard S. Rodberg, an aide to Gravel, to appear before it. Rodberg moved to quash his subpoena on the basis that he was protected by congressional immunity from such questioning; Gravel backed that motion. The Justice Department opposed it.

A federal district court held that no witness including Rodberg could be questioned about Gravel's conduct at the subcommittee meeting or about preparations for the meeting. The court of appeals, 1st circuit, held that Gravel and Rodberg could be questioned about the later publication of the subcommittee record.

Opinion. White, for the court, made clear that neither Gravel nor Rodberg could be questioned about the events at the subcommittee meeting. However, the majority agreed that this protection did not extend to cover arrangements that were made for publication of the papers nor information about the source of the classified documents. Gravel, as well as Rodberg, could be required to testify about these non-legislative matters, held the majority.

Stewart dissented from the ruling insofar as it held that a member of Congress could be forced to tell a grand jury about the sources of information used to prepare for legislative activity. Douglas, Brennan and Marshall would hold that the constitutional immunity protected Gravel and Rodberg and Beacon Press from questions concerning the publication of the papers. *(Details, chapter on Congress)*

Antitrust Law

Citizen Publishing Co. v. U.S., decided by a 7-1 vote, March 10, 1969. Douglas wrote the opinion; Fortas did not participate; Stewart dissented.

A joint operating agreement combining the advertising and circulation departments of two competing newspapers and involving price-fixing, market control and pooling of profits was clearly a restraint of trade in violation of the Sherman Antitrust Act. The "failing company" doctrine can serve as defense in antitrust suits only if acquiring company has been shown to be the only available purchaser; burden of proof that conditions of doctrine have been satisfied rested on those using doctrine as defense.

The court refused to hold that the First Amendment guarantee of freedom of the press bars application of antitrust laws to newspapers: "The First Amendment affords not the slightest support for the contention that a combination to restrain trade in news...has any constitutional immunity.

Utah Public Service Commission v. El Paso Natural Gas Co., decided by a 4-2 vote, June 16, 1969. Warren wrote the opinion; White and Marshall did not participate; Harlan and Stewart dissented.

Supreme Court's mandate that natural gas company divest itself of stock and assets of acquired pipeline company—and that district court reapportion gas reserves between two companies was not effectively implemented by court order permitting gas company to acquire stock in pipeline company and not returning divested company to same competitive premerger position.

U.S. v. Interstate Commerce Commission (ICC), Brundage v. U.S.; Auburn v. U.S.; Livingston Anti-Merger Committee v. ICC, decided by a 7-0 vote, Feb. 2, 1970. Burger wrote the opinion; Douglas did not participate.

ICC approval of merger of the Great Northern Railway Company and the Northern Pacific Railway Company was proper, despite the fact that the competitive merging lines were in sound financial health.

U.S. v. Phillipsburg National Bank, decided by a 5-2 vote, June 29, 1970. Brennan wrote the opinion; Blackmun and Stewart did not participate; Burger and Harlan dissented.

Anticompetitive effects of merger between small competing banks in town must be measured in same geographic area as are benefits of the merger.

U.S. v. Armour and Co., decided by a 4-3 vote, June 1, 1971. Marshall wrote the opinion; Black and Blackmun did not participate; Douglas, Brennan and White dissented.

A company with retail food subsidiaries can acquire majority stock of meatpacking company without violating Meat Packers Consent Decree of 1920 which prohibits meatpacking company from engaging in retail food operations.

U.S. v. Greater Buffalo Press Inc., decided by a 9-0 vote, June 1, 1971. Douglas wrote the opinion.

Acquisition of profitable major printer which results in concentration of 75 per cent of independent color comic supplement printing business violates Clayton Act; passage of time in itself is not barrier to divestiture of stock acquired as result of unlawful merger.

Hawaii v. Standard Oil of California, decided by a 5-2 vote, March 1, 1972. Marshall wrote the opinion; Powell and Rehnquist did not participate; Douglas and Brennan dissented.

State is not authorized by Clayton Act to sue for damages for economic interests of its citizens even if the alleged damage is attributed to violation of the antitrust laws.

Federal Trade Commission v. Sperry and Hutchinson Company, decided by a 7-0 decision, March 1, 1972. White wrote the opinion; Powell and Rehnquist did not participate.

Federal Trade Commission is empowered to protect consumers as well as competitors and to judge challenged practices against standards of fair competition and fair practices as well as against the letter and spirit of the antitrust laws.

Ford Motor Co. v. U.S., decided by a 5-2 vote, March 29, 1972. Douglas wrote the opinion; Powell and Rehnquist did not participate; Burger and Blackmun dissented.

Antitrust laws are violated by practice of cooperative and assets of second largest domestic independent spark plug manufacturer by nation's second largest automobile producer.

U.S. v. Topco Associates, decided by a 6-1 vote, March 29, 1972. Marshall wrote the opinion; Powell and Rehnquist did not participate; Burger dissented.

Antitrust laws are violated by practice of cooperative association of small supermarket chains in allocating territory among members to minimize competition between member stores, even if this territorial arrangement is needed to enable the small chains to compete with national chains; association limitations on resale of private label products are also in violation of antitrust laws.

Flood v. Kuhn, decided by a 5-3 vote, June 19, 1972. Blackmun wrote the opinion; Powell did not participate; Douglas, Brennan and Marshall dissented.

Professional baseball remains exempt from federal antitrust laws, an exception in which Congress has acquiesced, and therefore the reserve clause, which allows a monopoly over the services of an individual player, is allowed to stand.

Business

Anderson's-Black Rock Inc. v. Pavement Salvage Co., decided by a 7-0 vote, Dec. 8, 1969. Douglas wrote the opinion; Burger did not participate.

A useful combination of already-patented elements which added nothing to the nature and quality of the elements did not qualify as patentable invention.

First National Bank v. Dickinson, Camp v. Dickinson, decided by a 6-2 vote, Dec. 9, 1969. Burger wrote the opinion; Douglas and Stewart dissented.

A national bank operating within a state was subject to the same limitations which state law imposed upon banks chartered within the state.

City of Chicago v. U.S., decided by an 8-0 vote, Dec. 9, 1969. Douglas wrote the opinion.

Individual persons can obtain judicial review of orders of the Interstate Commerce Commission continuing investigation of termination or changes in operation of interstate passenger trains.

Ross v. Bernhard, decided by a 5-3 vote, Feb. 2, 1970. White wrote the opinion; Burger, Harlan and Stewart dissented.

Stockholders bringing suit in federal court on behalf of a corporation are entitled to a jury trial so long as the issues, if contested by the corporation in its own behalf, merit a jury trial.

U.S. v. Kordel, decided by a 7-0 vote, Feb. 24, 1970. Stewart wrote the opinion; Black did not participate.

Federal regulatory agencies have the right to demand information from manufacturers in civil suits under threat of forfeiting their products, even if the information so gained might incriminate the manufacturer.

Association of Data Processing Service Organizations v. Camp, decided by an 8-0 vote, March 3, 1970. Douglas wrote the opinion.

Data processing companies have standing to bring court challenge to 1966 ruling by currency comptroller which allowed national banks to sell data processing services to other banks and to businesses which were bank customers.

U.S. v. Key, decided by an 8-0 vote, March 30, 1970. Marshall wrote the opinion.

Insolvent corporation reorganizing under federal bankruptcy law must pay federal tax claims before other debts.

Investment Company Institute v. Camp, decided by a 6-2 vote, April 5, 1971. Stewart wrote the opinion; Burger did not participate; Harlan and Blackmun dissented.

Banks are barred by the Banking Act of 1933 from operating mutual investment funds.

Labor

Detroit and Toledo Shore Line Railroad Co. v. United Transportation Union, decided by a 6-2 vote, Dec. 9, 1969. Black wrote the opinion; Burger and Harlan dissented.

The "status quo" preserved by the Railroad Labor Act of 1927 pending resolution of labor-carrier disputes included all actual working conditions regardless of their inclusion in or omission from an existing collective bargaining agreement.

National Labor Relations Board (NLRB) v. Rutter-Rex Manufacturing Co., decided by a 5-3 vote, Dec. 15, 1969. Marshall wrote the opinion; Burger, Harlan and Douglas dissented.

Back wages ordered by NLRB to be paid to wrongfully discharged employees may not be reduced because of NLRB delay in issuing order.

Czosek v. Mara, decided by a 7-1 vote, Feb. 24, 1970. White wrote the opinion; Burger dissented.

Discharged railroad employees can seek damages against union officers for failing adequately to press their claims. Such a complaint is adequate allegation of the union's breach of its duty of fair representation.

H. K. Porter Co. v. NLRB, decided by a 4-2 vote, March 2, 1970. Black wrote the opinion; White and Marshall did not participate; Douglas and Stewart dissented.

NLRB cannot compel a party to agree to any substantive contractual provision of a collective bargaining agreement.

The National Labor Relations Act pre-empts state jurisdiction to enjoin peaceful pickets protesting substandard wages paid by foreign-flag ships to American longshoremen in American ports.

NLRB v. Raytheon Co., decided by an 8-0 vote, May 18, 1970. Marshall wrote the opinion.

Company found guilty of unfair labor practice does not automatically escape judicial proceedings in enforcement of NLRB cease-and-desist order because a valid election has intervened.

Boys Markets Inc. v. Retail Clerk's Union, decided by a 5-2 vote, June 1, 1970. Brennan wrote the opinion; Marshall did not take part; Black and White dissented.

Federal judges are empowered to halt strikes which occur in violation of no-strike provisions in labor contract when contract also provides for binding arbitration. (Reversal of *Sinclair Refining Co. v. Atkinson,* 1962 *(Congress and the Nation Vol. I p. 128a)*

Atlantic Coast Line Railroad Co. v. Brotherhood of Locomotive Engineers, decided by a 5-2 vote, June 8, 1970. Black wrote the opinion; Marshall did not participate; Brennan and White dissented.

Federal judge may not issue order blocking state court action—even if state court's authority to act is unclear—unless the federal court is specifically authorized to act or is obligated to act to protect its own jurisdiction.

NLRB v. Operating Engineers, decided by a 7-2 vote, Jan. 12, 1971. Marshall wrote the opinion; Douglas and Stewart dissented.

Union pressure on neutral contractor to bind all subcontractors to particular form of job assignment or suffer strike is unfair labor practice.

Boilermakers v. Hardeman, decided by an 8-1 vote, Feb. 24, 1971. Brennan wrote the opinion; Douglas dissented.

Federal court has jurisdiction over expelled union member's claim for damages for union's violation of his rights by failure to give him full hearing at disciplinary proceedings.

Chicago and Northwest Railway Co. v. United Transportation Union, decided by a 5-4 vote, June 1, 1971. Harlan wrote the opinion; Black, Douglas, Brennan and White dissented.

Railway Labor Act imposes judicially-enforceable duty on carriers and employees to exert every reasonable effort to reach agreement and legally obligates parties to negotiate with desire to reach agreement; federal court not barred from issuing strike injunction if injunction is only practical and effective means of enforcing duty to negotiate to agreement.

Chemical Workers v. Pittsburgh Plate Glass Co., decided by a 6-1 vote, Dec. 8, 1971. Brennan wrote the opinion; Douglas dissented.

Retired employees' benefits are not, under the National Labor Relations Act, a mandatory subject of bargaining.

NLRB v. Scrivener, decided by a 7-0 vote, Feb. 23, 1972. Blackmun wrote the opinion; Powell and Rehnquist did not participate.

Employer cannot lawfully discharge employees for giving sworn written statements to NLRB field examiner investigating charges against employer.

NLRB v. Burns International Security Services, decided by a 5-4 vote, *Burns v. NLRB,* decided by a 9-0 vote, May 15, 1972. White wrote the opinion; Burger, Brennan, Rehnquist and Powell dissented.

Successor employers are not bound to substantive provisions of collective-bargaining agreement negotiated by predecessors, held the court unanimously. But successor employers, the court held, 5-4, are bound to bargain with the union recognized by the predecessor employer.

Central Hardware Co. v. NLRB, decided by a 6-3 vote, June 22, 1972. Powell wrote the opinion; Douglas, Brennan and Marshall dissented.

Union organizer not representing employees is not entitled by First Amendment to solicit store employees in store parking lot unless he shows that he cannot otherwise communicate with them.

Pipefitters Local Union v. U.S., decided by a 6-2 vote, June 22, 1972. Brennan wrote the opinion; Blackmun did not participate; Burger and Powell dissented.

Corrupt Practices Act, which bars contributions by any labor organization to any federal election, does not bar union contributions and expenditures to campaigns from political funds financed by voluntary contributions from members; solicitation of contributions is not banned if conducted without deception or threat of reprisal.

Environmental Rights

Growing concern for the quality of the environment was reflected in the quadrupling of environmental law cases on the Supreme Court's docket from 1969 to 1972. In the most significant of these, the court ruled that:

• Federal highways can only be built through public parks in the most unusual situations. The court, 8-0 on March 2, 1971, directed a lower court to determine whether or not the secretary of transportation had acted arbitrarily or capriciously in authorizing the construction of a highway through a city park. Marshall wrote the opinion; Douglas did not participate. *(Citizens to Preserve Overton Park v. Volpe).*

• State courts were better equipped than the Supreme Court to rule on the local legal issues and matters of complex technical fact involved in a suit by Ohio against several chemical companies for allegedly polluting Lake Erie with mercury deposits. The court agreed, 8-1 on March 23, 1971; Harlan wrote the opinion; Douglas dissented *(Ohio v. Wyandotte Chemicals Corp.).*

• Federal law regulating the discharge of radioactive waste from nuclear power plants could not be superseded by stricter state pollution laws. Over the dissents of Douglas and Stewart, the court, 7-2, April 2, 1972, refused to review—and thus upheld—this ruling by a lower court *(Minnesota v. Northern States Power Co.)*

• The Sierra Club and other conservation groups could not mount a court challenge to federal action allowing development of a commercial ski resort in a national forest unless the club or its members claimed to suffer actual injury from the development. By a 4-3 vote, April 19, 1972, the court ruled in this case. Stewart wrote the majority opinion; Powell and Rehnquist did not participate; Douglas, Brennan and Blackmun dissented *(Sierra Club v. Morton).*

• Federal district courts were the proper original forums for a case brought by 18 states against the nation's four largest car manufacturers, charging them with conspiring to delay development of effective antipollution devices for car engines. The court unanimously sent the case to the lower courts on April 24, 1972; Douglas wrote the opinion *(State of Washington et al v. General Motors Corp. et al).*

• Lower federal courts had sufficient power to resolve a dispute between Illinois and four Wisconsin cities for allegedly polluting Lake Michigan with raw sewage. The court agreed unanimously on this point April 24, 1972; Douglas wrote the opinion *(Illinois v. Milwaukee)*

• A three-judge federal court had correctly refrained from ruling on a challenge to a state law requiring all Great Lakes vessels—even those with federal licenses operating in interstate commerce—to equip themselves with sewage holding tanks. The court reached this conclusion by a 7-2 vote; Brennan wrote the opinion; Burger and Powell dissented; the decision was announced May 30, 1972 *(Lake Carriers Association v. MacMullan).*

Chapter 6—Agriculture Policy

Key Votes

In this chapter, key roll-call votes are shown in bold-face type. The party breakdown on each of these votes and the position taken by each member of Congress may be found in the key vote charts which appear in the appendix to this book.

Agriculture Policy

Tension between the Republican administration and the Democratic-controlled Congress produced a halfway step toward a market-oriented national farm policy during President Nixon's first term. A battle in the second term, over whether to expand the shift in direction or reverse it, appeared inevitable.

The Agricultural Act of 1970 (PL 91-524) was the most significant farm legislation passed during the period 1969-72. Enacted after 16 months of controversy, the act constituted a compromise between Democratic advocates of continued crop and price controls and the administration and its allies, who sought a general loosening of government restrictions with increased emphasis on sales abroad. In the 1970 act, Congress retained the supply management approach of the preceding Democratic administrations, which had been reaffirmed most recently in the basic farm legislation in effect since 1965.

The intensified struggle in 1969 and 1970 between the two long-conflicting viewpoints pointed toward a major confrontation over agricultural policy during the second Nixon term. The stage was set by the scheduled expiration of the three-year price-support act at the end of 1973.

Basically, the 1970 act continued policies followed under the Kennedy-Johnson administrations, placing emphasis on keeping a check on supply and maintaining farm income through direct payments to farmers. However, the Republican administration obtained a key concession in what was known as the set-aside feature. Under this provision, the act permitted a farmer to be compensated for taking a certain amount of land out of production. He was free to raise what he wished on his other land. The set-aside feature constituted a significant step toward giving farmers greater freedom to plant what they desired, according to their assessment of market conditions, and it marked a relaxation of restraints imposed under Democratic administrations in the 1960s.

The Republican administration was prepared to go still further when the time came for another legislative move. It favored eventual elimination of direct government payments on cotton, wheat and other specified crops and of the crop-by-crop allotments in effect since the 1930s. But it wanted to retain the basic price-support loans and the authority to buy land taken out of production under the new set-aside program. Advocates of the administration approach, including the big American Farm Bureau Federation, pointed to increased farm exports and farm income as supporting their approach toward greater reliance on supply and demand.

On the other hand, a number of Democratic members of Congress from agricultural areas, backed by other farm organizations, argued for continued restraints (in combination with farm income aids) to curb overproduction. They maintained that the danger persisted that increasingly efficient American farming methods could, in the absence of adequate planning and controls along with price supports, produce huge surpluses which could drive prices down, eliminate farm profits and create serious problems for the whole economy.

Resentment which had been rising among urban members of Congress over large farm subsidy payments culminated in the inclusion in the 1970 bill of a provision imposing the first limitation on total payments. After efforts to limit payments to an individual farm to $20,000 a year failed, a compromise ceiling of $55,000 per crop was enacted. A few farmers had received subsidies of as much as $4-million in one year.

Another indication of future controversy came when the House in 1971 by a 12-vote margin passed a bill amended to raise price-support loan levels for wheat and feed grains by 25 per cent. The bill, which would have established a national reserve purchased by the government, so as to reduce oversupply of grains, died without action in the Senate. The issue, however, was far from dead.

In other actions during the four-year period, Congress extended the sugar quota program under the much-lobbied Sugar Act and continued such existing programs as those providing for food stamps, school lunches and Food for Peace—also called Food for Freedom.

Economic Trends

As the first Nixon term ended, the intensified debate over farm policy, and whether to move further away from the basic support-controls programs of some three decades, took place against a background which included:

• Record exports of farm products, including grains and soybeans, accompanied by the opening of a previously untapped market in the Soviet Union and growing

References

Discussion of agricultural policy for the years 1965-68 may be found in *Congress and the Nation*, Vol. II, p. 555-597; for the years 1945-64, *Congress and the Nation*, Vol. I, p. 665-767.

interest in underdeveloped countries.

• Record realized net farm income in 1972 of $19.2-billion.

• A continued trend toward fewer farms and a declining U.S. farm population, both in real terms and in relation to the overall population.

• A pronounced swing away from the family farm and toward larger farms which produced an ever larger share of the total farm production, required larger capital, and directed increasing attention to the term "agribusiness."

• Continued increases in mechanization and steadily rising production per acre.

Relation to Economy. While farming was one of the principal occupations in the nation, it continued in the early 1970s to produce directly only 3 per cent of total national income.

Both the number of farms and the farm population declined steadily over the 1969-72 period, continuing a trend which had been going on steadily since well before World War II.

Year	Farms	Farm Population	As % of Total Pop.
1935	6,814,000	32,161,000	25.3%
1945	5,967,000	24,420,000	17.5
1955	4,654,000	19,078,000	11.5
1960	3,962,000	15,635,000	8.7
1967*	3,146,000	10,875,000	5.5
1968	3,054,000	10,454,000	5.2
1969	2,971,000	10,307,000	5.1
1970	2,924,000	9,712,000	4.8
1971	2,876,000	9,425,000	4.6

Revised Agriculture Department figures.

Size of Farms. The average size of farms increased steadily. Government figures reflecting changes in farm definitions and revised counts showed that the average farm size rose from 167 acres in 1940 to 213 acres in 1950. By 1959, it had increased to 288 acres, by 1964 to 333 acres, and by 1969 to 378 acres. In 1971, the average was 389 acres, and preliminary 1972 figures indicated a rise to 394 acres.

Productivity. The long-term trend of increases in farm productivity, due to use of more machinery, fertilizer, lime and insecticides, continued in 1969-72. Corn yields, which averaged 32.7 bushels an acre in 1945 and 68.3 bushels over the 1962-66 period, reached 78.5 bushels an acre in 1968 and 86.8 bushels in 1971. Sorghum grain, a feed similar to corn, had average yields of 15.2 bushels an acre in 1945, 47.4 bushels over the period 1962-66, 52.9 bushels in 1968 and 53.9 bushels in 1971. Wheat rose from 17.0 in 1945 to 25.8 bushels an acre in the 1962-66 period, 28.4 bushels in 1968 and 33.8 bushels in 1971.

Exports. Agricultural exports showed a steady and accelerating climb. In 1961-65 they averaged $5.6-billion a year. In the period from 1966-70, farm exports averaged $6.5-billion annually. In 1970, they totaled $7.4-billion and in 1971, $7.9-billion. Exports passed $8-billion in 1972 and were expected to hit $10-billion in 1973.

In 1970, official figures showed that the United States produced 13 per cent of the world's wheat and provided 36.8 per cent of the world's wheat exports. The 1.1 billion bushels expected to be exported in 1973 greatly

Farm Program Tools

A combination of price support loans and direct payments to farmers make up the income-maintenance and supply control features of the existing farm program for wheat, feed grains and cotton.

Basic Price Support Loans. If a farmer cannot sell his crop at a favorable price, he can obtain a government loan, using his crop as collateral. Later, if the market price rises, he can sell his crop. If it fails to rise, he can keep the loan money; the government buys his crop. The loan available is placed at a certain dollar figure per bushel of grain or pound of cotton. It is expressed as a percentage of parity, an artificial price designed to reflect a fair relationship between farm income and farm costs. Basic price support loans in recent years have been fixed at or near the world price to allow the commodity to move in international trade. The Nixon administration favors keeping the loan mechanism.

Set-Aside Payments. These are direct payments to a farmer from the government for reducing a specified amount of his total farm from production, except for a small portion of land that must be idled for conservation purposes (the conserving base). On the rest of his land, a farmer is free to plant whatever crop he desires, even though payment formulas and production restrictions still must take into account a farm's historic allotments for individual commodities. The administration favors continued authority to make set-aside payments, but it wants a clean break from historic allotments.

Wheat Certificate Payments. These are special payments to a farmer participating in the program to assure him "full parity" on the wheat he produces for use in the United States. A payment amounted to $1.34 a bushel in 1972. To help finance the program, millers are required to purchase certificates from the government for 75 cents a bushel for the wheat they process for human domestic consumption. The administration classifies this payment as the type of "income supplement" it wants to phase out.

Cotton Payments. A cotton grower who participates in the program gets a payment of 15 cents a pound calculated on the acreage he plants up to his share of the national allotment on a yield representing his average yields in past years. The administration wants to phase out this "income supplement" as well as the wheat payments.

exceeded the previous U.S. record wheat export of 867 million bushels in 1966. This country produced 41.4 per cent of the world's corn for grain in 1970 and supplied 50.5 per cent of world corn exports, 73.0 per cent of world soybean production and 93.5 per cent of world soybean exports, 19.1 per cent of world cotton production and 22.5 per cent of world cotton exports.

Division of Market. The larger commercial farms continued to increase their share of the market and to grow in number. In 1959, some 2.8 per cent of the nation's farms had sales of $40,000 or more annually and accounted for 31.2 per cent of total farm income from sales. By 1967, they made up 5.8 per cent of all farms, with 47 per cent of all sales by value. By 1971, these farms made up 8.8 per cent of all farms, with 59.3 per cent of all sales by value. Agriculture Department figures divided farms in 1971, according to gross annual sales, as follows:

Class	Number	% of All Farms	% of All Sales
$40,000 and over	253,000	8.8	59.3
$20,000 to $39,999	365,000	12.7	19.2
$10,000 to $19,999	392,000	13.6	10.9
$ 5,000 to $ 9,999	385,000	13.4	5.5
$ 2,500 to $ 4,999	409,000	14.2	3.0
Under $2,500	1,072,000	37.3	2.1
Total	**2,876,000**	**100.0**	**100.0**

Chronology

Of Legislation

On Agriculture

1969

Proposals for a new omnibus farm program to replace the program expiring at the end of 1970 dominated congressional consideration of agricultural matters in 1969. Although there was little final legislative action, a squabble over subsidy payments to farmers during the debate on annual appropriations signaled new controversy ahead.

Urban members of Congress led a fight on the House floor to limit subsidy payments to individual farms to $20,000 and won the battle for the ceiling by a 225-142 roll-call vote. However, the limitation, which had also been tacked on to the omnibus farm bill by the House in 1968, was deleted by the Senate on a **key 53-34 roll-call vote.** The strong House vote for limitations led Secretary of Agriculture Clifford M. Hardin to suggest that some form of limitations might be worked into the 1970 farm program.

Since the omnibus farm program was due to expire at the end of calendar year 1970, the House Agriculture Committee began hearings in July on a committee bill (HR 12430) to make permanent existing commodity programs. Committee Chairman W. R. Poage (D Texas) announced that the committee would consider general farm legislation and food stamp proposals at the same time because the production and distribution of food were closely related.

Secretary Hardin described several tentative administration proposals for a new farm program and for wheat, cotton and feed grain programs. Basically, the administration sought more flexible price supports based on world market prices, with greater latitude for farms.

Alternative proposals were put forward during the year by the American Farm Bureau Federation—aiming at ending supports and controls and by a coalition of 24 farm organizations which favored permanent programs.

Congress enacted a $610-million food stamp authorization, an increase of $270-million over the fiscal 1969 total for the program which President Nixon had requested.

Farm Program Proposals

The House Agriculture Committee in 1969 worked on early drafts of a new farm program. The existing program, created by the 1965 Food and Agriculture Act (PL 89-321), had been extended in 1968 through the end of calendar 1970.

Three different plans were taken up during consideration of a replacement for the program expiring in 1970: an administration proposal which was presented to the committee in skeleton form so that the Department of Agriculture could develop a program in cooperation with the congressional committees; a program recommended by a 24-member organization of farm groups; and a plan advanced by the American Farm Bureau Federation.

Administration Bill. Secretary of Agriculture Clifford M. Hardin suggested the broad outlines of an administration program in testimony Sept. 24 before the House committee. Two alternative plans were described to cover the cotton, wheat and feed grain programs. Other programs were to be dealt with after Congress had set the pattern on these crops.

The administration recommendations employed acreage allotments, direct federal payments and price-support loans, as did existing programs, but operated these arrangements in different ways. The two proposals were:

• A "set-aside" plan under which a farmer agreed to leave unplanted part of his allotment (the amount of land he was assigned for production as part of the national allotment for the crop in question). The farmer also would have to agree to leave unplanted his "conserving base"—the acreage he had in permanent pasture or woods.

Hardin said wheat and cotton growers would have to divert for conservation uses crop acreage equivalent to perhaps 75 per cent to 100 per cent of the domestic allotment, and feed grain producers, 30 per cent to 50 per cent of their bases. Those who participated in the program would be eligible for price-support loans on all the crops raised. Cotton and wheat producers would also receive income-support payments based on domestic allotment production. Feed grain growers would be eligible for similar payments on half of their feed grain base.

• A domestic allotment and diversion program which would give direct payments to wheat and cotton producers on their domestic acreage allotment without requiring them to divert any acreage. There would be no domestic allotment for feed grain, but producers would receive payments if they took a certain percentage of their acreage out of production. The grain base would be determined by adding together the wheat base and the feed grain base.

Income From Farming

(in millions of dollars)

	Realized Gross Income	Production Expenses	Realized Net Income		Per farm, 1967 dollars*	Parity Ratio**
			Amt.	% of Gross		
1930	$11,472	$ 6,944	$ 4,528	39.5%	$1,538	83
1940	11,059	6,858	4,201	38.0	1,742	81(88)
1950	32,271	19,410	12,861	39.9	2,996	101(102)
1960	38,088	26,352	11,736	30.8	3,291	80(81)
1965	44,926	30,933	13,993	31.1	4,411	77(82)
1968	50,897	36,209	14,688	28.9	4,624	73(79)
1969	55,550	38,759	16,791	30.2	5,185	74(80)
1970	57,925	49,091	16,834	29.1	5,050	72(77)
1971	60,057	44,006	16,051	26.7	4,690	70(74)
1972	66,445	47,200	19,245	29.0	NA	74(79)

* *Dollars, not millions—revised to 1967 basis in government statistics.*
** *Adjusted parity ratio, reflecting government payments, shown in parentheses.*

COALITION BILL

Twenty-four general farm and rural groups and special commodity organizations sponsored legislation to extend permanently existing farm programs. The coalition group included the National Farmers Union, National Grange, Midcontinent Farmers Association and National Farmers Organization.

In addition to permanent extension of the 1965 act, the coalition urged the following changes in the programs:

Provide for export certificates for wheat comparable to domestic wheat certificates. Wheat accompanied by an export certificate would be supported at between 65 per cent ($1.90) and 90 per cent ($2.49) of parity, with a floor of 65 cents.

Establish consumer protection reserves of wheat, feed grains, soybeans and cotton.

Increase direct payments and price-support loans for corn and equivalent increases in other feed grains.

Establish a soybean program which would permit the secretary of agriculture to require acreage reductions and make diverted acreage payments. The proposal called for 75 per cent of parity price-support loans for participants in the acreage diversion program.

Extend market order authority to any commodity subject to approval by a majority of affected producers. (If producers agreed in a referendum, the secretary of agriculture was empowered to set minimum prices or market quotas on certain commodities which the processors must then honor.)

Extend existing cotton and wool programs.

FARM BUREAU

The American Farm Bureau Federation, which traditionally had espoused return to a completely free market system, proposed a five-year program to phase out acreage controls, base acreages, marketing quotas and direct payments for wheat, feed grain and cotton. Known as the Agricultural Adjustment Act, the program would:

Limit the total funds to be spent in all direct payments for wheat, feed grain and cotton under the 1965 act in

1971 to 80 per cent of the amount spent on 1969 crops, 60 per cent in 1972, 40 per cent in 1973 and 20 per cent in 1974. All payments would end after 1975.

Reduce the cost of wheat certificates to processors to 80 per cent of the 1969 level in 1971, 60 per cent in 1972, 40 per cent in 1973 and 20 per cent in 1974.

Direct the secretary of agriculture to retire at least 10 million acres per year from 1971 through 1975 as part of the cropland adjustment program.

Provide that loan rates for wheat, feed grains, cotton and soybeans be set at not more than 85 per cent of the previous three-year average price beginning with the 1971 crop year.

Authorize the secretary of agriculture to offer a special transitional program during the five-year period to small farmers to encourage them to transfer to nonfarm employment.

Appropriations Bill

The regular Agriculture Department appropriations bill for fiscal 1970 (HR 11612—PL 91-127) appropriated $7,488,903,150 in new budget obligational authority. The total was $251-million above the administration request ($7,237,562,050), and $716-million less than provided in fiscal 1969.

Although both houses passed the bill in early summer, the conference committee waited for congressional action on a higher fiscal 1970 food stamp authorization in order to incorporate the higher figure in the appropriations bill.

The two items which caused the amount appropriated to exceed the administration request were the continuation of the agricultural conservation program and the special milk program, both of which the administration had sought to end.

The bill provided $195.5-million in an advance program authorization for the agricultural conservation program, under which the government shared with farmers, ranchers and woodland owners the cost of carrying out approved soil-building and soil-and-water-conserving practices. The Johnson administration had consistently tried to cut the figure to $100-million, but Congress kept it at about $200-million. President Nixon had eliminated the whole fiscal 1970 budget request for that program.

The other program which Congress insisted on funding was the special milk program. The Nixon administration maintained that milk would be provided in an expanded school lunch program, but congressional supporters of the special milk program succeeded in including a separate $84-million appropriation for the program and included language in the bill reserving another $20-million in Section 32 customs receipts funds for the program. *(Box, p. 336)*

The conferees eliminated a House-passed amendment limiting to $20,000 the amount an individual farmer could receive in subsidy payments for the 1970 wheat, feed grains and cotton crops.

The fiscal 1970 appropriations total eventually rose from the $7,488,903,150 provided in PL 91-127 to $8,083,596,150. Included in the increase of $594,693,000 was $3.7-million appropriated for the Soil Conservation Service as part of the first fiscal 1970 supplemental appropriations bill (PL 91-166). A sum of $61,906,000 for the Department of Agriculture was included in the second fiscal 1970 supplemental (PL 91-305) as part of the $4,259,729,830 total in that bill for pay raises for federal employees. The bulk of the rest of the increase of $594,-693,000 represented the difference between what the department had estimated for reimbursement for net realized losses of the Commodity Credit Corporation (CCC) and what the actual figure was for fiscal 1970. The CCC lends farmers money against their crops so that the farmers will not have to sell when the market is glutted and the prices are low. If the farmer subsequently decides to sell his crop, he repays the loan; if he does not, the CCC keeps title to the crop and the farmer keeps the money.

The bill also:

• Authorized the following transfers of Section 32 funds to various agencies to be spent for their programs in addition to amounts provided through direct appropriations: Agricultural Research Service, for research, $15-million; school lunch program, $194,266,000; Foreign Agricultural Service, $3,117,000 (total Section 32 transfers: $212,383,000). *(Box, p. 336)*

• Reappropriated $2 million in unused fiscal 1968 funds for plant and animal disease and pest control activities of the Agricultural Research Service, in addition to its new appropriations.

• Authorized the transfer of $107,000 from the Commodity Credit Corp. (CCC) for salaries and expenses of the Foreign Agricultural Service, in addition to funds included in direct appropriations for the same purpose.

• Authorized the transfer of $62,483,000 from the CCC for expenses incurred by the Agricultural Stabilization and Conservation Service, in addition to direct appropriations.

• Authorized $366,700,000 for the Farmers Home Administration (FHA) direct loan account: $83-million for real estate loans, $275-million for operating loans and $8.7-million for soil conservation loans.

• Authorized $30-million for rural housing loans of the FHA.

• Authorized transfer of $2,250,000 from the Agricultural Credit Insurance Funds for salaries and expenses of the FHA, plus other transfers of $500,000, in addition to direct appropriations.

• Stipulated that $7.5-million of cooperative agricultural extension funds be used for professional workers to promote 4-H type programs in depressed urban areas.

Food Stamps

Congress, in reaction to a growing concern over the problem of hunger and to a presidential request, in 1969 provided additional funds for the food stamp program. The Senate passed two bills (S J Res 126, S 2547) further broadening the program, but the House Agriculture Committee did not take up the measures. The House committee, however, approved the President's request for additional funds, held hearings on various proposals to expand the food stamp program and began work on the administration's food stamp reform bill (HR 12222).

Farm Subsidies

On May 21, 1969, Rep. Paul Findley (R Ill.) placed in the *Congressional Record* a table showing how a total of $518,506,663 in farm subsidies was distributed in 1967 among 16,430 farms or farmers, each receiving $15,000 or more. The number of recipients, divided into groups according to the amounts received, ranged from 9,894 in the $15,000 to $24,999 category to five in the $1-million-and-over group:

• $15,000 to $24,999—9,894 receiving a total of $186,931,864.

• $25,000 to $49,999—4,843 receiving a total of $161,642,642.

• $50,000 to $99,999—1,285 receiving a total of $84,603,708.

• $100,000 to $499,999—388 receiving a total of $64,883,041.

• $500,000 to $999,999—15 farmers receiving a total of $9,556,372.

• $1 million and over—Five recipients and a total of $10,889,036.

A detailed listing by states and counties of payments of $25,000 or more in 1968 showed that the number of recipients in the $1-million-and-over category shrank that year from five to three, all in California. J. G. Boswell Co. of Kings County led the list with a subsidy of $3,010,042. It was followed by Giffen, Inc. in Fresno County with $2,772,187 and by South Lake Farms in Kings County with $1,177,320.

The three authorization bills on which action was taken were:

S J Res 126—Increased the fiscal 1970 authorization for the food stamp program from $340-million to $750-million. Passed by the Senate June 24 as reported. The House Agriculture Committee took no action.

S 2547—Increased authorization to $750-million for fiscal 1970 and to $1.5-billion for each of the following two fiscal years, reducing coupon costs for the neediest families and simplifying participation procedures. Passed by the Senate Sept. 24 with amendments to raise fiscal 1970 authorization to $1.25-billion and to provide free food stamps to families with incomes under $60 a month. The House took no action on S 2547 but began marking up the Administration's bill (HR 12222).

H J Res 934—Reported Oct. 14 by the House Agriculture Committee, increased fiscal 1970 authorization to $610-million, the amount of the President's request. Passed Nov. 5 by the House as reported. Passed Nov. 6 by the Senate without change (PL 91-116). Congress appropriated the full authorized amount of $610-million in the fiscal 1970 agriculture appropriations bill (HR 11612), cleared Nov. 19. *(Story on HR 11612 p. 334)*

House Agriculture Committee Chairman W. R. Poage (D Texas) insisted on considering the food stamp program only in connection with legislation dealing with the farm programs, which were due to expire in 1970. By tying the two together, Poage apparently hoped to gain support in 1970 from food stamp backers for extension of the farm programs. A similar "trade" had taken place in 1968.

Much of the Senate battle for an expanded food stamp program was led by the Select Committee on Nutrition and Human Needs, chaired by George McGovern (D S.D.). The committee highlighted the problem of hunger with hearings which centered on the food stamp program.

Other Bills

Rural Telephone. For the third year in a row, the House Rules Committee in 1969 blocked action on legislation to provide additional sources of financing for rural telephone systems.

The House Agriculture Committee reported a bill (HR 7) to supplement the existing program of 2 per cent loans to rural telephone systems by setting up a telephone bank to make 4 per cent loans, but the measure was bottled up in the Rules Committee.

The bill was supported by the Rural Electrification Administration (REA), a division of the Agriculture Department that administered the loan program, and by the lobbies for rural telephone systems. However, the measure was opposed by private power groups.

Peanut Allotments. Congress in 1969 passed an administration-backed bill (HR 14030—PL 91-122) extending for one year through crop year 1970 the authority in the Agricultural Adjustment Act for farmers to transfer peanut acreage allotments to each other within their own countries.

During House consideration, Rep. Maston O'Neal (D Fla.) said the legislation was needed to permit farmers to increase the size of their allotments to realize a more reasonable return on their investments. Most peanut acreage allotments were too small to constitute economic units, he said.

Migrant Workers' Health. The House Dec. 16 and the Senate Dec. 19 by voice votes passed different versions of a bill (HR 14733) to amend the Public Health Service Act (PL 78-410) to extend until June 30, 1973, health services programs for migrant farm workers. The bill had not been sent to conference before adjournment.

Under the program, started in 1962 and scheduled to expire June 30, 1970, grants were made to public agencies and private nonprofit groups to improve health conditions for migrant farm workers. The House version extended the programs to nonmigratory seasonal farm workers, while the Senate version did not.

CCC Supplemental Funds. Congress enacted a bill (H J Res 584—PL 91-7) which provided $1-billion in fiscal 1969 supplemental appropriations for the Agriculture Department's Commodity Credit Corp. (CCC), which administers the government's farm subsidy programs. The supplemental funds were needed to reimburse the CCC, which was running low on funds because of increased production of feed grains, wheat and soybeans over estimates and because of a national dock strike which had held up exports of CCC-held commodities.

1970

The most important farm legislation of the 1969-72 period was enacted in 1970. That year saw passage

Section 32 Funds

Section 32 of PL 74-320 earmarked 30 per cent of U.S. customs receipts from all sources each year for the secretary of agriculture to be used for various purposes, among them to encourage domestic consumption of commodities "among persons in low-income groups."

For several years, Congress had included language in agricultural appropriations bills pertaining to the use of Section 32 funds. Prior to fiscal 1969, restrictions on the use of Section 32 funds were interpreted as restricting their use for food assistance to low-income groups. An estimated $227 million of unused funds in fiscal 1968 was returned to the Treasury.

Final provisions worked out by conferees in the fiscal 1969 agriculture appropriations bill authorized the secretary to spend up to $45 million in Section 32 funds to provide direct distribution of food to needy children and low-income persons determined by him "to be suffering, through no fault of their own, from general and continued hunger resulting from insufficient food." The secretary was to consider the age, income, location and income of parents (if a minor) and employability. Such funds could be used whether or not needy cases occurred in areas already being served by the food stamp program or by the commodity distribution program.

of the Agricultural Act of 1970, establishing three-year price-support programs for wool, wheat, feed grains and cotton, beginning in January 1971. The bill was a compromise between the Nixon administration's request for more flexible price supports based on world market prices and the demand by many farm state members and farm organizations for higher parity guarantees. The 1970 act extended for three years, through 1973, the PL 480 (Food for Peace) program which made farm products available to underdeveloped countries.

Congress also enacted in 1970 a bill providing free food stamps to families of four with monthly incomes under $30, and a bill expanding and improving the program of free and reduced-price lunches for school children.

Agricultural Act

The Agricultural Act of 1970, a subject of major controversy among farm groups, Congress and the administration, took 16 months to make its way through hearings and floor action. The administration sought the end of parity guarantees for price supports, to be replaced by flexible supports based on world market prices. Farm groups fought for higher parity guarantees and argued that farm income would be lowered drastically by the administration proposals.

Another major issue in the debate was subsidy payments which urban members had sought to limit since 1968. The program had been criticized because individual farmers and farms had received payments as high as $4-million in one year.

The administration at first proposed a $110,000 ceiling per crop on the payments, but it agreed on a compromise $55,000 limitation in the face of strong congressional pressure to impose a $20,000 ceiling. The final bill included the $55,000 ceiling.

The final version contained administration provisions calling for farmers to set aside a certain acreage in order to qualify for price supports. They were free to plant whatever they wanted on the rest of their land. This feature marked a partial step toward a market-oriented farm policy.

PROVISIONS. As signed into law (PL 91-524) Nov. 30, HR 18546:

Title I—Payment Limitation

• Limited subsidy payments to $55,000 per producer per crop under the wheat, feed grain and cotton programs for the 1971 through 1973 crops.

• Exempted from the payment limitation lands owned by states and political subdivisions and their agencies, as long as the lands were farmed primarily in the furtherance of a public function.

Title II—Dairy

• Extended and amended the authority for the Class I Base dairy plans under federal milk marketing orders.

• Provided that any area which qualified to use the Class I Base plan authority had to do so by Dec. 31, 1973,

and if the federal marketing order were issued prior to that date, the order could remain in effect until Dec. 31, 1976. (Producers were assigned bases depending on their respective marketings during a representative period; under existing law a fixed representative period could be used in determining the producer's marketing history.)

• Continued the exemption of producer-handlers (individuals who produce, process and distribute milk of their own production) from all provisions of federal milk orders.

• Provided for a representative Class I Base period of one to three years, to be automatically updated each year.

• Set more flexible terms for entry of additional producers into the Class I Base plan, including a provision that dairy farmers outside a Class I plan market would within 90 days be entitled to competitive access and be treated the same as dairy farmers already within the scope of the order. (Entry was limited under existing law to new producers when the market's Class I sales were increasing.)

• Suspended from April 1971 through March 1974 mandatory requirements for support on butterfat and butterfat products.

Title III—Wool

• Extended the National Wool Act through Dec. 31, 1973.

• Continued the existing incentive price of 72 cents per pound for shorn wool and 80.2 cents per pound for mohair.

Title IV—Wheat

• Suspended marketing quotas and acreage allotments for the 1971, 1972 and 1973 crop years.

• Established a set-aside program under which wheat farmers, in order to be eligible for loans, certificates and payments under the marketing quotas and acreage allotment program had to set aside or divert from the production of wheat and other crops a certain amount of acreage determined by the secretary of agriculture.

• Provided that the 1971 set-aside program would cover 13.3 million acres and that the 1972 and 1973 set-aside program could not exceed 15 million acres.

• Provided domestic marketing certificates for farmers participating in the set-aside program.

• Set the face value of the domestic certificates at the difference between the wheat parity price (currently $2.85 per bushel) and the average price received by farmers during the first five months of the wheat-marketing year beginning on July 1.

• Provided for a preliminary payment to participating farmers as soon as possible after July 1 of each year in an amount estimated by the secretary to be 75 per cent of the value of the domestic certificate, and for payment of the remainder after Dec. 1 of each year.

• Continued the cost of certificates to wheat processors at 75 cents per bushel.

• Authorized price support loans to be set at a rate not less than $1.25 per bushel nor more than 100 per cent of the parity price for wheat.

• Authorized the secretary to make land diversion payments to farmers who devote additional acreage beyond the set-aside program to approved conservation uses.

Food for Peace

The Food for Peace—or Food for Freedom—program, started in 1954 as a means of getting rid of agricultural surpluses, from 1966 on was aimed at combating hunger and malnutrition, promoting economic growth in developing nations and expanding export markets for American agricultural products.

Originating under the Agricultural Trade Development and Assistance Act (PL 480), the program was extended in 1970 through 1973. Under the program, the United States sold on favorable terms or donated agricultural commodities to foreign countries.

Through June 30, 1972, sales agreements had been signed since 1954 with 55 countries covering sales on credit of commodities with a market value of $13-billion. Major items were wheat, cotton, fats and oils, rice and feed grains.

In addition, commodities valued at $3.5-billion were sold on long-term credit terms in that period. Under a third category of the law, providing for donations of agricultural commodities to meet famine and other urgent relief needs abroad, Congress from 1954 through calendar 1972 had authorized appropriations of $6.7-billion.

Outlays in the Food for Peace program were expected to drop gradually during the 1970s. The fiscal 1974 budget document and earlier budgets showed these outlays, with donations generally accounting for about one-third of the total:

Year	Outlay
1970	$937-million
1971	918-million
1972	993-million
1973	847-million (estimated)
1974	766-million (estimated), including $500-million in net sales and $266-million in donations).

The Reasons for Price Support System

The law of supply and demand can throw agriculture out of kilter, creating a need for some kind of intervention to stabilize production.

Take wheat, for an example, and assume that market forces alone will determine price.

Each of 1.3 million wheat growers is an independent decision-maker. Each has high fixed costs in land and equipment, which he naturally wants to use to produce as many bushels as he can.

The trouble is that 1.3 million wheat growers, operating on the same premise, will often overshoot demand by producing massive surpluses that have the potential to drive prices below production costs.

Contrast the situation of those 1.3 million wheat growers with three or four major U.S. automobile manufacturers who can make a survey of expected demand for cars and adjust supply accordingly and who moreover can attract sales with new styles and models. Wheat growers have neither option, because by themselves they cannot control supply, and because they produce a uniform or homogeneous product.

Wheat growers have the additional problem that consumer demand for bread and other wheat products (and for food in general) is relatively stationary—inelastic, in economic terms. A consumer in good times might buy more food, but not much more. He can eat only so much. The effect is that oversupply causes exaggerated price drops. A rule of thumb among agricultural economists is that a 1 per cent increase in excess supply will result in a 3 to 4 per cent drop in price to farmers.

In times of undersupply, as in 1973, exactly the opposite situation prevails. Because people always have to eat, they will bid up food prices to an exaggerated extent.

Because wheat growers (and other producers) are helpless in adjusting supply to demand in the short run, they have looked to the federal government for help in bringing supply and demand roughly into balance. The farm program basically is a cooperative effort of government planners and farmers to perform an economic function the free market cannot perform without severe disruption of the structure of the agricultural economy.

In February 1973, the Agriculture Department spelled out the consequences of abolishing the farm program: "...production increases, sharp drops in farm product prices and even greater drops in net farm incomes in the immediate years after removal of controls ...many marginal farm units (would) go out of production...it is by no means certain that farm prices and incomes at the end of the decade would have recovered to the levels of recent years. In additon, the social consequences...could be a source of considerable public concern...a free market system would be less equipped to cope with such unpredictable phenomena as the 1970 corn blight and the recent unusually strong export demand."

As ingenious as wheat growers—and other producers—have been in adapting new knowledge to increase their productivity, they have been singularly unsuccessful in getting together voluntarily to adjust total supply to demand. Their sheer numbers have prevented such cooperation. So have the conflicting interests of producers of different commodities and in different sections of the nation.

There are trends under way that may make it possible for producers to achieve supply and price stability other than through government programs. Increased farmer-processor bargaining and long-term contracting could assure guaranteed prices and reasonable production geared to expected demand, with pre-planned reserves for such outside factors as bad weather. Agricultural economists think that such alternatives may be down the pike, possibly covering many farm products in the 1980s.

Title V—Feed Grains

• Established a voluntary feed grain (corn, grain sorghum and barley) program for the 1971-1973 crop years.

• Established a set-aside program under which participating farmers would be required to set aside or divert feed grain or other cropland in order to become eligible for loans and payments.

• Provided that price support payments to participating farmers on one-half of their feed grain base would be based on the difference between the higher of $1.35 per bushel or 70 per cent of the parity price (for corn) and the average market price for the first five months of the marketing year (beginning on Oct. 1 for corn and grain sorghum and July 1 for barley).

• Stipulated that price support payments were not to be less than 32 cents per bushel for corn (with corresponding rates on grain sorghum and barley).

• Authorized the secretary to set the loan level for corn from a minimum of $1 a bushel to a maximum of 90 per cent of parity.

• Provided for a preliminary payment of 32 cents per bushel on corn to participating farmers as soon as possible after July 1 of each year and provided for an additional payment if the difference between the average market price and $1.35 were more than 32 cents during the first five months of the marketing year.

• Authorized the secretary to make land diversion payments to farmers who devote additional acreage beyond the set-aside program to approved conservation uses.

Title VI—Cotton

• Provided payments on the estimated crop yield from 11.5 million acres for the 1971 crop and authorized the secretary to set the base acreage allotment for 1972 and 1973 and adjust payments accordingly.

• Set a loan level of 90 per cent of the average world price for two previous years, and set payments at the difference between the higher of 65 per cent of parity or 35 cents and the average market price for the first five months following the beginning of the marketing year (beginning Aug. 1).

• Stipulated that payments were not to be less than 15 cents per pound.

• Authorized a payment bonus of 30 per cent to producers having allotments of 10 acres or less or producing 5,000 pounds or less.

• Provided for a set-aside program for cropland, not to exceed 28 per cent of the cotton allotment, as a condition of eligibility for benefits under the program.

• Established a voluntary program under which marketing quotas and penalties would be suspended for three years, through the 1973 crop year.

• Authorized the Commodity Credit Corporation (CCC) to divert to the Cotton Board not more than $10-million annually in 1971, 1972 and 1973 from cotton subsidy payments that would not be paid to producers because of the subsidy ceiling. Directed the Cotton Board to use the funds to develop and expand both domestic and foreign markets for upland cotton.

• Allowed the sale, lease and transfer of cotton allotments within a state.

Title VII—Public Law 480

• Extended for three years, until Dec. 31, 1973, the PL 480 (Food for Peace) program authorizing donations and long-term dollar credit and foreign currency sales of U.S. farm commodities to underdeveloped nations.

Title VIII—General and Miscellaneous

• Continued the cropland conversion and other long-term land retirement programs for three years, through 1973, at an authorized appropriation level of $10-million annually for each program.

• Permitted producers to plant, harvest and bale hay grown on wheat, feed grain and cotton set-aside programs or diverted under the wheat, feed grain or cotton programs and to store such hay for future emergency periods which may be declared by the secretary.

• Provided that funds appropriated for association loans and grants and for direct real estate loans and grants under the Farmers Home Administration (FHA) would remain available until expended; unused authorizations for appropriations could be carried over from year to year.

Title IX—Rural Development

• Committed Congress to a sound rural-urban balance and provided for reports on planning assistance, technical assistance, government services and utilities and financial assistance for rural areas. Required a federal policy that new offices and facilities be located, insofar as practicable, in communities of low population density.

LEGISLATIVE HISTORY

House. The House passed HR 18546 by a **key 212-171 roll-call vote** Aug. 5. Final passage came after the House rejected by a 167-218 roll-call vote a motion offered by Charles M. Teague (R Calif.) to recommit the bill with instructions to delete the provisions on payment limitations and wheat, feed grains, cotton and land retirement programs.

Limitations of subsidy payments to farmers was the most controversial and debated issue during the two-day consideration of the farm bill. Through a series of

votes, the House repeatedly defeated efforts to lower the ceiling on payments and attach conditions which farmers would have to meet to be eligible for the payments. An amendment to substitute a $20,000 ceiling on payments for the Agriculture Committee's recommendation of a $55,000 ceiling was defeated by a 134-161 teller vote.

Several members also sought to change provisions in the bill relating to price support payments and loans for wheat and feed grains. John Melcher (D Mont.) argued that the bill was an accommodation for cotton.

Senate. The Senate passed HR 18546 by a 65-7 roll-call vote Sept. 15.

"While the Senate bill is not all that it should be," said Milton R. Young (R N.D.), "it is a great improvement over the House bill," which would reduce farm income, Young charged.

Farm-state senators objected to House provisions based on administration recommendations to use world market prices as part of the formula for setting price-support loan levels. The secretary of agriculture was given authority by the House bill to set price supports from zero to 90 per cent of parity for feed grains and zero to 100 per cent for wheat.

The Senate version provided more generous price supports by placing a floor of $1.25 a bushel under the loan level for wheat and $1 a bushel for corn and by providing support for cotton at 65 per cent of parity.

But a number of farm-state senators said they still found the bill unsatisfactory. Two efforts, one successful, were made on the Senate floor to provide higher supports for feed grains.

The controversial subsidy payments issue arose when Ralph T. Smith (R Ill.) proposed a $20,000 ceiling per crop for wheat, feed grains and cotton, rather than the $55,000 limit in the bill. Smith's amendment was defeated by a 21-44 roll-call vote. But a similar amendment by Smith to the fiscal 1971 agricultural appropriations bill (HR 17923) had been accepted by a 40-35 roll-call vote July 8.

Conference. The final bill as agreed to by conferees adhered most closely to the House bill but included several of the parity guarantees proposed in the Senate version.

Before the House by a 191-145 roll-call vote adopted the conference report, House Agriculture Committee Chairman W. R. Poage (D Texas) read a letter from President Nixon calling the farm bill the "best compromise that could have been attained under the circumstances and one that this administration can accept."

Final action was delayed until after the congressional election recess when a messenger bringing the bill to the Senate from the House on Oct. 13 was barred from entering the chamber, and the messenger returned to the House with the undelivered document.

Mr. Nixon said refusal of the Senate Democratic leadership to allow action on the report was "a very grave disservice to the American farmer." Minority Leader Hugh Scott (R Pa.) claimed that at least 15 Democratic senators running for re-election were being protected from having to vote on the bill by Agriculture Committee Chairman Allen J. Ellender (D La.). By avoiding a vote, Scott said, the Democrats could campaign with any position they wanted on the issue.

Majority Leader Mike Mansfield (D Mont.) insisted the delay was not political.

During debate Nov. 19 on the conference report, Ellender said the report was signed by all of the House conferees but by only four of the seven Senate conferees. The three who did not sign were Ellender, Herman E. Talmadge (D Ga.) and Milton R. Young (R N.D.). The conferees "did not act freely," Ellender said, but were "more or less dominated by the Executive." Ellender particularly objected to a provision for the cotton acreage allotment for 1972 and 1973 to be left to the discretion of the secretary of agriculture.

The bill was cleared for the President Nov. 19 when the Senate by a 48-35 roll-call vote adopted the conference report.

Appropriations Bill

The regular Agriculture Department appropriations bill for fiscal 1971 (HR 17923—PL 91-566) appropriated $8,090,856,550 in new budget obligational authority. The total was $342-million more than the administration's revised request ($7,748,354,500) and $7.3-million more than the total eventually provided in fiscal 1970.

The original administration request had been for $7,531,755,500. On July 7, two days before the Senate acted on the bill, the President sent to the Senate a revised budget request for child nutrition programs. The revised request called for $301,974,000 for the programs —a $216,579,000 increase over the original request for $85,395,000.

The bill contained $185,000,000 to liquidate previously approved contract authorization. (Contract authority allows agencies to enter into contracts ahead of appropriations but requires appropriations in following years to liquidate the contracts.)

Although both houses passed the bill in early summer, a conference committee to resolve differences between the two versions did not meet until Congress had completed action on the Agricultural Act of 1970 (HR 18546—PL 91-524)—an omnibus farm bill which set a ceiling on subsidy payments of $55,000 per crop per producer. The Senate had amended the agriculture appropriations bill to include a $20,000 subsidy limit; the House bill had no such provision.

The increases over the administration's request were largely for continuation of the agricultural conservation program and the special milk program, both of which the administration had sought to end.

The bill provided $195.5-million in advance program authorization for the agricultural conservation program under which the government shared with farmers the cost of carrying out soil-and-water conservation practices.

The bill also:

• Appropriated $151,633,000 for general research under the Agricultural Research Service, representing a compromise between House and Senate figures.

• Appropriated $76-million for watershed works of improvement under the Soil Conservation Service and $6,066,000 for watershed planning.

• Appropriated $149,247,000 under the Consumer and Marketing Service for consumer protection, marketing and regulatory programs.

• Authorized $130-million for real estate loans under the Farmers Home Administration.

Support Price Payments

This table illustrates government payments to producers of cotton, feed grains and wheat in 1972. The wheat figures do not take into account the fact that the government recovered $390-million of payments to wheat growers from the processing tax on millers (bread tax).

(Amounts in dollars)

State	Cotton	Feed grain	Wheat
Alabama	$ 45,663,377	$ 14,401,968	$ 382,935
Alaska	——	——	——
Arizona	37,266,251	4,342,750	833,049
Arkansas	73,539,705	2,252,133	1,127,862
California	76,748,787	11,801,900	4,862,028
Colorado	——	23,644,209	29,895,587
Connecticut	——	113,599	542
Delaware	——	1,394,688	316,198
Florida	1,048,618	6,626,951	117,543
Georgia	35,228,488	34,483,359	1,299,148
Hawaii	——	——	——
Idaho	——	4,798,475	30,757,034
Illinois	112,086	211,250,592	23,964,491
Indiana	——	109,108,214	17,255,469
Iowa	——	304,947,571	1,173,259
Kansas	249	98,479,508	137,240,367
Kentucky	384,197	26,213,436	2,212,834
Louisiana	35,832,280	2,138,211	262,234
Maine	——	68,256	2,651
Maryland	——	6,524,139	1,748,636
Massachusetts	——	26,665	91
Michigan	——	34,496,082	16,009,705
Minnesota	——	147,890,208	17,762,451
Mississippi	108,985,481	9,207,249	593,491
Missouri	20,800,087	98,121,343	20,238,963
Montana	——	16,539,714	73,215,780
Nebraska	——	166,119,365	54,003,504
Nevada	245,137	70,759	424,097
New Hampshire	——	26,289	——
New Jersey	——	2,233,478	634,663
New Mexico	11,608,951	13,037,539	7,921,749
New York	——	8,997,813	4,911,110
North Carolina	14,636,933	30,520,335	4,801,980
North Dakota	——	53,587,067	141,243,764
Ohio	——	58,597,268	19,731,214
Oklahoma	20,936,518	19,259,312	70,637,073
Oregon	——	3,398,707	13,880,405
Pennsylvania	——	11,690,650	4,720,855
Rhode Island	——	1,517	——
South Carolina	29,641,579	12,534,656	2,125,605
South Dakota	——	57,713,566	40,719,532
Tennessee	31,246,287	18,365,954	1,541,565
Texas	263,805,941	153,621,378	54,157,238
Utah	——	1,197,602	3,964,560
Vermont	——	101,054	738
Virginia	308,608	9,894,587	3,176,372
Washington	——	5,823,497	41,542,398
West Virginia	——	662,104	169,353
Wisconsin	——	47,703,703	575,325
Wyoming	——	1,354,273	3,689,286
Total	$808,039,560	$1,845,383,693	$855,844,734

Food Stamps

Congress on Dec. 31 cleared for the President a bill (HR 18582—PL 91-671) extending the food stamp program for three years through fiscal 1973 and providing free stamps for families with monthly incomes under $30. The bill was a compromise between a liberal version passed by the Senate in September 1969 (S 2547) and a more restrictive bill (HR 18582) passed by the House on Dec. 16, 1970.

The final bill included a controversial work requirement under which an adult would become ineligible for food stamps and lose the benefits for his entire family if he refused employment. Many House and Senate liberals called the provision punitive and harsh. It had been part of the House-passed measure.

The House Agriculture Committee began hearings on the bill in June 1969, but did not report a bill until Aug. 10, 1970. Committee Chairman W. R. Poage (D Texas) reportedly hoped to win urban votes for the omnibus farm bill (HR 18546) by coupling it with the food stamp legislation and holding hearings on the two bills together. Urban members generally supported food stamps, but had in recent years objected to large farm subsidies in the agriculture program. *(Farm bill, p. 335)*

The Senate bill had authorized free stamps for families of four with monthly incomes under $60, adjusted the price of stamps so that no family was required to spend more than 25 per cent of its income on the stamps, provided that all families with incomes under $4,000 a year would be eligible for stamps, and authorized $2-billion for the program in fiscal 1971 and $2.5-billion in fiscal 1972.

The House bill had required a minimum payment of 50 cents per person per month for the stamps, required recipients to accept jobs, required states to share in the cost of the stamps, provided an open-ended authorization for the program and authorized the secretary of agriculture to set national eligibility standards.

Both houses adopted the conference compromise by voice vote. George McGovern (D S.D.), sponsor of a liberal food stamp bill which passed the Senate in 1969, said he had not signed the conference report on HR 18582 because of the work requirement which read "more like a declaration of serfdom for America's hungry poor."

Provisions. As cleared by Congress, HR 18582:

• Directed the secretary of agriculture in conjunction with the secretary of health, education and welfare to establish uniform national standards for participation by households in the food stamp program.

• Provided that the standards established by the secretary of agriculture, at a minimum, should prescribe the amount of household income and other financial resources to be used as criteria of eligibility.

• Required able-bodied adults in a household to register for and accept available employment in order for them and their families to be eligible to receive stamps.

• Stipulated that recipients be required to take only those jobs that paid at least the federal or state minimum wage, or $1.30 an hour if the job was not covered by a minimum wage law.

• Exempted from the work requirement mothers or persons who cared for infants or incapacitated family members, students or persons employed and working at least 30 hours a week.

• Authorized the secretary of agriculture to provide free food stamps to families of four whose income was less than $30 per month and specified that no family with income over $30 per month should be required to spend more than 30 per cent of its income for stamps.

• Established the value of the coupon allotment to food stamp recipients at a level which the secretary found would provide a "nutritionally adequate diet" ($106 per month for a family of four). Require the secretary to make an annual adjustment in the value of the coupon allotment to reflect increases for food in the cost of living index.

• Allowed states, if they requested, to operate both food stamp and surplus commodities programs, but prevented individual recipients from receiving benefits from both programs.

• Authorized $1,750,000,000 for the program for fiscal 1971 and open-ended authorizations for fiscal years 1972 and 1973.

School Lunches, Milk

Congress in 1970 enacted four bills providing food for needy school children. On May 4 Congress cleared for the President's signature a bill (HR 515—PL 91-248) to expand and improve the program of free and reduced-price lunches for needy school children. HR 515 provided an open-ended authorization for the special assistance program which furnished special funds for schools in impoverished areas; authorized $25-million for the school breakfast program for fiscal 1971; required that for fiscal years 1972 and 1973 states had to provide at least 4 per cent of the state matching requirement from state tax revenues; for fiscal 1974 and 1975, 6 per cent; for fiscal 1976 and 1977, 8 per cent; and for each fiscal year thereafter, 10 per cent.

The bill limited to 20 cents the cost of reduced-price lunches for children, required that first priority be given to providing free meals to the neediest children, and established the standard for "needy" after Jan. 1, 1971, as the federal income poverty guidelines prescribed by the secretary of agriculture.

The President March 12 signed into law a bill (HR 11651—PL 91-207) authorizing the transfer of an additional $30-million from Section 32 (customs receipts) funds to the national school lunch program during fiscal year 1970. The purpose of the bill was to provide free and reduced-price meals to needy children not being aided under the existing program.

Congress in 1970 completed action on an administration-opposed bill (HR 5554—PL 91-295) to make permanent the special milk program and to authorize the appropriation of up to $120-million annually for the program. The Nixon administration had asked no funds for the program in the fiscal 1970 or 1971 budgets, arguing that milk would be provided in expanded child nutrition programs, eliminating the need for a separate milk appropriation.

On June 30, the President announced he was allowing HR 5554 to become law without his signature because less than 10 per cent of the milk served in the program went to poor children. The major portion of funds authorized in the bill should be for the poor, he said.

Congress April 7 cleared for the President's signature a bill (S 2595—PL 91-233) to amend the Agricultural Act of 1949 to remove limitations on the donation of Commodity Credit Corporation (CCC) dairy products to school lunch programs and to charitable institutions. The administration supported the bill.

Section 416 of the Agricultural Act of 1949 authorized donations of dairy products only after the CCC had attempted to dispose of acquired stocks by sale. When the Senate passed S 2595 by voice vote, sponsor Gaylord Nelson (D Wis.) said the measure "assures that...(the) national school lunch program will receive first call in the distribution" of dairy products obtained by the Department of Agriculture through price-support programs.

Migratory Workers' Health

Congress Feb. 26 cleared a bill (HR 14733—PL 91-209) extending for three years, through fiscal 1973, the program of health services assistance for domestic migrant agricultural workers. The bill amended the Public Health Service Act (PL 78-410).

Provisions. As cleared by voice vote approval in each chamber of a conference report adjusting differing versions passed in 1969 by the House and Senate, HR 14733:

• Authorized appropriations for health services programs for migrant agricultural workers of $20-million in fiscal 1971, $25-million in fiscal 1972 and $30-million in fiscal 1973.

• Allowed the secretary of health, education and welfare to use funds appropriated under the authorization to provide health services to nonmigratory seasonal farm workers (and their families) if provision of such services would contribute to the improvement of the health conditions of migratory workers.

• Required the participation of migratory workers in the development and implementation of the health services program.

Miscellaneous Bills

ANIMAL QUARANTINE. Congress April 23 completed action on a bill (S 2306—PL 91-239) to provide for the establishment of an international animal quarantine station and to permit the importation of certain animals into the United States. Under existing law, livestock could not be imported directly from countries with problems such as hoof-and-mouth disease. The bill was intended to make possible the cross-breeding of imported livestock.

The estimated cost of construction of facilities was $2,500,000, with annual operating expenses of about $1,300,000. Most of the annual cost would be borne by user fees.

Provisions. As signed into law May 6, S 2306:

• Authorized the secretary of agriculture to establish and maintain an international animal quarantine station.

• Provided that the station be located on an island where, in the judgment of the secretary, maximum animal disease and pest security measures could be maintained.

• Permitted animals to be brought into the quarantine station from any country, including those in which hoof-and-mouth disease exists.

• Permitted animals from such countries to be moved into other parts of the United States in accordance with conditions determined by the secretary to be adequate to prevent the dissemination of livestock or poultry diseases.

• Imposed penalties against persons importing animals into the United States, the Virgin Islands, Puerto Rico or Guam contrary to conditions prescribed by the secretary of agriculture.

EGG INSPECTION. Congress Dec. 14 cleared a bill (HR 19888—PL 91-597) prohibiting distribution of unwholesome eggs and providing for mandatory inspection of egg processing plants to protect consumers.

Provisions. As cleared by Congress, HR 19888:

• Prohibited the distribution of unwholesome shell eggs and prohibited their use in food products. Made the prohibition applicable to intrastate as well as interstate and foreign commerce.

• Provided for mandatory continuous inspection of egg product processing plants by the Department of Agriculture.

• Exempted product processing at plants where the facilities met sanitary standards prescribed by the secretary of agriculture.

• Required identification of egg products not intended for human consumption.

• Established the same requirements for imported eggs and egg products as for domestic products.

• Permitted exemption from inspections for family farm operators who sell eggs from flocks of 3,000 or fewer hens.

• Authorized loans through the Small Business Administration to small businesses affected by the legislation and the Meat Inspection and Poultry Inspection Acts.

MEAT INSPECTION. Congress July 6 cleared for the President a bill (S 3592—PL 91-342) to amend the Federal Meat Inspection Act of 1967 (PL 90-201) to permit custom slaughterers to engage in the retailing and wholesaling of meat.

Provisions. As cleared July 6 by Congress, S 3592:

• Permitted the sale, under certain conditions, of inspected meat by custom slaughterers.

• Required the custom slaughterer to provide complete separation in his facility of those meat and meat parts that are slaughtered for the custom customer and those inspected meat products for sale to the public.

• Required the custom slaughtered or processed meat to be clearly identified as "not for sale."

• Provided authority for the custom slaughtering of game animals.

POTATO MARKETING. Congress Feb. 9 cleared for the President a bill (S 2214—PL 91-196) to exempt potatoes from the coverage of any federal marketing orders intended for certain types of processing, such as dehydration and chipping.

As signed by the President Feb. 20, S 2214 amended the Agricultural Marketing Agreement Act of 1937 to exempt from federal marketing orders potatoes for canning, freezing or other processing and provided that the exemption was to be effective for the two-year period beginning with the date of enactment of the bill.

RECLAMATION LANDS. Congress June 23 cleared for the President a bill (S 2062—PL 91-310) to exempt publicly owned lands from the 160-acre limit for which individuals could receive water from a federal reclamation (irrigation) project. The bill required that the exempted land be used only for nonrevenue producing functions (experimental farms, prison farms, hospital farms, etc).

1971

Congress in 1971 extended the Sugar Act of 1948, as amended, for another three years through 1974. The legislation, traditionally the center of much lobbying and attention from domestic and foreign sugar interests, extended the import quota system, adjusted production quotas for producers and made changes in some import quotas. Controversy in 1971 centered on the inclusion of a sugar quota for South Africa's apartheid regime.

In other action, Congress expanded the authority of the farmer-owned cooperative lending system to make loans to farmers and other rural residents and established a rural telephone bank to finance rural telephone facilities.

The President's nomination of Earl L. Butz as secretary of agriculture to succeed retiring Clifford M. Hardin led to a struggle over confirmation in the Senate. Butz found he was caught in the economic discontent that gripped farmers and their representatives in a lean year for agriculture. His close ties to corporate farming interests made some members fear he would be unwilling to use government policy to protect the small family farmer in time of need. However, after Butz met with senators in his own behalf, only four Republicans joined Democratic foes in opposing him on the floor. Butz was confirmed Dec. 2 by a 51-44 roll-call vote.

Sugar Act

Congress in 1971 enacted legislation (HR 8866—PL 92-138) extending the Sugar Act of 1948, as amended, for three years through Dec. 31, 1974, and adjusting production quotas for foreign and domestic producers. Final action came when the House, by a 194-91 roll-call vote on Oct. 4, agreed to a conference report on the bill. The Senate had approved the conference report by voice vote on Sept. 29.

SOUTH AFRICAN QUOTA

Opposition to the bill in both chambers focused primarily on the inclusion of a sugar quota for South Africa. In the House, efforts were made to defeat the closed rule under which the bill was reported, because it would bar amendments and thus prevent any move to cancel the South African quota. John G. Dow (D N.Y.), who led the attempt to defeat the closed rule, condemned South Africa's apartheid policy as "brutish subjugation of one race by another" and said he did not believe that "we should bestow regards upon a nation that blatantly offends transcendent principles of human relations." The House nevertheless adopted the closed rule by a roll-call vote of 213-136 and passed the bill June 10 by a roll-call vote of 229-128.

Most of the Senate debate, July 27-28, was likewise devoted to an attempt, led by Edward M. Kennedy (D Mass.), to delete the South African quota. Kennedy argued that South Africa practiced racial discrimination as a national policy, had been unfriendly to American citizens, and was not a developing nation in need of a sugar quota for its economic well-being. Russell B. Long (D La.), chairman of the Finance Committee that handled the bill, countered that social policy should not enter into consideration of the Sugar Act and that South Africa was a dependable supplier for U.S. markets. Long's position was that "if we undertook to say that we were not going to trade with somebody unless we agreed with their domestic policies about segregation or a number of other matters, we would find difficulty trading." Kennedy's amendment was rejected on a 45-47 roll-call vote. In a slightly different form the amendment was again defeated by a roll-call vote of 42-55. The Senate passed the bill July 28 by a 76-22 roll-call vote.

As it emerged from conference, the sugar bill preserved most of the features added by the House Agriculture Committee in June. Quota allotments for domestic producers were increased by about 300,000 tons, while the relative shares of several of the largest foreign suppliers were reduced. Three nations, Paraguay, Malawi and Uganda, received quotas for the first time, although the Malawi quota was not to take effect until 1973.

The administration, which earlier in 1971 hinted it might not want any sugar bill at all, had asked for a brief extension of the act, leaving the way open for major reassessment of the U.S. sugar program and the world sugar situation as international sugar agreements came up for renewal.

The quota mechanism had changed little since the Sugar Act was first passed in 1934. Domestic producers were granted a quota reflecting the amount they were able to produce—62 per cent of total U.S. consumption as provided by HR 8866. The remainder was allocated to various foreign countries depending on whether they were friendly to the United States, reliable as a source of sugar, reciprocal in their trade policies, or dependent on sugar markets for their economic survival or just in their treatment of sugar farmers.

Supporters of the program said it had brought stability to the American sugar industry while keeping the increases in the retail price smaller than those for other products. Critics complained that it artificially kept domestic prices higher than world market prices and funneled profits to large corporations rather than to workers or small producers.

FINAL PROVISIONS. As signed into law Oct. 14, HR 8866 in addition to setting quotas:

• Allowed the secretary of agriculture to reduce the importation of sugar during specified periods if in the 12-month period ending Oct. 31 of any year after 1972 the price of raw sugar averaged less than 99 per cent of a fixed price objective. (The price objective is based on the difference between sugar prices in 1967 and those in the current period.)

• Required the secretary to adjust his determination of consumer sugar needs whenever the price of raw sugar differed from the price objective by more than 3 per cent for seven consecutive days in November, December, January and February, or by more than 4 per cent in any other month.

- Established 11.2 million short tons as the prime reference point for determining consumer requirements, rather than a range between 9.7 and 10.4 million tons as specified in the existing act.

- Reduced to 23.74 per cent from 50 per cent the quota percentage set aside for Cuba which would be available should a government friendly to the United States assume control of that country.

- Distributed any increase in the unused Cuban quota to other supplying nations in the Western Hemisphere.

- Provided that when the President found it was no longer against the national interest to reinstate a foreign country's quota, he would be required to reinstate the quota within three years.

- Provided that the President could, at his discretion, suspend all or part of a nation's quota or levy a fine of up to $20 a ton on a nation's imports if the nation expropriated the property of an American business, imposed discriminatory taxes on such a business or violated any international agreement designed to protect such a business. This provision was to apply retroactively to expropriations occurring on or after Jan. 1, 1961.

- Specified that the act and the excise tax on sugar would expire if a law were enacted limiting payments to producers.

Sugar Quotas

As enacted, Oct. 14, 1971, HR 8866 set up the following annual quotas fixing the amount of sugar to be provided to the U.S. market by different producing areas during calendar years 1972 through 1974. The figures are based on a U.S. consumption level of 11.2 million short tons of sugar annually, rather than a range between 9.7 and 10.4 million tons as specified in the 1965 act. Quota amounts increase when consumption rises above the base.

Domestic Quotas

Domestic Supplies	Existing Act	House Bill	Senate Bill	Annual Quota, Tons
Domestic Beet Sugar	3,406,333	3,406,000	3,406,000	3,406,000
Mainland Cane Sugar	1,238,667	1,539,000	1,539,000	1,539,000
Hawaii	1,110,000	1,110,000	1,110,000	1,110,000
Puerto Rico	1,140,000	855,000	230,000	855,000
Virgin Islands	15,000	0	0	0
TOTAL	6,910,000	6,910,000	6,285,000	6,910,000*

Adjusted to 6,285,000 to reflect anticipated Puerto Rican deficit.

Foreign Quotas

Producing area	Existing Act	House Bill	Senate Bill	Annual Quota, Tons
Mexico	557,748	537,545	590,894	561,581
Dominican Republic	545,481	525,737	659,874	634,874
British Honduras	13,752	33,537	14,874	33,537
Bolivia	6,494	17,005	6,193	6,193
Honduras	6,494	17,005	6,494	11,750
Bahamas	10,000	33,537	10,000	27,000
Paraguay	0	15,116	0	6,193
Total, Western Hemisphere	2,893,354	2,881,866	3,104,516	3,016,751

Producing area	Existing Act	House Bill	Senate Bill	Annual Quota, Tons
Australia	203,785	206,025	196,162	203,785
Republic of China	84,910	85,844	81,734	84,910
India	81,514	82,494	77,973	81,514
South Africa	60,003	60,300	57,745	57,745
Fiji Islands	44,719	44,806	43,034	44,719
Brazil	545,581	525,737	577,905	547,905
Peru	435,087	418,982	391,839	391,839
West Indies	188,777	192,251	204,520	204,520
Ecuador	79,370	80,774	79,084	80,774
French West Indies	59,384	0	63,868	0
Argentina	67,102	76,050	67,062	76,050
Costa Rica	64,217	65,185	71,110	68,610
Nicaragua	64,217	65,185	64,217	64,217
Colombia	57,723	73,688	61,047	67,368
Guatemala	54,115	55,265	59,835	58,350
Panama	40,406	41,567	40,406	41,567
El Salvador	39,682	40,151	43,964	42,693
Haiti	30,305	30,704	30,305	30,704
Venezuela	27,419	36,845	61,025	61,026
Thailand	18,681	18,844	14,152	18,681
Mauritius	18,681	30,150	17,761	30,150
Malagasy Republic	9,623	15,075	9,223	12,149
Swaziland	7,359	30,150	7,084	30,150
Malawi	0	0	0	0
Uganda	0	15,075	0	15,075
Total, Eastern Hemisphere	529,275	588,763	504,868	578,878
Philippines	1,362,120	1,314,020	1,300,264	1,314,020
Ireland	5,351	5,351	5,351	5,351
Total Foreign	4,790,000	4,790,000	4,915,000	4,915,000
GRAND TOTAL	11,700,000	11,700,000	11,200,000	11,200,000

Appropriations Bill

Congress in appropriating funds for fiscal 1972 for the first time grouped appropriations for agriculture with appropriations for environmental projects and for consumer protection. The bill signed into law by President Nixon on Aug. 10, 1971, (HR 9270—PL 92-73), carried a grand total of $13,276,900,050 in appropriations for the three groups. Only slightly more than one-half of the total, or $6,811,573,550, was appropriated for strictly agricultural and rural development programs. A sum of $3,490,477,500 was earmarked for the Environmental Protection Agency and related services, including $500-million for water and sewer facilities. An appropriation of $2,974,849,000 was made for consumer services, the major part of that total to finance the food-stamp program.

The combined total of $13,276,900,050 came to almost $1.2-billion more than the President had requested ($12,104,813,850) in his fiscal 1972 budget message and to some $3.7-billion more than the amount appropriated for the same programs in fiscal 1971, a 28 per cent increase.

In previous years, environmental programs had been funded in the Public Works, Interior and Independent Offices-HUD appropriations bills; funds for consumer programs had been handled in the Independent Offices and Labor-HEW bills. The new arrangement gave major control of environmental and consumer funding for the first time to Jamie L. Whitten (D Miss.), chairman of the House Agriculture Appropriations Subcommittee. As it emerged from Whitten's subcommittee, the environmental section of the fiscal 1972 agriculture appropriations bill carried $209,-391,000 more than the President had requested. An additional $364,422,500 under later adjustments brought the environmental total to $573,813,500 more than the budget request of $2,916,664,000. The President's budget request for consumer programs was increased by $103,711,000 in Whitten's subcommittee and the final appropriation for the consumer sector amounted to $315,537,000 more than the initial request for $2,659,-312,000.

Other provisions of the agriculture appropriations bill:

• Provided that no crop subsidy payments could go to farmers who harvested marijuana or other drug-producing plants for illegal purposes.

• Retained the existing $55,000 annual per crop limitation on subsidy payments to farmers.

• Included $173,479,500 for research activities under the Agricultural Research Service.

• Appropriated $124,100,000 for telephone loan funds by the Rural Electrification Administration and $97,-665,000 for administrative expense of the Farmers Home Administration.

Rural Telephones

Congress in 1971 enacted a bill (S 70—PL 92-12) amending the Rural Telephone Electrification Act of 1936 by establishing a Rural Telephone Bank.

A similar bill (S 3387) had been passed by the Senate in 1970. Bills to create a rural telephone bank were reported by the House Agriculture Committee in both the 90th and 91st Congresses but because of opposition in the House Rules Committee were never considered by the House. A majority of the members of the Rules Committee opposed the bills because they objected to additional financing for telephone cooperatives at the low 2 per cent rate existing on Rural Electrification Administration loans. Rural telephone legislation was described by President Nixon on Jan. 26 in a special message to Congress as one of the measures which should be given priority consideration in the 92nd Congress.

Although the House and Senate rural telephone bills were similar, the administration preferred the Senate version. The House bill organized the telephone bank as a mixed-ownership government corporation but exempted it from Treasury approval in issuing its loans. The Senate bill treated the bank as a wholly owned government corporation requiring Treasury approval of its loans and periodic audits by the General Accounting Office. The final bill was closer to the Senate version.

As enacted, S 70 provided that loans would be made to existing or approved borrowers under the 2 per cent REA loan program.

Sugar Lobbying

Extension of the Sugar Act invariably touches off some of the hottest lobbying activity of the Washington scene and 1971 was no exception.

The United States depends upon imports for about 40 per cent of its sugar and provides a premium worth between $290-million and $342-million each year to foreign suppliers. Competition among foreign producers seeking shares of the U.S. sugar market lures agents and lobbyists, some of whom have held positions of influence in government.

Lobbyists testifying during House Agriculture Committee hearings early in 1971 included former Rep. Harold D. Cooley (D N.C. 1934-66), who was chairman of the House Agriculture Committee for 16 years and sponsored much sugar legislation; former Senate Republican Whip Thomas H. Kuchel (R Calif. 1953-69); former Rep. Charles H. Brown (D Mo. 1957-61), and Thomas Hale Boggs Jr., son of House Democratic Leader Hale Boggs (D La.).

The competition among foreign countries in 1965, the last time the act was extended, gave the House Agriculture Committee its reputation as the "little State Department."

Although the act had answered the needs of a great many interest groups, its renewal touched off considerable debate in 1971. Domestic producers, seeking larger quotas for mainland cane or beet production, fought a move in Congress to cut subsidy payments to growers. Thirty-eight countries sent representatives to petition for quota increases.

Chairman W. R. Poage (D Texas) of the House Agriculture Committee sent a letter March 4, 1971, to all lobbyists or agents registered on behalf of foreign countries seeking sugar quotas.

Poage outlined the criteria the committee would use in allocating new quotas. He wrote that it would not be possible for him to meet with everyone and it would be appreciated if representatives of foreign countries "would not seek a personal or private discussion." Some other members of the committee followed his example.

The loans were to bear interest based on the ability of the borrower to pay but not less than 4 per cent annually, and a borrower who could pay more than 2 per cent but not the market rate could receive a loan from the telephone bank for part of the amount to be borrowed and a 2 per cent REA loan on the remainder.

School Lunches

Congress adopted a resolution in 1971 (H J Res 923—PL 92-153) stating it to be the federal government's intention to ensure that every needy school child receive a free or reduced-price lunch as required by Section 9 of the National School Lunch Act of 1970 (PL 91-248).

The resolution set a minimum federal reimbursement rate to states of 40 cents for every free and reduced-price meal served. Additionally, it authorized a reimbursement to states of six cents for every meal served whether full-price, free or reduced-price.

The measure prohibited the secretary of agriculture from making changes in the standards of eligibility for free and reduced-price meals effective in the same year in which they were adopted. H J Res 923 prevented him from reducing the number of children to be served in any school district.

The Agriculture Department had stated that eligibility for the program would be restricted to children from families with an annual income of $3,940 or less. The department rescinded the new restrictions when the House adopted H J Res 923 on Oct. 18, followed two days later by the Senate.

School Lunch Authorization. Congress in June enacted a bill (HR 5257—PL 92-32) authorizing an additional $135-million through June 30, 1972, to provide free or reduced-price meals for needy children.

HR 5257 specified that the additional $135-million authorization was to be obtained through transfer of Section 32 funds, a mechanism set up by the Agricultural Adjustment Act of 1935 (PL 74-320). HR 5257 authorized the transfer of $35-million for the balance of fiscal 1971 and $100-million for fiscal 1972.

The Department of Agriculture in 1970 had underestimated the number of children eligible for the program under the new federal standards.

Non-School Food. Congress cleared for the President a joint resolution (H J Res 744—PL 92-35) appropriating $17-million for the 1971 summer non-school feeding programs. The sum was separated from HR 9270, the fiscal 1972 appropriations bill for the Department of Agriculture, because HR 9270 had not been enacted into law by the beginning of the new fiscal year.

Other Bills

Farm Loans. President Nixon Oct. 5 signed into law a bill (HR 10538—PL 92-133) making permanent the authority for insuring loans under the Consolidated Farmers Home Administration Act of 1961.

The bill was passed by the House Sept. 30 and by the Senate Oct. 1, both times by voice votes. Authority for the loans under the old act had expired at midnight Sept. 30. Programs financed by the act were the Farm Ownership Loan Program, the Water and Sewer Loan Program and the Association Loan Program.

Farm Credit. Congress Dec. 1 cleared for the President's signature the Farm Credit Act of 1971 (S 1483—PL 92-181) expanding the authority of the farmer-owned cooperative lending system to make loans to farmers and other rural residents. The act expanded the activities of the Farm Credit Administration of the Agriculture Department to grant it more flexible lending powers. The act authorized federal land banks and production credit associations to lend 15 per cent of their outstanding funds to rural non-farm residents for housing.

Burley Tobacco Quotas. Congress April 1 cleared a bill (S 789—PL 92-10) amending the tobacco marketing provisions of the Agricultural Adjustment Act of 1938. The bill established, subject to referendum, farm marketing quotas for burley tobacco by the pound rather than through restrictions on the number of acres on which

burley tobacco could be grown. S 789 was intended to provide equitable treatment for all growers regardless of the size of their operations.

Animal Disease Control. Congress Oct. 27 cleared a bill (HR 10458—PL 92-152) authorizing the secretary of agriculture to act with other countries in the western hemisphere to control livestock epidemics.

The bill was proposed after an outbreak of Venezuelan equine encephalomyelitis, a contagious form of horse sleeping sickness, killed more than 1,350 horses during the summer of 1971. HR 10458 gave the secretary authority to cooperate with other nations in Central and South America and with Canada to prevent the entry of communicable animal diseases into the United States.

Wheat and Feed Grains. The House Dec. 8 by a 182-170 roll-call vote passed a bill (HR 1163) creating a national reserve of wheat and feed grains to boost farm prices and ensure an adequate supply for consumers in times of shortage. The Senate did not act on the bill in 1971 and it died in 1972 in the Senate Agriculture Committee.

Before passing the bill, the House added an amendment raising the price-support loan levels for wheat and feed grains by 25 per cent. It rejected procedural efforts to bring about a vote on an amendment to limit farm subsidy payments to $20,000 per farmer per year.

The bill, sponsored by Rep. Neal Smith (D Iowa), was designed to reduce the oversupply of grains that had caused low farm prices in the Midwest markets. The grain purchased for the government reserve would be kept off the market during the coming year.

1972

Controversy over a major sale of American grain to the Soviet Union highlighted agricultural interest in Congress in 1972. The House Agriculture Committee's Subcommittee on Livestock and Grains held hearings on the transaction and reported a resolution to provide for special subsidy payments to wheat farmers who lost money in the market fluctuations that followed the deal. There was no floor action on the resolution, however.

Congress cleared a major bill—the Rural Development Act of 1972—in August. The act, designed to improve agricultural job opportunities and rural life, followed presidential messages in 1971 and 1972 calling for rural community development.

Agricultural interests joined in successful opposition to a measure to raise the federal minimum wage. The bill would have affected certain farm workers and was fought by producers of many products.

Soviet Grain Sale

The House Agriculture Committee in 1972 reported a resolution (H J Res 1300—H Rept 92-1484) providing for special subsidy payments to wheat farmers who lost money because of a controversial U.S.-Soviet grain deal announced in July. There was no floor action on the measure opposed by the Nixon administration, and it died at the end of the session. The administration maintained that all farmers would benefit from the multi-million-dollar sale.

The committee's action came after three days of hearings in September by the Agriculture Subcommittee on Livestock and Grains on alleged improprieties arising from the landmark sale of grains to the Soviet Union. The resolution was ordered reported Sept. 26 by a 23-10 roll-call vote. Sponsor of the resolution was Graham Purcell (D Texas), chairman of the subcommittee.

A similar resolution (S J Res 267), sponsored by Hubert H. Humphrey (D Minn.), was rejected Sept. 20 by a 7-1 vote of the Senate Agriculture and Forestry Committee.

Background. After months of negotiations, the U.S. and Soviet governments agreed July 8 to an historic grain credit arrangement. The U.S. government granted the Soviet Union a $500-million line of credit in return for a Soviet pledge to buy $750-million worth of U.S. grain over a three-year period, including at least $200-million in the first year.

As described by the Agriculture Department, the bulk of the transaction was to consist of feed grains, such as corn, which would be used by the Soviets to bolster their poultry and livestock production. By late summer, however, it had become apparent that the Soviet interest had shifted to wheat. Agriculture Secretary Earl L. Butz said Sept. 9 that Soviet purchases of wheat alone could come to 400 million bushels in 1972—more than one-fourth the total U.S. crop. And, Butz added, total U.S. grain sales to the Soviets were approaching $1-billion for the year—far more than the total value originally contemplated over the entire three-year life of the agreement.

Democratic presidential candidate George McGovern issued a statement Sept. 8 at Superior, Wis., linking the administration with large grain exporters and speculators who, he said, had made windfall profits from wheat sales to the Soviet Union. "Why did the Department of Agriculture join in a conspiracy of silence with the giant exporters? Why were the farmers the last to know how big the Soviet purchases were when they could have used that information to hold their wheat for a better price?" he asked.

Butz said Sept. 9 at a Washington press conference, "By attacking this historic sale with wild and inaccurate charges, Senator McGovern is engaging in another political flight of fancy and is jeopardizing a trade that is of great benefit to the nation." Cargill Inc., one of the chief exporters involved in the sale, issued a statement calling McGovern's charges "unfounded, uninformed, in many cases patently absurd and over-all damaging to the open, competitive U.S. marketing system."

Hearings. The House Agriculture Subcommittee on Livestock and Grains held hearings Sept. 14, 18 and 19 on the sale of U.S. wheat and other grains to the Soviet Union.

The main focus was on charges that the Department of Agriculture gave grain exporters an unfair market advantage by providing them advance notice of a temporary increase in U.S. export subsidies, to be followed by subsidy reductions. Other issues probed by the subcommittee included:

• Alleged improprieties in job shifts by three key officials between the Agriculture Department and leading export firms during the time of the U.S.-Soviet grain negotiations.

• Allegations that the department shortchanged farmers by withholding information about the extent of the Soviet purchases. Farmers in Texas, Oklahoma and Kansas, unaware of the dimensions of the Soviet demand, sold wheat at wholesale in July for as little as $1.32 per bushel. Domestic supply shortages created by the spiraling Soviet demand later pushed the price to $1.65.

• A related charge that grain dealers, by acquiring inside knowledge of the Soviets' purchase plans, were able to place future orders at considerably lower prices than they could have gotten when the scope of the deal became public.

• Allegations that the Soviets were granted a bargain-basement price for the wheat at the expense of American taxpayers.

Clarence D. Palmby, former assistant secretary of agriculture, who left the department June 7 to become vice president of Continental Grain, said his company had obtained an order from the Soviet Union for 150 million bushels of wheat on July 5, three days before the U.S.-Soviet agreement was consummated. (An order for another 37 million bushels was placed July 11, he said.) Palmby denied that his firm had any advance knowledge that the agreement would be reached or that he had taken an active part in the negotiations with the Soviets.

Rural Development Act

President Nixon on Aug. 30 signed into law the Rural Development Act of 1972 (HR 12931—PL 92-419). The act provided for expansion of various existing programs and authorized numerous new programs designed to improve job opportunities, increase incomes and generally enhance the quality of life in rural America. The President in a message to Congress on March 10, 1971, had proposed a $1.1-billion special revenue sharing plan for rural community development. Again, in a message on Feb. 1, 1972, he advocated rural community development revenue sharing and other measures "to help revitalize rural areas." The Senate included a modified revenue sharing plan in its version of the Rural Development Act, but it was deleted in conference.

BACKGROUND

Late in 1967, a National Advisory Commission on Rural Poverty appointed by President Johnson had recommended that the federal government put into effect immediately a policy designed to give rural Americans equal access to jobs, medical care, housing, education, welfare and other public services enjoyed by urban citizens. (*Congress and the Nation, Vol. II, p. 578*)

A law (PL 90-488) enacted Aug. 15, 1968, authorized the Farmers Home Administration (FHA) to make loans to farmers for projects that would supplement family income. The law also increased from $50-million to $100-million the maximum annual amount of matching grants which FHA could make to local agencies for construction of water supply and sewage disposal systems in rural areas. In addition, an omnibus housing act (PL 90-448) of Aug. 1, 1968, contained provisions authorizing funds for rural district planning and for subsidizing interest on loans for rural housing. But far-reaching plans for improving the conditions of rural life were still lacking.

A Senate bill (S 1612) embodying the rural revenue sharing program urged by President Nixon was given a hearing before the Senate Agriculture and Forestry Subcommittee on April 23, 1971. Secretary of Agriculture Clifford M. Hardin described the administration's plan as follows: "It provides for a consolidation of the funding of grant programs that currently operate in rural areas and smaller cities. Next, it provides for the allocation of funds to each state in accordance with a formula that has been developed to assure equitable treatment. The formula takes into account the size of each state's rural population, the income level of its rural residents and its rural population growth rate as compared with the national average. The lower the state's rate of rural growth, the greater its revenue share."

When the President repeated his $1.1-billion rural revenue sharing proposal in 1972, he added a proposal for rural community development credit sharing authority. Administration of both plans, along with that of other rural development programs currently under the Department of Agriculture (Farmers Home Administration, Rural Electrification Administration, Rural Telephone Bank, etc.) were to be moved to a new Department of Community Development. However, neither the revenue-sharing plan nor the proposed executive reorganization appealed to Congress.

When President Nixon signed HR 12931, the Rural Development Act of 1972, he commented that it "probably represents the best compromise which could be enacted by this Congress." But he added: "The most disconcerting feature of this act is that it does not include one of my most important proposals for rural development, the substitution of special revenue sharing for categorical grants and, instead, creates a number of new categorical grant programs."

PROVISIONS

As signed into law (PL 92-419) Aug. 30, HR 12931:

Title I

• Changed the title of the Consolidated Farmers Home Administration Act of 1961 (PL 87-128) to the Consolidated Farm and Rural Development Act.

• Authorized the Farmers Home Administration (FHA) to make loans to rural residents to acquire, establish or operate small businesses.

• Authorized FHA appraisal of rural properties at market value.

• Authorized FHA loans for community facilities such as firehouses and community centers.

• Increased the FHA water and waste disposal grant ceiling to $300-million, from $100-million under existing law.

• Established planning guidelines for FHA grants to require that proposed projects served areas not likely to decline in population, were adequate to meet growth and were consistent with community development plans and multi-jurisdictional plans.

• Extended to Oct. 1, 1973, FHA authority to make water and waste disposal grants before completion of final plans.

• Increased the rural water and sewer planning grant authority to $30-million annually, from $15-million annually under existing law.

Farm Problems Aired

"It is no secret that rural America has been declining for many decades. Rural poverty and powerlessness are facts of our time," said Rep. Lee H. Hamilton (D Ind.) in a March 1, 1971, speech before the House.

Hamilton's speech was part of a three-hour bipartisan caucus in the House on the problems of rural America. The purpose of the caucus was to discuss what one member termed "the sickest part of our economy, the most basic industry in this nation—agriculture."

Three major issues accounted for the seriousness of rural problems in America.

• Farm incomes were low relative to the incomes of nonfarmers.

• Population growth patterns reflected significant migration from rural to urban areas. This trend was not conducive to rural development and was creating vast socio-economic problems in rural and urban areas.

• The underdevelopment of rural America has resulted in rural poverty, high rural unemployment and inadequate housing, health services and education systems.

Low Income. Secretary of Agriculture Clifford M. Hardin told the Joint Economic Committee on Feb. 18, 1971, "Last year farm people got 78 per cent as much income as nonfarm people.... Income from nonfarm sources is becoming a larger and larger component of the net incomes of farm people." In 1970, 47.7 per cent of the farm population's income was from nonfarm sources.

Rural Outmigration. Hardin also told the joint committee, "We know from the census of last year that about half of all counties in the nation (most of them rural) lost population over the decade of the 1960s and that another one-quarter grew slowly. They experienced net outmigration and most outmigrants were young adults beginning their most productive years of life."

Rural Underdevelopment. Sen. Hubert H. Humphrey (D Minn.), chairman of the Senate Subcommittee on Rural Development, told a meeting of the Georgia Association of County Commissioners on April 19, 1971, "...Rural Americans are often discriminated against in many different ways. They are less likely than their city cousins to have the opportunity for quality education. They don't have the health and dental facilities that they desperately need. It's difficult to find jobs in rural America that pay a living wage."

During the farm caucus in the House, Rep. John Melcher (D Mont.) said: "In 1970, according to statistics available in the President's economic report, we produced 30 per cent more food, and farmers were paid $800-million less net for producing it than in 1950—20 years before. And what they were paid was in dollars of far less purchasing power than 1950 dollars."

• Defined "rural areas" as communities of 10,000 or fewer inhabitants, except for purposes of business and industrial loans and grants in which case such aid could be made to areas of up to 50,000 inhabitants.

• Repealed an existing ceiling on the maximum amount of indebtedness which could be incurred by rural water or sewer systems.

• Authorized grants of up to $10-million annually for the preparation of comprehensive rural development plans.

• Directed that top priority for rural water and sewer loans and grants be given to areas with populations of 5,500 or less where inadequate systems existed.

• Raised to $500-million, from $100-million, the maximum amount of new unsold loans that could be held in the Agricultural Credit Insurance Fund.

• Created a new rural development insurance fund to handle new guaranteed and insured rural development loans.

• Authorized insured watershed and resource conservation and development loans.

• Authorized the FHA to make and insure rural business and industrial loans, including pollution abatement and control loans, to improve the economy and environment of rural areas.

• Authorized up to $50-million annually in grants for pollution abatement and control projects, not to exceed 50 per cent of the project costs.

• Authorized up to $50-million annually in grants to public bodies for industrial development such as the establishment of industrial parks.

• Provided that the secretary of agriculture could finance such industrial development jointly with other agencies, but directed that such financing not work a hardship on other industrial areas through transfer of employment or business activity.

• Authorized the FHA to guarantee certain rural housing loans whether or not the recipient could obtain credit elsewhere.

• Authorized loans to rural youths for enterprises connected with the 4-H Clubs or Future Farmers of America.

• Authorized the FHA to make insured operating loans, and increased their maximum size to $50,000 from $35,000 under existing law.

• Authorized the FHA to contract for services incident to its loan-making activites, with the authority to expire on Dec. 31, 1974.

• Prohibited direct and insured loans for new rural development purposes (except for community facilities) if guaranteed loans could be obtained.

Title II

• Amended the Watershed Protection and Flood Prevention Act (PL 83-566) to include the conservation and utilization of land as well as water under the act.

• Authorized federal cost sharing for water quality management, land utilization and agricultural waste management.

• Authorized the federal government to share up to one-half the cost of water storage for municipal and industrial water supplies.

• Authorized local organizations to use other available federal funds, including those from the Interior Department or the Environmental Protection Agency, for acquisition of land, easements and rights-of-way for watershed improvement projects.

• Authorized the secretary of agriculture to enter into agreements for a period of up to 10 years with landowners to share the cost of conservation programs within watershed projects.

Title III

• Amended the Bankhead-Jones Farm Tenant Act of 1937 (PL 75-210) to authorize the secretary of agriculture to promote rural community development by furnishing technical assistance and cost sharing (up to 50 per cent) to public agencies and organizations carrying out plans for conservation of rural community water supplies, water quality management, control and abatement of agriculture-related pollution, disposal of solid wastes in rural areas and storage of water for rural fire protection.

• Directed the secretary to carry out a land inventory and monitoring program and prepare reports at least every five years on soil, water and resource conditions.

Title IV

• Directed the secretary of agriculture to provide financial and technical assistance to states to aid in rural community fire protection.

• Authorized the secretary to pay up to 50 per cent of the cost of fire protection programs.

• Authorized appropriations of $7-million for each of fiscal years 1973-75.

Title V

• Established a pilot program of rural development and small farm research and education to be administered through the land grant colleges.

• Authorized appropriations of $10-million for fiscal 1974, $15-million for 1975 and $20-million for 1976.

Title VI

• Directed the heads of all federal departments and agencies to give first priority to locating new offices and other facilities in rural areas.

• Required the secretary of agriculture to acquire and disseminate information on rural development and to coordinate activities within the executive branch.

• Provided for the creation of an additional assistant secretary of agriculture.

• Provided for 10-year contracts under the Rural Environmental Assistance Program (REAP) and authorized cost sharing under the program for agriculture-related pollution prevention or abatement not related to soil or water conservation.

LEGISLATIVE HISTORY

House Action. The House Agriculture Committee Feb. 16 by a 32-4 roll-call vote reported HR 12931 (H Rept 92-835), the Rural Development Act of 1972.

The purpose of the bill was to help halt "the steady flow of rural Americans to our nation's large population centers," the report stated. "Once this outmigration is checked, this legislation proposes to make it desirable for Americans to actually return to our rural areas, thereby lessening the burdens and problems of the modern big city."

Among general problems of rural areas revealed in committee hearings, the report included:

• Sixty per cent of the nation's substandard housing is located in rural areas.

• Per capita income is lower than that in cities.

• Fire protection and ambulance services often are inadequate.

- More water and sewer systems are needed.
- More jobs to provide employment are needed.

In his rural development message on Feb. 1, 1972, President Nixon cited "increasing mechanization of agriculture and other natural resource industries such as mining and lumber" as contributing to rural unemployment.

HR 12931 would provide new grant and loan authority for certain aspects of rural development under the Farmers Home Administration and the Soil Conservation Service. It would authorize funds for industrial and community development and pollution abatement and ease loan terms for farming and rural development purposes.

The House Feb. 23 by voice vote passed HR 12931 with amendments.

The President did not take a position on the bill, but the Department of Agriculture opposed some provisions of the measure on the ground that they would duplicate part of Nixon's proposed rural revenue-sharing program.

The House made two changes in the bill reported (H Rept 92-835) by the Agriculture Committee Feb. 16. The amendments:

- Increased the authorization for small community water and waste disposal project construction grants to $500-million from $200-million.
- Expanded programs of the Farmers Home Administration to permit loans to farmers and ranchers to help them comply with the Occupational Safety and Health Act of 1970 (PL 91-596).

The most controversial issue was an amendment offered by John G. Dow (D N.Y.) to prohibit profit-making organizations or individuals from receiving pollution abatement grants—thus restricting their availability to public bodies. Dow said:

"The bill would put the individual or corporate entity in the anomalous position of being punished for creating pollution under the Refuse Act of 1899 while accepting rewards for cleaning up the very same pollution. Indeed, one could pay off his fine with the money the government had given him to clean up his pollution."

W. R. Poage (D Texas), chairman of the Agriculture Committee, replied: "I have never understood the argument by my colleague from New York that somebody could make a profit on this deal because...he could not get more than 50 per cent assistance in the cost of any anti-pollution abatement. He would still have to pay a large share of the cost.... I think it is unfair to provide this help in the cities and withhold it, as this amendment would do, in rural areas."

The House rejected the Dow amendment by a 150-223 recorded teller vote.

Also controversial was an amendment offered by Henry S. Reuss (D Wis.) to provide that where public funds were used to build a reservoir or lake, and the secretary of the interior determined that it had potential value for recreation, the public would be guaranteed access. Reuss said:

"Precisely this is accomplished by all of the lake-building agencies of the government.... It is only the Soil Conservation Service which somehow balks at letting John Q. Public, under appropriate circumstances, in to visit the body of water which he has contributed to the building of with his taxpayer dollars."

Poage: "...it seems to be utterly unfair to require the landowner who furnished the land to open it up and give the public free access to it...no one can maintain a livestock operation very successfully if he is going to let the public come in there and use it, because when the public goes out, then the cows are going out too...."

The Reuss amendment was rejected by a standing vote of 12-80.

Senate Action. The Senate Agriculture and Forestry Committee April 7 reported S 3462 (S Rept 92-734), its own version of the rural development bill.

The main difference in S 3462 and the House-passed bill was that the committee's bill created an entirely new rural credit system, while the House bill expanded existing loan authority under the FHA and Soil Conservation Service.

The committee March 21 had voted 13-1 to report the bill.

S 3462, said the committee report, would "provide another large part of the financial investment, credit, educational, research, technical and institutional resources required" to implement the policy of rural revitalization set forth in the Agricultural Act of 1970 (PL 91-524). S 3462 "stems directly" from the 1970 act, the report said.

"Those wonderful conveniences of the big cities... seem to be fraying at the edges," noted the committee report. "Things don't quite work anymore."

Pointing to the problems of the over-urbanized society, the report took note of the "new town" movement but warned that "there are no bounds to the economic and social costs of such a proposal.

"But in rural America, thousands of small, viable towns already exist...a foundation on which can be constructed a new rural society that will provide jobs and services for those already living there, and for those who would return..." said the report.

"It would be foolhardy to propose a national policy of 'back to the farm,' " the report stated. "But a sensible policy of balanced national growth that would keep rural America strong and uniquely rural, while making better use of the land for all the people, is something that can be put together. It makes sense that it be implemented."

S 3462 as reported would:

- Establish a complete non-farm Rural Development Credit System modeled after the Farm Credit System and the Farmers Home Administration (FHA).
- Expand FHA loan and grant authority.
- Encourage private investment in rural areas.
- Authorize up to $500-million annually for a program of federal rural community development revenue sharing.
- Expand federal funding for small watershed development and resource conservation.
- Broaden rural environmental assistance programs to include pollution control.

The Senate April 20 passed an amended version of S 3462 by voice vote. The House then substituted the provisions of S 3462 for those of HR 12931, the House-passed companion bill, and passed the amended HR 12931 by a 78-0 roll-call vote.

On the floor, the Senate adopted 44-32 an amendment to S 3462 deleting provisions (Title I) which would have created a comprehensive rural development credit system modeled after the Farm Credit System and the Farmers Home Administration (FHA).

Supporters of the amendment, 33 of whom were Republicans, contended that Title I, if enacted, would create a vast new bureaucracy and be a severe financial drain on the federal government.

The Senate rejected an amendment to delete Title III, however, which would authorize funds for rural revenue-sharing. Instead, the amendment would have increased to $400-million from $100-million authorizations for FHA water and waste disposal programs.

Supporters of this amendment, who included 18 Republicans and 14 liberal Democrats, said that under the bill's percentage formula for revenue sharing, 39 states would receive a smaller share of the money than their percentage of the total rural population.

Conference Report. Conferees June 14 filed a conference report (H Rept 92-1129) on HR 12931. There were 52 specific points of difference between House and Senate versions.

Conferees took the following major actions:

• Deleted a Senate provision authorizing an additional $500-million annually for rural development revenue sharing with the states.

• Accepted a House provision extending FHA loan authority to include essential community facilities.

• Increased authorizations for water and waste disposal grants to $300-million, rather than to $500-million as in both the House and Senate versions.

• Included in the definition of rural areas towns of up to 10,000 population (and 50,000 for business loans), rather than towns of 5,500 as in the House version and areas having population densities of not more than 100 per square mile as in the Senate version.

• Created an additional assistant secretary of agriculture, as in the House bill; the Senate version reorganized the FHA into a Farm Development Administration and a Rural Enterprise and Community Development Administration.

Final Action. The House adopted the conference report on July 27 by a 340-36 roll-call vote.

The Senate adopted the conference report by a 73-0 roll-call vote Aug. 17 without debate, completing congressional action. Herman E. Talmadge (D Ga.), chairman of the Agriculture Committee, called HR 12931 "probably the single most significant rural development legislation ever considered by Congress."

Minimum Wage

Agricultural pressure groups were among forces which successfully opposed a bill (HR 7130) raising the federal minimum wage. The House Oct. 3, by a 188-196 roll-call vote, refused for a second time to submit to a House-Senate conference committee the differing versions of the measure. The action killed the bill for the 92nd Congress. *(Details, Labor chapter)*

Defeat of the measure was a severe disappointment for the House leadership, especially Speaker Carl Albert (D Okla.), who had pressed since 1971 for an increase in the wage floor. The hourly minimum under existing law—set in 1966—was $1.60 for most manufacturing and retail employees and $1.30 an hour for those farm workers covered by the Fair Labor Standards Act of 1938. Members representing rural and farm areas opposed provi-

sions in the Senate version repealing exemptions for certain agricultural workers. Also, the Senate version called for an increase in the minimum wage to an eventual $2.20 an hour by 1975 for agricultural workers covered, compared with the House version's eventual $1.70 the second year after enactment.

Among groups opposing the legislation or pushing for the House's lower wage levels were the Cotton Council of America and the American Sugar Cane League of the U.S.A., which sought to line up opposition to the bill from members representing agriculturally oriented districts.

Appropriations Bill

Congress in the general agriculture appropriations bill for fiscal 1973 (HR 15690—PL 92-399) appropriated $13,434,032,700 for the Agriculture Department, the Environmental Protection Agency (EPA) and a range of rural development and consumer protection programs. The bill signed into law on Aug. 22 also carried $195,500,-000 in appropriations to liquidate contract authority for previous fiscal years.

The new budget authority in the bill was $537,021,800 more than the House-passed figure, but $127,023,100 less than the Senate-approved amount. It was $481,842,300 more than the President's fiscal 1973 budget request but only $157,132,650 more than the amount appropriated for fiscal 1972. The final figure for liquidating contract authority was the same as the President requested.

Among other agencies funded by the bill were the Federal Trade Commission, Food and Drug Administration, National Industrial Pollution Control Council and the Council on Environmental Quality. In all, the bill carried $6,200,669,200 for agricultural programs, $1,026,-436,000 for rural development, $2,951,648,000 for environmental protection and $3,255,279,500 for consumer protection.

Subsidy Fight. HR 15690 was the forum for a bruising floor fight in both the House and Senate over proposals to reduce to $20,000—from the current $55,-000—the amount any single farmer could receive in annual per crop subsidy payments, except for sugar and wool. In the House, the amendment was rejected by only four votes (189-193). But in the Senate, opponents of the proposal overwhelmed it by a 2-1 margin (23-46). A similar amendment had been accepted by the House (214-198) but rejected by the Senate in 1971.

Silvio O. Conte (R Mass.), author of the amendment in both years, called the crop subsidies "a runaway farm program" during floor debate in the House June 29, 1972. He said the wealthiest 7 per cent of farms were currently receiving 63 per cent of total subsidies. Some farmers, he pointed out, were avoiding the $55,000 limit per crop by dividing farms among members of a family, or leasing acreage to other organizations, and he asked "Who knows that these agribusiness giants are planning now to evade the present regulations?"

House Agriculture Committee Chairman W. R. Poage (D Texas) and Appropriations Committee Chairman George Mahon (D Texas) both challenged Conte's arguments. Poage said: "Each year we are told how a few people control a whole lot of land and get a whole lot of payments. And certainly that is the way it works. If we want our farm program to be successful, it must work that way." In the same vein, Mahon added: "It is the larger operations that produce the quantity and quality of food and fiber that this nation requires. An attack upon those who are largely responsible for the dramatic job that is being done is wholly unjustified and indefensible."

Opponents of the Conte amendment, in 1972 as in 1971, insisted that because the $55,000 per crop limit on the subsidy payments had been instituted on a three-year basis by the Agricultural Act of 1970, that limit should continue without change through the final year. The same argument was made in Senate floor debate on a similar amendment by Birch Bayh (D Ind.) which, he said, was "designed to limit subsidies to large corporate farmers—not deny them to family farmers."

Funds appropriated by HR 15690 included:

• $188,036,000 for the Agricultural Research Service (ARS). One function of the ARS was predator control research. The conference report emphasized the need for research on non-lethal methods of predator control, but said "the conferees agree that there should be a complete review of the present executive decisions which prohibit dealing with predators in their sanctuaries on federal lands."

• $150-million for the Farmers Home Administration's water and sewer grant program. The House-Senate conference report said that in areas where full sewer service was not feasible, "a program of individual or small group loans shall be stressed with a view to full coverage in the future."

• $2.5-billion for the food stamp program.

Other Bills

Nutrition for Aged. Congress March 7 cleared a bill (S 1163—PL 92-258) amending the Older Americans Act of 1965 (PL 89-73) to provide grants to the states to establish nutrition programs for the elderly. The bill authorized grants to states to pay up to 90 per cent of the cost of establishing nutrition programs for the elderly, authorized $100-million in fiscal 1973 and $150-million in fiscal 1974 for the programs, and provided that nutrition projects were eligible to receive and use surplus commodities donated by the secretary of agriculture.

Coffee Pact. Congress March 13 completed action on a bill (HR 8293—PL 92-262) extending through Sept. 30, 1973, the President's authority to carry out the provisions of the International Coffee Agreement of 1968.

The agreement, which was negotiated in 1962 and extended for five years in 1968, was designed to keep coffee prices stable and prevent price fluctuations that had hurt Latin American producers—and American consumers as well. The treaty was due to expire on Sept. 30, 1973.

Strategic Exports. Congress April 24 completed action on a joint resolution (S J Res 218—PL 92-284) extending to Aug. 1, 1972, existing presidential authority to control U.S. strategic exports. The resolution extended the President's export control authority to Aug. 1 from May 1—the expiration date set by Congress in a previous extension approved on Oct. 29, 1971 (S J Res 167—PL 92-150). Congress twice in 1971 extened the authority, which was originally conferred by the Export Administration Act of 1969.

DES Ban. The Senate in 1972 passed a bill (S 2818) providing for an immediate ban on the growth hormone DES (diethylstilbestrol) in animal feed but permitting use of DES animal ear implants at least until Jan. 1, 1973. There was no House action on the bill, which died at the end of the 92nd Congress. DES, used in animal feed to stimulate rapid weight gain, had been found to cause cancer in mice. There was growing evidence, moreover, that occurrence of a rare form of vaginal cancer in young women might be linked to the fact that their mothers had been given DES, a synthetic hormone (estrogen), during pregnancy to prevent spontaneous abortion.

Rather than ban the use of DES outright, the Food and Drug Administration in early 1972 decided to permit its continued use pending a public hearing. On Aug. 2, however, the FDA banned immediately the production of DES used in feed for animals intended for human consumption. But it permitted continued use of existing supplies of DES as a feed additive until Jan. 1, 1973. The FDA ruling also permitted continued use indefinitely of DES ear implants.

Farm Bargaining. A controversial bill (HR 14987) regulating bargaining between farmers and purchasers of their products was killed Sept. 13 by a House subcommittee. By a 5-3 show-of-hands vote, the House Agriculture Subcommittee on Domestic Marketing and Consumer Relations rejected a motion to approve the measure, which would have given farmers more bargaining power by requiring food marketing and processing firms to negotiate in good faith with qualified farmers' associations. The bill was opposed by the National Farmers Organization and the National Farmers Union, as well as associations of food processors.

Chapter 7—Congress and Government

Key Votes

In this chapter, key roll-call votes are shown in bold-face type. The party breakdown on each of these votes and the position taken by each member of Congress may be found in the key vote charts which appear in the appendix to this book.

Congressional Affairs

Despite public opinion polls throughout the period of the 91st and 92nd Congresses indicating that the American public held Congress in low esteem, the first branch of government succeeded in enacting some noteworthy reforms of legislative procedures. The reforms had as their primary objectives the disclosure of more of the operations of Congress to the public and the modernization of outmoded congressional customs and institutions.

Major reforms along the lines of the first objective included a change in voting procedures on the House floor and in House and Senate committees which permitted the public for the first time to observe how representatives voted on amendments to legislation.

The second objective of the reform movement, a revamping of the institutions and legislative tools of Congress, included approval of an electronic voting system for the House, expansion of the role of the Library of Congress in furnishing members and congressional committees with information and expertise, expanded use of a data processing system, and creation of a Joint Committee on Congressional Operations to continue the study of the operations and organization of Congress.

Both goals were embodied in the provisions of the Legislative Reorganization Act of 1970 (PL 91-510). *(p. 382)*

Revision of the federal election laws was another area of reform that was realized during the period. After much vacillation on the issue of political campaign spending, and a Nixon veto of the first congressional effort to bring it under tighter control, the administration and Congress formed ranks behind the Federal Election Campaign Practices Act of 1971. *(p. 397)*

Ironically, the 1971 law, which was not cleared by Congress until early in 1972 and did not go into effect until April 7 of that year, was the motivation behind a concerted Republican fund raising campaign on behalf of President Nixon's re-election which subsequently got caught up in the Watergate scandal. *(Watergate affair, chapter on Presidency)*

Congressional Reform

On Jan. 2, 1971, the 182-year-old House tradition of disposing of crucial floor amendments to bills through hidden, non-recorded, voting came to an end with adjournment of the 91st Congress. Beginning in 1971 and used for the first time on March 3 was the vote by "tellers with clerks," or recorded teller vote, authorized by the 1970 Legislative Reorganization Act. Under the new procedure, representatives, at the request of 20 members, could require a recorded vote on any amendment introduced on the floor. Previously, a recorded vote normally could be expected only on the final passage or rejection of a bill. Members regularly missed votes on amendments on which they did not have great interest or on which there was heavy pressure on both sides of an issue. As he had nothing to lose since his vote went unrecorded, a member, by abstaining, could avoid antagonizing his colleagues.

In its first year of operation House voting participation on major amendments nearly doubled compared to the last year in which recorded votes were not permitted.

The other reforms in the 1970 law that were expected to have a lasting impact dealt with the committee system. With the purpose of opening up more of House and Senate committee proceedings to the public, Congress agreed to require that all roll-call votes taken in committee, along with each committee member's position, be made public and that committee reports on legislation contain the vote by which a committee ordered a bill reported.

In addition, the modest beginnings to what later, in 1973, became a major switch away from committee secrecy also was incorporated in PL 91-510. A provision applying to both chambers with only minor differences required all committee business meetings and hearings to be open to the public unless a committee by majority vote decided otherwise. In the year before the reform was enacted, 43 per cent of all House committee meetings and 28 per cent of all Senate committee meetings were closed to the public, according to Congressional Quarterly's annual survey. *(Secrecy 1953-72, p. 377)*

Seniority. The reorganization act did not touch upon many controversial subjects including seniority, tighter regulation of lobbying, the Senate filibuster, reorganization of committee jurisdictions, the "closed rule" in the House or the format of the *Congressional Record*.

In separate actions in 1971, however, House Republicans and House Democrats made the first inroads in the seniority system *(p. 366)*. Democrats agreed that:

• The Democratic Committee on Committees, consisting of the Democratic members on the Ways and

References

Discussion of congressional affairs for the years 1945-64 may be found in *Congress and the Nation, Vol. I,* p. 1407-1431; for the years 1956-68, *Congress and the Nation, Vol. II* p. 893-924.

Means Committee, would recommend to the party caucus nominees for the chairmanship and the Democratic members of each committee.

- The Committee on Committees' recommendations would be subject to a separate vote upon the demand of at least 10 House Democrats.
- Democrats also agreed that no member could be chairman of more than one legislative subcommittee.

Republicans agreed that:

- The Republican Committee on Committees, composed of one GOP representative from each state that had a Republican congressman, would nominate a member to be the ranking minority member of each committee or, if Republicans gained control of the House, the chairman of each committee.
- The Republican Conference would vote separately by secret ballot on each nomination.

Senate Filibuster. Although not part of the congressional reform package considered in 1970, six attempts were made in the Senate between 1969 and 1971 to modify the cloture rule (Rule 22) governing the filibuster, but a two-thirds vote was required to end debate on filibusters against a rules change before proponents could bring their proposal to the floor, and on none of the six tries did they come even close to obtaining the two-thirds majority. *(p. 356, 370)*

Events during the first Nixon term led to an unprecedented reassessment of the filibuster by some Senate liberals. Consistently the target of senators who had favored enactment of civil rights legislation in the past, Rule 22 was employed successfully in 1964, 1965 and 1968 to end filibusters on voting rights, open housing and ending racial discrimination.

Beginning in 1969, the issues for liberals changed from civil rights to administration-backed Vietnam war spending, accelerated military weapons development—such as the anti-ballistic missile (ABM)—and continued development of a supersonic transport (SST). Liberals and many moderates who questioned these priorities, or opposed them outright, began to see the filibuster as "a most useful tool" for blocking "accelerating concentration of executive power" by increasing public awareness of these issues. Three bills debated in 1971 were filibustered by moderates and liberals: an appropriation to continue development of an SST, a federal loan guarantee for the Lockheed Aircraft Corporation and extension of the military draft law.

Campaign Spending Reform

With the experience of the 1968 presidential election campaign behind it, an unequal financial competition that left the Democratic Party nearly $9-million dollars in the red, Congress early in 1972, after a three-year effort, completed action on a bill placing limits on the amount of money that candidates could spend on certain aspects of their campaigns and tightening requirements on reporting and disclosing political contributions and expenditures. Under the bill finally agreed upon, candidates for federal office—the House, Senate, President and Vice President—were restricted in the amount they could spend for advertising on television and radio, in newspapers, magazines, billboards and automatic telephone canvassing to 10 cents per eligible vote or $50,000, whichever was greater.

The new law, it was hoped, would plug many loopholes through which candidates had evaded earlier political spending regulations under the Corrupt Practices Act of 1925. Besides strengthening requirements for reporting contributions and campaign costs, the 1971 law defined more narrowly the roles unions and corporations, particularly those having business dealings with the federal government, could play in political campaigns and limited the amount a candidate or his immediate family could contribute to his own campaign.

The final version cleared by Congress did not contain two provisions vigorously opposed by President Nixon: repeal of the equal time requirement of the Communications Act of 1934, which was one of the key provisions in the earlier spending reform bill that caused him to veto it, and an over-all ceiling on the amount that could be spent in a single campaign.

Nixon also was successful in postponing until 1976 a provision, incorporated in another bill, providing for public financing of presidential campaigns by giving taxpayers the options of earmarking $1 of their annual income tax payments for use by the presidential candidate of the party of their choice.

Congressional Ethics

A former senator, two representatives and the chief aide of Speaker John W. McCormack (D Mass. 1928-71) were either convicted of or pleaded guilty to wrongdoing between 1969 and 1972.

Rep. John Dowdy (D Texas 1952-73) was convicted in 1971 of taking a bribe in return for attempting to halt a federal investigation of a Maryland home improvement company; part of the conviction subsequently was overturned by a U.S. appeals court. Rep. Cornelius E. Gallagher (D N.J. 1959-73) pleaded guilty in 1972 to income tax evasion; and former Sen. Daniel B. Brewster (D Md. 1963-69) was also convicted of bribery. *(p. 412)*

Revelations of corruption involving the office of speaker of the House made front page reading in American newspapers in 1969 with the disclosure that the top aide to Speaker McCormack, Martin Sweig, had been charged with using McCormack's office as a base from which to influence government contracts. Sweig later was convicted of influence peddling. McCormack was never implicated in the charges. He resigned at the end of the 91st Congress after serving 42 years in the House, nine as speaker.

The issue of congressional impropriety was raised in a different light by the release in June 1971 of portions of the then secret Pentagon Papers by Sen. Mike Gravel (D Alaska). Many of his colleagues saw Gravel's action as improper, unethical and even treasonous. The controversy also raised a basic constitutional question—to what extent does the Constitution protect members' activities under the Speech or Debate clause.

Financial Disclosures. The first disclosures ever by members of Congress of their income and financial worth, the result of legislation enacted in 1968 in reaction to the scandals that plagued Congress in the late 1960s, were reported in 1969. The disclosure requirement for representatives differed greatly from that relating to senators, but neither was comprehensive. The first reports covered calendar 1968 for House members and the period from July 1, 1968, for senators. *(p. 425)*

Chronology

Of Action

On Congress

The following chronology of action on the organization and procedures of Congress covers the years 1969-72. Excluded from the chronology but appearing as separate chapters are the following: the Legislative Reorganization Act of 1970 (p. 382), the Federal Election Campaign Act of 1972 (p. 397), congressional ethics, 1969-72 *(p. 412)* and financial disclosures 1969-72 *(p. 425)*.

1969

The first session of the 91st Congress, which convened at noon Jan. 3, 1969, adjourned Dec. 23, 1969. The session ran 355 days, making it the sixth longest in history up to that time and the longest since the first session of the 88th Congress (1963), which ran 356 days. *(Box, p. 370)*

Although the 1969 session ran for almost 12 months, Congress did not actually work all of that time. The Senate was in session for 176 days, while the House met on 186 days. Congress took numerous holidays, long weekends and a three-week vacation in August. The Senate was tied up for seven weeks with debate on the military procurement authorization bill (which contained the controversial antiballistic missile (ABM) system), almost three weeks on the tax reform measure, and over one week on President Nixon's nomination of Clement F. Haynsworth Jr. to be an associate justice of the Supreme Court.

There were 21,553 bills and resolutions introduced in the session, breaking the previous record set by the first session of the 90th Congress of 20,387 bills and resolutions introduced. Of the total introduced in 1969, only 190 became public law, the lowest in 36 years.

No bills were vetoed by President Nixon, though four measures were threatened with vetoes: tax reform (HR 13270—PL 91-172) and coal mine safety (S 2917—PL 91-173) subsequently were signed, while two bills threatened with vetoes were still pending at the close of the session— Labor-Health, Education and Welfare (HEW) appropriations (HR 13111) and federal salary comparability (HR 13000). (President Nixon Jan. 26, 1970, vetoed the Labor-HEW appropriations bills, and the House Jan. 28 by a 226-191 roll-call vote sustained the veto.)

The first session of the 91st Congress took 422 roll-call votes, fewer than in any year since 1964 when 418 roll-call votes were taken. The House had 177 votes and the Senate 245, of which 105, or 43 percent, were taken in December.

Two cloture votes were taken during the session, both at the beginning of the 91st Congress on motions to consider modification of the filibuster procedure (Rule 22). Both fell far short of the required two-thirds vote to invoke cloture. *(List of all cloture votes, box p. 358)*

Leadership Changes

Senate. In a major upset, Edward M. Kennedy (D Mass.) Jan. 3, 1969, defeated Russell B. Long (D La.) for the post of majority whip (assistant majority leader). The vote was 31-26. Long, who had 20 years of seniority and was chairman of the Finance Committee, was supported by an almost solid block of southerners and by many western Democrats.

Kennedy Dec. 30, 1968, had announced his candidacy for the whip's post after Edmund S. Muskie (D Maine), the 1968 Democratic vice presidential candidate, decided not to challenge Long for the job. Long was first elected Democratic whip in 1965.

Other Senate Democratic leaders were elected without opposition. *(Box, p. 356)*

In the first of two major Republican leadership contests in 1969, Republican senators Jan. 3 by a 23-20 vote elected Hugh Scott (R Pa.) to succeed Thomas H. Kuchel (R Calif. 1953-69) as Republican whip. Like Kuchel, Scott was considered a moderate among GOP senators. His conservative opponent, Roman L. Hruska (R Neb.), reportedly had the tacit support of Minority Leader Everett McKinley Dirksen (R Ill. 1951-69) in the effort to succeed Kuchel.

In another Republican leadership contest, Gordon Allott (R Colo.) by a 25-18 vote defeated Robert P. Griffin (R Mich.) for the chairmanship of the Senate Republican Policy Committee. The post was made vacant by the retirement of Bourke B. Hickenlooper (R Iowa 1945-69).

Other Senate Republican leaders were elected without opposition. *(Box, p. 356)*

Dirksen's death Sept. 7 set off a three-way race for the GOP Senate leadership post, which ended in the Sept. 24 election of Scott, 68.

The three announced candidates for the post were Howard H. Baker Jr. (Tenn.), Hruska and Scott.

Following the Sept. 24 election of Scott, the Republican Conference elected Griffin, 45, as assistant minority leader.

Selection of the top two leaders altered recent Republican practice of naming a conservative floor leader, and occasionally a moderate or liberal assistant. Scott received almost unanimous support among eastern state senators, gained an even break among senators from western states, and won vital votes from several veteran conservatives to defeat Baker by a 24-19 vote. Griffin also edged Baker, Dirksen's son-in-law, 23-20, on a third-round ballot for assistant leader. Hruska, a conservative, had withdrawn from the Senate minority leadership contest Sept. 20 and pledged his support to Baker.

House. The House Democratic Caucus Jan. 2, 1969, by a 178-58 vote formally nominated John W. McCormack (D Mass. 1928-71) as the Democratic candidate for speaker. McCormack, speaker since 1962, was opposed by Morris K. Udall (D Ariz.)

Udall's unsuccessful effort, supported primarily by relatively young liberals, provided a visible focus for widespread discontent with McCormack's leadership, but the liberal Democratic faction reportedly was disappointed by Udall's failure to get more votes among all Democratic members. In addition to the 58 votes for Udall, House Ways and Means Committee Chairman Wilbur D. Mills (D Ark.) received four votes.

Senate, House Leadership, 91st Congress

Senate Leadership

The following Senate officers were selected by their party caucuses during the first session of the 91st Congress:

President Pro Tempore—Richard B. Russell (D Ga.)
Majority Leader—Mike Mansfield (D Mont.)
Majority Whip—Edward M. Kennedy (D Mass.)
Democratic Conference Secretary—Robert C. Byrd (W.Va.)

Hugh Scott (R Pa.) was elected Minority Leader Sept. 24, replacing Everett McKinley Dirksen (Ill.), who died Sept. 7. Scott, a moderate, defeated freshman Howard H. Baker Jr. (Tenn.) for the post.

Robert P. Griffin (Mich.) replaced Scott as Minority Whip.

Republican Policy Committee Chairman—Gordon Allott (Colo.)

Republican Conference Chairman—Margaret Chase Smith (Maine)

Republican Conference Secretary—Milton R. Young (N.D.)

Russell replaced former Senator Carl Hayden (Ariz.), President pro tempore 1957-1969, who retired. Kennedy defeated Russell B. Long (La.) (Majority Whip 1965-1969). Scott at the beginning of the session had replaced Thomas Kuchel (R Calif. 1953-1969) as Whip. Allott replaced former Sen. Bourke B. Hickenlooper (R Iowa), who retired in 1969.

House Leadership

House officers in the 91st Congress—all but two the same as in the 90th—included:

Speaker—John W. McCormack (D Mass.)
Majority Leader—Carl Albert (D Okla.)
Majority Whip—Hale Boggs (D La. 1947-72)
Minority Leader—Gerald R. Ford (R Mich.)
Minority Whip—Leslie C. Arends (R Ill.)
Republican Policy Committee Chairman—John J. Rhodes (Ariz.)

Republican Conference Chairman—John B. Anderson (Ill.). He replaced former Rep. Melvin R. Laird (Wis.), who was named secretary of defense.

Republican Conference Secretary—Richard H. Poff (Va. 1953-72)

Republican Research and Planning Committee Chairman—Robert Taft Jr. (Ohio). He replaced Charles E. Goodell (N.Y.), who replaced the late Robert F. Kennedy (D) in the Senate Sept. 12, 1968.

Republican House members Jan. 2 elected John B. Anderson (R Ill.) to succeed Melvin R. Laird (R Wis. 1953-69) as chairman of the House Republican Conference. Unofficial reports credited Anderson with 116 votes, compared to 46 votes for Jackson E. Betts (R Ohio 1951-73) and 18 votes for Albert H. Quie (R Minn.). The GOP Conference, headed by Laird since 1965, was a policy group which included all House Republicans in its membership. The chairmanship was regarded as the third-ranking Republican House leadership post.

House Republicans Jan. 16 named Robert Taft Jr. (R Ohio, House 1963-65, 1969-71) to succeed former Rep. Charles E. Goodell (R N.Y., House 1959-68, Senate 1968-71) as chairman of the House Republican Committee on Research, after voting 91 to 61 to retain the committee. Taft, in a surprise victory, defeated Donald Rumsfeld (R Ill. 1963-69) for the chairmanship on a 76 to 74 vote.

All other members of the GOP leadership had been re-elected Jan. 2 without opposition.

Committee Secrecy

Congressional committees in 1969 held fewer meetings in closed sessions—from which the public was excluded—than at any time since 1964. *(Box, p. 377)*

Only 36 per cent of the 3,876 meetings of House, Senate and joint committees were held behind closed doors. The rate of closed hearings for 1969 represented a drop of 7 percentage points from the 1968 rate of 43 per cent.

Since Congressional Quarterly began the compilation of open and closed committee meetings in 1953, 37 per cent of all meetings had been in executive (closed) session. The highest rate for closed meetings in a single year was 43 per cent in 1968. The lowest rate was 30 per cent in 1959. Until 1965, the CQ study did not include the meetings of the House Appropriations Committee, all of which were closed. The 1969 closed hearings rate of 36 per cent was the lowest since House Appropriations hearings were included in the count.

During the first session of the 91st Congress House committees as usual held more of their meetings closed to the public than did Senate committees. House committees in 1969 held 974 (43 per cent) of their 2,267 meetings in closed session. The 1968 rate was 52 per cent. Senate committees closed 426 (28 per cent) of their 1,511 meetings. Joint committees in 1969 held only 14 of their 98 meetings in closed session, a rate of 14 per cent.

Senate Cloture Rule

In a series of parliamentary maneuvers between Jan. 16 and 28, the Senate twice rejected attempts by liberals to modify Rule 22. Senate liberals had tried to ease the requirements for cloture (limiting debate) at the beginning of each Congress beginning with the 1961 session. *(Congress and the Nation Vol. II, p. 904, 911)*

Rule 22 provided that the affirmative vote of two-thirds of senators present and voting was required to limit debate. Liberals proposed to reduce this to three-fifths of those present and voting. Filibusters frequently had been used to stall civil rights bills, labor bills and amendments to Rule 22 itself. *(Box p. 358)*

The Issue. Underlying the issue of changing Rule 22 was the question of whether the Senate could change its rules at the beginning of a new Congress without being subject to existing rules, particularly Rule 22. Supporters of modifying the filibuster argued that the Senate could adopt new rules by general parliamentary procedures— majority vote—at the beginning of each Congress, as did the House. Opponents of the rules change argued that the Senate was a continuous body and was required to act under its rules in making any changes to its rules. The authority for each chamber of Congress to determine the rules of its proceedings was set out in the Constitution and the issue of the procedure for changing the rules was seen as a constitutional one.

In 1969 the strategy of the liberals centered on obtaining a ruling from Vice President Humphrey, as presiding officer of the Senate until January 20, that a simple majority could vote cloture on debates involving a proposed change in Rule 22.

Support for a change was consolidated behind a bipartisan motion (S Res 11) to substitute a three-fifths vote for the existing two-thirds vote required to end a filibuster.

Senate Action. S Res 11 was debated on Jan. 10 and 13. A cloture motion was filed Jan. 14 and Humphrey said, in answer to a parliamentary inquiry, that if a majority, but less than two-thirds, of those present and voting voted for cloture he would rule that the majority prevailed. He said he believed that the majority had the right to cut off debate for the purpose of revising the Senate's rules. In the opinion of those senators supporting a change in Rule 22, the two-thirds requirement for limiting floor debate was an unconstitutional restriction on the right of the Senate to amend its rules. Humphrey said his decision would enable the Senate to decide the constitutional issue by a simple majority vote. He said that if he held that the cloture motion had failed because of the lack of a two-thirds vote, he would be inhibiting the Senate from deciding the constitutional question.

These issues had not been brought up in 1967 when a cloture motion on a motion to consider a change in Rule 22 was rejected because it fell short of the two-thirds vote, although a majority had supported it.

In explaining the ruling he proposed to make, Humphrey said: "On a par with the right of the Senate to determine its rules, though perhaps not set forth so specifically in the Constitution, is the right of the Senate, a simple majority of the Senate, to decide constitutional questions."

A slim majority, 51-47, Jan. 16 voted for cloture and Humphrey ruled that debate on the rules change issue would proceed under the provisions of Rule 22, which limits further debate to one hour per senator.

The Humphrey ruling was a major victory for proponents of the rules change but the ruling immediately was reversed when opponents of the change appealed the decision. The Senate voted to reverse the ruling by a 53-45 roll-call vote.

The reversal of Humphrey's ruling left the motion to consider the rules change open to further debate and liberals saw no possibility of obtaining the required two-thirds majority vote.

Secrecy Ground Rules

Statistics in Congressional Quarterly's open-closed committee study were derived primarily from information published in the daily digest section of the *Congressional Record,* the official journal of Senate and House proceedings. Section 221 of the Legislative Reorganization Act of 1946 required that:

"The Joint Committee on Printing shall provide for printing in the daily Record the legislative program for the day together with a list of congressional committee meetings and hearings, and the place of meetings and subject matter. It shall cause a brief resume of congressional activities for the previous day to be incorporated in the Record...."

In practice, however, not all committee meetings were listed in the Record. Committees used different criteria as to what constituted a meeting. Some did not report their meetings regularly to the Record; some said they reported their meetings but they were not carried in the Record.

For purposes of the CQ study, open meetings followed by closed meetings are counted twice—once in each category. Joint meetings of separate committees or subcommittees are counted as one meeting of each. A meeting of a subcommittee is counted as a meeting of the full committee.

The tabulations exclude meetings when Congress was not in regular session; meetings outside of Washington, D.C.; meetings of conference committees to reconcile conflicting Senate and House versions of bills; informal meetings without official status; and meetings of the House Rules Committee to consider sending legislation to the floor (but Rules Committee meetings for other purposes are included).

Meetings held by the House Appropriations Committee were not always reported in the Record. The CQ tally for the Appropriations Committee was made from a Record list of meetings scheduled.

The Senate Jan. 28 (after Spiro T. Agnew had become presiding officer of the Senate), defeated a second attempt by Senate liberals to invoke cloture on a motion to consider a modification of Rule 22. The cloture motion was rejected by a 50-42 roll-call vote—with 93 senators voting, 62 votes would have been required.

In debate Jan. 24, Frank Church (D Idaho), sponsor of S Res 11, acknowledged that the rules change was being sought under the existing rules, which meant that a two-thirds majority would be needed to invoke cloture. He said that the constitutional question of whether a simple majority of the Senate was sufficient at the beginning of the session to limit debate on rules changes was settled when the Senate voted to reverse Humphrey's ruling.

Spessard L. Holland (D Fla. 1946-71) said that the question of a rules change should be brought up "in the regular way as a resolution to be studied by the appropriate committee...." He said past modifications of Rule 22 were achieved through negotiation.

Church said that "whether the proposal is routed through the committee or whether it comes directly to the Senate at the commencement of a session...a filibuster is undertaken to preserve the filibuster rule."

Complete List of Cloture Votes Since Adoption of Rule 22

Following is a complete list through May 9, 1973, of the 72 cloture votes taken since Rule 22 was adopted in 1917. Only 13 of these (shown in **dark type**) were successful. In the right-hand column is shown the vote necessary to invoke cloture under a proposed 3/5-majority vote. Fourteen additional cloture votes (shown in *italics*) would have been successful using the proposed change.

Issue	Date	Vote	Yea Votes Needed 2/3 Majority	3/5 Majority
Versailles Treaty	Nov. 15, 1919	78-16	63	57
Emergency tariff	Feb. 2, 1921	36-35	48	43
Tariff bill	July 7, 1922	45-35	54	48
World Court	Jan. 25, 1926	68-26	63	57
Migratory birds	June 1, 1926	46-33	53	47
Branch banking	Feb. 15, 1927	65-18	56	50
Disabled officers	Feb. 26, 1927	51-36	58	52
Colorado River	Feb. 26, 1927	32-59	61	55
D.C. buildings	Feb. 28, 1927	52-31	56	50
Prohibition Bureau	Feb. 28, 1927	55-27	55	49
Banking Act	Jan. 19, 1933	58-30	59	53
Anti-lynching	Jan. 27, 1938	37-51	59	53
Anti-lynching	Feb. 16, 1938	42-46	59	53
Anti-poll tax	Nov. 23, 1942	37-41	52	47
Anti-poll tax	May 15, 1944	36-44	54	48
Fair Employment Practices Commission	Feb. 9, 1946	48-36	56	50
British loan	May 7, 1946	41-41	55	49
Labor disputes	May 25, 1946	3-77	54	48
Anti-poll tax	July 31, 1946	39-33	48	43
FEPC	May 19, 1950	52-32	64*	58*
FEPC	July 12, 1950	55-33	64*	58*
Atomic Energy Act	July 26, 1954	44-42	64*	58*
Civil Rights Act	March 10, 1960	42-53	64	57
Amend Rule 22	Sept. 19, 1961	37-43	54	48
Literacy tests	May 9, 1962	43-53	64	58
Literacy tests	May 14, 1962	42-52	63	57
Comsat Act	Aug. 14, 1962	63-27	60	54
Amend Rule 22	Feb. 7, 1963	54-42	64	58
Civil Rights Act	June 10, 1964	71-29	67	60
Legislative reapportionment	Sept. 10, 1964	30-63	62	56

Between 1949 and 1959 the cloture rule required the affirmative vote of two-thirds of Senate membership rather than two-thirds of senators who voted.

Issue	Date	Vote	Yea Votes Needed 2/3 Majority	3/5 Majority
Voting Rights Act	May 25, 1965	70-30	67	60
Right-to-work repeal	Oct. 11, 1965	45-47	62	55
Right-to-work repeal	Feb. 8, 1966	51-48	66	59
Right-to-work repeal	Feb. 10, 1966	50-49	66	59
Civil Rights Act	Sept. 14, 1966	54-42	64	58
Civil Rights Act	Sept. 19, 1966	52-41	62	56
D.C. Home Rule	Oct. 10, 1966	41-37	52	47
Amend Rule 22	Jan. 24, 1967	53-46	66	59
Open Housing	Feb. 20, 1968	55-37	62	55
Open Housing	Feb. 26, 1968	56-36	62	55
Open Housing	March 1, 1968	59-35	63	57
Open Housing	March 4, 1968	65-32	65	58
Fortas Nomination	Oct. 1, 1968	45-43	59	53
Amend Rule 22	Jan. 16, 1969	51-47	66	59
Amend Rule 22	Jan. 28, 1969	50-42	62	55
Electoral College	Sept. 17, 1970	54-36	60	54
Electoral College	Sept. 29, 1970	53-34	58	53
Supersonic transport	Dec. 19, 1970	43-48	61	55
Supersonic transport	Dec. 22, 1970	42-44	58	52
Amend Rule 22	Feb. 18, 1971	48-37	57	51
Amend Rule 22	Feb. 23, 1971	50-36	58	52
Amend Rule 22	March 2, 1971	48-36	56	50
Amend Rule 22	March 9, 1971	55-39	63	57
Military Draft	June 23, 1971	65-27	62	55
Lockheed Loan	July 26, 1971	42-47	60	54
Lockheed Loan	July 28, 1971	59-39	66	59
Lockheed Loan	July 30, 1971	53-37	60	54
Military Draft	Sept. 21, 1971	61-30	61	55
Rehnquist nomination	Dec. 10, 1971	52-42	63	57
Equal Job Opportunity	Feb. 1, 1972	48-37	57	51
Equal Job Opportunity	Feb. 3, 1972	53-35	59	53
Equal Job Opportunity	Feb. 23, 1972	71-23	63	57
U.S.-Soviet Arms Pact	Sept. 14, 1972	76-15	61	55
Consumer Agency	Sept. 29, 1972	47-29	51	46
Consumer Agency	Oct. 3, 1972	55-32	58	53
Consumer Agency	Oct. 5, 1972	52-30	55	49
School Busing	Oct. 10, 1972	45-37	55	49
School Busing	Oct. 11, 1972	49-39	59	53
School Busing	Oct. 12, 1972	49-38	58	53
Voter Registration	April 30, 1973	56-31	58	53
Voter Registration	May 3, 1973	60-34	63	57
Voter Registration	May 9, 1973	67-32	66	59

Capitol West Front

Congress in 1969 earmarked $2,275,000 in funds for studies of the west front of the U.S. Capitol, of which $250,000 was reserved for a study on restoring the original wall and as much as was necessary for emergency shoring and repairs. The remaining $2-million approximately was to be held for planning for extending the west front. Funds for the studies were contained in the legislative branch appropriations bill (PL 91-145) for fiscal 1970. The House by a 59-92 standing vote had rejected an amendment to delete all planning funds relating to the extension, and although the Senate had adopted, 53-24, a similar amendment, House-Senate conferees to the bill had agreed to appropriate the $2.275-million for the studies.

West Front Revival. The House Appropriations Committee's Subcommittee on the Legislative Branch held closed hearings Sept. 8, 1969, on a $2-million request to prepare contract specifications for an extension of the U.S. Capitol's historic west front, the central portion of the building that faces the Mall and the Washington Monument.

The revival of the project, a long-standing controversy in Congress, was disclosed Sept. 4, the same day that President Nixon announced a 75 per cent reduction in federal construction.

Congress previously had postponed the estimated $45-million project until the Vietnam war was concluded. But on Aug. 29, the Commission for the Extension of the Capitol received a report from a Massachusetts engineering company stating that the west front had badly deteriorated. Its sandstone walls had been declared unsafe in 1964 by the same firm, and temporary wood shoring was erected to support them.

The five members of the commission at the time were Vice President Spiro T. Agnew, House Speaker John W. McCormack (D Mass.), who resigned at the end of the 91st Congress, House Majority Leader Carl Albert (D Okla.), Senate Majority Leader Mike Mansfield (D Mont.), House Minority Leader Gerald R. Ford (Mich.), Senate Minority Leader Everett M. Dirksen (Ill.) (who died in September 1970) and Capitol Architect J. George Stewart, who died in May 1970.

Congress denied funds for the west front project in 1966 and 1967. A similar controversy arose in 1958 over the $24-million extension of the Capitol's east front, which was completed in 1962. *(Congress and the Nation Vol. I, p. 1428)*

The Commission for the Extension of the Capitol advanced a $34-million plan June 17, 1966, to rebuild the west front, altering its appearance and adding about 4.5 acres of space for restaurants, auditoriums, offices and a tourist center.

The American Institute of Architects led a strong attack on the proposed plans.

Contested House Elections

Congress Nov. 20 cleared a bill (HR 14195—PL 91-138) revising procedures for deciding contested elections to the House. The procedure for contested Senate elections was not altered in any respect by HR 14195.

The bill was reported by the House Administration Committee Oct. 14 and was passed by the House Oct. 20 on a 311-12 roll-call vote. The Senate cleared the bill on a voice vote Nov. 20.

The primary purpose of the legislation was to clarify the conditions under which a candidate could contest an election to the House of Representatives. No substantive grounds for upsetting an election were set forth in the bill, which was limited to setting up a framework for the procedural disposition of an election challenge patterned upon the Federal Rules of Civil Procedure.

Opposition to the bill was expressed by some members who objected to the failure of the bill to protect individuals who were unable to obtain a place on the ballot because of discriminatory action by state officials. Citing the challenge brought by contestants over the 1965 House elections in Mississippi, William F. Ryan (D N.Y. 1961-72) noted that the existing House law provided that "any person" could contest a House election, while PL 91-138 would require a contestant to be a candidate on the ballot.

Under HR 14195:

1) Only general and special elections to the House were covered.

2) Contestant was defined as a candidate whose name was on the official ballot for election to the House or who was a bona fide "write-in" candidate.

3) "Write-in vote" was defined to include all methods by which a state law permitted the casting of candidates whose names were not printed on the ballot.

Provisions. As cleared, HR 14195:

● Permitted any losing candidate for the House in general or special elections to challenge the election results by filing a sworn notice of contest with the clerk

---

Legislative Branch Expenditures
(Fiscal 1946-72)

The cost of running Congress more than doubled between fiscal 1969 and 1972. In 1968, expenditures for the legislative branch totaled $272-million; for 1972, it reached $567-million.

Between 1968 and 1972, Congress put into operation a new computer system, started its own television program, took over a 200-room hotel, bought an apartment building, installed an electronic voting system in the House and authorized an additional 214 policemen for Capitol Hill.

Although funds appropriated for the legislative branch are used to finance the operations of the Botanical Gardens, the Library of Congress, the Government Printing Office and the General Accounting Office, the bulk of the money goes for expenses directly related to congressional operations. In addition, Congress continued to fund congressional gymnasiums and swimming pools, chauffeured automobiles for the House and Senate leadership, a radio and television studio for each house, barber and beauty shops and such enterprises as a school for pages and 10 restaurants and cafeterias.

Fiscal Year	Amount
1946	$ 22,000,000
1947	40,000,000
1948	43,000,000
1949	47,000,000
1950	57,000,000
1951	61,000,000
1952	62,000,000
1953	61,000,000
1954	59,000,000
1955	65,000,000
1956	85,000,000
1957	97,000,000
1958	99,000,000
1959	118,000,000
1960	126,000,000
1961	133,000,000
1962	153,000,000
1963	147,000,000
1964	152,000,000
1965	179,000,000
1966	193,000,000
1967	261,000,000 [1]
1968	272,000,000 [1]
1969	307,000,000 [1]
1970	359,000,000 [1]
1971	436,000,000 [1]
1972	567,000,000 [2]

1 All figures beginning with 1967 include trust funds which averaged $4,000,000 per year.
2 Budget Bureau estimate.

SOURCE: Statistical Abstracts of the United States

of the House and serving it upon the newly elected member within 30 days after the official declaration of the election results.

• Provided that the newly elected member would have 30 days in which to either answer the notice or file a motion challenging the legal sufficiency of the notice or service of the notice.

• Provided both parties 70 days for taking depositions from witnesses.

• As under existing law, PL 91-138 provided that the House Administration Committee would consider each case and report its decision to the House in the form of a resolution. The full House either would uphold or overturn the committee's decision by a vote on the resolution.

Congressional Pay

Raises for members of Congress and other top legislative aides went into effect Feb. 14, 1969, after both houses tabled proposals that would have killed them.

A pay increase for congressional leaders and the Vice President was cleared by Congress Sept. 4, 1969.

Members of Congress. Members of Congress, as well as top officials in the executive and judical branches, for the first time received a pay increase without specific congressional approval. Under a procedure established by Congress in the 1967 federal pay raise bill (PL 90-206), every four years a commission of private citizens was to advise the President on salaries of top executive and judicial branch officials and members of Congress. The President then was to issue proposed salary revisions to go into effect within 30 days unless vetoed by either chamber of Congress. This procedure was put into practice in 1969 for the first time when President Johnson submitted proposed salary revisions with his fiscal 1970 budget. A veto resolution failed in the Senate by a 34-47 roll-call vote; while in the House, the Rules Committee prevented all veto proposals from reaching the House floor.

Opposition to the congressional pay increase continued to be heard throughout the session. During House debate in May on a fiscal 1969 supplemental appropriations bill, representatives unsuccessfully tried to cancel funds for the pay hike for the fiscal 1969.

The changes brought salaries to $42,500 for members of Congress, $60,000 for Cabinet members and Supreme Court justices, and $62,500 for the chief justice. Congressional staff members received a general salary increase of 10 per cent effective July 1, 1969. *(Box, this page)*

Congressional Leaders. A pay increase for the Vice President and congressional leaders was approved by Congress Sept. 4 after adverse Senate action earlier in the year had delayed passage of the legislation. The Senate Aug. 7, reversing its previous stand on the pay bill (HR 7206 PL 91-67), passed a compromise bill increasing the salary of the Vice President and the speaker of the House to $62,500 and the majority and minority leaders of the House and Senate and president pro tempore of the Senate to $49,500.

The salary increases were made retroactive to March 1, 1969. *(Federal pay, 447)*

Congressional Salaries

From 1789 to 1856, senators and representatives received per diem pay while Congress was in session, except for the period 1815-1817 when they received $1,500 a year. First established at $6 a day, per diem was raised to $8 in 1818 and remained there until 1856 when members of Congress were placed on annual salaries. Subsequent changes in pay scale, with the year the change became effective:

1856	$3,000	**1936**	$10,000
1866	5,000	**1946**	12,500 (plus $2,500 expense allowance)
1873	7,500		
1874	5,000	**1955**	22,500 (expense allowance eliminated)
1907	7,500		
1925	10,000	**1964**	30,000
1933	8,500	**1969**	42,500

Members' Retirement Benefits

Pension rates for former members of Congress were raised in 1969 in legislation (PL 91-93) changing the method by which the pensions were computed. Under the new system, former members received a pension based on their three highest wage-earning years, rather than on their five best as had been the law previously.

The bill amended the Civil Service Retirement and Disability Fund law and covered virtually all employees under the Civil Service system as well as members of Congress. *(Background, Congress and the Nation Vol. I, p. 1484, 1490; Vol. II, p. 932, 937)*

As it directly related to Congress, PL 91-93 also:

• Increased payroll contributions of members of Congress to the retirement fund to 8 per cent, from the previous 7.5 per cent, and contributions of congressional employees to 7.5 per cent, from the previous 6.5 per cent, beginning Jan. 1, 1970.

• Liberalized the method of computing annuities for congressional employees by eliminating the 15-year limitation under the previous law on the number of years of service for which the annuity would be computed at the rate of 2.5 per cent of average pay.

Related Action. Congress took no action on proposals introduced in 1971 to provide sizable retirement bonuses to elderly members of Congress who were not planning to seek re-election in 1972. Two such bills were reported July 28 by a House Post Office and Civil Service subcommittee. The bills (HR 9110, HR 10119) were introduced by Jerome R. Waldie (D Calif.) and Morris K. Udall (D Ariz.), both long-time opponents of choosing committee chairmen on the basis of seniority. Senior members of age 60 and over who retired before 1973 would have received an estimated $40,000-a-year pension and up to $50,000 paid life insurance.

Other 1969 Developments

PRIVATE BILLS. Senate Majority Leader Mike Mansfield (D Mont.) and Minority Leader Hugh Scott (R Pa.) on Oct. 1, 1969, took action to halt the practice of introducing private bills in the Senate by staff aides. Although no reason was given for the stricter interpretation of Senate rules, the decision may have been prompted by earlier allegations of impropriety in the handling of private immigration bills through various senators' offices. *(Story, see chapter on ethics p. 412)*

HUAC NAME CHANGE. The House Feb. 18, 1969, adopted a resolution (H Res 89—H Rept 91-15) changing the name of the House Un-American Activities Committee (HUAC) to the Internal Security Committee. The vote was 306-80.

Action on the name change came after the House by a 262-123 roll call had adopted a motion ending debate on and precluding amendments to H Res 89. Awaiting introduction, had the motion had defeated, were amendments to shift the functions of HUAC to the Judiciary Committee and thus abolish the Un-American Activities Committee.

HOUSE CRIME COMMITTEE. The House May 1, 1969, approved a resolution (H Res 172) establishing a select (temporary) House committee to investigate all aspects of crime in the United States. Rep. Claude Pepper (D Fla.), sponsor of the resolution, was named chairman. The committee was extended for two years in 1971, and on Feb. 28, 1973, the House extended the life of the committee to July 1, 1973, at which time the Judiciary Committee was to assume the crime-fighting function.

SENIORITY REVOKED. The House Democratic Caucus Jan. 29 voted 101-73 to strip Rep. John R. Rarick (D La.) of his seniority on the Agriculture Committee for having supported third-party candidate George A. Wallace in the 1968 presidential campaign. An earlier attempt on Jan. 2 to penalize him had been defeated by a vote of 85-87. Rarick was the lowest ranking Democrat on the committee in the 90th Congress but would have moved ahead in the 91st Congress.

1970

The second session of the 91st Congress, which convened at noon Jan. 19, 1970, adjourned Jan. 2, 1971. The session ran 349 days, making it the longest second session since the 1950 session of the 81st Congress, which ran 365 days.

Although the 1970 session ran for almost 12 months, Congress did not actually work all that time. The Senate was in session 208 days and the House was in session 164 days. Congress took several short vacations during the year. The House took a three-week recess from Aug. 14 to Sept. 9, and both houses took a recess from Oct. 14 to Nov. 16 for the 1970 election campaign. The return of Congress Nov. 16 marked the first post-election or "lame duck" session of both houses since 1950 and the first for the Senate since 1954.

A total of 505 bills became law in 1970.

President Nixon vetoed nine bills passed by Congress during the second session of the 91st Congress. Two vetoes were overridden by Congress. The veto of the $2.79-billion Hill-Burton hospital construction authorization for

---

Speaker McCormack Retirement

House Speaker John W. McCormack (D Mass. 1928-71), 79, retired at the close of the 91st Congress after serving nine years in the speaker's chair and 42 years as member of the House from Boston.

McCormack was speaker longer than any other man except Sam Rayburn (D Texas 1913-61), who served 17 years. On his retirement, Rep. Carl Albert (D Okla.), who succeeded him as speaker, called McCormack "the preeminent legislator of the world."

Speaker McCormack was born in Boston in 1891 and left school in 1904, after completing the eighth grade, following the death of his father.

Elected to Congress. McCormack's predecessor, James A. Gallivan (D 1914-28), was in poor health and McCormack decided to challenge him in 1926. McCormack was defeated but won a special election for the same seat after Gallivan died in 1928.

A loyalist to party and House leadership, McCormack helped Rayburn gain support for the post of Majority Leader in 1936. When Rayburn succeeded to the Speakership in 1940, McCormack became his choice for Majority Leader.

New Deal Liberal. McCormack consistently supported President Franklin D. Roosevelt's New Deal programs. His name was not attached to any major piece of legislation. However, McCormack actively promoted such programs as the Tennessee Valley Authority (1933) and the National Housing Act (1934) and Securities and Exchange Act (1934). He voted for the Social Security Act (1935), the Marshall Plan (1948), the Mutual Security Act (1958), the Peace Corps Act (1961), the anti-poll tax bill (1945), school construction aid (1956) and civil rights legislation (1957, 1960). He voted against overriding President Truman's veto of the Taft-Hartley bill (1947).

At age 70 in 1962, McCormack became the third oldest man elected speaker. At the time of his election he had served in the House for 34 years, longer than any other man who subsequently assumed the speaker's job.

---

fiscal 1973 was overridden June 22 by a 279-98 roll-call vote in the House and a 76-19 roll call in the Senate (HR 11102—PL 91-296). The veto of the $4.42-billion fiscal 1971 appropriations bill for the Office of Education was overridden Aug. 11 by a 289-114 roll-call vote in the House and a 77-16 roll call in the Senate (HR 16916—PL 91-380). *(For presidential vetoes, see p. 101a)*

Both the House and the Senate took record numbers of roll-call votes in 1970. The House took 266 roll-call votes, compared to the previous record of 245 in 1967. The Senate took 422 roll-call votes, compared to the previous record of 315 in 1967.

The lame-duck session, lasting from Nov. 16 to Jan. 2, 1971, was marked by intense controversy and filibusters on unfinished business. Congress debated several major appropriations bills, the controversial Cooper-Church amendment on Cambodia, the supersonic transport plane (SST), aid to Cambodia, welfare reform and import restrictions.

The 91st Congress ended with no final action on the President's request for trade legislation and welfare reform. On the SST, a compromise was reached; Congress cleared a continuing resolution providing funds for the SST and the Department of Transportation through March 31, 1971.

In a message Jan. 5, 1971, Mr. Nixon was critical of the lame-duck Congress, especially the Senate. "In the final month and weeks of 1970, the nation was presented with the spectacle of a legislative body that had seemingly lost the capacity to decide and the will to act," he said. "In probably no month in recent memory did the reputation of the whole Congress suffer more in the eyes of the American People."

Four cloture votes were taken in the Senate in 1970 —two in September in connection with a resolution (S J Res 1) to abolish the electoral college and two in December involving the appropriations bill (HR 17755) providing continued funding for the supersonic transport (SST) program. None of the 1970 votes was successful. *(Box, p. 358)*

Committee Secrecy

Forty-one per cent of all congressional committee meetings were held behind closed doors during 1970, an increase of five percentage points over 1969.

This was the third highest incidence of closed sessions since Congressional Quarterly started keeping records in 1953. The record was 43 per cent in 1968.

The committees in the House, as usual, had the highest percentage of closed meetings. Forty-eight per cent of all House committee meetings were held in executive session, as compared to 42 per cent in 1969.

Senate committees barred the public from 33 per cent of their meetings, an increase of five percentage points over the 28 per cent recorded in the first session of the 91st Congress.

Joint congressional committees continued to open most of their meetings to the public. During 1970, only 17 of 102 such meetings were held in executive session.

D.C. Representation

A bill giving the District of Columbia a nonvoting delegate in the House of Representatives was cleared for the President's signature Sept. 9, 1970, when the Senate passed the measure (HR 18725—PL 91-405) by voice vote. *(See also District of Columbia chapter, p. 459)*

PL 91-405 established the office of D.C. delegate to the House with all privileges except that of voting on the floor, and amended city election laws to provide for primary and general elections for the post. Washington, D.C., had had nonvoting representation in the House only once before in its history—from 1871 to 1875, when Congress established and then abolished a limited form of self-government for the city.

The bill also established a commission to study the organization of the District government.

Another D.C. delegate bill (HR 186195) passed by the House on Aug. 10, 1970, in conjunction with HR 18725, which would have given the city nonvoting delegates in both the House and the Senate, was not considered by the Senate.

On April 28, 1969, President Nixon had proposed a constitutional amendment giving the District voting representation in Congress. He recommended that the city be allowed to send a nonvoting delegate to the House until the amendment was ratified.

Pocket Veto Issue

President Nixon's pocket veto on Dec. 24, 1970, of two bills—a medical training assistance bill and a private bill dealing with the Foreign Claims Settlement Commission—brought immediate charges by Democrats in Congress that Nixon had misused his constitutional power to pocket veto legislation.

The President's pocket veto became controversial because it occurred over a brief six-day recess by Congress during the 1970 Christmas holidays. Democrats contended that the Constitution's provision for pocket vetoes was not intended to apply to brief adjournments of Congress.

"This bill has become a part of the law of the United States and was not killed by a pocket veto," Sen. Sam J. Ervin Jr. (D N.C.), chairman of the Senate Judiciary Subcommittees on Constitutional Rights and Separation of Powers, told reporters after the President's action.

Constitutional Question. Disagreement centered on interpretation of "adjournment" in the Constitution's pocket veto clause: "...if any bill shall not be returned by the President within ten days (Sundays excepted) after it shall have been presented to him, the same shall be a law, in like manner as if he had signed it, unless the Congress by their adjournment prevent its return, in which case it shall not be a law." *(Article I, Section 7)*

Attempts had been made on numerous occasions by members of Congress to pass legislation modifying or curtailing the President's veto power, but these efforts had failed. Because no existing legislation defined the terms of the pocket veto clause, the constitutional provisions stood alone with only two Supreme Court decisions to interpret them.

Contested Action. The President Dec. 14, 1970, received the Family Practice of Medicine Act (S 3418) and a private bill granting the Foreign Claims Settlement Commission jurisdiction to consider a dispute (HR 3571). The Family Practice of Medicine Act had been passed by a nearly unanimous vote, 64-1 in the Senate and 346-2 in the House. It authorized the appropriation of $225-million for a three-year program of grants to hospitals and medical schools to train general practitioners.

A return of the vetoed measure to the Congress would have resulted in an almost certain override, based on the near unanimity of the original votes. *(See chapter on health.)*

The 10-day period for both bills expired on Christmas day when Congress was in recess. The President refused to sign or return the two bills, thus killing them—at least according to the administration. Several members of Congress, however, claim that the measures became law.

Nixon's failure to act on the bills sparked immediate and heated debate in Congress. Sen. Edward M. Kennedy (D Mass.) called the President's use of the pocket veto an introduction of "an arbitrary element into the legislative process—an element never contemplated when the pocket veto provision was written into the Constitution by the Founding Fathers." Kennedy asked the Department of Justice to give the administration's side of the argument.

Court Cases. In defending Nixon's vetoes, the Justice Department had relied on the language of a 1929 Supreme Court decision and on the practice of previous administrations in using the pocket veto during brief adjournments.

There are only two Supreme Court cases dealing with the question. The so-called *Pocket Veto Case,* decided in 1929, was based on President Calvin Coolidge's veto of an Indian claims bill during a four-month congressional recess. The court, in a unanimous decision, held that the term "adjournment" applied to any congressional break preventing the return of the bill within the 10-day period.

Wright v. United States, decided in 1938, held that where only one house had adjourned, and only for a three-day period, Congress, as understood by the pocket veto provision, had not adjourned and a pocket veto could not be used.

Adjournment Defined. The Senate Judiciary Subcommittee on Separation of Powers, chaired by Sen. Sam J. Ervin Jr. (D N.C.), considered by many the Senate's leading constitutional scholar and a strict constructionist, held hearings Jan. 26, 1971, on the constitutionality of Nixon's vetoes.

Bills which would define "adjournment" to mean the final adjournment of both houses terminating the session of Congress, were introduced by Ervin in the Senate and by Representatives Emanuel Celler (D N.Y. 1923-73) and William M. McCulloch (R Ohio 1947-73) in the House (S 1642, HR 6225). Hearings on HR 6225 were held April 7, 1971, by a House Judiciary subcommittee at which the Assistant Attorney General at the time, William Rehnquist, testified for the administration. Neither bill was acted upon during the 92nd Congress.

Appropriations Test. Another strategy suggested by Kennedy and Ervin was not successful. During consideration in the House of a fiscal 1971 supplemental appropriations bill, an amendment was offered to appropriate $25-million to establish general medical practices at certain universities and hospitals, but a vote on the amendment was blocked when a point of order was sustained against it. The parliamentarian ruled that funds could not be appropriated for the program since there was no authorization in law. According to the ruling, "the chair may only refer to the statutes at large or the U.S. Code to find the authorization required to support this appropriation. Since no such statute can be cited, the chair must sustain the point of order."

Kennedy Suit. Kennedy Aug. 9, 1972, initiated a suit in federal district court in the District of Columbia against two administration officials—Arthur F. Sampson, acting administrator of the General Services Administration, and Thomas M. Jones, White House records chief —asking the court to declare Nixon's veto of S 3418 invalid and to order the defendants to publish the bill as law.

The district court's decision was expected to be appealed by either Kennedy or the Department of Justice; the Supreme Court eventually would have to settle the issue. Attorneys for the defendants moved for dismissal of the action Nov. 9, 1972.

Discharge Petitions

The discharge petition is a little-used device designed to enable a majority of representatives to bring to the House floor legislation blocked by a legislative committee or the Rules Committee.

The following table shows the extent to which the discharge petition was used between its adoption in 1910 and the close of the 92nd Congress in 1973. Although 25 bills were pried loose from committee by the discharge method and 20 of them ultimately passed the House, only two were finally enacted: the Fair Labor Standards Act of 1938 and a 1960 federal pay raise bill.

Congress	Petitions Filed	Bills Discharged	Discharged Bills That Passed House
61 (1909-11)	223	figures not avail-	
62-67 (1911-23)	241	able	
68 (1923-25)	4	1	0
69 (1925-27)	4	0	0
70 (1927-29)	2	0	0
71 (1929-31)	5	0	0
72 (1931-33)	12	1	1
73 (1933-35)	31	1	1
74 (1935-37)	33	2	0
75 (1937-39)	43	3	2
76 (1939-41)	37	2	2
77 (1941-43)	15	1	1
78 (1943-45)	21	3	3
79 (1945-47)	35	1	1
80 (1947-49)	20	1	1
81 (1949-51)	34	3	3
82 (1951-53)	14	0	0
83 (1953-55)	10	1	1
84 (1955-57)	6	0	0
85 (1957-59)	7	1	1
86 (1959-61)	5	1	1
87 (1961-63)	6	0	0
88 (1963-65)	5	0	0
89 (1965-67)	6	1	1
90 (1967-69)	4	0	0
91 (1969-71)	12	1	1
92 (1971-73)	15	1	0
TOTAL	850	25	20

In his suit, Kennedy said that what was at stake in the pocket veto issue was "nothing less than an opportunity to take a stand against one aspect of the continuing erosion of congressional power, and to vivify the fundamental principle of separation of powers in our government."

The Justice Department maintained that the suit was "an impermissible effort to involve" the federal courts in a constitutional dialogue between the executive and legislative branches of government. The department's memorandum in the suit added: "...this suit is uniquely of the type which is barred from judicial review since it involves a political question."

As to the veto itself, the department said Nixon was well within bounds of precedent: The practice of pocket vetoing legislation during a mid-session recess extended back "to the incumbency of President Andrew Johnson."

Kennedy Feb. 28, 1973, argued his own case before a U.S. district court in Washington, D.C., in what was believed to have been the first time a member of Congress had taken his complaint into court. During oral argument, Kennedy said S 3418 was "the most important piece of legislation" ever to be pocket vetoed and that the five-day congressional recess the shortest in which one had been used.

Other 1970 Developments

MADISON MEMORIAL LIBRARY. Congress in 1970 passed a bill authorizing an additional $15-million for construction of the James Madison Memorial Building of the Library of Congress. The bill (PL 91-214) amended PL 89-260 by increasing the authorization from $75-million to $90-million. The original authorization had been approved in 1965. PL 91-214 contained an amendment added by the House specifying that the law was not to be construed as authorizing construction "for general office building purposes." Some members were apprehensive that demands both in the House and the Senate would divert funds from construction of the library addition.

No funds for construction of the building were actually appropriated by Congress until 1970 when $15.6 million was added to the fiscal 1971 legislative branch appropriations bill (PL 91-382) to begin construction. Appropriations of $71.1-million were approved in 1971 (for fiscal 1972), and in 1972 (for fiscal 1973) Congress appropriated $4-million for initial outfitting of the building.

A late as 1971 members of Congress still were saying that the building ultimately would be transformed into a fourth House office building instead of being used for its original purpose as an annex of the Library of Congress.

SENATE AUTOMOBILE LEASES. The Senate Select Committee on Standards and Conduct Aug. 24, 1970, unanimously recommended that senators quickly terminate low-cost automobile leases.

Committee Chairman John Stennis (D Miss.) said on the Senate floor that the committee had decided "senators should not accept any favorable terms and conditions that are available to them only as senators."

All three major automobile companies had acknowledged leasing cars to senators at reduced rates.

Stennis: "Our committee found no evidence to suggest that these leases with senators were a means for the automobile companies to exercise improper influence. Nor did we find any indications that the automobile companies received any favorite treatment from senators or assistants to senators because of the favorable lease terms...."

The committee also discovered that some Senate committees had entered into contracts with an unnamed manufacturer for the private use of automobiles by senators on the committees, leases for which senators, not the committee, paid.

It had been disclosed earlier that one motor company, Ford, had been leasing insured Lincoln Continental sedans to at least 19 key House and Senate members for $750 a year. All but two of these 19 were committee chairmen or ranking minority members. The company said it was an arrangement designed to place its cars in the hands of prestigious drivers, including sports and entertainment figures.

1971

The first session of the 92nd Congress, which convened at noon Jan. 21, 1971, adjourned Dec. 17, 1971. The session ran 331 days.

Although the 1971 session ran for almost 11 months, Congress did not actually work all that time. The Senate was in session 186 days and the House was in session 163 days.

There were 13,146 bills and resolutions introduced in the session, far fewer than the record-setting 21,553 bills and resolutions introduced in the first session of the 91st Congress.

A total of 224 bills became law in 1971.

A total of 743 record votes were taken during the first session of the 92nd Congress, a record to that time. Votes in the House increased by 54, from 266 to 320, due in large part to the introduction of the recorded teller vote—the major procedural change brought about by the Legislative Reorganization Act of 1970. Of the 320 votes, 108 were recorded teller votes which, for the first time, forced members to go on record on major amendments to legislation. With anonymity no longer guaranteed, members voted in greater numbers than ever during the amendment stage of floor debate. Participation in amendment votes nearly doubled in 1971 after the introduction of the new procedure. *(1970 Reorganization Act, p. 382)*

Three bills were vetoed by the President during the sessions, and on each one his action was sustained.

Ten cloture votes were taken, of which only one was successful: on a bill extending the military draft for two years. The 10 votes set a record for a single session of Congress. *(Box, p. 357)*

Leadership Changes

HOUSE. The House of Representatives in 1971 elected Carl Albert (D Okla.) as the 54th speaker of the House. *(House Leadership, 92nd Congress, box p. 366)*

Albert, a slight, quiet veteran of 24 years in the chamber, was elected with only token Democratic opposition to succeed John W. McCormack (D Mass. 1928-71), who had retired.

Both McCormack, who had served as speaker since 1962, and Albert, who had succeeded McCormack as House Majority Leader that same year, had been proteges of the late Speaker Sam Rayburn (D Texas 1940-47, 1949-53, 1955-61) who died in 1961.

The retirement of McCormack and the elevation of Albert to succeed him as speaker created two other vacancies in the top of the Democratic hierarchy which were also filled in 1971. *(Box p. 361)*

Hale Boggs (D La. 1941-43, 1947-72) had to overcome strong liberal opposition within the party to move up from his assistant majority, or whip, position to claim Albert's former office as majority leader. In other moves, Thomas P. O'Neill Jr. (D Mass.) succeeded Boggs as whip, and Olin E. Teague (D Texas) became Democratic Caucus chairman. Teague defeated the incumbent, Dan Rostenkowski (Ill.), for that office.

In the House Republican organization, Minority Leader Gerald R. Ford (Mich.) and Leslie C. Arends (Ill.) were unopposed for re-election as minority leader and GOP whip. Other Republican leaders regained their positions without opposition, with one exception. In that contest John B. Anderson (Ill.) had to overcome a stiff challenge by conservative Samuel L. Devine (Ohio) for the chairmanship of the House Republican Conference. The vote was 89-81.

Albert was elected speaker Jan. 19 with only a token challenge by John Conyers Jr. (Mich.), who opposed Albert only at the last minute after Albert failed to support a bid to strip five Mississippi Democrats of their seniority. Albert defeated Conyers 220-20.

In his 24 years in the House, the 5-foot-4-inch former Rhodes scholar had traveled a careful political road that had earned him almost no enemies and had made him acceptable to all factions of the Democratic Party.

Boggs had built a successful House career by supporting the legislative goals of the national Democratic Party without violating the sensibilities of the New Orleans residents who elected him.

He was a consistent supporter of free trade and most social welfare legislation, and he had moderated the racial conservatism that led him to vote against civil rights bills in 1956, 1957, 1960 and 1964.

His increasingly moderate stand on these issues and his general backing for labor legislation won him acceptance among urban and northern Democrats that distinguished him from more orthodox southerners and helped him build the coalition he needed to become majority leader.

Albert and Boggs moved to build a bridge between the conservative and liberal factions of the party by selecting Thomas P. (Tip) O'Neill Jr. (D Mass.) as assistant majority leader.

O'Neill described himself as an establishment liberal, meaning one who combined the traditional emphasis on party loyalty and organization with the issue-oriented politics of younger liberals.

The issue on which O'Neill had been most controversial was the Vietnam war. In October 1967, he broke publicly with President Johnson and opposed continuation of the war. He supported Sen. Eugene J. McCarthy (D Minn. 1959-71) for President in 1968, and he advocated immediate withdrawal of U.S. troops in 1971.

Anderson was challenged by Devine on the grounds that his voting record on domestic issues—notably civil rights, consumer legislation and various social welfare programs—was too liberal. When he first came to the House in 1961, Anderson had a reputation as a conservative, but he had moved to a more moderate stance. Devine was the informal leader of conservative Republicans who backed his candidacy for conference chairman.

SENATE. In major intra-party contests Democrats replaced Edward M. Kennedy (Mass.) as assistant majority leader with Robert C. Byrd (W. Va.), and Republicans re-elected Hugh Scott (Pa.) in a close race for minority leader.

Byrd was elected majority whip Jan. 21. The vote was 31 for Byrd, 24 for Kennedy.

Russell Death

Sen. Richard B. Russell (D Ga. 1933-71), dean and one of the most powerful members of the Senate, died Jan. 21, 1971, at the age of 73.

Russell, Senate president pro tempore and chairman of the Appropriations Committee, regarded his support of strong U.S. military forces as his major career accomplishment.

An expert on defense, Russell served on the Senate Armed Services Committee from 1947 to 1969 and was chairman 1951-52 and 1955-69. He was a member of the former Naval Affairs Committee for 13 years.

A champion of states' rights, he was the undisputed leader of the southern bloc opposing civil rights legislation.

A knowledgeable politician with a complex personality, Russell was on nearly every list of the most powerful men in Washington for many years. His popularity extended even to his opponents, who respected his judgment and amired his integrity. Former President Harry S Truman once said of him: "If Russell had been from Indiana or Missouri or Kentucky, he may very well have been President of the United States."

Byrd's surprise win came after his covert but assiduous campaign for the job and was aided by a marked slippage in expected support for Kennedy.

Majority Leader Mike Mansfield (Mont.) was renominated without opposition for his post, and Sen. Frank E. Moss (Utah) was chosen—also without opposition—to be secretary of the Democratic Conference, the number three leadership post among Senate Democrats.

A self-described moderate conservative, Byrd had held more legislative elective offices than any other person in West Virginia history. When first elected to the Senate in 1958, he defeated Chapman C. Revercomb with more than 59 percent of the vote. In 1970, he won a record 78 percent of the vote in defeating Republican Elmer Dodson, the mayor of Charleston.

During four years as secretary of the Democratic Conference, Byrd built a wide base of support through energetic floor activity and careful attention to detail.

A long-anticipated fight for minority leader developed in the Republican caucus Jan. 21 between the incumbent, Hugh Scott of Pennsylvania, and youthful challenger Howard H. Baker Jr. of Tennessee. Scott won by a vote of 24-20.

The vote result was similar to the outcome of another contest between Scott and Baker in September 1969 for the same position, which ended in a 24-19 victory for Scott.

All other incumbent Republican leaders were re-elected, including Minority Whip Robert P. Griffin (Mich.), Gordon Allott (Colo. 1955-73), chairman of the Policy Committee, and Margaret Chase Smith (Maine 1949-73) as chairman of the Republican Conference.

The elected chairman of the Senate Republican Campaign Committee was Peter H. Dominick (Colo.), who was unopposed for the job.

Senate, House Leadership, 92nd Congress

The following officers were selected by their party caucuses as the 92nd Congress convened:

House Leadership

Speaker—Carl Albert (D Okla.)
Majority Leader—Hale Boggs (D La.)
Majority Whip—Thomas P. O'Neill Jr. (D Mass.)
Minority Leader—Gerald R. Ford (R Mich.)
Minority Whip—Leslie C. Arends (R Ill.)
Democratic Steering Committee Chairman—Ray J. Madden (D Ind.)
Republican Conference Comittee Chairman—John Rhodes (R Ariz.)
Republican Research and Planning Committee Chairman—Barber B. Conable Jr. (R N.Y.)

Senate Leadership

President Pro Tempore—Allen J. Ellender (D La.).
Following the death of Ellender July 27, 1972,
James O. Eastland (D Miss.) was elected July 28 as president pro tempore. Ellender had succeeded Richard B. Russell upon the latter's death Jan. 21, 1971.
Majority Leader—Mike Mansfield (D Mont.)
Majority Whip—Robert C. Byrd (D W. Va.)
Democratic Conference Secretary—Frank E. Moss (D Utah)
Minority Leader—Hugh Scott (R Pa.)
Minority Whip—Robert P. Griffin (R Mich.)
Democratic Conference Chairman—Mike Mansfield (D Mont.)
Republican Conference Chairman—Margaret Chase Smith (R Maine)
Democratic Policy Committee Chairman—Mike Mansfield (D Mont.)
Republican Policy Committee Chairman—Gordon Allott (R Colo.)
Democratic Steering Committee Chairman—Mike Mansfield (D Mont.)
Republican Committee on Committees Chairman—Wallace F. Bennett (R Utah)

Scott selected Norris Cotton (N.H.) to succeed Milton R. Young (N.D.) as secretary of the Republican Conference.

Seniority Challenged

Under renewed pressure in 1971 to modify the seniority system of selecting committee chairmen, Congress in January and February took some modest steps to reform the custom.

In the House, changes were adopted by the Democratic and Republican caucuses permitting their members to vote separately on nominations for committee chairmen and ranking minority members of each House committee.

In the Senate, a major challenge to the system was rejected in March; nevertheless party caucuses of Senate Democrats and Republicans approved changes to open up the system, under which members with the longest service automatically secured the top committee positions. *(Alternatives proposed, box p. 367)*

HOUSE CHANGES

During 1970, special committees had been set up by both parties to prepare recommendations for changes in the seniority system when the new Congress convened in January 1971.

Democrats. House Democrats Jan. 20, in caucus, adopted modest changes in the seniority system recommended by the special Committee on Organization, Study and Review headed by Julia Butler Hansen (D Wash.).

The principal changes in the seniority system agreed upon by the Democrats were:

• The Democratic Committee on Committees, which consisted of the Democratic members of the Ways and Means Committee, would recommend to the caucus nominees for the chairmanship and membership of each committee, and such recommendations would not have to be based on seniority.

• The Committee on Committees would make recommendations to the caucus, one committee at a time; upon the demand of 10 or more members, nominations could be debated and voted on.

• If a nomination was rejected, the Committee on Committees would submit another nomination.

The issue of seniority was first raised in the Democratic caucus Jan. 19 when Rep. John Conyers Jr. (Mich.) challenged the seniority rights of the all-Democratic Mississippi House delegation. Conyers pointed out that the five Mississippians had refused to run on the racially integrated Democratic ticket recognized by the national party, but had run instead on an all-white ticket. Conyers argued that if the Mississippians refused to adhere to the principles of the national Democratic Party, they should be stripped of their seniority and denied the right to hold committee chairmanships as Democrats. The challenge was rejected by a standing vote of 55-111.

Republicans. House Republicans on Jan. 20 agreed to allow the entire Republican membership to vote on nominations for ranking minority members of each House committee.

The Republican Conference, composed of members of the leadership including the minority leader and the minority whip, adopted without change recommendations of a Republican task force on seniority headed by Barber B. Conable J. (N.Y.). The major change accepted allowed the post of ranking Republican on each committee to be selected by vote, rather than by seniority. If Republicans gained control of the House, the change would apply to the selection of committee chairmen.

The report set up a procedure for the selection of ranking members: the Republican Committee on Committees, composed of one representative from each state which had in its congressional delegation at least one Republican member, would nominate a member to be the ranking Republican on each committee, but not necessarily on the basis of seniority. The Republican Conference would vote separately, by secret ballot, on each nomination; if the nomination were rejected, the Committee on Committees would submit another nomination.

There were no challenges in 1971 to the existing ranking members of the House committees.

Vote on Chairman McMillan. In party caucus Feb. 3, House Democrats voted 126-96 to retain John L. McMillan (S.C. 1939-73) as chairman of the District of Columbia Committee.

Brock Adams (D Wash.), a member of the D.C. Committee who led the caucus fight against McMillan, said he attempted to attack McMillan's procedures in chairing the committee rather than complain about McMillan's ideology, age or southern origin.

The House Feb. 4, by a 32-258 roll-call vote, rejected an attempt by liberal members to dislodge McMillan as chairman of the committee.

One hundred members did not vote and 42 members voted "present" on the question, a procedural vote that was preliminary to voting on Democratic committee assignments.

If House liberals had been successful on the procedural vote, Jerome R. Waldie (D Calif.) was prepared to offer an amendment to the resolution on Democratic committee assignments (H Res 193) that would have removed McMillan as chairman.

McMillan had been criticized increasingly as being unresponsive to the needs of Washington, D.C. He was defeated for re-election in 1972 after serving 24 years as chairman of the House District Committee.

Although the chairmanship of the D.C. committee was the principal target of the House reformers, floor debate indicated the real concern was whether the two parties should continue to make their own committee assignments, or whether the entire membership of the House should make the decisions. The question involved a fundamental change in the two-party system and the traditions of the House.

Debate on the McMillan question in the House Feb. 4 centered on whether the minority party should violate precedent by voting on the affairs of the majority party.

Majority Leader Hale Boggs (D La.) warned that "if a minority on the Democratic side and a majority on the minority side get together they could take over control of the entire committee system in the House."

"If by so doing the national interest were advanced," Waldie said, "I would not find that objectionable."

Minority Leader Gerald R. Ford (R Mich.) said the matter was "one for the Democrats to decide and not for us. The Democrats ought to have the right to choose their own chairman in caucus." Ford voted "present" on the question. Many of the liberal Democrats who voted in caucus Feb. 3 to unseat McMillan opposed

---

Alternatives to Seniority

Following is a selection of major alternatives to use of seniority in naming committee chairmen. The selection was compiled in 1970 by the Democratic Study Group, an informal organization of House liberals.

• Use the seniority system to nominate chairmen, subject to majority approval by the caucus.

• Have the caucus elect committee chairmen from among the three most senior members of each committee.

• Authorize the speaker to nominate chairmen, subject to approval by a majority of the caucus.

• Authorize the majority members of each committee to nominate the chairman, subject to caucus approval.

• Authorize the members of each committee—both majority and minority—to select the chairman, subject to approval of the House as a whole.

• Establish a new special committee to nominate chairmen, subject to majority approval by the caucus.

• Set an age limit, and require chairmen to give up their chairmanships when they reach that age.

• Set a limit on the number of years a member can serve as chairman and require that after serving as chairman, the member leave the committee and begin service on another committee.

• Rotate the chairmanship among the top three committee members every two years.

---

the Waldie proposal on the House floor. They argued that it could open the way for future conservative coalitions to unseat liberal chairmen or even block the majority party's choice of a speaker.

Chairmen Sidetrack Major Reform

At its Jan. 20, 1971, meeting the Democratic Caucus also agreed to a proposal that no members could be chairman of more than one legislative subcommittee. The change was intended to open up subcommittee chairmanships to some of the younger members. The change affected 16 Democrats who, at the end of the 91st Congress, held more than one subcommittee chairmanship.

Two House committee chairmen reorganized their committees Feb. 25 in such a way that other House Democrats said violated the spirit, if not the letter, of changes approved by the Democratic Caucus in January 1971.

The two chairmen were Chet Holifield (D Calif.) of the Government Operations Committee, and McMillan of the District of Columbia Committee.

Among its directives, the Hansen Committee on Organization, Study and Review recommended that a chairman of a full committee should not be chairman of more than one subcommittee of that committee and that no representative be chairman of more than one legislative subcommittee.

The changes—adopted after several months of investigation by the 11-member Hansen committee—opened approximately 40 subcommittee chairmanships to junior representatives.

In a meeting called Feb. 24 by Caucus Chairman Olin E. Teague (D Texas), many Democrats attacked reports that some chairmen had attempted to circumvent the earlier caucus decision.

Holifield Actions. Holifield, a member of the House since 1943 who ascended to the chairmanship of the House Government Operations Committee at the start of the 92nd Congress, notified members of his committee Feb. 22 that:

• Five of his subcommittees were chaired by members who also were subcommittee chairmen on other committees. But he said his subcommittees were investigative, not legislative, subcommittees. Therefore, he said, they were not covered by the caucus rule.

• He had consolidated the two most active subcommittees—Military Operations and Executive and Legislative Reorganization—into one subcommittee, which he would head.

By removing the legislative jurisdiction of the five subcommittees, all legislation referred to Government Operations would be handled by either Holifield's new subcommittee or a subcommittee on Government Activities headed by Jack Brooks (D Texas).

In another move in March that angered some committee members, Holifield abolished two of his investigating subcommittees—on consumer affairs and invasion of privacy.

The consumer panel, headed by Benjamin S. Rosenthal (D N.Y.), and the invasion of privacy inquiry, headed by Cornelius E. Gallagher (D N.J. 1959-73), had been established by the late William L. Dawson (D Ill. 1943-70), the previous committee chairman. Because they were select committees, both had to be re-established at the beginning of each new Congress.

McMillan Actions. House District of Columbia Committee Chairman McMillan Feb. 25 bypassed eligible senior liberals in namein four new chairmen for reorganized subcommittees.

McMillan disregarded sixth-ranking committee Democrat Donald M. Fraser (D Minn.) and seventh-ranking Andrew Jacobs Jr. (D Ind.) both of whom were in line to head subcommittees through the seniority system.

The four subcommittee chairmen selected by McMillan, and approved by a 12-3 committee vote, were John Dowdy (D Texas 1952-73), subcommittee on education; Earle Cabell (D Texas 1965-73), subcommittee on business, commerce and fiscal affairs; G. Elliott Hagan (D Ga. 1961-73), subcommittee on public health and welfare, and William L. Hungate (D Mo.), subcommittee on judiciary.

McMillan formed a fifth subcommittee which he indicated would be headed by Fraser. But the Minnesota representative delayed his acceptance, saying the post would be of questionable value until its jurisdiction was known.

Fraser and Jacobs criticized McMillan for relying on seniority to withstand a challenge to his own chairmanship and then disregarding it in the organization of the committee.

After the Feb. 25 committee meeting, McMillan said: "I don't think any chairman in the Congress who has any sense would appoint subcommittee chairmen who wouldn't back him up."

New D.C. Committee Rules. Having failed to oust McMillan from the chairmanship, House District

Committee members in 1971 succeeded in forcing the adoption of new committee rules to curb the chairman's power. In addition to giving the full committee veto power over staff hiring and firing, requiring better advance notice of meetings and opening more committee sessions to the public, the new rules provided for the creation of subcommittees with specific jurisdictions in order to deprive the chairman of his former power to assign bills to any subcommittee he chose.

SENATE ACTION

Senators Fred R. Harris (D Okla. 1964-73) and Charles McC. Mathias (R Md.) led an unsuccessful move to scrap the seniority system at the beginning of the new Congress.

Their proposal would have amended Senate Rule 24 to require that committee chairmen and ranking minority members be nominated individually by majority vote of the party caucuses and elected individually by majority vote of the full Senate at the beginning of each new Congress. Other committee members also would be elected individually, but a plurality would be sufficient for election. The proposal stipulated that the caucuses should not be "bound by any tradition, custom or principle of seniority."

Under existing practice, committee lists—based on seniority—were recommended by the party caucuses and usually approved by the Senate en bloc, although at the insistence of Harris and Mathias committee chairmen were individually elected in 1971.

The Harris-Mathias rules change proposal was adversely reported by the Rules and Administration Committee and tabled (killed) by the Senate March 16 on a 48-26 vote.

In a hearing on the resolution Feb. 12, Mathias said: "I fear that the seniority system as it currently exists in the Senate is dangerously close to creating a crisis of confidence." Mathias said his resolution did not seek to remove any ranking minority committee members in the Senate: "What we seek is not a change in faces but a change in attitude."

Harris, arguing for the resolution, said it "would grant the membership of each caucus and then the full membership of the Senate a real opportunity, and not the present illusory opportunity, to decide whether an incumbent chairman had been doing a satisfactory job, whether he had been responding to his own committee members and to the will of his caucus and the Senate itself on issues and legislation and selection of staff under his committee's jurisdiction."

Robert C. Byrd (D W.Va.), a member of the Rules and Administration Committee who was presiding at the hearing, said he saw "considerable value" in the seniority system, and contended that an open election of committee leaders would be fraught with "politicking" and "logrolling."

Byrd outlined his three major objections to the resolution. First, he said, it would recognize for the first time in the Senate rules the existence of majority and minority party caucuses, and it would set up standards governing their procedures. "I do not believe that there can be any justification whatsoever for a Senate rule governing the procedures of political party caucuses," Byrd said.

Further Seniority Changes

Major changes in the seniority procedure were instituted by House Democrats at the start of the 93rd Congress in January 1973. As approved by the Democratic Caucus Jan. 22, 1973, every committee chairman henceforth was required to win the support of all House Democrats at the beginning of a new Congress. The reform provided that every chairman was to be voted on separately, with a secret ballot required if requested by 20 per cent of the caucus.

Senate Republicans also adopted changes in the way they selected their top-ranking members on the committees. At a party caucus Jan. 9, Republicans approved a proposal requiring the election of each ranking committee member by a majority vote of the Republican membership of the committee. It also required that the person selected as the ranking member of each committee would have to be approved by the entire Republican membership of the Senate.

Second, adoption of the resolution would cause cumbersome, unwieldy and time-consuming delays in expediting Senate business. Byrd said. He said separate votes on the membership of the 17 standing Senate committees would be an exorbitant waste of time.

Third, Byrd said, the resolution would "open the way for such politicking, logrolling, buttonholing, pork-barreling, backslapping and trading in committee caucuses as has never been heard of." He added that it would be best to follow existing rules to "avoid these bloodletting and scar-leaving battles." The White House and special interest groups would apply pressure to have certain members appointed to various committees, he said.

Mathias, referring to the resolution passed by the Senate Republican Caucus when the 92nd Congress convened, said: "There have been changes this very year in the seniority system. This is a subject that no one would have even spoken about in this chamber a few years ago." The Republican Caucus resolution, passed Jan. 26, 1971, stated that each Republican senator could be ranking minority member or chairman of only one standing committee.

LEADERSHIP POSTS

Although the major effort to revise the seniority system failed, steps were made toward broadening access to positions of responsibility.

During consideration of the Legislative Reorganization Act of 1970, both the House and the Senate rejected proposals to modify or abandon the use of seniority in selecting committee chairman.

The 1970 act stipulated, however, that in the future no senator could hold the chairmanship of more than one full committee and one subcommittee of a major committee, but the provision did not apply to chairmanships currently held. The Senate Republican Conference in January 1971 accepted a proposal that each senator could be ranking member on only one standing committee.

The 1970 act's provision limited senators to one major committee chairmanship and subcommittee chairman-ship. Majority Leader Mike Mansfield (D Mont.) announced in February 1971 that in order to promote greater participation in the selection of chairmen, a meeting of the party caucus would be held at the request of any senator, and that any senator would be free to challenge any nomination of a committee chairman. Also, Mansfield said the practice of submitting Steering Commitee nominations of committee chairmen and members to the caucus would be continued as a regular procedure.

Democrats and Republicans alike established committees to study the seniority system. The three-member Democratic committee was composed of Senators Harris, Hubert H. Humphrey (Minn.) and Herman E. Talmadge (Ga.). The five-member Republican committee included Senators Wallace F. Bennett (Utah 1951-73), J. Caleb Boggs (Del. 1961-73), Clifford P. Hansen (Wyo.), Robert W. Packwood (Ore.) and Robert Taft Jr. (Ohio).

Committee Secrecy

1971 Closed Committee Meetings. Congressional committees conducted more than a third of their meetings in private during 1971, the year in which the Legislative Reorganization Act of 1970—aimed, in part, at opening proceedings to the public—went into effect. *(Reorganization act, p. 382)*

Thirty-six per cent of all congressional committee hearings and meetings were held behind closed doors in 1971. This marked a decrease from the 41 per cent recorded in 1970, but matched the secrecy score for 1969. The pattern of the past few Congresses had been to hold more open meetings in the first session than in the second.

The House, as in the past, had the higher percentage of closed meetings. It barred the public from 41 per cent of its committee sessions in 1971. This was down from the 48 per cent of 1970 but comparable to the 42 per cent figure for closed meetings in 1969.

Senate committees had an over-all secrecy score of 30 per cent—less than the 33 per cent of 1970, yet greater than the 28 per cent recorded in 1969. Joint committees continued to report a low number of executive meetings: 20 out of a total of 126.

House Appropriations. One of the noteworthy developments in 1971 was the opening of selected House Appropriations Committee hearings. Although only 8 per cent of its sessions—36 out of a total of 455—were open to the public, this was in contrast to the zero per cent recorded in the past.

The Reorganization Act stipulated that House appropriations budget hearings were to be held in open session, except when the committee determined that the testimony might affect national security.

Roll-Call Votes in Committee. The Legislative Reorganization Act contained a number of provisions affecting the conduct of congressional committee meetings. A main thrust was to bring committee proceedings under public scrutiny. The reform legislation provided for making public the outcome of committee roll-call votes.

The act stipulated that Senate committee business meetings were to be open except for markup (when a committee revises, amends and decides on the final language of a bill) and voting sessions. Senate committees were also permitted to close their business meetings by majority vote.

Ninety-seven per cent of these Senate committee meetings specifically designated in the *Congressional Record's* daily digest as business sessions—organizing, marking-up, voting, briefing sessions—were closed to the public in 1971.

The Reorganization Act also stated that House committee business meetings were to be open, except when a committee closed them by majority vote. Excluding the House Appropriations Committee, 79 per cent of the sessions listed as business meetings in 1971 were held behind closed doors.

Public markup sessions were rare. Most committees preferred to write legislation in private for a variety of reasons. One committee, which held open mark-up sessions in the past but not in 1971, found that the open meetings usually attracted more lobbyists than the public.

Radio and Television Coverage. The Reform Act contained provisions concerning hearings. It required that House and Senate committees, with the exceptions of the Senate Appropriations and House Rules Committees, announce the date, place and subject of hearings at least one week in advance, unless the committee found good cause for beginning them earlier. Provision for radio and television coverage of open committee meetings was contained in the act. Prior to the passage of the act, such coverage was permitted in the Senate but not in the House.

Three years later, in 1973, Congress continued the trend toward opening up committee business begun by the 1970 act. The House March 7 approved a change in its rules to require all House committee hearings to be open to the public unless they dealt with national security or the reputation of witnesses; it also permitted markup sessions to be closed only if a committee, in public session, voted in advance to close them.

(The Senate March 6 approved a much milder change giving each committee the authority to hold open mark-up sessions if it so chose. Previously, Senate Rule 25 prohibited committees from drafting bills in public session.)

Senate Cloture Rule

The almost ritualistic attempt by Senate liberals at the beginning of every Congress to relax the rules for cutting off filibusters failed again in 1971.

As in previous attempts, the effort to ease Senate Rule 22 was stifled by the device which was the target of the drive—the filibuster.

In 1971 four separate votes failed to choke off the filibuster being conducted by the forces defending the existing rule.

Cloture failed by 48-37 on Feb. 18, 50-36 on Feb. 23, 48-36 on March 2 and 55-39 on March 9. All the votes showed a majority in favor of modifying Rule 22, but none received the necessary two-thirds majority.

The debate in 1971 continued intermittently from Jan. 26 to March 9. The lengthy conflict revolved around a resolution (S Res 9) that would have allowed a three-fifths vote rather a two-thirds vote to end a filibuster.

With 51 senators as cosponsors of S Res 9, the anti-filibuster forces had a majority on the record in favor of modifying Rule 22.

Record of Long Sessions

The first session of the 91st Congress, which lasted 355 days, was the sixth longest session in history and the longest since the first session of the 88th Congress (1963). Comparative figures for the other sessions of the 1969-1972 period: 91st Congress, second session (1970)—349 days; 92nd Congress, first session (1971)—331 days; 92nd Congress, second session (1972)—275 days. Since 1961, only the 1968 session, which lasted 274 days, was shorter than the 1972 session. Below are the 20 longest sessions of Congress.

Congress	Session	Convened	Adjourned	No. of Days
76th	3rd	Jan. 3,	1940-Jan. 3, 1941	366
77th	1st	Jan. 3,	1941-Jan. 2, 1942	365
81st	2nd	Jan. 3,	1950-Jan. 2, 1951	365 [1]
80th	2nd	Jan. 6,	1948-Dec. 31, 1948	361 [2]
88th	1st	Jan. 9,	1963-Dec. 30, 1963	356
91st	1st	Jan. 3,	1969-Dec. 23, 1969	355 [3]
65th	2nd	Dec. 3,	1917-Nov. 21, 1918	354
79th	1st	Jan. 3,	1945-Dec. 21, 1945	353 [4]
80th	1st	Jan. 3,	1947-Dec. 19, 1947	351 [5]
78th	1st	Jan. 6,	1943-Dec. 21, 1943	350 [6]
91st	2nd	Jan. 19,	1970-Jan. 2, 1971	349 [7]
77th	2nd	Jan. 5,	1942-Dec. 16, 1942	346
40th	2nd	Dec. 2,	1867-Nov. 10, 1868	345 [8]
78th	2nd	Jan. 10,	1944-Dec. 19, 1944	345 [9]
90th	1st	Jan. 10,	1967-Dec. 15, 1967	340
92nd	1st	Jan. 21,	1971-Dec. 17, 1971	331 [10]
83rd	2nd	Jan. 6,	1954-Dec. 2, 1954	331 [11]
63rd	2nd	Dec. 1,	1913-Oct. 24, 1914	328
50th	1st	Dec. 5,	1887-Oct. 20, 1888	321
51st	1st	Dec. 2,	1889-Oct. 1, 1890	304

1 *Congress recessed from Sept. 23 to Nov. 27.*
2 *Congress recessed from June 20 to July 26 and Aug. 7 to Dec. 31.*
3 *Congress recessed from Aug. 15 to Sept. 3.*
4 *The House was in recess from July 21 to Sept. 5 and the Senate from Aug 1 to Sept. 5.*
5 *Congress recessed from July 27 to Nov. 17.*
6 *Congress recessed from July 8 to Sept. 14.*
7 *The House recessed from Aug. 14 to Sept. 9, and both houses recessed from Oct. 14 to Nov. 16 for the 1970 election campaign.*
8 *No business was transacted after July 27. Congress took three recesses between July 27 and Nov. 10.*
9 *Congress recessed from April 1 to 12, July 23 to Aug. 1 and Sept. 21 to Nov. 14.*
10 *Congress recessed from Aug. 6 to Sept. 8.*
11 *The House adjourned sine die on Aug. 20. The Senate was in recess from Aug. 20 to Nov. 8 and from Nov. 18 to Nov. 29, and adjourned sine die on Dec. 2.*

Senate Action. Opening the debate Jan. 26, James B. Pearson (R Kan.) said Rule 22 needed adjustment if the "two most fundamental rights possessed by members of the Senate—the right to debate and the right to vote—are to be justly balanced." Pearson said he would not support a change to permit cloture by a simple majority but that he believed the Senate had a constitutional right to change its rules at the beginning of a new Congress.

Frank Church (D Idaho) said Rule 22 constituted "a virtually insurmountable barrier." He added that "the record cannot disclose the many times that cloture had not even been attempted, due to the foreknowledge that the attempt would prove futile."

Initial opposition to the Church-Pearson proposal was led by Senators James B. Allen (D Ala.) and Sam J. Ervin Jr. (D N.C.) "Rule 22," said Allen, "protects the minority from the will of an arrogant majority. If we ever get to the point that 60 per cent of the Senate is to apply its will against an outvoted minority without debate, our country is in great danger."

A substitute to S Res 9 was offered Jan. 26 by Senators Jacob K. Javits (R N.Y.) and Philip A. Hart (D Mich.). The substitute would have permitted a simple majority of senators present and voting to cut off debate.

Proponents of the three-fifths requirement suffered a setback Jan. 26 when Vice President Agnew, presiding over the Senate, gave an opinion indicating that he would not rule that a simple majority could cut off debate and force a final vote on filibuster reform.

Church also termed unacceptable a plan mentioned by Robert C. Byrd (D W. Va.) to reduce the cutoff figure to three-fifths of the entire membership of the Senate (60 votes) instead of three-fifths of those present and voting.

Such a change, Church said, would hardly be an improvement on the current requirement of two-thirds, which—when there are absentees—can allow fewer than 60 senators to invoke cloture.

Opposition Arguments. Opponents of S Res 9 based their floor arguments on three main points:

• The Senate's tradition of unlimited debate was a vital element in the Senate's claim to being "the world's greatest deliberative body."

• The filibuster protected the minority against the will of an arrogant majority or a powerful presidency.

• Southern and small-population states were guaranteed a hearing on national issues because of the extended debate allowed by the two-thirds majority rule.

Tactics used in 1971 by senators opposed to a change in Rule 22 varied somewhat from those used in previous debates on attempts to modify the two-thirds requirement. The new arguments had as their basis the following points:

• During the 1960s, the filibuster was used primarily against civil rights legislation. Virtually all of the major civil rights bills eventually passed, although they were substantially improved because of the delay provided by extended debate. Thus, the pressure for altering Rule 22 had abated greatly.

• The possible ascendancy of conservative trends in the country could make the filibuster a necessary tool of liberal senators in working aginst "repressive" or "reactionary" legislation.

• The power of the executive branch had outgrown that of the legislative branch, particularly regarding war-making and foreign policy decisions. Congressional power would be diminished if the influence of the filibuster were weakened.

Alternative Cloture Proposals. Various alternatives were suggested to the three-fifths proposal for modifying Rule 22. All alternative plans were rejected by sponsors of S Res 9:

• A resolution (S Res 14) introduced by Jack Miller (R Iowa) to assure bipartisanship in any debate cutoff. It would have reduced the cloture requirement to three-fifths but required the three-fifths to include a majority of

---

Liberals and the Filibuster

A change of heart by many Senate liberals of their position on the filibuster occurred in December 1970 when opponents of the supersonic transport (SST) aircraft succeeded in killing a bill containing funds to continue development of the plane. This led in 1971 to a cancellation of the entire project.

Later that year, similar coalitions of liberal and moderate Democrats and Republicans used the filibuster against a bill extending the military draft, a proposed loan to the Lockheed Aircraft Corporation, President Nixon's nomination of William H. Rehnquist as an associate justice of the Supreme Court, further funding of the Vietnam war and funding for various military weapons programs.

Although liberal senators in the past occasionally used the filibuster, notably against a plan of the late Republican Minority Leader in the Senate Everett M. Dirksen (R Ill. 1951-69) to delay implementation of a Supreme Court decision requiring both houses of a state legislature to be apportioned on the basis of population, its use by liberals beginning in 1970 appeared to be the first widespread re-evaluation of their position on Rule 22, since the 1930s and 1940s when the filibuster came to be identified with the effort by southerners to block civil rights legislation.

In 1972 the trend continued as Senate liberals succeeded through use of the filibuster in killing a strong anti-busing bill actively pushed by President Nixon. It was also used, although unsuccessfully, against an amendment to add certain reservations to the agreement on offensive nuclear weapons.

1972 Votes Compared. The most dramatic change in senators' reconsideration of the filibuster came at the end of the 92nd Congress. Two major bills considered in the last month of the session—to set up an independent consumer protection agency and to curb the use of school busing to achieve integration—provoked filibusters supported by almost entirely different groups of senators. A talkathon backed by the traditional coalition of southern Democrats and Republicans successfully blocked cloture on the consumer protection bill, while northern Democrats and a few liberal and moderate Republicans succeeded in stoping the anti-busing bill.

Three cloture votes were taken on each bill. A total of only 49 senators voted for cloture on the busing issue. Stated another way, a majority of Democrats (32) and a significant minority of Republicans (19) refused to end a filibuster against it. These senators consisted of a majority of liberals and moderates in their party who in past years supported efforts to modify Rule 22.

A total of 53 senators voted for cloture at least once on the consumer agency bill. But of these 58 senators, only 17 had also voted for cloture on the busing issue.

---

each party. In the 12 successful attempts between 1917 and 1972 to end a Senate filibuster; a majority of senators from both major parties voted for cloture on all but

(Continued on p. 374)

1971 Capitol Bombing Caused Extensive Damage...

Early in 1971, the Capitol suffered extensive damage when a powerful bomb exploded in the original part of the building for which George Washington laid the cornerstone in 1793. Damage was estimated at $200,000, but there were no injuries.

Site of the explosion was an unmarked rest room on the ground floor of the Senate wing. The blast demolished the rest room and caused extensive damage to six other rooms, including the Senate barbershop, a hearing room of the Senate Appropriations Committee and hideaway offices used by several senators.

Telephone Warning

The explosion occurred at 1:32 a.m. on March 1— 33 minutes after a telephone caller warned the Capitol switchboard: "This building will blow up in 30 minutes. You will get many calls like this, but this one is real. Evacuate the building. This is in protest against the Nixon involvement in Laos."

Immediately after the warning call, a search of the Capitol building was conducted by the 15 members of the Capitol police force then on duty. Their search took them to the general area of the rest room, but they did not check the room itself, they said, because it had been inspected only a few minutes before the call was received.

Subsequently, an army munitions expert told a Senate subcommittee "it is our belief" that the explosive had been concealed behind a false wall in the rest room. He speculated the blast could have been caused by 15 to 20 pounds of dynamite connected to a "delayed timing device" and smuggled into the Capitol "in an ordinary briefcase." It was noted that the building had been open to tourists until 4:30 p.m. on the day preceding the bombing, a Sunday, and that while entrances to the Capitol were routinely guarded, no check of visitors or inspection of parcels was customary.

Responsibility for Explosion

Responsibility for the blast was promptly claimed by a group calling itself the Weather Underground. In identical letters to *The New York Times* and the Associated Press, the group wrote: "We have attacked the Capitol because it is, along with the White House and the Pentagon, the worldwide symbol of the government which is now attacking Indochina."

Some government officials, however, expressed doubt that the bombing was the result of a conspiracy. Attorney General John Mitchell said March 2 that the evidence pointed to "less than a conspiracy." "Every time we have one of these occurrences there are such communications," he said. "but it doesn't mean they were actually involved." The Federal Bureau of Investigation (FBI), which was investigating the explosion, had no comment.

Meanwhile, FBI questioning of Capitol employees prompted speculation that the bombing might have been the work of a congressional employee. Although access to the Capitol was free, the rest room where the bomb was placed was not only unmarked but opened off a small corridor not used by the general public. Even the janitor who cleaned the room reportedly did not know that the enclosure where the bomb was thought to have been hidden had a top that could be lifted off.

A week after the explosion, Senate leaders announced that an anonymous donor had offered a $100,-000 reward for information leading to the arrest and conviction of the bomber.

The first publicized move in the investigation of the bombing occurred April 27 when government agents took Leslie Bacon, 19, into custody as a material witness with a personal knowledge of the bombing. The FBI said Miss Bacon was also suspected of participation in the bombing.

Miss Bacon, whose home was in Atherton, Calif., was arrested in Washington, D.C., where she was working on plans for an antiwar protest. She was charged with no crime but was held under $100,000 bond as a witness for a grand jury in Seattle, Wash., which was investigating the bombing.

A letter signed "Weather Underground," made public May 3, said Miss Bacon was "completely innocent of any involvement in the bombing of the U.S. Capitol." The letter, addressed to Miss Bacon's mother, said: "We know this for a fact because as the FBI and Justice Department well know, our organization did the bombing."

Reaction to Incident

President Nixon and congressional leaders viewed the bombing as a symbolic attack on the government itself and agreed on the importance of keeping the Capitol open to the public. The President said that "necessary protective action" should be taken but that "the important thing is that these great buildings not be closed to the public." Senate Majority Leader Mike Mansfield (D Mont.) called the incident "outrageous and sacrilegious." Senate Minority Leader Hugh Scott (R Pa.) said it was a political act of terrorism by groups "who believe that if they cannot persuade by reason or by logic, perhaps they can terrify the American people." Sen. George McGovern (D S.D.) attributed the bombing to "our Vietnam madness."

Tighter Security Proposed

In the wake of the bombing, there was widespread agreement on the need for additional security measures on Capitol Hill. The Capitol was briefly closed to visitors on the morning following the bombing but was reopened at midday. Thereafter Capitol police were instructed to check all briefcases and large packages brought into the Capitol itself and the Senate and House office buildings by employees as well as tourists. The bombing site remained closed pending repairs.

...Incident Linked to Vietnam War Protests

On March 2, the Senate Public Works Subcommittee on Public Buildings and Grounds held a hearing on the bombing incident at which Senate Sergeant at Arms Robert G. Dunphy and Capitol Police Chief James M. Powell testified on the difficulties of protecting the Capitol. Powell said "200 to 300 bomb threats" had been received at the Capitol in the past few years, and "each call is treated as a real threat." However, said Dunphy, "Remember, we have six large buildings. The Capitol is like a Swiss cheese with all its tunnels and crannies and catacombs. We also have 150 acres of ground. When we say we conduct a search, we do the best we can."

Dunphy said that during the tourist season as many as 25,000 visitors pass through the Rotunda daily and that thorough inspection of all visitors would be extremely difficult. Powell recommended that certain out-of-the-way sections of the Capitol be closed to the public in the interest of security. He also suggested curtailment of patronage appointments to the Capitol police force. Patronage appointees constituted about 25 per cent of the authorized force of 622 officers, he said.

The bombing prompted a number of calls by members of Congress for installation of closed-circuit television systems and electronic devices to detect bombs or dangerous weapons. Dunphy said, however, that the Capitol Police Board had investigated such systems and had not found any that would be satisfactory.

Nevertheless, the incident gave impetus to the work of a special commission directed to plan and oversee the modernization of the House galleries, including the enclosure of the galleries with soundproof glass. The project was authorized under the Legislative Reorganization Act of 1970, but at the time of the bombing commission members had not been named by House Speaker Carl Albert (D Okla.). Although noise reduction was the stated purpose of the enclosure, 1970 House debate on the proposal made it clear that at least some representatives—recalling the March 1, 1954, shooting of five members by Puerto Rican nationalists—had security in mind as well.

Extent of Damage

During its March 2 hearings, the Senate subcommittee also heard testimony on the extent of the bomb damage from George M. White, newly appointed Architect of the Capitol. White said there was apparently no structural damage to the building and that the West Front had "not been damaged in any way," although it was only about 40 feet from the site of the explosion. White's predecessor, J. George Stewart, had contended that the West Front was so structurally weak as to be endangered by vibrations from aircraft flying overhead and had promoted a $34-million project to extend the West Front and add 4.5 acres of new space to the Capitol.

An earlier report by the Architect's Office said: "The damage consists primarily of cracked and otherwise damaged walls, blown-out doors and windows, destruction of trim, paneled jambs, weakened and damaged masonry floor, arch construction and damage to chandeliers." The report said that "some of the weakened arch construction undoubtedly will require shoring."

Antiwar Protests

The Capitol bombing occurred at a time when antiwar groups were mounting a new series of demonstrations against U.S. involvement in Southeast Asia. Although Washington had been the scene of numerous antiwar protests for several years, prior to 1971 most of the major protests had not focused on the Capitol itself.

The 1971 round of demonstrations began April 18-23 when about 2,300 Vietnam veterans came to Washington to participate in what they called Dewey Canyon III—"a military incursion into the country of Congress." Led by the Vietnam Veterans Against the War, the former soldiers camped on the Mall a quarter of a mile from the Capitol, marched to Arlington Cemetery to pay their respects to war dead, conducted guerrilla theater and a mock search and destroy mission on the steps of the Old Senate Office Building, threw away military medals and ribbons at the foot of the bronze statue of Chief Justice John Marshall on the west side of the Capitol and attempted to visit every member of Congress.

On April 24, a rally sponsored by the National Peace Action Coalition drew an estimated 175,000 persons to the steps leading to the Capitol's West Front, for what was believed to have been the largest demonstration ever held there. Although the event was peaceful, strict security was maintained at House and Senate office buildings, and the Capitol itself was protected by a barricade.

The April 24 demonstration was followed by 10 days of escalating protests that began April 26 with lobbying of Congress and disruption in the Senate galleries and congressional office buildings. In the days that followed, the protesters—who called themselves the Mayday Tribe—attempted work stoppages at the Departments of Justice and Health, Education and Welfare, the Internal Revenue Service and Selective Service headquarters.

On May 3, the protesters made an unsuccessful attempt to halt morning rush-hour traffic into Washington. They were met by 5,100 Washington policemen, backed by 10,000 federal troops; the result was an unprecedented mass arrest of approximately 7,000 persons. The following day an additional 2,700 demonstrators were arrested. The protest ended May 5 with the arrest of another 1,200 demonstrators on the steps of the Capitol's East Front during a rally attended by some members of Congress. Many groups called the procedures used in the week's arrests illegal.

one occasion—a majority of Democrats refused to end a filibuster against extension of the military draft on Sept. 21, 1971.

• A resolution (S Res 50) providing that the first cloture vote on a motion start with a two-thirds requirement, and that the requirement be reduced by one vote on each successive vote until, after eight attempts, it dropped to a three-fifths requirement.

• A proposal leaving the debate cutoff figure at two-thirds for the first three weeks of debate on any bill, then reducing it to three-fifths.

• A proposal that would have installed the three-fifths cutoff for filibusters against everything but further rules changes, for which the two-thirds requirement would be retained.

Javits' Motion. After the fourth and final cloture attempt failed March 9, Jacob K. Javits (R N.Y.) rose to appeal the ruling of President Pro Tempore Allen J. Ellender (D La.) that the vote had failed because it had not obtained a two-thirds majority.

Javits' challenge was in response to a Jan. 26 decision by Vice President Agnew that a two-thirds majority vote was needed to shut off debate before the Senate could consider a change in its own rules.

"We are really now tangled up in our own feet in a procedural mess that is unbelievable and one out of which the Senate cannot work its will except by action of the Vice President," Javits said.

A motion by Majority Leader Mike Mansfield (D Mont.) to table Javits' motion was approved by a 55-37 vote, thus killing the motion. Explained Mansfield: "I have said time and time and time again that I am against a mere majority vote to bring about a change in the rules, because I think to do so would alter the position of the Senate in our scheme of government. If the (Javits) appeal were upheld, then it would be only a matter of time before a majority would be able to cut off debate on any issue. That is the real issue at this time. The heart of the institution is at stake."

31-Day Rule

The House Jan. 22, 1971, voted to strip from a set of proposed House rules a provision that would have cleared the way for floor action on bills held up by the House Rules Committee. A coalition of Republicans and southern Democrats killed a proposed 31-day rule for bypassing the Rules Committee. The proposal had been approved by the Democratic caucus Jan. 21 and by Speaker Carl Albert (D Okla.).

The proposed rule would have provided a 10-day grace period for committee chairmen to file a request with the Rules Committee to report a rule on a specific measure. If such a rule were not given within 21 days after the request, the speaker could recognize a committee chairman for the purpose of calling up the bill.

Background. Virtually all major bills must receive clearance by the Rules Committee before they could be debated on the House floor. The committee, a traditionally conservative body, had been blamed by some liberals for bottling up legislation. The power of the committee lay in its role of scheduling time for debate on those important and usually controversial bills that were not disposed of by the more routine procedures of the House.

Although the Rules Committee could be bypassed by discharge petitions, suspension of the rules and certain seldom-used parliamentary techniques, these procedures were not normally successful.

The first adoption of a 21-day rule, in 1949, was one of a number of attempts by House reformers to curb the power of the Rules Committee. The rule provided that if the Rules Committee did not grant a rule for consideration of a bill by the House within 21 days of a request for a rule, the speaker could call upon the legislative committee that had favorably reported the bill to draft a rule for consideration of a bill. The 21-day rule was repealed in 1951 after the Democrats lost 29 seats in the 1950 elections.

At the beginning of the Kennedy administration in 1961, House Democrats, led by Speaker Sam Rayburn (D Texas 1913-61), enlarged the membership of the Rules Committee and filled the new seats in such a way as to give administration supporters a one-vote majority. The administration forces, however, did not always hold together, and several administration bills were defeated as a result. In 1965, the House adopted the 21-day rule again—the first time since 1949. But in 1967, on the opening day of the 90th Congress, the House voted to repeal the 21-day rule, and it has not been in effect since (through the January 1973 adoption of the rules for the 93rd Congress).

During the 89th Congress, the House used the rule successfully eight times. But most observers believed that the threat of its use was instrumental in bringing about release of other bills from the Rules Committee. *(Background, Congress and the Nation Vol. II p. 903, 911)*

Floor Action. Opposition to the 31-day proposal was led by Rep. William M. Colmer (D Miss. 1933-73), chairman of the Rules Committee. He said that "the language of the resolution...provides for what I consider the liquidation of the Rules Committee."

Richard Bolling (D Mo.), third-ranking Democrat on the Rules Committee and a long-time proponent of House reform, said the committee should be an adjunct to the majority leadership, with final power resting with the speaker. Bolling said the absence of a 31-day rule deluded the American public as to who was responsible for House action. "Why is it that the American people should be kidded? Why should not the majority party have the right to exercise its responsibility to bring to the floor of the House and have debated and voted up or down the legislation it favors? That is all this...rule will assure," Bolling said.

The House adopted an amendment offered by B. F. Sisk (D Calif.), deleting from the resolution (H Res 5) language containing the 31-day proposal. The vote was 234-153.

Other 1971 Developments

CIA SUBCOMMITTEE. The House Armed Services Committee in 1971 established a new Subcommittee on Intelligence Operations which was to be responsible for reviewing the programs of all intelligence operations paid for by the United States. Included on the list of agencies under the subcommittee's jurisdiction were the Central Intelligence Agency, the Defense Intelligence Agency of the Department of Defense and the National Security Agency. A CIA Oversight Subcommittee had been abolished by Chairman F. Edward Hebert when he replaced L. Mendel Rivers (D S.C. 1941-70).

SENATE GIRL PAGES. The Senate May 13, 1971, by voice vote passed a resolution (S Res 112) permitting the appointment of girl pages in the Senate. The first two girl pages were sworn in the following day.

A controversy over girl pages arose at the beginning of the 92nd Congress when three senators—Jacob K. Javits (R N.Y.), Charles H. Percy (R Ill.) and Fred R. Harris (D Okla. 1964-73)—attempted to appoint girl pages. Pages must be students and at least 14 years old; they were appointed on a patronage basis and paid $7,380 annually. Senate rules did not specify that the pages must be boys, but the Senate Sergeant at Arms in 1971, Robert G. Dunphy, had refused to enroll girls on the payroll without approval of the Senate Rules and Administration Committee or the full Senate.

The Rules Committee, which established an ad hoc subcommittee to consider the appointment of female pages in the Senate, on May 10 reported the resolution (S Rept 92-101). The committee amended the original language to allow the appointment of girl elevator operators, post office employees and Capitol policemen as well as pages. Another amendment specified that until a Capitol page school with dormitories was built, the senator who appointed a girl page must take responsibility for her. *(John W. McCormack Residential Page School, see provisions of 1970 reorganization act p. 382)*

S Res 112 also specified that the minimum age for pages be raised to 16 and that the Senate Appropriations Committee review page salaries.

HOUSE ALLOWANCES. The House in July 1971 passed a resolution providing procedural changes in allocating contingency funds. By a 233-167 roll-call vote, the House July 21 passed H Res 457 allowing the House Administration Committee to fix and adjust amounts of allowances for various perquisite expenses.

The resolution made possible the regulation by the committee of expenditures from the contingent fund in the House without bringing separate resolutions to the House floor for each proposed change. Expenditures from the contingent fund cover such areas as postage and stationery, telephone and telegraph charges, clerk hire, office space in the home district and travel to and from the home district.

SECRECY COMMITTEE. In the aftermath of Sen. Mike Gravel's (D Alaska) attempt in May 1972 to insert in the *Congressional Record* excerpts from a secret 1969 Vietnam war study, the Senate Aug. 15, 1972, voted to establish a special committee to study questions related to secret and confidential government documents.

By voice vote, the Senate passed S 299, authorizing the creation of a special 10-member committee to study "all questions relating to secrecy, confidentiality and classification of government documents committed to the Senate or any member thereof."

Jacob K. Javits (R N.Y.), sponsor of the resolution, said the committee would have authority to study the use of executive privilege to deny information to Congress, recommend creation of a permanent mechanism to consider members' requests to declassify documents and perform that function itself until a permanent mechanism was created.

The resolution was drawn up in May after the Senate spent parts of several days debating the propriety of making public information that had been classified by the executive branch. *(Congressional Ethics, p. 412)*

The Senate May 8 deferred action on S Res 299 after Roman L. Hruska (R Neb.) objected to Javits' request that the measure be considered immediately.

Before passing the resolution, the Senate by voice vote approved an amendment recommended by a Government Operations Subcommittee requiring the special committee to report its recommendations by Feb. 15, 1973. The Senate June 22 had referred S Res 299 to the Government Operations Committee with instructions that it be reported back by Aug. 7.

Ten senators were appointed Sept. 22, 1972, to the ad hoc committee created by S Res 299.

Majority Leader Mike Mansfield (D Mont.) and Minority Leader Hugh Scott (R Pa.) were named chairman and cochairman of the committee. Other members were Democrats John O. Pastore (R.I.), Harold E. Hughes (Iowa), Alan Cranston (Calif.) and Gravel; and Republicans Jacob K. Javits (N.Y.), Mark O. Hatfield (Ore.), Edward J. Gurney (Fla.) and Marlow W. Cook (Ky.).

HOUSE COMPUTER FUNDING. The House Nov. 9, 1971, by voice vote passed with amendments a resolution (H Res 601) authorizing $1.5-million for computer services for the House during the remainder of the 92nd Congress.

Passage of the resolution transferred computer operations in the House from the Data Processing Office of the House Clerk to the House Administration Committee.

The computer system eventually was intended to incorporate an electronic voting system in the House which was authorized by the 1970 Legislative Reorganization Act and put into operation at the beginning of the 93rd Congress. *(See p. 382)*

Besides the automatic floor voting system, the committee said it anticipated development of a bill status system, a bill drafting and editing system, a legislative search and retrieval system, an automated constitutent mail system and analytical assistance for committees.

Items already handled by computer included the House payroll, reports on members' allowance, office equipment inventory, the clerk's semi-annual report and a vote history system.

A House Administration Committee report cited a study made by the Stanford Research Institute early in 1971 that "emphasized the need and utility of a computer system which progressively strengthens and supports the legislative process in the House of Representatives." The report showed that the House utilized only one computer for its operations, compared to four computers for the Agency for International Development, 41 computers for the Veterans Administration and 2,668 for the Department of Defense.

The inability of the House to utilize computer-generated information is a serious handicap under which Congress, its committees and its members operate," the committee concluded.

CAPITOL POLICE EXPANSION. The House June 2, 1971, by voice vote passed a resolution (H Res 449) increasing the number of Capitol policemen by 214.

The resolution brought to 569 the number of policemen assigned to the House side of the Capitol and the House office buildings. No Senate action was required.

The Senate planned to add about 140 men to the force assigned to its side of the Capitol and the Senate

Hays' New Role as the Housekeeper of the House

Rep Wayne L. Hays (D Ohio), who became chairman of the House Administration Committee in 1971, distributed numerous fringe benefits available to House members, such as telephone, travel, postage and stationery allowances, and office space. One observer said of Hays' position: "His IOUs are piling up like paperwork at the Pentagon. He's built an empire out of that little committee."

Hays acknowledged the advantages of his new job when he first took over as chairman: "It's a great place. Every time a committee chairman comes in and you do him a favor, you're in a position to ask one in return."

The committee's jurisdiction also includes oversight over employment of all House personnel, the Library of Congress, Botanic Garden, Smithsonian Institution, printing and editing of the *Congressional Record*, data processing and matters related to federal elections such as corrupt practices, contested elections and qualifications for candidacy.

AUTONOMY OVER HOUSE OPERATIONS

The most severely criticized action by the committee under Hays' leadership was the introduction of a resolution (H Res 457), adopted by the House July 21, 1971, allowing the committee to bestow special allowances and benefits for House members without requiring any debate or vote by the House.

The resolution, which gave Hays' committee virtually autonomous authority over most House internal operations, was termed privately by some members as a "blatant power grab" which most members were afraid to vote against for fear of offending the committee chairman.

"The fundamental reason for this (the resolution) is to spare the House the time consumed each session in considering eight or 10 privileged resolutions on these various subjects...and to modernize a really ancient and absurd practice of bringing to the floor every bit of minutia with respect to the routine daily operations of this side of the Congress," said Rep. Frank Thompson Jr. (D N.J.), a member of Hays' committee.

The resolution was opposed by Rep. William L. Dickinson (R Ala.), who said "the taxpayers' interest is best protected by the scrutiny that comes from the searchlight of public disclosure on the floor of the House." Rep. James C. Cleveland (R N.H.), a member of Hays' committee, added: "It seems strange to me that with all the talk we hear about the public's right to know, we propose to hide from the public the matter of our allowances, some of which are already too generous." The resolution was approved by a 233-167 roll-call vote which divided closely on party lines.

OTHER COMMITTEE ACTIONS

During 1971, Hays' committee recommended and the House approved the addition of 214 policemen to the Capitol force. Through the authority granted by H Res 457, Hays' committee increased postage and home office rent allowances, altered travel and telephone allowances and made changes in the amount of extraneous material that could be printed in the *Congressional Record*.

Hays directed the removal from the House clerk's authority supervision of the new computer and data retrieval systems in the House, and he became involved in a dispute with House Clerk W. Pat Jennings (D Va., 1955-67) over enforcement of the 1971 campaign spending law.

Hays' colleagues were quick to give him credit for making long-overdue changes in the management of the House restaurants, which showed a deficit in fiscal 1971 of $379,000. Under Hays' supervision, the deficit was reduced substantially.

On Feb. 24, 1972, Hays announced another decision designed to cut costs—creation of the Special Subcommittee on Nonessential Employees. The body was to investigate how many unnecessary employees were on the House payroll. "Right now we don't even know for sure how many employees we have or what the payroll actually is," said Hays. One estimate by the House clerk's office showed about 7,500 House employees with a monthly payroll of $7.5-million.

---

office buildings, it was disclosed during the House debate on H Res 449. Such a move would increase the Capitol police force to about 1,000 officers.

Concern over the protection of the Capitol and other congressional buildings had increased since March 1 when a bomb exploded in a first-floor men's room in the Senate side of the Capitol. *(p. 372.)*

1972

The second session of the 92nd Congress, which convened at noon Jan. 18, 1972, adjourned Oct. 18, 1972. The session ran 275 days, compared to 331 days for the 1971 session. Since 1961, only the 1968 session, which lasted 274 days and adjourned on Oct. 14, was shorter than the 1972 session.

Although the 1972 session ran nine months. Congress did not actually work all that time. The Senate was in session 162 days and the House was in session 135 days. Congress took several short recesses during the year, and two longer recesses, from June 30 to July 17 for the Democratic national convention, and from Aug. 18 until Sept. 5 for the Republican national convention.

There were 7,208 bills and resolutions introduced in the session, a substantial decrease from the 18,146 measures introduced in the first session.

Decreases in the second year of a Congress were normal, since bills introduced in the first session remain pending in the second session.

The President signed 483 bills into law in 1972. He vetoed 16 public bills. Twelve of the vetoes were pocket vetoes after adjournment of the 92nd Congress on Oct. 18, 1972.

The Senate took 532 roll-call votes during the session, and the House took 329 recorded votes, a new record for each chamber. The previous records, set in 1971, were 423 for the Senate, and 320 for the House.

The Senate in 1972 voted 10 times on motions to invoke cloture. Of these only two were successful—votes on Feb. 23 and Sept. 14 to end debate on an equal job opportunity bill and the proposed U.S.-Soviet Strategic Arms Limitation (SALT) agreement. The vote on the equal jobs bill was 71-23; on the SALT agreement, 76-15.

The 10 votes in 1972 equaled the record set in 1971 for the most cloture votes in a single session; and the 20 votes for the two sessions set the record for an entire Congress.

Committee Secrecy

Congressional committees conducted 40 percent of their hearings and other meetings behind closed doors in 1972, the year after the Legislative Reorganization Act of 1970, aimed in part at opening such proceedings to the public, took effect.

In 1971, during the first session of the 92nd Congress, 36 per cent of all congressional committee meetings were held in secret. *(p. 369)* But, in recent years, more closed meetings had been held in the second session of a Congress when the number of mark-up meetings, during which bills are drafted and amendments voted upon, increases.

The percentage of committee meetings held in secret during second sessions remained relatively constant over the period beginning in 1966. The 40 per cent figure in 1972 compared with 42 per cent in 1966, 43 per cent in 1968 and 41 per cent in 1970.

As in the past, the House barred the public from its committee meetings more often than the Senate did. Forty-four per cent of all House meetings were closed, higher than the 1971 figure of 41 per cent but lower than the 1970 figure of 48 per cent.

Senate committees had an over-all secrecy rating of 36 per cent—up from 30 per cent in 1971 and 33 per cent in 1970. Joint committees continued to report a low number of executive sessions: 13 out of 90.

Challenge to House Procedure

In an unprecedented challenge to traditional parliamentary procedure, two members of the House on Feb. 29, 1972, effectively blocked consideration of 18 of 22 minor tax bills scheduled to be called up under the unanimous consent procedure by Chairman Wilbur D. Mills (D Ark.) of the Ways and Means Committee.

Such bills, known as members' bills because they were proposed by House members rather than drafted by a committee, previously had been approved with little or no debate. About fifty such bills were passed in 1971.

The bills were intended to correct alleged tax inequities which affected a single company, industry or other special interest. But often such bills authorized tax breaks exempting millions of dollars from federal taxes.

Chairman Wright Patman (D Texas) of the Banking and Currency Committee attacked the unanimous consent procedure used by Mills Feb. 29 to bring the bills to the floor. Bills called up under this procedure in the past

Closed Committee Meetings

Since 1953, when Congressional Quarterly began its annual study of open and closed committee meetings, 25,368—or an annual average of 37 per cent—of the 68,305 meetings reported have been closed to the public. In the period since 1965, when meetings of the House Appropriations Committee were added to the study, the percentage of meetings that have been closed increased to 40 per cent. Statistics on committee meetings are given below.

Year	Total Meetings	Number Closed	Percent Closed
1953	2,640*	892	35%*
1954	3,002*	1,243	41*
1955	2,940*	1,055	36*
1956	3,120*	1,130	36*
1957	2,517*	854	34*
1958	3,472*	1,167	34*
1959	3,152*	940	30*
1960	2,424*	840	35*
1961	3,159*	1,109	35
1962	2,929*	991	34*
1963	3,868*	1,463	38*
1964	2,393*	763	32*
1965	3,903	1,537	39
1966	3,869	1,626	42
1967	4,412	1,716	39
1968	3,080	1,328	43
1969	4,029	1,470	36
1970	4,506	1,865	41
1971	4,816	1,731	36
1972	4,073	1,648	40
TOTAL*	68,305	25,368	37%

*Meetings of the House Appropriations Committee, all reported to have been closed until 1971, were not included in the study until 1965.

had routinely been considered and passed in one step by voice vote if no objections were heard.

Patman said that members were not given the information needed to vote wisely on the bills because no hearings had been held. In many cases, he asserted, they involved changes in law or losses in tax revenue which should be given closer consideration.

Patman repeatedly complained that Mills had called up the bills under a gag rule prohibiting amendments. According to the House parliamentarian, however, floor amendments were permitted under unanimous consent. But Mills did not volunteer the information that such amendments were permissible.

Patman blocked consideration of two bills and Les Aspin (D Wis.), a member of the liberal Democratic Study Group, objected to a third; four were passed. Mills did not call up the 15 remaining measures.

Capitol West Front

Senate opponents of the west front extension succeeded in 1972 in adding language to the fiscal 1973 legislative branch appropriations bill (PL 92-342) prohibiting the use of any funds previously appropriated from being used for drawing up plans or for construction of the extension of the west front of the Capitol unless specificially authorized in subsequent legislation. The Senate Appropriations Committee had added the language after the Commission for the Extension of the Capitol *(see related 1969 action)* March 8, 1972, had recommended the extension and called for the drafting of final plans.

The Senate's action approving the prohibition, which followed the defeat by a 35-40 vote of a weakening amendment, held up the bill in a House-Senate conference committee for almost three months. Conferees never were able to reach a compromise and the prohibition was returned to the House which, after a lengthy debate and the failure of motions to alter the Senate's language, finally approved it by voice vote. The key action in the House was the defeat by a 181-197 recorded teller vote of a motion proposed by Rep. Bob Casey (D Texas) which would have permitted use of the $2-million-plus appropriation approved in 1969 for drawing up final plans for the extension.

The Senate victory by opponents of an extension was only temporary however. On April 17, 1973, the House approved an appropriation of $58-million which, along with the $2-million left over from 1969, was estimated by the House Appropriations Committee to be sufficient for the entire extension project. A vote on an amendment to delete the $58-million failed by a 189-195 recorded teller vote. There was no Senate action through May.

Senate Office Addition

The Senate in 1972 approved legislation (S 3917) to authorize construction of an addition to the New Senate Office Building and the purchase of land for additional parking facilities for senators and their staffs.

The House, however, took no action on the bill and it died at the end of the 92nd Congress. It was the second time in two years that the House had failed to approve the additional office space. In 1970 the House had failed to act on a bill (S 3594) passed by the Senate to authorize the purchase of property for the Senate addition.

S 3917 would have authorized the completion of the New Senate Office Building as originally planned when its construction was begun in 1955. Expansion of the building would double the number of offices and meeting rooms in the existing structure.

By a unanimous vote, the Senate adopted an amendment imposing a $53.5-million spending ceiling on building costs and directing the Public Works Committee to ensure "its economical construction."

The Architect of the Capitol estimated that the total cost of land purchases and construction authorized by S 3917 would be $53.5-million. Extension of the New Senate Office Building amounted to $47.9-million of the total.

Background. Congress originally authorized construction of the New Senate Office Building in 1948, but the onset of the Korean war delayed groundbreaking ceremonies until January 1955. First occupied in 1958, the building was completed with an authorization of $24,196,000. The existing structure fills one-half of a city block northeast of the Capitol building. Congress appropriated $1.25-million in 1969 and another $510,000 in 1970 for the purchase of most of the other half of the block as a site for the extension.

Voting Participation

Congress in 1972 easily surpassed its all-time high of 743 recorded votes set in 1971. Both the Senate and the House set new records. The Senate took 532 roll-call votes during the session; this was 109 more than the previous high of 423 set in 1971. The House surpassed its old record, also set in 1971, by nine.

The major procedural change in the 92nd Congress was the introduction of the recorded teller vote in the House, which provided a record of how each member voted on amendments to bills. The recorded teller vote was authorized by the Legislative Reorganization Act of 1970 (PL 91-510).

With anonymity no longer guaranteed on major amendments, members voted in greater numbers than ever before during the 92nd Congress. Of the 329 votes taken in 1972, 85 were recorded teller votes; this compared with 108 recorded teller votes in 1971, the first year in which the new procedure was in use.

Year	House	Senate	Total
1972	329	532	861
1971	320	423	743
1970	266	418	684
1969	177	245	422
1968	233	281	584
1967	245	315	560
1966	193	235	428
1965	201	258	459
1964	113	305	418
1963	119	229	348
1962	124	224	348
1961	116	204	320
1960	93	207	300
1959	87	215	302
1958	93	200	293
1957	100	107	207
1956	73	130	203
1955	76	87	163
1954	76	171	247
1953	71	89	140
1952	72	129	201
1951	109	202	311
1950	154	229	383

Congressional Record Changes

The Joint Committee on Printing May 24, 1972, announced changes in the procedure by which senators and representatives were permitted to insert speeches, articles and other materials in the *Congressional Record* that were not actually read from the floor of the House or the Senate.

According to the announcement, the changes were required by a law specifying that the Record must "be substantially a verbatim report of (House and Senate) proceedings" and calling on Congress to take all necessary action "for the reduction of unnecessary bulk."

In making the changes, the committee revived a procedure repealed in 1968 requiring members planning

(Continued on p. 380)

Capitol Expansion: Desecration or Needed Improvement?

Controversy over the architecture of the U.S. Capitol has been going on ever since George Washington and Thomas Jefferson first persuaded District of Columbia commissioners to accept Dr. William Thornten's original design for the Capitol in 1793.

The most recent issue has been whether to extend the building westward toward the Mall, adding office and restaurant space at a cost of between $50-million and $60-million, or to reinforce the 144-year-old wall and restore it to its original condition. Extension would cover up with marble the Virginia sandstone of the last visible portion of the building George Washington praised for "grandeur, simplicity and beauty of the exterior; the propriety with which the apartments are distributed, and the economy in the whole mass of the structure."

The issue pitted the Commission for Extension of the Capitol, a group created in 1955 and comprised of the Democratic and Republican leadership in the Senate and House and the Capitol Architect, against members opposed to enlarging the existing structure.

The west front had been a point of controversy since 1964 when Congress appropriated funds for an engineering study. In 1966, the commission unexpectedly approved an extensive plan to enlarge the west front—a decision the Senate decisively rejected in 1972.

The proposed extension was promoted by the late Capitol Architect J. George Stewart, who in 1963 said the wall was in imminent danger of collapse. Stewart, a former member of the House (R Del. 1935-37) who was not an architect by profession, came under attack for his promotion of several costly construction projects —including the extension of the east front of the Capitol and construction of the Sam Rayburn House office building. His plans for extension of the west front were still being discussed in Congress at the time of his death in 1970.

A professional architect, George M. White, was appointed to Stewart's position on Jan. 27, 1971.

The issue came to a head after the commission met in closed session March 8, 1972, and voted unanimously to direct the Capitol Architect to proceed with final plans to extend the west front. A commission report issued in 1967 and published in the March 28, 1972, *Congressional Record* said 285 rooms would be added by the proposed extension at an estimated cost of $35-million. But 1972 cost estimates by the Capitol Architect's office ranged between $50-million and $60-million.

Rep. Samuel S. Stratton (D N.Y.), a staunch opponent of the plan, suggested that the extension would "turn this nation's number-one historic shrine into a grand Howard Johnson's," and would "provide special, hideaway offices for senior members who do not want to walk or ride back to the Rayburn, Longworth or Cannon (House office) Buildings in between quorum calls or recorded teller votes."

Sen. Edward M. Kennedy (D Mass.) criticized the commission's "secret and unexplained decision" to proceed with the extension, and added: "I hope that we can rally the conscience of the nation to prevent this act of desecration of our Capitol."

Opponents also argued against the extension for aesthetic reasons. Sen. Ernest F. Hollings (D S.C.), chairman of the Legislative Branch Appropriations Subcommittee, March 28 questioned the need for what he termed "bunches of restaurants, committee rooms, bathrooms, lounges, tourist spots, sale of trinkets, Disneyland East—or are we going to maintain the Capitol for use as a capitol?"

Hollings said the plan would extend the central portion of the west front 44 feet, the former House and Senate wings 88 feet and the corridors joining the Capitol to the existing House and Senate chambers 56 feet. He said the Capitol dome would "look like the beanie on a freshman's head after the construction is done."

One writer, historian Charles C. McLaughlin, said the 36 tall, square windows that would embellish the west terrace under the commission's plan would "glitter in the western sun and, lighted up at night, would make the west front of the U.S. Capitol look like a five-story wedding cake, nearly twice the height of the east front."

McLaughlin said an access road for service vehicles would be cut across the west lawn to allow large trucks to pass under the stairways to loading docks. "Close scrutiny of the plan for the roadway level of the terrace discloses that there are 9,052 square feet of 'unassigned public space' between truck docks. This appears to be intended as a large, all-weather bus terminal for the seven million or more tourists who visit the building every year."

Sen. William Proxmire (D Wis.), citing a 1971 report by the New York City architectural firm of Praeger-Kavanagh-Waterbury, said the west wall could be restored to its original condition for $15-million. An extension, he said, would represent "a great waste of the taxpayers' money."

Proponents of extension of the building, including Senate Republican Leader Hugh Scott (Pa.), Senate Democratic Leader Mike Mansfield (Mont.) and White, contended the Capitol had undergone renovation many times in the past and had long been in need of additional committee and tourist facilities and improvements.

Debate on the issue during consideration of the fiscal 1973 legislative branch appropriations bill resulted in a three-month House-Senate conference deadlock during which Rep. Stratton called for White's resignation.

Hollings, promising to stand firmly against the extension plan in conference, said: "The House is engaged in a lot of trickery and gimmickry in trying to extend the west front." He accused the House of trying "a ransom move" involving Hollings' proposal to restore the old Senate and Supreme Court chambers in the Capitol.

to insert lengthy material to first obtain an estimate of the cost from the public printer.

Members then were required, when seeking unanimous consent for insertion of the material, to state "probable cost" but not the contents. Objection of any one member would prevent publication.

The 1968 format, agreed to unanimously by the committee, chaired by Rep. Wayne L. Hays (D Ohio), pertained to insertions that would fill more than two pages in the Record. The changes went into effect immediately; no further action by Congress was necessary.

The cost of printing a single page was estimated in 1972 at $140. Although a subscription cost $3.75 a month, 90 percent of the 41,200 subscribers got copies free.

On May 10-11, 1972, 88 pages of the Record were devoted to a 1969 National Security Council memorandum on Vietnam that was classified secret. Rep. Ronald V. Dellums (D Calif.) had obtained a copy of the document from Sen. Mike Gravel (D Alaska) and placed 30 pages of it in the Record May 10 after routinely getting unanimous consent to extend his remarks. The remaining two-thirds, taking up 58 pages, appeared in the Record the next day.

In addition to returning to the 1968 procedure, the committeee instituted other changes to prohibit the printing of all extraneous matter in the House and Senate proceedings (debate) section of the Record, with the following exceptions: a) excepts from letters, telegrams or articles presented in connection with a speech delivered in the course of debate; b) communications from state legislatures; c) addresses or articles by the President and members of his cabinet, the Vice President or a member of Congress.

Other 1972 Developments

GUAM, VIRGIN ISLANDS DELEGATES. Following its 1970 action giving the District of Columbia a non-voting delegate in the House, Congress in 1972 extended the same privilege to the U.S. territories of Guam and the Virgin Islands

As cleared by Congress March 28, 1972, the bill (HR 8787) allowed residents of the two U.S. territories to elect in November 1972 delegates to the 93rd Congress which convened in January 1973. Elected in November were Ronald de Lugo (D V.I.) and Antonio Won-Pat (D Guam).

The House already had two non-voting delegates from Puerto Rico and Washington, D.C.

Guam and the Virgin Islands previously had sent representatives to Washington, D.C., but they had no official status and functioned as lobbyists.

Provisions. As cleared by Congress, HR 8787 (PL 92-271):

• Provided that Guam and the Virgin Islands each was to be represented in the House by a non-voting delegate.

• Provided that each delegate was to be chosen in a general election for a two-year term starting Jan. 3, 1973. If no candidate received a majority, a runoff would be held two weeks later. Vacancies would be filled by interim election.

• Required that each delegate had to be at least 25 years old, a citizen for seven years and an inhabitant of the territory.

• Allowed each territory's legislature to establish alternative election procedures.

• Provided that each delegate, subject to change by the House, would receive the same compensation, allowances and benefits as members from the 50 states.

• Extended to each delegate, subject to change by the House, the same privileges and immunities granted to the resident commissioner from Puerto Rico with the exception of a vote in committee.

• Restricted the clerk hire allowance of each delegate to 60 percent of a member's allowance and his transportation expenses to his home to four round trips per year.

MUNDT ASSIGNMENTS. The Senate Feb. 23, 1972, unanimously approved Republican Conference decisions parceling out committee assignments of the incapacitated Karl E. Mundt (R S.D. 1948-73). Mundt had been ill for two years and was stripped of his committee assignments by the conference on Feb. 3.

Mundt, who had not appeared in the Senate since suffering a stroke in late 1969, was stripped of his assignments to three main committees in a 19-14 vote of the Senate Republican Conference on Feb. 3.

Mundt had been ranking minority member of the Government Operations Committee and second-ranking Republican on both the Appropriations and Foreign Relations Committees. Mundt ranked third in seniority among the 45 Senate Republicans.

The vote to remove Mundt from the three committees until such time as he might return to the Senate was along seniority lines, with most older and higher ranking senators voting against the move while younger, newer members voted for it.

In early 1971, the Republican conference had voted to relieve him temporarily of his committee seniority, in effect giving lower-ranking senators his powers as ranking minority member of the Government Operations Committee and several subcommittees. But the conference refused at that time to remove him from the committees altogether and thus open positions that other members could fill.

After a year of Mundt's additional absence, the Republican senators reversed themselves on the matter of committee membership.

The action by the conference apparently was without precedent in the history of the Senate, despite several instances where senators were absent for long periods due to disabling diseases.

HOUSE TRAVEL, STATIONERY FUNDS. The House Administration Committee Oct. 5, 1972, adjusted the travel and stationery allowances for representatives. (Under H Res 457, approved by the House July 21, 1971, the committee could make such adjustments itself; House approval was not required.) *(p. 376.)*

The committee increased to 36 from 24 the number of trips a representative could make at government expense between Washington and his congressional district during his term; increased to $2,250 from $1,500 the transportation payment that a representative could elect to receive instead of the trip reimbursement. The resolution also increased to six from four the number of round trips per Congress allowed employees of a representative. A representative's stationery allowance was increased to $4,250 from $3,500 for each regular session of Congress.

SELECT PRIVACY COMMITTEE. A bill (H Res 164) to establish a House select committee on privacy, human values and democratic institutions was rejected Feb. 8, 1972, by a 168-216 roll call.

Strong opposition to H Res 164 was expressed by Emanuel Celler (D N.Y. 1923-73), chairman of the Judiciary Committee, who said the proposed committee would have encroached upon his committee's jurisdiction.

TECHNOLOGY OFFICE. Congress Oct. 4, 1972, cleared a bill (HR 10234—PL 92-484) to establish an Office of Technology Assessment to aid Congress in evaluating scientific and technical proposals for legislation. *(Related action providing for computer services, see 1971 House action.)*

The bill amended the National Science Foundation Act of 1950 (PL 81-507).

Provisions. As cleared by Congress, HR 10243:

● Created an Office of Technology Assessment as a permanent agency to assist Congress in evaluating the impact of technology for the purposes of legislation.

● Established a 13-member Technology Assessment Board consisting of six members of the House and six members of the Senate, with the director of the office serving as an ex-officio member.

● Established a Technology Assessment Advisory Council to make recommendations to the board regarding activities to be undertaken by the office.

● Amended the National Science Foundation Act of 1950 to permit a closer working relationship between the office and the foundation.

● Authorized $5-million over two fiscal years (fiscal 1973-74) to implement provisions of the bill.

HOUSE CLOSED SESSION. House Speaker Carl Albert (D Okla.) ordered the House galleries closed to the public for nearly three hours during the session of May 10, 1972, to prevent a repetition of anti-war demonstrations that had occurred the previous day. It was the first time in memory that the public galleries in the House had been closed as a precaution. Albert told reporters he acted reluctantly on the advice of the Capitol police. House proceedings on May 9 had been interrupted three times by outbursts from anti-war protesters.

The House leadership the same day received unanimous consent to convene the House at 10 a.m. May 11—the second such meeting of the year; the House normally convenes at 12 noon. Michael Harrington (D Mass.) later told *The Washington Post* that the reason for the earlier start was to prevent a meeting of the House Democratic Caucus from voting on his motion to put Democrats on record against the President's mining of ports in North Vietnam.

FIRST MAJOR CONGRESSIONAL REFORMS SINCE 1946

Some major changes in legislative procedures were approved by Congress in 1970 with passage of the Legislative Reorganization Act (PL 91-510). The reforms were intended to improve the operations of Congress, particularly to open up many hitherto hidden procedures governing the way Congress conducted its committee meetings and disposed of legislation on the floor.

The bill was also designed to provide Congress with better tools for evaluating the federal budget along with improved research and information resources and services.

Under the new law, most provisions of which took effect with the convening of the 92nd Congress in January 1971, much of the secrecy surrounding the actions of members and their positions on various issues, particularly in the House, was peeled off. All roll-call votes taken in committee—where the vast majority of legislation is formulated—were to be made public; for the first time, House members' positions on amendments were to be individually recorded and printed in the *Congressional Record* in the same manner as senators' on roll-call votes (previously members had voted in virtual anonymity by non-recorded teller votes, and often a large percentage did not vote at all); and the televising of House committee hearings was authorized.

The product of a decade's effort by reform-minded senators and representatives, the 1970 act was the first substantial reorganization of congressional procedures since the Legislative Reorganization Act of 1946. That act was never fully enforced and had proved only partially successful.

Neither the 1946 act nor the 1970 act was really a comprehensive reorganization measure. Questions directly involving the distribution of power within Congress were largely excluded from both acts, and neither touched upon such sensitive and controversial subjects as the seniority system, the power of the House Rules Committee or the Senate filibuster.

Turning Point. The action of the House Rules Committee in reporting out a legislative reorganization bill in mid-1970 marked a turning point toward passage of the bill. But even after the House began consideration of the bill, hopes for its passage did not seem too bright. Three times the bill was laid aside to take up other business. In early August, as the House prepared to recess for several weeks, Thomas M. Rees (D Calif.), a leader of the reform group, accused the House leadership of stalling consideration of the bill: It had become, he said, "the ghost bill of 1970" and might become "the ghost bill of the century. One moment it surfaces and then the next it silently disappears. We hear rumors of an appearance (on the floor), but at the appointed time, it just never shows up."

But House Majority Leader Carl Albert (D Okla.) replied that there was no attempt to stall action on the bill (HR 17654), and action was completed on it Sept. 17.

Structure of HR 17654. HR 17654 contained six parts, the last five of which—fiscal controls (Title II), sources of information (Title III), Congress as an institution (Title IV), the House Office of Legislative Counsel (Title V) and effective dates (Title VI)—applied primarily to matters outside the internal operations of each chamber.

All of Title I and some of Title II dealt with the rules of the House and the Senate which govern committee and floor procedures. The Constitution gives each chamber the right to make its own rules.

Title I and the relevant parts of Title II thus followed a two-part style in HR 17654 to propose similar reforms in the rules of both houses without one house seeming to infringe upon the other's prerogatives. Each provision affecting the rules of both chambers had two sections: one amending the rules of the House directly; the other, in language identical or similar to that of the 1967 reform bill approved by the Senate, amending the Legislative Reorganization Act of 1946 to amend the rules of the Senate indirectly.

Effect of 1970 Reforms

The precedents for faithful implementation of congressional reform were not strong if the results of the post-war reorganization act of 1946 were any guide. Many provisions of that law were easily circumvented; others were merely ignored.

To cope with the multiplication of standing committees, the 1946 act cut the number in half—to 15 in the Senate and 19 in the House. At the beginning of the 91st Congress, there were 16 Senate committees and 21 in the House.

But subcommittees proliferated. At the beginning of the 91st Congress there were 122 subcommittees in the Senate and 145 in the House.

The 1946 act required all committees to fix a regular meeting day. But in 1969 a survey by Congressional Quarterly found that although most committees had set such a day, few observed it.

The 1946 act directed Congress each year to prepare a legislative budget fixing a ceiling on the amounts which could be appropriated for each function. This was unsuccessful and was dropped in 1949.

The test of the effectiveness of the 1970 reform measure would be the extent to which the new committee procedures were implemented—particularly in the House. With more members, more committees and more rules, the House of Representatives traditionally resisted rules reform more strenuously than the Senate.

And the key to implementation of the new procedures was the attitude of the House's senior members, who ruled its committees, and the amount of effort its junior

Principal Reforms

PL 91-510 opened to the public eye more of the operations of Congress and the positions of its members by:

- Encouraging more open committee meetings and hearings.
- Requiring that all committee roll-call votes be made public.
- Allowing radio and television coverage of committee hearings.
- Providing that House teller votes be recorded upon request, ending the secrecy surrounding members' positions on important amendments.

The bill expedited House proceedings by:

- Allowing all House committees to sit without special leave while the House was in session so long as it was not reading a bill for amendment under the five-minute rule.
- Dispensing with the reading of the Journal unless the speaker or a majority of the members present so ordered.
- Allowing the call of the roll for a quorum to be ended after a quorum was obtained.

The bill safeguarded the rights of the ideological or political minority by:

- Writing into the rules a specific time period for additional views to be added to a committee report.
- Allowing minority members of a committee to select two of a committee's six permanent professional staff.
- Stating that minority members could call witnesses of their choosing during at least one day of hearings on a measure or topic.
- Requiring that debate on a conference report be evenly divided between the majority and minority sides.

The bill provided more opportunity for members to base their votes on knowledge of a particular measure by:

- Providing that the committee report on a bill (and committee hearings on an appropriations bill) be available to members for at least three days before the House or Senate voted on the bill.
- Providing that there be 10 minutes' debate on any amendment offered on the floor of the House which had been printed in the *Congressional Record* at least one day prior to consideration.
- Providing that a conference report be available for three days before the House voted on its adoption.

The bill also provided for a modernized data processing system for federal fiscal and budgetary information, closer scrutiny by Congress of current and projected costs of all federal programs, increased staff assistance for congressional committees and a continuing study of the operations of Congress.

members were willing to exert to demand that the rules be observed.

Barber B. Conable Jr. (R N.Y.), who led the bipartisan effort to enact PL 91-510, said of the new law that it provided the basis for major improvements in committee procedures but that it all depended on the congressional will to enforce it. He added that the demand for observance of procedural safeguards was directly related to the degree of frustration that junior members of a committee felt—the extent to which they perceived themselves disenfranchised by the chairmen.

Thomas M. Rees (D Calif.), long an advocate of congressional reform, pointed out that even before the 1970 act the rules of the House contained many provisions designed explicitly to protect the rights of the ideological or political or chronological minority, but that these rules were rarely if ever invoked because of the repercussions which would follow such imprudent action.

Recorded Teller Votes. Despite an inauspicious start—Congressional Quarterly reported in 1971 that within two months of the date the new law went into effect Congress had disregarded or suspended at least four of its key provisions—the act's new procedure for voting on the House floor brought about some dramatic changes.

In the first full year of operation, 108 recorded teller votes were taken, most of them on amendments to bills which under the previous system would have been decided by a small number of anonymous members.

The 1970 act for the first time allowed recorded votes on amendments to bills when the House assembled as a Committee of the Whole. One fifth of the committee (20 members) could demand "tellers with clerks." Members would still file up the aisle, but would hand the tellers colored pieces of paper bearing their names and positions. *(Committee of the Whole, box p. 384)*

A survey by Congressional Quarterly based on the 108 recorded teller votes found that voting participation increased by more than 90 per cent compared to voting on amendments the previous year. The study showed that only 23 of the 108 recorded teller votes were decided by a margin of 150 votes or more.

Early in 1971 the potential importance of the recorded teller vote was realized when the House defeated funds for the controversial supersonic transport plane by a 217-204 vote on March 18. It was the first time House members had voted on SST funding by recorded vote. Another significant recorded teller vote, taken March 31, defeated an amendment cutting the President's authority to draft men into the armed services to one year from his request for a two-year extension; the amendment failed by a 198-200 vote.

Pressures were exerted to modify the recorded teller vote procedure by some disgruntled members who claimed that the procedure was being abused by small numbers of representatives seeking votes on minor issues. Although some members backed a move to modify the rule—perhaps by increasing the number of people who would have to request a recorded teller vote—support for the 1970 reform voiced by Speaker Carl Albert (D Okla.) early in 1972 effectively squelched the attack.

On Feb. 23, 1972, the Democratic Caucus voted to change the recorded teller vote rule to permit such votes to last 15 minutes rather than the existing 12 minutes. In addition, it voted to change the rules to allow quorum calls to be taken by a 15-minute teller vote procedure rather than by calling the roll. Both changes were adopted by the House by voice vote. No attempt was made during the caucus session to modify the procedure for having recorded teller votes.

(Continued on p. 385)

Pre-1971: Members Voted in Anonymity on Crucial Issues

Bells ring throughout the House of Representatives and its environs—from the chamber where Henry Clay presided as speaker to the handball court in the basement of the Rayburn Office Building—to summon representatives to vote on a piece of legislation or to answer a call for a quorum.

Privately owned restaurants and bars on Capitol Hill even announce the number of rings and one clangs a dinner bell, thanks to quick phone calls from obliging House doorkeepers.

One ring of the bells often will not budge a House member, even though the vote may be on important issues such as the antiballistic missile (ABM) system or American troops in Cambodia.

For two or three bells, though, the same members may show up to vote on the same or lesser issues on an empty stomach or wearing tennis shoes.

The difference is, one bell means only a vote listing total numbers—not names—of representatives. For two or three bells, members' names become a matter of record for constituents to see.

Issues Affected. Members voted in anonymity during the 1970 session of Congress on issues ranging from a measure to exempt potatoes for processing from federal marketing orders to the role of American troops in Cambodia, the antiballistic missile system and school desegregation.

An analysis by Congressional Quarterly showed that legislation upon which representatives voted in 1970 without the scrutiny of name-recording votes included:

• Eight amendments concerning the use of funds for American forces in Cambodia, Laos and Thailand.

• Two amendments offered April 30 by Rep. Robert L. Leggett (D Calif.) to cut funds for the antiballistic missile system, which were defeated by teller and standing votes (members stand and are counted but names are not recorded; also called division vote); amendments to cut funds for the C-5A plane, the MIRV missile, B-1 bomber, F-14 fighter plane and other military projects also were defeated by nonrecorded teller and standing votes.

• Amendments Feb. 19 to water down or knock out provisions in the Labor and Health, Education and Welfare Departments appropriations bill restricting the ability of the federal government to seek further school desegregation.

• Twenty-two amendments to the District of Columbia Court Reform and Criminal Procedures Act of 1970 which passed March 19; the amendments included votes on pretrial detention, "no-knock" search warrants, wiretapping and mandatory jail sentences.

• Amendments April 23 concerning the reduction of the National Aeronautics and Space Administration authorization for research and development for the Apollo program and for space flight operations.

• An amendment May 27 to the Department of Transportation appropriations bill to delete funds for the development of the supersonic transport (SST); defeated by an 86-102 teller vote.

COMMITTEE OF THE WHOLE. Senate rules permitted record votes on every issue. But the House took most of its votes while sitting as a Committee of the Whole House (all members of the House sit as a committee rather than as the House of Representatives), where record votes are prohibited to speed action by the large body.

The House's nonrecord vote practice was patterned after a centuries-old English system whereby members of Parliament could hide their individual votes from the king. In 1832, the English system was reformed to provide for a public record of votes. The House reform came 138 years later.

The Continental Congress frequently used the Committee of the Whole and in 1789 the first Congress adopted a system of rules for the House which provided for a Committee of the Whole. In 1840, a speaker ruled that record votes could not be taken in the Committee of the Whole and the ruling had been reaffirmed ever since. The rule provided that only amendments approved in the Committee of the Whole could be voted on by the full House. Amendments rejected in the Committee of the Whole and not reported to the House by the Committee were not considered by the full body and thus roll-call votes could not be taken.

The Committee of the Whole procedure had the advantage of allowing the House to conduct its business with fewer members present and more quickly since time-consuming roll calls were prohibited. A quorum was made in the Committee of the Whole with only 100 members present as opposed to a majority of the membership required to transact business for the House (218 members when there were no vacancies).

Technically, the Committee of the Whole considered only bills directly or indirectly appropriating money, authorizing appropriations or involving taxes or charges on the public, but actually it frequently considered other types of legislation, often in the form of amendments. When the full House resolved itself into the Committee of the Whole, it supplanted the speaker with a chairman. Measures were debated or amended, with non-record votes as needed. The votes could be voice (ayes and nays aloud), division (members stood and were counted), or teller (members filed past the tellers who counted those favoring and opposing a question but did not record names. It was almost impossible for observers to get an accurate list of members voting—and how they voted—on teller votes because the members passed by the tellers facing away from the press gallery and toward the public gallery where note-taking was forbidden.

Committee of the Whole action was tentative. Official and final approval of amendments and actual passage of bills occurred when the committee completed its work and resolved itself into the House of Representatives. For final House action on a bill, roll-call votes could be requested by one-fifth of the members present on amendments that were adopted in the Committee of the Whole.

(Continued from p. 383)

Richard P. Conlon, staff director of the Democratic Study Group, comprised of about 160 House Democrats, most of them liberals, said in 1972 that the recorded teller vote was "working beyond any expectations" of its original backers. He said that the House leaders "underestimated its potency" before the SST vote, but the popularity of that vote made it "untouchable."

Even more important than whether liberals or conservatives, Republicans or Democrats, benefited most from the recorded teller vote was the increase in House voting participation which resulted from the reform. Rep. Conable observed that it ensured majority participation in the amending process. Before its adoption, 100 members could usually amend a bill any way they sought—"a serious gap in the legislative process," Conable said.

Conlon said the new system had produced a few liberal cracks in the committee chairmen's control of the Committee of the Whole. That body was generally dominated by conservatives, and a committee chairman could usually guarantee success for his bill by getting his supporters on the floor during votes on amendments.

Chairmen must now "assess the entire membership of the House—the SST burned into their consciousness," Conlon said. He said during 1971 liberals prevailed on about 25 votes under the recorded teller system that they would probably have lost in earlier years under the non-record system.

Committee Secrecy. The 1970 reform act made little impact in opening up committee proceedings to the public in its first year of operation. Congressional Quarterly's annual survey of open and closed committee meetings showed that 36 per cent of all House and Senate committee hearings in 1971 were held behind closed doors, only a slight decrease from the 41 per cent recorded in 1970 and exactly the same as the 1969 percentage. *(See chronology for 1971)*

Provisions

As cleared for the President, HR 17654—PL 91-510:

Title I—The Committee System

The bill recognized the right of both the House and the Senate to change their own rules of procedure at any time. (The Constitution, Article I, Section 5, states: "Each House may determine the Rules of its Proceedings.")

HOUSE

It amended the rules of the House to:
• Provide that the ranking majority member of a committee would preside at any meeting in which the chairman was absent. (This was already the custom in most committees.)
• Provide that the ranking majority member of a ings were to be open to the public unless the committee by majority vote decided otherwise. (The House in 1973 moved to solidify and expand the language of the 1970 act. An amendment to the House rules, adopted March 7, required all House committee hearings to be open unless they dealt with national security or personal character. Markup sessions and other committee business meetings could be closed only by a majority vote in public session to close a future meeting or series of meetings.)

• Require that all roll-call votes taken in committee—and each member's vote—be accessible to the public and that committee reports on bills contain the vote by which the committee ordered the bill reported. (Under previous rules, such votes were not necessarily made public.)
• Provide that committee reports on bills be filed within seven calendar days (excluding days the House was not in session) after a majority of the committee filed a written request that the report be submitted. This provision did not apply to the House Rules Committee with regard to House rules and House business. (Under previous rules, the chairman had the responsibility of reporting a bill and arranging to get it scheduled for floor action.)
• Prohibit proxy voting in committee except when the committee's written rules permitted it, when the proxy was limited to a specific matter, and was in writing, designating the person to whom it was given. (Proxy votes were not mentioned under previous House rules; different committees allowed them in different circumstances.)
• Allow committee members three days (excluding Saturdays, Sundays and legal holidays) to file supplementary, minority or additional views to be included with the committee report on a bill or other matter. This provision did not apply to the House Rules Committee. (There was no similar provision previously; generally, time was allowed for the filing of such views.)
• Prohibit the House from considering any bill or other matter (except from the Appropriations, House Administration, Standards, or Rules Committees) unless the committee report on the measure had been available for at least three days (excluding Saturdays, Sundays and legal holidays) prior to consideration. This rule did not apply to declarations of war or emergency, or to legislative veto procedures or executive reorganization plans. (There was no such provision under previous rules.)
• Prohibit the House from considering any general appropriations bill until printed committee hearings and the report on the bill had been available for at least three days (excluding Saturdays, Sundays and legal holidays) prior to consideration. (A similar provision under previous House rules did not exclude Saturdays, Sundays and holidays.)
• Authorize the speaker—if no motion was offered for House consideration of a bill within seven days after a rule for its consideration had been granted—to recognize a member of the committee that reported the bill to move for its consideration, if so authorized by a majority the committee.
• Specify procedures by which funds were provided to meet committee expenses. (Previous House rules did not contain such provisions, but the procedures set forth were generally followed.)
• Require that no less than one-third of a committee's funds be used for minority staff. (There was no such provision under previous rules.) *(Later 1971 action, box p. 386)*
• Require committees to announce hearings at least one week in advance unless there was good reason to give shorter notice. This provision did not apply to the House Rules Committee. (There was no such provision under previous rules.)
• Provide that a majority of the minority party members of a committee were entitled to call witnesses during at least one day of hearings on a bill. (Many committees

by custom allowed minority members this opportunity but others did not, and when the Democrats early in the 92nd Congress passed a resolution which nullified the new rule, a partisan controversy developed. *(Jan. 22, 1971, vote deleting provisions, box this page)*

• Allow any open hearing to be broadcast over radio or television if majority vote of the committee involved permitted and if the broadcast was carried out in accordance with rules specifying that coverage would be live, without commercial sponsorship, subpoenaed witnesses would not be photographed or their testimony broadcast without their consent, and equipment would be limited so as not to obstruct the hearings. (Broadcasting was not permitted under previous House rules.)

• Provide that all committees could sit without special leave while the House was in session except when a bill was being read for amendment under the five-minute rule. The five-minute rule limitation would not apply to the Appropriations, Government Operations, Internal Security, Rules, and Standards Committees. (Under previous rules, only the Government Operations, Rules, Standards, and Internal Security Committees were allowed to sit without special leave while the House was in session.)

• Require each standing committee, except the Appropriations, House Administration, Rules, and Standards Committees, to report annually on legislation considered by the committee and on its oversight of enacted programs within its jurisdiction. (Committees already possessed this review function, but had not been required to report on it.)

• Allow 10 minutes of debate on any amendment offered on the floor—even if debate had been closed on the section of the bill to which the amendment was proposed—so long as the amendment had been printed in the *Congressional Record* at least one day before consideration. (Under previous rules, an amendment received no explanation at all during consideration of a bill when a majority of the House during consideration of the amendment agreed to cut off further debate on the section of the bill to which the amendment applied.)

• Provide that, upon request of one-fifth of a quorum, a teller vote be recorded by clerks or electronic devices, that the vote be taken in no less than 12 minutes, and that the record include the names of members voting for, voting against and not voting on the question. (Under previous rules, only the outcome of such votes was recorded, not the positions of members voting. All amendments were accepted or rejected in the Committee of the Whole by voice, standing, or teller votes, on which members' positions remained unknown.) *(1972 action on electronic voting, p. 387)*

• Provide that once a quorum was obtained, the call of the House for a quorum could be ended; that for 30 minutes from the beginning of the call, members could register their presence by signing in on tally sheets. (Under previous rules, once the call of the House for a quorum was begun, the entire roll had to be called, which took at least 30-35 minutes.)

• Provide for 10 minutes of debate on a motion to send a bill back to committee with instructions, with the time divided evenly between the person making the motion and the persons opposed. (In previous practice, a resolution issued by the Rules Committee for consideration of a

Minority Committee Staff

Before adopting the rules of the House for the 92nd Congress, the House Jan. 22, 1971, voted to eliminate a provision of the Legislative Reorganization Act of 1970 (PL 91-510) providing that one-third of committee investigative funds be used for minority party staff members. Members of the Democratic caucus had been bound to vote for the deletion. The proposed deletion had been introduced in the caucus by Chet Holifield (Calif.).

Republicans, led by Representatives William A. Steiger (Wis.), James C. Cleveland (N.H.), Robert McClory (Ill.) and Gerald R. Ford (Mich.), expressed outrage at the Democratic caucus action stripping the minority funding clause from the Legislative Reorganization Act.

John A. Blatnik (D Minn.), speaking in favor of the caucus action, said the one-third minority funding provision was "retrogression of the highest degree.... Once again staff appointments will depend on party activities and favors done for members of Congress rather than the real ability a person can bring to his job. Once again both parties will look to staff appointments for patronage purposes. Instead of reaping the benefit of a true career system that I thought we were developing among our professional staffs, we will be taking on all the headaches of a spoils system."

Deletion of the minority staffing provision was approved by a 226-156 vote.

Later Action. One hundred and fifty-five Republicans June 22 introduced a resolution (H Res 499) permitting up to one-third of committee investigative funds to be used for hiring minority party staff members. No action was taken on the resolution in 1971 and 1972.

bill usually specified that there would be no debate on a motion to recommit.)

• Require that every conference report be printed as a House report and be accompanied by an explanatory statement prepared jointly by House and Senate conferees. (In previous practice, the report was printed as a House report but only House conferees prepared a separate statement explaining the conferees' actions.)

• Divide debate on a conference report evenly between majority and minority. (In previous practice, such time was not formally divided and was controlled by the chairman of the conferees.)

• Forbid conferees to include any language in a conference version of a bill which concerned a topic which neither chamber sent to conference or to modify any topic beyond the scope of the differing versions of the bill sent to conference. (Previous rules stated that a conference report should not include matter not sent to conference by either chamber, but there was no flat prohibition.)

• Prohibit the House from considering a conference report unless the report and accompanying statement had been printed in the *Congressional Record* at least three calendar days (excluding Saturdays, Sundays and legal holidays) prior to consideration and that copies were available to all members. This rule did not apply during the last six days of a session. (Previous rules provided only that the House might not consider a conference report—except in the last six days of a session—until it had been printed in the *Congressional Record*, and conference reports were often brought up for a vote with little or no notice. However, the new rule did not end the practice by which the leadership could bring a conference report to the floor on the same day it was reported by getting the Rules Committee to draft a resolution suspending the rule.)

● Allow a separate House vote, upon the request of any member, on any nongermane amendment added by the Senate to a House-passed bill (approval of the amendment required only a majority vote); prohibit House conferees from agreeing to a nongermane Senate amendment unless authorized to do so by a vote on that amendment by the House. (In previous practice, the House had often been forced to vote on the bill as a whole, having to defeat the bill or accept the nongermane amendment.

The new rule was intended to apply to nongermane Senate amendments the same procedure (House Rule XX) already applied to certain types of Senate amendments added to general appropriations bills.

(The House in 1972 moved to clarify the intent of the new rule after several instances of confusion arose during the 92nd Congress over how the procedure was to operate. Varying interpretations by the House leadership, parliamentarian and the membership further muddled the intent of the rule allowing separate House votes on amendments added by the Senate that were in violation of the House's own rules. *(1972 modification of germaneness rule, p. 395)*

● Direct that the Journal (the official record of congressional proceedings) not be read daily unless the speaker so ordered, or there was a motion supported by a majority of the members present. (Such reading was omitted by unanimous consent under previous practice, but the objection of one member was enough to require that the Journal be read in full, a tactic occasionally used to delay or to force action on some measure.)

● Provide that the non-voting delegate from Puerto Rico be elected to standing committees and that he be allowed to vote in committee. (Under previous rules, the delegate was an additional, nonvoting member of the Agriculture, Armed Services and Interior Committees.)

SENATE

Amended the Legislative Reorganization Act of 1946 to amend the rules of the Senate to:

● Allow a majority of a committee to call a meeting when the chairman refused to upon request. (The House, but not the Senate, had this procedure available.)

● Authorize the ranking majority member of the committee to preside at any meeting from which the chairman was absent. (This was already the custom in most committees.)

● Require that Senate committees adopt and publish rules of committee procedure. (Under previous rules, there was no such requirement.)

● Provide that committee business meetings be open to the public except during sessions to mark up bills, to vote

Electronic Voting

The House Oct. 13, 1972, cleared the way for it to take its recorded votes electronically at the start of the 93rd Congress. The first recorded vote using the new system was taken Jan. 31, 1973.

By a voice vote it agreed to a resolution (H Res 1123) amending the rules of the House to require the use of an electronic voting system for quorum calls and all recorded votes unless the speaker invoked a call of the roll.

Under the new rules, members had 15 minutes to answer quorum calls and recorded votes (roll calls and recorded teller votes). Members were able to vote at any of 48 consoles in the House chamber by inserting a plastic card and pressing a button to indicate a yea or nay vote.

As members voted, boards installed on the walls of the chamber showed instantly how each member voted as well as a running breakdown of votes cast. Voting ceased when the speaker locked the vote total into the machine.

During the debate, Wayne L. Hays (D Ohio), chairman of the House Administration Committee, said the machinery for electronic voting was installed at a cost of $1,065,000. He said the machines would pay for themselves in a year because of the time they would save members. Quorum calls and recorded votes would take only 15 minutes, while a call of the roll by a clerk required about 35 minutes.

As part of the new system, the leadership tables on the majority and minority sides of the House floor were equipped with consoles to allow the leadership to see how members voted.

Members Changing Votes. Barber B. Conable Jr. (R N.Y.) said that he was concerned that the machinery did not record those members who changed their votes. "Under the present system, if a person changes his vote we keep a record of it, and it has had the effect of discouraging the changing of votes. I wonder if there is not a possibility that we will have a great deal of strategic maneuvering using this system when there is a close vote and the leadership does not wish the other side to know exactly where the votes are at a given time?"

But John M. Ashbrook (R Ohio) said the electronic voting could mean an end to "putting pressure on members to change their votes in the well," because a member could vote anywhere in the House chamber. Under the former roll call arrangement, members could vote or change their vote after the initial call of the roll by announcing it to the clerk in the well, the area surrounding the speaker's platform. Party leaders often pressured members to change their votes when the result appeared close.

Voting for Absent Members. In response to a question about members voting for absent members, B. F. Sisk (D Calif.), a member of the Rules Committee, said it was "a matter of the integrity of each member" not to give his voting card to someone else to cast his vote for him.

or when the committee by majority vote decided to conduct a hearing in executive (closed) session.

• Provide that committee hearings be open to the public except when the committee decided that the testimony might relate to national security, reflect adversely on an individual's character or reputation or contain confidential information.

• Require that all roll-call votes taken in committee on a measure or amendment—and the positions of senators voting—be published in the committee report on that measure, unless previously made public.

• Provide that committee reports on bills be filed (made available to members and other interested persons) within seven calendar days (excluding days the Senate was not in session) after a majority of the committee requested that the report be filed.

• Provide that no proxy vote might be cast on a motion to report a bill if a committee's rules forbade the use of a proxy on such a motion, and provided that a proxy could be used only upon the affirmative request of an absent member.

• Allow committee members three days to file supplementary, minority or additional views to be included with the committee report on a bill or other matter. (There was no similar provision under previous rules; generally, time was allowed for the filing of such views.)

• Prohibit the Senate from considering any bill or other matter reported from a standing committee unless the committee report on the measure had been available for at least three days (excluding Saturdays, Sundays and legal holidays) prior to consideration. This rule did not apply to declarations of war or emergency, to legislative veto procedures or to executive reorganization plans, and could be waived by agreement of the Senate majority and minority leaders. (There was no such provision under previous rules.)

• Specify procedures to govern procurement of funds for committee use in excess of an annual $10,000 ceiling.

• Require committees (except the Senate Appropriations Committee) to announce hearings at least one week in advance unless there was good reason that they begin earlier. (There was no such provision under previous rules.)

• Provide that the minority party members of a committee (except the Senate Appropriations Committee) were entitled to call witnesses during at least one day of hearings on a matter, as long as there was general agreement among the minority members on which witnesses would be called. (Many committees by custom allowed minority members this opportunity.)

• Allow any open hearing to be broadcast over radio or television under whatever rules the committee might adopt.

• Forbid Senate committees (except the Appropriations Committee) to sit while the Senate was in session unless special leave had been obtained from the Senate majority and minority leaders.

• Require each standing committee (except the Senate Appropriations Committee) to report annually on its activities reviewing the execution of laws and programs enacted within its jurisdiction. (Committees already possessed this review function but had not been required to issue reports on their activities.)

• Require that conference reports be printed as a Senate report and be accompanied by an explanatory statement prepared jointly by House and Senate conferees. (Under the previous custom, only House conferees prepared the statement of conferees and conference reports were usually printed only as House reports.)

• Divide debate on a conference report evenly between majority and minority. (Previously, such time was not formally divided, and it was controlled by the chairman of the conferees.)

• Require a quorum of the Senate Appropriations Committee to be present for a vote to report an appropriations bill from committee. (This was committee practice, except that previously, Senate rules exempted the Appropriations Committee from the requirement.)

• Rename the Senate Banking and Currency Committee the Senate Banking, Housing and Urban Affairs Committee.

• Reduce the size of certain Senate committees; provide that newly elected senators could be members of only two major committees and one minor, select, or joint committee; that no senator could serve on more than one of the following: Armed Services, Appropriations, Finance or Foreign Relations Committees; that no senator could hold the chairmanship of more than one full committee. (The provision would not deprive any senator of any committee position or chairmanship currently held, but would apply to all future assignments.)

• Create a Senate Committee on Veterans' Affairs.

Title II—Fiscal Controls

• Directed the secretary of the Treasury and the director of the Office of Management and Budget to set up and maintain a standardized data processing system for federal budgetary and fiscal data.

• Directed the secretary and director to furnish the congressional committees, upon request, information on the location and nature of available data on federal programs, activities, receipts and expenditures.

• Directed the comptroller general to review and analyze the results of government programs, make cost benefit studies of the programs at the direction of Congress or on his own initiative or upon request of any congressional committee, and assist congressional committees in analyzing cost benefit studies furnished by any federal agency or in conducting such studies.

• Required the President to send Congress—as part of the annual budget—five-year forecasts of the costs of every new or expanded federal program.

• Required that the President update the budget for the following fiscal year, as well as the five-year cost forecasts, at midyear, beginning with 1972, and transmit to Congress a supplemental summary of those revisions by June 1 each year.

• Required the comptroller general or a designated employee of the General Accounting Office (GAO) to explain to any congressional committee upon request any GAO report relevant to legislation, appropriations or programs within the committee's jurisdiction.

• Directed the comptroller general to deliver copies of GAO reports to the Appropriations and Government Operations Committees and to any other committee requesting them.

• Limited to one year the period in which a GAO employee could be assigned fulltime to work with any congressional committee.

• Required any federal agency to report to the House and Senate Government Operations Committees—no later than 60 days after a GAO report made recommendations concerning that agency—on what action had been taken to implement those recommendations.

• Required the House Appropriations Committee, within 30 days after the President sent the budget to Congress, to hold hearings on the budget and receive testimony from the director of the Office of Management and Budget, the secretary of the Treasury and the chairman of the Council of Economic Advisers; required such hearings to be open except when the national security required otherwise.

• Required committee reports on all measures—except revenue bills—to include cost estimates for the programs affected for that year and for the next five years. (The provision did not apply to the House Appropriations, Administration, Rules, and Standards Committees or to the Senate Appropriations Committee.)

Title III—Sources of Information

• Increased to six from four the number of permanent professional staff for each congressional standing committee, two of whom, in addition to one of the six permanent clerical staff members, might be selected by a majority of the committee's minority party members. (The provision did not apply to the House and Senate Appropriations Committees or to the House Standards of Official Conduct Committee.)

• Authorized standing committees, with the approval of the Senate Rules or House Administration Committees, to hire temporary consultants.

• Authorized standing committees, with the approval of the Senate Rules or House Administration Committees, to provide staff members with specialized training.

• Authorized salaries of Senate committee staff personnel to be comparable to those of House committee staff personnel.

• Redesignated the Legislative Reference Service of the Library of Congress the Congressional Research Service, redefining its duties to further assist congressional committees by providing research and analytical services, records, documents and other information and data, including memoranda on proposed legislation; authorized an expansion of its staff resources.

• Authorized the House parliamentarian, after the compilation of a new edition of the parliamentary precedents of the House (the first since 1934) was completed, to compile such precedents every five years.

Title IV—Congress as an Institution

• Created a Joint Committee on Congressional Operations to continue the study of the operations and organization of Congress and to recommend improvements, including possible uses of automatic data processing systems.

• Abolished the Joint Committee on Immigration and Nationality Policy which, established in 1952, had never met.

• Created a Capitol Guide Service to provide free tours of the Capitol.

Reform Amendments Rejected

Although the Legislative Reorganization Act was strengthened on the House floor by the addition of numerous amendments, a number of major reform proposals were either rejected or not brought to a vote.

Major amendments which were proposed but failed to pass included those to:

• Modify the seniority system by requiring each committee to elect its own chairman from the three most senior majority party members of the committee.

• Provide that seniority not be the sole consideration in the selection of committee chairmen.

• Limit the tenure of committee chairmen to eight years.

• Bar all proxy voting in committee.

• Require committees to decide by roll-call vote in open session whether each day's meeting would be open or closed. *(A similar proposal was approved in 1973, p. 370)*

• Prohibit the Rules Committee from sending a bill to the floor with a "closed rule" forbidding or placing limitations on the introduction of floor amendments to bills.

• Require the *Congressional Record* to be a verbatim account of House proceedings, with changes allowed to correct only grammatical and typographical errors, not content or meaning, and with any remarks inserted but not actually delivered printed in a typeface distinct from that used for remarks actually spoken on the floor.

• Make mandatory by the beginning of the second session of the 92nd Congress the use of electronic machinery to record votes. *(Approved in 1972 and put into effect Jan. 23, 1973; story, p. 387)*

• Allow a roll-call vote by the House on any amendment defeated by teller vote during the amendment stage of floor debate.

• Provide that a parliamentary precedent could not be used as the basis of a parliamentary ruling until the precedent had been printed and distributed to the members.

• Require that each chamber establish by resolution a legislative budget to set its priorities in considering authorization and appropriations bills.

• Authorized Congress to take a 30-day recess in August every non-election year, unless it had already adjourned or a state of war existed.

• Converted the House payroll system from the base pay standard using 1945 figures to a gross pay standard reflecting the 17 pay raises since 1945 and showing the actual amounts paid to House employees.

• Directed Senate pages to be between 14 and 18 years old and House pages to be between 16 and 18; and authorized the construction of the John W. McCormack Residential Page School.

• Authorized the speaker of the House to appoint a commission to plan and oversee the modernization of the House galleries, including the enclosure of the galleries with soundproof glass.

Title V—Office of the Legislative Counsel, House of Representatives

● Established the Office of Legislative Counsel for the House of Representatives, expanding existing functions and defining its duties.

Title VI—Effective Dates

● Provided that most of the provisions of HR 17654, with a few exceptions, would become effective as of noon Jan. 3, 1971; the remaining provisions would gradually take effect.

Background

Enactment in October 1970 of the Legislative Reorganization Act climaxed a five-year effort which began with the creation in 1965 of a joint House-Senate committee to study congressional operations and suggest reforms. Establishment of the committee and its subsequent recommendations marked the first major attempt to update congressional operations since passage of the Legislative Reorganization Act of 1946 (PL 79-601).

The 1946 act—the first comprehensive reorganization of congressional committees and procedures— reduced the number of standing committees, defined their jurisdiction, set certain rules for committee functioning, authorized a legislative budget, increased committee staff, set an annual July 31 adjournment date, increased salaries of senators and representatives, and required lobbyists to register and report their expenditures.

The reform effort which produced the Legislative Reorganization Act of 1970 began in the early 1960s and in 1965 Congress set up a Joint Committee on the Organization of Congress. The joint committee was headed by Sen. Mike Monroney (D Okla.) and by Rep. Ray J. Madden (D Ind.).

The joint committee in 1966 recommended a wide-ranging set of reforms, including tighter and more accountable committee procedures to curtail the powers of committee chairmen, a limit on the number of committee assignments, an increase in committee staff resources, better fiscal control by Congress, an expanded Legislative Reference Service in the Library of Congress, a revised *Congressional Record* format and stronger regulation of lobbying.

The Senate in 1967 passed a bill (S 355) embodying most of the joint committee's suggestions. That bill met stubborn opposition in the House and was never considered on the floor. But reform pressures persisted, and in 1970 the House finally passed a reform bill of its own. This measure was accepted by the Senate, which added reforms of its own, and the bill was signed into law Oct. 26, 1970.

1967 Bill. The Senate March 7, 1967, approved S 355, containing most of the joint committee's recommendations.

The bill would have revised committee procedures, established several new standing committees, required fuller federal budgetary data, established new procedures on appropriations bills, increased committee staffs and staffs for minority party members, made changes in jobs, Capitol police, pages and appointment of postmasters and revised the Regulation of Lobbying Act.

Reforms Disregarded

The 92nd Congress, within two months after it convened in January 1971, had disregarded or suspended at least four key provisions of the 1970 act.

● The House agreed to disregard a provision of the 1970 act that required one-third of each committee's investigative funds to be used to hire minority staff members.

● The Senate, in approving a resolution to create a Joint Committee on Environment, included language exempting appointments to the committee from a provision of the 1970 act that limited senators to one joint committee assignment.

● The House by unanimous consent waived a provision of the act barring the House from considering a conference report until it had been printed and made available to members for three days. The waiver, requested by Ways and Means Committee Chairman Wilbur D. Mills (D Ark.) in connection with a bill to raise the debt ceiling and increase Social Security benefits, also precluded any member from requesting a separate House vote on the nongermane Social Security amendment, which the Senate had added to the bill. A separate vote on nongermane Senate riders was authorized by the 1970 act.

● Committees varied in their compliance with a provision specifying that the results of all record votes taken by committees in reporting bills to the floor must be printed in the committee reports, and that the positions of individual members on such votes must be made available to the public. Some committees complied in full with these provisions. However, the House Agriculture Committee, in reporting one bill, did not include the vote in its report, although it made it available upon request. And the Ways and Means Committee, in its report on a debt limit bill, included in its report the 20-3 vote by which its action was taken but did not make the names available, stating that no record vote was taken.

S 355 did not deal with floor procedures, the *Congressional Record* or the seniority system, but its provisions concerning committee procedures aroused stubborn opposition in the House where it died at the end of the 90th Congress.

1969 Action. Sen. Karl E. Mundt (R S.D. 1948-73) introduced a bill (S 844) early in the 91st Congress which incorporated, with the exception of certain lobbying and housekeeping provisions, the provisions of S 355.

A special subcommittee of the House Rules Committee was set up in April 1969 to consider legislative reform.

The House Rules Committee held hearings on a draft bill to revise some of the House procedures, but no further action was taken in that chamber in 1969.

Senate. The Senate Government Operations Committee May 23 reported without amendment a bill (S 844 —S Rept 91-202) to revise the operation of the legislative branch of the federal government. However, the bill was never brought to the floor. The bill would have:

● Modified committee procedures on hearings, reporting out bills and proxy votes, all of which would reduce somewhat the powers of committee chairmen.

● Added new provisions providing for congressional review of the federal budget, increased use of the General Accounting Office by Congress and new fiscal responsibilities to the legislative standing committees.

● Provided for a data processing system to handle budgetary information, enlarged the staffs of members and committees and reorganized the legislative reference facilities of Congress, all intended to increase congressional access to and use of information.

● Established permanent joint committee on congressional operations, reorganized the Capitol police force and Capitol guide service, provided for appointment of postmasters in the competitive civil service without congressional intervention and reinstituted an annual July 31 adjournment date for Congress.

House. The Special Subcommittee of the Rules Committee held a series of hearings October-December 1969 on numerous proposals to revise House procedures and services.

For years political scientists and members had warned that Congress was losing power because its sources of information could not compete with those of the executive branch. They argued that Congress was overwhelmed with masses of data it found incomprehensible and thus ended up rubber-stamping most of what the executive requested and then losing track of the programs after they were established.

The House bill reorganized the Legislative Reference Service of the Library of Congress, which provided information for members, and added to it a pool of experts in many fields who would provide in-depth reports to committees which requested them. A new staff member would be added to each standing committee to serve as liaison between it and the research pool.

The reorganized LRS would also review the operation of programs authorized by Congress, a function currently performed by the General Accounting Office (GAO) which was supposed to be Congress' watchdog but whose head, the comptroller general, was appointed by the President.

The House bill also provided a new Joint Committee on Legislative Data Processing to coordinate the growing use of computers by Congress.

The bill was drafted by the Special Subcommittee of the Rules Committee, headed by Sisk. Other members were Richard Bolling (D Mo.), Delbert L. Latta (R Ohio), H. Allen Smith (R Calif. 1957-73) and John Young (D Texas).

The House bill lessened the power of committee chairmen by allowing the ranking majority member to call meetings if the chairman refused. It did not deal with the seniority system, however.

The bill set up a select committee to study changes in the lobby regulations.

It also:

● Provided that the precedents of the House be printed periodically. This had not been done since 1935.

● Granted two additional professional staff members and one additional clerk to the minority party members on each standing committee.

● Allowed the televising of House sessions and committee hearings, under stringent controls.

● Granted Congress an August recess annually.

● Made the fiscal year the same as the calendar year to give Congress six additional months to pass appropriations bills.

● Abolished several committees that no longer met.

● Authorized a dormitory for congressional and Supreme Court pages who were in high school.

An early witness at the hearings was Phillip S. Hughes, deputy director of the Bureau of the Budget (later reorganized into the Office of Management and Budget). He said the bureau favored changing the fiscal year to coincide with the calendar year to "help unscramble the present situation of hesitancy, confusion, and uncertainty over the government's program and budget...." He pointed out that "in every recent year it has been necessary for the government to start its fiscal year with many regular appropriations bills awaiting enactment."

To speed consideration of the budget, he said, authorizations might be made for four years or more instead of the usual one, thus eliminating the annual logjam of authorizing legislation that must be passed before funds can be appropriated. He urged that authorization bills be enacted early in the session.

In selected testimony during the three-month long hearings:

James C. Cleveland (R N.H.) criticized the minority staffing provision of the bill. He said the minority members of a committee should have the right to choose their own staff members. Under the draft bill, the minority could nominate two staff members, but final selection and control rested with the majority members.

William D. Hathaway (D Maine) contended that many of the bill's reforms did not go far enough. Among other points in a detailed statement, Hathaway said the bill:

● Made it too easy for committees to hold secret business sessions and hearings.

● Exempted the Appropriations Committee from several requirements, including the provision requiring open business meetings.

● Did not require committees to make public how members voted on amendments within committee.

● Allowed minorities on committees to outvote majorities if the majority members were not present, since it prohibited general proxy voting and allowed special proxies only under certain conditions.

● Did not allow the ideological minority (as opposed to the partisan minority) on a committee to call witnesses.

Richard H. Ichord (D Mo.), chairman of the Internal Security Committee, opposed a section of the bill which he said would prohibit committees from holding public hearings when testimony might "tend to reflect adversely on the character or reputation" of any person. He said the provision would hamper his committee.

Donald W. Riegle Jr. (R Mich.) said that because of archaic procedures, Congress was "no longer co-equal with the Executive Branch" and that its image had declined. He advocated:

● A permanent Joint Committee on Congressional Operations.

● Election of committee chairmen without regard to seniority.

● Opening to the public of all committee meetings that did not endanger national security or unduly violate personal privacy.

• Electronic voting.
• A systems analysis approach for appropriations which would budget funds by function rather than by agency.

1970 Action

The crucial decisions on legislative reform in 1970 came in the House, with Rules Committee approval of a compromise reorganization bill, which purposely ignored the major controversial reform proposals, and the successful efforts of reform backers to get the bill to a final vote on the floor after a debate that spanned a three-month period. Senate action after that was anti-climactic. Having prepared the ground in 1967 and 1969, senators readily agreed to the House-passed version with only minor revision after adopting some modest changes in Senate rules. The House acted quickly in approving the Senate changes without requesting a House-Senate conference.

HOUSE

Committee. The House Rules Committee June 17 reported a clean bill (HR 17654—H Rept 91-1215). It was the first major legislative reform bill to emerge from a House committee in 24 years.

HR 17654 did not propose any change in the seniority system, nor did it include provisions for electronic voting or reform of the way floor debates were presented in the *Congressional Record.*

The Rules Committee, unable to agree on reforms in two other controversial areas, approved a separate resolution (H Res 1931) turning over proposed amendments to tighten lobbying and political campaign financing to the House Committee on Standards of Official Conduct. *(See 1971 Federal Election Campaign Act, p. 397)*

Besides the changes in House procedures, in the operations of Congress as an institution and in the Legislative Reference Service of the Library of Congress, HR 17654 contained provisions applying to the Senate that were in most cases identical to those in S 844, reported by the Senate Government Operations Committee in 1969, and to provisions in S 355, which was passed by the Senate in 1967.

The bill was sent to the floor under a rule permitting any germane amendment to be offered, with the exception that no amendments to change the jurisdiction of any House committee—such as splitting the Education and Labor Committee—could be considered.

Floor. The House passed HR 17654 Sept. 17 after intermittent debate that lasted for more than three months. The vote was 326-19, with six Republicans and 13 Democrats voting against the bill. Fewer than half of the chairmen of the 21 standing committees voted for passage. During debate, the House adopted 36 amendments and rejected 29.

Most important among the 36 amendments adopted was the proposal permitting teller votes on amendments during floor debate to be recorded upon request of one-fifth of a quorum. (When the House meets to debate most bills it meets as the Committee of the Whole where a quorum is 100; meeting as the House, a quorum is a bare majority of the membership—218.) Therefore, the new change in the House rules made it possible for as few as 20 members to obtain a recorded vote on amendments which often drastically change the substance of a bill under consideration. Although the Senate had always had the opportunity of getting members' positions on amendments recorded, the new recorded teller vote in the House marked the first time representatives were forced to publicly disclose their positions on important amendments.

Other significant reforms approved were requirements to make public all roll-call votes taken in committee during the drafting of legislation, and to provide a minimum of three days between the date a conference report on a bill was reported and made available to members and the day it was brought up for a final vote. *(For major amendments rejected, see box p. 389)*

Another key change was made during the debate, which cleared away a major obstacle to Senate acceptance of the bill. By voice vote, the House agreed to modify a provision which required a two-thirds majority vote to approve any nongermane amendment added by the Senate to a House-passed bill. *(House confusion on application of the provision, see final provisions p. 387)*

Nine out of 10 amendments to streamline Congress and open up its operations to the public that were pushed by a bipartisan group in the House were approved.

Debate July 13

As debate began, B. F. Sisk (D Calif.), chairman of the special Rules subcommittee which wrote the bill, said that it was "not all I would like," but that the best reform proposals in the world were of no importance if there were not the votes to approve them in the House.

July 14

The House adopted two reform amendments and defeated two others in the first day of floor action on amendments.

By a teller vote of 71-54, the House approved an amendment by Fred R. Schwengel (R Iowa) to abolish voting by proxies in committee. By voice vote, the House also agreed to an amendment proposed by Dante B. Fascell (D Fla.), and backed by the bipartisan reform group, which required that all record votes taken in committee be made public along with the position taken by each voting member. *(Subsequent rejection of Schwengel amendment, Sept. 17 debate.)*

The House rejected an amendment proposed by William D. Hathaway (D Maine) to require a daily on-the-record vote in committee to determine whether a committee meeting or hearing for the day would be open or closed to the public. This amendment—endorsed by the bipartisan group—was rejected by a teller vote of 102-132.

The House also rejected by voice vote an amendment by Fascell to dilute the power of committee chairmen by providing that the majority of a committee could elect a temporary chairman if they determined that the chairman was unable to carry out his duties.

July 16

The House adopted an amendment proposed by Frank Thompson Jr. (D N.J.) to provide that no less than one-third of a committee's funds for personnel be used to furnish the minority party members of the committee with investigatory staff. The amendment was adopted by a teller vote of 105-63. A number of committee and subcommittee chairmen opposed the amendment; it was supported by the bipartisan reform group. *(Later controversy over repeal of the provision, see final provisions p. 385, box p. 386)*

July 20

House reformers narrowly won a major battle by defeating an amendment which would have struck from the bill the provisions allowing broadcasting of House committee hearings. Proposed by David W. Dennis (R Ind.)—who objected to the "physical disruption" of committee proceedings which he said broadcasting would entail—the amendment was defeated by a teller vote of 93-96.

July 27

Supporters of House reform won a major victory with adoption by voice vote of an amendment allowing votes of members on a teller vote during consideration of a bill in the Committee of the Whole to be recorded like roll-call votes at the request of one-fifth (20) of a quorum.

Under the former rules, tellers tallied the total number of members voting for and against an amendment, reporting the total but not the names of who voted and how. Under the new rule, one-fifth of a quorum could ask that clerks record the names of members voting on teller votes, how they voted, and the names of members who did not vote.

The amendment, cosponsored by Thomas P. O'Neill Jr. (D Mass.), Charles S. Gubser (R Calif.) and 182 other members, included a provision stating that members would have at least 12 minutes from the beginning of the teller vote to reach the floor and be counted. (Under the electronic voting procedure begun in January 1973, members have 15 minutes in which to vote.) The amendment had been rejected by a 6-6 vote in the Rules Committee.

O'Neill pointed out that the House disposed of many of its crucial and controversial issues by teller vote, thus concealing the positions which representatives took on those questions. "If we were recording these votes, if the people at home knew how we actually voted, I believe we probably would have had some different results," he said. "Probably we would have passed more pieces of legislation." *(Box, p. 384)*

Majority Whip Hale Boggs (D La. 1941-43, 1947-72) said that adoption of the O'Neill-Gubser amendment marked an "historic day...which will make the House of Representatives truly relevant." The existing system of nonrecorded teller votes, he said, was a major reason for absenteeism of members.

Prior to its adoption, the O'Neill-Gubser amendment was modified by amendments which required that the names of members not voting also be recorded and which provided that votes might be recorded by clerks or by electronic means.

The House by voice vote rejected an amendment to the O'Neill-Gubser amendment which would have provided that a recorded teller vote could not be demanded on an amendment unless the amendment had been printed in the *Congressional Record* at least 24 hours before its consideration. This amendment was proposed

by James C. Cleveland (R N.H.), who explained that it was needed to ensure that a member knew on what amendment he was voting.

Though stating that he sympathized with the problem presented by Cleveland, Donald M. Fraser (D Minn.) said the implication of arguments supporting the amendment was that it was "OK to be ignorant of what the amendment is as long as you are not on the record and only when you are going on the record is it essential that you understand what is being voted upon."

After lengthy debate on instituting an electronic system to record votes, the House by voice vote rejected an amendment proposed by H. Allen Smith (R Calif.) which provided for electronic recording of teller votes. The House then accepted an amendment authorizing the House in the future to adopt an electronic system for recording votes. *(Story, see p. 387)*

The House accepted by voice vote an amendment proposed by John N. Erlenborn (R Ill.), as amended by a substitute proposed by Tom Railsback (R Ill.), to provide for at least 10 minutes of debate upon any amendment offered on the floor provided the amendment had been printed in the *Congressional Record* at least one day prior to floor consideration. The purpose of the amendment was to guarantee some time for explanations of any proposed amendment even after House members, by a majority vote, had agreed to cut off further debate on a paragraph or a section of a bill. This amendment was one of those backed by the bipartisan reform group.

The House rejected by voice vote an amendment proposed by Paul G. Rogers (D Fla.) to require that all votes on passage of appropriations bills be by roll call. Barber B. Conable Jr. (R N.Y.) pointed out that in the previous four years the House had approved 30 of 72 appropriations bills by nonrecord votes.

July 28

The House defeated a major challenge to the seniority system through which committee chairmen were chosen, rejecting two amendments which attempted to modify the custom.

The first amendment was offered by Henry S. Reuss (D Wis.) and defeated by a 73-160 teller vote. It would have provided that seniority need not be the sole consideration in the selection of committee chairmen. *(For changes made by both Republicans and Democrats in the selection of committee chairmen, see 1971 chronology.)*

The House also rejected, by a 28-196 teller vote, an amendment proposed by Schwengel as a substitute for the Reuss amendment. The substitute provided that the majority party committee members should select their chairman from the three senior majority members of the committee.

Opponents of the Reuss and Schwengel amendments warned that campaigns for chairmanships would provide the opportunity for pressure groups to wheel and deal in support of their candidates for chairmen of various committees.

Ken Hechler (D W.Va.) said "the longer I serve in the Congress, the more evils I see in the seniority system, which puts a premium on those who can survive election after election, regardless of their ability, their responsiveness to public attitudes and their philosophy as it relates to the policies of their political party."

July 29

The House accepted an amendment proposed by Richard C. White (D Texas) to allow a quorum call to be dispensed with after a quorum had been obtained, and to allow members to answer the call by signing tally sheets for 30 minutes after the call had begun. The amendment, endorsed by the bipartisan reform group, was intended to shorten considerably the time consumed by the House in such calls. It was approved by a 68-20 standing vote.

A point of order was sustained against an amendment proposed by Andrew Jacobs Jr. (D Ind. 1965-73) to bar the Rules Committee from reporting bills under a closed rule which forbade any amendments from being offered on the floor.

The House also rejected by voice vote an amendment proposed by William A. Steiger (R Wis.) to require that the *Congressional Record* be a verbatim account of proceedings of the House. The amendment would have restricted extensions and revisions of remarks delivered on the floor to corrections of grammatical and typographical errors—with no changes in meaning or content of remarks. The proposed amendment allowed insertions in the Record of remarks not actually delivered on the floor but required that they be printed in a different typeface from that used for the verbatim remarks.

An amendment offered by Lloyd Meeds (D Wash.), and supported by the bipartisan reform group, to allow 10 minutes of debate on a motion to recommit a bill to committee with instructions, was accepted by a standing vote of 43-16.

Sept. 15

Debate resumed on HR 17654 after a six-week lag. A major obstacle to Senate approval of the reform bill was removed when the House by voice vote agreed to a compromise version of the controversial provision requiring a two-thirds vote to accept any nongermane amendment added by the Senate to a House-passed bill.

The House had a strict germaneness rule barring adoption of any amendment to a bill unless it was relevant to the bill's subject matter. The Senate did not have such a rule and frequently added nongermane amendments to measures which the House had passed.

The compromise provided that the House, upon request of any member, would vote separately on any nongermane amendment, with only a majority vote needed for approval.

The new rule made it possible for the House to vote upon a nongermane Senate amendment apart from the bill itself when considering a conference report.

The House also accepted by voice votes two amendments concerning conference reports. The first, proposed by Sisk, provided that conferees could not add new language or provisions to a bill not previously approved in some form by either chamber or modify any bill sent to conference beyond the scope of the provisions contained in the House and Senate versions.

The House then accepted an amendment which provided that the House would not consider a conference report until copies were available on the floor and unless the report and accompanying statement had been printed in the *Congressional Record* at least three calendar days, excluding Saturdays, Sundays and legal holidays, prior

to floor consideration. The rule would not apply during the last six days of a congressional session. This amendment had been endorsed by the bipartisan reform group.

Another amendment accepted by voice vote provided that the resident commissioner from Puerto Rico would be appointed by the speaker to standing committees in the same manner as were all elected members and that he would be able to vote in committee meetings. Under the previous rules, the resident commissioner was a nonvoting member of the Agriculture, Armed Services and Interior Committees. *(In 1970 the District of Columbia was given a similar elected nonvoting delegate; District of Columbia chapter.)*

An amendment to limit the tenure of committee chairmen to four terms, unless the House agreed by a two-thirds vote to make an exception to that rule, was rejected by voice vote.

Sept. 16

The House adopted by voice votes amendments providing for an annual 30-day August recess for Congress and continuing the use of high school boys as pages, rather than college-age boys as the committee bill had authorized.

The House also amended HR 17654 to delete provisions raising the salary of a representative's top aide to that of a senator's administrative assistant. Another amendment was adopted converting the House salary structure from a base to a gross pay standard. This latter amendment, proposed by Joel T. Broyhill (R Va.) and amended by Sam Gibbons (D Fla.), was first rejected on a standing vote, 20-26, but subsequently approved by an 84-73 teller vote. The base pay was established by a 1945 pay act. Since then, 17 staff pay increases had been enacted which were reflected in the gross pay standard.

Sept. 17

On the last day of debate on HR 17654, the House reversed its earlier action barring proxy voting in committee.

The House July 14 had adopted an amendment to prohibit the use of proxy votes in committee.

Before the final vote on the bill, Sisk asked for a separate vote on the Schwengel amendment, which then was rejected by a roll-call vote of 156-187.

Earlier, the House by voice vote had adopted an amendment deleting the section in the bill creating a joint committee to set up a coordinated automatic data processing and information retrieval system for the Congress.

Before passing HR 17654, the House by voice vote also adopted amendments authorizing construction of the John W. McCormack Residential Page School and creating a Joint Committee on Congressional Operations to carry out a continuing study of the Congress, including consideration of congressional use of automatic data processing systems.

SENATE

Committee. The Senate Government Operations Committee in May 1969 had reported its own congressional reorganization bill (S 844). *(See 1969 action, p. 390)*

(Continued on p. 396)

Nongermane Amendments: 1972 House Action Amended Rule

The House Oct. 13, 1972, passed by a 281-57 vote a resolution (H Res 1153) amending its rules governing consideration of committee reports, House-Senate conference reports and nongermane amendments added by the Senate. Under the new rules which took effect at the beginning of the 93rd Congress:

• Conference reports and provisions reported in disagreement by House-Senate conferees had to be printed in the *Congressional Record* when reported and could not be considered by the House until at least the third day thereafter. (Under the former rule, conference reports could not be considered until the fourth day. There was no provision dealing with voting on provisions reported by conferees in disagreement, therefore they could be considered immediately by the House. There was no requirement for printing conference reports in the *Congressional Record*, although in practice such reports were published in the Record on or before the report was considered by the House.)

• A bill could not be considered on the House floor until the third day a committee report on the bill had been available to members. (Previously, a bill could not be considered until the fourth day.)

• During House consideration of conference reports, any Senate amendment accepted by House conferees, which if introduced in the House would be ruled nongermane under House rules, was subject to 40 minutes debate and a majority vote on acceptance of the amendment. If a nongermane amendment was rejected, the entire conference report would be rejected and the bill, without the rejected amendment, would be returned to the Senate for further action.

Background. The primary impetus for the resolution was the issue of nongermane amendments added by the Senate—a long-standing irritant between the two chambers.

The House had strict rules forbidding consideration of amendments not germane to the bill before the House. The Senate, however, for years had attached nongermane amendments to House-passed bills. House members complained that the practice prevented them from considering these amendments because they were not considered in a House committee and, incorporated in conference reports, could not be voted separately.

During the 92nd Congress, the House operated under the new rule dealing with nongermane amendments to conference reports. The 1970 change was intended to rectify a problem which the previous House rule forbidding the House from considering nongermane amendments apart from the rest of a conference report had presented. But as written into the 1970 reorganization act, the new rule failed to achieve the desired result, partly because the 1970 act did not spell out the parliamentary procedure to follow in taking a separate recorded vote on nongermane portions of conference reports and partly because the new rule appeared to conflict with other House rules, that were not repealed, requiring an up-or-down vote on the entire bill with no chance to amend it.

Therefore, when a conference committee did agree to nongermane amendments, it was necessary in the House to obtain a special rule from the Rules Committee waiving points of order against nongermane amendments before bringing the conference report to the floor. On two major bills in the 92nd Congress—the fiscal 1972 military procurement authorization and the rural development bill—the germaneness issue was central.

On Nov. 10, 1971, the House agreed to a rule waiving points of order against the military procurement (HR 8687—PL 92-156) conference report and allowing separate votes on three sections of the conference report. The House actually voted on only one—allowing the importation of Rhodesian chrome—which it approved by a 251-100 roll-call vote.

On July 27, 1972, the House took up consideration of a Rules Committee resolution (H Res 1057) on the conference report of the rural development bill (HR 12931). The bill included eight provisions which Rules Committee members thought were nongermane. H Res 1057 waived points of order against the nongermane amendments and did not provide an opportunity to vote on the eight provisions separately.

H. Allen Smith (R Calif. 1957-73), ranking Republican on the Rules Committee, was ready to offer an amendment to H Res 1057 to provide for separate votes if the House defeated the previous question on the rule ordering an immediate vote on the conference report. However, the House voted 214-162 to order the previous question and then approved H Res 1057 by a voice vote. Subsequently, the House agreed to the conference report on HR 12931 by a 339-36 roll-call vote.

Under the newly adopted procedure for nongermane amendments, House members could make points of order against a conference report after it was read but before debate began on it. If any portion of the conference report was ruled nongermane, that portion was immediately subject to 40 minutes of debate and a separate vote on it. This could be repeated until all points of order were offered. If no points of order were sustained or if the House accepted all nongermane amendments, the House would then consider and accept or reject the conference report as a whole.

If any or all of the nongermane amendments were rejected by the House, the House then could consider a motion to accept the Senate version with an amendment—the amendment consisting of all provisions of the conference report not rejected by the House. If the House agreed to this motion, according to House Rules Committee members, the Senate could then agree to the House version, without the nongermane amendments, or request a second conference on the bill.

The House Rules Committee Sept. 26, 1972, reported H Res 1138 (H Rept 92-1451), but on Oct. 11 the committee held further hearings and reported another resolution (H Res 1153—H Rept 92-1573) revising some of the rules changes contained in H Res 1138.

On Oct. 13, the House by a 281-57 roll-call vote approved the rules changes set forth in H Res 1153.

S 844 incorporated the provisions of the congressional reform bill (S 355) which the Senate had approved in 1967 except for provisions of S 355 dealing with lobbying.

Almost all of the provisions of HR 17654 which affected the operations or the rules of the Senate were similar to provisions of S 844. Therefore HR 17654 was not considered by the Senate committee following House approval, but was placed on the Senate calendar Sept. 23 and brought to the floor Oct. 5.

Floor. The Senate spent only two days debating the bill before passing it Oct. 6 by a 59-5 roll-call vote. Five southern Democrats voted against HR 17654.

The Senate's version was essentially the same as that approved by the House except for the provisions pertaining only to the Senate.

As in the House, all attempts to revise the seniority system were soundly rebuffed, but the Senate did adopt amendments which limited the number of committees on which senators could serve in the future and the number of chairmanships which they could hold.

The Senate also approved amendments to rename the Committee on Banking and Currency the Committee on Banking, Housing and Urban Affairs, and to create a permanent Committee on Veterans' Affairs.

Debate Oct. 5

The Senate approved a series of amendments adding the provisions of S 844 to the bill.

Lee Metcalf (D Mont.), who had served as a member of the Joint Committee on the Organization of Congress, was floor manager of HR 17654. He said there were very few differences between Senate-related provisions of HR 17654, S 844 and S 355.

Metcalf pointed out that some provisions, pertaining only to the Senate, were not considered by the House and had to be added to HR 17654; the Senate in turn did not consider any provisions of the bill which dealt solely with the procedures of the House. Any major addition to or change in the bill, Metcalf warned, might mean the death of congressional reform in the 91st Congress.

The Senate Oct. 5-6 by voice vote adopted 13 amendments offered by Metcalf, including one which made the proposed August recess for Congress mandatory only in nonelection years. Metcalf said the House did not object to that change.

Jacob K. Javits (R N.Y.) proposed and then withdrew an amendment to establish a 30-day appropriations session for each chamber every year and to change the fiscal year to conform with the calendar year.

Oct. 6

The Senate defeated an attempt to eliminate the seniority system for selecting committee chairmen, and then passed HR 17654.

An amendment by Robert W. Packwood (R Ore.) to replace the seniority system (under which the entire Senate routinely approved as the chairman of each committee the member of the majority party with the most years of service on the committee, with a new system under which the majority members of each committee would select the committee chairman (and the minority members would select the ranking minority member) was rejected, 22-46. A voting majority in each party opposed the amendment.

Before voting to reject the amendment, the Senate by a 23-44 roll-call vote refused to allow the majority party caucus to select their committee chairmen. This alternate proposal was made by Charles McC. Mathias Jr. (R Md.) as an amendment to the Packwood amendment.

The Senate agreed by voice vote to create a Senate Veterans' Affairs Committee after defeating, 29-37, a motion by Russell B. Long (D La.) to table the amendment. The Senate Finance Committee, of which Long was chairman, the Interior and Insular Affairs Committee and the Senate Labor and Public Welfare Veterans' Affairs Subcommittee, of which Alan Cranston (D Calif.) was chairman, had jurisdiction over Senate measures concerning veterans. The House had established a Veterans' Affairs Committee in 1947.

The Senate also amended HR 17654 to require Senate committees to establish and publish certain rules of procedure, to retain the existing Joint Committee on the Library instead of substituting a new Joint Committee on the Library and Congressional Research and to provide that Senate pages must be between 14 and 18 years old.

The Senate by voice vote approved an amendment adding provisions of S 844 and S 355 which limited the work load that one senator might assume. The new provisions limited future work loads to membership on two major committees and one minor, select or joint committee to membership on only one of the following: Appropriations, Armed Services, Finance or Foreign Relations Committees, and to the chairmanship of one full committee and one subcommittee. No senator at the time the bill went into effect would be deprived of any chairmanship or committee position by the amendment; it applied only to future assignments.

Provisions. Only minor changes were made in the House version by the Senate; as passed by the Senate, provisions were the same as those enacted into law.

FINAL ACTION

The House Oct. 8, 1970, by voice vote agreed to the changes in HR 17654 made by the Senate, completing congressional action. The bill was signed by the President Oct. 26 (PL 91-510).

CQ Campaign Spending

CAMPAIGN FINANCING REFORM: COMPROMISE BILL ENACTED

The second of two major reforms in the area of Congress and politics went into effect early in 1972 with enactment of the Federal Election Campaign Act of 1971, a bill placing a ceiling on the amount of money a candidate for President, Vice President, the House or the Senate could spend for radio and television time, and other forms of political advertising, and requiring full disclosures of campaign contributions and expenditures.

The bill (S 382—PL 92-225) went into effect April 7, 1972, 60 days after it was signed by the President.

The heart of the new law was a provision placing a ceiling on the amount of money a candidate for federal office could spend on political advertising in the communications media, most important of which were radio and television. Under the new law, candidates were restricted to a maximum of 10 cents per eligible voter for all forms of media advertising—radio and television time, newspapers, magazines, billboards and automatic telephone equipment.

Attempts at reform began early in the 92nd Congress when numerous bills to reform election campaigning were introduced in the House and the Senate. The Senate bills were referred simultaneously to three committees—Commerce, which had jurisdiction over broadcasting, Rules, which had jurisdiction over election procedures, and Finance, which had jurisdiction over tax proposals.

Of the many proposals introduced, the one which came the closest to being a Nixon administration bill was S 956, cosponsored by Senate Minority Leader Hugh Scott (R Pa.) and Charles McC. Mathias (R Md.).

President Nixon himself was committed to a major overhaul of campaign practices. In October 1970, he had vetoed a bill (S 3637) that would have limited only broadcast spending by candidates for President, Congress and Governor. The bill set ceilings on general election campaign broadcast spending by candidates to seven cents per vote cast in the previous election. It also repealed the equal time provision of the 1934 Communications Act for presidential and vice presidential candidates.

In vetoing the bill, however, Nixon praised the "highly laudable and widely supported goals of controlling political campaign expenditures.... I am as opposed to big spending in campaigns as I am to big spending in government." Mr. Nixon's reasons for vetoing that bill were: 1) that it would have discriminated against broadcasters, 2) would have given an unfair advantage to incumbents and 3) would not have provided much needed over-all campaign reform.

Pressure for Reform. The 1968 and 1970 federal election campaigns saw a skyrocketing of political campaign spending by both major parties. There also was a profusion of affluent candidates which made political spending a major campaign issue in itself. By 1971, after Nixon's veto of the first reform bill, members came under considerable pressure to pass a bill that would be ap-

plicable to the 1972 presidential and congressional elections. Even as the proposals were being introduced, potential candidates from both major parties were collecting and spending sizable amounts to finance campaign organizations in preparation for the elections. *(Politics chapter, p. 1)*

Proponents of reform, cognizant of the partisan considerations that could have threatened any revision of campaign laws, worked to avoid writing a law that would favor any political party or candidate. Republicans, aware of the relatively healthy financial condition of their party in 1971, were eager to protect their coffers; Democrats did not want to jeopardize their large contributions from organized labor.

The reform thrust was also pushed by various groups outside Congress, including the National Commiteee for an Effective Congress, the chief pressure group, the citizens' lobby Common Cause, labor unions and some media organizations.

Eight months after enactment of the new law, legislation to modify one of its provisions—prohibiting corporations and labor unions having federal government contracts from making direct political contributions—was passed by the House. But the Senate refused to act on the bill and it died at the end of the 92nd Congress. *(p. 409)*

A plan to avoid the abuses of trying to raise money from private sources for running presidential election campaigns was reluctantly signed by the President Dec. 10, 1971. The bill (HR 10947—PL 92-178) established a federal election fund from public tax revenues to finance presidential campaigns. As a price for the President's acquiescence, however, sponsors were forced to change the effective date of PL 92-178 so that it would not apply to the 1972 presidential campaign. *(p. 410)*

Loopholes in New Law

The 1972 presidential and congressional elections highlighted some major failures of the new spending law. A loophole that existed previously that was not satisfactorily corrected was the "pass-through" political contribution. This occurs when a donor gives a sum of money to another person, committee or organization who in turn hands over the money, according to the wishes of the original donor, to a candidate for public office.

Although the pass-through tactic was prohibited under PL 92-225, a loophole was created which allowed an organization such as a social club, which was not established primarily to influence the outcome of an election, to use some of its dues for such purposes. If the organization contributed to a particular candidate an amount exceeding $1,000, it would have to report the total amount, but the names of the contributors would be shielded from public view. There was no requirement in the law to force such an organization to disclose the names of its members who had paid the dues which eventually became the political donation.

Another loophole was the loose definition of the word "candidate" in Title I of the law establishing media spending limitations for candidates. The language was construed in such a way as to permit persons to accept contributions and to spend money to aid their own prospects for public office and still not come under the law's spending ceiling for political advertising of 10 cents per eligible voter. The definition, moreover, was narrower than that contained in Titles II and III of the same law or that used by the Federal Communications Commission in dealing with requests for political broadcast time. Thus the Title I definition permitted unlimited spending during a time when a person might be a candidate in every way but name. Presidential candidates, for example, in recent years had made a habit of running unannounced for long periods before making an official announcement of candidacy, sometimes almost up to the eve of the first presidential primary.

A continuing tax loophole that was not plugged up was the exemption from federal gift taxes of political contributions under $3,000. It was evident from the 1972 campaigns that many persons had contributed substantially more than this amount to a single candidate—while avoiding the gift tax—by making more than one donation under $3,000 to numerous political committees working on behalf of the same candidate.

A big loophole that showed up during 1972 was in the use of loans to candidates. While the law provided that all debts had to be reported until they were terminated, it was silent on the means by which such loans were to be paid off. Thus a supporter of a particular candidate could forgive a debt to him or require only a token payment on the loan, and the report that was later made public would indicate only that the debt had been terminated. The source of the loan would not have to be named.

A related loophole involved the provision limiting the amount that a candidate or his immediate family could contribute to his own campaign. The restriction did not apply to relatives of the family, and there was no regulation against a member of a family giving the maximum contribution allowed and, in addition, making a loan to the candidate.

A serious flaw according to many observers was the failure of Congress to approve an independent election campaign commission to monitor and enforce the law, particularly Title I setting spending limits. Under the arrangement finally agreed to in PL 92-225, the clerk of the House was responsible for overseeing House elections, the secretary of the Senate for Senate elections and the comptroller general of the GAO for presidential elections.

One of the defects of this procedure was the way in which the Justice Department was given responsibility for prosecuting any violations brought to its attention by the House or Senate overseers or by the comptroller general. While Justice was required to act in any civil case, the language of the law allowed the department complete discretion in deciding whether or not to prosecute in criminal cases.

It was reported that during the 1972 campaigns the department had only one full-time attorney supervising enforcement of the act.

Enforcement was further impeded by another provision in the law requiring periodic reporting of contributions and expenditures. According to many members of Congress, the frequency required for the filing of these reports during election campaigns by all political committees of candidates—required for both primary and general elections—created monumental bookkeeping chores for the candidates. Correspondingly, the mammoth number of reports filed with the House clerk, the Senate secretary and the comptroller general made close scrutiny practically impossible.

Under the law, only contributions "in excess of $100" had to be reported and thus made public. Some members felt this language went counter to the intent of the act to open up the election process because it shielded from public view substantial sums donated in amounts of $100 and less.

Background

The cost of running for political office in America climbed to such dizzy heights in the 1960s that the task of bringing it down to something approaching a reasonable level—and keeping it there—came to seem almost beyond the bounds of legislative ingenuity. Many observers considered regulation of election campaign financing the most important unsolved problem of American democracy.

Mounting campaign costs increased the dependence of candidates on large contributions by wealthy individuals or special interest groups. This, in turn, nourished the image of the officeholder as indebted to these financial backers rather than being free to follow his conscience or represent the wishes of his constituents.

$400 Million in '72. Few topics in American politics were more obscure than the cost of election campaigns. But one fact was certain: modern political campaigns for Congress and the presidency were expensive. The most detailed and reliable figures showed that costs had risen with every presidential campaign.

The Citizens' Research Foundation (CRF) of Princeton, N.J., founded in 1958, was regarded as the most comprehensive source of itemized campaign contributions and expenditures.

In 1952, the total cost of campaigns for all elective offices in the United States was $140-million, according to CRF estimates. These costs rose to $155-million in 1956, $175-million in 1960, $200-million in 1964, $300-million in 1968 and were estimated at $400-million in 1972. Using 1952 as the base year, expenses in 1970 increased 185 percent. However, after economic and political adjustments, the increase was estimated at about 45 percent over the 20-year period. Cost per vote also increased, from 19 cents in 1952 to 60 cents in 1968.

Increased use of the broadcast media, particularly television, accented the growing problem of campaign costs. Television and radio, a major source of news for Americans, were ideally suited to large constituencies. Television emerged after 1952 as the dominant form of communications in presidential and many congressional campaigns. The spurt in spending on political broadcasts testified to the increased use of television and radio. Total charges for political broadcasts in general elections at all levels of government increased from $9.8-million in 1956 to $59.2-million in 1970.

Congressional Reaction. The rising costs of campaigning created in the late 1960s and early 1970s a favorable climate for the enactment of new legislation to regulate political spending. There was general agreement in both political parties that the existing law, the 1925 Federal Corrupt Practices Act, was inadequate to cope with the problems of contemporary political financing. A November 1970 Gallup Poll found that 78 per cent of adult Americans favored a law limiting the total amount of money spent in political campaigns; it had become difficult for a political figure to publicly oppose the need for new legislation on political spending.

Partisan politics also worked in favor of new legislation. The Democratic Party controlled Congress and was heavily in debt as the 1972 presidential campaign against President Nixon approached. Democrats looked upon laws regulating campaign financing as one way to narrow the financial odds against them. And although the Republicans were reluctant to lose the advantage that their well-stocked campaign war chest provided, they were also unwilling to come out on the wrong side of the campaign spending issue.

Congress worked on three major campaign spending bills in 1969-72:

• In 1970, Congress cleared a bill limiting spending on political radio and television broadcasting and repealing the "equal time" provisions of the 1934 Communications Act. President Nixon vetoed the bill, and the Senate failed to override it. In a letter to Minority Leader Hugh Scott (R Pa.), Mr. Nixon said he would endorse a "comprehensive election reform bill," *(p. 402)*

• In 1971, at the end of the first session of the 92nd Congress, House-Senate conferees had agreed on a compromise campaign spending bill regulating spending on all media—radio-television, printed material and billboards. The bill cleared the Senate before adjournment and was approved by the House in January 1972. Under the bill, presidential candidates in 1972 would be limited to $8.4-million for television spending—an amount less than that spent by the Republicans in 1968. However, the bill did not take effect until April 7, 1972, —60 days after it was signed into law. *(Box this page)*

• Also in 1971, Senate Democrats attached a campaign financing amendment to the Nixon administration's Revenue Act of 1971 (PL 92-178). The measure would have provided the two major parties in 1972 with a $20-million presidential campaign fund financed out of the U.S. Treasury from tax check-offs approved by individual taxpayers. House-Senate conferees, faced with a threatened veto by President Nixon because of the amendment, agreed to delay implementation of the plan until after the 1972 election. *(p. 410)*

FINAL PROVISIONS

As enacted into law Feb. 7, 1972 (S 382—PL 92-225):

Title I—Campaign Communications

• Limited the amount that could be spent by federal candidates for advertising time in communications media to 10 cents per eligible voter, or $50,000, whichever was greater. The limitation would apply to all candidates

Campaign Spending Limits

Under S 382 (PL 92-225) as cleared by Congress, the law allowed use of up to 60 percent of allowable funds (based on 10 cents per eligible voter in each state) for either broadcast or non-broadcast media advertising. Table below reflects spending ceilings permitted for 1972 Senate elections if candidates chose to spend the maximum on broadcast advertising (*Asterik represents minimum allowable*)

State	Broadcast 60 Percent	Non-Broadcast 40 Percent	Media Limit
Ala.	$137,460	$ 91,640	$229,100
Alaska	36,000	24,000	60,000*
Ariz.	73,620	49,080	122,700
Ark.	79,080	52,720	131,800
Calif.	854,220	569,480	1,423,700
Colo.	91,920	61,280	153,200
Conn.	127,020	84,680	211,700
Del.	36,000	24,000	60,000*
Fla.	305,280	203,520	508,800
Ga.	186,660	124,440	311,100
Hawaii	36,000	24,000	60,000*
Idaho	36,000	24,000	60,000*
Ill.	453,780	302,520	756,300
Ind.	209,220	139,480	348,700
Iowa	113,220	75,480	188,700
Kan.	92,340	61,560	153,900
Ky.	130,620	87,080	217,700
La.	141,360	94,240	235,600
Maine	39,720	26,480	66,200
Md.	162,900	108,600	271,500
Mass.	236,820	157,880	394,700
Mich.	352,500	235,000	587,500
Minn.	151,380	100,920	252,300
Miss.	84,720	56,480	141,200
Mo.	193,320	128,880	322,200
Mont.	36,000	24,000	60,000*
Neb.	60,120	40,080	100,200
Nev.	36,000	24,000	60,000*
N.H.	36,000	24,000	60,000*
N.J.	301,080	200,720	501,800
N.M.	37,980	25,320	63,300
N.Y.	762,840	508,560	1,271,400
N.C.	209,580	139,720	349,300
N.D.	36,000	24,000	60,000*
Ohio	429,900	286,600	716,500
Okla.	107,460	71,640	179,100
Ore.	88,380	58,920	147,300
Pa.	488,160	325,440	813,600
R.I.	40,260	26,840	67,100
S.C.	102,900	68,600	171,500
S.D.	36,000	24,000	60,000*
Tenn.	162,600	108,400	271,000
Texas	455,340	303,560	758,900
Utah	40,440	26,960	67,400
Vt.	36,000	24,000	60,000*
Va.	193,920	129,280	323,200
Wash.	142,860	95,240	238,100
W.Va.	70,500	47,000	117,500
Wis.	176,880	117,920	294,800
Wyo.	36,000	24,000	60,000*

SOURCE: Bureau of the Census Estimates, November 1972.

for president and vice president, senator and representative, and would be determined annually for the geographical area of each electon by the Bureau of the Census.

• Included in the definition of "communications media" were radio and television broadcasting stations, newspapers, magazines, billboards and automatic telephone equipment. Of the total amount permitted to be spent in a campaign, up to 60 per cent could be used for broadcast advertising time.

• Prohibited radio and television stations from charging political candidates more than the lowest unit cost for the same advertising time available to commercial advertisers. Lowest unit rate charges would apply only during the 45 days preceding a primary election and the 60 days preceding a general election.

• Required non-broadcast media to charge candidates no more than the comparable amounts charged to commercial advertisers for the same class and amount of advertising space. The requirement would apply only during the 45 days preceding the date of a primary election and 60 days before the date of a general election.

• Specified that candidates for president could spend during the period prior to the nomination convention no more in primary and non-primary states than the amount allowed under the 10-cent-per-voter communications spending limitation.

• Provided that broadcast and non-broadcast spending limitations were to be increased in proportion to annual increases in the Consumer Price Index over the base year 1970.

• Provided that amounts spent by an agent of a candidate on behalf of his candidacy would be charged against the over-all expenditure allocation. Fees paid to the agent for services performed also would be charged against the over-all limitation.

• Stipulated that no broadcast station could make any charge for political advertising time on a station unless written consent to contract for such time had been given by the candidate, and unless the candidate certified that such charges would not exceed his spending limit.

Title II—Criminal Code Amendments

• Defined "election" to mean any general, special, primary or runoff election, nominating convention or caucus, delegate selection primary, presidential preference primary or constitutional convention.

• Broadened the definitions of "contribution" and "expenditure" as they pertained to political campaigns, but exempted a loan of money by a national or state bank made in accordance with applicable banking laws.

• Prohibited promises of employment or other political rewards or benefits by any candidate in exchange for political support, and prohibited contracts between candidates and any federal department or agency.

• Placed a ceiling on contributions by any candidate or his immediate family to his own campaign of $50,000 for president or vice president, $35,000 for senator, and $25,000 for representative.

• Provided that the definitions "contribution" and "expenditure" did not include communications, non-partisan registration and get-out-the-vote campaigns by a corporation aimed at its stockholders or by a labor organization aimed at its members.

Key Provisions of S 382

The Federal Election Campaign Act of 1971 (S 382—PL 92-225) contained the following key provisions:

• Retained the "equal time" requirement of the Communications Act of 1934 for all candidates for federal office.

• Limited to 10 cents per voter the amount that could be spent by candidates for Congress and for President or Vice President for advertising on television, radio, newspapers, magazines, billboards and automatic telephone equipment. Up to 60 percent of the over-all ceiling on media spending could be spent on braodcasting.

• Required broadcasters to sell candidates advertising at the lowest unit rate in effect for the time and space used. The requirement would be in effect during the last 45 days preceding a primary election and the last 60 days preceding a general election.

• Provided for an increase in the media spending limit based on annual increases in the Consumer Price Index.

• Strengthened the requirements for reporting how much a candidate spent on his campaign and the sources of his contributions and other income.

• Specified that all candidates and political committees had to report names and addresses of all persons who made contributions or loans in excess of $100, and persons to whom expenditures in excess of $100 were made.

• Designated as the supervisory officers for collection of campaign reports the secretary of the Senate for Senate candidates, the House clerk for House candidates and the comptroller general of the General Accounting Office for presidential candidates. Copies of reports were required to be filed with the secretaries of state in those states where elections were held.

• Defined more strictly the roles unions and corporations could play in political campaigns.

• Limited the amount a candidate or his family could contribute to his own campaign to $50,000 for President or Vice President, $35,000 for senator and $25,000 for representative.

• Repealed the Corrupt Practices Act of 1925.

• Provided that the definitions "contribution" and "expenditure" did not include the establishment, administration and solicitation of voluntary contributions to a separate segregated fund to be utilized for political purposes by a corporation or labor organization.

Title III—Disclosure of Federal Campaign Funds

• Required all political committees that anticipated receipts in excess of $1,000 during the calendar year to file a statement of organization with the appropriate federal supervisory officer, which was to include the names of all principal officers, the scope of the committee, the names of all candidates the committee supported and other information as required by law.

- Required all political committees to have a chairman and a treasurer, and prohibited any expenditure by the committee without the authorization of the chairman or treasurer.

- Stipulated that the appropriate federal supervisory officer to oversee election campaign practices, reporting and disclosure was the clerk of the House for House candidates, the secretary of the Senate for Senate candidates and the comptroller general of the General Accounting Office (GAO) for presidential candidates.

- Required each political committee to report any individual expenditure of more than $100 and any expenditures of more than $100 in the aggregate during the calendar year.

- Required disclosure of all contributions to any committee or candidate in excess of $100, including a detailed report with the name and address of the contributor and the date the contribution was made.

- Required any committee that accepted contributions or made expenditures on behalf of any candidate without the authorization of such candidate to include a notice on the front page of all literature published by the committee stating that the committee was not authorized by the candidate and that the candidate was not responsible for the activities of the committee.

- Required the federal supervisory officers to prepare an annual report for each campaign committee registered and to make such reports available for sale to the public.

- Required candidates and committees to file reports of contributions and expenditures on the 10th day of March, June and September of every year, on the 15th and fifth days preceding the date on which an election was held and on the 31st day of January. Any contribution of $5,000 or more was to be reported within 48 hours after its receipt.

- Required reporting of the names, addresses and occupations of any lender and endorser of any loan in excess of $100 as well as the date and amount of such loans.

- Required reporting of the total proceeds from the sales of tickets to all fund-raising events, mass collections made at such events and sales of political campaign materials.

- Required any person who made any contribution in excess of $100, other than through a political committee or directly to the candidate, to report such contribution to the appropriate supervisory officer.

- Required a full and complete financial statement of the costs of holding a presidential nominating convention within 60 days after the end of the convention.

- Prohibited any contribution to a candidate or committee by one person in the name of another person.

- Authorized the office of the comptroller general of the GAO to serve as a national clearinghouse for information on the administration of election practices.

- Required political parties in states where a presidential nominating convention was held to file detailed reports on the financing of the convention with the office of the comptroller general.

- Required that copies of reports filed by candidates with the appropriate supervisory officer also be filed with the secretaries of state for the states in which the elections were held.

Title IV—General Provisions

- Repealed the Federal Corrupt Practices Act of 1925 (2 U.S. Code 241-256).

- Required the Civil Aeronautics Board, the Federal Communications Commission and the Interstate Commerce Commission to promulgate regulations with respect to the extension of credit without collateral by any person, business or industry regulated by the federal government to any person on behalf of any candidate for federal office.

- Prohibited funds appropriated for the Office of Economic Opportunity from being used for any political activity.

91st Congress (1969-70)

Both sessions of the 91st Congress showed signs of readiness to take action to regulate campaign spending. However, only one bill (S 3637), which concerned allocation of broadcasting time, was passed by both houses and it was vetoed.

Another bill (S 2876), to provide television time at reduced rates to candidates for the Senate and the House, died in a Senate committee. The bill would have allowed candidates to purchase a limited amount of spot advertising time at 30 per cent of commercial rates and a limited amount of program time at 20 per cent of commercial rates. Philip A. Hart (D Mich.) and James B. Pearson (R Kan.) introduced the bill, with 34 additional sponsors. A similar bill, having 34 sponsors, was introduced in the House. The Senate Commerce Subcommittee on Communications in October 1969 conducted hearings on S 2876 but submitted no report to the full committee. There were no hearings on the corresponding bill in the House.

A bill (S 734) allowing a tax credit for political contributions and requiring the secretary of the Senate and the clerk of the House to publicize reports filed by candidates and political committees was reported by a Senate committee in 1970, but no other action was taken.

Two House committees also conducted hearings on campaign financing reform proposals. In December 1970 hearings were held by the House Standards of Official Conduct Committee, headed by Melvin Price (D Ill.), on revision of the Corrupt Practices Act. A special subcommittee headed by Thomas P. O'Neill (D Mass.) made a formal report to the Justice Department on violations of the act during the 1970 election campaigns.

TAX CREDIT, REPORTING. Although a bill (S 734) was reported by the Senate Rules and Administration Committee, the Senate took no action in 1970 on it. It would have required comprehensive disclosure of political campaign contributions and expenditures and provide tax benefits for individuals who made contributions to candidates for federal office. *(Congress and the Nation Vol. II, p. 441)*

The "Election Reform Act of 1970" was substantially similar to a bill passed by the Senate in 1967 which later died in the House. Its most significant provisions would have required more frequent and detailed reporting of campaign finances by candidates and wider dissemination of such information by the secretary of the Senate and the clerk of the House.

In addition, the bill would have given tax benefits to contributors to candidates for federal offices. Persons could have had the option of taking a tax credit of up to $20 or a tax deduction of up to $100 in figuring federal income tax rates.

The measure would have amended portions of the Federal Corrupt Practices Act of 1925 and the Political Activities Act of 1939, known as the Hatch Act. It would have taken effect Jan. 1, 1971.

Provisions. As reported, S 734:

• Would have imposed a $1,000 fine and/or a prison sentence of one year on anyone who promised employment or other benefit to any person in exchange for political support.

• Would have imposed a $5,000 fine and/or a prison sentence of three years on anyone who solicited political contributions from any nonelected federal employee.

• Would have limited the amount which could be given by any individual to political candidates or commitees to $5,000 per year, and would have credited contributions of that individual's spouse or minor child to that individual.

• Would have prohibited contributions to candidates for federal office from government contractors.

• Would have repealed section 609, Title 18, of the U.S. Code, which limited contributions and expenditures by a political committee to $3-million per year.

• Would have required all political committees receiving or spending $1,000 or more a year to register with the clerk of the House or the secretary of the Senate and to provide detailed records of persons from whom contributions are received or to whom expenditures were made, including exact addresses and amounts.

• Would have required similar reports from individuals who contributed or spent at least $100 per year for political candidates.

• Would have imposed obligations on the secretary of the Senate and clerk of the House to provide wider dissemination of information disclosed by political committees and candidates.

• Would have required a copy of each statement to be filed with the House clerk or Senate secretary to be filed also with the clerk of the United States district court for the judicial district in which the principal office of the political committee or candidate was located.

• Would have prohibited any person from making a contribution in the name of another person.

• Would have allowed a credit against the tax liability of the contributor of an amount equal to one-half of the political contributions made by an individual within the taxable year, but in an amount not to exceed $20 in any taxable year.

• Would have allowed a contributor to take a tax deduction of not more than $100 in lieu of a tax credit.

1970 NIXON VETO. The one campaign financing bill cleared by Congress during the 91st Congress was limited to political broadcast advertising. President Nixon vetoed the bill (S 3637) largely on the ground that it was not comprehensive. More than half the senators voted to override the veto, but supporters of the bill fell four votes short of the two-thirds majority required for overridding a veto.

S 3637 would have limited spending on political broadcasts by candidates for election to the two houses of Congress, the presidency and state governorships. The limits for Senate and House candidates in the primaries would have been $10,000 or three and one-half cents per vote cast in the previous general election, whichever was greater, and, in the general election, $20,000 or seven cents per vote cast in the previous general election, whichever was greater. The bill also would have made possible television debates between the major parties' candidates for President by repealing the equal-time requirements of the Communications Act of 1934.

The Senate passed S 3637 on April 14, 1970, by a vote of 58-27. The House on Aug. 11 passed the bill with amendments which, among other things, applied the bill's restrictions to primary as well as general elections. Conferees accepted the House version after changing the effective date of the measure from Jan. 1, 1971, to 30 days after enactment. Neither the House nor the Senate Republican conferees signed the conference report. The House adopted the report by a vote of 247-112 on Sept. 16. By this time, it was too late for the measure's restrictions to be applied to the 1970 campaign. The Senate on Sept. 23 adopted the report by a vote of 60-19.

President Nixon vetoed S 3637 on Oct. 12, 1970, the last day on which he could sign or veto the bill. If he had not acted, it would have become law without his signature. Since the President had not made known his opposition, members of both houses were under the impression he would sign the bill.

S 3637, the President said in his veto message, represented "a good aim gone amiss." He called it a measure which "plugs only one hole in a sieve," and said he was vetoing it because it:

• "Discriminates against the broadcast media" by imposing spending limits on only one means of communication and leaving unrestricted campaign advertising in print media.

• "Might tend to increase rather than decrease the total amount that candidates spend in their campaigns." Wealthy candidates "would simply shift their advertising out of radio and television into other media."

• "Unfairly endangers freedom of discussion. By restricting the amount of time a candidate could obtain on television and radio, it "would severely limit the ability of many candidates to get their message to the greatest number of the electorate."

• "Gives an unfair advantage to the famous" over "the worthy but little-known" and to "the incumbent officeholder over the office-seeker."

Veto Sustained. On Nov. 20, before the Senate voted on the vetoed bill, the President wrote to Senate Minority Leader Hugh Scott (R Pa.) endorsing Scott's announced plan to propose a comprehensive election reform bill early in 1971. The President's letter said: "Reform is needed in this area, but this issue need not and should not be dealt with in a hurried and contentious fight over a veto. There will be no major elections between now and the time that Congress can consider this legislation in the next session."

The Senate on Nov. 23 sustained the President's veto by a four-vote margin. The vote was 58 for overriding (62 needed) and 34 against. Failure of the Senate to override made a House vote unnecessary.

92nd Congress (1971-72)

Following President Nixon's veto of the broadcast spending bill in 1970 and the Senate's failure to override the veto, Congress went to work early in the first session of the 92nd Congress to draft a new bill.

SENATE ACTION

The Senate Commerce Subcommittee on Communications began hearings in March 1971 on bills to revise federal election laws, lower the costs of political campaigns and reduce the rates of broadcast time to candidates for public office. One of these bills (S 382), placing limits on political campaign expenditures and contributions, was reported with amendments by the committee in May after 10 separate amendments offered by Republicans were defeated by record votes.

Title I of the committee-approved bill limited campaign spending by candidates for federal office to 5 cents per eligible voter for broadcast media and 5 cents per voter for non-broadcast media in both primary and general elections.

The committee said the limitation would allow an estimated $13,956,300 for all media spending by a presidential candidate in the 1972 general election.

For example, the 10-cent-per-voter formula set total media spending in 1972 Senate campaigns of $756,300 per candidate in Illinois, $394,700 in Massachusetts and $758,900 in Texas. Varying amounts were listed by the committee for other states, based on voting age population estimates of the Census Bureau.

Dissenting from the majority, five Republican committee members said the bill's defects were that it did not exempt all candidates for federal office from the equal time provisions, that it provided unrealistically low spending and contribution limits and that it failed to provide for an independent Federal Elections Commission.

Additional hearings on S 382 were held by the Senate Rules and Finance Committees in May, and the Rules Committee issued a second report on the bill in June endorsing S 382.

Democratic and Republican members of the committee, although voting to report S 382, split in their opinions on the bill. Senators Winston L. Prouty (R Vt.) and John Sherman Cooper (R Ky.) said the bill "represents effective, meaningful and workable election campaign reform legislation which is long overdue."

Sen. James B. Allen (D Ala.) said the bill "did not go far enough" in limiting campaign expenditures. "I feel that an over-all limit should be placed on the total amount of campaign contributions and expenditures that a candidate may receive or spend."

Allen listed expenditures on which the bill placed no limits as "mass mailings, telephone lines, postage, stationery, automobiles, trucks, telegrams, campaign headquarters, campaign workers, airplane rentals, buses, trains, campaign newspapers, movie theater film advertisements, campaign staffs, public relations firms, production expenses for broadcasts, public opinion polls, paid campaigners and poll watchers, novelties, bumper stickers and sample ballots."

After four days of debate, the Senate passed S 382 on Aug. 5 by an 88-2 vote. Voting against the bill were Arizona's two Republican senators, Barry Goldwater and Paul J. Fannin.

Passage came after 21 amendments were adopted, most of which were offered by Republicans to head off objections to the bill by President Nixon. The administration favored repeal of the equal time clause for all candidates for national office and did not want any limitation placed on the amount private individuals could contribute to any campaign. Both administration requirements were included in the Senate-approved version.

Election Campaign Commission. On Aug. 3 the Senate considered an amendment offered by James B. Pearson (R Kan.) to establish an independent federal regulatory agency to oversee election costs and campaign practices. "I do not think we ought to turn it over to an agency which is bound by long association to be highly responsive to Congress, as is the General Accounting Office. I think we need a truly genuinely independent commission."

Howard W. Cannon (D Nev.) said the commission would set up another federal bureaucracy and "would not be completely removed from politics," but he voted for the amendment and it was adopted by an 89-2 vote.

Extension of Credit to Candidates. Minority Leader Hugh Scott (R Pa.) introduced an amendment to prohibit extension of credit to candidates by federally regulated industries. "Because of their inability to protect themselves adequately, the airlines, telephone and telegraph companies have been placed in a position of unlawfully, unavoidably and unintentionally—and I might add illegally—subsidizing political campaign expenses," Scott said.

During the 1972 presidential election campaign, Republicans had charged that the Democrats' $1.5-million debt with the American Telephone and Telegraph Company, leftover from the 1968 campaign, was in effect a political contribution by a corporation and illegal under existing law.

The amendment was approved by voice vote after being modified to permit federal regulatory agencies to establish guidelines regarding extensions of credit to political campaigns.

Equal Time. An amendment was introduced by Prouty to repeal the equal broadcast time clause for all candidates for federal office and to give candidates "maximum flexibility" in the choice of television and radio program format. Although warning that the amendment "would place a campaign more or less at the whim of an affluent licensee," John O. Pastore (D R.I.) said he approved the change "because I think over-all the industry has reached the stage of maturity in which it can be trusted."

The amendment was approved 71-21.

Coverage. Charles McC. Mathias Jr. (R Md.) offered an amendment to bring under the requirements of the bill all candidates—announced or unannounced—who were allowing money to be collected on their behalf. "When we are talking about a man who has publicly announced his candidacy for office or who allows other people to puff up his candidacy with his knowledge and without any denial on his part, we are talking

(Continued on p. 105)

Conflicting Pressures On Campaign Spending Bill

Although not officially a lobby group, the National Committee for an Effective Congress (NCEC) served as the umbrella organization for groups attempting to create a strong campaign finance law in 1971. NCEC, a nonpartisan group formed in 1947, raised $236,231 for congressional campaigns in 1968.

"NCEC designated campaign finance reform as a major legislative goal about 2- and one-half years ago," said Susan King, representing the Washington office of the group. "When we saw that media budgets for campaigns were doubling and tripling with every election, we decided to concentrate on reducing the broadcast costs."

Congress agreed, but broadcasters and the Nixon administration didn't. The result was a veto of the 1970 bill because, Mr. Nixon said, the bill discriminated against the broadcast media.

NCEC initiated a 1971 reform attempt by working with Senate Republican Leader Hugh Scott (Pa.) on a bill (S 956) that removed all limitations on campaign spending but placed restrictions on the amounts that could be contributed by individuals. In testimony March 3, 1971, before the Senate Commerce Communications Subcommittee, Scott said: "If S 956 were passed as introduced, the President would sign it."

Administration Intervention

But then a confusing set of signals emanated from the Nixon administration. The first came in mid-March when *The Wall Street Journal* told of a visit by Eugene S. Cowen, special assistant to the President, to Rep. John B. Anderson (R Ill.), sponsor of House legislation to put money limits on campaign expenses.

Cowen was reported to have told Anderson to throw out specific limits on campaign spending and endorse the Scott plan. Anderson, however, did not revise his own bill.

No spokesman for the administration appeared during Senate hearings on campaign financing. But on March 22, in a television interview, President Nixon set forth another administration approach.

"We do favor a limitation on expenses. There is no question about that. The point is how can we have one which will do two things: One, it must be comprehensive, and the other is it must not give an advantage to incumbents over challengers," Mr. Nixon said.

The following day, Senate Republicans blocked a markup session by the Commerce Committee on a campaign finance bill. Committee Republicans then demanded that hearings be reopened because, as Sen. Marlow W. Cook (R Ky.) said: "There are a number of uncertainties as to the full effects of this legislation."

Regarding the administration's seeming vacillation on campaign financing, NCEC director Russell D. Hemenway charged March 31: "The administration has found itself caught in the noose of its own rhetoric and will be forced to publicly support reform while seeking behind the scenes to render any prospective legislation either toothless, or so riddled with controversial provisions as to defy congressional passage."

Broadcasters

The electronic media—radio and television—opposed the 1970 attempt to place limits on broadcast media spending by candidates. In 1971, they repeated the view that any limits placed on broadcasters should apply to all media, including newspapers, billboards and magazines. The bill reported by the Senate Commerce Committee April 23 complied with those stipulations.

The National Association of Broadcasters (NAB), representing 3,363 AM and FM radio stations, 537 television stations and all national radio and television networks, made its position clear March 5. "To require broadcasters to charge political candidates a lesser rate than charged other comparable purchasers of time would constitute an enforced subsidy for political broadcasting—a subsidy required of no other industry," said Vincent T. Wasilewski, president of the NAB.

Labor, Common Cause

Major labor organizations did not cite campaign finance revision as a prime legislative target in the 92nd Congress, although most supported the concept of reform.

Howard McGuigan, registered lobbyist for the AFL-CIO, said his organization was "waiting to see what is sent to the floor. In the meantime, we're making our views known to the committee members."

At the AFL-CIO's Executive Council meeting in Miami in February 1971, the group adopted a resolution calling for laws that would "give major party candidates equitable opportunities to reach the voters while at the same time minimizing dependence on wealthy individual contributors."

Evasion of legal restrictions on campaign financing was the motive for an action taken in 1971 by Common Cause.

Common Cause on Jan. 11, 1971, filed with the U.S. District Court for the District of Columbia a "class action" complaint as authorized by the Federal Rules of Civil Procedure alleging noncompliance with the Federal Corrupt Practices Act of 1925, with harmful results to members of the organization and others, and requesting "declaratory and injunctive relief."

Other groups which endorsed strong laws regulating political financing included Americans for Democratic Action, United Auto Workers, International Association of Machinists, American Association of Political Consultants and Twentieth Century Fund.

(Continued from p. 403)

about a man who ought to be covered," Mathias said. "I think the loophole is too big."

A motion to table, and thus kill, the amendment was accepted by a 51-40 vote which divided closely on party lines.

Rich Man's Amendment. Another hotly contested debate occurred over an amendment by Mathias and Lawton Chiles (D Fla.) to place a limit of $5,000 on the amount an individual could contribute to any one candidate or campaign committee. The proposal also limited the amount a wealthy candidate could contribute to his own campaign.

Scott, who early in 1971 publicly favored a limit on individual contributions, said the Mathias-Chiles amendment was "another rich man's amendment," that would not be constitutional, would be opposed strongly in the House and would be "unworkable and unenforceable."

The amendment eventually was agreed to after the $5,000 individual contribution limit was deleted. As approved, the amendment placed limits on the amounts candidates could contribute to their own campaigns.

Spot Advertisements. Vance Hartke (D Ind.) and Adlai E. Stevenson III (D Ill.) sponsored an amendment to prohibit television stations from selling advertising time to candidates in periods of less than one minute duration, thus reducing the use of "spot" advertising in campaigns.

Hartke said spot ads were "diabolical," promoted "superficial imagery" and were used "to cloud the issues and belie the truth." Hartke cited estimates that candidates for major offices spent 95 per cent of their broadcast funds on spot ads.

The amendment was tabled by a 74-17 vote.

Labor Fund. Dominick put forth an amendment to prohibit dues or assessments collected by any organization from its members to be used in support of any political candidacy.

Mike Gravel (D Alaska) called the amendment "sheer anti-labor legislation" and an "effort to gut the ability of organized labor to participate in the democratic process." Gravel said the amendment made "second class citizens out of people who belong to labor unions" and suggested that similar controls be placed on corporation executives who made political contributions.

The amendment was tabled by a 56-38 vote.

Possible Loophole. Edward M. Kennedy (D Mass.) in a brief exchange with Pastore at the close of debate said an escalator clause in the bill, which would permit increases in the limits on media spending, based on increases in cost of living, would allow "generous" increases in spending by 1972. Pastore conceded that the limit would be pushed up by the cost-of-living provision.

The escalator clause was inserted by Marlow W. Cook (R Ky.) during committee consideration. It allowed the limits to be increased and rounded to the next highest cent based on the annual increase in the Consumer Price Index.

HOUSE ACTION

Subcommittees of the House Interstate and Foreign Commerce and Rules and Administration Committees in June held hearings on related bills to reduce excessive campaign spending and require full disclosure of election financing.

Separate bills (HR 8628, HR 11060) were reported by the two committees on Oct. 13, 1971, and the bills then were combined before being passed by the House. Although similar in purpose, the bills differed in their approaches. HR 8628 placed limits on various media expenses in federal elections and repealed the equal time requirements for presidential and vice presidential candidates but not candidates for other federal elective offices. HR 11060 placed an over-all ceiling on the amount that could be spent on an election campaign and required detailed desclosure of all contributions and expenditures.

HR 8628 was reported by a 23-20 vote by the Commerce Committee after an amendment was adopted limiting broadcasting expenses to 5 cents per voter in federal elections. HR 11060 was reported by the Rules and Administration Committee by a 20-4 vote. Before reporting the measure, Republicans on the committee failed by an 8-15 vote to substitute the Senate-passed bill (S 382) for the committee version.

The committee defended its provisions which set an over-all spending limitation by labeling as "unfair" a legal cciling on media spending. "To insist that no more than a certain percentage may be spent in a particular manner is to operate unfairly as to those candidates who cannot utilize a pre-designated type of campaign spending effectively."

Three Democrats on the committee criticized provisions giving congressional employees supervisory authority over campaign disclosures, while seven Republicans attacked the spending ceiling as "arbitrary and unrealistic" and said it would constitute an "incumbent's bill.... Placing a limitation to total campaign spending amounts to a classic case of legislating in the dark," they added.

With overwhelming bipartisan support, the House approved the combined bill (HR 11060) by a 372-23 vote on Nov. 30 after three days of debate.

As passed by the House, the bill was a combination of the reporting and disclosure provisions of the Senate-passed bill, introduced in a House companion bill by Clarence J. Brown (R Ohio) and Bill Frenzel (R Minn.), and the media spending limitations provisions introduced by Torbert H. Macdonald (D Mass.), chairman of the Communications and Power Subcommittee. Most of the reporting and disclosure provisions in the original House bill (HR 11060) introduced by House Administration Committee Chairman Wayne L. Hays (D Ohio) were eliminated by the substitution of the Senate version.

Morris K. Udall (D Ariz.) and John B. Anderson (R Ill.), who headed a bipartisan movement in the House to reform campaign financing practices, praised the House action. Udall said: "It will stop millionaires from buying Senate seats and the Presidency. It brings this television monster under control."

Equal Time. The divisive issue of allowing candidates for the same political office equal air time on local and network broadcasts threatened during early consideration of the bill to delay final action.

The first of three amendments on the subject was offered by Lionel Van Deerlin (D Calif.). He recommended repeal of the equal time provision of the Communications Act of 1934 for presidential, vice presidential and Senate candidates, and sought a study of the effects of a repeal for House candidates.

But opponents, including both Republicans and Democrats, warned that members of Congress could not rely on the maturity and fairness of the nation's broadcasters.

Hays: "I do not trust them at all. I do not think you can trust them to be discreet about whom they give time to and whom they do not. I do not think you can trust them to be fair about how and to whom they give time and from whom they withhold it. I do not think there is a remote possibility that they would not be prejudiced and do exactly as they please."

Morris K. Udall (D Ariz.) said campaigns for the House were "special situations" that presented "435 special problems" of equal time considerations. "There are members on both sides of the aisle in this House who are under the thumb of just one broadcaster in particular situations," Udall said. "I do not trust (the broadcasters) either, but I support this amendment because it is a middle-ground position that puts us on the right track."

In a particularly strong attack on network television, Chet Holifield (D Calif.) said he had "no confidence in the integrity" of the networks and said candidates should have the protection of equal time because of broadcasters who "victimize the American people."

The Van Deerlin amendment was defeated by a non-record vote.

A second attempt to change the equal time clause was made by Louis Frey Jr. (R Fla.), who offered an amendment to repeal the requirement for all candidates —for President, the Senate and the House. Frey said the amendment would promote public interest in elections by giving major candidates the opportunity to debate on radio and television.

Macdonald called the Frey amendment "terribly dangerous" and said that if it passed "the broadcasters of this country are going to run our political life." The amendment was defeated by a 95-277 recorded teller vote.

An amendment by James Harvey (R Mich.) to retain the provision as written in the Communications Act subsequently won approval by voice vote after several hours of debate.

Speaking in support of the Harvey amendment, Udall warned that the entire reform bill could be jeopardized by modifying the equal time clause.

Lowest Unit Cost. An amendment by J.J. Pickle (D Texas) was approved by a 219-150 recorded teller vote permitting broadcasters and newspapers to charge political candidates the same rate charged to commercial advertisers.

Union Dues Restrictions. A successful attempt to tighten regulations on use of political funds by labor unions and corporations was made by Orval Hansen (R Idaho). He introduced an amendment to prohibit use of such money for active electioneering directed at the general public. Under the Hansen amendment, approved by a 233-147 recorded teller vote, unions could promote get-out-the-vote drives and voter registration activities only among union members, and corporations could sponsor such activities only among their stockholders.

Hansen said his amendment sought to clear up "undesirable confusion" of Section 610 of Title 18 of the U.S. Code pertaining to political activities by unions and corporations. He said deficiencies of the law had

---

Equal Time, Fairness

The "equal time" provision of the Communications Act of 1934—Section 315(a)—and the "fairness doctrine" of the Federal Communications Commission, although related to the federal regulation of broadcasting, differed significantly in their intent and effect.

The equal time provision required almost mathematical equality in television and radio broadcast treatment of legally qualified candidates for public office. The fairness doctrine, promulgated by the FCC after extensive hearings in 1949, required only fair or balanced treatment of community issues. Congress in 1959 added the fairness standard to Section 315(a) of the Communications Act by providing that broadcast licensees "must operate in the public interest and afford reasonable opportunity for the discussion of conflicting views on controversial issues of public interest."

The key distinction was between individuals, in equal time questions of law, and community issues, in fairness doctrine questions of policy. In no case under existing law or policy was there provision for equal time or fair broadcast treatment of political or social groups, organizations or institutions. That is, no group, organization, institution or individual—except legally qualified political candidates for public office—was guaranteed a right of access to the broadcast media.

Under the fairness doctrine, each licensee was compelled to seek responsible contrasting opinions on public issues once the broadcaster had provided time for raising an issue.

But the licensee was left with full discretion to determine what issues he would raise or permit to be raised on the air, who would be the "responsible spokesman" for opposing views, and at what length and in what context or format those issues would be raised and opposing views aired.

The FCC in 1964 said: "In passing on any complaint (under the fairness doctrine), the commission's role is not to substitute its judgment for that of the licensee as to any... programming decisions, but rather to determine whether the licensee can be said to have acted reasonably and in good faith."

"led to numerous charges that the law is defective or that it is not being observed."

Hansen added that his amendment would maintain the interpretation of existing law which "strikes a balance between organizational rights and the rights of those who wish to retain their shareholding interest or membership status but who disagree with the majority's political views."

Udall said the amendment would make it "very clear that labor unions and corporations are no longer going to be able to play unfair games, that there is a limited role for them in the political process."

Reporting—Disclosure. A prime target of campaign finance reformers was removal from the clerk of the House and secretary of the Senate the responsibility for collecting and compiling reports of campaign contributions and expenditures. A provision in the bill to place these duties with an independent federal elections commission was killed by an amendment introduced by Hays and approved by the House.

Hays objected to the independent commission because of its cost—which Hays estimated at $10-million to $20-million—and because it would transfer to the executive branch part of the control over congressional elections which, he contended, would be a violation of the separation of powers.

Frenzel objected strongly to the Hays amendment: "This is tantamount to putting the fox in charge of the chicken coop. The employees of the House and Senate are inappropriate people to be judging how this law is going to operate. I think they will not be credible in the eyes of the public."

Election Administration. An effort to improve the efficiency of election procedures was approved through an amendment by William J. Keating (R Ohio) to give the comptroller general's office authority to serve as a national clearinghouse for information on the administration of elections.

Under the amendment, the comptroller general would collect data and conduct research on the duties and makeup of local election boards, voter registration and voting and counting methods. The comptroller general could distribute information to local agencies when requested, but he could not advise local election boards on the conduct of elections.

Telephones. Jonathan B. Bingham (D N.Y.) introduced an amendment, subsequently approved, to control campaign expenditures through use of telephone "banks", by which potential voters could be called at home during a campaign, and computer systems used to send mass mailings of campaign literature to homes of voters.

Hays endorsed the amendment, saying it "plugs up the biggest loophole of all—computerized mail can be the most expensive thing and can put a candidate of modest means out of business."

Frenzel said the amendment "imperiled the bill because these expenditures are really not auditable. In addition, this amendment extends the advantages of the incumbent over the challenger. Incumbents have staff, we have telephone privileges, we have access to the media and we have a vast arsenal of weapons with which to campaign in a legitimate way."

$50,000 Campaign Ceiling. Bertram L. Podell (D N.Y.) attempted to place an over-all limit of $50,000 on total campaign expenditures for House candidates. The amendment was defeated after a heated floor discussion.

Podell called the proposal "a poor man's amendment" and said "there comes a point when more than enough money is spent on elections for public office."

Udall, while admitting that the Title I provisions were an "imperfect" answer to comprehensive expenditure limitation, said the Podell amendment was improper because "there are certain kinds of expenditures that cannot be effectively monitored or controlled, and you breed hypocrisy and evasion when you try to do so." Anderson (Ill.) added that "to impose that kind of ceiling on the challenger is to truly make this a pro-incumbent bill."

Individual Contributions. An amendment was offered by Jonathan B. Bingham (D N.Y.) to prohibit any individual running for federal office or any member of

---

Illegal Campaign Gifts

Rep. Melvin Price (D Ill.), chairman of the House Committee on Standards of Official Conduct, told Congressional Quarterly Sept. 11, 1970, his committee would use disclosures of illegal campaign contributions by two shipping companies "only...as background material" in a larger study of lobbying practices and campaign financing.

Price's committee was directed to investigate lobbying and campaign contributions and expenditures by a resolution (H Res 1031) approved July 8 that year by a 382-0 roll-call vote. The same resolution gave the standards committee continuing jurisdiction over those subjects. *(H Res 1031, p. 426)*

A news story naming 16 senators and representatives as recipients of the illegal contributions was distributed Sept. 9 by the *Associated Press.* The story reported that secret Justice Department files contained the names in connection with 10-count indictments against the American President Lines and the Pacific Far East Lines for violation of the 45-year-old Corrupt Practices Act. The act prohibits corporations from contributing to political campaigns.

The two corporations pleaded guilty and were fined $50,000 each in February 1970. Each of the indictments, the AP reported, listed contributions by the two shipping lines to 10 Republicans and 10 Democrats. Fifteen of the 16 members named by the AP received checks that figured in the indictments.

A spokesman said Sept. 11 that the Justice Department had no plans to release the names of the members involved. "The case is closed," he said.

The spokesman cited a "broad Justice Department policy" against releasing the names of any persons not charged with criminal activity. The AP quoted government attorneys as saying the Justice Department shielded the names because there was no indication the members knew the contributions were illegal.

Most of the 16 members were quoted by the AP as saying they had no idea they were receiving illegal campaign contributions.

---

his immediate family from contributing to his campaign more than $5,000 if he were running for Senator or Representative and $35,000 if he were running for President. The amendment, opposed by the Nixon administration, was defeated by a non record vote.

Harvey stated that the amendment was unconstitutional and that it was "violently opposed by the White House." He added that the amendment "discriminates against a person who chooses to exercise his political activity by making a contribution."

"I do not know which President it happens to be aimed at, but it looks like it is aimed at the incumbent," Frenzel said.

CONFERENCE ACTION

A House-Senate conference committee reached a compromise on the differing versions of S 382 on Dec. 14 and the Senate quickly adopted it the same day by voice vote. The House, however, waited until the convening of the second session of the 92nd Congress before approving the final version. Its concurrence came Jan. 19, by a 334-20 vote. The bill was signed by the President Feb. 7 (PL 92-225) and went into effect April 7. *(Controversy over Republican presidential campaign contributions received before April 7, see chapter on Politics and National Issues.)*

Compromise. The final version retained the "equal time" requirement for political candidates; the Senate bill would have repealed it.

The House-Senate conference adopted the Senate's formula requiring broadcast stations to charge candidates the lowest unit charge available to commercial advertisers. The House-passed version would have required broadcasters to charge no more than the actual charges levied on advertisers. However, for non-broadcast media the compromise incorporated a House provision requiring that candidates be charged no more than the actual charges assessed commercial advertisers.

Expenditures by candidates for broadcast time was limited to 10 cents per voter multiplied by the voting-age population of the candidates' district or state, as contained in the House version, rather than the Senate's plan placing a ceiling of 5 cents per voter for broadcast advertising and 5 cents per voter for print media advertising, with up to 20 per cent of either limitation transferable to the other.

Conferees adopted with only minor changes a Senate provision providing that the ceilings computed for campaign expenditures would be raised in proportion to increases in the Consumer Price Index over the base year, 1970. The House had required a raise in the ceiling to be based on computations made by a communications price index to be set up by the Department of Commerce.

The final bill contained a House provision not in the Senate version bringing under the spending limitation any commission given to an agent of a candidate for services performed.

Conferees also adopted a House provision defining more explicitly the roles that corporations and unions could take in political campaigns. There was no comparable Senate provision. In October 1972, less than six months after the act took effect, the House passed a bill to water down the restrictions against political activity by those corporations and labor organizations having government contracts, but the bill was shelved in the Senate and died at the end of the session. *(1972 House efforts to amend act, next page.)*

A key Senate provision establishing a federal elections commission was eliminated; instead, the final version contained a controversial House provision delegating supervision over campaign reports of House candidates to the clerk of the House, and to the secretary of the Senate for Senate candidates and the comptroller general of the GAO for presidential candidates.

A controversial Senate-approved provision which was eliminated when the bill got to the House floor was adopted in modified form by the conference committee. The Senate provision in question had required that copies of campaign reports be filed with the clerk of the U.S. District Court in the jurisdiction in which the election was held. Conferees simplified the procedure by requiring only that copies be filed with the secretary of state of the state in which the election was held.

In its final form, the bill did not contain computer mail postage within the communications media spending ceiling contained in the House version. However, expenses for telephone usage was retained. The Senate measure had no comparable provision.

Before giving its approval to the conference action, several members of the Senate conceded there were state of the state in which the election was held.

Of particular concern to Senate conferees, Pastore said, was the failure to repeal the equal time provision for candidates. Pastore said the House was "absolutely adamant" that the section be eliminated from the bill. "We were given the ultimatum that if we insisted on the equal time repeal we could forget about a bill," Pastore said.

Minority Leader Hugh Scott (R Pa.) said Congress had "missed the mark" in several respects in shaping true reform legislation. Scott said "ambiguous language" in the communications section of the bill would make these provisions unenforceable.

Peter H. Dominick (R Colo.), in a lengthy colloquy with Pastore, objected to numerous features of the bill and said the haste with which the conference report was considered did not allow members enough time to examine its provisions.

Dominick voiced concern for "protecting the constitutional free speech rights of candidates whose campaign tactics are strictly limited by this bill. In most campaigns, the restrictions will tend to aggravate rather that equalize campaign opportunities."

Objections by House members were even more numerous. Areas of the final bill that were questioned included labor and politics, enforcement and campaign staffs.

Labor Political Activity. A provision of the bill defining more explicitly the roles unions could play in financing political campaigns was challenged by Philip M. Crane (R Ill.). Crane said the bill "fails to come to grips with one of the major weaknesses of our election system, the labor union practice of spending millions of dollars of funds compulsorily contributed by union members for candidates or causes with which the members may be in total disagreement."

Samuel L. Devine (R Ohio): "This provision has the potential to allow widespread abuse of what would be a union member's right to prevent the channeling of his dues to political purposes against his wishes and will bear close watching."

Orval Hansen (R Idaho), sponsor of the labor union amendment which was adopted by the House, answered that the purpose of the amendment was "to codify and clarify the existing law. It merely writes currently accepted practices into clear and explicit statutory language." Hansen added that any contention that the amendment was intended to thwart prosecutions against labor unions was "completely without substance."

Lowest Unit Rate. A major provision of the bill added by the Senate requiring radio and television broadcasters, but not other communications media, to sell candidates for public office advertising at the lowest unit rate in effect for all other clients for the same period was opposed by members who preferred the House versions providing for "comparable" rates for advertising.

H. John Heinz III (R Pa.), who won a special election for his seat Nov. 2, 1971, said the provision "is discriminatory because it effectively destroys the media market-place by providing cut rates for candidates.... Congress in effect is starting a fire sale in one industry which could conceivably extend to other areas of political self-interest."

James T. Broyhill (R N.C.): "I feel that the distinction which has been made in the conference report between the broadcast and print media is unjustified and unfairly discriminates against the broadcasters."

Enforcement Power. The conferees' removal of the federal elections commission, established in the Senate version, was questioned. "The bill has flaws, omissions, and even a loophole or two," said Bill Frenzel (R Minn.). "Most significant is the omission of a federal elections commission."

John B. Anderson (R Ill.) added: "I think we must remember that thorough and timely reporting by candidates is only one side of the disclosure equation. The other half is an agency that can process, collate and disseminate these reports in an expeditious manner. I do not believe that the clerk of the House, as presently equipped, can possibly fulfill this important function. So, if we are determined to leave the supervisory responsibilities in that office, it seems to me that it is essential that we promptly provide...the additional resources and manpower...required to do the job effectively."

Campaign Staff. Peter A. Peyser (R N.Y.) and John Y. McCollister (R Neb.) asked if campaign staff workers were included under media spending limitations.

Jonathan B. Bingham (D N.Y.), sponsor of the successful amendment to include automated banks of telephones under the media limits, explained: "It was not my intention to include in the term 'paid telephonists' all staff that might use telephones incidentally to talk to voters. I had in mind people who are hired for the purpose of making telephone calls. These people are generally hired in considerable numbers and are a very distinct and recognizable category."

Efforts to Amend 1971 Act

The Senate in 1972 refused to consider a bill (HR 15276), passed earlier in the year by the House, to modify a provision of the Federal Election Campaign Act of 1971 prohibiting corporations and labor unions having federal government contracts from making direct political contributions to candidates for federal office.

The House-passed bill would have allowed these corporations and unions to engage in the same kinds of political activity as those not having government contracts.

The bill was shelved after a Senate filibuster threat developed late in the session. Howard W. Cannon (D Nev.), a member of the Rules and Administration Committee that had approved HR 15276, tried to call up the bill Oct. 14, but William Proxmire (D Wis.) objected because many senators opposed to the bill were absent. Proxmire said he was prepared to talk against HR 15276 as long as necessary.

Cannon said he would have liked to give the Senate a chance to vote, but Proxmire replied: "There's no chance—without cloture." Cannon withdrew the bill.

The "citizens' lobby" Common Cause fought the bill in both houses, maintaining it would give contractors an opportunity to exert influence on elected officials.

HR 15276 was passed by the House Oct. 2, 1972, by a 249-124 vote and was reported in the Senate Oct. 4 by the Senate Rules and Administration Committee.

1971 Act. The 1971 act (PL 92-225) prohibited corporations and labor organizations from making political contributions directly to candidates for President and Vice President, the Senate and the House. Exceptions were made for voluntary contributions by company employees and individual members of labor unions to a separate political fund managed and controlled by a corporation or union, contributions to nonpartisan voter registration drives, or contributions to pay for communications to stockholders, employees or members endorsing positions and candidates.

PL 92-225 made no exceptions, however, for those corporations and unions which held federal government contracts. The intent of HR 15276 was to exempt these companies and unions from that provision, thus entitling them to participate in the same political activities as corporations and labor unions not having government contracts.

HR 15276 was introduced in the House after Common Cause had filed suit on May 15 against TRW, Inc., a major aerospace firm with over $200-million in government contracts. The suit alleged that TRW had maintained an employee fund for political contributions in violation of the campaign spending law. The case was later settled out of court when TRW agreed to dissolve the fund, return unspent contributions and cease soliciting political donations from its employees.

Neither the House Administration Committee nor the Senate Rules and Administration Committee held hearings on HR 15276.

The House committee's rationale for approving the bill was that PL 92-225 was ambiguous and inconsistent since "corporations and labor organizations who happened to contract with the government were summarily prevented from being allowed the right to engage in even such limited political activities" as the act outlined.

"And certainly no attention was given to the constitutional issues that would arise under an outright prohibition against corporate and union political activities for their employees and members and their families."

But Pierre S. du Pont (R Del.) said during floor debate that "we speak here as if employees of corporations and members of labor unions had no other way of contributing their money to candidates and campaigns. That clearly is not the case. Anyone can make a contribution simply by calling up the local political party.... My proposal is that we tighten it up—that we get corporations and labor unions out of the political business."

Related Action. The House Administration Committee June 20, 1972, held a hearing on another bill (HR 15511) to amend the 1971 act.

HR 15511, introduced by Committee Chairman Wayne L. Hays (D Ohio), would have:

● Replaced the periodic report filing deadlines of March 10, June 10, Sept. 10 and Jan. 31 with two biannual reporting dates—March 15 and Sept. 15; replaced pre-election report filing dates of 15 and five days before each primary, convention and general election with filing dates of 10 days prior to and 30 days following each election.

● Defined "filed" as "postmarked on the date the report was due."

• Provided for pre-emption of state laws by the federal law.

No further action was taken on the bill during the 93rd Congress.

Tax Checkoff Campaign Fund

After a bitter partisan debate dominated by the approaching 1972 presidential election campaign, Congress on Dec. 8, 1971, approved legislation to establish a federal fund from public tax revenues to finance presidential election campaigns. The measure was initially adopted by the Senate as a non-germane amendment to the Revenue Act of 1971 (PL 92-178) reducing business and individual taxes to stimulate the economy.

A similar plan was cleared by Congress in 1966 but was rendered inoperative in 1967. *(Congress and the Nation Vol. II, p. 446)*

As approved by Congress, however, the campaign funding plan could become effective only in time for the 1976 election. House-Senate conferees, faced with a threat by President Nixon to veto the bill (HR 10947), delayed the effective date of the campaign financing provision until after 1972.

At the insistence of House conferees, the conference committee set up to iron out differences between House and Senate versions of HR 10947 also revised the Senate amendment by requiring Congress annually to appropriate to the campaign fund the money designated by federal taxpayers as contributions to presidential campaigns. Citizens first had an opportunity to contribute to the fund on their 1972 federal income tax returns.

Despite his continued opposition to the campaign funding provision, the President signed the bill Dec. 10. Nixon reportedly planned to leave further challenges to the plan to congressional action or the courts.

House Ways and Means Committee Chairman Wilbur D. Mills (D Ark.), leader of the House conferees, had been counted on by Democratic Party officials to insist that the conference approve the campaign funding amendment as passed by the Senate.

Mills, however, concluded that a campaign financing plan effective for the 1972 election would provoke a veto and kill the corporate and individual tax reductions requested by the administration to bolster the economy.

"...the administration has made it perfectly clear that it is opposed to the checkoff procedure and is willing to jettison the entire tax bill if it cannot have its way on this matter," Mills told the House in urging acceptance of the conference report.

Had the plan gone into effect before the 1972 election, about $20.4-million of federal funds would have been made available to each of the major party candidates. About $6.3-million would have been available for Gov. George C. Wallace (D Ala.) running for President as a third-party candidate.

The plan gave each taxpayer the option starting in 1973 of designating $1 of his annual federal income tax payment for use by the presidential candidate of the eligible political party of his choice or for a general campaign fund to be divided among eligible presidential candidates.

Democrats, whose party was $9-million in debt following the 1968 Presidential election, said the voluntary tax checkoff was needed to free presidential candidates from obligation to wealthy contributors to their election campaigns.

Republicans, whose party treasury was well stocked, charged that the plan was a device to rescue the Democratic Party from financial difficulty and assure a Wallace candidacy in 1972 that would lessen President Nixon's re-election chances.

Legislative Action. The campaign financing plan, proposed as a floor amendment by John O. Pastore (D R.I.), was adopted by the Senate Nov. 22 by a 52-47 roll-call vote which divided largely along party lines.

In an effort to win crucial Republican votes in the Senate, Pastore accepted an amendment by Charles McC. Mathias Jr. (R Md.) allowing each taxpayer to designate which party he wanted to donate his $1 to. The Mathias amendment was adopted by a 72-27 vote.

As introduced, the Pastore amendment would have divided the total amount designated for campaign contributions among eligible major and minor party candidates according to a formula based on the number of Americans 18 years old or over.

After acceptance of the Mathias modification, Mathias and Clifford P. Case (R N.J.) joined 50 Democrats in voting for adoption of the Pastore amendment.

Four Democrats—James O. Eastland (Miss.), Sam J. Ervin Jr. (N.C.), John L. McClellan (Ark.) and John C. Stennis (Miss.)—joined 42 Republicans and Harry F. Byrd Jr. (Ind. Va.) in voting against it.

Before adopting the plan, the Senate by a 82-17 roll call approved a related but less controversial Pastore amendment allowing income tax credits for contributions to candidates for any federal, state or local office.

Edward M. Kennedy (D Mass.) termed the Pastore proposals "the best investment the American taxpayer can possibly make to end the most flagrant single abuse in our democracy, the unconscionable power of money."

During the final day of debate Nov. 22, Wallace F. Bennett (R Utah) said he questioned "whether the federal Treasury and the U.S. taxpayer should be called upon to bail out the Democratic party from its present financial problems."

Mathias Amendment. Mathias said his modification of the Pastore proposal—to permit taxpayers to choose which candidate would receive their tax check-off contributions—"will be a voluntary designation, in contrast to the original scheme, which contemplated an involuntary subscription by every participating taxpayer to friend and foe alike."

CAMPAIGN FUND PROVISIONS

As approved by House-Senate conferees Dec. 4, 1971, HR 10947 included the following campaign financing provisions:

• Allowed a tax credit of $12.50 ($25 for a married couple) or, alternatively, a deduction against income of $50 ($100 for a married couple) for political contributions to candidates for local, state or federal office.

• Allowed taxpayers to designate on their federal income tax returns $1 of their tax payment as a contribution to the presidential and vice presidential candidates of the political party of their choice, beginning with the 1972 taxable year.

• As an alternative, allowed taxpayers to contribute to a general fund for all eligible presidential and vice presidential candidates by authorizing $1 of their annual income tax payment to be placed in such a fund.

• Required annual appropriation by Congress of payments into the presidential campaign fund not to exceed amounts checked off on tax returns.

• Directed the secretary of the Treasury to maintain a general account for presidential campaign contributions and separate accounts for candidates from eligible political parties.

• Provided that if any account for a specific party fell short of the amount to which its candidates were entitled, funds in the general account would be allocated to each party according to the ratio of contributions in their accounts. No party would receive from the general fund more than the smallest amount needed by a major party to reach the maximum amount of contributions to which it was entitled.

• Authorized to be distributed to the candidates of each major party (one which obtained 25 percent of the votes cast in the previous presidential election) an amount equal to 15 cents multiplied by the number of U.S. residents age 18 and over.

• Established a formula for allocating public campaign funds to candidates of minor parties whose candidates received 5 percent or more but less than 25 percent of the previous presidential election vote.

• Authorized payments after the election to reimburse the campaign expenses of a new party whose candidate received enough votes to be eligible or of an existing minor party whose candidate increased its vote to the qualifying level.

• Prohibited major party candidates who chose public financing of their election campaign from accepting private campaign contributions unless their shares of funds contributed through the income tax check-off procedure fell short of the amounts to which they were entitled.

• Prohibited a major party candidate who chose public financing as well as all campaign committees authorized by the candidate from spending more than the amount to which the candidate was entitled under the contributions formula.

• Prohibited any campaign committee not authorized by a candidate from spending more than $1,000 to promote his candidacy.

• Required candidates receiving public financing to submit weekly statements of campaign expenses to the Comptroller General of the General Accounting Office.

• Provided penalties of $5,000 or one year in prison, or both, for candidates or campaign committees which spent more on a campaign than the amounts they received from the campaign fund or which accepted private contributions when sufficient public funds were available.

• Provided penalties of $10,000 or five years in prison, or both, for candidates or campaign committees which used public campaign funds for unauthorized expenses, gave or accepted kickbacks or illegal payments involving public campaign funds or knowingly furnished false information to the Comptroller General.

• Created a Presidential Election Campaign Advisory Board made up of the Senate majority and minority leaders, the speaker and minority leader of the House, two members representing each major party and three public members.

• The bill went into effect Jan. 1, 1973.

CQ **Congressional Ethics**

MEMBERS, AIDES CONVICTED OF INFLUENCE PEDDLING

A number of members, former members and aides to members of Congress were convicted of illegal activities during the 92nd Congress. Others were accused of misconduct or unethical behavior.

Two cases which attracted nationwide attention involved a congressman, Rep. John Dowdy (D Texas 1952-73), and a former senator, Daniel B. Brewster (D Md. 1963-69), both of whom were convicted of taking bribes: in Dowdy's case, to stop a federal investigation of a Maryland home improvement company after complaints that the company defrauded scores of low-income homeowners in the Washington, D.C., area; in Brewster's case, to influence his vote on certain postal legislation in a manner favorable to a Chicago mail order firm. Some of the counts in the Dowdy conviction were overturned by a U.S. court of appeals in March 1973, and resolution of the case was still pending.

Corruption even reached the speaker's office in 1969 when disclosures of influence peddling led to the suspension of two trusted friends of Speaker John W. McCormack (D Mass. 1928-71). A news magazine tied the speaker himself to some of the allegations which were under investigation by two federal grand juries. McCormack, then 77, categorically denied having had any knowledge that his office was being used as a base for influence peddling. He was forced to suspend his top aide, Martin Sweig, and he barred his office to Nathan Voloshen, a lawyer-lobbyist McCormack described as a friend of at least 10 years' standing. McCormack was never implicated in the case.

Another case of national significance involved Sen. Mike Gravel (D Alaska), who was accused by some of his colleagues in the Senate with a serious violation of U.S. national security regulations and a breach of congressional ethics for his June 1971 release of portions of the classified Pentagon Papers dealing with U.S. involvement in the Vietnam war. His behavior raised a basic constitutional question of the extent to which members of Congress could claim immunity for their actions under Article I, Section 6, Clause 1 of the Constitution. *(Box, this page)*

A sequel to the case of Rep. Adam Clayton Powell (D N.Y. 1945-71) unfolded in January 1969 when the House voted to seat him, thus ending a two-year exile forced upon him by his colleagues in 1967. Five months later, the Supreme Court ruled, 7-1, that he had been excluded unconstitutionally from the 90th Congress. The court ruled that Powell, who was a duly elected representative in 1967 and was re-elected in 1968, met the constitutional requirements of age, residence and citizenship.

Dowdy Conviction

Rep. John Dowdy (D Texas 1952-73) was convicted ec. 30, 1971, of charges arising from acceptance of a

bribe, conspiracy and perjury by a U.S. District Court jury in Baltimore, Md.

On March 13, 1973, the 4th U.S. Court of Appeals reversed the conspiracy and bribery convictions but left standing the conviction on three counts of perjury. The Justice Department May 15, 1973, appealed to the Supreme Court to reinstate the convictions.

Dowdy, who was serving his 10th full term in the House, had been convicted of crossing state lines to receive a bribe, conspiracy to obstruct justice, conspiracy to violate conflict-of-interest statutes and five counts of perjury before the grand jury that indicted him March 31, 1970.

The verdict followed a 27-day trial in which Dowdy contended he never received a $25,000 payoff to thwart a federal investigation of a Maryland home improvement company in 1965.

Dowdy was sentenced Feb. 23, 1972, to 18 months in prison and fined $25,000. The court of appeals decision reduced his sentence to six months and $3,000 in fines. His attorneys could ask the Supreme Court to dismiss the three counts of perjury.

The court of appeals found that the first trial had violated the "speech or debate" clause of the Constitution, which provides that members of Congress cannot be questioned in any other forum for any speech or debate in which they participated in Congress. *(Box, this page)*

The court held that the evidence used in the first trial "was an examination of the defendant's actions as a congressman, who was chairman of a subcommittee investigating a complaint, in gathering information in preparation for a possible subcommittee investigatory hearing."

Dowdy was the first member of Congress to be convicted of a felony while still in office since 1956, when Rep. Thomas J. Lane (D Mass. 1941-62) pleaded guilty to willful evasion of income taxes. *(Congress and the Nation Vol. I, p. 1420)*

Background. A federal grand jury in Baltimore, Md., March 31, 1970, indicted Dowdy on charges of conspiracy, perjury and the use of interstate facilities to promote bribery. The indictment alleged Dowdy had accepted a $25,000 bribe on Sept. 22, 1965, to intervene in a federal

---

Congressional Immunity

Article I of the Constitution:

Section 6 (1) The Senators and Representatives shall...in all Cases, except Treason, Felony and Breach of the Peace, be privileged from Arrest during their Attendance at the Session of their respective Houses,...and for any Speech or Debate in either House, they shall not be questioned in any other Place.

investigation of the Monarch Construction Company of Silver Spring, Md.

Dowdy, 59, a high-ranking member of the House District of Columbia Committee, was the first incumbent member of Congress since 1962 to face criminal charges. He denied any wrongdoing.

Dowdy's trial was set for Sept. 14, 1970, but the opening of the case was delayed after Dowdy entered a Texas hospital Sept. 8 for treatment of a recurring back condition.

Lawyers for Dowdy attempted Sept. 1 to persuade the Fourth Circuit Court of Appeals to set aside the trial on grounds of congressional immunity. The lawyers agreed that federal prosecutors were attempting to question privileged legislative acts. The court turned down the petition.

The government's case against Dowdy was based on testimony that businessman Myrvin C. Clark, acting for his employer, Nathan H. Cohen, had delivered a briefcase containing $25,000 in cash to Dowdy at the Atlanta, Ga., airport on Sept. 22, 1965.

Cohen at that time was president of a home improvement company, Monarch Construction Company of Silver Spring, Md., and Clark was the firm's sales manager. Clark, Cohen and other government witnesses testified that the payment was for Dowdy's expected help in intervening with various federal and District of Columbia agencies that were investigating the firm in 1965. Cohen acknowledged in his testimony that Monarch had defrauded hundreds of Washington, D.C., homeowners.

A key part of the evidence in the case was a tape recording made by Cohen of a conversation which he had with Dowdy Jan. 20, 1970. The conversation, which took place in Dowdy's Capitol Hill office, was recorded without Dowdy's knowledge.

On the tape, which was played for the jurors, Cohen could be heard on four occasions mentioning the $25,000 he allegedly paid Dowdy in 1965. During the conversation, Dowdy failed to dispute Cohen's statements.

Dowdy appeared in his own defense Dec. 13 and told the jury he had never made any deal with Cohen to receive $25,000 for intervening in the government investigation of Cohen's firm.

Dowdy also maintained he had taken an earlier flight to Atlanta on Sept. 22, 1965, than the one government witnesses said he boarded. Dowdy's testimony later was refuted when federal prosecutor Stephen H. Sachs produced House records which showed that Dowdy was present during a roll-call vote at the time he claimed he was boarding a plane to Atlanta.

Five members and the clerk of the House of Representatives testified Dec. 15 at the trial that Dowdy's reputation for honesty was "good" or "excellent."

Besides House Clerk W. Pat Jennings, the members who appeared as character witnesses for Dowdy were Representatives Earle Cabell (D Texas 1965-73), Olin E. Teague (D Texas), W. R. Poage (D Texas), Kenneth J. Gray (D Ill.) and Andrew Jacobs Jr. (D Ind. 1965-73).

Despite his conviction, Dowdy continued to represent Texas' 2nd District in the House for the remainder of the 92nd Congress but declined to seek re-election to an 11th full term.

Impact on Congress. For the first time since its formation in 1967, the House Committee on Standards of Official Conduct April 26, 1972, initiated action to

---

Dowdy Votes

John Dowdy (D Texas 1952-73) voted three times in 1972 by proxy in the House District of Columbia Committee in June after he had promised House Speaker Carl D. Albert (D Okla.) he would refrain from voting in committee or on the House floor following his conviction on charges of bribery and perjury.

Dowdy told Congressional Quarterly he had given his proxy to the committee for use at a meeting scheduled for June 21, but that the session was postponed until June 22 without his knowledge. He said he did not intend to participate in any other committee or floor votes.

Dowdy's pledge to Albert was contained in a letter written the evening of June 21. However, John L. McMillan (D S.C.), chairman of the District Committee, used Dowdy's proxy vote three times in his committee. By promising not to vote on House business, Dowdy had acquiesced to the directive of H Res 933. (*"Impact on Congress," this page*)

---

punish a member of Congress. By a vote of 10-2, the committee approved a resolution (H Res 933) declaring that any representative convicted of a crime for which he might receive a sentence of two years or more in prison should refrain from participating in committee business or House voting. H Res 933 was formally reported by the committee May 3.

Dowdy was the only member to whom the resolution was applicable at the time, although he was not mentioned by name.

The resolution never was voted on by the House because the Rules Committee refused to recommend further action.

The committee's report said that "the preservation of public confidence in the legislative process" demanded that guidelines be established for House members who were convicted of "serious" crimes.

The Committee on Standards of Official Conduct, known as the ethics committee, was established by the House in April 1967. It was directed to draw up an enforceable code of ethics for House members and employees, but was given no enforcement powers.

The committee was set up in the wake of public furor over alleged misconduct on the part of several members of the 90th Congress. (*Congress and the Nation Vol. II, p. 893*)

The committee's six-week investigation of Dowdy was begun March 2 at the request of Representatives Jerome R. Waldie (D Calif.) and Charles E. Wiggins (R Calif.).

"The purpose of the proposed resolution is to express the sense of the House with respect to actions which it feels members who are convicted of certain serious crimes should take during the period of any appeals process when there is no presumption of innocence," the committee stated. "This point is reached in a criminal prosecution upon conviction by judge or jury."

House action is required under these circumstances, the report continued, because "in the absence of any other means of dealing with such cases short of reprimand, censure or expulsion—which would be totally inappropriate until final judicial resolution of the case—public

Dowdy Case Chronology

March 31, 1970—Indicted by federal grand jury in Baltimore, Md., on charges of conspiracy, perjury and using interstate facilities to promote bribery.

Sept. 8, 1970—Trial set to begin Sept. 14 delayed after Dowdy hospitalized for recurring back condition. Lawyers between Sept. 1970 and Dec. 1971 fail in numerous other attempts to set aside or delay the trial.

May 4, 1971—Dowdy relinquished his education subcommittee chairmanship on the District of Columbia Committee.

Nov. 3, 1970—Dowdy, running unopposed from his Texas district, re-elected to a 10th full term.

Nov. 28, 1971—Trial begins in Baltimore, Md.

Dec. 30, 1971—Dowdy convicted of accepting a $25,000 bribe on Sept. 22, 1965, to intervene in a Justice Department investigation of Monarch Construction Company of Silver Spring, Md.

Feb. 23, 1972—Dowdy sentenced to 18 months in prison and fined $25,000.

March 2, 1972—House Committee on Standards of Official Conduct begins six-week investigation of Dowdy.

April 26, 1972—The committee by a 10-2 vote approves a resolution (H Res 933) directing Dowdy to refrain from voting in the House and from participating in committee business. Although the resolution was formally reported by the committee May 3, H Res 933 was never voted on by the House because the Rules Committee refused to act on the measure.

June 21, 1972—Dowdy pledged in letter to Speaker Carl Albert (D Okla.) not to vote in committee or floor business, although his vote was used by District of Columbia Committee Chairman John L. McMillan (D S.C.) to defeat two amendments to legislation being considered by the committee. *(p. 386)*

Aug. 9, 1972—Lawyers for Dowdy appealed conviction to U.S. 4th Circuit Court of Appeals.

Oct. 31, 1972—Dowdy's lawyers argued before 4th circuit court that his conviction was based on inadmissible evidence.

March 13, 1973—The U.S. 4th Circuit Court of Appeals in Richmond reversed the conspiracy and bribery convictions against Dowdy and left it up to the federal government to decide whether to hold a new trial. The court left standing Dowdy's conviction on three counts of perjury.

"Even were it not for such constitutional limitation, the action taken here would still be improvident and indefensible on the basis of all Anglo-American concepts of due process," they continued. In the event of "an ultimate reversal and dismissal of the criminal charge... he would not then have been given the benefit of the presumption of innocence."

Brewster Conviction

Former Sen. Daniel B. Brewster (D Md. 1963-69), convicted in 1972 on three counts of accepting money to influence his vote on postal rate legislation before Congress, was sentenced Feb. 2, 1973, to a minimum of eight months and a maximum of two years in prison on each of the three counts and fined $30,000.

Also sentenced, following his conviction in 1972, was Cyrus T. Anderson, a lobbyist for the Chicago mail order firm of Spiegel Inc. Anderson was sentenced to one and one-half to four and one-half years in prison and fined $30,000.

Brewster was convicted Nov. 17, 1972, of accepting an "unlawful gratuity," a lesser bribery charge than the one for which he was indicted in 1969. The lesser charge meant that he received the money without corrupt intent.

Anderson was convicted on three bribery counts for paying Brewster $14,500 to influence his vote.

Spiegel Inc. had pleaded guilty to bribery charges following Brewster's and Anderson's conviction.

Only one other U.S. senator, Joseph R. Burton (R Kan. 1901-06), had been convicted since 1900 for a crime committed while in office.

Both Brewster and Anderson remained free on bond pending appeal of their convictions.

Background. A federal grand jury Dec. 1, 1969, indicted Brewster, Spiegel Inc. and Anderson on charges of violating federal bribery laws. A 10-count indictment, announced by Attorney General John N. Mitchell, charged that Brewster received $24,500 from Spiegel Inc. and Anderson to influence his "action, vote and decision" on postal rate legislation.

The grand jury said the payments were made in five installments between Jan. 10, 1966, and Jan. 31, 1968. Three of the payments, totaling $14,500, allegedly were made through the D.C. Committee for Maryland Education.

The indictment stated that Brewster "directly and indirectly, corruptly asked, solicited, sought, accepted, received and agreed to receive" contributions "for himself" and for his D.C. Committee for Maryland Education.

Brewster was a member of the Senate Post Office and Civil Services Committee during a 1967 debate on postal rate increases for regular third-class mail. Spiegel was a major user of such rates.

Brewster was charged on five counts. On four of the counts, he was charged with taking payments "in return for being influenced" on postal rate legislation "which might at any time be pending before him in his official capacity." The fifth count against Brewster charged that he received a payment "for and because of official acts performed by him" on postal rate legislation "which had been pending before him in his official capacity."

Spiegel Inc. and Anderson were charged jointly on four counts with making payments to influence Brewster

opinion could well interpret inaction as indifference on the part of the House."

The committee went on to warn that "any member... who violates the clear principles (this resolution) expresses will do so at the risk of subjecting himself to the introduction of a privileged resolution relating to his conduct."

In dissenting views, Representatives Olin E. Teague (D Texas) and Watkins M. Abbitt (D Va.) argued that the House had no authority to strip a member of his right to vote "without following the process sanctioned by the Constitution to expel a member (by) a two-thirds vote.

on postal rate legislation that might be before Congress and on one count with making a payment to Brewster after the Senate Committee had acted on a postal rate increase.

Spiegel Inc. issued a statement denying the charges. The statement said the firm had "openly and legally made contributions to various committees in Washington, D.C., under provisions of a District of Columbia law and after seeking and obtaining the advice of eminent legal counsel." Congress, in passing the Corrupt Practices Act of 1925, had not required financial reports from political campaign committees based solely in the District of Columbia.

During the 1967 congressional debate over a postal rate increase, a major controversy developed over bulk rate increases for regular third-class mail, mainly advertising matter often referred to as "junk mail." During Senate consideration of the rate increase measure (HR 7977), the activities of lobbyists for third-class mailers became a major issue.

Senate Post Office and Civil Service Committee Chairman A. S. Mike Monroney (D Okla 1951-69) accused bulk mailers of "some of the most vicious lobbying activities it has been my experience to witness in some 29 years in Congress."

Brewster voted for the rate hike after losing 27-64 on an amendment to HR 7977 which would have weakened a proposed rate increase for third class bulk mail—mainly advertising matter.

The indictment, which resulted from a grand jury investigation of Brewster that began several months before in Baltimore, Md., came 13 months after he had been defeated for re-election by Charles McC. Mathias Jr. (R).

Court Rulings. Ten months after Brewster's indictment, a U.S. district court judge dismissed it on the grounds that the senator was immune from prosecution because of Article I, section 6, clause 1 of the Constitution—that the immunity granted members of Congress by the Constitution shielded him from prosecution for bribery related to performance of a legislative act. (Box this page)

The government took an appeal directly to the Supreme Court, which issued a decision June 29, 1972, narrowing the category of protected actions under the immunity clause. A six-man court majority—made up of the Nixon appointees, Potter Stewart and Thurgood Marshall—ruled: "Taking a bribe is, obviously, no part of the legislative process or function."

Chief Justice Warren E. Burger, writing the opinion, continued: "The illegal conduct is taking or agreeing to take money for a promise to act in a certain way. There is no need for the government to show that (Brewster) fulfilled the alleged illegal bargain...for it is taking the bribe, not performance of the illicit compact, that is a criminal act." Brewster was ordered to stand trial, which began Oct. 30, 1972, and resulted in his conviction by a federal jury in Washington, D.C., on Nov. 17, 1972.

In its verdict, the jury found Brewster guilty of a lesser bribery charge, that of accepting an unlawful gratuity. Following the verdict, Spiegel Inc. pleaded guilty. The judge delayed sentencing of Brewster and Anderson. Lawyers for Brewster on Dec. 15, 1972, asked the district court to grant him an acquittal or a new trial.

Brewster Case Chronology

Dec. 1, 1969—Indicted by federal grand jury on charges of violating federal bribery laws. Also charged were Spiegel Inc., a Chicago-based mail order firm, and its registered congressional lobbyist, Cyrus T. Anderson. The indictment charged that Brewster received $24,500 from Spiegel and Anderson to influence his vote on postal rate legislation.

Oct. 9, 1970—U.S. district court judge dismissed 10-count indictment against Brewster on the grounds he was protected under the congressional immunity clause of the Constitution (Article I, Section 6).

Nov. 30, 1970—Justice Department appealed dismissal to the Supreme Court.

March 1, 1971—Supreme Court agreed to review Brewster case.

Oct. 12, 1971—Case argued before the Supreme Court; the case reargued in March 1972.

June 29, 1972—The Supreme Court, by a 6-3 vote, reversed district court's ruling and ordered Brewster to stand trial, ruling that the immunity clause of the Constitution did not protect a member of Congress from prosecution on bribery charges.

Oct. 30, 1972—Brewster trial began.

Nov. 17, 1972—Brewster convicted on three counts of accepting an unlawful gratuity to influence his vote on postal rate legislation. Anderson is found guilty on stiffer bribery charges.

Dec. 15, 1972—Lawyers for Brewster asked U.S. district court to grant Brewster an acquittal or a new trial, arguing that he had been "irrevocably tarred with the same sweeping brush" by the testimony at the trial against Anderson.

Jan. 26, 1973—U.S. district court judge denied Brewster's appeal for a new trial.

Feb. 2, 1973—Brewster sentenced to two to six years in prison and fined $30,000. Anderson sentenced the same day to one and one-half to four and one-half years in prison and fined $30,000. Brewster announced he would appeal the sentence.

Speaker McCormack's Office

A congressional scandal which attracted nationwide attention when it was revealed in 1969 involved the office of Speaker John W. McCormack (D Mass. 1928-71). In the end, one of his top aides was indicted and convicted of perjury in connection with influence-peddling from the speaker's office.

Martin Sweig, who until Oct. 20, 1969, had served as McCormack's administrative assistant, was convicted of perjury by a federal jury on July 9, 1970, and sentenced to two-and-a-half years in prison and fined $2,000. The presiding judge said after announcing the sentence that the trial had disclosed "a picture of corruption of a very profound kind.... I am convinced this is a grievous case of perjury," adding that it was linked to "an abuse of government trust."

After exhausting the appeals process, Sweig began serving his prison sentence July 22, 1971. On Nov. 3 of that year, a federal grand jury indicted him on a new charge of misusing the speaker's office to influence government decisions. He pleaded innocent before a U.S. district court but was convicted on Jan. 28, 1972. He was sentenced to three years in prison, with the sentence to run concurrently with the 30 month sentence he was already serving—thus adding six months to his period of confinement. Sweig was granted a parole and was released from the Lewisburg, Pa., penitentiary on July 17, 1972, after serving one-third of his three-year sentence.

Martin Sweig. In October 1969 it was revealed that McCormack's administrative assistant, Martin Sweig, was being investigated by federal authorities in connection with attempts to influence a case before the Securities and Exchange Commission (SEC).

McCormack announced on October 20, 1969, that he was suspending Sweig without pay but that he was unaware of any improper conduct in the office and had been guilty of nothing himself.

Sweig had been an employee of McCormack's for 24 years, with an annual salary in 1969 of $36,000.

On Oct. 16 the investigation of Sweig and Nathan Voloshen—a lawyer-lobbyist—was made public.

On that day the SEC filed suit against officers of the Parvin Dohrmann Company, naming Voloshen as co-defendant. Sweig, who was not named as a defendant, was placed on leave of absence without pay by McCormack. The speaker said Sweig, who supervised the office which handled matters related to McCormack's district in Massachusetts, had arranged an appointment with SEC officials without his knowledge or permission.

Columnist Jack Anderson and other sources reported Sweig could imitate McCormack's Boston accent and often posed as the speaker in telephone conversations. Anderson reported Sweig boasted he had once fooled President Johnson into thinking he was McCormack. *The Washington Post* reported that Sweig and Voloshen were being investigated by two federal grand juries. The newspaper said a grand jury in Baltimore was investigating reports the two men had aided a Boston contractor's efforts to be paid an additional $5-million for construction of underground parking for the House of Representatives.

Nathan M. Voloshen. Voloshen, New York City lawyer and long-time friend of McCormack, pleaded guilty June 17, 1970, to charges of conspiring to use the speaker's office to influence matters before federal government agencies. Voloshen also pleaded guilty to three counts of lying to a grand jury about the charges. Voloshen's guilty plea came at the start of the trial for both him and Sweig.

Voloshen was fined $10,000 and given a suspended one-year prison sentence on Nov. 24, 1970. Up to 25 years in prison could have been imposed.

On Oct. 23 *Life* magazine released an advance copy of an article concluding that the speaker's office had been used as a power base by Voloshen and Sweig. The article said "the evidence is that McCormack was more than naively involved in whatever took place in his office." *Life* said an unidentified friend of Voloshen told one of its investigators that Voloshen was willing to pay $50,000 if the article was not printed.

McCormack told a jammed news conference Oct. 24 he had no knowledge his office had been used for influence-peddling. He denied a *Life* charge implicating him in a number of allegations under grand jury investigation. The story said McCormack telephoned in May 1968 to Russell G. Oswald, chairman of the New York State Parole Board, to request an early parole for a convicted embezzler named Edward M. Gilbert.

The speaker said he had "no intention of passively letting a lifetime of public service, of which I am proud, be irreparably damaged by irresponsible journalism such as represented by *Life* magazine."

Later, McCormack reflected: "You don't know who's using your name or who's peddling your name around. You always find out after the fact. It could happen to anybody."

Voloshen was widely known as "the speaker's man," *Life* said, and with the "full compliance" of Sweig he "made free use of the official prestige, including the name, the stationery, the chair, the telephone—of McCormack." But the speaker's "precise involvement" was unknown, *Life* reporter William Lambert wrote. He added that *Life's* efforts had "uncovered literally dozens of fixed cases, near fixes and plain shakedowns emanating from Voloshen's power base in the speaker's office."

McCormack denied knowing some of the individuals involved in the *Life* allegations and denied making telephone calls which purported to come from him asking special treatment in certain cases.

Former California Gov. Edmund G. Brown (D 1959-67) said Oct. 25 that Voloshen visited him in 1966 and requested parole for a prisoner convicted of robbery. Brown said he called McCormack to verify his friendship with Voloshen. "He (McCormack) said Voloshen was a very good friend of his, but he said don't do anything that's not absolutely right," according to Brown. The prisoner was not granted parole.

Voloshen died Aug. 23, 1971, nine months after he was sentenced.

McCormack's Role. No charges were ever leveled against Speaker McCormack, despite speculation that he may have known of Sweig's and Voloshen's activities. During Sweig's trial, McCormack testified he had no knowledge of his aide's dealings with regulatory commissions, federal government departments, the Selective Service System or business firms.

On May 20, 1970, McCormack announced he would retire at the end of the 91st Congress, after first declaring in October 1969, when the case was first made public, that he would seek another term.

Other Aides Charged. Sweig and Voloshen were not the only congressional employees charged with wrongdoing.

● George A. Haag, former administrative assistant to Rep. James M. Collins (R Texas), Jan. 6, 1972, was indicted on charges of taking salary kickbacks from members of Collins' staff. Haag was employed by Collins from November 1968 to March 1970 when columnist Jack Anderson first made the charges public. On May 4, 1972, federal prosecutor Gene S. Anderson disclosed that a grand jury in the District of Columbia was investigating Collins and three other persons on allegations of obstructing justice and conspiring to obstruct justice. Collins was re-elected in November 1972 to a third full term.

● Robert T. Carson, former administrative aide to Sen. Hiram L. Fong (R Hawaii), former president of the Honolulu Stock Exchange and former chairman of the Hawaii Republican Party, was sentenced Jan. 4, 1972, to 18 months in prison and fined $5,000 on charges of perjury and conspiring to accept and offer bribes to help quash stock fraud indictments. Carson, who had worked for

Charges Involving Speaker's Office

Among charges cited by *Life* magazine in an article released Oct. 23, 1969, were the following. Speaker John W. McCormack (D Mass.) categorically denied knowing his office was used as a base from which to influence public officials' decisions and said the article subjected him to "unwarranted vilification." The magazine said:

• McCormack personally called New York Parole Board Chairman Russell G. Oswald in May 1968 seeking an early parole for Edward M. Gilbert, a New York financier convicted of embezzling $1.9-million from his own firm in 1962. The article said Gilbert paid Voloshen "at least $75,000" for his services, which presumably meant prompting the speaker to make the call.

Although previous stories reported that Sweig and Voloshen often imitated McCormack's voice on the phone, Lambert wrote that "there seems little doubt of the authenticity of this particular call. Oswald had frequently talked on the phone to McCormack during the years Oswald served as Corrections Commissioner in Massachusetts, and readily recognized his voice. The speaker said he was a friend of Gilbert's late father and that Eddie himself was a man of 'honesty and respectability.' McCormack recommended that Gilbert be granted an early parole."

• On Oct. 8, 1968, Sweig also called Oswald and told him that "Speaker McCormack wanted it called to Oswald's attention that two Massachusetts congressmen would like to have (Manuel) Bello released from prison because he was seriously ill," the article said. Bello was described as a "minor Mafia-connected thief."

Oswald did nothing. Later New York State Supreme Court Justice Mitchell D. Schweitzer, who originally had sentenced Bello, sentenced him again "to a shorter term that made him eligible for immediate release."

• Voloshen in late 1965 collected $5,000 in cash from Dr. Irving Helfert, a Dayton, Ohio, urologist, while sitting in the speaker's chair in McCormack's office. According to the article, Helfert was accused of non-payment of "more than $300,000" ($100,000 according

to Helfert) in taxes and had been referred to Voloshen for help. Voloshen told Helfert to meet him in the speaker's office and bring cash. After the payment, he said he would contact Helfert and send him a receipt. He never did either and Helfert subsequently was convicted, given a suspended sentence and fined $15,000.

• "Voloshen and Sweig," Lambert wrote, "waving the speaker's banner, met repeatedly with Capitol architects in an attempt to collect $5-million in dubious extra costs for construction of the new House garage." Voloshen was paid $20,000 for this service, the magazine said, by Victor J. Frenkil, president of the Baltimore construction firm that built the garage.

The House garage case also had involved Sen. Russell B. Long (D La.) and former Sen. Daniel B. Brewster (D Md. 1963-69). *(See p. 396)*

• Voloshen attempted unsuccessfully to arrange the release of Mafia leader Vito Genovese from an Atlanta prison.

• Vito's brother, Mike Genovese, paid Voloshen $5,000 for trying to block the transfer of Mafioso Salvatore Granello from the federal prison in Danbury, Conn., to the penitentiary at Lewisburg, Pa. Genovese never was transferred but only because his sentence was too short.

• Both Sweig and Voloshen in the fall of 1968 interceded unsuccessfully on behalf of Jack McCarthy at the Labor Department. A federal grand jury was investigating McCarthy at the time, and he later was convicted of 38 counts of violating labor laws and sentenced June 19, 1968, to three months in prison and fined $5,000.

• "In 1963," the article said, "Voloshen interceded successfully for Ben Cohen and Philip Simon, two New York and Miami entrepreneurs, in their takeover of the Bank of Miami Beach." Following a phone call "from a man who identified himself as Speaker McCormack," Lambert wrote, Florida State Controller Ray E. Green reversed a previous decision on the transaction.

• Finally, the *Life* article charged that McCormack "knew at least as far back as midsummer that not only *Life* but two federal grand juries were looking into Voloshen's affairs."

Fong since 1961, was suspended following his indictment Jan. 13, 1971.

Robert G. (Bobby) Baker, central figure in one of the most prominent congressional scandals of the past decade, was released from prison on parole June 1, 1972. Baker, who rose from Senate page to become right-hand man to Majority Leader Lyndon B. Johnson (D Texas 1949-61), entered prison Jan. 14, 1971, eight years after he left his $19,600 a year job as secretary to the Senate Democratic majority. While in that position, he had amassed a paper worth of $2-million.

Baker resigned under fire in 1963 after a suit was brought against him charging that he used his influence to obtain contracts for a vending machine concern in which he had a financial interest. Senate investigations conducted over the next two years concluded that Baker

had acted with "gross impropriety." *(Congress and the Nation Vol. I, p. 1430, 1773)*

Baker, meanwhile, was brought to trial on charges of income tax evasion, theft and conspiracy to defraud the government. Convicted in 1967, he began a series of appeals which ended Dec. 21, 1970, when the Supreme Court refused to review the case.

Baker was indicted in 1966 on charges that he had understated his income on federal tax returns, conspired to avoid paying taxes on legal fees, and retained for his own use about $100,000 in campaign contributions he was expected to give to his superiors in the Senate.

The Justice Department on July 15, 1969, moved to reopen the case. It filed a civil suit in federal district court seeking damages of up to $1.7-million. The department asked the court to order Baker to account for the increase in his net worth from $11,000 in 1956 to $1.7-million in 1963. The government contended that a portion of his net worth was obtained illegally by exploiting his influence as Senate Democratic secretary.

Gravel Immunity Case

The ethics issue was raised in different form by the behavior of Sen. Mike Gravel (D Alaska) surrounding his release June 29, 1971, of portions of the then-classified Pentagon Papers history of the United States' involvement in the Vietnam war. His action was seen by many senators as not just improper and unethical but even treasonous, since the 47-volume study was said to contain defense secrets the release of which would violate national security regulations.

The controversy also raised a key constitutional question for Congress: the extent to which the Constitution protected members' activities under the Speech or Debate clause (Article I, section 6). *(Box, p. 412)*

The Justice Department attempted to have Gravel's aide, Dr. Leonard S. Rodberg, testify before a federal grand jury in Boston about the subsequent publication of those portions of the papers in Gravel's possession. A staff member of the senator's Subcommittee on Public Buildings and Grounds, Rodberg was hired the night Gravel called the session of his subcommittee to read excerpts from the secret study. Rodberg then helped Gravel edit them and arrange to have the study published privately.

The department had argued that no immunity existed for either Rodberg or Gravel since the senator's action was not connected with a legitimate legislative purpose and, in any case, his negotiations to get the papers published divested him of any privilege. Legitimate legislative business did not include activity outside of Congress to inform the public on governmental matters.

The Senate took the position that a senator's constitutional immunities and the prerogatives of the Senate must be vigorously defended, regardless of any consideration as to the propriety of Gravel's act, against attempts of the executive branch to encroach on these protections. The Senate response took the form of a resolution authorizing it to file a friend of the court brief in the Supreme Court on the constitutional immunity issue raised by the Boston grand jury's probe into Gravel's actions.

Background. During the controversy over publication of the Pentagon Papers in 1971 by *The New York Times*, *The Washington Post* and several other newspapers, Sen. Gravel on June 29 convened a special meeting of the Public Works Subcommittee on Public Buildings, of which he was chairman. With the press and the public in attendance, Gravel read classified documents from the Pentagon Papers into the subcommittee record. Subsequently, the senator arranged for the verbatim publication of the subcommittee record by Beacon Press, the non-profit publishing arm of the Unitarian-Universalist Association.

In August of that year a federal grand jury in Boston, investigating the release of the Pentagon Papers, ordered Rodberg to appear before it. The grand jury also subpoenaed several persons associated with Beacon Press who were involved in publication of the papers.

Rodberg moved to quash the subpoena on the grounds he was protected from questioning by congres-

---

Supreme Court on Gravel

The Supreme Court June 29, 1972, in *Gravel v. U.S.*, defined the protections against having to testify before the grand jury in the Pentagon Papers case.

The court said no witness could be questioned concerning:

1) the conduct of Sen. Gravel or his aides at the meeting of the Subcommittee on Public Buildings and Grounds of the Senate Public Works Committee on June 29, 1971;

2) the motives and purposes behind the conduct of Sen. Gravel or his aides at the June 29 meeting;

3) communications between Sen. Gravel and his aides during the terms of their employment and related to the June 29 meeting or any other legislative act of the senator;

4) any act, in itself not criminal, performed by the senator or by his aides in the course of their employment in preparation for the subcommittee meeting, except as it proved relevant to investigating possible third-party crime.

---

sional immunity, contending such immunity extended to staff members.

Gravel filed a motion to intervene on Rodberg's behalf, claiming Rodberg was acting under the senator's orders, which were immune from judicial inquiry.

The Justice Department, in a brief filed in the case Sept. 8, 1971, said no immunity existed for either Rodberg or Gravel. While not saying so directly, the department's action left open the possibility it might subpoena Gravel himself to testify.

Regarding the senator's actions, the brief said his subcommittee meeting was "unauthorized and untimely." Congress, it said, "does not enjoy uncurbed power to conduct business; excursions of committee hearings into private lives unconnected with a legitimate legislative purpose have long been held unconstitutional. The reading of the paper in question can have no possible relationship to the legislative business with which Senator Gravel has sought to cloak himself."

Even if the reading was official business, the brief went on, his subsequent negotiations to publish the papers divested him of any privilege.

A lower court ruled in October that the grand jury could not question any witness about Gravel's conduct at the special meeting or about his preparation for the meeting. The grand jury was also prohibited from questioning Rodberg about his own actions taken at Gravel's direction relating to the meeting.

In January 1972 the court of appeals, 1st circuit, held that Gravel could be questioned about the subsequent publication of the subcommittee record by Beacon Press but not about the subcommittee meeting itself. The same immunities extended to Gravel were also to be applied to Rodberg, the court ruled. But third parties, the court ruled, could be questioned about any of their own actions regarding the publication and the ad hoc committee session.

The Supreme Court Feb. 22 agreed to hear arguments on *Gravel v. United States* and on June 29 issued its ruling on the extent of congressional immunity.

SUPREME COURT DECISION

In a 5-4 decision handed down June 29, 1972, the Supreme Court substantially narrowed the category of activities protected under the Constitution's Speech or Debate clause—which states that "for any speech or debate in either House...(senators and representatives) shall not be questioned in any other place." The ruling held that Sen. Gravel's constitutional immunity did not shield him or his aides from grand jury questioning regarding their activities not directly related to their legislative responsibilities. *(Box, p. 418)* "While the Speech or Debate Clause recognizes speech, voting and other legislative acts as exempt from liability that might attach," the court stated, "it does not privilege either senator or aide to violate an otherwise valid criminal law in preparing for or implementing legislative acts."

The court concluded that the immunity of Gravel's aide was identical to that of his employer and defined the latter's as immunity from "prosecutions that directly impinge upon or threaten the legislative process."

The court majority concurred with the lower court ruling that the negotiations leading to the unofficial publication of the committee record were outside the protection of the Speech or Debate clause; further, however, it also held that Gravel as well as Rodberg were vulnerable to grand jury questioning and possible liability regarding their role in the Pentagon Papers publication.

SENATE ACTION

Reacting to the Justice Department's contention that the scope of the Speech or Debate immunity was strictly limited to senators and representatives in carrying out their legislative duties, the Senate March 23, 1972, voted 55-27 in favor of a resolution (S Res 280) authorizing the Senate to file an amicus curiae—friend of the court—brief in the case when it came before the Supreme Court. Senators Sam J. Ervin Jr. (D N.C.) and William B. Saxbe (R Ohio) were designated to present the case for protection of the prerogatives of the Senate during oral argument before the court.

The resolution as amended on the floor also authorized the Senate to pay expenses of filing the brief (staff time and printing costs), but it did not cover Gravel's own legal fees as proposed in the original version of the resolution drafted by Mike Mansfield (D Mont.) and Ervin. *(Provisions, box this page)*

At issue in the Senate debate was the question of who was going to pay for the expenses involved in filing the brief and who would pay for Gravel's private legal fees, travel expenses and staff time involved in fighting the court case.

Majority Leader Mansfield said: "Regardless of how anyone may view the propriety of the specific act that gave rise to this controversy, such questions are simply not germane to the issue here at stake. What is at stake is whether the Senate's viewpoint concerning its constitutional role should be presented fully, adequately and effectively to the Supreme Court. It is my opinion that it should."

Sam J. Ervin Jr. (D N.C.), chairman of the Judiciary Subcommittee on Constitutional Rights, said: "The Justice Department would limit the protection of the clause (in the Constitution) to members (of Congress) only, and it characterizes judicial and executive inquiry of aides as only a hypothetical hindrance of the legislative process." Filing a friend of the court brief "is both proper and necessary...to ensure that the (Justice) Department's narrow view of legislative privilege and separation of powers does not prevail."

Senator Saxbe told the Senate he strenuously objected to paying Gravel's court expenses. "The minority is well aware of the challenges to the dignity of the Senate and its necessary immunities having to do with the freedom of members of this body as set out in the Constitution.... However, this resolution contains several items which we do not believe should be included. We do not believe that taxpayers' money should be expended for the purpose of perfecting an appeal."

Saxbe Amendment. To alleviate the objections of many Republicans to paying Gravel's legal expenses, Saxbe offered an amendment which sought to delete Senate funding of all expenses regarding the case—expenses of the Senate in preparing the friend of court brief and Gravel's expenses in presenting his own case.

Saxbe argued that the many qualified lawyers in the Senate could prepare the brief without costing the Senate anything. And as for Gravel's legal fees, Saxbe said: "The minority does not want to be included in any part of that."

Mansfield: "If the Senate wants to do something about Gravel, then the Senate should do it—not the executive or judicial branch. The senator (Gravel) is not on trial, but basically the Senate is on trial."

Provisions of Resolution on Gravel

The Senate March 23, 1972, adopted S Res 280 authorizing the Senate to intervene in certain ways in the Supreme Court case involving Sen. Mike Gravel (D Alaska). The resolution provided that:

• Members of the Senate would appear before the Supreme Court and file a brief on behalf of the Senate as a friend of the court.

• Although the Senate was filing such a brief, it was not meant to express any judgment on the propriety of Gravel's actions regarding release of the Pentagon Papers.

• Expenses involved in preparing the friend-of-court brief and the expenses for printing Sen. Gravel's personal brief and supporting documents—including costs to the Senate Public Works Committee of printing excerpts of the Pentagon Papers—would be paid for by the Senate.

The resolution stated: "In deciding this case the Supreme Court will consider the scope and meaning of the protection provided to members of Congress by...the U.S. Constitution...including the application of this provision to senators, their aides, assistants and associates and the types of activity protected....

"This case necessarily involves the right of the Senate to govern its own internal affairs and to determine the relevancy and propriety of legislative activity and the scope of a senator's duties under the rules of the Senate and the Constitution.... A decision in this case may impair the constitutional separation of powers between legislative branch and executive and judicial branches of government."

The Saxbe amendment was rejected March 23 by a 34-47 roll-call vote. Eight Republicans and all voting Democrats opposed the amendment.

Ervin Substitute. As a compromise, Ervin offered a substitute which excluded Gravel's legal fees as part of the costs to be absorbed by the Senate. The Ervin proposal, however, still included printing costs for Gravel's briefs and for supporting documents to his case. Also included in the Ervin substitute was authorization to pay for all Senate expenses contingent to filing the friend of the court brief.

After Saxbe's attempt to amend the Ervin proposal was rejected, the substitute language was adopted by voice vote. The Senate then approved the resolution 55-27. Fifteen Republicans and 40 Democrats supported S Res 280; all votes against were cast by Republicans.

After the Senate had adopted the resolution, there was a confrontation in which Saxbe described Gravel's action with regard to the Pentagon Papers as despicable and slippery. Saxbe said: "I can see such a man in wartime saying that the enemy was deserving of certain secrets that would give him advantage and that the degree of the kind of treason is only in the mind of the individual who applies it."

This was the only Senate action dealing with the Gravel case. Although some members at the time of the release of the Pentagon Papers had called for disciplinary action against him, the Democratic leadership in the Senate said no such action was warranted.

Minority Leader Hugh Scott (R Pa.) had declared in June 1971 that Gravel might have violated a Senate rule prohibiting the divulging of confidential communications from the President or an executive department as well as any classified information. If this was the case, Scott added, Gravel would be liable to expulsion if the Senate voted to censure him. But Scott said the Democratic majority should decide whether he broke the rule. Mansfield, however, on July 1, 1971, announced there would be no attempt to discipline the Alaskan senator. Gravel broke no rule of the Senate, Mansfield said.

Powell Case

Rep. Adam Clayton Powell Jr. (D N.Y. 1945-71), Jan. 3, 1969, was sworn in as a representative, ending a two-year exile from the House forced upon him by his colleagues in 1967. *(Congress and the Nation Vol. II, p. 893)*

Before permitting him to be seated, however, the House by a 254-158 roll-call vote adopted a resolution (H Res 2) fining Powell $25,000, purportedly for at least partial recovery of about $40,000 in congressional funds which Powell allegedly misused, and stripping him of his seniority.

The House, in adopting H Res 2, showed that its feelings about Powell had moderated considerably since 1967. Two years earlier, the chief proposal for seating Powell had called for a $40,000 fine, stripping his seniority, and formal censure by the House. And the House had rejected that harsh measure in 1967, opting instead to exclude him completely from the 90th Congress. In 1969, those who were influential in developing the compromise (H Res 2) never even proposed that Powell be censured, and those wanting to exclude him again were clearly a small minority.

Powell was initially elected to the House in 1944 and was returned regularly thereafter by large majorities of his Harlem constituency. He rose in seniority and became chairman of the House Education and Labor Committee in 1961; as such he earned a reputation as one of the more effective chairmen in the House.

In 1967, after a series of difficulties with his own committee and a preliminary investigation by a House subcommittee, Powell was investigated by a select committee, which found that he had misused congressional funds, acted contemptuously toward the courts of New York in a libel suit and kept his wife on the congressional payroll although she did not work in either his district or in the District of Columbia, as required by law. Rejecting the recommendations of the select committee, the House March 1, 1967, excluded Powell from the 90th Congress.

The Supreme Court June 16, 1969, ruled 7-1 in favor of Powell's contention that he had been excluded unconstitutionally from the 90th Congress.

Powell March 8, 1967, had sued the speaker and certain members and employees of the House, contending that he had been excluded unconstitutionally. He lost in district court in the District of Columbia and in the Court of Appeals. The Supreme Court Nov. 18, 1968, agreed to hear his appeal.

The central legal issues in the Powell suit were:

• Could the House add to the Constitution's three qualifications for House membership? The three are that the member be at least 25 years old, have been a U.S. citizen for at least seven years and be, when elected, an inhabitant of the state from which he was elected.

• Could the courts properly examine the actions of the House in such cases, order the House not to add to the Constitution's qualifications, and enforce this order?

Chief Justice Earl Warren, delivering the opinion of the court, ruled that the House had improperly excluded Powell, a duly elected representative who met the constitutional requirements of age, residence and citizenship. (A footnote to the opinion said the court expressed no view limiting Congress' power to expel or punish an already seated member.)

Having disposed of the procedural questions, the court moved to the major issues: Was the question of Powell's exclusion a "political question" which federal courts should not touch because of the separation of powers? Was House action excluding Powell from the 90th Congress unconstitutional?

The Constitution, the court ruled, in giving to the House the power to "be the Judge of the...Qualifications of its own Members" (Article I, Section 5, clause 1), left the House without the authority to exclude any duly elected representative who met the requirements for membership expressly stated in the Constitution. (Article I, Section 2, clause 2.) *(Box, next page)*

The court based its conclusion—that the House was powerless to exclude any member-elect who met the specific constitutional requirements of age, citizenship, and residency—in part upon a fundamental principle of representative democracy: the premise that the people should be able to choose whomever they wish to represent and govern them. This principle, Chief Justice Warren wrote, could be undermined as much by limiting whom the people could select as by limiting the vote itself.

The court did not deny the unquestionable interest of the Congress in maintaining its own integrity. In most cases, however, the court felt that that interest could be properly safeguarded by the use of each House's power to punish or expel its members. "Both the intention of the Framers, to the extent that it can be determined, and an examination of the basic principles of our democratic system persuade us," the court held, "that the Constitution does not vest in the Congress a discretionary power to deny membership by a majority vote."

The court dismissed the argument that the case presented a "political question" which, if decided by the court, could produce an explosive confrontation between the legislative and judicial branches. Determination of Powell's right to his seat in the 90th Congress, the court held, required only an interpretation of the Constitution, the traditional function of the court.

The Supreme Court Feb. 2, 1970, refused to order a federal district judge to award back pay and lost seniority to Powell.

Powell was defeated in the Democratic primary in his congressional district in a bid for re-election and died in 1971.

Gallagher Guilty Plea

Five months after being defeated in the Democratic primary in his congressional district, Rep. Cornelius E. Gallagher (D N.J. 1959-73) pleaded guilty Dec. 21, 1972, in U.S. District Court in Trenton, N.J., to tax evasion. He had been indicted April 7, 1972, by a federal grand jury in Newark, N.J., on charges of perjury and conspiracy to hide kickbacks. A trial had been set for Jan. 8, 1973.

Gallagher was also accused of evading payment of more than $102,000 in federal income taxes in 1966-67 and aiding two co-conspirators to evade taxes on an additional $326,000.

Federal judge George H. Barlow agreed to a five-month delay in sentencing Gallagher to give him the "opportunity to come forward and make known to the United States attorney such information as would be helpful to law enforcement authorities" regarding alleged political corruption in New Jersey.

The House Committee on Standards of Official Conduct, established in 1967 in reaction to mounting evidence of congressional wrongdoing by Rep. Adam Clayton Powell Jr. (D N.Y. 1945-71) and Sen. Thomas J. Dodd (D Conn. 1959-71), investigated charges against Gallagher raised by *Life* magazine in 1968. The magazine had called the congressman a "tool and collaborator" of a reputed Mafia figure in New Jersey. However, the committee chose not to release any information of its investigation into *Life's* allegations and no action was ever taken against Gallagher by the committee. Committee Chairman Melvin Price (D Ill.) said at the time that "there was no proof of any violation of the code (of ethics) which the committee had adopted." *(Congress and the Nation Vol. II, p. 902)*

Gallagher had been chairman of the House Government Operations Special Subcommittee on the Invasion of Privacy from its establishment in 1965 until March 1971, when it was abolished.

As chairman, Gallagher was a major opponent of the extensive use of computer data banks and eavesdropping.

Gallagher had announced April 11, 1972, that he would seek re-election to his eighth term in November, where he said he expected to be vindicated at the polls.

Powers of the House

Article I of the Constitution:

Section 2 (1) The House of Representatives shall be composed of Members chosen every second Year by the People of the several States....

(2) No Person shall be a Representative who shall not have attained to the Age of twenty-five Years, and been seven Years a Citizen of the United States, and who shall not, when elected, be an Inhabitant of that State in which he shall be chosen.

Section 5 (1) Each House shall be the Judge of the Elections, Returns and Qualifications of its own Members....

(2) Each House may determine the Rules of its Proceedings, punish its Members for Disorderly Behaviour, and, with the Concurrence of two thirds, expel a Member.

He won re-election both in 1968 and 1970, denying the *Life* charges as a "monstrous lie."

Gallagher was regarded as a prominent figure in the New Jersey Democratic Party and often was mentioned as a potential candidate for governor or senator.

Other Ethics Cases

● Rep. Martin B. McKneally (R N.Y. 1969-71) Dec. 20, 1971, was placed on one-year probation and fined $5,000 for failing to file an income tax return in 1965 on $24,000 of income. McNeally, who was defeated for re-election in 1970, pleaded guilty to the charges in October 1971. The Internal Revenue Service in September 1970 announced that it was investigating McKneally and on Dec. 16 indicted him on charges of income tax evasion.

● Sen. George Murphy (R Calif. 1964-71) confirmed March 11, 1970, that he had been receiving a $20,000-a-year private corporation retainer since coming to the Senate in 1965. The fee was paid by Technicolor Inc., a Hollywood, Calif., motion picture corporation, for Murphy's services as a "public relations consultant." Shortly after the development was reported by Washington columnist Jack Anderson, Murphy acknowledged receiving the fee from the firm which he served as a $40,000-a-year vice president before his election to the Senate. Murphy also was provided with a credit card for travel, and payment by the company of half the rent on his $520-a-month Washington apartment.

On March 11, Sen. John C. Stennis (D Miss.), chairman of the Senate ethics committee, said Murphy had asked him to review the Technicolor contract on Feb. 2, 1970. Stennis said he and Benjamin R. Fern, the committee's chief counsel, decided the employment "was reasonable and not a conflict of interest if carried out under the terms of the contract." The full committee did not consider the matter.

Murphy was ousted from Technicolor June 18, 1970, by an insurgent group of stockholders. The senator said June 19 he had planned to resign anyway. Murphy was defeated in the Nov. 3, 1970, elections by Rep. John V. Tunney (D), and was hired in December, 1970, as a consultant to Hill and Knowlton Inc., a public relations firm.

● Sen. Thomas J. Dodd (D Conn. 1959-71), who was censured by the Senate in June 1967 for allegedly diverting campaign contributions to his personal use, was spared having to face criminal charges when the Department of Justice Dec. 23, 1969, announced that prosecution was not warranted. The announcement was made in the form of a letter from Attorney General John N. Mitchell to Dodd's attorneys notifying them that prosecution would not be initiated. The Senate Select Committee on Standards and Conduct, which recommended censure of Dodd in 1967, had referred a number of allegations brought out in its investigation to the department and the Internal Revenue Service for review. *(Congress and the Nation Vol. II, p. 900)*

Dodd declined to seek the Democratic nomination for senator from Connecticut in 1970 but ran in the general election as an independent. He placed third, with 24 per cent of the vote. Dodd had served four years in the House and 12 years in the Senate. He died May 24, 1971.

Questions of Impropriety

Charges of conflict of interest and unethical behavior touched many other members who were not accused of violating any laws.

HALPERN'S DEBTS. The *Wall Street Journal* July 29, 1970, reported that Rep. Seymour Halpern (R N.Y.), the third-ranking minority member on the House Banking and Currency Committee, had debts "far exceeding $100,000" to banks in New York and Florida.

Halpern acknowledged that he had "a number of loans and several personal debts" but denied any conflict of interest between his finances and his role on the committee, which handles banking legislation.

In a statement issued in Washington, Halpern said:

"I have had my share of financial problems. Almost every American does at one time or another. But not one iota has rubbed off on my public life. There has never been an iota of conflict."

PAYMENTS TO THURMOND. *Life* magazine reported Sept. 19, 1970, that Sen. Strom Thurmond (R S.C.) received more than twice as much money as other nearby landholders for property condemned when the state of South Carolina in 1968 decided to build a highway on it.

Life said Thurmond and his former law partner, U.S. District Judge Charles E. Simons Jr., were paid $492 an acre for "rough, sandy land, mostly covered with scrub timber."

Other holders of similar property were paid an average of about $200 an acre, *Life* said.

Thurmond issued a statement saying he and Simons appealed the South Carolina Highway Department's original offer of less than $200 an acre because they felt the land was valuable as an industrial site. The case was settled out of court with the state agreeing to pay Thurmond and Simons $32,500, or $492 an acre.

Rep. John C. Watts (D Ky. 1951-71) and Securities and Exchange Commissioner A. Sydney Herlong Jr., who served as a Democratic representative from Florida from 1949 through 1969, were brought under the shadow of conflict of interest Aug. 6, 1970, in an article by Jerry Landauer in the *Wall Street Journal.*

Watts and Herlong were members of the tax-writing Ways and Means Committee. Watts was third-ranking Democrat on the committee at the time. The story charged

---

Conflicts of Interest

Beyond the criminal statutes there is a broad range of opinion on what constitutes conflict of interest. At one extreme is a general consensus that use of an official position to promote or carry on private business is a clear conflict of interest. At another extreme there is the contention that any activity that lessens a member's attention to official duties constitutes a conflict of interest.

The dilemmas are many, and avoidance of all conflict of interest impossible: members of Congress, for example, have until recently had to vote on increases in their own salaries.

Critics are fond of citing representatives of oil-producing states as prime examples of unethical conduct. The opposite point of view has been expressed by Sen. Russell B. Long (D La.), chairman of the Senate Finance Committee, whose jurisdiction included the celebrated depletion allowance for the oil industry.

"Most of my income is from oil and gas. I don't regard it as any conflict of interest. My state produces more oil and gas per acre than any state in the Union. If I didn't represent the oil and gas industry, I wouldn't represent the state of Louisiana." (Quoted by Erwin Knoll in the *New York Times Magazine,* March 8, 1970)

In contrast, Texas' two representatives on the tax-writing House Ways and Means Committee in the 91st Congress, Omar Burleson (D) and George Bush (R), reported in their first official financial disclosures in 1969 that they held no oil or gas stocks. Bush, in fact, disposed of large holdings in oil when he became a member of that committee.

---

that both men received loans of $37,937.50 to cover the purchase of $50,000 in West Virginia Turnpike bonds in 1967. Neither man invested any of his own money in the transaction, the article said. Watts was reported to have received at least $5,000 in profits in 1969 from the sale of the bonds. Herlong picked up capital gains of $8,700, according to the story. Both men declined to disclose the interest paid on the loans.

The loans were arranged by officers of the Winn-Dixie Stores Inc., a southern supermarket chain based near Jacksonville, Fla., the newspaper said.

"While doing favors for key members of Congress, Winn-Dixie embarked on a much more ambitions tax-saving plan for its own executives and other holders of its convertible stock. The tax saving in the end resulted from congressional action," the article said.

The paper contended that an action by the House Ways and Means Committee protected a Winn-Dixie stock issue from being brought under the tax reform bill of 1969, thus resulting in substantial tax savings for the firm's major stockholders.

No congressional or independent body undertook an investigation of the allegations made by the newspaper in 1970.

AUTOMOBILE LEASES. The Ford Motor Company for many years had been leasing insured Lincoln

Continental sedans to key lawmakers for $750 a year, it was reported Aug. 3, 1970, by United Press International. At least 19 House and Senate members, all but two of whom were committee chairmen or ranking minority members, accepted the offer.

Among the committees whose top members enjoyed the favorable lease arrangements with Ford were those responsible for auto safety and highway, consumer and tax matters that frequently were of direct interest to the auto industry.

A Ford spokesman said that 12-month Continental leases comparable to those made available to the top committee members could be obtained by private individuals in the Washington, D.C., area for an average of about $290 a month (about $3,480 a year). Ford said its offer was open only to committee chairmen and senior Republican members, that in no case was it initiated by Ford and that the cars were made available only upon request. The arrangement followed a Ford policy of placing its cars in the hands of prestigious drivers, including sports and entertainment figures, the company said.

Confirming that they leased Continentals under the special Ford offer at the same time the UPI report was made were the following Democratic House committee chairmen:

W. R. Poage (Texas), Agriculture; Thomas E. Morgan (Pa.), Foreign Affairs; Samuel N. Friedel (Md. 1953-71), House Administration; Harley O. Staggers (W.Va.), Commerce; Edward A. Garmatz (Md. 1947-73), Merchant Marine; Thaddeus J. Dulski (N.Y.), Post Office; George H. Fallon (Md. 1945-71), Public Works; William M. Colmer (Miss. 1935-73), Rules; and George P. Miller (Calif. 1945-73), Science and Astronautics

Those who leased Continentals in the Senate were Democratic Chairmen Russell B. Long (La.), Finance, and James O. Eastland (Miss.), Judiciary.

Also on the Continental list were these ranking Republican House members: Representatives Frank T. Bow (Ohio 1951-73), Appropriations; Leslie C. Arends (Ill.), Armed Services, and Robert J. Corbett (Pa. 1939-41, 1945-71), Post Office.

Ranking Senate minority members with Continentals were Senators Norris Cotton (N.H.), Commerce; Winston L. Prouty (Vt. 1959-71), District of Columbia, and Roman L. Hruska (Neb.), Judiciary.

In the House, Democratic Whip Hale Boggs (La. 1941-43, 1947-72) had a leased Continental. Sen. Robert P. Griffin, the GOP Whip in the Senate, used a leased Continental.

In addition to those legislators to whom new Continentals were supplied at the start of each model year, four chairmen or ranking members elected to take another Ford luxury car, the Thunderbird, also at $750 a year, or the Mercury, at $600.

House Armed Services Committee Chairman L. Mendel Rivers (D S.C. 1941-70) chose the Thunderbird. So did Rep. William C. Cramer (R Fla. 1955-71), senior Republican member of the Public Works Committee and a candidate for the Senate in Florida in 1970. Rep. Olin E. Teague (D Texas), chairman of the Veterans' Affairs Committee, used a Mercury as did Sen. Alan Bible (D Nev.), chairman of the Select Small Business Committee.

The Senate ethics committee Aug. 24, 1970, unanimously recommended that senators quickly terminate the low-cost automobile leases. Chairman Stennis said

Legal Restraints on Members

There are several existing restraints on the behavior of members of Congress dealing with questions of ethics. These include:

● Title 18 of the U.S. Code which makes it illegal for a member of Congress to accept a bribe or otherwise misuse the office for personal financial gain in certain specified ways.

● The Federal Election Campaign Act of 1971, which requires political parties and candidates for office to report campaign contributions and expenditures. The law (PL 92-225) places a ceiling on the amount of money federal candidates for elective office can spend on political advertising in the communications media and requires public disclosure of campaign contributions and expenditures. *(Complete list of provisions, p. 399)*

● General law applicable to all citizens such as income tax statutes.

● H Res 796, passed by the House May 26, 1970, requires House members to report annually sources of all honoraria of $300 or more and identify all creditors to whom $10,000 or more was owed for 90 days or longer without the pledge of specific security. *(Details, financial disclosures p. 425)*

● A code of ethics, approved in 1958, which covers all government employees, including members of Congress.

● The potential censure by the member's chamber should the member's conduct be judged reprehensible to his chamber as a whole. There is no clear-cut definition of what conduct is serious enough to merit censure.

that the committee had decided "senators should not accept any favorable terms and conditions that are available to them only as senators."

"From the facts available to us," the committee report said, "it appears that the price paid by a senator is considerably less than that which would have to be paid by the ordinary person making the same type of lease." The committee found that the leasing arrangement violated no law or Senate rule, and the report added: "We are confident that no favoritism either was given to or expected by the automobile companies." Ford later ended its participation.

RAYBURN HOUSE OFFICE BUILDING. The names of four members of Congress and a former member were involved in a year-long investigation in 1970 of a Baltimore contractor accused of trying to defraud the federal government. A grand jury in Baltimore alleged in its presentment that Victor H. Frenkil, a wealthy Maryland contractor and head of the company that built the parking garage for the Rayburn House office building, tried to use threats and political influence to win a $5-million claim against the government.

The grand jury and two successive U.S. attorneys recommended the case be prosecuted but Attorney General John N. Mitchell, citing lack of evidence, refused to authorize signature of the formal indictments.

The New York Times reported June 21, 1970, that Sen. Long and former Sen. Brewster were said to have been offered bribes of up to $125,000 each. The Times said there was no evidence that they accepted the offer or received any money.

A summary of the grand jury's presentment was made public June 22, 1970, at the order of Chief Judge Roszel Thomsen of U.S. District Court in Baltimore. The summary said Frenkil's firm remodeled at a cut-rate price the Bethesda, Md., home of Rep. Hale Boggs (D La.), House Majority Whip, in the hope of getting his aid. The report said Frenkil promised employment advances to congressional employees concerned with the claim in return for favorable action and threatened them with the loss of their jobs if the claim was disapproved. Boggs had denied he received special favors.

Two other House members were mentioned as urging a speedy review of the contractor's claim. Democrats Friedel and Clarence D. Long, both of Maryland, said subsequently that they had only made inquiries for a constituent about the case.

HOUSE 'GHOST' VOTING. The House Committee on Standards of Official Conduct in mid-1969 closed a case of alleged ghost votes in the House of Representatives.

The committee June 19 reported to Speaker John W. McCormack (D Mass.) that honest errors accounted for discrepancies in 1968 when members who were out of town were recorded as having voted. *(Congress and the Nation Vol. II, p. 903)*

The committee blamed the errors on overwork and exhaustion on the part of tally clerk Thomas V. Cooke, who later was dropped from the House payroll.

Cooke said at the time he had added extra names to the list of those voting at the request of another House employee. After an inquiry, the committee said this was not accurate and described the explanation as "an instinctively defensive reaction" on Cooke's part.

All other employees and members were absolved by the committee from complicity in the voting errors.

The committee urged installation at the earliest possible date of a modernized system of voting in the House.

IMMIGRATION BILLS. A newspaper investigation in 1969 which produced accusations of impropriety in the introduction of hundreds of private immigration bills to help Chinese seamen stay in the United States resulted in a Senate probe and a change in procedures.

The Senate Select Committee on Standards and Conduct said Sept. 29 it had begun a preliminary investigation into allegations that some senators or their aides received gifts and campaign contributions for introducing bills to help Chinese ship-jumpers escape deportation. Chairman John C. Stennis (D Miss.) asked the committee staff to make a study of all private relief bills introduced in recent years to determine whether there had been any abuse in handling them. Such bills automatically delay deportation while awaiting congressional action.

The Senate Majority and Minority Leaders took action Oct. 1 to halt the practice of staff aides' introducing private bills in the Senate. In a letter to Senate Secretary Francis R. Valeo, Mansfield and Scott instructed that "bills and resolutions should no longer be received at the desk by the Parliamentarian for reference to the appropriate standing committees unless they were signed by and delivered at the desk in person by the senator introducing them."

These developments followed publication of stories in August 1969 by Knight Newspapers, which after several weeks of investigation reported evidence that New York lawyers and Washington lobbyists had been getting $500 to $2,500 for each Chinese immigration bill involved.

Among those who figured in the upsurge of such bills since 1967 were Sens. Gaylord Nelson (D Wis.), Daniel K. Inouye (D Hawaii), Harrison A. Williams (D N.J.), and former Sen. Daniel Brewster (D Md. 1963-69). Although these senators said they had had little or no connection with the Chinese nationals, bills introduced by them constituted almost half the 700 Chinese immigration bills brought before Congress in the period 1967-69.

The immigration issue had become increasingly important since 1967, when U.S. immigration officials and federal courts began a crackdown on aliens who stayed in the country illegally.

By law, the U.S. Immigration and Naturalization Service must deport alien seamen who extend their stays beyond normal shore leave time. However, if private legislation is pending in Congress, immigration authorities generally allow the bills to be resolved in Congress before taking action against such aliens.

Introduction of private immigration bills was not uncommon, but the increase in such bills for Chinese after 1967 had been dramatic. During the preceding two years of the 89th Congress—in 1965 and 1966—there were bills for fewer than 25 such individuals. Beginning in 1967, 700 such bills had been filed by several dozen senators.

 **Financial Disclosures (1968-72)**

MEMBERS MAKE FINANCIAL DISCLOSURES UNDER 1968 ACT

Senators and representatives in 1969, for the first time in the history of Congress, were required to make a limited disclosure of their financial status under different rules adopted in 1968 by the House and the Senate. The new regulations differed considerably in the type of information to be reported and in the portions required to be made public. *(1968 Codes of Conduct, Congress and the Nation Vol. II, p. 921)*

While the new reporting requirements were generally considered a progressive development by those favoring fuller public disclosure by congressmen and their staff, the rules contained many loopholes, and the resulting reports provided a far from complete picture of members' financial holdings.

Disclosure Rules

Senate Reports. The Senate directed its members to make reports available to the public on the amount and source of each honorarium of $300 or more received during the preceding year. (For 1969 the new rule permitted senators to limit their accounting to the second half of 1968.)

Senators were also asked to list the sources, amounts and disposition of political contributions received by them, as well as the source and amount of any gift in excess of $50 from persons other than relatives.

The Senate reports produced little information, however, other than fees received by senators for speeches, writings, television appearances, or related activities. In some cases even this information was sketchy because senators merely listed booking agents as the source of large amounts of income. Sixty-one senators reported receiving honoraria in 1968.

House Reports. The House required a more detailed financial report to be made available for public inspection. Under the new House rule on disclosure, members were asked to list interests worth more than $5,000 in any business doing substantial business with the federal government or subject to federal regulatory agencies.

House members were also directed to disclose publicly the source of any income for services (other than congressional salaries) exceeding $5,000 annually and any capital gain from a single source exceeding $5,000. They were required to report associations with any professional organization from which an income of $1,000 or more annually was received.

Loopholes. Although the new Senate rules, required public accounting of contributions from fund-raising events and individuals, they had little meaning in practice. Most senators channeled campaign funds to committees exempted from the reporting requirements. The new rules did little to provide workable guidelines concerning financial transactions between senators and

persons or businesses with an interest in legislation before Congress.

Although the first House disclosure reports for the year 1968 revealed far more information about members' outside business activities than did the Senate reports, there were many loopholes in the House statements. No House member reported the source of any honorarium; instructions supplied by the House Committee on Standards of Official Conduct required disclosure of fees for speeches or writings only if they exceeded $5,000 in each case.

The House did not require members to list the amount or value of stock held in companies doing business with the federal government. Eighty members who were lawyers reported an active interest in law practices but were not directed to list the names of clients.

Ninety-four House members reported that they owned stock in banks or savings and loan associations or served on their boards of directors. Despite the large proportion (21.6 per cent) of House members reporting an interest in financial institutions, they were not required under the disclosure rule to reveal the amount of stock held in banks, savings and loan associations or bank holding companies.

Confidential Report. Both the Senate and the House rules directed members to file confidential financial reports in sealed envelopes to be held secure from public scrutiny.

Senators filed detailed information on income, assets and debts, including their 1968 U.S. income tax returns. House members merely had to report the dollar value of assets or sources of income listed in the public disclosure part of their reports.

The confidential Senate and House reports could be opened only by a majority vote of the Senate Select Committee on Standards and Conduct and the House Committee on Standards of Official Conduct respectively.

Background

The Senate March 22, 1968, passed a resolution (S Res 266) containing four new rules on standards of conduct. The House followed suit April 3, 1968, passing a resolution (H Res 1099) establishing a Code of Official Conduct for members and employees as well as the disclosure rule.

Pressures for creating the standards of ethical conduct and reporting of members' financial interests had been building for several years. Demands for action on congressional ethics had intensified in 1963 when charges of improprieties against Robert G. (Bobby) Baker, former secretary to the Senate Democrats, became public knowledge.

In 1967, the censure of Sen. Thomas J. Dodd (D Conn.) by the Senate and the exclusion of then member-elect Rep. Adam Clayton Powell Jr. (D N.Y.) by the House contributed to the growing pressures for action on ethical standards.

Ethics Committees. Before the passage of rules of conduct by the Senate and House in 1968, both chambers operated to a large extent without written standards for judging the conduct of their members.

The Senate in 1964 had authorized a six-member bipartisan Select Committee on Standards and Conduct. The committee made its first official report April 27, 1967, recommending censure of Dodd.

The House created its bipartisan Committee on Standards of Official Conduct April 3, 1968. The committee initiated its first action against a member in April 1972 when it voted to prohibit Rep. John Dowdy (D Texas) from participating in committee and floor activity. *(p. 412)*

Legislative Action, 1969-72

The House in 1970 added new provisions to the financial disclosure requirements adopted in 1968. For the first time, the House required members to report the source of honoraria of $300 or more if earned in a single year. Even more important, members were required to identify creditors to whom $10,000 or more was owed for 90 days or longer without the pledge of specific security.

A bill was introduced in the Senate in 1969 to require public disclosure of finances by top officials in all three branches of the federal government, but no action was taken by either house and the bill (S 1993) died at the end of the 91st Congress.

There was no action on financial disclosure legislation during the 92nd Congress.

Related to the movement to open to public scrutiny the sources of elected officials' wealth was the issue of reforming lobbying practices. The House Standards of Official Conduct Committee late in 1971 reported a bill to overhaul the 1946 Federal Regulation of Lobbying Act, but the House never acted on the bill.

HOUSE

HONORARIA AND LOANS. A resolution (H Res 796) requiring House members to report certain honoraria and loans was passed in 1970. H Res 796 was introduced by Melvin Price (D Ill.), chairman of the House Committee on Standards of Official Conduct. His committee also issued guidelines in 1970 for members in conducting business with governmental agencies on behalf of constituents. The guidelines did not require House approval.

The committee's guidelines said that members' conduct in such matters should be undertaken irrespective of political considerations and without suggestions of favoritism or reprisals. The committee said a member must be sure that actions made in his name by his employees conformed to his instructions. The committee noted that under existing law members or employees were prohibited from receiving compensation for services for constituents and warned of the need for caution in sharing fees charged by members' law firms.

The committee's action came in the wake of federal indictments against Martin Sweig, suspended administrative assistant of Speaker John W. McCormack (D Mass.) and lawyer Nathan Voloshen, a McCormack friend. *(p. 415)*

The loans provision followed reports in 1969 that Rep. Seymour Halpern (R N.Y. 1959-73), a member of the House Banking and Currency Committee, had owed banks more than $75,000. The proposed rule applied only to loans secured without the pledge of specific security. Loans made through the House bank specified that future salaries of congressmen would be used as collateral.

Provisions. As passed May 26, 1970, H Res 796:

● Amended House rule 44 on financial disclosure to require House members to report annually in statements filed with the standards committee: sources of all honoraria of $300 or more and the identity of creditors to whom $10,000 or more was owed for 90 days or longer without the pledge of specific security.

● The resolution would take effect with calendar year 1971, with 1972 the first reporting date. Amounts of honoraria and loans would be filed in sealed envelopes which would be available only for investigations by the standards committee.

LOBBYING STUDY. The House passed a second resolution (H Res 1031) in 1970 directing the House standards of Official Conduct Committee to investigate lobbying and campaign contributions and issue a report before adjournment of the 91st Congress. *(Committee recommendations, see chapter on lobbying, p. 469)*

William M. Colmer (D Miss. 1933-73), chairman of the Rules Committee, said his committee separated the lobbying and campaign contributions provisions from the Legislative Reorganization Act of 1970 (PL 91-510) because of "the depth and the complexity" of the subject. *(1970 act, p. 385)*

H. Allen Smith (R Calif. 1957-73), ranking Republican on Rules, said the committee had called for action on the subject in 1970 "because of the need to bring the Federal Regulation of Lobbying Act up to date now, rather than later." He said of the existing act (PL 79-601):

"The act has never been very successful in its primary intent, which was to require registration of all lobbyists and reporting of all expenditures made to influence legislation. All lobbyists have not registered during the years and all of their expenditures have not been reported. There are weaknesses in the language of the Act. Neither officer of the Congress has any way to verify the reporting."

Smith said he had received extensive briefs from the American Bar Association, the Washington Bar Association and many others "regarding the language which they think should be contained in any lobbying act." He added: "...The one difficult determination is regarding the word 'substantial.' Most bills introduced on lobbying require them to register and report if they spend a 'substantial' amount of their time in the activity. This will be one of the difficult decisions which the Committee on Standards of Official Conduct will have to make. It can only be determined after appropriate hearings and study of the court decisions interpreting the word 'substantial.' "

Provisions. As passed by the House July 8, H Res 1031:

● Granted the Committee on Standards of Official Conduct continuing jurisdiction over "measures relating to activities designed to: 1) assist in defeating, passing, or amending any legislation by the House, or 2) influence, directly or indirectly, the passage or defeat of any legislation by the House;" and "measures relating to the raising, reporting, and use of campaign contributions for candidates for the office of representative in the House ...and of resident commissioner to the United States from Puerto Rico."

• Authorized the committee to conduct investigations and hold hearings on "all pertinent matters which would assist Congress" with remedial legislation.

• Directed that the first investigation and study be made during the remainder of the 91st Congress, with a report and recommended legislation to be submitted by the end of the session.

1971 LOBBYING DISCLOSURE BILL. The House did not act on a comprehensive bill (HR 11453), reported in December 1971, to replace the 1946 Federal Regulation of Lobbying Act. The bill, the Legislative Activities Disclosure Act, was approved by the House Standards of Official Conduct Committee but never brought to the floor. *(Background to 1946 act, Congress and the Nation Vol. I, p. 1557-1570; loopholes, Vol. II, p.913)*

Hearings were held by the committee in October 1970 on bills to amend the 1946 law. Three witnesses, two of them attorneys for major business groups, said the law should be changed.

The witnesses variously described the law as "incomprehensible and unworkable," "vague and ambiguous" and "seriously deficient in many ways." They said it lacked definition, contained reporting requirements that were "simply a nightmare" and was "a sick statute" which posed "an almost insurmountable problem" for those seeking to comply with it.

Despite similar criticism of the law ever since its enactment in 1946, it had never been amended. All witnesses at the hearings emphasized that the Supreme Court narrowed its scope considerably in 1954. The dissenting views of three justices who would have held the law unconstitutional at that time were quoted frequently to the committee.

The hearings were the first held on the subject since House approval of H Res 1031, which gave the committee continuing jurisdiction over lobbying and campaign financing matters. As the first standing House committee to receive continuing lobby jurisdiction, it was authorized to investigate at its own discretion and to recommend any needed changes in lobby law. Melvin Price (D Ill.) headed the committee of six Democrats and six Republicans.

The House Committee on Standards of Official Conduct on Oct. 27, 1971, voted 9-3 to report HR 11453 as a clean bill differing only slightly from an earlier draft (HR 11019) introduced by Price and several other members. The reported version placed primary emphasis on disclosure without reference to regulation.

Price and the four other House committee chairmen serving on the Standards of Official Conduct Committee divided 3-2 on whether to report the bill to the House, with the majority favoring the report.

Voting to report HR 11453 were Price, Watkins M. Abbitt (D Va. 1948-73), Chet Holifield (D Calif.), Jackson E. Betts (R Ohio 1951-73), Lawrence G. Williams (R Pa.), Edward Hutchinson (R Mich.), Carleton J. King (R N.Y.) and Floyd Spence (R S.C.).

Voting against reporting the bill were Olin E. Teague (D Texas), Wayne N. Aspinall (D Colo. 1949-73) and James H. (Jimmy) Quillen (R Tenn.).

The committee issued its report (H Rept 92-714) Dec. 10 urging passage of HR 11453. Dissenting views were filed by three of the 12 members.

The committee said in its report that it did not seek to broaden or narrow provisions of the existing law. "It merely seeks to gain an understanding of the ways and means of those who attempt to influence the course of legislation and to devise a system which does not abridge rights guaranteed by the First Amendment, while protecting the over-all public interest," the report said.

Dissenting were Teague, Quillen and Aspinall. They said they favored "meaningful legislation" but felt the bill "suffers from many of the same shortcomings" as the 1946 law. They called the bill so complicated they did not understand it and predicted "nothing but difficulty" for many who would be covered.

Provisions. As reported by the House Committee on Standards of Official Conduct, HR 11453, the Legislative Activities Disclosure Act:

• Declared it Congress' purpose to provide for the disclosure of the activities, "and the origin, amounts, and utilization of funds and other resources, of and by persons who, for consideration, seek to influence the legislative process."

• Defined "covered communication to influence legislation" as any direct communication (other than an exempt communication) by any person for or on behalf of another person to influence legislation.

• Exempted from requirements of the act any communication by an individual acting solely on his own behalf.

• Exempted any communication relating only to the existence, status, purpose or effect of legislation.

• Exempted any communication to Congress made at the specific request of Congress, its members, committees or staff.

• Exempted any communication to an instrumentality of any branch of the federal government, the District of Columbia or the Commonwealth of Puerto Rico made at the specific request of the instrumentality or in exercise of a right of petition under the Administrative Procedure law.

• Exempted any communication by a government official or employee, acting in his official capacity.

• Exempted campaign finance activities.

• Exempted oral testimony and written statements to committees of Congress.

• Exempted general communications media and persons connected with them.

• Exempted communications to Congress or the General Accounting Office concerning regulations proposed under the act.

• Exempted any communication in connection with election candidates.

• Exempted any communication by political party units regarding their positions or activities.

• Defined as a "legislative agent" any individual or organization retained, for any consideration other than exempt travel expenses, "in a capacity other than as an officer or employee" of the employer, to make communications covered by the bill to influence legislation, acting by himself or through another.

• Defined "influence legislation" as meaning "to promote, effectuate, delay, or prevent the introduction, consideration, amendment, passage, approval, adoption, enactment, or defeat of legislation by Congress, or any member or any committee of Congress."

• Defined "direct communication" as meaning all methods of direct address to Congress, its members or staff, or the solicitation of an instrumentality of any branch of the federal government, the District of Columbia or the Commonwealth of Puerto Rico to make a direct address to Congress.

• Limited "exempt travel expenses" to actual transportation cost plus a per diem of up to 125 percent of the maximum allowance ($40 per day) provided government employees.

• Required each legislative agent to file a notice of representation with the comptroller general within five days after his first communication as defined by the bill to influence legislation.

• Specified that the notice shall include an identification of the agent, those who retained him and all for whom he was to act, the "financial terms and conditions" including contingent fee arrangements, the specific areas of legislative interest and an identification of each person acting for the legislative agent in the various areas of interest.

• Provided that the act should not be construed to require disclosure of membership rolls or dues structure of any voluntary membership association.

• Required a legislative agent to report changes in his status, including terminations, within five days of their occurrence.

• Required specified records to be maintained by:

1. A legislative agent.
2. The employer of a legislative agent.
3. A paid officer or employee of someone other than a legislative agent who on behalf of his employer makes a covered communication to influence legislation on all or part of six or more calendar days in a six-month filing period.
4. The employer of such an officer or employee.
5. A person who for consideration or as a paid officer or employee or through use of "funds contributed to him" solicits others to influence legislation by direct communication, if—

    a. the solicitation reasonably could be expected to reach at least 1,000 persons, or

    b. the solicitation was made to at least 25 persons who were paid or promised any consideration for their efforts to influence legislation.

6. Any individual or organization which publishes a house organ or trade or union journal not normally distributed to the general public and containing matter soliciting the reader to influence legislation by direct communication.

• Exempted from the requirements of provisions 5 and 6 *(above)* the reproduction or retransmission of a communication from someone required to maintain records if they were identified in the reproduction.

• Required maintenance and preservation for two years of records covering the first and second half of each calendar year showing: total income received to make covered communications to influence legislation; the name, address and amount for each person from whom the income was received; the total expenditures for that purpose, with itemization of all expenditures from $50 up.

• Specified that records should be open to inspection by the comptroller general upon request.

• Required those maintaining records to file reports each six months identifying the filer and his employers and providing the data required to be maintained, with the following exceptions.

• Exempted from the reporting requirement the identification of the contributors of less than $100 for the purpose of making covered communications to influence legislation.

• Exempted from the reporting requirement the identification of members of a voluntary membership organization who paid not more than 5 percent of the group's total expenditures for legislative purposes.

• Required the comptroller general to waive the identification of members whose payments exceeded 5 percent of the organization's expenditures for legislative purposes if he found the purpose of the act would not be impeded.

• Required the organization to report the number of members and totals involved below and above 5 percent of the voluntary membership organization's expenditures.

• Permitted the filer to estimate amounts chargeable to making covered communications.

• Authorized the comptroller general to permit joint filing of reports.

• Provided that compliance with requirements of the act would not be taken into consideration in determining, for enforcement of the Internal Revenue Code of 1954, whether a substantial part of an organization's activities were devoted to propaganda or other attempts to influence legislation.

• Required the comptroller general to prescribe forms for reports.

• Required him to summarize data in notices of representation and reports and issue a report to Congress within 45 days after the end of each six-month period.

• Required him to make all information filed under the act available for public inspection for two years.

• Required him to publish in the *Congressional Record* within three days after receipt each notice of representation and each amendment by a legislative agent.

• Required him to see that all persons required to file had done so.

• Required the comptroller general to draft proposed regulations, publish them in the *Federal Register,* allow 30 days for comments, then publish any changes in the regulations and, seven days later, to transmit them along with any comments he had received and additional changes he sought to the House Committee on Standards of Official Conduct and the Senate Government Operations Committee.

• Provided the regulations would become effective unless, within 30 days of continuous session of Congress, either committee by majority vote disapproved.

• Authorized the attorney general, upon request of the comptroller general, to seek a U.S. district court civil order requiring compliance with the act.

• Specified a fine of up to $5,000 for a legislative agent who knowingly and willfully violated the section requiring filing of notices of representation.

• Specified a fine of up to $5,000 and/or imprisonment of up to two years for willful falsification of any reports under the act.

• Specified a fine of up to $5,000 and/or imprisonment of up to two years for willful falsification or forgery of any part of a covered communication to influence legislation.

• Repealed the Federal Regulation of Lobbying Act.

SENATE

In 1969 Sen. Clifford P. Case (R N.J.) and a bipartisan group of 19 other senators introduced S 1993. Under the bill, all government employees, including members of Congress and federal judges who earned more than $18,000 a year, and candidates for the Senate or House would have to file public statements annually with the comptroller general.

The Case bill would require those covered to list sources and amounts of gross income, including gifts worth at least $100, fees and honoraria for public appearances or articles, and the monetary value of entertainment, travel and other facilities received, a statement of assets and liabilities, and dealings in securities or commodities and real estate. Failure to file, or filing a false report, could result in a fine of up to $2,000 or imprisonment for not more than five years.

On May 25, 1969, Senate Majority Leader Mike Mansfield (D Mont.) added his name to the Case bill as a co-sponsor and suggested the legislation go further and require public officials to make income tax returns public. Sen. Hugh Scott (R Pa.), Republican whip at the time, endorsed the bill two days later.

Case referred to the resignation of Abe Fortas from the Supreme Court after his financial dealings were questioned and said public confidence in the court and in government in general would not be restored until Congress required mandatory "full, regular, and most importantly, public reports of their income and financial activities."

The Case bill was opposed by Senate Minority Leader Everett McKinley Dirksen (R Ill. 1951-69), who said financial disclosure would make members of Congress "second class citizens."

The Justice Department answered a request to testify by stating that a decision had not been made about administration support of the bill.

Another bill (S 1510), which would require filing of financial reports by federal judges and Supreme Court justices, was before the Senate Improvements in Judicial Machinery Subcommittee. It was part of a package on judicial reform. Hearings were held in 1969 but no other action was ever taken.

Financial Disclosures 1968-72

1968

Sixty-one senators received a total of $302,920 in 1968 for speeches, writings, television appearances and related activities. But reports filed with the secretary of the Senate reveal only a small fraction of the actual outside income for most Senate members.

Detailed information on senators' business interests and outside income were kept in sealed envelopes, available only to the Senate Select Committee on Standards and Conduct.

Thirty-nine senators reported no income from speeches. Most reports covered the full 1968 calendar year, but several senators accounted only for the period July 1 through Dec. 31, as allowed for 1968 under the new rule.

Sen. Barry Goldwater (R Ariz.), who was a candidate and not a senator in 1968, easily had top honors for lecture circuit income with $66,873, Sen. Edward W. Brooke (R Mass.) reported $21,556 and Sen. J.W. Fulbright (D Ark.) $19,967—all three reporting for the full year.

Other senators receiving sizable amounts from honoraria were: Senate Minority Leader Everett McKinley Dirksen (R Ill.), $18,158 for half the year, Senate Majority Leader Mike Mansfield (D Mont.), $16,000 for the full year, and Sen. Eugene J. McCarthy (D Minn.), $11,500 for half the year.

More than one-third of the House members filing financial disclosure statements returned their report forms blank. Of 432 members who filed statements with the House Committee on Standards of Official Conduct, 274 disclosed financial interests in varying degrees of detail and 158 said they had no interests covered by the provisions of the disclosure rule. Eight days after the April 30 deadline for filing all but one member had filed reports, portions of which were open to public inspection.

Several members filed statements in which they disclosed financial interests in greater detail than required. But a large number of statements contained only the name of a member's law firm (about 56 per cent of the House members were lawyers) or other information already available to the public.

Under the new rule, campaign funds were not covered by the report. Although some members disclosed the size of certain stock holdings, details on the dollar value of assets were required only in a separate, confidential report kept by the committee in a sealed envelope.

1969

Seventy-five senators earned a total fo $640,662 in 1969 for speeches, public appearances, book royalties, magazine articles and newspaper columns.

Sen. Edmund S. Muskie (D Maine) was the top honoraria earner in 1969 with $80,183, almost twice his Senate salary of $42,500 a year.

Sen. George McGovern (D S.D.) was second with $63,501. Sen. Birch Bayh (D Ind.) was third with $38,800.

Of the top 10 honoraria earners, seven were Democrats. The leading Republican was Sen. Mark O. Hatfield (R Ore.) who reported earning $28,750, placing him fourth. Sen. Barry Goldwater (R Ariz.), who led the lecture circuit with $66,873 in income in 1968, received $27,635 in 1969.

Universities and colleges were the most lucrative source of honoraria with 43 senators receiving $186,338 for 194 speaking engagements.

Senate Republican leader Hugh Scott (R Pa.) received $500 and Norris Cotton (R N.H.) $1,000 for speeches before the International Seafarers' Union that was being investigated by a Baltimore grand jury for its methods of handling political contributions. The union also paid $1,000 honoraria to Senators Bayh and Charles McC. Mathias (R Md.).

One-hundred and eighty-five members of the House reported having a financial or management interest during 1969 in companies doing substantial business with the federal government or subject to federal agencies.

These representatives were among 268 House Members disclosing financial interests for the year.

Four-hundred and thirty-two members filed statements. More than one-third of the House members, 164, filed blank reports indicating they had no interests covered by provisions of the disclosure rule.

An analysis of the 1969 disclosures revealed:

• One-hundred and three members had an interest in or income from banks, savings and loan associations or bank holding companies, compared to 99 in 1968.

Nine of the 103 representatives with banking connections were members of the Banking and Currency Committee and seven were on the Ways and Means Committee, both of which handled laws concerning financial institutions.

• Sixty-two had an interest in companies ranked among the nation's top 100 defense contractors, compared to 63 in 1968. Four of the members were on the House Armed Services Committee, two were on the Joint Congressional Committee on Defense Production and one was on the Department of Defense Subcommittee of the Appropriations Committee.

• Forty-four reported an interest in oil and gas companies, compared to 41 in 1968. Four were on the Interior and Insular Affairs Committee which set national policy on natural resources.

• Twenty-three had interests in radio and television stations or corporations which owned stations, the same number as in 1969. One was on the Commerce Committee which played a major role in regulating the industry.

• Fourteen reported interests in airlines, eight in rail roads and five in trucking firms. In 1968, 13 members had interests in airlines, six in railroads and five in trucking. Three members holding stock in transportation companies were on the Commerce Committee, which handled legislation regulating the industry.

• Fourteen reported interests in farms or ranches, the same number as in 1968. Three were on the agriculture Committee.

• Eighty-one representatives reported being affiliated with law practice. Eleven of those said their law practice income exceeded $5,000 in 1969, compared to 24 who reported this in 1968.

1970

Seventy-three senators reported receiving a total of $642,316 for speeches and writing during 1970. This was $1,654 more than the figure of $640,662 reported for 1969.

Democrats earned the largest share of the fees, with 42 senators reporting income of $392,899 or 61 percent of the total. Thirty-one Republican senators reported receiving $249,417. Democrats outnumbered Republicans in the Senate 55-45.

Twenty-eight Senators reported no honoraria for 1970. Sen. David H. Gambrell (D Ga.), who was appointed Feb. 2, 1971, was not required to file.

Two defeated Senators, Charles E. Goodell (R N.Y.) and Joseph D. Tydings (D Md.) also filed reports. Tydings earned $9,500 and Goodell $8,800. Five other defeated incumbents did not file although required to do so under Senate rules. They were: the late Thomas J. Dodd (D Conn.), Ralph T. Smith (R Ill.), Albert Gore (D Tenn.), Ralph W. Yarborough (D Texas) and George Murphy (R Calif.)

Of the top 10 honoraria earners in 1970, five were Democrats and five Republicans.

Sen. Birch Bayh (D Ind.) led all senators in honoraria with $44,331.

The top Republican earner, and second over-all behind Bayh, was Sen. Mark O. Hatfield (R Ore.), with $41,956.

Sen. Edmund S. Muskie (D Maine) earned $40,866 to place third.

In fourth place was Sen. Abraham Ribicoff (D Conn.), who received $37,800 in 1970. Sen. Barry Goldwater (R Ariz.) received $30,050 in honoraria to place fifth.

Sen. John G. Tower (R Texas) was sixth in 1970 with $24,129 and Sen. George McGovern (D S.D.) received $24,035 to place seventh.

Completing the top 10 earners in 1970 were Sen. Harold E. Hughes (D Iowa), eighth with $20,579; Sen. Robert W. Packwood (R Ore.), ninth with $17,575, and Sen. Edward W. Brooke (R Mass.), 10th with $15,200.

Universities were again the most lucrative source of honoraria in 1970 with 45 senators receiving a total of $218,806 for 208 speaking engagements. In 1969, 43 senators were paid $186,338 for college and university appearances.

Democrats led Republicans in college honoraria with 116 speeches for a total of $125,415. Republican Senators gave speeches for $93,391. (These figures did not include some college fees paid to Senators Goldwater and Bayh. These Senators declined to itemize the sponsors of speeches handled by speakers' bureaus.)

The most popular college speaker in 1970 was Hatfield, who gave 27 speeches for $32,406. He was followed by Muskie, 15 speeches for $23,177, and Ribicoff, 14 speeches for $21,800.

The second highest source of honoraria during 1970 was writing. Nineteen senator-authors earned a total of $44,768 for magazine articles, newspaper columns and book royalties. In 1969, about $35,000 in writing fees was reported.

Of the 434 representatives who filed financial disclosure statements, 265 reported they had outside business or professional interests during 1970. More than a third, 169, filed blank reports indicating they had no interests covered by provisions of the limited disclosure rule.

Two hundred representatives reported income of more than $1,000 or financial or management interest in excess of $5,000 in business entities doing a substantial business with the federal government or subject to federal regulatory agencies.

All but seven members met the April 30 deadline for filing reports with the Commitee on Standards of Official Conduct.

Those who filed late were: Robert F. Drinan (D Mass.), Kenneth J. Gray (D Ill.), John E. Hunt (R N.J.), John C. Kluczynski (D Ill.), John M. Murphy (D N.Y.), Robert N. C. Nix (D Pa.) and Louis Stokes (D Ohio). The last report filed, that of Rep. Murphy, came in on May 11.

As in previous years, more House members reported an interest in banks and financial institutions than in any other type of business. A total of 102 members, one less than the 1969 total, reported an interest in or income from banks, savings and loan associations or bank holding companies.

Ten of the 102 were members of the House Banking and Currency Committee. One committee member, Rep. J. William Stanton (R Ohio), reported that he sold his bank holdings during 1970. Eight members were on the Ways and Means Committee, which originated laws controlling taxes paid by banks.

Of the 102 members with bank interests, 91 reported such holdings in 1969.

Four representatives who did not report owning bank stock in 1969 acquired banking stock during 1970 or reported family holdings which were not listed in 1969:

Rep. Mario Biaggi (D N.Y.) reported having common stock in Century National Bank and Trust Co., New York, N.Y., which he did not list in 1969.

Rep. Jonathan B. Bingham (D N.Y.) added First National City Corporation of New York to his list of securities holdings.

Rep. Edwin W. Edwards (D La.) reported interests in "state and federal banks" which he did not list in 1969.

Rep. Charles W. Whalen Jr. (R Ohio) reported that his five children owned common stock in Third National Bank & Trust Co. Whalen's report in 1969 did not include his family's holdings.

Of the 102 members who listed bank interests in 1970 reports, eight were defeated in primaries or general elections and one, J. Glenn Beall Jr. (R Md.), was elected to the Senate.

Eighty-one representatives reported at least $1,000 in income in 1970 from outside law practices. That compared with 81 in 1969 and 80 in 1968.

Based on the 1970 House financial disclosures, it appeared that although fewer members reported as much as $5,000 from outside practices, about the same number maintained contact with the legal profession as in years past.

Sixty-three representatives declared holdings in 1970 in companies ranked among the nation's top 100 defense contractors. This compared to 62 in 1969 and 63 in 1968.

1971

Seventy-six senators earned $787,438 in honoraria during 1971 compared to a total of $642,316 reported by 73 senators for 1970. The increase of $145,122 set a new record in honoraria income.

Another record was set by Hubert H. Humphrey (D Minn.), who led all senators in 1971 honoraria with $83,451. Humphrey's total was the highest recorded by a senator since the rules requiring honoraria to be reported went into effect in 1968.

Humphrey's 1971 earnings were nearly double his Senate salary of $42,500 and more than double the $39,338 earned by the second man in line, Sen. Mark O. Hatfield (R Ore.). Hatfield was also second in 1970.

An aide to Humphrey said that some of the money from honoraria went to pay expenses of his Senate office not covered by regular allowances for supplies and personnel, and some was regarded as personal income.

Sen. Birch Bayh (D Ind.), the leading recipient in 1970 with $44,331, dropped to fifth place in 1971 with $29,575.

Senators reporting the largest number of individual honoraria were Humphrey, 44; Bayh, 33; Hatfield, 32; Robert W. Packwood (R Ore.), 32; Robert Dole (R Kan.), 31; George McGovern (D S.D.), 31; Mike Gravel (D Alaska), 27, and Gale W. McGee (D Wyo.), 26.

Senators Warren G. Magnuson (D Wash.) and Barry Goldwater (R Ariz.) did not list the source of their honoraria. An aide to Magnuson said that detailed records of honoraria had been misplaced. Magnuson, whose 1971 honoraria totaled $3,500, had listed sources in reports for previous years.

Goldwater listed the sources of three honoraria—Time Inc., Florida Medical Association and Fawcett Publications—totaling $2,450. However, the remainder of his $17,390 in honoraria was listed as coming from Harry Walker Inc., a speaker's bureau, for "various speeches."

Advisory guidelines issued by the Senate Select Committee on Standards and Conduct state that, "If the honorarium service was arranged through a speaker's bureau, the sponsor of the event and not the bureau should be identified as the payer." Some senators listed both the speaker's bureau and the sponsor in their 1971 reports. Goldwater also failed to supply the names of sponsors for his 1970 honoraria in his 1971 statement.

Colleges and universities continued to be the most popular source of Senate honoraria, with 45 senators receiving a total of $201,148.56 for 203 speaking engagements. In 1970, 45 senators also spoke at various campuses, and were paid $218,206 for 208 appearances.

More than twice as many Democratic senators spoke at colleges than Republicans. Thirty-two Democratic senators made 127 college speeches for $130,751, while 13 Republican senators spoke 76 times for a total of $70,397.56. The most frequent college speakers, however, Hatfield and Packwood, were Republicans. They made 26 and 22 appearances respectively.

Among Democrats, those senators speaking most often at colleges were McGovern (14), Bayh (13), and William Proxmire (D Wis.) (12).

Of the 434 representatives who filed financial disclosure statements, 249 reported they had outside business or professional interests during 1971. The other 185 members filed either blank reports, indicating they had no interests covered by the limited disclosure rule, or reports listing only sources of honoraria or unsecured loans.

One hundred and ninety-three representatives reported income of more than $1,000 or financial or management interest in excess of $5,000 in business entities doing a substantial business with the federal government or subject to federal regulatory agencies.

All but 10 members met the April 30 deadline for filing reports with the Committee on Standards of Official Conduct. Those who filed late were: Mario Biaggi (D N.Y.), Shirley Chisholm (D N.Y.), Louis Frey Jr. (R Fla.), Richard Fulton (D Tenn.), Ray J. Madden (D Ind.), Ralph H. Metcalfe (D Ill.), John M. Murphy (D N.Y.), Alvin E. O'Konski (R Wis.), Louis Stokes (D Ohio) and Louis C. Wyman (R N.H.). The last report filed, that of Rep. Stokes, came in May 31.

The only member who had not filed by that date was District of Columbia delegate Walter E. Fauntroy (D).

For the first time, House members were required to report the source of honoraria of $300 or more. Amounts of honoraria were not required to be reported. The new requirement was contained in legislation approved by the House in 1970. *(p. 426)*

One hundred and forty-five representatives reported receiving honoraria in 1971. Of these, 38 reported the amounts of some or all of their honoraria.

Among members who listed the amounts of their honoraria, Rep. Ronald V. Dellums (D Calif.) led with $20,675. Second was Rep. Shirley Chisholm (D N.Y.), who received $14,300. Rep. Bella S. Abzug (D N.Y.) was next with $11,975 and Rep. Paul N. McCloskey Jr. (R Calif.) was fourth with $10,900.

Members in 1972 were also required for the first time to report each creditor to whom they were indebted through unsecured loans in an aggregate amount exceeding $10,000. Twenty-four House members reported that they had unsecured loans during 1971.

As in previous years, more House members reported an interest in banks and financial institutions than in any other type of business. A total of 101 members, one less than in 1971, reported an interest in or income from banks, savings and loan associations or bank holding companies.

Seven of the 101 were members of the House Banking and Currency Committee. Six were on the Ways and Means Committee, which originated laws controlling taxes paid by banks.

Of the 101 members with banking interests, 94 reported such holdings in 1970. Six representatives who did not report owning bank stock in 1970 acquired banking stock during 1971 or reported family holdings which were not listed previously.

Sixty-six representatives reported at least $1,000 income in 1971 from outside law practices. That compared with 81 in both 1969 and 1970. Six of these members reported at least $5,000 in 1971, although in three cases the payments were for old legal fees or sales of partnership interests. Nine members reported income of $5,000 or more from law practices in 1970, 11 in 1969 and 24 in 1968.

Of the 66 representatives reporting income from legal services, eight indicated on their statments that they had withdrawn from law firms or dissolved partnerships since being elected to Congress.

Fifty-nine representatives declared holdings in 1971 in companies ranked among the nation's top 100 defense contractors. This compared with 63 in 1970, 62 in 1969 and 63 in 1968.

Forty-four representatives listed holdings in the federally regulated oil and gas industries, compared with 45 in 1970. Four of these members were on the House Interior and Insular Affairs Committee which had jurisdiction over natural resources policy. They were John Dellenback (R Ore.), Craig Hosmer (R Calif.), Philip E. Ruppe (R Mich.) and Joe Schubitz (R Kan.).

Twenty representatives reported connections with radio or television broadcasting companies or with corporations which owned broadcasting firms. Twenty-one members reported such interests in 1970. Eighteen of these members also reported broadcast holdings in their reports for 1970.

The 1971 reports showed that 54 House members received at least $5,000 in capital gain transactions. In 1970 45 members showed such gains.

1972

Seventy-two senators reported receiving a total of $618,382.60 in honoraria during 1972, compared to a high of $787,438 reported by 76 senators in 1971. Fourteen of them—four Republicans and 10 Democrats—received over $15,000 each.

Sen. Robert Dole (R Kan.) topped the list with $33,500 earned from 26 speeches. Dole noted on his report that some of the money was received as a member of the Senate and some as Chairman of the Republican National Committee. He also said he returned a total of $1,500 to five of the sources of his honoraria.

The leading recipient in 1971, Sen. Hubert H. Humphrey (D Minn.), dropped to second place in 1972 with $29,135. Humphrey's 1971 total of $83,451 was the highest amount ever reported by a senator.

Senators reporting the largest number of individual honoraria payments were Mike Gravel (D Alaska), 33; Harrison A. Williams Jr. (D N.J.), 31; Dole, 26; Birch Bayh (D Ind.), 25, John V. Tunney (D Calif.), 24; Gale W. McGee (D Wyo.), 21; William Proxmire (D Wisc.), 20; and Harold E. Hughes (D Iowa), 18.

Sen. Barry Goldwater (R Ariz.) did not list the sources of his $3,150 in honoraria, saying only that he received the payments from Harry Walker Inc., a speaker's bureau, for "various speeches." It was the third year Goldwater had failed to comply with Standards Committee guidelines calling for disclosure of the original source of all honoraria.

Nineteen Senators listed some sources of contributions and gifts on their 1972 forms, although most said that all such funds were handled through their campaign committees and thus were not subject to the reporting rule.

Several senators referred anyone interested to campaign receipt and spending reports filed in compliance with the Federal Election Campaign Act of 1971.

Sen. Lawton Chiles (D Fla.) attached a 20-page statement detailing contributions and also expenditures for such things as office supplies, flowers and phone calls. Part of his statement was a list of contributions and expenditures required by elected officials in Florida. Chiles reported receiving $19,217.38 in contributions during the year, with the largest sum, $10,000 coming from a "Lawton Chiles Appreciation Dinner" held in Florida.

Nine senators included on their forms some explanation of how they used honoraria payments. Five of them said they donated all of their earnings to charitable organizations, two others donated part and two said they used the money to help pay for office expenses and other Senate-related activities such as air travel to and from their home states.

The largest amount paid to senators for speeches by any one organization was $10,000 spent by the National Association of Independent Insurers. The group paid $2,500 to four senators: Marlow W. Cook (R Ky.), Thomas F. Eagleton (D Mo.), Mark O. Hatfield (R Ore.) and Howard H. Baker Jr. (R Tenn.). In contrast, the Brookings Institution, a private Washington, D.C. research organization, lured nine senators to give 11 speeches during the year for only $150 apiece.

The highest single honorariums, $5,000 each, were paid to Humphrey by Golden Industries and by the Trade Policy Research Center, an organization of grain producers—and to Dole by administrators of the Tulane University Educational Fund.

Colleges and universities were, as in previous years, the most popular source of Senate honoraria, with 35 Senators receiving a total of $129,814 for 128 speaking engagements in 1972.

The over-all demand for Democrats was higher. But it was a Republican, Hatfield, who earned the most ($13,530) addressing students. After Hatfield came Bayh with $13,000 and Tunney with $11,210.

Of the 434 representatives who filed financial disclosure statements, 266 reported they had some sort of outside business or professional interest in 1972. (Two of the four delegates reported outside interests.) The other 168 members filed either blank reports indicating they had no interests covered by the limited disclosure rule or listed only sources of honoraria or unsecured loans. One new member, Rep. Cardiss R. Collins (D Ill.), sworn in June 7, 1973 to fill a vacancy created by the death of her husband, was not required to file a report covering 1972.

One-hundred and ninety-seven representatives— nearly one half of the House—reported income of more than $1,000 or financial or management interests in excess of $5,000 in companies doing a substantial business with the federal government or subject to federal regulatory agencies.

Seventy-one members who entered Congress in 1973 were required to file financial disclosure reports covering 1972. Some of these individuals later dropped business or professional connections listed in their reports.

As in previous years, more House members reported an interest in banks and other financial institutions than in any other kind of business. A total of 107 members, six more than in 1971, reported an interest in or income from banks, savings and loan associations or bank holding companies. Nine of those were members of the House Banking and Currency Committee and six others were on the Ways and Means Committee which initiates legislation controlling net-income taxes paid by banks.

Thirty-seven of the 107 members indicated they held some management position in financial institutions during 1972.

Sixty-nine representatives reported at least $1,000 in 1972 income from such practices—compared with 66 in 1971. But 20 of them were freshmen who were not in Congress during 1972.

Of the 69 members reporting law income, nine specified that they received more than $5,000 in 1972. Nine of the members noted on their forms that they had severed their connections with their law firms.

Legal practice by members of Congress had become a subject of debate, particularly since 1969 when the American Bar Association adopted a Code of Professional Responsibility that included a rule designed to discourage members from maintaining connections with law firms. The rule stated that a public official must withdraw his or her name from a law firm, or "actively and regularly practice law as a member of the firm." By 1973, most state bar associations had adopted the rule, which provided for grievance proceedings if violated.

One-hundred and sixty-seven representatives reported receiving honoraria for speeches, writings and media appearances in 1972, the second year such reporting was required. Forty-four of them listed the amounts they received, although that information was not required. In 1971, 145 House members reported receiving honoraria, and 38 included amounts.

The largest honoraria total of those members who listed amounts in 1972 was reported by Rep. Shirley Chisholm (D N.Y.), who said she received $30,491.41 from Harry Walker Inc., a lecture agency and from "others." The House disclosure form asked members to name original sources of honoraria, not speaker's bureaus.

The top recipient in 1971, Rep. Ronald V. Dellums (D Calif.), did not list amounts in 1972. Dellums had listed $20,675 in 1971.

Forty House members reported unsecured indebtedness for a period of 90 days or more in 1972, in an aggregate amount of more than $10,000. Of those, 27 were freshmen. Twenty-four representatives reported such indebtedness in 1971, the first year for which such information was required.

Sixty-five representatives declared holdings in 1972 in companies ranked among the nation's top 100 defense contractors.

Forty-two representatives, including four members of the Interior and Insular Affairs Committee, reported an interest in oil and gas companies, while thirty-one indicated a financial interest in power and light companies.

Twenty-two representatives reported connections with radio or television broadcasting companies or with corporations which own broadcasting firms, compared to 20 in 1971.

Seventy-four House members reported capital gains of more than $5,000 from a single transaction other than the sale of a residence occupied by the member, compared with 54 in 1971 and 45 in 1970.

Postal Policy

Congress in 1970 acted to halt the Post Office Department's "race with catastrophe" by converting the 141-year-old, cabinet-level institution into an independent government corporation that was expected to modernize the nation's mail delivery system.

As part of the historic reorganization, the reform legislation eliminated most congressional and other political influence in postal affairs—not only over the appointment of postmasters and all postal employees but also over postage rates, classes of mail and day-to-day operations.

Although the new agency was granted authority to set postage rates and issue revenue bonds, Congress did not make the Postal Service self-sufficient immediately. It provided for appropriation of public funds for an eight-year period and a declining federal subsidy for an additional five years to absorb the new agency's anticipated initial losses.

The landmark legislation brought to the final stage an effort begun in the Johnson administration to reestablish the ailing postal system on an efficient, financially sound, businesslike basis.

Kappel Commission Recommendations

In 1968, the Kappel Commission—a panel established by President Johnson to suggest ways to reform the nation's postal service and headed by Frederick R. Kappel, former board chairman of the American Telephone and Telegraph Co.—reported: "The United States Post Office faces a crisis. Each year it slips further behind the rest of the economy in service, in efficiency and in meeting its responsibilities as an employer. Each year it operates at a huge financial loss."

Former Postmaster General Lawrence F. O'Brien (1965-68) put it even more bluntly: The postal system, he said in a 1967 speech, was "in a race with catastrophe."

The Post Office Department's net operating loss in fiscal 1968 was more than $1-billion, of which $591-million was attributed to public service costs. The remaining $430-million, which according to law should have been covered by postal revenues, was termed the postal deficit.

The Kappel Commission issued its report, "Towards Postal Excellence," July 16, 1968. The commission made five recommendations, the first of which was the establishment of a government-owned corporation to operate the postal service on a self-supporting basis. Other recommendations were:

• The corporation should act immediately to improve the quality and kinds of services offered, and the physical conditions under which employees work. It should place the Post Office on a "sound financial footing" through operating efficiencies and increased revenues.

• Appointments and promotions should not be influenced by politics.

• Postal employees should be transferred to a new career service which would retain their wage scales and accrued civil service benefits.

• The board of directors of the corporation should be empowered to set postage rates.

Congressional Action

During the 1969-70 period, Congress considered a variety of postal reform bills, including one (HR 4) that would have left the Post Office in the executive branch, with Congress retaining control over postal rates and salaries. In mid-1970, however, Congress adopted the postal corporation format outlined by the Kappel Commission and sponsored by the Nixon administration—but only after settling the first postal strike in the nation's history.

Postal unions and the rank-and-file workers generally opposed the corporation plan because Congress, where they could exert political influence, was to be removed in large part from postal activities. The unions and workers mainly objected to Nixon administration plans to delay postal pay increases.

The terms settling the strike assured union support for a postal reorganization bill by providing an immediate 6 per cent raise for most federal workers, including postal employees, and an additional 8 per cent raise for the postal workers to be effective on enactment of a reform bill.

On Aug. 6, 1970, Congress cleared the Postal Reorganization Act; the Postal Service began operation on July 1, 1971.

Continuing Problems

The new corporation was not the immediate success its backers had predicted. During fiscal 1972, the agency's first year of operation, the Postal Service delivered 87.2

References

Discussion of postal legislation for the years 1945-64 may be found in *Congress and the Nation, Vol. I,* p. 1473-1494; for the years 1965-68, *Congress and the Nation, Vol. II*, p. 945-953.

billion pieces of mail. It also received several million complaints.

The postal problem, according to some observers, could be traced to the agency's attempt to run the nation's mail delivery system as a business. By trying to make the service operate on revenues it received from postage, by attempting to eliminate federal subsidies and by cutting operating expenses, the Postal Service left the public with inadequate service, they said. (Ironically, critics of the defunct Post Office Department had argued that its problems were due to its failure to operate on a "businesslike" basis.)

According to the Postal Service's first annual report, government appropriations in fiscal 1972 amounted to $1.36-billion, a 35 per cent decrease from $2.09-billion in fiscal 1971. Postmaster General E. T. Klassen conceded that "our service performance is still uneven," but he claimed "our service over-all continues to improve."

Members of Congress, who received hundreds of thousands of individual complaints about postal service each year, took issue with that assessment. Some even called for repeal of the 1970 reform act, contending that the old Post Office Department, despite its problems, offered better service than the new agency.

Chronology

Of Legislation

On Postal Policy

1969

Postal Reform

Proposals to reform the nation's postal system received thorough review in 1969 from House and Senate Post Office and Civil Service Committees and the Nixon administration, but major reform legislation was not enacted until the following year. *(Summary of action, p. 441)*

Activity in 1969 centered on two measures which authorized changes in postal management, labor relations and postal financing. HR 11750, the Nixon administration bill, proposed to turn the mails over to a nonprofit, government-owned corporation. HR 4, introduced by House Post Office and Civil Service Committee Chairman Thaddeus J. Dulski (D N.Y.), made major revisions in the operation of the Post Office while leaving it as a department in the executive branch.

NIXON PLAN

President Nixon May 27 asked Congress to create an independent, government-owned corporation to take over the duties of the Post Office Department.

"Postal reform is not a partisan political issue, it is an urgent national requirement," the President said in

Crisis Background

The Post Office Department was one of the earliest services established by the United States. In the young days of the nation's history, the Post Office was the only link between isolated communities and the government, and it provided the impetus for much expansion. The post roads, the famed Pony Express and the railway postal system all helped form a continent-wide communications network designed in large part to help deliver the mails.

Because of its interconnection with the country's development, operation of the Post Office historically has been shaped by tradition and a patchwork of changes in the law. Congress retained control of the operating and capital budgets. It dispensed pay raises and set postage rates, controlled appointments of postmasters and rural letter carriers, legislated labor-management relations and even limited the types of transportation available for moving the mails. The money the public spent on postage and other services went back to the U.S. Treasury and not the Post Office itself.

By the beginning of 1969, the Post Office Department had grown to a point where it employed more than 725,000 persons handling more than 82 billion pieces of mail a year; Post Office appropriations for fiscal 1969 amounted to nearly $7.13-billion.

A dramatic illustration of the growing postal crisis occurred in October 1966 when the Chicago post office, the world's largest postal facility, suffered a total breakdown that paralyzed postal service for nearly three weeks.

The postal crisis was traced by some critics to one fundamental problem: the Post Office was not run as a business. Up to 1958, the Post Office Department was instructed to operate on a "businesslike" basis, but not necessarily at a profit. The Postal Policy Act of 1958, however, established that the Post Office was a public service, not a business, and that public service costs should be borne by the government and nonpublic service costs should be met by periodic adjustments in rates.

The Post Office Department's net operating loss in fiscal 1968 was more than $1-billion, of which $591-million was attributed to public service costs. The remaining $430-million, which according to law should have been covered by postal revenues, was termed the postal deficit.

Postmaster General Lawrence F. O'Brien first proposed converting the Post Office Department into a corporation in a speech made April 3, 1967.

Five days later, President Johnson established a ten-man Commission on Postal Organization, headed by Frederick R. Kappel, former chairman of the board of American Telephone and Telegraph Co.

The Kappel Commission, as the panel became known, issued its report, "Towards Postal Excellence," July 16, 1968. The commission recommended the establishment of a government-owned corporation to operate the postal service on a self-supporting basis.

Post Office and Postal Service Highlights: Fiscal 1968-1972

(in millions of dollars)

	1968	1969	1970	1971	1972
Operating Revenue	$ 5,528	$ 6,142	$ 6,347	$ 6,665	$ 7,884
Per cent change	10.9	11.1	3.3	5.0	18.3
Govt. Appropriations	895	884	1,355	2,086	1,361
Per cent change	—12.9	—1.2	53.3	53.9	—34.8
Total Operating Expenses	6,544	7,168	7,867	8,955	9,522
Per cent change	6.6	9.5	9.8	13.8	6.3
Net Loss	120	143	166	204	175
Per cent change	—7.7	19.2	16.1	22.9	—14.0
Pieces of mail (millions)	79,517	82,005	84,882	86,983	87,156
Per cent change	1.5	3.1	3.5	2.5	0.2
U.S. population (millions), Jan. 1	200.2	202.3	204.4	206.7	208.1
Per cent change	1.1	1.0	1.0	1.1	0.7
Pieces of mail per capita	397	405	415	421	419
Per cent change	0.3	2.0	2.5	1.4	0.5

SOURCE: U.S. Postal Service

his message to Congress. He told reporters at the White House the same day that his postal recommendation was "one of the most significant proposals that will be made during the entire period of this administration."

The plan proposed by the President was similar to the general proposals of the Kappel Commission.

Nixon told Congress that in the current fiscal year, the postal deficit would exceed $1-billion. "It is bad business, bad government, and bad politics to pour this kind of tax money into an inefficient postal service," he said.

There were already more than a dozen government-owned corporations. The best-known ones probably were the Tennessee Valley Authority, the Federal Deposit Insurance Corporation and the Commodity Credit Corporation. But the Postal Service would be a far larger concern than any of the others, and would be the only important one which was converted from an executive department rather than started from scratch.

Reaction. The postal corporation proposal brought mixed reaction on Capitol Hill but was endorsed by a number of organizations, notably in the business community, such as the U.S. Chamber of Commerce and the National Association of Manufacturers.

Opposition to the corporation concept was registered by the labor unions representing postal employees. The unions' position was that if the Post Office became a corporation, union members should be given the right to strike. They also maintained that the new system would mean cuts in mail service, higher rates and the possibility that the board of directors could contract out to private enterprise work currently performed by civil service workers. Although not spelled out, a main reason the postal workers opposed the proposal was because they wanted their wages to continue to be set by Congress, where they could apply political pressure.

Proposal. According to the Nixon plan, the U.S. Postal Service would replace the existing Post Office Department. The service would have up to a year to prepare for the transition, after enactment of the bill, and would be required to be self-supporting within five years.

The Postal Service would be charged with operating the mails. It would be able to adopt its own regulations and procedures, sue and be sued, enter into contracts, handle its own funds, acquire and dispose of property, and in general hold all the powers and privileges of other government corporations.

DULSKI BILL

Chairman Thaddeus J. Dulski (D N.Y.) of the House Post Office and Civil Service Committee Jan. 3 introduced HR 4, a plan to overhaul the structure of the Post Office while retaining it as an executive department. In a floor speech Jan. 6 outlining his proposal, Dulski said, "My studies indicate that every major postal reform that a nonprofit corporation might achieve can be done more quickly and effectively within the present framework of government. Most important, I am convinced these can be done without the inevitable disruption and turmoil involved in a change-over to a corporation."

Under Dulski's plan, the Post Office Department would set its own budget and was expected to support itself from its revenues. The only exception to this would be retention of the existing "public service allowance" subsidizing certain services and classes of mail, requiring annual appropriations by Congress.

A quadrennial commission would be empaneled to review postal rates every four years. The body would make recommendations to the President, who could review them before submitting formal proposals to Congress. Either the House or the Senate could vote changes in part or all of the proposals before the new rates went into effect in 120 days.

To finance capital improvements, the bill would establish a Postal Modernization Authority which could borrow money and issue bonds up to a level of $20-billion outstanding at any one time. The authority would also carry on a research and development program and lease property and equipment as needed.

The labor-management section of HR 4 would establish compulsory arbitration, arrange for settlement of disputes by an independent labor-management relations panel, and establish guidelines for both management and labor. Patronage appointments would be prohibited, and residence requirements would be retained.

LOBBYING ON POSTAL REFORM

Lobbying in Congress in 1969 over President Nixon's proposal to convert the Post Office Department into a government-owned corporation pitted the men who deliver the mail against some of the country's biggest users of the mail.

Unions representing postal clerks and mail carriers opposed the change on the ground it would reduce their ability to get wage increases and other benefits. They preferred to deal with Congress, where they could exert political influence, rather than with the corporation.

Some of the nation's large mail users, particularly magazines, backed the change. They said the change might cost them more money initially but that they would receive better postal service in the long run. Not all the big mail users, however, supported the lobbied corporation proposal.

Two former postmasters general lobbied on opposite sides of the issue. Lawrence F. O'Brien, postmaster general during most of the Johnson administration, was one of two founders of a new lobby formed to push for the postal corporation concept.

J. Edward Day, postmaster general during most of the Kennedy administration, testified in opposition to the corporation plan and was a lobbyist for the Associated Third Class Mail Users. The association did not take a formal position on the subject.

Positions on the plan often were qualified by agreement or opposition to some of the specific provisions of a bill prepared by Postmaster General Winton M. Blount and endorsed by President Nixon.

Most unions and some large mailers challenged the idea that the Post Office should operate on a break-even basis. They said maintenance of a good mail system was a national responsibility and the Post Office should be allowed to operate at a deficit.

Some magazine spokesmen, however, said they were willing to pay higher rates for quicker service.

Magazine Position. Varying degrees of support for the postal corporation idea were reflected by views of two industry associations and two publishing companies which were among the largest users of second class mail.

Magazine Publishers Association Inc. Representing 125 companies which published about 400 magazines, the

Magazine Publishers Association approached the issue cautiously. In January the association's board of directors adopted a resolution calling the report of the Kappel Commission a progressive effort and asked Congress to hear the views of all interested parties. The board said this review would take time and therefore urged Congress to immediately remove restrictive laws which decrease postal efficiency "such as those involving the purchase of transportation, the appointment of postmasters and the promotion and transfer of personnel within the system."

The American Business Press. Composed of 111 companies which produced 537 publications, the American Business Press unanimously endorsed the Kappel report at a membership meeting April 23. It directed its officers and counsel to work toward reorganization of the Post Office and oppose any increase in mail rates "until postal reorganization along the lines of the Kappel Report shall have in fact been brought about."

About half the publications printed by the association were mailed at second class rates and the other half mailed at higher controlled circulation rates.

"Our view is that rates are going to go up under either system," said Robert A. Saltzstein, Washington attorney who was registered as lobbyist for the association. He said association members were willing to pay higher rates but wanted the mechanization and modernization promised by advocates of the postal corporation.

Time Inc. Publisher of three weekly magazines, one major monthly magazine and a membership book plan, Time Inc. was the nation's largest private mail user. The company spent about $31-million a year on postage, according to Evan Ingels, assistant treasurer. The largest share of this—$17-million—was spent on second class mail, with $5-million spent for first class, $7-million for third class and more than $2-million on fourth class.

"Everybody's ox is going to be gored in the short term but we believe in the long run we will all benefit from a more efficient operation," said Ingels.

Reader's Digest. With a once-a-month mailing of 17 million copies, the Reader's Digest spent only $4.5-million on second class mail but its total postage bill amounted to more than $30-million a year. It spent $11.7-million on first class mail, $7-million on third class and $7.1-million on fourth class. Much of the added cost was for its book and phonograph operations.

Unlike Time Inc., the Reader's Digest did not want to pay higher postage rates to get quicker service, even though company officials said it took an average of six days for their magazine to be delivered.

"We want to pay our fair share of the postal cost but we want to be quite sure whether everybody wants improved service," said Kent Rhodes, vice president of the Digest's publishing service. "We find the postal service we get on millions of pieces of mail is satisfactory."

Newspaper Groups. Newspapers were less active than magazines in taking positions on the postal corporation question.

American Newspaper Publishers Association. Most of the 1,030 members of the American Newspaper Publishers Association circulated most of their newspapers through home delivery and sidewalk sales. A few, however, were dependent on the mails for daily delivery. Among them were the *Wall Street Journal* and the *Christian Science Monitor*. The publishers' association studied

(Continued on p. 440)

Summary of Action on Postal Pay and Reform

1969

Jan. 3—HR 4, a bill to reform the Post Office within the executive branch (including a mechanism for adjusting salaries) introduced by Rep. Thaddeus J. Dulski (D N.Y.), chairman, House Post Office and Civil Service Committee.

April 22—House Post Office and Civil Service Committee began hearings on HR 4 and other postal reform bills. Subcommittee on Postal Operations the next day began hearings on a number of postal labor-management relations bills.

May 27—President Nixon sent message to Congress calling for reform of the Post Office Department and creation of government-owned postal corporation. The administration's bill (HR 11750) was introduced in House the next day.

June 16—House Post Office and Civil Service Subcommittee on Compensation began hearings on several pay bills concerning postal employees.

June 26—James H. Rademacher, president of the National Association of Letter Carriers (NALC), warned the House Post Office and Civil Service Subcommittee on Compensation that in many areas of the country "the possibility of a strike is imminent" because the 4.1 per cent automatic postal worker pay increase which was to take effect July 1 under the Postal Revenue Act of 1967 was smaller than the increase received by other federal employees.

July 1—Unofficial work stoppage occurred at New York's Kingsbridge station in the Bronx when 72 of the station's employees called in sick.

July 22—HR 13000, a committee bill to increase salaries of federal employees, including postal workers, was introduced by members of the House Post Office and Civil Service Subcommittee on Compensation.

Sept. 9—HR 13000 was reported by House Post Office and Civil Service Committee.

Sept. 23—House Post Office and Civil Service Committee agreed to make HR 4 its basic postal reform bill.

Oct. 6—Senate Post Office and Civil Service Committee began hearings on postal reform.

Oct. 8—House Post Office and Civil Service Committee, in closed session, rejected postal corporation proposal of HR 11750 on 13-13 vote.

Oct. 14—HR 13000 passed House on a 311-51 roll-call vote. During debate Minority Leader Gerald R. Ford (R Mich.) read a letter from the President implying a veto.

Dec. 8—Senate Post Office and Civil Service Committee reported a version of HR 13000 much different from the House bill.

Dec. 12—HR 13000 passed Senate, amended, by voice vote.

Dec. 17—House requested a conference on HR 13000 and appointed conferees. Senate appointed conferees the following day. Pay raises ultimately were enacted in other legislation.

1970

Feb. 2—President Nixon in his budget message proposed a six-month delay in federal employee pay increases.

Feb. 25—Rep. Dulski announced that his House Post Office and Civil Service Committee had failed to reach agreement on a postal corporation bill and that the committee would continue work on HR 4.

March 12—House Post Office and Civil Service Committee ordered HR 4 reported, including provisions for a postal pay raise and a plan for a postal corporation.

March 18—Postal strike began in New York City.

March 21—Strike spread across the country. The Post Office Department reported more than 600 postal offices were closed at the peak of the strike.

April 2—Strike settlement announced involving two-stage 14 per cent salary increase with 6 per cent for most federal employees and an additional 8 per cent for postal employees upon enactment of postal reorganization plan.

April 7—Senate Post Office and Civil Service Committee reported S 3690 providing for a 6 per cent pay raise for most federal employees.

April 8—Senate passed S 3690 on an 84-1 roll-call vote.

April 9—House Post Office and Civil Service Committee reported HR 16844 providing for a 6 per cent pay raise for most federal employees. House passed HR 16844 by a 372-7 roll-call vote. By voice vote the House substituted the provisions of HR 16844 for S 3690 and returned S 3690 to the Senate. Senate by voice vote concurred in House amendments and added its own technical amendments.

April 14—House by voice vote accepted Senate amendments to S 3690, clearing it for the President.

April 15—President Nixon signed S 3690 into law (PL 91-231).

May 19—House Post Office and Civil Service Committee reported HR 17070 providing for postal reorganization and an 8 per cent salary increase for postal workers.

June 3—Senate Post Office and Civil Service Committee reported S 3842 providing for postal reorganization and an 8 per cent postal pay raise.

June 18—House passed by a 359-24 roll-call vote HR 17070 embodying the postal reorganization proposal and an 8 per cent salary increase for postal workers.

June 30—Senate passed its version of HR 17070 by a 77-9 roll-call vote.

August 3—Conference report on HR 17070 filed. Senate approved the report by a 57-7 roll-call vote.

August 6—House adopted the conference report on HR 17070 by a 338-29 roll-call vote.

August 12—President Nixon signed HR 17070 into law (PL 91-375).

the postal corporation idea but took no position. The *Wall Street Journal*, which mailed more than 5 million copies per week, was probably the largest newspaper user of the mails. The Journal endorsed the postal corporation concept.

National Newspaper Association. Composed of about 7,000 small daily and weekly newspapers, this group had a particularly large stake in any change in postal rates. Existing regulations provided special rates for newspapers mailed within their home county.

Spokesmen for the group testified in favor of the corporation before the House and Senate Post Office Committees.

CHAMBER OF COMMERCE. One of the first national organizations to endorse the postal corporation concept was the Chamber of Commerce of the United States. The chamber announced its endorsement of the Kappel Commission report after polling 33,000 business members in October 1968. A total of 7,523 answered the poll.

The chamber said 96 per cent agreed with the commission's recommendation "that a postal corporation owned entirely by the federal government be chartered by Congress to operate on a self-supporting basis."

The chamber's national board of directors adopted this as its policy Feb. 28 but added two qualifications. These were that Congress appropriate money to make up losses caused by rate concessions, and that parcel post rates be, in the chamber's words, "competitively fair" with private shipment services.

UNION OPPOSITION. Most unions representing the 750,000 postal employees actively opposed the postal corporation concept, but intensity of opposition and viewpoint varied from union to union.

National Association of Letter Carriers. With 210,000 members, the letter carriers union was the most aggressive and adamant of the postal unions in fighting the proposal. Its Washington activities were financed by $16-a-year dues for active members and $7-a-year for retired workers.

James H. Rademacher, a letter carrier for 28 years before becoming union president, contended a self-supporting postal corporation would result in decreased service and higher rates. The union was also concerned that a corporation would contract with private firms to handle such things as parcel post and special delivery.

The union was opposed to the disputes panel and arbitration provisions of the Blount proposal.

The union contended the letter carriers would be at the mercy of postal directors in negotiating wages and working conditions if postal employes did not have the right to strike.

The United Federation of Postal Clerks. The right to strike was also a concern of the 165,000-member postal clerks union. Francis S. Filbey, union president, said the union would not object to binding arbitration on some issues but not wages. "We would have the public looking over our shoulder convinced that whatever we won would come out of their pocket," he said.

Like many organizations lobbying against the postal corporation, the postal carriers union said the Post Office should not be expected to operate on a break-even basis any more than the Department of Agriculture or other departments.

The Lobby Line-Up

Major lobby groups lined up as follows on proposed legislation to convert the Post Office into a federally chartered corporation.

For the Corporation

The American Business Press
The Chamber of Commerce of the United States
The Citizens Committee for Postal Reform
American Farm Bureau Federation
National Newspaper Association

Opposed to the Corporation

National Alliance of Postal and Federal Employees
National Association of Letter Carriers
National Association of Rural Letter Carriers
National Postal Union
Mail Advertising Education Committee
United Federation of Postal Clerks

CITIZENS' LOBBY. Formulation of a new lobby, the Citizens Committee for Postal Reform, was announced May 24 with passage of postal corporation legislation as its goal. Former Postmaster General Lawrence F. O'Brien and former Sen. Thruston B. Morton (R Ky.) were co-chairmen.

A number of the original backers of the new lobby were magazine publishing officials. These included David Brumbaugh, executive vice president and chairman of the finance committee of Time Inc.; Bayard E. Sawyer, senior vice president for corporate affairs of McGraw-Hill Inc.; Robert E. McKenna, president of the Chilton Co.; and Donald V. Buttenhein, president of Buttenhein Publishing Corp.

Other Postal Legislation

POSTMASTERS. The Senate in 1969 passed an administration bill (S 1583) to end political patronage in the selection of postmasters. The House held hearings on a companion bill (HR 8518) but took no action on the measure. However, the House Post Office and Civil Service Committee incorporated changes in the selection of postmasters in a broad postal reform bill (HR 4) which was reported in the House in 1970.

President Nixon early in the year announced he was ending the patronage system of appointing postmasters and rural letter carriers and requested Congress to enact legislation to end the requirement for presidential appointment and Senate confirmation of postmasters for first, second and third class post offices. Under the proposal, the postmaster general would appoint all postmasters from within the competitive Civil Service.

EMPLOYEES. The House Post Office and Civil Service Subcommittee on Postal Operations, chaired by Robert N. C. Nix (D Pa.), held hearings April 23-25 and May 22 on numerous postal employee labor-management bills as part of the committee's study in preparation for consideration of postal reform legislation.

Nearly 90 per cent of all postal employees belonged to one or more of a dozen organizations which dealt directly or indirectly with postal management. But under postal laws Congress, not management, set wages, hours, benefits and job descriptions.

In 1962 President Kennedy issued Executive Order 10988 which directed federal agencies to recognize employee representatives in order to negotiate agreements and consult on personnel matters. Federal employees were forbidden by law to strike, and the order prohibited binding third-party arbitration.

A number of bills were introduced in the 91st Congress to establish labor-management relations by law rather than by executive order. One of the most far-reaching was HR 4803, sponsored by Rep. Dominick V. Daniels (D N.J.), which authorized the department to grant recognition to unions and established third-party arbitration but prohibited strikes. In addition, a number of proposals being considered by the full committee to reorganize the Post Office Department contained provisions for labor-management relations. When the subcommittee's hearings began, more than 50 bills dealing at least in part with labor relations had been introduced.

RATES. The House Post Office and Civil Service Subcommittee on Postal Rates held numerous hearings between June 24 and Dec. 10 on President Nixon's request for an increase in postal rates. Action was delayed on the increases pending determination of postal reform legislation.

President Nixon April 24 sent Congress a message outlining his requests for postal rate increases in first, second and third class mail classifications.

The increases "can help in our efforts to control inflation by bringing federal revenues and expenditures into better balance," and they will allow the Post Office Department "to provide better postal service," Nixon said.

The rate increases announced by the President included one-cent increases starting July 1, 1969, for first-class letters and post cards, to seven cents per ounce and six cents each respectively, and for third class single piece rates, to seven cents. Air mail rates would remain at 10 cents per ounce.

The rates for second class mail (chiefly publications) outside the country in which they were published was already scheduled to increase by 8 per cent on Jan. 1, 1970, and Nixon recommended an additional increase of 12 per cent on July 1, 1970. Third class bulk rates, set for one increase July 1, should be increased again on Jan. 1, 1970, "so that the over-all level at that time would be some 16 per cent above present levels," Nixon said. The scheduled increases in second and third class rates were enacted by Congress in 1967 (PL 90-206).

1970

Postal Reform

Congress Aug. 6 cleared for the President a bill (HR 17070—PL 91-375) reorganizing the Post Office Department and the U.S. Postal Service into an independent

---

Major Provisions of Reform Act

The Postal Reorganization Act of 1970 (HR 17070), given final approval Aug. 6, included these major provisions:

● Created an independent U.S. Postal Service fully authorized to operate the postal system, a reorganization very similar to what President Nixon had requested in 1969.

● Granted an eight per cent pay raise to postal employees, in addition to the six per cent raise which they and most other federal employees received in April.

● Retained the Civil Service status and rights of postal workers and provided for faster attainment of top salary rates within grades but established collective bargaining between postal management and postal unions over pay and working conditions.

● Eliminated congressional and other political influence, not only over the appointment of postmasters and all postal employees but also over rates, classes of mail and postal operations.

Despite independent rate-making authority plus authority to issue bonds, the bill did not make the Postal Service self-sufficient immediately. It provided for appropriation of a fixed amount of public funds for an eight-year period and a declining appropriation for a further five-year period, after which Congress could appropriate a limited proportion of total postal costs or eliminate the public subsidy, according to its determination of the Postal Service's needs.

The bill did not raise postal rates. Mr. Nixon had requested rate increases to meet the cost of postal pay raises.

---

government agency, the U.S. Postal Service. The bill granted postal employees an eight per cent pay raise.

The landmark measure brought to the final stage an effort begun in the Johnson administration to re-establish the ailing postal system on an efficient, financially sound, businesslike basis.

Congressional action came after the first postal strike in U.S. history (March 18-25, 1970). Postal unions and the rank-and-file had salary grievances and generally opposed the corporation proposal sent to Congress by President Nixon on May 27, 1969. A negotiated settlement of the strike, announced April 2, 1970, called for a six per cent pay raise retroactive to Dec. 27, 1969, for most federal employees (including postal workers) and an eight per cent raise for postal employees to become effective when the postal corporation plan became law.

As cleared by Congress, HR 17070 differed only slightly from President Nixon's plan. The bill also followed closely the terms of the settlement negotiated with the postal unions.

HR 17070 emerged from a House-Senate conference Aug. 3. The most controversial issue resolved during conference negotiations concerned the status of the postal unions. The negotiated settlement of the postal strike permitted a "union shop"—where all workers must belong to a union or pay union dues—if it resulted from collective bargaining with the newly created postal authority.

But House-Senate conferees agreed to a House-passed "right to work" provision leaving each worker free to join or not to join a union.

The postal strike settlement provided for national recognition of unions organized on a "craft" basis as bargaining agents for postal employees. The settlement excluded two unions, the National Postal Union and the National Alliance of Postal and Federal Employees, organized on a service-wide or "industrial" basis. House-Senate conferees accepted the House-passed provision which left determination of recognized unions to the National Labor Relations Board.

HOUSE ACTION—HR 4

The House Post Office and Civil Service Committee April 8 reported a bill (HR 4) to convert the Post Office into a government-owned but independently operated corporation and to increase lower grade postal workers' salaries by an average 5.4 per cent retroactive to Jan. 1.

As introduced Jan. 3, 1969, by Committee Chairman Thaddeus J. Dulski (D N.Y.), HR 4 provided for major changes in the operation of the Post Office but would have left it as a department of the executive branch with Congress retaining control over postal rates and salaries.

The committee March 12, in what was regarded as a surprise action, ordered HR 4 reported. Dulski had announced Feb. 25 that the committee had failed to reach a compromise on the postal reorganization bill. The committee in October 1969 had rejected the administration-backed postal corporation plan on a 13-13 vote.

The committee reversal came in executive session March 12 when Rep. David N. Henderson (D N.C.) moved to delete the provisions of HR 4, as originally introduced in 1969, and report the bill with substitute postal corporation provisions and a salary increase for postal workers. Henderson's motion was approved on a 17-6 vote. His substitute closely paralleled President Nixon's total reform plan, which Henderson had voted against in October 1969.

In a statement March 13, President Nixon hailed the action on HR 4 as a "significant first step" in meeting postal needs. He expressed hope that Congress would enact the legislation promptly.

WILDCAT POSTAL STRIKE

Six days after HR 4 was ordered reported, a postal strike broke out March 18 in New York City and rapidly spread across the nation. Many postal union leaders and rank-and-file members regarded HR 4 as unacceptable. The bill did not include the additional pay raise they had expected July 1, 1970.

Events had been building toward a strike since Feb. 2 when the President's budget message for fiscal 1971 proposed that the next pay increase for postal and government employees be postponed from July 1, 1970 (the expected date of the raise), to Jan. 1, 1971. The budget message defended the postponement as an anti-inflationary measure.

Strike Issues. The long-term goals of federal employees and postal unions had been comparability of pay relative to similar work in private enterprise and a legally established bargaining position. A 1967 government em-

---

Postal Union Divisions

The wildcat strike revealed divisions, on one hand, among the postal unions and, on the other, between the striking letter carriers' union members and their leadership.

James H. Rademacher, who had headed the National Association of Letter Carriers (NALC) for only two years, appeared to be isolated from the other recognized unions involved in the negotiations. His alienation stemmed from his agreement with the postal corporation proposal together with a pay raise and compulsory arbitration of labor-management disputes. This was a switch for Rademacher, whose union previously had opposed the corporation proposal, as did the other unions.

Rademacher failed to win his rank-and-file to the new position. Many NALC strikers ignored his urging, first, not to leave, and later, to return to their jobs. As negotiations became imminent March 24, he was able to reverse himself and support separation of the salary issue from the corporation.

Independent Unions. Two postal unions were not represented in the negotiations between the administration and the postal unions. The bargaining sessions with the postmaster general were limited to officials of the seven postal unions having exclusive national recognition. Six of them were affiliated with the AFL-CIO, which led them in the negotiations. Together, those unions claimed to represent 620,000 of the 750,000 postal employees.

The negotiating sessions were picketed by members of the two unions not represented. Ashby Smith, president of the National Alliance of Postal and Federal Employees, a predominantly black union with 45,000 members, charged that it and the 90,000-member National Postal Union had been "dealt out" of the pay talks.

Neither independent union considered that its interests were being adequately protected in the negotiations, and neither felt bound by the outcome. Spokesmen for both said future walkouts by their unions were likely.

---

ployees pay act (PL 90-206) required that government employees receive salaries comparable to wages in private industry.

President Nixon granted comparability raises to all federal employees on July 1, 1969. The salary increases averaged 9.1 per cent for all civil service employees but only 4.1 per cent for postal employees.

Of the 750,000 post office employees, 80 per cent were in Postal Field Service grade five or a comparable level. Their beginning salary was $6,176; their top salary was $8,442. It took 21 years to reach the top of the grade scale, and there was little opportunity for advancement to higher grades. Postal workers compared their pay unfavorably with that of teachers, who averaged $8,560 nationwide; policemen, who in cities over 100,000, received a minimum of $7,773 on the average and a maximum of $9,247; and firemen in the same cities, with minimum of $7,464 and maximum of $8,778, and even United Parcel

Service delivery drivers, who received about $7,800, according to their employer.

Postal workers' frustration was heightened in 1969 when the President sought to link any postal pay increase to his postal reform proposal, HR 11750, to reorganize the Post Office Department into a government-owned corporate postal authority. The move was designed to blunt postal union opposition to his reorganization proposal. In opposing HR 11750, postal unions criticized the absence of a provision requiring the corporation to arbitrate disputes, although the bill did provide for collective bargaining. In addition, the postal unions regarded Congress as their most effective lobbying pressure point; under HR 11750, the proposed postal corporation would cease to be under direct congressional control.

Postal union leaders also were concerned that a federal comparability pay raise bill (HR 13000) had emerged from the two branches of Congress in 1969 in two greatly different versions. A House-Senate compromise appeared unlikely, and President Nixon had warned Oct. 14, 1969, the day HR 13000 cleared the House, that union officials regarded either form of HR 13000 as inadequate. *(HR 13000, chapter on federal pay, p. 447)*

Strike Settlement. Government and union negotiators April 2 announced a two-stage 14 per cent pay increase for postal workers.

Postmaster General Winton M. Blount and AFL-CIO President George Meany announced settlement of the postal wage dispute at the end of eight days of negotiations.

The first stage, a 6 per cent increase retroactive to Dec. 27, 1969, applied to all government workers including postal employees. The second stage, an 8 per cent increase applying only to postal workers, would become effective upon congressional enactment of a Post Office reform measure—to be negotiated by the administration, Congress and the postal unions.

The agreement would permit postal workers to reach top pay levels in eight years instead of 21 years and would allow no disciplinary action against postal workers who participated in the strike, without discussions between representatives of the Post Office and the postal unions.

Final settlement hinged on congressional approval of the agreement and union members' approval of the terms.

Blount said the plan would be submitted immediately to the President and recommended to Congress as legislation.

PAY RAISE

Congress April 14 enacted a bill (S 3690), the Federal Employees Salary Act of 1970, granting a 6 per cent pay increase for federal postal employees and most other civil service employees, military personnel and congressional employees, retroactive to Dec. 27, 1969. President Nixon signed the bill into law April 15 (PL 91-231).

S 3690, the first stage of the two-stage postal strike settlement, was rushed through Congress in one week; it was introduced in the Senate April 7 and cleared Congress April 14. Final action on the bill came when the House April 14 by voice vote accepted technical amendments added by the Senate. Prior to the voice vote, the House by a 309-65 roll-call vote adopted a motion cutting

off debate and preventing further amendment of S 3690. *(Details, chapter on federal pay)*

The estimated cost of the retroactive pay raise was $2.5-billion.

POSTAL CORPORATION, PAY RAISE

Committees in both the House and Senate in late April held hearings on postal reform bills and the second phase of pay and postal reform legislation resulting from the postal strike negotiations in March and April between the administration and major postal unions.

The House Post Office and Civil Service Committee April 22 began consideration of a new administration bill (HR 17070) which would combine postal corporation reform with collective bargaining and pay provisions.

In the Senate Post Office and Civil Service Committee, however, Chairman Gale W. McGee (D Wyo.) April 23 refused to consider postal reform in a bill encompassing the pay settlement. McGee's committee turned instead to a noncorporation-type reform bill (S 3613) which he and Hiram L. Fong (R Hawaii), the committee's ranking Republican, introduced in March.

McGee said he would introduce separate legislation based on the agreements resulting from the postal strike. He introduced a bill (S 3753) April 23 which was limited to the negotiated settlement issues, including an 8 per cent postal pay increase, more rapid advancement for workers in lower postal service grades and a mechanism for collective bargaining.

The House committee's postal corporation bill, HR 4, reported April 8, prior to consideration of the administration's new bill, was awaiting action by the House Rules Committee. Action on HR 4 was superseded by HR 17070.

House. The House June 18, by a 359-24 roll-call vote, passed a bill (HR 17070) converting the Post Office Department into an independent government agency to be called the U.S. Postal Service.

The bill before the House was the Post Office and Civil Service Committee bill. It had won committee approval narrowly over another version—later introduced as HR 17966—which was closer to the terms of the postal reorganization plan agreed to by the administration and the AFL-CIO postal unions.

The bill placed the Postal Service under an 11-member Commission on Postal Costs and Revenues, nine members of which were to be appointed by the President with Senate confirmation and the remaining two, the postmaster general and deputy postmaster general, were to be appointed by the other members. The aims of the legislation were not only to remove the Postal Service from the ranks of the cabinet departments and the postmaster general from the cabinet but also to remove the mail system from politics.

The bill created a new form of federal civil service for all postal employees, under which they retained existing rights, and granted them a retroactive 8 per cent pay increase. It authorized collective bargaining between postal unions and management and provided for mediation and compulsory arbitration in cases of protracted disputes, but explicitly outlawed strikes. It expressed the intent to make the Postal Service self-supporting within eight years and authorized the commission to set new postal rates, but made them subject to veto by either house of Congress.

Senate. The Senate on June 30, by a 77-9 roll-call vote, passed HR 17070 after substituting the language of a similar bill (S 3842) for the language of the House-passed HR 17070. S 3842 had been reported by the Post Office and Civil Service Committee June 3.

Both the Senate and House bills incorporated most of the provisions of the April 2 settlement of the postal strike, negotiated by the administration with the AFL-CIO and craft-organized postal unions.

S 3842 established a 15-member Board of Governors, including the postmaster general and deputy postmaster general plus four nonvoting members of Congress—two senators and two representatives (the House bill did not include the congressional members). The board was given full authority to operate the postal system.

The Senate bill included provisions for:

• Annual appropriations by Congress to equal approximately 10 per cent of the postal budget, continuing indefinitely (the House bill required appropriations to cover a declining proportion of postal costs and to terminate by 1978).

• Recognition of postal unions and establishment of pay rates and working conditions through collective bargaining (similar to the House bill, but the Senate did not outlaw, as the House did, a union shop agreement resulting from bargaining).

• Rates and classes of service to be established by the board on recommendation of an independent five-member Postal Rate Commission (the House bill provided for congressional veto of rate changes).

• Elimination of political influence in selection of postal employees (similar to the House bill).

Conference. Conferees Aug. 3 filed a conference report after three weeks of negotiations. Major issues in conference involved differing versions of provisions concerning postal unions, congressional influence on the Postal Service and the public subsidy of the postal system.

One of the most controversial provisions of the postal reform legislation was the administration's recommendation, based on the negotiated settlement of the strike, that a "union shop"—in which all workers must belong to or pay the equivalent of dues to the dominant union—be permitted if it resulted from collective bargaining.

Statutes called "right-to-work" laws in a number of states prohibited the union shop; under the Taft-Hartley Act, the administration bill would not have permitted a union shop in a state prohibiting it. Right-to-work advocates mounted campaigns to eliminate the union shop provision from the bill. The House, in a floor amendment, wrote a right-to-work provision into its bill. A similar effort in the Senate failed. The House subsequently voted to instruct its conferees to insist on the right-to-work provision. In the face of the inflexible House position, Senate conferees conceded, and the "right-to-work" provision was included in the final version.

The administration bill had provided for national recognition of unions organized on a "craft" or job basis—chiefly the AFL-CIO unions—as bargaining agents for postal employees, to the exclusion of service-wide or "industrially" organized unions, primarily the National Postal Union and National Alliance of Postal and Federal Employees. The House bill left determination of appropriate "units" or unions for representing the workers to the National Labor Relations Board, but provided that in the interim before the Postal Service went into full operation bargaining would be restricted to the craft unions which held exclusive national recognition under Executive Order 11491, issued by President Nixon on Oct. 31, 1969. The Senate bill followed the administration's recommendation but incorporated a floor amendment designed to open the subject in conference. The conference adopted the House version.

The Senate version had included two senators and two representatives as nonvoting members of the Board of Governors. The House bill had no such provision, but it gave either house of Congress a veto over rate and classification changes. The Senate bill lacked that provision. The conference deleted both from the bill, thereby eliminating any direct congressional intervention in the operation of the new Postal Service.

A measure of congressional control was retained in the provision authorizing appropriation of a public subsidy to the mail system until at least 1984. The House had authorized declining annual appropriations which were to have ended with calendar year 1977. The Senate authorized annual appropriations indefinitely, equal to the lesser of 10 per cent of total postal costs in the current fiscal year or in fiscal year 1971.

The conference authorized appropriations under a three-stage formula:

• A sum equal to 10 per cent of fiscal 1971 costs each year through fiscal 1979.

• One percentage point less in each of the succeeding fiscal years.

• After fiscal year 1984, 5 per cent of the fiscal 1971 total or less, as determined by the Postal Service.

Final Action. The Senate Aug. 3, by a roll-call vote of 57-7, adopted the conference report on HR 17070.

The House Aug. 6, on a roll-call vote of 338-29, adopted the report, completing congressional action.

FINAL PROVISIONS

As cleared by Congress, HR 17070:

General

• Established the U.S. Postal Service as an independent agency of the federal government and transferred to it the powers and duties of the Post Office Department.

• Removed the post of postmaster general from the President's cabinet.

• Established an 11-member Board of Governors to head the Postal Service, to be composed of nine public members appointed by the President with Senate confirmation (no more than five from the same political party); a 10th member, the postmaster general, to be appointed by the other nine members; and a deputy postmaster general, to be appointed by the other 10.

• Authorized the board to delegate its executive power to the postmaster general, except for rate and mail classification decisions.

• Provided that the nine presidentially appointed members of the board would serve staggered nine-year terms and that the postmaster general and deputy postmaster general would serve at the board's discretion.

• Established a 13-member Postal Advisory Council consisting of the postmaster general, the deputy postmaster general and 11 members appointed by the President, to advise the Postal Service on all postal matters.

● Continued existing laws governing mail services and criminal laws regarding the mail and postal employees.

● Required the Post Office Department to be phased out of existence and the Postal Service to take over its operation within one year after enactment, to the exact date to be set by the board.

● Continued existing rates and services until they were changed as provided for in the legislation.

Employees

● Granted an 8 per cent pay raise retroactive to April 16 for postal workers, the increase to be in addition to the six per cent raise granted most federal employees in legislation passed April 14 (PL 91-231).

● Created a Postal Career Service as a part of the U.S. Civil Service, retained existing civil service and veterans' benefits for postal employees, including retirement rights, but transferred responsibility for compensation and fringe benefits to the Postal Service.

● Prohibited political tests or qualifications in all postal personnel actions.

Labor-Management Relations

● Allowed compensation and working conditions to be set through collective bargaining.

● Provided that collective bargaining agreements negotiated by the Postal Service and postal unions would be effective for at least two years.

● Applied the National Labor-Management Relations Act (Taft-Hartley) of 1947 and the National Labor-Management Reporting and Disclosure Act (Landrum-Griffin) of 1959 to the Postal Service and postal unions.

● Provided for exclusive recognition of labor organizations selected by a majority of postal workers in bargaining units, as determined by the National Labor Relations Board (NLRB), as the workers' authorized collective bargaining agents, but explicitly left each worker free to join or not join a union.

● Continued the statutory prohibition on strikes by postal employees.

● Provided that if the Postal Service management and a union were unable to settle a dispute within 90 days the Federal Mediation and Conciliation Service would establish a fact-finding panel which would be required to make a report within an additional 45 days.

● Provided that if agreement on a dispute was not reached 90 days after termination of a collective bargaining agreement, the dispute would be submitted to a board for binding arbitration.

● Provided for union dues "check-off" collection, as in private industry.

● Provided that, in the interim before the Postal Service went into full operation, collective bargaining would be limited to those unions holding exclusive national recognition under executive order of the President.

Financial

● Transferred government equity in the Post Office Department to the Postal Service.

● Gave the Postal Service responsibility for financing its own operations and capital needs from revenues and securities issues.

● Authorized Congress to appropriate funds as a public subsidy to the Postal Service, equal to 10 per cent of total postal costs in fiscal year 1971 (July 1, 1970, to June 30, 1971), beginning in fiscal 1972 and continuing through fiscal 1979; after which Congress could appropriate 1 percentage point less each fiscal year for five years; after which Congress could continue the subsidy at 5 per cent of fiscal 1971 costs, modify the amount, or eliminate the appropriation.

● Provided that Congress could continue to appropriate indefinitely amounts equal to revenue lost through free and reduced-postage mail service as required by law.

● Authorized the Postal Service to issue and sell debt obligations not to exceed a $10-billion aggregate limit, of which not more than $2-billion could be issued in a single year.

● Authorized the Treasury to buy up to a total of $2-billion in Postal Service obligations, and authorized the Postal Service to require the Treasury to purchase up to $2-billion of its bonds.

Rates and Services

● Established an independent Postal Rate Commission of five members, appointed by the President, to make recommendations on rates, classifications of mail, and services.

● Required the board to request the commission to recommend changes when costs exceeded revenues plus the subsidy, and empowered the commission to initiate recommendations.

● Except for free and reduced-rate mail, empowered the commission to recommend any changes in postal rates and classifications, subject only to policies and guidelines established in the bill, including procedures to ensure that recommendations were reasonable and equitable, rights of all users were protected, costs would be apportioned fairly among users, and good service would be provided, as well as the requirement that at least one class of sealed mail (not to be opened except within prescribed judicial procedures) must be provided.

● Empowered the board to accept or reject the commission's recommendations; provided for legal appeal of changes; authorized the board to ask the commission to reconsider its recommendations; empowered the board to implement recommendations under protest and, when acting unanimously, to modify the commission's recommendations after reconsideration; and required the board to establish a new schedule of classifications within two years after going into operation.

● Provided transition periods of five years for rate and classification changes and 10 years for changes in existing preferential classes, during which new rates would gradually take effect.

● Required each class of mail to recover its costs through its rates, but continued existing free and reduced-rate mail for eligible mailers as long as Congress made up for the lost revenue with appropriations.

● Provided for prompt judicial review of rate and service proceedings.

● Authorized recipient of unsolicited merchandise to treat it as a gift.

● Prohibited mailing of sexually oriented commercial advertising to persons who specified they did not want to receive it.

Transportation

● Authorized the Postal Service to contract for transportation of mail by common carriers.

● Continued the legal obligations of railroads to provide mail transportation and extended the obligations to other carriers.

● Gave the Postal Service broad authority to transport mail by surface and air transportation, and included a number of specific provisions designed to give the board greater flexibility in contracting for mail transportation and greater incentive to expedite movement of mail, but left rates subject to approval of the Civil Aeronautics Board and the Interstate Commerce Commission.

Postal Rates

The House Post Office and Civil Service Subcommittee on Postal Rates held hearings in 1970, but it took no action on postal increases, leaving the issue to the newly created U.S. Postal Service.

President Nixon April 24, 1969, had requested a one-cent increase (to seven cents) for first-class mail, a 12 per cent increase for second-class mail and a five per cent increase for third-class mail. The requests were in addition to scheduled increases enacted in 1967 (PL 90-206) for second-class mail (effective Jan. 1, 1970) and third-class mail (effective July 1, 1969). The House Post Office and Civil Service Subcommittee on Postal Rates held hearings on the requests in 1969 but took no action.

In messages to Congress April 3 and 16, 1970, concerning the postal strike settlement and the proposed postal reorganization plan, President Nixon called for increased postal rates to pay for the salary increases which emerged from the settlement. In his April 16 message he revised downward from his April 3 message the requested rate increases for first-class mail but increased the rate request for second- and third-class mail. On April 3 he had asked for a 10-cent rate for regular first-class mail; on April 16 he asked for an eight-cent rate (existing rate: six cents). The revision in the request followed sharp and immediate opposition to the proposed increase by members of Congress.

1971-72

Postal Savings

Congress Aug. 5, 1972, completed action on a bill (HR 135—PL 92-117) authorizing the distribution of unclaimed postal savings accounts to the states and other jurisdictions.

Background. The Postal Savings System, established by Congress in 1910, was terminated on April 27, 1966 (PL 89-377). The system provided facilities, at designated post offices, for the deposit of savings. These savings accounts drew interest and were guaranteed by the U.S. government.

The Johnson administration recommended discontinuance on the grounds that the system was no longer needed and was not worth the cost.

PL 92-117 authorized the secretary of the treasury within 60 days of enactment of the bill and once in each of the four succeeding years to distribute to each state on a pro rata basis the remaining principal and interest of unclaimed postal savings deposits.

Federal Pay

During the Nixon administration's first term, Congress handed over to the executive branch its authority to adjust the pay scales of 4.5 million federal civilian and military employees. That action was based on the belief that pay raises should be granted on a regular basis—free from legislative whim and struggle—to assure that federal wages were comparable to those in private industry.

The Federal Pay Comparability Act (PL 91-656) passed by Congress in 1970 established a process first given recognition in 1962. In 1967, in an unprecedented move, Congress not only set higher pay levels for federal employees, but also provided for an automatic increase in 1968 and again in 1969 based on pay scales determined by the President. The mechanism giving the President authority to make pay adjustments, subject to congressional veto, lapsed, however, in 1969.

The 1970 legislation authorized the President, beginning in October 1972, to set wage rates for federal employees based on private industry pay surveys, recommendations from a federal employees' pay council and review by an executive advisory committee.

Since World War II Congress had steadily increased the federal pay levels. The trend continued through the Johnson administration, when the gap between federal and civilian pay scales was closed.

Between 1969 and 1972, various pay hikes raised the scale of the lowest-paid General Schedule (GS) federal worker from $3,889-$5,507 on July 1, 1969, to $4,798-$6,238 after Jan. 1, 1973. Pay of mid-range GS-9 employees rose in that period from $9,320-$12,119 to a range of $11,614-$15,097. Similarly, GS-15 workers' pay increased from $21,589-$28,069 in 1969 to $26,898-$34,917 in 1973.

President's Pay

In 1969, Congress doubled the President's salary to $200,000, starting with Richard M. Nixon's term in office, Jan. 20, 1969. The President's pay was last raised in 1949. In addition to his salary, the President was granted traveling and official allowances totaling $90,000 as well as funds for operation of the White House.

A pay increase for the Vice President and congressional leadership was also approved in 1969, after adverse Senate reaction was overcome. The legislation increased the salary of the Vice President and the Speaker of the House to $62,500 and the majority and minority leaders of the House and Senate and president pro tempore of the Senate to $49,500.

Under the 1967 pay procedure which allowed pay increases submitted by the President to go into effect unless vetoed by Congress, the salaries of members of Congress, cabinet officials and Supreme Court justices were increased in 1969.

The same year, President Nixon issued executive orders raising the pay of 2.3 million federal employees and nearly 3 million military personnel as of July 1. Classified civilian employees' raises averaged 9.1 per cent; military employees got flat 12.5-per cent increases.

In 1970, Congress granted a six per cent pay raise for federal postal employees and most other civil service workers, military personnel and congressional employees. The bill, the first step of a two-stage postal strike settlement, was rushed through Congress in one week following a nationwide mail carriers' strike. Later, in legislation that reorganized the Post Office Department, Congress granted postal workers an additional eight per cent pay raise.

Other wage increases for federal employees were granted in 1970, 1971, and 1972, becoming effective on Jan. 1, 1971, 1972 and 1973, respectively.

Blue Collar Employees

In 1972, Congress enacted legislation that established a revised system for adjusting the pay rates of federal blue-collar employees. The measure was similar to a bill President Nixon vetoed in 1971 because, he said, it would force the federal government to cut back its payrolls and would trigger inflationary wage pressures on private industry.

The 1972 bill created two additional wage steps in the federal blue-collar career ladder, adding an estimated $181-million annually to the federal payroll. Approximately 650,000 blue-collar workers were employed by the federal government, including carpenters, truck drivers, electricians, plumbers and aircraft personnel. Known also as wage board or prevailing rate employees, these workers represented about one-fourth of the total federal payroll.

References

Discussion of federal pay policy and legislation in the 1945-64 period may be found in *Congress and the Nation, Vol. I,* p. 1471-1494; for the years, 1965-68, *Congress and the Nation, Vol. II,* p. 929-943.

Chronology

Of Legislation

On Federal Pay

1969

Congressional and presidential action in 1969 provided pay raises for most categories of employees in the executive, legislative and judicial branches of the federal government.

New legislation passed during the year raised the salaries of the President, Vice President and the congressional leadership.

Salaries for members of Congress, top officials in the executive and judicial branches—including the President's cabinet and advisers and the Supreme Court justices— as well as the 2.3 million federal civil service employees, the 750,000 postal employees and the nearly 3 million military personnel were increased under a 1967 law.

Two of the pay raises, those for members of Congress and for the congressional leadership and the Vice President, ran into considerable controversy. Members of Congress, as well as top officials in the executive and judicial branches, for the first time received a pay increase without specific congressional approval. Under a procedure established by Congress in the 1967 federal pay raise bill (PL 90-206), every four years a commission of private citizens was to advise the President on salaries of top executive and judicial branch officials and members of Congress. The President then was to issue proposed salary revisions to go into effect within 30 days unless vetoed by either chamber of Congress. This procedure was put into practice in 1969 for the first time when President Johnson, shortly before leaving office, submitted proposed salary revisions with his fiscal 1970 budget. A veto resolution failed in the Senate by a 34-47 roll-call vote; while in the House, the Rules Committee prevented all veto proposals from reaching the House floor.

The Senate in April rejected a measure raising the salaries of the congressional leadership and the Vice President but then reversed itself in August and passed a compromise pay increase. Opponents of the bill argued that it contributed to inflation, an argument also heard over the President's 100 per cent salary increase in January. Opponents also complained about the automatic procedure by which members of Congress could receive pay raises without ever having voted on them, and an amendment was submitted to abolish the procedure. The move failed, however.

President Nixon June 17 issued executive orders raising the pay of 2.3 million federal employees and nearly 3 million military personnel as of July 1. The raises were designed to make government and military employees' pay comparable with wage scales in private industry and were also provided by the 1967 federal pay raise bill. PL 90-206 granted the President authority to implement raises on July 1, 1968, and July 1, 1969. With the 1969 executive order, the President's authority to implement raises lapsed. However, Congress in 1969 took up legislation to establish a permanent procedure for granting federal employees raises.

Congressional staff employees also received raises under authority provided by PL 90-206.

Taken together, the 1969 pay raises effected by Congress and presidential action benefited over six million persons at a cost of about $3.3-billion annually.

President's Pay

A bill (HR 10—PL 91-1) doubling the President's salary to $200,000, starting with Richard M. Nixon's term in office, Jan. 20, 1969, was passed by the Senate Jan. 15 and sent to the White House. The House had approved the measure Jan. 6. President Johnson signed the bill Jan. 17.

Background. The President's pay was last raised in 1949. In addition to his salary, the President had travel and official allowances totaling $90,000 annually. *(Box p. 449)* Yearly appropriations were also made for operation of the White House office and the Executive Mansion.

For the pay raise to go into effect for the new President, Nixon, action on HR 10 had to be completed before his inauguration Jan. 20. Article II, Section 1, clause 7 of the Constitution provides that the President's salary cannot be changed during his term of office. Because of the time element, no hearings were held and no commitee report was issued on HR 10.

House, Senate Action. The House Jan. 6 passed by voice vote and sent to the Senate HR 10. HR 10 was the first bill passed by the House in the 91st Congress.

The bill was sponsored by the majority and minority leaders of the House and by the chairman and ranking GOP member of the House Post Office and Civil Service Committee. They stated that the President's current salary was not commensurate with the importance of his office and cited the fact that the chief officers of large corporations often were paid more than the President of the United States. Majority Leader Carl Albert (D Okla.) said that HR 10 had originated in Congress and that neither Johnson nor Nixon had been asked for his views on the matter.

The only opposition came from Rep. H. R. Gross (R Iowa), who said he could "not understand how Congress can increase an executive's salary 100 per cent and yet talk about austerity and frugality.... I have had word indirectly that the President-elect takes a dim view of the 100 per cent pay increase."

Executive Branch Civilian Employment

Selected Agencies	1968	1972
Agriculture Department	122,715	123,299
Health, Education and Welfare Department	117,115	114,065
Interior Department	77,545	74,632
Postal Service	730,977	675,197
Treasury Department	89,125	105,326
Veterans Administration	175,688	187,561
Defense Department	1,317,049	1,073,471
All Executive Branch	3,032,817	2,756,744

The Senate by voice vote passed HR 10 Jan. 15. Senate Majority Leader Mike Mansfield (D Mont.) and Minority Leader Everett McKinley Dirksen (R Ill.) said that Nixon's take-home pay would amount to $78,000 with the pay increase, in contrast to the $51,500 after taxes at the existing salary level of $100,000.

Sen. John J. Williams (R Del.) said that the presidential pay raise would set a precedent for federal civilian employees, military personnel and private industry. He said the action paved the way for members of Congress to accept large pay boosts of their own.

Hours before the Senate voted on HR 10, President Johnson submitted his fiscal 1970 budget providing for a new salary scale for executive, legislative and judicial officials, which included a $12,500 pay raise (from $30,000 to $42,500) for members of Congress.

Vice President's, Leaders' Pay

A pay increase for the Vice President and congressional leaders was approved by Congress Sept. 4 after adverse Senate action earlier in the year had delayed passage of the legislation. The Senate Aug. 7, reversing its previous stand on the pay bill (HR 7206), passed a compromise bill increasing the salary of the Vice President and the Speaker of the House to $62,500 and the majority and minority leaders of the House and Senate and president pro tempore of the Senate to $49,500.

The salary increases were made retroactive to March 1, 1969.

PROVISIONS. As passed by Congress, HR 7206 (PL 91-67):

• Increased the salaries of the Vice President of the United States and the Speaker of the House of Representatives from $43,000 to $62,500 annually.

• Increased the salaries of the majority and minority leaders of the House and Senate and the president pro tempore of the Senate from $42,500 to $49,500 annually.

• Made the salary increases retroactive to March 1, 1969.

Prior to the 1969 action, the annual salary of the Vice President and the Speaker of the House had last been set in 1964 (PL 88-426) at $43,000 and the salaries of majority and minority leaders in the House and Senate in 1965 (PL 89-301) at $35,000. The president pro tempore had been paid no more than other members—$30,000 before the Feb. 14, 1969, increases.

A general pay increase for all members of Congress and for top officials of the executive and judicial branches went into effect Feb. 14, but it did not cover proportional increases for the congressional leadership nor for the Vice President *(Members increase, p. 550).*

House Action. The House March 18 by a 181-64 standing vote passed HR 7206 to raise the pay of the Vice President and the six top leadership positions of the Senate and House of Representatives.

Thaddeus J. Dulski (D N.Y.), chairman of the Post Office and Civil Service Committee, said in debate that HR 7206 was "essential to the maintenance of a proper relationship between the salaries of congressional officials and the salaries of executives and judges for whom adjustments have already become effective." Dulski cosponsored HR 7206 with the ranking Republican on the committee, Robert J. Corbett (R Pa.).

Presidential Salaries

Effective Dates	Annual Salary	Annual Allowances
1789-1873	$ 25,000	—
1873-1909	50,000	$25,000 (travel) [1]
1909-1949	75,000	40,000 (travel) [2]
1949-1969	100,000	40,000 (travel)
1969-	200,000	50,000 (official)

Note: The President's annual salary always has been taxable. The $50,000 official allowance, which as enacted in 1949 was tax-free, was made taxable by a 1951 law effective Jan. 20, 1953. The $40,000 travel allowance remained tax-free.

[1] Enacted in 1906.
[2] Increased to $40,000 in 1948.

Leader of the opposition to HR 7206 was Rep. H. R. Gross (R Iowa), who stated that members had not voted on their own pay raise which "was greased and slipped through the back door. I emphasize that this will be your only opportunity to vote on this whole ball of wax." Gross had also tried to block the pay increases of the President and members of Congress.

Senate Action. The Senate April 29 by a 64-21 roll-call vote recommitted HR 7206 to the Senate Post Office and Civil Service Committee, which had reported it April 25. The recommittal motion was agreed to following the adoption, by a 49-36 roll-call vote, of an amendment to do away with the automatic pay raise procedure for legislative, executive and judicial officials and during debate on an amendment to cancel all pay raises except that of the Vice President.

John J. Williams (R Del.) and Harry F. Byrd Jr. (D Va.) spoke against HR 7206 on the grounds that it contributed to inflation. Both also opposed the automatic pay raise procedure which could allow salary increases to go into effect without either chamber ever voting on them. Williams of Delaware was joined by Byrd of Virginia and two Nebraska Republicans, Roman L. Hruska and Carl T. Curtis, in offering an amendment to do away with that procedure.

Peter H. Dominick (R Colo.), with John O. Pastore (D R.I.) and Williams of Delaware as cosponsors, then proposed an amendment to raise only the Vice President's pay. During the debate on that amendment, McGee moved to recommit HR 7206.

But, on Aug. 7, the Senate by voice vote adopted a compromise version of HR 7206, increasing to $49,500 the salaries of the majority and minority leaders of the House and Senate and the president pro tempore of the Senate—a reduction of $5,500 from the House-passed version. Before passing the bill, members rejected by a 47-50 roll-call vote an amendment introduced by Williams (Del.) to do away with the quadrennial commission which recommends increases in executive, legislative and judicial salaries. The same amendment had been agreed to in April but the committee, in reporting HR 7206 for a second time June 5, had dropped this amendment from the bill.

The bill that the Senate passed and returned to the House for final approval increased the salaries of the Vice

President and the Speaker of the House from $43,000 to $62,500. The pay of the majority and minority leaders of the House and Senate and the president pro tempore of the Senate was increased from $42,500 to $49,500. The pay increases were retroactive to March 1, 1969.

Of the three senators absent during the voting on the Williams amendment, one had voted against the same amendment in April and the other two had not voted.

By a voice vote the Senate adopted an amendment by Peter H. Dominick (R Colo.) to set the salaries of the majority and minority leaders and president pro tempore at $49,500.

Final Action. The House Sept. 4 by voice vote accepted the Senate amendment to HR 7206 setting the new annual salary rates for the House and Senate majority and minority leaders and president pro tempore of the Senate at $49,500. The President signed the bill (PL 91-67) Sept. 15.

Congressional, Top Officials Pay

Top officials of the executive and judicial branches and members of Congress and other congressional officials received salary increases of 35 to 70 per cent beginning Feb. 14 after Congress failed to veto the increases. Prior to the Lincoln's Birthday recess, the Senate Feb. 4 defeated a veto resolution (S Res 82) by a 34-47 roll-call vote, and the following day the House Rules Committee refused to clear for floor action any of the 10 veto resolutions it was considering.

Under a new procedure established by Congress in 1967, President Johnson submitted a list of salary revisions with his fiscal 1970 budget that would go into effect automatically unless vetoed by Congress within 30 days.

The new salaries increased the pay of members of Congress to $42,500, cabinet members and Supreme Court justices to $60,000 and the chief justice of the United States to $62,500. The pay raise affected 2,047 persons and cost approximately $23-million annually.

BACKGROUND. In 1967, in order to avoid the politically thorny position of voting on its own pay rates, Congress established a system whereby new salaries would be recommended by the President and go into effect automatically unless vetoed. Under the law (PL 90-206), a quadrennial commission would make recommendations to the President, who would review those levels and include his own recommendations in the next budget. The recommendations would take effect within 30 days unless Congress vetoed them in whole or in part or enacted its own pay bill.

President Johnson appointed the first quadrennial commission June 3, 1968, and named Frederick R. Kappel, former chairman of the board of American Telephone and Telegraph Co., as its head. The commission, reporting in December 1968, recommended salary levels of $50,000 for members of Congress, $67,500 for the chief justice, $65,000 for associate justices, $60,000 for cabinet members, and a scale of $50,000 to $40,000 for Level II-V in the executive branch. With the exception of cabinet members, all salary recommendations were scaled down by Johnson in his Jan. 15, 1969, budget request. The last pay raise for top government officials had come in 1964.

President Nixon Jan. 28 endorsed the pay raises recommended in Johnson's budget.

Congress and Supreme Court Salaries

This table reviews the history of congressional and Supreme Court salaries.

Congress

From 1789 to 1856, senators and representatives received per diem pay while Congress was in session, except for the period 1815-1817 when they received $1,500 a year. First established at $6 a day, per diem was raised to $8 in 1818 and remained there until 1856 when members of Congress were placed on annual salaries. Subsequent changes in pay scale, with the year the change became effective:

1856	$ 3,000	1936	$10,000
1866	5,000	1946	12,000 (plus $2,500
1873	7,500		expense allowance)
1874	5,000	1955	22,500 (expense allowance
1907	7,500		eliminated)
1925	10,000	1964	30,000
1933	8,500	1969	42,500

Supreme Court

Year Enacted	Chief Justice	Associate Justices
1789	$ 4,000 per year	$ 3,500 per year
1819	5,000	4,500
1873	10,500	10,000
1903	13,000	12,500
1911	15,000	14,500
1926	20,500	20,000
1946	25,500	25,000
1955	35,500	35,000
1964	40,000	39,500
1972	62,500	60,000

SENATE ACTION. The Senate Feb. 4 by a 34-47 roll-call vote defeated a resolution (S Res 82), sponsored by Sen. John J. Williams (R Del.), to veto the pay raises. The vote was bipartisan, with senators from the larger states generally voting against the veto resolution and senators from the less populated states voting for it.

Opponents of the veto resolution pointed to the high salaries available to executives in private industry and to elective officials in state and local government. Supporters of the resolution claimed the raises would set off new demands by federal employees and other workers for higher wage levels. "If the members of Congress are to increase their own salaries by 40 per cent and the salaries of the executive branch by 35 to 70 per cent—that is, the top echelon—how can we in good conscience ask industry and organized labor to hold their price and wage increases down to approximately 5 per cent so that we can combat the serious threat of inflation?" asked Williams.

HOUSE ACTION. The House Rules Committee in executive session Feb. 5 voted 12-3 to table H Res 142 and nine similar veto resolutions, which assured the House would not vote on the matter before the Lincoln's Birthday recess of Feb. 7-17. (The increase automatically was set to go into effect Feb. 14.) Rep. H. R. Gross (R Iowa), sponsor of H Res 142, made a floor speech later Feb. 5, in which he objected to taking the recess before the House had a chance to vote on the pay raise issue. He later demanded a roll-call vote on adjournment for the Lincoln's Birthday holiday. The holiday recess was approved 240-125.

Twenty-five veto resolutions had been sent to the House Post Office and Civil Service Committee, but the committee had not yet organized itself and consequently did not act on any of them.

RELATED DEVELOPMENTS. Numerous bills were introduced in the House during 1969 to rescind the pay raises for top officials in the legislative, judicial and executive branches of the federal government.

The bills would have rescinded the raises, which increased salaries of members of Congress from $30,000 to $42,500, and abolished the quadrennial commission. The House Post Office and Civil Service Committee did not schedule any hearings on the measures in 1969.

A point of order raised by Gross and an amendment offered by Rep. Durward G. Hall (R Mo.) against the pay raise and an amendment to abolish the Commission on Executive, Judicial and Legislative Salaries were unsuccessfully sought during floor debate on the 1969 second supplemental appropriations bill.

Civilian, Military Pay Raise

President Nixon June 17 issued executive orders raising the pay of 2.3 million federal employees and nearly 3 million military personnel as of July 1.

Total cost of the pay raises was estimated at $3.3-billion annually. They were designed to make government and military employees' pay comparable to wage scales in private industry, as required by the 1967 government employees' pay raise bill (PL 90-206).

For classified civilian employees, raises averaged 9.1 per cent. Postal employees received raises averaging 4.1 per cent. Military employees got flat 12.5 per cent increases.

On June 18 House Speaker John McCormack (D Mass.) and Senate President Pro Tempore Richard B. Russell (D Ga.) authorized a 10 per cent pay raise for congressional staff employees, effective July 1. The basis for the raise was provided for in the 1967 federal pay raise bill (PL 90-206) which granted to the speaker and the president pro tempore power to set pay rates for congressional employees that were comparable to those established for federal civilian employees.

Supergrades

The Senate Dec. 20 cleared for the President's signature a bill (S 2325—PL 91-187) authorizing 222 more "supergrade" positions in the federal government.

The Senate agreed by voice vote to accept a House amendment to the bill which cut 53 positions out of the bill originally passed by the Senate.

The bill cleared by Congress contained the 222 positions (GS grades 16 through 18) originally requested by the Nixon administration. Cost of the bill was estimated

by the House Post Office and Civil Service Committee at $2.4-million annually.

Background. A bill authorizing new supergrade posts passed the Senate in 1968 and a similar measure was reported in the House but died when the rule by which it was being considered was defeated by a 135-221 roll-call vote.

Senate Action. The Senate Dec. 5 by voice vote approved a bill (S 2325) authorizing 275 more "supergrade" positions in the federal government. Before passing the bill, senators by voice vote adopted an amendment adding 45 positions to the 230 approved by the Senate Post Office and Civil Service Committee.

The Nixon administration originally had requested 22 additional posts in General Schedule (GS) grades 16 through 18, with salary ranges from $25,044 to $33,495. The Senate Post Office and Civil Service Committee reported the bill Nov. 26 with an amendment allowing eight additional supergrade jobs and a new assistant secretary for the Smithsonian Institution. The Senate agreed to the committee amendment by voice vote.

The bill passed by the Senate allowed 195 additional "quota" positions to be allocated by the Civil Service Commission, and 80 additional supergrade posts earmarked for specific agencies.

House Action. The House Post Office and Civil Service Committee Dec. 18 reported the Senate bill (S 2325) after holding hearings Nov. 5 on its own bill (HR 12476).

The House Dec. 19 by voice vote passed S 2325 after amending the bill by deleting the 45 supergrade positions for regional offices and the eight positions for the Smithsonian Institution added in the Senate.

Final Action. The Senate Dec. 20 agreed to the House amendment on a voice vote, completing congressional action. The bill was signed Dec. 30 (PL 91-187).

Pay Comparability

Congress in 1969 did not complete action on a bill (HR 13000) designed to establish a permanent apparatus whereby most federal civilian employees would be assured consideration of annual pay adjustments to bring their salaries in line with those in private industry. A temporary mechanism giving the President authority to make such comparability adjustments, subject to congressional veto, was passed by Congress in 1967 (PL 90-206). This authority, however, lapsed with the pay raise ordered by President Nixon June 17, 1969. *(Above)*

Comparability pay bills were passed by both chambers during the session, but in widely varying versions. A House bill providing a mechanism for future pay raises estimated to cost $4.3-billion when fully effective was threatened with a presidential veto, and a Senate bill authorizing a pay raise Jan. 1, 1970, and a further comparability raise July 1, at an estimated cost of $2.8-billion, was viewed by the House leadership as probably unacceptable to the House. The bill was sent to a House-Senate conference for further negotiations as the first session of the 91st Congress adjourned. HR 13000 did not clear Congress until Dec. 31, 1970.

Federal Salaries

Level (General Schedule Employees)	1969 [1]	1972 [2]
GS-1	$3,889—$ 5,507	$ 4,798—$ 6,238
2	4,360— 5,665	5,432— 7,061
3	4,917— 6,393	6,128— 7,964
4	5,522— 7,178	6,882— 8,943
5	6,176— 8,030	7,694— 10,007
6	6,882— 8,943	8,572— 11,146
7	7,639— 9,934	9,520— 12,373
8	8,449— 10,987	10,528— 13,687
9	9,320— 12,119	11,614— 15,097
10	10,252— 13,330	12,775— 16,609
11	11,233— 14,599	13,996— 18,190
12	13,389— 17,403	16,682— 21,686
13	15,812— 20,555	19,700— 25,613
14	18,531— 24,093	23,088— 30,018
15	21,589— 28,069	26,898— 34,917
16	25,044— 31,724	31,203— 36,000 [3]
17	28,976— 32,840	36,000 [3] —
18	33,495— — [3]	36,000 [3] —

1 *Effective the first pay period on or after July 1, 1969.*
2 *Effective the first pay period on or after Jan. 1, 1973.*
3 *The rate of pay for these levels is limited to $36,000—the rate for level V of the Executive Schedule, generally sub-cabinet political appointees.*

Civil Service Retirement

Congress in 1969 enacted legislation (HR 9825—PL 91-93) to strengthen the financing of the Civil Service Retirement and Disability Fund and liberalize some benefits.

HR 9825 was passed by the House July 23 and the Senate, amended, Oct. 3. The House approved the Senate version Oct. 7.

Although there had been speculation that President Nixon might veto the measure, he signed it into law Oct. 20, the deadline for action. The administration supported the financing provisions but opposed the inclusion of benefit increases in the bill.

One result of PL 91-93 was a large number of retirements by members of Congress in 1972.

The act was the culmination of two years of efforts by Congress and the executive branch to put the retirement fund on a sound financial footing. In recent years the fund had been incurring an increasingly large unfunded liability (the excess of the fund's liabilities or commitments to pay retirement benefits over the fund's projected assets). By July 1969, the unfunded liability had reached $61.1-billion, compared with $31.1-billion in 1960. Congressional experts predicted that under existing funding practices, disbursements from the fund would exceed the fund's annual income, beginning in 1975. By 1987, they said, the fund's balance would be entirely exhausted, and from then on Congress would have to make direct annual appropriations to meet benefit payments for retired federal workers. It was estimated that these appropriations would approach $5-billion annually by the turn of the century.

The main purpose of HR 9825 was to stabilize the unfunded liability. To accomplish this HR 9825 increased payroll contributions by employees and government agencies, authorized direct appropriations to the fund by Congress to cover certain types of costs and financial deficits experienced by the fund and provided permanent appropriations (automatic transfers from the Treasury to the fund) to make up the sums the fund was losing in interest because it was under-financed. These appropriations were expected to reach $2.7-billion by 1980.

The benefit increases included shortening the earnings period for computation of retirement benefits, providing retirement credit for unused sick leave, providing a 1 per cent "bonus" for each cost-of-living increase in annuities, improving survivor benefits and liberalizing the method of computing annuities for congressional employees.

The Senate Post Office and Civil Service Committee estimated that the bill would increase the normal cost of the retirement system from 13.86 per cent of payroll to 13.98 per cent—compared with a combined employee-agency payroll contribution of 14 per cent.

Background. The Civil Service Retirement and Disability Fund, created in 1920, covered virtually all employees in the civil service and, if they chose to participate, members of Congress and their employees.

The existing method of financing, which went into effect at the beginning of fiscal 1958, provided that each employing agency contribute to the retirement fund an amount equal to the employee's own contribution. Benefits were based on length of service, salary and age at retirement of the participant. Annuities ranged up to 80 per cent of the average annual salary (computed by finding the average of the salaries for the five consecutive years in which the recipient received his highest rate of pay).

Automatic cost-of-living increases were provided whenever the consumer price index rose by 3 per cent over the previous base period for three successive months.

Congress enacted a major pension increase, including the cost-of-living adjustments, in 1965 but did not raise contribution rates to cover the cost. Benefits were broadened further in the federal pay raise bill of 1966. In 1968, the House passed a bill that was generally similar to HR 9825, but there was no Senate action.

Provisions. As signed by the President, HR 9825:

Financing Provisions (Title I). Increased payroll contributions of civil service employees and their agencies from 6 1/2 per cent to 7 per cent each, beginning in January 1970, to meet "normal costs" of the retirement program.

Increased contributions of members of Congress from 7 1/2 per cent to 8 per cent and contributions of Congressional employees from 6 1/2 per cent to 7 1/2 per cent, beginning in January 1970.

Authorized direct appropriations to the Civil Service Retirement and Disability Fund, in equal installments over a 30-year period, to meet future unfunded liabilities resulting from liberalized benefits or salary increases.

Authorized permanent appropriations (automatic payments directly from the Treasury to the fund) to pay the interest on the existing unfunded liability and the additional costs of annuities for retired military personnel who transferred to the civil service. To minimize the impact on the budget, the payments would begin in fiscal

1971 at 10 per cent of the estimated interest and increase by 10 per cent annually until full interest payments were met in fiscal 1980 and thereafter.

Benefit Increases (Title II). Specified that the annuity computation formula would use an employee's average annual earnings during the highest consecutive three-year ("high-three") period rather than during a five-year period as provided by existing law.

Liberalized the method of computing annuities for congressional employees by eliminating the 15-year limitation on number of years of service for which the annuity would be computed at 2 1/2 per cent of average pay; limited military service that could be credited at 2 1/2 per cent to five years.

Allowed employees to credit unused sick leave toward retirement benefits.

Added 1 per cent to every cost-of-living increase in annuities to compensate for the delay between the time the consumer price index attained the required 3 per cent increase and the time the annuitant received his increased payment.

Eased rules regarding payment of benefits to surviving spouses who remarried.

Provided survivor benefits for spouses of employees with limited federal service (at least 18 months but less than five years) and increased benefits for surviving children.

1970

Federal Pay

Congress April 14 cleared for the President S 3690, the Federal Employees Salary Act of 1970, granting a 6 per cent pay increase for federal postal employees and most other civil service employees, military personnel and congressional employees, retroactive to Dec. 27, 1969. President Nixon signed the bill into law April 15 (PL 91-231).

S 3690 did not cover some 800,000 federal employees paid according to the prevailing wage rate for comparable work in private industry in their geographical area. Approximately 80 per cent of these employees worked for the Defense Department. Legislation to revise the system of pay for these employees was under consideration during the second session of the 91st Congress.

S 3690, the first stage of the two-stage postal strike settlement, was rushed through Congress in one week *(Postal Reorganization, p. 435)*; it was introduced in the Senate April 7 and cleared Congress April 14. Final action on the bill came when the House April 14 by voice vote accepted technical amendments added by the Senate. Prior to the voice vote, the House by a 309-65 roll-call vote adopted a motion cutting off debate and preventing further amendment of S 3690.

The estimated cost of the retroactive pay raise was $2.5-billion.

S 3690 delayed congressional action on HR 13000, which granted pay raises to federal employees and was passed in differing forms by both the House and the Senate in 1969. House-Senate conferees on HR 13000 had broken off negotiations March 26, 1970, to await the outcome of the postal strike negotiations. As finally enacted at year's end, HR 13000 provided a permanent method of adjusting federal employees' pay.

Provisions. As cleared by Congress S 3690:

● Granted a 6 per cent pay increase to civil service, military, foreign service and other Federal personnel (except employees whose rates of pay were set administratively) retroactive to Dec. 27, 1969, or the first pay period beginning after that date.

● Granted the same increase retroactively to congressional employees (Senate personal staff employees' raises took effect at the discretion of individual senators).

● Granted District of Columbia judges raises: from $29,000 to $36,500 for the chief judge of the Court of Appeals and from $28,500 to $36,000 for other judges. General Sessions judges received similar increases.

● Raised the aggregate allowances for staff for former Presidents Truman and Johnson from $80,000 to $96,000 for each.

● Authorized annual premium pay for employees whose duties did not permit their hours of work to be controlled administratively.

Postal Corporation, Pay Raise

Congress Aug. 6 cleared for the President's signature a bill (HR 17070—PL 91-375) reorganizing the Post Office Department and the U.S. postal system into an independent government agency, the U.S. Postal Service, and granting postal employees an 8 per cent pay raise retroactive to April 16, 1970. Postal employees earlier had been granted an additional 6 per cent pay increase by enactment of S 3690.

Prevailing Wage Veto

President Nixon Jan. 1, 1971, vetoed a bill (HR 17809) establishing a revised system for fixing and adjusting pay rates of federal blue-collar employees paid at prevailing wage rates for comparable work in private industry.

The bill cleared Congress Dec. 17, 1970, when the House by a 272-89 roll-call vote adopted a conference report on HR 17809. The Senate had adopted the report Dec. 16 by voice vote. HR 17809 had been passed by the House Sept. 9 and the Senate Sept. 10.

The action was Mr. Nixon's eighth veto of the 91st Congress. *(Vetoes, appendix, p. 101-A)*

In his veto message, the President said enactment of the bill would have adverse economic implications and would contribute to further inflation.

"At a time when the administration is most concerned about inflationary wage settlements in the private sector, this bill would mean that many federal employees... would be paid at much higher rates than those prevailing in the private sector of the same locality," he said.

The President added that most federal blue-collar workers were already being paid 4 per cent more than the prevailing wage in private industry.

Nixon signed a similar bill in 1972.

Background. The federal government employed about 800,000 wage-board, or blue-collar, workers who were paid according to prevailing wage rates for comparable work in private industry. About 80 per cent of these employees worked for the Department of Defense.

Since 1968, prevailing wage employees' pay rates had been fixed and adjusted under Civil Service Commission regulations. Before the regulations were issued, agencies employing these workers had different—and sometimes conflicting—systems of setting pay rates.

HR 17809 was designed to establish in law, with modifications, the system administered under the Civil Service Commission regulations.

Controversy over the bill was generated by the addition of one step to the prevailing wage schedule at an estimated cost of $95-million annually.

The Civil Service Commission, General Services Administration (GSA) and Veterans Administration (VA), as well as the Defense Department, opposed HR 17809. Unions for the employees affected supported the bill.

Defense Secretary Melvin Laird, in letters to Senate and House Post Office and Civil Service Committees, pointed out that pay increases for wage-board employees averaged 9.5 per cent in fiscal year 1969 and 8.1 per cent in fiscal 1970. He said the legislation would "make it necessary" for the Defense Department to lay off "thousands of additional employees" to absorb "hundreds of millions of dollars in unwarranted" wage hikes.

Federal Pay Comparability

Congress in 1970 completed action on a bill (HR 13000—PL 91-656), the Federal Pay Comparability Act, providing the President with authority to adjust the pay rates of 4.5 million federal employees.

Final action came when the House Dec. 31 agreed to a conference report on HR 13000. The Senate by voice vote had adopted the report Dec. 30.

The bill switched the responsibility for providing federal employees' pay raises from Congress to the executive branch. In 1962, the principle that federal salaries should be comparable with salaries in private industry was adopted by Congress in the Federal Salary Reform Act (PL 87-973).

The bill authorized the President, beginning in 1972, to set wage rates for federal employees based on private industry pay surveys, recommendations from a Federal Employees' Pay Council, established by the bill, and a review by an Advisory Committee on Federal Pay, also established by the bill.

The bill permitted the President to adjust the salaries of government workers in 1971 and 1972 (effective Jan. 1 of each of these two years) without following the review procedure authorized by HR 13000. (Based on 1970 private industry wage statistics, a six per cent pay comparability increase for 4.5 million government employees—including military personnel—would cost about $2.2-billion in 1971.)

On Oct. 14, 1969, the Federal Salary Comparability Act (HR 13000) was passed by the House. The Senate Dec. 12, 1969, approved an amended version of HR 13000. The House measure provided salary adjustments for federal employees, established a permanent method of adjusting pay rates of federal employees and included several miscellaneous employee fringe benefits. The Senate-passed version provided a flat percentage increase in pay for federal employees.

A House-Senate conference convened in March 1970 to resolve the differences between the Senate and House-passed versions of HR 13000, but no agreement was reached.

Subsequently, Congress in April 1970 approved a bill (S 3690—PL 91-231) providing a six per cent salary increase, retroactive to Dec. 27, 1969, for all federal employees under civilian and military pay systems, as well as for employees in the Agricultural Stabilization Service, and certain employees in the judicial, legislative and executive branches whose rates of pay were fixed by administrative action.

In August 1970, Congress approved the Postal Reorganization Act of 1970 (PL 91-375). It provided an 8 per cent pay increase for all employees of the Post Office Department, retroactive to April 16, 1970.

The question of a permanent method of adjusting pay rates for federal employees, however, was left unresolved.

Pay Comparability Bills. The Nixon administration submitted a proposal to Congress July 23 permitting the President to adjust the salaries of classified federal employees to correspond to private industry wages.

Sponsored by Robert J. Corbett (R Pa.), the Administration bill (HR 18603) differed from HR 18403 introduced by Morris K. Udall (D Ariz.) in the application of the pay comparability principle established by the Salary Reform Act of 1962.

Under the administration's pay comparability plan, the President by executive action would make annual salary adjustments based on three factors:

● Private industry salary levels compiled by the Bureau of Labor Statistics.

● Consultation between employee organizations, the Office of Management and Budget, and the Civil Service Commission.

● Recommendations of an impartial three-member committee of non-government advisers.

Provisions. As cleared by Congress, HR 13000:

● Provided that the President direct an agent each year to prepare a report based on surveys conducted by the Bureau of Labor Statistics comparing federal pay rates with pay rates in private enterprise for the same type of work and to make recommendations for appropriate adjustments.

● Established a Federal Employees Pay Council consisting of five members appointed from the largest federal employee unions to make recommendations on rates of pay to the President's agent.

● Established an independent Advisory Committee on Federal Pay composed of three members appointed by the President to review the agent's report and to make pay rate recommendations to the President.

● Authorized the President after considering the report of his agent and the findings of the advisory committee to make adjustments in the pay rates, which would take effect on Oct. 1 each year, beginning in 1972.

● Required the President to submit to Congress a report of the pay recommendations and reports of the President's agent and the advisory committee.

● Required the President to submit to Congress for approval before Sept. 1 of any year an alternative pay plan if he determined that national emergency or economic conditions made the required pay adjustment inappropriate.

● Provided that any alternative pay plan would take effect on Oct. 1 if Congress did not act on the alternative plan; provided that the original plan would take effect if either house rejected the alternative plan within 30 days after the date of transmittal to Congress.

● Authorized the President to adjust federal pay rates for 1971 and 1972 (effective Jan. 1 of each of 1971 and 1972) based on Bureau of Labor Statistics surveys. Designated the director of the Office of Management and Budget and the chairman of the U.S. Civil Service Commission to act as the President's agents for the 1971 and 1972 adjustments.

● Included the following government employees in the new pay adjustment system: Civil Service employees under the General Schedule (GS); officers, staff officers and employees in the Foreign Service; physicians, dentists and nurses in the Department of Medicine and Surgery of the Veterans Administration.

● Provided that pay rates fixed by the administrative action for employees in the legislative, executive and judicial branches of the federal government (except employees whose pay was disbursed by the secretary of the Senate or the clerk of the House of Representatives) and for employees of the District of Columbia may be adjusted by the appropriate administrative authority.

● Authorized the president pro tempore of the Senate to adjust the rates of pay of personnel whose pay was disbursed by the secretary of the Senate each time the President adjusted pay rates.

● Authorized the clerk of the House to adjust rates of pay for House personnel each time the President adjusted pay rates and to transmit the information to the appropriate pay-fixing authority (a member, committee chairman or the House Administration Committee) who could adjust pay rates as he considered appropriate.

Presidential Retirement

Congress Dec. 29 cleared for the President a bill (S 437—PL 91-658) authorizing a retired government employee to name a second spouse as beneficiary of his survivor annuity and increasing the annual retirement benefits of former Presidents.

Final action came when the Senate by a 37-35 roll-call vote agreed to a House amendment to S 437 increasing presidential retirement benefits. The House Dec. 7 by voice vote had passed an amended version of S 437 under suspension of the rules. The Senate had passed the bill Sept. 10:

Provisions. As cleared by Congress, S 437:

● Permitted the wife of a retired government employee to qualify for survivor benefits if she was married to the retiree for at least two years immediately before his death, or if a child was born by the marriage.

● Extended to widowers of deceased female employees the same survivor benefits accorded widows of male employees.

● Allowed a federal employee, unmarried at the time of retirement, to provide survivor benefits for a spouse whom he married after retirement.

● Increased the annual retirement allowance for former Presidents from $25,000 to an amount equivalent to the annual salary of cabinet officers. (Cabinet officers were paid $60,000 a year in 1970.)

● Increased the annual allowance for widows of former Presidents to $20,000 from $10,000.

Federal Firefighters Veto

President Nixon Jan. 4, 1971, pocket vetoed a bill (S 578) providing early retirement benefits for Federal firefighters. The bill would have benefited approximately 11,000 employees of various Government departments and agencies.

The bill cleared Congress Dec. 19, 1970, when the House by a 158-104 roll-call passed S 578 without amendment. The Senate had approved the measure Aug. 18 by voice vote.

In his veto message, the President said, "There is no demonstrated need for permitting Federal firefighters to retire at an earlier than normal age."

Mr. Nixon explained that Civil Service retirement laws had limited early retirement only to those occupations such as law enforcement in which there was a special need to maintain a young work force.

"This is not the case with Federal firefighters... because they are exposed to a lower incidence of fires... (and) do not face the same degree of hazard as employees of municipal fire departments...." he said.

Provision. As cleared by Congress, S 578:

● Provided that a Federal employee in a position connected with firefighting, who was separated from Government service after 50 years of age and who had completed 20 years of service, was entitled to an annuity if the head of his agency recommended his retirement and the Civil Service Commission approved the recommendation.

Foreign Service Retirement

The Senate Feb. 17 completed Congressional action on a bill (HR 14789) amending Title VIII of the Foreign Service Act of 1946, as amended, to provide for adjustments in the Foreign Service retirement and disability system. The purpose of the bill was to improve the financing and funding practices of the system, and to maintain parity between the Foreign Service and the Civil Service by making benefits comparable to those enacted in 1969 for civil service personnel under PL 91-93.

Provisions. As cleared HR 14789 (PL 91-201):

● Increased from 6 1/2 to 7 per cent the employee contribution rate and the matching Government contribution rate to the Foreign Service retirement fund.

● Carried forward the 7 per cent contribution rate into the computation of contributions due for prior service credit.

● Authorized appropriations to the retirement fund in equal annual installments over a 30-year period to finance any newly created unfunded liability incurred by enactment of future legislation, including benefit improvements for active employees, extension of coverage to new groups of employees, general salary increases and any new statutory annuity increases.

● Authorized direct appropriations, under permanent indefinite authority, to be made to meet Government obligations for present unfunded liability and the cost of military service credit.

● Directed the secretary of the treasury to pay into the fund each year (1) interest on the unfunded liability computed for that year at the interest rate used in the most recent valuation of the system; and (2) that portion of disbursements for annuities for that year which the secretary of state estimated was attributable to credit allowed for military service.

• Provided that annuities be based on the average salary during the highest paid three (rather than five) consecutive years of service.

• Increased children's basic survivor annuities by 50 per cent.

• Reduced from 5 years to 18 months the service eligibility requirement for a survivor annuity after death in service.

• Allowed employees to credit unused sick leave toward annuities.

• Provided an additional 1 per cent in each cost-of-living annuity increase.

1971

Federal Pay

The Senate Oct. 7, by a 32-51 roll-call vote, rejected a resolution (S Res 169) that would have allowed federal employees to receive salary increases beginning in January 1972.

A similar resolution (H Res 596) was defeated in the House Oct. 4 by a 174-207 roll-call vote.

President Nixon Aug. 31 ordered a suspension of a scheduled pay raise for approximately 4.5 million federal civilian and military personnel as part of his new economic policy. The estimated 5.5 per cent pay raise—totaling $1.4-billion—was ordered to be delayed to July 1, 1972.

Adoption of either the House or the Senate resolution would have allowed the pay raise to go into effect as scheduled on Jan. 1.

The administration had emphasized that a delay in federal pay increases was imperative to control inflation and stabilize the economy.

Reversal. In December Congress reversed itself on this point, including in a bill (S 2891) extending and expanding the President's economic control powers a provision allowing 5.5 per cent pay raises to go into effect for federal employees in January 1972. *(S 2891, Economy chapter)*

Background. Congress in 1970 passed the Federal Pay Comparability Act (PL 91-656) which transferred responsibility for providing federal employees' salary increases from Congress to the executive branch.

The 1970 law contained a provision allowing either house of Congress to veto a pay plan proposed by the President within 30 days from the date the plan was transmitted to Congress.

Blue Collar Wages

Congress in 1971 failed to complete action on a bill (HR 9092) establishing a revised system for fixing and adjusting the pay rates of federal blue-collar employees.

The House approved the bill July 28, but the Senate did not act on it during 1971. The bill was similar to one (HR 17809) approved by Congress in 1970 and vetoed by President Nixon Jan. 1, 1971. *(1970 action, p. 453)* Final action on a blue-collar pay system came in 1972.

Military Pay

After almost six months of debate which ranged over basic military and foreign policy, Congress Sept. 21, cleared for the President a bill (HR 6531—PL 92-129) extending the draft for two years and raising military pay. *(Details, National Security chapter)*

The over-all compensation package (pay increases, quarters allowances, subsistence allowances) which was adopted by the conference committee totaled less than either the House or Senate versions. The largest item was for basic pay increases for which conferees adopted the House provision, which called for $1.8-billion.

Conferees compromised on the amounts passed by the House for quarters allowances and dependent's allowances, but the conference version was still substantially greater than approved by the Senate. In the allowances sections, the compensation tended to be spread through all levels of the military, not just the low-ranking personnel at which the pay increases were aimed. The House had failed to adopt a provision providing for an enlistment bonus, while the Senate had established a $6,000 enlistment bonus ceiling. Conferees settled on a $3,000 bonus maximum.

1972

Federal Pay

President Nixon Aug. 31 postponed until Jan. 1, 1973, a federal pay raise scheduled to take effect Oct. 1, 1972.

In a message to Congress, Nixon said that pay increases for all workers had been limited to 5.5 per cent a year under existing wage guidelines. Since federal workers had received a 5.5 per cent wage boost Jan. 1, 1972, they were not eligible for another raise that year, he said.

The wage guidelines in question were set forth by the Pay Board, one of the committees proposed by Nixon Aug. 15, 1971, in his anti-inflation program. Nixon's requests were enacted into law as part of the Economic Stabilization Act Amendments of 1971 (PL 92-210). *(Economy chapter)*

The pay raise slated for Oct. 1 was authorized by the Pay Comparability Act of 1970 (PL 91-656). That law authorized the President to adjust pay rates for about 4.5 million federal workers in order to maintain pay scales comparable to those in private industry. The act provided that increases based on Labor Department wage surveys would become effective Oct. 1 of each year unless the President submitted an alternative plan to Congress by Sept. 1.

PL 91-656 did not apply to employees of the U.S. Postal Service or to the approximately 650,000 federal blue-collar workers whose pay rates were computed under a different formula.

Previous Wage Postponement. As part of his August 1971 economic policy announcement, Nixon had ordered that a federal pay increase scheduled for Jan. 1, 1972, under PL 91-656 be deferred for six months until July 1, 1972.

But in the Economic Stabilization Act Amendments of 1971, Congress directed that the 5.5 per cent pay adjustment permitted under the wage-price guidelines be made effective as scheduled on Jan. 1, 1972. *(Stabilization act, p. 105)*

House Employees' Pay

The House Jan. 27 by voice vote adopted a resolution (H Res 741) providing pay adjustments for certain House employees whose pay rates were fixed by the House.

The purpose of the bill was to provide comparable pay increases for House employees who were neither employees of members of Congress nor of the federal government.

In the Economic Stabilization Act Amendments of 1971 (PL 92-210), Congress directed that pay adjustments within the wage-price guidelines set forth by the government's Pay Board—5.5 per cent—be made effective for federal employees Jan. 1, 1972.

H Res 741 provided a 5.5 per cent pay raise for 33 House employees, excluding the official recorders of House floor and committee debates.

Annual cost of the raises was estimated at $23,587. The bill provided that the House contingency fund would be made available for this purpose.

Blue Collar Wages

Congress Aug. 15 cleared for the President a bill (HR 9092—PL 92-392) establishing a revised system for fixing and adjusting the pay rates of federal blue-collar employees.

The bill modified existing Civil Service Commission guidelines for determining the wages of certain federal workers and established them as law.

The measure was similar to legislation vetoed Jan. 1, 1971, by President Nixon, who then had stated that its "costly and unwarranted pay features" would force the federal government to cut back its payrolls and would trigger inflationary wage pressures on private industry. But electon-year pressures influenced the President to sign HR 9092.

HR 9092 created a fourth and fifth step in the federal blue-collar career ladder—to be paid at 108 per cent and 112 per cent of the prevailing wage rate of the surrounding industrial area. The two additional wage steps would add an estimated $181-million annually to the federal payroll, according to the Senate Post Office and Civil Service Committee report.

Under the existing system, each grade had three steps, the first paid at 96 per cent of the average private industry wage for that particular skill in the geographic area, the second at 100 per cent and the third at 104 per cent.

HR 9092 was passed by the Senate June 15 and by the House on July 28, 1971. Differences between the two versions were minor and were easily resolved by House and Senate conferees.

Background. The approximately 650,000 blue-collar workers employed by the federal government in early 1972 included carpenters, truck drivers, electricians, plumbers and aircraft mechanics. Known also as wage board or prevailing rate employees, these workers represented about one-fourth of the total federal payroll, excluding military personnel. Nearly 80 per cent of such blue-collar workers were employed by the Department of Defense.

A coordinated wage system was set up by the Civil Service Commission in 1968 as a result of an executive order issued by President Johnson. Designed to ensure equal pay for substantially equal work, the system established pay rates based on a survey of private industry wages in the labor market within a 50-mile radius of a government facility. Before the regulations were issued, agencies employing blue collar workers had different—and often conflicting—methods of establishing pay rates.

Provisions. As cleared, HR 9092:

• Provided a system of equal pay for substantially equal work for all blue-collar employees working under similar conditions in all government agencies within the same geographic area, keyed to the prevailing rate paid for similar work by local private industries.

• Defined a prevailing rate employee as an individual employed in a federal agency in a recognized trade or craft or in an unskilled, semi-skilled or skilled manual labor occupation or any individual, including foremen and supervisors, in a position having trade, craft or labor experience and knowledge as the chief requirement.

• Included employees of nonappropriated fund (PX system) activities of the armed services and employees of the Veterans Administration Canteen Service in the pay system.

• Established a Federal Prevailing Rate Advisor Committee—composed of a chairman appointed by the chairman of the Civil Service Commission, four representatives from executive branch agencies having the largest number of prevailing rate employees, a Civil Service Commission employee and five representatives from the employee organizations with the largest number of prevailing rate employees—to study the prevailing rate system and advise the Civil Service Commission.

• Required the Civil Service Commission to schedule wage surveys every two years, with follow-up surveys each two years thereafter, and authorized the commission to analyze data and develop wage schedules based on wages paid for comparable work in the private sector.

• Provided that where there were insufficient comparable private industry employees in a geographic area, wage levels in the nearest similar area could be considered for determining pay rates.

• Provided that each grade of a wage schedule would have five steps, the first at 96 per cent of the average private industry wage for that particular skill in that geographic area, the second at 100 per cent, the third at 104 per cent, the fourth at 108 per cent and the fifth at 112 per cent. (Existing law provided a three-step system with the third step at 104 per cent.)

• Provided that an employee would advance automatically to the next pay step within the grade after 26 weeks of service in step one, 78 weeks in step two and 104 weeks in steps three and four—but stipulated that advancement from step three to step four be deferred until the eonomic controls imposed by the President Aug. 15, 1971, were lifted or until April 30, 1973, whichever was earlier.

• Provided a 7 1/2 per cent pay differential, nationwide, for scheduled non-overtime work during the second shift (3 p.m. until midnight) and 10 per cent for the third shift (11 p.m. until 8 a.m.).

Federal Health Insurance

House and Senate conferees failed in 1972 to reach agreement on a bill (HR 12202) which would have raised the federal contribution to U.S. government employees' health insurance premiums. They remained deadlocked at the end of the session over whether to include the approximately 600,000 employees of the U.S. Postal Service.

The House bill would have gradually increased federal payments to 75 per cent (from 40 per cent) by 1976 for all civil service workers, including postal employees. The Senate bill would have reduced the proposed increase to 50 per cent and excluded postal workers from coverage.

Background. The federal government began contributing to the costs of its employees' health insurance program in 1960 (PL 86-724). The act set a fixed dollar limit on the government payment, which equalled 38 per cent of the existing cost.

The dollar limit was raised in 1966 but eliminated in 1970 (PL 91-418) when escalating health costs had reduced the federal payment of insurance premiums to 24 per cent of cost. PL 91-418 changed the government contribution to 40 per cent of the average cost of health insurance programs covering federal employees and their dependents.

The existing federal health program covered more than 8 million persons—including over 2.5 million employees, their dependents and many members of Congress.

Congressional Action. The House passed HR 12202 April 27, by a 238-110 roll-call vote. A floor amendment extending the increased benefits to postal employees was adopted on a 197-148 recorded teller vote, despite a warning by Postmaster General Elmer T. Klassen that the additional cost involved would require an increase in mail rates.

The Senate passed its version of HR 12202 by voice vote June 23. In an effort to avoid a threatened presidential veto, the Senate Post Office and Civil Service Committee had trimmed the increase in the federal contribution for health insurance premiums to 50 per cent and had excluded employees of the U.S. Postal Service from coverage under the bill.

Widows of Supreme Court Justices

Congress Aug. 9 cleared a bill (S 2854—PL 92-397) raising annuities for widows of Supreme Court justices to $10,000 annually from $5,000 annually and creating a contributory annuity system for serving and future justices. The Senate originally passed S 2854 on June 30. The House passed the bill June 7 after substituting the language of a similar bill (HR 12101), which it had approved on a 281-97 roll-call vote. The Senate accepted the House version Aug. 9, completing congressional action.

District of Columbia and

Island Dependencies

Visitors to the nation's capital at the end of 1972 were struck by the sight of heavy wooden planking on many of the District of Columbia's main streets. The planking covered construction of a subway system which was begun only after a long congressional struggle to approve construction funds was resolved in 1971.

During the first four years of Nixon's presidency, other changes not so readily apparent to the visitor's eye also occurred. For the first time since 1871-75, District residents were granted the right to elect a nonvoting delegate to the U.S. House of Representatives in 1971. And for the first time in its history, the city was granted the right to conduct presidential preference primaries. But the goal of many residents—self-government—was not attained.

Home Rule Background

It is not generally known that the District of Columbia enjoyed self-government for a good part of the 19th century. In 1802, Congress set up a city government consisting of a mayor and a 12-member, two-chamber council elected by the people. Two changes were made in the early years of the century in the direction of fuller self-government. In 1812, Congress authorized the popularly elected council to elect the mayor. Then, in 1820, Congress allowed the city's residents themselves to elect the mayor.

However, in 1871, Congress established a territorial form of government for the city and permitted its residents to elect only one chamber of the territorial assembly. Three years later, in 1874, Congress revoked even that partial self-government and temporarily placed the city under a three-member, appointed board of commissioners; in 1878, Congress made the commission permanent.

Thus, for nearly 100 years, Congress enacted for the District of Columbia laws usually enacted by a municipal government. The federal government also supplemented the District budget with annual payments to compensate the city for revenue lost due to the vast amounts of tax-free federally owned property in the city.

And for almost as many years, residents of the city sought the return of some measure of local control over city affairs—home rule, as it is commonly called.

Home rule advocates insisted that it was ridiculous for the national legislature to concern itself with such municipal minutiae as whether or not to raise dog-license fees from $3 to $5. Others objected that more important local problems suffered neglect because Congress could not spare enough time from national affairs to perform adequately the duties of a city council.

Defenders of the existing order pointed out that Washington had escaped the municipal corruption common in other big cities. In addition, they said, the constitutional precedents were not clear-cut and the role of the city as the national capital and the great variety of federal activities carried on in the city gave Congress a substantial interest in the conduct of its affairs. Home rule opponents also suggested that Congress might refuse to approve a federal contribution to the city if it did not exercise full control over District affairs.

The basic issue for decades, however, was racial. Southern members of Congress and many white Washingtonians and suburbanites were afraid that the black majority would win control of a local government. The 1970 census report showed that the District with a population of 756,510 was slightly more than 71 percent black.

House Objections. Despite the coequal status of the two chambers of Congress, the House during the period 1949-65 tended to outweigh the Senate in matters affecting the District. And the House traditionally proved itself to be more conservative than the Senate concerning D.C. affairs. With some notable exceptions—such as the nonvoting delegate bill—eight southern members had dominated the activities of the House District of Columbia Committee.

Six times between 1949 and 1965, the Senate passed home rule proposals. The first five died in the House District Committee. The sixth bill in 1965 was successfully discharged from the committee after it made no move to consider the legislation. But the final House version was so weakened from the Senate version that no compromise could be reached between the two chambers.

1967 Reorganization Plan. Frustrated by congressional failure to pass home rule legislation, President Johnson in 1967 used authority given him under the Reorganization Act to revamp the city government.

References

Discussion of legislation on the District of Columbia and Island Dependencies for the years 1945-64 may be found in *Congress and the Nation*, Vol. I, p. 1497-1516; for the years 1965-68, *Congress and the Nation*, Vol. II, p. 955-965. For additional background, *Guide to the U.S. Congress*, p. 353-365.

(A reorganization plan cannot be amended by Congress and can be rejected only if the House or Senate adopts a resolution disapproving the plan within 60 days after it is submitted.)

Between 1874 and 1967, the District's local government had consisted of three commissioners. Two, appointed by the President, were civilians and residents of the city. The third commissioner, nominally appointed by the President, was actually assigned by the Chief of Army Engineers. Either a brigadier general of engineers or a colonel, the commissioner was not required to live in the city. In 1952, a nine-member Citizen's Advisory Council was established by the commissioners as a guide to local opinions.

Under Johnson's Reorganization Plan No. 3, the three commissioners were replaced by a single commissioner who was afterward called "Mayor," a deputy commissioner and a nine-member city council. The new officials also were appointed by the President but the added number made the government more representative of a greater part of the city. Johnson subsequently named a black –Walter E. Washington—as the new "Mayor" and appointed five blacks—a majority—to the city council.

Home Rule, 1969-1972

Full self-government for the District of Columbia continued to be blocked during President Nixon's first term. The House District Committee relented somewhat in 1970 when it reported out a bill calling for the election of three members of the nine-member city council; however, the full House took no further action.

In 1971, the Senate again passed a home rule bill expanding the size of the city council and providing for election of the council and the mayor. However, in 1972, home rule supporters on the House District Committee failed repeatedly to obtain a quorum to consider any of the home rule proposals before it, including the Senate-approved measure which died at the end of the 92nd Congress.

Self-government proponents were buoyed somewhat by the defeat of John L. McMillan (D S.C.), chairman of the House District Committee since 1945 (with the exceptions of the Republican-controlled 80th and 83rd Congresses). McMillan, who was defeated in his state's 1972 Democratic runoff election, had consistently used the power of his post to block home rule legislation.

The man who succeeded McMillan to the chairmanship at the beginning of the 93rd Congress was Charles C. Diggs Jr. (D Mich.)—a black and a home-rule proponent. As 1972 drew to a close, Diggs announced that he wanted further study of the self-government issue, saying that he was looking for new solutions to old problems.

President Nixon, while supporting self-government in concept, said through aides in 1972 that he was awaiting completion of a study commission report before submitting a home rule proposal to Congress. The commission report, completed in late summer of 1972, did not touch upon the issue of home rule but centered on reform of the existing governmental structure. Nixon had not submitted a self-government proposal by the end of the 92nd Congress.

Delegate, Primaries

Although home rule was stymied, Congress did take action on two other closely-related fronts.

As a result of congressional action in 1970, the first nonvoting delegate from the city since 1875—Walter E. Fauntroy (D), a black—was elected to the U.S. House of Representatives March 23, 1971. Congress cleared the nonvoting delegate legislation in 1970 after the bill's supporters overrode attempts by House District Committee members to kill the measure. The Senate had passed the bill in 1969.

And, in 1971, Congress granted authority to the District to conduct presidential primaries. District residents had been permitted to vote for President and Vice President only since 1961 when the Twenty-third Amendment to the Constitution was ratified.

In 1972, the House Judiciary Committee proposed a constitutional amendment giving the district voting representation in both the House and the Senate but no further action was taken.

Congress cleared legislation in 1972 authorizing one nonvoting delegate each to the House from Guam and the Virgin Islands.

Crime, Subway Funds

Congress also dealt with two other controversial issues affecting the District which did not, at least directly, bear on the home rule issue. In 1970 Congress approved a D.C. crime bill which was proposed by the administration as a "model anticrime package" and attacked by its critics as unconstitutional. *(Crime Legislation p. 255)*

The other controversy concerned construction of a subway for the District metropolitan area. The city and its neighboring suburbs in Virginia and Maryland had backed a rail rapid transit system since the 1950s and the federal government had begun the initial planning.

However, beginning in the mid-1960s, Rep. William H. Natcher (D Ky.), chairman of the House Appropriations Subcommittee on the District of Columbia, repeatedly refused to recommend appropriations for subway construction of all city freeways proposed under the federally assisted Interstate Highway System.

When city officials voted to begin construction of a sixth bridge crossing the Potomac River between Virginia and the District, Congress in 1969 authorized almost $1.15-billion in federal funds and $216.5-million in District funds to begin construction of the subway.

In 1970, however, freeway opponents filed several court suits challenging freeway construction and in August 1970 a U.S. district court issued an injunction against continued construction of the bridge.

Subsequently, the House District Appropriations Subcommittee on the District of Columbia, repeatedly refused to recommend appropriations for subway construction until the District agreed to complete construction of all city freeways proposed under the federally-assisted Interstate Highway System.

(Continued on p. 462)

Constitution Silent on Home Rule and D.C. Representation

Constitutional issues and historical precedents had been used by both backers and opponents of home rule and congressional representation for the District of Columbia.

Article I, Section 8 of the Constitution reads, in part:

"The Congress shall have Power...To exercise exclusive Legislation in all cases whatsoever, over such District (not exceeding ten miles square), as may, by cession of particular states, and the acceptance of Congress, become the seat of Government of the United States...."

Madison's Views

Notwithstanding the comprehensiveness of this grant of power to Congress, self-government in local affairs was not precluded; rather, it seems to have been taken as a matter of course. James Madison indicated in No. 43 of *The Federalist Papers* what was in the minds of the drafters of the Constitution:

"The indispensable necessity of complete authority at the seat of Government carries its own evidence with it.... Without it not only the public authority might be insulted and its proceedings interrupted with impunity, but a dependence of the members of the general government on the state comprehending the seat of the Government for protection in the exercise of their duty might bring on the national councils an imputation of awe or influence...dishonorable to the Government..." Later in the essay Madison wrote: "A municipal legislature for local purposes, derived from their own suffrages, will of course be allowed them...."

Home rule advocates felt that the founding fathers wanted congressional control only to avoid conflicts between local and federal interests, and that where no conflict existed District citizens could control their own government.

The Constitution does not mention the District of Columbia (or the seat of the Federal Government) with respect to congressional representation. Article I, Section 2 reads: "The House of Representatives shall be composed of Members chosen every second year by the people of the several states." Article I, Section 3 reads: "The Senate of the United States shall be composed of two Senators from each State...."

To answer this, advocates of D.C. congressional representation cited another section of Federalist No. 43: "...the inhabitants (of the state areas to be ceded to the Federal government) will find sufficient inducements of interest to become willing parties to the cession; as they have had their voice in the election of the government which is to exercise authority over them...." This passage seems to refer to the time before cession.

Because the Constitution mentions only representatives and senators from the "states," a constitutional amendment was required to provide full voting representation for the District of Columbia in Congress. Nonvoting delegates from territories have sat in the House; only regular legislation was required to give the District a nonvoting delegate. Concerning home rule, the Constitution gives Congress the power to exercise "exclusive legislation" over the District. This power, however, could be delegated to local governments by legislation.

The actual 10-mile square site for the District of Columbia was chosen by President Washington. It consisted of land ceded by Maryland and Virginia on both banks of the Potomac River. The City of Washington, a much smaller area than the original District, was chartered in 1802. The charter provided for an elected council of two chambers and a mayor, who was first appointed by the President, later elected by the council, and, after 1820, elected by popular vote. Other areas of the District, Alexandria and Georgetown, also practiced local self-government.

Conflicts on racial and other issues between District residents and Congress erupted well before the Civil War. In 1846, both Georgetown and Alexandria, unable to obtain money from Congress for improvements, tried to return to their respective states, Maryland and Virginia. The Maryland legislature was unwilling, but Congress, the state of Virginia, and the citizens of Alexandria agreed that Alexandria should be returned to Virginia. The District was left with its present area, some 69.2 square miles on the Maryland side of the Potomac.

Washington was early a center for freed slaves, and, with the grant of universal suffrage in 1867, the Radical Republicans took control of the city. The strain on the city of the Civil War and postwar years led Congress in 1871 to establish a territorial form of government over the entire District.

D.C. Delegate: 1871-75

The new administration included an elected nonvoting delegate to the House of Representatives—Norton P. Chipman, a Republican—as well as an appointed governor, a territorial assembly, with one elected and one appointed chamber and a new board of public works. Gross financial mismanagement by Alexander Shepherd, board member and later the District governor, in his effort to modernize the District, led Congress to place the District temporarily under three commissioners appointed by the President with an Army engineer in charge of public works. The territorial assembly and the post of nonvoting delegate to the House were abolished. Chipman's term expired in 1875.

Although it was clear that permanent suppression of representative government was not intended, the changes then made were incorporated in the act of June 11, 1878, which established the government of the District of Columbia essentially as it remained until 1967.

The fact that independent local governments functioned in the District from 1802 until 1871 was cited as proof that local self-government in the District could work and not be contrary to the Constitution. The short-lived office of nonvoting delegate was cited as a precedent.

Chronology of
District of Columbia, Island
Legislation
1969

D.C. Subway

After nearly two decades of discussion and frustration, Congress passed legislation to provide a rail rapid transit system—Metro—for the District of Columbia and its Maryland and Virginia suburbs.

The bill (S 2185—PL 91-143) authorized appropriations of $1,147,044,000 in federal funds to build Metro and $216,500,000 out of the District's general funds to finance the city's local contribution toward construction of the system. The money was to remain available for the duration of construction. Metro was expected to be totally completed in 1990; however, sections of the system were scheduled to be operational by 1975.

Background. The District and its neighboring jurisdictions in Maryland and Virginia had backed a rapid rail transit system for nearly two decades. In 1960, Congress enacted legislation to create an interstate agency to oversee the system; in 1965 it passed another measure approving a basic 25-mile system and authorizing $100-million in federal and $50-million in District funds to begin construction.

However, a controversy involving construction of freeways arose in 1966, when the House initially denied all funds for the transit system in the D.C. appropriations bill on the ground that federal aid highway construction in and around the District had fallen behind and should be continued concurrently with construction of the subway. Although subway funds were added to the appropriations bill in conference, construction was stalled by continuing failure on the part of the Congress, the federal government and the local jurisdictions to settle the freeway dispute.

Then in 1968 Congress put strong pressure on the District to complete its freeway system by adding a provision to the Federal Aid Highway Act (PL 90-495) requiring that the District complete construction of all routes on the Interstate System within the District of Columbia. *(Congress and the Nation Vol. II p. 245, 962)*

Construction of interstate routes in the District was fought for by Rep. William H. Natcher (D Ky.), chairman of the District of Columbia Subcommittee of the House Appropriations Committee, and Rep. John C. Kluczynski (D Ill.), chairman of the House Public Works Subcommittee on Roads. Natcher threatened to block funds for the Metro system until the interstate projects were "beyond recall." Kluczynski told *The Washington Post* that "the District won't get a dime for a subway until it does what we want it to do to highways."

Four highway projects were at issue but the most controversial was the proposed Three Sisters Bridge

crossing the Potomac river into Virginia's northern suburbs. Five bridges already crossed the river from the District into Virginia. District and suburban citizen groups and many members of the District city council opposed construction of the freeways, arguing that the roads were not needed and that they would destroy not only park lands adjacent to the river but dislocate homes and neighborhoods. Civil rights groups were particularly concerned about potential dislocation of black neighborhoods, saying that blacks would have difficulty in finding new homes in the largely white suburbs.

The impasse was broken in August 1969 when the District city council formally approved construction of the Three Sisters Bridge in order to release subway construction money. In 1970, a court-ordered injunction against continued construction of the bridge led to a second funding stall in Congress. *(1971 chronology p. 464)*

Legislative Action. The Senate by voice vote and without debate July 8 passed S 2185. The bill specified that total federal contributions over 10 years would total the $1.1-billion figure or two-thirds of the net cost of the project, whichever was lower. It also authorized appropriations by the District of $216.5 million; this was accomplished by increasing the city's borrowing authority from the U.S. Treasury.

The House Nov. 24 by a 286-23 roll-call vote passed HR 11193, the National Capital Transportation Act of 1969. Then, by voice vote, the House substituted the language of its bill for the language of S 2185, then passed S 2185, as amended, by voice vote.

The House version of the bill differed from the Senate-passed measure in several minor, technical points. It had been reported by the House District of Columbia Committee on Nov. 20. The only amendment offered on the House floor—to eliminate a $150,000 study of a transit line to Dulles Airport in suburban Virginia—was defeated by a 52-256 roll-call vote.

The House also Nov. 24 approved the D.C. appropriations bill (HR 14916) for fiscal 1970 which provided $40.3-million in city funds for subway construction. On Nov. 18, the House had passed the Transportation Department appropriations bill (HR 14794) which contained nearly $43.2-million in federal funds for the subway system.

The Senate Dec. 2 by voice vote and without debate agreed to the version of S 2185 as amended by the House. Senate action cleared the bill for the President's signature.

D.C. Delegate

The Senate Oct. 1 by voice vote passed and sent to the House a bill (S 2163) providing for an elected but nonvoting delegate to the House of Representatives from the District of Columbia. The same day, the Senate also approved a bill (S 2164) establishing a Commission on Government for the District of Columbia to determine how to improve the city government's structure and how the city could best be given a greater measure of self-government.

The House did not act on either bill in 1969 but legislation (HR 18725) incorporating both bills cleared in 1970.

Background. Washington, D.C. had a nonvoting delegate in the House only once in its history: from 1871 to 1875. Congress abolished the position in 1874. *(Box p. 461)*

The Senate passed bills in 1952, 1953, 1955, 1958, 1959 and 1965; all provided for a nonvoting delegate in the House. But in all six instances, the bills were killed in the House.

Home Rule Study. On April 28, 1969, President Nixon proposed that Congress create a commission to draft a home rule plan for the District. He also recommended approval by Congress and ratification by the states of a constitutional amendment granting the District at least one representative in the House of Representatives. Until ratification of the constitutional amendment, Nixon said, Congress should provide the District with a nonvoting member in the House.

The Senate District Committee amended the President's commission proposal in S 2164 to provide that the commission also act as an investigative Hoover-type panel to study the operations of the city government as well as serving as a home-rule study commission. S 2163 and S 2164 were reported Sept. 25 by the committee and passed Oct. 1 with little debate and no amendment.

1970

D.C. Delegate

A bill giving the District of Columbia a nonvoting delegate in the House of Representatives for the first time since 1875 was cleared for the President's signature Sept. 9 when the Senate passed the measure by voice vote.

Final Senate action on the bill (HR 18725—PL 91-405) came after Edward M. Kennedy (D Mass.), the Senate Democratic Whip, met with top city officials and agreed to release his "hold" on the bill.

HR 18725 established an office of D.C. delegate to the House with all privileges except that of voting on the floor (he could vote in committee) and amended city election laws to provide for primary and general elections for the post. The bill also established a commission to study the organization of the city government.

Another D.C. delegate bill (HR 18619) passed by the House Aug. 10 in conjunction with HR 18725, which would give the city nonvoting delegates in both the House and the Senate, was not considered by the Senate Sept. 9.

House Action. The House District Committee Aug. 7 reported two bills: HR 18619 (H Rept 91-1384), giving the District of Columbia nonvoting delegates in the House and Senate; and HR 18725 (H Rept 91-1385), giving the District a nonvoting delegate in the House and establishing a commission to study the city's government.

Although the committee reported the two bills, Chairman John L. McMillan (D S.C.) made his disapproval of HR 17825 clear in the report.

The House Aug. 10 on roll-call votes of 338-23 (HR 18619) and 301-56 (HR 18725) passed the two bills giving the District of Columbia nonvoting representation in Congress.

D.C. Appropriations, Federal Payment

One stumbling block to achieving home rule for the District of Columbia is how the city government would raise enough revenue to finance city services, education and other public services. More than 40 percent of the District's land is owned by the federal government and is non-taxable. In addition, the seat of government attracts other tax-exempt property owners, such as foreign embassies and headquarters of patriotic organizations.

Congress sets a federal payment to the city to compensate for non-taxable, government-owned property. The Congress then appropriates funds, that is, tells the District how it may spend the money the city raises from local taxes and that it obtains from the federal payment.

Since the mid 1920's, Congress appropriated a specific amount for the federal payment each year. However, President Johnson in 1965 proposed a permanent annual federal payment to the District equal to the real estate, personal property and business income taxes which the federal government would pay if it were a taxable entity.

Taking a somewhat different tack, President Nixon in 1969 proposed that the federal payment to the city be established at a fixed percentage of the city's local taxes and other general revenue. Neither the Johnson nor the Nixon proposal was approved by Congress.

The Appropriations Committees in both the House and Senate and their District of Columbia Subcommittees wield a great deal of power over District spending activities. Members of the subcommittees have expressed concern about rising costs of welfare, community development and recreation in the District and have limited appropriations for such purposes to amounts which have often been criticized as far from adequate. Nonetheless, congressional appropriations for the District have been rising:

Fiscal Year	Appropriations (In millions)	Federal Payment (In millions)
1965	353.8	37.5
1966	369.1	44.3
1967	421.8	58.0
1968	518.9	70.0
1969	583.6	89.4
1970	700.4	116.2
1971	707.2	131.0
1972	1,014.2	173.7
1973	834.8*	181.5*

Does not include funds which may be included in Fiscal 1973 second supplemental: Nixon requested a supplemental of $8.5-million in the federal payment in his fiscal 1974 budget message.

SOURCE: District of Columbia Office of Budget and Financial Management.

The double-bill approach was adopted by members of the House District Committee opposed to giving the city a nonvoting delegate. McMillan first scheduled floor action on HR 18619, then supported a move to have the House delegate provision struck from HR 18725 on the grounds that such a post had already been provided in the other bill. The attempt to delete the House delegate from HR 18725 failed by a 31-104 standing vote.

HR 18619, the first bill considered, was sponsored by committee member Earle Cabell (D Texas 1965-73), who like McMillan in fact opposed a nonvoting delegate for the District. McMillan said the Senate had frequently voted to give the District a House delegate, but never a Senate delegate. "The majority of the members of the House District of Columbia Committee thought that if the House must have a delegate, we should also have one in the other body. There the delegate would have more freedom to talk," the chairman said.

Following passage of HR 18619 by a 338-23 roll call, HR 18725, sponsored by Ancher Nelsen (R Minn.), ranking Republican on the House District Committee, was brought before the House. Cabell immediately offered an amendment to delete from the bill the section on a nonvoting House delegate. Passage of both bills would "only add confusion," since the House had already voted to provide nonvoting delegates to both chambers, he said.

Committee member Brock Adams (D Wash.) responded that supporters of the amendment were trying to "trap and trick the House" into passing only a delegate bill the Senate would not accept. Gilbert Gude (R Md.), another committee member, called the Cabell amendment "some sophistry." The amendment failed on a 31-104 standing vote. HR 18725 was then adopted by a 301-57 roll-call vote.

Kennedy Tactics. Shortly after the House passed HR 18725 Aug. 10, Kennedy (D Mass.) requested that Senate action be held up until after the chamber considered his proposal to give the District voting representation in both the House and Senate. He maintained that passage of the nonvoting delegate bill would interfere with efforts toward real congressional representation—which would require an amendment to the Constitution.

In a subsequent meeting with city officials, Kennedy agreed to release his hold on the bill, saying the delay had "highlighted that the nonvoting delegate is important but only as an interim measure."

Senate Action. The Senate District of Columbia Committee reported HR 18725 Aug. 13. The committee made no changes from the House version. The Senate passed HR 18725 Sept. 9 by voice vote and with little debate but did not consider HR 18619.

The only objection to HR 18725 was voiced by James B. Allen (D Ala.) who called the measure "an entering wedge toward providing two U.S. senators and one or two U.S. representatives" for the District.

Home Rule

The House District Committee Oct. 12 reported a bill (HR 18782) providing for popular election of three of the members of the District city council. No further action was taken and the bill died at the end of the 91st Congress.

HR 18782 provided that the mayor and two other members of the nine-member council would be elected to three-year terms. Two council members would be appointed by the President and confirmed by the Senate. The chairmen of the House and Senate District Committees each would appoint members. The chairmen of the House and Senate Interior and Insular Affairs Committees jointly would appoint a council member, and the chairmen of the House and Senate Public Works Committees jointly would appoint one.

The new council would appoint a city administrator to manage the city's government. The duties of the present mayor and nine-member council—appointed by the President and confirmed by the Senate—would be assumed by the council.

1971

D.C. Metro Funds

A two-year impasse over funding construction of highways in the District was broken Dec. 15, when the House cleared a bill (HR 11932 — PL 92-202) appropriating $72.5-million for the city's share of the regional rapid transit system (Metro). The appropriation was contained in the fiscal 1972 District appropriation bill.

Highway-Subway Controversy. Having been assured by the District government that construction of the Three Sisters Bridge across the Potomac River would be begun, Congress in 1969 enacted a bill authorizing $1,147,044,000 in federal funds and $216,500,000 in city funds for construction of a Washington metropolitan area subway system. *(See 1969 chronology, p. 462)*

In 1970, however, opponents of the Three Sisters Bridge project filed several court suits and in August 1970, a U.S. district court issued an injunction against further construction.

In Congress, the scheduled fiscal 1971 payment to Metro of $34.2-million was rejected three times in 1970—in the regular D.C. appropriations bill and in the first and second fiscal 1971 supplemental appropriations bills.

William H. Natcher (D Ky.), chairman of the D.C. Appropriations Subcommittee, opposed release of any rapid transit funds until all highway projects were under construction. The full Appropriations Committee and the House consistently went along with Natcher's subcommittee, and the Senate always yielded to the House position in conference.

In May 1971, the first record vote was held in the House on funding the rapid transit system—made possible by a provision of the 1970 Legislative Reorganization Act providing for the recording of members by name on teller votes during the amending stages of House debate. An amendment to the second supplemental appropriations bill (HR 8190—PL 92-18), to restore the $34.2-million to the bill, failed by a 170-219 recorded teller vote.

The Senate approved the $34.2-million fiscal 1971 payment May 19, but conferees dropped it. The conference report said that both the $34,178,000 fiscal 1971 and the $34,308,000 fiscal 1972 payments would be appropriated in the regular fiscal 1972 D.C. appropriation bill The report cited a promise by Transportation Secretary John A. Volpe that the laws requiring construction of the highways would be complied with. Natcher said during floor debate on the conference report that if the Department of Transportation and the District government continued making a sincere effort to carry out the highway acts passed by Congress, the Appropriations Committee would have to approve the requested funds for the D.C. share of the rapid transit system.

(Congress had approved the full amount of the federal matching funds for Metro since authorizing legislation was passed in 1969. Only the funds in the D.C. appropriations bill to pay for the city's share, considered by Natcher's subcommittee, had ever been attacked.) *(See 1969 chronology p. 484)*

On Oct. 12, 1971, five months after Natcher made his promise to release the funds, a three-judge panel of the U.S. Court of Appeals voted 2-1 to continue the district court injunction until the Transportation Department completed a review of the Three Sisters Bridge project.

On Nov. 18, President Nixon asked the Justice Department to seek a rehearing before all nine judges of the Court of Appeals and, if that failed, to seek review by the Supreme Court.

While the House was debating the D.C. appropriations bill, the Court of Appeals decided, 4-3, not to rehear the case.

House Action. The House Appropriations Committee reported HR 11932 Nov. 29 after agreeing to delete the D. C. payment to Metro by a 31-13 roll-call vote, saying, "The impasse on freeway construction continues. Until it is resolved, no funds will be recommended" for the D.C. share of construction costs on the rail system.

The two-year impasse was broken Dec. 2 when the House, by a 195-174 roll-call vote, agreed to appropriate $72.5-million as the city's payment to the subway authority. The House subsequently passed HR 11932 by voice vote. The appropriation covered funds that would have been provided for fiscal 1971 as well as fiscal 1972.

The vote releasing the funds was a major legislative victory for President Nixon, who had put White House aides to work lobbying for the measure. It was a defeat for House Speaker Carl Albert (D Okla.) and Minority Leader Gerald R. Ford (R Mich.), both of whom asked House members not to overturn the Appropriations Committee's decision to withhold funds. Appropriations Committee Chairman George Mahon (D Texas) asked members not to "kick" his committee "in the teeth" or "topple" the leaders of the House.

The key vote on the controversial issue came earlier in the debate when an amendment to restore the Metro funds, introduced by Robert N. Giaimo (D Conn.), was tentatively adopted by a 196-183 recorded teller vote. Before passing the bill by voice vote, the House affirmed its earlier action by approving the amendment for a second time, 195 to 174.

Offering the amendment to reinstate the Metro funds for the second time in 1971, Giaimo said the city was in compliance with the highway laws requiring construction of roads and that court action—not refusal to comply by the city—was holding up the bridge project.

Minority Leader Ford said Congress should not release the funds until the Court of Appeals set a date for

Nonvoting Delegates

Democrat Walter E. Fauntroy, a black Baptist minister, easily defeated his major opponent March 23, 1971, to become the first nonvoting delegate in the House of Representatives from the District of Columbia since 1875.

Fauntroy defeated Republican John A. Nevius, a white city councilman and four other contenders, garnering 58.5 percent of the total vote. In November 1972, Fauntroy was elected to his first full term, receiving 62 percent of the vote.

As might be expected, Fauntroy was assigned to the House District of Columbia Committee. He was permitted to participate in committee votes but he could not vote on the House floor. Fauntroy concerned himself with District matters, particularly self-government and voting representation in Congress. Other major legislation introduced by Fauntroy included measures providing federal funds for treatment and prevention of sickle cell anemia, and a bill facilitating housing construction in the District of Columbia.

The first nonvoting delegates to the House from the Virgin Islands and Guam were elected Nov. 7, 1972. They were Ronald deLugo (D V.I.) and Antonio Won-Pat (D Guam).

a rehearing to review the injunction. Mahon said the dispute "is a question of the prestige and position of Congress, a question of orderly procedure, and a question of right or wrong, as I see it."

As the debate was drawing to an end, Silvio O. Conte (R Mass.) interrupted a member to announce that the Court of Appeals had voted 4-3 not to hold another hearing: "The Court of Appeals has just refused to review the petition, and therefore all these agreements that have been propounded here are *fait accompli.* The only appeal now is an appeal to the Supreme Court of the United States."

Natcher said: "I think there is no question at all but what this case must go to the Supreme Court. But the funds, $72-million, should now be refused until the law is enforced."

The Giaimo amendment was adopted on a 196-183 recorded teller vote. A majority of Republicans, 74-92, voted against their President's position favoring release of the funds. Northern Democrats approved the amendment by 113-35, while southern Democrats opposed it by 9-56.

In the vote May 11 on a similar Giaimo amendment, Republicans had voted against Metro funding by a much wider margin, 48-117; the margin among Democrats was about the same: northern Democrats, 114-36; southern Democrats, 8-66. The total number of Democrats voting for the amendment was the same on both votes—122.

Albert and Ford voted against release of the funds, while Majority Leader Hale Boggs (D La.) and Majority Whip Thomas P. O'Neill Jr. (D Mass.) supported it, as did Republican Conference Chairman John B. Anderson (R Ill.).

A majority of the chairmen and ranking minority members of the 23 legislative committees voted against the amendment, 16-22, with eight not voting.

Later, Natcher requested a roll-call vote on the amendment before final passage. It carried again, 195-174, with two members voting present. On that vote Republicans split 71-89, Democrats 124-85: northern Democrats 114-32, southern Democrats 10-53.

Senate, Final Action. The Senate passed HR 11932 Dec. 3 by an 85-0 roll-call vote. While the Senate amended some other aspects of the appropriations bill, there were no amendments offered and little debate on the subway funding.

House and Senate conferees filed their report Dec. 15. The same day, the House agreed to the conference report by a 260-79 roll-call vote and the Senate agreed to it by voice vote.

D.C. Presidential Primary

Congress Dec. 15 cleared a bill (S 2878—PL 92-220) establishing a presidential preference primary in the District of Columbia. District residents had been allowed to vote for President and Vice President only since 1961 when the Twenty-third Amendment to the Constitution was ratified.

S 2878 established a preference primary in May of each presidential election year to give voters an opportunity to choose presidential electors pledged to a particular candidate. It provided for election of delegates to party nominating conventions either pledged to particular candidates or listed on the ballots as uncommitted.

The bill also set D.C. residence requirements for voting at 30 days for presidential elections and 90 days for all other elections. It lowered the voting age to 18, to bring the District into compliance with the Twenty-sixth Amendment to the Constitution, ratified earlier in 1971.

S 2878 included the District of Columbia in the definition of a "state" under the Corrupt Practices Act of 1925, which required election campaign committees operating in two or more states to file periodic reports on campaign contributions and spending. That provision closed a loophole by which campaign committees for candidates in various states were established within the District. Such committees were exempt from national financial disclosure requirements since technically they did not operate in two or more states. The Corrupt Practices Act was repealed in 1972 and replaced by the Federal Election Campaign Act which also included the District within the definition of a state. *(Chapter on Campaign Finance p. 397)*

Legislative Action. The Senate passed S 2878 Nov. 20 by voice vote and without debate. A related bill (HR 11992) was passed by the House Dec. 13 by voice vote. The House then substituted the language of HR 11992 for that of S 2878 and passed the amended version of the Senate bill. The Senate Dec. 14 amended the House version of S 2878 and the following day both chambers agreed on the final version.

D.C. Home Rule

The Senate in 1971 approved a bill (S 2652) allowing the District of Columbia to elect its mayor and city council. S 2652 was the seventh Senate-passed home rule bill since 1949. The House did not act on the bill in 1971-72, and the bill died at the end of the 92nd Congress.

As passed by the Senate, S 2652 provided for partisan election of a mayor and an 11-member city council to serve for four-year terms. The bill empowered the council to legislate for the city but prohibited it from taxing federal property or incomes of non-residents who worked in the District. Either the House or the Senate could veto any action by the council within 30 days.

The bill required a referendum to be held within four months of enactment of the bill for voters to approve the charter establishing the elected mayor-council form of government. The new government would go into effect immediately if approved by a majority of the voters.

Senate Action. The Senate District Committee reported S 2652 Oct. 6 saying that the bill "would restore to the citizens of the District of Columbia some measure of self-government."

The Senate passed S 2652 without amendment Oct. 12 by a 64-8 roll-call vote. Six southern Democrats and two southern Republicans opposed the bill.

District Committee Chairman Thomas F. Eagleton (D Mo.) told the Senate that "the list of trivia involving the District of Columbia that this body is forced to consider is virtually endless.... Congress should delegate the making of these local regulations to a body elected by the citizens of the District of Columbia, with the continuing right to supervise such body to ensure that the federal interest in this, our nation's capital, is never violated."

Sam J. Ervin Jr. (D N.C.), who opposed the bill on legal grounds, said that the Constitution gave Congress exclusive legislative power over the District. "With some reluctance, I am compelled to vote against this bill. I would support it gladly if it were in the form of a constitutional amendment," he said.

1972

Island Delegates

Congress March 28 completed action on a bill (HR 8787—PL 92-271) providing for election of nonvoting delegates to the House from Guam and the Virgin Islands.

Final action came when the Senate by voice vote passed the bill without amendment. The House Jan. 18 had passed HR 8787 by a 232-104 roll-call vote.

As cleared by Congress, the bill allowed residents of the two U.S. territories to elect in November 1972 delegates to the 93rd Congress which was to convene in January 1973.

The House already had two nonvoting members: Jorge Luis Cordova (New Prog. P.R.), the resident commissioner from the Commonwealth of Puerto Rico, and Walter E. Fauntroy (D D.C.), delegate from Washington, D.C. *(1970 chronology p. 463)*

Guam and the Virgin Islands previously had sent representatives to Washington, D.C., but they had no official status and functioned as lobbyists.

Background. The United States acquired Guam from Spain in the Treaty of Paris after the Spanish-American War of 1898. The United States bought the Virgin Islands from Denmark in 1917.

Under acts passed by Congress, both territories are governed by locally elected legislatures. Congress in 1968 provided for the popular election of a governor and lieutenant governor for each territory. According to preliminary 1970 census figures, Guam had 86,929 residents and the Virgin Islands, 63,200.

Proposals for representation of the two territories had been considered by every Congress since the 84th.

Congress first authorized the election of a nonvoting delegate from a territory in the Northwest Ordinance of 1787, which provided for a delegate from the area northwest of the Ohio River. Excluding the District of Columbia and Puerto Rico, 31 territories had been represented by nonvoting delegates since the founding of the republic. Most of these territories subsequently gained statehood, with the exception of the Philippines which was granted independence in 1946.

House Action. The House Interior and Insular Affairs Committee reported HR 8787 June 10, 1971, by a 26-1 vote. James A. Haley (D Fla.), second-ranking Democrat on the committee, voted against reporting the bill. The House passed HR 8787 Jan. 18, 1972, by a 232-104 roll-call vote.

Debate on HR 8787 centered more on the method of paying the two new territorial delegates than on the need for such representation in the House.

The House by voice vote adopted an amendment by Wayne N. Aspinall (D Colo.), chairman of the Interior and Insular Affairs Committee, reducing the Guam and Virgin Islands delegates' allowances for clerical staff to 60 percent of funds provided elected House members and limiting each delegate's allowance for travel to and from his territory to the cost of four round trips per year.

The House by voice vote had substituted Aspinall's amendment for an amendment by John P. Saylor (R Pa.), ranking Republican on the committee, that would have required Guam and the Virgin Islands to pay the salaries and expenses of their own delegates.

The House by voice vote rejected an amendment by H. R. Gross (R Iowa) to authorize nonvoting delegates from Guam and the Virgin Islands to the Senate as well as the House.

Senate Action. The Senate Interior and Insular Affairs Committee unanimously reported HR 8787 March 23. The bill, as reported, was identical to the House-passed version. The Senate March 28 passed HR 8787 by voice vote without amendment, clearing the bill for the President's signature.

D. C. Representation

The House Judiciary Committee Feb. 29 reported H J Res 253, a constitutional amendment providing voting representation in Congress for the District of Columbia. Senate and House Judiciary Committees have jurisdiction for all proposed constitutional amendments.

The resolution was ordered reported by a 24-13 roll-call vote on Feb. 3. The House took no further action.

The proposed amendment would entitle Washington residents to elect two senators and the number of representatives—probably two—to which the city would be entitled if it were a state.

Background. The Constitution provided for a district outside the boundaries of any state as the seat of federal government and gave Congress the authority to pass

legislation for it. Elsewhere, representation in Congress was granted to the states but not to the district set aside as the capital.

Between 1871 and 1875, the District of Columbia elected a nonvoting delegate in the House. In 1970, Congress cleared legislation allowing the city to elect a nonvoting delegate. The 1970 census measured the city's population at 756,510—larger than that of nine states.

President Nixon in 1969 endorsed a constitutional amendment granting the city one House member, and other House and Senate members if Congress passed a subsequent law.

Committee View. The report on H J Res 253 said "In all fairness, the District's citizens should be accorded the full rights of citizenship and have a vote in the deliberations of their national government as do their fellow citizens who live outside the District."

The committee said that after the amendment was ratified, Congress would be required to enact laws settling such issues as whether the House would be temporarily or permanently enlarged beyond its current 435 members and what to do about the nonvoting delegate.

Minority Views. Nine committee members, in a joint statement, declared that the proposal "does violence to the fundamental structure of our government. It threatens the very federal system itself." They said that the District was entitled to representation in the House but not the Senate since the latter chamber represents states while the former represents people. If District residents want representation in the Senate, the District should either be ceded to another state or become a state, the members said.

Home Rule

The House District Committee held hearings in February on home rule for the District but failed several times subsequently to obtain a quorum to report out a bill.

The Senate had passed a bill (S 2652) in October 1971 which would have established elective positions of mayor and an 11-member city council. In addition to the Senate bill, the House committee considered a range of other bills, including a proposal to establish a partly elected city council and one to cede most of the District to Maryland.

At the beginning of the Feb. 8 hearing, District of Committee Chairman John L. McMillan (D S.C.) scheduled Rep. John R. Rarick (D La.), who was not a member of the committee and was known for his extreme views on racial questions, to testify first, despite the fact that two committee members wished to testify. It is customary to permit committee members to testify before other members of Congress.

In his remarks, Rarick backed a plan to cede most of the city to Maryland, which donated land for the city to the federal government in 1788. Rarick said that the present city government had made the city a "sinkhole, ...the laughing stock of the free and communist world." Rarick said the best solution would be to "remove all the people from the...District who are not here on government business and resettle them in areas of the country that have sparse population and living room."

Charles C. Diggs Jr. (D Mich.), a committee member and a black, said that Rarick's testimony was "racist" and "demeans the committee and the black community."

McMillan Defeated. McMillan, chairman of the House District of Columbia Committee since 1945 (with the exception of the Republican-controlled 80th and 83rd Congresses) was defeated for renomination in South Carolina's Democratic runoff primary Sept. 12. Home rule proponents both in and out of Congress were momentarily buoyed because Diggs, who had been counted in the pro-home-rule column, was next in line to succeed McMillan.

Diggs Sept. 26 called for a re-examination of the home rule question. Diggs said that the Senate-passed home rule bill would merely pass the city's problems from "one level of government to another.... I'm looking for new ways to solve old problems."

Eisenhower Center

Congress Oct. 14 cleared for the President a bill (S 3943—PL 92-520) amending the Public Buildings Act of 1959 (PL 86-249) to authorize the construction of the Dwight D. Eisenhower Memorial Bicentennial Civic Center in the District of Columbia.

Final action came when the Senate, by voice vote, agreed to a House amendment requiring approval by Senate and House District of Columbia and Appropriations Committees of the center's plans, specifications and cost estimates before construction contracts were awarded. The House passed S 3943 Oct. 3 by a 210-169 recorded teller vote. (On Feb. 24, 1970, the House had rejected by a 136-230 roll-call vote a bill (HR 10937) to study the feasibility of building the center.)

S 3943, as cleared, authorized $14-million with no fiscal year limitations to be spent to meet the center's financial obligations in its first years of operation.

All the funds to acquire the site and construct the center were to be provided by private sources. The city would pay the center's private developer in 30 annual installments to repay the initial outlay and provide a rate of return to private investors. The city would then own the center. No payments would be made until the center was ready for occupancy and the city was drawing revenue from it.

The District of Columbia government, not the federal government, would be the center's financial guarantor. The federal government's outlay for the center was limited to the $14-million authorization. "In no event will there be a recommendation by the committee for additional funds," said the House Public Works Committee report.

The total cost of the center was estimated by the House and Senate Public Works Committees at approximately $65-million, including site acquisition and relocation expenses for residents and businesses. The center was to be completed by July 4, 1976.

John F. Kennedy Center

The Senate by a 62-3 roll-call vote Oct. 6, 1969, agreed to increase the authorization for construction of the John F. Kennedy Center for the Performing Arts by $7.5-million. The bill (HR 11249) also authorized the sale of an additional $5-million in bonds to finance underground parking facilities for the cultural center. The Senate action cleared the bill for the President, who signed it Oct. 17 (PL 91-90).

American Bicentennial

Congress Feb. 15 cleared for the President a bill (S 1857—PL 92-236) increasing the membership on the American Revolution Bicentennial Commission and authorizing $4.3-million for expenses in fiscal 1972. The House Feb. 7 had passed S 1857 by a 328-66 roll-call vote.

The bill increased authorizations for the commission, set up an organizational framework and provided authority necessary to implement programs for the nation's 200th birthday in 1976.

S 1857 authorized $1.9-million for salaries and expenses of the commission and $2.4-million for grants-in-aid to states to assist in the establishment of local bicentennial commissions.

The national commission was established on July 4, 1966 (PL 89-491). The original act directed the commission to spend five years planning and five years developing and implementing programs to honor the nation's bicentennial.

Congress Oct. 11, 1972, cleared for the President a bill (HR 13694—PL 92-538) authorizing $3,356,000 for the Bicentennial Commission for the period July 1, 1972-Feb. 15, 1973. Not more than $1.2-million of the total was earmarked for grants to states and territories to assist in establishment of state bicentennial commissions. The bill also authorized a project grants program funded by the commission for nonprofit groups, including states and localities.

The House had passed the bill Sept. 28 by a 300-19 roll-call vote after adopting an amendment by House Judiciary Committee Chairman Emanuel Celler (D N.Y.) cutting in half the originally proposed $6.7-million authorization for the full fiscal year 1973. The cut followed criticism of the Bicentennial Commission by some members of Congress and the press for political bias and excessive commercialism of some of its planned activities.

Pending consideration of proposals for reorganizing the commission, the 93rd Congress authorized appropriation of an additional $3,359,000 through June 30, 1973.

Lobbies

Economic questions, two nominations to the Supreme Court, the Vietnam War, defense spending and environmental legislation were the most heavily lobbied issues in Congress during the first four years of the Nixon administration.

Business lobbies and labor unions, perennially the most active lobby groups on Capitol Hill, remained the most effective lobbyists. At times, however, their efforts were overshadowed by the noisier but less professional work of anti-war coalitions, environmentalists and "public interest" advocates.

The most spectacular lobbying effort of the four years came in 1971 when 175,000 people surrounded the Capitol to demand an end to the Vietnam War. The effectiveness of such mass efforts in influencing congressional opinion was doubtful, and some members of Congress reacted in anger. It was only after the signing of a cease-fire agreement in 1973 that a congressional majority could be marshaled to limit additional spending for the Indochina war.

Supreme Court Nominations. Two of the most fiercely fought lobbying battles of the period were over President Nixon's nomination of two conservative southerners to the Supreme Court—Clement F. Haynsworth Jr. of South Carolina in 1969 and G. Harrold Carswell of Florida in 1970. Both men were opposed by organized labor and civil rights groups. Senate refusal to confirm either of the men for posts on the high court was a major defeat for the Nixon administration and a victory for the AFL-CIO and the National Association for the Advancement of Colored People (NAACP).

The NAACP went on to fight the Nixon administration in 1972 over legislation which would have outlawed busing of school children to achieve racial integration. By 1972, however, the AFL-CIO had reached an unenthusiastic but workable accommodation with the administration and lobbying clashes between the two were less frequent and more restrained. The AFL-CIO maintained unprecedented neutrality during the 1972 Presidential election, strengthening President Nixon's re-election campaign.

Tax and Trade Legislation. Because of its complexity, the Tax Reform Act of 1969 drew the interest of perhaps more organizations and businesses than any legislation of the four-year period. Its hundreds of provisions affected every business and almost every individual in the country. Later, in 1970, many of the businesses that worked together on the tax bill fought against each other over legislation which would have curbed imports of many items. Some domestic industries and many labor unions favored the legislation; multinational corporations and foreign interests opposed it. The 1970 bill died but the issue of free trade vs. protection of domestic manufacturing continued to draw administration and congressional interest throughout the four years.

Regulation of Businesses. Lobbying battles were joined over a number of bills which sought to place additional regulation over various businesses. These included the Occupational Safety and Health Act, which passed in 1970; no-fault automobile insurance legislation, which was a lobbying issue in 1971 and was killed in the Senate in 1972; unsuccessful efforts to establish a Consumer Protection Agency in 1972, and passage of the Federal Water Pollution Control Act Amendments of 1972.

Welfare reform legislation drew the interest of many lobbyists in the last two years of the period, as provisions of the bill underwent hundreds of changes in the House and Senate—only to emerge with little change in the basic family welfare program.

Following are year-by-year highlights of lobbying activity during the 1969-72 period. (*Lobby registration and spending information p. 477*)

1969

Major pressure groups adjusted their lobby activities in 1969 to a shift in political alignment between the legislature and the executive.

For the first time in eight years a Republican occupied the White House, while reduced Democratic majorities continued to control both houses of Congress. The result was a rearrangement of alliances among lobbyists and executive branch officials and of the points of access through which interest groups influenced the governmental process.

Organized labor, civil rights advocates and anti-poverty activists—groups that worked closely from 1961 through 1968 with Democratic administrations generally sympathetic to their causes—spent much of 1969 battling proposals by Republican President Richard M. Nixon

References

Discussion of lobbying for the years 1945-64 may be found in *Congress and the Nation, Vol. I*, p. 1545-1593; for the years 1965-68, *Congress and the Nation, Vol. II*, p. 925-928 and index under Lobbying and Lobbyists.

Business and pro-military groups, on the other hand, found some Nixon administration policies more to their liking than those of the Kennedy and Johnson administrations.

The major lobby conflicts of the year, in fact, centered on disputes between Democrats in Congress and Republicans in the White House and executive agencies. The three most intensively lobbied issues of 1969—the antiballistic missile system, tax reform and the Haynsworth nomination—also were tests of the President's prestige and influence in Congress. Party affiliations took second place in a number of the year's confrontations to such factors as bipartisan coalitions along conservative and liberal lines.

Some of the most highly contested issues and groups involved included the following:

Tax Reform Act. The Tax Reform Act of 1969 (HR 13270—PL 91-172) attracted the largest number of lobbyists of the year in terms of registration specifically to influence provisions of the bill. *(p. 81)*

Lobbyists registered in 1969 to represent 141 organizations during consideration of the tax measure. Among them were corporations, foundations, labor unions, citizens' groups and private individuals.

Among groups that generally were unsuccessful in their attempts to change provisions of the bill were the real estate industry, which failed to win removal of new restrictions on accelerated depreciation of real estate; foundations and other tax-exempt organizations, which were subjected to tighter regulation; investment firms, which opposed the bill's changes in tax treatment of capital gains; and corporations, which opposed the capital gains provisions, other restrictions and repeal of the 7 per cent investment tax credit.

Organizations which had more success in the tax reform controversy included financial institutions, which persuaded the Senate and the conference committee to soften provisions of the House version of the bill; the mineral industry, including oil companies, which suffered some reductions in depletion allowances but was able to win removal of other House restrictions; state and local governments, which defeated attempts to remove exemptions for interest on state and local government bonds; and organized labor, which supported individual tax relief and elimination of some loopholes.

The American Petroleum Institute centered its efforts in 1969 primarily on the tax bill, proposing that the oil and gas depletion allowance be retained at 27.5 per cent. The act as passed lowered the allowance to 22 per cent.

The American Bankers Association met with mixed success. Provisions in the House-passed tax bill which substantially limited deductions by banks for bad-debt reserves, opposed by the bankers' group, were lightened in the final bill. The organization also opposed the House bill's treatment of bank income from bonds and other debt securities as ordinary income rather than capital gains—a provision which remained in the bill.

The Chamber of Commerce of the United States gave particular attention to the tax legislation. Provisions supported by the chamber included moving expenses deductions, deductions for gasoline taxes, existing treatment of capital gains, charitable trusts and charitable contributions, farm loss deductions and "adequate" depletion allowances. The chamber opposed an increase in the minimum standard deduction, a minimum income tax, changes in accelerated depreciation of real estate, deferred executive compensation, and tax treatment of interest on state and local government securities. The chamber supported extension of the income tax surcharge and repeal of the investment tax credit if federal spending were reduced.

Another major business association which made the tax bill its top priority in 1969 was the National Association of Manufacturers (NAM). NAM President W. P. Gullander in a statement after final action termed the measure "an incomplete and self-defeating response" to a public demand for tax relief.

By shifting much of the tax burden from individuals to business, Gullander said, the measure would retard economic growth. He called for a "moderation of business tax burdens—through rate reduction, depreciation and other reforms" and stricter control of government spending.

Provisions included in the final bill that were opposed by the NAM included a limit on deductions for moving expenses to moves of 50 miles or more; a 10 per cent minimum tax on tax preferences for corporations as well as for individuals; a 22 per cent oil depletion allowance; higher tax burdens on capital gains; elimination of accelerated depreciation of real estate; repeal of the 7 per cent investment tax credit; limitation of amortization of pollution control facilities to plants that were in operation before 1969; an increase in the personal income tax exemption; and limits on the deduction of recoveries of antitrust damages.

Anti-ballistic Missile System. Much of the lobby effort in support of ABM deployment was conducted by the Nixon administration and its allies in Congress. Administration officials urged support for the President's Safeguard proposal at meetings of organizations throughout the nation. The officials included Vice President Spiro T. Agnew, Secretary of Defense Melvin R. Laird, Secretary of State William P. Rogers, Secretary of the Interior Walter J. Hickel, presidential aide Robert Ellsworth and John S. Foster Jr., Defense Department director of research and engineering. *(ABM story p. 196)*

The nation's defense industries, including the major ABM contractors, avoided open lobbying for ABM deployment. Three of the 12 largest ABM contractors—Motorola Inc., General Electric Company and Lockheed Aircraft Corporation—were members of the American Security Council, an organization financed by private businesses which published a booklet supporting the ABM.

Citizens' groups supporting ABM deployment included the Liberty Lobby and the Committee to Maintain a Prudent Defense Policy, an ad hoc group headed by former Secretary of State Dean Acheson.

Opposition to ABM deployment was led by a variety of citizens' organizations that generally supported proposals they said would promote peace and international understanding. These included the Council for a Livable World, the National Citizens Committee Concerned About Deployment of the ABM and the Coalition on National Priorities, a loose alliance of 20 organizations including the Friends Committee on National Legislation, the National Committee for a Sane Nuclear Policy (SANE), Americans for Democratic Action, the Southern Christian Leadership Conference, United World Federalists and other church, youth and peace groups.

Haynsworth Nomination. Lobbying by organized labor and civil rights groups was a major force that contributed to the defeat of the Supreme Court nomination of Clement F. Haynsworth Jr. Senators attributed much of the anti-Haynsworth pressure to labor and civil rights groups critical of past decisions by Haynsworth, chief judge of the 4th U.S. Circuit Court of Appeals.

Active opposition to the nomination was led by the AFL-CIO, the National Association for the Advancement of Colored People (NAACP), International Union of Electrical, Radio and Machine Workers (IUE) and the Textile Workers Union of America.

Lobbying in support of the President's nomination was conducted primarily by the administration itself, with the help of pressure from state groups that contacted their senators. No major organized groups lobbied for the nomination. *(Court chapter p. 289)*

Civil Rights and Poverty. Civil rights and anti-poverty groups successfully sought to extend the life of the Office of Economic Opportunity without turning part of its authority over to state governments. They also were successful in their attempts to remove the Whitten amendment allowing freedom-of-choice school desegregation plans from the Labor-Health, Education and Welfare (HEW) appropriations bill. These groups failed to win House approval of a five-year extension of the 1965 Voting Rights Act.

Education. Education groups joined forces in 1969 to form the Emergency Committee for Full Funding of Education Programs, which won amendments to add $900-million to Labor-HEW appropriations recommended by the House Appropriations Committee and to set interim spending at higher levels in fiscal 1970 than in 1969.

Postal Reorganization. Opposition of postal workers' organizations helped slow congressional consideration of the Nixon administration's postal corporation proposal, which was supported by business groups, publishers and a new lobby, Citizens Committee for Postal Reform.

Airport/Airway Development. Proposals to finance development of air transportation through airway user charges were supported by airlines and opposed by private aircraft owners and pilots.

Communications. Lobbying on communications legislation during 1969 was marked by disputes between the National Association of Broadcasters (NAB) and the National Cable Television Association over cable television development and between the NAB and the tobacco industry over the timing of a ban on broadcast cigarette commercials.

1970

In 1970, some organized interests not only played their customary role in attempting to influence the results of the off-year congressional elections but also found in the elections of state legislatures a rare incentive for activity. The legislatures were to reapportion U.S. House districts on the basis of the 1970 Census, a significant factor in determining the makeup of the U.S. House of Representatives during the 1970s. The AFL-CIO's Committee on Political Education (COPE) and Americans for Democratic Action (ADA) were prominent among organizations which stressed this aspect. *(Box, 1970 elections, this page)*

Lobbies and 1970 Elections

Organized labor, which had described the 1970 congressional elections as a crisis for the future of labor unions, scored notable successes at the polls Nov. 3. Several other national pressure groups also had reason for satisfaction with many of the results, both in terms of numbers and in relation to key contests involving congressional leadership posts.

Election of endorsed candidates ranged as high as 91 per cent in the case of the United Mine Workers (UMW), which saw 50 of its 55 endorsed candidates elected. Other groups which endorsed a large number of successful candidates for House and Senate seats included Americans for Constitutional Action (ACA) with 83 per cent and Americans for Democratic Action (ADA) with 64 per cent.

By far the most successful in terms of numbers of endorsed candidates who won was the AFL-CIO's Committee on Political Education (COPE). Its state councils endorsed 361 House and Senate candidates, of whom 219—or 61 per cent—were elected. COPE endorsed 330 candidates in the House, winning 200. Of 31 COPE endorsements in the Senate, 19 won.

Of greater significance than numbers in many cases were the committee assignments involved in pressure group activities. COPE endorsed 19 of 20 Democrats on the House Education and Labor Committee, including the chairman and all subcommittee chairmen. They all won. COPE backed John F. Seiberling, the Democratic opponent of Rep. William H. Ayres (R Ohio), top Republican on the committee who was defeated.

In the Senate, COPE endorsed successful Harrison A. Williams Jr. (D N.J.), third-ranking Democrat on the Labor and Public Welfare Committee who was in line to become chairman. Sen. Ralph Yarborough (D Texas), the chairman, was defeated in the 1970 primaries in what was considered a serious blow by organized labor.

Americans for Constitutional Action endorsed 168 candidates, of whom 139 won. Americans for Democratic Action endorsed 58 candidates, of whom 37 won.

The second session of the 91st Congress was marked by the culmination of some legislative struggles which began the preceding year. A renewed buildup of organized pressure against continued U.S. involvement in the war in Southeast Asia also took place.

Among heavily lobbied topics which were carried over from 1969 and came to a climax in 1970 were controversies over bank holding companies, antiballistic missiles, trade policy, federal funding of education and hospital programs and postal reorganization. For the second year in a row, a confrontation occurred over a Nixon nomination to the Supreme Court.

Some of the contested issues and groups involved included the following.

Trade Policy. A move by domestic industries and organized labor to impose restrictions on certain foreign imports said to be injuring U.S. workers and businesses reached its highest peak in 1970 but failed late in the session. Among those opposing restrictive legislation were multinational corporations, free-trade organizations and foreign interests. *(International Economic chapter p. 119)*

A bill (HR 18970) to curb some kinds of imports and to increase U.S. aid to industries and workers harmed by foreign imports passed the House but died in the Senate after it was attached to the Social Security amendments bill (HR 17550).

Lobbyists for both foreign and domestic interests engaged in a fierce contest over the character and provisions of the bill. The primary issue was drawn in terms of continuation of the free-trade policy, which had prevailed since the New Deal, versus protection of American industry and labor from cheap foreign products and unfair international trade practices.

Many foreign interests had registered agents representing them in connection with the trade legislation. The countries involved in these interests included Algeria, Argentina, Austria, Belgium, Canada, England, France, Hong Kong, Iran, Italy, Japan, Korea, the Netherlands, New Zealand, Peru, Scotland, Switzerland and West Germany.

Among U.S. organizations supporting various forms of trade restrictions were the American Footwear Manufacturers Association, American Textile Manufacturers Institute, National Cotton Council of America, Nation-wide Committee on Import-Export Policy, Trade Relations Council of the United States, Liberty Lobby and the AFL-CIO.

Organizations working against restrictive legislation included the American Importers Association, Chamber of Commerce of the United States, Emergency Committee for American Trade, Committee for a National Trade Policy, Americans for Democratic Action, American Farm Bureau Federation, National Farmers Union and National Grange.

Carswell Nomination. A coalition made up largely of civil rights, labor and liberal forces staged a successful fight against Senate confirmation of President Nixon's appointment of G. Harrold Carswell of Florida to the Supreme Court. Many of these had taken part in the 1969 battle which led to Senate rejection of Clement F. Haynsworth Jr. of South Carolina for the high court.

Organizations whose lobbyists worked to block Carswell's confirmation included the AFL-CIO, United Auto Workers, National Education Association, Americans for Democratic Action, Leadership Conference on Civil Rights, National Association for the Advancement of Colored People and Southern Christian Leadership Conference.

With the help of members of Congress who opposed Carswell's appointment, the opposing groups stimulated letter-writing campaigns and visits to Capitol Hill by congressional constituents from across the country. Organized support for the nominee came largely from the Justice Department, which took an active role in promoting confirmation. *(Court chapter p. 289)*

Anti-War Amendments. Opposition to U.S. military involvement in Southeast Asia grew in Congress with debate of the Cooper-Church amendment to limit action in Cambodia, and of the McGovern-Hatfield amendment, to set a timetable for withdrawal of U.S. troops from South Vietnam. Peace groups and organizations dedicated to shifting national priorities toward greater government action at home pushed the war-limiting moves.

Among them were the Americans for Domestic Action, American Civil Liberties Union, Council for a Livable World, Friends Committee on National Legislation and, from its founding in August, the bipartisan pressure group Common Cause. *(Vietnam chapter)*

Health and Safety. A bill (S 2193—PL 91-596) called the Occupational Safety and Health Act providing for government enforcement of safety and health standards in places of employment was pushed heavily by labor organizations but met with mixed reactions from business groups. *(Health chapter p. 551)*

Among those basically supporting the legislation as enacted were the AFL-CIO, the AFL-CIO Building and Construction Trades Department and the Chamber of Commerce of the United States. Opposing the legislation were the Associated General Contractors of America and American Insurance Association. The National Association of Manufacturers and the American Petroleum Institute favored some provisions and opposed others.

Banking. Legislation enacted in 1970 to extend federal regulation to holding companies controlling a single bank (HR 6778—PL 91-607) was the center of intensive lobbying. Organizations active on the measure included the American Bankers Association (ABA), National Association of Real Estate Boards and National Federation of Independent Businesses. *(p. 135)*

The ABA favored the legislation but opposed certain provisions, such as the House version's restrictions on bank entry into specific business activities and its requirement that one-bank holding companies formed since the date of the 1956 Bank Holding Company Act divest themselves of nonbanking activities. These and a number of other provisions were made less stringent in the final version of the bill.

After Senate passage Sept. 16, but before the conference committee met on the bill, the ABA sent a request to a selected list of members in the states and districts of conference committee members asking them to contact the conferees and urge acceptance of several provisions of the Senate version which were more lenient than those of the House version. The conference bill differed substantially from both the House and Senate versions.

1971

Issues with political overtones setting the stage for the 1972 elections dominated much of the pressure group activity in 1971.

In most of the year's major pressure clashes, well-organized veterans of pressure politics were active on both sides. A notable exception occurred in one of the major lobby collisions of 1971—the battle over school prayer.

In that case, a grassroots campaign initiated by political amateurs gained formidable dimensions until a late opposition drive was organized by veteran lobby groups led by the National Council of Churches and most other politically active religious organizations. The result was victory in the House for opponents of a bid to overturn the impact of Supreme Court decisions which banned officially prescribed religious observances in tax-supported schools.

Politics marked major lobby fights over campaign financing, wage and price controls, national health insurance, federal welfare plans, the supersonic transport and anti-war or anti-military issues.

The year also saw attempts in Congress on two fronts to enact new legislation covering lobbyists and financial contributors to federal political campaigns. A controversial bill providing for public disclosure of campaign contributions neared final passage in 1971, ultimately becoming law in early 1972. A measure aimed at more stringent reporting requirements for lobbyists who sought to influence legislation failed to reach the floor in the House, where it originated. *(Campaign spending act, p. 397)*

Some of the more heavily lobbied issues and groups actively involved are discussed below:

Vietnam. If the number of persons mobilized to participate in rallies and to write letters to members of Congress was an indication of pressure group activism, then anti-war protests in Washington during the spring of 1971 represented the largest pressure group activity of the year. *(Vietnam chapter p. 899)*

The protest against U.S. participation in the Indochina war lasted nearly three weeks, groups of widely divergent political philosophies participated, and at one rally more than 175,000 persons surrounded the Capitol. More than 13,600 demonstrators were arrested in a show of civil disobedience during the three weeks.

Unlike previous years, anti-war leaders focused on Congress. Representatives of the Veterans Against the War and the National Peace Action Coalition appeared before Senate and House committees.

The demonstrations coincided with House passage and the beginning of Senate consideration of the draft extension bill (HR 6531—PL 92-129) but had no immediate effect on the consideration.

Less than two months after the demonstrations in Washington, however, the Senate adopted a proposal sponsored by Majority Leader Mike Mansfield (D Mont.) calling for the withdrawal of U.S. troops from Indochina within nine months. Although the nine-month deadline was dropped from the version of the bill that was signed by the President, Senate passage of such a measure was precedent setting.

SST. The environmental issue which generated the most lobbying during 1971 was the supersonic transport (SST) plane. During debate on the fiscal 1971 Department of Transportation appropriations bill, a Coalition Against the SST led the successful drive to delete development funds. Led by Friends of the Earth, the coalition also included such active environmental groups as the Sierra Club, Environmental Action, Wilderness Society and Zero Population Growth. Common Cause was also part of the coalition. *(Transportation chapter p. 147)*

On the pro-SST side, a National Committee for the SST and its adjunct, Industry and Labor for the SST, worked with the Nixon administration for congressional approval of continued funding. Spearheading the drive were SST contractors and subcontractors and labor unions representing workers in the aircraft industry, including machinists, steelworkers and airline pilots.

China. Lobbying for and against President Nixon's reversal of longstanding U.S. opposition to admission of Communist China to the United Nations involved many organizations. Among those actively supporting the Peking admission were the Committee for New China Policy, the National Committee on United States-China Relations, the Citizens to Change United States China Policy and Members of Congress for Peace Through Law. In

addition, various commercial and scholarly interests supported moves to open trade and other relations with mainland China. They included the American Farm Bureau Federation, the Emergency Committee for American Trade—made up of multinational corporations—the Council on Foreign Relations, General Motors, Xerox Corporation and several airlines.

Opposition to Peking's admission centered in the Committee of One Million—Against the Admission of Communist China to the United Nations and included the AFL-CIO, the American Legion, the Veterans of Foreign Wars, the American Security Council and the American Conservative Union.

No-Fault Insurance. One heavily lobbied measure never came to the floor of either chamber for a vote. A proposal to establish a national system of no-fault automobile insurance to cover drivers—without regard to fault—in accidents involving personal injury was opposed by the American Insurance Association, American Mutual Insurance Alliance, National Association of Independent Insurers, American Bar Association and American Trial Lawyers Association. *(p. 682)*

The insurance trade groups favored various forms of limited no-fault insurance—but on a state-by-state basis rather than a nation-wide system. The lawyers' groups favored retaining the present system of fault-finding. The Consumer Federation backed the national no-fault plan.

Welfare. Passage of HR 1, the Welfare Reform-Social Security bill, by the House June 22 involved the most intensive lobbying in the area of welfare legislation. *(p. 622)*

The bill provided for extensive revamping of the nation's welfare system, a five per cent increase in social security benefits and a liberalization of Medicare and Medicaid programs. It was supported by the administration and a variety of organizations.

A major reason for the wide support received was a feature of the bill's Family Assistance Plan which set a federally guaranteed $2,400-income floor for a family of four with no outside income. However, reasons for supporting the bill varied greatly, and there was some opposition. Despite the diversity of the coalition pushing Congress for enactment of welfare legislation and their divergent objectives, there was general agreement that current welfare programs were unsatisfactory and that change was necessary.

Some organizations supporting the welfare bill included: Common Cause, National League of Cities, National Governors Conference, National Welfare Rights Organization, AFL-CIO, League of Women Voters, National Association of Social Workers and National Association of Manufacturers.

The U.S. Chamber of Commerce was the most active opponent of the bill. The chamber vigorously opposed the provision for a guaranteed annual income and contended that the expense of the bill was too high.

The administration was happy with the House-passed bill because it contained many of the administration's original recommendations. The White House subsequently used its influence to convince many conservative Republicans to support the welfare bill.

School Prayer. One of the most intensely lobbied issues in the House in 1971 was the unsuccessful effort to amend the Constitution to undo the effect of Supreme

Court decisions outlawing officially prescribed religious observances in the public school.

The proposed amendment was brought to the floor by a discharge petition, forcing it out of the hands of the Judiciary Committee, whose chairman, Emanuel Celler (D N.Y.), who opposed any such amendment as an unnecessary modification of the Bill of Rights. Working for the discharge and for the amendment was a group of citizens mobilized into a Prayer Campaign Committee by an Ohio housewife, Mrs. Ben Ruhlin, and working in cooperation with similar groups including the Back to God movement, Project Prayer and Citizens for Public Prayer.

Belatedly aroused opposition to the amendment in 1971 was led by the National Council of Churches and included almost every major organized church group, including, for the first time on this issue, the U.S. Catholic Conference.

Lobbying. A proposed Legislative Activities Disclosure Act (HR 11453) reported by the House Standards of Official Conduct Committee late in 1971 drew no organized support but considerable organized opposition.

Organizations on record vigorously opposing the bill included the National Association of Manufacturers, the Chamber of Commerce of the United States and the Bar Association of the District of Columbia. The bill was intended to repeal the Federal Regulation of Lobbying Act of 1946, replacing it with a new law requiring reports on finances and backing by lobby groups and lobbyists covered.

Critics said the bill in attempting to cover indirect or grassroots lobbying—exempted by court interpretation from the Federal Regulation of Lobbying Act—might invade constitutional rights. Another criticism was that record-keeping and reporting requirements were excessive. Proponents disagreed on both counts.

George B. Mickum III of the Bar Association expressed doubts "whether somebody like Ralph Nader or John Gardner (chairman of Common Cause) would be covered under the bill." He said one loophole would permit unsalaried lobbyists who received expenses only to escape coverage.

Lambert H. Miller, senior vice president and general counsel of the National Association of Manufacturers, and Milton A. Smith, general counsel for the Chamber of Commerce, at hearings both questioned whether the subject of lobbying could be suitably dealt with by general legislation without infringing on constitutional guarantees.

Miller said: "A fair case can be made for the proposition that a reporting and disclosure statute will for the most part obtain information from the honest and forthright organization and individuals who have nothing to hide and that the sinister or corrupting influences, if any, will continue to function notwithstanding the requirements of reporting and disclosure."

1972

Business lobbies, with an occasional boost from the Nixon administration, chalked up a series of victories in fights over crucial legislation in the closing days of the 92nd Congress.

Capitalizing on the confusion of Congress' rush to adjourn, business interests persuaded legislators to kill or modify five key bills they considered unfavorable to business. These were measures to create a consumer protection agency, open up the Highway Trust Fund to aid urban mass transit systems, increase the federal minimum wage, strengthen federal controls over manufacture and use of pesticides, and provide regulation of coal strip mining and reclamation of strip-mined lands.

Top priority for the business lobbies went to killing a bill to create a Consumer Protection Agency that would be empowered to intervene in behalf of consumers before federal departments, agencies and courts.

An all-out effort by the highway lobby, aided by a surprise White House move not to intervene as had been promised in favor of environmental and municipal groups, resulted in adoption of a procedural motion in the House to block consideration of an amendment opening up the Highway Trust Fund to support urban mass transit.

As with the Consumer Protection Agency bill, a broad-based coalition of business interests worked together to kill legislation increasing the $1.60 an hour federal minimum wage for most non-farm workers to $2 immediately and $2.20 in 1974.

The agricultural products industry won a major victory in the closing days of the session when House-Senate conferees weakened a new pesticides control bill by adding language compensating a manufacturer if his product was found unsafe and was removed from the market.

Mining industry interests lobbied intensively against House and Senate bills to control strip mining of coal and other minerals. Interior Committees of both houses reported their bills in September. The House passed a tough control bill on Oct. 11 by a 265-75 roll call despite strong industry opposition. But there was no Senate floor action before adjournment.

Some of the heavily contested issues in 1972 and groups actively involved included the following:

General Revenue Sharing. Pressures by state and local government officials played a key role in winning congressional approval of a five-year plan to share $30,-236,400,000 in federal revenues with state and local governments. The proposal, first advanced by President Nixon in 1969, was one of the "six great goals" he proposed to Congress in 1971. *(p. 97)*

State and local government officials and their national organizations helped spur Congress to action on revenue sharing—perhaps helping to win a key convert in House Ways and Means Committee Chairman Wilbur D. Mills (D Ark.), who first opposed the plan.

Among organizations that helped devise the plan and later lobbied for enactment were the National Governors Conference, National Legislative Conference, National Association of Counties, National Conference of State Legislative Leaders, National Society of State Legislators, U.S. Conference of Mayors, International City Management Association and the National League of Cities.

Governors reportedly were instrumental in winning a conference compromise that eased restrictions placed on federal matching grants to state and local governments for social services. The compromise agreement raised to $2.5-billion from $1.6-billion an annual ceiling on such grants provided by Senate amendments to the revenue-sharing bill (HR 14370—PL 92-512).

Busing. Transportation of pupils to end segregated schools was among bitterly fought congressional battles in 1972, with action taken on two major bills. The National Association for the Advancement of Colored People (NAACP), Leadership Conference on Civil Rights, AFL-CIO and National Education Association (NEA) were among pressure groups fighting to retain busing as one of several means of desegregating schools. *(p. 512)*

Arrayed against them, though lacking organization, was the potentially most influential lobby of all—the people. According to public opinion polls, most of the country opposed busing, particularly citizens in areas under court orders requiring pupil transportation. Although busing for desegregation directly involved no more than three per cent of the 18 to 20 million students being transported, and opposition was not highly organized, the pressures on Congress to stop busing were enormous and resulted in some close legislative battles.

The first battle was fought over busing restrictions in the higher education bill (S 659—PL 92-318). The House had voted stronger restrictions than the Senate, but conferees, dominated by liberal members of the House and Senate education committees, succeeded in getting their respective chambers to approve relatively weak language postponing new busing orders until appeals had been exhausted.

The second battle was fought over the President's Equal Educational Opportunities bill (HR 13915). It was introduced with a ban on busing in grades one through six but emerged from the House with a ban on all busing, regardless of grade, except to the school closest or next closest to the pupil's home. The busing restrictions were the strongest in Congress' history and passed the House overwhelmingly.

Lobbyists for the NAACP and others opposing the measure concentrated their efforts in the Senate, which they knew was more receptive to busing and in which a filibuster could kill the bill. Although the Senate's anti-busing faction claimed to have a majority in favor of the bill and the President favored passage, liberally oriented senators—mainly from northern industrial states—succeeded in defeating three cloture votes aimed at cutting off debate, and the bill died.

Water Pollution. The most significant and far-reaching environmental measure in the nation's history—the Federal Water Pollution Control Act Amendments of 1972 (S 2770—PL 92-500)—aroused some of the most intensive lobbying efforts of the 92nd Congress. The bill became law Oct. 18 when Congress overrode President Nixon's veto. *(Environment chapter p. 743)*

Industry, environmental, labor, consumer, state and local government groups worked hard to influence the final version of the bill. Working to ensure that the bill was not too tough on industry were such groups as the National Association of Manufacturers, the American Petroleum Institute, the American Iron & Steel Institute, the American Paper Institute and the Manufacturing Chemists Association.

Lobbying for a strong bill from the environmental viewpoint was a coalition of about 30 diverse organizations, led by the League of Women Voters, the Environmental Policy Center and Ralph Nader's Task Force on Water Pollution Control. The coalition's members included the Amalgamated Clothing Workers, Common Cause, Environmental Action, Friends of the Earth, Izaak Walton League, National Consumers' League, National Wildlife Federation, Sierra Club, Trout Unlimited, United

Lobbies and 1972 Elections

Both business and labor organizations scored significant successes in the election held Nov. 7. Labor's traditional backing of Democratic aspirants was again pronounced, though the actual extent of union contributions to the Democratic victories in Congress in the face of President Nixon's landslide re-election was difficult to determine.

Following nomination of Sen. George McGovern (D S.D.) as the Democratic candidate, much of organized labor led by the AFL-CIO's Committee on Political Education (COPE) concentrated attention on congressional campaigns and the retention of Democratic control of both the House and Senate.

Some individual 1972 results which labor viewed as setbacks represented victories for business interests. For example, business favored Sen. John L. McClellan (D Ark.). McClellan won re-election after defeating Rep. David Pryor (D Ark.), who received top priority labor backing against McClellan in the primary. Business supported Dewey F. Bartlett (R Okla.), who defeated labor-backed Rep. Ed Edmondson (D Okla.) for the Senate.

Labor successes included:

• Victories of seven Senate candidates given high priority by unions: Senators Charles H. Percy (R Ill.); Claiborne Pell (D R.I.); Jennings Randolph (D W.Va.); Lee Metcalf (D Mont.); Clifford P. Case (D N.J.); Rep. William D. Hathaway (D Maine), who defeated Sen. Margaret Chase Smith (R Maine); and Floyd K. Haskell (D Colo.), victor over Sen. Gordon Allott (R Colo.). Allott was ranking Republican on the Interior and Insular Affairs Committee. Smith was ranking Republican on the Armed Services Committee and second-ranking on the Appropriations Committee.

• Victories of six high priority incumbents in the House: Peter W. Rodino Jr. (D N.J.), incoming Judiciary Committee chairman; Ray J. Madden (D Ind.), incoming Rules Committee chairman; Frank Thompson Jr. (D N.J.), chairman of the Special Labor Subcommittee; Melvin Price (D Ill.), second-ranking Democrat on the Armed Services Committee and chairman of the Standards of Official Conduct Committee; Donald M. Fraser (D Minn.) and Ella T. Grasso (D Conn.).

Sixty per cent of COPE's congressional endorsees won, including 218 of 361 endorsed in the House and 16 of 29 endorsed in the Senate. COPE endorsed predominantly Democrats, backing three Republicans in the Senate and 15 in the House.

The United Mine Workers won 93 per cent of their congressional endorsements, while the Business-Industry Political Action Committee (BIPAC) scored 74 per cent. BIPAC financially assisted 128 candidates in the House, of whom 97 won, and 13 in the Senate, of whom eight won.

Auto Workers, United Steelworkers, Wilderness Society and Zero Population Growth. Other groups which worked on the bill were the National League of Cities, U.S. Conference of Mayors, Association of Metropolitan Sewerage Agencies, Water Pollution Control Federation, Interstate

Conference of Water Problems, Consulting Engineers Council and the National Association of Regulatory Utility Commissioners.

Pesticide Control. Also subject to energetic lobbying pressure was the Federal Environmental Pesticide Control Act of 1972 (HR 10729—PL 92-516), a bill making the first major changes in federal regulation of pesticides in 25 years. The final version contained a controversial provision to compensate manufacturers if their products were found hazardous and taken off the market.

This indemnity clause, agreed upon by House-Senate conferees, was a victory for such groups as the National Agricultural Chemicals Association, the Manufacturing Chemists Association and the American Farm Bureau Federation, who also won a softening of several other tough provisions in the Senate version of the bill. Lobbying to strengthen the bill were such groups as the Sierra Club, National Farmers Union, National Farmers Organization and Agribusiness Accountability Project.

No-fault Insurance. A bill to establish a national no-fault auto insurance system was killed when the Senate, by a 49-46 roll-call vote, sent the bill (S 945) to the Judiciary Committee for further consideration.

One of the most heavily lobbied bills of 1972, the legislation was opposed by the Nixon administration which supported the concept but favored action at the state rather than federal level. Other opponents included the National Association of Independent Insurers, American Trial Lawyers Association, American Bar Association, and most governors and state insurance commissioners. Supporters of the legislation included the Consumer Federation of America, Consumers Union, Common Cause, American Insurance Association, Automobile Manufacturers Association, American Trucking Associations, rental car companies and several labor unions.

Consumer Protection Agency. An intensive lobbying effort blocked a bill that would have created an independent agency to represent consumer interests before other federal agencies and courts. Supporters of the bill (S 3970) said the administration was responsible for its defeat when the Senate failed a third and final time to invoke cloture limiting debate on the bill. The administration publicly supported a narrower version of the bill passed by the House in 1971. The bill's sponsors contended that administration lobbyists switched tactics and asked for no bill at all.

Major lobbying efforts against the bill were waged by the Grocery Manufacturers of America Inc., the National Association of Manufacturers, the Chamber of Commerce of the United States and Proctor and Gamble. Chief lobbyist for Procter and Gamble was Bryce N. Harlow, a former counselor to President Nixon and chief White House legislative representative in both the Nixon and Eisenhower administrations.

The brunt of an unsuccessful lobbying effort for the bill was carried by Ralph Nader's various organizations and most consumer organizations.

Welfare. Congress cleared a welfare-social security bill (HR 1—PL 92-603) Oct. 17 after prolonged controversy and heavy lobbying which resulted among other things in leaving the basic family welfare program—Aid to Families with Dependent Children—unchanged. *(p. 622)*

Although HR 1 included provisions liberalizing many Social Security, Medicare and Medicaid benefits, the intense lobbying concerned the family welfare section. The House version of HR 1 included a Family Assistance Plan strongly supported by the administration guaranteeing an annual federal payment of $2,400 to a family of four with no outside income.

When HR 1 passed the House in June 1971, the Family Assistance Plan was supported by many organizations, including Common Cause, the League of Women Voters, the AFL-CIO and the United Auto Workers. The U.S. Chamber of Commerce opposed the bill because of the guaranteed annual income provisions.

The Senate Finance Committee made hundreds of changes. It deleted the Family Assistance Plan from the welfare section and substituted a "workfare" plan making able-bodied family heads ineligible for welfare and requiring them to take a federally guaranteed job.

The National Welfare Rights Organization (NWRO) was critical of all three welfare proposals. It said the $2,400 backed by the administration and the $2,600 backed by Sen. Abraham Ribicoff (D Conn.) and other liberals for a Family Assistance Plan were inadequate. The NWRO favored an annual federal payment of $6,500 to a family of four with no outside income and adamantly opposed the "workfare" plan.

A divided Senate voted to test all three proposals for two to four years at a cost of $400-million per year. The Senate version contained strict child support provisions, personal restrictions on welfare recipients, and tough guidelines for the operation of the Office of Economic Opportunity legal services program.

After the Senate passed the bill, the child support and welfare restrictions were criticized by the NWRO. The American Bar Association was critical of a provision prohibiting legal services attorneys from representing the poor in welfare cases and requirements that the attorneys help prosecute paternity cases involving welfare recipients. The AFL-CIO, Common Cause and the League of Women Voters also opposed the provisions.

House and Senate conferees agreed to delete the family welfare provisions Oct. 14 when it became obvious they could not compromise in the short time remaining in the 1972 session. Restrictive child support and legal services provisions were also deleted by the conferees.

 **Lobby Registrations, Spending (1969-72)**

LOOPHOLES COLOR REGISTRATION, SPENDING STATISTICS

Although original backers of federal legislation covering individuals and groups who sought to influence Congress frequently spoke of exposing them to "the pitiless light of publicity," the main law in effect since 1946 was generally conceded to have failed in that purpose.

The Federal Regulation of Lobbying Act of 1946 proved to contain many loopholes and, as interpreted by the Supreme Court *(U.S. v. Harriss, 1954)* exempted many of those who attempted to influence legislation from registering or reporting their expenditures.

As a result, data on the numbers and identities of active lobbyists and their financial activities and backing are subject to error and at best reflect estimates based on official reports. In the case of spending, the amounts reported by organized interests represent minimum figures, with lobby groups differing widely in their interpretations of the requirements in reporting under the act. Those listing the highest totals in some instances interpret the law more strictly.

The 1946 act not only required paid lobbyists to register with officials of Congress but also required them and any organizations that attempted to influence legislation to file quarterly reports giving certain financial information and describing how much they spent for lobbying.

Since 1946, Congressional Quarterly has recorded lobbyist registrations and lobby spending reports filed under the 1946 act.

The following information based on Congressional Quarterly's records is given in this chapter:

- A list showing yearly spending totals, 1947-72.
- A list showing yearly lobby registration totals, 1946-72.
- A list of top lobby spenders for each of the years 1969 through 1972.

References. *Background on the 1946 act and its implementation, Congress and the Nation, Vol. I, p. 1557; lobby spending report highlights for 1946-63, Congress and the Nation, Vol. I, p. 1585; lobby spending for 1964-68, Congress and the Nation, Vol. II, p. 925.*

Spending Totals 1947-1972

Total spending reported by organizations under the Federal Regulation of Lobbying Act for each full year since the law's enactment:

Year	Spending	Year	Spending
1972	$ 6,138,717	1965	$ 5,484,413
1971	6,524,849	1964	4,223,277
1970	5,841,578	1963	4,223,605
1969	5,420,125	1962	4,211,304
1968	4,298,387	1961	3,986,095
1967	4,751,145	1960	3,854,374
1966	4,656,871	1959	4,281,468

Year	Spending	Year	Spending
1958	$ 4,132,719	1952	$ 4,823,981
1957	3,818,177	1951	8,771,097
1956	3,957,120	1950	10,303,204
1955	4,365,843	1949	7,969,710
1954	4,286,158	1948	6,763,480
1953	4,445,841	1947	5,191,856

Lobby Registration Totals

The 1946 Federal Regulation of Lobbying Act required any person or group (except public officials) who, for pay, attempted to influence federal legislation to register with the clerk of the House and the secretary of the Senate. The law did not provide any specific way to withdraw a registration once it was filed, and it was vague on other procedural points. Some lobbyists follow the practice of registering anew each session, even if they still represent the same client. Others register only once for each client.

The year-by-year breakdown of all registrations (including duplications) since the law was enacted is shown below.

Prior to 1964, years are calendar years unless otherwise indicated. Since 1964, the adjournment of Congress has marked the end of each year's total.

Year	Registrations	Year	Registrations
1946*	222	Jan. 1, 1964-	
1947	731	Oct. 3, 1964	255
1948	447	Oct. 4, 1964-	
1949	599	Oct. 23, 1965	450
1950	430	Oct. 24, 1965-	
1951	342	Oct. 22, 1966	332
1952	204	Oct. 23, 1966-	
1953	296	Dec. 15, 1967	449
1954	413	Dec. 16, 1967-	
1955	383	Oct. 14, 1968	259
1956	347	Oct. 15, 1968-	
1957	392	Dec. 23, 1969	647
1958	337	Dec. 24, 1969-	
1959	393	Jan. 3, 1971	498**
1960	236	Jan. 4, 1971-	
1961	365	Dec. 17, 1971	534
1962	375	Dec. 18, 1971-	
1963	384	Oct. 18, 1972	374
		TOTAL	10,694

* *Last four months only.*
** *Includes 1970 filings processed by officials early in 1971.*

TOP LOBBY ORGANIZATION SPENDERS 1969-72

1969

National Association of Letter Carriers (AFL-CIO)	$295,970
United Federation of Postal Clerks (AFL-CIO)	250,827
Realty Committee on Taxation	229,223
AFL-CIO (headquarters)	184,938
American Farm Bureau Federation	146,337
National Committee for the Recording Arts	139,726
National Association of Home Builders of the United States	138,472
United States Savings and Loan League	126,421
Record Industry Association of America Inc.	115,334
American Legion	114,609
Council for a Livable World	112,603
National Education Association, Office of Government Relations and Citizenship	97,537
National Housing Conference Inc.	95,562
American Medical Association	91,355
Railway Labor Executives Association	86,286
National Association of Theatre Owners	84,049
Citizens Committee for Postal Reform	83,951
Brotherhood of Railway, Airline & Steamship Clerks, Freight Handlers, Express and Station Employees (AFL-CIO)	80,985
American Trucking Associations Inc.	80,896
Liberty Lobby Inc.	79,927
National Federation of Independent Business Inc.	75,528
National Farmers Union	73,264
National Association of Postal Supervisors	68,365
National Council of Farmer Cooperatives	62,496
National Federation of Federal Employees	61,269

1970

Veterans of World War I, U.S.A. Inc.	$341,244
National Association of Letter Carriers (AFL-CIO)	277,125
United Federation of Postal Clerks (AFL-CIO)	228,325
Council for a Livable World	214,626
AFL-CIO (National headquarters)	197,493
American Farm Bureau Federation	163,553
American Hospital Association	153,241
National Association of Home Builders of the United States	151,605
United States Savings & Loan League	149,794
Citizens Committee for Postal Reform Inc.	138,545
Record Industry Association of America	123,286
Disabled American Veterans	117,134
National Committee for the Recording Arts	99,886
Livestock Producers Committee	96,945
American Medical Association	96,064
National Association of Postal Supervisors	94,661
National Council of Farmer Cooperatives	94,307
National Housing Conference Inc.	92,549
Farmers Educational and Cooperative Union of America	80,738

Common Cause (and Urban Coalition Action Council)	79,347
National Cotton Council of America	79,036
American Legion	78,939
Brotherhood of Railway, Airline & Steamship Clerks, Freight Handlers, Express and Station Employees (AFL-CIO)	75,056
American Trucking Associations Inc.	74,484
International Brotherhood of Teamsters, Chauffeurs, Warehousemen & Helpers of America	72,626

1971

Common Cause	$847,856
Veterans of World War I of the U.S.A Inc.	308,946
American Postal Workers Union (AFL-CIO)	257,093
AFL-CIO (National headquarters)	205,101
American Farm Bureau Federation	165,063
United States Savings & Loan League	158,727
National Association of Letter Carriers (AFL-CIO)	135,334
National Committee for an American SST	131,080
Disabled American Veterans	129,881
National Association of Home Builders of the United States	125,779
American Trucking Associations Inc.	115,287
American Medical Association	114,800
National Association of Postal Supervisors	102,795
New York Committee of International Committee of Passenger Lines	100,342
National Housing Conference Inc.	99,924
Farmers' Educational and Cooperative Union of America	97,438
United Mine Workers of America	93,352
Brotherhood of Railway, Airline & Steamship Clerks (AFL-CIO)	91,624
National Association of Real Estate Boards	74,952
Committee for Humane Legislation	74,241
National Federation of Federal Employees	67,856
American Insurance Association	65,812
International Brotherhood of Teamsters	63,716
American Hospital Association	62,496
National Citizens Committee for Revenue Sharing	61,720

1972

Common Cause	$558,839
American Federation of Labor-Congress of Industrial Organizations (AFL-CIO)	216,294
Veterans of World War I of the U.S.A. Inc.	213,743
American Postal Workers Union	208,767
United States Savings and Loan League	191,726
National Council of Farmer Cooperatives	184,347
Disabled American Veterans	159,431
National Association of Letter Carriers (AFL-CIO)	154,188
American Trucking Association Inc.	137,804
The Farmers' Educational and Cooperative Union of America	113,156

United Mine Workers of America	110,045	National Federation of Federal Employees	82,080
American Nurses' Association Inc.	109,643	National Housing Conference Inc.	77,906
National Association of Home Builders		International Brotherhood of Teamsters	76,897
of the United States	99,031	National Limestone Institute Inc.	75,777
American Medical Association	96,146	American Civil Liberties Union	73,131
Brotherhood of Railway, Airline &		National Association of Real Estate Boards	70,941
Steamship Clerks	88,540	Liberty Lobby Inc.	70,019
Recording Industry Association of America Inc.	88,396	New York Committee of International	
American Insurance Association	82,259	Committee of Passenger Lines	66,636

Chapter 8—Civil Liberties and Civil Rights

Key Votes

In this chapter, key roll-call votes are shown in bold-face type. The party breakdown on each of these votes and the position taken by each member of Congress may be found in the key vote charts which appear in the appendix to this book.

Civil Liberties
and
Internal Security

First Amendment guarantees of free speech, press religion and assembly were put to severe strain by the executive branch and by Congress during the 1969-72 period.

The Nixon administration seemed to set the tone for the period by strident criticism of the press and by widespread resort to electronic eavesdropping of domestic radicals and suspected criminals. The eavesdropping eventually broke out in the political sphere when, with the approval of officials in the Committee for the Reelection of the President, Democratic National Committee headquarters was bugged during the 1972 election campaign. *(Watergate chapter)*

Meanwhile, Congress showed less than due regard for First Amendment freedoms in several cases. But the potential infringement of those freedoms did not materialize. Attempts by Congress to clamp down on the mailing of supposedly obscene matter, to legalize prayer in the public schools, and to cite the Columbia Broadcasting System (CBS) for contempt all failed.

Congress came to the defense of civil liberties in repealing detention camp laws and in refusing to allow the President to expand the powers of the Subversive Activities Control Board (SACB), an agency which gained its fame in the 1950s as an identifier of alleged Communists and subversives. Congress' action on the SACB, led by the Senate, probably sounded the death knell of the board, because the President asked no money for it in his fiscal 1974 budget.

Free Press. Attacks on the press during 1969-72 were highlighted by Vice President Agnew's blasts at *The New York Times, The Washington Post* and network television news analysts, by an FBI investigation of a CBS television newsman and by an unsuccessful Justice Department attempt to ban publication of the Pentagon Papers, coupled with departmental success in obtaining court decisions requiring reporters to appear before grand juries to reveal their news sources.

The House, in a rare rejection of a committee recommendation, killed a contempt citation against CBS from its Commerce Committee. Members of Congress and the administration had been angered over a documentary on Pentagon public relations activities ("The Selling of the Pentagon") and wanted CBS to hand over non-televised material gathered in preparation of the documentary.

Still outstanding at the end of 1972 was the issue of how far grand juries could go in requiring reporters to yield to demands for their notes and to disclose sources of information. The House held hearings on so-called newsmen's privilege legislation, but no bill emerged.

On the matter of obscenity, hundreds of bills were introduced in Congress—and some passed one chamber or the other—to regulate the sending of allegedly obscene matter through the mails. The toughest action Congress took, however, was an amendment prohibiting the mailing of sexually oriented commercial advertising to persons who said they did not want to receive it.

In a related matter, the Commission on Obscenity and Pornography, created by Congress in 1967, issued its report in 1970 recommending the repeal of all laws regulating the sale, exhibition or distribution of sexual material to consenting adults. The Senate and the President rejected the report.

Religion. Despite intense grass-roots lobbying and the backing of a majority of the House, a proposed constitutional amendment to allow prayer in the public schools failed to gain the necessary two-thirds approval of the House in 1971. The proposal was similar to one defeated by the Senate by nine votes in 1966.

The amendment was aimed at overcoming a 1962 Supreme Court decision *(Engle v. Vitale)* which barred state-sponsored prayer in the public schools. If successful, the amendment would have represented the first change in the Bill of Rights. *(Court chapter p. 287)*

Electronic Eavesdropping. The Nixon administration relied heavily on wiretapping and bugging of suspected criminals and subversives in its first four years, a development which many critics considered not only unconstitutional but also impractical. Figures for 1971 showed that federal authorities installed 281 wiretaps at a cost of $1.8-million and thereby obtained 115 convictions.

But the 1971 figures failed to tell the whole story. They applied only to court-approved taps and bugs. Those the Justice Department installed without court approval on alleged domestic subversives and radicals were believed to be at least as numerous. The Supreme Court ruled unanimously in 1972 that such unauthorized wiretaps were unconstitutional. *(1971-72 wiretap box p. 491)*

Privacy Invasions. Senate hearings in 1971 revealed widespread Army surveillance of anti-establish-

---

References

Discussion of civil liberties and internal security for the years 1945-64, may be found in *Congress and the Nation Vol. I*, p. 1645-76; for the years 1965-68, *Congress and the Nation, Vol. II*, p. 409-19.

ment personalities, as well as members of Congress. Although spying on civilians actually began in the Johnson administration, it continued in the early Nixon years.

The Nixon administration refused to allow certain Defense Department officials, particularly generals, to testify at the hearings. But, conceding that the Army had gone too far, it transferred all of its domestic spying operations to the Justice Department. Administration officials maintained throughout, however, that Army spying on civilians did not run counter to the Constitution or the principle of civilian control of the military.

Chronology of

Legislation

1969

Emergency Detention

The Senate Dec. 22 passed a bill (S 1872) repealing the Emergency Detention Act of 1950 (Title II of the Internal Security Act of 1950, PL 81-831). The 1950 act allowed the President, in an "internal security emergency," to detain persons who might engage in espionage or sabotage. The legislation had been passed over President Truman's veto and the Nixon administration supported its repeal. The House did not act on S 1872, but the act eventually was repealed in 1971. *(Congress and the Nation, Vol. I, pp. 1651, 1654)*

Public Assembly

The House passed two bills (HR 1035, H J Res 247) aimed at preventing large-scale encampments on public land such as the 1968 Resurrection City camp-in by civil rights groups in Washington. HR 1035, passed June 11 by a roll-call vote of 327-51, applied to public land only in the District of Columbia. H J Res 247, adopted Sept. 9 by a 334-55 roll-call vote, provided that the interior secretary was not to issue camping permits in national parks except in areas regularly designated for camping. Although supporters of the bills insisted they were not aimed at a specific group or incident, debate kept returning to the activities at Resurrection City. That encampment cost the taxpayers more than $2-million, the bills' supporters said. The Senate did not act on either bill.

Obscene Mail

Three House subcommittees held hearings on various proposals, including an administration request, to curb obscene mail. None of the bills was reported. Nixon asked Congress to bar the mailing of offensive sex materials to persons under age 18, prohibit the mailing of sex-oriented advertising, and provide expanded protection against use of the mails for transmission of unsolicited "smut-advertising."

Members of Congress who testified at the hearings said they had received many complaints from constituents about the sexual nature of unsolicited advertising received in their homes and opened by their children, and in some cases addressed to the youngsters. Postmaster General Winton M. Blount said his department received more than 200,000 complaints about sex-oriented mailings in the first 11 months of fiscal 1969.

The American Civil Liberties Union opposed the administration bills as violative of the First Amendment. Emanuel Celler (D N.Y.) suggested that registration of households that did not wish to receive sex-oriented mail might be the best solution.

Student Violence

The Senate Government Operations Permanent Investigations Subcommitttee and the House Internal Security Committee held separate hearings on campus violence and militant groups. The Senate subcommittee did not allow testimony by members of SDS (Students for a Democratic Society), one of the larger radical youth groups.

Most of the witnesses were unsympathetic to protests by youths, whether peaceful or violent, and urged legislation to control them. Several witnesses testified that SDS was Communist-infiltrated. University administrators split on whether college authorities were more at fault than the students for campus protests.

The Internal Security Committee issued a report Dec. 15 indicating that American high schools had become a target for the "radical left" and the "recruiting grounds for future college radical activists."

HUAC-HISC

The House voted 305-79, Feb. 18, to change the name of its Un-American Activities Committtee (HUAC) to Internal Security Committee (HISC) and broaden its mandate. Richard H. Ichord (D Mo.), who took over as committee chairman in January, requested the changes. He said the term "un-American" in the committee's title was ambiguous. The new mandate, instead of empowering the committee to investigate un-American propaganda activities, directed it to probe groups which sought to overthrow or change the form of the federal government by violence or to obstruct the execution of internal security laws.

1970

Obscenity and Pornography

Congress in 1970 failed to complete action on proposed legislation to curb the distribution of sexually oriented advertising through the mails. House and Senate hearings were held in 1970 (following up earlier hearings in 1969) on several comprehensive administration-supported bills. Two of the bills were passed by the House during the session, one by the Senate. Neither chamber acted on the other's legislation, however, and the bills died with adjournment.

The urgency of such legislation was lessened somewhat by enactment in August 1970 of a provision prohibiting the mailing of sexually oriented commercial advertising to persons who specified they did not want to receive such material. The prohibition was passed in the form of an amendment, added by the Senate, to the Postal Reform Act of 1970 (PL 91-375). *(p. 435)*

Background. More than 300 bills to curb obscenity and pornography were introduced during the second session of the 91st Congress.

The law on obscenity has been made largely in the courts. The basic standard was set down in *Roth v. United States (1957)* and subsequent decisions by the Supreme Court. The test of obscenity under the First Amendment involved three elements: (1) the dominant theme of the material taken as a whole must appeal to a prurient interest in sex; (2) the material must be patently offensive because it affronts contemporary community standards relating to descriptions or representations of sexual matters; and (3) the material must be utterly without redeeming social value.

The Court subsequently ruled *(Ginzburg v. U.S., 1966)* that the origin of mailing (name of the town on the postmark), the advertising and the promotional matter in the distribution of books were proper legal aids in determining the issue of obscenity in "close cases."

The Warren Court also ruled that materials could be censored if they were offered for sale to minors.

Congress in 1967 enacted a law (S 188—PL 90-100) establishing a Commission on Obscenity and Pornography. The 18-member commission, appointed by the President, was charged with studying traffic in obscene materials, investigating the relationship between obscene matter and antisocial behavior and recommending action to control traffic in pornography. The group had no extraordinary investigative powers, such as the power to issue subpoenas. It was to go out of existence 10 days after filing its final report, which was due no later than Jan. 31, 1970. Congress later extended that deadline to Sept. 30, 1970.

The commission's 622-page report was released Sept. 30. The commission majority recommended the repeal of all legislation prohibiting "the sale, exhibition or distribution of sexual materials to consenting adults." The Senate by a vote of 60-5 adopted a resolution formally rejecting that recommendation and the findings upon which it was based. *(Box, this page)*

The White House also rejected the commission's stand. Press Secretary Ronald L. Ziegler told reporters that the President "believes pornography and obscenity relate to adverse social conduct."

Legislation. President Nixon had asked Congress on May 2, 1969, to ban the mailing of obscene material to minors and the mailing of sex-oriented advertising generally, and to expand protections against unsolicited "smut-advertising."

The first and third of Nixon's proposals were approved by the House April 28 as HR 15693. The bill, passed by a 378-8 roll-call vote, provided that certain pornographic literature could not be delivered or distributed by mail to persons under age 17 or to adults who requested that such mail not be delivered to them.

The second Nixon proposal was incorporated in a bill (HR 11032) passed by the House Aug. 3 by a 322-5 roll-call vote. It prohibited the intentional use of the mails or other interstate facilities to transport unsolicited salacious advertisements.

Pornography Report Rejected

The Senate Oct. 13 overwhelmingly rejected the findings and recommendations of the Commission on Obscenity and Pornography, released Sept. 30, 1970.

A Senate resolution (S Res 477), adopted by a 60-5 roll-call vote, said the commission failed to comply with the mandate of the Congress and specified that the findings and recommendations were not supported by evidence available to or considered by the commission.

Brought to the floor by John L. McClellan (D Ark.), and cosponsored by 26 Democrats and 24 Republicans, the resolution rejected the following commission conclusions:

(1) That there is "no evidence to date that exposure to explicit sexual materials plays a significant role in the causation of delinquent or criminal behavior among youths or adults";

(2) That "a majority of American adults believe that adults should be allowed to read or see any sexual materials they wish";

(3) That "there is no reason to suppose that elimination of governmental prohibitions upon the sexual materials which may be made available to adults would adversely affect the availability to the public of other books, magazines and films";

(4) That "nor is there evidence that exposure to explicit sexual materials adversely affects character or moral attitudes regarding sex and sexual conduct"; and

(5) That "Federal, state and local legislation prohibiting the sale, exhibition or distribution of sexual materials to consenting adults should be repealed."

Sen. Robert P. Griffin (R Mich.), expressing a concern of the resolution's cosponsors, said the real danger of the report was not that it would be accepted by Congress, but that it would serve to provide ammunition to those who advocated more pornographic permissiveness.

Urging adoption of the resolution rejecting the commission's report, McClellan said recognition of the conclusions, even by silence, would prove a direct threat to the nation's moral health.

The Senate Sept. 23 passed 79-0 a bill (S 3220) which prescribed specific language for labeling sexually oriented advertising sent through the mails. The bill provided that recipients of such mail could return it unopened at the sender's expense.

Defense Facilities

The House, by a 274-65 roll-call vote Jan. 29, passed a bill (HR 14864) to amend the Internal Security Act of 1950 to protect defense production facilities and classified information against subversives. The bill, reported by the Internal Security Committee, incorporated the provisions of a similar bill (HR 12699) on which the committee had held hearings in 1969. The Senate took no action on the bill.

As passed by the House, HR 14864 authorized the President to institute a personnel security screening program for defense facilities and provided for the safeguarding of classified information released to government contractors. An amendment to limit the situations in which the President might authorize inquiries into an individual's access to classified data, or his employment in a sensitive job, to cases in which the person knowingly belonged to a subversive organization was defeated by a 25-35 standing vote.

Hoover Testimony

FBI Director J. Edgar Hoover reported Nov. 27 that the bureau had uncovered a plot by a militant, anti-war group to blow up underground steam pipes serving federal buildings in Washington, D.C., and to kidnap a "highly placed government official." Hoover identified the principal leaders of the group as Philip and Daniel Berrigan, Catholic priests who at the time were serving sentences in a federal prison at Danbury, Conn., for participation in the destruction of draft board records in Baltimore, Md. He named the anti-war group as the "East Coast Conspiracy to Save Lives."

Hoover's statements were made before the Senate Subcommittee on Deficiencies and Supplemental Appropriations, which was holding hearings on an FBI supplemental appropriations request of $14,150,000. The session was closed to the press, but Hoover's testimony was made public the next day by the subcommittee.

The government official Hoover referred to was later identified as presidential national security adviser Henry A. Kissinger. Members of the "Conspiracy" held a press conference Nov. 30 to deny Hoover's allegations. Rep. William R. Anderson (D Tenn.) defended the Berrigans in a letter to Hoover.

The Rev. Philip Berrigan and six others, including Sister Elizabeth McAlister, were indicted Jan. 12, 1971, on several charges, including conspiring to kidnap Kissinger and blow up heating ducts in the nation's capital. On April 5, 1972, a mistrial was declared because of a hung jury which had voted 10-2 for acquittal on the conspiracy charges. But Berrigan and Sister McAlister were convicted of smuggling letters out of a federal penitentiary. The convictions were under appeal in the spring of 1973.

Military Spying

Sen. Sam J. Ervin Jr. (D N.C.) charged Dec. 16 that the army had conducted "surveillance" of more than 800 Illinois citizens, including politicians, newspaper reporters, religious figures and political contributors. Among those named by Ervin as targets of the surveillance were Sen. Adlai E. Stevenson III (D), Rep. Abner J. Mikva (D), and U.S. Circuit Court Judge Otto Kerner, former governor of Illinois (1961-68). Ervin's charges, plus others in later weeks, set the stage for extensive hearings in 1971 on army spying and use of data banks to keep records on certain citizens and groups. *(1971 chronology)*

Emergency Detention

The House Internal Security Committee on Oct. 13 reported a bill (HR 19163) amending the Emergency Detention Act of 1950 (PL 81-831). The amendments required that provisions of the act not go into effect in the case of an insurrection in aid of a foreign enemy unless Congress formally determined that such an insurrection existed, stated that no one could be detained under the act on account of race, color or ancestry, and assured counsel to those detained.

The Senate in 1969 had passed a bill (S 1872) to repeal the act, but the House committee refused to go along and the House itself did not act on the bill. Repeal of the 1950 act was accomplished by Congress in 1971.

Federal Employee Privacy

The Senate passed a bill (S 782) May 19 aimed at protecting civilian federal employees from unwarranted governmental invasion of their privacy. The bill specifically forbade the disclosure of an employee's race, religion, national origin, sexual habits, personal relationships, outside activities or political inclinations. The House did not act on the bill.

1971

School Prayer Amendment

Despite the support of a majority of the House, a proposed school prayer constitutional amendment failed Nov. 8 to win approval of the necessary two-thirds when it came to a vote.

The **key roll-call vote was 240-163,** with supporters of the amendment falling 29 votes shy of the necessary two-thirds of the 403 members voting. Republicans overwhelmingly supported the amendment (138-26), while northern Democrats opposed it (48-114).

(Constitutional amendments require approval of two-thirds majorities in the House and Senate and ratification by three-fourths of the states.)

The vote capped intense lobbying efforts for and against the amendment, designed to override Supreme Court decisions in 1962 and 1963 outlawing officially prescribed religious observances in the public schools. *(Congress and the Nation, Vol. I, p. 1675)*

As modified on the floor, the proposed amendment (H J Res 191) would have added to the Constitution a statement that voluntary prayer or meditation in public buildings, by persons lawfully assembled, was constitutionally permissible. *(Text of amendment, box p. 487)*

The resolution was introduced in 1971 by Rep. Chalmers P. Wylie (R Ohio) and was similar to one proposed in 1967 by then-Senate Minority Leader Everett McKinley Dirksen (R Ill. 1951-1969).

Wylie and supporters of the amendment—mobilized in a two-year grassroots lobbying effort by an Ohio housewife, Mrs. Ben Ruhlin—said that H J Res would restore the freedom of religious expression—through voluntary prayer in the schools—which the First Amendment was intended to guarantee.

Opponents of the amendment, led by the National Council of Churches, House Judiciary Chairman Emanuel Celler (D N.Y.), James C. Corman (D Calif.) and Fred Schwengel (R Iowa), said that the amendment was unnecessary, that it merely ensured that which the First Amendment already protected. Tampering with the Bill of Rights, they said, would "whittle down" the present freedom of religion enjoyed by Americans and would open a breach in the wall separating church and state.

The politically explosive proposal came to the House floor through the extraordinary procedure of a discharge petition. Mrs. Ruhlin asked Wylie to file such a petition to pry the resolution from Celler's committee, to which it had been referred. After a majority (218) of the members of the House sign such a petition, the committee is discharged from consideration of the measure which then can, on approval of a motion by a majority, be brought directly to the House floor.

Intense pressure on members to support the petition may have backfired. The motion to discharge the committee carried easily, 242-157, but when the amendment itself was voted on Nov. 8, 29 representatives who had signed the petition either did not vote or voted nay. Those 29 votes made the difference between success and failure for supporters of the amendment.

Debate. The amendment was opposed by Speaker Carl Albert (D Okla.) and Majority Leader Hale Boggs (D La.). Albert said he would not "let the meddling hand of government at any level in any degree be placed on any man's altar."

Schwengel pointed out that Wylie said local school boards would make the determination on what was a non-denominational prayer, subject to review by the courts. This, said Schwengel, would make it the business of government to decide the content of prayer.

An amendment by John Buchanan (R Ala.), a Baptist minister, substituting "voluntary" for "non-denominational" to describe the type of prayer allowed, was approved by voice vote.

Wylie argued in favor of the resolution. The Supreme Court, he said, had "for all practical purposes voided school prayer." G. V. (Sonny) Montgomery (D Miss.) warned members it would be politically unpopular to oppose the amendment. William J. Keating (R Ohio) said members would be acting in contradiction when they participate in prayer before each daily session of the House, yet say it is unconstitutional for their children to do the same in school.

Emergency Detention

Congress completed action Sept. 16 on a bill (HR 234—PL 92-128) repealing the Emergency Detention Act—Title II of the Internal Security Act of 1950 (PL 81-831).

Besides repealing Title II of the 1950 Act, HR 234 contained a proviso, added by the House Judiciary Committee, declaring that "no citizen shall be imprisoned or otherwise detained by the United States except pursuant to an act of Congress."

The administration supported a straight repeal of Title II, but the President signed the bill Sept. 25.

Final action came when the Senate with only about six senators present accepted the House-passed bill by voice vote without amendment. A similar Senate bill (S 592) had been reported by the Senate Judiciary Committee July 26. S 592 was identical to S 1872, passed by the Senate in 1969.

HR 234 was one of two bills considered by the House in 1971 on the same subject. Another bill (HR

School Prayer Amendment

H J Res 191 would have added the following amendment to the Constitution:

"Nothing contained in this Constitution shall abridge the right of persons lawfully assembled, in any public building which is supported in whole or in part through the expenditure of public funds, to participate in voluntary prayer or meditation."

Before the House amended the resolution on the floor, the language had provided for participation in non-denominational, rather than in voluntary, prayer.

---

820) was reported March 30 by the House Internal Security Committee. It would have amended the Emergency Detention Act in an attempt to ease the fears of minority groups and other critics who felt the act could become an instrument of repression against any group.

Background. The Emergency Detention Act provided that the President, in a self-declared "internal security emergency" such as invasion or insurrection in aid of a foreign enemy, or in case of war, could detain in detention camps persons whom the government suspected might engage in espionage or sabotage. *(Congress and the Nation, Vol. I, p. 1651)*

The specific language of the act provided that the President, acting through the attorney general, could, during the emergency, detain any persons "as to whom there is reasonable ground to believe that such persons probably will engage in, or probably will conspire with others to engage in, acts of espionage or of sabotage."

The act had never been used and the six camps established under the act had never been used for detention.

Nevertheless, members of minority groups, especially Negroes, felt threatened that such a law might be used against them. Their fears were fueled by a 1968 report of the House Committee on Un-American Activities (predecessor of the Internal Security Committee) recommending use of detention camps for certain categories of persons arrested in urban riots.

Particularly sensitive to the 1950 act were Americans of Japanese descent. After the Japanese attack on Pearl Harbor in 1941, more than 110,000 American citizens of Japanese origin were removed from their homes in the Pacific Coast states and transferred inland to relocation centers where they were detained for the duration of World War II. The reason for their detention was the belief of government leaders that some among them would aid Japan in an invasion of the West Coast by acts of espionage and sabotage against the United States.

House Debate. The House on Sept. 14, after two days of debate, passed HR 234 by a 356-49 roll-call vote. Attempts by opponents of repeal to water down the bill by amending instead of repealing Title II of the 1950 act, led by Richard H. Ichord (D Mo.), chairman of the Internal Security Committee, were beaten.

An Ichord try to substitute the provisions of his committee's bill (HR 820) for HR 234, was defeated on a 68-22 standing vote. An attempt by Ichord to water down the language in HR 234—that no person could be imprisoned by the United States except pursuant to congressional action—was beaten on a 124-272 recorded teller vote.

Obscene Mail

The House by a 356-25 roll-call vote, July 7, passed a bill (HR 8805) prohibiting the sending of obscene material through the mails. The bill defined obscene as appealing to the prurient interest when considered as a whole by contemporary standards. Prurient interest was defined in the bill as that which "includes a shameful or morbid interest in nudity, sex or excretion which goes substantially beyond limits of candor in description or representation."

Robert N. C. Nix (D Pa.), who introduced the bill, said existing law provided that obscene material could not be sent through the mails, but was not effective because it did not define obscene. The Senate took no action on the bill.

Privacy

The Senate Judiciary Subcommittee on Constitutional Rights held hearings in February and March on computers, data banks, Army spying and the right of privacy. Sam J. Ervin Jr. (D N.C.), subcommittee chairman, said data banks and computers posed a threat to privacy if improperly used.

The government had always kept dossiers on individuals—criminals and non-criminals alike—detailing their personal habits, associations, views and biographies. But the files in the past were handled manually and thus were laborious to locate and maintain. This had proved a partial bar against invasion of privacy. Computers and data banks changed that. Information now could be easily stored and rapidly transmitted to requesting parties.

By 1971, computerized information was flowing back and forth between government agencies, among the federal, state and local governments, and in some cases to such agencies in the private sector as credit bureaus.

Among government agencies identified by the Subcommittee as maintaining computerized files on individuals were the Departments of State; Health, Education and Welfare; Housing and Urban Development; Transportation; Justice; Defense; plus the Federal Bureau of Investigation, Census Bureau, Civil Service Commission, Secret Service and Internal Revenue Service.

Concern over army surveillance of the peaceful activities of individuals began early in 1970 with the disclosure by a former army intelligence officer, Christopher H. Pyle, that more than 1,000 plainclothes army investigators shadowed political dissidents.

The concern grew during the year as Ervin revealed that Illinois political figures had been under surveillance by the Army. After Ervin made his charges, other former Army intelligence specialists came forward to say they had been ordered to spy on civil rights leaders, college students, folk singers, welfare mothers and the Republican and Democratic conventions of 1968.

The reason for the surveillance, according to Ervin, was to determine the political leanings of the persons involved in order to predict their future behavior. The motivations behind the surveillance, said Ervin, "were directly counter to the principle that the Army is controlled by civilian constitutional authority—that it does not have a direct mandate to act independently of the appointed and elected civilian leadership of the country."

Army spying on civilians apparently stemmed from the urban riots of the late 1960s. Repeated calls for federal troops to help local police and national guardsmen quell riots meant that the Army needed certain information on cities: location of armories, police stations, power sources, potential detention facilities and names of persons who could help or hinder in restoring order.

Shakeup. Reacting to the disclosures, Defense Secretary Melvin R. Laird in late 1970 ordered a major shakeup in military intelligence operations to bring them under closer civilian control.

He called for a top-level civilian review of Pentagon policies regarding intelligence activities and ordered the director of the Defense Intelligence Agency (DIA) to report directly to him instead of through the Joint Chiefs of Staff. The DIA also was given increased control over the intelligence branches of the three services.

Also reacting to the criticism, the Army told its domestic intelligence commanders the Justice Department henceforward would handle domestic spying operations and they should "purge" some of the files at Fort Holabird, Md.

Robert F. Froehlke, assistant secretary of defense for administration, in day-long testimony March 2, insisted that the surveillance was constitutional, though perhaps inappropriate. He said the "culprit" for the Army spying was the Army Civil Disturbance Information and Collection Plan of May 2, 1968, which directed Army groups to provide civil disturbance information and called for cooperation among Department of Defense (DOD) and non-DOD agencies.

"So comprehensive were the requirements," he said, "that any category of information related even remotely to people or organizations active in a community in which the potential for a riot or disorder was present would fall within their scope." The plan was rescinded June 9, 1970, Froehlke said.

At another point, Froehlke told the subcommittee that "the highest level of civilian officials" in the Johnson White House and Justice Department were knowledgeable about the military spying, although little guidance in written form came from those officials. Prior to his testimony, it was believed only high military officers knew about the surveillance.

He confirmed that files were kept on Illinois Democratic Sen. Adlai E. Stevenson III and Rep. Abner J. Mikva (D Ill.) but denied that any file had been maintained on U.S. Circuit Court Judge Otto Kerner. This was contradicted by former Army intelligence agent John M. O'Brien, who told Congressional Quarterly he saw a dossier on Kerner in his office in Evanston, Ill.

Rehnquist Testimony. Assistant Attorney General William H. Rehnquist testified March 9 that utilization of modern data processing techniques was not harmful to privacy. The mere potential for abuse was no reason to restrict the use of computers and data banks, he said, adding, "I think it quite likely that self-discipline on the part of the executive branch will provide an answer to virtually all of the legitimate complaints against excesses of information gathering."

Testifying again on March 17, Rehnquist said government surveillance of persons for exercising their rights of speech under the First Amendment was not unconstitutional. He denied that such surveillance inhibited the exercise of First Amendment rights.

Various governmental officials testified on the use of computers by their agencies or departments. All assured the subcommittee they were sensitive to possible privacy invasions and that safeguards had been instituted to prevent unauthorized release of material.

Opponents of government computer files on personnel insisted there were no effective restraints on their use and that legislation was necessary to protect the threat to individual privacy posed by the computers and data banks.

Subversive Activities Control Board

The Senate Judiciary Subcommittee on Separation of Powers held a hearing Oct. 5 on S 2466 and S Res 163 relating to activities of the Subversive Activities Control Board (SACB).

S 2466 was designed to countermand President Nixon's Executive Order 11605 of July 2, 1971, which assigned new duties to the SACB. S Res 163 was a "sense of the Senate" resolution expressing the contention that Mr. Nixon had usurped legislative powers by his action. The bills were reported out by the subcommittee Oct. 28 but the full Judiciary Committee took no action in 1971.

The SACB was created by the Internal Security Act of 1950. It was composed of five members –appointed by the President and confirmed by the Senate—who were to determine whether any organization was a Communist-action or Communist-front group and whether any individual was a member of the former.

But Supreme Court decisions had so limited the constitutionally permissible activities of the SACB that its chairman, John W. Mahan, told the Senate Appropriations Committee July 6, "We do not have enough (to do) to fill our time."

The President's executive order gave the SACB the responsibility formerly held by the attorney general to keep a list of subversive groups. Persons belonging to

---

Nixon Expands SACB

President Nixon July 2, 1971, issued Executive Order 11605 expanding the role of the Subversive Activities Control Board.

Critics had long argued that the controversial board, which had been created in 1950 to identify Communist organizations, had been crippled by court rulings and was merely a repository for sinecures.

The presidential order made two significant changes in the duties of the board. It:

• Gave the board the responsibility formerly held by the attorney general to maintain a list of subversive groups.

• Directed the board to make determinations, upon petition by the attorney general and after hearings of whether a group was "totalitarian, fascist, communist, subversive, or whether it had adopted a policy of unlawfully advocating the commission of acts of force or violence to deny others their rights under the Constitution."

---

such groups could be barred from government jobs. The list—last updated in 1955—contained names of 283 groups, of which only 20 were believed to be active. *(Box this page)*

During the hearing on the bills, Subcommittee Chairman Sam J. Ervin Jr. (D N.C.) said Nixon's order went beyond his constitutional power and also violated First Amendment and due process rights of individuals. SACB Chairman Mahan argued that the President acted within his constitutional rights in expanding the jurisdiction of the board.

The SACB was the subject of intense Senate debate July 19 during consideration of the bill (HR 9272) containing its appropriation for fiscal 1972. The Senate voted to bar any use of SACB funds to carry out the executive order, but the provision was deleted by conferees.

1972

Freedom of the Press

The Senate Judiciary Subcommittee on Constitutional Rights resumed hearings in February on freedom of the press, with particular emphasis on broadcast journalism. Hearings had begun in 1971.

CBS television newsman Daniel Schorr testified that he was under investigation by the FBI in 1971, presumably because of critical stories he had broadcast on several subjects. The administration asserted that Schorr was under consideration for a high government job in the environmental field, but Schorr said he never was notified he was under consideration. The job itself was not identified by the government until the day Schorr testified.

Schorr said "an FBI investigation is not a neutral matter"—it affects the subject, his friends, family, relatives and business associates. He maintained that the Nixon administration had created "a climate of suspicion, hostility and nervousness" in the press corps. White House press officials declined to testify.

Bill Monroe, an NBC newsman, urged an end to licensing of broadcasters by the Federal Communications Commission. He said licensing was contrary to the First Amendment because it meant media answerability to government. Other witnesses complained of network television news bias and censorship of dramatic programs.

Clay T. Whitehead, director of the White House Office of Telecommunications Policy, discussed the federally funded Corporation for Public Broadcasting. He said the Nixon administration was promoting local control of public television in order to preclude the threat of government control.

Newsman's Privilege

House Judiciary Subcommittee No. 3 held hearings in September and October on bills designed to protect newsmen from compulsory disclosure of confidential information and sources in grand jury or other criminal proceedings.

Described as newsman's privilege legislation, the bills were an attempt to reconcile the constitutional guarantee of freedom of the press with the law enforcement system's need for information.

The issue arose in 1970 when federal and local prosecutors began securing subpoenas requiring newsmen to testify before grand juries about their sources for stories concerning criminal activities. Certain newsmen refused to testify, saying that their notes, tapes or films were protected by the constitutional guarantee of a free press and that disclosure would compromise their sources and shut off any further information from those sources because of the fear of disclosure.

The Justice Department issued guidelines in 1970 requiring approval, by the attorney general, of all federal subpoenas of newsmen and saying that such subpoenas should only be used when the information could not otherwise be obtained.

In three cases brought by protesting newsmen to the Supreme Court, the Court ruled 5-4 on June 29 that newsmen had no special right to refuse to answer relevant questions asked in a grand jury investigation. The majority opinion, however, appeared to leave open the possibility that Congress could legislate further on this question.

Witnesses differed on the amount of privilege the press needed to function effectively. Some said the privilege should be absolute—that is, there should be no condition under which a reporter would have to disclose confidential information. Others said the privilege should not apply to cases involving national security, libel, or certain crimes.

The Justice Department opposed all privilege bills. A witness said an absolute privilege was unwarranted because it might make it impossible to obtain information available from no other source, while a qualified privilege was unnecessary because the department had drawn up guidelines that gave the press adequate protection.

Government Information Policies

The House Government Operations Subcommittee on Foreign Operations and Government Information issued a report Sept. 20 on the administration and effectiveness of the Freedom of Information Act of 1966 (PL 89-487). *(Provisions, Congress and the Nation, Vol. II, p. 643)*

The act stated that all government papers, opinions, records, policy statements and staff manuals were to be made available upon request unless they were covered by one or more of nine exemptions. In addition, the person making the request could take the government to court if it refused disclosure, and the burden of proof for withholding information would be on the government. *(Exemptions, box)*

The report said effective operation of the act had been "hindered by five years of footdragging" by the federal bureaucracy. Major problem areas pinpointed by the committee were: bureaucratic delays in responding to requests for data, excessive fees for data, cumbersome legal remedies, lack of involvement in decision-making on requests for data by agency public information officers, and lack of priority given the enforcement of the act.

Nevertheless, the committee found that, in general, the act had helped thousands of persons to get access to information "when they have been able to overcome government roadblocks."

Information Act Exemptions

Certain types of information were made exempt from provisions of the Freedom of Information Act. The act reads:

"This section does not apply to matters that are—

"(1) specifically required by executive order to be kept secret in the interest of the national defense or foreign policy;

"(2) related solely to the internal personnel rules and practices of an agency;

"(3) specifically exempted from disclosure by statute;

"(4) trade secrets and commercial or financial information obtained from a person and privileged or confidential;

"(5) inter-agency or intra-agency memorandums or letters which would not be available by law to a party other than an agency in litigation with the agency;

"(6) personnel and medical files and similar files the disclosure of which would constitute a clearly unwarranted invasion of personal privacy;

"(7) investigatory files compiled for law enforcement purposes except to the extent available by law to a party other than an agency;

"(8) contained in or related to examination, operating, or condition reports prepared by, on behalf of, or for the use of an agency responsible for the regulation or supervision of financial institutions; or

"(9) geological and geophysical information and data, including maps, concerning wells."

One of the legislative changes recommended by the committee would require an agency to grant or deny the requested information within 10 working days of receipt of the request. An appeal from a denial would have to be answered in 20 days.

Subversive Activities Control Board

The House on May 30, by a 226-105 roll-call vote, passed an amended bill (HR 9669) to expand the powers of the Subversive Activities Control Board (SACB) and change its name to the Federal Internal Security Board. There was no Senate action on the bill.

The effect of the bill, requested by the administration, was to formalize an Executive Order (11605) issued by President Nixon July 2, 1971. The order gave the SACB the power formerly held by the attorney general to investigate and compile a list of groups which it considered subversive, totalitarian, fascist, or communist or any which sought to overthrow the government or advocated force or violence to deny others their rights. Persons belonging—or who had previously belonged—to such groups could be denied federal employment. *(Background, 1971 chronology)*

A floor amendment to the bill, reported May 9 by the Committee on Internal Security, was adopted by voice vote. Offered by Bob Eckhardt (D Texas), the amendment deleted a provision allowing the President to designate persons other than the attorney general to initiate investigations by the board.

An amendment offered by Richardson Preyer (D N.C.), to scrap the board entirely and substitute for it a completely new federal loyalty security act, was defeated by voice vote.

Richard H. Ichord (D Mo.), chairman of the Internal Security Committee, led the fight for the bill. He said the attorney general's list, last updated in 1955, was outmoded. By giving the responsibility for compiling the list to the board, Congress would both improve the effectiveness of security programs and breathe some life into the moribund agency, he said.

Liberals opposed the measure. Chairman Emanuel Celler (D N.Y.) of the Judiciary Committee said it was unconstitutional because of vagueness, because it delegated legislative authority to the executive branch, and because the Supreme Court had ruled that no one could be excluded from a federal job because of mere membership in a subversive group.

Even Preyer, who ultimately voted for the bill, said it made no contribution to federal security. "It merely tinkers with the security program—and in an unconstitutional way," he said.

Related Legislation. The State-Justice-Commerce Departments fiscal 1973 appropriations bill (HR 14989—PL 92-544), which contained funds for the board, provided that none of the money could be used to carry out Executive Order 11605.

The House version of the bill had reduced the board's funding request to $450,000 from $706,000. The Senate version excluded all money for the board. The conference agreement, which cleared Congress Oct. 13, contained $350,000 for the board plus the limit on its use. The final appropriation would enable the board to do little more than pay its five members at $36,000 apiece—and staff.

Travel Restrictions

The House on Oct. 2, under suspension of the rules procedure, rejected a bill (HR 16742) giving the President the power to restrict the travel of U.S. citizens to nations with which the United States was in armed conflict.

The **230-140 key roll-call vote** fell 18 short of the necessary two-thirds majority (248 in this case) required to pass a bill under the suspension procedure. Republicans largely supported the bill (130-27), but Democrats split (100-113) against it.

The Justice Department supported the bill. Its immediate application would have been to North Vietnam, the only country with which the United States was in armed conflict. The bill specified maximum penalties for unauthorized travel of 10 years in jail or a $10,000 fine or both.

Proposals to restrict Americans' travel, particularly to war zones, were introduced after actress Jane Fonda and former Attorney General Ramsey Clark toured North Vietnam in the summer of 1972 and made allegedly treasonable statements there. The Justice Department, however, refused to prosecute them upon their return.

Existing law required government approval for travel to North Vietnam, North Korea and Cuba, but did not prescribe penalties for violations of the law. In addition, the Supreme Court ruled in 1967 that travel to a re-

Court-Approved Eavesdropping

The Omnibus Crime Control and Safe Streets Act of 1968 authorized the use of electronic surveillance or wiretapping—when specifically approved by a federal or state judge—in a variety of circumstances relating to serious crimes. The same section of this law required judges who approved or disapproved wiretaps to report within 30 days of the end of the wiretapping to the Administrative Office of the U.S. Courts, informing them of the application, the action on the application and other related information. The Administrative Office was, each April, to provide Congress with a summary of this information. The first such report covered the last six months of 1968. The first full year report covered the year 1969. The following table shows the number of court-approved wiretaps and instances of electronic surveillance in each jurisdiction where such is authorized by law for the years 1969-72. The total cost of an intercept (manpower, equipment etc.) ranged from a low of $5.00 to a high of $146,300.00.

JURISDICTION	'69	'70	'71	'72
Federal	33	182	285	206
Arizona	8	7	6	10
Colorado	2	1	9	7
Connecticut	—	—	0	18
Delaware	—	—	—	1
Florida	2	12	15	7
Georgia	4	11	12	15
Kansas	—	0	1	3
Maryland	15	24	27	29
Massachusetts	0	7	6	8
Minnesota	—	3	1	2
Nebraska	—	0	0	4
Nevada	—	0	1	1
New Hampshire	—	1	0	0
New Jersey	45	132	187	235
New York	111	215	254	294
Oregon	—	0	0	1
Rhode Island	1	0	6	10
South Dakota	—	0	0	0
Washington	—	0	0	0
Wisconsin	—	1	6	4
TOTAL	301	596	816	855
(Number denied)	(2)	(0)	(0)	(4)

SOURCE: Annual reports on applications for orders authorizing or approving the interception of wire or oral communications. Administrative Office of the U.S. Courts, 1969, 1970, 1971, 1972.

stricted area with a valid passport was not illegal. HR 16742 was reported by the Internal Security Committee.

Committee On Privacy

The House Feb. 8 by a 168-216 roll-call vote, rejected a resolution (H Res 164) that would have created a Select Committee on Privacy, Human Values and Democratic Institutions. Under the resolution, the committee would have been composed of nine members appointed by the Speaker. They would have been empowered to investigate how technology, particularly computers, affected personal privacy, civil rights and democracy. The committee would not have been authorized to propose legislation but was to report its findings to the House by the end of the 92d Congress.

The resolution was sponsored by Cornelius E. Gallagher (D N.J.), who had headed the Government Operations Special Subcommittee on Invasion of Privacy that was abolished in 1971. Strong opposition to the resolution was expressed by Chairman Emanuel Celler (D N.Y.) of the Judiciary Committee, who said the proposed committee would encroach on his committee's jurisdiction.

HISC Budget

Reflecting increasing discontent with its Internal Security Committee, the House on March 1 voted 303-102 to approve a resolution (H Res 849) that reduced the committee's budget request by $71,500. The committee had requested $596,500 for the second session of the 92nd Congress, but the House vote backed the Administration Committee's recommendation of $525,000. HISC was the only committee to get less than it asked for in 1972.

The committee had long been the most controversial in the House. Critics contended that it did too little to justify its existence and accused it of treading on constitutional rights. Robert F. Drinan (D Mass.), HISC member, charged the committee with keeping more than 754,000 dossiers on Americans and sharing them with federal agencies in violation of House rules.

William F. Ryan (D N.Y.) said HISC was third among House committees in personnel (54) and seventh in appropriations in 1971, and Henry Helstoski (D N.J.) pointed out that it considered only seven bills in 1971 compared with an overall House committee average of 619.

Richard H. Ichord, HISC chairman, defended the committee. He said it held 60 days of hearings in 1971, conducted five major investigations and that most of the requested increase in funding was for minority staff made mandatory by the Legislative Reorganization Act of 1970.

Civil Rights

With the departure of Lyndon B. Johnson and the arrival of Richard M. Nixon at the White House in 1969, a watershed was marked out in the modern civil rights movement.

In the next four years, the character, the strength and the focus of the movement shifted. White House support for civil rights declined to an almost imperceptible level during Nixon's first term, perhaps in keeping with the attitude of 'benign neglect' urged on the President by one of his advisers.

Late in 1972 a civil rights symposium was held in Austin, Texas, at the new Lyndon B. Johnson Library. Gathered there, those men and women who had led the action in the 1960s looked back with pride—and forward with some foreboding. "We will either go forward to our announced goal of proving that all men are created equal... or we will denigrate the plural society we envisioned and developed, and revert to a 'house divided' which the prophetic Lincoln said 'cannot stand,'" warned retired Chief Justice Earl Warren.

And former President Johnson, in his last major address, seconded Warren's point: "By unconcern, by neglect, by complacent beliefs that our labors in the fields of human rights are completed, we of today can seed our future with storms that would rage over the lives of our children and our children's children."

These men and women had through their efforts placed firmly on the law books the Civil Rights Act of 1964, the Voting Rights Act of 1965, and the Fair Housing Act of 1968: There was little left to legislate the current need was for vigorous enforcement and implementation of these laws, carrying out of their spirit as well as their letter.

Legislation, 1969-72

The major civil rights bills of the 91st and 92nd Congresses were both amendments to these earlier landmark laws. In 1970 Congress amended the Voting Rights Act to extend its effectiveness for five more years. The extension was made over the opposition of the Nixon administration, which responded to southern pressure with a proposal to amend the 1965 law in such a way as to loosen the restrictions it placed on the areas it covered, all of which were in the South.

In 1972 Congress approved the Equal Employment Opportunities Enforcement Act, which gave the Equal Employment Opportunity Commission (EEOC) the power to back up its findings of job bias with a demand that the offender shape up. This measure remedied a deficiency in the 1964 Civil Rights Act, which had created the EEOC without enforcement powers. Although civil rights groups had pushed to equip the EEOC with the power to issue its own enforcement orders, there was general satisfaction with the alternative method suggested by the administration and approved by Congress—authorizing the agency to go to federal courts for enforcement orders.

The civil rights movement broadened in these four years. Young people, women, Mexican-Americans, Spanish-Americans and American Indians all moved within its scope, adding to its support even as they swelled its burden.

The voting rights law approved by Congress in 1970 lowered to 18 the voting age for all federal, state and local elections. President Nixon opposed this method of lowering the voting age—by federal statute rather than by constitutional amendment. Days before the new voting age was to become a reality on Jan. 1, 1971, the Supreme Court held that—since the change had been made by statute, not constitutional amendment—it was valid only for federal elections. Galvanized into unusually swift action, Congress by March 1971 had approved a constitutional amendment lowering the voting age for federal, state and local elections. Within a few months, the necessary 38 state legislatures had ratified it—and in the 1972 elections some 11 million young people were eligible to vote as a result.

And even as this amendment—the Twenty-sixth—went to the states for ratification, efforts were continuing to win congressional approval of the proposed Twenty-seventh, the long-sought Equal Rights Amendment, guaranteeing women equal legal rights with men. Approved for the first time—since its introduction in every Congress since 1923—by the House in 1970, the amendment finally won Senate approval and was sent to the states in 1972: the ratification process was under way at the end of that year.

Interestingly enough, both these measures—the language added to the voting rights bill in 1970 to lower the voting age and the equal rights amendment—had to be passed around and over the adamant and long-standing

References

Discussion of civil rights developments from 1945-64 may be found in *Congress and the Nation, Vol. I,* p. 1595-1642; for the years 1965-68, *Congress and the Nation, Vol. II,* p. 341-406.

The Court and Civil Rights

In its major pronouncements on civil rights matters from 1969-1972, the Supreme Court:

• Approved the use of busing, racial balance ratios, and gerrymandered school districts as interim means of erasing the vestiges of state-imposed school segregation. *Swann v. Charlotte-Mecklenburg County Board,* 9-0, April 20, 1971.

• Interpreted the Civil Rights Act of 1866 to ban a community swim club from denying membership to a black man leasing a home in the community served by the club. *Sullivan v. Little Hunting Park Inc.,* 5-3, Dec. 19, 1969.

• Held that the 1964 Civil Rights Act forbade an employer to require a high school diploma or general score on an intelligence test as a condition for employment or promotion if the test was not related to job skills and if it tended to disqualify more black than white applicants. *Griggs v. Duke Power Co.,* 8-0, March 8, 1971.

• Allowed states to make construction of low-income housing projects conditional upon approval of the project by a referendum in the area where the project is to be located. *James v. Valtierra,* 5-3, April 26, 1971.

• Held for the first time that the constitutional guarantee of equal protection of the laws applies to instances of sex discrimination, invalidating laws which require preference of one sex over the other. *Reed v. Reed,* 7-0, Nov. 22, 1971.

• Approved congressional action to lower, by legislation, the voting age for federal elections, to restrict state residence requirements for voting in presidential elections, and to ban literacy tests—but disapproved legislation approved by Congress to lower the voting age for state and local elections. *Oregon v. Mitchell,* 5-4, Dec. 21, 1970.

opposition of Emanuel Celler (D N.Y.), dean of the House and chairman of the House Judiciary Committee, the House committee with jurisdiction over both matters. Senate strategists circumvented Celler's opposition on the 18-year-old vote by attaching the language authorizing this expansion of the franchise to the extension of the 1965 Voting Rights Act, a measure which Celler strongly championed. And that same summer the House pulled the equal rights amendment from the Judiciary Committee—and Celler—by use of a petition discharging his committee from further consideration of the bill. Ironically, Celler in 1972 was defeated for re-election by a young woman lawyer.

School Desegregation

Definite retreat on civil rights in Congress was apparent during these years on only one major issue: school desegregation. Just as southern members had predicted, once federal pressure to desegregate public schools moved outside the South, the members of Congress from the areas newly feeling such pressure began to voice opposition. The specific issue was the use of buses to transport children to schools farther from their homes than they could walk. But the meaning behind the anti-busing movement was a general reaction of fear and resentment against federal pressure for a change in the racial composition of public schools.

Congress, backed solidly by the White House, began to approve strict limits on the use of busing for desegregation. Each time it cast a major vote on the issue, the House of Representatives found a larger number of non-southern votes on the anti-busing side.

But the Supreme Court—even with the Nixon-appointed members—stood firm behind the principles of its earlier decision. The first decision issued by the court after the new Chief Justice, Warren E. Burger, took his seat turned aside an administration request for further delay in school desegregation. And in the spring of 1971, the court directly rejected the administration's anti-busing stance to hold that busing was in some cases indeed a permissible tool for desegregating schools.

1969

Voting Rights

White House support for civil rights during Nixon's first term was in sharp contrast to the substantial backing from that source during the Johnson presidency. The first clear signal of the new administration's attitude came in 1969 on the issue of voting rights.

The Voting Rights Act of 1965, under which almost one million black citizens had been registered to vote, was described by Civil Rights Commission Chairman Theodore M. Hesburgh as the most effective civil rights law ever enacted. The act was to expire in August 1970. Civil rights advocates urged a simple five-year extension, but the Nixon administration proposed, and the House in 1969 approved, amendments to the law which would make it applicable nationwide and, critics said, dilute its impact. Civil rights advocates termed passage of the administration bill the worst defeat for civil rights suffered in the House in 10 years.

House Minority Leader Gerald R. Ford (R Mich.) said that the amendments would make the law more equitable because it would no longer apply only to certain areas. The purpose of the original "discriminatory legislation" had been accomplished, he said.

In the Senate, liberals, led by Philip A. Hart (D Mich.), blocked referral of the bill to the Judiciary Committee until they received assurances that the committee would report the bill back by March 1, 1970, and that it would immediately become the pending business of the Senate, thus preventing a filibuster on a motion to consider the bill.

The 1965 law (PL 89-110) had suspended the use of literacy tests and other voter qualification devices and authorized federal supervision of voter registration and new voting laws in certain states and counties.

An automatic "trigger" formula brought states and counties under the effect of the 1965 act. If a state or county had a literacy test or similar voter qualification device in effect on Nov. 1, 1964, *and* if less than 50 percent of the voting-age residents of the area were registered to vote on that date or actually voted in the 1964 presidential election, PL 89-110:

• Suspended literacy tests or similar voter qualification devices for that state or county.

• Authorized appointment of federal voting examiners to supervise voter registration in that state or county (Section 3).

• Required that any new voting law enacted in an area covered by the act be approved by the attorney general or a three-judge federal district court for the District of Columbia before taking effect (Section 5).

• Stated that any covered area could escape the effect of the act—and reinstate the suspended tests or devices and terminate the examiner process—by obtaining a judgment, from a three-judge federal district court in the District of Columbia, declaring that the state or county had used no such test or device during the preceding five years to discriminate against persons because of their race (Section 4).

This last provision permitted the act to terminate in August 1970. After that time the court could not refuse to grant such a judgment, because all such tests or devices would have been suspended for five years by PL 89-110. (Areas affected by the act as of 1969 were Alabama, Georgia, Louisiana, Mississippi, South Carolina, Virginia, and a number of counties in North Carolina.)

HOUSE ACTION

Two sets of amendments to the 1965 Voting Rights Act were the center of what was the major congressional battle over civil rights legislation in 1969.

Early that year, civil rights leaders began to urge extension of the act until August 1975. Such action was needed, they argued, to preserve the gains made by black voters in the South. Such a bill (HR 4249) was introduced Jan. 23 by House Judiciary Committee Chairman Emanuel Celler (D N.Y.). Hearings on the bill were held in May and June, but Attorney General John N. Mitchell repeatedly failed to appear to present the administration's position.

Finally, after five cancelled appearances, Mitchell appeared late in June and presented an alternative administration bill. It would amend PL 89-110 to:

• Impose a nationwide ban on literacy tests until Jan. 1, 1974.

• Delete provisions under which only certain areas were affected, thus making the act effective nationwide.

• Delete the requirement that affected areas obtain federal approval of all new voting laws.

• Set a minimum state residence requirement for voting in national elections.

The administration bill would eliminate from Section 5 the requirement that states covered by the bill file all election law changes with the Attorney General. Instead it would be up to the Justice Department to file suit against discriminatory laws. The bill would also remove exclusive jurisdiction over voting rights cases from the federal courts in the District of Columbia and assign it to the local federal courts.

Criticized as a "sophisticated but deadly" way to kill the 1965 act, the bill was opposed by Assistant Senate Minority Leader Hugh Scott (R Pa.) and House Judiciary Committee ranking minority member William M. McCulloch (R Ohio).

At the root of the dispute between proponents of the administration bill and the supporters of a simple five-year extension were differing assessments of the need to keep the seven southern states under special federal scrutiny.

In his testimony on July 11, the Attorney General contended that "the dangers to voting rights, which existed prior to the passage of the 1965 act, appear to have substantially decreased in the seven covered states."

Celler said the Mitchell proposal to ban literacy tests in all states was "like trying to stem a flood in Mississippi by building a dam in Idaho."

John Conyers Jr. (D Mich.), one of the nine blacks in the House, said "The whole thing is an approach toward Republicanizing the South. The political connotations are inescapable and reprehensible." Clarence Mitchell of the National Association for the Advancement of Colored People (NAACP) said "something had to be done to appease (Sen.) Strom Thurmond (R S.C.) and this is the appeasement."

But Attorney General Mitchell said that singling out the states now covered for continued coverage was unfair and unrealistic, when other areas had lower percentages of minority voting participation. He stated that a higher percentage of voting-age blacks voted in the Deep South in 1968 than in the Watts district of Los Angeles or Washington, D.C., and that little more than one-third of the voting-age Negro population of Manhattan, the Bronx or Brooklyn, New York City, voted in 1968.

Committee Action. However, the committee rejected the administration bill, and late in July it reported the Celler bill (HR 4249) extending the act for five years. The committee bill extended until August 1975 the period of time before certain states and counties could seek to reinstate literacy tests and other qualifying devices as prerequisites to voter registration.

The 1965 act provided that states and counties affected by the act, to become exempt from its provisions must obtain a declaratory judgment from the federal district court for the District of Columbia that no such test or device had been used "for the purpose or with the effect of denying or abridging the right to vote on account of race or color" for the preceding five years. The proposed amendment would provide that the court must find that no such test or device had been so used for the preceding ten years.

In its report, the committee noted that, during its deliberations, it had considered and rejected two amendments to the act proposed by the Nixon administration. Adoption of a nationwide ban on literacy tests, the report said, did not seem justified at the present time, since there was no evidence that literacy tests, outside the area already covered by the 1965 act, were used for discriminatory purposes. The committee report said that the proposal to set a uniform residence requirement for voting for President was not related to voting discrimination based on race.

Rules Committee Delay. HR 4249 as reported by the House Judiciary Committee remained pending before the House Rules Committee for three and one-half months. In November the Rules Committee provided a rule for consideration of the bill but specified that the administration bill could be offered as an amendment to HR 4249 during floor action.

Floor Action. In action seen as a defeat for civil rights forces, the House Dec. 11 approved, by a roll-call vote of

234-179, the administration-proposed voting rights bill. The administration's bill was approved in place of the version reported by Judiciary Committee.

Approval of the Nixon proposal by the House followed its adoption as an amendment in the nature of a substitute for the committee bill. After first rejecting the amendment on a voice vote, the House adopted it by a teller vote of 189-165 and by a **key voll-call vote of 208-204.**

House action followed heated debate which focused on the "regional" character of the 1965 Voting Rights Act and the need for continuing its selective application. Advocates of the five-year extension, led by Celler and McCulloch, argued that the effect of the act should be extended, without change, to preserve the substantial gains in black voter registration achieved since 1965 in the Deep South.

Supporters of the administration measure, offered by Minority Leader Gerald R. Ford (R Mich.), said that the act had accomplished its purpose—Negro registration in the covered areas had increased from 29 per cent to 52 per cent, with more than 800,000 blacks registered there since 1965—and should be amended to apply nation-wide, releasing the areas from "discriminatory legislation."

The administration proposal, attacked by Celler as "nothing but a sham and a subterfuge and misleading," was defended by Ford as a significant improvement over the 1965 act. Ford said it would eliminate the short-comings of the 1965 act while continuing federal surveillance of voting rights and practices.

Ford described the most significant change proposed in the administration measure as the shift from a presumption that covered areas were guilty of discrimination until proven innocent to the presumption that states were innocent of discrimination until proven guilty.

"Maybe, past sins justified such severity in past legislation," he said. "But this is not the Reconstruction Era and neither is this 1965. Four eventful years have passed; evils and errors of another time have yielded. Now, today, it is wrong and it is shameful for this House to perpetuate a punitive and discriminatory provision for another five years beyond the point where the original authors of the act intended it to expire.... Just as we do not want any second-class citizens in this country, neither do we want any second-class states."

McCulloch took issue with Ford concerning the effectiveness of the administration proposal. "The South," he said, "has not to any appreciable extent suffered a change of heart. Progress has been made only by impact of federal law and not through generosity of spirit."

The House by a teller vote of 189-165, reaffirmed on a roll-call vote of 208-204, agreed to the amendment to HR 4249 substituting the language of the Administration bill for the committee version. The House then passed the amended bill by a roll-call vote of 234-179.

SENATE ACTION

Committee Action. The Senate Judiciary Subcommittee on Constitutional Rights held hearings on the proposals in July, but Subcommittee Chairman Sam J. Ervin Jr. (D N.C.), who had voted against the 1965 act, had little enthusiasm for further action.

Floor Action. The Senate, by unanimous consent, Dec. 16 referred HR 4249, as passed by the House, to the Sen-

A Long Struggle for EEOC

The effort to create an effective federal agency to oversee and enforce equal job opportunity stretched back 30 years.

The Fair Employment Practice Committee (FEPC) was created by President Roosevelt in 1941 and directed to combat job discrimination within the federal government and by defense contractors. Four years later, Congress directed that the agency would expire in 1946 unless a law giving it permanent status was enacted. The FEPC died when a Senate filibuster and the House Rules Committee blocked action on a bill authorizing its continued existence.

Two years later, President Truman asked that Congress authorize a permanent FEPC, but it took two more years for a bill to reach the floor of either chamber. In 1950, the House bypassed the Rules Committee and took up a bill, but the conservative forces were able to substitute and pass a far weaker measure. A filibuster blocked Senate action on a similar bill that year.

During the next decade, the responsibility of supervising equal job opportunity was left to White House commissions. Twice the Senate reported a bill to strengthen the federal role in this area, but Congress took no further action.

A new drive for strong federal supervision of equal employment opportunities developed during the civil rights revolution of the late 1950s and early 1960s.

In 1961, the U.S. Commission on Civil Rights recommended that Congress grant statutory authority to a federal agency to encourage and enforce a policy of equal employment opportunity.

The first phase of this drive culminated in the creation by Title VII of the Civil Rights Act of 1964 of the Equal Employment Opportunity Commission. But in the bargaining process which won passage of that omnibus bill, the new EEOC lost any power of enforcement.

In 1962, a House committee had reported a bill creating an EEOC empowered to investigate and conciliate complaints of job discrimination. That bill allowed the EEOC, when conciliation failed, to haul discriminating employers into federal court. But the Rules Committee blocked further action.

In 1963, a House committee reported a bill creating an EEOC with the power to issue cease-and-desist orders to recalcitrant employers. But when the Judiciary Committee incorporated this measure into its omnibus civil rights bill, it watered down these enforcement powers. In the omnibus bill as passed by the House, the EEOC was only authorized to go to federal court to seek an injunction to enforce a halt to or a remedy for the discrimination it had found.

During Senate consideration in 1963, the still-to-be created EEOC lost even this enforcement power. The compromise version of the act which emerged transferred from the EEOC to the Attorney General the power to initiate court action against discriminatory employers.

ate Judiciary Committee with instructions that it be reported back by the committee by March 1, 1970. The instructions also specified that HR 4249 should be made the pending business of the Senate on March 1 or the first legislative day thereafter. The instructions were added to the motion referring the bill by liberal senators who feared that the committee might delay indefinitely sending the bill back to the floor.

Equal Employment Opportunity

"It shall be an unlawful employment practice for an employer to fail or refuse to hire or to discharge any individual or otherwise to discriminate against any individual with respect to his compensation, terms, conditions, or privileges or employment, because of such individual's race, color, religion, sex, or national origin," declared Title VII of the 1964 Civil Rights Act.

To oversee this law, the act created the Equal Employment Opportunities Commission (EEOC), but the compromises common to the legislative process resulted in this case in depriving the new agency of enforcement powers. The EEOC was authorized to use only conciliation in resolving problems of employment discrimination. *(Further background, box p. 496)*

Immediately upon enactment of the law creating the EEOC, the push was on for passage of a bill equipping the new agency with enforcement powers. President Johnson asked Congress repeatedly to authorize the agency to issue cease-and-desist orders.

The House in 1966 approved an EEOC enforcement bill, but the Senate, preoccupied with the abortive 1966 civil rights act, failed to act on that bill.

In 1968, the Senate reported an EEOC bill but took no further action in face of a filibuster threat by Everett McKinley Dirksen (R Ill. 1951-1969), who described the measure as "one of the most offensive pieces of legislation that could come before Congress."

With the change in administrations in 1969, White House support for such a measure dissolved. In March Dirksen threatened EEOC Chairman Clifford L. Alexander Jr. with loss of his post unless the EEOC stopped what Dirksen called its "punitive harassment" of businessmen. Within a month Alexander resigned, charging the administration with crippling the agency by its lack of support. William H. Brown III of Philadelphia was named as the new chairman.

The cease-and-desist proposal was reintroduced in 1969. The Nixon administration countered with a bill authorizing the EEOC to initiate suits in federal court against uncooperative employers. Both House and Senate subcommittees held hearings on the proposals, but that was the extent of congressional action on the matter in 1969. Alexander appeared before both subcommittees to urge adoption of the cease-and-desist powers approach.

Deputy Attorney General Richard G. Kleindienst and Brown advocated the administration position, stating that the courts were the proper forum for resolution of civil rights matters. The administration proposal, they said, would create powers which could immediately be put into use without the restructuring and expansion of staff which would be necessitated by adoption of the cease-and-desist powers approach.

Federally Subsidized Discrimination?

The federal government was using public funds to subsidize employment discrimination, charged the Civil Rights Commission in a report issued May 1, 1969. "Jobs and Civil Rights" was the title of the report, written by Richard P. Nathan, later assistant director of the Budget Bureau for human resources programs.

The commission called the federal government seriously deficient in enforcement of a 1965 executive order forbidding job discrimination by federal contractors. The commission said that "by continuing to contract with employers who practice discrimination, the federal government not only fails to use a powerful, readily available mechanism (contract cancellation) to help end discrimination in private employment, but in addition spends public funds actually to subsidize such discrimination."

The report recommended that the federal government begin "more determined application of sanctions" against contractors who fail to comply with federal policies on equal-opportunity employment. It also recommended transfer of the Office of Federal Contract Compliance (OFCC), which has primary responsibility for supervising compliance of federal contractors with federal employment policies, from the Department of Labor to the Equal Employment Opportunity Commission.

Administration Action. President Nixon March 28 sent a memorandum to the heads of all executive departments and agencies emphasizing his "official and personal endorsement of a strong policy of equal employment opportunity within the federal government. I am determined that the executive branch of the Government lead the way as an equal opportunity employer."

Nixon Aug. 8 issued Executive Order 11478 ordering federal leaders to take the initiative in eliminating job discrimination in Government agencies.

The order went beyond previous practices in demanding that the head of each executive department and agency must undertake "an affirmative program" to wipe out discrimination in recruiting, placement, advancement and on-the-job training. It required each department chief to allocate enough staff and money for the program and to make sure that all managers and supervisors on all levels carried it out.

The Civil Service Commission was authorized to oversee each department's program and to resolve complaints.

In a memorandum issued the same day, Nixon told all department and agency heads that "equal employment opportunity must become an integral part of the day-to-day management of federal agencies and interwoven with every action which has an effect on employees."

"Philadelphia Plan" Controversy. The Nixon administration's major initiative in civil rights—its "Philadelphia Plan" to increase minority employment on federal construction projects—survived a move in Congress in 1969 to kill it.

Named for the city in which the first agreement was reached with federal contractors, the plan was announced in June by the Labor Department; it took effect in September. Under the plan, federal contractors were required to work toward hiring a certain quota of minority employees on federal construction projects.

Controversy over the plan was ignited in August when Comptroller General Elmer B. Staats ruled it to be in violation of the 1964 Civil Rights Act, which forbade preference based on race or national origin. Attorney General John N. Mitchell disagreed: "The legal definition of discrimination is an evolving one, but it is now well recognized in judicial opinions that the obligation of nondiscrimination...does not require, and in some circumstances may not permit obliviousness or indifference to the racial consequences of alternative courses of action which involve the application of outwardly neutral criteria." The Labor Department announced late in September that similar plans would become effective in New York, Seattle, Boston, Los Angeles, San Francisco, St. Louis, Detroit, Pittsburgh and Chicago. By late 1972 approximately 55 such plans had been adopted.

The building trades unions and the AFL-CIO also opposed the plan. C.J. Haggerty, president of the building and construction trades department of the AFL-CIO, said that the unions opposed a quota system, regardless of its name. And AFL-CIO president George Meany complained that the Nixon administration was using the plan as a "horsewhip" against the building unions.

At October hearings before a Senate Judiciary subcommittee, Assistant Attorney General Jerris Leonard and Labor Secretary George P. Shultz defended the plan. Leonard called it "a major breakthrough in the fight for equality of opportunity in employment."

The issue came to the floor of the Senate in December: the Senate Appropriations Committee had added a rider to a fiscal 1970 supplemental appropriations bill barring the use of federal funds through contracts or agreements which the comptroller general found to be in violation of any federal law. The full Senate accepted the amendment, which would have nullified the "Philadelphia Plan," but the House refused Dec. 22 by a **key roll-call vote of 156-208** to accept the language and the Senate agreed to delete it.

1970

Voting Rights

The major civil rights measure of the 91st Congress became law June 22, 1970. On that day President Nixon signed a bill (HR 4249—PL 91-285) which extended the life of the 1965 Voting Rights Act until 1975 and granted the right to vote in federal, state and local elections to citizens between the ages of 18 and 21.

The President was dissatisfied with the bill. A five-year extension of the 1965 law had been approved by Congress instead of the revision of the law that he had proposed in 1969. And, as he pointed out in signing the bill, he was strongly of the opinion that Congress had overstepped itself in passing a law to lower the voting age. He believed that such a broad extension of the franchise should be accomplished by the process of amending the

---

Court Test on Voting Age

Early in its October 1970 term, the Supreme Court heard arguments challenging and defending the constitutionality of the provisions of PL 91-285.

The states of Oregon and Texas Aug. 3 asked the Supreme Court to declare the provision lowering the voting age to 18 unconstitutional. Congress had, the states charged, exceeded its authority in enacting a provision in conflict with state constitutions.

The Justice Department Aug. 17 brought two more cases before the court, filing suit against Idaho and Arizona. Both states had refused to comply with the 18-year-old vote provision. In addition, Idaho had refused to reduce its residence requirement to 30 days and Arizona had refused to suspend its literacy test for five years.

Days before the lower voting age became effective on Jan. 1, 1971, the Supreme Court ruled, upholding the lower voting age for federal elections, but striking it down—as enacted by the 1970 law—for state and local elections. The court upheld the literacy test suspension and the residence requirement reduction.

The court, in a curiously split decision, divided 5-4 on the issue of the 18-year-old vote provision. Justice Hugo L. Black, who wrote the majority opinion, stood alone in his belief that Congress could enact such a law governing federal elections but not regarding state and local elections.

Four justices—William J. Brennan Jr., William O. Douglas, Thurgood Marshall and Byron R. White—considered the 18-year-old vote provision constitutional for federal, state and local elections. Four others—Chief Justice Warren E. Burger, Harry A. Blackmun, John Marshall Harlan and Potter Stewart—considered it unconstitutional for any elections.

The reduction in residence requirements was upheld by an 8-1 vote, with only Harlan dissenting. The literacy test suspension was upheld unanimously.

Constitution—a process in which the states would participate through ratification or rejection. The lower voting age would add to the rolls approximately 11 million eligible voters between the ages of 18 and 21 by 1972.

Nixon asked Attorney General John N. Mitchell to move for a speedy court test of the validity of lowering the voting age by statute. He also urged Congress to continue work on a proposed constitutional amendment upon which a Senate subcommittee had held hearings early in 1970.

Six months later, on Dec. 21, the Supreme Court held, 5-4, that Congress had acted within its rights in lowering the voting age by statute for federal elections, but that it had exceeded its authority when it attempted to lower the voting age in that manner for state and local elections. *(Details, box this page)*

SENATE ACTION

As required in December 1969, the House-passed voting rights bill (HR 4249) arrived automatically on the Senate floor March 1, 1970. No committee vote had been taken on the bill; a subcommittee had held hearings in February. (Both the Civil Rights Acts of 1957 and 1964 were enacted without action by the Senate Judiciary Committee. The Senate bypassed committee consideration entirely by placing the House-passed bills directly on its calendar instead of referring them to committee. The Voting Rights Act of 1965 had been sent to the committee with a deadline for submission of the committee report.)

After substituting a five-year extension of the 1965 act for the House-approved administration bill, and adding the language lowering the voting age, the Senate on March 13 passed its version of the bill and sent it back to the House.

The substitute measure, extending the law for five years, was adopted March 13 by a vote of 51-22; the Senate had amended the substitute March 12 by a **64-17 key vote** to add the 18-year-old vote provision. The revised version of the bill was approved by a 64-12 roll-call vote.

Before final passage the Senate had rejected a series of amendments designed to weaken the provisions of the 1965 law, but it accepted an amendment which extended application of the law to states and counties that came within the triggering requirements as of Nov. 1, 1968. This amendment, first rejected by a 43-43 vote, was reconsidered and accepted by a vote of 50-37.

HOUSE ACTION

While the Senate was considering the amendment lowering the voting age, House Judiciary Committee Chairman Celler warned that he would oppose such an "extraneous" amendment. But the Senate's version of the bill placed Celler in a formidable dilemma.

Long a champion of civil rights—but even longer a foe of lowering the voting age—Celler had to choose between working against a civil rights bill similar to the one he had introduced and fought for in the House in 1969 and voting for the "extraneous" language lowering the voting age. He chose the latter.

Late in April President Nixon appealed to the House to separate the voting rights and voting age provisions and to consider the latter as a constitutional amendment instead. But early in June the Rules Committee voted 9-6 to send the bill back to the floor under a rule prescribing a choice between accepting the Senate version in its entirety or going to conference with the differing versions. Civil rights advocates, aware that most Senate conferees would come from the unfriendly Senate Judiciary Committee and would work to weaken—or kill—the bill, wished to avoid a conference.

The crucial vote came June 17 when the House agreed **by a key vote of 224-183** to vote on a resolution accepting the Senate version; the House then accepted the Senate bill 272-132. Had that resolution been rejected, the bill would have gone to conference.

Victory came as a result of the combined efforts of civil rights advocates, young lobbyists for the 18-year-old vote and retiring House Speaker John W. McCormack (D Mass.), who mounted a personal campaign for passage. Speaker McCormack noted that young people between 18 and 21 years old were far better educated than the young people of just 50 years ago, that the constitutional question would be reviewed by the Supreme Court and that "nothing would make John McCormack happier than to see this resolution adopted."

Celler warned that any change in the bill would send it to conference, where, he said, "there would be the death knell of the bill." He added that he was not worried about the rider lowering the voting age to 18 because the Supreme Court would review the provision before the 1971 elections.

Majority Leader Carl Albert (D Okla.) stated that if the House did not accept the Senate amendments, it "will have informed both the young and the blacks that there is no place for them in the orderly political process."

PROVISIONS

As signed by the President June 22, PL 91-285:

● Extended for five years, until August 1975, the life of the 1965 Voting Rights Act by lengthening from five to 10 years the period of time in which an area covered by the act must abstain from the use of any literacy test or qualifying device to discriminate against voters because of race or color.

● Amended Section 4 of the act to make the "trigger formula"—by which the act applied to a specified area—applicable to all states and counties with a literacy test in which less than 50 per cent of the voting age residents were registered on Nov. 1, 1968, or voted in the 1968 presidential election. (This would extend coverage of the Act to three Alaska districts; Apache County, Ariz.; Imperial County, Calif.; Elmore County, Idaho; Bronx, Kings (Brooklyn) and New York (Manhattan) counties, N.Y.; and Wheeler County, Ore.)

(Under the formula of the 1965 act—which was based upon November 1964 statistics—the act in 1969 affected Alabama, Georgia, Louisiana, Mississippi, South Carolina, Virginia and a number of North Carolina counties. These areas remained covered under the extension of the act.)

● Suspended the use of literacy tests in all states until Aug. 6, 1975.

● Provided that any person could vote in a presidential election in the place in which he had lived for 30 days immediately prior to a presidential election.

● Lowered from 21 to 18 the voting age for all federal, state and local elections, effective Jan. 1, 1971, "except as required by the Constitution."

Equal Employment Opportunity

The 91st Congress took a major step toward providing the Equal Employment Opportunity Commission (EEOC) with enforcement powers: the Senate in 1970 approved a measure authorizing the EEOC to issue cease-and-desist orders. But action was not completed; a similar House bill died in the Rules Committee when Congress adjourned, despite the efforts of its chief sponsor, Augustus F. Hawkins (D Calif.), to discharge the committee from consideration of the bill.

SENATE ACTION

Committee Action. Enforcement powers coupled with expanded responsibility were to be provided the EEOC by the Senate bill (S 2453), reported from the Senate Labor and Public Welfare Committee late in August. The bill granted the EEOC cease-and-desist powers—and transferred to it the power of the attorney general to sue persons or groups engaging in a pattern of employment discrimination. The bill also enlarged the coverage of federal civil rights law concerning job opportunity, thus expanding the field from which cases and complaints could come to the EEOC.

Floor Action. After two days of debate, the Senate Oct. 1 approved S 2453 by a 47-24 roll-call vote and sent the bill to the House. During floor debate, supporters of the committee bill defeated an effort to substitute the administration's proposed court enforcement language for that giving the EEOC cease-and-desist authority. The substitution was proposed by Peter H. Dominick (R Colo.) and was rejected Sept. 30 by a 27-41 vote.

The major amendment accepted during debate struck out a provision transferring to the EEOC from the Civil Service Commission responsibility for the federal equal employment program. Dominick also offered this amendment, adopted Sept. 30 by a 37-29 vote. The Senate inserted in the bill language creating a general counsel for the EEOC, whom the President would appoint with the advice and consent of the Senate.

The Senate rejected amendments proposed by Sam J. Ervin Jr. (D N.C.) which would have struck from the bill language extending the reach of federal civil rights laws concerning job opportunity—and therefore extending the authority of the EEOC—to employees of state and local governments and to employees of schools and colleges. It agreed to an Ervin amendment exempting most employees of religious organizations from such coverage.

HOUSE ACTION

Committee Action. On the same day in August that the Senate committee reported S 2453, the House Education and Labor Committee reported out a similar bill (HR 17555). The House bill granted cease-and-desist powers and extended the coverage of federal civil rights law and the EEOC to smaller businesses and unions than then covered, as well as to state and local governments and to employees of schools and colleges. The House version did not transfer the attorney general's "pattern or practice" lawsuit authority, but it did transfer to the EEOC the responsibility for supervising the equal opportunity program for federal employees.

The bill was referred to the Rules Committee, which effectively buried it for the duration of the 91st Congress.

Equal Rights Amendment

For the first time in history the House in 1970 approved a constitutional amendment guaranteeing equal legal rights for women. The bill (H J Res 264) was brought to the floor through a rarely used maneuver which allowed it to bypass the committee which ordinarily would have reported it. But Congress still failed to complete action on the amendment.

The bill was placed directly on the Senate calendar after House passage. The Senate began debate early in October, but the addition of two amendments effectively scuttled any chance of final congressional action on the measure in 1970. The Senate adjourned without taking a vote on passage of H J Res 264.

As passed by the House, the proposed constitutional amendment ensured that "equality of rights under the law shall not be denied or abridged by the United States or by any state on account of sex. Congress and the several states shall have power, within their respective jurisdictions, to enforce this article by appropriate legislation." To become a constitutional amendment, the bill required ratification by three-fourths of the states after passage in the House and Senate by two-thirds majorities.

HOUSE ACTION

Discharge Petition. No House committee hearings were held on H J Res 264. For 20 years House Judiciary Committee Chairman Emanuel Celler (D N.Y.) had consistently refused to hold hearings on such a measure. His opposition forced supporters of the bill to use the end-run tactic of the discharge petition to bring the bill to the floor. *(Chapter on Congress)*

In June 1970 Rep. Martha W. Griffiths (D Mich.), one of the Judiciary Committee members and the chief sponsor of the proposed amendment, filed a discharge petition. Within six weeks she had the requisite 218 signatures of a majority of the members of the House, and the Judiciary Committee was discharged of responsibility for the measure.

Floor Action. Facing off during floor debate, Griffiths and Celler each had their say. The Supreme Court had made the amendment necessary, said Griffiths, by failing to rule that women as a class were entitled to equal protection of the laws. She claimed that women were discriminated against by laws covering employment, divorce and alimony, property rights, pensions and inheritances, and by some criminal laws, among others. "The amendment would not change the substance of existing laws, except that those which restrict and deny opportunities to women would be rendered unconstitutional," she said.

Celler called the measure "a blunderbuss amendment" which would do away with necessary protective legislation for women. "Ever since Adam gave up his rib to make a woman, throughout the ages we have learned that physical, emotional, psychological and social differences exist and dare not be disregarded.... The equal rights amendment would eliminate all distinctions in legal treatment of men and women even when the fundamental reasonableness and common sense of such differences is apparent."

The House approved the amendment Aug. 10 by a 352-15 roll-call vote.

SENATE ACTION

Committee Action. The Senate Judiciary Subcommittee on Constitutional Amendments had held hearings in May on a proposal similar to H J Res 264; the full committee held hearings on the proposal in September but took no further action.

A number of witnesses appeared before the full committee opposing the amendment. Myra K. Wolfgang, vice president of the Hotel and Restaurant Employees and Bartenders International Union, AFL-CIO, said that the amendment would cause harm to working women by invalidating the protective laws and standards applying to them. These protective laws, countered Olga M. Madar, vice president of the United Auto Workers, discriminated against women: the equal rights amendment was no panacea, but neither was it a "Trojan Horse which would spread chaos and collapse of our legal system."

Floor Action. By tying on to the proposed equal rights amendment language exempting women from the military draft and guaranteeing a right to nondenominational prayers in public schools, opponents of H J Res 264 effectively foreclosed its final adoption in 1970.

The amendments required that the version approved by the Senate go to conference with the version approved without amendments by the House. Supporters of the equal rights amendment itself wished to avoid a conference, because they knew that the leader of the House conferees would be Celler, who would not be sorry to see the measure die in conference.

"The most important reason for enacting this amendment," said Birch Bayh (D Ind.), its chief Senate sponsor, Oct. 7, "is its symbolic value. The amendment will not eradicate, immediately upon passage, all the unduly discriminatory habits and customs of this country.... But I believe that passage of this amendment will go a long way toward providing the kind of dignity and legal status to which every American is entitled. It would prod the courts into taking long-overdue action. It would prod many employers into re-evaluating their employment practices, to see whether they, too, hire, assign work, and determine pay scales on the basis of sex, instead of making those decisions on the basis of an honest evaluation of each individual's personal abilities."

On the contrary, said Sam J. Ervin Jr. (D N.C.), not only was the amendment unnecessary, but it "will rob millions of wives, homemakers, mothers and widows of rights they now enjoy." He said approval of the amendment and its ratification by the states would result in years and years of litigation, which would be necessary in order to elucidate its meaning.

The amendment continuing the exemption of women from the draft was proposed by Ervin and adopted by the Senate Oct. 12 by a three-vote margin, 36-33. The school prayer amendment—designed to nullify earlier Supreme Court decisions—was proposed by Howard H. Baker Jr. (R Tenn.) and adopted by the Senate Oct. 13 by a 50-20 vote. The Senate took no further action on the matter in 1970.

Civil Rights Commission

Congress in 1970 approved an increase in the annual authorization ceiling for the U.S. Commission on Civil Rights, raising it to $3,400,000 from the level of $2,650,000 which had been set in 1967.

The Senate passed the bill in July by voice vote, after adding to it an amendment—adopted 44-40—which provided that any person defamed, degraded or incriminated by a commission report should be so notified before publication and given 30 days in which to file a rebuttal which should be printed as an appendix to the report. The House in November adopted the Senate bill without amendment.

School Desegregation

An amendment requiring uniform application of school desegregation standards North and South was incorporated in the law extending federal aid to elemen-

---

A "Shadow Cabinet"

Black members of the House of Representatives announced Oct. 14, 1970, that they were forming a so-called "shadow cabinet" to monitor federal enforcement of civil rights laws, in response to conclusions of a report of the U.S. Commission on Civil Rights.

The report, issued Oct. 12 by the commission, alleged a continuing failure of the federal government to put teeth into the civil rights laws which Congress had enacted over the past 15 years.

Charles C. Diggs Jr. (D Mich.), spokesman for the "shadow cabinet," said that the new body would include about 50 black officials serving in the Nixon administration. Diggs declined to identify members of the group but said they would not hesitate to expose any official who was guilty of lax enforcement of civil rights laws and policies.

Diggs was joined in his announcement by John Conyers Jr. (D Mich.), Shirley Chisholm (D N.Y.), Augustus F. Hawkins (D Calif.) and Louis Stokes (D Ohio). Adam C. Powell Jr. (D N.Y.), William Clay (D Mo.) and Robert N.C. Nix (D Pa.) supported the statement, according to Diggs' office. The other black member of the House, William L. Dawson (D Ill.), was in the hospital and could not be reached. Sen. Edward W. Brooke (R Mass.), the only black member of the Senate, was not invited to become a member of the group, according to one of Brooke's aides.

(The phrase "shadow cabinet" comes from British usage, in which it refers to a group of opposition members of Parliament who are expected to hold cabinet seats when their party comes to power.)

---

tary and secondary education (PL 91-230) passed by Congress in 1970. On the day that this language was first put into the bill by the Senate on a **key vote of 56-36,** a new special committee was created to examine all aspects of the effort to desegregate the nation's schools.

The Senate, after lengthy debate, accepted the amendment offered by John C. Stennis (D Miss.), which stated that such standards should be applied with equal force and "without regard to the origin or cause of such segregation." This last phrase would have eliminated the distinction between *de jure* and *de facto* segregation which Congress and the federal government had carefully maintained. House and Senate conferees eliminated this phrase, instead directing that two federal policies be established—one for *de jure* and one for *de facto* segregation—and that each be enforced uniformly across the states.

Supporters of the amendment admitted that it would legalize freedom-of-choice plans everywhere. Stennis said that when the same pressure to desegregate was placed on nonsouthern communities as on the South, citizens would rebel and insist that Congress modify the civil rights laws.

A surprising endorsement was given the Stennis amendment when Abraham A. Ribicoff (D Conn.), former secretary of HEW (1961-1962), said the North was guilty of "monumental hypocrisy" in its attitude toward the South, while refusing to face its own problems of discrimination in housing and jobs. This marked the first crack—since 1964—in the liberal Senate bloc which had pushed for vigorous enforcement of school desegregation.

Mondale Committee. The same day that the Senate approved the education bill with the Stennis amendment, it created a new Select Committee on Equal Educational Opportunity.

Walter F. Mondale (D Minn.), leader of the opposition to the Stennis amendment, became its chairman and promised that the committee would "reargue the case for integration." The failure of Senate liberals to defeat the Stennis amendment, Mondale said, had raised the question "whether this nation any longer believes in an integrated society."

Hearings began in April and continued until the end of the year. Testimony ranged over all aspects of equal educational opportunity. Late in the year the Senate extended the life of the select committee until Jan. 31, 1972; later its life was extended again until early 1973. *(Other 1970 action on administration proposals for aid to desegregating school districts, p. 512)*

1971

Voting Rights

Congress in March 1971 cleared and sent to the states a proposed 26th Amendment to the Constitution to lower the voting age to 18 in federal, state and local elections. The 26th Amendment was ratified by the required number of states by June 30, a record time for approval of a constitutional amendment. Three-fourths (38) of the 50 states had to ratify the proposal before it became part of the Constitution and Ohio became the 38th to do so on that date.

The speed with which the amendment became law, three months and seven days after passage by Congress, nearly cut in half the previous record speed.

The amendment was expected to grant the right to vote to an additional 11 million young Americans between the ages of 18 and 21. In the 1970 elections only three states, Georgia, Kentucky and Alaska, allowed 18-year-olds to vote. The amendment was the fourth to enlarge the electorate since the Constitution was adopted in 1789. The 15th amendment gave the vote to Negro citizens, the 19th to women and the 23rd permitted residents of the District of Columbia to vote for President.

Final congressional action on the 26th Amendment occurred March 23 when the House by a 401-19 roll-call vote approved H J Res 223. Immediately after the vote, the House by voice vote adopted the Senate measure (S J Res 7) and sent it to the states for ratification.

The Senate had given its unanimous approval March 10. A vote of two-thirds of the members of each chamber was required for a constitutional amendment. A joint resolution of Congress to amend the Constitution does not require the President's signature.

The congressional action and eventual ratification of the amendment cleared up the legal uncertainty which had hung over the right of 18-year-olds to vote. The uncertainty existed as a result of 1970 congressional action on the issue and subsequent Supreme Court decision rendering unconstitutional the part of the congressional action which applied to state and local elections. *(p. 498)*

The Twenty-Sixth Amendment

"The right of citizens of the United States, who are 18 years of age or older, to vote shall not be denied or abridged by the United States or by any state on account of age."

The 38 states whose ratifications put the amendment into effect were:

Alabama	Kansas	North Carolina
Alaska	Louisiana	Ohio
Arizona	Maine	Oregon
Arkansas	Maryland	Pennsylvania
California	Massachusetts	Rhode Island
Colorado	Michigan	South Carolina
Connecticut	Minnesota	Tennessee
Delaware	Missouri	Texas
Hawaii	Montana	Vermont
Idaho	Nebraska	Washington
Illinois	New Hampshire	West Virginia
Indiana	New Jersey	Wisconsin
Iowa	New York	

Background. In a 5-4 decision Dec. 21, 1970, the Supreme Court held that an amendment to the 1970 Voting Rights Act extension lowering the voting age to 18 was valid for federal but not state and local elections.

The decision created vast administrative difficulties for the 47 states that did not allow 18-year-olds to vote. State election officials and legislators said the task of producing dual registration books, ballots and voting machines could not be completed in time for the 1972 elections. Amendments to state constitutions to change voting age requirements would have been difficult to approve before 1972 without incurring enormous special election costs. Further, because of state requirements for amending state constitutions, 22 states could not act to lower their voting age laws before November 1972.

To resolve these difficulties, an amendment to the Constitution was reintroduced in both houses of Congress early in the 92nd Congress lowering the voting age to 18 in all federal, state and local elections.

Senate. The Senate Judiciary Committee March 4 unanimously approved S J Res 7, a proposed constitutional amendment lowering the voting age to 18 in federal, state and local elections. The resolution was cosponsored by 86 Senators.

The Senate March 10 approved the proposed amendment by a 94-0 roll-call vote. It killed, 68-23, an amendment to the proposed constitutional amendment granting full congressional representation to the District of Columbia.

House. The House Judiciary Committee March 2 voted 32-2 to report favorably H J Res 223, a proposed constitutional amendment lowering the voting age to 18 in federal, state and local elections. Opposed were Wiley Mayne (R Iowa) and Charles E. Wiggins (R Calif.).

The House March 23 voted 401-19 to approve the amendment and send it to the states for ratification. After adopting H J Res 223, the House then approved by voice vote the identical Senate resolution.

Equal Employment Opportunity

In 1971 Congress again moved part of the way toward giving the Equal Employment Opportunity Commission (EEOC) enforcement powers. The House, in a "slap in the face" for civil rights groups, approved the administration's court-enforcement approach (HR 1746) after rejecting a committee recommendation for cease-and-desist powers for the agency. Late in the year the Senate Labor and Public Welfare Committee reported out the House version without endorsement and its own bill (S 2515) granting cease-and-desist powers. No further action was taken in 1971.

HOUSE ACTION

Committee Action. During several days of hearings in March a subcommittee of the House Education and Labor Committee had heard arguments for and against the two types of enforcement powers. William H. Brown III, the EEOC chairman, said that he preferred the court-enforcement route but that "any type of enforcement powers" would help the agency to do a more effective job. Representatives of the Justice Department opposed transfer to the EEOC of its power to bring suits against persistent job discriminators, and the Labor Department opposed transfer to the EEOC of its power to enforce equal opportunity requirements with federal contractors. The Commission on Civil Rights, the AFL-CIO, and the National Association for the Advancement of Colored People backed the cease-and-desist approach and the transfer of powers.

The controversial Philadelphia Plan entered the discussion when certain members of Congress asserted that the transfer of contract compliance enforcement from the Labor Department would weaken such enforcement and therefore had won the support of organized labor for the bill. John T. Erlenborn (R Ill.), ranking minority member of the subcommittee holding the hearings, voiced this view during the hearings; he was backed by Shirley Chisholm (D N.Y.), who said that the Philadelphia Plan had alienated labor in general and the building trades unions in particular from the civil rights movement. She said that the building trades unions had pressured the AFL-CIO to back this transfer of powers from the Labor Department to the EEOC. *(Story p. 497)*

The Education and Labor Committee reported HR 1746 in June, granting the EEOC the authority to issue cease-and-desist orders. The committee had rejected, by a five-vote margin, the court enforcement approach. The committee extended the coverage of federal civil rights laws to smaller unions and businesses than those currently covered, to state and local government employees, and to persons employed by schools and colleges. It also transferred to the EEOC the lawsuit powers of the Department of Justice in this field, the responsibility of the Civil Service Commission for the federal employees' equal opportunity program, and the contract compliance responsibilities of the Labor Department.

Floor Action. The House in mid-September rejected the committee version of HR 1746 and instead adopted, by **a key roll-call vote of 200-195**, the administration's court-enforcement proposal. The revised bill was approved by a 285-106 roll call vote.

Fair Housing

Congress in 1968 enacted an open housing law (PL 90-284) barring discrimination in the sale or rental of most housing. President Nixon said June 11, 1971, that his administration would oppose housing segregation based on race, but would not interfere with local zoning laws whose effect was to exclude some persons for economic reasons.

The presidential statement confirmed what Nixon had stated several times in the past—that his administration would enforce open housing laws but would not "force" integration of neighborhoods. "Racial discrimination in housing is illegal and will not be tolerated," the President said. But he distinguished between housing segregation based on race and on economics. "We will not seek to impose economic integration upon an existing local jurisdiction," he said.

By barring action against "economic integration," Nixon meant that a community could exclude low-income or moderate-income housing through zoning. But, the President warned, "We will not countenance any use of economic measures as a subterfuge for racial discrimination." He said that when changes in land use are discovered to have been made for racially discriminatory purposes, the attorney general would seek legal action against the community.

The administration took such a step June 14 when it sued the St. Louis suburb of Black Jack, Mo., for racial discrimination in rezoning land to prohibit construction of a middle-income housing project.

Adoption of the administration substitute was a blow to civil rights advocates. The House action was "a slap in the face, but not a knockout punch" for civil rights groups, said Clarence Mitchell, director of the Washington bureau of the National Association for the Advancement of Colored People.

Adoption by the House of the administration bill, which critics considered far weaker than the bill reported by the Education and Labor Committee, capped an effort headed by Erlenborn and backed by a coalition of conservative Representatives.

The version of HR 1746 approved by the House was a much narrower measure than the committee version which, in addition to providing cease-and-desist powers, had enlarged the jurisdiction of the EEOC.

SENATE

Committee Action. After several days of hearings on the administration bill as passed by the House and on a Senate bill identical to the House committee version (S 2515), the Senate Labor and Public Welfare Committee reported them both late in October. It endorsed the cease-and-desist bill (S 2515) and merely sent the House-approved version (HR 1746) to the Senate floor without endorsement.

There was no floor action on either bill in 1971.

Equal Rights Amendment

In 1971, for the second time, the House approved a proposed constitutional amendment designed to ensure equal rights for women, but the Senate did not take final action on the measure.

The House approved the proposed amendment Oct. 12 by a margin substantially more than the necessary two-thirds. Senate action on a companion proposal was postponed until 1972, partly due to the illness of the wife of Birch Bayh (D Ind.), chief Senate sponsor of the amendment.

HOUSE ACTION

Committee Action. The House Judiciary Committee July 14 reported out an amended constitutional amendment (H J Res 208). Three members of the committee opposed H J Res 208: Chairman Emanuel Celler (D N.Y.), Edward Hutchinson (R Mich.) and David W. Dennis (R Ind.).

The committee amended the proposed constitutional amendment by adding language proposed by Charles E. Wiggins (R Calif.) which stated:

"This article shall not impair the validity of any law of the United States which exempts a person from compulsory military service or any other law of the United States or of any state which reasonably promotes the health and safety of the people."

The committee report noted a "substantial amount of confusion" over the legal effects of the resolution as originally introduced. Some proponents argued that Congress and state legislatures would be able to make "reasonable legal classifications in which sex is taken into account," while other proponents argued that the language required men and women to be given identical treatment under law.

"To obviate the possibility of such effects and of judicial chaos, your committee has recommended that the proposal be amended in such a way as to make it clear that Congress could exempt women from compulsory military service, and that neither Congress nor state legislatures would be paralyzed from taking differences between the sexes into account when necessary to promote the health and safety of our people."

Fourteen Democrats supported the original language of H J Res 208 and opposed the Wiggins amendment, "not only because of its refusal to grant full equality to women but also because it does violence to the concept of equality itself."

Floor Action. House consideration of the amendment, set initially for Sept. 22, was postponed because of the death of Wiggins' wife. When the House did take up the proposal, it voted 87-265 to reject the Wiggins amendment and then on Oct. 12 it approved the proposed amendment by a 354-24 vote. The text of H J Res 208 as approved in 1971 was identical to the text approved by the House a year earlier.

On final passage, nine of the 11 women members voted for the amendment. Leonor K. Sullivan (D Mo.) was the only woman to vote against passage, although she had supported the Wiggins modification; she also opposed the amendment in 1970. The other women member not voting for S J Res 208, Edith Green (D Ore.), was not present; she had supported the amendment in 1970.

SENATE

In the Senate, a companion equal rights amendment (S J Res 150) was introduced Aug. 6 by Birch Bayh (D Ind.) and placed directly on the Senate calendar on Sept. 18, bypassing the Judiciary Committee chaired by James O. Eastland (D Miss.). On the day the House acted on H J Res 208, Bayh, chief Senate sponsor of the amendment, announced he was withdrawing from the race for the Democratic presidential nomination to be with his wife while she recovered from a cancer operation. Due in part to this development, Senate action on the amendment was postponed until 1972.

Civil Rights Commission

Once again Congress approved an increase in the annual authorization for the Commission on Civil Rights, passing a bill (HR 7271) increasing that figure to $4,000,000 a year, $600,000 over the previously authorized level. *(Previous action, p. 501)*

The House passed the bill May 17 by a 262-67 roll call; the Senate passed the bill by voice vote without amendment July 24, and it was approved by the President on Aug. 4 (PL 92-64).

Spanish Speaking People

Congress in 1971 extended through fiscal 1973 the authorization for the Cabinet Committee on Opportunities for Spanish Speaking People. The House approved the bill (HR 7586) by voice vote June 21; the Senate followed suit Aug. 3, and President Nixon signed the bill into law (PL 92-122) on Aug. 16.

The cabinet committee had been established in 1969 (PL 91-181) to advise federal departments and agencies on actions to ensure that Spanish-speaking people were receiving needed federal aid and to advise departments and agencies on developing and carrying out programs focusing on the special needs and problems of Spanish-speaking and Spanish-surnamed Americans. It was created for a five-year period, but appropriations were authorized for only two years, through fiscal 1971. HR 7586 extended that authorization for two more years, through fiscal 1973.

Black Panthers

The House Committee on Internal Security unanimously issued a report Aug. 18, 1971, on the Black Panther party that said the group, while contributing to violence, was no danger to the government.

The 145-page report, titled "Gun-Barrel Politics: The Black Panther Party, 1966-1971," was based on two years of hearings and investigations by the committee. It traced the party from its origins in Oakland, Calif., on Oct. 15, 1966, through its confrontations with police and other acts of militancy, to its apparent disintegration in a leadership dispute in mid-1971.

The report concluded that the Black Panther party, "through its deliberately inflammatory rhetoric and through the actual arming and military training of its members, has contributed to an increase in acts of violence and constitutes a threat to the internal security of the United States.... (It) has never constituted a force, in

Shadow Cabinet to Black Caucus

The "shadow cabinet" of 1970 became the black caucus of 1971, as the 13 black members of the House of Representatives in the 92nd Congress organized to better serve black Americans. The members of the caucus said that they were congressmen-at-large, representing all black citizens. They pointed to 172 congressional districts which had at least a 25 per cent black population. The black caucus in 1971 consisted of:

Charles C. Diggs Jr. (D Mich.). Ninth term member from downtown Detroit; senior member and chairman of caucus; chairman of Africa subcommittee of House Foreign Affairs Committee.

Robert N. C. Nix (D Pa.). At 65, the caucus' oldest member; elected to eighth term in 1970 from northwest Philadelphia; chairman of Postal Operations Subcommittee of Post Office and Civil Service Committee.

Augustus F. Hawkins (D Calif.). Fifth term member from central Los Angeles and Watts.

John Conyers Jr. (D Mich.). Fourth term member from northern Detroit-Highland Park district.

Shirley Chisholm (D N.Y.). Elected from Brooklyn's Bedford-Stuyvesant district in 1968 as first black woman member of Congress; re-elected in 1970.

William (Bill) Clay (D Mo.). Second term member from north St. Louis.

Louis Stokes (D Ohio). Second term member from downtown Cleveland; brother of Cleveland Mayor Carl Stokes.

George W. Collins (D Ill.). Freshman member from West Side Chicago.

Ronald V. Dellums (D Calif.). Defeated incumbent Jeffrey Cohelan (D 1969-1971) in primary; from Berkeley-Oakland district.

Ralph H. Metcalfe (D Ill.). Succeeded the late William L. Dawson (D 1943-1970) as representative of Chicago's South Side.

Parren J. Mitchell (D Md.). Defeated incumbent Samuel N. Friedel (D 1953-1971) in close primary contest from Baltimore district.

Charles B. Rangel (D N.Y.). Defeated incumbent Adam C. Powell (D 1945-1971) in primary; from Harlem district.

Walter E. Fauntroy (D D.C.). First elected non-voting delegate to House from District of Columbia since 1875.

In a long-sought meeting with President Nixon at the White House March 25, the caucus urged him to commit himself unequivocally to the goal of equality for all citizens. Without this commitment on his part, they said, the goal would not be reached. In a reply characterized by the caucus as deeply disappointing, the President two months later said that his administration shared the caucus' goals.

When black Representatives in the 91st Congress first requested a meeting with President Nixon, they were informed—after several months—that such a meeting could not be fitted into the President's schedule. Late in 1970, they announced the formation of a "shadow cabinet" to oversee federal enforcement of civil rights laws. The black caucus was first officially organized in 1971. Its members stayed away from the joint session of Congress at which the President delivered his 1971 State of the Union message, in protest against his civil rights policies.

When they finally obtained the meeting in March 1971 which they had sought since February 1970, the black representatives spelled out to the President in 60 recommendations the first steps he might take to demonstrate his commitment to equality.

The general feeling in the black community was, they said, that the Nixon administration, by word and deed, was retreating at crucial points from the national commitment to equality. "Our people are no longer asking for equality as a rhetorical promise. They are demanding...the only kind of equality that ultimately has any real meaning—equality of results."

Mitchell said that the caucus told the President "the black community had not been blackjacked into silence or lulled into apathy...and that he might, therefore, be sitting on a powder keg."

Although all the black Representatives were Democrats, they denied their effort had any partisan flavor. "We have no permanent friends and no permanent enemies," said Clay, "only permanent interests."

and of itself, sufficient to threaten with immediacy the overthrow of the federal government.

"Fortunately, the Panthers' rhetoric regarding revolutionary activity has always exceeded performance," the committee said.

The four Republicans on the committee—John M. Ashbrook (Ohio), Roger H. Zion (Ind.), Fletcher Thompson (Ga.) and John G. Schmitz (Calif.)—complained that the report "does not give the reader a clear understanding of the Black Panther party as a subversive criminal group, using the facade of politics and Marxist-Leninist ideology as a cover for crimes of violence and extortion." The report, it said, sounded "more like a sociological rationalization for Panther violence than an investigative report .... The treatment of the Panther relationship to the Communist party is grossly inadequate," the minority said.

1972

Equal Employment Opportunity

Ending a seven-year struggle, Congress in 1972 finally granted the Equal Employment Opportunity Commission (EEOC) the authority to take corrective action in cases of job bias. On March 8, 1972, Congress cleared and sent to the White House the Equal Employment Opportunity Act of 1972 (HR 1746—PL 92-261), authorizing the EEOC to take cases of employment discrimination which could not otherwise be settled to federal district courts for a further finding of discrimination. If such a finding were made, the court would order an employer to cease discriminatory practices and to remedy the effects of past discrimination.

Created by the 1964 Civil Rights Act to oversee observance of federal laws barring discrimination in employment practices, the EEOC had never had any enforcement powers. Advocates of such powers for the agency were fairly well pleased with the 1972 law, although it basically embodied administration recommendations, giving courts the power to issue the orders, rather than the approach desired by civil rights groups, giving the agency the right to issue its own cease-and-desist orders.

Both chambers had once approved the more direct cease-and-desist approach—the House in 1966, the Senate in 1970. But in the 92nd Congress, although both House and Senate committees recommended the cease-and-desist approach, the more conservative court-enforcement approach was adopted by both chambers. The final version of the law was similar to that approved by the Senate in February 1972, expanding EEOC jurisdiction as well as giving it new powers. The House had approved the bill in 1971.

SENATE ACTION

After three motions to limit debate and more than 40 amendments, the Senate Feb. 22 approved, by a 73-16 vote, an amended bill (S 2515) providing the EEOC with court-enforcement powers.

Senate passage of S 2515 ended almost five weeks of debate during which the Senate substantially modified the bill. The major change was made Feb. 15—in an effort to end a filibuster against the bill—when the Senate, which had three times rejected the proposal, agreed to language authorizing the EEOC to go to the federal courts for enforcement of remedies for its findings of discrimination.

As reported by the Senate Labor and Public Welfare Committee in October 1971, S 2515 had authorized the EEOC to issue its own enforcement orders, subject to judicial review, directing discriminatory employers to cease their unfair practices. Critics of this type of enforcement power said it made the EEOC the prosecutor, judge and jury, denying due process to any employer haled before it. The court-enforcement approach was first suggested by the Nixon administration, which felt that the courts were the proper forum for resolving problems of discrimination in employment.

Civil rights advocates had backed cease-and-desist powers as the stronger alternative. But Harrison A. Williams Jr. (D N.J.), who with Jacob K. Javits (R N.Y.) managed S 2515 on the floor, said Feb. 22 that the bill, despite the weakening amendments, would assure a greater measure of equality in employment opportunities to women and minority groups and was "a major step forward."

The vote on passage came after the Senate Feb. 22 had approved, 73-21, a third cloture motion limiting further debate on the bill. A two-thirds majority vote (63) was required for approval. Two previous cloture motions had been rejected Feb. 1 and Feb. 3.

Most of the debate during the five weeks was conducted by five senators. Williams and Javits, the chairman and ranking minority member of the committee reporting the bill, were the floor managers and chief advocates of EEOC authority to enforce its own findings

through cease-and-desist orders. They were opposed by Sam J. Ervin Jr. (D N.C.) and James B. Allen (D Ala.), both of whom said the bill would create tyrannous power in the EEOC and would result in undue interference in state, local and individual affairs, and by Peter H. Dominick (R Colo.), chief advocate for the court-enforcement approach finally adopted. Their perseverance in lengthy and always germane discussion of the bill made adoption of the alternative court-enforcement powers possible.

Court-Enforcement Powers. The real issue at stake in the decision over the form that EEOC enforcement powers should take, said Dominick Jan. 20, was "whether we should put into one executive agency the power to make rules, the power to investigate whether or not those rules are being abided by, the power to charge violations of those rules and then the power to decide whether or not the violations are in fact in existence and, if they are, to issue appropriate judicial orders." This sort of "star chamber" proceeding is what the cease-and-desist measure would authorize, he said.

On Jan. 20, Dominick proposed his amendment to substitute the court-enforcement approach for the cease-and-desist powers. That amendment—when offered in committee in 1971—had been rejected 2-15.

The Senate Jan. 24 rejected the Dominick proposal 41-43. William B. Saxbe (R Ohio) immediately moved to reconsider the vote. A motion by Williams to table that reconsideration motion failed, 37-39; then the Senate agreed to the motion to reconsider, by a 40-39 vote.

Two days later on Jan. 26 the Senate voted again on the Dominick amendment; again it rejected it, 46-48. The Senate then agreed to a Williams motion to table a Javits motion to reconsider, 54-39.

The next day, for the third time the Senate rejected the court-enforcement approach. Ervin and Allen proposed that S 2515 be amended by substituting the language of the House-approved bill, adopting the court-enforcement approach, for the committee-approved cease-and-desist language. The amendment was rejected when the Senate adopted a motion by Javits to table the amendment: the vote was 45-32.

During a speech on Jan. 27 in support of his substitution proposal, Allen suggested that a filibuster might be waged to prevent the bill's coming to a final vote. In response Williams Jan. 28 filed a cloture petition. On Feb. 1 the Senate refused, 48-37, to cut off debate. Fifty-seven votes were needed for adoption of the cloture motion.

After the failure of the cloture move, Senate Majority Leader Mike Mansfield (D Mont.) suggested that the Senate proceed on a two-track basis, debating the equal employment bill for the first hour of each day's session and then moving on to other legislation. This system was begun Feb. 2.

The second cloture petition was filed by Williams Feb. 1. The Senate Feb. 3 failed, 53-35, to give two-thirds approval to the second cloture motion, thus allowing debate to continue. The vote fell six short.

Compromise. Admitting defeat in their effort to win Senate approval of cease-and-desist powers, Williams and Javits Feb. 8 announced that they would instead seek approval of a compromise version of the committee bill. Introduced Feb. 9, the compromise proposal would allow the EEOC, after hearings, to certify to a federal court its findings of discrimination; the court would then enforce these findings by issuing an order barring future discrimination. This modification, said Javits, was designed to win over enough votes to obtain approval of the third cloture motion.

This was no compromise at all, responded critics of the committee bill. Dominick met this suggestion with an amended version of his own court-enforcement amendment. Introducing his compromise on Feb. 14, he explained that it would authorize the EEOC general counsel —after the EEOC had failed to obtain a conciliation agreement—to bring a civil action in federal court against the offending employer.

If the general counsel certified to the judge that the case was in the general public interest, he could request that it immediately be heard before a three-judge court from which an appeal could go directly to the Supreme Court.

Dominick said that this procedure would allow speedier settlement of a job bias case than the procedure proposed by Javits and Williams. And further, he said, "if we do not adopt an amendment substantially similar to the one I have here, we will not get a bill out at all."

According to Javits, the two approaches were the same—both through the courts; the difference, he said, was the extent to which the burden thus imposed on the already overburdened judicial system could be minimized. His proposal would make the commission an official referee, making and certifying a decision that would then be enforced by the court's order, he said.

Allen spoke for the Dominick amendment, saying that the bill had an excellent chance of passing if the amendment was adopted.

On a **key roll-call vote of 45-39,** The Senate Feb. 15 voted to substitute Dominick's latest proposal for the Javits-Williams language in their compromise; it then adopted the amended compromise, 81-3.

A third cloture petition was filed Feb. 18. Four days later on Feb. 22 the Senate, 73-21, agreed to limit debate— only the eleventh time it had done so since adoption of the rule under which it was done, Rule 22, in 1917.

General Counsel. To meet the concern that EEOC in receiving and processing complaints of job bias would act as prosecutor and judge and jury, the Senate Jan. 20 agreed, 67-0, to an amendment creating a general counsel for the EEOC to handle its prosecutions. The counsel would be appointed by the President with the advice and consent of the Senate for a four-year term.

Jurisdiction. The extent to which coverage of federal job discrimination bans and the jurisdiction of the EEOC would be extended was the subject of lengthy debate and many amendments during Senate consideration of S 2515.

A major compromise in this area came Feb. 8. Existing law covered organizations employing 25 or more persons; the committee bill extended this coverage to organizations employing as few as eight persons. The compromise, proposed by Javits and Williams, and adopted 56-26, extended coverage to businesses and unions employing 15 or more persons.

On other jurisdictional points, the Senate refused:

• To restore the exemption from EEOC jurisdiction for some 10-million employees of state and local governments, who had been so exempted under the 1964 act. This amendment was rejected Jan. 31 by a 16-59 vote.

Ervin criticized this extension of EEOC jurisdiction as "the greatest grab for power ever made by the federal government." It would, he said, "make federal judges into employment bureaus for states" and would subject all employers to one government agency for the "supposed benefit" of only one segment of the American people.

Williams opposed the amendment, citing a report by the Civil Rights Commission which indicated that job bias was widespread among state and local governments.

The Senate also refused:

• To restore complete exemption for all employees of educational and religious institutions, who had been exempt under the 1964 act. This amendment was rejected by the Senate Feb. 1 by a 25-55 vote.

• To exempt hospitals, in their employment of physicians and surgeons, from EEOC jurisdiction. The Senate rejected this amendment Feb. 14 by voice vote.

• To exempt from coverage teachers and other faculty members employed by public schools. The Senate by voice vote rejected this amendment Feb. 22.

• To exempt from coverage all employment practices of educational institutions. The Senate rejected this amendment, 15-70, Feb. 22.

The Senate did agree on Feb. 17 to an Ervin amendment making clear that the anti-discrimination provisions would not preclude any state or local elected government official from selecting the persons he wished to have as his legal advisers. Four days later the Senate by voice vote agreed to another Ervin amendment which would allow schools or religious organizations to hire persons of a particular religion for all its activities. This exemption had originally applied only to persons hired for religious activies.

Transfer of Powers. Early in consideration of the bill on Jan. 26, the Senate agreed, 49-37, to cut out of the bill the language which transferred to EEOC the functions of the Office of Contract Compliance (OFCC) in the Labor Department. The shift had been opposed both by the Labor Department and by civil rights advocates who had feared that the transfer would weaken implementation of the Philadelphia Plan program for minority hiring.

After adoption of the amendment deleting this language, the Senate did approve language setting up an Equal Employment Opportunity Coordinating Council designed to correct the problem of inadequate coordination between OFCC and other government equal employment units.

Later in consideration of the bill, however, the Senate rejected an amendment cutting from the bill the language transferring to the EEOC the authority of the attorney general to file suits against persons engaging in a "pattern or practice" of job discrimination. This amendment was rejected Feb. 16 by a 33-43 vote.

Other Amendments. The Senate also:

• Amended the language to guarantee that contracts of federal contractors, whose job opportunity plans had won federal approval, would not be suspended or terminated for alleged job discrimination without a full hearing unless they had deviated substantially from their plan. This amendment was approved 77-0 on Jan. 27.

• Rejected an amendment, 33-33, Feb. 9 which would have foreclosed all other remedies for job bias to anyone filing such a charge with the EEOC.

• Agreed that the new procedures and powers authorized in S 2515 would apply to cases pending before the EEOC.

• Refused to expand the ban on preferential treatment of minority group employees to include action not only under the pending bill and Title VII of the Civil Rights Act of 1964, but also under any other executive orders or laws.

Javits opposed the amendment which, he said, would outlaw the Philadelphia Plan approach to increase minority employment by companies holding federal construction contracts. Javits noted that both Congress and the federal courts had upheld this approach. The amendment was rejected by a 30-60 vote Feb. 22.

• Agreed that a court should be allowed to refer a job bias case to a special master for hearing and recommendation if a judge had not acted on the case assigned to him within 120 days.

Move to Conference. After approving the amended version of S 2515 by a 73-16 vote, the Senate approved HR 1746 by a 72-17 vote after inserting the language of S 2515 in the House-passed bill.

The House Feb. 23 disagreed to the Senate amendments to HR 1746 and asked for a conference; the Senate agreed.

CONFERENCE REPORT

House and Senate conferees filed their report March 2. House conferees agreed to accept Senate provisions which:

• Expanded EEOC jurisdiction (and Title VII of the 1964 Civil Rights Act) to include businesses and labor unions with 15 or more employees or members and state and local government employees.

• Eliminated exemptions from the 1964 act for employees of educational institutions.

• Expanded the exemption for religious organizations to include all persons of a particular religion hired for any of the institution's activities.

• Allowed an aggrieved person to bring a private suit if the EEOC had entered into a conciliation agreement to which the aggrieved person was not a party.

• Authorized appointment of a special master to hear a job bias case.

• Transferred to the EEOC the Department of Justice's authority to bring suits against a "pattern or practice" of job discrimination.

• Established an Equal Employment Opportunity Coordinating Council.

• Specified the responsibility for equal job enforcement of the federal government concerning its own personnel; authorized enforcement of this policy through the Civil Service Commission and the federal courts.

• Provided that the new powers and procedures applied in pending cases.

• Provided for a full hearing before a government contractor with an approved equal opportunity plan could lose a contract for violation of equal job opportunity.

In resolution of other differences, conferees agreed:

• To drop a House provision stating that charges brought under Title VII were the exclusive remedy for job discrimination.

• To drop the Senate-passed provision for the appointment of a three-judge federal court in certain job bias cases; substituted language providing that the chief judge of the district would designate a judge to hear the case at the earliest practicable date and specify that the case was to be expedited.

• To include House language that to find an employer guilty, he must have been found to be intentionally engaging in an unlawful employment practice.

• To modify Senate language establishing an independent general counsel for the EEOC to make clear that the attorney general would conduct all cases before the Supreme Court to which the EEOC was a party.

Final Action. The Senate March 6 voted 62-10 to agree to the conference report on HR 1746.

The House March 8 by a 303-110 vote approved the report, completing congressional action on the bill.

PROVISIONS

As signed into law (PL 92-261) by the President March 24, HR 1746, the Equal Employment Opportunity Act of 1972:

• Extended coverage of Title VII of the 1964 Civil Rights Act to businesses and labor organizations with 15 or more employees or members, to state and local government employees (excluding elected officials, their personal assistants, appointed policy-making officials and legal advisers), and to employees of educational institutions.

• Established for the EEOC an independent general counsel appointed by the President for four years with the advice and consent of the Senate, to handle the prosecutions for the EEOC and to argue EEOC cases; provided that the attorney general of the United States would conduct all cases before the Supreme Court to which the EEOC was a party.

• Authorized the EEOC general counsel, after full investigation and hearings concerning a charge of job bias was filed under oath with EEOC, to bring a civil suit in federal court against an employer whom the EEOC had found was discriminating and with whom the EEOC had failed to secure a conciliation agreement. (If the employer concerned was a governmental agency or body, the attorney general would handle the case.)

• Required that EEOC cases be expedited in every way.

• Authorized the court, in a finding that an employer had engaged in discriminatory job practices, to order the employer to halt such practices and to remedy his past actions by reinstating or hiring the employees concerned with or without awarding them back pay and through any other remedial measures that might be needed. A back-pay award would be limited to the two-year period prior to the filing of the charge with the EEOC.

• Transferred to the EEOC from the Department of Justice—over a two-year period—the authority to bring suit against an employer or organization engaged in a pattern or practice of employment discrimination.

• Established an Equal Employment Opportunity Coordinating Council to coordinate and implement all federal equal employment efforts.

• Made clear that the federal government was required to make all personnel actions free from discrimination on the basis of race, color, religion, sex or national origin; authorized the Civil Service Commission to enforce this policy within the federal bureaucracy; expressly granted individual federal employees the right to seek relief from such discrimination in the federal courts.

• Provided that no government contract could be suspended or withheld from an employer without a full hearing if that employer had an equal opportunity program already approved by the federal government from which he had not substantially deviated.

Equal Rights Amendment

Forty-nine years after it was first introduced, a constitutional amendment guaranteeing equal rights for men and women (H J Res 208) was approved by the Senate March 22, 1972, and sent to the states for ratification.

The Senate vote was 84-8—22 more than the two-thirds majority required to adopt a proposed constitutional amendment. The House had approved it by a 354-24 roll-call vote on Oct. 12, 1971. The House margin was 102 more than was necessary. *(Text, box this page)*

If ratified by three-fourths (38) of the states, the measure would become the 27th Amendment to the Constitution. Less than two hours after the Senate acted, Hawaii became the first state to ratify it. States were given seven years to ratify H J Res 208—which would go into effect two years after the date of ratification.

Constitutional amendments do not require approval by the President, but Mr. Nixon notified Senate Minority Leader Hugh Scott (R Pa.) that he supported H J Res 208. In a letter dated March 18, he said that as a senator he had cosponsored a resolution in 1951 supporting an equal rights amendment. "Throughout 21 years I have not altered my belief that equal rights for women warrant a constitutional guarantee—and I therefore continue to favor the enactment of the constitutional amendment to achieve this goal," the letter stated. The amendment was supported by more than 50 women's groups, labor unions and civil liberties organizations.

Senate approval came after four days of debate during which Sam J. Ervin Jr. (D N.C.), leader of the opposition, offered nine proposed changes aimed at narrowing the impact of the amendment's coverage. All were rejected by substantial margins. Chief Senate advocate of the amendment was Birch Bayh (D Ind.), chairman of the Judiciary Subcommittee on Constitutional Amendments.

Ervin warned that adoption of the amendment would destroy the social fabric of America. During the debate he quoted the Bible, recited poetry, spun North Carolina tales and discoursed at length on constitutional law. Shortly before the Senate approved the amendment, he said women were being crucified "upon the cross of dubious equality and specious uniformity."

SENATE ACTION

Committee Action. The Senate Judiciary Committee March 14 reported H J Res 208 without amendments. The bill had been ordered reported by a 15-1 roll-call vote with only Ervin opposing it.

Earlier, the subcommittee on constitutional Amendments, by a 6-4 vote, had adopted language forbidding the federal government or states from making "any legal distinction between the rights and responsibilities of male and female persons unless such distinction is based on physiological or functional differences between them." But the committee later rejected such language by a 1-15 vote.

> ## Equal Rights Text
>
> "Equality of rights under the law shall not be denied or abridged by the United States or by any state on account of sex."

The committee also rejected five other proposed amendments to the language of the constitutional amendment approved by the House. Three of these, rejected by voice votes, would have continued certain legal distinctions between men and women, specified that the amendment did not affect the 5th or 14th Amendments and allowed higher educational institutions to continue to serve only one sex. By roll-call votes of 2-14 and 3-13 members rejected other amendments to allow women to be exempted from the draft.

There had been "some progress" toward equal rights for women in recent years, noted the committee report, but "there is overwhelming evidence that persistent patterns of sex discrimination permeate our social, cultural and economic life.... We cannot afford to wait any longer for Congress and each of the 50 state legislatures to find the time to debate and revise their laws. As in other areas where the Constitution has been amended, there is an imperative for immediate action. The nation has waited too long already—it has been 49 years since the equal rights amendment was first introduced. Only a constitutional amendment can provide the legal and practical basis for the necessary changes."

Ervin offered minority views 26 pages in length—five pages longer than the committee's own report. He claimed that a majority of both sexes did not want the amendment and that it was unnecessary because of the protections of the 14th Amendment.

Floor Action. The Senate by substantial margins rejected nine amendments offered by Ervin to modify the text of the constitutional amendment. Most were aimed at preserving state or federal laws granting women special protection or treatment. All were rejected by roll-call votes.

The amendments rejected March 21 would:
• Protect state or federal laws which "exempt women from compulsory military service." Rejected, 18-72.
• Protect state or federal laws which "exempt women from service in combat units of the armed forces." Rejected, 18-71. *(Box next page)*
• Protect state or federal laws "which extend protections or exemptions to women." Rejected, 11-75.

The first proposal would have exempted from coverage by the amendment any federal or state laws which exempted women "from compulsory military service."

Speaking in defense of the proposed change, Armed Services Committee Chairman John C. Stennis (D Miss.) said the equal rights amendment "proposes a very grave question from the standpoint of national security as well as the treatment of womanhood."

He said enactment of the amendment would indirectly abolish the draft. "Every senator who seriously considers the picture of our young women being taken prisoner in combat will know that we could not and will not subject them to military service on the same basis as men." He warned that the amendment "could seriously affect and impair the operation of our army in operating efficiently to defend our own country."

Bayh responded: "If a woman wants to volunteer, should she be treated differently from a man? ...There is an extremely small likelihood that any will really reach combat service."

After rejection of this proposal, Ervin offered a slightly different amendment which would protect laws exempting women from combat service. The proposed change, he said, "is designed to prevent the conversion of Annapolis and West Point and the Air Force Academy and the other service academies into co-educational war colleges. It is also designed to prevent sending the daughters of America into combat to be slaughtered or maimed by the bayonets, the bombs, the bullets, the grenades, the mines, the napalm, the poison gas and the shells of the enemy."

But Marlow W. Cook (R Ky.) opposed Ervin's exemption: "Combat today may be a lady sitting at a computer at a missile site in North Dakota. Does that mean that when it says she does not have to be in combat that she can get up and walk out?" He said that military nurses in Southeast Asia are currently in combat zones and receiving combat pay.

Ervin's next effort was to propose language protecting federal or state laws "which extend protections or exemptions to women."

He said that business and professional women "have the absolute legal right at the present moment, and without the equal rights amendment, to compete with men in all of the business or commercial activities of life." But working class women, he added, need the protection of laws which guarantee separate restrooms and dressing rooms, set minimum wages for women, set maximum hours of work, make husbands primarily responsible for supporting wives and children or grant divorced women alimony and child support.

Bayh said that many of the protective laws "were originally designed in a bygone era to provide special protection for women (but which) now...impose special penalties."

The Ervin amendment rejected March 22 would:

● Protect state or federal laws "which extend protections or exemptions to wives, mothers or widows." Rejected, 14-77.

● Protect state or federal laws "which impose upon fathers responsibility for the support of their children." Rejected, 17-72.

● Protect state or federal laws "which secure privacy to men or women, or boys or girls." Rejected, 11-79.

● Protect state or federal laws "which make punishable as crimes sexual offenses." Rejected, 17-71.

● Substitute for the text of the equal rights amendment the following: "Neither the United States nor any state shall make any legal distinction between the rights and responsibilities of male and female persons unless such distinction is based on physiological or functional differences between them." Rejected, 12-78.

● Substitute for the text of H J Res 208 language offering states the alternatives of accepting the House-passed text of the amendment or the following modification: "Equality of rights under the law shall not be denied or abridged by the United States or by any state on account of sex. The provisions of this article shall not impair the

Support for Military Exemptions

Fifteen senators who in 1970 supported an amendment to the equal rights constitutional amendment exempting women from the draft switched their positions 18 months later and in 1972 opposed such exemptions.

The 1970 amendment, sponsored by Sam J. Ervin Jr. (D N.C.), would have included in the constitutional amendment language upholding existing laws exempting women from the draft. The exemption was accepted by a 36-33 roll-call vote and, in effect, spelled doom for the entire measure.

In 1972, back-to-back amendments offered by Ervin March 21 would have exempted women from compulsory military service and from combat service. The first was defeated by an 18-73 roll-call vote, the second by an 18-71 roll call.

Thirteen senators who backed the 1970 exemption opposed the two related exemptions in 1972. They were:

James B. Allen (D Ala.), Gordon Allott (R Colo.), Clinton P. Anderson (D N.M.), Howard H. Baker Jr. (R Tenn.), Norris Cotton (R N.H.), Robert Dole (R Kan.), Thomas F. Eagleton (D Mo.), Len B. Jordan (R Idaho), Warren G. Magnuson (D Wash.), Lee Metcalf (D Mont.), James B. Pearson (R Kan.), William B. Spong Jr. (D Va.) and Milton R. Young (R N.D.).

In addition, two senators who voted for the 1970 exemption supported one of the two 1972 Ervin amendments: Peter H. Dominick (R Colo.) voted for the compulsory service exemption but against the combat exemption; Robert P. Griffin (R Mich.) voted against the compulsory service exemption but for the combat exemption.

validity, however, of any laws of the United States or any state which exempt women from compulsory military service, or from service in combat units of the armed forces; or extend protections or exemptions to wives, mothers or widows; or impose upon fathers responsibility for the support of children; or secure privacy to men or women, or boys or girls; or make punishable as crimes rape, seduction or other sexual offenses." Rejected, 9-82.

The Senate approved H J Res 208 by a **key 84-4 roll-call vote.** Voting against passage were two southern Democrats—Ervin and Stennis—and six Republicans—Norris Cotton (N.H.), Wallace F. Bennett (Utah), James L. Buckley (N.Y.), Paul J. Fannin and Barry Goldwater (Ariz.) and Clifford P. Hansen (Wyo.). James O. Eastland (D Miss.), chairman of the Judiciary Committee, gave a live pair against approval. The *Congressional Record* noted there were demonstrations in the galleries when the vote was announced.

Civil Rights Commission

Congress in 1972 approved a bill (HR 12652—PL 92-496) extending the life of the Civil Rights Commission to June 30, 1978. The commission was to go out of existence Jan. 31, 1973. The bill also authorized a total of $40.5-million for fiscal 1973-78, a substantially higher authorization level than the existing $4-million annual figure. For fiscal 1973 the bill authorized $5.5-million; for the succeeding years it authorized $7-million each.

The bill also expanded the jurisdiction of the commission, which already included discrimination due to race, color, religion or national origin, to include sex discrimination as well. The House had approved the bill May 1 by a 265-66 roll-call vote; the Senate approved an amended version by voice vote Aug. 4. Conferees filed their report on the bill Sept. 26; the Senate adopted the report that day by voice vote; the House followed suit Oct. 4.

Indians

Asking that the rights and property guaranteed to them by treaties with the United States be granted, a band of several hundred American Indians occupied the Washington, D.C., offices of the Bureau of Indian Affairs (BIA) from Nov. 2-8, 1972. The protest was staged to focus attention on the problems of American Indians and to protest current government policies.

A task force led by Leonard Garment, special consultant to the President, and Frank Carlucci, deputy director of the Office of Management and Budget, was, as a result of negotiations with the Indians, directed to review federal Indian policy and submit its recommendations to the President by June 1, 1973.

Also in 1972 the House and the Senate each approved a different bill geared to encourage the economic and social development of Indians, but neither bill cleared Congress. The Senate passed S 3157, the "Indian Self-Determination Act," Aug. 2, providing for full participation of Indian tribes in BIA programs and services; the House Oct. 13 passed HR 8063, the "Indian Financing Act," which provided for a revolving loan fund, a loan guaranty and insurance fund, a business grant program and interest subsidies for Indian economic development.

 **Busing and Desegregation**

BUSING: MAJOR SCHOOL DESEGREGATION ISSUE, 1969-72

When Massachusetts in 1852 became the first state to enact a compulsory education law, its legislators probably did not foresee all the complications that would ensue.

One of those complications resulted from the facts of a scattered population and a limited number of school buildings. Some way had to be provided for every pupil, particularly those in rural areas, to get to school. In 1869 Massachusetts became the first state to provide pupil transportation at public expense.

By 1919, all states were using tax revenues to transport pupils, and the most popular mode of transportation was the bus. The number of students bused to and from school grew steadily into the early 1970s. *(Table, next page)*

But since the mid-1960s, when federal courts began to order use of the school bus as one means of providing the quality education every state promised its pupils, busing has become such a controversial practice that its long history is often obscured.

The school bus has been bombed in Pontiac, Mich., overturned in Lamar, S.C., and damned around the country. Busing has become the symbol of federal interference in local affairs and the watering down of educational standards.

Busing was denounced as "massive" or "forced," despite estimates that busing for the purpose of desegregation accounted for only a very small percentage of total busing, according to official estimates.

A federal survey, for the 1969-70 school year, found a total of between 18 million and 19 million students, 43 per cent of all public school students, being bused. No figures were available for the number being bused for desegregation purposes, but the office of civil rights in the Department of Health, Education and Welfare (HEW) and the U.S. Commission on Civil Rights agreed on an estimate of only 2 to 3 per cent.

The Nixon administration articulated some of the complaints about busing in a statement accompanying its anti-busing measures sent to Congress March 17, 1972. Busing, said the administration statement, was widespread, costly, harmful to the educational process and it created unnecessary administrative burdens.

Stephen Horn, vice chairman of the Civil Rights Commission, expressed different views in testimony before the House Judiciary Committee May 10, 1972. Horn said that population growth accounted for almost all busing and that the cost of busing had held steady at between 3 and 4 percent of total educational expenditures for 40 years. He reminded the committee that Secretary of Health, Education and Welfare Elliot L. Richardson had told Congress in 1970 that there had been more busing in past years to preserve segregated schools than there was in 1970 to desegregate schools.

"Desegregation," said Horn, "actually can cause many children to spend less time on the bus...because children are no longer bused past one segregated school to get to another, and hence the trip is much shorter." As an example, he cited Georgia, where the number of pupils bused rose to 566,000 in 1971 from 517,000 in 1967, but where the miles logged in a year by Georgia buses dropped to 51.3 million from 54 million.

The presidential campaigns of 1972 provided a clear contrast on the busing issue. President Nixon's opposition to busing was well known; George McGovern, the Democratic nominee, supported the use of busing, and the party platform contained an endorsement of the transportation of students as one means of achieving equal educational opportunity.

The Courts

The federal courts—and the judges who manned them—took the brunt of the criticism of busing, for almost all busing resulted from some court's directive. Technically, courts did not order busing, but it was their approval of plans including busing that put those plans into effect.

Busing was approved as a means of desegregating schools by the Supreme Court's 1971 decision in *Swann v. Charlotte-Mecklenburg Board of Education.* Unanimously, the court held that "desegregation plans cannot be limited to the walk-in school." Busing was permissible so long as it did not risk the students' health or impinge on the educational process, it said.

The *Swann* decision was the latest in a series of Supreme Court rulings on school desegregation which began with its 1954 holding—in the case of *Brown v. Board of Education of Topeka*—that "separate educational facilities (for black and white students) are inherently unequal." This overturned an 1896 ruling *(Plessy v. Ferguson)* condoning separate-but-equal public facilities.

A year later, in a decision elaborating on the first *Brown* decision, the court called for desegregation "with all deliberate speed." But many southern school districts answered with delays and adopted plans which often did not achieve desegregation. In 1969 the court ruled that segregation must be eliminated "at once."

Black neighborhoods and white neighborhoods, found particularly in urban areas, result in black neighborhood schools and white neighborhood schools. In order to desegregate those schools some pupils must be assigned—and transported—away from their neighborhood schools.

New boundaries for attendance zones and the use of "magnet" schools often did not achieve results fast enough or completely enough to satisfy the requirement of desegregation "now."

National Pupil Busing Data: 1929-30 to 1969-70

School year	Total public school enrollment	Pupils transported at public expense		Expenditure of public funds for busing	
		Numbers	Percent of total enrollment	Total (excluding cost of new buses)	Average cost per pupil
1929-30	25,678,015	1,902,826	7.4	$ 54,823,000	$28.81
1931-32	26,275,441	2,419,173	9.2	53,078,000	24.01
1933-34	26,434,103	2,794,724	10.6	53,908,000	19.29
1935-36	26,367,098	3,250,658	12.3	62,653,000	19.27
1937-38	25,975,108	3,769,242	14.5	75,637,000	20.07
1939-40	25,433,542	4,144,161	16.3	83,283,000	20.10
1941-42	24,562,473	4,503,081	18.3	92,922,000	20.64
1943-44	23,266,616	4,512,412	19.4	107,754,000	23.83
1945-46	23,299,941	5,056,966	21.7	129,756,000	25.66
1947-48	23,944,532	5,854,041	24.4	176,265,000	30.11
1949-50	25,111,427	6,947,384	27.7	214,504,000	30.83
1951-52	26,562,664	7,697,130	29.0	263,827,000	34.93
1953-54	26,643,871	8,411,719	32.8	307,437,000	36.55
1955-56	27,740,149	9,695,819	35.0	353,972,000	36.51
1957-58	29,722,275	10,861,689	36.5	416,491,000	38.34
1959-60	32,477,440	12,225,142	37.6	486,338,000	39.78
1961-62	34,682,340	13,222,667	38.1	576,361,000	43.59
1963-64	37,405,058	14,475,778	38.7	673,845,000	46.55
1965-66	39,154,497	15,588,567	39.7	787,358,000	50.68
1967-68	40,827,965	17,100,873	42.1	981,006,000	57.27
1969-70	41,934,376*	18,200,000*	43.4*	$1,214,399,000*	$66.73*

*Preliminary figures

SOURCE: U.S. Office of Education, HEW

The South was the first region to feel the impact of the desegregation decisions and busing orders; its schools had been segregated by law *(de jure)*. The effects were dramatic in the late 1960s: Black pupils attending all-black schools in 11 southern states dropped to 14 per cent in 1970 from 68 per cent in 1968, according to HEW statistics. There was virtually no change in the racial isolation in northern and western schools during that same period.

But what was once a regional issue became a national controversy when federal courts began in 1970 to order busing in cities outside the South. Members of Congress from the North and West began giving their support to long-ignored antibusing proposals in Congress.

Yet undetermined by the Supreme Court in 1972 was the question of whether segregated schools resulting from residential segregation *(de facto)* were also unconstitutional. Attorneys for black parents in non-southern cities argued that what appeared to be *de facto* segregation was really the result of official action because of the backing of agencies like the Federal Housing Administration, whose loan guarantees supported much housing construction, and whose officials until the late 1940s had actively promoted racially restrictive covenants in property titles.

The Supreme Court had set arguments on the *de facto* issue for the fall of 1972.

In Denver Federal District Judge William Doyle had found in 1970 that its *de facto* segregation was in fact unconstitutional; he ordered implementation of a busing plan to overcome the segregation in that city's schools.

The Supreme Court June 21, 1973, ruled in the Denver case but declined to resolve the *de facto* issue directly. It decided, 7-1, to instruct Doyle to look again at the case, to decide if discriminatory policies of the school board with regard to one set of schools made the entire system a dual one, and if so, to order desegregation.

Adding to the national uproar was the 1972 decision of a Richmond, Va., federal district court requiring busing across city and county lines to desegregate schools. Judge Robert R. Merhige Jr.'s ruling—which was overturned in June by the U.S. Court of Appeals, 4th circuit,—would have merged the largely black Richmond city school system with the white suburban systems of Henrico and Chesterfield Counties, and required the busing of about 78,000 of the 104,000 pupils in the three systems, an increase of 10,000 over the number being bused in the three systems before the judge's order. The Supreme Court by a 4-4 decision on May 21, 1973, let stand the Court of Appeals ruling upsetting the Merhige plan for Richmond.

But in Detroit, Federal District Judge Stephen J. Roth, who earlier had found that city's schools deliberately segregated, had ordered in June 1972 the preparation of a desegregation plan for Detroit and 53 suburban districts. On July 10 Roth directed the state of Michigan to purchase 295 buses. The orders were appealed by the state and the suburbs of Detroit.

The National Association for the Advancement of Colored People adopted a resolution at its 63rd annual

(Continued on p. 516)

Anti-Busing Coalition: Non-Southern Representatives...

Long-time opponents of busing school children to desegregate public schools found themselves the core of a new majority in the House of Representatives in the early 1970s.

As some southern members had predicted, many representatives from outside the South—for the first time feeling real pressure for school desegregation in their districts—ignored past statements and voted to bar the use of busing for desegregation. A prime example of this shift was the position adopted by James G. O'Hara (D Mich.), for years one of the leaders of the floor fights to cut anti-busing language out of appropriations bills.

Late in September 1971, a federal judge ordered that a metropolitan-areawide desegregation plan be developed for Detroit, where he found the schools deliberately segregated. Within weeks, O'Hara was assuring his constituents—chiefly working-class Detroit suburbanites—that he felt court-ordered busing exceeded constitutional requirements.

Desegregation Pressure Moves North

Detroit was not the only non-southern city feeling pressure. The *de jure-de facto* distinction which had shielded the North from desegregation requirements was crumbling before the findings of federal courts. Judges were holding that school segregation in non-southern cities was often just as much the result of official action *(de jure)* as that in the South and was thus within the reach of court orders.

When school opened in the fall of 1971, the South —where statistics showed desegregation progress had moved far ahead of the rest of the country—was relatively quiet compared to bus bombings in Pontiac, Mich., protesting a desegregation plan and the Chinese-American led boycott of the San Francisco schools, which were desegregating through busing. Even before the Detroit ruling, a federal judge had found the city schools of Indianapolis, Ind., deliberately segregated.

The Department of Health, Education and Welfare (HEW) had begun proceedings to terminate federal funds to several non-southern school districts charged with violating federal school desegregation requirements. The districts included Ferndale, Mich., Wichita, Kan., Prince Georges County, Maryland, and Boston, Mass.

And as these moves kindled adverse reaction to desegregation outside the South, anti-busing sentiment was given additional impetus in August 1971, when President Nixon reaffirmed his opposition to busing for racial balance in the schools.

Mr. Nixon said Aug. 3, 1971, that he had instructed HEW Secretary Elliot L. Richardson and Attorney General John N. Mitchell to hold busing to the minimum required by law in all areas where their departments were involved—and that he was sending to Congress an amendment to his desegregation aid bill which would bar the use of any of its funds for busing students.

The new anti-busing majority showed its muscle on several votes in 1971, most impressively in November when it succeeded in adding strong anti-busing language to a massive higher education-desegregation aid bill passed by the House. These amendments:

• Postponed—until all appeals had been settled or the time for them had expired—the effective date of any federal court order requiring busing.

• Forbade the use of all federal education funds for busing to overcome racial imbalance and forbade federal pressure on local school agencies to spend state or local funds for busing.

A substantial majority of House members—235 and 233, respectively—approved these amendments. More than half of those votes were cast by representatives from states outside the South. Fifty-six Democrats from northern and western states—considered the most liberal voting group in the House—voted for the first amendment, which five of their number sponsored; 50 voted for the second. Only half that number had ever supported anti-busing proposals before those votes.

The Building of a Majority

Development of this anti-busing majority can be traced through the years 1968-1972 by comparison of several key House votes.

1968. The federal government began to move its desegregation efforts north in 1958. The Justice Department filed its first non-southern desegregation suit in April against an Illinois district, followed by suits against Indianapolis, Tulsa, Okla., and East St. Louis, Ill. HEW announced revised school desegregation guidelines, and for the first time they applied to northern as well as southern districts.

But on the key anti-busing vote in the House in October, only 71 non-southern members—12 of whom were Democrats—opposed a move to weaken anti-busing language. The House voted, 167-165, virtually to nullify a provision it had earlier approved as part of the Labor-HEW appropriations bill. The provision forbade HEW to withhold funds from districts in order to require them to move further, by busing or other methods, to desegregate their schools. This provision was called the Whitten amendment after its author, Jamie L. Whitten (D Miss.).

Among the non-southern supporters of the Whitten amendment were nine California members, 11 from Pennsylvania, eight from Ohio, Edward J. Derwinski (R Ill.)—in whose district the first non-southern desegregation suit had been filed—and William G. Bray (R Ind.)—whose district included part of Indianapolis.

1969. There was little significant change in members' positions on the busing issue in 1969, a fact not indirectly related to the ambiguity which surrounded the new administration's school desegregation policy. Aside from issuing a warning to Chicago that it must speed up desegregation and filing suits against the schools of Waterbury, Conn., and Madison, Ill., the

...Created a New Congressional Majority, 1969-1972

administration took little action outside the South on the matter.

Once again the House version of the Labor-HEW appropriations bill contained the Whitten amendment, but the House in December adopted Senate-added language to nullify it. On the key vote, the House rejected, 181-216, a motion to kill the nullifying amendment. Only 75 non-southerners backed the motion.

1970. The first key vote closely resembled the 1969 vote, coming during final House consideration of the second Labor-HEW appropriations bill for that year.

The second bill also contained the Whitten amendment to which the Senate had added weakening language. Once again anti-busing forces were defeated when the House voted 164-222 to reject a motion to kill the proposal that the House accept the weakening language.

Perhaps the most significant of the position changes registered by northern Democrats on this vote, in early March, was that of Roman C. Pucinski (D Ill.), a high-ranking member of the House Education and Labor Committee and—until 1966—champion of every civil rights measure which came to the House floor. In 1970, Pucinski cast his first record vote with anti-busing forces; by 1971 he was one of the leaders of the anti-busing majority.

In February, a desegregation order for Los Angeles was handed down, requiring substantial busing; in March, a similar plan was ordered for Pasadena, Calif.; in April, the HEW Department moved to cut off federal funds to Ferndale, Mich., schools, and the Detroit school board sparked vehement protest by changing school district boundaries to foster desegregation.

In June, the House cast its second key vote on the busing issue. For the first time on a significant vote, the anti-busing forces prevailed. The House agreed, 191-157, to kill a motion which required House conferees on the education appropriations bill to agree to Senate action dropping the modified Whitten amendment. The provision was retained.

Ninety-nine non-southern representatives—only 18 of them Democrats—joined the anti-busing forces in this victory. Significant among these were H. Allen Smith (R Calif.) who represented Pasadena and William S. Broomfield (R Mich.) who represented Ferndale.

1971. Anti-busing forces won again in April when the House refused, 149-206, to cut the Whitten amendment from the education appropriations bill for fiscal 1972. Among those voting with the opposition were 108 non-southern members.

By the time the House voted in November on the anti-busing amendment to the higher education-desegregation aid bill, the uproar in San Francisco and Pontiac, Detroit, Indianapolis and other urban and suburban neighborhoods had been translated into constituent pressure. The impact was obvious:

Michigan representatives voted 15-1 for the Broomfield amendment delaying the effect of court orders requiring busing. Six other Michigan representatives, including O'Hara, sponsored the amendment. Reflecting similar shifts, the delegations of Connecti-

cut, Illinois, Indiana, New York, Ohio, Pennsylvania and Wisconsin voted lopsidedly for the amendment.

Most long-time opponents of busing were delighted with the new majority position which they had attained with the votes of their northern allies. But some were disgruntled by the immediate success of the northern protest.

Jack Edwards of Alabama (R) cast one of the negative votes, explaining: "We are busing all over the 1st District of Alabama.... A lot of people say to me, 'How in the world are we ever going to stop this madness?' I say, 'It will stop the day it starts taking place across the country, in the North, in the East....'

"And so busing is ordered in Michigan and the first thing the members from Michigan do is come in with this amendment and ask us to delay it for them. But, my friends, we are not going to stop the busing as long as we let them off the hook the minute it hits them. Let it hurt them, and we will get their votes as we try to stop busing once and for all."

1972. Adding to the national uproar was the January 1972 decision of a Richmond, Va., federal district court requiring busing across city and county lines to desegregate schools. This ruling—which was overturned in June by the court of appeals, 4th circuit—merged the largely black Richmond city school system with two white suburban systems. And in Detroit, Federal District Judge Stephen J. Roth, who had earlier found that city's schools deliberately segregated, ordered in June the preparation of a desegregation plan for Detroit and 53 suburban districts.

In a major address March 16, President Nixon said the lower courts had gone beyond what the Supreme Court said was necessary in requiring pupil transportation. He asked Congress to approve bills allowing the use of busing only as a limited, last-resort remedy for segregation and barring implementation of all new busing orders until July 1, 1973, or until Congress passed the first bill, whichever was sooner. Neither bill was cleared by Congress in 1972.

But Congress did reaffirm the 1971 House action on the issue by approving its strongest anti-busing language in the higher education bill (PL 92-318). The language finally approved was a compromise between the stiff House language and the less rigid Senate provisions. Twice the House had voted to instruct its conferees not to accept any compromise in this language. On the first of these motions 272 members had approved such unusual instructions. Fifty-seven of these votes were cast by non-southern Democrats.

And the largest show of anti-busing strength ever in the House came when the House approved, in August, the President's proposal that busing be made a last-resort remedy. This bill passed the House by a vote of 283-103; 81 of these votes came from non-southern Democrats. As sent to the Senate, where it died with the end of the Congress, the bill barred busing except to the school closest or next closest to the student's home. It was the strongest anti-busing bill ever to pass either chamber.

convention in July condemning the President for his anti-busing views and asserting he had aroused "passions of hate and bitterness" among Americans.

Civil rights groups—127 of them—gathered under the umbrella of the Leadership Conference on Civil Rights to oppose the President and the trend in Congress.

Howard A. Glickstein, former staff director of the civil rights commission, directed the conference's battle to keep busing alive as a means of desegregating schools. People were "hysterical and irrational" over busing and the President "was anxious to make an issue of it," Glickstein said.

He predicted that the President would "keep the pot boiling" with attempts to stir Congress into action on the issue, and that Nixon would win points regardless of what Congress did. If Congress acted, Nixon could take the credit, and if it did not, he could blame them, Glickstein explained.

Other pressures on Congress and the President came from state legislatures. Voters in Florida on March 14 and in Tennessee May 4 voted overwhelmingly, in non-binding referendums, to support constitutional amendments barring busing. The Virginia Senate had voted 36-3 Feb. 15, 1972 in favor of a resolution asking Congress to amend the Constitution to bar busing to integrate schools.

Confusing the issue, Florida voters, at the same time they voted against busing, gave 78 per cent approval to another question on the ballot: "Do you favor providing an equal opportunity for quality education for all children, regardless of race, creed, color and place of residence, and oppose a return to a dual system of public education?"

Congress

The 92nd Congress responded to the busing pressures by approving its strongest anti-busing language in the Higher Education Act (S 659—PL 92-318). The amendments were a compromise between stronger House language and less rigid Senate provisions. They:

• Postponed until all appeals had been exhausted, or the time for them expired, the implementation of all federal district court orders requiring the transfer or transportation of pupils to achieve racial balance. The provision was to expire Jan. 1, 1974.

• Limited use of federal funds for busing intended to desegregate a school system to cases where the local officials requested the funds.

• Barred busing where it would risk the pupil's health or require him to attend a school inferior to his former school.

• Barred federal pressure on local school boards to induce them to use busing "unless constitutionally required."

But busing opponents were unsatisfied with these limitations and by mid-August were pressing for even stricter controls, specifically the President's proposals.

The President's moratorium was stronger than S 659 because it would put a complete ban on all new busing orders, whereas the anti-busing amendments to S 659 would bar implementation of busing orders until appeals—or the time for them—had been exhausted.

In order to get House action on stiffer busing control bills, proponents pulled off a rarely used power play through the Rules Committee that pried one bill out of the pro-busing Judiciary Committee and forced another out of the liberal Education and Labor Committee.

Under House rules, the Rules Committee was authorized to discharge a bill from a legislative committee by majority vote. This was seldom done.

But William M. Colmer (D Miss.), retiring chairman of the Rules Committee, was an ardent busing opponent who felt the Judiciary Committee was stalling action on the Lent amendment and the President's moratorium bill. The amendment had been in the committee for more than a year. Hearings were held, but no other action was taken. *(Details p. 517)*

Colmer issued an ultimatum to Chairman Emanuel Celler (D N.Y.) of the Judiciary Committee June 29 that one of the bills would have to be reported out of his committee by Aug. 1 or the Rules Committee would attempt to discharge them.

Celler and the Judiciary Committee refused to act and on Aug. 1 the Rules Committee voted 9-6 to discharge the amendment and send it to floor. The amendment read, "No public school student shall, because of his race, creed or color, be assigned to or required to attend a particular school." The language, seemingly egalitarian, had been denounced by constitutional experts as likely to bar desegregation as well as busing.

At the same time, the Rules Committee voted 11-4 to delay a discharge attempt on the President's moratorium proposal. It was clear, however, that there was enough strength on the committee to force anti-busing legislation out of the Education and Labor Committee. The Education and Labor Committee voted 21-16 Aug. 8 to report an amended version of the President's equal educational opportunities bill strictly limiting busing.

As ordered reported, the bill required that any pupil in the elementary grades (1-6) be allowed to attend the public school "closest or next closest" to his home. It also reserved $500-million annually for compensatory education from the sums appropriated for aid to desegregating school districts. The committee rejected an amendment which would have made the $500-million a newly authorized sum, instead of simply earmarking part of already authorized funds.

The committee also rejected a provision in the bill as proposed by Nixon that would have allowed reopening of school desegregation orders to determine whether they conformed with the provisions of the new legislation.

The Senate Judiciary Committee had not begun hearings on the moratorium proposal. Education Subcommittee Chairman Claiborne Pell (D R.I.) said after holding several days of hearings on the equal opportunity bill that he was having trouble finding witnesses who would testify in its favor. The committee did not report the bill in 1972.

In its largest show of anti-busing strength to date, the House in mid-August 1972 approved an amended version of the administration's equal opportunities bill. The bill was passed by a 283-102 vote after the House had restored the reopener language and had amended the bill to ban busing regardless of a child's grade in school except to the school closest or next closest to the student's home.

Anti-busing forces in the Senate used parliamentary tactics to hold the bill on the floor rather than to refer it to the liberally oriented Labor and Public Welfare Committee. The bill died in the Senate after three attempts to cut off debate on the measure failed.

Debate on the measure began Oct. 6. The first cloture vote came Oct. 10; it was 45-37—ten short of the necessary two-thirds; the second vote the next day was short by the same margin, 49-39; the third and final vote Oct. 12 was still nine short, 49-38. After the third failure the Senate agreed to move on to other business, and the bill was dead.

The Administration

President Nixon responded with sympathy to busing opponents. In a major address March 16, 1972, he said the lower courts had gone beyond what the Supreme Court said was necessary in requiring pupil transportation.

"All too often," the President said, "the result has been a classic case of the remedy for one evil creating another evil. In this case, a remedy for the historic evil of racial discrimination has often created a new evil of disrupting communities and imposing hardships on children—both black and white—who are themselves wholly innocent of the wrongs that the plan seeks to right."

The President followed up his speech with a two-part legislative proposal to slow, if not stop, the use of busing for desegregation. It consisted of:

• The "Equal Educational Opportunities Act" which would allow busing only as a limited last-resort remedy for segregation and would concentrate $2.5-billion in federal funds for compensatory education programs in poor schools.

• The "Student Transportation Moratorium Act" which would bar implementation of all new busing orders until July 1, 1973, or until Congress passed the equal opportunity bill, whichever was sooner.

The constitutionality of the proposals was a point of much discussion. The administration said that Congress had the constitutional authority to limit the jurisdiction of the federal courts. Opponents of the proposals questioned whether or not Congress could withdraw from the courts the power to order the use of a remedy necessary to secure to individuals their constitutional right to an equal educational opportunity.

The administration could have avoided this controversy by endorsing a proposed constitutional amendment barring the use of busing, but President Nixon declined to do so, saying that the amendment process (requiring two-thirds approval by both houses and ratification by three-fourths of the states) was too slow.

Clarence Mitchell, chief lobbyist for the NAACP, called the President's plan "a stunning example of government sanctioning hysteria and chaos." Nixon was standing in the school house door much as Alabama Gov. George C. Wallace did in the early 1960s to prevent blacks from entering the state university, he said.

Southerners were cool toward the proposals, recognizing them as fulfillment of their predictions that busing would be halted when it hit the North. "What about the old busing?" asked Rep. Joe D. Waggonner Jr. (D La.), referring to the busing already in effect which the moratorium would not touch.

And Mrs. Irene McCabe, a Pontiac, Mich., housewife and leader of the anti-busing National Action Group

(NAG), scolded the President for not endorsing the constitutional amendment route.

Many northerners regarded the President's proposals as saving them from carrying out busing orders in their section. House Minority Leader Gerald R. Ford (Mich.) and Rep. Norman F. Lent (R N.Y.) endorsed the moratorium. But Lent, the sponsor of a constitutional amendment barring busing, said he would press for that measure if Congress failed to pass the moratorium bill.

Some criticism came from within the administration itself. In April 1972, two-thirds of the lawyers in the Justice Department's civil rights division signed a letter to Congress calling on it to reject any measures that would limit the remedies available in the federal courts. And 40 black federal officials, calling themselves the Council of Black Appointees, criticized the proposals and called for major revisions.

The administration pressed ahead with its proposals, and by mid-year the Justice Department had intervened on the side of anti-busing forces in important busing cases in Detroit, Richmond, Nashville, Dallas, Oklahoma City and Fort Worth.

The President, signing the higher education bill which contained anti-busing amendments on June 23, scolded the legislative branch for refusing to act on his proposals. John D. Ehrlichman, the senior White House adviser on domestic affairs, said that if Congress failed to act on the administration's measures before it adjourned for the elections, the President would "go to the country" to rally support for a constitutional amendment.

Forces Pro and Con

Arrayed behind—and often ahead of—the politicians on the busing issue was a variety of pressure groups. Anti-busing forces were chiefly grass roots organizations.

Among them were the National Action Group (NAG) whose head, Mrs. McCabe, walked 600 miles from her home in Michigan to Washington, D.C., to dramatize her campaign for the Lent amendment. A group of parents from Richmond took part in a motor caravan to Washington to promote anti-busing legislation.

Also opposing busing was the Congress on Racial Equality (CORE), a leading black civil rights group. CORE's position was that only black-controlled schools could provide quality education for blacks, whereas busing would perpetuate white dominance of schools and school boards.

Other opponents included citizen action groups, school boards and local PTAs. A 1971 Gallup Poll had found 77 per cent national opposition to busing. Blacks split almost evenly on busing, it found.

Busing proponents counted on the support of labor, minority and civil rights groups. George Meany, president of the AFL-CIO, denounced the President's proposals as "political chicanery." The moratorium, he said, was "a cynical attempt to reward those who said 'never,' and to undermine the moral leadership of those citizens who endeavored to comply with the Constitution and the Supreme Court's 1954 decision."

The national PTA went on record supporting busing at its national convention in May—but by the slimmest of margins—302-296. The vote came on a resolution recommending "solutions that could, by rational means, reduce isolation through transportation."

Chapter 9—Space

Key Votes

In this chapter, key roll-call votes are shown in bold-face type. The party breakdown on each of these votes and the position taken by each member of Congress may be found in the key vote charts which appear in the appendix to this book.

Space Programs

A decade after President Kennedy launched the United States on a multi-billion dollar race to achieve the first manned moon landing, the future of American space exploration hung in the balance. Domestic priorities and needs took precedence over the moon and outer planets.

Indeed, the problems facing America's space program in 1972 stemmed in large measure from its very success. The nation's major space goal of the 1960s—to land a man on the moon and return him safely to earth—had been achieved within the period of time originally allotted for the task. In addition, unmanned spacecraft revolutionized global communications and performed such other tasks as mapping, military surveillance, observation of meteorological disturbances and examination of the surface of Mars.

In doing all this, the National Aeronautics and Space Administration (NASA) made the difficult seem commonplace. Live television coverage from Europe and Asia, an exciting novelty a decade ago, was taken for granted by 1972. The first manned moon landing—on July 20, 1969—held a worldwide television audience spellbound, but public interest in subsequent and more ambitious lunar missions declined as they became increasingly familiar.

At the close of President Nixon's first term in office, an era in space had ended. Apollo 16 and 17, launched in April and December 1972, were the last two manned flights in the moon program (originally there were to have been 19 Apollo flights, but two were canceled for budgetary reasons). Without a new long-range mandate to send men into space, NASA proposed—and the President endorsed—a program to construct a reusable space vehicle, commonly called the space shuttle, capable of ferrying men and equipment between earth and space.

The proposed space shuttle program, however, encountered stiff opposition in Congress, where critics contended that the funds requested for the project could be put to better use in solving human needs on earth. Terming the program a "senseless extravaganza in space," Sen. Walter F. Mondale (D Minn.), the leading opponent in Congress of the shuttle project, said Jan. 6, 1972, that "in the magnitude of its cost, in the folly of its concept and, thus, in its damage to the country, the space shuttle is many times worse than the SST (supersonic transport)." The money proposed for shuttle development, the senator added on Jan. 28, "should go to solve human problems such as mass transit, housing, education and the environment."

Nonetheless, despite repeated attempts by Mondale and others to cut off funding for the project, Congress in 1970, 1971 and 1972 authorized and appropriated research and development funds for the space shuttle and Skylab, the orbiting experimental space laboratory launched in May 1973.

The space shuttle, declared NASA, was "the key element in our program for the 1970s." It remained to be seen, however, whether the shuttle program could provide fresh impetus for the nation's space efforts in the 1970s.

Nixon Goals

By 1970, shifting priorities and budget restraints appeared to have caught up with the space program. On March 7 of that year, President Nixon outlined a series of six relatively modest specific objectives for the space program in the 1970s, including a "grand tour" mission by unmanned vehicles to explore the outer planets of the solar system, to be launched between 1977 and 1979.

"By no means should we allow our space program to stagnate," the President said in a statement. "But—with the entire future and the entire universe before us we should not try to do everything at once. Our approach to space must continue to be bold—but it must also be balanced."

The "bold" yet "balanced" space program outlined by Nixon no doubt was viewed as an austerity program by space agency officials. Six months earlier, on Sept. 15, 1969, a cabinet-level Space Task Group headed by Vice President Spiro T. Agnew had recommended a far more ambitious and specific set of space objectives for the 1970s. The principal recommendation of the task group report, entitled "The Post-Apollo Program: Directions for the Future," was that the United States "accept the long-range option or goal of manned Mars expedition before the end of the century as the first target."

The immediate response of the White House to the report was noncommittal. In his March 7 statement, Nixon said only that "we will eventually send men to explore the planet Mars." And he cautioned: "We must build on the successes of the past, always reaching out for new achievements. But we must also recognize that many critical problems here on this planet make high-priority demands on our attention and our resources."

References

Discussion of space developments from 1945-64 may be found in *Congress and the Nation*, Vol. I, p. 237-334, 531-551; for the years 1965-68, *Congress and the Nation*, Vol. II, p. 513-551.

Nixon Space Goals for 1970s

President Nixon outlined U.S. space objectives for the 1970s March 7, 1970, in a long-awaited statement on the future of the space program.

• Further exploration of the moon. The purpose of "future Apollo manned lunar landings" would be to "maximize our scientific return from each mission," said Mr. Nixon.

• Unmanned exploration of the planets and the universe. "In the late 1970s," said the President, "the 'grand tour' missions will study mysterious outer planets of the solar system—Jupiter, Saturn, Uranus, Neptune, and Pluto.... Preparations for this program will begin in 1972."

• Reduction in the cost of space operations. The President referred to studies of "the feasibility of reusable space shuttles as one way of achieving this objective."

• Extension of man's "capability to live and work in space." The President said that on the basis of experience with the 1972-1973 Skylab project "we will decide when and how to develop longer-lived space stations."

• Practical application of space technology. Mr. Nixon referred to the earth resources satellite program and called for further development of space-related technology in meteorology, communications, navigation, air traffic control, education and national defense.

• International cooperation in space.

Space Shuttle. There matters stood until Jan. 5, 1972, when the President declared that the United States "should proceed at once" with the development of a reusable space shuttle that would "take the astronomical costs out of astronautics." Such a vehicle, Nixon said, would "help transform the space frontier of the 1970s into familiar territory, easily accessible for human endeavor in the 1980s and 1990s." The cost of designing and building two test flight vehicles over a six-year period was estimated at $5.5-billion—around one-fourth the cost of the Apollo moon program.

The ultimate cost of the shuttle project, as outlined in the federal budget presented to Congress in early 1972, would reach $10-billion and possibly $14-billion, rather than the $5.5-billion previously estimated. For fiscal 1973, NASA requested $200-million for shuttle development—double the amount appropriated for fiscal 1972. Shuttle expenditures were expected to rise to $600-million in fiscal 1974 and to $1-billion in fiscal 1975.

Budget and Program Cutbacks

During the 1960s, as the moon program gathered momentum, congressional appropriations for the space agency steadily increased to a peak level of $5.25-billion in fiscal 1965. After that year, however, funds made available for space programs slowly declined. Congress authorized only $3.35-billion for the agency in fiscal 1972 and slightly more for fiscal 1973. Congress slashed the administration's request for fiscal 1969 by 8.6 per cent but appropriated more than was asked for in fiscal years 1971, 1972 and 1973.

NASA's budgetary cutbacks led to program delays and cancellations in manned and unmanned projects. Two of the remaining six Apollo moon landings were canceled in September 1970. The four other launches were rescheduled to go at six- rather than four-month intervals. The last Apollo flight, which had been rescheduled for June 1972, was later set back another five months to December 1972.

Budget cuts for fiscal 1971 also put the permanent space station in an "advanced studies stage." In 1972, NASA dropped plans for the "grand tour" to the outer planets proposed by Nixon in 1970. To replace the program, NASA budgeted $7-million for fiscal 1973 to study the feasibility of sending one or two spacecraft to Jupiter and possibly Saturn.

Another victim of budget-cutting was the NERVA nuclear space-engine project, on which $1.4-billion had been spent. Instead, NASA proposed to concentrate on development of a smaller nuclear-propulsion rocket that could be used for unmanned exploration.

Saturn V launch vehicle production was suspended after completion of the 15th Saturn V. The last Saturn was used as a launch vehicle for Skylab in May 1973. A smaller Saturn IB would be used for future missions.

The Tiros N weather satellite, which had been scheduled for a 1976 launch, was delayed for one year. The Orbiting Solar Observatories, OSO J and OSO K, scheduled for launch in 1974, were cancelled.

Stress on Environment

Diminished enthusiasm about the moon was reflected in the exploratory program itself, where changes in schedule resulted from budget cuts and altered priorities. A sign of the times was NASA's increasing stress on earth resources and ecology. Emphasizing the importance of observing the earth from space, John M. DeNoyer, director of the agency's Earth Observation Program, said in late 1970: "Perhaps the single most important event of the last decade which had made man aware of the urgent need to preserve his environment was his first view of his home from outer space."

NASA's chief manned vehicle for this job was Skylab, the experimental space station made of components from the Apollo program. It was planned that the earth-orbiting laboratory would be operated by three successive teams of three men each, living in the trailer-sized vehicle for up to 56 days at a stretch. One important task would be to search out hidden metal deposits on the earth; a second involved expanding existing surveys being made by satellite to aid in improving agriculture, fisheries and pollution control.

In a 1970 statement, Joseph B. Gavin Jr., senior vice president for space programs at Grumman Aerospace Corp., identified the source of the space agency's difficulties: "Our nation's space efforts today are searching for justification rather than providing solutions to accepted goals," he said. "The over-riding goal of the last decade, the lunar landing, has not been replaced. We do not seem to have clear-cut goals which are both sound and politically saleable. Hence, we lack wholehearted commitment to our goals by the present administration, the Congress and the public."

Chronology

Of Legislation

On Space

1969

AUTHORIZATION. Congress Nov. 7 cleared the fiscal 1970 National Aeronautics and Space Administration authorization bill (HR 11271—PL 91-119). The bill contained $3,715,527,000, matching the administration's request and including funds for three manned moon flights in fiscal 1970. This amount was $279.8-million below the amount authorized for fiscal 1969. It was the fifth year in a row that NASA authorizations declined. *(Box this page)*

The reduction in over-all authorizations below fiscal 1969 came despite the success of the Apollo 11 and 12 moon flights.

In the House, debate centered on national priorities and federal spending. However, the House-passed bill included $250 million more than the administration requested, primarily in the Apollo program and for space flight operations. The space flight operations program included the manned earth-orbiting space station and the space shuttle. Rep. Edward I. Koch (D N.Y.) offered an amendment, rejected by voice vote, which called for reductions in the authorizations of $204.9 million, of which $75.7 million was to come from the Apollo program and $129.2 million from the space flight operations program.

In other House action, debate on the NASA budget ranged from campus disorders to whether a U.S. flag should be placed on the moon. The House accepted by voice vote an amendment offered by Richard L. Roudebush (R Ind.) requiring that the U.S. flag—and no other flag be placed on the moon's, or any other planet's, surface by astronauts who land there as part of a program funded entirely by the federal government.

An amendment offered by Koch to delete a provision of the bill prohibiting the use of NASA funds by campus disrupters was defeated by a 15-83 standing vote.

The House by a 330-52 roll-call vote passed the bill June 10 and sent it to the Senate.

The Senate Aeronautical and Space Sciences Committee amended the House-passed bill, cutting it back to the Nixon administration's budget request of $3.7-billion. The committee omitted the House bill's denial of funds to campus rioters and the requirement that U.S. astronauts place only the U.S. flag on the moon.

During Senate floor debate, William Proxmire (D Wis.) introduced an amendment requiring high-level employees who transfer between similar jobs in NASA and the aerospace industry to disclose certain information to the NASA administrator. The amendment was adopted by voice vote.

HR 11271 passed the Senate by voice vote Sept. 19 and was sent to conference.

House and Senate conferees authorized the $3.7 billion contained in the Senate bill and requested by the

History of NASA Funding

(in millions of dollars)

Fiscal Year	Administration Request	Authorized Amount	Change (in %) From Request
1959	$ 280.5	$ 222.8*	—20.6%
1960	508.3	485.1*	— 4.6
1961	964.6	961.0	— 0.4
1962	1,940.3	1,825.3	— 5.9
1963	3,787.3	3,674.1	— 3.0
1964	5,712.0	5,100.0	—10.7
1965	5,445.0	5,250.0	— 3.6
1966	5,260.0	5,175.0	— 1.6
1967	5,012.0	4,968.0	— 0.9
1968	5,100.0	4,588.9	—10.0
1969	4,370.4	3,995.3	— 8.6
1970*	3,715.5	3,715.5	—
1971	3,333.0	3,410.9	+ 2.3
1972	3,271.5	3,355.0	+ 2.6
1973	3,407.6**	3,444.2	+ 1.1

* Funds actually available in first two years somewhat increased by transfers from other agencies.
**Budget request as amended.

administration, thereby cutting out the additional funds for Apollo and space flight operations approved by the House. The final version of the bill also retained the Proxmire amendment, the amendments requiring flag placement on the moon and the prohibitions on payment of NASA funds to campus rioters.

Final action on the bill came when the House Nov. 6 adopted the conference report by voice vote. The Senate Nov. 7 by voice vote also adopted the conference report on HR 11271, completing congressional action. The President Nov. 18 signed the bill (PL 91-119).

APPROPRIATION. Congress in 1969 for the fifth year in succession cut back appropriations for NASA. Monies for the National Aeronautics and Space Administration are included in the Department of Housing and Urban Development and independent offices and executive offices appropriations bill.

The $3,693,633,000 appropriated by Congress Nov. 18 (HR 12307—PL 91-126) was the lowest amount for the space agency since fiscal 1963 and a reduction of $18.9 million from the budget request.

Sen. William Proxmire (D Wis.) introduced an amendment to reduce the NASA appropriation by $100 million to show, he said, his concern with the "waste and extravagance" in the program. The amendment was rejected by a 22-46 roll-call vote.

The House and Senate Nov. 18 adopted the conference report on HR 12037 by voice votes. The President Nov. 26 signed the bill into law (PL 91-126).

1970

AUTHORIZATION. Congress June 22 cleared for the President's signature the fiscal 1971 National Aeronautics and Space Administration authorization bill (HR 16515—PL 91-303 containing $3,410,878,000. It included funds for the permanent space station/space shuttle project—

(Continued on p. 525)

Apollo 11: Man Sets Foot Upon The Moon in 1969

A manned moon landing, the goal of the American space program since 1961, came at 4:17 P.M. EDT, July 20, 1969. Astronauts Neil A. Armstrong and Edwin E. Aldrin Jr. of the Apollo 11 mission descended in their lunar module, the "Eagle," to a level rock-strewn plain near the southwestern edge of the moon's arid Sea of Tranquility.

The first words spoken by man on the moon were Armstrong's, radioed to Mission Control at the Manned Spacecraft Center, Houston, Texas, and heard by listeners around the world: "Houston, Tranquility Base here. The Eagle has landed."

Armstrong had been designated in advance to be the first man actually to set foot on the lunar surface. He did so six and one-half hours later, at at 10:56 P.M. EDT. A television camera attached to the lunar module recorded the event "live" for viewers on earth. They saw the astronaut slowly crawl backwards down a ladder, fixed to one of the lunar module's four legs. "That's one small step for man, one giant lep for mankind," he said as he stepped onto the moon.

Science Tasks. Within 20 minutes, Aldrin became the second human in history to plant a foot on the moon. He joined Armstrong at 11:14 P.M. EDT. Their moon exploration continued about two hours, until they re-entered the Eagle at 1:09 A.M. EDT. In that time they conducted a number of tasks on behalf of science and erected an American flag on a metal staff—while providing television pictures and a running commentary. They placed rocks and lunar soil in sealed boxes for the return trip to earth, where, it was hoped, scientists might examine the specimens free of exposure to the earth's environment. They left behind a package of seismometers to detect moonquakes and a reflector to bounce laser pulses back to earth.

Armstrong's first step onto the moon was planned originally to come about five hours lately than it did. Part of the intervening time after the Eagle's landing was scheduled for sleeping. But after making sure that their rocket engines could be refired for departure, the two astronauts decided to forgo rest. Houston concurred in their decision. They slumbered fitfully for a few hours after returning to the Eagle, according to signals received in Houston from medical monitoring devices.

The Eagle blasted off from the moon at 1:55 P.M. EDT, July 21, as flawlessly as it had alighted almost 21 hours earlier. It rejoined the command module, Columbia, at 5:35 P.M. EDT. The Columbia had been manned by the third Apollo 11 astronaut, Michael Collins, since the two spacecraft separated—"undocked"—shortly after 1:50 P.M. EDT the previous day. Collins circled the moon 31 times in all—on about half of the orbits he was without companions and was out of radio contact with anyone while on the moon's far side. His vigil was described as man's loneliest venture into space.

For several minutes after undocking, prior to the moon landing, Columbia and Eagle flew only a few feet apart in their moon orbit. Then Collins maneuvered the Columbia away while the Eagle began the first phase of its descent, from an altitude of 65.5 miles. At around 50,000 feet above the moon surface, about the lowest point reached by Apollo 10 in May 1969, the Eagle began descending in a steadily steepening trajectory toward the landing site 250 miles away. In the final minutes before landing, Armstrong took control manually when he saw that the computer-operated automatic control was guiding the craft down onto a football-field-size crater studded with large boulders. He flew the Eagle to a smoother site nearby and touched down with only enough descent fuel left in the engine's reserve to fly 30 seconds more.

Departure for Earth. Upon leaving the moon, Eagle rejoined Columbia in orbit so surely that only one mid-course correction was required. The reunited crew of Apollo 11 fired the propulsion rockets of their command ship and broke out of moon orbit at 12:56 A.M. EDT, July 22, for the return trip of about 245,000 miles. The astronauts splashed down in the Pacific at 12:50 P.M. EDT, July 24, eight days after their launching from atop a Saturn V rocket at Cape Kennedy, Fla.

The launching came precisely on schedule at 9:32 A.M. EDT, July 16. It was witnessed by Vice President Spiro T. Agnew, former President Lyndon B. Johnson, hundreds of Members of Congress, space officials, foreign dignitaries and by countless thousands of curiosity seekers who lined nearby beaches, highways and waterways. Millions more saw the launching on television. President Nixon was aboard the aircraft carrier Hornet to welcome the astronauts after their recovery from the sea. Their spacecraft splashed down some 210 miles south of tiny Johnston Island and 920 miles southwest of Honolulu.

Astronaut Quarantine. The returning astronauts were unable to greet the President directly, because of precautions taken to guard against the remote chance that they might be carrying some disease-producing organism from the moon. Upon reaching the Hornet, the three astronauts entered isolated living quarters—a mobile van that resembled a house trailer.

When the carrier reached Honolulu, the astronauts in their van were placed aboard a cargo jet and flown to Houston, where they were transferred to specially built quarters at the Manned Spacecraft Center for the remainder of the quarantine. They underwent detailed medical examinations.

The lunar materials that the astronauts brought back had meanwhile been flown ahead to an adjoining laboratory at the Manned Spacecraft Center for examination by scientists under conditions designed to keep the specimens free of earthly contamination. After study at the laboratory, some pieces of lunar rocks were due to be sent to scientists in several foreign countries. The bulk of the moon materials would remain in the laboratory.

First Moon Flight Renewed Debate Over National Priorities

The historic landing of Americans on the moon July 20, 1969, renewed the debate over national priorities. The U.S. civilian space program had cost an estimated $24.6 billion through 1969. The cost of the remaining scheduled Apollo missions was estimated at $350 million each. The fiscal 1970 authorization for the Apollo program was $1,691,100,000.

Future Space Policy

President Nixon July 22 indicated where he would like the thrust of U.S. space policy over the next 30 years: manned exploration of the solar system in the expectation of discovering life.

"In the year 2000 we on the earth will have visited new worlds where there there will be a form of life," he said. The American space effort, he said, represents "all of mankind.... It is not an adventure of conquest but an adventure of exploration which tends to unite us all."

Controversy which had swirled around the space program from the beginning had been rekindled even before Mr. Nixon's statement. Vice President Spiro T. Agnew July 16 called for establishment of a new national goal: a manned landing on Mars by the end of the century.

A report of the special Space Task Group made public Sept. 17 recommended that the United States adopt the goal of landing men on Mars before the end of the century. The Task Group, headed by Agnew, gave the President three "options" for a Mars landing —1983, 1986 or sometime in the 1990s. Agnew favored a 1986 Mars landing goal. Besides Agnew, the special Space Task Group was composed of Presidential Science Adviser Lee A. DuBridge, NASA head Thomas O. Paine, and Air Force Secretary Robert C. Seamans.

Paine told a House Appropriations subcommittee in April: "It is my view, and it is the view shared by the task group and President Nixon, as it was by President Johnson, that manned space flight must be a part of a balanced U.S. space program. We cannot conceive the United States turning over this whole new ocean of space to be traveled through exclusively by Soviet cosmonauts." Paine noted that the Nixon budget included funds, on which decision had been deferred by the Johnson administration, for continued exploration of the moon and for continued production of the Saturn V launch vehicle. These changes were in accord with the task group's views, Paine said.

'Needs on Earth'

Agnew's comments prompted Senate Majority Leader Mike Mansfield (D Mont.) to say July 16, "We have a lot of problems here on earth that we must face up to, and when we settle those we ought to consider future space ventures. I am interested in looking to the needs of people on earth, and particularly in this country. This should have priority."

Sen. Edward M. Kennedy (D Mass.) said the same day that after the Apollo program, space ventures should be "fitted in with other priorities in an orderly fashion. We have important and demanding needs on earth and they should have priority." And Sen. Clinton P. Anderson (D N.M.), chairman of the Senate Aeronautical and Space Sciences Committee, wrote constituents July 22 that the nation should go slowly with any plans for a manned flight to Mars. "We may not be ready for it," Anderson said. He said the project might cost $25 billion to $40 billion.

The July 20 landing of Neil A. Armstrong and Edwin E. Aldrin Jr. on the moon, followed by their rendezvous with moon-orbiting Michael Collins and the crew's return to earth, confronted U.S. policymakers with major decisions on the nation's future policies in space.

Benefits from Space

Some policymakers said man's problems on earth rated greater priority for American money and brainpower than space exploration. They cited space success as evidence of what can be done. "I will be arguing that we can have moon shots in the welfare field and some of these other areas," said Robert H. Finch. Secretary of Health, Education and Welfare. George Romney, Secretary of Housing and Urban Development, said, "It's time to revise and reverse the (space) policies and deal with the problems on earth."

Others said immense benefits to man will increasingly accrue from wealth-producing space activity. "The cumulative benefits in a decade or two will exceed space expenditures many times over...," Dr. Charles S. Sheldon II, director of research on science policy at the Library of Congress, said: "An analysis for NASA by IBM suggested that the return to civilian applications would reach $102 billion a year—compared to the $24 billion spent on the manned space program thus far."

(Continued from p. 523)
NASA's program for manned space flight after the scheduled completion of the Apollo series in 1974. Funds also were included for the 1972-1973 Apollo Applications flight (Skylab), a temporary space station in earth orbit using hardware developed for the Apollo lunar missions.

The authorization was $304,649,000 below the $3,715,-527,000 authorized in the fiscal 1970 NASA authorization bill, but it exceeded the administration's request by $77.9-million.

The major space event of the year, the abortive Apollo 13 mission (April 11-17), which threatened the lives of three astronauts, had little impact on congressional consideration of NASA's fiscal 1971 authorization request.

For the second year in a row the House Science and Astronautics Committee increased the amount asked for by the administration. The committee authorized $3,630,-875,000 ($297 million more than the administration requested). The biggest increases came in the manned space flight program (Apollo and Space Flight Operations, where the committee added $298.5-million).

On the House floor Joseph E. Karth (D Minn.) introduced an amendment to cut $240 million from the bill—all from the manned space program.

Karth's amendment would have cut $50 million out of the Apollo program and $190 million from space flight operations. The entire $190 million would have come out of the space shuttle and space station project.

In debate on Karth's amendment, opponents argued that the proposed $190-million cut would have eliminated work on the shuttle and station. Karth denied this, maintaining there was "$60 to $80 million" elsewhere in research and development funds in HR 16516 available for study and research on the shuttle and station.

Karth maintained that the $190 million contained in HR 16516 for the shuttle and space stations represented the "beginning of a manned Mars landing program," a program for which a "national policy determination...has not been made." Referring to testimony by NASA officials during hearings on the authorization bill, Karth said that for the space shuttle to be fully utilized it would be necessary to launch 60 flights and three million pounds (five times as much as in 1969) of payload into orbit each year.

In defense of the space shuttle and station program. Olin E. Teague (D Texas), chairman of the Manned Space Flight Subcommittee, said the "low-cost recoverable shuttle represents...the most significant aspect of the national space program in the late 1970s. Developing a reusable space transportation system operating much like commercial aircraft will provide broad new opportunities to utilize space and conduct scientific explorations at a significantly reduced cost."

The Karth amendment was defeated by a 53-53 teller vote.

An amendment offered by James G. Fulton (R Pa.), ranking Republican on the Science and Astronautics Committee, reducing authorizations for research and development for Apollo from $1,101,500,000 to $1,087,000,-000 and for space flight operations from $670,200,000 to $654,700,000 was accepted by voice vote.

HR 16516 passed the House April 23 by a 229-105 roll-call vote.

The Senate Aeronautical and Space Sciences Committee authorized $3,415,950,000 for NASA—$284.9-million less than authorized by the House and $17-million below the Administration's request.

Walter F. Mondale (D Minn.) proposed an amendment on the Senate floor to cut $110 million from space flight operations. Mondale's amendment would have reduced funds for the space shuttle/space station project.

Mondale said that the shuttle/station project, according to NASA estimates, "would cost $14 billion to complete" and would, by the year 1979, increase the annual spending level of about $3.5-billion to a spending level of $6.8-billion, thus nearly doubling the size of this nation's space program." Others supporting Mondale's amendment in the debate included William Proxmire (D Wis.) and J. W. Fulbright (D Ark.). Fulbright said he would support cuts even larger than those proposed by Mondale.

Opposing Mondale's amendment, Margaret Chase Smith (R Maine), ranking Republican on the Aeronautical

Manned Space Flight Costs

The manned space flight program—Mercury, Gemini, Apollo and post-Apollo planning—have consumed the largest percentage of NASA's research and development spending during the history of the U.S. space program.

(in millions)

Fiscal Year	Total NASA R&D Funds	Manned Flight Funds	Per cent Spent on Manned Flight Programs
1959	$ 195.3	$ 49.7	25.4%
1960	305.3	119.4	39.1
1961	617.7	296.3	48.0
1962	1,145.2	538.0	47.0
1963	2,509.7	1,502.0	59.8
1964	3,977.4	2,717.9	68.3
1965	4,285.3	2,961.0	69.1
1966	4,486.3	3,199.5	71.3
1967	4,175.7	3,024.0	72.4
1968	3,967.6	2,789.0	70.3
1969	3,201.4	2,177.5	68.0
1970	3,066.0	2,031.0	66.2
1971	2,606.1	1,474.2	56.6
1972	2,603.3	1,320.5	50.7
1973	2,637.4	1,224.4	46.4
TOTALS	$39,779.7	$25,424.4	63.9%

SOURCE: National Aeronautics and Space Administration

and Space Sciences Committee, and Carl T. Curtis (R Neb.) maintained that the $110 million budgeted by NASA for the space shuttle and station did not commit NASA to an expenditure of $14 billion. Mrs. Smith said there was "no commitment whatever in this bill for a trip to Mars," as contended by proponents of Mondale's amendment. The Mondale amendment was rejected by a 29-56 roll-call vote.

The Senate May 6 passed HR 16516, as reported by the committee, by a 69-15 roll-call vote.

House and Senate conferees June 15 filed a conference report (H Rept 91-1189) on HR 16516, authorizing $3,410,878,000 for the space program. The amount was $189,997,000 less than passed by the House and $94,-928,000 more than the total approved by the Senate. The conference total was also $77,878,000 more than the agency request.

The House and Senate June 22 by voice votes and with little debate adopted the conference report on HR 16516, completing congressional action.

The President July 2 signed the bill (PL 91-303).

APPROPRIATION. Congress Dec. 7 cleared for the President the second HUD-NASA Independent Offices appropriations bill (HR 1983—PL 91-556). President Nixon vetoed the first bill (HR 17548) because Congress had appropriated $541 million more than the budget request for HUD. *(Details, Presidential Vetoes, p. 97a)*

The $3,268,675,000 appropriated for NASA for fiscal 1971 in PL 91-556 was $480,541,000 below the appropriation for fiscal 1970 and $64,325,000 under the budget request for fiscal 1971.

HR 19830 passed the House Nov. 24 by a 375-10 roll-call vote. No floor amendments were offered.

The Senate Appropriations Committee reported the bill as passed by the House. On the Senate floor Walter F. Mondale (D Minn.) offered an amendment to cut $110-million from the space shuttle space station project.

Mondale called NASA's space station the beginning of a project bigger than the Apollo (moon landing) program, with a manned landing on Mars as the ultimate objective.

The space station, which would operate in a low-earth orbit and eventually support 50 to 100 men, would be a jumping-off point for flights to Mars, Mondale said.

He said the $110-million requested by NASA was the beginning of an ultimate $14-billion project.

"The amendment would strike from this program one of the most wasteful and indefensible items in the budget," Mondale said, "one that bears no relation to our many compelling domestic and human needs in our society; one which has little scientific yield: (and) one which would take enormous amounts of money from that part of the program which does have great scientific yield...."

James B. Allen (D Ala.), Edward J. Gurney (R Fla.). Alan Cranston (D Calif.), Theodore F. Stevens (R Alaska), John Stennis (D Miss.), Strom Thurmond (R S.C.) and Spessard L. Holland (D Fla.) defended the program, pointing to the spinoff benefits of NASA research for domestic uses, the space station's potential value as a safety device for U.S. astronauts stranded in orbit, the jobs that would be lost if the station were not built and the chance that the Russians might pass the United States in the space race.

The motion to reject the amendment was adopted by a 50-26 roll-call vote.

Final action came when the Senate Dec. 7 passed HR 19830. President Nixon Dec. 17 signed the bill into law (PL 91-556).

1971

AUTHORIZATION. Congress July 28 cleared a bill (HR 7109—PL 92-68) authorizing $3,354,950,000 for the National Aeronautics and Space Administration for fiscal 1972. The administration initially requested $3,271,-350,000 for NASA; subsequently, an amendment of $29,-285,000 to the budget request was submitted for a total of $3,300,635,000.

The House Science and Astronautics Committee authorized $3,433,580,000 ($162.2 million more than requested by the administration). This was the third year in a row that the committee reported an increase over the amount asked for by the administration.

On the House floor three amendments were offered to reduce the amount authorized by the committee. Only one—involving a one-half million dollar cut from the $135-million aeronautical research and technology program—was adopted by voice vote.

Rep. Peter A. Peyser (R N.Y.) offered an amendment to cut $300-milion from the Apollo program. "We have done much talking and thinking in this Congress dealing with priorities. It is for this reason that I am recommending an amendment to reduce the NASA authorization by $300-million. The $300-million would come from the Apollo 16 and 17 moonshots.... I would like to urge that the savings realized by the termination of these two shots

Apollo 13: Almost a Disaster

The abortive Apollo 13 mission, which almost cost the lives of three astronauts, was the major space event of 1970. The spaceship, carrying Comdr. James A. Lovell Jr., Fred W. Haise Jr. and John L. Swigert, was launched April 11 from Cape Kennedy.

Lovell and Haise were scheduled to descend to a valley in the moon's Fra Mauro Hills. This area is about 120 miles east of the area where Apollo 12 made its manned landing.

Two days after launch, one of the two oxygen tanks in the service module Aquarius exploded. The two tanks provided oxygen for breathing by the astronauts in the command module and for generating power for the command module through three fuel cells in the service module. Swigert radioed Houston's Manned Spacecraft Center "we've got a problem." There had been a complete loss of power on an electrical line hooked into a fuel cell and a second line was losing power quickly. Lovell said: "We're venting something into space; it's a gas of some sort."

Lovell later radioed Houston with the astronauts' decision to go to a LEM lifeboat. This is an emergency procedure under which oxygen and power supply from the lunar module is used and equipment in the command module is shut off. Swigert used the last fuel cell in the command module to charge the batteries needed for re-entry. The moon landing was cancelled.

During the rest of the trip, the astronauts used the limited oxygen and power of the lunar module. The small water supply was used and conserved to cool the spaceship's electronics systems.

With the heat turned down to temperatures as low as 38 degrees Fahrenheit to 45 degrees to save power, the astronauts found it almost impossible to sleep or eat for the next four days.

Apollo 13 continued around the moon before heading back to earth,. The astronauts April 17 jettisoned the service module. Lovell reported: "There's one whole side of the spacecraft missing. Right by the high-gain antenna the whole panel is blown out.... It's really a mess."

Apollo 13 splashed down April 17 about 610 miles southeast of American Samoa. The astronauts were then returned to Houston.

The same day NASA Administrator Thomas O. Paine announced that a special review board would be appointed to investigate the accident.

The eight-man board included Edgar M. Cortright, director of NASA's Langley Research Center, astronaut Neil A. Armstrong and six other NASA officials.

Paine and Cortright testified June 30 before the Senate Aeronautical and Space Sciences Committee on the results of NASA's investigation. Paine said: "We cannot in the case of Apollo 13 point to one individual or organization and say that they caused the accident. Nor have we...been able to formulate...a procedure which, had it been in effect for Apollo 13, would have guaranteed that such an accident could never happen."

could be directed in the area of mass transportation," Peyser said.

Peyser's amendment was defeated by voice vote.

Rep. Bella S. Abzug (D N.Y.) offered an amendment to cut $125-million for the space shuttle program. "The $125-million expenditure for the space shuttle system cannot be justified on economic grounds. Furthermore, the whole argument and discussion of the committee here today indicates that the committee is moving in the direction of phasing out the manned space program...Why should we want to spend money for a shuttle system when we are talking about lowering the effort for manned space activities?" Abzug said.

Alphonzo Bell (R Calif.), a member of the Science and Astronautics Committee, defended the space shuttle. "If we are to continue in space, a less costly launch system is essential....

"We are embarking into the age of space transportation.... The shuttle will itself carry spacecraft and men into orbit returning to earth for another payload.

"This reusable feature will allow a tenfold reduction in payload launch costs, from $1,000 per pound to $100."

Abzug's amendment was defeated by voice vote.

The House June 3 passed HR 7109 authorizing $3,433,080,000 for NASA by a 303-64 roll-call vote and sent the bill to the Senate.

The Senate Committee on Aeronautical and Space Sciences reported a bill authorizing $3,280,850,000 for NASA. The Senate authorization was $152.2 million below the $3.43 billion authorized by the House and represented the lowest Senate committee budget recommendation for NASA since 1962. The figure was $35.1-million less than the bommittee recommended in fiscal 1971.

On the Senate floor, Walter F. Mondale (D Minn.) offered the only amendment to HR 7109. His amendment would reduce the space shuttle program by $137.6-million.

Mondale stated: "When the American public realizes that we are trying to authorize a space shuttle and space station program that will cost $20-billion to $25-billion, they will begin to lose faith in the entire program—that part of the space program which is so vital and which we need in the United States.

"I am pro-space, but I am not pro-space waste. This is a wasteful project that will cost us $20-billion to $25-billion at least, before we complete development of the shuttle and the space station."

Frank E. Moss (D Utah) opposed the Mondale amendment: "The space shuttle will bring new capability to military and civilian space programs by replacing all present expendable launch vehicles and carrying spacecraft into orbit for the U.S. Weather Bureau, the communications industry, the NASA space program and the Department of Defense."

The amendment was defeated on a 22-64 roll-call vote.

The Senate June 29 by an 82-5 roll-call vote passed HR 7109.

House and Senate conferees agreed to a $3,354,-950,000 authorization for NASA—$54.3 million more than requested by the administration.

The House July 27 and Senate July 28 by voice votes adopted the conference report, clearing the bill for the President (PL 92-68).

Cosmonauts' Deaths

The crew of the Soviet orbiting laboratory Salyut, who set a record for time in space, died June 30, 1971, on their return to earth. The three Russian cosmonauts—Lt. Col. Georgi Timofeyevich Dobrovolsky, Vladislav Nikolayevich Volkov and Viktor Ivanovich Patsayev—spent 24 days in Salyut.

(In 1967 Russian cosmonaut Vladimir Komarov died when his spacecraft became tangled in its parachute cords and plunged four miles in the Ural Mountains. His was the first death reported by the Soviets during their space program.)

The cosmonauts linked their spaceship Soyuz to the orbital space station June 7. Salyut had been in space seven weeks without any crew.

The Salyut-Soyuz 11 mission appeared to be a success. The Soviet press agency Tass reported that the crew had "completed the flight program in full" and "had transferred the materials of scientific research and the logs to the transportation spaceship...for return to earth."

Upon landing, members of the recovery team opened the hatch and found the three cosmonauts lifeless in their seats. Soviet press sources said the dead cosmonauts appeared to be sleeping peacefully, and there were no signs of struggle for life.

A special Soviet inquiry commission appointed to study the sudden deaths of the three-man crew concluded that their deaths had been caused by a rapid air pressure drop due to "a loss of the ship's sealing" 30 minutes before landing.

APPROPRIATION. Congress Aug. 2 cleared a bill (HR 9382—PL 92-78) containing appropriations of $3,298,-035,000 for NASA in fiscal 1972. The administration had requested $3,300,635,000 for the agency.

On the House floor, two amendments offered by Bella S. Abzug (D N.Y.), which would have deleted funding for NASA's space shuttle, were defeated en bloc by voice vote. The first would have deleted $100-million for research and development of the shuttle, and the second would have added a provision to the bill barring the use of any other NASA funds for development of the shuttle.

Abzug said the scientific community was "doubtful" about the shuttle's feasibility, the military's interest in the shuttle might jeopardize the U.S. pledge of peaceful development of outer space and the ultimate cost of the manned space program of which the shuttle was a part would be $25 billion to $75 billion.

James G. Fulton (R Pa.), ranking Republican on the Science and Astronautics Committee, replied that the space shuttle would provide a 90 per cent savings in future space missions.

"We must realize," he said, "that the key to future space operations is economy and the key to that economy is the shuttle. This vehicle is a reusable space transportation system that will revolutionize present day space operations by furnishing an airline-type accessibility to space at low operational cost."

The House passed the bill by voice vote.

The appropriations bill passed the Senate by an 82-0 roll-call vote and was sent to conference.

Apollo: Eight Successful Lunar Missions, 1969-1972

The table below shows the Apollo flights between 1969 and 1972. The first American extravehicular activity (EVA) or spacewalk was performed by Edward H. White during the Gemini 4 mission in June 1965.

The first Apollo EVA occurred during the Apollo 9 flight in March 1969 by James A. McDivitt and lasted for 23 minutes. EVAs performed by Eugene Cernan and Harrison Schmitt during the last Apollo mission totaled 22 hours.

Project	Crew	Date	Duration	Revolutions/ EVAs	Material Recovered
Apollo 9	Air Force Col. James A. McDivitt Air Force Col. David R. Scott Civilian Russell L. Schweickart	Mar. 3-13, 1969	241:00:53	151 revs. of Earth 1 EVA 23 min.	
Apollo 10	Air Force Col. Thomas P. Stafford Navy Comdr. John W. Young Navy Comdr. Eugene A. Cernan	May 18-26, 1969	192:03:23	31 revs. of Moon	
Apollo 11	Civilian Neil A. Armstrong Air Force Lt. Col. Michael Collins Air Force Col. Edwin E. Aldrin, Jr.	July 16-24, 1969	195:18:35	First lunar landing; Sea of Tranquillity; 1 EVA 2 hrs. 31 min.	44 lbs. lunar material
Apollo 12	Navy Comdr. Charles Conrad, Jr. Navy Comdr. Richard F. Gordon, Jr. Navy Comdr. Alan L. Bean	Nov. 14-24, 1969	244:36:25	Second lunar landing; Ocean of Storms; 2 EVAs total 7 hrs. 39 min.	75 lbs. lunar material
Apollo 13	Navy Capt. James A. Lovell, Jr. Civilian Fred W. Haise, Jr. Civilian John L. Swigert, Jr.	Apr. 11-17, 1970	142:54:41	Planned lunar landing aborted after service module oxygen tank rupture	98 lbs. lunar material
Apollo 14	Navy Capt. Alan B. Shepard Air Force Maj. Stuart A. Roosa Navy Comdr. Edgar D. Mitchell	Jan. 31-Feb. 9, 1971	216:42:01	Third lunar landing; Fra Mauro; 2 EVAs total	98 lbs. lunar material
Apollo 15	Air Force Col. David R. Scott Air Force Lt. Col. James B. Irwin Air Force Maj. Alfred M. Worden, Jr.	July 26-Aug. 7, 1971	295:12	Fourth lunar landing; Hadley Apennine; 3 sur- face EVAs, totaling 18 hrs. 36 min.	173 lbs. samples
Apollo 16	Navy Capt. John W. Young Navy Lt. Comdr. Thos. K. Mattingly, II	Apr. 16-27, 1972	265:51:06	Fifth lunar landing; Descartes highlands; 3 surface EVAs totaling 20 hrs 14 min.	210 lbs. samples
Apollo 17	Navy Capt. Eugene A. Cernan Navy Comdr. Ronald E. Evans Harrison H. Schmitt, PhD.	Dec. 7-19, 1972	301:51	Sixth lunar landing; Taurus-Littrow; 3 surface EVAs totaling 22 hrs. 5 min.	250 lbs. samples

House and Senate conferees agreed to a final NASA appropriation of $3,298,035,000 for fiscal 1972.

The House July 29 adopted the conference report on HR 9382 by a 363-30 roll-call vote. The Senate Aug. 2 adopted the report by voice vote, completing congressional action. President Nixon signed the bill Aug. 10 (PL 92-78).

1972

AUTHORIZATION. Congress May 16 cleared for the President a bill (HR 14070—PL 92-304) authorizing $3,444,150,000 for NASA in fiscal 1973. The authorization included $227.9-million for the space shuttle program, unsuccessfully opposed in both houses. The shuttle was backed by the administration. *(Box p. 533)*

The House Science and Astronautics Committee authorized $3,428,950,000 for NASA—$49,950,000 more than the administration requested. It was the fourth year in a row that the committee authorization exceeded the budget request.

On the House floor, Les Aspin (D Wis.) offered an amendment to delete the authorization for the space shuttle. Aspin argued: "If we go ahead with the space shuttle, we will be committing ourselves to a very expensive and expanded space program....

"The figures paraded by NASA constitute a frail reed for fiscal support.... Aside from the inconclusive cost estimates, another question arises: What are the supposed savings to be derived from using the space shuttle?

"NASA asserts that this cost will be reduced from the present $1,000 per pound to lift a payload capacity— if this capacity is not used then the cost-per-pound increases and the supposed savings are lost....

"NASA continues to assert that launch savings of billions will accrue due to the relatively modest $10-million plus launch costs for the operative shuttle....

U.S.-Soviet Space Race: From Competition to Cooperation

President Nixon in an address before the United Nations in September 1969 said that the United States would take steps toward "internationalizing man's epic venture into space—an adventure that belongs not to one nation but to all mankind."

In October 1970, a delegation of U.S. space officials met in Moscow with a delegation of Soviet space experts for the first of a series of talks on U.S.-Soviet cooperation in space rescue.

The talks centered around such technical matters as linking vehicles in space and transferring crew members between space ships. The two delegations agreed that all spacecraft should have compatible docking systems so that any spacecraft could rescue occupants of any other spacecraft, regardless of nationality.

The delegates to the conference agreed to future meetings by three committees of space technicians from the U.S. and U.S.S.R.

The Soviets landed in November 1970 a driverless car on the moon. Lunokhod 1 was carried to the moon by the unmanned Soviet spacecraft Luna 17.

The solar-powered moon rover was the first wheeled vehicle to travel on the surface of the moon and was guided by radio signals from earth controllers for five days in a program of exploration and experiments. The spacecraft carried TV cameras and a French laser reflector used as a beacon for location purposes and for making precise measurements of distances, sizes and shapes on the moon.

The Soviet moon car stopped working in October 1971, 10 months after it landed on the moon. Lunokhod 1 ceased operation when the fuel of its nuclear heater was exhausted. The Soviets left the moon rover and Luna 17 on the moon's surface.

Tass, the Soviet news agency, reported that the interplanetary probe Venera (Venus) 7 had landed on Venus Dec. 15, 1970, and radio signals were "received for...23 minutes after landing." The announcement noted that this was "the first time that scientific information was relayed directly from the surface of another planet."

U.S. and Soviet scientific delegations met in Moscow in January 1971 and agreed to exchange about three grams of lunar surface material. The delegates also agreed to the formation of international working groups on synchronizing research.

In another demonstration of U.S.-Soviet cooperation, Dr. Aleksandr P. Vinogradov, vice president of the Soviet Academy of Sciences, attended the Lunar Science Conference held by NASA in Houston. At this meeting Vinogradov endorsed the moon-soil exchange.

NASA and the Soviet Academy of Sciences agreed in 1971 to exchange information on the biological effect of space flight.

The NASA announcement said that meetings of experts from both nations' space programs would include "the exchange of pre-, post- and in-flight data in sufficient detail to assure a full understanding of the flight experience of each country from a physiological and medical viewpoint."

U.S. and Soviet officials Oct. 20, 1971, announced agreement between the two nations to immediately report to the other findings of special interest made by their Mars probes—U.S. Mariner 9 and the U.S.S.R.'s Mars 2 and 3.

The biggest step toward cooperative ventures in space came on May 24, 1972. On that date President Nixon and Soviet Premier Alexei Kosygin signed an agreement in Moscow committing their countries to a joint flight with linked Soviet and U.S. spacecraft.

The pact called for each nation to "develop cooperation in the fields of space meteorology, study of the natural environment, exploration of near earth space, the moon and the planets, and space biology and medicine."

The two countries agreed to develop "compatible rendezvous and docking systems of U.S. and Soviet manned spacecraft and stations to enhance the safety of manned flights in space and to provide the opportunity for conducting joint scientific experiments in the future."

The docking system, called the Apollo-Soyuz Test Project, was scheduled for 1975.

NASA Administrator James Fletcher announced in June 1972 that the U.S. and U.S.S.R. had agreed to coordinate their separate Venus missions to avoid duplication of effort. The U.S. would concentrate on investigating the planet's upper atmosphere and the Soviets would concentrate on the planet's surface.

Venera 8, a Soviet unmanned spacecraft, landed in July on Venus' sunlit side and radioed data back to Soviet controllers for 50 minutes before the planet's intense heat made the probe's communications equipment inoperable.

Data indicated the temperature at the landing site was 840 degress Fahrenheit and the Venusian surface was the composition of granite rock.

Unless the space program is vastly inflated over the next 10 years we will not save money on launch costs with the shuttle."

Olin E. Teague (D Texas), chairman of the Manned Space Flight Subcommittee, opposed Aspin's amendment:

"NASA has conducted a study of anticipated shuttle economics...that assumes shuttle usage on 580 missions over a 12-year period from 1979...through 1990. That comes to an average of 48 flights annually. NASA terms the mission model realistic...

"The study concluded that the combined factors of a reusable delivery system, reusable payloads, design simplification and sharply reduced risk of failure add up to a savings averaging more than $1-billion a year...."

Possible military uses of the shuttle were seen by Aspin: "Recently announced dual facilities for the Air Force and for NASA...lend credence to an enhanced military program...it would appear that NASA is building something for the military that they feel would be nice to have but are unwilling to fund it from their own pocket.

(Continued on p. 532)

Major Unmanned Launches by U.S. Space Program

Following are the principal satellites, spacecraft and probes successfully launched by the United States between 1969 and 1972.

1969

OSO-5 (Jan. 22)—Fifth in Orbiting Solar Observatory series. Mission to study solar radiation and sun's influence on near-earth space. Data gathered expected to help predict solar flares and advance warning of intense solar activity that could affect scheduling of manned space flights.

Intelsat III F-3 (Feb. 5)—Operated by International Telecommunications Satellite Consortium. Relayed communications between North America, Hawaii, Philippines, Australia, Japan and Asian Mainland.

ESSA 9 (Feb. 26)—Operated by Environmental Science Services Administration. Carried two cameras to photograph cloud cover of entire earth once every 24 hours.

Nimbus 2 (April 14)—Launched as replacement for identical probe that failed to reach orbit in 1968. Carried seven meteorological research instruments. One experiment was to follow an elk in Yellowstone National Park. Movement relayed to satellite by means of radio that had been attached to the animal.

Intelsat III F-4 (May 21)—Launched to replace Intelsat III F-3, which had been troubled with interruptions in service.

OGO-6 (June 5)—Satellite, part of the Orbiting Geophysical Observatory. Carried 25 experiments to gather data on upper atmosphere and ionosphere, auroral regions around the poles and radiation surrounding earth.

Explorer 41 (June 21)—Satellite instrumented to measure charged particles and electric and magnetic fields in space.

Biosatellite 3 (July 7)—Carried monkey named Bonnie. Biomedical research capsule spent less than nine of planned 30 days in orbit when Bonnie's condition declined. NASA hoped experiment would provide data about mental, emotional and physiological processes in a man-like mammal during an extended space flight. Bonnie died shortly after return to earth.

OSO-6 (Aug. 9)—Similar to OSO-5. Solar probe looked at different parts of sun's spectrum.

ATS-5 (Aug. 12)—Applications Technology Satellite carried variety of experiments to test new ideas for future satellites. Primary mission to test gravity-stabilization system. System's function was to keep satellite pointed toward earth so its experiments always pointed in proper direction.

ESRO 1-B (Oct. 1)—Launched by U.S. for the European Space Research Organization. Satellite was equipped to study earth's ionosphere from a polar orbit that would make earth visible every 24 hours.

1970

Intelsat III F-6 (Jan. 14)—First of three global telecommunications satellites launched to complete an eight-satellite commercial system. **Intelsat III F-7** launched April 22. **Intelsat III F-8** launched July 23.

ITOS-1 (Jan. 23)—Weather satellite carrying TV, automatic picture transmission and scanning radiometers for global cloud data.

NATOSAT-1 (March 20)—Military communications satellite placed into stationary equatorial orbit by NASA for NATO.

Nimbus 4 (April 8)—Fifth in series of seven advanced weather satellites. Carried instruments to measure atmosphere's temperature and moisture content at different altitudes.

Skynet B (Aug. 19)—Communications satellite placed in orbit above the equator.

1971

Intelsat IV F-2 (Jan. 25)—First of three global communications satellites launched in 1971. **Intelsat IV F-3** launched Oct. 14. **Intelsat IV F-1** launched Dec. 19.

NATOSAT-11 (Feb. 2)—Military communications satellite placed in orbit over equator.

Explorer 43 (March 13)—Carried 12 instruments to collect data on cosmic rays, solar winds, electric and magnetic fields.

Explorer 44 (July 8)—Designed to monitor sun's X-rays and ultraviolet emissions in order to improve prediction techniques of solar activity.

OSO-7 (Sept. 29)—Seventh in series of orbiting observatories designed to study data on sun's corona, solar flares and other solar energy phenomena.

ITOS (Oct. 21)—Weather satellite.

1972

Pioneer 10 (March 2)—Unmanned vehicle launched on near perfect course to Jupiter. Fastest object to leave earth (speed of 31,431 mph in 16 min.) passing moon's orbit 11 hours after launch. Crossed Mars' orbital path May 24 and entered asteroid belt July 15th—first spacecraft to accomplish either feat. Expected to reach Jupiter in December 1973. Pioneer 10 to investigate Jupiter and fringes of solar system.

ERTS 1 (July 23)—First of Earth Resources Technology Satellites and first U.S. civilian satellite flown with primary objective to look at surface of earth. Equipped with three TV cameras (each sensitive to a different color). Satellite to transmit data on natural resources and earth's surface.

Copernicus (Aug. 21)—The last orbiting astronomical observatory satellite. Equipped with largest ultraviolet telescope ever orbited. Objective to study interstellar gas clouds.

Explorer 47 (Sept. 22)—Carried 13 sets of instruments to survey turbulent zone of wind from the sun and radiation and magnetic forces between earth and moon.

ESRO 4 (Nov. 22)—Seventh satellite of the European Space Research Organization launched by NASA. Principal mission to study the sun's effect on earth's environment.

Mars Probes Fail to Establish Life on Planet

In further efforts to determine whether Mars could sustain human life, NASA launched between 1969 and 1971 four Mariner television satellites to transmit photographs of the planet's surface. One, the Mariner 8 mission, was a failure. Scientists felt that Mars was the one other planet besides earth which could support life. The probes were conducted for NASA by the Jet Propulsion Laboratory.

However, scientific findings radioed back to earth led scientists to state at a Sept. 11, 1969, press conference held by the Jet Propulsion Laboratory that Mars was probably devoid of life and appeared to be "a cold desert by earth standards."

Mariners 6 and 7 were launched from Cape Kennedy on Feb. 24 and March 27, 1969. Each probe carried two television cameras and each took nearly 100 pictures and transmitted them back to earth. Instruments aboard the two Mariner ships provided data on surface temperatures and on the composition of the atmosphere. Temperatures ranged from 70 degrees Fahrenheit by day to minus 100 degrees Fahrenheit by night at the Martian equator. The probes also carried infrared spectrometers designed to determine the presence in the atmosphere of water, carbon dioxide and other molecules.

Mariners 6 and 7 flew past Mars July 31 and Aug. 5, 1971, at distances of 2,132 miles and 2,130 miles. Each sent back close-up photos of the planet and radioed back scientific findings.

Radio contact was lost with Mariner 7 for seven hours July 30-31. Jet Propulsion Laboratory scientists speculated that the probe had been hit by a meteoroid and thrown out of orientation. The impact did not damage Mariner 7's photographic abilities and high-quality photos were transmitted.

Mariner 8 was launched from Cape Kennedy May 8, 1971, and fell into the Atlantic because of a malfunction of the second stage of the two-stage Atlas-Centaur booster rocket.

Satellite Orbits Mars. Mariner 9 was launched May 30 and went into orbit around Mars Nov. 13. The satellite was the first man-made object to orbit another planet. Mariner 9 carried two cameras, instruments designed to measure Mars' surface temperature and provide data on the composition of the planet's surface and atmospheric temperatures.

The spacecraft started taking photos of Mars at a distance of 535,000 miles. Photos showed the planet to be obscured by a tremendous yellow dust storm.

Radio signals were transmitted back to earth at a rate of 6 minutes 43 seconds over 75-million miles.

The probe used up its attitude control gas Nov. 13 during its 698th revolution around Mars. Flight controllers at the Jet Propulsion Laboratory directed the spacecraft to turn off its radio.

Mariner 9's orbit was trimmed from a high point of 10,585 miles to a low point of 863 miles. This orbit took the probe between Mars' two small moons, Phobos and Deimos, and would keep Mariner 9 circling the planet for an estimated 17 years.

During nearly one year in Martian orbit, Mariner 9 transmitted 7,329 photos of Mars and other scientific data. The most important finding of the mission was that water helped shape much of the planet's surface. Water vapor was detected in some of the small clouds above volcanic mountains.

(Continued from p. 530)

Payload capacity and thrust and other technical changes nevertheless have been incorporated by NASA into the space shuttle in order to accommodate military missions."

The space shuttle received strong bipartisan support, and the leadership of both parties urged defeat of Aspin's amendment.

Majority Leader Hale Boggs (D La.): "I hope the House will reject this amendment. I say that with all the conviction I can command because, in my judgment, to delay and cut back this program at this time would really kill the space program."

Minority Leader Gerald R. Ford (R Mich.): "The cost of the program is high enough as it is, but a start and stop, peak and valley, operation would be astronomical in cost. We are prepared to proceed. We ought to do it on the schedule that has been announced."

The Aspin amendment was defeated by an 11-103 standing vote.

The House also rejected by voice vote an amendment introduced by Charles B. Rangel (D N.Y.) to prohibit the use of NASA funds for continued operation of a satellite tracking station in the Republic of South Africa.

The House April 20 passed HR 14070 by a 277-60 roll-call vote and sent the bill to the Senate.

The Senate Aeronautical and Space Sciences Committee authorized $3,420,150,000 for NASA. The figure was $12,500,000 more than the administration's amended budget request of $3,407,650,000. It included $28,650,000 for salary increases in a supplemental budget amendment which the House did not consider. The committee recommended $227.9-million for the space shuttle.

On the Senate floor, Walter F. Mondale (D Minn.) introduced an amendment to delete the entire authorization for the space shuttle.

Mondale said the shuttle would require an expanding commitment of limited federal resources. He called the $227.9-million the "tip of a multi-billion-dollar iceberg."

NASA estimated that the research and development cost of the space shuttle would be between $5.5- and $6.5-billion. Mondale criticized the $5.5-billion figure and said the cost of operating the shuttle after it was developed would be $35-billion. "We continue to hear the $5-billion figure. In fact, the total program cost over a 12-year period of operations is $35-billion."

He added: "It should be emphasized, moreover, that this $35-billion figure still does not include the multi-billion-dollar cost of developing a permanent manned station to be placed in earth orbit. Because the shuttle is inevitably linked to the eventual development of such a space station, the complete cost of this program—assuming no cost overruns—will approach $40-billion."

Space Shuttle: NASA Versus Domestic Needs

President Nixon announced Jan. 5, 1972, that he favored giving the National Aeronautics and Space Administration (NASA) $5.5-billion over the next six years to develop a space shuttle.

Supporters of the space shuttle hailed the decision as a milestone in America's space program while critics termed the program wasteful and an example of misplaced priorities.

Plans for the space shuttle called for a reusable two-stage vehicle consisting of a booster and an orbiter.

The orbiter would carry a two-man crew and two passengers with the capability—when modified—of carrying six to 12 passengers. It would be able to remain in space for up to 30 days.

NASA hoped to schedule the first manned space shuttle flight by April 1978 and expected the space shuttle to be entirely operational by the end of the decade.

The dispute over the space shuttle involved the future of the manned space program and competing domestic priorities.

Manned Space Program. Dr. James C. Fletcher, the NASA administrator, stated in a Jan. 5 press conference: "The shuttle is the only meaningful new manned space program which can be accomplished on a modest budget." Critics of the shuttle argued that the future U.S. space effort should concentrate on unmanned flights. Sen. Walter F. Mondale (D Minn.) commented Jan. 16 in a television interview on *Issues and Answers*: "I think that a space program of $2- to $3-billion a year, largely an unmanned, instrument flight, but also in some manned flight, could give us a fully sophisticated and very useful program."

Space vs. Domestic Needs. Supporters of the space shuttle described it as a logical extension of U.S. efforts in space and important for technological advancement. Sen. Edward J. Gurney (R Fla.) commented Jan. 16 on *Issues and Answers*: "It is extremely important to the United States to have a continuing and viable space program because technology, of course, is the strength of any great industrial nation.... We must continue in space and this is the next sensible and logical step."

Opponents criticized Nixon for requesting funds for the program instead of for domestic needs. Sen. William Proxmire (D Wis.) Jan. 8 in a press release called the decision "an outrageous distortion of budgetary priorities." He added, "...the President has chosen the space shuttle over money for schools, health, housing, mass transit, open space, environmental needs or other vital programs."

Supporters of the shuttle pointed to the reduced launching costs because of the shuttle's reusable features and the scientific benefits to be derived from the shuttle's mobility. They argued that the nation's space program had been cut back far enough because of an emphasis on social priorities.

Benefits. NASA estimated the research and development costs for the space shuttle at $5.5-billion over the next six years (fiscal 1973-78). Some $1-billion was added to that figure by NASA to serve as an increase allowance to cover unforeseen research and development problems. Two complete shuttles would be produced during the research and development stage.

NASA estimated that an additional $1.5 billion would be needed at a minimum for the procurement of three additional shuttles, facilities to launch and land the shuttles and extra equipment. The total investment cost of the shuttle was $7 billion and $8 billion when the contingency fund was included, according to NASA.

Cost Effectiveness Study. A NASA cost effectiveness study based on slightly more than 40 satellite launchings per year, the yearly average of the U.S. unmanned program over the last eight years, showed that the shuttle was economically feasible. It assumed NASA, the Defense Department and other agencies would fly 500 shuttle missions over a 12-year period between 1979 and 1990.

The study estimated that conventional launchings over the 12-year period using rockets would cost $11-billion. The total shuttle launching costs would be $5.8-billion or $5.2-billion less than the conventional method.

Payload development and procurement costs for the 500 missions during the 12-year period would be $29.8-billion for conventional launches. The comparable figure for the shuttle was set at $22.6-billion. The study said that the $7.2 billion savings with the shuttle system was due to payload reusability, design simplification and lower risk factors.

Priorities. Mondale, one of the most vigorous critics of the space shuttle, expressed anger at Nixon's veto of a $2.1-billion child care bill at the end of the first session of the 92nd Congress. After the President announced that the nation would develop a space shuttle, Mondale compared the decison and the child care veto in a Jan. 6 press release:

"Typically, this administration can squander $6.5-billion to fly four people in orbit, while it refuses to invest less than one third that amount to provide desperately needed day care and development programs for millions of pre-school children...."

Critics' Cost Estimates. Critics of the space shuttle said more expense was involved than the research and development costs. They set out to attack NASA's $5.5-billion to $6.5-billion research and development estimate and to emphasize long-range program costs.

Mondale stated in a Jan. 25 press release: "The briefings and materials on NASA's FY 1973 budget have exposed two myths concerning the proposed space shuttle.

"The first myth was that the shuttle would 'only' cost $5.5-6.5-billion.

"But even that figure is deceptive....

"It does not include the cost of the shuttle's payloads, which will add another $20-28-billion to the shuttle's total costs....

"The second myth has been that opponents of the shuttle are anti-space exploration...."

J. W. Fulbright (D Ark.), another opponent of the space shuttle, said: "If we had no urgent requirements for health, education, transportation, energy, pollution control and were just looking for something to do, perhaps we could say, 'Well this might be a nice interesting gift'.... But that is about the degree of urgency I attach to the space shuttle."

Edward J. Gurney (R Fla.) opposed the amendment: "The present amendment...is essentially a replay of amendments which he (Mondale) has introduced in past years. It seeks to have the Senate and the country turn its back on its future, on man's last and most important physical frontier...."

The Mondale amendment was rejected on a 21-61 roll-call vote.

The Senate adopted by voice vote an amendment introduced by Howard W. Cannon (D Nev.) to add $24-million to the authorization for aircraft noise reduction.

The Senate May 11 by voice vote passed HR 14070. The House May 16 adopted the Senate amendment by voice vote, completing congressional action. The President signed the bill May 19 (PL 92-304).

APPROPRIATION. Congress Aug. 3 cleared a bill (HR 15093—PL 92-383) containing appropriations for the National Aeronautics and Space Administration. Congress appropriated the full $3,407,650,000 requested by the administration for NASA. This amount included research and development funds for the space shuttle and Skylab, the orbiting space laboratory scheduled for 1973.

During House floor debate, Bella S. Abzug (D N.Y.) offered an amendment to delete $200-million from the $3,550,000,000 appropriation for NASA. The $200-million was earmarked for the Skylab and space shuttle programs.

"Our nation has other needs which are far more important than the shuttle," Abzug said. "When pushed to the wall on substantive reasons for not going ahead with the shuttle at this time, its proponents invariably take refuge in the claim that it is worth 50,000 jobs and that to delay it would put 50,000 individuals out of work.... We are fooling both ourselves and our constituents if we attempt to justify this program as a panacea for our massive unemployment crisis."

Robert McClory (R Ill.) opposed the amendment: "The benefits to be realized (from the program) extend far beyond those which are directly involved and may, indeed, help produce improvements in education, health, housing and many other fields of human interest which can benefit all mankind."

NASA Administrators

Thomas O. Paine resigned as administrator of the National Aeronautics and Space Administration July 28, 1970. Paine had served as the head of NASA since March 4, 1969. In leaving his post, Paine told reporters that budget cuts in the space program had nothing to do with his resignation.

President Nixon March 1, 1971, nominated James C. Fletcher to be the next NASA administrator. Fletcher had previously served as president of the University of Utah and College of Eastern Utah.

Fletcher became the fourth administrator for the agency since its founding.

NASA administrators (dates of Senate confirmation in parentheses):

T. Keith Glennan	(Aug. 15, 1958)
James E. Webb	(Feb. 9, 1961)
Thomas O. Paine	(March 4, 1969)
James C. Fletcher	(March 11, 1971)

The Abzug amendment was rejected May 23 by voice vote.

The House passed HR 15093 by a 367-10 roll-call vote.

The Senate Appropriations Committee recommended $3,431,650,000 for NASA in fiscal 1973. This figure represented $24,000,000 more than the budget request, $82,440,000 more than the House-passed bill and $121,-528,000 more than the fiscal 1972 appropriation.

The House cut $50.9-million from the NASA research and development request and the Senate committee restored the full amount in addition to adding $24-million which "has been specifically earmarked...for aeronautical research in the fields of noise abatement and aviation safety." The Senate committee also restored $7,560,000 to the NASA construction request which was cut by the House, making the Senate committee recommendation the same as the budget request.

The Senate June 14 passed HR 15093 by a 70-2 roll-call vote. No amendments were offered on the floor to alter the fiscal 1973 NASA appropriation.

House and Senate conferees agreed on a final figure of $3,407,650,000 for NASA—the same figure as the budget request.

The House and Senate Aug. 3 agreed to the conference report by voice votes. The President Aug. 14 signed the bill into law (PL 92-383).

Chapter 10—Veterans' Affairs

Key Votes

In this chapter, key roll-call votes are shown in bold-face type. The party breakdown on each of these votes and the position taken by each member of Congress may be found in the key vote charts which appear in the appendix to this book.

Veterans' Affairs

As the Vietnam war wound down and the military reduced its manpower rolls, the cost of services for veterans and their dependents mounted steadily.

A combination of more veterans, new services and cost-of-living increases in veterans' payments caused the Veterans Administration's (VA) share of the federal budget to climb to a projected 4.7 per cent for fiscal 1973 from an actual 3.8 per cent for fiscal 1968. Annual VA outlays rose by almost $5-billion from fiscal 1968 to fiscal 1973—to approximately $11.8-billion from $6.9-billion.

By June 30, 1972, the VA had spent a total of $62-billion in the eight years of the Vietnam era, defined in the Veterans' Pension and Adjustment Assistance Act of 1967 as beginning Aug. 5, 1964, the day President Johnson asked Congress to approve the Gulf of Tonkin resolution.

From fiscal 1969 to 1972, an average of almost one million servicemen returned to civilian life each year; the number swelled because the Department of Defense trimmed its manpower levels during those years.

Despite the increase in veterans' spending from 1969 to 1972, congressional critics charged that the Nixon administration was not doing enough to ease returning GIs into civilian society.

Vetoes of Veterans' Bills

President Nixon vetoed three veterans' bills during his first term. On Aug. 11, 1970, he vetoed the appropriations bill (HR 17548) for the VA, the Department of Housing and Urban Development and the National Aeronautics and Space Administration (NASA). The VA appropriation was $9,065,528,000, $105-million more than the administration had requested. The $105-million was for veterans' medical care. However, the VA appropriation was not cut in the second VA-HUD-NASA measure that the President did sign (PL 91-556) on Dec. 17, 1970. The cuts in PL 91-556 were made in HUD programs.

On Oct. 27, 1972, the President pocket vetoed the Veterans' Health Care Expansion Act of 1972 (HR 10880) and the National Cemeteries Act of 1972 (HR 12674). The health care act would have authorized expenditure of $85-million in fiscal 1973 for expanding health care services for veterans and their dependents. The cemeteries bill would have given the VA jurisdiction over most national cemeteries established for armed services members and veterans.

The President had threatened in 1970 to veto HR 11959 (PL 91-219)—a measure increasing veterans' monthly educational allowances by 34.6 per cent—if the final bill retained a Senate provision for a 46 per cent boost in benefits. Nixon had originally proposed that the allowance be increased by 13 per cent. He signed HR 11959 March 26, 1970, accepting the 34.6 per cent increase as "reasonable," in the words of press secretary Ronald L. Ziegler.

Problems Facing Vietnam Veterans

Unemployment. Perhaps the greatest obstacle facing the returning veteran was getting a job. Those who returned to the sluggish economy of 1970 and early 1971 often could not find work.

Not only did the numbers of unemployed veterans increase, but the rate of joblessness for these men exceeded that for nonveterans in the same age group. In February 1971, the jobless rate for 20- to 29-year-old veterans hit a high of 11 per cent, or 381,000 persons. By the last quarter of 1972, however, the jobless rate for this group had fallen to 5.6 per cent, or 241,000 persons.

Although the difference in the rate for veterans and nonveterans had been erased by September 1972 for the 20-29 age group as a whole, it persisted for the younger, more recently returned veterans (20-24 years old).

Black veterans, moreover, faced greater employment difficulties than did white veterans. The unemployment rate for black 20- to 29-year-old veterans in the fourth quarter of 1972 was 8.3 per cent, or 33,000 persons, compared to 5.3 per cent unemployment, or 208,000, for white veterans of the same age, according to Labor Department statistics.

When signs of declining unemployment overall began to appear in January 1972, Secretary of Labor James D. Hodgson had credited an improved labor market in an expanding economy and coordination of the employment efforts of government, business and veterans' organizations. Hodgson also cited President Nixon's personal efforts in reducing veterans' unemployment.

Nixon's Job Programs. The President on Oct. 15, 1970, announced a Jobs for Veterans Program and called for a nationwide effort to "highlight the quality of the American veteran whose blend of skills and self-discipline

References

Discussion of veterans' affairs from 1945-64 may be found in *Congress and the Nation, Vol. I*, p. 1335-1373; for the years 1965-68, *Congress and the Nation, Vol. II*, pp. 453-460.

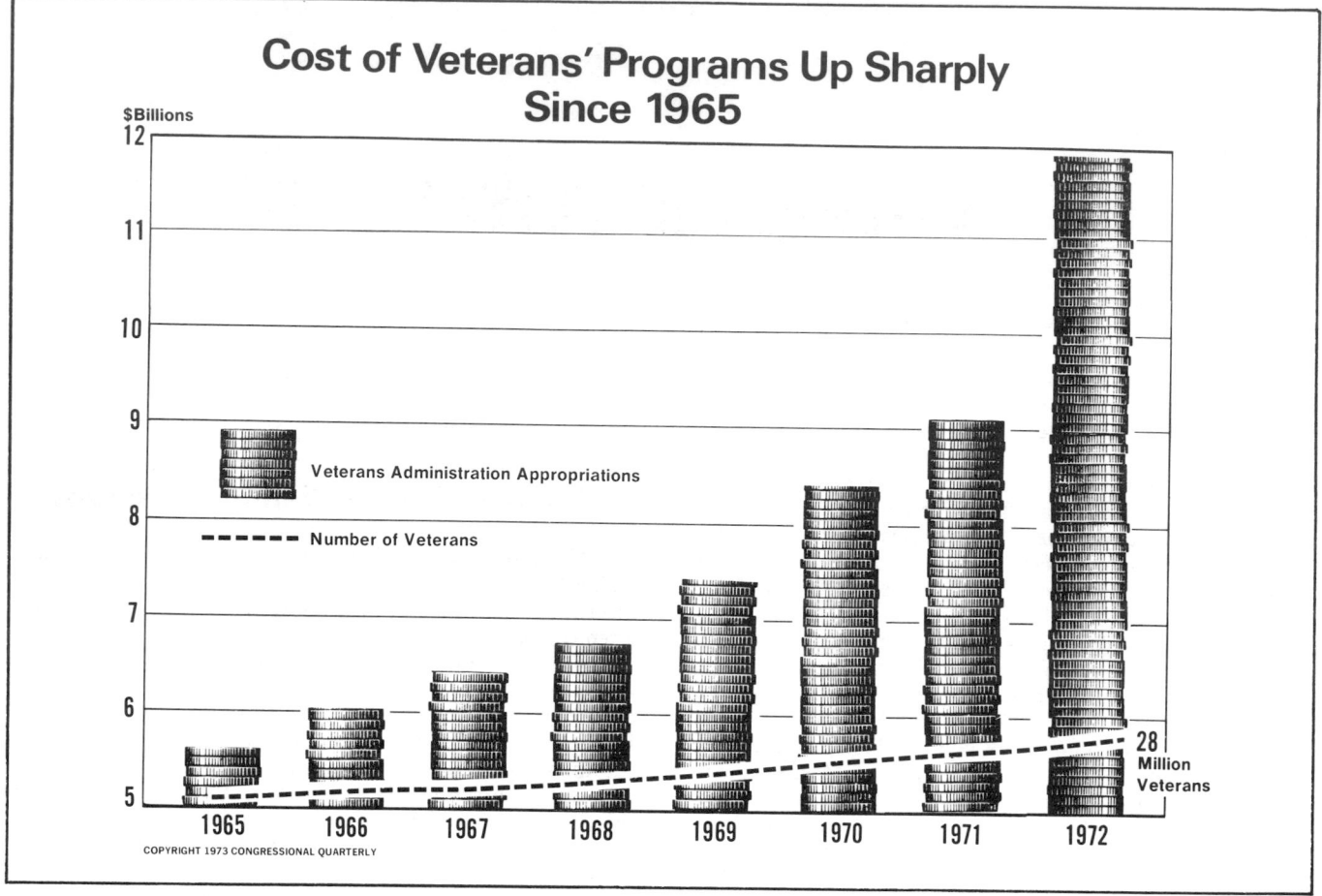

Cost of Veterans' Programs Up Sharply Since 1965

$Billions

Veterans Administration Appropriations

Number of Veterans

28 Million Veterans

1965   1966   1967   1968   1969   1970   1971   1972

COPYRIGHT 1973 CONGRESSIONAL QUARTERLY

make him an ideal candidate for employment." And on April 12, 1971, Nixon announced a pilot program to inform veterans of benefits available to them. The program was to be conducted in 10 cities with the aid of a $1-million grant to the Office of Economic Opportunity. Under the program, veterans were to be given priority for on-the-job training by the Labor Department, which continued to administer other veterans' manpower training and job placement programs.

Congress during Nixon's first term took no action on veterans' unemployment beyond holding hearings on the question in November and December 1970. Sen. Alan Cranston (D Calif.), whose Veterans Affairs subcommittee of the Senate Labor and Public Welfare Committee held the hearings *(Veterans' Affairs Committee, p. 544)*, asserted that what efforts the government had made up to that time to provide individualized help to job-seeking veterans had been "scant, diffused and uncoordinated." On the other hand, Assistant Secretary of Labor Malcolm R. Lovell Jr. testified that there was "a wide range of services directed toward helping the veteran move into and within the world of civilian work."

Major Legislation

Major veterans' legislation cleared by Congress in the 1969-72 period concerned pensions and other veterans' compensation, education allowances, and drugs.

Pensions. Since the first pension law was enacted in 1818 for needy Revolutionary War officers, pensions have been based in part on the recipient's income, which now includes Social Security and other benefits. A significant rise in income, therefore, might jeopardize pension eligibility or the amount of a pension. However, Congress established a pattern of raising pensions when income was increased, thereby avoiding a decrease in or loss of pensions.

Following a Social Security increase of 15 per cent in 1970, Congress raised monthly veterans' pensions by an average of 9.5 per cent. After a 20 per cent Social Security increase in 1972, the Senate Oct. 11, 1972, passed a bill which would have raised pensions by an average of 8 per cent, but the House took no action on the bill.

Education. During Nixon's first term, Congress increased GI education benefits for a single veteran with no disabilities enrolled in college by 34.6 per cent. In 1969 a single veteran enrolled in a VA-supported college program received $130 per month. Beginning October 1, 1972, he received $220 per month.

Married veterans or veterans with one dependent had their college education benefits increased 32.2 per cent from 1969 to 1972. Veterans with two dependents had theirs increased 31.4 per cent. Veterans with more than two dependents received $18 per dependent per month in 1972, an 80 per cent increase over $10 per dependent per month in 1969.

The laws which increased veterans' education benefits during the 1969-72 period were PL 91-219, approved March 26, 1970, raising the benefits to $175 per month for

Glossary of Veterans' Benefits Terms

Disability Compensation. A veteran suffering a service-connected disability in wartime or peacetime service is entitled to monthly compensation payments which differ according to the severity of the disability. Compensation is paid for service-connected disabilities rated at from 10 per cent disabling, based upon average impairment of earning capacity, to 100 per cent disabling. Additional or higher "statutory payments" are made for specific anatomical losses and for disabilities so severe as to render the veteran helpless or in need of attendance. A service-connected disability is one which is incurred or aggravated during military service, or presumed (by law) to have been incurred or aggravated during military service.

Death Compensation and DIC. Monthly support payments are made to the survivors of a person dying in service, or later of service-connected causes. Benefits under the death compensation system are payable to survivors of veterans who died of service-connected causes through Dec. 31, 1956. Survivors of veterans dying of service-connected causes after Dec. 31, 1956, receive benefits under the "Dependency and Indemnity Compensation" (DIC) provisions of the Servicemen's and Veterans' Survivor Benefits Act of 1956. DIC benefits are geared in part to the military pay of the deceased, and monthly payments are higher than under the old death compensation system.

Pensions. Pensions to war veterans are monthly support payments not based on service-connected disability. They are essentially a welfare payment made available to veterans as a reward for wartime military service in which, at least theoretically, the veteran risked extraordinary danger. Pensions are not and never were payable to veterans whose only service was in peacetime. Various different pension systems apply to veterans of wars before World War I. For veterans and their widows of World War I, World War II, the Korean War and the Vietnam War, there are three basic requirements for receipt of a pension: (1) 90 days of service during wartime and discharge under condi-

tions other than dishonorable; (2) need, as measured by annual income and net worth; and (3) a condition of disability (non-service-connected) which has made the veteran unable to work. For World War I, World War II and Korean War veterans, two different pension systems apply, both requiring a showing of need and disability. The first, the "old pension" system, applies to those who came on the pension rolls by June 30, 1960. The second, the "new pension" system, applies to those coming on the pension rolls after June 30, 1960. This category includes Vietnam veterans.

Death Pensions. Similar to pensions but limited to survivors of war veterans who die of non-service-connected causes. For survivors of World Wars I and II, the Korean War and the Vietnam War, need as measured by annual income is also a requirement for receipt of death pensions. An "old" and a "new" pension system based on the July 1, 1960, breakoff date, applies to death pensions for survivors of World War I, World War II and Korean War veterans. Vietnam veterans fall under the "new" system.

Medical Benefits. Veterans with service-connected disabilities of specified severity are entitled to free VA hospital, domiciliary, outpatient medical and dental care and prosthetic devices. Where space allows, war veterans are also permitted free hospital and domiciliary care for non-service-connected disabilities if in need.

Burial Benefits. All veterans are entitled to $250 in burial benefits, reimbursable to the person who bore the cost of the funeral. In addition, if the veteran dies in a VA facility, an amount equal to the cost of transporting the body by common carrier to the place of burial is paid.

Educational Benefits. While attending school or participating in job training programs, eligible veterans, veterans' widows or the wives of totally disabled veterans receive VA allowances to help pay for tuition, books, fees and living expenses.

---

a single veteran; and PL 92-540, approved Oct. 24, 1972, raising the benefits to $220 per month.

The Education Amendments of 1972, approved on June 23, 1972 (PL 92-318), provided for cost-of-instruction grants to institutions of higher education on the basis of $300 per veteran attending with GI bill educational aid or vocational rehabilitation assistance. *(Education chapter)*

Drugs. Congress failed to enact special drug legislation for veterans during the four years, although the use of marijuana and hard drugs was reported to be widespread in the military, especially in Vietnam and West Germany. The problem having become of serious concern and embarrassment, the services on June 17, 1971, instituted predischarge drug treatment and rehabilitation services.

The "Veterans' Drug and Alcohol Treatment and Rehabilitation Act of 1972" passed the House and Senate

in different versions in the summer of 1972 but was not sent to conference and so did not become law. However, the estimated 326,000 veterans with drug disabilities could seek treatment under a general drug abuse program authorized by a bill signed into law (PL 92-255) on March 21, 1972. *(Health chapter)*

VVAW. Large numbers of Vietnam veterans did not join traditional veterans organizations like the American Legion and the Veterans of Foreign Wars. The most visible veterans' organization from 1969-72 was the Vietnam Veterans Against the War. The group gained national attention in April 1971, when members camped out in Washington's Mall area, lobbied in Congress for peace in Southeast Asia and threw their medals on the Capitol steps.

John Kerry, a VVAW leader, testified before the Senate Foreign Relations Committee April 22. He said that the war had created "a monster, a monster in the

(Continued on p. 541)

Estimated Number of Veterans in Civilian Life, by State June 30, 1972

(in thousands)

State	Total Veterans	War Veterans Total	Vietnam Era	Korean Conflict	World War II	World War I	Service Between Korean Conflict and Vietnam Era Only
Alabama	425	376	93	93	200	17	49
Alaska	32	28	8	7	14	1	4
Arizona	251	225	51	55	124	11	26
Arkansas	225	201	43	40	115	15	24
California	3,149	2,822	649	735	1,566	125	327
Colorado	307	272	66	66	147	13	35
Connecticut	453	408	88	97	231	18	45
Delaware	78	69	17	16	38	2	9
District of Columbia	125	113	25	31	61	7	12
Florida	1,044	941	202	219	531	65	103
Georgia	498	444	105	105	245	19	54
Hawaii	72	61	21	16	27	2	11
Idaho	103	90	25	18	47	5	13
Illinois	1,629	1,461	324	324	813	74	168
Indiana	733	649	162	147	340	33	84
Iowa	390	346	83	75	180	24	44
Kansas	305	274	60	61	153	17	31
Kentucky	401	353	87	77	189	19	48
Louisiana	448	397	97	88	218	18	51
Maine	144	126	32	26	66	8	18
Maryland	547	491	111	122	275	19	56
Massachusetts	851	767	163	175	436	42	84
Michigan	1,217	1,076	269	238	570	49	141
Minnesota	548	482	126	108	244	29	66
Mississippi	223	200	42	44	116	12	23
Missouri	674	602	139	137	325	37	72
Montana	100	89	21	19	49	5	11
Nebraska	188	167	40	39	87	10	21
Nevada	69	62	14	17	36	2	7
New Hampshire	111	98	24	22	53	5	13
New Jersey	1,103	995	210	225	570	45	108
New Mexico	144	127	32	32	68	5	17
New York	2,619	2,365	486	516	1,358	118	254
North Carolina	557	496	115	116	272	21	61
North Dakota	74	63	20	13	30	3	11
Ohio	1,593	1,417	341	309	777	62	176
Oklahoma	352	313	74	71	172	20	39
Oregon	330	292	73	60	160	18	38
Pennsylvania	1,841	1,643	373	347	933	77	198
Rhode Island	131	119	23	28	71	6	12
South Carolina	273	242	58	58	132	11	31
South Dakota	85	75	18	18	38	5	10
Tennessee	506	449	108	102	243	22	57
Texas	1,430	1,277	293	294	718	59	153
Utah	137	121	32	30	62	5	16
Vermont	61	53	15	12	27	3	8
Virginia	567	507	114	128	287	21	60
Washington	500	443	111	104	238	25	57
West Virginia	275	237	68	47	121	13	38
Wisconsin	615	538	146	117	268	32	77
Wyoming	55	49	11	11	27	3	6
Outside U.S. - Total	213	177	68	53	54	14	36
Total	28,804	25,691	5,976	5,908	14,122	1,291	3,113
State Total	28,591	25,514	5,908	5,855	14,068	1,277	3,077

SOURCE: Veterans Administration

(Continued from p. 539)

form of millions of men who have been taught to deal and to trade in violence and who are given the chance to die for the biggest nothing in history, men who have returned with a sense of anger and a sense of betrayal which no one has yet grasped."

Chronology

of Veterans'

Legislation

1969

Survivors Benefits

Congress Oct. 13 cleared a bill (S 1471—PL 91-96) providing increased dependence and indemnity compensation (DIC) payments for widows and children of servicemen and veterans who died of service-connected causes.

The measure, approved Oct. 27, provided an over-all increase of 13 per cent in payments, or about $46-million the first year.

The Veterans Administration had recommended delaying action on all major sections of the bill.

The major provision raised the survivor benefits of families of enlisted servicemen who were killed or died while on active duty to a minimum of $167 per month for a single survivor from $134 per month. It revised the method of computing widow's benefits and provided increases in compensation varying according to the serviceman's grade and the number of dependents.

The Veterans Administration said total costs of the bill would be $61.6-million the first year, increasing to $67.9-million the fifth year. The VA declined to take positions on most sections of the bill. VA spokesmen at Senate Finance Committee hearings July 10 recommended a "comprehensive approach for remedial action" after a review of veterans programs was completed.

Education

Both houses of Congress passed a bill (HR 11959) which would vastly increase veterans' education and training benefits. However, disparities in the measures as passed by the House and Senate had not been reconciled by a conference committee when the session ended.

The House Aug. 4 approved a 27 per cent increase in education assistance benefits. A veteran attending college full time would have his monthly payment increased from $130 to $165. A veteran with one dependent would receive $197 monthly rather than $155.

The Senate Oct. 23 voted education assistance increases of 46 per cent. A veteran attending college full time would have his monthly payment increased from $130 to $190. A veteran with one dependent would receive $213 rather than $155.

Federal Budget Outlays for Veterans

Fiscal year	Amount (in billions)	% of Total Federal Budget
*1974	11.7	4.4
*1973	11.8	4.7
1972	10.7	4.6
1971	9.8	4.6
1970	8.7	4.4
1969	7.7	4.1
1968	6.9	3.8
1967	6.9	4.4
1966	6.0	4.4
1965	5.7	4.8

Estimates

SOURCE: Office of Management and Budget

The House Dec. 18 agreed to the Senate amendments with amendments. The Senate then asked for a conference. The Nixon administration opposed both increases, saying they were inflationary, but the President signed the bill into law (PL 91-219) March 26, 1970.

In debate Aug. 4, 1969, Rep. Fank Annunzio (D Ill.) had supported HR 11959 as a means of increasing the low rate at which Vietnam veterans were taking advantage of the education benefits for which they were eligible. He said only 21 per cent of Vietnam veterans had claimed such benefits, compared with 50 per cent of returning World War II servicemen.

In debate Oct. 23, Sen. Ralph W. Yarborough (D Texas) said the VA, the Department of Defense and the Bureau of the Budget were responsible for maintaining low education payments to veterans. "They fought this measure on a number of occasions.... They fought to keep the allowances low.... We have gone long enough in keeping 4.75 million veterans out of school."

Mortgage Rates

The House Sept. 29 passed by a 340-21 roll-call vote a bill (HR 13369) which would extend for two years the authority—due to expire Oct. 1, 1969—of the administrator of Veterans Affairs to set maximum interest rates for home loans to veterans.

The authority was provided in a law (PL 90-301) passed by Congress in 1968. *(Congress and the Nation, Vol. II, p. 225)*

The Senate did not act on HR 13369. However, Congress Sept. 24 had cleared a joint resolution (S J Res 152 —PL 91-78) that extended the authority along with other programs for 90 days. The Housing and Urban Development Act of 1969 (S 2864—PL 91-152), cleared Dec. 12, extended the authority to Oct. 1, 1970. Under the extended authority, the interest rate was raised in December from 7.5 to 8.5 per cent, effective in January 1970.

The Emergency Home Finance Act of 1970 (PL 91-351) extended the authority of the Secretary of Housing

Veterans Administration

The Veterans Administration was created by President Hoover in Executive Order 5398, issued July 21, 1930. It consolidated the functions of three existing agencies—the Interior Department's Pensions Bureau, the National Home for Volunteer Soldiers, and the Veterans Bureau (an independent agency which administered most benefits for World War I veterans). The first VA administrator was Brig. Gen. Frank T. Hines, who had previously headed the Veterans Bureau. The names and tenure of VA administrators are as follows:

Administrators of the Veterans Administration

Brig. Gen. Frank T. Hines	7/21/30 to 8/14/45
Gen. Omar N. Bradley	8/15/45 to 11/30/47
Carl R. Gray Jr.	1/1/48 to 6/30/53
Harvey V. Higley	7/22/53 to 12/9/57
Sumner G. Whittier	1/23/58 to 1/20/61
John S. Gleason Jr.	1/30/61 to 12/31/64
William J. Driver	1/2/65 to 5/31/69
Donald E. Johnson	6/5/69 to ——

and Urban Development to set maximum interest rates on VA mortgages from Oct. 1, 1970, to Jan. 1, 1972.

PL 92-213, cleared by Congress Dec. 13, 1971, to extend and modify HUD programs, extended the interest-setting authority from Jan. 1, 1972, to June 30, 1972. PL 92-335, which also extended HUD programs, cleared June 30, 1972, and extended the authority to June 30, 1973. *(Housing chapter)*

Other Legislation

Several other veterans' bills were signed into law during the first session of the 91st Congress. Below are brief histories and descriptions of some of them:

S 408—Modified eligibility for acquiring specially adapted housing necessitated by service-connected disabilities requiring use of wheelchairs. Senate passed March 17. House passed, amended, May 19. Senate agreed to House amendments with amendments May 26. House agreed to additional Senate amendment May 27. President signed June 6, 1969 (PL 91-22).

HR 684—Made certain technical changes and corrections in laws relating to veterans benefits. House passed Feb. 17. Senate passed June 2. President signed June 11 (PL 91-24).

HR 4622—Insured preservation of all veterans' disability compensation evaluations in effect for 20 years or more. House passed Feb. 17. Senate passed June 16. President signed June 23 (PL 91-32).

HR 2768—Eliminated the six-month limitation on nursing home care for veterans with service-connected disabilities. House passed June 2. Senate passed Oct. 21. President signed Oct. 30 (PL 91-101).

HR 3130—Authorized Veterans Administration to furnish medical services for nonservice-connected disability to veterans totally disabled from a service-connected disability. House passed June 2. Senate passed Oct. 21. President signed Oct. 30 (PL 91-102).

HR 9334—Increased federal payments to states for the care of veterans in state nursing homes. House passed June 2. Senate passed with amendment Oct. 21. House agreed to Senate amendment Dec. 18. President signed Dec. 30 (PL 91-178).

1970

Veterans' Pensions

Congress Dec. 17 cleared for the President, who signed it Dec. 24, a bill (HR 15911—PL 91-588) raising income ceiling limitations and nonservice-connected pensions for veterans and their dependents or survivors.

Final action came when the Senate by voice vote approved a substitute amendment. The House had passed HR 15911 Sept. 21 under suspension of the rules on a 315-0 roll call.

Earlier in the day, the Senate by voice vote had approved a substitute amendment to the House version recommended by the Senate Finance Committee.

But a subsequent motion by Vance Hartke (D Ind.) that the bill be reconsidered was accepted. The Senate by voice vote then accepted an amendment by Hartke rejecting the Finance Committee's amendment, thus leaving the way open for passage of the House version.

HR 15911 increased benefits for veterans disabled as a result of nonservice connected causes and their survivors. The House Veterans' Affairs Committee report said the bill applied to 1,575,286 persons.

Under the bill as passed, no pensioners eligible for a Social Security increase would lose their veterans' benefits. Pensions had been based on annual income, including Social Security and other benefits. Pensions were designed to be reduced as benefits increased; the inverse relationship continued after the payment of Social Security benefits began in 1940. Except when Congress specified exemption of Social Security benefits in computing annual income, an increase in Social Security benefits could force a drop in pensions.

When Congress did not enact an exemption for Social Security benefits, it raised income limitation scales or rates in order to protect pension levels.

A Social Security increase of 15 per cent, which became effective for the general population Jan. 1, 1970, became effective for VA pensioners Jan. 1, 1971. The Veterans Administration estimated that 1,230,000 pensioners would face pension losses if an increase was not enacted.

The Senate Finance Committee's substitute bill, while protecting most recipients, would have resulted in pension losses to about 160,000 pensioners who had received substantial Social Security increases.

Hartke, in asking that passage of the substitute bill be reconsidered, pointed out that while the substitute would give some persons increased pensions, about 160,000 veterans, widows and children would lose benefits and 440,000 would receive no increase at all.

He said that under his amendment—which retained provisions of the House bill—no pensioner would receive a cut in benefits and almost all would average a $7.47 per month increase.

Sen. Herman E. Talmadge (D Ga.), chairman of the Finance Committee's Veterans Legislation Subcommittee, said he had no objection to reconsidering the previously passed amendment and accepting the House bill.

He said the House bill would cost $230-million while the Finance Committee's bill would cost $160-million.

Provisions. As cleared by Congress, HR 15911:

• Provided across-the-board raises in monthly non-service-connected pensions for veterans and their dependents or survivors, to a maximum of $121 per month for a single person from a maximum of $110 per month.

• Raised annual income limitations for a veteran or his widow living alone to $2,300 from $2,000, and for a veteran or widow and one dependent to $3,500 from $3,200.

• Raised annual income limitations for dependency and indemnity compensation to one parent of a veteran to $2,300 from $2,000, to two parents living together to $3,500 from $3,200, and to two parents separated to $2,300 from $2,000.

• Established a $500 limit over the permissible annual income limitations in order to qualify for free drugs.

• Removed, effective Jan. 1, 1972, the requirement that nonservice-connected pensioners 72 years of age or older must file annual income and estate reports.

• Excluded certain income from reportable income under the nonservice-connected pension program.

• Included as beneficiaries those persons who served in the 1916-1917 Mexican border conflict or their survivors.

Education Assistance

Congress March 23 cleared a bill (HR 11959—PL 91-219) boosting educational benefits by 34.6 per cent for some 736,000 veterans who had served in the armed forces during the preceding 15 years (or after Jan. 31, 1955). Benefits in the bill were made retroactive to Feb. 1, 1970.

Different versions of the bill had been passed during the first session, but Congress adjourned without further action.

Provisions. As cleared by Congress, HR 11959:

• Raised to $175 a month from $130 a month the educational allowance for single veterans.

• Raised the allowance for those with one dependent to $205 a month, and for those with two dependents to $230 a month. For each additional dependent, $13 a month would be added.

• Authorized the Veterans Administration to pay eligible veterans $50 a month for up to nine months for "individualized tutorial assistance."

• Established a Predischarge Educational Program (PREP) which would subsidize the schooling of eligible servicemen with more than six months of active duty time to their credit. The Veterans Administration would pay up to $175 a month to institutions conducting the courses, which generally would be designed to lead to a high school diploma.

• Established an outreach program to seek out veterans with little education and inform them of the new programs.

Conference. The House version of the bill, passed Aug. 4, 1969, by voice vote, provided for a 27 per cent increase in educational and training benefits.

The Senate version of the bill, passed Oct. 23, 1969, by a 77-0 roll-call vote, provided for a 46-per cent increase. President Nixon, who had requested only a 13 per cent increase, threatened to veto the bill as "excessive and...inflationary."

A 34.6 per cent compromise figure was reached in the conference report (H Rept 91-918) filed March 18, breaking a five-month stalemate over the bill.

Final Action. The House March 18 and the Senate March 23, by voice votes, adopted the conference report on HR 11959.

In announcing the President's signing of the bill March 26, press secretary Ronald Ziegler called the compromise amount "reasonable." He said it would be "relatively easy to find" the estimated $186-million the bill would add to the fiscal 1971 budget by cutting other programs.

POW Dependents

Congress Dec. 10 cleared for the President a bill (S 3785—PL 91-584) authorizing education benefits and home loan assistance for dependents of U.S. servicemen who were prisoners of war, missing in action or interned by a foreign power.

Final action came when the House by voice vote approved the bill after first agreeing to four amendments added by the Senate Dec. 8. The Senate amendments dealt exclusively with the education benefits.

The amendments lowered to six months from two years the minimum time for GI bill school or training eligibility; expanded courses approved under the GI bill; clarified laws relating to assessment of college courses; and accelerated the date on which GI allowances were increased in the case of new dependents.

It was reported during House debate on the bill Nov. 16 that there were 2,859 dependents belonging to the 1,472 Americans estimated at that time to be missing in action or captured in Southeast Asia.

Provisions. As cleared by Congress, S 3785:

• Provided educational and training assistance and home loan benefits for wives and children of armed forces personnel missing in action, captured by a hostile force or detained or interned by a foreign government.

• Guaranteed up to 60 per cent of the amount of the home loan, but not more than $12,500.

• Authorized direct loans of up to $25,000 for purchase, construction or repair of housing in areas where GI loans from private lenders were not available.

• Set 120 hours a month as full-time attendance for on-the-job training courses.

• Clarified the method of computing educational allowances for correspondence courses.

• Provided that servicemen after more than 180 days of active duty could begin to use their GI bill entitlements for post-secondary school or training.

• Provided that a course required by the Small Business Administration for minority group entrepreneurs was covered by the GI bill.

• Clarified provisions of existing law relating to assessment of college courses for GI bill purposes.

• Provided that the GI bill's benefits for dependents would become effective from the date a veteran acquired a new dependent, rather than from the date the VA received notice of a new dependent.

Veterans' Affairs Committee

The Legislative Reorganization Act of (Oct. 26) 1970 (PL 91-510), which took effect on Jan. 3, 1971, established a standing Senate Committee on Veterans' Affairs. Creation of a Senate committee devoted exclusively to veterans' affairs had long been a goal of national veterans' organizations. Such a committee had been set up in the House of Representatives in 1924. Named originally the Committee on World War Veterans' Legislation, it had become the House Committee on Veterans' Affairs under the Legislative Reorganization Act of (Aug. 2) 1946 (PL 79-601).

Prior to 1971, handling of veterans' affairs in the Senate had been divided between the Finance Committee and the Labor and Public Welfare Committee. The Finance Committee appointed a subcommittee in 1944 to work on the GI Bill of Rights and in 1969 a general subcommittee on veterans' legislation. The Labor and Public Welfare Committee had a veterans' affairs subcommittee continuously from 1946 to 1970, when the new standing Senate Committee on Veterans' Affairs took over.

Vance Hartke (D Ind.) has been chairman of the standing committee since its creation. The committee has four subcommittees: Housing and Insurance (Harold E. Hughes, D Iowa, chairman); Readjustment, Education and Employment (Vance Hartke, chairman); Health and Hospitals (Alan Cranston, D Calif., chairman); and Compensation and Pensions (Herman E. Talmadge, D Ga., chairman).

Legislative History. The Senate Labor and Public Welfare Committee Sept. 23 reported S 3785. The Senate passed the bill Sept. 25 by voice vote. The House Veterans Affairs Committee reported the bill Oct. 14 with minor amendments dealing with on-the-job training and correspondence courses. The bill, with amendments, was passed by the House Nov. 16 by a 331-0 roll-call vote and returned to the Senate.

The Senate Dec. 8 passed the bill by voice vote after adding four amendments. There was no debate. The bill then went back to the House.

The House Dec. 10 agreed to the Senate amendments by voice vote. There was no debate on the amendments. Olin E. Teague (D Texas), chairman of the Veterans Affairs Committee, said the amendments were supported by the Veterans Administration. The President signed the bill into law Dec. 24.

Other Legislation

SERVICEMEN'S LIFE INSURANCE. President Nixon June 25 signed into law a bill (S 1479—PL 91-291) increasing to $15,000 from $10,000 the maximum coverage under servicemen's group life insurance.

Final congressional action came June 15 when the House approved the bill by voice vote and without debate. The Senate originally had passed the bill in 1969.

Provisions. As cleared by Congress, S 1479:

• Raised the maximum amount of automatic coverage under the Servicemen's Group Life Insurance program (SGLI) to $15,000 from $10,000 and set the cost to the serviceman at $1 per month for each $5,000 worth of insurance.

• Assured that the federal government would pay a portion of the cost of the policy for periods in which the insured serviceman was engaged in hazardous duty.

• Extended coverage to Reserve Officers Training Corps (ROTC) cadets and midshipmen attending field training or practice cruises of 31 days or more, and to Reserve or National Guard personnel on active duty or active duty for training for less than 31 days or certain inactive duty training and while traveling to and from such duty.

Background. Persons on active duty were not insured under federal legislation between 1956 and 1965 unless they retained government life insurance obtained prior to April 25, 1951. With the intensification of the war in Vietnam, however, Congress passed a bill (PL 89-214) in 1965 providing life insurance to military personnel on active duty.

A serviceman was automatically insured for the maximum, $10,000, unless he indicated he wanted $5,000 worth of insurance or none at all. The cost to the individual was $2 a month for $10,000 of insurance or $1 a month for $5,000. The program was administered by a commercial company supervised by the Veterans Administration. *(Congress and the Nation Vol. II, p. 838)*

HOSPITAL CARE. Congress Oct. 13 cleared for the President a bill (HR 693—PL 91-500) removing the requirement that veterans 65 years of age or older must certify that they were unable to pay hospital expenses in order to be treated for a nonservice-connected disability in a Veterans Administration hospital.

Final action on the bill came when the House agreed by voice vote to Senate changes in the bill.

Disability Compensation. Congress July 30 cleared for the President a bill (S 3348—PL 91-376) to increase by approximately 10 per cent the rates of service-connected compensation for disabled veterans.

Compensation rose to $25 per month for a 10 per cent disability from $23; and to $450 per month for a 100 per cent disability from $400.

The House by unanimous consent agreed to Senate amendments July 30, thus clearing the bill for the President, who signed it Aug. 12. The Senate amendments deleted clauses referring to the redemption of certain bonds held by the United Spanish-American War Veterans.

VIETNAM, PUEBLO POW BENEFITS. The House by a voice vote June 10 cleared a bill (HR 4204—PL 91-289) authorizing payments under the War Claims Act of 1948 (PL 80-896) to members of the armed forces held prisoner by North Vietnam and to the crew of the U.S.S. Pueblo held captive in North Korea in 1968.

The bill originated in 1969 and was reported by the House Interstate and Foreign Commerce Committee May 15, 1969. It passed the House by voice vote on May 28, 1969. HR 4204 was reported by the Senate Judiciary Committee May 18, 1970, with amendments, and was passed in the Senate by voice vote May 20.

The Senate amendments raised the payment to a prisoner of war from $1 to $2 for each day he was forced to exist on inadequate food and from $1.50 to $3 for each day he performed forced labor.

The bill also provided $60 per month for U.S. civilians held in captivity by North Vietnam.

The House then agreed to the Senate amendments by voice vote June 10. The President signed the bill into law June 24.

POW ALLOWANCES. President Nixon Dec. 7 signed into law a bill (HR 9486—PL 91-534) providing a family separation allowance to dependents of U.S. prisoners of war or servicemen missing in action in Vietnam.

Final congressional action came Nov. 23, when the Senate by voice vote passed the bill without amendment.

As passed HR 9486 authorized the payment of $30 a month to dependents of servicemen missing in action during the Vietnam conflict since Feb. 28, 1961. Some of those dependents, for a variety of reasons, had not been eligible for such an allowance.

Legislative History. HR 9486 had been reported by the House Armed Services Committee on Nov. 20, 1969. The bill passed the House by voice vote Dec. 1, 1969.

It was reported in the Senate Nov. 19 by the Armed Services Committee and passed the Senate by voice vote Nov. 23.

AUTO ALLOWANCES. Congress Dec. 31 cleared for the President a bill (HR 370—PL 91-666) increasing allowances for the purchase of specially equipped automobiles for disabled veterans to $2,800 from $1,600.

Provisions. As cleared by Congress, HR 370:

• Raised the allowance for purchase of specially equipped automobiles by disabled veterans to $2,800 from $1,600.

• Required the Veterans Administration to provide and maintain the necessary adaptive materials for such specially equipped cars.

• Limited coverage to World War II and Korean War veterans and to those veterans disabled during the period of the Vietnam war.

Legislative History. The bill was passed by the House June 15. The House-passed bill raised the disability allowance to $2,500. The Senate amended the bill Sept. 25 by increasing the limit to $3,000 from $2,500 and by requiring the Veterans Administration to provide and maintain essential adaptive materials for the disabled veterans' cars. The Senate also extended coverage to veterans of the Vietnam war era. The House Dec. 29 accepted the Senate amendments with modifications lowering the allowance to $2,800 and deleting coverage for Vietnam war era veterans if their disability had occurred before the Vietnam conflict and was only aggravated by service during the Vietnam war era (since 1964). The Senate Dec. 31 agreed to the House changes in the Senate amendments, completing congressional action. The President approved the bill Jan. 11, 1971.

HOUSING. Congress Oct. 14 cleared for the President a bill (HR 16710—PL 91-506), the Veterans Housing Act of 1970, removing time limits on housing and business loans for World War II and Korean war veterans and providing loans for purchase of mobile homes. HR 16710 also provided grants to certain disabled veterans.

Final action came when the Senate agreed by voice vote to House changes to the bill. The measure was signed into law Oct. 23.

1971

Survivor Benefits

The House Oct. 21, by a 372-0 roll-call vote, passed a bill (HR 10670) creating a survivor benefit plan to allow career military personnel to leave a portion of their retired pay to their survivors.

The Department of Defense supported the bill.

HR 10670 was structured to allow each military retiree to assure his widow an income of at least 55 per cent of his retired pay for the remainder of her life. The bill was intended to close the gap between retirement programs for Civil Service personnel and for armed forces personnel. Families of Civil Service employees were covered by a survivor annuity program, while 85 per cent of eligible retirees in the armed services, limited to self-financed programs, did not enroll because the plan was considered too expensive and complex.

HR 10670 replaced the retired servicemen's protection plan with a benefit program that supplemented Social Security benefits. On the average, the military retiree would pay 60 per cent of the cost of benefits provided to his survivors—the same percentage paid, on the average, by Civil Service retirees.

The bill also provided for attachment of up to 50 per cent of a military retiree's pay, by court order, for child benefits and support of a wife or former wife. The provision drew opposition from those members who said it would be unfair to military retirees because neither active duty personnel nor other government employees were subject to pay attachments.

The Armed Services Committee reported HR 10670 Sept. 16 without amendment.

The House Oct. 21, 1971, passed HR 10670 by a 372-0 roll-call vote after defeating an amendment offered by Charles S. Gubser (R Calif.) to allow attachment of the pay of active duty personnel as well as that of retirees.

The Senate passed the bill nearly a year later, Sept. 8, 1972, and it was signed into law (PL 92-425) Sept. 21, 1972.

Medical Care

The House Oct. 4 by voice vote passed a bill (HR 10880) providing improved medical care for veterans, their dependents and survivors. The Senate took no action on the bill in 1971, but cleared it Oct. 13, 1972. However, the President pocket vetoed the bill on Oct. 27, 1972.

The bill would have extended hospital and medical care benefits to wives, widows and children of veterans who were either totally and permanently disabled from service-connected causes or who had died as a result of a service disability.

Although the Veterans Administration supported most provisions of HR 10880, it did not endorse the provision extending hospital and medical care benefits to families of veterans who were totally disabled or had died from service-connected causes.

The estimated cost to the government of enactment of the bill was $271-million from fiscal 1972 through 1976.

Provisions. As passed by the House, HR 10880:

● Permitted outpatient treatment for any veteran with a non-service-connected disability.

● Provided pay differentials for nurses performing duty between 6 p.m. and 6 a.m.; from midnight Saturday to midnight Sunday and on federal holidays.

● Directed the VA to develop and carry out a training and education program for its health service personnel.

● Provided hospital and medical care to the wife or child of a veteran totally and permanently disabled as a result of a service-connected incident and to the widow and child of a veteran who died as the result of a service-connected disability.

● Authorized the appointment of two additional assistant chief medical directors in the VA.

● Prohibited payment for off-duty professional services performed by physicians, dentists or nurses.

● Permitted nursing home care for persons treated in any Armed Forces hospital.

● Authorized the VA to contract for scarce medical specialist services with non-government medical schools.

● Provided additional authority for temporary full-time appointments of medical personnel for a period not to exceed one year.

● Clarified and extended protection in malpractice suits brought against VA medical personnel.

● Permitted reimbursement to veterans in VA hospitals for loss of personal effects caused by natural disasters.

● Authorized reimbursement to veterans, under limited circumstances, for the value of hospital care or medical services provided when services were furnished from sources other than the VA.

● Delineated the authority of the VA to participate in programs under the Heart Disease, Cancer and Stroke Amendments of 1965 (PL 89-239).

Veterans' Compensation

The President Dec. 15 signed two veterans' dependents compensation bills (HR 11651—PL 92-198; HR 11652—PL 92-197) totaling $195-million in first-year costs.

HR 11651 provided an average increase of approximately 6.5 per cent in the rates of non-service-connected pensions and disability allowances payable to veterans and widows. First-year costs were estimated at $127.2-million rising to $136.9-million in the fifth year.

HR 11652 provided a cost-of-living increase to widows, dependent parents and children of veterans who died in the service or as a result of service-incurred disabilities—a 10 per cent increase to widows, a 5 per cent increase to children and a 6.5 per cent increase to dependent parents.

The House Veterans' Affairs Committee Nov. 10 reported HR 11651 and HR 11652. The House Nov. 15 passed HR 11651 by a 351-0 roll-call vote and passed HR 11652 by a 350-0 roll-call vote.

The Senate Veterans' Affairs Committee Nov. 30 reported HR 11651 and HR 11652. The Senate Dec. 2 passed HR 11651 by a 351-0 roll-call vote and passed HR ing the bills for the President's signature, which was attached to both measures Dec. 15.

Other Bills

Mortgage Life Insurance. The Senate July 30 passed by voice vote and cleared for the President

HR 943 (PL 92-95), a bill to provide government-backed mortgage protection life insurance for disabled veterans who purchased specially adapted housing costing up to $30,000. According to the committee report, 11,198 specially adapted housing grants had been given by the government which, when covered by insurance, would result in an expenditure of $1.6-million. The bill had been passed by the House March 1.

Dependents' Benefits. The House July 19 passed by voice vote and cleared for the President's signature S 421 (PL 92-58), a bill extending health care benefits to the handicapped children of a parent in the armed services who had been killed in the line of duty in a hostile fire zone. A 1966 law (PL 89-614) had provided benefits for the handicapped children but had inadvertently cut off the benefits when the parent died. Estimated cost of the program for the first year was $135,000. The bill had been passed by the Senate May 4.

Direct Loans. The Senate July 23 by voice vote passed and cleared for the President a bill (HR 3344—PL 92-66) authorizing the administrator of Veterans' Affairs to sell to any person, at prices he determined to be reasonable, direct loans made to veterans. The bill had been passed by the House by voice vote on July 6.

Private Hospitals. The House July 19 by voice vote passed HR 1409, a bill to remove certain restrictions on types of hospitals in which dependents of military personnel could receive treatment. The purpose of the bill was to permit the mentally retarded and physically handicapped spouses and children of active duty personnel to receive institutional care from private hospitals operated at a profit when it was determined that care from such institutions would be best for the patient. Estimated added cost for such care was $10,000 per year. There was no Senate action on the bill in 1971 or 1972.

Veterans' Care. The House March 1 by voice vote passed a bill (HR 460) designed to ease the patient load on Veterans Administration hospitals by extending government subsidies for disabled veterans in private nursing homes to nine months. Existing law provided six-month subsidies. The estimated cost of the bill was $6.9-million for the first year. There was no Senate action on the bill in 1971 or 1972.

1972

Education Benefits

President Nixon Oct. 24 signed into law a bill (HR 12828—PL 92-540) increasing the monthly allowances for veterans attending school or participating in vocational training programs under the GI education act of 1966.

Final action came when the Senate Oct. 13 agreed to a compromise version which raised the monthly payments for veterans enrolled in educational programs by 25.7 per cent and increased payments to veterans pursuing vocational training programs by 48 per cent. The increased rates were effective retroactive to Sept. 1, 1972, for all veterans and their dependents enrolled in an educational training program as of the date of the bill's enactment.

Members of the House and Senate Veterans' Affairs Committees met informally for several weeks to resolve differences between the two versions. The increases in educational allowances provided by the Senate version were scaled down and several Senate-added provisions were deleted in face of strong opposition by the administration. Those included a veterans' educational loan program and a requirement that federal departments and agencies develop a plan for the preferential employment of disabled veterans and veterans of the Vietnam war.

Under the unanimous consent procedure, the House Oct. 11 agreed to the Senate-passed amendments with an amendment substituting the language of the compromise bill.

Provisions. As cleared by Congress, major provisions of HR 12828:

• Raised the basic monthly rate for educational assistance for single veterans enrolled in full-time programs to $220 from $175, with proportionate increases for veterans with dependents and those enrolled in part-time programs, retroactive to Sept. 1, 1972.

• Increased the monthly allowance for single veterans participating in full-time apprenticeship or on-the-job training courses to $160 from $108, with proportionate increases for veterans with dependents.

• Authorized advance payment of up to two months' education allowances upon the receipt of evidence of a veteran's enrollment in an authorized program, effective no later than Aug. 1, 1973.

• Created the workstudy/outreach program in which veterans participating in educational or rehabilitative programs would be paid in advance up to $250 for work done for the Veterans Administration while enrolled.

• Permitted wives and widows of eligible veterans to enroll in apprenticeship or on-the-job training programs, correspondence courses, and, if applicable, secondary-level training.

Institutional Aid

The Education Amendments of 1972 (S 659—PL 92-318) provided for cost-of-instruction grants to institutions of higher education on the basis of the number of veterans (at $300 per veteran) attending each institution with GI bill educational aids or vocational rehabilitation assistance. The provision was adopted by the Senate on Feb. 28 and included in the conference version of the bill. Congress cleared S 659 on June 8, when the House agreed to the conference report by a 218-180 roll-call vote. *(Education amendments, p. 581)*

Drug Treatment

The Senate Sept. 7, 1972, by voice vote passed with amendments a bill (HR 9265), the Veterans' Drug and Alcohol Treatment and Rehabilitation Act of 1971.

As passed by the Senate, HR 9265 would establish a comprehensive treatment and rehabilitation program for veterans dependent on drugs or alcohol and relax existing program eligibility standards to include veterans with other than honorable discharges or whose maladies were not service-connected.

The program, which was estimated to cost $419-million in its first year of operation, would aid approximately 326,000 veterans with drug and alcohol disabilities, according to Alan Cranston (D Calif.), chairman of the

Veterans' Benefits and Services
(In millions of dollars)

Program or agency	Outlays 1972 actual	1973 estimate
Income security:		
Compensation and pensions:		
Service-connected compensation	3,485	3,797
Non-service-connected pensions	2,531	2,614
Other veterans benefits and services	85	94
Proposed legislation	—	—
Insurance programs:		
National service life insurance trust fund	720	501
U.S. government life insurance trust fund	81	66
All other insurance programs	—69	—47
Education, training, and rehabilitation:		
Readjustment benefits	1,918	2,542
Other	42	55
Housing:		
Loan guaranty revolving fund	—54	—165
Direct loan revolving fund	—246	—276
Other (HUD participation sales trust fund)	—17	—8
Hospital and medical care:		
Medical care and hospital services	2,229	2,522
Construction of hospital and extended care facilities	107	115
Medical administration, research, etc.	92	104
Proposed legislation	—	—
Other veterans benefits and services:		
Veterans Administration administrative expenses	284	321
Other VA programs	—3	2
Non-VA veterans support programs	36	45
Deductions for offsetting receipts:		
Intrabudgetary transactions	—2	—2
Proprietary receipts from the public	—489	—480
Total	10,731	11,795

SOURCE: Fiscal 1974 Federal Budget

subcommittee which had considered the Senate companion bill.

The House July 19, 1971, had initially passed HR 9265 by a unanimous 379-0 roll-call vote. The House measure, which authorized $89.3-million over five years for a drug abuse treatment program, did not cover alcohol disabilities.

There was no conference action on the bill, but a measure providing for a general drug abuse program had been signed into law (PL 92-255) March 21, 1972. *(Health chapter, p. 574)*

VA Medical Schools

President Nixon Oct. 24 signed into law a bill (H J Res 748—PL 92-541), the Veterans Administration Medical School Assistance and Health Manpower Training Act of 1972.

Final action came when the Senate Oct. 13 by voice vote agreed to a compromise version of the bill which authorized $75-million annually for fiscal years 1973-79 to expand the health manpower training programs operated by the Veterans Administration (VA) and by VA-affiliated schools.

The Nixon administration opposed the bill.

The House originally had adopted H J Res 748 July 19, 1971; the Senate approved a more liberal version April 27, 1972. Members of the House and Senate Veterans' Affairs Committee met informally for several weeks to resolve differences between the two versions. The House Oct. 11 by voice vote agreed to the Senate-passed amendments with an amendment substituting the language of the compromise bill. The Senate agreed to the House amendment Oct. 13 by voice vote, clearing the measure for the White House.

Provisions. As cleared, H J Res 748:

• Authorized appropriations of $25-million annually for fiscal years 1973-79 for matching grants to state colleges and universities to assist in the establishment of up to eight new medical and allied health professional schools operated in conjunction with Veterans Administration medical facilities.

• Authorized appropriations of $50-million annually for fiscal years 1973-79 for expansion of existing health manpower training facilities, up to 30 per cent of which was authorized for renovation and expansion of existing VA facilities and the balance was to be used for grants to nonprofit health manpower training institutions which were affiliated with the VA Department of Medicine and Surgery.

• Directed the VA administrator, when awarding grants to private institutions, to give special consideration to those schools which gave priority for admission to veterans with medical training acquired during their service.

Medical Care

President Nixon Oct. 27 pocket vetoed a bill (HR 10880), the Veterans' Health Care Expansion Act of 1972.

Final congressional action came when the Senate Oct. 13 by voice vote agreed to a compromise version of the bill which would have authorized about $85-million in fiscal 1973 for expanding the health care services provided to veterans and their dependents.

In his veto message, President Nixon said HR 10880 "runs counter to this administration's national health strategy which would...sharply reduce the federal government's role in the direct provision of services" and "unnecessarily adds hundreds of millions of dollars to the federal budget."

As cleared by Congress, HR 10880 would have made certain veterans and their dependents eligible for outpatient care and provided hospital and medical care to the wife or widow and dependents of veterans who were either totally and permanently disabled from service-connected causes or who had died as a result of a service-connected disability.

Members of the House and Senate Veterans' Affairs Committees had met informally for several weeks to resolve differences between the two versions of the bill—passed by the Senate May 4, 1972, and by the House Oct. 4, 1971.

The House Oct. 11 by voice vote agreed to the Senate version with an amendment substituting the language of the compromise bill; the Senate Oct. 13 by voice vote agreed to the compromise, completing congressional action.

Other Legislation

Other veterans' bills in 1972 included:

Pensions. The Senate Oct. 11 by voice vote passed a bill (S 4006) raising pension rates and income limitations by an average of 8 per cent for veterans receiving disability pensions, and for their survivors receiving pensions and other compensation. The House took no action on the bill.

As passed by the Senate, S 4006:

• Increased rates of monthly non-service-connected pensions for veterans and their dependents or survivors by an average of 8 per cent.

• Raised annual income limitations for an unmarried veteran or a veteran's widow living alone to $3,000 from $2,600, and for a veteran or widow with one dependent to $4,200 from $3,800.

• Raised annual income limitations for dependency and indemnity compensation to one parent of a veteran to $3,000 from $2,600; to two parents living together to $4,200 from $3,800; and to two parents separated to $3,000 from $2,600.

• Raised annual income limitations for a veteran or his widow living alone and receiving a pension under the Veterans Pension Act of 1959 (PL 86-211) to $2,600 from $2,200, and for a veteran or widow and one dependent covered under PL 86-211 to $3,900 from $3,500.

Disability Benefits. Congress June 29 cleared for the White House a bill (S 3338—PL 92-328) increasing by 10 per cent the rates of compensation for veterans with service-connected disabilities.

As cleared, the bill also authorized a clothing allowance of $150 per year for veterans whose disability required the wearing or use of a prosthetic or orthopedic device.

National Cemeteries. President Nixon Oct. 27 pocket vetoed HR 12674, the National Cemeteries Act of 1972, giving the Veterans Administration jurisdiction over most national cemeteries established for members and veterans of the armed forces.

The bill also would have authorized the payment of $150 for a plot, or an interment allowance, to veterans who were not buried in a national cemetery, and additional benefits of up to $800 for veterans who died of service-connected injuries.

HR 12674 also would have prohibited the transfer of any VA property of more than 100 acres or valued at more than $100,000, unless the transfer was approved by public law.

In his veto message, the President said, "The bill deals inconsistently with the serious problem of burial benefits for the nation's veterans and war dead. It commissions a study of this problem at the same time it preempts the results of such a study by authorizing new burial benefits which would annually add $55-million to the federal budget beginning next year."

The House Oct. 11 by voice vote had agreed to Senate amendments added Oct. 9.

Chapter 11—Health, Education and Welfare

Key Votes

In this chapter, key roll-call votes are shown in bold-face type. The party breakdown on each of these votes and the position taken by each member of Congress may be found in the key vote charts which appear in the appendix to this book.

Health Programs

One of the "six great goals" outlined by President Nixon in his 1971 State of the Union message was that of "improving America's health care and making it available more fairly to more people." A month later he submitted to Congress a wide-ranging package of health care proposals, saying: "We must recognize that we *cannot* simply *buy* our way to better medicine. We have already been trying that too long.... It must be our goal not merely to finance a more expensive medical system but to organize a more efficient one."

The major redirection of health programs envisaged by the President was not achieved during his first administration. Meanwhile, recurrent conflicts with Congress over spending levels for existing programs foreshadowed Nixon's proposals for termination of or drastic cutbacks in key government health programs in 1973.

Most of the action on health legislation by the 91st Congress consisted of extensions of the large number of programs enacted during the Kennedy-Johnson administrations. The 92nd Congress began to move in new directions. It authorized programs for stepped-up attacks on cancer and heart disease, and for research on little-known diseases such as sickle-cell and Cooley's anemia. As medical costs continued a steep and steady rise, serious attention was given to various proposals for some form of national health insurance. No action was taken, but the groundwork was laid for further consideration in the second Nixon administration.

During the period 1969-72, Congress and the Nixon administration were often quietly at odds on the direction of health programs. Congress usually refused to agree to administration proposals for changes in legislation. In turn, the administration asked for funding of many programs at levels well below those desired by Congress. *(Box, p. 567)*

In a 1970 veto of a bill designed to encourage doctors to go into general practice, President Nixon objected that the bill continued "the traditional approach of adding more programs to the almost unmanageable current structure of federal government health efforts." This was one of several conflicts between Congress and the administration; the administration often objected that Congress was authorizing unnecessary new programs for which sufficient authority already existed.

In another disagreement between the administration and Congress, the administration sought unsuccessfully to get Congress to move away from traditional categorical grant programs—grants for specific categories of health facilities—in favor of more flexible block grants which enabled states to spend money where they felt it was most needed. The administration was also unsuccessful in replacing formula grants for some programs with block grants and in switching from direct student loan programs to federally guaranteed loans.

In both the 91st and 92nd Congresses, conservatives and liberals were in unusual agreement on health legislation, and much of the congressional action was by unanimous or near-unanimous votes. Health legislation got strong new leadership in 1971 when Sen. Edward M. Kennedy (D Mass.) and Rep. Paul G. Rogers (D Fla.) became chairmen of the health subcommittees of their respective chambers.

Major Legislation

Here are highlights of the major actions by the 91st and 92nd Congresses on new health legislation:

Health Insurance. Senate and House committees in 1971 held lengthy hearings on proposals for some sort of national health insurance system. The administration proposed to require employers to provide comprehensive health insurance coverage including provision for catastrophic illness and office visits, and to replace the existing Medicaid program for families on relief with a broad government health insurance program. The other major proposal was a plan sponsored by Kennedy and Rep. Martha W. Griffiths (D Mich.) for a comprehensive federal national health insurance system for all Americans.

Health Maintenance Organizations. Allied to the health insurance proposals was a bill passed by the Senate in 1972 authorizing $5.2-billion for fiscal 1973-75 for establishment of health maintenance organizations (HMOs). HMOs were prepaid group practice organizations which provided a wide range of health services. The administration had proposed a more modest bill in 1971, and further action was expected in the 93rd Congress.

Cancer Research. The cancer research program at the National Institutes of Health (NIH) was substantially expanded in 1971 by a bill authorizing $1.59-billion over three years. A report by a special panel in 1970 had originally recommended that the expanded program be located outside of NIH, and this was what the bill pro-

References

Discussion of federal action in the field for the years 1945-64 may be found in *Congress and the Nation, Vol. I,* p. 1122-1194; for the years 1965-68, *Congress and the Nation, Vol. II,* p. 663-707.

vided as it originally passed the Senate. A major controversy then developed over placement of the program, with cancer specialists backing the Senate bill and other biomedical researchers opposing it on the grounds that it would dangerously isolate the program. The House eventually passed this bill leaving the program within NIH, and this was the disposition of the final bill.

Heart and Lung Disease. Congress in 1972 provided for the same kind of stepped-up research program on heart, lung and blood disease that it had voted for cancer research the year before. The bill authorized $1.38-billion through fiscal 1975 for research and control programs at NIH and 30 new regional centers.

Special Diseases. Congress in 1972 passed several bills for programs of research and control of neglected diseases. It passed separate authorizations for sickle cell anemia and Cooley's anemia and established a National Advisory Commission on Multiple Sclerosis.

Underserved Areas. Several bills enacted contained provisions aimed at bringing more health personnel to medically underserved areas. A Health Service Corps was established within the Public Health Service for assignment to health shortage areas. Health manpower programs were revised to provide for cancellation of loans to medical students who accepted service in shortage areas. Loans would be forgiven at the rate of 30 per cent for each of the first two years and 25 per cent for the third year of service.

Family Planning. Congress in 1970 increased family planning funding and established an Office of Population Affairs in the Department of Health, Education and Welfare (HEW) to oversee all HEW family planning programs. It also established a 20-man, independent Commission on Population Growth and the American Future.

Appropriations Bills Vetoed

During his first administration, President Nixon three times vetoed the annual appropriations bills for the Labor and Health, Education and Welfare (HEW) Departments. He vetoed the first fiscal 1970 appropriations bill (HR 13111) and, in 1972, two bills for fiscal 1973 (HR 15417, HR 16654). The veto of the last bill left the Labor-HEW appropriation for fiscal 1973 to 'be funded under a continuing resolution rather than a regular appropriations bill.

All of the bills contained substantial increases in requests for HEW, and the President's veto messages objected to the bills as inflationary. The veto message on the 1970 bill largely singled out education program fund increases as the objectionable features of that measure, but the 1972 veto messages also reflected congressional-executive conflict over the funding of health programs. *(Story on presidential vetoes, see p. 101a.)*

Both of the fiscal 1973 Labor-HEW bills contained nearly $1-billion more than the President had requested for health programs. He had requested $4,156,906,000; Congress voted $5,114,908,000. The two fiscal 1973 bills provided the same amount for all programs but differed in that the second permitted the President to impound a total of $1,238,919,500 from the over-all bill.

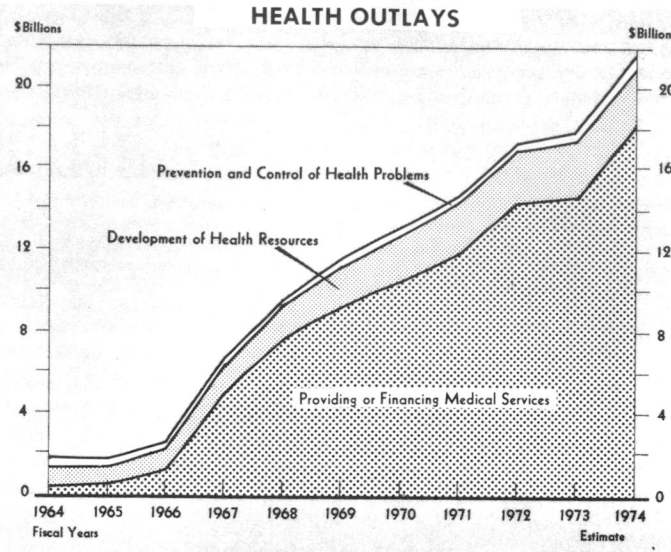

HEALTH OUTLAYS

Prevention and Control of Health Problems

Development of Health Resources

Providing or Financing Medical Services

The difference between the amounts requested and provided for health programs was the result of the fact that the President did not want to fund programs at what he felt were the unnecessarily high levels authorized by Congress. For the National Institutes of Health (NIH), the fiscal 1973 bills provided $2,723,670,000 against a request for $2,192,555,000. The biggest increases were $60 million for the National Cancer Institute and $64,720,000 for the National Heart and Lung Institute. The other part of the health budget, Health Services and Mental Health, was given $2,964,351,000, as against a $2,391,238,000 request. The bills provided $159,386,000 more than the request for health services planning and development and $52 million more than the request for preventive health services. The latter figure reflected the Congressional effort to get the administration to support a communicable disease program. *(p. 558)*

Chronology

Of Health

Legislation

1969

No major health legislation was enacted in 1969. Many basic health authorizations, such as the Hill-Burton hospital construction program, were due to expire in 1970. House and Senate health subcommittees worked on extensions of these various programs and some were passed by a single chamber, but there was no final action. *(For action on bills considered in both 1969 and 1970, see 1970 chronology, p. 553-562.)*

The new administration was slow to develop policies on health issues. The only presidential messages on health were on the peripheral areas of drug abuse and population growth. Part of the reason for the delay was a hold-up in the appointment of an assistant secretary for health and scientific affairs in the Department of Health, Education and Welfare (HEW). Dr. Roger O. Egeberg did not assume the position until September.

Appointment Controversy

Secretary of Health, Education and Welfare Robert H. Finch in April announced his intention to nominate Dr. John H. Knowles as assistant secretary for health and scientific affairs. The announcement met immediate opposition from elements of the American Medical Association (AMA) and from Senate Minority Leader Everett McKinley Dirksen (R Ill.). Knowles, director of the Massachusetts General Hospital in Boston, was reportedly opposed because his views on health care were too liberal. Dirksen said at a news conference April 22 that he had told Finch he would prevent confirmation if Knowles' nomination was sent to the Senate.

Knowles credited "certain political debts" of President Nixon for his failure to be nominated. The AMA's political arm contributed heavily in 1968 to many congressional candidates, most of them Republicans. The Knowles controversy produced strong criticism from several members of the Senate, who charged that the administration had improperly bowed to outside pressure against Knowles.

The Knowles nomination was never actually submitted. President Nixon July 12 nominated Dr. Roger O. Egeberg to the post. He was not confirmed until July and then did not take office until September. By December only three of his eight assistants had been selected.

1970

Hill-Burton Construction Program

Congress overrode a presidential veto for the first time in 10 years. The bill (HR 11102—PL 91-296) was a three-year extension of the 25-year old Hill-Burton program of federal grants for hospital construction and modernization. HR 11102 continued the program along the lines of past extensions except that it added new provisions for loan guarantees for construction and modernization of health facilities.

The administration had sought unsuccessfully to substitute a combination of direct block grants, direct loans and guaranteed loans for the Hill-Burton categorical grant (grants for different categories of health facilities) program. In vetoing the bill, President Nixon said it was inflationary and would restrict his options in managing federal expenditures.

Also turned down during 1970 action was an effort by Senate liberals to switch the program from its traditional formula which favored low-income rural states to a formula which would provide more aid for the deteriorating city hospitals. Such a provision was voted by the Senate but dropped in conference.

Background. The Hill-Burton Act (Title VI of the Public Health Service Act—PL 78-410), originally

---

enacted in 1946, was sponsored by Senators Lister Hill (D Ala.) and Harold H. Burton (R Ohio). As originally conceived, the program responded to what was at that time basically a rural problem. The American Hospital Association estimated that half the nation's counties had no hospital facilities. The program was therefore established with a formula for allocating hospital construction grants which favored low-income, rural states. The formula was based on population and per capita income, with the per capita income counting many times more than the population. Efforts by urban members of Congress to alter the formula in succeeding years were invariably unsuccessful.

Congress in 1964 did provide some special aid to urban areas when it amended the Hill-Burton Act to provide $160-million in federal grants for modernization of hospitals, with an allocation formula weighted in favor of urban areas and a provision that priority in modernization be given to urban hospitals. But a 1966 Johnson administration request for an expanded modernization program was not acted on. *(Congress and the Nation, Vol. II, p. 666)*

1969 Request. The Nixon administration requested extension of the Hill-Burton Act, which was due to expire June 30, 1970. In testimony before the Interstate and Foreign Commerce Committee, Secretary of Health, Education and Welfare Robert H. Finch proposed a "radical redirection" of the program.

Finch said the administration had "serious doubt that continuation of the categorical grants would assure the construction, replacement or modernization of other health facilities which are more urgently needed than general hospital beds." In place of continued categorical grants, Finch proposed a $500-million federally guaranteed loan program which "we believe would stimulate the private capital it will take to bring about modernization of acute care facilities." In addition, the secretary proposed a $150-million program of block grants to encourage state expansion and coordination of health facilities. He recommended that the Hill-Burton allocation formula be replaced with a system of allocation based on "financial need, population and need for construction and modernization of health facilities."

1969 House Action. The Interstate and Foreign Commerce Committee May 20 reported a clean bill (HR 11102) which rejected most of the administration proposals. The committee said it did not adopt the block grant approach because "existing transfer authority is adequate to permit the states to shift funds among categories as the needs of the state require."

The committee bill authorized $937.3-million for hospital construction and modernization grants for fiscal years 1971-73 and created a new program of federally guaranteed loans as proposed by the administration. It limited the loans to $300-million in fiscal 1971, $600-million in fiscal 1972 and $900-million in fiscal 1973.

HR 11102 was passed by the House June 4 by a 351-0 roll-call vote.

1970 Senate Action. The Senate Labor and Public Welfare Committee Feb. 5, 1970, reported HR 11102. Like the House, the Senate committee rejected the administration block grant proposal and voted the program of federally guaranteed loans. But its bill differed from the House version in extending the program for five years (instead of three), authorizing larger sums and amending the allotment formula for construction grants. The new formula was based on extent of need rather than per capita income and removed a requirement that rural areas have first priority in receiving grants. In turning down the block grant proposal, the committee said hospitals faced serious disadvantages in competing for private capital and that the grant program had been highly successful.

HR 11102 was passed by the Senate April 7 by a 79-0 roll-call vote. Before passage it accepted by voice vote an amendment modifying the new formula to include the square of per capita income as a factor in allocating grants. The amendment was a compromise which staved off an attempt to reinstitute the original Hill-Burton formula; even with the compromise the new formula was still considered more favorable to urban states.

Conference. The conference report, filed June 9, retained the existing construction allotment formula but provided for an HEW study and report of the formula by May 15, 1972.

The final bill extended the program for only three years and split the difference between House and Senate funds. It provided a total of $2.79-billion over three years for grants, loans and guaranteed loans to construct and modernize health facilities. Of the total, $1.29-billion was authorized for categorical grants and $1.5-billion for federally guaranteed or direct loans. The bill included a modified Senate provision requiring that funds appropriated for Hill-Burton and certain other health programs be spent only on those programs and be available only in the year for which they were appropriated.

Presidential Veto. President Nixon June 22 vetoed HR 11102 on grounds that the bill was too expensive and would hinder management of federal spending. He said HR 11102 would cost $350-million more than the $89-million requested for hospital construction in the administration's fiscal 1971 budget. He objected to the provision making certain health funds available for expenditure in the fiscal year for which they were appropriated. He said it would "significantly restrict" presidential options in managing federal expenditures and interfere with compliance with a congressional limitation on fiscal 1971 expenditures.

Veto Overridden. The House June 25 overrode the veto by a **279-98 key roll-call vote.** The Senate overrode the veto June 30 by a 76-19 roll call, and the bill thus became law over the President's objection.

PROVISIONS

As cleared by Congress, HR 11102 (PL 91-296):

Construction and Modernization

• Extended for three years, through fiscal 1973, the program of matching federal grants to states for construction of hospitals and other health facilities.

• Set grant authorizations for construction of hospitals and public health centers at $147.5-million in fiscal 1971, $152.5-million in fiscal 1972 and $157.5-million for fiscal 1973.

• For the three-year period, set grant authorizations for construction of long-term care facilities at $85-million annually; for outpatient facilities, $70-million annually; and for rehabilitation facilities, $15-million annually.

• Authorized appropriations of $65-million in fiscal 1971, $80-million in fiscal 1972 and $90-million in fiscal 1973 for modernization of health facilities.

• Removed existing limitations on the amounts that could be transferred from one grant category to another, except that total transfers from a given category could not exceed the minimum allotment for any category for any state.

• Raised the minimum allotment to a state for construction of rehabilitation facilities from $50,000 to $100,000, for outpatient facilities from $100,000 to $200,000 and for long-term care facilities from $200,000 to $300,000.

• Established a minimum allotment to a state for modernization of health facilities of $300,000.

• Authorized allotments to states for hospital construction on the basis of the population of the states and square of the state's allotment percentage (which was calculated on the basis of per capita income).

• Required the secretary of health, education and welfare (HEW) to study the effects of the formula whereby construction grants were allocated on the basis of population and per capita income. The secretary was to report the results by May 15, 1972.

• Provided that any funds appropriated for any fiscal year to carry out any program under the Public Health Service Act (PL 78-410) and the Mental Retardation Facilities and Community Mental Health Centers Construction Act of 1963 (PL 88-164) would remain available for obligation and expenditure until the end of the fiscal year for which appropriated (Section 601).

• Removed a provision of existing law requiring a state to give special consideration in making construction grants to projects for hospitals serving rural areas.

• Established new preferences to be used by the states in setting grant priorities, including facilities providing comprehensive health care, health training and treatment of alcoholism.

• Relaxed eligibility requirements for grants to outpatient (diagnostic and treatment) centers.

● Required that appropriate areawide health planning agencies have the opportunity to consider a Hill-Burton grant application before the application was approved by the HEW secretary.

● Increased from $50,000 to $100,000 the maximum amount available to a state for administration of its Hill-Burton program.

● Permitted a federal share of project costs of up to 90 per cent for projects with potential for reducing health care costs or projects serving poverty areas.

● Expanded eligibility for federal assistance to include additional health services (such as home health services) as long as the service was connected with a hospital.

● Permitted federal assistance for the purchase of equipment for a health facility even when no construction or modernization grant was involved.

Loan Guarantees and Interest Subsidies

● Authorized the secretary of HEW to guarantee payment of principal and interest on loans made by non-federal lenders to private nonprofit agencies for construction and modernization of health facilities.

● Authorized the secretary of HEW to make direct loans to public agencies for construction and modernization of health facilities.

● Authorized appropriation of $30-million for direct loans to public agencies.

● Limited the federal guarantee plus any federal grant or loan to 90 per cent of the cost of a project.

● Provided that the total amount of loan guarantees made to nonprofit private agencies and direct loans made to public agencies be allocated among states according to population, financial need and need for construction and modernization.

● Provided that the HEW secretary pay the holder of a guaranteed loan for a private nonprofit health facility amounts sufficient to reduce by three per cent per year the net effective interest rate otherwise payable on the loan.

● Limited the cumulative principal on loans that could be guaranteed to $500-million in fiscal 1971, $1-billion in fiscal 1972 and $1.5-billion in fiscal 1973.

● Authorized establishment of a fund in the Treasury Department composed of such sums as might be necessary to repay principal on guaranteed loans, to pay interest on guaranteed loans and to make direct loans.

● Required a public agency receiving a direct loan to pay interest comparable to the current rate of interest for guaranteed loans to nonprofit private agencies for the construction or modernization of similar facilities in the same areas, minus three percent.

● Authorized a program of project grants for construction and modernization of emergency rooms of general hospitals. Appropriations of $20-million in each of fiscal years 1971 through 1973 were authorized.

● Required the HEW secretary to report annually, beginning in 1971, on the health consequences of marijuana.

Community Mental Health Centers

Congress extended the Community Mental Health Centers Act through fiscal 1973. The bill (S 2523—PL 91-211) extended a 1963 act which provided for construc-

tion of community mental health centers on the theory that the mentally ill were more apt to recover if they were given treatment at locations close to their home communities.

S 2523 provided new aid for mentally ill children and centers in poverty areas. It also extended from 51 months to eight years the time period permitted for federal support for operation of community mental health centers. Existing authorizations for treatment and rehabilitation of alcoholics and narcotic addicts were expanded.

Background. Congress in 1963 enacted the Community Mental Health Centers Act authorizing appropriations of $150-million over fiscal years 1965-67 for grants to the states to pay from one-third to two-thirds of the costs of constructing public and private nonprofit community mental health centers for the prevention, diagnosis, treatment and rehabilitation of mentally ill patients in their own communities. The act was part of a comprehensive mental health package, the Mental Retardation Facilities and Community Mental Health Centers Construction Act of 1963 (PL 88-164), proposed by the Kennedy administration and in large part endorsed by Congress. An administration-backed section providing federal assistance for staffing centers was included in the Senate version but was deleted in the House and in conference. *(Congress and the Nation, Vol. I, p. 1147)*

In 1965, Congress reversed itself on the staffing issue and enacted a law (PL 89-105) amending PL 88-164 by authorizing federal grants to help pay for the salaries of professional and technical staff in the mental health centers. The measure was proposed by President Johnson. It authorized appropriations of $19.5-million in fiscal 1966, $24-million in fiscal 1967 and $30-million in fiscal 1968 for the grants. Such sums as were necessary were authorized for follow-up grants during fiscal 1967-72 to centers that had received initial staffing grants under the fiscal 1966-68 specific authorizations.

Congress in 1967 extended through fiscal 1970 the authorization for both the construction program and the staffing program. In 1968, in the Public Health Service Amendments (PL 90-574) it amended the Community Mental Health Centers Construction Act to authorize grants for construction and staffing of such facilities as halfway houses for alcoholics. The same bill for the first time contained a congressional declaration that alcoholism should be treated as a health problem rather than a criminal problem. *(Congress and the Nation, Vol. II, p. 669, 693, 699)*

1969 Action. The Senate Dec. 11 passed S 2523 by voice vote, extending the Community Mental Health Centers Act for three years. A similar but less expensive bill was passed by the House by voice vote Dec. 16.

1970 Action. The conference report on S 2523 was filed Feb. 25. The report was adopted by the House Feb. 26 by a 369-0 roll-call vote and by the Senate the same day by voice vote.

The final bill generally compromised the authorization amounts, but increased authorizations for treatment of addicts and alcoholics over the amounts in either the Senate or House bill.

PROVISIONS

As enacted, S 2523 (PL 91-211):

• Authorized appropriations of $80-million in fiscal 1971, $90-million in fiscal 1972 and $100-million in fiscal 1973 for grants to construct community mental health centers.

• Increased from 2 per cent to 5 per cent the amount of a state's construction allocation that could be applied to the cost of administration of the state plan. These funds could remain available for state use in the year following allocation.

• Permitted the federal share of construction costs to be as high as 90 per cent in poverty areas, as defined by the secretary of health, education and welfare (HEW). (Normally, the federal share could not exceed 66.6 per cent of costs.)

• Extended from 51 months to eight years the time period permitted for federal support for staffing of community mental health centers.

• Permitted federal support for any personnel performing technical functions in operating community mental health centers.

• Limited the federal share of staffing costs to 75 per cent the first two years after the first operational grant was made, 60 per cent the third year, 45 per cent the fourth year, and 30 per cent for the next four years.

• Permitted the federal share of staffing costs for centers serving poverty areas to be as much as 90 per cent during the first two years, 80 per cent the third year, 75 per cent the fourth and fifth years and 70 per cent for the next three years. (Normally, the federal share could not exceed 75 per cent during the first two years, 60 per cent for the third year, 45 per cent for the fourth year and 30 per cent for each of the next four years.)

• Permitted centers in poverty areas to begin service without all five "essential" services required for other centers. Centers in poverty areas were given 18 months to furnish the five services, after which grant payments would be suspended until the HEW secretary determined the center had met the requirement.

• Authorized appropriations of $45-million in fiscal 1971, $50-million in fiscal 1972 and $60-million in fiscal 1973 for grants for initial operating expenses for community mental health centers.

• Authorized appropriations of $15-million for the remainder of fiscal 1970, $30-million in fiscal 1971, $35-million in fiscal 1972 and $40-million in fiscal 1973 for construction, operation and special project grants to construct and staff facilities for rehabilitation of alcoholics and narcotics addicts.

• Increased the duration and amount of the federal share for construction grants and operating grants for facilities to treat narcotics addicts and alcoholics.

• Authorized $12-million in fiscal 1971, $20-million in fiscal 1972 and $30-million in fiscal 1973 for construction and staffing of facilities to provide mental health services for children and adolescents. Federal support for operation of these services was set at 80 per cent the first two years decreasing to 30 per cent by the end of eight years, with higher support permitted for centers serving poverty areas.

• Required that grants for the mental health of children be made only to facilities affiliated with a community mental health center.

• Permitted up to 5 per cent of money appropriated for initial operating grants for community mental health centers in poverty areas or initiation of rehabilitation programs for alcoholics and drug addicts to be used without any matching requirement.

Mental Retardation Facilities

Congress enacted the Developmental Disabilities Services and Facilities Construction Amendments of 1970. The bill (S 2846—PL 91-517) broadened and extended programs under the expiring Mental Retardation Facilities Construction Act of 1963 (PL 88-164). The bill was introduced by Sen. Edward M. Kennedy (D Mass.). Several of its provisions were opposed by the administration. In addition, the bill did not include an administration request to substitute project grants for formula grants (allotments based on state population and need) under the program.

Background. The Mental Retardation Facilities Construction Act of 1963 (Title I of PL 88-164) authorized grants to states to pay from one-third to two-thirds of the costs of constructing public and private nonprofit community mental retardation centers. Grants also were authorized to pay up to 75 per cent of the costs of constructing clinical mental retardation facilities associated with a college or university. The grants were allocated to the states according to population, need for facilities and financial need. Title III of PL 83-164 authorized grants to train teachers for mentally retarded and handicapped children.

The grant programs were extended in 1967 (PL 90-170) with the addition of a new grant program for staffing mental retardation centers and a new program for training teachers in physical education and recreation for the handicapped. (*Congress and the Nation, Vol. I, p. 1147; Vol. II, p. 692*)

Total appropriations for the mental retardation facilities programs were $158.7-million for fiscal 1964-70. The grant programs were due to expire June 30, 1970.

1969 Action. The Senate Labor and Public Welfare Health Subcommitttee in November held hearings on S 2846, extending for five years programs for construction of mental retardation facilities. The bill authorized $950-million for construction plus $53-million for university-affiliated facilities. It broadened the program to include persons with developmental disabilities, defined as illnesses such as cerebral palsy and epilepsy.

A spokesman for the Department of Health, Education and Welfare said the authorization level was unrealistically high in view of budget constraints, and would raise false expectations. He opposed extending the program to other developmental disabilities, on the grounds that they were under other programs and that too little had been done in the field of mental retardation to warrant broadening the focus of the programs. He proposed substituting consolidated project grants for formula grants under the program.

1970 Action. S 2846 was passed by the Senate April 13 by a 69-0 roll-call vote. The bill extended the programs for only three years but was not altered to meet administration objections. It authorized $100-million in fiscal 1971, $125-million in fiscal 1972 and $150-million in fiscal 1973 for grants to the states for planning, provision of services and construction and operation of facilities for the developmentally disabled. Additional funds were provided for university-affiliated facilities, demonstration programs and training programs. The bill established a National Advisory Council on Services and Facilities for the Developmentally Disabled. It retained the existing method of alloting grants.

A more modest version of the bill was passed by the House by a 338-0 roll-call vote July 30. The House bill provided $60-million for the primary grants in fiscal 1971, $85-million in fiscal 1972, and $105-million in fiscal 1973. The House committee report said it had rejected the administration proposal to substitute project grants for formula grants because the latter had "worked well in stimulating new state effort."

The conference report was cleared by voice votes of the House and Senate Oct. 13 and 14. The final bill contained most of the Senate provisions and provided authorizations of $60-million in fiscal 1971, $105-million in fiscal 1972 and $130-million in fiscal 1973 for services and facilities.

PROVISIONS

As cleared by Congress, S 2846 (PL 91-517):

• Amended the Mental Retardation Facilities Construction Act of 1963 to provide grants for planning, provision of services, and construction and operation of facilities for persons with developmental disabilities; authorized appropriations of $60-million in fiscal year 1971, $105-million in fiscal 1972 and $130 million in fiscal 1973 for these purposes.

• Defined developmental disability as a disability attributable to mental retardation, cerebral palsy, epilepsy or other neurological condition which originated before an individual reached age 18, which could be expected to continue indefinitely, and which constituted a substantial handicap to the individual.

• Entitled states to allotments (formula grants) from the sums appropriated based on population, need for services and facilities, and the financial need of the respective states, specified that the allotment for any state should not be less than $100,000 for any fiscal year.

• Authorized the secretary of health, education and welfare to use up to 10 per cent of authorized appropriations for project grants of national significance to assist the developmentally disabled.

• Established a National Advisory Council on Services and Facilities for the Developmentally Disabled to evaluate program effectiveness.

• Required states to assure that special financial and technical assistance is available for services and facilities for the developmentally disabled in poverty areas.

• Limited federal funds for any individual construction project to two-thirds of the costs of construction or 90 per cent for projects in urban or rural poverty areas.

• Limited the federal share of funds for planning, administration and services to 75 per cent of costs incurred by a state for fiscal years 1971 and 1972 and to 70 per cent for fiscal year 1973; limited the federal share to 90 per cent for fiscal years 1971-1972 in urban and rural areas and to 80 per cent in fiscal 1973 for the same areas.

• Established a new program of grants for administering and operating demonstration facilities and interdisciplinary training programs for personnel to serve the developmentally disabled and authorized for fiscal 1971, $15-million; fiscal 1972, $17-million; and fiscal 1973, $20-million.

• Authorized for construction of university-affiliated facilities: $20-million annually for fiscal 1971-1973.

• Permitted a state to consolidate grant funds functionally either within the state or by interstate pooling of allotments.

• Permitted a state which chose to provide services for developmental disabilities other than retardation to have its allotment increased proportionately.

Family Planning Services

Congress established an Office of Population Affairs in the Department of Health, Education and Welfare (HEW) to administer all HEW responsibilities in the area of family planning. The same bill (S 2108—PL 91-572) authorized $382-million for fiscal years 1971-73 for new and expanded family planning services and research programs. Additional family planning funds were provided through the budgets of the Office of Economic Opportunity and National Institutes of Health and other HEW offices.

Among the programs authorized under S 2108 were project grants to public and nonprofit agencies for voluntary family planning projects; formula grants to state health agencies for family planning services; and grants for personnel training, research and dissemination of information. The final bill did not include a Senate provision for grants for construction of research centers; the administration opposed it because such authority also existed under the Health Research Facilities program.

S 2108 was passed by the Senate July 14 by voice vote, authorizing $991-million over five years. As passed by the House Nov. 16 by a 298-32 roll-call vote, the bill provided $267-million over three years. The final version contained the same provisions and authorizations as the House bill except that it contained additional funds for the family planning services and population research programs. The bill was cleared by the House Dec. 8 and the Senate Dec. 10 by voice votes.

PROVISIONS

As enacted, S 2108 (PL 91-572):

• Established an Office of Population Affairs in the Department of Health, Education and Welfare (HEW) to administer all HEW responsibilities in the area of population and family planning.

• Required the HEW secretary to report to Congress within six months of enactment a five-year plan for extension of family planning services to all persons desiring them, for research programs and for training the necessary manpower, and to submit periodic reports thereafter showing progress under the plan.

• Provided that none of the funds appropriated could be used in programs where abortion was a method of family planning.

• Authorized project grants to public agencies and nonprofit organizations and institutions to assist in the establishment and operation of voluntary family planning projects.

• Authorized $30-million in fiscal 1971 and increased authorizations by $30-million a year up to fiscal 1973 for project grants.

• Authorized formula grants to state health agencies, allocated according to state population and financial need, to assist in providing family planning services, provided that a state plan for comprehensive family planning services was approved by the HEW secretary.

• Authorized $10-million in fiscal 1971 and increased authorizations by $5-million a year up to fiscal 1973 for formula grants.

• Authorized $2-million in fiscal 1971 and increased authorizations by $1-million a year up to fiscal 1973 to train personnel necessary to provide family planning services.

• Established a program of grants to promote research in fields related to family planning, authorized appropriations of $35-million in fiscal 1971, $50-million in fiscal 1972 and $65-million in fiscal 1973.

• Authorized project grants and contracts with public agencies and nonprofit organizations to assist in making available family planning information and educational materials to all persons desiring them; authorized appropriations of $750,000 in fiscal 1971, and increased authorizations by $250,000 a year up to fiscal 1973 to provide family planning and population growth information.

• Provided that low-income families would have priority in receiving cost-free family planning services.

Communicable Diseases

Congress cleared an administration-opposed bill authorizing a two-year program of grants to states for programs for communicable disease control and vaccination programs. The bill (S 2264—PL 91-464) said the grants were to be used to control tuberculosis, venereal disease, rubella, measles, poliomyelitis, diphtheria, tetanus, whooping cough and RH disease. S 2264 authorized $75-million in fiscal 1971 and $90-million in fiscal 1972.

During hearings on the proposal an administration spokesman opposed new categorical grants because funds for disease control were already covered by existing formula and project grant authorizations. He said another program would result in "overlapping and duplicatory grant authorizations and an impairment of effective health planning." S 2264 was designed to continue the programs of the Vaccination Assistance Act of 1962 (PL 87-868) which the Johnson administration had let lapse in 1968. *(Congress and the Nation, Vol. I, p. 1145)*

S 2264 was passed by the Senate Oct. 20, 1969, by voice vote and by the House Sept. 10, 1970, by a 313-1 roll-call vote.

Treatment For Alcoholism

One of several congressional efforts to aid alcoholics was a bill establishing a National Institute on Alcohol Abuse and Alcoholism in the National Institute of Mental Health. The bill (S 3835—PL 91-616) authorized $180-million for formula grants and $120-million for project grants to the states for programs for prevention and treatment of alcoholism in fiscal 1971-73.

Population Commission

Congress agreed to the request in President Nixon's 1969 population control message for establishment of a Commission on Population Growth and the American Future.

The bill (S 2701—PL 91-213) provided that the commission be composed of not more than 20 members, including one Republican and one Democrat each from the Senate and House. All members were to be appointed by the President.

S 2701 provided that the commission was to conduct an inquiry into (a) the probable course of U.S. population growth and internal migration; (b) government resources required to deal with population growth; (c) the effect of population growth on government activities; (d) the impact of population growth on environmental pollution and depletion of natural resources; and (e) means appropriate to American ethical values and principles by which the United States could achieve a population level suited to its resources.

S 2701 was passed by the Senate Sept. 29, 1969, by voice vote and by the House Feb. 18, 1970, by a 371-13 roll-call vote. As signed into law March 16, the final version was the same as the House bill. It had provided a somewhat broader mandate for the commission than had the Senate. John D. Rockefeller III was named chairman of the commission.

During testimony on the proposal an administration spokesman had objected to the formula grants and to the level of authorizations which he said were unrealistically high.

Congress, in the Community Mental Health Centers Amendments of 1970 (PL 91-211), also substantially raised authorizations for construction of facilities for the treatment of alcoholics. *(Construction authorizations, p. 555)*

S 835 was passed by the Senate Aug. 10 by voice vote and by the House Dec. 18 with minor amendments by voice vote. It was cleared by the Senate Dec. 19.

Provisions. As cleared by Congress, S 3835 (PL 91-616):

• Established a National Institute on Alcohol Abuse and Alcoholism in the National Institute of Mental Health.

• Required the secretary of health, education and welfare (HEW) to submit to Congress one year after enactment a report on the health consequences of alcohol consumption and recommendations for legislative and administrative action.

• Provided that no person may be denied or deprived of federal civilian employment solely on the basis of prior alcohol abuse and alcoholism.

• Provided that any individual who habitually uses intoxicating beverages to excess may not be employed in the Civil Service.

• Authorized formula grants totaling $180-million over a three-year period, beginning with $40-million in fiscal 1971, to help states develop and administer programs for the prevention of alcoholism.

• Authorized project grants totaling $120-million over a three-year period, beginning with $30-million in fiscal 1971, to states for prevention and treatment of alcoholism.

• Established an independent 15-member National Advisory Council on Alcohol Abuse and Alcoholism.

Family Medical Practice

President Nixon Dec. 24 pocket vetoed a bill (S 3418) authorizing $225-million for fiscal years 1971-73 for grants to hospitals and medical schools to provide departmental training to relieve a shortage of doctors in general practice. The secretary of health, education and welfare was authorized to appoint a 12-member Advisory Council on Family Medicine to consider application for grants.

During congressional consideration of the proposal a number of witnesses complained of the increasing shortage of doctors in general practice. The percentage of doctors in family practice had dropped from three out of four in 1931 to one out of five in 1967. The bill was supported by the American Medical Association but opposed by administration witnesses.

S 3418 was vetoed by the President on the grounds that "it simply continues the traditional approach of adding more programs to the almost unmanageable current structure of federal government health efforts." He said there were already "at least four" federal programs "that provide funds which can be used to promote the training of family medicine practitioners."

S 3418 was pocket vetoed during the six-day Christmas recess. Congressional Democrats charged that Nixon had misused the pocket veto because the Constitution's provision for pocket vetoes was intended to apply to permanent adjournment of Congress rather than brief recesses. A challenge to the veto was still in the courts when the first Nixon administration ended. *(Details, chapter on Congress, 1970 chronology)*

S 3418 had been passed by the Senate Sept. 14 by a 64-1 roll-call vote and by the House Dec. 1 by a 347-1 roll call.

Regional Medical Programs

Congress extended in one bill (HR 17570—PL 91-515) three expiring health programs which involved authorizations for regional medical programs, comprehensive health planning and services projects, and health research and development. The programs were extended for three years, through fiscal 1973.

Title I of HR 17570 extended the Heart Disease, Cancer and Stroke Amendments of 1965. The program had been set up to encourage localities to plan and establish regional medical programs for a specialized attack on those diseases. The programs were intended to serve as a framework for dissemination of the most advanced medical knowledge throughout the country. *(Congress and the Nation, Vol. II, p. 667, 699)*

The 1970 bill expanded the program to specifically include kidney disease and established a 20-member National Advisory Council on Regional Medical Programs.

Title II of HR 17570 authorized extension of programs for comprehensive health planning and services and for health research and development. These programs had been initiated by the Comprehensive Health Planning and Public Health Services Amendments of 1966 (PL 89-749). That act, known as the Partnership for Health, had amended the Public Health Service Act of 1944 to provide new authority to plan for public health services on a state- and area-wide basis. The planning was designed to identify imminent and pressing public health problems and establish priorities for health services. *(Congress and the Nation, Vol. II, p. 680, 690)*

The administration had requested a conglomerate bill "in order to improve the organization and delivery of health services and permit experimentation aimed at developing an integrated, comprehensive, consumer-oriented health care system."

Title I and Title II were originally passed by the House as two separate bills (HR 17570, HR 18110) Aug. 11 and 12. The votes were 365-0 and 376-1. The Senate combined the programs and passed HR 17570, providing for a five-year extension Sept. 9 by a 56-1 roll-call vote. The conference report, extending the programs for three years, was cleared by voice votes Oct. 13 and 14.

PROVISIONS

As signed into law Oct. 30, HR 17570 (PL 91-515):

Title I—Heart Disease, Cancer, Stroke and Kidney Disease Amendments of 1970:

• Authorized appropriations of $125-million in fiscal 1971, $150-million in fiscal 1972 and $250-million in fiscal 1973 for regional medical program grants for training, prevention, diagnosis, treatment and rehabilitation relating to heart disease, cancer, stroke, kidney disease or other related diseases.

• Provided that a maximum of $15-million of the amount appropriated in fiscal year 1971 be available for kidney disease activities.

• Authorized the secretary of health, education and welfare (HEW) to appoint a 20-member National Advisory Council on Regional Medical Programs.

• Authorized the secretary to make grants for use in two or more regional medical programs.

Title II—Amendments to Title III Public Health Service Act of 1944 (PL 78-410):

• Directed the HEW secretary to submit to Congress by Sept. 30, 1971, a systems analysis of national health care plans.

• Authorized appropriations of $71-million in fiscal year 1971, $82-million in fiscal 1972 and $94-million in fiscal 1973 for research and demonstrations relating to health facilities and services.

• Directed the secretary to conduct a study of each legislative proposal introduced during the 91st Congress which proposed to establish a national health insurance plan; authorized not less than $2-million of the above appropriation for fiscal year 1971 for this purpose.

• Authorized appropriations of $15-million in fiscal year 1971, $20-million in fiscal 1972 and $25-million in fiscal 1973 for national health surveys and studies.

• Authorized appropriations of $15-million in fiscal year 1970, $15-million in fiscal 1971, $17-million in fiscal 1972 and $20-million in fiscal 1973 for grants to states for comprehensive state health planning.

• Authorized appropriations of $15-million in fiscal year 1970, $20-million in fiscal 1971, $30-million in fiscal 1972, and $40-million in fiscal 1973 for project grants for area-wide health planning.

• Authorized appropriations of $7.5-million in fiscal year 1970, $8-million in fiscal 1971, $10-million in fiscal 1972 and $12-million in fiscal 1973 for grants for training, studies and demonstration projects to improve comprehensive health planning.

• Authorized appropriations of $100-million in fiscal year 1970, $130-million in fiscal 1971, $145-million in fiscal 1972 and $165-million in fiscal 1973 for formula grants for comprehensive public health services.

• Authorized appropriations of $109.5-million in fiscal year 1971, $135-million in fiscal 1972 and $157-million in fiscal 1973 for project grants for health services development.

• Simplified administration of projects funded under more than one statute administered by the HEW Department.

• Directed the secretary of HEW to report to Congress by Jan. 1 each year on the progress of comprehensive health activities.

• Created a National Advisory Council on Health Planning Programs to emphasize coordination of partnership for health programs with regional medical programs.

Health Training Aid

Congress extended the Allied Health Professions Personnel Training Act of 1966 (PL 89-751) for three years, through fiscal 1973. The administration had requested a one-year extension to bring the program's expiration date in line with that of the other health manpower authorizations.

PL 89-751 was designed to meet an urgent need for technical personnel to assist doctors, dentists and other health professionals. It included grants to allied health training institutions for construction, traineeships and improvement of health curriculums. It also authorized grants for nursing scholarships, but those provisions, extended in 1968, were not to expire until 1971. *(Congress and the Nation, Vol. II, p. 681, 697)*

The 1970 extension (S 3586—PL 91-519) was passed by the Senate July 13 by voice vote and by the House July 30 by a 343-1 roll-call vote. The conference report was cleared by voice votes of the House and Senate Oct. 13 and 14.

Provisions. As signed into law, S 3586 (PL 91-519):

• Authorized appropriations of $750,000 in fiscal year 1971, $1-million in fiscal 1972 and $1.25-million in fiscal 1973 for grants and contracts to assist individuals in need who have potential for education or training in the allied health professions.

• Authorized appropriations of $4-million in fiscal year 1971, $5-million in fiscal 1972 and $6-million in fiscal 1973 for scholarships in the allied health care field.

• Authorized $2-million in fiscal year 1971, $4-million in fiscal 1972 and $6-million in fiscal 1973 to assist in the operation of work-study programs for individuals in the allied health professions.

• Authorized $3.5-million in fiscal year 1971, $5-million in fiscal 1972 and $10-million in 1973 for allied health institutions to establish student loan funds.

• Authorized appropriations of $20-million in fiscal year 1971, $30-million in fiscal 1972 and $40-million in

fiscal 1973 to construct teaching facilities for allied health professions personnel.

• Authorized appropriations of $15-million in fiscal 1971, $15-million in fiscal 1972 and $15-million in fiscal 1973 for basic improvement grants for training for allied health professions.

• Authorized appropriations of $15-million in fiscal year 1971, $20-million in fiscal 1972 and $30-million in fiscal 1973 for special improvement grants to assist training centers for allied health professions.

• Authorized appropriations of $10-million in fiscal year 1971, $20-million in fiscal 1972 and $30-million in fiscal 1973 for special projects related to training allied health personnel.

• Authorized appropriations of $8-million in fiscal year 1971, $10-million in fiscal 1972 and $12-million in fiscal 1973 for advanced training of allied health professions personnel.

• Authorized special assistance to new schools of medicine, dentistry, osteopathy, pharmacy, optometry, veterinary medicine and podiatry.

• Provided that funds appropriated under section 772 of the Public Health Service Act for fiscal year 1971 remain available until expended or until June 30, 1972, for emergency grants to medical and dental schools in extreme financial distress.

Medical Libraries

Congress extended the Medical Library Assistance Act of 1965 (PL 89-291) for three years, through fiscal 1973. The original act had authorized a four-year program of matching grants to build medical library facilities and a five-year program of grants to expand medical library services, establish regional medical libraries and provide other assistance. *(Congress and the Nation, Vol. II, p. 673)*

The 1970 extension (HR 11702—PL 91-212) was passed by the House July 10, 1969, by a 370-3 roll-call vote and by the Senate Oct. 20 by voice vote. The House had continued authorizations at the existing level. The Senate increased authorizations, and the conference report was a compromise between the two. It was adopted by voice votes of the Senate and House Feb. 25 and 26, 1970.

Provisions. As cleared by Congress, HR 11702 (PL 91-212):

• Extended through fiscal 1973 grant assistance programs to public or private nonprofit agencies or institutions for medical library construction, providing $11-million for fiscal 1971, $12-million for fiscal 1972 and $13-million for fiscal 1973.

• Extended through fiscal 1973 grant assistance to individuals and institutions supporting training for service and research careers in medical library science and related fields, authorizing $1.5-million for fiscal 1971, $1.75-million for fiscal 1972 and $2-million for fiscal 1973.

• Extended through fiscal 1973 assistance to improve resources of medical libraries, authorizing $3.5-million for fiscal 1971, $4-million the following year, and $4.5-million for fiscal 1973.

• Extended through fiscal 1973 part of the Public Health Service Act providing grant assistance to develop a national system of regional medical libraries, authorizing $3-million the first year, $3.25-million the second, and $3.5-million for fiscal 1973.

● Allowed the secretary of health, education and welfare to make exceptions to the three-year limit on assistance for any publication in a library program.

● Retained law permitting funds appropriated for any purpose to remain available for only one year and beyond the year appropriated.

● Authorized the secretary to transfer funds from future appropriations for programs of medical library assistance to other medical library assistance programs, with certain limitations.

Other Bills

Among the large quantity of health legislation cleared in 1970 were these noncontroversial bills:

PUBLIC HEALTH SCHOOLS. The President March 12 signed a bill (S 2809—PL 91-208) extending the three existing grant programs for public health training for three years, through fiscal 1973. S 2809 authorized $36-million for formula grants to schools of public health, $45-million for project grants for graduate training in public health and $48-million for traineeships for professional public health personnel. *(Congress and the Nation, Vol. I, p. 1138)*

MIGRATORY WORKERS HEALTH. The President March 12 signed a bill (HR 14733—PL 91-209) extending the program of health services for domestic migrant agricultural workers for three years, through fiscal 1973. The bill provided $75-million for grants to public agencies and nonprofit groups to improve health conditions for migrants. *(Congress and the Nation, Vol. I, p. 1145)*

LEAD PAINT POISONING. Congress Dec. 31 cleared a bill (HR 19172—PL 91-695) authorizing $30-million over fiscal years 1971-73 to eliminate the causes and incidence of lead-based paint poisoning. The bill authorized: $5.01-million for the secretary of housing and urban development (HUD) to determine the extent of lead paint poisoning and methods by which the paint could be removed from residential housing; $15-million for grants to local governments to eliminate lead based paint hazards; and $9.99-million to assist local governments to detect and treat lead paint poisoning.

NATIONAL HEALTH SERVICE CORPS. President Nixon Dec. 31 signed a bill (S 4106—PL 91-623) authorizing the secretary of health, education and welfare (HEW) to assign medical and other health personnel of the Public Health Services to communities where medical personnel and services were inadequate to meet the residents' needs. The bill authorized $60-million for the program for fiscal 1971 through 1973.

FEDERAL HEALTH INSURANCE. President Nixon Sept. 25 signed into law a bill (HR 16968—PL 91-418) providing that the federal government pay an increased portion of the cost of health insurance for federal employees and annuitants.

Provisions. As cleared by Congress, HR 16968:

● Changed the government contribution from a fixed dollar amount to 40 per cent of the average cost of health insurance programs covering federal employees and their dependents, beginning Jan. 1, 1971.

● Extended the increased contribution to eligible retired federal employees.

Subcommittee Chairmen, 1971-72

Considerable health legislation was passed during 1971-72. Part of the explanation for the volume of health legislation cleared and the active health orientation of the Congress was due to two new subcommittee chairmen. They were Paul G. Rogers (D Fla.), chairman of the House Interstate and Foreign Commerce Subcommittee on Public Health and the Environment, and Edward M. Kennedy (D Mass.), chairman of the Senate Labor and Public Welfare Subcommittee on Health. Both men became chairmen of their subcommittees at the beginning of the 92nd Congress.

Kennedy and Rogers rapidly became "Mr. Health" in their respective chambers. They operated as active subcommittee chairmen by holding a number of hearings, reporting a great many bills to their full committees and vigorously fighting for their bills during floor debate.

Their high marks for getting health legislation through Congress also resulted from the fact that their expertise in health matters was widely accepted by colleagues on the full committees. In addition, health legislation often passed the House or Senate in a form similar to which it had been reported by a committee. Health bills supported by Rogers and Kennedy were not usually picked apart by other representatives or senators during floor debate.

Kennedy and Rogers operated in a dissimilar manner. With the exception of comprehensive legislation such as health maintenance organization bills, Kennedy preferred shorter hearings to spotlight the problems and then his subcommittee quickly prepared a bill for consideration by the full Labor and Public Welfare Committee.

Rogers favored longer, more in-depth hearings on health bills. The House subcommittee usually spent more time considering measures to report to the full Interstate and Foreign Commerce Committee. The Senate subcommittee was able to work more quickly because it had a much larger full-time professional staff. Rogers operated his subcommittee out of his office in the Rayburn House Office Building and his personal staff served double duty as his subcommittee staff. In some cases, the House subcommittee also used the services of the personal staffs of other subcommittee members.

The Senate also passed more health bills than the House because it was easier for Kennedy to have health legislation scheduled for floor action than it was for Rogers.

Rogers had to go through the powerful House Rules Committee to get a bill scheduled for floor debate. Toward the end of the second session, William M. Colmer (D Miss.), chairman of the Rules Committee, used his influence to prevent rules from being granted on health bills.

When a bill was not granted a rule, it could still be considered under suspension of the rules. But the suspension procedure requires a two-thirds majority vote, rather than a simple majority for passage.

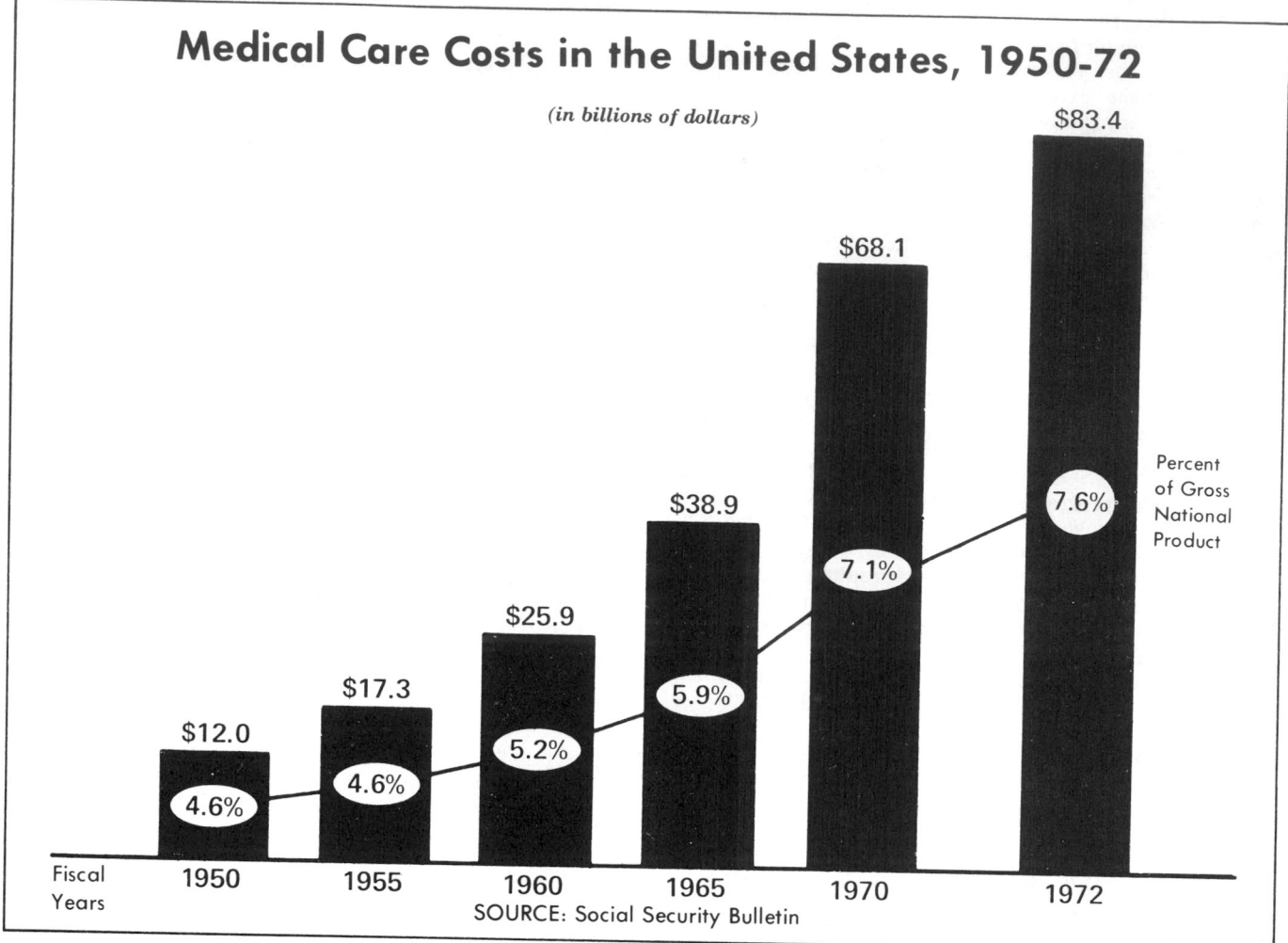

Medical Care Costs in the United States, 1950-72

(in billions of dollars)

SOURCE: Social Security Bulletin

Background. The federal government began contributing to its employees' health insurance programs in 1960 under legislation which established a fixed dollar limit on the government share. This equaled 38 per cent of the cost. Although increased in 1966, the fixed contribution equaled only 24 per cent of the average insurance cost in 1970. The administration favored an increase to 38 per cent of the insurance cost.

1971

National Health Insurance

The idea of national health insurance, once widely condemned as "socialized medicine," gained substantial respectability during the first Nixon administration. Interest in some sort of broad health insurance grew at a rate that workers in the long fight to enact medical care for the aging only a few years before did not think possible.

The reason for the growing acceptability of the concept was the soaring cost of medical care. Citizens were paying twice what they spent for health care in 1960,

and medical bills for Americans rose 12 per cent between June 1969 and July 1970.

Concern over health costs led to introduction of a variety of insurance proposals and to comprehensive hearings by the House Ways and Means Committee and the Health Subcommittee of the Senate Labor and Public Welfare Committee in 1971. Any legislation establishing a national health insurance program must start in the Ways and Means Committee, which has responsibility for originating all revenue-raising measures. The committee did not act on any of the complex proposals during the 92nd Congress.

In 1972 the Senate passed one feature of an administration health proposal—a bill for the establishment of health maintenance organizations to encourage prepaid comprehensive health care programs—but the bill died at the end of the 92nd Congress.

BACKGROUND

A report, Basic Facts on the Health Industry, prepared by the Ways and Means Committee in June 1971, discussed four important problems of the U.S. health system. The problems cited in the report showed why national health insurance was a key concern of many Americans and a political issue for the administration and Congress:

Manpower and Facilities. The supply of physicians increased faster than the population, but the number directly engaged in patient care did not increase relatively. More physicians became employed in research and administration.

Physicians located in metropolitan areas, particularly near university medical centers and in the suburbs, and many rural and inner-city areas had no physicians or inadequate numbers. Increasing specialization among new medical graduates sharply reduced the supply of physicians in general and family practice. The demand for general practice physicians exceeded the supply while the reverse often was true for specialists.

Organization and Delivery of Services. The life expectancy and infant mortality rates of the United States lagged behind many other Western nations. In 1967, the United States ranked 18th in male life expectancy, 11th for females, and 14th in infant mortality.

Within the United States, a wide disparity existed in the medical care received by different population groups. The poor and non-white groups experienced considerably higher rates of illness, disability and infant and maternal deaths, and received less medical care than other groups.

The organization of the U.S. health system was extremely fragmented. Medical care was rendered primarily by private physicians practicing alone or in small partnerships. Many hospitals were operated by voluntary organizations or local governments, and patients were usually placed in the hospital and treated there by private physicians. Other medical goods and services were supplied by independent firms. Physician and hospital fees were usually paid for separately, directly by the patient or by a third party such as an insurance company.

The committee summarized: "There is considerable evidence that these methods of organizing and delivering health services have resulted in considerable inefficiency in the delivery of services, fragmentation and poor quality of care, overuse of certain services and failure to use appropriate facilities. The system of delivering care is sometimes described as a non-system."

Financial Access to Medical Insurance. Eighty per cent of the population under age 65 had some insurance protection against health care costs. Most of the insurance was provided as a fringe benefit at places of employment.

Individuals not protected by employment-related insurance, including the self-employed and unemployed, can obtain insurance only by purchasing an individual policy. The Ways and Means Committee stated: "These policies are typically expensive because they pay relatively little in benefits compared to their premium cost."

The committee added: "For those with private health insurance, the scope and type of protection against hospital care costs and inhospital surgical and medical services—such as home and office visits, hospital outpatient care and diagnostic services—is relatively low. As a result, the insurance encourages use of expensive inpatient hospital care when ambulatory care would be more economical and suitable...."

The poor had little health insurance protection and the unemployed poor without access to employment-related health insurance rely on government medical care programs.

1971 PROPOSALS

Administration Plan. President Nixon in a special Feb. 18 message on health announced a "comprehensive national health insurance program...in which the public and private sectors would join in a new partnership to provide adequate health insurance for the American people."

The administration program had three main parts— a National Health Insurance Standards Act to require employers to provide basic health insurance coverage; a federal Family Health Insurance Plan to replace the Medicaid program for the poor and near-poor with children; and a proposal to encourage establishment of Health Maintenance Organizations (HMOs) which provided for prepaid comprehensive health care.

The proposed National Health Insurance Standards Act was designed to meet the failure of many current private insurance plans to cover either catastrophic illness costs or office visits. The bill (S 1632, HR 7741) required all employers to provide a minimum standard of health insurance for employees and dependents. For the first two and one-half years, the maximum premium for the employee would be 35 per cent of the total, dropping to 25 per cent. Coverage would include hospital services, doctor bills for treatment in and out of the hospital, well-baby care including immunizations, and laboratory costs. Each family member would have at least $50,000 worth of coverage.

The President proposed that the Family Health Insurance Plan replace the existing Social Security-financed Medicaid program for poor and near-poor welfare recipients under the Aid to Families with Dependent Children (ADFC) program. Beneficiaries under the three other relief programs (aid to the needy blind, aged and disabled) would continue to receive Medicaid. *(Further discussion of Medicaid, welfare chapter p. 605)*

Whereas the Medicaid program was administered on a joint federal-state basis with benefits varying widely from state to state, the new plan would be all-federal, providing health insurance to all poor families with children headed by self-employed or unemployed persons whose income fell below a certain level. The poorest families would pay no charges; other families would pay a graduated percentage of the premium.

These two parts of the administration program were introduced as the National Health Insurance Partnership Act by Sen. Wallace F. Bennett (R Utah) in the Senate (S 1623) and by John W. Byrnes (R Wis.) in the House (HR 7741).

In calling for action on the third part of his program, encouragement of Health Maintenance Organizations (HMOs) the President said "such organizations provide a strong financial incentive for better preventive care and for greater efficiency." He asked for a new $23-million program of planning grants to aid potential sponsors, a $300-million federal loan guarantee program to enable sponsors to construct facilities and sustain initial operating deficits; and a $22-million program of grants and loans to help locate HMOs in medically underserved areas. This was the one part of the President's program to see any congressional action. A bipartisan bill (S 3327) was passed by the Senate in 1972. *(1972 chronology, p. 570)*

Kennedy-Griffiths Plan. The other major program proposed in 1971 was the Health Security Act, intro-

(Continued on p. 565)

Comparison of Administration and Kennedy-Griffiths Plans

	National Health Insurance Partnership	Health Security Act
CONCEPT	Requires employer to provide private insurance for employees and their families. Provides federal family health insurance for low-income families with children.	Establishes national health insurance providing broad benefits administered by federal government and financed by payroll taxes and federal general revenues.
COVERAGE	Employees and their families covered under mandatory employment-related insurance. Special group plans for small employers and self-employed. Low-income families covered by federal health insurance.	Extends to all U.S. residents.
BENEFITS	Under employer plan, broad benefits with cost sharing of $100 annual deductible per person and 25 per cent of the balance. Under family plan, broad benefits with some cost sharing depending on annual income. No cost sharing for lowest income group.	Broad benefits with no cost sharing. Specific limitations on psychiatric, nursing home, dental services and prescription drugs.
ADMINISTRATION	Employer plan administered by private insurance carriers under federal supervision. Family plan administered by Department of Health, Education and Welfare.	Program administered totally by federal government. A special board in the Department of HEW operates program through regional and local offices.
OTHER PROGRAMS	Medicare would continue. Medicaid would be limited to the aged, blind and disabled.	Medicare would be abolished. Medicaid would not pay for services covered under national health plan.
FINANCING	Employer plan financed by employer-employee premium payments. Employer pays 75 per cent of cost. Administration bill in House includes federal subsidy payments for maximum of 10 employees to help small employers with high premium payments. Administration bill in Senate does not include subsidy. Family plan financed partially by premiums paid by enrollees and graduated by income class. No premiums paid by lowest class. Balance of cost paid from federal general revenues.	Taxes on payrolls, self-employed persons, unearned income. Payments from federal general revenues. The tax rates would be 1 per cent on employee wages and unearned income, 3.5 per cent for employers, 2.5 per cent for self-employed. Federal general revenues would equal total receipts from taxes. The first $15,000 of earnings and income of individuals and the total payroll of employers would be subject to taxation.
STANDARDS	Physician and hospital standards are the same as under Medicare. The bill would establish Professional Standards Review Organizations to review quality of services provided and payments claimed by professionals.	Physician and hospital standards are the same as under Medicare. Nursing homes must be affiliated with hospitals. Physicians must meet national standards. All providers' records subject to review by regional office.
PROFESSIONAL FEES	Payments to hospitals, physicians and other health care personnel based upon "reasonable charges" for services policy established under Medicare. Under employment-related insurance, physicians could make additional charges.	Hospitals and nursing homes would receive annual predetermined budget based on reasonable cost. Physicians, dentists and other professionals would get fees for service based on fee schedules or per capita payments or go on salary.
ESTIMATED COST	The additional cost for federal taxpayers of the plan in fiscal 1974 was estimated to be $3-billion for the House bill which includes the federal subsidy for small employers. Cost of the Senate bill estimated at $2.6-billion.	The additional cost for federal taxpayers of the plan in fiscal 1974 was estimated to be $59.4-billion. (Of the $67.2-billion spent for health and medical care in fiscal 1970, $44.3-billion came from private sources.)

SOURCE: Analysis of Health Insurance Proposals Introduced in the 92nd Congress prepared by the Department of Health, Education and Welfare and printed for the use of the Ways and Means Committee, August 1971.

(Continued from p. 563)

duced in the Senate as S 3 by Sen. Edward M. Kennedy (D Mass.) and in the House by Rep. Martha W. Griffiths (D Mich.) as HR 22. This plan proposed a comprehensive national health insurance system for all Americans financed partially from payroll taxes (3.5 per cent on employers and 1 per cent on employees) and partly from general revenues. The estimated federal cost was $68-billion. Kennedy said the crucial difference between his plan and the current system was "that the major part of the funds will flow through the federal government instead of through the private insurance industry."

The Kennedy-Griffiths plan had no deductibles and covered a broad range of services. There were limitations on psychiatric, nursing home and dental services. Physicians and other professionals would be salaried or get fees based on schedules or per capita payments. Hospitals and nursing homes would receive annual predetermined funding based on reasonable cost. The program would be federally administered and physicians and hospitals would meet national standards.

AMA, Insurance Industry Plans. In addition to the administration and Kennedy-Griffiths plans, Congress in 1971 also heard testimony on alternative programs proposed by the American Medical Association (AMA) and the health insurance industry.

The AMA proposal, known as Medicredit, was introduced in the Senate as S 987 by Sen. Clifford P. Hansen (R Wyo) and in the House as HR 4960 by Rep. Richard Fulton (D Tenn.). It provided income tax credits for the purchase of private health insurance on a sliding scale according to income level and provided for federally subsidized health insurance or group practice membership payments for low-income persons.

The plan proposed by the Health Insurance Association of America, the National Healthcare Act of 1971, was introduced in the Senate as S 1490 by Sen. Thomas J. McIntyre (D N.H.) and in the House as HR 4349 by Rep. Omar Burleson (D Texas).

It proposed establishment of federal standards for health benefits that would be provided by private insurance companies. It called for establishment of a system of health insurance in which employed individuals would have insurance provided through joint employer-employee contribution programs with government subsidies supporting state-sponsored insurance pools for the poor, the near-poor and substandard health risks.

HEARINGS ON INSURANCE

The Senate Finance Committee held hearings on the rival health insurance proposals during April, and the House Ways and Means Committee heard similar testimony in October and November. The administration program received support from a number of GOP members of Congress, but no substantial outside support because representatives of the medical profession and health insurance industry who might have backed it worked for approval of their own plans instead.

The Kennedy-Griffiths proposal had strong backing from organized labor, including the United Auto Workers and AFL-CIO.

During the hearings and other 1971 discussion of the health insurance proposals, two major areas of disagreement between the Kennedy-Griffiths and other programs continually appeared. These were the role of government in a national health insurance program and the capacity of the private health insurance industry to provide adequate health care coverage.

Role of Government. President Nixon said his program would build on the strengths of the existing health care system and that Kennedy's plan would tear the system apart.

The President told a meeting of the House of Delegates of the American Medical Association in June 1971: "When the government pays all the bills for health care, then the government becomes the only party with a strong interest in restraining costs. And this inevitably means that government officials must approve hospital budgets, set fee schedules and take other steps that would eventually lead to the complete federal domination of our medical system.

"Rather than freeing the doctor so that he can do more to help his patients, nationalized health insurance would burden him with the dead weight of more bureaucracy, more forms and more red tape.... Rather than encouraging more responsibility at the local level, it would concentrate more responsibility in Washington."

Kennedy said that the health crisis could not be met by modest patches and minor reforms such as the administration had proposed. He said that a major reform of the national health system was necessary and comprehensive legislation was needed.

Kennedy told the House Ways and Means Committee on Nov. 18: "Calls for health care as a right remain empty rhetoric unless the need for completely redesigning our ideas and methods concerning the organization and delivery of personal health services is recognized as the essential handmaiden of financing reforms.... If we do not harness the massive flow of public funding of medical care to the effort to refashion the delivery system, we will have abdicated our public responsibility....

"Only the leverage generated by the Health Security Act would effectively move our fragmented, disorganized health care services into organized systems of health care, where rational evaluation, planning and budgeting can occur."

Private Health Insurance Industry. President Nixon stated that his plan was one in which the public and private sectors would form a partnership to provide adequate health insurance for all Americans. Kennedy charged that the administration's plan relied too heavily upon the private insurance industry.

President Nixon said in his health message to Congress: "I believe that our government and our people, business and labor, the insurance industry and the health profession can work together in a national partnership to achieve our health objectives. I do not believe that the achievement of these objectives requires the nationalization of our health insurance industry.

"There simply is no need to eliminate an entire segment of our private economy and at the same time add a multi billion-dollar responsiblity to the federal budget. Such a step should not be taken unless all other steps have failed.

"Such action would be dangerous. It would deny the people the right to choose how they will pay for their health care. It would remove competition from the insurance system—and with it an incentive to experiment and innovate."

Kennedy told the Ways and Means Committee: "Both the history and current practices in this (insurance) industry, as well as the basic incentives and principles of operation of the industry, show that they cannot carry out this role.

"They can only serve as high overhead salesmen and money changers with no effective leverage over the providers. Indeed, even worse, while taking their profits and overhead, they serve as a misplaced buffer between the providers and the people which prevents the providers from feeling the full force of the people's outrage.

"I do not believe we can afford the health insurance industry in this country—nor do I believe we have any responsibility to maintain it at the public's expense now that its failure is apparent."

Cancer Research

Congress substantially expanded the cancer research program at the National Institutes of Health (NIH). It passed an administration-backed bill (S 1828—PL 92-218) authorizing $1.59-billion over three years to advance the national effort to find a cure for cancer.

During the legislative process, S 1828 became involved in a major controversy over whether the expanded research effort should be located within NIH or within an independent agency whose director reported directly to the President. The Senate passed a bill establishing an independent agency. During subsequent testimony before the House, the independent agency was supported by cancer research specialists. It was opposed by other biomedical researchers who cautioned that a cure for cancer could not be found through crash research and opposed isolation of the research effort.

The version of S 1828 passed by the House responded to this view. The research program remained within NIH although the National Cancer Institute budget was to be sent directly to the President. This was the provision which was contained in the final version; the entire final version of S 1828 was very close to the House-passed bill.

Background. The Senate April 27, 1970, adopted a resolution (S Res 376) creating a National Panel of Consultants on the Conquest of Cancer. The panel prepared a report which was released in December 1970.

The panel of 13 scientists and 13 laymen called for the establishment of an independent government agency, the National Cancer Authority, to coordinate a "national crusade" against cancer, the "number one health concern of the American people" and, after cardiovascular diseases, the second greatest killer.

The panel estimated that 50 million Americans alive in 1970 would develop cancer and 35 million would die of the disease if methods for treatment and prevention were not developed.

The amount spent on cancer research was "grossly inadequate," the report said. It recommended an appropriation for funding new programs of about $400-million in fiscal 1972 and increasing by $100-million to $150-million in subsequent years to a $1-billion level in 1976.

The National Cancer Institute within NIH received $182-million in federal funds in 1969 for cancer programs, and the American Cancer Society, a private group, spent $24-million a year for cancer research.

The National Cancer Institute "has done excellent work," the consultants said, but its research effort was fragmented and uncoordinated.

The panel suggested that all functions, personnel, facilities, appropriations, programs and authorities of the Institute be transferred to the National Cancer Authority which would coordinate research, assist clinics, disburse grants and develop cancer information storage and retrieval banks.

The report explained that the incidence of cancer was increasing, partly due to cigarette smoking, but that the cure rate was gradually improving. In 1930, one case in five was effectively treated; in 1970 one case in three was cured.

The new program should focus on the causes and cures of cancer rather than patient care, the report said.

Among the areas of special promise for cancer prevention and cure, the consultants listed: chemical, physical and other environmental factors, viruses, cell and tumor biology, radiotherapy and surgery.

Citing reasons for a stepped-up cancer research program, the report estimated that direct losses for hospitalization and medical care, coupled with losses of productivity and earning power, were in the range of $10-billion to $15-billion a year.

"In spite of these appalling facts, the 1969 allocations in our national budget, per citizen, were $410 for national defense and only 89 cents for cancer research," the panel said.

President Nixon in his 1971 State of the Union message announced that he would ask for an appropriation of an extra $100-million "to launch an intensive campaign to find a cure for cancer." The President said he would request "whatever additional funds can effectively be used." The $100-million was included in the fiscal 1971 second supplemental appropriations bill (PL 92-18).

1971 ACTION

Senate Action. The Senate Labor and Public Welfare Subcommittee on Health in March and June 1971 held extensive hearings on proposals that grew out of the 1970 panel report. Witnesses who agreed with the report's recommendation for an independent National Cancer Authority argued that the time had come when a coordinated, special assault on cancer through a new administrative design might have dramatic impact.

Witnesses from the medical profession who wished to keep cancer research within the National Cancer Institute at NIH argued that progress was dependent on advances in other bioscience fields, and that the cancer effort should not stand alone. They felt that the structure of the research effort should be suited to a basic biomedical research program rather than to a technological crash program. Some members of Congress also opposed the separate agency as the beginning of the dismantling of NIH. They said the National Heart and Lung Institute would request, and have as good reason for receiving, the same treatment.

As reported unanimously June 29, the Senate bill largely represented a victory for advocates of an independent agency. It provided that the research program would be handled by an independent agency with headquarters at the National Institutes of Health. The agency would absorb the existing National Cancer Institute within NIH and would have a separate budget

(Continued on p. 568)

Health and Welfare Program Funding, Fiscal Years 1970-73

	FY 1970	FY 1971	FY 1972	FY 1973*
Food and Drug Administration	$ 72,352,500	$ 89,549,000	$ 99,681,000[3]	$ 154,123,000
Health Services and Mental Health Administration				
Mental Health	353,177,000	379,516,000	612,201,000	743,823,000
St. Elizabeths Hospital	10,405,000	14,823,000	23,144,000	30,664,000
Health services planning and development	44,796,000	57,403,000	62,070,000	64,501,000
Comprehensive health planning and services	213,786,000	247,178,000	320,703,000	330,187,000
Regional medical programs	97,357,000	106,502,000	102,771,000	150,000,000
Communicable diseases	38,638,000	43,938,000	98,590,000	149,000,000
Maternal and child health [1]		255,659,000	330,151,000	252,676,000
Hospital construction	176,123,000	196,521,000	306,704,000	112,200,000
Patient care and special health services	72,224,000	79,889,000	85,700,000	93,952,000
National health statistics	8,841,000	9,668,000	15,900,000	18,514,000
Retirement pay of commissioned officers	16,700,000	19,501,000	23,196,000	29,163,000
Office of the Administrator	9,898,000	11,812,000	12,359,000	13,126,000
Total HSMHA	1,041,945,000	1,422,410,000	1,993,489,000	1,987,806,000
National Institutes of Health				
Biologics Standards	8,225,000	8,838,000	9,205,000	9,528,000
Cancer Institute	180,725,000	230,383,000	337,531,000	492,205,000
Heart and Lung Institute	160,513,000	193,479,000	232,107,000	300,000,000
Institute of Dental Research	28,590,000	35,257,000	43,388,000	46,991,000
Institute of Arthritis and Metabolic Diseases	137,254,000	138,339,000	153,164,000	167,316,000
Institute of Neurological Diseases and Stroke	100,407,000	105,807,000	116,590,000	130,672,000
Institute of Allergy and Infectious Diseases	100,904,000	102,249,000	108,710,500	113,414,000
Institute of General Medical Sciences	152,966,000	166,072,000	173,515,000	183,171,000
Institute of Child Health and Human Development	75,852,000	94,436,000	116,833,000	130,429,000
Eye Institute	23,283,000	30,986,000	37,255,500	38,562,000
Institute of Environmental Health Sciences	17,753,000	20,620,000	26,436,000	30,936,000
Research Resources	76,658,000	66,201,000	74,948,000	75,073,000
John E. Fogarty International Center for Advanced Study in the Health Sciences	2,954,000	3,582,000	4,288,000	4,666,000
Health manpower	212,715,000	275,934,000	180,620,000	738,628,000
National Library of Medicine	19,372,000	20,769,000	24,086,000	28,568,000
Buildings and facilities	1,615,000	141,100,000	3,565,000	8,500,000
Office of the director	7,093,000	8,206,000	11,422,000	12,042,000
Scientific activities overseas (special foreign currency)	3,455,000	32,444,000	25,545,000	25,619,000
Total NIH	1,428,579,000	1,539,868,000	1,679,209,000	2,536,340,000
Social and Rehabilitation Service				
Public assistance grants to states	7,351,551,000	8,651,950,000	11,411,693,000	13,344,704,000
Work incentives	102,000,000	98,000,000	259,136,000	259,198,000
Rehabilitation services and facilities	463,398,000	570,390,000	667,301,000	0
Programs for the aging	27,590,000	33,650,000	38,950,000	0
Youth development and delinquency prevention	10,000,000	15,000,000	10,000,000	0
Social and rehabilitation services overseas (special foreign currency)	2,000,000	4,000,000	8,000,000	8,000,000
Total SRS	7,956,538,700	9,372,990,000	12,395,080,000	13,611,902,000
Social Security Administration (Total)	2,014,564,000	2,599,886,000	3,109,546,000	4,001,985,000
Payments to disabled coal miners [2]			644,249,000	1,526,500,000
Grand Total Health and Welfare	$12,513,979,200	$15,024,703,000	$19,177,324,000	$22,138,033,000

* **Labor-HEW Funds, Fiscal 1973.** As a result of two presidential vetoes, Labor-HEW appropriations for fiscal 1973 were funded at a level provided by a continuing resolution (H J Res 1331) which expired Feb. 28, 1973. The resolution permitted maximum appropriations at the lower of either the Senate- or House-approved appropriation contained in the first fiscal 1973 bill (HR 15417).

1 *Started fiscal 1971.*

2 *Started fiscal 1972.*

3 *For fiscal 1972 and 1973 the FDA was funded under appropriations for the Agriculture Department.*

from other medical research programs and a director who would report directly to the President.

S 1828 was passed unchanged by the Senate July 7 by a 79-1 roll-call vote.

House Action. The Subcommittee on Public Health and the Environment of the House Interstate and Foreign Commerce Committee held hearings on S 1828 during September and October. The same arguments for and against an independent cancer research agency were presented at length. During committee consideration the American Cancer Society and the Citizens Committee for the Conquest of Cancer ran newspaper ads, paid for "by a group of concerned individuals", urging House members to support the Senate bill.

The full committee approved a clean bill Nov. 10 by a 26-2 vote. The bill placed the cancer attack program within the existing National Cancer Institute at NIH. The institute director was to report to the head of NIH. The agency was given some independence in that its budget was to be sent directly to the President; the director of NIH and the secretary of HEW were instructed to comment on but not revise it. The bill also established a three-man presidentially appointed panel to monitor the national cancer program and report directly to the President. The authorizations under the House and Senate bills were the same.

The House passed its version Nov. 15 by a 350-5 roll-all vote. Speeches on the floor were overwhelmingly in favor of the House approach. The bill's supporters said that while the administration had supported the Senate bill it was also willing to accept the House version.

Final Action. The conference report was adopted by the House Dec. 9 by voice vote and by the Senate Dec. 10 by an 85-0 roll-call. Its major provisions were the same as those of the House bill. On the Senate floor Edward M. Kennedy (D Mass.), chairman of the Health Subcommittee, said: "I believe...that this combination as between the program's relationship to the National Institutes of Health with direct access to the President is in the nation's interest and will result in a highly effective program."

Provisions. As cleared by Congress, S 1828 (PL 92-218):

• Established a cancer research program within the National Cancer Institute of NIH to coordinate intensified research efforts to find a cure for cancer.

• Authorized $1.59-billion over fiscal 1972-74 for the program, as follows: $400-million in fiscal 1972, $500-million in fiscal 1973, $600-million in fiscal 1974 and $90-million in additional funds over the three-year period for specific cancer control programs.

• Established a three-man presidentially appointed panel to monitor the national cancer research program and report directly to the President.

• Provided that the budget for the National Cancer Institute was to be sent directly to the President with the HEW secretary, the director of NIH and the National Cancer Advisory Board instructed to comment on, but not change, it.

• Provided that the director of NIH and the director of the National Cancer Institute were to be appointed by the President.

• Increased the number of cancer research institutes across the country by 15 and made them eligible to receive grants of up to $5-million annually from the director of the National Cancer Institute.

• Established a 23-member National Cancer Advisory Board. Eighteen of the 23 were to be presidential appointees.

Health Manpower

Congress extended and revised major existing health manpower programs. It passed a bill (HR 8629—PL 92-157), the Health Professions Educational Assistance Amendments of 1971. The major provisions of HR 8629 extended Title I of the Health Manpower Act of 1968 through fiscal 1974. *(Congress and the Nation, Vol. II, p. 697)*

In separate legislation, Congress also extended Title II of the 1968 act, providing for nurse's training aid. *(Nurse training, p. 569)*. In 1970 it had already extended Title III of the act, which provided for training aid for persons in the allied health professions. *(1970 action, p. 559)*

HR 8629 continued and increased authorizations for construction assistance grants for schools for the health professions, student grants to encourage schools to expand their enrollments and student loans and scholarship funds. Total authorizations for the period fiscal 1972 through 1974 were $2.9-billion. The sum was substantially above what some members of Congress thought the administration would request to be appropriated. In continuing the existing student loan program, the bill also turned down an administration proposal to phase out the program and make special provisions for loan guarantees for medical students under the Higher Education Act.

HR 8629 contained several new features. One was a provision cancelling loans to medical students who accepted service in designated medical shortage areas at the rate of 30 per cent for each of the first two years and 25 per cent for the third year of service. Another provision authorized a new $100-million program of financial incentives to medical schools to turn out more doctors who would go into family and general medical practice. President Nixon in 1970 had pocket-vetoed a bill providing $225-million for such a program. *(Vetoed bill, p. 559)*

During debate on HR 8629 there was general agreement on the need to increase personnel in the health professions. The bill was designed to increase the number of practicing physicians to 436,000 by 1977-78; there were 332,000 physicians in active practice in 1971.

HR 8629 was passed by the House July 1 by a 343-3 roll-call vote and by the Senate July 14 by an 88-0 roll call. The Senate bill provided for a five-year extension and higher authorizations than the House. The final version of the bill, which was close to the House bill, was cleared Nov. 9. Because the provisions for health scholarships had expired June 30, a stopgap bill was passed June 24 (HR 7736—PL 92-52). Its provisions were superceded by passage of HR 8629.

PROVISIONS

As cleared by Congress, HR 8629 (PL 92-157):

• Authorized for construction assistance grants to schools in the health professions $225-million in fiscal

1972, $250-million in fiscal 1973 and $275-million in fiscal 1974.

• Authorized $8-million in fiscal 1972, $16-million in fiscal 1973 and $24-million in fiscal 1974 for interest subsidies on loans to schools in the health professions. The funds were to be used for loan guarantees and interest subsidy payments on loans made by nonfederal lenders to public and nonprofit private schools.

• Provided that public or private nonprofit schools of medicine, osteopathy, dentistry, veterinary medicine, public health, pharmacy, podiatry or combinations of the above schools were eligible to apply for construction grant assistance, loan guarantees and interest subsidy payments.

• Provided per student grants to schools of medicine, osteopathy and dentistry of $2,500 for full-time first, second or third year students, $4,000 in the fourth year for graduating students, $8,500 in the third year for students who could graduate in three years, $1,000 for each student enrolled in a training program for physicians' assistants or dental therapists and $1,000 for each member of a class meeting increased enrollment standards.

• Provided that two-year schools of basic medical science converting to four-year medical schools could receive a one-time grant of $50,000 times the number of medical students enrolled in their first third-year class.

• Authorized per student grants of $200-million in fiscal 1972, $213-million in fiscal 1973 and $238-million in fiscal 1974 for schools of medicine, osteopathy and dentistry; $34-million in fiscal 1972, $37-million in fiscal 1973 and $41-million in fiscal 1974 for schools of veterinary medicine, optometry, pharmacy and podiatry.

• Authorized $10-million per year for each of fiscal 1972-74 for grants to new schools of medicine, osteopathy and dentistry.

• Authorized $118-million in fiscal 1972, $138-million in fiscal 1973 and $156-million in fiscal 1974 for special projects grants for schools in the health professions.

• Authorized $20-million in fiscal 1972, $15-million in fiscal 1973 and $10-million in fiscal 1974 for grants to schools with serious financial problems.

• Authorized $45-million in fiscal 1972, $90-million in fiscal 1973 and $135-million in fiscal 1974 for medical education initiative awards. These grants were to be utilized to identify and enroll persons who would practice in rural and other areas where there was a shortage of family doctors and to increase the admission and retention of qualified individuals from minority and low income groups.

• Authorized $50-million in fiscal 1972, $55-million in fiscal 1973 and $60-million in fiscal 1974 for loans to students of the health professions.

• Provided for cancellation of loans to students for professional service in designated medical-shortage areas at the rate of 30 per cent for each of the first two years of service and 25 per cent for the third year.

• Provided loans and scholarships for qualified U.S. students studying in foreign medical schools and authorized $1.75-million for loans and $150,000 for scholarships in each of fiscal 1972-74.

• Established a health professions scholarship program, to be administered by the schools, based on the number of full-time students from low-income backgrounds.

• Authorized $10-million in fiscal 1972, $15-million in fiscal 1973 and $20-million in fiscal 1974 for advanced traineeships and fellowships to permit teachers in the health professions to improve their teaching skills.

• Authorized $25-million in fiscal 1972, $35-million in fiscal 1973 and $40-million in fiscal 1974 in grants for medical schools to train doctors in family medicine.

• Authorized $5-million in fiscal 1972, $10-million in fiscal 1973 and $15-million in fiscal 1974 in grants for schools in the health professions to establish computer technology health care demonstration programs.

• Authorized the secretary of HEW to make scholarship grants of up to $5,000 per academic year directly to medical students who agreed to practice in areas with a shortage of physicians or in areas where migratory agricultural workers would receive care. Students failing to fulfill their obligation under the program would be required to repay the loans with interest within three years after graduation. Authorized $2.5-million in fiscal 1972, $3-million in fiscal 1973 and $3.5-million in fiscal 1974 for such scholarships.

Nurse Training

Congress extended for three years, through fiscal 1974, programs authorized by the Nurse Training Act of 1964. The programs had last been extended in the Health Manpower Act of 1968 (PL 90-490). *(Congress and the Nation, Vol. II, p. 697)*

The 1971 extension (HR 8630—PL 92-158) authorized $855.5-million for fiscal 1972-74. It extended existing student loan programs and programs of construction grants, loan guarantees and interest subsidies to encourage nursing schools to expand their facilities. It included a new program of per student grants to nursing schools designed to replace existing formula grant authority. The per student grant program was designed to give nursing schools financial incentives to increase their enrollments and expand their curriculums. The bill also included new student loan forgiveness provisions for service in a medical shortage area.

HR 8630 sought to increase the number of practicing nurses to 1.1 million by 1980. There were 700,000 nurses in active practice in 1971.

The measure was passed by the House July 1 and the Senate July 14. The conference report was cleared Nov. 9.

Provisions. As signed into law, HR 8630 (PL 92-158):

• Authorized for construction grants to nursing schools: $35-million in fiscal 1972; $40-million in fiscal 1973, and $45-million in fiscal 1974. The federal share for construction and modernization costs for schools was set at 75 per cent.

• Authorized $1-million in fiscal 1972, $2-million in fiscal 1973 and $4-million in fiscal 1974 for interest subsidies on loans to nursing schools. The funds were to be used for loan guarantees and interest subsidy payments on loans made by nonfederal lenders to nonprofit private schools of nursing.

• Authorized $20-million in fiscal 1972, $28-million in fiscal 1973 and $35-million in fiscal 1974 in special project grants to develop training programs and cooperative programs with hospitals and academic institutions.

• Authorized $15-million in fiscal 1972, $10-million in fiscal 1973 and $5-million in fiscal 1974 for special grants to nursing schools with serious financial problems.

• Provided per-student grants to nursing schools of $250 for each student other than students in their final year and $500 for each student to graduate. For this program the bill authorized $78-million in fiscal 1972, $82-million in fiscal 1973 and $88-million in fiscal 1974.

• Authorized $4-million in fiscal 1972, $8-million in fiscal 1973 and $12-million in fiscal 1974 for start-up grants to new nursing schools. Grants were limited to $100,000 annually per school.

• Authorized cancellation of up to 85 per cent of a loan for nurses working for a nonprofit agency for five years or serving for three years in an area designated as a medical shortage area.

• Authorized $25-million in fiscal 1972, $30-million in fiscal 1973 and $35-million in fiscal 1974 for nursing student loan programs.

• Permitted nursing students enrolled part-time in nursing studies to receive loans and scholarships.

• Established procedures for state or local educational agencies and other public or nonprofit organizations to apply for grants to establish nursing programs for needy students.

• The bill authorized $3.5-million in fiscal 1972, $5-million in fiscal 1973 and $6.5-million in fiscal 1974 for this program.

1972

Health Maintenance Organizations

The Senate passed a bill (S 3327) authorizing $5.2-billion over fiscal years 1973-75 for the establishment of health maintenance organizations (HMOs). The bill died at the end of the 92nd Congress.

The term health maintenance organization is a name for a prepaid group practice organization which provides a wide range of health care services. HMOs had been in existence for many years, particularly in the western states. Rising medical costs thrust the concept into political prominence in the 1970s.

President Nixon in his 1971 health care program for improved insurance had proposed a program of grants, loans and loan guarantees to help HMOs get started, especially in medically underserved areas. The proposal was introduced in the Senate as S 1182 and in the House as HR 5617. *(1971 proposal, p. 563)*

The bill voted on by the Senate was not the administration proposal, but a more expensive bipartisan bill (S 3327) introduced by Sen. Edward M. Kennedy (D Mass.). During testimony on the two bills Secretary of Health, Education and Welfare (HEW) Elliot L. Richardson supported the administration bill because it would provide a more "practical approach." He objected that S 3327 provided start-up grants only for "closed panel group practice" which offered varied services at one facility. The administration bill had also applied to medical foundations which permitted a group of individual practitioners, working in separate facilities, to make their services available to patients at certain prescribed rates.

The proposal was opposed by the American Medical Association, which objected that it favored one form of practice at the expense of another.

S 3327 was reported unanimously by the Senate Labor and Public Welfare Committee July 21 and passed by the Senate Sept. 20 by a 60-14 roll-call vote. The bill authorized for fiscal 1973 through 1975 $1,025,400,000 for initial development, construction and operation of HMOs $360,000,000 for initial development, construction and operation of Health Service Organizations (HSOs) in rural areas; and $2,930,000,000 for development and construction of area health education and service centers. The latter authorization, Title III of the bill, included funds for per capita grants to HMOs for care of indigents and high-risk individuals. The bill also established an independent Commission on Quality Health Assurance with a $285-million authorization and a new Institute of Health Care Delivery in HEW to carry out a research and development program on health care.

S 3327 also established a medical malpractice reinsurance program for insured health care providers which maintained approved quality control systems. The President's 1971 health message had cited rapidly increasing malpractice insurance rates as a factor in the rising cost of health care.

The House Interstate and Foreign Commerce Subcommittee on Public Health and Environment held hearings on bills to establish HMOs in April and May. The subcommittee reported a clean bill to the full committee Sept. 21, but no further action was taken.

Provisions. As passed by the Senate, the legislative provisions of S 3327:

• Authorized planning grants to study the feasibility of developing and expanding HMOs and HSOs.

• Authorized initial development grants to assist HMOs and HSOs.

• Authorized construction grants and loans to assist HMOs and HSOs, to construct ambulatory health care facilities and to meet capital investment costs for transportation equipment.

• Authorized initial operating grants and loans to assist HMOs and HSOs meet operating deficits incurred during their first three years of operation.

• Authorized grants to university health centers, regional medical programs and non-profit groups to develop area health education and service centers, and to construct and equip educational facilities for these centers.

• Authorized loan guarantees and interest subsidies to assist HMOs and HSOs construct ambulatory health care facilities, obtain transportation equipment and communications equipment (in the case of HSOs) and meet initial development and operating costs.

• Authorized loan guarantees to assist university health centers, regional medical programs and nonprofit groups develop, operate, and subsidize area health education and service centers.

• Pre-empted state legislation that would inhibit or restrict the operation of HMOs, HSOs or other health care providers receiving assistance under the bill.

• Authorized quality health care initiative awards to assist health care providers to maintain internal quality control systems.

• Authorized per capital grants to enable HMOs and HSOs to serve indigent and high-risk individuals.

• Established an independent Commission on Quality Health Care Assurance to encourage national systems for quality health care.

• Established a federal medical malpractice reinsurance program to make medical malpractice liability reinsurance available to insurers liable for malpractice damages incurred by insured health care providers that maintain approved quality control systems.

• Established a new Institute of Health Care Delivery within the Department of Health, Education and Welfare (HEW) to carry out a multidisciplinary research and development program to improve the delivery of health care.

Heart and Lung Disease

Congress in 1972 authorized a major expansion of programs of the National Heart and Lung Institute to combat heart, blood vessel, lung and blood diseases. The bill (S 3323—PL 92-423) authorized $1.38-billion through fiscal 1975 for research and control programs at the National Institutes of Health (NIH) and at 30 new regional centers.

S 3323 provided for the same kind of stepped-up attack on heart and lung disease as a bill enacted in 1971 had provided for cancer. *(Cancer bill, p. 566)* However, whereas the 1971 bill had gotten caught up in a major controversy over location of the program, S 3323 was noncontroversial and had broad bipartisan support.

Proponents said cardiovascular disease was the nation's leading health problem, afflicting more than 26 million Americans and killing more than one million persons annually. An additional 20 million persons were disabled with diseases of the lung, and chronic pulmonary disorders were the direct cause of more than 30,-000 deaths each year.

S 3323 was supported by the administration although it contained provisions opposed by the Department of Health, Education and Welfare during hearings. The administration had requested open-ended, rather than specific authorizations. It had also objected that S 3323 included "what we interpret as a program of services for heart and related diseases". It said delivery of services "should only be included in a research institute where essential to the achievement of the research."

S 3323 was passed by the Senate April 7 by a 62-0 roll call and by the House July 18 on a 380-10 roll-call vote.

Provisions. As cleared by Congress, S 3323 (PL 92-423):

• Required the director of the National Heart and Lung Institute to carry out a national heart, blood vessel, lung and blood disease program in coordination with other relevant programs within the National Institutes of Health.

• Required the institute to conduct research into the development and evaluation of techniques, drugs and devices, including computer, for the diagnosis, prevention and treatment of heart, blood vessel, lung and blood diseases.

• Established programs for conducting field studies on the diseases and specified that the studies were to include provision for emergency medical services.

• Authorized studies and research into blood diseases and the use of blood for clinical purposes.

• Authorized $25-million in fiscal 1973, $35-million in fiscal 1974 and $45-million in fiscal 1975 for prevention and control programs on the diseases.

• Authorized the establishment of 15 new centers for cardiovascular disease prevention programs and research and 15 new centers for chronic pulmonary disease prevention programs and research.

• Established a 23-member National Heart and Lung Advisory Council to advise the institute on programs formulated to combat the diseases.

• Authorized $375-million for fiscal 1973, $425-million for fiscal 1974 and $475-million for fiscal 1975 to carry out programs (other than prevention and control programs) specified in the bill.

Communicable Disease Control

Against the administration's wishes, Congress extended authorizations for grants to the states and local communities for communicable disease control. The bill (S 3442—PL 92-449) extended through fiscal 1975 a 1970 law which the administration had also opposed and which had never been funded. *(1970 law, p. 558)*

S 3442 for the first time earmarked funds for control of specific diseases. It authorized $62.5-million per year for venereal disease, $11-million per year for tuberculosis control, $6-million per year for measles control and $23-million per year for other diseases (such as polio and whooping cough). Applicants were required to present detailed plans for programs and to adequately publicize them.

During testimony on S 3442, an administration spokesman opposed it because it authorized categorical grant programs. The administration said existing authorities were adequate to meet the bill's purpose and proposed that Congress increase authorizations under the Partnership for Health law (PL 91-515). *(Regional medical programs, p. 559)*

In support of the legislation, members of Congress argued that funds for immunization programs had not been adequate and the nation had suffered an upturn in a number of communicable diseases, particularly venereal disease. They pointed out that Congress was currently committing huge sums for programs to combat diseases such as cancer which did not have a cure, and that it should continue to spend money to insure that diseases for which cures had been found were controlled.

S 3442 was passed by the House July 18 by a 386-2 roll-call vote and by the Senate June 7 by a 70-0 roll-call vote.

Health Service Corps

Congress cleared a bill (S 3858—PL 92-585) expanding the Emergency Health Personnel Act of 1970 (PL 91-623). PL 91-623 provided for assignment of Public Health Service personnel to medically underserved areas. *(1970 act, p. 561)*

The 1972 extension designated the persons assigned to medical shortage areas as the Health Service Corps. It authorized scholarships for students of the health professions who agreed to serve in the corps. The bill also required that any administration plan to close or transfer public health service hospitals and clinics be submitted to Congress 90 days in advance and contain assurances that the closure would not impair the capacity to deliver health services to medical shortage areas. The administration in 1971 had announced plans to close 8 hospitals and 30 clinics.

The administration in testimony opposed both the loan forgiveness and closure provisions.

S 3858 was passed by voice vote of the Senate Aug. 18 and by voice vote of the House Oct. 13.

Provisions. As signed into law, PL 92-585:

● Formally named the administrative unit established by the Emergency Health Personnel Act of 1970 (PL 91-623) as the National Health Service Corps.

● Required the secretary of HEW to use National Health Service Corps personnel to improve health care delivery and services in areas with a shortage of health personnel.

● Provided that health corps personnel were to be assigned to a medical shortage area solely on the basis of need and not upon the ability of an area to pay for services rendered.

● Required the secretary to conduct recruiting programs for the National Health Service Corps at health profession schools.

● Authorized $25-million in fiscal 1974 for the corps.

● Required that any plan by HEW to close or transfer Public Health Service hospitals and clinics contain assurances that the transfer would not impair the capacity to deliver health services to medical shortage areas.

● Required the secretary to give a detailed explanation to Congress 90 days in advance of the closure or transfer of any Public Health Service hospital or clinic.

● Authorized scholarships for students of the health professions who agreed to serve one year in the National Health Service Corps for each year in which they received federal schoarship assistance.

● Authorized a program of loan forgiveness providing federal repayment of educational loans made to health professionals who agreed to serve in medical shortage areas.

● Authorized $2-million in fiscal 1973 and $3-million in fiscal 1974 for scholarship training programs.

● Permitted the secretary of HEW to collect for services performed by the health corps by a fee-for-service or prepayment method.

Research On Aging

President Nixon Oct. 30 pocket vetoed a bill (HR 14424) establishing a National Institute of Aging within the National Institutes of Health (NIH) to conduct medical, social and behavioral research into the aging process. The bill also established a National Advisory Council on Aging within NIH. It amended the Community Mental Health Centers Act (PL 88-164) to establish a program for the mental health of the elderly and authorized $20-million for the program in fiscal 1973.

HR 14424 was passed by the House July 18 by a 380-10 roll-call vote and by the Senate Sept. 21 by voice vote. The chairman of the House committee which handled the bill said it was necessary because "there has not been sufficient emphasis given by NIH to research on the aging process and the problems of the aged." During hearings the administration opposed the bill on the grounds that it was unnecessary and would lead to duplicate work on diseases such as cancer.

In his veto message, Nixon objected that the bill would "fragment existing research efforts" and "create additional administrative costs without enhancing the conduct of biomedical research for the aging." He said authority already existed for the mental health program.

Nutrition For Aged

Congress passed a bill (S 1163—PL 92-258) amending the Older Americans Act of 1965 (PL 89-73) to authorize grants to the states to pay up to 90 per cent of the cost of establishing nutrition programs for the elderly. The bill authorized $250-million for fiscal 1973-74.

S 1163 was passed by the Senate Nov. 30, 1971, by an 89-0 roll-call vote and by the House Feb. 7 by a 350-23 roll-call. Later in the year the President vetoed a further expansion of the Older Americans Act. *(Welfare chapter p.605)*

Provisions. As cleared by Congress, S 1163 (PL 92-258):

● Amended the Older Americans Act of 1965 to authorize grants to states to pay up to 90 per cent of the cost of establishing nutrition programs for the elderly.

● Authorized $100-million in fiscal 1973 and $150-million in fiscal 1974 for the programs.

● Specified that funds for the programs were to be allocated by the HEW Department to the states on the basis of their proportionate share of the population aged 60 and over. Each state, Puerto Rico and the District of Columbia was to receive at least one-half of one per cent of the sums appropriated.

● Provided that each state had to designate a single state agency to administer the nutrition program within the state and coordinate such programs with other agencies providing services to the elderly.

● Provided that states were to disperse funds to public or nonprofit private nutrition projects, giving perference to those serving low-income elderly or minority groups, Indians and persons with limited English-speaking abilities.

● Provided that nutrition projects were eligible to receive and use surplus commodities donated by the secretary of agriculture.

Expiring Health Programs

With a large quantity of major health legislation coming up for extension in 1973, the Senate moved to avoid a "monumental legislative logjam" by extending some programs a year in advance. It passed a conglomerate bill (S 3716) extending a number of expiring acts, including authorization for the Hill-Burton hospital construction program and the community mental health centers program. S 3716 also included extensions of some minor programs which the Senate had already passed separately (medical libraries, aid to migrants, public health traineeships).

The administration refused to testify on extension of the programs because its "planning process was not sufficiently advanced" and the House did not act on S 3716. The House at the end of the session did pass a separate bill (HR 16676) extending the Community Mental Health Centers Act (PL 88-614) for one year and authorizing $279-million. The Senate passed HR 16676 authorizing $414-million. The House disagreed to the Senate amendments and the bill died.

S 3716 was passed by the Senate Sept. 20 by a 78-0 roll-call vote. It extended the following programs:

- Hill-Burton Hospital Construction Program (Title VI of PL 78-410). S 3716 extended Hill-Burton authorizations through fiscal 1975, providing $1.36-billion. *(1970 extension, p. 553)*

- Community Mental Health Centers Program (PL 88-164). S 3716 authorized $973-million for community mental health centers programs in fiscal 1973-75. *(1970 extension, p. 555)*

- Allied Health Training Act (PL 89-751). S 3716 extended for one year, through fiscal 1974, programs for training health technicians. It authorized $154.2-million. *(1970 extension, p. 560)*

- Medical Library Assistance Act (PL 89-291). S 3716 extended the program of assistance to medical libraries through fiscal 1977. *(1970 extension, p. 560)*

- Migrant Health Aid (PL 91-209). S 3716 extended programs of hospital care and health services for migrant workers for three years, through fiscal 1975. *(1970 extension, p. 561)*

- Public Health Schools (PL 91-208). S 3716 extended training programs for public health personnel for six years, through fiscal 1977. *(1970 extension, p. 561)*

In addition to these extensions of existing programs, S 3716 authorized $300-million over three years (fiscal 1973-75) for a national emergency medical services program to improve ambulance and hospital emergency room services. The House Oct. 2 by a 244-122 roll-call vote passed a separate bill (HR 15859) authorizing $255-million for a similar three-year program, but there was no further action on the bill.

Other Legislation

Congress in 1972 also cleared several bills designed to deal with specific health problems which members felt had been neglected.

SICKLE CELL ANEMIA. Congress May 3 cleared a bill (S 2676—PL 92-294) authorizing $115-million over three years (fiscal 1973-75) for programs to control and treat sickle cell anemia. The bill included $85-million for screening and counseling and $30-million for research on the disease.

Sickle cell anemia is an inherited blood disease which impedes the flow of blood to the body's vital organs. It is found almost exclusively among blacks. It afflicts one out of every 500 black children, and its victims frequently die before the age of 20. President Nixon in his 1971 health message said, "It is a sad and shameful fact that the causes of this disease have been largely neglected throughout our history."

COOLEY'S ANEMIA. Congress Aug. 18 cleared a bill (HR 15474—PL 92-414) authorizing $11.1-million over three years (fiscal 1973-75) to expand research, diagnosis, prevention and treatment of Cooley's anemia.

Cooley's anemia is an invariably fatal genetic blood disease which affects some 200,000 Americans, usually of Italian and Greek descent. It is caused by an impairment in the synthesis of hemoglobin which enables red blood-cells to carry oxygen to the tissues of the body.

MULTIPLE SCLEROSIS COMMISSION. Congress Oct. 17 cleared a bill (HR 15475—PL 92-593) establishing a National Advisory Commission on Multiple Sclerosis to determine the most effective means for finding the cause of and cure for the disease. The commission was to be comprised of five persons from the general public and four members of the National Institute of Neurological Diseases and Stroke Advisory Council.

Multiple sclerosis is a chronic, usually progressive disease of the nervous system which generally strikes adults between the ages of 20 and 40. It afflicts an estimated 200,000 Americans.

DIGESTIVE DISEASES. Congress May 5 cleared for the President a bill (HR 13591—PL 92-305) redesignating the National Institute of Arthritis and Metabolic Diseases as the National Institute of Arthritis, Metabolism and Digestive Diseases. The purpose of the bill was to place additional emphasis on research in the field of digestive diseases. The bill was opposed by the administration which said it would "create a precedent for other large areas which can claim that they have equally legitimate reasons for inclusion in a broadened name for individual institutes."

MAJOR ANTI-DRUG LEGISLATION CLEARED IN 1970, 1972

The need for new legislation to fight the increasingly serious problem of drug abuse was one area in which Congress and the first Nixon administration were in real agreement. The President sent Congress two major messages on drug abuse which resulted in two important conglomerate bills. The bills were enacted in 1970 and 1972.

In these bills, Congress, frequently by unanimous votes, gave the President all and more than he asked for to improve drug control and rehabilitation programs. The administration pronounced itself pleased with congressional actions, even when they went well beyond what had originally been requested.

The 1970 bill, the Comprehensive Drug Abuse Prevention and Control Act, grew out of a 1969 presidential message and request for what were essentially stronger enforcement tools and a more rational penalty structure. The House expanded this into a final bill which strengthened federal programs for drug rehabilitation and enforcement.

The rehabilitation provisions of the 1972 bill consisted largely of expansion of existing programs. The enforcement provisions of the measure revised the penalty structure for drug abuse, classified and set production quotas on drugs, beefed up the enforcement staff and provided for controversial "no-knock" search warrants which allowed entry without notice in drug cases. While the bill in general provided for tougher enforcement, it did eliminate mandatory penalties and make possession of marijuana a misdemeanor rather than a felony.

The bill passed in 1972 responded to a presidential request for a central office to coordinate and oversee the scattered federal anti-drug abuse programs. The bill created a Special Action Office for Drug Abuse in the Executive Office of the President. This helped to ease a jurisdictional dispute over whether the primary responsibility for drug control programs rested with the Department of Justice or Health, Education and Welfare.

The 1972 bill also created a National Institute on Drug Abuse within the National Institute of Mental Health, expanded drug research and treatment programs and established a program of formula grants to the states for drug control programs. The bill authorized a total of over $1-billion through fiscal 1975.

Among the research programs stepped up by the bill was an effort to develop nonaddictive synthetic substitutes for opium. The President's 1971 message on drug abuse said that heroin, an opium derivative, caused "the most difficult to control and the most socially destructive form of addiction in America today." No opium was produced in the United States and, in an internationally directed move to cut heroin addiction, the Nixon administration began programs to induce other countries to cease opium production. Congress appropriated $42.5-million for that purpose in fiscal 1973.

There was little additional drug abuse legislation beyond the two omnibus bills. However, a number of congressional committees held hearings on drug abuse and related problems. In particular, substantial attention was focused on heroin addiction among Vietnam servicemen and veterans. There were several proposals to deal with the problem, but none was enacted. *(National Security chapter, p. 222)*

1969

Congress in 1969 investigated a variety of problems involving drugs but did not clear any major legislation.

Congressional action was complicated by a jurisdictional question of whether to consider drug abuse a health problem or a law enforcement issue and whether the Justice Department or the Health, Education and Welfare (HEW) Department should have primary responsibility for drug control. Various congressional committees —Judiciary, Education and Labor, Crime, and Labor and Public Welfare—held hearings in the field. In the testimony before the committees, the disagreement between the Departments of Justice and HEW on the issue was made quite clear.

President Nixon July 14 sent Congress a special message on drug abuse and a comprehensive bill to revise and modernize the system for federal control of narcotics and other dangerous drugs. A bill was reported late in the session by the Senate Judiciary Committee (S 3246) but saw no further action. (A broader bill was cleared in 1970.)

The House Oct. 31 by a 294-0 roll-call vote passed a bill (HR 14252) authorizing a three-year program of grants to schools and public and private organizations for drug abuse education. The Senate did not act on the bill in 1969, but it was cleared in 1970. *(Drug abuse education, p. 577)*

The Justice Department Sept. 21 imposed an intensified car-by-car inspection program, Operation Intercept, to police the Mexican-American border and halt the flow of drugs there. The searches did not produce major finds, and violent protests concerning the delay and inconvenience brought modificaton of the program Oct. 10 into Operation Cooperation. The United States agreed to adjust its inspection procedures to eliminate the inconvenience, and Mexico promised to act more effectively to halt drug production and the smuggling of drugs into the United States.

Administration Request

President Nixon in his special July 14 message said drug abuse in the last decade had "grown from essentially a local police problem into a serious national threat to the personal health and safety of millions of Americans." He said juvenile arrests involving drug use had risen by 800 per cent between 1960 and 1967.

The President said existing drug abuse laws were inadequate and outdated. He proposed to replace them with a comprehensive bill, the "Controlled Dangerous Substance Act of 1969." *(Earlier drug legislation, box, this page)*

The administration proposal was designed to provide more meaningful regulation over legitimate sources of drugs, strengthen law enforcement against illicit drug traffic and eliminate inconsistencies in the existing regulation of drugs. The bill had the following eight titles:

● Title I to base federal jurisdiction over narcotics and dangerous drugs solely upon the power to control interstate commerce and to classify all drug traffic into three major categories—manufacture, distribution, dispensing.

● Title II to set up four "schedules" of drugs, classified according to their usefulness and effect, matched by four sets of federal registration and control requirements.

● Title III to provide uniform record-keeping requirements and to authorize the attorney general to suspend or deny a registration to deal in drugs.

● Title IV to authorize the attorney general to allow the importation of narcotics if necessary to insure a reasonable price to the consumer.

● Title V to revise the penalties for illicit traffic in and use of drugs. Possible revisions included providing more flexibility in penalties for illicit sale and possession of marijuana and LSD and in use of rehabilitative programs and medical treatment as alternatives to prison sentences.

● Title VI to create a Scientific Advisory Committee and provide for educational and research programs conducted by the Department of Justice.

● Title VII to expand the law enforcement powers of the agents of the Bureau of Narcotics and Dangerous Drugs, including a controversial "no-knock" provision to allow agents to enter without knocking and identifying themselves places suspected to house illegal drug activities.

● Title VIII to repeal laws which the act would supersede.

During hearings on the administration proposal before the Senate Judiciary Juvenile Delinquency Subcommittee, a number of witnesses advocated changes in the law to distinguish between the casual experimenter with drugs and the drug addict and to soften penalties for marijuana use. The administration agreed to alter its proposal to eliminate mandatory minimum penalties for drug possession and to make possession of marijuana a misdemeanor, not a felony.

Provisions of the administration bill which switched some authority for drug control programs from the HEW Department to the Justice Department were also softened. In changes in the draft bill, HEW was given full responsibility for drug research and the attorney general

Drug Law Background

Federal legislation controlling narcotic drugs and other dangerous substances, such as stimulant and depressant drugs, developed from the early 20th Century in patchwork fashion. The resulting body of laws lacked consistency, unity and, at times, logic.

The Federal anti-narcotics effort began in 1909 with the Opium Exclusion Act, barring the import of opium except for medicinal purposes. Subsequent laws enacted prior to World War II made it illegal to import or export narcotics in any form, or to make, sell, buy or transport narcotics unless for medicinal or scientific purposes and under approval of the Treasury Department's Narcotics Bureau. Under most of these laws, merely possessing a narcotic without being registered with the Treasury Department was considered evidence that some illegal act had been committed to obtain it.

The Bureau of Narcotics was created in the Treasury Department in 1930 to enforce these narcotics laws.

In the postwar period a number of new drug laws were passed, each one stiffening the penalties for violations of federal drug regulations. Mandatory minimum sentences were set for most narcotics offenses in 1951 (PL 82-255), and five years later another law (PL 84-728) increased the penalties and would allow the death sentence imposed upon someone convicted of selling heroin to a minor.

Drug legislation in the 1960s began to move in new directions with the expansion of federal control over depressant, stimulant and hallucinogenic drugs (including barbiturates, "pep pills" and LSD) in 1965 (PL 89-74) and passage of the Narcotics Rehabilitation Act (PL 89-793) the following year to provide that addicts convicted of drug offenses not be sent to prison, but instead be committed to medical institutions for treatment. In 1968 Congress amended the 1965 law to set penalties for the illegal possession of stimulant, depressant or hallucinogenic drugs (PL 90-639). *(Congress and The Nation, Vol. II, p. 673)*

An initial move toward coordination of the enforcement of all these various drug laws was the reorganization in 1968 of the federal agencies responsible for their enforcement. President Johnson, through an executive reorganization plan, combined the Bureau of Narcotics in the Department of the Treasury with the Bureau of Drug Abuse Control from the Department of Health, Education and Welfare, creating a Bureau of Narcotics and Dangerous Drugs in the Department of Justice.

was required to have written advice from the HEW secretary before he could classify a drug as dangerous.

A somewhat expanded version of the administration proposal was reported by the Judiciary Committee Dec. 16 (S 3246). The Senate passed it unanimously Jan. 28, 1970, but the House did not act. Instead it passed a much broader bill (HR 18583) dealing with rehabilitation as well as law enforcement. The Senate then passed it, and it became law in October 1970.

1970

Comprehensive Drug Control

Congress cleared a massive drug control bill, the Comprehensive Drug Abuse Prevention and Control Act of 1970 (HR 18583—PL 91-513). The bill provided expanded programs of rehabilitation, treatment and drug abuse education; unified and revised federal narcotics laws; revised the entire penalty structure for violations of those laws; and provided new tools for enforcement.

HR 18583 grew out of a 1969 administration request for a narrower bill, essentially a law enforcement measure, which would unify and revise federal drug laws and rationalize the penalty structure. A bill (S 3246), based on the administration proposals, was unanimously passed by the Senate in January 1970. But instead of acting on S 3246, the two House committees with jurisdiction over drug legislation jointly developed a much broader bill (HR 18583) which dealt with rehabilitation and treatment as well as law enforcement. *(1969 administration proposal, p. 574)*

HR 18583 was reported by the House Interstate and Foreign Commerce Committee, which wrote Titles I and II, and by the House Ways and Means Committee, which wrote Title III. The committee bill was close to the version finally enacted. Title I amended the Community Mental Health Centers Act (PL 88-164) to substantially enlarge programs for treatment of addicts. Title II increased the Justice Department's narcotics enforcement staff by at least 300; classified drugs in five schedules and set production quotas; revised the entire penalty structure and eliminated mandatory minimum sentences; and provided for search warrants which allowed enforcement officers to enter without notice ("no-knock" orders). Title III established a unified system of controls over the import and export of dangerous substances based on the schedules set forth in Title II.

HR 18583 was passed by the House Sept. 24 by a 341-6 roll-call vote. The bill's sponsors said the administration was highly pleased with the proposal. The House adopted one amendment; this authorized special sentencing procedures under which dangerous drug offenders would be given more severe sentences than the usual penalty prescribed for their offense. An amendment to eliminate the controversial "no-knock" provision was rejected by a 60-119 teller vote. *(Action on enforcement provisions, chapter on crime)*

HR 18583 was passed by the Senate Oct. 7 by a 54-0 roll-call vote after two days of debate. During debate it adopted by a 44-23 roll-call vote a sweeping new substitute for Title I proposed by Harold E. Hughes (D Iowa). The new title established a national health institute for dealing with drug dependence and set up an independent advisory council on drug abuse. It authorized grants totaling $190-million to state and local agencies to help finance drug dependence projects. Hughes said the proposal was the product of months of hearings before the Senate Labor and Public Welfare Committee.

The Senate also adopted an amendment to include two widely used tranquilizers (Librium and Valium) in the list of controlled substances. By a 20-42 roll-call vote

it rejected an attempt to strike the controversial "no-knock" section.

The conference report on HR 18583 was adopted by voice votes of the House and Senate Oct. 14. The conferees had restored Title I as approved by the House except that authorizations were increased from $164-million to $189-million. The conference report said the Senate substitute included a number of new concepts and that House hearings would be held on them in 1971. The Senate subsequently unanimously passed a bill (S 3562) containing its version of Title I, but the House did not act on it.

The other major Senate change, inclusion of Valium and Librium on the list of controlled drugs, was also dropped. A statement by Thomas J. Dodd (D Conn.) said the House conferees had "bludgeoned" the Senate into dropping the provision which was opposed by a powerful drug lobby.

PROVISIONS

As cleared by Congress, HR 18583, the Comprehensive Drug Abuse Prevention and Control Act of 1970:

Title I: Rehabilitation

● Authorized the Department of Health, Education and Welfare (HEW) to increase its programs of rehabilitation, treatment and prevention of drug abuse by:

Amending the Community Mental Health Centers Act (Title II of PL 88-164) to increase authorizations for funds for community facilities for treatment of narcotics addicts and drug dependent persons by $75-million for fiscal 1971, 1972 and 1973 (to $40-million from $30-million for 1971; to $60-million from $35-million for 1972; to $80-million from $40-million for 1973).

Amending PL 88-164 to authorize $29-million for drug abuse education projects for fiscal 1971, 1972 and 1973 ($3-million for 1971; $12-million for 1972, and $14-million for 1973).

Amending PL 88-164 to authorize $85-million for grants in fiscal 1971, 1972 and 1973 for special projects in the treatment and rehabilitation of addicts and drug dependent persons ($20-million for 1971; $30-million for 1972, $35-million for 1973).

Amending the Public Health Service Act (PL 78-410) to expand the direct patient care authority of the Department of HEW to include drug dependent persons as well as addicts, to grant the secretary of HEW new authority to protect the privacy of drug research subjects and to define "drug dependent person."

● Authorized the secretary of HEW, after consultation with the attorney general and professional organizations, to report to Congress on appropriate and legal methods of professional practice in the medical treatment of narcotics addicts.

Title II: Control and Enforcement

● Authorized the Bureau of Narcotics and Dangerous Drugs in fiscal 1971 to add at least 300 agents to its existing enforcement staff, and authorized an annual appropriation of $6-million for that purpose, beginning in fiscal 1971.

● Vested authority for the control of the dangerous substances specified in the title in the attorney general, empowered him to add, remove or transfer substances to, from or between categories (schedules), but required him to seek, and be bound by, the advice of the secretary of HEW before placing a substance under control or removing it from control.

• Classified drugs to be controlled into five schedules to be updated regularly. The schedules were based on the degree of abuse potential, the known effect or harmfulness and level of accepted medical use. Heroin, marijuana, LSD (lysergic acid diethylamide), mescaline and peyote were classified under Schedule I, which included substances with a high potential for abuse and no accepted medical use in the United States. Methadone, currently used in drug treatment programs as a substitute for heroin, and liquid injectable methamphetamine ("speed") were classified under Schedule II, which included substances with a high potential for abuse and a restricted medical use. Most other amphetamines and barbiturates were classified under Schedule III, which included substances with currently accepted medical uses and lower physical dependence than the drugs in Schedules I and II (although high potential psychological dependence).

• Authorized the attorney general to adopt rules for the registration and control of the manufacture, distribution and dispensing of substances classified as controlled, and to set production quotas for the amount of substances in Schedules I and II to be produced each year.

• Revised the entire penalty structure for unlawful manufacture, distribution, dispensing or possession with the intent to manufacture, distribute or dispense a controlled substance or counterfeit. All mandatory minimum sentences were eliminated except for professional criminals.

• Provided that possession of a controlled substance by a first offender, for his own use, be treated as a misdemeanor punishable by up to one year in prison and a fine of up to $5,000 or both.

• Provided that anyone 18 or older who distributed a controlled substance to someone under 21 should receive twice the authorized penalty for that offense.

• Provided that any professional criminal trafficking in drugs shall receive a mandatory minimum sentence of 10 years and a maximum fine of $100,000 for a first offense and a minimum term of 20 years and a maximum fine of $200,000 for a second.

• Provided that the penalty for distributing a small amount of marijuana for no remuneration be the same as that for mere possession.

• Authorized special sentencing procedures under which special dangerous drug offenders could be given more severe sentences—up to 25 years and not disproportionate in severity to the usual prescribed penalty for their offense. Defendants who might be found—in a special postconviction hearing—to fall into this category included a person convicted of a third serious drug offense, a professional criminal convicted of a serious drug offense, or an organized crime figure.

• Provided for search warrants which specifically allowed enforcement officers to enter without notice ("no knock") premises to be searched—if there was probable cause to believe that the property sought would be destroyed or someone's life or safety endangered if notice were given.

• Created a Commission on Marijuana and Drug Abuse to report to Congress, within one year, on marijuana, and, within two years, on the causes of drug abuse.

• Authorized $60-million for the Justice Department in fiscal 1972, $70-million in 1973 and $90-million in 1974 to carry out the provisions of Title II.

Title III: Import and Export

• Established a unified system of controls over the importation and exportation of dangerous substances listed in the act. No Schedule I or II substance or any narcotic drug in Schedules III, IV, or V could be imported without the special consent of the attorney general. No narcotic drug in Schedules I, II, III or IV, or other controlled substance in Schedules I or II could be exported without a permit from the attorney general.

• Provided stricter supervision over the importation and exportation of depressant and stimulant drugs.

• Revised the penalty structure for violations of these control laws, eliminating mandatory minimum sentences.

Title IV: Advisory Councils Report

• Directed the secretary of HEW to report annually —to the Senate Committee on Labor and Public Welfare and the House Committee on Interstate and Foreign Commerce—on activities of all advisory councils set up by the Public Health Service Act (PL 78-410) or the Mental Retardation Facilities and Community Mental Health Centers Construction Act of 1963 (PL 88-164).

Drug Abuse Education

Congress cleared a bill (HR 14252—PL 91-527) authorizing $58-million over three years (fiscal 1971-73) for drug abuse education programs.

The House had passed HR 14252 in 1969, carrying $29-million. The Senate passed it unanimously Nov. 17, 1970, with the $58-million authorization, and the House agreed to the Senate version.

Provisions. As cleared by Congress, HR 14252— PL 91-527):

• Authorized the secretary of Health, Education and Welfare to make grants to local educational agencies and other private and nonprofit organizations for community information programs on drug abuse. Grants could be used to develop curriculums, disseminate educational materials, provide training programs for teachers and law enforcement officials and offer community education programs to parents and others.

• Authorized $5-million in fiscal year 1971, $10-million in fiscal 1972 and $14-million in fiscal 1973 for drug abuse education programs.

• Authorized the secretary of HEW to make grants to public or private nonprofit agencies for community-oriented education projects on drug abuse.

• Authorized $5-million in fiscal year 1971, $10-million in fiscal 1972 and $14-million in fiscal 1973 for community education projects.

1971

As in 1969, the President sent Congress a major message on drug abuse. On June 17 he said: "We must now candidly recognize that the deliberate procedures embodied in present efforts to control drug abuse are not sufficient in themselves. The problem has assumed the dimensions of a national emergency. I intend to take every step necessary to deal with this emergency including asking the Congress for an amendment to my 1972 budget to provide an additional $155-million to carry out these steps. This will provide a total of $371-million for programs to control drug abuse in America."

The President asked Congress to create a Special Action Office of Drug Abuse Prevention in the Executive Office of the President to coordinate federal anti-drug abuse efforts. He said that such programs were currently scattered through nine agencies and a central office was needed to set program goals and evaluate performance. The message also requested additional funds for rehabilitation and enforcement.

Much of the message was devoted to the international implications of the drug abuse problem. The President said that America does not grow opium (from which heroin is made), but the U.S. had the largest number of heroin addicts in the world. It was estimated that less than 20 per cent of foreign-produced drugs aimed at the United States were being stopped. The message requested funds for training of foreign narcotics enforcement officers and for aid to opium-producing countries to induce and help them to end production. He also asked for stepped-up federal research efforts aimed at developing synthetic substitutes for all opium derivatives.

The President's proposal for a central drug control office in the executive offices was passed by the Senate in December and cleared in 1972. Otherwise, Congress in 1971 did not act on major drug abuse legislation. A number of committees, however, looked into various aspects of the problem. Hearings were held on heroin addiction, drug abuse in the armed forces, the effect of pep pills on truck drivers, barbituate abuse among young people, and the use of mood drugs.

1972

Drug Abuse Office

Congress completed action on the President's major 1971 proposal to create a Special Action Office for Drug Abuse Prevention in the Executive Office of the President. The bill (S 2097—PL 92-255) gave the director of the office authority to coordinate all federal drug abuse programs, with the exception of law enforcement, and to establish new ones. It authorized slightly more than $1-billion through fiscal 1975 to carry out the director's activities and to provide research funds and state grants.

In addition, S 2097 created a National Institute on Drug Abuse within the National Institute of Mental Health, a National Advisory Council for Drug Abuse Prevention and a National Drug Abuse Training Center,

and proposed the development of a long-term federal strategy to combat drug abuse.

House and Senate conferees made major changes in both the House- and the Senate-passed versions. The bill was passed unanimously by the Senate Dec. 2, 1971, authorizing $1.7-billion through fiscal 1976, with about $1.5-billion of that amount for grants to states and nonprofit agencies for drug control programs. The House Feb. 3, 1972, also passed the bill unanimously, but its version authorized only $411-million through fiscal 1974. The final bill authorized appropriations of $1,008,000,000 through fiscal 1975.

PROVISIONS

As cleared by Congress, S 2097 (PL 92-255):

Title I

● Declared that "the increasing rate of drug abuse constitutes a serious and continuing threat to the national health and welfare" requiring a response from the federal government.

● Provided that Title II, including the Special Action Office and the National Advisory Council for Drug Abuse Prevention established by the bill *(below)*, would be abolished on June 30, 1975.

Title II

● Established a Special Action Office for Drug Abuse Prevention, headed by a director, in the Executive Office of the President; provided that the placement of the office in the Executive Office "shall not be construed as affecting access" by Congress or the committees of either chamber to 1) information, documents, and studies in the possession of, or conducted by, the office, or 2) to personnel of the office.

● Provided that the attorney general of the United States must give the director notice before initiating any changes in the categories of drugs under the Controlled Substances Act.

● Authorized the director to make grants to any public or nonprofit private agency and to any federal department or agency to carry out his functions under the act.

● Provided that except for drug abuse functions, nothing in the act would restrict the authority of the secretary of defense or the administrator of veterans' affairs.

● Authorized $38-million for the Special Action Office.

● Gave the director authority to provide "over-all planning and policy and establish objectives and priorities for all federal drug abuse prevention functions"—including recommendations for changes in the organization or personnel of federal agencies and for modifying plans and budget requests of federal agencies for drug control programs.

● Created a special fund from which the director could distribute money among federal agencies to encourage new concepts of drug abuse prevention or to supplement prevention programs found to be especially effective; authorized $120-million for fiscal 1973-75 for the fund; provided that not more than 10 per cent of the fund could go to new concepts of drug abuse prevention.

Authorizations in 1972 Act

(in millions of dollars)

	Fiscal 1972	Fiscal 1973	Fiscal 1974	Fiscal 1975
Special Action Office (Operating Funds)	5	10	11	12
Special Action Office (Special Fund)	0	40	40	40
Pharmacological Research	0	20	25	30
Community Mental Health Centers Staffing Grants	0	60	60	60
Community Mental Health Centers Treatment Funds	0	25	75	0
State Formula Grants	15	30	40	45
Special Grants	25	65	100	160
National Drug Abuse Training Center	1	3	5	6
TOTALS	46	253	356	353

• Authorized the director to expand pharmacological research programs aimed at creating nonaddictive synthetic substitutes for opium in medical use, nonaddictive drugs for the treatment of heroin addiction and detoxification agents to ease the physical effects of withdrawal from heroin addiction; authorized $75-million for fiscal 1973-75 to provide research grants.

• Authorized the director to make recommendations to the President regarding drug abuse prevention in the law enforcement area. (The director was not authorized to make policy in this area.)

• Authorized the director to coordinate federal drug abuse prevention activities with state and local governments and provide a central clearinghouse for all governments, agencies and individuals seeking data on drug abuse prevention.

• Authorized the director, where necessary, to undertake a management oversight review, for not more than 30 days in one calendar year, of any federal drug abuse prevention program.

• Provided that the President could pick the director to represent the United States in meetings with foreign governments concerning drug abuse prevention or drug traffic prevention.

• Required the director to make annual reports by March 1 on activities of his office to the President and Congress.

• Established a 15-member National Advisory Council for Drug Abuse Prevention, consisting of the secretaries of defense and health, education and welfare, the VA administrator and 12 other members appointed by the President—the director was not specifically mentioned; the council was to make recommendations to the director on federal drug abuse prevention activities.

Title III

• Required the President to establish a strategy council in order to develop, within nine months after enactment of the bill, a "comprehensive, coordinated, long-term federal strategy" for all drug abuse prevention and drug traffic prevention activities conducted or supported by federal departments and agencies; the council would be be composed of the director of the Special Action Office, the attorney general, the VA administrator, the secretaries of defense, state and health, education and welfare, and other persons of the President's choice.

Title IV

• Amended the Community Mental Health Centers Act to allow grants for such centers to provide drug treatment and rehabilitation programs; authorized $180-million for fiscal 1973-75 for center staffing grants and $100-million in fiscal 1973-74 for center treatment programs.

• Amended the Public Health Service Act by providing drug abuse treatment and rehabilitation programs in facilities operated by the Public Health Service.

• Required that after June 30, 1973, state plans for grants for public health services have provisions for drug abuse prevention and treatment programs.

• Required the HEW secretary, within 90 days of enactment, to provide Congress and the director with a plan for the administration and coordination of all drug abuse activities in HEW; the secretary also was to maintain an information center on drug abuse prevention.

• Provided that no public or private hospital supported by federal funds could refuse emergency medical treatment to drug users; failure to provide such treatment could result in loss of funds.

• Provided for the confidentiality of patients' records prepared in connection with drug abuse programs affected by the act; disclosure of identity could come only with the patient's permission or pursuant to a court order.

• Established a formula grant program for assistance to states in planning, establishing, maintaining, coordinating and evaluating drug abuse projects; authorized $130-million for fiscal 1972-75 for the grants, to be administered by the HEW secretary.

• Provided that in order to be eligible for grants, each state must develop a drug abuse plan, designate a single agency to administer the plan, designate an advisory council for the agency and ensure coordination of state efforts against drug abuse.

• Established a special grant program to help public and private nonprofit agencies, organizations and individuals in drug abuse prevention, treatment and rehabilitation programs; authorized $350-million for fiscal 1972-75 for the grants, to be administered by the HEW secretary.

• Provided that the HEW secretary's decision to approve a special grant be based in part on an evaluation of the project filed with him by the agency created to administer the state's over-all drug abuse plan.

• Required the director of the Special Action Office to establish a National Drug Abuse Training Center to conduct training programs and other related activities to combat drug abuse; the center would be available to federal, state and local government officials, medical and related personnel, educators and others, including

Drug Traffic Report

In a report issued Oct. 24, 1971, by the House Foreign Affairs Committee, Rep. Seymour Halpern (R N.Y.) said international organizations had failed to use their authority to control the international drug traffic.

Reporting on an April 9-30 study mission in 11 countries in Southeast Asia, the Near East and Europe, Halpern said efforts to control dangerous drugs were hindered because high officials in some countries were involved in illegal drug traffic.

Halpern, a member of the Foreign Affairs Subcommittee on International Organizations and Movements, said international organizations, "despite having the authority to act on many aspects of narcotics control, have been unproductive, ineffective, and have failed to respond to this world crisis...."

drug users desiring training in drug abuse prevention; authorized $15-million for fiscal 1972-75 for the center; provided that the center would be transferred to the National Institute on Drug Abuse on Dec. 31, 1974.

• Provided that no person could be denied federal civilian employment because of prior drug use, except employees of or applicants to the Central Intelligence Agency, FBI, National Security Agency or any other department or agency designated by the President as dealing with national security.

Title V

• Established, effective Dec. 31, 1974, a National Institute on Drug Abuse in the National Institute of Mental Health, to administer the programs under the HEW secretary in the field of drug abuse.

• Amended the Public Health Service Act by creating a National Advisory Council on Drug Abuse to advise the HEW secretary about his functions in the field of drug abuse; the council would be composed of 15 members including the secretary, the chief medical officer of the VA, a medical representative of the Department of Defense and 12 other persons appointed by the secretary.

International Drug Traffic

Congress in 1972 took several steps which arose from the President's statement in his 1971 drug abuse message that greater effort must be made to get other countries to cease drug production.

Amendments added to three bills authorizing U.S. contributions to three international development lending institutions—the Asian Development Bank, PL 92-245; the Inter-American Development Bank, PL 92-246 and the International Development Association, PL 92-247—directed U.S. representatives to vote against loans to any nation that the President determined failed to take adequate steps to curb the sale of drugs to the United States or to U.S. personnel overseas.

The fiscal 1973 State Department appropriations bill (HR 14734—PL 92-352) included the full request of $42,500,000 for use by the President to help other nations and international organizations control narcotics traffic. The money had not been previously authorized. A major amount of the funds was used for payments to Turkish farmers for ceasing opium poppy production, and for enforcement of that effort. Turkey had been the major world supplier of opium, although it was also grown in other countries such as Pakistan, Afghanistan, Laos and Thailand.

Methadone Treatment

Congress amended the Narcotic Addict Rehabilitation Act of 1966—(PL 89-793) to permit the use of methadone in narcotic addiction treatment programs. The bill (HR 9323—PL 92-420) amended the definition of the word "treatment" (in PL 89-793) to include control of dependence (through use of synthetics such as methadone) in addition to elimination of dependence. *(Details of PL 89-793, Congress and the Nation, Vol. II, p. 315)*

Methadone is a synthetic drug that is addictive, like heroin, but which does not produce the euphoria or distorted behavior that heroin does. Persons undergoing controlled methadone maintenance programs were found to achieve functional normalcy impossible under heroin. President Nixon requested the bill in his 1971 message on drug abuse.

HR 9323 was passed unanimously by the House Nov. 1, 1971, and unanimously by the Senate Sept. 5, 1972.

Federal Education Programs

President Nixon's program for "fulfilling the federal role in education and meeting the educational needs of the 1970s" consisted of five major elements:

• Student assistance "to assure that no qualified person would be barred from college by a lack of money."

• A national institute "to bring energy and direction to educational research."

• A national foundation "to encourage innovation in learning beyond high school."

• Education revenue sharing.

• Emergency federal aid "to help local school districts desegregate wisely and well."

By the end of 1972, Congress had modified Nixon's student assistance plan, approved the institute, rejected the national foundation proposal, given perfunctory hearing to education revenue sharing, and authorized $500-million more than requested for desegregation aid.

And, critics noted, the Nixonian rhetoric endorsing educational improvement rang hollow when placed alongside the fact that he had, four times within his first term, vetoed bills providing funds to carry out federal programs of aid to education.

Education Funds Vetoes

One of the longest appropriations disputes in congressional history ended March 5, 1970—four months before the end of fiscal 1970—when President Nixon signed into law the fiscal 1970 appropriations bill (HR 15931—PL 91-204) for the Departments of Labor and Health, Education and Welfare (HEW). HR 15931 was the second bill for that purpose approved by Congress. The first, HR 13111, cleared Congress Jan. 26 but was vetoed by the President on nationwide television the same day.

The $19.7-billion contained in HR 13111—$1.1-billion more than the administration requested—Nixon said, was the "wrong amount for the wrong purposes for the wrong time." The veto, he said, "is in the vital interests of all Americans in stopping the rise in the cost of living."

The bill contained $717-million for elementary and secondary education, $312.5-million more than the administration request of $404.5-million. The White House maintained that only $15-million of the increase was necessary.

The House failed to override the veto, and Congress began work on a new bill (HR 15931). As finally enacted and approved by President Nixon, the measure contained $19.38-billion in appropriations—still $579.7-million over

the President's modified (compromise) request submitted Feb. 2 following the veto.

For the controversial impacted areas assistance, the final bill contained $80.4-million more than Nixon's compromise level, $318.4-million more than originally requested.

The Second Veto. In August 1970, President Nixon —proclaiming that his administration was determined "to hold the line against dangerous budget deficits"— vetoed HR 16916, a $4.4-billion appropriations bill for the Office of Education in fiscal 1971, because it appropriated $453-million over his request.

In his veto message, the President said the action meant "saying 'no' to bigger spending and 'no' to higher prices in the interest of all American people." The President argued that his budget request provided for a 28 percent increase in spending for education. Congress had appropriated $600-million more for education than in fiscal 1970, with major increases of $232-million for elementary and secondary education, $126-million for impact aid and $110-million for higher education.

Congress, however, overrode the President's veto by a 289-114 roll-call vote in the House, and a vote of 77-16 in the Senate.

Fiscal 1972. Although the bill (HR 7016—PL 92-48) appropriating $5.14-billion for the Office of Education and related agencies in fiscal 1972 contained $393-million more than requested by the administration, President Nixon signed the measure in July 1971.

Fiscal 1973. In mid-August 1972, President Nixon vetoed the Labor-HEW appropriations bill for fiscal 1973 (HR 15417) which contained $30.5-billion, an increase of $1.8-billion over the budget request. The bill, said Nixon, was "a perfect example of that kind of reckless federal spending that just cannot be done without more taxes or more inflation, both of which I am determined to avoid." The bill contained $2-billion for elementary and secondary education, $247.5-million more than requested; for impact aid it contained $681.4-million, $250.5-million more than requested. The House

---

References

Discussion of education policies for the years 1945-64 may be found in *Congress and the Nation, Vol. I,* p. 1195-1215; for the years, 1965-68, *Congress and the Nation, Vol. II,* p. 709-733.

failed to override the veto and work began immediately on a new bill.

A second bill (HR 16654) was cleared by Congress Oct. 14, providing almost exactly the same amounts of money for the Departments of Labor-HEW, but permitting the President to impound—not spend—up to $1.2-billion of the total, provided that no one appropriation was reduced by more than 13 percent. After Congress had adjourned, President Nixon again vetoed the bill Oct. 27.

ESEA Extension

A three-year, $24.6-billion extension of the 1965 Elementary and Secondary Education Act (ESEA) was signed by President Nixon in 1970, the largest authorization bill for education programs ever enacted. The administration had requested a two-year extension pending a full review of education programs.

Prior to final action, the Senate engaged in two major debates over equal enforcement of federal desegregation guidelines. The most heated Senate controversy centered around an amendment offered by John C. Stennis (D Miss.) and Abraham Ribicoff (D Conn.) which stated that federal guidelines on school desegregation must be applied equally to segregation in the North and South, whether *de jure* or *de facto*. Although the measure passed the Senate, House-Senate conferees required separate federal policies dealing with each type of discrimination.

The Nixon administration maintained a delicate position of neutrality on the amendment. In a formal statement, the President said (without endorsing the amendment) that "within the framework of the law, school desegregation problems should be dealt with uniformly throughout the land."

Major program revisions in the Elementary and Secondary Education Act extension (PL 91-230) included an increase to $4,000 from $3,000 in the maximum income level for determining eligibility of aid to school districts serving large numbers of poor children; and extension of impact aid to cover children living in federally financed public housing.

Budget requests and funding of these extended programs of aid to elementary and secondary education fell far below authorization levels in 1971 and 1972. *(Chart p. 585)*

Education Amendments of 1972

In mid-1972 Congress completed action on the most sweeping aid to education bill ever enacted. HEW Secretary Elliot L. Richardson praised the Education Amendments of 1972 (S 659—PL 92-318) as "truly a landmark in the history of education." The legislation differed significantly from President Nixon's original proposal for revising federal-aid-to-education programs.

The product of two and one-half years work, the bill authorized $19-billion for higher education programs through fiscal 1975, restructured existing higher education programs and established a new program of federal grants for qualified needy students. It also authorized a new program of federal aid to colleges and universities, and expanded federal aid for vocational education. The bill contained controversial provisions re-

---

Federal Outlays for Higher Education

(in millions of dollars)

Agencies	Fiscal 1971 actual	Fiscal 1972 estimate	Fiscal 1973 estimate
Department of Defense	516	535	543
Office of Education	1,388	1,469	1,394
Other HEW agencies	2,055	2,339	2,624
Housing and Urban Development	118	69	64
Veterans Administration	1,252	1,706	1,828
National Science Foundation	353	413	432
Others	472	519	560
TOTAL	6,154	7,050	7,445

SOURCE: Office of Management and Budget

---

stricting school busing and provided $2-billion in aid for desegregating school districts.

In 1970, Nixon sent Congress a special message proposing the refocusing of federal education aid to students from low-income families. He pointed out that a person whose family income exceeded $15,000 was five times more likely to attend college than one from a family with an annual income of less than $3,000.

Nixon also proposed that the financing of student loans be shifted to the private money market—phasing out the program of direct federal loans—and that Congress create a national foundation for higher education and a national institute of education to spark research and innovation in American education.

Critics of the administration's proposals said that they would substantially reduce aid to students from middle-income families, that the proposed shift to the private money market would reduce the amount of loan aid available and that aid should be provided to those already-strained colleges and universities which the additional government-aided students attended.

By late 1971, both the House and Senate had rejected the major thrusts of Nixon's student-aid proposals. The administration then supported the basic student grant program adopted by the Senate and a cost-of-education payment approach to general aid to colleges and universities. This payment would be based on the number of federally aided students attending an institution, to meet the cost of educating those students.

As cleared by Congress in June, the bill contained the Senate student-aid provisions which entitled any college student in good standing to a grant of $1,400 minus the amount his family could reasonably be expected to contribute toward his education expenses.

PL 92-318 also established a national institute of education within HEW, as requested by Nixon, to encourage educational research, and provided that direct federal aid be apportioned to higher education institutions on the basis of the amount of federal aid paid to students, the number of federal grant recipients attending each institution and the number of graduate students in attendance.

Desegregation Aid. President Nixon in 1970 requested $1.5-billion for improving schools in "racially impacted" areas and for aiding school districts to overcome problems caused by court-ordered desegregation.

Congress authorized $2-billion in desegregation aid as part of the 1972 education amendments.

School Financing

President Nixon April 6, 1971, sent Congress a special revenue sharing plan to consolidate into one program 33 existing categories of federal aid to elementary and secondary education. About $3-billion (roughly the same amount already provided in categorical grants) would be apportioned among the states on the basis of a formula taking into account the total school-age population in each state, the number of students from low-income families and the number of students whose families resided or worked on federal property.

Although the President stated in the expanded 1972 State of the Union address sent to Congress that he had "continuing confidence that special revenue sharing for education can do much to strengthen the backbone of our educational system...without compromising the principle of local control," Congress gave slight hearing to the proposal opposed by the education leaders.

Education interest groups were unenthusiastic about the proposal because it would erase existing categorical programs, which they considered effective, and provide only a small amount of additional funds.

Donald E. Morrison, president, National Education Association, told the Senate Labor and Public Welfare Subcommittee on Education Oct. 27, 1971:

"The problem with the federal aid programs is that they have never been fully funded, and the revenue-sharing proposal contains still-inadequate funds. It seems that the thrust of this bill is to provide administrative convenience and perhaps to bring political relief from the pressures for full funding of existing grant programs."

In his 1972 State of the Union message, the President committed himself to a solution to the growing problem involved in the financing of local school systems through property taxes, which he described as "one of the most inequitable and regressive of all public levies," but no firm proposals for reform were sent from the White House in 1972.

EDUCATION PROGRAMS: 1945-72

Support of elementary and secondary education is primarily a local responsibility; college education traditionally has been furnished by the states and private citizens. Yet in the 1971-72 school year, the federal government provided 7.9 percent of all funds spent on elementary and secondary education and 16.7 percent of higher education funds.

Direct federal contributions to education date back to the Morrill Act of 1862, establishing land-grant colleges in the states. But federal involvement grew slowly over the next 100 years. A dramatic change occurred in the middle 1960s—a landmark period in American education.

By 1966, the federal government was aiding education at all levels, from pre-school through graduate school to adult education for those bypassed along the way. From nursery schools to university campuses, it would be hard by the late 1960s to find a single pupil, teacher or classroom not in some way affected by the federal government's interest and assistance.

From the Morrill Act which helped establish colleges to the Smith-Hughes Act of 1917 which supported vocational training at the high school level, the government moved piecemeal into the education field. In the 1940s and 1950s Congress authorized the government to buy school lunches, to supply funds to improve the teaching of science, mathematics and foreign languages, to lend colleges money to build dormitories, to educate veterans and to grant funds for school construction, operation and teachers' salaries in areas "impacted" by tax-free federal property and the school-age children of federal employees.

Until 1965, however, no aid program was enacted which could be considered a general subsidy for education or for college students. The Elementary and Secondary Education Act of 1965 launched a federal program so broad in application as to constitute the first general aid-to-education program ever adopted by Congress. In the same year the government for the first time assumed responsibility, in the Higher Education Act, to pay for a college education for talented but needy students.

ELEMENTARY AND SECONDARY EDUCATION

Until the 1940s it was a truism that responsibility for the lower levels of education rested entirely in the states and local communities. But growing financial strains on local and state governments and the greater taxing power of the federal government led to slowly rising support in Congress for some general kind of federal contribution to education. A key portent was the conversion of the pre-eminent leader of conservative Republicanism, Sen. Robert A. Taft (R Ohio 1939-53). Taft declared in 1946 that the nation's schools no longer could provide an adequate education for all without federal assistance.

Two years later, the Senate for the first time passed a general school aid bill, but the House remained opposed to the concept. It did not give in until 1960, only to see

---

Federal Financial Aid

Federal aid to education comes in a variety of garbs—from the fellowship check to a graduate student to the non-profit, tax-exempt status enjoyed by most institutions of higher education.

Most existing federal aid to education consists of aid directly to the students—like fellowships and GI educational benefits—and of **categorical grants,** which provide aid for clearly defined categories of school needs.

Another form of aid, often advocated by Republican members of Congress, is the **block grant.** This type of grant is simply a chunk of money given to a state or institution which then decides how it should be divided up among various needs. **Education revenue-sharing,** as proposed by the Nixon administration, is an expansion of the block grant concept: under this proposal, each state would receive a certain amount of money—to be spent as the state decided within general areas of emphasis delineated by the federal government.

final action on the legislation stymied by the Rules Committee, which refused to let the House-passed bill be sent to conference with the Senate. Five years later, the first broad general-aid bill was enacted.

Over the years, opposition to general aid was based primarily on the contention that federal aid meant federal control of the schools, particularly if teachers' salaries and textbooks were part of the aid package. Two other basic issues added to the controversy: the government's position with regard to racially segregated schools and church-related schools.

The segregation issue reached its peak after the Supreme Court's 1954 decision outlawing the doctrine of "separate but equal" schools. It was largely resolved by the Civil Rights Act of 1964, which authorized federal court suits for desegregation of schools and the withholding of federal funds from institutions that practiced segregation.

The church-state issue, based on the First Amendment's ban on federal laws concerning religion, was not resolved until 1965. Legislation in the late 1940s had proposed to let the states spend federal education funds as they did their own tax revenues, supporting public schools and, in some states, parochial schools as well. Opposition to this proposal was too strong to overcome, and in the next decade Congress considered legislation that would specifically prohibit aid to private schools. Opposition then came from the Roman Catholic church and its spokesmen in Congress. The impasse continued until, in the 1965 Act, federal aid was focused on disadvantaged children no matter what kind of school they attended.

Elementary and Secondary

Education Act (ESEA)

This Act, the first general aid to education law (PL 89-10), was signed by President Johnson April 11, 1965, outside the former one-room schoolhouse at Stonewall, Texas, where he first attended classes. The President, a former school teacher himself, said no measure he had "signed, or will ever sign, means more to the future of America."

Enactment of the law took only three months—largely because old controversies were stilled by the new emphasis on aid to children, not schools, and because the Democratic party had achieved huge majorities in Congress in the November 1964 elections. To make sure there was no hang-up in conference, the Senate accepted the bill exactly as the House had passed it, which was almost as submitted by the Johnson administration.

The heart of the Act was Title I, which directed its funds to school districts on the basis of the number of children from low-income families in the area. Thus, although 95 percent of the nation's counties were eligible for aid, the bulk of the money was to be concentrated on the inner city and impoverished rural areas where the neediest children lived.

The appeal to all geographical segments was underlined by Title I's formula for providing federal funds, which was based on each state's average spending per student and its number of children from low-income families. Thus it appealed to the poorer states by taking into account their many poor children and to the richer states by recognizing their higher expenditures per child. The

formula was made more generous to the poorer states in 1966 by permitting them to use the national average expenditure per child instead of their own, smaller figure.

The church-state controversy which had blocked so many school bills in the past was overcome by ESEA's focus on aid to needy children rather than schools. The school districts were directed to include private school children in compensatory programs and to lend (but not give) federally funded school books to needy private school children. Such aid was not comprehensive enough to offend powerful opponents of private school aid and was satisfactory to lobbyists for aid to parochial schools.

SUMMARY OF ESEA PROVISIONS. Following are the main provisions of the Elementary and Secondary Education Act (ESEA) as passed in 1965 and amended in 1966, 1967 and 1970. Technically, the entire Act was an amendment to the "impacted area" school law of 1950 (PL 81-874), but it is generally treated as an entirely separate law.

Title I. This title allocated funds to local school districts (through state agencies) under a formula that multiplied the number of school children from low-income families (under $2,000 a year or on public assistance) by one-half of the state's average expenditure per school child. In 1966 Congress raised the low-income figure to $3,000, to take effect in fiscal 1968, but the next year this provision was made conditional upon the availability of sufficient appropriations to fulfill the goal. With appropriations for fiscal 1968 and 1969 falling far short of amounts authorized in the revised formula, the new income level was not put into effect.

The 1966 amendments to ESEA made another change in the formula, one that greatly benefited the poorer states. It allowed any state to use the national average expenditure per school child, instead of its own expenditure figure, in determining its Title I allotments. As a result, most Southern states received a substantial increase; the poorest state, Mississippi, went from $23.5 million in fiscal 1967 to $44.8 million in fiscal 1968.

"Incentive" grants were authorized but not funded. They were to go to states that spent a larger share of their resources on education than the national average.

The purposes for which Title I funds could be used were largely left up to the local school districts. The Act said only that the money was for programs "designed to meet the special educational needs of educationally deprived children." The schools could reduce their class sizes, hire remedial reading teachers, buy special equipment, serve breakfasts at school—the possibilities were endless.

Private school children, however, had to be included in some of the programs. The act said the local school agency must make provision for special services (such as dual enrollment, educational TV programs or mobile educational facilities) in which private school children could participate.

Reviewing the first three years of the program, HEW Secretary Wilbur J. Cohen said in January 1969 that the trend among participating schools was to put "increasing stress on activities most directly serving the student's needs: improving the quality of instruction and offering such services as medical care, guidance and counseling, and food." The percentage of money spent on construction and equipment had dropped sharply from the first year,

ESEA Appropriations-Authorization Gap

(figures in millions of dollars)

ESEA Titles	1969		1970		1971		1972	
	Authorized	Appropriated	Authorized	Appropriated	Authorized	Appropriated	Authorized	Appropriated
I-Educationally deprived children	$2,776	$1,123	$2,523.3	$1,339	$3,457.4	$1,500	$3,642.8	$1,597.5
II-Library resources, textbooks	165	50	206	42.5	206	80	216.3	90
III-Supplementary education centers	528	165	566.5	116.4	556.3	143.4	592.3	146.4
V-Strengthening state education departments	80	30	80	29.8	110	29.8	130	33
VI-Handicapped children	179	31	206	29.2	206	34	216.3	37.5
VII-Bilingual education	30	7	40	21.3	80	25	100	35
VIII-Dropout prevention	30	5	30	5	30	10	31.5	10
Total	$3,788	$1,411	$3,651.8	$1,583.1	$4,645.7	$1,822.2	$4,929.2	$1,949.4

SOURCE: HEW Office of Education, Budget Division

while the proportion spent on instruction and, to a much smaller extent, services had increased, Cohen said.

Over 9 million children participated each year in Title I programs, about 500,000 of whom were private school students. In addition, children of migrant farmworkers, residents in state institutions for neglected, handicapped or delinquent children, and those attending Indian schools received separate Title I allotments.

The failure to appropriate up to the level authorized, however, meant a reduction in per capita spending over the first three years. The number of poor children covered in the formula went up from 5,600,000 to 6,670,000 between 1966 and 1968 and to 7,900,000 by 1973 while the amount spent per child declined from $210 to $173. (The other children included in the 9,000,000 Title I total were attending the same schools as the "formula" children but were from families with incomes above the Act's poverty definition.)

Authorizations under the formula rose from $1-billion for fiscal 1966 to $3.6 billion for fiscal 1972, but appropriations were much lower and reached only $1.6 billion in fiscal 1972.

The most important change made by the 1970 act in Title I was an expansion of the program to include children from families earning up to $4,000 rather than $3,000 yearly.

Title II. Unchanged since its enactment in 1965, Title II authorized federal grants to the states for school library resources, textbooks and other printed material for the use of children and teachers in public and private schools. To avoid conflict with the First Amendment's clause guaranteeing freedom from any state "establishment" of religion, the ESEA specified that title and control of all materials furnished under Title II must remain with a public agency and that all ma-

terials, including books, must have been approved for use in public schools.

Because many states and school boards provide free textbooks for their schools, the emphasis under Title II has been on library resources. Almost $300 million was appropriated for the program in ESEA's first three years. In subsequent years the level of funding decreased.

Title III. This title was designed to introduce innovative programs into the schools. Federal grants were provided for supplementary educational centers and services that could serve as models for regular school programs or as centralized supplements to the curricula of individual schools.

The act specified a number of different services that might be offered, including: specialized equipment and instruction for students in advanced scientific subjects and foreign languages; art and music courses; production of educational radio and TV programs; special services for people in rural areas, including mobile units; and counseling and social services to encourage dropouts and adults to resume their education.

Originally, grants were made directly from the U.S. Commissioner of Education to the agencies applying for funds, although there was a general allotment of funds by state, based on their population.

In 1967 Congress rewrote the program to give most of the control to state education agencies. State plans for use of the funds were to be drawn up, and after fiscal 1969 the state agencies would distribute all of the money. However, 15 percent of the funds were to be spent on special programs for handicapped children. (Title VI of ESEA, which was added in 1966, was directed entirely at handicapped children.)

In 1970 Congress consolidated Title III of ESEA and Title V (a) of the National Defense Education Act (guidance, counseling and testing) and authorized programs under Titles III and V for gifted and talented children.

Authorizations for Title III programs, like those for Title I, increased sharply over the years but appropriations remained relatively stable. The program began with a $100 million authorization increasing to $556-million for fiscal 1971 and $592-million for fiscal 1972. Appropriations for 1971 and 1972, however, were only $143-million and $146-million, respectively.

Title IV. The Cooperative Research Act of 1954, providing federal construction aid for educational research facilities, had funded research centers on a pilot basis at four universities. In 1965 the program was written into ESEA as Title IV and was expanded to permit contracts or grants to various kinds of research groups. A five-year authorization of $100 million for cooperative research construction was provided.

The 1970 act extended the $100-million authorization through fiscal 1974, and the Education Amendments of 1972 authorized additional funds; but total appropriations were far below these levels.

Title V. To strengthen state departments of education, Title V of ESEA authorized direct federal grants for such purposes as statewide planning, reporting of educational data and programs to improve the competence of employees of educational agencies and of teacher training efforts.

Originally, 85 percent of each appropriation was to be alloted directly to the states and 15 percent reserved for allotment by the U.S. Commissioner for experimental projects or services that might help state agencies on a regional or nationwide basis. In 1967 the Commissioner's share was reduced to 5 percent. About $30 million a year was appropriated under the title although the authorization permitted $110-million in fiscal 1971 and $130-million in 1972.

The 1970 act authorized new programs of grants for strengthening local education agencies, grants to aid planning and evaluation on local and state levels and of advisory councils on quality education.

Title VI. Enacted in 1966, this title authorized federal funds to assist the states in the education of mentally and physically handicapped children. It was expanded in 1967 to include funds to improve the recruitment of personnel for the field, to establish regional resource centers and model centers for deaf-blind children.

Under the state grant program a number of services were provided for the first time: mobile units for rural areas, work-study programs, and special transportation arrangements, for example. Nearly 225,000 children were helped under the program in its first years.

Title VII. At the initiative of Congress, particularly the delegations from California and Texas, a program to improve the education of children from non-English-speaking families was authorized in 1967. About 3 million children of school age were expected to benefit from special programs funded under this Bilingual Education title.

However, although $100-million was authorized for aid to school districts and teacher training in fiscal 1972, the appropriation was only $35-million.

Title VIII. Two other Congressionally initiated programs were added to this title in 1967. One authorized grants for local programs to cut school dropout rates. The demonstration programs were to focus on schools which have a high concentration of children from low-income families and a high dropout rate. The authorization was for $30 million a year, but the first appropriation, granted in fiscal 1969, was for only $5 million, which was expected to finance five projects; by 1972 the appropriation had risen to $10-million.

The second new program in Title VIII authorized a small technical assistance project for rural schools to help them apply for federal aid. In 1968 this was replaced by a more general provision for collection and dissemination of information which was written into the Vocational Education Amendments of 1968.

Federal Control. The 1965 Act stated that there was to be no federal control over the curriculum, selection of books or personnel of any school aided by the ESEA, nor was there to be any payment of funds for religious worship or instruction.

Desegregation. After a bitter battle in 1966, Congress wrote into the law language prohibiting the Federal Government from requiring the assignment or transportation of students or teachers to overcome racial imbalance—in other words, to alter de facto segregation. The provision left intact the Government's authority to require desegregation of schools that were run on a discriminatory basis; it also permitted school districts, if they wanted, to use federal funds for busing students in order to improve the racial balance of their schools.

A time limit was set for determination by the U.S. Commissioner of Education of a district's compliance with the nondiscrimination requirements of the 1964 Civil Rights Act. Title VI of that Act authorized the Commissioner, after holding hearings, to withhold federal funds from any school district found in noncompliance with the Act.

Adult Education. The community action program authorized in the 1964 Economic Opportunity Act, the basic antipoverty law, included as one of its many undertakings projects to upgrade the education of adults. In 1966 Congress transferred this activity to the U.S. Commissioner of Education. Specific authorization of funds for the program was made, and the Federal Government's share of the cost of each local undertaking was set at 90 percent. Most of the money was to go to state agencies for distribution, but 20 per cent was reserved for experimental projects funded directly by the commissioner.

In 1972 the Adult Education Act was amended to authorize grants for projects and programs of adult education specifically for American Indians. For fiscal 1973, $5-million was authorized; for fiscal 1973-74, $8-million each.

Teacher Corps

The National Teacher Corps was first proposed in 1965 by Sens. Edward M. Kennedy (D Mass.) and Gaylord Nelson (D Wis.). Kennedy had noted the success of trained volunteers who taught Negro students in Prince Edward County, Va., when the public schools were closed to avoid integration. Nelson was impressed with the impact of former Peace Corps volunteers who participated as teacher interns in ghetto schools in Washington, D.C.

The two Senators offered their Teacher Corps proposal as an amendment to the Higher Education Act. The idea was quickly endorsed by President Johnson and became labeled a Great Society program.

The National Teacher Corps was created by Title V, Part B of the Higher Education Act of 1965 (PL 89-329). The Corps had no difficulty in the Senate, but it survived in conference with the House only after a motion by Albert H. Quie (R Minn.) to delete it was rejected on a 152-226 roll-call vote of the House.

The Corps was designed to improve elementary and secondary education in city slums and impoverished rural areas by sending in teams of an experienced teacher and several young college graduates to strengthen local school programs. The Act authorized the Commissioner of Education to recruit teachers and interns to serve in the Corps for up to two years.

There were two stages in the program—a three-month summer training period at a designated college, followed by an in-service period during which a team was assigned to a local school. The interns had their tuition paid for part-time graduate work at a nearby university.

The primary goal of the program was to improve public education in poverty areas. But the program was also intended to encourage idealistic college graduates to enter training in the country.

PL 89-329 authorized $36,100,000 for fiscal 1966 and $64,715,000 for fiscal 1967. In 1967, in PL 90-35, the Teacher Corps was extended for three years, through fiscal 1970, and the word "National" was removed from its name. Authorizations for the Corps were set at $33 million in fiscal 1968, $46 million in 1969 and $56 million in 1970. In 1970 the authorization for fiscal 1970 was increased to $80 million and to $100 million for fiscal 1971. The Education Amendments of 1972 reduced the authorization level through fiscal 1975 to $37.5-million (the amount appropriated for fiscal 1972) or one-quarter of the total appropriation under Title V of the 1965 Higher Education Act, whichever figure was greater. The reduced level of authorization in the 1972 amendments reflected low levels of appropriation—rising from only $9.5 million for fiscal 1966 to $37.5 million for fiscal 1972.

Opposition to the Teacher Corps was always something of a mystery. It was extremely popular with school authorities; it provided direct assistance to the neediest schools while at the same time training young school teachers to cope with the most difficult of educational problems. To overcome opposition, Congress specified that not only the local schools but also the state agencies must request the assignment of Teacher Corpsmen and that 10 percent of their salaries must be furnished by the schools they were serving. The opposition came from the "conservative coalition" of Republicans and Southern Democrats and was generally based on the need to economize in federal spending.

Impacted Area Schools

Although no general school aid program was approved by Congress until 1965, from 1950 on there were two highly popular programs of federal grants to build and operate schools and pay teachers in federally "impacted" areas. The programs were begun as the outgrowths of federal commitments in the Lanham Act of 1940 to provide school aid in areas where federal activities brought in more families and reduced taxable property. Amendments raising the amount of federal support and liberalizing the qualifications for aid over the following 10 years led to a broad program which some Congressmen, mainly those from recipient areas, said merely honored a federal commitment to supplant lost taxes, and which others, mainly those from non-recipient areas and those who supported general school aid, said had developed into a massive "pork barrel."

Repeatedly, Presidents Eisenhower, Kennedy and Johnson were rebuffed in attempts to cut back the impacted areas program to what they said would represent more accurately the need of each "impacted" district.

The two 1950 laws (PL 81-815 and 81-874) authorized federal grants to areas "impacted" by tax-free federal property and installations, Indian reservations or Government contractors. PL 815 authorized federal payments for school construction; PL 874 authorized federal payments for building maintenance and teachers' salaries. The two laws did not authorize specific money appropriations but set criteria for determining whether a school district was entitled to assistance and, if so, how much it could receive.

Under PL 874 the Government paid 100 per cent of the local share of the cost of educating each child whose parents both lived and worked on federal property (Section A). It paid 50 per cent of the local share of the cost of educating children whose parents lived or worked on taxable property (Section B). It also authorized payments of 100 per cent the first year and 50 per cent the second where there were sudden increases in federal contract activity (Section C).

Under PL 815, the Government paid 95 per cent of the cost per pupil of construction for Section A children, 50 per cent for Section B children and 45 per cent for Section C children.

Section A of both laws was permanent; the others carried expiration dates.

In 1970 the program was amended to include children living in federally financed public housing, but through fiscal 1972 this part of the program had not been funded.

COLLEGE AND GRADUATE EDUCATION

Unlike the elementary and secondary field, federal aid to institutions of higher education was well established before 1965. But the late 1960s and early 1970s produced a dramatic new emphasis on aid to college students, especially those from families who could not afford a college education for their children.

Federal scholarships were authorized in the Higher Education Act of 1965, though they were disguised as "educational opportunity grants," not scholarships. The same Act also authorized interest subsidies on private loans to middle-income students and transferred the anti-poverty agency's work-study program for college students to the Office of Education.

Federal financing of direct loans to students dated back to the 1958 National Defense Education Act (NDEA); the subsidized-interest program was intended to replace NDEA loans, but Congress insisted on retaining both pro-

(Continued on p. 590)

Major Trends in Education: Projections of . . .

Population is increasing less rapidly or declining.

(change in millions)

	1958	1968	1978
Elementary school age	30.9	37.2 (+20%)	35.5 (— 5%)
Secondary school age	10.9	15.1 (+39%)	16.8 (+11%)
Higher education undergraduate age	9.0	14.3 (+59%)	16.9 (+18%)

The high school graduation rate is increasing.

Graduates as percent of 18-year-olds

1958-59	64%
1968-69	77%
1978-79	88%

The proportion of high school diplomas awarded to boys is increasing and is expected to exceed 50 percent before 1979.

Boys as percent of all graduates

1958-59	48.2 % (790,000 of 1,639,000)
1968-69	49.8 % (1,408,000 of 2,839,000)
1978-79	50.6 % (1,908,000 of 3,773,000)

Proportionately more people are earning college degrees.

Bachelor's degrees as percent of graduation age population

1958-59	17.5 %
1968-69	22.0 %
1978-79	25.4 %

A larger proportion of degrees earned are advanced degrees.

	Master's as percent of total	Doctor's (except first-professional) as percent of total
1958-59	15.6% (72,500 of 462,000)	2.0% (9,400 of 462,000)
1968-69	19.4% (188,600 of 969,700)	2.7% (26,100 of 969,700)
1978-79	24.9% (368,400 of 1,481,400)	3.8% (57,000 of 1,481,000)

The proportion of bachelor's and first-professional degrees awarded to women is increasing.

Women as percent of bachelor's and first-professional-degree recipients (numbers)

1958-59	33.5% (127,000 of 380,000)
1968-69	42.5% (321,000 of 755,000)
1978-79	46.8% (494,000 of 1,056,000)

*SOURCE: *Projections of Educational Statistics to 1978-79,* Office of Education.

... Enrollment and Expenditures from 1958 to 1979*

Degree-credit enrollment in 2-year institutions is growing faster than in 4-year institutions.

Degree-credit students in 2-year institutions as percent
of all degree-credit students (members)

1958	11.9% (386,000 of 3,236,000)
1968	18.6% (1,289,000 of 6,928,000)
1978	21.1% (2,176,000 of 10,318,000)

The ratio of public elementary and secondary students to classroom teachers is declining.

Ratio of students to classroom teachers

	Total	Elementary	Secondary
1958	26.1	28.7	21.7
1968	23.1	25.4	20.3
1978	22.4	24.5	20.2

The cost of educating elementary and secondary students is increasing.

	Current expenditure per pupil in average daily attendance (1968-69 dollars)	Total expenditures by school systems (in billions)
1958-59	$440	$20.7
1968-69	696	39.8
1978-79	885	52.0

The cost of educating college students is increasing.

Current expenditures per full-time-equivalent student
for student education (1968-69 dollars)

	Total	Publicly controlled institutions	Privately controlled institutions
1958-59	$1,355	$1,350	$1,361
1968-69	1,772	1,638	2,100
1978-79	2,089	1,865	2,833

Expenditures by higher education institutions is increasing.

(billions of 1968-69 dollars)

	Total	Publicly controlled institutions	Privately controlled institutions
1958-59	$7.8	$ 4.4	$ 3.4
1968-69	21.3	13.6	7.7
1978-79	35.4	22.8	12.6

grams. As interest rates zoomed up in 1966 and again in 1968, the private, subsidized program fell far below expectations in the number of students it helped.

The principal laws aiding colleges and universities were the 1950 Housing Act, the 1963 Higher Education Facilities Act, the 1958 National Defense Education Act, the Economic Opportunity Act of 1964 and the Higher Education Act of 1965, as amended in 1972.

College Housing and Classrooms

The 1950 Housing Act authorized 40-year, low-interest Government loans to public and private colleges and universities for construction of dormitories and infirmaries. The program was operated through a revolving fund administered by the Housing and Home Finance Agency, which became the Department of Housing and Urban Development. The agency was authorized to borrow $300 million from the Treasury to set up the fund, and this authorization was regularly reviewed. In 1965 a flat 3 percent interest rate was set on the loans. In 1968 Congress enacted a program of debt service grants (i.e., subsidized interest on private loans). Since 1968 this program has financed construction of college housing. The direct loan revolving fund also continues and is used for those colleges which cannot get market loan financing.

A more controversial program of federal aid for college classroom construction was included in the Higher Education Facilities Act of 1963. The Act authorized $1.2 billion over three years in federal grants and loans for facilities at public and private colleges and universities. The funds for grants were earmarked for libraries and classrooms where science, engineering, mathematics or modern language courses were taught.

When the program was extended in 1965, these categorical restrictions, similar to those in the original NDEA law, were removed.

By fiscal 1971 annual authorizations for the program had reached $936-million for grants for undergraduate facilities, $120-million for graduate facilities and $400-million in loans. But authorization levels were sharply cut for fiscal 1973 and 1974—to $200- and $300-million for undergraduate facilities, to $40- and $60-million for graduate facilities, and $100- and $150-million in loans.

National Defense Education Act (NDEA)

Enacted in 1958 in reaction to Russian achievements in space technology, symbolized by the 1957 orbiting of the first earth satellite (Sputnik), and in awareness of the country's need for more scientists, the NDEA focused on encouraging the study of science, mathematics and foreign languages. All school levels were covered by the Act. Its major titles provided equipment for elementary and secondary schools; financed loans for college students; and authorized three-year graduate fellowships, with preference for prospective college teachers.

By the end of 1968, after several extensions, NDEA's focus on limited, mainly scientific, categories was ended and aid for study of almost all subjects was authorized under the Act. For the principal programs the 1968 extension authorized: $130-million in fiscal 1970 for purchase of equipment for lower schools, plus an additional $160-mil-

lion for schools receiving ESEA Title I funds (those in disadvantaged areas); $275-million for student loans; and 7,500 new graduate fellowships a year, with matching payments to the graduate schools of $3,500 per fellow.

The NDEA student loans grew out of a proposal by President Eisenhower in 1958 for 10,000 federal scholarships a year. The House Education and Labor Committee reported a bill providing 23,000 scholarships and, in addition, $220-million for a federal student loan fund. The scholarship provision was stripped from the bill on the floor, and the $120 million authorized for the scholarships was added to the loan fund. The Senate version was accepted in conference and became law. Under its provisions, the Federal Government provided 90 per cent and the individual schools 10 per cent of the money in loan funds set up and administered by each participating college.

Under the original NDEA, undergraduates were eligible for loans of up to $1,000 a year, not to exceed $5,000 during a student's undergraduate years. The 3-percent interest rate did not go into effect until the repayment period began, nine months after the student left college. The repayment could be deferred up to a total of three years while the recipient was attending graduate school or serving in the armed forces, the Peace Corps or Volunteers in Service to America (VISTA). Repayment could extend over a 10-year period.

If the borrower became a full-time school teacher or college professor, half of the loan was cancelled at 10 per cent for each year of teaching. If he taught at designated "hardship" schools in low-income areas or was a teacher of handicapped children, he could have the additional 50 per cent cancelled at 15 per cent a year.

To receive a loan, students had to sign an oath of loyalty to the United States.

Since the loans were made directly by the institutions, students applied directly to their colleges.

Office of Education figures showed that through the end of the 1966-67 college year, one million students had borrowed more than $1 billion since the program began.

The Education Amendments of 1972 increased authorizations for direct student loans to a level of $375-million for fiscal 1972 and $400-million annually for 1973-1975 and set a $2,500 aggregate limit on direct loans to an undergraduate student in his first two years of study (replacing a $1,000 per year ceiling).

The 1972 act also restricted the kinds of jobs or service in the armed forces for which part of these loans could be cancelled, eliminating forgiveness for teaching unless the teacher taught handicapped children, students in a Head Start pre-school program or students in a school with a high concentration of disadvantaged children. Cancellation for military service was restricted to time of service in an area of hostilities.

Work-Study Program

The Economic Opportunity Act of 1964 (PL 88-452), the basic anti-poverty law, authorized grants to colleges to pay 90 per cent of the wages of students with part-time jobs in the college or other nonprofit institutions. The grants were to support students from low-income families.

The Higher Education Act of 1965 transferred the work-study program to the Office of Education, removed the requirement that students be from low-income families and permitted colleges to provide their matching share through services and equipment, including tuition and books. The Act authorized $129-million in fiscal 1966, $165-million in fiscal 1967 and $200-million in fiscal 1968. A further extension was made in 1968, raising the authorization to $285-million by fiscal 1971 and setting the federal matching share at 80 per cent of the grants. The Education Amendments of 1972 authorized $330-million for fiscal 1972, $360-million for 1973, $390-million for 1974 and $420-million for 1975. It also allowed half-time students to participate.

The work-study program was administered by the colleges, which passed upon the applications of their students and received the matching funds from the Government.

Work under the program was limited to an average of 15 hours a week while classes were in session and 40 hours a week during summers and vacation periods. The on-campus work could be anything from running the soda fountain in the student union to acting as faculty aides or laboratory assistants.

Higher Education Act of 1965

Enacted with wide bipartisan support in Congress, the Higher Education Act (PL 89-329) was revolutionary in several aspects, particularly in its student aid provisions. For the first time in U.S. history Congress approved federal scholarships for undergraduate students. The $70 million authorized annually for first-year scholarships was estimated to provide 140,000 students of "exceptional financial need" with scholarships each year. Scholarships had been approved by the Senate in past years only to die in the House. When HR 9567 was first debated by the House, an amendment to remove scholarships from the bill was defeated on a 58-88 standing vote. No further efforts were made to delete the provision.

Another new aid program for college students was insurance on loans, with federal subsidies on interest payments. Federally insured loans had been proposed by President Johnson when he was in Congress, and were subsequently requested by President Kennedy in 1963. Insured loans and scholarships, combined with the expanded work-study program also authorized by the Act, were expected to help students from middle-income as well as low-income backgrounds. They were designed to supplement NDEA loans.

Five titles of the 1965 Act provided aid for colleges and universities. For the first time, funds were voted ($50 million a year) to buy library materials, including books. Other programs in the Act provided grants to develop university extension courses related to community problems and funds to raise the academic quality of impoverished small colleges. The latter program was authorized for only one year because the Senate insisted on making junior colleges eligible, and the House was opposed.

Another key program established by the Act was the Teacher Corps (*see above*).

Title I of the Education Amendments of 1972 incorporated in the 1965 Act, as amended, certain programs established by the National Defense Education Act of 1958, and the provisions of the Higher Education Facilities Act of 1963. The 1965 Act thereby became the basic federal-aid-to-higher-education law covering almost all programs with the exception of veterans' benefits.

HIGHER EDUCATION ACT PROVISIONS. The principal programs in the Act, as amended by Congress in 1966, 1968 and 1972 were:

Title I. Matching grants to the states were authorized for community service programs conducted by public or private nonprofit colleges and universities. They were to give particular emphasis to urban and suburban problems, including housing, poverty, employment, transportation, health and other local issues.

Beginning at a $25 million level, the grants rose to an authorized $60 million for fiscal 1971, but the failure of appropriations to reach this level resulted in reduction of authorizations to $10-million for fiscal 1972 and $30-million for 1973, $40-million for 1974 and $50-million for 1975.

Title II. The library title of the Act, this section authorized basic grants for college library books and materials, special purpose grants for colleges with special needs, training grants to increase the supply of college librarians and to develop new techniques, and a small amount for the cataloging service of the Library of Congress. The 1968 extension of the Act authorized $75-million for this title in fiscal 1970 and $90-million in fiscal 1971. Authorizations for fiscal 1972 and 1973 were $39-million and $87-million, for 1974, $100-million; and for 1975, $109-million.

Title III. Colleges which "are struggling for survival and are isolated from the main currents of academic life," defined as "developing institutions," received special help under this title. The colleges, many of them small, largely Negro institutions in the South, could apply for federal grants to raise the academic quality of their programs. Faculty and student exchange programs with more established colleges were part of the offering, along with national teaching fellowships for graduate students and junior faculty members who wished to strengthen the developing colleges' faculties. Two-year colleges and technical institutes were eligible for aid as well as institutions that grant B.A. degrees. For fiscal 1970 and 1971, $70 million and $91 million, respectively, were authorized for this title of the Higher Education Act. The 1972 Act authorized $91-million for fiscal 1972 and $120-million, for 1973-75.

Title IV. The Student Assistance title of the Act authorized federal scholarships ("educational opportunity grants"), federally insured loans and subsidies on interest for full-time college students and transferred the work-study program authorized in the 1964 Economic Opportunity Act to the Office of Education.

The scholarships section authorized (in Part A) $70 million annually in fiscal 1966-68 for grants to institutions of higher education for first-year scholarships to full-time students "of exceptional financial need," plus whatever sums were necessary to continue scholarships beyond the first year.

It limited the amount of each scholarship to the lesser of $800 or half the amount of financial aid provided the student by the college or a state or private scholarship program, including loans and scholarships under the Act but excluding aid under work-study programs. (To be eligible for a federal scholarship, a student had to receive an equal amount of other financial aid.) A $200 bonus could be awarded scholarship students who in their preceding college year placed in the upper half of their class. In 1968 the bonus was dropped and the maximum scholarship was raised to $1,000, in 1972 the maximum grant was increased to $1,500.

Scholarship funds were allotted to the states according to the ratio of the number of each state's college students to the number nationally. The colleges receiving funds were forbidden to cut back their other student aid below the average amount furnished in the preceding three years.

Funds provided for these scholarships allowed 296,-800 new grants to students for the 1971-72 academic year and 266,700 for 1972-73.

The 1972 Act redesignated the educational opportunity grant program the "supplemental educational opportunity grant program," and established a new basic educational opportunity grant program under which any college student in good standing was entitled to a grant of $1,400 minus the amount his family would reasonably be expected to contribute to his educational expenses.

Upward Bound—A provision in the 1965 act authorized the U.S. commissioner of education to contract with public or private groups for the singling out of talented students who needed encouragement to attend college. This program, known as Talent Search, was directed in the 1968 law to take over, beginning in fiscal 1970, the better known Upward Bound program of the Office of Economic Opportunity, which had similar goals. Funds for the merged programs, including special services to help disadvantaged students stay in college, were set at $56.7 million for fiscal 1970 and $96 million for fiscal 1971. Under the 1972 act authorizations were $96-million for fiscal 1972 and $100-million annually for fiscal 1973-75.

Guaranteed Loans—Part B of Title IV established a guaranteed, interest-subsidized loan program designed for middle-income families. The program was proposed by the Johnson administration in the hope that private loans could replace the direct federal cost of NDEA student loans, but Congress clung to the popular NDEA program as well as approving the new program.

The new program sought to encourage state and private nonprofit insurance for student loans and authorized the Federal Government to pay the interest costs while a student was in college and 3 percent during the repayment period on loans made by private sources at a maximum percentage rate. The subsidy was available to families with net income, before taxes, of less than $15,000. The 1972 Act allowed students from families earning more than $15,000 to obtain loans in some cases.

In its first three years, the program fell far below its predicted scope as banks and other lenders found the interest rate too low and the administrative details too cumbersome to be profitable. By the end of 1968 the number of students receiving loans under the program was about 750,000 whereas the goal for the first year alone had been 950,000.

In 1968 Congress set the maximum interest rate at 7 percent and removed the interest subsidy during the after-college repayment period.

In 1969 Congress approved the Emergency Insured Student Loan Act, which authorized special payments to lenders in times of high interest rates. The 1972 act extended this act through 1974.

The 1972 Act also set up a student loan marketing association backed by the federal government through fiscal 1981 to provide a secondary market and warehouse for student loans.

Work-Study—The work-study program, originally part of the antipoverty law, became Part C of the Higher Education Act of 1965.

Cooperative Education—In 1968 Part D was added to Title IV. Entitled Cooperative Education, the program was to encourage alternate periods of full-time study and full-time employment. Beginning in fiscal 1970, grants of $8-million the first year and $10-million the second year could be made to colleges and universities to plan and carry out these programs.

Direct Loans. The 1972 Act added to Title IV of the Higher Education Act language authorizing the direct loan program established by Title II of the National Defense Education Act. *(Details in NDEA p. 590)*

Title V. This title established the Teacher Corps (described in the preceding section on Elementary Education) and a number of programs to improve teacher education, mainly by fellowships for graduate study.

The title was expanded in 1967 and given the name of the Education Professions Development Act. It added special grants for the educational upgrading of persons teaching or preparing to teach in elementary and high schools, and for the recruitment of qualified personnel in areas of critical teacher shortages. In 1972, $200-million was authorized for the title in fiscal 1973; $300-million in 1974, and $450-million in 1975.

Title VI. This title, the equipment section of the Higher Education Act, authorized 50-50 matching grants to the states for laboratory and audiovisual equipment and closed-circuit television equipment. The program was generally funded at $10- to $15-million a year.

Title VII. This title, completely revised in 1972 to contain the provisions of the Higher Education Facilities Act, authorized grants for construction of classrooms and other academic facilities by undergraduate and graduate institutions and authorized loans for this construction.

Title VIII. Added to the Act in 1968, this title was given the name Networks for Knowledge. It was intended to encourage colleges to share educational facilities and resources such as closed-circuit TV, computers and special library collections. The Commissioner of Education was authorized to make contracts to facilitate such sharing. Planning funds were authorized for fiscal 1969, plus grants of $4-million in fiscal 1970 and $15-million the next year; lack of any appropriations for the program brought cut-backs in authorization levels to $5-million for fiscal 1972, $10-million for 1973, and $15-million each in 1974 and 1975.

Title IX. The 1972 Act consolidated into a new Title IX a number of categorical programs of aid to graduate students. They included: aid to improve graduate programs (previously Title X) aid for graduate programs in public service, graduate fellowships for students intending to be college teachers (previously Title IV, NDEA), graduate fellowships for students intending to follow careers in state, local or federal governmental service and fellowships for students interested in mineral resource conservation.

Title X. The 1972 Act created a new Title X which contained a new program of aid to states for the planning of the expansion of their community college systems and of aid to the community colleges to assist their development and expansion. For planning grants, the bill authorized $15.7-million; for grants to colleges, the bill authorized $50-million in 1973, $75-million in 1974 and $150-million in 1975. In addition the newly written title also contained a new and expanded program of federal grants to improve post-secondary occupational education and to increase the preparation for such training in elementary and secondary schools. For these purposes, $100-million was authorized in 1973; $250-million in 1974, $500-million in 1975.

Title XI. This title authorized contracts with law schools to pay 90 per cent of the cost of programs providing clinical experience for law students. The hope was to train more trial lawyers. The authorization was $7.5-million annually in fiscal 1970 and 1971, but lack of funding resulted in a drop of authorization to $5-million for fiscal 1973 and $7.5-million each in 1974-75.

Title XII. As in other education acts, this title specified that nothing in the Act authorized any federal control over curriculum or personnel or any aid to religious instruction or departments of divinity. In addition, it specified that there was to be no federal control over college organizations, such as fraternities, which were financed entirely by private funds and whose facilities were not owned by the college.

NATIONAL SCIENCE FOUNDATION

The National Science Foundation was established by Congress in 1950 (PL 81-507) to promote basic scientific research and education of future scientists and to establish and coordinate national scientific policies.

The 1950 Act directed the NSF to "develop and encourage the pursuit of a national policy for the promotion of basic research and education in the sciences." The NSF was authorized to (1) make grants and loans for basic research in the mathematical, physical, medical, biological, engineering and other sciences; (2) undertake military research for national defense; (3) award scholarships and graduate fellowships to U.S. citizens; (4) aid the interchange of information among scientists in the United States and other countries; (5) correlate its programs with private and other public research projects; and (6) maintain a roster of scientific and technical personnel and in other ways provide a central clearinghouse for information on such personnel.

The Act authorized appropriation of $500,000 to establish the Foundation and get its program under way, and eventual appropriations of $15 million. In the first year of operation, fiscal 1951, the NSF received an appropriation of $225,000. In 1953, the $15-million ceiling was removed, but total appropriations did not exceed that level until 1956. In the next 11 years, appropriations increased rapidly until, in fiscal 1968, they reached a total of $495 million, reflecting a vast enlargement of the Foundation's activities. In fiscal 1969, however, over objections in the Senate, NSF appropriations dropped to $400 million.

Authorizations for NSF increased from $477.6 million in fiscal 1970 to $703.9-million for fiscal 1973. Appropriations for fiscal 1972 were $622-million, and for 1973, $626-million.

Only minor amendments to the 1950 Act were made between 1952 and 1959. Major changes came in 1962,

by Presidential initiative, and in 1968, by congressional order. President Kennedy's 1962 Reorganization Plan No. 2 established a new Office of Science and Technology in the Executive Office of the President and transferred to the new Office the NSF's responsibility for shaping, evaluating and coordinating Government scientific policy. Under the Plan, the NSF could continue to originate policy proposals and make recommendations, but the policy was actually set by the Office.

The House Subcommittee on Science, Research and Development, headed by Rep. Emilio Q. Daddario (D Conn.), began the first comprehensive legislative review of the NSF late in 1964. The review resulted in proposed legislation to expand NSF's scope. The House passed the bill in 1966 and again in 1967, only to have the Senate fail to act. But in 1968 Congress gave the Director greater authority over NSF management and enlarged the Foundation's scope so that it could support applied science as well as basic science and research in the social sciences as well.

FOUNDATION ON ARTS AND HUMANITIES

After several years of growing Congressional and private support for federal aid for the study, development and presentation of the arts and humanities, Congress in 1965 established a National Foundation on the Arts and Humanities. The final bill was based on an Administration proposal.

The National Foundation established in PL 89-209 consisted of two autonomous subdivisions, a National Endowment for the Arts and a National Endowment for the Humanities. Each endowment had a chairman and a 26-member advisory council—one on the arts and one on the humanities. Each endowment was authorized to make grants—most of them to be matched—for a wide range of activities. The operations of the National Foundation were to be coordinated with other federal activities through a nine-member Federal Council on the Arts and the Humanities, made up of representatives of various agencies.

In addition to establishing the Foundation, Pl 89-209 (S 1483) authorized two small programs of financial assistance to be carried out by the Office of Education. These were to help schools buy equipment for teaching the humanities and the arts and to finance training institutes for teachers of these subjects.

The bill authorized appropriations for each endowment of $5 million for each of three fiscal years, 1966, 1967, and 1968. An additional annual maximum of $5 million for the Humanities Endowment and $2.25 million for the Arts Endowment were authorized to match gifts or bequests. Another $2.75 million was authorized for the Arts Endowment for matching grants to state arts agencies of $50,000 annually to each state. States without such an agency could receive a one-time grant of $25,000—without matching requirements— to establish arts councils.

In 1968 Congress extended the Foundation for two years. PL 90-348 (HR 11308) authorized appropriations of $34 million over the two years, plus sums to match up to $13.5 million in private gifts to the Foundation.

Appropriations for the Foundation in its first four years remained around the $10-million level annually.

In 1970 Congress authorized a three-year extension of the Foundation with authorizations set at $40-million for fiscal 1971, $60-million for fiscal 1972 and $80 million for fiscal 1973. Appropriations for fiscal 1972 were $61.2 million; for fiscal 1973, Congress appropriated $81.5-million.

Chronology Of Education Legislation 1969

Congress failed to complete action on any major education measures in 1969. Even the bill (HR 13111) providing fiscal 1970 funds for education programs remained unfinished business to be considered again by Congress in 1970.

Also left for completion in the second session of the 91st Congress was a bill to extend the Elementary and Secondary Education Act (ESEA) and aid to federally impacted areas programs. The House in April passed a bill (HR 514) to extend ESEA programs for two years, through fiscal 1972, to consolidate several of its programs and to extend impact aid to cover children living in federally financed public housing.

The Senate Labor and Public Welfare Committee in December ordered reported its own version of the ESEA extension (HR 514). HR 514 as reported by the Senate committee would extend ESEA programs for four years and increase authorizations but would not consolidate programs. The Senate bill also contained provisions concerning programs for the education of disabled and gifted children. These programs had been approved by the House as separate bills.

Congress raised the effective interest rates on guaranteed loans for college students by voting to allow "special allowances" of up to 3 per cent on top of the 7 per cent interest ceiling available on government-backed loans to college students.

Congress also enacted four provisions attempting to deal with campus riots but killed several other efforts to take action against students or the institutions where disruptions occurred. Congressional committees conducted investigations of student violence.

Major battles over funding and desegregation were waged in connection with HR 13111, the appropriations bill for the Departments of Labor and Health, Education and Welfare. But final action on the bill itself was delayed until January 1970. The House had added more than $1-billion in education funds to the amount requested by the administration and provided, in the second continuing resolution for the year, that education spending could continue at that increased level set by the House version of HR 13111. The Senate approved both House actions in raising education spending levels, making the bill a likely candidate for a presidential veto.

Expenditures of Public and Private Schools

(in billions of dollars)

Year	Including college	Primary and secondary
1959-60:		
Total 32.8		23.9
Public 26.1		21.1
Private 6.7		2.8
1964-65:		
Total 49.2		33.3
Public 38.1		29.2
Private 11.1		4.1
1970-71		
Total 77.6		49.6
Public 62.7		44.6
Private 14.9		5.0

Future Projections

Year	Including college	Primary and secondary
1974-75:		
Total 84.1		50.1
Public 67.6		45.2
Private 16.5		4.9
1979-80:		
Total 97.4		55.2
Public 78.4		49.7
Private 19.0		5.5

Source: U.S. Office of Education.

Elementary and Secondary Education

Elementary and Secondary Education Act. The House April 23 approved the administration's proposal to extend Elementary and Secondary Education Act programs for two years, through fiscal 1972, in place of the five-year extension recommended by the House Education and Labor Committee.

The Senate Labor and Public Welfare Committee Dec. 19 ordered reported its version of HR 514 to extend Elementary and Secondary Education Act programs for four years, through fiscal 1974. The report was to be filed after the beginning of the second session Jan. 19, 1970.

The House April 23 by a 400-17 roll-call vote passed an amended bill (HR 514), the Elementary and Secondary Education Amendments of 1969, extending the Elementary and Secondary Education Act (ESEA) programs for two years, through fiscal 1972, consolidating into a single package two ESEA programs (Title II—books and materials—and Title III—supplemental services) and two programs contained in the National Defense Education Act (NDEA) (Title III(a)—equipment—and V(a)—counseling) and extending the impacted areas aid program to children living in federal-aid public housing.

The major vote came just before passage, when a coalition of 227 Republicans and southern Democrats helped adopt, by a 235-184 roll-call vote, an amendment offered by Rep. Edith Green (D Ore.) rewriting the entire bill. The major change between the Green bill and the one reported by the Education and Labor Committee (H Rept 91-114) was the two-year extension sought by the Nixon administration rather than a five-year continuation favored by a majority of committee members.

Education-Aid Authorizations for Fiscal Years 1968-72

	1968	1969	1970	1971	1972
Elementary and Secondary					
Education Act:					
Title I—Educationally deprived children	$2,563,067,584	$2,725,959,699	$2,862,175,945	$3,547,396,000	$3,642,835,000
Special incentive grants	— —	50,000,000	50,000,000	50,000,000	50,000,000
Title II—Libraries and textbooks	154,500,000	167,375,000	206,000,000	200,000,000	210,000,000
Title III—Supplementary education	515,000,000	527,875,000	566,500,000	550,000,000	575,000,000
Title IV—Cooperative research [1]	— —	— —	— —		— —
Title V—State education departments	65,000,000	80,000,000	80,000,000	80,000,000	85,000,000
Title VI—Handicapped children	171,500,000	187,125,000	234,000,000	348,000,000	399,000,000
Title VII—Bilingual education	26,000,000	40,000,000	50,000,000	80,000,000	100,000,000
Title VIII—Dropout prevention, Rural Area Information, Demonstration Projects [2]	3,500,000	33,700,000	36,000,000	40,000,000	47,500,000
Adult Education Act	— —	70,000,000	80,000,000	160,000,000	225,000,000
Impacted Areas:					
Construction	62,000,000	66,000,000	66,000,000	15,000,000	20,004,000
Operation-maintenance	477,384,000	510,000,000	545,000,000	536,068,000	592,580,000
TOTALS	$4,037,951,584	$4,458,034,699	$4,775,675,945	$5,606,464,000	$5,946,919,000

1 Title IV—$100-million authorized for fiscal 1966 and available through fiscal 1974.
2 Title VIII—Authorization for fiscal 1968 was for the Rural Area Information program. Authorizations for fiscal 1969 were for Rural Area Information and Dropout Prevention. Fiscal 1970: Rural Area Information, Dropout Prevention and Demonstration Projects. Fiscal 1971 and 1972: Dropout Prevention and Demonstration Projects.

The House action on the ESEA was the first vote on a major social welfare issue in the 91st Congress. It was considered a legislative victory for the Republican administration.

The bill as passed by the House would continue for two more years the fiscal 1970 authorizations, which amount to an estimated $5.3-billion for all ESEA programs and programs of aid to federally impacted areas. This amounted to $4,368,500,000 for all ESEA programs, $702,407,000 for existing impact aid programs and $235,-000,000 for the new public housing impact aid programs.

The Senate Labor and Public Welfare Subcommittee on Education held hearings in June and July on its ESEA extension proposal, but not until six months later did it report a bill. During the hearings, on June 11 Secretary of Health, Education and Welfare Robert H. Finch asked for a two-year extension of existing programs while the Nixon administration conducted a thorough review of all federal aid-to-education programs. By mid-1972, Finch said, 1970 census figures would be available for use in revising the formula for distribution of funds under ESEA Title I (aid to educationally deprived children, the largest program in the act).

The second major change requested by Finch would consolidate five state grant programs—the four already combined by the House plus the educational equipment program administered by the National Foundation on the Arts and Humanities. This would eliminate red tape, the secretary said, and would make available to students in non-public schools all the programs to be consolidated.

Finch opposed the public housing amendments enacted by the House.

The full committee Dec. 19 ordered reported an amended bill (HR 514) extending the Elementary and Secondary Education Act for four years, through fiscal 1974, and increasing authorization for its programs by more than 25 percent. The bill as ordered reported contained provisions expanding school aid to federally impacted areas to cover students living in federally financed public housing and providing programs for gifted children and children with learning disabilities. It did not consolidate existing library and counseling programs.

Special Education. The House passed and sent to the Senate in 1969 two bills (HR 13304, HR 13310) amending the Elementary and Secondary Education Act (ESEA) to provide programs for gifted and talented children with learning disabilities.

HR 13304, for gifted and talented children, authorized the U.S. commissioner of education to make grants to state educational agencies to provide services and assistance to local school districts for such programs. It also provided fellowships for teachers and required the commissioner to conduct studies of such programs.

No additional funds were authorized for the program, which was an amendment to Title V of ESEA.

The Senate Labor and Public Welfare Committee, which held hearings on a similar bill (S 718) in July, incorporated the provisions of S 718 in a bill (HR 514) to extend Elementary and Secondary Education Act programs. *(See above)*

HR 13310 amended Title VI of ESEA to provide programs for children with specific learning disabilities, authorizing grants for research, teacher training and model centers. Authorizations were $6 million for fiscal

1971, $12 million for fiscal 1972 and $18 million for fiscal 1973.

The Senate, Labor and Public Welfare Committee also incorporated its provisions into the bill (HR 514) to extend Elementary and Secondary Education Act programs.

Higher Education

Student Loans. The Emergency Insured Student Loan Act (HR 13194—PL 91-95), cleared by Congress Oct. 16 authorized the payment of "special allowances" by the federal government on guaranteed student loans under the insured student loan program of the Higher Education Act of 1965. The bill was made necessary by rising interest rates that were preventing thousands of students from obtaining loans for the school year beginning September 1969.

Under the existing student loan program, the federal government guaranteed student loans of up to $7,500 per student carrying a maximum interest rate of 7 percent. The special allowance provision in HR 13194 permitted the government to pay a direct interest subsidy of up to 3 percent to lending institutions providing loans under the guaranteed loan program.

The bill authorized $20-million for fiscal 1970, $40-million for fiscal 1971, and as much as needed thereafter to meet the cost of the special allowances on loans made before the expiration date of the law.

It also increased authorizations for the national defense student loan program by $50-million to $325-million in fiscal 1970 and by $75-million to $375-million in fiscal 1971; for the college work-study program by $25-million to $275-million in fiscal 1970 and by $35-million to $320-million in fiscal 1971; and for the educational opportunity grant program by $25-million to $125-million for fiscal 1970 and by $30-million to $170-million for fiscal 1971.

Campus Disorders. Widespread and violent campus disorders early in the year brought on strong reaction from Congress and the administration during 1969.

In Congress, a rash of bills was introduced to cut off federal aid to disruptive students; and anti-student riot provisions were included in three pieces of legislation. Both chambers held hearings on campus disturbances.

President Nixon said student disorders endangered academic freedom and that school officials should "have the backbone to stand up against" campus violence. Attorney General John N. Mitchell warned that "the time has come for an end to patience."

A bipartisan band of liberals, most of them members of the House Education and Labor Committee, joined forces three times to block action aimed at disruptive college students.

The first instance came in June and July, when liberals on the committee for four weeks used a variety of parliamentary tactics to prevent a campus disorders bill (HR 11941) from being reported to the full House.

The bill, as introduced by committee member Edith Green (D Ore.), required all colleges and universities receiving federal aid to file with the U.S. commissioner of education plans of action for dealing with campus upheavals and allowed schools to end virtually all forms of federal aid to students convicted in court or found by the university to have violated its rules in connection with student riots.

Mrs. Green argued that HR 11941 would stall off more repressive action on the floor. However, the liberals, led by John Brademas (D Ind.) and Ogden R. Reid (R N.Y.), countered that the bill would be used on the floor as a vehicle for more repressive action.

The committee July 1 voted to send the bill to the Special Subcommittee on Education, thus in effect killing the measure.

On July 31, the same members were the leaders in a floor fight on a student unrest provision included in the appropriations bill (HR 13111) for the Departments of Labor and Health, Education and Welfare (HEW). Again using parliamentary strategy, they knocked out the section of the bill, although the House added another amendment, generally considered to be weaker.

And in mid-August, committee liberals agreed to report an emergency college student loan bill (HR 13194) only on the condition that no floor amendments such as an anti-student riot amendment could be added by the full House.

Provisions to cut off federal aid to students who participated in campus disturbances were included in other bills, including the appropriations bill for the Departments of State, Justice and Commerce (HR 12964) and the authorization bills for the National Aeronautics and Space Administration (HR 11271) and the National Science Foundation (S 1857).

Other congressional action in this area centered on investigations by the Senate Government Operations Committee's Permanent Investigations Subcommittee and the House Internal Security Committee into activities of militant student groups such as the Students for a Democratic Society (SDS).

Throughout the session, House members were more concerned with taking action against students engaged in campus disruptions than were senators. For instance, House action on the student loan bill was held up for a month over a dispute about adding student rioting amendments, while in the Senate the issue never arose.

Smaller disputes centered about the Reserve Officers Training Corps (ROTC) and military recruitment on campus after anti-military demonstrations occurred on several campuses in the spring.

National Science Foundation. Congress approved an authorization of $477.6 million for the National Science Foundation (NSF) in fiscal 1970 (S 1857—PL 91-120). The bill contained a provision similar to one in the Higher Education Amendments of 1968 (PL 90-575) requiring that institutions receiving NSF funds deny for two years aid from those funds to students or employees found to have been convicted of violent crimes against the institution or to have willfully refused to obey a regulation of the institution, provided that the student's action was of a serious nature and contributed to a substantial disruption of the administration of the institution.

1970

Congress in 1970 enacted the largest elementary and secondary education authorization bill in its history (HR 514—PL 91-230), and spent much energy in conflict with the White House over appropriations to carry out these education programs.

PL 91-230 extended for three years the 1965 Elementary and Secondary Education Act, aid to federally impacted areas and related education aid programs. Its total authorizations and entitlements for the three years amounted to $24.6-billion.

President Nixon in January vetoed the fiscal 1970 appropriations bill for the Departments of Labor and Health, Education and Welfare (HEW). Congress failed to override the veto and in March completed action on a compromise bill—just three months before the end of the fiscal year. Again in August education funds for fiscal 1971 were vetoed by the President, but Congress overrode that veto.

Desegregation replaced campus unrest as the chief education-related controversy especially during consideration of HR 514. This resulted in creation of a new Senate Select Committee on Equal Educational Opportunity, which immediately began a long series of hearings on the subject of educational opportunity. Congress failed to complete action on any revision of higher education programs, as requested by President Nixon, or on his proposed program of emergency federal aid to desegregating school districts.

Education Funds

First Veto. During a nationwide television and radio address, President Nixon Jan. 26, 1970, vetoed the $19.7-billion Labor-HEW appropriations bill (HR 13111) which contained $3,265,302,700 for the Office of Education. This amount was actually $207.5-million less than the budget request, but Congress had allocated funds differently than requested among the various programs. The administration asked $202.2-million for impact aid; Congress voted $600.2-million. The administration asked 404.6-million for elementary and secondary education (in addition to $1.01-billion already available); Congress voted $717-million.

The House Jan. 27 by a **226-191 key roll call vote** sustained the veto. The White House and congressional leaders negotiated a compromise on additional spending for education and health programs, on which was based the second Labor-HEW appropriations bill for fiscal 1970, enacted March 5, 1970 (HR 15931—PL 91-204). It contained $3,005,219,700 for the Office of Education, which included $638.6-million for elementary and secondary education (in addition to the $1.01-billion already available) and $520.6-million for impact aid.

Second Veto. For fiscal 1971 education appropriations were separated from HEW appropriations into a separate appropriations bill. A $4,420,145,000 appropriations bill (HR 16916—PL 91-380) for the Office of Education was enacted into law Aug. 18 notwithstanding a presidential veto. The $4.4-billion bill included $4,345,145,000 in appropriations for fiscal 1971 and $75-million in emergency school assistance for fiscal 1970. It exceeded the President's final budget request (including the $150-million request for fiscal 1970 for emergency school assistance) by $453,321,000, and it exceeded his requests for fiscal 1971 alone by $528,321,000.

Congress rejected, however, an administration request of $1,339,050,000 for advance funding for fiscal 1972 of Title I programs under the Elementary and Secondary Education Act.

The House Aug. 13 by a **key 289-114 roll-call vote** overrode the veto—a margin of 20 more than the two-thirds majority needed to pass a bill over the President's objection.

Senate action enacted the bill into law Aug. 18 on a 77-16 roll-call vote.

The bill had been sent to the President for his signature July 28. On August 11, Nixon announced that he had vetoed the bill, "saying no to bigger spending and no to higher prices in the interest of all of the American people."

As enacted, the bill contained $1,846,968,000 for all elementary and secondary education programs and $551,068,000 for impact aid.

HR 16916 as passed also contained two controversial sections aimed at limiting the federal government's desegregation authority. Known as the Whitten amendments after their original sponsor, Rep. Jamie L. Whitten (D Miss.), the provisions stipulated that no funds in the bill could be used to force schools or school districts already considered "desegregated" under the 1964 Civil Rights Act to bus students, abolish schools or set attendance zones either against the choice of students' parents or as a prerequisite for obtaining federal funds. Federal officials repeatedly said that the Whitten amendments would serve to confuse the public but would not change enforcement of the administration's desegregation policy.

Elementary and Secondary Education

Elementary and Secondary Education Act. The President April 13 signed into law (HR 514—PL 91-230) a three-year, $24.6-billion extension of the 1965 Elementary and Secondary Education Act, aid to federally impacted areas and other educational legislation.

Final congressional action came when the House April 7 adopted the conference report on HR 514 (J Rept 91-937).

Prior to final action, the Senate engaged in two major debates over equal enforcement throughout the nation of federal desegregation guidelines. The most heated Senate controversy on HR 514 centered around an amendment offered by John C. Stennis (D Miss.) and Abraham Ribicoff (D Conn.), which stated that federal guidelines on school desegregation must be applied equally to segregation in the North and South, whether *de jure* (the result of law) or *de facto* (the result of housing patterns).

Although the amendment passed the Senate, a House-Senate conference committee reinstated the distinction between *de jure* and *de facto* discrimination.

As cleared for the President's signature, HR 514 extended for three years, through fiscal 1973, the programs of the Elementary and Secondary Education Act (ESEA), the programs of aid to school districts "impacted" by large numbers of children of government employees, and numerous other education programs.

The most important change made by the 1970 legislation in Title I of ESEA—which provided per-pupil aid to school districts serving large numbers of poor children—expanded the program to include children whose families earned up to $4,000 rather than $3,000 a year. The law also stipulated that Title I funds could not be used in place of non-federal funds and that state and local funds in areas with Title I programs must be comparable to those available in other areas.

The law fixed the authorization for the special incentive grant program for states exceeding the national effort for public education at $50-million annually and changed the distribution formula from a state-by-state allotment to an entitlement. The 1970 law set up a new program of grants for urban and rural school systems serving the largest concentrations of low-income families.

PL 91-230 increased authorizations for other titles of ESEA, consolidated Title III of ESEA (supplemental educational centers and services) and Title V(a) of NDEA (guidance, counseling and testing) and authorized programs under Titles III and V for gifted and talented children.

The 1970 law established new programs of grants for strengthening local education agencies, grants to aid planning and evaluation on local and state levels, of advisory councils on quality education, and of demonstration projects to improve nutrition and health services in public and nonpublic schools serving many poor children.

PL 91-230 also expanded the bilingual education program to cover Indian children living on reservations and attending Interior Department or tribal schools.

Impacted Area Laws. PL 91-230 amended the basic impact aid laws (PL 81-815 and PL 81-874) to cover children living in federally financed public housing.

House hearings on administration proposals to revise this aid program did not result in any action in Congress on the proposals to change criteria by which a district was judged eligible for this aid.

Other Programs. PL 91-230 also increased authorizations for programs under the Adult Education Act of 1966, extended loan forgiveness provisions in the direct student loan program to include forgiveness for military service, established a new program of aid for children with specific learning disabilities, authorized funds for education of the handicapped and extended vocational education programs, with increased authorizations, through fiscal 1972.

PL 91-230 also provided for an automatic one-year extension of authorization for any existing education program for which Congress had failed to complete action on an extension bill by the expiration date of the current authorization.

Authorization for the Teacher Corps was increased to $80-million for fiscal 1970 and $100-million for fiscal 1971; and a student Teacher Corps was established by PL 91-230.

Higher Education

President Nixon March 19, 1970, called for a shift in federal spending on college education to emphasize the needs of poor youths.

In a special message to Congress, Nixon proposed increasing grant-and-loan aid to students from low-income families so that they would have the same ability to pay as students from families earning at least $10,000.

Federally guaranteed loans would be available to every qualified student, regardless of family income level. But direct federal subsidies would go to the students who need them the most.

"Something is basically unequal about opportunity for higher education," the President said, "when a young

person whose family earns more than $15,000 a year is nine times more likely to attend college than a young person whose family earns less than $3,000."

Under the President's proposed program, youths whose families have an annual income of $4,500 or less would be guaranteed a total of $1,300 each in grants and subsidized loans. The $1,300 could be supplemented by earnings, other scholarships and access to unsubsidized loans.

The President also recommended the creation of a National Student Loan Association to purchase student loan paper from banks and other financial institutions. Since the association would be privately financed, Nixon said, it would make more money available for the student loan paper from banks and other financial institutions.

Both House and Senate committees held hearings on the administration proposals and related bills, but took no further action on them in 1970.

In Congress during 1970, no major legislation involving campus unrest reached the floor of either chamber.

The Higher Education Act expired in mid-1971, so Congress was not under immediate pressure to act on a bill during 1970. Partly because of the press of other business—but in great measure in order to avoid a campus unrest fight in the Congress—the leadership in both chambers decided to put off higher education legislation until the 92nd Congress.

Campus unrest provisions restricting the spending of Federal funds were inserted in a number of bills. The Office of Education appropriations bill (HR 16916—PL 91-380) prohibited funds from being used for loans or salaries for students or school employees who had engaged in conduct involving the use or threat of force or seizure of property to interfere with school activities.

Other legislation with campus unrest clauses included the appropriations bills for the State, Justice and Commerce Departments and the Department of Defense and authorization bills covering military procurement and the National Science Foundation.

Veterans' Benefits. A bill enacted in 1970 (HR 11959—PL 91-219) boosted educational benefits by 34.6 percent for some 736,000 veterans who had served in the armed forces after Jan. 31, 1955. PL 91-219 increased to $175 a month the educational allowance for single veterans, to $205 a month for those with one dependent, and to $230 a month for those with two dependents.

National Science Foundation. Congress in 1970 approved a bill (HR 16595—PL 91-356) authorizing $537.7-million for the National Science Foundation for fiscal 1971. In addition Congress extended through 1973 (HR 11766—PL 91-349) the Sea Grant program established in 1966 to encourage "aquaculture" in the same way that the land grant aid system had encouraged agriculture.

Desegregation and Equal Education

A New Committee. The Senate Select Committee on Equal Educational Opportunity was established Feb. 19.

On Dec. 11, the Senate unanimously approved a resolution extending the life of the select committee for one year, setting Jan. 31, 1972, as the date for its final report. The date originally had been set at Jan. 31, 1971.

The resolution establishing the committee, cosponsored by Walter F. Mondale (D Minn.) and Jacob K. Javits (R N.Y.), was originally offered as an amendment to HR 514, the bill extending the Elementary and Secondary Education Act. Mondale and Javits both opposed the Stennis amendment to HR 514—introduced by John Stennis (D Miss.)—which attempted to eliminate the distinction between *de jure* and *de facto* school desegregation in Federal enforcement of desegregation.

The Mondale-Javits proposal was withdrawn as an amendment and enacted separately to avoid going to conference with the House or to the President for his signature. Traditionally, internal matters such as the establishment of a Senate committee are not subject to action by the House or the President.

The Committee, chaired by Mondale, was composed of 15 members: From the Labor and Public Welfare Committee, Democrats Jennings Randolph (W Va.), Mondale, and Harold E. Hughes (Iowa), and Republicans Javits and Peter H. Dominick (Colo.); from the Judiciary Committee, Democrats John L. McClellan (Ark.)—who served as the second ranking Democrat—Thomas J. Dodd (Conn.), and Birch Bayh (Ind.) and Republicans Roman L. Hruska (Neb.)—who was the Select Committee's ranking minority member—and Marlow W. Cook (Ky.); and from the Senate at large, Democrats Warren G. Magnuson (Wash.), Daniel K. Inouye (Hawaii), and William B. Spong Jr. (Va.) and Republicans Edward W. Brooke (Mass.) and Mark O. Hatfield (Ore.).

The committee was directed to study all aspects of school segregation, to make an interim report by Aug. 1, 1970, and a final report by Jan. 31, 1971 (which later was extended first to Jan. 31, 1972, then to Dec. 31, 1972). Mondale said that the committee would try to "re-argue the case for integration."

Emergency School Aid. Congress did not complete action on a bill (HR 19446), the Emergency School Aid Act of 1970, which would have authorized $1.5-billion in Federal aid in fiscal 1971 and 1972 to school districts which were desegregating or attempting to overcome racial imbalance.

Following more than a year of controversy over his position, President Nixon issued a statement on March 24 which pledged that his administration would continue to move against school segregation required by law or established by official actions. In the statement, he promised to spend $1.5-billion in fiscal 1971 and 1972 for improving schools in "racially impacted areas" and for aiding school districts to overcome problems caused by court-ordered desegregation.

Specific legislation (HR 17846, S 3883) was sent to Congress on May 21. As written, the bill was aimed chiefly at approximately 1,400 school districts, the majority of them in the South, which were desegregating or had recently desegregated.

It also was designed to aid *de facto* segregated schools, in which racial separation stemmed from neighborhood residence patterns and other factors, and large school districts in which minority students comprised over half the enrollment.

Each state would receive $100,000 initially under the administration bill. Remaining funds would be allocated in proportion to minority enrollments in each state. Students in the first category—districts under

Desegregation Report

As members of Congress studied and argued about the extent and methods of school desegregation—and as the Supreme Court pondered crucial questions concerning the standards by which desegregation should be measured—the pace of desegregation in southern schools outstripped that of the rest of the country.

Statistics released by Elliot Richardson, Secretary of Health, Education and Welfare (HEW), Jan. 14, 1971—based on data collected in the fall of 1970—showed that the number of black pupils attending majority white public schools in the South doubled from the fall of 1968 to the fall of 1970.

More than one of every three black pupils in the South attended a majority white school in 1970, according to the HEW figures, a sharp increase over the fewer than one in every five who did so two years earlier.

But there was little comparable change outside the South. *(Table below)*

In the South, the percentage of black students in all-black schools decreased dramatically from 68 per cent in 1968 to 18.4 per cent in 1970. Outside the South, this percentage showed only minimal change, from 12.3 per cent to 11.9 per cent.

In revealing the figures, Secretary Richardson said that the administration's commitment to desegregation was to "more than a numbers game." He declared that the real goal was "equal educational opportunity and (that the administration was) committed to a uniform effort throughout the country to achieve it."

The HEW statistics showed that nationwide, there had been substantial progress in desegregation—from approximately one of every four black children attending majority white schools in 1968 to approximately one of every three doing so in 1970. Here is a summary of the report:

Geographical Area	***PER CENT OF NEGRO PUPILS ATTENDING:**		
	0-49.9% Minority Schools	80-100% Minority Schools**	100% Minority Schools
CONTINENTAL U.S.			
1968	23.4	68.0	39.7
1970 est.	32.8	50.2	16.0
(1) 32 NORTH & WEST			
1968	27.6	57.4	12.3
1970 est.	27.7	57.4	11.9
(2) 11 SOUTH			
1968	18.4	78.8	68.0
1970 est.	38.1	41.7	18.4
(3) 6 BORDER +D.C.			
1968	28.4	63.8	25.2
1970 est.	29.6	60.3	22.0

(1) Alaska, Ariz., Calif., Colo., Conn., Idaho, Ill., Ind., Iowa, Kan., Maine, Mass., Mich., Minn., Mont., Neb., Nev., N.H., N.J., N.M., N.Y., N.D., Ohio, Ore., Pa., R.I., S.D., Utah, Vt., Wash., Wis., Wyo.
(2) Ala., Ark., Fla., Ga., La., Miss., N.C., S.C., Tenn., Texas, Va.
(3) Del., D.C., Ky., Md., Mo., Okla., W.Va.
* Districts with fewer than 300 pupils are not included in the survey. 1970 figures are estimates based on latest available data and are subject to variation upon final compilation.
** Percentage figure includes percentage shown in 100% minority schools.

court order or HEW-approved plan—would be counted twice.

The House passed its version of the bill (HR 19446) Dec. 21, but opposition from both liberal and conservative members blocked Senate passage.

Conservatives criticized HR 19446 as a "busing bill"; they said it also was too lax in its requirements for Northern school districts.

Liberals opposed the House-passed bill as not stringent enough in the degree of desegregation required of recipients. As Congress adjourned, an alternative desegregation aid bill—awaiting action by the Senate Labor and Public Welfare Committee—also died. The alternative bill set stricter requirements for its recipients and stronger guidelines for use of authorized funds.

Other Programs

Congress in 1970 also enacted legislation (S 3318— PL 91-600) extending programs of federal aid to public libraries for five years, through fiscal 1976, and authorizing $1.14-billion during that time. It consolidated several programs of services and construction aid, set up new programs for poor people and metropolitan libraries.

A bill (HR 14252—PL 91-527) was also passed by Congress authorizing $58-million over fiscal years 1971-1973 for drug abuse education programs.

1971

Congress in 1971 failed to complete action on any aid-to-education bill beyond the bill providing appropriations in fiscal 1972. Most major programs of federal aid to higher education expired June 30, 1971, but the automatic one-year extension of all education programs by the language of PL 91-230 released Congress from the pressure of that deadline for enactment of extension legislation.

The administration's proposed revisions of aid to higher education and its program of emergency aid to desegregating school districts were linked late in the year when the House added the emergency school aid bill as a title of the by-then omnibus education bill revising programs of aid to college students. Further loaded down with antibusing provisions, the bill was before a Senate committee for reconsideration at the end of the year.

Education Funds. Congress passed, and the President signed, a bill (HR 7016—PL 92-48) providing $5,146,-311,000 for the Office of Education in fiscal 1972. The total included $612.6-million for impact aid; $1,993,-278,000 for elementary and secondary education; and $1,341,784,000 for higher education.

Higher Education

In its deliberations on financing of higher education in 1971, Congress considered several aspects of the issue and in the end combined several different bills into one omnibus measure.

The measure (S 659), after being passed by the Senate and the House, was reconsidered by the Senate Labor and Public Welfare Committee because of the major alterations made in the Senate-passed bill in the House.

Supreme Court Decisions, 1969-1972

In decisions affecting schools and colleges, the Supreme Court in 1969 ruled:

● That a public school could not constitutionally bar the wearing of black arm bands in protest of the Vietnam War—when such protest did not substantially disrupt school activities. (*Tinker v. Des Moines Independent Community School District*).

● That a federal district judge could direct a desegregating school board to desegregate faculties and school staff personnel according to a specific mathematical ratio (*U.S. v. Montgomery County Board of Education*).

● That a "monkey law"—forbidding public school teachers to teach the Darwinian theory of man's evolution—was an unconstitutional violation of the 1st Amendment (*Epperson v. Arkansas*).

● That the time for "all deliberate speed" in school desegregation was past and that schools should desegregate immediately (*Alexander v. Holmes County Board of Education*).

In decisions affecting schools and colleges in 1971, the Supreme Court ruled that:

● Busing of school children was a permissible interim method of desegregating still-segregated schools (*Swann v. Charlotte-Mecklenburg Board of Education*).

● A state could require teachers to take an oath to uphold the state and federal constitutions, but could not dismiss, without a hearing, a teacher who refused to swear that he did not believe in forcible overthrow of the government (*Connell v. Higginbotham*).

● That the 1st Amendment bars state laws allowing the state to reimburse nonpublic schools for the cost of teachers' salaries, books, and other instructional materials in certain secular subjects and state laws authorizing supplementary salary grants to nonpublic elementary school teachers of secular subjects (*Lemon v. Kurtzman, Earley v. DiCenso, Robinson v. DiCenso*).

● That the 1st Amendment does not bar federal construction grants (under the Higher Education Facilities Act of 1963) to church-related colleges or universities so long as the buildings constructed are to be used exclusively for secular educational purposes (*Tilton v. Richardson*).

In education-related decisions in 1972, the Supreme Court held that:

● Federal courts could intervene to halt state or local action to create a new school district with the effect of impeding desegregation (*Wright v. Emporia City Council*).

● Children of members of the Amish sect were exempt under the 1st Amendment from state compulsory attendance laws (*Wisconsin v. Yoder*).

As originally passed by the Senate just before the August congressional recess, S 659 was already the most sweeping aid-to-education bill ever considered by Congress. The product of two years' work in the Senate Labor and Public Welfare Committee, it extended exist-

Federal Spending on Education and Manpower Programs

(in millions, by fiscal year)

	1959	1965	1966	1968	1971	1972*
Elementary and secondary education	$259	$ 478	$1,646	$2,430	$3,164	$ 3,383
Higher education	225	413	701	1,392	1,429	1,442
Vocational education	38	132	136	265	415	531
Manpower training	4	336	731	1,263	2,602	3,643
Science education and basic research	106	309	368	449	522	538
Other education and manpower aids	451	850	925	1,227	757	957
Veterans readjustment benefits	864	50	211	673	1,659	2,240
Deductions for offsetting receipts	—3	—9	—11	—16	—12	—29
TOTALS	$1,944	$2,559	$4,707	$7,683	$10,536	$12,705

* Estimated

SOURCE: Office of Management and Budget

ing programs of federal aid to colleges and students and established new ones—including a new basic grant program for students and a cost-of-instruction payment program for institutions attended by federally aided students—at a cost of $19-billion for the following four years.

The House revised provisions of the bill to extend existing programs for five years, to expand the existing student grant program, to provide a new program of general federal aid to colleges and universities, and to provide a new program of federal aid to occupational education.

It also added the contents of a major bill providing aid to desegregate school districts. The bill (S 1557—HR 2266) had passed the Senate in April and been reported by the House Education and Labor Committee but was refused clearance for floor consideration by the House Rules Committee.

In an attempt to bypass the Rules Committee, floor managers of the desegregation bill sought to get House consideration under suspension of the rules, a maneuver usually reserved for noncontroversial bills which requires a two-thirds majority of the House. The House on Nov. 1, however, refused to consider the measure under such circumstances. It did agree (three days later) to add the desegregation aid provisions, accompanied by anti-busing amendments, to S 659. The total amount authorized by the bill rose to $24-billion.

The measure was then referred back to the Senate Labor and Public Welfare Committee. That committee ordered S 659 reported Dec. 3 with amendments which included the provisions of S 659 and S 1557 as approved by the Senate, the provisions of an Indian education bill (S 2482) already approved by the Senate and provisions creating a foreign service scholarship program.

Mr. Nixon on Feb. 22, 1971, again asked Congress to equalize the opportunity for a higher education by directing most federal aid to students from low-income families and to shift the financing of student loans entirely to the private money market.

Democratic-sponsored counter proposals would extend and expand existing aid programs, and some added a new program under which eligible students were entitled—as a matter of right—to a certain basic federal grant. A separate cost-of-education payment would to to institutions for each federally aided student in attendance.

Nixon renewed his request that Congress authorize creation of a national foundation for higher education and a national institute of education.

Critics of the administration's proposals in Congress and in the education community said that the Nixon plan would substantially reduce aid to students from middle-income families and that the proposed shift to the private money market would cut the amount of aid available through loans.

One million additional low-income students would receive aid under the administration plan, said U.S. Commissioner of Education Sidney P. Marland. The higher education community reacted with alarm at the prospect.

Colleges and universities were already stretched to their financial breaking point, a panel of educators told the Senate Education Subcommittee in March. The push for institutional aid—general federal aid to colleges and universities to help them meet general operating expenses—gained momentum in 1971.

The administration opposed general formula institutional aid, but pressure from members of Congress and the education community did bring forth a mid-year endorsement for federal payments to meet the costs of educating federally aided students.

Elementary and Secondary Education

National Science Foundation. Congress approved authorization of $655.5-million for the National Science Foundation in fiscal 1972 (HR 7960—PL 92-86).

Education Revenue-Sharing. President Nixon April 6, 1971, sent Congress the sixth of his special revenue-sharing plans—one to consolidate into one program 33 existing categories of federal aid to elementary and secondary education. He had included $2.8-billion in the fiscal 1972 budget for the combined programs.

Nixon proposed including an additional $200-million for the first year of the plan's operation. The total amount would be apportioned among the states on the basis of a formula taking into account the total school-age population in each state, the number of students from low-income families and the number of students whose families reside or work on federal property.

No state would receive less under the new plan, Nixon said, than under the existing structure. Funds would be used in five broad areas: education of the disadvantaged, education of handicapped children, vocational education, impact aid and supporting materials and services.

Education interest groups were unenthusiastic about the proposal because it would erase existing categorical programs, which they considered effective, while providing only a small amount of additional funds. Senate hearings were the only congressional action on the proposal in 1971.

Desegregation and Equal Education. For the second year in a row Congress failed to complete action on a $1.5-billion program to aid the desegregation of the nation's public schools.

The plan, originally proposed by the Nixon administration in 1970, would have channeled the funds to school districts which were desegregating or attempting to overcome racial imbalance.

In 1971 a compromise version of the administration bill (S 1557) was passed by the Senate in April but a similar bill (HR 2266) stalled in the House when the Rules Committee refused to grant a rule for floor consideration.

The House in November agreed to incorporate similar desegregation aid provisions into the major aid-to-education bill (S 659) then being considered in the House. That bill was then returned to the Senate Labor and Public Welfare Committee which further amended it and had not reported it out by the end of the session.

School Prayer. The House Nov. 8 rejected an attempt to amend the Constitution to add language stating that voluntary prayer or meditation, by persons lawfully assembled in a public building, was not unconstitutional. The proposed amendment (H J Res 191) failed by 28 votes to win the necessary approval of two-thirds of the members present and voting.

The proposed amendment, introduced in 1971 by Rep. Chalmers P. Wylie (R Ohio), was similar to one introduced in 1967 by then-Senate Minority Leader Everett McKinley Dirksen (R Ill.). Wylie introduced the amendment at the urging of an Ohio housewife and mother, Mrs. Ben Ruhlin, who marshalled nationwide support for the amendment through a Prayer Campaign Committee.

The opposition to the amendment was led by the National Council of Churches, House Judiciary Committee Chairman Emanuel Celler (D N.Y.), James C. Corman (D Calif.) and Fred Schwengel (R Iowa). They argued that the amendment tampered with the Bill of Rights to diminish the present freedom of religion.

Indian Education. The Senate approved a bill (S 2482) amending existing programs of aid to education to improve the educational opportunity available to Indian children and adults. The provisions of the bill were added to the omnibus education bill (S 659) by the

Senate Labor and Public Welfare Committee late in the year.

1972

Congress completed action on the $21-billion Education Amendments of 1972 (PL 92-318), which extended existing programs of aid to postsecondary education through fiscal 1975 at a total level of $19-billion and which authorized a new program of $2-billion in aid to desegregating school districts. The new education act also contained several provisions restricting the use of federal funds for busing and delaying the effective date of federal court orders requiring busing.

The administration's bill to curb the use of busing as a court-ordered remedy for school desegregation did not clear Congress. Liberals filibustered in the Senate and killed the bill which the House had stiffened and approved earlier.

President Nixon vetoed two bills containing funds for federal aid to education programs in fiscal 1973. Congress sustained his first veto; the second money bill was pocket vetoed after adjournment.

Congress cleared a bill increasing veterans' educational benefits by more than 25 per cent.

Education Funds

Congress again, under threat of yet a third veto of education funds, added large amounts of money to the administration's request for education programs in the Labor-HEW appropriations bill (HR 15417) for fiscal 1973. The Senate provided $5,283,043,000, almost $950-million more than requested; the House provided $3,999,-885,000. Neither version of the bill contained funds for higher education programs, because at the time of consideration by the committees, the education amendments authorizing that aid had not been enacted. House-Senate conferees agreed on a bill containing a total of $30.5-billion in appropriations.

President Nixon Aug. 16 vetoed the bill and the House sustained the veto on a **key 203-171 roll-call vote.**

Two months later Congress cleared a second bill appropriating the same amount of money for the Departments of Labor and HEW but allowing the President to impound up to $1.2-billion of the total, provided that no one appropriation was cut by more than 13 per cent. But after Congress adjourned this bill was pocket vetoed by Nixon Oct. 27 as part of his effort to hold down federal spending. Programs covered under the vetoed Labor-HEW bills were funded for the entire fiscal year under a continuing appropriations resolution.

Funds for some of the new and expanded higher education programs and for desegregation aid escaped the vetoes. They were included in a supplemental appropriations bill which cleared Congress in October and was signed by the President. They were not included in the regular Labor-HEW appropriations bill because the law authorizing them was not enacted until June, after Congress had begun its consideration of the HEW budget.

Higher Education

President Nixon June 23 signed into law the Education Amendments of 1972, (S 659—PL 92-318), a three-year, $19-billion extension of existing programs of federal aid to postsecondary education. PL 92-318 also consolidated the various federal laws authorizing the programs into one basic statute—the Higher Education Act of 1965.

In addition, PL 92-318 established two new basic programs of federal aid—a program of basic educational opportunity grants to which every qualified student in need of aid was entitled and a program of federal cost-of-education payments to which every institution attended by federally-aided students was entitled.

PL 92-318 also authorized expanded aid to programs of career education, Indian education, and a new $2-billion program of federal aid to desegregating or racially impacted school districts.

The President's signature ended speculation that he might veto the bill, primarily because of his dissatisfaction with the anti-busing language it contained. Final congressional action had come more than two weeks earlier when the House June 8, by a **key 218-180 roll-call vote,** had adopted the conference report on the bill. The relatively narrow margin by which the report was approved reflected dissatisfaction with the compromise reached by conferees on the anti-busing provisions of the bill.

The House had added language to the bill late in 1971 which virtually prohibited the use of busing altogether; the Senate, before sending the bill to conference early in 1972, had added more moderate language. The House twice took the unusual step of voting to instruct its conferees to insist on the more severe language; despite such instructions, however, the House conferees compromised. The Senate adopted the final bill May 24, 63-15, after rejected another effort to toughen the anti-busing language.

When Nixon finally signed the bill, he criticized the anti-busing language as "inadequate, misleading, and entirely unsatisfactory." *(Further details on busing controversy, p. 512)*

Student Aid. Based on a new premise of entitlement, the program of basic educational opportunity grants would provide—as a matter of right for any qualified college student—an annual grant of $1,400 less the amount his family could reasonably be expected to contribute each year toward his educational expenses. No new grants were to be awarded in any year when appropriations for certain other major student aid programs fell below a certain level, directed the bill. The maximum grant would be pro-rated if appropriations for the basic grant program were insufficient to provide every eligible student with the amount to which he was entitled.

Also created by the act was a student loan marketing association, a secondary market for student loans. The act extended through 1974 the Emergency Insured Student Loan Act allowing special interest payments to lenders in times of high interest rates. Other student aid programs extended included: supplemental grants (at an annual level of $200-million), special programs for disadvantaged students, insured student loans (with an increase in the total of loans insured to $2-billion by 1975), work-study and cooperative education programs, direct student loans (at an annual level of $400-million), graduate fellowships for students interested in college teaching or public service, and grants for area studies.

Institutional Aid. For the first time, a program of direct general federal aid to institutions of higher education was provided by the 1972 Amendments, which authorized annual payments to colleges and universities based in part upon the total amount of federal aid going to students in attendance at each school and in part upon the total number of students and students in attendance receiving the basic educational opportunity grants. In addition, the law provided for $40-million in emergency grants to rescue institutions on the verge of bankruptcy.

Furthermore, the 1972 law provided for a new program of $850-million in federal aid over fiscal years 1973-75 to encourage improved programs of occupational education and better counseling and guidance efforts to direct students into these programs. It also authorized a $290-million program of grants for the planning, establishment and improvement of community colleges in fiscal 1973-75.

Other programs extended by the bill included aid for programs of: community service, library improvement, developing institutions, education professions development, acquisition and construction of equipment and facilities, improvement of graduate education, and existing programs of vocational education.

Busing and Desegregation Aid. The 1972 Amendments authorized $1-billion in each of fiscal years 1973-74 in federal aid for desegregating school districts. Forty-one per cent of the funds was earmarked for special purposes such as bilingual education and metropolitan areas projects, the remaining 59 per cent was to be allocated among eligible districts in the 50 states.

In the most controversial provisions of the entire massive bill, the new law:

• Barred the use of federal funds for busing—unless they were expressly and voluntarily requested by local officials for this purpose—and then only so long as the busing did not risk the health or education of the children concerned and did not send any child to a school inferior to that he would otherwise attend.

• Barred federal pressure for the use of state or local funds for busing—unless busing was constitutionally required—and then only so long as the health and education factors mentioned above did not preclude busing.

• Postponed—until Jan. 1, 1974—the effective date of any federal court order requiring busing until all appeals of the order—or the time for them—had been exhausted.

Education Division. The bill also created an Education Division within the Department of Health, Education and Welfare (HEW), to be headed by an assistant secretary of education—who could not also be the commissioner of education—and which would consist of the existing Office of Education and the new National Institute of Education. The Institute, also created by the bill, would lead in supporting education research by channeling a total of $550-million in grants to persons and institutions conducting such research in fiscal 1973-75.

Almost $1-billion in appropriations to carry out these extended and expanded programs was included in a supplemental appropriations bill enacted late in the 92nd Congress: of the total $577.5-million was for higher education and $270.6-million for aid to desegregating school districts.

Veterans' Benefits. Congress in 1971 again increased the monthly allowances for veterans attending school or participating in vocational training programs under the GI bill. The basic monthly rate for single veterans who were fulltime students was increased to $220 from $175; veterans with dependents or who were part-time students received proportionate increases in allowances.

National Science Foundation. Congress in 1972 approved a bill (HR 14108—PL 92-372) authorizing $703.9-million for the National Science Foundation in fiscal 1973.

Elementary and Secondary Education

Desegregation and Equal Education. President Nixon March 17 asked Congress to enact his Equal Educational Opportunities Act which would establish that busing was strictly a last-resort remedy for segregation to be used only in certain circumstances and to target $2.5-billion in federal aid (authorized under other law) upon areas with the greatest need for improving their schools.

Congress moved deliberately on this proposal (HR 13915, S 3395) in 1972; both houses held hearings and the House committee in late July reported out a bill which reduced the targeted aid to $1-billion. The House Aug. 18 passed HR 13915 with stronger restrictions on busing than requested by the President. As passed by the House, the bill banned busing for students except to the school nearest or next nearest to their homes, allowed the reopening of cases involving desegregation orders already in effect in order that they might be modified in keeping with these busing curbs, and provided for the termination of any desegregation order once a court found that a unitary school system existed.

When the bill reached the Senate, liberal opponents of the busing curbs took up the conservatives' old weapon—the filibuster—and talked the bill to death. After the third effort to end the filibuster failed, supporters of the bill conceded that it was dead for the 92nd Congress.

President Nixon also March 17 asked Congress to approve his Student Transportation Moratorium Act which would halt all new busing until July 1, 1973, or until passage of the equal opportunities bill. House hearings on the moratorium proposal (HR 13916, S 3388) were the only action on this proposal in 1972.

The House Rules Committee in August discharged the House Judiciary Committee from further consideration of a constitutional amendment barring school busing. The Rules Committee sent the proposed amendment to the House floor, but no further action was taken on the proposal during the 92nd Congress.

Education Revenue-Sharing. The House held hearings in early 1972 on the President's proposal for special revenue-sharing for education, but no further action was taken in 1972.

Tuition Tax Credits. Both President Nixon and Democratic presidential nominee George McGovern endorsed the idea of tuition tax credits for parents of children who attend non-public schools. The House Ways and Means Committee held hearings on such proposals and approved the language of a draft bill providing such tax credits, but no further action was taken on the matter in the 92nd Congress.

Welfare Legislation

If there was one subject upon which leaders of all political persuasions agreed in 1969, it was the "welfare mess"—a term that embraced soaring welfare rolls, skyrocketing costs and imperfect and uneven administration. Welfare reform became one of the "six great goals" of the first Nixon administration, but the goal was never realized and by the time of his 1972 re-election campaign President Nixon was talking more about the "work ethic" than about welfare reform.

At the beginning of his second term in 1973, Nixon formally abandoned his own welfare reform proposals. He also moved to dismantle the Office of Economic Opportunity (OEO), the umbrella agency for the antipoverty program which had been launched by Congress at President Johnson's behest in 1964.

The record of the 91st and 92nd Congresses in the field of welfare legislation was undistinguished. Congress refused to give President Nixon the welfare system overhaul he wanted. The President refused to let Congress do what it wanted with the antipoverty program, a new child development program and expanded programs for the aging. The result was a largely unproductive standoff.

After working for three years on the proposed Family Assistance Plan, the President's overhaul of the mammoth Aid to Families with Dependent Children (AFDC) program, Congress saw Senate intransigence let it die in conference. *(Family Assistance Plan p. 622)*

In other action in the field of Social Security legislation, Congress did raise Old Age, Survivors and Disability Insurance (OASDI) benefits three times to keep up with the cost of living and eased various OASDI requirements. It also made one major welfare change—consolidating, federalizing and raising benefits under the three "adult" welfare programs. And it generally expanded federal programs providing food for the hungry. *(Hunger programs, p. 628)*

The President wrested the initiative for action on the antipoverty program from Congress. The result was a fairly steady level of funding and few changes in the direction of the program. A 1971 OEO authorization containing a new $2-billion child development program was vetoed, as was a 1972 expansion of the Older Americans Act.

Social Security Changes

The continuing high rate of inflation led Congress to raise Old Age, Survivors and Disability Insurance (OASDI) benefits three times between 1969-72. In 1969 benefits were raised 15 per cent, in 1971 they were raised 10 per cent, and a further 20 per cent increase was voted in 1972. The 1972 law also provided for future automatic increases in Social Security benefits when the cost of living rose more than 3 per cent.

To finance the changes, the amount of earnings subject to Social Security taxes (the taxable earnings base) was substantially increased. The base had been $4,800 in 1969; by 1973 it had been raised to $12,000. Increases in the tax rate itself, which caused greater hardship for the poor, were not as substantial. It was raised from 4.6 per cent to 5.8 per cent, and part of the increase was to put the Medicare trust fund on a more stable basis. *(Social Security taxes, p. 610)*

All three benefits increases were voted as amendments to bills dealing with other subjects. Not until the last days of the 1972 session did Congress pass an over-all Social Security bill making other changes in the program. President Nixon had requested a number of noncontroversial liberalizations of OASDI programs in 1969, but the proposals got tied up with his controversial welfare reform plan and were not enacted until the end of the 92nd Congress. Among the changes finally enacted were a further liberalization of the retirement test and increased benefits for widows and widowers.

Medical Care. The same Social Security bill included a number of changes in the Medicare program for the aged and the Medicaid program for welfare recipients and the borderline poor. With soaring medical care costs, both programs were far more expensive than Congress had anticipated. As a result, Congress rescinded the requirement that all states have comprehensive Medicaid programs and attempted to tighten up administration of both programs to cut costs. However, it made no major changes, and the problem of the high U.S. medical costs remained for the second Nixon administration.

Welfare Issue. The over-all welfare caseload rose from 9.6 million in 1969 to 13.5 million in 1972. Costs went from $6.2-billion in 1969 to over $9-billion in 1971. Most of the increase was in the Aid to Families with Dependent Children (AFDC) program. AFDC benefits and eligibility requirements varied widely from state to state, and the

References

Discussion of welfare policies and legislation in the years 1945-64 may be found in *Congress and the Nation Vol. I*, p. 1225-1330; for the years 1965-68, *Congress and the Nation Vol. II*, p. 745-778.

program was unevenly administered by 1,152 separate state and local welfare jurisdictions. The administration and many members of Congress were in agreement that the AFDC program should be completely overhauled, but they could not agree on how to do it.

The administration's Family Assistance Plan (FAP), which would have provided for the first time benefits for the working poor (at reduced rates), was passed twice by the House but got caught between liberals and conservatives in the Senate. It finally died in conference at the end of the 1972 session, leaving the family welfare system much bigger and more expensive but in the same framework as when President Nixon took office. *(Family Assistance plans, p. 622)*

Congress did ease two controversial restrictions in the AFDC program. In 1969 it repealed a provision which would have frozen the proportion of children in each state eligible for AFDC assistance at the percentage of children on the rolls in January 1968. In 1971 it altered the Work Incentive Plan (WIN) for the adult AFDC recipients. This brought the plan closer to the work-training program proposed under the President's Family Assistance Plan.

While it failed to make substantial revisions in the AFDC program, Congress in 1972 did make an important change in the other three federal-state welfare programs —Old Age Assistance (OAA), Aid to the Blind (AB) and Aid to the Permanently and Totally Disabled (APTD). It consolidated them into one federally administered "supplemental security income" program with a guaranteed minimum federal payment of $130 a month ($195 per couple). The new program both raised benefits to the needy and helped to take some of the increasingly difficult welfare burden from the states.

Antipoverty Program

During the Johnson administration, Congress had taken the initiative from the administration in shaping the antipoverty program. In addition, each new authorization had faced a stiff fight from opponents who sought to dismantle its parent agency, the Office of Economic Opportunity (OEO).

During the Nixon administration, this changed. The first authorization, in 1969, did meet a strong challenge from opponents in the House. But after that the opposition faded and the President took the upper hand. A comfortable majority in Congress wanted to extend and enlarge the program, but Nixon permitted its continuation only on his own terms. He vetoed the 1971 authorization, leaving the OEO without legal authority for 14 months, although funds were appropriated. In 1972 Congress carefully tailored the bill to avoid a veto, including calling back the conference report to reduce the authorization and strike a section on the legal services program opposed by the administration.

President Nixon in 1969 asked for extension of the OEO pending an administration study of how the programs should be revised. He recognized the value of "an agency whose special concern is the poor" but said "much has been tried that has not worked."

The 1969 authorization extended the agency for two years and provided $2.19-billion for fiscal 1970 and $2.8-billion for fiscal 1971. Congress earmarked funds for a number of programs. The bill did not clear the House until the tail end of the session. Its supporters had post-

poned action while they rounded up strength to defeat a substitute proposal to hand over authority held by regional OEO offices to state governors. When the bill finally came to the floor this was rejected by a **163-231 key roll-call vote**.

The President's 1971 request to extend the OEO was described as temporary until the President's proposed cabinet reorganization could take place. However, it became clear early in the session that Congress was unlikely to go along with the extensive reorganization.

The authorization became involved in controversy over the congressional addition of a special $2-billion child development plan. The $6.3-billion final bill also contained provisions transferring the OEO's legal services program to a new public corporation, prohibiting transfer of programs out of the OEO without congressional consent and earmarking funds for many of the OEO programs. The President vetoed the bill with a long message. He objected particularly to the child development program but also opposed earmarking, the transfer prohibition and the make-up of the board of the Legal Services Corporation. *(Explanation of issues, below)*

Congress in 1972 wrote a new bill extending the OEO through fiscal 1974. The bill was written to avoid most of the administration objections to the vetoed bill, but as first sent to conference it did contain a controversial provision which limited the President's flexibility in appointing members of the Legal Services Corporation board. When it became clear that the President was likely to veto the bill if that provision remained, the entire plan for the legal services transfer was dropped. Also to satisfy the administration, the level of authorization in the final bill was substantially below that of the bill as passed by either chamber—$2.36-billion for fiscal 1973 and $2.39-billion for fiscal 1974.

Child Development. The Senate in 1971 added a special $2-billion child development program to the OEO authorization, providing a range of educational, day care and health services for pre-school children. Children from families with incomes under $6,900 would have been eligible to participate without charge; others would have paid on a sliding scale. A similar program was added to the House bill on the floor, setting the income level for free services at $4,320. During months of conference sessions the administration opposed the program and said it certainly would not accept anything above the $4,320 income level. That figure was contained in the final bill.

The President vetoed the bill, objecting to a number of its features and singling out the child development program. He said it would "commit the vast moral authority of the federal government to the side of communal approaches to child rearing."

The Senate in 1972 passed separately a modified version of the plan but the House took no action.

Earmarking. Another feature of the vetoed 1971 bill to which the President objected was a provision earmarking funds. Congress had begun this practice in 1966 in an effort to take more control over the direction of the program. The Johnson administration, faced with congressional opposition that could have killed the legislation altogether, was resigned to the earmarking. The Nixon administration also accepted earmarking in the first (1969) OEO bill, but in the 1971 veto message Nixon objected to it as "reactionary." Congress did not earmark funds in 1972.

Public Assistance: Recipients and Payments, 1940-72

Period	Old-age assistance [1]	Aid to the blind [1][2]	Aid to the permanently and totally disabled [1]	Aid to families with dependent children		
				Families	Total recipients [3]	Children
Number of recipients (in thousands)						
December:						
1940	2,070	73.4	—	372	1,222	895
1945	2,056	71.5	—	274	943	701
1950	2,786	97.5	69	651	2,233	1,661
1955	2,538	104.1	241	602	2,192	1,661
1960	2,305	106.9	369	803	3,073	2,370
1961	2,229	102.7	389	916	3,566	2,753
1962	2,183	98.7	428	932	3,789	2,844
1963	2,152	96.9	464	954	3,930	2,951
1964	2,120	95.5	509	1,012	4,219	3,170
1965	2,087	85.1	557	1,054	4,396	3,316
1966	2,073	83.7	588	1,127	4,666	3,526
1967	2,073	82.7	646	1,297	5,309	3,986
1968	2,027	80.7	702	1,522	6,086	4,555
1969	2,074	80.6	803	1,875	7,313	5,413
1970	2,082	81.0	935	2,552	9,659	7,033
1971	2,024	80.3	1,068	2,918	10,653	7,707
1972	1,933	80.0	1,168	3,122	11,064	7,983
Average monthly payment						
December:						
1940	$20.25	$ 25.35	—	$ 32.40	$ 9.85	—
1945	30.90	33.50	—	52.05	15.15	—
1950	43.05	46.00	$ 44.10	71.45	20.85	—
1955	50.05	55.55	48.75	85.50	23.50	—
1960	58.90	67.45	56.15	108.35	28.35	—
1961	57.60	68.05	57.05	114.65	29.45	—
1962	61.55	71.95	58.50	119.10	29.30	—
1963	62.80	73.95	59.85	122.40	29.70	—
1964	63.65	76.15	62.25	131.30	31.50	—
1965	63.10	81.35	66.50	136.95	32.85	—
1966	68.05	86.85	74.75	150.10	36.25	—
1967	70.15	90.45	80.60	161.70	39.50	—
1968	69.55	92.15	82.65	168.15	42.05	—
1969	73.95	98.75	90.20	176.05	45.15	—
1970	77.65	104.35	97.65	187.95	49.65	—
1971	77.50	106.50	102.25	190.90	52.30	—
1972	80.01	112.83	106.05	191.15	53.95	—

1 *Represents data for payments to recipients of the specified type of assistance under separate programs and under the combined State adult assistance programs.*
2 *Beginning September 1965, excludes State blind pension program in Pennsylvania administered under State law without Federal participation.*

3 *Includes as recipients the children and 1 or both parents or 1 caretaker relative other than a parent in families in which the requirements of such adults were considered in determining the amount of assistance.*

SOURCE: Social and Rehabilitation Service

Transfer of Programs. President Nixon in 1969 transferred the OEO's Foster Grandparents program to the Department of Health, Education and Welfare (HEW) and delegated two others—Head Start to HEW and the Job Corps to the Labor Department. Delegation did not have to be approved by Congress because it left a program under the over-all supervision of the OEO). In 1971 he proposed and Congress agreed to the merging of OEO's volunteer programs (VISTA and the Auxiliary and Special Volunteer Programs) with other federal volunteer programs in a new agency called ACTION.

The vetoed 1971 bill contained a provision prohibiting further transfers or delegations without prior congressional approval. The President in his veto message said the administration should have the flexibility to shift tried and proven programs to established agencies and concentrate OEO efforts on testing new ideas. The transfer prohibition was not voted in 1972.

Legal Services. The vetoed 1971 bill contained a provision transferring the legal services programs to a new nonprofit Legal Services Corporation. The board of the corporation was to be appointed by the President, but he could freely choose only six of 17 members. The balance was to be picked from lists submitted by professional and client groups. The President's veto message said he should have a free hand to appoint all board members and that the provision as it stood was "an affront to the principle of accountability to the American people."

Congress included a similar provision in the 1972 OEO authorization, but dropped the entire legal services transfer in conference when it appeared it might lead to another veto. Behind the specific issue of the make-up of the board there appeared to be considerable Republican dissatisfaction with the operation of the legal services program.

New Programs. The result of the 1971 veto and administration-directed 1972 bill was that Congress made few changes in the OEO program during the first Nixon administration. It did not write new restrictions or revise programs as it did during the Johnson years. It did add a few new programs. In 1969 it voted new alcoholic counseling and drug recovery programs, and in 1972 it added an OEO consumer action program for low-income persons.

Chronology

Of Legislation

On Welfare

1969

The major 1969 action in the field of welfare was a two-year extension of the antipoverty program along existing lines. The bill for a while appeared to be in serious trouble in the House, but was passed by a comfortable margin late in the session.

President Nixon asked for a 10 per cent increase in Social Security benefits coupled with a number of improvements in the system. Congress added a 15 per cent benefits increase to the Tax Reform Act and promised consideration of the other proposals in 1970.

Congress also extended the Older Americans Act, repealed a controversial welfare restriction and permitted states to cut back the increasingly expensive Medicaid program.

Antipoverty Program

Six months after the old authorization had run out, Congress extended the antipoverty program for two years. The bill (S 3016—PL 91-177) authorized $2,195,500,000 for fiscal 1970—slightly more than the administration request and the amount voted by the previous Congress for fiscal 1969. For fiscal 1971, the bill authorized $2,831,900,000.

President Nixon, who had said little about the controversial antipoverty program during his election campaign, Feb. 19 had sent Congress a rather skeptical message on the program. He asked for a one-year extension pending administration study and recommendations on how the program should be revised. He announced delegation of two programs (Head Start and Job Corps) to existing agencies and the outright transfer of two more (Foster Grandparents and Comprehensive Health Centers). Later in the year, in June, he revised his request and asked for a two-year extension. The decision to transfer the health program was also rescinded.

In April the administration announced the closing of 59 of the Job Corps centers which took unemployed and poorly educated youths away from their home environments to residential conservation camps or training centers. The program had probably been the most unpopular antipoverty measure with Congress. The Senate in May considered a measure (S J Res 194) to postpone the closings until antipoverty legislation had been considered; it was rejected by a 40-52 roll call.

Although committee hearings were completed in early summer and the program authorizations expired, the Senate did not pass a bill (S 3016) until October. Its version gave the administration what it wanted for fiscal 1970 but almost $600-million above the request for fiscal 1971. The only controversial legislative provision allowed state governors to veto legal services projects in their states.

In the House, the antipoverty program was stalled for months in an Education and Labor Committee fight between its supporters and several members of the committee who wanted to make major changes. It finally reached the floor in December. As passed, it carried more than the request for fiscal 1970 and an open-ended authorization for fiscal 1971. Before passage the House defeated the strongest attempt ever made to turn the entire program over to state control.

The final version of the bill split the difference on funds and did not contain the Senate veto amendment.

The fiscal 1970 Labor-HEW appropriations bill (HR 15931—PL 91-204) provided $1,948,000,000 for the Office of Economic Opportunity. For fiscal 1971 Congress provided a total of $1,323,400,000 for all antipoverty programs run by the OEO or delegated to other departments (HR 18515—PL 91-667).

Request. In his Feb. 19 message President Nixon said the Urban Affairs Council was conducting an intensive study of how the antipoverty program could be made more effective. He said that from the OEO "we have learned the value of having in the federal government an agency whose special concern is the poor" but that "even those most thoroughly committed to the goals of the antipoverty effort recognize now that much that has been tried has not worked." He said he would be sending Congress reorganization proposals before the Economic Opportunity Act of 1964 expired in June 1970. In the meantime, he requested authorization of appropriations until that date.

Congress in the Vocational Education Amendments of 1968 had directed the executive branch to study the placement of the popular Head Start and controversial Job Corps programs. In his February message, the President announced that this had been completed, and that Head Start was to be delegated to the HEW Department "to strengthen it by association with a wide range of other early development programs within the department and also with the research programs of the National Institutes of Health and related agencies." The Job Corps was to be delegated to the Labor Department to be coordinated with other manpower services "at the point of delivery."

Delegation of programs did not require congressional approval; it left the program under the over-all supervision of the OEO. The President also proposed transferring entirely to HEW two additional antipoverty programs, the Foster Grandparents program and the Comprehensive Health Centers programs. The former was later transferred in the Older Americans Act (PL 91-69). The administration changed its mind about transfer of the latter, and instead expanded it under the OEO.

The President in June revised his request for a one-year extension and instead asked Congress to authorize funds for the OEO through fiscal 1971. He said this would provide a better framework for necessary improvements in the program.

Senate Action. The Senate passed the fiscal 1970 and 1971 anti-poverty authorization (S 3016) Oct. 14, by a 72-3 roll call. The bill authorized $2.048 billion for fiscal 1970 (the amount requested by the administration) and $2.732 billion for fiscal 1971 ($584.2 million more than the administration request).

S 3016 contained extra funds for eight anti poverty programs "considered to be of special importance": Head Start, legal services, health services, emergency food and medical services, Special Impact, senior opportunities and services, migrant and seasonal farmworkers, and day care projects. It also authorized two new community action programs—an alcoholic counseling and recovery program and a drug addiction rehabilitation program.

The Senate on a 45-40 roll-call vote accepted an amendment by George Murphy (R Calif.) giving state governors the power to veto legal service projects in their states. This was the latest in a long line of congressional actions on veto power over antipoverty programs. (*Box, this page*)

House Action. The House version of S 3016 (HR 12321) was not reported to the floor until Nov. 22. Apparently Education and Labor Committee Chairman Carl D. Perkins (D Ky.) had for months unsuccessfully sought unanimous committee agreement that no major amendments would be offered to the bill on the floor. The bill was finally ordered reported by a 21-12 vote.

Veto Power

The power of a governor of a state to veto an antipoverty project in his state, a controversial issue since the start of the war on poverty, emerged again as a topic of debate in the Senate as it considered S 3016.

The Johnson administration antipoverty measure as introduced in 1964 stipulated that no VISTA volunteers be referred to a state without the consent of the governor. But the draft bill contained no other veto powers for the governors.

The issue quickly became a significant point of controversy, however, as Republicans and Southern Democrats charged that the antipoverty bill ignored "states' rights."

The conservative coalition in the Senate sought to reduce the authority of the director of the OEO by requiring that he obtain the consent of state governors before initiating any antipoverty projects in their states. Although unsuccessful on several amendments, they did succeed in adding to the bill a veto for the governor over the establishment of a Job Corps camp or other work-training projects in his state.

The House added an amendment permitting governors to veto any project under the community action program. As finally enacted, therefore, the Economic Opportunity Act of 1964 (PL 88-452) gave the governors absolute veto power over Title I (Job Corps, Neighborhood Youth Corps, and other work programs), Title II (all community action programs) and VISTA projects.

Modifications in the veto power were approved, however, in the Economic Opportunity Amendments of 1965 (PL 89-253). The director of the OEO was given the authority to override the veto in the case of Neighborhood Youth Corps or community action programs. The governor's absolute veto power was retained in Job Corps programs and VISTA projects which was the situation in 1969 during consideration of S 3016, even with the Job Corps delegation to the Department of Labor. (*Congress and the Nation, Vol. II, p. 761*)

From the beginning of the antipoverty program to October 1969 there had been 70 vetoes of poverty programs by governors. Of the total, 19 vetoes were subsequently withdrawn by the governors. 25 were sustained by the OEO director, 15 were overridden and 11 were still pending.

California had registered the highest number of vetoes—15—all exercised by Gov. Ronald Reagan (R). Six vetoes were withdrawn by the governor, four were overridden, four sustained by the OEO director and one was pending. Alabama had 13 vetoes, made by three different governors, Mississippi had nine and Louisiana and Florida each had four. A total of 20 states were responsible for the 70 vetoes.

House floor action on HR 12321 was scheduled for early December and then indefinitely postponed after a bipartisan group of Education and Labor Committee members announced plans to offer a substitute bill.

The committee bill authorized $2,343,000,000 for fiscal 1970 and provided an open-ended authorization for fiscal 1971. It earmarked funds for only a few programs— Operation Mainstream, New Careers, Head Start, Follow Through and emergency food and medical services.

The substitute proposal transferred all authority held by the regional offices of the Office of Economic Opportunity to state governors. The governors would have the option of taking over the programs or of vetoing all antipoverty activities in their states. States were to develop state plans for antipoverty activities. Funds were to be channeled through state agencies which were to take over OEO functions of reviewing and approving local antipoverty applications.

HR 12321 was finally brought to the floor Dec. 12 and passed with minor amendments by a 276-117 roll-call vote. It supporters had worked for two weeks to round up support and to defeat the substitute. The substitute was rejected by a **163-231 key roll-call vote** on a motion to recommit with instructions to report back the substitute bill. In the crucial vote on the proposal, it had earlier been defeated on a 167-186 teller vote.

Conference Report. The House adopted the conference report on S 3016 Dec. 20 by a 243-94 roll-call vote and the Senate adopted it the same day on a 54-21 roll call.

The final version split the difference between the House and Senate on fiscal 1970 funds, providing $2,195,500,000. It authorized $2,831,900,000 for fiscal 1971. House conferees accepted the earmarking of funds made by the Senate and the final bill also contained special funds voted by the House for Operation Mainstream and New Careers. The Senate governors' veto amendment was dropped.

Provisions. As cleared for the President, S 3016 (PL 91-177):

• Authorized a total of $2,195,500,000 for fiscal 1970 and $2,831,900,000 for fiscal 1971.

• Reserved $328.9-million in each fiscal year authorization for Title II local initiative (community action) programs.

• Established new alcoholic counseling and recovery and drug rehabilitation programs and earmarked funds for each in fiscal 1970 and 1971.

• Permitted the OEO director to reallocate funds within the various programs by up to 10 per cent in fiscal 1970 and by up to 15 per cent in fiscal 1971.

• Limited the amounts that the director could add to existing programs to 100 per cent for programs of $10-million per year or less and up to 35 per cent for programs of over $10-million.

• Provided that children not in low-income families be permitted to participate in Head Start programs, and required their families to be charged fees for their participation.

• Required counseling, education and other services under the legal services program to be limited to legal matters.

• Added a new title to the act to provide for special work and career-development programs.

• Allocated funds for the two fiscal years in the following manner:

	Fiscal 1970	Fiscal 1971
Work and training programs	$ 890,300,000	$ 890,300,000
Special Impact	46,000,000	60,000,000
Special work and career development	20,000,000	54,700,000
Title II Community Action (subtotals)	(811,300,000)	(1,234,000,000)
Head Start	398,000,000	578,000,000
Follow Through	90,000,000	90,000,000
Legal services	58,000,000	90,000,000
Health services	80,000,000	160,000,000
Emergency food and medical services	62,500,000	175,000,000
Family planning	15,000,000	30,000,000
Senior opportunities and services	8,800,000	12,000,000
Alcoholic counseling and recovery	10,000,000	15,000,000
Drug rehabilitation	5,000,000	15,000,000
Unearmarked Title II funds	84,000,000	69,000,000
Rural loans	12,000,000	12,000,000
Migrant and seasonal farmworkers	34,000,000	49,000,000
Day-care projects	——	50,000,000
Administration and coordination	16,000,000	16,000,000
Volunteers in Service to America (VISTA)	37,000,000	37,000,000
Subtotal	**$1,866,600,000**	**$2,403,000,000**
Unearmarked funds	——	100,000,000
Special reserved funds for Title II local initiative	328,900,000	328,900,000
TOTAL	**$2,195,500,000**	**$2,831,900,000**

Social Security Benefits

The immense 1969 Tax Reform Act (HR 13270—PL 91-172) included among its many provisions a 15 per cent across-the-board increase in all Social Security payments. The increase, which was to cost an estimated $4.4 billion a year, was to be financed for the time being out of surplus balances in the Social Security trust fund. *(Tax chapter, p. 77)*

President Nixon in September had asked for a 10 per cent increase in Social Security benefits to make up for the rise in the cost of living. The increase was to be financed by an immediate rise in the taxable wage base. He also asked for a number of other changes in the system, including future automatic benefit increases to match the cost of living.

The Senate Dec. 5 adopted amendments to the tax bill raising Social Security benefits by 15 per cent and making certain liberalizing changes in the retirement system. The same day the House Ways and Means Committee reported a bill (HR 15095) which also provided for a 15 per cent increase. It promised early consideration of the other administration Social Security proposals in 1970.

HR 15095 was passed by the House unanimously, and its provisions were incorporated into the final version of the omnibus tax bill. Other Senate Social Security amendments to the tax bill were dropped in conference.

Request. President Nixon Sept. 25 proposed a 10 per cent across-the-board increase in Social Security benefits to make up for cost-of-living increases since benefits were last raised in February 1968. He also asked that the Social Security system be revised to provide for automatic cost-of-living increases in the future. He said this could be coupled with and financed by automatic increases in the taxable wage base, and that an increase in Social Security tax rates would not be necessary. Automatic adjustments, the President said, would depoliticize the Social Security system and make it more stable.

The message proposed an immediate increase in the wage base from $7,800 to $9,000; an increase in the amount a retired person could earn and still receive benefits; and additional reforms to benefit widows, recipients over 72, veterans, persons disabled in childhood and dependent parents of the disabled.

Senate Action. During debate on the Tax Reform Act the Senate adopted an amendment increasing all Social Security benefits by 15 per cent effective Jan. 1, 1970. The amendment, sponsored by Finance Committee Chairman Russell B. Long (D La.), was approved by a 73-14 roll-call vote. It included provisions increasing minimum retirement payments for single persons to $100 and for married couples to $150 and providing larger payments for some three million disabled. The Senate the same day adopted another amendment permitting persons aged 60 to retire with reduced Social Security benefits; the minimum retirement age under existing Social Security law was 62.

The administration opposed the 15 per cent increase in benefits and lobbied unsuccessfully for its own 10 per cent proposal. An amendment substituting a 10 per cent increase failed, 34-56.

House Action. The House Ways and Means Committee Dec. 5 reported a clean bill (HR 15095), a substitute for the administration Social Security proposal, increasing Social Security benefits by 15 per cent. The report said the need for the increase was urgent, and that further Social Security changes would be considered early in 1970. It said there was a substantial surplus in the Social Security retirement trust fund, so that no increase was currently needed in the Social Security tax or taxable wage base.

HR 15095 was passed by the House unanimously Dec. 15. House Ways and Means Committee Chairman Wilbur D. Mills (D Ark.) said it was "unique to present a bill increasing benefits while withholding action on other needed improvements," but the increase was necessary immediately in light of a 9.1 per cent increase in the cost of living since the last benefits increase went into effect in February 1968.

Because it already had voted to increase Social Security benefits in the tax reform act, the Senate did not act on HR 15095.

Final Action. House-Senate conferees agreed to include a 15-per cent across-the-board Social Security benefits increase in the Tax Reform Act. The other Social Security provisions the Senate had added to the tax bill were deleted in conference.

In signing the tax bill into law Dec. 30, President Nixon expressed disappointment that Congress had not enacted his Social Security proposals, but said "the overriding consideration is that 25 million recipients of Social Security benefits have fallen behind financially, which makes my approval of this short-range revision necessary."

Older Americans Act

Congress extended the Older Americans Act of 1965 (PL 89-73) for three years and substantially expanded authorizations. It also added a new provision to the law creating a Retired Service Volunteer Program (RSVP) for persons aged 60 and over to provide community services without compensation. The foster grandparents program, under which people over 60 care for retarded and orphaned children, was expanded and transferred from the Office of Economic Opportunity to the Department of Health, Education and Welfare.

The Older Americans Act was enacted in 1965. It established an Administration on Aging in HEW and authorized a five-year program designed to coordinate federal activities related to the elderly and to expand programs for the aging on both the federal and state levels. It authorized federal grants for such programs totaling $17.5-million for the first two years. In 1967 Congress authorized grants totaling $42.9-million for fiscal years 1968 and 1969. *(Congress and the Nation, Vol. II, p. 762, 776)*

The 1969 bill (HR 11235—PL 91-69) set total authorizations at $62-million for fiscal 1970, $85-million for fiscal 1971 and $105-million for fiscal 1972. The administration had requested open-ended authorizations. During House debate William A. Steiger (R Wis.), author of the administration bill, called HR 11235's funding unrealistically high.

HR 11235 was passed by the House June 16 by voice vote and by the Senate Aug. 13 by voice vote with minor amendments. The House accepted the Senate amendments Sept. 3.

Provisions. As signed into law, HR 11235:

● Set total authorizations at $62 million for fiscal 1970, $85 million for fiscal 1971 and $105 million for fiscal 1972.

● Authorized appropriations over the three years of $75 million for state and community projects and $47 million for research, demonstration and training projects.

● Authorized a Retired Service Volunteer Program (RSVP) for persons aged 60 and over to provide community services without compensation. The bill authorized $30 million over three years for reimbursement of out-of-pocket expenses incident to RSVP services.

● Authorized appropriations totaling $60 million over the three years for the foster grandparents program under which people over 60 care for retarded and orphaned children.

● Established new requirements for statewide planning of programs for older people and separated authorizations for such planning from the grant funds available to states. Planning authorizations totaled $15-million through fiscal 1972.

● Provided for reallotment of unused funds granted under the Older Americans Act for administration of state plans. The funds would go to states which could use them, with the exception that, through fiscal 1971, a state lacking legal authority to use all its yearly allotment could carry over unused funds to the next fiscal year.

● Permitted continuation of federal support to states for community projects and services beyond the fiscal years 1967-1969 provided for in the 1967 Older Americans Act Amendments (PL 90-42). The federal share would continue at 50 per cent.

● Authorized $25 million over a three-year period for areawide model community projects to be conducted through the secretary of HEW.

Welfare Freeze Repeal

Congress repealed a controversial provision of the 1967 Social Security Amendments (PL 90-364) which had been scheduled to take effect July 1. Already postponed in 1968, the provision would have frozen the future proportion of children in each state who could receive federal assistance under the Aid to Families with Dependent Children (AFDC) program at the percentage of children on the rolls in January 1968. *(Congress and the Nation, Vol. II, p. 746, 776)*

The repeal was added to a minor House-passed bill (HR 8644—PL 91-41) by the Senate Finance Committee. The committee said it was necessary because up to 200,000 additional families were eligible for AFDC assistance as a result of an April 21 Supreme Court ruling that residency requirements for the program were unconstitutional. It said the states would have to provide for these families solely with state funds unless the provision was repealed.

HR 8644 was passed by the Senate by voice vote. The House agreed to the amendment by a 269-65 roll call, although it had been the originator of the restriction.

Medicaid Cutback

Congress held hearings on Medicaid costs and passed a bill (HR 5833—PL 91-56) permitting states to cut back certain assistance under the program. The actions were a continuation of congressional concern over steadily rising costs under Medicaid since it was created in 1965.

Background. As enacted in 1965, the Medicaid program extended the Kerr-Mills program of medical aid to the needy aged to include all persons on public assistance plus other borderline poor whom the state judged "medically needy." The program was funded by federal and state contributions with the amount of federal aid varying from 50 to 83 per cent and based on state per capita income.

Within a year after the program began, it was clear that it was costing far more than Congress had intended, both because of rising medical costs and the rather generous interpretation of the income limits of the "medically needy" in some states. In the 1967 omnibus Social Security bill Congress set income levels for the eligibility of the medically needy, but Medicaid costs continued to increase substantially. *(Congress and the Nation, Vol. II, p. 748)*

1969 Action. The Senate Finance Committee in July held hearings on rising costs under both the Medicare and Medicaid programs. Finance Committtee Chairman Russell B. Long (D La.) said Medicaid costs had increased 57 per cent in three years, three times as fast as the number of Medicaid patients.

The Senate June 30 added a nongermane rider to a minor House bill (HR 5833) permitting states to cut back certain medical assistance under Medicaid. States could not reduce cash payments for medical services or eliminate basic services such as hospital care but could reduce or eliminate such peripheral services as payment for drugs or dentistry. The bill also extended the deadline for requiring states to establish comprehensive medical assistance programs from July 1, 1975 to July 1, 1977.

HR 5833 with the Senate amendments was cleared by the House by voice vote.

The administration in 1969 also took a step toward reducing Medicaid costs when it issued new regulations limiting payments to doctors to 75 per cent of January 1969 average costs. The administration also eliminated contingency allowances to hospitals and nursing homes under both Medicaid and Medicare.

1970

Social Security Benefits

Proposed Social Security benefit increases failed to clear Congress despite passage of bills by both the House and Senate. The Senate bill got caught in end-of-the-session filibusters on two other sections its Finance Committee had added to the bill—the Trade Assistance Act and the President's proposal for a Family Assistance Plan. Those sections were eventually dropped and the benefits increase passed; by that time (Dec. 29) House Ways and Means Committee Chairman Wilbur D. Mills (D Ark.) said it was too late in the session for conferees to reconcile the differences between the two versions.

House. The House passed the bill (HR 17550) May 21 by a 344-22 roll-call vote. The bill provided for a 5-per cent increase in Old Age, Survivors and Disability Insurance (OASDI) payments, and made a number of other changes in the OASDI, Medicare and Medicaid programs. Many of the changes had been requested by President Nixon in a September 1969 message on the Social Security system; Congress in 1969 had not had time to act on them and had simply provided a 10 per cent benefits increase in the Tax Reform Act. *(Details, p. 77)*

Among the President's recommendations included in the House bill was one added as a floor amendment by a 233-144 roll-call vote. This provided for automatic future increases in Social Security benefits when the Consumer Price Index rose 3 per cent or more in the previous year. Raising benefits was traditionally a congressional prerogative and Chairman Mills had consistently opposed proposals for automatic increases.

Other provisions included a controversial section reducing by one-third the federal share of matching federal-state Medicaid payments after the first 90 days of patient care in a nursing home or mental hospital. The House bill also included administration proposals which increased the amount a beneficiary could earn and still receive OASDI payments; increased widows benefits; and liberalized provisions benefiting the blind, divorced and childhood disabled.

Medicare provisions allowed persons ineligible for the program to purchase hospital insurance for $27 a month and authorized the secretary of health, education and welfare to set limits on health provider costs and to terminate payments to providers found abusing the system. The bill repealed the requirement in existing law that states begin comprehensive Medicaid programs by 1972.

To finance the changes, the House bill increased the Social Security taxable wage base from $7,800 to $9,000 and provided a new schedule of OASDI tax rates. It increased the portion of taxes going into the hospital insurance trust fund (Medicare) to 1 per cent.

Senate. The Senate version of HR 17550 was not reported until Dec. 11. It provided for a 10 per cent increase in OASDI benefits and included the provision for future automatic benefit increases. Among the many other Social Security provisions were an increase in the minimum monthly benefit from $64 to $100 and a special new Social Security program of catastrophic health insurance which covered 80 per cent of costs above a $2,000 annual deductible. In addition, the committee tacked on its version of the controversial trade bill and a trial run of the President's proposed reform of the welfare system.

During two weeks of debate on HR 17550 there was little discussion of Social Security increases or changes in the Medicare programs. Instead, the bill was caught in filibusters over the trade provisions and welfare reform. On Dec. 29 a motion was adopted, 49-21, deleting the trade, welfare reform and catastrophic illness sections of the bill. The other Social Security changes were passed, 81-0. Mills then refused to take the bill to conference and it died with the 91st Congress. He said it would be "utterly impossible" to work out differences between the two versions before the session's end.

1971

The President took the initiative in the formulation of the antipoverty program when he vetoed a two-year extension late in the session. He objected to a number of the bill's provisions, including an expensive new child development program and limitations on the administration's flexibility in managing the antipoverty effort. The program continued without an authorization.

Final action on comprehensive Social Security changes once again was postponed when it got tied up with the welfare reform issue. Congress did, however, raise benefits another 10 per cent to keep up with increases in the cost of living. It also made some changes in the work incentive program under the welfare system.

Antipoverty Program

President Nixon late in the session vetoed a $6.3-billion, two-year OEO extension (S 2007) chiefly because of objections to the bill's new comprehensive child development program. OEO's legal and fiscal authority expired June 30. Funds to keep its programs operating in fiscal 1972 were appropriated, without being previously authorized, in a supplemental appropriations bill (HR 11955—PL 92-184) cleared Dec. 10. The bill provided $741,380,000 for programs administered directly by OEO.

President Nixon March 18 requested a two-year extension of the OEO. On March 25 it became clear that he hoped it would be the last extension. His long-range government reorganization plan, released that day, called for splitting existing OEO activities between the proposed Departments of Community Development and Human Resources. OEO manpower training programs, administered by the Department of Labor, would be switched to the administration's special manpower revenue-sharing programs. By the end of the session however, it was equally clear that Congress was unlikely to go along with either the new departments or manpower revenue sharing.

The President in 1971 also proposed the immediate merging of the OEO's volunteer programs (VISTA and the Auxiliary and Special Volunteer Programs) with other federal volunteer programs in a new agency called ACTION. Congress agreed to this.

Whereas in earlier years there had been considerable criticism of the OEO during action on its authorizations, controversy in 1971 centered on the new special child care program. Dissatisfaction with the program by the administration and GOP members of Congress seemed to intensify during the session. Early in the year major objections were that the program should be considered as separate legislation and that the income level for free entrance into the program was too high. By the end of the year GOP opponents were viewing it as an intrusion on the rights and responsibilities of parents.

The child care plan was first endorsed by the Senate Labor and Public Welfare Committee in July when it reported S 2007 with a special $2-billion program providing a broad range of day care, nutritional, education and health services for pre-school children. Children of poor families (under $6,960 annual income in the Senate bill) would be eligible for free services and children of middle-income families would be charged a fee based on annual income. The administration was unenthusiastic about the program, and supported a move to delete it on the Senate floor. The motion was defeated, 17-46.

The House after three days of debate adopted an amendment encompassing a program similar to the one voted by the Senate. The amendment set the income ceiling for free participation at $4,320. It was adopted by a 186-183 roll-call vote.

The conference agreement was not filed until two months after the House had passed the bill. For a long time conferees tried to reach a compromise between the Senate and House figures for free qualification for the child care program. The administration indicated that it opposed the program and that any figure above the $4,320 House level was totally unacceptable. Conferees finally settled on that, although GOP conferees from both the House and Senate refused to sign the conference report.

The conference report was adopted in the Senate by a 63-17 roll-call vote and in the House on a 211-187 roll call. During debate on the conference report opposition to the child care program was more vehement than it had been during earlier floor action. Opponents denounced the plan as radical and socialistic and compared it to programs in the Soviet Union. Supporters pointed out that it was voluntary and structured to permit full parental involvement.

President Nixon vetoed S 2007 Dec. 9 on the grounds that it demonstrated "fiscal irresponsibility, administrative unworkability and family-weakening implications." An attempt to override the veto the next day in the Senate failed by seven votes; 13 Republicans who had voted for the bill a week earlier switched positions.

In its other provisions, the $6.3 billion final bill had provided for transferring the legal services program to a new public corporation. It established new Environmental Action and Rural Housing Development and Rehabilitation programs. The bill earmarked funds for 15 OEO programs and prohibited administration transfer of the antipoverty programs out of the OEO without congressional consent. In his veto message, the President also objected to earmarking, to the transfer prohibition and to a provision restricting his authority to appoint the board of directors to the new Legal Services Corporation.

Request. President Nixon March 18 requested a two-year extension for the OEO. During House and Senate hearings on the extension, new OEO Director Frank Carlucci made clear that the administration wanted the extension only until Congress enacted the proposed departmental reorganization and manpower revenue-sharing programs; if they had been approved, the administration wanted the OEO programs divided among them.

On March 24 the President sent a reorganization plan to Congress merging the two OEO volunteer programs (Volunteers in Service to America and Auxiliary and Special Volunteer Programs) with the Peace Corps and other federal volunteer programs in a new agency called ACTION. Congress did not veto the plan, and it took effect automatically June 3.

Senate Action. The Senate Labor and Public Welfare Committee July 30 reported a two-year OEO extension combined with a new comprehensive child development program. The committee estimated the cost of the bill at $3.03 billion for fiscal 1972 and $3.12 billion for fiscal 1973.

The complex child development program provided that local governmental units or public or non-profit agencies in communities of over 5,000 could be designated as a "prime sponsor" of a child development program and would receive a federal grant. Each prime sponsor would be required to establish a special advisory council with half its membership drawn from parents with children participating in the programs. The program would, in effect, have strengthened and expanded the Head Start program by providing a range of educational, nutritional and health services for pre-school children. Funds would also be provided for training personnel to work in the programs. Children from families with incomes of under $6,900 would be eligible to participate in the program without charge; others would be charged on a sliding scale based on family income.

Other provisions of the Senate bill included earmarking of funds for many of the specific OEO programs; a provision that no more programs could be transferred out of the OEO without specific congressional approval;

and establishment of a private nonprofit National Legal Services Corporation to replace the legal services program administered by OEO. The Legal Services Corporation was to be administered by a 17-member board of directors. Of these, six would be appointed by the President and the balance would be chosen from lists provided by various professional, client and special interests groups.

The Senate passed S 2007 without significant changes Sept. 9 by a 49-12 roll-call vote after administration spokesmen failed to modify it.

Sen. Robert Taft Jr. (R Ohio) unsuccessfully offered a number of amendments to bring the bill in line with administration wishes. Amendments to limit the child development program were defeated, as was a motion to recommit the bill with instructions to delete the program altogether. The recommittal motion failed 17-46. Taft had argued, "We believe that the child care provisions of S 2007 are of such importance and character that they should comprise a separate piece of legislation."

Taft also offered an amendment to delete the provision prohibiting the transfer or delegation of OEO programs without congressional approval. He called the prohibition "a wholly undesirable limitation on the goals and the objectives which the President of the United States seeks for the Office of Economic Opportunity." The amendment was defeated on a 26-31 roll-call vote.

Taft offered an amendment to delete another section of provisions which particularly rankled the administration. This was the earmarking of funds for specific programs. Earmarking had also been an issue during the Johnson administration when Congress, attempting to take more control over the direction of antipoverty programs, had also been more specific about funding than the administration wanted. Taft said earmarking "strips OEO of flexibility and robs the agency of its greatest potential, the research and development potential." That amendment was defeated, 17-47.

House Action. The House Education and Labor Committee Sept. 8 reported its version of a two-year antipoverty program extension (HR 10351). The House bill was more modest than the Senate version; its estimated cost was $2.19 billion for fiscal 1972 and $2.75 billion for fiscal 1973.

Like the Senate bill, HR 10351 transferred the legal services program to a new independent corporation. It also contained provisions creating new Environmental Action and Rural Housing Development programs. It did not contain any of the provisions that had caused controversy on the Senate floor—the child development program, earmarking of funds or prohibition of transferral of OEO programs.

The House passed HR 10351 Sept. 30 by a 251-115 roll-call vote after three days of debate.

Before passage it added to the bill a child development program similar to the Senate program. The amendment was adopted by a 186-183 roll-call vote. Originally very close to the Senate program, before passage it was amended to provide free services to families with an income level under $4,320 (instead of $6,900). Supporters of the lower level wanted to make the income ceiling for free federal services the same as the ceiling for free day care services in the administration's welfare reform bill *(HR 1, p. 622)*

Considerable time during debate was devoted to transfer of the legal services program. As written by the committee, the legal services provisions permitted the new corporation to assist the indigent in criminal cases. After considerable debate, a motion to prohibit corporation involvement in criminal cases was adopted by voice vote. There was also substantial discussion of whether the Legal Services Corporation had been adequately considered; a motion to delete it was rejected by a 152-210 teller vote.

Conference Action. House and Senate conferees Nov. 29 filed separate reports on S 2007 two months after the House had passed the bill. Three of five Senate Republican conferees and five of the six House Republican conferees refused to sign the conference report.

Conferees for many meetings had sought a compromise between the House and Senate figures for free services under the child development program. The administration repeatedly emphasized that it did not like the program and that anything above the smaller $4,320 House figure was totally unacceptable; finally the conferees agreed on that.

In other respects, the conference version carried most of the provisions of both the House and Senate bills—the controversial Senate provisions earmarking funds and prohibiting transfer of OEO programs and the new programs added by the House.

The conference report was adopted by the Senate Dec. 2 by a 63-17 roll-call vote and by the House Dec. 7 by a 211-187 roll-call vote. There was intensive lobbying on behalf of the administration to defeat the conference report because of objection to the child care sections. Opponents denounced the program at length as costly and radical—more appropriate for the Soviet Union than for the United States.

VETO SUSTAINED

President Nixon with a lengthy message Dec. 9 vetoed S 2007. He objected to a number of the bill's provisions but said the "most deeply flawed" was the child development program which he called "the most radical piece of legislation to emerge from the 92nd Congress." He said that "for the federal government to plunge headlong financially into supporting child development would commit the vast moral authority of the national government to the side of communal approaches to child rearing against the family-centered approach." He asked Congress to pass his welfare reform bill instead.

The President also objected to the amendment prohibiting delegation of OEO programs. He said the OEO should be able to shift tried and proven programs to old-line agencies and concentrate its resources on testing new ideas and programs. He also objected to earmarking as "reactionary legislation" which inhibited experimentation and objected that the President could appoint only six directors of the 17-member National Legal Services Corporation.

The Senate the next day failed to override the President's veto by a 51-36 roll-call vote—seven short of the two-thirds vote needed.

Social Security Increase

Congress granted a 10 per cent across-the-board increase in Social Security benefits and raised the taxable wage base and OASDI tax rate to finance it. The action was taken as an amendment to a bill increasing the national debt (HR 4690—PL 92-5).

For the third straight year Congress failed to complete action on proposals making further changes in the Social Security system. In 1969 it also had enacted only a benefits increase on the grounds that there was not enough time for consideration of additional changes proposed by the President. *(1969 action, p. 610)* In 1970 both houses passed a bill making extensive changes in Social Security programs, but it died because Senate passage came too late in the session for conference action. *(1970 action, p. 612)* In 1971 Social Security changes other than the increase in benefits were voted in June by the House as part of a bill containing the President's controversial welfare reform plan (HR 1). The Senate took no action. *(Family assistance p. 622)*

The 1971 benefits increase was added on the Senate floor to the House-passed bill (HR 4690) increasing the ceiling on the public debt. The amendment was offered by Finance Committee Chairman Russell B. Long (D La.). Long said it was urgently needed to help recipients meet the rising cost of living. He said other provisions of the bills passed by the Senate and House in 1970 but not enacted (such as automatic benefits increases to meet cost-of-living increases) would be considered as part of a more comprehensive bill later in the 92nd Congress.

The Senate amendment, adopted 82-0, did make a few other changes. It increased the minimum monthly payment from $64 to $100; increased the amount a beneficiary could earn and still receive full benefits from $1,680 to $2,400; and provided a 5 per cent increase in special benefits to persons over 72 who were not eligible for regular benefits. The provisions were to be financed by a rise in the taxable wage base from $7,800 to $9,000.

Old-Age, Survivors' Insurance

Year	Workers with taxable income (in millions)	Average taxable earnings	Average monthly OASI benefits		
			Individual retired worker	Worker and wife	Widow and child
1937	$32.9	—	—	—	—
1940	35.4	$ 932	$ 22.60	$ 36.40	$ 33.90
1943	47.7	1,310	23.42	37.50	34.20
1946	48.8	1,414	24.55	39.00	36.60
1949	46.8	1,748	26.00	41.40	36.50
1952	59.6	2,159	49.25	81.60	87.50
1955	65.2	2,416	61.90	103.50	106.80
1958	69.8	2,577	66.35	111.20	117.00
1961	72.8	2,879	75.65	126.60	135.00
1964	77.5	3,050	77.57	130.70	141.60
1967	87.4	3,769	85.37	144.20	155.90
1970	93.6	4,482	118.10	198.90	213.00

SOURCE: Social Security Administration

In conference, Ways and Means Committee Chairman Wilbur D. Mills (D Ark.) said he was willing to accept the Social Security increase as part of the debt ceiling bill since the House had passed a benefits increase in 1970. Conferees accepted the 10 per cent benefits increase but reduced the $100 minimum monthly payment passed by the Senate to $70.40. They adopted the Senate provisions raising special benefits for persons over 72 by 5 per cent but deleted the Senate provisions raising the earnings limitation.

To finance the increases, conferees agreed to the rise in the taxable wage base to $9,000 but modified the Senate provision increasing tax rates. They provided for a 5.15 per cent rate in 1976 and dropped the rate increase for 1981.

Provisions. As signed into law, the Social Security provisions of HR 4690:

• Provided a 10 per cent across-the-board increase in Old Age, Survivors and Disability Insurance (OASDI) benefits, retroactive to Jan. 1, 1971.

• Raised the minimum monthly payment to $70.40 from $64.00.

• Provided a 5 per cent increase in special benefits payable to individuals age 72 and over who were not insured for regular benefits. Provided that the increases would be retroactive to Jan. 1, 1971.

• Increased the taxable wage base to $9,000 from $7,800 effective Jan. 1, 1972.

• Increased the tax rates on employers and employees to 5.15 per cent from 5 per cent beginning in 1976. (Under existing law, the tax rate was scheduled to remain at 4.6 per cent through 1972 and to increase to 5 per cent in 1973.)

Work Incentive Programs

With the administration's welfare reform program tied up in the Finance Committee, Congress made a few changes in the work incentive program (WIN) under the existing Aid to Families with Dependent Children (AFDC) program.

The controversial WIN program, established by Congress in 1967, was a mandatory work-training program for welfare recipients over 16. States were to decide who was an appropriate candidate for training; in a controversial provision, the law did not exclude mothers of pre-school children from participating if the state chose to so require. Those taking training were allowed a $30 monthly allowance, and recipients could keep $30 plus one-third of their income without reduction in payments. *(Congress and the Nation, Vol. II, p. 775)*

The 1971 amendments (HR 10604—PL 92-223) spelled out specifically who was eligible for the WIN program instead of leaving the determination to the states. Existing law had resulted in widely differing rates of referrals and program participation. HR 10604 gave priority for program participation to unemployed fathers, followed by dependent children over 16 and mothers who volunteered for participation. It specifically excluded a number of persons from the work requirement, including mothers of pre-school children if they did not choose to work. The amendment was expected to bring more participants into the WIN program.

Other provisions of HR 10604 increased federal matching for the WIN program from 80 per cent to 90

per cent for expenses under the program, and from 75 per cent to 90 per cent for child care, family planning and other services needed to permit an individual to participate in the program. The bill required that at least 40 per cent of funds spent for the program be used for on-the-job training and public service employment. It provided that states which referred less than 15 per cent of welfare registrants to the WIN program would be subject to a decrease in federal matching funds for the AFDC program.

The work incentive amendments were added to a minor House-passed bill (HR 10604) on the Senate floor and agreed to with modifications in House-Senate conference. All actions were by voice votes.

1972

Congress passed a two-year antipoverty extension in the form the President wanted. A bill making a number of liberalizations in the Social Security program was finally cleared, as was a separate 20 per cent benefits increase. The Social Security changes included federalization of the three "adult" welfare programs. The President vetoed an extension of the Older Americans Act. A modified version of the child development program in the vetoed 1971 antipoverty bill was passed by the Senate but got no further.

Anti-poverty Program

President Nixon in September signed a two-year OEO extension. The action came more than 14 months after the OEO's legal authority had expired June 30, 1971, and nine months after he had vetoed an earlier OEO authorization. *(Veto, p. 613)*

Congress wrote the new bill (HR 12350—PL 92-424) to avoid most of the administration objections to the bill vetoed in 1971. HR 12350 did not contain controversial provisions of the 1971 bill earmarking funds, prohibiting transfer of programs or establishing a comprehensive child care program. (A child care program was passed as a separate measure by the Senate and reported to the House, but the House did not act. *Child Development, p. 620)*

But despite congressional efforts to avoid a veto, the 1972 bill also looked for a while as if it was in trouble. The issue was a dispute over transferring the OEO's legal services program to a new National Legal Services Corporation; this also had been one of the controversial sections of the bill vetoed in 1971.

While the administration originally had proposed the legal services transfer, it objected to the bill's selection procedure for the directors of the corporation. This permitted the President to freely appoint only some of the corporation directors. The balance were to be chosen from nominations submitted by professional and client groups. The administraton objected that the directors appointed from these lists would be accountable to the organizations that proposed them rather than to the public. The administration, House and Senate conferees were unable to come to agreement on appointment of the board, and the legal services program transfer was finally dropped altogether to avoid a veto. Beyond this specific problem, there also appeared to be general dissatisfaction with the legal services program among many Republicans.

As enacted, HR 12350 retroactively extended the OEO authorization through fiscal 1972, although the year had already ended. It also authorized funds for fiscal 1973 ($2.36-billion) and fiscal 1974 ($2.39-billion). The funds were for programs directly operated by OEO and programs such as manpower training, Head Start and VISTA, which had been delegated to other agencies. A fiscal 1973 HEW appropriations bill, which should have contained OEO funds, was never enacted and programs were actually funded under a continuing resolution at the fiscal 1972 level.

HR 12350 also established a new environmental action program to put low-income persons to work on jobs to protect the environment. Another new program was an OEO consumer action and education program to help the poor obtain credit at reasonable cost.

House Action. The House Education and Labor Committee reported HR 12350 Feb. 2, extending the OEO through fiscal 1973. The committee estimated the cost of its bill at $2.3-billion for fiscal 1972 and $3-billion for fiscal 1973. The Nixon administration's fiscal 1973 budget request was $2.1-billion.

The bill did not contain the controversial child development title of the 1971 bill, but instead proposed a major expansion of the Head Start program. It recommended $1.5-billion for Head Start in fiscal 1972 and 1973, about double the administration request and the level at which the program had been operating. Children from families in the "near poor" category were allowed to enter the program by paying a fee based on a sliding scale.

Other provisions of the committee bill reduced funds for other programs from levels of the vetoed bill, and set up a new environmental action program to provide payment for low-income persons working on projects to combat pollution. Like the 1971 bill, HR 12350 transferred OEO's legal services program to a new nonprofit Legal Services Corporation. It retained a controversial 1971 provision requiring the President to select 11 of the 17 directors of the corporation from lists submitted by legal and antipoverty groups.

HR 12350 was passed by the House Feb. 17 on a 234-127 roll-call vote. No major floor amendments were adopted.

The administration was opposed to the bill as passed because it objected to the high level of funding and the Legal Services Corporation Board selection procedures. It supported an attempt by Albert H. Quie (R Minn.) to amend the bill by simply extending the program for two years at its current level of funding— $1.2-billion less than proposed by the committee. The amendment was defeated on a 159-206 teller vote.

During debate liberals argued that Head Start was reaching only about 20 per cent of the children who needed it and that the proposed expansion was crucial. Opponents said the increased funds were a "poorly disguised attempt" to pass off a child development program and warned that funds should be cut to prevent a presidential veto. House Majority Leader Hale Boggs (D La.) expressed resentment over the warning that the House should legislate on the basis of a threat to veto: "I just

(Continued on p. 618)

Fiscal 1970-73 Funding of OEO Programs

(in millions)

Programs Administered by OEO

	Actual Obligations			New Obligational Authority
	FY 1970	FY 1971	FY 1972	FY 1973
Research, Development and Evaluation	$ 65	$ 84	$ 45	$ 70
Community Action Operations	387	410	348	390
Local Initiative	336	356	298	330
Training, Technical Assistance	19	17	11	3
State Economic Opportunity	10	12	12	12
Senior Opportunities	7	8	8	11
Operations Support	15	17	18	19
Summer Recreation	—	—	—	15
Health and Nutrition	157	195	177	146
Comprehensive Health	74	99	107	96
Family Planning	22	19	24	15
Food and Medical Services	46	49	23	8
Drug Rehabilitation	5	13	18	24
Alcoholic Counseling	9	12	2	—
Health Support	2	3	3	3
Community Economic Development (Special Impact)	36	37	27	36
Migrant and Seasonal Farmworkers	34	36	36	36
Legal Services	55	61	68	76
General Direction & Administration	16	19	18	19

Programs Delegated by OEO to Other Agencies

Health Education and Welfare Department	398	431	3	17
Head Start	325	360 [1]	—	—
Follow Through	70	68 [1]	—	—
Summer Recreation	3	3	3	3
Alcoholic Program	—	—	—	14
Labor Department	753 [2]	—	—	—
Job Corps	169	—	—	—
NYC-In School	59	—	—	—
NYC-Summer	124	—	—	—
NYC-Out-of-School	98	—	—	—
DOL Program Support	18	18	—	—
JOBS	47	—	—	—
Public Service Careers	47	—	—	—
Operation Mainstream	51	—	—	—
Concentrated Employment	139	—	—	—
ACTION				
VISTA	34	38	38 [3]	—
Agriculture Department	10	9	—	—
Rural Loans-Program Administration	4	6	—	—
Rural Loans-Revolving Fund	6	3	—	—
Unobligated	3	3	2	—
TOTAL APPROPRIATION	1,948	1,323	762	790

(Details may not add due to rounding.)

1 Funds were appropriated directly to HEW in FY 1972.
2 Funds were appropriated directly to Labor in FY 1971.
3 VISTA program administered by OEO in FY 1970-71. Funds were made available to ACTION by OEO in FY 1972 through an appropriation transfer and was not considered a delegated program in 1972. Funds were appropriated directly to ACTION in FY 1973.

SOURCE: Office of Economic Opportunity

do not believe the time has come in this body when we are required to legislate on the theory that someone in the executive branch, the President, is going to veto what we do. If that is the case, then we really do not need a legislative body. All we really have to do is to find out exactly what the executive wants and just put an OK on it and send it down there."

Senate Action. The Senate Labor and Public Welfare Committee May 16 reported its version of the bill (S 3010). The committee explained that it had sought to meet the President's objections to the 1971 bill by reporting the child development legislation separately and by limiting earmarking and the prohibition on transfer of programs (only transfer of community action and community economic development programs was prohibited). It increased the number of members on the board of the Legal Services Corporation to 19 and authorized the President to nominate a majority, 10 of his own choice.

S 3010 extended the OEO for three years, through fiscal 1974. The committee estimated the cost of the bill at $3.05-billion for fiscal 1972, $3.32-billion for fiscal 1973 and $3.32-billion for fiscal 1974. It authorized $500-million annually for Head Start—half-way between the House bill and administration proposal—and proposed a major expansion of the Neighborhood Youth Corps with emphasis on educational and vocational rehabilitation.

The Senate passed its version of HR 12350 June 29 by a 75-13 roll-call vote. Passage came after five days of debate during which the Senate adopted 22 floor amenments, none of them major.

During debate a number of Republicans made a strong attack on the legal services program transfer, despite the insistence of the bill's sponsors that those provisions had been written to respond to the administration's point of view. Opponents objected that the new corporation would not be accountable to the public. They expressed dissatisfaction with the way the program was currently operating, and said it should be kept within the OEO to reform it. A major objection was that lawyers involved in the legal services program did not have adequate federal supervision and had engaged improperly in political activities. Two attempts to delete the legal services transfer were defeated on roll-call votes, 37-46 and 34-56.

For awhile debate on the bill was sidetracked to an amendment to bar federal courts from issuing busing orders. The amendment was withdrawn after some senators charged it was being offered to obstruct passage of the bill. *(Busing amendments, p. 512)*

Conference Report. Conferees Aug. 18 filed a revised conference report on HR 12350—nearly two months after the Senate had passed the bill. An earlier report had been filed July 26 with a provision establishing an independent legal services corporation. It was recommitted by the Senate Aug. 11 when it became likely that the provision would lead to a presidential veto. House conferees had insisted on their position that more than half of the Legal Services Corporation directors be chosen from lists submitted by organizations, and this was unacceptable to the administration.

The final bill dropped the fiscal 1972 authorization because the year had ended. It authorized $4.75-billion for OEO programs in fiscal 1973-74—nearly $2-billion

below the Senate figure. The House had not voted funds for fiscal 1974 but had voted $3-billion for fiscal 1973. Like the elimination of the legal services transfer, the cut in funds was a concession to the administration.

There was no provision prohibiting transfer of programs. The final bill also did not earmark funds for programs, thus in effect eliminating the big House increase for Head Start and the Senate expansion of the Neighborhood Youth Corps. The final bill provided for fee schedules for participation of children from families above the poverty level in Head Start. It authorized the new environmental action and consumer action programs within the OEO.

The second conference report was adopted by the Senate Sept. 5 by voice vote and by the House the same day on a 223-97 roll call.

Provisions. As signed into law, HR 12350 (PL 92-424):

● Authorized $2.36-billion in fiscal 1973 and $2.39-billion in fiscal 1974 for programs administered under the Economic Opportunity Act of 1964.

● Extended programs authorized under the act through fiscal 1974.

● Authorized the secretary of HEW to establish procedures to make at least 10 per cent of Head Start enrollment available for handicapped children.

● Established guidelines for the secretary to follow in setting Head Start fee schedules for children from families with annual incomes over $4,320.

● Created a new environmental action program and required that persons with low incomes hired for the program were to be employed on projects which would not otherwise be carried out. (The restriction on work that could be done by individuals hired under the new program was made to avoid displacing persons already employed.)

● Prohibited the use of funds appropriated for the Teacher Corps or ACTION from being used to finance activities designed to influence the outcome of an election, voter registration project or salary of any employee engaged in such activities.

● Provided that contracts and agreements for programs in which federal funds were awarded must prohibit discrimination because of race, creed, national origin, sex, political affiliation or beliefs.

● Authorized the director of an agency administering a program funded under the Economic Opportunity Act to conduct an independent evaluation of the program administered by his agency.

● Retained the existing legal services program within OEO.

● Established OEO consumer action and education programs for low-income persons to help them obtain financial credit at a reasonable cost and to improve the delivery and lower the cost of goods and services.

Social Security Increase

With proposals for a variety of changes in the Social Security system tied up with the President's welfare reform plan, Congress at mid-year passed a separate 20 per cent increase in Social Security benefits. The increase was added to a House-passed bill raising the debt limit (HR 15390—PL 92-336). The proposal also provided for future automatic increases in Social Security benefits

Effect of 20 Per Cent
Increase on Social Security Benefits

Category	Average monthly amounts	
	Before increase	After increase
Retired worker alone	$129	$156
Retired worker and wife*	224	271
Disabled worker alone	144	173
Disabled worker, wife and children	295	354
Aged widow alone	115	138
Widow and 2 children	322	386
Average of all retired workers**	134	162
Average of all disabled workers**	148	178

*Both receiving benefits.
**With or without dependents.

SOURCE: Social Security Administration

when the cost of living rose more than 3 per cent. The taxable wage base and OASDI tax were raised to finance the increases. Later in the year Congress made other changes in the Social Security system. *(Social Security Benefits, below)*

Senate Action. The Senate June 30 by an 84-2 roll-call vote adopted an amendment to a debt ceiling increase (HR 15390) granting a 20 per cent across the board increase in Social Security benefits. The bill raised the tax rate from 5.2 per cent to 5.5 per cent and the taxable wage base from $9,000 to $10,800 in 1973 and $12,000 in 1974, and authorized an automatic increase in Social Security benefits whenever the cost of living rose more than 3 per cent in a given year. The latter provision had been proposed by President Nixon in 1969 and passed by both houses in 1970 in a bill that was never enacted. It had been opposed by Ways and Means Committee Chairman Wilbur D. Mills (D Ark.). *(1970 action, p. 612)*

President Nixon June 29 had opposed the 20 per cent increase as "highly inflationary." A compromise proposal for a 10 per cent increase was defeated on the Senate floor June 30, 20-66.

Final Action. House-Senate conferees June 30 on a party-line vote accepted the Senate-passed version of HR 15390. The House then concurred in the Senate amendments, 302-35, clearing the bill for the White House. An effort to reduce the increase to 10 per cent had failed, 83-253.

Mills had initially opposed attaching the increase to a debt limit bill. However, he changed his mind after a June 22 statement by President Nixon that he would not compromise with Senate liberals on the House-passed welfare reform bill (HR 1) that also contained a Social Security benefits increase. After that it appeared that HR 1 might be held up indefinitely. Mills felt the benefits increase was urgent because of the very high rate of inflation in 1971, and decided to go along with the Senate amendment.

Social Security Benefits

More than three years after President Nixon had asked for a number of liberalizations of OASDI and

Medicare programs, a bill containing many of them was cleared. The bill was HR 1 (PL 92-603), which, as passed by the House in 1971, had also contained the President's controversial family welfare reform plan. In the Senate it became entangled for more than a year in controversy over welfare reform. The Senate finally approved HR 1 with provision for tests of rival welfare plans, but in conference all family welfare provisions were dropped. *(Welfare controversy, p. 622)*

The final version of HR 1 did contain welfare provisions federalizing and consolidating "adult" relief programs for the needy blind, aged and disabled in a new "supplementary security income" program, and substantially increasing benefits. The federal payment to a single person would be $130 a month; it had been as low as $70 in the poorest states.

Ways and Means Committee Chairman Wilbur D. Mills (D Ark.) said the bill contained more amendments to the Social Security Act than any bill he had ever managed. The final version had 45 sections relating to the OASDI program and 99 sections relating to the Medicare and Medicaid programs in addition to the new adult welfare provisions. Many of the amendments were comparatively minor, but there were some important changes in existing law. OASDI amendments included: increased benefits for widows and widowers; an increase in the amount an OASDI beneficiary could earn; and an increase in Social Security benefits for persons who delayed retirement past 65. Medicare provisions included extension of coverage to OASDI disability benefits recipients and establishment of a professional standards review organization to oversee certain program operations. The bill repealed the requirement in existing law that states have comprehensive Medicaid programs by 1972.

HR 1 raised the Social Security tax rate to 5.85 per cent for 1972-78. Of that, 1 per cent was set aside for Medicare.

Many of the above provisions were the same as those of a bill (HR 17550) which was passed by the House and Senate in 1970. HR 17550 got tied up in the welfare controversy and was never enacted. *(HR 17550, p. 612)*

As passed by the House, HR 1 had also increased Social Security benefits across the board by 5 per cent. That provision was dropped in 1972 after Congress added a 20 per cent benefits increase to a debt limit bill (HR 15390). Congress took the action at a time when the rate of inflation was very high and HR 1 appeared tied up indefinitely over the family welfare controversy. *(Details, p. 622)*

HR 1 was passed by the House June 22, 1971, by a 288-132 roll-call vote. It was passed by the Senate Oct. 6, 1972, by a 68-5 roll call, and the conference report was cleared Oct. 17. The provisions other than the family welfare provisions were not controversial and the House and Senate were basically in agreement, although Senate benefit levels were sometimes higher. There was little debate on them in either chamber.

Provisions. As signed into law, PL 92-603:

• Increased to $2,100 from $1,680 the amount that a Social Security beneficiary under age 72 could earn and still receive full Social Security benefits.

• Increased Social Security benefits for widows and widowers to 100 per cent from 82.5 per cent of the amount received by a deceased spouse.

- Provided every person who has worked in Social Security-covered employment for at least 30 years a minimum monthly benefit of $170 a month ($255 for a couple.)
- Increased Social Security benefits by 1 per cent per year for each year after 65 an individual delayed retirement.
- Extended Medicare coverage to an additional 1.7 million disabled Social Security beneficiaries.
- Replaced existing federal-state programs of assistance to the aged, blind and disabled with a program fully financed and administered by the federal government effective Jan. 1, 1974.
- Guaranteed aged, blind, or disabled persons with no outside income a minimum federal payment of $130 per month ($195 for a couple). Up to $20 a month in Social Security benefits and $65 in earnings would be disregarded in determining eligibility for this assistance.
- Increased Social Security taxes for employers and employees to a maximum of $702 each in 1974 (5.85 per cent on $12,000) and $632 each in 1973 (5.85 per cent on $10,800) from $468 each in 1972 (5.2 per cent on $9,000).
- Enabled Medicare beneficiaries to enroll in health maintenance organizations providing comprehensive prepaid health care with the government paying the premiums if the plans provided federally approved services.
- Established professional standards review organizations representing local practicing physicians to review Medicaid and Medicare services.
- Covered payments to chiropractors under Medicare.
- Provided coverage for almost all Americans afflicted with chronic kidney disease under Medicare with specific protection against the costs of hemodialysis or kidney transplants.
- Required that individuals eligible for Medicaid and welfare assistance in September 1972 not be made ineligible for Medicaid from October 1972 through September 1973 because of the 20 per cent increase in Social Security benefits.

Child Development

The Senate in June passed a bill (S 3617) authorizing almost $3-billion in fiscal 1973-75 to begin a comprehensive child development program for pre-school children. The program would have provided a broad range of day care, educational and health services.

S 3617 was similar to the child development title of an Office of Economic Opportunity authorization vetoed by President Nixon in December 1971. The program was modified to meet some of the objections listed in the veto message, but the basic framework was the same.

The House did not act on S 3617. Shortly before adjournment the House Education and Labor Committee reported a more modest bill that it had approved before a child development program was tacked onto the OEO extension in 1971. No further action was taken.

Strongly held philosophies were expressed during the two-day Senate debate on S 3617. Conservatives echoed the President's comment in his veto message that such a program "would commit the vast moral authority of the federal government to the side of communal ap-

proaches to child-rearing as against the family-centered approach." They saw such a program as an encroachment on family life. Supporters argued that Head Start, which reached only a limited number of children, had proven the value of well thought out programs for disadvantaged pre-schoolers. They pointed out that the program was voluntary and designed to involve parents.

Senate Action. The Senate Labor and Public Welfare Committee May 16 reported S 3617. The bill strengthened and expanded the Head Start program, which provided pre-school training for disadvantaged children, and established child care and family services programs for children from low- and middle-income families. Free services under the programs could be granted to a family of four with an annual income of $4,320 or less. Families with higher incomes would be charged a fee based on ability to pay.

The bill provided federal grants to state or local governments of at least 25,000 population which were chosen as prime sponsors of child care and family services programs. Each prime sponsor would have been required to establish and maintain a child and family services council with half its membership drawn from parents of children participating in the program. The child care program would include day care, education and health services. The family services program would include prenatal services and classes in child-rearing. The bill authorized $150-million in fiscal 1973 for personnel training and planning for the programs.

Child Development Debate

During Senate debate on S 3617, Robert Taft Jr. (R Ohio), who had led a floor fight to have the child development program dropped from the 1971 OEO bill, supported S 3617 and explained that it was a compromise between Democratic and Republican-sponsored bills. He said the program had the "potential to expand and achieve an additional amount of good over and above present efforts being carried out by Head Start."

Jennings Randolph (D W. Va.) said the bill was aimed at "the 4.3 million children who may not now be cared for in America. Is their development to be restricted to the mindless viewing of television programs all day long, or can we provide these youngsters with some quality care, education and development? That is the issue. Innuendoes suggesting that this measure will in some way break up families or create little communists are mischievous, unfair and untrue."

The bill was opposed primarily by western Republicans and two southern Democrats. Paul J. Fannin (R Ariz.) summed up their concern that the program encroached upon family life and was not a responsibility of the federal government: "In this bill we are speaking of establishing a centrally controlled chain of schools.... Moreover, these schools, unlike the established elementary and secondary schools, would begin with the assumption that they would not simply train a child's intellectual capacities, but they would be responsible for his whole being, his emotional, psychological and physical welfare."

In its report, the committee enumerated a number of ways the program had been modified to meet President Nixon's objections to the child development program contained in the OEO authorization vetoed in 1971. It said the authorization had been lowered, the number of eligible localities substantially reduced and provisions for training staff members increased. It objected to the President's comment that the bill would weaken the family, and said that it was designed to involve the family and that the programs were voluntary. *(Details of vetoed bill, 1971 chronology)*

The Senate passed S 3617 June 20 by a 73-12 roll-call vote. Six amendments were adopted, none of them major. An amendment to reduce the authorization by $600-million failed by a 25-61 roll-call vote and an amendment to increase the minimum city population level for program sponsorship to 100,000 was defeated by voice vote.

House Action. The House took no action on S 3617. However, a week before adjournment the Education and Labor Committee reported a more modest bill (HR 6748). The committee had actually approved HR 6748 in September 1971 but had never issued a report because the program had been tacked on to the OEO extension by a House floor amendment.

HR 6748 differed from the Senate bill in providing that only governmental units with a population of over 100,000 could qualify as prime sponsors of a child development program. It provided for a federal payment of 80 per cent to prime sponsors for costs of child development programs for the disadvantaged and 50 per cent for other children. The bill authorized $40-million to train professional and paraprofessional personnel.

Older Americans Act

President Nixon Oct. 30 pocket vetoed a bill (HR 15657) to amend and extend the Older Americans Act of 1965. HR 15657 added new programs and substantially increased authorizations over the amounts provided when the act was last extended in 1969. *(p. 611)*

HR 15657 was passed by the House July 17 by a 351-3 roll-call vote and by the Senate Oct. 3 by an 89-0 roll call. The main difference between the two versions was Senate inclusion of a new Americans community service employment program for persons 55 and older. This was included in the final bill, which authorized $100-million for the program in fiscal 1974 and $150-million in fiscal 1975.

Other provisions of HR 15657 transferred the Administration on Aging from HEW's Social and Rehabilitation Service to the office of the HEW secretary and established a 15-member federal-level Council on Aging. Among the bill's authorizations was $600-million over a three-year period for grants to states and communities for social service programs for the aged. The bill also established special programs directed at problems confronting the elderly in areas of housing, transportation, employment and pre-retirement guidance.

President Nixon in a March 23 message to Congress on older Americans had requested on open-ended extension of the act with appropriations of $100-million for the office of Aging in fiscal 1973, an additional $100-million for nutrition programs and $57-million for other programs under the act. In his veto message on HR 15657 the President said it would authorize new funding of more than $2-billion through fiscal 1965—"far beyond what can be used effectively and responsibly."

C **Family Assistance**

NIXON ADMINISTRATION WELFARE PLAN NOT ENACTED

At the start of the first Nixon administration in 1969, liberals, conservatives and the executive were in agreement that the principal welfare program—Aid to Families With Dependent Children (AFDC) was in trouble and in need of change. Four years later this was still the consensus, but the system remained because a majority could not agree on how to change it. The administration's proposal, the Family Assistance Plan, was dead, killed by liberals who argued that it provided too little and conservatives who found it too far-reaching and too costly.

As proposed by the President in 1969, the Family Assistance Plan would have replaced AFDC. The AFDC program had been plagued by rapidly rising numbers of recipients and costs, and great inequities in benefits and eligibility from state to state. Heavy welfare costs were becoming a major problem in northern states.

As set forth in 1969, the Family Assistance Plan (FAP) would have provided a basic federal payment of $1,600 a year for a family of four. This would have increased welfare benefits above the levels currently existing in 18 states. The remaining states would have been required to supplement the federal floor so that benefits did not fall below their current level, but the federal government would have paid a percentage of the supplement. For the first time the "working poor" as well as the unemployed would have been eligible for benefits (at a reduced rate). The unemployed were required to take job training or lose their portion of the family benefit.

The above is only a bare description of a very complex program which administration witnesses found hard to describe and some legislators apparently found hard to grasp. Throughout the four-year consideration of the program there was controversy over whether it constituted a "guaranteed annual income," a concept strongly opposed by conservatives. The administration vigorously denied that it did, but many were unconvinced.

FAP first passed the House with surprising ease in April 1970. It was cosponsored by the chairman and ranking minority member of the House Ways and Means Committee, Wilbur D. Mills (D Ark.) and John W. Byrnes (R Wis.). But when the bill reached the Senate it failed to find an advocate in the Finance Committee. Chairman Russell B. Long (D La.) was skeptical and ranking minority member John J. Williams (R Wis.) was an articulate and powerful opponent. Liberals said that the payments floor was too low, despite administration insistence that even a small increase would make millions more eligible for payments and be prohibitively expensive. In late 1970 the committee finally reported a bill providing for trials of alternative welfare proposals. On the Senate floor the welfare provisions were caught in a filibuster and dropped from the bill, ending action on welfare reform in the 91st Congress.

A revised version of the plan was reintroduced in the 92nd Congress as HR 1, and the President labeled it his "first priority." The new bill excluded recipients from eligibility for food stamps but raised the federal floor by roughly their cash equivalent, from $1,600 to $2,400 for a family of four. It contained more comprehensive training requirements for the unemployed and unskilled, establishing a new program administered by the Department of Labor.

As in 1970, the House in June 1971 easily passed the Family Assistance proposal. But once again it got caught in the Finance Committee. When HR 1 was finally reported 16 months later, FAP had been dropped. Substituting for it was a "workfare" program sponsored by Chairman Long excluding families headed by employable adults from welfare but guaranteeing them jobs. On the Senate floor the workfare program was also dropped and after days of debate the Senate finally approved an administration-opposed proposal for trial runs of three alternative welfare proposals. HR 1 reached conference late in the session. It became obvious that House and Senate conferees could not work out their differences in the short time remaining, and all welfare provisions affecting the AFDC program were dropped.

Among the provisions that remained in HR 1 was an important but little-noticed change in the direction of the three other U.S. welfare programs—Aid to the Blind (AB), Old Age Assistance (OAA) and Aid to the Permanently and Totally Disabled (APTD). While the rolls of these three so-called "adult" welfare programs had not had the huge increases of the AFDC program, the programs had also suffered from wide disparities in state benefits and uneven administration. HR 1 combined them into one federalized program. Benefits were substantially increased and states could supplement payments if they wished. *(Details, p. 623)*

The President's welfare proposal never found its constituency, and at the end of the battle many liberals questioned even the depth of Nixon's own commitment to it. Writing in *The New Republic* in 1973, Sen. Abraham Ribicoff (D Conn.), leader of the fight for a more liberal program, said: "Everyone engaged in the battle has his own perceptions of what went wrong, but one thing is clear: after Pat Moynihan left the White House, the leadership expected of the Nixon administration was not forthcoming."

Daniel P. (Pat) Moynihan, a major advocate of FAP and counselor to the President in 1969-70, in 1973 published a book on the FAP battle, *The Politics of a Guaranteed Income*. Moynihan put much of the blame for FAP's failure on Senate liberals and welfare organizations who he said hurt the plan by not giving it their full support, backing instead what he felt were unrealistically expensive alternative proposals. He pointed out that the bill also got little support from southerners although it would have provided the greatest fiscal relief to southern states.

Whatever the reasons for its defeat, the defeat was thorough. President Nixon in February 1973 announced he would not resubmit FAP to the 93rd Congress.

Background

A Nixon task force on public welfare recommended to the President-elect on Jan. 12, 1969, that major changes be made in the welfare system. The nine-man task force, headed by Richard P. Nathan of the Brookings Institution, called for the federal government to assume a much greater share of welfare costs and to impose national minimum standards on payments to the poor.

Momentum for reform had been building for years as the number of welfare recipients climbed higher and higher. Welfare costs, which were shared by local and state governments and the federal government, had soared as the number of recipients increased.

There were four basic federal-state welfare programs under the Social Security Act. These were Aid to the Blind (AB), Old Age Assistance (OAA), Aid to the Permanently and Totally Disabled (APTD) and Aid to Families with Dependent Children (AFDC). Relief payments under the programs varied widely depending on how much each state decided to spend on welfare.

Under the old-age, blind and disabled programs, the federal share in 1970 was $31 of the first $37 in payments. The federal government also paid 50 to 65 per cent of the remaining state cost, with the percentage depending on state per-capita income. The lower the income, the higher the percentage paid by the federal government.

For Aid to Dependent Children, the federal share was five-sixths of the first $18 for each recipient and 50 to 65 per cent of the balance, with the percentage again depending on state per-capita income. The maximum federal share for each recipient was $32.

Although the term welfare actually covered all four programs mentioned above, the program which caused the welfare controversy and inspired the Brookings proposal was the AFDC program. The steadily rising number of participants in the program had caused a startling increase in costs. It took 25 years—from 1935 to 1960—for the program to reach the billion-dollar mark in cost. But in only seven more years, the program was costing an additional billion dollars. In 1968 alone, benefit costs rose by another half-billion. Benefit payments for a female-headed family of four varied from state to state from $39 to $263 a month. Moreover, state regulations for eligibility under the program varied widely; in some states only families headed by a woman were eligible for payments. In no state were the employed eligible for payments, no matter how low the family income. *(Congress and the Nation Vol. I, p. 1225; Congress and the Nation Vol. II, p. 745)*

The Nathan report, the essence of which was adopted by the Nixon administration, called for ending the existing uneven welfare system and providing for the first time benefits for the working poor.

Request. President Nixon Aug. 8 in a nationally televised speech proposed replacing the AFDC program with a complex new nationally administered Family Assistance Program aimed at ending the "unfairness in a system that has become unfair to the welfare recipient, unfair to the working poor and unfair to the taxpayer." The President pointed out that currently benefit levels were "grossly inequal" from state to state; that under many state laws a father who could not find work had to leave home in order that his wife and children could qualify for welfare; and that the current system made it possible to receive more money on welfare than on a low-paying job.

The new proposal had two main parts—aid to families of the unemployed and aid to families of the working poor. For aid to the unemployed, the administration proposed a basic federal payment of $1,600 a year per family of four, in addition to food stamps ($500 per person for the first two family members and $300 per person thereafter up to seven). States were required to supplement the federal floor so that payments did not fall below their current level, with the federal government giving the states some relief from the welfare burden by paying 10 per cent of the supplement. In 18 states (all in the South or West except Maine) the federal minimum payment would be higher than the existing AFDC payment. Those states would have to reimburse the federal government for 50 per cent of the amount they had been spending on the AFDC program.

The bill required adult recipients of the family assistance payments to register with the U.S. employment service for work or job training, except for mothers of pre-school-age children or the mother of a family in which the father was working. Any adult who refused to accept work or training was to lose his share of the family assistance benefit paid to his family.

For the working poor, the President proposed that "for the first time the government would recognize that it has no less of an obligation to the working poor than to the nonworking poor; and for the first time, benefits would be scaled in such a way that it would always pay to work." The proposal called for a family assistance supplement under which families of four with earnings up to $3,920 per year would be eligible for payments reduced from the $1,600 a year for the unemployed by a formula applied to the amount of income. Under the formula, a working head of a household could retain the first $720 of his earnings and 50 per cent of his income above that amount and still receive welfare payments until his income reached $3,920.

The bill provided for 90 per cent federal grants to public or nonprofit agencies for day care services for 450,000 children of working mothers. The President said this would "bring new opportunities along several lines: opportunities for the further involvement of private enterprise in providing high quality child care service; opportunities for volunteers; and opportunities for training and employment in child-care centers of many of the welfare mothers themselves."

In addition to these major changes in aid to families with children, the President also called for changes in the benefit levels in the programs for the needy blind, disabled and aged. He said the current system varied benefit levels from $40 per month for an aged person in one state to $145 per month for the blind in another. He proposed a minimum payment of $65 per month for all three categories, with the federal government contributing the first $50 and sharing in payments above that amount.

The cost of the proposals was estimated at $4-billion per year—$2.5-billion for aid to families; $.4-billion for the three adult welfare programs; $.6-billion for training and day care and $.5-billion for administration and fiscal relief to states. This was in addition to existing federal spending of $4.2-billion for public assistance. The new Family Assistance Program was expected to benefit about 3.3 million families—2 million white and 1.3 million non-white.

1970 Action

House. The House Ways and Means Committee held hearings in October and November 1969 on the Family Assistance Program and then began closed-door consideration of the proposal. On March 11, 1970, it reported a clean bill (HR 16311) embodying the administration proposal without major change. The bill was co-sponsored by Committee Chairman Wilbur D. Mills (D Ark.) and by ranking minority member John W. Byrnes (R Wis.). Mills in 1969 had indicated reservations about the plan.

The committee made a few important revisions in the proposal. One gave more relief to the states with high welfare payments and big welfare bills. It provided that the government would pay 30 per cent of the difference between the federal floor of $1,600 and the amount currently paid by the states for welfare; the administration had proposed only 10 per cent.

The committee increased the amounts proposed for the other federal relief programs for the blind, aged and disabled. It combined the programs and required the states to provide a payment sufficient to bring an individual's income up to at least $110 a month. The government would pay 90 per cent of the first $65 of average payments and 25 per cent of the remainder.

HR 16311 was passed by the House April 16 by a **243-155 key roll-call vote.** Democrats voted 141-83 in favor of the bill, Republicans 102-72 in favor. Of 102 votes cast by Southerners, 17 were for and 85 against.

At the beginning of debate the previous day, conservative opponents of the bill lost an attempt to open up the bill to amendments when a closed rule was adopted on a close 205-183 roll call. During the two-day debate, opponents argued that it inaugurated a guaranteed annual income system which would increase greatly in cost over the years, creating an army of bureaucrats to administer the plan and leaving too many loopholes by which recipients could escape work or training.

Supporters of the bill argued that it was a necessary alternative to what one called "the colossal welfare mess." No one could be sure it would work perfectly, they said, but it was a step in the right direction. Mills said the program for the working poor was not a guaranteed annual income but a "supplement to an individual who is working and not making enough to supply his family with the ordinary needs of life."

Senate. The Family Assistance Plan ran into immediate obstacles in the Senate when the Finance Committee began hearings on the bill. Opposition was strong among both Republicans and Democrats on the committee—either because of a belief that the benefit level was too low, the plan was too costly or that it was badly drawn and would be impossible to administer.

After only three days of hearings in late April and early May, the committee, under Chairman Russell B. Long (D La.), sent the measure back to the White House

for reworking. The action came after initial questioning of then Secretary of Health, Education and Welfare (HEW) Robert H. Finch.

Both Democratic and Republican senators complained that the administration had failed to provide adequate cost estimates on the proposal and to prove that the measure would encourage welfare recipients to seek work.

The administration sent the revised plan back to the Senate June 10. The basic structure of the original welfare bill—a minimum income guarantee of $1,600 for a family of four and scaled-down benefits for the working poor—remained intact in the administration proposal.

The revised bill contained new recommendations, however, for meshing Medicaid, food stamp and housing programs with the welfare system. Under the original proposal, it was possible for poor persons to lose their eligibility for these programs because of a higher income from welfare benefits.

The committee resumed hearings on the bill in July, but it continued to encounter strong opposition from many committee members.

In an effort to speed Senate action on the bill, President Nixon Aug. 28 said he would accept a proposal by Abraham Ribicoff (D Conn.) to test the plan for one year in three areas of the country. The amendment also deferred the date for the program to take effect nationwide from July 1, 1971, to Jan. 1, 1972.

In a statement issued at San Clemente, Calif., Mr. Nixon said, "The present legislation is too far advanced, the need for reform is too great," for time to run out on the proposal.

But when the committee voted on Family Assistance on Nov. 20, it rejected both the full program and the Ribicoff amendment to test the plan for a year before making it a national program. The vote against the full program was 10-6. The committee finally approved a limited test run of the plan, with no provision for putting the system into effect nationwide after the pilot program.

The test run provision was added onto a conglomerate House-passed bill (HR 17550) which included Social Security benefit increases, veterans' pensions, import quotas and catastrophic illness health insurance.

The Senate committee also added to HR 17550 several controversial welfare restrictions reestablishing rules which the Supreme Court had struck down—a one-year residency requirement for welfare recipients and the "man-in-the-house" rule under which welfare benefits were denied to a family if a man capable of supporting the family was living in the house.

When HR 17550 came to the Senate floor in December, Senate liberals, led by Ribicoff, sought on the floor to revive the plan. The administration had agreed to a series of compromises which Ribicoff had proposed to secure more liberal votes for the plan. However, the conglomerate bill got tied up in a two-week filibuster, and Ribicoff was unable to get a vote on his amendment. Finally, on Dec. 29 the Senate voted 49-21 to delete the Family Assistance and several other controversial sections from the bill, killing welfare reform for the 91st Congress. It then passed the remaining provisions 81-0, but the action came only a few days before the end of the session and the House Ways and Means Committee refused to take the bill to conference. *(Social Security benefits, p. 610)*

(Continued on p. 626)

Broad Coalition Lobbies for Family Assistance Plan

A coalition of about 20 diverse organizations sharing the belief that the $10-billion welfare system needed overhauling but frequently disagreeing about how to go about it was formed in December 1970 to produce a welfare reform bill in the 92nd Congress.

Despite their divergent views which defied an agreement over what the bill should contain, the coalition's broad aim was to prevent a repeat of 1970 when the administration's Family Assistance Plan and other welfare proposals stalled in the Senate.

The coalition included such widely diverse groups as the National Association of Manufacturers and the National Welfare Rights Organization.

Each organization had its own major goal. They admitted that their different objectives hampered their effectiveness as a working coalition.

The National Welfare Rights Organization was fighting for a $6,500 minimum income for poor families. The AFL-CIO insisted that welfare recipients be paid at least $1.60 an hour and be given suitable protections if they were required to take jobs. States, counties and cities were looking for relief from skyrocketing welfare budgets.

Pressure built up from some of the groups for federalization of the welfare system.

Despite their objections to different features of the Family Assistance Plan, the organizations sought a welfare bill passed in the 92nd Congress. They believed political pressure for change was so strong that Congress had to act.

The National Association of Counties, the National Governors Conference and the National League of Cities-U.S. Conference of Mayors had occasional meetings. Then NACO took the lead in calling together about 10 groups to meet weekly. Their aim: to pool intelligence about their positions and their activities.

The list of organizations grew as the initial 10 suggested other groups which might be interested in attending or the groups themselves contacted NACO when they heard about the meetings. Close to 20 organizations eventually sent representatives from time to time to the meetings.

The groups attending included: Common Cause (successor to the Urban Coalition Action Council), National League of Cities, National Governors Conference, National Welfare Rights Organization, AFL-CIO, League of Women Voters, National Rehabilitation Association, National Association of Social Workers, American Jewish Committee, Goodwill Industries, National Assembly for Social Policy and Development, National Conference of Catholic Charities, National Association of Manufacturers, American Vocational Association, Center for Community Change, Committee for Economic Development, American Federation of State, County and Municipal Employees and American Public Welfare Association.

One major participant in the meetings was John Montgomery, assistant to the secretary of health, education and welfare (HEW) and director of the HEW Family Planning Assistance Office.

The organizations within the coalition also took different approaches on lobbying. Common Cause, for instance, aimed at providing the public with enough information on the legislation to mobilize nationwide support for welfare change. Common Cause sought to organize its members into congressional districts so they could press their representatives. Other groups, such as the AFL-CIO and other labor organizations, were more concerned with specific points in the bill, such as work requirements, job protection and minimum wage guarantees.

The coalition also adopted a strategy of waiting until a bill emerged from the House Ways and Means Committee before concentrating on the contents of the bill.

The Opposition

When the President unveiled his Family Assistance Plan, many major organizations acclaimed its two principal features—a federally guaranteed minimum income and assistance for the working poor. Citizen, labor, civil rights and public interest groups argued that the $1,600 benefit level was too low, but they applauded many of the concepts in the plan.

One major exception was the U.S. Chamber of Commerce. The chamber objected that the plan would increase welfare rolls to almost 24 million persons.

"Adding 14 million more people to the relief rolls and guaranteeing a minimum family income," said chamber vice president Arch N. Booth, "is not the way to clean up the monumental welfare mess."

Chamber officials said the organization supported some features of the Family Assistance Plan. "One of our most serious disagreements is bringing in the working poor."

Congressional action committees were formed by the chamber in congressional districts. The chamber encouraged the committee members to let their representatives know their positions on welfare change.

Chamber officials were worried at the beginning of 1971 that the Ways and Means Committee was going to rush a welfare bill to the House floor early in the session. The chamber wanted the committee to hold public hearings on the welfare provisions.

Administration Lobbying

Apart from the National Welfare Rights Organization which claimed it "zapped FAP" at the end of 1970, the welfare lobbyists said much of the battle for the bill was fought out between the administration and Senate liberals.

Many welfare change supporters believed the administration was inept in its own lobbying by trying to win over Senate conservatives who were not going to support the bill anyway. At the same time, the administration was losing liberal senators who would have worked for the bill, the lobbyists said, if the administration had agreed to some of their proposals.

1971 Action

Revised Request. President Nixon in his Jan. 22 State of the Union message listed six legislative priorities of which the "most important" was welfare reform. In a March 13 letter to Ways and Means Committee Chairman Wilbur D. Mills (D Ark.), Nixon said the existing system was a "demoralizing disgrace." He expressed support for recent moves within the committee to strengthen the employment and work incentive provisions of the proposal. He endorsed proposals for a special program within the Labor Department for training and employment of the working poor; increased penalties for refusal to accept work or training; and substitution of increased welfare payments for food stamps.

House Committee Action. The Ways and Means Committee May 26 reported HR 1, an omnibus Social Security bill containing a somewhat revised version of the welfare reform plan. While the essence of the proposal was the same as the plan submitted to the 91st Congress, there was more distinction between the programs for the employable and the unemployable. The income level for a family of four with no income was raised from $1,600 to $2,400 because the value of food stamps was included.

For families in which the adult members were incapacitated or headed by women with children under age three, HR 1 established a Family Assistance Plan administered by the Department of Health, Education and Welfare. The program would pay welfare benefits of $2,400 to a family of four with no income, and the maximum benefit for a family of eight or more would be $3,600. Families eligible for these benefits would no longer be eligible for food stamps.

For working poor families with incomes of under $2,400 (for a family of four) and for families of the able-bodied unemployed, HR 1 established another program, administered by the Department of Labor. This plan was called the Opportunities for Families Program. All persons whose families received benefits under the program would be required to register for work or training. This included the working poor who might be retrained or helped to find better jobs. The unemployed would receive the same benefits as persons enrolled in the Family Assistance Plan. Benefits would be reduced for the working poor, but the first $720 of earned income each year would not be used to reduce the benefit, nor would one-third of any earned income above $720.

A range of supportive services would be provided with the Opportunities for Families Program. The bill authorized $750-million for child care services; $800-million for public service employment; $540-million for manpower training and placement and $100-million for minor medical services, family planning and transportation to help individuals find jobs.

HR 1 provided federal benefit levels that were higher than the existing levels of assistance in 22 states. Unlike the welfare proposal approved by the House in the 91st Congress, it did not require states that had welfare payment levels higher than the guaranteed federal payment to continue them at existing levels. It included a new "hold harmless" clause to ensure the states that their welfare costs would not be increased over 1971 levels because of the bill.

For the three "adult" relief programs, HR 1 proposed repealing the existing federal-state programs and substi-

tuting a single new federal program for the needy aged, blind or disabled. For the starting period, income limits were graduated from $130 a month to $150 a month.

HR 1 also contained a 5 per cent across-the-board increase in Social Security benefits and made a number of other changes in Social Security retirement, Medicare and Medicaid benefits. (Unlike the Family Assistance Plan, many of these provisions were eventually enacted in 1972.)

House Floor Action. HR 1 was passed by the House June 22 by a 288-132 roll-call vote after two days of debate. Urging passage of the bill June 21 in a letter to Speaker of the House Carl Albert (D Okla.), President Nixon called it "the most important social legislation in thirty-five years."

HR 1 was brought to the floor under a modified closed rule which prohibited floor amendments but permitted a separate record vote on a motion to delete Title IV (the Family Assistance Plan and Opportunities for Families Program). That motion was also offered June 22 and defeated by a **187-234 recorded teller key vote.** A majority of both Democrats and Republicans opposed the move.

Most of the debate on the 687-page bill was concentrated on Title IV. Chairman Mills said he took "as much pride in Title IV as I have taken in any bill that I have ever had the privilege of having my name affixed to."

Other members speaking in support of Title IV emphasized the problems of the existing welfare system, and HR 1's strong training provisions and provisions for fiscal relief for the states.

Opposition to Title IV came from a mixture of the most conservative and most liberal members of the House. Conservatives objected to the concept of federal aid for the working poor and to the increased federal costs under the program. Some liberals considered the federal floor for relief payments much too low, and objected that because recipients would be excluded from food stamp programs and states were not required to keep the level of existing benefits, some welfare recipients could be worse off than they currently were.

Senate Committee Consideration. The Senate Finance Committee began hearings on HR 1 July 27. Congressional momentum to pass a welfare bill in 1971 was stopped Aug. 15 when the President announced a major new economic policy to combat inflation which included postponement of implementation of welfare reform for one year. After that the Finance Committee put aside HR 1 to work on other requests in the Aug. 15 economic message.

1972 Action

Senate Committee Action. The Senate Finance Committee resumed hearings on HR 1 in January and February. On Sept. 26 it reported out its version of HR 1, which dropped entirely the Opportunities for Families Program and Family Assistance Plan.

Instead, the committee adopted an alternative proposal by Chairman Russell B. Long (D La.) to exclude all families headed by employable adults with children over 6 years of age from eligibility for the Aid to Families with Dependent Children (AFDC) program. For such persons, the bill established a new guaranteed job opportunity program known as "workfare." Under this program employable persons would either be given a guaranteed job with a new Federal Work Administration at $48 a week or wage supplements and work bonuses for low-paying jobs outside the government. A Bureau of Child Care would be established within the Work Administration.

Persons remaining in the AFDC program would be eligible for the workfare and child care programs. The method of federal funding for AFDC would be changed from a flat percentage of state per capita income to a block grant. The committee estimated that its welfare changes would provide $800-million per year in fiscal relief to the states.

Senate Floor Action. HR 1 was passed by the Senate Oct. 6 by a 68-5 roll-call vote. Before passage the workfare program was dropped. Instead, the Senate voted, 46-41, to test three rival welfare plans for two to four years—workfare, the welfare proposal in the House version of HR 1, and a proposal to set a guaranteed annual income of $2,600 for a family of four with no outside income with future raises tied to the cost of living.

The third proposal was sponsored by Abraham Ribicoff (D Conn.), a former secretary of health, education and welfare. The Ribicoff plan was offered earlier as a substitute for the test programs but was defeated by a **key 52-34 roll-call vote.** Ribicoff had originally supported a $3,000 guaranteed income but had modified this to $2,600 after consultation with HEW officials in hopes of gaining administration support. The President, however, refused to support a figure above the $2,400 provided by the House bill. Ribicoff and other liberals were highly critical of the President for refusing to compromise. They

also criticized him for not working to defeat workfare, and questioned the genuineness of his desire for welfare reform.

In support of his own proposal, Ribicoff argued that the administration $2,400 floor was simply too low. He opposed the test proposal because it would leave the current welfare system in existence for another two to four years: "Allowing the present welfare system to continue for that length of time is intolerable.... (It) is bankrupting state and local governments and is not helping the truly needy." Ribicoff called the workfare provisions slavefare. He objected that the Finance Committee bill had concentrated on the employable when the "vast majority" of welfare recipients were unemployable.

The other important vote on welfare was the 51-35 defeat of a proposal by Adlai E. Stevenson III (D Ill.) which essentially would have substituted the House-passed welfare provisions for the test plan. Stevenson said his motion would "give the administration and the Senate our last chance in this session of the Congress to support welfare reform and perhaps the last chance for a long time to come."

HR 1 went to conference with only 10 days remaining in the second session. Senate conferees were unwilling to accept the House Family Assistance provisions and House conferees were unenthusiastic about the Senate test plan. It became obvious that they could not compromise their differences in the short time remaining, and all family welfare provisions were dropped from the bill. Consolidation and federalization of the three adult relief programs remained. *(Details of this and other Social Security provisions in HR 1, p. 619)*

 **Feeding the Hungry**

EXPANSION OF FEDERAL NUTRITIONAL AID PROGRAMS

The 91st and 92nd Congresses continued the efforts begun in the Johnson years to reach more of the nation's poor through federal food programs. Both the food stamp and school lunch programs were greatly expanded.

Public understanding of hunger and nutrition in America was increased between 1969 and 1972 by well-publicized and lengthy hearings by the Senate Select Committee on Nutrition and Human Needs. The committee was headed by 1972 presidential candidate George McGovern (D S.D.). It looked into such subjects as federal food programs, the role of the food industry in meeting nutritional needs and nutritional problems of the elderly.

A White House Conference on nutrition was held December 2-4, 1969, attended by about 2,500 educators, scientists, medical people, food processors and government officials. The conference recommended a presidential declaration of a national hunger emergency, greatly expanded federal food programs, free lunches for all school children, transfer of food programs from the Agriculture Department to the Department of Health, Education and Welfare and a guaranteed minimum family income of $5,500.

Food Stamps. Appropriations for the food stamp program jumped from $610 million in fiscal 1970 to $2.5 billion in fiscal 1973. A 1970 bill (HR 18582—PL 91-671) extended the program through fiscal 1973 with an open-ended authorization, and for the first time provided free food stamps for families with monthly incomes below $30. It also included a controversial House provision making adults lose benefits for their entire family if they refused employment on jobs paying $1.30 or more an hour.

The Nixon administration's 1971 revised version of its welfare reform plan (HR 1) proposed making recipients of its Family Assistance Plan (FAP) benefits ineligible for food stamps and giving cash payments in their place. This was adopted by the House, but the entire plan died in conference in 1972.

School Lunch. Congress passed legislation expanding the school lunch program in 1970 and in 1972. In 1971 it barred the Agriculture Department from cutting the program back.

The 1970 bill (HR 515—PL 91-248) was designed to impose uniform eligibility standards on the program and to bring all needy children into it. In 1971, when the Agriculture Department tried to reduce the federal contribution and eligibility for the program, Congress passed a bill (H J Res 923—PL 92-153) blocking it. In 1972, in HR 14896 (PL 92-433), it raised the federal contribution to the program; established a new funding system designed as an incentive for states to bring more schools into the program; and permitted states to further ease eligibility requirements. Nearly

25 million children were involved in the school lunch program by 1972.

Other Child Feeding Programs. Congress continued the school breakfast program, established in 1966, through fiscal 1975. In 1972 it put the breakfast program on the same method of "performance funding" as the school lunch program. The non-school feeding programs for low-income children established in 1968 were also extended until fiscal 1975.

Milk Program. President Nixon, like President Johnson, was unsuccessful at ending the special milk program. He did not request funds for the program in the fiscal 1970 or 1971 budgets, arguing that milk would be provided through other expanded programs. Congress voted the money anyhow, and in 1970 it made the milk program permanent.

Hunger Legislation 1969

FOOD STAMPS. Although substantial agreement developed in Congress during 1969 that federal food programs were not reaching enough of the poor, a food stamp reform bill had not cleared Congress by year's end.

President Nixon May 6 recommended that fiscal 1970 funds for food stamps be increased from $340-million to $610-million and that fiscal 1971 spending for the program reach about $1-billion. He also proposed that free stamps be provided for families with incomes under $30 a month.

Hearings throughout the year by the Senate Select Committee on Nutrition and Human Needs highlighted the difficulties faced by the poor in trying to apply for and receive food under the federal programs. Witnesses complained about encountering endless administrative red tape in applying for the stamps, of having to travel miles to pick up their stamps or food under the surplus commodities program and of having the food run out before the end of the month.

The Senate Sept. 24 passed a food stamp bill (S 2547) which provided free stamps to families with incomes under $60 a month and authorized the secretary of agriculture to set eligibility standards for participation in the program. The bill also placed a ceiling on the purchase price of stamps so that no family had to spend more than 25 per cent of its income for the stamps and permitted the purchase with the stamps of such non-food items as soap.

Passage of the bill marked a major victory for Senate supporters of food stamp reform. The bill was liberalized considerably on the Senate floor from the version reported by the Senate Agriculture Committee under Chairman Allen J. Ellender (D La.). The committee bill had authorized $750-million for the fiscal 1970 program and

$1.5-billion for the two succeeding fiscal years; as passed, the bill authorized $1.25-billion for fiscal 1970, $2-billion for fiscal 1971 and $2.5-billion for fiscal 1972. The committee had not provided for free food stamps for the neediest of the poor.

Action in the House on food stamp reform was delayed because of the insistence of Agriculture Chairman W. R. Poage (D Texas) that food stamp reform had to be considered along with hearings on extension of basic farm programs. (Food stamp and farm commodity programs are all administered by the Department of Agriculture.) Poage was known to believe that he would have difficulty getting continuation of farm commodity programs, including subsidy payments to farmers, without trading for the votes of urban members by use of the food stamp bill. Poage also indicated his opposition to any kind of free stamp program.

But Congress Nov. 6 cleared a bill (H J Res 934—PL 91-116) authorizing an increase in the fiscal 1970 food stamp program from $340-million to $610-million, as the President had requested. The Senate June 24 had passed a $750-million fiscal 1970 authorization for food stamps (S J Res 126) but accepted the House-passed bill when it became apparent the House would not approve a higher authorization in 1969.

Child Feeding Programs

The federal government began donating surplus foods for use in elementary and secondary school lunch programs in 1936. *(Congress and the Nation, Vol. I, p. 739; Vol. II, p. 587-594)*

The National School Lunch Act (PL 79-396) was passed in 1946. The act authorized a grant-in-aid program to states and placed responsibility for the expansion and improvement of school lunch programs in the state educational agencies.

In return for federal cash payments and commodity assistance, schools participating in the program were required to operate the lunch program on a non-profit basis, serve lunches meeting specified nutritional requirements and serve free and reduced-price lunches to needy children.

The act was amended in 1962 (PL 87-923) and special cash assistance was authorized for schools which drew their attendance from low-income areas. These schools were given special cash payments in addition to the basic federal payments authorized by the 1946 act because they served a higher proportion of free and reduced-price lunches.

The Child Nutrition Act of 1966 (PL 89-642) strengthened the school lunch program and established a program aimed at improving the nutrition of needy children. It established a pilot school breakfast program primarily for schools with a high percentage of needy students who traveled long distances to school.

PL 90-302, passed in 1968, extended federal child food assistance to programs serving needy children in non-school settings such as day-care institutions and summer camps. It also removed the pilot status of the school breakfast program and extended the program for three years.

The agriculture appropriations bill (HR 11612—PL 91-127), which was held up pending final action on the food stamp authorization, when passed Nov. 19 included the full $160-million for food stamps. Total fiscal 1970 appropriations for food assistance programs in the bill were $1.8-billion, an increase of $577-million over 1969.

SCHOOL LUNCH OPERATIONS. The House passed a bill (HR 515) changing the operation of the federal school lunch program. The bill made three major changes in the National School Lunch Act of 1946 and the Child Nutrition Act of 1966. It established eligibility standards by which needy children would be selected for free or reduced-price lunches; it provided that appropriations for the program could be made a year in advance; and it changed the requirements on state matching funds to require additional contributions from the states.

The latter change required states to begin to provide at least 4 per cent of the state matching requirement from state tax revenues. The program was funded by 3-1 federal-state matching and the states had relied almost entirely on children's payments to provide the funds for their share.

The committee report on HR 515 said the bill was the result of extensive hearings which had established that there were wide variations across the country in the problems of undernutrition among children and in the operation of child food service programs.

HR 515 was passed by the House March 20 by voice vote. *(1970 action, p. 630)*

Program Funding. The total for food assistance programs in the agriculture appropriations bill (HR 11612—PL 91-127) was $1,820,343,000. This was an increase of $89-milion over the administration request, $84-million of which was to fund the special milk program the administration had wanted to end. Included in the total for food assistance was $316,766,000 for child nutrition programs and $610-million for food stamps.

Legislation 1970

FOOD STAMPS. Congress completed action on a bill passed by the Senate in 1969 enlarging the food stamp program and extending it for three years, through fiscal 1973. The final bill (HR 18582—PL 91-671) included a new administration proposal for free stamps for families with monthly incomes under $30, but also contained a restrictive new work requirement.

The bill was a compromise between a liberal version passed by the Senate in September 1969 (S 2547) and a more restrictive bill (HR 18582) passed by the House on Dec. 16, 1970.

The final bill included a controverisal work requirement under which adults would become ineligible for food stamps and lose the benefits for their entire family if they refused employment on jobs paying $1.30 or more an hour. Many House and Senate liberals called the provision punitive and harsh. It had been part of the House-passed measure.

Delay in final passage of the bill was due to slow action on the legislation by the House Agriculture Committee. The committee began hearings on the bill in June 1969, but did not report a bill until August 10, 1970. Agriculture Committee Chairman W. R. Poage (D Texas) reportedly hoped to win urban votes for the omnibus farm bill (HR 18546) by coupling it with the food stamp legislation and holding hearings on the two bills together. Urban members generally supported food stamps, but had in recent years objected to large farm subsidies in the agriculture program. The Agriculture Committee reported the farm bill on July 23.

The Senate bill had authorized free stamps for families of four with monthly incomes under $60, adjusted the price of stamps so that no family was required to spend more than 25 per cent of its income on the stamps, provided that all families with incomes under $4,000 a year would be eligible for stamps and authorized $2-billion for the program in fiscal 1971 and $2.5-billion in fiscal 1972.

The House bill had required a minimum payment of 50 cents per person per month for the stamps, required recipients to accept jobs, required states to share in the cost of the stamps, provided an open-ended authorization for the program and authorized the secretary of agriculture to set national eligibility standards.

The final conference report authorized $1.75-billion for the program in fiscal 1971 and provided an open-ended authorization for fiscal years 1972 and 1973.

Conferees also dropped the state-sharing provisions of the House bill and approved the work requirement. They agreed to allow free stamps for families with monthly incomes under $30.

Provisions. As cleared by Congress, HR 18582:

• Directed the secretary of agriculture in conjunction with the secretary of health, education, and welfare to establish uniform national standards for participation by households in the food stamp program.

• Provided that the standards established by the secretary of agriculture, at a minimum, should prescribe the amount of household income and other financial resources to be used as criteria of eligiblity.

• Required able-bodied adults in a household to register for and accept available employment in order for them and their families to be eligible to receive stamps.

• Stipulated that recipients be required to take only those jobs that paid at least the federal or state minimum wage, or $1.30 if the job was not covered by a minimum wage law.

• Exempted from the work requirement mothers of persons who cared for infants or incapacitated family members, students, or persons employed and working at least 30 hours a week.

• Authorized the secretary of agriculture to provide free food stamps to families of four whose income was less than $30 per month and specified that no family with income over $30 per month should be required to spend more than 30 per cent of its income for stamps.

• Established the value of the coupon allotment to food stamp recipients at a level which the secretary found would provide a "nutritionally adequate diet" ($106 per month for a family of four). Required the secretary to make an annual adjustment in the value of the coupon allotment to reflect increases for food in the cost of living index.

• Permitted a household to elect to have the food stamp purchase charge deducted from any federally aided grant or public assistance payment and to have its coupon allotment distributed with its grant or payments.

• Permitted public assistance recipients to certify for the food stamp program by means of an affidavit.

• Allowed states, if they requested, to operate both food stamp and surplus commodities programs, but precluded individual recipients from receiving benefits from both programs.

• Permitted persons 60 years of age or older who were participating in the program to use stamps to purchase meals delivered to them by a nonprofit organization or local government agency.

• Authorized $1,750,000,000 for the program for fiscal 1971 and open-ended authorizations for fiscal years 1972 and 1973.

SCHOOL LUNCH OPERATIONS. Congress completed action on a bill (HR 515—PL 91-248), passed by the House in 1969, amending the operation of the school lunch program. As passed by the House, the bill had established eligibility standards and required additional state tax contributions to fund the program. *(House version, p. 629)*

Senate floor amendments substantially expanded the bill, and most of them were retained in the final version. As passed by the Senate Feb. 24, by an 85-0 roll-call vote, the bill included new provisions authorizing funds for the school breakfast program; authorizing funds for equipment for school food service programs; limiting the cost of reduced-price meals to 20 cents; and providing that any child whose family had an income of $4,000 or less be eligible for free lunches. Conferees altered the latter provision to make eligible children whose family income was not above poverty guidelines to be prescribed by the secretary of agriculture.

Provisions. As signed into law, HR 515:

• Authorized appropriations one year in advance for child nutrition programs.

• Provided an open-ended authorization for the special assistance program which furnished special funds for schools in impoverished areas.

• Authorized $25-million for the school breakfast program for fiscal 1971.

• Authorized the following sums for nonfood assistance (equipment for school food service programs): $38-million for fiscal 1971; $33-million for fiscal 1972; $15-million for fiscal 1973; and $10-million for each succeeding fiscal year.

• Required that for fiscal years 1972 and 1973 states had to provide at least 4 per cent of the state matching requirement from state tax revenues; for fiscal 1974 and 1975, 6 per cent; for fiscal 1976 and 1977, 8 per cent; and for each fiscal year thereafter, 10 per cent.

• Limited to 20 cents the cost of reduced-price lunches for children.

• Required that first priority be given to providing free meals to the neediest children.

• Established the standard for "needy" after Jan. 1, 1971, as the federal income poverty guidelines prescribed by the secretary of agriculture at the beginning of each fiscal year. Until that date, the determination of need was to be made by local school authorities on the basis of criteria including family size and income and the number of children in school.

• Allocated special assistance funds to the states according to the ratio of children in families with incomes of $4,000 and under to total number of children in the state.

• Required every state as a condition for receiving funds for child nutrition programs to submit an annual report to the secretary of agriculture on its program for the following fiscal year. The state was to detail how it intended to furnish a free or reduced-price lunch to every needy child and how it proposed to extend the lunch program to every school in the state.

• Limited the special assistance funds disbursed to each school to a maximum per meal amount established by the secretary of agriculture for all states.

• Established a National Advisory Council on Child Nutrition.

SPECIAL MILK PROGRAM. Against the President's wishes, Congress made the special milk program permanent and authorized appropriations of up to $120-million annually to finance it.

The bill (HR 5554—PL 91-295) was passed by the House May 6, 1969 on a 344-2 roll-call vote and by the Senate May 11, 1970, by voice vote. The Nixon administration had not requested funds for the milk program in the fiscal 1970 or 1971 budgets, arguing that milk would be provided in expanded child nutrition programs and that the special program was no longer necessary. This was strongly opposed by members of Congress from dairy states.

The President June 30 announced he was allowing HR 5554 to become law without his signature because less than 10 per cent of the milk served in the program went to poor children.

Congress appropriated $104-million for the special milk program in both fiscal 1970 and 1971.

PROGRAM FUNDING. The agriculture appropriations bill (HR 17923—PL 91-566) provided $1,420,000,000 for food stamps—more than double the amount provided for fiscal 1970. It provided a total of $540,332,000 for child nutrition programs and $104-million which the President had not wanted for the special milk program.

Legislation 1971

SCHOOL LUNCH. The Agriculture Department in 1971 moved first to reduce the average federal contribution to the school lunch program and later to tighten eligibility requirements. Both actions brought howls of protest from Congress, which passed a resolution (H J Res 923—PL 92-153) reversing them.

The Agriculture Department Aug. 13 issued regulations reducing the average federal contribution to states for schools participating in the school lunch program to 35 cents per meal. The national average in the preceding school year had been 42 cents.

In response to this, the Senate Oct. 1 by a 75-5 roll-call vote passed S J Res 157, authorizing an increase in the minimum federal contribution to states in the program to 40 cents per meal. Senators said the regulation would force school districts out of the program and was in direct opposition to congressional intent in a 1970 school lunch bill (PL 91-248) to see that lunches were provided to all needy children. *(1970 bill, p. 630)*

The Agriculture Department Oct. 6 rescinded its Aug. 13 regulations but said it was tightening eligiblity requirements for participation in the program. Under new rules, states would no longer receive federal funds for free lunches for children from families with annual in-

Section 32 Funds

The question of the use of "Section 32" funds for child feeding programs came up a number of times in the 91st and 92nd Congresses. Section 32 funds are derived from a 1935 law (PL 74-320) which authorized the secretary of agriculture to use 30 per cent of U.S. customs receipts for various purposes, including utilization of commodities among "low income groups." Several hundred million dollars are usually available.

Until 1968 Congress was reluctant to use large amounts of Section 32 funds to finance feeding programs despite administration requests that it do so. The reason apparently was that Section 32 funds originally had been used extensively to buy up fresh fruits, vegetables and other perishables in areas threatened by a surplus; these items were then donated to food programs. Members of Congress from areas producing perishable commodities thus opposed tying up Section 32 funds in feeding programs because that would make them unavailable for spot purchases of perishables. *(Congress and the Nation, Vol. II, p. 588)*

By 1968-69 members of Congress who wanted to hold back Section 32 funds instead of using them to finance feeding programs had lost much of their control over the issue. The agriculture appropriations bills passed by the 91st and 92nd Congresses provided for extensive use of Section 32 funds to directly finance feeding programs. The fiscal 1970 bill, for example, provided that $194,266,000 out of $311,766,000 appropriated for child feeding programs was to come from Section 32.

Moreover, Congress began to direct the agriculture secretary in bills that were not appropriations bills to use Section 32 funds for child feeding. This situation occurred several times between 1970 and 1972 when it appeared that regular appropriations were inadequate to fund feeding programs because Congress had expanded eligibility for them.

A bill enacted in March 1970 (HR 11651—PL 91-207), provided for transfer of $30-million in Section 32 funds for school feeding. In 1971 Congress passed authorizing legislation (HR 5357—PL 92-32) extending several child feeding programs and directing use of $135-million in Section 32 funds. Later in the session another bill (H J Res 923—PL 92-153) which grew out of a congressional dispute with the Agriculture Department over the size of the school lunch program, directed the secretary to use Section 32 as necessary to insure that every needy schoolchild received a free lunch. Legislation passed in 1972 (HR 14896—PL 92-433) set aside an additional $25-million in Section 32 funds for summer non-school food programs.

comes above $3,940. The department estimated this would eliminate 584,000 children from the program.

The House Education and Labor Committee Oct. 14 reported a new resolution (H J Res 923) prohibiting the secretary from making changes in the eligibility standards for free and reduced-price meals effective in the same year in which they were issued and preventing him from reducing the number of children already being served. The resolution established a minimum federal reimbursement rate to states of 40 cents for every free and reduced-price meal served plus a six-cent reimbursement on every meal served.

H J Res 923 was passed by the House Oct. 18 on a 354-0 roll-call vote and was agreed to and cleared by the Senate Oct. 20 by voice vote. The Agriculture Department Oct. 18 rescinded the eligibility requirement.

CHILD FEEDING PROGRAMS. Congress extended the school breakfast program for two years, through fiscal 1973, at an authorized level of $25-million annually. It extended the special food service program for children through fiscal 1973 with a $32-million annual authorization. *(Background on the two programs, box, p. 629)*

The same bill (HR 5257—PL 92-32) authorized the use of Section 32 funds ($35-million in fiscal 1971 and $100-million in fiscal 1972) for child feeding programs. The authorization was necessary because new eligibility requirements set by Congress for the school lunch program in 1970 (in Pl 91-248) had substantially increased participation in the program. *(Explanation of Section 32 funds, p. 631)*

HR 5257 was passed by the House May 17 by a 331-0 roll call and by the Senate June 18 by voice vote.

Provisions. As cleared by Congress, HR 5257:

• Authorized the secretary of agriculture to commit an additional $35-million in fiscal 1971 and $100-million in fiscal 1972 from Section 32 funds to provide free and reduced-price meals for needy children.

• Extended the school breakfast program for two years at an authorized level of $25-million annually.

• Extended the school breakfast program for two years at an authorized level of $25-million annually.

• Extended the special food assistance program for children for two years at an authorized level of $32-million annually.

• Provided that in circumstances of severe need, the secretary could authorize financial assistance up to 100 per cent (instead of 80 per cent as provided under existing law) of the operating costs of food programs, and that in such cases schools could receive prepayment in lieu of reimbursement.

• Provided the same eligibility requirements for free and reduced-price meals in the breakfast program as in the lunch program.

• Authorized the use of up to $20-million in Section 32 funds for supplemental food programs in fiscal 1972.

• Added a new criterion for the selection of the schools participating in the school breakfast program to include schools in which there was a need to improve the nutrition and dietary practices of children of working mothers and those of low-income families.

PROGRAM FUNDING. The fiscal 1972 agriculture appropriations bill (HR 92-70—PL 92-73) provided $531,-594,000 for child nutrition programs. In addition, Congress in other legislative bills twice directed the agriculture secretary to use Section 32 funds for the school lunch program when it developed that new regulations had brought more children into the program than there was money to feed. *(Box, p. 631)*

(Continued on p. 633)

National School Lunch Program

(figures are for month of April 1972)

State	Schools Approved	Average Daily Lunches Served	Children Involved*	Lunches Served April 1972	% of Total Free and Reduced-Price
Ala.	1,375	566,943	618,933	11,326,204	44.0
Alaska	269	37,269	39,189	747,534	38.6
Ariz.	677	212,015	245,957	3,795,788	26.5
Ark.	966	312,476	344,515	5,809,452	39.4
Calif.	5,530	1,233,087	1,350,588	24,223,208	46.8
Colo.	1,178	258,614	289,926	4,735,412	23.0
Conn.	842	196,351	214,123	2,970,195	21.7
Del.	181	70,592	77,916	1,060,880	22.5
Fla.	1,851	878,193	1,005,948	15,806,002	33.7
Ga.	1,814	840,221	944,068	15,248,256	38.1
Hawaii	229	137,899	147,801	2,765,553	10.6
Idaho	485	91,642	100,484	1,694,247	17.0
Ill.	4,024	720,416	791,665	15,127,558	34.2
Ind.	2,199	622,202	694,421	12,700,508	14.4
Iowa	2,209	425,999	467,104	8,186,818	15.2
Kan.	1,705	272,051	318,188	5,081,048	15.9
Ky.	1,608	535,811	591,402	8,472,778	35.3
La.	1,658	708,989	790,400	13,396,605	45.1
Maine	720	117,657	125,836	1,807,519	31.4
Md.	1,257	324,397	371,163	5,210,441	27.5
Mass.	1,801	592,000	654,143	8,739,486	18.4
Mich.	2,943	672,061	730,501	11,610,531	25.4
Minn.	2,225	567,832	628,828	10,724,342	18.6
Miss.	938	424,175	471,305	8,398,439	59.7
Mo.	2,590	562,831	666,072	10,579,138	22.4
Mont.	521	66,198	73,308	1,315,833	21.8
Neb.	879	183,374	197,814	3,503,147	20.7
Nev.	193	31,726	37,995	602,324	24.6
N.H.	365	74,908	83,977	1,198,528	16.8
N.J.	1,560	433,140	496,720	7,105,019	33.6
N.M.	657	163,766	184,629	2,893,421	47.8
N.Y.	4,626	1,424,600	1,568,942	22,280,350	44.9
N.C.	2,016	883,579	945,004	15,462,634	30.9
N.D.	511	92,660	100,281	1,725,413	22.9
Ohio	3,961	1,018,924	1,088,594	18,884,347	22.0
Okla.	1,872	334,050	369,933	6,442,379	29.9
Ore.	1,156	227,227	258,212	4,487,453	20.1
Pa.	3,815	1,019,434	1,108,080	19,748,867	18.9
R.I.	270	53,500	62,867	804,950	38.8
S.C.	1,122	469,801	517,401	8,204,128	49.3
S.D.	654	103,797	113,812	1,887,738	23.0
Tenn.	1,742	584,938	638,578	11,698,164	37.2
Texas	4,813	1,316,260	1,470,681	24,949,520	40.2
Utah	536	180,313	195,355	3,547,237	11.2
Vt.	343	53,067	57,431	795,228	24.6
Va.	1,820	638,689	708,080	11,367,252	32.3
Wash.	1,557	304,613	323,368	5,544,546	26.4
W.Va.	1,277	226,422	248,542	4,089,410	45.7
Wis.	2,296	438,506	497,172	7,519,664	17.5
Wyo.	277	38,493	41,524	716,739	18.0
D.C.	195	63,040	75,406	950,228	79.3
Samoa	33	7,823	8,521	154,351	100.0
Guam	44	16,305	19,137	326,100	22.8
Puerto R.	2,446	350,597	388,688	6,490,433	99.2
Virgin I.	45	17,341	19,056	310,538	100.0
U.S. Totals	82,876	22,198,814	24,579,584	405,223,883	33.4

Child participation figures include absentees based on attendance rate information supplied by the Department of Health, Education and Welfare.

SOURCE: U.S. Department of Agriculture.

(Continued from p. 632)

For the food stamp program the President had requested just above $2 billion. The Senate raised the figure to $2.5 billion and the final bill provided $2.289 billion.

Legislation 1972

SCHOOL FEEDING PROGRAMS. Congress again raised the level of basic federal assistance for school lunches and established new eligibility requirements for free and reduced-price meals. The same bill (HR 14896—PL 92-433) extended federal non-school child food programs and school breakfast programs for three years, through fiscal 1975. The school lunch program was permanent.

As passed by the House June 29 by voice vote, HR 14896 was described as a combination of measures to correct inadequacies in funding nutrition programs. Major provisions of the House-passed bill permitted states to provide free lunches to families whose total incomes were as much as 25 per cent above the poverty level. Children from families with incomes up to 50 per cent above the poverty level could receive reduced-price lunches if a state to chose. The level of basic federal assistance for school lunches was increased to eight cents from six cents per lunch served.

HR 14896 was passed by the Senate Aug. 16 by an 82-0 roll-call vote. It included a number of amendments that were retained in the final bill. Among these was adoption of an administration-proposed "performance funding structure" designed to establish a positive incentive for states to bring more schools and children into the school lunch and breakfast program. Another major amendment retained in the final bill established a pilot program to provide supplemental food assistance for pregnant and lactating women and infants up to age four.

HR 14896 was one of a number of bills passed by the 91st and 92nd Congresses which authorized use of Section 32 funds for child feeding programs. *(Box p. 631)*

Provisions. As cleared by Congress, HR 14896:

• Amended the National School Lunch Act to authorize the secretary of agriculture to utilize up to $25-million in Section 32 funds between May 15, 1972, and Sept. 15, 1972, for summer non-school food programs; directed that Section 32 funds would be reimbursed through a supplemental appropriation.

• Extended the non-school food programs for three years, through fiscal 1975.

• Amended the Child Nutrition Act of 1966 to extend the school breakfast program for three years, through fiscal 1975.

• Authorized the secretary of agriculture to use Section 32 funds to reimburse schools at the rate of eight cents for every lunch served.

• Established eligibility standards for school lunch programs under which all children below the federal poverty level would receive free lunches, but permitted states to provide free lunches to families whose total incomes were as much as 25 per cent above the poverty level.

• Permitted children from families with incomes up to 50 per cent above the poverty level to receive reduced price lunches.

• Provided for "performance funding," beginning with fiscal 1974, of the school breakfast program and the basic eight-cents per meal payments to the school lunch program. (Under performance funding, each state agency would receive an average basic payment for each meal served in a fiscal year, with additional payments for free and reduced-price meals.) States would have the authority to vary the rates of assistance among schools.

• Authorized schools with more liberal eligibility requirements than the new federal standards *(above)* prior to July 1, 1972, to continue operating under the higher requirements until July 1, 1973. (The schools would be eligible for reimbursement by the federal government at these levels through fiscal 1973.)

• Authorized $40-million for food equipment assistance for each of fiscal 1973-75.

• Waived the requirement for rural and urban low-income schools to pay 25 per cent in matching funds for the purchase of school food equipment.

• Permitted the sale of competitive foods if the proceeds from the sale were to benefit the schools or be given to approved student organizations.

• Authorized $20-million in each of fiscal 1973-74 for a pilot program to provide supplemental food assistance for pregnant and lactating women and for infants up to age four.

PROGRAM FUNDING. The fiscal 1973 agriculture bill (HR 15690—PL 92-399) provided $2.5-billion for the food stamp program; the administration had requested $2.3-billion. For child nutrition programs, the bill carried $471,296,000. It also provided $97,123,000 for the special milk program.

Housing

and

Community Development

Congress made few major changes in federal housing programs during the years 1969-72. It expanded new housing subsidy programs established by the landmark 1968 Housing Act, and it significantly altered the public housing program.

As interest rates began to spiral upward in late 1969 and 1970 and housing production decreased, Congress cleared legislation which helped reduce interest rates and made more mortgage money available.

President Nixon in 1971 proposed legislation to consolidate urban community development grant programs and to establish a Department of Community Development. Neither proposal was enacted.

Housing and Rent Assistance. Modest, programmatic changes in housing law in 1969 and 1970 were built largely upon the 1968 Housing Act, expanding authorizations for the direct-payment housing subsidy programs for homeownership (Section 235) and for rental (Section 236) assistance for moderate and low-income families. *(Sections 235, 236, box p. 644)*

At the same time as authorizations under the 1968 act were being expanded, problems in administration of housing programs began to develop. Twenty-eight Housing and Urban Development Department (HUD) employees were indicted in 1972 for criminal activity relating to programs established in 1968. Large numbers of mortgage foreclosures made HUD the largest landowner in several central cities. Local public housing authorities became increasingly reliant on federal support and many persons for whom the programs were intended became victimized. *(HUD scandals, p. 653)*

In 1969 and 1970, Congress liberalized the eligibility requirements for residents of public housing, first by agreeing to pay the difference between 25 per cent of a family's income and the rent (for a family with no income, the government paid the entire rent), and then by mandating that no rents shall be higher than 25 per cent of a family's income and that the federal government would assume the cost of any operating deficits.

Until 1969, under housing legislation enacted in 1937, 1949 and 1965, public housing was occupied principally by the elderly and by the working poor who could afford the low rents (1968 median monthly rent: $55). The effect of the legislation enacted in 1969 and 1970 was a large increase in the percentage of lowest and no-income tenants in public housing, and a decrease in the percentage of elderly and other persons at the top end of the income limits as many of these families moved to take advantage of other federally-assisted housing programs such as the Sections 235 and 236 direct subsidy programs, established in the 1968 act. With rising costs for increased

vandalism and a lower paid revenue from the tenants of public housing, the annual federal outlay for the public housing program increased from $362-million in fiscal 1969 to $889-million in fiscal 1972.

Perhaps the most striking example of the problems of the public housing program was the St. Louis Public Housing Authority's Pruitt-Igoe complex. Completed in 1955, the Pruitt-Igoe complex had 33 high-rise buildings on a 57-acre site housing some 10,000 persons. By 1972, many of the buildings had been vandalized to the point of being uninhabitable and abandoned, and the area was crime-ridden. The population had decreased to 2,000 persons in nine buildings, and the St. Louis Housing Authority by mid-1972, and on June 5, 1973, the St. Louis Housing Authority voted to close Pruitt-Igoe as soon as its residents could be relocated.

Community Development. Congress increased authorizations for the seven grant programs for community development in 1969 and 1970 instead of enacting the Nixon administration proposal for consolidation of the programs into a broader $2.3-billion urban community development revenue sharing program. Large increases for the water and sewer grant program were authorized by the 1970 Emergency Community Facilities Act, a direct federal crime insurance program was established in the 1970 Housing Act for those states where no effective solution was possible through state law; and Congress in the 1970 act expanded programs of guaranteed loans and grants for the development of new communities.

Mortgage Money. Since the economy—principally through interest rates and therefore mortgage rates—had a substantial effect on homebuilding, Congress saw its goal (set forth in the 1968 act) of producing 26 million new or rehabilitated homes by 1978 in trouble as interest rates shot up to the highest levels since the Civil War. In 1970 FHA maximum interest rates reached 8.5 per cent. Analysts saw no immediate downturn in the costs of construction or financing with the result that fewer persons could afford to purchase a house.

By mid-1970 Congress acted to provide additional funds to ease the home mortgage problem. It authorized

---

References

Discussion of housing legislation for the years 1945-64 may be found in *Congress and the Nation, Vol. I*, p. 459-515; for the years 1965-68, *Congress and the Nation, Vol. II*, p. 183-226.

HOUSING STARTS, APPLICATIONS FOR FINANCING, 1967-73

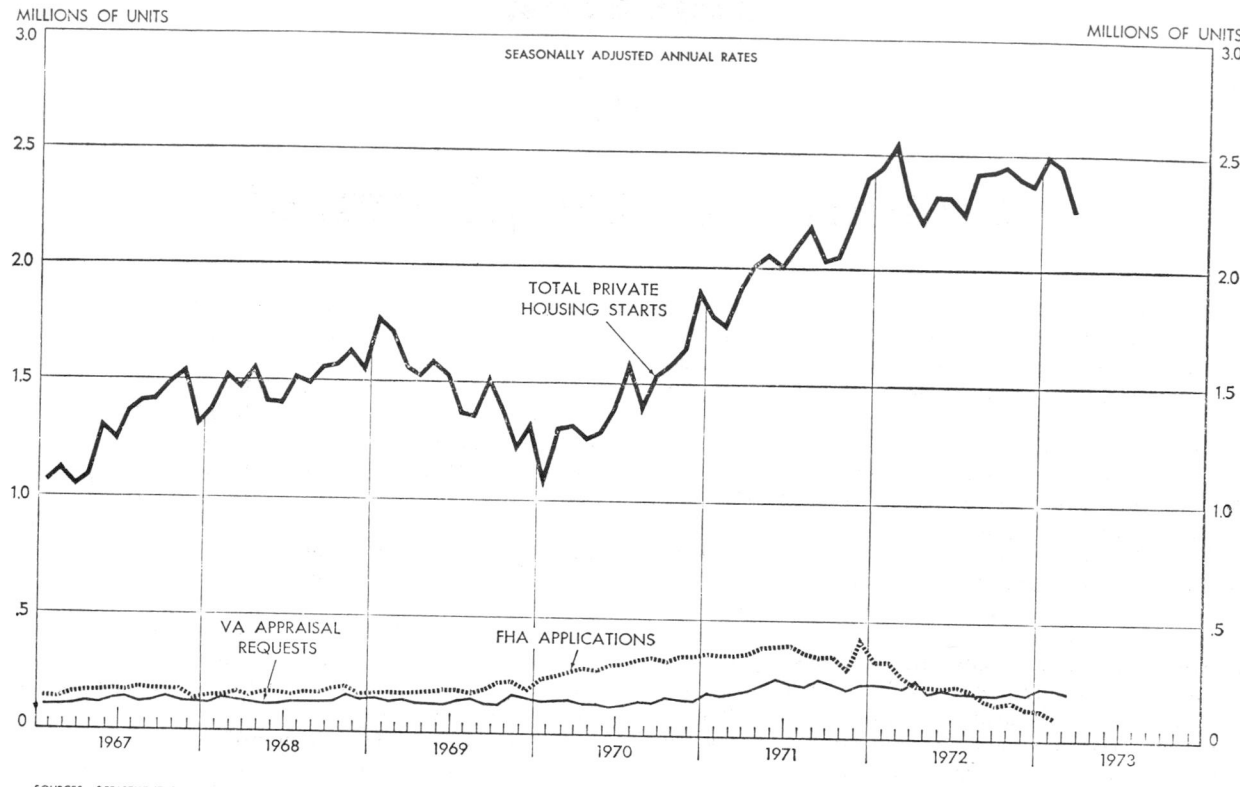

MILLIONS OF UNITS

SEASONALLY ADJUSTED ANNUAL RATES

TOTAL PRIVATE HOUSING STARTS

VA APPRAISAL REQUESTS   FHA APPLICATIONS

1967   1968   1969   1970   1971   1972   1973

SOURCES: DEPARTMENT OF COMMERCE, DEPARTMENT OF HOUSING AND URBAN DEVELOPMENT, AND VETERANS ADMINISTRATION   COUNCIL OF ECONOMIC ADVISERS

appropriations for federal home loan banks to reduce interest rate costs for savings and loan banks—the primary mortgage lender for single family homes. It also established and funded a Federal Home Loan Mortgage Corporation to purchase mortgages, thus freeing private lenders to incur further mortgage obligations. These actions helped bring down mortgage and interest rates, but not to the six per cent level of the mid-1960s. As a result of the decline in interest rates, housing starts rose and reached record levels in 1971 and 1972. In 1970, there were 1.47 million housing starts; in 1971, 2.09 million, and in 1972, 2.38 million.

New Housing Proposals. Congress in 1970-71 extended most housing programs through mid-1972 with the intention of completing a comprehensive review of housing and urban development programs. President Nixon and the Housing and Urban Development (HUD) Department pressed for several changes in existing programs, notably the consolidation of various categorical grant programs into urban community development special revenue sharing. At the same time, many members of Congress sought administrative changes to rectify problems in the administration of subsidized housing and public housing programs.

Many hearings on different aspects of urban problems culminated in two massive bills—one from the House Banking and Currency Committee and the other from the Senate Banking, Housing and Urban Affairs Committee. The two bills were reported in 1972. Both bills adopted the consolidation approach of the urban revenue sharing proposal—called block grants in each of the bills—and

made some changes in the housing programs. For the most part, the changes were aimed at the administration, not the cost or thrust. Both bills also authorized operating subsidies for mass transit.

The Senate committee bill passed the Senate in March 1972. The House committee bill, bogged down by internal committee politics, was not ready for House floor action until late September 1972 near adjournment time, at which point the House Rules Committee voted to defer action on the controversial bill—in effect killing it for the 92nd Congress.

On Jan. 5, 1973, with no reform likely from Congress for at least a year, the Nixon administration halted all new commitments for federal housing subsidy programs until the administration could complete a six-month study cf alternatives to them, and halted most new commitments for the categorical grant programs. The funds for the categorical grant programs were to be included as part of the initial funds for the President's proposed 1973 urban community development revenue sharing program.

Programmatic reforms in housing and community development programs largely failed during the first Nixon term and so did the major structural reform proposed by the President. In his 1971 State of the Union address, President Nixon proposed, in addition to revenue sharing, a sweeping reorganization of the executive branch. It involved consolidating seven existing cabinet departments into four.

Proponents of government reorganization chose the proposed Department of Community Development as an appropriate first objective, primarily because its two large components would have been the existing Housing and Urban Development (HUD) and Transportation Departments. Both departments established in the 1960s had less ingrained constituencies among the lobbyists and in Congress who could oppose the new department, supporters thought. However, the strategy did not work; rural interests successfully opposed the proposed department because part of the Agriculture Department was included in the plan. The Community Development Department bill was reported from the House Government Operations Committee but died at the end of the 92nd Congress after the House Rules Committee failed to act.

Chronology of Housing

And Community Development

Legislation

1969

Congress made few major changes in housing laws in 1969, but focused its attention on funding programs authorized under the 1968 Housing and Urban Development (HUD) Act. The $4.8-billion Housing and Urban Development Act of 1969 cleared in December. It extended major programs through fiscal 1971, required for the first time that each slum dwelling razed as part of an urban development project be replaced by a new low-income dwelling and sought to prevent interference with the use of technological innovations in experimental HUD programs. The provision of the bill supporting the new technology was strongly opposed by the AFL-CIO and construction unions, which may have been instrumental in confining its authority to experimental, rather than all, HUD programs.

Funding for the Model Cities program, a controversial issue each year since 1966, included authorization of an additional $600-million, to be added to a carryover of $712.5-million, for a total authorization of $1,312,500,-000 for Model Cities in fiscal 1971. The House had authorized $750-million by fiscal 1971. The Senate had approved additional authorization of $287.5-million for fiscal 1971 and $1.5-billion for fiscal 1972. The 1972 authorization was deleted from the final bill.

Congress authorized in the bill $1.7-billion for the urban renewal program in fiscal 1971 and reserved not less than 35 per cent of the fiscal 1970 and 1971 funds for Neighborhood Development Projects (NDP). HUD Secretary George W. Romney had signaled a slow-down in the program with an Oct. 3 announcement that a shortage of money would prevent HUD from approving more than a limited number of NDP grants in 1969, but congressional enthusiasm for the program resulted in the earmarked funds. Romney announced in December that more than $330-million in NDP funds frozen for almost seven months would be released in the fiscal year ending June 30, 1970.

FHA-VA Interest Rates

The following figures show the maximum interest rates permitted by law on Federal Housing Administration (FHA) and Veterans' Administration (VA) housing programs and the actual rate that was prescribed by each agency within the maximum. The 1968 Housing Act allowed a flexible ceiling.

Period	Federal Housing Admin.		Veterans Admin.	
	Pre-scribed	Maxi-mum	Pre-scribed	Maxi-mum
November 1934—June 1935	5-1/2	6	—	—
June 1935—July 1939	5	6	—	—
July 1939—June 22, 1944	4-1/2	6	—	—
June 22, 1944—Aug. 10, 1948	4-1/2	6	4	4
Aug. 10, 1948—April 1950	4-1/2	6	4	4-1/2
April 1950—May 1953	4-1/4	6	4	4-1/2
May 1953—Dec. 3, 1956	4-1/2	6	4-1/2	4-1/2
Dec. 4, 1956—Aug. 5, 1957	5	6	4-1/2	4-1/2
Aug. 6, 1957—April 1958	5-1/4	6	4-1/2	4-1/2
April 1958—June 1959	5-1/4	6	4-3/4	4-3/4
June 30—July 2, 1959	5-1/4	6	4-3/4	5-1/4
July 2—Sept. 23, 1959	5-1/4	6	5-1/4	5-1/4
Sept. 23, 1959—Feb. 1, 1961	5-3/4	6	5-1/4	5-1/4
Feb. 2—May 28, 1961	5-1/2	6	5-1/4	5-1/4
May 29, 1961—Feb. 6, 1966	5-1/4	6	5-1/4	5-1/4
Feb. 7—April 10, 1966	5-1/2	6	—	—
March 3—April 10, 1966	5-1/2	6	5-1/2	6
April 11—Oct. 2, 1966	5-3/4	6	5-3/4	6
Oct. 3, 1966—May 6, 1968	6	6	6	6
May 7, 1968—Jan. 23, 1969	6-3/4	—	6-3/4	—
Jan. 24, 1969—Jan. 4, 1970	7-1/2	—	7-1/2	—
Jan. 5, 1970—Dec. 1, 1970	8-1/2	—	8-1/2	—
Dec. 2, 1970—Jan. 11, 1971	8	—	8	—
Jan. 12, 1971—Feb. 17, 1971	7-1/2	—	7-1/2	—
Feb. 18, 1971—	7	—	7	—

SOURCE: FHA, VA

Congress authorized an additional $225-million in fiscal 1970 and $170-million in fiscal 1971 in annual contribution authority to public housing projects.

Congress cleared Nov. 18 an appropriations bill signed into law Nov. 26, which included $1.8-billion for HUD programs in fiscal 1970.

The Senate Dec. 19 cleared for the President's signature a bill to slow down inflation and increase the supply of mortgage credit. The House approved the measure Dec. 18. The bill, which granted the President sweeping authority to instruct the Federal Reserve Board (FRB) to regulate terms, amount and interest rates on all forms of credit if he deemed it necessary to prevent or control inflation, was opposed by members of Congress who claimed the measure did not contain adequate controls, and that the President did not request or desire the additional power.

Housing Program Extension

Congress Dec. 12 cleared for the President's signature a bill (S 2864—PL91-152), the Housing and Urban Development Act of 1969, extending programs for one- and two-year periods under the Housing and Urban Development Act of 1968 and authorizing $4.8-billion for housing
(Continued on p. 638)

Housing and Urban Development Appropriations, 1969-73

(Thousands of dollars)

Housing Production and [1] Mortgage Credit—FHA	FY 1969	FY 1970	FY 1971	FY 1972	FY 1973 [3] estimate
Rent supplement program:					
Approval of contract authority	($30,000)	($50,000)	($55,000)	($55,000)	($48,000)
Cumulative authority approved	(72,000)	(122,000)	(177,000)	(232,000)	(280,000)
Homeownership assistance (Section 235):					
Approval of contract authority	(70,000)	(125,000)	(130,000)	(170,000)	(170,000)
Cumulative authority approved	(70,000)	(195,000)	(325,000)	(495,000)	(665,000)
Rental housing assistance (Section 236):					
Approval of contract authority	(70,000)	(120,000)	(135,000)	(200,000)	(175,000)
Cumulative authority approved	(70,000)	(190,000)	(325,000)	(525,000)	(700,000)
College housing:					
Borrowing authorization	300,000	———	———	———	———
Participation sales insufficiencies	53,929	53,152	35,904	22,752	13,284
Approval of contract authority	(5,500)	(11,500)	(9,300)	(9,300)	(5,000)
Housing for elderly or handicapped:					
Loan fund	25,000	———	10,000	———	———
Participation sales insufficiencies	2,789	2,786	2,755	———	———
Mortgage insurance programs:					
Treasury borrowings (net increase)	—	—	—	253,400	759,121
Nonprofit sponsor assistance:	500	2,000	3,000	4,000	1,000
Government National Mortgage Association					
Special assistance function:					
Treasury borrowing authority	565,090	2,750,000	—	—	—
Participation sales insufficiencies	—	—	6,079	9,600	10,258
Restoration of capital	—	—			
Payment of participation sales insufficiencies (unused balance of appropriation)	—	8,992	20,720	—	—
Subtotal, housing production and mortgage credit	**947,308**	**2,816,930**	**82,458**	**289,753**	**783,663**
Housing Management					
Housing payments	385,000	525,500	851,600	1,371,705	1,800,000
Revolving fund (liquidating programs)	8,250	3,500	—	—	—
Counseling services	—	—	—	3,250	—
Subtotal, housing management	**393,250**	**529,000**	**851,600**	**1,374,955**	**1,800,000**
Community Planning and Management					
Comprehensive planning grants	43,838	50,000	50,000	100,000	100,000
Community development training and urban fellowship programs	3,500	3,500	3,500	3,500	3,500
New communities assistance grants	—	2,500	5,000	10,000	7,500
Subtotal, community planning and management	**47,338**	**56,000**	**58,500**	**113,500**	**111,000**
Community Development					
Model cities programs	312,500	575,000	575,000	150,000	500,000
Neighborhood facilities grants	35,000	40,000	40,000	40,000	40,000
Open space land programs	—14,708 [2]	75,000	75,000	100,000	100,000
Grants for basic water and sewer facilities	165,000	135,000	350,000	500,000	—
Urban renewal programs	1,062,500	1,000,000	1,200,000	1,250,000	1,450,000
Rehabilitation loan fund	—	45,000	35,000	90,000	70,000
Public facility loans:					
Participation sales insufficiencies	3,161	3,147	2,971	3,131	2,512
Subtotal, community development	**1,563,453**	**1,873,147**	**2,277,971**	**2,133,131**	**2,162,512**
Federal Insurance Administration					
National flood insurance	1,500	2,428	5,000	6,000	10,000
1969 recision	—250,000	—	—	—	—
National (riot) insurance development	250,000	—	—	—	—
Interstate Land Sales Registration	262	521	555	745	885
Research and Technology	11,000	23,000	45,000	45,090	53,000
Fair Housing and Equal Opportunity	2,000	6,266	8,000	8,411	9,489
Departmental Management (including salaries)	59,975	76,461	78,441	109,780	117,433
Deductions for offsetting receipts	—12,905	—23	—52,420	—30	—30
GRAND TOTAL BUDGET AUTHORITY, HUD	**3,013,181**	**5,383,730**	**3,355,105**	**4,081,335**	**5,047,952**

1 Figures in parentheses are not added to the totals. They represent the amounts approved in each year for multi-year housing contracts. The actual payments on these outstanding contracts are included in the housing payments category under Housing Management.

2 Negative figure for 1969 represents cancellation of previous appropriations.
3 1973 figure represents appropriations through January 1973.

(Continued from p. 636)

and urban development programs. The bill increased funds and relaxed cost ceilings for housing programs for low- and moderate-income families.

Although the bill largely extended existing programs covering mortgage loans and insurance, urban renewal and public housing assistance, model cities and urban development, it also contained a new provision, which had been added on the House floor, to require that for each slum home razed as part of an urban renewal project, a new low-income dwelling unit had to be constructed.

The $4.8-billion authorization for fiscal 1970 and 1971 in the bill was $100-million less than the House authorization of $4.9-billion and $1.4-billion less than the $6.2-billion total the Senate had approved for fiscal years 1970, 1971 and 1972.

The conferees extended the authority for the programs in the act for only one year, in most cases through fiscal 1971 for programs scheduled to expire in fiscal 1970, rather than for two years as the Senate had provided. House members said that the administration was preparing a comprehensive housing bill for 1970 consideration that could modify or change existing programs.

The bill contained a number of provisions aimed at increasing housing for low-income persons. It increased the fiscal 1971 and 1972 contract authority for the home-ownership and rental assistance programs; raised room-cost limitations for public housing projects; reduced rentals for very low-income tenants of public housing projects; and increased direct loan authority for housing of the elderly.

A Senate proposal to establish flexible mortgage rate ceilings on Federal Housing Administration (FHA) programs and public housing was dropped by the conferees in favor of a House provision establishing percentage increases over the ceilings in existing law.

PROVISIONS

As signed by the President on Dec. 24, S 2864 (PL 91-152):

• Extended until Oct. 1, 1971, the authority of the FHA to insure mortgage loans in homeownership programs for low-income families and in construction or rehabilitation of multifamily housing projects for low-income families, and extended other mortgage credit authorizations until Oct. 1, 1970.

• Lowered the down payment required on FHA-insured homes valued at $25,000 from 20 per cent to 10 per cent.

• Authorized FHA financing of mobile homes for up to $10,000 with repayment over 12 years.

• Increased by 10 per cent the dollar limitations on FHA-insured sales and rental housing; by 15 per cent on FHA-insured multifamily dwelling units for low- and moderate-income families; and by 20 per cent for FHA-insured low-income homeownership and rental assistance housing and low-to-moderate income housing.

• Increased from $100-million to $125-million the amounts authorized in fiscal 1970 and 1971 in contract authority for the Section 235 low-income homeownership program and the Section 236 low-income rental assistance program. Authorized $170-million in contract authority for each program for fiscal 1972.

• Authorized the secretary of HUD to increase from 20 per cent to 40 per cent the maximum number of rent supplement units in any Section 236 single-family dwelling project.

• Raised from $17,500 to $22,000 the per-dwelling-unit limitation on low-income housing mortgages purchased by the Government National Mortgage Association.

• Authorized $1.7-billion for the urban renewal program in fiscal 1971 and reserved not less than 35 per cent of the fiscal 1970 and 1971 funds for neighborhood development programs.

• Prohibited unreasonable restraints by contract, practice, building codes or zoning ordinances against the use of new technologies for experimental housing programs under Section 1010 of the 1966 Demonstration Cities and Metropolitan Development Act.

• Raised from $2,400 to $2,800 the basic room-cost limits for public housing and from $3,150 to $4,200 the room-cost limits for public housing in high-cost areas.

• Authorized unit-for-unit replacement of low-income homes razed or destroyed in urban renewal projects; if the percentage of vacancies for all existing housing in the area was 5 per cent or more, the new units could be built anywhere in the city or county, rather than in the immediate urban renewal area.

• Authorized $225-million in fiscal 1970 and $170-million in fiscal 1971 in annual contribution authority to public housing projects.

• Limited rents fixed by public housing agencies to no more than 25 per cent of a tenant's income, and permitted very low-income tenants to be charged less if the secretary of HUD determined that paying 25 per cent of their income would reduce their welfare assistance.

• Authorized $150-million in direct loans for housing for the elderly to become available upon enactment of the bill.

• Extended through fiscal 1971 and authorized an additional $100-million for the water and sewer facilities program.

• Authorized an additional $600-million for the fiscal 1971 model cities program. (The program had a carryover of $712.5-million for fiscal 1971; the total of the new authorization and carryover meant a fiscal 1971 authorization of more than $1.3-billion.)

• Extended through fiscal 1971 the authorization for grants for comprehensive planning, open space land acquisition, urban beautification, historic preservation, new community supplementary assistance, neighborhood facilities and advance acquisition of land.

• Authorized $300-million for the urban mass transportation program in fiscal 1971.

• Extended to Oct. 1, 1970, the authority of the secretary of HUD to set maximum interest rates on FHA and Veterans Administration mortgage loans.

Background. Congress in 1968 had established a major new program for low and moderate income housing and made substantial reforms in many other then-existing programs.

The 1968 act authorized federal subsidies to help poor persons buy their own homes and rent apartments (Sections 235 and 236), federal underwriting of the insurance industry against riot losses and a new urban renewal program. It also set as a goal for the 1968-78 decade the construction or rehabilitation of 26 million housing units of which six million would be for lower income families. *(Sections 235, 236, box, p. 640)*

The Nixon administration assumed office without at first seeking major changes in the Housing and Urban Development Department (HUD) programs. In testimony before the House Banking and Currency Housing Subcommittee on May 12, 1969, new HUD Secretary George W. Romney said he accepted the goals of the 1968 act as "a reasonable expression of our national need," but that he was not ready to endorse that goal as a realistic production schedule.

Romney cited inflation, "backward" methods of housing production and inadequate funding of housing programs as obstacles blocking attainment of the 1968 goals. He also asked for funding for housing programs. He said the "stop and go" dependence on yearly appropriations was one of the most serious problems his department and the housing industry faced.

SENATE ACTION. The Senate Banking and Currency Committee Sept. 5 reported a bill (S 2864—S Rept 91-392) extending most programs under the 1968 act, which were scheduled to expire in fiscal 1970, for two years, through fiscal 1972.

The Committee recommended $5,489,500,000 in new authorizations for fiscal 1971 and 1972 and also approved $702.5-million in new contract authority for housing programs.

The bill was a substitute for the administration proposal (S 2620) on which the committee held hearings in July.

The committee made three major amendments, proposed by Sen. Edward W. Brooke (R Mass.), in the public housing program:

• Provided that families with no income could move into public housing with the government paying their rent.

• Provided that the government would make up the difference if rent for a low-income family in public housing was more than 25 per cent of that family's income.

• Raised the ceiling on the amounts that could be spent for per-room construction costs.

The Brooke amendments, as they came to be known after being enacted, were to have substantial effect on the socio-economic composition of public housing, as it absorbed the poorest families. Vandalism increased; many of the "working poor" families near the income limit moved out. There was increased reliance by local housing authorities on annual federal payments to cover the rents.

The Senate Sept. 23 by a voice vote passed and sent S 2864 to the House.

Only minor changes were made in the bill on the Senate floor. The Senate left unchanged the $6.2-billion authorized by the committee, but raised the ceilings on conventional home mortgages and the mortgage limits on dollar-per-room limitations in public housing.

The only floor controversy developed over an amendment by John G. Tower (R Texas) to prevent government approval of housing construction contracts that sought to restrict the use of new technologies in construction. The amendment was adopted on a voice vote.

Tower said that attempts by labor unions to prevent the use of new techniques held back government efforts to encourage the production of mass housing at low cost. William Proxmire (D Wis.) argued that the amendment was unnecessary because the 1968 Housing Act directed the HUD secretary to require the use of new methods wherever possible. Proxmire also objected to the amend-

---

Housing Goals

The Housing Act of 1949 established a National Housing Policy that sought "realization as soon as feasible of the goal of a decent home and a suitable living environment for every American family."

In the 1968 Housing Act, Congress gave the old goal new meaning as it set as a target the construction or rehabilitation of 26 million housing units during the decade from 1968 to 1978 with six million of them for low and moderate income families.

The act required an early 1969 report by the President on a program to meet the goal and reports by the President each year thereafter.

The anticipated production figures were modified slightly in the First Annual Report on National Housing Goals. The changes included a small increase in projected private housing starts balanced by a decrease in assisted starts.

The first annual report predicted some difficulty in meeting anticipated 1969 and 1970 goals as a result of insufficient funding of government programs and pressures on the housing industry caused by unfavorable market conditions, but on the whole it was optimistic: "From a long-range point of view, the economic resources to meet the specified housing requirements over the next decade should be available."

Total private and public starts and rehabilitation in 1969 came close to the 1.7 million goal outlined in the first annual report, largely because of mortgage financing available before a credit squeeze began.

Housing starts in 1970 fell dramatically, but rebounded to record levels in 1971 and 1972 as interest rates on mortgages dropped. The FHA-VA maximum allowable interest rate dropped from a record 8½ per cent in mid-1970 to 7 per cent by early 1971. Increases above projected goals for subsidized housing helped ease the 1970 shortfall but fiscal 1970 actual housing production was some 55,000 units below target. *(Interest rates, p. 637)*

In the Fourth Annual Report on National Housing Goals, the President on June 29, 1972, said that after four years the nation had produced 8,865,700 units, somewhat ahead of the 8,221,000 goal for the first four years.

By Jan. 8, 1973, however, the Nixon administration had called a halt to all new commitments for federal housing subsidy programs, and Housing and Urban Development (HUD) Secretary James T. Lynn announced a six-month comprehensive review of federal housing programs. Lynn said he believed firmly in the 1949 policy, but said he wanted to review targets set by the 1968 act to see if they should be retained, raised, or lowered.

---

ment on the grounds that it gave the HUD secretary "sweeping and ill-defined powers" without adequate legal safeguards and that it was unfair and discriminatory by focusing on restrictive union practices and ignoring restrictive building codes.

HOUSE ACTION. The House Banking and Currency Committee Sept. 30 reported a bill (HR 13827—H Rept 91-539) with amendments, extending existing housing and urban programs for one year—those that expired in fiscal 1969 through fiscal 1970, and those that expired in fiscal 1970 through fiscal 1971; and authorized $3,074,200,000 for the programs. (The Senate bill had authorized a two-year extension.)

The House Oct. 23 by a 339-9 roll-call vote passed HR 13827.

The House-passed bill authorized some $4.9-billion in housing programs, $1.8-billion above the committee bill.

Following passage of the bill, the House by voice vote substituted the language of HR 13827 for the language of S 2864 as passed by the Senate Sept. 23. The House then passed S 2864, as amended, by voice vote.

The House passed S 2864 after three days of debate during which $1.8-billion was added to the $3.1-billion recommended by the House Banking and Currency Committee. Of the increase, $1.5-billion was authorized for the Government National Mortgage Association (GNMA) to purchase mortgages on low-cost housing insured by the Federal Housing Administration (FHA) and the Veterans Administration (VA).

The largest single item in the House-passed bill was $2-billion for the fiscal 1970 urban renewal program. Another $300-million was added by the House for urban mass transit programs.

Before final passage of the bill, the House by a 116-92 teller vote adopted an amendment, offered by Lowell P. Weicker Jr. (R Conn.), requiring that urban renewal projects provide for an equal amount of housing to replace any housing demolished.

CONFERENCE, FINAL ACTION. House and Senate conferees Dec. 10 filed a report (S Rept 91-740) on S 2864, authorizing $4.8-billion for fiscal 1971 housing and urban development programs. The House and Senate Dec. 12 with little debate approved the conference report.

The conferees accepted the one-year extension through fiscal 1971 which had been approved by the House for most of the programs, but added the Senate provision extending the interest subsidy programs for home ownership and rental housing through fiscal 1972.

Retained in the compromise bill was the House provision requiring one-for-one replacement of housing demolished by urban renewal.

Conferees authorized $1.7-billion for urban renewal for fiscal 1971, compared to the House figure of $2-billion and the Senate provision for $1.3-billion for fiscal 1971 and $1.7-billion for fiscal 1972. (With a carryover of $587.5-million for fiscal 1971, the authorization for the program that year would total $2,287,500,000.)

For the Model Cities program, the compromise in the final bill provided an additional $600-million for the program in fiscal 1971, to be added to a carryover of $712.5-million for a total of $1,312,500,000. The House had approved $750-million; the Senate, $287.5-million for fiscal 1971 and $1.5-billion for fiscal 1972.

Both the House and Senate had sought to raise ceilings on FHA mortgage insurance programs after local officials had argued that existing ceilings were unrealistic in the face of rising housing costs. The House had increased all FHA-insured per-dwelling-unit and per-room dollar ceilings by 10 per cent; the Senate based increases in mortgage limits for single- and multifamily housing on the percentage change in average sales price of new homes since 1965. The Senate had also provided for a 45-per cent increase in per-room cost ceilings for low-income housing in high-cost areas. The conferees compromised on percentage increases ranging from 10 per cent to 20 per cent for different housing programs.

The conferees dropped a House provision which reduced from 25 per cent to 20 per cent the amount of a tenant's income for maximum rent under the Section 236 and rent supplement programs.

Retained in the final bill was an amendment added by both the House and Senate which prohibited "unreasonable restraints" against the use of new technologies in housing under federal programs, but conferees accepted the House version which applied the restriction only to experimental housing programs such as Operation Breakthrough.

Fiscal 1970 Appropriations

In contrast to the appropriations fights in the mid-1960s, there was little controversy over the 1969 appropriations bill containing funds for the Department of Housing and Urban Development.

Congress Nov. 18 cleared a bill (HR 12307—PL 91-126), the fiscal 1970 regular appropriations bill for 20 independent agencies and executive offices and the HUD department. Congress appropriated $1,869,026,000 for HUD, an amount $173,612,000 less than requested by the administration. The principal decrease was for the Model Cities program, which received $100-million less than the $675-million request. Also approved was $231.5-million in contract authority for housing programs. *(Full-year HUD appropriations, including supplemental bills, for fiscal 1969-73, p. 638)*

Mortgage Interest

Congress in 1969 passed legislation (S 2577—PL 91-151) to increase the supply of credit during tight money periods and to strengthen the execution of monetary policies.

The bill in its major provisions authorized the President to instruct the Federal Reserve Board to regulate terms, amounts and interest rates on all forms of credit when he deemed it necessary to combat inflation; authorized an alternative system of controls under which the President could ask the credit industry to work out restraints voluntarily; and raised maximum insurance protection on deposits in federally chartered banks and savings and loan institutions from $15,000 to $20,000. The measure also extended flexible authority for federal banking regulatory agencies to set interest rates for fixed maturity deposits (such as "certificates of deposit") in banks and savings and loan institutions.

Background. Congress first authorized regulatory agencies to set maximum interest rates on deposits in commercial banks and savings and loan associations in 1966 to curb excessive competition for deposits between financial institutions. Unrestrained bidding was reducing the savings flow into thrift institutions, the main suppliers of mortgage credit. As a result the institutions were forced to cut back mortgage lending, contributing to a rapid decline in new building projects. The authority was extended in 1967 and 1968.

Controversy arose in 1968 over an amendment offered by Sen. William Proxmire (D Wis.) directing the Federal Reserve Board (FRB) to purchase directly obligations of government agencies when such actions would aid the housing market. The amendment, adopted in committee, was dropped after the Treasury Department and the FRB strongly opposed the proposal.

1970

In mid-December 1970, Congress finished action on a $2.8-billion housing bill including a new program of federal crime insurance and creating a Community Development Corporation to carry out loan and grant programs for development of new communities. The bill continued existing programs of public housing, urban renewal and model cities. Other 1970 housing legislation authorized $250-million to reduce the interest rates charged by federal home loan banks on loans to member savings and loan associations.

Congress in December cleared for the second time the fiscal 1971 HUD-Independent Offices appropriations bill containing $3,343,081,000 for HUD programs. The first fiscal 1971 HUD-Independent Offices appropriations bill contained an additional $300,000,000 for HUD programs. That bill was vetoed by the President Aug. 11 because the entire appropriation was $541-million over his budget request. The veto was sustained by the House.

HR 19830 was identical to the vetoed bill except for $150-million taken out of each of two HUD programs, urban renewal and sewer and water facilities grants.

HUD appropriations contained in HR 19830 included $1.2-billion for urban renewal, $350-million for water and sewer facilities grants, $575-million for model cities, $40-million for neighborhood facilities, $115-million for home-ownership and rental assistance and $43-million for rent supplements.

The Emergency Home Finance Act of 1970 was cleared by Congress July 20. The bill authorized $250-million for the Federal Home Loan Bank Board to reduce interest rates charged by federal home loan banks on short- and long-term loans to member associations.

The administration asked for a sweeping consolidation and simplification of public housing programs in 1970. Hearings were held in both chambers, but the bills were never reported.

Housing Programs Extensions

President Nixon Dec. 31 signed into law a bill (HR 19436—PL 91-609), the Housing and Urban Development Act of 1970, authorizing $2,884,500,000 for various housing and related programs.

The $2.8-billion 1970 act was a compromise reached by a conference committee (H Rept 91-1784). The original Senate bill (S 4368) passed Sept. 23, authorized $3.9-billion for Department of Housing and Urban Development (HUD) programs. The House version (HR 19436), which omitted the new communities title and authorized only $2.4-billion for HUD programs, was passed Dec. 3.

New insurance provisions authorized the HUD secretary to write insurance against such crimes as theft, burglary and robbery when the federal reinsurance pro-

gram or state or private plans were unavailable or available only at unreasonable rates.

In addition to establishing the five-member Community Development Corporation (CDC) within HUD, the bill called for development of new communities within existing cities and suburban towns, adjacent to them and in rural areas.

A national urban growth policy was recommended and a biennial report on urban growth was required to be prepared by the President for Congress.

A total of $178-million was authorized for new community facilities and planning. Other authorizations included $200-million for model cities, $1.5-billion for urban renewal and $375-million for public housing.

PROVISIONS

As cleared by Congress, HR 19436, the Housing and Urban Development Act of 1970:

Title I—Mortgage Credit

● Amended the National Housing Act of 1934 by extending until Oct. 1, 1972, all programs of the Federal Housing Administration (FHA).

● Amended Section 235 of the act by increasing the total amount of homeownership contracts the HUD secretary could sign by $25-million in fiscal 1971 and by an additional $30-million in fiscal 1972.

● Amended Section 236 of the act by increasing the total amount of rental assistance contracts the HUD secretary could sign by $25-million in fiscal 1971 and an additional $30-million in fiscal 1972.

● Amended the Housing and Urban Development Act of 1965 by increasing the amount of contracts for rent supplements by $40-million in fiscal 1972.

● Provided that 10 per cent of the Section 235 contracts (home ownership assistance) authorized for fiscal 1972 shall be available for use for rehabilitated dwellings.

Title II—Urban Renewal and Housing Assistance Programs

● Authorized $1.5-billion for urban renewal programs in fiscal 1972 and reserved a minimum of 35 per cent of the funds for neighborhood development programs.

● Authorized increases in grants for low-rent public housing program of $150-million (to $320 from $170-million) in fiscal 1971 and by $225-million (to $575-million) in fiscal 1972. Provided that of the $150-million authorized for fiscal 1971, $75-million was to be used exclusively for operation and maintenance expenses.

● Authorized increases of $12-million in fiscal 1972 for annual debt-service grants for college housing.

● Amended the Housing Act of 1937 to define family income for the purpose of establishing maximum rentals at one-fourth of a tenant's total income. Family income under the definition would include all money received by each member of the family in the household who was at least 18 years of age, except (1) income which was determined by HUD to be nonrecurring, as well as the income of full-time students; (2) an amount equal to the sum of $300 for each dependent, $300 for each secondary wage earner, 5 per cent of the family's gross income (10 per cent in the case of elderly families), and extraordinary medical expenses; and (3) further deductions as allowed by HUD for unusual circumstances.

● Authorized HUD to assure low-rent public housing and assist local housing authorities in maintaining operating and maintenance services by paying the difference between annual expenses and rental income.

Title III—Model Cities and Metropolitan Development Programs

● Authorized $200-million for model cities and $30-million for comprehensive planning grants in fiscal 1972.

● Authorized $50-million for neighborhood facilities in fiscal 1972.

● Increased guarantee authority for new community development projects to $500-million from $250-million and extended the availability period of unexpended funds to July 1, 1974.

Title IV—Consolidation of Open-Space Land Programs

● Amended the Housing Act of 1961 to authorize $100-million in fiscal 1972 for a single program of grants for purchase and development of open space land in urban areas for uses such as parks and historic preservation.

Title V—Research and Technology

● Authorized $10-million for each of fiscal years 1972 and 1973 for HUD research to demonstrate the feasibility of providing low-income families with allowances to assist them in getting existing standard rental housing of their choice.

● Authorized $20-million for fiscal 1971-1972 for HUD to begin grant programs to assist public bodies in testing methods aimed at ending housing abandonment.

Title VI—Crime Insurance

● Authorized HUD to provide crime insurance beginning on Aug. 1, 1971, on a direct basis, where the federal reinsurance program or state and private plans were unavailable or were available at unreasonable rates. Coverage would include burglary, theft, robbery and larceny.

Title VII—Urban Growth and New Community Development

● Set forth congressional findings that the nation's population would increase by about 75 million persons by the year 2000 and declared that new communities must be established to accommodate them.

● Provided that the President make biennial reports to Congress, beginning in February 1972, on assessments of federal, state and local policies affecting urban growth; analyses of future needs resulting from urbanization and steps being taken to meet those needs, and recommendations for programs to carry out a national urban growth policy.

● Contemplated four types of new communities under the act: (1) communities within metropolitan areas as alternatives to urban sprawl; (2) additions to existing smaller towns and cities; (3) major in-town develop-

---

Major Provisions of 1970 Act

The 1970 Housing and Urban Development Act included these major innovations:

Crime Insurance. Direct federal insurance was authorized, which took effect Aug. 1, 1971, where state and federal reinsurance programs did not provide crime insurance coverage or where existing coverage rates were prohibitive.

Public Housing. A maximum rent—25 per cent of a family's income—was established for public housing, and annual federal contributions to cover the difference between the rent income and operating costs were authorized.

New Communities. Required a biennial report by the President on urban growth, provided new federal assistance for the establishment of new communities and authorized a Community Development Corporation within HUD to coordinate new-community development.

---

ments to help renew central cities, and (4) free-standing communities.

● Established the Community Development Corporation (CDC) within HUD to administer the secretary's guarantee and loan functions under the title. The CDC would be headed by a five-member board consisting of the secretary, a general manager appointed by the President with the advice and consent of the Senate and three persons appointed by the secretary.

● Authorized the HUD secretary, acting through the CDC, to guarantee $500-million in bonds to help finance new community programs.

● Authorized HUD to make supplementary grants to states and local public bodies to carry out public facilities projects in support of new communities. The authorizations for appropriations for these grants would not exceed $36-million for fiscal 1971 and $66-million for each of fiscal 1972 and 1973.

● Authorized the CDC to make loans to new community developers to assist them in making interest payments on indebtedness for HUD approved programs. The interest loans outstanding in fiscal 1971 could not exceed $20-million for a single program and $240-million for all programs.

● Authorized $5-million in fiscal 1971 and $5-million in fiscal 1972 for planning grants to new community developers.

Title VIII—Farm Housing

● Amended the Housing Act of 1949 to authorize HUD to insure loans for farm labor housing made by private lenders to public or private nonprofit groups of farmworkers.

● Amended the 1949 act to authorize an increase in the maximum loan allowable for a project under the rural rental housing program for the elderly to $750,000 from $300,000.

(Continued on p. 646)

Federal Housing Assistance: Wide Variety...

Federal assistance for housing takes many forms. They include the direct cash payments for mortgages and rents, secondary-market mechanisms to reduce interest rates, loan funds, special risk programs and tax advantages.

The principal federal programs in housing are carried out by the Federal Housing Administration (FHA) of the Department of Housing and Urban Development (HUD), the Farmers Home Administration (FmHA) of the Agriculture Department and the Veterans Administration (VA), all of which provide mortgage insurance or guarantees.

Other federal agencies are also important to housing finance. The Federal Home Loan Bank Board supervises savings and loan institutions which are the largest mortgage lenders for single family homes. The Federal Home Loan Mortgage Corporation, the Government National Mortgage Association (GNMA), another part of HUD, and the private, government-supported Federal National Mortgage Association (FNMA) operate in a secondary market to buy and sell various kinds of mortgages to keep funds available for mortgages.

Housing Subsidy Programs

The primary federal programs to assist low and moderate income persons in obtaining housing are programs with direct federal contributions toward rent and mortgage payments.

The Federal programs are: public housing, rental payments, rent supplements, home ownership assistance and college housing. All these programs were suspended by President Nixon in January 1973, pending a six-month review.

Public Housing. Authorized by the U.S. Housing Act of 1937, the low-rent public housing program provides federal loans and annual contributions for construction and maintenance of housing owned or leased by local housing authorities created by state law. The program was amended in 1969 to include subsidy payments as part of the annual federal contribution to pay for part or all of rents for lowest income and no-income persons. During fiscal 1973, an estimated 1,071,000 dwelling units of public housing were eligible for federal payment.

Rent Supplements. First authorized by the Housing and Urban Development Act of 1965, the rent supplement program provides federal payments to owners of certain private housing to make up the difference between a tenant's rent and the 25 per cent of his income he is required to pay toward rent. To be eligible for rent supplements, a tenant must be elderly, physically handicapped, displaced from his home by a government action, (relocation program), living in substandard housing or be serving in the Armed Forces.

Section 236 Rentals. Under Section 236 of the 1968 Housing Act, periodic payments are made by the mortgage holder (typically, a saving and loan as-

sociation) to reduce the monthly payment which the owner of a rental or cooperative project is required to pay. These savings are in turn passed on to the renting family in the form of reduced rent. The family is still required to pay 25 per cent of its income for rent.

Section 235 Homeownership. Authorized by Section 235 of the 1968 Housing Act, periodic payments are made by mortgage holder on behalf of families purchasing their own homes. The family is required to pay 20 per cent of its income toward the mortgage payment, insurance and taxes.

College housing. First authorized in 1950, the program authorizes grants to colleges to assist them in paying mortgage interest rates for college dormitories and certain other student facilities.

Section 202 loans. This program providing direct loans for housing for elderly and handicapped persons was phased out as similar housing was available under the Section 236 rental housing assistance program.

Mortgage Insurance, Guarantees

Federal Housing Administration. The primary function of the FHA is to insure loans for housing production, purchase, repair, and improvement. FHA has four basic insurance funds established by statute: (1) The mutual mortgage insurance fund which handles most single family homes, a cooperative management housing insurance fund insuring most cooperative type management mortgages; (2) the general insurance fund which covers the insurance of loans on property repairs and improvements, and the special risk insurance fund for mortgages on homes in declining neighborhoods; (3) mortgages for persons who without counseling would be considered unacceptable credit risks; (4) mortgages on which the government makes interest reduction payments.

Farmers Home Administration. The FmHA through its rural housing insurance fund insures rural housing site loans, farm labor housing loans, rural rental housing loans, low-income building loans an' moderate income building loans.

Veterans Administration. The VA through its GI home loan program guarantees to lender a portion of a veteran's mortgage. In mid-1973, the VA guaranteed up to 60 per cent of the mortgage to a maximum of $12,500 if the veteran defaulted.

Housing Finance

Congress has established several mechanisms to keep mortgage money plentiful. The federal home loan bank system was an early direct attempt to establish institutions to deal in home mortgages. More recent congressional actions have been in the **secondary mortgage market.** The secondary market consists of institutions and individuals buying and trading already executed, valid mortgages. In what are called **participation sales,** certain agencies offer bonds secured by

...of Subsidy and Loan Guarantee Programs

pools of mortgages for which investors bid. With the purchase of the bonds, more mortgage capital is generated since the original obligations are sold and new obligations can be assumed by the original mortgage holders. The availability of secondary markets and investors provides a better flow of funds for mortgages.

The secondary market was the first vehicle for supporting reduced interest rate mortgage programs before most of the direct payment programs were established. The Below Market Interest Rate (BMIR) program, for example, which was authorized by the Housing Act of 1961 and phased out in 1972, permitted below market interest rate mortgages which would be purchased by the Federal National Mortgage Association which would then sell the mortgage-backed bonds.

Because in that program and others after it, the interest paid on the bond was higher than the interest being collected from the mortgage, the difference—or so-called **participation sales insufficiencies**—were made up from **special assistance funds** appropriated by Congress. Participation sales and provisions for insufficiencies were authorized by the Participation Sales Act of 1966. *(Background, Congress and the Nation, Vol. II, p. 130)*

Federal Home Loan Bank. The Federal Home Loan Bank Act of 1932 first authorized a system of financial institutions called federal home loan banks which supply credit for member institutions—principally savings and loan type operations and savings banks—to assist their operations as savings media and home mortgage lenders in their own communities. The 12 regional banks operate under the aegis of the Federal Home Loan Bank Board (FHLBB) and are owned by the member banks. The FHLBB also directs for the member banks the **Federal Savings and Loan Insurance Corporation (FSLIC)** which insures savings in the federal home loan system.

The FHLBB also directs for the federal home loan banks the **Federal Home Loan Mortgage Corporation (FHLMC)** created in 1970 which purchases, sells and otherwise deals in mortgages on residential properties as a secondary market.

Federal National Mortgage Association. The FNMA, often called Fannie Mae, is a government-sponsored private corporation to provide supplementary assistance to the secondary mortgage market by attracting more capital to mortgage investment. FNMA invests in FHA-insured, VA-guaranteed and conventional mortgages and certain Farmers Home Administration obligations. In 1968, Congress authorized its removal from the Department of Housing and Urban Development and establishment as a private corporation. The special assistance functions of the pre-1968 FNMA were continued as part of the newly-established Government National Mortgage Association in HUD.

Government National Mortgage Association. GNMA, often called Ginnie Mae, is the main instrument by which the government has aided the liquidity of its low-income housing programs, principally by using the special assistance funds to cover participation sales insufficiencies. GNMA, part of the HUD, is responsible for managing and liquidating its original mortgage holdings.

Community Development

The principal vehicle for federal assistance to state and local governments for urban development has been the Housing and Urban Development Department's community development grant and loan programs.

These programs are ones that the Nixon administration first in 1971 sought to consolidate into Urban Community Development Revenue Sharing, or, as it was called in a later proposal introduced in 1973, the Better Communities Act. *(Background on grant programs and revenue sharing p. 97)*

Model Cities. Authorized by the Demonstration Cities and Metropolitan Development Act of 1966, the Model Cities program was designed as a demonstration of coordinated and comprehensive use of federal, state and other existing funds together with loans and grants authorized by the act, for the planning and carrying out of plans for improvement of city life.

Neighborhood Facilities Grants. Grants authorized by the Housing Act of 1965 to local public bodies and agencies for part (generally two-thirds) of the development costs of multipurpose neighborhood facilities designed to provide education, health, recreation, social and other community service programs.

Open Space Land Programs. Authorized by the 1961 Housing Act and amended by the 1970 Housing and Urban Development Act, the open space land program offers grants to state and local public bodies to acquire and develop open space land.

Basic Water and Sewer Facilities. Grants (generally up to 50 per cent) to local governments to finance construction of water and sewer facilities other than waste treatment works. The grant program was authorized by the 1965 Housing Act.

Urban Renewal. Funds for slum clearance were first authorized in 1949, and since then urban renewal programs have come to support a large number of activities including slum clearance, enforcement of local housing codes, demolition, rehabilitation, and construction of community facilities.

Section 312 Rehabilitation Loans. Section 312 of the 1964 Housing Act authorized loans to assist owners or tenants finance the rehabilitation of residential and business properties. To be eligible for these loans, the property had to be within urban renewal or other certified areas.

Public Facility Loans. Loans for up to 40 years for municipalities and other political subdivisions (including Indian tribes) with populations under 50,000 were first authorized by the 1955 Housing Amendments for water and sewer facilities, gas distribution systems, streets, and public works.

Title IX—Miscellaneous

• Authorized $5-million for aid to low- and moderate-income tenant organizations and nonprofit sponsors of multifamily housing.

• Authorized $1.5-million for each of fiscal 1971-73 for HUD to provide technical assistance to construction contractors or subcontractors working through the Small Business Administration.

1970 HOUSING PROPOSALS

An overhaul of the public housing program and major changes in mortgage law represented the main thrust of the Housing and Urban Development Department's 1970 legislative recommendations.

The Housing and Urban Development Act of 1970 (S 3639) was introduced March 25 by John J. Sparkman (D Ala.), chairman of the Senate Banking and Currency Committee.

At a March 19 press conference, Secretary George Romney of the HUD department said the act would, if approved:

• Reduce down payments on Federal Housing Administration (FHA) insured home mortgages to closing costs or a $200 minimum on homes costing up to $20,000.

• Allow public housing occupants to buy their homes, as individuals or members of tenants' organizations.

• Lower rental payments of many public housing tenants to 20 per cent of the first $3,500 and 25 per cent of additional income.

• Streamline FHA programs and reduce them from 50 to 8, and replace 40 existing HUD programs with 4: one each for subsidized and unassisted home mortgages, and one each for subsidized and unassisted rental projects.

Major goals of the new legislation, according to HUD officials, were to make more efficient programs providing low, moderate and middle income dwellings, to eliminate unnecessary bureaucratic requirements and establish uniform criteria for low income housing programs, to make assistance programs more responsive by basing eligibility limits and construction requirements on factors in the community area, and to ensure that an optimum number of low income families participate in rental and home-ownership programs.

SENATE ACTION. The Senate Banking and Currency Committee reported Sept. 21 that it did not have time to consider a major program overhaul, but would take up the major HUD-proposed reforms in 1971. Instead, it reported a bill (S 4368—S Rept 91-1216) that it described in the report as "essentially a bill to extend and fund existing federal housing programs authorized by previous acts of Congress" and "to make them more workable and more effective in carrying out the intent of Congress."

The bill extended for three years those programs due to expire in fiscal 1971—Federal Housing Administration (FHA) mortgage insurance and loans, and home improvement and mobile home loans, but specific funding was authorized for the programs only for one year. A direct federal crime insurance program was established for states where no effective solutions were available through state laws. Subsidies to states to develop new communities and mass transit systems were authorized for the first time. It also required a biennial presidential report on urban growth.

The Senate Sept. 23 by a 59-2 roll-call vote passed S 4368 which authorized $3,988,500,000 for housing and urban development programs. The bill granted three-year extensions, through fiscal 1973, to programs due to expire in fiscal 1971 but extended authorizations for only one year, through fiscal 1971.

Much of the Senate debate on the bill focused on the public housing program. The bill also established 25 per cent of a family's income as the maximum income in public housing projects and spelled out standards for determining a family's income.

Carl T. Curtis (R Neb.) argued that some persons were able to pay more than 25 per cent of their income for rent, and they should not be prevented from doing so. He offered an amendment to allow local housing authorities to fix rents without regard to the 25 per cent rule if such housing was for the elderly and had no more than 200 units.

Edward W. Brooke (R Mass.) argued that the Curtis amendment could deny the benefits of the 25 per cent limit to some persons who were not able to pay as much rent. The Curtis amendment was defeated by a 9-59 roll-call vote.

HOUSE ACTION. The House Banking and Currency Committee held hearings in June on the administration housing bill (HR 16643), the Housing and Urban Development Act of 1970, and other housing legislation.

On Sept. 29 the committee reported a bill (HR 19436 —H Rept 91-1556), authorizing $7,015,350,000.

HR 19436 incorporated features of four major bills: HR 16643, the administration's consolidation proposal; HR 16647, the Urban Growth and New Community Development Act of 1970; HR 17845, which provided extensions and funding authorizations for all Housing and Urban Development (HUD) programs, and HR 13666, the Urban Property Protection and Reinsurance Amendments of 1970.

However, the committee bill failed to include major administration proposals calling for consolidation and simplification of public housing programs. The committee said limited time and the press of other business prevented it from examining the administration proposals.

The House Dec. 3 by a 328-30 roll-call vote passed HR 19436, the Housing and Urban Development Act of 1970, authorizing $2,416,000,000 for housing, urban renewal, model cities programs, and a new program for federal crime insurance.

The bill as passed was a substitute offered by Robert G. Stephens Jr. (D Ga.) for the committee version reported Oct. 5.

Major Reductions. The Stephens substitute cut $4,599,350,000 from the $7,015,350,000 authorized in the committee bill. The substitute cut a $1.8-billion section of the bill establishing a new community development program and reduced authorizations for other programs in the bill by $2.8-billion. The substitute cut by half the urban renewal fiscal 1972 authorization from $3-billion to $1.5-billion and deleted fiscal 1973 and 1974 authorizations for all federal housing subsidy programs. It also reduced from $500-million to $250-million the fiscal 1972 authorization for the model cities program and deleted a $500-million authorization for the fiscal 1972 water and sewer facilities grant program.

CONFERENCE, FINAL ACTION. House and Senate conferees filed a report on HR 19436 (H Rept 91-1784) Dec. 17. Differences in funding authorizations between House and Senate versions were compromised in almost every case by taking a figure midway between the House and Senate amounts. The Senate adopted the conference report Dec. 18 by voice vote; the House cleared the bill for the President Dec. 19 by a roll-call vote of 168-104.

Following were the major actions taken by conferees to resolve differences:

● **Homeownership Assistance.** The House bill contained a provision barring the use of homeownership assistance (Section 235) in a situation in which a family could qualify for an unsubsidized mortgage on existing housing. Conferees dropped the provision because "the limitation would have made it difficult, if not impossible, to build needed new housing units in many areas of the country, and it would have created serious administrative problems and inequities among families otherwise eligible to participate in the Section 235 program." Conferees urged HUD to exclude administratively Section 235 assistance to any family which could afford to buy a home without a subsidy.

● **Crime Insurance.** The Senate bill provided that the provision would become effective Aug. 1, 1971, or at the close of the first full regular session of a state legislature, whichever was later. The House bill specified that the program would become effective upon enactment of the bill. Conferees set the effective date at Aug. 1, 1971.

● **Mass Transit Aid.** The Senate bill authorized $750-million in fiscal years 1971-75 for grants to public mass transit systems to defray annual operating deficits, interest charges and other annual obligations. The House bill contained no such provisions. Conferees dropped the provision, saying Congress should wait for the results of a Transportation Department feasibility study on assistance to mass transit systems, due on Oct. 15, 1971.

● **New Communities.** The Senate bill included a title setting forth a national growth policy, requiring a biennial report on urban growth to be sent by the President to Congress, and establishing a greatly expanded program of guarantees, loans and grants for new community development. The House bill contained no such provisions. Conferees included the Senate version with minor changes.

Fiscal 1971 Appropriations

Congress Dec. 7 cleared for the President a bill (HR 19830—PL 91-556) appropriating $17,709,525,300 for fiscal 1971 for the Department of Housing and Urban Development (HUD) and 23 independent offices and agencies, including the Veterans Administration and the National Aeronautics and Space Administration (NASA).

The $17.7-billion appropriation exceeded the President's request ($17,468,223,500) for fiscal 1971. He signed the bill into law Dec. 17.

Action on HR 19380 came after Nixon Aug. 11 had vetoed an earlier HUD-Independent offices bill (HR 17548) which contained $18,009,525,300. The House Aug. 13 failed to override the veto on a **key 204-195 roll-call vote,** 62 less than the necessary two-thirds vote.

Housing and Urban Funds. HR 19380 contained $3,343,081,000 for Housing and Urban Development programs, $300-million less than the $3,643,081,000 contained in HR 17548. The President had requested $2,993,021,000 for housing and urban programs—$300-million less than contained in the bill he signed Dec. 17.

The major differences in housing and urban programs between the vetoed bill and the one signed into law were in urban renewal programs and in grants for water and sewer facilities. HR 17548 contained $1,350,000,000 for urban renewal; HR 19380 contained $1,200,000,000. The President had requested $1-billion.

HR 17548 contained $500,000,000 for water and sewer grants; HR 19380 contained $350,000,000. The President had requested $150,000,000. *(Chart p. 638, for fiscal 1971 funds including supplemental appropriations)*

FIRST BILL, VETO

HOUSE ACTION. The House Appropriations Committee May 7 reported HR 17548 (H Rept 91-1060), appropriating $17,015,212,300 for fiscal 1971.

The committee recommended appropriations of $2,929,081,000 for HUD, a reduction of $63,940,000 from the Nixon budget request of $2,993,021,000. The largest single cut in budget requests for the department was a $25-million reduction in funds for research and technology.

In addition, the committee approved $322.2-million in new contract authority for housing programs, a reduction of $407.1-million from the budget. The reduction consisted largely of $360-million in new contract authority requested by the administration for housing programs in fiscal 1972.

The House May 12 by voice vote pased an amended HR 17548, appropriating $17,390,212,300 for fiscal 1971.

House Amendments. The House added $375-million on the floor to the total recommended by the Appropriations Committee. The increases came through two amendments. The first amendment added $25-million to veterans' medical care. The second added $350-million to the water and sewer program of the Department of Housing and Urban Development. By adding $350-million to the $150-million proposed by the committee, the House brought the total fiscal 1971 appropriation up to $500-million. The President had requested only a $150-million appropriation.

The amendment adding the $350-million was offered by Robert G. Stephens Jr. (D Ga.) and was adopted by a 73-63 teller vote. The $350-million brought the housing and urban development appropriations in the House bill to $3,279,081,000.

SENATE ACTION. The Senate Appropriations Committee June 24 reported an amended HR 17548 (H Rept 91-949), appropriating $17,919,603,500. The total recommended was $529,391,200 more than the $17,390,212,300 appropriated by the House.

As considered by the Senate committee, HR 17548 included an additional $251,400,000 in administration requests that had been submitted after House passage of the bill on May 12. The bulk of the increase—$250-million—was for interest adjustment payments by the Federal Home Loan Bank Board.

The committee recommended housing and urban development appropriations of $3,321,871,000—an increase of $42,790,000 over the House appropriation of $3,279,081,000 and $328,850,000 more than the budget request of $2,993,021,000.

Floor Amendments. The Senate July 7 by a 68-4 roll-call vote passed an amended HR 17548, appropriating $18,655,019,500 for fiscal 1971.

As passed by the Senate, HR 17548 exceeded the President's request by $1,186,796,000 and the amount appropriated by the House by $1,264,807,200.

The Senate-passed bill included an amendment increasing funds for HUD's urban renewal program by $400-million.

Philip A. Hart (D Mich.) at first sought to add $987.5-million to the urban renewal program to bring it up to its full authorization of $2,287,500,000 for fiscal 1971. The administration had requested and the House had approved a $1-billion appropriation. Hart's amendment was defeated by a 33-38 roll-call vote.

Hart then offered another amendment, this one increasing urban renewal funds by $587.5-million—the same increase he had asked for in 1969.

John O. Pastore (D R.I.) asserted that the House was unlikely to accept an increase of more than $400-million in urban renewal funds.

At that point, Allen J. Ellender (D La.) offered a substitute for Hart's second amendment which reduced the proposed increase from $587.5-million to $400-million. Ellender's substitute immediately was accepted on a 43-30 roll-call vote and the modified Hart amendment was passed on a 49-22 roll call.

An amendment increasing HUD's water and sewer facilities program by $300-million (from $200-million in the committee bill to $500-million), passed on a 55-17 roll call, was introduced by Charles E. Goodell (R N.Y.) and cosponsored by Russell B. Long (D La.). The $500-million figure was identical to the House-passed amount and was $350-million more than the administration's request.

Conference Action. House and Senate conferees July 28 filed a report (H Rept 91-1345) on HR 17548. The final version of the bill contained appropriations of $18,009,525,300.

In the major action on HUD programs, conferees cut $350-million from the $1.7-billion approved by the Senate for urban renewal appropriations.

The House July 29 by voice vote and the Senate Aug. 4 by a 70-8 roll-call vote cleared HR 17548.

Veto. On Aug. 11, President Nixon announced that he had vetoed both HR 17548 and the Office of Education appropriations bill (HR 16916)—the third and fourth vetoes of his administration.

The President said he was determined "to hold the line against a dangerous budget deficit." The vetoes, he added, meant "saying no to bigger spending and no to higher prices in the interest of all the American people."

Congress had appropriated for HUD programs alone $650-million more than the President had requested.

The House Aug. 13 voted to sustain President Nixon's veto of HR 17548, killing the measure by his action. The **key roll-call vote was 204-195**, or 62 less than the necessary two-thirds needed to override.

SECOND BILL

Congress Dec. 7 cleared for the President a bill (HR 19830—PL 91-556) appropriating $17,709,525,300 in fiscal 1971 funds for the HUD and independent agencies. President Nixon signed the bill Dec. 17.

The compromise bill was $300-million less than the first bill with the reduction coming out of housing and urban programs. Cuts of $150-million in the urban renewal program and $150-million in water and sewer facilities programs. Even with the cuts, urban renewal funds of $1.2-billion exceeded the President's request by $200-million and water and sewer facilities funding at $350-million exceeded the request by $200-million.

Emergency Home Finance

President Nixon July 24 signed into law a bill (S 3685—PL 91-351), the Emergency Home Finance Act of 1970, to provide additional funds for the home mortgage market.

Congress cleared the bill July 20, when the House adopted the conference report on S 3685 (H Rept 91-1311) by voice vote. The Senate had adopted the report by voice vote July 17.

PROVISIONS

As signed by President Nixon July 24 (PL 91-351), the Emergency Home Finance Act of 1970:

• Authorized appropriations of $250-million for the Federal Home Loan Bank Board to reduce the interest rates charged by federal home loan banks on short-term and long-term loans to member associations.

• Provided that no more than 20 per cent of the $250-million appropriated to the Federal Home Loan Bank Board be disbursed in any one federal home loan bank district.

• Expanded the purchase authority of the Federal National Mortgage Association (FNMA) to include conventional mortgages in addition to the federally underwritten mortgages it had been purchasing and selling.

• Authorized the establishment of a secondary mortgage market facility, called the Federal Home Loan Mortgage Corporation, under the direction of the Federal Home Loan Bank Board, with initial maximum capital stock of $100-million, subscribed to by member banks of the Federal home loan bank system.

• Authorized the corporation to purchase residential mortgages from members of federal home loan banks and financial institutions insured by an agency of the U.S. government.

• Prohibited the purchase of a conventional mortgage by FNMA or of a residential mortgage by the Federal Home Loan Mortgage Corporation if the outstanding principal balance of the mortgage at the time of purchase exceeded 75 per cent of the value of the property, unless the seller agreed to retain a participation of at least 10 per cent or to repurchase the mortgage within a stipulated time, or if the excess above 75 per cent was privately insured.

• Provided for an increase of $750-million in special assistance authority for the Government National Mortgage Association (GNMA) and reallocated an additional $750-million to GNMA to increase its purchase of mortgages underwritten by the federal government for low-cost housing.

• Permitted GNMA to purchase Federal Housing Administration (FHA) low-income housing mortgages in excess of the existing $22,000 per unit statutory limit where such mortgages had the benefit of a local tax abatement program for low-income housing.

• Authorized a new interest subsidy program for single-family housing for middle-income families under which the Department of Housing and Urban Development (HUD) would subsidize interest rates to achieve an effective borrowing rate as low as 7 per cent per year.

• Provided that the housing units assisted under the program have an appraised value of not more than $20,000 (or up to $30,000 in high-cost areas) and eligible families have an income no higher than the median for the area in which the property was located.

• Authorized $105-million annually for the program for a three-year period, with no more than 25 per cent of the funds under the program available to subsidize interest pryments on existing housing.

• Extended from Oct. 1, 1970, to January 1, 1972, the authority of the HUD secretary to set maximum interest rates on FHA-VA (Veterans Administration) mortgages as necessary to meet mortgage market conditions.

• Directed the HUD secretary and the VA administrator to prescribe standards governing the amounts of settlement costs allowable in any area in connection with the financing of FHA- and VA-assisted housing.

• Raised the statutory lending limit for savings and loan associations from $40,000 to $45,000 per single-family dwelling.

• Authorized an additional $2.1-million in contract authority in fiscal 1971 for college housing.

Background. In late 1969 and early 1970 with interest rates rising and mortgage money scarce, there was great pressure on Congress to take action to ease the home mortgage market.

On Dec. 30, 1969, Secretary of Housing and Urban Development (HUD) George Romney announced that interest rates on Federal Housing Administration (FHA) loans would be raised from 7½ per cent to 8½ per cent.

The action brought immediate criticism from some members of Congress. In the Senate, Albert Gore (D Tenn.) called the increase "another nail in the coffin of homebuilding." Wright Patman (D Texas), chairman of the House Banking and Currency Committee, announced that he would hold hearings in February to examine the effects of inflation and rising interest rates on the housing industry.

President Nixon Jan. 21, 1970, promised to take every possible step to solve the housing problem "consistent with the overriding need to contain inflation."

In a slight easing of the anti-inflation fiscal policy he had established at the outset of his administration, the President lifted the five-month ban on federally assisted state and local construction March 17, 1970. The ban had been imposed Sept. 4, 1969, as part of a $3.5-billion cut in spending to offset rising uncontrollable expenditures and congressional action which did not conform to Mr. Nixon's budget recommendations.

In a further move relaxing economic restraints, Chairman Arthur F. Burns of the Federal Reserve Board hinted March 18 to the Senate Banking and Currency Committee that the board had relaxed its longstanding tight money policy.

The President's March 17 announcement was included in a long statement listing his administration's efforts on behalf of the depressed housing industry. He urged congressional enactment of measures including

S 3685 to increase available financing for housing construction.

SENATE ACTION. The Senate Banking and Currency Committee April 7 reported a bill (S 3685—S Rept 91-761), to provide additional funds for the home mortgage market and to reduce interest rates and other expenses of homebuyers.

The bill included a provision by William Proxmire (D Wis.), chairman of the committee's Financial Institutions Subcommittee, authorizing the Federal Home Loan Bank Board (FHLBB) to issue obligations up to $3-billion annually to provide lower-interest mortgage funds through the federal home loan banks to member savings and loan associations and other member institutions for loans to middle-income home buyers. The obligations would be sold to member banks of the Federal Reserve System under discount procedures which would require the Federal Reserve to absorb interest costs above 6 per cent. President Nixon, the Federal Reserve Board, and the chairman of the FHLBB, Preston Martin, opposed the provisions as inflationary.

The primary objection was that to increase its holdings of FHLBB obligations the Federal Reserve would have to reduce its holdings of Treasury obligations, forcing their sale in the market. That could have inflationary effects and, in addition, defeat the purpose of issuing the FHLBB obligations, since the Treasury obligations would compete for funds with housing and other capital improvements. Another objection was that use of Federal Reserve credit for one special purpose could lead to other special-purpose uses—small business, or state and local financing, for example—which would frustrate the Federal Reserve Board's conduct of monetary policy. Still another was that the provision was a "backdoor financing" mechanism.

The committee bill authorized $250-million in appropriations to the Federal Home Loan Bank System to reduce interest charges on advances by home loan banks to savings and loans. It also established within the home loan bank system a secondary market facility—the Federal Home Loan Mortgage Corporation, and expanded the authority of the Federal National Mortgage Corporation (FNMA) to allow it to purchase conventional mortgages in addition to government-insured or guaranteed mortgages. The bill also reallocated special assistance funds of the Government National Mortgage Association (GNMA). The bill also authorized a new housing subsidy program for middle-income families to keep the interest rate at 7 per cent.

The Senate April 16 by a 72-0 roll-call vote passed an amended bill and sent it to the House.

During Senate debate Sen. Sparkman, the floor manager for S 3685, said the bill was an effort to counter effects that the administration's anti-inflation policy was having on the housing industry.

"Unless something substantial is done right away—at the beginning of the 1970 home-building season—" Sparkman said, "to bring relief, a far worse housing crisis than is presently being experienced will occur later this year."

Sparkman said that new housing starts in 1969 dropped each month from a seasonally adjusted annual rate of 1.9 million in January 1969 to 1.3 million in December.

The Alabama Democrat quoted Sherman J. Maisel, a governor of the Federal Reserve Board, as having said that during a similar inflationary period in 1966 the housing industry, which comprises about 3.5 per cent of the Gross National Product, absorbed 70 per cent of the impact of the Federal Reserve Board's tight money policy.

An important change was made in the bill when the Senate accepted an amendment by William Proxmire (D Wis.) providing for mandatory appropriations to subsidize Federal National Mortgage Association (FNMA) and Federal Home Loan Mortgage Corporation loans during periods of tight money.

The Proxmire amendment deleted a provision that he himself had included in the committee report which would have required the Federal Reserve Board to buy all housing certificates presented to it by the Federal Home Loan Bank Board (FHLBB) at 6 per cent interest. The administration opposed the Federal Reserve Board provision.

HOUSE ACTION. The House Banking and Currency Committee May 28 reported its version of the Emergency Home Finance Act (HR 17495—H Rept 91-1131). The House bill forbid FNMA and FHLMC secondary market operations when the HUD secretary determined it would harm GNMA special assistance functions. The House bill also increased by $1.5-billion the special assistance funds authorized for GNMA. The committee bill deleted a provision authorizing creation of a National Development Bank to provide a minimum $4-billion annually to purchase 200,000 housing units for low-income and moderate-income families. Chairman Patman opposed the deletion.

The House June 25, by a 323-2 roll-call vote passed HR 17495 with floor amendments and then by voice vote substituted the language of HR 17495 for the language of the Senate-passed bill (S 3685) and passed S 3685, as amended, by voice vote, and sent S 3685 to conference.

During the House debate on the bill, a main issue was the committee amendment to delete from the bill the Title V provisions to create a National Development Bank.

Patman, who proposed creation of the bank, argued that HR 17495 would not provide "a realistic answer to the nation's housing crisis" without Title V. The crisis was focused, Patman said, on the lack of available mortgage funds at reasonable rates, which had resulted in a reduction in housing starts to an annual average rate of 1.2 million units. The total was only 46 per cent of the volume required to meet the country's annual housing goals, Patman observed.

Patman said the administration was "operating under a system of double standards" over housing credit. In 1969, Congress gave the President authority for credit controls, Patman said, but the President had refused to exercise that authority and also had opposed Title V. "Yet, at the same time, the administration has shown itself willing to bend over backwards in its attempts to bail out the big bank creditors and wealthy stockholders of Penn Central railroad," he added.

Opponents of Title V argued that it could take as long as a year to set up the bank, which was not consistent with the aim of the bill to provide immediate emergency relief to the housing market. They also questioned the constitutionality of the proposal.

The amendment to delete Title V was approved by a 215-113 roll-call vote.

Final Action. The Senate July 17 and the House July 20 by voice votes adopted the conference report on S 3685.

Conference, Final Action. House and Senate conferees July 20 filed a conference report (H Rept 91-1311) on S 3685. Both chambers adopted the report on voice votes.

The following were the major agreements reached by conferees on differing provisions:

• The House bill prohibited FNMA and the Federal Home Loan Mortgage Corporation from offering securities to finance conventional secondary market operations when the HUD secretary determined that such borrowing would unduly inhibit the financing of GNMA special assistance functions. The Senate bill contained no similar provision and it was dropped from the final version of the bill. The conferees indicated, however, that they intended to secretary of HUD to exercise his authority to prohibit the borrowings if such borrowings would inhibit the financing of GNMA special assistance functions.

• The Senate bill reallocated $750-million in GNMA special assistance funds from congressional to presidential authority. The House had provided an additional $1.5-billion in special assistance authority for GNMA. The final bill contained new authority of $750-million and a reallocation of $750-million.

• Conferees amended a new interest subsidy program for middle-income families which was contained in the Senate but not the House version of the bill. The interest subsidy payments were made available for the financing of cooperative housing as well as single-family housing and for mortgages guaranteed by the VA. Conferees also set an annual authorization of $105-million for a three-year period, rather than the Senate-approved $60-million, and provided that up to 25 per cent of the funds for the program could be used for existing housing, rather than 10 per cent.

(The middle-income housing subsidy program never became a reality since interest rates dropped in 1971 to the 7 per cent level authorized by the program. The administration never sought an appropriation for the program and Congress never appropriated any funds for it.)

• Conferees accepted the Senate provision extending to Jan. 1, 1972, the authority of the HUD secretary to set maximum interest rates on FHA-VA mortgages as necessary to meet mortgage market conditions, rather than the House provision which extended the authority to Oct. 1, 1971.

Family Relocation

Sensitive to the charge that the federal government was displacing a million or more families every ten years with no uniform policy on how to help them relocate, Congress in 1970 passed the Uniform Relocation Assistance and Real Property Acquisition Policies Act.

The act (S 1—PL 91-646) established a single uniform policy for relocating persons forced to move from their homes or businesses located in the path of federal or federally assisted programs.

Previously, residents in one area might receive fair negotiated prices for their properties and relocation payments and assistance, while residents elsewhere might be offered below-market prices and no assistance.

The relocation act also provided for additional compensation over and above any condemnation award to enable a person to purchase a "comparable" replacement that is "decent, safe and sanitary."

Provisions. As signed by President Nixon on Jan. 2, 1971, S 1:

• Provided a moving-expense allowance not to exceed $300 and a dislocation allowance of $200 for persons displaced from their dwellings who did not wish to go through the process of administrative determination of what constituted a fair and reasonable payment.

• Provided that the owner of a business or a farm could elect to receive a fixed relocation payment equal to the average annual net earnings of the business or farm operation in lieu of payments for actual expenses and losses, except that the payment could not be less than $2,500 or more than $10,000.

• Authorized a payment of up to $15,000 (in addition to the amount paid for the property) to a displaced homeowner for the following reasons:

1. To bridge the gap between the acquisition payment paid to an owner and the actual reasonable cost which he had to pay for a comparable replacement housing, or

2. To compensate the displaced homeowner for the present worth of any loss of favorable financing.

• Authorized a payment up to $4,000 for persons renting housing displaced by federal programs.

• Required heads of federal agencies providing relocation assistance advisory programs for persons displaced by federal programs and projects to include measures to assure relocation housing.

• Provided that no person should be required to move from his dwelling to make way for a federal project unless the head of the federal agency was satisfied that replacement housing was available to the person.

• Required state and local agencies administering federally assisted programs to provide the relocation payments and provide all assistance required of federal agencies, as a condition for receiving the federal assistance for the programs involved.

• Stipulated that the federal agency should pay the full amount of the first $25,000 of the cost to a state agency of providing relocation payments and assistance for any displacement prior to July 1, 1972. After that date, states were to include relocation costs as part of the total cost of the project for which federal assistance was available and were to be reimbursed by the federal government for those costs in line with the formulas in the programs.

• Provided seed money loans for planning and obtaining federally insured mortgage financing to stimulate the construction or rehabilitation of housing for persons displaced by federal projects. Stipulated that such loans could be made to nonprofit, limited-dividend or cooperative organizations and public bodies for up to 80 per cent of the preliminary expenses involved in obtaining the federally insured mortgage financing.

• Outlined nine policy provisions to guide federal agencies in acquiring real property, which included requiring the head of a federal agency to make every reasonable effort to acquire real property expeditiously by negotiation and providing that the property should be appraised before the initiation of negotiations.

Background. The Senate first passed a relocation assistance bill in 1968 as part of the Intergovernmental Cooperation Act. The Senate provisions were dropped in conference, however, because of a jurisdictional dispute: the Senate Government Operations Committee had jurisdiction over land acquisition and relocation assistance, while its House counterpart did not.

On Oct. 27, 1969, the Senate passed S 1. The House passed the bill Dec. 7, 1970, with amendments and sent it back to the Senate which amended it further Dec. 17 and returned it to the House. The House cleared the bill for the President Dec. 18.

1972 Extension Failed. The 1970 act provided that state and local governments would begin sharing the costs of relocation on July 1, 1972.

Testimony in 1972 House and Senate hearings generally opposed the July 1 date because:

• Cost sharing would impose financial hardships on state and local governments that they were not prepared to bear.

• Sharing would tend to undermine the uniform treatment in relocation assistance, producing varied assistance for different federal programs.

• Sharing would represent a step away from the funding arrangements that have been in operation in major federal programs for nearly a decade—urban renewal, public housing, mass transportation and model cities, for example.

On March 28, 1972, the Senate Government Operations Committee reported a bill (S 1819—S Rept 92-721) to extend indefinitely federal relocation payments of up to $25,000. The Senate passed the bill April 12. On Aug. 7, the House passed an amended version of the bill extending the payments through July 1, 1974.

House-Senate conferees Oct. 18 filed a conference report (H Rept 92-1616) on S 1819 extending payments through July 1, 1976. The conference report failed, however, when the House and Senate adjourned at the end of the 92nd Congress without acting on it.

Emergency Community Facilities

Congress Sept. 21 cleared for the President a bill (HR 17795—PL 91-431), the Emergency Community Facilities Act of 1970, authorizing an additional $1-billion for construction of water and sewer facilities in fiscal 1971. Final action came when the Senate by voice vote approved the House-passed bill.

The bill amended Title VII of the Housing and Urban Development Act of 1965 (PL 89-117), which provided matching grants to public agencies. A 1969 extension (S 2864—PL 91-152) of Title VII provided an authorization of $500-million for fiscal 1971.

President Nixon's fiscal 1971 budget asked $150-million for continuation of the program. The fiscal 1971 HUD-Independent Offices appropriation bill (HR 17548), which was vetoed Aug. 11, contained $500-million for the program. The 1969 authorization combined with the $1-billion in HR 17795 totaled $1.35-billion more than the amount the President requested for water and sewer facilities construction in fiscal 1971.

Mr. Nixon criticized Congress for what he called "lavish spending" but allowed HR 17795 to become law Oct. 6 without his signature.

As cleared by Congress, HR 17795:

• Authorized an additional $1-billion in fiscal 1971 for construction of water and sewer facilities.

• Extended for one year, to Oct. 1, 1971, the time in which a community could qualify for a grant under the program, even though its plans for a water or sewer system had not been completed.

• Provided that any funds authorized but not appropriated could be appropriated for fiscal 1972.

Alaska Urban Renewal

President Nixon July 31 signed into law a bill (S 778 —PL 91-367) to amend the 1964 amendments to the Alaska Omnibus Act (PL 88-451) to permit the expenditure of appropriated but unobligated funds for urban renewal projects in Alaska.

Final action came July 20 when the House by voice vote cleared S 778 for the White House. The Senate had acted on the bill in late 1969.

As signed into law, S 778 permitted the Department of Housing and Urban Development (HUD) to authorize the use of $850,628 in urban renewal funds which had not been allocated or expended prior to the expiration on June 30, 1967, of the authority for the program. The money was the unused portion of a special $25-million grant for urban renewal projects in Alaskan communities damaged by the 1964 earthquake.

1971

The House and Senate held hearings on new housing and community development proposals submitted by the administration in 1971. One proposal would consolidate many Department of Housing and Urban Development and Federal Housing Administration programs. A second called for a $2.3-billion program of urban special revenue sharing funds to be distributed free of federal control for community development purposes. A third measure would have set up a new cabinet-level Department of Community Development. Hearings in both chambers were held on these proposals but no final action was taken.

In August, Congress cleared the annual HUD-independent offices appropriations bill containing $3.27-billion for housing and urban development programs for fiscal 1972. In December, Congress cleared a simple extension of various HUD programs.

New Housing Proposals

Congress in 1971 began consideration of two of President Nixon's key legislative initiatives relating to urban development that he laid out in his 1971 state of the union message.

A $2.3-billion program of special urban community development revenue sharing and a government reorganization plan that included a Department of Community Development were both the subject of hearings in 1971, but no action occurred on either until 1972. And in 1972 neither proposal became law. (p. 652)

Community Development Legislation. In his state of the union message the President offered an expanded program to share $25-billion in federal revenues with the states and cities for general purposes with no strings attached. This proposal became known as general revenue sharing. In addition he proposed to consolidate 105 narrow-purpose grant programs into six broad area special revenue sharing programs. One of the six proposed was urban community development revenue sharing which was to have consolidated funds for model cities, open space grants, urban renewal, public facility and rehabilitation loan programs, neighborhood facilities and water and sewer grant programs. The urban special revenue sharing program was to be divided up among the cities and states according to a formula for use as they wished within the area of community development. *(Background on revenue sharing p. 73)*

Urban community development special revenue sharing was considered along with other administration and congressional ideas for reform of housing and urban development law. In 1972, the revenue-sharing proposal was modified in a Senate-passed bill which died when the House Rules Committee blocked action on a companion measure.

The Senate Banking, Housing and Urban Affairs Subcommittee on Housing and Urban Affairs held hearings in August and September on housing and community development legislation. The House Banking and Currency Subcommittee on Housing held hearings in August and September on housing and community development.

The major bills before Congress were:

• S 1618 (HR 8853)—The administration's $2.3-billion proposal for urban revenue sharing. It would distribute money to cities with almost no strings attached for programs of urban renewal, model cities, rehabilitation grants and neighborhood facilities. There was no matching requirement for the cities. Distribution would be automatic, based on population, overcrowdedness and extent of poverty.

• S 2049 (HR 9331)—The administration's proposal to simplify and consolidate many Department of Housing and Urban Development (HUD) programs.

• S 2333—The Senate subcommittee's bill introduced by Chairman John Sparkman (D Ala.). It proposed $8.8-billion over three years for block grants to cities for programs of urban renewal, water and sewer facilities, neighborhood facilities and open space. Fund distribution would be based on past performance and future plans, with the federal share set at 90 per cent of project costs. HUD would have to take action on each grant application within 90 days. (HUD estimated it took 15 months to process an urban renewal application.)

• HR 9688, the House subcommittee's housing and urban development proposals for 1971.

Department of Community Development. In his 1971 State of the Union message, President Nixon proposed reducing the present twelve cabinet departments to eight.

The proposed Community Development Department would have included housing, community development, metropolitan development and renewal and transportation programs. It would have included certain functions at that time performed by Housing and Urban Development, Health, Education and Welfare, Commerce, Agriculture and Transportation departments, the Appalachian Regional Commission and disaster relief programs of the Office of Emergency Preparedness and the Small Business Administration.

The full Senate Government Operations Committee and the House Government Operations Subcommittee on Legislation and Military Operations both held hearings in November on bills to create a Community Development Department. No bills were reported.

In the hearings, proponents of the new department argued for a streamlining of the executive branch to eliminate the fragmentation of government policy-making. Opponents insisted it would dilute various constituencies which under the existing structure could have more of a voice in policy. Agriculture spokesmen stressed the need for a strong Agriculture Department to allow significant farmer input in policies.

Fiscal 1972 Appropriations

In the fiscal 1972 HUD-independent offices appropriations bill (HR 9382—PL 92-78), which cleared Aug. 2, Congress appropriated $3,274,824,000 for HUD, $882,721,-000 more than requested by the President ($2,557,177,-000). Of that increase, $150-million was for the Model Cities program and $650-million was for the urban renewal program. (In all, Congress appropriated $1,250,-000,000 for urban renewal.) *(Chart p. 638, for fiscal 1972 funds including supplemental appropriations)*

The House bill, which was approved by voice vote June 30, included $3,206,324,000 for housing and urban programs. The Senate measure, approved July 20 on an 87-0 roll-call vote, included $3,532,234,000.

In the major compromise by House-Senate conferees, the Senate-approved $1.5-billion for urban renewal was cut $250-million to $1.25 billion.

The $882.7-million increase in the final bill over the administration's budget request for fiscal 1972 paralleled to a large extent Congress' failure to act on the administration's budget request for $850-million for fiscal 1972 to launch the proposed urban special revenue sharing program. The administration's January 1971 budget request of $2,557,177,000 for HUD appropriations for fiscal 1972 had been submitted with the expectation that Congress would approve the program of special revenue sharing. *(Special revenue sharing proposal, p. 73)*

Housing Program Extensions

Congress Dec. 13 cleared a bill (S J Res 176—PL 92-213) extending and modifying certain Department of Housing and Urban Development (HUD) programs.

Final action came when the House and Senate adopted a conference report on the bill by voice votes.

The purpose of the bill was to extend HUD programs due to expire by Jan. 1, 1972, and to permit certain exemptions and modifications in other laws.

Final Provisions. As cleared for the President, S J Res 176:

• Added church property used for religious purposes among those properties eligible for coverage under the federal flood insurance program.

• Extended for six months, to June 30, 1972, the authority of the Government National Mortgage Association to purchase FHA or VA mortgages up to 150 per

Housing Program Scandals

Revelations of scandals in government-subsidized, privately built low-income housing projects in 1971 and early 1972 provoked demands for review and revision of the four-year-old, multi-million-dollar effort to provide low-cost housing in the inner cities.

Abuses involving programs administered by the Federal Housing Administration were brought to light in a number of cities, including New York, Boston, Chicago, Detroit, Newark and Philadelphia.

In these cities speculators purchased ghetto homes cheaply, made cosmetic repairs and, often with FHA approval, sold them to poor families at inflated prices. Many of these families, unable to meet FHA mortgage payments and undertake needed but costly repairs, eventually abandoned the homes.

By virtue of the resulting soaring foreclosure rate, thousands of dilapidated houses in the ghetto fell into government hands. At the end of fiscal 1972, HUD owned title to 51,917 single-family homes and 195 multifamily properties with 25,006 dwelling units.

In addition to mortgage foreclosures, other problems besetting the government's low-income housing programs included skyrocketing construction costs, excessive fees and settlement costs, mismanagement of rental units, shoddy construction, inflated land prices and malpractice by FHA officials.

During 1972, 28 HUD employees were indicted on a variety of fraud and conspiracy charges, compared with seven during the years 1968 through 1971. In 1971 and 1972, 48 persons were imprisoned for a total of over 70 years and 84 persons put on probation totaling over 180 years.

The charges against realtors and HUD officials included submitting false claims and statements to the government in connection with repair work on FHA-rehabilitated houses, accepting bribes to alter FHA appraisals, submitting false inspection reports and conspiracy to defraud the government.

House Banking Committee Reports. The House Banking and Currency Committee reported in December 1970 that administration of the house-ownership assistance program by HUD and the Federal Housing Administration bordered on a "national housing scandal" due to "sheer fraud" on the part of builders and real estate operators and FHA carelessness.

HUD Secretary George Romney initially labeled the staff report "inaccurate and misleading," but on Jan. 14, 1971, said that abuses were more prevalent than he previously had thought. On that day he suspended the portion of the program dealing with rehabilitated housing. The program subsequently was reinstituted in areas where HUD determined reforms had been made.

Moratorium. Partly because of the criminal conduct and continuing unworkability of some parts of the federal housing subsidy programs, the Nixon administration Jan. 5, 1973, halted all new commitments under the program in order to conduct a comprehensive review, concentrating on alternatives to the 1968 Housing Act subsidy programs.

cent of the limits prescribed by section 302(b)(1) of the National Housing Act of 1954.

• Delayed for one year, to Jan. 1, 1973, the date when states could tax the intangible personal property of national banks in their jurisdictions; provided that the Board of Governors of the Federal Reserve System were to study the fiscal impact of the loss of revenue from the delay and issue a report to Congress within six months of enactment of S J Res 176.

• Extended to June 30, 1972, the deadline for communities to meet comprehensive planning requirements to be eligible for basic water and sewer grants.

• Made nonprofit organizations eligible for supplementary grants under the new communities assistance program of the 1970 HUD act.

• Increased authorizations for comprehensive planning program by $50-million and the open spaces land program by $100-million.

• Barred a reduction in welfare assistance to recipients living in low-rent housing who had their rent reduced because it exceeded 25 per cent of their income.

• Clarified the authority of the Small Business Administration to guarantee debentures issued by small business investment companies.

• Extended for six months, to June 30, 1972, the authority for the secretary of HUD to set interest rate ceilings on VA and FHA mortgages.

• Reduced the statutory requirements for insurance reserves held by the Federal Savings and Loan Insurance Corporation to 1-3/5 per cent from 1-3/4 per cent.

• Suspended for two years, to Dec. 31, 1973, a requirement that federal disaster assistance would not be available to property owners in an area eligible for flood insurance if the owner had not taken advantage of the insurance.

1972

The Senate in March overwhelmingly approved an omnibus housing bill which included the administration's 1971 proposal for consolidation of 50 separate housing and community development programs into eight sections of the federal housing law. The Senate bill, however, contained a modification of the administration's proposed revenue sharing proposal by stipulating specific objectives and procedures for urban renewal funds. The companion House bill died at the end of the 92nd session following a Rules Committee vote to defer action.

The administration's proposal for a new Department of Community Development was reported in the House, but no further action was taken.

Simple extensions of existing housing programs were cleared by Congress: in June a bill extending six HUD programs was approved; in October, the Federal Housing Administration's authority was extended through June 1973.

The fiscal 1973 HUD-Independent offices appropriations bill cleared in August containing $4.3-billion for housing and urban development programs.

Omnibus Housing Bill

The House Rules Committee Sept. 27, by a 9-5 roll-call vote, decided not to grant a rule for floor considera-

tion of HR 16704, the Housing and Urban Development Act of 1972, in effect killing the omnibus bill for the 92nd Congress.

House action came after the Senate had voted overwhelming approval of a similar bill (S 3248) on March 2. The two bills were the first major housing measures considered by Congress since enactment of the Housing and Urban Development Act of 1968. S 3248 sailed through the Senate by a 80-1 roll-call vote.

The House version of the housing bill had been reported (H Rept 92-1429) Sept. 21 by the Banking and Currency Committee which had ordered the bill reported Sept. 19 by a 9-3 roll-call vote.

Approximately 50 existing federal housing assistance programs—including those to aid low-income persons—were revised and consolidated under eight sections of the federal housing law by HR 16704.

The bill also consolidated several urban development categorical programs into a system of block grants and authorized $5.5-billion over a two-year period for those grants. It established regulations for closing costs and settlement of real estate transactions and authorized $400-million for operating subsidies for public mass transit systems.

HR 16704 authorized a total of $11,004,000,000 for housing and urban development programs in fiscal years 1973 and 1974 and an additional $33-million for fiscal years 1975-1977. The Senate bill authorized $11,588,000,-000 for fiscal 1973 through 1975.

The proposed 1972 omnibus housing bill was the result of two and a half years of committee consideration in both the House and Senate. Committees in both chambers held extensive hearings on housing and community development legislation during 1971. *(p. 652)*

SENATE ACTION

The Senate Banking, Housing and Urban Affairs Subcommittee on Housing and Urban Affairs held hearings in 1971 on bills concerning housing and other urban programs, and the subcommittee met in February 1972 to mark up a bill. Early action in the Senate had been expected since John Sparkman (D Ala.), chairman of the full committee and the housing subcommittee, was a candidate for re-election in 1972 and sought to begin campaigning full time for another six-year term.

On Feb. 28, the Senate Banking, Housing and Urban Affairs Committee reported its bill (S 3248—S Rept 92-647) without a recorded vote. The Senate passed the bill on March 2 by an 80-1 roll call.

The lone vote against the bill was cast by Bill Brock (R Tenn.).

The bill, the first major housing legislation since 1968, consolidated into eight programs about 50 existing federal housing assistance programs, expanded low-income housing programs, authorized $5.9-billion in new federal block grants to local governments to support community development activities, overhauled the FHA mortgage insurance program and authorized $800-million in operating subsidies for deficit-ridden mass transit systems across the country. Included in the bill were provisions providing criminal penalties for giving or receiving kickbacks or title insurance commissions at real estate settlements in which the government guaranteed the mortgage.

Authorizations contained in S 3248 totaled $9.16-billion over three years, fiscal 1973-75.

As passed, S 3248 would permit more flexibility in the use of federal housing money at the local level. The block-grant provisions were presented by the Senate committee reporting the bill as a compromise similar to that proposed in the President's revenue-sharing plan for community development.

The bill would set guidelines to encourage a mix of middle- and low-income families in federally subsidized housing. It would also decrease the down-payments required for conventional FHA-insured housing.

During the two days of debate (March 1-2), 16 floor amendments were adopted by the Senate, adding $800-million to total authorizations in the bill. The additional funds, for payment of operating expenses of urban mass transit systems, were included in an amendment offered by Jacob K. Javits (R N.Y.). Another amendment that was adopted, introduced by William Proxmire (D Wis.), would prohibit kickbacks from real estate settlements on properties where the mortgages were guaranteed by the federal government.

While the primary purpose of S 3248 was to consolidate and simplify FHA mortgage insurance and low-rent public housing programs, its far-reaching block-grant community development program would, if enacted, give priority in the use of federal funds to the elimination of slums and blight and to make the nation's cities more attractive and viable places in which to live.

The block-grant approach lumped together existing separate grants for urban renewal, neighborhood development, water and sewer assistance, neighborhood facilities, open space, public works and land acquisition.

Revenue-Sharing Modification. S 3248 would alter the administration's proposed urban renewal revenue-sharing proposal to distribute federal funds automatically to the nation's cities without first requiring state and local planning and federal guidelines. The bill as passed by the Senate outlined specific objectives and procedures for urban renewal funds; it required a locality requesting funds to provide adequate housing for the community, take steps to eliminate its slums and assist residents who were adversely affected by community development projects.

HOUSE ACTION

Banking Committee. Action did not come as early in 1972 in the House as in the Senate. The House Banking and Currency Subcommittee on Housing held hearings and reported an omnibus housing bill to the full committee on May 9, 1972, by a 15-0 vote.

The full committee then held more hearings and considered the bill for a six-week period from late July to mid-September. On Sept. 21, the committee reported the bill (HR 16704—H Rept 92-1429) to the House by a 19-3 recorded vote.

The delay and long deliberation in the full committee was attributed in part to a power dispute between Chairmand Wright Patman (D Texas) and Housing Subcommittee Chairman William A. Barrett (D Pa.).

During mark-up, Patman chided the subcommittee: "Some might suggest that the mere fact that there are dozens and dozens of amendments being offered—with many more to come—could indicate that the bill which came forward from the subcommittee was far from perfected."

Dissatisfaction with the bill as reported was reflected in the fact that 25 of the committee's 37 members offered supplementary views to the committee report.

Major points of controversy regarding the bill were its provisions concerning federal subsidies for rent or mortgage payments by low-income persons, providing an operating subsidy for mass transit, permitting localities to veto federally subsidized housing projects, forbidding the Department of Housing and Urban Development (HUD) to withhold water and sewer grants if a community refused to accept certain housing programs, and allowing kickbacks in connection with real estate settlements.

"Administration of federal housing and urban development programs has been so singularly inadequate that even soundly conceived congressional programs have been called into question," said the committee report. An underlying cause of the dissatisfaction with current housing programs was "the lack of a rational and coherent national growth policy," it said.

The committee "considered but emphatically rejected the administration's revenue-sharing approach" to urban development programs, adopting the block grant program instead. The committee particularly objected to the fact that the administration proposed that block grants under revenue-sharing not be contingent on an application or preconditions.

In a supplementary view, Patman said he favored adoption of the bill but that he was disappointed that such a "massive bill that defies thorough understanding by members" was being brought to the floor.

Patman also charged HUD Secretary George Romney with an "astonishing lack of leadership.... While the committee wrestled with extremely complex elements of the bill, the secretary was wandering around the nation making political speeches on behalf of the President's re-election.... Under these circumstances, it is little wonder that HR 16704 fails to reflect any meaningful effort to bring reform and new direction to federal housing programs which have been all but crippled by abusive and fraudulent real estate transaction practices."

Rules Committee. The House Rules Committee Sept. 27, by a 9-5 roll-call vote, adopted a motion to defer action on HR 16704. The committee's action did not come as a great surprise. Rules Committee members pointed to the length of the bill (314 pages), its complexity and objections to many sections of the bill raised by both liberals and conservatives.

Rules Committee Chairman William M. Colmer (D Miss.) said that it would be a "Herculean task" to consider the bill on the floor before adjournment. Ray J. Madden (D Ind.) Sept. 26 asked Patman: "Why did (the bill) bob up a few weeks before adjournment?" Patman replied that the bill's complexity and the Banking and Currency housing subcommittee were responsible for the delay.

However, William B. Widnall (R N.J.), ranking Republican on the Banking and Currency Committee, Sept. 27 told the Rules Committee that Patman had "made a mockery" of the legislative process by his "dilatory" handling of the bill during full committee consideration.

In seeking a rule for the bill, Patman appeared less than enthusiastic: "It's a good bill in many instances. You do what you want. I'd like to see a bill."

On the motion to defer action on the question of providing a rule for floor consideration of the bill, voting "aye" (in favor of deferral—killing the bill) were five Democrats and all four of the Republican members present. Voting against the motion—and therefore for moving the bill to the floor—were five Democrats.

Rep. Thomas L. Ashley (D Ohio), second-ranking Democrat of the housing subcommittee told Congressional Quarterly that "there was more to the Rules Committee decision than the fact that it was late in the session.

"There was a total lack of interest on the part of the Republican members of the Rules Committee. It was suggested by John Anderson (R Ill., second-ranking Republican on Rules) that, if we cropped the bill, parts of it could go through—parts they would gladly furnish.

"Dick Bolling (D Mo.) was against it six weeks before it even came to them. He and several other Democratic members thought the bill as it was emerging did violence to families living in public housing, and the fact that the 235 and 236 (subsidized housing) programs had emerged as high visibility programs and were attracting animosity and this was not the time to extend them."

Rep. Robert G. Stephens Jr. (D Ga.) said, "The chairman (Patman) just didn't want a bill this year. How can you go to Rules Committee and ask for a bill and tell them at the same time that it's a bad bill but they ought to grant (a rule) anyway. That's damning it with faint praise."

Community Development Department

The House Government Operations Committee May 23 reported a bill (HR 6962—H Rept 92-1096) to create a Department of Community Development. No further action was taken on the bill.

The committee voted 27-7 May 10 to report the bill.

The new department would have included the entire Department of Urban and Housing Development (HUD), and elements from the Departments of Health, Education and Welfare (HEW), Transportation (DOT), Commerce and Agriculture, the Office of Economic Opportunity (OEO), the Small Business Administration and the Office of Emergency Preparedness.

Background. In his 1971 state-of-the-union message, President Nixon proposed reducing the number of cabinet departments from twelve to eight. The Departments of State, Defense, Treasury and Justice would remain; functions of the Post Office Department would be turned over to a public corporation under legislation passed in 1970. The functions of the remaining seven departments would be divided among four new departments: Natural Resources, Human Resources, Community Development and Economic Development.

Nixon sent these proposals to Congress in March 1971. In November 1971, he announced that the Agriculture Department would remain largely intact. HR 6962 was the first of these proposals to be reported from committee.

Committee Views. In its report, the committee said that the bill offered a "new concept of community devel-

opment" as a primary purpose of government and would reduce "fragmented administration, diffusion of responsibility and the confusion and delay caused by departments and agencies working at cross-purposes."

HUD Programs Extensions

Congress June 30 cleared for the President a bill (S J Res 250—PL 92-335) extending the authorization for certain programs administered by the Department of Housing and Urban Development.

S J Res 250 extended six programs for which new authorizing legislation had not yet been passed. The six programs were contained in the omnibus housing bill approved by the Senate but still in committee in the House and ultimately killed by the House Rules Committee Sept. 27.

As cleared, S. J. Res 250:

• Extended to June 30, 1973, the authority of the HUD secretary to establish maximum interest rates on insured mortgages at levels necessary to meet the mortgage market.

• Extended to Sept. 30, 1972, authorizations for appropriations for the model cities program, the water-sewer and neighborhood facilities grant program and the comprehensive planning program.

• Extended to Sept. 30, 1972, the waiver of certain planning requirements under the basic water and sewer facilities grant program.

• Extended to Sept. 30, 1972, the authorization for the open-space land program.

• Extended for an additional three months the authority of the HUD secretary to purchase mortgages with principal obligations in excess of statutory limitations when the secretary determined such purchase was necessary to avoid excessive discounts.

FHA Extension

Congress Oct. 14 cleared for the President a bill (H J Res 1301—PL 92-503) extending through June 30, 1973, the authority of the Federal Housing Administration (FHA) to insure loans and mortgages.

The extension was necessary after the House rules Committee Sept. 27 refused to grant a rule for floor consideration of the 1972 omnibus housing bill. *(p. 654)*

FHA's authority expired Oct. 1.

The bill increased by $250-million the authorization for urban renewal to provide additional funds for flood relief and increased by $150-million the amount authorized for public housing.

The increase in funds for public housing may be used by Housing and Urban Development (HUD) Secretary George Romney to finance additional units of public housing or increase subsidies to meet rising operating costs. The bill repealed provisions in the existing law requiring that subsidies be based on the original financing of the project.

Romney announced Oct. 6 that he would increase public housing authority subsidies by more than $100-million when this legislation is enacted and outlined standards on which the subsidies would be based.

Legislative History. Before the House Rules Committee killed the omnibus housing bill, the House Banking and Currency Committee reported H J Res 1301 (H Rept 92-1409) on Sept. 19 extending FHA authority for one month. On Oct. 2, the House passed, by voice vote under suspension of the rules, the bill as amended to extend the authority to June 30, 1973.

The Senate Banking, Housing and Urban Affairs Committee on Oct. 3 reported the bill to the floor extending the programs to April 30, 1973, and adding funds for public housing and urban renewal (S Rept 92-1261).

The Senate on Oct. 6 passed the bill by voice vote after accepting an amendment by Sen. Wallace F. Bennett (R Utah). Bennett's amendment, accepted by a voice vote, changed the term of the extension from April 30, 1973, as reported by committee, to June 30, 1973, as passed by the House.

The House Oct. 14 agreed to the Senate amendments to H J Res 1301, clearing the bill for the President.

Fiscal 1973 Appropriations

In the regular fiscal 1973 HUD-Independent offices appropriations bill (HR 15093—PL 92-383), which cleared Congress Aug. 3, Congress appropriated $4,034,065,000 for HUD programs. The administration had requested $4,657,807,000. *(Chart p. 638 for fiscal 1973 funds including supplemental appropriations)*

The major reductions made from the administration's request were in the special risk insurance fund, the Government National Mortgage Association special assistance functions and in urban renewal programs.

The administration had requested $314-million for the special risk fund and the special assistance fund. Congress cut the entire $314-million from the bill. House-Senate conferees agreed that HUD borrowing from the Treasury could meet the needs of the two funds. The other major cut came in urban renewal funds; the administration had requested $1,450,000,000, and Congress appropriated $1,200,000,000.

Public Utilities

The Senate July 21, by a 60-11 roll-call vote, passed a bill (S 1991) authorizing the Securities and Exchange Commission (SEC) to permit companies subject to regulation under the Public Utility Holding Company Act of 1935 to participate in federally assisted low- and moderate-income housing projects. The House did not act on the bill.

S 1991 would have affected 17 multi-state utility holding companies which were prohibited from engaging in business not reasonably necessary or incidental to the operation of a public utility. If enacted, S 1991 would have been the first amendment to the 1935 act.

An identical bill was approved by the Senate in 1970 as an amendment to the Housing and Urban Development Act but it was deleted in a House-Senate conference.

S 1991 was introduced by Commerce Committee Chairman Warren G. Magnuson (D Wash.) at the request of the Department of Housing and Urban Development (HUD). The Commerce Committee held hearings on the bill in 1971 and reported it (S Rept 92-961) on June 28.

Emergency Community Facilities

The House July 19 refused to go along with a $5 billion emergency grant program for construction of water and sewer and other community facilities. The bill (HR 13853), strongly supported by the House Democratic leadership, was defeated by a 189-206 roll-call vote.

According to supporters of the bill, most of whom were Democrats, the funds were intended primarily for building water and sewer systems. They said the bill was vital to help reduce water pollution, create jobs for construction workers and combat unemployment.

Opponents of the bill, mostly Republicans and southern Democrats, argued that HR 13853 was inflationary, duplicative and politically inspired. They said a pending water pollution control bill would provide sufficient funds for construction and pollution abatement, and called HR 13853 part of an election year tactic to force President Nixon to veto a popular bill.

Consumer Legislation

The nation's consumers gained a stronger voice during the years 1969-1972, and, as a group, commanded more attention from both Congress and the business community than they had in the past.

Congress acted positively on several important consumer issues during President Nixon's first term: it approved legislation banning cigarette advertisements from radio and television, requiring fair credit reporting legislation, setting toy, tire and auto bumper safety standards and enacting poison prevention legislation. And, in its most far-ranging action, Congress in 1972 moved away from its piecemeal approach to product safety by creating an independent agency to set standards for a myriad of consumer products.

But what Congress did not do in the realm of consumer legislation was as significant as what it did. It did not approve the creation of an independent agency to advocate consumer interests before other federal agencies and courts. It did not pass measures providing for product warranty standards or for consumer class-action suits. It did not approve legislation strengthening the powers of the Federal Trade Commission. It did not pass legislation establishing a national system of no-fault auto insurance. And it did not approve legislation setting standards for fair credit billing.

In short, consumer advocates in Congress were able to push through legislation dealing with relatively narrow consumer issues but were unable, in most instances, to muster enough support to pass measures that would give consumers a strong voice in government or that would substantially affect wide areas of business or the way business is conducted.

Business also made concessions to consumerism, as evidenced by the increased consumer services offered by a growing number of firms and corporations. But business and industry groups continued to oppose federal consumer legislative proposals that, in their opinion, would have led to harassment of businesses or to broad sweeping changes in the marketplace.

Consumers themselves grew more organized and cohesive during the four year period. Research groups affiliated with consumer advocate Ralph Nader specialized in specific consumer areas—auto safety, health, food and clean air, for example. The Consumer Federation of America, created in May 1968 and composed of approximately 200 consumer organizations across the country, increased its visibility on Capitol Hill while serving as a clearinghouse for its member groups.

President Nixon's consumer policy was widely criticized by consumer groups as disappointing and at times in direct opposition to consumer interests.

The President submitted two consumer messages in his first four years. The first, delivered Oct. 30, 1969, proposed a "buyer's bill of rights" and called for a new program of consumer protection based primarily on creation of a Justice Department consumer protection division, a revitalization of the Federal Trade Commission and creation of an Office of Consumer Affairs in the Executive Office of the President.

In the second message, submitted Feb. 24, 1971, Nixon reiterated many of the proposals of the first message but made three major changes:

- Announced the creation of an Office of Consumer Affairs in the White House by executive order and named Virginia H. Knauer, his special assistant for consumer affairs, as its head.
- Shifted his position on a consumer advocate from his 1969 proposal of a consumer protection division in the Justice Department; in his 1971 message he said he would defer legislative proposals until the recommendations of the Advisory Council on Executive Reorganization had been fully examined.
- Proposed creation of a product safety division within the Department of Health, Education and Welfare.

Nixon called his proposals "the most significant set of presidential recommendations concerning consumer interests in our history." Consumer advocates called them disappointing. And consumer supporters in Congress charged the administration with supporting consumer proposals publicly but working against their passage privately.

In an Oct. 6, 1972, press release, Sen. Frank E. Moss (D Utah), chairman of the Senate Commerce Consumer Subcommittee and a strong supporter of consumer measures, said that "the blatant role the Nixon administration has played in protecting big business has cast a pall over the nation."

Apparently undaunted by past failures, consumer groups at the end of 1972 were gearing up to try once again for congressional passage of legislation aimed at ensuring fair play for the consumer in government and the market place.

References

Discussion of legislation on consumer issues for the years 1945-64 may be found in *Congress and the Nation Vol. I*, p. 1159-1185; for the years 1965-68, *Congress and the Nation Vol. II*, p. 779-823.

Following is a summary of the major legislation considered during the 1969-72 period:

Product Safety. In a significant move away from its piecemeal approach to product safety, Congress in 1972 cleared a bill establishing an independent Consumer Product Safety Commission authorized to set safety standards for a wide range of consumer products and to ban those products presenting an unreasonable risk of injury. The measure was opposed by Nixon, who preferred that a product safety division be placed within the Health, Education and Welfare Department. The only significant piece of consumer legislation to be passed within one year, the commission's creation grew out of a recommendation by the National Commission on Product Safety.

In other product safety actions, Congress in 1969 approved a bill designed to protect children from potentially unsafe toys due to electrical, mechanical or thermal hazards. The following year, in 1970, Congress passed a measure requiring safety closures on potentially dangerous household products, such as polishes, cleansers and medicines, to prevent children from accidentally poisoning themselves. And in 1972, Congress cleared a bill extending the Flammable Fabrics Act for another year.

Jurisdiction over the Toy Safety Act, the Poison Prevention Packaging Act and the Flammable Fabrics Act was transferred to the new Product Safety Commission.

Consumer Protection. Congress, however, failed to approve the creation of another independent agency—this one to represent consumer interests before other federal agencies and before courts. The Senate in 1970 approved a bill creating an independent agency, but the House Rules Committee killed a weaker version reported out of a House committee and the measure died at the end of the 91st Congress.

In 1971, the House approved its version of the measure, but in 1972, a well-coordinated lobby campaign waged by more than 150 business organizations helped to kill the bill in the Senate. The legislation was set aside for the remainder of the 92nd Congress after Senate supporters failed three times to muster enough votes to invoke cloture (limit debate) on the bill. Supporters charged that the administration, which had announced support for the House version, lobbied covertly against cloture.

Congress also failed to complete action on two other consumer protection bills. In both 1970 and 1971, the Senate passed measures setting minimum federal standards for consumer product warranties but the House did not take action on either measure. The Senate had also included provisions strengthening the Federal Trade Commission in the 1971 warranty measure.

A Senate committee reported a bill in 1970 that would have allowed consumers to join together as a class to sue for damages. However, neither chamber took any further action. Nixon had recommended similar legislation.

Auto Safety, Insurance. Congress approved two bills designed to improve auto and tire safety and to reduce repair costs. But a move to establish a national system of no-fault insurance was quashed in the Senate in 1972.

In 1970, Congress completed action on a bill extending the National Traffic and Motor Vehicle Safety Act of 1966 for three years and requiring tire manufacturers to notify purchasers of safety-related tire defects. The 1966 act had required automobile manufacturers to recall cars having safety-related defects.

And in 1972, Congress cleared a bill authorizing the secretary of transportation to set automobile bumper standards aimed at reducing damage incurred in low-speed accidents.

The concept of no-fault auto insurance, under which the victim of an accident is compensated for his damages by his own insurance company regardless of who caused the accident, had been under consideration for several years by congressional committees and the Department of Transportation. A bill establishing minimum federal standards for no-fault auto insurance to be adopted by states and included in all auto insurance policies came to the Senate floor in August 1972. But the measure was killed when its opponents succeeded in having it committed to the Judiciary Committee for further study. The measure was opposed by the Nixon administration, the American Trial Lawyers Association, several insurance companies and associations and many governors and state insurance commissioners.

Consumer Credit. During 1969-72, Congress also became involved with consumer credit problems. In 1970, Congress approved two bills (attached as riders to a bill concerning secret foreign bank accounts) restricting the issuance of unsolicited credit cards and allowing persons to look into and challenge or correct their credit dossiers. In 1972, the Senate passed a bill to protect consumers against unfair billing practices. The House took no action on the measure. As passed by the Senate, the bill was so weakened from the original legislation that its chief sponsor, Sen. William Proxmire (D Wis.), voted against final passage.

Cigarette Advertising. Congress in 1970 completed action on a bill that banned cigarette advertisements from radio and television. Passage of the measure ended six years of controversy over whether the federal government should regulate the advertisement of cigarettes which had been found to be hazardous to health.

Bans. The House in 1972 approved a measure allowing food manufacturers, processors and distributors to sue the federal government for payment of losses incurred as a result of a 1969 ban on cyclamates, artificial sweeteners. The Senate failed to take action on that bill, but it did pass in 1972 a bill calling for the immediate ban of DES (diethylstilbestrol), a growth-promotant for cattle and sheep, if DES residue from ear implants was found. The Food and Drug Administration had banned the use of DES in cattle feed in August after the hormone was found to cause cancer in test animals. But the agency action allowed continued use of DES in ear implants.

Meat, Fish Inspections. Congress in 1970 cleared a bill permitting custom slaughterers to engage in the retailing and wholesaling of meat. In 1972, the House rejected a measure that would have increased the amount the federal government could pay toward state meat and poultry inspection programs. The Senate had passed the bill in 1971.

The Senate in 1971 also passed a bill establishing a federal inspection program to regulate fish products, processing plants and fishing vessels. The bill died at the end of the 92nd Congress when the House failed to take action on it.

Chronology

Of Legislation

On Consumer Issues

1969

Congress enacted no major consumer legislation in 1969. Instead, efforts centered on how to reorganize government agencies charged with protecting the consumer rather than on passing additional consumer protection laws. Consumer advocates maintained that the great need was not for more laws but for more money, manpower, efficiency and organization to enforce the already existing laws.

The first session of the 91st Congress did enact two consumer measures, although neither was considered a broad step. They were: an amendment to the Federal Hazardous Substances Act to protect children from electrical, mechanical and thermal hazards in toys, known as the Toy Safety Act of 1969, and a measure extending the life of the National Commission on Product Safety.

In addition, two other consumer-oriented bills were passed in differing versions by both the House and Senate in 1969 but final resolution did not occur until the 1970 session. They were a tire-safety bill, which was included in legislation extending the National Traffic and Motor Vehicle Safety Act of 1966, and a bill to regulate cigarette advertising.

The Fair Credit Reporting Act passed the Senate but not the House. Other proposals which Congress considered but did not take action upon were: federal-state fisheries inspection; safe packaging to protect children from poisons; and a bill permitting consumers to seek court action as a group (class-action).

House and Senate committees held investigative hearings on auto insurance and auto repair costs, the effectiveness of the Fair Packaging and Labeling Act of 1966 (Truth in Packaging), the use of chemical sprays and promotional games.

Government agencies involved with consumer protection came under fire in 1969. In a 58-page confidential report, the Food and Drug Administration acknowledged it was "not equipped to cope" with the myriad consumer protection problems with which it was faced. And the Federal Trade Commission was the subject of a report prepared by the American Bar Association (ABA) and one prepared by a group of law students associated with consumer advocate Ralph Nader. Both reports were highly critical of the agency's activities. The agency was called "a failure on many counts" in the ABA report, prepared at the request of President Nixon.

Executive Action. Nixon April 9 appointed the former director of the Pennsylvania Bureau of Consumer Protection, Virginia H. Knauer, as his special assistant for consumer affairs. An earlier appointee, Willie Mae Rogers, had resigned Feb. 15 following charges of "conflict of interest." Rogers, director of the Good Housekeep-

ing Institute, had been appointed Feb. 11 to be a part-time, unpaid consultant to the President.

Nixon delivered his first consumer message to Congress Oct. 30. In it, he proposed:

● A statutory Office of Consumer Affairs in the White House.

● A consumer protection division in the Justice Department to represent the consumer before federal regulatory agencies and in judicial proceedings.

● Legislation to permit consumers to band together in groups (class-action) to sue in federal courts for damages resulting from fraudulent or deceptive business practices.

● Reactivation and revitalization of the Federal Trade Commission.

● Re-examination of the Food and Drug Administration including a review of food additives listed as "generally recognized as safe."

Consumer advocates called the program "inadequate and disappointing," while Nixon said his recommendations were "the most significant set of presidential recommendations concerning consumer interests in our history."

Toy Safety

Spurred by the interim report of the National Commission on Product Safety, released Feb. 24, 1969, Congress overwhelmingly approved a bill (S 1689—PL 91-113) extending federal control over toy safety. The bill amended the Federal Hazardous Substances Act to protect children from potentially unsafe toys due to electrical, mechanical or thermal hazards.

Background. The 1966 Child Protection Amendments (PL 89-756) to the Federal Hazardous Substances Act permitted federal officials to require a warning label on all hazardous household items and on hazardous toys and children's articles. It also allowed the government to ban from sale household items and children's toys if they were found to be too dangerous for general use, regardless of whether a warning label was attached.

The interim report of the product safety commission maintained that "existing legislation...is in critical need of amendment.... The commission believes that the categories of hazards related to toys and other articles intended for use by children should be extended and expanded to include three additional categories of hazards, namely, electrical, mechanical and thermal." (The commission was authorized by Congress in 1967 and was directed to review categories of products used in or around American households to determine whether or not the products were hazardous. *(Congress and the Nation Vol. II, p. 803)*

Toys considered hazardous by the commission in its interim report included children's ovens which heated up to 600 degrees internally, hotter than most cooking ranges, and metal casting sets which reached temperatures of 800 degrees.

Provisions. As signed into law (PL 91-113) Nov. 6, 1969, S 1689, the Children Protection and Toy Safety Act, amended the Federal Hazardous Substances Act as follows:

● Provided a one-step regulation process for excluding from the market children's articles and toys presenting electrical, mechanical or thermal hazards.

- Provided that determination of a children's article as a hazardous substance automatically would make it a banned hazardous substance unless the secretary of health, education and welfare (HEW) determined that an article served a functional purpose which required the inclusion of such a hazard and was appropriately labeled.

- Provided that the secretary could exclude an article from the market for a limited period before or during determination proceedings if he found that its distribution presented an imminent hazard to the public health and safety.

- Provided that any person adversely affected by a determination of the secretary could within 60 days seek review in the United States court of appeals; required the repurchase of banned hazardous substances by their manufacturers, distributors or dealers.

- Defined electrical hazard as one which would cause personal injury or illness by electric shock through normal use resulting from current leakage, accessibility of live parts and inadequate insulation; defined mechanical hazard as one which presented an unreasonable risk of personal injury or illness through any aspect of the article's design or manufacture; defined thermal hazard as one which presented unreasonable risk of personal injury or illness by heat; no specific temperatures were set.

Legislative History. The bill, as cleared for the President, embodied most of the recommendations of the commission. S 1689 was reported by the Senate Commerce Committee June 17 with two major amendments. "Thermal hazard" was more specifically defined and maximum temperatures were set. And a liability clause was inserted stating that the manufacturer upon having to recall an article must reimburse the distributor or dealer. The Senate passed the bill June 30 by voice vote.

On July 24, the House Interstate and Foreign Commerce Committee reported its own toy safety bill (HR 7621). The bill was similar to the Senate version; the only major difference dealt with the procedure for banning toys. Whereas the Senate bill provided a more direct and immediate formula for removing hazardous toys from the market, HR 7621 provided greater procedural protection to the toy industry. The House bill set no specific temperatures for thermal hazards. The House Sept. 4, by a 327-0 roll-call vote, passed HR 7621 as reported from committee. It then passed S 1689 after substituting the language of the House bill for the Senate-approved provisions.

House-Senate conferees resolved the major difference between the two versions by providing a regulation process in which only one proceeding to determine if an article was hazardous to children was necessary to exclude the article from the market. Definitions of electrical, thermal and mechanical hazards set out in the House version were retained. The House Oct. 23 and the Senate Oct. 27 adopted the conference report.

The act went into effect Jan. 6, 1970; between then and Christmas of that year, the Food and Drug Administration (FDA) took action to make 24 specific toys safer. However, no order to ban a toy under terms of the act became final until Dec. 28, 1970, and only after a court challenge against several allegedly hazardous toys had been filed by Consumers Union and the Children's Foundation. By the end of 1972 FDA had banned more than 800 toys.

Cigarette Advertising

The House and Senate in 1969 passed differing versions of a bill (HR 6543) regulating cigarette advertisement. However, the bill was not sent to conference until 1970. *(1970 chronology, p. 671)*

The Senate measure, passed Dec. 12, banned cigarette advertising on radio and television and strengthened the warning on cigarette packages. The House version, passed June 18, contained no reference to advertising of cigarettes on radio and television and provided for a weaker label warning.

The Senate bill prohibited the Federal Trade Commission (FTC) from regulating cigarette advertising only until July 1, 1971. However the House measure extended for six years a clause (which expired June 30, 1969) in the Cigarette Labeling and Advertising Act of 1965 prohibiting federal agencies from requiring any health warning in cigarette advertising.

The FTC and the Federal Communications Commission (FCC) throughout the year announced plans to impose new restrictions on cigarette advertising but delayed such regulations pending the outcome of the legislation.

BACKGROUND

In January 1964, the U.S. Surgeon General's Advisory Committee on Smoking and Health reported a probable relationship between smoking and certain diseases, such as lung cancer, chronic bronchitis, emphysema and coronary artery disease. The first government agency to act was FTC; it ruled in June 1964 that cigarette packages and advertising had to contain a health warning as of July 1, 1965. But the FTC postponed implementation of its ruling when Congress indicated its intention to consider legislation.

The Cigarette Act was signed into law July 27, 1965. It required a health warning on cigarette packages which read: "Caution: Cigarette Smoking May be Hazardous to your Health." But the legislation nullified the FTC's proposed restrictions by prohibiting local, state or federal agencies from requiring similar health warnings in cigarette advertising or from imposing a health labeling requirement beyond what was contained in the bill (preemption clause).

No further legislation affecting cigarette labeling or advertising was enacted from 1966 through 1968, although several bills were offered that would have imposed warning requirements in cigarette advertising and a listing of tar and nicotine contents on packages.

Periodic reports were issued, as required by the 1965 Act, by the Department of Health, Education and Welfare (HEW) on the consequences of smoking and by the FTC on the effectiveness of the package label. HEW cited more statistics to establish that cigarette smoking does cause certain diseases. The FTC continued to recommend that Congress require warnings in advertising.

While the preemption clause restricted the FTC and the FCC from requiring health warnings, it did not affect any other powers of the commissions. The FCC, therefore, was able in 1967 to order radio and television stations to allow time for antismoking advertisements, and the FTC continued to watch cigarette advertising for false or misleading claims. *(Background, Congress and the Nation Vol. II, p. 675, 694, 703)*

1969 Developments. The FCC Feb. 5, 1969, proposed rules to prohibit the broadcasting of cigarette advertising on radio and television. The action was taken, the commission said, because federal studies had shown a "serious, unique danger to public health" from smoking. FCC Chairman Rosel H. Hyde said the FCC wanted to advise Congress of the agency's plans in "the absence of a contrary congressional direction."

The FTC March 7 reported that new laboratory tests had shown increases of "statistical significance" in the tar and nicotine content of many cigarettes. The FTC said 32 cigarette varieties had increased in tar content and 78 in nicotine content between October 1968 and February 1969, while decreases occurred in the tar content of 14 varieties and in the nicotine content of only one.

Sen. Frank E. Moss (D Utah) said the test held the "sinister" implication that cigarette companies might be attempting to increase the addictive power of their product by raising nicotine content. The Tobacco Institute, a spokesman for the tobacco industry, denied Moss's suggestion, saying that deficiencies in FTC testing procedures or normal crop variation could account for the increases.

HEW Secretary Robert H. Finch announced April 25 that representatives of the department and the tobacco industry were developing a cooperative research program on tobacco and health.

The FTC May 20 proposed that all cigarette advertising carry warnings of health hazards from smoking. The warning would read: "Cigarette smoking is dangerous to health and may cause death from cancer, bronchitis, pulmonary emphysema and other diseases."

The House, moving to head off the FTC and FCC plans while placating the antismoking forces, June 18 passed a bill (HR 6543) toughening the wording of the existing health warning required on cigarette packages but continuing the prohibition against any other regulation of cigarette advertising by federal and state agencies. *(Legislative history, below)*

The FTC on July 1—one day after the restriction ban expired—held hearings on its proposal to require all cigarette advertising to carry a health warning.

The first witness, Surgeon General William H. Stewart, said it was "indefensible" that cigarettes were advertised "in a context of happiness, vigor, success and well-being without even a hint appearing anywhere that the product may also lead to disease and death."

Stewart noted the argument that the proposed FTC warning would drive cigarette advertising off radio and television. "If this is so—if the truth about a product cannot be told—then I think it perfectly clear there should be no advertising," he said.

In opening the hearings, FTC Chairman Paul Rand Dixon said the commission would hold up final action on the regulation until Congress had expressed its will.

In a radio interview July 27, Moss urged the Nixon administration to cut off tobacco farm price supports and to stop advertising U.S. cigarettes abroad. Moss also said he opposed the House-passed measure to extend a ban on federal regulation of cigarette advertising, despite the industry's announcement that it would stop all radio and TV advertising by September 1970.

The Public Health Service (PHS) July 28 released a report presenting new evidence that cigarette smoking was bad for the heart, lungs and mouth and for the unborn babies of pregnant women who smoke.

HOUSE ACTION

The House Interstate and Foreign Commerce Committee June 5 reported HR 6543 by a 22-5 vote. The bill strengthened the warning on cigarette labels and extended for six years a provision of the 1965 Federal Cigarette Labeling and Advertising Act (PL 89-92) which prevented federal regulatory agencies from making further restrictions on cigarette advertising. That provision was set to expire June 30.

The warning adopted by the committee read: "Warning: The Surgeon General has Determined that Cigarette Smoking is Dangerous to your Health and may Cause Lung Cancer and Other Diseases." The effect of the bill as reported was to nullify FCC and FTC proposals which included strengthening the warning to add the phrase "may cause death" and banning all cigarette advertising on radio and television.

The Commerce Committee June 10 held an unusual additional day of hearings after the reported HR 6543 had been challenged on the grounds that the broadcasting industry might have misled Congress concerning the industry's self-regulating process.

Warren Braren, who was manager of the National Association of Broadcasters (NAB) Advertising Code Authority in New York City until May 1, charged at the hearing that the NAB's television and radio code authority had a history of failure in controlling cigarette commercials with appeals to young people. This assertion contradicted testimony given at committee hearings April 21 by Vincent T. Wasilewski, who told the committee then that the industry's codes on cigarettes "were designed to prohibit any advertising of cigarettes in such a manner as to indicate to youth that the use of cigarettes contributes to individual achievement or social acceptance."

Braren charged that the NAB Code Authority virtually abandoned review of cigarette commercials, in April of 1969. He said the strategy of the industry had been "to avoid meaningful self-regulatory action as long as the possibility exists that Congress will enact legislation favorable to the broadcasting and tobacco industries." At a June 8 meeting with newsmen in the office of Rep. Brock Adams (D Wash.), Braren said that the broadcasting industry stopped enforcing its own cigarette guidelines in April because of pressure from cigarette companies and the broadcast industry.

Rep. Harley O. Staggers (D W.Va.), chairman of the committee, said that the bill was approved partly because Wasilewski had assured the members that the NAB was doing its own policing of cigarette commercials.

At the June 10 hearing, Wasilewski told Staggers that he had told the truth at the April hearings and that the self-regulatory efforts of the NAB were effective in dealing with the cigarette advertising issue.

FLOOR ACTION. The House rejected all efforts to place curbs on cigarette advertising, passing HR 6543 as reported by voice vote on June 18. A motion to recommit the bill failed on a 138-25 roll-call vote.

Repeated attempts by anti-cigarette members to require advertising warnings or to permit regulatory agencies to act on advertising were defeated. Rep. John

E. Moss (D Calif.), who led the fight for advertising curbs, described the House action as a "disgraceful performance" which served the tobacco industry rather than the public interest.

Passage of the bill without the restrictions was a victory for tobacco-state representatives and other members opposed to what they called usurpation of congressional authority by federal regulatory agencies.

Rep. Bob Eckhardt (D Texas) argued that nothing in the bill prevented the FCC from going ahead with its ban since the language of HR 6543 related only to health warnings. Supporters of the bill countered that the FCC understood the intent of Congress that it should not act.

Eckhardt offered an amendment specifically prohibiting the FCC from banning commercials to show, he said, congressional intent. The amendment was defeated, both by the votes of the supporters and opponents of the bill.

Shorter Term. Anti-cigarette members, led by Moss and Adams, tried to convince House members to shorten to three years the period during which federal regulatory agencies were prohibited from requiring warnings in cigarette advertising. Moss said that during his 13 years on the Interstate and Foreign Commerce Committee, it had always been the custom to require termination of legislation in three years so that Congress could review its actions.

If HR 6543 was a bill to serve the public interest, Moss said, a three-year period should be set for its provisions. Otherwise the legislation could be viewed as an industry protection bill, he said.

An amendment offered by Rep. Robert O. Tiernan (D R.I.) to extend the preemption clause until 1972 rather than 1975 as the bill provided was defeated by the closest vote of the day—an 87-114 teller vote.

Other key amendments which were rejected included proposals by Moss and Adams to require health warnings in advertising or to free the FTC to require such warnings and to require a listing on packages of the tar and nicotine content of the cigarettes.

Three Arguments. Consideration of the bill ran for two days during which supporters of the legislation argued for passage on three main grounds: that advertising restrictions would harm the cigarette industry and destroy the livelihood of thousands of tobacco farmers; that federal regulatory agencies should not be allowed to usurp the power of Congress; and that neither Congress nor the regulatory agencies had the right to discriminate against one product which was legally produced and sold.

In opening the debate June 17, Staggers said it was important that the House itself act on cigarette labeling and advertising and "not abrogate its responsibility" by letting the regulatory agencies move into a vacuum created by Congress. The FTC and FCC had assumed policy-making roles, Staggers said, which Congress never intended them to have.

Anti-Cigarette Bloc. The anti-cigarette bloc on the House floor remained small during the debate. On standing votes, they were never able to command more than about 40 votes. Moss said the amendments they offered were mainly aimed at protecting young people who had not yet begun to smoke but were subject to powerful inducements to smoking via television advertising of cigarettes.

When Moss offered an amendment to require the package warning in advertising as well, he said that "lit-

erally thousands" of radio and television commercials every day brought cigarette smoking forcefully to the attention of young men and women who had not yet started to smoke. "Is the warning label," he asked, "designed only to protect the industry against liability or to protect the American public?"

Rep. Albert W. Watson (R S.C.) countered that no other legal product was required to label itself as dangerous. Even if cigarettes did cause health problems, Watson said, the individual who smoked harmed only himself. Products like automobiles were dangerous to many people, he said.

"Let's be practical," Watson said. If Congress required warnings in advertising, he said, it would be forcing the industry to spend more time degrading its product than trying to sell it. The effect would be, Watson added, to bar advertising of any cigarettes. Besides, Watson said, the amendment was not necessary. "We could shout from the rooftops that smoking is harmful and we would not be telling anyone anything that they did not know."

PROVISIONS. In addition to strengthening the warning on cigarette labels and extending for six years the restriction prohibiting local, state or federal agencies from requiring any health warning in cigarette advertising, HR 6543, as passed by the House, also provided that nothing in the bill apart from the preemption clause limited or restricted the authority of the FTC to regulate unfair practices in cigarette advertising. The bill also required a report from the HEW secretary within 18 months of enactment of the bill and annually thereafter on the health consequences of smoking and a similar report from the FTC on the effectiveness of cigarette labeling and current cigarette advertising practices.

SENATE ACTION

The Senate Commerce Committee July 22 held a hearing on HR 6543.

Paul Rand Dixon, chairman of the FTC, said his agency would suspend—at least until July 1971, its attempt to require a strict health warning in all cigarette advertising including publications if broadcast advertising stopped by September 1970. Dixon said that if broadcast advertising were discontinued, "the principal form of promotion would have been eliminated."

But he attached two conditions to the FTC's willingness to suspend its efforts to require health warnings. First, he said that the FTC did not want to see cigarette makers switch their TV advertising budget to newspapers and magazines. Second, he said that broadcasters should continue to air antismoking messages.

Dixon also argued that his agency needed standby powers in case the promised voluntary withdrawal of broadcast advertising was not carried out. He said that after a two-year interval the commission would examine the situation and report to Congress.

Vincent T. Wasilewski, president of the NAB, contended that the sudden shut-off of cigarette advertising money, which constituted 10 per cent of broadcasters' advertising revenue, would cause "economic disruption and chaotic conditions in the broadcasting industry." If cigarette advertisements were banned from one medium, he said, they should be banned from all.

Wasilewski told the subcommittee that it would be "somewhat unfair" for the tobacco companies to try to cancel their advertising contracts nine months before the termination date of September 1970.

The Commerce Committee Dec. 5 reported a version of HR 6543 that was far stronger than the House-passed measure. The bill made it unlawful to advertise cigarettes on radio and television as of Jan. 1, 1971, and changed the mandatory wording on cigarette packages to read: "Warning: Excessive Cigarette Smoking is Dangerous to your Health." The bill also prohibited health-related regulation or prohibition of cigarette advertising by any state or local authority and prohibited FTC regulation of printed cigarette advertising for 18 months after the end of broadcast advertising.

Nine committee members joined in objecting to the provision barring the FTC from regulating cigarette advertising. If the FTC was barred from requiring a warning in advertising, the nine senators wrote, "the public would have no meaningful defense, even against a massive onslaught of print advertising employing themes designed to obscure the medical verdict against cigarette smoking and designed to make cigarette smoking appealing to young people."

In addition, the dissenting senators objected to the use of the word "excessive" in the committee's version of the package warning. "Smoking is dangerous in normal use," the senators contended, calling the committee warning "a misleading half-truth."

FLOOR ACTION. By a roll-call vote of 70-7 the Senate Dec. 12 passed and sent to conference a bill (HR 6543) to ban cigarette commercials on radio and television by Jan. 1, 1971.

Frank E. Moss (D Utah), a leader of Senate antismoking forces, successfully offered two amendments. One strengthened the proposed package warning to read: "Warning: Cigarette Smoking Is Dangerous To Your Health." The Commerce Committee-approved language had said: "Excessive Smoking Is Dangerous To Your Health." Moss protested that the committee language would imply that moderate smoking was not harmful. His amendment to delete "excessive" was adopted, 38-35.

The Senate also accepted, by voice vote, an amendment, introduced by Moss and modified by Norris Cotton (R N.H.), to delete the committee provision which would have prevented the FTC from requiring health warnings in printed advertisements until 18 months after the broadcast ban went into effect. As modified, the amendment allowed the FTC to require warnings in newspapers, magazines or billboards after July 1, 1971, but specified that the regulatory agency could act sooner if it determined that cigarette advertising practices constituted "a gross abuse" of the nonbroadcast media. Under the amendment, the FTC would be required to notify Congress six months before acting. This would mean that Congress was "the last judge of what constitutes 'gross abuse'," Cotton said.

Sam J. Ervin Jr. (D N.C.) opposed the bill and the Moss amendments, asserting that there was "no evidence of any clinical character and no proof based on research of any causal relationship between smoking and lung cancer, or emphysema or heart disease. The whole case," Ervin said, "is based on statistics collected in unreliable ways."

The House-Senate conference on HR 6543 occurred in 1970. *(1970 chronology, p. 671)*

Lobbying Campaign

In 1964 the tobacco industry, in anticipation of the surgeon general's report and the FTC regulations, chose former Rep. and Sen. Earle C. Clements (D Ky.) to supervise its lobbying activities. Clements became president of the Tobacco Institute, which represented the major cigarette producers in the country.

At the same time, the tobacco companies announced that beginning in January 1965 their advertising would be controlled by a voluntary cigarette advertising code. Moreover, the broadcast networks agreed to prohibit appeals to young smokers.

The industry's strategy for 1969 was to emphasize arguments similar to those of 1965: that the health charges against cigarette smoking had not been scientifically established and that federal regulatory agencies had no authority to impose more stringent restrictions.

In early 1969, the Tobacco Institute appointed former Rep. Horace R. Kornegay (D N.C.) to its staff. Kornegay, a member of the House Interstate and Foreign Commerce Committee during the 1965 antismoking debate, had retired from Congress after the 1968 session.

The Tobacco Institute began a six-week advertising campaign in February 1969 aimed at challenging the health charges against cigarette smoking. It purchased full-page advertisements in large newspapers to contend that a causal relationship between smoking and disease had not been proved.

The broadcast industry was also interested in the 1969 legislation, since expiration of the preemption clause could permit the FCC to ban advertising.

The effect of such a restriction was clear. A 1968 report of the National Clearinghouse for Smoking and Health showed cigarettes to be the number-one product advertised on television. Television revenue from cigarette advertising in 1966, the report stated, was $194.1-million, leading the second product (automobiles) by $65.3-million. Cigarette advertising on both radio and television in recent years had been about $226.9-million, representing about 10 per cent of network revenues.

During House consideration of HR 6543, the Americans for Democratic Action (ADA) wrote the representatives that the bill would prevent effective regulation of cigarette advertising and "...put the federal government into the position of promoting lung cancer and other diseases caused by cigarette smoking." The ADA urged defeat of the bill, leaving regulation of cigarette advertising to the FTC and FCC.

LASH (Legislative Action on Smoking and Health) placed an advertisement in Washington newspapers calling HR 6543 "ludicrous...if not downright biased."

"Gentlemen, no one wants to see any unnecessary or unreasonable infringement of the selling of wares in a free enterprise system," the advertisement read. "But next time you're in your own home town, visit the cancer ward in your local hospital and tell those patients how you voted. And why."

Auto, Tire Safety

The House and Senate in 1969 passed different versions of a bill (HR 10105) extending the National Traffic and Motor Vehicle Safety Act of 1966 (PL 89-563), but final action did not come until May 1970. *(1970 chronology, p. 672)*

Included in HR 10105 were provisions requiring manufacturers of auto tires to notify purchasers by certified mail of safety-related tire defects.

The 1966 act had authorized $51-million over a three-year period for implementing federal auto safety standards, $5.8-million for implementing tire safety standards and $3-million for study of the need for a federal research and testing facility.

Background. Under the National Traffic and Motor Vehicle Safety Act of 1966 (PL 89-563), automobile companies were required to recall defective cars. More than 12 million cars had been recalled by mid-1969. But tire manufacturers were not subject to a similar requirement.

Government tests by the National Highway Safety Bureau in 1969 disclosed that 18 per cent of the tires tested for compliance with the minimum tire safety standards failed one or more of the tests. *(Congress and the Nation Vol. II, p. 782, 804)*

Authorizations for appropriations to carry out the auto and tire safety provisions of the 1966 act expired June 30, 1969. As introduced, HR 10105, the administration bill, provided for a two-year extension of authorizations, and expanded the 1966 act to include $10-million in authorizations for safety research and a broader definition of "motor vehicle equipment." Another bill, HR 11092, required the manufacturers of defective auto tires to notify purchasers of defective tires.

In March 1969 the Department of Transportation asked two U.S. tire companies to show cause why they should not be penalized for apparent violations of PL 89-563 based on the government tests. This was the government's first such action since federal auto and tire safety laws were enacted in 1966. Under the law, violators of tire standards could be subjected to civil penalties of up to $1,000 for each violation, or a maximum of $400,000 for a related series of violations.

House Action. As reported by the House Interstate and Foreign Commerce Committee July 8, HR 10105 was amended to extend authorizations for three years and to incorporate the tire notification requirement of HR 11092.

The House Sept. 3 by a 322-0 roll-call vote passed HR 10105 after adopting by voice vote two amendments offered on the floor. The first was a committee amendment authorizing the secretary of transportation to set a limit on the age of tire carcasses that could be retreaded and resold; the second amendment authorized the secretary of transportation to prepare a report on farm tractor accidents.

Major provisions of HR 10105, as passed by the House, authorized appropriations of $23-million in fiscal 1970, and $35-million in each of fiscal 1971 and 1972 to carry out the auto and tire safety provisions of the National Traffic and Motor Vehicle Safety Act of 1966; required manufacturers of motor vehicles to notify purchasers and prospective buyers of performance and technical data as deemed necessary by the secretary of

transportation; and required manufacturers of tires to notify purchasers by certified mail of safety-related tire defects.

HR 10105 also authorized the secretary to plan facilities for testing in traffic safety and to establish national standards for protective headgear although the secretary was not authorized to require the use of such equipment.

Senate Action. The Senate Commerce Committee reported HR 10105 with several amendments Nov. 25. Major changes from the House-passed version included reducing the three-year authorization to two years ($23-million in fiscal 1970 and $40-million in fiscal 1971) and extending the authority of the transportation secretary to set minimum federal standards for all safety equipment intended to protect highway users rather than limiting the authority to helmets and headgear.

The bill, as reported, also required that manufacturers of motor vehicles and equipment remedy defects free of charge.

The Senate by voice vote passed HR 10105 Dec. 2 after accepting the committee amendments, also by voice vote.

Consumer Reorganization

Momentum appeared to be building in 1969 for a major reorganization of the federal machinery for protecting the American consumer. Although no reorganization legislation was enacted in 1969, hearings on a variety of proposals set the stage for enactment in 1972 of a bill creating a consumer product safety agency and for the drive to create an independent agency to represent consumer interests before other federal agencies and courts.

Major proposals under consideration in 1969 included:

Consumer Department. Sen. Gaylord Nelson (D Wis.) and Rep. Benjamin S. Rosenthal (D N.Y.) Feb. 4 introduced identical bills (S 860, HR 6037) to establish a cabinet-level Department of Consumer Affairs. The proposal was first introduced in 1959 by the late Sen. Estes Kefauver (D Tenn. 1949-63) and was the subject of House hearings in 1966. The Nelson-Rosenthal bills had nearly 100 cosponsors. Major provisions of the bills would:

• Transfer into the new department existing agencies which currently dealt with cost-of-living statistics, home economics research, nutrition research and enforcement of the Fair Packaging and Labeling Act.

• Create an Office of Consumer Counsel to represent public interests before regulatory agencies, federal departments and courts.

• Establish an Office of Consumer Safety to make a continuing study of measures designed to protect consumers from hazardous household products.

During hearings on the bills, Virginia H. Knauer, special assistant to the President for consumer affairs, told a Senate subcommittee July 15 that a cabinet-level department would be premature. Other witnesses said a consumer affairs department was necessary because the government was not adequately responsive to the needs of consumers.

Dwyer-Sullivan Bill. Rep. Florence P. Dwyer (R N.J.), ranking Republican on the House Government Operations Committee, Sept. 23 introduced a bill (HR 13947) to establish a permanent Office of Consumer Affairs in the White House. The bill also gave the office the right to represent consumer interests before federal agencies. Dwyer's bill was cosponsored by Rep. Leonor K. Sullivan (D Mo.), a strong defender of consumer interests. The measure was introduced in the Senate (S 3097) by Charles H. Percy (R Ill.) on Oct. 30, the day of Nixon's consumer message.

Nixon Administration Bill. Dwyer Nov. 12 introduced the administration bill (HR 14758) to establish a statutory Office of Consumer Affairs in the Executive Office of the President. The bill also called for creation of a consumer protection division in the Justice Department with authority to represent consumer interests before other federal agencies. Nixon had outlined the proposal in his Oct. 30 consumer message. In the Johnson administration a consumer counsel existed briefly in the Justice Department, but Nixon did not fill the position when he took office.

Consumer Council. Sens. Frank E. Moss (D Utah) and Philip A. Hart (D Mich.) Sept. 25 introduced a bill (S 2959) establishing an independent consumer council, a nongovernmental organization to represent the consumer before other federal agencies.

Class Action Suits

The Senate Commerce Consumer Subcommittee held hearings in December on three related bills designed to give full legal recognition in federal courts to consumers as a class and to protect consumers from fraudulent or deceptive practices. No further action was taken.

In closing the hearings Dec. 17, chairman Frank E. Moss (D Utah) said the areas of the administration bill most criticized by witnesses were: the role of the Federal Trade Commission in relation to the Justice Department, the narrow definition of unfair and deceptive business practices and the restrictions on initiations of private remedies.

Auto Insurance, Repair Costs

The Senate Judiciary Subcommittee on Antitrust and Monopoly continued hearings on the automobile insurance industry and on automobile repair costs. Previous hearings were held during the 90th Congress.

Background. In response to complaints made by the American driving public of allegedly "unfair and arbitrary" insurance company practices, Congress in 1967 set the stage for several full-scale investigations into the insurance industry.

Critics of the automobile insurance system had charged that it was unduly cumbersome and expensive, practiced discrimination against certain drivers because of race, age or place of residence, and frequently was unfair in awarding judgments. Another concern was that the states were unable to regulate the industry, and many critics advocated "total, full and complete federal regulation." Congress in 1945 exempted insurance companies from federal antitrust laws and left regulation of them to the states. *(Congress and the Nation Vol. I, p. 454)*

The companies, on the other hand, were requesting additional rate increases and were refusing to insure a growing number of people they deemed to be poor risks. They also claimed they were losing money, although figures introduced at subcommittee hearings, in June 1968, showed that in 1967 the 10 largest stock property

---

Insurance Costs vs. Benefits

An analysis prepared by the Senate Antitrust and Monopoly Subcommittee for the hearings on automobile insurance showed that in the 1959-69 decade, motorists paid premiums totaling $81.5-billion and received less than 60 per cent of that sum in benefits. Of the $33.8-billion difference between the pay-in and the pay-out, lawyers' fees accounted for $10-billion, or almost one-third.

The staff study revealed that $47.7-billion was disbursed to claimants as net benefits, $33-billion went for expenses and $800-million was underwriting profit after taxes. Investments of the $81.5-billion yielded an additional after-tax profit of $3.2-billion.

Of the $47.7-billion in net benefits, $5-billion or nearly 10 per cent went to claimants' lawyers. Of the $33-billion in expenses, $5-billion—or 15 per cent—went to defense lawyers.

Since 1959, the study reported, 1,200 firms, selling all kinds of insurance, had average after-tax earnings of 10.5 per cent. This, the exhibit said, was 0.3 per cent less than that of the nation's 50 largest banks, 0.7 per cent more than that of the 50 largest public utilities, and 1.5 per cent less than that of the 500 largest industrial corporations.

The insurance industry figures showed that in the period 1955-1968 property and liability insurance earned 3.7 per cent, a rate "substantially below a standard prescribed by 59 other major industry sectors."

---

and casualty companies made a profit of $55-million. These figures did not include $1.7-billion net income from investment. The subcommittee also was told that insurance companies were earning greater rates of profit than 90 per cent of some 640 leading American corporations.

Congressional action began on July 25, 1967, when Emanuel Celler (D N.Y.), chairman of the House Judiciary Committee, asked a Judiciary subcommittee to prepare a study of the auto insurance industry. The 183-page report released Oct. 24, 1967, was a clear indictment of the industry. The report led to an announcement by Sen. Philip A. Hart (D Mich.), chairman of the Senate Judiciary Antitrust and Monopoly Subcommittee, that his subcommittee would hold hearings on auto insurance problems. Hearings began in 1968. *(Congress and the Nation Vol. II, p. 805, 820)*

Auto Insurance Hearings. Hart's auto insurance industry hearings, continued in February and March 1969, covered a wide range of problems in the industry. A spokesman for the National Association of Insurance Commissioners cited three external problems which had a fundamental impact on the cost and operation of the insurance system: traffic safety, the economic climate and the liability system upon which the system rested. Several other witnesses proposed tighter automobile licensing laws, more comprehensive and uniform safety regulations, improvement of road conditions and better automobile construction to cut down on the costs of auto repairs.

Auto Repairs Hearings. Hart's subcommittee in April and October held hearings on the high cost of auto repairs. The hearings grew out of the subcommittee's investigation of auto insurance; three days of hearings were held in December 1968.

During the 1969 hearings, a spokesman for the National Association of Independent Insurers said that super-powered cars, increases in the cost of automobile repair parts, increases in repair garage charges and the extreme vulnerability of automobiles to costly damage in even low-speed collisions were the major underlying reasons for the inflation in automobile damage losses.

An American Mutual Insurance Alliance spokesman said that high auto repair costs could be lowered by reducing the number of accidents, changing auto design to make cars less vulnerable to damage and developing cheaper methods of repairing auto damage including changing auto design, standardization of parts and improved garage efficiency.

Insurance Company Insolvency. The Senate Commerce Committee held hearings in November on a bill to create a Federal Insurance Guaranty Corporation to protect customers from insolvency of certain insurance companies, but took no further action. Under the bill the corporation would be patterned after the Federal Deposit Insurance Corporation (FDIC).

The corporation would have the power to regulate property and casualty insurance companies and would be authorized to examine applicable insurance companies and require them to report on their financial condition. It also would assume the liability for insurance obligations of an insolvent company.

Consumer Credit Bills

FAIR CREDIT REPORTING. A bill (S 823)—the Fair Credit Reporting Act—to allow persons to look into and to challenge or correct their credit dossiers was passed by the Senate Nov. 6. The House did not act on the bill in 1969. *(Final action, 1970 chronology, p. 673)*

The bill was introduced by Sen. William Proxmire (D Wis.), chairman of the Senate Banking and Currency Subcommittee on Financial Institutions, and nine cosponsors. S 823, which would amend the Truth-in-Lending Act (PL 90-321), was supported by the administration.

During the May hearings on the bill, Proxmire said that although consumer credit and the insurance industry were subject to state and federal regulation to protect the consumer, credit reporting agencies had no public supervision. Proxmire said that the trend toward use of computers could result in creation of a gigantic national data bank including extremely personal information on everybody. He added that existing law provided no public safeguards against such a system.

The Senate Nov. 6 passed the bill as reported by the Banking and Currency Committee Nov. 5 by voice vote.

Major Provisions. As passed, S 823:

• Limited the furnishing of credit reports to purposes of credit, insurance, employment, obtaining a governmental license, or other legitimate business need involving a business transaction with the consumer; prohibited reporting of adverse information from investigative reports which was more than three months old unless the information was reverified; prohibited the reporting of most adverse information older than seven years, or 14 years in the case of bankruptcies.

• Required reporting agencies to restrict disclosure of information to authorized recipients, to disclose upon request all information in the consumer's file to the consumer, the source of the information and all persons who received the information during the past six months or two years for employment purposes and to reinvestigate and delete disputed information.

• Required those who order reports to notify the consumer that an investigative report was being made; required those who reject a consumer for credit to advise the consumer and identify the reporting agency.

Federal Reserve Board Regulations. Regulations to carry out the 1968 Truth-in-Lending Act were published by the Federal Reserve Board Feb. 7 and went into effect July 1. The rules, formally known as Regulation Z, required businesses offering credit to explain clearly the terms of that credit to their customers.

CREDIT UNION AGENCY. The House July 28 passed a bill (HR 2) to establish an independent National Credit Union Administration to supervise federally chartered credit unions. The administration would replace the existing Bureau of Federal Credit Unions, an arm of the Social Security Administration. The House passed the bill without amendment by a 357-10 roll-call vote.

HR 2 was reported in the Senate Nov. 5 by the Banking and Currency Committee, but did not reach the Senate floor in 1969. The Nixon administration opposed the measure. HR 2 was enacted in 1970. *(1970 chronology, p. 673)*

CREDIT CARD PROBLEMS. Senate and House subcommittees held hearings late in the year on the problems of unsolicited credit cards but neither subcommittee took further action. Legislation restricting the issuance of unsolicited credit cards was enacted in 1970. *(1970 chronology, p. 672)*

Truth in Packaging

In 1969, three years after enactment of the landmark truth-in-packaging law, the federal government moved toward oversight of the act's effectiveness. Meanwhile, a House subcommittee held hearings on the effectiveness of the legislation.

The law—the Fair Packaging and Labeling Act of 1966 (PL 89-755)—authorized the Food and Drug Administration (FDA) and the Federal Trade Commission (FTC) to establish standards and regulations for package information and identification. The FDA was to handle most foods, drugs and cosmetics, and the FTC was responsible for other household commodities, generally kitchen and bathroom items. *(Congress and the Nation Vol. II, p. 792)*

The House Government Operations Subcommittee on Special Studies held three days of oversight hearings June 3-5 on the truth-in-packaging act.

Subcommittee Chairman Benjamin S. Rosenthal (D N.Y.), in opening remarks, said that available information suggested that three years after enactment of the Fair Packaging and Labeling Act, consumers were still confronted with packages which concealed content shrinkage and with food labels which failed to provide accurate information as to contents.

Hot Dog Contents. Rosenthal also said that while the Department of Agriculture was proposing a higher allowable percentage of fat content in hot dogs, it was encouraging their increased use in the school lunch program. "They are really being party to harming the health of American children who are supposed to be the beneficiaries of the program," he said.

The Agriculture Department had pending a proposal of a fat content limitation requirement for sausage products higher than an earlier proposal which was not acceptable to the meat industry. The department proposed in December 1968 to limit fat contents to 30 per cent. The limitation was changed in April 1969 to 33 per cent and also included a proposal not to disclose the fat content percentage on the label.

Virginia H. Knauer, special assistant to the President for consumer affairs, and Edward Berlin, general counsel for the Consumer Federation of America, both told the subcommittee they opposed the 33 per cent limitation proposal. In subsequent action, the Agriculture Department revised its proposal, setting a 30 per cent limit on the fat content in hot dogs, effective Oct. 16.

FDA Consumer Report

A study panel of the Food and Drug Administration (FDA) concluded in 1969 that the agency was not equipped to protect the American consumer from bad food, bad drugs, bad cosmetics or faulty products. The evaluation was contained in a 58-page confidential report on FDA objectives and programs. A House subcommittee held hearings on the report in August and September.

The internal assessment of the FDA was made public Aug. 11 after United Press International obtained a copy of the report and broke the story Aug. 8. The previously secret document, prepared by a seven-member study panel of FDA officials at the request of FDA Commissioner Herbert L. Ley Jr., had been completed July 14.

In an introduction to the report sent to Ley, the panel said: "The American public's principal consumer protection is provided by the Food and Drug Administration, and we are currently not equipped to cope with the challenge."

Ley set up the panel May 1, asking it to define the consumer protection objectives of the FDA, identify its shortcomings and suggest changes. Its official title was the Study Group on Food and Drug Administration Consumer Protection Objectives and Programs. Ley told the panel to approach the task "without regard to the present restraints of law, budget, personnel or facilities."

"We want to know first what we should be doing for the people of this country; later we will see how much of what should be done is practical...," Ley said in a memorandum to the panel.

In its report, the study group said the FDA had been limited by legislation, manpower and money and as a result had been unable to deal adequately with the problems of pesticide residues, food sanitation, chemical additives, microbiological contamination, drug and device safety and efficacy, hazardous household products, medicated animal feeds and many other problems.

"There is a fairly common view held by consumers that 'they' (the consumer isn't really sure who) are taking care of all potential hazards associated with the products he ingests and uses," the report said.

"This misconception should be dispelled to the greatest extent possible. The consumer must be exposed to the

---

Cyclamate Ban

Secretary of Health, Education and Welfare Robert H. Finch ordered a ban on the sale of all beverages containing cyclamates, an artificial sweetener, after Jan. 1, 1970. The original order, issued Oct. 18, also applied to general purpose foods, but Finch Nov. 20 eased the ban to permit marketing of foods containing cyclamates provided they were labeled to show the cyclamate content in an average serving. He also allowed the use of cyclamates in tablet or liquid form. The action followed pressure from weight-watchers and diabetics.

The Oct. 18 order was based on reports of a high incidence of cancer in rats that were fed large daily doses of cyclamates. The action was taken under the 1958 Delaney amendments to the Food, Drug and Cosmetic Act of 1938. The Delaney amendments required the removal from the market of any food additive shown to cause cancer when fed to humans or animals. *(Congress and the Nation, Vol. I, p. 1176)*

Finch and Food and Drug Administration Commissioner Herbert L. Ley Jr. stressed that there was no evidence to indicate that cyclamates had caused tumors or malformations in humans.

---

realities of what FDA can and cannot do both from the standpoint of legal authority and resources allocation."

The officials said the problem facing the FDA could be stated simply: "Increasing volume and sophistication in types, production and marketing of consumer goods under our jurisdiction has outstripped our ability to assure the public that all is well...."

The industries regulated by the FDA had annual sales of more than $130-billion, with some 60,000 companies involved. The agency budget for fiscal 1970 was $72-million and provided for about 4,500 employees.

Hearings. The House Interstate and Foreign Commerce Subcommittee on Public Health and Welfare held hearings in August and September on the FDA report. During testimony Sept. 12, Ley called the report "a very thoughtful document." Ley said the FDA was developing minimum standards to serve as guidelines for drug companies. In the area of food, he said the agency did not have the authority to require the type of reports required of drug manufacturers. And, Ley said, some types of reporting on harmful or ineffective drugs, such as physicians' reports of adverse effects, were poor.

In other testimony, Maurice D. Kinslow, director of the Baltimore FDA district and chairman of the study group, said the agency spent about 44 per cent of its manpower on drugs, 35 per cent on food and the remainder on cosmetics, medical devices and other consumer products.

Reorganization. Secretary of Health, Education and Welfare Robert H. Finch Dec. 10 announced an extensive reorganization of FDA, beginning with Ley's ouster. Dr. Charles C. Edwards, a former surgeon and management expert, was named to replace Ley. Finch also announced that the agency would be made independent of the Consumer Protection and Environmental Health Service and reorganized into product-related bureaus, instead of functional ones.

FTC Under Fire

The Federal Trade Commission (FTC), an agency with broad antitrust and consumer-protection powers, came under increasing criticism in 1969. The year began with publication of a highly critical report on the FTC, prepared by law students associated with consumer advocate Ralph Nader. Later in the year, further criticism was voiced in a report prepared by the American Bar Association at the request of President Nixon.

The FTC also was the subject of September hearings before the Senate Judiciary Subcommittee on Administrative Practice and Procedure.

Nader Report. Seven students from Harvard and Yale Law Schools who spent three months during 1968 investigating the FTC Jan. 5 issued a report highly critical of the commission and its chairman, Paul Rand Dixon. The students, organized by Nader, said that "alcoholism, spectacular lassitude and office absenteeism, imcompetence by the most modest standards and lack of commitment to their regulatory missions are rampant" at high levels within the FTC. *(Nader profile, p. 699)*

Specifically, the student report stated that the FTC shied away from investigating large industries and was preoccupied with trivia.

Dixon Jan. 9 said that the student investigators used "invective and smear" in criticizing the FTC. He said that the report emanated from "a group with a self-granted license to criticize a respected government agency by the use of a type of invective and 'smear technique' that newspapermen inform me is unusual even for Washington."

ABA. A panel of lawyers and economists Sept. 15 called the FTC "a failure on many counts." The study group was organized in May 1969, by the American Bar Association (ABA) at the request of the President.

The 16-member study group said that the FTC had been preoccupied with trivial matters, such as the technicalities of labeling practices. The group blamed misallocation of priorities on the commission's leadership and said there were "too many instances of incompetence in the agency, particularly in senior staff positions."

The ABA group urged that the FTC concentrate more effort on retail consumer fraud; also, that pilot programs be established in major cities to detect and attack local frauds against consumers and to identify areas of consumer concern.

Hearings. The Senate Judiciary Subcommittee on Administrative Practice and Procedure heard testimony Sept. 12 and 16 from five FTC commissioners on the question of agency responsiveness to the public's needs.

Dixon Sept. 12 told the subcommittee that the FTC would be more able to enforce the many consumer protection acts for which it had jurisdiction if Congress would appropriate enough money for an adequate staff. Dixon vigorously defended his selection of top commission officials against charges that the appointments were politically inspired. Those allegations were made by another commissioner, Philip Elman, who, in his lengthy reply to a subcommittee questionnaire, had said that many of the FTC's problems stemmed from political "cronyism" in top appointments.

Replying to charges that FTC wasted its resources on comparatively trivial matters, Dixon said "that's hog-wash." He added, however, that the FTC could not ignore any complaint that came from the public.

Concerning secrecy in commission proceedings, Dixon said that it would not be in the public interest for the commission to operate "in a fishbowl." A public listing of complaints would not be beneficial to consumers with grievances, he said.

Elman said that he thought the main role of the FTC should be "quasi-legislative"; that it should concentrate on rule-making rather than case-by-case prosecution.

Elman said he would prefer to see appointments to the FTC made on the basis of "intrinsic merit" in order to give the FTC an "atmosphere of professionalism." Elman also said the public received inadequate information about product violations of advertising or safety regulations because of poor coverage of the FTC's findings by the general press.

Other Action

PRODUCT SAFETY. Congress cleared for the President's signature a bill (S 1590—PL 91-51), extending the life of the National Commission on Product Safety until June 30, 1970. Final action came when the House approved the bill July 21 by voice vote. S 1590 was passed by the Senate by voice vote May 8.

The measure extended to June 30, 1970, the deadline for the seven-member commission to complete its study of hazardous merchandise and make legislative recommendations to Congress. Without the extension, the commission would have gone out of existence Nov. 20, 1969. The bill was backed by the Nixon administration. *(Congress and the Nation, Vol. II, p. 803)*

PROMOTIONAL GAMES. The House Select Small Business Subcommittee on Activities of Regulatory Agencies Relating to Small Business conducted three days of hearings Nov. 12-14 on "sweepstakes" (drawings) promotional games and contests. Chairman John D. Dingell (D Mich.) said that replies to a subcommittee questionnaire indicated that in "sweepstakes" with pre-selected winners, only about 10 per cent of the advertised prizes were actually awarded and that 90 per cent of the awarded prizes were of nominal value. This was because few consumers checked to see whether their numbers had won.

Dingell castigated pre-selected games as "flagrantly deceptive and misleading" and threatened companies with strict enforcement of existing laws or a new law banning such promotions entirely, if the companies would not drop them voluntarily.

The FTC Aug. 12 adopted regulations intended to eliminate deception in promotional games of chance used by food stores and gasoline stations.

The regulations required retailers to disclose "clearly and conspicuously" the exact number of prizes in a contest, the odds of winning, the geographic area covered by a game, the total number of participating stores and scheduled termination date of the promotional program. The regulations said winning game pieces must be distributed solely on a random basis throughout the contest area and records must be maintained to show that this was done.

FISHERIES INSPECTION. The Senate Commerce Consumer Subcommittee held hearings on two bills providing for continuous inspection of fisheries and fish products and providing financial assistance to the commercial fishing industry to meet inspection requirements, but no further action was taken. The Senate passed a fish inspection bill in 1971 but the House took no action. *(1971 chronology, p. 684)*

POISON PREVENTION. The Consumer Subcommittee also held hearings on a bill (S 2162), the Poison Prevention Packaging Act of 1969, to require the safe packaging of hazardous household substances, including the use of safety catches or "closures" that were "childproof."

Subcommittee Chairman Frank E. Moss (D Utah), when introducing the bill, said that as many as 400 deaths resulted from the one million accidental poisonings of children each year, and more than 40,000 children under five years of age were hospitalized. No further action was taken in 1969 but the bill was approved by Congress in 1970. *(1970 chronology, p. 674)*

UTILITY CONSUMERS. The Senate Government Operations Subcommittee on Intergovernmental Relations held hearings, but took no further action, on S 607, the Utility Consumers' Counsel Act of 1969. As introduced by Sen. Lee Metcalf (D Mont.) and 10 other senators, the bill established a federal office of utility consumers' counsel to represent private consumers and the federal government as a consumer before federal and state agencies and courts regulating privately owned electric, gas, telephone and telegraph utilities. The bill also provided grants to state and local governments to establish their own consumers' counsels, provided grants to universities and other nonprofit organizations for study of regulatory problems, and required utility companies to make annual reports to the Federal Communications Commission or the Federal Power Commission describing their earnings, rate structures, officers and stockholders.

1970

Congress in 1970 completed action on two bills passed in differing versions by the House and Senate in 1969. They were a bill banning cigarette advertisements from radio and television and a bill extending the National Traffic and Motor Vehicle Safety Act of 1966 and requiring tire manufacturers to notify purchasers of safety-related tire defects.

Other consumer bills cleared by Congress in 1970 were the Fair Credit Reporting Act and a bill restricting the issuance of unsolicited credit cards. Both measures were attached as nongermane amendments (riders) to legislation relating to secret foreign bank accounts. Congress also approved three other consumer credit measures and a bill requiring safety closures on household products with which children might accidently poison themselves.

In the most controversial consumer matter before Congress in 1970, the Senate passed a bill creating an independent federal agency to advocate consumer interests before other federal agencies and courts. The House Government Operations Committee reported a similar measure, but the House Rules Committee, by a 7-7 vote, refused to grant a rule for floor consideration, thus killing the legislation for the 91st Congress.

In other action, the Senate approved a bill providing minimum federal standards for product warranties; the measure died in a House committee. President Nixon made no major consumer recommendations in 1970.

In its final report issued June 30, 1970, the National Commission on Product Safety called for the creation of an independent consumer product safety agency authorized to set standards for products harboring unreasonable risks of injury. The commission, established by Congress in 1967, said that "federal authority to curb hazards in consumer products is virtually nonexistent."

Cigarette Advertising Ban

Congress March 19 ended six years of controversy over federal government efforts to regulate or prohibit cigarette advertising by clearing legislation (HR 6543—PL 91-222) banning all cigarette commercials on radio and television, or on any other medium of electronic communication subject to the jurisdiction of the Federal Communications Commission, effective Jan. 2, 1971.

The bill was passed 13 months after HR 6543 was introduced in 1969 with the intention of extending a provision of the Cigarette Labeling and Advertising Act of 1965 (PL 89-92) that prohibited any federal, state or local government from requiring health warnings in cigarette advertising.

1969 Action. The Senate and House in 1969 passed differing versions of HR 6543. The Senate measure, passed Dec. 12, banned cigarette advertising on radio and television and strengthened the warning on cigarette packages. The House version, passed June 18, contained no reference to advertising on radio and TV and provided a weaker label warning. *(Background, 1969 chronology, p. 662)*

Conference Report, Final Action. House-Senate conferees March 3 unanimously agreed to file a report on HR 6543 which differed only slightly from the Senate version of the bill. The conference report prohibited the Federal Trade Commission (FTC) from acting in the event of "gross abuse" of advertising through the printed media by cigarette advertisers until on or after July 1, 1971. The Senate version would have permitted FTC action before that date. The House version extended for six years a clause (which expired June 30, 1969) in the Cigarette Labeling and Advertising Act of 1965 prohibiting federal agencies from requiring any health warning in cigarette advertising.

The conference report also banned all regulation of cigarette advertising by state governments, as in the Senate bill, changed the Senate label warning slightly, and moved the effective date for a ban on radio and TV commercials from Jan. 1, 1971, as in the Senate bill, to Jan. 2, 1971. The later cutoff date, considered a concession to broadcasters and tobacco companies, would permit cigarette advertisements on the telecasts of the widely viewed football bowl games on New Year's Day, 1971.

The Senate March 10 adopted the conference report on HR 6543 by a 75-9 roll-call vote. The House March 18 by voice vote and with little debate adopted the conference report with a minor amendment. A day later the Senate agreed to the House amendment, clearing the measure for the President.

Provisions. As cleared by Congress, HR 6543 (PL 91-222):

• Made it unlawful to advertise cigarettes on radio or television, beginning Jan. 2, 1971.

• Changed the mandatory wording on cigarette packages from: "Caution: Cigarette Smoking May Be Hazardous to Your Health" to: "Warning: The Surgeon General Has Determined That Cigarette Smoking Is Dangerous To Your Health."

• Prohibited any affirmative action by the FTC on printed cigarette advertising until July 1, 1971, and outlined a detailed formula for congressional approval which the FTC would have to follow before issuing any health-related regulation of such advertising.

• Prohibited all state and local health-related regulation or prohibition of cigarette advertising.

Auto, Tire Safety

President Nixon May 22 signed into law a bill (HR 10105—PL 91-265) extending the National Traffic and Motor Vehicle Safety Act of 1966 for three years, through June 30, 1972, and requiring tire manufacturers to notify purchasers of safety-related tire defects. *(Subsequent extension, 1972 chronology, p. 698)*

Under the 1966 Act (PL 89-563), automobile companies were required to recall defective cars. More than 12 million cars had been recalled by early 1970. However, tire manufacturers were not subject to similar requirements with regard to tire defects.

Government tests by the National Highway Safety Bureau in 1969 disclosed that 18 per cent of the tires tested for compliance with the minimum tire safety standards failed one or more of the tests. The results of the test spurred congressional efforts to require tire manufacturers to notify purchasers of defects.

1969 Action. The House passed HR 10105, extending authorizations under the act for three years, on Sept. 3, 1969. The Senate passed HR 10105 Dec. 2, 1969, after amending it to extend authorizations for only two years. Grant authorizations had expired June 30, 1969. Both versions of the bill required tire manufacturers to notify purchasers of defective tires. *(1969 chronology, p. 666)*

Conference Report. House-Senate conferees filed a report April 20, agreeing to a three-year extension of the National Traffic and Motor Vehicle Safety Act as provided in the House-passed bill. Conferees further agreed to a compromise provision authorizing the establishment of standards for motor vehicle equipment exclusively related to safety. The House version covered only motorcycle helmets and other protective headgear. The conference agreement covered such accessories as motorcycle goggles, tire repair equipment and tire inflation equipment.

Final Action. The Senate April 23 by voice vote adopted the conference report on HR 10105. The House May 5 adopted the conference report with a technical amendment. The Senate May 11 agreed to the House amendment, clearing the bill for the President's signature.

Provisions. As cleared by Congress, HR 10105:

• Authorized appropriations of $23-million in fiscal 1970, $40-million in fiscal 1971 and $40-million in fiscal 1972 to carry out the auto and tire safety provisions of the National Traffic and Motor Vehicle Safety Act of 1966.

• Authorized the secretary of transportation to set minimum standards for the manufacture or sale of equipment intended exclusively to safeguard motor vehicles and their passengers.

• Required manufacturers of motor vehicles to notify purchasers and potential purchasers of performance and technical data at all dealer locations. The information was to include printed material which could be retained by the prospective purchaser and accompany the motor vehicle when it was sold.

• Required manufacturers of tires to notify purchasers by certified mail of safety-related tire defects.

• Required the secretary of transportation to set limits within one year of enactment on the age of tire carcasses that could be retreaded.

• Authorized the secretary of transportation to plan facilities for testing in traffic safety. No appropriation of more than $100,000 for such a facility could be made without the concurrence of House and Senate Commerce and Public Works Committees.

Unsolicited Credit Cards

Congress Oct. 13 cleared a conglomerate bill (HR 15073—PL 91-508) which included provisions that restricted the issuance of unsolicited credit cards (S 721) and provisions regulating credit information reporting and use (S 823).

The provisions of both S 721 and S 823 were added by the Senate on Sept. 18 as nongermane amendments (riders) to HR 15073, a bill to curb violation of U.S. laws and avoidance of taxes through use of secret foreign bank accounts. *(Action on HR 15073, International Economic Policy chapter, p. 119)*

Background. There were more than 50 million credit cards in the hands of the American public in 1970 as compared to fewer than 5 million in circulation in 1965. Approximately 3,000 different types were available and they were expected to be used to purchase goods and services valued at more than $50-billion during the year.

But complaints about jumbled accounts, computer errors and the theft of cards from the mail also were increasing. A stolen credit card sold for $100 or more on the black market in New York City. In Washington, D.C., one credit card firm reported losses up to $290,000 in the first four months of 1970 alone.

The Federal Trade Commission (FTC) May 18 banned unsolicited mailings of credit cards. But the Federal Reserve Board, the traditional regulator of banking, argued that there was no authority for such restrictions. The Nixon administration, after initially favoring the FTC ban, reversed itself, saying it gave banks already in the credit card business a virtual monopoly.

Senate Action. The Senate Banking and Currency Committee reported an amended version of S 721 March 13. Hearings had occurred in 1969. Major provisions prohibited the issuance of credit cards except in response to a request or application and set the maximum liability of a cardholder for unauthorized use of his card at $50 if the use occurred prior to his notifying the company. The Senate passed S 721 April 15 by a 79-1 roll-call vote.

Before final passage, the Senate adopted four amendments, including one by Russell B. Long (D La.) which made unauthorized use of credit cards a federal crime and one by Harrison A. Williams Jr. (D N.J.) exempting cards issued as renewals or substitutes from the provision outlawing unsolicited credit cards.

House Action. The House Post Office and Civil Service Committee March 26 reported a far more limited bill (HR 16542) which simply declared a credit card non-mailable matter unless the card had been solicited, was a replacement for one previously issued, was a lost or stolen card being returned or was sent by registered mail. The House passed HR 16542 Sept. 9 on a 302-0 roll-call vote.

Second Senate Action. On Sept. 15, the Senate passed the House bill by voice vote after substituting the language of its own version. Three days later, on Sept. 18, the Senate added the provisions of the credit card bill along with the provisions of the Fair Credit Reporting Act *(below)* to HR 15073, the foreign bank account bill.

Conference Report, Final Action. The conference report on HR 15073 left the Senate version of the credit card bill substantially intact. The bill prohibited issuance of unsolicited credit cards and placed financial liability for unauthorized use of a credit card on the issuer and the merchant involved. The Senate Oct. 9 and the House Oct. 13 by voice votes agreed to the conference report. The President signed the bill Oct. 26.

Major provisions of HR 15073 relating to restriction of unsolicited credit cards (S 721) as cleared by Congress:

• Prohibited issuance of unrequested credit cards except as renewals or substitutes for cards previously held.

• Set maximum liability of a cardholder for unauthorized use of his card at $50 unless a lesser amount of liability had been agreed upon by the issuer and cardholder; placed the burden of proof in liability questions on the issuer of credit cards.

• Made unauthorized use of a credit card to obtain goods or services totaling $5,000 or more a crime punishable by a fine of up to $10,000 or five years in prison or both.

Fair Credit Reporting

HR 15073 *(above)* also contained provisions of a bill (S 823) regulating credit information reporting and use.

Background. American consumers in 1969 owed $116-billion in outstanding credit. Because of the trend toward credit buying, a vast organization of credit bureaus maintained files on more than 110 million individuals and in 1967 issued more than 97 million credit reports to 400,000 creditors in 36,000 communities. These agencies had no public supervision. With the trend toward use of computers, there was a fear that a gigantic national data bank including extremely personal information on nearly all consumers would be created with no public safeguards to protect the American buyer.

The Senate, which originally passed S 823 in November 1969, added the provisions of the bill to HR 15073 Sept. 18 as a nongermane amendment (rider).

Although the House Banking and Currency Committee had held hearings on a number of credit reporting bills, including S 823, it did not report any of them. House conferees agreed to accept the Senate-approved credit reporting provisions of HR 15073 Oct. 8 after making a number of changes in the provisions of S 823.

Conference Report. The conference version of the Fair Credit Reporting Act required all agencies reporting credit information—not just investigative agencies, as in the Senate bill—to follow reasonable procedures to assure accuracy of their information. The conference agreement required any user of a report who rejected a consumer for credit, insurance or employment to inform the consumer of the source of the report. The Senate version required the consumer to request identification of the source in writing.

The Senate Oct. 9 and the House Oct. 13 agreed to the conference report on HR 15073 by voice votes.

Provisions, S 823. Major provisions of HR 15073 relating to the Fair Credit Reporting Act (S 823) as cleared by Congress:

• Authorized the furnishing of credit information by reporting agencies only: (1) in connection with credit, insurance, employment or a government license for which a person had applied; (2) for a business transaction in which the subject of the information was involved; (3) by written consent of the subject; or (4) in compliance with a court order.

• Prohibited reporting of adverse information more than seven years old regarding suits, arrests and other matters except bankruptcies, for which information could be available for 14 years.

• Required a reporting agency, on request, to disclose to a consumer all information about him in the agency's files, other than medical, and its sources.

• Required a person or business rejecting a consumer for credit, insurance or employment on the basis of a credit report to advise the consumer and identify the reporting agency.

• Permitted civil actions in federal courts to recover damages resulting from willful and negligent noncompliance.

• Made obtaining information under false pretenses for credit reporting and willfully giving credit information to unauthorized persons punishable by a fine of up to $5,000 and imprisonment for up to one year.

Federal Credit Unions

Congress Feb. 24 cleared for the President's signature a bill (HR 2—PL 91-206) establishing a National Credit Union Administration to supervise federally chartered credit unions. The bill established the credit union administration as an independent agency, replacing the existing Bureau of Federal Credit Unions—an arm of the Social Security Administration in the Department of Health, Education and Welfare.

The Nixon administration had opposed the measure.

Background. The House Banking and Currency Committee June 27, 1969, reported HR 2. The bill was then passed by the House July 28, 1969, without amendment. The bill as amended by the Senate Banking and Currency Committee was reported Nov. 5, 1969, but it did not reach the Senate floor before adjournment of the first session of the 91st Congress. *(1969 chronology, p. 668)*

1970 Senate Action. The Senate Feb. 4 by a 73-15 roll-call vote passed HR 2 as previously reported by the committee.

Supporters of the bill argued that credit unions were the only financial institutions not regulated by an independent agency. They also charged that the existing Bureau of Federal Credit Unions was too deeply buried in the federal bureaucracy.

Wallace F. Bennett (R Utah), who led the opposition to the bill, argued that the measure would not help credit unions overcome their difficulties with federal regulation and that it was opposed by many individual credit unions.

An amendment offered by Bennett to provide federal insurance coverage of deposits in all federally chartered credit unions and to make similar coverage available on a voluntary basis to state-chartered credit unions was defeated by a roll-call vote of 35-52.

Final Action. House-Senate conferees Feb. 18 filed a conference report on HR 2.

Conferees resolved the major difference in the House and Senate versions of the bill by establishing control over the agency with an administrator who "shall seek the advice, counsel and guidance" of a seven-man National Credit Union Board. The Senate had provided that an administrator would run the regulatory agency assisted by an advisory board. The House would have established a board of governors and an administrator who was responsible to the board.

The Senate Feb. 19 and the House Feb. 24 by voice votes adopted the conference report.

Credit Union Insurance

Congress Oct. 5 cleared for the President a bill (S 3822—PL 91-468) establishing a federal insurance system for state and federally chartered credit unions.

As signed into law, S 3822 required the administrator of the newly created National Credit Union Administration to insure the accounts of all federally chartered credit unions, and authorized him to insure state-chartered credit unions which apply for coverage and which maintain the same reserves as federally chartered credit unions. Deposits of up to $20,000 would be insured.

S 3822 was reported Aug. 19 by the Senate Banking and Currency Committee; the provisions of the bill as reported were the same as those that cleared Congress. The Senate approved S 3822 Sept. 2 by voice vote. S 3822 was then reported unchanged Sept. 21 by the House Banking and Currency Committee and passed the House by voice vote Oct. 5. House passage cleared the bill for the President.

Consumer Finance Commission

Congress extended the reporting date of the National Commission on Consumer Finance in 1970. The date was extended in a joint resolution (S J Res 201—PL 91-344) from January 1, 1971, until July 1, 1972.

The commission had been established as part of the Consumer Credit Protection Act (PL 90-321), passed May 29, 1968, to study the functioning and structure of the consumer finance industry and consumer credit transactions. *(1969 chronology, p. 668)*

S J Res 201 was reported by the Senate Banking and Currency Committee on June 23. It passed the Senate June 25. The House passed the joint resolution on July 6 by voice vote and without debate. There had been no committee action.

Poison Prevention

Congress Dec. 16 cleared for the President's signature a bill (S 2162—PL 91-601) requiring special packaging of potentially dangerous household goods to protect children from serious injury or illness resulting from handling, using or ingesting such substances.

The bill pertained to polishes, cleansers, drugs and other common household substances that had caused accidental poisonings.

Background. Swallowing toxic household substances was the most common medical emergency facing young children. More than 70,000 emergency cases and 300 deaths were reported annually to poison control centers. Surveys showed only one in five serious poisoning accidents were reported. About 50 per cent of the cases were caused by drugs and medicines with the rest caused by household products such as furniture polishes, electric dishwasher detergents, drain cleaners, paints and turpentine, cosmetics and kerosene.

In 1966, hearings were held in the House on a bill that would require safety closures on drug containers. No action resulted, but a joint industry professional-governmental committee was established to develop methods for measuring the capacity of various types of packaging to prevent access by children.

There were relatively few child-resistant containers on the market, but some were being developed. A large-scale two-year field test involving more than 600,000 containers had shown that 90 per cent of poisoning due to medicines could be prevented by dispensing medicines in child-resistent containers.

S 2162, the Poison Prevention Packaging Act of 1970 was introduced by Frank E. Moss (D Utah) in 1969. *(1969 chronology, p. 671)*

Senate Action. The Senate Commerce Committee reported S 2162 May 6. The bill amended the Federal Hazardous Substances Act (PL 86-612) to require household substances that were accessible to young children and that could cause injury or illness to be contained in special packaging that was difficult for children under the age of six to open within a reasonable period of time.

S 2162 provided that substances for which special packaging standards had been established could be marketed in one ordinary container size not complying with the standards for the use of the elderly and the handicapped. These containers must be labeled: "For households without young children." The bill empowered the secretary of health, education and welfare to establish package standards after consultation with an advisory committee.

The Senate passed S 2162 May 11 by voice vote.

House Action. The House Interstate and Foreign Commerce Committee reported S 2162 Dec. 1 with one major change from the Senate version.

The House committee adopted language requiring the manufacturer to produce only one size of safety package. Conventional packages were required to contain on the label: "This product is also available in special packaging which is recommended for use in households with young children." The committee said that since 75 per cent of the nation's households do not have children under the age of five, "it seems illogical to...require that all sizes of a substance except one be marketed in special packaging."

The House passed S 2162 Dec. 7 by voice vote.

Conference Report. House-Senate conferees agreed to the Senate version of S 2162 requiring all containers of dangerous substances to have safety openings except for one conventional size intended for the use of the elderly and handicapped.

The House and Senate adopted the conference report Dec. 16 by voice votes, clearing the measure for the President.

Provisions. As cleared by Congress, S 2162, the Poison Prevention Packaging Act of 1970:

• Authorized the secretary of health, education and welfare (HEW), after consultation with a technical advisory committee, to establish regulations for special packaging of substances dangerous to children if such a container was technically feasible. The secretary must publish an explanation of his actions.

• Authorized the HEW secretary to prohibit any type of package he determined was unnecessarily attractive to children.

• Allowed manufacturers to produce a single size of package in a conventional container, to benefit elderly or handicapped people, if the nonsafety package bore a label stating, "This package for households without young children." Prescription drugs could only be dispensed in nonsafety packages if specifically authorized either by the doctor or the purchaser.

• Authorized the HEW secretary to require manufacturers to market their products in safety containers.

• Established a technical advisory committee of up to 18 members, including representatives of the HEW and Commerce Departments, manufacturers, scientists, doctors and consumers.

• Provided that violators of the packaging law would be subject to the penalties contained in the Hazardous Substances Act, the Insecticide, Fungicide and Rodenticide Act and the Food, Drug and Cosmetic Act.

Consumer Protection Agency

1970 marked the beginning of a long congressional battle over creation of an independent agency to represent consumer interests before other federal agencies and courts.

The Senate passed its version of a consumer protection agency bill Dec. 1, but the legislation died at the end of the session when the House Rules Committee refused to clear a similar House bill for floor debate.

The Senate bill (S 4459), passed by a 74-4 roll-call vote, created an independent Consumer Protection Agency and established a Council of Consumer Advisers in the Executive Office of the President to coordinate consumer programs, develop policy and resolve interagency conflicts regarding consumer matters.

Similar legislation (HR 18214) was reported July 30 by the House Government Operations Committee. The Rules Committee held one hearing on the bill Oct. 8, but delayed further action until the post-election session. On Dec. 2, the day after the Senate approved S 4459, the Rules Committee failed by a 7-7 vote to grant a rule to the House bill. *(Box this page)*

The Nixon administration opposed the establishment of an independent consumer agency. It had offered another bill (HR 14578) to create a statutory Office of

---

House Rules Committee Action

The House Rules Committee refused by a 7-7 vote Dec. 2 to grant a rule for floor consideration of HR 18214, the House version of the consumer agency bill. The vote killed further House action on consumer agency legislation in the 91st Congress.

One member of the Rules Committee, Richard Bolling (D Mo.), supported the bill but was on vacation in the Caribbean and did not vote.

The House Government Operations Committee had reported HR 18214 by a 31-4 vote on July 30.

Voting to grant a rule on HR 18214 were Rules Committee members Ray J. Madden (D Ind.), Thomas P. O'Neill Jr. (D Mass.), B. F. Sisk (D Calif.), Claude Pepper (D Fla.), Spark M. Matsunaga (D Hawaii), William R. Anderson (D Tenn.) and John B. Anderson (R Ill.). Opposing the rule were Chairman William M. Colmer (D Miss.), James J. Delaney (D N.Y.), John Young (D Texas), H. Allen Smith (R Calif.), Dave Martin (R Neb.), James H. Quillen (R Tenn.) and Delbert L. Latta (R Ohio).

Bolling, according to his press aide, was in St. Barthelemy on a vacation planned before the post-election session of Congress was announced. He had gone to the West Indies on Nov. 20 and was scheduled to return Dec. 20. His office was notified of the Rules Committee meeting on the afternoon of Dec. 1, the day before the vote, the aide said.

Bolling was the author of two books dealing with reforming the House of Representatives.

Benjamin S. Rosenthal (D N.Y.), cosponsor of the bill, said after the Rules Committee hearing, "It is outrageous that seven men can now prevent the House from working its will."

Consumer Affairs in the Executive Office and a consumer protection division in the Justice Department.

House Action. The House Government Operations Committee July 30 reported the Consumer Protection Act of 1970 (HR 18214) a bill establishing an independent Consumer Protection Agency, a statutory Office of Consumer Affairs in the White House, and a Consumer Advisory Council to oversee the operations of the other two agencies.

The report said that although numerous federal agencies had programs affecting the consumer, they had been "far less than adequate" in protecting him. "The doctrine of *caveat emptor* (let the buyer beware) by itself is no longer a sufficient safeguard against modern technology, sophisticated mass advertising and buying stimulation," the report stated.

The new Consumer Protection Agency and the Office of Consumer Affairs would not assume any important authority already delegated by law to an existing federal agency, the report said. But giving existing agencies authority to regulate and promote commercial activities, and also to guard the consumer, "has proven singularly unsuccessful." The purpose of the new agency and office would be to split up these dual functions. The committee said no new, large bureaucracy was contemplated in the bill. "If personnel and programs mushroom, the organizational structure herein designed

(Continued on p. 678)

Who Should Protect the Consumer: The White House,...

President Johnson in early 1964 created by executive action the position of special assistant for consumer affairs, to provide "more effective representation at the presidential level." He appointed Esther Peterson, then an assistant secretary of labor, as his first assistant and later replaced her with television personality Betty Furness.

President Nixon's first action on consumer affairs turned out to be embarrassing for the new administration. On Feb. 11, 1969, he appointed Willie Mae Rogers, director of the Good Housekeeping Institute, as a part-time consultant on consumer affairs. She resigned four days later, after criticism of potential conflicts of interest between her public and private roles. A month later, Mr. Nixon named Virginia H. Knauer, director of the Pennsylvania Bureau of Consumer Protection, as full-time assistant for consumer affairs.

Proposals to establish a cabinet-level Department of Consumer Affairs had been circulating on Capitol Hill for more than a decade. In the late 1960s, the chief advocate of the department had been Rep. Benjamin S. Rosenthal (D N.Y.). In the 88th Congress, his proposed legislation had only a handful of supporters, but it picked up support and in the 91st Congress his consumer department bill (HR 6037) had almost 100 cosponsors.

The consumer department would have assumed numerous consumer functions currently scattered throughout the federal government. A 1969 Congressional Quarterly study found that at least 39 different agencies had responsibility for administering consumer aspects of hundreds of federal laws. Often responsibility for a single law was split among several agencies. The truth-in-lending provision of the 1958 Consumer Credit Protection Act (PL 90-321) was enforced by nine departments and agencies; three agencies enforced the Fair Packaging and Labeling Act of 1966 (PL 89-755).

Rep. Florence P. Dwyer (R N.J.), ranking Republican on the Government Operations Committee, introduced a bill (HR 13793) in 1969 with about 60 cosponsors. The bill proposed a White House consumer affairs office to promote consumer interests and provide representation before other federal agencies.

Nixon Message

President Nixon, in an Oct. 30, 1969, message on consumer affairs, outlined his legislative proposals. This included a statutory Consumer Affairs Office in the Executive Office, and a consumer protection division in the Justice Department "to act as a consumer advocate before federal regulatory agencies, in judicial proceedings and in government councils." Dwyer introduced the administration bill (HR 14758) two weeks later.

In the Senate, in addition to the consumer department bill and the Nixon administration proposal, hearings were held in 1969 on a bill (S 2959) to establish an independent consumer council, a non-governmental organization representing the consumer and appearing on his behalf before federal departments and agencies.

A number of other developments affected the drive for increasing the consumer's voice in federal agencies in 1969 and 1970. An internal report by the Food and Drug Administration (FDA) and a review of the Federal Trade Commission (FTC) conducted by the American Bar Association both criticized the performances of those agencies. The National Commission on Product Safety, appointed by President Johnson, in its final report in June 1970 called for establishment of an independent agency with authority to set and enforce product-safety standards.

Ralph Nader, the free-lance consumer advocate, organized teams of "Nader's Raiders" to study various aspects of government policy. Well-publicized reports were issued which were highly critical of the FTC and federal air pollution efforts, among others.

Rosenthal-Dwyer Compromise

After hearings before the House Executive and Legislative Reorganization Subcommittee, Rosenthal revised his bill to substitute an independent agency for a cabinet-level department. The new agency would have retained the advocacy functions envisioned for the proposed department, but responsibilities for enforcing laws would have remained in the agencies where they already were.

Testifying before the hearings in September 1969, Nader listed four reasons the regulatory functions should be separated from the "unabashed...partisan" consumer advocacy powers of an independent agency:

● "First of all, such a department would tend to refocus the entire lobby structure" away from individual agencies and onto the new department.

● "It would weaken the strong advocate role, because the department would have to assume a referee role between competing interests in its rulemaking and administrative processes...."

● "Such a department would lighten any public interest burdens from other departments and agencies...."

● "It would generate needless opposition by the agencies which feel their functions are being stripped for transfer to the Department of Consumer Affairs."

Subsequently, a compromise was worked out between the Rosenthal and Dwyer bills which gave the proposed agency power to intervene on behalf of consumers in federal proceedings while the White House office was authorized to develop policy and coordinate activities carried out by the departments and agencies. The bill (HR 18214) was ordered reported June 23 by the House Government Operations Committee on a 31-4 committee vote, but was killed Dec. 2 by the House Rules Committee.

...Justice Dept., or an Independent Consumer Agency?

Senate Legislation

In the Senate, jurisdiction over the bill fell originally to the Executive Reorganization and Government Research Subcommittee of the Senate Government Operations Committee, headed by Abraham A. Ribicoff (D Conn.). On June 30, 1970, the subcommittee approved in principle an independent agency bill.

The full Government Operations Committee Oct. 12 reported its bill (S 4459) to establish an independent Consumer Protection Agency and a Council of Consumer Advisers in the White House.

Before it could come to the floor, the bill had to be cleared by the Senate Commerce Committee as well. That committtee reported S 4459 (S Rept 91-1365) on Nov. 25, two days after its deadline. The final version of the bill approved by the Senate on a 74-4 roll call Dec. 1 differed in detail but generally agreed in substance with HR 18214.

Administration Bill

The administration opposed the concept of an independent agency serving as a consumer advocate within the federal government.

HR 14758, the administration bill, would have created a new Justice Department consumer protection division with its own advocacy powers. The director of the division could have petitioned another federal agency to take certain actions on behalf of consumers, participated as a party in agency proceedings (except those concerned solely with the imposition of penalties, when he could have filed briefs stating the division's position), and initiated and participated in court proceedings reviewing agency actions.

The bill would have expanded the powers of the FTC to deal with consumer violations, including power to obtain preliminary injunctions against deceptive practices. It contained a list of specific practices which had been found to be deceptive by the FTC and which would be outlawed.

Testifying before a House subcommittee in November 1969, Richard W. McLaren, assistant attorney general, antitrust division, backed the administration bill: "The consumer protection division will be armed with power to get information needed to determine consumer needs, with power to represent the consumer and his needs before federal agencies which set government policy, and with power to go into the marketplace and restrain consumer fraud and deception."

Advocacy functions should not be placed in the White House, "where all agency conflicts must eventually be resolved," McLaren said. He opposed establishing a separate agency, "with all the difficulties, duplication and expense which usually attend such an effort."

On Dec. 15, 1969, the Justice Department announced it was setting up a consumer affairs section in its antitrust division, to be headed by Bruce B. Wilson.

Mrs. Knauer, the President's consumer adviser, said that the move was not a substitute for the administration's proposal. She called the new section "a laying of the foundation for what we would hope would grow into something similar to our earlier approach."

Opposition Campaign

Opposition to the consumer agency bill was led by the U.S. Chamber of Commerce. Kenneth F. Stinger, chamber consumer issues attorney, said that the group had made the bill "a top priority issue" on its roster of legislative interests for the year. He said the lobbying effort probably would concentrate on eliminating the agency provisions from the bill and getting its functions transferred to the White House adviser's office.

The chamber sent numerous mailings to its affiliates trying to drum up grass roots support for its position.

The chamber backed legislation which would establish a statutory office of consumer affairs in the White House, authorized to appear as a witness—not a party—in proceedings of other agencies. Rather than giving the Justice Department greater jurisdiction, the chamber said that the Federal Trade Commission should be revitalized to defend consumers from fraud more effectively. The group opposed legislation giving a consumer agency authority to conduct product testing or set safety standards.

The chamber felt that "there has to be more consumer representation than there is," Stinger said. But such representation should be "close to the President where it is liable to get more direction from the President."

Support

Taking a diametrically opposing view, Rosenthal said that was exactly why consumer advocacy functions should be in an independent agency. The White House was too politically sensitive, he maintained: It must balance consumer interests against the interests of businessmen and other special interest groups. What the consumer needed was a partisan advocate to represent the buyers of goods and services without taking into consideration the positions of those other groups. The White House was the place for formulation and coordination of policy, he said, but the agency should have the freedom to oppose any policy it felt was detrimental to consumers.

Working for enactment of consumer agency legislation were several consumer groups and organized labor, chiefly the consumer committee of the AFL-CIO. The other group most active in its behalf was the Consumer Federation of America, which registered as a lobbyist for the first time in 1969.

One of the problems sponsors of the bill confronted, said Rosenthal, was that the consumer groups at the grass roots level were not well organized, especially on an issue like establishing a new agency.

will no longer be serving its intended purpose," the report said.

Senate Action. The Senate Government Operations Committee reported its version of the bill (S 4459) Oct. 12. The bill then went to the Senate Commerce Committee with instructions to report it back to the full Senate by Nov. 23. As reported by the Government Operations Committee, S 4459 was similar to the House version.

The Senate Commerce Committee, which reported S 4459 Nov. 25—two days after its deadline—made several substantive changes in the bill previously approved by the Government Operations Committee.

Major changes included a provision specifying that the annual report of the agency go to the President and Congress simultaneously to prevent "prior screening" by the White House or the Office of Management and Budget; elimination of any references in the bill to product testing, and elimination of a standing consumer advisory committee within the agency.

The Senate Dec. 1 approved S 4459 by a 74-4 roll-call vote following two days of debate, after rejecting a series of amendments designed to strengthen the agency and enhance its independence.

The amendments, submitted by Philip A. Hart (D Mich.), would have made the proposed agency more independent of presidential control and given it more authority to intervene in agency or court proceedings. Although Hart had said in views attached to the Commerce Committee report that no bill at all would be preferable to S 4459, he voted for the bill on final passage.

Provisions. As passed by the Senate Dec. 1, major provisions of S 4459:

• Established a Council of Consumer Advisers in the Executive Office of the President, composed of the director of the consumer protection agency and two other members appointed by the President and confirmed by the Senate, to coordinate federal consumer programs, resolve conflicts between agencies, conduct investigations regarding consumer protection and develop federal consumer policies.

• Established an independent Consumer Protection Agency with a director, deputy director and consumer counsel appointed by the President and confirmed by the Senate.

• Authorized the agency to intervene as a party representing consumer interests in the proceedings of other federal agencies or federal courts under certain circumstances: when the pending matter did not affect the agency's internal operations; when the matter substantially affected consumer interests.

• Authorized the agency to appeal to the federal courts agency rulings in matters which it initiated or in which it intervened. Intervention or appearance as *amicus curiae* (friend of the court) in other cases would be left to the discretion of the courts.

• Authorized grants to state and local governments and to private nonprofit organizations to foster consumer protection programs.

• Authorized appropriations for the independent agency of $10-million in fiscal 1971, $15-million in fiscal 1972, $25-million in fiscal 1973, opened-ended appropriations thereafter; authorized open-ended appropriations for the Council of Consumer Advisers.

Consumer Warranties

In addition to the consumer protection agency, congressional and consumer interests also began to focus on product warranties in 1970. A bill (S 3074) providing minimum standards for manufacturers' warranties passed the Senate July 1 by voice vote but died in the House Interstate and Foreign Commerce Committee.

As passed, S 3074 required manufacturers who offered warranties on any products worth $5 or more to specify whether the warranty was full or partial and to spell out the terms and conditions, including duration, of the warranty. The bill also required a supplier warranting or guaranteeing a product to repair or replace defective products within a reasonable time and without charge (unless the warrantor could show that the customer failed to provide adequate maintenance for the product or subjected it to unreasonable use).

The administration supported controls on warranties for consumer products worth more than $25.

Other Action

FLAMMABLE FABRICS. Congress in 1970 did not complete action on a bill (S 3765) extending through fiscal 1972 the Flammable Fabrics Act of 1953, as amended in 1967. *(Congress and the Nation, Vol. II, p. 802)*

S 3765 would have required manufacturers or importers to subject their fabric products to a testing program conducted by manufacturers or importers and approved by the secretary of commerce. Fabrics had to be certified that they met the requirements of the tests, and sale of uncertified fabrics was made a violation of the Federal Trade Commission Act.

Authorizations contained in the 1967 amendments to the original act expired June 30, 1970. The 91st Congress adjourned without the House having considered the measure. The Senate passed S 3765 Sept. 23.

As passed by the Senate S 3765:

• Required certification by the commerce secretary of an approved testing program (rather than a "reasonable testing program" approved by the FTC) designed to prevent or minimize the manufacture or distribution of any fabric, product or related material not in compliance with flammability standards established by the 1967 amendments.

• Modified certain of the penalty provisions to provide a defense of "due care" in applying an approved testing certification program. Set an effective date one year after enactment of the bill for the provision dealing with certification and other penalties.

FIRE PREVENTION RESEARCH. Although passed by the Senate and reported by a House committee, Congress did not complete action in 1970 on legislation (S 3766, HR 16538) authorizing up to $5-million in fiscal years 1971 and 1972 to carry out federal fire research programs.

In 1968, Congress authorized a two-year, $5-million federal program of research by the Department of Commerce on the causes of fire and methods for reducing loss of life and property from fire. The measure (S 1124—PL 90-259) provided for the establishment of a 20-member National Commission on Fire Prevention and Control. *(Congress and the Nation, Vol. II, p. 816-818)*

The $5-million authorization was for the period ending June 30, 1970. A Commission on Fire Prevention and Control was never created.

Senate Action. The Senate Commerce Committee reported S 3766 on July 29.

The Senate July 31 by voice vote passed the bill, which authorized $5-million for fiscal years 1971 and 1972 to carry out the federal fire research program in the Department of Commerce.

PRODUCT SAFETY COMMISSION. Declaring that the "federal authority to curb hazards in consumer products is virtually nonexistent," the National Commission on Product Safety called for the creation of an independent consumer product safety agency. The commission, created in 1967, made its recommendations in a final report released June 30, 1970.

"Federal product safety legislation," the report said, "consists of a series of isolated acts treating specific hazards in narrow product categories. No government agency possesses general authority to ban products which harbor unreasonable risks or to require that consumer products conform to minimum safety standards."

To remedy the situation, the commission called for the establishment of an independent agency with authority to develop and set mandatory safety regulations, to enforce compliance with those standards and to ban those products which do not conform or which present unreasonable hazards. (A consumer product safety agency was created by Congress in 1972; *p. 685*)

CLASS ACTION SUITS. Legislation allowing consumers to bring class-action suits in federal courts died at the end of the 91st Congress without reaching a vote in either chamber.

The Senate Commerce Committee Aug. 14 reported a modified administration bill (S 3201) allowing joint suits against fraudulent businessmen and strengthening the authority of the Federal Trade Commission (FTC). The Senate Judiciary Committee subsequently held hearings on S 3201, approving the bill Oct. 5 without issuing a written report.

In the House, a subcommittee of the House Interstate and Foreign Commerce Committee held hearings and June 1 approved a bill allowing consumer class-action suits without prior Justice Department action, but the full committee did not act.

Background. Consumer class-action suits would allow a group of consumers affected by similar practices to file suit collectively, sharing lawyers' fees and court costs. If they won their case, every injured consumer could collect damages whether or not he was a party to the suit.

But existing federal court rulings and regulations made class-action suits prohibitively difficult. Federal courts required a claim of more than $10,000 in order to file a class-action suit. They also required that the case involve citizens of different states, citizens of different countries, or a combination of the two. And in March 1969, the Supreme Court ruled that a consumer could not satisfy the jurisdictional amount ($10,000) by pooling the claims of individual members of the class. *(Snyder v. Harris)*

The 91st Congress considered numerous bills to permit class-action suits and to revamp the FTC to provide greater protection for consumers. In 1969, two Senate subcommittees held hearings on class-action bills. *(1969*

In October, 1969, President Nixon sent to Congress legislation (S 3201) providing for class-action suits. The administration bill allowed consumer suits only after the Justice Department had brought successful suits against offending businessmen. The same bill revamped the powers of the FTC. The requirement that the Justice Department act first, Mr. Nixon said, "will prevent harassment of legitimate businessmen by unlimited nuisance lawsuits."

Consumer advocates criticized the President's proposal as far too limited, claiming the federal government's efforts in prosecuting fraudulent merchants and manufacturers often had been ineffective and that the new bill gave no protection to consumers when the government chose not to act.

Supporters of the administration position claimed that unlimited class-action suits would jam federal court dockets and encourage consumers to bring frivolous suits.

Senate Report. The Senate Commerce Committee "rejected the proposition that the governments should be the sole agent to bring suit on behalf of classes of consumers injured by unfair or deceptive acts or practices." If the government chooses to sue there is no need for class-action suits covering that particular product or practice, the report said.

But, the report added, "the necessity to allocate (limited) legal resources will necessarily leave unsatisfied hundreds, if not thousands, of valid cases in which consumers have suffered significant damages but which the government might choose not to prosecute."

MEAT INSPECTION. Congress July 6 cleared for the President a bill (S 3592—PL 91-342) to permit custom slaughterers to engage in the retailing and wholesaling of meat.

Final action came when the House July 6 by a 296-2 roll-call vote passed the administration-supported bill. The Senate passed S 3592 June 5 by voice vote.

Custom slaughter was performed for hire for the owners of meat animals who wished to use the meat in their own households. The 1967 Federal Meat Inspection Act (PL 90-201) exempted custom slaughtering from inspection but also prohibited custom slaughterers from buying or selling any carcasses, parts of carcasses, meat or meat food products.

PL 90-201 greatly strengthened federal meat inspection standards under the Meat Inspection Act of 1906. The 1967 act authorized the secretary of agriculture to provide assistance to states for the purpose of bringing their inspection standards to a level "at least equal" to federal standards applicable to plants in interstate commerce. *(Congress and the Nation, Vol. I, p. 1161; Vol. II, p. 799)*

As cleared by Congress, S 3592 amended the Federal Meat Inspection Act of 1967 to permit the sale, under certain conditions, of inspected meat by custom slaughterers.

● Required the custom slaughterer to provide complete separation in his facility of meat and meat parts slaughtered for the custom customer and those inspected meat products for sale to the public; require that custom slaughtered meat be clearly identified as "not for sale."

EGG INSPECTION. Congress cleared a bill (HR 19888—PL 91-597) prohibiting distribution of unwholesome eggs and providing for mandatory inspection of egg processing plants to protect consumers.

Final action came when the Senate Dec. 14 by voice vote passed HR 19888. The House approved the measure Dec. 11 by voice vote.

As cleared by Congress, HR 19888:

• Prohibited the distribution of unwholesome shell eggs and prohibited their use in food products. Made the prohibition applicable to intrastate as well as interstate and foreign commerce.

• Prohibited states from imposing requirements conflicting with those in the bill, but permitted states to require that all shell eggs sold within their boundaries be labeled with the name, address and license number of the packer of the egg.

• Provided for mandatory continuous inspection of egg product processing plants by the Department of Agriculture. Required all shell egg packer plants to be inspected at least once during each calender quarter. Permitted exemption from inspections for family farm operators who sell eggs from flocks of 3,000 or fewer hens.

• Authorized loans through the Small Business Administration to small businesses affected by HR 19888 and the Meat Inspection and Poultry Inspection Acts.

1971

No consumer legislation was cleared by Congress in 1971, although both chambers passed a variety of consumer measures and held hearings on legislation establishing a product safety commission.

The Senate passed four major bills dealing with consumer product warranties, meat and fish inspection systems and auto repair costs. It also held extensive hearings on no-fault automobile insurance, an issue that was to embroil the Senate in bitter controversy in 1972.

In its only major consumer action of the year, the House passed a bill creating an independent Consumer Protection Agency to advocate consumer interests before other federal agencies and courts. Similar legislation had been killed by the House Rules Committee in 1970.

Virginia H. Knauer, special assistant to the President for consumer affairs, endorsed the House measure; her approval represented yet another administration position shift on creation of the agency. In 1969, President Nixon proposed that a consumer protection division be established in the Justice Department.

In his second consumer message, delivered Feb. 24, 1971, Nixon asked Congress to postpone action on the agency until further White House study of recommendations made by the Advisory Council on Executive Reorganization could be completed. If Congress felt it must take action before receiving his recommendations, Nixon said, he would support placing an advocate within the Federal Trade Commission as an interim measure.

Other highlights of Nixon's 1971 consumer message included:

• Creation by executive order of a new Office of Consumer Affairs within the executive branch to analyze and coordinate federal consumer activities. Knauer was named director of the new office.

• Establishment of a product safety program within the Department of Health, Education and Welfare.

• Legislation providing for clearer warranties and barring the issuance of deceptive warranties.

• Legislation making a number of unfair and deceptive business practices unlawful.

Consumer Protection Agency

Legislation establishing an independent agency to represent consumer interests before other federal agencies and courts passed the House Oct. 14 by a 345-44 roll-call vote. The bill (HR 10835) also granted statutory status to the newly created Office of Consumer Affairs in the Executive Office of the President.

However, the legislation died at the end of the 92nd Congress when the Senate in 1972 failed three times to invoke cloture (limit debate) on a stronger version of the legislation. *(1972 chronology, p. 691)*

Before final passage in the House, members rejected by recorded teller votes amendments aimed at both broadening and restricting the authority granted to the agency under HR 10835.

Background. In 1970, the Senate passed a bill granting the agency far greater powers by a 74-4 roll-call vote. But the House Rules Committee refused to grant a rule for floor consideration to a bill similar to HR 10835. *(1970 chronology, p. 675)*

In his 1971 consumer message, President Nixon asked Congress to postpone action on the independent agency until the White House could make further studies of recommendations made by the Advisory Council on Executive Reorganization. If Congress felt it must take action, Nixon said, he would support placing a consumer advocate within the Federal Trade Commission as an interim measure. Nixon also announced the creation by executive order of an Office of Consumer Affairs in the White House.

House Action. The House Government Operations Committee reported HR 10835 Sept. 30 by a 24-4 roll-call vote.

The bill was immediately endorsed by Virginia H. Knauer, the President's special adviser for consumer affairs, and denounced by consumer advocate Ralph Nader. Knauer called HR 10835 a "balanced and responsible proposal which will go far toward guaranteeing the consumer a strong voice in government activities affecting consumer interests."

Nader said Knauer's comment was "a reflection on how weak the bill is." Nader endorsed efforts by Rep. Benjamin S. Rosenthal (D N.Y.) to strengthen the bill by allowing the agency to intervene in informal investigations and proceedings of other federal agencies.

The House Rules Committee granted a rule to HR 10835 by voice vote Oct. 6, clearing the bill for floor action.

The House Oct. 14, after three days of debate, passed the bill by a 345-44 roll call. During the first day of debate Oct. 12, Chet Holifield (D Calif.), chairman of the Government Operations Committee, called HR 10835 "a strong and effective bill...carefully balanced by safeguards to ensure that trade secrets will not be improperly disclosed, test data will not be misrepresented, duplicative works will be avoided, and governmental operations will not be disrupted. These safeguards are needed, not because the bill is weak, but because the bill is strong."

The key vote came on an amendment sponsored by William S. Moorhead (D Pa.), which was rejected by a **160-218 recorded teller vote.**

Cosponsored by 17 of the 39 Government Operations Committee members, the Moorhead amendment would have allowed the agency to intervene in more informal activities than HR 10835 as reported would permit; the amendment also would have given the agency additional authority to act when other federal agencies refused to investigate consumer complaints.

Moorhead said the bill as reported by the committee had two defects which would be corrected by his amendment. "First, the bill prohibits the Consumer Protection Agency from participating in most adjudicatory proceedings because most of such proceedings involve, in the words of the bill, a 'fine, penalty or forfeiture,' and second, the bill does not give the Consumer Protection Agency any powers where a federal agency either refuses to act or, as is the practice with most agencies, acts through an informal proceeding."

Holifield said the wording in the bill gave the agency more power than supporters of the Moorhead amendment would admit. The imposition of penalties has generally occurred in courts and not in the proceedings of other federal agencies, he said. "If the critics who want the language changed are serious about it, then they are asking to move against persons who violate the law."

Shortly after Moorhead formally introduced his amendment Oct. 13, Don Fuqua (D Fla.) offered a substitute amendment to limit the new agency's powers to that of advising other government agencies and intervening in court suits only on an *amicus curiae* basis.

Fuqua said his major concern was "that we not create an agency to go in and formally intervene in other agencies' proceedings, whether they be formal or informal, and thereby create internal fights within the federal government." He said the primary function of the agency should be to publicize "wrongs being done where the interest of consumers is not being considered."

Holifield said Fuqua's amendment would "in effect cause the agency administrator to have one hand tied behind his back and with his hat in the other hand, to come before agencies to plead the consumer's cause."

The Fuqua substitute amendment was defeated Oct. 14 by a 149-240 recorded teller vote. Moorhead's amendment was then defeated on a 160-218 recorded teller vote.

Provisions. As passed by the House, HR 10835:

• Granted statutory status to the Office of Consumer Affairs, with a director and deputy director appointed by the President and confirmed by the Senate, to assist in coordinating federal programs affecting consumers, assure that consumer interests were observed in setting policy and operating programs, and investigate consumer problems not being dealt with by other federal agencies.

• Established a Consumer Protection Agency with an administrator and a deputy administrator appointed by the President and confirmed by the Senate.

• Authorized the agency to represent consumers in formal proceedings conducted by other federal agencies and in certain court suits. In the case of agency proceedings, the consumer agency could intervene as a party in any adjudicatory proceeding which was not seeking primarily to impose a fine, penalty or forfeiture. In the case of adjudications leading to fines, penalties or forfeitures, the consumer agency could submit information or evidence or appear as *amicus curiae.*

• Authorized the agency to intervene as a party in or institute a court review of a proceeding by another federal agency in which it participated. If it did not participate in the proceeding, it could enter the suit if it was eligible to intervene and if the court found that the other agency's actions adversely affected consumers and if consumers were not otherwise adequately represented.

• Authorized the administrator to request another federal agency to initiate a proceeding or takes an action in the interest of consumers. If the other agency failed to do so, it must specify its reasons in writing. The consumer agency could request another agency to provide information or summon witnesses.

• Authorized the agency to seek review in a federal court of another federal agency's action or refusal to act, to the extent that the right of judicial review was allowed by law.

• Established a Consumer Advisory Council, composed of 15 members appointed by the President for staggered five-year terms, to work with both the consumer agency and the White House Office.

• Made open-ended authorizations for carrying out the provisions of the act.

Consumer Warranties

In 1971, the Senate again passed a consumer warranty bill (S 986) incorporating the provisions of its 1970 bill and adding provisions to strengthen the consumer protection powers of the Federal Trade Commission (FTC). The House did not take action on S 986 in either 1971 or 1972, and the measure died at the end of the 92nd Congress.

S 986, as passed by the Senate Nov. 8 by a 76-2 roll-call votes did not require manufacturers to offer warranties, but, if they chose to do so, warranties for goods valued at $5 or more had to explain clearly what was covered and what was excluded. S 986 provided remedies for consumers if manufacturers or merchants failed to live up to the warranty agreements. It also prohibited dealers from disclaiming implied warranties—those that implied without specifically stating that a product would do what it was intended to be used for.

The FTC provisions (Title II) gave the commission broader powers to define unfair or deceptive acts and practices, and to take action against businessmen who violated those standards. It could issue orders on its own and go to court to obtain penalties against anyone who violated those orders. The FTC was also authorized to initiate court actions to obtain redress for consumers affected by fraudulent merchants.

A third section of S 986, approved as a floor amendment, provided for a new study of consumer grievance procedures.

The bill was introduced by Sen. Warren G. Magnuson (D Wash.), chairman of the Commerce Committee. The Nixon administration had introduced a warranty bill covering items costing more than $10.

Background. In 1970, the Senate passed a warranty bill (S 3074) but the measure died in the House.

Another bill (S 3201), combining FTC provisions with provisions allowing consumers to band together to bring class-action suits against fraudulent businessmen, was reported in the Senate but never came to a vote on the floor. In 1971, advocates of the measures decided to combine the warranty and FTC provisions in a single package. The FTC provisions had been part of the 1970 class-action bill. *(1970 chronology, p. 678)*

President Nixon advocated legislation in his Feb. 24 consumer message—but less broad than the provisions of S 986.

Auto Repair Costs

Legislation setting minimum federal standards for limiting property loss on automobiles involved in crashes passed the Senate Nov. 3. Although the House Interstate and Foreign Commerce Committee held hearings in November, the House did not consider the measure until 1972. *(1972 chronology, p. 689)*

The Senate bill (S 976) was aimed at curbing auto repair costs by either requiring manufacturers to produce vehicles that were more resistent to damage in collisions or by lowering the expense of repairs. As passed, S 976 required the transportation secretary to set property loss reduction standards; the costs of implementing those standards, however, had to be lower than benefits to consumers. Where cost standards conflicted with safety standards, the safety standards would take precedence.

S 976 authorized a federal government study of ways to provide consumers with information on the operating costs and safety features of cars and set up a system of demonstration inspection centers. Tampering with odometers—devices which record the total mileage a car has been driven—was prohibited.

The bill was originally introduced by Sen. Philip A. Hart (D Mich.) as part of a five-bill package aimed at reducing costs of car insurance and repairs. Among the other bills in the package was one (S 945) establishing a national system of no-fault auto insurance covering personal injuries arising out of auto accidents. A Senate subcommittee chaired by Hart had held hearings on auto repair costs in 1969 and 1970. *(Chronology, p. 667, 689)*

Senate Action. The Senate Commerce Committee reported S 976 Oct. 28 by voice vote, saying that "the need to reduce property loss resulting from motor vehicles is critical." In 1970, auto owners paid more than $5.5-billion to repair cars damaged in accidents, the report said. Of the total, $4.6-billion was reimbursed by insurance companies—which collected $7.9-billion in premiums for this coverage—and the remainder was absorbed by the car owners.

"Because of this great and unnecessary economic loss, there is a need to authorize the government to set minimum property loss reduction standards which would protect the fragile exteriors of motor vehicles," the report said.

The Senate Nov. 3, by a 89-4 roll-call passed S 976. No changes were made in the bill on the Senate floor.

Most of the floor debate centered on an amendment, offered by Robert P. Griffin (R Mich.) to eliminate Title I of the bill, which would allow the transportation secretary to set federal standards to reduce property damage resulting from accidents or to lower repair costs. The amendment failed on a 29-64 roll call.

Griffin called Title I "mischievous meddling with the free market system; it carries with it very serious implications because, if the federal government is to go so far as to regulate the design and manufacture of automobiles purely for the purpose of trying to affect so-called property loss and property value, then I wonder to what extent, as a logical result of such a precedent, the federal government would eventually go in regulating the design and manufacture of other major consumer products."

He said that consumers were willing to pay increased car costs for safety and anti-pollution features. "The question now before the Senate is: do they want to pay an even higher price to enforce a set of standards that have nothing to do with pollution or safety, that are supposedly going to reduce the damageability of the car and, in general, to increase the prices of new cars still further?"

Warren G. Magnuson (D Wash.), chairman of the Commerce Committee which reported the bill, said that S 976 "specifically provides that only regulations saving consumers money can be required."

No-Fault Auto Insurance

The push for a national no-fault auto insurance bill, which was to embroil Congress in one of its most heated consumer contests in 1972, began in earnest in 1971 with hearings in both the House and Senate.

Sen. Philip A. Hart (D Mich.), a leading congressional advocate of auto insurance change, introduced on Feb. 24 and 25 a package of five bills aimed at reforming the system and lowering costs. The package contained a bill (S 945) establishing a no-fault insurance system covering personal injury and property damage to be available throughout the country.

S 945 would eliminate the existing "tort liability" system under which the person who caused an accident—or his insurance company—paid for damage inflicted on others. Insurance claims should be paid without regard to who caused the accident, Hart said; the finding of fault should be a separate concern handled by police and courts, not insurance companies.

Less than a month later, on March 18, Transportation Secretary John A. Volpe released the final recommendations revolving from a two-year, $2-million Department of Transportation (DOT) study of auto insurance. The study was authorized by Congress in 1968. *(DOT study, Congress and the Nation, Vol. II, p. 805; other background, 1969 chronology, p. 667)*

Hart Bills. In introducing the insurance change bills, Hart said insurance companies provided insufficient payments to claimants and the "delivery system for this pittance is expensive and wasteful." He cited statistics compiled by the Senate Judiciary Subcommittee on Antitrust and Monopoly (which Hart headed) and various government agencies showing that only 42 per cent of all premiums paid for personal injury liability insurance in 1969 actually went to claimants. *(Chart, p. 683)*

Of that 42 per cent, he said, only 14 per cent accounted for out-of-pocket losses. Seven per cent was in duplicate payments (for benefits received from such sources as health insurance, Social Security and sick leave benefits) and the remaining 21 per cent was in excess of out-of-pocket losses (for pain and suffering and other general damages.).

Two-Fifths of Auto Insurance Premiums Paid Out in Claims

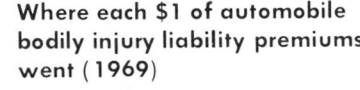

Where each $1 of automobile bodily injury liability premiums went (1969)

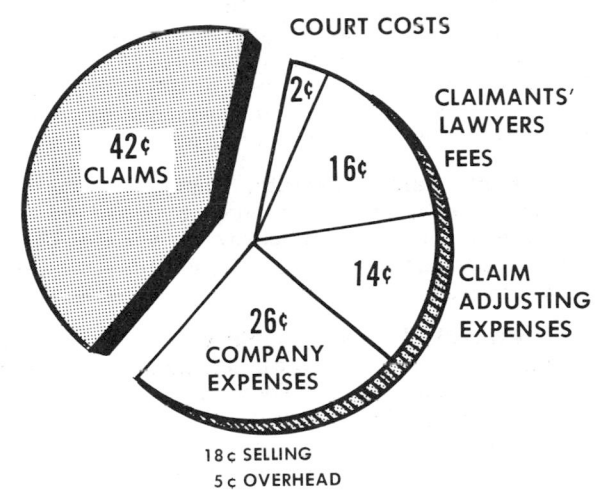

COURT COSTS

2¢

42¢ CLAIMS

CLAIMANTS' LAWYERS FEES

16¢

14¢   CLAIM ADJUSTING EXPENSES

26¢ COMPANY EXPENSES

18¢ SELLING
5¢ OVERHEAD
3¢ STATE TAXES

	Amount	%
Premiums*	$5,768,000,000	100
Company expenses:		
Selling	1,043,286,000	(18)
Overhead	295,374,000	(5)
State taxes	167,817,000	(3)
Total company expenses	1,506,477,000	26
Claim adjusting expenses	789,586,000	14
Claimants' lawyers fees	947,839,000	16
Court costs	111,102,000	2
Total expenses, fees and costs	3,355,004,000	58
Net benefits to claimants	2,412,996,000	42

* Earned by over 1,000 stock, mutual, and reciprocal insurers on automobile bodily injury liability insurance premiums, 1969.

SOURCE: U.S. Senate Antitrust and Monopoly Subcommittee

Chapman

In order to deliver a claimant $1 in benefits, the insurance company accumulated expenses of $1.40, Hart said. In comparison, $1 of workmen's compensation cost 50 cents in administrative costs; $1 of group accident and health insurance cost 22 cents.

Hart said enactment of his bill "would result in more benefits speedily delivered and would take a fantastic burden off our courts." The new system, he added, would not increase premiums even though more claims would be compensated. "All that is necessary is to change the present system so that monies paid in go to victims instead of being consumed by the present extremely inefficient system itself."

Hart's bill, the Uniform Motor Vehicle Insurance Act, required insurance policies to provide auto accident victims all "net economic losses"—those not covered by such things as health insurance, hospitalization or sick leave. Lost wages must be reimbursed at the rate of 85 per cent of salary or $1,000 per month, whichever was lower, up to 30 months of payment. Maximum payment in the case of death was $30,000.

The bill allowed the secretary of transportation to assign liability to trucks and other heavy vehicles which would cause more extensive damage in an accident than a passenger car would. It provided optional coverage for catastrophic accidents up to $50,000 for any one person and $300,000 for all personal claims.

The bill prohibited insurance companies from refusing to issue or renew policies or to cancel coverage, except for nonpayment of premiums or loss of the driver's license. It required companies to report statistics regarding claims and payments to the DOT, which must publish them regularly.

The other bills introduced by Hart would allow the establishment of group auto insurance, which would be offered to employees of a business or other concern similar to group health or life insurance. One of the bills (S 976) would require that all cars manufactured after July 1, 1974, have bumpers which would withstand a five-mile-per-hour collision with another car without suffering damage. The Senate passed S 976 in November 1971; the House did not take final action until 1972. *(1971 chronology below, 1972 chronology, p. 694)*

DOT Study. The massive DOT study shed more light on the problems of the existing auto insurance system. One of the reports, Public Attitudes Toward Auto Insurance, found during a public opinion survey that: 44 per cent of insurance holders would prefer no-fault insurance, compared with 36 per cent who preferred the fault-finding system; 14 per cent of those surveyed had policies cancelled or had trouble obtaining renewals, and half of the rest had heard of other people with the same difficulties; more than half of those surveyed said payments for pain and suffering should be eliminated if that would make rates go down; 58 per cent said that the prospect of being held liable for damages did not make any difference in the way people drive, while only 14 per cent said that such liability did in fact lead to careful driving.

Another DOT study, called Economic Consequences of Automobile Accident Injuries, examined the impact on people of accidents involving property damage, personal injuries or fatalities. It found that on the average, about half of total personal and family economic loss due to serious injuries or fatalities was recovered. But when the loss was small—less than $500—more than twice the amount was recovered on the average; when it was large—more than $25,000—recovery averaged only 30 per cent of total losses. The study found that the time lapse between the date of the accident and final settlement of tort claims averaged about 16 months—with less time necessary for small claims and more for large ones.

Administration Position. During his testimony before the Senate Commerce Committee March 18, Volpe said the Nixon administration opposed federal legislation, preferring instead that all states adopt their own no-fault auto insurance laws. Volpe urged Congress to enact only a "sense of the Congress" resolution calling for state action. If the states failed to act, the federal government could then step in to set standards below which the states could not go. Volpe recommended giving the states at least 25 months to enact their own laws.

The Senate Commerce Committee held further hearings on S 945 in May; the House Interstate and Foreign Commerce Subcommittee on Commerce and Finance held hearings in April on HR 4994, similar to S 945. No further action was taken by either committee.

Other Bills

MEAT INSPECTION. The Senate July 29 by voice vote passed a bill (S 1316) increasing to 80 percent from 50 per cent the amount the federal government could pay toward state meat inspection programs. The House rejected the bill in 1972. *(1972 chronology, p. 700)*

Before passing S 1316, the Senate rejected, on a 38-52 roll-call vote, an amendment by Charles McC. Mathias Jr. (R Md.) to allow meat to be transported in interstate commerce without federal inspection if it had passed state inspection equal to that carried out by the federal government.

FISH INSPECTION. A bill (S 2824) establishing a federal inspection program to regulate fish products, fish processing plants and fishing vessels passed the Senate Dec. 2 by a 67-4 roll-call vote. The House failed to take action on the bill.

S 2824, the Wholesome Fish and Fishery Products Act of 1971, required regular surveillance of fish processors and continuous inspection where necessary by the Food and Drug Administration. It also required FDA to certify all plants and fishing vessels for compliance with sanitation standards.

Government inspection of fish and fish products is carried out under two basic programs. The Food and Drug Administration (FDA), part of the Department of Health, Education and Welfare, samples fish in retail stores as part of its regular food inspection efforts. The Interior Department's Bureau of Commercial Fisheries offers a voluntary continuous inspection service for shore fishery establishments. Both programs together covered only a small percentage of the fish and fish products industries.

Revelations of high concentration of mercury and other poisonous chemicals in tuna and swordfish in 1971 increased demands for stronger fish inspection programs. *(Background, Congress and the Nation, Vol. II, p. 822; previous hearings, 1969 chronology, p. 670)*

Insurance Components

There are six basic components of automobile insurance; bodily injury liability, property damage liability, medical payments, comprehensive physical damage, collision, and protection against uninsured motorists. Insurance customers can buy these components in different combinations and for varying costs.

Only the first two—bodily injury and property damage liability—are subject to redress by the tort system by which the person causing the injury or his insurance company pays costs to the injured parties. In the other four categories, payments are made regardless of who caused the accident.

Bodily Injury Liability. This protects the insurance holder against claims brought by or on behalf of persons injured or killed by his vehicle. This includes passengers in his car, persons in other cars or pedestrians.

Property Damage Liability. This covers claims against the driver if his car damages other property —usually another car. Bodily injury and property damage generally are discussed by a series of three numbers representing thousands of dollars. The first number represents the maximum amount an insurance company will pay to any individual person in an accident; the second refers to the total amount the company will pay for all bodily injury claims, and the third refers to the total property damage limit. Thus 10/20/5 means the company will pay up to $10,000 to any person injured in an accident, $20,000 in claims for all injured persons, and $5,000 for total property damage claims.

Medical Payments. This covers medical costs for the driver and all other passengers in his car involved in an accident—regardless of whether he caused the accident.

Comprehensive Physical Damage. This covers a wide range of possible losses including theft, fire, glass breakage, flood, falling objects, vandalism and storms.

Collision. This protects the owner against upset or collision with a car or another object without regard to which driver was at fault. This allows a car owner to be reimbursed immediately by his own insurance company for damages caused by another car without waiting for a settlement or suit to get payment from the other driver. Collision and comprehensive physical damage insurance are usually written on a $50 or $100 deductible basis, which means the driver must pay the first $50 or $100 in repairs and the insurance company pays for the rest.

Uninsured Motorist Protection. This applies to accidents caused by uninsured or hit-and-run drivers. It provides coverage by the insurance holder's company up to the limits of his policy. The uninsured motorist must be legally liable for the injuries suffered by the insured driver and his passengers.

Provisions. As passed, S 2824, contained the following major provisions:

● Required the FDA to develop adequate processing standards at plants and on vessels and set a timetable for implementation of the standards.

● Provided continuous and effective surveillance by the FDA of all fish processing plants and continuous (daily) inspection of plants where deemed necessary by the secretary of health, education and welfare. Procedures would be set for inspection, fish labeling and condemnation. Imported fish and fish products were required to meet the same standards established for domestic fish.

● Required the FDA to cooperate with state agencies in developing fish inspection programs which were at least as strong as the federal program and allowed federal grants of up to 50 per cent of the cost of the state programs.

FLAMMABLE FABRICS. A bill (HR 5066) authorizing $4-million for fiscal 1972 to carry out the provisions of the Flammable Fabrics Act of 1953, as amended, which set standards for apparel and certain household articles, passed the House April 28. The Senate completed action in 1972. *(p. 698)*

The previous authorization of funds for administering the act expired at the end of fiscal 1970.

HR 5066 was passed as reported April 19 by the House Interstate and Foreign Commerce Committee. The bill made no changes in the flammable fabrics program other than the authorization of funds. *(Background, 1970 chronology, p. 679)*

PRODUCT SAFETY. The Senate Commerce Committee held hearings in July on two bills establishing federal machinery to set consumer product safety standards.

The administration's proposal, S 1797, directed the secretary of health, education and welfare to set up a consumer product safety program. A bill, S 983, sponsored by Warren G. Magnuson (D Wash.), chairman of the Commerce Committee, and Frank E. Moss (D Utah), would establish an independent consumer product safety agency. Congress in 1972 cleared legislation establishing an independent agency. *(1972 chronology, this page)*

CLASS-ACTION SUITS. The Senate Commerce Consumer Subcommittee held hearings on April 27 and 29 on numerous bills allowing consumers to band together and bring class-action lawsuits. No further action was taken. A class-action bill was reported in 1970 by the Senate Commerce Committee but the measure never reached the floor for a vote. *(1970 chronology p. 679)*

1972

In a dramatic legislative year for consumer affairs, Congress in 1972 approved the most significant consumer measure of President Nixon's first term—the creation of an independent Consumer Product Safety Commission authorized to set standards for a wide variety of consumer products and to ban those products that presented an unreasonable risk of injury.

The Nixon administration did not support the measure, preferring instead that a product safety agency be established within the Department of Health, Education and Welfare.

Congress also approved a bill promoting safer automobiles and making them less costly to repair. The measure authorized the secretary of transportation to set standards for automobile bumpers to reduce or eliminate low-speed collision damage.

But two other consumer-supported measures were killed in the Senate, in both cases after intensive lobby pressure was brought to bear.

In August, the Senate recommitted a strong no-fault auto insurance bill to the Judiciary Committee; the move effectively killed the legislation for the year. The measure, which would have established minimum federal standards to be incorporated into state no-fault laws, was opposed by the administration, trial lawyers and several insurance companies and associations.

And, in the last days of the 92nd Congress, Senate supporters of a bill establishing an independent Consumer Protection Agency were unable to muster enough votes to cut off a filibuster on the measure. After the third vote to invoke cloture (limit debate), the Senate leadership agreed to set aside the legislation for the remainder of the session.

A large coalition of business associations worked diligently among members of the Senate to defeat the consumer protection bill. The measure's supporters also charged that the administration covertly lobbied against adoption of cloture. The administration had publicly announced its support for a weaker House version of the bill approved in 1971.

In other 1972 action, the House, by a seven-vote margin, passed a bill allowing food processors, growers, packers and distributors to sue the federal government for damages incurred as a result of the 1969 ban on cyclamates, artificial sweeteners used in a wide variety of foods. Cyclamates had been banned after they were found to cause cancer in rats.

The Senate took no action on the cyclamate bill but it did approve a bill banning DES (diethylstilbestrol), a synthetic hormone used as a growth promotant in meat animals. In August, the Food and Drug Administration set up a phase-out on the use of the hormone which had been found to cause cancer in test animals. The Senate measure would have banned immediately some uses of DES and banned other uses after Jan. 1, 1973 unless further tests found those uses to be safe for humans. The House took no action on the measure.

The Senate also approved a measure calling for fair credit reporting while the House rejected legislation increasing federal participation in state meat inspection programs. The Senate had passed that bill in 1971.

Product Safety Agency

The Senate Oct. 14 by voice vote cleared for the President a bill (S 3419—PL 92-573)—the Consumer Product Safety Act—one of the two major pieces of consumer legislation approved by Congress in 1972.

Impetus for creation of the product safety commission stemmed largely from the final report of the National Commission on Product Safety recommending a new agency.

The independent agency, to be headed by a five-member commission, would have the authority to set safety standards for consumer products and to ban those products presenting an unreasonable risk of injury.

The House adopted the conference report by voice vote Oct. 13. House-Senate conferees agreed on a compromise that was much closer to the narrower House version than to the measure passed by the Senate. In addition to transferring to the new agency the functions of several federal safety standard laws, the Senate measure would have transferred the functions of the Food and Drug Administration (FDA) out of the Department of Health, Education and Welfare (HEW) into the new agency. Conferees deleted that provision. (*Transfers, box, this page*)

Conferees, however, modified a Senate provision to permit a private citizen to petition the agency to promulgate a safety standard for a product he considered dangerous. If the agency failed to issue a regulation, the citizen could appeal the agency's failure to act in court. If the court found in favor of the citizen's case, the agency would be required to begin the rule-making procedure. Conferees added a proviso that would not make that section effective until three years after enactment of S 3419.

The Nixon administration did not support S 3419, preferring instead that a consumer product safety agency be established within the HEW department.

Burger Aide. Prior to adoption of the conference report, columnist Jack Anderson Oct. 5 charged that Chief Justice Warren E. Burger sent Rowland F. Kirks, chief administrative officer of the federal courts, to discuss the consumer product safety bill with House Speaker Carl Albert (D Okla.). Kirks was accompanied by Thomas Corcoran, a Washington attorney and one-time aide to President Franklin D. Roosevelt, who represented several drug firms opposed to the bill. According to Albert's office, Corcoran was the spokesman of the two at the late summer meeting, where he contended that the bill would add significantly to the number of cases before federal courts.

On Oct. 13, Kirks said that Burger was unaware of his visit to Albert's office. Kirks added that he considered his visit a routine one to inform Congress of the impact of legislation on the courts. Albert said that neither Kirks nor Corcoran represented themselves as being sent by Burger.

Also on Oct. 13, Burger released a letter he had sent to Albert in which he declared that he had taken no position with regard to the consumer product safety bill. "However," Burger added, "I do have and always will have a strong view about when Congress considers legislation that will add a substantial volume of cases in the federal courts the Congress should also provide the means to handle those cases."

John E. Moss (D Calif.), the bill's major House sponsor, said Burger's letter was a "highly evasive response," adding that Burger had not satisfactorily answered whether he had sent Kirks to speak with Albert.

Consumer Legislation Transfers

Following is a list of major consumer legislative programs which were transferred to the Consumer Product Safety Act (S 3419).

Federal Hazardous Substances Act of 1960 (PL 86-613) as amended by the Toy Safety Act of 1969 (PL 91-133) (*1969 chronology, p. 661*) as amended by the 1966 Child Protection Amendments (PL 89-756) (*Congress and the Nation, Vol. II, p. 796*)

Poison Prevention Packaging Act of 1970 (PL 91-601) (*1970 chronology, p. 674*)

Flammable Fabrics Act of 1953 as amended (PL 90-189) (*Congress and the Nation, Vol. II, p. 802; 1970 chronology p. 678; 1971 chronology, p. 685*)

Radiation Control for Health and Safety Act of 1968 (PL 90-602) (*Congress and the Nation, Vol. II, p. 818*)

See also: National Commission on Product Safety (PL 90-146) (*Congress and the Nation, Vol. II, p. 803; 1970 chronology, p. 679*)

PROVISIONS

As cleared by Congress, S 3419:

• Established an independent five-member commission to protect consumers from unreasonable product hazards; the commissioners were to be appointed by the President and confirmed by the Senate for seven-year terms; the President would designate one commissioner as chairman for the duration of his term; no more than three commissioners could be from the same political party.

• Established an injury information clearinghouse within the commission to collect information relating to the causes and prevention of death, injury or illness associated with consumer products and to conduct studies and investigations.

• Authorized the commission to conduct safety studies and tests of consumer products.

• Prohibited the commission from disclosing information which dealt with trade secrets or sensitive costs and competitive data to the public; required the commission to give notice to the manufacturer or distributor of a product at least 30 days before releasing information that might identify the manufacturer or distributor; required the commission to print a retraction if it had released inaccurate or misleading information.

• Authorized the commission to promulgate mandatory safety standards to prevent or reduce unreasonable risk of injury associated with consumer products; required the standard to relate to performance, composition, content, design, construction, finish or packaging of the product or to relate to warnings or instructions for use; delineated the procedure to be used by the commission in promulgating such regulations; permitted the commission to allow persons outside the commission to develop safety standards; if the sole person outside the commission developing a standard was the manufacturer, distributor or retailer of the product for which the standard was being developed, the commission could independently develop standard proposals.

• Permitted the commission to ban a consumer product if it determined that product presented an unreasonable hazard and that no safety standard would adequately protect the public from that hazard.

• Authorized the commission to prohibit a manufacturer from stockpiling a product before a safety standard becomes effective.

• Permitted private persons to petition the commission to issue, amend or revoke a safety standard; if the commission denied the petition, the petitioners could appeal the denial to a U.S. district court; if the court found in favor of the petitioners, the commission would be required to initiate the action petitioned for; the petition provision would not be effective until three years after enactment of the bill.

• Provided for judicial review of commission safety standards.

• Allowed the commission to seek a court order against a product constituting an imminent public hazard and any manufacturer, distributor or retailer of it.

• Authorized the commission to require manufacturers to furnish notice and a description of any new consumer product to the commission before marketing.

• Required manufacturers to certify that a product met all applicable safety standards, permitted the commission to test for compliance and to investigate factory facilities; permitted the commission to require labels for consumer products carrying the date and place of manufacture, the name of the manufacturer and certification of compliance with safety standards.

• Permitted the commission upon determining that a product presented a substantial hazard, to require the manufacturer, distributor or retailer to give public notice of the hazards, to bring the product into conformity with applicable safety standards or to repair it, to replace the product or to refund its purchase price.

• Required that imported consumer products meet safety regulations applicable to domestically produced consumer products, but exempted products from complying with safety standards if they were labeled for export.

• Set civil penalties of $2,000 for each violation with the maximum amount at $500,000; set criminal penalties at $50,000 or a year in prison or both if a person continued to violate the law after being informed of noncompliance.

• Permitted private persons to sue for damages if injury resulted from use of a consumer product not complying with safety standards; permitted private persons to seek court action to enforce a safety standard.

• Prohibited states from establishing or continuing in effect consumer product safety standards not identical with federal standards.

• Required the commission to submit duplicate copies of budget requirements and legislative recommendations to Congress as well as to the President or the Office of Management and Budget.

• Established a 15-member Product Safety Advisory Council within the commission to propose and advise on safety standards.

• Instructed the commission to set up programs for federal-state cooperation with regard to consumer products.

• Transferred to the commission the functions, orders and regulations under the Federal Hazardous Substances Act, the Poison Prevention Packaging Act, the Flammable Fabrics Act and the Refrigerator Safety Act.

• Prohibited the commission from having authority to regulate tobacco products, firearms, motor vehicles, pesticides, aircraft, boats regulated by the Federal Boat Safety Act of 1971, drugs, cosmetics, and food; the commission was also prohibited from issuing regulations for products that could be regulated under the Occupational Safety and Health Act of 1970, the Atomic Energy Act of 1954, the Clean Air Act of 1963 or certain products emitting electronic radiation.

• Authorized appropriations of $55-million for fiscal 1973, $59-million for fiscal 1974 and $64-million for fiscal 1975; authorized appropriations of up to $100,000 for planning and constructing research, development and testing facilities.

Background. The National Commission on Product Safety, created by Congress in 1967, in mid-1970 issued a report calling for a comprehensive law covering all products and for a new independent agency to devise and enforce safety standards. In effect, these changes would strip the Food and Drug Administration of authority to police standards prescribed by Congress for specific products. *(Congress and the Nation, Vol. II, p. 803; 1970 chronology, p. 675)*

In 1971, President Nixon proposed "legislation providing broad federal authority for comprehensive regulation of hazardous consumer products." He called for a new division within the HEW Department to set standards for products not already covered by specific safety laws.

The Senate Commerce Committee had extensive hearings in 1971 on the administration bill (S 1797), the Product Safety Commission bill (S 983) and other consumer safety proposals. The House Interstate and Foreign Commerce Subcommittee on Commerce and Finance began hearings on product safety legislation in December 1971. *(1971 chronology, p. 685)*

SENATE COMMITTEE ACTION

Three different committees—Commerce, Labor and Public Welfare, and Government Operations—held jurisdiction over various titles of S 3419. The bill first was reported by the Commerce Committee on April 13. Then under a unanimous consent agreement of the Senate, the measure was referred to the other two committees.

Commerce. The Commerce Committee ordered S 3419 reported March 21 by a 17-1 roll-call vote, with Norris Cotton (R N.H.), ranking minority member of the committee, casting the lone dissenting vote.

As reported from the Commerce Committee, S 3419 contained three titles. Title I established the agency and defined the duties of the commissioners. Title II transferred into the agency the functions of several existing product safety laws as well as the FDA. Title III established the procedures by which the agency would formulate safety standards.

An amendment offered by Cotton to delete Titles I and II and give product safety authority to the HEW secretary was defeated, 4-11.

In a 13-page statement, Cotton objected to the bill because, he said, the federal consumer safety agency in addition to the proposed Consumer Protection Agency would be redundant, regressive and a waste of tax-payers' money.

Government Operations. The Government Operations Committee's Subcommittee on Executive Reorganization and Government Research held two days of hearings on Titles I and II of S 3419. However, the full committee failed three times to obtain a quorum to report the bill by a May 31 deadline set by the Senate. The panel thus forfeited its right to act on the bill.

Labor and Public Welfare. The Labor and Public Welfare Committee reported an amended version of S 3419 June 5. Major changes made by the committee included changing the name from the Consumer Safety Agency to the Food, Drug and Consumer Product Agency, expanding the definition of the agency's duties to include protection of consumers against misbranding, adulteration and illegal distribution of food, drugs, cosmetics and medical devices, making five additional transfers to the new agency and extending regulations for cosmetics labeling.

SENATE FLOOR ACTION

The Senate June 21, by a 69-10 roll-call vote, passed an amended version of S 3419.

During floor debate on S 3419, the Senate defeated attempts to 1) strip the agency of its independence and place it under HEW jurisdiction and 2) relieve the agency of most of its enforcement powers.

The Senate approved an amendment adding a new title to the bill bringing inspection of food, drugs, cosmetics and certain household fuels under the scope of the act and requiring registration and labeling of consumer products containing corrosive or toxic substances.

In other changes made in the bill, the Senate added a commission of veterinary medicine to the new agency and retained responsibility for administering certain existing laws within the Department of Agriculture rather than transferring their functions to the new agency.

The Senate considered 18 amendments, adopting 14 by voice vote and rejecting four by roll-call votes.

Independent Agency. Cotton offered an amendment to vest the functions proposed for the new agency in the HEW Department. He said this would attain the same end result "without tearing FDA out by its roots from HEW and separating it from the National Institutes of Health and from all of the other agencies in the (HEW) Department whose work must be closely coordinated in the enforcement of this very meritorious act we are considering this afternoon."

Commerce Consumer Subcommittee Chairman Frank E. Moss (D Utah) opposed the amendment: "We can cite many gaps in the administration of the laws under the HEW Department. To compound these by including additional authority in this agency would be a bungling disaster and an insult to the American people."

Cotton contended that there was no demonstrated need for a new agency, particularly in view of pending legislation (HR 10835) which would create an independent Consumer Protection Agency to represent consumers in government proceedings. He cited administration opposition to creation of a new agency and said enactment of his amendment would prevent the confusion which inevitably would arise during the transition of functions and personnel to a new agency.

Joseph M. Montoya (D N.M.) said an independent agency was "a healthy concept for the reason that the director of this agency is going to be responsible.... For any mistakes that he makes and for any omissions in his duties, he will be responsible and he will be charged with them.... However, if we immerse again the protection and enforcement in a vast agency such as HEW, we will lose sight of the responsibility vested in any public official with respect to enforcement." Cotton's amendment was rejected by a 32-51 vote.

Enforcement. Edward J. Gurney (R Fla.) offered an amendment making the enforcement proceedings of the new agency a responsibility of the Justice Department, with the exception that the agency itself could seek a temporary injunction against a product which it determined might constitute an imminent threat to consumers. (Under S 3419, the new agency would have responsibility for enforcing its regulations.)

Gurney said the issue was whether the enforcement powers of the new agency should be administered differently from those of other agencies. "The Justice Department and the courts should enforce consumer protection decisions as they do in the case of other agencies," Gurney maintained. He added that an enforcement division within the new agency would be duplicative and uneconomical.

Magnuson countered: "It does little good to equip an agency with the authority and personnel to locate defective or nonconforming products and then not equip it to take action against manufacturers or processors of those products." Gurney's amendment was rejected by a 31-51 roll-call vote.

Criminal Penalties. Cotton then offered an amendment deleting provisions for criminal penalties from S 3419, thus prohibiting attorneys for the agency from prosecuting criminal cases. Magnuson said that routing cases through the Justice Department often took too long, particularly in instances where the agency must have the ability "to take emergency measures." The Cotton amendment was rejected by a 39-41 roll-call vote.

Title V. The Senate approved an amendment by Montoya adding the new title (Title V) to the bill amending the Federal Hazardous Substances Act to include food, drugs, cosmetics and certain household fuels under the regulations of the act. The amendment was approved by voice vote without substantive debate.

Voting on Amendments. The three amendments by Cotton and Gurney seeking to narrow the authority of the proposed new agency were supported by a majority of Republicans and, with the exception of the Gurney amendment, by a majority of southern Democrats. Six southern Democrats voted for the Gurney amendment while seven opposed it. All voting northern Democrats opposed all three amendments.

HOUSE ACTION

The House Interstate and Foreign Commerce Committee reported a bill (HR 15003) June 20. As reported, HR 15003 was a much narrower version of S 3419.

The House bill did not transfer into the new agency the functions of the FDA, changed the composition of the agency members and did not include provisions extending regulations relating to misbranding of cosmetics or establishing a registration mechanism for products containing toxic or corrosive substances.

Floor Action. The House Sept. 20, by a 319-50 roll-call vote, passed an amended version of S 3419, the Senate's Product Safety Commission bill.

Before the vote on passage, the House by voice vote passed a companion bill (HR 15003) reported by the Interstate and Foreign Commerce Committee. The House then substituted the provisions of HR 15003 as amended on the floor for the provisions of the Senate-passed version (S 3419).

Provision Changes. Major provisions of HR 15003 as reported were not substantially changed by the nine amendments adopted during floor debate.

Adopted on the floor was an amendment by Committee Chairman Harley O. Staggers (D W.Va.) permitting the date of manufacture to appear in coded form on certain consumer products, and an amendment by Commerce Subcommittee Chairman John E. Moss (D Calif.) guaranteeing that no person would be subject to a civil suit for disclosing information to the commission. An amendment to require that warning of products constituting substantial hazards be written in Spanish as well as English was withdrawn.

Amendments that would have added guns and ammunition to the list of consumer products covered under the bill and authorized the commission to establish safety regulations for nonmedical products that emitted radiation were rejected.

Debate. As in the Senate, debate on the bill in the House centered on the need for creating an independent agency. James T. Broyhill (R N C), ranking minority member of the Commerce Subcommittee, supported creation of the independent commission: "An independent commission can give more objective, single-minded attention to consumer safety. An independent agency has undivided responsibility for product safety and can be more easily held responsible for any failures that occur.... And, significantly, an independent agency would combine existing fragmented programs which are currently dispersed through approximately 30 different federal organizations."

William L. Springer (R Ill.), ranking minority member of the full committee, disagreed: "Past dealings with such commissions indicate serious weaknesses in their operations. Many commissions are fraught with internal bickering.... Most commissions do not have the clout... with the budget process nor access to the White House."

George A. Goodling (R Pa.) said the bill would harm the free enterprise system: "Are we going to stifle the expertise responsible for our inventive genius that brings countless new and improved products to our marketplace? Are we going to...discourage costly research, so necessary to the development of any new product, when the developer must first secure permission from a government agency to sell his product?"

No member, however, offered an amendment to place the commission within HEW.

CONFERENCE ACTION. Conferees filed their report on S 3419 Oct. 12. The House agreed to the conference report Oct. 13 by voice vote and the Senate adopted it Oct. 14 by voice vote. More than five months after its creation, President Nixon April 4, 1973, named four of the five commissioners to the Consumer Product Safety Commission. The fifth was to be named at a later date.

The four nominees, subject to Senate confirmation, were: Richard O. Simpson, acting assistant secretary of commerce for science and technology, who was to serve as chairman; Lawrence M. Kushner, acting director of the National Bureau of Standards; Constance E. Newman, director of Volunteers in Service to America (VISTA); and Barbara A. Hackman Franklin, White House adviser on the employment of women in government.

Auto Repair Costs

Congress Oct. 6 cleared for the President a bill (S 976—PL 92-513), the Motor Vehicle Information and Cost Savings Act, to promote safe automobiles and make them less costly to repair.

Final action came when the Senate by voice vote approved a conference report on S 976.

The bill, as cleared, required the secretary of transportation to establish front and rear bumper standards for passenger motor vehicles to reduce low-speed collision damage. S 976 defined a bumper standard as one which eliminated or reduced substantial physical damage to the front and rear ends of automobiles involved in low-speed collisions, or reduced the cost of repairing autos involved in such collisions. Bumper standards could not take effect before July 1, 1973.

The bill did not establish a minimum speed under which bumpers would have to withstand impact. However, hearings in both the Senate and the House, and debate on the House floor, indicated that the minimum probably would be set at five miles per hour.

S 976 also set up a consumer information program which would compare various models of cars as to their susceptibility to damage and their relative repair costs and authorized the establishment of five to 10 motor vehicle diagnostic inspection demonstration centers throughout the nation to test for compliance with safety and emission standards. Tampering with odometers, devices that record the total mileage driven, was made a federal offense.

S 976 authorized appropriations of $108-million for fiscal years 1973-75 to carry out provisions of the bill.

The Nixon administration opposed both the House and Senate versions of the bill, preferring instead its own bill (HR 9353) which would have required publication of insurance company statistics and test results on all cars.

House-Senate conferees adopted the major provisions of the House version of the bill (HR 11627). The Senate version, passed in November 1971, was broader, requiring the transportation secretary to set standards for the costs of auto repairs and auto susceptibility to damage when involved in a collision. *(Senate action, p. 682)*

The conference report stated that it was "likely that a bumper standard which requires protection of the external sheet metal of motor vehicles in low-speed collisions would provide the maximum cost savings to the public.... It is not as clearly defined...what other property loss reduction standards may be feasible or what cost savings would be achieved from their implementation."

Background. Consumers and the insurance industry had long sought some kind of relief from the rising costs of

Estimated Repair Costs for Slow-Speed Car Crashes

SEDANS	2.5 MPH Rear/Barrier	5 MPH Front/Barrier	5 MPH Rear/Barrier	10 MPH Front/Barrier	10 MPH* Front/Rear	10 MPH** Front/Side	15 MPH Front/Barrier
Chevrolet Impala	$112.60	$153.75	$197.05	$576.65	$163.35 261.70	$173.90 719.25	$1,133.52
Ford Galaxie	20.00	402.10	242.60	917.17	265.65 423.81	341.70 598.65	1,243.30
Plymouth Fury	96.50	331.15	224.50	722.15	269.35 151.25	310.20 524.75	1,035.10
AMC Ambassador	12.00	168.25	159.10	830.50	220.00 280.40	338.65 421.65	1,095.90
Average	60.28	263.81	205.81	761.62	229.59 279.29	291.11 566.08	1,126.96
SMALL CARS							
Chevrolet Vega	71.70	190.90	274.45	619.20	250.53 273.75	128.35 218.30	777.41
Ford Pinto	36.80	125.20	267.50	667.05	176.55 263.10	145.92 197.50	805.25
AMC Gremlin	44.80	334.65	235.65	653.35	243.74 108.85	233.70 314.95	861.15
Toyota	8.36	251.46	214.78	657.00	206.62 368.28	209.91 328.34	872.20
Average	40.42	225.55	248.10	649.15	219.36 253.50	179.47 264.77	829.00

In this test, one car of the model listed hit the rear of a similar car which was stationary in neutral with the brake off. The price listed first for each car model is the estimated repair cost for the striking car (front-end damage); the second price is for the struck car (rear-end damage).

**In this test, one car of the model listed hit the side of a similar car. The price listed first is the estimated repair cost for the striking car (front-end damage); the second price is for the struck car (side damage).*

SOURCE: Insurance Institute for Highway Safety

auto repair. Tests conducted by the Insurance Institute for Highway Safety found that for 1972 sedans hitting a barrier head-on going five miles an hour, the average cost of repair—for parts and labor—was $263.81. At 15 miles an hour, the average repair costs for the same model cars were $1,126.96. *(Box, this page)*

The American Insurance Association estimated that automobile owners would save $1-billion a year in repairs if cars were equipped with front and rear bumpers that could withstand impacts of up to five miles an hour without suffering damage.

In March 1970, Allstate Insurance Co. announced that it would reduce collision premium rates by 20 per cent on cars that could withstand front or rear end collisions up to five miles an hour without damage. Allstate also provided lesser reductions for automobiles meeting less rigid bumper standards. The Insurance Service Organization, to which about 1,000 insurance companies subscribed, had recommended a 10-per cent

reduction on premium rates for 1973 model cars meeting certain federal safety standards.

During debate prior to House passage of the bill, Charles A. Vanik (D Ohio) said he was "shocked" that S 976 did not require standardized bumper heights. A spokesman for the National Highway Traffic Safety Administration told Congressional Quarterly that a regulation, promulgated in April 1971, requiring most 1974 model cars to pass a pendulum impact test, would go far in establishing uniform bumper heights.

PROVISIONS

As cleared by Congress, S 976:
● Authorized the secretary of transportation to set bumper standards for domestic and imported passenger motor vehicles to reduce low-speed collision damage; required the secretary to permit interested parties to

comment on proposed bumper standards.

- Provided judicial review procedures for persons adversely affected by the bumper standards.
- Prohibited the secretary from disclosing trade secrets except to the appropriate congressional committees and to other persons involved with implementing provisions of S 976.
- Required manufacturers to keep records and make reports; authorized the secretary to inspect manufacturing plants to ensure compliance with federal standards; required manufacturers or distributors to certify that each vehicle complied with federal standards.
- Set civil penalties of up to $1,000 for each violation of the bill; set a maximum of $800,000 for multiple violations; set criminal penalties of up to $50,000 or one year in prison, or both.
- Authorized automobile owners to sue manufacturers in federal court if damages to their cars resulted from noncompliance with federal standards; provided that the suits must be brought within three years of an accident.
- Permitted states to enforce their own bumper standards until federal bumper standards were promulgated, provided that the state standards were in effect when S 976 was enacted and were not in conflict with other federal standards.
- Authorized $5-million in fiscal 1973, $9-million in fiscal 1974 and $10-million in fiscal 1975 for carrying out the bumper standard provisions.
- Authorized the secretary to carry out a one-year study to determine the degree of passenger protection, damage susceptibility, ease of diagnosis and repair and operating costs of passenger motor vehicles and to furnish that information to the public.
- Required the secretary to develop and distribute to dealers by Feb. 1, 1975, information comparing differences in insurance costs for different makes and models of cars based on their damage susceptibility and degree of passenger protection; required the dealers to give the information to prospective buyers.
- Authorized the secretary to request information from automobile insurers, including accident claims data relating to personal injury and costs of repairs for all makes and models of cars; set civil penalties of up to $1,000 for failure to comply with the request.
- Authorized $3-million per year for fiscal years 1973-75 to carry out the consumer information provisions.
- Directed the secretary to establish between five and 10 motor vehicle diagnostic inspection demonstration projects; authorized appropriations of $15-million for fiscal 1973; $25-million for fiscal 1974 and $35-million for fiscal 1975 to establish the centers; prohibited the secretary from granting more than 20 per cent of the amount authorized to any one state.
- Made it unlawful do disconnect or alter the odometer of any motor vehicle, to sell or use any device which changed odometer readings or knowingly to drive an automobile with a nonfunctional odometer.
- Set civil penalties of three times the amount of actual damages sustained or $1,500, whichever was greater, for violations of the odometer provision.

HOUSE ACTION

The House passed its version of the bill (HR 11627) May 22 by a 254-38 roll-call vote. No changes were made

in the bill as reported by the House Interstate and Foreign Commerce Committee April 28.

George E. Danielson (D Calif.) offered an amendment to permit states to enforce their own bumper standards if those standards were the same as or higher than the federal standards to be established by the bill.

Lionel Van Deerlin (D Calif.), a member of the committee, offered a substitute for the Danielson amendment to permit states to enforce their own standards if such standards were in effect before Jan. 1, 1972, unless a federal standard of "at least equal stringency" were in effect.

Bob Eckhardt (D Texas), also a committee member, opposed the amendment: "Who determines what is equal stringency?" Eckhardt contended that the Van Deerlin amendment would "place a burden on the automobile manufacturer" and on "ourselves" by requiring manufacturers to produce a different product for those states which already had bumper standards." Both the Danielson amendment and the Van Deerlin substitute were defeated by voice votes.

Charles A. Vanik (D Ohio) said he was shocked that HR 11627 did not require standardized bumper heights. "Thousands of accidents and physical injuries result from the haphazard mixing of vehicles and trucks which have bumpers which mix instead of match," Vanik said.

Robert McClory (R Ill.) opposed the bill, asserting that it represented "governmental interference in the private industry the like of which...we have never had before.... It seems to me that when the government of the United States substitutes itself for the consumer and goes into the business of dictating to the manufacturers and purchasers of merchandise details of construction ...it causes injury and permanent harm to the American people."

After passing HR 11627, the House by voice vote passed the companion Senate bill (S 976) in lieu after amending it to contain the language of the House version.

Final Action. The House Oct. 4 and the Senate Oct. 6 by voice votes and without debate adopted the conference report on S 976.

Consumer Protection Agency

After the Senate failed three times late in the session to shut off debate on a bill (S 3970) to establish an independent consumer advocacy agency, the Democratic leadership agreed to shelve the bill for the remainder of the 92nd Congress.

The death of the bill was viewed as a major victory for members of the business community who believed the proposed Consumer Protection Agency would cause undue government harassment.

The third and last effort to invoke cloture (limit further debate) was made Oct. 5, but the vote, **a key roll call of 52-30,** was three short of the two-thirds majority of those present and voting needed for approval.

The Senate Sept. 29 rejected the first cloture motion by a 47-29 roll-call vote—four votes short. The second motion, rejected Oct. 3 by a 55-32 roll call, was three votes short.

S 3970, sponsored by Abraham Ribicoff (D Conn.), Charles H. Percy (R Ill.) and Jacob K. Javits (R N.Y.), would have created an independent non-regulatory agency authorized to represent consumer interests in formal and informal actions of other federal agencies and before courts; if invited, the agency, under S 3970, could intervene in state and local proceedings.

The bill also would have replaced the Office of Consumer Affairs with a Council of Consumer Advisers charged with formulating and coordinating consumer programs.

Opponents contended that the agency administrator would be permitted to intrude in any federal agency activity that could be construed to be in the interests of consumers. Supporters said the bill contained numerous safeguards designed to prevent the administrator from interfering with or delaying agency activities.

Led by Government Operations Committee Chairman Sam J. Ervin Jr. (D N.C.), opponents began to filibuster the bill after the Senate Sept. 26 rejected an amendment by James B. Allen (D Ala.) to weaken the agency's authority to participate in court proceedings and other advocacy activities.

The Allen amendment would have allowed the agency to submit oral and written briefs but not to intervene as a party in formal agency proceedings. The proposed agency would also have the right to present written views on all written data upon which the other federal agency would base its final decision, the right to seek a rehearing or reconsideration of any final agency action and to appear in court as an *amicus curiae.*

The administration publicly supported the House version of the bill, approved in October 1971, which was more limited in scope. That bill (HR 10835) would not have permitted the Consumer Protection Agency to participate in as many kinds of proceedings and activities as outlined in the Senate version. *(1971 Chronology, p. 680)*

However, in the last days of debate, the bill's sponsors charged that the administration opposed enactment of any bill and that its acquiescence to the filibuster finally killed the bill for 1972.

Percy Oct. 5 said he had approached administration officials to offer a compromise on amendments to the bill proposed by the White House, but to no avail.

(The five administration amendments, according to Percy, would have eliminated 1) the Council of Consumer Advisers, 2) the state grant program, 3) a provision permitting the agency to participate in state and local proceedings, 4) a provision permitting the agency to gather information to ensure consumer health and safety and to prevent consumer fraud and, 5) a provision authorizing the agency to seek judicial review in certain instances. Adoption of the five amendments would have put the Senate bill more in line with the House version.)

In a statement issued after the third cloture vote, Ribicoff said: "The bill is dead for the year and there should be no doubt where responsibility for killing it rests: squarely on the Nixon administration. The administration position was simply that it wanted no bill at all, not even the House bill which it previously supported."

Debate on the bill began Sept. 21; the filibuster did not begin in earnest until Sept. 26.

In a related development, Ribicoff Oct. 6 offered both the Senate and House versions of the Consumer

Lobbying Against Consumer Bill

During debate Sept. 21 on the Consumer Protection Organization bill (S 3970), Sen. Charles H. Percy (R Ill.), a cosponsor of the bill, described the lobbying efforts made by opponents of the bill:

"Having myself spent 25 years in the business community...I was a natural target for businessmen to seek out to stop what some called 'dreadful legislation' and...others categorized as a 'super-agency.' I can say without hesitation that there has been no piece of legislation that I have encountered in my years in the Senate as to which there have been more misstatements of fact and misrepresentations.... I know of no legislation (about) which more lobbyists have tried to see me.

"It reached almost ludicrous proportions when I would receive letters addressed 'Dear Chuck' from friends of mine in business...saying that from their personal experience this is their reaction to this bill; and I had to...remind them that it could not be very personal when I had received exactly the same letter, word for word, comma for comma, period for period... from another good friend of mine who had spoken about his personal reaction to this bill."

Indeed, killing S 3970 was a top priority of the business lobbies in 1972. And, after more than three months of sustained lobbying against the bill, a coalition of more than 150 business groups emerged successful.

To coordinate pressures against the bill, participating industries formed a "Members of the Consumer Issues Working Group," which met throughout the summer to map lobbying strategy. Among the leading participants in the group were representatives of the Chamber of Commerce of the United States, General Mills, American Cyanamid, Procter and Gamble and the Grocery Manufacturers of America. The coalition's key contact with Congress was Procter and Gamble lobbyist Bryce N. Harlow, a former counselor to President Nixon and chief White House lobbyist in both the Nixon and Eisenhower administrations.

The brunt of an unsuccessful lobbying effort for the bill was carried by Ralph Nader's various organizations and an array of consumer groups, many of them organized at the local level. The groups argued that the agency was necessary because no other federal agency adequately represented consumer interests in governmental proceedings. Business and industry groups saw the bills as unnecessary harassment.

Protection Agency bill as amendments to the school anti-busing bill (HR 13915). However, the Senate failed three times to end another filibuster on that bill, thus killing the measure.

Background. In 1970, the Senate, by a 74-4 roll-call vote, passed a bill (S 4459) creating a strong Consumer Protection Agency but related legislation was killed in the House Rules Committee.

In October 1971, the House, by a 345-44 roll-call vote, approved a much less extensive consumer protection bill (HR 10835). Major differences between HR 10835 and S 3970, the bill reported in the Senate in 1972 *(below)*, were that the House-passed measure would permit the Consumer Protection Agency to intervene only in formal agency proceedings, prohibited the agency from intervening in state and local proceedings and did not provide for planning and program grants to the states.

In his Oct. 30, 1969, consumer message, President Nixon opposed creation of an independent agency and suggested that a consumer protection division be established within the Justice Department. In his Feb. 24, 1971, consumer message, Nixon asked Congress to postpone action on the Consumer Protection Agency until after further White House study of the recommendations of the Advisory Council on Executive Reorganization. At that time, he urged Congress to make the proposed agency part of the Federal Trade Commission if the Congress felt it must take immediate action.

SENATE COMMITTEE ACTION

The Senate Government Operations Committee ordered S 3970 reported Aug. 17 by a 11-2 roll-call vote. Ervin and Allen voted against reporting the bill.

Provisions. As reported, major provisions of S 3970:

• Established a three-member Council of Consumer Advisers in the Executive Office of the President to replace the existing Office of Consumer Affairs, the Consumer Advisory Council and the President's special assistant for consumer affairs; authorized appropriation of such sums as the council might need to carry out its duties.

• Created an independent nonregulatory Consumer Protection Agency to be headed by a three-member commission appointed by the President with Senate approval; authorized the President to designate one as agency administrator.

• Authorized the administrator to intervene as a party or to participate in any federal agency proceeding (rule-making, adjudication and licensing) when he determined that the result of the proceeding might substantially affect consumer interests.

• Authorized the administrator to participate in informal agency activities which he determined might substantially affect consumer interests.

• Gave the administrator standing to obtain judicial review of any agency action reviewable under law and to intervene as a party or to participate in any federal court civil proceeding; required the administrator, if he did not participate or intervene in the original agency activity or proceeding, first to petition the agency for a rehearing before seeking judicial review.

• Provided that a private citizen could seek judicial review if he believed that the administrator's intervention or participation in a final federal agency action was prejudicial to such person but prohibited judicial review of the administrator's determination that the agency proceeding or activity substantially affected consumer interests or of his decision to intervene or participate in any agency proceeding or activity.

• Authorized the administrator, to the extent necessary to ensure consumer health and safety and to prevent consumer fraud, to submit specific questions to any person engaged in business that substantially affects interstate commerce and consumer interests unless the information sought was for use in a pending agency proceeding; authorized the administrator to seek an order in federal district court for compliance.

• Authorized the administrator to make available to the public pertinent information on consumer interests but prohibited him from disclosing trade secrets or other confidential business matters or information which any federal agency specified could not be disclosed; required the administrator to notify any person or company if he released information that might be injurious to that person, his products or services.

• Authorized appropriations of $15-million for fiscal 1973, $20-million for fiscal 1974 and $25-million for 1975 for the Consumer Protection Agency.

• Authorized appropriations of $20-million for fiscal 1974 and $40-million for fiscal 1975 for consumer protection grants to the states.

Committee Views. The committee said a Consumer Protection Agency was necessary "because the interests of consumers have lacked the continuing effective representation that other interests have had before federal agencies and courts." The committee emphasized that the consumer agency would have no regulatory authority, nor would it be permitted to overrule actions of other federal agencies or alter another agency's regulatory functions.

In a minority view, Ervin opposed S 3970, saying that the bill "puts the federal government directly into every transaction relating to goods or services consummated or contracted for anywhere in the United States.... It proceeds on the ideal that we must do for the people what the people ought to do for themselves."

Ervin said he favored the so-called "amicus amendment," defeated in committee, which would permit the agency to present oral and written briefs on matters affecting consumers but not to intervene as a party. Allen, Bill Brock (R Tenn.) and Edward J. Gurney (R Fla.) also favored adoption of the amicus amendment.

SENATE FLOOR ACTION

During nine days of debate on S 3970, the Senate rejected Allen's amicus amendment and then failed three times to invoke cloture (limit debate) on the bill. Following the third vote on cloture, the Democratic leadership decided to drop the bill for the rest of the 92nd Congress.

Amicus Amendment. Debate began Sept. 21. On Sept. 22, Allen introduced his amicus amendment. "Rather than protect the consumer, the agency fashioned by S 3970 is nothing...more than a disruptive force empowered to wander to and fro through the halls of government, and, whenever it takes a mind to, to engage administrative agencies in guerrilla warfare....Instead of pitting agency against agency, the amicus amendment will grant the...agency the right to always...bring consumer interests before any federal agency in a similar but actually stronger way than an *amicus curiae* now presents a view to a court."

On Sept. 26, the Senate, by a 49-31 roll-call vote, agreed to a motion by Ribicoff to table (kill) the Allen amendment. A motion to reconsider that action was tabled 45-30. Following defeat of the Allen amendment, opponents of S 3970 began their filibuster.

First Cloture Vote. The Senate Sept. 29, by a 47-29 roll call, defeated the first motion to invoke cloture (cut off debate) on S 3970. The vote was four short of the required two-thirds majority.

Javits filed the second motion for cloture Sept. 30. (A motion to invoke cloture must be signed by at least 16 senators and is put to a roll-call vote one hour after the Senate meets on the second day following introduction of the motion.)

Second Cloture Vote. The Senate Oct. 3 rejected the second motion to invoke cloture by a 55-32 roll-call vote; the vote was three short of the number needed.

During debate, Ervin said that in essence the proposed agency would provide the federal government with a second prosecuting attorney—one from the Consumer Protection Agency and one from the other agency or department involved. "I have long fought for the rights of the public against the oppression of the government," Ervin said, "...and I fight now for the protection of the people against two government prosecutors."

Third Cloture Vote. The Senate Oct. 5 by a **52-30 key roll-call vote,** rejected the third attempt to invoke cloture. Again, the vote fell three short of the number needed for approval.

Allen urged the Senate to vote down the motion, contending that Senate business would be expedited if cloture were defeated: "Since I have been in the Senate there never have been more than three efforts to invoke cloture on a particular bill. I would feel that in all likelihood if the Senate...votes against applying cloture (this time), that the bill will be set aside and the Senate will be allowed to dispose" of the pending welfare bill (HR 1) and anti-busing legislation (HR 13915).

Javits predicted that if (S 3970) were "repulsed," any future Consumer Protection Agency bill would be "tougher, meaner and more difficult so far as those elements of business are concerned who think they are scoring a victory now."

No-Fault Auto Insurance

Opponents of a national no-fault auto insurance law won a major victory when the Senate Aug. 8, by a **49-46 key roll-call vote,** sent a bill (S 945), the National No-Fault Motor Vehicle Insurance Act, to the Judiciary Committee for further consideration. The move killed the bill for the year.

S 945, as reported by the Commerce Committee, required all motorists to carry insurance providing compensation for bodily injury regardless of who caused an accident in which they were involved. To ensure that such insurance was available, S 945 required each state to enact no-fault laws meeting minimum federal standards (outlined in the bill) within two years of its enactment or become subject to more stringent standards.

One of the more controversial standards would have abolished tort liability (the right to sue) except in cases of an uninsured owner; a person engaging in criminal conduct; damage to property other than motor vehicles in use; intangible damages involving death, permanent serious disfigurement or injury resulting in six months of "complete inability of an injured person to work in his

---

State No-Fault Laws

Although Puerto Rico has had a no-fault auto insurance law since 1969, only nine states had enacted such laws by the end of 1972: Massachusetts in 1970, Delaware, Florida, Illinois and Oregon in 1971, and Connecticut, Maryland, Michigan and New Jersey in 1972. The Illinois plan was ruled unconstitutional in 1972 by the state supreme court.

In addition, three states—Minnesota, South Dakota and Virginia—required insurance companies to offer first-party (no-fault) benefits to policy purchasers.

President Nixon, the American Trial Lawyers Association, and many insurance companies opposed federal legislation that would establish minimim federal standards for no-fault policies to be incorporated in all auto insurance policies.

Nixon and some insurance companies preferrred that states enact their own laws; the American Trial Lawyers Association and some other insurance companies opposed any legislation—federal or state—that would restrict the right to sue.

Movement toward enactment of no-fault laws was frustrated in several states in the 1970-72 period because of the competing interests of lobbyists.

However, proponents of state laws, rather than federal legislation, were aided considerably when representatives of nine major insurance companies met at the Camelback Inn in Scottsdale, Ariz., in December 1972 to work out a model state no-fault law that most insurance companies could and would support.

Between January and mid April 1973, seven states enacted their own no-fault laws: New York, Arkansas, Utah, Hawaii, Kansas, Texas and Nevada. The New Mexico state legislature passed a no-fault bill but the governor vetoed it. The Arkansas plan only required insurance companies to offer first-party benefits to clients, while the Texas law retained all right to sue. The laws of the five other states provided for some level of first-party benefits and abolition of the right to sue under certain cirsumstances.

---

occupation," or tangible damages not covered by a no-fault policy nor accruing as a loss of monthly earnings.

Opponents of the motion said recommittal was a parliamentary move to kill the bill. Supporters of the motion charged that several sections of the bill appeared to deny constitutional rights and should be reviewed by the Judiciary Committee.

S 945 originally was introduced by Commerce Committee Chairman Warren G. Magnuson (D Wash.) and Philip A. Hart (D Mich.) in February 1971. The committee held extensive hearings on the bill in 1971 and 1972 and substantially revised the original bill. *(1971 Chronology, p. 682)*

Extensive lobby efforts, both for and against the national no-fault law, had been waged during consideration of S 945. Passage of a national no-fault law was favored by the American Insurance Association, Consumers Union,

Consumer Federation of America, Common Cause, Automobile Manufacturers Association, American Trucking Associations, Hertz and Avis rental car companies and labor unions. Opponents of a national no-fault law included the Nixon administration, which preferred that individual states write their own no-fault laws, the National Association of Independent Insurers, the American Trial Lawyers Association, governors and most state insurance commissioners.

COMMITTEE ACTION. The Senate Commerce Committee ordered S 945 reported May 25 by a 13-4 roll-call vote. The committee report contained a summary of testimony by three insurance associations estimating insurance costs to motorists under the no-fault plan in comparison with existing costs. Two associations estimated a slight savings; the third projected an increase.

"Even though an over-all savings is projected under S 945, it is possible, even probable, that some premiums... will increase," the report cautioned.

Minority Views. Howard H. Baker Jr. (R Tenn.) opposed S 945 because it forced "the repeal of all existing state programs," it produced "a very discouraging cost picture," it "discriminated against rural states" and it penalized "the middle-income, middle-aged average driver by severely limiting safe driver discounts." Marlow W. Cook (R Ky.) agreed with Baker's views.

Norris Cotton (R N.H.) opposed S 945, saying that "the states...are proceeding (with no-fault insurance systems)...on a trial-and-error basis and a delay of only a few months in framing federal standards may well demonstrate to us some of the expedients that work and some of the mistakes to be avoided." Cotton also said he believed the bill would work to the disadvantage of rural states.

Ernest F. Hollings (D S.C.) agreed with Cotton that states should have more time in which to formulate their own no-fault laws. William B. Spong Jr. (D Va.) supported S 945 with reservations. The limitations on tort liability, Spong said, "are unnecessarily rigid and could deprive individuals of a fundamental legal right with no commensurate benefits in return." J. Glenn Beall Jr. (R Md.) also supported S 945 with reservations regarding the cost of insurance and the extent of the minimum federal standards.

FLOOR ACTION. The motion to commit S 945 to the Judiciary Committee was offered Aug. 8 by Roman L. Hruska (R Neb.), ranking minority member of that committee. It was adopted by a **49-46 key roll-call vote.** General debate on S 945 had taken place Aug. 7.

Hruska said he was very frankly extremely disappointed" that the Commerce Committee report was "almost bare" of any discussion of the constitutionality of S 945.

He contended that the Judiciary Committee should review the bill because the sections abolishing tort liability in certain instances raised serious questions with regard to the guarantee of jury trials in civil suits involving more than $20 and with due process of the law. He added that the Commerce Committee had not adequately studied the impact S 945 might have on the judicial mechanism. The Judiciary Committee, he said, had jurisdiction over matters relating to the McCarran-Ferguson Act which provided for states to retain jurisdiction over the insurance industry.

Lowell P. Weicker Jr. (R Conn.) responded: During the course of testimony and committee work on S 945, "where were the cries of those who felt this was being done by the wrong committee? Where were those who said it should have been before the Committee on the Judiciary? Not a word, except when the bill comes before the Senate for action. Then, all of a sudden, the question arises as to whether it was before the appropriate committee."

Cook, one of the four Commerce Committee members who voted against reporting the bill, agreed with Hruska's arguments, suggesting that sections of the bill requiring insurers to invest 2 per cent of their annual premiums for construction and maintenance of rehabilitation centers and emergency medical response systems could be considered a tax.

"Can a federal statute," he asked, "impose a tax, not to be collected by the federal government but...by the state government and then not even to be paid into the state treasury and not even to be allocated by the state legislatures, but to be allocated by the commissioner of insurance in the state?"

Speaking in opposition to the motion to refer S 945 to the Judiciary Committee, Magnuson and Hart both said adoption of the motion would effectively kill the bill. Hart said that additional study by the Judiciary Committee was not needed. "We are all as aware as we can possibly be before passage of the impact of this legislation," he said.

Saying that the existing automobile insurance system "is bordering on a national scandal," Magnuson contended that recommittal would postpone meaningful action for at least two more years. "In those two years," he continued, "consumers will have to spend $28-billion for automobile insurance and receive back in benefits only $14-billion."

Twenty-one Democrats and 28 Republicans voted for the motion; 33 Democrats and 13 Republicans voted against.

Cyclamate Compensation

The House July 24, by a **177-170 key roll-call vote,** passed a bill (HR 13366) permitting domestic food growers, processors, packers and distributors to sue for payment by the federal government of losses sutained as a result of a 1969 ban on cyclamates.

A Senate Judiciary subcommittee held hearings on the bill in September but took no further action.

Six House members changed their vote from nay to yea at the completion of the initial roll call on passage, thus providing the winning margin—Democrats Robert H. Mollohan (W.Va.), John Brademas (Ind.) and Harley O. Staggers (W.Va.) and Republicans William H. Harsha (Ohio), Sherman P. Lloyd (Utah) and William L. Dickinson (Ala.).

The cost to the U.S. Treasury of expected claims was estimated at $100-million to $120-million.

Background. Cyclamates, a class of artificial sweeteners made by cyclamic acid and its salts, were banned by the Department of Health, Education and Welfare (HEW) on Oct. 18, 1969. A schedule for phasing out cyclamates in foods and other substances was set, and on

Aug. 14, 1970, a total ban went into effect. *(1969 chronology, p. 669)*

Cyclamates were used as sweeteners in a wide variety of diet foods and drinks, as a cheaper substitute for sugar in processed foods and as a coating or sweetener for numerous drug products.

The sweeteners were placed by the Food and Drug Administration (FDA) on its "generally recognized as safe" (GRAS) list in the 1950s. But the substances were found through subsequent testing to cause cancer in laboratory animals; federal law required substances producing cancer in test animals to be banned from human consumption.

The use of cyclamates had grown substantially during the decade preceding the ban. According to the committee report on HR 13366, consumption increased from five million pounds six years before the ban was announced to 17 million pounds in 1969. Production of at least 20 million pounds had been projected for 1970.

Provisions. As passed by the House, HR 13366:

• Authorized the U.S. Court of Claims to grant relief to domestic growers, manufacturers, packers or distributors who suffered damages, resulting from the federal ban on cyclamates, because of good-faith reliance on their inclusion on the "safe" list. Such damages, to be paid by the federal government, would be set by the court after considering the amount of loss resulting from direct or indirect costs and damages but not lost profits.

• Required manufacturers and other affected parties to file claims within one year of enactment of the law.

House Action. The House Judiciary Committee ordered the bill reported April 25 by a 17-7 roll-call vote with three members voting present.

No changes were made in HR 13366 on the floor although the measure was debated at length.

Supporters of the bill argued that the FDA had banned cyclamates without adequate prior warning to users of the sweeteners. Opponents contended there was adequate warning by federal officials. They further argued that the language of the bill virtually assured that all claims would be granted by the U.S. Court of Claims.

Several California members from areas having small farmers and fruit growers, that were most affected by the cyclamate ban, led debate in support of HR 13366. Jerome R. Waldie (D Calif.) said the manner in which the ban was processed "misled people, led them to a position in which they incurred losses.... It is to be noted, first, that when cyclamates were added to the GRAS list they were generally recognized as safe by the scientific community. Second, the list never carried any warning that the substances could at any time be found unsafe and removed from the list. Third, it is obvious that the GRAS list was relied upon by the industry as an official assurance that cyclamates were safe in fact."

Judiciary Committee Chairman Emanuel Celler (D N.Y.) called the bill a boondoggle: "The government is right in banning the use of cyclamates after laboratory testing established that they cause cancer in animals. There were numerous danger signals flashed upon the cyclamate users, yet they continued to use this sugar substitute and they...thumbed their nose at these warnings. There were any number of warnings, yet they paid not a jot nor jit of attention to these warnings and continued to reap profits from the use of cyclamates."

Fair Credit Billing

The Senate April 27 passed S 652, a bill intended to protect consumers against unfair billing practices. As passed, S 652 contained fewer safeguards for the consumer than were included in the original legislation, and its sponsor, William Proxmire (D Wis.), voted against final passage. There was no House action on the bill.

S 652 would have amended the Truth in Lending Act enacted in 1968 (PL 90-321) to correct problems arising in the administration of that act and to increase criminal penalties for the fraudulent use of credit cards.

Background. The Truth in Lending Act was designed to allow consumers full, honest and comparable information about the cost of credit they were obtaining for loans and installment buying.

The law required that lenders and consumer creditors disclose the cost of loans and installment purchase plans in terms of an annual rate calculated under certain specified procedures for all lenders and creditors. It also required the lender or creditor to tell customers the total cost in dollars of the credit that was being extended. The act fixed no minimum or maximum charges for credit, and gave the Federal Reserve Board responsibility for drafting regulations to implement the law. *(Congress and the Nation, Vol. II, p. 807)*

In 1970 Congress passed a law (also an amendment to the Truth in Lending Act) prohibiting issuance of unsolicited credit cards and setting maximum liability of a cardholder for unauthorized use of his card at $50 in most cases. The bill was attached as a rider to a conglomerate measure regulating use of secret foreign bank accounts. *(1970 chronology, p. 673)*

Provisions. As passed by the Senate, S 652:

• Required creditors to acknowledge customer billing disputes within 30 days and to resolve them within 90 days by correcting the customer's bill or by explaining why the original bill was correct. Creditors who failed to do so would forfeit the amount in dispute up to $50, whether or not the bill was in error. Creditors were prohibited from sending dunning letters, taking other actions or reporting such amounts as delinquent before explaining to the customer why the bill was correct. If a customer continued to dispute a bill, the creditor could not report the disputed amount as delinquent to a credit reporting agency unless he also notified the customer of his action. The creditor was required to inform the credit agency of the amount in dispute and of any subsequent settlement of the dispute.

• Required creditors to identify each transaction contained in billing statements, to include an address for handling disputes, and to inform customers twice each year of their right to have these disputes resolved.

• Required creditors to mail monthly bills at least 14 days prior to the date that finance charges are imposed on unpaid balances and to record customers' payments promptly.

• Prohibited credit card issuers from requiring merchants to maintain deposits or purchase other services as a condition for participating in the credit card plan.

• Prohibited financial institutions from offsetting a consumer's credit card debt against a checking or savings account unless the customer had agreed to such offsets.

• Limited any creditor's liability for punitive damages under the Truth in Lending Act or the Fair Credit Billing Act to a minimum of $100 in an individual action, and to a maximum of $100,000 or 2 per cent of net worth (whichever is less) in a class-action suit. No limit was placed on the amount of actual damages which could be recovered.

• Increased criminal penalties for fraudulent uses of credit cards in transactions of $1,000 or more to a maximum of 10 years' imprisonment and fines of $10,000.

• Required that when a seller agreed to the return of goods or to forgiveness of a debt for services or goods purchased with a credit card he must arrange with the company issuing the credit card to have the amount of the transaction credited to the account of the purchaser.

• Provided that where state law afforded greater protection to consumers than the provisions of S 652, state laws could remain in force.

SENATE ACTION

The Senate Banking, Housing and Urban Affairs Committee reported S 652 April 17 with substantial amendment. The committee had agreed by voice vote March 15 to report the bill.

The committee cut from the bill provisions specifying a method for computing finance charges on certain open-end accounts and prohibiting creditors from imposing minimum charges on open-end accounts.

The committee also voted 8-7 to drop a provision which would have allowed consumers to refuse to pay disputed amounts to three-party credit card concerns. Those concerns primarily operated by banks—were those in which consumers used credit cards at a variety of different stores but paid all their bills through a central account.

The provisions that were cut would have given credit card holders the right to assert the same claims or defenses against a card issuer that they could assert against a merchant honoring the card, such as withholding payment because of defective merchandise or failure to perform services.

In a lengthy statement, Proxmire said that the committee had "substantially weakened" his original bill and that it should be titled the Bank Protection Act. Unless the measure were strengthened on the floor, it should be defeated, Proxmire said. "No bill is better than a bogus bill."

The Senate April 27 rejected four major strengthening amendments to S 652, then passed the bill by a 51-15 roll-call vote.

The conservative coalition, consisting of a majority of voting Republicans and southern Democrats, succeeded in defeating each of the four amendments.

Proxmire and other proponents of the original bill charged that the banking lobby had gutted S 652 during committee consideration. But Bill Brock (R Tenn.), a member of the Financial Institutions Subcommittee of the Banking, Housing and Urban Affairs Committee, labeled the charges "misleading."

Brock said the bill "in its original form...would have been extremely costly for the consumer. Its effect would have been to deprive many small businesses of the ability to extend credit to their customers...and stifled the growth of the technology to enable us to live in a cashless society...."

"Because there was an obvious need for amending the original legislation, the majority...acted favorably upon the suggestions to improve the bill made by the banking panel, retail groups and small business interests."

First Proxmire Amendment. Proxmire offered two amendments, both of which were rejected. The first would have allowed a consumer to refuse to pay disputed charges over $50 to a credit card company. S 652 permitted refusal in the case of a two-party (customer-store) credit account, but not when the credit card was issued by a third party, such as a bank.

Wallace F. Bennett (R Utah), ranking Republican on the Financial Institutions Subcommittee, opposed the amendment: "To try and force this bank-consumer relationship into the same pattern as the bank-dealer relationship is not a wise thing.... The relationship of the bank is completely outside that of the credit card issuer and completely outside of the relationship between the buyer and the seller of the merchandise."

The amendment was rejected by a 35-46 roll-call vote. Seven Republicans and 28 Democrats voted for the amendment; 34 Republicans and 12 Democrats voted against.

Second Proxmire Amendment. The second amendment would have forbidden a creditor to charge interest on an original amount after the balance had been reduced by partial payment. That amendment was rejected on a tie vote, 38-38. Ten Republicans and 28 Democrats voting for the amendment were opposed by 27 Republicans and 11 Democrats.

Tunney Amendments. Three amendments were then introduced by John V. Tunney (D Calif.). The first, to guarantee that state laws giving greater protection to the consumer would not be pre-empted by passage of S 652, was adopted by voice vote without opposition.

His second amendment which would have added a new section to the bill prohibiting billing for undelivered goods or services was rejected by a 30-42 roll call. The third amendment would have prohibited minimum finance charges on open-end credit plans, such as revolving charge accounts. It was rejected by a 19-47 vote.

Consumer Finance Commission

The House June 19 by voice vote cleared for the President's signature a bill (S J Res 211—PL 92-321) extending the life of the National Commission on Consumer Finance through Dec. 31, 1972.

S J Res 211 authorized an additional $500,000 for the commission's work, bringing the total authorization to $2-million.

The commission was established by the Consumer Credit Protection Act of 1968 (PL 90-321), better known as the Truth in Lending Act, to study the functioning and structure of the consumer finance industry and consumer credit transactions in general. A report on the commission's findings and recommendations was scheduled to be submitted by Jan. 1, 1971. However, Congress in 1970 extended the reporting date to July 1, 1972.

In 1972, the commission requested a further six-month extension to compensate for delays on a study made for the commission by the Census Bureau.

The Senate passed S J Res 211 May 23 by voice vote without amendment or debate. The House approved the resolution June 19 by voice vote without amendment, thus completing congressional action.

Flammable Fabrics

Congress Oct. 14 cleared for the President a bill (HR 5066—PL 92-542) extending the 1953 Flammable Fabrics Act, as amended, and authorizing appropriations of $4-million for fiscal 1973.

The 1953 act authorized the secretary of commerce to set federal standards to reduce the flammability of fabrics for clothing and certain household items.

Final action came when the Senate Oct. 14 agreed to House deletion of an amendment that would have broadened coverage of the act to include children's sleepwear for sizes 7 through 14 by July 1973.

In 1970, the secretary had issued a fire-resistant standard for sleepwear in sizes 1 through 6X. Sleepwear not meeting that standard after July 29, 1972, was required to be labeled as such; sleepwear not meeting the standard after July 29, 1973 could not be sold.

Harley O. Staggers (D W.Va.), who offered the House motion Oct. 13 to reject the Senate amendment including the larger sizes in the standard, said in floor debate that he saw no need to impose a statutory mandate on the secretary.

The House had passed HR 5066 April 28, 1971. The Senate originally passed the bill, amended, June 16, 1972, and then reconsidered and passed the bill June 19 after the addition of a technical amendment. *(House passage, 1971 chronology, p. 685)*

Other Bills

MOTOR VEHICLE SAFETY. President Nixon Oct. 25 signed a bill (HR 15375—PL 92-548) authorizing $52,714,000 in fiscal 1973 for motor vehicle safety programs under the National Traffic and Motor Vehicle Safety Act of 1966.

As passed by the House Aug. 15, the bill authorized only $37.5-million. The Senate, which passed HR 15375 Oct. 6, boosted the authorization and added a provision temporarily exempting certain classes of motor vehicles from safety standards required by the Transportation Department. The final bill followed the Senate version.

Existing authority under the 1966 act expired June 30, 1972. The Nixon administration had requested an open-ended authorization. *(Previous extension, 1970 chronology, p. 672)*

DES BAN. The Senate Sept. 20 passed a bill (S 2818) providing for an immediate ban on the growth hormone DES (diethylstilbestrol) in animal feed but permitting use of DES animal ear implants at least until Jan. 1, 1973.

There was no House action on the bill which died at the end of the 92nd Congress.

Background. DES, used in animal feed to stimulate rapid weight gain, had been found to cause cancer in mice. A growing body of evidence indicated a direct link between young women having a rare form of vaginal cancer and their mothers who were given DES, a synthetic hormone (estrogen), during pregnancy to prevent spontaneous abortion.

DES residues had been detected with increasing frequency in beef and lamb livers despite regulations established by the Food and Drug Administration (FDA) designed to eliminate such residues. The Delaney clause, a provision of the Food Additive Amendments (to the Food, Drug and Cosmetic Act) of 1958 stated that a food additive could not be tolerated or approved if the substance caused cancer in laboratory animals—even if some presumably safe level for human food use could be established. *(Congress and the Nation, Vol. I, p. 1176)*

The clause did not forbid the use of a cancer-causing substance in animal feed; but it did require that all such substances be eliminated from the animal before it was slaughtered.

Rather than ban the use of DES outright, the FDA in early 1972 decided to permit its continued use pending a public hearing. On Aug. 2, however, the FDA banned immediately the production of DES used in feed for animals intended for human consumption. But it permitted continued use of existing supplies of DES as a feed additive until Jan. 1, 1973. The FDA ruling also permitted continued use indefinitely of DES ear implants.

Senate Action. After one day of hearings July 20, the Senate Labor and Public Welfare Committee ordered the bill reported Aug. 15 by a unanimous voice vote.

S 2818 was passed in the Senate by voice vote and without amendment Sept. 20. As passed, the bill banned immediately the use of DES in the feed of any animal intended to be used for human consumption and banned, as of Jan. 1, 1973, DES ear implants in any animal to be used for food unless Agriculture Department tests showed that ear implants did not leave residues in slaughtered meat. If the tests showed residues at any time prior to Dec. 31, 1972, the bill provided that immediate steps be taken to ban the use of ear implants.

In a later development, the FDA April 25, 1973, banned the use of implants containing DES after tests showed residues of DES remaining in slaughtered meat. The beef cattle tested had been implanted with DES 120 days prior to their slaughter.

FIRE SAFETY. President Nixon June 22 signed into law a bill (HR 13034—PL 92-317) authorizing funds for research on fire prevention and safety programs and scientific research data programs.

Final action came when the House June 14 under the unanimous consent procedure agreed to amendments added by the Senate June 6. The House originally had passed the bill April 25 by voice vote.

As cleared, HR 13034 authorized appropriations to the Commerce Department for fiscal years 1973-75 of $24.5-million to conduct research into fire control and prevention, and an additional $13-million for the operation of standard reference data programs.

Background. The Fire Research and Safety Act of 1968 (PL 90-259) declared that a comprehensive fire research and safety program was needed and authorized the secretary of commerce through the National Bureau of Standards to carry out such a program. Funds authorized in HR 13034 would be used for investigations into the causes of fires, development of improved techniques for fire control and prevention, public education on fire hazards and safety, and education and training programs for firefighters.

The Standard Reference Data Act, which was passed in 1968, stated that critically evaluated reference data

(Continued on p. 700)

Ralph Nader: Consumer Advocate, Critic of Congress

The rising level of consumer consciousness during the 1960s and early 1970s was due in large part to the activities of a young lawyer, Ralph Nader. Nader's concern for consumer issues dated back at least to his undergraduate days at Princeton in the mid-1950s, when he opposed the spraying of campus trees with DDT. Nader, a graduate of Harvard Law School, was born Feb. 27, 1934.

Nader's career as the nation's foremost consumer advocate began in November 1965 with the publication of his book *Unsafe at Any Speed: The Designed-In Dangers of the American Automobile.* Although he attacked the whole Detroit automobile industry for emphasis on profits and styling over safety, he concentrated his fire on the Chevrolet Corvair, "one of the nastiest-handling cars ever built." The book became a best-seller and the demise of the Corvair was attributed to its influence.

Meanwhile congressional support was growing for the passage of auto-safety legislation, and Nader testified in behalf of such a bill early in 1966. Effective legislation probably would have been passed that year in any event, but within the next few weeks a news story broke that aroused public opinion to the point where swift passage was virtually assured. On March 6, 1966, newspapers published Nader's complaint that for the past few months he had been under investigation by private detectives hired by the auto industry. Three days later, General Motors conceded that it had initiated "a routine investigation."

Then, in a nationally televised hearing on March 22, GM President James M. Roche told the Senate Government Operations Subcommittee on Executive Reorganization that there had been "some harassment," publicly apologized to Nader and agreed with Chairman Abraham Ribicoff (D Conn.) that the inquiry had been "most unworthy of American business." Final passage of the National Traffic and Motor Vehicle Safety Act of 1966 came five months later. (Subsequently, GM agreed to pay Nader $425,000 in an out-of-court settlement of his invasion of privacy suit.)

Having won his initial victory on auto safety, Nader turned his attention to other areas where he felt the public interest was threatened. These included health hazards in mining, safety standards for natural-gas pipelines, the lot of American Indians, indiscriminate use of X-rays in dental examinations and meat inspection.

Nader's method of attack on meat inspection was typical. In the summer of 1967, he obtained from the Department of Agriculture a forgotten study of conditions—some of them gruesome—in intrastate meat-processing plants not subject to federal inspection. He passed the report to the press, helped to organize a letter-writing campaign directed at Congress, addressed groups in cities from coast to coast and wrote several hard-hitting articles for *The New Republic.*

Nader Organizations. After June of 1969, Nader greatly expanded the scope of his activities on behalf of consumers. To this end, he set up a number of organizations staffed largely by idealistic young people. With few exceptions, those who worked for the Nader groups received small salaries and worked exceptionally long hours, following the example set by Nader.

The parent Nader organization, dating from June 1969, was the Center for the Study of Responsive Law, a Washington-based tax-exempt organization, best known as a staging area for the activities of "Nader's Raiders"—groups of young people who descended on Washington during the summer months to do the digging for subsequent investigative reports.

Public Interest Research Group (PIRG), established in July 1970, has been described as Nader's public interest law firm, although in recent years the actual court room work as been assumed by the Public Citizen Litigation Group. PIRG staff members testified on Capitol Hill, petitioned regulatory agencies and prepared investigative reports on consumer interests.

The third major organization in the Nader network, the Center for Auto Safety, was set up on an informal basis in 1968 and incorporated two years later. It monitored the operations of the National Highway Traffic Safety Administration, a federal agency established under the 1966 auto-safety legislation. The center was the source of many of the safety defect charges Nader made against Volkswagen, Volvo and Cadillac automobiles.

Congress Project. Perhaps Nader's most ambitious and controversial undertaking was his investigation of the United States Congress. Announced in November 1971, the project involved more than 1,000 persons—most of them volunteers—who conducted interviews, wrote studies of the congressional process and compiled detailed information on election statistics, financial disclosures, campaign spending and congressional biographies.

Almost a year later, on Oct. 3, 1972, Nader released the first product of the project—a paperback book entitled *Who Runs Congress,* which partially summarized and partially previewed the results of the massive study.

On Oct. 22, the project released its individual profiles of all senators and all representatives except those retiring or defeated in primaries. The 494 profiles, ranging in length from 20 to 40 pages each, marked the completion of the second phase of the project.

The third phase, scheduled for release in 1973, consisted of separate studies on congressional committees and an analysis of the congressional process.

According to Nader staffers, response from members of Congress to the profiles was in general, favorable. An aide to Sen. Barry Goldwater (R Ariz.), who had opposed the project and declined an interview, said: "I was quite surprised at the high quality of the profile."

Although several members of Congress pointed to errors of fact and charged the study of bias, the sharpest criticism, came from Rep. John R. Rarick (D La.) who likened Nader to an "Arab terrorist" and termed the profiles "yellow journalism."

should be readily available to scientists, engineers and the general public. The secretary of commerce was directed to provide for the collection, compilation, critical evaluation, publication and dissemination of standard reference data.

CIGARETTE REGULATION. The Senate Commerce Consumer Subcommittee held two days of hearings in 1972 on regulation of the cigarette industry. No legislation resulted. The bill under consideration (S 1454) was introduced by Frank E. Moss (D Utah) to limit the content of tar, nicotine and other substances which are considered health hazards in cigarettes.

Robert Pitofsky, director of the Bureau of Consumer Protection in the Federal Trade Commission, said his bureau would prefer legislation which would foster competition within the industry to reduce quantities of tar and nicotine but said that S 1454 might be necessary. Horace R. Kornegay, president of the Tobacco Institute, Inc., said there was no place "for governmental limitation of what type cigarettes may be made legally available."

SOFT DRINK FRANCHISES. The Senate Judiciary Antitrust and Monopoly Subcommittee held hearings in August and September on a bill (S 3133) amending the Federal Trade Commission Act of 1914 to permit exclusive territorial arrangements for soft drink manufacturers.

S 3133 and similar bills were introduced after the Federal Trade Commission (FTC) in July 1971 issued complaints against seven national-brand soft drink syrup manufacturers, and against an eighth early in 1972, charging that it was illegal for them to issue licenses restricting soft drink bottlers of their brand to selling their product in a specific and limited geographical territory.

The eight companies were The Coca-Cola Company, PepsiCo. Inc., Royal Crown Cola Co., The Seven-Up Co., Beverages International Inc., Dr. Pepper Co., Canada Dry Corp. and Cott Corp.

In its complaints, the FTC charged that territorial restrictions violate the Sherman (Antitrust) Act of 1890 and the Federal Trade Commission Act. The FTC said such restrictions prohibited intra- and inter-brand competition, raised the cost to consumers and harmed small bottlers. The FTC proposed that for a 10-year period after the restrictions are prohibited the small bottlers be permitted to market in the territories of larger bottlers but that larger bottlers be prohibited from marketing in small bottler territories.

S 3133, which was intended to have the effect of foreclosing FTC action, was introduced by James O. Eastland (D Miss.) and had 31 cosponsors. Authors of the legislation worked closely with the National Soft Drink Association (NSDA) in drafting the bill. NSDA was conducting an extensive lobby effort in favor of the proposed legislation.

In a subsequent development, *The Washington Post* Sept. 13 reported that two soft-drink bottlers suffered cutbacks in their supplies after testifying against S 3133 in August.

William Pope Foster, a Coca-Cola bottler from Taft, Calif., told the subcommittee that a large bottler in nearby Los Angeles had been permitted to indirectly sell Coca-Cola in Foster's territory but that Foster had been prevented from indirectly selling Coca-Cola in the Los Angeles territory. Upon returning to California Foster was told by a Coca-Cola Company official that his supply of syrup would be cut back by two-thirds, according to the Post. Foster told Antitrust and Monopoly Subcommittee Chairman Philip A. Hart (D Mich.) of the cutback. On Sept. 8, a Coca-Cola official told Foster that his syrup supply would be restored to the previous level.

TRUTH IN ADVERTISING. The Senate Commerce Consumer Subcommittee held hearings May 16 and 18 on a bill (S 1461) to require that documentation of advertised claims concerning the safety, performance, efficacy, characteristics and comparative prices of a product or service be made available to the public. No further action was taken.

The subcommittee held one hearing on the truth-in-advertising legislation Oct. 4, 1971. At that hearing, the Federal Trade Commission (FTC) announced that it had recently undertaken an advertising substantiation pilot program to study the impact public documentation might have on consumer purchasing competition and the quality of substantiation. The FTC asked that further hearings on the legislation be deferred until the pilot program could be evaluated.

The subcommittee was also considering a related bill (S 1753) to establish a National Institute of Advertising, Marketing and Society to study the effect of advertising and marketing on society.

MEAT INSPECTION. The House Oct. 4, by a 172-169 roll-call vote, killed a bill (S 1316) to increase to 80 per cent from 50 per cent the amount the federal government could pay toward state meat and poultry inspection programs.

The final vote was on a motion to strike the enacting clause, offered by Hugh L. Carey (D N.Y.). The motion was adopted first by a 104-97 standing vote and a 172-170 recorded teller vote. The House then reaffirmed its earlier action on a final roll-call vote of 172-169.

S 1316 would have amended the Federal Meat Inspection Act of 1967 (PL 90-201) and the Poultry Products Inspection Act of 1957 (PL 85-172). These two acts, as amended, required states to develop meat and poultry production inspection programs meeting federal standards and to pay 50 per cent of the costs. If states did not develop programs meeting federal standards, the Department of Agriculture assumed inspection jurisdiction and program costs.

The Senate passed S 1316 by voice vote on July 29, 1971. *(1971 chronology, p. 684)*

Related Development. A Sept. 26 U.S. district court ruling required the Agriculture Department to open its records on state-operated meat inspection programs in Ohio, Missouri, Nebraska, Massachusetts, Kentucky and Texas. The Center for the Study of Responsive Law, an organization affiliated with consumer advocate, Ralph Nader, filed the suit in May 1971.

During House debate on S 1316, Thomas S. Foley (D Wash.), who opposed the bill, said that he did not have access to the Agriculture Department records of state inspection programs. "I suggest," he said, "the reason is the department is afraid that a public audit of its actions in certifying state systems would show in fact there was not such an adequate basis to show that they were certified as equal (to federal standards)."

Chapter 13—Labor

Key Votes

In this chapter, key roll-call votes are shown in bold-face type. The party breakdown on each of these votes and the position taken by each member of Congress may be found in the key vote charts which appear in the appendix to this book.

Labor Legislation

The nation's economic problems dominated congressional consideration of labor legislation in the first Nixon administration. In a period of high unemployment and sustained inflation, organized labor focused its attention on bread-and-butter issues—public service employment programs, extension of unemployment compensation benefits, increased retirement benefits and a higher minimum wage. Administration economic policies were an issue of continuing labor concern.

The administration's principal legislative initiative in the labor field was its proposed manpower revenue sharing program, under which federal manpower training programs would be consolidated and turned over to state and local control. Labor leaders and congressional Democrats argued that at a time when unemployment was running close to 6 per cent of the labor force the need was for new jobs rather than training for jobs that did not exist. The government, they said, should act as "employer of last resort."

President Nixon, contending that "WPA-type jobs are not the answer," vetoed two bills containing public service employment provisions, but in 1971 he signed a measure designed to provide about 150,000 public service jobs for the unemployed at the state and local levels. Nixon's manpower revenue sharing program was sidetracked by the debate over the public service employment issue. (Manpower, p. 733)

In 1970 Congress approved an extension of unemployment benefits to about 4.8 million additional workers and provided an additional 13 weeks of benefits for workers who had exhausted their regular benefits during periods of high unemployment. Subsequent legislation provided for temporary federal financing of this program.

Disregarding warnings of an impending financial crisis in the railroad retirement system, Congress also approved three increases in retirement benefits for railroad workers. The third of these bills was enacted over President Nixon's veto in 1972. Although the percentage increases voted for rail workers paralleled increases voted for Social Security beneficiaries, the dollar value of the increases was far higher for rail retirees. (Social Security, chapter on Welfare)

Legislation on two key labor issues was frustrated during Nixon's first term. Two years of hearings on minimum wage legislation and a final push for passage in 1972 were nullified when the House refused to send its bill to conference. Bills providing for federal regulation of private pension plans never reached the floor in either chamber.

Congress enacted two major pieces of legislation dealing with worker protection. The Occupational Safety and Health Act of 1970 established a comprehensive on-the-job safety program for 55 million industrial, farm and construction workers employed by firms engaged in interstate commerce. The Coal Mine Health and Safety Act of 1969 established federal safety standards at coal mines and authorized a compensation program for miners suffering from black lung disease. That program was liberalized in 1972.

The administration's "Philadelphia Plan" to increase minority employment on federal construction projects led to a clash between labor and government in 1969, but a labor-backed move to kill the plan failed to win congressional approval. The coalition that lawmakers had come to expect from labor and civil rights groups was broken on this issue, and some Democratic members of Congress accused President Nixon of engineering the break.

Meany vs. Nixon on Economy

The most dramatic encounters between labor and government during the years 1969-72 occurred outside the legislative process, in the shifting relationship between President Nixon and George Meany, venerable president of the AFL-CIO.

Meany's long-standing antipathy toward Nixon culminated in his 1968 effort to win the presidency for Nixon's Democratic opponent, Hubert H. Humphrey. Yet as Nixon took office in 1969, it seemed possible that the AFL-CIO chief might not oppose him strenuously. This was due largely to Nixon's firm Vietnam policy and his refusal to be influenced by anti-war demonstrators.

Renewed Rift over Economics. Meany was Nixon's guest of honor at a 1970 Labor Day dinner, but he had already become a severe critic of the President's economic policies.

Initially he rejected the administration's effort to curb inflation through budget-cutting and tight money. As the economy slipped into a recession in late 1969 and unemployment began a year-long rise that reached 6 per

References

Discussion of labor legislation for the years 1945-64 may be found in Congress and the Nation, Vol. I, p. 563-657; for the years 1965-68, Congress and the Nation, Vol. II, p. 601-622.

Selected Unemployment Rates 1961-1972

(Percent of Labor Force Categories)

	1961	1962	1963	1964	1965	1966	1967	1968	1969	1970	1971	1972
All Civilian Workers	6.7	5.5	5.7	5.2	4.5	3.8	3.8	3.6	3.5	4.9	5.9	5.6
All Male Workers	6.4	5.2	5.2	4.6	4.0	3.2	3.1	2.9	2.8	4.4	5.3	4.9
All Female Workers	7.2	6.2	6.5	6.2	5.5	4.8	5.2	4.8	4.7	5.9	6.9	6.6
Men (20 and over)	5.7	4.6	4.5	3.9	3.2	2.5	2.3	2.2	2.1	3.5	4.4	4.0
Women (20 and over)	6.3	5.4	5.4	5.2	4.5	3.8	4.2	3.8	3.7	4.8	5.7	5.4
Married Men	4.6	3.6	3.4	2.8	2.4	1.9	1.8	1.6	1.5	2.6	3.2	2.8
Married Women	6.5	5.4	5.4	5.1	4.5	3.7	4.5	3.9	3.9	4.9	5.7	5.4
All 55 and over	5.3	4.3	4.1	3.7	3.2	2.6	2.5	2.2	2.0	2.8	3.4	3.3
Insured Workers*	5.6	4.4	4.3	3.8	3.0	2.3	2.5	2.2	2.1	3.4	4.1	3.5

Insured unemployed as percent of all insured workers.

Source: U.S. Labor Department

cent of the labor force at the end of 1970, Meany repeatedly scored the President for failing to act forcefully to cope with either the slowdown or continuing inflation.

On Aug. 15, 1971, Nixon inaugurated his new economic policy with a 90-day wage-price freeze and other measures. Meany joined most other labor leaders in denouncing the program. Angered by a statement by Labor Secretary James Hodgson that he was "out of step with the needs and desires" of working men and women, Meany assailed the President for "mismanagement" of the economy.

His criticism of the freeze was concentrated on its effect on labor contracts calling for raises. The AFL-CIO would not cooperate with the freeze, he said, urging that unions cancel contracts if negotiated benefits were withheld.

As consideration of Phase Two, the post-freeze period of the new economic policy, began, Meany urged Nixon to establish an independent, tripartite wage-control board, representing labor, business and the public. Nixon accepted the proposal, and Meany, backed by the AFL-CIO Executive Council, agreed to serve on the board.

Phase Two began in mid-November 1971. The five labor Pay Board representatives quickly differed with public and business members over the size of pay increases and retroactive payment of raises due under existing contracts.

The labor members charged the public and business members were actually representing the administration. They expressed dissatisfaction with the price control effort, charging that it was ineffective. Labor eventually got most of what it wanted on retroactive pay, because Congress wrote appropriate provisions into an extension of the Economic Stabilization Act, under which Nixon had established his stabilization program. *(Details, chapter on Economic Stabilization Policy p. 105)*

On Nov. 18, 1971, Meany addressed the AFL-CIO convention in Bal Harbour, Fla. It was a scathing attack on the new economic policy. The previous day the White House accepted an invitation for the President to address the convention. Nixon's Nov. 19 speech was a strong defense of his program. It included a statement that labor's interests could not be placed before the public interest.

Nixon got a cool reception at Bal Harbour, and White House aides publicly denounced what they considered discourteous treatment. Treasury Secretary John B. Connally called Meany boorish and arrogant.

Meany later claimed to have evidence that the White House had planned the appearance at the convention as a televised confrontation between Nixon and Meany. In a televised interview Meany read from what he called a White House telephone memorandum:

"President Nixon is going to speak at 10:30 a.m. They will chastise him, and that will be the best thing that could happen. George Meany will be trying to make himself look like a big deal, but the American people will see the spectacle and decide for themselves on the merit of what Nixon is trying to do."

Break Over Dockworkers' Contract. Four labor members, including Meany, resigned from the Pay Board March 22-23, 1972. The issue was a decision by public and business members to scale down a pay increase won by the International Longshoremen's and Warehousemen's Union after a long strike. But the statement adopted by the AFL-CIO Executive Council March 22 announcing the withdrawal of its three members (the fourth was Leonard Woodcock, president of the independent United Auto Workers) made clear the labor leaders' dissatisfaction was with trends of both pay and price policy.

Labor had a strong case. The cost of living, as measured by the consumer price index, rose .5 per cent in February. The food price index, representing items most of which were not controlled, rose 2 per cent.

Meany's Anti-Communism. Ironically, the Meany-Nixon split in 1972 was based as much on international politics as it was on economic differences. An old fighter of communism in the labor movement, Meany was unable to tolerate the President's peaceful overtures to China and the Soviet Union.

Communist domination of some CIO unions was an obstacle to reunification of the AFL and CIO from 1937, when the CIO unions were expelled from the AFL, until 1955, when the merged AFL-CIO was created.

As a long-time leader of the AFL, named secretary-treasurer in 1940, Meany played an active role in keeping Communists out of positions of authority.

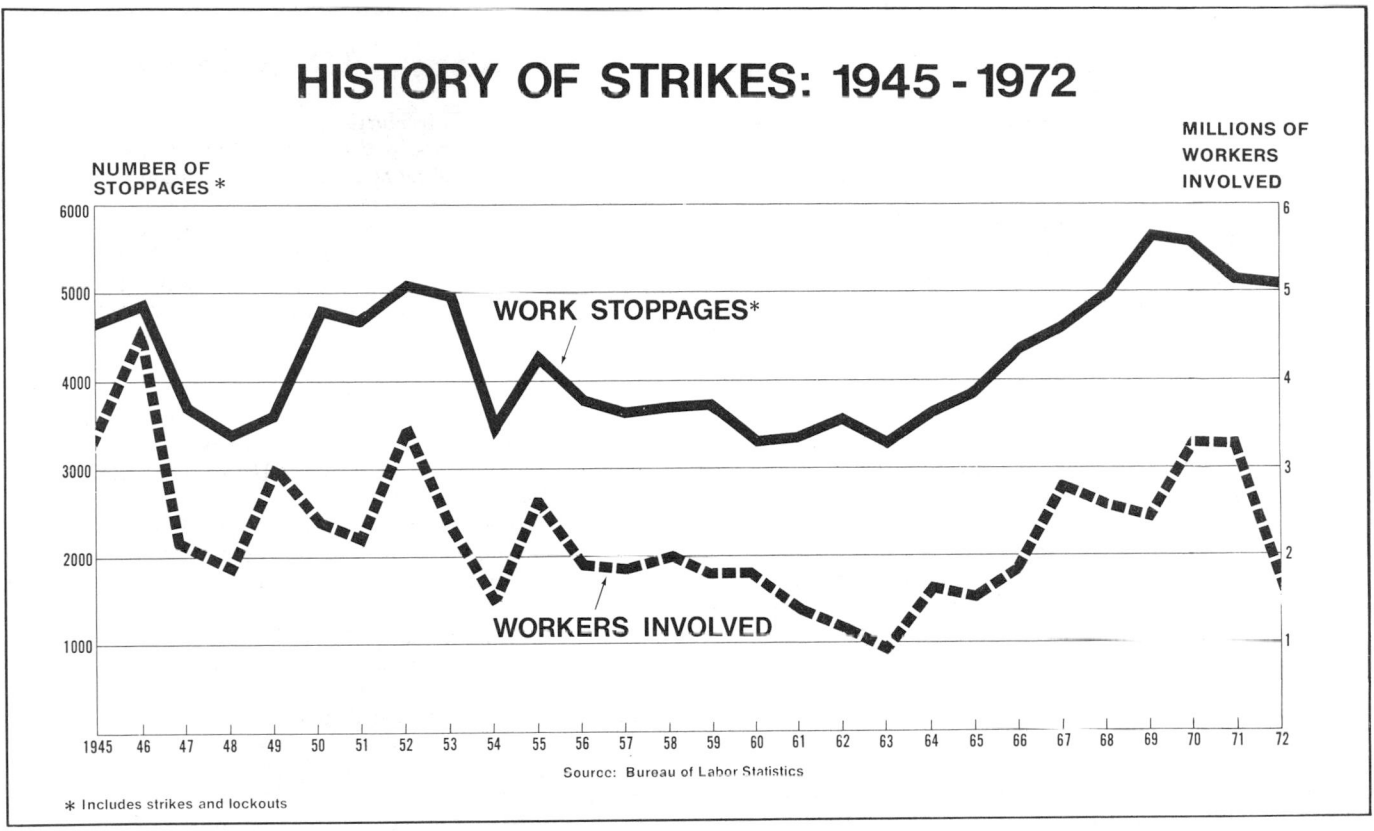

HISTORY OF STRIKES: 1945 - 1972

NUMBER OF
STOPPAGES *

MILLIONS OF
WORKERS
INVOLVED

WORK STOPPAGES*

WORKERS INVOLVED

Source: Bureau of Labor Statistics

* Includes strikes and lockouts

In 1945 the AFL refused to join the World Federation of Trade Unions because of Communist organizations it enrolled, principally the government-dominated Russian trade unions. In 1949, when the CIO and the British Trade Union Congress withdrew from the World Federation, the AFL joined with them in establishing the International Confederation of Free Trade Unions. But the AFL also continued to operate its own anti-Communist information agency, the Free Trade Union Committee. It was headed by Jay Lovestone, a former Communist who became a firm anti-Communist and remained one of Meany's principal advisers.

An AFL-CIO Executive Council statement Aug. 10, 1971, in language sounding much like Meany, posed a number of questions prompted by Nixon's announced plan to visit China and the consequent effect on Peking's bid for United Nations membership:

"Has Communist China provided any proof that, in line with the charter, it is now qualified for UN membership? Can the Nixon administration give the American people and the nations of the world any evidence that, in contrast to a year ago, the Mao Tse-tung regime is today qualified for UN membership in accordance with the aforementioned charter requirements?"

Meany was reported to have been particularly angered that Nixon, while in Peking Feb. 21, 1972, signed a bill (PL 92-235) providing for mandatory settlement of the West Coast dock strike.

The signing was a symbolic act, since a settlement had been ratified by the dockworkers Feb. 19, but Meany reacted negatively to the symbolism.

The Election and After. The AFL-CIO Executive Council July 19, 1972, voted to withhold endorsement from either Nixon or Sen. George S. McGovern, the Democratic candidate, during the presidential campaign. It was the first time in the federation's 17-year history that it had not endorsed the Democratic presidential candidate. Meany said that he personally would not support or vote for either man.

Throughout the campaign, Meany criticized McGovern's Vietnam position as one of "surrender."

In spite of the wage-price dispute between labor and the Republicans, the election returns showed that much of big labor had deserted the top of the Democratic ticket. In a post-election interview, McGovern called Meany one of the "wreckers" of the Democratic party. At the end of 1972, the Republicans appeared to have cemented labor support—at least among the more conservative craft unions—to a degree unparalleled since the beginning of the New Deal.

The coalition continued after the election. On Nov. 19, 1972, Peter J. Brennan, a building trades union official, was nominated as secretary of labor. The nomination had been cleared with Meany and Frank E. Fitzsimmons, president of the International Brotherhood of Teamsters, whose union supported Nixon in the 1972 campaign.

Meany rejoined the President's economic team Dec. 16 as a member of the Productivity Commission. On Dec. 30, the *New York Times* reported that Nixon had pledged to appoint labor representatives to the assistant secretary level in all relevant departments.

In early January 1973, Meany was appointed to Nixon's Labor-Management Advisory Commission to the Cost of Living Council, a group which was to determine if the administration's price stabilization standards

(Continued on p. 707)

Confrontations of Presidents and Labor—1935-1972

1935—President Roosevelt was threatened with strike by John L. Lewis, president of United Mine Workers (UMW) who wanted passage of Bituminous Coal Conservation Act. Coal strikes were postponed four times on Roosevelt's request, pending congressional action. Passage averted immediate strike.

1937—Lewis, who had become president of CIO, vainly pressured Roosevelt to endorse General Motors sit-down strikes in return for labor's 1936 campaign contributions.

1941—Roosevelt clashed with Lewis over UMW strike. National Defense Mediation Board rejected union demands. CIO representatives on board resigned. Dispute settled by Roosevelt-appointed three-man commission, including Lewis, which granted UMW demands.

1941—Roosevelt threatened by march on Washington by A. Philip Randolph, president of black Brotherhood of Sleeping Car Porters. Randolph charged black labor supply for war effort was going untapped. Roosevelt established Commission on Fair Employment Practice.

1943—Roosevelt clashed with Lewis over refusal of National War Labor Board to grant wage increases to miners. UMW struck; government seized mines. Settlement was reached after two more work stoppages.

1945—President Truman asked general labor-management conference at White House to continue "no strike" and "no lockout" wartime policies. Conference could not agree. United Auto Workers struck soon afterwards, setting off series of major strikes by electrical workers, meatpackers, steelworkers and miners.

1946—Truman seized coal mines during UMW tions with Brotherhoods of Railroad Trainmen and Locomotive Engineers over wage increases and work rules. Unions struck but agreed to Truman's conditions before army was to take over railroads.

1946—Truman seized coal mines during UMWs strike and negotiated new contract. When union struck again and ignored back-to-work injunction, Lewis was charged with contempt of court. Union was fined $3.5-million; Supreme Court reduced fine to $700,000.

1950—Truman ordered army seizure of railroads to prevent nationwide strike by Order of Railroad Conductors and other unions during Korean war. When new contract between unions and railroads was signed in 1952, railroads returned to private control.

1951—Labor representatives withdrew in February from participation in government's mobilization and stabilization programs in protest over what they described as labor's secondary role. They voted to return in April after being promised a strong policy-making voice.

1952—Truman seized steel mills after companies rejected Wage Stabilization Board settlement accepted by United Steelworkers. Supreme Court ruled Truman's action unconstitutional. Government returned mills to private ownership, and steelworkers struck. Truman asked Congress for legislation authorizing seizure to

avoid invoking Taft-Hartley Act, which Congress had passed over Truman's veto and which labor bitterly resented. Congress refused to comply. Union and companies later reached settlement.

1954—President Eisenhower's proposal for compulsory strike ballot amendment to Taft-Hartley Act was sharply opposed by Walter Reuther, president of CIO, and other labor leaders. Proposal killed in Senate.

1959—Eisenhower disagreed with AFL-CIO, UMW and Teamsters over Taft-Hartley reforms he favored on secondary boycotts, "blackmail" picketing, "no-man's-land" cases and "hot cargo" contracts. Reforms were included in Labor-Management Reporting and Disclosure Act of 1959.

1963—President Kennedy and five operating railroad unions clashed over Kennedy's proposed legislation on compulsory arbitration of dispute over elimination of jobs. Congress subsequently passed nation's first peacetime compulsory arbitration law. Arbitration board created by act ruled for management.

1964—Teamsters president James R. Hoffa accused Attorney General Robert F. Kennedy of conducting "personal vendetta" against him. Hoffa was convicted in 1964 of both jury tampering and fraud and conspiracy in misuse of union pension funds. Hoffa was released from federal prison December 1971 after President Nixon commuted his sentence; he had served almost five years.

1967—President Johnson and six railroad shopcraft unions disputed plan for imposed settlement of threatened nationwide rail strike. Mediation board could not achieve voluntary settlement after two-day strike, so its recommendations went into effect instead.

1970—President Nixon ordered federal troops to run postal system when National Association of Letter Carriers, supported by National Postal Union, went on nation's first postal strike. Government and unions negotiated settlement, which Congress approved by passing Postal Reorganization Act (PL 91-375).

1971—Nixon won passage of legislation (PL 92-110) ordering striking Brotherhood of Railway Signalmen and sympathizing unions back to work after two-day strike.

1972—Nixon gained legislation (PL 92-235) to settle longshoremen's five-month West Coast dock strike. President signed law Feb. 21, while on China trip, as "symbolic act." Dock workers ratified new contract Feb. 19.

1972—Longstanding labor dissatisfaction over Nixon's wage-price stabilization program erupted March 16 when Pay Board, by 8-5 vote, ordered sharp cuts in dock workers' wage increases under strike settlement ratified Feb. 19. Board's five labor members denounced decision; four of five, including AFL-CIO President George Meany, resigned March 22-23. Nixon March 23 restructured board, which had been composed of 15 members, five each representing labor, business and public. New Pay Board consisted of seven members representing public.

(Continued from p. 705)
under Phase Three of Nixon's economic plan should be changed.

The President's decision to drop most mandatory wage-price controls during Phase Three was reported to have been influenced in part by Meany's talks with Secretary of the Treasury George P. Shultz. According to the *New York Times*, Shultz agreed to a voluntary controls program if labor pledged to participate in the stabilization program and to cooperate in seeking non-inflationary wage hikes during 1973.

The honeymoon between Meany and the Nixon administration was short-lived, however. By April 1973 Meany was once again blasting the administration on a variety of issues, ranging from its minimum wage proposals to its trade policy.

Chronology of

Labor

Legislation

Note: In addition to the legislation discussed below, other proposals considered by Congress involved matters of interest to labor. These are dealt with in other chapters. For information on farm labor, see Agriculture chapter; for guaranteed income, see Welfare chapter; for specific information on transportation strikes, see Transportation chapter; for wage-price controls, see Economic Stabilization chapter; see also chapter on Manpower.

1969

Congress in 1969 took little action in the field of labor, while President Nixon initiated a number of studies as the basis for future legislative recommendations.

Congress cleared a strong coal mine safety measure, a bill setting safety standards for construction workers on federally assisted projects and a bill permitting employers to contribute to trust funds to provide scholarships and child care centers.

Legislation (HR 12625) embodying the administration request to expand the unemployment insurance program was passed by the House. Congressional hearings were held on bills to legalize "common site" picketing and to permit farm workers to unionize and on equal employment and problems of migratory labor.

The President asked Congress for legislation to consolidate and expand various manpower training programs and by executive action he reorganized the manpower programs in the Department of Labor. *(Manpower programs, p. 733)* He also asked Congress for legislation to establish a National Occupational Safety and Health Board with the power to set standards for the protection of most of the nation's workers. A similar request by President Johnson was successfully opposed by powerful business interests.

Nixon established a commission to deal with "strife and tensions" in the construction industry and he invoked provisions of the Railway Labor Act to delay a railroad strike.

The administration instituted mandatory quotas—called the Philadelphia Plan—in the hiring of minority group workers by federal contractors. The plan evoked strong criticism from labor unions and conservatives.

Coal Mine Safety

Congress Dec. 18 cleared for the President's signature the most comprehensive mine health and safety bill (S 2917—PL 91-173) in U.S. history. The White House, which had indicated that the President might veto the bill, announced Dec. 29 that Nixon would sign despite misgivings about a federal compensation provision in the bill for miners suffering from black lung disease. The White House estimated the provision could cost the government from $150-million to $300-million a year. The bill was signed Dec. 30.

The President, in a special message to Congress March 3, recommended a new mine health and safety bill but did not recommend federal compensation for black lung victims. Approximately 10 per cent of the nation's active coal miners and 20 per cent of inactive miners suffered from the disease, according to estimates.

As passed, the bill provided that for the first three years of the act the federal government would pay totally disabled pneumoconiosis or "black lung" victims who were single $136 a month and married miners with three dependents $272. Widows of victims would get $136 a month. After Dec. 31, 1972, the states would take over all compensation for new victims. The program was expanded in 1972. *(1972 Chronology, p. 725)*

Just prior to the announcement that the President would sign the bill, 1,200 miners at four West Virginia mines went on strike to protest the threatened veto. They returned to work following the President's decision.

Among other major provisions, the act set safety standards of 3 milligrams of coal dust per cubic meter six months after the bill became law, and 2 milligrams per cubic meter after three years. It also required the use of non-sparking electrical equipment to prevent gas explosions.

Background. Concern over coal mine health and safety and related federal legislation mounted in 1968 following a West Virginia coal mine accident which killed 78 workers. In addition, widespread attention was focused on another mining problem, pneumoconiosis or "black lung"—a lung disease which afflicted miners as a result of coal dust inhalation.

Existing legislation in the mining field included laws passed in 1941 (PL 77-49) and 1947 (PL 80-328) which permitted federal safety inspection of mines. In 1952, federal inspectors were given the right to order unsafe mines to shut down (PL 82-552). However, small mines, employing less than 15 workers underground, were exempted and could not be shut down. After several unsuccessful attempts to remove the exemption for small mines, Congress in 1966 extended inspection and safety requirements to these mines. (PL 89-376). *(Congress and the Nation, Vol. I, p. 642; Vol. II, p. 688, 703)*

President Johnson Sept. 11, 1968, proposed new health and safety legislation. The measure, which extended coverage of existing regulations, provided penalties and covered limitations on permissible amounts of coal dust, was not enacted in the 90th Congress but was reintroduced in the 91st.

Nixon Proposals. President Nixon, in his March 3 message to Congress, emphasized the need for safety requirements. Workers in the mining industry, he said, "too long endured the constant threat and often sudden reality of disaster, disease and death."

In addition to submitting legislative proposals, the President by administrative action increased the number of mine inspectors, ordered a study of a possible reorganization of the Bureau of Mines, expanded research on black lung disease, initiated previously authorized grants to states for their health and safety programs and ordered programs of federal-state and labor-management cooperation in the field.

At the time Nixon submitted his proposals, congressional committees were considering other plans to promote mining safety and health, including the one submitted by the Johnson administration.

PROVISIONS

As signed into law Dec. 30, S 2917 (PL 91-173):

• Required the secretary of interior to establish mine safety standards and the secretary of health, education and welfare (HEW) to set health standards.

• Required a minimum of four inspections of each mine annually and a minimum of one spot inspection every five working days of a mine in known dangerous gas-generating areas or which the secretary believed had especially hazardous conditions. A miners' representative could obtain an immediate inspection of a mine in which he believed there was a violation of health or safety standards or where an imminent danger existed.

• Provided for issuance of withdrawal orders—withdrawal of all persons except those needed to correct deficiencies—in mines where dangerous conditions or violations of standards existed.

• Established civil penalties of up to $10,000 for operator violations of the act and civil penalties of up to $250 to a miner violating the act.

• Established criminal penalties of up to $25,000 in fines and one year imprisonment for willful violations of the act by coal mine operators for first conviction, and for subsequent convictions, penalties of up to $50,000 and five years imprisonment.

• Established interim mandatory health and safety standards which included a permissible coal-dust level of 3 milligrams per cubic meter six months after enactment and reduction to 2 milligrams after three years.

• Provided free periodic X-rays for miners and reassignment to relatively dust-free areas for miners showing black-lung symptoms.

• Eliminated the existing classification of mines as "non-gassy." Required conversion to non-spark electrical equipment within one year after enactment at all mines formerly classified as gassy. Mines not previously so classified were given extensions of up to three years under certain conditions. Mines above the water table were given four years to convert, with provision for extensions of up to two years. All hand-operated equipment was required to be non-sparking after one year.

• Provided compensation ranging from $136 a month for a miner totally disabled with pneumoconiosis (black lung) or to his widow and up to $272 for a miner with three dependents. (Total compensation to be paid by the federal government through Dec. 31, 1972, after which the states would take over all compensation for new victims. Further, where a state lacked an adequate compensation law, provided that the coal mine operators pay miner disability benefits.)

• Authorized appropriation of federal funds for health and safety research.

• Provided limited pay guarantees for miners idled by a withdrawal order.

• Established an interim compliance panel—composed of the assistant secretary of labor for labor standards, director of the Commerce Department's Bureau of Standards, HEW's administrator of Consumer Protection and Environmental Health Service, and the director of the National Science Foundation—authorized to grant temporary waivers of standards and relief from closing orders except in cases of imminent danger.

SENATE ACTION

Committee. The Senate Labor and Public Welfare Committee Sept. 17 unanimously reported S 2917. The committee bill was considered tougher than the administration proposal (S 1300).

Floor. The Senate Oct. 2 passed S 2917 on a 73-0 roll-call vote.

The bill was sent to the House after two days of deadlocked debate over a requirement that all mines use non-spark producing equipment.

The deadlock was broken after Harrison A. Williams Jr. (D N.J.) successfully offered an amendment giving small mines which normally do not contain methane gas extra time to convert to the new equipment.

The Williams amendment was a substitute for an amendment by John Sherman Cooper (R Ky.) which would have established two categories of mines—gassy, which would have to use the non-spark-producing equipment, and non-gassy, which would not.

The Williams amendment provided that small mines in which gas is not expected to be present would have five years to convert to new equipment. But other mines would have to convert in four years. The amendment was passed on a 45-31 roll call.

Under the original bill, all mines would be treated as gassy and, after a transition period, be required to operate with non-spark equipment. Existing law treated as non-gassy those mines where methane gas was present in quantities of less than 0.25 per cent of the total volume of air. Those mines were permitted to use equipment which was not permissible in the gassy mines where methane was present in larger volumes. Methane is explosive when the volume of the gas is 5 to 20 per cent of the air.

Cooper argued that non-spark-producing equipment was not necessary in the mines already classified as non-gassy. He said the cost of converting to such equipment by small operators of non-gassy mines would be prohibitive.

Although the gassy and non-gassy mine distinction was crucial throughout most of the debate, two days of debate were taken up with discussion of a 4-cent-per-ton assessment on coal producers. The assessment was to finance coal mine health and safety research.

Questions over the research assessment arose Sept. 26 when Winston L. Prouty (R Vt.) charged that the provision in S 2917 covering the assessment was unconstitutional. He argued that such an assessment was essentially a tax and the Constitution requires tax bills to originate in the House.

A compromise was reached Sept. 30 after Jennings Randolph (D W.Va.) offered an amendment providing that federal funds rather than assessment on mine operators be used to finance the research. The amendment set an appropriation ceiling of $20-million for the current fiscal year and $30-million each year thereafter. The amendment was approved on a 91-0 roll-call vote.

The Randolph amendment also provided for compensation of miners for disability caused by contraction of pneumoconiosis, so-called "black lung." The amendment established federal responsibility for funding the program in fiscal 1970 and 1971. In succeeding years the states would bear half the cost. The bill authorized $70-million to partially pay for the program.

Provisions. As passed by the Senate, S 2917 set a maximum coal dust level of 3.0 milligrams per cubic meter of air to be achieved six months after enactment and 2 milligrams three years later; removed the distinction between gassy and non-gassy mines, giving owners of gassy mines 16 months after enactment to convert to non-sparking equipment and giving non-gassy mine owners four to five years to convert, depending on the mine's size; provided federal compensation for miners and widows of miners disabled by contraction of pneumoconiosis; and abolished the Coal Mine Safety Board of Review.

HOUSE ACTION

Committee. The House Education and Labor Committee Oct. 13 reported a clean bill (HR 13950).

Floor. The House Oct. 29 by a 389-4 roll-call vote passed HR 13950 with amendments. After passing the bill, the House substituted the language of HR 13950 for that of S 2917 and passed the amended S 2917 by voice vote.

The House action came on the third day of debate on the measure after a compromise was reached off the floor on the most controversial issue, whether to retain the Coal Mine Safety Board of Review, created under the 1952 Mine Safety Act and considered by critics a buffer for mine owners and operators against strict enforcement of existing legislation.

Supporters of the board accepted assurances by Democratic supporters of the bill and Bureau of Mines officials that mine owners and operators would be given adequate time to meet standards before closing orders took effect. Passage of a strong bill appeared assured when John N. Erlenborn (R Ill.), leader of the opposition and a member of the Education and Labor General Labor Subcommittee which drafted the bill, said he would not offer an amendment to empower the board to override closing orders.

Chairman Carl D. Perkins (D Ky.) of the Education and Labor Committee offered an amendment to the committee bill to eliminate the board and substitute an interim compliance panel composed of five administration officials, only one of whom would be from the Interior Department.

Perkins explained that, under the 1952 act, the board had equal representation of miners and mine owners and operators, with a neutral chairman. He said the United Mine Workers of America, representing the miners, had recently announced that it would not take part in the board's activities as contemplated in the bill. His amendment was accepted by voice vote.

Floor opposition concentrated on the grant of compensation for miners afflicted with black lung disease (pneumoconiosis). John H. Dent (D Pa.) said some 100,-000 miners and former miners suffered from the disease. He said about half would be eligible for funds. But opponents objected to creation of a special workmen's compensation program for coal miners.

Perkins said in rebuttal that most state workmen's compensation programs evaded or ignored the problem of miners suffering from the disease.

William J. Scherle (R Iowa) moved to recommit the bill to committee with instructions to delete the compensation provision. The motion was defeated by voice vote.

Erlenborn offered an amendment, accepted by voice vote, providing for an open authorization of federal funds for health and safety research and for medical examinations for miners. This replaced a controversial proposed levy of 2 cents per ton of coal against mine owners and operators for research. The amendment was agreed to by voice vote. The Senate had deleted a similar provision on the floor.

Provisions. As passed by the House, HR 13950 set maximum coal dust levels at 4.5 milligrams per cubic meter of air within six months after enactment and 3 milligrams six months later; removed the distinction between gassy and non-gassy mines, requiring owners of gassy mines to convert to non-sparking equipment 15 months after enactment and owners of non-gassy mines to convert within four years; provided federal grants to states for compensation of black lung victims and their dependents; and established an interim compliance panel to grant temporary waiver of standards and relief from closing orders except in cases of imminent danger.

CONFERENCE, FINAL ACTION

Conferees Dec. 16 filed a report on S 2917. Major differences between the two versions of the bill were reconciled as follows:

Black Lung Compensation. Resolved a conflict over federal support for financing assistance to victims of pneumoconiosis by providing full federal support of the program during the first three years after enactment, (through Dec. 31, 1972) and state support thereafter. Language requiring mine owners to accept responsibility for miners benefits in states which did not have approved workers' compensation laws was also incorporated in the provision. The program was placed under the administration of the secretary of HEW.

Non-Spark Equipment. Adopted the Senate language with technical changes and changes in the time requirements for converting to non-spark equipment. Gassy mines as well as all mines using small hand-operated equipment were required to convert within one year. Mines formerly labeled non-gassy were given extensions of up to three years. Non-gassy mines above the water table were permitted four years to convert with provision for two-year extensions under certain conditions.

Coal Dust. Incorporated in the health and safety standards section the Senate language limiting permissible coal dust levels in mines to 3.0 milligrams per cubic meter six months after enactment of the bill and 2.0 milligrams 36 months after enactment. The House had established limits of 4.5 milligrams six months after enactment and 3.0 milligrams within one year.

Civil Penalties. Adopted the $10,000 civil penalty limits for mine operator violations of the act as provided in the House-passed bill. The Senate had provided a maximum civil penalty of $25,000.

Criminal Penalties. Adopted the $25,000 fine and maximum prison term of one year provided in the Senate bill. The House had provided penalty limits for criminal violations by mine operators of $10,000 and six months in prison for first violations.

Standards. Accepted, with modification, the House provision that health standards would be set by the secretary of health, education and welfare. Under the bill as passed by the Senate, health standards would have been set by the surgeon general. Both bills provided that safety standards would be set by the secretary of interior and that regulations developed incorporating health and safety standards would be promulgated by the secretary of interior.

Conferees said the act was to be "construed liberally" when executing provisions relating to the need to eliminate unsafe and unhealthful conditions and practices.

The House adopted the conference report Dec. 17 by a **334-12 key roll-call vote.**

The Senate adopted the conference report Dec. 18 by voice vote, clearing the bill for the President's signature.

'Philadelphia Plan'

The administration's "Philadelphia Plan" to increase minority employment on federal construction projects survived a strong move in Congress late in the session to kill it.

The plan—named for the city in which the first agreement with federal contractors was made—was announced in June by the Department of Labor and went into effect for Philadelphia in September. Under the plan, federal contractors were required to work toward hiring a certain quota of minority employees on federal construction projects.

Controversy over the plan arose when Comptroller General Elmer B. Staats, who worked for Congress and not the executive branch, in August ruled it to be in violation of the 1964 Civil Rights Act. Attorney General John N. Mitchell denied it was a violation. The plan was opposed by the AFL-CIO and the building trade unions. Their opposition strained the long established and politically effective labor-civil rights coalition.

The issue hit the floor of the Senate in December after the Appropriations Committee had added to the fiscal 1970 supplemental appropriations bill (HR 15209) an amendment forbidding the use of any federal funds as direct aid or through contracts or agreements which the comptroller general "holds to be in contravention of any federal statute." The Senate in a series of roll-call votes accepted the amendment, which in effect would nullify the plan. However, after a call by the President for the Senate amendment to be killed, the House refused to accept the provision; and the Senate agreed to delete the

language. President Nixon had threatened to veto the bill unless the Senate amendment was knocked out.

Background. When the American Federation of Labor was founded in 1886, it held to a policy of nondiscrimination against Negro workers. But it believed that the growth of independent trade unionism should be based on craft autonomy rather than centralized control. Each of the federation's constituent unions had its own governing body and determined its own policies.

Many locals began to back away from the federation's nondiscrimination policy in the mid-1890s, a period when racial segregation was becoming institutionalized in many sectors of American life. At the same time, the federation decided it would grant charters to all-Negro unions, partly to minimize the possibility that Negroes would be used as strikebreakers.

Restrictive membership practices and strict union control over certain skilled jobs worked to exclude Negroes from the ranks of organized labor beyond the end of World War I. A. Philip Randolph, the Negro organizer and leader of the Sleeping Car Porters, argued as early as 1919 that the structure of craft unionism was discriminatory. "The present American Federation of Labor is the most wicked machine for propagation of race prejudice in the country," he said.

With the Depression and the coming of the Roosevelt era in the 1930s, political influence of black workers began to increase. Trade unionists determined to unionize the mass-production industries realized that they could not succeed without winning the support of black workers. The Congress of Industrial Organizations, formed in 1938, made overt attempts, with some success, to win black support during World War II.

President Franklin D. Roosevelt realized the political benefits that would accrue to the Democratic party with an amalgamation of black and white workers. He conveyed a sense of commitment to the cause of Negroes, who had been largely apolitical or Republican.

The Roosevelt coalition of Negroes, blue-collar workers, urban residents and the South was cemented by common economic and social goals. It survived through 1955, when the American Federation of Labor merged with the Congress of Industrial Organizations (AFL-CIO). At that time, out of 15 million organized workers, 1.5 million were black.

During the terms of Presidents Kennedy and Johnson in the 1960s, new forces developed in the civil rights movement. Black consciousness and militancy began to emerge within labor organizations, and labor responded by giving political support to such legislation as the Civil Rights Acts of 1964 and 1968 and the Voting Rights Act of 1965.

Charges of racial discrimination in organized labor were aimed primarily at craft unions—those consisting of workers possessing a specific skill or a closely related set of skills. Construction trades came in for particularly harsh criticism. Industrial unions, which attempt to organize all workers in a given industry regardless of their particular skills, generally escaped charges of racial discrimination.

Erbin Crowell Jr., an editor of *Civil Rights Digest*, wrote in 1969: "The dilemma of labor unions is in many ways the dilemma of the nation: Words don't match deeds; pronouncements by leaders are ignored or even opposed by large numbers of the citizenry; the sham of

tokenism is revealed by continuing injustice and prejudice."

Criticism of Plan. The AFL-CIO and the building
trades unions adamantly opposed the Philadelphia Plan.

Much of the pressure on union leaders came from
rank-and-file white workers who feared that such moves
as the Philadelphia Plan would cost them jobs, and who
saw themselves paying for social change at the cost
of personal and family security.

G.C. Haggerty, president of the construction and
building trades department of the AFL-CIO, speaking
for the federation on Sept. 23, 1969, said, "We are 100
per cent opposed to a quota system, whether it be called
the Philadelphia Plan or whatever."

AFL-CIO President George Meany, speaking in
January 1970 several months after the plan took effect,
termed it "a concoction and contrivance of a bureau-
crat's imagination" to offset criticism of the administration's civil rights record.

Meany said the plan would not bring a single
added black worker into the Philadelphia work force.
Contractors would merely switch existing Negro workers
from private to government projects, he said.

Civil rights leaders said the plan pitted black
workers against white workers. Clarence Mitchell, Washington lobbyist and director of the National Association
for the Advancement of Colored People (NAACP), said
Dec. 23, 1969, the day after Congress upheld the plan,
that it was a "calculated attempt coming right from the
President's desk to break up the coalition between Negroes and labor unions. Most of the social progress in this
country has resulted from this alliance."

"Nixon's people are forcing employers to lay off
workers and then telling them to put in a certain
quota of blacks into those vacancies. It is a strategy designed to increase friction between labor and Negroes,"
said black Rep. Augustus F. Hawkins (D Calif.) in November 1970.

SENATE ACTION

The Senate Appropriations Committee Dec. 17 reported HR 15209, the House passed supplemental appropriations bill, with an amendment upholding the comptroller general in his dispute with the Labor and Justice Departments over the legality of the Philadelphia
Plan. The amendment barred the use of any federal
funds as direct aid or through contracts or agreements
which the comptroller general "holds to be in contravention of any federal statute." The AFL-CIO and the
building trades unions had lobbied for inclusion of
such a provision in the bill.

The Senate passed HR 15209 Dec. 18, 74-0. Prior to
passage, the Senate in a series of roll-call votes acted to
uphold the committee restrictions on the Philadelphia
Plan. The crucial vote came on a 52-37 roll call, when
senators agreed that the committee provision was germane to the bill.

Jacob K. Javits (R N.Y.) led the fight to delete the
committee's amendment on the Philadelphia Plan
from the bill. He said the language of the provision
gave the comptroller general "absolute power—the
power to even defy courts."

Instead of just killing the Philadelphia Plan, "which
is the real purpose of the provision," Javits said, senators

"would be killing a lot of other things with the same
shot."

Javits read a letter from Attorney General John N.
Mitchell to Senate Minority Leader Hugh Scott (R Pa.)
in opposition to the committee amendment. "It provides
that the comptroller general's determination as to the
legality of any contract is binding whether or not such
determination is later upheld by the courts," the letter
said.

Roman L. Hruska (R Neb.) said the committee
amendment was designed to "reaffirm congressional support for the authority already invested in the comptroller general" when his authority over appropriations and
expenditures was challenged.

Javits responded that the comptroller general had
asked the committee for congressional action confined
only to the Philadelphia Plan. "He did not want any
broad sweeping authority like the one contained in this
supplemental," Javits said.

Javits made a point of order that the committee
amendment was legislation in an appropriations bill
(prohibited by Senate rules). Under Senate rules, the
full Senate had to decide whether the provision was
germane to the appropriations bill.

Robert C. Byrd (D W. Va.), floor manager of HR
15209, raised the question of germaneness. The question
was sustained by a 52-37 roll-call vote, and the provision was left in the bill.

Byrd (W Va.) then offered an amendment stipulating
that the provision "shall not be construed as affecting or
limiting" the scope of judicial review of any decision made
by the comptroller general. That amendment was accepted, 73-13.

FINAL ACTION

The conference report on HR 15209 was filed Dec.
20. The Senate's Philadelphia Plan provision was reported
in disagreement.

The House Dec. 22 by voice voted adopted the conference report, after which it rejected the Philadelphia
Plan amendment by a **156-208 key roll-call vote.**

Earlier in the day, the President had issued a statement calling on the House to kill the Philadelphia Plan
amendment. The President said such action would be
"an historic and critical civil rights vote" and said he
would have to consider vetoing the entire bill unless the
section was deleted.

Later that day, the Senate by a 39-29 roll-call vote
reversed its earlier position and agreed to delete the
Philadelphia Plan amendment from HR 15209.

Construction Safety

Congress July 28 completed action on a labor-
backed bill (HR 10946—PL 91-54) to set safety standards
for construction workers on all federal and federally
assisted or financed projects.

HR 10946 was an outgrowth of what was called an
oversight in federal statutes which provided safety
standards for workers in supply and service industries
under federal contract but not in the construction industry. It also was an outgrowth of work accident statistics.

In 1969, it was estimated, work accidents would cost the construction industry approximately $3-billion. In 1968, 2,800 construction workers were killed on the job, the highest annual death rate for any one industry in the United States. Since 1959, there had never been fewer than 209,000 construction workers disabled per year.

Labor and business interests clashed on the bill. The construction industry said that federal regulations on safety measures would result in higher prices for construction work and would cause state and local governments to withdraw from taking responsibility for construction safety. Organized labor supported the bill.

Provisions. As signed into law Aug. 9, HR 10946 (PL 91-54):

• Required the secretary of labor, after consulting with a nine-member advisory committee, which included members representing contractors, construction workers, and the general public, to set minimum safety and health standards for federal and federally aided construction work.

• Authorized the secretary of labor to inspect places and practices of construction employment and to seek compliance with the safety standards through the U.S. district courts if necessary.

• Authorized the federal agency for which work was being done to cancel the contract of any contractor or subcontractor found guilty by the secretary of non-compliance with the standards.

• Prohibited the awarding of contracts for a three-year period to any contractor found guilty of noncompliance.

• Allowed the blacklisted contractor the right to petition the U.S. court of appeals for review of the ruling.

• Permitted the blacklisted contractor, after complying with the safety requirements, to petition the secretary before the end of the 3-year period to be removed from the blacklist.

• Authorized the secretary to set up programs for the education and training of employees and employers in construction safety.

• Authorized the secretary to require reporting of construction injuries and accidents and their causes and costs.

Legislative History. The House Education and Labor Committee May 14 reported HR 10946, and the House passed the bill June 4 by voice vote. The Senate Labor and Public Welfare Committee reported HR 10946 July 15. The Senate July 24 passed the bill by voice vote and without debate. The House July 28 by voice vote agreed to technical amendments added by the Senate.

Other Bills

LABOR-MANAGEMENT TRUST FUND. The Senate Oct. 1 accepted by voice vote a House amendment and cleared for the President's signature a bill (S 2068—PL 91-86) to amend the Labor-Management Relations Act of 1947 to permit employers to contribute to trust funds to provide scholarships for employees and their dependents or establish child care centers for dependents of employees. The Senate originally passed S 2068 by voice vote on Sept. 12.

The House Sept. 29 passed a similar bill (HR 4314) by a 354-1 roll-call vote. The House bill limited payments to trust funds. The Senate bill permitted payments to individuals also. The House then substituted the language of HR 4314 for that of S 2068 and passed the amended S 2068 by voice vote.

RAILROAD RETIREMENT. Responding to the possibility of a bankrupt pension fund for retired railroad workers, the House Sept. 30 by a 372-17 roll-call vote passed a bill (HR 13300) to provide financing for the continuation, through June 1975, of supplemental payments under the Railroad Retirement Act of 1937. Final action came in 1970. *(1970 chronology, p. 716)*

A supplemental pension fund established in 1966 (PL 89-699) was supposed to last until 1971, but there had been an underestimation of the number of retiring railroad workers. *(Congress and the Nation, Vol. II, p. 765)*

As passed by the House, HR 13300 provided for an increase in the excise tax levied on railroads to finance supplemental annuities for pensioned railroad workers. It also required compulsory retirement of all railroad employees at age 65.

PRESIDENT'S YOUTH COUNCIL. Congress in 1969 enacted legislation (H J Res 764—PL 91-176) providing an open-ended authorization for the President's Council on Youth Opportunity.

The council was established by President Johnson by Executive Order 11333, issued March 5, 1967, on the recommendation of an interagency task force which had studied existing youth programs in the summer of 1966. The council was responsible for the coordination, evaluation and encouragement of the various federal youth programs. It was chaired by the Vice President and consisted of certain cabinet members.

H J Res 764 was passed by the House Aug. 4 and the Senate Dec. 20. During House debate on the measure, Rep. Carl D. Perkins (D Ky.), chairman of the Education and Labor Committee, said: "We have tried to concentrate and provide employment opportunities, training opportunities and educational opportunities. That is the purpose of this legislation."

Appropriations of $300,000 for the council were included in the fiscal 1970 Labor-Health, Education and Welfare appropriations bill (HR 15931—PL 91-204), which cleared Congress March 4, 1970.

UNEMPLOYMENT COMPENSATION. The House Nov. 13 by a 337-8 roll-call vote passed an administration-backed bill (HR 14705) to extend coverage and benefits of unemployment compensation to an additional 4.5 million workers. The Senate, passed the bill in 1970. *(1970 chronology, p. 715)*

Background. The Federal Unemployment Tax Act was enacted in 1935. Under it in 1969 employers of 79 per cent of the labor force paid taxes pased on their payrolls, up to a maximum amount per worker, to finance benefits for workers who became unemployed. State unemployment taxes were offset against the federal tax, and benefits were paid according to eligibility standards, in amounts and for time periods established under state programs.

President Nixon July 8 proposed that an additional 4.8 million workers be covered by unemployment insurance and that the duration of benefits be extended in periods of high unemployment.

In a message to Congress, Nixon also urged states to provide unemployed workers with benefits equaling at least 50 per cent of their pay when working. The President promised federal action if the states failed to act voluntarily within the next two years to meet that goal.

Nixon said most states provided about 26 weeks of benefits. When the national unemployment rate reached 4.5 per cent or higher for three consecutive months, the President said, unemployed workers should receive benefits for up to 13 additional weeks.

To meet the increased costs of the program, the President proposed raising the taxable wage base over a five-year period to $6,000. In a majority of states, Mr. Nixon said, the base was the first $3,000 of wages.

As passed by the House, HR 14705 increased the wage base only to $4,200. It also excluded farm workers, whom the administration had proposed bringing under the unemployment compensation program for the first time.

1970

Occupational Safety

After a three-year dispute between labor and business forces over how the federal government should adopt and enforce safety standards, Congress in 1970 passed a comprehensive on-the-job safety program, the Occupational Safety and Health Act (S 2193—PL 91-596). *(1968 proposal, Congress and the Nation, Vol. II, p. 821)*

The act covered about 55 million industrial, farm and construction workers employed by firms engaged in interstate commerce. *(1972 hearings on administration of act, p. 731)*

The legislation gave the secretary of labor authority to set safety and health standards for the protection of workers and created a three-member commission to enforce regulations.

Organized labor and most liberal Democrats had wanted the secretary to set and enforce safety standards while business interests backed by Republicans and the administration had requested that two presidentially appointed boards be created, one to set standards and the other to enforce them.

Labor groups contended that independent boards could become captives of the industries they were supposed to regulate. Business interests argued that due process would be violated if the secretary were allowed to set, monitor and enforce safety rules.

The Senate Nov. 17 passed a bill which provided a compromise by giving the secretary standards-setting authority and a three-member commission enforcement power.

The House, however, Nov. 24 adopted the administration- and business-backed approach by establishing two independent boards.

House-Senate conferees followed the Senate version, giving the secretary the rule-making responsibilities.

But on another key provision, conferees deleted a Senate provision allowing the secretary to close a plant if an "imminent danger" threatened the lives of workers.

Occupational Accident Facts

"The on-the-job health and safety crisis is the worst problem confronting American workers," reported the House Committee on Education and Labor in October 1970.

The following annual statistics compiled by the Bureau of Labor Statistics (BLS) were cited by the committee for the nation's 80 million workers:

- 14,500 killed, an average of 55 per day during a five-day work week.
- 2.2 million injured.
- 390,000 cases of occupational diseases (lung cancer, asbestosis, heart disease and others).
- 250 million man days of work lost, 10 times as many as from strikes.
- More than $1.5-billion lost in wages.
- More than an $8-billion loss to the Gross National Product.

A report submitted on contract to the Labor Department Sept. 20 by the Delphic Systems and Research Corporation concluded that the annual BLS survey of work-related accidents was "seriously restricted" by survey-sampling and data-collection procedures at state levels.

The Delphic validation of work injuries reported to the BLS by the state of California—a state with rigorous accident reporting procedures—revealed that more than 36 per cent of firms reporting "no injuries" actually had employee accidents. On a national basis, the report projected approximately 200,000 disabling work injuries beyond the 2.2 million reported in 1969.

House conferees insisted that the secretary should obtain a court order before a plant could be closed.

Although the conference version drew mixed reactions from labor and business interests, final passage was assured when the Labor Department as well as some business and labor groups endorsed the bill.

PROVISIONS

As signed into law Dec. 29, S 2193 (PL 91-596):

Duties of Employers

- Required employers to furnish a work place free from recognized hazards that had caused or were likely to cause death or serious physical harm to employees.

Safety and Health Standards

- Required the secretary of labor within two years after enactment to promulgate national consensus safety standards and established federal safety standards.
- Provided that when the secretary of labor wished to promulgate, revise or revoke an occupational safety and health standard, he could appoint an ad hoc advisory committee to submit recommendations within three to nine months, but not after that period.

● Required the secretary of labor to schedule a hearing on objections to a proposed standard within 30 days after the last day for filing recommendations.

● Authorized the secretary of labor to promulgate, revise or revoke a standard within 60 days after the completion of hearings or within 60 days after the last day for filing comments.

● Provided for exemption from standards for any employer who applied to the secretary of labor and met certain requirements.

● Required posting of labels or warnings to apprise employers of safety and health hazards to which they were exposed.

● Permitted any person to file for judicial review of a standard within 60 days after it was promulgated.

Advisory Committee

● Established a National Advisory Committee on Occupational Safety and Health consisting of 12 members representing management, labor and occupational safety and health professions to make recommendations on the administration of the act.

Inspections

● Authorized federal inspections and investigations of working conditions.

● Allowed employer and employee representatives to accompany a federal official during his inspection.

● Permitted employees to request an inspection if they believed a safety or health violation existed.

Appeals Commission

● Established an Occupational Safety and Health Appeals Commission consisting of three members appointed by the President with the consent of the Senate.

Enforcement

● Authorized the federal inspector to issue a citation if he believed an employer violated a standard.

● Required posting of the citation near the violation site.

● Authorized the commission to conduct a hearing if an employer contested a violation and to issue orders and penalties to enforce the act; if the employer did not give notice that he planned to contest a citation, the citation and the penalty assessment would be considered a final order of the commission and not subject to review.

● Provided that any person affected by a commission order could obtain review in a U.S. court of appeals.

Imminent Danger

● Required the secretary of labor to petition a U.S. district court to issue an order restraining any practices in a plant where an imminent danger existed to employees.

● Required the inspector to notify the affected employees and employers of the danger.

Penalties

● Assessed a civil penalty of not more than $10,000 for each willful or repeated violation of the Act.

● Assessed a penalty of not more than $1,000 for a serious violation of the act.

● Assessed a penalty of not more than $10,000 or six months imprisonment or both for any employer who willfully violated any standard and if the violation resulted in an employee death; doubled the penalty after the first conviction.

State Standards

● Authorized the secretary of labor to approve a state plan to develop and enforce standards if he found the plan complied with the Act.

● Authorized federal grants for up to 90 per cent of costs to states to identify needs, develop plans and improve administration and enforcement of standards.

● Authorized federal grants for up to 50 per cent of costs to assist states in carrying out occupational safety and health standards.

Research and Training

● Authorized the secretary of health, education and welfare (HEW) to conduct research on occupational safety and health problems to produce criteria which would assist the secretary of labor in formulating standards.

● Directed the secretary of labor to develop occupational safety and health training programs.

● Established a National Institute for Occupational Safety and Health in the HEW Department to conduct research on job safety.

Workmen's Compensation

● Established a 15-member National Commission on State Workmen's Compensation Laws to study such laws and report to Congress by July 31, 1972, with recommendations for improving them.

Assistant Secretary

● Provided for an additional assistant secretary of labor, to be given the title of assistant secretary of labor for occupational safety and health.

LEGISLATIVE HISTORY

As reported by the Senate Labor and Public Welfare Committee Oct. 6, S 2193 gave the secretary of labor responsibility for both setting and enforcing safety standards. The Senate passed the bill Nov. 17, after adopting, on a 43-38 roll-call vote, an amendment establishing a presidentially appointed panel to enforce regulations. The amendment provided a crucial compromise between Democratic and Republican versions of job safety legislation.

The House Education and Labor Committee, in reporting its version of the bill July 9, also had given both standards-setting and enforcement powers to the secretary of labor. But the committee recommendation was rejected on the House floor Nov. 24, when the House adopted, on a 220-173 roll-call vote, a substitute amendment that established two independent panels to set and enforce safety standards. This was the approach endorsed by the administration.

The conference report was filed Dec. 16. Conferees generally followed the Senate version of the bill. The conference report was approved by the Senate Dec. 16 by voice vote and the House Dec. 17 by a 309-60 roll call.

Unemployment Compensation

The Senate completed action on an unemployment compensation bill (HR 14705—PL 91-373) that had been approved by the House in 1969. Passage came during a period of almost unbroken rise in the unemployment rate, which reached 6.2 per cent of the labor force in December 1970.

The Emergency Security Amendments of 1970 extended unemployment compensation to about 4.8 million additional employees and provided extended benefits to all eligible workers during periods of high unemployment. *(1971 and 1972 action on extended unemployment benefits, p. 718, 723)*

Background. The House Nov. 13, 1969, passed HR 14705 to extend unemployment insurance coverage to an additional 4.5 million workers. The House bill did not go as far as the administration bill. It trimmed approximately 800,000 workers from the coverage sought by President Nixon. Among the workers not included in the House-passed bill were agricultural workers whom the administration had asked be brought under the unemployment compensation program for the first time.

The Federal Unemployment Tax Act was enacted in 1935 and amended in 1954 (PL 83-767). Under it in 1969 employers of 79 per cent of the labor force paid taxes based on their payrolls, up to a maximum amount per worker, to finance benefits for workers who became unemployed. State unemployment taxes were offset against the federal tax, and benefits were paid according to eligibility standards, in amounts and for time periods established under state programs. *(Congress and the Nation, Vol. I, p. 1289)*

Existing federal law required coverage of employees by all employers having four or more workers on their payrolls during any 20-week period. Some states covered firms with fewer employees for shorter periods. Agricultural employees had never been covered.

About 58 million workers were covered; about 17 million were not. The wage maximum on which the tax was paid was $3,000, established in 1939 when it was almost equal to average wages paid in employment covered under the act. Amount and duration of benefit eligibility rules varied considerably among the states.

Average compensation was only about one-third of average lost wages for the same period. Even during 1968, a year of high employment, about one unemployed worker in five exhausted his benefits before finding work.

Both the Kennedy and Johnson administrations sought to broaden the unemployment compensation system. Congress came close to revamping the system in 1966 when both chambers passed a bill making changes in the program. However, the legislation died at the end of the 89th Congress when Senate-House conferees were

unable to resolve their differences. *(Congress and the Nation, Vol. II, p. 616)*

President Nixon July 8, 1969, proposed that an additional 4.8 million workers be covered by unemployment insurance and that the duration of benefits be extended in periods of high unemployment.

In a message to Congress, Nixon also urged states to provide unemployed workers with benefits equaling at least 50 per cent of their pay when working. The President promised federal action if the states failed to act voluntarily within the next two years to meet that goal.

Nixon said most states provided about 26 weeks of benefits. When the national unemployment rate reached 4.5 per cent or higher for three consecutive months, the President said, unemployed workers should receive benefits for up to 13 additional weeks.

To meet the increased costs of the program, the President proposed raising the taxable wage base over a five-year period to $6,000. In a majority of states, Nixon said, the base was the first $3,000 of wages. *(1969 chronology, p. 712)*

Provisions. As signed into law Aug. 10, HR 14705 (PL 91-373):

• Required states to extend benefits at regular rates for periods of at least 13 weeks to unemployed persons who, during periods of high unemployment, had exhausted their regular benefits.

• Provided that the extended benefits would be "triggered" nationally by an unemployment rate of 4.5 per cent of the labor force for three consecutive months and, additionally, in individual states where the unemployment rate over a three-month period was 20 per cent higher than during the corresponding period in the preceding two years.

• Authorized federal financing of half the cost of extended unemployment benefits.

• Gave states until Jan. 1, 1972 (July 1, 1972, in states whose legislatures were not scheduled to meet during 1971) to amend their unemployment compensation programs to provide extended benefits.

• Extended coverage of the Employment Security Act to 4.8 million additional workers: 3.1 million employees of non-profit organizations, state hospitals and state institutions of higher learning; 200,000 employees not previously classified as "employees," such as agent drivers and outside salesmen; 200,000 employees of agricultural processing plants, such as food processing plants; 160,000 U.S. citizens employed abroad by American firms; and 1.1 million employees of businesses with only one or more workers and a quarterly payroll of $1,500. (Existing law included workers in small firms which had four employees and quarterly payrolls of $800 or more.)

• Extended coverage, at the option of local governments, to a possible additional 436,000 employees of municipal and county hospitals and institutions of higher learning.

• Increased the federal payroll tax for unemployment compensation from 3.1 per cent to 3.2 per cent (against tax credits of up to 2.7 per cent) retroactive to Jan. 1, 1970, and increased the taxable wage base from $3,000 to $4,200 for calendar years beginning in 1972.

• Authorized judicial review of adverse rulings of the secretary of labor affecting state unemployment programs.

• Required state laws to provide that eligibility depended on employment of the beneficiary during the benefit year; to prohibit denial of compensation to a worker undergoing training; to prohibit denial of benefits to a worker who lived or worked in another state when applying; to make illegal the cancellation of wage credits to a worker discharged for reasons other than misconduct.

SENATE ACTION

The Senate Finance Committee, in reporting HR 14705 March 26, made several changes in the provisions of the House-passed bill—including the addition of unemployment coverage for farm workers. Under the committee amendment, workers on farms that employed eight or more workers during 26 different weeks of the year—nearly one-fifth of U.S. farm labor—would be brought under the unemployment compensation program.

The committee deleted a House provision which would have extended coverage to 1.3 million employees of businesses employing less than four workers. It extended coverage, at the option of local governments, to employees of county and municipal hospitals and institutions of higher learning. It also extended coverage to handicapped persons who worked in nonprofit sheltered workshops.

The Senate passed HR 14705 April 7 by a 77-0 roll call. It accepted, 42-36, an amendment to include migratory workers under the extension of benefits to farm workers. It rejected, 29-47, an amendment that would have provided federal standards for state unemployment compensation programs. The AFL-CIO had pressed for establishment of a minimum federal benefit standard.

CONFERENCE, FINAL ACTION

A conference report on HR 14705 was filed May 5. In major actions, conferees:

• Dropped a Senate amendment which would have extended unemployment insurance coverage to 270,000 farm workers. Conferees, however, did agree to a study on extending coverage to farm workers as the first item of research authorized under the bill.

• Adopted a House amendment in modified form extending coverage to 1.1 million employees of small firms employing one or more workers and having quarterly payrolls of $1,500. (Original House version had retained the existing payroll figure of $800.)

The conference deleted a Senate-passed extension of coverage to 100,000 workers in nonprofit sheltered workshops—such as craft shops for the blind.

The House July 23 adopted the conference report 388-3, after rejecting, on a 270-219 roll call, a motion to recommit the bill to conference with instructions to accept the Senate amendment extending coverage to farm workers.

The Senate adopted the conference report Aug. 4 by a 50-19 roll call. Walter F. Mondale (D Minn.) and others unsuccessfully urged rejection of the report with the aim, ultimately, of restoring coverage for farm workers to the bill.

Railroad Retirement Annuities

Congress in 1970 enacted two bills relating to railroad retirement benefits.

One bill (HR 15733—PL 91-377) amended the Railroad Retirement Act of 1937 to provide a 15 per cent increase in annuities and changed the method of computing interest on investments of the railroad retirement accounts. Provisions of the measure were retroactive to Jan. 1, 1970, and extended through June 30, 1972. *(Further increases were voted in 1971 and 1972, p. 719, 724)*

The other bill (HR 13300—PL 91-215) amended the Railroad Retirement Act of 1937 and the Railroad Retirement Tax Act of 1946 to finance supplemental annuities for pensioned railroad workers and contained provisions designed to encourage retirement at age 65.

Background. During 1966, Congress approved (PL 89-699) changes in the Railroad Retirement Act of 1937 to establish a supplemental pension program for career railroad employees and to increase certain annuities under the regular retirement program as well. The supplemental pension was financed by an excise tax levied on the carriers, while the increased annuities were financed by an increased tax on both the carriers and the employees. Because of an underestimation of the number of retiring railroad workers, the pension fund, which was supposed to have lasted until after fiscal year 1971, ran out of money by the end of 1969. *(1966 legislation, Congress and the Nation, Vol. II, p. 765)*

INCREASED ANNUITIES

HR 15733 provided a 15 per cent increase in railroad retirement benefits, retroactive to Jan. 1, 1970. The bill brought railroad retirees' benefits into line with Social Security beneficiaries, who received a 15 per cent increase Jan. 1, 1970. *(Social Security increase, chapter on Welfare)*

The 15 per cent increase extended only through June 30, 1972. HR 15733 established an independent commission to study the railroad retirement system and report to Congress and the President one year before that date. The bill also changed the method of computing interest on railroad retirement investments in a way that was estimated to increase interest income of railroad retirement accounts by $27.5-million over an eight-year period.

HR 15733 was passed by the House April 7 and the Senate June 30. The conference report was cleared July 30.

Provisions. As signed into law Aug. 12, HR 15733 (PL 91-377):

• Raised payments, retroactive to Jan. 1, 1970, under the Railroad Retirement Act of 1937 by 15 per cent, but not by more than $50 monthly for a retiree or $25 monthly for his spouse. If a retiree also received benefits under Social Security, the new increase was reduced by the amount he received under a 15 per cent increase in Social Security benefits enacted in December 1969 (PL 91-172); however, a retiree would receive at least a $10 monthly increase under railroad retirement and his spouse at least a $5 monthly increase, regardless of their increased benefits under Social Security.

• Increased survivor annuities by 15 per cent, but not by more than $25 monthly. This increase would also be subject to an offset by the survivor's Social Security benefits, but would be no less than $5 monthly.

• Established an independent five-member Commission on Railroad Retirement to be appointed jointly by the President and Congress and required the commission to make a report to both by June 30, 1971. The commission was designated to study the railroad retirement system and provide guidelines for its future management and financing.

• Provided that the rate of interest to be borne by investments in the railroad retirement account would be computed on the basis of U.S. "notes" rather than "obligations," increasing the interest rate payable on such investments prior to enactment of HR 15733.

• Provided that the increase in benefits should cease to apply as of June 30, 1972.

SUPPLEMENTAL ANNUITIES

HR 13300 provided for an increase in the excise tax levied on railroads to finance supplemental annuities for pensioned railroad workers. It also contained provisions designed to encourage retirement at age 65. The measure was passed by the Senate Feb. 4. The House had passed HR 13300 in 1969. *(1969 chronology, p. 712)* The conference report was cleared March 5.

Provisions. As signed into law March 17, HR 13300 (PL 91-215):

• Provided an excise tax on railroads beginning April 1, 1970, at a rate calculated by the Railroad Retirement Board to cover the costs of the supplemental annuities program negotiated in 1966 between the railroads and the unions.

• Made the annuities program permanent; it had been scheduled to lapse at the end of October 1971.

• Eliminated the supplemental payments for employees who reached age 68 in 1970 and worked into 1971. The cutoff age would drop one year annually until an employee reached age 65 in 1973.

• Gave the Railroad Retirement Board authority to borrow from the Railroad Retirement Account enough money to pay pensioners to whom annuities were overdue.

• Provided a moratorium on changes in the program until July 1, 1974.

Vocational Rehabilitation

Congress extended the Vocational Rehabilitation Act for one year and authorized $1,010,000 to assist in the rehabilitation of handicapped persons in fiscal 1972. The bill (HR 19401—PL 91-610) was passed by the House Dec. 7 and the Senate Dec. 17.

First authorized in 1920 and slowly expanded thereafter, the Vocational Rehabilitation Act provided federal grants to state rehabilitation agencies for services that would enable the disabled to gain employment. The grants were administered by the Health, Education and Welfare Department's Rehabilitation Services Administration.

At first the program concentrated on the physically handicapped. But 1965 amendments brought the mentally handicapped into the program in large numbers, and in 1968 a new category was added, the "socio-economic disadvantaged"—in other words, the hard-core unemployed. *(Congress and the Nation, Vol. II, p. 737-43)*

In 1972 a further extension of vocational rehabilitation programs was pocket vetoed by President Nixon. *(1972 chronology, p. 726; Congress and the Nation, Vol. II, p. 737-43)*

Provisions. As signed into law Dec. 31, HR 19401:

• Extended for one year, through fiscal 1972, programs to assist in the rehabilitation of handicapped persons.

• Authorized appropriations of $700-million in fiscal 1972 for grants to states, $10-million for innovation of rehabilitation services, $140-million for special project grants, $30-million for construction and staffing of facilities, $30-million for improvement of rehabilitation facilities and $100-million for vocational evaluation and work adjustment programs.

Other Bills

JOINT INDUSTRY PROMOTION. Although passed by the House and reported by a Senate committee early in 1970, Congress failed to complete action on a bill (HR 860) amending the Taft-Hartley Act to permit employer contributions for joint industry promotion of construction products.

Court decisions had held that employer contributions to product-promotion programs administered jointly by trustees representing both employers and employees were prohibited by the 1947 Taft-Hartley Act.

HR 860 was passed by the House Jan. 27, by a 189-186 roll call vote. Sponsors of the bill contended that it would merely remove a legal barrier of the Taft-Hartley Act which prohibited joint union-management funds from promoting construction products and materials. Opponents of the bill argued that it would allow unions to intrude into management functions and complicate collective bargaining.

The Senate Labor and Public Welfare Committee Jan. 28 reported S 1369, containing the same provisions as the House-passed bill. There was no Senate floor action.

MINIMUM WAGE. The House Education and Labor Committee's Subcommittee on Labor held hearings between July and September on proposals to amend the Fair Labor Standards Act to increase minimum wages and broaden coverage. Minimum wage legislation was passed by both chambers in 1972 but died when the House refused to send it to conference. *(1972 chronology, p. 720)*

The proposals were opposed by business interests ranging from the Council of State Chambers of Commerce and National Federation of Independent Business to the Automatic Car Wash Association, International and Motel Association of America. Spokesmen for the groups said that if they were forced to pay higher straight time wages and premium pay for overtime, the employee would be the one most affected by the resultant price increase.

Organized labor and women's rights groups supported the proposals. "The present federal minimum wage is clearly obsolete," said George Perkel, research director of the Textile Workers Union of America, AFL-CIO. "A wage of $1.60 an hour is a poverty wage. It is not even sufficient to provide a family with an annual income of about $3,900, which is the current benchmark for the so-called poverty level of income for a family of four."

The women's rights groups recommended extension of the Fair Labor Standards Act to include domestic workers and extension of the Equal Pay Act to cover executive, administrative and professional employees. There is a "consistent, massive and vicious pattern of sex discrimination in the academic community," said Dr. Bernice Sandler of the Women's Equity Action League.

FARM LABOR. The Senate Agriculture Subcommittee on Agricultural Research and General Legislation held hearings on a bill that would have imposed restrictions on farm labor strikes. No further action was taken on the bill, which would have limited strikes to a single farm and outlawed strikes that would have resulted in permanent loss or damage to the crops.

Agricultural workers were not covered by the National Labor Relations Act of 1935, which guaranteed workers' rights to organize and join labor unions, bargain collectively and strike.

A farm organizing group in California had some success in 1970 in organizing grape and lettuce workers. Led by Cesar Chavez since 1966, the United Farm Workers Organizing Committee (UFWOC) was successful in signing up some of the largest grape growers after a nationwide consumer boycott against table grapes. By the end of 1970, the UFWOC had launched a similar boycott against lettuce. (*Congress and the Nation, Vol. II, p. 595*)

The Senate Labor and Public Welfare Subcommittee on Migratory Labor continued hearings, begun in 1969, on the problems of migrant and seasonal farm labor. (*Details, chapter on agriculture*)

YOUTH CONSERVATION CORPS. Congress established the Youth Conservation Corps, a three-year pilot program providing for the employment of teenagers in summer conservation jobs. The bill (S 1076—PL 91-378) was passed by the Senate June 26, 1969, and the House June 15, 1970. The Nixon administration opposed the measure on grounds that the corps would duplicate existing summer job programs and would be unable to provide adequate job training in the 90-day employment period envisioned by the bill.

MINE WORKERS ELECTION. The Senate Labor and Public Welfare Subcommittee held hearings from February through May on the 1969 election of the United Mine Workers Union. The election ultimately was voided and a new election was held in 1972. (*Box, this page*)

1971

Emergency Unemployment Aid

Congress Dec. 15 cleared a bill (HR 6065—PL 92-224) providing for full federal financing of extended unemployment benefits in states with a high rate of joblessness. The bill provided for 13 weeks of extended com-

---

Mine Workers Election

The Labor Department March 5, 1970, filed suit in federal district court in the District of Columbia to set aside the Dec. 9, 1969, election of the United Mine Workers (UMW). In that election, incumbent W. A. "Tony" Boyle, a protege of John L. Lewis, defeated Joseph A. "Jock" Yablonski, a member of the international union's executive board, for the union presidency by a margin of almost two to one. In early January, 1970, Yablonski and his wife and daughter were found murdered in their house near Clarksville, Pa.

During Senate hearings in 1970, Joseph "Chip" Yablonski, son of the slain UMW official, charged that the union spread "a reign of fear and terror... into every coal mining patch in Appalachia" during the campaign. Boyle, in a prepared statement, denied that there had been nomination irregularities in the 1969 election, that there was a union blacklist and that a 1969 miners' pension increase had been politically motivated.

Five persons were convicted in the Yablonski slayings and two UMW officials were indicted in 1972. Boyle was not implicated, but he was convicted March 31, 1972, of illegally converting $79,000 in union funds to the 1968 presidential campaign of Sen. Hubert Humphrey (D Minn.) and to congressional candidates; removed from the UMW pension fund board of trustees on the grounds of misusing the funds; and found guilty of illegally appointing many UMW district officers rather than permitting their elections.

On May 1, 1972, Judge William Bryant issued a court order for another election on the grounds of improper use of the union newspaper to promote Boyle in 1969, improper campaign expenditures and failure to provide adequate safeguards for a fair election.

In the new election Dec. 1-8, 1972, Boyle ran against Arnold R. Miller, 49, a West Virginia miner backed by a union faction called Miners for Democracy, the ideological heirs of Yablonski. Miller, campaigning on a platform of $200-per-month pensions, election of all union officers, sick pay, improved vacation time, cost-of-living salary increases and lower salaries and pensions for UMW officials, defeated Boyle by more than 14,000 votes. Final returns gave Miller 70,373 votes and Boyle, 56,334.

Miller's running mates, Mike Trbovich and Harry Patrick, were elected vice president and secretary-treasurer.

Boyle supporters depicted the Miller slate as "three stooges" who wanted to wreck the union and had no experience at union administration beyond the local level.

The 1972 election was held under extremely tight security. The ballots were under continuous custody of over 1,000 Labor Department officials, who supervised the election under authority from the 1959 Landrum-Griffin Act (PL 86-257), which contained federal guarantees of fair union elections.

---

pensation at 50 per cent of the regular benefits rate. (*Previous action, 1970 chronology, p. 715*)

The bill was expected to provide an estimated $274-million to approximately 538,000 persons who had exhausted their eligibility for unemployment payments from states. Jobless workers generally were allowed 39 weeks of payments before their eligibility expired.

The measure would apply to states whose rate of unemployment totaled at least 6.5 per cent for a 13-week period. At the time the bill cleared, 11 states were qualified for the added benefits—Alaska, California, Connecticut, Maine, Massachusetts, Michigan, New Jersey, Rhode Island, Vermont, Washington and Nevada.

The unemployment compensation provisions were added Dec. 6 by the Senate to a House-passed bill making minor changes in the Social Security Act. HR 6065 passed the House Nov. 17 by voice vote.

Major Provisions. As signed into law Dec. 29, HR 6065, the Emergency Unemployment Compensation Act of 1971:

• Extended for 10 years the period during which states may obligate, for administrative purposes, certain funds transferred from excess federal unemployment tax collections.

• Extended to jobless persons who had exhausted their regular unemployment benefits an additional 13 weeks during which to receive payments. Benefits would equal 50 per cent of the regular compensation payable to the unemployed person and would be financed from general federal revenues.

• Provided that the additional benefits could be paid only in those states whose rate of unemployment equaled or exceeded 6.5 per cent for a 13-week period.

• Barred payments under the act for any week ending after June 30, 1972. (A six-month extension was voted the following year. *1972 chronology, p. 720*)

Legislative History. As reported by the Ways and Means Committee Oct. 27 and passed by the House Nov. 17, HR 6065 made technical changes in the Social Security Act regarding use of federal funds at state levels.

The Senate, in passing the bill Dec. 6, amended it to grant additional unemployment benefits. House conferees accepted the Senate provision, although the House had refused to accept a similar addition to the tax bill (HR 10947) cleared Dec. 9.

During House debate on the conference report, Rep. Wilbur D. Mills (D Ark.), said the measure would prevent families of unemployed workers from entering welfare rolls. "The amendment is designed to furnish some additional relief in states that have been particularly hard hit by cutbacks in national programs, including defense and space programs," Mills said.

John W. Byrnes (R Wis.), ranking minority member of the committee, called the unemployment compensation provisons "a Rube Goldberg-type discriminatory welfare program in the guise of an extended unemployment insurance program.

The House Dec. 15 adopted the conference report on HR 6065 by a 194-149 roll-call vote. The Senate then cleared the bill by voice vote.

Other Bills

RAILROAD RETIREMENT. Congress June 24 cleared a bill (HR 6444—PL 92-46) amending the Rail-

---

Hoffa Freed

President Nixon Dec. 23, 1971 commuted the 13-year prison sentence of former Teamsters Union President James R. Hoffa. Hoffa, target of an intense investigation during the Kennedy presidency, served four years and nine months of his sentence.

Eight of the 13 years stemmed from a 1964 conviction of jury tampering; the other five were from a 1964 Teamsters' pension fraud conviction.

Hoffa was convicted March 4, 1964, of a government charge of jury tampering in his 1962 Nashville trial for accepting illegal payments from an employer. He was sentenced to an eight-year jail term and a $10,000 fine. On Dec. 13, 1966, his conviction was upheld by the Supreme Court, which in February 1967 refused to reconsider its decision.

Hoffa was also convicted July 26, 1964 on four counts of fraud and conspiracy in connection with alleged misuses of Teamster pension funds.

Hoffa began his prison sentence at the Lewisburg, Pa., federal prison on March 7, 1967. Before Nixon granted him executive clemency, Hoffa had applied three times for parole to the Federal Parole Board and had been refused each time.

Hoffa received a conditional commutation of sentence that specified that he could not "engage in the direct or indirect management of any labor organization" until March 6, 1980—the date when his prison term would have been completed.

Some critics charged that Nixon freed Hoffa in an effort to win Teamsters support for his 1972 reelection bid. Whatever Nixon's motivation, the Teamster Union did in fact support him in 1972. It was the second time in four decades that the Teamsters had deserted the Democratic presidential nominee. The only other time the Teamsters failed to back the Democratic candidate was in 1960 when the union supported Nixon against John F. Kennedy.

---

road Retirement Act of 1937 to provide a 10 per cent increase in retirement benefits for railroad employees.

Final action came when the House by voice vote agreed to the bill as amended and passed by the Senate June 21. The House originally passed the bill April 28.

Congress March 16 granted a 10 per cent increase in Social Security benefits to 26 million recipients; HR 6444 provided a proportional increase in railroad retirement benefits retroactive to Jan. 1.

Congress had enacted a 15 per cent increase in railroad retirement benefits in 1970. It enacted a 20 per cent increase in 1972.

Final Provisions. As signed into law July 2, HR 6444:

• Granted a 10 per cent increase in retirement benefits for railroad employees to June 30, 1973, retroactive to Jan. 1, 1971.

• Extended to June 30, 1972, the time given the Commission on Railroad Retirement to conduct a thorough study of the railroad retirement system.

BLACK LUNG AID. The House Nov. 10, by a 312-78 roll-call vote, passed a bill (HR 9212) extending disability benefits to dependents of coal miners disabled or killed by pneumoconiosis (black lung disease). A more liberal version of the bill became law in 1972. *(1972 chronology, p. 725)*

HR 9212 encountered strong Republican opposition after provisions were added that broadened the intent of the bill beyond its original purpose, which was to provide benefits to orphans of families in which both the miner and his widow were deceased.

In an earlier vote Oct. 18, the House failed to pass HR 9212 under suspension of the rules. The 227-124 roll-call vote was seven votes short of the two-thirds majority necessary to pass the bill under the suspension procedure.

MINIMUM WAGE. Hearings were held in both the House and Senate on bills to raise the minimum wage and extend coverage under the 1938 Fair Labor Standards Act to additional workers. No legislation was reported in the Senate. *(Previous hearings, p. 717)*

The House Education and Labor Committee Nov. 17 reported a bill (HR 7130) that increased the minimum wage for most non-agricultural workers to $2 an hour, effective Jan. 1, 1972, and extended coverage to about six million additional workers. The Nixon administration favored a two-step increase, to $1.80 an hour in 1972 and $2 in 1974.

HR 7130 was passed by both chambers in 1972, but the measure died when the House refused to send it to conference. *(1972 chronology, below)*

1972

Minimum Wage

Organized labor suffered a large defeat when a push to pass minimum wage legislation in 1972 was frustrated by a coalition of conservative House Republicans and Southern Democrats. The House Oct. 3, by a **188-196 roll-call vote**, refused for a second time to submit the bill (HR 7130) to a House-Senate conference committee. The action killed the bill for the 92nd Congress.

Defeat of the measure was a severe disappointment for the House leadership, especially Speaker Carl Albert (D Okla.), who had pressed since 1971 for an increase in the wage floor. The hourly minimum under existing law—set in 1966—was $1.60 for most manufacturing and retail employees and $1.30 an hour for those farm workers covered by the Fair Labor Standards Act of 1938.

House conservatives particularly feared that a House-passed provision permitting the employment of youths at wages below the applicable adult minimum would be rejected in conference. And members representing rural and farm areas opposed provisions in the Senate version repealing exemptions for certain agricultural workers.

The House May 11 had rejected a comprehensive version of HR 7130 in favor of a narrow substitute bill—backed by the White House—which cut the proposed wage boost and greatly narrowed the scope of the bill. The substitute was adopted by a **217-191 recorded teller vote.** But the Senate—by one vote—July 20 defeated a similar attempt to pass a less liberal version.

Action on Strikes

Congressional action on strikes, 1969-72:

Postal Service. In 1970 Congress approved a two-stage, 14 per cent pay increase for postal workers as part of the settlement of the first postal strike in U.S. history. *(Details, chapter on Postal Policy)*

Transportation. In April 1970 Congress imposed a settlement in a 17-month dispute between the railroads and four shopcraft unions. Earlier it had acted to postpone the threatened strike.

In December 1970 Congress attempted to avert a nationwide rail strike by imposing an 80-day moratorium, but the action came too late to stop a brief walkout by four railroad operating unions. Emergency legislation provided a 13.5 per cent increase for union members.

A two-day nationwide rail strike in May 1971 ended when Congress passed emergency legislation that sent railmen back to work and gave members of the striking Brotherhood of Railway Signalmen a 13.5 per cent wage increase.

Congress in 1972 acted to end a lengthy West Coast dock strike by establishing a three-member board to settle all issues in the dispute by compulsory arbitration. However, striking longshoremen and the shipping industry reached agreement on a new contract before the bill was signed, thus voiding the legislation. The voluntary settlement subsequently was scaled down by the Pay Board, leading four of the five labor members of the board to resign.

President Nixon asked Congress in 1970 and 1971 for legislation to prevent strikes in the transportation industry, but Congress did not act on the request. The administration subsequently withdrew its support for the legislation, which was opposed by organized labor. *(Details, chapter on Transportation)*

Lobbying. HR 7130 was the target of intensive lobbying efforts by a coalition of business interests which sought to kill the bill or ensure, at the least, that any measure that cleared conference included the House's lower minimum wage levels together with the payment differential for employment of youths.

Among the groups lobbying for those objectives were the Chamber of Commerce of the United States, the National Association of Manufacturers, the Cotton Council of America, the American Sugar Cane League of the U.S.A., and a number of mammoth carry-out restaurant and drive-in food chains such as McDonald's Hamburger, Toddle House, and Seven-Eleven Food Stores.

Background. Following two years of hearings, the House Education and Labor Committee reported HR 7130 Nov. 17, 1971. As reported, the bill increased the minimum wage for most non-agricultural workers to $2 an hour, effective Jan. 1, 1972, and extended coverage to about six million additional workers. *(1971 chronology, this page)*

After delaying minimum wage legislation for nearly six months, the Rules Committee May 9, 1972, approved a resolution (H Res 968) sending HR 7130 to the floor under an open rule—permitting amendments. It was made in order to consider a Republican-sponsored amendment introduced by John N. Erlenborn (R Ill.) as a substitute bill.

HOUSE FLOOR ACTION

The House May 11 passed an amended version of HR 7130 by a 330-78 roll-call vote.

As amended, the measure postponed the immediate increase in the minimum wage to $2 an hour for non-farm workers and substituted an increase to $1.80 in 1972 and $2 in 1973. The amended version also dropped the extension of coverage provided in the committee bill. It retained the two-stage increase in the committee bill for farm workers.

The decision to narrow the scope of the bill and stretch out the wage increase came when members adopted, by a **217-199 recorded teller vote**, an amendment introduced as a substitute bill by Erlenborn.

Approval of the stretchout was the result of a bipartisan drive led by Erlenborn and Don Fuqua (D Fla.), cosponsor of the substitute bill. Their drive rallied a conservative coalition consisting of a majority of Republicans (148) and southern Democrats (63) to accept the Erlenborn substitute. It dropped from the committee version all provisions expanding coverage under the act as well as a controversial section (Title III) permitting import restrictions on foreign goods. *(Box, p. 722)*

In a key test of sentiment on the committee's version, the House adopted, by a 216-187 recorded teller vote, an amendment to the substitute sponsored by John B. Anderson (R Ill.), which stretched out the wage boost in two steps, one 60 days after enactment and the second a year later.

Anderson told the House that his measure would add only $400-million in payroll costs while the Democratic-sponsored bill would raise wages $2.4-billion a year.

Supporters of the committee version argued that an immediate raise in the hourly wage floor was necessary to compensate for the increase in the cost of living since the original act last was amended in 1966.

Opponents of the comprehensive measure contended that a 25 per cent increase in the hourly minimum would spark a renewed round of inflation and would force many employers to cut payrolls, thus creating further unemployment in an already tight job market.

Provisions. As passed by the House, HR 7130:

• Raised the minimum wage for non-agricultural employees covered under the Fair Labor Standards Act of 1938 prior to its amendment in 1966 to $1.80 an hour within 60 days after enactment and $2 the following year.

• Increased the hourly wage floor for non-farm workers first covered under the 1966 amendments to the act to $1.70 within 60 days after enactment, $1.80 the following year and $2 two years later.

• Raised the minimum hourly wage for agricultural workers covered under the act to $1.50 within 60 days after enactment and $1.70 the following year.

• Authorized the employment of youths at either 80 per cent of the applicable minimum adult hourly wage, $1.60 an hour for non-agricultural workers or $1.30 an hour for farm laborers, whichever was higher.

Minimum Wage Background

The first successful federal attempt to regulate working hours and establish a "floor" for wages was the 1938 Fair Labor Standards Act (FLSA). This law, which provided the basis for all subsequent legislation, set a minimum hourly wage for covered workers of 25 cents, to be raised to 40 cents in 1945. It also made 40 hours the normal workweek for most covered workers and required employers to pay time-and-a-half for overtime.

Congress raised the minimum to 75 cents in 1945 and to $1 in 1955. However, the majority of American workers did not receive protection, and efforts to amend the act to bring more workers under its protection failed through 1960.

In 1961 Congress concluded a bitter struggle by passing landmark legislation raising the hourly minimum wage and, for the first time, extending the categories of coverage. The Fair Labor Standards Amendments of 1961 (PL 87-30) extended the minimum wage and (with some exceptions) the overtime provisions to an estimated 3.6 million additional workers. The act also raised the minimum wage for workers already covered from $1 an hour to an eventual $1.25 an hour. The newly covered workers were to reach the $1.25 hourly minimum and the 40-hour standard work week in three steps over four years.

In 1966 Congress raised the minimum wage to $1.40 an hour on Feb. 1, 1967 and to $1.60 per hour on Feb. 1, 1968. The legislation extended coverage to an additional 9.1 million workers, including 2 million employees of hospitals and nursing homes and 1.3 million workers in public and private educational institutions.

• Exempted from minimum wage and overtime requirements newsboys delivering shopping newspapers, certain husband-and-wife teams employed by nonprofit educational institutions which served as house parents for orphans and high-salaried employees of retail and service operations during peak sales periods.

SENATE

Committee. The Senate Labor and Public Welfare Committee refused to recommend HR 7130 June 12. Instead the committee June 8 reported a bill (S 1861) raising the minimum wage for most non-agricultural workers to $2 an hour upon enactment and $2.20 the following year. The bill also provided a four-stage increase for farm workers, culminating in a $2.20 wage in 1975.

Floor. The Senate July 20, by a 65-27 roll-call vote, passed the minimum wage bill in substantially the same form as reported by the Labor and Public Welfare Committee except for a year's delay—to 1974—in the effective date of the increase in the non-farm wage floor to $2.20. As passed, the bill bore the number (HR 7130) of the House-passed bill although it was vastly different from that measure. Prior to passing the legislation, the Senate substituted the number of the

the House bill for that of its own bill (S 1861) to conform with parliamentary procedures for subsequent conference action.

Prior to passing the bill, the Senate July 20, by a **46-47 roll-call vote,** rejected a Republican-sponsored substitute proposal reducing to $2 and sharply limiting the coverage of the committee bill. The substitute was defeated by a coalition of 34 Democrats and 13 Republicans. Sixteen Democrats, all but two of whom were southern Democrats, and 30 Republicans voted for the substitute.

Two major changes agreed to were:

• An amendment, introduced by Charles H. Percy (R Ill.), delaying for an additional year, to 1974 from 1973, the effective date of the second step in the two-stage raise of the wage floor to $2.20, by a 87-6 roll call.

• An amendment, sponsored by Robert T. Stafford (R Vt.), deleting from the committee version a provision extending wage and hour coverage under the act to business establishments with gross sales of $150,000 or more a year, by a 91-0 roll-call vote. (Existing law, which was retained by the Senate action, covered operations grossing in excess of $250,000.)

But Democrats rallied to defeat several amendments incorporating various provisions of the substitute bill that was rejected earlier, including:

• An amendment, sponsored by Peter H. Dominick (R Colo.) which would have set the wage floor at $1.80 in 1972 and $2 in 1973, by a 42-52 roll-call vote.

• An amendment, introduced by James L. Buckley (Cons-R N.Y.), which would have authorized the employment of youths under age 18 and students under age 21 at wages below the applicable adult minimum, by a 36-54 roll call.

• An amendment, introduced by Robert Taft Jr. (R Ohio), which would have deleted from the committee version minimum wage coverage for approximately 1.2 million domestic household workers, by a 40-52 roll call.

Provisions. Following are the major features of the proposed amendments to the Fair Labor Standards Act of 1938 in the Senate-passed version of HR 7130:

Changes in Minimum Wage Coverage

• Total number of workers covered by the Fair Labor Standards Act after the 1972 amendments: 51.9 million (under existing law 45.4 million were covered).

Breakdown in New Coverage

• 1.7 million federal government employees.
• 3.2 million state and local government employees.
• 1.2 million domestic household workers.
• 75,000-150,000 agricultural employees.
• 45,000 in manufacturing.
• 24,000 in transportation, communications, utilities.
• 25,000 in finance, insurance, real estate.

Minimum Wage Increase

• For workers covered under the act prior to the 1966 amendments: to $2.00 an hour 60 days after enactment and $2.20 two years later, from $1.60 an hour under existing law.

• For workers first covered in 1966 and additional non-farm workers who would be covered under the proposed 1972 amendments: to $1.80 an hour 60 days after enactment, $2 one year later and $2.20 two years later, from $1.60 an hour under existing law.

House Versions Compared

The two House versions of the proposed amendments to the Fair Labor Standards Act—the bill approved by the House Education and Labor Committee and the Erlenborn substitute bill—differed greatly in scope and intent.

Wage Increase. The Erlenborn amendment as introduced contained the same wage schedule provided by the committee bill—an immediate raise to $2 an hour for most non-agricultural workers covered under the bill—but was amended on the floor to establish a two-step wage increase. The wage increase for farm workers was the same under both bills—to $1.50 in 1972 and $1.70 in 1973.

Coverage. The committee version would have extended coverage under the act to about 6 million additional workers—including employees of federal, state and local governments; hotel, restaurant and domestic workers; persons employed by transit industries, nursing homes, sugar processing plants, seasonal industries and laundry and cleaning establishments, and certain employees in Puerto Rico and the Virgin Islands.

The Erlenborn substitute provided no new coverage but authorized three additional exemptions.

Youth Employment. Under HR 7130 as reported, employers were permitted to hire full-time students at wages equal to 85 per cent of the applicable minimum wage or $1.60 an hour ($1.30 for agricultural labor), whichever was higher. Employment of youths in hazardous occupations was prohibited, and certification by the labor secretary stating that the student worker would not displace an adult employee was required.

The Erlenborn substitute permitted the employment in any field of youths under the age of 18 and students under age 21 at 80 per cent of the applicable minimum wage or $1.60 an hour ($1.30 for agricultural labor), whichever was greater.

Import Restrictions. The Erlenborn amendment deleted a section (Title III) of the committee bill which would have prohibited the procurement—if financed in whole or in part by federal funds—of foreign goods from industries employing persons working under conditions which did not meet U.S. wage and hour standards.

The committee bill had also authorized the President to impose higher tariffs or import quotas on foreign goods which threatened the economic well-being of any group of U.S. workers.

• For agricultural workers covered under the act: to $1.60 an hour 60 days after enactment, $1.80 in 1973, $2 in 1974, and $2.20 in 1975, from $1.30 an hour under existing law.

Most of the 51.9 million workers to be covered by the revised act were already earning more than the proposed minimums of $1.60, $1.80 and $2 which would go into effect 60 days after enactment of the bill; however, an estimated 4.1 million workers were earning less and would receive wage increases on the effective date.

HOUSE REJECTS CONFERENCE

The House twice rejected motions to send differing versions of HR 7130 to a House-Senate conference committee. Several Republicans said the House conferees to be appointed would not uphold the House position in conference.

The first vote was Aug. 1, on a 190-198 roll call. The second was Oct. 3 on a **188-196 roll-call vote.**

Unemployment Compensation

Congress June 29 cleared for the White House a bill (HR 15587—PL 92-329) extending the Emergency Unemployment Compensation Act of 1971 for six months.

The Emergency Unemployment Act of 1971 (PL 92-244) authorized the disbursement of federal funds to any state with an unemployment rate exceeding 6.5 per cent for the payment of additional unemployment compensation for up to 13 weeks to individuals who had exhausted their regular unemployment benefits.

As cleared by Congress, HR 15587 extended for six months—to Dec. 31 from June 30, 1972—the period during which an unemployed individual could apply for the additional 13 weeks' benefits. The bill extended the termination date of the program to March 31, 1973, from Sept. 30, 1972.

The six-month extension was requested by the administration. The bill was passed by the House June 28 and the Senate June 29.

An estimated 300,000 to 400,000 persons were expected to receive between $120-million and $220-million in additional benefits under the measure. Individuals received benefits equal to the weekly rate provided by the state's program.

At the time HR 15587 cleared, 18 states—Alaska, California, Connecticut, Idaho, Maine, Massachusetts, Michigan, Minnesota, Montana, Nevada, New Jersey, New York, North Dakota, Oregon, Rhode Island, Vermont, Washington and West Virginia—and Puerto Rico qualified for the added benefits.

Payments under the extension were to be financed by a one-year increase of .08 per cent—to .58 per cent—during calendar 1973 in the net federal unemployment tax paid by all employers. According to Labor Department estimates, the temporary tax increase would raise an additional $220-million in revenue, equal to or greater than the projected cost of the program's extension.

As enacted in 1971, the program had been financed from general federal revenues.

Provisions. As signed into law June 30, HR 15587:

• Extended for six months—to Dec. 31 from June 30, 1972—the period during which an unemployed individual would be eligible for the additional 13 weeks' unemployment compensation benefits authorized by the Emergency Unemployment Compensation Act of 1971.

• Extended the termination date of the program for six months—to March 31, 1973, from Sept. 30, 1972.

• Raised for one year, during calendar 1973, the net federal unemployment tax paid by all employers—to .58 per cent from .5 per cent.

• Provided that the additional benefits could be paid only in those states whose rate of unemployment equaled or exceeded 6.5 per cent for a 13-week period.

Minimum Wage: Political Impact

Sen. George McGovern (D S.D.), spurred by organized labor's cool reception to his presidential candidacy, flew to Washington from his home state of South Dakota July 20 to vote for the wage increase sought since 1970 by labor leaders.

McGovern arrived in Washington barely an hour before the 11:15 a.m. roll call on a Nixon administration substitute bill reducing the size of the wage increase and the coverage proposed by the Senate Labor and Public Welfare Committee.

The substitute was defeated by a 46-47 roll-call vote, with McGovern voting against it.

In 1972, as in 1960, a minimum wage boost backed by the Democratic presidential nominee overcame staunch Republican opposition in the Senate but failed of enactment because of strong House opposition.

House and Senate conferees in 1960 had failed to reach a compromise on another minimum wage bill when confronted with a Senate bill far more liberal than its House counterpart. The bill (HR 12677) died in a conference committee during a special August session of Congress that year held after the national political party conventions.

The House Education and Labor Committee's bill was similar to that later passed by the Senate.

But a conservative coalition of Republicans and southern Democrats greatly altered the committee recommendations by adopting a substitute bill sponsored by A. Paul Kitchin (D N.C., 1957-63) and William H. Ayres (R Ohio, 1951-71).

The Kitchin-Ayres substitute would have limited the wage increase to $1.15 an hour for workers previously covered under the act and authorized a raise to $1 for about 1.4 million newly covered workers.

The Senate-passed measure, sponsored by Sen. John F. Kennedy (D Mass., 1953-60), the Democratic presidential nominee, would have raised the hourly wage floor to $1.25 and extended both wage and overtime coverage to about 4 million new workers.

After meeting for nearly a week, the conference broke up in disagreement Aug. 30, 1960, despite repeated attempts by Senate conferees to reach a compromise. Kennedy later complained that House conferees wanted their bill "or nothing" and during his presidential campaign blamed the defeat of the bill on Republican intransigence.

Congress in May 1961 handed the newly elected President one of his major legislative victories of that year by clearing substantially the same bill (HR 3935 —PL 87-30) he had advocated as a senator. *(Congress and the Nation, Vol. I, p. 643-48)*

Background. The Emergency Unemployment Compensation Act cleared Congress Dec. 15, 1971. It was intended to meet the needs of persons whose unemployment was caused primarily by changes in the nation's economic policies. Federal cutbacks in national defense and space expenditures produced high unemployment rates in those and supportive industries. The program attempted to counteract local as opposed to national joblessness by limiting coverage to states whose unemployment rates exceeded 6.5 per cent.

Progress reports filed on the program in May and mid-June 1972 by the labor secretary revealed that most beneficiaries under the program were regular full-time workers, often the primary wage-earner in a family. Benefits totaling $270-million had been given to more than 500,000 unemployed persons by May 1972. The national average weekly benefit totaled $54.65.

Related Action. Congress included in the third 1972 debt limit bill (HR 16810—PL 92-599) language that permitted states to repeal the provision in the 1970 unemployment compensation law which authorized payment of an additional 13 weeks of unemployment benefits to be paid to persons who had exhausted their regular 26 weeks of benefits, provided the insured unemployment rate of the state was at least 120 per cent of the average the previous two years—thereby preventing the disqualification of states whose unemployment rates had persisted at a high but unchanging level for more than two years.

Railroad Retirement

Almost 900,000 retired railroad workers won increases of 20 per cent in their pensions when Congress Oct. 4 overrode President Nixon's veto of HR 15927 (PL 92-460).

The 20 per cent increase, which would expire June 30, 1973, followed two other temporary increases in benefits authorized by Congress in 1970 and 1971 and totaling 25 per cent. *(Previous action, p. 716, 719)*

The financial soundness of a further 20 per cent increase was hotly debated in light of a report prepared by the Commission on Railroad Retirement which predicted that, unless revised, the railroad retirement system would be bankrupt by 1988. *(Box, this page)*

The Railroad Retirement Act of 1937 (PL 75-162) established an independent pension system for the 1.3 million persons then employed by the nation's rail carriers. The pension was to be financed by joint contributions of the railroads and their employees.

Under existing law, each party paid 9.5 per cent on the first $750 a month of each employee's earnings. Under the existing Social Security benefit formula, employers and employees each paid a 5.2 per cent tax on the first $9,000 of annual earnings—about half the tax levied on the same total income of the railroad workers.

The 1972 increase in Social Security benefits (PL 92-336) raised the payroll taxes for both retirement systems. As of Jan. 1, 1973, the employer and employee contributions to the railroad retirement fund would rise to 10.25 per cent a month on the first $900 earned, while the Social Security tax rate would go to 5.5 per cent on the first $10,800 in earnings. *(Social Security, chapter on Welfare)*

The average 1971 pension for railroad workers who retired at 65 was $233 a month, about 75 per cent more than the average Social Security benefits of $133 monthly.

Provisions. As cleared by Congress, HR 15927:

• Provided a temporary 20 per cent increase in railroad retirement benefits with respect to annuities ac-

---

Retirement System in Crisis

The 35-year-old railroad retirement system was on the brink of a serious financial crisis in 1972—it appeared to be headed for bankruptcy by 1988 and $11-billion in debt by the year 2000.

These predictions were part of the preliminary findings of the five-man commission on Railroad Retirement appointed by the President and Congress in 1970 to investigate the railroad retirement system. The commission delivered its report to Congress Sept. 7, 1972.

As currently structured, the commission stated, the retirement plan could not handle the growing burdens imposed by the increasing cost of benefits, the expanding number of retirees and the dwindling pool of employed workers to finance the fund.

The commission rejected a plan to restore full funding of the existing system because it would have required payroll taxes to be doubled—"a very costly solution."

Instead, it recommended an immediate increase in payroll taxes of 3.9 per cent, to 13.4 per cent from 9.5 per cent. Extension of the existing 15 per cent and 10 per cent temporary benefits increases, or the proposed 20 per cent benefits increase, must be accompanied by further tax increases, the commission declared.

The commission proposed two long-range solutions:

• Railroad employees should be brought under the existing Social Security system, which would provide basic pension benefits.

• Rail workers and their employers should negotiate a second retirement benefit plan to supplement joint employer-employee contributions.

A federal subsidy to the railroad retirement fund was not justified on economic or social grounds, the commission concluded.

---

crued after August 1972; the temporary increase would expire June 30, 1973.

• Declared it congressional policy that the three temporary benefit increases slated to expire June 1973 would be made permanent only if changes were made in the retirement program to ensure the collection of sufficient funds to pay out all benefits due in the foreseeable future.

• Directed representatives of employees, retirees and management of the rail carriers to report to the Senate Labor and Public Welfare and the House Interstate and Foreign Commerce Committees no later than March 1, 1973, with their recommendations for sound funding of the plan, and required the railroad retirement board to comment on their report by April 1, 1973.

• Made technical amendments in the Railroad Retirement Act of 1937 (PL 75-162) to simplify the computation of benefits.

Legislative History. The House Committee on Interstate and Foreign Commerce reported the measure July 31. The House Aug. 9 passed HR 15927 without amendment by a 399-4 roll-call vote.

The Senate Labor and Public Welfare Committee reported HR 15927 Sept. 14. The committee added an amendment requiring railroad employers and employees to determine ways to finance permanent increases in retirement benefits. The provisions of a companion bill (HR 15922) containing technical amendments to the Railroad Retirement Act of 1937 were also added by the committee. The House passed HR 15922 Aug. 14 by voice vote. The Senate passed HR 15927 Sept. 19 by voice vote, and the House cleared the bill Sept. 20.

Nixon Veto. President Nixon vetoed the bill Oct. 4. In his veto message, Nixon said the bill would "jeopardize the fiscal integrity of the railroad retirement system" and "contribute to inflation."

He said the bill contained "the third...benefit increase in three years...to be made without any accompanying increase in taxes to finance the benefits." Nixon had approved both previous temporary increases, in 1970 and 1971, without warning he would veto future unfinanced raises.

Nixon had proposed in his message that Congress enact a bill giving rail retirees a pension increase about equal in dollar value to that approved for Social Security beneficiaries in June. HR 15927 raised railroad pensions by the same percentage as the Social Security boost, but provided far larger dollar increases, because railroad pensions generally were larger than those provided under the Social Security program.

Final Action. The House Oct. 4, by a 353-29 roll-call vote, and the Senate the same day, by a 76-5 roll call, approved motions to override the President's veto of HR 15927.

Both the House and Senate, under pressure to wind up legislative business by Oct. 14, were reluctant to consider an alternative proposal.

Black Lung Aid

A bill (HR 9212—PL 92-303) liberalizing eligibility standards for benefits to coal miners stricken by pneumoconiosis (black lung disease) cleared Congress May 10.

HR 9212 amended Title IV of the landmark Coal Mine Health and Safety Act of 1969 (PL 91-173) which established federal safety standards at coal mines and authorized a compensation program for miners and widows of miners totally disabled or killed by pneumoconiosis. *(1969 chronology, p. 707)*

The disease, which is caused by the inhalation of fine coal dust particles, leads in its advanced stages to severe breathing difficulty and premature death.

As cleared by Congress, HR 9212 enabled a miner to more easily establish his entitlement to black lung benefits by vastly broadening the definition of total disability and forbidding the denial of benefits solely on the basis of a negative chest X-ray.

The bill also delayed until 1974 the responsibility of industry to start paying new lifetime claims. And it made benefit payments available to orphans of miners, who were inadvertently excluded under the 1969 law.

Provisions. As signed into law May 19, HR 9212:

● Provided disability benefits to orphans of deceased miners, and permitted dependent parents, brothers or sisters of a deceased miner to receive such benefits, where no widow or child survived him, if they had been totally dependent on the miner and had lived in his household for one year prior to his death.

Pressures on Nixon

Despite speculation that he might veto HR 9212, President Nixon signed the measure May 19, on the eve of his departure for the Moscow summit.

White House budget advisers had urged a veto on fiscal grounds, citing the bill's estimated $4-billion cost to the federal government. During Senate hearings, an administration witness had described extension of federal responsibility for disability payments as "an unwarranted subsidy to the coal-mining industry." Nixon himself, in signing the original 1969 law, had expressed reservations about federal intrusion into the field of workmen's compensation and had emphasized that the program was only "temporary." (States traditionally have been responsible for workmen's compensation laws, under which costs are borne by industry owners.)

But the President's political advisers cautioned that a veto could become a damaging election-year issue for the Republicans. Coal-state members of Congress, led by Senate Republican leader Hugh Scott (Pa.) and Majority Whip Robert C. Byrd (D W. Va.), urged Nixon to sign the bill. The President was warned that a veto could put Pennsylvania and other coal-producing states in the Democratic column in the November election.

In his statement on signing HR 9212, Nixon did not mention the bill's costs to the taxpayers. He did say he had "mixed emotions" about signing the measure "because of the precedent it tends to establish" of federal involvement in workmen's compensation. "Responsibility for black lung compensation clearly should lie with the owners and operators of the mines," he said, and he urged the states to update their workmen's compensation laws before 1974.

● Extended for 18 months—to July 1, 1973, from Jan. 1, 1972—the filing period for claiming disability benefits during which the federal government would assume responsibility for the cost of such benefits for the remainder of a beneficiary's life; authorized federal payment of claims filed during the period July 1, 1973—Dec. 31, 1973, for that period only. Beginning Jan. 1, 1974, claims were to be filed under state workmen's compensation laws.

● Extended the program for five years, to Dec. 30, 1981, and authorized the payment of disability benefits on all claims filed prior to that date for the remainder of a beneficiary's life.

● Prohibited the denial of a claim solely on the basis of a negative chest X-ray, and provided that miners with 15 years' service prior to July 1, 1971, who were disabled by a respiratory disease would be presumed disabled by pneumoconiosis unless proven to the contrary.

● Broadened the definition of total disability to include any respiratory impairment which prevented a miner from engaging in his usual occupation.

● Authorized the payment of benefits to miners working on surface or strip mine operations.

● Prohibited discrimination by employers against any miner solely because he had contracted pneumoconiosis.

• Authorized the secretary of the Department of Health, Education and Welfare to issue grants for construction of pneumoconiosis treatment facilities and directed him to initiate research on devices to test for the presence of black lung disease.

Legislative History. The House passed HR 9212 Nov. 10, 1971, over strong Republican opposition to provisions which sought to ease benefit-eligibility standards. *(1971 chronology, p. 719)*

HR 9212 was reported by the Senate Labor and Public Welfare Committee April 10 and passed by the Senate April 17 by a 73-0 roll-call vote. In a major change from the House-passed version, the Senate added a provision permitting dependent parents, brothers and sisters of a deceased miner to receive his disability benefits where no widow or child survived him. It also broadened the definition of total disability to include any respiratory ailment which prevented a miner from engaging in his usual mining occupation.

Conferees generally agreed to the more liberal language and intent of the Senate version of the bill. The conference report was approved by the Senate May 4 by voice vote. The House approved it May 10 on a 275-122 roll call.

Vocational Rehabilitation

President Nixon Oct. 27 pocket vetoed the Rehabilitation Act of 1972 (HR 8395).

In his veto statement, Nixon declared that "the bill would authorize funding far in excess of the budget request and far beyond what can be made available and used effectively." Nixon the same day vetoed eight other measures which, he said, would "breach the budget by $750-billion in 1973."

As cleared by Congress, HR 8395 would have authorized $800-million in fiscal 1973 and $975-million in fiscal 1974 to assist states in providing vocational rehabilitation services to handicapped individuals. The budget had projected a $610-million funding level for fiscal 1973. Other provisions of the bill brought total authorizations for fiscal 1973-75 to nearly $3.48-billion.

In explaining his reasons for withholding approval of HR 8395, Nixon said that the "numerous committees and independent commissions" which would have been established by the bill would "waste the taxpayers' dollars"; he criticized provisions of HR 8395 which would have authorized "activities that have no vocational element... or are essentially medical in character."

New programs for persons who are confined to their homes or institutionalized and those with spinal cord injuries or end-stage renal disease—as well as several commissions to study employment, transportation and housing problems encountered by disabled persons— would have been set up under the vetoed measure.

Authority for existing rehabilitation programs expired June 30, 1972. *(1970 extension, p. 717)* Funds for these programs were provided at fiscal 1972 levels through Feb. 28, 1973, under a continuing resolution.

PROVISIONS

As cleared, major provisions of HR 8395 would have:
• Provided a statutory basis for the existing Rehabilitation Services Administration in the Department of Health, Education and Welfare (HEW).

• Permitted pursuit of non-vocational goals and provision of goods and services to enable a handicapped individual to live more independently.

Title I

• Authorized a payment to a state of 80 per cent of the cost of basic rehabilitation services, up to the state's allotment under existing law; authorized appropriations of $800-million in fiscal 1973 and $975-million in fiscal 1974.

• Required that first priority for services under the program be given to the most severely handicapped.

Title II

• Created a new program to provide supplementary grants to the states for payment of up to 90 per cent of the cost of services for severely handicapped persons for whom no vocational goal was possible, with authorizations of $30-million in fiscal 1973, $50-million in fiscal 1974 and $80-million in fiscal 1975.

Title III

• Continued authority in existing law for construction of rehabilitation facilities and vocational training programs for the handicapped.

• Established a new program to pay interest charges on funds borrowed by states for construction of rehabilitation facilities and created special programs for the deaf, the deaf-blind and older blind individuals as well as persons with spinal cord injuries and end-stage renal disease.

• Established in the Department of HEW a national policy and performance council and a national advisory council on rehabilitation of handicapped individuals.

Title IV

• Authorized appropriations of $125-million in fiscal 1973, $175-million in fiscal 1974 and $250-million in fiscal 1975 for federal assistance to states for research and training of vocational rehabilitation personnel.

Title V

• Directed the secretary of HEW to evaluate all rehabilitative programs annually and to report to the President and Congress.

Title VI

• Created an Office for the Handicapped within the Department of HEW charged with the preparation of a long-range plan for the delivery of services to disabled persons.

Title VII

• Repealed the existing Vocational Rehabilitation Act of 1968 90 days after enactment of HR 8395.

• Established a new federal interagency committee on handicapped employees to devise an affirmative action plan for the hiring of handicapped persons by the federal government, a national commission on transportation and housing for the handicapped and an architectural and transportation barriers compliance board.

HOUSE ACTION

Committee. The Education and Labor Committee unanimously reported HR 8395 March 16. As reported, the bill authorized $800-million in fiscal 1973, $950-million in fiscal 1974 and $1.1-billion in fiscal 1975 for the basic state grant program. It also authorized $160-million for a supplementary grant program to help states develop and implement comprehensive rehabilitation services for severely handicapped individuals for whom no vocational goal was possible.

"During the last four or five years the meaning of vocational rehabilitation has, by regulations, been broadened to include services to those individuals handicapped in the social sense rather than in the traditional manner (physically or mentally)," the committee observed.

But "given the limited number of dollars available for vocational rehabilitation programs and the amount of resources available in other federal programs designed to serve those who are socially handicapped, the first priority should be assigned to serve those persons who are severely physically and mentally handicapped," the committee stressed in its report.

The committee urged Congress to fully fund the programs, noting that since 1970 "the administration has been recommending, and Congress has been accepting, amendments to the act in the annual appropriations bills which establish allotment bases lower than those mandated in the law."

Floor. The House March 20, by a 327-0 roll-call vote, passed HR 8395 under suspension of the rules.

During debate on the bill, Chairman Carl D. Perkins (D Ky.) of the Education and Labor Committee declared: "In my judgment, the Congress will not pass a more important piece of legislation this year than the Vocational Rehabilitation Act Amendments of 1972."

"I consider this bill to represent the most significant advance in assistance to handicapped persons in half a century," declared John Brademas (D Ind.), chairman of the Education and Labor Select Subcommittee on Education which had held hearings on HR 8395.

Durward G. Hall (R Mo.) criticized the bill: "We are considering a multibillion-dollar bill under a suspension of the rules procedure, without amendments being available except those brought by the committee, with certainly inadequate debate and with some question about a roll-call vote...."

"We are duplicating programs, especially in the kidney dialysis and other kidney programs," he continued. "We are running out of people to rehabilitate.... The vocational rehabilitation counselors are at the present time going into the highways and byways in order to seek these people out...and they are given point credits and demands are placed upon them to handle so many cases a year."

Albert H. Quie (R Minn.), ranking Republican on the Education and Labor Committee, countered: "The committee has recommended that quotas and case balancing be abandoned and some system developed to cope with difficult cases,"

Perkins: "It has been a disappointment to me, as it has been to many of you, that the administration has not been recommending the full amount authorized in the law (for these programs)."

Ogden R. Reid (R N.Y.), a member of the Education and Labor Committee: "In 1970 we appropriated $525-million, in 1971 $603-million and in 1972 $687-million. The budget submission for fiscal 1973 calls

for $768-million. The actual appropriations have evidently followed fairly closely the authorizations with the exception of the fact that the authorizations have exceeded the appropriations by about $200-million or $300-million.... The administration itself asked for an increase of almost $100-million between 1972 and 1973."

SENATE ACTION

Committee. The Senate Labor and Public Welfare Committee reported its version of the bill Sept. 15. It authorized appropriations of $900-million in fiscal 1973, $1.15-billion in fiscal 1974 and $1.35-billion in fiscal 1975 for the basic state grant program, plus an additional $185-million in fiscal 1973-75 for grants for innovation and expansion of services. It authorized $550-million in fiscal 1973-75 for federal assistance to states for research and the training of vocational rehabilitation personnel.

The committee bill paralleled the House version in providing services for the severely disabled, including persons suffering from spinal cord injuries and end-stage renal disease. The major Senate committee change was a revision in the formula for computing funds allocated to each state under the bill. That provision was dropped on the Senate floor.

The committee emphasized the need to make certain that all handicapped individuals have access to rehabilitative services. "While the committee expects fully that the program will remain vocationally oriented, it does believe that there are handicapped individuals whose handicaps are so severe, or because of other circumstances such as age, that they may never achieve employment.... They should not be denied services."

At the same time, the committee cautioned that "the program should be serving only handicapped individuals whose handicap constitutes a substantial handicap to employment... Witness after witness during the hearings raised questions regarding the population that state agencies are serving, and whether the program was being as effective as it might be in delivering services to those...most in need."

Floor. The Senate Sept. 26 unanimously approved HR 8395 by a 70-0 roll-call vote.

Jennings Randolph (D W.Va.), a member of the Labor and Public Welfare Committee which had reported the bill: "Many persons who are handicapped are on the welfare rolls solely because they have not been rehabilitated so that they may engage in gainful employment.... An expanded federal program of vocational rehabilitation will have the effect of taking thousands of handicapped welfare recipients out of poverty and providing them with a livelihood."

The most controversial amendment approved by the Senate, offered by Randolph, restored to the bill the formula contained in existing law for allocating appropriations among the states. The bill reported by the committee changed the formula for distributing appropriations in excess of $700-million to give more weight to states with large populations—effective in fiscal 1974. Randolph accepted language offered by Jacob K. Javits (R N.Y.) extending the formula in existing law through fiscal 1974, and the Randolph amendment as modified was approved by voice vote.

(Continued on p. 730)

Growing Pressure for Regulation of Private...

Despite growing pressure for federal regulation of private pension plans, Congress failed to enact pension plan legislation in the 1969-72 period. Extensive hearings were held in both the Senate and House, however, and a pension plan bill was reported in the Senate in 1972. That measure died in a jurisdictional dispute between the Senate Labor and Public Welfare Committee and the Finance Committee.

Proponents of pension plan regulation were optimistic about the outlook for 1973 action. They predicted that if legislation reached the floor of Congress, it was all but assured of passage. Pension plan regulation, they said, was "an idea whose time has come."

Private pension plan funds constituted the largest sum of unregulated capital in the United States. Pension plans were an important element of the total compensation package offered by most employers, yet few workers understood their complex provisions and many learned with bitter disappointment after years of service that they were not entitled to the pensions they had counted on. A report issued by the Senate Labor Subcommittee in March 1971 revealed that, since 1950, 92 per cent of the persons in plans requiring 11 or more years of service for pension eligibility and 73 per cent of those in plans requiring 10 years or less did not qualify for pension benefits when they left their jobs.

Background

Private pension plans would celebrate their centennial in 1975. One hundred years earlier, in 1875, the American Express Company established, if not the first, one of the first private plans on record. It provided retirement benefits to employees 60 years of age or older with 20 years of company service. Benefits equaled one-half the average salary earned during the retiree's last 10 years of work but could not exceed $500 a year.

Many factors contributed to the spectacular growth of private pension plans in the 20th century.

As America moved from an agricultural to an industrial society, the elderly worker was no longer assured secure retirement on the family farm. Yet families in the city had no room for parents or in-laws.

The devastating effects of the Great Depression, which wiped out the life savings of millions, prompted concern about the capability of personal savings and investments to provide adequately for old age.

Congress in 1935 recognized the need for public underwriting of retirement when it passed the Social Security Act. And since the 1920s Congress had encouraged the expansion of the private pension system by offering increasingly generous tax advantages for contributions by employers to employee pension funds.

Pension plans grew slowly, however, until World War II, when wage freezes held down pay increases but did not limit fringe benefits such as pensions. In 1949 the Supreme Court declined to review—and thus upheld—a lower court ruling allowing labor unions to negotiate pensions under collective bargaining laws.

Union demands escalated as a result of both these factors; total pension assets jumped from $2.4-billion in 1940 to $52-billion in 1960.

In 1963 pension plans fell under harsh public scrutiny when the Studebaker automobile factory in South Bend, Ind., stopped production, throwing thousands of persons out of work. In that incident, 4,500 workers under the age of 60 with fully vested pension rights received only 15 per cent of the retirement benefits they had earned under the Studebaker plan. The average age of persons in the group was 51, their average length of service 23 years. Many other employees received nothing.

The public outcry at this incident was largely responsible for renewing congressional interest in the adequacy of existing federal regulations governing private pension plans.

Private pension plans covering more than 30 million workers held assets totaling about $129-billion in 1970, but no comprehensive federal law governed the operation of such funds.

The Welfare and Pension Plan Disclosure Act of 1958 required plan administrators to report annually on the structure and operations of the funds but did not regulate vesting and funding practices. *(Congress and the Nation, Vol. I, p. 601, 616)*

Issues

Congress had been urged to regulate private pension plans at least since 1965, when a presidential advisory committee recommended legislation to require fuller funding of pension plans and to guarantee worker's rights to at least part of their accumulated benefits. *(Congress and the Nation, Vol. II, p. 610, 622)*

There was also opposition to such proposals. The major issues were:

Vesting. Reformers argued that some federal standard must be established for the vesting of pension plan benefits—giving a worker the irrevocable right to receive at least part of his accumulated pension benefits whether or not he continued to work for the sponsoring company until retirement.

Existing standards for vesting under private plans varied widely. Some employers vested workers after 10 years of employment; others viewed pensions as a reward for lengthy service and held off vesting any part of an employee's benefits until he reached the age of 50 or even 65. Often plans required continuous service or permitted only short interruptions due to layoffs or unemployment. Consequently, many workers never received all or even part of the benefits they accrued over their years of service.

Administration of Trust Funds. Existing law required only disclosure of the provisions and financial operations of a pension plan.

There was almost universal support on the part of business and labor leaders, the administration and Congress for proposals which would regulate:

...Pension Plans, but Congress Failed to Act, 1969-72

● Investments—Some plans invested a large portion of their funds in the company's own stock or placed money in questionable investments. Critics said such practices curbed the growth of a fund and often risked the loss of millions of dollars by directly linking the fund to the welfare of the corporation.

● Loans—Some companies in a financial pinch dipped into their pension funds for short- or long-term loans to meet operating costs. The use of pension funds for working capital increased during tight money periods of the late 1960s. Other funds made loans— frequently not repaid—to underworld or gambling figures.

● Trustees—Trustees administering some pension plans paid themselves exorbitant fees for their services. Others had been accused of using pension funds for their personal investment gain.

Full Funding. Under existing law, sponsors of private pension funds were not required to maintain a level of assets sufficient to pay the claims of all vested workers if the plan terminated due to business failure, plant shutdown, transfer or merger.

Labor Department statistics revealed that approximately 500 pension plans ceased each year, affecting about 25,000 workers. Some of the employees received partial benefits or vesting in new plans; others lost all claims to retirement benefits.

Critics of existing conditions suggested that the federal government establish a schedule for pension plan funding, requiring that plans set aside enough cash or assets to pay all the benefits promised to workers. Some proposals gave plans 40 to 50 years to reach the full-funding level.

Opponents of funding schedules said federal regulation would be unnecessary if trusteeship standards and a system of fund insurance were established.

Pension Fund Insurance. Closely related to the issue of full funding were proposals to give corporations the option—or require them—to purchase insurance on all unfunded liabilities from a federal agency patterned after the Federal Deposit Insurance Corporation. The FDIC insured bank deposits up to $20,000 against loss due to bank failure.

Such an agency would guarantee payment of benefits to vested workers, the proponents said, if the sponsoring company could not pay them, due to inadequate funding or bankruptcy. Insurance premiums would be based on the existing level of the plan's funding.

Portability. Reformers called for voluntary establishment under federal guidelines of a central clearinghouse where vested workers would deposit credits for benefits as they moved from job to job. The credits would earn additional income until the depositor reached retirement age or was eligible to collect them.

Certain union plans, such as those of construction workers, offered a form of portability—the ability to transfer vested pension rights from one employer to another.

Opponents argued that both Social Security and personal savings were completely portable and that private plans were designed to supplement, not duplicate them. They said existing variations among pension plans would make it virtually impossible to match the values of various company benefits.

Administration Proposals

President Nixon in 1970 proposed legislation to establish strict standards for administration of pension plan funds and broaden disclosure requirements under the Pension Plan Disclosure Act.

In a special message to Congress Dec. 8, 1971, Nixon called for legislation to:

● Establish minimum federal standards for the vesting of pension plan benefits.

● Provide further tax deductions for self-employed persons who contributed to pension plans for themselves and their employees.

● Provide a tax deduction for personal funds set aside by individuals for their retirement, up to a limit of 20 per cent of earned income, or $1,500, whichever was less.

Nixon was waiting for the results of a study ordered in his December 1971 message before considering legislation regulating funding standards and plan insurance.

1972 Senate Action

The Senate Labor and Public Welfare Committee Sept. 15 reported a bill (S 3598) that would have provided the first comprehensive regulation of private pension plans in their 100-year history.

S 3598 was referred to the Finance Committee Sept. 19 at the request of its chairman, Russell B. Long (D La.). The Finance Committee objected that S 3598 as reported by the Labor Committee infringed upon its jurisdiction over tax legislation and complained that the bill would be difficult and costly to enforce.

The Finance Committee reported S 3598 Sept. 25. As reported, the bill would have stiffened existing federal standards for the selection and conduct of pension plan administrators.

The Finance Committee stripped the bill of provisions which would have:

● Required that employees receive an irrevocable right to 30 per cent of the pension after eight years of service, with an additional 10 per cent guaranteed each following year. A worker would have been entitled to his full pension after 15 years of service.

● Directed employers to set aside within 30 years enough money to pay all benefits owed to workers.

● Established a federal program of pension plan insurance to pay pension benefits if a plan were cancelled or bankrupt.

● Set up a voluntary system for the transfer of certain pension benefits from job to job.

CONFERENCE ACTION

House and Senate conferees Oct. 11 reached agreement on a compromise version.

In major actions, conferees reduced Senate-passed authorizations for the basic state grant program and deleted as nongermane to the bill Title VII of the Senate version which expanded opportunities for blind persons to operate vending facilities in federal buildings.

The conference report was approved by the Senate Oct. 13 and the House Oct. 14.

Longshoremen's Compensation

Congress Oct. 14 cleared for the President a bill (S 2318—PL 92-576) amending the Longshoremen's and Harbor Workers' Compensation Act of 1927 to improve benefits, extend coverage to additional workers, provide a specified course of action for obtaining damages against third parties and make certain administrative reforms.

S 2318, the first updating of the original act since 1961, more than doubled existing compensation levels by setting the maximum weekly payment at $167 compared with a $70 maximum that had been provided since 1961.

The law applied not only to longshoremen and harbor-workers but to some workers in private industry in the District of Columbia and other areas of federal interest including defense bases overseas, PXs and commissaries.

Provisions. As signed into law Oct. 27, S 2318:

● Allowed a disabled worker to receive two-thirds of his average weekly salary, subject to a phased-in maximum starting at 125 per cent of the national average weekly wage and rising in three years (by 1975) to 200 per cent; increased the minimum benefits to not less than 50 per cent of the national average weekly wage or the average weekly wage of the longshoreman, whichever was less.

● Provided for annual increases in compensation benefits based on increases in the national average wage, an upgrading of benefits payable for injuries incurred before the effective date of the act, elimination of the $24,000 ceiling on compensation for certain types of disabilities and expansion of survivors benefits and of dependents entitled to receive such benefits.

● Expanded coverage of the act to include injuries incurred in the immediate area of docks related to ship loading, shipbuilding and repair work.

● Provided that third-party actions could be brought against shipowners on the basis of negligence but eliminated the doctrine of seaworthiness as a basis for claiming damages; indemnity claims against stevedoring companies were prohibited.

● Provided that all hearings under the act be conducted in conformity with the Administrative Procedure Act and established an Administrative Benefits Review Board to review decisions.

● Provided that the federal government would pay 50 per cent of the cost of increases in benefits to permanently disabled workers injured prior to enactment of the bill or to widows and survivors.

Legislative History. The Senate Labor and Public Welfare Committee unanimously reported S 2318 Sept. 14 and the Senate passed the measure by voice vote the same day without debate or amendment.

The House Education and Labor Committee Sept. 19 by voice vote reported HR 12006. The House Oct. 14 by a roll-call vote of 198-71 passed the bill under suspension of the rules—19 more than the two-thirds majority required for passage.

Subsequently, the House passed the related Senate bill (S 2318) in lieu, after amending it to contain the provisions of HR 12006. Differences between the two bills were minor.

The Senate Oct. 14 agreed to the House amendments by voice vote, completing congressional action.

Summer Jobs for Youth

President Nixon Oct. 27 signed into law a bill (S 2454—PL 92-597) providing for employment of youths in summer conservation jobs.

The Senate passed S 2454 May 23, and the House approved a less comprehensive version Oct. 11. The Senate accepted the House version Oct. 12.

As cleared by Congress, PL 92-597 extended for two years the pilot program established by the Youth Conservation Corps Act of 1970 (PL 91-378). *(1970 chronology, p. 718)*

During the summers of 1971 and 1972, nearly 5,600 young persons employed by the project cleared and built trails and campsites, planted trees and prevented or repaired streambed erosion on federal lands. A similar program, the Civilian Conservation Corps, was set up in the 1930s to provide jobs for unemployed youths. *(Congress and the Nation, Vol. I, p. 1053)*

PL 92-597 authorized $30-million in fiscal 1973, increasing to 25,000 the number of persons to be hired under the program. Thirty per cent of the funds were earmarked for a separate program granting states up to 80 per cent of the costs of operating similar projects on state and local lands.

Provisions. As signed into law, S 2454:

● Authorized $30-million in fiscal 1973 and $60-million in fiscal 1974 for programs employing persons between the ages of 15 and 19 to develop, preserve and maintain the public lands under the administration of the Departments of Agriculture and Interior.

● Earmarked 30 per cent of the funds for a pilot program of grants to the states to pay 80 per cent of the costs of operating similar programs on state and local lands.

Nonprofit Hospital Employees

A bill (HR 11357) guaranteeing to employees of nonprofit hospitals the right to organize and strike was passed by the House Aug. 7 under suspension of the rules by a 285-95 roll-call vote.

A two-thirds majority of members present and voting (253 in this case) is needed for passage under suspension of the rules.

HR 11357 would include employees of nonprofit hospitals in the definition of persons guaranteed by the National Labor Relations Act of 1935 the right to form unions, bargain collectively and strike.

Approximately 48 per cent of U.S. hospitals were considered nonprofit, according to Frank Thompson Jr. (D N.J.), chairman of the subcommittee which had considered the bill. The 1,387,000 workers they employed handled 66 per cent of all admissions.

Profit-making hospitals, which represented about one-fourth of American hospitals, already were included under HR 11357.

There was no Senate action on the bill.

Occupational Safety and Health

Three congressional committees held hearings in 1972 on the administration and enforcement of the Occupational Safety and Health Act of 1970 (PL 91-596). *(1970 chronology, p. 713)*

Congressional interest in the 1970 act was spurred by widespread complaints by labor and business interests over administration of the act by the Department of Labor. The act provided for federal establishment and enforcement of safety and health standards for the protection of about 55 million industrial, farm and construction workers employed by firms engaged in interstate commerce.

The three committees which held hearings were the following:

● The House Select Small Business Subcommittee on Environmental Problems which held hearings in June and issued a report on occupational safety Aug. 15. *(Box, this page)*

● The Senate Labor and Public Welfare Subcommittee on Labor held hearings in July and September.

● The House Education and Labor Select Subcommittee on Labor held hearings in July and September.

Amendments to Labor-HEW Bills. In addition to hearings on occupational safety, Congress in 1972 responded to business complaints about the administration of the 1970 act by attaching a rider concerning the Labor Department to the first fiscal 1973 Labor-HEW appropriation (HR 15417) which was vetoed Aug. 16 by President Nixon. The provision would have prohibited use of funds in the bill for inspection of businesses employing 15 or fewer workers.

The 2nd Labor-HEW bill (HR 16654) which cleared Congress Oct. 14 contained an exemption through June 30, 1973, from compliance with the 1970 act for businesses employing three or fewer employees. Nixon, however, vetoed that bill Oct. 27 on the grounds that it exceeded his requests for Labor-HEW funds. The effect of the veto was to leave the 1970 safety act unchanged through the end of the 92nd Congress.

A major issue at the hearings was whether small businesses should be exempted from the act. Organized labor opposed the idea. Leonard Woodcock, president of the United Auto Workers (UAW), said that excluding small businesses would "doom millions of workers to the continued presence and the insidious escalation of hazardous materials and hazardous conditions of employment." Organized labor also attacked the act's implementation by the Labor Department.

Operators of small businesses, criticized administration of the law as unfair to establishments lacking safety engineers and legal departments skilled in interpreting the bulky and highly technical regulations. They protested a lack of concise information outlining their obligations and complained of what one spokesman called "the whims of the Occupational Safety and Health Administration."

Occupational Safety Report

Extensive revision of existing "grossly inequitable" administrative procedures was necessary to forestall congressional moves to amend the Occupational Safety and Health Act of 1969, concluded the first congressional study of the impact on small businesses of the 1969 act.

In its report released on Aug. 15, the Select Small Business Subcommittee on Environmental Problems declared: "Businessmen have a deep and sincere desire to provide safe working conditions. However, their efforts are being met with a variety of obstacles—primarily from the federal government."

Citing the testimony of 83 witnesses—including 22 members of Congress and representatives of 48 trade associations—received during five days of hearings in June, the subcommittee noted that "voluntary compliance" with the standards set forth by the Labor Department under the 1969 act "cannot be achieved under the existing approach. The present system is similar to a hypothetical situation where a police officer issues traffic tickets to motorists who voluntarily seek vehicle inspections."

"If understandable and accurate information could be made available to small businessmen, if initial or requested on-site inspections could be made without incurring a penalty, if standards could be promulgated for separate industries and categories within industries and, finally, if standards have a direct and meaningful and not merely illusory relationship to employee safety," the committee said, small businesses should continue to be included under the act, as recommended by "nearly all of the witnesses testifying before the subcommittee."

The subcommittee urged the Labor Department to gather and classify data on injuries and deaths resulting from work-related accidents according to the size and class of business involved and directed the department to report to the subcommittee within 90 days on actions taken to meet its recommendations.

The appropriate legislative committees of Congress should consider amending the act to permit the Labor Department to make inspections without issuing citations unless an imminent danger existed and to follow penalties to be given to employees willfully violating safety standards, the subcommittee concluded.

Some witnesses sought compromise. Sen. Bill Brock (R Tenn.) said, "One of the major defects in the present law is that there is no provision for cooperation between government and business to work out voluntary compliance programs.... The emphasis should be shifted from citations and fines to one of cooperation."

Rep. Orval Hansen (R Idaho) favored changes in the act and regulations that would "take into consideration differences between large and small industries so that small employers may comply with the basic objectives of the law without undue economic hardships."

Manpower Programs

Congress and the Nixon administration grappled inconclusively during the 1969-72 period with the issue of manpower training programs. Although there was substantial agreement that the existing plethora of categorical federal grant programs was inefficient and lacking in focus, the two branches were unable to agree on a basic overhaul of the system.

President Nixon's approach—embodied in his proposed Manpower Training Act of 1969 and Manpower Revenue Sharing Act of 1971—was to decentralize control over manpower assistance programs. This was a key element in the administration's "new federalism" concept.

In a 1971 message to Congress, Nixon said: "Manpower Revenue Sharing is a partnership. Washington puts up the purse and sets out the broad purposes of authorized spending, while program decisions are turned over to the statehouses, county governments and city halls. My proposal neither mandates nor terminates any programs. It provides that the continuation, expansion or modification of each program would be determined, as it ought to be, by the test of performance alone—and determined by the state or community which the program serves. Programs that have proved themselves in practice could be continued with the use of the federal funds provided."

During congressional hearings on manpower reform, the goal of decentralization and decategorization of manpower programs won broad support. A number of witnesses, however, urged the retention of some federal programs to protect special groups that lacked political influence at the state and local level.

Rising unemployment figures injected another issue into the manpower reform controversy. Unemployment in December 1969 was 3.5 per cent of the labor force, seasonally adjusted. That was the average for the year. But in January 1970 unemployment began an almost unbroken rise, reaching 6.2 per cent in December. The unemployment rate hovered around 6 per cent of the labor force throughout 1971. Thereafter it declined gradually to 5.1 per cent in December 1972—still well above the accepted full employment level of 4 per cent of the labor force.

Against this background, congressional Democrats maintained that the primary need was not for job training but for job creation, through a federally subsidized public service employment program. The administration countered that over the long run, improved training would help poorly skilled workers more than subsidized jobs at low-level salaries.

President Nixon vetoed a 1970 manpower training bill that authorized a massive federal public service employment program. "WPA-type jobs are not the answer" to unemployment, he said. In 1971 he vetoed a bill that provided $2-billion for accelerated public works projects on grounds that such a program would be the most costly and least effective method of cutting unemployment. But he signed another bill that authorized $2.25-billion to create about 150,000 public service jobs. House Republicans failed in their efforts to substitute the administration's manpower revenue sharing plan for the provisions of that measure.

Although the House defeated the administration's manpower revenue sharing proposal in 1971 and neither a Senate nor a House committee reported the proposal after hearings in 1972, the administration announced early in 1973 that it planned to implement the program anyway under an extension of existing law. The administration also said it would phase "down" programs under the Emergency Employment Act of 1971.

Background

In the Employment Act of 1946, Congress declared it the national purpose to "use all practicable means to promote maximum employment."

But large-scale federal manpower programs did not come into being until the early 1960s when the government sought to create special programs for persons left jobless through technological change or the move of industries to other parts of the country. Under the Area Redevelopment Act of 1961, for example, the federal government provided $4.5-million a year for four years for vocational training programs for unemployed and underemployed workers in depressed areas.

The major piece of manpower legislation was the Manpower Development and Training Act of 1962—the first comprehensive peacetime effort by the federal government to assess the economy's labor needs in the face of technological and structural changes.

The Department of Labor was directed to make annual surveys and studies on manpower needs and

References

Discussion of manpower training programs for the years 1945-64 may be found in *Congress and the Nation, Vol. I,* p. 1220-1224; for the years 1965-68, *Congress and the Nation, Vol. II,* p. 734-743.

trends and employment problems. Testing, counseling and training were to be provided for the unemployed and underemployed who could not reasonably expect to get full-time jobs without training.

The program consisted of both on-the-job training and vocational education.

Other training programs were created as part of the Economic Opportunity Act of 1964 which set up the poverty program. These included the Job Corps and Neighborhood Youth Corps (which was created under provisions in the bill authorizing federal assistance for state and local work-training programs for in-school and out-of-school youths).

The Neighborhood Youth Corps was, in effect, a public-service program in its reliance on public agencies for the jobs for youths in the program. Another prototype of public-service employment was Operation Mainstream, sponsored by Sen. Gaylord Nelson (D Wis.) in 1965, to put the unemployed to work on conservation projects.

Two other programs added in the 1966 amendments to the poverty program were New Careers to train the poorly skilled and unemployed for para-professional jobs and Special Impact to concentrate training efforts on the unemployed in slum areas of the country.

Under the 1967 Economic Opportunity Act Amendments, the JOBS program was created (Job Opportunities in the Business Sector). The program was operated by private employers and financed in part by the federal government. The goal of the plan had been to have 50,000 hard-core unemployed on the job by June 1971, employed and trained by the private sector, with the government paying only for above-normal training costs (literacy training, counseling and health services, for example).

Former Labor Secretary George P. Shultz told a congressional hearing in 1970 that the economic slow-down had affected the Department's "short-term expectations" of what could be accomplished through the JOBS program. For fiscal 1970, the Labor Department listed 140,000 training opportunities in the JOBS program, but from the beginning of the program in 1968 through January 1970, only 84,703 persons had been hired.

The President had projected $420-million for the program in fiscal 1971 which Congress cut to $280-million. But department officials later said they would spend only $175-million on the program with the additional $105-million shifted to other programs.

Another new manpower effort created by the 1967 poverty program amendments was the Concentrated Employment Program. This was designed to bring together a variety of manpower services and focus them in a unified effort in designated target areas—usually large cities. Administered by the Labor Department's Manpower Administration, the programs were usually controlled by community action agencies, financed by the Office of Economic Opportunity, acting as the prime local sponsor.

In 1967, Congress added, through amendments to the Social Security Act, a work-incentive program for persons on welfare. The program required persons over the age of 16 in households receiving Federal Aid to Families with Dependent Children to register for work or training except those who were ill or too old or whose presence was required at home to care for another family member. *(Chapter on Welfare, p. 605)*

The Unemployed. Federal job-training programs began to focus in the mid-1960s on youths and the ghetto poor as labor statistics revealed the extent of unemployment within these two groups.

The National Advisory Commission on Civil Disorders (the Kerner Commission) estimated in 1968 that 20 per cent of the participants in the 1967 riots did not have jobs. The persons in the most critical need of help, the commission said, were the 500,000 "hard-core unemployed" in the central cities of the country.

It had been estimated that 10 per cent of the males in the ghetto dropped out of the job market altogether for a variety of reasons including discouragement at finding suitable jobs at adequate pay.

Black unemployment had increased every month since December 1969, a spokesman for the Urban League told a Senate committee in May 1970. The existing unemployment rate for blacks, he said, was 8.7 per cent or 691,000 persons. Another witness at the same hearing said unemployment for black teeenagers in Los Angeles poverty neighborhoods was 45 per cent and the rate in Detroit, 40 per cent.

Public Service Employment. In 1965, a private consulting firm, Greenleigh Associates, did a national survey for the Office of Economic Opportunity of needed public-service jobs that could be filled by unskilled workers. They found 4.3 million jobs, they said, in 12 different categories.

In 1966, the National Commission on Technology, Automation and Economic Progress said there were 5.3 million public-service jobs in six categories. The commission recommended that "the government become an employer of last resort, providing work for the 'hard-core unemployed' in useful community enterprises."

The Urban Coalition, which had been advocating a public-service-employment program since 1966, had a survey undertaken in January 1969 of cities of 100,000 or more population. The survey turned up 280,000 possible jobs in 130 cities, in 13 municipal public-service functions. At least 140,000 of the jobs, the coalition said, could be filled quickly by inner-city residents.

During hearings in early 1970 by the Senate Subcommittee on Employment, Manpower and Poverty, Los Angeles county officials testified that there were some 2,000 jobs that needed to be filled and could be performed by low-skilled persons. The county could not budget funds for the jobs, however, because of lack of tax revenue, they said.

Manpower Programs. Statistics on how many individuals actually had been aided by federal manpower programs were difficult to compile because the programs were the responsibility of a number of different federal agencies. The Labor Department estimated, however, that federal spending on manpower programs had risen from $245-million in 1961 to $2.2-billion in 1968.

The federal government was estimated to be spending $1.6-billion a year on existing manpower training programs which served 425,000 persons.

In arguing for the administration manpower bill in 1970, Shultz said most of the manpower programs had "their own authority, separate appropriation, special target group, different delivery system." The result, he said, was often "rigidity, lack of coordination, duplication of effort and wide gaps in services."

Under the Manpower Training Act, the administration proposed the elimination of the cateogrical program, allowing local planners to choose what kind of training programs they wished to utilize.

The administration emphasized the role of the United States Employment Service, Shultz said, because with 2,200 local offices, it was the only nationwide manpower organization.

Chronology

Of Legislation

On Manpower Programs

1969

President Nixon in 1969 presented to Congress a new manpower training program that ultimately would replace federal programs to train the unemployed with state programs funded by the federal government. Opposition to the plan was voiced by big city mayors, directors of community action programs and antipoverty workers on grounds that it would weaken local programs.

Late in the year Senate and House subcommittees began hearings on the plan. In 1970 Congress approved a manpower training bill, but Nixon vetoed the measure.

Nixon Proposals

As a first step toward consolidating responsibility for manpower programs, President Nixon March 13 announced plans to reorganize manpower programs within the Department of Labor.

The plans would place greater authority for all manpower programs with the Department's manpower administration, streamline procedures ranging from field offices to Washington, D.C., and establish a single office to consolidate eight training programs and the job-placement and recruitment functions of the U.S. Employment Service, which was to be eliminated.

The President proposed a further consolidation of manpower programs in his Aug. 12 message to Congress on manpower training.

He had announced his proposals in an Aug. 8 television address in which he also asked for changes in the welfare system and the sharing of federal tax revenue with the states. He called the package "The New Federalism."

The new manpower program would initially consolidate manpower training programs run by the Office of Economic Opportunity (OEO) with those of the Department of Labor. OEO would remain only as a planning agency with no operational control over programs.

As states developed manpower training programs of their own, they would administer more and more of the federal funds apportioned them. Ultimately, the states would run their own programs funded by the federal government.

The Nixon program would also:

● Provide incentive for a trainee to choose training best suited for him rather than training that paid more.

● Pay welfare recipients $30 a month more if they went into job training.

● Create a comprehensive career development plan for trainees to help them get and keep jobs.

● Set up a computerized job bank to match job seekers with job vacancies.

● Increase manpower spending by 10 per cent whenever unemployment reached at least 4.5 per cent for three consecutive months to help stabilize the economy.

1970

The Senate Dec. 21 voted to sustain President Nixon's veto of a bill (S 3867) authorizing $9.5 billion for fiscal years 1971-1974 for federal manpower training and public service employment programs.

The roll call was 48-35 in favor of overriding the President's action—eight votes short of the two-thirds (56) majority necessary to override the veto.

Because the Senate sustained the President's veto, House action became unnecessary; however, had the Senate overriden the veto, chances of similar House action would have been slim. The House Dec. 10 had agreed to the conference report by a narrow 177-157 vote. The Senate the same day had adopted the conference report by a 68-13 roll call.

Veto. The President vetoed S 3867—his sixth veto since taking office—on Dec. 16. Nixon said the bill failed to link public jobs with training opportunities, increased the number of special federal programs such as Mainstream and New Careers and restricted individual job opportunities.

The bill had been supported by the U.S. Conference of Mayors, National League of Cities, AFL-CIO, Urban Coalition, Common Cause, Congress of American Indians, National Association of Counties, National Farmers Union, Leadership Conference on Civil Rights and state governors.

As cleared for the President, S 3867 authorized $2-billion in federal funds for manpower training, $2.5-billion for a public service employment program and $3-billion to prepare employees for better jobs and for special federal programs. In addition, the bill carried a special $2-billion authorization over fiscal years 1971-1974 for a federally supported employment program.

The total $9.5-billion authorization was $2.5-billion less than the Senate had provided and $2-billion more than approved by the House. The $2.5-billion cut from the Senate-passed version came from funds for the public job program; the House had provided no special funding for the program.

The measure consolidated authority for manpower programs in the Department of Labor and decentralized federal control over manpower programs administered by the states and by cities with populations of 75,000 or more. The bill, however, retained a number of federally administered training programs, including Operation Mainstream, New Careers and the Job Corps.

PROVISIONS

As cleared by Congress, S 3867 would have:

• Authorized appropriations of $2-billion in fiscal year 1972, $2.5-billion in fiscal 1973 and $3-billion in fiscal 1974 to carry out provisions of the act.

• Allocated funds not reserved for specific purposes in the following manner: one-third for comprehensive manpower services (Title I), one-third for public service employment programs (Title III) and one-third for occupational upgrading (Title II) and special federal responsibilities (Title IV).

• Allowed the secretary of labor to transfer up to 25 per cent of funds authorized for any program to another activity under the act.

• Established a National Manpower Advisory Committee (13 to 17 members) appointed by the President and composed of representatives of labor, management, education and agriculture.

Title I—Comprehensive Manpower Services

• Authorized the secretary of labor to develop and carry out a program of comprehensive manpower services.

• Provided that the following would be eligible as prime sponsors of manpower programs: any state; any city with a population of 75,000 or more; any county or unit of local government with a population of 100,000 or more having governmental powers similar to those of a city; any unit or combination of units of local government, without regard to population, in rural areas with substantial population decreases and unemployment.

• Required prime sponsors to appoint a manpower services council with representation from community and social agency groups to plan manpower programs. Authorized the secretary of labor to give preference to a local unit of government as the prime sponsor in cases where both the local unit and the state applied for the designation; authorized the secretary of labor to determine a prime sponsor if two or more units of local government applied for the designation.

• Provided that local government manpower plans must be submitted to the governor for his comments and that the secretary of labor should consider the comments and confer with the applicants to resolve any differences.

• Provided that a community action agency could submit a prime sponsorship plan if the unit of local government did not submit an approvable plan for the area.

• Allocated 70 per cent of the funds reserved for Title I to the states based on a formula including total number of persons in the labor force, number of persons unemployed and number of low-income persons.

• Provided that an area within a state would have its percentage of the total state allotment computed on the basis of the above formula.

• Approved not less than $1.5-million of Title I funds to any state.

• Reserved 5 per cent of Title I funds for the secretary of labor to use as incentive money to encourage area-wide coverage by single prime sponsors and reserved another 5 per cent as an incentive for establishment of procedures for cooperation with vocational education agencies in the area served by the prime sponsor.

• Reserved the remaining Title I funds for allocation by the secretary of labor according to his discretion.

Title II—Occupational Upgrading

• Authorized the secretary of labor to provide financial assistance to private or public employers to help them prepare employees for better positions.

• Specified that applications submitted by prime sponsors and employers contain assurances regarding selection of trainees, training program content and other program elements.

• Provided that employers would receive payment equal to 90 per cent of instruction and training expenses, less the value of productive services provided by the trainees.

Title III—Public Service Employment

• Authorized the secretary of labor to assist public and private nonprofit agencies to provide employment for unemployed and underemployed persons in public service jobs.

• Authorized special appropriations of $200-million in fiscal year 1971, $400-million in fiscal 1972, $600-million in fiscal 1973 and $800-million in fiscal 1974 for the public service employment program.

• Allocated 80 per cent of funds reserved for Title III to states and areas on the basis of unemployment and number of low-income persons. (The conferees agreed to the Labor Department's criteria for low-income, but expected regional and rural-urban differences to be taken into account.)

• Reserved the remaining Title III funds for allocation by the secretary of labor according to his discretion.

• Limited Title III funds to 15 per cent for those training and manpower services that were unavailable but related to public service employment.

• Specified that public service job employees could receive wages not lower than the highest of the following: the national minimum wage, state or local minimum wage or the prevailing wage rate.

• Specified that employees be assured of workmen's compensation, retirement benefits, health insurance, unemployment insurance and other benefits.

Title IV—Special Federal Responsiblities and Programs

• Authorized the secretary of labor to provide financial assistance to public and nonprofit agencies for the following programs: New Careers, to provide the unemployed with jobs and the low-income worker with greater career opportunity; Mainstream, for work by the chronically unemployed; Community Environment Service, for jobs which will improve the physical environment and recreation facilities in poverty communities; Jobs for Progress, for comprehensive employment services for the unemployed.

• Authorized the secretary of labor to provide funds for the establishment and operation of Opportunities Industrial Centers, to provide comprehensive employment services and job opportunities for low-income persons who are unemployed or underemployed; management training programs, to train individuals in business management, and manpower programs in correctional institutions, to provide training and work experience for inmates.

• Authorized the secretary of labor to establish and operate Job Corps centers for low-income, disadvantaged young men and women.

• Authorized the secretary of labor to provide financial assistance to Neighborhood Youth Programs and to provide part-time employment and training for students from low-income families.

• Authorized the secretary of labor to establish a comprehensive program of manpower research and to develop a comprehensive system of labor-market information.

• Authorized the secretary of labor to develop a national computerized job bank program to match persons seeking jobs with available positions.

• Established a program to determine the level of employment generated by federal grants and assistance programs and to what extent such programs could provide a source of opportunities for the employment of the disadvantaged.

Title V—Programs for Indian, Bilingual, Migrant and Older Workers

• Established in the Department of Labor a National Indian Manpower Advisory Council and a Migrant and Seasonal Farmworker Manpower National Advisory Council.

• Authorized the Secretary of Labor to reserve funds for Indian and seasonal farmworker programs based on the proportion of Indians and migrant workers to the total low-income population.

• Authorized the Secretary of Labor to reserve funds for manpower programs for persons with limited English-speaking ability and for middle-aged and older workers.

• Established a comprehensive midcareer development service program in the Department of Labor.

Title VI—Emergency Employment Assistance

• Authorized the secretary of labor to provide financial assistance for employment and training activities in areas of high unemployment in the following amounts: $200-million when the national rate of unemployment equaled or exceeded 4.5 per cent for three consecutive months and an additional $200-million when the rate equaled or exceeded 5 per cent for three consecutive months.

SENATE ACTION

S 3867 was reported by the Senate Labor and Public Welfare Committee Aug. 20 and passed by the Senate Sept. 17 on a 68-6 roll-call vote. The Senate version of the bill carried total authorizations of $12-billion.

As passed, S 3867, the Employment and Training Opportunities Act of 1970, consolidated authority for most manpower training programs in the Department of Labor and decentralized project control to states and metropolitan areas.

The Senate-passed bill authorized federal funds to cover 80 per cent of the cost of hiring up to 250,000 unemployed and underemployed persons to work in state and local hospitals, schools, police and fire departments and other agencies. The administration opposed the public service employment provision.

The bill authorized appropriations of $2-billion in fiscal 1972, $2.5-billion in fiscal 1973 and $3-billion in fiscal 1974. One-third of the total amount authorized under the act was earmarked for manpower services, one-third for public service employment, and one-third for manpower programs administered by the Labor Department.

The following additional amounts were authorized for public service employment: $750-million in fiscal 1971; $1-billion in fiscal 1972; $1.25-billion in fiscal 1973; and $1.5-billion in fiscal 1974.

The administration recommended placing manpower projects under the control of states and metropolitan areas; S 3867 extended the proposal by specifying that communities with a population of 75,000 or more could run their own programs. Mayors, organized labor and antipoverty agency spokesmen had expressed concern that state governments would not be sensitive to the job needs of the city poor.

The bill also required mayors and governors to set up manpower service councils composed of representatives from community and social agency groups to plan manpower programs.

The administration proposed dropping most of the federal training programs to permit states to administer their own projects with federal funds. However, S 3867 retained several federal programs including the Neighborhood Youth Corps, Operation Mainstream and New Careers. The bill also authorized new programs for Indian, bilingual, migrant and older workers.

The only major change in the bill on the floor involved a provision allowing the secretary of labor to transfer funds from one program to another. A successful amendment offered by Jacob K. Javits (R N.Y.) allowed a transfer of 25 per cent of authorized funds; the committee version had allowed a transfer of 15 per cent of such funds.

Debate. Peter H. Dominick (R Colo.) offered an amendment designed to reallocate program funds to allow states and local communities to propose and the secretary of labor to decide amounts to be used for manpower training, public service employment, and special work and training programs.

Opposing the amendment, Gaylord Nelson (D Wis.), chairman of the Senate Subcommittee on Employment, Manpower and Poverty, said, "Congress has yet to accept the concept that we just appropriate money and the executive branch spends it, and I do not think we should." The amendment was defeated by a 19-55 roll-call vote.

A second amendment offered by Dominick provided that state governors be given increased authority over manpower training plans submitted by mayors. But Nelson objected saying, "What we would have is a confrontation between mayors of large cities and governors around the country." The amendment was rejected by a 28-46 roll-call vote.

A third amendment proposed by Dominick limited an individual's public service employment to two years and wages to 80 per cent of the rate paid for comparable jobs held by nonsubsidized workers. "The purpose...is to assure that public service employment would be used only as one part of an over-all manpower training program," Dominick said. The amendment was defeated by a 29-43 roll-call vote.

Jacob K. Javits (R N.Y.), in an effort to tie the public service employment section of the bill to manpower training, proposed that subsidized employment be limited to transitional jobs between training and regular employment. The amendment was defeated by a 27-46 roll-call vote.

Before final passage of the bill by a 68-6 roll call, Javits said S 3867 was a monumental measure in the manpower training field. But Dominick insisted that the bill would "inject the federal government into every city and county in the country."

HOUSE ACTION

The House Education and Labor Committee reported its version of the bill Oct. 5, and the measure was passed by voice vote of the House Nov. 17. The House bill authorized a total of $7.5-billion in fiscal years 1972-74. Unlike the Senate version, the House bill did not carry a special authorization for public service employment. It did, however, require that 18.75 per cent of all funds appropriated under the act be used to support public service employment programs.

Before passing the bill, the House by an 80-275 roll-call vote rejected a motion proposed by William J. Scherle (R Iowa) to recommit the bill to the Committee on Education and Labor.

Scherle offered an amendment to remove the public service employment title from the bill. He said the provision would initiate a "vast new program where the federal government acts as an 'employer of first resort' and not of last resort."

Carl D. Perkins (D Ky.), in opposing the amendment, said the public service provision was the most important part of the bill "because we are trying to do something about rising unemployment in this country." The amendment was defeated by a 31-59 standing vote.

An amendment to give the unemployed special consideration for job placement was introduced by John H. Buchanan Jr. (R Ala.) who said the measure would simply give preference to the unemployed.

But James G. O'Hara (D Mich.) said he did not think it was wise or helpful to confine the public employment service to serving only the unemployed. The amendment was defeated by a 42-46 standing vote.

CONFERENCE, FINAL ACTION

The conference report on S 3867 was filed Dec. 9 and approved the next day by the Senate, on a 68-13 roll call, and the House, on a 177-159 roll call. The conference bill closely resembled the version passed by the Senate Sept. 17.

General Provisions. The conferees agreed to allocate $7.5-billion of the $9.5-billion total authorized in the bill in the following manner: one-third for manpower services, one-third for public service employment and one-third for occupational upgrading and special federal programs. The Senate had earmarked one-third of the funds for manpower services, one-third for public service employment and one-third for special training programs and special federal responsibilities. The House had allocated three-quarters of the funds for manpower, occupational upgrading and public service employment and one-quarter for special federal responsibilities. The House

had also specified that not less than 18.75 per cent of the total amount appropriated under the act could be used for the public service employment program. Under the agreement, the secretary of labor was authorized to transfer up to 25 per cent of the funds from one title to another, thus providing a minimum of 25 per cent ($1,875,000,000) for public service employment. This transfer authorization was included in both House and Senate versions.

The conferees agreed that members of the National Manpower Advisory Committee, included in both the Senate and House versions, would be appointed by the President—as provided in the Senate-passed bill. The House had authorized the secretary of labor to appoint the committee members.

Comprehensive Manpower Services. The Senate had specified that a city, county or combination of units of local government with a population of 75,000 or more was eligible to be a prime sponsor. The House raised the population base requirement to 100,000. The conferees retained the House population requirement for a county or combination of units of government but adopted the Senate figure with respect to a city.

In addition, the conferees agreed to accept a House provision permitting a unit or combination of units of government in rural areas to qualify as prime sponsors without regard to population requirements. The Senate-passed bill contained no similar provision.

The conferees agreed to apportion 70 per cent of manpower funds among the states, as provided by the House. The Senate had specified that 75 per cent of the funds would be granted to the states.

Occupational Upgrading. Conferees adopted a House provision establishing a program of occupational upgrading under a separate title. The Senate-passed bill contained provisions relating to job upgrading but they dealt with the subject in less detail.

Public Service Employment. The Senate bill contained a special authorization for public service employment in the following amounts: $750-million in fiscal 1971, $1-billion in fiscal 1972, $1.25-billion in fiscal 1973 and $1.5-billion in fiscal 1974. The House-passed measure did not contain a special authorization. The conferees agreed to a special authorization of $200-million in fiscal 1971, $400-million in fiscal 1972, $600-million in fiscal 1973 and $800-million in fiscal 1974 for public service employment.

The conferees agreed to apportion public service employment funds among the states and areas with consideration given to the percentage of unemployed and low-income persons. The Senate bill contained a separate allocation for public service employment while the House-passed version had no state or area allocation but required that 18.75 per cent of all funds appropriated under the act be reserved for public service employment programs.

Special Manpower Programs. The Senate-passed bill contained authorizations for a number of manpower activities including New Careers, Mainstream, Community Environment Services and the Job Corps. While the House provided funding by the secretary directly to public and private agencies for these programs, it did not emphasize them. Conferees agreed to "highlight existing activities and to emphasize the secretary's right to deal directly with applicants other than prime sponsors" by placing the federal manpower programs under a separate title (IV).

Emergency Employment Assistance. Conferees agreed to accept a Senate provision providing for an Emergency Employment Assistance Program. The House-passed bill did not contain a provision for this program.

VETO MESSAGE

In his Dec. 16 veto message, President Nixon said the conference bill failed to link public jobs with training or other employment opportunities. "WPA-type jobs are not the answer," he said.

Nixon also objected to authorizations for such federal programs as Mainstream and New Careers which, he said, would "hamstring" communities trying to adjust to local needs.

The President announced he would have signed the version of the manpower program passed by the House Nov. 17. The House bill streamlined the categorical grants programs, linked public jobs to training and contained no special funding above an 18.75-percent authorization for public service jobs. The conference-adopted version allocated $200-million to create 40,000 public service jobs by mid-1971.

VETO UPHELD

The Senate's Dec. 21 48-35 roll-call vote to sustain the veto divided along liberal-conservative lines, with 39 Democrats and 9 Republicans voting to override and 9 Democrats—all but one from the South—and 26 Republicans, voting to uphold the veto. On the 68-13 roll-call vote Dec. 10 adopting the conference report on S 3867, 7 Democrats—all southerners—and 6 Republicans voted against the bill.

Senators who supported the President's veto maintained that the public service program would result in WPA-type, make-work employment. They also contended that the public jobs program was not adequately tied to training and other employment opportunities.

Opponents of the President's action said that rising unemployment dictated a need for giving the jobless useful government work. The bill, they said, would tie public service to training and would give the secretary of labor authority to ensure that the jobs for the unemployed were meaningful.

George Murphy (R Calif.), the ranking Republican member of the Senate Subcommittee on Employment, Manpower and Poverty which drafted S 3867, said state and local governments should be required to move public service employees onto locally supported payrolls.

Murphy, who voted for the conference version but against the attempt to override, said, "Federally subsidized public jobs should lead to career opportunities. They must not be a path to nowhere."

Edward M. Kennedy (D Mass.) replied that the President had neglected to mention that the bill provided for training programs for those interested in public service employment.

Vance Hartke (D Ind.) added that the secretary of labor could reject any plan submitted by a state or community which failed to include provisions for encouraging trainees to move into better paying jobs and could

cut off funds to any program which had a WPA-type purpose.

Challenging the President's statement that state and local government employment would be make-work, Kennedy said, "This assumption flies in the face of everything we know about the current crisis in municipal government. As the Kerner Commission found in 1968, there are vast unmet needs in education, health, recreation, public safety, sanitation and municipal services."

Kennedy added that it must come as a surprise to the unemployed to learn that working for a state or city is a limitation on individual opportunity, as the President declared.

John Stennis (D Miss.), who voted against the conference report and the attempt to override the veto, said the President indicated the manpower program Congress had cleared "was not in the ball park with his ideas of what we need...."

"Any kind of manpower training program that is going to be successfully carried out by the federal government certainly must have the administration behind it...in order to organize it and to make it bring a return," Stennis said.

Although the President's veto came too late for drafting new legislation in the 91st Congress, no manpower programs were scheduled to expire immediately. The existing programs in the Office of Economic Opportunity were authorized through June 30, 1971, and others in the Departments of Labor and Health, Education and Welfare were established through June 30, 1972.

1971

President Nixon, in a message to Congress March 4, proposed a program of manpower revenue sharing—one of six special revenue sharing programs recommended by the administration in 1971. (*Revenue sharing p. 97*)

The President's proposed Manpower Revenue Sharing Act was intended to replace the Manpower Development and Training Act and the manpower provisions of the Economic Opportunity Act on Jan. 1, 1972. Under the proposal, $2-billion would be provided in the first full year. Of that amount 85 per cent would be distributed to the states and to cities and counties with a population of 100,000 or more. The remaining 15 per cent would be reserved for use by the secretary of labor to support and assist state and local programs.

Nixon said his proposals would provide "$4 for every $3 now being spent...to help move men and women into productive employment." Manpower training programs were funded at about $1.4-billion in fiscal 1971.

Manpower revenue sharing made little headway in Congress. Republicans succeeded in forcing floor consideration of the proposal during House consideration of a Democratic-backed bill (HR 3613) to provide public service jobs for the unemployed. A motion to recommit HR 3613 with instructions to substitute the provisions of the administration's manpower revenue sharing plan was rejected on a 184-202 roll-call vote June 2.

President Nixon ultimately signed the employment bill, although its provisions were similar to the public service employment provisions of the manpower training bill he had vetoed in 1970. *(Emergency employment bill, p. 735; 1970 manpower training veto, p. 739)*

Late in the year a House subcommittee began hearings on over-all manpower reform legislation. To permit more time for consideration of this issue, the House Dec. 6 passed (HR 11570) a one-year extension of Title II of the Manpower Development and Training Act, which was scheduled to expire June 30, 1972. Title II authorized establishment of on-the-job and vocational training programs for the unemployed and underemployed.

That extension was enacted in 1972. *(Below)* Congress in 1972 also extended the Office of Economic Opportunity for two years, through fiscal 1974.

Emergency Employment Act

President Nixon July 12 signed into law a bill (S 31—PL 92-54) authorizing $2.25-billion to provide public service jobs for the unemployed at the state and local level.

The bill was one of several attempts during 1970 and 1971 by Congress and the administration to cope with prolonged unemployment. The two branches were frequently at odds over their approaches to the problem. During that period President Nixon vetoed two bills providing public service jobs and S 31 was originally opposed by the administration.

The administration and its congressional supporters instead favored the President's revenue-sharing approach to manpower training. But President Nixon approved S 31 and praised its provisions in contrast to the proposals contained in S 575 which he had rejected June 29. *(Comparison of bills, box this page)*

Final congressional action came July 1 when the House by a 343-14 roll-call vote adopted the conference report on the bill. The Senate had adopted the conference report by a 75-11 roll-call vote June 29.

The House had passed a similar bill (HR 3613) June 2 after defeating Republican and southern Democratic attempts to substitute the administration manpower revenue-sharing bill (HR 8141). The House had then substituted the provisions of HR 3631 for those of S 31 passed April 1 by the Senate.

As finally passed, S 31 was expected to provide approximately 150,000 jobs in recreation, education, health, housing, public safety and environmental improvement, at an average annual cost of between $5,000 and $6,000 per job.

Congress Aug. 6 completed action on an emergency supplemental appropriations bill (H J Res 833—PL 92-72) appropriating the full $1-billion authorized under S 31 for fiscal 1972.

Provisions. As signed into law July 12, S 31 (PL 92-54):

● Authorized $750-million for fiscal 1972 and $1-billion for fiscal 1973 to provide transitional public service employment at the state and local levels. The funds would be released when the national unemployment rate reached 4.5 per cent for three consecutive months.

● Authorized $250-million for fiscal 1972 and $250-million for fiscal 1973 for a "special employment assistance program" to be used in local areas where the unemployment rate was 6 per cent or higher, regardless of the national unemployment rate.

Vetoes Over Job Bills

In 1970 and 1971, Congress and the White House clashed repeatedly over differing approaches to unemployment and the concept of public service jobs.

During that period, President Nixon vetoed two measures (S 3867) and (S 575) but approved other bills containing proposals in the rejected bills.

As cleared by Congress, S 31, the Emergency Employment Act, was similar to the public service employment provisions of the manpower training bill (S 3867) vetoed by President Nixon in December 1970. Mr. Nixon signed S 31 July 12 (PL 92-54).

Title III of the 1970 vetoed bill would have provided a total of $2-billion through fiscal 1974 for public service jobs.

In his veto message, Mr. Nixon said, "WPA-type jobs are not the answer for the men and women who have them, for government which is less efficient as a result, or for the taxpayers who must foot the bill." He added that public employment that was not linked to real and permanent jobs was a "self-defeating concept."

The bill enacted in 1971 contained authorizations totaling $2.25-billion for public service jobs in fiscal years 1972 and 1973.

A major provision of the vetoed 1970 bill incorporated in S 31 was a "trigger" feature that would release funds when the national employment level reached 4.5 per cent for three consecutive months. S 31 also created a Special Employment Assistance Fund administered by the secretary of labor, for use where the unemployment rate exceeded 6 per cent for three consecutive months. The jobless rate hovered near 6 per cent of the labor force throughout 1971.

S 31 was part of a two-pronged effort by Democrats in Congress to stimulate the economy and create jobs. A sister bill, S 575, providing $5.7-billion for public works projects and regional economic development, was vetoed by President Nixon June 29—his first veto of the 92nd Congress. *(Veto of S 575, p. 180)*

The Nixon administration originally opposed both S 31 and S 575. But in his veto message of the public works acceleration bill, Mr. Nixon praised S 31 and urged its enactment.

Administration officials had consistently opposed the Title I provisions of S 575 that provided $2-billion for accelerated public works projects. Mr. Nixon reasoned that such a program would be the most costly and least effective method of cutting unemployment.

Titles II and III of S 575, extending federal aid for Appalachia and other regional development programs, also were vetoed by Nixon, but were then cleared by Congress July 30 and signed by the President Aug. 5 (S 2317—PL 92-65).

● Authorized the secretary of labor to approve applications from state and local governments for federal assistance in providing jobs to fill needs in environmental quality, health care, housing and neighborhood improvements, recreation, education, public safety, maintenance of streets, parks and public facilities, rural development, transportation, beautification, conservation, crime prevention and prison rehabilitation.

- Permitted only 15 per cent of authorizations to be used for training or administrative purposes and required that 85 per cent of funds be used for wages and direct job benefits to persons employed under the bill.

- Stipulated that veterans of the Korean war and those who served in Indochina after Aug. 5, 1964, would be given preference in filling jobs under the act, and that no more than one-third of the jobholders could be professionals or executives.

- Provided that applicants for funds would be assured that jobs would offer prospects for advancement, training and continued employment; that jobs would be in expanding occupational fields, and that barriers to employment, such as Civil Service requirements, would be nullified.

- Stipulated that persons employed under the bill would receive not less than the prevailing minimum wage rates for similar occupations in the locality, but that no person would be paid more than $12,000 annually from federal funds.

- Stipulated that 80 per cent of the funds were to be apportioned among the states on a scale determined by the percentage of unemployed persons in a state compared to the national average. Twenty per cent of the funds would be distributed at the secreatary of labor's discretion. Each state would be given a minimum allotment of $1.5-million.

- Provided that not more than 90 per cent of funding for jobs under the bill be provided by federal apporpriations unless the secretary of labor determined that the local agency could not pay 10 per cent of the costs.

SENATE

Committee. The Senate Labor and Public Welfare Committee reported S 31 March 27.

The committee said S 31 was "stopgap legislation" offered to deal promptly with an extremely serious national problem. "This legislation, by virtue of being a temporary and limited program, could take effect almost immediately and serve a great public need until more comprehensive legislation is enacted."

"The proposals advanced in S 31," said Winston L. Prouty (R Vt.), chief sponsor of the administration's manpower bill, "sound the death knell to the President's revenue-sharing concept."

Floor. The Senate April 1, by a 62-10 roll-call vote, passed S 31, authorizing up to $1.75 billion in federal assistance for public service jobs during periods of high unemployment.

HOUSE

Committee. The House Education and Labor Committee May 4 reported HR 3613, authorizing $3.95-billion through fiscal 1975 for emergency public service jobs.

Floor. The House June 2, in a major setback for the Nixon administration, rejected a Republican-sponsored manpower revenue-sharing plan and then passed, by a 246-142 roll-call vote, HR 3613 providing public service jobs for the unemployed.

The revenue-sharing proposal (HR 8141), introduced by Rep. Marvin L. Esch (R Mich.), was initially defeated by a 182-204 recorded teller vote. The vote represented the first defeat by either the House or Senate of an administration-backed revenue-sharing bill.

The Republican substitute would have consolidated a dozen manpower programs into a single flexible authorization of federal funds to be shared with the states for use in manpower training under specific plans drawn up by the states and communities. It contained a $500-million authorization to be used until Jan. 1, 1972, and an estimated $2-billion for the next fiscal year. No committee hearings had been held on the Esch (administration) bill.

An even closer vote came on a motion to recommit HR 3613 to the Education and Labor Committee with instructions to report the bill back with the provisions of the Esch substitute. The motion was defeated by a 184-202 roll-call vote.

Republicans voted 160-5 in favor of the revenue-sharing proposal, while Democrats voted against it by 24-197. Southern Democrats voted against it by 22-51.

Following passage of HR 3613 June 2, the House substituted its provisions for those of the Senate bill, then passed S 31 by voice vote.

Earlier House Action. A coalition of House Republicans and southern Democrats May 18, in three roll-call votes, succeeded in forcing floor consideration of the Nixon administration's manpower revenue-sharing proposal. The action was the first floor consideration in either chamber of any of the six special revenue-sharing programs proposed by the President in 1971.

Republican strategists, led by Rep. H. Allen Smith (R Calif.), engineered defeat of a previous-question motion (to cut off debate and foreclose any amendments) to the rule (H Res 437) permitting consideration of HR 3613. The motion, offered by Rep. Ray J. Madden (D Ind.), was rejected by a 182-210 roll-call vote.

Only three of 167 Republicans voted for the motion and 42 of 46 Democratic votes against the motion were cast by southern members. Defeat of the motion opened the rule to amendment.

Democratic proponents of the emergency public service employment bill charged that southern Democrats had voted with Republicans in exchange for promises of Republican help in attacking a bill (HR 1746) to give enforcement powers to the Equal Employment Opportunity Commission (EEOC).

Smith then offered an amendment to permit substitution of the text of HR 8141, the revenue-sharing plan, for the Education and Labor Committee's version of HR 3613. Smith said the administration plan was "a new approach for trying to restructure the manpower grant-in-aid programs."

Speaking against the amendment, Rep. Carl D. Perkins (D Ky.), chairman of the Education and Labor Committee, said: "We should not waive the rules of the House to permit the substitute of a bill with a much broader purpose than the bill the committee reported. No one knows what the full consequence will be."

Madden, referring to HR 8141, said: "This so-called mysterious bill, that was written in the dead of night down at the White House" should be scheduled for hearings "at the proper time."

The Smith amendment to the rule was adopted by a 210-177 roll-call vote, again with strong southern Democratic support. The House then adopted the amended rule by a 349-34 roll-call vote.

CONFERENCE, FINAL ACTION

Senate and House conferees filed a report June 28 on S 31.

Conferees stipulated that jobs created under S 31 must be "transitional" by leading to permanent positions in the public or private sectors. The report said this requirement "is intended to make it crystal clear that public service employment shall not be of the 'dead end, make work' sort that is feared by the critics of public service employment."

Conferees provided that funds under the bill could not be used for contracts with nonprofit agencies and required that at least 85 per cent of the funds should be used for wages and employment benefits.

House conferees accepted with modifications a Senate provision authorizing $750-million for fiscal 1972 and $1-billion for fiscal 1973 for public service jobs. The House had authorized a total of $3.95-billion through fiscal 1975.

Funds would be triggered when the national unemployment rate rose to 4.5 per cent or more for three consecutive months. Funding would cease when the national unemployment rate fell below 4.5 per cent for three consecutive months.

In addition, conferees accepted a House provision with minor changes creating a Special Employment Assistance Program and authorizing a total of $500-million for fiscal years 1972-1973. The funds, to be used separately from the main program of public service employment, were authorized for local areas where the unemployment rate reached 6 per cent or more.

Senate conferees accepted a House provision requiring that preference in filling public service jobs be given to veterans who served in Korea or Indochina after Aug. 5, 1964.

The Senate June 29 adopted the conference report on S 31 by a 75-11 roll-call vote. The House July 1 approved the report by a 343-14 roll-call vote.

1972

Senate and House subcommittees held extensive hearings on manpower reform legislation in 1972, but the only measure enacted (S 3054—PL 92-277) was a stopgap one-year extension, through fiscal 1973, of Title II of the Manpower Development and Training Act of 1962.

As cleared, S 3054 deleted a provision of the 1962 act that prohibited the disbursement of funds for manpower programs after Dec. 30, 1972. This action was intended to permit the Labor Department to enter into long-term grants or contracts extending beyond 1972.

The final bill also included a nongermane provision, added as a Senate floor amendment, relating to federal impact aid to school districts where large numbers of parents work on federal property.

Provisions. As signed into law April 24, S 3054:

• Extended Title II of the Manpower Development and Training Act of 1962 for one year, through fiscal 1973.

• Deleted a provision of the act prohibiting disbursement of funds for manpower programs after Dec. 30, 1972.

• Provided that government post offices treated as federal property which were transferred to the U.S. Postal Service would continue to be regarded as federal property for two years, thereby qualifying certain school districts for impact aid given to areas where large numbers of persons worked on federal property.

Legislative History. As reported by the Senate Labor and Public Welfare Committee Feb. 10, S 3054 contained only the provision relating to disbursement of funds. The Senate, in passing the bill Feb. 15, added the impact aid provision. The House passed S 3056 March 16 after substituting for the Senate provisions the language of HR 11570, the one-year manpower extension it had approved in 1971. Conferees included all three provisions in the final bill.

Chapter 13—Environmental Programs

Key Votes

In this chapter, key roll-call votes are shown in bold-face type. The party breakdown on each of these votes and the position taken by each member of Congress may be found in the key vote charts which appear in the appendix to this book.

Environmental Programs

The environmental alarums that were sounding throughout the country began reverberating in Washington in early 1969. On Jan. 28, just eight days after the inauguration of Richard M. Nixon, an oil well located on land leased by the federal government off the coast of Santa Barbara, Calif., burst its seams below the ocean floor and began pumping hundreds of thousands of gallons of crude oil into the Pacific Ocean. The spill formed an 800-square-mile slick that coated 30 miles of southern California beaches, causing major damage to boats and an estimated 600 waterfowl.

At the same time, such well-known environmentalists as biologist Barry Commoner and French oceanographer Jacques Cousteau were warning of broader, perhaps irreversible damage that industrial man was doing to his surroundings. Popular interest in ecology snapped into focus on April 22, 1970, with the celebration of Earth Day: Millions of Americans attended environmental teach-ins, antipollution protests and various cleanup projects, all under the green-and-white banner of the new ecology flag. Congress adjourned for the day while members addressed rallies throughout the nation.

The President's response to what had become a public clamor came during his Jan. 22, 1971 State of the Union address to Congress. Among the six "great goals" he listed, the third was "to continue the effort so dramatically begun this year: to restore and enhance our natural environment."

The race to clean up America had begun, and the mood was one of urgency and commonality of interest. Who, it seemed, could be against the environment?

Four years after Nixon took office, Congress had exceeded his most ambitious goals, producing the broadest and most expensive environmental legislation in the nation's history. Acting sometimes over strenuous objections from the White House itself to the cost of the new laws, Congress had:

● Established firm deadlines for the reduction of pollutants from automobiles;

● Overridden Nixon's veto of a comprehensive water pollution control measure aimed at cleaning up the nation's waters by 1985;

● Made petroleum companies liable for oil spill cleanup costs;

● Shifted the President's own priorities, appropriating more money for pollution control than he had asked for and less than he had proposed for defense;

● Acted on a host of other environmental issues, including the banning of hunting from aircraft; conser-

vation of wildlife; reforestation of national forests; protection of national forests; and numerous others creating or expanding national wilderness, historical or recreational areas;

● Set the stage for further action on other issues, including controlling toxic chemicals and strip mining.

By the end of Nixon's first term, environmental concern had become bureaucratized and a bundle of new laws were on the books; but a new set of problems by then was emerging, which cast doubts on the future of ecology as a politically easy, one-dimensioned issue.

Energy vs. Environment

At the same time Congress was churning out unprecedented environmental legislation, the energy shortage was emerging as a counter problem. In several instances the solutions to America's dwindling supply of power seemed diametrically opposed to the concerns of the environmentalists. *(Energy chapter p. 841)*

The energy issue became real for millions of Americans during the winter of 1972-73. After decades of dependence on cheap and plentiful energy, the United States suddenly seemed unable to muster enough fuel to heat its homes and power its factories. Schools shut down in Denver, factories idled, forcing thousands of workers off their jobs in Alabama and Louisiana, and a major oil supplier announced that it would ration heating oil in four eastern states.

"We've come to a turning point—we've reached the end of the road on cheap energy," a Senate Commerce Committee aide told Congressional Quarterly. Former Commerce Secretary Peter G. Peterson commented, "Popeye is running out of cheap spinach."

Among the complex and interacting forces many observers cited in the energy problem was the nation's increased environmental consciousness, which forced cutbacks in the use of certain polluting fuels and stymied efforts to construct what some experts were pointing to as the solution to the problem: nuclear power plants.

References

Discussion of legislation on environmental programs for the years 1965-68, *Congress and the Nation Vol. II*, p. 463-528; for the years 1945-64, *Congress and the Nation Vol. I*, p. 771-1109.

Nuclear Plants. Although properly operated nuclear plants produce less air pollution than conventional plants, they present unique safety and waste disposal problems. Haunting environmentalists and scientists who opposed continued construction was the fear of an accidental break in the nuclear reactor's cooling system, which it was theorized could release deadly radioactive materials up to 75 miles downwind from a plant.

Byproducts of the plants presented additional problems. The water used to cool reactors—released into surrounding rivers or streams at temperatures as much as 12 degrees higher than normal—endangered plants and aquatic life. Environmentalists feared that human life as well as wildlife was threatened by the highly toxic radioactive waste products of nuclear plants, which must be isolated for 1,000 years or more before being rendered harmless. Existing practices of underground storage required surveillance for centuries to ensure that unwary future generations did not unearth the poisons.

In 1971, a federal appeals court halted construction of a nuclear plant at Calvert Cliffs, Md. The court ruled that the Atomic Energy Commission was required by the National Environmental Policy Act of 1969 to consider fully the environmental impact of the plant—including, but going beyond, the radiological impact—before proceeding with construction. The court said that "the spectre of a national power crisis" did not justify a "black-out of environmental consideration."

Later in the year a federal district court halted AEC licensing of a nuclear plant in Illinois on similar grounds. These decisions dampened the industry's hopes that nuclear power would substantially ease the burden of heating and cooling the nation as early as 1985.

Strip Mining. The continuing controversy over strip mining was another example of the environment-energy dichotomy. On the one hand, stripping was the easiest and cheapest method of supplying the nation with coal—America's most abundant natural resource. More than half the total electric output of the nation came from coal, and nearly 60 per cent of that coal came from strip mines.

On the other hand, the stripping process—tearing away trees, brush and topsoil with bulldozers or giant earthmoving machines, and blasting clawing and boring out the coal—left the land gashed and piled with discarded earth. The results were landslides, erosion, water pollution and esthetic blight. Stripping was anathema to plant life, wildlife, fish, and ultimately to humans. West Virginia Democrat Ken Hechler, who fought strip mining interests in his state and in Congress, called stripping "a cancer of the earth...a menacing disease—a pathology deriving from. Our lust for energy at the cheapest monetary cost regardless of the social cost."

The failure of Congress to pass any legislation on strip mining by the end of Nixon's first term in office reflected the growing awareness that concern for the environment thenceforth would have to be tempered by consideration of the growing fuel shortage. "I have no desire to stop it (strip mining), because I realize the need for coal," remarked Rep. Wayne L. Hays (D Ohio), the original sponsor of an anti-stripping bill in the 92nd Congress.

Secretaries of Interior

Two prominent Republicans served as secretary of interior, a key environmental post, during the first Nixon administration. President Nixon's original choice, former Alaska Gov. Walter J. Hickel, was dismissed in November 1970. He was succeeded by Rogers C. B. Morton, former representative from Maryland and Republican National Chairman.

Hickel. The Hickel nomination became controversial in January 1969, after conservation groups questioned his dedication to natural preservation and others criticized his ties with oil companies. He was confirmed Jan. 23, 1969, by a 73-16 roll-call vote in the Senate. All of President Nixon's other cabinet nominations had been confirmed by voice vote Jan. 20.

Hickel stirred controversy again in May 1970 when, shortly after the U.S. move into Cambodia, he wrote a letter to Nixon suggesting the administration tone down the rhetoric of Vice President Agnew and show greater concern for the attitudes of young people. The letter became available to the press.

Hickel was removed from his post by the President Nov. 25, 1970. White House Press Secretary Ronald L. Ziegler said the dismissal was not related to any specific incident but that "the President felt that the required elements for a good and continuing relationship which must exist between the President and his cabinet members did not exist in this case."

Hickel's dismissal drew protests from many of the same conservationists and members of Congress who had opposed his confirmation in 1969. Sen. Gaylord Nelson (D Wis.), a member of the Senate Interior and Insular Affairs Committee who opposed Hickel's confirmation, said he was "astonished" by the ouster.

Morton. At the time of Hickel's dismissal, the White House announced that Morton would be nominated as secretary of interior. The Senate confirmed his nomination by voice vote Jan. 28, 1971. Although Morton had built a reputation as a conservationist while still a member of the House, national conservation groups opposed his nomination, claiming that his voting record on conservation issues had been poor.

Morton served as secretary of interior throughout the remainder of the first Nixon administration and was retained in that post when the second Nixon administration began in 1973.

Nevertheless, action taken by a galvanized Congress during the four-year period signaled at least the beginning of a halt to the thoughtless befouling of the water and the air, and brightened the prospects for a substantially cleaner America during the next decade.

Clean Water

One of the two most far-reaching environmental bills to be enacted was the Federal Water Pollution Control Act Amendments of 1972, more comprehensive and expensive than any environmental legislation ever considered by Congress.

In vetoing the measure, President Nixon called its price tag "staggering, budget-wrecking;" but Congress overrode the veto by substantial margins.

The bill initiated a major change in the basic approach to water pollution control in the United States by limiting effluent discharges as well as setting water quality standards. It set a national goal of eliminating all pollutant discharges into U.S. waters by 1985 and an interim goal of making the waters safe for fish, shellfish, wildlife and people by 1983. The measure contained authorizations of $24.7 billion, including more than $18-billion in federal grants to the states for construction of waste treatment plants.

Under the bill, citizens would be allowed to sue polluters, the federal government or the Environmental Protection Agency if the citizens had interests—economic or recreational—which were adversely affected.

An important earlier step had been the Water Quality Improvement Act of 1970, which made petroleum companies liable for up to $14-million in cleanup costs for oil spills. The legislation outlawed the flushing of raw sewage from boat toilets; strengthened restrictions on thermal pollution from nuclear power plants; and ordered development of criteria covering the effects of pesticides in streams, rivers and other waters. The bill also created an Office of Environmental Quality to act as a staff for the Council on Environmental Quality, established under the National Environmental Policy Act of 1969.

In two related areas, Congress passed a bill banning the unregulated dumping of waste materials into the oceans and coastal waters, and a bill to establish a national program for the management, use, protection and development of U.S. coastal zones. Areas covered included coastal waters, bays, sounds, lagoons and estuaries, the Great Lakes, and adjacent shorelands such as tidal areas, salt marshes, wetlands and beaches. The measure declared a national policy of preserving, protecting, restoring and developing the coastal zones in the national interest.

Clean Air

The other of the two environmental heavyweights that cleared Congress was the Clean Air Amendments of 1970, which established specific deadlines for a 90 per cent reduction of certain pollutants from new automobiles. The bill specified that by law automobiles by model year 1975 must emit 90 per cent less carbon monoxide and hydrocarbons than did model year 1970 cars; by model year 1976 they must emit 90 per cent less nitrogen oxides compared with model year 1971 cars. Manufacturers could seek a one-year extension of each deadline.

The bill set up new research programs and aid to states to establish abatement programs. It established primary air quality standards, which affect public health, to be administered nationally, and secondary air quality standards, pertaining to public welfare, which must be administered by the states. The measure also established controls on emission by new stationary sources of pollution and set new antipollution regulations for auto fuels and for aircraft engines and fuels.

The law was greeted with expressions of doubt by the automobile industry, which, along with the White House, had lobbied vigorously against it. "Unless the science and technology of emission control move ahead much faster than we believe is possible, we will not be able to meet the standards prescribed by the bill," said L. A. Iacocca, then executive vice president (later president) of Ford Motor Company. Others pointed to the cost of emission control, which they said would have to be passed on to the consumer.

Cost, whether through higher prices for consumer items or through higher taxes, became a recurring theme—along with the fuel shortage—whenever the environment was discussed.

As 1972 drew to a close, the future of emission control appeared as clouded as the exhaust fumes themselves. General Motors Corporation filed a request that the U.S. Court of Appeals for the District of Columbia review a denial by the Environmental Protection Agency of a one-year delay in the new standards. An extension ultimately was granted. *(Box, p. 758)*

As for the broader question of just how the legislation of the past four years would affect American life, environmentalists were in a mood to settle down to a long, hard fight for adequate enforcement of existing laws as well as for the writing of new ones. "We must make some drastic changes in priorities, lifestyles and fundamental values," said the architect of Earth Day, Sen. Gaylord Nelson (D Wis.) in early 1973. Nelson saw resistance to such change as "the new challenge facing the environmental issue as it moves from awareness to action."

Chronology

Of Legislation

On Environmental Programs

1969

Congress and the Nixon administration late in 1969 turned much of their attention to the nation's environmental and pollution problems. The move came in the face of growing public concern and the threat of possible ecological disaster.

Existing federal programs to curb pollution in the nation's cities were plagued with a shortage of funds and were sprawled across several departments and agencies creating an overlap of responsibilities.

In December, Congress cleared the National Environmental Policy Act (NEPA), which made environmental protection a matter of national policy. The measure required federal agencies to issue environmental impact statements before taking action or making recommendations having environmental consequences. And it established a three-man Council on Environmental Quality to advise the President and Congress on environmental matters. President Nixon earlier had created a cabinet level environmental council by executive order.

The council created by Congress was authorized to do research, studies and surveys relating to the ecological systems, natural resources and the quality of the human environment. It was aimed at preventing environmental problems on an anticipatory basis rather than dealing with environmental pollution after it had occurred.

Antipollution efforts in Congress centered on cleaning up the nation's waterways. One of the major pieces of legislation before the 91st Congress was the proposed Water Quality Improvement Act of 1969 (HR 4148) amending the Federal Water Pollution Control Act (PL 80-845). After extensive hearings, the House and the Senate reported and passed diverse bills and the measure remained in conference at the close of the session. The bill was an omnibus clean water bill which not only would clean up the nation's waterways but also would prevent further water pollution by upgrading federal water quality standards. It also made those responsible for oil spills pay the costs of cleanup. This provision, a costly one for the oil industry, received mass public support after a leaking well off the coast of Santa Barbara, Calif., spewed oil and caused major damage on Jan. 28. The area continued to suffer from pollution from the off-shore wells throughout 1969. The bill also had provisions for vessel pollution control and standards for federal licensees.

Congress attacked the shortage of federal funds to combat water pollution and rebuked the Nixon administration when it approved an $800-million appropriation to finance waste treatment plants throughout the nation. The amount was part of the public works appropriations bill (HR 14159—PL 91-144) and was cleared Dec. 4. The President, in his budget request, had asked for only $214-million out of a $1-billion authorization. The Senate had recommended the entire $1-billion and the House $600-million.

No other major congressional action took place in the area of water pollution, but hearings were held on phosphate pollution caused by synthetic detergents and on the effects of the use of nuclear energy.

On Nov. 4, 1969, the General Accounting Office (GAO) issued a report to Congress criticizing the nation's water pollution efforts and calling them "inadequately financed, badly organized, poorly planned and undermined by industrial and municipal pollution."

Little congressional action occurred on air pollution problems in 1969. An amendment to the Clean Air Act (PL 91-137) cleared Congress extending for one year research grants totaling $45-million for air pollution studies in fuel combustion. The administration had requested $18.7-million.

In November, President Nixon ordered a Task Force on Pollution created to evaluate federal efforts to keep the air clean and to curb further pollution.

No major push for new air pollution control legislation had been expected in 1969. Instead, Congress continued to study air pollution problems, investigating alternatives to the internal combustion engine. Efforts continued in the Department of Health, Education and Welfare (HEW) to designate air quality control regions called for under the Air Quality Act of 1967 (PL 90-

148). Testimony in December 1969 revealed that 20 control regions out of a total of 57 regions had been designated. Federal air quality standards were to be enforced in the regions by the state and local governments under the bill.

In other environmental actions, Congress strengthened laws limiting the importation and sale of endangered wildlife species, and the Senate passed bills to set up a commission on population growth and to establish a national mining and minerals policy. Both measures became law in 1970. Senate and House committees held hearings on bills to provide for settlement of the land claims of Alaskan natives, but their only action was a temporary suspension of an order freezing further transfer of Alaska federal lands to state hands.

National Environmental Policy Act

Congress in 1969 enacted landmark legislation in the environmental field when it approved the National Environmental Policy Act (NEPA) Dec. 22. Signed into law (S 1075—PL 91-190) by President Nixon Jan. 1, 1970, as his first act of the new decade, the measure set as national policy the goal of creating and maintaining "conditions under which man and nature can exist in productive harmony." The bill also set up a three-man Council on Environmental Quality to advise the President and Congress on environmental matters.

The bill declared that it was the continuing policy of the federal government "to use all practicable means and measures, including financial and technical assistance, in a manner calculated to foster and promote the general welfare, to create and maintain conditions under which man and nature can exist in productive harmony, and fulfill the social, economic, and other requirements of present and future generations of Americans."

In what was to become the most far-reaching provision of the new law, the bill directed federal agencies to consider the impact on the environment of all major activities and to include in every recommendation a written analysis of that effect as well as alternatives to the proposal.

S 1075 was passed by the Senate July 10 and the House Sept. 23. The conference report was approved by the Senate Dec. 20 and the House Dec. 22.

Administration Proposal. Congress imposed its version of an environmental advisory group on the administration.

President Nixon May 29 by executive order had created a cabinet-level Environmental Quality Council to coordinate and direct a governmental attack on all forms of pollution. Nixon, who was to head the new council, said it would "provide the focal point for this administration's efforts to protect all of our national resources." Members included Vice President Spiro T. Agnew, as vice chairman, and the secretaries of agriculture, commerce, health, education and welfare, housing and urban development, interior and transportation.

During hearings on bills to create a separate environmental council, administration witnesses indicated that—although they did not oppose a new council—one would be of little value. Congressional supporters, however, argued that the value of the administration's interagency body was limited.

The executive order also established a 15-member Citizen's Advisory Committee on Environmental Quality, headed by Laurance S. Rockefeller. It replaced the Johnson administration's Advisory Committee on Recreation and Natural Beauty, but members of the Johnson committee were carried over to the new Nixon committee.

Provisions. As cleared for the President, S 1075:

• Established as national policy that federal, state and local governments act to protect the environment.

• Directed agencies of the federal government to consider environmental factors in decision-making and include in every recommendation or report on proposals for legislation and other major federal actions affecting the environment a statement on the environmental impact of and alternatives to the proposed action.

• Established in the Office of the President a three-member Council on Environmental Quality to assist the President in the preparation of an annual report on the environment, to review federal activities affecting natural resources and to conduct studies on the environment. The members were subject to Senate confirmation.

• Directed that beginning July 1, 1970, the President submit an annual environmental quality report to Congress, describing the state of the environment, current and foreseeable trends in the management of the environment and federal environmental programs.

• Authorized expenditures for the council of up to $300,000 in fiscal 1970, $700,000 in fiscal 1971 and $1-million each following year.

AIR QUALITY

AIR QUALITY ACT AMENDMENTS. An amendment to the Clean Air Act of 1967 (PL 90-148) extending for one year research grants for studies of air pollution caused by automobile fuel combustion was approved by Congress Nov. 25.

As signed into law Dec. 5, the bill (S 2276—PL 91-137) extended section 104 of the 1967 act through June 30, 1970, and authorized $45-million for research on the control of pollution resulting from fuel combustion in gasoline- and diesel-powered vehicles. The final funding level was a compromise between a Senate version asking for $90-million for research programs and a House authorization of $18.7-million as requested by the administration.

The only other controversy over enactment developed over an effort to set exhaust emission levels to be met by automobiles sold or imported after Jan. 1, 1978. The House rejected an amendment sponsored by Leonard Farbstein (D N.Y.), which would have banned automobiles exceeding certain emission levels after Jan. 1, 1978.

AIR POLLUTION STANDARDS. Secretary of Health, Education and Welfare (HEW) Robert H. Finch Feb. 10 announced federal guidelines to control air pollution from sulphur oxides and particulates (dirt particles) in 10 areas designated by Finch as air quality control regions.

The HEW secretary was permitted to set criteria for the control of certain pollutants under the 1967 Air Quality Act. Under provisions of the 1967 law, the states in which the air quality control regions were

---

Council on Environmental Quality

President Nixon Jan. 29, 1970, named the three members of the newly created Council on Environmental Quality (CEQ). They were Under Secretary of the Interior Russell E. Train, former head of the Conservation Foundation, chairman; Robert Cahn, an environmental reporter for the *Christian Science Monitor*, and Gordon J. F. MacDonald, vice chancellor of the University of California at Santa Barbara.

The council submitted its first annual report to Congress Aug. 10.

The 241-page report catalogued in detail a number of problem areas—water and air pollution, weather modification, solid wastes, pesticides, noise, radiation, population, land use and international cooperation.

For the most part, it made few new recommendations for solving the problems beyond further research, stricter enforcement of existing regulations and enactment of environmental bills already pending before Congress.

One major recommendation was the formulation of a national land use policy to direct the types, location and timing of future land development. The report also called for formulation of national policies on energy and transportation.

---

located had three months to indicate that they intended to comply with the guidelines. The states then had six months to set standards in compliance with the guidelines and an additional six months to formulate a plan of implementation. Should a state fail to meet its deadlines, or should it fail to keep to its plan of implementation, the federal government was authorized to step in.

WATER AND MARINE RESOURCES

Water Quality Improvement Act

For the third consecutive year, Congress in 1969 failed to complete action on a major water pollution control bill to help clean up the nation's waterways.

Both houses approved different versions of HR 4148, the Water Quality Improvement Act of 1969, but the two versions differed so widely in strength that conferees were unable to resolve the differences by the end of the session. After a five-month deadlock, conferees in 1970 worked out a compromise that closely resembled the stiffer Senate-passed version. *(p. 765)*

National concern over water pollution reached a new level in January 1969 when a leaking offshore oil well off the coast of Santa Barbara, Calif., spread oil over 800 square miles of the Pacific Ocean, coating beaches, killing marine life and damaging property. *(Details, energy chapter)*

HR 4148, aimed primarily at oil spills, was designed to protect public waters from polluting discharges and place the onus of cleanup on polluters.

The biggest task faced by conferees in trying to resolve the disagreements between the two versions of

HR 4148 was over the conditions and extent of liability to be required to cover costs and damages resulting from vessel, offshore and onshore oil spills.

The House-passed bill stated that when an owner or operator of a vessel "willfully or negligently" discharged oil into U.S. navigable waters the amount the federal government could recover from the owner for cleanup costs "shall not exceed $10-million or $100 per gross registered ton, whichever is the lesser amount."

As amended and passed by the Senate, HR 4148 provided "absolute liability" of the owner of a vessel except where the spill was the result of an act of God or of war or certain other circumstances. The Senate version set a limitation on the amount of absolute liability at $125 a gross ton, or $14-million, whichever was less.

The administration had supported the House bill.

Background

The Federal Water Pollution Control Act (PL 80-584), passed in 1948, and its several amendments set forth the basic legal authority for federal regulation of water quality.

The first major water pollution control legislation approved by Congress, the 1948 act provided funds for sewage plant construction loans, permitted the Justice Department to file suits against polluters and set up a Water Pollution Control Advisory Board. Congress in 1952 extended the program for three additional years. *(Congress and the Nation Vol. I, p. 1132, 1137, 1139, 1143, 1150)*

Early Efforts. Subsequent amendments vastly broadened federal authority to curb water pollution. Legislation approved in 1956 (PL 84-660) strengthened enforcement provisions by allowing the federal government to sue to stop polluters upon the request of a state. Where health was involved, state consent was not necessary.

The 1956 amendments also added a $50-million annual grant for sewage treatment plant construction. Three years later, President Dwight D. Eisenhower asked Congress to reduce, and after 1960, to eliminate the grants. He said responsibility for sewage treatment costs should be returned entirely to states and localities. But Democrats, in control of Congress by almost a 2-1 majority, favored federal aid. They passed a bill providing $90-million in annual grants over 10 years. Eisenhower vetoed the bill Feb. 23, 1960, and an attempt two days later to override the veto failed, leaving the earlier grant program in effect.

In February 1961, President John F. Kennedy asked for a substantial increase in the federal grants program and a strengthening of enforcement proceedings against polluters. PL 87-88, authorizing higher grants and permitting federal contributions to single projects to total 30 per cent or $600,000, whichever was less, instead of 30 per cent or $250,000, was passed. Under the bill, half of each year's grants was restricted to communities of fewer than 125,000 persons. The secretary of health, education and welfare (HEW) was given authority to prosecute polluters without state government permission.

In 1964, a new Federal Water Pollution Control Administration was created in the HEW Department to administer antipollution activities, and the HEW secre-

---

Water Programs Scored

The federal government's long and costly effort to control water pollution and clean up the nation's rivers was found ineffective by the General Accounting Office (GAO).

A report issued Nov. 4, 1969, said efforts to combat pollution were inadequately financed, badly organized, poorly planned and were undermined by industrial and municipal pollution. Little or nothing had been accomplished despite the expenditure of $5.4-billion on waste treatment facilities since 1957, the report found. The federal government had contributed $1.2-billion of the $5.4-billion that had been spent to construct 9,400 waste treatment projects.

Existing funding levels were totally inadequate to meet the problems of waste-choked streams and rivers, the GAO said. But before more money was spent, a new basis for awarding grants should be developed, the agency recommended.

---

tary was authorized to recommend water quality standards for interstate waters.

Water Quality Standards Enacted. In 1965 and 1966, two pieces of legislation were enacted which made the 89th Congress the most important to date in dealing with the problems of water pollution—the Water Quality Act of 1965 (PL 89-234) and the Clean Waters Restoration Act of 1966 (PL 89-753). In addition, President Lyndon B. Johnson signed an executive order requiring federal departments and agencies to install water pollution controls for federal installations. *(Congress and the Nation Vol. II, p. 497, 503)*

The 1965 law required states to set water quality standards for interstate waters within their boundaries and authorized the federal government to act where states failed to do so. It established the Federal Water Pollution Control Administration within the Department of Health, Education and Welfare. (The water pollution administration was subsequently transferred to the Interior Department and renamed the Federal Water Quality Administration.)

The establishment of water quality standards was designed to prevent pollution before it occurred: Under previous laws, there were no pre-established purity levels, and, as a result, abatement action was not usually taken until the pollution had reached an advanced stage. Although water quality standards, according to the 1965 act, would differ from stream to stream and even for parts of the same stream, for the first time there would be a recognizable standard for all cases arising in a specific region.

The water quality standards, however, did not have as wide a coverage as the general pollution-abatement procedures of the 1948 Water Pollution Act, with its amendments. The standards were to cover only interstate bodies of water or portions of such waters within a state.

The Clean Waters Restoration Act of 1966 provided money to help communities pay the costs of meeting the water quality standards which they were required to establish and enforce, and provided financial incentives for states to establish purity standards on intrastate waters. For fiscal years 1967-71, $3,908,000,000 was authorized for federal water pollution control activities. Most of the money ($3.550-billion, rising from the existing level of $150-million a year in fiscal 1967 to $1.250-billion in fiscal 1971) was for grants to help communities defray the costs of building sewage treatment plants.

The 1966 act also required that enforceable standards be set for intrastate waters (although not subject to formal federal review) before a state's communities could qualify for the highest level of federal grants. This incentive was intended as an important step toward a system of comprehensive controls over the purity of the nation's waterways.

Oil Spill Legislation. Since enactment of those far-reaching bills, little congressional action had been taken on additional water pollution control legislation.

In 1967, the Senate passed an omnibus water pollution control bill (S 2760) to combat lake, mine and oil pollution, but Congress did not complete action on the measure. *(Congress and the Nation Vol. II, p. 512)*

In 1968, the House and Senate passed different forms of a water pollution control bill (S 3206), but the two chambers were unable to reconcile differences prior to adjournment and the bill died with the close of the 90th Congress. S 3206 included provisions relating to oil pollution controls, pollution from marine vessels, and compliance with water pollution standards by federal licensees, and would have provided additional financial aid to local governments for waste treatment facilities. *(Congress and the Nation Vol. II, p. 521)*

1969 Action

House. The House Public Works Committee March 25 reported HR 4148 with an amendment in the nature of a substitute bill.

The bill specified that the federal government was responsible for the cleanup of any polluting discharge regardless of the cause of the discharge. To reimburse the government for cleanup costs, the owner or operator of a vessel responsible for the pollution was held liable for up to $10-million or $100 per gross ton, whichever was less. The owner or operator of onshore or offshore facilities responsible for pollution was liable for up to $8 million.

The bill set up a $20-million revolving fund to cover federal cleanup costs prior to reimbursement and a $15-million fund to finance research on solutions to aid mine drainage pollution and authorized appropriations totaling $348-million over a three-year period: $173-million for 1970, $150-million for 1971 and $25-million for 1972.

The reported version of HR 4148 was a major revision of the original bill which had been introduced at the request of the Department of Interior.

The reported bill lowered the amount of liability insurance required for vessels and onshore and offshore facilities engaged in activities which might pollute the national waters. Insurance company spokesmen had said, in hearings, that the higher liability limits would have been uninsurable.

Much tighter restrictions were placed on applicants for federal licenses to conduct any activity which might result in pollution of U.S. waters in the reported version of HR 4148. Applicants were required to receive certification from each affected state stating that the activity would not reduce the quality of that state's waters below designated water standards. The original bill required a report on each application by the secretary of interior.

After a two-day debate, the House April 16 passed HR 4148 by a 392-1 roll-call vote. Opponents of the measure contended it was not strong enough, but only minor changes were made on the floor in the bill as reported.

Senate. By a unanimous vote, the Senate Public Works Committee Aug. 7 reported an omnibus bill (S 7) to curb water pollution, particularly by oil spills.

The bill required operators of oil tankers and drilling rigs which spilled oil into the nation's waters to pay the costs of cleanup. Liability would be without limit if the owner or operator was negligent. The burden of proving non-negligence would be on the operator.

Owners and operators of tankers, oil drilling rigs, storage depots and other such facilities located along the shore or in the water between the shore and the three-mile limit, would not be liable for spills if they were a result of an unanticipated "act of God" or war or government or by a vandal, saboteur or other third party.

In all other cases, owners or operators of offshore oil wells in state-controlled waters would be liable for $8-million cleanup costs.

Owners of tankers would be liable for $125 per gross ton of the vessel, or a maximum of $14-million for any one spill.

The bill authorized a $50-million Interior Department revolving fund for emergency oil cleanup action for federal agencies.

By an 86-0 roll-call vote, the Senate Oct. 8 passed HR 4148. Prior to final passage, the Senate had substituted the language of S 7, with amendments, for that of HR 4148.

Nine amendments to the Senate bill resulted in some major changes from the bill as reported. An amendment by Gaylord Nelson (D Wis.) required the interior secretary to develop water quality criteria for all pesticides.

The Senate also approved a compromise reached between Edmund S. Muskie (D Maine) and Henry M. Jackson (D Wash.) to clarify the role of the Office of Environmental Quality set up by Title II of S 7.

That title had led to a dispute between Muskie and Jackson over jurisdictional matters. Muskie was chairman of the Public Works subcommittee which had handled S 7, while Jackson—who headed the Interior Committee—had sponsored a bill (S 1075) creating a Board of Environmental Quality Advisers to advise the President on environmental issues. The Jackson bill had been passed by both houses but was not sent to conference until agreement was reached between the two Democrats to prevent a floor showdown.

Under the compromise worked out by the senators, Muskie's Office on Environmental Quality would serve as staff support for Jackson's Board of Environmental Advisers. S 1075, the National Environmental Policy Act, cleared Congress Dec. 22. *(Details, p. 748)*

Conference. HR 4148 was sent to a House-Senate conference Oct. 9, but no agreement had been reached when Congress adjourned.

Other Water Legislation

MARINE SCIENCE COUNCIL. Congress voted a one-year extension (HR 8794—PL 91-15) of the National Council on Marine Resources and Engineering Development—through June 30, 1970—pending establishment of a new federal agency to do the council's work.

Established by the Marine Resources and Engineering Development Act of 1966 (PL 89-454), the council was a coordinating body for all governmental marine science activities. Its life was to have expired June 30, 1969. *(Congress and the Nation Vol. II, p. 482)*

The Commission on Marine Science, Engineering, and Resources, also created by the 1966 act, in a report to Congress in January 1969, recommended creation of a National Oceanic and Atmospheric Agency to oversee the national marine science program. *(Hearings on report, below)*

Because legislation incorporating this recommendation (HR 13247) could not be acted upon before June 30, 1969, the House Merchant Marine and Fisheries Committee asked that the life of the council be extended for one year until the new agency was established to take over the council's responsibilities.

HR 8794 also reduced the annual authorized appropriation for the council from $1.5-million to $1.2-million.

MARINE COMMISSION REPORT. The Marine Science Commission in January called on the United States to undertake a mammoth expansion of its oceanography programs.

The commission released its report, "Our Nation and the Sea," on Jan. 11, 1969. It called for the United States to make a major investment in understanding, exploiting and preserving the oceans through major scientific research, conservation, technological development and industrial and food-producing exploitation.

The commission urged that the United States—which was expected to spend $773-million during the 1969 fiscal year on ocean study and development—increase that sum to $2-billion a year by 1980. The report forecast a total cost of $8-billion for the first 10 years of the effort.

The report charged that the sea was not sufficiently understood and that the seas, coast and estuaries were used haphazardly, inefficiently and often destructively by the nation either through ignorance or indifference. *(Marine protection legislation, 1972 chronology, p. 798)*

It recommended creation of the National Oceanic and Atmospheric Agency (NOAA) which would incorporate the Coast Guard, the Commerce Department's Environmental Science Services Administration (the Weather Bureau and Coast and Geodetic Survey), the Interior Department's Bureau of Commercial Fisheries, the National Sea Grant Program, the U.S. Lake Survey and the National Oceanographic Data Center.

At the time of the report, 22 bureaus in nine federal agencies were involved in matters concerning the nation's oceans.

Background. In June 1966 Congress had created an independent Commission on Marine Science, Engineering and Resources to make a survey of the nation's needs as related to the seas and to work out an over-all plan for the reorganization of the government's oceanography program. The commission was authorized under the Marine Resources and Engineering Development Act of 1966 (PL 89-454). *(Congress and the Nation Vol. II, p. 482)*

President Johnson appointed the commission on Jan. 9, 1967. Its 15 members included men from federal and state governments, industry, universities and marine laboratories. Chairman of the commission was Dr. Julius A. Stratton, chairman of the Ford Foundation.

Hearings. A House Merchant Marine and Fisheries subcommittee held hearings intermittently between April and October on the commission's recommendations, including a bill (HR 13247) to establish the centralized agency (NOAA) to manage nonmilitary oceanic and atmospheric programs recommended in its report. The committee took no action on the bill, although a similar agency was set up by executive order in 1970. *(p. 757)*

Administration witnesses appearing before the subcommittee opposed HR 13247, while members of the scientific community in general approved of the proposed consolidation of maritime programs.

Testifying in September, James M. Beggs, under secretary of the Department of Transportation, said he was in favor of some kind of reorganization to coordinate federal ocean programs, but suggested putting the programs into an existing department rather than creating the NOAA.

Myron Tribus, assistant secretary of commerce, science and technology, said the proposed NOAA might "not be the best vehicle for the nation's effort in the marine environment." It was preferable, Tribus said, to defer to the President in the matter of reorganization.

A month later, Lee A. DuBridge, director of the Office of Science and Technology, said it would be improper for a member of the administration to comment on the NOAA until the President's Council on Executive Organization had completed organization studies. DuBridge said that, although the NOAA was a radical proposal in that it would "disrupt" portions of the existing government structure, it was also too conservative a proposal because it failed to include many closely related programs of the environment.

Agnew Proposals. In his role as chairman of the National Council on Marine Resources and Engineering Development, Vice President Spiro T. Agnew Oct. 19 suggested five priorities for ocean activities. Their cost was estimated at $30-million in fiscal 1971, with a total of $200-million over a five-year span. Among the projects Agnew suggested for immediate action in the long-range maritime study program were:

● Coastal zone management—Authorizing federal grants to be matched by the states for setting up or expanding state planning and regulatory authorities to protect resources of coastal areas.

● Coastal laboratories—Establishing federal research centers to develop a data base, map, analyze, monitor and assess the impact of different land uses on coastal zones and to advise and assist in coastal management.

● Lake restoration—Mounting a pilot program using a lake of several hundred square miles in area to study lake-pollution processes and reclamation methods.

● Arctic environmental research—Studying pollution problems posed by development of arctic areas where low temperatures vary the natural processes normal to the rest of the world.

• International Decade of Ocean Exploration (IDOE)—Funding the U.S. contribution to the IDOE, which the United States proposed and the United Nations General Assembly endorsed in 1968.

Related Hearings. Three Senate committees held separate hearings on the use of ocean space but took no action on bills under consideration.

A Senate Foreign Relations subcommittee in July heard testimony on a resolution (S Res 33) setting forth detailed principles regarding use of oceans. It declared that ocean space should not be subject to national appropriation by claim of sovereignty and the seabed should be used for peaceful purposes only. S Res 33 was closely related to negotiations being conducted at the Geneva Disarmament Conference on proposals to ban nuclear weapons from the ocean floor.

The policies of the United States at the United Nations with respect to the exploitation of the resources of the ocean beyond the limits of national jurisdiction were the subject of hearings in the fall by a Senate Commerce subcommittee. A special Senate Interior subcommittee conducted hearings on similar issues in December.

DESALINATION PROGRAM. Congress completed action on a bill (S 1011—PL 91-43) authorizing a slight increase in funds for the saline water conversion program for fiscal 1970 but denied an administration request for authority to engage in research programs with foreign countries.

As signed into law July 11, the bill authorized appropriations totaling $26-million for programs under the the Saline Water Conversion Act of 1952 (PL 82-448) with a restriction that none of the funds be used in foreign operations. The programs were aimed at developing low cost methods for desalting brackish water and seawater into fresh water. *(Congress and the Nation Vol. I p. 939)*

The Senate version had broadened the authority of the Office of Saline Water (within the Interior Department) to engage in activities in foreign countries but the House deleted that language. Conferees adopted the House position.

LAND USE

ALASKAN LAND CLAIMS. Late in 1969 the House and Senate Committees on Interior and Insular Affairs agreed to a temporary modification of the order freezing further transfer of Alaska federal lands to state hands.

The land-freeze order had been issued in 1966 by then Interior Secretary Stewart L. Udall to halt further transfer of lands until Congress could settle conflicting land claims by the state and Alaskan natives. The approval of the congressional Interior Committees to a temporary modification of the land-freeze order was needed for Interior Department action because Interior Secretary Walter J. Hickel had agreed, during his confirmation hearings in January 1969, to continue the freeze until Congress could act to resolve the land claims dispute. *(Confirmation, p. 746)*

The temporary modification of the land-freeze order cleared the way for work on a pipeline from northern Alaskan oil fields to a warm water port by allowing the interior secretary to issue construction permits. *(Trans-Alaskan pipeline controversy, p. 807)*

Alaska Lands Issue

The United States purchased Alaska from Russia for $7.2-million under the terms of an 1867 treaty. The treaty by which the United States acquired sovereignty was with Russia on the theory that Russia, by acquiring sovereignty, had extinguished aboriginal title. Native rights in specific lands were not confirmed in that treaty. They were acknowledged, however, as a future obligation of the United States in the Organic Act of 1884, which established a civil government for Alaska.

In the 1884 act, Congress provided that Alaska natives should not be removed from lands they used or claimed, but that the terms by which they could acquire title to those lands would be the subject of future legislation. No such law had been enacted as of 1969, and some groups of natives had sought redress in the courts.

Thus, the situation of the Alaskan natives was different from that of the Indian tribes in the 48 contiguous states who were granted lands for their own use by treaty with the United States and whose subsequent claims were limited to monetary compensation in payment for rights in other lands taken. The Alaskan natives continued to live by sufferance on federal lands; native claims to the land were never extinguished through any legal action.

Statehood. When Alaska became a state in 1958, more than 99 per cent of its 375 million acres was owned by the federal government. The Alaskan Statehood Act of 1958 (PL 85-508) provided for the transfer of more than 103 million acres of federal unreserved lands to the state government over a 25-year period.

According to a report issued that year by the House Interior and Insular Affairs Committee, the government had withdrawn many of the more valuable resources of the territory through the creation of tremendous federal reservations for the furtherance of the programs of the various federal agencies. At that time, about 95 million acres—more than one-fourth of the total land area—were enclosed within various types of federal withdrawals or reservations. Much of the remaining area, the report said, was covered by "glaciers, mountains and worthless tundra."

Approximately 23 million acres of land out of the 103 million acres to be transferred had been selected by the state when, in December 1966, then Secretary of Interior Udall (1961-69) imposed a freeze on further selection because of conflicting claims between the state and the natives over the land. Udall ruled that disposal of the remaining 80 million acres of federal land would be held up until Congress settled the native land claims.

Both the House and Senate Interior Committee held hearings in 1969 on measures to provide for settlement of the land claims of Alaskan natives, but neither committee reported out a bill. The measures under consideration differed on the amount of public land to be distributed to Alaskan villages and on the sources of federal revenue for the settlement of native claims.

The Federal Field Committee for Development Planning in Alaska, created by President Johnson after the 1964 Alaskan earthquake, provided the recommendations embodied in HR 10193. That bill would have provided for the distribution of 23,040 acres of federal land, the equivalent of one township, to each village. The bill also provided that 10 per cent of all federal revenue realized from timber sale and oil, gas and land leases in Alaska be used to settle land claims.

The administration's proposal (HR 13142) would have distributed two townships of land to each village and authorized $500-million over a 20-year period to settle land claims.

The Senate in 1970 passed a broader bill (S 1830) authorizing payments for and grants of land to the Alaskan natives but the House took no action on the measure. Congress approved a final settlement of the century-old claims in 1971. *(p. 774, 783)*

TIMBER SUPPLY. Congress in 1969 conducted extensive studies of the causes and effects of the nation's escalating lumber prices but stopped short of enacting legislation to encourage more timber production.

Late in the session, the House Agriculture Committee reported a bill (HR 12025) designed to cut prices by increasing production from national commercial forest lands, but further action on the measure was put off until 1970. The primary beneficiary of the bill was to be the lumber industry.

Despite heavy pressure from lumber interests, the House in 1970 refused to take up the bill, and it died at the end of the session. *(p. 770)*

The House Agriculture Subcommittee on Forests held hearings in May on a proposed timber supply bill (HR 10344). In June, John L. McMillan (D S.C.), subcommittee chairman, offered a new bill (HR 12025) said to incorporate suggestions made at the hearings by conservation groups and the Forest Service.

The full committee reported HR 12025 in November. W. R. Poage (D Texas), committee chairman, abstained.

The committee's report described the bill as one answer to housing conditions that "are a disgrace to this nation, degrading to our citizens, costly to our economy and extremely dangerous to the health of the country." Only nine of the committee's 33 members had voted for the 1968 Housing and Urban Development Act (PL 90-448). *(Congress and the Nation Vol. II p. 215)*

In dissenting views filed with the committee report, Charles M. Teague (R Calif.) said the bill would lower lumber prices and encourage housing "only incidentally, if at all."

Provisions. As reported by the committee, HR 12025:

• Directed the secretary of agriculture to revise immediately allowable annual national forest harvesting rates subject to the Multiple Use-Sustained Yield Act of 1960 (PL 86-517) in order to develop optimum timber productivity.

• Credited all unallocated receipts from the sale of timber from national forests to a High Timber Yield Fund to be established in the United States Treasury.

• Provided that the use of money from the fund be under the regular appropriations process; allowed money appropriated to be available until expended and provided that money credited to the fund and not appropriated within two years following the year it was credited would be transferred to the Treasury.

• Provided that the fund be allocated as determined by the secretary of agriculture.

• Required that the use of the money be in conformity with the Multiple Use-Sustained Yield Act of 1960 which directed the secretary of agriculture to administer the national forests for the development of outdoor recreation, range, watershed and fish and wildlife resources as well as timber. The 1960 act further directed the secretary to manage the resources in order to maintain a perpetually high level of renewable resources. *(Congress and the Nation Vol. I, p. 1057)*

• Required that the fund be used only to increase the timber yield through a number of specified management practices.

• Directed the secretary to submit to Congress within one year from enactment of HR 12025 a program for development and management of all national forest resources.

Related Actions. In a related administrative move, President Nixon March 19 ordered the sale of publicly owned timber increased by 1.1 billion board feet over a 15-month period in an effort to dampen the lumber price spiral. The President announced the action after his Council of Economic Advisers had reported that softwood and plywood prices had risen 92 per cent over the past year.

The increase in lumber prices was held by George Romney, secretary of housing and urban development, to be partially responsible for the inability of government to meet the 1969 goal of 225,000 subsidized housing units set under the 1968 housing act. Under the existing price structure, Romney said, no more than 175,000 units could be built.

By the end of 1969, however, the President's move had had little visible effect. Actual construction of subsidized housing units for the year came to only 165,000.

MINING AND MINERALS POLICY. A bill (S 719) to establish a national mining and minerals policy was approved by the Senate Sept. 5, but the House took no action on the measure. The bill became law in revised form in 1970. *(p. 774)*

S 719 would have encouraged a strong domestic mining industry and the orderly development of domestic mineral resources to meet the nation's needs. The bill also would have fostered mining, mineral and metallurgical research to promote the efficient use of domestic mineral resources. Responsibility for carrying out the provisions of the bill, called the Mining and Minerals Policy Act of 1969, was given to the interior secretary.

SOLID WASTE DISPOSAL. Legislation to expand the federal role in solid waste disposal was the subject of hearings in the fall of 1969 before a Senate Public Works Subcommittee. Under consideration were measures to boost federal funds for the construction of waste treatment facilities and research and planning programs, but the committee failed to report out a bill. Congress in 1970 enacted a comprehensive revision of existing federal solid waste programs. *(p. 769)*

WILDLIFE PROTECTION

ENDANGERED SPECIES. Congress in 1969 moved to more closely protect endangered species of animals when it approved a bill (HR 11363—PL 91-135) designed to strengthen laws limiting the importation and sale of animals, fish and amphibians in danger of becoming extinct both in the United States and abroad.

The bill barred importation of endangered species of fish or wildlife and prohibited shipment in interstate commerce of amphibians, reptiles, mollusks or crustaceans if they were obtained in violation of any federal, state or foreign law.

In its report on the bill, the House Merchant Marine and Fisheries Committee noted that the International Union for the Conservation of Nature and Natural Resources had listed 275 mammals and more than 300 birds as endangered species. But it was the problem of the poaching of alligators that brought pressure for the bill.

At hearings in February of that year, an Interior Department spokesman said about 1,000 poachers were active in southern Florida despite a state law banning the killing of alligators.

The House, which had passed HR 11363 July 21, concurred Nov. 20 in a number of Senate amendments. The most significant among these revised the enforcement procedures and required the federal government to seek a multinational conference by June 30, 1971, to draw up an international convention on the conservation of endangered species. The Senate had passed the bill Nov. 10.

Background. The first comprehensive endangered species legislation was enacted in 1966. The Endangered Species Preservation Act (PL 89-669), gave the interior secretary authority to protect native species threatened with extinction and expanded his authority to manage the national wildlife refuge system.

The Endangered Species Conservation Act of 1969 (PL 91-135) expanded the 1966 law by giving the secretary authority to develop a list of species threatened with worldwide extinction and to prohibit their import into the United States. It also gave him authority to protect reptiles, amphibians, mollusks and crustaceans.

OTHER LEGISLATION

POPULATION COMMISSION. At the President's request, the Senate Sept. 29 passed a bill (S 2701) to set up a commission on population growth and the American future. A similar measure (HR 15165) was reported in the House in December, but no further action was taken in 1969. The bill became law in revised form in 1970. *(p. 776)*

President Nixon July 18 proposed an expanded government effort to meet the problems of population growth, including creation of a high-level commission to study the effects of U.S. population growth on government activities. *(Box, this page)*

In its report on S 2701, the Senate Government Operations Committee noted that the Senate May 27 had passed S J Res 60 establishing a commission on Balanced Economic Development. The committee recommended that the Commission on Population

---

Population Growth

President Nixon July 18, 1969, proposed an expanded government effort to meet the problems of population growth.

In what the White House said was the first message on population ever sent to Congress by a President, Nixon, said "One of the most serious challenges to human destiny in the last third of this century will be the growth of the population. Whether man's response to that challenge will be a cause for pride or for despair by the year 2000 will depend very much on what we do today."

Nixon pledged U.S. cooperation with international bodies dealing with population problems and a continuation of unilateral assistance to developing nations.

To deal with American population problems, the President proposed creation of a Commission on Population Growth and the American Future. He also committed the administration to providing voluntary family planning services within five years to an estimated 5 million low-income women, setting as a national goal "the provision of adequate family planning services within the next five years to all those who want them but cannot afford them."

Unwanted Births. Elimination of unwanted births, adopted by the administration as a national goal, would alleviate problems for all economic classes, but especially for the poor.

A study by Charles F. Westoff, professor of population research at Princeton University, found that from 1960 through 1968, between 35 and 40 per cent of the natural increase in U.S. population could be attributed to unwanted fertility. Thus, prevention of unwanted births might be expected to contribute considerably to a lessening of population growth.

But the poor, who wanted about the same number of children as the nonpoor, were less able to support an extra child and had less access to family planning services. HEW statistics showed the average number of children wanted by a wife was between 3.2 and 3.4 from the lowest to the highest income families. But only about 1 million of the 5 million targeted poor women were receiving help in preventing births in 1970.

Birth control had been called an attempt on the part of rich whites to control the number of the poor and blacks. But family planning services were nonetheless eagerly received where they were available.

Growth set up under S 2701 consider a balanced geographic distribution of population in its study of population growth.

As passed by the Senate, S 2701 directed the commission to investigate the probable course of population growth and internal migration, the government resources that would be required to deal with anticipated population growth and the effect of population growth on government activities.

The House Government Operations Committee in December reported HR 15165, a clean bill establishing a Commission on Population Growth and the American Future. The House measure was similar to the Senate-passed version but expanded the commission's mandate to include a study of the effect of population growth on environmental pollution and natural resources. HR 15165 also directed the commission to study the means "appropriate to the ethical values and principles of this society" by which the desired population level could be achieved.

According to news reports, the bill was opposed by House Speaker John W. McCormack (D Mass.), a Catholic, who kept the measure from going to the floor for a vote. The Rules Committee had not given the bill a rule when the session ended.

Related Hearings. In related hearings, a Senate subcommittee held hearings on population research activities of the federal government, a House subcommittee explored the effects of population growth on natural resources and another House subcommittee conducted hearings on legislation to establish an Office of Population Problems.

1970

1970 was a landmark year for environmental action. In a symbolic gesture emphasizing the importance of the environment, President Nixon signed the National Environmental Policy Act on Jan. 1 as his first official act of the new "decade." The act, which Congress had cleared the preceding December, made environmental protection a matter of national policy and established a Council on Environmental Quality to advise on ecological matters.

In February, Nixon sent Congress a major environmental message outlining a 37-point program of legislative and administrative actions. What was needed, he stressed, was "total mobilization" to clean up the environment.

In July, Nixon sent Congress a reorganization plan establishing an independent Environmental Protection Agency (EPA). The new agency, which came into being Dec. 2, consolidated major antipollution programs that previously were scattered among existing government agencies. William D. Ruckelshaus was confirmed by the Senate Dec. 2 as the first EPA administrator. At the time of his appointment, Ruckelshaus was serving as assistant attorney general, civil division.

Congress in 1970 cleared two far-reaching pollution abatement measures. The Clean Air Amendments of 1970, cleared Dec. 18, established specific deadlines for a 90 per cent reduction of certain pollutants from new automobiles. Both the administration and the automotive industry opposed the deadlines; the administration backed a provision leaving authority for setting the deadlines in the executive branch, and the industry claimed it could not meet the deadlines required by the bill. The measure also set up new research programs and established national air quality standards. It established controls on emission by new stationary sources of pollution and set new antipollution regulations for auto fuels and for aircraft engines and fuels.

"Earth Day"

Observance of "Earth Day" in 1970 by millions of Americans marked the peak of national harmony on environmental issues. Celebrated April 22, the day was devoted to study and protest of environmental problems, including several large rallies in New York City and Washington, D.C., environmental "teach-ins" and various community clean-up projects.

Congress adjourned for the day as at least 23 senators and 15 representatives spoke on environmental issues at gatherings across the nation.

President Nixon took no formal role in the proceedings, but a White House spokesman released a statement saying the President "feels the activities show the concern of people of all walks of life over the dangers to our environment."

The effort, originally suggested by Sen. Gaylord Nelson (D Wis.), was designed to focus national attention on environmental problems, just as the 1969 demonstrations against the Vietnam War sharpened public opinion on that issue. Nelson and Rep. Paul N. McCloskey Jr. (R Calif.) sponsored a group, the Environmental Teach-In, formed early in 1970 to organize Earth Day activities. The group estimated that at least 2,000 colleges, 10,000 primary and secondary schools and 2,000 communities undertook Earth Day observances.

Earth Day was lengthened to Earth Week by presidential proclamation in 1971 and again in 1972. But enthusiasm for "save the earth" activities dwindled each year as the public began to question the economic costs of cleaning up the environment.

Earlier in the year, Congress completed action on the Water Quality Improvement Act, which set liability for cleanup costs of oil spills and established controls on acid mine drainage. Related legislation to help communities build water sewage treatment plants did not get out of committee in either chamber.

President Nixon Aug. 11 vetoed the first fiscal 1971 appropriations bill (HR 17548) for the Department of Housing and Urban Development (HUD) and various independent agencies, in part because it contained $500-million—$350-million more than his budget request—for HUD's basic water and sewer facilities grants. He signed a second bill (HR 19830—PL 91-556) that appropriated $350-million for the program. *(Chapter on Housing)* Congress also appropriated, in the fiscal 1971 public works appropriations bill (HR 18127—PL 91-439), $1-billion for construction grants to states and localities for sewage treatment works.

Congress Oct. 13 cleared a major bill, the Resource Recovery Act of 1970, that contained a three-year, $463.75-million authorization for solid waste disposal programs. The measure gave greater emphasis than existing federal programs to the recycling and recovery of materials from solid waste. Other bills enacted in 1970 established a national minerals and mining policy and created a commission to study population growth.

Concluding a five-year study, the Public Land Law Review Commission June 23 recommended stringent controls over the environment on the 775 million acres of federally owned public land—one-third of the nation's land area. Action on the recommendations was held over for the 92nd Congress.

Environmental Agencies

President Nixon in July 1970 sent to Congress two reorganization plans to establish an independent Environmental Protection Agency (EPA) and a National Oceanic and Atmospheric Administration (NOAA). Congress did not approve resolutions vetoing the proposals, thereby endorsing formation of both agencies.

The Environmental Protection Agency (EPA) consolidated all major programs to combat pollution in a single agency independent of existing departments. It was comprised of the Federal Water Quality Administration and certain pesticide research programs, formerly in the Interior Department; the National Air Pollution Control Administration and parts of the Environmental Control Administration and Food and Drug Administration, all formerly in the Department of Health, Education and Welfare; the pesticides registration authority of the Department of Agriculture; the standard-setting functions of the Atomic Energy Commission; the Federal Radiation Council's functions, and certain research authority of the Council on Environmental Quality.

The National Oceanic and Atmospheric Administration (NOAA) assumed the functions of the Environmental Science Services Administration, then in the Commerce Department; the Bureau of Mines' Marine Minerals Technology program, most of the Bureau of Commercial Fisheries, and the marine sports fishing program of the Bureau of Sports Fisheries and Wildlife, all in Interior; the Office of Sea Grant Programs of the National Science Foundation; parts of the Army's U.S. Lake Survey; the Navy's National Oceanographic Data and Instrumentation Centers; and the national data buoy program of the Transportation Department.

House Action. The House Government Operations Committee endorsed both reorganization plans in September and issued reports recommending that the veto resolutions be defeated.

Regarding Reorganization Plan No. 3 establishing an Environmental Protection Agency, the report said the new agency would be "a favored step in the federal government's effort to improve our environment" even though it did not include several existing pollution control programs.

The report on Reorganization Plan No. 4 establishing the National Oceanic and Atmospheric Administration expressed some reservations about transferring sport fishing and commercial fisheries programs from the Interior Department to the Commerce Department. But it added that Commerce "does now seem to be moving in the direction of becoming a scientific and technologic services agency with less emphasis than formerly on commerce and business." The committee said it would "closely watch" the performance of the new unit.

Later that month the House defeated veto resolutions (H Res 1209 and H Res 1210) by voice votes.

Most members who spoke defended the proposed changes. The only major opposition came from John D. Dingell (D Mich.), one of the House's leading conservationists. Dingell recommended that the House establish a cabinet-level Department of Environmental Quality rather than let a new agency be established through a reorganization plan.

Senate Action. Only one veto resolution—pertaining to the establishment of the National Oceanic and Atmospheric Administration—was filed in the Senate. The Government Operations Committee reported the resolution (S Res 433) with the recommendation that it be defeated and that the plan be allowed to go into effect.

The committee also issued a special report explaining the reasons it endorsed Reorganization Plan No. 3 establishing the new environmental agency.

The report on S Res 433 said that the Commerce Department was the proper place for the new division. "It will be associated with the department already having primary responsibility for research, monitoring and development regarding the sea and atmosphere."

The Senate in October by a 5-47 roll-call vote defeated S Res 433.

Leading the opposition to the National Oceanic and Atmospheric Administration was Gaylord Nelson (D Wis.). He said the plan did not make clear "where the responsibilities will be placed." The plan did not establish jurisdiction over such important problems as wetlands development, handling oil spills, dumping of solid wastes in the oceans or proposed construction of floating airports, he said.

AIR QUALITY

Air Pollution

After a year of aroused public concern over the declining quality of the air, Congress Dec. 18 completed action on the most comprehensive air pollution control bill in U.S. history. The $1.1-billion, three-year program (HR 17255—PL 91-604), which set specific deadlines for the reduction of certain hazardous automobile emissions, was signed into law by President Nixon Dec. 31 despite his disapproval of one portion of the bill.

The Nixon administration and the automobile industry had both exerted pressure on Congress to allow the executive agency in charge of air pollution abatement to set deadlines for cleaning up potentially hazardous exhaust fumes in new model cars. Despite the strenuous lobbying effort by automobile manufacturers, Congress agreed to a provision which required by law that model year 1975 cars must emit 90 per cent less carbon monoxide and hydrocarbons than did model year 1970 cars. The bill also specified that nitrogen oxides in 1976 model cars must be reduced by 90 per cent compared with model year 1971 levels.

A one-year extension of the deadlines could be granted by the administrator of the new Environmental Protection Agency (EPA), which in early December assumed control over the air pollution programs formerly administered by the Department of Health, Education and Welfare (HEW). Such an extension was granted in 1973. *(Box, p. 758)*

(Continued on p. 759)

One-Year Extension of Auto-Emission Standards

After three tries, auto makers in April 1973 won a one-year extension of the strict auto emission standards imposed by Congress in the Clean Air Act of 1970. The postponement marked the resolution of one of the most controversial environmental issues debated in 1971-72.

Under the 1970 legislation, automobile manufacturers were required to reduce engine emissions of carbon monoxide and unburned hydrocarbons by 1975 by 90 per cent compared with 1970 model year levels. A similar reduction in nitrogen oxides was prescribed by 1976.

The law permitted the administrator of the Environmental Protection Agency (EPA) to grant a single one-year extension of the deadline if he determined that the suspension was essential to public interest or health; manufacturers had made a good faith effort to meet the deadline; the applicant had proved that the necessary technology was not available, and that a study by the National Academy of Sciences indicated that such alternatives were not available.

But auto makers' requests for the postponement could not be made until January 1972 for the carbon monoxide and hydrocarbon standards or until January 1973 for the nitrogen oxide standard.

Extension Twice Denied. On March 13, 1972, the first automobile manufacturers requested a one-year extension of the 1975 model year deadline. The three top auto makers—the Ford Motor Company, the Chrysler Corporation and the General Motors Corporation—April 5 petitioned William D. Ruckelshaus, the EPA administrator, to grant the delay.

The companies argued that the standards were unreasonable and impossible to meet under existing technology. Even if devices to clean up auto exhaust were perfected in time, the industry contended, they would reduce automobile performance and add up to $860 to the price of a new car.

Contending that a combination of catalysts—to convert hydrocrabons and carbon monoxide into harmless carbon dioxide and water vapor—and other technological devices would meet the exhaust standards, Ruckelshaus turned down their request May 12.

The auto companies appealed his decision June 8. The appellate court remanded the issue to Ruckelshaus Dec. 19, directing him to consider a report issued Jan. 1, 1972, by the National Academy of Sciences which stated that technology was "not available at this time" and could be perfected and implemented only if several conditions were met.

Ruckelshaus reaffirmed his earlier decision Dec. 30, stating that his conclusion was consistent with the academy's findings.

EPA Case Not Proven. In a second appeal of the EPA decision, the auto companies asked the U.S. Court of Appeals for the District of Columbia to order a year's extension of the 1975 deadline. The court refused to do this, noting that the administrator had not determined that such a delay was in the public interest or that manufacturers had acted in good faith.

But the court ordered Ruckelshaus to reconsider his refusal to grant the postponement, saying his "reliance on technological methodology to offset the actual tests raised serious doubts and failed to meet the burden of proof which, in our view, was properly assignable to him."

Technology Questioned. During 12 days of hearings in March 1973 on the proposed delay, auto manufacturers argued that they could not meet the emission-control standards on a mass-production basis in time for the start-up of 1975 model year production, set to go on the market in September 1974.

But three foreign manufacturers—the makers of Mazda, Honda and Mercedes-Benz—already had met the 1975 emission standards and showed great promise for meeting the tougher 1976 standards. In addition, a report released Feb. 16, 1973, by the National Academy of Sciences concluded that the auto makers probably would be able to meet the 1975 standards but were focusing on the most costly and least satisfactory technology.

Extension Granted. Ruckelshaus April 11 gave the manufacturers the additional year to meet emission standards they had requested, but imposed interim standards far stricter than the industry had contended were feasible. Ruckelshaus said he had granted the extension to avoid the "potential societal disruptions" which auto makers had threatened would result—including a shutdown of the industry—if pollution-abatement equipment was required on all 1975 model year cars.

Instead, Ruckelshaus—using authority granted by the 1970 law—set interim standards for California which in effect required antipollution devices on all cars sold there, about 10 per cent of the national market. He ordered less stringent standards for the rest of the nation.

The following table shows the levels of exhaust emissions of hydrocarbons and carbon monoxide, in grams per mile, permitted for pre-1968 (uncontrolled) vehicles, under the original 1975 standards, the California 1975 interim standards and the national 1975 interim standards:

	Hydrocarbons	Carbon Monoxide
Pre-1968	8.7	87
1975	.41	3.4
California	.9	9.0
National	1.5	15

Other Recommendations. In his statement, Ruckelshaus also recommended that Congress reconsider the nitrogen oxide emission standards slated to go into effect in 1976 because EPA studies "no longer support the reduction standard." He also asked Congress to give the EPA administrator "additional flexibility to handle distortions in the implementation of the act," such as occurred in Los Angeles, where EPA scientists in January 1973 suggested a drastic cutback in auto traffic as the only way the area could meet air pollution standards by 1977.

(Continued from p. 757)

While the bill was in a House-Senate conference, HEW Secretary Elliot L. Richardson, reflecting President Nixon's sentiments, requested that the power to set the emission deadlines be conferred on the EPA administrator rather than written into law.

The prevailing deadlines on passenger car emissions were included in the Senate version of the bill, passed Sept. 22 by a 73-0 roll-call vote. A far weaker House version of the bill, which contained no deadlines, was passed June 10 by a 374-1 roll-call vote. In conference, the Senate version was adopted. *(Comparison of bills, p. 762)*

Other provisions of the bill as cleared included establishment of new research programs and assistance to states to set up pollution control programs. It required the EPA administrator to devise national primary—pertaining to public health—and secondary—pertaining to welfare—air quality standards. It also put controls on emissions by new stationary sources of pollution. The final bill established new antipollution regulations for auto fuels and for aircraft engines and fuels.

When President Nixon signed the bill in a ceremony before newsmen, he called it a "cooperative effort" of both parties. Conspicuously absent from the group of senators and representatives who had been invited to witness the signing, however, was the bill's chief architect, Sen. Edmund S. Muskie (D Maine). Muskie, a potential candidate for the presidency in 1972, had not been invited. A Nixon aide explained the ceremonial room was too small to accommodate all 40 sponsors of the bill and when asked why Muskie had not been invited to witness the signing of what had been called the "Muskie bill," the aide said, "I don't believe it's been called that—in this room."

Background

Most air is contained in the first two thousand feet of the troposphere. Since man discovered fire, this shallow layer of air surrounding the earth has become a giant wastebasket for the byproducts of massive combustion. The atmosphere does have a natural self-cleansing process which operates as long as there is enough time and space allowed. But scientists have warned that we have not been allowing nature sufficient time to catch its breath between our assaults on the purity of the air. It would be a mistake, scientists claimed, not to take the air pollution problem seriously. Some said it would be fatal.

Pollution Sources. Air polluters were divided into two categories—stationary (factories) and mobile (automobiles). Each year the stationary polluters were discharging two million tons of carbon monoxide, nine million tons of sulfur oxides, two million tons of nitrogen oxides, four million tons of hydrocarbons and six million tons of particulate matter. *(Box, p. 760)*

The big three industrial polluters were petroleum refineries (4.2 million tons of pollutants), smelters (4.15 million tons) and iron foundries (3.7 million tons). Power plants and the heating systems used in homes were also high on the list of stationary polluters.

Mobile polluters, a man driving the family car, composed the largest single contributor to pollution in the atmosphere. Exhaust from cars, trucks and buses spewed about 90 million tons of contaminants into the atmosphere every year—about 60 per cent of the total air pollution.

Previous Legislation. The federal government became involved in the problems of air pollution just after the Korean War, long before the public had heard of ecology. First congressional action came in 1955 with the passage of a bill (PL 84-159) which authorized the Public Health Service to conduct air pollution research. The $5-million authorized by the act was to cover expenses for fiscal years 1956-60.

The Clean Air Act of 1963 (PL 88-206) increased air pollution authorizations to $95-million for fiscal years 1964-67 and provided for a series of steps—culminating in legal action—that states, municipalities and the federal government could take to end interstate and intrastate air pollution (although for intrastate pollution the federal government could act only at the request of the state's governor). *(Congress and the Nation Vol. I, p. 1136-50)*

A second title (PL 89-272) was added to the Clean Air Act in 1965 directing the secretary of health, education and welfare to establish emission standards for new motor vehicles. The first standards for hydrocarbon and carbon monoxide exhaust emissions were published in 1966 and were applicable to most new gas-powered motor vehicles beginning with the model year 1968.

Legislation enacted in 1967 (PL 90-148) substantially strengthened the powers of local, state and federal authorities. It authorized the secretary of the Department of Health, Education and Welfare to designate air quality regions throughout the country; provide full federal financing for regional control commissions to be established by state governors; and empowered the HEW secretary to enforce air quality standards in the control regions, if the states failed to adopt such standards and an acceptable pollution abatement plan within 15 months after receiving federal guidelines on air purity. The act also empowered the HEW secretary to go to court to prosecute violation of standards in an air quality region after 180 days' notice of violation. By the end of 1970 no state had full-scale standards and implementation plans in effect for any pollutants. As of May, 1970, 34 metropolitan air quality regions out of a projected 109 had been designated by the National Air Pollution Control Administration.

Airlines Agreement. A "gentlemen's agreement" between the Nixon administration and 31 of the nation's airline companies to install pollution control devices on most of 1,000 jetliners by the end of 1972 was announced Jan. 20. The airlines originally had sought until 1974 to make the necessary changes, which they said would cost $13-million to $15-million.

The devices would eliminate about 70 to 80 per cent of solid pollutants spewed into the air daily by flying jets. A government study estimated that about 34,500 pounds of solid pollutants were emitted each day by jet engines.

Health, Education and Welfare Secretary Robert H. Finch, announcing the agreement, said it eliminated any need for legislative or regulatory action by Congress. "I do not favor further legislation for an industry which has met its responsibility," he said.

Administration Request

In his Feb. 10, 1970, environmental message, President Nixon strongly urged Congress not only to extend appropriations for the 1967 act (which were set to expire June 30), but also to add further pollution-abatement authority to the provisions that were already law. He asked that the Clean Air Act be amended to:

• Give the federal government authority to set nationwide air quality standards for specific pollutants or combinations of pollutants from stationary sources. Under existing law, the states set air quality standards subject to federal approval, using federal criteria.

• Require the states to include emission standards in their implementation plans, subject to federal approval.

• Allow the federal government to set federal emission standards for stationary sources which "contribute substantially to endangerment of the public health or welfare."

• Strengthen and speed the federal enforcement process, doing way with the system of public hearings.

In regard to automobile emission control, the Nixon proposal would:

• Require federal testing of emission control devices on motor vehicles. Existing law provided for testing of prototypes only.

• Required federal regulation of fuels and fuel additives, and permit the federal government to establish standards for the composition of fuel and fuel additives to assure that they "will not cause or contribute to emissions which would endanger the public health or welfare, or impair the performance of any emission control device or system." Existing law required only that fuel additives be registered.

Finally, the President proposed that industries or municipalities failing to meet air quality standards and correction standards be subject to court action, ranging from injunctions to fines of up to $10,000 a day.

The President's proposal would abolish the existing system under which the federal government approved air quality standards set by the states to be applied within air quality control regions embracing major industrial and metropolitan areas.

In his environmental message, Nixon said that a national standard for emissions was necessary because the program established in 1967 for creating air quality control regions had "not gone far enough or fast enough.... There are no provisions for controlling pollution outside of established air quality regions. This is unfair not only to the public but to many industries as well, since those within regions with strict requirements could be unfairly disadvantaged with respect to competitors that are not within regions."

Nixon's proposal for national standards was questioned by Muskie, chief architect of the 1967 act, who said that the "minimum standard" of air quality would tend to become, under industry pressure on state governments, a maximum standard.

HOUSE ACTION

Committee. Following extended hearings on air pollution in March and April, the House Interstate and Foreign Commerce Committee June 3 reported a bill (HR 17255) that was similar in many respects to the administration recommendations.

The major deviation from the administration proposal concerned spot checks of pollution control devices in automobile assembly lines.

Constituents of Air Pollution

Pollutants fall into two main types, particles and gases. The particles include fly ash, the unburnable leftover of ordinary coal; soot, an incompletely burned carbon; and lead, the unburnable additive in gasoline. The brilliant red sunsets admired in New York City and Los Angeles are caused by large particles in the air, most of them produced by incomplete combustion in the generation of heat and power.

Less visible, but more damaging, are the gases. These include:

Sulphur dioxide. A product of the combustion of coal or oil that contains sulphur. Some 30.4 million tons are expelled into the air yearly, two-thirds from burning coal. In combination with moisture, including rain, or even the moist membranes of the lungs, sulphur dioxide can form sulphuric acid, a poison.

Hydrocarbons. Any of a class of compounds containing only hydrogen and carbon. They interact with nitrogen dioxide and the sun's ultraviolet rays to form smog. The most dangerous product of this process is the gas ozone. Levels of ozone in the atmosphere above .3 parts per million can cause eye, nose and throat irritations.

One hydrocarbon, benzo-a-pyrene, causes cancer in laboratory animals.

Carbon monoxide. Produced when carbon-containing substances, such as gasoline and tobacco, are burned. Reaches the highest relative concentrations of any gaseous pollutant in urban areas. Relatively small amounts of carbon monoxide can have harmful effects ranging from headaches to blackouts.

Carbon dioxide. Not usually classified as a pollutant, carbon dioxide has worried scientists because of its possible effects on the weather. Unlike carbon monoxide, sulphur dioxide and the other pollutants, carbon dioxide is the inevitable result of carbon combustion, the end product of even the cleanest burning, and a normal component of expired breath.

Hundreds of millions of tons of carbon dioxide are discharged into the atmosphere every year. Since 1860, fossil fuel burning has increased the atmospheric content of carbon dioxide about 14 per cent. It is expected to increase another 25 per cent by the year 2000, because of the growing combustion of petroleum and coal.

The annual increase has led to speculation about a possible "greenhouse effect," by which the warming properties of carbon dioxide will cause the planet to warm up enough so that the ice caps will slowly begin to melt. Carbon dioxide in the air allows less of the earth's heat to escape into outer space and could, a National Air Pollution Control Administration official said, cause a rise of the oceans by as much as 400 feet, submerging coastal cities.

The committee report concluded that progress in controlling air pollution since the enactment of the 1967 legislation had been "regrettably slow." The report blamed lack of progress on cumbersome and time-consuming procedures outlined in the act, inadequate funding on all levels, lack of skilled personnel and inadequacy of testing and control procedures.

Floor. By a 374-1 roll call vote, the House June 10 approved HR 17255, after adopting one technical amendment and rejecting eight others aimed at strengthening various sections of the bill.

Leonard Farbstein (D N.Y.), a proponent of higher standards, urged Congress to adopt standards which would drastically reduce pollution caused by vehicles and virtually eliminate it by the mid-1970s. "HR 17255 fails to achieve this objective. Indeed, it appears to bend over backward to accommodate the auto and oil industries," he said.

Farbstein offered an amendment which would have phased out the internal combustion engine on newly built vehicles in stages, starting with automobile engines with the greatest horsepower. The amendment failed by voice vote.

Another unsuccessful amendment rejected by voice vote also concerned vehicle emissions. Lionel Van Deerlin (D Calif.) proposed establishing voluntary inspection of pollution devices for vehicles after they had been driven 4,000 miles. He argued that defects might not show up on assembly line inspections, as provided by the bill, but would become evident after the cars had been driven for a while.

John P. Saylor (R Pa.) recommended allowing states to set higher vehicle emission standards than federal levels if the secretary of HEW found that extraordinary circumstances existed. California had permission to set such standards, but other states were specifically forbidden to impose more stringent regulations regarding auto exhausts. Daniel E. Button (R N.Y.) proposed another amendment which would have applied the California levels to the rest of the nation. Both amendments were rejected.

Robert O. Tiernan (D R.I.) offered an amendment which would have substituted the language of the administration bill's section on fuel and fuel additives for the language in the bill reported by the committee. Tiernan said the committee version put all responsibility for improving emissions on auto manufacturers and none on fuel manufacturers.

Before debate began, proponents of stricter standards attempted to defeat the rule granted by the Rules Committee for consideration of the bill. They complained of the "undue haste" with which the bill was brought to the floor. But the resolution on the rule was adopted by a 335-40 roll-call vote.

Senate Action

Committee. The Senate Public Works Committee Sept. 17 reported S 4358, authorizing $1.27-billion for air cleanup programs. The bill as reported included a controversial provision that automobiles must cut back their pollution by 90 per cent from existing levels by 1975.

Final committee action had been held up while members worked out a compromise on the deadline for low-pollution cars. The bill reported by the Subcommittee on Air and Water Pollution had set 1975 as the final deadline, with no extensions. After heavy lobbying by officials of the automobile industry, the full committee Sept. 10 voted 10-3 to include a one-year extension and a provision allowing for judicial review of the extension. The next day, the committee voted unanimously to order the bill reported.

In addition to the automobile section, the committee bill set up a schedule for establishing and implementing air quality standards, beginning 30 days after enactment of the bill and proceeding in stages until pollution emission was controlled in about five and a half years.

The bill would "provide a much more intensive and comprehensive attack on air pollution, the committee declared in its report. It would establish that the air is a public resource, and that those who would use that resource must protect it from abuse, to assure the protection of the health of every American."

Floor. By a unanimous 73-0 roll call, the Senate Sept. 22 approved a three-year, $1.27-billion extension (HR 17255) of the Clean Air Act, including a requirement that auto exhaust emissions be curbed by 90 per cent by 1975.

Before passage, the Senate had substituted the language of the committee recommendations (S 4358) for that of HR 17255.

The Senate version of HR 17255 was far more stringent than that passed by the House June 10. The House version contained no low-pollution deadline for automobile engines and weaker requirements for testing new cars and controlling vehicle fuels. It also contained lower authorizations for research and other activities.

The automobile pollution deadline was the chief focus of the two days' debate on the bill. The controversial provision required automobile manufacturers to comply by Jan. 1, 1975, with standards lowering engine exhaust emissions by 90 per cent from 1970 model year levels. But a one-year postponement of the deadline could be granted to manufacturers who proved that, despite a good-faith effort, they could not meet the 1975 cut-off date. Edmund S. Muskie (D Maine), floor manager of the bill, declared, "Detroit has told the nation that Americans cannot live without the automobile. This legislation would tell Detroit that if that is the case, then they must make an automobile with which Americans can live."

The only major opposition to the deadlines came from Robert P. Griffin (R Mich.), who represented the home state of the auto industry. He called the deadline "the concept of brinkmanship—an industry pivotal to the U.S. economy is to be required by statute to meet standards which the committee itself acknowledges cannot be met with existing technology." The auto industry supported 800,000 jobs directly and more than 14 million other jobs indirectly—28 per cent of private nonfarm employment in the nation. Cars and trucks accounted for 10 per cent of all tax revenues and expenditures for automotive transportation accounted for 16 per cent of the gross national product, he said. "This bill holds a gun at the head of the American automobile industry in a very dangerous game of economic roulette."

Two other Republicans offered amendments aimed at softening the impact of the 1975 deadline—but not doing away with it entirely. Robert Dole (R Kan.) offered an amendment eliminating the provision for judicial re-

(Continued on p. 763)

Administration, House, Senate Air Pollution Bills Compared

President Nixon included numerous legislative proposals on air pollution in a Feb. 10 message on the environment. The administration bill (S 3466), extending the Clean Air Act for three years, through fiscal 1973, was introduced Feb. 18 by Senate Minority Leader Hugh Scott (R Pa.). The House June 10 by a 374-1 roll-call vote passed HR 17255, a three-year air pollution bill, and the Senate passed a different version by a 73-0 roll-call vote Sept. 22. A comparison of major provisions of the three bills follows:

Air Quality Standards

Administration—Required the secretary of the Department of Health, Education and Welfare (HEW) to devise national standards for pulluting agents within six months of enactment, and to publish information on recommended control techniques. Required states or interstate agencies to devise and implement plans for putting the standards into effect. Authorized the secretary to regulate emissions from stationary sources of pollution and to request that the Justice Department take action against violators of those regulations. Maximum penalties were set at $100 per day.

House—Required national standards for polluting agents, made each state an air quality region and authorized the secretary to designate interstate air quality regions. Allowed the secretary to regulate emissions from new stationary sources of pollution. Allowed the Justice Department to bring suit against violators, and set maximum punishment at $10,000 per day. Allowed federal inspections for pollution violations.

Senate—Required national standards for polluting agents and completion of the designation of air quality control regions, both under set timetables. Set timetables for state implementation of the plans, and authorized states to adopt local standards stricter than national ones. Established a new category of extremely hazardous pollutants which must be banned entirely. Allowed the HEW secretary to bring action against violators, and set maximum penalties at $25,000 per day and one year in prison for the first convictions, $50,000 and two years, thereafter. Required federal installations to comply with local pollution standards.

Limitations on Vehicles

Administration—Authorized certification and testing of new vehicles and engines (standards would be set by administrative action, not law) and of imported vehicles and engines.

House—Required the federal government to test new motor vehicles or engines coming off an assembly line to determine if they conform with emission standards, and authorized the HEW Department to revoke certification of any violators. Required the states to establish inspection programs if the federal government determined it was necessary and feasible. Directed the HEW Department to conduct re-

search to develop low-cost instruments to measure vehicle emissions. (The House defeated by nonrecorded votes amendments to allow states to set standards higher than national ones, set specific emission standards, phase out the internal combustion engine, and establish voluntary programs of vehicle inspection after 4,000 miles of actual use). The bill allowed the HEW Department and the Federal Aviation Administration to devise emission standards for aircraft and aircraft engines.

Senate—Required that by Jan. 1, 1975, or with model year 1975 all automobiles and other light duty vehicles and their engines must lower emissions by 90 per cent, compared with 1970 levels. Allowed manufacturers to obtain a one-year extension of the deadline, subject to judicial review. Allowed states to implement more stringent standards. Required certification of all new vehicles and engines, testing procedures, and a pollution warranty system including cost information for the devices. Applied standards to life of car or engine, and established controls for used cars and antipollution devices. Established a federal procurement program for low-emission vehicles. Authorized standards for aircraft, vessels and other types of vehicles and their engines.

Fuel Regulation

Administration—Allowed the HEW secretary to regulate fuel and fuel additives and to establish standards for fuel composition. Established maximum punishment for violators at $10,000 per day.

House—Authorized the HEW secretary to set limitations on or provide for elimination of ingredients of fuels, including additives, which endanger public welfare or interfere with emission control devices in vehicles. Such action must be based on relevant medical and scientific evidence, and the evidence must show that equivalent standards could not economically or technically be achieved through higher emission standards for vehicles rather than changes in fuel composition. (The House by voice vote rejected an amendment substituting the administration provision for this one.)

Senate—Authorized the secretary to prohibit the use of any fuel in commerce which may provide emissions that would endanger the public health, and established maximum punishment for violators at $10,000 per day.

Authorizations

Administration—Open-ended.

House—$755-million over three years, including $300-million for research and $475-million for other activities.

Senate—$1.27-billion over three years, including $465-million for research, $775-million for other activities, and $30-million for a new program of noise pollution research.

(Continued from p. 761)
view of the one-year extension and instead allowing it to go into effect automatically unless vetoed in 60 days by either chamber of Congress. "While I have no quarrel with judicial review as an orderly procedure, in this instance... why should not Congress have the final word on whether or not the extension should be granted?" he asked. "If we are willing to impose deadlines today we should be willing to determine in the future whether the deadlines should be extended."

Muskie supported the amendment, but it failed by a 32-43 roll call.

The key vote during Senate consideration of the bill came on an amendment offered by Edward Gurney (R Fla.) as an amendment to Dole's proposal. Gurney's amendment would have eliminated the requirement that a manufacturer's request for extension of the 1975 deadline must be made 12 months to 24 months prior to the expiration of the five-year time limit. Gurney said the manufacturers might need additional time "to jell...the elements that go into the (car) model as well as the anti-pollution device." The amendment was rejected by a **key 22-57 roll-call vote.**

Conference Action

House and Senate conferees Dec. 17 filed a report on HR 17255. The biggest single issue in dispute between House and Senate versions of the bill dealt with the establishment of specific deadlines for a 90 per cent reduction of specified automobile emissions. Conferees agreed to retain the 1975 deadlines for carbon monoxide and hydrocarbons and a 1976 deadline for nitrogen oxides. Each was subject to a one-year extension if the EPA administrator decided that the earlier dates were not feasible. The Senate bill had specified a 1975 deadline, with a one-year extension for hazardous emissions, but it did not include in the bill a description of what those emissions were. There was no comparable House provision.

Conferees agreed to grant auto manufacturers a three-year period in which to apply for extension of the first deadlines; the Senate bill had allowed them only 24 months in which to make this request.

Conferees also agreed to limit automobile anti-pollution requirements to five years or 50,000 miles, whichever came first, rather than the life of the car. They also modified the provisions concerning inspections, warranties and testing.

Fuel. Conferees agreed to a provision allowing the administrator to control or prohibit fuels or fuel additives which harm public health or welfare, or impair a device or system to control emissions. Before taking this step, the administrator must consider certain technical and cost factors; states, except for California, were not allowed to devise standards for fuels stronger than federal regulations. (California had already enacted stricter laws regarding air pollution.) The House provision strictly limited prohibitions on fuel components, and the Senate gave the administrator virtual blanket authority to control fuels.

Air Quality Standards. The conference version allowed the federal government to set "primary" quality standards—those which affect public health—but left to states chief control over "secondary" air standards pertaining to public welfare. The bill set procedures and timetables for federal and state action, and required regulation over new stationary sources of pollution. It established grant programs for planning and implementing state pollution control plans with special emphasis on programs serving more than one locality. It also required federal installations to comply with such regulations.

The House bill included provisions setting up national standards for designated pollutants and control of new stationary sources of pollution. The Senate bill did not make a differentiation between primary and secondary air quality standards.

Authorizations. The final version of the bill included authorizations of $1.1-billion over three fiscal years. In contrast, the House had voted $775-million over three years (fiscal 1971-73); the Senate had approved $1.27-billion over the three-year period.

Final Action. The Senate Dec. 18 by voice vote adopted the conference report on HR 17255. Muskie, chief sponsor of the measure, called it "a tough bill." He stressed that the bill "intends that all Americans in all parts of the country shall have clean air to breathe within the 1970s."

The House adopted the conference report on the bill the same day by voice vote, thus clearing it for the President's signature.

Final Provisions

As signed by the President Dec. 31, HR 17255 (PL 91-604) contained the following major provisions:

Air Quality Standards

- Required the administrator of the Environmental Protection Agency (EPA) to publish a list of air pollution agents for which air quality criteria would be issued; the first such list must be published within 30 days of enactment of the bill. Specific criteria must be issued within 12 months after the pollutants were designated.

- Required the administrator to publish national primary and secondary ambient (average) air quality standards for each agent which was already cited as a pollutant when the bill went into effect. For other pollution agents, the administrator must publish national standards at the same time pollutants are designated. (Primary standards specify the minimum air quality needed to protect public health and secondary standards promote public welfare.) The administrator must promulgate primary air quality standards; states must devise plans for secondary standards.

- Authorized the administrator to specify and set emission standards for hazardous air pollutants—those having a proven relationship to increased human death rates or serious illness. The administrator could grant waivers of up to two years for compliance with the standards. The President also was authorized to grant such waivers if he found technology did not exist or if national security required such action. States had the primary task to enforce the regulations.

- Required the administrator to publish periodically, starting within 90 days of enactment of the bill, lists of the categories of new stationary (non-mobile) pollution sources and set emission standards. The administrator could formulate or enforce plans where states failed to act.

• Required the administrator to emphasize research on the effects of air pollution agents, singly and in combinations, on public health and welfare.

State Implementation Plans

• Required each state, after public hearings, to adopt plans for implementing, maintaining and enforcing the standards and goals promulgated for each air control region, or portion of a region, within that state. Such plans must be submitted to the federal government within nine months after the standards and goals were promulgated and were to be approved or disapproved within four months. The administrator could approve the plan if it provided for attainment of primary air quality standards in three years; included emission requirements and schedules of compliance; included provisions for monitoring devices; included effective procedures to control new pollution sources; provided for intergovernmental cooperation; provided that each state would have adequate personnel, funding and authority to enforce the plan, and provided for periodic inspection and testing of motor vehicles. The administrator could grant extensions of up to 18 months for submission of plans, and up to three years for implementation of plans.

• Authorized the administrator to formulate plans for states which did not submit plans or which submitted plans that were not approved; the administrator could also provide for hearings if the states made no such provision, or he could require the revision of already approved plans if he later found them to be inadequate.

• Required each state to be responsible for air quality within its boundaries. Existing interstate and intrastate air quality control regions were maintained; the administrator was directed to designate other control regions within 90 days.

• Authorized the EPA to provide up to two-thirds of the planning costs and up to half of the operating costs of establishing or improving air quality control programs serving a single municipality, or up to 75 per cent of planning costs and 60 per cent of operating costs for programs serving two or more municipalities. Part of these grants could be in the form of technical aid provided by federal personnel.

• Authorized the EPA to provide 100 per cent of costs for two years, and 75 per cent of costs thereafter, for implementation plans for interstate air quality control regions.

Automobile and Fuel Regulations

• Authorized the administrator to set emission standards for all potentially dangerous pollutants from new motor vehicles and engines.

• Required that engines of automobiles and other light duty vehicles, beginning with model year 1975, must comply with standards lowering emissions of carbon monoxide and hydrocarbons by 90 per cent compared with the model year 1970 levels; and by model year 1976 with standards lowering emissions of nigrogen oxides by 90 per cent compared with the model year 1971 level. The administrator must report annually to Congress on matters relevant to control systems.

• Permitted manufacturers to apply for one-year extensions of the carbon monoxide and hydrocarbon deadlines after Jan. 1, 1972, and for the nitrogen oxide deadline after Jan. 1, 1973. The administrator must act on the requests within 60 days; if he granted the requests, he was required to establish interim standards at the same time. The National Academy of Sciences was authorized to study the technological feasibility of meeting the standards.

• Required passenger car pollution control standards to be effective for five years or 50,000 miles, whichever was less, according to regulations set by the administrator. He could also set standards for other types of vehicles and engines.

• Prohibited the sale of new cars or engines not in compliance with standards; prohibited the removal of pollution control devices. Violations would be subject to a civil penalty of up to $10,000.

• Required the administrator to conduct tests on new vehicles or engines submitted by manufacturers or new pollution abatement devices and to issue one-year certifications of conformity. The administrator could also perform assembly line tests and suspend or revoke certification of non-conforming vehicles manufacturered after that date or produced prior to that date and still in the manufacturer's possession. The suspension would continue until conformity was again achieved. EPA employees could inspect plants and records.

• Required warranties, under standards set by the administrator, which would cover all purchasers and would require the manufacturer to bear costs of repairs to achieve compliance. After a vehicle had been sold, an inspection of its pollution abatement devices could be made only with the owner's permission.

• Authorized the administrator to control or prohibit sale of any fuel or fuel additive if he found that emissions from it would endanger public health or interfere with passenger cars' pollution control devices. The administrator must take into account technical and cost factors. No state could implement regulations regarding fuels which were stricter than federal levels unless such regulations were part of its air quality plan. Civil penalties were set at $10,000 per day.

• Authorized the administrator to grant states up to two-thirds of the cost of developing and maintaining effective vehicle inspection programs and emission testing and control programs.

• Established a federal low-emission vehicle procurement program in the federal government. The government was authorized to purchase any vehicles certified to be low-polluting at a premium price of up to 150 per cent of the lowest cost of conventional car models which they were replacing. The premium could be raised to 200 per cent for especially innovative cars. The bill authorized $5-million for fiscal 1971 and $25-million annually for fiscal 1972 and 1973.

• Authorized the administrator to encourage research on air pollution in relation to fuels and low-emission alternatives to the existing internal combustion engine with authorizations of $75-million for fiscal 1971; $125-million for fiscal 1972, and $150-million for fiscal 1973.

Enforcement

• Authorized the administrator to seek injunctions to stop pollution sources which endangered public health, if local or state authorities had not acted to seek abatement.

• Authorized citizens or groups to bring suits in federal courts against either the administrator—for failure to perform specified duties—or alleged violators, including government agencies.

• Authorized the attorney general to go to court to require that the owner of any patent relating to emission limitations make the information available to any person who needed it in order to comply with standards set by the bill. The court would determine payments to the patent owner.

• Set punishments for violations of implementation plans. The administrator was required to give prior notification to both the person violating the plans and the state in which the violation occurred. If corrective action was not taken, he could issue an order requiring compliance or bring civil suits against the violator. A person who knowingly violated an implementation plan or an abatement order could be punished by a fine of up to $25,000 for each day of violation and a year in prison, or up to $50,000 per day and two years in prison for persons with previous violations. Anyone convicted of falsifying information or tampering with monitoring devices was subject to a fine of up to $10,000 and six months in prison.

Aircraft

• Required the administrator, following a study and hearings, to formulate standards for aircraft emissions. The secretary of transportation was to help formulate the standards and enforce them. States could not implement standards more stringent than those set by the federal government. The administrator of the Federal Aviation Administration must set aviation fuel standards, following consultation with the EPA administrator.

Noise Pollution

• Established within the EPA a new Office of Noise Abatement and Control to study noise pollution and its effect on the public health and welfare. The office would be authorized to look into problems associated with all types of noise, including sonic booms. One year after enactment of the bill, the administrator would be required to report on the study to the President and Congress, and to request new legislation. The bill authorized $30-million for the noise program. *(Report, legislation, p. 817)*

Funds

• Authorized for carrying out provisions of the act other than those specified above: fiscal 1971, $125-million; fiscal 1972, $225-million, and fiscal 1973, $300-million.

RELATED LEGISLATION

As part of the intense congressional focus on air cleanup programs in 1970, the Senate March 20 passed but the House failed to consider legislation to encourage the development of low-emission cars. But a similar program was set up under the Clean Air Act of 1970 *(above)*.

The bill (S 3072) would have required the federal government to purchase available low-emission vehicles thereby assuring a market for innovative pollution abatement technology.

A vehicle certification board would have been authorized to purchase low-polluting vehicles for federal use at between 25 and 50 per cent above the average retail purchase and maintenance price for comparable commercial vehicles.

In its report on the bill, the Commerce Committee argued that adoption of national auto exhaust emission standards would not solve the nation's auto pollution problem. In the committee's view, the best solution was to develop a new low-polluting propulsion system.

WATER AND MARINE RESOURCES

Water Quality Improvement Act

After a five-month deadlock between House and Senate conferees Congress March 25 approved a major water pollution control bill (HR 4148) to help clean up the nation's waterways. The bill, aimed primarily at oil spills, was signed into law April 3 (PL 91-224) by President Nixon as the Water Quality Improvement Act of 1970.

The bill authorized the federal government to clean up disastrous oil spills which seriously jeopardized the nation's waters and beaches, with the polluter paying the costs, and placed new controls on sewage coming from vessels which fouled many of the nation's marinas, harbors and ports.

In addition to making petroleum companies liable for up to $14-million in cleanup costs for oil spills, HR 4148 also outlawed the flushing of raw sewage from boat toilets; strengthened restrictions on thermal pollution from nuclear power plants, and ordered development of criteria covering the effects of pesticides in streams, rivers and other waters. The bill also created an Office of Environmental Quality to act as a staff for the President's Council on Environmental Quality. The council had been established by Congress in 1969 to advise the President and Congress on environmental issues. *(p. 748)*

In 1969, the House and Senate had approved differing versions of HR 4148. The two versions varied so widely concerning the conditions of owner liability that conferees were unable to resolve differences during the first session of the 91st Congress—the third consecutive year that Congress had failed to complete action on a major water quality bill. *(1969 action, p. 749)*

National concern over water pollution—especially over numerous offshore oil spills in 1969 which coated beaches, killed marine life and damaged property—was credited with overcoming the vigorous opposition of the oil and gas lobbies to antipollution legislation. Failure of water pollution control bills to clear Congress in previous years had been attributed to the lobbies.

Conference Action. HR 4148 was sent to a House-Senate conference committee Oct. 9, 1969, but conferees were unable to resolve differences between the two versions when Congress adjourned.

The deadlock continued for five months—until March 24. A series of oil spills off the coasts of Florida, California and Louisiana preceded the conference committee's reaching an agreement and possibly contributed to the House conferees' acceptance of the Senate's "absolute liability" provision. (One staunch opponent of that principle had been Rep. William C. Cramer (R Fla.), the House Public Works Committee's ranking Republican. One of the oil spills just prior to the conference agreement was in Cramer's district, St. Petersburg, Fla. If absolute liability had been in effect, the federal government would have quickly stepped into the St. Petersburg situation because it would have been assured of reimbursement. The cleanup measures taken by the Humble Oil Company, owner of the cargo, were considered slow and ineffective by area residents.)

The chief hurdle faced by conferees was to work out differences over the liability issue. The House version, generally considered a weaker measure, held owners or operators of vessels which "willfully or negligently" discharged oil or other matter into a waterway responsible for up to $10-million or $100 per gross ton—whichever was less—for the costs of a federal government cleanup.

As approved by the Senate, HR 4148 provided absolute liability of the owner of a vessel except where the spill was the result of an act of God or certain other circumstances. Its version set a limit of $14-million or $125 a gross ton—whichever was less—on the amount of liability.

Conferees reached a compromise liability figure for the costs of cleanup of an amount not to exceed $14-million for a vessel and $8-million for an onshore or offshore facility. In the case of a vessel, the liability was further limited to $100 per gross ton.

In a case in which the United States could show that the discharge was the result of willful negligence or willful misconduct, the owner or operator was absolutely liable.

The owner or operator would not be liable if he could prove that the oil spill was caused solely by (a) an act of God, (b) an act of war, (c) negligence on the part of the United States, or (d) an act of omission of a third party, whether or not negligent. In the latter case, a third party would be liable for the actual costs of the oil cleanup.

Both House and Senate bills provided for a revolving fund in the U.S. Treasury to cover emergency oil cleanup costs. The House bill allocated $20-million and the Senate $50-million for the funds. Conferees agreed to $35-million.

Final Action. On March 24 the House-Senate conferees reached agreement and filed a conference report on the antipollution bill. The report was adopted by the Senate on the same day and by the House on March 25.

PROVISIONS. As signed into law April 3, HR 4148:

Oil Pollution. Declared it to be U.S. policy that there should be no oil discharges into navigable waters of the United States or adjoining shorelines.

• Authorized the President to act to remove an oil spill unless properly done by the owner or operator responsible for such spill.

• Established a liability to the United States for an oil spill of up to $100 per gross ton of oil or $14-million, whichever was lower, for a vessel and $8-million for an onshore or offshore facility, unless the spill resulted from an act of God, war, U.S. Government negligence or an act or omission of a third party.

• Established unlimited liability if an oil spill resulted from willful negligence or misconduct.

Hazardous Polluting Substances. Authorized the President to designate those discharges, other than oil, which constituted dangerous substances and to remove such substances, unless accomplished immediately by an owner or operator of a vessel or onshore or offshore facility.

Control of Sewage From Vessels. Provided means for the establishment of federal standards for marine sanitation devices to prevent discharge of untreated sewage into navigable waters of the United States.

Great Lakes Pollution. Authorized the federal government to enter into agreements with states or other political subdivisions or agencies to carry out demonstration projects on new methods and techniques for the elimination or control of pollution within the watersheds of the Great Lakes.

Federal Government Cooperation. Required compliance with water quality standards and the purposes of the Act by all federal agencies and departments engaged in public works activities of any kind.

• Required any applicant for a federal license or permit involving the construction or operation of facilities which could result in the discharge of substances into navigable waters to obtain a certification from the state in which the discharge would originate that there was reasonable assurance that such activity would not violate water quality standards.

• Provided means for revocation of federal licenses or permits for violation of water quality standards.

Office of Environmental Quality. Established in the Executive Office of the President an Office of Environmental Quality, to be directed by the chairman of the Council on Environmental Quality established in 1969 by PL 91-190. *(p. 748)*

Other Water Legislation

WATER POLLUTION CONTROL. Neither the House nor the Senate Public Works Committees completed action in 1970 on related water pollution legislation intended to aid communities building water sewage treatment plants. Bills—including an administration proposal—were considered which would have increased aid to communities for construction of facilities, streamlined existing programs and strengthened enforcement. The existing authorizations for water pollution programs were to expire June 30, 1971. A comprehensive water pollution abatement bill was approved by Congress in 1972. *(p. 792)*

Administration Requests. In a special message to Congress Feb. 10, President Nixon presented a program to clean up water pollution from municipal and industrial wastes.

"Federal appropriations for constructing municipal treatment plants have totaled about one-third of authorizations," Nixon declared, and municipalities have been unable "to finance their share of the construction costs."

Magnitude of Water Pollution Problem in 1970

During the 1960s, the water pollution problem had become increasingly severe. The United States had invested about $15-billion since 1952 in building 7,500 municipal sewage treatment plants and other water treatment facilities. But in 1970 some 1,400 U.S. communities and hundreds of industrial plants still dropped untreated waste into waters.

Only 140 million of the country's more than 200 million persons in 1970 were served by any kind of sewer system. The nation's water needs were constantly increasing—from 23.7 billion gallons per day in 1965 to 74.3 billion by 2020, according to the U.S. Water Resource Council. But expenditures of $1.2-billion in federal grants and $4.2-billion by localities had resulted in no improvement in water quality, according to a General Accounting Office (GAO) report issued in November 1969.

The Cuyahoga River in Cleveland, Ohio, caught fire in 1969; arsenic was found in the Kansas River; mercury pollution put a halt to fishing along the shores of Lake St. Clair on the Canadian border. Ohio banned commercial fishing in Lake Erie; conservationists contended millions of fish were dying in Lake Superior as a result of industrial pollutants.

"In the last 10 years, the quality of the nation's water has probably degenerated," commented David D. Dominick, commissioner of the Federal Water Pollution Control Administration.

Cost of Controls. Former Secretary of Interior Stewart Udall estimated that a water pollution control program through 1973 would cost almost $30-billion, including $8-billion for sewage treatment plants, and about $6-billion each for sewer lines, industrial treatment, and new operating and maintenance costs.

An estimate in *Fortune* magazine placed sewer and treatment plant costs at $10-billion, and the cost of ending industrial pollution at $33-billion.

Congress—and the taxpayers—seemed increasingly willing to face the challenge. An April 20 Louis Harris Poll reported that, in a dramatic switch of position over the past three years, 54 per cent of the American people in 1970 said they would be willing to pay $15 a year more in taxes to finance federal pollution control programs.

Treatment Methods. Debris, organic wastes and chemical effluents are the three major types of pollutants which can be removed with proper sewage treatment. Organic waste, as it decays, removes oxygen from water, diminishing the supply for marine life. Death of fish and production of noxious gases by bacteria that can live without oxygen may result from improper treatment of organic waste. Chemical wastes, like acid residue, DDT and some dyes can destroy marine organisms outright or in lesser quantities can affect their life processes.

Sticks, papers and the dust picked up by rain can be removed from waste water through simple primary sewage treatment-screens and settling chambers where filth falls out of water as sludge.

Secondary treatment, which effectively removes 90 per cent of degradable organic waste, utilizes a trickling filter, a bed of rocks three to ten feet deep, covered with bacteria which consume the organic matter. Chlorination kills 99 per cent of the germs in the water.

Tertiary sewage treatment, utilizing filtration, flocculation and other mechanical and chemical processes, removes almost all contaminants from water. Although existing water pollution abatement program goals called for establishing secondary treatment in 90 per cent of the communities in the U.S. and in most factories, tertiary treatment ultimately would be required to deal with the ever-increasing flow of chemical pollutants.

Nixon proposed a two-part program to help communities build the estimated $10-billion worth of waste treatment plants and interceptor lines needed to meet national water quality standards over the next five years:

• A Clean Water Act with a $4-billion authorization for fiscal 1971 to cover the federal share of the $10-billion projected for plant construction costs, to be allocated over the next four years at a rate of $1-billion annually.

• Creation of an Environmental Financing Authority to ensure that all municipalities would be able to sell plant construction bonds and thereby finance their share of the cost of treatment plants.

Nixon also proposed amendment of all federal-state water quality standards to impose precise effluent standards on all industrial and municipal sources and measures to ensure that the new funds were well invested.

Appropriations. In December 1969, Congress had staged its most open revolt against the President in the environment field that year when it cleared the fiscal 1970

public works appropriations bill (PL 91-144). In the bill, Congress appropriated $800-million out of a $1-billion authorization for waste treatment facilities, although President Nixon had requested only $214-million. The House had fallen two votes short of approving the full $1-billion, as had been voted by the Senate.

The fiscal 1971 public works appropriations bill (HR 18127—PL 91-439), which cleared Congress Sept. 23, included $1-billion for direct construction grants to states and localities for sewage treatment works. Congress rejected President Nixon's recommendation that contract authority of $1-billion be substituted for direct grants. *(Chapter on Public Works, and Flood Control)*

Hearings. The Senate Public Works Subcommittee on Air and Water Pollution held hearings in the spring on several bills dealing with financing, enforcement and other aspects of water pollution control but took no action on any legislation.

Walter J. Hickel, secretary of the interior, told the subcommittee that the administration's proposals would provide $4-billion of the $9.9-billion needed for municipal waste treatment plants according to estimates of a 1970 study, "The Economics of Clean Water."

But representatives of state and local governments termed the administration's proposed funding level "inadequate" and called for $10-billion in federal funds over five years.

WATER RESOURCES INSTITUTES. A bill (S 3553) to increase authorizations for water resources research was approved by the Senate in 1970, but the House took no action on the bill. A similar measure cleared Congress in 1971. *(p. 783)*

The Water Resources Research Act of 1964 (PL 89-379) had provided for grants of $100,000 annually for each state and Puerto Rico for water resources research centers. For each of fiscal years 1972-1976, $10-million was authorized for research grants to educational institutions, private foundations and other organizations. *(Congress and the Nation Vol. I, p. 897; Vol. II, p. 499)*

As passed by the Senate Sept. 1, S 3553 would have boosted annual authorizations for each center to $200,-000 annually and made the District of Columbia, the Virgin Islands and Guam eligible to receive water resources research grants.

The Interior Department had opposed S 3553 because the 1964 act did not grant the department authority to control the research conducted by each center and as a result their programs did not always comply with national objectives. But the Senate Interior and Insular Affairs Committee replied in its report that the act had intended that research in each center be responsive to local needs.

The Interior Department also opposed the inclusion of Guam and the Virgin Islands in the bill because of the limited resources of educational institutions there.

SEA GRANT PROGRAM. As requested by the administration, Congress extended (HR 11766—PL 91-349) the Sea Grant program through fiscal 1973 with authorizations totaling $75-million over three years.

The Sea Grant program—established in 1966 under Title II of the Marine Resources and Engineering Development Act of 1966 (PL 89-454)—was intended to encourage the development of "aquaculture" in the manner that the land grant college program had fostered the development of agriculture. The 1966 act authorized the National Science Foundation to initiate and support programs of education and research in fields relating to the development of marine resources. It had been extended for two years in 1968. *(Congress and the Nation Vol. II, p. 482)*

DESALINATION PROGRAM. Congress completed action on a bill (HR 15700—PL 91-221) authorizing $28.9-million in fiscal 1971 for the Interior Department program to convert salt water into fresh water, an increase of almost $3-million over the fiscal 1970 authorization of $26-million. *(p. 753)* The bulk of the boost was intended for construction of a new saline water conversion plant module.

Approximately $183-million had been spent on the program since it first was established in 1952 (PL 82-488). *(Congress and the Nation Vol. I, p. 939)*

OCEAN POLICY. A Senate Commerce subcommittee in 1970 considered but took no action on a bill to establish a national oceanic program and create an independent national oceanic and atmospheric agency, as well as other legislation on coastal zone management.

A National Oceanic and Atmospheric Administration was created later that year through executive reorganization. *(p. 757)*

Ocean Dumping. President Nixon told Congress Oct. 7 that he would seek legislation in 1971 regulating all dumping of wastes into the oceans, the Great Lakes and estuaries.

About 48 million tons of dredging, sludge and other materials were dumped annually off the coastlines of the United States.

Nixon's message was accompanied by a report by the Council on Environmental Quality outlining a national policy on ocean dumping. The President said he endorsed the council's recommendations and would ask for laws to implement them during the next Congress. The council's report backed new legislation to:

• Require a permit from the administrator of the new Environmental Protection Agency for the transporting or dumping of all materials in the oceans, the Great Lakes and estuaries (areas of mixed fresh and salt water).

• Authorize the administrator to ban ocean dumping of specific materials and to designate safe sites.

The report also outlined a national policy on ocean dumping:

• Ocean dumping of materials harmful to man or marine life should be stopped immediately, and other dumping phased out unless research shows it does not damage the environment.

• Biologically critical areas—chiefly estuaries and shallow, nearshore areas—should be designated and protected.

• Dumping of untreated sewage should be stopped immediately and no new sources allowed. Dumping of treated sewage should be phased out and no new sources allowed. Dumping of existing sources of solid waste and industrial waste should be stopped as soon as possible.

• Dumping of polluted dredge spoils should be phased out as soon as alternatives can be devised.

• The existing prohibition on ocean dumping of high-level radioactive wastes should be continued; low-level radioactive wastes should continue to be controlled by federal regulations and international standards.

• Dumping of chemical and biological warfare materials should be prohibited.

Ocean Resources. U.S. policies concerning regulations governing exploitation of the continental shelf and deep sea mineral resources were examined during hearings by a Senate Interior subcommitttee. At issue were the seaward limits of the legal continental shelf and the extent of coastal nations' jurisdiction over the mineral resources on the ocean floor adjacent to their shores.

On May 23, President Nixon announced the administration's proposals for regulating ocean resource exploitation. Nixon called on all nations to adopt "as soon as possible" a treaty under which they would renounce all national claims over the natural resources of the seabed beyond a 200-meter (656 feet) depth. Beyond that limit, the treaty would establish an international regime for exploiting seabed resources.

"The regime should include the collection of substantial mineral royalties to be used for international community purposes, particularly economic assistance to developing countries," the President said. "The regime should also establish general rules to prevent unreasonable interference with other uses of the ocean, to protect the ocean from pollution, to assure the integrity of the investment necessary for such exploitation and to provide for peaceful and compulsory settlement of disputes."

The President's proposals were similar in many respects to recommendations made by the Commission on Marine Science, Engineering and Development in its 1969 report on "Our Nation and the Sea." *(p. 752)*

In endorsing the narrow, 200-meter limit of national jurisdiction which was proposed in the 1958 Geneva Convention on the Continental Shelf, the United States was acting in its national interests, Elliot L. Richardson, under secretary of state, told the subcommittee May 27. "A concept of broad extension of national jurisdiction would have indirect, but serious, national security implications and would impede the freedom of scientific research and other uses of the high seas," he declared.

LAND USE

Solid Waste Management

Increased concern for environmental protection prompted Congress to shift the focus of federal solid waste programs to the recovery and reuse of resources and energy from the materials discarded by society. Most earlier federal efforts had concentrated on the disposal of solid wastes.

Congress Oct. 13 sent to the President a three-year, $462.75-million extension (HR 11833) of federal solid waste disposal programs. The new legislation, the Resource Recovery Act of 1970, set up a program of demonstration and construction grants for innovative solid waste management systems, provided technical and financial assistance to state and local agencies in planning and developing resource recovery and waste disposal systems and established major research programs to develop methods of dealing with solid wastes.

HR 11833 also established a two-year, $2-million study by a new National Commission on Materials Policy.

President Nixon signed the measure into law on Oct. 26 (PL 91-512). In announcing the signing, White House Press Secretary Ronald L. Ziegler said the President had considered vetoing the bill because he had "some concern about the ability of the federal government to effectively spend at the research and development level which is called for in this legislation." But, Ziegler said, "his concern for dealing with problems of the environment was the overriding factor in his signing the bill."

The administration had proposed legislation containing open-ended authorizations, rather than the year-by-year figures set in HR 11833, and a study of the reclamation and reuse of solid wastes to be made by the Council on Environmental Quality.

For fiscal 1971, President Nixon had made budget requests of about $15.3-million for solid waste programs administered by the Department of Health, Education and Welfare (HEW), compared to $41.5-million authorized by the bill, and no new funds for solid waste programs in the Interior Department's Bureau of Mines, for which HR 11833 authorized $8.75-million. The bill also authorized $172-million for the two programs in fiscal 1972 and $238.5-million in fiscal 1973.

HR 11833 expanded HEW's authority, but after the establishment of the Environmental Protection Agency on Dec. 2, 1970, all HEW solid waste programs were to be transferred to the new agency.

The House passed the bill June 23 by 339-0 roll-call vote, and the Senate passed its version Aug. 3 by voice vote. The House version stressed research and established a program of construction grants; it extended solid waste programs for three years. The Senate adopted a four-year extension including research funds and a program of development grants.

House and Senate conferees rewrote the bill to include the major provisions of both versions. The final bill extended programs for three years, and contained the authorizations set by the House bill, which were more than double the amount approved by the Senate. The Senate adopted the conference report Oct. 7 by voice vote; the House by voice vote Oct. 13.

Background. The Solid Waste Disposal Act (PL 89-272) was passed by Congress in 1965 to begin a national research and development program for improved methods of solid waste disposal, and to provide technical and financial aid to state and local governments in developing, establishing and conducting solid waste disposal programs. It authorized up to 50 per cent of the cost of state or interstate surveys of disposal practices and grants for demonstration projects, including up to two-thirds of a project's construction costs. Responsibility for the program was split between the HEW and Interior Department, with Interior having responsibility over problems of solid waste resulting from mineral or fossil fuels, and HEW have jurisdiction over all other aspects. In 1968, Congress extended the act through fiscal 1970 (PL 90-574). *(Congress and the Nation Vol. II, p. 679, 699)*

On April 10, 1970, President Nixon sent a message to Congress outlining the administration's plans for "total mobilization" to save the environment of the nation. In addition to proposals for air and water pollution control and parks and recreation, he recommended:

● Extension of the Solid Waste Disposal Act with redirection of research "to place greater emphasis on techniques for recycling materials and on development and use of packaging and other materials which will degrade after use."

● Development of a bounty payment or similar system "to promote the prompt scrapping of all junk automobiles" by the Council on Environmental Quality.

● Development of other incentives or regulations for submission to Congress by the Council on Environmental Quality in conjunction with "appropriate industry and consumer representatives."

The first proposal required action by Congress; the second and third needed only administrative action.

The message stressed a program of incentives, regulations and research for reducing the amount of wastes by making products more easily disposable and reusing a large proportion of waste materials. Existing packaging methods, with all emphasis on "nonreturnable" bottles and cartons had created an increasing volume of waste and refuse, the message stated. The traditional method of dealing with the problem was to continue spending money on collection and disposal of wastes, which "amounts to a public subsidy of waste pollution," it continued.

Provisions. Major provisions of HR 11833, the Resource Recovery Act of 1970:

• Directed the secretary of the Department of Health, Education and Welfare (HEW), to promote research on health and welfare effects of waste, operation and financing of solid waste disposal programs, reduction of the amount of waste, development and application of better methods of collecting and disposing of solid waste and of processing and recovering materials and energy from solid wastes and components of solid waste.

• Directed the secretary of HEW to conduct studies on economic means of recovering useful materials from solid waste; uses of such materials and the market impact of such recovery; appropriate incentive programs, including tax incentives, to aid in solid waste disposal; reasonable changes in existing production and packaging methods to reduce the amount of solid waste; waste collection and containerization; and proposals for imposing disposal charges. The Secretary was to report annually on such studies to the President and Congress.

• Authorized the HEW Department to establish demonstration projects on techniques developed through its special studies.

• Authorized planning grants of up to two-thirds of the cost for single municipalities, and three-quarters of the cost for other areas, for making surveys of solid waste problems, preparing solid waste disposal plans (with emphasis on recycling wastes), developing proposals for pilot projects and planning programs for collecting and processing abandoned vehicle hulks.

• Authorized grants to public agencies for demonstration of resource recovery systems or construction of innovative solid waste disposal facilities. The federal share of demonstration grants would be 75 per cent; the federal share of construction grants would be 50 per cent if the project served only a single municipality and 75 per cent in other cases. Federal funds would be used only for design and construction, plus first-year operation and maintenance costs in the case of demonstration grants. Funds could not be used for land acquisition. No more than 15 per cent of the annual authorization could be used in any one state.

• Authorized the secretary of HEW, as soon as practicable, to formulate guidelines for solid waste recovery, collection, separation and disposal systems, as well as model codes and ordinances.

• Authorized $41.5-million for all HEW solid waste programs for fiscal 1971.

• Authorized for HEW demonstration and construction grants: fiscal 1972, $80-million; fiscal 1973, $140-million. For other HEW programs (including research): fiscal 1972, $72-million; fiscal 1973; $76-million.

• Authorized for Interior Department solid waste programs: fiscal 1971, $8.75-million; fiscal 1972; $20-million; fiscal 1973, $22.5-million.

• Created a seven-member National Commission on Materials Policy to develop by June 30, 1973, a national materials policy. The commission would study national and international materials requirements, relationship of materials policy to population and environmental quality, means of using more materials which could be recycled, or reused, or which would self-destruct, and means of improving and coordinating information on materials usage. The bill authorized $2-million for the study.

Timber Supply

The House handed embryo environmental lobby groups a major victory Feb. 26 when it rejected the rule under which the National Forest Timber Conservation and Management Act (HR 12025) was to be considered. Refusal to take up the bill came on a 150-228 roll-call vote. No further action was taken on the measure in 1970, and it died when Congress adjourned.

The purpose of the bill was to increase the yield of timber from national forest lands. When hearings on HR 12025 began in May 1969, timber prices were unusually high, but subsequently declined. The House Agriculture Committee had reported HR 12025 in November 1969. *(p. 754)*

The bill, which was endorsed by Secretary of Agriculture Clifford M. Hardin and Secretary of Housing and Urban Development George Romney, directed the U.S. Forest Service to develop "optimum timber productivity" on the 97 million acres of commercial timber in the national forests.

"Without the substantial increase in timber production which the enactment of this legislation will encourage, it will be difficult, if not impossible, to build the homes America needs," Romney said Feb. 12.

The lumber industry's tactics in support of HR 12025, which included alliances with builders' associations and urban lobby groups, produced a debate over which of two national needs—adequate housing or preservation of the environment—should be given priority.

Opponents, led by an ad hoc alliance of 10 conservation groups called the Conservation Coalition, rejected the housing argument as an industry attempt to lend moral weight to a measure to its own economic benefit. High interest rates, not lack of lumber, hindered housing construction, they argued. *(Major arguments, box p. 771)*

Background. A primary reason for introduction of the timber supply bill was pressure on the timber industry from the housing industry in late 1968 and early 1969 after a shortage of timber drove prices up.

The tight timber supply was prompted partly by seasonal and short-term problems—a dry summer in 1967 caused a shut-down of some logging operations due to fire hazard, while heavy snows in the Northwest in January 1969, coupled with a boxcar shortage and an East Coast dock strike, slowed deliveries. Another factor was the continued export of logs—primarily to Japan. Exports to Japan and other nations represented nearly 7 per cent of the total domestic production of softwood saw logs and veneer logs.

But prices began to go down in March 1969, a phenomenon which the National Association of Home Builders attributed to the "present slowdown in housing, particularly the drop in single-family housing."

Lobbying. In early 1970, the Conservation Coalition began an intensive campaign against HR 12025, stressing that the emphasis in the bill was on logging at the expense of all other uses of the national forests.

The members of the Conservation Coalition, who joined forces to fight the timber measure, included traditional conservation groups and the United Auto Workers.

Volunteers and officers of five of the organizations—the National Audubon Society, the Sierra Club, the Wilderness Society, Friends of the Earth and Trout Unlimited—were active in canvassing congressional offices. They operated out of a room in the Rayburn (House Office) Building. Workers for the Sierra Club delivered an information kit Dec. 21, 1969, to members of Congress. The kit contained articles on the environmental impact, the housing effect and the forestry implications of the bill.

Eight of the national conservation organizations sent a telegram Jan. 28, 1970, to all members of Congress contending, among other things, that the bill "threatens America's national forests, scuttles historic multiple-use practices and undermines prospective parks, wilderness, open space and recreation areas."

Lobbying in support of HR 12025 was led by the National Forest Products Association and the National Association of Home Builders.

E. F. Behrens, executive assistant to Agriculture Secretary Clifford M. Hardin, was employed by the National Forest Products Association from 1958 to 1967. His last position with the association was manager for general operations.

The two trade organizations agreed to make a united effort to increase national forest timber cuttings at a joint meeting at Houston, Texas, in 1969. Several legislative proposals developed at the meeting were included in HR 12025.

On Jan. 28, 1970, the two associations jointly published a 36-page booklet, "Housing Goals and the Future Course for the National Forests," urging enactment of HR 12025. Ralph N. Hodges Jr., vice president of the National Forest Products Association, said 5,000 copies were mailed to members of Congress, newspaper editors, editorial writers and radio and television journalists. He estimated the cost of printing and mailing the publication at $2,000.

The National Forest Products Association also urged urban lobby groups to support HR 12025. The National Urban League, the National Association of Housing and Redevelopment Officials and the National Housing Conference all endorsed the measure.

Floor Action. In a sharp defeat for the lumber industry, the House Feb. 26 by a roll-call vote of 150-228 rejected the rule (H Res 799) under which HR 12025 was to be considered. The action had the effect of defeating the measure.

W. R. Poage (D Texas), chairman of the Agriculture Committee which had considered the bill, had indicated earlier that month that he would vote against the bill. "I think it opens the door to destroy multiple use," he said, referring to a policy established by the Multiple Use-Sustained Yield Act of 1960 (PL 86-517) under which national forests were to be managed to provide a broad range of uses, including recreation and other non-commercial activities. *(Congress and the Nation Vol. I, p. 1057)*

During debate on HR 12025, a few members expressed skepticism about claims that more intensive harvesting of national forests would help realize the 10-year goal of 26 million units of new and rehabilitated housing set by the 1968 Housing and Urban Development Act (PL 90-448). The administration in 1969 had blamed timber shortages and high prices for its failure to meet the 1969 goal under the act.

James H. Scheuer (D N.Y.) declared that the bill "...is not only a poor conservation measure, but it is also a poor housing measure." He suggested that alter-

(Continued on p. 774)

Arguments on Timber

Supporters of the timber bill argued that the nation's chronic housing shortage was due in large part to a recent shortage of timber.

Opponents maintained that the housing shortage was a result of high interest rates, high land prices and high labor prices.

Supporters said the worsening housing situation justified emphasizing increased timber production. Opponents contended that HR 12025 would sacrifice the national forests to maximum timber cutting without regard for protection of watershed, fish and wildlife, grazing or scenic and recreation values.

Supporters of HR 12025 contended that almost any wood substitute required the development of depletable resources and the production of water and air polluting wastes in the manufacturing process.

Opponents argued that the timber industry—whose real worry, they said, was that wood would be displaced by lower-priced substitutes—was trying to hold on to the construction material market.

Supporters of HR 12025 contended that almost any reduction in exports of timber to Japan would shift the balance of trade to the disadvantage of the United States.

Those in favor of the timber supply bill argued that higher levels of management would benefit national forest land in that proper harvesting would enhance a forest's watershed capacity by preventing compacted soil and controlling erosion.

Opponents contended that the largest increase in logging under the bill would occur in the virgin timber of the Pacific Coast and Rocky Mountains where, they said, the mountainous terrain is ecologically fragile.

Further, they said, the Forest Service was already selling timber at a rate about 50 per cent in excess of that which can be sustained while maintaining a good forestry.

Supporters of HR 12025 maintained that under the bill the Forest Service would be able to protect areas which should be left as wilderness. Opponents said that a provision requiring intensive forestry on all land capable of supporting marketable timber would make it possible to withdraw the six to eight million acres which have their highest value as wilderness.

Supporters of HR 12025 said that the bill would increase the funds available to the Forest Service. Opponents said it would not alleviate the Forest Service's funding problems because the service would still have to go through the appropriations process every two years.

The Forest Service favored having at its disposal proceeds from timber sales rather than having to rely entirely on appropriations from the general Treasury.

The agency estimated that under the bill it would have received $229-million from the timber fund in fiscal 1971 for reforestation and forest management. The bill required, however, that unused funds be transferred to the Treasury after two years.

Public Land Law Review Commission Recommends...

Stringent controls over the environment on the 755 million acres of federally owned public land—one-third of the nation's land area—should be put into effect without delay, the Public Land Law Review Commission recommended to President Nixon and Congress June 23, 1971.

Concluding five years of study, the commission made more than 350 recommendations, providing guidelines to help Congress overhaul outmoded laws and unsnarl the often conflicting regulations governing the use and sale of federal lands. Action on the commission's report was held over for the 92nd Congress.

The 19-member commission—the fifth such group in the nation's history—was created by Congress in 1964 but did not organize until 1965. Its chairman was Rep. Wayne N. Aspinall, (D Colo.) chairman of the House Interior and Insular Affairs Committee. *(Congress and the Nation Vol. I, p. 1044; Vol. II, p. 488)*

In 1964, there were about 5,000 public land laws on the statute books pertaining to 770.8 million acres of federally held land in the 50 states and perhaps 1,000 administrative rules and regulations. Of that amount, the commission was charged with studying the law and regulations governing some 719 million acres of federal land which were or had been in public domain status. This was about one-third of the entire land area of the country, located mainly in the West. Both public land users and conservationists generally agreed in 1964 that the public land laws should be updated, for many had become archaic, obsolescent, conflicting and unrelated.

In its 343-page report, entitled *One Third of the Nation's Land,* the commission recommended that enhancement and maintenance of the environment, with rehabilitation where necessary, be defined as objectives for all classes of public lands, and federal standards for environmental quality be established.

Public lands should be managed under statutory guidelines "to enhance the quality of the environment, both on and off public lands" where feasible, the report said. Thus, public land users would not only be required to meet high standards in removing resources such as timber and minerals from public lands but also in processing them off public lands.

Congress should require land management agencies to classify public lands for environmental management into four basic categories: water, air, biosystem and quality of experience, the commission said. Then, as a precondition to certain kinds of uses on public lands, Congress should require the agencies to make impact studies. These uses would include, it said, transmission lines, roads, dams, open-pit mining, timber harvesting, extensive chemical control programs (such as use of DDT and other pesticides), mineral operations on the outer continental shelf, and high density recreation developments such as major reservoir areas built by the Army Corps of Engineers and the Bureau of Reclamation.

Responsibility

To provide "the maximum benefit for the general public," the commission recommended that the bulk of the public lands be retained in federal ownership and managed in a new Department of Natural Resources. This would be an expanded Department of Interior to which the U.S. Forest Service would be transferred from the Department of Agriculture. Congressional jurisdiction over public lands should be centered in one committee (presumably Interior) in both the House and Senate.

Because existing revenue-sharing programs in effect were neither fair nor equitable to the public land states and counties, located mainly in the West, the commission recommended that they be replaced by federal tax payments to the states. These should be the equivalent of what the states and counties could get in taxes to repay them for services which they render the public lands, less 10 per cent to 40 per cent for the benefits which they derive from public lands. The reimbursement tax formula should assure that the states return the tax payments to the public land counties and require both states and counties to make the necessary effort to raise taxes from non-federal sources, the commission said.

If and when the in-lieu tax payments were authorized by Congress, the commission recommended that existing revenue-sharing programs with public land states be ended. Since 1907, the federal government had returned to public land counties 25 per cent of its timber stumpage sale receipts. And under the 1920 Mineral Leasing Act, the states of origin (except Alaska) received 37.5 per cent of the receipts from oil and gas leases and the reclamation fund received 52.5 per cent. Alaska received 90 per cent of oil and gas lease revenues.

Acquisition, Withdrawals and Disposal

All past land classifications, reservations and withdrawals of public land by the executive branch should be reviewed at once and periodically in the future, the commission recommended. It said that Congress should reserve to itself authority to make large-scale withdrawals and reservations of public land for the purpose of establishing and enlarging units such as national parks and forests.

In the future, it said, withdrawal authority should be delegated by Congress solely to the secretary of interior, acting for the executive department. The effect of this recommendation would be to keep the President, the Federal Power Commission, the director of the Bureau of Land Management and the director of the National Park Service, among others, from making further land withdrawals. Withdrawals could be made, however, by assistant interior secretaries, under this recommendation.

...Strict Environmental Controls on Federal Lands

The commission took a stiff line on withdrawals because its hearings and contract study of the problem indicated "they have been used by the executive in an uncontrolled and haphazard manner," it said. When lands were withdrawn, they could not be used for settlement, mineral leasing, or other types of entry on public lands.

Escalating land costs were such a major problem in buying more federal land that the commission recommended the federal land management agencies "should be authorized to employ a broad array of acquisition techniques on an experimental basis" when buying land.

But generally it opposed major new land acquisitions by federal agencies of timber land, for watershed management, for outdoor recreation, for multiple purpose use, or to enlarge grazing districts.

The commission said Congress should reserve to itself decisions about large public land disposals, either by dollar or acreage amount. It generally favored sales of public lands and resources from such lands at fair market value. It opposed artificial restraints on land sales, but it said "in cases of competing applicants, we favor a statutory preference for state and local governmental units or nonprofit entities."

Long-Range Planning

With competition for public lands escalating, Congress should establish by statute "a continuing dynamic program of land-use planning," the commission said. The goals of such a program should be management of public lands by dominant use, with secondary uses permitted where they were compatible with the dominant use, and in such a manner that federal, state and private land uses were complementary.

The commission endorsed the multiple-use concept so long held to be the key to public land management, and it said the Bureau of Land Management should be given permanent multiple-use management authority. But as a planning tool it "has little practical meaning" the commission said.

It recommended that "Congress provide for a dominant use zoning system" on public land, and that the federal land management agencies develop long-range comprehensive land-use plans, based on this system, for each state and region.

Specific Uses

The following were some of the other key recommendations of the commission, by category or commodity use of public land. Most were recommendations directed to Congress because the commission favored their enactment into statutory law.

Timber. The most highly productive timber on public lands should be classified and managed with commercial timber production as the designated dominant use by a federal timber corporation, the commis-

sion said, presumably within the yet-to-be-consolidated public land management agency in Interior. A revolving fund should be established to assure proper investments in these "big timber production units."

Mining and Mineral Leasing. With a sharp dissent from commission members Robert Emmet Clark of the University of Arizona, former Gov. Philip H. Hoff (D Vt.) Maurice K. Goddard of Pennsylvania and Rep. Morris K. Udall (D Ariz.), the commission recommended that the claim-location-patent system for hardrock mining be continuing but modified. Extralateral rights, however, would be terminated. (Extralateral rights extend to the end of a vein whose apex starts on a miner's claim on public land.)

For hard-rock mining, the commission spelled out these new procedures:

• Claims would have to be filed with the nearest federal land office as well as with the county where they must now be filed after they are staked. Rents would be charged for claims, but would be credited against exploration and development. The claimholder would sign a contract with the government to secure producing rights; at the same time he must agree to stringent environmental controls of his mining operation.

• After he started producing minerals, he would be eligible to obtain a patent only for the mineral deposits. He would have to pay a fair value for his patent and a royalty on the minerals which he produced and marketed before and after patent.

Grazing and Agriculture. The homestead laws and the 1877 Desert Entry Law should be repealed, the commission said. Grazing permits should be issued for statutory periods, with compensation to the permittee for termination of his permit prior to the end of the term. Cost of the permit should be fair market price value, considering other uses of public land and type of forage on the range.

Outdoor Recreation. An annual permit of $1-$3 should be charged each citizen aged 12-65 who used federally held land for outdoor recreation. The commission said an additional charge should be made for fishing and hunting on federal lands. Once these charges were instituted, the Golden Eagle "passport" should be phased out. To prevent overloading national parks and wilderness areas, the commission said the federal government should institute a fair and equitable rationing system for those who visited them.

The commission recommended that states and local governments should own and operate intensive-use recreation areas. But federal funding would be necessary in some instances in operating and maintaining such area to protect the land, it stated.

native materials to replace wood were the answer to housing problems.

B. F. Sisk (D Calif.) of the House Rules Committee said that the bill had been "completely rewritten" since it had first been proposed and was acceptable to "a number of members of the Sierra Club in my district." John P. Saylor (R Pa.), ranking minority member of the House Interior Committee and a leader of conservationist opponents of the bill, replied: "I know of no conservation group and I know of no one who knows what is in this bill who is for it, outside of a few people who have a special interest or who will gain a special benefit."

Wayne N. Aspinall (D Colo.), chairman of the House Interior Committee, said he opposed the provisions of the measure, although its objectives were correct. Aspinall said further consideration of a bill dealing with timber production in the national forests should wait until recommendations had been made by the Public Land Law Review Commission. The Commission, created in 1964 to study public land laws, recommend over-all revision and establish principles of national policy on the public lands and national forests, released its report on June 23. *(Box, p. 772)*

Other Land Use Bills

MINING AND MINERALS POLICY. Congress called for the development of a strong domestic mining industry when it enacted legislation (S 719—PL 91-631) establishing a national mining and minerals policy. The Senate had approved the measure in 1969. *(p. 754)*

Major provisions of S 719:

• Encouraged in the private sector economically sound and stable domestic mining, minerals, metal and mineral reclamation industries.

• Encouraged the orderly and economic development of domestic mineral resources, reserves and reclamation of metals and minerals for industrial, security and environmental needs.

• Encouraged mining, mineral and metallurgical research, including the use and recycling of scrap.

• Encouraged development of methods for the disposal, control and reclamation of mineral waste products, and the reclamation of mined land, in order to lessen harm to the environment that may result from mining and mineral activities.

• Expanded the definition of minerals to include mineral fuels including oil, gas, coal, oil shale and uranium.

• Gave the interior secretary responsibility for carrying out the provisions of the act.

During consideration of S 719 in the House, the Interior and Insular Affairs Committee made three major changes in the bill. It gave more stress to the role of private enterprise in the development of a sound, stable industry, expanded the definition of the mining and minerals industry to include metals and mineral reclamation and broadened the definition of mineral to include energy minerals—or fuels.

After adopting the committee's recommended changes, the House passed S 719 Sept. 21; the Senate agreed to the House amendments Dec. 18, clearing the bill for the President. The bill was signed into law Dec. 31.

RECLAMATION LANDS. Congress June 23 cleared for the President a bill (S 2062—PL 91-310) to exempt certain publicly owned lands from the 160-acre limit for which individuals could receive water from a federal reclamation (irrigation) project. The bill required that the exempted land be used only for non-revenue producing functions such as experimental farms, prison farms and hospital farms. *(Congress and the Nation Vol. I p. 800, 903)*

Under existing law, the Reclamation Act of 1902, no landowner in a federal reclamation project could receive water for lands in exess of 160 acres for each individual (320 acres for man and wife). The justification for the limitation was that the federal reclamation program was intended primarily to aid the family farmer—the small farmer working his own land.

An administrative interpretation of the 160-acre limit was made in 1967. The Department of the Interior held Jan. 23, 1967, that the restriction applied equally to land held by public authorities and private individuals. States, municipalities, public universities and hospitals were required by the department's ruling to dispose of lands in excess of 160 acres that were irrigated by federal reclamation projects.

LAND USE POLICY. In the last weeks of the session, the Senate Interior and Insular Affairs Committee reported a bill (S 3354) to encourage states to set in land use planning policies. No further action was taken on S 3354 in 1970.

The bill, the National Land Use Policy Act of 1970, as reported would have authorized $100-million annually for grants to state and interstate and river basin commissions to develop and implement statewide land-use plans. Hawaii was the only state in 1970 having such a plan, although Colorado was the process of developing one.

Under the proposal, federal agencies would have been prohibited from undertaking or aiding state projects which would require the commitment of substantial land or water resources in any state which had not submitted a land-use plan within five years of the bill's enactment.

S 3354 also would have set up a cabinet-level Land and Water Resources Council to study federal policies and programs relating to land use.

ALASKAN NATIVE CLAIMS. The Senate July 15 passed a bill (S 1830), the Alaska Native Claims Settlement Act of 1970, authorizing the payment of $1-billion and the grant of up to 10 million acres of land to the natives to cancel their claim to land in Alaska.

However, the House took no action on the bill and it died at the end of the 91st Congress. Congress approved a final settlement of the century-old land claims in 1971. *(p. 783)*

The bill as passed by the Senate was more generous than the administration proposal. The administration had supported a payment of $500-million over 20 years and a grant of about 10 million acres of land to the Alaskan natives.

Background. In the Organic Act of 1884, which provided a civil government for Alaska, Congress had provided that the Alaskan natives should not be removed from the lands they used or claimed but that the terms under which they could acquire title to the lands would be the subject of future legislation. No such law had been enacted.

The value of the land in the interim had sky-rocketed—particularly due to the discovery in 1968 of huge oil reserves on the northern Alaska slopes—and settlement of the outstanding claims was critical to the fortunes of both the state and its estimated 53,000 native Eskimos, Aleuts and Indians. The original native request had been for 40 million acres of land. *(Background, 1969 action, p. 753)*

Provisions. As passed by the Senate, major provisions of S 1830:

• Extinguished all existing native claims to Alaskan lands.

• Provided that persons eligible for benefits under the act had to be at least one-fourth Alaskan Indian, Eskimo or Aleut, who were citizens of the United States.

• Authorized the appropriation of $500-million to the natives over a 12-year period as compensation for lands taken in the past or to which their rights and claims were extinguished by the act.

• Authorized the native people to receive, in addition to the $500-million, two per cent of the revenues derived from the disposition of leasable minerals on the public lands in Alaska until a total of $500-million had been paid.

HERBICIDES. The effects of the herbicide 2, 4, 5-T on man and the environment were probed by a Senate Commerce subcommittee during hearings from April through June.

The chemical 2, 4, 5-T, developed during the 1940s, had been applied to the environment for nearly 20 years, but until 1969 few if any studies had been conducted by any government agency on the possible carcinogenic (cancer-producing) or teratogenic (fetus-deforming) properties of the herbicide or on the ecological consequences of its use. The most common defects produced by 2, 4, 5-T in test animals were kidney abnormalties and cleft palates.

A week after the 1970 hearings began, Agriculture Secretary Clifford M. Hardin, Interior Secretary Walter J. Hickel and Robert H. Finch, secretary of the Department of Health Education and Welfare (HEW) announced April 15 the immediate suspension by the Agriculture Department of the registrations of the liquid formulations of the weed killer 2, 4, 5-T for use around the home and for registered uses on lakes, ponds and ditch banks.

The three cabinet officials also announced that the Agriculture Department intended to cancel registered uses of non-liquid formulations of 2, 4, 5-T around the home and for all food crops for human consumption for which it had been registered at that time.

The suspension actions were based on the opinion of the HEW Department that contamination resulting from uses of 2, 4, 5-T around the home and in water areas could constitute a hazard to human health, according to a department official.

Background. In February 1969, preliminary results of tests performed by the Bionetics Research Laboratories, under a contract from the National Cancer Institute, showed that 2, 4, 5-T caused birth defects in mice. The chemical herbicide had been used in Vietnam as a defoliant and in the United States as a brush and weed killer.

On Oct. 29, 1969, Dr. Lee A. DuBridge, Director of the White House Office of Science and Technology, acted "to assure the safety of the public while further evidence is sought." The Department of Agriculture, DuBridge said, would cancel manufacturers' registrations of 2, 4, 5-T for use on food crops, effective at the beginning of 1970, "unless by that time the Food and Drug Administration (FDA) has found a basis for establishing a safe legal tolerance in and on foods," and the Departments of Agriculture and the Interior, in their own programs, would stop the use of 2, 4, 5-T in populated areas, and in all other areas where residues of the substance could reach man.

Testimony. Harrison Wellford, an associate of the Center for the Study of Responsive Law, a group established in 1969 by consumer advocate Ralph Nader, told the subcommittee April 7 that herbicides containing 2, 4, 5-T—widely marketed for use by the individual consumer in residential areas—were causing "a grave and unnecessary risk to public health." Following the government's April 15 actions to restrict use of the herbicide, Wellford termed the move "a sham which misleads the public" and criticized existing laws to regulate pesticides.

DuBridge, science adviser to the President, testified June 18 that existing laws were inadequate to protect the public completely against all hazards of pesticides and other dangerous substances sold commercially. "There is not sufficient flexibility...to allow the government to take action" where new information of potential health hazards becomes available, he said. (Congress in 1972 cleared a comprehensive pesticide control measure. *p. 800*)

The same day, Dr. Jesse L. Steinfeld, U.S. surgeon general, stressed that studies conducted on animals left uncertainties as to the significance of the results when applied to man. The evidence available "does not in my judgment" support a conclusion that under current uses the herbicides in question pose a health hazard, he declared.

Related Hearings. Rep. Richard D. McCarthy (D N.Y.) held two days of informal hearings in February in Globe, Ariz., where local residents had complained that animals in an area where 2, 4, 5-T spray was used produced deformed offspring. The chemical was one of several used by the U.S. Forest Service in a 1900-acre area of the Tonto National Forest in eastern Arizona to increase water runoff by killing underbrush.

During March hearings on several bills to control the use of pesticides, herbicides and fungicides which were harmful to fish and wildlife, the administration opposed a bill (HR 11477) authorizing the interior secretary to prohibit the use of certain pesticides. Charles H. Meacham, commissioner of fish and wildlife within the Interior Department, told a House Merchant Marine and Fisheries subcommittee that the administration was reviewing pesticide problems and would take water quality into consideration—as would have been directed by HR 11477—when making its recommendations.

WILDLIFE PROTECTION

WILDLIFE RESTORATION ACTS. Congress completed action on a bill (HR 12475—PL 91-503) revising and clarifying the Federal Aid in Fish and Wildlife Restoration Acts.

The bill made numerous housekeeping changes in both the fish and wildlife restoration programs, and gave states the alternative of using comprehensive long-range plans rather than plans made on a project-to-project basis. It also amended the wildlife program by applying certain firearms excise taxes directly to the wildlife restoration fund, and gave states the option of using up to three-quarters of their shares of the fund for hunter safety programs.

The administration opposed the provision that transferred revenues from certain firearms taxes from the general fund of the Treasury to the wildlife restoration fund.

Background. The Federal Aid in Wildlife Restoration Act, called the Pittman-Robertson Act, was enacted in 1937. The law authorized the proceeds from an 11 per cent federal excise tax on sporting arms (excluding pistols and revolvers which were subject to a 10 per cent tax) and ammunition to be used for grants to the states for 75 per cent of state costs for cooperative programs in wildlife research, management and development. Through fiscal 1969, the program had made available to the states more than $355-million.

A similar program was established for fisheries in 1950. The Federal Aid in Fish Restoration Act—the Dingell-Johnson Act—authorized proceeds from a 10 per cent Federal excise tax on fishing rods, reels, lures, bait and flies to be used for grants to states to cover up to 75 per cent of state costs for cooperative programs in fisheries research, management and development. Through fiscal 1969, more than $100-million had been allocated for this program. *(Congress and the Nation Vol. I, p. 1064)*

Provisions. As signed into law (PL 91-503) Oct. 23, major provisions of HR 12475:

• Allowed the wildlife restoration fund in the Treasury to receive receipts of the 10 per cent tax on pistols and revolvers, in addition to the 11 per cent tax on other types of firearms and ammunition already deposited in the fund.

• Authorized states to use up to one-half of wildlife funds obtained from the tax on pistols and revolvers to conduct a hunter safety program, including construction, operation and maintenance of public outdoor target ranges. Federal funds could be used to finance up to 75 per cent of the costs of such programs. If a state did not wish to establish safety programs, funds would be available for regular wildlife restoration projects on a federal-state ratio of 75-25.

ANADROMOUS FISH. Congress approved legislation (HR 1049—PL 91-249) to extend and expand the federal-state program for conservation and improvement of anadromous fish resources.

Anadromous fish are born in fresh water, migrate to salt water and then return to fresh water to spawn and die. They include salmon, shad, striped bass and various kinds of trout. Considered valuable for both commercial and sport fishing, the fish had been depleted in recent years by pollution, dams, channel improvements, ship traffic and over-fishing.

The Anadromous Fish Conservation Act of 1965 (PL 89-304) authorized the secretary of the interior to initiate with states or other non-federal interests a cooperative program for the conservation of the nation's anadromous fish resources. The bill authorized $25-million in federal funds over the period ending June 30, 1970, to pay up to one-half of the cost of projects such as fish hatcheries, habitat improvement and artificial spawning research. Thirty-one states participated in the program in 1970. *(Congress and the Nation Vol. II, p. 493)*

As signed into law (PL 91-249) May 14, HR 1049 extended the 1965 act until June 30, 1974, and authorized maximum spending for the programs of $6-million in fiscal 1971, $7.5-million in fiscal 1972, $8.5-million in fiscal 1973 and $10-million in fiscal 1974.

WILDLIFE AND WATERFOWL. President Nixon Dec. 19 signed a bill (HR 15770—PL 91-559) authorizing the secretary of agriculture to contract with landowners to preserve major migratory waterfowl nesting and breeding areas. The bill provided that the contracts with landowners would specify that wetlands could not be drained or filled and that owners would be compensated for resulting loss of income. The bill authorized $10-million annually for this purpose.

HUNTING FROM AIRCRAFT. A bill imposing criminal penalties on hunting for wildlife from aircraft died at the end of the 91st Congress. The House in December passed a bill (HR 15188) making it a crime to shoot, attempt to shoot or harass any bird, fish or other animal from an aircraft, and setting maximum penalties of $5,000 and a year in prison. The Senate Commerce Committee reported the bill but it never came to a floor vote. Congress completed action on a similar measure in 1971. *(p. 789)*

OTHER LEGISLATION

POPULATION COMMISSION. Acceding to an administration request, Congress in 1970 set up a commission to study the effects on the United States of its booming population, but it tacked on a directive to investigate birth control methods to curb population growth.

The legislation (S 2701—PL 91-213) was the outgrowth of a request by President Nixon in 1969 for the creation of such a commission. President Nixon in 1972 disavowed the commission's final recommendations.

The Senate in 1969 had approved an administration bill (S 2701) establishing a commission on population growth, while the House Government Operations Committee later that year reported a broader version (HR 15165) of the bill. HR 15165 expanded the authority of the commission to include studies of the environmental effects of population growth and the means "appropriate to the ethical values and principles of this society" by which the desired population level could be maintained. *(p. 755)*

The House on Feb. 18, 1970 approved HR15165 by a 371-13 roll-call vote. Following the vote, the House substituted the language of HR 15165 for that of the Senate bill and passed S 2071, as amended, by voice vote. The Senate March 3 agreed to the House amendments, clearing the measure for the President.

Provisions. As signed into law March 16, PL 91-213:

• Established a Commission on Population Growth and the American Future.

• Provided that the commission be composed of not more than 20 members, including one Republican and one Democrat each from the Senate and the House of Representatives.

Overpopulation and Health: Hazards of the Pill Explored

The popularity of the "pill"—oral contraceptives—was dealt a major blow by hearings before the Senate Monopoly Subcommittee on Small Business early in 1970.

Spurred by public confusion about the risks, dangers and efficacy of the pill and its alternatives following a series of conflicting reports on the medication, Gaylord Nelson (D Wis.), subcommittee chairman, called the hearings to determine "the truth" about birth control pills.

Although no consensus developed during the hearings, a Gallup Poll completed while they were taking place found that 36 per cent of the women surveyed considered the pill unsafe, compared with 22 per cent in 1967. One witness estimated that there would be as many as 100,000 "Nelson babies" born as a result of the testimony.

Background. Introduced on the market in 1960, the birth control pill soon became the most popular form of contraceptive because of the ease with which it could be taken and because of its effectiveness. Some 8.5 million American women were estimated to be taking the "pill" in 1970, plus an additional 10 million women in other parts of the world.

Some scientists and physicians, however, had warned that too little was known about the side effects of the pill and the possibility of women developing cancer or blood clots from its use. Proponents of the pill argued that health hazards from the pill were no greater than the hazards to many women of pregnancy or the danger to the world of overpopulation.

The risk of death from blood clotting disorders, first reported in British medical literature in 1962 and considered well-documented, was three per hundred-thousand pill users. This was approximately 10 times the rate of death from the same cause for nonusers.

In 1966, a committee studying reports of the side effects from the pills for the Food and Drug Administration (FDA) said it had found "no adequate scientific data at this time" to prove that the pills were "unsafe for human use." The committee recommended, however, that more extensive studies be made. In 1968 the FDA sent a warning to physicians about a "definite association between the use of oral contraceptives and the incidence of thromboebolic disorders."

FDA Warnings. The FDA Jan. 19, 1970, urged physicians to advise their patients of potential ill effects from use of birth control pills. In a letter to 381,000 doctors, hospital pharmacies and administrators, the FDA said "full disclosure" by the physician to his patients of potential adverse effects from the pill was advisable. Such disclosure would "permit participation of the patient in assessment of risks," the FDA said.

In the absence of an adequate replacement for the pill, the FDA advised physicians to prescribe, whenever possible, oral contraceptives containing the lowest amounts of estrogen, the ingredient blamed for blood problems.

Hearings. Several witnesses appearing before the subcommittee emphasized the health hazards associated with reliance on birth control pills.

Dr. Hugh J. Davis, an assistant professor of gynecology at Johns Hopkins Medical School, warned that birth control pills might cause breast cancer that might not be detected for years. Other witnesses pointed to increases in blood clotting, high blood pressure, and other effects after use of the pill.

Proponents of the method noted that it was the most effective way of preventing pregnancy. Dr. Allan F. Guttmacher, president of Planned Parenthood World Population, told the subcommittee that pregnancy carried greater health risks than use of the pill and there was no acceptable substitute for oral contraceptives. Intrauterine devices (IUDs) had a failure rate of five pregnancies per one hundred users and a death risk of one to two per hundred-thousand users. Other methods posed an even higher failure rate, he indicated.

At one point during the hearings—on Jan. 23—proceedings were interrupted by members of a Washington, D.C., women's liberation group, who protested that no women had testified before the subcommittee and that there was no contraceptive pill for males.

Since the panel was only investigative in nature, it could not send bills to the floor.

• Provided that members of the commission and the chairman and vice chairman be appointed by the President.

• Stated that the commission was to conduct an inquiry into (a) the probable course of U.S. population growth and internal migration; (b) government resources that would be required to deal with anticipated population growth; (c) the effect of population growth on government activities; (d) the impact of population growth on environmental pollution and depletion of natural resources; and (e) means appropriate to American ethical values and principles by which the United States could achieve a population level suited to its resources.

POPULATION CONTROL AND RESEARCH PROGRAMS. Congress in 1970 also approved a plan to coordinate and expand family planning services and federal population research activities. As enacted into law (PL 91-572), S 2108 authorized $382-million over three years for grants to public agencies and private organizations to help set up and operate voluntary family planning services and to promote research in related fields.

In a House-Senate conference over differences between the versions of the bill as passed by both houses, conferees accepted the more generous funding level approved by the Senate. Other provisions of the bill were substantially the same in both versions.

Little controversy arose during consideration of the measure, which was passed by the Senate July

14 and the House Nov. 16. The measure was cleared by Congress Dec. 10.

Provisions. As cleared by Congress, S 2108:

• Established an Office of Population Affairs in the Department of Health, Education and Welfare (HEW) to administer all HEW responsibilities in the area of population and family planning.

• Required the HEW secretary to report to Congress within six months of enactment a five-year plan for extension of family planning services to all persons desiring them, for research programs and for training the necessary manpower, and to submit periodic reports thereafter showing progress under the plan.

• Provided that low-income families would have priority in receiving cost-free family planning services.

• Provided that none of the funds appropriated could be used in programs where abortion was a method of family planning.

• Authorized project grants to public agencies and non-profit organizations and institutions to assist in the establishment and operation of voluntary family planning projects, with authorizations of $30-million in fiscal 1971, to be increased by $30-million a year up to fiscal 1973.

• Authorized formula grants to state health agencies, allocated according to state population and financial need, to assist in providing family planning services, provided that a state plan for comprehensive family planning services was approved by the HEW secretary, with authorizations of $10-million in fiscal 1971, to be increased by $5-million annually up to fiscal 1973.

• Established a program of grants to promote research in fields related to family planning; authorized appropriations of $35-million in fiscal 1971, $50-million in fiscal 1972 and $65-million in fiscal 1973.

ENVIRONMENTAL EDUCATION. A bill (HR 18260—PL 91-516) setting up a new program of environmental education was approved by Congress. With authorizations of $45-million for fiscal years 1971-73, the U.S. Office of Education was to award grants for the development of elementary, secondary and adult education programs in the field of environment.

Provisions. As cleared by Congress, HR 18260, the Environmental Education Act:

• Established in the U.S. Office of Education a program of grants for environmental education. Funds could be used for curriculum development, teacher training, establishment of community education programs (especially for adults), support for state and local educational agencies for elementary and secondary school programs, preparation and distribution of materials suitable for the mass media and planning of outdoor ecological study centers.

• Stipulated that the federal share of the cost of these programs could not exceed 80 per cent for the first year, 60 per cent for the second year and 40 per cent for the third year. Programs of curriculum development, dissemination and evaluation were exempted from this cost-sharing provision.

JOINT ENVIRONMENT COMMITTEE. A resolution (H J Res 1117) establishing a Joint Committee on the Environment died at the end of the 91st Congress after House and Senate conferees failed to reach agreement on differing versions of the resolution.

The House in May and the Senate in November approved similar resolutions to establish a 22-member committee to review environmental matters. The committee would have no legislative mandate—similar to the Joint Economic Committee—but could advise other committees on their legislation.

Similar resolutions were passed by the House and the Senate in 1971, but no further action was taken on the measures, which died at the close of the 92nd Congress. *(p. 790)*

ENVIRONMENTAL DATA SYSTEM. Although the House voted in 1970 to set up a national environmental system to consolidate all the government's information relating to the environment, the Senate took no action on the bill (HR 17436), and it died when the 91st Congress adjourned. The bill authorized $9-million over three years for a national clearinghouse for environmental information to service federal, state and local governments as well as private individuals and institutions.

Congress in 1972 completed action on similar legislation (HR 56) but President Nixon pocket vetoed the bill after Congress adjourned. *(p. 820)*

1971

President Nixon, in his Jan. 22 State of the Union address, cited environmental protection as one of the "six great goals" of his administration's domestic policy. In a special message Feb. 8, Nixon called for stiffer pollution controls including the imposition of taxes on sulfur emission and lead gas additives, strengthening of federal pesticide laws, regulation of ocean dumping, noise control legislation, land use controls and other programs of research and international cooperation.

Nixon proposed setting authorizations for the federal share of water pollution programs administered by the Environmental Protection Agency (EPA) at $2-billion annually for fiscal years 1972-74. The Senate in November unanimously passed a major water pollution bill that authorized $16.8-billion over four years. The bill set the goal of making the nation's waterways virtually pollution-free by 1985, and established a new program of granting permits to control discharge of wastes. The bill was criticized by the White House on grounds that it gave too much power to the federal government and not enough to the states. The House did not act on the measure in 1971, but similar legislation was enacted over the President's veto in 1972.

In other major environmental actions, Congress approved a bill settling a century-old claim by Alaskan natives to land ownership and two measures designed to protect wildlife from slaughter by commercial or recreational hunters; a bill to control ocean dumping was passed by both houses, although Congress did not complete action on the measure until 1972; the House passed a bill—which was enacted in revised form in 1972—tightening federal pesticide laws and setting up a class of "restricted use" pesticides which required a federal permit for use.

Congress dealt the administration a major defeat when it voted to end federal funding of the controversial supersonic transport (SST) airplane. Charges that the SST presented environmental hazards were a major factor in the vote. *(Chapter on Transportation)*

Meanwhile, as the year progressed, there were signs that an ecological backlash was setting in, as the public began to weigh the costs of cleaning up the environment. President Nixon's public statements reflected this shift. In his "clean energy" message in June, Nixon stressed the importance of developing a fast-breeder nuclear reactor by 1980 and maintained that it was possible to "balance environmental and energy needs." On Aug. 6, he warned against seeking "ecological perfection at the cost of bankrupting the very taxpaying enterprises which pay for the social advance the nation seeks." And in an address before the Economic Club of Detroit a month later, Nixon said: "We are not going to allow the environmental issue...to destroy the industrial system that made this the great country it is."

Concern over the economic effects of environmental protection was reflected by the House Appropriations Committee in its report on a bill (HR 9270—PL 92-73) providing funds for the Agriculture Department, environmental assistance and consumer protection in fiscal 1972. (In 1971, for the first time, environmental funding was consolidated in the agriculture appropriations bill; in previous years funding for environmental programs was scattered among the public works, Interior Department and Independent Offices-Department of Housing and Urban Development (HUD) appropriations bills.)

In recommending the full $2-billion requested by the administration for Environmental Protection Agency (EPA) grants, the Appropriations Committee warned that economic effects must be studied before the EPA laid down environmental rules.

"The estimated total cost of cleaning up the environment is so great," the committee said, "that we must establish priorities to make sure that we take care of those environmental problems which are dangerous to human health first, dangerous to our general environment second and those which are merely undesirable third."

The environmental portion of the final bill contained nearly $3.5-billion, including $2,448,400,000 for EPA, $500-million for HUD's water and sewer facilities grant program and $539.3-million for agricultural conservation programs.

WATER AND MARINE RESOURCES

Water Pollution

Legislation aimed at making the nation's waterways virtually pollution-free by 1985 and authorizing $16.8-billion to do the job passed the Senate unanimously in 1971 but was not acted upon in the House.

The new legislation (S 2770) would dramatically increase the federal investment in construction of sewer treatment plants and require local governments to charge user fees to pay for the treatment of wastes of industrial polluters. It would also require federal permits for discharging any wastes into navigable waters; industrial polluters would be required to install the most up-to-date abatement equipment available.

Although the $14-billion federal share for sewage treatment plants for fiscal years 1972-75 was more than double the President's request of $6-billion for the period 1972-74, no attempts were made on the Senate floor to reduce the scope of the bill.

One indirect attempt to limit spending—switching most of the $14-billion authorization from the contract authority procedure (which allows agencies to enter into

contracts ahead of appropriations but requires appropriations in following years to liquidate the contracts) to the traditional authorization-appropriation method—was defeated by a 34-58 roll-call vote. Under the latter method, appropriations often fall far short of authorizations, while funding comes closer to the maximum amount allowable through contract authority financing.

Shortly after Senate approval, the Nixon administration announced its opposition to the bill on the grounds it gave too much authority to the federal government and not enough to the states. The White House called upon the House Public Works Committee to reopen hearings on the measure, and hearings were held shortly before Congress adjourned. The committee ordered reported its version of the water bill in mid-December, but the report was not filed until the following March. Congress completed action on a similar measure in 1972. (p. 792)

Existing federal water pollution control programs had expired June 30, but Congress passed two temporary extensions. A third extension of the programs was not enacted in 1971, however, and existing legislation technically expired Oct. 31. (Box, p. 780)

Senate Action

Committee. The Senate Public Works Committee Oct. 28 unanimously reported S 2770, the Federal Water Pollution Control Act Amendments of 1971.

Its Air and Water Pollution Subcommittee had held extensive hearings on several bills in February and March, including a measure (S 523) sponsored by its chairman, Edmund S. Muskie (D Maine), which would have authorized $2.5-billion annually for fiscal years 1972-76 for pollution control programs. Also under consideration were four administration-backed bills—S 1012, authorizing funds for state grants; S 1013, authorizing $2-billion annually for fiscal years 1972-74 for construction of facilities; S 1014, setting water quality standards and enforcement, and S 1015, establishing an Environmental Financing Authority.

The committee's recommendations changed the thrust of federal water cleanup efforts from water quality standards (regulating the amount of pollutants in a given body of water) to effluent limitations (controlling the amount, rate and concentration of pollutants discharged from a given source).

The bill would establish a two-phase program for applying effluent limits. The first, to be implemented by 1976, required industrial polluters to use the best practicable technology to control discharges; the second, to be implemented by 1981, required the best available technology in cases where discharge could not be completely eliminated.

Besides setting a goal of eliminating all pollutant discharges by 1985, an interim goal of making the nation's waters suitable for swimming and fish propagation by 1981 was established.

"This legislation would clearly establish that no one has the right to pollute—that pollution continues because of technological limits, not because of any inherent right to use the nation's waterways for the purpose of disposing of wastes," the report said.

Total authorizations in the bill came to $2.4-billion for fiscal 1972; $3.6-billion for fiscal 1973; $4.8-billion for fiscal 1974, and $5.7-billion for fiscal 1975. In addition, $2.8-billion was authorized without limitation on fiscal year spending.

Floor. The Senate Nov. 2 unanimously approved S 2770, by an 86-0 roll-call vote. Although a number of amendments were adopted on the floor, none made major changes in the measure as reported by the committee.

An amendment offered by Allen J. Ellender (D La.) would have restored the Army Corps of Engineers' existing authority to grant permits for the dumping of dredged materials into waterways. Under the Refuse Act of 1899, the corps had authority to issue such permits, but S 2770 removed the issue-granting authority from the corps and transferred it to EPA.

Ellender said that shifting permit authority to EPA and requiring the corps to follow strictly the effluent standards to obtain permits for dumping sludge in its harbor dredging activities, "would result in 90 per cent of the ports and harbors of the United States being closed" until land disposal sites were designated.

Muskie said Ellender's amendment would exempt dredging by the corps from the effluent limitations imposed by the bill.

He then proposed a substitute for Ellender's amendment which specified that any application for discharging dredged material into the waterways must be accompanied by a certificate from the secretary of the Army that such dumping was the only reasonable alternative available. Muskie's substitute required that the permit be granted unless the EPA administrator found that dumping would harm municipal water supplies, wildlife, fisheries or recreation areas. The Muskie substitute for the Ellender amendment was adopted by voice vote.

A proposal offered by William Proxmire (D Wis.) to tax anyone dumping effluent into the waterways and to allow the funds collected to be used for water pollution control programs was rejected by voice vote. Proxmire argued that an economic incentive was missing to make factory owners comply with antipollution laws.

Another unsuccessful amendment, offered by J. Caleb Boggs (R Del.), ranking Republican on the Air and Water Pollution Subcommittee, would have deleted the provision providing funding for construction of waste treatment plants for fiscal years 1973-75 by contract authority. Instead, it would substitute the regular authorization-appropriation procedure for funding programs included in the bill.

(Under contract authority, the EPA administrator could enter into agreements with localities to provide grants without awaiting for Congress to enact an appropriations bill. Under the authorization-appropriation procedure, Congress would appropriate a specific sum—often much less than the amount authorized—and the administrator could not make agreements with localities until after Congress acted.)

Provisions. As passed by the Senate, S 2770 contained the following major provisions:

Title I—Research

• Established as federal policy the goal of making the nation's waters suitable for fish propagation and recreation by 1981 and of eliminating completely by 1985 the discharge of pollutants in navigable waters.

• Gave the administrator of the Environmental Pro-

Program Extensions

Federal water pollution control programs technically expired Oct. 31, 1971. Congress had approved two temporary extensions of the programs after existing legislation expired June 30. But a third bill which would have further extended the Federal Water Pollution Control Act was not acted upon by the Oct. 31 expiration date.

First Extension. On July 9 President Nixon signed into law a bill (S 2133—PL 92-50) extending through Sept. 30 authorizations for expiring federal water pollution control programs.

The major program authorized under the act was the program of grants to local governments for construction of sewage treatment facilities. The fiscal 1970 authorization for that program was $1.25-billion. President Nixon had proposed setting new authorizations at $2-billion annually through fiscal 1974, while other proposals pegged funding as high as $3-billion.

The interim extension set the three-month authorization at $500-million—the amount requested by the President. Total authorizations under the bill were $2.5-million—25 per cent of the fiscal 1971 authorization.

Second Extension. Congress in September voted a one-month extension (S 2613—PL 92-137) of the water programs, through Oct. 31. The measure increased authorizations by $150-million to $650-million for grants to local governments for waste treatment facilities.

Third Extension Failed. The House Oct. 28 passed a bill (HR 11423) extending the water pollution programs through Jan. 31, 1972, but the Senate Nov. 3 amended HR 11423 to extend the programs through Nov. 30. No further action was taken on the bill.

1972 Extension. Congress did not complete action on a further extension of the water programs until February 1972. The bill approved then (S 3122—PL 92-240) authorized a $1-billion increase in the state construction grant program through April 30, 1972.

---

tection Agency authority to plan programs to eliminate pollution from navigable waters and ground waters in cooperation with state and interstate water pollution agencies, municipalities, industries and the public. Fifty per cent federal-state matching grants for planning of pollution control in river basins were authorized.

• Authorized the administrator to conduct various types of research including the establishment of six field laboratories around the nation, a one-year study of problems associated with disposing of waste oils, a national monitoring and surveillance system, the measurement of social costs and benefits, methods to reduce unnecessary water consumption and control of agricultural pollution.

Title II—Construction Grants

• Authorized for construction grants of water pollution treatment plants under a formula based on population: fiscal 1972, $2-billion; fiscal 1973, $3-billion; fiscal

1974, $4-billion; fiscal 1975, $5-billion. (Fiscal 1972 funds would be provided by appropriations; fiscal 1973-75 funds would be provided by contract authority.)

• Set the federal share for construction of sewage treatment facilities at 60 per cent, which would be raised to 70 per cent if states agreed to contribute 10 per cent by grants to localities.

• Required applicants for construction grants to obtain from each industrial user a promise to repay the federal government for its share of the capital outlay required to dispose of the user's wastes. The applicant must adopt user charges by July 1, 1973, to guarantee that each type of user would pay its share of operating and maintenance costs of the facility.

• Authorized $2-billion in retroactive construction grants for all projects begun after June 30, 1966, to raise the federal share to at least 50 per cent; the funds must be spent to retire the project's indebtedness or to finance the local share of a new project. In addition, $400-million was authorized to reimburse projects built between 1956 and 1966, raising the federal share to 30 per cent.

Title III—Standards and Enforcement

• Specified that discharge of any pollutant was illegal, except as permitted under procedures set by the bill. By Jan. 1, 1976, all "point" sources of pollution (single sources, such as factories), except publicly owned treatment works, must use the "best practicable control technology currently available." Effluents sent through a publicly owned treatment works must meet specified pre-treatment standards. A timetable was set for public facilities to utilize secondary treatment. By 1981, non-public point sources must eliminate the discharge of pollutants; if the owner presented evidence to the administrator that compliance could not be attained at a reasonable cost, the source had to make use of the "best available technology." All discharge limitations must be reviewed every five years.

• Prohibited discharge into navigable waters of any radiological, chemical or biological warfare material, or any high-level radioactive waste.

• Required the administrator to publish within a year of enactment of the bill criteria on water quality and effluent-limitation guidelines. Other information would also be required on methods of pollution reduction, procedures for controlling pollution from "non-point" sources (pollution not confining its discharge to a specific location; would include run-off and accumulation from agriculture, mining or construction work), and pre-treatment standards for certain types of pollutants.

• Required the administrator to report to Congress by July 1, 1973, on the specific quality of all U.S. waters, including the identity of all point sources of pollution; required an inventory of waters currently suitable for swimming and fish propagation and waters which would meet those standards by 1976, 1981 or at some later date. States must report annually, beginning July 1, 1974, on existing water quality levels within their borders, including cost-benefit analyses of achieving water quality standards and reviews of non-point sources of pollution.

• Required the EPA administrator to promulgate new standards to eliminate or reduce pollution from new plants in various types of industries (the bill specified

Administration's Views

The Nixon administration opposed S 2770 in the form in which it passed the Senate Nov. 2 and began a campaign to have the bill rewritten in the House to return more controls to the states.

White House press secretary Ronald L. Ziegler told reporters Nov. 8 that the administration felt the states should have more control over water quality standards than S 2770 granted. Ziegler called for new hearings in the House "in which the states that are very much involved in this bill can make their views known."

S 2770 would abolish the existing system by which states set water quality standards, subject to federal approval, and reduce pollution within their borders to levels which would not exceed over-all pollution control standards. In its place, the bill would establish a system which would limit—and eventually abolish—effluents from any source of pollution. The new system would be supervised by the federal government unless a state demonstrated it could manage stricter controls.

Edmund S. Muskie (D Maine), chief sponsor of S 2770 and a prospective Democratic presidential candidate in 1972, said: "The Senate's unanimous vote to chart a new course of action in our fight to clean the nation's waters should have encouraged the White House environmentalists. Unfortunately, it appears that the administration has undergone an environmental metamorphosis, emerging from the cocoon not as a butterfly but as a moth."

Other major differences between S 2770, as passed by the Senate, and administration proposals included:

• The administration requested $2-billion annually for three years as the federal share of constructing water treatment facilities, with local governments qualifying for reimbursement of up to 50 per cent of construction costs. S 2770 contained a $14-billion authorization over four years and set the federal share at 60 per cent, with provision for raising the level to 70 per cent.

• The administration recommended funding the bill through the regular authorization-appropriation procedure. S 2770 authorized $2-billion for fiscal 1972 and provided that the remaining $12-billion proposed for fiscal 1973-75 would be funded by the contract authority procedure.

28 types) through use of the latest available control technology.

• Required the administrator to establish a roster of toxic substances and to set procedures to eliminate them and to set pre-treatment standards for the dumping of industrial discharges into public treatment facilities.

• Set procedures for dealing with violations and gave EPA authority to bring civil or criminal charges against violators and to assume enforcement over all facilities in a state if that state refused to act.

• Required EPA to designate hazardous materials which presented imminent hazards to public health or welfare.

Title IV—Permits and Licenses

● Established a system for granting EPA permits to discharge pollutants in navigable waters and allowed states to establish comparable programs.

● Specified that any application by the Corps of Engineers for a permit to discharge dredged material must be accompanied by a certificate from the secretary of the Army stating that the dumping of such material in navigable waters was the only reasonable alternative available; the permit would be granted unless the EPA administrator found that such discharge would harm municipal water supplies, wildlife, fisheries or recreation areas.

● Set procedures for granting EPA permits to dump materials into the oceans or coastal waters.

Title V—General Provisions

● Specified that if a pollution source presented an imminent or substantial danger to health, the EPA could issue an immediate abatement order.

● Allowed any citizen to bring a civil action against a person for violating an effluent limitation or a federal or state abatement order, or against the EPA administrator for failure to comply with the provisions of the bill. A state governor could bring suit against the administrator for failure to act on pollution in another state which adversely affected his state.

● Retained the rights of states and interstate agencies to set stricter standards than those contained in federal law.

House Action

The House Public Works Committee held intermittent hearings from May through September on numerous measures extending and expanding the federal program of water pollution control.

Following Senate passage in November of a far-reaching, multibillion-dollar pollution abatement bill, the House, in response to an administration request, reopened hearings on water cleanup. The White House was sharply opposed to the Senate version of the bill.

The House committee ordered reported its version of the water pollution control legislation in December, but the measure was not reported until 1972. *(p. 792)*

Ocean Dumping

A bill (HR 9727) to control the dumping of waste materials in the oceans passed both houses but was lodged in conference at the end of 1971. Congress completed action on the measure in the final week of the 1972 session. *(p. 798)*

The major differences between the two versions concerned the definition of waters covered, the dumping of dredge material and designation of marine sanctuaries to be preserved for recreational, ecological and esthetic values. The House bill had extended coverage under the act to oceans, estuaries and the Great Lakes. The Senate language covered the oceans, coastal waters and other waters beyond U.S. jurisdiction.

The House version had given the Army Corps of Engineers primary responsibility for controlling the dumping of dredged material, while the Senate had placed chief responsibility in the Environmental Protection Agency.

In addition, the Senate bill contained no marine sanctuaries provisions, while the House version added a third title to name and protect such areas.

In his environmental message Feb. 8, President Nixon had recommended banning unregulated ocean dumping of all materials and placing strict limits on ocean disposal of any materials harmful to the environment. In 1970, a report by the Council on Environmental Quality had indicated that while ocean dumping was not then a critical problem, dumping of materials harmful to man or marine life should be stopped at once and other dumping phased out unless research showed it posed no threat to the environment.

House Action

Committee. The House Merchant Marine and Fisheries Committee July 17 unanimously reported HR 9727, the Marine Protection, Research and Sanctuaries Act of 1971, with provisions similar to those in President Nixon's ocean-dumping legislation (HR 4723).

HR 9727 would prohibit the unregulated dumping of waste materials into the oceans, coastal waters or the Great Lakes, and would ban the transportation or dumping of chemical or biological warfare (CBW) agents or radioactive wastes. It set up a permit program under the direction of the Environmental Protection Agency (EPA) to control waste dumping.

Floor. After two days of debate, the House Sept. 9 passed HR 9727 by a 304-3 roll-call vote. The only major amendment to the bill adopted on the floor allowed states to maintain jurisdiction over ocean dumping occurring off their shores.

An amendment offered by Wayne N. Aspinall (D Colo.) to delete language authorizing the commerce secretary to name and protect marine sanctuary areas was rejected, as well as a proposal to delay the issuance of new mineral leases over the outer continental shelf until after studies on proposals for establishing new marine sanctuaries were completed.

Senate Action

Committee. The Senate Commerce Committee Nov. 12 reported HR 9727 with an amendment in the nature of a substitute bill. In a major change from the House version, the committee dropped the marine sanctuaries provisions (Title III) from the bill.

Floor. Later that month the Senate adopted four amendments to the bill before unanimously approving HR 9727 Nov. 24. None made major changes in the bill as reported.

An amendment offered by Gaylord Nelson (D Wis.) which would have reinstated the marine sanctuaries program was withdrawn after Henry M. Jackson (D Wash.), chairman of the Interior and Insular Affairs Committee, promised to hold hearings on the issue.

Related Action. Two international agreements dealing with ocean pollution caused by oil spills were ratified by the Senate in September.

Other Water Legislation

WATER RESOURCES INSTITUTES. Congress enacted a bill (HR 10203—PL 92-175) increasing authorizations for 51 existing water resources research institutes in the United States and establishing three new ones. A similar measure had died at the end of the 91st Congress. *(p. 768)*

HR 10203 increased the annual authorizations for each of the water resources research institutes in all 50 states and Puerto Rico to $250,000 from the previous level of $100,000 annually. In addition, it established new institutes in the District of Columbia, the Virgin Islands and Guam; authorizations for each of the new institutes were set at $125,000 for fiscal 1973, $200,000 for fiscal 1974 and $250,000 annually thereafter. The bill also made administrative changes in the operation of the program.

The Water Resources Research Act of 1964 had established in all 50 states and Puerto Rico research institutes on water resources. Authorizations for each institute were set at $100,000 annually. *(Congress and the Nation Vol. I, p. 897; Vol. II, p. 499)*

OCEANS AND ATMOSPHERE COMMITTEE. A National Advisory Committee on the Oceans and Atmosphere was established (HR 2587—PL 92-125) by Congress. The role of the 25-member committee was to improve the monitoring of the nation's efforts in marine and atmospheric science. It was expected to provide guidance in determining what kinds of research should be undertaken by the government and what types should be left to private maritime industries. The committee, whose members were to be appointed by the President, was to submit an annual report on or before June 30 of each year.

DESALINATION PROGRAMS. Congress in 1971 extended existing saline water conversion programs for five years, but instructed that they be phased out over an additional three-year period. The bill (S 991—PL 92-60), the Saline Water Conversion Act of 1971, extended through fiscal 1977 programs begun in 1952 to develop methods for the conversion of sea water and inland brackish water to water suitable for human consumption. *(Congress and the Nation Vol. I, p. 939; Vol. II, p. 499, 510, 519)*

As cleared by Congress, the bill made two major changes in previous extensions of authorizations approved by Congress in 1969 and 1970. *(p. 753, 768)* It expanded the program to cover chemically contaminated water as well as saline water and allowed up to 2 per cent of the funds to be used for research and development in foreign countries.

The bill set open-ended authorizations for research and development for fiscal years 1973-77. In addition, PL 92-60 provided three additional years beyond fiscal 1977 for phasing out research and completing other aspects of the program. The bill was signed into law July 29.

MARINE SAFETY. Congress did not complete action on legislation to promote marine safety and protect the environment in harbors and navigable waters. The House approved a bill (HR 8140) to establish federal controls in marine areas to reduce the increasing frequency of vessel accidents and to avoid pollution of ports, waterways and adjoining shorelines. As passed by the House Oct. 18, HR 8140 authorized the Coast Guard to supervise vessel traffic to encourage safety and prevent water pollu-

tion, but the measure did not apply to recreational and pleasure craft. The Senate took no action on the bill in 1971, but the measure cleared Congress in revised form in 1972.

LAND USE

Alaskan Native Claims

A century-old claim by Alaskan natives to land ownership was settled Dec. 14 when Congress cleared a bill (HR 10367—PL 92-203) granting them $962.5-million and 40 million acres of land.

The Alaska Native Claims Settlement Act provided the state's estimated 53,000 Eskimos, Aleuts and Indians with $462.5-million in federal grants and $500-million from state and federal mineral revenues. HR 10367 established a series of native corporations to administer the grants and other revenues.

The bill allowed native villages to choose 22 million acres of land, while the regional corporation could select an additional 16 million acres and the secretary of the interior would confer the remaining 2 million acres on the villages and regional corporations. The villages would hold only surface rights to the lands, while the regional corporations would retain mineral rights to all 40 million acres.

Settlement of native land claims would allow the state of Alaska to complete selecting an additional 80 million acres to which it was entitled under the Alaskan Statehood Act of 1958. The state was given the power to select 103 million acres from federal holdings, but state selection was frozen in 1966 pending settlement of native land claims.

Provisions were written into the bill to protect existing parks and wildlife refuges and to allow the federal government to claim an additional 80 million acres for national parks, forests or refuges.

Land claim settlement would also prevent legal challenges by native groups to drilling and transporting oil located in a massive field in the northern part of the state. Although the bill did not specifically authorize construction of the controversial trans-Alaska oil pipeline, it did guarantee that neither the state nor the natives could select lands set aside by the interior secretary for a pipeline corridor. *(Details, p. 807)*

The Senate in 1970 had passed a bill (S 1830) authorizing the payment of $1-billion ($500-million in cash and $500-million from a 2 per cent royalty on the sale of leasable minerals) and the grant of up to 10 million acres of land to the natives. The measure approved by the Senate in 1971 was identical to S 1830. *(p. 774)*

Legislative History

House Action. The House Interior and Insular Affairs Committee Sept. 28 by voice vote reported HR 10367 providing $925-million and 40 million acres of land for Alaskan natives to settle land claims.

Under the bill, Alaskan natives—Indians, Eskimos and Aleuts—would receive $425-million from the Treasury over a 10-year period, and $500-million from mineral revenues that would otherwise have gone mainly to the state government. Native assets would be administered through 12 regional corporations and a network of village corporations.

The report said that the $925-million assigned to the natives by the bill "is an arbitrary one...based on the following considerations: the extreme poverty and underprivileged status of the natives generally, and the need for adequate resources to permit the natives to help themselves economically." It said that the 40-million-acre land grant provision "is a generous grant by almost any standard."

The committee said the bill would cost the federal government $425-million in outright grants, and about $280,000 for the allotment of 2 per cent of its share of mineral revenues from federal lands in Alaska.

Twelve conservation groups objected to the bill in a letter to President Nixon Sept. 30. They said the House Interior Committee had responded to the "speculators and exploiters" who lobbied for "enormous grants of public land and some money for the natives, but no restraints upon the commercial exploitation of the public lands of Alaska."

The House approved the bill Oct. 20 in essentially the same form reported by the committee.

The key vote during the two days of debate came on an amendment sponsored by Morris K. Udall (D Ariz.) and John P. Saylor (R Pa.) and supported by a coalition of environmental groups. The Udall-Saylor amendment required that about 125 million acres be set aside as "national interest study areas" for possible inclusion in the future in various Alaskan national parks and established a federal-state planning commission to review land selection by natives and by the state. The amendment, rejected by a 177-217 recorded teller vote, was opposed by the Alaska Federation of Natives and the National Council of American Indians, both of which supported the committee version.

Senate Action. The Senate Interior and Insular Affairs Committee Oct. 21 unanimously reported S 35, authorizing the payment of $1-billion ($500-million in cash and $500-million from a 2 per cent royalty on the sale of leasable minerals) and the grant of up to 10 million acres of land to the natives.

The bill set up a system of native corporations to engage in business activities to benefit the natives and to implement social reforms. It also specified that the federal government would retain jurisdiction over a corridor across the North Slope "for recreation and transportation purposes." The North Slope corridor was the subject of a controversial proposal to pipe oil and gas across the state.

The report said that settlement of native land claims and the proposed trans-Alaska pipeline "are separate issues. Their relationship should not be confused and the reasonable and long-delayed expectations of the Alaska native people for a settlement of their land claims should not be further frustrated by efforts to address the questions raised by the pipeline proposal."

The committee emphasized that the provision dealing with federal jurisdiction over the North Slope recreation and transportation corridor did not grant approval for the pipeline. The provision merely guaranteed that any activities in that area "will be compatable with public recreation and stringent environmental controls," the committee said.

No opposition to HR 10367 was voiced during debate prior to its approval by the Senate Nov. 1. Before passage, however, the Senate had substituted the provisions of the committee-reported bill (S 35) for those of HR 10367. As passed, HR 10367 established two options for land selection by the natives, who would choose between plans in a statewide election held within a year of enactment of the bill.

Conference and Final Action. House and Senate conferees filed a report on HR 10367 in the closing days of the session. Both the size of the money settlement and the land selection procedure were altered by conferees from the House and Senate versions.

Conferees agreed to $462.5-million as the total federal payment to the natives. The House originally had voted $425-million and the Senate $500-million. The $500-million payment from mineral leasing revenues was identical in both versions.

The final version of the bill granted the natives title to 40 million acres of land—the same amount as in the House bill and one of the two options in the Senate measure—but modified the land selection system. The method settled on by conferees allowed the native villages to choose 22 million acres and the regional corporations to select 16 million acres, with the remaining 2 million acres to be picked by the interior secretary.

The House originally had voted to let the native villages pick 18 million acres of land, then allowed the state to select the remaining 80 million acres as provided in the Statehood Act. After state selection was completed, the regional corporations could choose their remaining 22 million acres.

The system outlined in the Senate version established two different methods of selection and provided for a statewide election by natives to decide their preference. The first option gave the natives 40 million acres near their villages, while the second option gave natives title to 30 million acres and control over an additional 20 million.

The system of regional development corporations outlined in the bill was similar to the House-passed provision, but it added one additional corporation to the 12 provided in the House bill. The 13th corporation, which was to receive money grants but no land, was for the benefit of natives living outside the state.

The Senate version had provided an Alaska Native Investment Corporation, an Alaska Native Services Corporation, seven regional corporations, an urban corporation for native residents of Alaskan cities and a national corporation for natives outside the state.

Other changes in the conference report included:

• Park lands—The conference report allowed the interior secretary to withdraw for seven years up to 80 million acres for possible inclusion in federal park or wildlife systems. The House had not provided any land to be set aside for parks; the Senate version provided for lands to be considered for parks, but had not set any maximum limit on the acreage.

• Pipeline—The final version of the bill specified that if the interior secretary chose to withdraw a transportation and utility corridor across the state—presumably for the trans-Alaska pipeline—then natives and the state could not select lands in the corridor. The House bill contained no provision for protecting a pipeline corridor. The Senate bill had withdrawn the corridor—giving the interior secretary no option—and specified that it remain under federal jurisdiction and subject to environmental protection laws.

The Senate adopted the conference report on HR 10367 Dec. 14 by voice vote. Although no dissent was voiced on the floor, Henry M. Jackson (D Wash.), Interior Committee chairman, inserted a statement in the *Congressional Record* listing reservations about the final version of the bill, including its failure to include provisions requiring competitive leasing of all public lands.

Although sharp objections to the land settlement were expressed on the floor, the House approved the conference report earlier the same day. John P. Saylor (R Pa.), ranking Republican on the Interior Committee, criticized the cost to the federal government of the bill as too high.

John H. Kyl (R Iowa), another committee member, defended the bill as "a step in the right direction to solve the problem of aboriginal people in one of our states. Ultimately we will find that the cost is very much less than it has been per capita for the natives in the lower 48. More than that, we give these people their birthright of individuality, of freedom and dignity."

Major Provisions

As signed by the President Dec. 18, major provisions of HR 10367, the Alaska Native Claims Settlement Act:
• Extinguished all aboriginal titles to Alaskan land and all claims based on such titles.
• Granted title to 40 million acres of land to be divided among native villages and 12 regional corporations. Villages must be incorporated and membership in village corporations was limited to natives. Villages would receive surface rights to about 18.5 million acres in the township areas surrounding their villages, divided on a population basis, and an additional 3.5 million acres divided among the villages by the regional corporations. The 12 corporations would hold mineral rights to the village-owned 22 million acres, plus full title (surface and subsurface rights) to an additional 16 million acres located in the township areas around the villages, divided on a land-area basis.

The natives would receive an additional 2 million acres, selected by the interior secretary and composed of the following: the regional corporations would get existing cemetery sites and historical sites; any native group too small to qualify as a village would receive surface rights of up to 23,040 acres, while the mineral rights would be held by the regional corporations; any individual native living outside a village would receive surface rights of up to 160 acres, while the mineral rights would be held by the regional corporations; natives in four towns which were originally native villages but were currently composed chiefly of non-natives would receive surface rights of up to 23,040 acres, while the mineral rights would be held by the regional corporations; and the balance of the 2 million acres, if any would go to the regional corporations.
• Authorized the payment of $462.5-million in federal funds, over an 11-year period, to the regional and village corporations and $500-million from mineral revenues received from lands acquired by the state under the Statehood Act and from remaining federal lands. The mineral revenues would take the form of a 2 per cent royalty on minerals extracted and 2 per cent of bonuses and rentals, with no time limitation.
• Required the establishment of 12 regional corporations and allowed natives living outside of Alaska to form a 13th regional corporation if they wished. All 13 corporations would share the $962.5-million grant on a population basis. The first 12 corporations would hold title to lands they were entitled to, plus mineral rights for lands held by the villages. (The non-resident corporation would receive no land and would not share in mineral revenues of other corporations.)

Each regional corporation would distribute at least half of its share of the $962.5-million grant and half of all revenues from the mineral rights among the village corporations. Each corporation must share 70 per cent of its mineral revenues with the other corporations. For the first five years, 10 per cent of the mineral revenues and cash settlement must be distributed among individual native stockholders.
• Established a 10-member joint federal-state land use planning commission, with at least one native member, with advisory duties but no regulatory or enforcement powers. The commission was to go out of existence in five years.
• Allowed the secretary of the interior to withdraw from selection by either the state or natives up to 80 million acres of unreserved lands for possible inclusion in the national park, forest, wildlife refuge or scenic river systems. The withdrawal was to last for seven years.
• Specified that if the secretary of the interior set aside a utility and transportation corridor for the trans-Alaska pipeline, neither the state nor the natives could select lands in the corridor.
• Set open-ended authorizations to carry out the provisions of the act.

Pesticide Regulation

Legislation regulating the manufacture, distribution and use of pesticides was approved by the House but the Senate took no action on the bill (HR 10729) in 1971. The measure cleared Congress in revised form in 1972. *(p. 800)*

As approved by the House, the Federal Environmental Pesticide Control Act of 1971 would make the first major changes in pesticide regulations in nearly 25 years. HR 10729 for the first time required all pesticides to be registered with the Environmental Protection Agency (EPA), which would regulate their use.

Under HR 10729, pesticides were divided into two categories—"general use" and "restricted use." Pesticides which would not cause "substantial adverse effects" on the environment when applied according to directions were classified for general use. Restricted-use pesticides could cause such harm and could be applied only by EPA-certified persons or companies.

New procedures were set up by the bill for the EPA administrator to register and to suspend registration of all pesticides, subject to judicial review. It set civil penalties of up to $5,000 and criminal penalties of up to $25,000 in fines and a year in prison for violating the pesticide control law.

HR 10729 also provided for indemnity payments to manufacturers of pesticides whose registrations were canceled by EPA because the substances were found to be hazardous, and provided for protection of trade secrets and other confidential data.

Growing concern since the early 1960s over the effect of pesticides on humans, wildlife and the environment in general had produced pressure for stricter federal control over certification and use of pesticides. Existing legislation, enacted in 1947, was primarily a labeling law. *(Box, p. 787)*

Administration Proposal. President Nixon proposed new legislation to regulate pesticides on Feb. 8, 1971. Provisions of the 1947 act were "cumbersome and time-consuming," he said, and lacked authority to deal with the actual use of pesticides. "A comprehensive strengthening of our pesticide control laws is needed," Nixon said.

Nixon proposed that pesticides be classified for registration in three categories: "general use," "restricted use" and "use by permit only," with strict controls over the latter two groups. He also proposed improving procedures for canceling registrations and authorizing EPA to stop the sale of illegal pesticides.

Bills containing these proposals were introduced in the House and Senate. Both the House Agriculture Committee and the Senate Agriculture and Forestry Committee held hearings in 1971.

House Action

Committee. The House Agriculture Committee reported HR 10729 Sept. 25 by a 13-6 non-recorded vote—with only a bare majority of the 37-member committee voting on the measure.

The act was neither a farmer's, a manufacturer's nor an environmentalist's bill, but rather "a mixture of each, a composite of all," the committee stated in its report.

But in additional views, John G. Dow (D N.Y.), criticized the bill for failing to establish a balanced approach to the pesticides problem, limiting information disclosure and placing the burden of proof of adverse effects on the EPA rather than the manufacturer.

As reported the bill did not contain a provision opposed by the Nixon administration which would have banned the import of pesticides from any nations which did not have pesticide restrictions at least as strict as the U.S. law. While marking up the bill, the committee originally voted to include the import provision but subsequently voted to delete it by an 18-6 non-recorded vote. The report said the matter should be covered by separate legislation.

Floor. The House passed HR 10729 Nov. 9, after two days of vigorous debate during which House environmentalists unsuccessfully attempted to strengthen the bill.

As approved by the House, the bill contained only one change in the committee version. An amendment adopted on the floor would allow states to administer their own laws if they were stricter than federal standards. Several states, notably Michigan, Wisconsin and Massachusetts, already had stringent pesticide laws in effect.

Numerous conservation groups opposed the Agriculture Committee's bill and supported a substitute offered during the floor debate by Dow. Among the changes in

Dow's substitute were preservation of stricter state laws, continuation of existing law allowing citizen suits challenging pesticide registration, a requirement that manufacturers prove environmental effect or lack of effect and elimination of provisions in the committee bill directing that the lack of an established need was not to be considered in granting certification.

Among the groups supporting the Dow substitute were the Sierra Club, National Wildlife Federation, Wilderness Society, Izaak Walton League, Friends of the Earth, Environmental Action, American Association of Pesticide Control Officials, International Association of Game, Fish and Conservation Commissioners, Sport Fishing Institute and Wildlife Management Institute. Supporting the committee version of the bill were the EPA, the Department of Agriculture and the American Farm Bureau Federation.

No direct vote was taken on the Dow amendment, but several of the changes which he recommended in the committee bill were rejected in a series of recorded and non-recorded votes. Also defeated were three amendments which would have restricted or eliminated indemnity payments for banned pesticides. The amendment that was approved, allowing states to administer their own laws, was sponsored by John H. Kyl (R Iowa), a member of the Agriculture Committee, with the assent of the committee chairman, W.R. Poage (D Texas).

Provisions. As approved by the House, the bill contained major provisions which:

- Required all pesticides to be registered with EPA. (Existing law applied only to pesticides in interstate commerce.)

- Established two classifications of pesticides—general use and restricted use. General use pesticides were those which the EPA administrator determined would not cause substantial adverse effects on the environment when applied according to directions. Restricted use pesticides were those which could cause adverse effects on the environment if used without restrictions.

- Specified that restricted use pesticides could be used only by or under the supervision of a certified pesticide applicator or subject to other regulatory restrictions. The EPA administrator was required to set standards for certifying both commercial and private applicators. (Most private applicators were expected to be farmers.) The states could certify applicators if EPA approved plans, to be administered by the states, which were at least as strict as federal standards.

- Set new procedures for the EPA administrator to register and to suspend registration of all pesticides. Lack of essentiality could not be used as a criterion to deny certification of a pesticide.

- Allowed states to regulate the sale or use of a pesticide as long as they did not permit the sale or use of substances prohibited by the federal government. Gave the federal government sole authority to set labeling or packaging requirements.

- Exempted exported pesticides which did not meet U.S. standards but met the standards of the foreign purchaser.

(Continued on p. 788)

Pesticides Use: Background on Controversy

Public attention was first focused on pesticides by the publication, in 1962, of *Silent Spring* by Rachel Carson. This influential book argued that many pesticides had unknown and cumulative effects which could be determined only by many years of tests. Since so little was known about the effects of these chemicals on plants, animals and humans, their use should be curtailed, Carson said. She also criticized the U.S. Department of Agriculture's endorsement of increased pesticide use, and contended that farmers often exceeded permitted tolerances without detection.

Wide Use, Long History. The use of chemicals in agriculture began in the mid-19th century, when the trend toward intensive farming and specialized crops created imbalances in nature which sometimes led to great increases in pest population. As agriculture became a commerical production industry, pesticides began playing an increasingly important role.

According to the U.S. Department of Agriculture the average corn yield increased about three times between 1940 and 1972, and rice yields more than doubled. U.S. production of 17 major crops in 1969, if produced with the average yields of 1940, would have required use of an area equal to Texas, New Mexico and Arizona combined, department spokesmen said. Without pesticides, the department estimated that there would be a 25 per cent loss of livestock and a 30 per cent drop in crop production.

Pesticides also were widely used in the production of lumber and cotton.

In 1947, Congress enacted the Insecticide, Fungicide and Rodenticide Act (PL 80-104) to replace the Insecticide Act of 1910. The way law required registration of economic poisons or chemical pesticides prior to their sale in interstate or foreign commerce. It also specified that labels must include poison warnings or other warnings of possible injury and instructions for use. Subsequent amendments in 1954 required pretesting of pesticides used on food crops and in 1959 widened the definition of pesticides. Another law in 1964 provided for the removal of unsafe pesticides from the market. *(Congress and the Nation, Vol. I, p. 1169, 1173, 1178, 1184)*

More than 1 billion pounds of pesticides and related products were produced in the United States in 1970. In all, approximately 60,000 products made from one or more of the 900 chemical compounds were registered with the Environmental Protection Agency (EPA). All sterilizing, disinfecting, sanitizing, germicidal and bacteria-killing chemicals—except those sold exclusively for use on or in the living bodies of people or animals—were classified as "pesticides" and must be registered.

Possible Hazards. Since 1962, warnings of the possible dangers of pesticides had received increasing public attention. Their effects on wildlife had been the subject of hundreds of research projects since discovery in the late 1960s of harmful buildups of DDT and other chemicals in brown pelicans, bald eagles, peregrine falcons, fish and other animals.

Some pesticides moved up the food chain through a process called biological magnification, in which minute quantities of chemicals absorbed by plankton or insects were transferred in constantly increasing quantities to fish, birds and larger animals feeding on one another, and stored in body fat and tissues.

Scientists also began examining the possible accumulation of pesticides in human beings. They discovered that Americans carried in their bodies an average of 12 parts per million of pesticide residues, nearly twice the level allowed for most foods in interstate commerce. Evidence presented in 1970 showed that even very small quantities of DDT could affect the human metabolism. The National Cancer Institute reported in 1969 that 11 of 123 pesticides tested caused increased incidence of tumors in laboratory animals.

Studies and Recommendations. "Pesticides are now affecting individuals, populations and communities of natural organisms.... Within the organochlorine group of pesticides, there is a wide range of potential for acute toxicity of man. The organophosphate pesticides...are health hazards because of their high toxicity and ease of absorption by ingestion and the dermal or respiratory routes," concluded a 1970 study by a commission on pesticides which had been created in the Department of Health, Education and Welfare (HEW). The commission recommended that many pesticides be restricted to specific essential uses.

The recommendation was not new. As early as 1963, a presidential commission recommended orderly reduction in—and eventual elimination of—the use of persistent pesticides.

But a 1968 study by the General Accounting Office (GAO) showed that federal agencies—particularly the Agriculture Department's pesticide regulation division—took little action to enforce the Federal Fungicide, Insecticide and Rodenticide Act of 1947 which required registration and proper labeling of pesticides.

The GAO study said the department had not initiated a single criminal prosecution for 13 years despite evidence of repeated violations. Of 2,751 pesticides tested in 1966, 750 were found to violate the law and 562 of these were major violations, the report said. But the Agriculture Department acted to remove pesticides from the market only 106 times, and in many cases merely seized products from the initial site where they were discovered without recalling them from other locations.

The House Government Operations Committee held hearings in 1969 on enforcement of the 1947 act and issued a report which severely criticized the pesticides regulations division. The report cited numerous deficiencies in the division's operations which it said should be corrected.

After creation of the Environmental Protection Agency (EPA) in 1970, the registration and monitoring responsibilities were transferred to EPA, whose enforcement division was somewhat more active in enforcing the 1947 law.

• Provided indemnity payments to owners of pesticides for which registrations were canceled by EPA after a determination that the substances were hazardous.

• Set civil penalties for violations of the act at up to $5,000 per violation. Violations by private pesticide applicators would be punishable by fines of up to $1,000. Persons who knowingly violated the act would be subject to criminal charges of up to $25,000 in fines and a year in prison; in the case of private applicators, criminal charges would be up to $1,000 in fines and 30 days in prison. EPA could issue warnings, seek court injunctions, and seize pesticides and devices.

Other Land Use Bills

COASTAL MANAGEMENT. In the closing weeks of the session, the Senate Commerce Committee reported a bill establishing a grant program for states to develop and operate coastal zone management programs. No further action was taken on the measure (S 582) in 1971, but the bill cleared Congress in revised form in 1972. (*p. 799*)

As reported by the committee Dec. 1, the program would allow states along the Atlantic and Pacific Coasts, the Gulf of Mexico, Long Island Sound and the Great Lakes to establish coastal zone management programs and to acquire and operate estuarine sanctuaries.

The bill authorized $12-million for fiscal 1972 and open-ended authorizations for fiscal 1973-76 for development of management programs for the land and water resources of the coastal and estuarine zone. Federal funds would finance up to two-thirds of the program. After management programs were developed, the federal government would finance up to two-thirds of the operating costs for such programs. For operations, the bill authorized $50-million for fiscal 1973 and open-ended authorizations thereafter. The bill authorized $6-million for grants of up to 50 per cent to finance state estuarine sanctuary programs and $1.5-million annually for administration of the program.

The report said, "By providing grants-in-aid to the states bordering the Atlantic and Pacific coasts, the Gulf of Mexico, Long Island Sound and the Great Lakes, the bill provides financial incentive to those states to undertake the responsibility for establishing management programs for each state's coastal and estuarine zone. No attempt is made to diminish state authority by federal pre-emption, but rather to enhance it by encouraging and assisting the states to assume planning and regulatory powers over their coastal and estuarine zones."

NATIONAL FOREST SAFETY. Congress approved legislation (HR 3146—PL 92-82) authorizing the Agriculture Department to cooperate with state and local law enforcement agencies in the enforcement of state or local laws on National Forest system lands. The bill also covered reimbursement to states and localities for expenses of protecting federal forest lands. The cost of the legislation was estimated at $4.7-million for fiscal 1972; $7.5-million, fiscal 1973; $8.3-million, fiscal 1974; $9.1-million, fiscal 1975 and $9.4-million, in fiscal 1976.

FOREST MANAGEMENT. Congress failed to complete action on a bill boosting authorizations for the forest management and fire-fighting programs of the U.S. Forest Service (within the Agriculture Department). The House approved a bill (HR 8817) increasing to $15-million from $5-million the annual authorization for the cooperative forest management program in which the federal government helps finance state programs providing technical forest management aid to private landowners, forest operators, wood processors and public agencies. The bill cleared Congress in 1972. (*P. 811*)

The House-passed bill also doubled the annual authorization for grants to states to combat forest fires—raising the level to $40-million.

Congress in 1950 had cleared the Cooperative Forest Management Act (PL 81-729) which set up programs of forest management aid. (*Congress and the Nation Vol. I, p. 1054*)

WILDLIFE PROTECTION

MARINE MAMMALS. The House failed to pass legislation (HR 10420) setting up a federal permit program for the killing of marine mammals. By a 199-150 recorded teller vote, the House Dec. 6 refused to pass HR 10420, the Marine Mammal Protection Act, under suspension of the rules.

Although a majority of House members voted in favor of the measure, passage under suspension of the rules requires a two-thirds majority—and proponents fell 34 votes short of the 233 needed in that case for passage.

The bill provided for a permit system for the killing of marine mammals, including polar bears, whales, porpoises, seals, sea otters and others—some of them in danger of extinction because of commercial slaughtering or hunting for recreation. The permit program would have been administered jointly by the secretaries of the Departments of Commerce and Interior.

The bill had the support of some environmental groups, but others—including Friends of the Earth, Defenders of Wildlife, Fund for Animals and World Federation for the Protection of Animals—lobbied strenuously for another bill imposing a moratorium on the killing of ocean mammals. Congress in 1972 banned most marine mammal killings. (*Background, 1972 action, p. 812, 814*)

Committee Action. The House Merchant Marine and Fisheries Committee Dec. 4 unanimously reported HR 10420.

The committee considered a two-year moratorium on the killing of such animals, but rejected it—"not because the committee was unsympathetic with its objectives, but rather because it was felt that the situation of the animals demanded a more flexible means of handling problems that may arise. As a practical matter, with regard to practically all of the species and stocks involved, there will exist a de facto moratorium for at least two years, and very probably longer."

Floor Action. The House Dec. 6 under suspension of the rules failed to give the bill the two-thirds vote necessary for passage.

John D. Dingell (D Mich.), floor manager of the bill, said that HR 10420 contained numerous safeguards for public participation in setting limitations on the killing of various types of marine mammals. "I simply do not believe that any administrator, forced to operate in that kind of goldfish bowl, can abuse the discretion that the committee has given him."

David Pryor (D Ark.), sponsor of another bill banning the killing of marine mammals, said, "This legislation falls far too short of what we must do and what we know we must do...I would doubt very seriously that those people who are involved in the seal killings are going to inquire as to whether that seal is two months old, eight months old, one year old, or two years old."

Provisions. As reported, major provisions of HR 10420, the Marine Mammal Protection Act of 1971 would have:

• Prohibited the importation of any marine mammal for commercial purpose which is pregnant, nursing (either parent or baby), less than eight months old, classified as an endangered species or taken inhumanely.

• Authorized the secretaries of interior and commerce to set limitations on the killing of marine mammals based on scientific evaluations of what is best for that species or stock of animals. Public participation was provided for. Permits would be issued for the taking of any marine mammal, and no one—with the exception in some cases of Eskimos and Alaskan natives—would be allowed to kill any animal without a permit.

• Set civil penalties up to $10,000 per violation and criminal penalties up to $20,000 or a year in jail for violation of the act or of permits or regulations issued under the act. Vessels engaged in violations of the act could be seized. The Coast Guard was given authority for enforcement.

• Established a three-member Marine Mammal Commission appointed by the President to review laws and treaties, review information on management of stocks, conduct research, recommend new administrative procedures and treaties, recommend new policies and advise on additions to the endangered species list.

HUNTING FROM AIRCRAFT. Spurred by reports of wild animals shot from aircraft, Congress in 1971 made it a federal crime to shoot, harass or hunt any bird, fish or animal from an airplane.

The new legislation (HR 5060—PL 92-159) set maximum penalties of up to $5,000 in fines and a year in prison for violations. Exceptions were permitted for employees or agents of the federal or state governments or holders of state or federal permits to protect land, water, animals, people or crops. Permit holders, however, were required to report quarterly on the number and type of animals they killed.

Congress had failed to complete action on a similar bill in 1970. *(p. 776)* In 1972, Congress amended PL 92-159 to give enforcement authority to the Interior Department. *(p. 813)*

Background. Public outrage over widely publicized instances of hunting animals from airplanes prompted congressional action. In November 1969, a television documentary on North American wolves which included several scenes of shooting from aircraft aroused strong public support for the prohibition. A Wyoming pilot testifying before a Senate subcommittee in August 1971 revealed that sheep ranchers had killed about 500 bald and golden eagles in a similar manner.

Congress in 1972 voted stiffer penalties for violations of law protecting bald and golden eagles. *(p. 814)*

WILD HORSES. Congress Dec. 3 cleared for the President a bill designed to protect the estimated 9,000 to 10,000 unclaimed wild horses and about 10,000 wild burros on public lands. At the beginning of the 20th century, an estimated two million wild free-roaming horses existed in the West.

The bill (S 1116—PL 92-195) put all free-roaming horses and burros under the jurisdiction of the Interior Department's Bureau of Land Management and the Agriculture Department's Forest Service. It required management of the animals "in a manner that is designed to achieve and maintain a thriving natural ecological balance on the public lands."

Animals could be destroyed—in a humane manner— for population control or to aid maintenance. Animals could not be destroyed if they strayed onto private lands, except by federal agents.

A joint advisory board would be established to make recommendations about the animal program. Penalties of up to $2,000 in fines and a year in jail were set for violations of the act.

The bill was signed into law Dec. 15.

CONSERVATION OF FISHERIES. Congress completed action on a bill (HR 3304—PL 92-219) amending the Fishermen's Protective Act of 1967 to enhance the effectiveness of international fishery conservation programs.

The bill authorized the President to prohibit the importation of fish products from nations which conducted fishing operations detrimental to international conservation programs.

As originally introduced in the House, HR 3304 was intended primarily to conserve and protect Atlantic salmon of North American origin. But the scope of the legislation was expanded in committee to include all fish species protected by international programs.

Provisions. As signed into law (PL 92-219) Dec. 23, major provisions of HR 3304:

• Directed the secretary of commerce, whenever he determined that foreign nationals were conducting fishing operations which diminished the effectiveness of international fishery conservation programs, to certify this fact to the President.

• Authorized the President to direct the secretary of the treasury to prohibit the importation into the United States of fish products of the offending country for such time as he believed warranted and to the extent sanctioned by the General Agreement on Tariffs and Trade (GATT).

• Required the President within 60 days after certification to notify Congress of any action he took, or to explain his reasons if he failed to take action.

OTHER LEGISLATION

WEATHER MODIFICATION. Congress imposed limited restrictions on persons attempting to change the weather and gave the Commerce Department new responsibility for keeping track of such activities.

Congress approved legislation (HR 6893—PL 92-205) requiring anyone engaging in weather modification activities to report those actions to the federal government. Authority to authorize, prohibit or otherwise regulate weather modification activities, however, remained with the states; 29 had enacted legislation relating to weather modification by 1971.

Until 1969, the National Science Foundation (NSF) was charged with the responsibility of maintaining reports on weather modification activities. But in 1968,

Congress enacted a bill (PL 90-407) making changes in the organization and operation of the NSF, and its responsibility for weather modification information was dropped. This authority was not transferred to any other agency and since then there had been no central source of information on weather modification research being carried out in the United States. *(Congress and the Nation Vol. II, p. 718)*

During consideration of HR 6893, the House Interstate and Foreign Commerce Committee made two substantive changes in the bill as introduced with the support of the administration. The committee replaced language authorizing open-ended appropriations with fixed authorizations for fiscal 1972-74 (totaling $550,000) and added a provision requiring the commerce secretary to make information received by him available to the public to the fullest practicable extent. The committee's recommendations were included in both the House and Senate versions of the bill.

Provision. As cleared by Congress, major provisions of HR 6893:

• Required persons engaged in welfare modification activities to file a report on those activities with the secretary of commerce, unless those persons were acting on behalf of the federal government.

• Required the secretary to maintain a record of all weather modification research and activities and to publish periodically summaries of such information to be made available to the public to the fullest extent practicable. Trade secrets and other confidential information would be available only to other government agencies, in judicial proceedings under court order and to protect public health and safety.

• Set fines up to $10,000 for deliberate violations of the act.

NOISE CONTROL. An administration proposal (S 1016) to reduce pollution by noise was the subject of hearings in June and July by a Senate Commerce subcommittee, but the committee took no action on the bill in 1971. Congress enacted comprehensive noise control legislation in 1972. *(p. 817)*

In his Feb. 8 environment message, President Nixon proposed establishing a noise pollution control program which would authorize the Environmental Protection Agency (EPA) to set noise limits on transportation, construction and other equipment and require labeling of certain other products.

Aircraft Noise. Also in July, another Senate Commerce subcommittee held a hearing on legislation to reduce and control aircraft noise, but failed to report out a bill in 1971. The problem of aircraft noise was addressed by the comprehensive noise control bill which cleared Congress in 1972.

In 1968, Congress enacted a bill (HR 3400—PL 90-411) to provide for aircraft noise abatement. The measure, which applied only to non-military aircraft, gave the Federal Aviation Administration (FAA) power to set aircraft noise and sonic boom standards as part of its authority to certify aircraft for use. *(Congress and the Nation Vol. II, p. 250)*

The administration's bill, S 1016, would remove the FAA's independent authority to establish standards for aircraft noise control by allowing the Environmental Protection Agency to veto standards, rules and regulations set by the FAA.

S 1566, introduced by Alan Cranston (D Calif.), would require significant aircraft noise reduction by Jan. 1, 1976. The bill would authorize funds for research and development and would provide guaranteed loans to airlines to finance costs of noise reduction.

John H. Shaffer, the FAA administrator, told the subcommittee that the requirement to reduce noise levels for all aircraft by standards set in S 1566 was arbitrary and "beyond our technological capacity to accomplish." He supported the administration's proposal.

ENVIRONMENTAL DATA SYSTEM. Congress in 1971 failed to complete action on a bill (HR 56) establishing a national environmental data system. The measure cleared Congress in revised form in 1972 but was pocket vetoed by President Nixon after the Congress adjourned. *(p. 820)*

As passed by the House May 17, HR 56 established a central facility to serve as a clearinghouse for new and existing information on environmental matters to be gathered from the federal, state and local governments and private institutions. The information would be available without charge to Congress and federal, state and local governments and upon payment of a reasonable fee to private persons or groups. A total of $6-million was authorized for operations of the system over three years.

Numerous government agencies, including the Council on Environmental Quality and the Environmental Protection Agency, had opposed the bill, recommending that no action be taken pending further study of the need for such a system.

HR 56 was similar to a measure (HR 17436) passed by the House in late 1970. The Senate took no action on the bill and it died at the end of the 91st Congress. *(p. 778)*

NATIONAL ENVIRONMENTAL CENTER. A bill (S 1113) establishing a national environmental center and a network of independent environmental laboratories was approved by the Senate Dec. 7, but the House took no action on the measure and it died at the end of the 92nd Congress. By taking an interdisciplinary approach, the national center was to supplement existing federal research.

ENVIRONMENT COMPACT. Legislation granting advance congressional consent to interstate agreements to combat joint environmental problems was reported late in the session by the Senate Judiciary Committee. The bill (S 907) was known as the Interstate Environment Compact.

Under existing procedures on interstate compacts, each affected state legislature and Congress had to agree to such an arrangement before it could be put into effect. The Interstate Environment Compact, if approved by Congress and any state legislature that wanted to participate, would allow states to enter into joint pollution abatement agreements without specific approval by Congress. Such projects by two or more states would be known as supplementary agreements.

After it was reported by the Judiciary Committee, S 907 was sent to the Public Works Committee, which had to give its approval to the measure before it could be brought to the Senate floor for a vote.

The Public Works Committee approved S 907 in 1972 and the Senate later passed the bill, but the House took no action on the measure and it died at the end of the 92nd Congress. *(p.821)*

Background. The Southern Governors Conference originated the compact proposal and recruited the support of Sen. John L. McClellan (D Ark.), chairman of the Government Operations Committee and second-ranking Democrat on the Judiciary Committee. In the House, Rules Committee Chairman William M. Colmer (D Miss.) and 20 cosponsors introduced a companion bill (HR 5446).

Led by the Southern Governors Conference, many governors and state government organizations argued that states would be more than willing to tackle joint pollution problems if the procedure were simpler. But getting approval by state legislatures and Congress took years—an average of eight to nine years, one expert estimated—while the pollution continued unabated or joint programs operated without legal standing. The compact would allow interstate projects to be put into action in far less time and would stimulate interest in more joint efforts, proponents asserted.

The opponents, led by Friends of the Earth, an environmental group, feared that such a device would allow an end-run around strict federal standards in such areas as air and water pollution and solid waste disposal. If delays occurred in the past, they argued, it was because the proposed interstate compacts were defective—not because Congress was failing to do its duty. Each proposed compact should be required to stand or fall on its own merits; Congress should not give blanket approval in advance for so broad a range of programs, they contended.

JOINT ENVIRONMENT COMMITTEE. Differing versions of a joint resolution establishing a Joint Committee on the Environment passed both the House and the Senate in 1971. But the resolution was never sent to conference to resolve differences between the House (H J Res 3) and Senate (S J Res 17) versions, and the bill died at the end of the 92nd Congress. Congress had failed to complete action on a similar resolution in 1970.

The chief difference between the House and Senate versions of the resolution was a provision in S J Res 17 which exempted appointments to the new joint committee from a provision of the Legislative Reorganization Act of 1970 (PL 91-510) restricting to one the number of joint committees on which a senator could serve. House conferees in 1970 had objected to amending the reorganization act through another bill on a different topic.

As approved by the Senate, S J Res 17 established a non-legislative Joint Committee on the Environment to study environmental matters.

The only controversy arose over an amendment proposed by Lee Metcalf (D Mont.) to delete from the resolution language exempting members appointed to the new committee from a provision of the Legislative Reorganization Act which limited each senator to membership on only one joint committee. (A resolution adopted by the Senate late in 1970 provided that a senator serving in the 92nd Congress on more than one joint committee could exchange one of these positions for membership on another joint committee without giving up all other joint committee assignments.) The effect of the Metcalf amendment would be to bar from service on the proposed joint environment committee 70 senators, including Edmund S. Muskie (D Maine), Jennings Randolph (D W.Va.), chairman of the Public Works Committee, Henry M. Jackson (D Wash.), chairman of the Interior Committee and Warren G. Magnuson (D Wash.) who headed the Commerce Committee.

The Metcalf amendment was defeated by a 36-43 roll-call vote.

As passed by the House, H J Res 3 set up a Joint Committee on the Environment to investigate environmental issues, but specified that it had no authority to propose legislation or investigate any subject which was already being studied by a House or Senate legislative committee.

Before passing the resolution, the House rejected an amendment prohibiting any member of the proposed congressional committee from becoming a candidate for President "until the issuance of the commission's (joint committee's) last press release."

The amendment, offered by H.R. Gross (R Iowa), was an obvious swipe at Senator Muskie, an undeclared Democratic presidential contender and a leader of Senate forces to establish the new committee.

1972

Six major environmental measures cleared Congress in the final days of the 1972 session, which along with numerous other bills in the fields of conservation and natural resources, helped give the 92nd Congress the most productive record for environmental protection in the nation's history.

The six bills—setting up federal controls over water pollution, ocean dumping, coastal zones, noise, pesticides and sea mammals—were passed after months of conferences and compromises which culminated in a rush of action during the two weeks before adjournment Oct. 18.

Perhaps the most dramatic vote came on the last day of the session when Congress overrode President Nixon's veto of the Federal Water Pollution Control Act Amendments of 1972, a comprehensive $24.7-billion measure aimed at cleaning up the nation's waters by 1985. The bill had cleared Congress Oct. 4 but was vetoed Oct. 17.

The other five measures were cleared in the last week of the session when both houses adopted conference reports or agreed to changes made during eleventh-hour negotiations between members of corresponding House and Senate committees.

In addition, the 92nd Congress set the stage for further action early in 1973 on other important environmental legislation. A toxic chemicals control bill passed both bodies but died when the House refused to accept a few late Senate changes. A tough strip mining control bill passed the House by a wide margin, but the Senate took no floor action. And one land use bill passed the Senate while another was reported out of committee; a House bill also was reported but did not reach the floor.

Among other environmental bills cleared by Congress in 1972 were measures to make hunting from aircraft a federal crime, to make surplus federal lands available for wildlife conservation use, to provide funds for accelerated reforestation of national forests, and to extend indefinitely the golden eagle passport program for admission into national parks. When added to the six major bills and to the numerous other bills creating or expanding national wilderness, recreation or historic areas, they made the 1972 environmental legislative record an impressive one.

President Nixon, in a special message Feb. 8, urged Congress to complete action on the proposals outlined in his environmental message the year before. Nixon said "the necessary first steps" had been taken in such broadly based areas as air pollution, water pollution and pesticide hazards. "Now," he said, "as we press on with that work in 1972, we must also come to grips with the basic factors which underlie our more obvious environmental problems —factors like the use of land and the impact of incentives or disincentives built into our economic system."

Nixon also cautioned that "the temptation to cast technology in the role of ecological villain must be resisted—for to do so is to deprive ourselves of a vital tool available for enhancing environmental quality."

The fiscal 1973 Agriculture Department-environmental protection appropriations bill (HR 15690—PL 92-399) carried nearly $3-billion for environmental programs, including $2,371,014,000 for the Environmental Protection Agency (EPA).

In its report on the bill June 26, the House Appropriations Committee warned that "Congress in recent years has been passing environmental laws that are difficult if not impossible not to support, but which may be impossible to carry out." The report listed phosphate restrictions, automobile emission control requirements, power plant construction delays and pesticide bans as actions which had produced as many problems as they solved. "Perhaps with all good intentions we are moving too fast," the report said.

The use of resources and the discard of waste materials were vitally important, the report said, and the ability to control them "is the power to control how we live. Yet, under present law and several more under consideration, we are investing more and more of this power in a single agency (EPA) with a single head without the means of setting priorities in public debate and where the costs and the effects of a decision to clean up a river or clean up the air can be assessed by those workers who must seek other employment, by the consumers who must pay higher prices and by those industries which must fund better locations and manufacturing processes."

WATER AND MARINE RESOURCES

Water Pollution

On the last day of the session, Congress overrode President Nixon's veto of the Federal Water Pollution Control Act Amendments of 1972 (S 2770—PL 92-500), the most comprehensive and expensive environmental legislation in the nation's history.

The amendments initiated a major change in the basic federal approach to water pollution by adding strict limits on what could be discharged into waterways to existing standards for water quality. (*Previous water quality legislation, p. 765*)

The bill set a national goal of eliminating all pollutant discharges into U.S. waters by 1985 and an interim goal of making the waters safe for fish, shellfish, wildlife and people by July 1, 1983. S 2770 contained authorizations of $24.7-billion over three years, through fiscal 1975, including more than $18-billion in federal grants to the states for construction of waste treatment plants.

Stockholm Conference

Growing worldwide concern over the state of the environment culminated in the United Nations Conference on the Human Environment, held in Stockholm, Sweden, June 5-16, 1972. Among the major results of the conference were:

• Adoption of the Declaration on the Human Environment containing new principles to guide future international action on environmental issues, including the principle that states are responsible for damages to the environment of other states or international areas.

• Recommendation of a permanent high-level UN environmental unit to coordinate activities, headed by Conference Secretary-General Maurice Strong of Canada.

• Creation of a five-year, $100-million UN environmental fund for pollution control and other activities, with a 40 per cent U.S. share.

• Establishment of a global "Earthwatch" program to monitor environmental trends including air and water pollution, land use and human health.

• Implementation of a worldwide environmental information service to help countries exchange knowledge and data.

• Creation of "genetic pools" to collect and preserve the planet's animal, plant, insect and microorganism resources.

• Agreement on an ambassadorial meeting in London in October 1972 to initiate an ocean-dumping treaty pending final consideration at the UN law of the sea conference in 1973.

• Urging of a shift from chemical control of agriculture pests to a more integrated approach emphasizing biological controls instead of pesticides.

The bill was strongly opposed by major industries and by some state and local officials, but was endorsed by most environmental organizations.

Nixon had withheld approval of the controversial measure awaiting the outcome of an executive-legislative tussle over the extensive powers to curb federal spending he had requested. (*Details, p. 74*) When the Senate Oct. 17 balked at granting such broad authority, Nixon vetoed the water bill, shortly before midnight. In his veto message, Nixon, who had proposed a $6-billion federal program, called S 2770 "staggering, budget-wrecking." (*Impoundment of funds, box, 794*)

The measure automatically would have become law at midnight Oct. 17 without the President's signature. Had Congress adjourned before midnight, Nixon could have pocket vetoed the bill, as had been widely predicted. The President has 10 full days, excluding Sundays, to sign a bill or it becomes law, unless Congress adjourns in the interim, when he may pocket veto it.

The Senate promptly voted to override the veto in the pre-dawn hours of Oct. 18. The House rejected the veto later the same day on a **key 247-23 roll call**. The votes in both houses were well over the two-thirds majority required by the Constitution.

1899 Refuse Act Used to Control Polluters

Dusting off an old statute, President Nixon late in 1970 issued an executive order requiring industries to acquire a permit before dumping certain wastes into the nation's waterways—or face prosecution.

In 1899—long before the development of modern environmental consciousness—Congress approved language in the Rivers and Harbors Act of that year declaring it unlawful to dump any refuse matter "other than that flowing from streets and sewers...in a liquid state" into navigable waters. The law—known as the Refuse Act of 1899—provided that the secretary of the Army could permit such deposits under limits and conditions he prescribed.

The President's Dec. 30 action set up the first formal permit program under the 1899 act and marked the beginning of a broad federal attempt to use the act as a prime weapon in its water clean-up efforts.

Russell E. Train, chairman of the Council on Environmental Quality, praised the President's move as "the single most important step to improvement of water quality that this country has taken."

Under the new program, a discharger was required to apply to the Army Corps of Engineers for a permit to dump wastes into the nation's navigable waters, specifying the type and amount of effluent to be discharged. Before the permit was granted, the state or interstate pollution control agency had to certify that the dumping would meet state water quality standards. If the proposed discharges failed to meet those standards, an abatement plan and compliance schedule also were required as part of the application.

The permits then were reviewed and approved by the Environmental Protection Agency (EPA).

Violators of water quality standards and compliance schedules as well as dischargers without permits were subject to enforcement action.

In a little more than a year, criminal and civil actions filed under the act had increased to 198 from 129.

Problems. But the ambitious program ran into snags scarcely a year after its initiation. On Dec. 21, 1971, the U.S. District Court of the District of Columbia blocked further granting of permits until corps regulations were amended to require that environmental impact statements—mandated under the National Environmental Policy Act (NEPA) of 1969 for all major federal actions—be filed for permits issued. *(Kalur v. Resor)* On the basis of the legislative history of the bill, the corps had determined that its pollution abatement actions were not covered by NEPA.

No further permits were issued under the 1970 program, although the EPA continued to process applications up to the point of issue. Out of a total of approximately 20,000 applications received, only about 20 permits were issued.

Six months later, all prosecutions under the act were halted following a May 30, 1972, federal appeals court ruling. The court held that a company prosecuted under the 1899 act for discharges prior to the establishment of the permit program could not be held criminally responsible for its actions.

The federal government had charged the Pennsylvania Industrial Chemical Corporation with violating the dumping ban in August 1970 by depositing industrial waste in the Monongahela River without a permit. The company, in turn, argued that the corps had consistently read the 1899 language to prohibit only the dumping of deposits which would impede navigation.

Enforcement actions under the 1970 program up to May 1972 totaled 371. No further enforcement actions were initiated pending a federal appeal of the ruling.

The Supreme Court held on May 14, 1973, that the 1899 act was operative regardless of the existence of a formal permit program, reversing the appeals court decision. But the court also directed the lower courts to reexamine arguments of the company, indicating that "traditional notions of fairness" would prevent the government from proceeding if the company could prove that it had been seriously misled by the corps.

New Permit Program. The Water Pollution Control Act Amendments of 1972 (PL 92-500) set up a new permit program to supplant the 1970 procedures. The new program provided two major expansions of coverage—to include all (not just interstate) waters and all discharges (including previously exempt municipal discharges).

Applications for permits under the new discharge program initially were to be submitted directly to the EPA, but the agency over the long term was to delegate responsibility for permit issuance to the states.

S 2770 set up a new pollutant discharge permit program under stiff guidelines administered by the Environmental Protection Agency (EPA), replacing an old program established under the Refuse Act of 1899. States could operate their own permit programs if EPA approved, but the agency could take over state programs which failed to meet federal standards and veto individual permits under certain circumstances.

Citizens were allowed to sue polluters, the federal government or the EPA if they had interests—economic or recreational—which were adversely affected.

Industry—the nation's largest user of water—was particularly affected by the legislation. Industries were required by mid-1977 to use the "best practicable" technology for treatment of any discharges into U.S. waters. By mid-1983, they were directed to install the "best available" equipment. The bill established a 15-member national commission to study the costs and benefits of achieving the 1983 deadline and to report to Congress.

In a major departure from the language of both the House and Senate versions of the bill, the final version exempted most EPA actions under S 2770 from provisions of the National Environmental Policy Act of 1969 (PL 91-190) which required the filing of detailed environmental impact statements for federal projects significantly affecting the environment.

Senate approval of a tough water cleanup bill in 1971 had prompted concerted lobby efforts on the part of the administration and industry to soften the abatement deadlines and grant more power to state authorities. But the final version of the bill paralleled Senate language in many respects and was far stiffer than the administration-backed measure approved by the House in 1972. *(Background, p. 779)*

House Action

Committee. The House Public Works Committee March 11 reported a bill (HR 11896), the Federal Water Pollution Control Act Amendments of 1972, to provide a comprehensive program to clean up the nation's waters in the next two decades.

In its key provision, HR 11896 set national goals of eliminating all discharge of pollutants into U.S. waters by 1985, and of making the waters safe for fish, wildlife and recreation by 1981.

The bill required the National Academy of Sciences, within two years, to conduct a study of the environmental, technological, economic and social feasibility of meeting these goals, which could then be implemented by further congressional action.

The bill also established a federal-state discharge permit program and required the Environmental Protection Agency to set guidelines for state permit programs. No new permits would be issued under the 1899 Refuse Act.

Industries were required to use the "best practicable" technology to eliminate discharges by 1976 and the "best available" technology by 1985.

Local citizens were allowed to file suit against violators of the act only if their economic interests were directly affected or if they had been actively engaged in the administrative process prior to the suit.

HR 11896 authorized total spending of $24.6-billion over three years, including $18.4-billion in federal grants for new municipal waste treatment plants.

Despite the bill's additional grant funds, environmentalists attacked the measure as being weaker than the Senate version, particularly those House provisions which made implementation of the 1981 and 1985 goals dependent on further congressional action and restricted citizen suits.

Floor. By a 380-14 roll-call vote, the House March 29 passed HR 11896 in much the same form as reported by the Public Works Committee. It then passed S 2770, after substituting the text of HR 11896 for the language of the Senate bill. Passage came after extensive efforts by environmentalists, most of them unsuccessful, to toughen the committee version.

Only four substantive amendments were accepted on the floor, during three days of debate, out of 20 amendments which were offered.

Those accepted:
• Increased authorizations in fiscal year 1972 for programs covered by the bill from $6-million to $11-million.
• Guaranteed public hearings by the Environmental Protection Agency in investigations of employee firings or lay-offs resulting from effluent limitations or orders.
• Required the EPA to encourage recycling, spray irrigation, land disposal and integrated facilities in waste treatment management.

Sewage Funds Impounded

President Nixon ordered the Environmental Protection Agency to allot to the states less than half of the $11-billion authorized by Congress in the 1972 water pollution bill for new sewage treatment plants in fiscal 1973 and 1974. Acting on orders from the President, EPA Administrator William D. Ruckelshaus announced Nov. 28 that only $2-billion of the $5-billion authorized for fiscal 1973 and $3-billion of the $6-billion authorized for fiscal 1974 would be made available to the states.

Ruckelshaus acknowledged that there was some legal question concerning Nixon's authority to impound the funds authorized by Congress, but said the President's action represented the "soundest, most defensible" place to cut expenditures.

The administration's action was challenged in the courts, and in May 1973 a federal district court judge ordered the release of the impounded $6-billion. Judge Oliver Gasch of the U.S. District Court for the District of Columbia ordered EPA to release the funds immediately and begin allocating them to cities across the country. He also ordered that applications be accepted for an additional $11-billion authorized for the same purpose over the next two years. *(Impoundment controversy, p. 74)*

• Allowed states to prohibit the discharge of all sewage by vessels in their navigable waters.

Among amendments that were rejected were those offered by House environmentalists to allow any citizen or public interest group to bring suit against polluters or the federal government, to require industry to use the "best available" waste treatment technology by 1981 and to give the EPA veto power over state-issued discharge permits.

George Mahon (D Texas), chairman of the House Appropriations Committee, offered an amendment to delete from the bill the $18-billion, three-year contract authority for construction of new municipal waste treatment plants and substitute annual funding by Congress on a one-year advance basis. (Contract authority allows federal agencies to enter into contracts ahead of appropriations but requires appropriations in following years to liquidate the contracts.)

Chief opponents of several major provisions in the version of the bill reported by the House Public Works Committee were Henry S. Reuss (D Wis.), chairman of the Government Operations Subcommittee on Conservation and Natural Resources, and John D. Dingell (D Mich.), chairman of the Merchant Marine Subcommittee on Fisheries and Wildlife Conservation. Reuss and Dingell proposed a Clean Water Package of six amendments to HR 11896.

None of the original amendments offered on the floor was adopted, however.

The Nixon administration, including the Environmental Protection Agency and the Council on Environmental Quality, opposed most of the amendments to the bill and strongly endorsed the committee bill. The National Association of Manufacturers and most industries also opposed efforts to amend the House bill.

The coalition of environmental, labor, consumer and citizen groups which had lobbied for the Reuss-Dingell package of amendments criticized the bill passed by the House. Their leaders issued a statement saying HR 11896 "does not represent the will of the people or the majority of Americans. Rather it represents the will of campaign contributors who are the major polluters of this country."

Provisions. As approved by the House, HR 2770 contained major provisions which:

Title I

- Declared the bill's objective to restore and maintain the chemical, physical and biological integrity of the nation's waters.
- Declared national goals of eliminating discharge of pollutants into navigable waters by 1985, and achieving an interim goal of water quality safe for fish, shellfish, wildlife and recreation by 1981.
- Directed the administrator of the Environmental Protection Agency (EPA) to help develop comprehensive programs for water pollution abatement by federal, state, interstate, municipal and industrial groups.
- Authorized the administrator to make research and development grants to states and municipalities, not to exceed 75 per cent of the cost of projects.

Title II

- Authorized grants for construction of publicly owned treatment works applying the best practicable technology, with the federal share not to exceed 75 per cent of costs.
- Authorized some reimbursements of states and municipalities for treatment work construction begun since 1956.

Title III

- Required the establishment by Jan. 1, 1976, of effluent limitations for point sources (other than publicly owned treatment works) demanding the best practicable pollution control technology.
- Required publicly owned treatment works to have effluent limitations based on secondary treatment.
- Established an Environmental Financing Authority to help finance the non-federal share of the costs of any waste treatment construction project, with a five-member board of directors whose chairman would be the secretary of the treasury.

Conference Action

House and Senate conferees Sept. 28 issued their reports on S 2770. The final agreement, which came Sept. 14 in the 40th meeting of the conference committee (the first was held May 11), represented a major compromise by the conferees. The House and Senate versions of S 2770 were so divergent that some predicted the bill would die in conference.

Among the major compromises, conferees:

- Declared the 1985 and 1981 deadlines for eliminating pollution and achieving certain water quality levels as national "goals," as provided by the House, not "policy," as voted by the Senate—but dropped House language making their implementation dependent on further congressional action.

House, Senate Differences

There were several basic differences between the water pollution control bill passed by the House in 1972, HR 11896, and S 2770, the version approved by the Senate in 1971.

Zero Discharge. The House bill declared national goals of eliminating the discharge of pollutants into navigable waters by 1985 and of achieving water quality safe for fish, wildlife and recreation by 1981. These goals would be implemented only by further congressional action after the National Academy of Sciences completed a two-year study. The Senate bill called the achievement of zero discharge by 1985 national policy rather than a national goal and did not make implementation of the goal dependent on the results of an NAS study.

Spending. The House bill authorized total spending of $24.6-billion, including $18.4-billion in federal grants for construction of waste treatment works. Grants would be allotted to states on the basis of need, with a maximum federal share of 75 per cent. S 2770 authorized $20-billion in total spending, including $14-billion for waste treatment construction grants which would be allotted on the basis of population with a federal share of 70 per cent.

Permit Program. The House version established a federal-state discharge permit program in which the states could issue permits under federal guidelines established by the EPA. The EPA could veto state permits during the interim period before the guidelines were issued, but thereafter approved state permit programs would be subject only to cancellation of the entire program by EPA, not a permit-by-permit veto. The House bill also would prohibit issuance of new waste discharge permits under the authority of the 1899 Refuse Act. The Senate version also established a federal-state permit program under EPA guidelines but gave EPA continuing permit-by-permit veto power. The Senate bill left intact the 1899 Refuse Act permit program.

Citizen Suits. The House bill narrowly limited citizen suits against polluters, the federal government or the EPA; it defined citizens as residents of the geographic area who were affected by the pollution, or groups which had been actively engaged in the administrative process concerning the alleged violation. The effect of the provision was to limit future legal action by such national groups as the Sierra Club and Friends of the Earth. The Senate bill would allow any citizen to bring suit against violators of the act.

Financing Authority. The House version established an Environmental Financing Authority, with an initial authorization of $100-million, to help localities pay the non-federal share of treatment plant construction projects. S 2770 had no comparable provision.

- Adopted the higher House-passed authorization of $24.7-billion over three years for programs under the bill.
- Required all industries discharging pollutants to install the best practicable control technology by July

1977 and the best available technology by July 1983, rather than by Jan. 1, 1976, and Jan. 1, 1981, respectively, as provided by the House and Senate versions.

• Gave the EPA administrator discretion in initiating legal actions against polluters, as in the House bill, dropping Senate language making such actions mandatory.

• Allowed citizen suits against violators of the act if they had an interest which was adversely affected, a broader grant than in the House bill but more narrow than the Senate version.

• Added new language not contained in either version exempting EPA actions from the environmental impact statements required under the National Environmental Policy Act, with two exceptions.

Conference Report Adopted. Before adopting the conference report Oct. 4, the House approved a resolution (H Res 1146) waiving points of order against the report. The resolution was necessary because conferees added substantive language to the bill that was in neither the House nor Senate versions. The Senate unanimously adopted the report the same day with little floor debate.

Members in both houses emphasized that conferees had attempted to avert the possibility of a presidential veto by adding amendments loosening expenditure requirements. The bill was sent to the White House Oct. 5.

Presidential Veto

Veto Message. In his veto message, shortly before midnight Oct. 17, the President said S 2770 was "a bill whose laudable intent is outweighed by its unconscionable $24-billion price tag," which he called "staggering, budget-wrecking."

The veto message came shortly after the Senate, by a 39-27 roll-call vote, rejected the House-Senate conference report on a bill (HR 16810) setting a federal spending ceiling and giving the President authority to decide where spending cuts should be made.

In an 11:30 p.m. press conference, domestic affairs adviser John D. Ehrlichman said the President had instructed him to deliver the veto message if the spending ceiling was rejected.

In his message, Nixon prepared for the possibility that the veto might be overridden: "I have nailed my colors to the mast on this issue; the political winds can blow where they may.... Even if this bill is rammed into law over the better judgment of the executive...certain provisions of S 2770 confer a measure of spending discretion and flexibility upon the President, and if forced to administer this legislation I mean to use those provisions to put the brakes on budget-wrecking expenditures as much as possible."

Although the bill's price tag more than tripled the President's 1971 proposal, there was immediate speculation that the veto was motivated by other than fiscal considerations, particularly since the bill contained authorizations over a three-year period but did not actually appropriate the money.

The veto came against the advice of Environmental Protection Agency Administrator William D. Ruckelshaus, who "strongly" recommended the bill's approval in an Oct. 11 report to the Office of Management and Budget, copies of which circulated on Capitol Hill.

Veto Overridden. Congress handed the President a resounding defeat Oct. 18 by voting overwhelmingly to override his veto of the water pollution bill. The Senate vote, 52-12, came at 1:30 a.m. on Oct. 18 (legislative day Oct. 17), several hours after the President's veto. About 12 hours later, in the afternoon, the House voted to override on a **key 247-23 roll call**, enacting the bill into law.

Floor debate on the veto in the Senate alternated between criticism of the President's action by his opponents and defense of the veto by his supporters. House floor statements were mostly critical.

In his veto message, Nixon said the action was tied to the Senate's rejection of a bill (HR 16810) setting a federal spending ceiling and giving the President authority to decide where spending cuts should be made. But on Oct. 19, the day after Congress adjourned, Nixon announced that he intended to withhold or impound appropriated funds despite the legislators' refusal to grant him specific authority. He said this power was implicit in a section of HR 16810 requiring the President to tell Congress when funds were impounded, which ones and for what purpose.

Final Provisions

As cleared by Congress over the President's veto, S 2770 contained major provisions which:

Title I—Research

• Declared it the act's objective to restore and maintain the chemical, physical and biological integrity of the nation's waters.

• Established as a national goal elimination of pollutant discharges into U.S. waters by 1985 and as an interim goal achievement of water quality safe for fish, shellfish, wildlife and recreation by July 1, 1983.

• Established as a national goal elimination of discharges of toxic pollutants in toxic amounts, providing federal financial aid to build public waste treatment works, developing areawide waste treatment management plans and making a major research effort to develop technology to eliminate pollutant discharges.

• Directed the administrator of the Environmental Protection Agency (EPA) to administer the act and provide for public participation in development of regulations.

• Authorized the administrator to make a maximum of 50 per cent federal grants to states for administrative expenses of planning agencies (for a maximum of three years) developing comprehensive water quality control plans for river basins, bays or lakes.

• Directed the administrator to study the special water pollution problems of oil spills, marine sewage equipment (especially on small boats), pesticides, waste oil, estuary pollution, total sewage, agricultural and other rural pollution, fresh water aquatic ecosystems, river systems and thermal discharges.

• Authorized the administrator to make a maximum of 75 per cent research and development grants (for demonstration purposes only) for storm sewers, joint municipal-industrial treatment systems, water recycling methods and agricultural pollution.

• Directed the administrator to set up special demonstration projects (with a maximum of 75 per cent federal participation) to eliminate pollution of the Great Lakes, with particular attention to the rehabilitation and environmental repair of Lake Erie.

• Authorized a one-year study of Lake Tahoe and the Tahoe Basin ecosystem and the need for federal oversight.

• Directed the administrator to identify and eliminate stationary toxic pollution sources in ports and harbors.

Title II—Construction Grants

• Declared the purpose of the title to require waste treatment management plans and practices which applied the best practicable technology, were on an areawide basis, encouraged recycling and reclamation and integrated facilities.

• Authorized the administrator to make grants to state or local agencies for the construction of publicly owned treatment works, with a maximum 75 per cent federal share.

• Authorized grants to be allotted to the states on the basis of need, as determined by the EPA.

• Authorized some reimbursement of states and municipalities for treatment work construction begun between 1966 and 1972 (not more than 80 per cent) and between 1956 and 1966 (not more than 30 per cent).

• Directed the President to prepare a water resources plan for all U.S. basins; plans must be completed by Jan. 1, 1980, with annual progress reports to Congress required.

Title III—Standards and Enforcement

• Made the discharge of any pollutant by any person unlawful except as authorized by a discharge permit (*Title IV*).

• Provided that existing interstate and intrastate water quality standards remain in effect subject to EPA approval and revision.

• Directed the administrator to develop and publish detailed water quality information and guidelines for effluent limitations.

• Required industrial dischargers by July 1, 1977, to meet effluent limitations based on use of the "best practicable control technology currently available," as defined by the EPA administrator. Required publicly owned treatment works to meet effluent limitations based on secondary treatment (the second step in waste treatment in which bacteria consume the organic parts of the wastes) by the same date.

• Required industrial discharges by July 1, 1983, to meet effluent limitations based on use of the "best available technology economically achievable" as determined by the administrator: limits would be based on categories or classes of industries, and would be aimed at elimination of discharges if technologically and economically achievable. Industries could seek relief based on economic capability. Public treatment works must use best practicable technology over the life of the works by the same date.

• Directed the administrator to list categories of industrial pollution sources and set national performance standards—including zero-discharge, if practicable—for each new source. States could take over enforcement if laws were as strict as federal standards. If new factories complied with provisions of the bill, they would not be subject to more stringent standards for at least 10 years.

• Directed the administrator to submit a water quality inventory report to Congress by Jan. 1, 1974, and required states to submit such reports by Jan. 1, 1975.

Total Authorizations in S 2770

(Fiscal years 1972-1975)

Research, investigations, training and information	$260,000,000
Research and development grants	150,000,000
Pollution control program grants	135,000,000
Mine water pollution control	15,000,000
Lake Erie study	5,000,000
Training grants, contracts, scholarships	50,000,000
Alaska village demonstration projects	1,000,000
Lake Tahoe study	500,000
Toxic pollutants	15,000,000
Construction reimbursements	2,750,000,000
Waste treatment works construction	18,000,000,000
Areawide waste treatment management	300,000,000
Areawide technical assistance	100,000,000
Water Resources Council, basin planning	200,000,000
Supplemental funds	200,000,000
Clean lakes programs	300,000,000
National study commission	15,000,000
Financing study	1,000,000
General authorization	900,000,000
Waste treatment works (fiscal 1972)	350,000,000
Research (fiscal 1972)	6,000,000
Small business loans	800,000,000
National policies and goals study	5,000,000
Environmental Financing Authority	100,000,000
GRAND TOTAL	**$24,658,500,000**

• Directed the administrator to list toxic (seriously harmful to human or other life) pollutants and to set effluent limitations—including prohibition of discharge, if needed—to provide "an ample margin of safety."

• Prohibited discharge of radiological, chemical or biological warfare agents or high-level radioactive waste.

• Required the administrator to set effluent limitations for thermal discharges (discharge of water at different temperature from receiving waters) that would ensure a balanced population of fish, shellfish and wildlife.

• Provided criminal penalties of between $2,500 and $25,000 per day or one year in prison or both; $50,000 per day or two years or both for second offenses; and civil penalties of up to $10,000 per day.

• Declared it to be U.S. policy that there should be no discharges of oil or hazardous substances into U.S. waters, adjoining shorelines or contiguous zone waters.

• Set civil penalties for oil or hazardous substance discharges of up to $50,000 (per discharge), with no limit for willful discharges.

• Directed the states to prepare plans to restore fresh water lakes and authorized federal grants for clean lakes projects.

• Established a 15-member national commission to investigate the technological aspects of achieving the 1983 economic, social and environmental goals in the act.

Title IV—Permits and Licenses

• Required applicants for federal discharge licenses or permits to first obtain state, interstate agency or EPA certification that the discharge would comply with effluent limits set under the act.

• Authorized the EPA administrator, after opportunity for public hearings, to issue permits for pollutant discharges, including previously exempt municipal discharges, under certain conditions and if they met other requirements of the act.

- Authorized states to conduct their own discharge permit programs if approved by the EPA.
- Declared existing permits issued under the 1899 Refuse Act to be valid, but provided that no new permits could be issued after the bill's enactment.
- Authorized the administrator to suspend state programs which did not meet federal guidelines; but the administrator could veto individual state permits only during the interim period before the guidelines were issued.

Title V—General Provisions

- Established a 10-member water pollution control advisory board.
- Gave the administrator emergency powers to bring suit in district court to stop pollution presenting an imminent health or welfare hazard.
- Authorized citizen suits against the U.S. government, other federal agencies or the EPA administrator. Defined citizens as persons having an interest adversely affected.
- Forbade the firing of or discrimination against the employees who filed proceedings or testified under provisions of the act, with procedures for review by the secretary of labor.
- Provided for judicial review of the administrator's actions in circuit courts of appeals.
- Provided that nothing in the act would deny the right of states or interstate agencies to set pollution control standards at least as stringent as federal standards.
- Directed the President to study the feasibility of a separate environmental court system and to report to Congress within one year.
- Directed the President to study the national policies and goals in the bill and to report within two years.
- Established an Environmental Financing Authority to help finance the non-federal share of the costs of any waste treatment construction project.
- Exempted EPA actions under the act from the requirements for filing a statement detailing the impact on the environment of major federal projects as mandated by the National Environmental Policy Act of 1969 (PL 91-190), except for federal grants for construction of publicly owned sewage treatment plants and permits issued for pollutant discharges from new sources.

Ocean Dumping

After being tied up in conference for nearly a year, a bill (HR 9727—PL 92-532) banning the unregulated dumping of waste materials into the oceans and coastal waters cleared Congress in the last week of the 1972 session.

The bill declared a national policy of regulating ocean dumping to protect human health and welfare, the marine environment and the economic potential of ocean resources. It banned the transportation out to sea or dumping under any circumstances of radiological, chemical or biological warfare agents or high-level radioactive wastes. And it set tough civil and criminal penalties of up to $50,000, with each day of a violation to be considered a separate offense.

The bill also provided for the designation of marine sanctuaries to be preserved for recreational, ecological or esthetic values.

Differing versions of HR 9727 were passed by each house in 1971, but the measure was lodged in a House-Senate conference committee for nearly a year. *(1971 action, p. 782)*

Conference and Final Action. The conference report on HR 9727 was filed Oct. 9. In resolving the differences between the House and Senate versions, conferees:

- Extended coverage of waters under the bill to the "base line," or that line from which U.S. territorial limits are measured. The House bill had extended coverage to oceans, estuaries and the Great Lakes, while the Senate language included the oceans, coastal waters and other waters beyond U.S. jurisdiction.
- Gave the Army Corps of Engineers power to issue dumping permits under guidelines to be established by the Environmental Protection Agency (EPA). The House had lodged primary responsibility in the corps while the Senate granted such authority to the EPA.
- Adopted House language authorizing the designation and protection of marine sanctuaries. The Senate bill contained no such provision.

The House and Senate adopted the conference report on Oct. 13.

Provisions. As signed into law (PL 92-532) Oct. 23, HR 9727:

Title I—Ocean Dumping

- Prohibited the transportation out to sea or dumping into the territorial waters or contiguous zones (the area outside the coastal zone but within the 12-mile territorial limit) of any radiological, chemical or biological warfare agent or any high-level radioactive waste.
- Authorized the Environmental Protection Agency (EPA) administrator to issue permits, after opportunity for public hearings, for the transportation out to sea and dumping of waste materials if it would not unreasonably endanger human health and welfare or the marine environment.
- Authorized the secretary of the Army, through the Corps of Engineers, to issue permits for the transportation out to sea and dumping of dredged or fill material, under similar restrictions contained in EPA permits; gave the EPA administrator veto power over Corps of Engineers permits.
- Required permits to designate the type and amount of material to be dumped, dumping location, permit expiration date and other information; authorized issuance of general permits; required all permits to be reviewed periodically and all information to be made public.
- Set civil penalties of up to $50,000, after notice and opportunity for public hearings; set criminal penalties of up to $50,000 or a year in prison or both; provided that each day of violation would be considered a separate offense; exempted from penalties emergency dumping to safeguard life at sea.
- Pre-empted state authority to regulate ocean dumping, but allowed states to adopt dumping criteria and issue regulations if approved by the EPA administrator.
- Authorized appropriations of $3.6-million for fiscal year 1973 and $5.5-million for 1974 to administer Title I.

Title II—Research

- Authorized $6-million annually for three years for research programs on ocean dumping and the long-range effects of pollution and other man-induced changes of ocean systems.

Title III—Marine Sanctuaries

• Directed the secretary of commerce, after consultation with the secretaries of state, defense, interior, transportation, the EPA administrator, and the governors of adjacent states, to designate marine sanctuaries in coastal waters as far seaward as the outer edge of the continental shelf.

• Defined the purpose of marine sanctuaries as the preservation or restoration of such areas for their conservation, recreational, ecological and esthetic values.

• Authorized the commerce secretary to set regulations to control activities within marine sanctuaries, and set civil penalties of up to $50,000 for violations, after notice and opportunity for hearings.

• Authorized appropriations of up to $10-million annually for three years to carry out Title III.

RELATED ACTION. An international convention prohibiting the dumping of poisonous materials into the oceans was signed by the United States Dec. 29, 1972. Hammered out by representatives of 91 countries, including all of the world's major maritime nations, the Convention on the Prevention of Marine Pollution by Dumping of Wastes and Other Matter forbade the unloading at sea of high-level radioactive wastes, biological and chemical warfare agents, crude oil, some pesticides and durable plastics; it also required a permit for the discharge of less harmful materials such as cyanides and flourides. The convention was more comprehensive in the number and types of substances whose discharge was prohibited than the Marine Protection, Research and Sanctuaries Act (HR 9727—PL 92-532) as cleared by Congress in 1972.

Other Water Bills

COASTAL ZONE MANAGEMENT. Congress established a national program for the management and protection of U.S. coastal waters and adjacent shorelines in the Coastal Zone Management Act of 1972 (S 3507—PL 92-583).

The $186-million measure authorized federal grants to the states to help them develop coastal management programs under federal guidelines. The grants would pay up to two-thirds of the cost of state programs each year.

The bill was designed to protect the resources of coastal waters in face of increasing population and other pressures on the areas. Areas covered under the bill included coastal waters, bays, sounds, lagoons and estuaries, the Great Lakes, and adjacent shorelands such as tidal areas, salt marshes, wetlands and beaches. The measure declared a national policy of preserving, protecting, restoring and developing the coastal zones in the national interest.

A House committee report called the U.S. coast "the nation's most valuable geographic asset" and said it probably was the area "most threatened with deterioration and irreparable damage." There are about 100,000 miles of U.S. coastline and 75 per cent of the population lives in coastal states, the report said.

A Senate committee report said that according to some projections, more than 80 per cent of the population would live within 50 miles of a coast by the year 2000.

Populations near the Atlantic and Pacific Oceans, the Gulf of Mexico and the Great Lakes were growing more rapidly than in the interior, the report said.

Legislative History. The Senate April 25 unanimously approved its version of S 3507, which gave primary administrative authority to the secretary of commerce.

The Commerce Committee originally had reported a different measure (S 582) in 1971 *(p. 788)*, but that bill was recommitted to the committee in early 1972 at the request of Ernest F. Hollings (D S.C.), chairman of the subcommittee which held hearings on the bill in 1971.

As sent to the floor in 1972, S 3507 was a clean bill incorporating sections of S 582 and S 638. According to its report, the committee rewrote certain provisions of S 582 to clear up matters of conflicting jurisdiction and other issues.

During consideration of a similar bill (HR 14146) on the House floor, members adopted an amendment which transferred all coastal zone management authority to the interior secretary rather than the commerce secretary as recommended by the House Merchant Marine and Fisheries Committee. The House Aug. 2 passed S 3507 after amending it to contain the language of HR 14146.

In resolving differences between the House and Senate versions, conferees adopted the Senate language which gave primary administrative authority for the bill to the secretary of commerce. In their report on the bill, conferees noted that "it was expected that actual administration would be delegated to the administrator of the National Oceanic and Atmospheric Administration (NOAA)" and cited that agency's "capability to assist state and local governments in the technical aspects of coastal problems."

Both the House and Senate adopted the conference report on the bill Oct. 12, in the final week of the session.

Provisions. As signed into law Oct. 27, S 3507 contained major provisions which:

• Declared it the national policy to preserve, protect, develop and, wherever possible, restore the nation's coastal zone resources.

• Defined coastal zones as coastal waters and adjacent shorelands, including tidal areas, salt marshes, wetlands and beaches; defined coastal waters to include the Great Lakes and their connecting waters or sounds, bays, lagoons and estuaries.

• Authorized the secretary of commerce to make annual grants to coastal states to help them develop and administer coastal zone management programs under federal guidelines, but provided that individual grants could not exceed two-thirds of the cost of a program.

• Required the secretary to review state management programs and performance, and authorized him to terminate financial assistance in cases of poor performance.

• Authorized the secretary to make grants of up to 50 per cent of the costs (not to exceed $2-million) for acquisition, development and operation of estuarine sanctuaries for research purposes.

• Authorized appropriations of $9-million annually for fiscal years 1973-77 for program planning grants, $30-million annually for 1974-77 for administrative grants, up to $6-million for fiscal 1974 for estuarine sanctuary grants and $3-million annually for 1973-77 for general administrative expenses.

MARINE SAFETY. Congress in 1972 moved to prevent oil spills and other accidents in the nation's ports and waterways when it approved legislation (HR 8140—PL 92-340) authorizing the Coast Guard to supervise marine traffic in congested areas.

Approved by the Senate in 1972 without debate, HR 8140 included the same water safety provisions as those adopted by the House in 1971. *(p. 783)*

The Senate Commerce Committee, however, added a new title to the bill requiring design and construction standards for vessels carrying hazardous bulk materials such as inflammable or combustible liquids and oil of any kind. In its report on the bill, the committee upheld the new provisions as placing "appropriate emphasis" on prevention of marine accidents.

Conferees agreed to the vessel design standards approved by the Senate, but excluded from those regulations vessels carrying dry cargoes and deferred until Jan. 1, 1976, the latest date for which initial standards must be applied to vessels in foreign trade.

Provisions. As signed into law (PL 92-340) July 10, HR 8140, the Ports and Waterways Safety Act:

• Authorized the secretary of transportation to establish comprehensive regulations for the design, construction, maintenance and operation of vessels carrying bulk cargoes for the purpose of protecting the marine environment. (Bulk cargoes were defined as materials such as inflammable or combustible liquids, oil of any kind, hazardous polluting liquids; bulk dry cargoes were excluded from provisions of the act.)

• Set Jan. 1, 1976, as the latest day by which initial design and construction standards would have to be applied to vessels in foreign trade or foreign registry.

• Authorized the secretary of transportation to establish and operate marine traffic systems and controls for congested waterways and to prescribe safety equipment and procedures for docks and other structures.

• Provided a maximum civil penalty of $10,000 and criminal penalties of not less than $5,000 nor more than $50,000 or five years imprisonment, or both, for violations of the act.

DESALINATION PROGRAMS. Congress without controversy authorized (HR 12749—PL 92-273) appropriations of $26.9-million for salt water conversion projects in fiscal 1973—the exact amount of the President's request. The desalting program was established by the Saline Water Conversion Act of 1971 (PL 92-60) which made it subject to annual authorizations through fiscal 1977. *(p. 783)* Before 1971, the program had been conducted under the Saline Water Conversion Act of 1967, which consolidated all earlier legislation dealing with research and development programs in low-cost desalting methods and authorized construction of demonstration desalting plants.

WATER RESOURCES COUNCIL. Congress in 1972 voted increased funds for the Federal Water Resources Council. HR 14106, signed into law (PL 92-396) Aug. 20, amended the Water Resources Planning Act of 1965 to authorize a $3.5-million increase in appropriations for the council in fiscal 1973. The funds were earmarked for the assessment of national water resources and demands ($2.5-million) and to provide direction and coordination in regional comprehensive water resource planning ($1-million). The council, set up under the 1965 act, was directed to assess regional water supplies and establish standards and procedures for federal water projects. *(Congress and the Nation Vol. II, p. 498)*

SAFE DRINKING WATER. A bill to assure that the public was provided with an adequate supply of safe drinking water was approved by the Senate in 1972. The House, however, took no action and the measure (S 3994) died when Congress adjourned.

The bill would have established a program within the Environmental Protection Agency (EPA) to regulate drinking water. The federal government at that time only possessed authority to monitor for possible contamination drinking water aboard interstate carriers, and regulation of drinking water was primarily a state responsibility.

In its report on the bill, the Senate Commerce Committee declared that "cleaning up our rivers and lakes through pollution control will not result in adequate water for drinking.... Drinking water is not perfect in nature and even if pollution were to stop immediately, problems in drinking water supply would still exist."

Provisions. As passed by the Senate, major provisions of S 3994:

• Authorized the EPA to establish minimum federal drinking water standards prescribing maximum limits for contaminants as well as standards for the operation and maintenance of drinking water systems.

• Placed primary responsibility upon the states for enforcement of the standards with federal enforcement when states failed to act in cases of imminent hazard.

• Authorized $6-million in fiscal 1973, $11.25-million in fiscal 1974 and $15.98-million in fiscal 1975 for the EPA to make grants to states to defray the cost of state water programs.

• Authorized $10.5-million in fiscal 1973, $17.25-million in fiscal 1974 and $23.25-million in fiscal 1975 for the EPA to conduct and promote research, technical assistance and train water supply personnel.

• Authorized $6-million in fiscal 1973, $8.25-million in fiscal 1974 and $9.75-million in fiscal 1975 for other EPA activities on drinking water programs.

OIL POLLUTION ACT. Although the House approved legislation (HR 15627) to implement 1969 amendments to a 1954 international oil pollution convention, the Senate took no action on the measure, killing it for the 92nd Congress.

HR 15627, passed by the House Oct. 11, would have amended the Oil Pollution Act of 1961 (PL 87-167) to implement the 1969 amendments to the 1954 International Convention for the Prevention of the Pollution of the Sea by Oil.

The purpose of the bill, known as the Oil Pollution Act Amendments of 1972, was to expand penalty provisions of the 1961 act and to reflect changes in the 1954 convention adopted by the Inter-Governmental Maritime Consultative Organization (IMCO) in 1969. The 1961 act was the domestic law implementing the 1954 convention, which was the first international effort to control ocean oil pollution.

LAND USE

Pesticide Regulation

Congress in 1972 replaced existing laws regulating the use of pesticides with new legislation (HR 10729—PL 92-516) giving the government broader authority to control the vast array of pesticides and other pest killers.

In the first major change in federal regulation of pesticides in 25 years, Congress required that all pesticides be registered with the Environmental Protection Agency (EPA) which would control the manufacture, distribution and use of pesticides. Only those involved in interstate commerce had been regulated by existing law—the Insecticide, Fungicide and Rodenticide Act of 1947—which was primarily a labeling law.

The new legislation, the Federal Environmental Pesticide Control Act of 1972, made it easier to ban hazardous pesticides and imposed penalties for their improper use. Under existing law, the government had to complete a long and complicated procedure before banning a pesticide it found dangerous. And while it could require proper labeling, no penalties were prescribed for improper use.

As cleared by Congress, HR 10729 divided pesticides into two categories—general use and restricted use. Restricted pesticides would have to be clearly labeled and could be used only by certified applicators. The bill required pesticide manufacturers to submit detailed information to the EPA with their registration applications, including labels, claims to be made, directions for use, the chemical formula and test results.

Under a controversial provision originally added by the House Agriculture Committee, pesticide manufacturers or retailers were compensated if their products were declared an imminent hazard by EPA and removed from the market. No payment would be made, however, if the pesticide owners knew in advance that their products were harmful and still continued to use or produce them. Original House action had been completed in 1971. *(p. 785)*

Senate Committee Action

HR 10729 was reported separately by two Senate committees—the Agriculture and Forestry Committee in June and the Commerce Committee in July. The Commerce Committee adopted 15 amendments to the Agriculture Committee version, including most of those originally introduced by Philip A. Hart (D Mich.), chairman of the Commerce Subcommittee on Environment, and Gaylord Nelson (D Wis.) which strengthened the bill from an environmental viewpoint.

According to newspaper reports, Agriculture Committee Chairman Herman E. Talmadge (D Ga.) and Commerce Committee Chairman Warren G. Magnuson (D Wash.) had made a "deal" to give the Commerce environment subcommittee a chance to strengthen HR 10729 in return for a promised effort by Magnuson to delete from the Consumer Safety Act of 1972 (S 3419) a provision which would transfer the Agriculture Department's meat, poultry and egg inspection duties to a new consumer safety agency.

Senate farming interests, according to *The Washington Post*, wanted the tough food inspection clause out of S 3419, and Magnuson felt the bill could not pass the House if the provision stayed in.

Agriculture Committee. The Senate Agriculture Committee June 7 unanimously reported a heavily amended version of HR 10729.

Among the amendments added to the House-passed bill, the committee deleted a provision providing for

Pesticides

Pesticide is a general term for all chemical pest killers. They are divided into insecticides (insect killers), rodenticides (rodent killers), fungicides (fungus killers), miticides (mite killers) and herbicides (plant killers).

More than 60,000 pesticides products were registered with the Environmental Protection Agency by 1972. They were all made from one or more of approximately 900 basic chemical compounds.

Every formulation of a pesticide must be registered for every intended use; consequently, many registrations are for new uses of existing products. Few new pesticide compounds had been registered in recent years.

U.S. production of pesticides and related products in 1970 totaled 1.03 billion pounds, while sales reached 881 million pounds and a value of $870-million.

Farmers use by far the largest volume of pesticides produced in this country, but about half of registered pesticide products are intended for home, institutional or industrial use. All sterilizing, disinfecting, sanitizing, germicidal and bacteria killing chemicals—except those sold exclusively for use in or on the living bodies of men or animals—are classified as pesticides and must be registered.

Among the major types of chemical pesticides are:

● **Chlorinated hydrocarbons, or organochlorines** —"Hard" pesticides, which break down chemically quite slowly and can remain in the environment for some time. Pesticides of this type include: DDT, DDD, DDE, dieldrin, chlordane, toxaphene, aldrin, endrin and helptachlor.

● **Organic phosphates, or organophosphates**— Not persistent in the environment, but highly toxic to human beings. They include; parathion, malathion, chlarethion, thimet, phosdrin, methylparathion and trichlorphone.

● **Pyrethins**—Natural or botanical insecticides essentially non-toxic to warm-blooded animals.

● **Carbamates**—Of low toxicity to human beings.

● **Dessicants**—Kill insects by penetrating and drying up, and kill plants by causing leaves to dry out and fall.

● **Plant regulators**—Produce seedless fruits and vegetables, cause plants to mature uniformly or prevent premature dropping of fruit.

indemnity payments to owners of pesticides for which registrations were cancelled by the Environmental Protection Agency (EPA) as too hazardous. It added to the definition of "misbranded" pesticides those which caused substantial adverse effects on the environment even when used normally.

The committee also rejected amendments to permit citizen suits against the federal government or other parties for alleged violations of the act and to require increased protection of farmers and farm workers from hazardous pesticides.

Pesticides Bill: Lobbying for Indemnities

The agricultural products industry won a major victory in the closing days of the session when House-Senate conferees weakened a new pesticides control bill by adding language compensating a manufacturer if his product is found unsafe and removed from the market.

The indemnity provision, included in a bill passed by the House in November 1971, was omitted from the original Senate version, passed by a 71-0 roll-call vote in September 1972. Pressure for the provision came from the National Agricultural Chemicals Association (NACA), which supplied conferees with a detailed fact sheet on the kind of bill it hoped would emerge. While adding the indemnification provision, conferees agreed to drop Senate provisions calling for more liberal disclosure policies on trade secrets and other confidential information, requirements to make more data public, a prohibition against exporting any pesticides which might ultimately cause adverse effects on the U.S. environment and a requirement that imported agricultural products be screened for pesticide residues.

Prior to Senate passage in September, NACA also won a softening of Commerce Committee amendments, which had been added to the bill after the Senate Agriculture Committee—a panel more favorably inclined to the pesticide manufacturers—had originally reported the measure. (Because of overlapping jurisdictions, both committees had considered the bill.) The compromise bill that emerged from negotiations between NACA and the Commerce Committee deleted a provision raising fines against violators to $10,000 from $1,000, a provision giving local governments authority to control pesticides with standards tougher than state or federal requirements, and a provision giving EPA inspectors the right of entry into establishments where they suspected pesticides were being used or kept unlawfully.

Leonard Bickwit, staff counsel to the Commerce Subcommittee on Environment, told Congressional Quarterly that the subcommittee had invited NACA representatives in "almost as parties to the legislation" in order to hammer out a bill that could pass the Senate. "We were fully aware that if there was to be any difference in our bill and in the NACA-backed bill that went through the Agriculture Committee, it would have to be slight," he said, "so we thought inviting the NACA people in was the most expeditious way of proceeding. We felt it was more expeditious to have them in there than negotiating with the Agriculture Committee."

Asked by CQ if that procedure were not unusual for a Senate committee, Bickwit said: "I can't say it's as unusual as it should be. It does happen, but it's seldom so blatant. The industry was talking as though they owned the committee. We were distinctly under the impression that no bill was going to come out that didn't have industry approval."

Bickwit added: "There were threats by the administration to come out in favor of the Agriculture Committee bill if we (Commerce) didn't give in. We were constantly threatened. I was yelled at a lot. They put the pressure on what the felt was the weakest link, which was us.... The industry set the rules; the administration agreed to play by them. They were so eager for the ends (passage of a bill) that they were willing to accept means that we found disgusting."

Environmental lobbies worked hard but ineffectively against the weakening amendments. Linda Billings of the Sierra Club, which led the opposition to the amendments, told CQ that "It's been terribly hard work on this bill because we just haven't had any (administration) support." Although the Environmental Protection Agency (EPA) had publicly opposed the indemnity provision in March, it buckled in the end, Billings said. "EPA completely sold us out. They gave up on the indemnity provision in order to get a bill."

Commerce Committee. Following two days of hearings on the bill as reported by the Agriculture Committee, the Senate Commerce Committee July 19 reported the bill with 15 additional amendments.

Among the major changes made by the committee were actions which permitted the EPA to ban pesticides which posed "unreasonable" but no "substantial adverse" effects on the environment; deleted language which stated EPA should not make "lack of essentiality" a criterion for denying a pesticide registration, and added provisions allowing citizen suits against violators of the act and requiring increased protection of farmworkers from hazardous products.

Agriculture Committee Rebuttal. In late July the Agriculture Committee issued a committee print of a report which detailed the committee's opposition to most of the amendments added by the Commerce Committee.

Senate Floor Action

The Senate Sept. 26 unanimously passed a compromise version of HR 10729 which had been worked out during nearly two months of negotiations between the Agriculture and Commerce Committees.

Before the 71-0 roll call, the Senate by voice vote adopted the compromise version as a substitute for the entire bill, and the Commerce amendments were withdrawn. The compromise was sponsored by all members of the Agriculture Committee and most of the Commerce Committee members.

The compromise substitute made the following major changes in the bill:

• Accepted Commerce Committee amendment on registration criteria, changing description to "unreasonable" from "substantial."

• Authorized citizen suits against the EPA administrator but not against manufacturers, distributors or users of pesticides.

• Made it unlawful to use pesticides in tests on farm-workers or other human beings without disclosure of foreseeable consequences and voluntary participation.

Conference and Final Action

House-Senate conferees filed their conference report on Oct. 5. According to the report, there were more than 50 points of disagreement between House and Senate versions of the bill.

Among the major compromises, conferees:

• Approved the Senate definition of the criterion for rejecting a pesticide application, requiring "unreasonable" adverse effects on the environment, instead of "substantial" adverse effects as in the House version. The conference report said: "This change from the House language is a matter of clarification only. There is absolutely no difference in substance...."

• Provided for mandatory licensing of test data, which was similar to the Senate provision, but allowed data to be sold to another applicant with the original applicant's permission. The report said: "The conferees concluded that the (EPA) administrator is in the best position to determine the proper amount of reasonable compensation for producing the test data."

• Protected manufacturers' trade secrets or commercial or financial information, as in the House version. The Senate version had provided more liberal disclosure policies in certain situations.

• Deleted a Senate provision prohibiting the export of those pesticides which could result in unreasonable adverse effects on the U.S. environment.

• Adopted a Senate provision prohibiting tests on human beings without adequately informing them and obtaining their voluntary participation.

• Included a House provision for indemnity payments, except that indemnities would be denied manufacturers who withheld essential information showing that a product was illegal.

• Deleted a Senate provision allowing citizen suits against the EPA administrator.

Final Action. Both the House and Senate adopted the conference report in October. Several members in each house spoke against the provision allowing compensation for banned pesticides, warning that the action would set a precedent for compensation of manufacturers of other products barred from the market. *(Cyclamate bills, consumer chapter)*

Provisions. As signed into law Oct. 21, major provisions of HR 10729:

• Required all pesticides in U.S. commerce to be registered with EPA.

• Required registration applicants to submit detailed information on the pesticide, including labeling, claims to be made, directions on use, chemical formula and test results.

• Allowed test data supporting one application to be used in support of another application if the original registrant agreed and was paid a reasonable amount for the information.

• Required all information in support of an application (except trade secrets) to be made public 30 days after the registration.

• Provided that the lack of a proven need for a pesticide could not be a criterion for denying registration.

DDT Decision

Environmental Protection Agency Administrator William D. Ruckelshaus June 14, 1972, announced a ban on almost all remaining uses of the pesticide DDT, to take effect Dec. 31, 1972.

The decision was a victory for environmental groups which had fought DDT in the courts for at least three years. However, a coalition of chemical manufacturers almost immediately appealed to a federal court to set aside the Ruckelshaus order. Their several challenges were consolidated into a single case which was pending before the U.S. Court of Appeals for the District of Columbia at the close of 1972. *(Coahoma Chemical Co. et al* v. *William D. Ruckelshaus).* The ban, however, went into effect as scheduled.

DDT still could be used for public health and disease control, but only under stringent conditions. It also could be used on green peppers, onions and sweet potatoes in storage, three crop uses for which there were no effective pest control alternatives.

DDT (dichloro-diphenyl trichloroethane) had been hailed as a revolutionary panacea and damned as a persistent poison.

The EPA decision was ordered by the federal district court for the District of Columbia in January 1971, the result of a lawsuit filed against EPA by the Environmental Defense Fund and the Sierra Club. The court ordered EPA to cancel all uses of DDT and undertake a "fresh determination" of its registration status. After a series of appeals by both sides, EPA began seven months of public hearings.

On April 25, 1972, EPA hearing examiner Edmund M. Sweeney declared that the proceedings did not prove that DDT caused severe environmental damage and its essential uses should be continued.

An EPA spokesman said DDT use in the United States had declined by about two-thirds in the past two decades, from a high of 80 million pounds in 1959 to about 33 million pounds in 1971.

DDT was still widely used abroad to control diseases such as malaria. Much of the DDT produced in the United States was purchased by UNICEF, AID and the World Health Organization.

• Authorized the EPA administrator to cancel the registration, change the classification or hold hearings on pesticides which, when used in accordance with commonly recognized practice, caused "unreasonable" adverse affects on the environment.

• Authorized the EPA administrator to suspend registrations of pesticides which presented an imminent hazard to health or the environment, with opportunity for hearings and judicial review.

• Authorized indemnity payments to pesticide manufacturers or owners in cases of imminent hazard, unless they knew in advance that the products were illegal under the act.

• Provided that exported pesticides had to meet the laws of the foreign purchaser only, and that imported pesticides had to meet U.S. standards.

- Established two classifications of pesticides: 1) general use and 2) restricted use; restricted pesticides would have to be clearly labeled and could be used only by certified applicators.
- Required EPA to set standards for federal or state certification of private and commercial applicators, and gave the EPA administrator the authority to reject state programs.
- Allowed states to impose stronger regulations on the sale or use of pesticides than those enforced by the federal government, but prohibited different state packaging or labeling requirements.
- Set civil penalties of up to $5,000 for each offense or up to $1,000 for pesticide applicators; set criminal penalties for manufacturers of up to $25,000 or a year in prison or both, or up to $1,000 or 30 days in prison for private applicators.
- Authorized appropriations of whatever sums were necessary to carry out provisions of the act.

Surface Mining

Comprehensive legislation to regulate the strip mining of coal was a casualty of Congress' race to adjournment in 1972.

In the last week of the session, the House gave its approval to a measure (HR 6482) generally regarded as a tough control bill by environmentalists and mining interests alike. It applied to coal mining on the surface and to the surface effects of underground mining.

But the Senate took no action on a related bill (S 630), reported in mid-September.

Under HR 6482, the secretary of the interior would have administered a federal regulatory and permit program, but states would have been able to run their own programs if they met federal standards; state programs which failed to comply would have been taken over by the Interior Department.

For the first time, mine owners would have been required to obtain permits for strip mining operations and to submit reclamation plans and purchase reclamation bonds. No strip mining would have been permitted on slopes greater than 20 degrees unless the mine owner could prove that environmental damage would be prevented and the land reclaimed.

The House bill was endorsed by most environmental groups, including the Coalition Against Strip Mining, but was opposed by the National Coal Association and the American Mining Congress.

House Action

Committee. The House Interior and Insular Affairs Committee Sept. 28 reported a bill (HR 6482), the Coal Mine Surface Area Protection Act of 1972, to provide for the regulation of strip coal mining and the reclamation of strip mined lands.

The bill was ordered reported by voice vote Sept. 27. It had previously been ordered reported on Sept. 6, but during the three-week interim the committee decided to meet again to reconsider a last-minute amendment which had been added to the bill, apparently without full knowledge of its potential impact.

The controversial amendment, sponsored by Teno Roncalio (D Wyo.), required the secretary of the interior to deny permits for strip mining on slopes steeper than 20 degrees. This would have effectively ended strip mining in much of Appalachia and other mountainous areas.

After the amendment was adopted Sept. 6, Ed Edmondson (D Okla.), chairman of the Mines and Mining Subcommittee which drafted the bill, said: "This hits Appalachia right between the eyes." Edmondson and other committee members said they had thought the permit denial was discretionary with the interior secretary, not mandatory.

In its Sept. 27 meeting, the committee changed the provision to allow the secretary to waive the prohibition if the mine operator can "affirmatively demonstrate" that he can prevent sedimentation, landslides or water pollution and that the land can be reclaimed. Roncalio agreed to the new language.

Roncalio had agreed Sept. 21 to "acquiesce" to the committee amendment, according to *United Press International*, which reported that word of Roncalio's change of mind came from Carl E. Bagge, president of the National Coal Association. The industry had been outraged by the amendment, which Bagge said "threatens blackouts in six months for more than 15 per cent of American homes and industries." Bagge said the industry was in "a state of seige" over "this environmental orgy... for reclamation."

Committee Views. "If surface mining is to continue as an accepted method of modern mineral extraction then the utmost effort must be made to bring the land back into a productive and useful condition or the condition the land was in prior to mining. If there is either a lack of ability or a lack of desire to engage in this type of rehabilitation and restoration...mining must be either severely restricted or prohibited," said the report.

Because of the nation's "critical energy situation," the committee focused on means for regulation and control of surface coal mining rather than outright prohibition. "The latter would create an intolerable situation in the presently over-strained energy supply picture," the report said. "In addition, the committee was not unmindful of the economic and unemployment problems that would be created by outright prohibition of surface coal mining, nor was it unaware that the accident rate is much higher in underground coal mining than in surface mining."

The committee emphasized the need for proper reclamation of stripped lands, saying: "Much of the land that is technically considered as restored has been restored in name only.... For all practical purposes, it is little better than land that entirely escaped any efforts of restoration."

Separate Views. In a 4½-page statement, lame duck Interior Committee Chairman Wayne N. Aspinall (D Colo.), defeated in a Sept. 12 Democratic primary, and committee member James Kee (D W.Va.), defeated by Rep. Ken Hechler (D W.Va.) in a May 9 primary, expressed their specific objections to the reported bill. While agreeing with its general purpose, they said they could not support the bill.

Some features "reflect an unfortunate over-reaction and lack of balance," they said, taking an approach which was "too narrow." Reclamation was necessary, they said, but "instead of focusing on the end result of reclamation, (the bill) focuses on the specifics of the mining operation, imposing absolute and arbitrary prohibitions."

Aspinall and Kee said the 20-degree slope provision could shut down about half of the surface coal mines in Appalachia and reduce production by about 20 per cent.

Floor. After a bitter debate, the House Oct. 11 approved HR 6482 without amendment. The bill was considered under suspension of the rules, a procedure requiring a two-thirds majority vote for passage and precluding floor amendments. Several members deplored this procedure, saying the bill needed to be amended before it was passed. Other members, while admitting the measure contained imperfections, contended it was the best possible at the time and deserved support.

Ed Edmondson (D Okla.), chairman of the Interior Subcommittee on Mines and Mining which drafted the bill, said it was "best recommended by the fact that it is under attack from two flanks. Some extreme environmentalists will say that it does not do everything that it should do...some industry people are saying that the bill is too tough in its reclamation requirements."

Aspinall said it was the first time since he became chairman that he was unable to support a bill reported to the floor by his committee. If the bill cleared Congress, he declared, it would not be "an environmental bill, which all of us desire, but this practically becomes a prohibitive bill."

The most lengthy and detailed floor statement on HR 6482 was made by Hechler, a longtime advocate of abolishing strip mining and the winner over Kee in the May 9 West Virginia primary in which strip mining was a crucial issue. Hechler said he would vote for the bill "because it will slow down some of the worst devastation, yet I vote for it without much enthusiasm because I firmly believe the only answer to this giant rip-off that strip mining constitutes is a complete abolition."

On the 265-75 roll call suspending the rules and passing the bill, 108 Republicans and 157 Democrats voted for the bill—38 more than the two-thirds majority required; 36 Republicans and 39 Democrats voted against it. Strip mining was a state-wide issue in 1972 in Kentucky and West Virginia. All of Kentucky's representatives voted for the bill, while three of West Virginia's five representatives—Kee, Robert H. Mollohan (D) and John M. Slack (D)—voted against it; the other two—Hechler and Harley O. Staggers (D)—voted for it.

Provisions. As reported by the committee and passed by the House, HR 6482 contained major provisions which:

• Declared the purpose of the act to be the regulation of surface coal mining to prevent adverse environmental effects, restoration of stripped lands and prevention of further devastation through enforcement of federal standards and state programs.

• Authorized the secretary of the Interior Department to make rules, conduct inspections, hold hearings, issue cease-and-desist orders, revoke permits, designate some areas unsuitable for surface mining and other duties.

• Provided that areas could be designated as unsuitable for surface mining if the secretary found reclamation economically or physically impossible or if such mining would cause lasting injury to the environment.

• Prohibited any surface coal mining without a permit and required permit applicants to submit a reclamation

---

Background on Surface Mining

Surface mining—stripping off the face of the earth to extract minerals—surpassed underground mining in 1971 as the nation's leading method of coal production for the first time in history.

The controversial mining technique of removing the earth from the coal, rather than the coal from the earth, produced 276.3 million short tons in 1971 compared with 275.9 million from underground mines, according to the Interior Department's Bureau of Mines.

According to spokesmen for the American mining industry, surface mining—which included both strip mining with giant earth mover machines and auger mining with huge power drills—was more efficient, less costly and much safer than underground, or deep mining. In addition, they said strip mining was vital to ensure that the nation had a sufficient supply of coal to generate electric power during the impending "energy crisis."

But opponents of strip mining (which accounted for by far the largest percentage of surface mining) said it was a devastating process which destroyed vast amounts of land, caused severe landslides and soil erosion, polluted water with silt and mine acid, and drove away wildlife and—ultimately—humans. They urged that strip mining be abolished in favor of deep mining and that research on alternate forms of energy be increased. They cited U.S. Geological Survey reports that an area of land the size of Delaware and Rhode Island combined already had been disturbed by strip mining, and that unreclaimed lands would represent a barren swath one mile wide from New York to San Francisco.

But stripping proponents countered that proposals to abolish the practice were unrealistic and irresponsible considering the nation's enormous coal reserves and dwindling domestic supplies of oil and gas. Existing domestic coal reserves totaled more than 3 trillion tons, according to the Geological Survey, of which about 128 billion tons in 27 states could be strip mined and 750 billion tons could be deep mined. The U.S. Bureau of Mines estimated that only about 45 billion tons were economically strippable, however.

---

plan and detailed information on the mine site and operations. Also required operators to buy public liability insurance, pay a $500 fee and be subject to public hearings if local residents raised objections.

• Authorized the secretary to approve or disapprove permit applications and required him to disapprove any permit at a slope greater than 20 degrees unless the operator could prove that sedimentation, landslides or water pollution could be prevented and the area reclaimed.

• Authorized states to run regulatory programs if they were not less stringent than federal standards; required the secretary to maintain close oversight of state enforcement and to take over inadequate programs.

• Authorized the secretary to make grants to states to help them administer programs; such grants not to exceed 80 per cent of costs during the year before approval or 60 per cent thereafter.

• Authorized appropriations of whatever sums were necessary to carry out provisions of the act.

Reclamation

• Required all plans for reclamation to include the best land use prior to mining, the proposed future use, future mining plans and provisions to maintain water quality, reclaim land, prevent air or water pollution, preserve top soil and estimate time and costs involved.

• Required approved permit applicants to file performance bonds with the secretary of not less than $5,000 or $500 per acre, whicher was greater, and to pay a special reclamation fee of $100 per acre; authorized him to set the amount of the reclamation bond per acre.

• Required reclamation operations to remove and separate top soil, backfill excavations, grade and replace top soil to support stable and diverse vegetation, remove or bury waste material, prevent permanent spoil banks (waste deposits) on slopes greater than 14 degrees, and restore the land to the same purpose or for an equally useful purpose.

• Established a $100-million revolving reclamation fund to restore previously stripped lands.

• Authorized the secretary to acquire such lands and to restore them, and then to sell them or administer them in the public interest.

Senate Action

In the rush to adjourn prior to the 1972 congressional elections, the Senate failed to act on strip mining curbs (S 630) recommended Sept. 18 by its Interior and Insular Affairs Committee.

Titled the Surface Mining Reclamation Act of 1972, S 630 provided federal guidelines, technical assistance and grants-in-aid to the states to help them regulate strip mining. It would apply to all forms of surface mining— stripping, auger (drill) mining, open cast mining, hydraulic (placer) mining, quarrying and dredging. S 630 would apply to all coal and all other minerals, with the exceptions of oil, natural gas or others extracted in liquid or gaseous form.

A committee aide said S 630 as reported was an "unfinished" bill which had been written by the Subcommittee on Minerals, Materials and Fuels but had not been considered in detail by the full committee. It was ordered reported in response to a Senate leadership ultimatum that bills must be out of committee by mid-September to reach the floor before adjournment.

Environmental organizations considered S 630 a weak bill and urged adoption of many strengthening amendments. Mining industry groups generally preferred S 630 to the more restrictive House bill.

Provisions. As reported by the committee, S 630 contained major provisions which:

• Declared congressional findings that surface mining was a significant and essential industrial activity for the nation's economic well-being; declared the purpose of the act to prevent or reduce the adverse effects of surface mining.

• Prohibited any new coal mining or significantly increased mining at existing operations without a state or federal permit; required ongoing coal mines to obtain a permit within one year of enactment and other mineral mines to obtain a permit within two years.

• Authorized prohibition of mining in areas of critical concern, issuance of stop orders and civil or criminal actions against violators.

• Set specific federal guidelines for surface mining of coal; required the interior secretary to publish federal guidelines for coal surface mining and reclamation within 90 days and for all other minerals within one year, with provision for public hearings.

• Required permit applications to provide a reclamation bond of at least $500 per acre.

• Established a $100-million abandoned mine reclamation fund and authorized the secretary to acquire such lands by purchase, donation or condemnation, to reclaim the lands and to administer them or sell them.

• Provided federal ssistance for state plans which met the federal guidelines for reclamation enforcement, financing, training, reports, permits, sanctions and inspections.

• Authorized grants to the states to help them develop, administer and enforce plans, not to exceed 80 per cent of costs the first year and 50 per cent thereafter.

• Authorized the secretary and other federal agencies to provide aid to the states in the form of technical assistance, personnel training, mining operation inventories, and evaluation of state plans and needs.

• Authorized appropriations of $10-million for fiscal year 1973 and $20-million for fiscal 1974 and 1975 and whatever sums were necessary thereafter.

Related Action. The Senate Oct. 12 adopted a sense of the Senate resolution (S Res 377) calling for a temporary moratorium on federal coal leasing, prospecting and exploring in Montana. The resolution asked the secretary of the interior to apply the moratorium for coal deposits owned by the federal government that could be mined only by surface mining methods. The resolution set the moratorium for a period of one year or until Congress enacted comprehensive surface mining legislation, whichever came sooner.

Land Use Policy

Although Congress in 1972 focused considerable attention on the nation's land use policy, it failed to complete action on bills to encourage states to develop their own land use programs.

The Senate approved a bill (S 632), the Land Use Policy and Planning Assistance Act of 1972, which set up a program of grants and technical assistance to the states in the area of land use.

If cleared by Congress, S 632 would have represented the first significant federal involvement in land use regulation and would have been a major departure from traditional control and enforcement by private, local and state agencies. The bill emphasized state programs of land use planning for areas of critical environmental concern, key facilities, regionally beneficial or large-scale developments and coastal zones.

(Continued on p. 808)

Trans-Alaskan Pipeline: Environment vs. Economy

Whether and how to bring oil from Alaska's northern slopes to the lower 48 states was one of the major environmental issues debated during the Nixon years.

Immediately at stake was what industry termed the costliest private construction project ever—a proposed 48-inch pipeline to haul the oil 789 miles south across Alaska. Estimated construction costs had swollen to well above $2-billion in three years of struggle.

But a deeper controversy centered on whether the economy or the environment would play a dominant role in national policy decisions which impinged on both areas.

Oil Struck. An Atlantic Richfield Company well struck oil commercially on Alaska's North Slope in the summer of 1968. The major obstacle to large-scale development of the field was the difficulty of transporting the oil at economical cost from the frozen north to markets far to the south.

In October 1968, eight companies based in the United States, Canada and Great Britain set up the Trans-Alaska Pipeline System as a joint enterprise. The major participants, directly or through subsidiaries, were Atlantic Richfield, Humble Oil & Refining Company and British Petroleum. Humble is a subsidiary of Standard Oil Company (New Jersey), world's largest oil company.

The oil companies applied for permits to build an access road and a four-foot pipeline to Valdez in south Alaska. Tankers would carry the oil from that point.

The state of Alaska, which included 2 million acres of North Slope land in its selections for state ownership in compliance with the Alaska Statehood Act of 1959, auctioned leases Sept. 11, 1969, netting $900-million from oil companies.

By January 1972, about 15 billion barrels of proven reserves had been located on the Beaufort Sea, site of the Atlantic discovery. Of these, Atlantic Richfield's proven reserves were about 1.9 billion barrels. Some estimates were that Alaskan oil reserves might exceed 100 billion barrels, far beyond known U.S. reserves.

Heated Argument. Opposition to the proposed pipeline crystalized in 1969. Opponents attacked on several fronts in the courts, Congress and administrative agencies. They opposed the building of a road—first step toward actual pipeline construction and toward opening up the Alaska interior—and pressed Alaskan native land ownership claims.

Various groups said the heated oil could melt the terrain along the pipeline, causing changes in a delicately balanced environment lacking the capability of regenerating itself because of climate. They said caribou migrations might be interfered with by fear of crossing the pipe where it was above ground. Ecologists cited dangers of pollution from oil spills in Alaskan waters and in Washington's Puget Sound to which oil would be hauled. Some challenged the need for the oil and suggested Japan would become the major recipient.

Pipeline proponents, on the other hand, argued that the Alaskan oil was vital to meet the nation's skyrocketing energy needs and curb its increasing dependence on foreign sources of oil. Proposed alternative routes would cost more and cause an equal amount of environmental damage, they argued, while application of the most advanced technology could hold environmental harm to a minimum.

Blocked Since 1970. Construction of the pipeline first was halted in April 1970 when three environmental groups won an injunction barring the interior secretary from granting the permits requested by the oil companies. (The Trans-Alaska Pipeline System was succeeded by the Alyeska Pipeline Service Company in August 1970.)

A federal district court judge held that the Interior Department had not complied with provisions of the National Environmental Policy Act (NEPA—PL 91-190) which required every federal agency to file a detailed statement of the impact on the environment of any major decision.

The injunction was lifted in August 1970 following the department's five-month study of the environmental consequences of the pipeline, but construction halted when conservationists appealed the decision.

After nearly two years' work, the department in March 1972 released a nine-volume study of the impact of the proposed pipeline on the Alaskan wilderness. The report concluded that some environmental damage was inevitable but that the trans-Alaska route was the most feasible economically.

Less than two months later, on May 11, Interior Secretary Rogers C. B. Morton announced he would issue a permit for the pipeline construction, and environmentalists in August again asked a federal appeals court to block issuance of the permit.

No Right-of-Way. But—barring congressional action—construction of the pipeline was blocked permanently by a federal appeals court Feb. 9, 1973. The U.S. Court of Appeals for the District of Columbia barred the interior secretary from granting the oil companies a permit to begin construction, holding that the right-of-way across public lands they had requested—146 feet in some stretches—was far greater than the 25 feet on either side permitted under the Mineral Leasing Act of 1920. The court did not address the environmental questions posed by the suit, noting that the environmental data presented with the case might be outdated should Congress amend the 1920 act in the future or otherwise permit a wider right-of-way.

The Supreme Court April 2, without comment or dissent, upheld the lower court's ruling.

In a press conference April 5, Morton said President Nixon had directed him to "go all out working with Congress...in pursuing the construction of the trans-Alaska pipeline which he feels is vital to the national interest."

The House took no action on S 632. Its Interior and Insular Affairs Committee reported a similar bill (HR 7211) in August.

Under both the House and Senate measures, federal approval of a state land use program would be based upon establishment of a process to determine land use policies and methods of implementation rather than upon the substance of the policies and methods used.

Senate Action

Committee. As reported by the Senate Interior and Insular Affairs Committee June 19, S 632 would have authorized federal spending of $100-million annually over eight fiscal years to cover up to 90 per cent of the cost of state land use programs.

All states would have been required to develop, within three years, a land-use planning process for state and private lands, and within five years, a land use program which concentrated on areas of environmental importance; key facilities, such as major airports and highway interchanges; land use and development of regional benefit; and large-scale development.

If states did not comply with the federal guidelines, they could be subject to sanctions, including the withholding of grant-in-aid funds or the phased withholding of other federal aid.

In all parts of the country, the committee report said, "conflicting demands over limited land resources are placing severe strains upon economic, social and political institutions and processes and upon the natural environment."

Land use planning too frequently focused on local problems while neglecting regional and national needs, the report said. Most plans were "single-purpose or mission-oriented" to support a single demand and seldom reflected non-economic factors such as long-range environmental impact or recreational needs.

Paul F. Fannin (R Ariz.) and Clifford P. Hansen (R Wyo.), who voted against reporting the bill, said that state responsibility for land use planning should not be usurped by the federal government.

Floor. S 632—attacked by opponents as being both too weak and excessively stringent—was heavily amended on the Senate floor. A total of 14 substantive amendments were adopted before passage Sept. 19; four others were rejected.

Henry M. Jackson (D Wash.), committee chairman and floor manager of the bill, said in opening debate that S 632 "embodies a recognition that our country is experiencing a land use crisis which has been caused by increasingly competitive economic, social and environmental demands upon a very finite land resource."

He said the bill was intended to provide alternatives for "the chaotic, ad hoc, short-term, crisis-by-crisis, case-by-case land use decision-making employed all too frequently today."

Edmund S. Muskie (D Maine) criticized the bill, which he said might have greater implications "than any domestic legislation we have yet considered in this session of Congress." Muskie said S 632 "creates an outline for national land use policy with no substance; declares a national policy but concedes to the several states responsibility to determine what that policy should be, subject only to procedural review by the Department of Interior. Federal legislation of this magnitude, with far-reaching impact on many federal programs—at least 112 by the Interior Committee's count—must provide some federal policy guidance. This legislation provides none."

Muskie offered three amendments aimed at strengthening the bill, but the only one adopted was a guarantee that other federal laws would not be superseded by the act, that state efforts to implement pollution control laws would not be compromised and that states would be able to set more restrictive controls on land use development if they so desired. Rejected by the Senate were two other Muskie amendments which would have transferred responsibility for administration of the act to the Executive Office of the President from the Interior Department, as provided by the bill, and would have prohibited private or public land development which did not conform with the Clean Air Act of 1970 and the Federal Water Pollution Control Act and banned certain other development.

Jackson offered seven amendments en bloc which were accepted unanimously. The most controversial provided economic sanctions against states which failed to develop land use programs within five years by withholding federal funds for all programs which might have a substantial adverse environmental impact or which would significantly affect land use. The committee bill had provided for withholding of funds only for airport development, highway construction and land and water conservation.

But the Senate later adopted an amendment by Clifford P. Hansen (R Wyo.) which stripped all economic penalties from the bill. Hansen's amendment was "reluctantly" supported by Jackson, who said he wished to "proceed expeditiously so we can complete action on this bill."

The Senate unanimously adopted an amendment sponsored by Herman E. Talmadge (D Ga.) providing that nothing in the bill could be construed as giving the federal government any constitutional authority possessed by state and local governments to zone non-federal lands. "There is nothing that is more peculiarly local than the authority to determine whether a man can build a dairy, a poultry house, a home, a filling station or how he can use property that he owns...," Talmadge said. "The bureaucrats will say that this bill gives them the authority to tell state and local officials how they will utilize their land.... I want to make it clear that no federal official can sit here in Washington and determine how every acre of land in the United States will be used."

Provisions. As passed by the Senate, major provisions of S 632:

● Declared the purpose of the Act to establish a national land use policy and to help the states develop land use programs through grants-in-aid and technical assistance under federal guidelines.

● Established an office of land use policy administration in the Interior Department and gave the interior secretary authority to conduct a land use study, develop a federal land use information and data center, coordinate land use programs and administer the grant-in-aid program.

● Authorized the interior secretary to make annual grants to states to help them develop land use programs.

● Required states to develop statewide land use planning processes within three fiscal years as a condition of continued federal grant eligibility, including an inventory of state land and natural resources, population density, economic characteristics and urban and rural growth.

● Required states to develop within five fiscal years statewide land use programs establishing state authority over use and development of lands in areas of critical environmental concern, locations of key facilities, development of regional benefit and large-scale development.

● Required the secretary to review state programs to make sure they did not exclude any areas of critical environmental concern, a list of which must be submitted at the governor's request.

● Authorized technical assistance to states through federal contracts or grants.

● Authorized the secretary to make grants to the states not to exceed 66-2/3 per cent of the cost of developing state land use programs during the first two fiscal years and not more than 50 per cent during the next three fiscal years.

● Authorized appropriations of $40-million annually for the first two fiscal years and $30-million annually for the next three fiscal years for state grants, and $10-million annually for five fiscal years for administration by the interior secretary.

House Action

The House Interior and Insular Affairs Committee Aug. 7 reported a bill to establish a comprehensive national policy and program for federal and non-federal land use in the United States, but the House took no further action on the bill following the primary defeat of its chief sponsor, Wayne N. Aspinall (D Colo.), committee chairman.

The bill (HR 7211), the National Land Policy, Planning and Management Act of 1972, would have established a public land policy and provided guidelines for its administration. It would have authorized grants to the states to help them develop land use programs for private, state and local lands.

Committee Views. In its report on the bill, the committee said that HR 7211 was intended to "translate into law" the June 1970 recommendations of the Public Land Law Review Commission in its report, *One Third of the Nation's Lands.* The commission recommended that Congress establish public land policies and goals and provide the federal land management agencies with the necessary authority to implement the policy.

"Our nation has gone too long without an over-all plan," the report said. "We have treated symptoms often without considering the causes. Any action taken frequently has been on a piecemeal, *ad hoc* basis.... There is scant consistency in the pattern of land use in the United States. Ownership varies widely. Land use controls are uneven in character and they often are nonexistent or subject to the frequent granting of 'variances'.... There is a lack of coordinated effort among the federal land management agencies and between those agencies and other landowners.... There is a similar absence of coordination between the federal agencies and the state and local governments and...private individuals.... Because of this, a major objective of HR 7211 is to secure coordination among the federal agencies and between those agencies and the non-federal owners and planners."

Land Squeeze

Deciding how to use land traditionally has been a private or local decision in the United States. From the pioneer days, land was viewed as a commodity to be bought or sold, used and depleted as the owner saw fit, with a minimum of governmental interference or guidance.

But as the nation grew more crowded, it became evident that some regulations were needed. Especially in urban areas, unrestricted private land use began to create conflicts. Cities and states adopted zoning ordinances, building codes, subdivision laws and other regulations.

The nation's burgeoning population and accompanying demands for increased land development produced clashes among various groups—and a growing awareness that some guidelines were needed to resolve such conflicts. Farm and environmental groups were pitted against real estate developers and highway planners, while cities and suburbs quarreled over the use of increasingly scarce land in urban areas, a Senate committee report noted.

According to federal estimates, between 1972 and the year 2000 the nation must build again all that had been constructed earlier—as many homes, office buildings and hospitals in the next three decades as had been erected in the past three centuries.

Who Decides? According to a 1968 report of the National Commission on Urban Problems, there were about 10,000 local governments exercising some form of land use controls in the United States. This fragmentation of authority followed the pattern of the nation's growth. But few land use decisions considered more than immediate local or private interests.

The increasing potential for a land use crisis led to numerous studies of land use patterns and policies. The largest and most controversial was the June 1970 report of the Public Land Law Review Commission, *One Third of the Nation's Lands.*

The report was severely criticized by many environmental organizations which said that it was too commercially oriented and that the dominant use concept it recommended would sacrifice values such as soil, water, wildlife and esthetics to mining, grazing and logging interests. *(Details, p. 772)*

Another report, *The Quiet Revolution in Land Use Control,* was prepared for the Council on Environmental Quality by Chicago attorneys Fred Bosselman and David Callies and released in December 1971. This report analyzed laws in the several states where land use controls already had been enacted and outlined issues in state land use regulations.

"This country is in the midst of a revolution in the way we regulate the use of our land," the report said. "...The *ancien regime* being overthrown is the feudal system under which the entire pattern of land development has been controlled by thousands of individual local governments, each seeking to maximize its tax base and minimize its social problems, and caring less what happens to all the others."

The report said the bill would give the United States "an opportunity to rethink its management practices" on the more than 761 million acres of public land, and also "allow the federal government to set an example" for land use planning.

Provisions. As reported, major provisions of HR 7211:

• Authorized the secretary of the interior to make land use planning grants to states which have eligible planning agencies.

• Defined eligible state land use planning agencies as those with primary responsibility for developing and administering comprehensive state land use planning processes.

• Authorized land use planning grants to states at the rate of 90 per cent of costs during fiscal 1973, 75 per cent during fiscal 1974 and 1975 and 50 per cent thereafter.

• Authorized the secretary to terminate assistance to states not making progress, and for states which do not qualify by July 1, 1976, to withhold federal grant-in-aid funds (for airport development, highways, land and water conservation fund) at the rate of 7 per cent the first year, 14 per cent the second year and 21 per cent the third year.

• Established an Office of Land Use Policy and Planning in the Interior Department to develop a federal land use information and data center, administer the grant program and coordinate federal land use planning.

Public Lands

• Declared national policy that public land classifications be reviewed to determine uses of maximum public benefit; that executive withdrawals (for national parks, forests and wildlife refuges) be reviewed and protected from encroachment; that Congress generally exercise withdrawal authority; that statutory public land use planning guidelines be set on the basis of multiple use and sustained yield; that public lands be managed for protection, to provide fish and wildlife habitat and outdoor recreation; that fair market value be received for public land and resource use; that equitable compensation be provided to present users of public lands who are forced to change plans; that an equitable system be devised to compensate state and local governments for burdens borne by federal land tax immunity; that persons such as coal miners be required to have a land reclamation plan and a performance bond; and that public lands be administered uniformly.

• Required public land management agency heads to inventory lands under their jurisdiction, to develop land use plans, to involve the public in planning and to coordinate their plans with states.

Funding

• Authorized total appropriations of $204-million over five fiscal years for grants to states, at the rate of $54-million during fiscal 1973, $45-million during fiscal 1974 and 1975, and $30-million during fiscal 1976 and 1977.

• Repealed, effective July 1, 1974, all open-ended appropriation authorizations for administration of public lands.

Federal Lands

Entwined in the controversy over national land use legislation were the policies of the nation's largest land owner—the federal government—which held about one-third of the nation's land area. Congress in 1972 failed to complete action on legislation which would have set guidelines for the management of certain public lands.

1972 Action. The Senate Interior and Insular Affairs Committee in September reported a bill (S 2401) to provide land use management goals and guidelines for the more than 450 million acres of federally owned lands administered by the Interior Department's Bureau of Land Use Management.

Known as the National Resource Lands Management Act of 1972, the bill would have established a national policy of preserving, protecting and managing these lands for multiple use and sustained yield in the long-term public interest.

The bill defined multiple use as the utilization of natural resources to accommodate present and public needs for both quantifiable (timber, minerals, grazing) and non-quantifiable (scenic, recreational, historic) values. It defined sustained yield as a high level of regular periodic output of nonrenewable resources without permanent damage to the environment.

The House Interior Committee had combined management policy guidelines for federal and non-federal land use in a single bill (HR 7211) which it sent to the House floor in August. Title IV of the bill directed that public land use planning guidelines be set on the basis of multiple use and sustained yield and implemented a number of the June 1970 recommendations of the Public Land Law Review Commission.

There was no Senate floor action on S 2401, and the measure died when the 92nd Congress ended. The full House never acted on HR 7211, and that bill also died. *(p. 809)*

Long Overdue. Disposal and development of public lands had long been the thrust of public lands management. But in 1964 Congress established the Public Land Law Review Commission to reassess the body of law governing the approximately 775 million acres owned by the federal government.

After five years' study, the commission in 1970 recommended that "the policy of large-scale disposal of public lands reflected by the majority of statutes in force today (should) be revised and that future disposal should be of only those lands that will achieve maximum benefit for the general public in non-federal ownership."

In addition, the commission noted the need for "a clear set of goals for the management and use of public lands, particularly for lands administered by the Bureau of Land Management." The report called for a congressional policy statement. *(Details, p. 772)*

Other Land Use Bills

FOREST PROGRAMS. Congress in 1972 enacted three separate bills dealing with management and protection of the nation's forests but failed to complete action on a fourth.

Reforestation. Congress voted $65-million each year for 15 years to fund an accelerated reforestation program on national forest lands. The new legislation (HR 13089—PL 92-421) made additional funds available to the U.S. Forest Service for tree-planting and seeding projects on the estimated 5 million acres of land in need of reforestation.

As signed into law Sept. 18, HR 13089 also directed the secretary of agriculture to report to Congress on reforestation needs and submit plans for reforestation programs.

The House and Senate versions had contained different funding methods for programs authorized under the bill. While the House had earmarked a portion of the funds collected through import duties on wood and paper products under section 32 of the Agriculture Adjustment Act of 1934, the Senate voted direct appropriations.

In resolving differences between the two versions, conferees adopted the Senate language, with the stipulation that "this approach should first be tried for a reasonable period of time," and if reforestation needs were not being met "the search for more direct financing methods will resume."

The only opposition to the conference report on the bill came from Charles A. Vanik (D Ohio), who criticized the measure as "a complete subsidy of the timber industry at the taxpayers' expense."

Forestry Programs. Congress approved without controversy legislation (HR 8817—PL 92-288) to expand cooperative forestry and fire prevention programs administered by the secretary of agriculture. Original House action had been completed in 1971. *(p. 788)*

The measure amended the Cooperative Forest Management Act of 1950 (PL 81-729) to extend Forest Service technical aid to trees and shrubs in urban communities. In addition, HR 8817 boosted authorizations for technical assistance to state forestry officials under the 1950 act by $15-million, to $20-million, and increased to $40-million from $20-million authorizations for cooperative forest fire protection programs under the 1924 Clarke-McNary Act. *(Congress and the Nation Vol. I, p. 1054)*

The bill was signed by the President May 5.

National Forest Volunteers. A new program to allow volunteers to work in the nation's national forests also was established (S 1379—PL 92-300) by Congress in 1972. The volunteers would provide information to visitors, develop programs, plant trees, construct trails, maintain campgrounds, lead youth activities, do research and write brochures.

As signed by the President May 18, S 1379 authorized the agriculture secretary to recruit and train volunteers for activities in areas administered by the U.S. Forest Service and to reimburse them for meals, transportation, lodging and uniforms. The measure authorized annual appropriations of $100,000 to fund the program.

Forestry Incentives. Legislation to encourage better forest protection methods and management in small private and non-federal public forests died at the end of the 92nd Congress.

Clearcutting "Action Plan"

The U.S. Forest Service June 24 adopted a new "action plan" to restrict clearcutting and improve management practices in the nation's national forests.

Clearcutting is the controversial logging method of harvesting an entire stand of trees at one time. Environmentalists charge that it damages soil, water, wildlife and scenery. Foresters counter that, when properly used, it actually helps forests regenerate.

According to Forest Service Chief John R. McGuire, the new plan was in direct response to guidelines set forth in a Senate Interior Public Lands Subcommittee report, "Clearcutting on Federal Timber Lands," released March 29, 1972.

Many of its features were similar to those in a proposed presidential order on clearcutting, written by the Council on Environmental Quality but cancelled in January 1972, under apparent pressure from the timber industry.

Key features of the action plan included:

● Increased Forest Service sensitivity to esthetic values in planning and carrying out timber harvests, road construction and preparation of harvest sites for new planting.

● Withdrawal of land that would be harmed by clearcutting from harvesting.

● Deferral of clearcutting on any tract where there was no assurance a new stand of trees would be established within five years.

● Preparation of environmental impact studies for proposed conversion of land from one type of vegetation to another.

● Closer supervision of timber sale contracts to obtain high quality performance in logging and road building.

Facts and Figures. There was a total of 187 million acres in America's 154 national forests in 1972. Of this total, 97 million acres were classified as commercial forest land, which was defined as land capable of producing timber crops. Logging was carried out by private companies which bid for sales contracts with the Forest Service to harvest timber.

The Forest Service calculates an annual "allowable cut," which is the amount of timber which may be harvested from national forest lands without depleting the forests. This figure is computed in "board feet," which is a measurement equal to a piece of wood one foot by one foot by one inch thick. In 1950, the allowable cut on national forests was 6 billion board feet. In 1960, it had increased to almost 11 billion board feet. In 1970, the figure was 13.5 billion board feet. The Forest Service attributed the increase to technological improvements, changes in classification and increased reforestation.

In 1970, 11.5 billion board feet were harvested. Of this total, 6.4 billion, or almost 60 per cent, was removed by clearcutting. Selection cutting accounted for 2 billion board feet, or 19 per cent, and intermediate cutting took 1.2 billion board feet, or 11 per cent.

The Senate approved a bill (S 3105), the Forestry Incentives Act of 1972, authorizing federal cost sharing, loans and technical aid, but the House Agriculture Committee voted to table—and thereby kill—a similar bill (HR 12873). Both measures would have authorized the agriculture secretary to help forest land owners to plant more trees, increase productivity, protect watersheds and improve fish and wildlife habitat in their forests. The Nixon administration had opposed the bills.

MINERAL RESEARCH CENTERS. Legislation (S 635) to establish mining and mineral research centers in each of the 50 states was approved by Congress but pocket vetoed by President Nixon after the session ended. S 635 would have authorized $25.2-million in fiscal 1973 (rising to $40.4-million in fiscal 1978) for grants to the states for research and training of mineral scientists in the fields of mining, mineral resources and technology. The programs were to be administered by the interior secretary.

In his veto message, Nixon said S 635 would "fragment our research effort and...preclude us from taking advantage of the best research talents of the nation—wherever they may be."

WILDLIFE PROTECTION

Marine Mammals

A highly emotional conflict over the protection of ocean mammals was at least partially resolved by Congress in 1972 when it imposed a permanent moratorium on most killing of ocean mammals and on importation of their products.

The new legislation (HR 10420—PL 92-522) was designed to protect the warm-blooded animals which inhabit the oceans—seals, sea lions, whales, porpoises, dolphins, sea otters, manatees, walruses and polar bears —which were, in 1972, steadily declining in population. Many of them were in danger of extinction and had been placed on the Interior Department's endangered species list.

The bill generated a great amount of controversy, with some environmentalists endorsing complete protection for sea mammals and others preferring a scientific program of wildlife management. The bill that finally emerged was a compromise which emphasized protection but granted several exceptions.

Permits could be granted for the killing or capture of ocean mammals for scientific research or for public display in zoos or commercial marine exhibits, for example. The Alaska fur seal harvest in the Pribilof Islands, administered by the Commerce Department, would continue under a one-year study. Alaskan Indians, Aleuts and Eskimos would be allowed to continue taking ocean mammals for subsistence or for the manufacture and sale of traditional handicrafts and clothing.

The most controversial exemption was granted to the commercial fishing industry, primarily tuna fishing, in which hundreds of thousands of porpoises were inadvertently killed each year when they became entangled in tuna nets and drowned. The industry would be exempt from the moratorium for two years while a comprehensive research and development program aimed at reducing porpoise mortality was undertaken. In addition, the moratorium could be waived in certain cases by the secretaries of commerce and interior in cases of "undue economic hardship" or "in accord with sound principles of resource protection and conservation."

House Action. As passed by the House March 9, HR 10420 placed a five-year moratorium on most taking of ocean mammals and on the importation of their products. Exceptions to the moratorium authorized the tuna fishing industry to kill porpoises and dolphins when incident to fishing operations and allowed the capture of ocean mammals for research and public display in zoos.

The five-year moratorium and the exceptions to it were included in one of the two amendments approved during floor debate. House members rejected two separate proposals to ban the killing of certain mammals incident to tuna fishing.

In 1971, the House had refused to pass HR 10420 under the suspension of the rules procedure. As reported that year by the House Merchant Marine and Fisheries Committee and turned down by the House, HR 10420 would have prohibited the granting of permits to kill ocean mammals for only 60 days after enactment rather than for the five-year period agreed to in 1972. *(Details, p. 788)*

Senate Action. The Senate July 26 approved a far stiffer version of HR 10420 after adopting during floor debate several strengthening amendments to a companion bill (S 2871) reported by the Senate Commerce Committee.

While the committee had recommended a 15-year moratorium on ocean mammal killing, the Senate approved a permanent moratorium. Also agreed to was an amendment calling for reduction to "insignificant levels" of the killing of dolphins and porpoises incidental to commercial tuna fishing operations.

The Senate rejected amendments which would have prohibited for five years the issuance of federal permits granting additional exceptions to the moratorium and would have reserved to the states the right to conserve, control and manage marine mammals unless the interior secretary determined a species was endangered.

Conference and Final Action. In their efforts to resolve differences between the House and Senate versions of the bill, conferees accepted the Senate provision for a permanent moratorium on killing and importation, rather than the five-year ban imposed by the House. Conferees adopted House language requiring the secretary to determine that any permits issued would not harm a marine mammal species and would be consistent with the act. "In some circumstances it would be to the advantage of a species or stock to allow (killing) as part of a scientific management program," the report said.

Concerning commercial fishing operations, conferees adopted the Senate approach of a two-year exception to the moratorium while the problem was being studied, rather than the House provision granting general permits to commercial fishermen. On the goal of zero mortality and injury, the report said: "It may never be possible to achieve this goal, human fallibility being what it is, but the objective remains clear."

The conference report was adopted by the House and Senate during the last week of the session.

Provisions. As signed into law Oct. 21 (PL 92-522) by the President, major provisions of HR 10420:

• Declared the finding of Congress that some marine mammals were in danger of depletion or extinction and should be protected and managed primarily for the health and stability of the marine ecosystem rather than for commercial exploitation.

• Gave the secretary of commerce responsibility for whales, porpoises, dolphins, seals and sea lions; gave the secretary of the interior responsibility for polar bears, walruses, manatees and sea otters.

• Defined "taking" as harassing, hunting, capturing or killing; defined "humane" as taking which involved the least possible degree of pain and suffering.

Title I—Conservation and Protection

• Declared a permanent moratorium on the taking and importation of marine mammals or their products, with certain exceptions *(below)*.

• Directed the secretary of the treasury to ban the importation of fish or products caught in a manner which caused death or injury in excess of federal standards set forth in the act.

• Made it unlawful for any person subject to U.S. jurisdiction or using a vessel, port or harbor subject to U.S. jurisdiction to take or import any marine mammal.

• Made it unlawful, except for scientific research, to import any marine mammals who were pregnant, nursing, less than eight months old, on the endangered or depleted species lists, or taken inhumanely.

• Set civil penalties of up to $10,000 per violation, and criminal penalties of up to $20,000 or a year in prison or both.

• Directed the secretary of state to initiate international negotiations on agreements for the protection and conservation of marine mammals worldwide, and to seek an international meeting before July 1, 1973.

• Required a one-year study of the Alaska fur seal harvest and a report to Congress on proposed changes in the North Pacific Fur Seal Convention of 1957.

Title I—Exceptions

• Allowed for two years after enactment of the bill the killing of marine mammals incidental to commercial fishing operations, so long as techniques were used which produced the least possible hazards and were aimed at reducing deaths or injury to insignificant levels approaching a zero mortality and serious injury rate.

• Granted an exception to the moratorium to Indians, Aleuts and Eskimos who killed marine mammals for subsistence or for the manufacture of native clothing or handicrafts for sale, if not done in a wasteful manner.

• Authorized additional one-year exceptions for those who might otherwise suffer undue economic hardship, and additional exceptions consistent with the act if based on the best available scientific evidence and after con-

sultation with the marine mammal commission to be established. *(Title II)*

Title I—Permits and Regulations

• Authorized the issuance of permits by the interior and commerce secretaries for the killing or capture of sea mammals; required that in order for permits to be issued to decrease overpopulation, transplanting of some animals to different locations must first be considered; authorized general permits for fishermen or Eskimos.

• Allowed permits to be issued by the secretaries for scientific research and public display, after review by a marine mammal commission and a scientific advisory committee. *(Title II)*

• Forbade issuance of permits to take any marine mammals on the endangered or depleted species lists, except for scientific research.

• Authorized the issuance of regulations on the taking and importation of marine mammals—including restrictions on the number, age, size and sex of animals which could be taken as well as the season of the year, method and locations of hunting such animals.

Title I—Funding

• Authorized marine mammal research grants to state or federal agencies, public or private institutions, and authorized $2.5-million annually for fiscal years 1973-77.

• Directed a two-year research and development program in commercial fisheries gear to devise improved methods of reducing the incidental kill of marine mammals; authorized $2-million, and required the issuance of regulations after the study was completed.

• Authorized $10-million over five years for the Commerce Department and $2.8-million for the Interior Department.

Title II—Marine Mammal Commission

• Established a three-member marine mammal commission to be appointed by the President to review all aspects of marine mammal protection and make recommendations to Congress.

• Directed the commission to establish a nine-member committee of scientific advisers knowledgeable in marine ecology.

• Authorized up to $1-million per year for five years to carry out Title II.

POLAR BEAR MORATORIUM. Congress failed to complete action on a related bill (H J Res 1268) calling for a moratorium on the killing of polar bears. The resolution would have required the President to seek a treaty or other appropriate arrangement with the Soviet Union, Canada, Denmark, Norway and other interested nations to curb the killing of polar bears.

A provision of the Marine Mammal Protection Act of 1972 directed the secretary of state to initiate negotiations with other nations on agreements for the protection and conservation of marine mammals.

Other Wildlife Legislation

HUNTING FROM AIRCRAFT. Congress gave the Interior Department authority to enforce a 1971 act (PL 92-159) making it a federal crime to shoot at birds, fish or other animals from aircraft. Since no federal agency was given specific enforcement authority by the 1971

Two Approaches to Ocean Mammal Protection . . .

Efforts to protect ocean mammals produced friction between persons who advocated a total ban on killing of the animals and those who sought to establish a program of scientific management.

Conservationists who wanted to stop all killing accused the other side of brutality and even murder. But proponents of wildlife management argued that since man had already upset the balance of nature, he had to continue to both protect and harvest the world's wild animals for their own good. They pointed to situations in which a species left alone overpopulated its habitat until the animals died of starvation and disease.

Ocean mammals faced threats from a variety of sources, ranging from hunting to pollution. This is how the situation appeared as Congress prepared to consider protective legislation in 1972:

Seals. Of all species of ocean mammals, seals probably have been the subject of the most prolonged controversy. Pictures of young seals being clubbed to death during annual hunts have appeared in the mass media. Opponents of the hunt have called it immoral and inhumane.

However, the issue is clouded because there are many types of seals and several different hunts. The United States has no jurisdiction over the Canadian harp seal hunt in the Gulf of St. Lawrence where thousands of white-coated baby seals are taken for their skins. Some 240,000 harp seals were killed in 1971. Some Canadian biologists believe the kill should be cut by at least 100,000.

The other widely publicized seal hunt is for Alaskan fur seals on the Pribilof Islands in the Bering Sea. The Department of Commerce administers this hunt and hires Aleut Indians and other Alaskans as hunters. Bachelor male seals are driven away from the large males and their harems of females, where they are killed with wooden clubs and skinned. The method of killing has been defended by the federal government as the most humane possible, but conservationists have protested that several blows often are necessary to kill an animal, that females are killed accidentally and some seals are skinned alive.

The lucrative fur seal harvest has gone on for decades. The Aleuts have killed seals in the Pribilofs since the 18th century, when they were brought to the islands as slaves by Russian fur traders. The United States acquired Alaska in 1867, and in 1911 a four-nation treaty was signed in which the United States and Russia each agreed to give 15 per cent of their fur seal skins to Canada and Japan in return for cessation of pelagic, or open sea, sealing by the latter two countries.

Advocates of the hunt maintain that the seal herd is being managed to its own benefit, and that the herd has increased from its depleted state of about 200,000 in 1911 to a present size of some 1.5 million. However, conservationists point out that the herd reached a peak of nearly 4 million in 1948, so it actually has decreased by about 75 per cent.

Sea Lions. Also endangered by pollution are the some 50,000 sea lions which live off the coast of California. Frequent abortions of infant sea lions have been documented in recent years, and scientists have blamed a combination of DDT and PCB deposits. The Alaskan sea lion herd, which is estimated at 500,000, is hunted by Eskimos who take several thousand animals each year for food and hides. State laws forbid sportsmen to hunt sea lions for other purposes.

Whales. More than a century of widespread whaling has brought many kinds of whales close to extermination. In the 19th century, when whale oil was used primarily for lamps, the United States dominated the world whaling industry with a fleet of some 700 sailing ships. However, modern whaling methods, such as helicopter and sonar tracking, explosive harpoons and huge factory ships, made the 1960s the most efficient decade in whaling history. In 1966 nearly 58,000 whales were killed, yielding 1.5 million barrels of oil. When 29,000 whales were killed in 1933, they yielded 2.6 million barrels of oil. Conservationists argue that such evidence proves modern whale hunters are killing smaller whales in larger numbers.

One of Walter J. Hickel's final acts as secretary of interior was to place eight kinds of whales on the department's endangered species list. Seven of them—the blue, grey, bowhead, right, fin, sei and humpback—are baleen whales, which feed by straining plankton through sieve-like plates of whalebone, or baleen. The other basic class, the toothed whale, includes sperm and killer whales, porpoises and dolphins. Of these, only the sperm whale is on the endangered species list.

Until 1972, the United States imported nearly a third of the world's whale products. Whale oil is used for paint, transmission oil, cosmetics and in tanning leather. Whale meat is used in dog and cat food and on

---

act, enforcement had been the general responsibility of the Federal Bureau of Investigation. *(Background, details, p. 789)*

The new legislation (HR 14731—PL 92-502) gave the interior secretary authority to issue regulations implementing and enforcing the provisions of the 1971 act and to designate enforcement officials. Those officials were authorized to conduct searches without warrants and to arrest and bring to court any person they witnessed violating the act. In its report on the bill, the Senate Commerce Committee noted that the provision for warrantless searches if authorized by law was intended to supersede recent court decisions which held that federal game agents had no authority to search beyond that expressly granted by statute. "This provision would not authorize a search not otherwise permissible under the Constitution," the committee stated.

BALD EAGLE PROTECTION. Following the revelation in 1971 of instances of mass eagle killings, Congress in 1972 strengthened the penalties imposed by the Bald Eagle Protection Act of 1940, which prohibited the shooting or molesting of bald and gloden eagles.

. . . Ban All Killing or Permit Managed Harvest

mink farms. But effective December 1971, the United States banned importation of all whale products.

The last remaining United States whaling operations were terminated in 1971, although these consisted of only three small boats owned by the Del Monte Fishing Company of San Francisco, Calif. Most of the whaling done today is by Japan and the U.S.S.R., which each have three fleets of whaling ships. The Japanese and Russians combined take some 20,000 whales a year. Norway has one factory ship

Porpoises and Dolphins. In the same family with whales are the air-breathing dolphins and porpoises, which probably are the most intelligent of all ocean mammals. In the 2nd century A.D., Oppian wrote: "It is an offense to the gods to kill dolphins...because the gods hold the massacre of the monarchs of the depths to be as execrable as the murder of a human." After the dolphin population in the Black Sea was wiped out, the U.S.S.R. in 1966 prohibited the capture or killing of dolphins.

The primary threat to these animals today is from the commercial tuna fishing fleets of the United States and Japan. Porpoises often swim with schools of tuna, and fishermen drop their huge purse-seine nets when they see porpoises feeding near the surface. But the porpoises dive when frightened, their flippers or snouts become entangled in the nets and they drown. The National Marine Fisheries Service estimates that from 250,000 to 400,000 porpoises are inadvertently killed each year in this manner.

Sea Otters, Walruses. Inhabiting the waters off the California and Alaska coasts, sea otters were nearly extinct at the beginning of this century because of fur hunters who killed them by the thousands for their skins. A federal policy of complete protection began in 1911 and the population recovered to a level of between 30,000 and 50,000 today.

The only American stocks of walruses are found in the Bering Sea off the coast of Alaska, where they inhabit shifting ocean ice floes. Eskimos are the primary walrus hunters, and there is no limit on the number they can take for food, either for themselves or for dog sled teams. There is also a demand for ivory walrus tusks, and some walruses are taken each year by trophy-hunting sportsmen.

The main threat to the walrus is modern rifles. Eskimos often fire indiscriminately into a herd of walruses and keep only those which are killed. The wounded animals swim away but usually die later. Alaskan newspapers have carried reports of hundreds of dead walruses washing ashore on beaches.

Nonetheless, estimates of the present number of walruses indicate the population has increased since the beginning of this century. According to the Interior Department, the primary need is for education of Eskimos in better hunting practices.

Manatees. The manatee or American sea cow (known in Europe and Asia as the dugong) today is found only in Florida, although it once ranged all along the Gulf and East Coasts from Mexico to the Carolinas. Manatees were slaughtered for their meat, which was considered a delicacy, but now are protected by Florida state law.

Still, manatees are on the endangered species list because their population has been diminished by motorboats, whose whirling propellers kill or maim the animals in shallow waters. Another threat to manatees is pollution, as waters contaminated by herbicides, dredging silt, or industrial phosphate effluents destroy the vegetation on which they feed. One species, Stellar's sea cow, became extinct during this century.

Polar Bears. Although they spend less time in the water than other animals covered by the proposed legislation, polar bears are considered ocean mammals because they inhabit the flowing Arctic ice pack. Because knowledge of polar bear population and movement is limited, the Interior Department has not placed the species on the endangered list, despite a suit by Friends of Animals Inc. to force this listing.

Hunting by American and Scandinavian sportsmen is the primary threat to polar bears, but there also is a large illegal market for their hides. Alaska's Fish and Game Department manages the hunt in the United States and in 1971 issued 300 permits. Although shooting bears from small aircraft was prohibited by November 1971 legislation (HR 5060—PL 92-159), the animals still are hunted from spotter aircraft which chase the bears to a hunter on the surface. Alaska plans to ban this practice in 1973, but hunting from dog sleds, boats and snowmobiles still will be allowed.

Estimates of polar bear population today range from 5,000 to 20,000 with about 1,300 being killed each year. The U.S.S.R. banned all killing of polar bears in 1956, and now blames the United States for killing Russian bears which migrate to Alaska.

The new legislation (HR 12186—PL 92-535) increased the maximum fines and prison sentences for violations of the act, authorized rewards for information leading to conviction and increased the responsibility of offenders to know the law.

The bald eagle population in the continental United States was estimated in 1971 at only 2,519, while the golden eagle population had dropped to 702.

In the House, Representatives of sheep ranching areas argued that ranchers had a right to protect their stock from attacks by eagles and that already stiff penalties against killing eagles were sufficient to discourage their destruction.

Provisions. As signed into law Oct. 23 by the President, major provisions of HR 12186:

• Made it unlawful for anyone knowingly or with negligent disregard to kill, possess, sell or transport any bald or golden eagle, alive or dead, or any eagle part, nest or egg.

• Increased the penalties from a $500 fine or 6 months imprisonment or both to a $5,000 fine or 1 year imprisonment or both for a first offense and $10,000 or 2 years imprisonment or both for a second offense, and provided that one-half of any fine, up to a maximum of $2,500, be paid to persons providing information leading to a conviction.

• Prohibited the poisoning of bald or golden eagles.

PREDATOR CONTROL. Congress failed to complete action on two related bills dealing with the control of predatory wildlife.

Poison Restrictions. An administration proposal to restrict the use of poisons in predator control programs was approved by the House but the Senate took no action on the measure (HR 13152). The bill also was aimed at reducing loss of livestock and poultry, especially in the West where such damage often was costly for ranchers and farmers.

A January 1972 study prepared for the Council on Environmental Quality and the Interior Department had recommended stopping the use of poisons for control of predatory wildlife, increased use of traps and expanded ecological and economic research. A presidential order Feb. 8 banned the use of poisons for predator control on federal lands and the Environmental Protection Agency (EPA) on March 10 halted interstate shipment of all pesticides registered for predator control.

As passed by the House July 17, HR 13152 banned the field use of chemical toxicants for predator control on federal lands and declared illegal the use of poisons which had secondary effects on other animals. Federal officials were authorized to allow emergency use of chemical toxicants, however, in cases where use was essential for protection of human health or safety, preservation of a species threatened with extinction or prevention of damage to natural resources or major damage to domestic livestock.

The measure also authorized the interior secretary to set up a program to help develop predator control methods consistent with principles of wildlife management and environmental quality and to aid state predator control programs.

Rancher Indemnity. Prior to passage of HR 13152, the House had refused to consider a bill (HR 14163) providing indemnity payments to owners of livestock killed by predators. Many cattle and sheep owners believed such losses would increase as the result of administration actions to restrict use of poisons in predator control.

Members June 29 rejected a rule (H Res 1019) permitting the House to take up the rancher indemnity bill.

Opponents of HR 14163 argued that taxpayers should not be called upon to help private livestock owners make a profit. Supporters contended that recent federal actions restricting predator control efforts to trapping and hunting would result in great financial losses for livestockmen. The measure would have compensated owners for the loss of poultry, cattle, sheep, swine, goats, horses, mules or other equines.

ENDANGERED SPECIES. Congress failed to complete action on legislation (S 3818) reported by the Senate Commerce Committee to provide for the conservation and protection of fish, wildlife and plant life threatened with extinction. The Senate took no floor action on the bill before adjournment.

As reported, S 3818, the Endangered Species and Conservation Act of 1972, would prohibit the hunting, killing or capture of endangered species in the United States or on the territorial or high seas, and for the first

time make such taking (killing) a federal crime. It would give the secretaries of the Commerce and Interior Departments expanded authority to place species on the endangered list, including those likely to be threatened with extinction.

Congress in 1969 had strengthened laws limiting the importation and sale of animals, fish and amphibians in danger of becoming extinct both in the United States and abroad. *(p. 755)*

FISH RESOURCES. Congress in 1972 extended authorizations for research into the conservation of commercial fisheries and set up a new program to develop tuna and other fisheries resources in the Pacific Ocean. Another measure continued programs to control jellyfish and other ocean pests.

A bill (HR 9501—PL 92-471) authorizing the secretary of commerce to administer the International Convention for High Seas Fisheries of the North Pacific Area also was approved in 1972.

Commercial Fisheries. Congress voted to continue programs to coordinate state and federal efforts in research for the conservation of fisheries for five years when it approved legislation (S 3524—PL 92-590) extending the provisions of a 1964 law, the Commercial Fisheries Research and Development Act (PL 88-309). S 3524 authorized $6.6-million annually for fiscal years 1974-78 to carry out the provisions of the act. The bill was signed into law Oct. 27. *(Congress and the Nation Vol. I, p. 1070; Vol. II, p. 492)*

Tuna Fisheries. Congress approved a three-year, $3-million program (HR 12207—PL 92-444) to develop the tuna and other fisheries resources in the Pacific Ocean. The measure was intended to encourage development of a skipjack tuna fishing industry in American Samoa, Guam and the Trust Territory of the Pacific Islands. Proponents of the bill argued that the tuna fishing industry appeared to be the only important private enterprise capable of development that would give the islanders of the central and western Pacific a viable industry.

As signed into law Sept. 29, HR 12207 authorized the secretary of commerce, beginning July 1, 1973, to carry out a program for fisheries resource development in the area, including exploration and stock assessment, improvement of harvesting techniques, gear development and economic evaluation. The secretary was directed to submit to Congress a report on his activities no later than June 30, 1976.

Jellyfish Control. In a related effort to guard fish resources, Congress extended (HR 16074—PL 92-604) for an additional four years the program to provide for the control or elimination of jellyfish and other ocean pests. The purpose of the program, set up in 1966, was to conserve and protect fish and shellfish resources in U.S. coastal waters and to promote and safeguard water-based recreation.

In 1966 Congress had enacted PL 89-720 authorizing the secretary of the interior to cooperate with and assist the states in controlling and eliminating jellyfish and other pests and in conducting research for the purposes of controlling floating seaweed in U.S. coastal waters. The program was to continue through June 1970. *(Congress and the Nation Vol. II, p. 494)*

In 1970 the program was extended for three years, until June 30, 1973 (PL 91-45). HR 16074 amended the act to extend the program for an additional four years, to June 30, 1977, at a cost of $400,000 per year.

Studies authorized by the original act were not accomplished because of the low numbers of jellyfish and other marine pests in the waters in recent years.

WILDLIFE RESTORATION. In the closing days of the session, Congress boosted funding for wildlife restoration projects and hunter safety programs. It approved a bill (HR 11091—PL 92-558) providing for an 11 per cent sales tax on bows and arrows and other archery accessories. Revenues from this tax, which would not apply to bows and arrows manufactured by Indians on reservations, were earmarked for the Wildlife Restoration Fund. The secretary of the interior administers the fund, which calls for matching state grants.

The bill was signed into law Oct. 25.

WILDLIFE CONSERVATION LANDS. Congress liberalized the authority of the General Services Administration to transfer surplus federal land to state agencies or the Department of Interior for wildlife conservation use.

The new legislation (HR 13025—PL 92-432) amended a 1948 act (PL 80-537) authorizing such transfers without reimbursement if the land were "chiefly valuable" for that purpose. HR 13025 was designed to place use for wildlife conservation on an equal footing with alternative public uses for the property.

The bill was signed into law Sept. 26.

OTHER LEGISLATION

Noise Control

On the last day of the session, Congress set up the first comprehensive federal program aimed at curbing noise harmful to the human environment.

The Noise Control Act of 1972 (HR 11021—PL 92-574) gave the federal government authority to set standards limiting certain commercial sources of noise, such as construction and transportation equipment, motors, engines and electric or electronic devices. It also directed the Environmental Protection Agency (EPA) to propose noise standards for aircraft but gave the Federal Aviation Administration (FAA) final authority to review and reject standards which it found unsafe or impractical.

The EPA-FAA jurisdictional problem was resolved in a last-minute compromise by House and Senate sponsors of differing noise control measures. The House version of HR 11021 had given primary authority for aircraft noise regulation to the FAA, with a consulting role for EPA. The Senate version (S 3342) had placed chief authority in EPA, with veto power for the FAA.

The compromise was reached without a House-Senate conference after five days of intensive negotiations between members of the Senate Public Works and Commerce Committees and the House Interstate and Foreign Commerce Committee.

House Action

Acting in the belief that most major soures of excessive noise in the United States could be reduced with application of existing technology, the House Interstate and Foreign Commerce Committee, in reporting HR 11021

Noise: Annoying and Dangerous

Research amassed by 1972 indicated that noise, which had grown markedly in previous years, was not only annoying but dangerous.

Medical Aspects. Researchers were unanimous on only one thing: noise caused hearing loss. Permanent damage occurs when a person is exposed to a sound level of 85 decibels (a decibel is a measure of sound) over a period of years, although he is not likely to notice the hearing loss until it is too late to do anything about it.

While normal conversation occurs at about 60 decibels, heavy traffic operates at about 90 decibels, a riveting machine blasts away at 110 decibels and the noise level at a discotheque reaches 120 decibels. The threshold of pain is put variously at between 130 and 150 decibels.

Other research implicated a variety of other ailments besides hearing loss, ranging from nervous tension headaches to neurosis. Doctors at the December 1969 meeting of the American Association for the Advancement of Science reported experiments indicating that noise:

- Causes blood vessels to constrict, cutting the flow of blood to key parts of the body.
- Affects the whole autonomous nervous system, which controls the involuntary functions of the heart, blood vessels, muscles and glands.
- Can cause seizures in epileptics.
- Disturbs unborn children and may harm them.

A four-year study at the University of Tennessee revealed increasing hearing problems among young people. A survey of incoming freshmen in 1968 found that about 33 per cent had high-frequency hearing difficulty. A later survey indicated that more than 60 per cent had the same problem. The report concluded that most of the hearing disorders probably were the result of exposure to music played too loudly.

EPA Report. In January 1972, the Environmental Protection Agency (EPA) reported that noise had a significant impact on persons in the United States, with physiological and psychological effects including speech interference, hearing impairment, sleep disturbance and stress reactions. Repeated exposure to high noise intensity could cause permanent hearing loss, the report said, while lesser noise might produce irritation and annoyance.

Another EPA estimate indicated that noise subjected about 40 million Americans to hearing damage or other mental or physical hazards, and that up to 64 million people lived in homes which were affected by aircraft, traffic or construction noise.

Prior Congressional Action. Despite widespread discussion of the detrimental effects of noise, the only measures enacted by Congress prior to 1972 were a 1968 bill providing for aircraft noise abatement (PL 90-411) and a section of the Clean Air Act Amendments of 1970 (PL 91-604) which required EPA to conduct a study of noise and report its findings. *(Details, p. 765)*

Feb. 19, recommended establishment of federal noise emission standards for commercial products.

The House Feb. 29 approved the committee version of the bill, after rejecting five floor amendments. The chief controversy developed over an amendment offered by John W. Wydler (R N.Y.) to give the EPA primary regulatory power to control aircraft noise as well as other sources of noise listed in the bill. The committee version provided only that the FAA must consult with the EPA before issuing aircraft noise control standards.

The House rejected the Wydler amendment as well as another sponsored by Abner J. Mikva (D Ill.) to prohibit sonic booms over the United States by commercial jets.

Senate Action

Public Works Committee. The Senate Public Works Committee Sept. 15 reported a similar bill (S 3342) designed to control the emission of excessive noise.

The bill would have required the Environmental Protection Agency (EPA) to issue noise emission standards for newly manufactured products, railroads, trucks and buses, and, with the Federal Aviation Administration (FAA), for aircraft.

The bill as reported by the committee was a combination of the original S 3342, sponsored by Edmund S. Muskie (D Maine) and John V. Tunney (D Calif.), the Nixon administration bill (S 1016) and the House-passed bill (HR 11021).

In minority views appended to the committee report, however, Muskie objected to the bill as reported on grounds that it did not recognize state and local responsibility. Under the committee version, the federal government would assume (pre-empt) states' authority to enforce noise emission standards against manufacturers, although state and local governments still could set and enforce limits on environmental noise from the use of products.

S 3342 was endorsed in mid-September by eight environmental organizations—Friends of the Earth, Sierra Club, Citizens Committee on Natural Resources, Citizens Against Noise, Environmental Policy Center, Environmental Action, Trout Unlimited and the Federation of American Scientists.

Commerce Committee Action. Later that month the Commerce Committee unanimously agreed to offer an amendment to S 3342 to delete provisions dealing with aircraft noise. The proposed committee amendment would insert instead the aircraft noise provisions of the House bill (HR 11021), which directed the FAA to consult with the EPA in setting aircraft noise standards and gave the EPA administrator review (but not veto) authority.

Environmental groups had feared the Commerce Committee would ask for re-referral of S 3342, which probably would have killed the bill for the 1972 session. The committee's action increased the bill's chances for Senate floor action and final passage by the 92nd Congress.

Floor Action. The Senate approved S 3342 on Oct. 13 after two days of heated debate. The Senate then passed HR 11021 after inserting the language of S 3342.

Sharply critical of the bill as reported, Muskie offered two amendments which were later rejected. One would have required the EPA and FAA to curb cumulative noise exposure levels around airports, while another would have given states and localities authority to regulate the sale of products through noise emission controls more stringent than federal standards.

The Senate adopted four amendments to the bill, including language which barred the landing of supersonic civil aircraft at airports within U.S. jurisdiction unless they met noise standards for subsonic aircraft and called for a study of means to finance the retrofitting—adaptation—of existing aircraft.

Final Action

On the last day of the session, both the House and Senate approved certain changes the other body had made in the bill, clearing it for the President. Compromises on the differences between the two versions of the bill were hammered out without a House-Senate conference after five days of negotiations between members of the two committees which had considered the measure.

The major stumbling block was resolved when the Senate agreed to drop its ban on supersonic aircraft landings and compromised on jurisdiction over general aircraft noise. The final bill gave the EPA power to propose aircraft noise standards but gave the FAA final authority to review and reject any which it found unsafe or impractical.

In addition to the EPA-FAA question, negotiators agreed to delete a Senate-passed provision requiring a study by the Transportation Department on methods of financing the retrofitting of existing aircraft engines with equipment to reduce noise. Also deleted was a Senate-passed provision requiring any supersonic transport (SST) aircraft landing at U.S. airports to meet noise emission standards for subsonic aircraft.

But the final version contained some provisions of the Senate bill which were not in the House version: a requirement that the EPA publish criteria on the maximum levels of environmental noise which could be tolerated without having adverse effects on public health, welfare or safety and authority for the EPA to set regulations for noise control on interstate carriers, including railroads, trucks and buses.

Both Senate and House bills amended and expanded provisions of the Clean Air Act Amendments of 1970 (PL 91-604), but the final version established a separate act.

The House agreed to certain Senate amendments by voice vote on Oct. 18. A House vote was initially blocked by Durward G. Hall (R Mo.), who protested "the procedural press of year-end legislation," criticized "federal pre-emption of states rights," objected to the absence of a House-Senate conference and criticized the newly granted right of citizens "to bring civil suits leading to these too severe penalties." Hall finally relented and dropped his objection to considering the measure under a unanimous consent motion.

The Senate later that same day agreed to other House amendments by voice vote, completing congressional action.

Provisions

As signed into law Oct. 27, HR 11021 contained major provisions which:
● Declared it national policy to protect the public health and welfare from detrimental noise, to coordinate

federal research and activities in noise control, to set federal noise emission standards for commercial products and to provide information to the public.

• Exempted military combat weapons, rockets or experimental federal equipment from the act's requirements.

• Required the EPA administrator, within nine months of enactment, to issue noise criteria based on scientific knowledge; within 12 months, to publish noise levels to protect public health, welfare and safety; and within 18 months, to identify products which were major sources of noise and give techniques for controlling their emissions.

• Required the administrator, within 18 months, to set noise emission standards for products distributed in interstate commerce designated as major noise sources, including construction and transportation equipment, motors and engines, and electrical and electronic equipment.

• Required EPA standards to be based on the reduction in noise emissions achievable with the best available control technology, taking into account the cost of compliance.

• Required product manufacturers to warrant new products to conform to the federal regulations.

• Pre-empted state and local authority to set noise emission standards that would be enforceable against manufactured products, but allowed states to set and enforce limits on environmental noise through licensing, regulation or restriction on use.

• Directed the EPA administrator, within nine months of enactment, to report on the adequacy of FAA flight and operational noise controls, the adequacy of emission standards on new and existing aircraft (including recommendations for retrofitting engines and phasing out existing aircraft), cumulative airport noise exposure levels and other airport noise control measures.

• Required the FAA, after consultation with the EPA and the Transportation Department, to set or amend standards for measurement, control and abatement of aircraft noise and sonic booms.

• Required the EPA to submit to the FAA proposed regulations to control and reduce aircraft noise and sonic booms; required the FAA to begin proposed rule-making procedures within 30 days and to hold hearings within 60 days. Required FAA to approve, modify or reject EPA's proposed rules; however, if any EPA rules were rejected FAA would have to explain its reasons publicly and in detail, including information on safety, public interest, economics and technology; required all interagency communications to be printed in the *Federal Register*.

• Directed the EPA administrator to issue labeling requirements for products which emitted excessive noise or were intended to reduce noise.

• Required the secretary of the treasury to regulate imported products for noise emissions.

• Required the administrator to issue, within nine months of enactment, noise emission standards for railroads and motor carriers (trucks and buses) in interstate commerce; gave the secretary of transportation authority to enforce these standards; allowed states to set higher standards or restrict movement if made necessary by special local conditions.

• Directed the EPA administrator to identify low-noise-emission products with the help of an advisory committee and to certify them for preferential use by federal agencies if the General Services Administration determined that their costs were not more than 125 per cent of the retail price of the least expensive alternate produce; authorized $1-million for fiscal year 1973 and $2-million per year for 1974 and 1975 to help purchase such products.

• Authorized citizen suits in federal courts against violators or against the EPA or FAA for failure to carry out mandatory provisions of the act.

• Authorized $3-million for fiscal 1973, $6-million for 1974 and $12-million for 1975 to carry out the act.

Toxic Substances

A bill (S 1478) to establish a federal regulatory system for potentially hazardous chemicals died in the final days of the 92nd Congress when the House failed to agree to changes made by the Senate in the original House-passed version.

Among the potentially harmful elements to be regulated under the legislation were asbestos, lead and mercury, as well as mixtures of organic chemicals such as polychlorobiphenyls (PCBs) and phosphate detergents —substances which are not widely recognized as hazardous until harm had already been done.

Two million recognized chemical compounds were in existence in 1972; nearly 250,000 new compounds were added each year. The major difference between the House and Senate versions involved pre-market testing requirements for those new chemical substances. Unlike the original Senate version, the House bill would have exempted from pre-market testing by the Environmental Protection Agency (EPA) new chemicals with no known potential hazards.

The House bill also prohibited the EPA administrator from exercising authority under the bill if environmental or health risks could be prevented through other laws.

Four days before adjournment, the Senate amended the House-passed version to make it conform more closely to the original Senate bill, but the House took no further action on the Senate amendments.

Administration Proposal. The legislation was originally proposed by President Nixon in his 1971 environmental message to Congress, and was introduced at the request of the administration by Philip A. Hart (D Mich.), chairman of the Commerce Subcommittee on Environment, Warren G. Magnuson (D Wash.), chairman of the Commerce Committee, and Edward M. Kennedy (D Mass.). The environment subcommittee made several major changes in S 1478 as originally introduced, including a pre-market certification requirement of test results, authority to require testing of certain existing chemicals and a citizen-suit provision.

The Nixon administration opposed the pre-market screening provision of S 1478, although it endorsed the general concept of the bill.

Senate Action

The Senate Commerce Committee reported S 1478 May 5 by a unanimous vote.

"It is possible that most...new chemical compounds will never be produced commercially," the committee report said. "However, several hundred will find their way into the market place and subsequently into the environment.... As man continues to develop and produce chemicals at an increasing rate, the risk of producing a chemical which will cause serious environmental or health problems also increases."

The Senate passed S 1478 unanimously May 30, after rejecting two amendments which would have weakened or eliminated EPA's pre-market testing authority.

Provisions. As approved by the Senate, major provisions of S 1478:

• Declared it national policy to test all new and some existing chemical substances and to curb use of those which posed unreasonable threats to human health and the environment.

• Authorized EPA to require testing of existing chemical substances whose manufacture, processing, distribution, use or disposal posed an unreasonable threat to human health or the environment.

• Authorized EPA to restrict use or distribution of some chemicals, to seize substances which posed an imminent hazard and authorized federal district courts to restrain substances presenting imminent hazards.

• Exempted chemical substances intended solely for export from most provisions of the bill, except that none could be exported which posed unreasonable threats to the human health or the environment of the United States.

• Authorized citizen suits against alleged violators of the act.

• Authorized appropriations of $6.3-million in fiscal 1973, $10.4-million in fiscal 1974 and $9.6-million in fiscal 1975.

House Action

The House Interstate and Foreign Commerce Committee reported an amended version of S 1478 Sept. 28.

The bill would have given the Environmental Protection Agency (EPA) comprehensive authority to require pre-market testing of new and some existing chemicals, to screen test results prior to commercial production and to regulate use and distribution.

Five days before adjournment, on Oct. 13, the House approved S 1478 under suspension of the rules, a procedure which requires a two-thirds majority vote for passage and precludes floor amendments. Considerable opposition was expressed on the floor both to the procedure and to the bill itself.

Harley O. Staggers (D W.Va.), chairman of the Interstate and Foreign Commerce Committee and floor manager of the bill, said S 1478 had the "active support of the EPA and several major chemical manufacturers."

But Durward G. Hall (R Mo.) opposed the bill: "We need this additional legislation just to prove that we are in favor of a good environment like we need extra holes in the head. This is one of the worst pieces of legislation that I have heard of in 12 years here. The report itself admits it is duplicative, overlapping, biased and not thought out as to whose responsibility is what.... But the main thing wrong with this bill is that it will take all chemical manufacturing, research, development and production of needed toxic substances out of the United States and send them overseas because of the require-

ment of pre-market screening and because of the need for clearances in advance."

Provisions. As reported by the committee and passed by the House, major provisions of S 1478:

• Declared it national policy to test adequately all hazardous or potentially hazardous chemicals.

• Required the EPA to list chemicals which were likely to post substantial danger to health or environment and require stricter pre-market screening procedures for them.

• Authorized the EPA to prescribe rules prohibiting the manufacture or distribution in commerce of some chemicals, to limit amounts, restrict uses or require adequate label warnings and instructions.

• Authorized the EPA to file actions in federal district courts against "imminently hazardous" chemicals in order to seize substances to prevent "imminent and unreasonable" risk to health or the environment.

• Authorized citizen suits against the federal government, manufacturers or other alleged violators of the act.

• Authorized appropriations of $8-million for fiscal 1973, $11-million for fiscal 1974 and $10-million for fiscal 1975.

Senate Changes

The following day, Oct. 14, the Senate agreed to a motion concurring in the House changes, but adding several amendments offered by Frank E. Moss (D Utah), chairman of the Commerce Committee's Consumer Subcommittee.

The major Senate changes, Moss said, dealt with the pre-market testing provisions and with the bill's relationship to existing laws. One would have authorized pre-market screening for new chemicals whose "dangers are unknown" as well as those "which are likely to pose substantial danger to the health or the environment." The other exempted from the provisions of the bill tobacco and tobacco products, all foods, drugs, devices and cosmetics subject to the Food, Drug and Cosmetic Act, and pesticides regulated by the Pesticide Control Act. But it gave the EPA administrator authority in situations where dangers could not be prevented by other laws.

The House did not act on the Senate amendments prior to adjournment Oct. 18.

General Environmental Bills

ENVIRONMENTAL DATA SYSTEM. Congress voted to set up a national data system to serve as a clearinghouse for information on environmental matters, but the bill (HR 56) was pocket vetoed by President Nixon after Congress adjourned. Nixon objected that the bill would "lead to the duplication of information or would produce results unrelated to real needs." The bill had been opposed by the Environmental Protection Agency.

As cleared, HR 56 would have established a central facility to store, analyse and disseminate environmental data provided by federal, state and local governments and private institutions and individuals. Appropriations of $1-million for fiscal 1974 were authorized under the measure. In addition, HR 56 would have provided for the establishment of state and regional environmental centers to conduct and coordinate the environmental research and teaching facilities of educational institutions in the area, with authorizations of $7-million in fiscal 1974.

Initial House action had been completed in 1971. *(p. 790)*

ENVIRONMENTAL COMPACTS. Although the Senate March 1 approved a bill (S 907) granting advance congressional consent to interstate compacts on pollution control, the House took no action on the bill and it died at the close of the 92nd Congress. S 907 had been reported by the Senate Judiciary Committee in 1971. *(p. 790)* It was then referred to the Public Works Committee which reported it Feb. 24 with amendments that limited the pre-consent authority.

The bill would have permitted two or more states to enter into cooperative intergovernmental agreements to protect the environment if they did not conflict with existing federal laws. Such a compact then would be subject to approval by either the Senate or House. States have had difficulty making legally binding arrangements because Article I, section 10 of the Constitution requires that Congress approve all interstate compacts in advance.

EXPO '74. President Nixon Oct. 27 signed into law a bill (S 4022—PL 92-598) authorizing $11.5-million for the construction and operation of a U.S. pavilion at the 1974 International Environmental Exposition in Spokane, Wash.

Sponsored by the two Washington senators, Henry M. Jackson (D) and Warren G. Magnuson (D), PL 92-598 provided federal funds for a theater and auditorium which were expected to be used by the Interior Department upon completion of the exposition.

Four countries—Russia, Japan, Iran and Canada—had agreed as of early October to participate in the fair, whose theme was to be "how man can live, work and play in harmony with his environment."

In a message to Congress Sept. 22, Nixon had requested approval of the funds.

Background. On at least two previous occasions, Congress authorized U.S. participation in a federally recognized domestic or international exposition. A total of $9.9-million was authorized for a U.S. pavilion at Century 21, the Seattle world's fair held in 1962. The cost of federal participation in Hemisfair, an exposition which took place in San Antonio in 1968, was $6.75-million.

Since 1962, the U.S. pavilion erected in Seattle had been leased at an annual rent of $1 to the Pacific Science Center Foundation, a non-profit organization, as an exhibition center. Although the federal government retained title to the property, no federal use for the center had been devised. The U.S. pavilion at San Antonio was being converted for use as a federal courthouse.

Congress in 1970 cleared the International Exposition Act (PL 91-269) which provided permanent standards for all U.S. international expositions seeking federal endorsement and support. The act required that state and local governments and business and civic organizations guarantee financial or other support and called for preparation of a detailed plan outlining proposed federal participation, including potential uses of the area after the exposition closed.

The International Environmental Exposition, known as Expo-74, was scheduled to be held from May through October, 1974. The state of Washington had appropriated $7.5-million for a state pavilion and exhibit, and the city of Spokane had provided $5.7-million for purchase of a site and a development program. Expo-74 was the first U.S. fair to seek an endorsement under PL 91-269.

Parks and Recreation

Expansion of parks and recreation facilities was an increasingly expensive but largely uncontroversial activity during the 91st and 92nd Congresses. New legislation added more than 2.4 million acres to the nation's park systems (including the incorporation of federal parks already established by executive orders). Congress also doubled the size of the Land and Water Conservation Fund for fiscal 1970-1973, compared to the previous four-year period. The fund financed acquisition of new park lands by federal, state and local agencies, and development of these properties for recreation use. *(Box p. 827)*

The centennial year of the National Park Service, oldest of the agencies which administer federal parks, forests, wildlife refuges and recreation areas, came in 1972. Originally, parks were created from undeveloped federal lands. As the centennial year approached, Congress and the Nixon administration placed increasing emphasis on the provision of parks and recreation areas in the major urbanized regions of the nation. This policy reflected a record growth in demand for outdoor recreation space, the overcrowding of many existing parks and the nation's growing demands for protection of the natural environment. The National Park Service, which operated most of the federal parks and recreation sites, recorded a near doubling of visits to its parks from 121.3-million in fiscal 1965 to 212-million in 1972.

Both policy and demand were reflected in the rising costs of new park developments. Much of the existing open space near urban areas which could be used for parks was in private hands. Land acquisition costs in many cases reached several thousand dollars an acre, particularly in the San Francisco Bay area, where new parks involved the purchase of land with the potential for commercial exploitation. The Golden Gate National Urban Recreation Area and the adjoining Point Reyes National Seashore together represented nearly $120-million in estimated land costs.

Intensive use of parks also drove up costs for development. The new Gateway National Recreation Area in New York and New Jersey, which was located mostly on public lands, cost $92.8-million for development of park facilities alone. In all, more than $1-billion in federal funds were appropriated from the Land and Water Conservation Fund during the four years.

To assist the identification and development of smaller parks in urban areas, the administration instituted a "Legacy of Parks" program in 1971. At the President's request, Congress in 1971 and 1972 appropriated a total of $200 million to the open space program of the Department of Housing and Urban Development for matching grants to state and local governments for the acquisition and development of parks in urban areas. In addition, the President ordered all federal agencies to review federal properties and identify ones which could appropriately be used for parks and recreation. In his Feb. 8, 1972, environmental message Nixon announced that 151 properties had been identified as being well suited for park use. Of these, some 83 properties were immediately available for such use, he reported. They totaled 14,585 acres, with an estimated fair market value of more than $56-million, and were located in 31 states and Puerto Rico.

Major Units Authorized

Among the major park units authorized by Congress between 1969 and 1972 were three National Parks—Voyageurs, Minn.; Arches, Utah; and Capitol Reef, Utah—five National Recreation Areas—Gateway, N.J.-N.Y.; Golden Gate, Calif.; Glen Canyon, Ariz.-Utah; Sawtooth, Idaho; and Oregon Dunes, Oregon—(the latter two under the Forest Service, Agriculture Department)—the Chesapeake and Ohio National Historical Park, D.C.-Md.-Va.; the Apostle Islands National Lakeshore, Wis.; the Sleeping Bear Dunes National Lakeshore, Mich.; the Gulf Islands National Seashore, Fla.-Miss; the Cumberland Island National Seashore, Ga.; and the Buffalo National River, Ark.

Congress also authorized a large number of small park units. Many of these were historic sites, including ones located in urban areas.

At the end of the 92nd Congress, only one major administration proposal had not been acted on. This was the Big Cypress National Fresh Water Reserve, Fla., a 547,000-acre tract largely in private hands which controlled the water supply for a large section of the Everglades. With an estimated land acquisition cost of $156-million, Big Cypress ranked as the most expensive national park ever proposed to Congress by the executive.

While generally encouraging the expansion of the park system, President Nixon in 1972 pocket vetoed one

References

Discussion of legislation on the National Park System for the years 1945-64 may be found in *Congress and the Nation, Vol. I*, p. 1074-1093; for the years 1965-68, *Congress and the Nation, Vol. II*, p. 465-473.

Major Units of the National Park System

bill which would have created a 125,000-acre national recreation area on the South Big Fork River in Kentucky and Tennessee. The park would have been operated by the Department of the Army's Corps of Engineers. The President vetoed the bill (S 4018) because he opposed numerous river, harbor and flood control projects which it authorized the Corps of Engineers to build.

Park Use Controversy

As the first century of the National Park Service drew to a close, a major policy debate developed between conservationists and officials responsible for development of the parks for public use. At the heart of the unresolved debate was a paradox. The park system was established by statute to preserve natural areas for public use. But how, asked the conservationists, could any natural area be preserved when at the same time it was being used by hordes of visitors, who demanded access roads, created traffic jams, polluted the air and water, brought drugs and crime to the parks and discarded billions of pieces of litter.

The debate over park use was given a sharp focus with the 1970 publication of *One Third of the Nation's Land*, a report of the Public Land Law Review Commission. Chairman of the commission was Rep. Wayne N. Aspinall (D Colo.), chairman of the House Interior and Insular Affairs Committee.

The report recommended establishment of a new Natural Resources Department—in effect, an expanded Interior Department to which the U.S. Forest Service would be transferred from the Agriculture Department. Regarding the national parks, the commission recommended that a "fair and equitable rationing system, in line with the carrying capacity of parks and wilderness areas, should be adopted now to assure adequate controls over visitor use."

Although none of the major recommendations of the commission had been enacted by the end of the 92nd Congress, there was increasing discussion of the need for some rationing of park use.

Wilderness Areas

One approach to preserving large park tracts from development was to put them into the National Wilderness Preservation System established by the Wilderness Act of 1964. *(Congress and the Nation,* Vol. I, p. 1095)

The act placed in the Wilderness System about 9.1 million acres of National Forest System land that had not yet been commercially exploited and was still in a natural state. Other federal lands were to be added later, after review by the executive branch and approval by Congress. Lands subject to later review totaled over 53 million acres, including 5.5 million acres of National Forest lands classified as "primitive" by the secretary of agriculture; 24.4 million acres of roadless lands in federal wildlife and game ranges; and 22.2 million acres of roadless National Park System areas.

Land placed in the wilderness system was to be safeguarded permanently (subject to existing rights) against commercial use, such as cutting of timber, extensive livestock grazing, construction of buildings and permanent roads and, with important qualifications, mineral extraction. Recreational facilities that would mar the wild character of the landscape (hotels, lodges, motorboats, sports fields, bathhouses, for example) also were forbidden.

Expansion of the wilderness system proceeded slowly because of opposition from commercial mining, lumbering and cattle-grazing interests. A major obstacle was the House Interior and Insular Affairs Committee. In 1968, Congress made the first additions to the system since the 1964 act—some 800,000 acres, bringing the total to 9.9 million. *(Congress and the Nation,* Vol. II, p. 473)

During the 91st and 92nd Congresses another 1.1 million acres were added. But there was no action on another 7.5 million acres requested by President Nixon. Of these, 1.7 million were under Forest Service jurisdiction, 5 million under National Park Service jurisdiction and about 800,000 in wildlife areas administered by the Interior Department's Bureau of Sport Fisheries and Wildlife. The President in 1971 called for completion of the Wilderness system, including the review of over 50 million additional acres, as a "major goal within the drive for environmental protection."

In 1972, the Forest Service declared that none of its remaining eastern forest lands were suitable for inclusion in the wilderness system. A bill to create a new, less stringent system of "wild areas" in national forests passed the Senate but not the House in 1972.

Withdrawals

In the last official act of his administration, President Johnson Jan. 20, 1969, added 384,500 acres to the National Parks System. The new parklands, however, were but a small fraction of the 7.5 million acres which Secretary of the Interior Stewart L. Udall reportedly had asked the President to withdraw from public lands for the purpose of enlarging park system acreage.

The President explained his reluctance to withdraw the full 7.5 million acres saying that it would pre-empt the right of Congress to review the action and would "strain the Antiquities Act (of 1906) beyond its intent." The Antiquities Act authorizes the President by proclamation to set aside federal lands, if they were outstanding for some scenic or historic quality, as "national monuments," to be administered under the general laws applicable to national parks and to be safeguarded from commercial exploitation or ruin. Only Congress can create new national parks.

The last time the Presidential authority under the 1906 act had been used was in 1965 to make Ellis Island —the former immigration depot in New York harbor— a part of the Liberty Island National Monument.

The new parklands created by President Johnson included the 26,000-acre Marble Canyon National Monument in Arizona, the addition of 49,000 acres to the existing Arches National Monument in Utah, the addition of 215,000 acres to the existing Capitol Reef National Monument in Utah and the addition of 94,500 acres to the existing Katmai National Monument in Alaska. Parklands which Udall had requested, but which the President did not create, included a proposed 4.1 million-acre Gates of the Arctic National Monument in Alaska, a

2.2-million-acre Mount McKinley National Monument in Alaska and a 911,700-acre Sonoran Desert National Monument in Arizona.

Partly in reaction to these moves, the Public Land Law Review Commission in 1970 declared that Congress should reserve to itself authority to make large withdrawals of public lands for the purpose of establishing national monuments and other units of the park system, wildlife refuges and defense reservations.

(In a related development, Congress in 1970 authorized the secretary of the interior to withdraw from selection by the state of Alaska or Alaskan natives up to 80 million acres of unreserved public lands for possible inclusion in the national park systems. The authority was included in the Alaska Native Claims Settlement Act (HR 10367).

Chronology of
Legislation on
Parks and Recreation
1969

PADRE ISLAND NATIONAL SEASHORE: Congress June 30 cleared a bill (HR 11069—PL 91-42) authorizing the appropriation of $4,129,829 plus interest to complete the acquisition of land for Padre Island National Seashore in Texas. The bill provided authority to settle judgments against the U.S. government brought by former landowners of the southern 11,000 acres of Padre Island.

HR 11069 brought total expenditures on the island seashore, which stretches for approximately 80 miles between Brownsville and Corpus Christi, Texas, to over $16-million, more than triple the $5-million estimated when the purchase was first approved by Congress in 1962.

EVERGLADES NATIONAL PARK. Congress Oct. 8 cleared a bill (S 2564—PL 91-88) authorizing $700,200 for purchase of 6,640 acres of the Flagler tract, privately owned land in a principal drainage area of the Everglades National Park in Florida.

FLORISSANT FOSSIL BEDS. Congress Aug. 7 cleared a bill (S 912—PL 91-60) authorizing the Interior Department to acquire a 6,000-acre tract near Pike's Peak, Colorado, and to establish the Florissant Fossil Beds National Monument. The new park would cover part of an ancient lakebed, 36 million to 38 million years old, which preserves more fossil species than any other known site.

HISTORIC SITES. Congress in 1969 enacted four bills establishing national historic sites at the Gettysburg, Pennsylvania, farm of former President Dwight D. Eisenhower (S J Res 26—PL 91-133); the Texas birthplace and the boyhood home of former President Lyndon B. Johnson (S 2000—PL 91-134); the Cincinnati, Ohio, home of former President William Howard Taft (HR 7066— PL 91-132), and the Washington, D.C., home of the 19th century Negro abolitionist orator and writer Frederick Douglass (HR 5968—PL 91-109).

WILDERNESS SYSTEM. Congress added two tracts to the National Wilderness Preservation System in 1969: the 63,469-acre Desolation Wilderness of the Eldorado National Forest, California (S 713-PL 91-82), and the 98,000-acre Ventana Wilderness in the Ventana Primitive Area, about 120 miles south of San Francisco in Monterey County (S 714—PL 91-58).

1970

Land Conservation Fund

For the second time in little more than two years, Congress cleared legislation (S1708—PL 91-485) increasing annual authorizations for the Land and Water Conservation Fund. The bill, which was prompted by the rising cost of land acquisition resulting from the effort to establish parks near populated areas, raised the level of the fund from $200-million a year to $300-million. It also permitted the transfer of surplus federal properties to state or local governments for public recreation.

Background. The Land and Water Conservation Fund was established in 1964 to finance acquisition of outdoor recreation areas. Revenues were derived from sales of federal surplus real property, proceeds of a federal motorboat tax and a system of uniform admission and user fees at federal recreation areas. These were expected to bring in up to $140-million a year, but by fiscal 1967 had reached only $94.8-million.

In 1968, Congress approved a modified administration bill to shore up the fund and provide additional monies in view of rising land costs. It repealed the uniform user fees, which had proved unpopular, and permitted direct appropriation in the amount necessary to bring the fund to an annual level of $200-million. An alternative source of funding was also provided by allowing use of receipts from federal oil and gas leases on the outer continental shelf.

However, in a move discouraging to conservationists, the Johnson administration limited fund outlays to $154-million just before leaving office, and the Nixon administration pared it back further to $124-million for fiscal 1970.

This move prompted one of the earlier exchanges in what later became a full-scale "battle of the budget" between the Democratic-controlled Congress and the Republican White House. House Interior and Insular Affairs Committee Chairman Wayne N. Aspinall (D Colo.) Sept. 18, 1969, denounced the Budget Bureau as "the usurper of the power of Congress" for impounding Land and Water Conservation Fund outlays. He released a letter from Budget Bureau Director Robert P. Mayo stating that there would be insufficient funds through fiscal 1973 for even some of the more modest land acquisition proposals already authorized by Congress. Both the House and Senate Interior Committees promptly cancelled pending parks legislation.

But the Nixon administration made a dramatic turnaround. In a Feb. 10, 1970, message to Congress, President Nixon proposed full use of the $327-million in un-

---

National Park System

The various park system units fall into three main groupings in terms of principles of management. There are natural areas, historic and commemorative areas, and recreation areas.

Natural. *National Parks,* created by Congress, are the highest category of natural or park-type units in the system. They are usually large areas combining natural scenic, wildlife, geologic and recreational features of outstanding quality. *National Monuments,* designated by the President, are often as large as national parks, or larger, and are used for many of the same purposes. Sometimes a monument is elevated to park status by act of Congress.

Historical and Commemorative. This grouping includes *National Historical Parks, National Battlefields, National Military Parks, National Historic Sites, National Memorials* and *National Cemeteries.* These areas differ from natural park areas in one major respect: grazing, farming or timber cutting might be permitted in historical areas if, for instance, a farm was being preserved as the birthplace of a famous man.

Recreation. *National Seashores, National Lakeshores* and *National Recreation Areas* are virtually identical to national parks except for their heavier emphasis on recreational use and development. This grouping also includes *National Parkways,* which frequently follow historic trails, and *National Scenic Riverways.*

All of these facilities except National Recreation Areas are administered by the National Park Service. The Recreation Areas come under the Park Service or the Bureau of Sport Fisheries and Wildlife, also in the Interior Department, or the Agriculture Department's Forest Service.

---

expended Land and Water Conservation funds, placed increased emphasis on acquiring lands close to urban areas, and ordered surplus federal lands in urban areas to be made available for park and recreation use.

1970 Legislation. Congress cleared S 1708 Oct. 8. The bill increased the Land and Water Fund authorization to $300-million annually through 1989, and authorized the transfer through donation or sale of surplus federal property to local and state governments for parks and recreational purposes. Action in both House and Senate was by voice vote. President Nixon signed the bill into law on Oct. 22.

Other Legislation

POINT REYES SEASHORE. The most expensive land acquisition programs of the National Park Service came from the establishment of the Point Reyes National Seashore, in Marin County, California (HR 3786-PL 91-223). Authorized in 1962, Point Reyes included some 26,000 acres of privately owned "pastoral land" as well as other private properties. Over the years, subdivision of the private lands, speculation, and general price increases drove the estimated cost of acquiring private lands in the park up 400 per cent over the $14-million original estimate. PL 91-223 increased authori-

New National Park and Recreation Units, 1969-72

Name and Location	Acres	Date Authorized	Name and Location	Acres	Date Authorized
			National Historic Sites		
National Parks			Mar-A-Lago Site, Fla.	17	1/16/69 [5]
			Eisenhower Site, Pa.	493	12/2/69
Voyageurs, Minn.	219,431	1/8/71	Lyndon B. Johnson Site, Texas	7	12/2/69
Arches, Utah [1]	73,233	11/12/71	William Howard Taft Site, Ohio	1	12/2/69
Capitol Reef, Utah [2]	241,672	12/18/71	Ford's Theatre, D.C.	—	6/23/70
			Andersonville, Ga.	495	10/16/70
National Seashores			Fort Point, Cal.	96	10/16/70
			Lincoln Home, Ill.	12	8/18/71
Gulf Islands, Fla.-Miss.	124,425	1/8/71	Puukohola Heiau, Hawaii	77	8/17/72
Cumberland Island, Ga.	39,494	10/23/72	Grant-Kohrs Ranch, Mont.	1,564	8/25/72
			Longfellow Site, Mass.	2	10/9/72
National Recreation Areas			Thaddeus Kosciusko National Memorial, Pa.	—	10/21/72
Oregon Dunes, Oregon	32,000	3/23/72	Benjamin Franklin National Memorial, Pa.	—	10/25/72
Sawtooth, Idaho	537,500	8/22/72			
Gateway, N.J.-N.Y.	26,172	10/27/72			
Glen Canyon, Ariz.-Utah [3]	1,285,310	10/27/72	**National Historical Parks**		
Golden Gate, Calif.	34,201	10/27/72	Chesapeake and Ohio Canal, D.C.-Md.-W.Va.	20,239	1/8/71
National Lakeshores			Sitka, Alaska	108	10/18/72
Apostle Islands, Wisconsin	42,826	9/26/70	**National Scenic Rivers**		
Sleeping Bear Dunes, Mich.	71,105	10/21/70	Buffalo National River, Ark.	95,840	3/1/72
National Monuments			Lower St. Croix National Scenic Riverway, Minn.-Wis.	7,845 [6]	10/25/72
Marble Canyon, Ariz. [4]	32,665	1/20/69			
Florissant Fossil Beds, Colo.	5,992	8/20/69			
Hohokam Pima, Ariz.	1,555	10/21/72			
Fossil Butte, Wyo.	8,178	10/23/72			

1. *Name changed from Arches National Monument. On Jan. 20, 1969, outgoing President Lyndon B. Johnson more than doubled the size of Arches National Monument by a proclamation adding 48,943 acres.*

2. *Name changed from Capitol Reef National Monument. On Jan. 20, 1969, President Johnson, by proclamation, enlarged Capitol Reef National Monument from 39,185 acres to 254,241 acres, an addition of over 215,000 acres. In converting the Capitol Reef Monument to a National Park, Congress reduced its size by 12,570 acres.*

3. *The Glen Canyon National Recreation Area included 1.1 million acres already*

administered by the National Park Service under an agreement with the Bureau of Reclamation dated April 18, 1958.

4. *Marble Canyon National Monument was authorized by proclamation of President Johnson on his last day in office, Jan. 20, 1969.*

5. *Mar-A-Lago was designated an historic site by the secretary of the interior. On Oct. 21, 1972, President Nixon signed a bill (PL 92-527) giving congressional authority for the designation.*

6. *Additional acreage is administered by Minnesota and Wisconsin.*

zation for land acquisition in Point Reyes park from $19.1-million to $57.5-million. Signed by President Nixon on April 3, it prohibited the Park Service or other owners of land within the boundaries of the park from conveying land for residential or commercial development or subdivision. This freeze on new development eliminated Park Service plans, disclosed during hearings, to sell 9,200 acres, or one-sixth of the park area, to a private developer for residential use as a restricted subdivision with related commercial facilities, including shopping centers.

CAPE COD SEASHORE. Congress April 30, cleared a bill (HR 1187—PL 91-252) authorizing an additional $17.5-million, covering 7,519 acres, to complete acquisition of land for the Cape Cod National Seashore established in 1961.

EVERGLADES. Congress Sept. 22 cleared a bill (S 2565—PL 91-428) authorizing an additional $20-million to purchase the remaining 58,398 acres of privately held land within the boundaries of the 1.4-million-acre Ever-

glades National Park in Florida. Previous appropriations for land in the park totaled about $2.7-million. The measure was signed into law Sept 26.

VOYAGEURS NATIONAL PARK. Congress Dec. 29 cleared a bill (HR 10482—PL 91-661) creating a major new national park, the Voyageurs National Park in Minnesota. The new unit consisted of about 139,000 acres of land and about 80,000 acres of lake area. The bill authorized $26,014,000 for land acquisition and $19,179,000 for development.

APOSTLE ISLANDS LAKESHORE. Congress Sept. 16 cleared a bill (S 621—PL 91-424) creating the Apostle Islands National Lakeshore on Lake Superior in northern Wisconsin.

The park was first proposed in 1930 and was revived as a legislative proposal in 1963. The lakeshore, under the management of the Interior Department's National Park Service, included 20 of the 22 Apostle Islands, totaling 39,497 acres, plus 2,469 acres on the Bayfield, Wis., peninsula section of the mainland. The bill provided that no Indian trust lands could be acquired for the park, except for two parcels on the lakefront which could be purchased only if a majority of the owners wanted to sell them. State-owned lands would be donated to the national park. The bill authorized $4.25-million for land acquisition and $5-million for development.

SLEEPING DUNES LAKESHORE. Congress Oct. 7 cleared a bill (HR 18776—PL 91-479) establishing the Sleeping Bear Dunes National Lakeshore on Lake Michigan near Traverse City, Mich.

The 60,748-acre lakeshore included a mainland unit of about 41,000 acres, with 31.5 miles of shoreline along Lake Michigan, and two offshore islands, the largest about 14,500 acres and the other about 5,300 acres. The bill authorized $19.8 million for land acquisition and $18,769,000 for development.

GULF ISLANDS NATIONAL SEASHORE. Congress Dec. 29 cleared a bill (HR 10874—PL 91-660) establishing the Gulf Islands National Seashore in Mississippi. The bill authorized $3,120,000 for land acquisition and $14,799,000 for development of about 7,800 acres of shoreline and several off-shore islands totaling more than 10,000 acres.

C & O CANAL NATIONAL PARK. Congress Dec. 22 cleared a bill (HR 19342—PL 91-664) establishing the Chesapeake and Ohio Canal National Historical Park in Maryland, West Virginia and Washington, D.C.

The bill authorized $20.4-million for land acquisition and $17-million for development of the park.

The federal government already owned the 184.5-mile canal and its towpath, which stretches between Georgetown in Washington, D.C., and Cumberland, Md. The existing park totaled about 5,250 acres.

The funds authorized by the bill would permit the purchase of about 12,000 more acres of privately owned land between the canal and the Potomac River.

The canal was initially planned by George Washington, who helped gain a charter for the original canal company in 1784. It was under construction for more than 50

years. It was used heavily during the second third of the 19th century and was closed to commercial traffic in 1924.

MINOR PARK BILLS. Congress approved a bill (HR 13934—PL 91-548) authorizing $5.9 million to complete land purchases for the Minuteman National Historic Park in Massachusetts. The park commemorates the first battle of the American Revolutionary War. Congress also completed action on a bill (HR 1160—PL 91-554) authorizing $2,285,000 for development of Wilson's Creek Battlefield National Park near Springfield, Mo. The park commemorates a Civil War battle.

HISTORIC SITES. Congress cleared and the President May 9 signed a bill (HR 14896—PL 91-243) to extend through fiscal 1973 the national historic preservation program (PL 89-665) passed in 1966 to coordinate and provide financial aid for identification and preservation of sites significant in national, regional, state or local history.

● Extended the national historic preservation program for three years; authorized appropriations of $7 million for fiscal 1971, $10 million for 1972 and $15 million for 1973.

● Added the secretaries of agriculture and transportation and the director of the Smithsonian Institution to the Advisory Council on Historic Preservation which reported annually to Congress and the President.

● Authorized appropriations of $100,000 a year for three fiscal years for limited U.S. participation in the International Centre for the Study of the Preservation and Restoration of Cultural Property, an independent organization established by UNESCO in 1958 to disseminate technical information on the preservation of historically important objects.

Congress Oct. 7 cleared three bills establishing national historic sites at Andersonville, Georgia; Fort Point, San Francisco, California; and Ford's Theatre, Washington, D.C.

The Andersonville National Historic Site (HR 140—PL 91-465) would commemorate the prison camp maintained by the Confederacy during the Civil War where 50,000 Union soldiers were imprisoned and about 11,000 died. Part of the land was already federally owned; the bill authorized $362,000 for acquisition of an additional 294 acres and $1,605,000 for development of the site.

The Fort Point National Historic Site (HR 18410—PL 91-457) would preserve a mid-19th century military fort which was in use intermittently through World War II. The land was already federally owned; the bill authorized $5.25 million for development of the site.

The Ford's Theatre National Historic Site legislation (HR 12860—PL 91-288) authorized $94,000 for purchase and $176,000 for development of property next to the theatre, to be used for administrative offices and theatre-related support facilities. HR 12860 also designated Ford's Theatre, the House Where Lincoln Died, the Lincoln Museum and the new property as the Ford's Theatre National Historic Site.

PARKS CENTENNIAL. Congress June 20 cleared a bill (H J Res 546—PL 91-332) designating 1972 as National Parks Centennial Year and establishing a 15-member commission to host an international conference on national parks. The date was selected to commemorate the establishment of Yellowstone National Park, the first national park, on March 1, 1872.

Land and Water Conservation Funds

(millions of dollars)

Fiscal Year	State Grants	Federal Appropriations
1965	$10.4	$5.6
1966	82.4	38.3
1967	56.5	35.9
1968	61.5	48.8
1969	44.9	116.7
1970	61.8	65.8
1971	185.2	167.2
1972	255.0	101.7
1973	181.0	113.0
Total *1*	939.6	693.3

1 Totals do not add due to rounding.

SOURCE: Department of the Interior

The commission was to be composed of four senators, four representatives, the secretary of the interior and six presidential appointees. H J Res 546 authorized $250,000 for the commission, but funds could not be released until the commission collected at least $300,-000 from non-federal sources.

NATIONAL PARK TOURISM. President Nixon Dec. 14, 1970, signed into law a bill (HR 14714—PL 91-549) to increase financing for the promotion of tourism in the national parks.

Final congressional action came when the Senate passed the bill Dec. 1 by voice vote and without debate. The law increased the budget of the National Park Service travel program from $100,000 to $250,000 for fiscal year 1971 and $750,000 for fiscal year 1972.

KING RANGE CONSERVATION AREA. Congress Oct. 8 cleared a bill (HR 12870—PL 91-476) establishing the King Range National Conservation Area in California.

The conservation area would comprise about 44,500 acres of rugged, chiefly undeveloped land along the westernmost bulge of California's Pacific coast. About two-thirds of this area was already owned by the federal government under the management of the Interior Department's Bureau of Land Management. The bill allowed the interior secretary to purchase or exchange the remaining acreage for other federal holdings. HR 12870 authorized $1.5 million for acquisition and $3.5 million for inprovements.

NEW WILDERNESS AREAS. With the passage of one bill (S 3014—PL 91-504), Congress Oct. 7 designated 23 new wilderness areas in 12 states.

The new wilderness areas totaled 201,212 acres. They included national parks, national monuments, wildlife refuges, national forests and other lands already owned by the federal government. The bill required no new expenditures.

S 3014 designated the following as wilderness areas:

• Bering Sea Wilderness, Alaska; three islands totaling 41,113 acres in the Bering Sea about 200 miles from the Alaska mainland.

• Bogoslof Wilderness, Alaska; two islands totaling about 390 acres in the Bering Sea north of the Aleutian Islands.

• Tuxedni Wilderness, Alaska; two islands located in the Tuxedni National Wildlife Refuge, Cook Inlet, totaling 6,402 acres.

• St. Lazaria Wilderness, Alaska; three islands totaling about 62 acres in Sitka Sound.

• Hazy Island Wilderness, Alaska; five islands totaling about 42 acres 30 miles south of St. Lazaria Island.

• Forrester Island Wilderness, Alaska; five islands and numerous rocky outcrops totaling about 2,630 acres in southeastern Alaska.

• Three Arch Rocks Wilderness, Oregon; nine rocky areas totaling about 17 acres near Oceanside, Ore.

• Oregon Islands Wilderness, Oregon; one island totaling about 21 acres one-half mile off the coast from Brookings, Ore.

• Washington Islands Wilderness, Washington; composed of Copalis, Flattery Rocks and Quillayute National Wildlife Refuges, including numerous small islands, rocks and reefs extending for more than 100 miles and totaling 5,174 acres.

Historic Preservation

As the Revolutionary War bicentennial drew closer, the nation began to express a new interest in preserving buildings and other man-made landmarks of the American past. Congress responded in 1970 by passing a three-year extension of the National Historic Preservation Act of 1966, and authorizing increased amounts of money for preservation efforts. *(p. 828)*

The organization which served as the catalyst for the growing preservationist movement was the National Trust for Historic Preservation, chartered by Congress in 1949. In 1972, it had 31,000 members and a budget of $3.1-million, 40 per cent of it supplied by the National Park Service.

A major focus of the modern-day preservation effort was to save not just historic sites and buildings in scattered locations, but to protect the total environment of urban areas of historic interest, such as parts of Charleston, S.C., the Georgetown section of Washington, D.C., and the French Quarter of New Orleans. President Nixon noted in his 1971 message to Congress on the environment that "for most of us, the urban environment is the one in which we spend our daily lives." America's cities, he said, "reflect in the architecture of their buildings a uniqueness and character that is too rapidly disappearing."

Beginning in 1966, the federal government, through the National Historic Preservation Act, offered matching grants to the states and the trust for a variety of preservation projects. Other laws passed in that year allocated federal housing funds to cover a portion of the cost of identifying and restoring historic properties, and provided statutory protection for historic sites threatened by highway construction.

In the Omnibus Housing and Urban Development Act of 1970, Congress found that "there is a need for timely action to preserve and restore areas, sites, and structures of historic or architectural value in order that these remaining evidences of our history and heritage shall not be lost or destroyed through the expansion and development of the nation's areas...." The act merged three HUD programs—historic preservation, open-space lands and urban beautification—into a single open-space land program.

Congress in 1972 enacted legislation authorizing the free transfer of surplus historic buildings owned by the federal government to states or localities for revenue-producing use. Previously such surplus buildings could only be used for museums or other non-revenue-producing functions. Known as "the bill to save the old St. Louis Post Office," the measure gave legislative sanction to a plan to turn that 1873 structure into a commercial center.

• Salt Creek Wilderness, New Mexico; located within the Bitter Lake National Wildlife Refuge, comprised of two separate tracts along the Pecos River in Chaves County totaling about 8,500 acres.

• Island Bay Wilderness, Florida; comprised of about 20 acres of the upland portion of several small islands and keys, located off the west coast of Florida within Charlotte Harbor.

● Passage Key Wilderness, Florida; an area at the mouth of Tampa Bay totaling about 20 acres.

● Wichita Mountains Wilderness, Oklahoma; two tracts located in the Wichita Mountains National Wildlife Refuge, totaling 8,900 acres, in Comanche County.

● Seney Wilderness, Michigan; located in the northwest corner of the Seney National Wildlife Refuge, totaling about 25,150 acres.

● Huron Islands Wilderness, Michigan; seven islands in the Huron Islands National Wildlife Refuge totaling 147 acres, located three miles off the south shore of Lake Superior.

● Michigan Islands Wilderness, Michigan; three islands totaling about 12 acres.

● Wisconsin Islands Wilderness, Wisconsin; comprised of the Gravel Island and Green Bay National Wildlife Refuges in Door County, totaling 29 acres of limestone islands in Lake Michigan.

● Moosehorn Wilderness, Maine; comprised of parts of the Edmonds and Birch Islands units of the Moosehorn National Wildlife Refuge, totaling 2,782 acres.

● Pelican Island Wilderness, Florida; comprised of Pelican Island, a three-acre island in the Pelican Island National Wildlife Refuge, located in Indian River County, about 75 miles north of West Palm Beach.

● Monomoy Wilderness, Massachusetts; comprised of 2,340 acres in the Monomoy National Wildlife Refuge, located on Monomoy Island nine miles south of Cape Cod.

● Craters of the Moon Wilderness, Idaho; comprised of 43,243 acres in the Craters of the Moon National Monument in Idaho.

● Petrified Forest Wilderness, Arizona; comprised of two tracts in the Petrified Forest National Park, 43,020 acres in the Painted Desert and 7,240 in the Petrified Forest.

● Mount Baldy Wilderness, Arizona; comprised of 6,640 acres in the Mount Baldy Primitive Area and 335 contiguous acres in the Apache National Forest, located 225 miles northeast of Phoenix.

1971

CANYONLANDS NATIONAL PARK. The major congressional action expanding the national park system in 1971 came on a bill (S 26—PL 92-154) which cleared Oct. 4. The bill added 79,718 acres of mostly federal land to the existing Canyonlands National Park in Utah. The addition brought the total acreage in the park to 337,258 acres. The bill authorized $16,000 for land acquisition and $5,102,000 for development.

ARCHES NATIONAL PARK. Congress Oct. 29 cleared a bill (S 30—PL 92-155) converting the Arches National Monument in Utah into a national park, and reducing the size of the park by 9,719 acres. Arches National Monument was established by proclamation of President Johnson on Jan. 20, 1969.

CAPITOL REEF NATIONAL PARK. Congress Dec. 9 cleared (S 29—PL 92-207) converting the Capitol Reef National Monument in Utah into a national park, reducing the size by 12,570 acres. Like Arches Na-

tional Monument, Capitol Reef had been established by presidential proclamation on Jan. 20, 1969.

LINCOLN HOME HISTORIC SITE. Congress Aug. 18 cleared a bill (HR 9798—PL 92-127) establishing the Lincoln Home National Historic Site on a 12-acre tract in Springfield, Ill.

REDWOOD NATIONAL PARK. The House Nov. 15 rejected by a 148-203 roll-call vote a bill (HR 11080) which would have given special tax advantages to taxpayers whose property was taken by the government to form the Redwood National Park in California. The park was established in 1968. *(Congress and the Nation, Vol. II, p. 471)*

Background. Congress in 1968 vested ownership in the federal government of all large segments of private lands within the boundaries of Redwood National Park. This "legislative taking" provision was designed to forestall speculative or other increases in land acquisition costs, a problem which plagued a number of other parks created from private land during the 1960s, and to bring an immediate end to cutting timber on such lands. Most of the large tracts belonged to lumber companies which harvested redwood. The bill also authorized exchange of Forest Service lands for privately owned lands within the park boundary.

1971 Action. HR 11080 would have relieved taxpayers—mostly the lumber companies—whose lands were taken under the 1968 law of having to pay capital gains taxes.

The House Ways and Means Committee reported that it was not possible to obtain redwood tracts as large, or of the quality, as those taken under the 1968 law. The proposed legislation would allow the owners to invest in other businesses, even if not related to lumbering, in which they were engaged at the time the land was taken.

The major opposition to HR 11080 came from Rep. Jerome R. Waldie (D Calif.), who identified four companies qualified to receive tax benefits and listed the amounts offered them by the government for their property: Arcata Lumber Co.—$22.1-million in cash and $40-million in land; Georgia Pacific Lumber Co.—$27.6-million in cash; Simpson Lumber Co.—$783,000 in cash and $1.45-million in land; and Miller Lumber Co.—$3,78-million in cash and $8-million in land.

"No other taxpayer in the United States except for these...companies by this special legislation will receive this sort of tax treatment...." Waldie said. "However, they want more than that right which every other taxpayer has. They want a special privilege above and beyond that so that they incur no tax whatsoever.

"Could you ask for anything better than that, to get the proceeds from a condemnation without one dime of taxes, and not only that, but you (could) describe where you want to invest and the Congress of the United States will enact legislation to permit you to do that."

Joe D. Waggonner Jr. (D La.), a member of the Ways and Means Committee, told Waldie that if he were a part of the Arcata lumber company and, against his will, his property were taken, he might feel differently.

Waldie replied: "I would be just as selfish in that instance as Arcata is here, but if I were representing the people of the United States as I purport to do, I would oppose it."

1972

GOLDEN GATE RECREATION AREA. Congress Oct. 12 cleared a bill (HR 16444—PL 92-589) establishing one of the most costly national parks on record: the 34,000-acre Golden Gate National Urban Recreation Area. It would be administered by the National Park Service and included three units. The San Francisco County unit, of some 7,000 acres, would include a number of existing county and city parks, plus other state and federal lands. The Marin County unit of some 27,000 acres would stretch 22 miles north from the Golden Gate Bridge to the Point Reyes National Seashore, providing a continuous green belt. Most of the land in the Marin County unit was privately owned, causing high land acquisition costs. The third unit would be comprised of Alcatraz and Angel islands in San Francisco Bay, both publicly owned. Congress authorized $60,610,000 for land acquisition and estimated that an additional $58-million would be required to develop public facilities.

Related Development. Congress June 16 cleared a bill (HR 12143—PL 93-330) establishing a 21,662-acre San Francisco Bay National Wildlife Refuge in California. The purpose was to preserve and enhance the wildlife habitat of south San Francisco Bay, protect the migratory waterfowl which frequented the marshes, mudflats, open waters and salt ponds of the area, protect a colony of 400 harbor seals and provide for recreational and educational use of the area. Land acquisition costs were limited to $9-million, and costs for recreation development and conservation and management of wildlife to $11.3 million.

GATEWAY NATIONAL RECREATION AREA. Congress Oct. 13 cleared an administration urban park proposal, the 26,250-acre Gateway National Recreation Area in New York and New Jersey (S 1852—PL 92-592). The bill authorized the secretary of the interior to combine lands in five separate units—Breezy Point, Jamaica Bay, Staten Island, Sandy Hook and Hoffman and Swinburne Islands—to create one park under National Park Service administration. Creation of the park would involve transfer of federal and state lands, including several existing parks, and acquisition of some private holdings. Acquisition costs were limited to $12,125,000; development costs to $92,813,000. The House on Sept. 26 voted to name the park in memory of Rep. William Fitts Ryan (D N.Y., 1961-1972). But conferees later recommended retaining the Gateway name and proposed instead that a visitor center at the new park be named for Ryan.

DELAWARE RECREATION AREA LAND COSTS. Congress Oct. 14 cleared a bill (HR 13396—PL 92-575) authorizing an increase in land acquisition funds for the Delaware Water Gap National Recreation Area in New Jersey and Pennsylvania. The bill raised the ceiling to $65-million from $37.4-million. The Delaware Water Gap National Recreation Area was authorized in 1965. *(Congress and the Nation Vol. II, p. 467)*

SAWTOOTH RECREATION AREA. Culminating a decade of effort by Idaho conservationists, Congress Aug. 14 cleared a bill (HR 6957—PL 92-400) creating a 754,000-acre park tract—roughly the size of Rhode Island—in the south central area of the state, 40 miles from Sun Valley. The bill created the 537,000-acre Sawtooth National Recreation Area and the 216,400-acre Sawtooth Wilderness, both under Forest Service administration.

Background. Creation of a Sawtooth national park was first proposed in 1911, but interest lagged until the 1960s, when renewed mining activity in the area aroused concern by conservationists. In 1969, the Senate passed a bill (S 853) to create a Sawtooth National Recreation Area under the National Park Service, but the House took no action during the 91st Congress. The Senate bill would have protected the area from commercial subdivision and mining. In 1970, the Greater Sawtooth Preservation Council, an Idaho citizens' group, proposed a combined national park and national recreation area to protect the Sawtooth country. The proposal was widely supported within the state and by the Sierra Club, Wilderness Society, Friends of the Earth and Federation of Western Outdoor Clubs. It was opposed by mining, logging and cattle-grazing interests, whose existing rights to use the federal lands would be curtailed. A principal opponent was the American Smelting and Refining Co., which held claims on molybdenum deposits in the area and was planning an open-pit mine.

1972 Action. The chief controversy over the 1972 proposal to create a Sawtooth National Recreation Area and a Sawtooth Wilderness under the secretary of agriculture involved mining rights. The House proposed a five-year moratorium on new mining in the recreation area only. Under the 1964 Wilderness Act (PL 88-577), mining in the wilderness area would have been allowed until 1983. The Senate, however, voted to withdraw both areas from new mining operations permanently, and authorized the secretary of agriculture to issue regulations governing the use of motorized and mechanical equipment in order to protect the parklands and wilderness. During House debate, Rep. Orval Hansen (R Idaho), whose district included the Sawtooth area, said existing federal authority to protect water quality, plus the regulations governing the environment of the new parklands, "will have a direct impact on the economics of mining in the area and will likely have the effect of significantly reducing or eliminating those activities which are causing the despoliation of the area."

OREGON DUNES. Congress March 14 established another major park under Forest Service administration when it cleared a bill (S 1977—PL 92-260) authorizing the Oregon Dunes National Recreation Area. The area included more than 32,000 acres, of which almost 19,000 were part of the existing Siuslaw National Forest. Land acquisition funds were set at $2.5-million and development costs at $12.7-million. Massive, shifting sand dunes along approximately 40 miles of the Oregon coast were a major feature of the area.

CUMBERLAND NATIONAL SEASHORE. Congress Oct. 12 cleared a bill (S 2411—PL 92-536) setting aside 39,494 acres of islands and water off the Georgia coast as the Cumberland National Seashore.

BUFFALO NATIONAL RIVER. Congress Feb. 9 cleared, and the President March 1, signed, a bill (S 7—PL 92-237) to establish the Buffalo National River in the state of Arkansas. The bill created a corridor of 132 miles along the river, starting in the Ozark National Forest, and incorporated a total of 95,730 acres in the national river.

ST. CROIX RIVER. Congress Oct. 13 cleared a bill (S 1928—PL 92-560) designating a segment of the lower

St. Croix River in Minnesota and Wisconsin as part of the national wild and scenic rivers system.

A 1968 act included the Upper St. Croix River and its tributary, the Namekagon, in the wild and scenic rivers system, and provided that the lower segment of the river be studied for possible inclusion in the system.

Public hearings held in 1972 revealed that because of the many separate jurisdictions controlling land use along the river, a single governmental entity was needed to provide effective control of future development.

GLEN CANYON RECREATION AREA. Congress Oct. 14 cleared a bill (S 27—PL 92-593) establishing the Glen Canyon National Recreation Area in Arizona and Utah.

The bill gave permanent, statutory protection to 1,285,310 acres of land and water which had been administered under an agreement between the National Park Service and the Bureau of Reclamation.

The principal use of the area would be recreational, but mineral exploration and development and grazing and hunting would be permitted, subject to regulations of the secretary of the interior to protect the scenic, scientific and historic values of the area.

"GOLDEN EAGLE" PARKS PASSPORT. Congress June 29 cleared a bill (S 1893—PL 92-347) to extend indefinitely the golden eagle passport program for admission into areas of the national park system.

The bill amended the Land and Water Conservation Fund Act (PL 88-578) by restoring the $10 annual camping permit for entrance into national parks, monuments, historic sites and battlefields. The golden eagle program had expired on Dec. 31, 1971. The bill:

• Provided that $10 golden eagle passports would admit the holder and those accompanying him in a single, private, non-commercial vehicle into any national park area.

• Provided that reasonable admission fees could be charged at designated national parks and recreation areas for non-permit holders.

• Authorized the sale of golden eagle passports through the offices of the secretaries of agriculture and interior and at U.S. post offices.

• Provided for special golden age passports to be issued free of charge to citizens over 62 years of age.

• Authorized special additional charges for use of recreation sites such as large campsites and boat launching ramps (half price for golden age passport holders).

• Provided that funds from permit sales would be used in conjunction with land and water conservation funds for outdoor recreation purposes.

• Set penalties of up to $100 for violations of permit regulations, or up to $250 and six months in prison for false manufacture of golden eagle passports.

NATIONAL PARK SYSTEM. Congress March 29 cleared an omnibus bill (S 2601—PL 92-272) providing for increases in appropriations ceilings and for boundary changes in certain existing units of the national park system.

The purpose of S 2601 was to include such changes in a single bill rather than requiring separate legislation for each change.

Final action came when the House March 29 by voice vote agreed to a Senate amendment to the House-passed version of the bill.

Everglades Jetport Blocked

A major concern of conservation groups during 1969-72 was a series of threats to the water supply for the Everglades Swamp in South Florida. The biggest threat was a proposed major international jetport, which would have cost $250-million to build. It was to be located six miles north of the Everglades on 39 square miles of land and fill in the middle of the Big Cypress Swamp, which supplied 38 per cent of the water flowing into the Everglades National Park.

The issue was settled when the White House on Jan. 15, 1970, announced an agreement between federal, state and local authorities prohibiting construction of the jetport.

Under the agreement local authorities could use a single runway, already constructed at a cost of $14-million, but only under strict federal supervision. The agreement further specified that the training runway would be closed as soon as an acceptable alternative site was found.

Among environmental safeguards required in the use of the training strip were prohibition of the use of detergents and pesticides, a ban on aircraft fueling, prohibition of the disposal of solid wastes at the site and maintenance of the park's water supply.

On Sept. 17, 1969, the Interior Department had released a report concluding that the jetport would "inexorably destroy the South Florida ecosystem and thus the Everglades National Park." The report also declared the existing training strip "intolerable" because it would lead to "urbanization and drainage, which would destroy the ecosystem."

In 1969 and 1970, Congress passed bills authorizing approximately $20.8-million for purchase of the remaining private land tracts in the Everglades National Park.

In his 1972 message on the environment, President Nixon asked Congress for authority to acquire and set aside 547,000 acres of the Big Cypress Swamp in order to protect the water source of the Everglades. Land acquisition for the Big Cypress National Freshwater Reserve, which was not acted on by the 92nd Congress, was estimated to cost $156-million, making the park by far the most expensive ever proposed.

S 2601 consisted of three titles:

• Title I—Increased statutory ceilings in land acquisition appropriations at eight areas: Assateague Island National Seashore, Maryland; Big Hole National Battlefield, Montana; Bighorn Canyon National Recreation Area, Wyoming and Montana; Effigy Mounds National Monument, Iowa; Fort Donelson National Military Park, Tennessee; Lincoln Boyhood National Memorial, Indiana; Ozark National Scenic Riverways, Missouri; Shiloh National Military Park, Tennessee.

• Title II—Increased appropriations ceilings for development at four areas: Herbert Hoover National Historic Site, Iowa; Booker T. Washington National Monument, Virginia; Johnstown Flood National Memorial, Pennsylvania; Wolf Trap Farm Park, Virginia.

• Title III—Authorized the secretary of the interior to revise the boundaries of 11 areas: Adams National Historic Site, Massachusetts; Cowpens National Battleground Site, South Carolina; Fort Caroline National Memorial, Florida; George Washington Birthplace National Monument, Virginia; Glacier National Park, Montana; Isle Royale National Park, Michigan; Johnstown Flood National Memorial, Pennsylvania; Lassen Volcanic National Park, California; Muir Woods National Monument, California; Ozark National Scenic Riverways, Missouri; Petersburg National Battlefield, Virginia.

RECREATION LANDS. Congress Oct. 14 cleared a bill (HR 10384—PL 92-534) ending certain restrictions on land acquisition for recreational development at fish and wildlife areas.

The bill applied to lands adjacent to areas within the national wildlife refuge system, national fish hatcheries and other conservation areas administered by the Interior Department for fish and wildlife purposes.

MINOR PARK BILLS. Congress in 1972 passed six bills establishing, extending or otherwise affecting the park system: (1) a bill (HR 8756—PL 92-525) to preserve the remains of the ancient Hohokam Indian Community in the Gila River Indian Reservation, Arizona, by creating the 1,555-acre Hohokam Pima National Monument; (2) a bill (S 141—PL 92-537) to protect roughly 8,200 acres of Eocene era fossil fishbeds in Wyoming as the Fossil Butte National Monument; (3) a bill (S 1497—PL 92-501) to add 53 acres to the Sitka National Monument, Alaska, and to change its name to Sitka National Historic Park; (4) a bill (HR 15597—PL 92-533) to allow an additional $1.5-million for acquisition of scenic easements within the Piscataway National Park, Maryland; (5) a bill (S 3153—PL 92-275) to expand the Gulf Islands National Seashore, established in 1970, to include the 266-acre Magnolia State Park in Mississippi; and (6) a bill (S 2441—PL 92-948) authorizing the secretary of the interior to conduct a study to determine the feasibility of preserving the Great Dismal Swamp and the Great Dismal Swamp Canal in Virginia and North Carolina.

HISTORIC SITES. Congress in 1972 enacted a number of bills authorizing historic sites and memorials. They were: S 3129—PL 92-475, establishing the Longfellow National Historic Site on 2 acres in Cambridge, Mass. HR 13067—PL 92-527, giving statutory approval to the administration of a Florida estate, Mar-A-Lago, as a National Historic Site, and to authorize use of the property as a retreat for visiting foreign dignitaries or executive branch officials; S 1973—PL 92-524, authorizing the acquisition of a Philadelphia, Pa., boarding house once occupied by Polish patriot and American Revolution Gen. Thaddeus Kosciusko as a national memorial; HR 1462—PL 92-388, authorizing the preservation of three Hawaiian temples and other property as the Puukohola National Historic Site; S J Res 221—PL 92-551, establishing the Benjamin Franklin National Memorial in Philadelphia, Pa.; S 2166—PL 92-406, establishing the 1,564-acre Grant-Kohrs Ranch National Historic Site in Montana; S 3159—PL 92-404, establishing the John D. Rockefeller Memorial Parkway of 23,700 acres in Wyoming; and HR 10595—PL 92-333, changing the name of the Custis-Lee Mansion in Arlington National Cemetary, Virginia, to Arlington House, The Robert E. Lee Memorial.

WILDERNESS AREAS. Congress enacted nine bills expanding the national wilderness system by 912,-637 acres. They were the 19,500-acre Pine Mountain Wilderness, Arizona (PL 92-23); the 48,500-acre Sycamore Canyon Wilderness, Arizona (PL 92-241); the 375-acre Cedar Keys National Wildlife Refuge Wilderness, Florida, (PL 92-364); the 240,000-acre Scapegoat Wilderness, Montana (PL 92-395); the 216,400-acre Sawtooth Wilderness (PL 92-400); addition of the 208,000-acre Stratified Primitive Area to the Washakie Wilderness, Wyoming (PL 92-476); 28,460-acre wilderness in the Lava Beds National Monument (PL 92-493); a 78,982-acre wilderness in the Lassen Volcanic National Park, California (PL 92-510); and addition of the 72,420-acre Minam River Canyon in Oregon to the Eagle Gap Wilderness (PL 92-521).

INCOMPLETE ACTION. At the end of the 92nd Congress, four major parks and recreation bills had been passed by at least one chamber, but nevertheless failed to become law. They were:

Montana Wilderness Tracts. In both the 91st and 92nd Congresses, the Senate passed bills to designate 240,500 acres of the Lincoln Back Country in three national forests in Montana as part of the Bob Marshall wilderness. The House took no action. The 1971-72 Senate bill was S 484.

Connecticut Historic Waterway. The Senate Dec. 9, 1971, passed a bill (S 36) to establish a Connecticut Historic Riverway of about 23,500 acres along the Connecticut River between East Haddam and Old Saybrook. The House took no action on the proposal, which did not have administration backing.

National Forest Wild Areas. In 1972, the Agriculture Department declared that none of its forest lands east of the Mississippi could qualify as wilderness areas under the 1964 Wilderness Act. It endorsed a Senate bill to create a new category of "wild areas" in national forests during 1972. The bill (S 3973) passed the Senate Sept. 26, 1972, but was not acted on in the House. During Senate hearings, the proposed legislation was opposed by both conservation groups and lumber interests. If enacted, S 3973 would have placed legislative responsibility for establishing "wild areas" in the Senate and House agriculture committees. Responsibility for wilderness proposals rested with the Senate and House interior committees.

Big South Fork Veto. President Nixon vetoed a bill (S 4018) authorizing the Department of the Army, Corps of Engineers to establish and operate the 125,000-acre Big South Fork National River and Recreational Area in the Cumberland region of Kentucky and Tennessee. The authorized cost of $32.8-million would have been borne by the Land and Water Conservation Fund. The Recreational Area was the major project in S 4018, the biennial rivers, harbors and flood control bill. Normally such legislation was not controversial because it contained projects carefully bargained between the administration and interested members. But President Nixon pocket vetoed the bill Oct. 27, arguing that it would "ultimately cost taxpayers hundreds of millions of dollars" and contained many projects not approved by the administration.

Water, Power
and
Flood Control

Numerous federal water projects, some with power-generating features, were authorized and funded during the years 1969-72, but Congress took little action of major national significance dealing with federal water and power projects.

Similarly, although Congress became increasingly aware of the growing national energy crisis, it did little during the four-year period to deal with the problem. *(Details in energy resources chapter, p. 841)*

Congress did, however, place new emphasis on the potential environmental effects of federal public works projects, particularly during consideration of the annual public works appropriations bills.

In 1971, Congress forced President Nixon to make a direct decision on the merits of a controversial underground nuclear test to be conducted beneath an Alaskan wildlife refuge by barring funds for the blast unless it was given express presidential approval.

In 1970 and 1972, environmentalist-minded members unsuccessfully sought to cut funds for a cross-Florida barge canal and an advanced nuclear power plant using highly toxic plutonium.

Aside from major hydroelectric power projects funded in the appropriations measures, Congress paid little attention to power projects, although it did in 1970 give final approval to legislation allowing private utility companies to share in the development of the Tocks Island power project.

The years 1969-72 also saw the emergence of an executive-legislative squabble over which branch would establish water project standards and determine those to be approved and funded. Congress in 1970 enacted an omnibus flood control bill which authorized 11 projects not approved by the President's Office of Management and Budget. Two years later, Congress cleared similar legislation authorizing projects never approved or recommended by the executive branch. Nixon vetoed the bill, citing his disapproval of congressional initiatives in that area as well as budget restrictions in explaining his refusal to approve the measure.

The controversy over federal spending also figured in consideration of the annual public works appropriations bills. In 1971 the House Appropriations Committee criticized the administration for impounding funds voted by Congress in 1970. It said such action was not "good business" because it increased long-term costs and decreased benefits. Another view was expressed by Sen. William Proxmire (D Wis.) in 1972. Congress must cut spending or raise taxes, he said, adding: "The public works pork barrel is a classic example of where we should save taxpayers' money."

A number of public works measures considered by Congress during the years 1969-72 were aimed primarily at stimulating the economy and reducing unemployment. Those measures are discussed elsewhere in this volume. *(Chapters on miscellaneous economic legislation, labor, p. 177, 703)*

Chronology Of Legislation 1969

Appropriations

The annual public works-Atomic Energy Commission (AEC) appropriations bill (HR 14159—PL 91-144) appropriated a total of $4,756,007,500 for public works projects, water pollution control, power development, the AEC and related independent agencies in fiscal 1970.

The bill included $1,141,683,000 for river, harbor and flood control projects of the Army Corps of Engineers and $267,701,500 for the irrigation and power activities of the Interior Department's Bureau of Reclamation. It carried $118-million for the Bonneville Power Administration, a power marketing agency for the Interior Department, and $50.6-million for the Tennessee Valley Authority. Total AEC appropriations of $2,217,769,000 included $38-million for a controversial 200-billion electron volt (BEV) nuclear accelerator at Weston, Ill.

For the third year, the Dickey-Lincoln School hydroelectric project in Maine received no funds. The project, which would bring public power to the New England area, had received $1.9-million in planning funds since it was authorized by Congress in 1965. *(Congress and the Nation Vol. II, p. 511)* The Senate voted $807,000 for the project, but House conferees insisted that the funds be removed from the bill.

References

Discussion of legislation on water, power and flood control for the years 1945-64 may be found in *Congress and the Nation, Vol. I,* p. 769-969; for the years 1965-1968, *Congress and the Nation, Vol. II,* p. 495-528.

The final bill included $800-million for construction of waste treatment plants under the Federal Water Pollution Control Administration. Passage ended nearly eight months of controversy over the gap between the $1-billion authorized for 1970 under the Clean Waters Restoration Act of 1966 (PL 89-753) and the Nixon administration's budget request of $214-million. The Senate had recommended the entire $1-billion, the House $600-million.

Tocks Island, Basin Projects

Both the House and the Senate in 1969 approved measures to allow private utility companies to share in the development of a pumped-storage hydroelectric power project at Tocks Island Dam and Reservoir in the Delaware River Basin. Congress completed action on the legislation in 1970.

The Tocks Island project, located in a section of the Delaware River which divides Pennsylvania from New Jersey and lower New York state, would be a multipurpose project for recreation, water supply, flood control and power benefits with an estimated cost of $214-million.

Conservationists opposed the measures, contending that expansion of the hydroelectric power facilities at Tocks Island would damage an important wilderness area. Advocates of the measures pointed to the densely populated area's need for more electrical power. (The Tocks Island Dam is located along the upper Delaware River 65 miles from New York City and 80 miles from Philadelphia.)

The Senate July 30 approved S 2678 to amend the Flood Control Act of 1962 (PL 87-874)—which authorized construction of the Tocks Island Dam—to permit private companies to share in power development there. S 2678 also provided that payments of at least $1-million annually be made to the government by the companies.

The House Dec. 15 approved a bill (HR 15166) which included language identical to S 2678. HR 15166 also authorized additional appropriations of $830-million for continued work on 13 river basin flood control projects.

The Senate took no action on HR 15166 in 1969, and the House did not act on S 2678.

Background. Federal planning for the development of the Delaware River Basin began in 1961, when Congress approved an interstate-federal compact (PL 87-328) establishing the Delaware River Basin Commission to administer the basin's water resources.

The compact provided that before the commission could initiate any project, except for one financed wholly by state funds, it must receive congressional approval. The four state legislatures approved the compact before congressional passage. *(Congress and the Nation Vol. I, p. 1090)*

The commission's development plans provided for construction of a dam five miles north of the Delaware Water Gap. This would create a new lake (Tocks Island Reservoir) suitable for recreational purposes. The lake would be 37 miles long and one-half to 1½ miles wide.

Under the 1962 Flood Control Act (PL 87-874), Congress authorized $192.4-million for construction of the dam and reservoir.

The 1962 Flood Control Act provided for the use of the dam and reservoir by a federal power plant as part of a large pumped-storage facility. Pumped storage is a method of guaranteeing sufficient hydroelectric power during peak demands.

In August 1965, Congress passed a bill (PL 89-158) establishing the Delaware Water Gap National Recreation Area and authorized $55,612,000 for acquisition and development of 47,675 acres of land by the Corps of Engineers and the National Park Service. *(Congress and the Nation Vol. II, p. 467)*

Power Companies' Proposal. Controversy over the Tocks Island development project centered on the dispute between conservation groups and three private utility companies.

The conservationists contended the proposed development of pumped storage power would seriously damage Sunfish Pond and adjoining areas as a natural beauty spot ideal for outdoor recreation.

The power companies, supported by the governors of the four states represented on the Delaware River Basin Commission and by many other government officials, said safeguards would prevent substantial deterioration of Sunfish Pond. Furthermore, they contended the project would provide urgently needed electrical power to all of New Jersey, the most urban state in the nation and frequent victim of power shortages.

A proposal by three New Jersey power companies would make the Tocks Island Reservoir and Dam part of a much larger pumped storage project than the facility authorized in the 1962 legislation. The yield of the expanded project would reach 1.3 million kilowatts daily, about 30 times the original forecast.

1970

Appropriations

The fiscal 1971 public works-Atomic Energy Commission appropriations bill (HR 18127—PL 91-439) appropriated a total of $5,244,265,000, including $5,748,000 for the Bureau of Reclamation to liquidate previously approved contract authority. Contract authorization allows government agencies to enter into contracts which later must be paid for through appropriations.

The bill provided $1,295,933,000 in new budget authority for the Army Corps of Engineers, $310,185,000 for the Bureau of Reclamation, $115.2-million for the Bonneville Power Administration, $56,180,000 for the Tennessee Valley Authority and $2,282,760,000 for the AEC. Appropriations for construction grants for waste treatment projects totaled $1-billion.

As in 1969, the House refused to accept funds voted by the Senate for the Dickey-Lincoln School hydroelectric project in Maine. The Senate rejected an amendment to suspend funding of the controversial Cross-Florida Barge Canal, being built by the Corps of Engineers, pending completion of ecological and economic reviews by federal agencies. The project was blocked early in 1971 by executive order.

Tocks Island, Basin Projects

Congress in 1970 completed action on a bill (HR 15166—PL 91-282) authorizing $835-million in additional appropriations for continued work on 13 river basin flood control projects for calendar years 1970-71, and $9-million to complete a comprehensive study of the Chesapeake Bay basin. The bill was signed into law June 19.

HR 15166 also included a section that amended the Flood Control Act of 1962 (PL 87-874)—which authorized the construction of the Tocks Island Dam and Reservoir in the Delaware River Basin—to permit private power companies to share in the power development project there. The modification provided that payments of $1-million annually be made to the government by the companies.

Final action came when the House June 4 by voice vote accepted amendments added by the Senate. The Senate had passed an amended version of the bill by voice vote on May 28. The House had originally passed its version of HR 15166 on Dec. 15, 1969. Also in 1969, the Senate had approved a bill (S 2678) to allow private utility companies to share in the development of the Tocks Island power project.

The Chesapeake Bay basin study was authorized in 1965 and was not to exceed $6-million. The study was to include navigation, flood control, fisheries, control of noxious weeds, water pollution, water quality control, beach erosion and recreation. In 1969, it was found that completion of the study would cost $15-million as compared with the original $6-million.

The chief change made by the Senate during its consideration of HR 15166 in 1970 was the addition of $5-million over the House authorization level for construction of works to meet the water requirements of the Everglades National Park in Florida. The Everglades National Park, which includes about 2,300 square miles of land and water, is located at the southern end of a southwestern Florida flood control project under construction by the Army Corps of Engineers since 1950. The park's plant and animal life is dependent on a steady flow of water from the north. Critics charged that a good part of that water had been diverted by the corps for the benefit of farmers and developers.

This was the second major conservation action taken by Congress in a six-month period affecting the Everglades Park. In December 1969 Congress added a provision to the fiscal 1970 Department of Transportation appropriations bill specifying that no funds could be used to build a jetport near the park until the Interior and Transportation Departments could show there would be no adverse effects on the environment. The White House announced Jan. 15, 1970, a compromise which ended further construction of the jetport.

Provisions. As signed into law June 19, HR 15166 contained the following authorizations for basin projects:

Basin	Authorization through 1971
Alabama-Coosa River	$45,000,000
Arkansas River	89,000,000
Brazos River	5,000,000
Central and Southern Florida	25,000,000
Columbia River	263,000,000
Lower Mississippi River	167,000,000
Missouri River	109,000,000
Ohio River	69,000,000
Quachita River	18,000,000
San Joaquin River	18,000,000
South Platte River	21,000,000

Upper Mississippi River	2,000,000
White River	4,000,000
Total, river basins	**$835,000,000**
Chesapeake Bay Basin Study	9,000,000
Grand Total	**$844,000,000**

Rivers and Harbors

Congress completed action on an omnibus bill (HR 19877—PL 91-611), signed by the President Dec. 31, authorizing $693,018,000. The authorizations included $596,215,000 for 31 public works projects—$169,341,000 for 11 projects to aid navigation, $426,634,000 for 19 flood control projects and $240,000 for a Florida beach erosion project.

HR 19877, the Rivers and Harbors and Flood Control Acts of 1970, was passed by the House Dec. 7 and the Senate Dec. 9. The conference report on the measure was cleared by Congress Dec. 19.

Aside from rivers and harbors and flood control projects, the conference agreement directed the Army's Corps of Engineers to survey the Great Lakes and St. Lawrence Seaway to determine the feasibility of extending the navigation season by de-icing waterways and locks; to clean up the polluted Cuyahoga River (Cleveland) and to promulgate guidelines to assure that final decisions on public works projects take into account environmental as well as economic and social effects. The bill also established a new position of assistant secretary of the army for civil works to oversee rivers and harbors and flood control projects.

Eleven of the 31 projects approved by conferees were authorized despite lack of approval by the President's Office of Management and Budget (OMB). The conference report specified, however, that work could not begin on the projects until such approval had been given.

Authorizations contained in HR 19877 for omnibus rivers and harbors and flood control were the smallest in 20 years, said Rep. John A. Blatnik (D Minn.), chairman of the House Rivers and Harbors Subcommittee on Public Works. The previous omnibus bill, passed in 1968 (PL 90-483), had authorized $1.8-billion in public works projects. *(Congress and the Nation Vol. II, p. 519)*

Provisions. As cleared by Congress, HR 19877 contained the following navigation and flood control authorizations (asterisks denote projects not approved by the OMB):

Title I—Rivers and Harbors (Navigation)

Pleasant Bay, Mass.	$ 10,221,000
Baltimore Harbor	40,000,000*
Atlantic Intracoastal Bridges	11,220,000*
Manteo Bay, N.C.	10,769,000
Pamlico River, N.C.	2,642,000*
Tampa Harbor, Fla.	40,000,000
Freeport Harbor, Texas	13,710,000*
Coos Bay, Ore.	9,100,000
Nawiliwili Harbor, Hawaii	1,952,000*
New York Harbor	16,227,000
Ouachita and Black Rivers, Ark. and La.	13,500,000*
Total	$169,341,000

Title II—Flood Control

Deep Fork River, Okla.	24,900,000
Lower Mississippi River, La.	15,333,000
Blue River, Kansas City, Mo.	40,000,000
Oahe Dam, N.D.	732,000
Wild Rice River, Minn.	8,359,000
Cheyenne River, N.D.	20,000,000
Burlington Dam, N.D.	29,240,000
Atascadero Creek, Calif.	13,830,000
Sabine River, Texas and La.	40,000,000
Mississippi River, Davenport, Iowa	12,263,000*
Mill Creek, Ohio	36,642,000
Red Run Drain, Mich.	40,000,000
Sandridge Dam, N.Y.	19,070,000*
Portugues Dam, Puerto Rico	11,110,000
Carrillos Dam, Puerto Rico	16,351,000
Ponce, Puerto Rico	14,295,000
Cottonwood Creek, Calif.	40,000,000*
Merced County Streams, Calif.	37,260,000*
Kaneohe-Kailua Area, Hawaii	7,249,000*
Total	$426,634,000

Walla Walla Project

Congress June 23 cleared a bill (S 743) authorizing the secretary of the interior to construct and maintain the Touchet division of the Walla Walla project serving Oregon and Washington. The purpose of the division was to develop the local water supply and to provide flood control, fish and wildlife enhancement and recreation.

As signed into law (PL 91-307) July 7 by the President, S 743 authorized appropriations to the Bureau of Reclamation of $22,774,000 for the construction and maintenance of the division, less the costs to be allocated to enhancement of anadromous fish—those which migrate from the sea up rivers to spawn.

1971

Appropriations

The fiscal 1972 public works—Atomic Energy Commission appropriations bill (HR 10090—PL 92-134) appropriated a total of $4,706,625,000, including $31.5-million for the Bureau of Reclamation to liquidate contract authority approved in previous bills.

New budget authority (NBA) provided by the bill included $1,482,640,000 for the Army Corps of Engineers, $352,929,000 for the Bureau of Reclamation, $118,825,000 for the Bonneville Power Administration, $298,113,000 for the Appalachian Regional Commission, $67,150,000 for the Tennessee Valley Authority and $2,294,380,000 for AEC.

Controversy over the bill centered on efforts to block a planned Amchitka Island, Alaska, underground nuclear test (Project Cannikin) by the AEC. The House accepted an amendment added in the Senate to ban the test "unless the President gives his direct approval for such test." Nixon subsequently authorized the blast, and on Oct. 2 a nuclear device was exploded beneath the surface of the island, which was part of a wildlife refuge.

Appropriations for the Corps of Engineers included $12.3-million to initiate construction on 22 projects at an estimated total cost of $252.3-million, along with 24

projects to be completed during fiscal 1972 at an estimated total cost of $468.8-million. Conferees said they had "given priority to the provision of more adequate funding of projects under construction and have agreed to a very restrictive policy in the provision for new construction starts."

The measure provided funds for termination costs on four existing contracts for the Cross-Florida Barge Canal. About one-third of the controversial project had been completed when environmentalists prevailed upon President Nixon to halt further construction. Nixon issued an order stopping the project on Jan. 19, 1971.

Funds for the Dickey-Lincoln School hydroelectric project were refused for the fifth year. Conferees eliminated $800,000 originally approved by the Senate for a restudy of the feasibility of designing a small-scale project to meet the needs of the state of Maine only.

Not included for the first time in the annual public works bill were funds for waste treatment grants under the Federal Water Quality Administration, which was transferred to the Environmental Protection Agency (EPA) in 1970. EPA funding was included in the Agriculture Department appropriations bill.

Impoundment Issue. The House Appropriations Committee, in its report on HR 10090, expressed concern over what it termed the Nixon administration's "action of impounding the planning and construction funds" added by Congress to the fiscal 1971 public works appropriations bill in 1970. Such action, the committee said, increased long-term costs and decreased benefits. "The committee just does not believe that it is good business to freeze $63.4-million in funds when the project delays will entail added costs and benefit losses totaling $242-million."

Such impoundment, the committee said, "is considered in effect an unconstitutional item veto of the projects authorized and funded by Congress."

The committee noted that in many other cases, unrequested funds provided by Congress were not frozen but involved "less urgent" projects. Of more concern, the committee said, was disclosure that in several instances the funds added for the Reclamation Bureau's programs "are being diverted" in the fiscal 1972 budget for purposes other than those specified by Congress. (*Impoundment controversy, p. 74*)

Other Legislation

RIVER BASIN PROJECTS. Congress in 1971 boosted (S 2887—PL 92-222) authorizations for construction of 14 river basin projects by $628-million through 1973.

The projects, for flood control, navigation and other purposes, came under the jurisdiction of the Army Corps of Engineers. Although Congress had previously authorized the projects, their funding authorizations were scheduled to expire in calendar 1972 and 1973.

Additional authorizations contained in the bill included:

Alabama-Coosa River	$ 38-million
Arkansas River	57-million
Brazos River	20-million

Central and Southern Florida	$18-million
Columbia River	130-million
Mississippi River and Tributaries	97-million
Missouri River	101-million
North Branch Susquehanna River	17-million
Ohio River	62-million
San Joaquin River	44-million
South Platte River	37-million

The bill also authorized $52,103,000 for numerous other projects.

BIG BLUE RIVER COMPACT. The House in 1971 approved a bill (HR 8116) giving the consent of Congress to the Kansas-Nebraska Big Blue River Compact, but the Senate took no action on the measure that year. Congress completed action on the bill in 1972. *(p. 840)*

The compact, negotiated between the two states and ratified by the state legislatures in April 1971, would provide a workable formula for apportionment of the waters in the river basin, set limits on conservation storage in the state of Nebraska, encourage continuation of state pollution control programs, and create an administrative body for management of compact affairs.

1972

Appropriations

The fiscal 1973 public works-Atomic Energy Commission appropriations bill (HR 15586—PL 92-405) appropriated $5,557,914,000, including $53-million in appropriations to liquidate contract authority. New budget authority of $5,504,914,000 was nearly $830-million more than the amount provided by the fiscal 1972 bill.

AEC appropriations totaled $2,633,410,000, including $285-million for research, development and demonstration of the liquid-metal fast breeder nuclear reactor, a more efficient type of nuclear power plant which had been strongly endorsed by the President in his 1971 energy message. *(Details, p. 844)* Other major AEC programs funded by the bill were a plutonium recovery factory at Rocky Flats, Colo.—$12.2-million—and a prototype nuclear propulsion plant at West Milton, N.Y.—$56-million.

Among other funds carried by HR 15596 were $467,-817,000 for the Interior Department's Bureau of Reclamation, most of it for construction and rehabilitation, $328,217,000 for the Appalachian Regional Commission and $125,520,000 for the Bonneville Power Administration, of which $94.5-million was for construction. The Army Corps of Engineers was allotted $1,815,671,000 for public works and other projects, including an environmental impact study of the controversial Cross-Florida Barge Canal. No funding for the Dickey-Lincoln School project was proposed by either the House or Senate.

Debate on the bill featured little controversy, except for a heated House discussion over the nuclear power project and a $150,000 allotment for the Florida canal study. Environmentalist-minded members—who saw the canal investigation as a ploy to resurrect the project, which had been terminated in early 1971 by President

Nixon—sought to cut the two programs, but they lost floor fights on both issues.

During Senate debate, William Proxmire (D Wis.), chairman of the Joint Economic Committee, said Congress must cut back on spending or taxes would have to be increased. "The public works pork barrel is a classic example of where we should save taxpayers' money," he said. "We must reorder our priorities and stop wasting taxpayers' money on projects which benefit only a small special interest group."

SUPPLEMENTAL APPROPRIATIONS. Congress Aug. 16 cleared a bill (HR 16254—PL 92-393) making supplemental appropriations of $1,587,300,000 for disaster relief in fiscal 1973, including $1.3-billion for Small Business Administration (SBA) low-interest loans. The measure was designed to help repair the damage caused by Hurricane Agnes, which caused extensive flood damage throughout the eastern United States June 19-24.

The amount was $17.5-million more than the President had requested. The increase included $16-million for flood control and coastal emergency activities of the Corps of Engineers and $1.5-million for general construction projects of the corps. *(Chapter on miscellaneous economic legislation, p. 177)*

Other Legislation

RIVERS AND HARBORS. President Nixon Oct. 27 pocket vetoed a bill (S 4018) authorizing $593-million for the construction, repair and preservation of public works flood control projects on rivers and harbors. Congress had cleared the bill Oct. 13.

In his veto message, Nixon said the bill would have "ultimately cost hundreds of millions of dollars" by stimulating demand for full funding of approved water projects, including "projects never approved or recommended by the executive branch." Funds for water works customarily are not appropriated for several years, however, and many projects are authorized but never funded.

The bill would have authorized funds for the Army Corps of Engineers to carry out desilting operations in rivers and streams, projects to alleviate streambank and shoreline erosion and flood protection projects in any area that had been declared a disaster area in the past five years.

S 4018 would have canceled the authorization of projects which had been authorized for eight years but on which work had never begun, unless Congress acted to reverse cancellation.

COLORADO RIVER BASIN. Congress in 1972 voted (HR 13435—PL 92-370) authorizations of $352,-195,000 through fiscal 1977 for continued construction of the Upper Colorado River basin storage project and for other projects authorized in 1956. The bill was signed into law Aug. 10.

The initial act gave the secretary of the interior authority to construct, operate and maintain four major storage units, a power transmission and marketing system, 11 water use projects and certain fish and wildlife and recreation, programs, in the Upper Colorado River basin. Initial appropriation of $760,000,000, authorized by the 1956 act, was considered to be only partial funding. *(Congress and the Nation Vol. I, p. 850; Vol. II, p. 513)*

MISSOURI RIVER BASIN. Further appropriations of $114-million to complete construction of the Pick-Sloan Missouri basin were authorized (S 3284—PL 92-371) by Congress in 1972.

The bill, signed into law Aug. 10, was proposed by the Interior Department to complete development of the project, formerly known as the Missouri River basin project, which was authorized by the Flood Control Act of 1944.

The 1944 act had authorized $200-million for initial development of the plan. Additional authorizations had been approved in subsequent years.

BIG BLUE RIVER COMPACT. Congress in 1972 gave its consent to the Kansas-Nebraska Big Blue River compact when it approved HR 8116 (PL 92-308). The Senate in May approved legislation which had been passed by the House in 1971.

The compact, negotiated between Kansas and Nebraska and ratified by the state legislatures in April 1971, divided the waters of the Big and Little Blue Rivers in the Big Blue River basin. The basin drains an area of about 9,700 square miles, of which about three-quarters is in south central Nebraska and one-fourth is in north central Kansas.

In addition, HR 8116 set limits on conservation storage in the state of Nebraska, encouraged continuation of state pollution control programs and created an administrative body for management of compact affairs.

The compact also provided that it would become binding when Congress consented to have the United States joined as a party litigant in any action in the Supreme Court resulting from the compact in which either or both states were involved.

The bill was signed into law June 2.

SAN LUIS VALLEY PROJECT. Congress Oct. 5 cleared for the President a bill (S 520—PL 92-514) authorizing the construction, operation and maintenance of a multi-purpose water resource development in the San Luis Valley of south central Colorado.

The northern portion of the San Luis Valley forms a closed basin. Water supply to the basin is derived primarily from snowfall and amounts to an average of 1,466,400 acre-feet annually in several small streams. Quantities of groundwater are lost from the basin through evaporation and transpiration by nonbeneficial plants.

The closed basin division of the San Luis Valley project would salvage an average of 100,800 acre-feet of groundwater per year. Much of this would be used to fulfill Colorado's obligations under the Rio Grande Compact of 1938 which provided that Colorado deliver certain flows of water to New Mexico each year. The bill was signed into law Oct. 20.

DAM SAFETY INSPECTION. In the wake of two disastrous dam failures, Congress in 1972 authorized the secretary of the Army to undertake a national dam inspection program.

The measure (HR 15951—PL 92-367) applied to the more than 28,000 nonfederal dams in the United States, but did not cover dams under the jurisdiction of the Bureau of Reclamation, the Tennessee Valley Authority, the International Boundary and Water Commission or the Federal Power Commission. Dams which had been inspected in the previous 12 months or which posed no threat to human life and property also were exempted from the bill.

State programs for licensing and inspection of non-federal dams varied widely in scope and effectiveness. Dam failures at Buffalo Creek, W.Va., and Rapid City, S.D., in 1972 had taken the lives of nearly 350 persons, and inflicted millions of dollars in damage.

As signed into law Aug. 8, HR 15951:

• Authorized the secretary of the Army, through the Army Corps of Engineers, to undertake a national dam inspection program.

• Defined dams as any artificial barrier which impounded or diverted water and which was at least 25 feet high or had an impounding capacity of at least 50 acre-feet.

• Directed the secretary to give results of dam inspections to state governors and notify governors during inspections of any hazardous conditions.

• Directed the secretary to issue a report to Congress by July 1, 1974, which would include an inventory of all dams, a review of inspections and recommendations and a suggested national program for dam safety regulation.

Energy Policy

Lulled by seemingly abundant supplies of fuel to fill the nation's current power needs, Congress during the first Nixon administration enacted few bills concerning energy. But the years 1969-72 did witness a growing awareness of potentially severe shortages of fuel in the future.

During Nixon's first term, the nation's energy demands grew steadily while output of fossil fuels levelled off or declined. The United States, with 6 percent of the world's population, devoured one third of the globe's energy production in 1972, yet federal authority over energy policy remained fragmented among 64 different departments and agencies.

The nation's energy policies, of minor concern in 1969 and 1970, received increased congressional attention in the following two years.

President Nixon in 1971 highlighted the nation's growing concern over energy resources in the first message of an American President on energy needs. Warning that "we cannot take our energy supply for granted any longer," he proposed accelerated offshore leasing and stepped-up development of an advanced nuclear power plant. The same year both houses attempted to launch investigations of the energy situation, though the effort succeeded in the Senate only. *(Box, p. 844)*

Extensive hearings held in Congress in 1972 on all aspects of the energy supply were marked by warnings that unless energy policies were revised and coordinated, the nation in the future would be unable to meet its fuel needs. The unusually bitter winter of 1972-73 brought those concerns to a peak. Shortages of fuel oil and natural gas—which forced some midwestern companies to shut down while others were compelled to find alternative fuel supplies—brought an abrupt recognition of the tenuous balance between the nation's power supply and its economic stability.

Nuclear Power. In the field of energy policy, Congress became most deeply involved in the furor over construction of nuclear power plants, brought to a virtual standstill in 1971 by environmentalists. In 1972 Congress enacted legislation facilitating the licensing of nuclear reactors but refused to free the licensing process of all environmental considerations.

Petroleum Policy. Congress also scrutinized the oil policies implemented during the Nixon years. The President's decision in 1970 to retain the oil import quota system provoked a storm of protest from members concerned with petroleum scarcities and high prices, though his action was well-received by the petroleum industry and members representing states in which oil

was produced. The administration's efforts to boost domestic oil supplies by increasing offshore leasing and building a pipeline across Alaska to carry its oil to the "lower 48" states were assailed by members of Congress who feared the adverse impact on the environment of those moves.

Natural Gas. The most controversial question concerning the nation's gas reserves during this period concerned effort to approve a merger between El Paso Natural Gas Co. and a natural gas supplier. Bills to authorize the merger were lodged in committee at the end of 1972 pending a Supreme Court decision on El Paso's appeal to keep its acquisition. Congress did, however, extend for two years the deadline by which states were to adopt gas pipeline safety legislation.

Other Sources. Increased attention was focused on undeveloped sources of energy which promised to meet the nation's future fuel needs. Funds for the fast breeder nuclear reactor—hailed by Nixon as the nation's "best hope" for economical fuel in the next decade—were boosted in 1971 and 1972. Congress enacted a bill in 1970 to encourage development of geothermal resources and to monitor the formation of a similar oil shale leasing program.

Legislation, 1969-72

(NOTE: The following chronology is organized by subject matter. When action occurred in different years, it is reported entirely within the story about the bill and not in different places in the chronology.)

Nuclear Power

Shrinking domestic supplies of fossil fuels and the nation's booming demand for electric power produced great pressures during the Nixon years to harness nuclear power, which accounted for less than one per cent of the nation's power in 1972.

References

Discussion of legislation on energy, power for the years 1965-68, *Congress and the Nation Vol. II,* p. 495-528; for the years 1945-64, *Congress and the Nation Vol. I,* p. 800-907.

Congress considered several measures—and in 1972 enacted a bill—to expedite the construction of nuclear power plants, which had been brought to a virtual standstill by environmentalists in 1971.

In a related action, Congress cleared a bill requiring the Atomic Energy Commission (AEC), to view nuclear power plants as profit-making commercial operations subject to antitrust laws.

POWER PLANT LICENSING

Disturbed by power brownouts and blackouts caused in part by delays in construction of nuclear power plants, Congress during the Nixon years considered several bills to expedite power plant licensing procedures.

Environmentalists opposing nuclear power plant construction focused their efforts on the requirements of the National Environmental Policy Act of 1969 (NEPA—PL 91-190). That act directed all federal agencies to prepare and weigh seriously in its considerations a detailed description of the impact on the environment of any proposed project.

Carrying their objections to the federal courts, conservationists succeeded in blocking construction of several power plants. In a landmark decision, handed down in July 1971, the U.S. Circuit Court of Appeals for the District of Columbia in *Calvert Cliffs Coordinating Committee v. AEC,* halted construction of the Calvert Cliffs, Md., nuclear plant on the grounds that the AEC had not fully complied with PL 91-190.

In December 1971, in *Izaak Walton League v. Schlesinger* (James R. Schlesinger, chairman of the AEC), the same court granted an injunction against licensing of the Quad Cities nuclear plant near Cordova, Ill., on similar grounds.

These court interpretations of NEPA spurred congressional efforts to free power plant license applications from the environmental considerations imposed by the act.

Licensing Criteria. Congress in December 1970 cleared a bill (HR 18679—PL 91-560) requiring the AEC to regard nuclear power plants as profit-making commercial ventures subject to licensing in accordance with the competitive criteria of the antitrust laws. A controversial provision which effectively would have stripped from the Environmental Protection Agency (EPA) its newly acquired authority to set radiation standards was deleted prior to final passage of the bill.

As cleared by Congress, PL 91-560 eliminated from the Atomic Energy Act of 1954 the provision which required the AEC to find a "practical value" before licensing a plant for commercial or industrial purposes. During hearings on a similar measure held by the Joint Committee on Atomic Energy in November 1969, Sen. George D. Aiken (D Vt.) had charged that a small group of utility companies were seeking a monopoly in the field of nuclear power plants. Aiken said that under existing practices the AEC licensed nuclear power plants under a "medical therapy" provision of the law which permitted them to avoid being found in violation of antitrust laws.

A provision of HR 18679—approved by the House but removed in the Senate—would have required the federal agency overseeing radiation standards to commission studies of the standards from the National

---

Atomic Energy Commission Funding

Congress July 1, 1969, cleared a bill (HR 12167—PL 91-44) authorizing fiscal 1970 appropriations of $2,448,052,000 for the Atomic Energy Commission (AEC). On Dec. 4, Congress sent to the White House a bill appropriating $2,217,769,000 of that total—$353,105,000 less than the amount appropriated for the same purposes in fiscal 1969. Of the final total, 53 per cent was for military applications and 47 per cent for civilian programs. Such a breakdown was not provided by the administration after 1969.

In 1970, Congress May 19 completed action on a bill (S 3818—PL 91-273) authorizing $2,290,907,000 for the commission's fiscal 1971 programs. Congress Sept. 23 cleared the annual AEC appropriations bill (HR 18127—PL 91-439), carrying $2,282,760,000 for the agency in fiscal 1971—$64,991,000 more than the fiscal 1970 appropriation.

Congress Dec. 10 approved $25.5-million in supplemental appropriations (S 4557—PL 91-580) for fiscal 1971 for fire prevention operations at AEC nuclear weapons facilities.

Congress in 1971 voted fiscal 1972 appropriations of $2,294,380,000 for the agency (HR 10090—PL 92-134), $30,807,000 less than had been approved in the annual authorization bill (HR 9388—PL 92-84).

Friction developed during consideration of the appropriations measure over AEC plans for an underground test (called "Project Cannikin") of the Spartan warhead component of the Safeguard antiballistic missile system. A House-Senate Conference approved a provision to ban the test without direct approval by the President, but after Nixon's consent, the test was carried out with little noticeable environmental effects.

Except for a brief House floor fight over nuclear weapons testing, little controversy developed during 1972 as Congress acted on the AEC's fiscal 1973 program. Congress Aug. 10 cleared appropriations of $2,633,410,000 for the agency (HR 15586—PL 92-405)—$29,935,000 more than the sum allotted in the fiscal 1973 AEC authorization measure (S 3607—PL 92-314).

The floor battle in the House developed when Bella S. Abzug (D N.Y.) offered an amendment to the authorization bill—later rejected—which would have deleted certain funds for nuclear weapons testing because the ecological effects of the 1971 Cannikin test were not yet known.

Council on Radiation Protection and Measurements and the National Academy of Sciences.

Authority to set radiation protection standards had been transferred to EPA from the AEC and the Federal Radiation Council when EPA was established in December 1970. The AEC frequently had been attacked by environmentalists for being more concerned with the promotion of atomic energy than with the promulgation of stringent radiation standards. Both the council and the academy were known to be close to the AEC position on those matters.

Interim Licensing. Responding to warnings of future power blackouts and brownouts, Congress May 17,

1972, cleared for the President a bill (HR 14655—PL 92-307) authorizing the AEC to issue temporary operating licenses for certain nuclear power plants whose operation was necessary to ensure an adequate power supply. About 13 power plants were affected by the bill.

A provision for public hearings with "expedited procedures" on applications for temporary licenses was included in the bill. The AEC and the power industry opposed the provision, contending that speedy licensing could not be achieved unless the hearing requirement was waived.

PL 92-307 amended the Atomic Energy Act of 1954 (PL 83-703) by adding a new section authorizing the issuance of interim operating licenses until Oct. 30, 1973, for reactors whose applications for a full operating license had been contested. The bill specified that all applications filed before Sept. 1, 1971, must meet the NEPA requirements. (A related bill allowing the AEC to issue temporary licenses before having filed the environmental statements required under NEPA passed the House but died at the end of the session when the Senate took no action.)

NEPA Waiver. A major effort to free nuclear power plant licensing procedures from the environmental considerations imposed under PL 91-190 failed in 1972 when the Senate took no action on a House-passed measure to permit licensing of nuclear power plants prior to completion of environmental impact statements by the AEC.

The House approved the bill (HR 13752) in April but the measure was bottled up in a Senate committee at the session's end.

Many House environmentalists warned that HR 13752 marked the first step in weakening the strict provisions of the 1969 act. The bill would have amended NEPA to authorize temporary licensing of nuclear power plants whose license applications were filed before Sept. 1, 1971, and construction permit applications were filed before Jan. 1, 1970. The interim licenses were to expire no later than Oct. 30, 1973.

AEC Chairman Schlesinger had questioned what he called the "rigid proceduralization" of the NEPA requirements in testimony in March at Senate hearings. The act's "sweeping scope, broadly stated social goals and meager legislative history combine to leave both the agencies and the courts with a formidable task of devising a workable implementation regime," he said.

ENVIRONMENTAL EFFECTS

Attempts by environmentalists to delay construction of nuclear power plants were berated by the AEC chairman during hearings conducted by the Joint Committee on Atomic Energy in October 1969.

AEC Chairman Glenn T. Seaborg charged some foes of nuclear power with engaging in "unsubstantiated fearmongering" and said that "today's outcries about the environment will be nothing compared to cries of angry citizens who find power failures due to lack of sufficient generating capacity have plunged them into prolonged darkness." The environmental problems associated with nuclear energy were "manageable," he said.

Project Rulison. An underground nuclear explosion—code-named Project Rulison—was conducted in western Colorado in September 1969 to release natural gas located below the surface. Sponsored jointly by the AEC and Austral Oil Co. of Houston, the 40-kiloton nu-

---

Federal Regulations: Pre-1969

Although Congress during the Nixon years made few moves to expand federal control over fuel supplies and prices, the government already exerted considerable influence on the nation's petroleum, natural gas and nuclear power.

Since 1959 the oil import quota system had limited the amount of foreign oil brought into the United States, allegedly to protect the national security. The Federal Power Commission set the price of gas sold in the interstate market under the mandate extended by the Natural Gas Act of 1938. License applications for all nuclear power plants were approved by the Atomic Energy Commission.

Federal authority itself was circumscribed by a far-reaching law, the National Environmental Protection Act, enacted in 1969. The act—which required all federal agencies to consider the impact on the environment of all proposed projects—forced the government to consider the environmental consequences of offshore oil and gas leasing, the trans-Alaskan pipeline and nuclear power plants.

---

clear device was detonated to pulverize heavy formations of shale and sand trapping an estimated six to 10 trillion cubic feet of gas. Attempts to block the explosion by court orders failed. The AEC said no radioactivity was released above ground, while the oil company reported in October that damage caused by the blast was minor.

The explosion was the second in the AEC project Plowshare series to develop peaceful uses of atomic power. The first blast, Project Gasbuggy (also to release natural gas), had taken place in New Mexico in December 1967.

A bill setting up a commission to investigate the potential environmental effects of underground uses of nuclear energy was the subject of hearings in November 1969 before a Senate Public Works subcommittee. Academic opinion on the danger of such activities was divided. C. L. Comar, professor of physical biology at Cornell University, told the subcommittee that the benefits to be derived from the peaceful uses of nuclear energy in a controlled situation might outweigh the often-exaggerated risks of radioactive contamination. Lamont C. Cole, professor of ecology at Cornell, said that he regarded many proposed underground nuclear projects as "hazardous to the point of being irresponsible." He emphasized the difficulty of ensuring that no radioactive debris from such an explosion escaped through porous rock or in water.

OTHER ATOMIC ENERGY BILLS

Nuclear Compact. Congress Oct. 5, 1970, approved a bill (S 1628—PL 91-461) consenting to the creation of an interstate nuclear compact to improve cooperation among 13 western states on nuclear matters. The pact was a voluntary agreement by the 13 state governors to cooperate in the development of nuclear energy and in case of a nuclear incident.

Death Penalty Ended. Congress in 1969 cleared a bill (S 3169—PL 91-161) ending the death penalty for violations of the Atomic Energy Act of 1954. The measure also extended until Sept. 1, 1974, the AEC's authority to require the licensing of atomic energy patents, although the commission had never used its authority to compel patent licensing to guard against monopolies.

Petroleum

The major controversies which erupted concerning energy programs during the years 1969-72 concerned the nation's oil policies and efforts to secure an adequate future supply of petroleum, which provided about 45 per cent of the nation's fuel in 1972.

Congress reacted strongly to the Santa Barbara oil spill and the administration's oil import policies, but it enacted little legislation in the area aside from a three-year extension of the oil and gas compact.

Conservationists, consumers and other spokesmen assailed the oil import quota system, which was retained by the President through the end of 1972 despite strong recommendations to the contrary.

Administration attempts to speed up offshore oil drilling to bolster dwindling domestic petroleum supplies were strongly contested by environmentalists. Early in 1969 the massive oil spill at Santa Barbara pointed up the environmental dangers involved in the nation's hunt for oil.

Administration-backed efforts to construct a pipeline across the Alaskan tundra to carry oil to the "lower 48" states also were opposed by environmentalists. At the close of Nixon's first term, construction of the pipeline was blocked pending a federal appeals court decision on whether the Interior Department had considered alternate means of shipping the Alaskan oil when it approved construction of the pipeline earlier in 1972.

OIL IMPORT QUOTAS

In the most controversial decision related to energy in his first administration, President Nixon in 1970 deferred any major changes in the oil import quota system and scrapped a report urging its replacement. Both House and Senate subcommittees held extensive hearings on oil import controls following his action.

President Nixon Feb. 20 announced he would retain the controversial quota system until the United States had consulted with foreign governments. At the same time, the White House released a 400-page report by a seven-member Cabinet task force which recommended replacing the quota system with a variable, gradually reduced tariff on oil imports.

Background. During the immediate postwar period, there had been a world shortage of oil. But by the mid-1950s, excess producing capacity developed as new deposits were discovered in the Middle East and Venezuela. Restrictions on oil imports had originated as a means to protect the U.S. domestic oil production from disruptions of world petroleum markets and thereby, according to Eisenhower administration spokesmen, to assure national security. Following administrations retained the quota system.

The system of oil import quotas first was introduced in 1955 in a clause to the Reciprocal Trade Agreements Act (PL 84-86) which authorized the President to impose

Nixon Energy Message

Warning that "we cannot take our energy supply for granted any longer," President Nixon June 4, 1971, outlined his proposals on a "broad range of actions to ensure an adequate supply of clean energy" for the future.

Increased leasing of oil-rich lands in the outer continental shelf and stepped-up development of an advanced nuclear power plant were among the major actions proposed in the first message of an American President on the nation's energy needs.

The President's message requested supplemental appropriations of just under $100-million for fiscal 1972—most of it earmarked for the new breeder reactor. He called for congressional action on earlier administration requests but did not propose any new programs requiring authorization by Congress.

Among the supplemental requests made by Mr. Nixon were: $27-million in operating funds for the nuclear reactor program and an additional $50-million for the federal contribution to construction of a demonstration plant; $15-million additional for developing methods of removing sulfur from the stack gases of power plants and industrial plants burning coal and oil; $2-million for controlled thermonuclear fusion research, and $3-million for research in nuclear-reactor safety.

Department of Natural Resources. Nixon called upon Congress to approve his recommendation—first made in his 1971 state of the union message—to place responsibility for most energy programs in a single agency within the proposed Department of Natural Resources. "Our present structure is not equipped to handle the relationships between (energy) problems and the emergence of new concerns," Nixon declared. Under his reorganization plan, the Atomic Energy Commission would retain authority over nuclear programs and related energy research while energy-related operations of the Interior and other departments would be consolidated in an Energy Administration.

Fast Breeder Reactor. "Our best hope today for meeting the nation's growing demand for economical clean energy lies with the fast breeder reactor," Nixon declared. He requested an additional $27-million in fiscal 1973 for construction of a breeder demonstration plant in Oak Ridge, Tenn. The reactor was prized as a partial solution to the nation's dwindling fuel supplies because it would produce more fuel than it consumed.

Offshore Leasing. Referring to the vast quantity of oil and natural gas reserves lying untapped off the U.S. coast, Nixon called for accelerated leasing of federal lands on the outer continental shelf. He directed that sales be made "not only in the highly productive Gulf of Mexico" but also in "some other highly promising areas," foretelling administration moves to open lands off the Atlantic Coast to drilling for the first time. Nixon emphasized that the proposed sales were to be undertaken within "clear limits" including strict regulations to avoid oil spills.

restrictions on products entering the country in such volume as to impair national security. While voluntary limits on oil imports were begun in 1957, President Eisenhower in 1959 ordered mandatory controls on imports of crude and residual oil. The 1962 Trade Expansion Act (PL 88-794) established a formula regulating oil imports. *(Congress and the Nation Vol. I, p. 203)*

By early 1969, criticism of oil import controls had become widespread. In a Jan. 14 report to the President, the Special Representative for Trade Negotiations recommended a re-examination of the oil import policy to determine whether there was still a need to protect national security through quotas and, if so, whether the administration of the program might be improved.

A critical investigation of the oil industry also was undertaken that year by the Senate Judiciary Subcommittee on Antitrust and Monopoly, chaired by Philip A. Hart (D Mich.). An underlying issue was the pending proposal to create a free-trade zone in Machiasport, Maine, and set up a large refinery to provide New England with low-cost fuel from imported Libyan crude oil.

Nixon Task Force. On Feb. 20, 1969, President Nixon announced that he was assuming responsibility for all decisions relating to oil, and on March 26 he named a Cabinet-level task force to review oil import policy. (President Johnson, to avoid suspicion that he would favor the Texas oil industry, in 1963 had given authority to determine oil quotas to the Secretary of the Interior.)

The Nixon task force was headed by Secretary of Labor George P. Shultz. The other members were Secretary of State William P. Rogers, Defense Secretary Melvin R. Laird, Treasury Secretary David M. Kennedy, Secretary of the Interior Walter J. Hickel (the Interior Department administers the oil quota system), Commerce Secretary Maurice H. Stans and George A. Lincoln, director of the Office of Emergency Preparedness.

The task force was swamped with advice from members of Congress, executive agencies, foreign governments, state governments, and lobby groups. The Justice Department's Antitrust Division wanted to abolish quotas, but the Interior Department recommended keeping them, with modifications to make them fairer and more efficient. The two Departments also took issue with the argument that oil quotas were needed for national security. Assistant Attorney General Richard W. McLaren called the quota system expensive and unnecessary for national security, but Interior Secretary Walter J. Hickel said the national security basis for the quota system was a "reasonable concept."

Task Force Recommendations. In their report Feb. 20, 1970, the majority on the presidential task force recommended phasing out the quota system and replacing it with a system of variable duties on foreign oil imports, effective Jan. 1, 1971. Initially, the tariff for Middle Eastern oil would be set at $1.45 a barrel, with Canadian and Mexican oil entering at 10 cents a barrel and oil from other Western Hemisphere nations entering at $1.25 a barrel. After further review, the tariff schedule would be liberalized in 1972. The initial effect of the proposed tariff system would be a 30-cent reduction, to $3.00 a barrel, in the domestic crude oil price.

Laird and Rogers, while agreeing with the majority recommendation, submitted supplementary views stating that implementation should be postponed pending full consultation with other governments.

Stans and Hickel, joined by Federal Power Commissioner John N. Nassikas (an official observer) filed a separate report arguing for retention of the present system, but proposing an expansion of the quota by more than 100,000 barrels a day annually through 1974.

New Review. In his Feb. 20, 1970, statement rejecting the recommendations the President had announced that he was establishing an interdepartmental Oil Policy Committee "to consider both interim and long-term adjustments that will increase the effectiveness and enhance the equity of the oil import program."

Nixon said, however, that "major long-term adjustments must necessarily await the outcome of discussions with Canada, Mexico, Venezuela and other allies and affected nations...."

Reaction. Spokesmen for the U.S. oil industry generally praised the President's announcement. The American Petroleum Institute issued a statement terming the President's statement "encouraging" and declaring: "In our opinion the elimination of import controls would seriously weaken this country's ability to meet its energy needs from domestic sources and would have a grave impact on the economy of many areas of the United States."

Sens. Clifford P. Hansen (R Wyo.) and John G. Tower (R Texas)—both from oil-producing states—said they were pleased with the President's decision. Sen. Russell B. Long (D La.), chairman of the Senate Finance Committee, said he would hold hearings on oil import policy.

Criticism of the President's decision came primarily from New England members of Congress, who had led the fight to liberalize the oil quota system. Nine New England Senators Feb. 20 made public a letter to the President demanding an overhaul of oil import policy and calling attention to the high price of fuel oil in New England.

One effect of Nixon's decision to continue the review of oil import policy was to defer once more a decision on granting Occidental Petroleum Co. a quota to import oil into a refinery it planned to construct in the free-trade zone of Machiasport, Maine.

Senate Hearings. In March 1970 a Senate Judiciary Subcommittee on Antitrust and Monopoly, chaired by Philip A. Hart (D Mich.), began hearings on the report of the presidential task force on oil import quotas.

George P. Shultz, secretary of labor and chairman of the task force, endorsed the majority view recommending abolition of the quota system. The oil import quota system "does not reflect national security needs, present or future, and is no longer acceptable," he told the subcommittee. "Besides costing consumers an estimated $5-billion each year, the quotas have caused inefficiencies in the market place." A tariff system as proposed by the task force would protect national security at a much lower cost to the consumer, he said.

Joseph J. Simmons, administrator of the Oil Import Administration within the Interior Department, defended the existing oil quotas. If the country had elected to satisfy its energy needs with cheap foreign oil, the oil-rich Alaskan North Slope would almost certainly have remained unexplored, Simmons asserted. The use of tariffs to replace quotas as a control mechanism was an unworkable suggestion, he concluded.

(Continued on p. 847)

Congressional Studies of Energy Crisis: 1971-72

Growing concern in Congress over the sufficiency of the nation's energy resources was evidenced by attempts in both houses in 1971 to initiate studies of the nation's resource base and future fuel needs. The following year committees in both houses conducted hearings on the domestic energy supply and several proposals to coordinate responsibility for energy-related decisions on the federal level.

The most exhaustive congressional investigation in recent years of the nation's energy policy was launched by the Senate in May 1971. The task force—which included representatives of the Interior, Commerce, Public Works and Joint Atomic Energy Committees—set up under a resolution (S Res 45) held hearings in 1971 and 1972 on a broad range of issues. Its report was to be published in the fall of 1973.

In the House a related proposal to establish a select committee to investigate energy resources was defeated in 1971. A bill (H Res 155) was rejected by a 128-218 roll-call vote less than a month after Senate approval of S Res 45. Defeat followed a debate in which numerous committee chairmen charged that the proposed unit would interfere with the jurisdiction of several existing committees, particularly the Interstate and Foreign Commerce Committee.

The resolution would have established a seven-member committee to study the availability and ownership of domestic oil, gas, coal and nuclear energy reserves; reasons and possible solutions for the delay in new starts on fossil-fueled power plants, and other issues.

Energy Supplies

Under the mandate granted by S Res 45, the Senate Interior and Insular Affairs Committee held hearings intermittantly between January and August 1972 on the nation's fuel policies.

Administration spokesmen testified in January in support of the President Nixon's proposal to establish an Energy Administration within a Department of Natural Resources. "We lack the qualities of stability, coherence and centered responsibility in our policies addressed to energy matters," Hollis M. Dole, assistant interior secretary, told the committee.

A series of hearings in June focused on potential future sources of energy. Dr. Alfred J. Eggers Jr., assistant director for research applications within the National Science Foundation, termed solar energy the most promising of the unconventional energy sources.

Oil and natural gas exploration and production was examined in August hearings before the committee. Clifford P. Hansen (R Wyo.), a committee member, told his colleagues that "the solution to our energy crisis... is to stimulate domestic (oil) production." Sen. John G. Tower (R Texas) noted that in 13 years or less, the nation will be forced to rely on foreign sources for at least one-half of its petroleum needs. Tom B. Medders Jr., president, Independent Petroleum Association of America, recommended increased tax incentives for domestic oil and gas exploration.

During seven days of hearings in April 1972, the House Interior Committee was told by several witnesses that a continuation of existing policies toward energy issues would likely result in critical shortages of fuel in the future.

"We are facing a fuel and power crisis," Interior Secretary Rogers C.B. Morton told the committee. "Its implications for our economy, our environment...and our foreign policy...are broad and pervasive."

John B. Connally, treasury secretary, ticked off a list of projects to bolster domestic fuel supply which had been blocked or delayed by environmentalists, including increased oil imports and leasings on the outer continental shelf, surface mining of coal and construction of the trans-Alaskan pipeline, east coast refineries, deep-water ports to service supertankers and nuclear power plants. "There have been enough delays. Let us start leasing, exploring, drilling...and using more prudently the resultant clean energy this country needs to keep...our society alive."

Representatives of the coal, oil and natural gas industries supported programs to promote use of their products while conservationists urged that the nation conserve its energy resources.

Hearings focused on the nation's energy reserves were conducted by the House Public Works Committee in August 1972.

Assistant Interior Secretary Dole told the committee that the existing "scarcity will widen as time goes by to include nearly every form and category of energy."

Nuclear power was touted as the answer, over the long term, to the nation's energy shortages. "In the decade of the 1970s nuclear capacity is expected to increase from 2 per cent of the total electric generating capacity to 23 per cent, to 38 per cent by the end of the 1980s and to 50 per cent by the year 2000," William O. Doub, commissioner, Atomic Energy Commission, said.

Council on Energy Policy

Various bills to establish a three-person Council on Energy Policy to advise the President and Congress on energy issues were considered in 1972 but none was reported out of committee.

During hearings in August held jointly by the Senate Commerce and Interior Committees, John W. Larson, assistant interior secretary, endorsed the objectives of the bill but said that "President Nixon's proposal for the creation of a Department of Natural Resources will more effectively serve these objectives than the Council on Energy Policy. The proposed (council) would impose yet another bureaucratic layer of government on top of the large number of federal agencies which already exist."

Rep. Hastings Keith (R Mass. 1959-73), sponsor of one of the bills, asserted: "We don't have one, concrete national energy policy. We have instead bits and pieces of policies for each segment of the energy spectrum (which) need to be consolidated."

(Continued from p. 845)

House Hearings. A second investigation of the oil import controls was conducted in March and April 1970 by the House Interior Subcommittee on Mines and Mining, chaired by Ed Edmondson (D Okla.).

George A. Lincoln, director, Office of Emergency Preparedness, told the subcommittee that changes were needed in the existing system. "I personally believe that a tariff system can be devised which is workable and will safeguard the national security as adequately as a quota system, at less cost to the consumer." Lincoln had been a member of the President's task force and was director of the Oil Policy Committee named by Nixon in February.

Barry J. Shillito, assistant secretary of defense for installation and logistics, declared that the oil task force analysis "clearly indicated that a relaxation of import controls over time, coupled with appropriate Western Hemisphere preferences and a security adjustment to prevent undue Eastern Hemisphere imports would... satisfactorily protect security of (oil) supply."

Several spokesmen for the petroleum industry testified on the need to retain the oil import quota system and criticized the presidential task force recommendations on replacing the quota with a tariff system.

1971-72 Developments. As U.S. dependency on foreign sources of oil increased, pressures began to build in 1971 and 1972 to further restrict petroleum imports. Proponents of that view argued that reliance on oil supplied by the politically unstable nations of the Middle East opened the nation to supply uncertainties and a possible embargo by Arab states. In 1972, the United States imported 1,735,256,000 barrels of crude and refined petroleum, 580 million more than in 1969 (1,155,551,000 barrels), according to the Bureau of Mines.

But strict import curbs were regarded as impractical in view of the increasingly scarce domestic oil reserves. The heating oil shortages which plagued the nation during the unusually bitter winter of 1972-73 provoked sharp criticism of the import controls which acted to restrict petroleum supplies.

The administration in late 1972 appeared to support that line of reasoning at least in the short run. The Office of Emergency Preparedness announced Dec. 8, 1972, that it was suspending through May 1973 import curbs on the type of crude oil—No. 2—used primarily for home heating.

SANTA BARBARA OIL SPILL

The adverse environmental effects of offshore oil production were dramatized in January 1969 when an oil well blowout off the California coast poured 235,000 gallons of oil into the Pacific Ocean, forming an 800-square mile slick.

A well off the coast of Santa Barbara—located on a tract leased by the federal government to the Union Oil Co.—burst its seams below the ocean floor during a routine maintenance operation, spewing crude oil from Jan. 28 to Feb. 8 and causing major damage to wildlife, boats and beaches. An estimated 600 birds were affected by the oil, which blackened 30 miles of southern California's beaches. The event mobilized conservationist sentiment as photographs of oil-coated wildfowl and beaches dominated the nation's publications.

Background. Seventy-two leases in the Santa Barbara channel were auctioned to private oil companies by the Department of the Interior in 1966 and 1968, netting $623-million in federal revenue. The Outer Continental Shelf Lands Act of 1953 (PL 81-212) authorized federal control of oil and gas resources on offshore lands, which extend outward underwater from U.S. shorelines as far as 150 miles in some areas. The act authorized the Interior Department to grant leases on a competitive bid system for oil and gas extraction, with lease proceeds and subsequent royalties to go to the general fund of the Treasury. At the close of 1972, the department had auctioned off 1,778 oil and gas tracts. *(Congress and the Nation Vol. I, p. 1036)*

Administration Reaction. Interior Department Secretary Walter J. Hickel suspended all drilling and pumping operations in the channel Feb. 7. Ten days later he announced new department regulations compelling all firms drilling on offshore federal tracts to be responsible for cleaning up any pollution caused by their operations. Other regulations issued by the department tightened safety rules in an effort to prevent further blowouts and pollution from offshore rigs.

Hickel appeared before a Senate Public Works subcommittee hearing on Feb. 27 to defend his decision announced that day to allow Union Oil Co. to resume drilling in the channel.

Following the recommendations of a presidential task force, Hickel in June authorized resumption of unlimited offshore drilling in the channel by all oil companies having leases in the area. The task force concluded that the only way to prevent further leaks was to pump the field dry.

In 1971 the Supreme Court backed up lower courts' refusal to order a halt to government action allowing the drilling of new oil wells in the channel. But the government later voluntarily imposed a moratorium on all drilling on federal leases in the channel. The oil companies affected sued the government and won in federal district court; the government appealed the ruling and the moratorium continued in early 1973. *(County of Santa Barbara v. Malley; Gulf Oil v. Morton)*

Senate Bill. A bill to terminate certain leases and suspend others in the Santa Barbara channel was considered by the Senate Interior Committee in May. The administration opposed the bill as unnecessary in light of stricter drilling regulations established by the Interior Department. The committee in July rejected a proposal banning all oil drilling in the channel and took no further action on the related bills.

In the first federal attempt to buy back offshore tracts it had leased, President Nixon in June asked Congress for legislation to establish a federal marine sanctuary in the Santa Barbara Channel. His recommendation would have canceled 20 federal leases in the area of the proposed sanctuary, which was to cover about 198,000 acres. Congress took no action on the administration's proposal.

Long-Term Effects. The most long-lasting result of the Santa Barbara spill was seen in the successful efforts of environmentalists concerned with the potential damage to the environment of offshore drilling to delay certain federal lease sales pending completion of environmental impact statements by the Interior Department.

President Nixon in June 1971 called for accelerated sale of offshore oil leases in the Gulf of Mexico and "other promising areas" in an effort to bolster domestic fuel supplies. A leasing program announced that month by Interior Secretary Rogers C. B. Morton scheduled at least two major oil and gas sales each year through 1975. The leases were to be offered chiefly in the Gulf of Mexico but also in the Gulf of Alaska and—for the first time—on the Atlantic outer continental shelf.

In November 1971 a group of 60 congressmen from eastern states demanded that the department cancel its planned sales off the Atlantic coast.

Three weeks before a major sale scheduled for December 1971, environmentalists filed suit contending that the Interior Department had failed to prepare adequate statements detailing the impact upon the environment of the proposed sales as required by the National Environmental Policy Act of 1969 (NEPA—PL 91-190). A federal district court for the District of Columbia upheld the conservationists' claim and blocked the lease of 366,000 acres off the coast of Louisiana. The court held that the department had not given adequate consideration to other ways to meet the nation's energy needs which posed less of a threat to the environment.

The Interior Department, however, announced in March 1972 that it was considering granting two Louisiana leases later that year after drafting new environmental impact statements. The following month it revealed that the U.S. Geological Survey would conduct "core drilling" on the Atlantic outer continental shelf as part of its "continuing mission to gather basic geological data."

Rep. Norman F. Lent (R N.Y.) criticized the department's Atlantic drilling plans as a "large-scale research effort undertaken at taxpayers' expense, the results of which will be freely available to private industry."

As a result of the district court's December 1971 ruling, no offshore leases were offered by the government until September and December 1972, when 178 tracts were auctioned for a total of $2.2-billion.

During hearings on offshore leasing before the Senate Interior and Insular Affairs Committee in April 1972, petroleum and natural gas industry officials encouraged expanded leasing of lands on the outer continental shelf. John M. Houchin, deputy chairman, Phillips Petroleum Co., noted that only 25 of the 14,000 wells drilled in U.S. waters had created a pollution hazard as a result of a "blowout." The three major oil spills which resulted caused no lasting harm to the environment, he indicated.

OIL AND GAS COMPACT

Congress in 1969 cleared a bill (S J Res 54—PL 91-158) extending for two years—through Sept. 1, 1971—the Interstate Oil and Gas Compact. A further three-year extension—through Sept. 1, 1974—was approved (S J Res 72—PL 92-322) by Congress June 1972. The consent of Congress had expired in the intervening 10 months.

The compact, first approved in 1935, set up a program among the oil producing states to conserve oil and natural gas—the product of a growing public concern in the 1930s that precious reserves of oil and gas were being wasted or destroyed. Under practices flourishing at that time, petroleum was left unused on the ground at well sites and natural gas was burned off at the wellhead. A commission set up under the act fostered the exchange of information concerning conservation practices and related problems among the 29 member states and the petroleum industry.

Trials of a Policymaker

Secretary of the Interior Rogers C. B. Morton told a congressional hearing April 10, 1972, there had been plenty of advice on dealing with energy and the environment.

The advice came, he told the House Interior and Insular Affairs Committee, from conservationists, industry, consumers and some of the 61 federal entities involved in energy policy. Morton testified:

"This advice together has said: Give us an energy policy that is intelligent and concise and, above all, responsive to the interests of the nation as a whole. Give us a policy that can apply to the short-term and to the longer term as well.

"Give us an energy policy, they say, that will provide the consumer with the type of fuel he wants, in the amounts he needs, at the time he must have it and at the lowest possible price. Assure us this energy will be from secure and reliable sources.

"But don't drill offshore of my coastline, don't build any pipelines across my land, don't strip mine any coal, don't build any refineries or storage facilities in my area, abolish the oil import program but don't move oil in by tanker for this might pollute our waters.

"Give us an energy policy that guarantees protection of the environment, where the use of energy does not intrude upon our esthetic values nor damage the ecology of the land. Give us an energy policy that will maximize national security yet not impinge upon normal trade between nations."

Pointing out that there was no easy solution, Morton added: "Unlike the advocate for a cause, the decision-maker must recognize that any particular course of action may have extremely detrimental reactions in other areas."

Natural Gas

The steady growth in the use of natural gas led to concern throughout the first Nixon administration that the nation ultimately would face severe shortages of the popular clean-burning fuel, which supplied approximately 32 percent of the nation's power needs in 1972. Although Congress considered several bills to ensure an adequate supply, no measures were enacted to achieve that goal.

GAS SUPPLY

In September 1969, a Federal Power Commission (FPC) staff report cautioned that a "major new government-industry program was needed to ensure the continued growth of natural gas service during the next decade."

Programs to avert a possible shortage of natural gas were the subject of hearings November 1969 by the Senate Interior Subcommittee on Minerals, Materials and Fuels. Hollis M. Dole, assistant interior secretary, told the subcommittee that "a serious supply problem will be fully upon us by 1975 if current trends persist and immediate corrective action is not taken." Dole indicated

El Paso Pipeline

A 16-year struggle by El Paso Natural Gas Company to retain control of a huge natural gas market in the West ended March 5, 1973, when the Supreme Court directed El Paso to sell $290-million in assets of the old Pacific Northwest Pipeline Corporation.

In a 6-0 ruling, the court affirmed without opinion a federal district court plan under which El Paso was required to sell Pacific Northwest's gas reserves, pipeline facilities and other property to a combine of four companies known as the Apco Group. The holdings ensured Apco access to the lucrative natural gas markets of the northwest and California and provided major incentives to develop new gas supplies in Canada.

Contested Since 1957. The Justice Department in July 1957 challenged El Paso's acquisition earlier that year of Pacific Northwest, contending that the merger violated antitrust laws by reducing potential competition in the California region. In 1964, the Supreme Court held the merger illegal and ordered El Paso to sell the pipeline, but divestiture was delayed for nine years as the high court in 1967 and again in 1969 rejected proposals to carry it out.

The divestiture plan approved by the court March 5 was issued by a federal district court in June 1972, but was modified in August to name the Apco Group—Apco Oil Corp., Alaska Interstate Co., Gulf Interstate Co. and Tipperary Land and Exploration Corp.—to operate the new company created under the ruling. El Paso in November 1972 asked the Supreme Court to review the decision.

Congressional Action. At the same time teams of lawyers argued in the courts over the El Paso merger, a decade-long struggle directly affecting the issue was waged off and on in Congress.

As early as 1962, after the Supreme Court's first ruling in the dispute, the FPC proposed legislation giving it sole jurisdiction over natural gas pipeline mergers and exempting FPC-approved mergers from antitrust laws.

Identical bills (S 2404, HR 10331) were introduced in the Senate and House in 1971-72 to permit El Paso to retain the pipeline by holding the merger immune from antitrust requirements.

Proponents contended that conditions had changed since 1957 and the public interest in an adequate supply of natural gas would be best served by upholding the merger.

Congress in September 1972 completed hearings on measures—strongly opposed by the Justice Department—to legalize the El Paso acquisition, but no bill was reported by the committees involved. Hearings held that month before the House Interstate and Foreign Commerce Subcommittee on Communications and Power dealt with El Paso's expenditures in 1971 of $893,862 on efforts to promote the legislation.

The Supreme Court's decision appeared to rule out further congressional efforts to legalize the merger.

the administration was increasing gas and oil leasing on the outer continental shelf while awaiting supply boosts expected from completion of the trans-Alaska pipeline and perfection of a technique to extract gas from coal. Industry officials urged the FPC to permit higher gas prices to encourage further exploration and production.

The Senate Commerce Committee in 1972 held hearings on—but did not report—three bills to help alleviate the nation's natural gas supply shortage. Two measures would have amended the Natural Gas Act of 1938 to provide incentives to producers for increasing natural gas reserves. Under the 1938 act, the terms of a producer's contract may be changed by the FPC at any time. The proposed bills would have guaranteed the sanctity of such contracts so that a producer would know what price he would receive and the amount of gas he must deliver. FPC chairman John N. Nassikas told the committee in March that sanctity of contract bills "should induce an increase in gas exploration" while an attorney from Ralph Nader's Public Interest Group, David W. Calfee, opposed the legislation as "an attempt to achieve indirectly the decontrol of natural gas prices."

A third bill considered by the committee would have directed the FPC to make an independent evaluation of proven natural reserves and update their findings annually.

GAS PIPELINE SAFETY

Congress in 1972 enacted a bill (HR 5065—PL 92-401) extending for two years—to Aug. 12, 1973—the deadline for states to enact natural pipeline safety legislation.

The 1,287 individual gas pipeline failures reported to the Transportation Department in 1971 had resulted in 45 deaths, 391 injuries and an estimated $2.6-million in property damage, according to a Senate Commerce Committee report (S Rept 92-829).

As signed into law Aug. 22, Pl 92-401 provided mandatory federal grants-in-aid of up to 50 percent for the costs of establishing state safety programs and enforcing federal interstate pipeline safety standards. Appropriations totaling $11.8-million over three years were authorized by the act. The bill amended the Natural Gas Pipeline Safety Act of 1968 (PL 90-481) which authorized the secretary of transportation to set standards for more than 760,000 miles of transmission, distribution and gathering pipelines in residential and commercial areas.

Geothermal Steam Resources

Congress in 1970 took a major step toward commercial development of geothermal steam as a power source when it cleared a bill (S 368—PL 91-581) authorizing the interior secretary to lease public lands in order to develop geothermal resources. Geothermal resources occur naturally underground in two forms—dry steam and hot water—both of which can be used to generate electricity. The first federal geothermal tracts were expected to be leased by the Interior Department in 1973.

Another geothermal steam bill had cleared Congress in 1966 but was vetoed by President Johnson who criticized provisions he said ran "counter to public policy." *(Congress and the Nation Vol. II p. 952)*

Chapter 14—Foreign Policy

Key Votes

In this chapter, key roll-call votes are shown in bold face type. The party breakdown on each of these votes and the position taken by each member of Congress may be found in the key vote charts which appear in the appendix to this book.

Foreign Policy

President Nixon capped his first term in the White House with a series of foreign policy spectaculars—a dialogue with Communist China, improved relations with the Soviet Union and an imminent cease-fire in Vietnam. The televised views of an American President chatting with Chinese Communist party chairman Mao Tse-tung in Peking and meeting with Soviet Communist party leader Leonid I. Brezhnev in Moscow dazzled a world grown accustomed to decades of cold war tensions.

But it was Indochina which dominated foreign affairs in the first four years of the Nixon presidency. The Vietnam conflict had been the longest war in U.S. history—11 years at the time of the cease-fire agreement signing in Paris in January 1973. And, as events in the first half of 1973 were to show, U.S. involvement in Indochina was not terminated by the signing nor were its effects erased.

In 1964, Lyndon Johnson had told the American people of his opposition to "committing a good many American boys to fighting a war that ought to be fought by the boys of Asia." But American boys were committed. By the time the last U.S. troops came home in March 1973, nearly nine million Americans had seen service in the Vietnam conflict. Almost 46,000 had been killed in combat, more than 300,000 wounded. Estimates of Vietnamese deaths—South, North, Vietcong, civilian—reached to more than a million.

Beyond the death counts, casualties, refugees, military costs, bombs dropped, assistance figures and other statistics were the factors which defied cost analysis and line graphs. Profound changes had taken place in the country which had become bogged down in what at times seemed an endless land war on the far side of the globe.

It had been impossible to escape the war. It was on the front page almost daily, in radio broadcasts and, more importantly, it was brought home every night on the television screen. A nation that had seen death tolls flashed before it weekly, that had seen the bodies of My Lai, the fatalities of Kent State, the marches on Washington, the burning of American flags, the tortures suffered by prisoners of war could not be the same.

Repercussions of the war touched almost every aspect of American life from the military establishment to the economy to traditional mores. The toll was high, the divisions deep and, once the cease-fire agreement had been signed, nearly everyone—war critic and administration supporter alike—had had enough. There was no dancing in the streets; no champagne corks popped. There was only relief—and an apparent national commitment to avoid other Vietnams.

Congress, which left to 5 Presidents the decisions once U.S. troops and prisoners of war had returned—the number on Capitol Hill willing to say "no" to the White House grew substantially. Amid signs of increasing involvement in Cambodia, the House in May 1973 for the first time went on record in opposition to continued military activity. A similar but stronger stance by the Senate was less surprising.

Direct congressional challenges to the President had been a long time in coming. Congress—like the people it represented—had supported the search for peace with honor. And, although the many congressional votes on measures to curtail the war did demonstrate growing disillusionment with America's role in Indochina, Congress—up until 1973—continued to give both President Johnson and President Nixon full support in funding military operations in Southeast Asia.

End-the-War Legislation

Congress, which left to five Presidents the decisions by which the United States began and pursued its involvement in the Vietnam war, also left to President Nixon the decision on how that involvement should end.

From the mid-1960s through the signing of the cease-fire agreement, 94 roll-call votes had been taken on the question of limiting or halting American involvement in the Indochina war. Anti-war amendments were attached to bills dealing with defense procurement, foreign aid, defense appropriations and military sales, among others. But no matter what the package, congressmen against the war were unable to muster enough strength to send an explicit policy directive to the President.

Although Congress approved several measures to curtail U.S. activities in Laos, Cambodia and Thailand, and twice urged the President to set a date for withdrawal of American troops from the conflict, no provisions actually cutting off funds or setting a specific deadline for withdrawal ever cleared both houses.

In 1972, in the most serious challenge to the President's conduct of the war up to that time, the Senate voted to cut off funds for the war. The amendment was deleted in conference, at the House's insistence, and in the end, support for President Nixon's Vietnamization policy—coupled with reluctance to challenge the execu-

---

References

Discussion of foreign policy for the years 1945-64 may be found in *Congress and the Nation, Vol. I*, p. 91-232; for the years 1965-68, *Congress and the Nation, Vol. II*, p. 52-116.

tive conduct of diplomacy—killed all end-the-war legislation during the President's first term.

The President's strategy and the Congress' acquiescence appeared to pay off early in 1973. A cease-fire agreement—providing for military solutions now and political solutions later—was signed in Paris Jan. 27, 1973.

All U.S. troops and known prisoners of war returned home within 60 days. And once they were home, Congress became increasingly defiant of the administration's Indochina policies. Requests to provide funds within a supplemental appropriations bill for continued bombing in Cambodia were turned down by both the House and the Senate early in the President's second administration.

Foreign Aid

Reluctant to challenge the President on his war policy, Congress found other targets for its frustrations. The foreign aid program was among the most popular.

In its first four years in office, the Nixon administration moved to redirect the U.S. foreign aid program, long a cornerstone of the nation's foreign policy. Military assistance in particular was assigned an important role in the U.S. strategic posture under the Nixon doctrine of helping other nations defend themselves by providing the equipment and supplies but not the manpower.

But Congress, increasingly disenchanted with the results produced by 24 years of foreign assistance, was challenging the necessity and wisdom of pouring billions of dollars overseas through the existing program. In some quarters, in the Senate Foreign Relations Committee in particular, sentiment grew for abandoning the program— at least its military components.

While Congress kept funding the program, in three out of the first four Nixon years it failed to complete action on foreign aid legislation until many months after the beginning of the fiscal year. The program stayed in operation, however, with funds provided by continuing resolutions.

In both 1971 and 1972, moreover, the Senate rejected foreign aid authorization bills. Although the Senate in each year subsequently revived the legislation, the initial defeats served notice that the program's future was in doubt.

While the program continued, the Senate Foreign Relations Committee made clear its determination to use its control over foreign aid authorizations to work its will on administration foreign policies with which it disagreed. The committee's objectives—withdrawal from Indochina, reduced overseas commitments and more congressional participation in foreign policy decisions—all were addressed by policy amendments to foreign aid bills.

War Powers

The various war-powers proposals introduced during the first Nixon administration reflected congressional concern over the way the United States had entered its costly involvement in the Vietnam war. Adoption of the Tonkin Gulf resolution in 1964 and subsequent disclosures concerning it portrayed a convincing picture of congressional impotence. Approved overwhelmingly on the basis of what later emerged as a distorted account of a minor

naval engagement, the resolution became the primary legal justification for the Johnson administration's escalation of the war.

By the time Congress learned that the naval incident had been misrepresented and moved to repeal the resolution in 1970, President Nixon had already shifted to another legal rationale—his constitutional powers as Commander in Chief—for his Vietnam policies.

Unwilling to challenge the conduct of the current war, Congress began to look to future entanglements. In its 1969 "national commitments" resolution, the Senate made a bid to reassert a congressional voice in decisions committing the United States to the defense of foreign countries. The House passed war-powers measures in 1970, 1971 and 1972.

The furthest step toward codifying war powers was taken by the Senate in 1972, when it passed a bill defining the powers of Congress and the President in decisions involving the use of the armed forces in hostilities. Despite opposition from the White House, the bill was supported by a broadly-based coalition of Republicans and Democrats, northerners and southerners, advocates and opponents of higher defense spending in the Senate. The House, however, passed a weaker measure and the bill died in conference.

Overseas Commitments

Revelations in 1969 and 1970 of previously unknown U.S. military activities abroad provided a major impetus to the movement to reassert congressional influence. Secret executive agreements with potential for future military entanglements were uncovered in hearings by the Senate Foreign Relations Subcommittee on U.S. Security Agreements and Commitments Abroad. At the conclusion of a two-year inquiry, the special subcommittee warned that the United States had assumed "creeping commitments" blurred by secrecy and threatening to trap the nation in global responsibilities. Recipients of "creeping commitments" cited by the subcommittee included the Philippines, Laos, Thailand, Korea, Ethiopia and Spain.

The proliferation of executive agreements—which do not require congressional sanction—was central to the debate over powers and prerogatives in foreign affairs. As of the beginning of 1973, the United States was party to 910 treaties and 4,589 executive agreements. And in recent years some of those agreements dealt with issues formerly considered sufficiently important to require Senate ratification by treaty—notably military base and joint defense agreements.

Fears of future Vietnams prompted passage in 1972 of legislation requiring the administration to submit to Congress the texts of all international agreements. The secretary of state had been required by law to publish annually the contents of all treaties and executive agreements. In practice, however, agreements considered by the executive branch to be sensitive to national security were withheld. As a result, Congress was not informed of many agreements, even on a classified basis.

Several of the more controversial agreements were given individual attention. Although the administration had assured Congress that a 1970 base agreement with Spain represented no defense commitment to Spain, there were enough doubts in the Senate to assure passage of a resolution confirming that the agreement did not constitute a national commitment.

In 1972, the Senate passed a resolution urging the President to submit base agreements concluded with Portugal and the Persian Gulf state of Bahrain. Senate approved amendments requiring congressional sanction of executive agreements blocked conference clearance of the fiscal 1973 military assistance authorization bill.

Vietnam Aftermath

The challenges to the executive branch during the first Nixon administration were mixed. Some were so timid that "challenge" was probably a misnomer. Others, mostly in the Senate, were more forceful. Still others, particularly those generated by the Senate Foreign Relations Committee, were defiant.

But the message from Congress was still the same: The Vietnam experience must not be repeated; war powers must be shared; overseas commitments must be reviewed.

Chronology

Of Action

On Foreign Policy

1969

U.S. involvement in Vietnam and the nation's global defense commitments provided the focus of administration and congressional concern in foreign affairs in 1969. These issues were, in turn, closely related to mounting criticism of the defense establishment and a desire to curb military and foreign expenditures.

While discontent with the war in Vietnam gave principal impetus to congressional debate on American military commitments and expenditures, the war in Vietnam did not itself become a subject of prolonged controversy on Capitol Hill until the fall of 1969. Until that time, the attention of Congress had focused on investigating the Pentagon's programs and budget, national priorities and other defense issues.

One result of congressional dissatisfaction with the direction of U.S. foreign policy was an attempt to reassert the legislature's prerogatives in the foreign policy field through the overwhelming passage of a two-year-old "national commitments" resolution (S Res 85) by the Senate. It declared that a national commitment—defined as the use or promise to use armed forces to assist a foreign government—could be made only by affirmative action of both Congress and the executive branch. Although the resolution was simply a declaration by the Senate without the force of law, its passage characterized the tenor of the first session of the 91st Congress.

In a more specific effort to limit the use of U.S. troops abroad, the Senate added a provision to the defense

---

Nixon's Trips Abroad

President Nixon made 11 major trips abroad during his first term as Chief Executive, visiting a total of 23 countries or their possessions. (Dates below are official departure and return days.

1969: Feb. 23-March 2—Belgium, Britain, Germany, Italy, France, the Vatican.

June 7-10—Midway Island, a U.S. possession (meeting with South Vietnamese President Nguyen Van Thieu).

July 22-Aug. 3—Philippines, Indonesia, Thailand, India, Pakistan, Rumania, Britain.

1970: Aug. 20-21—Mexico.

Sept. 27-Oct. 5—Italy, the Mediterranean (to visit the Sixth Fleet), Yugoslavia, Spain, Britain, Ireland.

Nov. 11-12—France (funeral of President Charles de Gaulle).

1971: Dec. 13-14—Azores, a Portuguese possession (meeting with French President Georges Pompidou).

Dec. 20-21—Bermuda, a British colony (meeting with British Prime Minister Edward Heath).

1972: Feb. 17-28—People's Republic of China.

April 13-15—Canada.

May 20-June 1—Austria, Soviet Union, Iran, Poland.

---

appropriations bill prohibiting the use of U.S. ground combat troops in Laos or Thailand.

Congressional action on the foreign aid program was yet another sign of Capitol Hill's emerging sentiment for retrenchment. In late 1969, Congress passed a bill authorizing the lowest amount in the history of the foreign aid program. Congress considered President Nixon's proposals for reforming the aid program, but a dispute over additional military aid funds for South Korea and Taiwan stalled approval of fiscal 1970 appropriations.

A detailed review of U.S. military commitments and their relationship to foreign policy was launched in the fall of 1969 by the Senate Foreign Relations Subcommittee on U.S. Security Agreements and Commitments Abroad. The subcommittee, organized in February with a two-year life span, examined during its first year U.S. commitments to the Philippines, Laos, Thailand and Taiwan, but only a censored transcript of the hearings on the Philippines had been released by the end of 1969.

Congressional attempts to exercise an oversight role in the Spanish base agreement negotiations and to obtain details of a U.S. military contingency plan with Thailand were further evidence of discontent on Capitol Hill.

The troubled Congress reflected the country's weariness with U.S. involvements abroad—a situation which did not go unnoticed by the new occupant of the White House. President Nixon in 1969 formulated a policy aimed at lowering the U.S. military profile abroad. The Nixon Doctrine, which declared the United States would avoid military involvement in remote parts of the world and instead would give economic and military aid for self-determination, became the cornerstone of the administration's foreign policy.

National Commitments Resolution

The Senate June 25, by a roll-call vote of 70-16, passed a "national commitments" resolution (S Res 85), designed to reassert a congressional voice in decisions committing the United States to the defense of foreign nations. As a sense of the Senate resolution, however, it did not have the force of law or require any House action.

Passage of the measure came after five days of debate, during which almost all members spoke in support of the move. Opinion divided concerning the scope of the resolution and the definition of "national commitments," however.

The actual effect of the resolution on the nature of U.S. foreign commitments was limited by the fact that the measure did not alter existing arrangements, such as treaties. Moreover, S Res 85 was only an admonition to the President to consult with Congress; he still was not bound to do so.

However, S Res 85 could have an indirect impact on the direction of U.S. foreign policy by constraining the President to consult Congress before undertaking significant national commitments—particularly in view of the fact that some members had been increasingly critical of what they consider America's over-extension in the world.

As passed, S Res 85 represented a substitute version of the text originally introduced on the floor for debate. The first version was similar to a resolution authored in 1967 by J. W. Fulbright (D Ark.), chairman of the Senate Foreign Relations Committee. Fulbright reintroduced the resolution Feb. 5, 1969, and the Committee reported the measure April 16, with one dissenting vote cast by a new member of the committee, Gale W. McGee (D Wyo.).

During the floor debate, however, several Senators said they considered the Fulbright version, which did not define a "national commitment," to be too ambiguous.

An alternate version was offered June 24 by two members of the committee—Karl E. Mundt (R S.D.) and Thomas J. Dodd (D Conn.). The Mundt-Dodd substitute defined "national commitment," for the purposes of the resolution, as a promise to a foreign government to use the U.S. armed forces in hostilities.

The Mundt-Dodd amendment was considered too restrictive by most supporters of the original resolution and was defeated by a roll-call vote of 36-50.

The final form of the resolution represented a compromise between the two versions and was offered on June 25 by John Sherman Cooper (R Ky.), with the endorsement of Fulbright and Majority Leader Mike Mansfield (D Mont.).

Background. Fulbright's first "national commitments" resolution had been unanimously reported by the Foreign Relations Committee in November 1967, following public hearings in August. No floor action was taken, however, since Democrats feared it would be considered a rebuke to the Johnson administration's Vietnam policy. (*Congress and the Nation, Vol. II, p. 83*)

In introducing the new resolution, Fulbright said that it would not affect the U.S. involvement in Vietnam, nor would it prevent the President from responding "immediately and appropriately" to an attack on the United States. It would, however, if honored, "inhibit the President from making politically significant foreign commitments solely on his executive authority, and initiating

hostilities, limited or unlimited, with any foreign country or organized force without the prior and explicit authorization of Congress." S Res 85 would not, however, be legally binding on the President.

Nixon View. While President Nixon had not vigorously opposed the resolution itself, the State Department had reiterated the objections of the Johnson administration in a March 10 letter to the Foreign Relations Committee.

However, in his June 19 press conference, the President had remarked that it would not be in the best interests of the country "for the President...to have his hands tied in a crisis" by an admonition to consult with the Senate. The President gave two examples of situations which, in his view, had required immediate executive response: President Eisenhower's decision to send troops to Lebanon in 1958 and President Johnson's 1964 decision to send planes to the Congo to evacuate missionaries.

The President's remarks were challenged by two strong supporters of the resolution—Fulbright and Mansfield. Fulbright doubted that there was an emergency crucial enough to justify immediate U.S. intervention in Lebanon, and Mansfield said the Congo action was the very one which had led him to conclude "we were jumping in everywhere without any consultation." Mansfield said he thought Nixon had misinterpreted the intent of the resolution, "which is to strengthen the hand of the President through an accommodation with the Senate."

Dirksen Opposition. The most vigorous opposition to S Res 85 came within the Senate itself and included, in addition to McGee, Minority Leader Everett McKinley Dirksen (R Ill.).

He told reporters June 17 it was "a bundle of mischief" which would represent "an invasion of the constitutional prerogatives of the President."

Dirksen's opposition was indicative of the feeling of some Republicans that the resolution might be viewed as an affront to the Nixon administration. But all Republican members of the Foreign Relations Committee had voted to approve the resolution.

In reporting the bill April 16—with McGee's dissent —the committee said that the executive branch had acquired "virtual supremacy over the making as well as the conduct" of foreign relations and that the division of war powers between the executive and legislative branches specified by the Constitution should be restored.

The committee said that much of the responsibility for the "erosion of legislative authority" since World War II lay in congressional acquiescence to the transfer of power.

The report cited several instances of executive commitment of U.S. troops without congressional authorization as well as several resolutions adopted by Congress authorizing executive discretion in the conduct of foreign affairs. The report warned against a "process of commitment by accretion," which it illustrated by referring to a series of policy statements contributing to the "widely held view that the United States is committed to the defense of Israel even though we have no security treaty with that country."

Finally, the committee criticized the terms of a 1953 executive agreement with Spain (renewed in 1963), and the manner in which it had been negotiated. Noting the committee's concern that the current talks on renewing the agreement might lead to an "upgrading" of the U.S. commitment, the report stated that a military commitment "could only be binding on the United States if it were the result of a treaty approved by the Senate." *(Spanish base agreement, p. 861)*

Supporting the Resolution. The debate on S Res 85 opened June 19 with a plea by Mansfield: "The question is not partisan; it is not even bipartisan," he said. "It is one of all-Senate concern which goes to the nature of the constitutional responsibilities of this body.... What is involved is a view of the responsibilities of the Senate in foreign affairs, now and in the future. What is involved is how obscure national commitments can lead from one step to another and eventually to tens of billions of dollars of cost and the tragic loss of lives in armed conflict."

Terming S Res 85 "one of the most important of its kind that has ever been before the Senate since I have been here," Fulbright stated June 19 that there was "almost no restraint" on the President's power "to commit the country to dangerous and often irreversible courses of action in foreign policy."

After rejecting the Dodd-Mundt substitute resolution June 24, the Senate June 25 accepted a modified version of the Fulbright resolution which contained a more precise definition of "national commitment."

Resolution Text. The following revised version of S Res 85 was approved by the Senate June 25 on a 70-16 roll-call vote:

"Whereas accurate definition of the term 'national commitment' in recent years has become obscured: Now, therefore, be it

"Resolved, that a national commitment for the purpose of this resolution means the use of the armed forces on foreign territory, or a promise to assist a foreign country, government or people by the use of the armed forces or financial resources of the United States, either immediately or upon the happening of certain events, and

"That it is the sense of the Senate that a national commitment by the United States results only from affirmative action taken by the legislative and executive branches of the United States government by means of a treaty, statute, or concurrent resolution of both houses of Congress specifically providing for such commitment."

Commitments Hearings

U.S. global commitments came under close scrutiny in the fall of 1969—just a few months after Senate approval of a "national commitments" resolution. The Senate Foreign Relations Subcommittee on U.S. Security Agreements and Commitments Abroad, organized in February 1969 with a two-year life span, began its "detailed review of the international military commitments of the United States and their relationship to foreign policy."

In 1969, countries studied by the subcommittee, chaired by Stuart Symington (D Mo.), included the Philippines, Laos, Thailand and Taiwan. Only a censored transcript of the hearings on the Philippines had been released by the end of 1969. *(Further details, 1970 chronology, p. 866)*

Philippines. During four days of hearings, Sept. 30-Oct. 3, on U.S. defense activities in the Philippines, the subcommittee heard testimony from six Pentagon and State Department officials. Release of the hearings transcript was held up on request of the State Depart-

---

Thai Contingency Plan

A four-month attempt to obtain a copy of a U.S. military contingency plan with Thailand was capped Nov. 7, 1969, in an unannounced, executive session of the Senate Foreign Relations Committee when Pentagon officials brought the text of the plan for members to examine. *(Commitments hearings, this page)*

The controversy had surfaced July 8, when Committee Chairman J. W. Fulbright (D Ark.) charged that the plan (known as COMUSTAF Plan 1/64), negotiated in 1964-65, went far beyond U.S. treaty commitments to Thailand. Subsequently, the Defense Department had offered to show the plan to members of the panel who were willing to go over to the Pentagon to examine it.

Following the Nov. 7 session, Fulbright said "there were really no surprises" and that he continued to believe the plan "comprised more of a treaty than just a 'contingency plan.'" Frank Church (D Idaho), a member of the committee, said he thought the decision to produce the document before the panel "reaffirms the constitutional authority of the Senate to be fully informed on matters that could vitally affect the country abroad."

---

ment until after the Philippine presidential election Nov. 11, because the administration feared subcommittee revelations could prejudice the election outcome.

As finally made public, the testimony was riddled with deletions, which frequently came at points in the discussion concerning Philippine internal security and high crime rates in areas surrounding U.S. military facilities. At Clark Air Base alone, the subcommittee was told, the Communist-led Huk group stole about $1-million a year in civilian and military goods.

In the course of the Philippine hearings, members of the subcommittee and its staff pursued several lines of questioning. But all sessions stressed one theme: was it necessary to retain such extensive and costly military operations in and commitments to foreign countries; and if not, should they not be scaled down?

Among the major topics pursued by the subcommittee were the following:

• The nature and extent of U.S. defense commitments to the Philippines, as established in treaties, executive agreements and communiques. Had the commitments been broadened by successive administrations, and if so, was the United States receiving reciprocal benefits? As the hearings continued, many members indicated they considered that the reply to the first question was "yes" and to the second, "no."

• The military value of numerous U.S. bases in the country as compared to their dollar cost, possible political cost in exacerbating U.S.-Philippine relations and possible military cost in leading to unwarranted involvements. This issue was also related to "reciprocity" in the U.S.-Philippine defense arrangement. Testimony showed that revising the base agreement to require "prior consultation" had the possible effect of prohibiting Vietnam bombing missions because the Philippine government had indicated its aversion to using the bases for this purpose. If

(Continued on p. 859)

Mid-East Policy: Peace Proposals, Aid to Israel

Continued U.S. support for Israel, diplomatic initiatives designed to bring about an Arab-Israeli peace settlement and strong opposition to an expanded Soviet presence in the region were the principal ingredients of the Nixon administration's Middle East policy.

Four years after he took office, however, the President could point to only partial success. While a fragile, and frequently violated, Arab-Israeli cease-fire had been in effect since August 1970, prospects for achieving a lasting peace settlement in the region appeared as remote as they had been in 1969. Neither the Arabs nor the Israelis had accepted U.S. proposals for an interim agreement, while U.S.-Soviet bilateral talks and four-power negotiations which included France and Britain failed to lay substantial ground for international guarantees of a peace settlement.

Arms Aid. With the Soviet Union providing military assistance to the Arab governments, the United States moved in to fill a vacuum created by the French government's 1967 decision to end its role as principal supplier of armaments to Israel. In the last days of the Johnson administration, the United States announced the sale of 50 Phantom F-4 fighter jets to Israel. The sale had been advocated by Congress, which had added a provision to the fiscal 1969 foreign aid bill directing the President to negotiate the aircraft sale.

The legislative mandate to support Israeli military strength was renewed several times throughout the first term of the Nixon administration. An amendment to a 1970 arms sale bill (PL 91-672) called on the President to seek an arms limitation with the Soviet Union in the Middle East and declared that arms would be made available and credits provided to Israel.

In 1972, Congress added a provision to the defense procurement bill (PL 92-436) that extended, through Dec. 31, 1973, the President's authority to provide direct sales and credit sales of military aircraft and supporting equipment to Israel. The bill also extended a section of the 1970 defense act (PL 91-441) stating, "The Congress views with grave concern the deepening involvement of the Soviet Union in the Middle East and the clear and present danger to world peace resulting from such involvement...."

Following the French government's decision in December 1969 to supply Libya—an ally of Egypt—with 110 Mirage jets, congressional insistence on providing additional combat aircraft to Israel intensified. A further catalyst was provided when the Soviet Union began deploying military personnel, aircraft and surface-to-air missiles in Egypt.

While the President and administration officials offered repeated assurances of continued support for Israel, the President announced in March 1970 that an Israeli request for 125 fighter planes had been turned down on an "interim basis." At the same time, Nixon emphasized that the decision would be "constantly reappraised" if the Arab-Israeli arms balance shifted. Eight months later, on Nov. 18, 1970, the President requested—and Congress subsequently approved—a $500-million authorization to finance credit sales of arms to Israel.

Israel renewed its request for aircraft in late 1971, and, on Feb. 7, 1972, it was confirmed that the United States had agreed to sell Israel 42 Phantom and 90 A-4 Skyhawk jets over the next two to three years. At the same time, it was disclosed March 31, 1972, that the United States had agreed to sell 12 to 24 F-5 jet fighters to Jordan over the next two years on the grounds that U.S. aid would have a stabilizing effect by enabling King Hussein to curtail the Palestine commando threat in his country.

In January 1972, Congress cleared the fiscal 1972 foreign aid bill (PL 92-226) earmarking $50-million in security supporting assistance funds and $300-million in foreign military credit sales funds for Israel.

A major change in the Mid-East military balance occurred in July 1972, when Egypt's President Anwar Sadat requested the departure of Soviet military advisers from his country.

Diplomatic Initiatives. Along with its implicit commitment to support Israeli air superiority, the administration sought to defuse the explosive Middle East situation by moving on the diplomatic front. In a departure from previous U.S. policy, the administration agreed early in 1969 to a series of bilateral talks with the Soviet Union as well as four-power talks which included Britain and France. The talks were carried on sporadically throughout the year, but little was achieved.

The major elements of the U.S. diplomatic position were outlined by Secretary of State William P. Rogers on Dec. 9, 1969. Rogers called on Israel to withdraw from Arab territories occupied in the June 1967 war in return for Arab assurances of a binding commitment to a Middle East peace. He also put on record for the first time more detailed peace proposals made by the United States in October during bilateral talks with the Soviet Union. The proposals were rejected by Israel and scorned by the Arabs.

Meanwhile, the United States continued to support the efforts of United Nations envoy Gunner V. Jarring to mediate a settlement between the Arabs and Israelis. On Jan. 25, 1970, Nixon reaffirmed U.S. support for Israel's insistence on direct peace negotiations with the Arabs. On Jan. 30, he asserted that the United States was "neither pro-Arab nor pro-Israel. We are pro-peace."

The Arab-Israeli conflict was potentially more dangerous than the Indochina war and could result in a direct U.S.-Soviet clash, Nixon warned in a televised interview July 1, 1970. He reiterated that the United States would not allow the military balance to shift against Israel.

The United States had "not excluded the possibility" of participating in a Mid-East peacekeeping role, Rogers said Dec. 23, 1970, but he ruled out any joint U.S.-Soviet force as "totally impractical."

In late 1971 and early 1972, the United States put forward a new proposal for indirect, American-mediated talks between Israel and Egypt on an interim peace settlement that included a troop pullback and reopening of the Suez Canal; but negotiations made little headway by the end of 1972.

(Continued from p. 857)

the bases were not used extensively for direct Vietnam operations, and if American policy was aimed to scale down U.S. presence in Asia to avoid involvement in "future Vietnams," then—queried some members—what was the justification for maintaining such extensive facilities in the Philippines? The answers that emerged were unclear.

U.S. support of a Philippine noncombat force (known as PHILCAG) serving in Vietnam provoked sharp criticism by several senators. The subcommittee heard testimony that the U.S. Military Aid Command in Vietnam had spent about $35-million, the official estimate, since the beginning of 1966 to support the group, compared with about $9-million appropriated by the Philippine government. Although the latter paid the PHILCAG salaries, the United States contributed extensive "extras," including overseas allowances that ranged from $33 a month for a private to $210 for a brigadier general, equipment, and troop replacement costs. (Soon after the hearings, the Philippine government announced that the PHILCAG would gradually be withdrawn due to "lack of funds.")

Testimony concerning Vietnam-related payments to the Philippines revealed that South Korea and Thailand also were receiving U.S. support in return for participation in the Vietnam war. "This seems to me to be the ultimate in corruption for us to make deals like this in pursuit of an illusory policy all designed to prove to the world that we have great support in Vietnam, which we do not have at all," said Fulbright.

Other areas examined by the subcommittee during its Philippines study included U.S. assistance to counter-insurgency operations and the costs of relocating several bases.

Subcommittee Membership. In addition to chairman Symington, members of the subcommittee were: J. W. Fulbright (D Ark.), John J. Sparkman (D Ala.), Mike Mansfield (D Mont.), George D. Aiken (R Vt.), John Sherman Cooper (R Ky.) and Jacob K. Javits (R N.Y.).

Foreign Aid

The U.S. foreign aid program entered a period of re-examination and revision in 1969 amid proposals for reform and growing reluctance by Congress to provide the money to continue assistance to other nations.

In preparation for extensive revamping of the program, the Nixon administration submitted its first foreign aid message, making the lowest appropriations request ($2.6-billion) in the program's history. Following up recommendations submitted in January by a presidential commission, the administration proposed new legislation putting greater reliance on technical assistance and private investment in helping other nations develop.

In anticipation of further reform proposals, Congress approved an unusual two-year (fiscal 1970 and 1971) foreign aid authorization—again the lowest in the program's history—but a Senate dispute over military aid to Nationalist China and South Korea stalled approval of fiscal 1970 appropriations until January of 1970.

Aid Study. When he took office in January, Nixon had before him recommendations by the President's General Advisory Committee on Foreign Assistance Programs "to reorganize and revitalize" assistance to developing nations.

The seven proposals made by the committee were:
• The creation of a "streamlined successor" to the Agency for International Development (AID). The new agency should be authorized to make long-term loans on liberal terms for capital assistance, grants for technical assistance and grants for reconstruction and emergency assistance.
• The expansion of contributions to multinational agencies "as rapidly as their managements can handle additional resources competently."
• The separation of military assistance from development assistance and the transfer of the former to the budget of the Department of Defense.
• The establishment of an overseas investment corporation to take over the present investment guarantee and investment promotion functions of AID and to undertake new initiatives for more rapid expansion of private investment in less developed countries.
• The focusing of U.S. assistance on improvements in agricultural, family planning, scientific and educational, and popular participation programs.
• The restoration of U.S. development assistance to "at least the share of our income reached in 1965," with expansion in the future "as our income and tax revenues rise."
• The prompt study of longer-term innovations.

Nixon Proposals. In his May 28 foreign aid message to Congress, the President proposed new legislation in three principal areas:
• Creation of an Overseas Private Investment Corporation (OPIC) to assume investment promotion functions carried on by AID. The corporation, expected to become self-sustaining over time, would stimulate private investment in developing countries through pre-investment assistance, loans and political-risk insurance against expropriations.
• More emphasis on technical assistance programs providing training, research, institution-building and advisory services.
• Appointment of an AID auditor to keep track of how U.S. assistance funds were used.

Authorization. Congress did not act on Nixon's proposals until December. With fiscal 1970 nearly half over, Congress Dec. 19 cleared a measure (HR 14580—PL 91-175) authorizing foreign economic and military aid appropriations of $1,972,525,000 in fiscal 1970 and $1,936,525,000 in fiscal 1971. The authorization bill, signed by Nixon on Dec. 30, created a number of new programs, including OPIC.

Final congressional approval of HR 14580 came only after conferees dropped House amendments authorizing an additional $104.5-million for military aid to South Korea and Taiwan. In reporting HR 14580 on Nov. 6, the House Foreign Affairs Committee added $50-million for military aid to South Korea that had not been requested by the administration.

During floor action on HR 14580, the House added another $54.5-million in military aid funds for the Nationalist Chinese air force. In all, as passed by the House the bill authorized appropriations of $2,193,900,000 in economic and military assistance for fiscal 1970—a reduction of $436.5-million from the administration's request.

When the bill went to the Senate, the Foreign Relations Committee made major changes. In reporting a substitute version of HR 14580 on Dec. 10, the committee

(Continued on p. 861)

U.S.-Latin America Relations: Dissatisfaction on Both Sides

U.S. relations with Latin America were exacerbated by a number of crises during 1969, including expropriation of certain U.S. oil interests, seizure of fishing vessels and the kidnapping of the U.S. ambassador to Brazil, who was held captive for three days before being released. There was dissatisfaction on both sides. Latin America was struggling to strike a satisfactory balance between a rapidly spreading mood of nationalism and its dependence upon the United States for developmental assistance. Congressional discontent with foreign aid led to cuts in Alliance for Progress funds.

Rockefeller Mission Report. Gov. Nelson A. Rockefeller (R N.Y.) undertook a series of four fact-finding missions to Latin American nations during the spring and summer of 1969. He encountered several anti-American demonstrations and was barred from visiting Peru, Chile and Venezuela. Most of the Rockefeller report—"The Quality of Life in the Americas"—was made public Nov. 10.

Among the 83 specific recommendations made in the far-reaching report:

• Establishing an Institute of Western Hemisphere Affairs which would conduct all government-to-government aid programs under three- to five-year contracts.

• Doubling U.S. trade with Latin America by 1976.

• Assigning greater responsibility to multilateral organizations in planning aid programs.

• Suspending or modifying the Hickenlooper amendment which required a cutoff of aid to nations refusing to negotiate compensatory payment within six months after nationalizing a U.S.-owned firm.

The report also emphasized the Communist threat to the region (the mission had encountered strident anti-U.S. feeling in many countries), and recommended increased military aid, training and sales. The military recommendations of the report were criticized by J. W. Fulbright (D Ark.), chairman of the Senate Foreign Relations Committee, and Frank Church (D Idaho), chairman of the panel's Subcommittee on Western Hemisphere Affairs.

The Rockefeller Report recommendations formed part of the basis for President Nixon's first major Latin American policy address.

Nixon Policy. The address, delivered Oct. 31, called for a new "more mature partnership" between the United States and Latin America. President Nixon offered a number of more specific policy proposals, some of which had been suggested by Latin American governments on June 11, when they had presented the administration with a statement (the "Consensus of Vina del Mar") demanding changes in U.S. aid and trade policies. Major Nixon proposals included: giving increased responsibility for development assistance decisions to multilateral agencies, establishing an under secretary of state for inter-American affairs, a commitment to lead a vigorous effort to reduce non-tariff barriers and to press for a liberal system of generalized tariff preferences for all developing nations and an immediate untying of U.S. aid to purchases in the United States.

Previously (in June), the administration had eliminated the controversial aid policy of "additionality," which required recipient countries to purchase in the United States specific items that they probably would otherwise not buy or would buy elsewhere.

Alliance for Progress. The House Foreign Affairs Subcommittee on Inter-American Affairs held 14 days of hearings on the Alliance for Progress and issued a report calling for new directions in the Alliance. Among its major proposals:

• Reduction of the "strings" on U.S. aid, including the tying of loans to purchases of American goods.

• Increased emphasis on long-term technical assistance, education, agriculture and family planning programs.

• Better coordination of private investment, trade and government aid activities.

• A redirection of programs toward long-range social development.

• A thorough review of U.S. military aid programs.

U.S.-Peruvian Relations. The Senate Foreign Relations Subcommittee on Western Hemisphere Affairs held three days of hearings on U.S. relations with Peru. Relations between the United States and Peru in late 1968 and early 1969 became strained by a series of episodes involving expropriation of the International Petroleum Co. (IPC), a subsidiary of Standard Oil of New Jersey, and the seizure by Peru of U.S. fishing vessels.

The subcommittee also held hearings on U.S. military policies and programs in Latin America. Charles A. Meyer, assistant secretary of state for inter-American affairs, told the subcommittee the U.S. military aid program for Latin America was "sharply diminishing." He said the administration believed there was "very little likelihood of a major external threat to the area in the foreseeable future." He acknowledged that this assessment, combined with a reduced danger of "formidable insurgencies," raised legitimate questions concerning the desirability or need to continue the military program. Nonetheless, Meyer said, the administration considered it necessary to help maintain the counterinsurgency capabilities of Latin military forces.

Subcommittee chairman Church said he was struck by the "bland quality" of the official statements in view of private witnesses' critical testimony, calling for an urgent reappraisal of U.S. policy. Church said he thought the "political costs were all out of proportion with the practical gains" of a military aid program, since the mere existence of such a program prompted many Latin Americans to believe the United States was closely allied with the military sector and was thereby interfering with internal politics.

Fulbright challenged Assistant Defense Secretary G. Warren Nutter's observation that "the progress (in the area's economic development) should not, however, lull us into a sense of complacency." Fulbright said he questioned the degree of progress achieved and wondered whether officials really had a sense of complacency after the anti-American demonstrations which greeted the Rockefeller missions.

(Continued from p. 859)

eliminated the provisions creating OPIC, deleted the additional funds for Nationalist China and South Korea and cut the over-all authorization to $1,967,650,000.

In floor action, the Senate accepted most of the Foreign Relations Committee's changes but restored the authorization for OPIC. The Senate also struck out a committee provision forbidding military aid to Greece.

In conference compromises on HR 14580, the Senate agreed to two-year authorizations for most programs. The House provisions authorizing the extra funds for Taiwan and South Korea were dropped at Senate insistence.

Appropriations. Although the compromise foreign aid authorization bill was cleared, Senate opposition to the extra military assistance funds for Taiwan and South Korea delayed enactment of fiscal 1970 foreign aid appropriations.

Final action on appropriations was stalled Dec. 20, when the Senate in a **key 30-29 roll-call vote** tabled a conference report appropriating an additional $54.5-million for Nationalist China and earmarking $50-million from military grant assistance funds for South Korea.

As approved narrowly by the House in a **key 200-195 roll-call vote**, the appropriations measure (HR 15149) included separate line-item appropriations for military grant aid of $50-million for South Korea and $54.5-million to Nationalist China.

The Senate, which had dropped authorizations for the funds from HR 14580, deleted the $54.5-million for Nationalist China and earmarked the $50-million for Korea from other military assistance funds.

After conferees restored a separate $54.5-million for Taiwan, the Senate adopted the tabling motion, offered by Majority Leader Mike Mansfield (D Mont.), and directed Senate conferees to insist that the extra funds be eliminated.

Final action on fiscal 1970 appropriations thus was delayed until Congress returned for its second session in January 1970. House-Senate conferees then reported a second conference report earmarking $50-million for South Korea but omitting the $54.5-million for China. Both houses accepted the second conference effort.

The second conference report, like the first, provided no fiscal 1970 appropriation for foreign military credit sales. The $275-million administration request was omitted from the bill because separate authorizing legislation had not been cleared.

Treaties

NONPROLIFERATION. The Senate March 13, by a **key roll-call vote of 83-15**, consented to the ratification of the Nuclear Nonproliferation Treaty (Exec H, 90th Congress, 2nd Session). Approval of the landmark treaty, submitted to the Senate in the summer of 1968, came after four days of debate during which the Senate rejected six reservations and understandings.

AIR CRIMES AGREEMENT. The Senate May 13, by a 93-1 roll-call vote, consented to the ratification of the Tokyo Convention of 1963 (Exec L, 90th Congress, 2nd Session) which was submitted to the Senate by former President Johnson on Sept. 25, 1968. The convention, signed by 35 nations at the time of Senate approval, required ratification by 12 nations to bring it into force. It provided that the country in which a civil aircraft was

registered had criminal jurisdiction over offenses committed aboard that aircraft anywhere in the world.

Article II required that the contracting country in which a hijacked aircraft landed "shall permit its passengers and crew to continue their journey as soon as practicable, and shall return the aircraft and its cargo to the persons lawfully entitled to possession." The convention did not provide for the punishment or extradition of hijackers, however.

The United States formally ratified the convention Sept. 5. It was the 12th nation to do so and the convention went into effect Dec. 4. *(1970 implementing legislation, crime chapter)*

NIAGARA FALLS AGREEMENT. The Senate May 13, by a 94-0 roll-call vote, approved an agreement (Exec C, 91st Congress, 1st Session) between the United States and Canada providing for temporary diversion of water from the Niagara river that would stop the flow over the American falls for as long as six months. The agreement required the approval of the Senate because it would authorize a departure from the limitations on minimum flow prescribed in the Niagara River Treaty of 1950. The agreement was signed by the governments of Canada and the United States on March 21.

Spanish Base Agreements

Renewal of the U.S.-Spanish executive agreement on military base rights sparked controversy in the first two years of the Nixon administration. Members of the Senate Foreign Relations Committee voiced concern that the United States had committed itself to the defense of Spain in return for leasing military bases in that country. They questioned whether the value of the bases was worth their price and argued that any commitment to Spain should take the form of a treaty, requiring Senate advice and consent. *(Commitments hearings, p. 867; executive agreements, p. 880)*

Committee members also feared that the U.S. presence alone constituted a *de facto* commitment to support the Franco regime, particularly in light of reports of joint U.S.-Spanish maneuvers to suppress a theoretical internal revolt there. Executive assurances that the U.S. commitment to Spain had not been upgraded by the Nixon administration failed to quiet critics.

Two-year Pact. The United States and Spain June 20, 1969, signed an agreement which would extend U.S. military base rights in the country from Sept. 26, 1968, to Sept. 26, 1970, in return for $50-million worth of military equipment and a loan from the Export-Import Bank for the purchase of an additional $35-million of American equipment.

The two-year extension substituted for an earlier five-year extension proposal which had met with congressional opposition. Senate Foreign Relations Committee Chairman J. W. Fulbright (D Ark.) called the two-year agreement "infinitely better than the early (five-year) proposal," and added, "My hope is that this is a step toward liquidation of the military bases.... I personally think the national interest does not require them."

Five-year Pact. However, the following year, the United States and Spain signed a five-year agreement of friendship and cooperation which entered into force Sept. 26, 1970. The agreement permitted the United States to lease air bases at Torrejon and Saragossa, a standby

(Continued on p. 863)

Foreign Aid Appropriations, Fiscal 1970-73

(thousands of dollars)

	Fiscal 1970		Fiscal 1971		Fiscal 1972		Fiscal 1973	
	Request	Appropriation	Request	Appropriation	Request	Appropriation	Request	Appropriation
ECONOMIC ASSISTANCE								
Worldwide technical assistance	$ 224,500	$ 166,750	$ 183,500	$ 166,750	$ 232,929	$ 160,000	$ 166,408	$ 155,000
Development loans	675,500	300,000	570,000	420,000	400,000	200,000	415,500	250,000
Alliance for Progress								
Technical assistance	116,000	81,500	90,750	82,875	129,745	80,000	88,500	77,500
Development loans	437,500	255,000	337,500	287,500	235,000	150,000	206,500	150,000
International organizations	122,620	105,000	122,620	103,810	141,000	127,000	124,835	105,000
Population control	—	—	—	—	—	125,000	125,000	100,000
American schools and hospitals abroad	12,900	25,900	8,895	12,895	10,175	20,000	15,575	25,500
Indus Basin Development Fund								
Grants	7,530	7,530	5,850	4,925	15,000	10,000	25,000	10,000
Loans	820	—	7,960	6,980	12,000	12,000	18,000	12,000
Contingency fund	40,000	12,500	15,000	15,000	100,000	30,000	30,000	25,000
International narcotics control	—	—	—	—	—	—	42,500	—[2]
Bangladesh refugee relief	—	—	—	—	250,000	200,000	100,000	100,000
Administrative expenses								
Agency for International Development	54,250	51,000	51,125	51,000	60,200	50,000	50,000	50,000
State Department	3,800	3,700	4,200	4,100	4,555	4,221	4,775	4,221
Israeli desalting plant	—	20,000	—	—	—	—	—	—
Total, economic assistance	$1,695,420	$1,028,880	$1,397,400	$1,152,835	$1,590,604	$1,168,221	$1,412,593	$1,064,221
MILITARY ASSISTANCE								
Military grant aid	425,000	350,000	350,000	350,000	705,000	500,000	780,000	550,600
Security supporting aid	514,600	395,000	414,600	414,600	764,614	550,000	844,000	600,000
Military credit sales	275,000	70,000 [1]	272,500	200,000	510,000	400,000	527,000	400,000
Latin American naval training center	—	—	—	—	—	—	—	2,500
Total, military aid	$1,214,600	$ 815,000	$1,037,100	$ 964,600	$1,979,614	$1,450,000	$2,151,000	$1,553,100
OTHER ASSISTANCE								
Peace Corps	101,100	98,450	98,800	90,000	82,200	72,000	88,027	81,000
Cuban refugee assistance (HEW)	87,282	87,282	112,000	112,000	144,103	139,000	161,000	145,000
Refugee and migration assistance (State Department)	5,511	5,511	5,787	5,649	8,690	8,690	8,644	8,500
Soviet refugee assistance	—	—	—	—	—	—	—	50,000
Overseas Private Investment Corp. reserves	—	—	37,500	18,750	25,000	12,500	85,000	12,500
International financial institutions								
Inter-American Development Bank	300,000	300,000	—	—	261,760	211,760	836,760	418,380
International Development Association Bank	160,000	160,000	160,000	160,000	—	—	320,000	320,000
Asian Development Bank	20,000	20,000	20,000	20,000	—	—	100,000	—
World Bank	—	—	—	—	246,100	123,050	—	—
Okinawa administration (Army)	20,651	18,790	6,952	6,476	4,564	4,216		[3]
Total, Other Assistance	$ 694,544	$ 671,243	$ 441,039	$ 412,875	$ 772,417	$ 571,216	$1,599,431	$1,035,380
GRAND TOTAL	$3,604,564	$2,515,123	$2,875,539	$2,530,310	$4,342,635	$3,189,437	$5,163,024	$3,652,701

1 Funded by continuing resolution.
2 Separate line item deleted but funds remain available from other foreign aid programs at $42.5-million annual rate.
3 Okinawa returned to Japan in 1972.

(Continued from p. 861)

air base at Moron and a naval base at Rota. In return, the United States agreed to provide Spain with $60-million in military grants and $120-million in Export-Import Bank loans. Other provisions covered the loan of naval vessels and provision of $15-million for educational, scientific, technical, cultural and agricultural cooperation.

The new agreement specifically stated that "each government will support the defense system of the other and make such contributions as are deemed necessary and appropriate to achieve the greatest possible contingencies." It also called for a U.S.-Spanish defense committee to coordinate "reciprocal defense support."

Although the administration insisted that the agreement represented no commitment by the United States to defend Spain, the pact met with some severe criticism on Capitol Hill.

Senate Action. The Senate Dec. 11, 1970, by voice vote adopted a resolution (S Res 469) stating that the United States held no national commitment to Spain as a result of the Agreement of Friendship and Cooperation signed Aug. 6, 1970, by the United States and Spain. As a "sense of the Senate" resolution, it did not carry the force of law.

The resolution, which was introduced Sept. 22 by Frank Church (D Idaho), was reported unanimously by the Senate Foreign Relations Committee Nov. 23.

The committee report indicated that the resolution was necessary "in view of certain language in the agreement drafted in a deliberately ambiguous form.... To foreclose any possibility that the Agreement of Friendship and Cooperation with Spain might later be given an expanded application, it is incumbent upon us, now, at the outset, to place an authoritative construction upon it."

The committee held an unusual open hearing Aug. 26 on the new executive agreement between the United States and Spain.

U. Alexis Johnson, under secretary of state for political affairs, told the committee that "so far as the military aspects of the agreement are concerned, it is substantially the continuation of the arrangements that existed since 1953." He denied it was a defense commitment.

Peace Corps Authorization

Congress authorized appropriations of $98,450,000 for the Peace Corps in fiscal 1970 (HR 11039—PL 91-99). The administration had requested $101.1-million. Congress had appropriated $102-million for the Peace Corps in fiscal 1969.

Conferees accepted a House-approved amendment eliminating funds for the Volunteers to America program, or "exchange Peace Corps." The administration had proposed using about $100,000 of Peace Corps funds to bring foreign volunteers to America for training through work in service projects. Wayne L. Hays (D Ohio), sponsor of the amendment, said he opposed the program because it would overlap with the cultural exchange activities of the State Department. Administration of the Volunteers to America program had already been transferred from the State Department to the Peace Corps, which still could continue to operate the program under executive authority with funds from other sources.

HR 11039 also authorized up to $300,000 in fiscal 1970 in contributions to an international register of volunteers to encourage development of international service programs.

Appropriation. Congress set Peace Corps funds for fiscal 1970 at $98,450,000, as part of the foreign aid package which cleared in January 1970. *(Fiscal 1970 foreign aid bill, p. 860)*

Immigration Act

Congress cleared for the President Nov. 20 a bill (HR 3666—PL 91-136) amending Section 336(c) of the Immigration and Nationality Act to eliminate the prohibition which barred petitioners from taking the final oath and acquiring citizenship within 60 days preceding general elections. In its report on HR 3666, the Senate Judiciary Committee noted, "This prohibition was added to the naturalization laws many years ago at a time when election frauds were being committed by persons who were alleged to seek out aliens for the purpose of procuring their votes...the aliens were rushed through the naturalization process on election day in order to vote as directed by political bosses. The five-year residence requirement and other safeguards since written into the Immigration Act...now effectively prevent such abuses."

Recognition of Governments

The Senate Sept. 25 by a roll-call vote of 77-3 passed a resolution (S Res 205) declaring that "when the United States recognizes a foreign government and exchanges diplomatic representatives with it, this does not of itself imply that the United States approves of the form, ideology, or policy of that foreign government."

The resolution was a simple "sense of the Senate" declaration which required no further action by Congress and did not have the force of law. The resolution, however, was supported by the Department of State. It was intended to clarify existing U.S. recognition policy and spell out the Senate's interpretation of the implications of recognition.

State Department Appropriations

Congress appropriated $404,132,100 for the State Department in fiscal 1970, as part of a $2,550,247,700 appropriation for the Departments of State, Justice and Commerce, the Judiciary and 13 other government agencies (HR 12964—PL 91-153). The administration had requested $408,381,000 for State Department funding.

The bill also included $9,500,000 for the Arms Control and Disarmament Agency (the amount requested by the administration) and $174,150,000 for the U.S. Information Agency (the administration had requested $177,650,-000).

A controversial non-germane amendment added by the Senate had been deleted in conference. The amendment would have expressed the "sense-of-the-Senate" that no agreement which the President might make to change the status of a territory which was part of the World War II peace treaty with Japan could take effect without the advice and consent of the Senate. The amendment was specifically concerned with the future status of Okinawa which the Japanese wished restored to their jurisdiction.

The amendment, offered by Harry F. Byrd Jr. (D Va.), was approved by the Senate Nov. 5 by a roll-call vote of 63-14, but conferees deleted it from the final version of HR 12964 on the grounds that such language should be part of a legislative measure, rather than an appropriations bill.

1970

Signs of an expanded U.S. role in Indochina heightened congressional concern over executive supremacy in foreign affairs and cast some doubt on the meaning of the Nixon Doctrine in 1970.

An outcry was raised among war critics on Capitol Hill and around the country when U.S. troops were sent into Cambodia in April 1970 to attack Communist sanctuaries along the Cambodian border with South Vietnam. The Senate reacted by attaching a restrictive amendment to the foreign military sales bill. The amendment, which prohibited the introduction of U.S. ground combat forces in Cambodia, was dropped from the military sales bill but was included in a supplemental foreign aid appropriations bill which cleared Congress in December. *(Details, p. 868)*

The Cambodian incursion precipitated the introduction of a number of bills and resolutions on the President's war-making powers—one of which was passed by the House. The resolution directed the President to consult "whenever feasible" with Congress before committing U.S. troops and to report to Congress on such a commitment when he had not received prior authorization. The Senate took no action on the measure.

Congressional concern over U.S. activities abroad was intensified by revelations from the Senate Foreign Relations Subcommittee on U.S. Security Agreements and Commitments Abroad, which concluded its two-year inquiry in 1970. The hearings—which in 1970 delved into U.S. commitments to Japan-Okinawa, Korea, Greece-Turkey, Ethiopia, Morocco-Libya, Spain and the North Atlantic Treaty Organization—uncovered a considerable amount of information previously unknown.

The subcommittee warned that the United States had assumed "creeping commitments" which were being blurred by excessive executive secrecy. The final report recommended a greater oversight role for Congress.

Release of the transcript of 1969 hearings on Laos came only ten days before the United States entered Cambodia and served to further congressional discontent. The transcript, although riddled with the censors' deletions, provided the first detailed official account of the growth of U.S. military involvement in Laos since 1962. In particular, the testimony made public the key role the United States had played in the war in northern Laos, in addition to the more generally known U.S. bombing of the Ho Chi Minh trail in southeast Laos.

Congress in 1970 repealed the Gulf of Tonkin resolution; the Senate did this twice. The resolution, passed in 1964, was widely considered as having given congressional approval to the Johnson administration's escalation of U.S. involvement in Vietnam. Its repeal was largely symbolic since President Nixon, basing his conduct of the war on his prerogatives as Commander-in-Chief, did not oppose the repeal.

Yet another attempt at asserting some influence on foreign policy could be seen in the Senate passage of a resolution stating that the five-year agreement of friendship and cooperation signed with Spain in 1970 did not constitute a national commitment to Spain.

The foreign aid program became a hostage of war critics in 1970. After clearing fiscal 1970 foreign aid funding in January—halfway through the fiscal year—Congress encountered a deadlock over amendments to fiscal 1971 appropriations which delayed action until the end of the year. The amendments sought to restrict U.S. involvement in Cambodia.

War Powers

U.S. entry into Cambodia in 1970 prompted a reexamination of executive powers. In November, the House passed by a 288-39 roll-call vote a joint resolution (H J Res 1355) defining the war-making powers of the President. The Senate took no action on the measure and it died at the end of the session.

The resolution reaffirmed the right of Congress to declare war and stated the sense of Congress that the President should consult with Congress "whenever feasible" before sending U.S. troops into conflict. It also directed the President to report to Congress whenever he committed troops into combat, sent combat-ready troops into foreign territory or enlarged the number of U.S. troops in another nation "without specific prior authorization by Congress."

Debate. During consideration of the resolution, Clement J. Zablocki (D Wis.), floor manager of H J Res 1355, said the bill represented a reassertion of congressional responsibility in the matter of war-making and was not being put forward as a reflection of criticism of or as a reprisal against the actions of Presidents, past or present.

Zablocki said the provision requiring Presidents to report to the Congress was not unusual as "fully 100 reporting requirements have been imposed in the past on the executive branch by Congress as part of foreign affairs and national security affairs legislation." These reports should be an effective way of keeping Congress informed and "may lead to increased harmony and cooperation between Congress and the President in national security matters," he said.

Jonathan B. Bingham (D N.Y.), who voted against the measure, said he opposed the provision declaring that it is the sense of Congress that whenever feasible the President consult with the Congress before involving the armed forces of the United States in armed conflict. The wording, he said "may be construed by the President in such a way as to justify a failure to consult with the Congress before embarking on some military adventure."

Roman C. Pucinski (D Ill.) said: "The fact of the matter is that it (the resolution) does not mean very much. We have not done much. This is a good resolution, an expression of some concern," but the Constitution generally has been interpreted differently by the President, Congress and the Supreme Court.

Provisions. As passed, H J Res 1355:

● Stated that the Congress reaffirms its power under the Constitution to declare war but recognizes that the President in certain "extraordinary and emergency circumstances" has the authority to defend the United

(Continued on p. 866)

State of the World: Four Presidential Reports

Early in his first administration, President Nixon called for a lowering of the U.S. profile abroad through a greater sharing of responsibilities and increased self-reliance by U.S. allies. The so-called "Nixon Doctrine" became the cornerstone of the administration's foreign policy. *(Nixon Doctrine, p. 869)*

Formal enunciation of the doctrine came in President Nixon's first foreign policy message to Congress and remained the recurring theme of the annual messages during his first administration.

The practice of submitting a foreign policy report —which has become known as the "state of the world" message—was inaugurated by President Nixon in February 1970. The first report and its succeeding ones outlined the events of the previous year, objectives for the current year and the administration's basic foreign policy philosophy.

1970

The Nixon Doctrine dominated the first foreign policy message, submitted to Congress Feb. 18, 1970, and entitled "United States Foreign Policy for the 1970s: A New Strategy for Peace." The President described the report as a "monumental task," the "most comprehensive statement on United States foreign policy ever made in this century." It marked, he said, a "watershed" in U.S. foreign policy out of the cold war era.

Stressing the beginning of a new era, the report maintained that U.S. relations with allies would change from one of "predominance" to one of "partnership." The United States would aid in the defense of other allied and friendly nations, would maintain its treaty commitments but would not assume a primary responsibility as a world policeman.

The President outlined the three principles which were to guide U.S. foreign policy: partnership with allies, strength with regard to potential enemies and a willingness to negotiate with the Communist powers.

1971

Worldwide application of the Nixon Doctrine remained a keynote of administration policy, according to the President's second annual foreign policy message, "United States Foreign Policy for the 1970s: Building for Peace," submitted to Congress Feb. 25, 1971. The United States would continue to encourage greater participation by all countries in their own development and defense.

The Nixon Doctrine sought to reflect the need for continuity as well as the mandate for change, the President said. "There are two concurrent challenges: to carry out our new policy so as to maintain confidence abroad; to define our new policy to the American people and to elicit their support."

Partnership, strength and negotiation—major themes in the first special message on foreign policy— were repeated. "It will take many years to shape the new American role," the President stated. "The transition from the past is under way but far from completed. During this period the task of maintaining a balance abroad and at home will test the capacity of American leadership and the understanding of the American people."

1972

"1971 was the watershed year," according to the President's third annual foreign policy report. The document, entitled "United States Foreign Policy for the 1970s: The Emerging Structure of Peace," was submitted to Congress Feb. 9, 1972.

Among the "changes in our foreign policy of historic scope and significance" cited in the report were rapprochement with the People's Republic of China, initiation of a new relationship with the Soviet Union, a foundation for improved relations with Europe and Japan, and creation of a new environment for the world's monetary and trade activities.

The "breakthrough with our adversaries" dominated the report. President Nixon, looking forward to a February 1972 visit to Peking, said that although the rapprochement with China was "fragile," it "could have greater significance for future generations than any other measure we have taken this year."

The President cautioned that some Soviet activities—its weapons deployment, expanded naval operations, arms policy in the Middle East and behavior during the India-Pakistan crisis—raised serious questions as to the Soviet Union's fundamental commitment to a stable international system. Nevertheless, he cited a series of concrete agreements reached in 1971 as providing "serious grounds for believing that a fundamental improvement in the U.S.-Soviet relationship may be possible."

1973

The fourth annual foreign policy report—"United States Foreign Policy for the 1970s: Shaping a Durable Peace"—was written against a backdrop of detente with the Soviet Union and the People's Republic of China, as well as the conclusion of a cease-fire agreement in Vietnam. Although admitting that peace in Indochina was "not yet solid or comprehensive," the President called the cease-fire "the most satisfying development of this past year." The report was submitted to Congress May 3, 1973.

The administration appeared prepared to turn to new challenges in foreign policy. Relations with traditional allies in Western Europe, Japan and Latin America were to have high priority in 1973.

The report indicated that monetary and trade questions would dominate the foreign policy picture in 1973—the year the administration had proclaimed to be the "year of Europe." Hard bargaining with U.S. allies —with the United States linking economic, military and political issues—appeared likely.

States and its citizens without specific prior authorization by the Congress.

• Declared that it is the sense of Congress that whenever feasible the President should seek appropriate consultation with the Congress before involving U.S. armed forces in armed conflict.

• Stated that such consultation should continue periodically during such conflict.

• Stated that in any case in which the President without prior authorization by Congress commits U.S. military forces to armed conflict or commits military forces equipped for combat to foreign territory or substantially enlarges military forces already located in another nation, the President shall promptly report to the Congress in writing setting forth:

1. The circumstances necessitating his action.

2. The authority—constitutional, legislative and treaty—under which he took such action.

3. His reasons for not seeking prior congressional consultation.

4. The estimated scope of activities.

5. Such other information as the "President may deem useful to the Congress in the fulfillment of its constitutional responsibilities with respect to committing the nation to war and to the use of United States armed forces abroad."

• Stated that "Nothing in this joint resolution is intended to alter the constitutional authority of the Congress or of the President, or the provisions of existing treaties."

Commitments Hearings

The special Senate Foreign Relations Subcommittee on U.S. Security Agreements and Commitments Abroad concluded in 1970 its inquiry into U.S. military activities overseas. Some 2,500 pages of hearings had been released by early 1971. *(1969 chronology, p. 857)*

The subcommittee, chaired by Stuart Symington (D Mo.), was created in January 1969 for the duration of the 91st Congress. Its establishment coincided with Senate consideration of S Res 85, defining national commitments, and spanned a period during which Congress became increasingly preoccupied with U.S. foreign military involvements. It was reestablished in the 92nd Congress.

During its hearings and in releasing its reports, the subcommittee was critical of the secrecy surrounding U.S. commitments and bases abroad. In the course of its investigations, the subcommittee uncovered a considerable amount of information which previously had been unknown about overseas military activities.

Of particular concern to the subcommittee were the political arrangements and obligations of the United States relative to placement of nuclear weapons abroad. The subcommittee said it had difficulty obtaining information about the disposition of nuclear weapons overseas. It said that secrecy veiled not only U.S. activities abroad but also blurred the extent of defense commitments.

Asked if the subcommittee had concluded that the United States was overcommitted to foreign nations, Symington said the report indicated "not that we were overcommitted, but just that we did not know how we were committed. In some cases, I think we are."

The report criticized the executive branch and various government agencies for denying disclosure of information the subcommittee deemed necessary for intelligent evaluation of foreign policy. "Accordingly," it said, "the public was kept ill informed."

In its final report Dec. 21 the subcommittee said the United States had assumed "creeping commitments" that threatened to trap the nation in global responsibilities.

"The basic thrust of the report is the people's right to know—what are the facts?" Symington told a news conference on Dec. 18.

The report, which summarized a two-year investigation and the findings of 2,500 pages of hearings on the Philippines, Laos, Thailand, Taiwan, Japan-Okinawa, Korea, Greece-Turkey, Ethiopia, Morocco-Libya, NATO and Spain, questioned the implications of U.S. military presence abroad and stressed the need for frequent re-evaluation of U.S. defense needs and interests.

"Any lasting impact of this report will not be made by what it says in terms of current foreign policy, but rather in the continuation of active oversight of foreign military policy through on-the-scene inquiry and hearings by the proper committees of the Congress," the report said.

Proposals. Recommendations in the report focused upon "continuing, objective review of all aspects of military and military-related programs and activities overseas." The subcommittee report placed this responsibility on the President and on Congress:

"Specifically, the Congress should undertake, on some regular schedule, inquiries in areas of foreign policy interest, particularly including the political aspects of military activities, such inquiries to be based on facts ascertained at first hand overseas."

The report recommended regularly scheduled hearings that would include testimony from government and nongovernment witnesses, and that appropriate committees of the Congress would receive full information on security agreements and on foreign negotiations.

"Finally, and perhaps, most important," the subcommittee said, "the Congress should take a realistic look at the authority of the President to station troops abroad and establish bases in foreign countries. Notwithstanding the general authority which is contained in treaties and in congressionally authorized programs, no U.S. forces should be stationed abroad or bases established abroad without specific prior authority of the Congress in each case. The political importance of such programs as joint military exercises and joint planning should be recognized, and these programs should be reviewed for their political as well as their military impact."

COUNTRIES STUDIED

The subcommittee reported on commitments in the following countries:

The Philippines. Development of the Philippine-U.S. Mutual Defense Treaty is an example of "creeping commitment" due to expansion of the original relationship by executive action without the consent of Congress. *(Details, p. 857)*

The 1951 treaty with the Philippines provided for each party to respond to an attack on the other's territory in the Pacific area "in accordance with its constitutional process." The subcommittee report maintained that a note sent by Secretary of State John Foster Dulles to the Philippine Foreign Secretary in 1954 initiated the concept of "instantaneous response" by the executive branch rather than moving through congressional channels.

Laos. Congress did not inquire into nor was it kept informed of U.S. military activities in and over Laos, and initial efforts to get the facts "were either blocked, or the responses were misleading." *(Details, p. 908)*

"The United States, without any treaty commitment, nevertheless is deeply involved in Laos. We provide Laos with three-quarters of its foreign exchange needs plus food, AID advisers at all levels of government, public road experts, even personnel to run the Lao information agency. All this expense, along with direct and indirect military assistance, adds up each year to far more than the Laotian $150-million gross national product."

Thailand. U.S. relations with Thailand had increased as the United States sought to use Thailand to meet threats to Laos and to South Vietnam. *(Details, p. 908)*

Formal agreements between the United States and Thailand included the 1954 SEATO agreement, which established a multilateral defense commitment; the 1962 Rusk-Thanat communique, which turned SEATO into a bilateral United States-Thai defense agreement; and the 1965 United States-Thai contingency plan which provided the military relationship implied in the 1962 agreement.

"With each step, the United States increased both its military presence and its military activities in Thailand.

"After Thai approval of U.S. use of Thai bases for bombing in Laos and Vietnam, insurgent elements surfaced in Thailand. In turn, the United States increased its counterinsurgency activities. Thailand, with its small, isolated insurgent forces, became the testing ground for programs which later were to be employed in Vietnam."

Taiwan. Information provided by the subcommittee's hearings demonstrated that U.S. policy toward Nationalist China was in a period of transition, marked by several apparent inconsistencies. For example, although U.S. military and economic assistance was being phased out, there seemed to be a possibility that the U.S. commitment to Taiwan might be indirectly—and perhaps unintentionally—upgraded by the relocation of U.S. military facilities to Taiwan. And although the administration had stated its intention of trying to improve relations with Peking, both the United States and Taiwan were simultaneously engaging in activities which could appear provocative to the Communist mainland regime.

The United States has never expressed "public disapproval of provocative action by the Nationalist Chinese" against the Communist mainland, the subcommittee reported.

"Despite official denials in the subcommittee hearings, the series of unconventional warfare joint exercises held between U.S. and Nationalist special forces over the past years had the scenario of 'return to the mainland.' This could only give the appearance of tacit approval by the United States of such a military goal, and it must be assumed such exercises were known by the Peking government.

"Through the use of excess military equipment and defense repair programs, the Departments of State and Defense in recent years have been able to keep the military assistance provided the Nationalist government at a high level. During this period, however, the Congress believed that such aid was being diminished by means of reductions in the regular military assistance program which it had approved."

Japan-Okinawa. Large numbers of military bases in Japan and Okinawa resulted in a relationship "more akin to that of victor and vanquished" and fostered increasing anti-American feeling.

Korea. Although the United States is in the process of removing American troops from South Korea, military assistance funds to Korea under a 1966 agreement pay for commercial consumables and not for new weapons which the Koreans will need. "This 1966 agreement means, therefore, that Congress will be called upon to appropriate additional funds for new equipment for the Korean army, despite the fact Congress knew nothing about the agreement at the time it was made and learned about it later only with great difficulty."

Ethiopia. "Neither the Congress nor the public was informed about the details of the commitment to Ethiopia made in 1960. The facts were only disclosed some ten years later by the investigation of this subcommittee.

"Involved in this agreement was not only a commitment to support a 40,000-man Ethiopian Army, but also a pledge for continued military assistance (running $12-million a year; $147-million through 1970); economic assistance ($97.2-million in loans; $131.5-million in grants through the fiscal year 1969); and what is even more significant, a statement reaffirming the United States' 'continuing interest in the security of Ethiopia and its opposition to any activities threatening the territorial integrity of Ethiopia.' "

U.S.-Ethiopia relations evolved primarily from a "declared need" for Kagnew Station, a communications base in northern Ethiopia. Arab-supported Eritrean insurgents operating around the base have further complicated U.S. involvement there.

NATO. Although the report did not question the validity of U.S. commitment to NATO, it suggested reviewing the role of the U.S. military in Europe and the possibility of withdrawal of some U.S. forces.

Spain. Under the 1963 defense agreement between Spain and the United States—which was extended Aug. 6, 1970—the United States was permitted use of air bases at Torregon and Zaragosa, a Polaris naval base at Rota and a standby air base at Moron. In return, the Spanish government was granted between $300-million and $400-million in grants, loans and improvements to be paid over the next five years.

The subcommittee's investigations of the negotiations between Spain and the United States hinged on its concern with defense commitments that are created by executive agreements without the advice or consent of Congress.

The subcommittee questioned the continued validity of an outside military threat to Spain, the necessity for continued use of the Spanish bases when apparently in some cases their functions were duplicated by other overseas bases, and the nature of U.S. commitments to Spain.

"Spain is a good example of a commitment which has not only creeped but which has also in the process generated new justifications as old ones became obsolete.

"The Spanish base agreements, which have never been submitted to the Senate as treaties, have had secret annexes which limit the manner in which the bases can be used. Prior to the subcommittee inquiry, these limitations were not brought to the attention of the proper committees of the Congress, let alone the American people."

During the inquiry, the subcommittee discovered that since 1967 the United States had participated in joint military exercises that were directed toward the possibility of anti-government guerilla forces emerging in northern Spain. After the subcommittee raised political questions inherent in such an exercise, all joint exercises were reviewed by the State Department, USIA and the White House.

Deployment of Tactical Nuclear Weapons. The subcommittee found it had been many years since political implications of nuclear weapons deployment had been considered and called for a thorough congressional inquiry.

"The stationing of nuclear weapons in foreign countries represents a special kind of commitment between the United States and the host country. In almost every one of these countries a veil of secrecy hides the presence of such weapons. Nowhere is this veil stronger than in the United States.

"Most people here are unaware of the fact that United States tactical nuclear warheads have been and are stationed in countries all around the world, a pattern of deployment which results in arousing deep concern in both the Soviet Union and Communist China....

"The placement of these weapons abroad was undertaken at a time when relationships between the super powers was one of inequality; when the vast preponderance of nuclear power rested with the United States. In the future, however, that situation promises to be far different, if that is not already the case.

"Should the Soviet Union or Communist China seek parity in the placement of tactical nuclear weapons...we could face an international crisis comparable to the Cuban missile crisis of 1962. The United States went to the brink of nuclear war when faced with the possibility that the Soviet Union was putting missiles in a country 90 miles from the United States. We must assume that the Soviets, as they view our placement of tactical nuclear weapons in countries far closer to their borders than Cuba is to ours, will seek to break out of the nuclear ring that has been drawn around them."

Intelligence Activities Abroad. A committee composed of representatives of the Armed Services, Foreign Relations and Appropriations committees should begin an in-depth and continuing study of intelligence activities, the subcommittee stated.

● "Costly and unnecessary duplication exists among the various U.S. intelligence agencies operating abroad. In at least one situation, two of our agencies were working with competing local agencies of a foreign country.

● "As is true of other more visible political-military activities abroad, there appears to be no objective inter-agency oversight in the executive branch of overseas intelligence activities....

● "In the past the Senate Foreign Relations Committee has been totally unaware of many intelligence activities which had profound foreign policy implications."

Secrecy. The "executive branch consistently over-classified information relating to foreign policy that should be a matter of public record." Contributing to the process of "creeping commitments," the report found that "one secret agreement or activity led to another, until the involvement of the United States was raised to a

level of magnitude far greater than that originally intended."

The executive branch sought by the use of classification to prevent discussion in a closed session of the Foreign Relations Committee of the placement of tactical nuclear weapons abroad. Although the subcommittee later acquired the information through the Joint Atomic Energy Committee and from the executive branch, it recommended that basic legislation regarding classification be reviewed.

Foreign Aid

Although regular fiscal 1971 foreign aid funds had been authorized in the two-year authorization bill passed in 1969, it took Congress until the end of 1970 to complete action on fiscal 1971 appropriations for the aid program.

The delay was caused by Senate efforts to restrict U.S. involvement in Cambodia in the wake of the President's April 30 announcement that American forces had joined South Vietnamese troops in an attack on Communist border sanctuaries in that nation.

The point of dispute was the President's request for appropriations of $272.5-million for foreign military credit sales. Authorization of a continued military sales program—considered separately from programs authorized for two years in the 1969 legislation—was delayed six months by a House-Senate deadlock over Cambodia restrictions.

The arms sales authorization bill (HR 15628) was kept in conference from June 30 to Dec. 31 by House conferees' refusal to accept a Senate amendment—drawn up by John Sherman Cooper (R Ky.) and Frank Church (D Idaho)—barring funds for the support and maintenance of U.S. ground combat forces and advisers in Cambodia.

That conference deadlock was broken only when the House accepted the Cooper-Church restriction as an amendment to separate legislation (HR 19911) authorizing the President's request for $550-million in supplemental foreign aid funds.

Approval of the conference report on HR 19911 on Dec. 22 cleared the way for final congressional action on three foreign aid bills: the supplemental appropriations on Dec. 28 and the military sales authorization and regular foreign aid appropriations on Dec. 31.

Military Sales. The Cooper-Church amendment debate obscured other issues raised by legislation extending the arms sales programs, a source of controversy during the Johnson administration. *(Congress and the Nation Vol. II, p. 85-86, 107-110)*

In 1969, no action was taken on the administration's request for a $275-million appropriation for the arms sales program. Funding was continued in fiscal 1970 through a series of continuing resolutions.

In considering further arms sales funding in 1970, Congress made clear that it would insist on limits to the amount of military hardware the United States could sell to developing nations.

As passed by the House, for example, HR 15628 set permanent limits on annual arms sales to Latin America ($75-million) and Africa ($40-million), broadened an existing prohibition on sales to dictators and urged the President to initiate discussions with other arms-supplying nations to curtail the armaments trade.

Nixon Doctrine: 'More Realistic American Role'

"...the United States will participate in the defense and development of allies and friends, but... America cannot—and will not—conceive all *the plans, design* all *the programs, execute* all *the decisions and undertake* all *the defense of the free nations of the world."*

The Vietnam war—and its lessons—dominated the first four years of the Nixon administration. Congressional attempts to reassert an influence on foreign policy, to limit the President's war powers and to exercise a veto on further commitments abroad were symptomatic of a "no-more-Vietnams" sentiment which had begun to permeate the country.

The White House recognized the need to reduce the U.S. profile abroad. Early in the first Nixon administration, the so-called "Nixon Doctrine," as stated above in the President's February 1970 foreign policy message to Congress, was formulated.

Many observers considered the administration's Vietnamization program as the first test of the viability of the policy aimed at a low-level U.S. profile in Asia. The Vietnamization strategy, whereby the United States would withdraw as it turned over its combat role to the South Vietnamese troops, was at the core of the administration's policy for extracting the United States from the Indochina conflict.

The agreement between the United States and Japan for the return of Okinawa to Japan by 1972 was seen as another early application of the Nixon Doctrine's thesis of a low-level military posture.

Long-range prospects for the success of the Nixon Doctrine remained questionable because its foundation —foreign aid—was shaky. Throughout the first Nixon administration, the foreign assistance program—particularly military aid—came under ever increasing fire on Capitol Hill.

Background. During 1969, Mr. Nixon frequently repeated his desire to mute the U.S. military presence in Asia and to push back the moment when the United States felt obliged to intervene militarily. A statement by the President in Guam July 25, 1969, was widely heralded as a first step in a reassessment of U.S. policy in order to avoid future Vietnams. The President said that future U.S. policy in Asia would aim to avoid military intervention which could involve the country in situations like Vietnam, would encourage Asian nations to assume greater defense responsibilities and would place increasing emphasis on the concept of self-help and the creation of a partnership between the United States and Asian nations for the region's economic development. During his July Asian trip, however, the President emphasized that as long as turmoil in Asia posed a significant threat to world peace, the United States would continue to play a major (though no longer front-line) role there and would abide by its existing defense arrangements (though they might be interpreted more strictly).

Mr. Nixon restated the self-help concept when South Korean President Chung Hee Park visited the United States Aug. 21-22.

Understanding of the doctrine was complicated by the manner in which the President had presented it: reporters were forbidden to quote him directly and the administration's interpretation of the doctrine remained unclear.

However, in a Nov. 3, 1969, address on Vietnam, the President put on record the Nixon Doctrine. The three key principles as explained by the President were:

- "The United States will keep all of its treaty commitments."
- "We shall provide a shield if a nuclear power threatens the freedom of a nation allied with us or of a nation whose survival we consider vital to our security."
- "In cases involving other types of aggression, we shall furnish military and economic assistance when requested in accordance with our treaty commitments. But we shall look to the nation directly threatened to assume the primary responsibility of providing the manpower for its defense."

Message to Congress. A more formal statement of the doctrine's thesis was given in the President's Feb. 18, 1970, message to Congress entitled "United States Foreign Policy for the 1970s: A New Strategy for Peace." In the document, widely described as a "state of the world" message, President Nixon called for partnership with U.S. allies and pledged U.S. participation in— rather than primary responsibility for—their defense and development.

"A more responsible participation by our foreign friends in their own defense and progress means a more effective common effort toward the goals we all seek. Peace in the world will continue to require us to maintain our commitments—and we will," the President stated in his report. "But a more balanced and realistic American role in the world is essential if American commitments are to be sustained over the long pull."

Throughout the first four years of the Nixon administration, the President reaffirmed his commitment to the "Nixon Doctrine" of shared responsibilities, particularly in the annual "state of the world" messages to Congress. *(Box, p. 865)*

The House-passed bill authorized the full administration requests of $275-million for fiscal 1970 arms sales and $272.5-million for each of fiscal 1971 and fiscal 1972.

The Senate, however, accepted a Foreign Relations Committee recommendation in cutting the President's request to $250-million for each of fiscal 1970 and fiscal 1971 and omitting authorization for fiscal 1972.

As passed by the Senate, moreover, the bill included additional arms sales restrictions and a floor amendment repealing the 1964 Gulf of Tonkin resolution used by President Johnson to justify intervention in the Vietnam war.

As cleared for the President on Dec. 31, the conference version of HR 15628 authorized $250-million for each of fiscal 1970 and fiscal 1971 and included both House and Senate restrictive amendments, as well as the Tonkin Gulf resolution repeal.

Regular Appropriations. With House approval of the Senate's Cooper-Church amendment as part of the supplemental foreign aid authorization, action proceeded on the previously authorized regular foreign aid appropriations measure. Final action, however, required a second conference and floor maneuvering on the arms sales appropriation.

As passed by the House on June 4, the regular appropriations bill (HR 17867) provided $2,220,961,000 for foreign aid and related programs in fiscal 1971, including the full $272.5-million requested for military credit sales. In adopting the rule governing floor action on HR 17867, the House waived points of order against consideration of military sales appropriations before authorizing legislation had been enacted.

With the authorizing legislation stalled in conference over the Cooper-Church provision, however, the Senate deleted the $272.5-million arms sales appropriations from HR 17867.

In conference, Senate conferees agreed to include $200-million for arms sales, but the Senate Dec. 22 by voice vote rejected the conference report in protest against the arms sales funds.

The House agreed to another conference the same day, and a second conference report was filed Dec. 29. In their second report, the conferees deleted the $200-million for arms sales and reported the provision in disagreement.

With the arms sales authorization bill nearing final action, the Senate Dec. 30 adopted the second conference report. By a 60-12 roll call, the Senate then approved the $200-million for arms sales after adding language specifying that none of that amount could be spent until authorizing legislation had been enacted.

The House completed congressional action on the regular appropriations bill Dec. 31 by a voice vote accepting the Senate's qualifying language to the arms sales appropriation.

Supplemental Appropriations. With the arms sale and regular appropriations bills still under consideration, President Nixon Nov. 18 asked Congress for a supplemental $1,035,000,000 appropriation for additional military and economic assistance.

Nixon's request included $500-million for military credit sales for Israel, $340-million for grant military assistance and $195-million for defense-related economic supporting assistance to U.S. allies.

The President's requests included $65-million for the Vietnamization program in South Vietnam, $85-million in grant aid and $70-million in economic aid for Cambodia, $100-million to replace economic and military aid funds earlier transferred to Cambodia from other programs, $150-million in grant aid to South Korea and other funds for Jordan, Lebanon, Indonesia and East Pakistan flood relief.

The $500-million request for credit sales to Israel had been authorized in 1969 as part of a defense procurement authorization bill.

In considering authorizations for the rest of Nixon's request, the House Foreign Affairs Committee rejected an amendment requiring that aid to Cambodia be used only to further the withdrawal of U.S. troops from South Vietnam. The House Dec. 9 passed legislation (HR 19911)

authorizing $550-million in supplementary foreign aid appropriations.

In the Senate, the Foreign Relations Committee amended HR 19911 with a variant of the Cooper-Church amendment. On the floor, the Senate cut the military aid authorization for South Korea by $5.8-million.

In conference, the South Korean funds were restored, but House conferees accepted the Cooper-Church amendment, breaking the foreign aid logjam that followed the Cambodia invasion.

Following enactment of the authorizing legislation, on Dec. 22, Congress Dec. 28 cleared a $1.9-billion fiscal 1971 supplemental appropriations bill (HR 19928) including most of Nixon's supplemental foreign aid request. The appropriations bill provided the President's full requests for military grant aid and credit sales but reduced his supporting assistance requests by $40-million.

Treaty

The Senate Sept. 21 by a 66-0 roll-call vote ratified a Supplementary Extradition Convention with France (Exec F, 91st Cong., 2nd Session). The convention added hijacking, traffic in narcotics and hallucinogenic drugs, use of the mails to defraud the public and offenses against the laws relating to bankruptcy to the list of crimes and offenses for which extradition would be granted.

The convention had been signed Feb. 12, 1970, in Paris and would become effective 30 days after ratification by both nations; it could be terminated by either country by giving six months' notice.

United Nations

Congress authorized a U.S. contribution of $20-million for the expansion of United Nations headquarters in New York (S J Res 173—PL 91-622). To meet building and expansion costs estimated at $80-million, the UN Secretary General worked out an arrangement whereby $25-million was to be paid from the regular UN budget; $15-million from the UN Development Program and UN Children's Fund; $20-million from the City of New York, which was also donating land valued at $12-million; and $20-million from the United States.

During consideration of the bill in the Senate and House, UN critics raised the issue of the continuation of U.S. financial support for the UN, while some members of the organization remained delinquent in their dues. *(UN funds, fiscal 1973 State Department appropriations, p. 890)*

UN 25th Anniversary. The House Foreign Affairs Subcommittee on International Organizations and Movements held hearings in February and March to review the United Nation's performance, operations and future goals.

In February, the House Foreign Affairs Committee released an assessment of UN activities, written by Dante B. Fascell (D Fla.) and J. Irving Whalley (R Pa.) who were members of the U.S. delegation to the 24th General Assembly. The two concluded that the United Nations, on the eve of its 25th anniversary, stood "long on promise but short on performance." The 24th General Assembly session, they wrote, "did not feature any spectacular achievements or great controversies. In many respects, it was a holding operation."

(Continued on p. 872)

Foreign Aid Review: Task Force and Nixon Message

A thorough reorganization of U.S. development assistance programs, a complete separation of military and economic aid, greater U.S. contributions to international lending institutions, and a multiyear, partially independent, funding basis for American foreign aid were among the principal recommendations submitted by a presidential task force on March 8, 1972.

The 16-member panel, composed of private citizens and headed by former Bank of America President Rudolph A. Peterson, was appointed by President Nixon Sept. 24, 1969, to undertake a comprehensive review of past U.S. aid programs and chart new directions for the 1970s.

The establishment of a task force was first mentioned by Nixon in his May 28, 1969, annual foreign policy message to Congress. The action was taken in response to an amendment to the 1968 Foreign Assistance Act (PL 90-554), which required the President to initiate the review and present his findings by March, 1970.

Receiving the report, the President hailed the proposed "sweeping changes in foreign assistance programs" as "fresh and exciting."

Greater Support for International Efforts. The task force recommended redesigning U.S. aid policies so that international lending institutions "become the major channel for development assistance."

Specifically, the task force urged increases in funds for the International Development Association (the soft-loan window of the World Bank group) to $1-billion annually by 1972, with the U.S. share 40 per cent of the total. It proposed increasing Inter-American Development Bank lending by 50 per cent—from $600-million to $900-million annually.

Also recommended was an increase of $500-million in annual U.S. contributions to international financial institutions by 1972. Such increases were then being considered by members of the World Bank group.

Separation of Military and Economic Aid. The task force recommended that all types of "security assistance"—including military assistance and sales, supporting assistance and contingency fund—be combined in one legislative act, separate from economic aid, with the State Department exercising "firm policy guidance" over military programs. The panel also recommended phasing out grant military assistance and gradually replacing it with military credits.

Reorganizing U.S. Economic Aid. The report suggested establishing new organizations which would assume the functions exercised by the Agency for International Development (AID):

- A U.S. International Development Bank to administer the U.S. development loan program, with initial capitalization of $2-billion through congressional appropriations and authority to borrow another $2-billion on the public market through sale of bonds. The bank would be an independent government agency.

- A U.S. International Development Institute to administer the technical assistance program, assuming the functions of AID's Technical Assistance Bureau established by the President in 1969. The new institute would be an independent government agency, receiving an initial congressional authorization of $1-billion, with the funds to be available over the life of the institute.

- A U.S. International Development Council, composed of top administration officials connected with American international economic policy, to coordinate all U.S. aid activities and formulate basic international development strategy.

Trade Policies and the Private Sector. The task force expressed full support for current administration efforts to obtain international agreement on nondiscriminatory tariff preferences for developing countries. It urged larger U.S. quotas for products important to developing countries.

Endorsing the establishment (in 1969) of the Overseas Private Investment Corporation (OPIC), the task force recommended eliminating current restraints on U.S. direct private investment in developing countries.

The task force urged congressional approval of U.S. participation in an international investment insurance program against the risks of expropriation, as has been proposed by the World Bank.

Size of Aid. The task force called for a reversal of the downward trend in U.S. development assistance appropriations, but expressed reservations "about the usefulness of any formula to determine how much assistance the industrial countries provide...." (The October 1969 report of the Pearson Commission to the World Bank had proposed a target of one per cent of GNP for aid by 1975.)

Nixon Message

On Sept. 15, 1970, President Nixon sent a 6,000-word message to Congress outlining planned changes in foreign military and economic assistance programs. The changes closely paralleled the recommendations made by the Peterson task force.

The most significant reform in the message would begin the channeling of the bulk of U.S. development assistance funds through international financial institutions.

The President said he would send Congress legislation in 1971 to create two independent institutions, a U.S. International Development Corporation to "enable us to deal with lower income nations on a businesslike basis," and a U.S. International Development Institute to utilize U.S. scientific and technological expertise to solve development problems abroad.

The existing Agency for International Development would be abandoned. The message said the number of overseas U.S. personnel working on development programs could be reduced significantly.

Military aid would be funneled through a new international security assistance program which, the message said, would "help other countries assume the responsibility of their own defense..."

The President particularly emphasized the conclusion of the Peterson task force that "the downward trend of U.S. contributions to the development process should be reversed."

Immigration

The Senate Select Standards and Conduct (Ethics) Committee reported that its investigation, begun in 1969, into alleged improprieties surrounding private immigration bills in the Senate had disclosed no evidence of misconduct by any senator or Senate employee. *(Ethics chapter, p. 412)*

However, the committee found indications of law violations by some of the lawyers and lobbyists who sought introduction of immigration bills. Chairman John Stennis (D Miss.) was directed to refer evidence to the Justice Department and Internal Revenue Service.

Background. Allegations of misconduct arose from a series of newspaper articles in 1969 which implied that bribes were paid to Senate employees for the introduction of hundreds of private immigration bills to help Chinese seamen stay in the United States.

Thirteen senators and two former senators were named in the articles as among those whose offices were used to submit the bills, but several dozen senators were estimated to have filed such private relief bills.

The ethics committee launched its closed-door inquiry in September 1969. In October, the Senate was informed by Senate Majority Leader Mike Mansfield (D Mont.) and Minority Leader Hugh Scott (R Pa.) that no private bills could be introduced by Senate staff aides or other Senate employees but only by the senators themselves.

During 1967 to 1969, bills for 657 Chinese ship jumpers had been placed into consideration. "The committee was struck by the fact that bills for about 80 per cent of the total of 657 beneficiaries introduced in the relatively short period of May 1967 to September 1969 originated in or were referred through the offices of only four lawyers in New York City and were handled in Washington, D.C., by not more than nine lobbyists," the report said.

"The amounts of payments made to the lobbyists for their services in obtaining the introduction of bills varied, but the committee had obtained documentary evidence revealing that payment to a lobbyist as high as $750 for a bill for a single beneficiary was not uncommon," the report said.

The committee report named none of the senators involved in the inquiry, but those named in press accounts included Harrison A. Williams Jr. (D N.J.), George McGovern (D S.D.), Gaylord Nelson (D Wis.), Joseph M. Montoya (D N.M.), Daniel K. Inouye (D Hawaii), Lee Metcalf (D Mont.), Frank E. Moss (D Utah), Alan Bible (D Nev.), Gale W. McGee (D Wyo.), Hiram L. Fong (R Hawaii), Charles E. Goodell (R N.Y.), Jacob K. Javits (R N.Y.) and Clifford P. Case (R N.J.).

Former senators mentioned were Ernest Gruening (D Alaska 1959-69) and Daniel Brewster (D Md., House 1959-63, Senate 1963-69).

Immigration Amendments. Congress sent to the President in 1970 a bill (S 2593—PL 91-225) amending the Immigration and Nationality Act of 1952 (PL 82-414) to facilitate the temporary entry into the United States of executive, managerial and specialist personnel of international organizations, fiances and fiancees (and their children) of U.S. citizens and persons of distinguished merit and ability. The bill also amended provisions of the Immigration and Nationality Act dealing with the two-year foreign residence requirement for aliens in the United States as exchange visitors.

Treatment of Soviet Jews

Concern for the treatment of Soviet Jews was widespread on Capitol Hill. In 1970, the House and the Senate passed similar resolutions (H Res 1336, S Res 501) requesting the President to convey to the Soviet Union concern over alleged injustices to Jewish citizens. Both resolutions merely expressed the sense of the House and the Senate, respectively, and did not carry the force of law.

Refugee Funds. In the fiscal 1973-74 State Department authorization bill, approved in 1972, Congress earmarked $85-million for assistance to Israel and other nations for resettlement of Jewish refugees from the Soviet Union. A resolution continuing foreign aid appropriations until Feb. 28, 1973 (H J Res 1331—PL 92-571)—approved because of a conference deadlock over the fiscal 1973 foreign aid funds—included $50-million for Soviet refugee assistance.

Jackson Amendment. In October 1972 Sen. Henry M. Jackson (D Wash.) introduced an amendment to an East-West trade bill which would have made most-favored-nation tariff treatment (nondiscrimination in customs matters) for the Soviet Union contingent upon an end to restrictions on emigration. In addition to other restrictive policies, the amendment was aimed at an August 1972 Soviet decree permitting the levying of exit taxes on holders of high academic degrees. The burden of the taxes fell primarily on Jewish citizens, since Jews were among the most highly educated in the Soviet Union and formed the bulk of those wishing to leave.

The amendment—with the support of a commanding majority in both the Senate and the House—was reintroduced the following year and, early in 1973, despite signs of Soviet relaxation of restrictive policies, appeared to threaten implementation of the U.S.-Soviet trade agreement reached in October 1972. *(Trade agreement, p. 897)*

Peace Corps Authorization

Congress authorized appropriations of $98.8-million for the Peace Corps in fiscal 1971 (S 3430—PL 91-352). The authorization was the exact amount requested by the President. Congress had appropriated $98.45-million for the Peace Corps in fiscal 1970.

In accepting the House version of S 3430, the Senate also approved a House-added provision permitting the Peace Corps director to prescribe such rules as necessary governing conduct of volunteers. The final version of the bill retained language enacted in 1969 prohibiting the use of Peace Corps funds to finance the Volunteers to America program or any similar program for bringing volunteers from foreign countries to serve in the United States in a "reverse Peace Corps" program.

PL 91-352 contained provisions (requested by the administration) extending educational, health care and other benefits to dependents of married volunteers as well as raising the readjustment allowance of one volunteer in the family.

The measure also removed the $75-per-diem ceiling paid by the Peace Corps to consultants and simplified and broadened a provision relating to encouragement of voluntary service programs and participation in international voluntary service programs. Congress authorized the use of up to $300,000 for the latter purpose in fiscal 1971, the same amount as provided for in fiscal 1970.

Appropriation. Congress set Peace Corps funds for fiscal 1971 at $94.5-million, as part of the foreign aid package which cleared in December 1970. *(Fiscal 1971 foreign aid bill, p. 868)*

Illegal Fishing

The penalty for illegal fishing in U.S. coastal waters was raised from $10,000 to $100,000 for each offense in legislation approved by Congress in 1970 (HR 14678—PL 91-514). The measure amended a law enacted in 1964 (PL 88-308) which made it illegal for any foreign vessel to fish within a three-mile zone of the U.S. coast. In 1966, the act was amended to extend to 12 miles the exclusive fisheries zone of the United States.

PL 91-514 also included a provision warning that all fish found aboard a seized vessel would be considered caught in violation of the act. This new "presumption" would subject the entire catch of the vessel to forfeiture and place upon the seized vessel's captain the burden of proving that all fish aboard were not illegally caught.

Exchange Program

The Senate approved, by a 38-28 roll-call vote, a bill (S 3127) amending the Mutual Educational and Cultural Exchange Act of 1961 (PL 87-256) to include a program for the exchange of government officials between the United States and the Soviet Union. The measure would have authorized $5-million over a five-year period for up to 1,000 elected U.S. officials and their spouses to visit the Soviet Union. Some senators criticized the bill as unnecessary. The House Foreign Affairs Committee held hearings on the bill but took no further action.

Naval Ship Loans

Congress approved a bill (HR 15728—PL 91-682) authorizing five-year loans of surplus U.S. Navy vessels to Greece, Pakistan, South Vietnam and Turkey. A Senate amendment to the House-passed version deleted authorization for the loan of three submarines to the Republic of China which had not been requested by the administration.

Background. Since 1951, Congress had authorized the loan of inactive U.S. warships to friendly foreign countries. In recent years, about 75 ships, usually destroyers or submarines, were loaned to 17 countries.

Military aid and sales, particularly to Nationalist China and Greece, had been the subject of controversy in previous years. Such shipments to Greece had been attacked in Congress since the establishment of the military dictatorship in that country in 1967. In 1969, an

Biafra Relief

Congressional and public pressures for more action by the Nixon administration mounted early in 1969, as the civil war between Nigeria and its secessionist eastern region of Biafra entered its third year.

Members of Congress received increasingly heavy mail from their constituents calling for more relief efforts. Resolutions were introduced in the House and Senate, proposing various relief and diplomatic measures. One resolution which urged the administration to "increase significantly" U.S. assistance was sponsored by 52 senators. Several congressional fact-finding missions visited Nigeria-Biafra in early 1969.

In February President Nixon responded to congressional pressures by naming Clarence C. Ferguson Jr. as special coordinator for Biafran relief. The administration also increased U.S. contributions to international relief agencies, including the Red Cross. Like his predecessor, however, Nixon firmly rejected U.S. military involvement or direct political intervention, despite suggestions by some members to use diplomatic measures in seeking an immediate cease-fire. Administration witnesses restated their opposition to any military involvement in testimony in July before the Senate Judiciary Subcommittee on Refugees and Escapees, whose chairman, Edward M. Kennedy (D Mass.), had urged the United States "to assume some leadership in this area."

Biafran Surrender. With the surrender Jan. 12, 1970, of the secessionist state of Biafra after 30 months of bitter civil war, the administration announced its readiness to assist the Nigerian government in providing food and medicine to avert possible widespread starvation among the rebel tribes. On Jan. 15, Under Secretary of State Elliot L. Richardson said U.S. aid would be given through the Nigerian government which was assuming full responsibility for providing relief.

However, the Senate refugee subcommittee heard administration witnesses express concern about relief to Biafra in hearings Jan. 21 and 22. Conflicting reports continued to flow out of Nigeria on the magnitude of assistance required, the ability of the Nigerian government to provide it and the conduct of federal troops in the former Biafran enclave.

Rogers Report. In February 1970, Secretary of State William P. Rogers visited 10 African countries, including Nigeria. In his foreign policy report on the period 1969-1970, Rogers reported that the United States had provided relief at a total value of over $40-million in 1970. He said that the need for relief had ended and the United States had shifted assistance to the Nigerian program of rehabilitation and reconstruction.

attempt in the House to include funds in the annual foreign aid authorization and appropriation bills (PL 91-175, PL 91-194) for a squadron of F-4 Phantom jet aircraft for Taiwan aroused widespread congressional debate. *(Fiscal 1970 foreign aid authorization, p. 860; fiscal 1970 foreign aid appropriation, p. 862)*

State Department Appropriations

Congress appropriated $445,431,800 for the State Department in fiscal 1971, as part of a $3,108,074,500 appropriation for the Departments of State, Justice and Commerce, the Judiciary and 13 related agencies (HR 17575—PL 91-472). The administration had requested $454,434,000 for State Department funding.

The bill also provided $8,250,000 for the Arms Control and Disarmament Agency—$50,000 less than the administration request of $8,300,000. Funds for the U.S. Information Agency were set at $183,398,000; the budget request had been $187,888,000.

ILO Funds. The House approved the full contribution of $7,458,875 for the International Labor Organization (ILO) in fiscal 1971. Later, the House Appropriations Committee heard AFL-CIO President George Meany and Edwin Neilan, one of the three American representatives to the ILO, advise that this contribution not be made. Meany said the organization had become "a forum for Russian political propaganda."

Founded in 1919 as a League of Nations agency, the ILO later became an agency of the United Nations. The United States' contribution was assessed at 25 per cent of the ILO annual budget.

When the bill reached the Senate, ILO funds were cut nearly in half. The Senate, by a roll-call vote of 49-22, accepted a Senate Appropriations Committee amendment reducing ILO funds to $3,758,875. Conferees accepted the lower Senate figure.

1971

A diplomatic revolution in U.S. policy took place in 1971. Announcement that President Nixon would visit Peking and Moscow the next year was heralded as opening a new era in U.S. foreign policy.

The President's initiatives toward the People's Republic of China—including support of China's admission to the United Nations—were generally well received in Congress and throughout the country. But UN rejection of the United States' two-China proposal through its expulsion of Taiwan set off an angry response on Capitol Hill, the ripples of which later were to touch other foreign policy areas, including foreign aid and U.S. financial support of the United Nations.

Senate defeat of a proposal to repeal the 1955 Formosa Resolution, authorizing the President to defend Nationalist Chinese territory, was part of the congressional reaction to the UN decision.

Although U.S. policy toward China and the Soviet Union provided the drama and captured headlines in 1971, there were other ongoing issues. Foreign aid, the Vietnam war, executive powers and overseas commitments continued to trouble relations between Congress and the President.

Foreign aid, an instrument of U.S. foreign policy since 1948, had assumed an important role in administration policy when the President in 1969 proclaimed the Nixon Doctrine of providing money and arms but not men to help other nations defend themselves. However, in 1971, the strategy was placed in jeopardy.

Growing congressional disenchantment with foreign aid, coupled with events that strained U.S. relations with aid recipients, culminated in a startling Senate vote defeating a foreign aid authorization measure. Although the Senate subsequently revived the bill, final approval of fiscal 1972 foreign aid funding—nearly $962-million below the administration's request—was delayed beyond the end of the year by a dispute over an end-the-war amendment.

After a bitter conference battle, the amendment—setting a policy of complete withdrawal of troops from Vietnam within six months—was finally deleted. But two other end-the-war amendments—weakened because they lacked a specific withdrawal deadline—cleared Congress. This marked a major breakthrough for the anti-war forces in the House and Senate. It was the first legislative action by Congress urging a change of policy by the President in South Vietnam.

Anti-war sentiment, as well as concern over congressional prerogatives, were fanned in June 1971 by the *Pentagon Papers'* disclosures. The Defense Department's secret history of the Vietnam war raised questions as to the events leading up to the alleged Tonkin Gulf incident, although publication of the papers did not directly affect President Nixon's handling of the war.

Perhaps more important in the long run was the study's dramatization of the comparative impotence of Congress in making foreign policy. The *Pentagon Papers* also demonstrated the executive branch's general indifference to the constitutional prerogatives of Congress in the conduct of defense and foreign affairs.

In 1971 the House again made an attempt at reasserting congressional war-making powers. Although the resolution approved was stronger than the one the House passed in 1970, the Senate took no action on the measure.

Vietnam was not the only place where there were attempts to cut back U.S. military involvement. Senate Majority Leader Mike Mansfield (D Mont.) twice offered amendments to reduce the number of U.S. troops stationed in Europe. Both were rejected. *(European troop cuts, p. 214)*

War Powers

The House Aug. 2 by voice vote under suspension of the rules (requiring two-thirds majority vote for passage) approved a resolution (H J Res 1) reaffirming the constitutional war-making powers of Congress and the President. The Senate held hearings on various war-powers bills in 1971 but took no action.

H J Res 1 would have required the President to submit a written explanation to Congress if he acted without prior congressional consent in committing U.S. troops to combat, sending combat-equipped forces to foreign countries or significantly enlarging military forces already stationed abroad.

The resolution also urged the President to consult Congress before sending Americans into armed conflict but recognized the President's authority to defend the nation and its citizens without specific legislative approval in extraordinary and emergency circumstances.

Supporters of the resolution said that if enacted it would make it difficult in the future for a President to take actions committing the United States to a foreign conflict without the knowledge of Congress. The reporting requirement, they said, would ensure that congressional and public reaction would be weighed in decisions on the use of U.S. forces abroad.

H J Res 1 was similar to a resolution which was passed by the House in November 1970 (H J Res 1355) but died at the end of the 91st Congress. When the measure was reintroduced in 1971, the phrase "whenever feasible" was deleted from a provision declaring it the sense of Congress that the President should seek consultations with Congress before sending U.S. forces into armed conflict. (*1970 war powers resolution, p. 864*)

Committee Report. The House Foreign Affairs Committee said the most significant provision of the resolution was the requirement that the President report to Congress on any commitment of military forces without prior congressional consent.

"While not tying the President's hands, a reporting requirement would place congressional influence far closer to the points and moments of great decision," the committee said. "It would require the President and his advisers to give thorough consideration to the judgment and reaction of Congress" as well as to legal authority for military action.

Had it been in effect during the last decade, H J Res 1 would have required reports to Congress on the 1970 U.S. incursion into Cambodia, the U.S. bombing of Laos which began in the 1960s, the dispatch of Marines to Thailand in 1962 and the decision to raise the number of U.S. advisers in Vietnam to 16,000 from 700 in 1962, the committee said.

China Policy

Dramatic developments in the U.S. China policy sparked a variety of reactions on Capitol Hill.

The year 1971 saw three major changes in American policy toward Communist China: the end of the trade embargo (June 10); announcement of the President's 1972 trip to Peking for discussions with Red Chinese leaders (July 15), and support for the seating of Communist China in the United Nations (Aug. 2).

The first two changes met with general approval throughout the nation. The Senate Aug. 2 by voice vote passed a resolution (S Con Res 38) commending President Nixon for accepting the invitation to undertake "a journey for peace" to Mainland China and offering its support for his efforts to establish normal relations with Peking. No action was taken by the House on the resolution.

UN Controversy. The same day the Senate approved the resolution commending the President's "peace" journey, Secretary of State William P. Rogers announced the U.S. would abandon its opposition to seating Communist China in the UN. That action, coupled with fear that Taiwan would be thrown out of the UN when Mainland China entered, angered many members.

The official U.S. position was that the two Chinas should be seated in the UN, with the majority of members deciding which would hold the Security Council seat reserved for China. The United States said it would oppose any attempt to expel Taiwan from the world body.

On Sept. 28, 21 senators and 33 House members of both parties joined in issuing a statement declaring that if the Republic of China were expelled from the United Nations, "we would feel compelled to recommend a complete reassessment of U.S. financial and moral support of the UN."

China and the UN Issue

From 1950 to 1970, Congress expressed its opposition to the seating of Communist China in the United Nations at least 30 times.

Every year, statements expressing this opposition have been attached to appropriations bills and enacted into law.

Every year, that is, until 1971.

The last time Congress went on record opposing admission of the People's Republic of China into the UN was in 1970, when it cleared a bill signed by President Nixon Oct. 21 (PL 91-472) providing appropriations for the Departments of State, Justice and Commerce. That routine bill, along with the annual foreign aid appropriations measure, had been used in past years as the vehicle for the China resolution.

In 1970, the section on China stated: "It is the sense of Congress that the Communist Chinese Government should not be admitted to membership in the United Nations as the representative of China."

A more extensive policy statement on the China question had been included in the foreign aid bill since 1956. But it was stricken for the first time in 1970 as one of several deletions granted by point of order. In the past, the appropriations bill had been submitted to the House under a rule waiving points of order.

The deleted provision was similar to that included in the fiscal 1970 foreign aid appropriations bill (PL 91-194), signed by the President on Feb. 9, 1970. That bill included the traditional statement as Section 105:

"The Congress hereby reiterates its opposition to the seating in the United Nations of the Communist China regime as the representative of China, and it is hereby declared to be the continuing sense of Congress that the Communist regime in China has not demonstrated its willingness to fulfill the obligations contained in the Charter of the United Nations and should not be recognized to represent China in the United Nations."

That provision, which was rendered obsolete by omission from the later (fiscal 1971) bill, asked the President to inform Congress of the implications for U.S. foreign policy in the event the Peking regime was seated in the UN.

1971 Deletion. On June 24, 1971, as the House was considering the State, Justice, Commerce appropriations bill for fiscal 1972 (HR 9272—PL 92-77), Rep. Sidney R. Yates (D Ill.) made a point of order against the China resolution "as being legislation on an appropriation bill."

In reply, the floor manager of the bill, Rep. John J. Rooney (D N.Y.), stated: "This provision has been in this bill for many, many years. It goes back to the time that the late senator from Nevada, Pat McCarran (D 1933-54), was chairman of the Senate appropriations for this bill. However, I am constrained to have to concede that the point of order has merit."

The point of order was sustained and the resolution was deleted from the bill.

On Oct. 13, President Nixon received a petition signed by 336 of the 430 members of the House (there were five vacancies) opposing "strongly and unalterably" the expulsion of Taiwan from the UN. According to the White House, the President thanked the members who presented him with the petition—most of them among the more conservative members of the House—for their "support of the administration on this issue."

Taiwan Expulsion. The expulsion of Nationalist China from the United Nations Oct. 25 produced immediate response—mostly angry and accompanied by threats of retaliation—from members of Congress. Action, statements and floor speeches Oct. 26 included:

• A move by senators from both parties for a reduction in U.S. financial support of the United Nations, and specifically in the $141-million authorization for UN funds in the $3.2-billion foreign aid authorization bill on which debate began Oct. 26.

• A demand by Sen. Barry Goldwater (R Ariz.) that the United States withdraw from UN membership.

• Announcement by Sen. James L. Buckley (Cons-R N.Y.) the night of the UN vote that he was drafting legislation calling for a major reduction in U.S. financial contributions to UN activities.

• A promise by Rep. John J. Rooney (D N.Y.), chairman of the State-Justice-Commerce Appropriations Subcommittee, to reduce UN funds in the bill when it came up again in 1972. UN funds totaled $107.9-million in the fiscal 1972 appropriation.

• A proposal, made by Rep. Philip M. Crane (R Ill.), to base UN contributions from each country on population. If applied to total contributions, the overall U.S. outlay in 1972 would have been reduced to approximately $80-million.

Senate Reaction. Senate defeat of the proposal to repeal the 1955 Formosa Resolution, attached as a committee amendment to the fiscal 1972 foreign aid authorization bill, and the subsequent defeat of the aid bill itself were closely tied to dissatisfaction, particularly among Senate conservatives, with the expulsion of Taiwan from the United Nations. *(Fiscal 1972 foreign aid authorization, this page)*

Formosa Resolution

The Senate Foreign Relations Committee Sept. 21 by voice vote reported a resolution repealing the 1955 Formosa Resolution. The committee's subsequent attempt to include the repealer in the fiscal 1972 foreign aid authorization was defeated on the Senate floor Oct. 28.

As reported, S J Res 48 revoked the President's power, granted by Congress on Jan. 29, 1955 (H J Res 159 —PL 84-4), to commit U.S. forces "as he deems necessary" to defend Taiwan, the Pescadores and offshore Chinese islands occupied by the Chinese Nationalists.

S J Res 48 did not alter U.S. commitments to Taiwan under the Mutual Defense Treaty of 1954, the committee said in its report. But since U.S. action to protect Taiwan under the treaty's terms required specific authorization by Congress, repeal of the Formosa Resolution would "restore the constitutional balance of authority with regard to the use of armed forces in this area," the committee added.

The resolution "would clear away a legislative obstacle to a new China policy" and be "a timely recognition of the changed conditions" in Southeast Asia, the committee said.

Background. The United States signed a mutual defense treaty with the Republic of China (Taiwan) on Dec. 2, 1954. The Senate had not acted on the treaty, however, when President Eisenhower requested the authority provided by the Formosa Resolution.

The 1955 resolution gave the President authority to employ U.S. armed forces "as he deems necessary for the specific purpose of securing and protecting Formosa and the Pescadores against armed attack, this authority to include the securing and protection of such related positions and territories of that area now in friendly hands...."

The resolution said its provisions would remain in effect until the President determined and reported to Congress "that the peace and security of the area is reasonably assured by international conditions...."

"The crisis which precipitated passage of the Formosa Resolution has long since passed," the committee said in recommending repeal. "Since 1964, artillery activity in the area has been limited to ritualistic exchanges of shells containing propaganda leaflets. Despite the developments of the past 16 years and radically changed conditions, the President has not made the report" required to terminate the resolution.

The Senate Foreign Relations Committee attached S J Res 48 to the fiscal 1972 foreign aid authorization (HR 9910) when it reported the aid bill, but the repealer provision was deleted on the Senate floor Oct. 28 by a 43-40 roll-call vote. *(Fiscal 1972 foreign aid authorization, this page)*

Foreign Aid

Delayed by a startling Senate vote and stymied by an end-the-war dispute, Congress in 1971 failed to complete action on extending the foreign aid program.

Although the U.S. assistance program was kept going by interim funding resolutions, the drawn-out 1971 debate on fiscal 1972 authorizations and appropriations cast doubt on the future of foreign aid.

The primary challenge to continuation of foreign assistance efforts came from the Senate. In a **key 27-41 roll-call vote** on Oct. 29, the Senate rejected a House-passed bill (HR 9910) authorizing appropriations for both economic and military aid in fiscal 1972 and 1973.

The bill's defeat—the first outright rejection of foreign aid legislation in the program's 24-year history— was the result of disenchantment with foreign aid among both conservative and liberal senators, some of whom previously had supported the program.

Conservatives argued that the billions poured by the United States into foreign aid had failed to gain international support for U.S. policies. On the other hand, liberals contended that the aid mechanism had been taken over by military considerations, that it was not effective in its humanitarian efforts and should be funneled through international organizations.

These differences were heightened by numerous international events. World conditions affecting the foreign aid dispute included the smoldering Pakistan-India conflict over the rebellion in East Pakistan, the overwhelming vote Oct. 25 in the United Nations for the entry of Communist China and the expulsion of Taiwan, the controversy over U.S. support of the Greek military government and the continuing policy debates over U.S. Indochina policy, especially the growing involvement in Cambodia. These developments were seized upon by opponents of foreign aid of differing ideologies as reasons for cutting off foreign aid.

Another factor was heightened determination by the Senate Foreign Relations Committee—a center of opposition to Nixon administration foreign policies—to use its control over foreign aid authorizing legislation as leverage to change those policies.

The committee made the annual authorization measure a vehicle for various policy amendments, most notably provisions restricting U.S. military activity in Indochina.

The amendments were opposed by the administration and its backers in Congress. If unable to delete such provisions on the floor, therefore, administration supporters who otherwise backed foreign aid were reluctant to vote for the entire bill.

Some Foreign Relations Committee members, notably Chairman J. W. Fulbright (D Ark.) and Majority Leader Mike Mansfield (D Mont.), on the other hand were questioning the usefulness of foreign aid and thus welcomed its defeat.

In an Oct. 29 floor speech entitled "Farewell to Foreign Aid: A Liberal Takes Leave," Sen. Frank Church (D Idaho), a Foreign Relations Committee member, told the Senate that he no longer could "endorse with my vote a foreign aid program which has been twisted into a parody and a farce."

"The experience of 20 years of aid shows that we can neither bring about fundamental reform in tradition-encrusted societies nor prevent revolution in those countries where the tide of change runs deep and strong," Church contended. "All we can do is to service the status quo in countries where it is not strongly challenged anyhow."

Arguing a conservative's case against foreign aid, John L. McClellan (D Ark.) asserted that "for too long (the nation) has attempted to export democracy abroad to unwilling and unready recipients, while neglecting the obvious needs of our people and democratic institutions at home.... Foreign aid as an instrument of international diplomacy is a flop and we should stop it."

Minority Leader Hugh Scott (R Pa.) defended foreign aid as an essential instrument for implementing the Nixon doctrine. Defeat of the bill, he argued, "will serve only one objective: that of making isolationism respectable again in the United States."

After the Senate defeated HR 9910, Congress went to work almost immediately to keep the foreign aid program going while fundamental reforms were considered.

Continued disputes over foreign aid—in particular over a Senate end-the-war amendment—nevertheless kept the program's future in doubt until the final day of the 1971 session.

The Senate Nov. 10-11 adopted a two-bill package (S 2819 and S 2820) authorizing $1,144,000,000 for economic assistance and $1,503,000,000 for military aid in fiscal 1972.

The House, in an unusual procedure, revived the $3.4-billion bill beaten in the Senate and sent it to conference with the two Senate-passed bills. Conferees resolved most differences but after nearly a month were deadlocked over the Senate-added Mansfield amend-

Foreign Aid Side Issues

Under challenge on its own merits, the U.S. foreign aid program during the Nixon administration's first four years was frequently threatened by unrelated disputes between Congress and the executive branch.

Opposed to many administration foreign policies, the Senate Foreign Relations Committee attempted to use its control over foreign aid authorization measures to exact changes in those policies. In 1971 and again in 1972, measures authorizing continued foreign aid became hostages in conference as the Senate conferees tried to win House acceptance of Foreign Relations Committee policy amendments declaring military withdrawal from South Vietnam and requiring Senate ratification of military base agreements with other nations. *(1971 and 1972 chronologies, p. 876, 884)*

In two other instances, moreover, the Foreign Relations Committee threatened to cut off foreign aid funds as a sanction against administration use of executive privilege and impoundment of funds.

In 1971, the committee invoked a provision of the Foreign Assistance Act of 1961 cutting off funds 35 days after administration refusal to furnish documents on foreign aid requested by the committee unless the President gave reasons for turning down the request. The committee was seeking a copy of a five-year plan for military assistance.

President Nixon Aug. 31 averted a fund cut-off—scheduled to go into effect the next day—by invoking executive privilege. Nixon said he denied the request because the information sought by the committee was contained in internal executive branch documents based on tentative planning data.

In 1972, Congress cleared a foreign aid authorization bill (S 2819—PL 92-226) including a Foreign Relations Committee amendment requiring a cutoff of foreign aid funds unless the President by April 30 released an estimated $2.3-billion in funds for the Agriculture, Housing and Urban Development and Health, Education and Welfare Departments that had been impounded by the administration.

On May 2, however, Comptroller General Elmer B. Staats certified to Congress that all funds appropriated to those departments had been released, leaving foreign aid funding uninterrupted.

ment, which declared a national policy of withdrawal of all troops from Indochina within six months.

The dispute delayed adjournment as senators opposed to continuation of the program without reform held up action on a resolution providing interim foreign aid funding.

In a **key 130-101 roll-call vote** on Dec. 16, the House defeated a motion to instruct House conferees to accept the Senate-passed Mansfield amendment calling for withdrawal from Indochina within six months. Senate Majority Leader Mike Mansfield (D Mont.) accepted this roll call as an expression of House sentiment on the end-the-war amendment, and the conference committee reached agreement on remaining differences between the House and Senate versions of the bill. This broke the deadlock, clearing the way for passage of a continuing resolution and a $2.75-billion authorization bill.

Peace Corps

Congress authorized appropriations of $77.2-million in fiscal 1972 for the Peace Corps (S 2260—PL 92-135). The amount authorized was $5-million less than the $82.2-million requested in the administration's revised fiscal 1972 budget estimate. Congress had appropriated $94.5-million for the Peace Corps in fiscal 1971.

Merger with Action. Under Executive Order 11603 issued June 30, 1971, the Peace Corps was transferred to Action, a volunteer agency created by Reorganization Plan No. 1 of 1971. Action, which came into being July 1 in the absence of disapproval by Congress, included the Peace Corps, Volunteers in Service to America (VISTA) and other volunteer programs. Peace Corps Director Joseph H. Blatchford was appointed director of the new agency.

Under the Nixon administration, the Peace Corps had shifted from an emphasis on youthful, enthusiastic but inexperienced volunteers to more skilled recruits who could offer greater technical competence. This new direction of the Peace Corps came in for some criticism from the Senate Foreign Relations Committee, which had concluded that "all is not well with the Peace Corps."

Pointing out that the Peace Corps never was intended to provide the skilled technicians sought by developing nations, the committee said it had "therefore reached the point of questioning seriously whether the Peace Corps has an effective role to play in the 1970s." It asked "...whether better results might not be obtained by putting equivalent resources in the technical assistance and educational exchange programs and in the budding United Nations effort which will continue to offer Americans an opportunity to serve abroad in a Peace Corps-like setting."

Appropriation. Congress set Peace Corps funds for fiscal 1972 at $72-million, as part of the foreign aid package which cleared in March 1972. *(Fiscal 1972 foreign aid bill, p. 876)*

Immigration

The House April 19 suspended the rules and passed HR 1534 and HR 1535 amending the Immigration and Nationality Act of 1952. *(Congress and the Nation Vol. I, p. 222)*

HR 1534, reported from the House Judiciary Committee March 30, was passed by voice vote. It raised to 18 from 16 the age at which children could still acquire automatic United States citizenship through the naturalization of their parents.

HR 1535, reported from the House Judiciary Committee March 30, was passed by a 192-84 roll-call vote. It exempted from the requirement of understanding English any alien over age 50 who had lived in the United States for 20 years at the time he files for naturalization.

The Senate did not act on either bill in 1971.

Fishing Protocols

Congress July 30 completed action on a bill implementing two new protocols regarding international fishing agreements for the northwest Atlantic area (HR 9181—PL 92-304). The protocols covered investigation, protection and conservation of the fisheries in that region of the ocean in order to maintain a maximum sustained catch without depleting stocks.

Treaties

OKINAWA REVERSION. The Senate Nov. 10, by an 84-6 roll-call vote, ratified the Okinawa Reversion Treaty (Exec J, 92nd Congress, 1st session) returning control of the Ryukyu and the Daito Islands in the Pacific to Japan.

The treaty was debated over a two-day period (Nov. 9-10). Approval of two-thirds of senators present and voting (60 in this case) was required for ratification.

Voting against ratification were James B. Allen (D Ala.), Harry F. Byrd Jr. (Ind Va.), Barry Goldwater (R Ariz.), Clifford P. Hansen (R Wyo.), Warren G. Magnuson (D Wash.) and Milton R. Young (R N.D.).

Major Provisions. As ratified by the Senate, Exec J, 92nd Congress, 1st session, included the following provisions:

• The United States relinquished its rights and responsibilities to the Ryukyu and Daito Islands and Japan assumed full authority to govern the islands. (Okinawa was the largest of the Ryukyu Islands.)

• Treaties and agreements between the United States and Japan were made applicable to the islands.

• Japan agreed to grant the United States use of military facilities on Okinawa in accordance with the 1960 U.S.-Japan Treaty of Mutual Cooperation and Safety.

• Japan agreed to pay the United States $320-million, in installments within five years from the date of reversion, as compensation for the transfer of assets and extra costs borne by the United States.

• The reversion was scheduled to go into effect two months after exchange of the instruments of ratification.

Background. The United States, whose forces captured the Ryukyu and Daito Islands during World War II, assumed all powers of "administration, legislation and jurisdiction" over the islands under the 1951 Peace Treaty with Japan.

President Johnson and Japanese Prime Minister Eisaku Sato in 1967 agreed that reversion should take place within a few years. President Nixon and Sato Nov. 21, 1969, announced an agreement to begin negotiations on reversion, which was to be accomplished by 1972.

Several weeks before the Nixon-Sato talks, the Senate had added an amendment to the State-Justice Departments appropriations bill instructing the President to obtain the Senate's advice and consent on any agreement or understanding which changed the status of Okinawa (HR 12964—PL 91-153). The amendment—the first concrete application of the Senate's "national commitments" resolution—was deleted in conference.

After detailed negotiations, U.S. and Japanese officials June 17, 1971, signed the treaty (the Agreement Between the United States of America and Japan Concerning the Ryukyu Islands and the Daito Islands) in Washington, D.C., and in Tokyo.

(The United States and Japan exchanged documents ratifying the treaty March 15, 1972. The island reversion took place May 15, 1972, in accordance with an agreement reached between President Nixon and Premier Sato early that year.)

U.S.-MEXICAN BOUNDARY. The Senate Nov. 29, by a 79-0 roll-call vote, ratified a treaty (Exec B, 92nd Congress, 1st session) settling U.S.-Mexican boundary disputes. The treaty, signed Nov. 23, 1970, resolved a dispute over land known as the Presidio-Ojinaga tracts along the Rio Grande border between Texas and the Mexican state of Chihuahua and established the international boundary in the middle of the river. Under its terms, the United States and Mexico exchanged several islands in the river and other lands nearby. The nations also agreed to share equally the cost of relocating the river channel to place all U.S. territory north of the river and all Mexican territory south.

Background. Starting in 1884, the United States and Mexico tried in a series of treaties to resolve boundary differences caused by the changing courses of the Rio Grande and Colorado River. Previous treaties failed to establish a procedure for settling new disputes that arose.

Several years of discussion through the International Boundary and Water Commission at El Paso, Texas, and Ciudad Juarez, Chihuahua, led to an agreement on basic principles that were approved by President Nixon and Mexican President Gustavo Diaz Ordaz Aug. 20, 1970, at Puerto Vallarta, Mexico.

U.S.-MEXICAN COOPERATION. The Senate Feb. 10 by a 72-0 roll-call vote approved a resolution of ratification consenting to a treaty (Exec K, 91st Congress, 92nd Congress, 1st session) settling U.S.-Mexican boundand Mexico providing for the recovery and return of stolen archeological, historical and cultural properties.

The treaty was signed at Mexico City on July 17, 1970, and will run for a minimum of two years and continue thereafter unless 30 days notice is given by either country to terminate.

Under the treaty, both countries are required to take all legal means at their disposal to recover stolen properties covered in the treaty.

OCEAN POLLUTION. Two international agreements (Exec G, 91st Congress, 2nd session) dealing with oil pollution were ratified by the Senate Sept. 20, by separate 75-0 roll-call votes.

The agreements ratified were the Convention Relating to Intervention on the High Seas in Cases of Oil Pollution Casualties and amendments to the 1954 Convention on the Pollution of the Sea by Oil.

The Convention Relating to Intervention on the High Seas established the right of a coastal nation to take action against the threat of oil pollution after a maritime accident such as a collision at sea.

The amendments to the 1954 convention altered existing international law governing the intentional discharge of oil and specified a rate-of-discharge formula to limit the amount of oil a ship was legally permitted to discharge into the sea.

At the recommendation of the Foreign Relations Committee, the Senate deferred action on a third agreement, the Convention on Civil Liability for Oil Pollution Damage, until the Inter-Governmental Maritime Consultative Organization (IMCO) completed work on a supplementary convention to set up an international oil pollution fund.

Background. The agreements were aimed at resolving legal uncertainties surrounding the prevention and cleanup of oil pollution in the seas. The issue had been raised in 1967 when the oil tanker S.S. Torrey Canyon ran aground in international waters off the southwest coast of England. The supertanker's oil tanks ruptured spilling 60,000 tons of crude oil into the English Channel, causing severe ecological damage and costing millions of dollars to clean up. Work on the oil pollution agreements was completed in 1969, and the United States signed both in November 1969.

LATIN NUCLEAR TREATY. The Senate April 19, by a 70-0 roll-call vote, approved a resolution of ratification of Protocol II to the Treaty of Tiatelolco (Exec H, 91st Congress, 2nd session), a treaty for the prohibition of nuclear weapons in Latin America.

Twenty-two Latin American nations had signed the treaty since Feb. 14, 1967. The signatories agreed under the treaty to prohibit the production, testing or possession of nuclear weapons in Latin America. The treaty did not prohibit peaceful uses of nuclear energy.

Protocol I of the treaty, signed by the Latin American countries, declared the agreement to be a step toward general disarmament.

Protocol II, which the United States signed April 1, 1968, was intended for countries already possessing nuclear weapons. The only other signatory of Protocol II, the United Kingdom, signed Dec. 20, 1969. Under Protocol II, the United States agreed, with reservations, to forego the use of nuclear weapons or to threaten the use of nuclear weapons in Latin America.

AIRCRAFT HIJACKING. The Senate Sept. 8, by a 53-0 roll-call vote, adopted a resolution (Exec A, 92nd Congress, 1st session) ratifying the Convention for the Suppression of Unlawful Seizure of Aircraft, signed at the Hague in December 1970. *(Details, chapter on crime)*

CONVENTION WITH NICARAGUA. The Senate Feb. 17 by a 66-5 roll call vote approved a resolution of ratification (Exec L, 91st Congress, 2nd session) on a Convention with Nicaragua terminating the Bryan-Chamorro Treaty of 1914.

The convention, which was signed July 14, 1970, in Managua, Nicaragua, terminated a treaty that had provided for construction of a Nicaraguan interoceanic canal route, a 99-year lease to the Corn Islands off the coast of Nicaragua and the right to establish a naval base on the Pacific coast of Nicaragua.

Nicaragua received $3-million in payment for the U.S. options, but the United States never exercised any of its rights under the treaty.

EXTRADITION TREATY WITH SPAIN. The Senate Feb. 17 by a 72-0 roll-call vote approved a resolution of ratification on an extradition treaty with Spain (Exec N, 91st Congress, 2nd session).

The treaty authorized extradition for 23 offenses including airplane hijacking and crimes against laws relating to narcotic drugs.

The treaty was signed May 29, 1970, and replaced an extradition treaty between Spain and the United States signed in 1904 and a protocol signed in 1907.

Radio Free Europe

In 1971, Congress for the first time approved open U.S. funding for Radio Free Europe and Radio Liberty. For about 20 years the stations had depended on funds covertly supplied by the Central Intelligence Agency (CIA). Both the government and the stations, however, had maintained that the radio operations were financed by public contributions.

After a four-month deadlock in conference, Congress in March 1972 cleared a bill (S 18—PL 92-264) authorizing an appropriation of $36-million through June 30, 1972, for Radio Free Europe and Radio Liberty.

Both the Senate and House had passed differing versions of S 18 during 1971. The Senate approved an authorization of $35-million for fiscal 1972 only for the two stations. The House version would have created a presidential commission to study the stations' operations and authorized $36-million for fiscal 1972 and $38,520,000 for fiscal 1973.

The version which came out of conference was almost identical to the Senate measure. The only concessions were that Senate conferees agreed to the House appropriation of $36-million instead of its chamber's own allotment of $35-million and agreed to consider a fiscal 1973 authorization measure before fiscal 1972 ended. The Senate concession on the amount of the authorization was meaningless, however, because Congress already had appropriated (HR 11955—PL 92-184) only $32,225,000 in fiscal 1972 for the stations pending enactment of the authorization bill.

Adoption of the conference report left the stations' futures in doubt and, thus, was a victory for Senate Foreign Relations Committee Chairman J. W. Fulbright (D Ark.) who argued that the radio stations were cold war vestiges that threatened improvement of East-West relations.

Fiscal 1973. However, opponents of the stations were unable to block a fiscal 1973 authorization. In August 1972 Congress cleared for the President a bill (S 3645—PL 92-394) authorizing an appropriation of $38,520,000 in fiscal 1973 for the two radio stations.

Background. Radio Free Europe, which broadcasted to Eastern Europe, and Radio Liberty, which broadcasted to Russia, were incorporated in 1949 and 1951, respectively, as private, nonprofit corporations.

In 1967, at the time the Central Intelligence Agency was criticized for allegedly contributing funds to the National Student Association, President Lyndon B. Johnson made a policy statement declaring that "no federal agency shall provide covert financial assistance or support, direct or indirect, to any of the nation's educational or voluntary organizations." *(CIA secret financing, Congress and the Nation Vol. II, p. 852)*

Clifford P. Case (R N.J.) touched off a debate Jan. 24, 1971, when he recalled the Johnson policy statement and tried to apply it as reason for adopting his bill (S 18) calling for congressionally authorized funding of Radio Free Europe and Radio Liberty. On Jan. 25, the Nixon administration, speaking through the State Department, announced that the two radio stations were "not educational or private voluntary organizations" within the United States and, therefore, the Johnson policy statement was not applicable to the situation.

While the administration refused to accept the argument that the radio stations should not be funded by the CIA because of the 1967 Johnson statement or, indeed, that any such relationship existed, the Case proposal itself attracted attention in the State Department. The administration proposed in 1971 an alternative to S 18 which would create a single, non-profit private corporation to operate both stations through funds authorized and appropriated by Congress.

Before the Foreign Relations Committee could act on either of the proposals, the Senate Appropriations Committee, under Chairman Allen J. Ellender (D La.), reported June 25 a routine resolution (H J Res 742) providing for the continued funding of certain government agencies until regular fiscal 1972 appropriations could be cleared through Congress. Contained in the resolution as amended by the committee was the first mention ever made in an official public document that the U.S. government was connected with Radio Free Europe or Radio Liberty. The committee had inserted language providing for the continued funding of the two stations, at a level equal to what they had been receiving from the CIA, under provisions of the U.S. Information Act being used by the Case proposal. The committee also included a restraining clause which provided that funds from other government agencies could not be used to support the stations.

State Department Appropriations

Congress appropriated $495,363,000 for the State Department in fiscal 1972, as part of a $4,067,116,000 appropriation for the Departments of State, Justice and Commerce, the Judiciary and 14 related agencies (HR 9272—PL 92-77). The administration had requested $509,598,000 for State Department funding.

The bill also included $9,000,000 for the Arms Control and Disarmament Agency, as compared to a budget request of $9,064,000. Funds for the U.S. Information Agency were set at $196,806,000; the administration had requested $198,130,000.

During House consideration of HR 9272, a provision was deleted expressing the sense of Congress against the admission of Communist China in the United Nations as the representative of China. The language, carried in similar bills for years, was removed through a point of order against legislation in an appropriations bill. Congress in 1971 failed to enact any expression of sentiment against the seating of Communist China in the UN as it had repeatedly in the past. *(Box, p. 875)*

The major issue on the House floor was International Labor Organization (ILO) funding. The House Appropriations Committee had not recommended any funds for payment of $11,600,749 in dues owed the ILO.

The report said the committee was dissatisfied with the performance of the ILO. It quoted testimony by George Meany, president of the AFL-CIO, before the Subcommittee on State, Justice, Commerce and the Judiciary, on July 31, 1970, in which the labor leader said the organization had become "a forum for Russian political propaganda." It also complained that the ILO was in the process of building a $25-million office in Geneva, Switzerland, without asking approval from Congress of a 25 per cent American contribution.

In 1970, Congress had cut ILO funds in half for fiscal 1971. Failure of the United States to pay its dues would eventually result in loss of voting rights in the ILO. *(1970 chronology, p. 874)*

A floor amendment to restore ILO funds, offered by Sidney R. Yates (D Ill.), was defeated on a recorded teller vote of 147-227.

The Senate approved $7,816,337 for ILO dues but the funds were deleted by conferees who said, nonetheless, that they had "not the slightest intention of ever abandoning our membership in the ILO. We do not lose our voting rights until we are two years in arrears. The conferees recommend that no payment at all be made at this time pending further improvement of our position."

1972

A dialogue with Communist China, an arms limitation agreement with the Soviet Union, an imminent cease-fire in Vietnam—1972 was a year of spectaculars. *(Details of the President's trip to Peking and Moscow, p. 893)*

But it was also a year of congressional challenges to the executive branch—challenges which seemed to come with greater frequency and intensity. The Senate took both its toughest stand on terminating U.S. involvement in Indochina and its furthest step toward restoring what it saw as the constitutional balance in war-making powers.

The foreign aid program remained a popular vehicle for mounting challenges. After completing action on fiscal 1972 foreign aid funds, Congress was unable to reach agreement on fiscal 1973 appropriations. With both the House and Senate refusing to compromise their difference over Senate amendments requiring Senate approval of overseas military base agreements, the aid program was kept going only by continuing resolutions.

During consideration of the first of two fiscal 1973 military aid authorization bills, the Senate attached an end-the-war amendment. It was the first provision cutting off funds for the war ever approved by either the House or Senate. But supporters of the administration joined with traditional military aid foes to defeat the entire measure.

The Senate attached a similar war funds cut-off to a defense procurement authorization bill but it was dropped in conference at House insistence. Earlier in the year the Senate had defeated an end-the-war amendment to the State-USIA authorization bill.

The fiscal 1973 military aid authorization bill was resurrected—only to die in conference at the end of the session. This time its fate had been sealed by amendments dealing with executive agreements rather than war. The amendments were among several congressional attempts at exercising some type of oversight role. Disclosures that some agreements had been kept secret had provided added impetus to those in Congress already deeply troubled over U.S. commitments abroad.

A requirement that the administration submit to Congress the texts of all international agreements passed both houses and was signed into law in 1972. The Senate also passed a resolution urging the President to submit the basic agreements included with Portugal and Bahrain for Senate approval.

Background: Executive Agreements

Executive agreements, which unlike treaties are not reviewed by the Senate, became paramount in U.S. foreign policy beginning with World War II.

Before the war, treaties predominated in the agreements reached with foreign countries. In 1930, for example, the United States concluded 25 treaties and nine executive agreements. In 1972, on the other hand, the United States entered into 21 treaties and 282 executive agreements.

The Constitution made no mention of a specific presidential authority to negotiate executive agreements. Beginning with President Washington, however, such agreements customarily were used to handle routine understandings such as tariff agreements and postal conventions. The President's authority was derived primarily from his constitutional powers as chief executive and Commander in Chief (Art. II, Section 2) and from implementation of congressional statutes or treaties approved by the Senate.

In recent years, however, executive agreements had dealt with issues formerly considered sufficiently important to require Senate ratification by treaty. Some, notably military base and joint defense agreements, involved a U.S. commitment to future action, including the possibility of war.

As of Jan. 1, 1973, according to the State Department, the United States was party to 910 treaties and 4,589 executive agreements.

Under a law enacted in 1950 (PL 81-821), the secretary of state was directed to compile and publish annually the contents of all treaties and executive agreements made during the preceding year.

In practice, however, agreements considered by the executive branch to be sensitive to national security were withheld. As a result, Congress was not informed of many agreements, even on a classified basis.

In addition, the Senate passed the most far-reaching war-powers bill yet. The measure marked the first attempt at actually codifying war powers. The House passed a less restrictive version of the bill and the measure died in conference.

Executive Agreements

Executive agreements were a dominant issue in the tug-of-war between the administration and Congress over powers and prerogatives. Disclosures that some executive agreements with other nations had been kept secret and fears that these agreements could lead to new military commitments for the United States sparked legislative moves—spearheaded by Clifford P. Case (R N.J.)—in the Senate.

Congress cleared legislation requiring the administration to submit to Congress the texts of all international agreements. The Senate approved a resolution urging the President to submit agreements concluded with Portugal and the Persian Gulf state of Bahrain. Hearings were held by the Senate Judiciary Subcommittee on Separation of Powers, introduced by subcommittee chairman Sam J. Ervin Jr. (D N.C.), which would have required congressional consideration of executive agreements.

A conference dispute over Senate-approved amendments requiring congressional approval of executive agreements blocked passage of a fiscal 1973 military assistance authorization bill. *(p. 885)*

AGREEMENTS TEXTS

Congress approved legislation (S 596—PL 92-403) requiring the executive branch to submit to Congress the texts of all international agreements.

As signed into law, S 596 would ensure that Congress or its foreign affairs committees had knowledge of national commitments made to other nations through executive agreements.

Commitments made by treaty were made known to Congress through the Senate's exercise of its constitutional power of approving ratification. In recent years, however, the number of executive agreements—some kept secret from Congress—had proliferated.

Congressional action on S 596 was largely a response to secret agreements uncovered by the Senate Foreign Relations Subcommittee on Security Agreements and Commitments Abroad. *(Hearings, p. 866)*

Sen. Case, chief sponsor of S 596, and other members contended that Congress could not adequately perform its role in foreign policymaking without knowledge of commitments made by the executive branch.

By passing S 596, the full Senate and House gave their support to efforts led by the Senate Foreign Relations Committee to assert a larger congressional role in foreign policy decisions. In the early stages of action, the State Department had bucked that tide by opposing S 596. The opposition was dropped, however, after the bill won unanimous approval of the Senate. The bill was similar to a measure proposed in 1954 and passed by the Senate in 1956. *(Congress and the Nation Vol. I, p. 119, 110)*

Provisions. As cleared by Congress, S 596 directed the secretary of state to transmit to Congress within 60 days of execution the text of any agreement—other than a treaty—with another nation.

If the President determined that public disclosure would prejudice national security, the bill required that the text be sent to the Senate Foreign Relations and House Foreign Affairs Committees under an injunction of secrecy.

Senate Passage. The Senate Feb. 16, by an 81-0 roll-call vote, passed S 596 with amendments.

No opposition to S 596 was voiced during the debate, although Case, the bill's sponsor, expressed reservations about the ability of Congress to maintain secrecy.

Sen. Ervin, chairman of the Judiciary Subcommittee on Separation of Powers, said S 596 "...fills a need which has existed for a long time.... If the executive branch...is entirely free to determine what it will submit to the Senate in this area, then the constitutional provision requiring Senate participation in the treaty-making field is no more than a piece of dead parchment."

Foreign Relations Committee Chairman J. W. Fulbright (D Ark.) cited President Nixon's offer of U.S. aid to rebuild both North and South Vietnam after a peace settlement and an agreement negotiated by the administration with the sheikdom of Bahrain for a U.S. naval base

Overseas Base Agreements

Agreements with Portugal and the Persian Gulf sheikdom of Bahrain were central to the debate in 1972 over executive agreements.

The Senate approved a resolution urging the administration to submit the two agreements, concluded in December 1971, to the Senate as treaties. Later the Senate attempted to add legislative force to this resolution by attaching amendments to the fiscal 1973 foreign military aid authorization that would have required submission of the Azores agreement, as well as all future base agreements. (Committee-added language requiring approval of the Bahrain agreement had been deleted on the Senate floor during consideration of S 3390, the military aid authorization which the Senate defeated, and, therefore, was not included in the substitute bill, HR 16029.)

Conferees were unable to break a deadlock over the amendments and HR 16029 died at the end of the 92nd Congress. *(Fiscal 1973 foreign military aid authorization, p. 885)*

Azores Agreement. In an exchange of diplomatic notes with Portugal in 1951, the United States obtained rent-free use of Lajes Field in the Azores, owned by Portugal. The agreement lapsed in 1962 after negotiations for an extension broke down over U.S. support for self-determination by Portuguese African territories, but U.S. use of the airfield continued under an informal understanding.

On Dec. 9, 1971, the U.S. and Portuguese governments reached an agreement extending U.S. rights to use the field until Feb. 3, 1974.

In exchange, although no formal rent was required, the United States agreed to provide Portugal with $30-million in Food for Peace (PL 83-480) credits in fiscal 1972-73, $400-million in Export-Import Bank financing, the loan of a hydrographic vessel at no cost, $1-million in Defense Department funds for educational projects and excess Pentagon equipment for non-military purposes worth $5-million.

Bahrain Agreement. The United States had no previous agreements with Bahrain, an independent sheikdom on the Persian Gulf under British protection until 1971. Since 1949, however, several U.S. Navy vessels, designated as the Middle East Force, had been deployed in the area, sharing British base facilities at Bahrain.

Great Britain in August 1971 decided to withdraw from the area, and the administration subsequently decided to keep the Middle East Force in the gulf and negotiate a direct agreement with Bahrain.

The agreement, concluded by an exchange of notes on Dec. 23, 1971, provided for annual leasing by the United States of facilities occupying about 10 per cent of the area of the former British base.

The Bahrain government and the Nixon administration said no political or military security commitment was involved.

in the Persian Gulf as agreements that should be approved by treaty. *(Box, p. 882)*

Senate approval of S 596 "...in no way gives validity to such agreements, which...should be treaties," Fulbright said. "The Constitution did not anticipate that matters of this importance should be done secretly by executive agreement."

House Passage. The House Aug. 14, by voice vote under suspension of the rules, passed S 596 without amendments. (A two-thirds majority of members present and voting was required for passage under that procedure.) House acceptance of the Senate bill without change cleared the measure for the White House.

During a brief floor debate on the bill, Clement J. Zablocki (D Wis.) said that if executive agreements were binding on the nation "then Congress must know about them. To keep them entirely secret from Congress is a distortion of our constitutional system. Yet, that is what happened in the past and may well happen in the future unless S 596 is enacted into law."

ACCORDS WITH PORTUGAL, BAHRAIN

The Senate March 3, by a 50-6 roll-call vote, passed a resolution (S Res 214) urging the Nixon administration to submit executive agreements with Portugal and Bahrain to the Senate as treaties for ratification.

S Res 214 expressed the sense of the Senate that agreements with Portugal on the use by the U.S. government of an airbase in the Azores Islands and with Bahrain for naval base facilities on the Persian Gulf, should be concluded as treaties requiring ratification by the Senate. *(Box, p. 882)*

Although S Res 214 did not have the force of law, it complemented S 596 which required the executive branch to submit to Congress the texts of all international agreements. Case, principal sponsor of those two measures, said, during floor consideration of S Res 214, that the agreements with Portugal and Bahrain were "simply too important to be left to an exchange of diplomatic notes.... Both of these agreements represent significant foreign policy moves. They both involve the stationing of American military forces abroad. As we have learned in the past, this can lead ultimately to war."

War Powers

The Senate, by a 68-16 roll-call vote, passed a bill (S 2956) defining the powers of Congress and the President in decisions involving the armed forces of the United States in hostilities.

Passage of the bill marked the first time that either house of Congress had undertaken to codify the war powers left vague by the Constitution.

It also marked the furthest step taken by the Senate in an effort to restore to Congress constitutional powers involving decisions of war and peace which many senators believed had been usurped by successive Presidents since World War II.

Despite opposition by the Nixon administration, the bill was supported on final passage by a broadly based coalition of Republicans and Democrats, northerners and southerners, and advocates and opponents of higher defense spending.

The House passed an amended version of S 2956, but the bill died in conference.

SENATE ACTION

The Senate Foreign Relations Committee Feb. 9 by unanimous vote reported S 2956 setting limits to the President's use of armed forces without specific congressional authorization.

The bill was another in a series of measures by which the Foreign Relations Committee challenged the assumption of larger foreign policy powers by the President.

Chief sponsors of S 2956—a synthesis of war powers bills introduced in 1971—were Senators Jacob K. Javits (R N.Y.) and John C. Stennis (D Miss.), chairman of the Senate Armed Services Committee.

Reflecting congressional concern over the way the United States entered its costly involvement in the Vietnam war, the bill defined emergency conditions in which the President could commit forces "in the absence of a declaration of war by the Congress."

S 2956 also prescribed procedures by which Congress could terminate the emergency use of American forces if it disapproved of the President's action.

The committee bill exempted U.S. participation in the Indochina fighting from its provisions—an omission that drew protests in separate views filed by Chairman J. W. Fulbright (D Ark.) and John Sherman Cooper (R Ky.).

Fulbright, while endorsing the bill's intent, also objected that the emergency conditions defined by S 2956 "...may have the unintended effect of giving away more power than they withhold."

Provisions. As reported, S 2956:

• Provided that, in the absence of a declaration of war by Congress, armed forces could be committed to hostilities or to "situations where imminent involvement in hostilities is clearly indicated by the circumstances" only:

1. To repel an armed attack on the United States or to forestall the "direct and imminent threat of such an attack."

2. To repel an armed attack against U.S. armed forces outside the United States or to forestall the threat of such attack.

3. To protect and evacuate U.S. citizens and nationals in another country if their lives were threatened.

4. Pursuant to specific statutory authorization by Congress (not to be inferred from any existing or future law or treaty unless specific authorization was provided; specific statutory authority also was required for assignment of U.S. military personnel to assist a foreign nation's forces in hostilities or situations where hostilities were imminent).

• Required the President to promptly report to Congress the commitment of forces for such purposes.

• Limited to 30 days the length of involvement of U.S. forces unless Congress by specific legislation authorized their continued use.

• Provided that Congress by act or joint resolution could terminate the use of U.S. forces by the President before the end of the 30-day period.

• Set procedures to require prompt consideration in both houses of any bill or joint resolution authorizing or terminating use of U.S. forces committed by the President.

• Made the bill's provisions effective on the date of enactment but exempted hostilities in which U.S. forces were involved on the effective date.

In its report on S 2956, the Senate Foreign Relations Committee dwelt at length on "the intent of the framers" of the Constitution that Congress exercise the power to declare war and how Presidents gradually had taken over the war-making power.

The purpose of S 2956 was "...to fulfill—not to alter, amend, or adjust—the intent of the framers of the...Constitution in order to assure that the collective judgment of both the Congress and the President will be brought to bear in decisions" involving U.S. forces in hostilities, the committee said.

Floor Debate. After seven days of debate, the Senate April 13 approved S 2956 with the same provisions as reported by the Foreign Relations Committee, plus three floor amendments offered by Javits.

Adopted en bloc by a 59-0 roll-call vote, the Javits amendments added language spelling out the President's authority to:

• Protect and evacuate U.S. citizens and nationals whose lives were threatened on the high seas.

• Permit U.S. military officers to continue to participate in joint headquarters operations by NATO, the United Nations forces in Korea and the U.S.-Canadian North American Air Defense Command.

• Continue to use the armed forces in combat if, after the 30-day limit on actions not authorized by Congress expired:

1) "...unavoidable military necessity" required protection of troops "in the course of bringing about a prompt disengagement...."

2) an armed attack physically prevented Congress from convening to consider legislation extending the President's authority or ordering a troop withdrawal.

Amendments Rejected. A series of motions and amendments were rejected during the seven days of debate on S 2956. A motion by Roman L. Hruska (R Neb.) to refer the bill to the Judiciary Committee for a study of constitutional issues involved was rejected on a 26-60 roll-call vote. The amendment had the support of Sam J. Ervin Jr. (D N.C.), chairman of the Judiciary Subcommittee on Separation of Powers. Ervin opposed the bill on constitutional grounds.

Also defeated during the debate were amendments, offered by J. W. Fulbright (D Ark.) and Mike Gravel (D Alaska), making the bill's provisions apply to the war in Indochina.

HOUSE ACTION

The House Aug. 14, by a 344-13 roll-call vote under suspension of the rules, passed an amended version of S 2956.

A two-thirds majority of members present and voting (238 in this case) was required for passage under suspension of the rules.

The House Foreign Affairs Committee had deleted the provisions of the Senate-passed bill and substituted legislation less restrictive of the President's war powers which had been passed twice before by the House.

As passed by the House, S 2956 was similar to H J Res 1, passed by the House by voice vote on Aug. 2, 1971, and

---

Constitutional Powers

The Constitution divided authority to make war between Congress and the President, giving Congress the power to declare war and the President command of the armed forces.

Art. I, Sec. 8: "The Congress shall have the power ...to declare war...to raise and support armies, but no appropriation of money to that use shall be for a longer term than two years; to provide and maintain a Navy; to make rules for the government and regulation of the land and naval forces...to make all laws which shall be necessary and proper for carrying into execution the foregoing powers, and all other powers vested by this Constitution in the government of the United States, or in any department or officer thereof."

Art II, Sec. 2: "The President shall be Commander in Chief of the Army and Navy of the United States ...he shall have power, by and with the advice and consent of the Senate, to make treaties, provided two-thirds of the senators present concur; and he shall nominate, and by and with the advice and consent of the Senate, shall appoint ambassadors, other public ministers and consuls...."

---

to H J Res 1355, passed by a 288-39 roll-call vote on Nov. 16, 1970. It required only that the President report to Congress whenever he acted without prior congressional authorization to commit U.S. forces to hostilities, to send combat-equipped troops overseas or to enlarge forces already stationed abroad. It urged but did not require the President to consult Congress before taking such action. (*H J Res 1, p. 875; H J Res 1355, p. 864*)

The Nixon administration was firmly opposed to the Senate bill but said it could accept the House provisions as approved in H J Res 1355 and H J Res 1.

After the Senate passed S 2956 on April 13, the Senate Foreign Relations Committee April 20 reported H J Res 1 adversely. Opponents of the Senate bill blocked a request for unanimous consent to amend H J Res 1 with the Senate-approved provisions of S 2956.

The legislation died in conference.

Foreign Aid

Congress in 1972 finished up action on fiscal 1972 foreign aid funds that had been left hanging when its 1971 session adjourned. But unable to agree on fiscal 1973 appropriations, Congress kept the assistance program going beyond the end of 1972 only through continuing resolutions.

In 1971, the obstacle to final action had been the Mansfield end-the-war amendment to the fiscal 1972 authorization bill. That roadblock had been removed by Senate agreement in December 1971 to drop the Mansfield provision, clearing the way for final action on March 2.

In 1972, the obstacle was disagreement over two Senate amendments cutting off funds for military base agreements not approved by the Senate as treaties. This time, however, both House and Senate conferees refused proposed compromises, and the conference committee

Oct. 11 gave up efforts to reach agreement on authorizing legislation for military aid and Bangladesh relief.

Although Congress had authorized fiscal 1973 appropriations for economic aid as part of the fiscal 1972 bill, the House refused to act on economic assistance appropriations separately from military aid funds. The Senate, on the other hand, refused to act on appropriations for military aid and Bangladesh relief without enactment of authorizing legislation for those programs.

The military aid impasse—and Senate rejection of an initial military assistance authorization bill—kept the entire foreign aid program's future in doubt.

Fiscal 1972 Funds. With eight months of the fiscal year already gone, Congress March 2 cleared legislation appropriating $3.2-billion for foreign aid and related programs for fiscal 1972.

On Jan. 25, Congress had completed action on a measure (S 2819) authorizing $2.6-billion in fiscal 1972 for bilateral economic and military assistance programs. House approval on Jan. 25 of the conference report on S 2819—adopted by the Senate on Dec. 17, 1971—ended a long struggle over fiscal 1972 authorizations that included the 1971 Senate defeat of the original fiscal 1972 authorization bill.

Although the Mansfield end-the-war amendment had been dropped, the final authorization bill included several Senate policy amendments—including a $341-million ceiling on aid to Cambodia. Making important changes in congressional procedures, the bill transferred military assistance authorizations for Thailand to the Foreign Relations and Foreign Affairs committees' jurisdictions and required periodic authorizations of State Department and U.S. Information Agency appropriations.

Both provisions gave the Foreign Relations Committee greater opportunity for future challenges to administration policies. *(State Department-USIA authorization bill, p. 891)*

The fiscal 1972 authorization bill also authorized $984-million for economic aid in fiscal 1973.

Fiscal 1973 Funds. As in 1971, Congress in 1972 was unable to reach agreement on legislation extending the foreign aid program. With authorizing legislation stalled in conference—again over Foreign Relations Committee policy amendments—final action on foreign aid appropriations was impossible.

House and Senate conferees Oct. 11 gave up efforts to reach agreement on a bill (HR 16029) authorizing fiscal 1973 appropriations for military aid and Bangladesh relief.

The stalemate—which marked the third time in the four years of the Nixon administration that Congress had failed to complete action on either a foreign aid authorization or appropriation—resulted from a disagreement on two Senate Foreign Relations Committee amendments sponsored by Clifford P. Case (R N.J.). One would have cut off funds to implement a 1971 executive agreement with Portugal for a U.S. air base in the Azores Islands unless it was approved by the Senate as a treaty. The other, applying the same principle of congressional participation in foreign policy decisions, would have barred use of funds to carry out any future agreement with another nation for military base rights unless the agreement was approved as a treaty by the Senate. *(Executive agreements, p. 884)*

Both sides rejected proposed compromises offered in conference. House conferees rejected a Senate offer to drop the Azores provision and revise the base agreement provision to require approval by both houses of Congress by simple majorities.

Senate conferees turned down a House substitute proposal requiring the executive branch to submit all base agreements to Congress.

The Senate had deleted appropriations for military aid and Bangladesh relief from the House-passed appropriations bill (HR 16705) on the ground that funds for those programs had not been authorized. Although both houses had approved versions of HR 16705 appropriating funds for economic aid and related programs, the House refused to separate those programs from military aid.

Failure of conferees to work out a compromise bill made it necessary for Congress to include the foreign aid program under a resolution providing continued funding for various departments and agencies. Foreign aid was continued at an annual rate of $3,652,701,000 through the end of the fiscal year on June 30, 1973.

Late in September it had appeared that action on the aid bill might be completed in 1972 when the Senate reversed an earlier decision to kill its own bill and decided instead to pass an amended version of the House-passed measure (HR 16029). The Senate version authorized appropriations of $1,822,500,000 in fiscal 1973 for foreign military aid and Bangladesh relief. The House bill, passed Aug. 10, authorized $2,131,000,000.

With one major exception, the new Senate bill's provisions were nearly identical to the aid measure (S 3390) that the Senate rejected by a **key 42-48 roll call** on July 24. In an action assuring passage of HR 16029, the Senate Sept. 26 by a 45-42 roll call deleted a provision cutting off funds for the Vietnam war which had been attached to the bill by the Foreign Relations Committee.

Bangladesh Recognition

Several weeks before the United States extended formal diplomatic recognition to Bangladesh, the Senate passed a resolution (S Con Res 55) urging President Nixon to do so. The resolution, which was not binding on the President, was approved March 21 by voice vote and formal recognition was extended April 4.

The House took no action.

Background. Bangladesh declared independence from Pakistan after Indian troops seized control of the area—formerly known as East Pakistan or East Bengal—during the India-Pakistan war of November-December 1971.

The Pakistani government's repressive policies against advocates of East Bengal autonomy were a factor in provoking the war. Sheik Mujibu Rahman, who was imprisoned in West Pakistan after his Awami (People's) League won a majority of East Pakistani national assembly seats in 1970 elections, became the Bangladesh prime minister after his release.

Members of Congress in 1971 said the administration had failed to use U.S. influence in Pakistan to end the repression in East Pakistan and had taken Pakistan's side during the war with India. *(U.S. aid to Pakistan, p. 886)*

U.S. Aid to Pakistan: Opposition in Congress

U.S. assistance to Pakistan created an ongoing controversy in Washington during 1971 and 1972. Pakistan's seizure in early 1971 of the rebel-held East Pakistani capital of Dacca and other events which erupted into open war between Pakistan and India in November-December 1971 prompted several congressional moves to cut off arms to the war-torn area.

In May 1971 the Senate Foreign Relations Committee reported a resolution (S Con Res 21) calling for the suspension of U.S. military assistance and licenses for military sales to Pakistan until the conflict in East Pakistan was resolved. The committee added two amendments to the resolution which stipulated that the military assistance and sales should be suspended until "the distribution of relief supplies in that area is undertaken."

The committee report said that when the Pakistan army took control of Dacca, the capital of East Pakistan, on March 25, 1971, the army engaged in "indiscriminate killing of civilians with military equipment furnished by the United States." Initially the State Department did not confirm the information, but on April 23, the committee received a letter from the State Department stating that "some M-24 tanks and F-86 aircraft have been observed in use in East Pakistan in recent weeks."

The report stated that the involvement of U.S. military equipment in an internal dispute over the political autonomy of East Pakistan violated the Foreign Assistance Act of 1961, which was intended to restrict the use of U.S. military assistance to Pakistan to combat external Communist aggression or internal Communist subversion.

No further action was taken on the resolution. However, arms bans were written into several foreign aid bills.

Refugee Assistance. The fiscal 1972 foreign aid authorization bill (S 2819—PL 92-226), which cleared Congress in January 1972, suspended all economic and military aid to Pakistan, except for food and humanitarian assistance distributed by international agencies. The measure authorized $250-million for refugee and humanitarian relief.

The fiscal 1972 foreign aid appropriations bill (HR 12067—PL 92-242), which cleared Congress in March 1972, barred aid to Pakistan and India while the two countries were involved in armed conflict with each other, except for humanitarian and refugee relief. The President could waive the ban if such action was required by national security. He was to report the waiver to Congress within 30 days.

Appropriations of $200-million for East Pakistani refugee relief were included in the fiscal 1972 appropriations bill. Fiscal 1973 appropriations totaled $100-million.

Additional bans were written into other foreign aid legislation which never cleared Congress.

Background. Before 1965, the United States furnished grant military aid to Pakistan amounting to hundreds of millions of dollars. In 1965, as a result of the India-Pakistan war, the United States embargoed future shipments of military equipment to both countries and ended all grant military assistance. In 1966 and 1967 the United States modified the embargo to permit the cash sale of ammunition, military communications, medical and transportation equipment and spare parts for equipment provided before the embargo.

In April 1971, shortly after the outbreak of fighting in East Pakistan, the United States held up any further new authorization of arms for Pakistan, but permitted sales for which export licenses had been issued prior to March 25, 1971. In November, the United States announced the cancellation of existing export licenses. The following month, the United States suspended arms shipments and economic aid to India. Previously approved licenses for military exports were revoked.

Throughout 1971, critics on Capitol Hill said the administration had failed to use U.S. influence in Pakistan to end the repression in East Pakistan and had taken Pakistan's side during the war with India. The administration countered that India had started the open fighting as behind-the-scenes U.S. efforts to persuade Pakistan to grant East Pakistan autonomy were about to succeed.

Disclosures in late 1971 and early 1972 by columnist Jack Anderson of discussion during White House strategy sessions on policy in the India-Pakistan war added fuel to the controversy. The classified documents containing the minutes from meetings of the Washington Special Action Group, a top-level strategy planning group, indicated the President had ordered a strong pro-Pakistan policy and a tough stand against India. Anderson received a Pulitzer Prize in May 1972 for his disclosures on administration policymaking.

In February 1972 President Nixon notified Congress that the fiscal 1972 foreign aid legislation's ban on military and economic aid no longer applied because conditions in Pakistan were returning to normal. In March 1973 the United States announced the partial lifting of the arms embargo against India and Pakistan. (*Recognition of Bangladesh, p. 885*)

Seabed Arms Treaty

The Senate Feb. 15, by an 83-0 roll-call vote, ratified a treaty (Exec H, 92nd Congress, 1st session) prohibiting the deployment of nuclear weapons on the ocean floor.

The treaty pledged the United States and other nations not to place nuclear weapons or other weapons of mass destruction on the seabed outside a 12-mile territorial limit recognized by most nations.

In addition to the United States, 85 nations had signed the treaty including the Soviet Union and Great Britain, both nuclear powers.

France and the Peoples Republic of China, the other nations known to possess nuclear weapons, had not signed the treaty.

The treaty prohibited the construction of launching installations and storage or testing facilities for such weapons, but it did not apply to submarines anchored or resting on the seabed.

Background. The Senate Foreign Relations Committee in 1967 held hearings on resolutions introduced by Claiborne Pell (D R.I.) urging the United Nations to study rules governing activities in the oceans and proposing a draft treaty prohibiting nuclear weapons. The Johnson administration opposed the resolutions as premature.

The United States in 1967 began an examination of seabed weapons control, and the United States and the Soviet Union in 1969 agreed on a draft treaty which was submitted to the Conference of the Committee on Disarmament at Geneva, Switzerland.

After four revisions, the UN General Assembly Dec. 7, 1970, endorsed the treaty by a 104-2 vote. The United States signed the treaty on Feb. 11, 1971, and President Nixon submitted it to the Senate on July 21, 1971.

Other Treaties

PLANTS. The 1951 International Plant Protection Convention, drawn up to increase international cooperation in controlling pests and plant diseases and preventing their spread across international boundaries. Exec D, 84th Congress, 2nd session, ratified 74-0, June 12.

TERRORISM. The 1971 Convention to Prevent and Punish the Act of Terrorism Taking the Form of Crimes Against Persons and Related Extortion That Are of International Significance, excluding kidnapping and other violent acts against diplomats from treatment as political offenses rather than crimes. Exec D, 92nd Congress, 1st session, ratified 74-0, June 12.

HONDURAS. The 1971 Treaty with Honduras on the Swan Islands, recognizing Honduran sovereignty over the Caribbean islands but maintaining U.S. rights to operate a telecommunications and meteorological facility there. Exec H, 92nd Congress, 2nd session, ratified 74-0, June 12.

EVIDENCE. The 1968 Convention on the Taking of Evidence Abroad in Civil or Commercial Matters, drawn up to simplify the process of gathering evidence abroad for lawyers and courts from nations with differing legal systems. Exec A, 92nd Congress, 2nd session, 84-0, June 13.

ARGENTINA. The 1972 Treaty on Extradition Between the United States of America and the Republic of Argentina, which replaced an 1896 extradition treaty and listed 30 extraditable offenses including narcotics violations and aircraft hijacking. Exec F, 92nd Congress, 2nd session, 84-0, June 13.

TELECOMMUNICATIONS. The 1971 Partial Revision of the 1959 Radio Regulations Relating to Space Telecommunications, which updated existing regulations to accommodate new technology and uses of radio communications in space. Exec E, 92nd Congress, 2nd session, 84-0, June 13.

CULTURAL PROPERTY. The 1970 Convention on the Means of Prohibiting and Preventing the Illicit Import, Export and Transfer of Ownership of Cultural Property. Exec B, 92nd Congress, 2nd session, 79-0, Aug. 11.

NORWAY. The 1971 Convention for the Avoidance of Double Taxation with Norway, replacing a 1949 tax treaty with Norway. Exec D, 92nd Congress, 2nd session, 79-0, Aug. 11.

METROLOGY. The 1955 Convention Establishing an International Organization of Legal Metrology. The United States previously was not a member of the organization, which was made up of most of the major trading partners of the United States and provided for cooperation in the science of measurement. Exec I, 92nd Congress, 2nd session, 79-0, Aug. 11.

COPYRIGHT. A 1971 revision of the Universal Copyright Convention. The revised convention permitted developing nations to reproduce and translate works by other nations' authors sooner than permitted under existing copyright regulations. Exec G, 92nd Congress, 2nd session, 67-0, Aug. 14.

FISHERIES. A 1970 protocol to the 1949 Convention of the Northwest Atlantic Fisheries, allowing amendment of the convention 120 days after approval by three-fourths of the contracting governments. The resolution of ratification was approved with a reservation directing the secretary of state to object to any proposed amendment that went into effect without approval of its ratification by the Senate. Exec C, 92nd Congress, 2nd session, 89-0, Oct. 3.

SEA SAFETY. Eleven amendments to the 1960 Convention for the Safety of Life at Sea, setting new standards for navigational equipment, use of automatic pilots, charts and publications and safety equipment. Exec O, 92nd Congress, 2nd session, 89-0, Oct. 3.

BRAZIL. A 1972 agreement between the United States and Brazil regulating shrimp fishing by U.S. boats in water claimed by Brazil. Exec P, 92nd Congress, 2nd session, 89-0, Oct. 3.

AVIATION SAFETY. A 1971 Convention for the Suppression of Unlawful Acts Against the Safety of Civil Aviation, providing for the punishment of violent acts on or against civilian aircraft. Exec T, 92nd Congress, 2nd session, 89-0, Oct. 3.

Protection of Foreign Officials

Congress Oct. 11 completed action on a bill (HR 15883—PL 92-539) strengthening the protection of foreign officials and diplomatic missions in the United States.

The bill was designed to deter increasing harassment of and violence against foreign officials, particularly from the Soviet Union and Middle East nations. The scope of the bill was broadened to include protection for official guests, after the Sept. 5 and 6 killing in Munich, Germany, of 11 members of the Israeli Olympic team by Arab terrorists. *(Terrorist resolution, p. 890)*

Kidnapping Penalty. The House Judiciary Committee had originally reported a bill (HR 10502) which included a provision revising the kidnapping law to permit the death penalty whether the defendant was tried by jury or by a judge. However, on the same day the bill was reported, the Supreme Court ruled the death penalty unconstitutional as currently imposed in the United States. In light of the decision, the committee withdrew HR 10502 for reconsideration and subsequently reported

Genocide Convention: Pending in Senate Since 1949

In 1970—after a delay of 22 years—the Senate Foreign Relations Committee recommended that the Senate consent to the ratification of the 1948 United Nations convention against genocide (Exec O, 81st Congress, 1st session). No action was taken in the 91st Congress or in the 92nd Congress, when it was reported for a second time.

President Nixon, in early 1970, called for Senate ratification of the International Convention on the Prevention and Punishment of the Crime of Genocide which had been adopted unanimously by the UN General Assembly in 1948 and had been ratified by 75 nations, including the Soviet Union.

President Harry S Truman submitted the genocide treaty to the Senate for ratification in 1949, and hearings were held by a Senate Foreign Relations subcommittee in 1950. The subcommittee recommended ratification, but the treaty got caught up in 1953-54 during Senate debate over the proposed, narrowly defeated Bricker amendment to the Constitution and the question of whether such treaties infringed on national and state laws. *(Bricker amendment, Congress and the Nation Vol. I, p. 110)*

The convention, which went into force in 1951, prohibited killing or forcible action with the intent to destroy national, ethnic, racial or religious groups and deliberate attempts to cause "serious bodily or mental harm" to large numbers of members of such groups.

In the past there had been reluctance to bring the genocide pact to a vote on the floor because of opposition from more conservative senators. The American Bar Association had opposed ratification, although a group in the ABA urged reversal of the position. In 1970, the ABA House of Delegates voted 130-126 against recommending ratification.

ABA spokesmen have argued that the agreement failed to cover the Soviet Union's extermination of political opposition. The ABA also contended friction, perhaps war, might result if an international forum attempted to pass judgment on a crime committed within a state's domestic jurisdiction.

Committee Action. In July 1970 the Senate Foreign Relations Committee voted 7-5 to delay action on the genocide convention. The committee first had voted 6-5 to approve the treaty, but reversed its decision when floor manager Frank Church (D Idaho) decided it would be unwise to report it with such narrow committee support.

Citing the My Lai massacre, Church said most of the members objecting were concerned about the definition of genocide and the possibility that other nations could charge the United States with genocide before the International Court of Justice.

In December 1970, however, the full Foreign Relations Committee voted 10-2 to report the convention favorably with four separate statements clarifying the U.S. government's understanding of the meaning of certain provisions of the treaty.

The majority report said that racial intolerance and minority harassment, no matter how deplorable, would not be outlawed by the convention. It added that approval would probably have only limited impact since implementing legislation would be required, extradition accords had to be worked out and an international tribunal would have to be established to deal with the crime.

"The committee is not as convinced as the executive branch that ratification will make a significant contribution to (the) goal" of buttressing U.S. moral leadership and promoting international law and order, the report said. "But it can scarcely do any harm and on balance could well represent a modest step forward."

The understandings and declaration approved by the committee included statements emphasizing that acts involved meant those against a substantial part of an attacked group, provided a definition of mental harm, reserved the right to try U.S. citizens for acts committed outside the country and stated that the United States would not complete the ratification process until after implementing legislation had been enacted by Congress.

In March 1971, the Senate Foreign Relations Committee again recommended ratification of the genocide convention but no action was taken by the 92nd Congress. The treaty was favorably reported for a third time in March 1973.

HR 15883, which eliminated the death penalty. *(Court decision, p. 311)*

Foreign Service Grievances. During floor debate on the bill, the Senate dropped a committee-added provision that would have created a grievance procedure for personnel of the State Department and others covered under Title VI of the Foreign Service Act of 1946. The Senate had made two previous attempts in 1972 to legislate a grievance procedure for State Department employees. Provisions similar to those in HR 15883 had been incorporated into the State Department authorization bill but were deleted in conference. The Senate later passed a bill identical to the grievance provisions in the authorization measure. *(Fiscal 1973-74 State-USIA authorization, p. 890)*

Fishing Boat Seizures

Congress Oct. 11 completed action on a bill (HR 7117—PL 92-569) expediting federal reimbursements to fishing-boat owners for fines incurred by unlawful seizure of U.S.-flag vessels by other nations.

As cleared, HR 7117 created a revolving fund to provide funds for reimbursement of boat owners for fines paid to free vessels seized by other nations in territorial waters not recognized by the United States. The fund would eliminate the need for Congress to appropriate funds separately to meet each claim, a process that caused delays of more than a year in most cases.

Background. Under a law passed in 1954, the federal government reimbursed fines paid to free boats seized while fishing in waters claimed by other nations but considered open sea by the United States. The United States recognized a 12-mile limit on territorial waters, but other nations—notably Ecuador and Peru—claimed more extensive limits and frequently seized U.S. boats operating within those waters.

The conference report on HR 7117 included a Senate amendment allowing the President to waive a provision requiring that the amount of any fine or damages reimbursed by the federal government be deducted from foreign assistance payments to the nation that had seized a U.S. boat and refused to pay for damages or refund the fine.

A 1968 law (PL 90-482) had required such deductions from foreign aid, but the State Department had interpreted the law as giving the secretary of state discretion to decide whether or not to withhold the money. As a result, fishing boat owners had to wait long periods for reimbursement by the federal government until Congress appropriated the money in supplemental appropriations bills. HR 7117 was introduced to remedy those complaints.

North Pacific Fisheries

Congress cleared legislation (HR 9501—PL 92-471) amending the North Pacific Fisheries Act of 1954. In addition to provisions dealing with the appointment of commissioners to international fishery commissions, the bill authorized the secretary of commerce to administer the International Convention for High Seas Fisheries of the North Pacific Area.

UN Environmental Fund

The Senate Foreign Relations Committee June 8 reported a resolution (S Con Res 82) requesting the U.S. government to support the establishment of a $100-million United Nations fund for the environment.

The resolution expressed the sense of Congress that the U.S. delegation to the United Nations Conference on the Human Environment, held June 5-16 in Stockholm, Sweden, should urge creation of the fund.

The voluntary UN fund was originally proposed by President Nixon in his Feb. 8, 1972, environmental message to Congress. He said the United States should "commit itself to provide its fair share of the fund on a matching basis." The U.S. share would be about 40 per cent.

No further action was taken on the resolution.

Immigration Amendments

Several amendments to the Immigration and Nationality Act were considered in 1972.

• Congress Oct. 14 cleared a bill (HR 8273—PL 92-584) amending the Immigration and Naturalization Act, to reduce the residency requirements for retention of U.S. citizenship by persons born abroad with one American parent and one alien parent.

• The House Feb. 22 by voice vote passed a bill (HR 6420) increasing the maximum amount of naturalization fees that could be kept by clerks of state courts.

• The House March 16 by voice vote passed a bill (HR 9615) authorizing the issue of special immigrant visas to Eastern Hemisphere countries for a four-year period.

Pacific Trust Territories

In 1972, Congress approved legislation (S 860—PL 92-257) aimed at promoting the economic development of the U.S. Trust Territory of the Pacific Islands (Micronesia). The bill authorized an appropriation of $3.1-million to the islands' development fund —raising total U.S. contributions to $5-million—and set conditions for loans granted to stimulate economic development on the islands.

Background. Since 1947, the United States had administered about 2,200 islands in the western Pacific under a UN trusteeship. Before World War II, the islands—which include the Mariana, Caroline and Marshall Islands—were held by Japan under a League of Nations mandate.

The islands' economy, which had been exploited by Japan mainly for copra oil, stagnated under the U.S. trusteeship. Although U.S. assistance during the 1960s created a government superstructure and public works facilities, the islands' economy lacked the capital to develop large enterprises. The population of about 91,000 living on 97 scattered islands, depended mainly on government jobs, trade and tourism.

An economic development fund created in 1964 grew through appropriations by Congress to about $1.9-million by 1972. The Nixon administration in its fiscal 1973 budget requested appropriation of an additional $1-million for the fund.

Other Bills. Congress passed several other bills dealing with the Pacific Trust Territory during the first Nixon administration:

• In 1969, Congress approved a bill (S 3479—PL 91-578) providing a three-year authorization to finance civil government in the trust territories. The bill authorized $60-million a year for fiscal 1972 and 1973 to support construction of educational and health facilities for the Caroline, Marshall and Mariana Islands. The bill also increased the authorization for fiscal 1971 to $60-million from $50-million.

• In 1971, Congress approved a joint resolution (H J Res 617—PL 92-39) authorizing $25-million in World War II and postwar damage claim payments to inhabitants of U.S. trust territories.

• The House Sept. 12 by voice vote passed a bill (HR 16188) amending the Immigration and Nationality Act (PL 82-414) to make it illegal to knowingly hire aliens who had not been admitted for permanent residence.

Naval Ship Loans

Congress approved a bill (HR 9526—PL 92-270) authorizing five-year loans of military ships to five allied countries: Spain, Turkey, Greece, South Korea and Italy. The final version of the bill contained a Senate-added provision stating that "any loan to a country under this act shall not be construed as a commitment by the United States to the defense of that country." It also provided that renewal of any of the loans must be approved by Congress (previously the President determined renewals).

Boundary with Mexico

Congress Oct. 13 completed action on a bill (HR 15461—PL 92-549) authorizing implementation of a 1970 treaty with Mexico settling boundary disputes along the Rio Grande. *(Treaty, p. 879)*

As cleared, the bill gave the federal government authority to buy land from U.S. owners for transfer to Mexico, to dispose of land acquired from Mexico and to undertake engineering and construction projects to relocate the Rio Grande channel to comply with the treaty. HR 15461 also authorized the State Department to negotiate and share the cost of an agreement with Mexico for flood control along the Rio Grande in the Presidio Valley of Texas.

The cost of land acquisition and channel relocation authorized by the bill was estimated at $12,868,000, with annual operating costs expected to be about $400,000. If undertaken simultaneously with channel relocation, the Presidio flood control project was expected to cost $2.5-million.

Terrorist Sanctions

The Arab terrorist killing of 11 Israeli Olympic team members in Munich, Germany, Sept. 5 and 6 sparked a heated reaction on Capitol Hill.

The Senate and House Sept. 6 unanimously passed resolutions calling for suspension of aid to nations that support or sanction terrorism. The resolutions did not specify particular nations or aid to be suspended, but in debate—during which over 100 senators and representatives spoke in support of the resolutions—Syria, Lebanon, Libya and Algeria were named as having provided refuge for terrorists in the past.

The resolutions were advisory and required no action from the President. They asked "that all means be sought by which the civilized world may cut off from contact with civilized mankind any people or any nation giving sanctuary, support, sympathy, aid or comfort to acts of murder and barbarism such as those just witnessed at Munich." The Senate vote was 82-0 and the House vote, 346-0.

On Sept. 28, the Senate passed by voice vote and without debate a resolution (S Con Res 100) requesting the President to consider sanctions against nations which harbor terrorists.

Also in reaction to the Munich killings, Congress broadened the scope of a bill providing protection for foreign officials and diplomatic missions in the United States to include official guests, before clearing it Oct. 11. *(Protection of foreign officials bill, p. 887)*

Foreign Travel Restriction

The House Oct. 2, under suspension of the rules procedure, rejected a bill (HR 16742) giving the President power to penalize U.S. citizens who travel to nations with which the United States was engaged in armed conflict.

The 230-140 roll-call vote fell 18 short of the necessary two-thirds majority (248 in this case) required to pass a bill under the suspension of the rules procedure.

The bill's immediate application would have been to North Vietnam, the only nation with which the United

States was in armed conflict. The President could delegate his authority, under the bill, to the secretary of state. In addition, the bill would have provided maximum penalties for unauthorized travel of 10 years in prison or a $10,000 fine, or both.

Background. Proposals to restrict travel of Americans, particularly to war zones, were introduced in Congress after actress Jane Fonda and former Attorney General Ramsey Clark toured North Vietnam in the summer of 1972.

Existing law required federal government approval for travel to North Vietnam, North Korea and Cuba but did not contain penalties. Hence travel to those countries could be denied, but violators could not be punished. In addition, the Supreme Court ruled in 1967 that travel to a restricted area with a valid passport was not illegal.

HR 16742 had the support of the Justice Department.

State Department Appropriations

Congress appropriated $533,671,750 for the State Department in fiscal 1973, as part of a $4,681,017,850 appropriation for the Departments of State, Justice and Commerce, the Judiciary and 15 related agencies (HR 14989—PL 92-544). The administration had requested $569,848,000 for State Department funding.

The bill also included $10,000,000 for the Arms Control and Disarmament Agency, down from the administration request of $10,253,000. Funds for the U.S. Information Agency were set at $206,803,000; the administration had requested $207,209,000.

Among the bill's provisions was a section restricting the U.S. share of the United Nations budget to not more than 25 per cent of the total UN budget, beginning Jan. 1, 1974. The International Atomic Energy Agency and the joint financing program of the International Civil Aviation Organization were excepted from the provision.

UN Contributions. During consideration of HR 14989, the House Appropriations Committee added a provision immediately (July 1, 1972) reducing U.S. contributions to the United Nations and its affiliated agencies from 31.52 per cent to 25 per cent of the total annual budget. The provision would have resulted in a $25,103,500 reduction in the over-all budget request of $100,978,319, the committee said. "The recommended reduction serves notice that the Congress means what it has been saying" about reducing U.S. contributions to international organizations.

The United Nations determined each member's contribution for a three-year period. Opponents of an immediate, unilateral reduction in U.S. payments argued that the United States was obligated by international agreement to continue its 31.52 per cent contribution through calendar 1973 and that defaulting on this obligation could precipitate UN bankruptcy.

A proposal to restore the $25,103,500 and to delete the reduction provision was defeated 156-202 on a recorded teller vote.

The Senate Appropriations Committee, however, restored $24,070,500 and delayed to Jan. 1, 1973, the House-approved provision limiting U.S. contributions to 25 per cent. The committee exempted the International Atomic Energy Agency and the joint financing program of the International Civil Aviation Organization. During floor debate, the Senate, by a 39-28 roll-call vote, accepted an amendment offered by Roman L. Hruska (R Neb.) to extend from Jan. 1, 1973, to Dec. 31, 1973, the date after which U.S. contributions to the United Nations could not exceed 25 per cent of the annual UN budget.

On Dec. 13, the UN General Assembly, by a vote of 81-27, with 22 abstentions, agreed to accept a UN Finance Committee's recommendation that the U.S. assessment be reduced to 25 per cent.

ILO Dues. Appropriation of funds for U.S. dues to the International Labor Organization (ILO) had sparked controversy in 1970 and 1971 because of allegations that the organization had become a forum for Soviet propaganda. Appropriations in 1970 had been cut nearly in half and no funds were appropriated in 1971. *(Fiscal 1972 State-Justice bill, p. 880; fiscal 1971 State-Justice bill, p. 874)*

In 1972, the House had approved $4-million for ILO dues and the Senate $12.6-million. Conferees agreed to the House-approved figure which would cover dues for the second half of 1971 and the first few weeks of 1972.

In 1973, in the second supplemental appropriations bill for fiscal 1973, Congress appropriated $8,617,000 for the ILO, thus completing payment of U.S. dues through calendar 1972.

State-USIA Authorization

Congress authorized appropriations of $1,001,130,000 in fiscal 1973-74 for U.S. foreign policy agencies and activities (HR 14734—PL 92-352), after a wide-ranging debate on such issues as the Vietnam war and executive privilege.

The measure included authorizations for fiscal 1973 appropriations of $648,354,000 for the State Department, $200,249,000 for the United States Information Agency (USIA) and $88,027,000 for the Peace Corps. It authorized fiscal 1973-74 appropriations of $22,000,000 for the Arms Control and Disarmament Agency.

In addition, the bill provided $42,500,000 in fiscal 1973 for use by the President to assist narcotics control efforts by other nations and international organizations.

The House and Senate had approved identical amounts for the four agencies. The Senate had added the narcotics control authorization—requested as part of the fiscal 1973 foreign aid bill—as a floor amendment to the State Department-USIA measure. The House accepted the amendment in conference.

Each house had increased the administration's State Department request by approving an additional $85-million for aid to Israel and other nations in resettlement of Jewish refugees from the Soviet Union. The bill also provided $8,212,000 for migration and refugee aid to other groups.

Each house also had approved a single-year authorization of $88,027,000—the proposed fiscal 1973 program expenditures—for the Peace Corps. The President had asked Congress for a permanent, open-ended Peace Corps authorization.

HR 14734 authorized the full amounts requested for the USIA, arms control agency and narcotics control program.

Before fiscal 1973, State Department and USIA Appropriations had been funded under a permanent authorization. In 1971, however, a Senate Foreign Relations Committee amendment to the fiscal 1972 foreign aid bill required regular authorization of the department's and agency's funds. *(Fiscal 1972 foreign aid bill, p. 873)*

Indochina Amendment. In reporting the State-USIA bill, the Senate Foreign Relations Committee had attached a series of legislative amendments, including an end-the-war provision, authored by Clifford P. Case (R N.J.) and Frank Church (D Idaho). Their amendment kept the bill before the Senate for more than a month. The proposal was revised, amended further and then deleted on a voice vote May 31.

USIA Funds. Angered by USIA information policies and by the President's invocation of executive privilege to deny congressional access to USIA planning documents, the committee recommended a reduction of $45.6-million—nearly 23 per cent—in the agency's fiscal 1973 budget request.

The committee had requested the agency's country planning memoranda and related information. However, in a memorandum to Secretary of State William P. Rogers and USIA Director Frank Shakespeare, President Nixon directed them not to make available to Congress "any internal working documents...which would disclose tentative planning data...which are not approved positions."

The committee argued that the planning documents "may provide a full and adequate justification for the $200-million authorization request.

"In the absence of such information and justification," the committee added, "the taxpayers of the country should be given the benefit of the doubt.... If the agency decides at a later date to furnish the information requested, the committee of course would consider a supplemental authorization request."

The money was restored by a floor amendment offered by Gale W. McGee (D Wyo.) and accepted May 1 by a roll-call vote of 57-15.

USIA Material. The Senate Foreign Relations Committee also adopted an amendment prohibiting distribution of USIA materials within the United States without specific congressional authorization.

Committee Chairman J. W. Fulbright (D Ark.), in a March 28 letter to Acting Attorney General Richard G. Kleindienst, questioned the showing of the USIA film "Czechoslovakia 1968" during a taped television report by Sen. James L. Buckley (Cons-R N.Y.) for a number of New York television stations.

During the show, Bruce Herschensohn, assistant USIA director of motion pictures and television, termed Fulbright's foreign policy views "naive and stupid." Herschensohn resigned on April 3, and Shakespeare and Buckley apologized to Fulbright.

Fulbright argued that domestic showing of the film was a violation of the United States Information and Educational Exchange Act of 1948. Kleindienst, however, ruled that the law prohibited USIA from actively distributing its materials in the United States but required the agency to make materials available upon request by the press or by members of Congress. *(Congress and the Nation Vol. I, p. 208)*

Terming Kleindienst's ruling "a distortion of the legislative intent concerning the domestic distribution of USIA materials," the committee approved what it termed "a blanket prohibition."

The final version of the bill forbade the distribution in the United States of USIA materials, except for study by students and scholars in Washington, D.C., and for examination but not distribution by members of Congress.

Grievances. Another major provision added by the Senate Foreign Relations Committee was a proposal for creating a State Department grievance procedure.

The committee in 1971 blocked the nomination of Howard W. Mace, former State Department director of personnel, to be ambassador to Sierra Leone after former Foreign Service officers criticized the way Mace handled the "selection-out" of employees who were passed over for promotion.

The committee recommended creation of a semi-autonomous three-member board to hear employee grievances. The secretary of state could reject the board's recommendations for resolution of disputes over promotions, assignments or dismissals only if he determined "that the foreign policy or security of the United States will be adversely affected."

The provision was deleted in conference when House conferees argued that the Foreign Affairs Committee should have the opportunity to hold hearings on the proposal, which was opposed by the State Department.

The Foreign Relations Committee reported the grievance procedure as separate legislation (S 3722) and the Senate passed the bill June 22, but no action was taken in the House. The committee made another attempt at setting up a Foreign Service grievance procedure during its consideration of legislation to protect foreign officials and diplomatic missions in the United States. However, the proposal was deleted from the bill on the Senate floor. *(Foreign officials protection bill, p. 887)*

Rhodesian Chrome. The Foreign Relations Committee approved an amendment by Gale W. McGee (D Wyo.) repealing a provision enacted in 1971 that required the President to disregard a United Nations embargo against Rhodesia in order to import Rhodesian chromium ore.

The provision, an amendment to the fiscal 1972 defense procurement authorization bill (HR 8687—PL 92-156), ended U.S. support of sanctions decreed by the UN Security Council in 1966 after Rhodesia's white supremacist government declared independence from Great Britain.

The committee amendment was deleted on the floor by a roll-call vote of 40-36.

Other Provisions. In addition to the authorized appropriations and the restriction on dissemination of USIA material, PL 92-352:

• Extended Civil Service retirement benefits to foreign government employees who represented U.S. interests in nations with which the United States had no diplomatic relations.

• Required the Arms Control and Disarmament Agency to prepare a report for Congress on the international transfer of conventional arms.

• Abolished the Peace Corps National Advisory Council.

• Permitted persons appointed to positions in foreign affairs agencies to express their own views and recommendations upon request by congressional committees.

• Created a Commission on the Organization of the Government for the Conduct of Foreign Policy to study foreign operations by all U.S. government agencies.

• Required that all persons given the title of ambassador or minister be confirmed by the Senate, with an exception for persons given the personal rank of ambassador or minister while undertaking a special mission for the President of six months or less duration.

• Established the positions of deputy secretary of state and under secretary of state for economic affairs.

• Increased to $350,000 from $300,000 the ceiling on Peace Corps funds used during any fiscal year to assist the development of international voluntary efforts by other nations and international organizations.

• Excluded certain trust funds and similar accounts from a provision in the fiscal 1972 foreign aid bill (S 2819 —PL 92-226) requiring regular authorization of State Department and USIA appropriations.

Historic Trips to Moscow and Peking

NEW RELATIONSHIP WITH COMMUNIST SUPERPOWERS

In major foreign policy initiatives, President Nixon in 1972 paid visits to the Communist world's two major capitals—Moscow and Peking. The trips were the first state visits by a U.S. President to either country.

The President's conferences with leaders of the Soviet Union and the People's Republic of China had a common goal: stabilization of U.S. relations with the two vast countries vying for power and influence as leader in the Communist world.

In terms of substantial results, the President's journeys were vastly different. Returning from China after his February visit, the President brought home only the prospect of formal relations with Peking—by itself a significant departure from U.S. policy followed since 1949.

Returning from Moscow on June 1, however, the President brought seven agreements with the Soviet government, including two nuclear arms control accords. Both accords—a treaty limiting anti-ballistic missile sites and an agreement limiting offensive missiles—received congressional approval.

The Moscow agreements brought formal recognition by the two superpowers of their mutual interests in arms control, trade, scientific development and preservation of the environment. The Peking discussions brought only recognition by estranged rivals of the need for better understanding of each other, with the specific issues dividing them left for future resolution.

China

Nixon's Feb. 21-28 stay in mainland China ended more than 20 years of official U.S. hostility toward the People's Republic, an attitude proclaimed in 1949 after the Communists drove the government of Chiang Kai-shek from the mainland to Taiwan.

Led by Premier Chou En-lai, Chinese officials gave Nixon a restrained welcome upon his arrival in Peking. Later that day, however, the President met four hours with Communist Party Chairman Mao Tse-tung—an indication of the importance the Chinese leadership assigned Nixon's visit.

After a week of private conferences, public banquets and sightseeing tours, Nixon and Chou Feb. 27 issued a joint communique indicating agreement on the need for increased contacts between their nations.

(During a February 1973 visit to Peking by national security adviser Henry A. Kissinger, the United States and the People's Republic of China agreed to set up liaison offices as a step toward "normalization of relations." The liaison offices in Peking and Washington opened in May 1973.)

The communique's most controversial part gave U.S. acceptance to Peking's contention that Taiwan was part of China. Conceding that Taiwan's fate should be determined only by the Chinese, the United States pledged

ultimate withdrawal of its military forces from Taiwan.

For its part, the Chinese government in the communique repeated its claim to sovereignty over Taiwan, governed by the Nationalist Chinese since 1949 with U.S. military and diplomatic support. Settlement of the Taiwan question, Peking maintained, was crucial to normal relations with the United States.

Nixon returned Feb. 28 and was met by a chorus of praise for establishing contacts with the Chinese Communist government.

The praise was not unanimous, however. Nixon's agreement that Taiwan was a part of China and that its future was a matter to be determined by the Chinese, evoked bitter criticism from some sources.

The statement was interpreted by some conservatives as meaning the abandonment of the Nationalist Chinese government. Criticism came from such disparate candidates for President as Rep. John M. Ashbrook (R Ohio), Nixon's conservative opponent for the Republican nomination, and Sen. Hubert H. Humphrey (D Minn.).

"For over two decades," Ashbrook said, "it is we who have fostered and supported, both by words and deeds, the concept of an independent Republic of China on Taiwan. Now, in a single week, we have abandoned that position—and in so doing we have set up the framework to abandon 15 million people to the tender mercies of a regime that during its tenure in office—its 23 years of enlightenment and progress—has managed to slay, at conservative estimate, 34 million of its own citizens."

Humphrey's concern was more for the native Taiwanese, as distinct from the Nationalist Chinese who came from the mainland.

"It is now clear," he said, "that the rug has been pulled out from under the Taiwanese, though the people of the island of Formosa once aspired to determine their own destiny."

Humphrey also took issue with Nixon's statement (in his arrival speech) that no other nation's fate was negotiated behind its back in the talks with Chou and that no American commitment to another country was given up.

"It is apparent from the communique as I read it," Humphrey said, "that concessions were made by the President and by Dr. (Henry A.) Kissinger (Nixon's national security adviser), but not any, insofar as I have been able to interpret, were made by the Chinese."

Ashbrook's view was echoed by four House conservatives, Philip M. Crane (R Ill.), John R. Rarick (D La.), John G. Schmitz (R Calif.) and Robert L. Sikes (D Fla.).

Further criticism came from two other candidates for the presidency, Rep. Paul N. McCloskey Jr. (R Calif.) and Sen. Henry M. Jackson (D Wash.). McCloskey welcomed the limited renewal of relations with China but said that, despite Nixon's trip, "we did not progress one inch toward settling the major problem of today, ending the Vietnam war." Jackson expressed disappointment that Nixon had not gained concessions on Vietnam from the Chinese government.

Sen. James L. Buckley (Cons-R N.Y.), said that relaxation of the U.S. commitment to defend Taiwan would "vastly diminish" his regard for Nixon. But he said he still would support Nixon for re-election.

Sen. George McGovern (D S.D.), the eventual Democratic nominee for President, praised the Nixon trip, as did Sen. Edward M. Kennedy (D Mass.). Chairman J. W. Fulbright (D Ark.) of the Senate Foreign Relations Committee, a persistent critic of Nixon's Vietnam policy, indicated he was satisfied with the results of the trip. So did Sen. Barry Goldwater (R Ariz.), the unsuccessful Republican presidential candidate in 1964. Goldwater said he was satisfied that "we have not given away one single thing to the Red Chinese" and that "we will uphold our treaty commitments to the Taiwan government."

During Nixon's visit, U.S. officials arranged for high-level visits to China by congressional leaders. Senate Majority Leader Mike Mansfield (D Mont.) and Minority Leader Hugh Scott (R Pa.) visited six Chinese cities, from April 19 to May 3, and House Majority Leader Hale Boggs (D La.) and Minority Leader Gerald R. Ford (R Mich.) followed June 23-July 8.

Soviet Union

Back in the United States for less than half an hour from his mission to Moscow, the President reported June 1, 1972, to Congress and the American people on the results of his agreements with the Soviet leaders.

The President had been in the Soviet Union from May 22-30. On May 26, he and Soviet Communist Party General Secretary Leonid I. Brezhnev signed a treaty limiting construction of antiballistic missile sites to two and an agreement limiting the number of offensive strategic missiles each side would have.

He urged the assembled lawmakers to "seize the moment so that our children and the world's children live free of the fears and free of the hatreds that have been the lot of mankind through the centuries."

He assured them that "the present and planned strategic forces of the United States are without question sufficient for the maintenance of our security and the protection of our vital interests."

"No power on earth is stronger than the United States of America today," he said. "None will be stronger than the United States of America in the future."

He added: "It is clear the agreements forestall a major spiraling of the arms race—one which would have worked to our disadvantage."

The President encouraged "the fullest scrutiny of these accords," and said he was confident that "such examination will underscore...that this is an agreement in the interests of both nations."

As the President urged Congress to approve the accords, the Soviet news agency, Tass, reported that the Soviet Politburo, the Council of Ministers and the Presidium of the Supreme Soviet all had "entirely approved" the summit pacts. U.S. endorsement required action by Congress.

Partisan feelings were evident in the House chamber as the President spoke. The American success in the strategic arms and other negotiations, the President said, "came about because, over the past three years we have

---

Nuclear Pacts and Congress

Congressional approval was required on both the offensive and defensive aspects of agreements on nuclear arms reached by the President with the Soviets.

A provision in the 1961 law establishing the Arms Control and Disarmament Agency, which negotiated the pacts, specifies that any agreement to limit U.S. armed forces or armaments must be approved by legislation or treaty.

President Johnson June 13 submitted the two accords to Congress together with documents explaining U.S.-Soviet agreements and disagreements on interpretations of the accords.

The disagreements concerned mainly the ultimate size of nuclear submarine fleets and the size of certain offensive weapons. The explanation of the differences was designed to head off reservations on the part of the Senate to the treaty.

The President urged approval "without delay" promising that U.S. defense capabilities would remain "second to none." He called for "a sound strategic modernization program" as the nation moved to negotiate further arms accords.

The explanatory statements, drawn up in Moscow by U.S.-Soviet negotiators, emphasized U.S. concern over development of large Soviet missiles and envisaged future negotiations on nuclear limitations.

The document recorded a unilateral Soviet statement, not agreed to by the United States, that the Soviets would increase the number of their nuclear submarines, if Washington's NATO allies increase theirs.

The President said the two Moscow agreements were "a significant step into a new era of mutually agreed restraint and arms limitation between the two principal nuclear powers." The agreements did not, he said, "close off all avenues of strategic competition." They "open(ed) up the opportunity for a new and more constructive U.S.-Soviet relationship, characterized by negotiated settlement of differences, rather than by the hostility and confrontation of decades past."

---

consistently refused proposals for unilaterally abandoning the ABM (antiballistic missile), unilaterally pulling back our forces from Europe and drastically cutting the defense budget."

Nixon said Congress deserved "the appreciation of the American people for having the courage to vote such proposals down and to maintain the strength America needs to protect its interests."

Past Summits. The President alluded to past meetings of Soviet leaders and American Presidents. "One meeting after another," he said, "produced a short-lived euphoric mood—the spirit of Geneva, the spirit of Camp David, the spirit of Vienna, the spirit of Glassboro —without producing significant progress on the really difficult issues."

But this summit was different, he said. "This was a working summit. We sought to establish not a superficial spirit of Moscow, but a solid record of progress on solving the difficult issues which for so long have divided our two nations and the world." That goal was accomplished, the President added. (Soviet leader Brezhnev visited Washington in June 1973 for another round of summitry with President Nixon.)

Seven Agreements. The President returned to Washington with seven agreements he had signed with Soviet leaders.

They included pacts on joint space missions, technology, the environment, medical research, trade, accidents at sea and the limitation of strategic arms.

But it was the arms accord that overshadowed every other aspect of the dramatic week in Moscow. The agreement was based on three premises:

• That development of offensive weaponry clearly was more advanced than the development of defensive weapons systems. Therefore, the freeze on both offensive and defensive weapons would leave both nations naked to a first attack.

• That both powers were confident they could survive a first strike to the extent they could retaliate with enough force to totally destroy the opposing nation.

• That the threat of nuclear obliteration—the "balance of terror" that had prevailed for almost a quarter century—was an adequate deterrent to all out war.

Two Arms Agreements

There were two elements to the arms agreement worked out by the American and Soviet leaders: a treaty that would limit the deployment of antiballistic missiles (ABMs) and an executive agreement limiting the number of offensive weapons to those already under construction or deployed when the agreement was signed. The executive agreement also placed limitations on the number of missile-carrying submarines that could be constructed.

Under the defensive arms treaty, both the United States and Soviet Union would be limited to one ABM site for the defense of their capital cities, plus one additional site each for the defense of an ICBM (intercontinental ballistic missile) field.

Defense critic Senator William Proxmire (D Wis.) argued that the treaty did not require construction of the two ABM sites.

Under the offensive arms agreement, the Soviet Union would be permitted to field about 300 of its new giant SS-9 missiles in silos occupied by older models. But the total number of the larger variety could not be increased.

Both sides would be able to construct new submarine-launched ballistic missiles (SLBMs) of the Polaris or Poseidon variety if they dismantle an equal number of land-based ICBM launchers or older submarine launchers. Thus, while the number of submarines could increase, the total of warheads would not.

Although the Russians were left with more land- and sea-based missiles in their arsenal, the United States—because it had developed systems whereby one missile delivers a number of independently targeted warheads—would have more than three times the Soviet number of deliverable warheads.

The Soviets had not yet tested a multiple warhead weapons system, although the treaty would allow them to do so.

Fact Sheet on Agreements

Following is the text of a White House fact sheet, released May 26, 1972, on the strategic arms limitation agreement:

The ABM Treaty

• Limits each side to one ABM site for defense of their national capital (Moscow and Washington) and one site for each side for the defense of an ICBM field.

• There will be a total of 200 ABM interceptors permitted each side, 100 at each site.

• Radars will be limited to Modern ABM Radar Complexes (called MARCs) six for each side within a circle of a 150 kilometer radius around the national capitals; (MARCs are a circle of 3 km diameter, in which radars can be deployed; in practice they can accommodate about one large radar or a few smaller ones).

• For the ICBM defense fields there will be a total of twenty radars permitted; two of them can be about the size of the two larger radars deployed at Grand Forks; the other eighteen radars will be much smaller.

• The Soviet ICBM protection site will be at least 1300 km from Moscow. Our comparable site will be at Grand Forks, North Dakota.

• Other large non-ABM radars that may be built in the future will be restricted to space tracking or early warning and limited in size so as not to create a clandestine ABM potential.

• The treaty will be of unlimited duration with withdrawal rights if supreme interests are jeopardized, and on six months notice.

The Interim Offensive Agreement

• Limits ICBMs to those under construction or deployed at the time of signing the treaty or July 1. (This will mean about 1618 ICBMs for the USSR and 1054 for the United States. The USSR will field about 300 large SS-9s, but they will be prohibited from converting other ICBM silos to accommodate the large SS-9 types. Other silos can be modified, but not to a significant degree. Modernization is permitted.)

• Construction of submarine launched ballistic missiles on all nuclear submarines will be frozen at current levels. The further construction of SLBMs on either side, can only be accomplished by dismantling of an equal number of older land based ICBMs or older submarine launchers.

• The Interim Agreement will run for five years (compared to the original Soviet proposal of 18 months), and both sides are committed to negotiating a permanent and more comprehensive agreement.

• Both sides will abide by the obligations of the agreement once it is signed, though formal implementation will await ratification of the ABM treaty.

The agreement did not provide for any on-site inspection. Both sides apparently were satisfied that satellite reconnaissance was adequate for monitoring the other's activities. But there was an unusual agreement whereby each side pledged not to interfere with the other's gathering of technical data. Both promised not to conceal their missile deployments or tests.

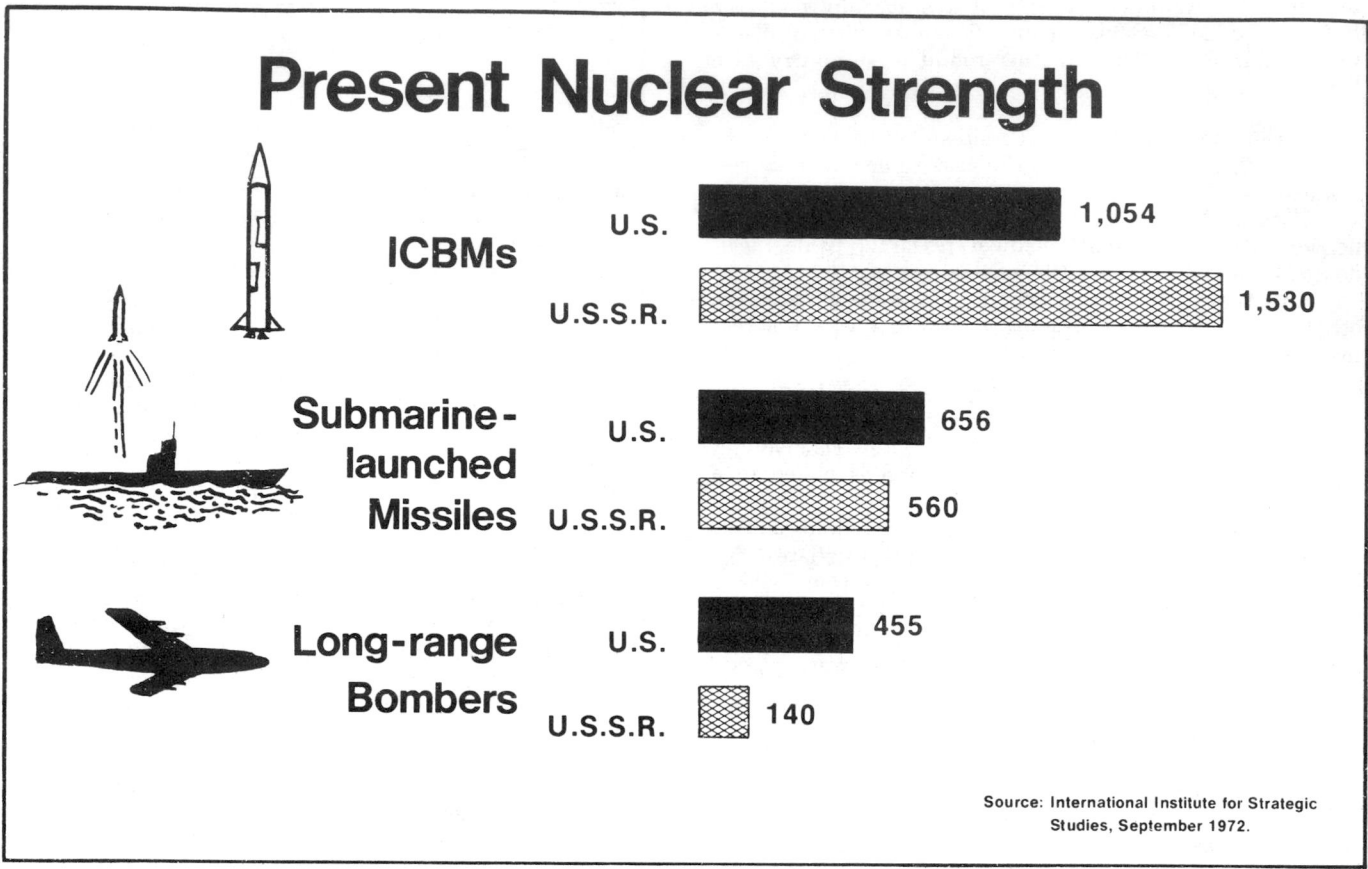

Present Nuclear Strength

ICBMs
U.S. — 1,054
U.S.S.R. — 1,530

Submarine-launched Missiles
U.S. — 656
U.S.S.R. — 560

Long-range Bombers
U.S. — 455
U.S.S.R. — 140

Source: International Institute for Strategic Studies, September 1972.

Debate in Congress

For both President Nixon and his Soviet counterparts, the road from the conference table promised a few more obstacles. Communist Party chief Brezhnev had to contend with some of the more reluctant members of the Soviet hierarchy.

President Nixon had to face the Congress.

The offensive arms agreement required approval by simple majorities in both the House and Senate; the ABM treaty had to be ratified by a two-thirds majority in the Senate. *(Box, p. 894)*

President Nixon had several advantages going into congressional hearings in the summer of 1972 on the nuclear arms pacts he negotiated with the Soviet Union. Though sentiment was mixed, the President hoped to avert an all-out battle like the one when the Senate ratified the 1963 nuclear test ban treaty.

By contrast with 1963, the 1972 agreements:

• Were produced by a President with a long record of militant anti-communism.

• Received early approval of the Joint Chiefs of Staff. In 1963 the joint chiefs qualified their endorsement with insistence on four safeguards eventually incorporated. In 1972 they insisted on weapons progress.

• Were supported by a secretary of defense (Melvin R. Laird) with a congressional record of backing a strong military posture. In 1963 Secretary of Defense Robert S. McNamara was widely criticized by defense-oriented sources.

• Were negotiated in a period of comparatively relaxed tensions between the United States and Soviet Union. In 1963 the memory of the 1962 Cuban missile crisis was fresh in congressional minds.

On the other hand, Congress had not abandoned support for a strong military defense. Proxmire and others succeeded in trimming military funds by several billion dollars in 1969, but Congress in 1971 resisted defense-cutting attempts.

Many members of Congress who voiced basic approval of the 1972 pacts, as well as some who criticized them, emphasized they would be influenced by disclosures at committee hearings. A chief complaint by early critics was the lack of details and lack of clarification of complex technical questions affecting U.S. security.

Senate Approval

The Senate Aug. 3 gave its approval to ratification of the ABM treaty by a **key roll-call vote of 88-2.**

The Senate acted after the Foreign Relations Committee unanimously approved both the treaty and the interim agreement. In urging Senate support for the accords, however, the committee made clear that a majority of its members questioned the need for an ABM site to protect Washington, D.C., and for accelerated development of offensive weapons as requested by the administration.

James B. Allen (D Ala.) and James L. Buckley (Cons-R N.Y.) cast the only votes against approval of the ABM treaty. Both argued that the treaty, by limiting each nation to two ABM sites, would expose their civilian populations to destruction in the event of nuclear war.

Allen also questioned whether the United States could trust the Soviet Union to live up to the treaty and the agreement.

Interim Agreement. Congress Sept. 25 cleared for the President a bill (H J Res 1227—PL 92-448) authorizing his approval of a five-year U.S.-Soviet agreement limiting offensive nuclear weapons, but only after inclusion of a controversial amendment offered by Sen. Henry M. Jackson (D Wash.).

The House had given routine consideration to H J Res 1227. The resolution was passed Aug. 18, by a 329-7 roll-call vote, after about one hour of debate. No changes were made on the floor.

But when the measure reached the Senate the going was rougher. Breaking a six-week deadlock, the Senate Sept. 14 demanded a stiff U.S. bargaining stance in upcoming nuclear arms talks with the Soviet Union when it passed H J Res 1227 by an 88-2 roll-call vote.

The hard-line instructions for negotiators in the strategic arms limitation talks (SALT) were contained in an amendment sponsored by Jackson which requested that any future permanent treaty on offensive nuclear arms "not limit the United States to levels of intercontinental strategic forces inferior to" those of the Soviet Union, but rather be based on "the principle of equality." The amendment stipulated that failure to negotiate a permanent treaty limiting offensive arms would be grounds to abrogate the U.S.-Soviet ABM agreement. It also endorsed the maintenance of a vigorous research, development and modernization program.

The Jackson amendment was adopted by a **key 56-35 roll-call vote** after its supporters had beaten back several attempts to weaken it.

The White House Aug. 7 endorsed Jackson's effort after he modified his proposal by dropping a stipulation that any Soviet action or deployment that threatened U.S. deterrent capability would be grounds for repudiating the interim agreement.

In its place, Jackson and the White House agreed on the statement that failure to negotiate an offensive arms treaty by 1977 would be grounds for repudiating the ABM treaty—a position taken previously by the administration.

Controversy over the Jackson proposal had threatened to delay the resumption of strategic arms control talks, formerly scheduled to begin in Geneva in mid-

October. The House accepted the Senate changes rather than risk further delay.

The Jackson and other amendments added to the bill had no effect on the accord itself as signed in Moscow. But they served to emphasize the disquiet of many members of Congress—and a majority of the Senate, which must ratify any permanent treaty—concerning the terms of the interim agreement.

Final action came Sept. 25 when the House, by a 308-4 roll-call vote, approved a resolution (H Res 1133) concurring with Senate amendments.

Trade Mission

Following up on Nixon's Moscow visit, the administration and the Soviet leaders sought agreements to broaden trade between the two nations.

The first major result was an agreement by the Soviet Union to buy at least $750-million in American grains over a three-year period.

Secretary of Commerce Peter G. Peterson in July led a delegation of American officials to Moscow to discuss further trade accommodations. The discussions were the first formal meeting of the U.S.-Soviet commercial commission created as a result of the Moscow summit.

A major stumbling block at issue in the bargaining was settlement of the Soviet Union's World War II lend-lease debts to the United States. Administration officials were insisting on settlement of the debts as part of any broad trade arrangement.

Agreement was reached the following fall. On Oct. 18, the United States and Soviet Union signed a three-year trade pact, as well as an agreement on repayment of the lend-lease debts.

Implementation of the trade agreement hinged on congressional approval of most-favored-nation status (nondiscrimination in customs matters) for Soviet products. If it was not granted, the pact would not enter into force and the Soviet Union, in accordance with the second agreement, would not have to repay the balance of its lend-lease debt of $722-million. According to the agreement, the Soviet Union would repay $48-million by July 1975, but the remaining debt would be deferred until most-favored-nation treatment was granted.

(In the spring of 1973, the administration's plans to extend most-favored-nation treatment to the Soviet Union appeared to be in trouble on Capitol Hill. A majority in both the Senate and the House had pledged to make such tariff treatment for Soviet products contingent upon an end to Soviet restrictions on emigration.)

Vietnam War Policy

During his 1968 election campaign, Nixon repeatedly pledged to end U.S. involvement in the Vietnam war. More than four years later, on January 27, 1973, a cease-fire agreement was signed in Paris. *(Cease fire, p. 928)*

During the intervening period, the President generally managed to defuse the issue of the war so that anti-war sentiment in the country did not ride at the steadily high level of the last years of the Johnson administration. Early abandonment of the concept of a "purely military victory" and formulation of a policy which regularly reduced U.S. ground troops and turned the ground fighting over to the South Vietnamese helped to ease the country's frustration over the war.

War opponents and an increasing number of Congressmen did, however, quarrel unsuccessfully with the slow pace of the winding down of the war—a pace the President justified as being necessary to give the Paris peace talks time to work and to achieve "peace with honor."

This quarrel became a full-scale protest whenever the President directed any widening of the war. A ground incursion into Cambodia in April 1970, U.S.-backed invasion of Laos in February 1971, renewed bombing of North Vietnam in April 1972 and the mining of North Vietnamese harbors in May 1972 caused major anti-war protests. The latter two actions were partially responsible for winning the Democratic nomination for the candidate most closely associated with the peace issue—Sen. George McGovern (D S.D.).

The protests no doubt helped to underscore the political desirability of achieving a settlement before the November 1972 election. Such a settlement came very close in October 1972. It slipped away temporarily, but by that time the war was erased as an election issue.

Nixon Strategy

When Nixon became President it was clear that if he did not want to be brought down by the Vietnam war, as his predecessor had been, he would have to find a way out. This the President promised, and he moved away from earlier U.S. policy which sought a clear-cut military victory for South Vietnam. However, he ruled out a "precipitous" withdrawal, and said the rate of U.S. troop reductions would depend on progress in Paris peace negotiations, a decline in the level of enemy military activity and the rate at which South Vietnamese forces were trained to assume the major combat responsibilities.

The latter point became known as "Vietnamization," and it was the centerpiece of the administration's plan to end direct U.S. involvement in the war. After the program

was given time to work the Nixon administration claimed major successes for it, and U.S. troops were steadily withdrawn. When President Nixon was inaugurated in 1969 there were 542,500 U.S. servicemen in Vietnam; at the end of 1972 there were 24,200.

Vietnamization was in a sense the pilot project for a new policy, enunciated in February 1970, termed the Nixon doctrine. As set forth by the President, the central thesis of the new policy was that the United States would "participate in the defense and development of allies and friends, but that America cannot—and will not—conceive all the plans, design all the programs, execute all the decisions and undertake all the defense of the free nations of the world."

But the President did not restrict himself to a policy of gradual withdrawal from involvement in Indochina. He also took several strong aggressive actions, such as invasion of Cambodia in 1970 and of Laos in 1971, which he insisted were necessary to disrupt Vietcong sanctuaries and supply routes. There was a rise in anti-war sentiment after each of these incidents, but it always subsided as U.S. troops continued to leave and U.S. casualties continued to fall.

The President had to deal with hawks as well as doves. A peripheral aspect of the administration's Vietnam strategy was the rapprochement with Communist China which began in 1971 and was capped by the President's visit to Peking in February 1972. One of the Johnson administration rationales for involvement in Vietnam had been the threat posed to the United States by a hostile Communist China which supported North Vietnam. Once the hostility between the two nations was eased there was less justification for a U.S. presence in Indochina. *(China policy p. 893)*

While the administration followed its strategy of Vietnamization mixed with strong action, the Paris peace talks went on. Begun in 1968 when the Johnson administration ordered a partial halt to the bombing of North Vietnam, talks between representatives of the United States, North Vietnam, South Vietnam and the National Liberation Front went on for 174 sessions until January 1973. In addition, there were numerous secret meetings

References

Discussion of Vietnam policy for the years 1945-64 may be found in *Congress and the Nation, Vol. I,* p. 127-141; for the years 1965-68, *Congress and the Nation, Vol. II,* p. 49, 53-54, 67-70, 78-82, 101-103.

between national security affairs advisor Henry Kissinger and Le Duc Tho of North Vietnam.

Until mid-1972 the Paris talks showed few public results. New peace plans offered by both sides were revealed and rejected in early 1972. The talks were suspended in March and a major communist offensive and U.S. bombing followed. The talks resumed with intensified negotiations in July and Hanoi, in an Oct. 26 broadcast, revealed that they had finally resulted in a nine-point peace settlement. The communists apparently then changed their position on several issues and in December the talks again stopped and the heaviest U.S. bombing of North Vietnam of the war followed. In January the talks resumed, ending with the formal signing of the cease-fire agreement Jan. 27.

The agreement provided for an internationally-supervised cease-fire in place, and return of all American prisoners within 60 days. All foreign military troops were to be removed and bases dismantled. The South Vietnamese were to decide their political future "through genuinely free and democratic general elections under international supervision." A National Council of National Conciliation and Concord was to be established, with equal membership from both sides, to set up the elections.

After the agreement was signed, many critics wondered if it had been worth the agony and whether a similar result could have been achieved earlier in the Nixon administration. In a May 3, 1973, "State of the World" message, President Nixon emphasized that until late 1972 the North Vietnamese had insisted on negotiating a political settlement as well as a military settlement, whereas the United States refused to impose a political solution on South Vietnam. The President said: "Until the final stage the North Vietnamese and their allies insisted on a settlement that would effectively guarantee that the future of South Vietnam would be communist. Public speculation and commentary to the contrary they never agreed to separate military from political issues until the end of 1972.... This basic philosophical clash, not the failure to find precise formulas, delayed a settlement for four years."

Congress and the War

As the war dragged on and expanded into Cambodia and Laos, congressional opposition grew. Increasingly, members of both the House and Senate questioned the right of the President to wage war without congressional consent or guidance. From 1966-72 a total of 94 roll-call votes were cast on the war. Over 80 of these votes occurred during Nixon's first term.

But, for all the time spent on the issue, Congress was not united or effective in anti-war efforts. This was particularly true of the House where, despite many complaints about aggrandizement of presidential war powers, a majority of members were consistently unwilling to challenge the President's preeminence in the conduct of the war or its diplomacy. At the peak of anti-war strength in Congress only one out of three representatives voted to back end-the-war proposals. Of the 94 roll calls on the war, only a few were cast by the House, and House conferees almost invariably were responsible for deleting or emasculating Senate anti-war amendments.

The attitude in the Senate was different, but the result was similar. There was a great deal of complicated

---

Anti-War Amendments

The primary method by which Congress attempted to legislate policy concerning the Vietnam war from 1969-72 was in the form of amendments to annual or recurring pieces of major legislation such as foreign aid, defense appropriations and the extension of the military draft.

This chapter discusses this legislation only insofar as it pertains to the Vietnam war. For details on other aspects of these bills, the researcher is directed to the foreign policy and national security chapters of this volume. (p. 853, 191)

Major Vietnam Legislation. For a quick overview of congressional action on Vietnam in each of the four years, the researcher is directed to the "Legislative Action" summaries appearing on pages 903, 910, 916, and 925 of this chapter.

legislative action on proposals to control or end the war, but most of the proposals were deleted in conference or did not carry the force of law. Those which became law were largely moot since they placed restrictions on military activity the executive no longer intended to pursue. Defense appropriations bills covering the cost of the war were approved each year by overwhelming majorities.

A number of Senators became familiar to U.S. newspaper readers as they sponsored a succession of anti-war proposals. Chief among them were Majority Leader Mike Mansfield (D Mont.), and Sens. John Sherman Cooper (R Ky.), Frank Church (D Idaho), George McGovern (D S.D.), Mark O. Hatfield (R Ore.) and Edward W. Brooke (R Mass.).

The Senate first disputed administration policy in 1970 when it twice passed a Cooper-Church amendment barring use of U.S. funds for U.S. military operations in Cambodia. A weakened version of the amendment—barring use of ground but not air forces—was eventually carried in a supplemental foreign aid authorization.

Other action on anti-war proposals in 1970 included repeal of the 1964 Tonkin Gulf resolution which President Johnson had claimed provided congressional authority for stepped-up U.S. military action in Indochina. A Hatfield-McGovern amendment, providing for withdrawal of U.S. troops by Dec. 31, 1971, was twice defeated by the Senate. *(Tonkin Gulf text, p. 947)*

In 1971, the Senate adopted amendments to three bills by Majority Leader Mansfield calling for withdrawal of troops from Indochina by a certain deadline. Two of these survived House-Senate conferences—with the withdrawal deadline deleted—the first time the House had gone on record urging the end of the war. The President said the provision was not binding and he would not follow it. A new Cooper-Church amendment, limiting use of U.S. funds in Indochina to troop withdrawal, was defeated on the Senate floor in a series of close votes.

No end-the-war legislation won final congressional approval in 1972. The Senate barely passed a Brooke amendment cutting off funds for the war four months after enactment. It was the first time a funds cut-off had been approved, but the proposal died in conference.

In spring 1973 there was an important postscript to the congressional action on the Vietnam war. Although it had pulled out of Vietnam after Jan. 27, the United States had continued bombing in Cambodia and Laos in support of anti-communist activities there. In action on a supplemental appropriations bill in May, both chambers made it clear that they believed the United States should get out of Indochina altogether. The House for the first time voted to cut off funds for military activity there. On May 10 it voted 219-188 to prohibit transfer of funds from other defense programs for U.S. military activity in Southeast Asia. It then voted 224-172 to prohibit use of funds in the bill for combat activity in Cambodia. The House votes were followed by even stronger Senate action prohibiting use of any funds appropriated by Congress for combat activities in Laos or Cambodia. The Senate voted May 31, 55-21, that the amendment was germane to the appropriations bill.

Chronology of

Vietnam Policy

And Legislation

1969

Hopes were high when the Nixon administration came into office. A U.S. halt of bombing raids on North Vietnam had been in effect since November 1968. Preliminaries to the Paris peace talks were completed in mid-January when the United States and North Vietnam agreed on the shape of the negotiating table. Formal peace talks with representatives from South Vietnam, North Vietnam, National Liberation Front (Vietcong) and the United States opened Jan. 25. The very newness of the administration was a psychological plus—even the most vocal war critics appeared willing to give the new leadership a chance.

The first year of the Nixon administration saw a gradual scaling down of the U.S. military presence in Vietnam. The President abandoned the concept of a "purely military victory." In mid-year he began bringing U.S. troops home, amid talk of his "Vietnamization" program to prepare the South Vietnamese to take over the U.S. combat role.

Nixon responded to public weariness with sustained involvement in remote regions with a popular policy (the "Nixon Doctrine") aimed at avoiding future Vietnams by assisting but not assuming primary responsibility for resisting aggression. *(Box p. 869)*

But 1969 was also a year of disappointments and frustrations. Hopes for the Paris negotiations soon dropped. No breakthroughs occurred and the year ended with the chief U.S. negotiator's resignation and a pessimistic prognosis for the future of the talks.

It was a year of ever-widening divisions in the country. The "silent majority" and "middle America"—which Nixon saw as his constituency—were pitted against the war protestors—the "impudent snobs" as the Vice President tagged them—who resumed marching in the streets,

U.S. Troop Levels in Vietnam

As of Jan. 31, 1973, several days after signing of the cease-fire agreement, U.S. military personnel in Vietnam had been reduced to 21,500. The peak level of U.S. military strength—543,500—was reached April 30, 1969.

The last U.S. combat forces left South Vietnam Aug. 12, 1972, reducing military personnel to 43,500. The last troops, except for U.S. members of the Joint Military Commission (JMC) and several hundred detailed to the defense attache's office, were withdrawn March 29, 1973. JMC withdrawal was completed March 31.

Given below are the U.S. troop levels as of Dec. 31 of each year.

Year	Total
1960	900
1961	3,200
1962	11,300
1963	16,300
1964	23,300
1965	184,300
1966	385,300
1967	485,600
1968	536,100
1969	475,200
1970	334,600
1971	156,800
1972	24,200

SOURCE: Department of Defense

as well as their fellow critics on college campuses and in the halls of Congress.

The scars of the war—in Vietnam and at home—were deepened in 1969 by revelations of the "Green Beret" case and the My Lai massacre. In June the Army charged six members of the U.S. Special Forces (or Green Berets) with murdering a South Vietnamese double intelligence agent. The Army, offering little explanation, dropped the charges in September.

Horror, incredulity and dismay were registered in Congress and throughout the country with the revelation in November 1969 of an alleged massacre of Vietnamese civilians by U.S. forces in March 1968. In November the Army announced the court-martial of First Lt. William L. Calley on charges of the premeditated murder of at least "109 Vietnamese civilians." *(Box p. 905)*

Military Activity

Renewed enemy offensives, increasing toward the end of the year, broke the intermittent lulls on the battlefield in 1969. But enemy attacks never reached the intensity of the 1968 Tet offensive.

Troop Withdrawals. The U.S. troop level in Vietnam was at 542,500 when Nixon came into office. His timetable for their withdrawal became a focal point of controversy between the administration and its critics. The administration repeatedly ruled out a "precipitous" or immediate troop withdrawal, and declared that the rate of U.S. troop reductions would depend on developments on three fronts: progress in the Paris negotiations; a decline in the level of enemy military activity; and the rate at which South Vietnamese forces were trained and equipped to assume major combat responsibilities.

The first withdrawal of 25,000 was announced June 8 by Nixon and South Vietnamese President Nguyen Van Thieu after a meeting on Midway Island. The second withdrawal of 35,000 was announced Sept. 16, after having been deferred Aug. 23 following the outbreak of major enemy fighting Aug. 10-11. The President, in a brief televised report to the nation Dec. 15, announced a reduction by mid-April, 1970, of 50,000 more U.S. troops.

Vietnamization. The President said Dec. 15 he was basing his decision for the third troop cut on progress in the "Vietnamization" program—the administration's plan to end direct U.S. involvement in the war. During a trip to Saigon in early March, Defense Secretary Melvin R. Laird said he would ask Congress for a $70-million increase in the Vietnam budget to carry out the program.

Although administration officials continued to point to successes in the program, it was difficult to assess results with certainty. After a July briefing by Gen. Earle G. Wheeler, Joint Chiefs of Staff chairman, who had just recently returned from Saigon, Sen. John C. Stennis (D Miss.) said it appeared it would take several years before South Vietnamese combat troops could assume most of the fighting.

In October Laird confirmed reports that U.S. commanders had received new orders to give "highest priority" to the program. At that time, he said the Vietnamization plan had "achieved a real momentum." In November Nixon stressed that the program was a means of ending the war "regardless of what happens on the negotiating front."

Peace Negotiations

Nixon's comment indicated the pessimism surrounding peace negotiations. In March the President predicted that progress in Paris would be made through private rather than public talks; in November, he revealed that secret meetings had been held but without results. South Vietnamese President Thieu's offer in March of private unconditional talks with the National Liberation Front was rejected. North Vietnam scorned a proposal by U.S. chief negotiator Henry Cabot Lodge to hold private talks outside the large formal sessions.

Frustrations in Paris led Secretary of State William P. Rogers to suggest in October that the conflict could gradually "fade away" without ever being formally resolved at the negotiating table.

In November, Lodge and his deputy, Lawrence E. Walsh, announced their resignations effective Dec. 8. Both expressed pessimism concerning the course of the negotiations. Nixon named Philip C. Habib, former chief advisor to Lodge, as acting head of the U.S. delegation. But, despite speculation to the contrary, the White House formally discounted any intention of down-grading the talks.

Nixon Peace Proposal. In his first nationwide policy address on Vietnam, the President May 14 offered an eight-point proposal to bring about a settlement, which included: mutual withdrawal of all non-South Vietnamese forces to designated bases over a 12-month period, after which remaining troops would be totally withdrawn from the South; creation of an international body to supervise and verify the withdrawal and ceasefire; internationally supervised free elections in the South; and agreement by all parties to observe the 1954 Geneva Accords regarding Vietnam and Cambodia and the 1962 Laos Accords.

The President's speech was viewed as a public reply to a 10-point peace proposal offered in Paris May 8 by the National Liberation Front and endorsed by Hanoi. The communist proposal reiterated demands for a unilateral unconditional withdrawal of all U.S. forces.

Nixon restated his proposals and programs in a Nov. 3 nationally televised address, during which he asked for support from "the great silent majority" and stated the U.S. position as "anything is negotiable except the right of the people of South Vietnam to determine their own future."

In his Dec. 15 address, Nixon said there had been "no progress whatever" in the Paris peace negotiations since his November speech. The President also noted the "disturbing new development" of substantially increased enemy infiltration, and restated his November warning to Hanoi that he would "not hesitate to take strong and effective measures" to counter renewed enemy offensives.

War Protests

During the early months of the Nixon administration only one major anti-war demonstration occurred (April 5-6). But by the fall the mood of war critics had changed.

Vietnam Moratorium. The desire for peace, frustration with an apparent impasse in reaching any settlement and a wish to see the President move more quickly in extricating the United States from Vietnam culminated in the "Vietnam moratorium" Oct. 15, when an estimated million Americans participated in anti-war demonstrations, protest rallies and peace vigils across the nation.

Considerable debate arose over Vice President Spiro T. Agnew's Oct. 19 characterization of anti-war protesters as an "effete corps of impudent snobs." Agnew's charges—"if the moratorium had any use whatever, it served as an emotional purgative for those who feel the need to cleanse themselves of their lack of ability to offer a constructive solution to the problem"—met with vigorous counter-criticism in the press and among congressional doves.

Administration Response. The President said he recognized the right of all Americans to express their opinions, but he said that to abandon policies "based on exhaustive study of all available evidence...because of a public demonstration would...be an act of gross irresponsibility on my part." Nonetheless, a series of Vietnam policy consultations among high-level officials took place in the days preceding the moratorium, and administration spokesmen sought to deflate criticism by pointing to the successes of the President's policy. In other moves, the White House Oct. 10 announced the planned replacement of Lt. Gen. Lewis B. Hershey, chief of the Selective Service for 28 years and a target of antidraft and antiwar protesters. The administration also took the unusual step of announcing three weeks in advance that the President would address the nation on Vietnam Nov. 3.

The President's address failed to placate war protesters. In mid-November an estimated 250,000 converged in Washington for a 40-hour "march against death," capped by a mass march and rally. The generally peaceful demonstrations were concentrated in the capital, with fewer activities across the nation than in October.

Supporters of the administration's policy held numerous "unity rallies" throughout the United States, the largest of which was at the Washington Monument on Veterans' Day Nov. 11.

Congressional Action

Congress also adopted a "wait-and-see" attitude during the first part of 1969, reflecting a widespread feeling that the new administration should be given time to work out its policies.

By May, however, several members—including Sens. George D. Aiken (R Vt.), Mike Mansfield (D Mont.), Jacob K. Javits (R N.Y.), Edward M. Kennedy (D Mass.), Charles H. Percy (R Ill.) and Hugh Scott (R Pa.)—were beginning to call for substantial reductions of U.S. troops. But the President's Midway meeting with Thieu and announcement of the initial troop pullout raised expectations that the President was committed to withdrawal and consequently dampened criticism for a time.

War critics on Capitol Hill quickened their pace in the fall. A number of resolutions related to Vietnam were introduced. On the eve of the Oct. 15 moratorium, war opponents kept the House in session late into the night, while they engaged in a spirited contest with supporters of the Nixon administration's policy.

Reaction to Nixon Address. While some doves expressed disappointment that the President had offered no new peace initiatives or major policy shifts in his Nov. 3 address, the predominant congressional reaction was one of support for the President. The leadership of both parties introduced resolutions supporting the withdrawal policy.

One such resolution (H Res 613), endorsing the administration's efforts to achieve "peace with justice," sparked a spirited debate on the scope of the endorsement before House passage in early December. Several other Vietnam-related resolutions were passed in 1969.

Laos-Thailand Involvement. Widening of the U.S. role in Indochina came under close scrutiny in the fall of 1969, when the newly created Senate Foreign Relations Subcommittee on U.S. Security Agreement and Commitments Abroad held closed hearings on Laos and Thailand. Transcripts of the hearings—with deletions for security reasons—were not made public until 1970. *(Story p. 908, 922)*

Legislative Action

In 1969 three major bills were vehicles for efforts to limit U.S. participation in the Indochina war. The three bills and action on key war-related amendments were (details in legislative chronology immediately following):

• **Supplemental Appropriations** (HR 11400—PL 91-47)—Congress rejected efforts to cut back or eliminate appropriations for Southeast Asian operations.

• **Defense Procurement Authorization** (S 2546—PL 91-121)—Congress placed a $2.5-billion ceiling on U.S. support of South Vietnamese and other free world forces

in Vietnam, and local forces in Laos and Thailand; killed in conference was a Senate-passed amendment to limit U.S. support to local forces in Laos and Thailand to supplies, materiel, equipment, facilities and training, except when protection of U.S. personnel was directly involved.

• **Defense Appropriations** (HR 15090—PL 91-171)—Congress approved a Senate-passed amendment to prohibit use of any funds in the bill to finance introduction of U.S. ground combat troops in Laos or Thailand.

SUPPLEMENTAL APPROPRIATIONS

Congress July 9 cleared a bill (HR 11400—PL 91-47) appropriating $4.3-billion in additional funds for fiscal 1969 programs, including $1.27-billion for Southeast Asian operations. The House had approved $1,234,000,000 for activities in Southeast Asia, but conferees settled on the Senate-approved amount of $1,272,000,000. The administration had requested $1,496,900,000.

Several attempts were made to amend the supplemental appropriations bill on the House floor. William F. Ryan (D N.Y.) proposed an amendment to eliminate the Vietnam appropriation. Noting that for the fifth straight year the House was being asked to appropriate supplemental funds because of under-estimates in war costs, Ryan said the only way Congress could express its concern about the war was by its action on such legislation.

Appropriations Committee Chairman George Mahon (D Texas), Robert L. F. Sikes (D Fla.) and Glenard P. Lipscomb (R Calif.) voiced opposition to Ryan's amendment. They argued that some of the funds were to upgrade South Vietnamese combat forces to enable a cutback in U.S. forces. The amendment was rejected on a 25-140 standing vote.

Another anti-war amendment introduced by Bob Eckhardt (D Texas) sought to eliminate $640.1-million in procurement funds for the Army. Eckhardt said his amendments would not jeopardize the lives of U.S. soldiers in Vietnam but would curb spending on the war. Roman C. Pucinski (D Ill.), commenting on both amendments, saw "serious incongruity" in members seeking a U.S. withdrawal from the war by attempting to cut off funds to strengthen the South Vietnamese army.

Minority Leader Gerald R. Ford (R Mich.) said adoption of the amendment would "slow down and materially hinder and hamper" the attempt to turn over more of the fighting to the South Vietnamese. The amendment was rejected on a 23-134 standing vote.

DEFENSE PROCUREMENT AUTHORIZATION

The Senate in September approved an amendment, offered by John Sherman Cooper (R Ky.), to the defense procurement authorization bill (S 2546—PL 91-121) which its backers hoped would bar the use of U.S. troops in Laos and Thailand, but the provision was deleted in conference. Another Senate amendment, however, setting a $2.5-billion ceiling on support, as determined by the secretary of defense, of South Vietnamese and other free world forces in Vietnam, and local forces in Laos and Thailand, was in the final version which cleared Congress Nov. 6.

Support Ceiling. The amendment to limit funds for support of the allied and local forces was offered by Sen. J. W. Fulbright (D Ark.) who argued that the traditional type of blanket authority to support these troops in past years could lead to almost unlimited support. His amendment, which also required that actions under the provisions be supported by presidential authority, was approved by voice vote Aug. 12. It had the backing of Sen. John Stennis (D Miss.), chairman of the Armed Services Committee, who reduced Fulbright's original $3-billion limit to the final $2.5-billion. House-Senate conferees accepted the $2.5-billion ceiling.

Laos-Thailand Restriction. Cooper, calling for tighter restrictions to prevent other Vietnam-type involvements, proposed an amendment that would limit U.S. support to local forces in Laos and Thailand to supplies, materiel, equipment, facilities and training. After accepting the amendment by an 86-0 vote, the Senate Sept. 17 approved by voice vote an amendment by Jack Miller (R Iowa) which exempted situations directly involving the protection of U.S. personnel.

Despite the unanimity of the vote, the meaning and possible effect of the measure was in dispute. Cooper had intended it to prevent the use of U.S. troops in Laos and Thailand, but the Defense Department and Stennis said it would not have that effect. Stennis argued that because Cooper's amendment would be attached to a provision in the bill affecting only U.S. aid and support to local forces in those countries, it would not affect the use of U.S. troops. House and Senate conferees deleted the Cooper amendment.

DEFENSE APPROPRIATIONS

Cooper continued his efforts to limit U.S. activities in Laos and Thailand, when the Senate took up the fiscal 1970 defense appropriations bill. The final measure, cleared by Congress Dec. 18, included $23.2-billion for Vietnam activities and prohibited the introduction of U.S. combat troops in neighboring Laos and Thailand (HR 15090—PL 91-171).

When Cooper's amendment to the defense procurement authorization was deleted in conference, he had indicated that he would raise the issue again during the debate on defense appropriations. Although Cooper was absent when the bill came to the Senate floor because of a family illness, Majority Leader Mike Mansfield (D Mont.) Dec. 15 introduced the same amendment, limiting the support of local forces in Laos or Thailand to supplies, materiel, equipment, facilities, maintenance and training.

Secret Session on Laos. The bill's acting floor manager, Allen J. Ellender (D La.), agreed to accept the Cooper-Mansfield amendment, but a prolonged discussion about the amendment and U.S. operations in Laos ensued. During that discussion, Ellender revealed that the bill contained $90-million for support of the Royal Laotian Army. Shortly afterwards, it was decided that the rest of the discussion on the subject should be held in private, whereupon the Senate was sealed off to all persons except Senators and key staff members who were sworn to secrecy. *(Box p. 922)*

In the public segments of the debate, Foreign Relations Committee Chairman J. W. Fulbright (D Ark.) repeatedly expressed concern that the Senate would have to vote on the appropriations for that purpose without being informed on how far the United States was involved in Laos and what its intentions were. He also said there was no authority for the Laos involvement.

Mansfield and Fulbright discussed the acknowledged U.S. bombing of the Ho Chi Minh trail in Laos in connection with the Vietnam operations, the training of Laotian military personnel and the President's public statements that no U.S. combat troops were in Laos. Also discussed were reports that the United States was conducting aerial operations in other parts of Laos in support of Royal Laotian forces against North Vietnamese and Pathet Lao rebels and might be advising, leading or paying Laotian government or irregular troops.

Fulbright introduced into the record letters from soldiers and Agency for International Development employees training for or already stationed in Southeast Asia indicating an intensification of U.S. activity in Laos.

Church Version. When the doors to the Senate chamber and gallery were opened again after the more than two-hour secret session, the Senate was taking a roll call on a motion introduced by Gale W. McGee (D Wyo.) to table (or kill) the Cooper-Mansfield amendment. The motion, however, was rejected on a 41-48 vote.

Following that vote, Frank Church (D Idaho) introduced for himself a substitute for the pending Cooper-Mansfield proposal. The substitute would have replaced the Cooper-Mansfield limitation on aid to materiel and supplies with language stating, "In line with the expressed intention of the President of the United States," no funds in the bill could be used to finance "the introduction of American ground combat troops into Laos or Thailand without the prior consent of Congress."

Church later dropped the requirement for prior congressional consent because it was pointed out such language would constitute legislation in an appropriations bill, which is prohibited by Senate rules. Church argued that the Cooper-Mansfield proposal was unclear. Other Senators, however, contended that the Church amendment was also vague because it made no mention of existing troops and aerial operations or of future aerial operations. Church and Charles E. Goodell (R N.Y.), however, said it granted no authority, approval or disapproval for any other actions. And Church said the amendment was well drafted to prevent another Vietnam situation.

The Church substitute was first approved by a **key roll-call vote of 73-17** and the Cooper-Mansfield amendment, with Church's substitute language, was adopted on an 80-9 roll call Dec. 15.

When the measure went to conference, House members accepted the Senate prohibition on the introduction of U.S. troops into Laos and Thailand.

OTHER ACTIONS

VIETNAM POLICY DECLARATION. In 1969 the House considered its first major Vietnam policy declaration since the 1964 Gulf of Tonkin resolution. Following a two-day debate which ranged over a number of Vietnam war issues, the House, by a **key roll-call vote of 334-55**, Dec. 2 approved a resolution (H Res 613) endorsing the President's efforts to achieve "peace with justice."

The debate was touched off by a parliamentary controversy initiated by House "doves" who attempted to open the resolution to amendments. The House, however, by a 225-132 roll call Dec. 1, accepted the Rules

(Continued on p. 906)

My Lai Massacre Influenced U.S. Public Opinion

One event during the Vietnam war which severely tarnished the image of U.S. fighting men and affected public opinion concerning the war was the disclosure in November 1969 of the 1968 massacre of Vietnamese civilians at My Lai village, and the ensuing trial of platoon leader Lt. William Calley.

The nation's first reaction to the massacre of more than 100 Vietnamese peasants by U.S. soldiers was one of shocked disbelief, disgust and anger. But when it became apparent, nearly two years later, that the only GI who was going to pay for the massacre was Lt. Calley, the mood of the nation split. Some said the Army was using Calley as a scapegoat and urged that he not be punished unless everyone involved was also punished. Others said Calley should pay for what he did regardless of all other circumstances.

Disclosure. Seymour M. Hersh, who won a Pulitzer Prize for his reporting of the massacre, gave the My Lai story to the press Nov. 13, 1969.

Eight days after the Hersh account of My Lai appeared in the national press, the Army announced it was investigating 26 men, 15 of them civilian, in connection with the massacre. Lt. Calley was court martialed Nov. 24 on charges of premeditated murder of at least 109 Vietnamese civilians "of various ages and sexes."

Two days after Calley was court martialed, the House and Senate Armed Services Committees began hearings on the incident.

Sixteen months after the initial charges were brought against Calley, he was convicted of premeditated murder of at least 22 Vietnamese civilians and on March 31, 1971, Calley was sentenced to life imprisonment.

Congressional Reaction. Immediately after Calley's conviction there was an outpouring of protest from Congress. Sen. Abraham Ribicoff (D Conn.) said: "The tragic events at My Lai are reflective of the tragedy of the entire Vietnam war. All sides have committed horrible atrocities. Lt. Calley should not be made to bear the sole responsibility for all wrong-doing."

Sen. Herman Talmadge (D Ga.) said: "Most Americans believe that he (Calley) is assuming the burden for the entire war, including the errors of his superiors.... I am saddened to think that one could fight for his flag and then be court martialed and convicted for apparently carrying out his orders."

In the House, Rep. Joe D. Waggonner Jr. (D La.) said: "Lt. William Calley was convicted...for criminal responsibility in the death of 22 of the Vietcong enemy... Lt. Calley has been made a scapegoat and there is no honor in that course. The Army does not know what it is doing. I protest the verdict and urge others to join me."

President Nixon intervened twice on behalf of Calley in the days after the conviction. On April 1, 1971, Nixon ordered that Calley be removed from the stockade and placed instead under house arrest in his apartment. On April 3 the President announced through one of his aides that he would personally review the Calley case when all avenues of appeal were exhausted.

Sen. Hugh Scott (R Pa.), minority leader, said that Nixon intervened "in response to enormous public reaction to this case."

But another Republican, Jacob Javits (N.Y.), told the Senate: "If the nation really is encouraged to believe that he (Calley) did nothing wrong—indeed he is a hero—then we have changed as a people during the course of this tragic war even more disastrously than I had imagined."

Draft Debate. The conviction of Lt. Calley was announced during the middle of House debate on the military draft extension bill.

Minutes before the final roll-call vote on the bill Edward J. Derwinski (R Ill.) told the House: "I do not believe that good judgment was shown by the majority leadership in bringing this bill to the floor this week. It is difficult to maintain composure and objectivity with the debate over the Calley case reaching a peak as a result of the decision and sentencing...."

Rep. M. G. Snyder (R Ky.) told the House: "There is no question but that we must maintain an adequate military force to defend our country and I can and will support legislative efforts to do this. But I cannot in good conscience vote to send American boys to fight a 'no win' war for a government that then allows the American boys to be tried for discharging that obligation."

Post-mortem. Calley's original life sentence was commuted Aug. 20, 1971, to 20 years during his first appeal. Calley then appealed to the Army Court of Review.

Rep. Samuel S. Stratton (D N.Y.), a member of the Armed Services Committee and its My Lai investigating subcommittee, told the House Feb. 8, 1972: "I am profoundly dissatisfied with the way the Army has allowed this complex, tragic and highly damaging case to simply peter out. If the Army leaves this case unresolved, unexplained, unexamined and uncommented upon...then its failure can only have the most damaging impact on the Army and the American defense establishment."

"Twenty-five officers and men were originally charged in connection with the killings at My Lai and their subsequent coverup within the Army," Stratton continued. "Charges against 19 of the 25 were dropped without trial. Five were acquitted. Only one, Lt. Calley, was convicted."

Rep. Les Aspin (D Wis.) told the House April 4, 1972: "The most distressing aspect of this entire tragic chapter in the history of the Vietnam war is that the Pentagon is covering up its own investigation which first unearthed the initial conspiracy guide of the truth about My Lai. The military is guilty of a double coverup—first with the massacre and now with the investigation."

The Army Court of Review Feb. 16, 1973, upheld the conviction and sentencing. Calley could still appeal to the Civilian Court of Military Appeals and the Supreme court.

Committee's resolution recommending a four-hour, no-amendment debate (99 Democrats—all but five northern Democrats—and 33 Republicans opposed).

H Res 613 encountered opposition from members of the House who questioned the circumstances surrounding its introduction and passage. The resolution, authored by Jim Wright (D Texas) and Wayne L. Hays (D Ohio), was introduced Nov. 4, one day after the President's nation-wide address on Vietnam. It was drafted and circulated before the speech, however. Although the draft was sent to the White House for clearance, sponsors of the measure said repeatedly that the administration played no role in its formulation.

Nixon Visit. During an unexpected visit to both chambers, coinciding with the Nov. 13-15 anti-war protests, President Nixon expressed his appreciation to the approximately 300 members who had sponsored the resolution, declaring that such support for the administration could "hasten the day when just peace might come."

Although H Res 613 had the active support of the leadership of both parties, liberal Democrats and some Republican doves objected to the speed with which the measure was sent to the floor, as well as possible ambiguities in the resolution. Some felt that consideration of the resolution could place them in the uncomfortable political position of being pressed either to oppose a widely endorsed peace measure, or to support what could be construed as "blank check" approval of presidential actions and policies.

OTHER RESOLUTIONS. On Dec. 15, the House passed two additional resolutions dealing with the war. One (H Con Res 454), approved by a 405-0 roll-call vote, called on North Vietnam and the National Liberation Front of South Vietnam to observe the Geneva Convention on prisoners of war.

The second resolution (H Res 661), passed by voice vote, commended American servicemen and Vietnam war veterans for their efforts. Neither resolution required the President's signature or had the force of law.

A joint resolution, passed in both chambers by voice votes, called for a National Prayer Day for Vietnam prisoners of war. It was signed into law Nov. 6 (H J Res 910—PL 91-111).

1970

The year began quietly. The nation had turned inward to domestic problems—inflation and pollution of the environment.

The administration had partially defused the issue of the Vietnam war. President Nixon's troop withdrawals and transfer of combat responsibilities to the South Vietnamese ("Vietnamization") had come to be regarded by many as a workable formula for disengaging the United States from Southeast Asia.

In addition, the President placed renewed emphasis on his policy (the "Nixon Doctrine") to avoid direct U.S. military involvement in remote corners of the globe. In his Feb. 18 "State of the World" message, the President said that his doctrine's "central thesis is that the United States will participate in the defense and development of allies and friends, but that America cannot—and will not—conceive all the plans, design all the programs,

execute all the decisions and undertake all the defense of the free nations of the world." *(Nixon Doctrine, p. 869; State of the World message, p. 865)*

But the calm was deceptive, the silence shortlived. Several events in the early spring rekindled controversy over the war and brought into question the meaning of the Nixon Doctrine. In March and April, details on increased U.S. involvement in Laos and Cambodia surfaced when the transcripts of Senate hearings held in 1969 were made public. *(Details, p. 908)*

A second key development was the President's decision, announced April 30, to send U.S. forces into Cambodia to clean out communist sanctuaries along that country's border with South Vietnam. The Cambodian "incursion" sent anti-war protesters back into the streets and plunged Congress into a session-long debate over congressional war powers and the Indochina war.

Military Activity

President Nixon went on nationwide television April 20 to report on the Vietnam war and to announce further troop withdrawals. In reviewing the military situation in Vietnam, the President noted in several areas the level of enemy activity had increased "substantially" since December 1969. But, despite this upsurge of enemy operations in Vietnam, Cambodia and Laos, the President reported that "progress in training and equipping South Vietnamese forces has substantially exceeded our original expectations last June" and that there had been "very significant advances" in the pacification programs.

The President said that the United States was ready to move from short-range testing of troop withdrawals to a longer-range program for the replacement of Americans by South Vietnamese troops. He announced the withdrawal of 150,000 additional American troops over the next 12 months. This would bring the total reduction in American forces to 265,000 since the Nixon administration took office and, when completed, would leave 284,000 troops in Vietnam.

But Nixon added the following warning: "If I conclude increased enemy action jeopardizes our remaining forces in Vietnam, I shall not hesitate to take strong and effective measures to deal with that situation."

Cambodian Incursion. Within 10 days the President followed through on his threat. In an April 30 address to the nation, Nixon announced a joint U.S.-South Vietnamese combat force had launched an attack against communist border sanctuaries in Cambodia. He said the operation (which initially involved several thousand U.S. troops) was "not an invasion" of the country but was necessary to protect American forces in Vietnam. Nixon defended the decision as "indispensable for the continuing success of the (Vietnam) withdrawal program." He asserted, "We will not be defeated. We will not allow American men by the thousands to be killed by an enemy from privileged sanctuaries."

The situation in Cambodia had been deteriorating rapidly. In mid-March Cambodian chief of state Norodom Sihanouk was deposed in a bloodless coup by Lon Nol, premier and defense minister. Lon Nol was granted full power by the Cambodian National Assembly.

A month later, Lon Nol issued calls for international assistance, including a personal appeal to President Nixon for extensive military equipment. When he announced the Cambodian operation, Nixon said that, while the administration had decided against "massive military assistance," the United States would "provide the small arms and other equipment which the Cambodian army needs and can use now for its defense."

Progress Reports. In a June 3 interim report, President Nixon characterized the Cambodian operation as "the most successful of this long and very difficult war." He assured the American public that the June 30 deadline for the withdrawal of U.S. forces would be met. The President's speech was accompanied by a film of arms, ammunition and food said to have been captured during the allied operations. Nixon issued a final report June 30. *(Box, p. 912)*

Air Strikes. In early May and late November, the United States conducted extensive air strikes over North Vietnam. The air operations in November coincided with a U.S. helicopter commando raid on a prisoner-of-war camp Nov. 21 at Sontay, some 20 miles west of Hanoi. The commando team found no prisoners at the camp site. Defense Secretary Laird, revealing the raid several days later, said that it had been carried out with the approval of President Nixon who had been informed earlier in the month that some American prisoners were dying.

In a Dec. 10 press conference, President Nixon indicated there might be more air strikes. He said, if there was increased fighting in South Vietnam and if North Vietnamese infiltration was considered a threat to U.S. forces, "I will order the bombing of military sites in North Vietnam, the passes that lead from North Vietnam into South Vietnam, the military complexes and the military supply lines." *(Box on bombing, p. 925)*

Paris Negotiations

The peace talks in Paris remained stalemated throughout the year. Each side came up with a new peace proposal only to be rebuffed by the other.

It was not until the second half of the year that a successor to Henry Cabot Lodge, who resigned as the chief U.S. negotiator in December 1969, was sent to Paris. Philip C. Habib served as acting chief negotiator until the arrival of David K. E. Bruce in August.

On Sept. 17, the Vietcong presented an eight-point peace plan which was sent as the first substantive initiative in the talks since Nixon offered his peace plan in May 1969. *(1969 plan, p. 902)*

Among the Vietcong's proposals were the withdrawal of U.S. forces by June 30, 1971, with talks on prisoner exchanges to begin when withdrawal was agreed to. The plan also called for purging of the top three members of the Saigon regime and arrangement of a cease-fire after agreement had been reached on all points of the plan.

President Nixon announced a new five-point plan on Oct. 7. The administration's plan called for a cease-fire in place; the convening of an Indochina peace conference to deal not only with South Vietnam, but also Cambodia and Laos; a timetable for U.S. troop withdrawals as part of an overall settlement; communist cooperation in searching for a political settlement of the conflict, while respecting the South Vietnamese right to self-determination; and immediate, unconditional release of all prisoners of war.

Major Anti-Vietnam Marches

1965 April 17—First large anti-Vietnam war demonstration in Washington—Students for a Democratic Society.
Nov. 27—Demonstration in Washington—National Committee for a Sane Nuclear Policy and Women's Strike for Peace.

1967 April 15—Demonstrations in New York and San Francisco—Spring Mobilization Committee (later became National Mobilization Committee) and Student Mobilization Committee to End the War in Vietnam (SMC).

Oct. 21—Rally at Lincoln Memorial and march on the Pentagon—National Mobilization Committee to End the War in Vietnam (NMC).

1968 Aug. 26-29—Demonstration at the Democratic National Convention in Chicago—NMC and Youth International Party (Yippies).

1969 Oct. 15—Demonstrations in major cities and towns—Vietnam Moratorium Committee.

Nov. 15—Demonstration in Washington—Vietnam Moratorium and the New Mobilization Committee to End the War in Vietnam (New Mobe, successor of NMC).

1970 May 9—Rally at the Ellipse in Washington—New Mobe and SMC.

1971 April 24—Demonstrations in Washington and San Francisco—National Peace Action Coalition (NPAC).

April 25-May 5—Civil disobedience in Washington culminating in a moratorium on "business as usual" nationwide—Peoples Coalition for Peace and Justice (PCPJ).

Oct. 26—Demonstrations in Washington, other cities and college campuses—PCPJ.

1972 April 22—Demonstrations in New York, San Francisco, Los Angeles and other cities—NPAC.

1973 Jan. 20—Anti-inaugural demonstration in Washington—NPAC and PCPJ.

War Protests

The U.S. incursion into Cambodia inspired an outcry from opponents on Capitol Hill and throughout the country.

College campuses were once again thrown into ferment. On May 4, four college students were shot to death by Ohio National Guardsmen during an anti-war protest on the Kent State University campus. Demonstrations continued throughout the week, with tens of thousands of students protesting widening U.S. involvement in Indochina and the shootings at Kent.

Protest moved into the halls of Congress following a demonstration May 9 which attracted an estimated 60,000 to 100,000 persons to Washington.

(Continued on p. 910)

1969 Closed Senate Hearings Examined...

The widening role of the United States in Indochina jumped into the headlines and congressional limelight in the fall of 1969. U.S. operations in Laos and Thailand were closely scrutinized during closed hearings held by the Senate Foreign Relations Subcommittee on U.S. Security Agreements and Commitments Abroad. The hearings resulted in a successful campaign by Sen. John Sherman Cooper (R Ky.) for a legislative ban on the introduction of U.S. combat troops in those two countries. *(Details, p. 904)*

Nixon on Laos

The Nixon administration held to the policy of official secrecy on Laos, which it had inherited, until March 6, 1970. Then, as a result of a North Vietnamese offensive in Laos, wide press coverage of U.S. military involvement and pressure from senators, particularly those on the Foreign Relations Committee, President Nixon released a 3,000-word statement on U.S. involvement.

The President made these points in his statement:

• The total number of Americans involved on the ground in Laos was 1,040—616 government employees and 424 hired on a contractual basis. Of the total, 320 were engaged as military advisers and 323 were involved in logistics. "U.S. personnel in Laos," the President said, "during the past year has not increased, while during the past few months, North Vietnam has sent over 13,000 additional ground troops (bringing the total to 67,000)." (The last official disclosure of U.S. personnel in Laos was made Sept. 23, 1968, by the State Department; at that time 830 Americans were serving in Laos.)

• "There are no American ground combat troops in Laos. We have no plans for introducing ground combat forces into Laos.... No American stationed in Laos has ever been killed in ground combat operations."

• Regarding air action over Laos, Nixon repeated earlier administration statements that U.S. action was meant to "interdict the...flow of troops and supplies... on the Ho Chi Minh trail." He added that "we have continued to carry out reconnaissance flights in north Laos and fly combat support missions for Laotian forces when requested...by the Royal Laotian government."

The President gave no figures on U.S. air sorties against North Vietnamese forces in Laos, nor did he mention the widely reported role of the Central Intelligence Agency in Laos.

Nixon coupled his partial disclosure of U.S. activity in Laos with letters to British Prime Minister Harold Wilson and Soviet Premier Aleksei Kosygin calling on them in their capacity as cochairmen of the 1962 agreements on Laotian neutrality to "help in restoring the 1962 Geneva Agreements for that country."

Laos Hearings

One of the most significant hearings held by the U.S. Security Agreements and Commitments Abroad Subcommittee concerned the largely undercover U.S. activities in Laos. The subcommittee had been set up in 1969 to conduct a two-year investigation of U.S. military commitments to foreign nations. The transcript was released April 20, 1970, after five months of delay. The long delay in the release of the Laos transcript—during which the subcommittee staff had 100 negotiating sessions with administration officials—stemmed from the policy of official secrecy on military involvement in Laos which the United States had maintained since 1962. At that time, agreements guaranteeing Laotian neutrality were signed in Geneva by 14 nations, including the United States and North Vietnam.

The Laos hearings, although riddled with the Executive Branch censor's deletions, provided the first detailed official account of the growth of U.S. military involvement in Laos since 1962. In particular, they brought to light the key role the United States played in the war in northern Laos as opposed to the more generally known U.S. bombing of the Ho Chi Minh trail in southeast Laos.

The main administration witness was William H. Sullivan, deputy assistant secretary of state for east Asian and Pacific affairs. Sullivan participated in the negotiation of the Geneva agreements and was ambassador to Laos from November 1964 to April 1969. CIA Director Richard Helms testified, but all references to the CIA role in Laos and even to the fact that he testified were deleted from the record.

No 'Legal Obligation'

The United States did not have "any legal obligation for...any commitment that requires us...to insist that the independence of Laos must be preserved," said Sullivan. Laos, a protocol state under the eight-nation Southeast Asia Treaty Organization (SEATO), renounced SEATO's protection in its 1962 declaration of neutrality. Since the United States agreed at Geneva to honor Laotian neutrality, Sullivan explained, there was no military commitment to defend Laos. The defense of Laos, he said, was "a policy decision made by various political leaders of the country" since 1962.

"Our policy is founded on the assumption that the interests of the United States are best served by an independent and neutral Laos," said Sullivan.

Maintaining Laotian independence and neutrality presented the United States with a dilemma in the light of North Vietnam's refusal to observe the 1962 neutrality agreements. To defend Laotian independence against North Vietnam, explained Sullivan, meant that U.S. military assistance could compromise Laotian neutrality. "This consideration...had a significant influence upon the way in which we have responded to the Royal Lao government's requests for assistance in the face of North Vietnamese military attacks on Lao soil," he said.

...Expanded U.S. Military Role In Laos, Thailand

The military witnesses who appeared after Sullivan explained the strategic importance of Laos to the conduct of the Vietnam war. In the southeastern part of Laos, the Ho Chi Minh trail was the main infiltration route into South Vietnam; and in the northeastern part of Laos, the United States maintained aircraft navigational sites on mountain peaks as close as 17 miles from the North Vietnam border.

U.S. Involvement

The most heavily censored portions of the testimony concerned the extent of U.S. military involvement.

Despite these deletions, the testimony indicated a growth in U.S. military involvement in Laos from 1962-1969 and demonstrated U.S. officials in Laos played a key role in formulating the requests for assistance submitted by the Laotian government.

The Air War. The first U.S. "reconnaissance flight" over southern Laos took place May 19, 1964, said Sullivan, after consultation the previous day between Souvanna Phouma and U.S. Ambassador Leonard Unger. Flights were extended May 21 to cover the Plain of Jars to monitor Pathet Lao and North Vietnamese activity.

On June 6, 1964, when an unarmed U.S. reconnaissance plane was shot down over the Plain of Jars, Souvanna approved the addition of "armed escorts" to reconnaissance flights. At a June 16 meeting, Unger and Souvanna agreed that "escorted reconnaissance flights would be acknowledged," but that "firing on ground targets by escort aircraft would not be acknowledged and would be kept out of discussions with the press," said Sullivan. The U.S. "bombing of the Lao territory along the Ho Chi Minh trail (began) in early 1965," Sullivan said.

Vietnam Bombing Shifted. The testimony showed that when the United States temporarily stopped bombing North Vietnam from Dec. 24, 1965, through Jan. 31, 1966, U.S. air strikes were redirected over Laos.

The testimony also demonstrated that after Nov. 1, 1968, when U.S. bombing of North Vietnam was terminated by President Johnson, U.S. aircraft shifted to targets in Laos. Air Force Col. Robert L. F. Tyrrell, U.S. Air Attache in Vientiane, acknowledged Symington's point that "in north Laos—in some months in 1969 the strikes doubled, in others tripled." At the same time, Symington said there had been a "marked deceleration in U.S. efforts against the Ho Chi Minh trail...." The explanation, said Tyrrell, was that North Vietnamese and Pathet Lao activities had increased in north Laos, "coupled with the increased availability of USAF aircraft," resulting from the cessation of bombing of North Vietnam.

Military Assistance. Since the Geneva agreements did not permit establishment of a U.S. Military Advisory Group in Laos, a covert operation, described by Col. Peter T. Russell, Deputy Chief, Joint U.S. Military Advisory Group, Thailand, was set up. Russell's command was "an integral part of the U.S. Military Advisory Group, Thailand." Since it could not operate in Laos, a special group called the Requirements Office was established in the Agency for International Development (AID) in Laos. The office was "staffed by retired military personnel."

The Requirements Office in Laos ascertained the needs of the Laotian army and forwarded requests based on these needs to Russell's command in Thailand. Russell sent supplies to Laos and arranged for training of Laotian personnel in Thailand. "My authority ends on the Thai side of the Mekong," said Russell. "We have no functions in Laos proper."

U.S. Personnel. Sullivan introduced into the record a breakdown of all U.S. personnel permanently assigned in Laos in September 1969. The total was 558 U.S. direct hire employees and 333 contract personnel. AID personnel accounted for 338 of the direct hire; military attaches totalled 127; Department of State personnel were 59. Two hundred and seven of the contract personnel were employees of Air America, described in the press as a Central Intelligence Agency front.

Casualties. Information included in the hearings noted that "something under 200 U.S. military personnel were killed in Laos between 1962-1969 and another 200 were missing or were prisoners of war."

Costs of the War. Twice in the hearings, Fulbright said Laos did not justify spending "a billion dollars." However, when he apparently used a more precise figure, the figure was deleted.

Military assistance to the Royal Laotian Government, according to testimony, cost $90 million in fiscal 1969. No other yearly figure was given, nor was there a cumulative figure. The $90-million figure did not include assistance to the 36,000 Meo tribesmen fighting under Gen. Vang Pao in the Plain of Jars region.

Thailand

The Subcommittee June 8 released the testimony it had received in November 1969, on U.S. activities in Thailand. The testimony revealed that under secret accord entered into in 1967, the United States had been paying $50 million a year to Thailand for sending a combat division to South Vietnam.

In addition, the United States agreed to increase its military assistance by $30 million for two years and to supply Thailand with a battery of Hawk anti-aircraft missiles in return for the 11,000-man Thai unit in Vietnam.

A military aid agreement between the United States and Thailand was first signed in 1950 and the U.S. presence increased from 300 in 1960 to 48,000 in mid-1969. In 1967, B-52 bombers were stationed in Thailand for operations in Vietnam and Laos. It was also disclosed that the United States had invested $702 million in construction of military bases in Thailand.

The generally peaceful demonstration—held at the Ellipse across the street from the White House grounds—capped a week of frequently more violent protests on college campuses across the nation.

In contrast to the Oct. 15, 1969, Vietnam "moratorium," only a handful of members of Congress attended the May 9 rally. More than 50 had participated in anti-war activities across the nation in October, while fewer than a dozen were present at the May 9 demonstration.

White House Response. Immediately preceding the May 9 rally, the administration made a number of conciliatory gestures to deflect possible violence and indicate sympathy with the protesters. Administration officials muted their criticism of campus demonstrators, and the administration moved to accommodate organizers' demands for a rally site close to the White House by allowing the event to take place on the Ellipse. Administration officials were available throughout the day to discuss the protesters' grievances.

The President met with reporters on the eve of the demonstration to express his sympathy with the protester's objectives. During a May 8 televised news conference, which dealt almost entirely with the Cambodia and student protest issues, Nixon made these points:

• He defended the Cambodia decision, but insisted that "what I have done will accomplish the goals" demanded by the protesters by hastening the end of U.S. involvement in Southeast Asia. "I think I understand what they want. I would hope they would understand somewhat what I want."

• He restated his May 5 pledge to members of Congress that "all Americans of all kinds" would be out of Cambodia by the end of June, and said the first contingent of Americans would be withdrawn during the week of May 10.

• He defended the operation as essential to save the lives of American troops in Vietnam and to "buy time" for the Vietnamization program. If the enemy should return to the Cambodian sanctuaries, he said, the South Vietnamese army would be able to "handle it alone."

• He said his use of the word "bums" in informal remarks at the Pentagon May 1 was not intended to refer to all student protesters, but only those who "burn buildings," "engage in violence," "terrorize their fellow students and terrorize the faculty."

• In other actions, the President paid a surprise pre-dawn visit to the Lincoln Memorial on May 9 to discuss the Cambodian issue with a small group of students. He met with the nation's governors on May 11 to discuss the student strikes and Cambodian decision.

Congressional Action

The Cambodia issue revived debate on the questions of congressional consultation and constitutional foreign policy-making powers. These issues stood out:

• Did the Cambodian operation represent a qualitatively new U.S. military involvement in Southeast Asia and, if so, was congressional action or further consultation required?

• Did briefings by high administration officials before congressional committees serve to inform Congress of all contemplated military actions?

Nixon Meets Committees. Chairman J. W. Fulbright (D Ark.) announced May 1 that the Foreign Relations Committee had unanimously requested a meeting with President Nixon on his decision to send U.S. forces into Cambodia.

The President deflected the committee's request by inviting the members of four congressional committees to the White House May 5—the Senate and House Armed Services Committees in the morning and the Senate Foreign Relations Committee and the House Foreign Affairs Committee in the afternoon.

Reaction to the meeting was mixed. Senate Armed Services Committee Chairman John C. Stennis (D Miss.) said the information presented indicated that U.S. operations in Cambodia were "going right well." But Sen. Stuart Symington (D Mo.) said he had "grave reservations" which had not been dispelled by the meeting. Fulbright termed the meeting "unproductive."

In other immediate reactions to the decision to send U.S. forces into Cambodia:

• Senators George McGovern (D S.D.), Harold E. Hughes (D Iowa), Alan Cranston (D Calif.), Charles E. Goodell (R N.Y.) and Mark O. Hatfield (R Ore.) announced May 2 they planned to offer an amendment (termed the "end-the-war" amendment) to eliminate spending for military operations in Vietnam, Laos and Cambodia.

• Senators Frank Church (D Idaho) and John Sherman Cooper (R Ky.) introduced an amendment (known as the Cooper-Church amendment) to the foreign military sales bill (HR 15628) to prohibit military assistance to Cambodia and to bar funds for U.S. military operations in Cambodia.

Legislative Action

In 1970 four major bills were vehicles for efforts to limit U.S. participation in the Indochina war. The four bills and action on key war-related amendments were (details in legislative chronology immediately following):

• **Foreign Military Sales** (HR 15628—PL 91-672)—Congress repealed the 1964 Tonkin Gulf resolution; killed in conference was a Senate-passed Cooper-Church amendment banning funds to retain U.S. forces in Cambodia, to pay for U.S. instructors there or to conduct any combat activity in the air above Cambodia in support of Cambodian forces.

• **Supplementary Foreign Aid Authorization** (HR 19911—PL 91-652)—Congress approved a Senate-passed revised Cooper-Church amendment prohibiting the use of all funds to finance introduction of U.S. ground combat troops into Cambodia or to provide U.S. advisers to or for Cambodian military forces in Cambodia.

• **Defense Procurement** (HR 17123—PL 91-441)—Congress placed a ceiling of $2.8-billion on U.S. aid to the South Vietnamese, and other free world forces in Laos and Thailand, and approved a ban on funds for military operations by the South Vietnamese or other allied troops in support of the Cambodian or Laotian governments; Congress rejected a McGovern-Hatfield amendment to set a deadline of Dec. 31, 1971, for withdrawing all U.S. troops from Vietnam.

• **Defense Appropriations** (HR 19590—PL 91-668)—Congress approved a ban on financing military operations by the South Vietnamese or other allied troops in support of the Cambodian or Laotian governments, except to promote the safe and orderly disengagement of U.S. troops from Southeast Asia or to aid in release of American prisoners of war, as well as a ban on the use of the act's funds to finance introduction of U.S. ground forces into Laos or Thailand. Congress rejected amendments to eliminate or reduce funds for Southeast Asian operations; killed in conference was a Senate-added ban on use of funds for the introduction of U.S. ground forces into Cambodia, but the same prohibition became law in the supplementary foreign aid authorization *(above).*

FOREIGN MILITARY SALES

Congress Dec. 31 cleared for the President the foreign military sales bill (HR 15628—PL 91-672), containing a repeal of the 1964 Tonkin Gulf resolution which former President Johnson had construed as providing congressional authority to step up U.S. military operations in Vietnam.

HR 15628 had been deadlocked for six months in House-Senate conference because of a Senate-adopted Cooper-Church amendment barring funds for the support and maintenance of U.S. ground combat forces and advisers in Cambodia. Congress on Dec. 22 accepted a modified restriction on U.S. military activities in Cambodia as part of a supplemental foreign aid authorization bill (HR 19911). Enactment of the Cooper-Church restrictions in HR 19911 permitted the Senate supporters of such restrictions to relinquish their insistence on its inclusion in the military sales bill, thus clearing the way for final action. *(Story on HR 19911, p. 912)*

Cooper-Church Debate

Consideration of the bill and of the Cooper-Church amendment to it plunged the Senate into heated debate on the administration's Asia policy, U.S. military involvement in Indochina and the issue of constitutional powers to commit U.S. troops to foreign combat.

The measure would have prohibited the use of any funds to retain U.S. forces in Cambodia, to pay for U.S. instructors there, or to conduct any combat activity in the air above Cambodia in support of Cambodian forces, unless Congress enacted legislation to authorize such operations.

The seven-week Senate debate—from May 13 through June 30—on the amendment produced contradictory assessments of the intention and actual impact of the Cooper-Church measure. Supporters argued that the provision was intended to limit broader-scale involvement in Cambodia. On the other hand, seeking additional votes for the measure, sponsors emphasized equally that its passage would not prevent U.S. retaliation or protective reaction in response to enemy attacks originating from across the border and hot pursuit of enemy forces which crossed into Cambodia.

The seven-week debate prevented Senate action on all other major legislation. Numerous amendments to the Cooper-Church amendment by Senate supporters of the administration were submitted attempting to defeat, weaken or dilute the restrictions the Cooper-Church measure would place on military actions in Cambodia. In addition, the strategy of those supporting the administration was to delay Senate voting on the Cooper-Church measure until June 30, the day the President had pledged during a May 8 press conference to remove all U.S.

troops from Cambodia. The amendment was adopted June 30 by **a key roll-call vote of 58-37.**

The Senate June 3 had rejected by a 36-54 roll-call vote an amendment, offered by Robert Dole (R Kan.), which would have allowed the President to overrule provisions of the Cooper-Church amendment during any period he determined that U.S. citizens were held as prisoners of war in Cambodia by the North Vietnamese or the National Liberation Front. Defeat of the amendment was regarded as the first test of Senate sentiment on the Cooper-Church amendment. The vote came a few hours before the President appeared on national television to present an interim report on the Cambodian operation.

The Senate, by a 47-52 roll-call vote June 11, had defeated an amendment, offered by Sen. Robert C. Byrd (D W.Va.) and supported by the administration, which would have allowed the President to take such action as he considered necessary in Cambodia in order to protect U.S. troops in South Vietnam. The close vote was considered a critical test of Senate support for the Cooper-Church amendment.

Tonkin Gulf Repeal. During debate on the Cooper-Church amendment, Dole—a leader of the anti-Cooper-Church forces on behalf of the administration—offered an amendment June 22 to repeal the 1964 Tonkin Gulf resolution. The Dole amendment was viewed as an attempt by Senate administration supporters and the Republican leadership to seize the initiative from the largely Democratic Cooper-Church forces by demonstrating that they, too, were opposed to expansion of the Indochina war. At the same time, repeal of the resolution did not clash with the administration's position, which was neutral on the Tonkin Gulf matter but opposed to the Cooper-Church measure. *(Administration's evolving views on the Tonkin Gulf resolution, p. 946)*

The Senate Foreign Relations Committee May 15 had reported a resolution (S Con Res 64) to repeal the Tonkin Gulf measure. It had been expected that the committee resolution would be the vehicle for repeal and that it would be brought up for debate later in the session.

When Dole June 22 offered the repealer as an amendment to the military sales bill, Fulbright—a leading advocate of repealing the resolution—immediately objected that repeal was "improper in this form" and should be secured instead through passage of S Con Res 64, which had been fully considered by the committee. Fulbright's position was overruled June 24, when by an 81-10 roll-call vote, the Senate adopted the Dole amendment to HR 15628. The repeal was to take effect at the end of the 1970 congressional session.

The Senate also passed S Con Res 64 July 10, 57-5, but it was not voted on by the House.

"End-the-War" Amendment. Gordon Allott (R Colo.), third ranking Senate Republican and chairman of the Republican Policy Committee, June 25 offered—in an attempt to defeat it—the "end-the-war amendment," authored by McGovern, Hatfield, Cranston, Hughes and Goodell.

The measure would have prohibited funds for use in Vietnam after Dec. 31, 1970, except for purposes of withdrawal; for military operations or advisers in Laos after the same date, and for military aid or operations in Cambodia 30 days after enactment. Sponsors had introduced the measure as an amendment to the defense authorization bill, which would be taken up later in the session.

Allott's strategy in bringing up the amendment was part of an effort by administration supporters to clean up debate on all Southeast Asia legislation during consideration of the foreign military sales bill.

Those who wish to call up the amendment now "want to see it defeated," said McGovern June 29. Agreeing with McGovern's criticism of the procedure were several members who strongly opposed the "end-the-war amendment."

Supporters of the "end-the-war amendment" thus joined forces with those who questioned Allott's procedure in voting, 62-29, June 29 to table (kill) the measure. The amendment was rejected in action on the defense procurement bill. *(p. 913)*

House, Conference Action. An effort to instruct House conferees to agree to the Cooper-Church amendment failed July 9 when the House by a **key roll-call vote of 237-153** tabled (killed) a motion to this effect offered by Donald W. Riegle (R Mich.).

House and Senate conferees remained locked in disagreement over the amendment for six months. After a revised Cooper-Church amendment was included in HR 19911, the supplementary foreign aid authorization bill, they agreed to drop the amendment from HR 15628.

SUPPLEMENTARY FOREIGN AID AUTHORIZATION AND APPROPRIATION

After eight months of intense debate, Congress agreed to prohibit the use of U.S. ground troops in Cambodia. Unlike the first Senate-passed Cooper-Church amendment to the foreign military sales bill, the modified amendment which did become law did not bar U.S. air activity over Cambodia.

The revised amendment was attached to a fiscal 1971 supplemental foreign aid authorization bill (HR 19911—PL 91-652). The bill cleared Congress Dec. 22, nearly six months after U.S. ground troops had been pulled out.

Senate restrictions on U.S. military activity in Cambodia had been incorporated in two other bills during the session in varying forms and had run into trouble in conference. Then, in an agreement between the administration and liberal senators advocating restrictions, the compromise language contained in HR 19911 was accepted. As a result the curbs contained in the foreign military sales bill (HR 15628) and the defense department appropriations bill (HR 19580) were dropped. *(p. 911, 913)*

Cambodia Restrictions. As cleared by Congress, HR 19911 contained the following Cambodia restrictions:

• Prohibited the use of funds to finance introduction of ground combat troops into Cambodia or to provide U.S. advisers to or for Cambodian military forces in Cambodia.

• Provided that military and economic assistance could not be construed as a defense commitment to Cambodia.

• Stipulated that the President must inform the Speaker of the House of Representatives and the chairman of the Senate Foreign Relations Committee 30 days in advance if he intended to provide any additional assistance to Cambodia. In case of emergency, the President must inform the Congress 10 days in advance.

Background. President Nixon Nov. 18, two days after Congress returned from its election recess, sent Congress a message requesting $1.035-billion for supplementary foreign aid for fiscal 1971. At the time, the Cooper-Church amendment to the foreign military sales

---

Nixon Report on Cambodia

President Nixon issued a written report on the 60-day U.S. operation in Cambodia June 30, 1970, a day after the last American ground units, except for some advisers, left Cambodia. The report stated that the operation had been successfully concluded and that no American ground personnel would be returned to the country in the future.

According to the President, 32,000 American troops and 48,000 South Vietnamese had participated at various times in the ten major operations launched against a dozen of the "most significant" bases. Nixon said that the operations had assured the continued withdrawal of American forces from Vietnam. The President's report emphasized the need to negotiate a settlement of the Indochina war as well as the need for flexibility in the American position at the bargaining table.

Nixon set down certain guidelines for future U.S. policy toward Cambodia, including a prohibition on sending U.S. advisers on ground personnel, other than regular embassy staff, into Cambodia. The President said that the United States would conduct air interdiction missions against enemy supply and troop routes in Cambodia and would provide military assistance in the form of small arms and relatively unsophisticated equipment in types and quantities suitable for the Cambodian army.

---

bill had been tied up in conference deadlock for nearly five months.

Included in the request was $255-million for Cambodia—$70-million for economic support, $85-million for military assistance and $100-million to "restore funds" which the President said he had already shifted to Cambodia from aid programs in Taiwan, Greece and Turkey.

The major obstacle to Nixon's request was the Senate Foreign Relations Committee, which had jurisdiction over military assistance authorization for most countries. South Vietnam, Laos and Thailand were exceptions to this rule. The committee was chaired by J. W. Fulbright (D Ark.), who was hostile to the war policy.

In 1966, Congress placed military assistance for South Vietnam under the regular Defense Department appropriations act (PL 89-374). The following year, Congress brought military assistance for Laos and Thailand under the regular Defense Department appropriations (PL 90-22). Since the Armed Services Committee dealt with the annual Defense Department authorization legislation, the 1966 and 1967 actions by Congress—renewed annually since 1967—shifted jurisdiction for military assistance for three Southeast Asian countries (Vietnam, Laos and Thailand) from the Foreign Relations to the Armed Services Committee.

Under neutralist Prince Sihanouk, Cambodia did not receive U.S. military assistance. The Lon Nol government's request for aid and Nixon's subsequent message presented an unusual situation: Cambodia became the one country involved in the Indochina conflict for which military assistance remained within the jurisdiction of the Foreign Relations Committee.

Revised Cooper-Church. Fulbright was overruled Dec. 14 when his committee voted 8-4 to defeat a motion by Stuart Symington (D Mo.) to delete the $255-million for Cambodia from HR 19911.

But the committee did agree unanimously to adopt an amendment which embodied some of the provisions of the Cooper-Church amendment passed by the Senate June 30. The committee amendment barred use of funds for introduction of U.S. ground combat troops and advisers into Cambodia and declared that aid to Cambodia should not be "construed as a commitment by the United States to Cambodia for its defense."

The stronger June 30 version of the amendment also barred U.S. support for third countries' forces in Cambodia (South Vietnamese troops) and U.S. combat air activity over Cambodia in 'direct support of Cambodian forces.'

On the Senate floor Dec. 15-16 Fulbright renewed his opposition to Cambodian aid but was defeated Dec. 16 as HR 19911 cleared the Senate on a 72-22 roll-call vote.

When the bill went to conference, the House agreed to the Senate restrictions on U.S. activities in Cambodia.

Appropriations

On Dec. 28 Congress completed action on the first fiscal 1971 supplemental appropriations bill (HR 19928—PL 91-665) which included $85-million in military aid and $70-million in economic aid for Cambodia—the amounts requested by the President. It also contained $75-million to restore funds originally intended for military and economic aid to other nations but spent instead for Cambodia. The Present had requested a $100-million allocation for restoration of funds in his original overall request of $255-million for aid to Cambodia.

DEFENSE PROCUREMENT

The McGovern-Hatfield "end-the-war" amendment, considered during Senate debate on the military sales bill, was rejected Sept. 1 during debate on the fiscal 1971 defense procurement authorization bill (HR 17123—PL 91-441). However the Senate, in action on HR 17123, did approve several other restrictions on U.S. activities in Indochina. Although the House had turned back attempts to curtail U.S. involvement in Southeast Asia during its consideration of HR 17123, House conferees agreed to most of the Senate restrictions.

Provisions. The final version of HR 17123 placed a ceiling of $2.8-billion on U.S. aid to the South Vietnamese and to other free world forces in Laos and Thailand. Financing of military operations by the South Vietnamese or other allied troops in support of the Cambodian or Laotian governments was prohibited.

Other Indochina-related provisions included a ban on U.S. payment of special combat or overseas duty pay to U.S. allies in Southeast Asia which was higher than that received by U.S. servicemen for the same purpose, except to fulfill agreements negotiated before July 1, 1970. The transfer to third parties of weapons or military equipment furnished to Southeast Asian allies, except by approval of the United States, was also prohibited.

"End-the-war" Debate. The McGovern-Hatfield proposal would have limited U.S. troop strength in Vietnam to 280,000 men by April 30, 1971, close to the 284,000 figure projected April 20 by the administration; limited the use of funds after that date to finance the complete withdrawal of remaining troops by Dec. 31, 1971, and authorized the President to extend the withdrawal date not to exceed 60 days in case of a clear and present danger to U.S. troops.

As first announced May 2 by its cosponsors, the amendment sought to cut off funds by the end of 1970. It was modified in the hope of gaining support.

In debate on the amendment, proponents argued that a U.S. withdrawal would hasten a Vietnam peace by meeting conditions for progress at the Paris peace talks and by forcing the Saigon government to adopt a more flexible attitude. Thomas F. Eagleton (D Mo.) and Jacob K. Javits (R N.Y.) said Aug. 31 that the Nixon policy of gradual de-escalation was leading to a wider war in Indochina. Church said Congress needed to keep pressure on the President to hasten the withdrawal.

Robert Dole (R Kan.), Strom Thurmond (R S.C.) and Minority Leader Hugh Scott (R Pa.) attacked the amendment. They expressed concern over the fate of U.S. prisoners if U.S. troops were removed and said the United States would lose its bargaining pressure if the amendment were passed.

On the final day of debate, two Senators who had previously been uncommitted on the issue, Cooper and George D. Aiken (R Vt.), ranking Republican on the Foreign Relations Committee, emerged as opponents. Aiken said the amendment would bring no assurance that its objectives could be attained. Cooper said peace negotiations would have a better chance without the amendment.

Fifteen senators who voted for Cooper-Church voted to reject the Hatfield-McGovern proposal. The proposal was defeated Sept. 1 by a **key roll-call vote of 39-55.**

DEFENSE APPROPRIATIONS

The fiscal 1971 defense appropriations bill (HR 19590—PL 91-668) cleared Congress Dec. 29, after going to conference two times in disagreement over U.S. military activity in Cambodia. As cleared, the $66.6-billion measure contained three restrictions on U.S. support for, or participation in, the Vietnam war. The bill:

● Prohibited payment of special combat duty pay to U.S. allies in Southeast Asia in excess of pay received by U.S. servicemen, except to fulfill agreements entered into prior to July 1, 1970.

● Prohibited financing of military operations by the South Vietnamese or other allied troops in support of the Cambodian or Laotian governments, except to promote the safe and orderly disengagement of U.S. troops from Southeast Asia or to aid in the release of American prisoners of war.

● Prohibited—in line with the expressed intention of the President—the use of funds to finance introduction of U.S. ground forces into Laos or Thailand.

Controversial Provision. Two conferences—Dec. 15 and Dec. 29—were required because Senate liberals refused to allow a floor vote on the first report, which contained a House-added provision permitting U.S. military operations in Cambodia for the purpose of aiding U.S. withdrawals from Vietnam or the release of U.S. prisoners of war. At the second conference, held shortly before the Jan. 2, 1971, legal end of the session, House conferees agreed to drop the provision.

Legislative History. HR 19590, as reported Oct. 6 by the House Appropriations Committee, contained provisions, identical to those in the fiscal 1970 defense appropriations act, reaffirming U.S. support for U.S. allies in Indochina and barring the use of funds for U.S. ground combat troops in Laos and Thailand.

The House passed the bill Oct. 8 by a 274-31 roll-call, turning back by voice votes two amendments introduced by Donald W. Riegle Jr. (R Mich.)—the first amendment would have limited spending on the war to $15-billion in fiscal 1971; the second would have cut off funds for U.S. ground combat troops in Vietnam after June 20, 1971. Defeated on a 23-65 standing vote was a proposal by Donald M. Fraser (D Minn.) providing that Vietnam funds could only be spent for withdrawal from that country.

The Senate Appropriations Committee reported HR 19590 Dec. 3 with an amendment adding Cambodia to the other two countries (Laos and Thailand) barred to U.S. ground combat troops by the fiscal 1970 defense appropriations bill.

It added language enacted in the fiscal 1971 defense procurement authorization bill prohibiting financing by the United States of combat duty pay for Southeast Asian allies at a higher level than that paid to U.S. servicemen and the financing of allied support to the Cambodian and Laotian governments. The committee also placed a ceiling of $2.5-billion on aid to U.S. allies in Southeast Asia.

Senate, Conference Action. After a brief debate, the Senate Dec. 8 passed HR 19590 with the committee restrictions by an 89-0 roll-call vote.

Both chambers approved a second conference report Dec. 29. The House conferees agreed to delete the language permitting the entry of U.S. ground combat troops into Laos, Thailand or Cambodia. In return, Senate conferees agreed to delete Cambodia from the Southeast Asian countries barred to U.S. troops. A ban on U.S. troops in Cambodia had already been written into the fiscal 1971 supplemental foreign aid authorization bill. *(p. 912)*

A prohibition on U.S. troops in Laos and Thailand had been included in the fiscal 1970 defense appropriations bill (PL 91-171) and the conference action left that provision unchanged.

OTHER ACTION

POW RESOLUTIONS. American prisoners of war were the topic of several congressional resolutions in 1970. On Feb. 18, the Senate by voice vote approved H Con Res 454, passed by the House in 1969, calling for humane treatment and release of the prisoners.

In April, the House and Senate, by voice votes, approved H Con Res 582, designating May 1, 1970, as a day for an appeal for justice for Americans captured and missing in Southeast Asia, and May 3 as a national day of prayer for the prisoners.

Both the House and Senate in December passed resolutions (H Res 1282 and S Res 486) commending participants in the Nov. 21 military raid into North Vietnam to rescue U.S. prisoners of war believed to be held captive at a camp near Hanoi.

CON SON PRISON. The House in 1970 dispatched a 12-member select committee to Southeast Asia to report on the situation there. The study group issued a report in July which generally was optimistic about the May-June U.S. military action in Cambodia and the progress of the Vietnamization policy. However, the report was overshadowed by two members' disclosures of the South Vietnamese government's harsh treatment of political and war prisoners at the Con Son Island prison.

William R. Anderson (D Tenn.) and Augustus F. Hawkins (D Calif.), along with a committee staff aide, visited the prison July 2. They reported that about 400 civilian political prisoners were crammed in five-by-eight-foot "tiger cage" type cells, with three to five people in each one.

Anderson said July 7 that since the U.S. government had involved itself (through the aid program) in the Saigon prisons, it should "insist on immediate prison reforms." Replying to the charge, a U.S. Embassy information staff official, Roy W. Johnson, July 7 issued a statement that although the United States had been aware of the "tiger cages," it had no responsibility for the administration of the Vietnamese prison system.

Both Anderson and Hawkins issued individual reports on the fact-finding mission.

1971

Laos dominated controversy over the war in 1971. Throughout the year and early in 1972 the United States stepped up its participation in the air war over Laos and the Central Intelligence Agency (CIA) continued to train and advise guerrilla forces.

The U.S.-assisted invasion of Laos by South Vietnam Feb. 8 provoked months of debate and criticism. Although the reaction to the Laos operation was moderate compared with the aftermath of the Cambodian invasion of 1970, U.S. participation still served to fan growing concern over the widening role of the United States in Indochina. It intensified war critics' drive for greater details on the extent of U.S. involvement in Southeast Asia.

Publication of the Pentagon Papers in June did little to allay suspicions. The study—a secret 7,000 page history of the policy decisions which led the United States into the Indochina quagmire—rocked Congress, the White House and the nation, and helped further diminish government credibility. *(Details, p. 946)*

Congressional critics continued to press for withdrawal of U.S. forces. Congress for the first time went on record urging the President to accelerate his policy of gradual withdrawal of U.S. troops from South Vietnam. Three times the Senate approved amendments offered by Majority Leader Mike Mansfield (D Mont.) declaring specific withdrawal deadlines: once a nine-month deadline, twice a six-month deadline. The House twice agreed to weakened versions of the amendment calling for an end of U.S. military operations in Indochina "at the earliest practicable date" and the setting of a "date certain" for withdrawal—once as a sense-of-Congress statement and once as a national policy declaration.

The President signed the measures to which they were attached but, in signing the policy declaration, he stated it "will not change the policies I have pursued." *(Box, p. 919)*

The protests continued. Demonstrators ranged from Vietnam veterans to big-name lawyers and student militants—tactics from marches to peaceful lobbying to disruptions of rush-hour traffic in Washington.

Military Activity

On Feb. 8, South Vietnamese ground troops, with United States air support, launched a major drive into Laos against North Vietnamese supply bases along the Ho Chi Minh trail.

At the outset it was said that the operation would be ended before the rainy season which usually began about two weeks before or after May 1. However, the South Vietnamese, suffering heavy losses and facing strong North Vietnamese counterdrives, ended the operation March 24. Both the South Vietnamese and United States denied charges of retreat and claimed the troops had succeeded in disrupting enemy logistic supply routes.

Nixon Speech. In an April 7 nationwide television address President Nixon, assessing the invasion of Laos, concluded that "the South Vietnamese demonstrated that without American advisers they could fight effectively against the best troops North Vietnam could put in the field."

Although the South Vietnamese suffered heavy casualties, he said "by the most conservative estimates the casualties suffered by the enemy were far heavier." Most important, he added, "the disruption of enemy supply lines and the consumption of ammunition and arms in the battle has been even more damaging to the capability of the North Vietnamese to sustain major offensives in South Vietnam than were the operations in Cambodia 10 months ago."

"Consequently tonight I can report that Vietnamization has succeeded," Nixon said. In the same speech, the President announced the planned withdrawal of an additional 100,000 American military personnel from South Vietnam between May and December 1971.

During his message to the nation, Nixon also criticized a number of congressional bills and resolutions that would set a specific date for total American withdrawal from Indochina. The President said an announcement for total withdrawal, despite its great appeal to the American people, would "serve the enemy's purpose, not our own."

The withdrawal announcement was the fifth Nixon had made since assuming office. From a high of 540,000 men, the President previously had authorized the withdrawal of 265,000 troops, dropping the number still there to 284,000 by May 1.

The President noted that he had pledged to end American involvement in the Vietnam war during his campaign for the presidency: "I am keeping that pledge. You should hold me accountable if I fail."

On Nov. 12 Nixon announced a troop withdrawal of 45,000 more U.S. troops by Feb. 1, 1972. He told reporters that with the reduction of troops "it is particularly important for us to continue our air strikes on the infiltration routes." He warned that a "substantial step-up" in enemy infiltration would necessitate a step-up in U.S. air strike activity.

There had been intermittent air strikes over North Vietnam throughout 1971. The year ended with five days of heavy air strikes on military installations in North Vietnam. U.S. officials said the strikes were in response not only to an extensive supply build-up by the North Vietnamese, possibly in preparation for an offensive, but also to air and missile attacks on U.S. bombers over Laos. *(Box on bombing p. 925)*

Peace Negotiations

A new Vietcong peace plan broke the tedium of deadlock and rhetorical exchanges in the fourth year of the Paris peace talks.

On July 1, the Vietcong, with North Vietnam's support, proposed the return of all American and allied prisoners held in North and South Vietnam by the end of 1971, if all U.S. troops were withdrawn within that same period. A cease-fire would go into effect once agreement on withdrawal had been reached.

The U.S. reaction was cautious. Chief negotiator David K. E. Bruce criticized various points in the plan, such as its call for unconditional withdrawal and exclusion of South Vietnamese President Nguyen Van Thieu from a transition government in Saigon. However, he called for further exploration of the plan in a restricted session "free from the glare of publicity." His suggestion was rejected as "a perfidious maneuver" by the communist delegations. The stalemate continued through the year.

In late July, Bruce resigned for health reasons as chief U.S. delegate to the Paris talks. He was replaced by William J. Porter, U.S. ambassador to South Vietnam at the time.

War Protests

Allied operations in Laos sparked more demonstrations in Washington. A bomb was exploded in the Capitol March 1 as a protest. An unidentified caller told the Capitol switchboard, about 30 minutes before the explosion, that a bomb was about to go off and said it was planted in "retaliation for the Laos decision." The explosion occurred at 1:32 a.m. and no one was injured. *(Box p. 372)*

Three weeks of antiwar demonstrations in the spring intensified feelings on both sides. About 2,300 members of the Vietnam Veterans Against the War camped on the Mall near the Capitol and lobbied Congress for an end to the war during a six-day protest in mid-April. Some members flung down their war medals on the Capitol steps.

Other demonstrations followed, lasting until May 5. These protests began with peaceful lobbying on Capitol Hill, but ended in increasingly militant acts of civil disobedience which led to mass arrests.

Congressional Action

In the Senate, most of the criticism of the Laotian operation came from Democrats, although a few Republicans also questioned President Nixon's handling of the war.

George D. Aiken (Vt.), the ranking Republican on the Senate Foreign Relations Committee, Feb. 10 recommended convening an Indochina conference to negotiate a settlement of the area's disputes.

"The time has come for someone other than the President of the United States or the great powers of Europe to convene a conference of nations concerned with Southeast Asia to consider collective action in support of the people there," Aiken said.

House Democrats. In an unprecedented action, House Democrats, meeting in caucus March 31, voted 138-62 to adopt a compromise resolution stating that the House "should work to end the military involvement in Indochina and to bring about the release of all prisoners" by the end of the 92nd Congress, which probably would come in late 1972.

Perhaps more significant, however, was an earlier vote to substitute the compromise version of the original resolution, which called for the withdrawal of all U.S. troops by the end of 1971. The stronger resolution lost out by only one vote, 101 to 100. There were 254 Democrats in the House.

The resolution closely paralleled action taken by Senate Democrats Feb. 23 when they voted 38-13 with two abstentions and two reservations to adopt a "resolution of purpose" for the 92nd Congress to end United States involvement in Indochina and "bring about the withdrawal of all U.S. forces and the release of prisoners in a time certain."

And on March 24, the Democratic Policy Council unanimously had passed a stronger resolution setting Dec. 31, 1971, as the date to cut off all funds for U.S. military operations in Indochina.

President Nixon's April 7 address in which he told the nation that the invasion of Laos was a success and announced further troop withdrawals did little to quiet the war critics.

The Senate met June 7 behind closed doors to discuss United States involvement in Laos. A censored version of what was said during the secret session was printed in the *Congressional Record* in early August.

Later in the month Senate war critics began in earnest their session-long campaign to legislate an end to the Southeast Asian conflict.

Legislative Action

In 1971 five major bills were vehicles for efforts to limit U.S. participation in the Indochina war. The five bills and action on key war-related amendments were:

● **Draft Extension** (HR 6531—PL 92-129)—Congress modified a Mansfield amendment that would have set a nine-month withdrawal deadline to make it a sense-of-Congress statement that the United States should end its military operations in Indochina "at the earliest practicable date" and a "date certain" should be set for troop withdrawal. Congress rejected an amendment cutting off funds for the war (McGovern-Hatfield amendment).

● **Defense Procurement** (HR 8687—PL 92-156)—Congress modified a Mansfield amendment that would have set a six-month withdrawal deadline to make it a policy declaration that the United States should end its military operations in Indochina "at the earliest practicable date" and that a "date certain" should be set for troop withdrawal. Congress approved a $350-million

ceiling on U.S. expenditures in Laos, excluding air support, and rejected an attempt to cut off funds for the war.

● **Foreign Aid Authorization** (HR 9910)—Before Senate defeat of the entire bill, the House had rejected two war-related amendments and the Senate had deleted the committee-added Cooper-Church provision cutting off funds for the war. The bill, which included such Senate-added policy provisions as a six-month troop withdrawal deadline (Mansfield amendment) and a $341-million ceiling on aid to Cambodia, was defeated by the Senate Oct. 29.

● **Substitute Foreign Aid Authorization** (S 2819—PL 92-226, cleared by Congress in January 1972)—Congress approved a $341-million ceiling on fiscal 1972 aid to Cambodia and rejected a six-month troop withdrawal deadline (Mansfield), as well as a requirement for specific congressional approval of all U.S. funds used to finance military operations by third-country forces in Laos, North Vietnam or Thailand.

● **Defense Appropriations** (HR 11731—PL 92-204)—Congress rejected two amendments cutting off funds for the war.

DRAFT EXTENSION

The primary vehicle for end-the-war legislation during 1971 was the military draft extension bill (HR 6531—PL 92-129). The President's draft authority, last extended in 1967, expired June 30, 1971. Conference deadlock over a Mansfield troop withdrawal amendment and a subsequent Senate delay in acting on the conference report resulted in a lapse of that authority until Sept. 28, when the new draft extension was signed into law.

Before final passage June 24, the Senate June 22 voted to attach an amendment setting an Indochina withdrawal deadline of nine months from enactment of the measure. The bill, having been approved by the House April 1, went to conference June 28.

Within two days, only one of 28 differences between the House and Senate versions of the bill remained in contention—the withdrawal provision. The deadlock was not broken until July 30, when conferees agreed to modify the Mansfield amendment to make it a sense-of-Congress statement that the United States should end its military operations in Indochina "at the earliest practicable date."

The House adopted the conference report Aug. 4. But disagreements over conference action on military pay increases and the withdrawl amendment stalled Senate action until Sept. 21, when the bill was cleared for the President's signature. Despite the weakened version of the Mansfield amendment, the provision did mark the first time Congress had expressed a desire to withdraw troops from Indochina.

HOUSE ACTION. During House consideration of the draft bill March 30-April 1, four amendments were offered that dealt directly with restricting U.S. troop deployment in Indochina or setting a withdrawal date for troops. All the proposals were rejected.

Donald M. Fraser (D Minn.) offered an amendment providing that no person drafted after Dec. 31, 1971, could be required to serve in Indochina. The amendment was defeated by a 122-260 recorded teller vote.

Immediately following rejection of Fraser's amendment, Henry B. Gonzalez (D Texas) offered a proposal to prohibit the use of draftees in any armed conflict outside the United States except during a war declared by Congress. The Gonzalez amendment was rejected by voice vote.

A similar amendment, offered by Sam Gibbons (D Fla.), provided that no person drafted after June 30, 1971, could be required to serve in combat outside the United States unless the President declared war or told Congress that an attack on the United States was imminent. The amendment was defeated by a 96-278 recorded teller vote.

Finally, William F. Ryan (D N.Y.) offered an amendment that called for the total withdrawal of U.S. military forces from Indochina and surrounding waters by Dec. 31, 1971. It was rejected by voice vote.

Opposition to the amendments was led by F. Edward Hebert (D La.), chairman of the House Armed Services Committee. "The Joint Chiefs of Staff came before our committee...and they said they could not live with it (manpower restrictions in Indochina), that it would destroy our ability to meet our commitment in Indochina," Hebert said.

SENATE DEBATE. Twice during consideration in June of the draft bill the Senate came to major votes on end-the-war proposals, rejecting the tough McGovern-Hatfield amendment and one week later adopting the weaker Mansfield proposal with its nine-month troop withdrawal amendment.

McGovern-Hatfield. The Senate June 16 rejected by a 42-55 roll-call vote the anti-war amendment sponsored by Senators George McGovern (D S.D.) and Mark O. Hatfield (R Ore.) after one week of debate.

The McGovern-Hatfield amendment sought to cut off funds for support of U.S. troops in Indochina for any purpose other than withdrawal as of Dec. 31, 1971. With one exception, the major issues debated were not appreciably different from those discussed prior to the 1970 vote on a similar proposal offered by McGovern and Hatfield.

The one major new topic which figured heavily in the presentations by supporters of the amendment was the soaring rate of drug addiction among soldiers and veterans who had served in Indochina.

Mansfield Amendment. The Senate June 22 broke with historical precedents, reversed the position it had upheld six days earlier on the McGovern-Hatfield amendment and adopted by a **key roll-call vote of 57-42** and a 61-38 roll-call vote a proposal calling for the withdrawal of all U.S. troops from Indochina within nine months.

After a series of six consecutive roll-call votes on a tangle of troop withdrawal amendments and modifications considered during debate, the Senate adopted a withdrawal proposal offered by Mansfield.

The fifth vote of June 22, on which the Mansfield proposal was tentatively adopted by a 57-42 roll-call vote, was the crucial test for supporters of a withdrawal amendment. The final 61-38 roll-call vote, officially adopting the Mansfield amendment, was a procedural formality on which four additional senators voted "yea" when it became apparent the measure was certain to pass.

Mansfield termed his proposal a national policy declaration. It was adopted in lieu of an amendment sponsored by Marlow W. Cook (R Ky.) that had been weakened by modifications adopted on the floor prior to consideration of the Mansfield substitute.

The Mansfield amendment declared it the policy of the United States that the withdrawal of all U.S. troops from Indochina would be completed within nine months of enactment of HR 6531. The amendment urged the President to set his own date for complete withdrawal within the nine-month period set by the proposal, and that the President should begin negotiations for the release of all U.S. prisoners of war immediately. The withdrawal of troops, the proposal stated, was subject to the successful negotiation for the release of the prisoners.

The Mansfield proposal, which called for the phased withdrawal of all U.S. troops along with a phased release of U.S. POWs, was not legally binding. The policy declaration language, however, carried more weight than the standard sense of Congress resolution. If the Mansfield amendment had been accepted by the House en toto—which it was not—it would have acted as a policy directive for the administration although the President would have been within the rights granted to him under the Constitution to ignore it—which he did. *(Box, p. 919)*

The six roll calls which resulted in the adoption of the Mansfield withdrawal declaration were preceded by a heated debate on the Senate floor and a last-minute lobbying effort by the administration to stem the growing support for setting a withdrawal date.

White House Press Secretary Ronald L. Ziegler told reporters after the vote June 22 the President would regard the amendment as a sense-of-the-Congress resolution and nothing more if it emerged from the House-Senate conference as part of the bill and was adopted by both chambers. Ziegler said the amendment was simply the view of 57 senators, not the will of the people.

Adoption of the Mansfield proposal represented the first time in modern U.S. history that either chamber of Congress had urged an end to a war in which the country was still actively involved.

Conference, Final Action. After a one-month deadlock, conferees agreed to soften the Mansfield amendment, declaring it to be the sense-of-Congress—rather than national policy—that U.S. terminate military operations in Indochina "at the earliest practicable date"—rather than nine months from enactment. The provision urged the President to begin negotiations for an immediate cease-fire and for establishing a definite withdrawal deadline along with the release of U.S. prisoners. The conference report was filed July 30.

The House accepted the conference report Aug. 4, but the Senate delayed its approval until after the August recess because of disagreements over military pay increases and the watered-down version of the Mansfield amendment. The Senate Sept. 17 rejected an attempt to send the bill back to conference and on Sept. 21 cleared the measure for the President's signature.

DEFENSE PROCUREMENT

A second Mansfield amendment received congressional approval Nov. 11 when Congress cleared the fiscal

1972 defense procurement authorization bill (HR 8687—PL 92-156). The amendment declared to be U.S. policy that the United States end military operations in Indochina "at the earliest practicable date" and set a "date certain" for withdrawal. As originally adopted by the Senate Sept. 30 and included in the Senate-passed version of HR 8687, the Mansfield amendment set a six-month withdrawal deadline, pending the release of U.S. prisoners.

Another Senate-added provision which was included in the final version of the legislation was a $350-million ceiling on U.S. expenditures in Laos excluding air support.

HOUSE ACTION. Although the bill authorized funds for development, research and procurement of weapons for fiscal 1972, much of the floor debate as well as nine of the 21 amendments considered by the House in June were related to the war in Indochina—not armaments.

The most highly publicized amendment dealing with the war, which was similar in its intent to the Senate McGovern-Hatfield amendment, was a proposal by Lucien N. Nedzi (D Mich.) and Charles W. Whalen Jr. (R Ohio). The Nedzi-Whalen amendment sought to cut off funds as of Dec. 31, 1971, for all items covered in the bill that could be used in Indochina, thus signaling to the President, the amendment's supporters said, that the House was requesting an expedited withdrawal of U.S. forces from Indochina.

Even the authors of the Nedzi-Whalen amendment freely admitted the proposal was ambiguous and carried almost no legal authority to force the President to do anything. They blamed the House germaneness rule—which prohibited sweeping end-the-war amendments barring use of funds in Indochina other than those in HR 8687—for the narrowness of their amendment.

Despite the questionable power of the amendment to legally force the President to set a date for U.S. withdrawal from Indochina, it was regarded by the White House as an attempt to undermine public support for the President's withdrawal policy. Small groups of representatives were ushered in and out of the White House during the days prior to June 17 when the amendment was voted down. Members were briefed on the President's position and were allowed to discuss the matter with congressional liaison White House staff members.

Although the Nedzi-Whalen amendment was rejected by a 158-254 recorded teller vote, the vote reflected growing dissatisfaction in the House with the Indochina war.

For the first time, a majority of House Democrats (135-105) supported a position which could be described as both against the war and dissatisfied with the administration's withdrawal program. Twenty-three Republicans supported the amendment and 149 voted against it.

The 158 votes supporting the amendment also amounted to the largest House protest vote against the war to that date. A vote to prohibit the use of draftees in Indochina was rejected by a 122-260 recorded teller vote April 1.

After debate began on the Nedzi-Whalen amendment June 17, four proposals aimed at modifying the amendment were introduced, debated and rejected. Another four amendments dealing with Indochina were

also debated and rejected. The House passed HR 8687 June 17.

SENATE ACTION. The Senate Oct. 6, by an 82-4 roll-call vote, approved HR 8687, after adding nine amendments—two dealing with Indochina.

Vietnam. For the second time in 1971, the Senate passed a Vietnam troop withdrawal proposal offered by Majority Leader Mansfield. The amendment declared it to be national policy that all U.S. troops would be withdrawn from Indochina within six months after the bill became law pending the release of U.S. prisoners of war. It was adopted Sept. 30 on a 57-38 roll-call vote.

With the exception of the six-month withdrawal deadline, Mansfield's amendment was identical to one adopted June 22 as part of the draft extension bill (HR 6531—PL 92-129). That amendment was weakened in a House-Senate conference, however, and the final version signed by the President contained no withdrawal deadlines.

Laos. The Senate imposed a $350-million ceiling on U.S. expenditures on Laos. Although the action set a precedent for Congress, the spending ceiling figure was the same as that recommended by the administration for fiscal 1972. The amendment, proposed by Sen. Stuart Symington (D Mo.), excluded from the expenditure ceiling all U.S. air actions over Laos.

The White House opposed the Laos amendment, however, and Henry A. Kissinger, special assistant to the President for national security affairs, urged John C. Stennis (D Miss.), floor manager of the bill, to oppose the amendment. Stennis supported the proposal despite White House pressure. but only after the ceiling was raised from $200-million to $350-million.

The Symington amendment was adopted Oct. 4 by a 67-11 roll-call vote. Two additional Indochina amendments were rejected in early October, before final Senate passage Oct. 6.

HOUSE ANTI-WAR ACTION. During the usually routine procedure of appointing House members to a House-Senate conference, an anti-war faction attempted to obtain a direct vote on the Senate-passed Mansfield troop withdrawal amendment. But the Oct. 19 move was blocked by the House leadership of both parties.

Instead of a straight up or down vote on the Mansfield amendment—a direct vote which the Nixon administration lobbied strenuously to avoid because it opposed any withdrawal deadline—the House voted on two separate procedural motions, neither of which directly confronted the Mansfield amendment.

The issue, as it was presented to the House by Republican Whip Leslie C. Arends (Ill.) and Minority Leader Gerald R. Ford (Mich.), was one of germaneness. The House, they claimed, was being bullied by the Senate into approving a bill containing nongermane amendments which violated House rules established by the 1970 Reorganization Act. Supporters of the Mansfield amendment charged that the leadership was making a mockery of the House rules and using the germaneness issue as a ploy to avoid confronting the more basic question of ending U.S. involvement in the Indochina war.

The House first voted, by a **key roll-call vote of 215-193,** to end further debate on the conference instructions offered by Arends; the vote also ended any opportunity to amend the Arends proposal, particularly by anti-war members to get a vote on the Mansfield amendment.

On a second vote, an almost complete reversal of the first one, the House by a 192-216 roll-call vote proceeded to throw out the set of instructions offered by Arends, thus giving conferees a free hand to negotiate on all Senate-passed amendments—whether they were germane to the House version of the defense authorization bill or not.

CONFERENCE REPORT. Conferees removed from the Senate-passed amendment the six-month withdrawal deadline, replacing it with the language "at a date certain." House conferees tried to make the amendment a sense of Congress proposal instead of a declared policy statement, but the Senate language prevailed. House conferees added language to the provision, however, requiring that all Americans missing in action who had been held or were known to be held by North Vietnam or its allies had to be accounted for by those governments before the policy statement would take effect.

On the Laotian aid ceiling, the conference report stated that House conferees "intend that the $350-million limitation should include all assistance-related activities in Laos." According to the report, however, "the conferees wish to make it understood that it is not the intent to place a ceiling on, or reduce, funds available for vital non-assistance-related activities in programs which must be carried on...."

The House approved the conference report Nov. 10 by a voice vote. The Senate adopted the report Nov. 11 on a 65-19 roll-call vote.

FOREIGN AID AUTHORIZATION

A third Mansfield amendment, identical to the six-month deadline provision added to the defense procurement bill, was attached by the Senate Foreign Relations Committee to the fiscal 1972 and 1973 foreign aid authorization bill (HR 9910). But it, along with other Indochina policy amendments, went down with HR 9910, when the Senate Oct. 29 rejected the entire measure, as liberals and conservatives frustrated with the foreign aid program joined forces to defeat the measure.

HOUSE ACTION. There was little debate on the war when the House considered HR 9910. The House rejected by voice vote an amendment offered by John G. Dow (D N.Y.) to reduce the U.S. military assistance by $195,200,000 for both fiscal years.

Dow said his amendment was intended to reduce the $200-million in military aid which the House Foreign Affairs Committee had recommended for Cambodia to the $4,800,000 provided in fiscal 1970. Asking the House to "repudiate adventurism in Cambodia," Dow said the United States "sould substitute dollars for GIs so as to encourage the war in Cambodia to escalate, not subside."

Phoenix Program. The House rejected by voice vote an amendment offered by Ogden R. Reid (R N.Y.) barring aid to any nation "for programs which encompass the assassination or torture of persons, or which violate the standards set forth in the Geneva Conventions."

Reid said the amendment was aimed primarily at "the outrageous abuses which have taken place

Effect of Mansfield Amendment

In September 1971, when Congress cleared a modified version of the Mansfield amendment as part of the draft extension bill (HR 6531), the provision stated that it was the "sense of Congress" that U.S. military operations in Indochina should cease "at the earliest practicable date" and a "date certain" should be set for U.S. troop withdrawal. *(Details, p. 920)*

A nearly identical end-the-war provision was sent to the President in November 1971 as part of the defense procurement authorization bill (HR 8687). But this time the provision stated that it was the "policy of the United States" rather than the sense of Congress. *(Details, p. 920)*

The effect of that distinction was subject to dispute. Proponents, opponents and legal experts differed as to whether the policy declaration was legally binding.

The real distinction appeared to be more psychological than legal, since the policy declaration contained no specific date for withdrawal nor legal imperatives. Since a sense-of-Congress statement had already been approved, the broader national policy declaration was the next step.

Before signing the $21.3-billion defense procurement authorization, President Nixon explained how he viewed the troop withdrawal amendment:

"To avoid any possible misconceptions, I wish to emphasize that Secton 601 of this Act—the so-called Mansfield amendment—does not represent the policies of this administration. Section 601 urges that the President establish a 'final date' for the withdrawal of all U.S. forces from Indochina, subject only to the release of U.S. prisoners of war and an accounting for the missing in action. Section 601 expresses a judgment about the manner in which the American involvement in the war should be ended.

"However, it is without binding force or effect and it does not reflect my judgment about the way in which the war should be brought to a conclusion. My signing of the bill that contains this section, therefore, will not change the policies I have pursued and that I shall continue to pursue toward this end."

under the Phoenix program in South Vietnam." Under the program, Reid said, the South Vietnamese government was trying to eliminate the Vietcong infrastructure by methods that included torture and assassination.

The House Aug. 3 passed HR 9910 by a 202-192 roll-call vote.

SENATE COMMITTEE ACTION. Before reporting HR 9910 by an 11-5 vote Oct. 20, the Foreign Relations Committee attached a series of amendments renewing the committee's challenge to the Nixon administration's policies in Southeast Asia. The committee added two legislative amendments which, it said, would commit the United States to withdrawing its troops from Indochina within six months of their enactment.

One, the Vietnam troop withdrawal amendment sponsored by Majority Leader Mansfield, already had been approved twice—in nearly identical versions—by the Senate in 1971 as amendments to the draft extension bill (HR 6531) and defense procurement authorization (HR 8687). It declared it to be the policy of the United States that all U.S. troops would be withdrawn from Indochina within six months, contingent on release of all Americans held prisoners of war by the North Vietnamese and the Vietcong. The amendment was approved by a 12-4 vote.

Cooper-Church. The second withdrawal amendment proposed by Frank Church (D Idaho) and John Sherman Cooper (R Ky.), required that all funds authorized for U.S. forces in Indochina be used only for the purpose of completing the withdrawal of all U.S. troops from South Vietnam. Under its terms, U.S. forces could not engage in fighting in North Vietnam, South Vietnam, Cambodia or Laos except to protect withdrawing Americans from "imminent danger."

The Cooper-Church amendment would permit U.S. forces to remain in Thailand, the committee said, but they could not be used in combat in neighboring countries except to protect the U.S. withdrawal. Military assistance to South Vietnam, Laos and Cambodia would be permitted, however.

The Cooper-Church provision, adopted in committee by an 11-5 vote, "is a logical culmination of the committee's principal policy efforts over the last several years," the report said. "It is also a logical extension of the committee's efforts in recent years to restore the proper constitutional balance between Congress and the executive branch in matters of war and peace."

Cambodia Aid. Going beyond attempts to force a quick withdrawal of U.S. troops from the Indochina fighting, the committee added other amendments the purpose of which was to limit what the committee viewed as a growing U.S. commitment to Cambodia's defense.

The principal Cambodia amendment, a combination of provisions proposed by Stuart Symington (D Mo.) and Clifford P. Case (R N.J.), placed limits on the amount of money and the number of men the United States could allocate to Cambodia.

The proposal by Symington would limit to $250-million fiscal 1972 economic and military aid to Cambodia. The ceiling applied to spending by all executive branch departments and agencies.

The $250-million—$93-million below the total projected for Cambodia by the administration—did not apply to funds for air operations over Cambodia. Some members had argued that a limit on air operations would jeopardize withdrawal from Vietnam.

Beginning with fiscal 1973, the amendment would require specific congressional authorization for funds to be spent in Cambodia and would require the President to explain to Congress the purpose for which such funds were requested.

The committee included with the fund ceiling a proposal by Case to impose a 200-man ceiling on the number of U.S. military and civilian personnel who could be stationed in Cambodia.

The provision also placed a 50-man ceiling on the number of third country nationals that the United States could support in Cambodia.

Other Restrictions. Taking note of the process by which the American role in Indochina was started and expanded, the committee included in HR 9910 several restrictions on the President's discretion in allocating assistance funds. Their provisions:

• Required specific congressional approval before the President could use U.S. funds to finance military operations in Laos, South Vietnam, North Vietnam, Thailand, Cambodia or Burma by the armed forces of a third nation.

• Prohibited U.S. government personnel from advising Cambodian police and paramilitary forces or security and intelligence units. The provision expanded the existing prohibition, enacted by the Cooper-Church amendment to the fiscal 1971 supplemental foreign aid authorization bill, against assigning U.S. advisers to Cambodian military forces.

• Tightened provisions in existing law by requiring the President to give prior notice to Congress before using his authority to waive restrictions on military aid to other nations.

• The committee also inserted provisions requiring publication of presidential findings that aid limits should be waived and requiring that Congress have access to information while a presidential determination was being considered.

• Required the President to supply Congress at least 30 days after final passage of the annual foreign aid appropriation with the projected country-by-country breakdown of the assistance funds.

• Prohibited giving any country more than 10 per cent over the amount specified by the President unless he determined that additional aid was vital to U.S. national security and gave Congress at least 10 days prior notice. (Under existing law, the President had unlimited authority to increase or decrease funds to a particular country—by transferring funds from one intended recipient to another—regardless of the amounts he had justified to Congress during committee consideration of the entire aid program.)

"By using this waiver authority last year," the committee said, "Cambodia was allocated a total of $110-million in military aid by the President, without a specific authorization by Congress, through transfer of funds from other economic and military aid programs."

• In an effort to assert greater control over U.S. spending in Southeast Asia, the committee added a provision requiring all military aid to South Vietnam, Laos and Thailand be funded out of the regular military assistance program under the Foreign Assistance Act of 1961.

The effect of the provision was to transfer congressional oversight of foreign military grant assistance to those countries from the Armed Services Committees of both houses to the Senate Foreign Relations and House Foreign Affairs Committees. (Congress in 1966 had approved a transfer of all assistance to South Vietnam to the Defense Department budget as an interim measure during the war buildup. In 1967, military aid to Laos and Thailand was also placed in the defense budget. Thus the oversight function was transferred to the Armed Services Committees since they considered the defense budget.)

SENATE FLOOR ACTION. In a series of three close roll-call votes, the Senate Oct. 28 deleted the Cooper-Church amendment:

• A **key roll-call vote of 47-44** adopting an amendment by Minority Leader Hugh Scott (R Pa.) deleting the Cooper-Church provision.

• A 44-45 roll-call vote defeating Scott's motion to kill a motion by Fulbright to reconsider the vote approving Scott's amendment.

• A 44-48 roll-call vote rejecting Fulbright's motion to reconsider the amendment.

Cambodia. The Senate Oct. 28 by a 35-52 roll-call vote rejected an amendment by Gale W. McGee (D Wyo.) increasing military grant aid and supporting assistance to Cambodia by $62-million and eliminating the $250-million Cambodian aid ceiling approved by the Foreign Relations Committee.

The Senate Oct. 29 by a 45-36 roll-call vote adopted an amendment by Stuart Symington (D Mo.) raising the ceiling imposed on all forms of aid to Cambodia to $341-million from $250-million.

Though he sponsored the $250-million limit amendment in the committee, Symington had announced Oct. 28 that he would introduce an amendment increasing the ceiling to $341-million.

Before approving Symington's modification, the Senate by a 26-53 roll-call vote rejected a substitute amendment by Mike Gravel (D Alaska) lowering the ceiling on aid to Cambodia to $150-million.

Other Indochina Amendments. The Senate Oct. 29 by separate voice votes adopted four other amendments relating to the Indochina war:

The first, offered by Bill Brock (R Tenn.), and accepted by Mansfield on behalf of the Foreign Relations Committee, barred aid to a nation that the President determined had failed to actively support the provisions of the 1949 Geneva Convention on treatment of prisoners of war.

The remaining three amendments were compromises between the Foreign Relations and Armed Services Committees on provisions added in committee.

The Foreign Relations Committee had added a provision requiring specific congressional approval for all U.S. funds used to finance military operations by third-country forces in South Vietnam, North Vietnam, Laos, Thailand, Cambodia and Burma.

An amendment offered by Case after consultation with Stennis deleted South Vietnam, Cambodia and Burma from the provision's language, leaving the requirement in effect for North Vietnam, Laos and Thailand.

An amendment offered by Fulbright, also with Stennis' agreement, left committee oversight of military funds for South Vietnam and Laos in the Defense Department budget under the Armed Services Committee's jurisdiction. Although Laos and South Vietnam were exempted, the amendment left in the bill a provision returning oversight of military aid to Thailand to the Foreign Relations Committee and placing such aid in the foreign assistance bill.

The third amendment, offered by Stennis with Fulbright's concurrence, clarified language in HR 9910 to ensure that certain reports required by the Foreign Relations Committee from the State Department did not overlap the jurisdiction of the Armed Services Committee.

The Senate Oct. 29, by a 27-41 roll-call vote, rejected HR 9910. The reasons for its defeat were as varied as the liberals and conservatives who voted against it. Opposition to the Vietnam war and continued military involvement, a desire to assert congressional influence over foreign policy and concern over increasing military aid, especially the aid to Cambodia planned by the administration, were among the reasons for the bill's defeat.

SUBSTITUTE FOREIGN AID AUTHORIZATION

A substitute foreign aid authorization bill for fiscal 1972 failed to gain final congressional approval until the 92d Congress returned for its second session in 1972 (S 2819—PL 92-226). The Senate had defeated Oct. 29 the original authorization bill (HR 9910).

A month-long conference deadlock was broken when conferees agreed to drop the Mansfield Indochina-withdrawal amendment. The Senate adopted the conference report Dec. 17 and the House Jan. 25, 1972.

Although the Mansfield amendment was dropped, the conference version included several Senate amendments limiting the President's authority to commit aid funds in Southeast Asia, including a $341-million ceiling on aid to Cambodia.

SENATE ACTION. The Senate Foreign Relations Committee Nov. 4 reported a two bill package: S 2819 (military assistance) and S 2820 (economic and humanitarian assistance).

The committee incorporated in S 2819 many of the legislative provisions it added to HR 9910 to limit the President's authority to use U.S. money, arms and men abroad, especially in Indochina.

As reported, S 2819 included the Vietnam troop withdrawal amendment sponsored by Mansfield. It declared U.S. policy to be withdrawal of all U.S. troops from Indochina within six months, contingent upon release of all Americans held prisoners of war by the North Vietnamese and Vietcong.

In drawing up S 2819, the committee accepted Senate floor actions on HR 9910 that:

• Raised to $341-million from $250-million a ceiling recommended by the committee on all U.S. aid to Cambodia.

• Transferred military assistance authorizations for Thailand from the Defense Department budget to the foreign aid authorization bill effective in fiscal 1973, but left military funds for South Vietnam and Laos within the defense budget.

• Required specific congressional approval for all U.S. funds used to finance military operations by third-country forces in Laos, North Vietnam or Thailand, omitting similar requirements for forces in South Vietnam, Cambodia and Burma.

Floor Action. Senate debate on S 2819 Nov. 11 reflected differences in points of view over the adequacy and necessity of the foreign military assistance program.

Supporters of existing U.S. policy in Indochina argued that the bill reported by the Foreign Relations Committee authorized insufficient funding of military aid programs, which they called essential for implementation of the Nixon Doctrine. Without additional military aid, they said, the withdrawal of U.S. troops from Indochina and the reduction in the U.S. military presence in other areas would be in jeopardy.

Senators opposed to the administration's Indochina policy said the military assistance would increase U.S. commitments overseas.

Secret Senate Session on Laos

The Senate met June 7 in secret session, to be briefed on the Laos situation by Sen. Stuart Symington (D Mo.) from a top secret Foreign Relations Committee staff report. The staff report was sanitized and released Aug. 3. *(Additional details on Laos, Thailand, p. 908)*

In a June 7 statement, Symington said he had requested the secret session because of "the increasingly grave situation in (Laos), along with the implications of that situation for the United States."

Thai Guerrillas. Included in the published staff report was a section dealing with Thai irregular forces fighting in Laos. "The Central Intelligence Agency supervises and pays for the training of these irregulars in Thailand," the report stated, "and provides their salary, allowances (including death benefits) and operational costs in Laos.... The Thai irregulars are transported from Thailand to Laos by Air America (private airline sponsored by the CIA) and are returned to Thailand when their tours are up again."

Sen. Clifford P. Case (R N.J.), a member of the Foreign Relations Committee, had sent a letter to the State Department April 23 requesting information on any agreements between the United States and Thailand by which Thai troops were being imported into Laos against the provisions of United States law. *(Fiscal 1971 Defense Department appropriations, p. 913, 914)*

Assistant Secretary of State David M. Abshire replied to Case's letter May 19: "We believe that it has been made clear that this is not a question of U.S. support for regular Thai forces in Laos. The irregular forces involved, while raised and trained in Thailand, are all one-year volunteers who go to Laos to serve under the command of the Royal Lao government. These guerrilla forces are therefore considered to be local forces in Laos."

After reading Abshire's letter to the Senate, Symington said: "Common sense forces one to ask, how can these Thai irregulars in Laos be described as local forces? They are Thai not Lao. They are recruited in Thailand, not Laos."

Sen. Robert P. Griffin (R Mich.), assistant minority leader, argued in behalf of the administration: "There is no question, I suppose, under the language here, that if the Thai government sent forces into Laos under a Thai military command and they fought, that there would be a violation (of the law)."

"But are we going to say that the Laos military command cannot recruit volunteers...should limit the recruiting of troops in its own country?" Griffin said.

Safe and Orderly Withdrawal. The justification advanced on the Senate floor for B-52 bombings in northern Laos and along the Ho Chi Minh trial in southern Laos was that it was part of overall U.S. strategy to ensure the safe and orderly withdrawal of U.S. troops from South Vietnam.

By a 24-64 roll-call vote, the Senate rejected an amendment by Sen. J. W. Fulbright (D Ark.) which would have reduced authorizations by $185-million—military grant aid by $50-million, supporting assistance by $85-million and military credit sales by $50-million.

John C. Stennis (D Miss.) said the Fulbright amendment would bring the military aid program to an immediate halt because the United States already had spent nearly as much as the amount the amendment would authorize for all of fiscal 1972.

Stennis offered an amendment, adopted by a 46-42 roll-call vote, increasing authorizations in the bill for military grant assistance to $566-million, from $350-million, and for supporting assistance to $537-million from $435-million.

The Senate, by a 43-46 roll-call vote, rejected an amendment by Gaylord Nelson (D Wis.) reducing the ceiling on all forms of aid to Cambodia to $263,500,000 from $341-million.

On Nov. 1, the Senate passed S 2819 by a 65-24 roll-call vote. The economic aid bill (S 2820) had been passed Nov. 10 by a 61-23 roll-call vote.

HOUSE, CONFERENCE ACTION. The House Nov. 18, in an unusual procedure, adopted by a 269-115 roll-call vote a resolution (H Res 710) which revived the House-passed version of HR 9910, the original bill rejected by the Senate. A conference with the Senate was then requested to iron out differences between HR 9910 and the two Senate-passed bills.

Senate and House conferees filed identical reports on S 2819, in which they had combined authorization for both economic and military assistance funds.

A month-long deadlock over the Senate-approved Mansfield amendment was broken Dec. 16, when the House, in a **key roll call vote of 130-101**, tabled a motion to instruct House conferees on the bill to accept the amendment. Conferees, interpreting this as a vote on the merits of the proposal, dropped the amendment and worked out their remaining differences.

Among the Senate amendments accepted by House conferees, some in modified form, were provisions that:

• Placed a $341-million ceiling on fiscal 1972 aid to Cambodia (accepted with amendments excluding from the ceiling funds for operations in Cambodia by South Vietnamese troops).

• Placed ceilings of 200 on the number of U.S. personnel and 85 on the number of third-country nationals paid by the United States who could be deployed in Cambodia (Senate bill had limited third-country nationals to 50).

• Transferred military assistance authorizations for Thailand from the Defense Department budget to the foreign aid authorization bill effective in fiscal 1973.

• Prohibited the deployment of U.S. advisers to Cambodian military, paramilitary, police or other security or intelligence forces.

In addition to deleting the Mansfield amendment, conferees dropped the Senate amendment requiring specific congressional approval of all U.S. funds used to finance military operations by third-country forces in Laos, North Vietnam or Thailand.

DEFENSE APPROPRIATIONS

Several Indochina-withdrawal amendments were turned back by the House during consideration of the fiscal 1972 defense appropriations bill (HR 11731—PL 92-204).

When the bill was reported by the 55-member House Appropriations Committee Nov. 11, one Republican and 13 Democrats filed an additional statement pledging their support to a so-called end-the-war amendment setting a June 1, 1972, date for cutting off funds for use in U.S. military operations in Indochina. The fund cutoff would apply only to those funds provided in the defense appropriations bill.

The most controversial issue during floor consideration of HR 11731 was an amendment submitted by Edward B. Boland (D Mass.). The Boland amendment called for the withdrawal of all U.S. troops from Indochina subject to the release of all U.S. prisoners of war and an accounting for those missing in action. The amendment urged a withdrawal "at the earliest practicable date" and set a June 1, 1972, deadline for the cutoff of funds provided in HR 11731, which would be spent for military operations in or over South and North Vietnam, Laos, Cambodia. The amendment was rejected by a 163-238 recorded teller vote.

Andrew Jacobs Jr. (D Ind.) offered an amendment which sought to cut off funds effective Nov. 7, 1972, for U.S. military operations in Indochina pending the release of all U.S. prisoners of war. The amendment was rejected Nov. 17 by a 52-161 standing vote.

Vietnam was not a key issue during Senate and conference consideration of HR 11731 which cleared Congress Dec. 15.

OTHER ACTIONS

VIETNAMESE ELECTION. The House Oct. 20 in a separate voice vote tabled (killed) identical resolutions (H Res 632 and 638) directing the secretary of state to provide information on U.S. activities in events prior to the uncontested Oct. 3 presidential election in South Vietnam.

President Nguyen Van Thieu ran unopposed and was re-elected with more than 90 per cent of the vote. Vice President Nguyen Cao Ky and Gen. Duong Van Minh earlier dropped out of the race amid charges that Thieu had rigged the election.

The House Sept. 30 by voice vote tabled a similar resolution (H Res 595) requiring the secretary of state to furnish complete texts of all communications pertaining to the Vietnamese election between the State Department and the U.S. embassy in Saigon and between the embassy and the presidential candidates. *(Other resolutions of inquiry, box this page)*

POW RESOLUTIONS. The House Oct. 4, by a 370-0 roll-call vote, passed under suspension of the rules a concurrent resolution (H Con Res 374) calling for humane treatment of American servicemen held prisoner by North Vietnam and its allies and endorsing efforts to win their release.

At the recommendation of the Foreign Affairs Committee, the House sidestepped the issue of setting a withdrawal date for all U.S. forces in Indochina in exchange for release of the prisoners. The committee deleted a provision added by its Subcommittee on National Security Policy and Scientific Developments urging President Nixon to follow up a July 1 North Vietnamese

---

Resolutions of Inquiry

The House turned back several attempts in 1971 to force the administration to supply Congress with information on U.S. activities in Indochina.

On July 7, the House by a roll-call vote of 261-118, tabled (killed) a resolution directing the secretary of state to give Congress documents on policy governing U.S. military operations in Laos.

The House then tabled by voice votes resolutions instructing the secretary of state to turn over to Congress the secret Pentagon Papers, as well as documents concerning U.S. bombing of northern Laos and the U.S. role in the "Phoenix" program of relocation and rehabilitation in Laos.

---

offer to begin release of American prisoners in return for setting a withdrawal date.

No Senate action was taken on the resolution.

The House March 3 and the Senate March 5 by voice votes approved a bill (H J Res 16) authorizing the President to proclaim the week of March 21-27 as "National Week of Concern for Prisoners of War/Missing in Action."

1972

It was a year of extremes. Promises of peace were on a seesaw with escalating military operations.

Early in the year both the United States and North Vietnam offered new peace plans. Within two months the communists launched their biggest offensive since 1968. The United States responded with the first air raids against Hanoi and Haiphong since that same year.

In late April the Paris peace talks resumed—only to be canceled in early May. The U.S. mining of North Vietnam's harbors and waterways followed.

During the summer and fall, national security adviser Henry A. Kissinger and chief North Vietnamese negotiator Le Duc Tho held bargaining sessions in Paris—meetings which led to Kissinger's ill-fated October statement "peace is at hand." Instead, peace slipped away—temporarily—and as the year neared its end U.S. bombers pounded North Vietnam with its heaviest aerial bombardment of the war.

Military Activity

Despite intense military activity in 1972, President Nixon continued to withdraw U.S. troops from Vietnam. In January he announced the seventh withdrawal: 70,000 servicemen by May 1, reducing the authorized troop level to 69,000.

Several months into 1972 the North Vietnamese launched a major offensive across the demilitarized zone into South Vietnam. The operation—begun March 30—was their biggest military thrust since the Tet offensive in 1968. In retaliation, President Nixon ordered the bombing of the Haiphong-Hanoi area.

In a televised speech April 26, the President said that the bombing would not be stopped until the

---

Supreme Court: Hands Off the War

The Supreme Court steadfastly refused to rule on the question of the constitutionality of American involvement in Vietnam. This refusal stood despite repeated attempts by various individuals and groups, including the state of Massachusetts, to persuade the court to meet the issue head on. As late as October 1972, the court voted, 7-2, to decline to hear a case in which taxpayers challenged the use of foreign aid funds to finance American operations in Vietnam. *(Sarnoff v. Schultz)*

Justices William O. Douglas and William J. Brennan Jr. disagreed with the court's hands-off-attitude, arguing that the case should be heard: the Constitution specifically gives Congress the power to declare war, they said, and thus "impliedly bars its exercise by the executive branch."

Although the court did not deal directly with the issue of war, the ferment created in the United States by protest over the American role in Southeast Asia brought to the court a number of related cases. In these the court did often rule to set standards and limits for the operation of the selective service system; to define more clearly the requirements for certain draft exemptions and conscientious objector status; and to spell out the limits on action which could be taken against those who protested the war, whether that protest was demonstrated by the destruction or turning in of draft cards, by making public classified documents as in the case of the Pentagon Papers, by desecrating the American flag or by wearing a black armband.

---

enemy withdrew its troops from South Vietnam. However, he also announced the withdrawal of 20,000 more troops by July and the Paris peace talks resumed the following day.

But the hopeful signs were shortlived. The peace talks were broken off once again and Nixon took what many critics considered a major step in escalating the Indochina conflict. In a nationally televised address May 8, the President announced his decision to mine North Vietnam's ports and interdict land and sea routes to prevent the delivery of war supplies to North Vietnam.

Two further troop withdrawals were announced during the summer. In June, President Nixon said that 10,000 more servicemen would be withdrawn by September. In late August, the President stated that 12,000 more men would be withdrawn by December. The White House told reporters in November that, with the U.S. force level reduced to 27,000, there would be no further public announcements on troop withdrawals.

In the fall of 1972, peace negotiations picked up momentum. On Oct. 26, when Kissinger met with reporters to discuss what appeared to be an impending peace settlement, he confirmed reports that all bombing north of the 20th parallel in North Vietnam had been halted.

But the peace settlement proved elusive and within two months the United States was engaging in its heaviest bombing of North Vietnam of the war. A White House

statement warned that the bombing "will continue until such a time as a settlement is arrived at." On Dec. 30, the President ordered an indefinite halt to bombing above the 20th parallel.

Peace Negotiations

Very early in the year, both the United States and North Vietnam made public new plans for ending the war. In a Jan. 25 nationwide address, President Nixon revealed that Kissinger had had 12 secret meetings with North Vietnamese representatives during the period from August 1969 to August 1971. Nixon made public an eight-point peace proposal which the United States had offered in secret negotiations in October 1971. Proposals included an internationally supervised cease-fire that would go into effect upon the signing of an agreement. Within six months, all U.S. and allied forces would be withdrawn from South Vietnam, all prisoners of war would be released and there would be a presidential election run by an independent commission representing all political forces in South Vietnam.

A few days later North Vietnam made public the nine-point plan it had offered in the secret negotiations. North Vietnam called for unconditional withdrawal of U.S. allied forces from all Indochinese countries, as well as withdrawal of support for the current Saigon regime. A tripartite coalition government would be established that would set up and run the presidential elections.

Neither plan was acceptable to the other side. The Paris peace talks were suspended indefinitely in March and were not resumed until late April, following the communist offensive and heavy U.S. bombing of the North. They were canceled once again May 4—two days after Kissinger met with Tho in Paris and several days before the President announced his decision to mine North Vietnam's ports. The peace plan which accompanied Nixon's announcement was rejected.

In mid-July, after a 10-week suspension, both the public Paris talks and private meetings between Kissinger and Tho resumed. The negotiations intensified in the fall and, in a Hanoi broadcast Oct. 26, a nine-point peace settlement was revealed. Later that day Kissinger confirmed at a White House press conference that the United States and North Vietnam were in substantial agreement on a peace settlement, which included a cease-fire in place, withdrawal of all U.S. forces and release of all American prisoners within 60 days, and establishment of a three-part commission to supervise elections in South Vietnam.

Kissinger told reporters "we believe peace is at hand" and that unresolved provisions in the agreement were minor details that could be settled at one more negotiating session "lasting no more than three or four days."

The national security adviser confirmed that the breakthrough in the talks had come Oct. 8, when, according to Kissinger, the communist side agreed to the American position on ending the military aspects of the war and establishing general principles within which the South Vietnamese forces could work out a political solution.

Kissinger said there was a "misunderstanding" over a claim by Hanoi that the United States had agreed to sign the accord by Oct. 31. He told reporters that, while the United States had agreed to "make a major effort to end the negotiations by Oct. 31," American negotiators had insisted they could not set a definite date for conclusion of the talks.

North Vietnam kept pressuring for an early signature of the agreement but the United States refused to accept any deadline. The Kissinger-Tho talks were continued in late November and the first part of December, but no final agreement was reached.

Talks were recessed and, on Dec. 16, Kissinger told a White House press conference that the talks in Paris had been suspended because Hanoi had changed its position on several points—a charge the communists also leveled against the United States.

Two days later the heavy bombardment of North Vietnam began. When it was halted Dec. 30, the White House announced that Kissinger and Tho would resume talks in Paris Jan. 8—meetings which proved to be the final stage in negotiations leading to the signing of a Vietnam cease-fire agreement Jan. 27, 1973. *(Details, p. 932)*

Congressional Activity

After President Nixon April 15 ordered U.S. planes to bomb Haiphong and Hanoi, Congress came alive with a new round of heated debates over U.S. participation in the Indochina war—debates that were further fueled by the President's May 8 announcement of the mining of North Vietnam's harbors.

With public opinion against the war and presidential-election year pressures on their side, anti-war members in Congress won several victories in 1972. In the end, however, support for the President's Vietnamization policy—coupled with reluctance to challenge executive conduct of diplomacy—killed all end-the-war legislation during the 92nd Congress.

Legislative Action

In 1972 five major bills were vehicles for efforts to limit U.S. participation in the Indochina war. The five bills and action on key war-related amendments were:

- **State-USIA Authorization** (HR 14734—PL 92-352) —Congress rejected an amendment cutting off funds for the war (Case-Church).

- **Military Aid Authorization** (S 3390)—Before rejecting the entire bill, the Senate—for the first time—approved an amendment cutting off funds for the war.

- **Military Aid Authorization** (HR 16029)—Before the bill died in conference, Congress rejected an amendment setting a troop withdrawal deadline and one cutting off funds for the war.

- **Defense Procurement** (HR 15495—PL 92-436)— Congress approved a ceiling of $375-million on aid to Laos and rejected amendments cutting off funds for the war.

- **Defense Appropriations** (HR 16593—PL 92-570)— Congress rejected an amendment cutting off funds for the war and one urging the President to end U.S. involvement in Indochina.

Bombing Pattern, 1966-1972

Defense Department statistics on U.S. air strikes in Southeast Asia, published by the Senate Armed Services Committee in July 1973 documented the pattern of U.S. bombing during the war. The figures did not include bombing sorties in Cambodia from 1969 up to the April 1970 incursion.

President Lyndon B. Johnson on March 31, 1968, ordered a partial halt to the bombing of North Vietnam. No U.S. planes were to strike targets north of the 20th parallel—61 miles south of Hanoi and 225 miles north of the demilitarized zone (DMZ). Johnson announced on Oct. 31, 1968, that effective Nov. 1 the U.S. would halt all bombing of North Vietnam.

By and large, President Nixon maintained this bombing halt through April 15, 1972. The Defense Department statistics revealed that there was a total suspension of B-52 sorties over North Vietnam from November 1968 through April 1972. U.S. bombs dropped on North Vietnam from January 1966 through October 1968, totaled 602,623 tons.

After October 1968, the United States did occasionally attack surface-to-air missile installations within North Vietnam on the grounds that the attacks were necessary to protect U.S. reconnaissance planes operating over North Vietnam. During the suspension period, U.S. fighter-bomber attack sorties over North Vietnam totaled 3,774 with a total bomb tonnage of 4,580. These attacks were almost exclusively below the 20th parallel.

Laos Bombing. During the 1969 hearings by the Senate Foreign Relations Subcommittee on U.S. Security Agreements and Commitments Abroad, testimony showed that when the United States temporarily stopped bombing North Vietnam from Dec. 24, 1965, through Jan. 31, 1966, U.S. air strikes were redirected over Laos. *(Box, p. 908)*

Testimony also demonstrated that after the Nov. 1, 1968, bombing halt U.S. aircraft were again shifted to targets in Laos. B-52 sorties in Laos rose from 1,718 in 1967 to 3,377 in 1968; 5,567 in 1969; 8,518 in 1970 and 8,876 in 1971. They dropped to 2,644 in 1972, the year the United States resumed intensive bombing of North Vietnam. Fighter-bomber attack sorties followed this same pattern.

Bombing Resumption. On April 15, 1972, the United States resumed the systematic bombing of military targets above the 20th parallel. The administration said the attacks were in response to North Vietnam's violation of a 1968 understanding that they would not move forces across the DMZ.

U.S. air strikes over North Vietnam remained steady through Oct. 23 when, with a cease-fire agreement seemingly imminent, Nixon ordered a temporary cessation of all bombing north of the 20th parallel. But the agreement was not forthcoming and the bombing suspension was broken Dec. 18. The United States resumed strikes above the 20th parallel and conducted the war's heaviest aerial bombardment of North Vietnam. A halt to the bombing above the 20th parallel was announced Dec. 30.

North Vietnamese Ports Mined

President Nixon announced May 8, 1972, his decision to mine North Vietnam's ports and waterways.

In his nationally televised speech, Nixon played down his escalation of the war, the risk of confrontation with the Soviet Union and the threat his action posed to his own global strategy for peace. He outlined a plan of "decisive military action to end the war" and offered a peace plan. The military action was clear-cut:

• Entrances to Haiphong and other harbors were to be mined to stop the flow of Soviet, Chinese and East European supplies and equipment to Hanoi and prevent naval operations from the ports, a step long advocated by Vietnam "hawks" and proposed by Nixon himself as early as 1965.

• U.S. forces were to interdict the delivery of material in the internal and in the claimed territorial waters (12 miles offshore) of the North.

• Rail and all other communications were to be cut off to the greatest extent possible.

• Air and naval strikes were to continue against military targets.

• Ships in the ports had three daylight periods (ending at 7 p.m. May 11 Hanoi time, 6 a.m. May 11 Washington time) to leave safely, after which the mines were set to become active and ships trying to enter or leave the ports did so at their own risk.

Nixon said two conditions had to be met before the military plan would be suspended. Return of all American prisoners of war and an internationally supervised ceasefire throughout Indochina.

When those conditions were met, Nixon said, the United States would stop "all acts of force throughout Indochina" and would withdraw "all American forces from Vietnam within four months." The fixed withdrawal deadline in exchange for return of the prisoners was essentially what war opponents in Congress had been urging Nixon to offer.

Congress Ignored. In contrast to the Cuban missile crisis of 1962, during which congressional leaders were consulted before the major decisions were made, Nixon in reaching his decision ignored Congress.

An hour before his 9 p.m. television speech, Nixon met with the Democratic and Republican leadership of the House and Senate and the chairmen and ranking minority members of four committees of each chamber. "We were told after the fact," Senate Majority Leader Mike Mansfield (D Mont.) said of the President's decision, adding that he did not consider that as consultation with Congress.

1973 Development. The United States and North Vietnam Jan. 27, 1973, signed a separate protocol to the Vietnam cease-fire agreement which dealt with the removal of the mines. On Feb. 6, the Defense Department announced that U.S. Navy minesweepers had been ordered to begin clearing operations on the approaches to Haiphong harbor.

STATE-USIA AUTHORIZATION

For more than a month the fiscal 1973-74 authorization for the State Department, United States Information Agency (USIA), Peace Corps and Arms Control and Disarmament Agency was bogged down in debate over the Vietnam War (HR 14734—PL 92-352). A controversial end-the-war amendment to the measure, added in the Senate Foreign Relations Committee, was modified by its sponsors, amended by its opponents and, finally, deleted May 31 on the Senate floor. HR 14734 cleared Congress June 30.

Committee Action. The Senate Foreign Relations Committee used S 3526, the Senate-version of the State-USIA authorization bill, as a vehicle for an end-the-war amendment, sponsored by Frank Church (D Idaho) and Clifford P. Case (R N.J.). It was adopted in committee by a 9-1 vote, with George D. Aiken (R Vt.) dissenting.

The amendment prohibited the expenditure of funds to maintain or support U.S. forces in or over North or South Vietnam, Cambodia or Laos after Dec. 31, 1972— if an agreement was reached for release of U.S. prisoners of war and an accounting was made for all Americans missing in action who had been held by or known to the North Vietnamese or Vietcong.

The provision did not terminate military assistance to the countries of Indochina or require the withdrawal of regular military assistance advisors.

Floor Action. When the authorization measure reached the Senate floor in late April, opponents of the end-the-war clause were reported to be pushing for an early vote on the amendment in hopes that the deteriorating South Vietnamese military situation, in an enemy offensive launched March 30, would unify the Senate behind the President.

John C. Stennis (D Miss.) offered an amendment to delete the Indochina provision, but it was another month before the Senate finally agreed to the Stennis proposal.

On May 9, Case and Church modified the language to make their proposal partially conform to the peace plan set forth by President Nixon May 8, during his announcement of the U.S. mining of North Vietnam's harbors.

The Case-Church perfecting amendment—approved by the Senate Democratic caucus—would have forbidden the use of funds to maintain, support or engage U.S. forces in Indochina four months after an agreement was reached on the return of all Americans held prisoner by North Vietnam and the Vietcong.

Majority Whip Robert C. Byrd (D W.Va.) subsequently offered an amendment to the Case-Church perfecting amendment to make a U.S. withdrawal contingent also on "an internationally supervised cease-fire"— a condition included by the President but ignored by Church and Case.

Adoption of the Byrd amendment May 16, by a 47-43 roll-call vote, killed the effect of the Case-Church amendment.

The Senate May 31 adopted by voice vote the Case-Church amendment, as modified by the Byrd amendment. It then proceeded to adopt by voice vote the Stennis amendment deleting the entire end-the-war provision.

Passage came after the Senate, under an unanimous consent agreement, discharged the companion House-passed bill from the Foreign Relations Committee and substituted the language of S 3526, the Senate version as amended.

MILITARY AID AUTHORIZATION

In July 1972, the Senate—for the first time—voted to cut off funds for continuing U.S. participation in the Vietnam war. Earlier end-the-war provisions—for example, the 1971 Mansfield amendments—had expressed the judgment of Congress that the war should end but none had had the force of law.

Inclusion of the fund cutoff sealed the fate of S 3390, a fiscal 1973 military aid authorization. The bill was defeated July 24.

In September, the Senate assured passage of a second authorization bill (HR 16029)—the House version—by deleting a committee-added provision cutting off funds for the war. However, the measure died in conference because of a dispute over Senate-added amendments requiring approval of executive agreements.

Action on S 3390

Committee Action. The Senate Foreign Relations Committee reported S 3390 with an amendment, offered by Mansfield, that would have required a two-stage U.S. disengagement from the Indochina war. Specifically, the amendment would have prohibited:

hibited:
- Use of funds to keep U.S. forces in South Vietnam after Aug. 31, 1972.
- Participation by U.S. forces in hostilities in or over Indochina upon completion of a cease-fire agreement between U.S. and communist forces, release of all U.S. prisoners of war and an accounting for all Americans missing in action held or known by North Vietnam and its allies.

Other Indochina-related provisions in the committee bill dealt with reducing the ceiling on aid to Cambodia; curtailing the use of U.S. funds for foreign forces operating in Laos, Thailand or North Vietnam; and transferring committee jurisdiction over military aid to South Vietnam and Laos from the House and Senate Armed Services committees back to the Senate Foreign Relations and House Foreign Affairs committees.

Floor Action. After more than three weeks of debate, the Senate July 24, by a 42-48 roll-call vote, rejected an amended version of S 3390.

The stage for rejection of S 3390 had been set when the Senate, in a series of roll-call votes earlier on July 24, turned back attempts by supporters of President Nixon's Vietnam policy to drop or neutralize the bill's end-the-war provisions.

Their efforts to make the bill acceptable to the President failed when the Senate, by a 46-49 roll call, rejected an amendment by Armed Services Committee Chairman John C. Stennis (D Miss.) that would have deleted the entire end-the-war provision.

Rejection of the Stennis amendment left in the bill a fund cutoff provision approved by the Senate as a substitute for a two-stage withdrawal plan introduced by Mansfield and approved by the Foreign Relations Committee.

Classified Information

Uncertainty over how to handle secret information about the Vietnam war became a major issue before Congress in 1972.

The controversy, raised by attempts by Mike Gravel (D Alaska) to publish a secret 1969 National Security Council memorandum on Indochina in the *Congressional Record*, centered on the right of members of Congress to make public information classified secret by the executive branch. *(Details, p. 418, 419)*

After the Senate in two secret sessions failed to act on Gravel's request to print the memorandum in the *Record*, the Senator proceeded on May 9 to read on the Senate floor portions of the 1969 study that he said cast doubt on the wisdom of the President's decision to mine North Vietnamese ports. Following are excerpts:

Department of State—"On a volume basis, about 85 per cent of communist aid to the DRV (North Vietnam) arrives by sea: rail deliveries from China account for the remaining 15 per cent, including the military equipment provided by the Soviets and Chinese.

"To begin with, it must be noted that in practical terms it would be impossible to deny all imports by sea. Even if the one principal port (Haiphong) and the two secondary ports (Cam Pha and Hon Gai) were closed, there would still be 12 minor ports as well as numerous coastal trans-shipment points suitable for over-the-beach off-loading. Lightering operations (small boats bringing in supplies from ships anchored off-shore) would permit an indeterminate amount of supplies to enter North Vietnam from the sea....

"We therefore believe that interdiction of Haiphong and heavy attacks on the rail lines from China would over time prevent North Vietnam from receiving sufficient economic and military aid to continue the war effort....

"On the other hand, one important point should be kept in mind. The North Vietnamese surprised many observers and confounded many predictions by holding the North together and simultaneously sending ever-increasing amounts of supplies and personnel into the South during 3½ years of bombing....

"With this experience in mind, there is little reason to believe that new bombing will accomplish what previous bombings failed to do unless it is conducted with much greater intensity and readiness to defy criticism and risk of escalation....

"It should be noted, in conclusion, that this paper does not address the advisability of closing Haiphong, nor the question of the Soviet and Chinese responses...."

Central Intelligence Agency. "In addition, the overland capacity (by trucks), an airlift from Chinese airfields could potentially provide a means for importing a large volume of high-priority goods. Moreover, total interdiction of seaborne imports would be difficult because shallow-draft lighters could be used to unload cargo from ocean-going ships anchored in waters outside the mined major harbor areas....

"The multiplicity of modes and transport routes in the North would make it necessary to sustain interdiction (by bombing) at a larger number of points than in the Panhandle....

"All of the war-essential imports could be brought into North Vietnam over rail lines or roads from China in the event that imports by sea were successfully denied."

Vietnam Peace Terms

The House Foreign Affairs Committee June 13, by a 19-18 vote, ordered reported an amended resolution (H J Res 1225) expressing congressional support for President Nixon's latest Vietnam peace terms.

The resolution never was taken up on the House floor. And it never received consideration in the Senate.

H J Res 1225 was the first end-the-war measure reported by the House Foreign Affairs Committee. It fell far short, however, of the independent congressional initiative to end U.S. participation in the Vietnam war that had been sought by House Democrats.

On the contrary, its provision stated the sense of Congress that U.S. troops should be removed from Vietnam not later than four months after an internationally supervised cease-fire, release of American prisoners of war and accounting for Americans missing in action. Similar terms were stated by the President in his May 8 speech announcing the mining of North Vietnamese ports.

Acting under orders from the House Democratic caucus, committee Democrats had drafted a resolution requiring termination of U.S. military involvement in or over Indochina by Oct. 1, contingent only on the release of prisoners and accounting for men missing in action. That resolution was shelved when the committee, by a one-vote margin, approved a substitute offered by John Buchanan (R Ala.).

However, less than two months later, the committee reversed its position and, by a 18-17 vote, attached to the fiscal 1973 military and authorization bill (HR 16029) a provision terminating U.S. involvement in the Vietnam war on Oct. 1, subject to certain conditions.

The floor substitute for the Mansfield amendment—a combination of amendments by John Sherman Cooper (R Ky.) and Edward W. Brooke (R Mass.)—forbid the use of funds for U.S. participation in the Indochina fighting except to protect withdrawal of remaining troops from South Vietnam, Laos and Cambodia within a four-month period from the date of enactment.

The fund cutoff was subject to a single condition: release of American prisoners of war. President Nixon, in his May 8 address announcing the U.S. mining of North Vietnam's ports, had posed a second condition: an internationally supervised cease-fire throughout Indochina.

As proposed by Cooper, the floor substitute would have cut off funds for the U.S. role in the war, except for withdrawal, four months after enactment with no conditions—the strongest end-the-war proposal ever given serious consideration in Congress.

Unwilling to impose an end to the war without provision for release of the prisoners, the Senate by a 63-32 roll call adopted Brooke's amendment to the Cooper substitute requiring their release before the cutoff took effect.

The Senate earlier had rejected amendments by Howard W. Cannon (D Nev.) and James B. Allen (D Ala.) that would have put the bill's peace terms more in line with the President's own proposals.

The revised Cooper amendment was accepted on a 50-45 roll call.

Before defeating the bill, the Senate had also deleted a committee provision transferring U.S. military grant aid to South Vietnam and Laos to the foreign military assistance program from the Defense Department budget.

It exempted foreign mercenary forces operating in Laos and North Vietnam from a provision requiring congressional authorization for use of U.S. funds to support such operations. Amendments dealing with humanitarian assistance to Indochina had been added.

Action on HR 16029

Both the House Foreign Affairs and the Senate Foreign Relations Committees reported HR 16029, a fiscal 1973 military aid and Bangladesh relief authorization, with end-the-war amendments—and both provisions were deleted in floor action.

House Committee. In a departure from its usual practice, the House Foreign Affairs Committee used the foreign aid authorization measure as a vehicle for several policy amendments, including an end-the-war provision. Approval of that provision, in response to a request by the House Democratic Caucus, marked the first time the House committee had taken a stand on the war differing from the President's policy. *(Box, this page)*

The amendment, adopted by an 18-17 vote, called for an end to participation by U.S. forces in hostilities in or over Indochina by Oct. 1, 1972, and required their withdrawal by that date. The provision would be subject to a cease-fire between U.S. and communist forces assuring safe withdrawal of U.S. troops. It also would be subject to release of all U.S. prisoners of war and an accounting for men missing in action (to be verified by the International Red Cross or another international body agreed to by the President and the North Vietnamese government).

The committee also adopted amendments dealing with narcotics traffic in Thailand and a ceiling on aid to Cambodia.

House Floor. Before passing HR 16029, the House, in a **key recorded teller vote of 229-177,** stripped from the bill the committee's end-the-war amendment.

The vote on the provision had promised the clearest House challenge to President Nixon's policy for ending the war. The issue was made less clear-cut, however, by a dispute among anti-war members over the effective date of the withdrawal required by the committee amendment.

An amendment by war critic Charles W. Whalen Jr. (R Ohio) postponing the effective date to Dec. 31 from Oct. 1 was rejected by a 109-304 recorded teller vote. Several leading sponsors of the committee provision supported Whalen's amendment, but other anti-war members joined administration supporters to oppose it.

The President insisted on a cease-fire throughout Indochina as a condition for withdrawing U.S. troops from South Vietnam. The administration also opposed on principle congressional action forcing withdrawal from the war.

The House accepted by voice vote an amendment offered by Louis C. Wyman (R N.H.) to require release of U.S. prisoners before the end-the-war provision would go into effect. But then the House proceeded to approve an amendment by Richard Bolling (D Mo.) deleting the entire provision.

Senate Committee. The major Indochina-related provision in HR 16029, as reported by the Senate Foreign Relations Committee, was an end-the-war amendment.

Like the Brooke amendment to HR 3390, the committee-approved end-the-war provision prohibited use of funds for U.S. forces in Vietnam, Laos and Cambodia for any purpose except withdrawal within four months of enactment. The committee amendment was contingent on release during the four-month period of all American prisoners of war and an accounting for men missing in action. The Brooke amendment to S 3390 required release of the prisoners but made no mention of men missing in action.

Senate Floor. The Senate dropped the end-the-war amendment prior to passing HR 16029 on Sept. 26.

By a 45-42 roll call, the Senate Sept. 26 adopted an amendment by Armed Services Committee Chairman John C. Stennis (D Miss.) deleting from HR 16029 the committee-approved end-the-war amendment.

Removal of the end-the-war provision was assured by the absence of several anti-war senators, including George McGovern (D S.D.), the Democratic presidential candidate.

The Senate accepted policy amendments protesting the narcotics traffic in Southeast Asia and the alleged repressive policies adopted by South Vietnamese President Nguyen Van Thieu.

Senate amendments requiring congressional approval of executive agreements stymied House and Senate conferees who Oct. 11 abandoned efforts to reach a compromise.

DEFENSE PROCUREMENT

The major point of dispute between the Senate and House versions of the fiscal 1973 defense procurement authorization bill (HR 15495—PL 92-436) was a Senate-passed amendment calling for the withdrawal of U.S. troops from Indochina four months after enactment of the bill. House conferees prevailed in conference and the provision was dropped from the final bill.

The legislation, cleared by Congress Sept. 15, established a ceiling of $375-million on U.S. economic and military assistance to Laos. The ceiling did not apply to U.S. or South Vietnamese air combat operations over Laos.

House Action. Several attempts to add Indochina-related amendments were made when the bill was brought to the House floor.

Michael Harrington (D Mass.) offered two amendments dealing with Vietnam. The first sought to delete a provision which if enacted would allow the Pentagon to spend $2.7-billion for support of local forces in Vietnam, Laos, Thailand and Korea during the final quarter of fiscal 1972. The Pentagon told the House

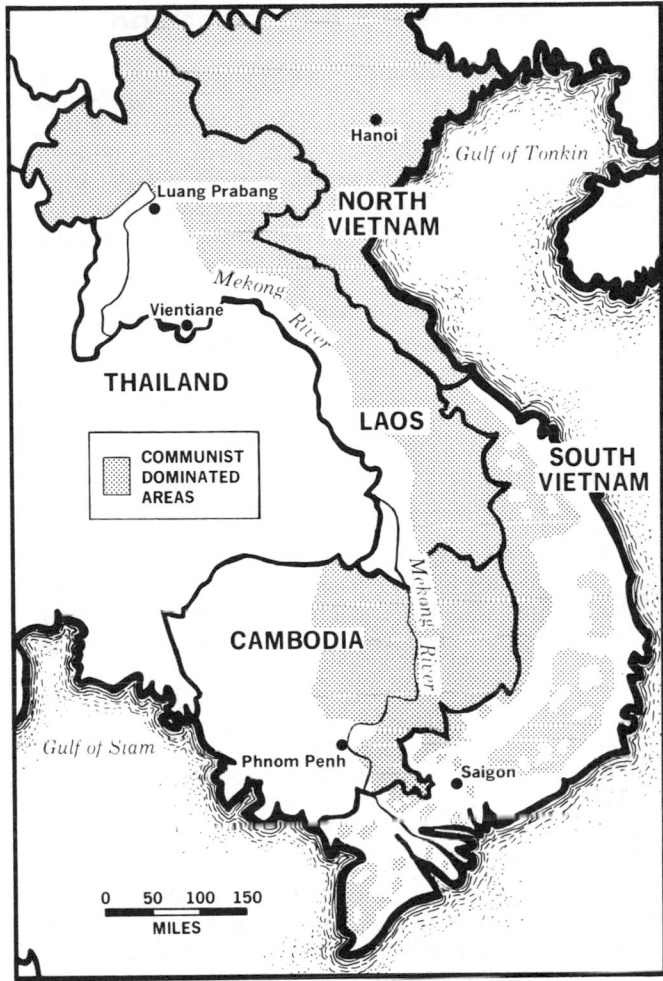

SOUTHEAST ASIA FEBRUARY 1973

COMMUNIST DOMINATED AREAS

0   50   100 150
MILES

Armed Services Committee during hearings in 1972 that it would go over its $2.5-billion ceiling for fiscal 1972 because of increased enemy activities and a corresponding increase in South Vietnamese military activities. The amendment was rejected by voice vote June 27.

Harrington's second Vietnam amendment sought to cut off funds authorized in the bill as of Sept. 1, 1972, for U.S. activities in or over North and South Vietnam, Cambodia, Laos and the territorial waters surrounding those nations, pending the release of U.S. prisoners of war. The amendment was rejected by a 152-244 recorded teller vote.

Senate Action. The Senate Armed Services Committee rejected an administration request for $973.4-million for procurement funds related to increased U.S. activities in Vietnam because the request was received "too late for consideration."

When the bill reached the floor, the Senate Aug. 2 adopted by a **key roll-call vote of 49-47,** a tough Vietnam war fund cut-off amendment, introduced by Brooke, calling for the withdrawal of all U.S. ground, naval and air forces from Laos, Cambodia and Vietnam within four months of enactment of the bill, pending the release of U.S. prisoners of war. A second amendment adopted stipulated that those missing in action must be accounted for by the North Vietnamese.

War Powers and Indochina

Although frustration with the Indochina war was obviously the driving force behind Senate passage of war powers legislation (S 2956) in 1972, amendments making the bill's provisions apply to the Southeast Asian conflict were defeated. Adoption of the amendments would have jeopardized support of the bill among many senators, including John C. Stennis (D Miss.), chairman of the Senate Armed Services Committee.

On April 11, the Senate defeated amendments:

• By Mike Gravel (D Alaska) making the bill's provisions apply to the war unless Congress within 15 days declared war on North Vietnam. *(Roll call: 11-74)*

• By Gravel deleting the provision exempting ongoing fighting and substituting a declaration of war on North Vietnam. *(Motion to table adopted by 78-7 roll call)*

• By J. W. Fulbright (D Ark.) specifying that the bill by exempting the war did not imply any authority to pursue hostilities not otherwise conferred on the President by the Constitution or by law. *(Roll call: 28-56)*

The amendments by Gravel and Fulbright relating the provisions of S 2956 to the Indochina war (expressly excepted by the language of the bill) were debated more on their effect on the bill's chances of passage than on the merits of U.S. policy in Southeast Asia. *(War powers bill, p. 883)*

It was the second time in two weeks that the Senate had voted to cut off funds for U.S. involvement in Indochina. As an amendment to the foreign military aid bill (S 3390), the Senate July 24 voted to set an Oct. 1, 1972, date for the withdrawal of all U.S. troops. But the Senate then rejected the entire foreign military aid authorization because of general resentment toward the foreign aid program and because the bill included the end-the-war mandate.

The two troop withdrawal amendments added to HR 15495 differed in one respect from the proposal added to the foreign aid bill. The Aug. 2 version, due to an amendment sponsored by Jack Miller (R Iowa), required an accounting for those men missing in action as well as the release of U.S. POWs, while the July 24 version stipulated only the release of prisoners.

The Senate took 11 consecutive roll-call votes on troop withdrawal amendments and numerous modifying proposals. Only one major change was made in the Brooke amendment—the requirement for an accounting of those missing in action by the North Vietnamese.

Conference Action. At the insistence of the House conferees, the Senate-approved end-the-war amendment was dropped.

"It is safe to say that the conferees spent more time on this particular subject than any other of the differences in the House and Senate versions of HR 15495," according to the report. House conferees argued that the amendment was not germane to the bill and therefore, under House rules, the conferees could not accept it. (They did accept two other non-germane amendments,

however, dealing with aid to Israel and seamen's hazardous duty pay.) House conferees also pointed out that no anti-war amendment had ever been adopted by the House, which they said clearly indicated a lack of support for the Senate-passed amendment in the House. Congress cleared the measure Sept. 15.

DEFENSE APPROPRIATIONS

The Senate attached a watered-down Indochina-withdrawal amendment to the fiscal 1973 Department of Defense appropriations bill, but the provision was dropped in conference (HR 16593—PL 92-570).

House Action. An attempt to add an end-the-war amendment to the legislation had been turned back in the House Sept. 14 by a 160-208 recorded teller vote. The amendment, sponsored by Joseph P. Addabbo (D N.Y.), would have cut off funds appropriated by the bill for support of U.S. military activities in Vietnam, Laos and Cambodia within four months of the bill's enactment, pending the release of U.S. prisoners of war and an accounting for those missing in action.

Senate, Conference Action. For the first time since Congress began considering proposals to extricate the United States from the Indochina war, the Senate Oct. 2 adopted an end-the-war amendment by voice vote. The amendment, sponsored by Charles McC. Mathias Jr. (R Md.), set no precedents for toughness, but rather reaffirmed the watered-down anti-war amendment passed by Congress in 1971. The amendment declared that U.S. policy was to terminate U.S. involvement in Indochina at the earliest date possible and that the President was supposed to set a date for the total withdrawal of U.S. forces and to seek a multilateral cease-fire. When President Nixon signed into law the bill containing the 1971 anti-war amendment, he said the provision was in no way binding and that he would ignore it.

The Senate rejected by a 26-55 roll-call vote an amendment offered by William Proxmire (D Wis.) which would have cut back the appropriation by $2-billion and barred use of funds in the bill for bombing operations in and over Vietnam, Laos and Cambodia.

House and Senate conferees agreed to drop the Mathias amendment from the final version of the appropriations bill which cleared Congress Oct. 13.

OTHER ACTIONS

VIETNAMESE CIVILIANS. Two Senate committees—Foreign Relations and Judiciary—held hearings in 1972 on effects of the war on the Vietnamese civilian population. The Foreign Relations panel's hearings were limited to the bill (S 2497) creating a temporary U.S. agency to assist Vietnamese orphans, while the Judiciary Committee probed the broader topic of the impact of the war on the civilian population of North Vietnam.

Background. The Vietnam war produced uncounted casualties among the South Vietnamese civilian population, nearly half of whom were 14 years old or younger. Some were maimed, others left homeless. While North Vietnamese and Vietcong attacks inflicted many civilian casualties, part of this toll was exacted by U.S. bombing and shelling.

Harrison A. Williams Jr. (D N.J.), Mark O. Hatfield (R Ore.) and Harold E. Hughes (D Iowa) introduced legislation that would have declared that the United States had a moral responsibility to help South Vietnam care for its children, particularly children fathered by Americans serving in that nation.

The bill would have created a Vietnam Children's Care Agency, a temporary, independent executive branch agency to administer a program assisting Vietnamese children 16 years old or younger.

The Senate Judiciary Subcommittee on Refugees held hearings focusing on the impact of the Indochina war on the civilian population of North Vietnam.

Edward M. Kennedy (D Mass.), chairman of the subcommittee, said that the purpose of the hearings was "to provide accurate information on humanitarian problems that exist among the people of North Vietnam.... There can be little doubt today that we are witnessing a human disaster of historic proportions in Indochina. The plight of civilians is worse today than at any time since the war began—including the Tet experience in 1968."

WEATHER MODIFICATION. The Senate Foreign Relations Subcommittee on Oceans and International Environment held hearings in July on a resolution (S Res 281) proposing an international treaty to ban weather modifications as a weapon of war.

Subcommittee Chairman Claiborne Pell (D R.I.) said he proposed the resolution "because it was becoming increasingly clear that the potential for offensive military uses of environmental and geophysical modifi-cation is very real...(and) that development and use of these modification techniques, without limitation, could have awesome consequences."

Since late 1971, Pell said, he had tried unsuccessfully to acquire information on the weather modification activities of the Defense Department as they might have been used in the Indochina war.

There was a passing reference to the military use of weather modification in the Pentagon Papers—a reference which gave the impression that the United States was already engaged in rainmaking experiments over Indochina during the mid-1960s. A March 1967 rainmaking project, called Operation Pop Eye, was designed to reduce traffic along the Ho Chi Minh trail in Laos. "Authorization (is) required," stated the Pentagon Papers, "to implement operational phase of weather modification process previously tested and evaluated in same area."

Defense Secretary Melvin R. Laird repeatedly denied that the United States was engaged in weather modification over North Vietnam, but refused to make similar categorical statements about South Vietnam, Laos and Cambodia.

INFORMATION ON VIETNAM. The House Aug. 16 by voice votes rejected two House resolutions which sought to force the Defense Department to disclose details of U.S. bombing activities over North Vietnam and information about U.S. prisoners of war.

The two resolutions, sponsored by Paul N. McCloskey Jr. (R Calif.), were adversely reported from the Armed Services Committee Aug. 10 by roll-call votes of 5-27 and 1-31.

Cease-Fire Agreement

VIETNAM WAR OFFICIALLY ENDED JANUARY 27, 1973

Over the years, American officials more than once returned from Vietnam to report that they had spotted the "light at the end of the tunnel." On Jan. 27, 1973, after 11 years of fighting, false hopes and frustrations, the journey out of that seemingly endless tunnel was officially ended.

Representatives of the United States, South Vietnam, North Vietnam and the Vietcong's Provisional Revolutionary Government formally signed a cease-fire agreement in Paris. At 7 p.m. (EST) that day, an internationally supervised cease-fire went into effect.

The truce was made public Jan. 23, when President Nixon announced an agreement "to end the war and bring peace with honor in Vietnam and Southeast Asia."

Within 60 days from the start of the cease-fire, Nixon said in his televised announcement, all American prisoners in Indochina would be returned home. "There will be the fullest possible accounting of those missing in action," he added. *(Prisoner release, p. 934)*

During the same period, said the President, the 25,000 American troops remaining in South Vietnam would be returned. He said the people of South Vietnam "have been guaranteed the right to determine their own future without outside interference."

These features of the agreement were described by Nixon as conditions he had laid down that had been met. The agreement was initialed in Paris on Jan. 23 by Henry Kissinger, the President's national security adviser, and chief negotiator Le Duc Tho of North Vietnam. The initialing, announced simultaneously in the United States and in North and South Vietnam, ended three months of intensive negotiating.

The settlement, Nixon said, "meets the goals and has the full support of President Thieu and the government of the Republic of Vietnam, as well as that of our other allies who are affected." He said the United States would continue to recognize the regime of President Nguyen Van Thieu "as the sole legitimate government of South Vietnam."

Assistance Sought. Nixon indirectly asked other nations—the implication was that he referred to China and Russia in particular—to help make the settlement stick. "All parties must now see to it that this is a peace that lasts, a peace that heals—and a peace that not only ends the war in Southeast Asia but contributes to the prospects of peace in the world," he said.

The agreement, he continued, "must be scrupulously adhered to. We shall do everything the agreement requires of us, and we shall expect the other parties to do everything it requires of them. We shall also expect other interested nations to help ensure that the agreement is carried out and the peace maintained." The agreement included provisions for a four-party international supervisory commission and a 13-party international conference on peace in Indochina.

Details of Agreement

On Jan. 24, the day after Nixon's announcement, the text of the agreement was released. Kissinger, at a lengthy press conference, went into the details of the document, which contained 23 articles, and of the four protocols that went with it. He predicted the settlement of hostilities in Cambodia and Laos soon after the Vietnam agreement had been signed. Following are highlights of the agreement and of Kissinger's comments:

Cessation of Hostilities. At the time of the cease-fire, both sides were to stop all military activities. The United States agreed to remove, deactivate or destroy the mines it had planted in North Vietnamese ports.

Removal of American and other foreign troops and dismantlement of military bases would be completed within 60 days of the signing. North Vietnamese troops already in South Vietnam would be allowed to remain in place but not to be replaced. Replacement of arms, munitions and other war materials—but not men—would be permitted for both sides on a one-for-one basis but would not be allowed to increase.

Kissinger pointed out that U.S. economic advisers and civilian technicians, some attached to military units, would be allowed to stay in Vietnam.

Personnel Return. Captured military personnel and foreign civilians would be returned in 60 days. Lists of these personnel were to be exchanged by the two sides at the time of the signing. The two sides were to cooperate in getting information about persons missing in action. On the basis of an agreement signed in 1954, the North and South Vietnamese would resolve the question of repatriating captured Vietnamese civilians within 90 days.

American prisoners were to be released in equal installments at 15-day intervals, Kissinger said. They would be returned to U.S. medical evacuation teams at Hanoi and flown on American planes "to places of their own choice, probably Vientiane (Laos)," he said.

South Vietnam Self-Determination. One article of the agreement stated that the right of the South Vietnamese to self-determination was "scared, inalienable, and shall be respected by all countries." The people would decide their political future "through genuinely free and democratic general elections under international supervision."

To help the South Vietnamese achieve self-determination, a National Council of National Conciliation and Concord would be established, within 90 days if possible. The council, with members appointed equally by the two sides, would be responsible for setting up the elections.

One significant part of this section of the agreement, said Kissinger, "is that the United States has consistently maintained that we would not impose any political solution on the people of South Vietnam." The Saigon government can remain in office, he said, but the political future

The Basic Elements of the Vietnam Agreement

MILITARY PROVISIONS

Cease-fire

• Internationally-supervised cease-fire throughout South and North Vietnam, effective at 7:00 pm EST, Saturday, Jan. 27, 1973.

American Forces

• Release within 60 days of all American servicemen and civilians captured and held throughout Indochina, and fullest possible accounting for missing in action.

• Return of all United States forces and military personnel from South Vietnam within 60 days.

Security of South Vietnam

• Ban on infiltration of troops and war supplies into South Vietnam.

• The right to unlimited military replacement aid for the Republic of Vietnam.

• Respect for the Demilitarized Zone.

• Reunification only by peaceful means, through negotiation between North and South Vietnam without coercion or annexation.

• Reduction and demobilization of communist and government forces in the South.

• Ban on use of Laotian or Cambodian base areas to encroach on sovereignty and security of South Vietnam.

• Withdrawal of all foreign troops from Laos and Cambodia.

POLITICAL PROVISIONS

• Joint United States—Democratic Republic of Vietnam statement that the South Vietnamese people have the right to self-determination.

• The Government of the Republic of Vietnam continues in existence, recognized by the United States, its constitutional structure and leadership intact and unchanged.

• The right to unlimited economic aid for the Republic of Vietnam.

• Formation of a non-governmental National Council of National Reconciliation and Concord, operating by unanimity, to organize elections as agreed by the parties and to promote conciliation and implementation of the Agreement.

INDOCHINA

• Reaffirmation of the 1954 and 1962 Geneva Agreements on Cambodia and Laos.

• Respect for the independence, sovereignty, unity, territorial integrity and neutrality of Cambodia and Laos.

• Ban on infiltration of troops and war supplies into Cambodia and Laos.

• Ban on use of Laotian and Cambodian base areas to encroach on sovereignty and security of one another and of other countries.

• Withdrawal of all foreign troops from Laos and Cambodia.

• In accordance with traditional United States policy, U.S. participation in postwar reconstruction efforts throughout Indochina.

• With the ending of the war, a new basis for U.S. relations with North Vietnam.

CONTROL AND SUPERVISION

• An International Commission of Control and Supervision, with 1160 international supervisory personnel, to control and supervise the elections and various military provisions of the Agreement.

• An International Conference within 30 days to guarantee the Agreement and the ending of the war.

• Joint Military Commissions of the parties to implement appropriate provisions of the Agreement.

---

remains to be worked out between the two sides in Vietnam.

A second significant provision in the section was the requirement for a reduction and demobilization of Vietnamese armed forces, Kissinger said.

Reunification. South and North would set their own timetable for reunification, "without coercion or annexation by either party, and without foreign interference," the agreement stated. The demilitarized zone at the 17th parallel was, in accordance with the 1954 Geneva agreement, "only provisional and not a political or territorial boundary."

Enforcement Machinery. Two international commissions would oversee the peace agreement. Supervising the cease-fire and withdrawal of troops would be the Four-Party Joint Military Commission. It would have a ceiling of 3,300 members, divided equally among the United States, the South Vietnamese, the North Viet-

namese and the Vietcong. This commission would cease to exist after withdrawals are completed in 60 days. It was to be replaced by a Two-Party Joint Military Commission comprised of South Vietnamese and Vietcong troops.

Assisting in the supervision of the cease-fire would be a 1,160-member International Commission of Control and Supervision. Its members would be from Canada, Poland, Hungary and Indonesia. The commission was to post 12 teams at points along the border and coast of Vietnam, with a double-sized team at the demilitarized zone to watch for infiltrators. Seven other teams were to supervise points of entry for replacement military equipment.

Within 30 days after the signing of the agreement, an international peace conference was to be held to, among other things, "contribute to and guarantee peace in Indochina." Invited to participate, besides the four parties involved in the Paris negotiations, would be China,

France, Russia, Great Britain, the four countries on the international supervisory commission and the secretary general of the United Nations.

Cambodia, Laos. The seventh of the agreement's nine chapters was devoted to Cambodia and Laos—protection of their "fundamental rights," respect for their neutrality. The Paris conference participants pledged not to use the two countries "to encroach on the sovereignty and security of one another and of other countries."

Other parts of the chapter required an end to foreign military activities in Laos and Cambodia and self-determination for their people. "It is our firm expectation that within a short period of time there will be a formal cease-fire in Laos which, in turn, will lead to a withdrawal of all foreign forces from Laos and, of course, to the end of the use of Laos as a corridor of infiltration," said Kissinger. He said the situation in Cambodia was more complex but that "it is our expectation that a de facto cease-fire will come into being over a period of time relevant to the execution of this agreement."

Kissinger's Observations. Kissinger, the United States' chief negotiator in Paris and the man who had to live with his erroneous report of Oct. 26, 1972, that "peace is at hand," said at a Jan. 24 news conference that this country "is seeking a peace that heals. We have had many armistices in Indochina. We want a peace that will last."

He recalled his Dec. 16 report of a stalemate in Paris. The deadlock applied to the protocols, he said. There was disagreement over the demilitarized zone and the role of South Vietnam in the settlement, he added. When the negotiators returned on Jan. 8, the atmosphere was cool, but by the next day it was apparent that both sides wanted to break the deadlock, said Kissinger.

On Oct. 26, according to Kissinger, he did not want to provide a complete check list against which both sides could be measured. The "substantial adaptations" the United States asked for on Oct. 26 have been achieved, he said. "We did not increase our demands after Oct. 26, and we substantially achieved the clarifications which we sought...it is obvious that a war that has lasted for 10 years will have many elements that cannot be completely satisfactory to all the parties concerned."

He was asked if the heavy 12-day bombing of the north in December was the key to achieving the agreement. He replied that he would not speculate on North Vietnamese motives, "but I will say that there was a deadlock which was described in the middle of December, and there was a rapid movement when negotiations resumed.... These facts have to be analyzed by each person for himself."

A reporter asked Kissinger how the agreement differed from one that might have been reached four years earlier. At that time, he answered, the North Vietnamese refused to separate military and political issues and insisted on the dismemberment of the South Vietnamese government as a prelude to negotiation.

Relieved Reaction. Leaders of North and South Vietnam and members of Congress responded to the cease-fire announcement with relief, sometimes tempered by skepticism over the durability of the peace it would bring. Both Le Duc Tho, the chief negotiator for the North Vietnamese, and President Thieu of South Vietnam claimed victory for their side.

POW Release, Second Cease-Fire

If any date could be attached to an end to American military involvement in Vietnam, it would be March 29, 1973. On that day, the remaining 67 U.S. prisoners of war held by North Vietnam were freeded in Hanoi. The same day, the United States withdrew its remaining 2,500 troops from South Vietnam. The troop pull-out and prisoner exchange were completed one day after the 60-day deadline agreed to in the Jan. 27 cease-fire agreement.

Between Jan. 27 and March 29, a total of 587 American military and civilian prisoners had been released and 23,500 U.S. troops withdrawn from South Vietnam. Also completed was a large-scale exchange between Saigon, Hanoi and the Vietcong of more than 30,000 prisoners of war. Morever, as of mid-June, little progress had been made in accounting for more than 1300 Americans missing in action.

The U.S. pull-out left about 210 military personnel attached to the American embassy in Saigon. By mid-June, less than 7,000 Americans—mostly civilian technicians and construction workers—remained in South Vietnam.

With termination of U.S. combat involvement in Vietnam, and a cease-fire in Laos signed Feb. 21, attention shifted in early April to the continuing war in neighboring Cambodia, where central government forces, aided by intensive U.S. bombing raids, battled against Communist-led insurgents. As prospects for a cease-fire in Cambodia remained elusive throughout the spring of 1973, congressional pressures to legislate a prohibition on American bombing operations intensified, spurred by apprehensions that U.S. military activities in Cambodia might lead to re-involvement in Indochina.

Faced with the stalemate in Cambodia and numerous reports of cease-fire violations in South Vietnam, presidential national security adviser Henry A. Kissinger and chief North Vietnamese negotiator Le Duc Tho met in Paris May 17-23 in an attempt to shore up the fragile Jan. 27 accord. At the end of their discussions, Kissinger announced that "significant progress" had been made in ironing out differences.

The two negotiators met June 6 for a second round of discussions which resulted in a June 13 joint communique, signed by the United States, North and South Vietnam and the Vietcong, designed to reinforce the cease-fire accord. The 14-point communique reiterated the basic framework of the Jan. 27 accord; it called for a strictly observed cease-fire to begin at midnight EDT June 14 in South Vietnam but established no new mechanisms for enforcement nor any solution for Cambodia. Although the level of fighting in South Vietnam dropped after the renewed cease-fire went into effect, the South Vietnamese government and Vietcong remained deadlocked over the terms and implementation of a political settlement.

 **Vietnam War Statistics**

WAR COSTS: BUDGET FIGURES EASY, OTHERS IMPOSSIBLE

It is impossible to put a price tag on war. The 11-year Vietnam conflict—the longest in this nation's history—was no exception.

The Defense Department budgeted expenditures are easily identified. Costs from fiscal 1965 through fiscal 1973 were estimated at more than $135-billion and were guaranteed to climb. But these were only a part of the true cost of the war. Economic aid and veterans' benefits had already added sizable sums by 1973 and those also would climb.

After the cease-fire in Southeast Asia, Nixon administration proposals for a massive post-war aid program to both North and South Vietnam were expected although aid to the North faced strong opposition on Capitol Hill in early 1973. On Jan. 27, 1972, a White House official said Henry A. Kissinger in his talks with the North Vietnamese in Paris had mentioned a figure of $7.5-billion in aid, with $2.5-billion earmarked for North Vietnam. These same figures were included in President Nixon's Feb. 9, 1972, foreign policy message. However, after that date U.S. officials backed off from making firm estimates and have indicated that the $7.5-billion figure had been used for illustrative purposes. There was also some question as to whether the administration had been referring to a $7.5-billion multi-nation or to a unilateral effort.

Long-range veterans' payments were difficult to estimate. In 1969, James L. Clayton, a University of Utah professor, told a subcommittee of the Joint Economic Committee that veterans' costs from the Vietnam war could range from a low of $110-billion to as high as $330-billion—and those estimates were made on the assumption that the war would end in fiscal 1970.

In 1972, the Veterans Administration estimated that Vietnam veterans' benefits payments, excluding administrative costs, would cost about $33-billion by 1980. Total costs, including administrative costs, were set at $7.3-billion through fiscal 1972. At that time, World War II veterans' payments had cost $96.5-billion.

Beyond these items are the intangibles which defy cost analysis—lost human lives, disabled bodies, displaced people, devastated countrysides.

Defense Costs. Defense Department budgeted costs for the Vietnam war from fiscal 1965 through fiscal 1973 were officially estimated at $135.5 billion, as of Dec. 31,

---

U.S. Economic and Military Aid to Indochina

(In millions—by fiscal year)

	1953-61	1962-65	1966	1967	1968	1969	1970	1971	1972
South Vietnam									
Military[1]	$ 526.3	$ 957.8	$ 862.0	$1,203.5	$1,054.5	$1,608.2	$1,692.6	$1,882.5	$2,382.6
Economic	1,548.2	851.6	736.5	568.1	536.7	413.5	476.7	575.7	454.6
Cambodia									
Military[2]	67.6	23.8					8.6	188.1	186.9
Economic	219.9	57.5	5	5	5	5	5	76.8	57.6
Laos									
Military[3]	98.4	161.8	54.3	56.0	80.1	77.5	74.2	160.8	219.3
Economic	267.1	142.8	57.6	57.8	64.4	52.2	53.8	49.5	52.2
Thailand									
Military[4]	299.4	244.9	31.4	33.1	56.3	167.1	96.8	72.0	55.0
Economic	272.5	130.8	61.7	59.3	50.3	40.6	32.4	24.8	36.2

1 Since fiscal 1967, military aid to South Vietnam has been included in defense appropriations rather than in the regular foreign aid program. The transition from the regular foreign aid program was begun in fiscal 1963.

2 Military assistance to Cambodia is almost exclusively part of the foreign aid program.

3 Since fiscal 1968, military aid to Laos has been included in defense appropriations rather than in the regular foreign aid program. Before then, almost all military assistance came from the regular foreign aid program.

4 Since fiscal 1968, military aid to Thailand has been included in defense appropriations rather than in the regular foreign aid appropriations program. Before then, almost all military assistance came from the regular foreign aid program. Authorization for Thailand's military assistance program was returned to the foreign aid budget beginning with fiscal 1973.

5 Less than $50,000.

SOURCE: Agency for International Development

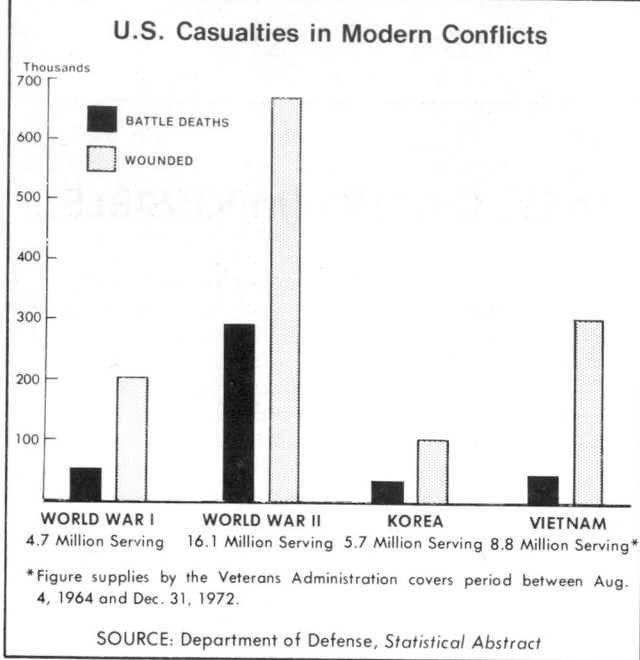

U.S. Casualties in Modern Conflicts

BATTLE DEATHS

WOUNDED

WORLD WAR I — 4.7 Million Serving

WORLD WAR II — 16.1 Million Serving

KOREA — 5.7 Million Serving

VIETNAM — 8.8 Million Serving*

*Figure supplies by the Veterans Administration covers period between Aug. 4, 1964 and Dec. 31, 1972.

SOURCE: Department of Defense, *Statistical Abstract*

1972. However, that figure was expected to go up because the fiscal 1973 estimate did not reflect the costs of U.S. bombing in Cambodia in 1973.

Within the full cost figures, the Defense Department identified what it called the incremental cost of conducting the war and set it at $107.8-billion. The Defense Department set a baseline figure which it regarded as the normal peacetime defense expenditure. Costs above the baseline were incremental costs which came about because of the war. The baseline and incremental costs added up to the full budgeted war costs.

Bomb Tonnage. In Southeast Asia the allied forces dropped more than three times the bomb tonnage dropped in World War II. From 1966 through 1972, it was estimated that the allied forces dropped 7,078,032 tons of bombs over North Vietnam, South Vietnam, Laos and Cambodia. The total tonnage for World War II was 2,057,244. In the Korean conflict, 635,000 tons were dropped. *(Year-by-year breakdown of U.S. bombing in Southeast Asia, chart p. 937)*

Figures Disputed. Vietnam war critics charged that the defense figures did not accurately reflect the cost of the Vietnam war. As part of the Cornell University Program on Peace Studies, a small group of professors and students examined the Indochina air war.

In their report, *The Air War in Indochina,* published in 1972, the group estimated the cost of the Vietnam war from fiscal 1966 to 1971 as about $200-billion—almost double the Defense Department's incremental figures which the group used as its beginning point.

In addition to these incremental costs, the group included what it saw as additional costs due to such things as money deferred from peacetime defense investments (e.g., research and development), the value of potential goods and services lost by drafting men from civilian life at lower pay and the loss in the labor force due to war-related casualties.

U.S. Aid Programs. United States involvement in Indochina through its aid programs dates back to the early 1950s. At that time, France was receiving vast amounts of assistance, much of which was being funneled into that country's effort in Indochina.

In May 1950, Secretary of State Dean Acheson announced in Paris that the United States would give arms aid to the French-sponsored states in Indochina. In March 1954, several months before the French defeat at Dienbienphu, a defense report to the French National Assembly said that the United States was paying 78 per cent of the cost of the fight against the communist Viet Minh.

The United States supplied large sums of economic aid to the war-zone countries. A Library of Congress report on the impact of the Vietnam war prepared for the Senate Foreign Relations Committee in 1971, said that, while it was probable that there would have been some aid program if there had been no war, the economic dislocation caused by the war increased the amount of aid which was necessary for these nations.

After 1966 the military aid program for Vietnam was included in Defense Department appropriations rather than the regular foreign aid budget. After 1967, military aid for Laos and Thailand was also included in defense appropriations. The defense estimates of war costs given above included the Military Assistance Service Funded (MASF) program which provided, from the defense budget, grant assistance to Vietnam and allied forces serving there: South Korea, Laos and Thailand. Fiscal 1972 estimates set MASF for Vietnam at $1.8-billion, Laos, $240.3-million and Thailand, $66.1-million. None of the military aid provided to Cambodia was included in the defense war cost estimates. *(Foreign economic and military aid to Indochina, chart p. 935)*

In addition to official foreign assistance, U.S. volunteer agencies were involved in providing social welfare funds. They contributed an estimated $106.3-million to Vietnam during fiscal years 1968 through 1972.

War Casualties. Estimates of lives lost in the Indochina conflict reached more than one million by the end of 1972. U.S. combat losses were set at 45,929 from

(Continued on p. 938)

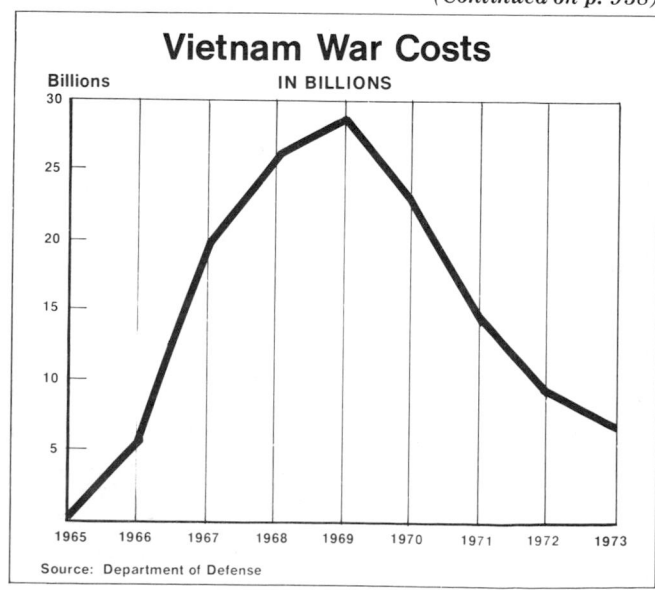

Vietnam War Costs

IN BILLIONS

Billions

Source: Department of Defense

Selected Statistics on the War in Indochina

Combat Casualties in Southeast Asia [1]

YEAR	UNITED STATES			SOUTH VIETNAMESE		ENEMY
	Killed	Wounded		Killed	Wounded	Killed
		H[2]	NH[3]			
1960				2,223	2,788	5,669
1961	11	2	1	4,004	5,449	12,133
1962	31	41	37	4,457	7,195	21,158
1963	78	218	193	5,665	11,488	20,575
1964	147	522	517	7,457	17,017	16,785
1965	1,369	3,308	2,806	11,243	23,118	35,436
1966	5,008	16,526	13,567	11,953	20,975	55,524
1967	9,378	32,370	29,654	12,716	29,448	88,104
1968	14,592	46,799	46,021	27,915	70,696	181,149
1969	9,414	32,940	37,276	21,833	65,276	156,954
1970	4,221	15,211	15,432	23,346	71,582	103,638
1971	1,380	4,767	4,169	22,738	60,939	98,094
1972	300	587	634	39,587	109,960	131,949
TOTALS	**45,929**	**153,291**	**150,307**	**195,137**	**495,931**	**927,168**

1 *S.E. Asia includes South Vietnam, North Vietnam, Laos and Cambodia.*
2 *Required hospital care.*
3 *Did not require hospital care.*

SOURCE: Department of Defense

U.S. Prisoners/Missing

Year	POWs	MIAs
1964	3	4
1965	74	54
1966	97	204
1967	179	226
1968	95	294
1969	13	176
1970	12	86
1971	11	79
1972	103	204
1973*	2	8
TOTALS	**589**	**1,335****

*As of Jan. 13, 1973.
**The Defense Department lists a total of 1,222 MIAs. The difference between the two totals can be attributed to several causes: men missing in action could have been declared dead, found to be prisoners or returned.

SOURCE: Department of Defense

Allied Bomb Tonnage in S.E. Asia [1]

Year	Tonnage
1966	496,319
1967	932,119
1968	1,437,370
1969	1,387,259
1970	977,446
1971	763,160
1972	1,084,359
Total	**7,078,032**

Comparison with Previous Wars

World War II	2,057,244
Korea	635,000
Vietnam	7,078,032 [2]

1 *S.E. Asia includes South Vietnam, North Vietnam, Laos and Cambodia.*
2 *As of the end of 1972.*

SOURCE: Department of Defense

The Longest Talks Finally End the Longest War

Not only was the Vietnam war the longest in America's history, but so were the peace talks leading to its conclusion. The fifth anniversary of the U.S.-North Vietnamese talks would have been marked on May 10, 1973.

By way of comparison, the Korean war truce talks, which seemed interminable, lasted only two years and 17 days.

The 174th plenary session of the Vietnam talks took place Jan. 18. Those sessions involved representatives from the United States, North Vietnam, South Vietnam and the National Liberation Front (NLF).

In addition, numerous secret sessions were held between U.S. and North Vietnamese negotiators. The exact number has not been made public, but President Nixon said on Jan. 25, 1972, that his national security adviser, Henry A. Kissinger, had made 12 trips to Paris for secret talks beginning Aug. 4, 1969. Secret meetings between Kissinger and Le Duc Tho of North Vietnam continued right up to the announcement of the agreement.

Chronology. Following is a chronology of major events surrounding the Paris peace talks:

March 31, 1968—President Johnson announces a partial bombing halt of North Vietnam so that negotiations can begin.

May 10, 1968—U.S. and North Vietnamese negotiators meet for the first time, and the talks immediately bog down over whether South Vietnam and the NLF can participate.

Oct. 31, 1968—President Johnson announces a total halt to the bombing of North Vietnam. He says talks will resume Nov. 6 with participation open to South Vietnam and the NLF. Negotiators fail to agree on technical details, such as the shape of the conference table.

Jan. 25, 1969—First plenary session of four parties is held.

Aug. 4, 1969—First secret meeting between U.S. and North Vietnamese negotiators.

May 14, 1969—President Nixon unveils an eight-point peace plan calling for an internationally supervised election in South Vietnam with a coalition government to follow if the communists win representation.

July 1, 1971—NLF proposes to free all American and allied POWs in North and South Vietnam by the end of the year if all U.S. troops are withdrawn by that date.

Jan. 25, 1972—President Nixon announces he has passed to the communists, through secret channels, an eight-point peace proposal. North Vietnamese and NLF delegates in Paris denounce the plan the next day.

March 24, 1972—President Nixon calls for an indefinite suspension of the Paris talks.

May 8, 1972—President Nixon orders mining of North Vietnamese ports and increased bombing.

July 13, 1972—Peace talks resume.

July 19, 1972—Kissinger holds private meetings with Tho in Paris through Oct. 11.

Oct. 26, 1972—North Vietnamese announce they and United States have reached agreement on a nine-point peace plan, including withdrawal of all U.S. forces from South Vietnam and return of U.S. prisoners. Kissinger confirms North Vietnam's announcement, but says details still need to be worked out in one more session lasting three or four days. "We believe peace is at hand," Kissinger says. Bombing of North Vietnam is suspended.

Nov. 20, 1972—Negotiators meet again secretly in Paris through Dec. 13, but no agreement is reached.

Dec. 18, 1972—U.S. resumes bombing of North Vietnam through Dec. 30, when it is announced that Paris talks will begin anew.

Jan. 8, 1973—Kissinger and Tho begin five days of secret discussions in Paris on cease-fire arrangements.

Jan. 13, 1973—Kissinger returns to Washington to brief Nixon amid speculation that a cease-fire agreement is near.

Jan. 22, 1973—Kissinger flies to Paris for another meeting with Tho.

Jan. 23, 1973—President announces peace accord.

(Continued from p. 936)

1961 through the end of 1972. Total U.S. wounded for that period was 303,601. South Vietnam battle deaths were set at 195,137. Enemy deaths were given as 927,168. *(Year-by-year breakdown, chart p. 937)*

Figures on American casualties are compiled by the Defense Department. The South Vietnamese command provides its own and enemy casualty estimates.

The greatest number of battle deaths in U.S. history was recorded in World War II, when 291,557 were said to have lost their lives. In other modern conflicts the death toll was recorded as 53,402 in World War I and 33,629 in the Korean conflict. *(Chart p. 936)*

The war toll among civilians is much more difficult to estimate. Statistics are sparse. According to the State Department, terror killings or assassinations of South Vietnamese civilians in 1971 and 1972 were estimated at 8,271. The number of civilians wounded as a result of terrorism rather than accidentally was set at 17,104 and abductions at 18,746.

The following chart, a composite of estimates made by the Agency for International Development and the Senate Judiciary Subcommittee on Refugees and Escapees, indicates some of the war's effects on the civilian population in South Vietnam.

Year	AID Est. War Casualty Hospital Admissions	Subcommittee Casualty Est. Including Deaths	Subcommittee Death Estimates
1965	—	100,000	25,000
1966	—	150,000	50,000
1967	48,734	175,000	60,000
1968	84,492	300,000	100,000
1969	67,767	200,000	60,000
1970	50,882	125,000	30,000
1971	39,395	100,000	25,000
1972	53,781	200,000*	65,000*

* *Through October, 1972.*

CQ **Indochina Chronology 1950-1973**

TWO DECADES OF U.S. INVOLVEMENT IN SOUTHEAST ASIA

United States involvement in Indochina dated back to 1950 when Washington initiated a program of military assistance to French Indochina. Following is a chronology of major developments through the signing of the Vietnam peace agreement in January 1973:

1950

May 8—Secretary of State Dean Acheson announces in Paris that the United States will give arms aid to the French-sponsored states in Indochina.

Aug. 10—The first shipload of U.S. arms aid to pro-French Vietnam arrives.

Oct. 17—The United States and Thailand sign an agreement on U.S. arms assistance and technical military advice.

1951

Sept. 7-9—Vietnam, Laos and Cambodia sign pacts to receive U.S. economic aid.

1953

Feb. 18—At his first news conference, Secretary of State John Foster Dulles says that U.S. aid to Korea and Indochina will build up native forces so that they will be able to take over the fighting and release U.S. and French forces.

Dec. 23—In a report on his world tour, Vice President Richard M. Nixon supports U.S. aid to Indochina and predicts that the communists will take over if the French withdraw. He says: "If Indochina goes under communist domination, the whole of Southeast Asia will be threatened."

1954

April 16—In remarks to the American Society of Newspaper Editors in Washington, Nixon says that U.S. troops may have to be sent to Indochina if there is no other way to prevent its fall to the communists.

May 7—Viet Minh overrun French fortress at Dienbienphu. First time in war that the French stronghold is taken by direct assault.

Sept. 8—Eight nations sign the U.S.-sponsored Southeast Asia Collective Defense Treaty (SEATO) which pledges joint action against "armed attack" on any state or territory in the area. (South Vietnam was included in a protocol to the treaty).

Oct. 23—President Eisenhower, in a letter to South Vietnamese Premier Ngo Dinh Diem, promises U.S. aid "in developing and maintaining a strong, viable state capable of resisting attempted subversion or aggression through military means," in return for the effecting of "needed reforms" by Diem.

1955

Feb. 12—First American military advisers are dispatched by the Eisenhower administration for the purpose of training the South Vietnamese army.

Oct. 23—National referendum in South Vietnam deposes Emperor Bao Dai and elevates Premier Ngo Dinh Diem to chief of state.

Oct. 26—Diem declares South Vietnam a republic and proclaims himself president.

1956

July 6—Nixon flies to Saigon and praises the administration of Diem in a speech before the Constituent Assembly.

Sept. 5—Eisenhower tells a news conference that the French are "involved in hopelessly losing war in Indochina."

1957

May 10—Eisenhower pledges additional aid to South Vietnam within U.S. "constitutional processes."

1959

July 8—Two Americans are killed and one wounded during a Viet Minh attack 20 miles north of Saigon. The Americans were members of the U.S. Military Assistance Advisory Group in South Vietnam.

July 30—A subcommittee of the Senate Foreign Relations Committee holds hearings on allegations of "serious waste" and "outrageous scandal" in the Vietnam aid program.

1960

Dec.—North Vietnam announces the formation of the National Liberation Front (NLF) of South Vietnam.

1961

May 5—President Kennedy tells reporters the dispatch of troops to Vietnam is "one of the matters Vice President Johnson will deal with" on his May 9-24 fact-finding mission to Asia.

May 12—At a reception in Saigon, Johnson says the United States is ready to stand "shoulder to shoulder" with South Vietnam in its fight against communism.

May 13—Kennedy orders 100 specially trained jungle fighters (Special Forces) to South Vietnam. An agreement for increased military and economic aid to South Vietnam is made public.

June 16—The United States and South Vietnam agree on a program for direct training and combat supervision by U.S. instructors.

Oct. 15—Gen. Maxwell D. Taylor leaves Washington for South Vietnam, Thailand and Laos. Before departing he says: "Any American would be reluctant to use troops (in Vietnam) unless absolutely necessary."

Oct. 26—Kennedy in a message to Diem says the United States is "determined to help Vietnam preserve its independence, protect its people against communist assassins and build a better life."

Dec. 8—Secretary of State Dean Rusk announces that the United States is consulting with its allies on the provision of joint economic and technical defense support for Vietnam. Rusk says that South Vietnam is in "clear and present danger" of communist conquest.

Dec. 11—U.S. aircraft carrier *Core* arrives in Saigon with 33 U.S. Army helicopters and 400 air and ground crewmen assigned to operate them for South Vietnam.

Dec. 22—Specialist 4 James Davis of Livingston, Tenn., killed by Viet Cong; later called by Johnson "the first American to fall in defense of our freedom in Vietnam."

1962

Jan. 4—The U.S. and South Vietnamese governments announce that the two countries have agreed to launch "a broad economic and social program aimed at providing every Vietnamese with the means of improving his standard of living."

Feb. 14—Kennedy tells a news conference that the United States has enlarged its training mission and its logistics support and is attempting to prevent a communist take-over in Vietnam.

Feb. 15—In commenting on charges that Kennedy concealed the extent of U.S. involvement, former Vice President Nixon states: "I don't agree at all with any partisan or other criticism of the U.S. build-up in Vietnam. My only question is whether it may be too little and too late.... I support President Kennedy to the hilt, and I only hope he will step up the build-up and under no circumstances curtail it because of possible criticism."

March 9—The State Department confirms that U.S. pilots are flying combat-training missions with South Vietnamese airmen over Viet Cong areas, but refuses to confirm or deny news reports that these missions involve bombing and strafing attacks.

March 14—Kennedy tells a news conference that Americans serving in Vietnam cannot be called combat troops. He adds that "if there were a basic change in that situation in Vietnam which calls for a constitutional decision (on sending troops), I...would go to the Congress."

May 15—Kennedy orders an immediate buildup of U.S. troops in Thailand to a total of 5,000 and says the move is "considered desirable because of recent attacks in Laos by communist forces and the subsequent movement of communist military units toward the border of Thailand."

July 23—Defense Secretary Robert S. McNamara says the war will be long and costly. "It will take years rather than months, but the communists eventually will be defeated."

Dec. 2—Sen. Mike Mansfield (D Mont.), concluding a visit to South Vietnam as Kennedy's personal representative, rejects using a departure statement prepared for him by the U.S. embassy. The statement contained an optimistic assessment of the fight against the communists.

1963

Feb. 24—A report on U.S. aid to Southeast Asia, prepared under Mansfield's direction, requested by Kennedy in 1962, is submitted to the Senate Foreign Relations Committee. The report concludes "there is no interest of the United States in Vietnam which would justify, in present circumstances, the conversion of the war...primarily into an American war to be fought primarily with American lives."

Sept. 2—Kennedy discusses the Vietnam war and says: "In the final analysis it's their war. They are the ones who have to win or lose it. We can help them, give them equipment, send our men out there as advisers, but they have to win it, the people of Vietnam against the communists."

Oct. 2—McNamara and Chairman of the Joint Chiefs of Staff Taylor report to the President after their Sept. 24 trip. The White House announces that in their judgment the major part of the U.S. military task (in Vietnam) can be completed by the end of 1965, although there may be a continuing requirement for a limited number of training personnel.

Nov. 1—Diem and his brother are assassinated outside of Saigon. One coup d'etat follows another and weakens the nation's ability to maintain its war effort.

1964

April 15—Arriving home from a 24-day Asian trip, Nixon says: "We should strengthen our policy toward communist activities in Asia rather than move along the lines suggested by Sen. Fulbright." In a speech the following day, Nixon calls for military action against communist bases in Laos and North Vietnam.

May—Secret American bombing begins in Laos.

Aug. 2—U.S. destroyers Maddox and C. Turner Joy are reported attacked by North Vietnamese torpedo boats in the Gulf of Tonkin.

Aug. 4—U.S. destroyers are again reported attacked in the Gulf of Tonkin. Johnson announces retaliatory air action was being taken against military facilities in the North.

Aug. 7—Congress approves Gulf of Tonkin resolution affirming support of "all necessary measures to repel any armed attack against the forces of the United States...to prevent further aggression...(and) to assist any member or protocol state of the Southeast Asia Collective Defense Treaty requesting assistance...." The Senate vote was 88-2; the House vote was 414-0.

Fall—United States turns down secret peace talks with North Vietnam. The administration disclosed this offer in November 1965, explaining that Hanoi was not prepared for serious talks in 1964.

1965

Jan. 26—In a speech in New York City, Nixon proposes using the navy and air force to interdict communist supply lines and to destroy staging areas in North Vietnam and Laos.

Feb. 7—President Johnson announces joint U.S. and South Vietnamese air attacks against the North Vietnamese staging areas "in response to provocation ordered and directed by the Hanoi regime."

May 12-18—United States calls for a moratorium on bombing of the north in order to elicit peace feelers from Hanoi.

May 20—Hanoi restates its peace proposal which Washington has already rejected. (Revealed by State Department Nov. 17, 1965.)

June 8—The State Department announces that U.S. military commanders in Vietnam have been given authority to commit U.S. ground troops to combat if their assistance is requested by the South Vietnamese Army.

Sept. 5—On visit to Saigon Nixon states: "There is only one basis for negotiations on South Vietnam, and that is for a communist withdrawal of their forces and for the communists to agree to quit infringing on the independence and territorial integrity of South Vietnam."

Dec. 24—United States begins bombing moratorium over North Vietnam.

1966

Jan. 31—Johnson announces that U.S. aircraft have resumed bombing targets in the North after a 37-day pause.

Feb. 4—Johnson meets with leaders of the South Vietnamese government in Hawaii.

Feb. 8—Johnson issues a communique, after Hawaii meeting, stressing a new plan combining civil reform and military progress.

March 1—Attempt to repeal the Gulf of Tonkin Resolution defeated in the Senate.

June 29—United States begins bombing in the immediate vicinity of Hanoi and Haiphong—considered to be a major escalation of air war.

Oct. 17-Nov. 2—Johnson visits seven Pacific and Asian nations and participates in a conference in Manila to discuss the conflict in South Vietnam.

1967

Jan. 10—Johnson's state of the union message warns that the United States faces a long, costly war.

Feb. 2—Johnson, in a letter to North Vietnamese President Ho Chi Minh, proposes "direct talks" to end the war.

Feb. 15—Ho rejects direct talks.

Sept. 3—Chief of State Nguyen Van Thieu elected president of South Vietnam.

Sept. 29—Johnson, in a speech in San Antonio, says the U.S. bombing of North Vietnam would be stopped "when this will lead promptly to productive discussions."

Nov. 16—In testimony before the Senate Armed Services Committee, Gen. William C. Westmoreland, U.S. commander in Vietnam, expresses "cautious optimism" but does not see an early termination of the war.

1968

Jan. 30—Communist troops start Tet offensive which escalates into one of the major battles of the war, including attacks on almost all the capitals of South Vietnam's 44 provinces.

March 31—Johnson announces he will not seek reelection and orders a halt in the bombing over about three-quarters of North Vietnam in which about 90 percent of the population lives.

May 13—First substantive meeting between the United States and North Vietnam in Paris.

Oct. 31—Johnson announces a complete halt of the bombing of the North effective Nov. 1.

1969

Jan. 18—Expanded peace talks open in Paris with representation by the United States, South Vietnam, North Vietnam and the National Liberation Front (Viet Cong).

Jan. 27—At his first news conference, Nixon said that "it is not helpful in discussing Vietnam to use such terms as 'cease-fire' because cease-fire is a term...that really has no relevance...to a guerrilla war.... When you have a guerrilla war, in which one side may not even be able to control many of those who are responsible for the violence in the area, the cease-fire may be meaningless. I think at this point this administration believes that the better approach is...mutual withdrawal of forces on a guaranteed basis by both sides from South Vietnam."

May 8—NLF offers 10-point peace proposal in Paris, calling for unilateral U.S. withdrawal and demanding political participation in the south before elections.

May 14—Nixon announces eight-point program to end the war, including phased mutual troop withdrawal over a 12-month period, free elections as soon as possible and an internationally supervised cease-fire.

June 8—At a conference with Thieu on Midway Island, Nixon announces the first planned troop withdrawal.

July 25—In a news conference on Guam, Nixon enunciates his Asian Doctrine which maintains that the United States should continue its alliances in the Pacific, but should not become involved in future wars on the mainland.

Sept. 3—Ho Chi Minh dies. A group of communist party leaders assumes control.

Nov. 3—Nixon says he plans withdrawal of all U.S. ground combat forces on a secret timetable. He discloses that secret peace initiatives to Ho Chi Minh had been "flatly rejected."

1970

April 30—President Nixon announces incursion by U.S. and South Vietnamese forces into Cambodia to destroy border area sanctuaries.

June 30—U.S. forces withdraw from Cambodia.

Sept. 17—Viet Cong delegates at Paris talks call for withdrawal of all U.S. forces by June 30, 1971, and the ouster of top South Vietnamese leaders.

Oct. 7—Nixon proposes a standstill cease-fire throughout Indochina and general Indochina peace negotiations.

1971

Jan. 13—President signs bill repealing Gulf of Tonkin Resolution.

Feb. 8—South Vietnamese troops, with U.S. air and artillery support, launch 44-day attack on the Ho Chi Minh trail in Laos.

July 1—Viet Cong advances a new peace plan.

Oct. 3—Thieu re-elected president of South Vietnam.

Dec. 26-30—United States carries out the heaviest air raids on North Vietnam since 1968 in retaliation for communist buildup and offensive.

1972

Jan. 25—Nixon, in a nationwide television address, announces that he has submitted to the communists through secret channels an eight-point program to end the war in Vietnam.

Jan. 26—North Vietnamese and Viet Cong delegations at the Paris talks denounce the President's plan.

March 23—U.S. delegation announces an indefinite suspension of the Paris peace talks.

March 30—North Vietnamese troops launch a major offensive across the DMZ.

April 15—Nixon orders bombing of Hanoi and Haiphong in retaliation for North Vietnamese offensive.

April 27—Peace talks resume.

May 4—United States suspends peace talks.

May 8—Nixon announces the mining of North Vietnamese ports and interdiction of land and sea routes to North Vietnam in a move to prevent delivery of war supplies to that country. He also announces that air strikes against the north will continue.

July 19—Presidential adviser Henry A. Kissinger holds private meeting with Le Duc Tho, North Vietnamese politburo member and chief adviser to the North Vietnamese delegation to the Paris peace talks.

Aug. 12—The last units of U.S. combat troops leave South Vietnam.

Oct. 12—Kissinger returns to Washington after his latest meeting with Le Duc Tho in Paris. Speculation increases that both sides are near an agreement.

Oct. 23—The White House orders a temporary cessation of all bombing north of the 20th parallel in North Vietnam.

Oct. 24—Kissinger returns to Washington after five days of talks with North Vietnamese Foreign Minister Tran Van Lam and Thieu.

Oct. 26—Kissinger announces at a White House press conference that the United States and North Vietnam are in substantial agreement on a nine-point peace settlement, disclosed earlier the same day in a Hanoi broadcast. The settlement includes a cease-fire "in place," withdrawal of all U.S. forces and release of American prisoners of war within 60 days, and a three-part commission to supervise elections in South Vietnam. Kissinger says "we believe peace is at hand," and that unresolved details will be worked out at a final negotiating session. But he denies Hanoi's contention that the United States had agreed to sign the accord by Oct. 31.

Nixon expresses optimism about an early settlement of the war in campaign speeches at Huntington, W.Va., and Ashland, Ky.

Oct. 27—Soviet Premier Alexei N. Kosygin tells envoys of North Vietnam and the Viet Cong in Moscow he hopes the negotiations will "lead soon to the signature of an agreement ending the war."

South Vietnamese Foreign Ministry announces its willingness "to accept a cease-fire" but expresses reservations about a political settlement.

Oct. 29—North Vietnamese Foreign Minister Nguyen Duy Trinh charges that since the conclusion of the talks between Kissinger and North Vietnamese negotiator Le Duc Tho Oct. 8-11 in Paris, the United States had "repeatedly insisted on altering provisions of the draft agreement."

Oct. 30—The United States is reported to have halted all naval bombardment north of the 20th Parallel in North Vietnam.

Oct. 31—A White House statement reaffirms Nixon's "firm intention" to eschew all deadlines for signing the peace agreement, although North Vietnam insisted on an Oct. 31 deadline.

Nov. 1—In a broadcast marking South Vietnam's National Day, President Thieu denounces the draft peace agreement as "a surrender of the South Vietnamese people to the Communists."

Nov. 2—In his first paid political broadcast of the presidential campaign, Nixon asserts that he will not sign a peace accord until all remaining differences with the North Vietnamese are resolved. He says he will not "allow an election deadline or any other kind of deadline to force us into an agreement, which would be only a temporary peace and not a lasting peace."

Nov. 20—Kissinger and North Vietnamese negotiator Le Duc Tho resume private discussions in Paris aimed at working out a final Indochina peace agreement.

The Defense Department announces it has completed a buildup of emergency arms shipments to South Vietnam's armed forces.

The South Vietnamese Senate approves a resolution supporting President Thieu's opposition to the U.S.-North Vietnamese draft peace accord unless it contains the following three conditions: withdrawal of all North Vietnamese troops from South Vietnam, re-establishment of the demilitarized zone and Saigon government approval.

Nov. 25—Private Kissinger-Tho talks recess.

Nov. 30—White House announces that, with the U.S. force-level reduced to 27,000, there will be no further public announcements on American troop withdrawals from South Vietnam.

Dec. 4—Kissinger and Tho resume private peace talks in Paris.

Dec. 13—Kissinger-Tho talks recess with no agreement.

Dec. 16—Kissinger tells White House press conference that the secret talks in Paris were suspended because Hanoi changed its position on several points in the agreement negotiated by the two sides.

Dec. 18—U.S. begins heaviest bombing of North Vietnam, resuming strikes above the 20th Parallel in North Vietnam and mining of North Vietnamese harbors. A White House statement warns that the bombings "will continue until such a time as a settlement is arrived at." White House Press Secretary Ronald Ziegler defends the action as necessary to prevent a North Vietnamese offensive in the South.

The official Soviet news agency Tass calls for "immediate stoppage of the actions (bombing) and speedy signing of an agreement on ending the war."

Dec. 20—A statement by the Chinese Foreign Ministry calls the bombing "a new barbarous crime," which "has threatened to wreck a peace agreement which is close at hand."

Dec. 28—Chinese Premier Chou En-lai tells a *Washington Post* reporter in Peking that the U.S. bombing of North Vietnam will adversely affect U.S.-Chinese relations.

Dec. 30—The White House announces that President Nixon has ordered an indefinite halt to the bombing above the 20th Parallel in North Vietnam, and that Kissinger and Tho will resume negotiations in Paris Jan. 8. Bombing continues in the southern "panhandle" section of North Vietnam. (From Dec. 18 to Dec. 30, twenty-six planes, including 15 B-52's, were destroyed as a result of the bombing.)

1973

Jan. 8—Kissinger and Tho resume private talks.

Jan. 11—At a news conference near Minsk, Soviet Communist Party Chief Leonid I. Brezhnev expresses confidence that a settlement will be reached soon. "From the moment that talks begin it means the two sides are determined to settle the affair peacefully," he says.

Jan. 13—Kissinger returns to Key Biscayne to brief President Nixon on progress of the talks.

Jan. 14—Gen. Alexander M. Haig Jr., Army Vice-Chief of Staff, travels to Saigon to consult with President Thieu on the progress of the cease-fire negotiations.

Jan. 16—The White House announces the suspension of bombing, mining, shelling and all other offensive action throughout North Vietnam, citing "progress" in the Paris negotiations.

Jan. 27—Formal signing of peace agreement in Paris by U.S., South Vietnam, North Vietnam and Viet Cong's provisional revolutionary government.

Congressional Roll-Call Votes

CONGRESS TOOK 94 ROLL-CALL VOTES ON WAR 1966-72

The chronology below sets forth the major congressional votes on the question of limiting or halting American involvement in the Indochina war.

From 1966 through 1972, Congress took 94 roll-call or recorded teller votes on Indochina war-related measures. At least 45 other non-record (voice or standing) votes were taken during this period on similar proposals. The tally of recorded votes included votes on all amendments to curtail U.S. military activity as well as efforts to weaken these amendments. *Excluded* from the tally were votes on sense-of-Congress (House or Senate) resolutions and votes on *final passage* of legislation covering substantially more than Vietnam-related provisions—for example, the annual defense appropriations bill and the 1971 draft bill.

Only nine of the recorded votes took place during the years 1966, 1967 and 1968. The remaining 85 were cast from 1969 to 1972. Seventy-nine of the recorded votes were cast by the Senate; 15 by the House.

In 1969 Congress for the first time voted to restrict U.S. military activities in Laos and Thailand to support of only local forces; in 1970 Congress imposed similar limits on U.S. activities in Cambodia.

In 1971 Congress twice approved measures urging the President to set a date for withdrawal of American troops from the conflict; in both instances President Nixon stated that he was not bound by such congressional action. In 1972—although Congress cast a record number of 32 recorded votes on war-related measures—it failed to complete action on any one which restricted U.S. military action in Southeast Asia.

Peak Anti-War Sentiment. At the peak of anti-war strength in the Congress, almost three out of five senators and one of every three representatives voted to back end-the-war proposals. In the House, the largest number of representatives ever to vote against the war was the total of 177 mustered on August 10, 1972, to oppose a move to kill a provision terminating American involvement in the war by Oct. 1, 1972. Despite this show of strength, the opponents of the war were defeated, 229-177, and the anti-war language was killed. The second largest show of strength in the House came a year earlier on June 28, 1971, when 175 members backed a motion telling House conferees to agree to a Senate amendment calling for a withdrawal of all American troops from Indochina within nine months.

Anti-war sentiment reflecting disagreement with administration policy in the Senate hit its peak of voting strength on June 30, 1970, when 58 senators approved an amendment barring funds for U.S. military operations in Cambodia after July 1. A year later on June 22, 1971, 57 senators backed an amendment declaring it U.S. policy that American troops be completely withdrawn from Indochina within nine months. The same amendment—but with a six-month deadline—was again approved by 57

...But They Still Approved the Funds

The many congressional votes on measures to curtail the war did demonstrate growing disillusionment with America's role in Indochina. But despite that fact, Congress continued to give both President Johnson and President Nixon full support in funding military operations in Southeast Asia. The various defense appropriations bills and Vietnam supplemental appropriations bills were approved each year by overwhelming majorities and no limit was set on the amount of money which the Defense Department could funnel into the Indochina war effort. From 1965, when the first Vietnam supplemental was enacted, through the end of 1972, between 95 and 96 per cent of the members of Congress present and voting approved the war-related appropriations bills on final passage, providing an estimated $135.5-billion for the war during that time.

senators on Sept. 30, 1971. But by Aug. 2, 1972, the anti-war strength had dropped to a bare majority, and the Senate voted 49-47 to adopt an amendment cutting off funds for the war within four months.

Votes appearing in bold face type below refer to key vote charts appearing in the appendix. *(p. 5a)* Other references below are to vote charts appearing in 1969-1972 Congressional Quarterly *Almanacs.*

1969

SENATE. Major votes during the session were directed toward defining the U.S. military role in Laos and Thailand. In riders attached to two defense spending bills, the Senate stipulated that the United States would not introduce combat troops into the two countries and would support only local forces.

Aug. 12—Fulbright (D Ark.) amendment to defense procurement authorization bill—adopted by voice vote—stipulated that the United States would support only local forces in Laos and Thailand.

Dec. 15—Church (D Idaho) amendment to defense appropriations bill—barred the introduction of U.S. ground combat troops into Laos or Thailand. Adopted, **on a key vote, 73-17.**

HOUSE. The House acquiesced to most of the amendments passed by the Senate concerning Laos and Thailand.

1970

SENATE. On the 22 record votes taken during the session on matters relating to the Indochina war, 14 dealt with Cambodia. The Senate adopted strict limits on U.S. military involvement in Cambodia (later weakened by the House) and the Senate repealed the Gulf of Tonkin Resolution.

June 30—Cooper (R Ky.)—Church (D Idaho) amendment to the military credit sales bill—sought to bar use of funds for U.S. military operations in Cambodia after July 1, 1970, unless authorized by Congress. Adopted on a **key vote 58-37.**

July 10—Repeal of Gulf of Tonkin Resolution by 57-5 roll-call vote. *(1970 Almanac p. 39-S)*

Sept. 1—McGovern (D S.D.)—Hatfield (R Ore.) amendment to defense procurement authorization bill—sought to limit U.S. troops in Vietnam to 280,000 men by April 30, 1971, and to provide for the complete withdrawal of troops by Dec. 31, 1971. Rejected on a **key vote, 39-55.**

HOUSE. After refusing to accept even a modified version of the Senate-passed Cooper-Church amendment, the House finally relented after a six-month delay of several foreign assistance bills in conference.

Dec. 22—The House by voice vote passed the foreign aid bill with provisions prohibiting the use of funds to finance U.S. ground combat troops or military advisers to Cambodia. The House refused to accept a Senate provision barring U.S. airpower over Cambodia.

1971

SENATE. During the session the Senate took 20 record votes on proposals which sought to halt or restrict U.S. involvement in Indochina. Although the Senate did not adopt any measures which sought to cut off funds for U.S. involvement, two amendments adopted on the floor set a specific deadline for the withdrawal of troops pending the return of POWs. In each case the Senate removed the deadlines and otherwise weakened the language.

June 16—McGovern (D S.D.)—Hatfield (R Ore.) amendment to draft extension bill—sought to cut off funds for U.S. military activities in Indochina effective June 1, 1972, pending the release of U.S. POWs. Rejected, 44-52. *(1971 Almanac p. 15-S)*

June 22—Mansfield (D Mont.) amendment to draft extension bill—sought the withdrawal of U.S. troops from Indochina nine months after enactment pending the release of POWs. Adopted on a **key vote, 57-42.**

Sept. 30—Mansfield amendment to defense procurement authorization bill—sought the withdrawal of U.S. troops from Indochina six months after enactment pending the release of POWs. Adopted 57-38. *(1971 Almanac p. 37-S)*

HOUSE. Each time the Senate adopted the Mansfield amendment, the House voted not to accept it. Later, the House accepted weakened versions of the Mansfield proposals as parts of various defense bills.

June 17—Nedzi (D Mich.)—Whalen (R Ohio) amendment to defense procurement authorization bill—sought to bar use of funds included in the bill for U.S. activities in and over Indochina, giving the President the right to change the Dec. 31, 1971, fund cutoff date if he could gain the support of Congress. Rejected, 158-255. *(1971 Almanac p. 32-H)*

Oct. 19—A procedural motion, ordering the previous question, was offered which had the effect of blocking a direct vote on the Senate-passed Mansfield amendment. Adopted 215-193. *(1971 Almanac p. 71-H)*

Nov. 17—Boland (D Mass.) amendment to defense appropriations bill—sought to cut off funds for U.S. involvement in Indochina effective July 1, 1972, pending the release of POWs. Rejected, 163-218. *(1971 Almanac p. 90-H)*

Dec. 16—A procedural motion to table (kill) a proposal which instructed House conferees on the Foreign Military Assistance authorization bill to accept the Senate-passed Mansfield amendment. Adopted on a **key vote, 130-101.** *(1971 Almanac p. 105-H, 68)*

1972

SENATE. Twenty-eight roll-call votes were taken during 1972 on war-related issues, but no end-the-war language won final congressional approval. Early in the session concern in the Senate focused on preventing future involvements entered into without congressional participation by limiting the President's war powers. The Senate passed a war powers bill April 13. The House approved an amended version but the bill died in conference.

Later in the session the Senate barely approved an amendment, offered by Edward W. Brooke (R Mass.) which called for a cutoff of funds for the war pending the release of POWs. The House dropped the amendment during conference on the bill to which it was added. Late in the year, the Senate rejected an amendment to cut off funds for bombing in Vietnam.

April 13—Passage of war powers bill—sought to require the President in the future to obtain the advice and consent of Congress before committing U.S. troops to hostilities. Passed, 68-16. *(1972 Almanac p. 22-S)*

Aug. 2—Brooke (R Mass.) amendment to defense procurement authorization bill—sought to require cut-off of funds for conduct of war within four months, pending release of U.S. POWs. Adopted on a **key vote, 49-47.**

Oct. 2—Proxmire (D Wis.) amendment to defense appropriations bill—sought to bar use of funds for continued bombing of Vietnam, Laos and Cambodia, and to reduce the appropriations by $2-billion to reflect savings from bombing ban. Rejected, 26-55. *(1972 Almanac p. 71-S)*

HOUSE. Only four recorded teller votes were taken in the House during 1972 on issues relating to the Vietnam war. Of the four, two were efforts to cut off funds for the war; both failed.

June 27—Harrington (D Mass.) amendment to defense procurement authorization bill—sought to cut off funds as of Sept. 1, 1972, for U.S. military activity in and over Vietnam, Laos and Cambodia subject to release of POWs and accounting for persons missing in action. Rejected, 152-244. *(1972 Almanac p. 49-H)*

Aug. 10—Bolling (D Mo.) amendment to foreign military aid authorization bill—deleted provision terminating U.S. involvement in the Indochina war by Oct. 1, subject to release of U.S. POWs, accounting for persons missing in action and a cease-fire as needed to protect U.S. withdrawal. Adopted on a **key vote, 229-177.**

Sept. 14—Addabbo (D N.Y.) amendment to defense department appropriations bill—sought to cut off all funds in bill for support of U.S. involvement in Indochina. Rejected, 160-208. *(1972 Almanac p. 80-H)*

 Tonkin Gulf Resolution

PENTAGON PAPERS REVEALED MANIPULATION OF CONGRESS

For congressional critics of U.S. involvement in the Indochina war, the most galling experience was the wide disparity between the manner in which the Johnson administration in August 1964 sought congressional authorization for military action through the Tonkin Gulf resolution and the later disclosures which strongly suggested that Congress had been manipulated into granting that authorization. *(Text of Tonkin resolution, p. 947)*

An additional congressional frustration emerged in 1969-1970. With increasing numbers of members in both chambers favoring repeal of the 1964 resolution, the Nixon administration adroitly withdrew its opposition to repeal and maintained that its authority for pursuing the war rested on the President's constitutional power as Commander-in-Chief.

A touch of irony was added in June 1970 when Sen. Robert Dole (R Kan.), a staunch supporter of Nixon's Vietnam policies, introduced an amendment repealing the 1964 resolution. Dole's amendment became law at the end of the 91st Congress, preempting an earlier effort at repeal by Sen. J. W. Fulbright (D Ark.), chairman of the Foreign Relations Committee and one of the severest critics of U.S. involvement in the war.

Background

Criticism of President Truman's decision in June 1950 to commit U.S. forces to battle in Korea without seeking a declaration of war or requesting congressional approval led Truman's successors to seek advance congressional authority for the use of armed forces overseas.

In the Cold War atmosphere of the 1950s and 1960s, U.S. policymakers envisioned primarily two types of military engagements—a brush fire war or a nuclear holocaust. They believed that a constitutional declaration of war by Congress was inappropriate for either of these contingencies. A new formula, called the policy resolution, was developed by the Eisenhower and Kennedy administrations.

Eisenhower requested and was granted congressional authority in January 1955 to use armed forces in the event of a communist attack on Taiwan; in January 1957, he obtained similar authority to meet alleged communist aggression in the Middle East. Kennedy followed suit: in 1961 he obtained authority to protect West Berlin by force, and in September 1962 Congress gave him authority to use force to meet communist threats from Cuba.

The Tonkin Gulf resolution, modeled on the four resolutions and presented to Congress in August 1964, became the fifth—and through early 1973 the last—policy resolution obtained by the executive.

1964: The Incident

In the spring of 1964 the Vietnam war was going badly for the Saigon government. The Vietcong controlled the countryside. In June, when Henry Cabot Lodge resigned as U.S. ambassador to Saigon, President Johnson named a military man, Gen. Maxwell D. Taylor, at that time the chairman of the Joint Chiefs of Staff, as his replacement. One month later, it was announced that the U.S. military contingent in Vietnam would be increased by 5,000 men—to 21,000.

Politically, Johnson was under fire from the Republicans whose party platform, adopted July 14, charged him with having "encouraged an increase in (communist) aggression in South Vietnam...."

This atmosphere of a deteriorating military situation in South Vietnam formed the backdrop as U.S. destroyers patrolling in the Gulf of Tonkin reported attacks by North Vietnamese torpedo boats Aug. 2 and 4. The President ordered a retaliatory air strike, which destroyed 25 boats at their bases. He announced the action to a nationwide television audience later on Aug. 4 while the attack was underway. He stressed the action as a "positive reply" to "repeated acts of violence" against U.S. forces.

The next day, Aug. 5, he asked Congress to enact a policy resolution to "give convincing evidence to the aggressive communist nations...that the peace and security of the area will be preserved."

On Aug. 7 the Senate by a 88-2 vote and the House by a 414-0 vote passed a resolution (H J Res 1145) declaring support for "determination of the President, as Commander-in-Chief, to take all necessary measures to repel any armed attack against the forces of the United States and to prevent further aggression." Senators Wayne Morse (D Ore.) and Ernest Gruening (D Alaska) voted against the resolution.

A 'Declaration of War'?

The meaning of the Tonkin Gulf resolution became a source of intense debate as the war grew in scope and prospects of a quick military or political solution faded.

Testifying in January 1966 before the Foreign Relations Committee, Secretary of State Dean Rusk said the broad language of the resolution authorized "all necessary steps, including the use of armed force" to protect U.S. forces in Southeast Asia. In April 1967, in testimony before the committee, Under Secretary of State Nicholas deB. Katzenbach described the resolution as the "functional equivalent" of a "declaration of war."

President Johnson, who reportedly carried a copy of the Tonkin Gulf Resolution in his pocket continually to use against his critics, described the resolution at an April 1967 news conference:

"We stated then, and we repeat now, we did not think the resolution was necessary to do what we did and what we're doing. But we thought it was desirable, and we thought if we were going to ask them (Congress) to stay the whole route and if we expected them to be there on the landing, we ought to ask them to be there on the takeoff."

Initial Disclosures

The first major assault on the Tonkin resolution came in February 1968, when the Foreign Relations Committee held closed hearings on the 1964 incident. (A censored transcript was made public Feb. 24.) Defense Secretary Robert S. McNamara and Chairman of the Joint Chiefs of Staff Gen. Earle G. Wheeler testified that the reported attacks had in fact occurred and were unprovoked. Senator Fulbright quoted from cables between the ships involved and the Pentagon and concluded there were "uncertainties" about the attack. One cable from the commander of the destroyer task force, dated Aug. 4, 1964, stated: "No actual visual sighting.... Suggest complete evaluation before any further action."

McNamara denied there was coordination between the destroyer mission and South Vietnamese attacks by patrol boats on North Vietnamese islands in the Gulf of Tonkin. Fulbright quoted from another cable which stated that one of the purposes of the mission was "to draw NVM (North Vietnamese) PGMs (patrol boats)...away from areas of 34-A operations." (34-A was the code name for South Vietnamese attacks on North Vietnamese held islands.)

Tonkin Gulf Repeal

In a December 1969 State Department letter to Fulbright, the administration "oppose(d) the repeal of the Tonkin Gulf resolution....The existence of the... resolution...must be considered carefully in terms of our other international obligations in the area, particularly the Southeast Asia Collective Defense Treaty which the Tonkin Gulf Resolution specifically cites."

In March 1970, however, the State Department modified its position by informing Fulbright that the President's legal authority for carrying out the war did not depend on the resolution.

Commenting on the administration's shift in position, the Foreign Relations Committee report on the repealer (S Con Res 64—S Rept 91-872) stated that termination of the Tonkin Gulf resolution would "leave the executive in the legal position of continuing to conduct an unauthorized war."

During a six-week Senate debate in May and June on an administration-opposed amendment, dealing with Indochina, to the Foreign Military Sales bill (HR 15628), Dole, leader of the administration supporters in the Senate, offered an amendment to repeal the 1964 Tonkin Gulf resolution. His action was viewed as an attempt to seize the initiative from the Democrats by demonstrating that the Republicans also were opposed to the Vietnam war.

Tonkin Resolution Text

Following is the complete text of the "Gulf of Tonkin" resolution (PL 88-408) adopted by Congress in August 1964 after reported attack by North Vietnamese torpedo boats on U.S. destroyers in the Gulf of Tonkin on August 2 and 4.

The resolution was subsequently used by the Johnson administration as legal justification for escalation of the Vietnam war.

The text follows:

Whereas naval units of the Communist regime in Vietnam, in violation of the principles of the Charter of the United Nations and of international law, have deliberately and repeatedly attacked United States naval vessels lawfully present in international waters, and have thereby created a serious threat to international peace;

Whereas these attacks are part of a deliberate and systematic campaign of aggression that the Communist regime in North Vietnam has been waging against its neighbors and the nations joined with them in the collective defense of their freedom;

Whereas the United States is assisting the peoples of Southeast Asia to protect their freedom and has no territorial, military or political ambitions in that area, but desires only that these peoples should be left in peace to work out their own destinies in their own way; Now, therefore, be it

Resolved by the Senate and House of Representatives of the United States of America in Congress assembled, That the Congress approves and supports the determination of the President, as Commander in Chief, to take all necessary measures to repel any armed attack against the forces of the United States and to prevent further aggression.

SEC. 2. The United States regards as vital to its national interest and to world peace the maintenance of international peace and security in Southeast Asia. Consonant with the Constitution of the United States and the Charter of the United Nations and in accordance with its obligations under the Southeast Asia Collective Defense Treaty, the United States is, therefore, prepared, as the President determines, to take all necessary steps, including the use of armed force, to assist any member or protocol state of the Southeast Asia Collective Defense Treaty requesting assistance in defense of its freedom.

SEC. 3. This resolution shall expire when the President shall determine that the peace and security of the area is reasonably assured by international conditions created by action of the United Nations or otherwise, except that it may be terminated earlier by concurrent resolution of the Congress.

Fulbright objected to Dole's repeal amendment as "improper in this form" and said repeal should have been accomplished by S Con Res 64. Fulbright was overruled June 24 on an 81-10 roll-call vote as the Senate adopted the Dole amendment. The repeal took effect at the end of the 1970 session when HR 15628 was signed by the President (PL 91-672).

Pentagon Papers

Further light on the Tonkin Gulf incident emerged in June 1971 with publication of the Defense Department's secret history of the Vietnam war. The study revealed that:

● South Vietnamese patrol attacks and naval commando raids (code-named 34-A) on North Vietnamese islands in the Gulf of Tonkin on the night July 30-31, 1964, were under the over-all command of Gen. William C. Westmoreland, U.S. commander in Vietnam.

● A May 25, 1964, administration draft document existed which in a modified form later became the Tonkin Gulf resolution.

● Preparation of the draft document was part of a scheduled step-up of military pressure against North Vietnam in the summer and fall of 1964.

● On June 1-2, 1964, a high-level meeting in Honolulu attended by Westmoreland, Rusk and McNamara was held at which a major subject discussed was the obtaining of a congressional resolution "prior to wider U.S. action in Southeast Asia," according to the Pentagon study.

Mobilize 'Public Support.' The Pentagon study summarized the Tonkin Gulf incident and the resolution as follows: "The Tonkin Gulf reprisal (ordered by Johnson) and the Tonkin Gulf resolution set U.S. public support for virtually any action."

Quite apart from the background on the Tonkin Gulf incident and the Tonkin resolution, the *Pentagon Papers* demonstrated a general indifference to the constitutional prerogatives of the legislative branch in the conduct of defense and foreign policy: conspicuously absent throughout the 47-volume study detailing the actions of four administrations in Southeast Asia was any discussion of the role Congress should have in the formulation of U.S. Southeast Asian policy.

Congressional Reaction

Initially, the *Pentagon Papers* disclosures provoked a wave of dismay among members of Congress at the manner in which they and the public had been kept in the dark about the growing military involvement in Vietnam.

Fulbright said the published documents demonstrated a "deliberate and flagrant deception" by the Johnson administration. Sen. Barry Goldwater (R Ariz.), 1964 Republican presidential candidate, considered himself vindicated: "...all the time Johnson was saying he'd never send American boys, I knew damn well he would."

Two weeks after the initial *New York Times* publication on June 13, congressional interest was waning. The only formal action in either chamber was the June 30 rejection in the House of a motion by Rep. Bella S. Abzug (D N.Y.) requiring the President to turn over the study to Congress. The issue became moot when the administration directed the Government Printing Office to print sufficient copies of a declassified version of the study, which was delivered to members of Congress Sept. 27.

In the Senate, the Foreign Relations Committee initiated a $250,000 study of the documents. By the end of 1972, the committee had produced a series of scholarly reports on the Vietnam war and conducted three days of hearings in May 1972 on the origins of the war. Leslie H. Gelb, chairman of the Pentagon task force that prepared the Pentagon papers, testified and placed heavy responsibility on Congress for continuation of the war. He said "the war can only be ended here in Congress. Congressmen and senators for years have hidden behind the President.... If the war continues, it will be as much the responsibility of Congress as of the President."

Chapter 15—The Presidency

The Presidency, 1969-72

On Nov. 5, 1968, Richard M. Nixon was elected 37th President of the United States in one of the closest contests of the century for that office. Four years later he won a remarkable re-election victory, carrying every state except Massachusetts and the District of Columbia. In the years between, Nixon's popularity seesawed, affected by instability of the economy, by developments in the Vietnam war and by changes in relations with the leading Communist powers.

In the year that counted most—1972—the President looked best. But within six months of the 1972 election, his popularity had dropped to an all-time low. A war settlement of sorts had finally been achieved in Vietnam and the American troops and prisoners of war had come home, but attainment of those long-sought goals was overshadowed by unfavorable economic trends and by disturbing disclosures in the Watergate affair. Renewed inflation and the unfolding story of discreditable GOP tactics in the 1972 campaign raised many questions about the President's judgment and about his choice of advisers. *(Watergate story, p. 978)*

Much of President Nixon's first term was dominated by the two main problems he inherited from his predecessor—the Vietnam war and deeply rooted inflation. In 1969 Nixon initiated the popular policy of Vietnamization—a gradual shift, from Washington to Saigon, of responsibility for fighting the ground war in Indochina.

Antiwar dissent rose in 1970 when the fighting was extended to Cambodia, and in 1971 Congress for the first time called for an end to the war. In late 1972 it appeared that years of negotiations were finally about to end in a cease-fire, although national security adviser Henry Kissinger's October promise that "peace is at hand" was not immediately realized. The cease-fire agreement was signed at last in January 1973.

The economic news during the first two and a half years of the Nixon administration was almost all bad. The President's course of "gradualism" in the effort to control inflation did not work, a tight money policy helped send the economy into a recession at the end of 1969, and unemployment rose steadily. Poor economic performance was cited as one reason for a mediocre Republican showing in the midterm 1970 elections.

Then, on Aug. 15, 1971, the President won applause when he announced a major new policy of wage, price and rent controls. New measures announced the same day to check a steadily worsening U.S. balance of international payments led to an 8.5 per cent devaluation of the dollar in December 1971, which also won praise for the President. In early 1973, the President announced a more flexible system of controls. *(Economy chapter p. 53)*

Foreign Affairs Gains

The achievement most prominently identified with Nixon's first term was a general improvement in relations with the communist bloc. Success in that direction was made possible in part by the President's past reputation as a strong anti-communist.

In 1972 Nixon became the first President to pay state visits to the People's Republic of China and to the Soviet Union. The China trip opened communications between the two countries. The trip to Moscow resulted in the conclusion of a number of agreements, including a major arms accord.

Legislative Record

President Nixon put a substantial share of his energy into foreign affairs, leaving to others much of the responsibility for developing domestic proposals and dealing with Congress. His failure to give more personal attention to domestic matters and to cultivate closer relations with Capitol Hill no doubt had something to do with the administration's legislative record.

The amount of legislation requested and the legislative output of Congress were considerably smaller than they had been during the Johnson administration. Congress spent much of its time arguing with the administration over spending priorities.

The White House sought to cut back some of the social welfare programs developed during the 1960s and to "turn power back to the people." This policy was reflected in one of the few new pieces of major administration legislation enacted—a 1972 bill to share federal revenues with the states and local communities. Other important administration bills passed during the four years were a military draft lottery bill, several anti-crime measures, a proposal to convert the Post Office Department into a government-owned corporation and two strong bills to combat drug abuse. Both the 91st Congress and the 92nd Congress had excellent records on environmental protection, going well beyond what the administration asked.

During his first term, Nixon increasingly gave the impression of being a very private man, remote from all

References

Discussion of the Presidency for the years 1945-64 maybe found in *Congress and the Nation, Vol. I* p. 1432-1433, 1455-59; For the years 1965-1968, p. 625-660.

but his closest advisers, unwilling to reveal a great deal of himself to the public. Even GOP members of Congress found him extremely hard to approach. Relations with the news media were often poor. The administration also specialized in "government by surprise." Henry Kissinger engaged in a number of important secret missions, and major decisions (the China visit, new economic policy) were announced unexpectedly with no advance hints to the public or even to Congress.

Relations With Congress

1969. The Nixon administration and its lieutenants on Capitol Hill faced a political situation in Washington unique in this century. Not since the inauguration of Zachary Taylor in 1849 had a President entered office facing opposition majorities in both houses of Congress. The President experienced numerous difficulties in working with a Democratic-controlled Congress, and he also had trouble keeping liberal members of his own party in line.

The administration was criticized for delays in submitting specific program proposals and for failure to provide witnesses to testify on the administration's position when hearings were scheduled early in the session. Once proposals did get to Congress, a majority of members disagreed with the White House on national priorities. Moderates and liberals wanted to spend less for defense and more on education, health and pollution control than the President had requested.

Particularly in the Senate, members of the President's own party opposed him on a number of issues. This was the case with the President's narrowest victory of the year—a 50-50 vote on an amendment to stop deployment of the Safeguard ABM system—and with his major defeat —the Senate's rejection of his nomination of U.S. Circuit Court of Appeals Judge Clement F. Haynsworth of South Carolina as a Supreme Court justice. All three of the Senate Republican leaders voted against the Haynsworth nomination.

The sentiments of the Republican liberals probably were best expressed by Sen. Charles McC. Mathias Jr. (Md.), who referred to the President's advisers as "the Prussians" and added: "I suppose they're bright in their way. But they just don't understand this body. They just haven't found any way to communicate effectively." Sen. Jacob K. Javits (R N.Y.) spoke of a need for the White House to "buttress its liaison machinery" with Congress, but poor liaison was a problem which was to continue throughout Nixon's first term.

1970. The second session of the 91st Congress was unusually long, acrimonious and not particularly productive. Congress spent most of its time quarreling with the President over spending priorities. It sliced funds from his military, foreign aid and space requests and added money to numerous domestic programs, primarily education, health, manpower training and pollution control.

Nixon met with greatest resistance from Congress on his military and foreign policy stands concerning Vietnam and Cambodia. He also suffered another embarrassing defeat when a second Supreme Court nominee—U.S. Circuit Court of Appeals Judge G. Harrold Carswell of Florida—was rejected by the Senate.

'Six Great Goals'

President Nixon's 1971 State of the Union message was devoted entirely to setting forth "six great goals" which he said would "reform the entire structure of American government so we can make it again fully responsive to the needs and the wishes of the American people."

Of the six goals, five required legislation. In the order presented, these were welfare reform, environmental initiatives, health insurance reform, revenue sharing and government reorganization. When the 92nd Congress adjourned in October 1972, only revenue sharing had been enacted in the form desired by the President. The Congress had a good record on environmental protection, but the President's own priorities had shifted somewhat. He vetoed a major water pollution control bill that Congress had substituted for one of his anti-pollution proposals, and then refused to spend the funds after Congress overrode the veto.

Of the three other legislative goals, welfare reform and reorganization of cabinet-level departments were clearly dead. The first seemed to have been killed in part by the administration, which had refused to move an inch toward compromise with Senate liberals who wanted a more generous plan. Government reorganization, which did not get beyond the hearings stage, had considerable liberal support but was strongly opposed by the business and labor groups that had a comfortable relationship with the existing bureaucracy. The last legislative goal, health insurance reform, also did not get beyond hearings but appeared likely to reappear in the 93rd Congress.

The remaining goal—"full prosperity in peacetime"—had to be achieved by a combination of policies rather than by specific legislation. Progress toward this goal was mixed. By the end of 1972 the economy was expanding rapidly, but inflation still threatened and unemployment—an economic ill that seemed to defy the Nixon administration— remained relatively high.

The President's Senate spokesman, Minority Leader Hugh Scott (R Pa.), asserted that Congress had "dawdled, postured, delayed" for two years, leading to "confusion and loss of confidence in government" and to "embarrassment" of the Congress.

But presidential vetoes had contributed partly to the slow legislative pace. Four of the President's six vetoes during the year were sustained. Two of the four were appropriation bills which had to be rewritten. Despite the unusual length of the 1970 session—the longest since 1950—Congress did not complete action on some of the President's major requests: welfare reform, revenue sharing, consumer protection and Social Security increases.

Among proposals enacted into law, there were some major victories: postal reform, environmental measures and crime legislation. For the second time, Congress approved further deployment of the controversial antiballistic missile system (ABM), but only after Nixon's request was cut back substantially.

1971. Nixon began his third year of the presidency with a pledge to restructure government and turn power "back to the people." In his state of the union message, he introduced "six great goals" of his administration: welfare reform, revenue sharing, health insurance reform, environmental initiatives, government reorganization and full employment. All but the last required legislation. Achievement of all six, Nixon said, would bring about "a new American revolution."

By the end of the year, none of the first five goals had been reached. They were bogged down in what the President called a lagging Congress controlled by Democrats. His two major domestic proposals—welfare reform and revenue sharing—were locked in committee, partly because the President himself had asked that they be delayed so that Congress could consider his new economic program.

Nixon had other difficulties with Congress. It spent more for domestic programs than he wanted, resulting in three vetoes of legislation the administration considered too costly. It also turned down his requests for funding of the supersonic transport (SST) and the foreign aid program.

Many members of Congress were alienated by what they called the President's method of "government by surprise." The President often announced policies to Congress at the same time he announced them to the nation—via television.

1972. The 92nd Congress adjourned Oct. 18 after two acrimonious encounters with the White House. By lopsided margins, Congress overrode a Nixon veto of a Democratic-inspired $24.7-billion water pollution control bill. And House acquiescence to a Senate vote rejecting a $250-billion ceiling on federal spending in fiscal 1973 killed the President's proposal that Congress grant him the authority to slash whatever he wanted from any congressional appropriation.

To the President, the issue was spending, and votes to override his midnight veto of the "staggering, budget-wrecking" anti-pollution measure were votes for "higher prices and higher taxes." In his veto message, the President noted: "I have nailed my colors to the mast on this issue; the political winds may blow where they may."

Only one of Nixon's "great goals" *(above)* was acted upon by the 92nd Congress—general revenue sharing. But the blame for inaction rested with the administration as well as Capitol Hill since the White House had been unwilling to work very hard for some of its proposals (welfare reform) and to accept congressional substitutes for others (environmental legislation).

Generally, the administration received what it wanted in foreign affairs and national security, while the Democratic-controlled Congress was successful in strengthening some domestic programs. In a sense, then, it was a standoff, with Nixon having the final word: after Congress adjourned, he pocket vetoed nine bills on the ground that they would cost too much.

The Economy

1969. The Nixon administration's effort to slow down the pace of the economy's inflationary growth met with little tangible success in 1969. The President and his financial advisers pursued a policy of "gradualism" in

Presidential Support

President Nixon in 1972 won 66 per cent of the 83 recorded votes in Congress that represented a clear-cut test of support for his views. This was a four-year low for the President and the lowest score since 1960 when President Dwight D. Eisenhower won only 65 per cent of the congressional votes involving questions on which he had taken a position.

Nixon's 66 per cent in 1972 was nine points below his 1971 figure of 75 per cent and 11 points under his best score—77 per cent in 1970. In 1969, the first year of his administration, the President scored 74 per cent.

Compared with past years, in 1972 the Nixon position was hard to pin down on many of the major pieces of legislation considered by Congress. Congressional Quarterly's tabulation showed that the Nixon stand was clear in the case of only 83 recorded votes—the lowest number since presidential support studies began in 1953. In 1971, by comparison, Nixon's views were known in the case of 139 recorded congressional votes.

an attempt to halt inflation without bringing on a recession. Unlike some previous administrations, President Nixon maintained an official hands-off policy toward labor and industry concerning wage and price increases.

But by the end of the year, the administration's actions showed—at best—limited success in holding down government expenditures and the wage-price spiral.

When he submitted his revised budget to Congress in April, Nixon promised to hold federal spending to $192.9-billion and to produce an anti-inflationary surplus for fiscal 1970 of nearly $6-billion. But action and inaction by Congress, coupled with increases in uncontrollable spending, quickly made those goals illusory.

In a move initiated on Capitol Hill instead of by the White House, Congress in 1969 cleared legislation providing the most comprehensive reform of the nation's tax statutes in history and the largest tax cut since 1964. The measure, passed over the threat of a presidential veto, resulted in a net annual loss to the Treasury of $2.5-billion.

1970. The economy, which reached the trillion-dollar level in its annual output of goods and services, continued to be plagued by inflation. The Nixon administration, its critics charged, had achieved recession, unemployment and inflation simultaneously.

The outcome of the Nov. 3 off-year elections, which left Congress under firm Democratic control, was widely attributed to the state of the economy. By the end of the year, Democratic leaders in Congress were calling for stringent controls. (Congress had passed legislation over the President's opposition authorizing credit controls and a wage-price freeze.)

Late in the year, Nixon appeared to be moving decisively away from previous policy in three broad areas: federal expenditures, monetary policy and private wage and price decisions. In a major economic speech Dec. 4, he confirmed a widespread expectation of new tactics.

The President announced he would use deficit spending to stimulate economic growth. He said he was planning the new budget "on the basis that it would be balanced if we were at full employment and the economy were producing full revenues." He announced measures taken to offset oil price increases and plans to intervene in wage negotiations in the construction industry if strikes and rising costs were not limited.

1971. After two and a half years of unsuccessful attempts to curb inflation, the President Aug. 15 imposed wage and price controls on the economy and sought to reverse growing deficits in the U.S. balance of trade. Under authority voted by Congress in 1970 (despite opposition from the White House), Nixon froze wages, prices and rents for 90 days ("Phase I") and then set up mechanisms for continued limitations during the post-freeze "Phase II."

The President also called for tax reductions to stimulate economic growth and reduce unemployment, a tax credit for business investment, a step-up in scheduled increases in personal tax exemptions and a repeal of the excise tax on cars. He suspended convertibility of the dollar into gold at the $35-an-ounce fixed price which had pegged the value of the dollar in international exchange for nearly 40 years, and imposed an indefinite 10 per cent surcharge on imports. He established a Cost of Living Council to oversee the program.

In addition to new tax laws, Nixon asked Congress to extend his authority to control wages, prices and rents and to add powers to regulate interest rates and dividends. Congress cleared such a bill Dec. 14.

The President established his Phase II program by executive order under existing authority. He established a Pay Board of five members each from the public, labor and management and a seven-member Price Commission to devise guidelines to take effect after the freeze ended.

Imposition of the freeze and subsequent actions of the Pay Board widened a rift between the Nixon administration and organized labor. Labor objected chiefly to the Pay Board's action limiting wage increases scheduled by existing contracts.

The international aspects of the President's Aug. 15 actions—suspension of dollar convertibility and the new import surcharge—by design precipitated a monetary crisis. They led to a meeting of the principal world finance ministers at the Smithsonian Institution and, on Dec. 18, to the announcement of a revaluation of stronger currencies and a devaluation of the dollar by 8.5 per cent. The import surcharge was rescinded.

In keeping with his state of the union pledge, the President Jan. 29 had sent Congress a record $229.2-billion budget with an $11.6-billion deficit for fiscal 1972. "By operating as if we were at full employment," Nixon predicted in his budget message, "we will help to bring about that full employment."

1972. The economic news in 1972 generally was favorable. The gross national product was increasing at the rate of $100-billion a year. Wages were rising faster than prices, thereby swelling the real income of workers. Farmers were making profits. And, according to the Census Bureau, for the first time more than half the the country had incomes of more than $10,000. The bureau noted, however, that because of inflation, the increase in 1971 income over 1970 was illusory.

On the other hand, unemployment was still high (5.5 per cent in September), and the administration had decided to abandon its goal of 4 per cent unemployment. On election day, 4.8 million Americans did not have jobs, 2 million more than when President Nixon took office. Prices also continued to rise (0.5 per cent in September, or at an annual rate of 6 per cent). And the deficit in the federal budget was looming larger than had been expected. (One report said the Nixon experts predicted a deficit of at least $34-billion for fiscal 1973, or $8.5-billion more than had been expected in January. The cumulative deficit for Nixon's four years in office was expected to reach $75-billion.)

So, even as it appeared that the economy was emerging from the doldrums, the President still faced serious problems. *(Early 1973 developments p. 59)*

Vietnam and Foreign Policy

1969. The Nixon administration in 1969 attempted to shape a policy on Vietnam which would gradually shift responsibility for fighting the ground war from Washington to Saigon.

In an address to the nation Nov. 3, the President reported that virtually no progress had been made at the Paris peace talks. U.S. policy, he said, would stress "Vietnamization" of the war, whereby American combat troops would be withdrawn according to an "orderly scheduled timetable."

Nixon restated earlier peace proposals, and—for the first time—put on record his so-called Asian Doctrine. The doctrine maintained that the United States should continue its alliances in the Pacific but should not become involved in future wars on the Asian mainland. Greater stress would be placed on self-help and on economic development of the region, he said.

On March 13, the Senate ratified the Treaty for Non-Proliferation of Nuclear Weapons. By the end of the year, 24 of the 40 countries required to put the treaty into effect had ratified it, including the major nuclear powers—Britain, the Soviet Union and the United States—which agreed not to furnish nuclear weapons to non-nuclear countries.

1970. Despite the President's efforts in Vietnam, extension of the war to neighboring Cambodia gave rise to the fear that the United States would become further bogged down in Southeast Asia.

When Nixon ordered U.S. combat troops into Cambodia April 30, he claimed his move did not constitute a widening of the war or an invasion of Cambodia. U.S. troops, he said, would only enter border areas held by the North Vietnamese and Viet Cong. He claimed the incursion was necessary to protect U.S. forces during the prolonged withdrawal process from Vietnam.

In the Senate, the President's decision precipitated a seven-week debate which ended June 30 with the passage (58-37 roll-call vote) of an amendment sponsored by Senators John Sherman Cooper (R Ky.) and Frank Church (D Idaho) prohibiting re-entry of U.S. ground forces into Cambodia. A revised version of the amendment was included as part of the supplemental foreign aid authorization bill, which cleared Congress Dec. 31. The substitute still contained a clause prohibiting U.S. ground troops from participating in combat operations in Cambodia.

Aside from Vietnam, the President had set forth a new policy (termed the Nixon Doctrine) which had as its goal avoiding direct U.S. military involvement in remote corners of the globe. The Nixon Doctrine was formally stated by the President Feb. 18 in a 40,000-word message to Congress entitled "United States Foreign Policy for the 1970s: A New Strategy for Peace." In the document, widely described as a "state of the world" message, the President said that the Nixon Doctrine's "central thesis is that the United States will participate in the defense and development of allies and friends, but that America cannot—and will not—conceive all the plans, design all the programs, execute all the decisions and undertake all the defense of the free nations of the world."

The President trod a cautious path in the tense Middle East arms race during 1970. In March, he announced that Israel's request to purchase additional combat aircraft had been turned down on an "interim basis," but he emphasized that the decision would be "constantly reappraised" if the Arab-Israeli arms balance shifted.

When the Soviet Union began deploying military personnel, aircraft and surface-to-air missiles in Egypt, pressure built up on the President, particularly from Congress, to supply Israel with additional aircraft.

In the closing days of the 1970 session, Congress approved an administration request for $500-million to finance credit sales of arms to Israel.

1971. President Nixon, who made his early political reputation as a strong anti-communist, jolted the world in 1971 with announcements that he would visit both Peking and Moscow the following year. After two decades of hostility and non-recognition of the People's Republic of China, the administration made three dramatic shifts in U.S. policy toward the Peking regime:

• On June 10, the President ended a 21-year embargo on trade with mainland China.

• On July 15, Nixon announced he would visit Peking in 1972.

• On Aug. 2, Secretary of State William P. Rogers announced that the United States would support the seating of Communist China in the United Nations.

In thus abandoning the long-standing policy of non-recognition of the communist regime in Peking, the President cast himself in the role of a statesman seeking new roads to world peace. Reaction in Congress and the nation generally was favorable, although the move did arouse fears among some conservatives that the United States would abandon its alliance with the Chinese communists' bitter enemy, the Chinese Nationalist government on Taiwan.

The United States officially supported both the seating of Communist China in the United Nations and the continued membership of the Nationalist government, which had occupied China's permanent seat in the Security Council since the United Nations was founded. This two-China strategy failed when the General Assembly voted Oct. 25 to transfer China's membership to the Peking government, thereby terminating representation of Taiwan in the world organization. Taiwan's expulsion produced an immediate angry response from many members of Congress.

Dissent over the Vietnam war—which seemed on the rise in the spring of 1971—had waned by midyear following further troop withdrawal announcements. At year's end, 45,000 additional troops were scheduled for withdrawal, practically bringing to an end the offensive combat involvement of U.S. ground forces.

But in Congress total U.S. withdrawal from Southeast Asia remained a major issue. For the first time, Congress in 1971 called for an end to the Indochina war. Yet Nixon, when signing the bill containing the withdrawal amendment, told reporters the measure was not binding and would not change his policies.

In keeping with the Nixon Doctrine, the President proposed increased military aid for Southeast Asia in his foreign aid request. But in the Senate, doubts about the doctrine were among a variety of conflicting ideas and positions that endangered the future of the foreign aid program. For the first time in the program's history, a foreign aid bill was defeated as the Senate rejected the legislation authorizing fiscal 1972 funds.

The Senate revived the authorization legislation in a two-bill package in reduced form, and Senate and House

---

The China Visit

At the end of President Nixon's first term, many observers believed that the achievement of which he was most proud was the detente with Communist China. It seemed likely that that was also the achievement for which the first term would be best remembered.

The President's February 1972 visit to mainland China was the first ever by a U.S. President. It ended more than 20 years of hostility toward the People's Republic, which began in 1949 after the Communists drove the Nationalist Chinese government of Chiang Kai-shek from the mainland to Taiwan.

The groundwork for the Nixon visit was established in June 1971 by the President's national security affairs adviser Henry A. Kissinger. While on a visit to Pakistan to discuss the troubled political situation there, Kissinger feigned illness and, with the cooperation of then President Yahya Khan, made a secret trip to Peking. It was one of a number of secret diplomatic trips for which Kissinger became known.

The President's week-long visit to China the next year ended with issuance of a joint communique with Premier Chou En-lai indicating agreement on the need for increased contacts between the two countries. The communique included a controversial statement whereby the United States accepted Peking's contention that Taiwan was a part of China, agreed that Taiwan's fate should be determined by the Chinese, and pledged ultimate withdrawal of American forces from Taiwan.

The new relationship between China and the United States was further strengthened in February 1973 following another visit by Kissinger to Peking. That trip resulted in establishment of liaison offices in Washington and Peking. David K.E. Bruce, former U.S. ambassador successively to France, West Germany, and Great Britain, was named as the U.S. representative in China. Gen. Huang Chen, formerly the People's Republic's ambassador to France, was named to head China's liaison office in Washington.

Moscow Trip, Arms Pacts

While not so glamorous as his journey to China two months earlier, a trip by President Nixon to the Soviet Union in May 1972 brought more substantive results. Like the China visit the trip to the Soviet Union was the first state visit to that country by a U.S. President. Nixon returned from Moscow with seven agreements he had signed with Soviet leaders. They included pacts on joint space missions, technology, the environment, medical research, incidents at sea and two agreements on the limitation of strategic arms. A trade agreement, not completed during the President's visit, followed in October.

The arms accord overshadowed every other aspect of the Moscow trip. It involved two parts: a treaty limiting construction of anti-ballistic missile sites to two in each country and an interim agreement limiting the number of offensive strategic missiles each side could have during the following five years to those under construction or deployed when the agreement was signed.

The ABM treaty had to be submitted to the Senate for approval. It was ratified Aug. 3 by an 88-2 vote. As a courtesy, the offensive arms executive agreement was submitted to both houses of Congress, although no further action was necessary to consummate that accord. It ran into trouble from Senate proponents of a hard line toward the Soviet Union, but was finally approved after six weeks of debate and modification in several respects. *(p. 895)*

---

conferees engaged in a bitter struggle to resolve differences over a Senate amendment setting a policy of complete withdrawal of troops from Vietnam within six months. The amendment finally was deleted.

After war broke out between Pakistan and India, as an offshoot of the civil war in East Pakistan, members of Congress criticized the President for failing to make more vigorous efforts to settle the India-Pakistan differences and for treating India as the aggressor. The administration countered that India had started the open fighting just as behind-the-scenes efforts by Washington to persuade Pakistan to grant partial autonomy to East Pakistan seemed about to succeed. In January 1972 East Pakistan declared its independence as Bangladesh.

1972. By October, it appeared that a settlement of the Vietnam war, or at least a cease-fire and the return of U.S. prisoners of war, was imminent. Presidential adviser Henry A. Kissinger and North Vietnamese officials had hammered out a nine-point agreement, but final details were not settled to the satisfaction of both sides until early in 1973.

In other respects, 1972 was at times a spectacular year in foreign policy. Nixon made successful trips to Peking in February and to Moscow in May. Both were historic; both were highly praised throughout the nation. And together they contributed to the President's stature among the voters.

The first American President to visit Moscow, Nixon returned to Washington June 1 with seven agreements he

had signed with Soviet leaders. Most important were two arms agreements: a treaty that would limit the deployment of anti-ballistic missiles (ABMs) and an interim agreement limiting the number of offensive weapons to those already under construction or deployed when the agreement was signed. The interim agreement, to remain in effect for five years, also placed limitations on the number of missile-carrying submarines to be constructed.

The President submitted the interim executive agreement to Congress, which gave its approval, and the Senate ratified the ABM treaty. The arms agreements were followed in October by a trade agreement and a settlement of the Soviet Union's World War II lend-lease debt to the United States. Implementation of the trade agreement depended on action by Congress extending most-favored-nation treatment to imports from the Soviet Union. That action was delayed by efforts to make it dependent on lifting of Soviet exit taxes on emigrants to Israel. Meanwhile, Moscow made large purchases of American wheat and other grains.

National Security

1969. The Nixon administration and Congress engaged in a protracted debate in 1969 over priorities: whether increased weight should be given to national security needs or domestic programs. In the end, Congress cut $5.6-billion from budget requests for defense spending.

The most dramatic fight came in the Senate over the administration's Safeguard anti-ballistic missile system (ABM). Senators debated the issue for two months before defeating by a 50-50 vote a proposal to block all work on the Safeguard system. The Aug. 6 vote was a central, if shaky, victory for the administration, which had extensively revised former President Johnson's Sentinel ABM system.

In an attempt to shave funds from defense spending, the administration dropped requests for the Manned Orbiting Laboratory (MOL), the Cheyenne helicopters and the controversial F-111 fighter-bomber. Responding to mounting criticism from Congress and the public, the President announced near the end of the year a halt to the biological aspects of chemical-biological warfare (CBW).

Congress enacted the President's top legislative request which established a lottery system for selection of Army draftees. The new system was aimed at inducting 19-year-olds first and reduced the period of prime draft eligibility from seven years to one.

1970. Congress in 1970 cut $2-billion from the President's $68.7-billion budget request for the military for fiscal 1971. Final action on the $66.6-billion defense appropriations bill came late in the session after months of debate on the ABM, the Indochina war and procurement of new weapons systems.

Nixon asked congressional approval of plans to enlarge the ABM system and add five additional sites for defense against an attack by China. A total of $1-billion for non-construction costs and $357-million in construction appropriations was finally allocated by Congress, but only after cutting out the anti-Chinese portion of the President's request.

Late in the year, Defense Secretary Melvin R. Laird indicated that defense spending would have to increase in the near future "in order to meet urgent requirements, many of them too long deferred."

1971. The President asked Congress for a $73.5-billion defense appropriations bill which would cover all Defense Department expenses during fiscal 1972 except building programs. Congress cut $3-billion from the administration request with more than half the cuts coming from the weapons procurement budget. On two different occasions, the White House mounted lobbying efforts to defeat attempts in the Senate to reduce the number of U.S. troops stationed in Europe. Both times, the administration was successful.

The administration also succeeded in thwarting all efforts in Congress to shorten the two-year draft extension requested by the Pentagon, although the House turned back a one-year extension amendment to the draft bill by a margin of only two votes. The bill was a major battleground on the question of changing to an all-volunteer army.

1972. The Nixon administration's request for military spending shot up to $82.3-billion for fiscal 1973. Congress approved $74.4-billion in defense appropriations and $2.3-billion for military construction during the year.

The Defense Department accelerated its plans for development of weapons systems not covered by the U.S.-Soviet arms accords, including the B-1 bomber and the Trident submarine.

In mid-July, the General Accounting Office reported that cost overruns on 77 weapons systems had increased by $28.7-billion despite "measurable progress" in the Pentagon's arms-purchasing procedures.

Civil Rights

1969. President Nixon was elected to office with little support from Negroes and other non-white minorities. Although he promised early in his presidency "to rectify" his reputation of indifference to black aspirations, the new administration took few public actions in 1969 to back up the promise.

The administration's policy statement on school desegregation guidelines, made public July 3, stated that plans for dismantling dual school systems must be carried out by September unless "bona fide educational and administrative problems" warrant delay. But in late August, HEW Secretary Robert H. Finch asked a federal court to delay implementation of HEW plans scheduled to go into effect in September. Later, the Justice Department aligned itself with southern school officials and against civil rights advocates in defending the delay before the Supreme Court. This marked the first split in the Justice Department-civil rights partnership since the 1954 Supreme Court decision which declared that segregated schools were illegal. The court refused to delay the desegregation plans.

In June, the Labor Department drew up what became known as the "Philadelphia Plan," a scheme for increasing the employment of black laborers in the highly segregated construction industry unions. The plan survived a strong move in Congress late in the session to kill it.

In August the President issued an executive order designed to eliminate job discrimination in the federal government.

1970. The Nixon administration's second year was marked by continued evolution of a more cautious federal stance in regard to school desegregation enforcement. The President made it clear that he saw the nation's schools primarily as instruments of education, not integration. Nixon went on record as opposing busing and favoring neighborhood schools. Many of the more activist officials with desegregation responsibilities left the administration during the year.

In a defeat related to civil rights, Congress passed over the President's objections a bill extending the Voting Rights Act of 1965. The administration had proposed a revision of the voting rights legislation in what civil rights advocates called an attempt to water down the act to take some of the burden of the legislation off the South.

1971. After the Supreme Court decision in April sanctioned the use of busing and other methods of pupil assignment to desegregate schools, the administration moved quickly to carry out such a policy. By mid-summer, HEW had warned 64 school districts that they should move to increase the desegregation of their schools when sessions started in the fall. But in a statement issued in August, the President reiterated his opposition to busing.

On June 11, in a long-awaited statement on equal opportunity in housing, President Nixon said he would enforce federal laws barring racial discrimination in the sale, rental or construction of housing—but that he would not approve a federal policy of forcing cities and neighborhoods to accept low-income housing.

1972. In March, Congress passed and the President signed a bill providing court-enforcement powers for the Equal Employment Opportunity Commission. The measure authorized the EEOC to institute suits in federal court to enforce U.S. laws against job discrimination.

Nixon also signed the higher education bill containing compromise busing provisions which postponed the effective date of court orders requiring busing until 1974 and limited the use of federal funds for busing intended to overcome racial imbalance or to desegregate schools.

The President, responding to strong anti-busing sentiment throughout the country, had proposed (1) that a moratorium be established on new, court-ordered busing orders until July 1, 1973, or until Congress legislated limits on busing, whichever came first, and (2) that busing be made a last-resort and strictly limited means of achieving school desegregation.

Supreme Court

Because of three retirements and one resignation, the President was given the opportunity to reshape the Supreme Court in a more conservative image—as he had promised in 1968. Reshaping the court, however, gave him his two most embarrassing defeats in Congress.

The Senate Nov. 21, 1969, by a 45-55 roll-call vote refused to confirm Clement F. Haynsworth Jr. of South

Carolina and chief justice of the 4th U.S. Circuit Court of Appeals to be an associate justice. Opponents questioned his sensitivity to the appearance of ethical impropriety.

On April 8, 1970, the Senate on a 45-51 roll call turned down the nomination of G. Harrold Carswell of Florida. Carswell, a judge of the 5th U.S. Circuit Court of Appeals, was opposed by key senators who did not like his record on civil rights.

Of the four men confirmed, the first was the new Chief Justice Warren Earl Burger. The Senate confirmed the nomination June 9, 1969, by a roll-call vote of 74-3. Burger, a judge of the U.S. Court of Appeals, District of Columbia, was known in legal circles for his conservative stance on questions of criminal law.

In 1970, after the Carswell nomination was rejected, Nixon nominated Harry A. Blackmun, a Minnesotan from the 8th U.S. Circuit Court of Appeals. His nomination was confirmed unanimously May 12.

The two remaining judges were appointed in 1971. The appointments virtually assured a conservative majority on the Court. The nomination of Lewis F. Powell Jr., a Virginia lawyer and past president of the American Bar Association, was confirmed Dec. 6 by an 89-1 roll-call vote. The second nomination, that of Assistant Attorney General William H. Rehnquist, ran into more trouble. He was opposed by a group of liberal senators and interest groups who criticized him as insensitive to the rights of the individual and of minority group members. The nomination was confirmed Dec. 10 after four days of debate by a 68-26 roll-call vote.

Federal Judgeships. President Nixon during his first year in office had an opportunity to make an unusually large number of appointments to the federal bench. He appointed 177 federal district and appeals court judges and four Supreme Court justices. The total moved Nixon within easy striking distance of the record set by Franklin D. Roosevelt, who in his 12 years placed 194 men on the lower federal courts and nine men on the Supreme Court.

At the end of 1972, there were 400 federal district judgeships and 97 courts of appeals seats—almost exactly double the number when Harry S Truman took office in 1945. Congress six times since 1945 enacted bills creating additional judgeships, including a bill passed in 1970 adding new positions to the judiciary. *(p. 303)*

Of the 176 men and one woman named to the lower federal courts during the first Nixon term, 165 were Republicans, many with long records of service to the GOP.

Presidential Power

Major clashes between President Nixon and Congress during the first Nixon administration refocused public attention on the long-debated issue of presidential power.

Presidential power has been slowly and steadily enhanced with the passive consent of Congress. It derived from somewhat vague wording in the Constitution; from precedents established by activist presidents; and from laws, never repealed, which gave the executive special powers in emergencies. Scholars have long argued over the proper extent of presidential power in a number of areas. (For a detailed discussion of the basic issues, see *Congress and the Nation, Vol. II, p. 628)*

During the years 1969-72, Congress was in direct conflict with the Executive in three areas involving presidential powers: the power as commander in chief to wage war, the power deriving from executive privilege and the power to impound funds voted by Congress. Of the three, only the power to wage war was directly established by the Constitution, and that was ambiguously set forth.

WAR POWERS

Dissatisfaction with the conduct of the Vietnam war caused controversy over presidential war powers during the Johnson administration. The controversy both continued and expanded during the Nixon administration. The Senate in 1972 moved to limit and define those powers, but the House refused to go along.

Background. Article II, Section 2, of the Constitution contains the only authority for the President's role in foreign affairs. It provides that "The President shall be Commander in Chief of the Army and Navy of the United States and of the Militia of the several states, when called into the actual service of the United States," and it gives the President authority to appoint ambassadors and make treaties. These powers were modified by other sections of the Constitution which gave Congress the power to "provide for the common defense," declare war, raise and support armies and ratify the treaties negotiated by the executive.

The President's power to direct the conduct of war has been spelled out and substantially strengthened over the years by precedents established by strong activist Presidents such as Lincoln and Theodore Roosevelt. The growth of presidential prerogatives in foreign policy accelerated during World War II and its aftermath as the United States attained—and exercised—worldwide power.

Recent years witnessed increasingly frequent examples of presidential moves which involved the country in armed conflicts without the authorization of Congress. "Five times in the past 10 years," historian Henry Steele Commager told the Foreign Relations Committee in 1971, "Presidents have mounted major military interventions in foreign nations without prior consultation with the Congress: the Bay of Pigs, the invasion of the Dominican Republic, the attacks on North Vietnam, Cambodia and Laos." Until it became clear that the war in Vietnam would not be easily or quickly won, most members of Congress were of the view that modern diplomatic and military conditions required that the President have the free exercise of his powers to conduct foreign policy and defend the nation.

Vietnam Impact. As opposition to the Vietnam war grew both among the public and in Congress, a number of members of Congress began to question the authority of the Johnson administration to involve the United States so heavily in Vietnam. The administration maintained that Article II of the Constitution gave the President authority to undertake armed intervention there. Moreover, it claimed congressional authorization from the Gulf of Tonkin resolution (H J Res 1145—PL 88-408), approved by Congress on Aug. 7, 1964. The resolution, passed after the United States reported that two U.S. destroyers had been attacked by North Vietnamese PT boats, declared congressional support for the President's "determination

...to take all necessary measures" to repel attacks on U.S. forces and to prevent further aggression.

During the Nixon administration continuing opposition to the war led Congress in 1970 to repeal the Tonkin resolution and to begin consideration of bills to force an end to U.S. involvement in the war. Then, in 1972, the Senate passed a more general bill (S 2956) designed to place restrictions on the President's use of armed forces without prior congressional approval and providing procedures whereby Congress could overrule the President's decision to commit troops to combat in undeclared wars. The bill also defined the emergency circumstances in which the President could act on his own; sponsors said it was intended as a supplement to the Constitution.

S 2956 was strongly opposed by the Nixon administration which lobbied unsuccessfully to defeat it in the Senate. The administration was successful in the House, which passed a much modified version of S 2956. The House version dropped the Senate restrictions and "urged" the President to consult with Congress before sending Americans into armed conflict. Conferees met only once on the disparate versions. They made no headway toward resolving the differences and S 2956 died at session's end. The outcome indicated that a majority of members of Congress still conceded the need for executive supremacy in the area of war powers.

EXECUTIVE PRIVILEGE

Related to the war powers issue was a growing debate over the right of the executive branch to withhold information from Congress under the claim of executive privilege. The argument over executive privilege arose as Congress disputed the right of White House advisers to refuse to testify on the conduct of the Vietnam war. Executive privilege became a major issue at the start of the second Nixon term, in 1973, when the President at first indicated that his aides would invoke executive privilege rather than give testimony in the Watergate case.

Background. Executive privilege is not specifically sanctioned by the Constitution although some scholars feel that it is justified by the principle of separation of powers.

Because executive privilege is not usually invoked in writing, statistics on its historical use are scanty. It is known that it was first invoked by President Washington in 1796 when he refused a request by the House of Representatives for correspondence relating to the controversial Jay Treaty with Great Britain. After that the privilege was invoked by at least 18 of Washington's successors, usually only a few times.

The most common justification for resort to executive privilege has been the need for secrecy in military and diplomatic activities. The privilege has been invoked also by Presidents to avoid unwarranted exposure of individuals to unfavorable publicity, especially when documents or files contain incomplete, inaccurate or unsubstantiated information. Other reasons cited for invoking executive privilege have been the need for confidential exchange of ideas within the executive branch and fear that disclosures would interfere with criminal or security investigations.

Recent Controversy. During Nixon's first term, members of Congress were distressed by refusal of the President's national security adviser, Henry A. Kissinger, to testify before committees on the conduct of the Vietnam war. Congressional concern about the limits of executive privilege intensified after publication of the "Pentagon Papers" in 1971 disclosed that Johnson administration war decisions had been made with extraordinary secrecy.

In July and August 1971 the Senate Judiciary Subcommittee on Separation of Powers held hearings on executive privilege and on a bill introduced by Sen. J.W. Fulbright (D Ark.) to require that executive privilege be claimed only in person with a written assertion of the privilege from the President. The bill (S 1125) also provided that funds for the agency represented by the official be cut off until the written claim of executive privilege had been made.

During the hearings, Fulbright observed that "The elaborate new foreign policy apparatus in the White House is not an oddity or innovation of the present administration but rather the consummation of a long-term trend toward the centralization of foreign policy powers in a small elite of experts and intellectuals surrounding the President." A number of members of Congress voiced support for the bill; it was opposed by spokesmen for various Cabinet-level departments.

There was no action on S 1125. Shortly after the hearings ended, the President invoked executive privilege on a Foreign Relations Committee request for a five-year plan for military assistance to foreign countries. In a letter to the committee, Nixon spelled out his philosophy of executive privilege. He said he had told department heads that it was to be invoked only "in the most compelling circumstances." The letter continued: "The precedents on separation of powers established by my predecessors from first to last clearly demonstrate, however, that the President has the responsibility not to make available any information and material which would impair the orderly function of the executive branch of the government, since to do so would not be in the public interest."

IMPOUNDMENT OF FUNDS

Another old controversy between Congress and the executive resurfaced in 1972 when President Nixon refused to spend funds voted for several programs. Congresss argued that the President did not have the authority to refuse to spend appropriated funds, but Nixon found many precedents for his action and justified impoundment as a necessary anti-inflationary device.

Background. The Constitution, in assigning legislative powers to Congress and executive powers to the President, made no mention of impoundment. It provided, however, that "No money shall be drawn from the Treasury but in Consequence of Appropriations Made by Law...."

To the President, on the other hand, the Constitution gave the task of making sure that "the Laws be faithfully executed...."

What the Constitution did not spell out, at least not beyond debate, was whether the President was required to spend funds appropriated by Congress or whether he could make independent judgments on the timing and need for federal spending.

Congress gave some legislative authority for impoundment in passing the Anti-Deficiency Act of 1905. That act required the executive branch to subdivide appropriations to ensure that government agencies would not make commitments in excess of amounts appropriated. In 1950, an omnibus appropriations act provided additional authority for the executive branch to create reserves to provide for contingencies or for savings made possible by developments after appropriations were voted.

Presidential precedents for impoundment go back to the administration of Thomas Jefferson. After the New Deal, as the federal budget grew larger and the American economy more complex, impoundment more and more came into use as a presidential fiscal policy tool.

Recent examples of impoundment include President Truman's decision to ignore a rider on an Omnibus Appropriations Act providing for a loan to Spain. During the Kennedy and Johnson years, Congress provided funds for new weapons systems opposed by Defense Secretary Robert S. McNamara, but in most cases the administration simply refused to develop the systems.

Nixon Impoundments. As Nixon ended his first term in 1972, the impoundment debate heated up amid congressional charges that the President was impounding funds not only to avoid inflation but also to assert his own priorities for the federal government over those of Congress.

The issue was joined in October 1972, in the waning days of the 92nd Congress, when the Senate killed Nixon's request for legislation setting a $250-billion ceiling on fiscal 1973 outlays. His request denied, Nixon set out to meet that goal anyway be vetoing bills and impounding funds.

According to estimates gathered by Rep. Joe L. Evins (D Tenn.) and made public Jan. 15, 1973, the administration had impounded $12-billion in funds appropriated by Congress. The amount included $6-billion in sewage treatment funds voted by Congress over Nixon's veto.

Executive Branch Reorganization

The Reorganization Act of 1949, which grew out of the recommendations of the first Hoover Commission, authorized the President to reorganize the executive branch through the medium of a reorganization plan. Unlike a bill, a reorganization plan cannot be amended by Congress. It takes effect automatically 60 days after being submitted to Congress unless either chamber passes a resolution of disapproval by majority vote.

As originally enacted, the Reorganization Act allowed the creation of cabinet-level departments by reorganization plan. That authority was rescinded by Congress in 1964 following a controversy over a plan by President Kennedy to create a Department of Housing and Urban Affairs. (*Congress and the Nation Vol. I, p. 1455; Congress and the Nation Vol. II p. 655*)

Between 1949 and the end of 1972, 91 reorganization plans were submitted to Congress. Of these, 71 became effective and 19 were rejected. President Nixon submitted six plans (in contrast to 17 submitted by President Johnson). Nixon submitted one in 1969, four in 1970 and one in 1971; all were accepted.

In addition to the reorganization plans, President Nixon sent Congress an ambitious plan for reorganization of the cabinet-level departments, which would have to be accomplished through legislation. The proposal, submitted in 1971, was widely praised by political scientists but was generally unpopular with Congress. By the end of 1971, the plan was clearly dead. Hearings were not resumed in 1972, although the President's state-of-the-union message urged congressional action on executive branch reorganization.

1969

Congress granted President Nixon's request for extension of presidential authority to submit executive reorganization plans to Congress. It also let the only reorganization plan he submitted that year go into effect. The plan authorized the President to designate the chairman of the Interstate Commerce Commission.

Reorganization Act Extension. Congress early in the session passed a bill (S 1058—PL 91-5) extending the 1949 Reorganization Act through April 1, 1971. The act had expired Dec. 31, 1968. The Senate passed S 1058 by voice vote and without debate. The House passed it on a 335-44 roll-call vote.

ICC Chairman. Reorganization Plan No. 1 extended to the President the authority to designate the chairman of the Interstate Commerce Commission (ICC) from among its members and gave the chairman administrative authority. Previously, the chairmanship had rotated annually among the 11 commissioners. The ICC had been the only major regulatory agency whose chairman the President could not designate.

1970

The President submitted four reorganization plans to Congress. All were important, and the Congress agreed to all of them.

The four plans established an Office of Telecommunications Policy in the Executive Office of the President; an Office of Management and Budget (OMB) and a Domestic Council to replace the Bureau of the Budget in the Executive Office; an Environmental Protection Agency independent of the cabinet departments; and a National Oceanic and Atmospheric Agency in the Department of Commerce.

Congress also passed an administration bill converting the Post Office Department into a public corporation. (*Details, p. 441*)

Telecommunications Policy. Reorganization Plan No. 1 of 1970 abolished the Office of Telecommunications Management in the Office of Emergency Preparedness and established an Office of Telecommunications Policy in the Executive Office. The House Government Operations Committee recommended against adoption of a resolution to disapprove the plan and the resolution was never brought to the House floor for a vote. No resolution to veto the plan was introduced in the Senate.

The new office was to advise the President on issues involving telecommunications (telephone, telegraph, broadcasting, etc.) and help formulate policies and coordinate the government's own telecommunications systems. It was to be headed by a director and deputy director appointed by the President and confirmed by the Senate.

Office of Management and Budget. Reorganization Plan No. 2 made the first administrative rearrangement of a President's traditional relationship with his cabinet officers and budget officials in more than 30 years. It established an Office of Management and Budget which was to be built around the nucleus of the existing Bureau of the Budget and both carry on and expand its functions. The plan also established a Domestic Council, consisting chiefly of the Vice President and cabinet members heading the domestic departments, which was to advise the President on programs and policies outside the foreign and military areas. To a considerable extent, it was to be a domestic counterpart of the National Security Council. The executive director of the Council was to be an Assistant to the President and not subject to Senate confirmation.

The House defeated a resolution disapproving the plan by a 164-193 roll-call vote. Opponents of the plan said the reorganization should be accomplished through legislation and that the proposal, as it stood, reduced the congressional role in management of programs. No resolution of disapproval was submitted in the Senate.

The plan said the OMB would broaden the existing functions of the Bureau of the Budget to create greater executive capability for analyzing, coordinating, evaluating and improving the efficiency of government programs. It would coordinate the complex system of federal grants, which often involved not only more than one federal agency in a particular area but also various agencies at the state and local levels. It would assist in implementing major legislation under which several agencies shared responsibility for action.

The Domestic Council, supported by its own permanent professional staff of 40 to 50, would formulate domestic policy positions on broad questions as well as specific programs. The council would not work as a committee but would be divided into subcommittees formed to deal with particular problems. The subcommittees would eliminate the need for special advisory groups and task forces. The Council, the White House said, was not designed to deprive cabinet members of access to the President. Rather, it was intended to involve them more directly in the formulation of domestic policy and provide them with new perspectives.

Mr. Nixon appointed John D. Ehrlichman, who had been an Assistant to the President for domestic affairs, as executive director of the Domestic Council. Robert P. Mayo, the director of the Bureau of the Budget, was appointed to head the OMB. Neither job was subject to congressional confirmation.

Environmental Protection Agency. Reorganization Plan No. 3 established the Environmental Protection Agency (EPA) and consolidated in it all major programs to combat pollution. The plan was generally popular with Congress and a resolution of disapproval was turned down in the House by voice vote. No such resolution was submitted in the Senate.

The EPA was to be composed of the Federal Water Quality Administration and certain pesticide research programs from the Interior Department; the National Air Pollution Control Administration and parts of the Environmental Control Administration and the Food and Drug Administration from the Department of Health, Education and Welfare; the pesticides registration authority of the Department of Agriculture; the standard-

---

President's Advisory Council

The 1970 Reorganization Plans were recommended to the President by the President's Advisory Council on Executive Organization. The special council was named by President Nixon in April 1969 to advise him on ways to increase the effectiveness of the Executive Branch.

Roy L. Ash, president of Litton Industries, was chairman of the Advisory Council. Other members were Walter N. Thayer, president of the Whitney Communications Corp. and a partner in the Whitcom Investment Co.; Richard M. Pagot, senior partner in the New York City management consultant firm of Cresap, McCormick and Paget; Frederick R. Kappel, former chairman of the board of American Telephone and Telegraph Co.; George P. Baker, retired dean of the Harvard Graduate School of Business Administration; and John B. Connally, governor of Texas from 1962 until 1968.

---

setting functions of the Atomic Energy Commission; the Federal Radiation Council's functions; and certain research authority of the Council on Environmental Quality.

Reorganization Plan No. 4 established the National Oceanic and Atmospheric Agency as a division of the Commerce Department. Resolutions to disapprove the plan were turned down in the House by voice vote and in the Senate by a vote of 5-47.

The NOAA assumed the functions of the Environmental Science Services Administration, already in the Commerce Department; the Marine Minerals Technology program of the Bureau of Mines; most of the programs of the Bureau of Commercial Fisheries and the marine sports fishing program of the Bureau of Sport Fisheries and Wildlife, all in Interior; the Office of Sea Grant Programs of the National Science Foundation; parts of the Army's U.S. Lake Survey; the Navy's National Oceanographic Data and Instrumentation Center; and the national data buoy program of the Transportation Department.

1971

President Nixon sent Congress one Reorganization Plan in 1971. The proposal, to merge federal voluntary programs into a new agency, was accepted. After the President submitted the plan, the authority to propose reorganization plans expired. Congress let it lapse for eight months and then extended it through April 1, 1973.

Nixon also proposed a major reorganization of the cabinet departments which would have reduced the current 12 departments to eight. The proposal, which could only be accomplished by legislation, had considerable support from both Democratic and Republican liberals. There was strong opposition from business and labor groups which had a comfortable relationship with the bureaucracy as it was. There was also concern in Congress that such a reorganization would force a dismantling and reorganization of congressional committees. Hearings were held on the proposals, but no action was taken, and it was clear that none was likely.

ACTION. Reorganization Plan No. 1 of 1971 merged the Peace Corps, VISTA and other federal volunteer pro-

Gardner Testimony

John W. Gardner, former secretary of HEW and chairman of Common Cause, in testimony on the President's departmental reorganization proposals, summed up the arguments for the proposals and the trouble they ran into.

The President's recommendations "distill some of the best thinking of a generation of thoughtful students of government. The reorganization is long overdue.

"Structurally speaking, most organizations, public and private, are designed to solve problems that no longer exist. There is no better example than our federal government. It is a museum in which all our past purposes are displayed under the glass of anachronistic bureaucratic compartments.

"Perhaps the most common question about the President's proposals is whether the four new agencies will be too big to manage effectively. I do not regard the question as crucial. We are stuck with bigness. The critical question is how we manage bigness, how we devolve authority to lower levels, how we force our big institutions to remain responsive, how we prevent them from smothering individuality and creativity.

"It is a fact, unknown to the general public, that some elements in Congress and some special interest lobbies have never really wanted the departmental secretaries to be strong. Questions of public policy nominally lodged with the Secretary are often decided far beyond the Secretary's reach by a trinity consisting of 1) representatives of an outside lobby, 2) middle-level bureaucrats and 3) selected members of Congress, particularly those concerned with appropriations. In a given field these people may have collaborated for years. They may have formed deep personal and family friendships. They have traded innumerable favors. They have seen secretaries come and go. Often they couldn't care less about White House messages, or pronouncements from the top of the department. They have a durable alliance that cranks out legislation and appropriations in behalf of their special interest.

"When a reorganization plan comes up, the special interests move in like hornets, and most of our leaders tend to come down on the side of one or another of those special interests. And the reorganization plan fails to come off."

---

grams into a new agency called ACTION. The new agency came into existence July 1 after the House defeated a resolution to disapprove the plan by a 131-224 roll-call vote and the Senate defeated a similar resolution by a 29-54 roll call.

The plan initially would consolidate in ACTION the following programs: Volunteers in Service to America (VISTA), from the Office of Economic Opportunity (OEO); Auxiliary and Special Volunteer Programs, from OEO; Foster Grandparents, from the Department of Health, Education and Welfare (HEW); Retired Senior Volunteer Program (RSVP), from HEW; and Service Corps of Retired Executive (SCORE) and Active Corps of Executives (ACE), both from the Small Business Administration.

In addition, the President in his message proposing the reorganization said that after ACTION was established he would "delegate" to it the Peace Corps and the Office of Voluntary Action (then in the Department of Housing and Urban Development). Unlike outright transfers, delegations did not have to be approved by Congress.

In his message, the President said consolidation of volunteer services would enable the government to expand testing and development of innovations in voluntary programs and would provide a more effective system of recruitment, training and placement than the existing division permitted. These arguments were also put forward by congressional supporters of the plan. Its opponents in Congress unsuccessfully argued that because there was little similarity among the programs, nothing was to be gained from merging them except an additional layer of bureaucracy.

Reorganization Act Extension. Congress Dec. 1 cleared a bill (HR 6283—PL 92-179) extending the 1949 Reorganization Act through April 1, 1973. HR 6283 amended the Act to prohibit the submission of more than one plan within any 30-day period and plans dealing with more than one subject. It also authorized any member of the House or Senate Government Operations Committee to file a motion to discharge the committee from further consideration of any reorganization bill not reported by the committee within 20 calendar days from the date it was submitted to Congress.

The Reorganization Act temporarily expired April 1, 1970. The House passed HR 6283 May 3 by a 301-20 roll-call vote and the Senate passed the bill Nov. 19 by voice vote and without debate.

Cabinet Reorganization Proposed. Congress in 1971 held hearings but took no action on President Nixon's proposals to consolidate several cabinet departments. In his 1971 state of the union message, the President proposed reducing the present 12 cabinet departments to eight. The Departments of State, Treasury, Defense and Justice would remain; functions of the Post Office Department would be turned over to a public corporation under legislation passed in 1970. The other seven that would be consolidated into four were: Labor, Agriculture, Transportation, Interior, Commerce, Health, Education and Welfare, and Housing and Urban Development.

The four new departments and their functions would be:

● Department of Natural Resources—Land, recreation, water resources, energy and mineral resources, and marine resources.

● Department of Human Resources—Health services, income maintenance and security, education, manpower, and social and rehabilitation services.

● Department of Economic Development—Food and commodities, domestic and international commerce, science and technology, labor relations and standards, and statistical economic development.

● Department of Community Development—Housing, community development, metropolitan development and renewal and transportation.

President Nixon said his proposal would organize departments around "the great purposes of government." Rather than scatter responsibility by adding new levels of bureaucracy, he said, "we would focus and concentrate the responsibility for getting problems solved."

The executive reorganization proposal grew out of a two-year study by the President's Advisory Council on Executive Reorganization, headed by Roy L. Ash, president of Litton Industries.

The President repeated his recommendations in a special cabinet reorganization message on March 25. This time he renamed the proposed new economics department a Department of Economic Affairs (instead of Economic Development); there was no change in the names of the three other proposed new departments. Clark MacGregor, counselor to the President for congressional liaison, acknowledged March 28 that the cabinet reorganization plan would be the most difficult of the five major Nixon administration programs to move through the 92nd Congress. "It's the most difficult because it steps on the most special-interest toes" he said.

Hearings on the proposal were held in May and June by the Senate Government Operations Committee and in June by the House Government Operations Subcommittee on Legislation and Military Operations. Although the proposal was supported by a number of cabinet secretaries and some others, it made no headway in either chamber. Some members of Congress were dubious because they feared the plan would entail a shifting of jurisdictions among congressional committees or that it might do away with some government jobs. The most entrenched obstacles to reform were business and labor groups that had a comfortable relationship with the bureaucracy as it was.

Sen. Abraham Ribicoff (D Conn.), testifying Nov. 16 before the Senate Government Operations Committee on a separate bill (S 1430) to create a Department of Community Development, voiced opposition on a broader basis. "The President," he said, "has failed to provide us with a vision of where we are going and how reorganization will help us move there. What are the administration's community development goals for 1975 and 1980? In short, what are we organizing for? We do not know." The President himself announced Nov. 11, when he nominated Earl Butz as Secretary of Agriculture, that he had changed his mind about splitting the Department of Agriculture among the four proposed new departments. That old-line department would remain intact, he said, except for some peripheral programs not directly connected with farm production.

 **Nixon Cabinet, Staff**

WHITE HOUSE STAFFERS OUTSTRIP CABINET AS KEY FIGURES

Several weeks prior to his first term, President Nixon introduced his newly named cabinet members in an event televised across the nation. Each nominee was listening as Mr. Nixon praised the team and cited its superior leadership ability. He asserted that "every one is an independent thinker," and pledged he would never accept a cabinet of yes men.

But as the first term unfolded, it was clear that President Nixon's closest advisers were senior members of his White House staff. The cabinet had obviously yielded much of the influence it once had. By 1970, no fewer than six of the original twelve were being talked of as potential dropouts. Despite a number of early meetings, cabinet officials soon began to make regular complaints that the President was isolated.

Turnover Rate

After an initial flurry of activity, including one meeting with the wives present, the importance of the cabinet seemed to fade. Soon there were complaints that the President—guarded by his White House staff—was inaccessible to cabinet members.

When President Nixon began his second term, only two of the original cabinet members remained. In fact, the Nixon cabinet posted the greatest four-year turnover rate in the history of the Republic.

Only Secretary of State William P. Rogers remained in his original position at the start of Nixon's second term. Treasury Secretary George P. Shultz began as Secretary of Labor, rose quickly in the President's eyes, and after a stint as Director of the Office of Management and Budget, was named to the Treasury post in December 1972.

Interior Secretary Walter Hickel was fired in November 1970, following disagreements with Nixon and his top aides.

Treasury Secretary David M. Kennedy became an ambassador at large after his inexperience in dealing with Congress and the press became a problem for the administration.

Agriculture Secretary Clifford M. Hardin, a former chancellor at the University of Nebraska, also had problems mastering the political end of the job and was replaced in late 1971 by the more savvy Earl L. Butz.

Housing and Urban Affairs Secretary George Romney, considered the most liberal member of the President's original cabinet, stayed the full four years, but expressed a sense of relief when it was over. Postmaster General Winton M. Blount left after reorganizing the postal system. He was defeated in a bid for an Alabama Senate seat in the November, 1972, elections.

Attorney General John N. Mitchell, the President's 1968 campaign director, emerged as the strongest cabinet member early in the administration. But after three stormy years in the job, he resigned to manage the 1972

Nixon campaign. When his name became implicated in the Watergate scandal, he left that post, too.

The President's chief fund-raiser in 1968, Maurice H. Stans, became Commerce Secretary but failed to establish a meaningful role for the department. He returned to raising funds in the 1972 Nixon campaign.

Robert H. Finch, a long-time friend of the President's and the lieutenant governor of California, was named secretary of health, education and welfare. Finch was unable to bring the government's largest bureaucracy under control and was moved to a less sensitive job as adviser to the President.

Defense Secretary Melvin R. Laird survived the entire four years, but had made it clear that he would not stay more than one term.

Three of the President's "second" cabinet appointees also had left by 1973. John B. Connally, named treasury secretary in 1971, stayed just one year, after emerging as one of the President's top advisers.

The resignation of Commerce Secretary Peter G. Peterson was accepted by the President in December, 1972, reportedly because some White House aides felt he was too close to some journalists and liberals, including Sen. Charles H. Percy (R Ill.).

Labor Secretary James Hodgson served 18 months. He never managed to become a presidential "insider" and failed to establish a workable relationship with union leaders.

Former Governors. The original Nixon cabinet included four former governors who had commanded smaller budgets and staffs in their home states, but who at least had been in charge. In the cabinet they found their control was not as great as they had anticipated.

Transportation Secretary John A. Volpe—who left the cabinet after the first term—remarked in 1970, "Being a governor (of Massachusetts, 1961-68) can be tough, but at least when you made a decision you just put it into practice.... I didn't realize that there would be quite so many people to check with on everything."

CABINET BIOGRAPHIES, 1969-1972

AGRICULTURE

Clifford M. Hardin was nominated and confirmed by the Senate Jan. 20, 1969, and remained secretary of agriculture until he resigned on Nov. 11, 1971.

Hardin was chancellor of the University of Nebraska for 14 years prior to his appointment to President Nixon's cabinet.

Hardin was born on a farm near Knightstown, Ind., on Oct. 9, 1915. He participated in 4-H club activities and won a club scholarship to Purdue University, where he earned his B.A., M.S. and Ph.D. degrees. After teaching at the University of Wisconsin and Michigan State University, he became director of the agricultural experiment station at Michigan State and later dean of its School of Agriculture. In 1954, Hardin became chancellor of the University of Nebraska. During his tenure, the school quadrupled in size to 30,000 students and played an active role in the development of a new university in Turkey and agricultural assistance programs in Latin America.

Earl L. Butz was nominated as secretary of agriculture on Nov. 11, 1971, replacing Clifford M. Hardin. He was confirmed by the Senate Dec. 2, 1971 and continued in that capacity into the President's second term.

Butz was no stranger to the Washington political scene at the time of his appointment. As assistant secretary of agriculture for marketing and foreign affairs from 1954-57, Butz served under Ezra Taft Benson, President Eisenhower's agriculture secretary.

The Butz nomination encountered stiff Senate opposition from both farm-belt Republicans and liberal Democrats. Senate critics accused Butz of maintaining too close ties with corporate farming or "agribusiness." Butz also had earned a reputation as a conservative opposed to price supports as well as to the food stamp program and President Nixon's proposed welfare reform.

Despite the political storm surrounding Butz' nomination, the Senate confirmed him by a 51-44 vote.

Born in Albion, Ind., on July 3, 1909, Butz attended public schools in Wawaka, Ind. He earned a B.S.A. degree from Purdue University in 1932, and his doctorate from Purdue in 1937. Upon completing graduate work, he worked for one year as a research economist with the Federal Land Bank in Louisville, Ky.

For the next 16 years, Butz taught agricultural economics at Purdue, chairing the agricultural economics department from 1946-54. In 1954, President Eisenhower appointed Butz assistant secretary of agriculture. While assistant secretary, he headed the American delegation to the United Nations Food and Agriculture Organization three times.

In 1957, Butz was named dean of the School of Agriculture at Purdue, a post he held for more than 10 years. From 1968-71, he served as Purdue's dean of continuing education.

ATTORNEY GENERAL

John N. Mitchell was nominated and confirmed as attorney general on Jan. 20, 1969. President Nixon accepted Mitchell's resignation on Feb. 15, 1972.

Mitchell, considered one of the nation's leading specialists in municipal and state financing, never had been in politics until Mr. Nixon tapped him as his campaign manager in May 1968. A Wall Street lawyer, Mitchell became one of Mr. Nixon's law partners after their two firms merged in January 1967. Associates said the two men achieved an unusual rapport almost from the day they met, and Mitchell eventually became one of the main draftsmen of the calm, no-excitement political campaign that won Mr. Nixon the presidency.

After his resignation as attorney general, Mitchell became director of the Committee for the Re-election of the President on April 13, 1972. He left the re-election campaign on July 1, 1972, and on May 10, 1973, was one

---

Vice President Agnew Biography

Profession: Attorney.

Born: Nov. 9, 1918, Baltimore, Md.

Home: Towson, Md.

Religion: Episcopal.

Education: Attended Johns Hopkins University, Baltimore, for three years; Univ. of Baltimore, B.L., 1947.

Offices: Baltimore County Board of Appeals, 1958-61; Baltimore County executive, 1962-66; governor of Maryland, 1967-69; vice president since 1969.

Military: Army, 1942-46; Bronze Star; discharged as 2nd lieutenant; one year in reactivated reserve during Korean war.

Memberships: AHEPA, Kiwanis, American Legion.

Family: Wife, Elinor (Judy); four children.

Career Highlights: Agnew, who changed his political affiliation from Democratic to Republican in 1946, got his earliest taste of politics working in the four successful House races of Rep. James P.S. Devereux (R Md. 1951-59), a Marine Corps war hero. In 1960, Agnew made his first bid for elective office, campaigning unsuccessfully for judge of Baltimore County Circuit Court.

In 1961, Agnew was ousted by the Democrats from the post he had held since 1958 on the County Board of Zoning Appeals. The following year, he was elected Baltimore County executive.

As the county's chief executive officer, Agnew supported and signed into law an ordinance barring discrimination in some public accommodations, one of the first such ordinances in the nation.

In 1966, Agnew waged an aggressive campaign for the Republican gubernatorial nomination, stressing his experience with urban and suburban problems. He supported a limited open-housing bill, one that would cover "only new housing developments or new apartment ventures." Agnew easily defeated four nominal primary opponents with an 80,651-vote plurality (83.5 percent).

Agnew was aided in the November election by a serious split in the Democratic party (Maryland is registered more than 3-1 Democratic).

In what was regarded as a victory over the "white backlash," Agnew won the election with an 81,775-vote plurality (49.6 percent) over George P. Mahoney, the anti-open-housing Democratic nominee, to become the fifth Republican governor in Maryland's history.

In 1967 and early 1968, Agnew was a leading supporter of New York Gov. Nelson A. Rockefeller for the Presidency, repeatedly urging him to declare his candidacy for the Republican nomination. But after Rockefeller temporarily declined to run on March 21, 1968, Agnew moved toward the candidacy of Richard M. Nixon. His final break with the Rockefeller candidacy did not come, however, until the opening day of the Republican national convention, when he announced his support for Nixon.

---

of four men indicted by a federal grand jury in New York on charges of conspiring to arrange a secret $200,000 contribution to the President's 1972 campaign.

Mitchell was born Sept. 5, 1913, in Detroit, Mich. He gained his undergraduate and law degrees from Fordham University, N.Y. During World War II he was a Navy commander of motor torpedo boats in the Pacific, and John F. Kennedy was one of his junior officers. As an expert on public finance, he helped shape many of New York Gov. Nelson A. Rockefeller's revenue-raising proposals, including housing and university construction plans. When his law firm merged with that of President-elect Nixon, Mitchell became a senior partner in the renamed firm of Nixon, Mudge, Rose, Guthrie, Alexander and Mitchell.

Richard G. Kleindienst was nominated Feb. 15, 1972. Following one of the most prolonged fights in history over a presidential cabinet appointment, he was confirmed June 9, 1972, by **a key 64-19 roll-call vote** as attorney general of the United States.

The Senate debate, which raged for four months, centered on charges accusing Kleindienst of involvement in an out-of-court settlement of antitrust charges against International Telephone and Telegraph Corp. (ITT).

Nixon announced his selection of Kleindienst when John N. Mitchell stepped down from the post to assume new duties as head of Nixon's re-election campaign. Kleindienst had been acting attorney general since that time.

Kleindienst was approved by the Senate Judiciary Committee by a 13-0 vote on Feb. 24, and the way seemed clear for quick Senate confirmation.

However, the issue was re-opened after columns by syndicated columnist Jack Anderson appeared in newspapers on Feb. 29 and March 1. The columns strongly implied that Nixon administration officials had agreed to settle the antitrust case against ITT on terms favorable to the company, in return for a $400,000 contribution by ITT's Sheraton subsidiary to the costs of the Republican national convention, then scheduled for San Diego.

Kleindienst demanded the Senate Judiciary Committee re-open its hearings so that he could clear himself; however, evidence presented at the committee hearings proved inconclusive as to Kleindienst's role in the ITT dispute.

At the swearing-in ceremony on June 12, Nixon expressed new confidence in Kleindienst for the way he conducted himself during the long ordeal of Senate confirmation, saying, "Only when a man has been through adversity do you find out how really strong he is...a great ship is not tested by smooth sailing, but only by rough seas."

Kleindienst served under Mitchell as deputy attorney general from the beginning of the Nixon administration.

Prior to that position, he was a member of the Arizona legislature from 1953-54, and in 1964 he ran unsuccessfully as the Republican candidate for governor. In 1968, Kleindienst served as the national director of field operations for Nixon's presidential campaign.

The son of a brakeman on the Santa Fe Railroad, Kleindienst was born in Winslow, Arizona, on August 5, 1923.

Kleindienst served during World War II as a navigator in the 15th Air Force division and achieved the rank of first lieutenant. After graduating Phi Beta Kappa from Harvard in 1947 and from Harvard Law School, Kleindienst returned to Arizona in 1950.

He joined the firm of Jennings, Strouss, Salmon, and Trask in Phoenix, which he left to form Shimmel, Hill, Kleindienst and Bishop in 1958.

Kleindienst resigned from the cabinet April 30, 1973, in the wake of charges that the Justice Department had not conducted an adequate investigation of the Watergate break-in.

COMMERCE

Maurice H. Stans was nominated and confirmed as part of the original Nixon cabinet on Jan. 20, 1969. He served until Jan. 27, 1973.

Stans, Director of the Budget Bureau in the Eisenhower administration, was an accountant and banking executive by profession and a strong advocate of fiscal restraint.

Stans was born in Shakopee, Minn., March 22, 1908, the son of an immigrant Belgian house painter. He left his home town at the age of 17 with a saxophone and $151 he had earned from playing at dances. He became an office boy in the Chicago accounting firm of Alexander Grant & Co. in 1928 and rose to executive partner in 10 years.

By 1955, he had made the once small company the nation's tenth largest in its field and amassed enough wealth to create his own charitable foundation.

As a young man, Stans studied accounting at night at Northwestern University. He later studied at Columbia University, but his only degrees are honorary ones.

Stans moved back briefly into politics in 1962 to raise money for Mr. Nixon's attempt to win the California governorship. In the 1968 presidential campaign, he helped Mr. Nixon raise more than $20-million for campaign expenses.

After his resignation from the cabinet, Stans served as chairman of the Finance Committee to Re-elect the President.

On May 10, 1973, Stans was indicted, along with former Attorney General John N. Mitchell and two others, on charges of conspiring to arrange a secret $200,000 contribution to the President's campaign.

Peter G. Peterson was nominated to be secretary of commerce Jan. 27, 1972, and confirmed by the Senate Feb. 21, 1972. On Dec. 6, 1972, press secretary Ronald L. Ziegler announced that Peterson would be leaving the cabinet at the end of the President's first term.

Peterson, called "the economic Kissinger," replaced Maurice Stans who resigned to become the chief money raiser for Nixon's re-election campaign.

Peterson came to Washington in 1971 when Nixon appointed him executive director of the newly created Council on International Economic Policy.

Born in Kearney, Nebraska on June 5, 1926, Peterson received a B.S. degree from Northwestern University, graduating summa cum laude in 1947. He went to work in 1948 for Market Facts Inc., a Chicago company specializing in market counsel and research. He became executive vice president of the firm in 1952. While engaged in market analysis, Peterson took night courses at the University of Chicago and received his master's in business administration in 13 months.

Peterson joined Bell and Howell in 1958 as an executive vice president. He was elected president in 1961 at the age of 34, and two years later became chief executive officer. He was elected chairman of the board in 1968.

Peterson believed that the United States needed at least limited government planning if it was to compete with relatively regimented economies, such as Japan's. He had a major voice in the international component of the economic controls which Nixon announced Aug. 15, 1971.

DEFENSE

Melvin R. Laird was nominated and confirmed on Jan. 20, 1969, and resigned four years later on Jan. 20, 1973. On June 6, 1973, the White House announced Laird would become the President's chief domestic adviser.

Laird was the first elected politician to head the Defense Department since it was established in 1949. Previously, the department had been headed mainly by lawyers, financiers and business executives. Elected to Congress in 1952, Laird established a reputation in the House as one of his party's leading theoreticians and work-horses. At the time of his selection to head the Defense Department, he was the powerful chairman of the House Republican Conference, the party's caucus, and a member of the Republican Coordinating Committee, the party's highest policy-making body.

Laird's prestige and power were acquired largely because of his participation on Republican National Convention Platform Committees since 1952. He was vice chairman of the committee in 1960, when he assumed a crucial role in guiding through a controversial Nixon-Rockefeller platform accord which had threatened to disrupt the platform operation. As full chairman of the 1964 platform group, he was instrumental in the writing of a platform acceptable to presidential candidate Barry M. Goldwater in the face of stiff resistance from the party's liberal wing.

He also emerged as a top party spokesman and ideologist through his service as chairman of a joint House-Senate GOP committee which in 1962 drafted a 2,500-word declaration of Republican principles and policy to dispel the party's "negative" image, and as editor of two books, *The Conservative Papers* and *Republican Papers* in 1964 and 1968, respectively. He also wrote *A House Divided: America's Strategy Gap* in 1962, in which he advocated foreign and military policy unity, a firm policy of deterrence, continued testing of nuclear weapons, training for guerrilla warfare and a reduction in taxes accompanied by a cut in nondefense spending.

Laird was born Sept. 1, 1922, in Omaha, Neb., but was reared and educated in Marshfield, Wis. He received a bachelor's degree from Carleton College, Northfield, Minn. During World War II, he served with the Navy in the Pacific. In 1946 he was elected to the Wisconsin senate to succeed his father, who had died. He continued as a state senator, becoming an expert on taxation, until his election to Congress in 1952.

HEALTH, EDUCATION AND WELFARE

Robert H. Finch was nominated and confirmed on Jan. 20, 1969. He was named counsellor to the President on June 6, 1970, and left the White House staff at the end of the President's first term. At the time of his cabinet appointment, Finch was the lieutenant governor of California. President Nixon described him as "a first-class strategist as well as a good tactician." Others who know him say Finch is "ambitious and brainy." He was the youngest member of the original Nixon cabinet.

Finch served as Mr. Nixon's national campaign manager in the 1960 presidential race and was active in Mr. Nixon's unsuccessful 1962 bid for the California governorship. He also was statewide campaign manager for Sen. George Murphy (R Calif.) in 1964. Finch was elected lieutenant governor in 1966 with the largest vote of any statewide candidate, leading a Republican ticket which captured all but the attorney general's post.

Finch was born Oct. 9, 1925, in Tempe, Ariz., but moved to California when he was a child. He was graduated from Occidental College in 1947 and from the University of California Law School in 1951. He organized a Young Republican Club at Occidental and went on to establish similar clubs at a dozen other colleges in southern California. Finch served in the Marine Corps during 1943-45 and was recalled to service during the Korean war.

Elliot L. Richardson was confirmed as secretary of health, education and welfare June 15, 1970. Nominated June 6 by Mr. Nixon to replace Robert H. Finch, Richardson had been appointed assistant secretary for legislation at HEW in 1957 by President Eisenhower and during his two year's stay he was responsible for major legislation affecting public welfare, social security, public health and juvenile delinquency. For four months during this period he served as acting secretary.

Appointed by President Nixon in 1969 as under secretary of state, Richardson earned a reputation as a creative manager. He was referred to as "probably the most effective administrator at Foggy Bottom in the last 10 years."

Richardson was born July 20, 1920, to a prominent Boston family that has made notable contributions in the fields of medicine, law, education and banking.

Richardson was graduated from Harvard and from Harvard Law School with honors. At law school he was student president of the Harvard Law Review. During World War II he rose from private to first lieutenant and was decorated with the Bronze Star. Richardson was law clerk to both Judge Learned Hand from 1947 to 1948 and to Supreme Court Justice Felix Frankfurter from 1948 to 1949.

A Republican, he was active in Massachusetts politics. In 1964 he won the lieutenant governorship, serving under John A. Volpe, now secretary of transportation. In 1962 he lost a GOP primary race for Massachusetts attorney general, but won election to that office in 1966, which he held until his 1969 appointment as under secretary at the State Department. He also served as an aide to Sen. Leverett Saltonstall (R Mass. 1945-67).

In 1959 and 1960 as a federal district attorney, he gained a reputation for fighting corruption. At that time he prosecuted the late Bernard Goldfine, key figure in the political case involving Sherman Adams, President Eisenhower's White House chief of staff.

On Nov. 28, 1972, President Nixon announced his intention to nominate Richardson as Secretary of Defense. Richardson was confirmed by the Senate Jan. 29, 1973. On April 30, 1973, following Richard G. Kleindienst's resignation, the President nominated Richarson to become attorney general, a post to which he was confirmed May 23, 1973.

HOUSING AND URBAN DEVELOPMENT

George Romney was part of the original Nixon cabinet, nominated and confirmed on Jan. 20, 1969. The President accepted Romney's resignation Nov. 27, 1972. Romney, a three-term governor of Michigan, brought to his job a first-hand knowledge of urban problems. He once described himself as a "realistic idealist," and he sees himself as bringing the idealism of his Mormon religion to business and politics in general.

A man of driving energy, Romney was one of the biggest Republican vote-getters in Michigan history. He first was elected governor in 1962 by 80,000 votes—becoming the state's first Republican governor in 14 years. He won again in 1964 by 383,000 votes and in 1966 by 568,000 votes. He was the first serious announced candidate for the GOP presidential nomination. However, he withdrew early in 1968, saying his candidacy had not "won wide acceptance."

Romney was born July 8, 1907, in a Mormon settlement in Chihuahua, Mexico. He and his family lived at various times in Idaho, Texas and California and eventually moved to Salt Lake City where Romney attended public school. He spent two years of required Mormon missionary duty abroad and then attended the University of Utah for one semester (1929). He later moved to Washington, D.C., where he attended George Washington University for a semester.

In 1930, Romney became an apprentice with the Aluminum Co. of America (Alcoa) and later became its Washington lobbyist. In 1939, he became director of the Detroit office of the Automobile Manufacturers Assn. (AMA) and in 1942 was named its general manager. He joined the Nash-Kelvinator Corp. in 1948 as a special assistant to the president and became vice president in 1950. Through a 1954 merger, the company became the American Motors Corp., and the subsequent death of the firm's president moved Romney into the presidency. He also was named general manager and chairman of the new corporation.

It was with American Motors that Romney won the respect of industrialists everywhere. Cutting out larger, uncompetitive lines and concentrating on the compact Rambler car, Romney led the company from its money-losing status to its peak by 1960. He startled the automobile world in 1961 by signing a three-year contract with the United Automobile Workers which included the first employee profit-sharing plan in the industry.

INTERIOR

Walter J. Hickel, nominated and confirmed on Jan. 23, 1969, was removed from his post by President Nixon on Nov. 25, 1970. Hickel was the most controversial cabinet nominee of the original Nixon cabinet and the only cabinet appointment which the Senate did not confirm unanimously. Final Senate consent, after four days of hearings, was by a 73-16 roll-call vote.

Hickel's opponents had charged he was more attuned to land utilization than to conservation and depicted him as a millionaire with close ties to the oil industry. Hickel, as governor of Alaska, where more than 95 per cent of the state's land is under federal ownership, favored the freeing of public lands for economic development.

Raised on a tenant farm in Claflin, Kan., where he was born Aug. 18, 1919, he left home at 20, armed with a high school diploma and the Kansas Golden Gloves welterweight championship. He arrived in Alaska in 1940 with only 37 cents in his pocket, took a job as a dishwasher, fought several professional prize fights, and worked at odd jobs including bartending, railroad work and building inspection for the Army Air Corps. In 1946,

he began a contracting and real estate business that later included ownership of a number of hotels.

In 1966, Hickel sought and won his first elective office—the governorship—when he defeated Gov. William A. Egan (D 1959-67). His only previous political experience was 10 years of service on the Republican National Committee (1954-64). He was one of the first GOP governors to endorse Mr. Nixon for the 1968 presidential nomination.

Hickel's departure from the cabinet was believed to have stemmed from his public disagreement with the administration over anti-war dissent.

Following President Nixon's April 30, 1970, announcement of the Cambodian incursion, Hickel, in a private letter to the President, expressed deep disagreement with what he regarded as a mistaken administration policy of alienating the nation's youth. The letter was leaked to the press May 6.

"We must win over our philosophical enemies by convincing them of the wisdom of the path we have chosen rather than ignoring the path they propose," Hickel wrote.

Hickel suggested the President consult with his own cabinet "on an individual and conversational basis" so that "we can gain greater insight into the problems confronting us all."

Rogers C. B. Morton was nominated Jan. 25, 1971, and confirmed Jan. 28, 1971. Morton left an eight-year political career in the House of Representatives and the chairmanship of the Republican National Committee to replace Walter J. Hickel as secretary of the interior. Hickel was removed from his Interior Department post by the President in November, 1970, and Morton assumed his new duties on Jan. 29, 1971.

Morton, 56, won a reputation as a successful conciliator during his political career. After the unsuccessful presidential bid of Barry Goldwater (R Ariz.) in 1964, he stumped the country pulling the Republican party together. He served as Richard Nixon's floor manager at the 1968 Republican national convention.

After Nixon won the election, Morton openly courted the job of interior secretary, but Nixon had promised that the position would go to a western governor. Morton accepted the Republican chairmanship instead at Nixon's request and succeeded Ray C. Bliss of Ohio to the post in April 1969.

Morton was born Sept. 19, 1914, in Louisville, Ky., into a family whose lineage goes back to Gen. George Rogers Clark, an explorer of the West. He was graduated from Yale University in 1937.

LABOR

James Day Hodgson was nominated June 10, 1970, by Mr. Nixon to replace George Pratt Shultz whom Nixon had named director of the newly created Office of Management and Budget.

Hodgson was confirmed June 17, 1970. He submitted his resignation Nov. 29, 1972. He moved up from under secretary of labor, a position he had held since the beginning of the Nixon administration. *(Shultz biography, p. 970)*

Before coming to Washington, Hodgson was vice president in charge of industrial relations at Lockheed Aircraft Corporation. In this position he bargained in labor negotiations with the 55,000 men of the International Association of Machinists.

Hodgson, a Democrat, joined Lockheed in 1941 as a personnel clerk, remaining there until 1969. He served as an air combat intelligence officer in the Navy for three years during World War II.

Born in Dawson, Minn., on Dec. 3, 1915, Hodgson received an A.B. degree from the University of Minnesota in 1938. He did graduate work at the University of Minnesota and the University of California at Los Angeles, where he was an instructor in labor relations for five years.

Hodgson has served as supervisor of youth employment for the state of Minnesota, as a consultant on manpower matters for the state of California, and as a member of the Los Angeles Mayor's Labor-Management Executive Committee.

POSTMASTER GENERAL

Winton M. Blount was nominated and confirmed on Jan. 20, 1969. He resigned from the cabinet Oct. 29, 1971, after which he unsuccessfully sought the Senate seat from Alabama held by Sen. John Sparkman (D).

Blount was the only southerner in the Nixon cabinet from 1969 to 1971. In making the appointment, Mr. Nixon said he had pledged to back Blount (pronounced Blunt) in "efforts to modernize the Post Office Department and to bring modern business techniques into it." Blount had a reputation for aggressiveness and managerial wizardry.

Blount helped formulate an administrative proposal made in May 1969 to convert the Post Office Department into a government-owned independent postal corporation.

The proposal took effect July 1, 1971, when the U.S. Postal Service took formal control from the defunct Post Office Department of delivering the nation's mail. Blount, who lost his post in the Nixon cabinet as of that date, remained in charge of the new corporation and retained the title of Postmaster General.

Blount was born Feb. 1, 1921, in Union Springs, Ala., and attended public schools there, Staunton (Va.) Military Academy and the University of Alabama. He served in World War II as an Army Air Corps bomber pilot. In 1946, he and his brother founded the Blount Brothers Corp., general contractors in Montgomery, Ala., with $28,000 worth of surplus earth-moving equipment and then built it into a multimillion-dollar enterprise. The firm has constructed space development projects at Cape Kennedy and several missile defense installations. In 1964, Blount helped form a biracial community affairs commission in Montgomery.

STATE

William P. Rogers was nominated and confirmed as secretary of state on Jan. 20, 1969. He was the only member of the original Nixon cabinet to remain in the same position into the President's second term.

Rogers brought to the office only limited experience in foreign affairs but a reputation as an able administrator and good lawyer. He also had a close relationship with President Nixon as a friend and long-time political adviser.

Prior to his appointment as secretary of state, Rogers had only brief assignments dealing with foreign affairs.

In 1955 he went to Geneva as chief American delegate at a United Nations conference on prison conditions and treatment of offenders. In 1960 he headed the American delegation to the independence ceremonies of Togo. After serving on the American delegation to the 20th UN General Assembly in 1965-66, he was given ambassadorial rank by President Johnson and assigned to a 14-nation UN ad hoc committee on Southwest Africa.

Rogers was born June 23, 1913, in Norfolk, N.Y., and attended public schools there and in Canton, N.Y. He received an A.B. degree in 1934 from Colgate University and an LL.B. in 1937 from the Cornell Law School.

After a short term with a Wall Street law firm, he was appointed assistant district attorney for New York County, a post he left in 1942 for a four-year stint in the Navy. This was followed by another brief term as assistant district attorney in New York. In 1947, he was appointed counsel to the Senate Special Committee to Investigate national defense programs. From 1948 to 1950, he was chief counsel of the Investigations Subcommittee of the Senate Committee on Expenditures in Executive Departments. It was during this period that Rogers first met Mr. Nixon, then a freshman congressman.

Rogers returned to private law practice in 1950. In the 1952 presidential campaign, he actively supported the Eisenhower-Nixon ticket. Rogers was traveling with Mr. Nixon when a furor arose over a political expense fund that had been set up for Nixon by some wealthy California backers. Rogers urged Nixon to stand fast and helped arrange the television speech which influenced Dwight D. Eisenhower to retain Nixon on the Republican ticket.

Rogers was named deputy attorney general in the new Eisenhower administration. In 1957, he was chosen to succeed Herbert Brownell as attorney general and became known for his strong stand on civil rights. He played a principal role in drafting the Civil Rights Act of 1957 and supervised the establishment of the Civil Rights Division in the Justice Department. In 1958, he was the chief architect of the agreement between Mr. Eisenhower and Mr. Nixon on the continuity in functions of the presidency in the event of presidential disability—an issue finally resolved by the 25th Amendment to the Constitution, approved by Congress in 1965 and ratified in 1967.

TRANSPORTATION

John A. Volpe was nominated and confirmed on Jan. 20, 1969. He was nominated Jan. 4, 1973, to become ambassador to Italy, a position to which he was confirmed Feb. 1, 1973.

Volpe had a background both in politics and the construction industry that stood him in good stead as head of the Department of Transportation. The department, established in 1966, coordinates the functions of various federal agencies involving safety and other matters in the aviation, automotive, highway, railway and pipeline sectors. One of Volpe's major jobs was supervising the vast Interstate Highway System, which he helped launch.

Volpe, three-time governor of Massachusetts, founded the Volpe Construction Co. in Malden, Mass.—now a multimillion-dollar firm conducting business in many of the eastern states. His public career began in 1953, when he became commissioner of public works in Massachusetts. As a member of the American Assn. of State Highway

Officials, he helped in the effort to get Congress to approve the interstate highway program in 1956. He was appointed that same year by President Eisenhower as the first federal highway administrator.

Volpe was born Dec. 8, 1908, in Wakefield, Mass., of immigrant Italian parents. After graduating from high school, he went to work as a hod carrier, became a plasterer and studied at night school to gain a degree in architectural engineering in 1930 from the Wentworth Institute in Boston. He founded his construction company in 1933 and served as its president until he became chairman of the board in 1960. During World War II, Volpe served in the Navy.

He first was elected to public office in 1960, when he won the governorship by 139,000 votes. He lost a bid for re-election by 5,000 votes to Democrat Endicott Peabody in 1962 but was re-elected in 1964 and won a four-year term in 1966. Volpe's administration was marked by steps to stamp out corruption and to streamline governmental machinery.

TREASURY

David M. Kennedy was nominated and confirmed as secretary of the treasury on Jan. 20, 1969. He served until Dec. 14, 1970, when he resigned to become an ambassador at large.

Kennedy spent the first 16 years of his working career with the Federal Reserve Board in Washington. At the time of his cabinet appointment, Kennedy was chairman of the board of the Continental Illinois National Bank and Trust Co. in Chicago, the nation's eighth largest bank.

Kennedy was born July 21, 1905, at Randolph, Utah, and received his bachelor's degree from Weber College, Ogden, Utah, in 1928. He earned master's and law degrees at George Washington University, Washington, D.C., in 1935 and 1937, respectively, and was a 1939 graduate of the Stonier Graduate School of Banking at Rutgers University. He joined the Federal Reserve Board in 1930, where he rose from a technical assistant on bank operations to special assistant to former "Fed" Chairman Marriner Eccles. He joined the staff of the Continental Bank in 1946, was elected a director and president 10 years later and became chairman and chief executive officer in 1959.

Kennedy served as assistant to former Treasury Secretary George M. Humphrey in 1953-54. President Johnson in 1967 appointed him chairman of a 15-man Commission on Budget Concepts, whose recommendations resulted in the present "unified" federal budget hailed by economists as a major breakthrough in fiscal planning.

John B. Connally was nominated Jan. 25, 1971, and confirmed Feb. 8, 1971. He resigned June 12, 1972, and headed Democrats for Nixon during the presidential campaign.

Connally had only limited experience in banking and finance when he was chosen in December, 1970, by President Nixon to replace Secretary of the Treasury David M. Kennedy. Connally did bring to the post an extensive legal and business background and the skills of an accomplished politician.

The nomination of Connally, a southern Democrat, former three-term Texas governor and close political associate of former President Lyndon B. Johnson, surprised many Republicans and Democrats. President Nixon characterized the appointment as a move to approach problems in a "bipartisan spirit."

Connally was born Feb. 27, 1917, in Floresville, Texas, and attended public schools before entering the University of Texas in Austin, where he earned a law degree in 1941.

In 1961, Connally was appointed Secretary of the Navy by President John F. Kennedy. A year later he resigned to campaign for the first of his three terms as governor of Texas (1962-67).

Connally gained national prominence on Nov. 22, 1963, when he was seriously wounded in Dallas during the assassination of President Kennedy.

George P. Shultz was nominated May 17, 1972, and confirmed June 8, 1972.

Shultz had served as Nixon's first secretary of labor and resigned to become the director of the Office of Management and Budget (OMB) in 1970. Shultz had served as secretary of labor from January 20, 1969, to July 2, 1970, when he was succeeded by James Dan Hodgson.

Shultz became Nixon's third secretary of the treasury, following the resignation of Democrat John B. Connally in May. Nixon's first treasury secretary was David Kennedy who served until December 1970.

The only son of the founder of the New York Stock Exchange Institute, a training school for people employed in the securities field, Shultz was born in New York City on December 13, 1920. He spent his childhood in Englewood, N.J., and received his first lesson in economics when he was twelve and the country was at the depths of the Depression. Shultz tried to launch a mimeographed newspaper of his own, but the business enterprise collapsed when a neighbor refused to pay five cents for the paper, arguing he could get a *Saturday Evening Post* for the same price.

Shultz attended Loomis Institute, a private school in Connecticut, and graduated from Princeton with a degree in public and international affairs. He joined the U.S. Marines in 1942 and served as an officer in the Pacific until 1945.

Following his military service, Shultz received his Ph.D. from Massachusetts Institute of Technology (MIT) and remained at the institution as an assistant professor of industrial relations. From 1954-55, Shultz was the acting director of the industrial relations section of MIT.

In 1955, he was promoted to the rank of associate professor and granted a leave of absence to serve as senior staff economist for the President's Council of Economic Advisers. Shultz also served as an economic adviser to both Presidents Kennedy and Johnson.

In 1957, Shultz resigned from the MIT faculty to accept an appointment as professor of industrial relations at the University of Chicago Graduate School of Business, where he was appointed dean in 1962. He held that position until his appointment to the Nixon cabinet in 1969.

WHITE HOUSE STAFF

Not since the 1960 election of John F. Kennedy had a President faced the staff-building task Richard M. Nixon faced in November 1968—that of putting together a White House staff from scratch. This staff is composed of key men the President selects to advise and assist him, a group with much influence in government. *(Box, p. 973)*

President Johnson, when he was sworn in Nov. 22, 1963, after the assassination of President Kennedy, inherited a staff assembled by Mr. Kennedy. Mr. Johnson kept those who chose to stay, replacing them with his own appointments as the Kennedy men gradually resigned. By late 1968, only one member of the Kennedy staff remained as a presidential adviser.

Initial Staff. By Jan. 20, 1969, the date of his inauguration, President Nixon had selected his staff with one exception. And although a key aide predicted it would be smaller than previous White House staffs, the Nixon staff with 26 men and one woman was larger than those of recent administrations. President Johnson averaged 22 on his staff and Mr. Kennedy had 16 at the time of his death.

Nixon's original White House staff could be described as a campaign staff. Nineteen of the 27 appointees were key people in his 1968 presidential campaign, and 13 of the 19 were veterans of previous campaigns.

One of the most striking characteristics was the staff's general lack of government experience. Just seven of the 27 had had previous government experience. Nearly half of the staff were newspaper, advertising or public relations men when chosen by the President to be his advisers. One woman and one Negro were among the 27 members of the White House staff.

Burgeoning Numbers. Nearing the end of his first term in office, the President in November 1972 complained that the White House Staff had grown "rather like Topsy" and promised to reduce it. The staff was said then to number 510, of whom 147 were considered to be presidential advisers; that is, full-time, non-career professionals. The remaining 363 positions were filled by career clerical and supportive personnel, such as mail handlers.

A personnel list released Jan. 26, 1973, showed 47 of the 147 advisers had left the President's staff for other government departments or private life—a reduction of 32 per cent.

Impact of Watergate. The April 1973 departure of top presidential aides H. R. Haldeman and John D. Ehrlichman—as well as several other White House officials—in the wake of the Watergate scandal put a severe crimp in executive branch operations. Their resignations led to a major reshuffling of high-level White House personnel that heralded significant changes in the President's relations with his cabinet (which, some observers felt, had suffered during the first term from Nixon's tendency to rely heavily on his closest White House advisers—to whom he had delegated far-reaching authority) and with Congress (many members had complained that their accessibility to the President had been severely restricted by his White House aides during Nixon's first term). *(Watergate chapter, p. 978)*

Biographies of White House
and Key Executive Branch Personnel

Following are biographies of key White House and executive branch officials who served during the first Nixon administration. Where dates of service include the phrase "to present," the official was still serving in June 1973, when this chapter went to press.

Patrick J. Buchanan, b. Nov. 2, 1938. A speechwriter, Buchanan had been a close associate of Nixon since 1966 when he left his job as an editorial writer for the *St. Louis Globe Democrat* to become an executive assistant to the President. In addition to his White House speechwriting duties which began in 1969, Buchanan was in charge of preparing a daily news summary for the President. Buchanan had a reputation as a conservative and a harsh critic of alleged liberal bias in the press and television networks. He was reported to have been one of the authors of Vice President Agnew's 1969 speech in Des Moines attacking television news analysts.

Frank Carlucci, b. Oct. 18, 1930. Carlucci joined the White House in 1971 as associate director of the Office of Management and Budget and in July 1972 Nixon named him deputy director of the office. A former director of the Office of Economic Opportunity, Carlucci was assigned by Nixon in August 1972 to take on-the-spot charge of federal aid to victims of the tropical storm Agnes in eastern Pennsylvania. Carlucci gained credit from the Nixon administration for his role in dispensing aid to the flood victims and in January 1973 Nixon named him as under secretary of health, education and welfare. Carlucci served from September 1971 to January 1973.

Ken W. Clawson, b. Aug. 16, 1936. Clawson joined the White House in February 1972 as deputy director of communications. He had previously worked as a reporter for the *Washington Post*. Clawson was the coordinator of the 1974 budget campaign in the White House. Clawson served from Feb. 17, 1972 to present.

Kenneth R. Cole Jr., b. Jan. 27, 1938. Cole, who left his job as an account executive for the J. Walter Thompson advertising agency to join Nixon's 1968 campaign, was appointed special assistant to Nixon in January 1969. In November 1969 Cole was named deputy assistant for domestic affairs and in December 1972 Nixon appointed Cole as executive director of the Domestic Council. Cole, who reported directly to the President, considered the development of new sources of energy and housing for the poor to be domestic issues of the highest priority. Cole served from Jan. 20, 1969 to present.

Charles W. Colson, b. Oct. 16, 1931. Special counsel to the President from late 1969 until February 1973, Charles Wendell Colson was known in White House circles as a tough troubleshooter and key political adviser. In charge of liaison with outside groups, Colson hammered out agreements between administration officials and lobbies and took charge of public relations efforts to garner support for presidential policies. From 1956-61, Colson was administrative aide to former Sen. Leverett Saltonstall (R Mass. 1945-67), and after several years in private law practice, he played a marginal role in Nixon's 1968 presidential campaign.

During the 1972 campaign, Colson rode herd on the campaign efforts of White House staff members, while reportedly trying to influence re-election committee activities. Watergate conspirator E. Howard Hunt worked as a consultant for Colson in early 1972. In an August 1972 memo to White House staffers, Colson wrote that it was correct he once said "I would walk over my grandmother if necessary" to assure the President's re-election. He served from Nov. 6, 1967 to March 1, 1973.

John W. Dean III, b. Oct. 14, 1938. Dean, the President's counsel appointed in July 1970, was largely responsible for the legal work on the unprecedented positions the President took on executive privilege and impoundment of funds voted by Congress.

It was Dean who supposedly conducted the first Watergate investigation for the President in the summer of 1972 and reported that no one then at the White House was involved. Later events, however, led Nixon to ask for Dean's resignation, which he received and accepted April 30, 1973.

Dean's rise to the important job of the President's White House lawyer was rapid. He was minority counsel for the House Judiciary Committee in 1967, associate director of the National Commission on Reform of the Criminal Laws from 1967 to 1969, and associate deputy attorney general from 1969 to 1970 before replacing John D. Ehrlichman as counsel to the President.

Harry S. Dent, b. Feb. 21, 1930. Dent, a former administrative assistant to Sen. Strom Thurmond (R S.C.) and former chairman of the South Carolina Republican party, played a key role in bringing some southern states into the Republican column for the 1968 presidential election. He joined the White House in January 1969 and soon became the President's political coordinator. He was responsible for removing more than 2,000 Democrats from top government positions and replacing them with Republicans. He also aided in raising money for Republican candidates. After leaving the White House staff Dent was named as chief counsel to the Republican National Committee. Dent served from 1969 to 1972.

John D. Ehrlichman, b. March 20, 1925. Directed the White House organization for domestic affairs. Ehrlichman rose rapidly in the Nixon administration. He was counsel to the President from January to November 1969, when he became assistant to the President for domestic affairs.

Ehrlichman—like White House staff chief H.R. Haldeman, another principal in the Watergate case who also resigned April 30—was an advance man during Nixon's 1960 presidential campaign. He was a classmate of Haldeman at the University of California at Los Angeles.

Ehrlichman served as Nixon's "tour director" during the 1968 campaign. Before joining the campaign, he was associated with the law firm of Hullin, Ehrlichman, Roberts and Hodge in Seattle, Wash. He held no official post in the 1972 Nixon re-election campaign. Ehrlichman served from Jan. 20, 1969 to April 30, 1973, when he resigned following allegations that he was involved in the Watergate affair.

Robert H. Finch, b. Oct. 9, 1925. Finch had been a close associate of the President, having worked for him when Nixon was vice president and in his three presidential campaigns. Finch, a former lieutenant governor of California, was a member of Nixon's original cabinet as secretary of health, education, and welfare. In 1970 Nixon removed Finch from his cabinet position and appointed him special counsel to the President. As counselor Finch became the ombudsman for Latin America in the White House. He travelled to Latin countries as the President's emissary and was Nixon's liaison officer with the Cabinet Committee on Opportunity for the Spanish Speaking. Finch returned to a private law practice in Los Angeles after leaving the White House. He served from June 6, 1970 to Dec. 15, 1972.

Peter M. Flanigan, b. June 21, 1923. Flanigan joined the White House in 1969 as an assistant for commercial and economic matters and in 1972 Nixon named him executive director of the Council on International Economic Policy. He was the principal architect of Nixon's trade and energy messages of 1973. Flanigan had the reputation of "business' man" in the White House. His refusal (later rescinded) to testify about his role in the Justice Department's out-of-court settlement of anti-trust cases against International Telephone and Telegraph Corp. (ITT) almost cost Attorney General Richard G. Kleindienst his nomination for the post. Flanigan served from April 16, 1969 to present.

Leonard Garment, b. May 11, 1924. Garment was named acting White House counsel April 30, 1973, after serving as special consultant to the President since May, 1969. Garment first met President Nixon when Nixon, in 1965, joined the law firm of Mudge, Rose, Guthrie and Alexander, in which Garment had been a partner since 1957. Generally considered the "house liberal" in the Nixon administration, Garment was one of the few advisers to whom the President turned for counsel on the Watergate affair. Garment served from June 11, 1969 to present.

Gen. Alexander M. Haig Jr., b. Dec. 2, 1924. On June 6, 1973, the White House announced Haig would become assistant to the President and would retire from active duty in the Army effective Aug. 1, 1973. Since May 4, Haig had been acting assistant to the President. President Nixon in early January 1973, named Haig as Army Vice Chief of Staff, passing over 240 senior generals to place Haig in the job. Before that time, Haig had served as deputy assistant to the President for national security affairs, more commonly referred to as Henry Kissinger's right-hand man. In that role, he travelled to Vietnam more than a dozen times. As White House chief of staff, Haig took over the responsibilities of H.R. Haldeman, including supervision of the day-to-day operations and responsibilities of the White House staff. Haig served from Feb. 7, 1969, to present.

H.R. (Bob) Haldeman, b. Oct. 27, 1926: Haldeman was generally considered the most powerful man in the White House after the President until his resignation April 30, 1973, following allegations of involvement in the Watergate affair. The crew-cut Haldeman, who had been an assistant to the President since 1969, was charged with running the White House, passing the President's ideas to subordinates and jealously guarding the President's schedule.

Haldeman was an advance man in Nixon's 1960 presidential campaign, managed his 1962 try for the governorship of California and was chief of staff in Nixon's 1968 presidential campaign. Although he took no official part in the 1972 campaign, it was reported Haldeman played a major role in directing the Committee for the Re-election of the President from the White House.

Many of the personalities in prominent White House jobs had either worked for Haldeman when he managed the J. Walter Thompson advertising agency's Los Angeles office in the 1960s or were recruited by him. Among them were John D. Ehrlichman, Haldeman's college classmate, and Dwight Chapin and Ronald Ziegler from the advertising firm.

Bryce N. Harlow, b. Aug. 11, 1916. Harlow was President Nixon's first staff appointee in late 1968, when he was named assistant for legislative and congressional affairs. He had held the same position during most of the Eisenhower administration. In late 1969, Nixon named Harlow as one of three cabinet-ranking counsellors to the President. Harlow took a leave of absence from his job as chief of governmental relations for Procter & Gamble when he joined the Nixon campaign in 1968. He returned to the company after he resigned from the White House late in 1970. He rejoined the White House staff in June 1973.

Henry A. Kissinger, b. May 27, 1923. A foreign policy specialist, Kissinger had counseled Presidents Kennedy and Johnson and Republican presidential candidate Nelson Rockefeller before becoming Nixon's assistant for national security affairs in 1969. Author of six books and over 40 articles on foreign policy, the German-born scholar was a member of the faculty of his alma mater, Harvard University, from 1954 until 1972. As Nixon's principal adviser on matters of foreign policy, he gained the reputation of being "number two man in Washington." He was the key U.S. negotiator in the Paris peace talks that eventually led to the Vietnam cease-fire agreement. Kissinger also played a major part in the arrangements surrounding President Nixon's 1972 trips to the People's Republic of China and the U.S.S.R. Kissinger served from Dec. 2, 1968 to present.

Herbert G. Klein, b. April 1, 1918. Klein was a reporter and then editor with the San Diego-based Copley Newspapers for 20 years before assuming the position of director of communications for the President—a post created for Klein. One of Nixon's oldest associates, Klein met the future President in 1946 and handled his press relations in all his political campaigns since that date. As spokesman for the executive branch Klein coordinated information policies. His most important achievement for the administration from a public relations point of view was to bring the President into meetings with newsmen throughout the country rather than holding Washington press conferences exclusively. He also encouraged cabinet officials to make television appearances. Klein resigned June 5, 1973, to become a vice president of Metromedia, Inc. Klein served from Jan. 20, 1969 to July 1, 1973, the effective date of his resignation.

Clark MacGregor, b. July 12, 1922. A Republican representative from Minnesota from 1961 to 1971, MacGregor was the first former member of Congress to act as Nixon's principal assistant for congressional affairs. In this position Mr. MacGregor acted not only as Nixon's chief lobbyist but as intermediary between the executive and legislative branches, attempting to sensitize administration officials and White House aides to the moods of Congress. The reputation he earned as friendly persuader helped convince Nixon to name him successor to John N. Mitchell as campaign director for the Committee for the Re-election of the President, a position he gave up one day after the 1972 elections to become a vice president for the United Aircraft Corporation. MacGregor served from Jan. 1, 1972 to July 3, 1972.

Jeb S. Magruder, b. Nov. 5, 1934. Magruder, the first administration official to resign over the Watergate affair, was another of the California advertising and management types who served in the White House in the first Nixon term. He was in line for a high administration job in the second term, but was implicated in the Watergate scandal.

White House Aides, 1969-73*

Name	Appointed	Resigned
Kenneth E. BeLieu	1969	1971
Patrick J. Buchanan	1969	present
Dr. Arthur F. Burns	1969	1970
Frank Carlucci	1971	1973
Dwight L. Chapin	1969	1973
Ken W. Clawson	1972	present
Kenneth R. Cole Jr.	1969	present
Charles W. Colson	1969	1973
Dr. Edward E. David Jr.	1970	1973
John W. Dean III	1970	1973
Harry S. Dent	1969	1972
Dr. Lee A. DuBridge	1969	1970
Robert Ellsworth	1969	1969
John D. Ehrlichman	1969	1973
Robert H. Finch	1970	1972
Peter M. Flanigan	1969	present
Leonard Garment	1969	present
Alexander Haig Jr.	1969	present
H. R. Haldeman	1969	1973
Bryce N. Harlow	1969	1970
Gen. Lewis B. Hershey	1970	1973
Stephen Hess	1969	1969
Dr. Jerome H. Jaffe	1971	1973
James Keogh	1969	1970
Dr. Henry A. Kissinger	1969	present
Herbert G. Klein	1969	1973
Virginia H. Knauer	1969	present
Tom C. Korologos	1971	present
Frederick C. LaRue	1969	1972
Clark MacGregor	1971	1972
Jeb S. Magruder	1969	1971
Frederick V. Malek	1970	1972
Robert A. Mayo	1969	1970
Clark R. Mollenhoff	1969	1970
Edward L. Morgan	1969	1972
Daniel P. Moynihan	1969	1971
Peter G. Peterson	1971	1972
Raymond K. Price	1969	present
Donald Rumsfeld	1970	1971
William L. Safire	1969	1973
John A. Scali	1971	1973
William E. Timmons	1969	present
Clay T. Whitehead	1969	present
Ronald L. Ziegler	1969	present

* Through June.

At the White House, which he joined in 1969, Magruder worked for Haldeman and Herbert G. Klein, communications director for the executive branch. He left the executive mansion in late 1971 to become deputy director of the Committee for the Re-election of the President.

He was regarded as a top-notch administrator, having worked in advertising and management before heading a small cosmetics firm in Santa Monica, Calif. He was a volunteer for Nixon, Sen. Barry Goldwater (R Ariz.) and former Rep. Donald Rumsfeld (R Ill.). Magruder served from Oct. 7, 1969 to late 1971.

Robert P. Mayo, b. March 15, 1916. In January, 1969 Mayo was appointed director of the Bureau of the Budget.

Prior to that he had been in the Treasury Department, an officer of the Continental Illinois Bank, and a member of President-elect Nixon's budget task force. In the spring of 1970 when the cabinet was organized George Shultz became head of the new Office of Management and Budget. Mayo moved to the White House to become a counsellor to the President but resigned soon after. He served from January 20, 1969 to July 28, 1970.

Clark R. Mollenhoff, b. April 16, 1921. After more than twenty years as an investigative reporter Mollenhoff was appointed deputy counsel to the President in July, 1969. Described as the White House trouble-shooter, his job was to find and solve problems of corruption and mismanagement inside the government before they could be found by outsiders. During the ten-month period that he served he repeatedly came into conflict with newsmen, top administration officials and many congressmen. In early 1970 it was revealed that he had virtually unlimited access to the Internal Revenue Service's supposedly confidential tax returns. During March of 1973 he testified at the Civil Service hearings concerned with the firing of A. Ernest Fitzgerald, a former Pentagon management analyst. He served in the White House from July 2, 1969 to May 30, 1970.

Daniel P. Moynihan, b. March 16, 1927. Moynihan took a leave of absence from the faculty of Harvard University to become assistant to the President for urban affairs and executive secretary of the Council on Urban Affairs in January, 1969. Nine months later he was named counsellor to the President. An urbanologist and economist, Moynihan served both Presidents Kennedy and Johnson. Although considered a liberal in the broad sense, he had crossed swords with liberals and gained a reputation as a pragmatist. The author of a proposal for a family assistance program which would have guaranteed a basic income for every American family, he also coined the controversial phrase "benign neglect" in a 1970 memorandum to the President outlining what he thought the administration's attitude on race issues should be. He returned to Harvard in January 1971 but remained a consultant to the President. He was named ambassador to India, Dec. 11, 1972. Moynihan served from Jan. 23, 1969 to Jan. 20, 1971.

William L. Safire, b. Dec. 17, 1929. Safire left his public relations firm to write speeches for Nixon's 1968 campaign. He had worked in three previous elections including 1960 when he was chief of special projects for the Nixon-Lodge volunteers. On January 20, 1969 he became special assistant to the President and was one of the chief speech writers on domestic and economic policy. In the 1970 off-year elections, while writing for the Vice President, he coined the phrase "nattering nabobs of negativism." In the 1972 presidential campaign he specialized in writing speeches on Nixon's political philosophy. In April, 1973 he resigned to write a column for the *New York Times.*

Herbert Stein, b. Aug. 27, 1916. After serving on the Council of Economic Advisers for two years Stein became chairman when Paul McCracken resigned on January 1, 1972. Although he was in charge of the task force that worked out the details of the wage-price controls that took effect in August, 1971, he has long been known as a con-servative, opposed to government intervention in the private sector. During 1972 he broke with the tradition of his predecessors by actively engaging in the presidential campaign. He remained chairman of the Council although with less influence as a result of the rising power of Treasury Secretary George Shultz. He served from February 4, 1969 to present.

William E. Timmons, b. Dec. 27, 1970. Timmons joined the White House staff in January, 1969, as deputy assistant to the President for congressional relations. In February of that year, after Bryce Harlow became counselor to the President, Timmons replaced him as head of congressional relations. Before coming to the White House, Timmons was an aide to the late Sen. Alexander Wiley (R Wis. 1939-63) and administrative assistant to then Rep. Bill Brock (R Tenn.). In the President's 1968 campaign, Timmons served as director of congressional relations. Timmons was selected the "Outstanding Young Republican" by the national Young Republicans in 1965. Timmons served from Jan. 20, 1969 to present.

Caspar W. Weinberger, b. Aug. 18, 1917. A former assemblyman and director of finance of California, Weinberger was appointed by Nixon in 1969 to head the Federal Trade Commission (FTC). He worked to upgrade its role as a protector of consumer rights. Weinberger was named deputy director of the Office of Management and Budget (OMB) in June 1970 and became its director in May 1972. He emphasized balancing the budget by cutting federal spending. This action earned him the nickname "Cap the Knife." Weinberger described himself as a "fiscal Puritan." In November 1972 Nixon named him to succeed Elliot Richardson as secretary of health, education and welfare (HEW). He served from July 1, 1970 to Feb. 8, 1973, when he was confirmed as HEW head.

Clay T. Whitehead, b. Nov. 13, 1938. Following the 1968 election Whitehead served on the President-elect's task force on budget policies. After the inauguration he became a special assistant to the President concerned with space, energy, maritime and communications policies. On September 22, 1970 he was named director of the newly formed Office of Telecommunications Policy, making him the President's chief adviser on the government's use of and policy towards the media. Late in 1972, he gained much notoriety by being the main spokesman for the administration's proposed changes in the regulation of public television stations and the public television network. Critics contended that some of the proposals amounted to censorship. Whitehead served from January 20, 1969 to present.

Ronald L. Ziegler, b. May 12, 1939. Ziegler, the President's press secretary since 1969, took much of the heat from reporters over the Watergate affair—mainly because he was the only administration spokesman on the subject. His credibility was damaged badly by 10 months of denials of Watergate news stories as "fiction," "shabby journalism" and "character assassination," only to turn around after the President's April 17, 1973, statement and declare his past remarks "inoperative."

Ziegler, was a protege of H.R. Haldeman, for whom he worked in the J. Walter Thompson advertising agency in Los Angeles. He worked on Nixon's unsuccessful gubernatorial campaign in 1962 and was campaign press secretary for Nixon in 1968. He also aided in the 1964 campaign of former Sen. George Murphy (R Calif. 1965-71). Ziegler served from Jan. 20, 1969 to present.

CQ **Executive-Press Rivalry**

NIXON ADMINISTRATION AND THE NEWS MEDIA

The President and the press in the United States are traditional adversaries, but critics charged the Nixon administration with exceeding constitutional limits in attempting to influence newsmen and networks to give administration actions and views favorable treatment.

The exercise of press freedom guaranteed by the First Amendment was chilled during the Nixon years, the critics said, by:

• Vice President Agnew's blasts at the networks and certain newspapers, criticism backed by the implied threat of government action through its licensing and antitrust powers.

• The administration's attempt—foiled by the Supreme Court—to halt permanently the publication in *The New York Times* and *The Washington Post* of information taken from the classified Pentagon Papers, and the subsequent grand jury investigation of the manner in which the documents were obtained and used.

• The Justice Department's argument that it did not adversely affect freedom of the press to require a reporter to appear before a federal grand jury.

• The FBI investigation of Columbia Broadcasting System (CBS) newsman Daniel Schorr.

Press Problems. Richard M. Nixon had his share of problems with the press before he reached the White House in 1969. Years earlier, newsmen had named him "Tricky Dick," and to them he attributed part of the blame for his 1960 defeat.

The nadir of his relationship with the press was reached in 1962. Conceding his defeat in the race for governor of California, Nixon blasted the press for its coverage of his campaign and concluded: "You won't have Nixon to kick around anymore, gentlemen, because this is my last press conference."

When Nixon returned to the campaign trail as a presidential candidate in 1968, he skillfully used the media, television in particular. He promised, in campaign speeches and in his inaugural address, that his administration would be "open to ideas from the people and in its communication with the people."

In times of national stress, the adversary relationship of the President and the press most often erupts. It was from the tensions arising from American involvement in Indochina, from concern about race relations, drugs and militant revolutionary groups that most of the administration's criticism of the media came—and its efforts to influence the way in which the press dealt with news of these problems.

1969: 'Querulous Criticism'

In November 1969, tension was rising. A massive anti-war demonstration was planned for Washington Nov.

15; more than 250,000 persons were expected to converge on the nation's capital.

Two weeks before the scheduled demonstration, on Nov. 3, the President made a nationally televised address, asking support for his policy of winding down the war in Indochina. After the speech, newsmen on all three major networks analyzed the speech and concluded it was a restatement of administration policy.

Ten days later Vice President Agnew loosed the opening salvo in administration criticism of the news media. At a Republican gathering in Des Moines, Iowa, Agnew complained that the President's Nov. 3 speech had been subjected to "instant analysis and querulous criticism...by a small band of network commentators and self-appointed analysts, the majority of whom expressed in one way or another their hostility to what he had to say."

The television newsmen, Agnew continued, wield "a concentration of power over American public opinion unknown in history." This concentration "in the hands of a tiny enclosed fraternity of privileged men elected by no one and enjoying a monopoly sanctioned and licensed by government" should be questioned, he said. Viewers should urge the networks to bring their views into accord with those of the majority, telling them "that they want their news straight and objective." Agnew disclaimed any desire for censorship.

Three days later on Nov. 16, White House Communications Director Herbert F. Klein appeared on a television interview program and expanded Agnew's criticism to include newspapers. He warned, "If you look at the problems you have today and you fail to continue to examine them, you do invite the government to come in. I would not like to see that happen."

Agnew unleashed a second blast at the media on Nov. 20 in an address before the Alabama Chamber of Commerce in Montgomery. He repeated his disclaimer of any intent to impose censorship and then attacked the trend he saw toward monopolization of the news media. He pointed to the fact that one company controlled *The Washington Post, Newsweek,* and a radio and television station in Washington. He criticized the way in which *The New York Times* had treated certain stories and said that when the media became unjust in its criticism, "we shall invite them down from their ivory towers to enjoy the rough and tumble of public debate."

Speaking for the news industry Nov. 25, CBS President Frank Stanton replied: "No healthy society and no governing authorities worth their salt have to fear the reporting of dissenting or even of hostile voices." The licensing power which means life or death of the broadcaster, Stanton continued, makes any official's attack on the press an ominous threat. No more serious threat has been made to freedom of the press in the United States, he said, since the enactment of laws in 1798 that made criticism of the government cause for punishment and exile.

Stanton warned that "it does not take overt censorship to cripple the free flow of ideas." Irreparable harm could be done merely by the threat of reprisal dangling over news executives and newsmen making decisions about what to cover and include in their presentations.

But the administration stood firm behind Agnew's comments: Mr. Nixon said Dec. 8 that the Vice President has rendered a public service by his discussion of the news media.

1970: Newsmen and Investigators

Freedom of the press appeared threatened by another form of government pressure in 1970—subpoenas issued to newsmen ordering them to provide grand juries with information.

In two cases, state courts ruled that newsmen must provide the information; the Justice of Department asked the U.S. Supreme Court to sustain the decisions of the state appeals courts concerning:

• Paul M. Branzburg, investigative reporter for the Louisville *Courier-Journal,* who wrote several articles based on personal observation of drug users, whom he had promised not to identify, and who was then subpoenaed by two grand juries to testify on what he had observed.

• Paul Pappas, television newsman, who was allowed to visit a Black Panther headquarters during a period of civil unrest on the condition that he not report what he saw, and who was later subpoenaed by a grand jury in Massachusetts to testify about that visit.

But a reporter won his case before the U.S. Court of Appeals, 9th Circuit—and the Nixon administration appealed to the Supreme Court to have that ruling overturned. Earl Caldwell, black reporter for *The New York Times,* gained the confidence of Black Panthers in the San Francisco area and wrote several articles about them. In 1970, he was ordered to appear before a federal grand jury to testify; he refused, was held in contempt by a federal district court, and that contempt ruling was reversed by the Court of Appeals.

The administration argued that Caldwell would not have to disclose any confidential information or sources and therefore should not be allowed immunity from the subpoena on the ground that his appearance alone might impair his functioning as a newsman.

Initially the Justice Department said that issuance of subpoenas for unpublished or unbroadcast material was consistent with past policy. Former Attorney General Ramsey Clark immediately disagreed, and Attorney General Mitchell admitted Feb. 5 that the sweeping subpoenas resulted from a breakdown in department procedures. There would be negotiations with the media, he said, before any other subpoenas were issued.

In August, Mitchell announced new guidelines for the issuance of subpoenas to the media. None would be issued without prior negotiation, he said, or without the **express approval of the attorney general.** *(Box, this page)*

In September 1971, CBS and NBC disclosed that between January 1969 and July 1971, they had been served 122 subpoenas—52 of them from governments.

Guidelines for Subpoenas

(Aug. 10, 1970)

"The Department of Justice recognizes that compulsory process...may have a limiting effect on the exercise of First Amendment rights. In determining whether to request issuance of a subpoena to the press, the approach in every case must be to weigh that limiting effect against the public interest....

"The department...does not consider the press 'an investigative arm of the government'....

"It is the policy of the department to insist that negotiations with the press be attempted in all cases in which a subpoena is contemplated....

"If negotiations fail, no Justice Department official should request or make any arrangements for a subpoena to the press without the express authorization of the Attorney General.

"If a subpoena is obtained...without this authorization, the department will—as a matter of course—move to quash the subpoena....

"In requesting...authorization for a subpoena....

A. There should be sufficient reason to believe that a crime has occurred.... The department does not approve utilizing the press as a springboard for investigations.

B. There should be sufficient reason to believe that the information sought is essential to a successful investigation....

C. The government should have unsuccessfully attempted to obtain the information from alternative non-press sources.

D. Authorization requests for subpoenas should normally be limited to the verification of published information....

E. Great caution should be observed in requesting subpoena authorization...for unpublished information...."

1971: Disturbing Victories

In 1971, the news media faced and overcame major threats to its independence—from Congress as well as from the Nixon administration—but not without disturbing implications:

• Daniel Schorr, a CBS television reporter, was investigated by the FBI. The administration said a routine background investigation had been initiated because Schorr was being considered for a high government job. But no post was offered Schorr and he was never told he was being considered. The probe, it was found out later, began in August as a result of White House displeasure caused by Schorr's disclosure that the President's endorsement of financial aid for parochial schools had caught Catholic educators and federal officials off guard.

• The newspapers defeated the administration's effort to halt publication of material contained in the classified Pentagon Papers, but not until they had been restrained from publishing it for two weeks. *(Details, Supreme Court chapter)*

● Broadcasters won when the House of Representatives killed a contempt citation issued by a committee against CBS after that network refused to supply the committee with unbroadcast film ("out-takes") taken in composing a particularly controversial program—but broadcast news continued under congressional scrutiny.

The **key vote** on the contempt citation was **226-181 (R 95-76; D 131-105).** This key vote came on a motion to reject the citation, with a majority of both parties approving the motion.

The citation stemmed from a Feb. 23 CBS broadcast of a documentary called "The Selling of the Pentagon," which portrayed an elaborate public relations campaign carried out by the Defense Department.

The documentary was criticized by members of Congress and administration officials, some of whom charged that the film had been edited to alter the meaning of certain remarks. Agnew charged that the documentary was "a clever propaganda attempt to discredit the defense establishment."

In April, the investigations subcommittee of the House Commerce Committee, which has jurisdiction over communications, subpoenaed all materials from CBS related to the making of the documentary. CBS supplied a transcript and film of the televised program but refused to provide any non-televised material.

CBS President Stanton, appearing under subpoena before the subcommittee, in June, refused again to provide the so-called "out-takes." The FCC said that the network appeared to have presented all sides of the issue fairly, but the Commerce Committee voted to cite Stanton and CBS for contempt for their refusal to cooperate.

1972: Easing Off

Government pressure on newsmen appeared to ease off in 1972. Vice President Agnew had little to say publicly about the press. At the Republican National Convention he indicated to reporters that his press-baiting days were over and that his future criticisms would be toned down.

The election itself may have had something to do with the lowering of government voices. It made little sense to antagonize journalists before and during campaigns.

Perhaps more important, the administration won a significant victory in the Supreme Court, which ruled in the three grand jury subpoena cases brought by the Justice Department that newsmen had no special rights to refuse to appear before a grand jury or refuse to answer questions. *(Details, Supreme Court chapter)*

The Court's decision left open the possibility that Congress could legislate on the matter of newsman's privilege, and a House subcommittee held hearings on the subject in the fall. No legislation was recommended, however.

1972 BREAK-IN CLOUDED NIXON ADMINISTRATION AURA

A break-in at an office building in Washington, D.C., early in the morning of June 17, 1972, has developed into one of the best-publicized pieces of political skulduggery in American history. The name of the building in which five men were arrested at 2:30 a.m. that day became the word commonly used to describe not only the break-in itself but the widening circle of events surrounding it. The name was Watergate.

The five men were arrested in Democratic national headquarters, offices occupying a suite on the sixth floor of the Watergate office-apartment-hotel-shopping complex, one of the smartest in Washington. The men were carrying electronic surveillance equipment. They were wearing surgical gloves to prevent leaving fingerprints.

Incredulity, sometimes accompanied by cynical laughter, typified the initial public reaction to the bungled break-in. But, as one disclosure followed another, the laughter faded and the Watergate incident was recognized for what it was: one segment of a much larger political spy puzzle involving espionage and sabotage, implicating White House officials and financed with hundreds of thousands of dollars in secret campaign funds.

During the spring of 1973, developments surrounding the Watergate scandal captured headlines in newspapers acorss the country. There were reports of widespread Republican sabotage and espionage efforts during the 1972 campaign; revelations of domestic surveillance efforts and possible wiretaps on reporters as a result of the 1971 Pentagon Papers leak; and numerous allegations linking the highest ranking officials in the White House and the Committee for the Re-election of the President in the Watergate cover-up. Controversy flared over the extent and role of the Central Intelligence Agency's (CIA) involvement in the cover-up operations. By mid-June there were allegations—made principally by former White House Counsel John W. Dean III—that the President himself knew of the cover-up. Nixon and his White House spokesmen emphatically denied the charges.

Operations at the White House and throughout the government suffered a slowdown as a result of the widening Watergate affair. The shake-up involved the resignations of three top White House aides, the Attorney General, the acting director of the Federal Bureau of Investigation (FBI) and a score of other presidential assistants and former campaign officials (many of whom held administration positions).

Grand juries in New York, Washington, D.C., Los Angeles, Houston, Texas, and Orlando, Fla., continued their probes of 1972 presidential campaign practices, handing down indictments—with more expected throughout the summer and fall of 1973. In less than a year after the Watergate break-in, the five burglars and two of their accomplices had either pleaded guilty to or been convicted of felonies. And two former Nixon cabinet officers were indicted for obstructing justice.

Finally, exactly 11 months after the Watergate break-in, the Senate Select Committee on Presidential Campaign Activities opened a series of dramatic public hearings on the Watergate affair before a nationwide television audience. The investigation opened "in an atmosphere of the utmost gravity," with appearances by a battery of top former White House and campaign aides.

The following background summarizes developments in the Watergate case through late June of 1973.

Senate Investigation

All the still-undisclosed facts, it was hoped, would be brought to light by public hearings to be conducted by a bipartisan, seven-member select committee of the Senate. The committee, chaired by Sen. Sam J. Ervin Jr. (D N.C.), was established by a unanimous vote of the Senate Feb. 7. The resolution establishing the committee (S Res 60) provided subpoena powers and authorized $500,000 for expenses of the investigation and the writing of a report by Feb. 28, 1974. *(Committee members and staff, p. 981)*

Samuel Dash, a Georgetown University law professor who is chief counsel for the investigative committee, discussed a few of the committee's ground rules with Congressional Quarterly. Without committing himself to a timetable, Dash said that public hearings would begin "as quickly as possible." Private investigation by him and minority counsel Fred Thompson was underway, he added, and "This is going to be, as far as I'm concerned, a very careful, a very thorough investigation."

Dash said he and Thompson were assembling a staff, starting with a "core team of specialists," that might number "in the 30s or 40s" when the investigation reached its peak. Although he expected the committee to complete its work within the allotted time, he mentioned the possibility that, if necessary, the investigators might have to exercise their option for an extension of time and money to finish their job.

Arrangements were made for a hearing room large enough to accommodate the large crowds expected to attend the hearings. One ground rule, Dash said, was that the hearings would be open to press and public. A one-day closed hearing on March 28 produced so many leaks to the press from unidentified sources that further closed hearings were canceled.

"The success of the investigation will depend on the staff," Dash said. He expected the initial public hearings to last about a month, followed by continued investigation by the staff through the summer and more extensive hearings in the fall, he said. The investigation was expected to be broad in scope, exploring not only the details of the Watergate but other charges of political wrong-doing by both the Republican and Democratic parties.

The ultimate goal of the committee, said Dash, was to discover "what impact (all this) has on the election process in a Democratic country." The final report, he said, may contain recommendations to reform existing election laws.

The Bugging and Break-in

After the initial reports on the June 17 break-in, the Watergate incident dropped temporarily from the headlines. Not until late summer did the story of the broader scandal start to unfold. But, even during its absence from the news, a federal grand jury was conducting a secret investigation that led to the indictment of seven men. Many of the revelations that gradually came to light were the result of diligent digging by and occasional leaks to the press.

The Conspirators. These were the five men arrested by Washington police in the Democratic offices:

James W. McCord Jr.

• Bernard L. Barker, a Miami, Fla., realtor and a former Central Intelligence Agency (CIA) employee who reportedly had a role in the Bay of Pigs invasion of Cuba in 1962.

• Virgilio R. Gonzalez of Miami, a locksmith who emigrated from Cuba during Fidel Castro's rise to power.

• Eugenio R. Martinez, a member of Barker's real estate firm and an anti-Castro Cuban exile with CIA associations.

• James W. McCord Jr. of Washington, security coordinator for the Republican National Committee and the Committee for the Re-election of the President, a former FBI agent and CIA employee. He was fired the day after the break-in.

E. Howard Hunt Jr.

• Frank A. Sturgis of Miami, an associate of Barker who had connections with the CIA and had participated in anti-Castro activities.

The five were charged with attempted burglary and attempted interception of telephone and other communications. On Sept. 15, the grand jury indicted them and two other men for conspiracy, burglary and violation of federal wiretapping laws. The two others were:

• E. Howard Hunt Jr. of Washington, a former White House consultant, writer of spy novels and former CIA employee. Hunt's consulting work included declassification of the Pentagon Papers and intelligence work in narcotics enforcement.

• G. Gordon Liddy of Washington, counsel to the Finance Committee to Re-elect the President, former FBI agent, former Treasury Department official and former member of the White House staff. Liddy was fired for refusing to answer the FBI's questions during an investigation of the Watergate incident.

At a trial in January 1973, Hunt, Barker, Sturgis, Gonzalez and Martinez pleaded guilty. Liddy and McCord were convicted.

Partisan Reaction. Lawrence F. O'Brien, Democratic national chairman at the time of the break-in, called it "an incredible act of political espionage." John N. Mitchell, former attorney general and, until July 1, President Nixon's re-election campaign manager, said the five men arrested at the Watergate "were not operating either in our behalf or with our consent."

G. Gordon Liddy

More Bugging. On Sept. 7, O'Brien, then the campaign manager for Democratic presidential nominee George McGovern, charged that Republican-sponsored surveillance of Democratic headquarters had been going on before the June 17 arrests. He said that his phone and that of R. Spencer Oliver, executive director of the state chairmen's association of the Democratic National Committee, had been tapped for several weeks. Information from the taps had, he claimed, been monitored and transcribed in a motel across the street from the Watergate.

O'Brien said the five men arrested on June 17 had come to repair a faulty tap on his phone and to install a bugging device nearby. On May 27, he said, the presence of campaign workers had prevented some men from setting up eavesdropping equipment in McGovern campaign headquarters on Capitol Hill.

News stories on Sept. 16 identified Alfred C. Baldwin III, a former FBI agent and an alleged participant in the Watergate bugging, as the source of O'Brien's information. In a copyrighted interview published in *The Los Angeles Times* Oct. 4, Baldwin said he had delivered eavesdropping logs to the President's re-election committee less than two weeks before June 17. He said the material was sent to someone besides the seven men indicted, but he did not name that person.

The Washington Post reported on Oct. 6 that Baldwin, who was granted immunity from prosecution in return for his cooperation with investigators, told the FBI that memos describing wiretapped and bugged conversations in Democratic headquarters had been sent to three persons: William E. Timmons, Nixon's assistant for congressional relations; Robert C. Odle Jr., director of administration for the re-election committee, and J. Glenn Sedam Jr., the committee's general counsel. The charges were denied.

The Money Morass

As the grand jury was hearing witnesses throughout the summer of 1972 in connection with the Watergate bugging, reports began to appear about enormous sums of money, obtained under unusual circumstances, for use in the Republicans' intelligence operations.

GAO Investigation. An investigation by the FBI and the General Accounting Office's (GAO) Office of Federal Elections began Aug. 1 on the finances of the President's re-election committee. The investigation was started after *The Washington Post* reported that a $25,000 check intended for Nixon's campaign had been deposited to the Miami bank account of Bernard Barker, one of the men arrested at the Watergate.

Maurice H. Stans

Kenneth H. Dahlberg, midwestern finance chairman for the Nixon campaign, said he had given a cashier's check for $25,000 to Maurice H. Stans, the former secretary of commerce who was Nixon's finance chairman in 1972, as he had been in 1968.

The Washington Star-News reported on Aug. 10 that additional contributions of $89,000 had been deposited in installments in Barker's account, bringing the total to $114,000. The article quoted investigators as saying the Republicans had a "security fund" for their national convention.

A GAO report released Aug. 26 cited five "apparent" and four "possible" violations of the Federal Election Campaign Act of 1971 by the re-election finance committee. The report was turned over to the Justice Department for further action. These were among its disclosures:

• The committee failed to keep a detailed account of the $25,000 contribution. It was given anonymously, but the donor was revealed to be Dwayne Andreas, a Minneapolis, Minn., grain executive. Andreas and Dahlberg, it was later revealed, were both directors of a bank that was granted a federal charter on Aug. 22. Both denied any connection between the contribution and the charter.

• The committee did not disclose details of the $25,000 contribution in accordance with the 1971 campaign law.

• The committee failed to keep a detailed account of the money spent from the $25,000 Dahlberg check or from the four checks totaling $89,000, drawn on a Mexico City bank and eventually deposited to Barker's account. Stans told the GAO that the four checks were from donors in Texas who wished to remain anonymous by contributing before April 7—the deadline for anonymous contributions before new reporting requirements took effect under the 1971 law.

• The committee kept inadequate records, not only on the $114,000 in anonymous contributions, but on the balance of $350,000 deposited on May 25 to the credit of the Media Committee to Re-elect the President. Hugh W. Sloan Jr., former treasurer of the finance committee, said the $350,000 had been kept in a safe in Stans' secretary's office. Only Stans and Sloan had access to the safe. Stans told the GAO that the funds had been collected before the April 7 deadline and that any records pertaining to them had been destroyed after April 7.

Indictment, Settlement. The GAO investigation led to the indictment of the re-election finance committee on eight counts of campaign spending violations. The committee was fined $8,000 on Jan. 26, 1973, in U.S. District Court in Washington after pleading nolo contendere—no contest—to the charges.

Barker Trial. Another trial that resulted from one of the Republican financial transactions was that of Barker, the Miamian in whose bank account the secretly contributed money had been deposited. Barker was indicted in Dade County (Florida) Criminal Court on a charge of fraudulently using his notary public seal to indicate that the $25,000 check from Dahlberg—the Dwayne Andreas contribution—had been endorsed in his presence.

Barker pleaded guilty on Sept. 15. He was found guilty on Nov. 1 and given a 60-day suspended sentence on the condition that he surrender his notary license.

Banking Committee Probe. But the Barker trial and conviction were only subsidiary elements in the movement of much larger amounts of money through his firm's account.

The House Banking and Currency Committee staff distributed to committee members on Sept. 12 a report claiming that finance chairman Stans knew of the transfer of $100,000 in contributions from Texas donors through a Texas bank and into the campaign treasury. The report was leaked to the press.

According to the report, the money was delivered, along with an additional $600,000 in contributions, to the re-election committee on April 5, two days before the deadline for identifying donors. Included in the $100,000, said the report, was the $89,000 deposited to Barker's account on April 20.

The report said that Stans had denied knowledge of the Mexican bank transfer at first but later had admitted knowing about the transaction when he was confronted with conflicting testimony from a Texas fund-raiser. Stans issued a statement denying any knowledge of the Mexican transactions and calling the committee report "rubbish" and "transparently political."

By a 20-15 vote on Oct. 3, the Banking and Currency Committee rejected a probe of Nixon campaign finances. The rejection was bipartisan; six Democrats joined 14 Republicans in preventing the investigation. It was opposed by the Justice Department on grounds that it would interfere with the criminal trial of the seven Watergate defendants.

A report by Democratic members of the House committee was released Oct. 31, making additional charges of campaign fund mishandling by the Nixon re-election committee. A re-election committee spokesman said the report was a "dishonest collection of innuendo and fourth-hand hearsay." Among the allegations in the report:

• The re-election committee had developed the capability of monitoring the bank accounts of Democratic senators and representatives. The charge was attributed to a friend of Hugh Sloan, the former campaign treasurer. Sloan's attorney called it an "absolute lie."

• Alfred Baldwin, the Watergate bugger who had been granted immunity, was hired for $18,000 a year to record not only political discussions but personal conversations.

• At least $30,000 had been channeled to the Nixon committee through a Luxembourg bank before the new campaign spending law took effect.

• The campaign finance committee had committed massive bookkeeping errors and omissions, including one $800,000 discrepancy between committee records and bank records of cash on hand in April 1972.

(Continued on p. 982)

Biographies of Senate Select Committee's Members, Counsels

Sen. Sam J. Ervin Jr. (D N.C.), 76, chairman of the committee, is considered the Senate's leading constitutional scholar. In his nearly 19 years in the Senate, he

has sided sometimes with the conservatives, sometimes with the liberals. He was chosen to head the committee because of his reputation for fairness and nonpartisanship. Ervin is a member of the Judiciary and Armed Services Committees and chairman of the Government Operations Committee.

When President Nixon ordered presidential aides not to honor subpoenas issued by the select committee, Ervin responded by saying, "I'd recommend to the Senate they send the sergeant at arms of the Senate to arrest a White House aide or any other witness who refuses to appear and...let the Senate try him."

Sen. Howard H. Baker Jr. (R Tenn.), 47, the committee vice chairman and ranking minority member, was elected to the Senate in 1966. His father was the late

Rep. Howard H. Baker (R Tenn. 1951-64), and his father-in-law was the late Sen. Everett McKinley Dirksen (R Ill. 1951-69).

Baker unsuccessfully challenged Sen. Hugh Scott (R Pa.) for the minority leadership in 1969 and 1971 as the candidate of Senate conservatives. He serves on the Commerce and Public Works Committees, the Republican Committee on Committees and the Republican Personnel Committee.

Baker has said he favors "a full, thorough and fair investigation with no holds barred, let the chips fall where they will."

Sen. Edward J. Gurney (R Fla.), 59, elected in 1968, is the first Republican senator from Florida since Reconstruction. He is a member of the Government Oper-

tions, Judiciary and Select Small Business Committees. In 1972, Gurney was the chief defender of the Nixon administration during the Judiciary Committee's investigation of the International Telephone and Telegraph Corporation.

He has said of the Watergate investigation, "I want to see that it is as nonpartisan as possible, but I certainly want to bring out every last piece of information." When the investigation resolution was de-

bated Feb. 7, Gurney read information from political polls indicating that the public did not have much interest in the Watergate matter.

Sen. Daniel K. Inouye (D Hawaii), 48, has represented Hawaii in Congress since the islands gained statehood in 1959. He served in the

House for four years and has been a senator since 1963. He is a member of the Appropriations, Commerce and District of Columbia Committees.

In 1972, as chairman of the D.C. Appropriations Subcommittee, he conducted full-scale investigations of the District of Columbia government. He is one of four assistant majority whips and vice chairman of the Democratic Senatorial Campaign Committee.

Sen. Joseph M. Montoya (D N.M.), 57, came to the Senate in 1964 after spending eight years in the House. He is a member of the Appropriations and Public Works Committees.

When first appointed to the investigating committee, he said he expected that the members "will be able to sift through the facts and come up with a complete story of just what was involved and just who was involved, in addition, if any, to those already named."

Sen. Herman E. Talmadge (D Ga.), 59, a senator since 1957, was governor of Georgia for the nine years preceding his election to the Senate. In the Senate, he is chairman of the Agriculture and Forestry Committee and ranking Democrat on the Finance Committee. He also

serves on the Veterans' Affairs, Select Standards and Conduct and Select Nutrition and Human Needs Committee and is a member of the Democratic Policy Committee.

Talmadge, considered by some senators to be one of their most intelligent colleagues, has said he plans to do no investigating on his own but will depend on the committee's hearings for his knowledge. "I see myself as a juror," he said, "and a juror doesn't background himself."

(Watergate—Continued from p. 980)

Sen. Lowell P. Weicker Jr. (R Conn.), 41, was elected to the Senate in 1970 after spending one term in the House. He is a member of

the Banking, Housing and Urban Affairs and Aeronautical and Space Sciences Committees. He is also on the Republican Senatorial Campaign Committee.

Weicker has been particularly outspoken about the Watergate investigation and has said he is conducting his own studies on the matter. He has charged that offices of members of Congress were next in line to be bugged. Weicker said he sought membership on the investigating committee because "I'm a professional politician. Because of things like the Watergate, people have lost faith in politicians, and I want to see that changed. The only thing that will convince them to respect politicians is to bring dirty business like the Watergate out in the open."

Samuel Dash, 48, a Georgetown University criminal law professor, is the majority counsel for the select com-

mittee. He is director of Georgetown's Institute of Criminal Law and Procedure and is considered a leading authority on wiretapping. He is a former Philadelphia District Attorney and was a trial attorney for the Justice Department's criminal division in 1951 and 1952.

Dash has characterized the Watergate investigation as "the most important ever undertaken by the Senate because it goes to the heart of the democratic process."

Fred D. Thompson, 30, a Nashville lawyer, is the committee's minority counsel.

Thompson is a former U.S. attorney for Tennessee's middle district and served as Sen. Baker's re-election campaign manager for that area in 1972. As a federal prosecutor, Thompson was known chiefly for his handling of bank robbery and moonshine whisky cases.

Thompson said he views his role as minority counsel as ensuring that the committee staff "keeps within the scope of the investigation" and does not delve into matters unrelated to political espionage.

Funds Returned. The contributor of the mysterious $100,000 identified himself early in 1973. He was a Texas oilman, Robert H. Allen. He acknowledged that $89,000 of his donation had been deposited to the Barker account. In a letter to Stans, he asked that the $100,000 be returned for personal reasons.

The return of Allen's $100,000 was announced on March 9 by the re-election finance committee. Also returned to its donors, the re-election committee said, was another $555,000. Of this amount, $305,000 was given back to Walter T. Duncan, a Texas land speculator, and $250,000 to Robert L. Vesco, a New Jersey financier. Duncan needed the money to pay off debts. Vesco had been accused by the Securities and Exchange Commission of a $224-million stock fraud. His contribution of $200,000 to the Nixon campaign was the object of another GAO investigation. The other $50,000 was not involved in the investigation.

Vesco's Role. The interaction of Vesco with the President's finance committee was brought to light in a court deposition made public in New York City on Feb. 27. His $200,000 contribution was delivered to the committee in cash on April 10, 1972, three days after the new reporting law took effect. But it was never reported to the GAO.

Vesco was accused of swindling investors in IOS Ltd., an overseas mutual fund corporation. Although the $200,000 contribution and another $50,000 contribution—given after April 7 and reported as required—were returned to Vesco on Jan. 31, the finance committee claimed the law had not been violated, because Vesco had intended to contribute the money before the deadline and it was "constructively in the hands" of the committee before April 7.

John N. Mitchell

The court deposition, made by an attorney who was an associate of Vesco and was Nixon's campaign manager in New Jersey in 1972, linked John Mitchell, Maurice Stans and the President's younger brother, Edward Nixon of Edmonds, Wash., to the Vesco contribution. The deposition stated that:

● Late in 1971, then Attorney General Mitchell phoned the U.S. embassy in Geneva, Switzerland, expressing interest in the jailing of Vesco on the complaint of a former IOS customer. Vesco was freed on bond within a day. Mitchell later denied any wrongdoing; he said he made the call at the request of the attorney who gave the deposition, Harry L. Sears.

● Vesco said that Stans had asked for the contribution in cash. This request was later confirmed by Edward Nixon. A re-election committee spokesman denied these statements; Stans and Edward Nixon were unavailable for comment.

More 'Apparent Violations.' A GAO report charging the President's re-election finance committee with four new "apparent violations" was referred to the Justice Department on March 12 for possible prosecution. The chief subject of the report was the $200,000 Vesco contribution. It was "undisputed," said the GAO, that the contribution was not delivered to the finance committee until after the April 7, 1972, deadline.

The committee labeled the GAO report "irresponsible" and said the committee's handling of the Vesco contribution had a "conclusive precedent." That precedent was the $25,000 Andreas contribution of April 10, 1972, which, according to the committee, had been ruled within the law in a Justice Department report on Jan. 11, 1973.

The Secret Fund. Recurrent references had been made since the fall of 1972 to a secret fund, kept in a safe in Maurice Stans' office, that allegedly was used to finance the Watergate bugging and broader espionage and sabotage operations. Press reports said that high Republican officials in the re-election campaign and on the White House staff had knowledge of the fund. Many of these reports were denied, but full details on the fund and its uses had yet to be revealed by mid-June of 1973.

In September 1972, *The Washington Post* quoted sources involved in the Watergate investigation as saying that John Mitchell, while attorney general, personally controlled a secret fund used to finance intelligence-gathering operations against the Democrats. Mitchell denied the charge.

Quoting federal investigators and grand jury testimony, the Post reported on Oct. 25 that H. R. Haldeman, the White House chief of staff, was one of five men authorized to approve payments from the fund. The cash fund, according to the story, fluctuated between $350,000 and $700,000. The White House said the reference to Haldeman was untrue and the report was "based on misinformation."

The first acknowledgment by a campaign official that the fund existed was made in a Washington television interview on Oct. 26 by Clark MacGregor, who had replaced Mitchell as Nixon's campaign manager on July 1. MacGregor said no money from the fund had been used for illegal purposes. And he repeated the denial of Haldeman's authority for making disbursements from the fund.

In its August report, the GAO asked the Justice Department to investigate the fund. The department took no action. In its March 12 report, the GAO repeated its request for a Justice Department investigation of the fund, which included Vesco's $200,000 contribution.

Espionage and Sabotage

Reports of an alleged widespread Republican network of espionage and sabotage against the Democrats, paid for out of the secret cash fund, began to appear in the fall of 1972. The first article, published in the Oct. 10 *Washington Post*, was dismissed as a "collection of absurdities" by a re-election committee spokesman. Information in the article was attributed to FBI and Justice Department files. Among the activities described in the Post article were:

- Following members of Democratic candidates' families and assembling dossiers on their personal lives.
- Forging letters and distributing them under Democratic candidates' letterheads.
- Leaking false and manufactured items to the press.
- Throwing campaign schedules into disarray.

- Investigating Democratic campaign workers.
- Planting provocateurs at the national political conventions.
- Seizing confidential campaign files.
- Investigating potential contributors to the Nixon campaign.

Muskie Campaign. According to the Post story, one of the targets of Republican sabotage was Sen. Edmund S. Muskie of Maine, a candidate for the Democratic presidential nomination. One of the incidents most damaging, and perhaps fatal, to his campaign was a well-publicized letter alleging his use of the pejorative word "Canuck" to describe Americans of French-Canadian descent. That incident made headlines in February 1972, before the New Hampshire primary.

The Post account said that one of its reporters had been told by Ken W. Clawson, deputy director of White House communications, that he had written the letter, which had been attributed to a man in Florida. Clawson denied the charge.

An interview with Muskie (conducted before the Oct. 10 report) was published in the Oct. 13 Post, quoting him as saying that he had been victimized by a "systematic campaign of sabotage," including:

- Theft of documents from his files.
- Middle-of-the-night telephone calls to voters from impostors claiming to be Muskie canvassers.
- False items planted in newspapers.
- Facsimiles of his envelopes used to mail embarrassing material under his name—including one assertion that two of his opponents for the nomination had engaged in illicit sexual acts.

A Tampa, Fla., secretary said that she had participated in a scheme to disrupt Muskie's primary campaign in Florida, *The New York Times* reported on Oct. 25.

Enter Segretti. The alleged recruiter of the provocateurs for the Nixon campaign was a young California lawyer and former Treasury Department attorney, Donald H. Segretti. He denied knowing anything about such an operation and called the report "ridiculous."

But that was only the first of many reports alleging that Segretti was involved in undercover rascality. The allegations of sabotage and espionage were regularly denounced as false by spokesmen for the White House and the re-election committee.

The Post reported on Oct. 15 that Segretti, one of more than 50 alleged undercover operators for the Nixon

campaign, had named Dwight L. Chapin, then the President's appointments secretary, as one of his contacts. The source of the charges was a sworn statement from another California attorney, Lawrence Young. Segretti, Young and Chapin had been college classmates. Chapin said the story was "based on hearsay and is fundamentally inaccurate."

Time magazine Oct. 23, citing Justice Department files, wrote that:

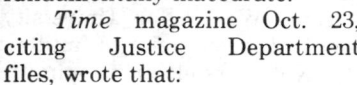

Dwight Chapin

• Segretti was hired by Chapin and Gordon Strachan, a White House staff assistant, and was paid by Herbert W. Kalmbach, Nixon's personal attorney.

• Segretti received more than $35,000 between Sept. 1, 1971, and March 15, 1972, "to subvert and disrupt Democratic candidates' campaigns."

• The FBI began an investigation after discovering a record of phone calls between Segretti and Howard Hunt, one of the seven Watergate defendants.

Records showed that Segretti had made calls to the White House and Chapin's home, *The New York Times* reported Oct. 18. A Times report Oct. 19 said that Segretti apparently volunteered to work for Democratic candidate McGovern in the California primary campaign in June. Although there was evidence that a man named Segretti had appeared at McGovern headquarters, there was no evidence that he actually had worked on the campaign, the Times said.

The Los Angeles Times reported on Oct. 23 that Segretti had told a San Francisco attorney that "he was trying to develop an organization to infiltrate the primary campaigns of two candidates for the Democratic nomination, Senators Muskie of Maine and Henry M. Jackson of Washington. His purpose, it was reported, was to prevent a sweep of the primaries by one candidate.

Segretti Investigation. A Justice Department investigation of Segretti was confirmed by an administration source on Feb. 11, 1973, *The New York Times* reported. Earlier, the department had said that Segretti's efforts appeared to be legal and did not warrant an investigation. But the Times quoted a source as saying that Segretti might have violated a statute making it illegal to distribute political literature that is unsigned or contains an unauthorized signature.

On May 4, a grand jury in Orlando, Fla., indicted Segretti and Tampa accountant George Heagins on charges of distributing a bogus letter under the letterhead of Sen. Muskie containing derogatory charges against two of his Democratic presidential rivals.

Other Incidents. James McCord, one of the defendants in the criminal case, investigated syndicated columnist Jack Anderson in the spring of 1972, *The Washington Post* reported on Sept. 27. An alleged confidential memorandum from McCord dealt with Anderson's business and social relationship with Anna Chennault of Washington, D.C., a member of the Republican National Finance Committee.

Another Watergate defendant, E. Howard Hunt Jr., had tried to recruit a government employee to investigate the private life of Sen. Edward M. Kennedy (D Mass.), the Post reported on Feb. 10. Clifton DeMotte, a General Services Administration employee at Davisville, R.I., said the incident had occurred in July 1971, when Kennedy was considered a leading contender for his party's presidential nomination.

The GAO said on March 12 that it would investigate some $150-a-week payments reportedly made to Theodore T. Brill, chairman of the Young Republicans at George Washington University. Brill told the Post that he had been paid to infiltrate radical groups in 1972 for Nixon's re-election committee.

Criminal and Civil Trials

The criminal trial of the seven Watergate defendants began on Jan. 8 and ended on Jan. 30, 1973. Sentencing was March 23. Still to be tried were three civil suits related to the Watergate. The U.S. District Court in Washington was where the criminal trial was held and where the civil suits would be tried. Chief Judge John J. Sirica tried the criminal case. Judge Charles R. Richey will try the civil cases.

John J. Sirica   **Charles R. Richey**

Criminal, civil trial judges

Pre-trial Activity. A federal grand jury indicted Liddy, Hunt, McCord, Barker, Martinez, Sturgis and Gonzalez on eight counts Sept. 15. The seven were charged with breaking into the Watergate offices for the purpose of stealing documents and installing electronic listening devices to intercept telephone and oral communications.

Sirica on Oct. 4 enjoined all parties connected with the bugging from making public statements about it. His injunction covered law enforcement officials, defendants, witnesses, alleged victims and attorneys. Sirica's order was greeted with a protest from several Democratic officials. He responded by amending the order to remove references to "witnesses, potential witnesses, complaining witnesses and alleged victims." And he said, "It is not the intention of this court to affect congressional activity, political debate or news media reporting."

On Oct. 11, the final day for filing motions, attorneys for Liddy, Hunt and McCord filed affidavits charging that they had been followed and their telephones had been tapped. They asked for a change of venue, which was denied.

The trial was supposed to start on Nov. 15. But on Oct. 27, Sirica postponed the trial until Jan. 8, 1973. The judge had a pinched nerve, and his doctor advised the postponement.

Trial Opening. A jury was chosen in two days. Sirica warned prospective jurors that he expected the trial to last four to six weeks. Jurors were sequestered from the start.

Defense and government attorneys made their opening statements on Jan. 10. Earl J. Silbert, the chief prosecutor, charged that a broadly ranging political espionage operation had been ordered by top officials of the Committee to Re-elect the President in 1972. He said Liddy had received $235,000 in cash from the re-election committee to carry out various assignments. Only $50,000 of the money could be accounted for by the prosecution, Silbert said. He also described the hiring by Hunt of a Brigham Young University student, Thomas J. Gregory, to infiltrate the campaign organizations of candidates McGovern and Muskie.

Two defense attorneys, Gerald Alch and Henry Rothblatt, acknowledged in their opening statements that their clients had been in the Watergate the night of June 17. But both said their clients were innocent of the charges.

Guilty Pleas. Within a few days, the seven defendants had been reduced to two. On Jan. 11, Sirica accepted a guilty plea from Hunt on all six counts with which he was charged. On Jan. 15, Barker, Sturgis, Martinez and Gonzalez pleaded guilty. Hunt was freed after posting $100,000 bond. The other four remained in the District of Columbia jail.

Gerald Alch, McCord's attorney, made a motion for a mistrial after the guilty pleas had been made. The absence of the five men from the courtroom would lead the jurors to conclude that guilty pleas had been made and would prejudice the rights of McCord and Liddy, the two men still on trial, he argued. Sirica denied Alch's motion and advised him that he could appeal the ruling to the U.S. Court of Appeals.

Few Answers. Several times during the trial, Sirica personally questioned defendants and witnesses in an effort to get to the bottom of the Watergate affair. He interrogated Barker, Sturgis, Martinez and Gonzalez Jan. 15 about who had planned the bugging and where the money to pay for it had come from.

The four denied press reports that they had been under pressure to plead guilty, that they still were being paid by an unnamed source and that they had been promised a cash settlement as high as $1,000 a month if they pleaded guilty and went to jail.

Anti-communism and anti-Castroism figured in the testimony of the four, two of whom had been linked to the Bay of Pigs invasion. "When it comes to Cuba and the communist conspiracy involving the United States, I will do anything to protect this country," Sturgis said. Gonzalez said he had been told by Barker and Hunt that "we're solving the Cuban situation" by breaking into the Watergate.

'Law of Duress.' Alch, McCord's lawyer, wrote in a memorandum to the court Jan. 17 that his client's participation in the break-in and other activities had been justified because McCord feared violence against Nixon and other Republicans. He explained the "law of duress" to reporters in these words: "If one is under a reasonable apprehension—regardless of whether that apprehension is in fact correct—he is justified in breaking a law to avoid the greater harm..." Alch cited "potentially violent groups" that supported Democratic candidates in 1972 and might have indicated their plans to the Democrats.

Baldwin Testimony. A key government witness, Alfred Baldwin, testified in secret session Jan. 17 about the persons whose conversations he had overheard while tapping phones at the Democratic National Committee. Before the trial went into secret session, Baldwin described how McCord had hired him in May 1972 and how his wiretapping apparatus had been set up in the motel room across from the Watergate. He said he was instructed to take notes on monitored conversations through the day and into the evening, turning over his logs to McCord.

Sloan Testimony. Hugh W. Sloan Jr., the former treasurer of the President's re-election finance committee, said John Mitchell and Maurice Stans had approved spending money that the government claimed was used for espionage against the Democrats.

In testimony Jan. 23, Sloan said that he had given $199,000 in cash to Liddy at the direction of Jeb Stuart Magruder, deputy campaign chairman for the President. Magruder testified that the committee budgeted about $235,000 for intelligence operations directed by Liddy. He said he knew nothing about illegal bugging activities.

Jeb. S. Magruder

Convictions. Liddy and McCord were found guilty on Jan. 30 of conspiracy, burglary and wiretapping violations. Liddy was convicted on six counts, McCord on eight. Their attorneys said they would appeal.

Alch, McCord's attorney, was bitingly critical of Sirica on the trial's last day. Sirica, he said, "did not limit himself to acting as a judge. He has become, in addition, a prosecutor and an investigator. Not only does he indicate that the defendants are guilty, but that a lot of other people are guilty. The whole courtroom is permeated with a prejudicial atmosphere." Alch claimed on Jan. 31 that Sirica had committed at least nine errors providing grounds for the reversal of McCord's conviction.

The judge had been critical of the prosecution for failing to ask more questions about the motivation of the men. He had sought to compensate for what he felt was this shortcoming by doing extensive interrogating of his own. Questions left unanswered by the trial would, he said, have to be answered by the Senate investigation.

Sentencing. Liddy was given the heaviest sentence by Sirica on March 23. He was sentenced to a minimum of six years and eight months to a maximum of 20 years in prison and was fined $40,000.

The judge left open the final sentence, pending a three-month study by the U.S. Bureau of Prisons, for Barker, Hunt, Sturgis, Martinez and Gonzalez. The five were jailed until the study was completed, at which time Sirica would, he said, uphold the "provisional" maximum sentences he had imposed, reduce the sentences or place the men on probation. For Barker, Sturgis, Martinez and Gonzalez, the potential maximum sentence was 40 years; for Hunt, 35.

One of the most unusual twists of the trial occurred the day of sentencing, when Sirica read a letter written to him by McCord earlier that week. In the letter, McCord wrote that other persons besides those convicted had been involved. Perjury had been committed, he charged. And he claimed that political pressure had been applied to make the defendants plead guilty.

Sirica postponed sentencing of McCord for one week and freed him on $100,000 bond. On March 30, Sirica deferred sentencing until June 15 so that McCord would have the opportunity to testify further before a federal grand jury and before the Senate investigating committee.

Civil Suits. Remaining to be tried before Judge Richey were three civil suits, one filed by Democrats against Republicans and two by Republicans against Democrats. The actions:

• Attorneys for the Democratic National Committee filed suit against the President's re-election committee on June 20, 1972—three days after the break-in—seeking $1-million in damages. Damages sought were increased to $3.2-million on Sept. 11 and increased again to $6.4-million on Feb. 28, 1973. Defendants were expanded to include Liddy, Hunt, former campaign treasurer Sloan, finance chairman Stans, Magruder and Herbert L. Porter, a former Nixon campaign aide.

• Stans and Francis I. Dale, chairman of Nixon's re-election committee, filed a $2.5-million countersuit on Sept. 11.

• Stans filed a $5-million libel suit against former Democratic Chairman O'Brien on Sept. 14 on the grounds that O'Brien had falsely accused him of political espionage on Sept. 11.

Probes, Leaks, Denials

The longest and most penetrating probe of the Watergate and related matters was expected to be conducted by the Senate select committee. But, in the months since the bugging arrests, other investigations as well as those by the House Banking and Currency Committee were conducted by the FBI, the GAO, the White House and a federal grand jury. Leakage of information from these probes led to denials, countercharges and recriminations. As the Senate committee was preparing for public hearings, Chairman Ervin and the White House appeared to be headed toward a showdown over the right of White House staff members to refuse to testify before congressional committees.

White House. At an Aug. 29 news conference, Nixon said that no one then employed in his administration had been involved in the Watergate bugging. He said

that a complete investigation of the incident by John W. Dean III, his counsel, permitted him to declare "categorically that his investigation indicates that no one in the White House staff, no one in this administration, presently employed, was involved in this very bizarre incident."

The President claimed that "technical violations" of the federal election campaign law had "occurred and are occurring, apparently, on both sides." He refused to discuss what possible violations had been committed by the Democrats, saying only that "I think that will come out in the balance of this week."

John W. Dean III

Nixon added, "What really hurts in matters of this sort is not the fact that they occur, because over-zealous people in campaigns do things that are wrong. What really hurts is if you try to cover it up."

At a news conference the next day, Aug. 30, Nixon said he would not comply with a Democratic suggestion that a special, nonpartisan prosecutor instead of a Justice Department attorney be assigned to the Watergate case.

Ronald L. Ziegler, the White House press secretary, said on Sept. 8 that the report on Dean's Watergate investigation would not be released. Lawrence O'Brien, then McGovern's campaign manager, had requested its release.

Justice Department. Attorney General Kleindienst pledged on Aug. 28 that the FBI investigation of the Watergate would be "the most extensive, thorough and comprehensive investigation since the assassination of President Kennedy." When completed, he said, "no credible, fair-minded person is going to be able to say that we whitewashed or dragged our feet on it."

Nixon expressed confidence in the FBI investigation on Oct. 5. He said it made the 1948 Alger Hiss probe, which had helped him build a reputation as a young representative, look like "a Sunday school exercise."

The Washington Post reported on Oct. 11 that FBI investigators in the Watergate case had been hindered by resistance from middle- and lower-level White House officials and by witnesses who gave incorrect or incomplete information.

Judiciary Committee. The Senate Judiciary Committee began confirmation hearings Feb. 28 on L. Patrick Gray III, Nixon's nominee for permanent director of the FBI. Out of the hearings came new disclosures about espionage and the Watergate. FBI records submitted by Gray to the committee sometimes corroborated some earlier news reports. These were among the statements in the records:

• Herbert Kalmbach, Nixon's personal attorney, told the FBI he and Dwight Chapin, then the President's appointments secretary, arranged to pay between $30,000 and $40,000 to Donald Segretti, the alleged saboteur.

• Re-election committee officials tried to impede an FBI investigation of the Watergate.

• Dean, the President's counsel, sat in on all interviews of White House personnel conducted by FBI investigators. Gray told the committee on March 6 that he had opposed Dean's presence at the interviews but had permitted him to be present because the alternative would have been to have no interviews.

• Liddy and Hunt, two former White House consultants, "traveled around the United States contacting former CIA employees for the purpose of setting up a security organization for the Republican Party dealing with political espionage."

• An unnamed official of the Republican re-election committee told the FBI that Hugh Sloan "allegedly disbursed large sums to various committee officials for unknown reasons." The disbursements included $50,000 to Jeb Stuart Magruder, $100,000 to Herbert Porter and $89,000 to Liddy.

The Judiciary Committtee hearings resulted in the withdrawal of Gray's nomination, at Gray's request, by the President on April 5. Confirmation of the nominee had appeared increasingly unlikely.

Among the factors that damaged Gray's chances were his testimony before the committee that he had turned over FBI files to John Dean and his statement to the committee that Dean probably had lied to the FBI in saying he did not know that E. Howard Hunt had a

White House office. Gray also was damaged by Dean's refusal to testify before the committee, claiming executive privilege.

Select Committee. The executive privilege issue was an important one in the impending hearings of the Senate investigating committee, too, and by mid-April it was not resolved. Chairman Ervin, considered the Senate's foremost constitutional expert, threatened to subpoena White House staff members and have them arrested by the Senate sergeant at arms if they did not appear.

The White House promised to cooperate with the committee by answering questions in writing. Ervin rejected that offer and a later White House suggestion that informal testimony, not under oath, might be permitted. "That is not executive privilege," said Ervin at a news conference April 2. "That is executive poppycock."

As a result of the letter he had written to Judge Sirica, conspirator James McCord had arranged to meet with the judge several days after the sentencing. Instead, he met privately with Samuel Dash, the committee counsel, on March 23 and 24. Dash briefed reporters on the meeting on March 25 but would not discuss the substance of the conversations.

Quoting unidentified sources, *The Los Angeles Times* said that McCord had told Dash that Magruder and Dean had prior knowledge of the Watergate bugging. The report was denied—as it had been before—and Nixon reaffirmed his confidence in Dean.

McCord testified in secret before the select committee on March 28. Another leak, again attributed to an unidentified source by *The Washington Post,* quoted McCord as telling the committee that John Mitchell had approved the bugging personally and that Charles W. Colson, former special counsel to Nixon, knew in advance of the plot. More denials were forthcoming.

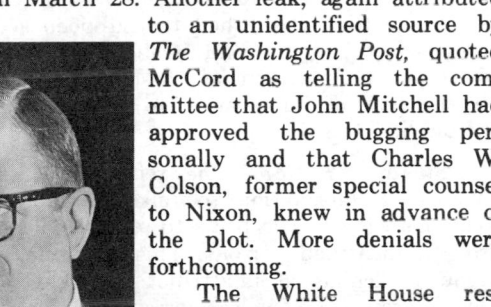
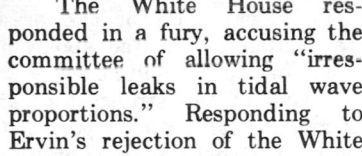

Charles W. Colson

The White House responded in a fury, accusing the committee of allowing "irresponsible leaks in tidal wave proportions." Responding to Ervin's rejection of the White House offer of informal testimony by its staffers, press secretary Ziegler said: "I would encourage the chairman to get his own disorganized house in order so that the investigation can go forward in a proper atmosphere of traditional fairness and due process."

Ervin announced on April 3 that the full committee would suspend closed hearings. Colson reinforced his assertion of innocence by taking a lie detector test which indicated, according to press reports April 8, that he was telling the truth.

Grand Jury. While the select committee was conducting its leaky investigation, the federal grand jury was continuing to hear witnesses in secret. E. Howard Hunt Jr. invoked the 5th Amendment (against self-incrimination) when he appeared before the jury on March 27. The next day, Judge Sirica granted the government's request to grant Hunt immunity from further prosecution, and he testified for nearly four hours.

G. Gordon Liddy, too, had been granted immunity and ordered by Sirica on March 30 to testify before the grand jury. He refused to answer the jury's questions and was sentenced to an additional jail term for contempt of court. Sirica sentenced Liddy to serve until the end of the grand jury term—the end of 1973 unless extended—or 18 months, whichever came first.

Four other conspirators—Barker, Martinez, Sturgis and Gonzalez—were ordered to testify after being given immunity. Sirica indicated their cooperation, and McCord's, would be a factor when he sentenced them and McCord in June.

Partisan Repercussions

If the Watergate scandal dropped any ominous fallout on Republican candidates in the 1972 elections, it apparently did no damage to the President, who won a second term by a landslide. Watergate simply was not an important issue in most places.

McGovern. George McGovern made several speeches about it. In a Los Angeles speech Oct. 16, he called the Republican activities "the shabbiest undercover operations in the history of American politics." On Oct. 25, in a nationwide television speech, he accused the administration of corruption and sabotage and said the nation was confronted with "a moral and a constitutional crisis of unprecedented dimensions." Earlier that day in Cleveland, McGovern had said a report linking White House staff chief Haldeman with the affair "places the whole ugly mess of corruption, espionage and sabotage squarely in the lap of Richard Nixon."

Republicans. As the Senate investigation drew closer and the administration-Congress disagreement grew sharper, Republican leaders showed more signs of worry.

Senate Republicans were becoming more concerned about the political impact, said Senate Minority Leader Hugh Scott (R Pa.) on March 29. The same day, Senators Robert W. Packwood (R Ore.) and Charles McC. Mathias Jr. (R Md.) urged Nixon to appoint a prominent outsider to head a special White House investigation. "The most odious issue since the Teapot Dome," said Packwood in describing the matter.

George Bush, the Republican national chairman, called the Watergate bugging "grubby" and said the incident should be "promptly and fully cleared up" to prevent adverse effects on the party.

But the shrillest attack on the White House was launched by Sen. Lowell P. Weicker Jr. (R Conn.), the junior Republican on the investigating committee. He said in a television interview April 1 that a paid agent of the Nixon re-election committee had spied on nine congressional offices in 1972. Two days later, he called for Haldeman's resignation because, said Weicker, he "clearly has to accept responsibility" for a broad range of alleged espionage activities during the 1972 campaign.

Senators Ervin and Howard H. Baker Jr. (R Tenn.), the select committee's vice chairman, issued a statement on April 4 saying that the committee had "received no evidence of any nature" connecting Haldeman with illegal activities. To which Weicker responded: "I concur with the statement."

Martha Mitchell's Phone Calls

Former Attorney General John N. Mitchell resigned as President Nixon's campaign manager on July 1, 1972. He said he had been spending too much time away from his wife, Martha, and their daughter.

His resignation came a week after Mrs. Mitchell had telephoned a wire service reporter twice. In both calls, she threatened to leave Mitchell if he did not give up politics.

Mrs. Mitchell phoned *The New York Times* on March 27, 1973, and said, according to the Times' report: "I fear for my husband. I'm really scared. I have a definite reason. I can't tell you why. But they're not going to pin anything on him. I won't let them, and I don't give a damn who gets hurt. I can name names.... If you hear that I'm sick or can't talk, please, please, get your reporters out to find me. Somebody might try to shut me up."

Mrs. Mitchell was quoted as saying, in another call to the wire service on March 31: "I think this administration has turned completely against my husband. In other words, they're desperate, and I will not under any circumstances let them pin it on my husband. I think my husband has become the whipping boy for the whole administration, and they want to hide who is really involved."

Newspaper Poll. A poll conducted by Political Surveys and Analyses Inc., Princeton, N.J., and commissioned by *The Wall Street Journal,* indicated that the Republicans might find the Watergate affair a serious liability. The poll, published April 6, found, in 501 telephone interviews around the country:

• Ninety-one per cent of those questioned had heard or read about the Watergate incident.

• Thirty-eight per cent believed some top Nixon aides knew in advance about the bugging; 33 per cent did not; 29 per cent were unsure.

• Seventy-one per cent said the affair would not affect their votes; 29 per cent said they would be less likely to vote Republican in 1974.

• Fifty-three per cent thought Nixon was unaware of the bugging plans; 21 per cent thought he was; 26 per cent were unsure.

• Fifty-four per cent believed the White House had tried to prevent a full investigation of the case; 23 per cent thought the White House had done "everything it should to bring out all the facts"; 23 per cent were unsure.

• Fifty-four per cent felt press coverage had been fair; 30 per cent thought the press had been "making too much" of it.

• Sixty per cent wanted the congressional investigation to continue; 26 per cent thought the case should be dropped; 14 per cent were unsure.

Bouts with the Press

Two court tests involving the press coverage have been byproducts of the Watergate affair.

Los Angeles Times. The first test resulted from the tape-recorded interview of Alfred Baldwin in Oc-

tober by two *Los Angeles Times* reporters, Jack Nelson and Ronald J. Ostrow. The Times had promised Baldwin that it would not divulge details of the interview without his approval.

In December, attorneys for E. Howard Hunt sought the tapes for use in the forthcoming criminal trial. Judge Sirica rejected the Times' contention that being forced to turn over the tapes would inhibit its ability to report the news and would violate the Constitution's first Amendment protection for a free press.

Sirica cited the newspaper for contempt of court and ordered its Washington bureau chief, John F. Lawrence, jailed. He was in jail for only a few hours before the impasse was broken by an agreement between Baldwin and the court. Baldwin and his attorneys agreed to make the recordings available to Sirica for private inspection, with the understanding that Sirica would edit out any remarks by Baldwin's attorneys or the two reporters.

Civil Suits. The second court action against the press occurred on Feb. 26, when attorneys for Nixon's re-election committee subpoenaed nine reporters, two newspaper executives and three other persons with knowledge of the Watergate. The publications involved were *The Washington Post, The Washington Star-News, The New York Times* and *Time* magazine.

The re-election committee attorneys sought materials such as notes, tapes and other private records from the reporters. The material was sought in connection with the three civil suits before the U.S. District Court.

Judge Richey quashed the subpoenas on March 20. "This court cannot blind itself to the possible chilling effect the enforcement of these subpoenas would have on the flow of information to the press and, thus, to the public," he said.

Steady Friction. The refusal of many potential sources of information to talk to reporters about the Watergate forced the press to rely heavily on statements from unidentified persons. This situation brought about frequent denials of unattributed accusations and occasional castigation of the press by administration and re-election committee spokesmen. Their favorite target was *The Washington Post.*

One of the strongest attacks came from campaign manager Clark MacGregor on Oct. 16, just after the reports on Donald Segretti and his alleged associations with the White House. "Using innuendo, third-person hearsay, unsubstantiated charges, anonymous sources and huge scare headlines—the Post has maliciously sought to give the appearance of a direct connection between the White House and the Watergate—a charge which the Post knows—and half a dozen investigations have found—to be false," MacGregor said.

MacGregor accused the Post of "hypocrisy" for not investigating allegations that the McGovern campaign organization was responsible for isolated incidents of violence at Nixon campaign offices. The Post reported on Oct. 18 that police and both parties' campaign workers had failed to link the McGovern organization with the incidents.

After a Post report on Oct. 25 linked Haldeman, the White House staff chief, with the secret cash fund, press secretary Ziegler accused the Post of "character assassination" and "the shoddiest kind of journalism."

SPRING 1973 WATERGATE DEVELOPMENTS: TOP AIDES RESIGN

Throughout the spring and early summer of 1973, investigations of the Watergate affair and related activities continued on many fronts. Involved in the probes were several grand juries, the Justice Department, an independent special prosecutor and several congressional committees in addition to the select Senate panel.

Reports leaked to newsmen from grand jury and Capitol Hill proceedings implicated officials at the highest level of the Nixon administration in cover-ups, illegal campaign sabotage and espionage activities and questionable domestic surveillance operations undertaken for the stated reason protecting national security. Many of the President's top aides denied the allegations; but others publicly admitted their roles and offered possibly damaging testimony against their former colleagues. By mid-June, the question had arisen whether the President himself should testify before grand juries and Congress; but the White House stated that to do so would be "constitutionally inappropriate" and a violation of the separation of powers.

Nixon Actions

Amid mounting speculation about White House involvement in the Watergate affair, the President April 17, in a dramatic reversal of previous policy, said that all members of the White House staff would appear voluntarily when requested by the Senate committee. "They will testify under oath and they will answer fully all proper questions," he said.

The President also told reporters that he had begun "intensive new inquiries" into the Watergate affair on March 21 "as a result of serious charges which came to my attention." Without further elaboration he said there had been "major new developments in the case."

All previous statements from the White House were "inoperative," said Press Secretary Ronald L. Ziegler April 17. "The President's statement today is the operative statement."

During the next two weeks, the burgeoning Watergate scandal unreeled with breathtaking speed. Among the developments:

● Attorney General Richard G. Kleindienst April 19 disqualified himself from further involvement in the case and announced that Assistant Attorney General Henry E. Petersen would take full control of the Justice Department's criminal investigation of the Watergate.

● With reports predicting his imminent resignation, White House counsel John W. Dean III issued a statement that he would not "become a scapegoat in the Watergate case."

● On April 27, L. Patrick Gray III, acting director of the FBI, announced his resignation effective immediately. Gray, whose name had been withdrawn as Nixon's nominee for permanent FBI director April 5, resigned amid reports that he had been directed by Ehrlichman and Dean to destroy documents belonging to conspirator E. Howard Hunt early in July 1972.

Haldeman, Ehrlichman Resignations. In a dramatic series of events, Nixon April 30 announced the resignation of four of his closest aides: H.R. Haldeman, White House chief of staff; John D. Ehrlichman, chief counselor for domestic affairs; John W. Dean III, presidential counsel; and Attorney General Richard G. Kleindienst. The President said he accepted with regret the resignations of Haldeman, Ehrlichman and Kleindienst. Of his counsel, Nixon only stated, "I have requested and accepted" Dean's resignation.

In the same statement, Nixon announced the nomination of Defense Secretary Elliot L. Richardson as attorney general and the appointment of Leonard Garment as presidential counsel.

Addressing the nation that night, Nixon said he took full responsibility for any improper activities connected with his 1972 campaign and pledged that "justice will be pursued fairly, fully and impartially." The President said Richardson would have full charge of the administration's Watergate investigations and would have authority to appoint an independent special prosecutor in the case.

Cox Appointment. With pressures in Congress building up for speedy appointment of a prosecutor and assurances that he would have broad independent powers, Attorney General-designate Richardson May 18 announced the selection of former Solicitor General and Harvard law professor Archibald Cox as the special prosecutor for the Watergate case. Promising that he would have no compunctions in pursuing the trail of any federal crime involved in the Watergate-presidential campaign scandal, Cox said he would follow all leads to their conclusion.

Nixon Statement on Cover-up. The President followed up his April 30 address with a 4,000-word statement released May 22. In the statement and another summary statement, Nixon admitted that there had been a White House cover-up in the Watergate affair but asserted he was innocent of any planning or knowledge of it.

In his first public remarks on Watergate since April 30, the President sought to explain his and the White House's roles in the Watergate affair and related activities. He also made these points:

● He would not resign.
● Some of his directives may have led to the coverup.
● He did not authorize or know of offers of executive clemency or money to Watergate defendants.
● He did not attempt to implicate the Central Intelligence Agency (CIA) in the Watergate affair.

"To the extent that I may in any way have contributed to the climate in which they (the Watergate and any other illegal campaign activities) took place, I did not intend to; to the extent that I failed to prevent them, I should have been more vigilant," he said.

Pentagon Papers Trial

Meanwhile, the Watergate scandal took a bizarre turn on April 27, 1973, when it was revealed that two of the convicted conspirators—E. Howard Hunt Jr. and G. Gordon Liddy—had burglarized the files of Daniel Ellsberg's former psychiatrist. Ellsberg was one of the defendants in the Pentagon Papers trial in Los Angeles.

It was disclosed May 1 that Ehrlichman had told FBI interviewers April 27 that the President had directed him in 1971 to undertake an independent investigation of the Pentagon Papers leak. Ehrlichman hired Hunt and Liddy to conduct the probe, which led to the burglary of the psychiatrist's office. Ehrlichman said he had not authorized the burglary and that when he learned about it, he instructed Hunt and Liddy "not to do this again."

In a second FBI interview May 2, Ehrlichman contended that he had not seen anything about the secret probe for more than a year and that the results of the investigation were probably in the hands of former White House aides Egil Krogh Jr. and David Young. Both Krogh and Young were members of a group known at the White House as "the plumbers" (Hunt and Liddy also were members). The group was set up on orders from Nixon in July 1971, after publication of the Pentagon Papers in several newspapers, with the publicly announced mission of stopping any more such leaks.

In a statement filed as part of an affidavit in the Pentagon Papers trial, Krogh May 5 said he took full responsibility for the September 1971 break-in at the psychiatrist's office. Krogh May 9 resigned as under secretary of transportation.

Meanwhile, CIA Director James L. Schlesinger May 9 conceded that the agency had cooperated with former CIA agent Hunt in the burglary. He described the agency's role as an "ill-advised act."

Following a May 10 disclosure of an FBI wiretap on Ellsberg's telephone, Judge W. Matthew Byrne Jr. May 11 dismissed all charges of espionage, theft and conspiracy against Ellsberg and codefendant Anthony J. Russo and declared a mistrial because of government misconduct.

The President linked the Watergate case with the Pentagon Papers in his May 22, 1973, statement. Discussing his actions that may have led to the Watergate cover-up, Nixon said that when the Watergate scandal broke in June, 1972, he feared that an investigation of the break-in might lead to a probe of the White House "plumbers" unit that he had established in 1971 to investigate leaks to newsmen—and, from there, to the CIA, which he said he mistakenly believed may have been involved in Watergate.

CIA's Role Questioned

In a related development, the question of alleged White House pressure on the CIA to help cover up the Watergate case unfolded before several congressional committees during the spring of 1973.

In testimony before the Senate Armed Services Committee May 14, 1973, Lt. Gen. Vernon Walters, deputy director of the CIA, revealed that the White House tried to pressure the CIA into assisting in a cover-up of the Watergate scandal. Walters reportedly said Haldeman, Ehrlichman and former acting FBI director Gray were directly involved in the attempt.

During hearings before the Senate Foreign Relations Committee May 22, former CIA Director Richard Helms said he assumed the White House aides who requested aid from the CIA were doing so on orders from Nixon. Asked why he did not consult the President when the requests proved questionable, Helms answered:

"My interest was to keep the CIA out of this (Watergate). Frankly, I wanted to stay as head of the agency and keep it out of all this." Helms was replaced as head of the CIA after the 1972 elections.

The CIA officials' statements were contradicted in testimony by Haldeman and Ehrlichman May 30 and 31. They confirmed that a meeting with Helms and Walters took place June 23, 1972, during which a discussion occurred concerning the FBI investigation of Nixon campaign funds that passed through a Mexican bank and ended up in the Miami bank account of one of the Watergate burglars. But Ehrlichman denied that the meeting was designed to pressure the CIA into blocking an FBI investigation of the "Mexican connection."

According to Haldeman, the meeting was called to discuss in general terms whether the CIA had any involvement in the Watergate break-in. In his statement, Haldeman referred to White House concern that a Watergate investigation might lead to disclosure "of non-Watergate-related covert CIA operations or other national security activities." These same concerns for national security were the primary reasons he ordered Haldeman and Ehrlichman to meet with CIA officials, Nixon said in his May 22 speech.

(In a related development, former acting FBI Director Gray told a Senate Appropriations subcommittee May 24 that he had warned Nixon July 6, 1972, that "people on your staff are trying to mortally wound you" by hampering the FBI's investigation of the Watergate.)

Vesco Indictments

The grand jury investigation of the Vesco case climaxed May 10, with the indictments of former Attorney General John N. Mitchell and former Secretary of Commerce Maurice H. Stans. The two were accused of obstructing justice by interfering with a federal investigation and lying to the grand jury. They were charged with obtaining a secret $200,000 cash contribution to the Nixon campaign in return for promises to intercede with the government on behalf of the contributor, financier Robert L. Vesco, who already was in trouble with the Securities and Exchange Commission (SEC) over an alleged mutual fund swindle. Vesco also was indicted, along with Harry L. Sears, a New Jersey lawyer and Republican politician. All but Vesco denied the charges. (Background p. 982)

Senate Hearings

Exactly 11 months after the break-in and bugging of Democratic national headquarters, the seven-member Senate Select Committee on Presidential Campaign Activities opened hearings on the Watergate scandal "in an atmosphere of the utmost gravity." The incident on June 17, 1972, was only a pebble at the center of a still-widening circle of disclosures of governmental and political corruption.

Chairman Sam J. Ervin Jr. (D N.C.) described the atmosphere as testimony began May 17 in front of the television floodlights that filled the pillared, chandeliered, marble-walled caucus room of the Russell Senate Office Building. "If the allegations that have been made in the wake of the Watergate affair are substantiated, there has been a very serious subversion of the integrity of the electoral process," he said.

The first round of hearings dealt with the planning and execution of the wiretapping and break-in and the alleged cover-up of the incident. A second round of hearings was to explore allegations of broader campaign espionage and sabotage. And a third would probe alleged violations of campaign spending laws.

McCord Testimony. The hearings got off to a slow start the first day. But they sprang vividly to life on the second day, with testimony from convicted Watergate conspirator James W. McCord Jr. His testimony implicated President Nixon himself in alleged offers of executive clemency in return for a guilty plea by McCord at the January 1973 criminal trial of seven Watergate defendants.

McCord, a stocky veteran of 19 years with the CIA, read a statement in which he said presidential pressure was conveyed to him in January by John J. Caulfield, a former presidential staff assistant whose immediate supervisor was former White House counsel Dean.

Caulfield told him, McCord said, "to remain silent, take executive clemency by going off to prison quietly, and I was told that while there I would receive financial aid and later rehabilitation and a job. I was further told in a January meeting in 1973 with Caulfield that the President of the United States was aware of our meeting...."

Caulfield Testimony. McCord's testimony that he believed President Nixon had direct knowledge of the clemency negotiations was contradicted by Caulfield, who took the witness chair May 22. According to Caulfield, he never referred to the President himself but to "the highest levels of the White House." His White House contact, he said, was counsel John Dean.

Sloan Testimony. As the committee prepared to resume hearings June 5, controversy flared up between the committee and special prosecutor Cox, who had requested a delay in the hearings on the ground that testimony from some witnesses might interfere with their later prosecution. The committee rejected the request.

The single most important witness to come before the committee on June 6 was Hugh W. Sloan Jr., former treasurer of the Nixon re-election campaign. Sloan gave the senators a detailed accounting of nearly $1.8-million in cash disbursements by the President's finance committee before a tighter reporting law took effect on April 7, 1972. Sloan also described in some detail the efforts of campaign officials to force him to perjure himself. Rather than do so, he explained, he resigned from the campaign committee in July 1972.

Sloan described his role as chiefly that of a conduit for funds. He said he seldom questioned what the money would be used for.

Magruder, Stans Testimony. The most detailed account thus far of high-level Nixon administration involvement in the Watergate affair and its cover-up emerged from testimony before the committee during the week ended June 16. The most damaging statements came from former deputy director of the Nixon campaign, Jeb Stuart Magruder, who testified under a grant of partial immunity from further prosecution.

Implicated most strongly in Magruder's testimony, both in the planning and cover-up, was John N. Mitchell, Nixon's former attorney general and law partner who later became his campaign director.

In a full day of testimony June 14, Magruder freely admitted his own complicity in the well-financed scheme to spy on the Democrats. His implications reached as high in the White House hierarchy as H.R. Haldeman, the President's former chief of staff. But they stopped at the door of the oval office. Magruder stated repeatedly that, to his knowledge, Nixon was unaware of the crimes or their cover-up.

Besides naming Mitchell as the official who authorized espionage activities against the Democrats, Magruder revealed that Gordon Strachan, an aide to Haldeman, had advanced knowledge of the Watergate plan. Under intense and repeated questioning, however, Magruder stopped short of saying that Haldeman knew about the Watergate operation in advance.

Magruder was preceded in the witness chair June 12 and 13 by Maurice H. Stans, Nixon's former commerce secretary and later his campaign finance director. Stans denied any advance knowledge of the Watergate, describing himself as only a fund-raiser and a conduit for money that went to the political side of the operation.

But Stans was contradicted by Magruder. June 24, 1972, became a date of contention, because Magruder claimed Stans had been briefed by Mitchell that day on the burglary at Democratic national headquarters. Stans could recall no such briefing.

Dean Testimony. The committee had been scheduled to hear from former White House counsel Dean on June 19, but was pressured into postponing the hearings until after the state visit of Soviet Communist Party leader Leonid I. Brezhnev. Dean appeared before the committee June 25, testifying under a grant of immunity.

In his long-awaited and somewhat predictable (due to previous grand jury and committee staff leaks) testimony, the fired White House aide testified that he and President Nixon had discussed the Watergate cover-up at a series of personal meetings—the first in September 1972, and many more in late March and April of 1973.

Dean also said the orders to burglarize the office of Ellsberg's psychiatrist had come "right out of the oval office." And he testified that it had been reported to him that Haldeman "had cleared" Watergate conspirator G. Gordon Liddy's "activities" with the President prior to the Watergate bugging.

During the six-hour reading of his 245-page formal statement, Dean said both the FBI and Justice Department had been pressured by the White House to ease up on certain aspects of their Watergate probe.

Concerning the President's Aug. 29, 1972, announcement that an investigation by Dean had cleared all those presently employed at the White House or in the administration from any complicity in the Watergate matter, Dean said he had no advance knowledge that Nixon would make that statement and, had Dean been consulted in advance, he "would have strongly opposed" issuing such a statement. Dean said he was involved in a cover-up rather than an investigation and "had never been able to determine whether Haldeman had advance knowledge or not" of the Watergate break-in.

Dean's testimony conflicted sharply with the President's May 22 statement on several points. In subsequent appearances before the committee, Dean's credibility was tested in close questioning by several senators.

Chapter 16—Election Laws and Procedures

Chapter 16—Election Laws and Procedures

 **Reapportionment and Redistricting**

1970 CENSUS LED TO EQUITABLY DRAWN HOUSE DISTRICTS

The Supreme Court's landmark decisions of the 1960s on apportionment and districting set the stage for a massive redrawing of congressional district lines following the 1970 census.

The standard, as laid down in *Kirkpatrick v. Preisler* (1969) was that states must strive to create congressional districts of precisely equal population. Any variance, no matter how small, had to be justified by the state or be shown to result despite a good-faith effort to reach precise mathematical equality, said the court.

Kirkpatrick v. Preisler was the culmination of the liberal Warren court's "one person—one vote" decisions. It was the decision which determined the standards by which the new congressional districts would presumably be judged by the courts. Consequently, once the 1970 census figures became available, state legislators worked very closely with the new data to minimize population variances between districts. The result was that for the first time in history, Americans in November 1972 elected representatives to the U.S. House from districts of nearly equal population within each state.

In June 1973, the court reaffirmed its decision in *Kirkpatrick v. Preisler* by overturning a Texas congressional redistricting plan having a variance of 4.1 per cent between the largest and smallest districts. The court substituted a plan with a variance of only 0.159 per cent.

Court Decisions

Before 1962, the Supreme Court had shunned involvement with apportionment and districting problems. In *Colegrove v. Green* (1946), in which Kenneth Colegrove, a political science professor at Northwestern University, alleged that Illinois' congressional districts were so unequal that they violated the 14th Amendment's guarantee of equal protection of the laws, the court said the issue was "of a peculiarly political nature and therefore not meet for judicial determination.... Courts ought not to enter this political thicket. The remedy for unfairness in districting is to secure state legislatures that will apportion properly, or to invoke the ample powers of Congress."

Historic 1962 Decision. But in 1962, a group of Tennessee city dwellers successfully broke the long-standing precedent against federal court involvement in apportionment and districting problems. For more than half a century, since 1901, the Tennessee legislature had refused to reapportion itself, even though a decennial reapportionment based on population was specifically required by the state's constitution. In the meantime, Tennessee's population had grown and shifted dramatically to urban areas. By 1960, the House legislative districts ranged from 3,454 to 36,031 in population, while the Senate districts ranged from 39,727 to 108,094. Appeals by urban residents to the rural-controlled Tennessee House and Senate proved fruitless. A suit brought

in the state courts to force reapportionment was rejected on the ground that the courts should stay out of legislative matters.

The urban interests then appealed to the federal courts" into a "mathematical quagmire." Frankfurter inhad refused to act for more than half a century; the state courts had refused to intervene; Tennessee had no referendum or initiative laws. The city dwellers charged that there was "a debasement of their votes by virtue of the incorrect, obsolete and unconstitutional apportionment" to such an extent that they were being deprived of their right to "equal protection of the laws" under the 14th Amendment. (The 14th Amendment reads, in part: "No state shall...deny to any person within its jurisdiction the equal protection of the laws.")

The Supreme Court on March 26, 1962, handed down its historic decision in *Baker v. Carr,* ruling in favor of the Tennessee city dwellers by a 6-2 margin. In the majority opinion, Justice William J. Brennan Jr. emphasized that the federal judiciary had the power to review the apportionment of state legislatures under the 14th Amendment's equal protection clause. "The mere fact that a suit seeks protection as a political right," Brennan wrote, "does not mean that it presents a political question" which the courts should avoid.

In a vigorous dissent, Justice Felix Frankfurter said the majority decision constituted "a massive repudiation of the experience of our whole past" and was an assertion of "destructively novel judicial power." He contended that the lack of any clear basis for relief "catapults the lower courts" into a "mathematical quagmire." Frankfurter insisted that "there is not under our Constitution a judicial remedy for every political mischief." Appeal for relief, he maintained, should not be made in the courts, but rather "to an informed civically militant electorate."

Terminology

Apportionment. The decennial computation and assignment of U.S. House seats to the individual states; within a state, the computation and assignment of seats in the state legislature.

Districting. The process of drawing boundaries for congressional districts or state legislative districts.

Gerrymandering. Manipulation of the boundaries of a district to suit the purposes of a political party or interest.

Ideal Population. The average population of all districts in a state.

Variance. The difference between a district's actual population and ideal population.

'One Man, One Vote.' Shortly after the Baker decision was handed down, James P. Wesberry Jr., an Atlanta resident and a member of the Georgia Senate, filed suit in a federal court in Atlanta claiming that gross disparity in the population of Georgia's congressional districts violated 14th Amendment rights of equal protection of the laws. At the time, Georgia districts ranged in population from 272,154 in the rural 9th district in the northeastern part of the state to 823,860 in the 5th district in Atlanta and its suburbs. District lines had not been changed since 1931. The state's number of House seats remained the same in the interim, but Atlanta's district population—already high in 1931 compared with the others—had more than doubled in 30 years, making a 5th district vote worth about one-third of that of a vote in the 9th.

On June 20, 1962, the three-judge federal court divided 2-1 in dismissing Wesberry's suit. The majority reasoned that the precedent of *Colegrove* still controlled in congressional district cases. The judges cautioned against federal judicial interference with Congress and against "depriving others of the right to vote" if the suit should result in at-large elections. They suggested that the Georgia legislature (under court order to reapportion itself) or the U.S. Congress might better provide relief. Wesberry then appealed to the Supreme Court, which heard arguments on the case in November 1963.

On Feb. 17, 1964, the Supreme Court ruled in the case of *Wesberry v. Sanders* that congressional districts must be substantially equal in population. The court, which upheld Wesberry's challenge by a 6-3 decision, based its ruling on the history and wording of Article I, Section 2, of the Constitution providing that representatives shall be apportioned among the states according to their respective numbers and be chosen by the people of the several states. This language, the court stated, meant that "as nearly as is practicable, one man's vote in a congressional election is to be worth as much as another's."

The majority opinion, written by Justice Hugo L. Black and supported by Chief Justice Earl Warren and Justices Brennan, William O. Douglas, Arthur J. Goldberg and Byron R. White, said that "While it may not be possible to draw congressional districts with mathematical precision, that is no excuse for ignoring our Constitution's plain objective of making equal representation for equal numbers of people the fundamental goal for the House of Representatives."

Predictably, the decision referred to the findings of the Baker case to show that districting questions were justiciable and to the *Gray v. Sanders* case to establish the principle of "one man, one vote." (*Gray v. Sanders, 1963,* overturned Georgia's county unit system of voting in statewide and congressional primary elections.) Unlike those two decisions, however, *Wesberry* did not attempt to use the 14th Amendment as its justification.

In a strongly worded dissent, Justice John M. Harlan asserted that the Constitution did not establish population as the only criterion of congressional districting and that the subject was left in the Constitution to the discretion of the states, subject only to the supervisory power of Congress.

Justice Potter Stewart said he found that the Constitution gave "no mandate to this Court or to any court to ordain that congressional districts within each state must be equal in population," but he disagreed with Harlan in that he thought the matter was justiciable.

Justice Tom C. Clark also found the matter justiciable but rejected the idea that Article I, Section 2, required a "one man, one vote" standard in congressional elections. Clark said the case should be returned to the lower court for a hearing on the merits based on the 14th Amendment's equal protection requirements set down in *Baker.*

Wesberry established no precise standards for districting beyond declaring that districts must be as nearly equal in population "as is practicable." In his dissent, Harlan suggested that a disparity of more than 100,000 between a state's largest and smallest districts would "presumably" violate the equality standard enunciated by the majority. On that basis, Harlan estimated, the districts of 37 states with 398 representatives would be unconstitutional, "leaving a constitutional House of 37 members now sitting."

Gerrymandering Excluded. The court's *Wesberry* decision did not make any reference to gerrymandering, since it discussed only the population, not the shape of districts. In a separate districting opinion handed down the same day as *Wesberry*, the court dismissed a challenge to congressional districts in New York City, which had been brought by voters who charged that Manhattan's 17th "silk-stocking" district had been gerrymandered to exclude Negroes and Puerto Rican citizens.

Tighter Standards

The Supreme Court tightened its standards for congressional district populations in *Kirkpatrick v. Preisler* (April 17, 1969). It held a Missouri congressional redistricting statute producing districts with a maximum population variance of 3.1 per cent from perfect mathematical equality was unconstitutional without justification or proof that such variation was unavoidable despite a "good-faith effort" by the state to create districts of precisely equal population.

On the basis of the *Wesberry* ruling of 1964, a district court in 1965 had declared Missouri's 1961 redistricting statute unconstitutional because it did not create equally populated districts. A 1965 redistricting statute was also declared unconstitutional by the district court, a ruling affirmed by the Supreme Court in 1967.

The Missouri legislature in 1967 enacted a third redistricting plan, producing ten districts with a maximum deviation of 3.1 percent from the precise mathematical average population. The district court again declared this law unconstitutional, and Missouri appealed the decision to the Supreme Court.

The court in 1968 stayed the judgment of the lower court pending the appeal and authorized the 1968 elections in the districts as created by the law in question.

Justice Brennan, for the court, affirmed the lower courts ruling and held that states must strive to create congressional districts of precisely equal population. Any variance in population, "no matter how small," must be justified by the state or shown to result despite a "good-faith effort."

In *Wesberry*, Justice Brennan stated, the court held that the Constitution required "as nearly as is practicable one man's vote in a congressional election... to be worth as much as another's."

Defining the phrase "as nearly as practicable," the court ruled in *Kirkpatrick* that there is no fixed population variance small enough to be considered negligible. The *Wesberry* standard, the Court held, directed states to create districts absolutely equal in population. The court said:

"Equal representation for equal numbers of people is a principle designed to prevent debasement of voting power and diminution of access to elected representatives. Toleration of even small deviations detracts from these purposes."

The only permissible variances in population the court ruled, were those unavoidable despite the effort to achieve absolute equality or those which could be legally justified. The variances in Missouri, the court said, could have been avoided. The court noted that the legislature rejected a plan which would have created more equal districts and that it did not use accurate data in forming the plan enacted in 1967.

None of Missouri's argument for the plan qualified as "legally acceptable" justifications. The court rejected the argument that population variance was necessary to allow representation of distinct interest groups. The court held acceptance of such variance in order to produce districts with specific interests as "antithetical" to the basic purpose of equal representation.

The court also rejected the argument that political reality—legislative compromise and the integrity of existing political boundaries—justified population variance. It dismissed arguments that nonvoting military personnel and students inflated census figures for certain districts, that post-1960 population trends were reflected in the new districts, and that geographical compactness dictated the new boundaries and some population inequality.

Justice Abe Fortas, concurring in the rejection of the Missouri plan, disagreed with the standard of mathematical precision announced in the court's opinion. Agreeing that there should be a "high degree of correspondence" between population and district divisions, Justice Fortas said he would accept districts with "small disparities" in population.

"The majority's pursuit of precision is a search for a will-o'-the-wisp," Justice Fortas said. He pointed out that legislatures implementing the standard "might have to ignore the boundaries of common sense, running the...district line down the middle of the corridor of an apartment house or even dividing the residents of a single-family house between two districts."

Justice Fortas agreed that the Missouri plan should not be accepted because of the legislature's failure to comply with the directions of the district court or to use accurate data in constructing the new districts.

Justice White said that some "acceptably small" population variance could be established. He indicated that considerations of existing political boundaries and geographical compactness could justify to him some variation from "absolute equality" of population.

Justice Harlan, joined by Justice Stewart, objected that "whatever room remained under this Court's prior decisions for the free play of the political process in matters of reapportionment is now all but eliminated by today's Draconian judgments."

The court, Justice Harlan declared, had transformed "a political slogan into a constitutional absolute." He said: "Straight indeed is the path of the righteous legislator. Slide rule in hand, he must avoid all thought of county lines, local traditions, politics, history and economics, so as to achieve the magic formula; one man, one vote."

In June 1973, after the new congressional districts had been drawn for the 1972 elections, the Supreme Court reaffirmed its strict standards of mathematical equality in *White v. Weiser*. It threw out a Texas congressional districting plan enacted in 1971 and substituted for it one with minimal population variances. The state's original plan had a variance of 4.1 per cent between the largest and smallest districts; the court's plan reduced it to 0.159 per cent.

Writing for the court, Justice White conceded that the percentage variances in the Texas congressional districts were smaller than those invalidated in *Kirkpatrick*, "but we agree that, under the standards of (that case), they were not as mathematically equal as reasonably possible."

But the court specifically avoided going beyond the question of equal population to those of gerrymandering and compactness and contiguity of congressional districts. Two alternative congressional district plans had been devised by Dan Weiser, a Dallas mathematician, and presented to the courts along with his suit against the legislature's plan. The first, known as Plan B, took the legislature's plan and made small territorial adjustments to it to achieve greater equality in population.

The second, Plan C, ignored the state legislature's districting policy and constructed districts solely on the basis of population considerations. The legislature's plan had contained other considerations—avoiding throwing too many sets of incumbents together in the same districts, maintaining the districts in the same general geographical shape and area as before redistricting, etc.

A lower court had preferred Plan C, but the Supreme Court favored Plan B, affirming the state legislature's right to draw lines as it saw fit, as long as the resulting districts were very close to equal in population.

The decision was unanimous, although Chief Justice Burger, Justices Lewis F. Powell Jr. and William H. Rehnquist said they were going along reluctantly because a majority had not seen fit to modify the *Kirkpatrick* standards.

1970: New Apportionment

Following the 1970 census, the Census Bureau calculated the new distribution of U.S. House seats for each state.

Regular reapportionment of the House based on a complex mathematical formula, called the Method of Equal Proportions, was provided by the Reapportionment Act of 1929, as amended in 1941. *(Description of Method of Equal Proportions, CQ Guide to Congress, p. 509)*

The act requires the President to transmit to Congress, within the first week of the regular January session following every decennial census, the new apportionment based on census figures and computed according to the Method of Equal Proportions. Within 15 days of receipt of the President's message, the clerk of the House auto-

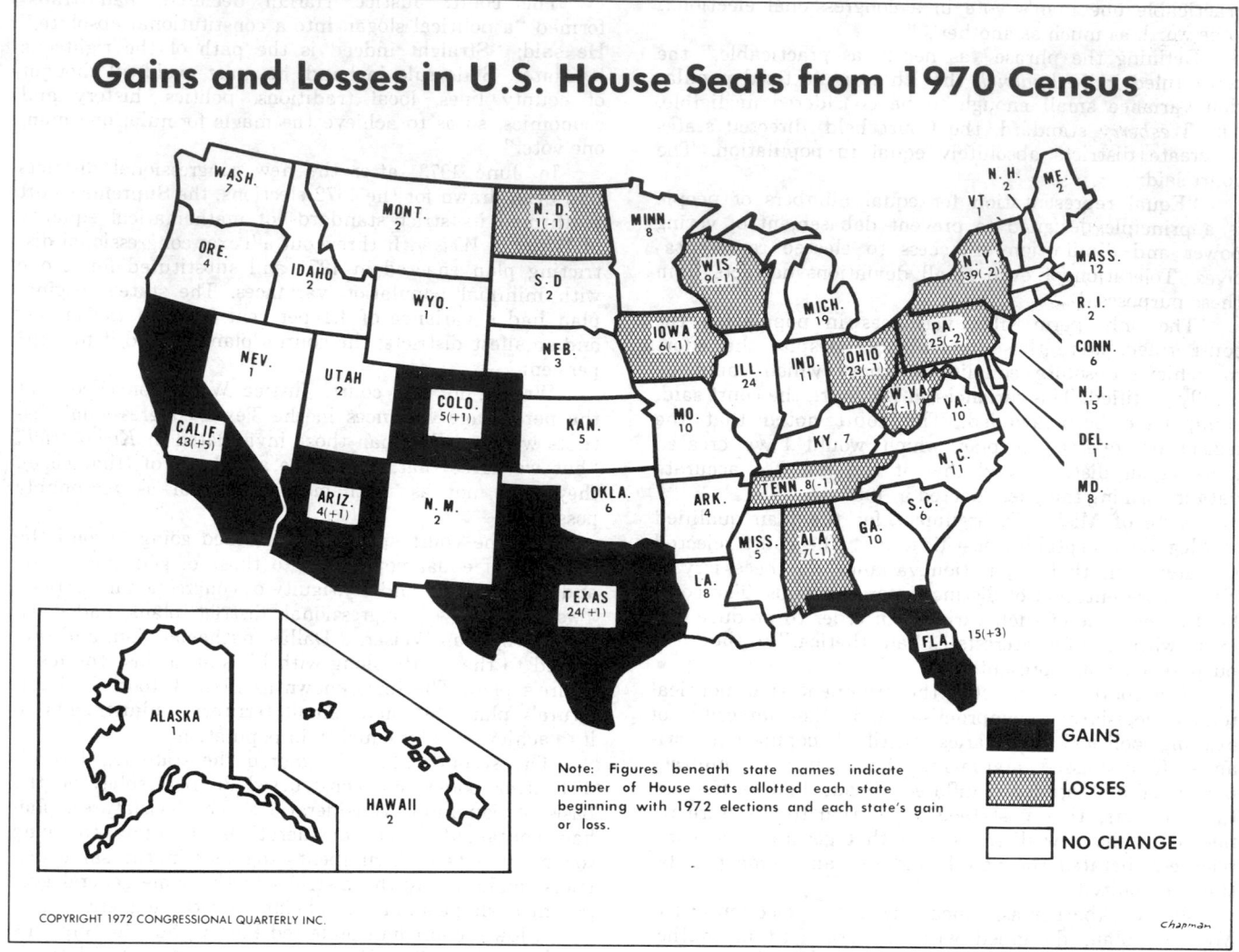

Gains and Losses in U.S. House Seats from 1970 Census

Note: Figures beneath state names indicate number of House seats allotted each state beginning with 1972 elections and each state's gain or loss.

GAINS

LOSSES

NO CHANGE

COPYRIGHT 1972 CONGRESSIONAL QUARTERLY INC.

Chapman

matically informs the executive of each state of the number of members to which his state is entitled in the following Congress.

The act also requires the Bureau of the Census to submit the new population figures, broken down by states, to the President before Dec. 1 of the year of every decennial census. *(Map this page for 1970 apportionment, gains and losses)*

Five states gained seats in the House of Representatives and nine states lost seats based on final 1970 Census figures.

California gained five seats for a total of 43. The four other gainers were Florida (3 seats), Arizona (1), Colorado (1) and Texas (1).

Two states lost two seats each: New York and Pennsylvania. Seven more states lost one seat each: Alabama, Iowa, North Dakota, Ohio, Tennessee, West Virginia and Wisconsin. North Dakota's loss left the state with only one representative for the first time since 1900.

According to the Census Bureau, Oregon would have gained a fifth seat in the House if the state had only 235 more people. Connecticut missed gaining a seventh seat by 8,502 people.

For the first time, armed forces personnel overseas, other U.S. Government personnel overseas, and their dependents were allocated to their home states for use in the reapportionment calculations. *(Table, p. 1001)*

Small states also had a disproportionately large share of the overseas population—for instance, Maine, New Hampshire, North Dakota, South Dakota, Montana. Large states, such as New York, Illinois and California were well below the national average.

The addition of the overseas population for apportionment purposes affected one seat. Without the addition of this population, Connecticut would have gained a seat and Oklahoma would have lost a seat.

In 1970, the District of Columbia was granted the right to elect one non-voting delegate. The delegate is not involved in the reapportionment process—i.e., the District has one delegate regardless of its population.

Redistricting: 1971-72

State legislatures began to struggle with congressional redistricting in early 1971. The first state to enact a plan was Arkansas, whose legislation was signed by

Gov. Dale Bumpers (D) on January 28, 1971. Arkansas was followed by Utah, whose plan was signed by Gov. Calvin L. Rampton (D) on February 8, 1971. (Arkansas passed a second redistricting bill in March 1971, making some minor changes.) On July 18, 1972, Connecticut became the last state to redistrict when a federal court imposed new congressional district lines.

A total of forty states changed their congressional district lines during 1971 and 1972. Six states had only one seat—Alaska, Delaware, Nevada, North Dakota (down from two), Vermont, and Wyoming—and so did not have to draw new lines. Four states—Hawaii, Maine, Nebraska, and New Mexico—did not redraw congressional district lines because the variances between their districts were minimal.

Before 1970, Republicans were optimistic that they could pick up large numbers of House seats in the following decade. But when all the redistricting had been done, it appeared that the Republicans had gained very little advantage in the process.

Democratic gains in state legislatures and governorships in 1970 were the main factor in this change of fortune. These gains gave the Democrats leverage to do several things, depending on the state: they could pass a redistricting plan of their own; prevent the passage of any plan, leaving it to the courts; hold out for an "incumbent bill," favoring the re-election of all or almost all of the state's representatives in both parties; or a Democratic governor could threaten the use of his veto power. Republicans, where they retained power, employed the same tactics. *(State party lineups following the 1970 elections, box this page)*

Redistricting action in 1971-72 fell into three general categories: incumbent plans, partisan plans and court plans.

INCUMBENT PLANS

Incumbent plans often were enacted where the legislature and governor were of different parties. In order to enact any redistricting legislation at all, the parties had to compromise. The most obvious compromise was to keep the status quo: give all incumbents of both parties safe seats—or at least new districts little changed from the old districts. Twenty-six states, with 207 incumbent representatives, elected members of the 93rd Congress under plans generally favorable to incumbents. In addition, other states had partisan plans or court plans that favored many incumbents. Thus a majority of the 435 House members were able to run in 1972 in districts favorable to their re-election, or at least little changed in political balance from 1970.

Largest States. California, Ohio and Pennsylvania were the largest states with incumbent plans. California's plan was evolved after Democrats captured both houses of the state legislature from the Republicans in 1970. Negotiations between Democratic legislative leaders and Republican Gov. Ronald Reagan came close to establishing a mutually acceptable compromise but broke down at the last minute. Democrats then passed their version of the plan, which made all but one of the 38 old districts relatively safe for the party then holding them. The five new seats were divided between the parties—two Democrats, two Republicans, one tossup.

State Legislative Control

(January 1971)

	Upper House	Lower House	Governor
Alabama 2	D	D	D
Alaska	Tie √	D	D √
Arizona 3	R	R	R
Arkansas 2	D	D	D √
California	D √	D √	R
Colorado 3	R	R	R
Connecticut	D	D	R √
Delaware 3	R	R	R
Florida 2	D	D	D √
Georgia 2	D	D	D
Hawaii 2	D	D	D
Idaho	R	R	D √
Illinois	Tie √	R	R
Indiana 3	R	R	R
Iowa 3	R	R	R
Kansas	R	R	D
Kentucky	D	D	R
Louisiana 2	D	D	D
Maine	R	R	D
Maryland 2	D	D	D
Massachusetts	D	D	R
Michigan	Tie √	D	R
Minnesota	NP1	NP1	D √
Mississippi 2	D	D	D
Missouri 2	D	D	D
Montana	D	R	D
Nebraska	NP1		D √
Nevada	D	R	D √
New Hampshire 3	R	R	R
New Jersey 3	R	R	R
New Mexico 2	D	D	D √
New York 3	R	R	R
North Carolina 2	D	D	D
North Dakota	R	R	D
Ohio	R	R	D √
Oklahoma 2	D	D	D √
Oregon	D	R	R
Pennsylvania 2	D √	D	D √
Rhode Island 2	D	D	D
South Carolina 2	D	D	D
South Dakota	R	R	D √
Tennessee	D	D √	R √
Texas 2	D	D	D
Utah	R	D √	D
Vermont 3	R	R	R
Virginia	D	D	R
Washington	D	R	R
West Virginia	D	D	R
Wisconsin	R	D √	D √
Wyoming 3	R	R	R

√ *Switched party control as a result of 1970 elections.*
1 *Nonpartisan.*
2 *Both legislative chambers and governship controlled by Democrats.*
3 *Both legislative chambers and governorship controlled by Republicans.*

Republicans objected on the grounds that the new seats would favor the Democrats, three to two, and that one old district (the 11th) that had been represented by a Republican was favorable to the Democrats. Reagan vetoed the redistricting bill, contending that the new districts contained "a random disregard for preservation of communities of interest...with many communities arbitrarily divided—sometimes solely for political purposes."

Failing to override the governor's veto, Democratic legislators took their case to the state supreme court, asking it to uphold their redistricting plan. In response, the court adopted as a "temporary court plan" for the 1972 elections the bill passed by the legislature and vetoed by the governor. But the court retained jurisdiction to draw new congressional district lines if the legislature did not come up with a new and acceptable plan for the 1974 elections.

Ohio was another example of political compromise benefiting most incumbent representatives, but one that worked out more smoothly than California's. The state's Republican legislature faced two main problems in designing new congressional district boundaries: eliminating one district due to reapportionment and designing a plan acceptable to Democratic Gov. John J. Gilligan.

A threatened deadlock over which seat to eliminate was resolved when Rep. Jackson E. Betts (R) announced his retirement in January 1972. His district was then divided among neighboring districts. The remaining 23 districts were designed to remain in the hands of incumbents.

In Pennsylvania, an unusual situation developed. Although the Democrats were in control of both houses of the state legislature and the governorship, they were not able to enact a redistricting plan to their advantage. Such a plan was drawn up and adopted by the state House. It provided for a 15-10 Democratic advantage, costing the Republicans three seats. But Democratic factionalism in the Senate prevented that body from approving the House plan. Instead, the Senate adopted a bill more acceptable to the Republicans. The House concurred one day before the deadline—the first day for congressional candidates to file nomination papers. The plan was designed to yield a 13-12 Democratic margin, a loss of one seat for each party (the state lost two seats through reapportionment).

Combination Plans. Incumbent plans were also in several instances partisan plans. When one party controlled an overwhelming majority of a congressional delegation, simply ensuring their continued preponderance became both an incumbent plan and a partisan plan.

This type of redistricting legislation was enacted in Florida and Oklahoma, among other states. Before 1972, Florida had nine Democrats and three Republicans in the House. All twelve districts were designed to stay in the incumbent party's hands, thus preserving a large Democratic majority; one weak Democratic district was strengthened for this purpose. The state's three new districts were drawn to favor one Democrat, one Republican, with one tossup. In Oklahoma, which had a four-to-two Democratic edge in the House, legislators drew lines to try to maintain this advantage with one Republican district weakened somewhat.

PARTISAN PLANS

Partisan plans were simply those enacted by one party for that party's advantage. When one party was in solid control of both houses of the state legislature and the governor's chair and was reasonably united, it could make considerable gains by redrawing congressional district lines.

New York enacted a Republican-slanted redistricting plan in March 1972. Designed to give Republicans three additional seats, the plan created a new district on populous Long Island and added Republican voters to two upstate Democratic districts. In addition, two Democratic seats in New York City were eliminated to reduce the state's total delegation from 41 to 39, in accordance with reapportionment.

In two fast-growing western states—Arizona and Colorado—which gained one seat each through reapportionment, Republicans were able to design legislation to their advantage. Both new districts were dominated by strongly Republican suburban and new urban areas, one around Phoenix and the other near Denver.

COURT PLANS

Democrats had good luck in the courts, which accepted Democratic plans as official court plans in several states. Courts found themselves in the business of establishing congressional districts in seven states for the 1972 elections. In all seven cases, state legislatures had failed to meet deadlines for drawing new district lines, and the courts assumed jurisdiction. The seven were California, Connecticut, Michigan, Missouri, Illinois, New Jersey and Washington.

Despite the removal of redistricting from the legislatures, most plans adopted by the courts were partisan. Democrats managed to get their congressional district plan adopted for the 1972 elections by the California Supreme Court, although the court stipulated that new lines be drawn for the 1974 elections.

In Connecticut, a federal court accepted a plan proposed by John M. Bailey, the state Democratic chairman and former chairman of the Democratic National Committee. In Michigan, a federal district judge adopted a plan based on a Democratic proposal that failed to pass the legislature. And in Missouri, an incumbent plan favoring the state's nine-to-one Democratic delegation was selected by a court.

Republicans also benefited from court decisions. In Illinois and New Jersey, where closely divided legislatures had bogged down in their efforts to enact redistricting legislation, Republican lines were adopted by the courts.

Only in the state of Washington was a non-political court plan drawn. There, the special master appointed by the court to draw new lines was enjoined to "...carefully avoid contracts of any kind—formal or informal—with any incumbent congressman or state legislator, any person who has announced (or plans to announce) his candidacy for public office..." and "...any representative of a political party and anyone representing or acting for any of the aforesaid persons." Furthermore, the master was charged to ignore existing precinct borders and voting patterns while drawing the new districts. Despite the non-political na-

1970 Population and Number of Representatives

State	Resident Population	Overseas Population	Population used as basis for apportionment	Overseas population as a percentage of apportionment population	No. of Rep. based on 1970 Census	Change from 1960 apportionment
United States	203,184,772	1,580,998[1]	204,002,799[2]	0.77%	435	
Alabama	3,444,165	31,720	3,475,885	0.91	7	—1
Alaska	302,173	1,894	304,067	0.62	1	
Arizona	1,772,482	15,138	1,787,620	0.84	4	+1
Arkansas	1,923,295	19,008	1,942,303	0.97	4	
California	19,953,134	145,729	20,098,863	0.72	43	+5
Colorado	2,207,259	19,512	2,226,771	0.87	5	+1
Connecticut	3,032,217	18,476	3,050,693	0.60	6	
Delaware	548,104	3,824	551,928	0.69	1	
District of Columbia	756,510	6,461	—	—	—	
Florida	6,789,443	66,259	6,855,702	0.96	15	+3
Georgia	4,589,575	37,731	4,627,306	0.81	10	
Hawaii	769,913	14,988	784,901	1.90	2	
Idaho	713,008	6,913	719,921	0.96	2	
Illinois	11,113,976	70,344	11,184,320	0.62	24	
Indiana	5,193,669	34,487	5,228,156	0.65	11	
Iowa	2,825,041	21,879	2,846,920	0.76	6	—1
Kansas	2,249,071	16,775	2,265,846	0.74	5	
Kentucky	3,219,311	27,170	3,246,481	0.83	7	
Louisiana	3,643,180	28,828	3,672,008	0.78	8	
Maine	993,663	12,657	1,006,320	1.25	2	
Maryland	3,922,399	31,299	3,953,698	0.79	8	
Massachusetts	5,689,170	37,506	5,726,676	0.65	12	
Michigan	8,875,083	62,113	8,937,196	0.69	19	
Minnesota	3,805,069	28,104	3,833,173	0.73	8	
Mississippi	2,216,912	16,936	2,233,848	0.75	5	
Missouri	4,677,399	40,635	4,718,034	0.86	10	
Montana	694,409	7,164	701,573	1.02	2	
Nebraska	1,483,791	13,029	1,496,820	0.87	3	
Nevada	488,738	3,658	492,396	0.74	1	
New Hampshire	737,681	8,603	746,284	1.15	2	
New Jersey	7,168,164	39,871	7,208,035	0.55	15	
New Mexico	1,016,000	10,664	1,026,664	1.03	2	
New York	18,190,740	96,789	18,287,529	0.52	39	—2
North Carolina	5,082,059	43,171	5,125,230	0.84	11	
North Dakota	617,761	6,420	624,181	1.02	1	—1
Ohio	10,652,017	78,183	10,730,200	0.72	23	—1
Oklahoma	2,559,253	26,233	2,585,486	1.01	6	
Oregon	2,091,385	19,425	2,110,810	0.92	4	
Pennsylvania	11,793,909	90,405	11,884,314	0.76	25	—2
Rhode Island	949,723	8,075	957,798	0.84	2	
South Carolina	2,590,516	26,804	2,617,320	1.02	6	
South Dakota	666,257	6,990	673,247	1.03	2	
Tennessee	3,924,164	36,896	3,961,060	0.93	8	—1
Texas	11,196,730	102,057	11,298,787	0.90	24	+1
Utah	1,059,273	8,537	1,067,810	0.79	2	
Vermont	444,732	3,595	448,327	0.80	1	
Virginia	4,648,494	42,248	4,690,742	0.90	10	
Washington	3,409,169	34,318	3,443,487	0.99	7	
West Virginia	1,744,237	19,094	1,763,331	1.08	4	—1
Wisconsin	4,417,933	29,080	4,447,013	0.65	9	—1
Wyoming	332,416	3,303	335,719	0.98	1	

1 Includes (a) members of the Armed Forces; (b) civilian employees of any federal department or agency who are citizens of the United States or who have a home state; (c) spouses and children who are living abroad with persons classified in groups (a) and (b); (d) other relatives living abroad with persons in groups (a) and (b) who are citizens of the United States or have a home state.

2 Excludes the District of Columbia. The total including the District of Columbia is 204,765,770.

ture of the construction of the new districts, none of the state's seven incumbent representatives—six Democrats and one Republican—received districts which hurt their reelection prospects.

Black Beneficiaries. Blacks generally did well in redistricting. All 12 incumbent black representatives were given relatively safe seats. However, some blacks complained that black voters were concentrated in single districts, whereas, if their strength had been apportioned equally between two districts, they would have had a good chance of capturing both seats.

At least five districts were created in which blacks hoped to capture a seat in 1972 or some other time in the 1970s: California 37th (Los Angeles), Georgia 5th (Atlanta), New Jersey 10th (Newark), Tennessee 8th (Memphis) and Texas 18th (Houston). Black candidates won in 1972 in the Los Angeles, Atlanta, and Houston districts. In many other districts, especially in the South, blacks make up a large percentage of the population and can hold the balance of power if they mobilize and unite their potential voting strength.

1972 Election Impact

The overall political impact of reapportionment and redistricting favored the Republicans, but only minimally. A Congressional Quarterly study just after the 1972 elections showed that 18 of the seats that moved into Republican hands for the 93rd Congress did so largely because of redistricting or reapportionment. Democrats won eight of their new seats for this reason. With redistricting and reapportionment eliminated, the 1972 House elections would probably have resulted in a change of only a handful of seats in the 92nd Congress.

In terms of equalization of population however, the impact of redistricting was considerable. In 385 of the 435 House districts in effect for the 1972 elections, the population differed less than one per cent from the state ideal district population. In 41 districts, the deviation ranged from one to five per cent, and in three the deviation was between five and ten per cent. The remaining six seats were in states with only one House member.

In contrast, the results of the redistricting following the 1960 census and reapportionment (and before the Supreme Court decisions) revealed much greater variances from the state's ideal district population. Only nine districts in the 88th Congress (elected in November 1962) deviated less than one per cent from the state ideal; 81 were between one and five per cent, 87 from five to ten, and in 236 districts, the variance was ten per cent or greater. There were 22 at large seats in the 88th Congress.

The average variance from the ideal district size was less than one half of one per cent for the 93rd Congress, compared with 17 percent for the 88th Congress.

Congressional Action

In 1971, Rep. Emanuel Celler (D N.Y.), chairman of the House Judiciary Committee, introduced a new version of his proposed redistricting legislation.

Since 1951, Celler had attempted to enact comprehensive legislation regulating the redistricting pro-

cess. His proposals included requirements for compact and contiguous congressional districts, a limitation on the size of variances and mandatory redistricting after every census.

Celler regularly introduced his bill throughout the 1950s and early 1960s, but it made no headway until the Supreme Court handed down the *Wesberry* decision in 1964. On June 24 of that year, a Celler bill finally was approved by a House Judiciary subcommittee. But the full committee did not act on the bill before adjournment.

Bills were again introduced in 1965 and 1967. They made more headway, the 1967 bill actually passing both houses although not in the same form (HR 2508). But the two houses could not agree on a compromise and in the end the only legislation enacted was a ban on at-large elections in states with more than one U.S. representative. This was in the form of a rider which the Senate added to a House-passed private bill (HR 2275—PL 196). The states of New Mexico and Hawaii, which had a tradition of electing their two representatives at large, were exempted for the 1968 elections only. Both of them, however, soon passed districting laws—New Mexico for the 1968 elections, and Hawaii for 1970.

Celler's 1971 bill was reported from the full Judiciary Committee on Sept. 22, 1971 (HR 10645). As reported, the bill:

• Required that each congressional district be composed of contiguous territory in as reasonably compact a form as practicable and that districts within each state contain substantially equal numbers of persons, as determined by the most recent decennial or statewide census. The provision was adopted to outlaw the practice of "gerrymandering" districts.

• Provided that federal courts could not refuse to assume jurisdiction over a state's redistriction procedure on the ground that a state legislature needed more time to draw up a redistricting plan.

• Required states to complete their redistricting on or before Feb. 1 of the first congressional election year (except 1972) after a decennial apportionment. In the case of calendar year 1972, the redistricting must be completed on or before the 30th day after the convening of a general or special state legislative session.

In reporting the measure favorably by voice vote, the Judiciary Committee said of the bill:

"HR 10645 responds to the prospect of imminent, complex and time-consuming redistricting litigation in both 1971 and 1972. The committee has concluded that the state legislatures, the courts, candidates for office, and above all, the electorate, are entitled to a declaration of congressional policy on redistricting. The committee believes HR 10645 furnishes reasonable and appropriate procedures to govern redistricting and, accordingly, urges its enactment."

The committee noted that 28 states had not completed their redistricting for the 93rd Congress at the time the bill was reported and admonished the courts to act "sufficiently in advance of filing dates and before primary elections so that the districting process will be completed in time to assure the orderly operation of election machinery."

But no further action was taken on the bill and it died at the end of the 92nd Congress.

CONSTITUTIONAL AMENDMENT GAVE VOTE TO 18-YEAR OLDS

More than 25 million young Americans became eligible to vote for President for the first time in 1972. It was the biggest influx of potential new voters since the 19th Amendment to the Constitution gave women the right to vote in 1920.

Of the 25 million new voters, more than 11 million were given the franchise by the 26th Amendment, which lowered the voting age to 18 in all the states. The amendment was ratified in 1971. The remaining 14 million potential presidential voters were men and women between the ages of 21 and 25 who had been too young to vote in 1968.

Approval of the amendment was by far the most important action taken in the United States from 1969 through 1972 to extend the franchise. The right to vote was given to 18-year-olds for state and local as well as federal elections.

The emphasis on the youth vote was a shift from the drive in the previous decade, culminating in passage of the Voting Rights Act of 1965, which added nearly one million black voters to registration rolls in southern states by 1970. *(Earlier data on franchise, Congress and the Nation, Vol II, p 436)*

According to a U.S. Census Bureau report, the projected voting-age population in the United States in November 1972 was 139,642,000. This was an increase of nearly 20 million over the 120,006,000 estimated in 1968, the previous presidential year, and more than 15 million over the 1970 off-year estimate of 124,498,000.

Thus it was predictable that the voter turnout in 1972 would, consistent with the steadily expanding American population, set a record. And it did—the official total vote for President, based on the records of secretaries of state, was 77,734,330, an increase of more than four million over the 73,211,562 of 1968.

In percentage, however, the 1972 presidential vote was the lowest since 1948. Only 55.6 per cent of the eligible voters cast votes for President, compared with 61 per cent in 1968. Although nearly 78 million Americans went to the polls, some 62 million did not. In 1948, the percentage was 51.7.

One of the reasons for the disappointing turnout was the failure of new voters to participate in the numbers expected. Considerable effort was made by both political parties, and by organizations outside the parties, to sign up young voters. But the Census Bureau found, in its post-election study, that only about 48 per cent of those eligible for the first time reported that they had voted, and—because some of those surveyed said they had voted when they had not—the actual figure was even lower.

Despite the indifference of large numbers of Americans to their right to vote, both Congress and the Nixon administration showed an interest in increasing the number of prospective voters. Approval of the 26th Amend-

ment was expedited by passage of legislation lowering the voting age to 18 in 1970 that was partly upheld and partly rejected by the Supreme Court. The court limited the coverage of the 1970 law to federal elections.

The same 1970 legislation that lowered the voting age also helped expand the franchise by extending the life of a civil rights law that banned discriminatory literacy tests. And the new law relaxed residency requirements, clearing the way for even more persons, especially college students, to vote.

Some headway was made toward liberalizing voter registration procedures. A bill creating a nationwide voter registration system was defeated narrowly in the Senate in 1972. Similar legislation was scheduled to be brought up again in 1973, although it was opposed by the Nixon administration and its chances for enactment appeared doubtful.

18-Year-Old Vote

1970 LEGISLATION. President Nixon June 22, 1970, signed into law HR 4249 (PL 91-285) amending the Voting Rights Act of 1965 (PL 89-110) to extend its effect until 1975 and lowering the voting age to 18 beginning Jan. 1, 1971. The Voting Rights Act was scheduled to expire Aug. 6, 1970.

On signing the bill—the major civil rights measure of the 91st Congress—Nixon restated his belief that the 18-year-old-vote provision was unconstitutional because Congress had no power to extend the suffrage by simple statute. It should initiate such action by constitutional amendment, he said, which would require ratification by three-quarters of the states before it could take effect.

At the time of enactment of HR 4249, voters in three states—New Jersey, Ohio and Oregon—already had rejected proposals to lower voter ages in 1969 and 1970. Fifteen more states had scheduled referenda on the issue in the November elections. Only four states allowed persons to vote under the age of 21. They were Georgia and Kentucky, 18; Hawaii, 20, and Alaska, 19.

The President immediately directed Attorney General John N. Mitchell to cooperate in a swift court test of the provision's constitutionality. Until the Supreme Court had made such a ruling, the results of any national, state or local election after Dec. 31, 1970, would remain in doubt.

Nixon urged Congress to continue work on a constitutional amendment to lower the voting age, in the event the provision did not survive a court test.

The President explained that he did not veto the bill because such action would have blocked extension of the 1965 Voting Rights Act. If the 18-year-old vote provision were declared unconstitutional, the rest of the bill would not be affected.

The Growing Franchise in the U.S., 1920-1972

YEAR	ESTIMATED POPULATION OF VOTING AGE	VOTE CAST FOR PRESIDENTIAL ELECTORS		VOTE CAST FOR U.S. REPRESENTATIVES	
		Number	Per cent	Number	Per cent
1920	60,581,000	26,769,000	44.2	25,080,000	41.4
1922	62,984,000	———	———	20,409,000	32.4
1924	65,597,000	29,095,000	44.4	26,884,000	41.0
1926	67,912,000	———	———	20,435,000	30.1
1928	70,362,000	36,806,000	52.3	33,906,000	48.2
1930	72,602,000	———	———	24,777,000	34.1
1932	75,048,000	39,759,000	53.0	37,657,000	50.2
1934	77,215,000	———	———	32,256,000	41.8
1936	79,375,000	45,655,000	57.5	42,886,000	54.0
1938	81,514,000	———	———	36,236,000	44.5
1940	83,512,000	49,900,000	59.8	46,951,000	56.2
1942	85,759,000	———	———	28,074,000	32.7
1944*	89,517,000*	47,977,000*	53.6	45,103,000*	50.4
1946	91,497,000	———	———	34,398,000	37.6
1948	94,470,000	48,794,000	51.7	45,933,000	48.6
1950	96,992,000	———	———	40,342,000	41.6
1952	99,016,000	61,551,000	62.2	57,571,000	58.1
1954	101,097,000	———	———	42,580,000	42.1
1956	103,625,000	62,027,000	59.9	58,426,000	56.4
1958**	105,727,000**	———	———	45,655,000**	43.2
1960	107,949,000	68,838,000	63.8	64,133,000	59.4
1962	110,266,000	———	———	51,304,000	46.5
1964	113,931,000	70,645,000	62.0	66,044,000	58.0
1966	115,882,000	———	———	52,874,000	45.6
1968	120,006,000	73,212,000	61.0	66,109,000	55.1
1970	124,498,000	———	———	54,169,000	43.5
1972	139,642,000	77,734,000	55.6	71,139,000	50.9

*Includes 4,342,000 members of the armed forces serving abroad.

**Includes Alaska, which voted for representative in November 1958, although it did not achieve statehood until January 1959.

(Voting age starting in 1972 is defined as resident population 18 years and over. Before 1972, it was defined as resident population 21 years and over, with these exceptions: 18 years and over in Georgia since 1944; 18 years and over in Kentucky since 1956; 19 years and over in Alaska, and 20 years and over in Hawaii.)

Congressional Action. Final congressional action on HR 4249 came June 17 when the House, by a roll-call vote of 272-132, agreed to the Senate amendments to the bill. One of those amendments, not previously considered by the House, lowered to 18 the voting age for all federal, state and local elections as of Jan. 1, 1971.

HR 4249, as cleared for the White House, extended until August 1975 the enforcement provisions of the 1965 Voting Rights Act, under which 900,000 black voters in the affected southern states had been registered. By lowering the voting age, HR 4249 also would have added approximately 11 million eligible voters between the ages of 18 and 21 to the rolls in 1972.

Final passage of the Senate version of the bill was a major victory for civil rights forces, which had waged a year-long battle for extension of the 1965 act, the most successful civil rights legislation ever enacted.

The Nixon administration had opposed extension of the act, which it labeled "essentially regional legislation." The administration in mid-1969 had proposed amendments to the act to allow its enforcement provi-

sions to expire in August 1970 and to delete the "trigger formula" under which it applied only to certain states and counties.

Nixon April 27, 1970, asked the House to separate from HR 4249 the provision lowering the voting age and to act on it separately as a constitutional amendment. During debate preceding the final House vote, Minority Leader Gerald R. Ford (R Mich.) hinted that Nixon might veto the bill.

But Vice President Agnew June 17 spoke in favor of lowering the voting age to 18. "I believe," he said, "that once our young people can sound off at the polls, there will be less need to sound off in the streets."

Provisions. As cleared for the President, HR 4949:

● Extended for five years the period of time for which an area covered by the act must abstain from the use of any literacy test or qualifying device to discriminate against voters because of race or color.

● Amended the Voting Rights Act to make the "trigger formula"—by which the act applied to a specified area—

applicable to all states and counties with a literacy test in which fewer than 50 per cent of the voting-age residents were registered on Nov. 1, 1968, or voted in the 1968 presidential election. (This extended coverage of the act to three Alaska districts; Apache County, Ariz.; Imperial County, Calif.; Elmore County, Idaho; Bronx, Kings (Brooklyn) and New York (Manhattan) counties, New York, and Wheeler County, Oregon. Under the formula of the 1965 act—which was based upon November 1964 statistics—the act in 1969 affected Alabama, Georgia, Louisiana, Mississippi, South Carolina, Virginia and a number of North Carolina counties. These areas remained covered under the extension of the act.)

● Suspended the use of literacy tests in all states until Aug. 6, 1975.

● Provided that any person could vote in a presidential election in the place in which he had lived for 30 days immediately prior to a presidential election.

● Lowered from 21 to 18 the voting age for all federal, state and local elections, effective Jan. 1, 1971, "except as required by the Constitution."

SUPREME COURT RULING. The Supreme Court Dec. 21, 1970, by a 5-to-4 decision upheld the new law lowering the voting age to 18 in presidential and congressional elections but ruled the change unconstitutional as it applied to state and local elections. Also upheld were other provisions of the voting rights amendments of 1970 that abolished residency requirements of longer than 30 days for presidential elections and outlawed literacy tests for all voters.

Five separate opinions, comprising 184 pages, were issued by the justices on the decisions. Four states—Arizona, Idaho, Oregon and Texas went before the Court to argue various aspects of the cases.

The majority opinion was written by Justice Hugo L. Black, who cast the pivotal vote on the voting age case, entitled *Oregon v. Mitchell.* Justice Black's position was that Congress is empowered to establish laws governing federal elections but that state and local elections must be regulated by the states themselves.

Four justices—William J. Brennan Jr., William O. Douglas, Thurgood Marshall and Byron R. White—considered the 18-year-old vote provision fully constitutional for federal and state elections. Four others—Chief Justice Warren E. Burger, Harry A. Blackmun, John Marshall Harlan and Potter Stewart—believed it was unconstitutional as to both state and federal elections. None agreed completely with Black's position.

In his majority opinion, Black cited Article I, Section 4 of the Constitution as a basis for the ruling on the 18-year-old vote. This section reads in part: "The Times, Places and Manner of holding Elections for Senators and Representatives, shall be prescribed in each State by the Legislature thereof; but the Congress may at any time by Law make or alter such Regulations...."

CONSTITUTIONAL AMENDMENT. In February and March 1970, while Congress was considering HR 4249, the Senate Judiciary Subcommittee on Constitutional Amendments held hearings on S J Res 147. The resolution would have amended the Constitution to extend voting rights to 18-year-olds. It was not reported from committee and died at the end of the 91st Congress.

The 92nd Congress wasted little time early in 1971 in approving and sending to the states a proposed 26th Amendment lowering the voting age in all elections.

Voter Registration Background

The first voter-registration law in the United States was enacted in 1800 in Massachusetts, but the practice of registering prospective voters did not become widespread until the early 20th century. According to a November 1970 study by a Democratic National Committee task force, the original justification for the introduction of registration requirements was the attempt to ensure the integrity of elections by freeing them from fraudulent manipulations.

Some students of state registration systems cited a twofold purpose in gathering information on eligible voters before voting day: to disenfranchise blacks and some whites in the South and to prevent election abuses—such as duplicate voting and stuffed ballot boxes—by political machines in the growing cities of the North during the early 1900s.

Sen. Edward M. Kennedy (D Mass.) charged that "arbitrary, obsolete and unfair" registration systems act as impediments to voting in many states. Critics contended that many voters did not turn out in elections because of a maze of state and local obstacles—closing of registration books months before an election, obscure absentee-voting laws, lengthy residency requirements (except for presidential elections) and arbitrary purging of registration books.

In 1968, 47 million eligible Americans did not vote in the presidential election, a figure that continued a downward trend in voter participation since the turn of the century, creating what the Democratic task force report called "a profound failing of the democratic system." Reformers called for a system of "universal voter enrollment" that would automatically register voters for federal elections through computers, postcards or door-to-door registrars.

Final congressional action on H J Res 223 was taken on March 23, by a 401-19 roll call vote in the House. Immediately after the vote, the House by voice vote adopted the Senate measure (S J Res 7) and sent it to the states for ratification.

The Senate had given its approval March 10 by a 94-0 roll call. A vote of two-thirds of the members of each chamber is required for a constitutional amendment. A joint resolution of Congress to amend the Constitution does not require the President's signature.

The 26th Amendment was ratified by the required number of states by June 30, a record time for approval of a constitutional amendment. Three-fourths (38) of the 50 states had to ratify the proposal before it became part of the Constitution, and Ohio became the 38th to do so on that date. The speed with which the amendment became law, three months and seven days after passage by Congress, nearly cut in half the previous record speed.

The amendment was the fourth to enlarge the electorate since the Constitution was adopted in 1789. The 15th Amendment gave the vote to Negro citizens, the 19th gave it to women and the 23rd permitted voting for President in the District of Columbia.

Impact of Youth Vote: Much Smaller Than Expected

Election day 1972 was payoff day for the new youth vote. Those who had counted on a significant impact came away disappointed.

The turnout was lowest among first-time voters in the 18-to-24 age group, for one thing. The potential was some 25 million new votes. A U.S. Census Bureau survey found that only 12.2 million at most—one-sixth of the total vote for President—went to the polls. And that figure, the bureau noted, was probably high, because some persons who did not vote said they did.

The actual percentage of all eligible persons who voted was about 55.6, the lowest since 1948. But the Census Bureau survey showed that 63 per cent of those eligible said they voted.

Only 48 per cent of the 18-to-20-year-olds—those enfranchised by the new 26th Amendment to the Constitution—reported that they voted. Slightly higher was the 51 per cent of new voters aged 21 to 24, who reached the previous minimum voting age of 21 after the 1968 election.

Both groups of new voters, however, suffered by comparison with their elders. Among voters over age 25, 66 per cent said they voted. The highest participation, said the Census Bureau, was the 71 per cent reported by persons 45 to 64 years old.

Vote Drive. Organizers for both President Nixon, the incumbent Republican, and Sen. George Mc-Govern, his Democratic challenger, set out to capture a large share of the youth vote. An estimated 30 per cent—7.5 million—of the 25 million newly eligible voters were students. McGovern youth strategists concentrated on them, relying on their regular canvassing organization to reach the non-student youth.

The estimated 17.5 million non-students were a majority of potential new voters. These workers, housewives, soldiers and job-seekers were the special target of Nixon campaigners.

According to a profile prepared by the Department of Commerce, the typical young person voting for the first time in November 1972 was white, single, living in a family, not going to school but having a high school diploma, holding a job and living in a metropolitan area. His impact was expected to be most apparent in the congressional races, where young persons were concentrated in several districts. Young people were expected to be a less cohesive force on the state and national levels, where most races probably would be determined by a combination of factors, according to the profile.

Presidential Results. A Gallup Poll published Oct. 21, 1972, found that votes of college students were almost evenly split between McGovern and Nixon. McGovern's share of the college vote had dropped sharply from the 26 per cent edge he held over Nixon in a similar poll published July 22. At that time, 61 per cent of students polled supported McGovern, while 35 per cent favored Nixon.

Between Sept. 25 and Oct. 8, the Gallup organization found that 49 per cent of the students surveyed indicated they would choose McGovern, while 47 per cent preferred Nixon and 4 per cent were undecided.

McGovern forces, desperately sagging in the public opinion polls, had counted on the new voters to swing the election in their favor. Their premature hopes of a 10-million-vote plurality, expressed in the spring, were based on a view of a youth bloc as a cohesive force in the national campaign.

But McGovern's early lead among the young disappeared on the night of Nov. 7. A jubilant Nixon told crowds at his victory celebration: "We have accomplished what was thought to be impossible...we won a majority of the votes of young Americans."

House Contests. In a half dozen House districts containing large universities, Democratic challengers tried to cash in on the assumption that liberal first-time student voters would get behind them in opposition to more conservative Republican opponents.

It turned out to be a shaky assumption. The only winners among the six were Edward Mezvinsky of Iowa and Ike F. Andrews of North Carolina. Neither attributed his victory to the student vote.

The congressional action and ratification of the 26th Amendment cleared up the legal uncertainty that had hung over the right of 18-year-olds to vote. One issue not settled by the amendment, however, was whether or not newly enfranchised college students could register and vote in their college communities. Most states would not allow students temporarily residing within their borders to vote there. Other complications were the difficult absentee requirements in many jurisdictions which might discourage many absent students from voting in their permanent residence. Lawsuits were initiated in many states to allow college students to register where they were attending school.

Voter Registration

Congress in 1971 did not complete action on proposals for a national voter registration system. A bill setting up such a system (S 2574) was reported out of committee in the Senate, but a jurisdictional dispute prevented action by the whole Senate.

By a 6-3 vote of the Post Office and Civil Service Committee, S 2574 was reported on Nov. 9, 1971. It was defeated by four votes in the Senate March 15, 1972, after five days of debate.

By a 46-42 roll-call vote, the Senate adopted a motion introduced by James B. Allen (D Ala.) to table (kill) S 2574. The evening of March 14, Senate Majority Leader Mike Mansfield (D Mont.) had forestalled an attempt to vote on the pending Allen motion by introducing a series of seven motions to recess or adjourn. His move won time for two Democratic presidential aspirants, George McGovern (S.D.) and Vance Hartke (Ind.), to return from campaigning; both voted against Allen's motion. But six announced supporters of S 2574—including Democratic presidential hopefuls Hubert H. Humphrey (Minn.), Henry M. Jackson (Wash.) and Edmund S. Muskie (Maine)—failed to appear for the crucial vote.

Party Reform (1972)

BIG CHANGES FOR THE DEMOCRATS AND REPUBLICANS

Far-reaching political reforms, initiated by the Democratic and Republican Parties after the 1968 national conventions, were finished in time for their biggest test—at the 1972 conventions.

Political observers generally believed the reforms, covering delegate selection processes and convention procedures, would have a liberalizing effect on the makeup of state delegations. But opponents of reform warned that implementation of the changes could narrow party appeal and result in the nomination of weak candidates.

The most comprehensive changes in party structure were made by the Democrats through the Commission on Party Structure and Delegate Selection, headed first by Sen. George McGovern (S.D.) and later by Rep. Donald M. Fraser (Minn.), and the Commission on Rules, headed by Rep. James G. O'Hara (Mich.). Republican reform recommendations were issued by the Delegates and Organizations Committee, headed by Mrs. M. Stanley Ginn, national committeewoman from Missouri.

In the months after the chaotic 1968 Democratic convention, the reform commissions worked to democratize the nominating process, remove control from party insiders and return it to the grass-roots level. Recommendations made by the two commissions were adopted virtually intact by the national committee in 1971.

Democratic Delegate Selection

Because the 1972 Democratic nomination was contested by numerous candidates, the delegate selection reforms had a greater impact on Democrats than Republicans, who appeared certain to renominate President Nixon. The most apparent result was a growth in primaries—23 presidential primaries in 1972, compared with 17 in 1968.

The primary states accounted for nearly 1,900 convention votes (63 percent) in 1972. In 1968, primary states comprised 42 percent of convention votes. At least 1,509 votes were required to nominate at the 1972 Democratic convention.

The 23 primaries, some occurring on the same days, produced exhausting, divisive and expensive campaigns that would guarantee a divided convention at a time when party unity was necessary, said some detractors. They pointed out that under the old rules, an early front-runner, such as Sen. Edmund S. Muskie (D Maine), would have had the nomination locked up because of his early broad support among governors, senators and other key Democrats. But with the delegate selection process shifted to the grass-roots level, the traditional strength of national party leaders was diluted.

Primaries vs. Conventions. Although presidential primaries capture public attention, they did not in 1972 represent a solid bloc vote at the Democratic convention and thus were not the determining factor in the nomina-

tion. In 1972, only four states—California, Massachusetts, Oregon and South Dakota—were "winner-take-all" states able to bring blocs of delegates to the convention. Most other primary states chose their delegates through a combination of congressional district apportionment and at-large selection.

Thus winning the primaries would not necessarily guarantee the nomination under the new reforms. For instance, a candidate could win a majority of votes in all 23 primaries in 1972 and still fall as many as 250 votes short of the number needed to nominate.

About 75 to 80 percent of the delegates selected in primaries were chosen at the district level; the remainder were to be chosen at large. A candidate who won a district would get that district's delegates, while at-large delegates would go to statewide winners.

Because early primary results indicated that no candidate would take a commanding lead into the Democratic convention, there were incentives to win delegates in states that held party conventions. Such delegates are generally selected in a three-tiered convention system at the precinct, county and state levels, a process usually governed by state party rules.

McGovern-Fraser Commission guidelines stipulated that the delegate selection process be open to all enrolled party members. Before this change, many states permitted only party officials to participate in the process. The guidelines also required that at least 75 percent of the delegates be chosen at the congressional district level and that delegations include representatives of minorities, women and young persons "in reasonable proportion to their representation in the party as a whole in that state." *(Box p. 1008)*

Delegate Challenges. Monitoring of the delegate selection process at each stage was done by the Womens' Political Caucus, the Congressional Black Caucus, the National Farmers Union and Common Cause. Challenges of state delegations occurred at the Democratic convention.

Placed in charge of handling the challenges were Patricia Roberts Harris, chairwoman of the Credentials Committee, and a panel of 36 lawyers, headed by Yale Law School Professor Burke Marshall.

Lawrence F. O'Brien, Democratic national chairman, spoke in January 1972 of possible credentials challenges and offered the following warning: "Those states that remain in non-compliance with the delegate-selection guidelines must make the necessary changes, promptly. Any state delegation that comes to Miami Beach having been selected by procedures that violate the delegate-selection rules of the 1972 call is certain to be challenged. The issue is clear and beyond debate."

O'Brien also cautioned candidates for the nomination to insist upon strict compliance with the rules and to "make sure every delegate is challenge-proof."

(Continued on p. 1009)

Eighteen McGovern Commission Guidelines

1. Discrimination Against Race, Color, Creed or National Origin. The commission required state parties to adopt six antidiscrimination standards in their party rules. These "six basic elements," accepted by the 1968 Democratic national convention as official policy, ask state parties to open all public meetings at all levels of the party to all members of the Democratic Party.

2. Discrimination Against Age and Sex. The commission required state parties to "eliminate all vestiges of discrimination" on grounds of age and sex. Any Democrat at least 18 years old is to be encouraged to participate in all party affairs. State parties were required to "make all feasible efforts to repeal, amend or otherwise modify state laws to accomplish this purpose."

3. Voter Registration. The commission urged state parties to "remove or alleviate" restrictive voter registration laws and practices, including annual registration, literacy tests and untimely registration periods.

4. Costs and Fees. No party member could be assessed more than $10 to participate or run as a delegate in the delegate selection process. All mandatory assessments of delegates and alternates were recommended to be abolished by the commission. In addition, any petition requirement that calls for a number of signatures in excess of 1 percent of the standard used for measuring Democratic strength was termed "excessive."

5. Statewide Party Rules. Wide disparity in the accessibility and use of rules governing state party processes prompted the commission to require that readily available party rules be adopted by each state.

Explicit, written provisions should be made in the rules covering (1) the apportionment of delegates and votes within the state; (2) the allocation of fractional votes; (3) the selection and responsibilities of convention committees; (4) the nomination of delegates and alternates; (5) the succession of alternates to delegate status and the filling of vacancies; (6) credentials challenges; (7) minority reports.

6. Proxy Voting. The commission required state parties to forbid proxy voting in all procedures incidental to the delegate selection process.

7. Clarity of Purpose. The commission required state parties to make clear to participants in party meetings whether they are participating solely in a process that will nominate their party's candidate for President, or if other business unrelated to delegate selection is being considered.

8. Quorum Provisions. The commission required that state parties adopt rules setting quorums at not less than 40 percent.

9. Selection of Alternates; Filling of Delegate and Alternate Vacancies. Many states allowed state chairmen to choose alternates and fill vacancies without consultation with other party members. The commission required state parties to prohibit such practices and required all vacancies on the delegation to be filled by: (1) a timely and representative party committee; (2) a reconvening of the body that selected the delegate and/or alternate whose seat was vacant; or (3) the delegation itself acting as a committee.

10. Unit Rule. In light of the 1968 Democratic national convention directive that "the unit rule not be used in any stage of the delegate selection process," the commission required state parties to add to their standing rules provisions that explicitly forbid the use of the unit rule.

11. Adequate Representation of Minority Political Views at Each Stage in the Delegate Selection Process. The commission urged each state to adopt procedures to encourage as full a representation of minority views on candidates as possible. It recommended that the 1972 convention adopt a rule requiring fair representation of minority political views in the delegate selection process in all states "to the end that minority views be preserved to the highest level of the nominating process." Under the provision, direct district election of delegates would be permissible.

12. Apportionment. The commission required that state parties apportion their delegations to the national convention on a basis that gives equal weight to the size of the Democratic vote in the previous presidential election and the latest reliable population figures in each state. Those states using a convention system would be required to elect at least three-fourths of their delegation at congressional district or smaller unit levels.

13. Adequate Public Notice. The commission required publicizing the times, places and rules for all public meetings of the party. Such meetings would have to be held in easily accessible places. Public notice would have to supply as much information as practical about the presidential preferences of candidates for delegate.

The commission said favorite-son candidates "tend to obscure the serious presidential preferences of candidates for delegate." The group recommended that state parties discourage favorite-son candidates.

14. Automatic (Ex-Officio) Delegates. States would have to repeal laws allowing certain public or party officeholders to be delegates to county, state and national conventions by virtue of their official positions.

15. Open and Closed Processes. State parties were urged to provide for party enrollment that (1) allows non-Democrats to become party members, (2) provides easy access and frequent opportunity for unaffiliated voters to become Democrats and (3) assures identification of the party membership of each voter.

16. Premature Delegate Selection. To assure timeliness in delegate selection, the commission required state parties to prohibit any practices by which officials chosen before the calendar year of the convention choose nominating committees or propose a slate.

17. Committee Selection Processes. The commission required state parties to limit that portion of any national convention delegates chosen by committee procedures to not more than 10 percent of the total number of delegates and alternates.

18. Slate-Making. The commission required state parties to assure that the bodies making up candidate slates permit widespread participation and establish appeal safeguards.

(Continued from p. 1007)

There were several bases from which challenges of delegations could be brought, but most observers agreed that fair representation for women, youth and minorities was the predominant criterion. "The idea of the reform guidelines was to assist those party members who traditionally had been under-represented at the national conventions," said Ken Bode, director of the Center for Political Reform and former director of research for the McGovern-Fraser Commission. "If the Credentials Committee determines a case of discrimination exists, it will have no choice but to unseat a delegation until it complies with the rules."

O'Brien stressed that the reform commission rules did not require the establishment of quotas. "What the rules do require," O'Brien said, is "the most imaginative and persistent efforts to carry this message of an open party and an open convention to all persons who might wish to participate" in the nominating process.

When it opened its deliberations June 26, the Credentials Committee was faced with resolving a record 82 challenges to 1,289 delegates from 30 states and one territory—about 41.5 per cent of the elected delegates. More than 80 per cent of the challenges had been filed on grounds of non-compliance with reform commission guidelines regarding adequate representation of women, youth and minorities.

Decisions by the committee added about 103 delegates to the convention rolls for a new total of 3,203 delegates. About 90 of the new delegates were women.

Another factor in the challenge process was that minority reports filed by at least 15 members of the Credentials Committee could be brought to the floor and debated, a tactic that promised to be useful to disgruntled delegates. Two of the most controversial challenges—involving the California delegation and part of the Illinois delegation controlled by Chicago Mayor Richard J. Daley—were resolved by dramatic votes on the convention floor during the early morning hours of the convention's first session.

Delegate Makeup. When the Democrats convened in Miami Beach July 10, 1972, there was little doubt that the McGovern-Fraser reform commission had changed the face of the Democratic Party. And it was clear that the changes had favored McGovern's candidacy by expanding the party's base and bringing more youth, women and minorities into the process.

Nine out of 10 of the delegates had never before attended a national convention. Most had been chosen by open and democratically run elections and caucuses. A breakdown of delegate makeup issued by the Democratic National Committee July 10—before that night's credentials votes made minor changes—listed these delegate figures (1968 figures in parentheses): 1,173 women—38 per cent (13 per cent); 649 youths—21 per cent (4 per cent); 468 blacks—15 per cent (15 per cent).

Democratic Rules Changes

In October 1971, the O'Hara Commission on Rules adopted changes in convention procedures intended to produce better-informed delegates, more floor order, reduced confusion and less favoritism.

The reforms assured the 1972 convention of being markedly different from past conventions: Roll-call order determined by lot rather than by alphabet, favorite-son candidacies prohibited, nominating and seconding speeches limited to a total of 15 minutes and floor demonstrations banned. "If a candidate's supporters jump up and raise hell after the nominating speech, it comes out of his 15 minutes," said O'Hara.

A significant reform of convention policy required that the Platform, Rules and Credentials Committees submit their reports in writing to delegates before the convention began. "In the past," O'Hara said, "written copies of the platform sometimes were not available until after the convention. Credentials reports usually were simply presented orally from the podium."

New Democratic Charter

The chairmen of two Democratic reform commissions March 26, 1972, proposed a drastic reshaping of the party that went beyond any previous party reorganization. Representatives O'Hara and Fraser said the plan would transform the party from a loose federation of state parties into a tightly structured body with more continuity and a stronger ideological identity. They claimed it would give the party a measure of independence from presidential politics and policies and free it from the "strait jacket" that had hampered its operations between national elections.

Under the existing system, O'Hara said, "we get caught in four-year cycles during which we're helpless.... We're trying to make the party independent of the vicissitudes of national elections."

Compromise and Delay. After a short and spirited floor fight, the Democratic national convention the night of July 13 voted overwhelmingly to delay for two years consideration of a proposed new party charter. The charter, which was criticized by both liberals and conservatives in the party and condemned by the House Democratic caucus June 28, was put off by a roll-call vote of 2,418.45 to 195.10.

Weary of fights over credentials, platform and the presidential nomination, the convention adopted a compromise, creating a commission to recommend an overhaul of the party at a conference to be held in 1974. The compromise also enlarged the Democratic National Committee and revised its membership to reflect Democratic strength in the various states.

The compromise accepted by the convention mandated that a "new party structure" should be "established and implemented." Although the resolution stipulated that the national committee "shall have the same powers and duties" previously assigned to the committee, the size of the body was significantly increased.

Under the adopted plan, the national committee would consist of:
- The chairman and the highest-ranking officer of the opposite sex of each recognized state Democratic Party, who will share one vote to be divided equally when both are present.
- Additional national committee members with a total vote of 150 apportioned to each state on the basis of that state's representation on the standing committees of the 1972 Democratic national convention.
- The chairman and two others designated by the Democratic Governors' Conference.

• The Democratic leaders in the U.S. Senate and House of Representatives and one more from each body designated by a caucus of the Democratic members of each house.

• Additional members not to exceed 25 could also be added to provide balanced representation of all Democratic voters.

Thus the size of the national committee was increased to a maximum of 303 from the previous membership of 110. The resolution directed the national chairman to appoint a commission before Jan. 1, 1973, which would draw up a permanent charter for the party. In addition, the proposal called for a "conference on Democratic Party organization and policy" to be held in 1974.

In addition to the charter commission, chaired by former Gov. Terry Sanford (D N.C. 1961-65), the Democrats set up a 51-member Commission on Delegate Selection, headed by Leonard Woodcock, president of the United Auto Workers, as a successor to the McGovern-Fraser panel. And a smaller commission under Sen. Hubert H. Humphrey (D Minn.) was formed to study improved methods for selecting vice presidential nominees.

The convention did not act on other proposals recommended for consideration by the Rules Committee. These included abolition of crossover voting and winner-take-all primaries in 1976, creation of a special fund to subsidize expenses of poor delegates to the national conventions and a proposal to hold the 1976 convention on the campus of a large university so that needy delegates could use dormitory rooms and cafeterias.

Republican Reforms

The Republican delegate selection reform movement was not as well publicized as that of the Democrats, but in July 1971, the Delegates and Organizations Committee proposed 10 recommendations that, if adopted, would make comprehensive and workable changes in party procedures. The suggested reforms included broadened participation in the delegate selection process; broadened representation of women, youths and minority groups on national convention committees; equal representation of men and women in state delegations to the national convention; and representation on state delegations of youths under 25 in proportion to their numerical voting strength in the state.

Ginn, chairwoman of the committee, said in June 1971, "We found there are no great problems with state (party) structures. No basic structural changes are needed. Any changes will have to come from within the states themselves."

Anne Armstrong, cochairman of the Republican National Committee, said in December 1971, "Many of the reforms the Democrats are just now getting around to discussing were accomplished without fanfare years ago by our own party." She acknowledged that "our record in the past in providing recognition and particularly delegate representation to the young voters, to women and to members of minorities has not been good enough. But it is getting better...."

Sen. Robert Dole (Kan.), the Republican national chairman in 1971-72, said in April 1972 that the party was trying, through voluntary efforts in the states, to "make certain that half the delegates are male, half are female, that we have young and minority representation

in every delegation. We know we're the minority party. We know we must build the base of our party and attract Democrats and independents."

Delegate Selection. The 1972 Republican National convention declined to accept all of the 10 recommendations proposed by the Delegates and Organizations Committee. Four days before the convention opened, the Republican National Committee Aug. 17 approved without debate a rules change adding sex and age to race, religion, color and national origin as factors in not discriminating in selecting convention delegates. "The Republican state committee or governing committee of each state shall take positive action to achieve the broadest possible opportunity for everyone to participate in party affairs," the section concluded. Another section, in a concession to those who opposed a flat requirement that men and women on convention delegations be divided equally, stated: "Each state shall endeavor to have equal representation of men and women in its delegation to the Republican national convention."

Other rules changes accepted without dissent by the convention included: elimination of excessive fees as a condition for serving as a delegate or alternate to the Republican national convention; elimination of proxy votes in delegate selection; and elimination of automatic convention delegates such as party officials or holders of high office.

Finally, the convention adopted the following resolution: "The Republican National Committee and the Republican state committee of each state shall take positive action to achieve the broadest possible participation by women, young people, minority and heritage groups and senior citizens in the delegate selection process."

1972 Delegate Makeup. Compared to the 1972 Democratic convention, the Republican mix of delegates was not as noticeable. Nonetheless, the increased role of women and youths was apparent throughout the Republicans' Aug. 21-23 convention in Miami Beach. A breakdown of Republican delegate makeup in 1972 showed these changes from 1968 (1972 Republican figures were based on statistics available Aug. 7, 1972, from 45 states—1,158 delegates of the 1,348 total). In 1972, youth representation climbed to 8.7 per cent from 1 per cent in 1968; and the percentage of women delegates—17 per cent in 1968—reached 30.1 per cent.

Impact of Reform

Would the reform efforts undertaken by Republicans and Democrats be a step forward in making the parties strong or more representative and more responsive? Most party professionals believed they would after a number of credentials challenges and other fights.

William B. Welsh, Democratic Party executive director, contended that the party's situation would have been far worse without reform. "The best situation for a Democratic nominee is a one-to-one confrontation with Richard Nixon—no third party, no fourth party. And the reform rules are working toward that end, to keep everyone within the party. If people are inside the convention hall, it's easier to deal with them, and compromise, and make the system work, than if they're outside. What the new rules have done is to bring a lot of people under the tent and then keep them there to play out the game within the party."

But challenges of the rules and procedures brought about by the reforms were inevitable, and some of them reached the courts. One suit was brought in 1971 by a coalition of Democratic reform groups and party leaders challenging the Democratic National Committee's formula for apportioning convention votes to the states.

U.S. District Court Judge June L. Green of the District of Columbia upheld the reformers June 16, 1971, ruling that delegates should be apportioned strictly on party strength in each state. Her decision was overturned Sept. 30, 1971, by the U.S. Court of Appeals, but the challenge set a precedent for taking challenges beyond the convention and into the courts.

In early 1972, challenges were made by women's groups in Arizona and civil rights groups in Illinois, and challenges were being prepared in several other states. Geri Joseph, former Democratic national committeewoman from Minnesota, wrote in April that challenges would be based mainly on two grounds: electing women, young people and minorities in proportion to their numbers in the states, and electing delegates in a timely process that took place within the convention year.

On the Republican side, a challenge was mounted against the delegate apportionment formula for 1976 that was adopted Aug. 22 at the 1972 Republican convention. The formula generally favored small southern and western states as against representation for most large states. Despite denials from both sides, the dispute was in part a battle between party liberals and conservatives. On Sept. 12, 1972, the Ripon Society, an organization of liberal young Republicans, filed a brief in the U.S. Court of Appeals in Washington, D.C., seeking rejection of the formula.

"We're a strong minority party, but that's not enough," said outgoing Republican National Committee chairman Dole in a January 1973 interview with Congressional Quarterly. Before 1974, "we've got to reach out and take in some of these people—blacks and Spanish speaking Americans—and we've got to elect some good candidates."

 **Electoral College**

SENATE FILIBUSTER KILLED POPULAR VOTE FOR PRESIDENT

In 1969, the House passed a constitutional amendment eliminating the electoral college and providing for direct popular election of the President. But the proposal died in a Senate filibuster in 1970. Twice, the Senate voted on cloture motions to cut off debate, but each vote failed by a narrow margin—six votes on Sept. 17 and five votes on Sept. 29. *(p. 1019)*

The merits of the venerable electoral college method of electing a U.S. President produced growing national debate in the period since 1945. But Congress made no changes, despite—or perhaps because of—the profusion of conflicting proposals to reform the sytem.

Background

The method of selecting a President was the subject of long debate at the Constitutional Convention of 1787. Several plans were proposed and rejected before a compromise solution, which was modified only slightly in future years, was adopted.

Facing the Convention when it convened May 25 was the question of whether the Chief Executive should be chosen by direct popular election, by the Congress, by state legislatures or by intermediate electors. Direct election was opposed because it was generally felt that the people lacked sufficient knowledge of the character and qualifications of possible candidates to make an intelligent choice. Many delegates also feared that the people of the various states would be unlikely to agree on a single person, usually casting their votes for favorite-son candidates well-known to them. Southerners opposed direct election for the additional reason that suffrage was more widespread in the north than in the south, where negro slaves did not vote.

The possibility of giving Congress the power to pick the President also received consideration. However, this plan also was rejected, largely because of fear that it would jeopardize the principle of executive independence. Similarly, a plan favored by many delegates, to let state legislatures choose the President, was turned down because it was feared that the President might feel so indebted to the states as to allow them to encroach on federal authority.

Unable to agree on a plan, the Convention Aug. 31 appointed a "Committee of Eleven" to propose a solution to the problem. The committee Sept. 4 suggested a compromise under which each state would appoint presidential electors, equal to the total number of its Representatives and Senators. The electors, chosen in a manner set forth by each state legislature, would meet in their own states and cast two votes for President. The votes would be counted in Congress, with the candidate receiving a majority elected President, and the second highest candidate becoming Vice President.

This plan constituted a great concession to the less populous states, since they were assured two extra votes (corresponding to their Senators) regardless of how small their population might be. The plan also left important powers with the states by giving complete discretion to state legislatures to determine the method of choosing electors.

Only one provision of the committee's plan aroused serious opposition—that giving the Senate the right to decide elections in which no candidate received a majority of electoral votes. Some delegates feared that the Senate, which already had been given treaty ratification powers and the responsibility to "advise and consent" to all important executive appointments, might become too powerful. Therefore, a counterproposal was made, and accepted, to let the House decide in instances when the electors failed to give a majority of their votes to a single candidate. The interests of the small states were preserved by giving each delegation only one vote in the House on roll calls to elect a President.

The system adopted by the Constitutional Convention was a compromise born out of problems involved in differing state voting requirements, the slavery problem, big-v.-small state rivalries and the complexities of the balance of power between different branches of the government. It also was apparently as close to a direct popular election as the men who wrote the Constitution thought possible and appropriate at the time. Some scholars have suggested that the electoral college, as it came to be called, was a "jerry-rigged improvisation" which really left it to future generations to work out the best form of presidential election.

Only once since ratification of the Constitution has an amendment been adopted which substantially altered the method of electing the President. In the 1800 presidential election, the Republican (anti-Federalist) electors inadvertently caused a tie in the electoral college by casting equal numbers of votes for Thomas Jefferson, whom they wished to be elected President, and Aaron Burr, whom they wished to elect Vice President. The election was thrown into the House of Representatives and 36 ballots were required before Jefferson was finally elected President. The 12th Amendment, ratified in 1804, sought to prevent a recurrence of this incident by providing that the electors should vote separately for President and Vice President.

Other changes in the system evolved over the years. The authors of the Constitution, for example, had intended that each state should choose its most distinguished citizens as electors and that they would deliberate and vote as individuals in electing the President. But, as strong political parties began to appear, the electors came to be chosen merely as representatives of the parties; and after 1800 independent voting by electors almost disappeared. From 1820 through 1972, only ten of the 15,092 electoral votes cast were cast contrary to "instructions." The instances since 1945 occurred in 1948, when Preston Parks, a Truman elector in Tennessee, voted for Gov. Strom Thurmond (D S.C. 1947-51); in 1960, when Henry D. Irwin, a Nixon elector in Oklahoma, voted for Sen. Harry F. Byrd (D Va.); in 1968, when Dr. Lloyd W. Bailey, a Nixon elector in North Carolina, voted for George C. Wallace: and in 1972 when Roger L. Mac-Bride, a Nixon elector in Virginia, voted for John Hospers, the presidential candidate of the Libertarian party.

The original system underwent further change as democratic sentiment mounted early in the 19th century, bringing with it the demand that electors should be chosen by direct popular vote of the people, instead of by the state legislatures. By 1804, the majority of state legislatures had adopted popular-vote provisions.

Initially, most "popular election" states provided that electors should be chosen from districts similar to congressional districts, with the electoral votes of a state split if the various districts differed in their political sentiment. This "district plan" of choosing electors was supported by the leading statesmen of both parties, including Jefferson, Alexander Hamilton, James Madison, John Quincy Adams, Andrew Jackson, Martin Van Buren and Daniel Webster.

The district plan, however, tended to dilute the power of political bosses and dominant majorities in state legislatures, who found themselves unable to "deliver" their states for one candidate or another. These groups brought pressure for a change and the unit rule system evolved, under which all of a state's electoral votes went to the party which won a plurality of the popular votes statewide.

When some states began to adopt the unit vote, the others soon followed suit. Jefferson explained in 1800: "All agree that an election by districts would be the best, if it could be general; but while 10 states choose, either by their legislatures (or by unit rule popular vote), it is folly and worse for the other six not to follow." A Senate committee report in 1826 said, "When the large states consolidate their votes to overwhelm the small ones, those, in their turn, must concentrate their own strength to resist them. A few states may persevere, for some time, in what they believe to be the fairest system, but when they see the unity of action which others derive from the (unit rule), they cannot resist the temptation of following the same plan."

By 1804, seven of the 10 "popular election" states cast their electoral votes under the unit rule; by 1824, 13 out of 18. By 1836, the district plan had vanished from the scene. However, no mention of unit rule voting was ever written into the Constitution, and the state legislatures retained the power to specify any method of choosing presidential electors and to determine how their votes would be divided.

Pros and Cons

The existing electoral college system, under which the entire electoral vote in a state is given to the candidate whose electors have won a plurality of the popular vote, has long been a matter of controversy.

Major objections to the current system:
● It has permitted the election of three Presidents who trailed their opponents in the national popular vote.

● The founding fathers never intended that the states would cast their electoral votes en bloc. Under the unit rule, minority popular votes not only are not reflected in a state's electoral votes but are added to those of the majority and given to the candidate against whom they were cast.

● The unit system offers no incentive for a heavy voter turnout in supposedly "safe" states.

● In large states which are fairly evenly divided between the major parties, the unit system inflates the bargaining power of splinter parties and pressure groups.

● The system puts a premium on fraud because juggling of a few votes can swing the electoral votes of an entire state.

● The current electoral system gives state legislatures the power to direct any method they wish of selecting presidential electors. While moral pressures have forced the legislatures to authorize a popular vote within the respective states, the possibility of abuse of power by state legislatures exists.

● There is no legal way to force an elector to vote for the candidate to whom he pledged himself. In a close election, several electors could be bribed, or simply change their minds, and the selection of the President thus altered.

● If an election is thrown into the House of Representatives because of the failure of a candidate to win a majority of electoral votes, an archaic and totally unrepresentative system goes into operation. Each state has a single vote, in total disregard of its population. Furthermore, the votes of evenly split delegations are not counted at all.

The current electoral system has been defended as follows:

● With minor amendment, it has successfully withstood the test of almost two centuries. Former President Kennedy, defending the current system as a Senator during a 1956 floor debate, said it was one "under which we have, on the whole, obtained able Presidents capable of meeting the increased demands upon our executive.... No urgent necessity for immediate change has been proven."

● Only once, in 1876, did a man who actually had a majority of the popular vote fail to win the presidency. The other "minority" Presidents were opposed by men who also failed to win an absolute majority.

● Any method of electoral reform which preserves the federal system by according each state two extra electoral votes could result in the election of a candidate who did not receive the majority of popular votes. The only alternative would be direct popular election of the President.

● Weighing the composition of the electoral college to give adequate representation to the small and sparsely settled states had been necessary if the authors of the Constitution were to reconcile those states to the idea of federation.

● The choice of President has fallen into the House of Representatives only twice (in 1800 and 1824), a remarkably low average.

● The unit rule's "winner-take-all" feature discourages the growth of splinter parties, which have been an impediment in the path of democratic growth in some European countries.

• The current system's exaggeration of the winner's majority should not be considered an unmitigated evil. After a bitterly fought election campaign, such as that of 1960, the appearance of nationwide backing for the winner of the electoral vote and elimination of doubt about the certainty of his election may help him win broader acceptance of his assumption of the powers of the presidency.

Reform Proposals

In light of criticism leveled at the existing electoral college, a number of proposals for alternate methods of choosing the President have been suggested. Since Jan. 6, 1797, when Rep. William L. Smith (F S.C.) introduced in Congress the first proposed constitutional amendment to reform the electoral college system, hardly a session of Congress has passed without the introduction of one or more resolutions of this nature. The majority of the proposed changes fit into three major categories.

DISTRICT PLAN

The district plan of choosing electors was the most popular reform proposal in the early years of the Republic, having been proposed at one time or another by most of the state legislatures and passed by the U.S. Senate more than once in the early 19th century. Following World War II, the provisions of the district plan were embodied in proposals offered by a number of Senators and Representatives. Those introduced by Rep. Frederic R. Coudert Jr. (R N.Y.) and Sen. Karl E. Mundt (R S.D.), known as the Mundt-Coudert plan, became the most widely known but, were not enacted.

The Mundt-Coudert plan would have preserved the office of elector, but provided that electors be chosen in the same manner as Representatives and Senators. The presidential candidate with a plurality in each electoral district, the lines of which would be set by the state legislatures, would receive the vote of its elector. The candidate with a plurality in a state would receive the electoral votes equal to its two Senators. The candidate receiving a majority of the total electoral votes would become President; but if no one received a majority, the new Senators and Representatives, sitting jointly and voting as individuals, would choose the President from the three candidates having the most electoral votes.

Proponents of the district plan argued that it would extend to presidential elections the same principles of representation that applied to congressional elections, with popular vote results reflected more accurately in electoral vote totals than under the existing method. Supporters also claimed that the district plan would encourage the minority party in currently one-party states by the hope of winning one or more districts. In addition, it was said that the system would give equal weight, based on population, both to rural and urban, and predominantly Democratic and Republican, districts; make it impossible for localized bad weather, vote frauds or other accidental circumstances to swing the entire electoral vote of a state; remove the method of choosing presidential electors from control of the state legislatures; and mark a return to the system contemplated by the founding fathers.

Opponents of the district plan responded that it might lead to gerrymandering of elector district lines by

'Minority' Presidents

Under the electoral college system, 15 Presidents who did not receive a majority of the popular votes cast in the election have been elected, either by the electoral college itself or by the House of Representatives. Three of them—John Quincy Adams, Rutherford B. Hayes and Benjamin Harrison—actually trailed their opponents in the popular vote.

The following table shows the percentage of the popular vote received by candidates in the 15 elections in which a "minority" President was elected:

Year	Elected		Opponents	
1824	Adams 30.54	Jackson 43.13	Clay 13.24	Crawford 13.09
1844	Polk 49.56	Clay 48.13	Birney 2.30	
1848	Taylor 47.35	Cass 42.52	Van Buren 10.13	
1856	Buchanan 45.63	Fremont 33.27	Fillmore 21.08	Smith .01
1860	Lincoln 39.79	Douglas 29.40	Breckinridge 18.20	Bell 12.60
1876	Hayes 48.04	Tilden 50.99	Cooper .97	
1880	Garfield 48.32	Hancock 48.21	Weaver 3.35	Others .12
1884	Cleveland 48.53	Blaine 48.24	Butler 1.74	St. John 1.49
1888	Harrison 47.86	Cleveland 48.66	Fisk 2.19	Streeter 1.29
1892	Cleveland 46.04	Harrison 43.01	Weaver 8.53	Others 2.42
1912	Wilson 41.85	T. Roosevelt 27.42	Taft 23.15	Others 7.58
1916	Wilson 49.26	Hughes 46.12	Benson 3.16	Others 1.46
1948	Truman 49.51	Dewey 45.13	Thurmond 2.40	Wallace 2.38
1960*	Kennedy 49.71	Nixon 49.55	Unpledged .92	Others .27
1968	Nixon 43.42	Humphrey 42.72	Wallace 13.53	Others .33

*1960 percentages total more than 100 because of double-counted Alabama votes (both under Kennedy and Unpledged columns).

SOURCES: Library of Congress, Historical Statistics of the U.S., and Congressional Quarterly Records

state legislatures, and that election of a "minority" President would still be possible. They also argued that the district plan might concentrate presidential campaigns in marginal congressional districts and minimize the influence of minority groups by isolating them in individual districts. Finally, opponents saw little advantage in substituting a district-wide unit rule for the state-wide rule of the existing system.

PROPORTIONAL METHOD

Under the proportional method of dividing each state's electoral votes, the office of the elector would be abolished but the electoral vote retained, with each candidate receiving the same proportion of the electoral vote as his share of a state's popular vote. This method was first introduced by Rep. Levi Maish (D Pa.) in 1877, when he proposed that each state's electoral votes be divided proportionately, but rounded off to whole numbers. Later in 1877, Rep. Jordan E. Cravens (D Ark.) introduced a similar plan but provided for a proportional division of the state's electoral votes to the third decimal place. More recent proportional method proposals were introduced by Sen. Henry Cabot Lodge (R Mass.) and Rep. Ed Gossett (D Texas) and by Sens. Price Daniel (D Texas) and Estes Kefauver (D Tenn.)

The major argument for the proportional distribution of electoral votes was that it would tend to reflect more accurately the popular strength of the various candidates, with the electoral vote count conforming far more closely to the actual vote count than under the existing system. Supporters also contended that it would encourage the two-party system in one-party states because each citizen's vote would have some effect on the national outcome; that state legislatures or individual electors would not have the power to frustrate the will of the people; that the influence of organized minorities would be lessened, inasmuch as their strength would be measured by their numbers rather than their bargaining power; and that accidental circumstances or fraud would be less likely to defeat the choice of the people because the entire electoral vote of a state would not hinge on a few questionable votes. Finally, proponents argued that the proportional plan would set the mode of electing a President on a uniform and permanent principle, at the same time giving the people a feeling that they had a more direct voice in the selection of the President.

Opponents argued that it would still be possible under the proportional method to elect a man who lost in the popular vote. They pointed out that had the system been in effect in 1880, it is probable that Winfield S. Hancock would have been elected, although he trailed James A. Garfield in the popular vote. Likewise, William Jennings Bryan would probably have scored an electoral victory over William McKinley in 1896, even though he received four percent less of the popular vote. Opponents also contended that the proportional distribution of electoral votes might weaken the power of the major parties by making it relatively easy for minority parties to win electoral votes.

DIRECT ELECTION

The direct election plan of choosing the President, considered at the Constitutional Convention in 1787, was first introduced in Congress as a constitutional amendment by Rep. William McManus (N.Y.) in 1826.

Supporters of direct election argued that it would be the most simple and direct way of having the President elected by the people. They said that a direct vote for President would sweep away all the possible abuses of the current method, including the right of state legislatures to direct methods of choosing electors, the right of electors to disobey instructions, the advantages of big states over smaller states or small states over big states, and the possibility that the popular vote winner would not become President. Finally, advocates of direct election argued that such a method would promote political activity in the supposedly "safe" states and invigorate the two-party system.

Arguments against the direct vote were that it would deprive the small states of the slight advantage they enjoyed through the two extra electoral votes accorded each state, regardless of size; lead to irresistible pressure for national laws governing qualifications for voting, which would constitute a blow to state power and jeopardize the states' control over voting for all other offices; and be impossible to ratify because of opposition by small states and by southern states, where many blacks had been barred from voting in the past and the white population had, in effect, cast the vote for both themselves and the blacks under the existing system. By the late 1960s, however, several factors—including the widening of suffrage, implementation of the Civil Rights Act and the Voting Rights Act and the growth of effective two-party competition in states where it had previously been weak or non-existent—were tending to cancel out some of the arguments against direct election of the President.

Congressional Action

None of the proposed reforms of the electoral college in the period between 1945 and 1973 were enacted. However, hearings were held on a number of the many bills that were introduced, and several were passed by either the House or the Senate.

1948

Sen. Lodge (R Mass.) and Rep. Gossett (D Texas) introduced legislation (S J Res 200, H J Res 9) calling for a proportional system of electing the President and Vice President. H J Res 9 was reported March 26 by the House Judiciary Committee and S J Res 200 on May 3 by the Senate Judiciary Committee, but no further action was taken in either House.

1950

The Lodge-Gossett proportional-method amendment was passed by the Senate but died in the House Rules Committee. S J Res 2, introduced by Lodge in 1949, was reported by the Senate Judiciary Committee on June 30, 1949. The Senate Feb. 1, 1950, rejected four amendments—including substitute amendments by William Langer (R N.D.), rejected 31-60 (D 11-39; R 20-21), and Hubert H. Humphrey (D Minn.), rejected 28-63 (D 13-37; R 15-26)—which provided for election of the President and Vice President by direct vote. The Senate then accepted by voice vote an amendment by Sen. Scott Lucas (D Ill.) making 40 per cent of the electoral vote, instead of a majority, the minimum necessary to elect a candidate. If no candidate received at least 40 per cent of the electoral vote, the Senate and House in joint session would choose the president from the three candidates receiving the highest number of electoral votes. S J Res 2 was adopted Feb. 1 by a 64-27 (D 46-4; R 18-23) roll-call vote, which was more than the two-thirds majority required for a proposal to amend the Constitution.

H J Res 2, an identical plan introduced by Rep. Gossett and approved July 21, 1949, by the House Judiciary Committee, was bottled up in the House Rules Committee. Gossett July 17, 1950, moved to suspend the rules and bring the resolution to the floor, but the motion—which required a two-thirds majority—was rejected 134-210 (D 87-116: R 47-93; Ind. 0-1).

1951

Bills constituting the same Lodge-Gossett plan which had passed the Senate in 1950 were reported in both houses but received no further action. S J Res 52, introduced by Lodge, was reported July 30 by the Senate Judiciary Committee, H J Res 19 (Gossett's) was reported Oct. 17 by the House Judiciary Committee.

1956

S J Res 31, introduced by Daniel and Kefauver, was reported May 19, 1955, by the Senate Judiciary Committee and brought to the floor March 27, 1956. The plan, known as the "original Daniel plan," contained provisions similar to the Lodge-Gossett proportional proposals.

By the time S J Res 31 was called up for Senate floor action, supporters of the proportional and the district systems had joined forces in an effort to gain enough votes for passage. Their amendment, known as the "Daniel substitute," would have divided each state's electoral votes by the proportional method, unless the state legislature voted to employ the district method of choosing electors—in other words, giving each state the choice between the Daniel-Kefauver and the Mundt-Coudert plans for casting its electoral vote. The Senate rejected four amendments—including one by Langer, rejected 13-69 (D 11-28; R 2-41), and one by Sen. Herbert H. Lehman (D N.Y.), rejected 17-66 (D 16-25; R 1-41)— providing for direct popular election of the President. The Senate then approved the Daniel substitute by a 48-37 (D 26-18; R 22-19) roll-call vote. This was enough to carry it as a substitute, but was short of the two-thirds favorable vote required for a constitutional amendment. Rather than face defeat on the vote for final passage, Daniel moved, and the Senate voted by voice, to recommit S J Res 31 to the Judiciary Committee, where it died.

Among the leading opponents of electoral reform during the 1956 Senate debate was Sen. John F. Kennedy (D Mass.). Speaking in opposition to changes in the existing system, Kennedy said, "It is not only the unit vote for the Presidency we are talking about, but a whole solar system of government. If it is proposed to change the balance of power of one of the elements of the solar system, it is necesary to consider the others."

By "solar system" Kennedy was referring to the entire governmental structure of the United States—state legislatures, the two houses of Congress and the presidency. He argued that because the state legislatures and

Congress were disproportionately represented by rural areas and the small states, it was proper for the urban areas, with their liberally oriented minority groups, to have a larger role in electing the President. Liberals tended to shift to opposition of electoral reform when it became clear that the consequence could be a weakening of comparatively liberal and minorities voting strengths.

1961

The Senate Judiciary Constitutional Amendments Subcommittee held hearings between May 23 and July 13 on proposals for reform of the electoral college but took no further action. Sentiment for basic reform was expressed by former Presidents Hoover, Truman and Eisenhower, 17 Senators, one state Governor, the chairman of the Republican National Committee, professors of law and political science from a number of universities and several private citizens. However, there was a lack of agreement on how reform should be achieved.

The only principal witnesses opposing a basic overhaul of the current system were representatives of the Kennedy administration, the chairman of the Democratic National Committee and two Senators. They all recommended some limited type of amendment designed chiefly to prevent individual electors from breaking their pledges to vote for a certain presidential candidate.

1963

The Senate Constitutional Amendments Subcommittee June 4 held hearings, a continuation of the 1961 hearings. Subcommittee Chairman Kefauver said the hearings had been called to assess recent change in the U.S. political balance of power, including the reduction of conservative-rural influence by rapid state legislature reapportionments in the wake of 1962 Supreme Court decision in *Baker v. Carr (p. 1017)* and a diminishing of conservative one-party states and areas—all occurring, Kefauver pointed out, without a concurrent change in the unit vote electoral system, which was generally felt to give political priority to the votes of big states with liberally oriented urban populations.

Prof. James MacGregor Burns of Williams College testified that reform of the electoral college, though long a pressing problem, "has proved impossible because politicians have feared that it might upset or threaten political arrangements that they have found congenial or at least predictable and dependable."

1966

The Senate Judiciary Constitutional Amendments Subcommittee again held hearings on electoral reform, with initial emphasis on the proposal of the Johnson administration—first put forth in 1965 and reiterated by the President in 1966—to abolish the office of elector while confirming the existing state unit vote system of casting electoral votes. But little enthusiasm was expressed for the administration proposal, which had been sponsored by subcommittee chairman Birch Bayh (D Ind.). Most reform advocates considered the presidential proposal a substitute for true reform since it would "freeze" into the Constitution what they found the most undesirable element of the existing system—the "winner-take-all"

Varied Factors Spurred Reform Efforts

Public interest in a change in the electoral college system was promoted by the close 1960 and 1968 elections, a series of Supreme Court rulings and introduction of unpledged elector systems in the South.

Court Decisions

The "one man-one vote" decisions of the Supreme Court intensified dissatisfaction with the electoral college. Critics maintained the electoral college violated the "one man-one vote" and equal representation principles in several ways: the two extra votes given to each state, no matter their size; the winner take all method of casting each state's vote; the possibility that a winner in the popular vote could be a loser in the electoral college, etc.

In *Baker v. Carr,* the Court March 26, 1962, ruled that Tennessee citizens had the right to challenge the apportionment of their state legislatures in the federal courts, thus for the first time opening the apportionment and districting established by state legislatures to review by federal courts.

This was followed on June 15, 1964, by a series of decisions in *Reynolds v. Sims* and related cases in which the Supreme Court ruled that the equal protection clause of the 14th Amendment "requires that the seats in both houses of a bicameral state legislature must be apportioned on a population basis," and that while "mathematical exactness of precision" in carving out legislative districts may be impossible, apportionments must be "based substantially on population."

In a March 18, 1963, decision in *Gray v. Sanders,* the Court ruled that Georgia's county unit system of voting in statewide and congressional primary elections deprived citizens of equal protection of the laws and was therefore unconstitutional. The majority opinion set forth the principle of "one person, one vote," and went on to refuse to justify Georgia's unit system on analogy to the electoral college, saying that the electoral college was based on a "conception of political equality that belongs to a bygone day."

On Feb. 17, 1964, the Supreme Court declared that congressional districts must be as equal in population as practicable. In *Wesberry v. Sanders,* in which the congressional districts of Georgia were challenged, the Court relied on the findings of *Baker* to show that districting questions were justiciable and on *Gray* to establish the principle of "one person, one vote."

The Court April 7, 1969, in *Kirkpatrick v. Preisler,* ruled that no numerical or percentage population variance between districts within a state could be considered negligible. Any variance—"no matter how small"—must be justified by the state or shown to be unavoidable, the Court said. *(Details Redistricting Chapter)*

In 1966, Delaware, joined by 12 other states, asked the U.S. Supreme Court to hear a suit challenging the constitutionality under the 14th Amendment of the unit vote—the "winner-take-all" method of casting state electoral votes. Delaware asked the Court to "open the door" to reform by granting a type of interim relief that would require the states to divide their electoral votes in a way that would reflect popular vote sentiment. The suit acknowledged that a direct vote would be the only permanent remedy to the inequalities built into the electoral college system. The Court refused to hear the case, giving no reasons for its action. Delaware's brief, however, served to dramatize the shortcomings of the electoral college when compared with the "one-man, one-vote" standard being required by the courts in the state legislatures and congressional districts.

Unpledged Electors

Unpledged electors also caused increasing doubts about the value of the electoral college. The selection of unpledged electors could remove the choice of the president from the people altogether by having electors cast their votes for whomever they chose.

Support for changes in the electoral college also increased as a result of efforts to affect the out-come of presidential elections by means of unpledged electors. The laws of five southern states—Alabama, Georgia, Louisiana, Mississippi and South Carolina—permitted the election to the electoral college of a slate of independent of unpledged electors. Other states provided a place on the ballot for slates representing new or minor political parties. Some states allowed the use of petition procedures to qualify electoral slates pledged to an independent candidate.

In 1960, an unpledged elector movement was successful in two states—Mississippi and Alabama. In electoral college balloting, all of the Mississippi electors and six of Alabama's 11 electors withheld their votes from both Republican candidate Richard M. Nixon and Democrat John F. Kennedy, casting them instead for Sen. Byrd (D Va.) for President and Sen. Thurmond (D S.C.) for Vice President. Byrd received an additional vote from an Oklahoma elector who had pledged to Nixon.

In 1968, a North Carolina elector, Dr. Lloyd W. Bailey, who had been elected as a Republican elector, cast his vote for George C. Wallace. Objection to the vote was raised in the Jan. 6, 1969, Joint Session of Congress for the counting of the electoral votes, but the challenge was rejected by a 33-58 (R 13-30; D 20-28) roll-call vote of the Senate and a 170-228 (R 50-125; D 120-103) roll call of the House.

system of casting each state's electoral votes. About all the administration measure would have accomplished would have been to frustrate the southern unpledged elector strategy. *(Box, this page)*

The death knell for the administration plan was apparently sounded May 18 when Bayh announced he was abandoning his support of it and switching to backing for direct popular election of the President. Bayh said he had changed his position, "after a great deal of soul-searching," because he doubted whether it would be worthwhile to go through the complex steps necessary to amend the Constitution just "to rectify and legalize the status quo" and achieve a reform that was "second best."

Bayh introduced a bill (S J Res 163) providing a constitutional amendment to substitute a direct popular election in which the people would choose between slates of candidates running together for President and Vice President. In the event that no candidate slate received 40 per cent of the national popular vote, the Senate and House in joint session would be required to choose, by majority vote, one of the two President-Vice President slates that had received the most popular votes.

Bayh said he was "not speaking for the administration" and that "at least the Justice Department is not at all happy with this." He said Justice Department officials had asked him why he was shifting to the direct popular vote solution when similar amendments had been soundly beaten on the Senate floor in 1956. Bayh said his reply was that "a lot of history has been made since 1956, and a lot of freedoms given to our people since 1956." Specifically, he noted the 24th Amendment abolishing the poll tax in federal elections, the Civil Rights Acts of 1957, 1960 and 1964 and the Voting Rights Acts of 1965. "Today, for the first time in our history, we have achieved the goal of universal suffrage regardless of race, religion or station in life," Bayh said. "Today, we are witnessing a political development in our states where for the first time in decades, legislatures fully represent people.... We have only one election remaining wherein some votes are not equal to others and wherein millions of votes do not count in the final result—and that is in the election of the most powerful political officer in the world, the President of the United States."

While no action was taken on Bayh's proposal, several developments took place in 1966 and 1967 supporting reform of the electoral college system:

• The Chamber of Commerce of the United States, following a policy referendum of its member organizations, Jan. 31, 1966, announced it favored abolishing the electoral college and shifting to either a nationwide popular vote or a district system of choosing presidential electors. The final vote of the Chamber members for approving the new policy position was 91.5 per cent in favor.

• The Gallup Poll May 18, 1966 reported 63 per cent of the American people would like to do away with the electoral college and substitute a direct vote of the people for President.

• Sen. Quentin N. Burdick (D N.D.) conducted a poll of all members of the 50 state legislatures and found 58.8 per cent in favor of direct election of the President and only 9.7 per cent in favor of continuing the existing system. Another 21.2 per cent favored a proportional method of casting state electoral votes, while 10.2 per cent were in favor of a district system. Results of the Burdick poll showed that in 44 states, direct election was favored by 50 per cent or more of the legislators responding. Support for direct election was almost as strong among legislators from small states as those from large states.

• A special electoral college commission of the American Bar Association Jan. 7, 1967, recommended that the President and Vice President be elected as a team by popular vote of the people, with the entire electoral college mechanism discarded. The commission suggested

that the winning candidate must receive at least 40 per cent of the vote to be elected. A national runoff election would be held if no candidate reached the 40 per cent mark.

The ABA's House of Delegates Feb. 13, 1967, voted 171-57 to approve the Commission's report.

1967

The Senate Judiciary Constitutional Amendments Subcommittee again held hearings on various proposals for reforming or abolishing the electoral college. One proposal, (S Res 6), introduced by Sen. Margaret Chase Smith (R Maine) called for a direct vote for President and also proposed a national nominating primary for presidential candidates. But no further action was taken.

1969-70

Efforts to reform or eliminate the electoral college came to a head during the 91st Congress after the 1968 presidential election. George Wallace, who ran as the American Independent Party candidate, received the support of 46 electors who pledged to vote for him or for whomever he directed them to vote.

Those who wanted to abolish the electoral college said that if President Nixon had not received a majority of electoral votes, Wallace (or any other third party candidate in a similar situation) could have bargained his electoral votes to Nixon or Vice President Humphrey in exchange for certain favors.

Nixon, in a Feb. 20, 1969, message to Congress asking for prompt action on electoral college reform, said he would support any plan which would eliminate individual electors and distribute among the presidential candidates the electoral vote of every state and the District of Columbia in a manner more closely approximating the popular vote. He said that while previously he had supported the proportional method, "I am not wedded to the details of this plan or any other specific plan."

House Action. Hearings were held before the House Judiciary Committee during February and March, 1969. On May 16, the committee reported a bill (H J Res 681) proposing a constitutional amendment to provide for direct popular election of the president and vice president. It also provided for a runoff election between the top two candidates for the presidency if no candidate received 40 per cent of the vote.

The House passed the proposal on Sept. 18, 1969, by **a key 338 to 70 roll-call vote** and sent it to the Senate. The vote was well over the required two-thirds majority for constitutional amendments.

House debate on the constitutional amendment centered on which of three main proposals for changing the current voting system was the best. The two most popular alternative plans to the direct popular vote were the district and proportional plans. The district plan required that the presidential candidate with a plurality in each electoral district would receive the vote of its elector and the candidate with a state-wide plurality would receive the electoral votes equal to that state's two senators. Under the proportional plan, each candidate would receive the same proportion of a state's electoral vote as he received of the popular vote in that state.

In the House vote, 184 Democrats and 154 Republicans voted for the amendment; 44 Democrats and 26 Republicans voted against it. Prior to passage, opponents of the plan were defeated in a last-minute bid to recommit the amendment and substitute for it the district plan. The vote on recommittal was 162-246. A conservative coalition of 100 Republicans and 62 Democrats voted for recommittal; 80 Republicans joined 166 Democrats to vote against the motion.

The voting on the recommittal motion pointed up the geographic divisions and philosophical differences which permeated debate on the proposed amendment. The direct vote plan which was approved was viewed by its supporters as the most simple and democratic method and won the backing of not only the more liberal members but also the Republican leadership. The district plan, which would retain a geographical electoral system, was favored by conservative members, including southerners and some midwesterners. The proportional plan, regarded as more of a middle-ground, was viewed by many—including President Nixon—as the plan most likely to win over-all approval both in Congress and in the states

Nixon Statement. Following House approval of the direct vote plan, the President Sept. 30, 1969 issued a statement supporting that action. He said that, "because the ultimate goal of electoral reform must prevail over differences as to how best to achieve that goal, I endorse the direct election approach and urge the Senate also to adopt it." He said he believed that "contrary views are now a luxury" and the need for electoral reform was "urgent and should be our controlling consideration."

SENATE ACTION. The proposed constitutional amendment (S J Res 1) died in 1970, the victim of filibusters by southern and small state senators.

The Senate bill, sponsored by Birch Bayh (D Ind.), was similar to the one passed by the House in 1969, except for the date each would become effective.

The Senate bill would have become effective a year after the April 15 following ratification by 38 of the 50 states; the House version set the effective date at one year after the Jan. 21 following ratification.

But a coalition of southern and some small state senators was able to prevent the resolution from coming to a vote by filibustering.

Opponents generally feared direct elections would destroy the two-party system and encourage numerous splinter parties. Southerners, in addition, saw national voting requirements, at the expense of state laws, as a natural outgrowth of direct elections.

Some senators from small states feared the influence of their voting populations in a direct election would be less than the influence of their electoral votes under the existing system.

Carl T. Curtis (R Neb.), a leading opponent of direct elections, explained that his state had 92/100ths of 1 per cent of the total electoral vote. But based on the 1968 election, it would have had only 73/100ths of 1 per cent of the popular vote. "I'm not authorized to reduce the voting power of my state by 20 per cent," he said.

Cloture Attempts. The filibuster, led by Sam J. Ervin Jr. (D N.C.), lasted intermittently from Sept. 8 to Oct. 5. Attempts by Majority Leader Mike Mansfield (D Mont.) to invoke cloture (end debate) under Rule 22 failed on two occasions. Under the rule, debate can be ended by two-thirds approval of those senators present and voting.

The first cloture attempt failed Sept. 17 on a **key 54-36 roll-call vote,** six votes short of the required 60. The second attempt failed Sept. 29 on a 53-34 vote, five short of the required 58.

In the Sept. 17 vote, 21 Republicans and 33 Democrats voted for cloture; 18 Republicans joined 18 Democrats in defeating cloture. In the Sept. 29 vote, the breakdown was as follows: for cloture, 19 Republicans and 34 Democrats; against cloture, 19 Republicans and 15 Democrats.

On the first cloture attempt 20 of 26 southern senators voted against ending debate, while the small state (eight or fewer electoral votes) senators split almost evenly: 25 for cloture, 21 against and 6 not voting. On the second cloture attempt, 20 of 26 southern senators again voted against ending debate, while small state senators split evenly: 23 for, 23 against and one not voting.

Mansfield filed a third cloture motion Oct. 2, but withdrew it Oct. 5 when it became clear that the attempt to end debate would fail for a third time. In approving Mansfield's unanimous consent request to withdraw his cloture motion, the Senate also agreed to postpone further action on the bill until after an election recess from Oct. 14 to Nov. 16. The resolution, however, never came up again in the 91st Congress.

The Appendix

Pages in this Appendix are numbered, 1a, 2a, 3a, etc.
It consists of the following sections:

The Appendix

Pages in this Appendix are numbered, 1a, 2a, 3a, etc.
It consists of the following sections:

Key Votes 1969-1972

Congressional Quarterly each year selects a series of key votes on major issues.

Selection of Issues. An issue is judged by the extent it represents one or more of the following:

- A matter of major controversy.
- A test of presidential or political power.
- A decision of potentially great impact on the nation and lives of Americans.

Selection of Votes. For each series of related votes on an issue, only one key vote is ordinarily chosen. This vote is the roll call in the House or Senate that in the opinion of Congressional Quarterly was the most important in determining the outcome.

In the descriptions of the key votes, the designation ND denotes northern Democrats and the designation SD denotes southern Democrats.

TAX REFORM AND REDUCTION, VOTING RIGHTS MAJOR ISSUES

House Key Votes

1. POWELL SEATING. The House Jan. 3 ended the two-year exile it had forced on Rep. Adam C. Powell (D N.Y.) in 1967. Before permitting him to be seated, however, the House fined him $25,000 and stripped him of his seniority. The key vote was on a motion by Judiciary Committee Chairman Emanuel Celler (D N.Y.) to move the previous question on the resolution (H Res 2) to seat Powell, fine him the $25,000 at the rate of $1,150 per month and to commence his seniority as of the date of his swearing-in. The previous question was ordered by a 249-171 vote with the Republicans divided almost evenly on the question, 96-89 and the Democrats voting 153-82 (ND 136-12; SD 17-70).

2. SURTAX. President Nixon's tax package, designed to fight inflation and give tax relief to the poor, squeaked by the House June 30 by a 210-205 party-line vote. Four Republicans switched their votes to aid passage. The bill (HR 12290) extended the surtax at 10 percent through Dec. 31, 1969, and at 5 percent through June 30, 1970, repealed the 7-percent investment credit and provided a low income allowance for individuals. The bulk of the opposing votes came from liberals who had insisted upon meaningful tax reform as a price for the one-year surtax extension, and conservatives who were against increased federal spending implied by higher taxes. Voting for the bill were 154 Republicans and 56 Democrats; against the bill were 26 Republicans and 179 Democrats. The breakdown of the Democratic vote was ND 22-129; SD 34-50.

3. EDUCATION FUNDS. Despite Administration efforts to hold the line on spending for federal programs to help curb inflation, the House July 31 voted to increase spending on education programs by more than $1 billion over the amounts requested by the Administration. The bulk of the increase—$894.5 million—was added through an amendment to the Labor-HEW appropriations bill (HR 13111) by Charles S. Joelson (D N.J.), supported by almost all Democrats and a majority of the Republicans. Nearly half of the increase ($398 million) was for the politically popular program of aid to federally impacted areas, which reaches more than 375 Congressional districts. The amendment was adopted 294-119: R 99-81; D 195-38 (ND 147-2; SD 48-36).

4. TAX REFORM. Climaxing seven months of work by the House Ways and Means Committee, the House Aug. 7 overwhelmingly approved a major tax reform bill (HR 13270). The legislation lowered individual tax rates by an average of 5 percent, provided a low-income allowance to remove most poor persons from tax rolls and contained provisions to ensure that persons with large nontaxable incomes and large deductions did not totally escape tax liability. The comprehensive measure, approved by a 395-30 vote, also tightened tax treatment of private foundations, other tax-exempt organizations, charitable contributions, income from oil and other minerals, capital gains and real estate. The investment tax credit was repealed and the surtax extended at 5 percent through June 30, 1970. Only 10 Republicans and 20 Democrats voted against passage: R 176-10; D 219-20 (ND 150-1; SD 69-19).

5. ELECTORAL COLLEGE. With the memory of the 1968 Presidential election fresh in their minds and the possibility that the election could have been thrown into the House of Representatives for selection of the Presidency, the House Sept. 18 passed a proposed constitutional amendment to abolish the electoral college system. By a 338-70 vote, the House passed H J Res 681 to provide for the direct popular election of the President and Vice President. Opposition to the measure came largely from Southern Democrats—R 154-26; D 184-44 (ND 142-3; SD 42-41). The President did not take a position on the resolution.

6. SELECTIVE SERVICE REFORM. The President scored a major victory Oct. 30 when the House passed the Administration's draft lottery proposal (HR 14001). Action on the bill came after the President Sept. 19 threatened to "take unilateral action by executive order" if Congress failed to act in the 1969 session. The House passed the Administration proposal by a lopsided 383-12 vote: R 175-1; D 208-11 (ND 126-11; SD 82-0). On Nov. 19, the Senate, which earlier had been divided over the Administration proposal, approved it by a voice vote.

7. VIETNAM RESOLUTION. The second major policy declaration on Vietnam by Congress since the 1964 Gulf of Tonkin resolution was approved Dec. 2 by the House. During a two-day debate on a number of issues related to the war in Vietnam, the House by a 334-55 vote passed a resolution (H Res 613) commending President Nixon's efforts to achieve "peace with justice" in Vietnam. Only one Republican—Ogden R. Reid (N.Y.)—was among the 55 opponents. Although H Res 613 had the active support of the leadership of both parties, liberal Democrats and some Republican doves objected to the speed with which the measure was sent to the floor shortly after the President's Nov. 3 address to the nation on Vietnam. The breakdown of the vote was R 172-1: D 162-54 (ND 89-54; SD 73-0).

8. FOREIGN AID. By a narrow 200-195 vote, the House Dec. 9 passed a bill (HR 15149) appropriating $1.6 billion for foreign aid in fiscal 1970. Those who voted against the bill—the lowest appropriation in the history of foreign aid—included supporters of the program who objected to the addition of $104.5 million in military assistance to South Korea and Nationalist China. A majority of Republicans and Southern Democrats voted against the measure—R 79-91; D 121-104 (ND 92-52; SD 29-52).

9. VOTING RIGHTS. Another close victory for the Administration came when the House Dec. 11 approved by a 208-204 vote the Administration voting rights bill (HR 4249). Southern Democrats joined Republicans to pass the measure to extend the Voting Rights Act of 1965 nationwide rather than to extend the Act unamended. The Administration bill had the effect of weakening the Act, particularly by deleting a provision in the Act which required federal approval before state laws on voting could take effect. The key vote was on an amendment in the nature of a substitute (HR 12695) by Minority Leader Gerald R. Ford (R Mich.) to the committee bill. The amendment was adopted 208-204: R 129-49; D 79-155 (ND 10-141; SD 69-14).

10. POVERTY PROGRAM. The strongest effort in the history of the poverty program to turn its control over to the states was beaten Dec. 12 after House leaders delayed action on the bill for several weeks to rally support behind a straight two-year extension of the program. The Administration had requested the two-year extension, but had been opposed largely by Republicans and Southern Democrats who argued that states should be given the option to run the program. The state-control effort was defeated when the House rejected by a 163-231 vote a motion by William H. Ayres (R Ohio) to recommit the bill (HR 12321) to committee with instructions to report back the substitute bill providing for state administration of the program. The breakdown of the vote was R 103-63; D 60-168 (ND 7-139; SD 53-29).

11. COAL MINE SAFETY. Despite the threat of a Presidential veto, the House Dec. 17 adopted the conference report on the bill (S 2917) to improve health and safety conditions of persons working in the coal mining industry. The Administration objected to provisions to compensate victims of black lung disease because, it argued, the assistance would cost up to $385 million a year. The vote on adoption of the conference report was 334-12: R 144-12; D 190-0 (ND 128-0; SD 61-0).

12. MINORITY HIRING. The House sided with the Administration late in the session in a dispute over whether the Government should require federal contractors to set targets for hiring minority workers. After the Administration had developed the so-called "Philadelphia Plan" for minority hiring, the Comptroller General ruled that the quota system violated the Civil Rights Act of 1964. In passing the fiscal 1970 supplemental appropriations bill, the Senate had added language allowing the Comptroller General to refuse federal funds to any programs he considered illegal. When the measure came back to the House, a motion to agree to the Senate amendment (and thus, in effect, to kill the Philadelphia Plan) was defeated Dec. 22 by a 156-208 vote, with a majority of Democrats voting for the Senate amendment and a majority of Republicans voting against the amendment. The breakdown of the vote was R 41-124: D 115-84 (ND 54-78; SD 61-6).

Senate Key Votes

1. NONPROLIFERATION TREATY. After months of delay during which approval became a political issue, the Senate on March 13 overwhelmingly consented to the ratification of the treaty to ban the spread of nuclear weapons. The accord drafted by the United States and Soviet Union had been signed and sent to the Senate in July 1968. After the Soviet invasion of Czechoslovakia in August, Presidential candidate Richard M. Nixon and others opposed action on the treaty at that time although they supported its contents. On Feb. 5, 1969, President Nixon called for "prompt" Senate action. The treaty, regarded as a milestone in arms-control efforts, barred the transfer of nuclear devices to countries which did not possess such equipment. The treaty was approved 83-15: R 34-8; D 49-7 (ND 38-0; SD 11-7).

2. NATIONAL COMMITMENTS. The Senate June 25 moved to regain active participation in foreign policy by approving a two-year-old declaration of intent defining national commitments and reasserting the Congressional role in making such commitments. This resolution, which did not carry the force of law, nevertheless represented a clear expression of Senate sentiment opposed by Presidents Johnson and Nixon as a restriction on the President. The measure had been originally introduced in 1967 as a result of the expanding controversy over growing involvement into the undeclared war in Vietnam. The Senate passed the resolution, which did not require House action, by a vote of 70-16: R 27-13; D 43-3 (ND 28-3; SD 15-0).

3. FARM SUBSIDY CEILING. For the second year in a row, the Senate blocked House attempts to limit farm subsidies to individual farmers. Such an amendment was attached to the omnibus farm bill in the House in 1968 but deleted in conference with the Senate. In 1969, the House against accepted a floor amendment to the agriculture appropriations bill (HR 11612) limiting federal farm subsidy payments to $20,000. The Senate Appropriations Committee June 25 removed the limitation. It argued the limitation would increase the cost of the cotton program and that such action should be considered thoroughly as part of a pending review of farm legislation. On July 7, the Senate by a vote of 53-34 specifically approved the Committee's deletion and later rejected a separate move to impose an even lower subsidy limit. A majority of Republicans and Democrats opposed the limitation although a majority of Northern Democrats favored it in a victory for the conservative coalition (ND 13-17; SD 15-4; R 25-13).

4. SURTAX EXTENSION. Despite earlier attempts by the Senate Democratic leadership to block extension of the 10-percent income tax surcharge, the Senate on July 31, voted such an extension until Dec. 31, 1969, by a vote of 51-48 (ND 27-10; SD 18-1; R 6-37). Senate Democratic leaders had sought to link the Administration-sought extension with tax reform proposals they favored. President Nixon March 26 requested an extension of the 10-percent surtax through June 30. On April 21 he offered his tax reform plan. In his proposal, the surtax would be extended at 10 percent through Dec. 31, and at 5 percent through June 30, 1970. When the Democratic leadership relented to allow an extension without tax reform, Sen. Russell B. Long (D La.) offered the 10-percent extension to Dec. 31 as an amendment to a House-passed bill on collection of federal unemployment taxes (HR 9951). Although Republicans generally opposed the Long proposal as not going far enough to brake inflation, the

Senate approved the partial extension by a narrow margin. The House agreed to the Senate proposal a few weeks later and a provision extending the surtax at 5 percent until June 30, 1970, was contained in the tax reform bill (HR 13270).

5. SAFEGUARD ABM. In 1969, as in 1968, a significant debate involved construction of a defense against enemy missiles. In 1968, President Johnson's Sentinel ABM program to defend U.S. cities was the subject of several votes supporting the plan. President Nixon decided March 14 to protect the U.S. retaliatory missile arsenal instead. Opposition continued, and an intense lobbying campaign on both sides was waged in the Senate, where an extremely close vote was foreseen. Sen. Margaret Chase Smith (R Maine) introduced an amendment to the Defense Procurement Bill (S 2546) to knock out all funds for the program. When that proposal was rejected 11-89 Sen. Smith and other opponents drafted a compromise amendment to block any work on the President's Safeguard ABM system but allowing development of other ABM defenses. On that crucial vote the Senate Aug. 6 divided evenly 50-50 thus rejecting the proposal. On a subsequent vote to limit Safeguard work to research, Sen. Smith sided with the Administration to form a 49-51 vote supporting Safeguard. The ABM was approved by larger margins in the House and later in the Senate. The 50-50 vote was a victory for the conservative coalition as a majority of Republicans and Southern Democrats sided with the President for the ABM. R 14-29; D 36-21 (ND 31-7, SD 5-14).

6. HAYNSWORTH NOMINATION. Perhaps the Administration's worst Congressional defeat of 1969 occurred Nov. 21 when the Senate, by a 45-55 vote, rejected the President's nomination of Clement F. Haynsworth Jr. for the Supreme Court. The rejection, largely over Haynsworth's financial dealings while on the 4th Circuit Court of Appeals, climaxed three months of debate and lobbying over the nomination. The Aug. 18 nomination of Haynsworth was actively opposed by organized labor and civil rights groups on the grounds that Haynsworth had sided against them in decisions before his court. Revelation by opponents also indicated that he had had financial ties with organizations involved in cases before him. The Administration waged an aggressive lobbying campaign in support, and several Senators complained of the pressure. Ultimately, the Senate rejected the nomination by a 45-55 vote (ND 3-35; SD 16-3; R 26-17).

7. OIL DEPLETION ALLOWANCE. Senate liberals won a sizable victory over a traditional target as the chamber Dec. 1 defeated an attempt to retain for tax purposes the 27.5-percent depletion allowance for oil and gas companies. In rejecting by a 30-62 vote an amendment to the tax reform bill by Allen J. Ellender (D La.) to restore the full depletion allowance, the Senate sided with the Finance Committee, which had recommended a reduction to 23 percent (ND 5-30; SD 8-10; R 17-22). However, a subsequent 38-52 vote rejected an attempt to reduce the depletion allowance to the 20-percent level recommended by the House. Although the President favored retention of the 27.5-percent allowance, the final version of the bill (HR 13270) reduced the figure to 22 percent.

8. PERSONAL EXEMPTION. In another blow to the Administration, the Senate Dec. 3 voted 58-37 to raise the personal exemption for the income tax from $600 to $800: R 10-32; D 48-5 (ND 35-0; SD 13-5). The in-

crease came over Presidential threats to veto the tax reform bill as not "fiscally responsible" if the exemption increase was added. The sponsor, Albert Gore (D Tenn.), had originally sought a $1,000 exemption but switched to the $800 figure in a move that undermined Senate Republican moves to offer their own exemption increase and left liberal Republicans critical of the Administration. In a compromise move in the House-Senate conference on the tax bill, the personal exemption was increased to $750.

9. TAX REFORM. Disregarding a Presidential promise to veto the bill, the Senate Dec. 11 climaxed a year of tax reform deliberations by passing HR 13270 by a 69-22 vote (ND 35-0; SD 16-2; R 18-20). The President had threatened such a veto if the Senate measure contained the increase to $800 for personal exemption and the 15-percent increase in Social Security benefits. In the final version of the bill worked out in conference, the personal exemption was scaled down to $750 but the Social Security increase was retained.

10. LAOS TROOP CURB. In another move to restore the Congressional role in foreign affairs, the Senate Dec. 15 voted to prohibit the introduction of U.S. ground combat troops into Laos and Thailand by a vote of 73-17. The proposal was a substitute to a pending amendment to the defense appropriations bill (HR 15090) which would have limited U.S. aid to those countries to equipment and material. The President had earlier stated no U.S. combat troops were involved in Laos. It was supported by a majority of both parties (ND 25-7; SD 10-8; R 38-2).

11. SCHOOL DESEGREGATION. The Senate Dec. 17 backed the Administration by watering down a House-passed attempt to legalize freedom-of-choice school desegregation plans. The House provision would have impeded federal enforcement of school desegregation by forbidding termination of funds to districts which had a freedom-of-choice plan. This House language was opposed by the Administration and liberal and civil rights forces. An Administration-backed amendment to the House rider to the Labor-HEW appropriations bill (HR 13111) weakened the House restriction by adding the words "except as required by the Constitution." This action received Senate endorsement 52-37: R 22-19; D 30-18 (ND 28-3; SD 2-15). A day later, the House agreed.

12. AID TO CHINA. Although the concept of foreign aid has repeatedly been a controversial issue in the past, in 1969 the most vehement debate centered around an unbudgeted item for Nationalist China which was added in the House. As a result of efforts by key Members of Congress the House approved an additional $54.5 million in the foreign aid authorization for Taiwan to purchase additional jet aircraft. Although the amount was stricken from the authorization measure, it was nevertheless included in the foreign aid appropriations bill (HR 15149). Numerous Members objected to the appropriations without authorization and specifically to additional unrequested military assistance. Liberal Senators Dec. 20 won a last-ditch move to block the appropriation when the Senate backed a motion by Mike Mansfield (D Mont.) to table the conference report on HR 15149 by a 39-29 vote: R 8-19; D 31-10 (ND 23-4; SD 8-6). The chamber later voted to send the conferees back to negotiate with the House with instructions that the amount appropriated not exceed the authorization, a move which delayed final acceptance of the appropriations until 1970.

SENATE RATIFIES NUCLEAR NONPROLIFERATION TREATY; VOTES ABM DEPLOYMENT; TURNS DOWN HAYNSWORTH

1. Exec. H, 90th Congress, 2nd Session. Nuclear Nonproliferation Treaty. Approval of the resolution consenting to the ratification of the treaty to ban the spread of nuclear weapons. Approved 83-15: R 34-8; D 49-7 (ND 38-0; SD 11-7), March 13, 1969. A "yea" was a vote supporting the President's position.

2. S Res 85. National Commitments Resolution. Passage of the resolution defining a national commitment as the use of armed forces on foreign territory or a promise to assist a foreign country by armed force or financial resources, and affirming the role of the Congress with respect to making national commitments. Passed 70-16: R 27-13; D 43-3 (ND 28-3; SD 15-0), June 25, 1969. A "nay" was a vote supporting the President's position.

3. HR 11612. Agriculture Appropriations. Adoption of the Senate Appropriations Committee amendment eliminating the House-passed $20,000 ceiling on subsidy payments to individual farmers. Adopted 53-34: R 25-13; D 28-21 (ND 13-17; SD 15-4), July 7, 1969. The President did not take a position on the amendment.

4. HR 9951. Unemployment Tax Collection. Adoption of Long (D La.) amendment to extend the surtax at 10 percent through Dec. 31. Adopted 51-48: R 6-37; D 45-11 (ND 27-10; SD 18-1), July 31, 1969. A "yea" was a vote supporting the President's position.

5. S 2546. Defense Procurement Authorization. Second Smith (R Maine) amendment to prevent funds from being used on the Safeguard antiballistic missile (ABM) system while allowing development of other ABM or weapons systems. Rejected 50-50: R 14-29; D 36-21 (ND 31-7; SD 5-14), Aug. 6, 1969. Vice President Agnew also voted "nay." A "nay" was a vote supporting the President's position.

6. Haynsworth Nomination. Rejection of President Nixon's nomination of Clement F. Haynsworth Jr. as an Associate Justice of the Supreme Court. Rejected 45-55; R 26-17; D 19-38 (ND 3-35; SD 16-3), Nov. 21, 1969. A "yea" was a vote supporting the President's position.

	1	2	3	4	5	6
ALABAMA						
Allen	N	Y	Y	N	N	Y
Sparkman	Y	‡	Y	Y	N	Y
ALASKA						
Gravel	Y	Y	√	Y	Y	Y
Stevens	Y	Y	Y	N	N	Y
ARIZONA						
Fannin	N	N	Y	N	N	Y
Goldwater	N	N	Y	N	N	Y
ARKANSAS						
Fulbright	Y	Y	Y	Y	Y	Y
McClellan	?	Y	Y	Y	N	Y
CALIFORNIA						
Cranston	Y	Y	Y	Y	Y	N
Murphy	N	-	Y	N	N	Y
COLORADO						
Allott	Y	N	Y	N	N	Y
Dominick	N	N	Y	N	N	Y
CONNECTICUT						
Dodd	Y	N	Y	Y	N	N
Ribicoff	Y	‡	X	Y	Y	N
DELAWARE						
Boggs	Y	Y	N	N	N	Y
Williams	Y	Y	N	N	N	N
FLORIDA						
Holland	Y	Y	Y	N	Y	Y
Gurney	N	N	√	N	N	Y
GEORGIA						
Russell	N	‡	Y	Y	N	Y
Talmadge	Y	Y	Y	Y	N	Y
HAWAII						
Inouye	Y	Y	Y	Y	Y	N
Fong	Y	?	Y	N	N	Y
IDAHO						
Church	Y	Y	N	Y	Y	N
Jordan	Y	Y	Y	N	N	Y
ILLINOIS						
Percy	Y	Y	N	N	Y	N
Smith	*	*	*	*	*	Y
INDIANA						
Bayh	Y	?	N	Y	Y	N
Hartke	Y	Y	N	Y	N	Y
IOWA						
Hughes	Y	‡	N	Y	Y	N
Miller	Y	Y	Y	N	N	N
KANSAS						
Dole	Y	Y	Y	N	N	Y
Pearson	Y	Y	Y	N	Y	Y
KENTUCKY						
Cook	Y	Y	Y	N	Y	Y
Cooper	‡	Y	Y	N	Y	N
LOUISIANA						
Ellender	Y	Y	Y	Y	Y	Y
Long	N	Y	Y	Y	N	Y
MAINE						
Muskie	Y	Y	Y	Y	Y	N
Smith	Y	N	Y	N	Y	N
MARYLAND						
Tydings	Y	?	X	Y	Y	N
Mathias	Y	Y	N	Y	N	N
MASSACHUSETTS						
Kennedy	Y	Y	N	Y	N	N
Brooke	Y	Y	-	N	Y	N
MICHIGAN						
Hart	Y	‡	N	N	Y	N
Griffin	Y	N	-	N	N	N
MINNESOTA						
McCarthy	Y	Y	Y	Y	Y	N
Mondale	Y	Y	N	Y	Y	N
MISSISSIPPI						
Eastland	N	Y	Y	Y	N	Y
Stennis	N	Y	Y	Y	N	Y
MISSOURI						
Eagleton	Y	Y	Y	Y	Y	N
Symington	Y	Y	Y	Y	Y	N
MONTANA						
Mansfield	Y	Y	N	Y	N	N
Metcalf	Y	Y	√	Y	Y	N
NEBRASKA						
Curtis	N	Y	Y	N	N	Y
Hruska	Y	Y	Y	N	N	Y
NEVADA						
Bible	Y	Y	Y	N	N	N
Cannon	Y	Y	‡	N	Y	N
NEW HAMPSHIRE						
McIntyre	Y	Y	N	Y	Y	N
Cotton	Y	Y	?	N	N	Y
NEW JERSEY						
Williams	Y	?	N	N	Y	N
Case	Y	Y	N	Y	Y	N
NEW MEXICO						
Anderson	Y	Y	?	Y	N	N
Montoya	Y	Y	Y	N	Y	N
NEW YORK						
Goodell	Y	?	N	Y	Y	N
Javits	Y	Y	N	Y	Y	N
NORTH CAROLINA						
Ervin	N	Y	Y	Y	N	Y
Jordan	Y	Y	Y	N	Y	N
NORTH DAKOTA						
Burdick	Y	Y	Y	N	Y	N
Young	Y	Y	Y	N	N	Y
OHIO						
Young	Y	Y	N	N	Y	N
Saxbe	Y	Y	N	Y	N	N
OKLAHOMA						
Harris	Y	Y	N	Y	N	N
Bellmon	Y	N	N	N	N	Y
OREGON						
Hatfield	Y	Y	N	N	Y	N
Packwood	Y	Y	N	N	N	N
PENNSYLVANIA						
Schweiker	Y	Y	N	N	Y	N
Scott	Y	Y	N	N	N	N
RHODE ISLAND						
Pastore	Y	Y	N	N	N	N
Pell	Y	Y	N	Y	Y	N
SOUTH CAROLINA						
Hollings	N	?	Y	Y	N	Y
Thurmond	N	N	Y	N	N	Y
SOUTH DAKOTA						
McGovern	Y	Y	N	?	Y	N
Mundt	Y	Y	Y	N	N	Y
TENNESSEE						
Gore	Y	‡	N	Y	Y	N
Baker	Y	Y	Y	Y	N	Y
TEXAS						
Yarborough	Y	Y	Y	Y	Y	N
Tower	N	N	Y	N	N	Y
UTAH						
Moss	Y	?	N	Y	Y	N
Bennett	Y	N	Y	N	N	Y
VERMONT						
Aiken	Y	Y	Y	Y	Y	Y
Prouty	Y	Y	X	N	N	Y
VIRGINIA						
Byrd, Jr.	Y	Y	N	Y	N	Y
Spong	Y	Y	N	Y	N	Y
WASHINGTON						
Jackson	Y	N	N	Y	N	N
Magnuson	Y	Y	√	Y	Y	N
WEST VIRGINIA						
Byrd	Y	Y	Y	N	Y	Y
Randolph	Y	Y	Y	Y	Y	Y
WISCONSIN						
Nelson	Y	Y	X	N	Y	N
Proxmire	Y	Y	N	N	Y	N
WYOMING						
McGee	Y	N	Y	Y	N	N
Hansen	Y	N	Y	N	N	Y

- KEY -

Y   Record vote for (yea).
√   Paired for.
‡   Announced for or CQ poll for.
N   Record vote against (nay).
X   Paired against.
-   Announced against or CQ poll against.
?   Absent, general pair, "present" or did not announce or answer poll.

Democrats in this type; *Republicans in italics*   *Member had not been sworn in when vote was taken.

SENATE REDUCES OIL-GAS DEPLETION ALLOWANCE; VOTES TAX REFORM; OPPOSES PLANES FOR NATIONALIST CHINA

7. HR 13270. Tax Reform. Ellender (D La.) amendment restoring to 27.5 percent the depletion allowance on oil and gas. Rejected 30-62: R 17-22; D 13-40 (ND 5-30; SD 8-10), Dec. 1, 1969. A "yea" vote was a vote supporting the President's position.

8. HR 13270. Tax Reform. Gore (D Tenn.) amendment to increase the personal income tax exemption to $800. Adopted 58-37: R 10-32; D 48-5 (ND 35-0; SD 13-5), Dec. 3, 1969. A "nay" was a vote supporting the President's position.

9. HR 13270. Tax Reform. Passage of the Tax Reform Act of 1969. Passed 69-22; R 18-20; D 51-2 (ND 35-0; SD 16-2), Dec. 11, 1969. A "nay" was a vote supporting the President's position.

10. HR 15090. Defense Appropriations. Church (D Idaho) substitute for pending Cooper (R Ky.)-Mansfield (D Mont.) amendment stating that in line with the expressed intention of the President, no funds in the bill could be used to finance the introduction of U.S. ground combat troops into Laos and Thailand. Adopted 73-17: R 38-2; D 35-15 (ND 25-7; SD 10-8) Dec. 15, 1969. The President did not take a position on the substitute.

11. HR 13111. Labor-HEW Appropriations. Scott (R Pa.) amendment adding the words, "except as required by the Constitution," at the beginning of the section barring use of funds to force a school district to take action involving busing of students, abolition of any school, or assignment of any student to any particular school against the wishes of his parents. Adopted 52-37: R 22-19; D 30-18 (ND 28-3; SD 2-15), Dec. 17, 1969. A "yea" was a vote supporting the President's position.

12. HR 15149. Foreign Aid Appropriations. Mansfield (D Mont.) motion to table the conference report on foreign aid appropriations for fiscal 1970. Mansfield and other Senators objected to the fact that the appropriations bill contained an amount higher than authorized. The most objectionable item from the Mansfield group's standpoint was $54.5 million for Nationalist China to purchase fighter aircraft. The item had been included by the House although the Administration had not requested it. Adopted 39-29: R 8-19; D 31-10 (ND 23-4; SD 8-6), Dec. 20, 1969. The President did not take a position on the bill.

State / Senator	7	8	9	10	11	12
ALABAMA						
Allen	N	Y	Y	N	N	Y
Sparkman	N	Y	Y	N	N	Y
ALASKA						
Gravel	√	Y	Y	Y	Y	?
Stevens	Y	Y	√	Y	Y	?
ARIZONA						
Fannin	Y	N	N	Y	N	N
Goldwater	?	N	X	Y	N	?
ARKANSAS						
Fulbright	Y	†	Y	N	N	Y
McClellan	Y	Y	Y	Y	N	N
CALIFORNIA						
Cranston	N	Y	Y	Y	Y	Y
Murphy	Y	N	N	Y	N	?
COLORADO						
Allott	Y	N	N	Y	N	N
Dominick	Y	N	Y	Y	Y	N
CONNECTICUT						
Dodd	N	Y	Y	Y	Y	N
Ribicoff	N	Y	Y	Y	Y	Y
DELAWARE						
Boggs	N	N	Y	Y	Y	?
Williams	N	N	N	Y	N	?
FLORIDA						
Holland	N	N	N	Y	N	N
Gurney	Y	N	N	Y	N	N
GEORGIA						
Russell	N	N	N	?	X	?
Talmadge	N	Y	Y	Y	N	?
HAWAII						
Inouye	N	Y	Y	Y	√	?
Fong	N	Y	Y	Y	Y	N
IDAHO						
Church	N	Y	Y	Y	Y	Y
Jordan	N	N	N	Y	N	?
ILLINOIS						
Percy	-	N	N	Y	Y	-
Smith	X	N	Y	Y	N	X
INDIANA						
Bayh	N	†	Y	Y	Y	Y
Hartke	N	Y	Y	Y	Y	Y
IOWA						
Hughes	N	Y	Y	Y	Y	Y
Miller	N	N	Y	†	N	N
KANSAS						
Dole	Y	N	N	Y	N	N
Pearson	Y	N	N	Y	Y	?
KENTUCKY						
Cook	N	Y	Y	Y	Y	Y
Cooper	N	N	Y	?	?	?
LOUISIANA						
Ellender	Y	N	X	N	N	N
Long	Y	N	Y	N	N	?
MAINE						
Muskie	N	Y	Y	N	Y	Y
Smith	N	N	N	Y	N	N
MARYLAND						
Tydings	N	Y	†	?	Y	?
Mathias	N	N	√	N	Y	Y
MASSACHUSETTS						
Kennedy	N	Y	Y	N	†	Y
Brooke	N	N	N	Y	Y	√
MICHIGAN						
Hart	N	Y	Y	N	Y	Y
Griffin	N	N	N	Y	Y	N
MINNESOTA						
McCarthy	N	Y	Y	N	Y	?
Mondale	N	Y	Y	Y	Y	Y
MISSISSIPPI						
Eastland	Y	Y	Y	N	N	?
Stennis	Y	Y	Y	N	N	N
MISSOURI						
Eagleton	N	Y	Y	Y	Y	Y
Symington	X	†	√	?	†	?
MONTANA						
Mansfield	Y	Y	Y	N	Y	Y
Metcalf	N	Y	Y	Y	Y	?
NEBRASKA						
Curtis	Y	N	N	Y	N	N
Hruska	Y	N	N	Y	N	N
NEVADA						
Bible	Y	Y	Y	Y	N	Y
Cannon	N	Y	Y	Y	N	-
NEW HAMPSHIRE						
McIntyre	N	Y	Y	Y	Y	Y
Cotton	Y	N	N	Y	N	N
NEW JERSEY						
Williams	N	Y	Y	†	Y	Y
Case	N	N	Y	Y	Y	?
NEW MEXICO						
Anderson	√	?	†	?	?	?
Montoya	Y	Y	Y	Y	Y	N
NEW YORK						
Goodell	N	N	N	Y	Y	Y
Javits	N	N	Y	Y	Y	N
NORTH CAROLINA						
Ervin	N	Y	Y	N	N	N
Jordan	N	Y	Y	N	N	N
NORTH DAKOTA						
Burdick	Y	Y	Y	Y	Y	Y
Young	Y	Y	Y	Y	N	N
OHIO						
Young	N	Y	Y	N	Y	?
Saxbe	N	N	X	Y	Y	Y
OKLAHOMA						
Harris	Y	Y	Y	Y	N	Y
Bellmon	Y	Y	Y	Y	Y	N
OREGON						
Hatfield	N	Y	Y	Y	Y	Y
Packwood	N	N	Y	Y	Y	N
PENNSYLVANIA						
Schweiker	N	Y	Y	Y	Y	Y
Scott	N	N	Y	Y	Y	N
RHODE ISLAND						
Pastore	N	Y	Y	Y	Y	-
Pell	N	Y	Y	Y	Y	Y
SOUTH CAROLINA						
Hollings	?	Y	Y	Y	X	?
Thurmond	Y	N	N	Y	N	N
SOUTH DAKOTA						
McGovern	N	Y	Y	Y	Y	Y
Mundt	-	?	?	?	?	?
TENNESSEE						
Gore	N	Y	Y	N	N	Y
Baker	N	Y	Y	Y	N	?
TEXAS						
Yarborough	Y	Y	Y	Y	Y	Y
Tower	Y	N	N	Y	N	-
UTAH						
Moss	N	Y	Y	Y	Y	Y
Bennett	Y	N	N	Y	N	?
VERMONT						
Aiken	N	Y	Y	N	Y	Y
Prouty	N	Y	Y	Y	Y	Y
VIRGINIA						
Byrd, Jr.	N	N	Y	Y	N	?
Spong	N	Y	Y	Y	N	Y
WASHINGTON						
Jackson	N	Y	Y	†	√	N
Magnuson	N	Y	Y	Y	X	Y
WEST VIRGINIA						
Byrd	N	Y	Y	Y	Y	Y
Randolph	N	Y	Y	†	√	Y
WISCONSIN						
Nelson	N	Y	Y	Y	Y	Y
Proxmire	N	Y	Y	Y	Y	Y
WYOMING						
McGee	Y	Y	Y	N	Y	N
Hansen	Y	N	N	Y	N	N

- KEY -

Y Record vote for (yea).
√ Paired for.
† Announced for or CQ poll for.
N Record vote against (nay).
X Paired against.
- Announced against or CQ poll against.
? Absent, general pair, "present" or did not announce or answer poll.

Democrats in this type; *Republicans in italics*

HOUSE SEATS ADAM CLAYTON POWELL; GREATLY BOOSTS EDUCATION FUNDS; VOTES TO END ELECTORAL COLLEGE

1. H Res. 2. Powell Seating. Celler (D N.Y.) motion to move the previous question on the resolution to seat Adam C. Powell (D N.Y.), to fine him $25,000 and to strip him of seniority. Adopted 249-171: R 96-89; D 153-82 (ND 136-12; SD 17-70), Jan. 3, 1969. The President did not take a position on the motion.

2. HR 12290. Surtax. Passage of the bill extending the surtax at 10 percent through Dec. 31 and at 5 percent through June 30, 1970, repealing the 7-percent investment credit, postponing reductions in certain excise taxes and providing a low-income allowance to ensure that poor families paid no income taxes. Passed 210-205: R 154-26; D 56-179 (ND 22-129; SD 34-50), June 30, 1969. A "yea" was a vote supporting the President's position.

3. HR 13111. Labor-HEW Appropriations. Joelson (D N.J.) amendment to add $894,547,000 to the appropriations for elementary and secondary education, aid to federally impacted areas, higher education and vocational education. Adopted 294-119: R 99-81; D 195-38 (ND 147-2; SD 48-36), July 31, 1969. A "nay" was a vote supporting the President's position.

4. HR 13270. Tax Reform Act of 1969. Passage of the bill reducing individual income taxes by an average of 5 percent, extending the income surtax at 5 percent through June 30, 1970, repealing the 7-percent investment tax credit, reducing mineral and oil depletion allowances and making other changes in the Internal Revenue Code of 1954. Passed 395-30: R 176-10; D 219-20 (ND 150-1; SD 69-19), Aug. 7, 1969. The President did not take a position on the bill.

5. H J Res 681. Electoral Reform. Passage of the bill to amend the Constitution by abolishing the electoral college and providing for the direct popular election of the President and Vice President. Passed 338-70: R 154-26; D 184-44 (ND 142-3; SD 42-41), Sept. 18, 1969. An affirmative vote of two-thirds of those present and voting was required for passage of the constitutional amendment. The President did not take a position on the bill.

6. HR 14001. Selective Service Reform. Passage of the bill amending the Selective Service Act of 1967 by removing a provision prohibiting the President from instituting a random selection (lottery) system for induction into the armed forces. Passed 383-12: R 175-1; D 208-11 (ND 126-11; SD 82-0), Oct. 30, 1969. A "yea" was a vote supporting the President's position.

- KEY -

Y Record vote for (yea).
√ Paired for.
† Announced for or CQ poll for.
N Record vote against (nay).
X Paired against.
- Announced against or CQ poll against.
? Absent, general pair, "present" or did not announce or answer poll.

	1	2	3	4	5	6
ALABAMA						
3 Andrews	N	N	N	Y	N	Y
7 Bevill	N	N	Y	Y	N	Y
5 Flowers	N	N	Y	Y	N	Y
8 Jones	N	Y	Y	Y	N	Y
4 Nichols	N	N	Y	Y	N	Y
6 Buchanan	N	Y	N	Y	Y	Y
2 Dickinson	N	Y	N	Y	Y	Y
1 Edwards	N	Y	N	Y	Y	Y
ALASKA						
AL Pollock	N	Y	Y	Y	X	?
ARIZONA						
2 Udall	Y	Y	Y	Y	Y	Y
1 Rhodes	Y	Y	N	Y	Y	Y
3 Steiger	N	Y	N	Y	Y	Y
ARKANSAS						
1 Alexander	N	Y	Y	Y	Y	Y
2 Mills	Y	Y	Y	Y	Y	?
4 Pryor	Y	Y	Y	Y	Y	Y
3 Hammerschmidt	N	Y	Y	Y	Y	Y
CALIFORNIA						
5 Burton	Y	N	Y	Y	Y	X
7 Cohelan	Y	N	Y	Y	Y	Y
9 Edwards	Y	N	?	?	Y	N
34 Hanna	*	N	Y	Y	Y	Y
2 Johnson	Y	N	Y	Y	Y	Y
4 Leggett	Y	N	Y	Y	Y	Y
15 McFall	Y	N	Y	Y	Y	Y
8 Miller	Y	N	Y	Y	Y	Y
3 Moss	Y	N	Y	Y	Y	Y
16 Sisk	Y	N	Y	Y	√	Y
38 Tunney	Y	N	Y	Y	Y	Y
37 Van Deerlin	Y	N	Y	Y	Y	Y
14 Waldie	?	N	Y	Y	Y	Y
1 Clausen	N	Y	Y	Y	Y	Y
10 Gubser	Y	Y	Y	Y	Y	Y
11 McCloskey	Y	Y	Y	Y	Y	Y
6 Mailliard	Y	Y	Y	Y	Y	Y
18 Mathias	N	Y	Y	Y	Y	Y
33 Pettis	Y	Y	Y	Y	Y	Y
12 Talcott	Y	Y	Y	Y	Y	Y
13 Teague	Y	Y	Y	Y	?	Y
35 Utt	N	Y	N	N	?	Y
36 Wilson	Y	Y	N	N	Y	Y
Los Angeles Co.						
17 Anderson	Y	N	Y	Y	Y	Y
29 Brown	Y	N	Y	Y	Y	X
22 Corman	Y	N	Y	Y	Y	Y
21 Hawkins	Y	N	Y	Y	Y	N
19 Holifield	Y	N	Y	Y	Y	Y
26 Rees	Y	N	Y	Y	Y	N
30 Roybal	Y	N	Y	Y	√	Y
31 Wilson	Y	N	Y	Y	Y	Y
28 Bell	Y	Y	Y	Y	Y	?
23 Clawson	N	X	N	Y	Y	Y
27 Goldwater	*	Y	N	Y	N	Y
32 Hosmer	N	Y	Y	Y	Y	Y
24 Lipscomb	N	√	?	?	?	?
20 Smith	N	N	Y	N	N	Y
25 Wiggins	Y	Y	N	Y	Y	Y
COLORADO						
4 Aspinall	N	Y	Y	Y	Y	Y
3 Evans	Y	N	Y	Y	Y	Y
1 Rogers	Y	N	Y	Y	Y	Y
2 Brotzman	Y	Y	Y	Y	Y	Y
CONNECTICUT						
1 Daddario	Y	Y	Y	?	Y	?
3 Giaimo	Y	N	Y	Y	Y	Y
5 Monagan	Y	Y	Y	Y	Y	?
2 St. Onge	Y	N	Y	Y	Y	Y
6 Meskill	Y	N	Y	Y	Y	Y
4 Weicker	Y	N	Y	Y	Y	Y
DELAWARE						
AL Roth	Y	Y	N	Y	Y	Y
FLORIDA						
3 Bennett	N	N	N	Y	Y	Y
4 Chappell	N	N	X	Y	N	Y
12 Fascell	Y	Y	Y	Y	Y	Y
2 Fuqua	N	N	?	Y	N	Y
6 Gibbons	N	N	Y	Y	Y	Y
7 Haley	N	N	N	Y	N	Y
11 Pepper	Y	Y	†	Y	Y	Y
9 Rogers	N	Y	N	Y	Y	Y
1 Sikes	N	Y	N	Y	N	Y
10 Burke	N	N	N	Y	Y	Y
8 Cramer	N	Y	N	Y	Y	Y
5 Frey	N	Y	N	Y	N	Y
GEORGIA						
3 Brinkley	N	N	Y	Y	N	Y
7 Davis	N	N	Y	Y	Y	Y
6 Flynt	N	N	N	Y	N	Y
1 Hagan	N	N	N	Y	N	Y
9 Landrum	N	N	Y	Y	Y	Y
2 O'Neal	N	N	N	Y	N	Y
10 Stephens	N	?	Y	Y	Y	Y
8 Stuckey	N	N	Y	N	N	Y
4 Blackburn	N	Y	N	Y	N	Y
5 Thompson	N	Y	Y	Y	Y	Y
HAWAII						
AL Matsunaga	Y	N	Y	Y	Y	Y
AL Mink	Y	N	Y	Y	Y	Y
IDAHO						
2 Hansen, O.	Y	Y	Y	Y	Y	Y
1 McClure	N	Y	Y	Y	N	Y
ILLINOIS						
21 Gray	Y	N	Y	Y	Y	Y
24 Price	Y	N	Y	Y	Y	Y
23 Shipley	N	N	Y	Y	Y	Y
16 Anderson	Y	Y	N	Y	Y	Y
17 Arends	Y	N	Y	Y	Y	Y
14 Erlenborn	Y	Y	N	Y	Y	Y
20 Findley	Y	N	Y	Y	Y	Y
12 McClory	Y	Y	Y	Y	Y	?
18 Michel	N	N	N	Y	Y	Y
19 Railsback	Y	Y	Y	Y	Y	Y
15 Reid	N	Y	N	Y	Y	Y
22 Springer	Y	Y	Y	Y	Y	Y
Chicago-Cook Co.						
7 Annunzio	Y	Y	√	Y	Y	Y
1 Dawson	Y	Y	Y	Y	√	?
5 Kluczynski	Y	Y	?	Y	Y	Y
2 Mikva	Y	N	Y	Y	Y	?
3 Murphy	Y	Y	Y	Y	Y	Y
11 Pucinski	Y	N	Y	Y	Y	?
6 Vacancy						
8 Rostenkowski	Y	Y	Y	Y	Y	Y
9 Yates	Y	N	Y	Y	Y	Y
10 Collier	Y	Y	N	Y	Y	Y
13 Vacancy						
4 Derwinski	Y	Y	N	Y	N	Y
INDIANA						
3 Brademas	Y	N	Y	Y	Y	?
9 Hamilton	Y	Y	Y	Y	Y	Y
11 Jacobs	Y	N	Y	Y	Y	Y
1 Madden	Y	N	Y	Y	Y	Y
4 Adair	N	N	Y	Y	Y	Y
6 Bray	N	Y	N	Y	Y	Y
10 Dennis	N	Y	N	Y	N	Y
2 Landgrebe	N	Y	N	N	N	Y
7 Myers	Y	Y	N	Y	Y	Y
5 Roudebush	N	N	N	Y	Y	Y
8 Zion	N	N	Y	Y	Y	Y
IOWA						
2 Culver	N	N	Y	Y	Y	Y
5 Smith	N	N	Y	Y	Y	Y
3 Gross	N	N	N	Y	Y	Y
4 Kyl	N	N	N	Y	Y	Y
6 Mayne	N	Y	N	Y	N	Y
7 Scherle	N	N	N	Y	Y	Y
1 Schwengel	Y	Y	Y	Y	Y	Y
KANSAS						
2 Mize	N	Y	Y	Y	N	Y
1 Sebelius	N	Y	N	Y	N	Y
4 Shriver	N	Y	Y	Y	Y	Y
5 Skubitz	N	Y	Y	Y	Y	Y
3 Winn	N	Y	Y	Y	Y	Y
KENTUCKY						
2 Natcher	N	N	Y	Y	Y	Y
7 Perkins	Y	N	Y	Y	Y	Y
1 Stubblefield	N	N	Y	Y	Y	Y

Democrats in **this type**; Republicans in *italics*   *Member had not been sworn in when vote was taken.*

Member	1	2	3	4	5	6
6 Watts	N	Y	Y	Y	Y	
5 Carter	N	Y	Y	Y	Y	
3 Cowger	N	N	N	Y	Y	
4 Snyder	N	N	?	Y	Y	
LOUISIANA						
2 Boggs	Y	Y	Y	Y	Y	
3 Caffery	N	N	N	N	Y	
7 Edwards	N	N	N	N	Y	
1 Hebert	N	√	N	N	N	
8 Long	N	N	N	N	N	
5 Passman	N	N	N	N	N	
6 Rarick	N	N	N	N	N	?
4 Waggonner	N	N	N	N	N	
MAINE						
2 Hathaway	Y	N	Y	Y	Y	
1 Kyros	Y	N	Y	Y	Y	
MARYLAND						
4 Fallon	Y	Y	Y	Y	Y	
7 Friedel	Y	Y	Y	Y	Y	
3 Garmatz	Y	N	Y	Y	Y	
2 Long	Y	N	Y	Y	Y	
6 Beall	Y	Y	Y	Y	Y	
8 Gude	Y	Y	Y	Y	Y	
5 Hogan	N	Y	Y	Y	Y	
1 Morton	Y	Y	N	Y	Y	
MASSACHUSETTS						
2 Boland	Y	N	Y	Y	Y	
11 Burke	Y	Y	Y	Y	Y	
4 Donohue	Y	N	Y	Y	Y	
6 Harrington	*	*	*	*	*	Y
7 Macdonald	Y	N	Y	Y	Y	
9 McCormack						
8 O'Neill	?	?	Y	Y	Y	√
3 Philbin	Y	N	Y	Y	Y	
1 Conte	Y	Y	Y	Y	Y	
10 Heckler	Y	Y	Y	Y	Y	
12 Keith	Y	Y	Y	Y	Y	
5 Morse	Y	Y	Y	Y	Y	
MICHIGAN						
12 O'Hara	?	N	Y	Y	Y	Y
18 Broomfield	Y	Y	√	Y	Y	
3 Brown	Y	Y	Y	Y	Y	
10 Cederberg	Y	Y	?	Y	Y	?
6 Chamberlain	N	X	Y	Y	Y	Y
2 Esch	Y	Y	Y	Y	Y	
5 Ford	Y	Y	N	Y	Y	
8 Harvey	Y	Y	Y	Y	Y	
4 Hutchinson	Y	Y	N	Y	N	Y
19 McDonald	Y	Y	Y	Y	Y	
7 Riegle	Y	N	Y	Y	Y	
11 Ruppe	Y	Y	Y	Y	Y	
9 Vander Jagt	Y	Y	Y	Y	Y	
Detroit-Wayne Co.						
1 Conyers	Y	N	Y	Y	N	
13 Diggs	Y	N	Y	Y	N	N
16 Dingell	Y	N	Y	Y	Y	
15 Ford	Y	N	Y	Y	Y	
17 Griffiths	Y	N	Y	Y	√	Y
14 Nedzi	Y	N	Y	Y	Y	
MINNESOTA						
8 Blatnik	Y	N	Y	Y	Y	
5 Fraser	Y	N	Y	Y	Y	
4 Karth	Y	N	Y	Y	Y	
7 Langen	N	Y	N	Y	Y	
3 MacGregor	Y	Y	Y	Y	Y	
2 Nelsen	N	Y	N	Y	Y	
1 Quie	Y	Y	Y	Y	Y	
6 Zwach	Y	N	Y	Y	Y	
MISSISSIPPI						
1 Abernethy	N	N	N	Y	N	
5 Colmer	N	Y	N	Y	N	?
3 Griffin	N	N	N	N	Y	
4 Montgomery	N	N	N	Y	N	
2 Whitten	N	N	N	Y	N	
MISSOURI						
5 Bolling	Y	Y	Y	Y	?	Y
10 Burlison	N	N	Y	Y	Y	
1 Clay	Y	N	N	Y	N	N
6 Hull	N	N	?	Y	Y	
8 Hungate	Y	N	Y	Y	Y	
8 Ichord	Y	N	Y	Y	Y	
4 Randall	N	N	Y	Y	Y	
3 Sullivan	?	N	Y	Y	√	

Member	1	2	3	4	5	6
2 Symington	Y	N	Y	Y	Y	
7 Hall	N	Y	N	Y	N	Y
MONTANA						
2 Melcher	*	N	Y	N	X	Y
1 Olsen	Y	N	Y	Y	Y	
NEBRASKA						
2 Cunningham	Y	Y	Y	Y	Y	
1 Denney	N	Y	N	Y	Y	
3 Martin	N	Y	N	Y	Y	Y
NEVADA						
AL Baring	N	N	Y	Y	N	?
NEW HAMPSHIRE						
2 Cleveland	Y	Y	N	Y	N	Y
1 Wyman	Y	Y	N	Y	Y	
NEW JERSEY						
14 Daniels	Y	N	Y	Y	Y	√
13 Gallagher	Y	?	?	Y	Y	?
9 Helstoski	Y	N	Y	Y	Y	N
11 Howard	Y	N	Y	Y	Y	
15 Patten	Y	Y	Y	Y	Y	
10 Rodino	Y	N	Y	Y	Y	
8 Vacancy						
4 Thompson	Y	X	Y	Y	Y	
6 Cahill	Y	?	Y	Y	Y	?
12 Dwyer	?	Y	Y	Y	Y	
5 Frelinghuysen	Y	Y	Y	Y	Y	
1 Hunt	N	N	N	Y	Y	
2 Sandman	Y	Y	Y	Y	Y	
7 Widnall	Y	Y	Y	Y	Y	
NEW MEXICO						
2 Foreman	N	N	Y	N	Y	
1 Lujan	N	?	N	Y	Y	?
NEW YORK						
41 Dulski	Y	N	Y	Y	Y	
34 Hanley	Y	N	Y	Y	Y	
5 Lowenstein	Y	N	Y	Y	Y	N
39 McCarthy	Y	N	Y	Y	Y	
25 Ottinger	Y	N	Y	Y	Y	
1 Pike	Y	Y	Y	Y	Y	
35 Stratton	Y	Y	Y	Y	Y	
3 Wolff	Y	N	Y	Y	Y	
29 Button	Y	N	Y	Y	Y	
37 Conable	Y	Y	N	Y	Y	
28 Fish	Y	Y	Y	Y	Y	
2 Grover	?	Y	N	Y	Y	
38 Hastings	Y	Y	?	Y	Y	
36 Horton	N	N	Y	Y	Y	
30 King	N	Y	N	Y	Y	
31 McEwen	Y	Y	N	Y	Y	
27 McKneally	Y	Y	Y	Y	Y	
32 Pirnie	Y	√	Y	Y	?	
26 Reid	‡	Y	Y	Y	Y	
33 Robison	Y	Y	Y	Y	Y	
40 Smith	Y	N	Y	Y	Y	
4 Wydler	Y	N	Y	Y	Y	
New York City						
7 Addabbo	Y	N	Y	Y	Y	
24 Biaggi	Y	N	Y	Y	Y	
23 Bingham	Y	N	Y	Y	Y	
11 Brasco	Y	N	Y	Y	Y	
15 Carey	Y	N	?	Y	X	
10 Celler	Y	N	Y	Y	Y	
12 Chisholm	Y	N	Y	Y	Y	N
9 Delaney	Y	N	Y	Y	Y	
19 Farbstein	Y	N	Y	Y	Y	
22 Gilbert	Y	N	Y	Y	Y	
17 Koch	Y	N	Y	Y	Y	
16 Murphy	Y	Y	Y	Y	Y	
13 Podell	Y	N	Y	Y	Y	
18 Powell	*	?	?	?	?	X
14 Rooney	Y	N	Y	Y	Y	
8 Rosenthal	Y	N	Y	Y	Y	N
20 Ryan	Y	N	Y	Y	Y	N
21 Scheuer	Y	N	Y	Y	Y	
6 Halpern	Y	Y	?	Y	Y	
NORTH CAROLINA						
2 Fountain	?	N	N	Y	Y	
4 Galifianakis	N	N	Y	Y	Y	
3 Henderson	N	N	Y	Y	Y	
1 Jones	N	N	Y	Y	Y	
7 Lennon	N	X	N	N	Y	
6 Preyer	N	Y	Y	Y	Y	

Member	1	2	3	4	5	6
11 Taylor	N	N	Y	Y	Y	
10 Broyhill	N	Y	N	Y	Y	
9 Jonas	N	Y	N	N	Y	
5 Mizell	N	Y	N	Y	Y	
8 Ruth	N	Y	N	Y	Y	
NORTH DAKOTA						
1 Andrews	Y	N	Y	N	Y	
2 Kleppe	N	Y	Y	Y	N	Y
OHIO						
9 Ashley	N	Y	Y	Y	Y	
20 Feighan	Y	N	Y	Y	Y	
18 Hays	Y	N	Y	Y	Y	
19 Kirwan	?	?	?	?	√	?
21 Stokes	Y	N	Y	Y	Y	
22 Vanik	Y	N	Y	Y	Y	
17 Ashbrook	N	N	N	N	Y	
14 Ayres	Y	Y	Y	Y	Y	
8 Betts	N	N	Y	Y	Y	
16 Bow	Y	N	Y	Y	Y	
7 Brown	Y	Y	Y	Y	Y	
2 Clancy	N	N	N	Y	Y	
12 Devine	N	Y	X	√	Y	
6 Harsha	N	Y	N	Y	Y	
5 Latta	N	N	Y	Y	Y	
24 Lukens	*	Y	Y	Y	N	Y
10 McCulloch	N	Y	Y	Y	Y	
23 Minshall	N	Y	N	Y	Y	
13 Mosher	*	Y	Y	Y	Y	
11 Stanton	Y	Y	Y	Y	Y	
1 Taft	*	Y	?	?	Y	Y
3 Whalen	Y	Y	Y	Y	Y	
15 Wylie	N	Y	N	Y	Y	
OKLAHOMA						
3 Albert	Y	Y	Y	Y	Y	
2 Edmondson	Y	N	Y	Y	Y	
5 Jarman	N	N	N	Y	Y	
4 Steed	Y	Y	Y	Y	√	
1 Belcher	N	Y	Y	N	Y	
6 Camp	N	Y	N	Y	Y	
OREGON						
3 Green	Y	N	Y	Y	Y	
2 Ullman	Y	N	Y	Y	Y	
4 Dellenback	Y	Y	Y	Y	Y	
1 Wyatt	Y	Y	Y	Y	?	
PENNSYLVANIA						
25 Clark	Y	N	Y	Y	?	
21 Dent	Y	N	Y	Y	√	
11 Flood	Y	N	Y	Y	Y	
20 Gaydos	Y	Y	Y	Y	Y	
14 Moorhead	Y	Y	Y	Y	Y	
26 Morgan	Y	N	Y	Y	Y	
15 Rooney	Y	Y	Y	Y	Y	
24 Vigorito	Y	N	Y	Y	Y	
6 Yatron	Y	N	Y	Y	Y	
8 Biester	Y	Y	Y	Y	Y	
18 Corbett	Y	Y	Y	Y	Y	
13 Coughlin	Y	Y	Y	Y	Y	
16 Eshleman	Y	Y	Y	Y	Y	
27 Fulton	Y	Y	Y	Y	Y	
19 Goodling	N	?	N	Y	Y	
23 Johnson	Y	Y	Y	Y	Y	
10 McDade	Y	Y	Y	Y	Y	
22 Saylor	Y	N	N	Y	Y	
17 Schneebeli	Y	Y	Y	Y	Y	
9 Watkins	N	Y	N	Y	Y	
12 Whalley	Y	Y	Y	?	?	
7 Williams	N	Y	N	Y	Y	
Philadelphia City						
1 Barrett	Y	N	Y	Y	Y	
3 Byrne	Y	N	Y	Y	?	
4 Eilberg	Y	N	Y	Y	Y	
5 Green	Y	N	Y	Y	Y	
2 Nix	Y	N	Y	Y	Y	
RHODE ISLAND						
1 St. Germain	Y	N	Y	Y	Y	
2 Tiernan	Y	N	Y	Y	Y	
SOUTH CAROLINA						
3 Dorn	N	Y	Y	Y	Y	
5 Gettys	N	N	Y	N	?	
6 McMillan	N	N	N	X	N	
4 Mann	N	Y	Y	N	Y	

Member	1	2	3	4	5	6
1 Rivers	N	Y	N	Y	N	Y
2 Watson	N	Y	N	Y	N	Y
SOUTH DAKOTA						
2 Berry	N	Y	N	Y	Y	
1 Reifel	Y	Y	Y	N	Y	
TENNESSEE						
6 Anderson	N	N	Y	Y	Y	
7 Blanton	N	N	Y	Y	Y	
4 Evins	Y	√	?	Y	N	Y
5 Fulton	N	N	Y	Y	Y	
6 Jones	*	N	Y	X	X	Y
3 Brock	N	Y	N	Y	Y	
2 Duncan	N	Y	N	Y	Y	
9 Kuykendall	N	Y	N	Y	Y	
1 Quillen	N	Y	Y	N	Y	
TEXAS						
9 Brooks	Y	Y	Y	Y	Y	
17 Burleson	N	N	N	N	Y	
5 Cabell	N	Y	N	Y	Y	
22 Casey	N	Y	N	Y	Y	
15 de la Garza	N	Y	?	Y	?	
2 Dowdy	N	N	N	N	N	
8 Eckhardt	N	N	Y	N	Y	
21 Fisher	N	Y	N	Y	N	Y
20 Gonzalez	Y	N	Y	Y	Y	
23 Kazen	Y	N	Y	Y	Y	
19 Mahon	Y	N	Y	Y	Y	
1 Patman	N	N	Y	Y	Y	
10 Pickle	Y	Y	Y	Y	Y	
11 Poage	N	Y	N	?	Y	
13 Purcell	N	Y	N	?	Y	
4 Roberts	N	N	N	Y	Y	
6 Teague	N	N	Y	Y	Y	
16 White	N	Y	Y	N	Y	
12 Wright	Y	N	Y	Y	Y	
14 Young	N	Y	Y	Y	Y	
7 Bush	N	Y	N	Y	Y	
3 Collins	N	Y	N	N	Y	
10 Price	N	N	?	√	?	
UTAH						
1 Burton	N	Y	Y	N	?	
2 Lloyd	N	Y	N	Y	Y	
VERMONT						
AL Stafford	Y	Y	Y	Y	Y	
VIRGINIA						
4 Abbitt	N	N	N	Y	N	Y
5 Daniel	N	N	N	Y	N	Y
1 Downing	N	Y	N	Y	Y	
7 Marsh	N	Y	Y	Y	Y	
3 Satterfield	N	Y	N	Y	Y	
10 Broyhill	N	Y	Y	Y	Y	
6 Poff	Y	Y	Y	Y	Y	
8 Scott	N	N	N	Y	Y	
9 Wampler	N	Y	Y	Y	Y	
2 Whitehurst	N	Y	Y	Y	Y	‡
WASHINGTON						
7 Adams	Y	N	Y	Y	Y	
5 Foley	Y	N	Y	Y	Y	
3 Hansen	Y	N	Y	Y	Y	
6 Hicks	Y	N	Y	Y	Y	
2 Meeds	Y	N	Y	Y	Y	
4 May	Y	Y	N	Y	Y	
1 Pelly	Y	Y	Y	Y	Y	
WEST VIRGINIA						
4 Hechler	Y	N	Y	Y	Y	
5 Kee	Y	N	Y	Y	Y	
1 Mollohan	Y	N	Y	Y	Y	
3 Slack	N	N	Y	Y	Y	
2 Staggers	Y	N	Y	Y	Y	
WISCONSIN						
2 Kastenmeier	Y	N	Y	Y	Y	
7 Obey	*	N	Y	Y	Y	
5 Reuss	Y	N	Y	Y	Y	
4 Zablocki	Y	N	Y	Y	Y	
8 Byrnes	Y	Y	Y	Y	Y	
9 Davis	Y	Y	N	Y	Y	
10 O'Konski	N	?	Y	Y	?	N
1 Schadeberg	Y	N	N	Y	Y	
6 Steiger	Y	Y	Y	Y	Y	
3 Thomson	N	Y	Y	Y	Y	
WYOMING						
AL Wold	Y	Y	Y	Y	Y	

HOUSE SUPPORTS PRESIDENT ON VIETNAM COURSE; ALTERS
VOTING RIGHTS ACT; REJECTS STATE POVERTY CONTROL

7. H Res 613. Vietnam Resolution. Passage of the resolution affirming the support of the House of Representatives for the President in his efforts to negotiate a "just peace" in Vietnam. Adopted 334-55: R 172-1; D 162-54 (ND 89-54; SD 73-0), Dec. 2, 1969. A "yea" was a vote supporting the President's position.

8. HR 15149. Foreign Aid. Passage of the foreign aid appropriations bill, fiscal 1970, appropriating $1,649,380,000 for economic and military assistance; $275 million for the Foreign Military Credit Sales Program; and $683,640,000 for other related foreign aid programs. Passed 200-195: R 79-91; D 121-104 (ND 92-52; SD 29-52), Dec. 9, 1969. The President did not take a position on the bill.

9. HR 4249. Voting Rights. Ford (R Mich.) amendment substituting the Administration bill to extend nationwide the provisions of the Voting Rights Act of 1965 in place of the Committee bill extending the law in its existing form. Adopted 208-204: R 129-49; D 79-155 (ND 10-141; SD 69-14), Dec. 11, 1969. A "yea" was a vote supporting the President's position.

10. HR 12321. OEO Authorization, fiscal 1970. Ayres (R Ohio) motion to recommit the bill to committee with instructions to report a substitute bill turning control of the antipoverty program over to the states. Rejected 163-231: R 103-63; D 60-168 (ND 7-139; SD 53-29), Dec. 12, 1969. A "nay" was a vote supporting the President's position.

11. S 2917. Coal Mine Safety. Adoption of the conference report on the bill to improve the health and safety conditions of persons working in the coal mining industry, including provisions to compensate victims of black lung disease. Adopted 334-12: R 144-12; D 190-0 (ND 128-0; SD 62-0), Dec. 17, 1969. A "nay" was a vote supporting the President's position.

12. HR 15209. Supplemental Appropriations, fiscal 1970. Mahon (D Texas) motion to recede from disagreement to Senate amendment which had the effect of killing the Philadelphia Plan to eliminate job discrimination. Rejected 156-208: R 41-124; D 115-84 (ND 54-78; SD 61-6), Dec. 22, 1969. A "nay" was a vote supporting the President's position.

	7	8	9	10	11	12
ALABAMA						
3 Andrews	Y	N	Y	Y	?	√
7 Bevill	Y	N	Y	Y	Y	√
5 Flowers	Y	X	Y	Y	Y	Y
8 Jones	Y	Y	Y	N	Y	N
4 Nichols	Y	X	Y	Y	Y	√
6 Buchanan	Y	Y	Y	Y	?	N
2 Dickinson	?	N	Y	Y	Y	N
1 Edwards	Y	N	Y	Y	Y	N
ALASKA						
AL Pollock	?	N	Y	N	Y	X
ARIZONA						
2 Udall	Y	Y	N	N	Y	N
1 Rhodes	Y	Y	Y	Y	Y	N
3 Steiger	Y	N	Y	Y	Y	Y
ARKANSAS						
1 Alexander	Y	Y	Y	N	Y	Y
2 Mills	?	N	Y	N	?	?
4 Pryor	Y	Y	Y	Y	Y	Y
3 Hammerschmidt	Y	N	Y	Y	Y	X
CALIFORNIA						
5 Burton	N	N	N	N	Y	N
7 Cohelan	N	N	N	N	Y	N
9 Edwards	N	N	N	N	?	?
34 Hanna	?	Y	N	N	?	N
2 Johnson	Y	Y	N	N	Y	Y
4 Leggett	N	N	N	N	Y	N
15 McFall	Y	Y	N	N	Y	N
8 Miller	Y	Y	N	N	Y	Y
3 Moss	N	N	N	N	?	?
16 Sisk	Y	Y	N	N	?	N
38 Tunney	N	?	N	N	?	N
37 Van Deerlin	Y	N	X	N	?	N
14 Waldie	N	N	N	N	Y	N
1 Clausen	Y	N	Y	Y	?	N
10 Gubser	Y	Y	Y	Y	Y	N
11 McCloskey	Y	Y	N	N	?	N
6 Mailliard	Y	?	?	N	Y	N
18 Mathias	?	Y	Y	Y	Y	N
33 Pettis	Y	N	Y	Y	N	N
12 Talcott	Y	Y	Y	Y	Y	N
13 Teague	Y	Y	Y	Y	Y	N
35 Utt	?	X	√	√	?	N
36 Wilson	Y	Y	Y	√	?	N
Los Angeles Co.						
17 Anderson	Y	Y	N	N	Y	N
29 Brown	X	N	N	X	Y	Y
22 Corman	Y	Y	N	N	?	N
21 Hawkins	N	?	N	N	Y	N
19 Holifield	?	Y	N	X	Y	Y
26 Rees	N	N	N	N	?	?
30 Roybal	N	Y	N	N	Y	N
31 Wilson	Y	Y	N	N	Y	N
28 Bell	Y	Y	N	?	Y	N
23 Clawson	Y	N	Y	Y	Y	Y
27 Goldwater	Y	N	Y	Y	Y	Y
32 Hosmer	?	√	√	√	?	N
24 Lipscomb	?	X	√	Y	?	?
20 Smith	Y	N	Y	Y	?	N
25 Wiggins	Y	Y	Y	N	Y	N
COLORADO						
4 Aspinall	Y	Y	Y	N	Y	N
3 Evans	Y	N	N	N	Y	N
1 Rogers	Y	Y	N	N	?	N
2 Brotzman	Y	Y	Y	Y	Y	N
CONNECTICUT						
1 Daddario	N	Y	N	N	Y	N
3 Giaimo	?	Y	N	Y	Y	Y
5 Monagan	Y	Y	N	N	Y	N
2 St. Onge	N	Y	N	Y	Y	Y
6 Meskill	?	N	Y	Y	N	N
4 Weicker	Y	Y	Y	N	?	N
DELAWARE						
AL Roth	Y	Y	N	Y	Y	N
FLORIDA						
3 Bennett	Y	N	N	Y	Y	Y
4 Chappell	Y	N	Y	Y	?	Y
12 Fascell	Y	√	X	X	?	?
2 Fuqua	Y	N	Y	Y	Y	Y
6 Gibbons	Y	Y	N	N	Y	N
7 Haley	Y	N	Y	Y	Y	Y
11 Pepper	?	Y	N	N	Y	N
9 Rogers	Y	N	Y	Y	Y	Y
1 Sikes	Y	Y	Y	Y	?	Y
10 Burke	Y	N	Y	Y	Y	N
8 Cramer	Y	X	Y	Y	Y	Y
5 Frey	Y	N	Y	Y	Y	Y
GEORGIA						
3 Brinkley	Y	N	Y	Y	Y	Y
7 Davis	Y	N	Y	Y	Y	Y
6 Flynt	Y	N	Y	Y	?	Y
1 Hagan	Y	N	Y	Y	Y	Y
9 Landrum	Y	?	Y	Y	?	?
2 O'Neal	?	N	Y	Y	Y	√
10 Stephens	Y	N	Y	Y	Y	?
8 Stuckey	?	N	Y	Y	Y	Y
4 Blackburn	Y	N	Y	Y	Y	Y
5 Thompson	Y	N	Y	Y	Y	Y
HAWAII						
AL Matsunaga	Y	Y	N	X	Y	N
AL Mink	N	N	N	Y	Y	N
IDAHO						
2 Hansen, O.	Y	Y	Y	N	Y	N
1 McClure	Y	N	Y	Y	Y	N
ILLINOIS						
21 Gray	Y	Y	N	N	Y	Y
24 Price	Y	Y	N	N	Y	N
23 Shipley	Y	N	N	N	Y	Y
16 Anderson	Y	Y	N	N	Y	N
17 Arends	Y	Y	Y	Y	Y	Y
14 Erlenborn	Y	Y	Y	Y	N	N
20 Findley	Y	Y	N	N	Y	?
12 McClory	Y	Y	N	Y	Y	?
18 Michel	Y	N	Y	Y	N	N
19 Railsback	?	Y	N	N	Y	N
15 Reid	Y	N	Y	Y	Y	N
22 Springer	Y	Y	Y	Y	Y	N
Chicago-Cook Co.						
7 Annunzio	Y	Y	N	N	Y	N
1 Dawson	?	?	?	X	?	?
5 Kluczynski	Y	Y	N	X	Y	Y
2 Mikva	N	N	N	N	Y	N
3 Murphy	Y	Y	N	N	Y	Y
11 Pucinski	Y	√	N	N	Y	N
6 Vacancy						
8 Rostenkowski	Y	Y	N	X	Y	?
9 Yates	N	N	N	N	?	N
10 Collier	Y	N	Y	Y	Y	?
13 Crane	Y	N	Y	Y	Y	N
4 Derwinski	Y	N	Y	Y	Y	Y

	7	8	9	10	11	12
- KEY -						

	7	8	9	10	11	12
INDIANA						
3 Brademas	Y	?	N	N	Y	N
9 Hamilton	Y	Y	N	N	Y	N
11 Jacobs	Y	Y	N	N	Y	N
1 Madden	Y	Y	N	N	Y	N
4 Adair	Y	N	Y	Y	Y	?
6 Bray	Y	N	Y	Y	Y	Y
10 Dennis	Y	Y	Y	Y	N	N
2 Landgrebe	Y	N	Y	Y	Y	N
7 Myers	Y	N	Y	Y	Y	Y
5 Roudebush	Y	N	Y	Y	Y	Y
8 Zion	Y	N	Y	Y	Y	N
IOWA						
2 Culver	Y	Y	N	N	Y	N
5 Smith	Y	Y	N	N	Y	Y
3 Gross	Y	N	Y	N	Y	N
4 Kyl	Y	X	?	Y	Y	N
6 Mayne	Y	Y	Y	Y	Y	N
7 Scherle	Y	N	Y	N	Y	N
1 Schwengel	Y	N	N	N	Y	N
KANSAS						
2 Mize	Y	Y	Y	N	Y	N
1 Sebelius	Y	N	Y	√	Y	N
4 Shriver	Y	Y	Y	N	Y	N
5 Skubitz	Y	N	Y	Y	Y	Y
3 Winn	Y	N	Y	√	?	N
KENTUCKY						
2 Natcher	Y	N	Y	N	Y	Y
7 Perkins	Y	Y	N	N	Y	N
1 Stubblefield	Y	N	Y	N	Y	Y

	7	8	9	10	11	12
6 Watts	Y	N	Y	N	?	Y
5 Carter	Y	N	Y	N	Y	N
3 Cowger	Y	?	N	X	?	N
4 Snyder	Y	N	Y	✓	Y	Y
LOUISIANA						
2 Boggs	Y	Y	Y	N	?	N
3 Caffery	Y	N	Y	Y	Y	?
7 Edwards	?	N	Y	N	Y	?
1 Hebert	✓	Y	Y	✓	?	✓
8 Long	Y	N	Y	Y	?	Y
5 Passman	Y	Y	Y	Y	Y	Y
6 Rarick	?	N	Y	Y	Y	Y
4 Waggonner	Y	N	Y	Y	Y	Y
MAINE						
2 Hathaway	N	Y	N	N	Y	N
1 Kyros	Y	Y	N	N	Y	Y
MARYLAND						
4 Fallon	Y	Y	N	N	?	?
7 Friedel	Y	Y	N	N	Y	N
3 Garmatz	Y	Y	N	N	Y	N
2 Long	?	Y	N	N	Y	Y
6 Beall	Y	Y	N	Y	Y	N
8 Gude	Y	Y	N	N	Y	N
5 Hogan	Y	Y	Y	Y	Y	N
1 Morton	Y	Y	Y	?	Y	N
MASSACHUSETTS						
2 Boland	Y	Y	N	N	Y	N
11 Burke	Y	Y	N	N	Y	Y
4 Donohue	Y	Y	N	N	Y	Y
6 Harrington	N	Y	N	N	Y	N
7 Macdonald	N	✓	N	N	Y	Y
9 McCormack						
8 O'Neill	N	Y	N	N	Y	N
3 Philbin	Y	Y	N	N	Y	Y
1 Conte	Y	N	N	N	Y	N
10 Heckler	Y	Y	N	N	?	N
12 Keith	Y	Y	N	N	Y	N
5 Morse	Y	Y	N	N	Y	?
MICHIGAN						
12 O'Hara	Y	Y	N	N	Y	Y
18 Broomfield	Y	Y	Y	Y	Y	N
3 Brown	Y	N	Y	N	Y	N
10 Cederberg	Y	Y	Y	✓	?	N
6 Chamberlain	Y	N	Y	Y	Y	N
2 Esch	Y	Y	N	N	N	N
5 Ford	Y	Y	Y	Y	Y	N
8 Harvey	Y	N	N	N	Y	?
4 Hutchinson	Y	N	N	Y	Y	N
19 McDonald	Y	N	N	N	Y	Y
7 Riegle	Y	✓	N	N	Y	N
11 Ruppe	Y	X	?	N	Y	N
9 Vander Jagt	Y	✓	?	N	Y	N
Detroit-Wayne Co.						
1 Conyers	N	N	N	N	?	X
13 Diggs	N	Y	N	N	Y	N
16 Dingell	?	Y	N	N	Y	Y
15 Ford	N	N	N	N	Y	Y
17 Griffiths	Y	Y	N	N	Y	?
14 Nedzi	N	N	N	N	Y	Y
MINNESOTA						
8 Blatnik	N	Y	N	X	Y	N
5 Fraser	N	Y	N	N	Y	N
4 Karth	N	N	N	N	Y	Y
7 Langen	Y	N	Y	Y	Y	N
3 MacGregor	Y	Y	N	N	Y	N
2 Nelsen	Y	Y	Y	Y	Y	N
1 Quie	Y	Y	Y	Y	Y	N
6 Zwach	Y	Y	Y	Y	Y	N
MISSISSIPPI						
1 Abernethy	Y	N	Y	Y	Y	Y
5 Colmer	Y	N	Y	Y	Y	?
3 Griffin	?	N	Y	Y	Y	Y
4 Montgomery	Y	N	Y	Y	Y	✓
2 Whitten	Y	N	Y	Y	?	Y
MISSOURI						
5 Bolling	Y	Y	N	N	?	?
10 Burlison	Y	N	Y	N	Y	Y
1 Clay	N	N	N	N	Y	N
6 Hull	Y	N	Y	Y	Y	?
9 Hungate	N	N	N	N	Y	Y
8 Ichord	Y	N	Y	Y	?	Y
4 Randall	Y	N	N	Y	Y	Y
3 Sullivan	Y	Y	N	N	?	?

	7	8	9	10	11	12
2 Symington	Y	Y	N	N	Y	Y
7 Hall	Y	N	Y	✓	?	?
MONTANA						
2 Melcher	Y	Y	N	N	Y	Y
1 Olsen	Y	N	N	N	Y	Y
NEBRASKA						
2 Cunningham	Y	Y	Y	Y	?	N
1 Denney	Y	N	Y	Y	?	Y
3 Martin	Y	N	Y	Y	?	?
NEVADA						
AL Baring	Y	N	Y	Y	?	Y
NEW HAMPSHIRE						
2 Cleveland	Y	N	N	Y	Y	N
1 Wyman	Y	N	Y	Y	Y	N
NEW JERSEY						
14 Daniels	Y	Y	N	N	Y	Y
13 Gallagher	?	Y	N	N	Y	N
9 Helstoski	N	Y	N	N	Y	N
3 Howard	Y	N	N	N	Y	N
11 Minish	Y	Y	N	N	Y	N
15 Patten	Y	Y	N	N	Y	N
10 Rodino	Y	Y	N	N	Y	N
8 Roe	Y	N	N	N	Y	Y
4 Thompson	N	N	N	N	Y	N
6 Cahill	?	✓	X	X	?	?
12 Dwyer	Y	Y	N	N	?	?
5 Frelinghuysen	Y	Y	N	N	Y	N
1 Hunt	Y	N	Y	Y	Y	N
2 Sandman	?	Y	N	Y	Y	N
7 Widnall	Y	Y	N	N	?	N
NEW MEXICO						
2 Foreman	Y	N	Y	Y	Y	Y
1 Lujan	Y	N	Y	N	Y	N
NEW YORK						
41 Dulski	Y	Y	N	N	Y	N
34 Hanley	Y	Y	N	N	Y	N
5 Lowenstein	N	N	N	N	Y	N
39 McCarthy	N	Y	N	N	Y	N
25 Ottinger	N	N	N	N	Y	N
1 Pike	Y	Y	N	N	Y	N
35 Stratton	Y	Y	N	N	Y	N
3 Wolff	N	Y	N	N	Y	?
29 Button	?	Y	N	N	Y	N
37 Conable	Y	Y	N	N	Y	N
28 Fish	Y	Y	N	N	Y	N
2 Grover	Y	N	Y	Y	Y	Y
38 Hastings	Y	Y	Y	Y	Y	N
36 Horton	Y	Y	N	N	Y	N
30 King	Y	N	Y	Y	Y	Y
31 McEwen	Y	Y	Y	Y	Y	N
27 McKneally	Y	Y	N	N	Y	N
32 Pirnie	Y	Y	N	N	Y	N
26 Reid	N	Y	N	N	Y	N
33 Robison	Y	N	N	N	Y	N
40 Smith	Y	Y	N	N	?	N
4 Wydler	Y	?	Y	N	Y	N
New York City						
7 Addabbo	Y	Y	N	N	Y	Y
24 Biaggi	Y	Y	N	N	Y	Y
23 Bingham	N	Y	N	N	Y	N
11 Brasco	N	Y	N	N	Y	N
15 Carey	N	Y	N	N	Y	?
10 Celler	Y	Y	N	N	?	X
12 Chisholm	N	N	N	N	?	N
9 Delaney	Y	N	Y	N	?	?
19 Farbstein	N	Y	N	N	Y	X
22 Gilbert	N	Y	N	N	Y	N
17 Koch	N	N	N	N	Y	N
16 Murphy	Y	Y	N	N	Y	N
13 Podell	N	Y	N	N	?	N
18 Powell	?	?	?	?	?	?
14 Rooney	Y	Y	N	N	?	N
8 Rosenthal	N	Y	N	N	Y	N
20 Ryan	N	Y	N	N	Y	N
21 Scheuer	N	N	N	N	Y	N
6 Halpern	Y	Y	N	N	Y	N
NORTH CAROLINA						
2 Fountain	Y	N	Y	Y	Y	Y
4 Galifianakis	?	N	Y	Y	Y	Y
3 Henderson	Y	N	Y	Y	Y	Y
1 Jones	Y	N	Y	Y	Y	Y
7 Lennon	Y	N	Y	Y	?	Y
6 Preyer	Y	Y	Y	N	Y	Y

	7	8	9	10	11	12
11 Taylor	Y	N	Y	Y	Y	Y
10 Broyhill	Y	N	Y	Y	Y	Y
9 Jonas	Y	X	Y	Y	?	Y
5 Mizell	Y	X	Y	Y	Y	Y
8 Ruth	Y	N	Y	Y	Y	Y
NORTH DAKOTA						
1 Andrews	Y	Y	X	N	Y	?
2 Kleppe	Y	N	Y	Y	Y	N
OHIO						
9 Ashley	Y	Y	N	N	Y	N
20 Feighan	Y	Y	N	N	Y	N
18 Hays	Y	✓	?	N	Y	Y
19 Kirwan	?	✓	?	X	?	?
21 Stokes	N	N	N	N	Y	N
22 Vanik	N	N	N	N	Y	N
17 Ashbrook	Y	N	Y	✓	N	Y
14 Ayres	Y	Y	Y	Y	Y	N
8 Betts	Y	N	Y	Y	Y	N
16 Bow	?	X	Y	Y	Y	N
7 Brown	Y	N	Y	N	Y	N
2 Clancy	Y	N	Y	Y	Y	Y
12 Devine	Y	N	Y	✓	Y	Y
6 Harsha	Y	N	Y	Y	Y	Y
5 Latta	Y	N	Y	Y	Y	N
24 Lukens	Y	N	Y	N	Y	N
4 McCulloch	Y	N	N	N	Y	N
10 Miller	Y	N	Y	Y	Y	N
23 Minshall	Y	N	Y	?	Y	Y
13 Mosher	Y	X	N	N	?	N
11 Stanton	Y	Y	N	N	?	N
1 Taft	Y	Y	N	N	?	N
3 Whalen	Y	N	N	N	Y	N
15 Wylie	Y	N	Y	N	Y	N
OKLAHOMA						
3 Albert	Y	Y	N	N	Y	N
2 Edmondson	Y	Y	N	N	Y	Y
5 Jarman	Y	N	Y	Y	Y	Y
4 Steed	Y	N	?	N	?	Y
1 Belcher	Y	Y	Y	Y	Y	N
6 Camp	Y	N	Y	Y	Y	N
OREGON						
3 Green	Y	Y	Y	Y	?	?
2 Ullman	N	N	Y	Y	?	Y
4 Dellenback	Y	Y	N	N	?	N
1 Wyatt	Y	N	Y	N	Y	N
PENNSYLVANIA						
25 Clark	Y	✓	N	N	Y	Y
21 Dent	?	N	N	N	Y	?
11 Flood	Y	Y	N	N	Y	Y
20 Gaydos	Y	N	N	N	Y	Y
14 Moorhead	N	Y	N	N	Y	N
26 Morgan	Y	Y	N	N	Y	Y
15 Rooney	Y	?	N	N	Y	Y
24 Vigorito	Y	Y	N	N	Y	Y
6 Yatron	Y	Y	N	N	Y	Y
8 Biester	Y	Y	N	N	Y	N
18 Corbett	Y	Y	Y	N	Y	Y
13 Coughlin	Y	Y	N	N	?	N
16 Eshleman	Y	N	Y	Y	Y	N
27 Fulton	Y	Y	N	N	Y	Y
19 Goodling	Y	N	Y	Y	Y	N
23 Johnson	?	N	Y	Y	Y	?
10 McDade	Y	Y	N	N	Y	N
22 Saylor	?	N	Y	N	Y	N
17 Schneebeli	Y	Y	X	X	Y	N
9 Watkins	Y	N	Y	✓	Y	?
12 Whalley	Y	?	Y	?	?	N
7 Williams	Y	N	Y	Y	?	Y
Philadelphia City						
1 Barrett	Y	Y	N	N	?	N
3 Byrne	Y	Y	N	N	Y	N
4 Eilberg	?	✓	X	N	Y	Y
5 Green	N	Y	N	N	Y	N
2 Nix	Y	Y	N	N	Y	N
RHODE ISLAND						
1 St. Germain	Y	N	N	N	Y	Y
2 Tiernan	Y	N	N	N	Y	Y
SOUTH CAROLINA						
3 Dorn	Y	N	Y	Y	?	Y
5 Gettys	?	X	Y	Y	Y	Y
6 McMillan	Y	N	Y	Y	?	Y
4 Mann	Y	Y	Y	Y	Y	Y

	7	8	9	10	11	12
1 Rivers	?	Y	Y	Y	?	Y
2 Watson	Y	N	Y	✓	Y	Y
SOUTH DAKOTA						
2 Berry	Y	N	Y	✓	?	?
1 Reifel	?	-	?	✓	Y	?
TENNESSEE						
6 Anderson	Y	Y	Y	X	?	Y
7 Blanton	Y	N	Y	Y	?	Y
4 Evins	Y	Y	Y	N	?	?
5 Fulton	?	✓	?	X	?	?
8 Jones	Y	N	?	N	Y	Y
3 Brock	Y	N	Y	Y	N	?
2 Duncan	Y	N	Y	Y	Y	Y
9 Kuykendall	?	N	Y	Y	Y	N
1 Quillen	Y	N	Y	Y	Y	Y
TEXAS						
9 Brooks	Y	Y	N	N	?	Y
17 Burleson	Y	N	Y	Y	Y	Y
5 Cabell	?	Y	Y	Y	Y	Y
22 Casey	Y	N	Y	N	Y	Y
15 de la Garza	Y	Y	N	N	Y	Y
2 Dowdy	Y	N	Y	Y	Y	Y
8 Eckhardt	Y	N	N	N	Y	N
21 Fisher	Y	Y	Y	Y	Y	Y
20 Gonzalez	Y	Y	N	N	Y	N
23 Kazen	Y	Y	N	N	Y	Y
19 Mahon	Y	Y	Y	?	Y	Y
1 Patman	?	Y	N	N	?	Y
10 Pickle	Y	Y	Y	N	Y	Y
11 Poage	Y	N	Y	Y	?	?
13 Purcell	Y	Y	✓	Y	Y	Y
4 Roberts	Y	N	Y	Y	?	Y
6 Teague	?	Y	✓	Y	Y	?
16 White	Y	N	N	N	Y	N
12 Wright	Y	Y	Y	N	?	?
14 Young	Y	✓	Y	N	Y	Y
7 Bush	Y	Y	Y	Y	Y	N
3 Collins	Y	N	Y	Y	N	Y
18 Price	Y	N	Y	Y	Y	N
UTAH						
1 Burton	Y	N	Y	Y	Y	?
2 Lloyd	Y	Y	Y	Y	Y	N
VERMONT						
AL Stafford	Y	Y	N	N	Y	N
VIRGINIA						
4 Abbitt	Y	N	Y	?	?	?
5 Daniel	Y	N	Y	Y	Y	Y
1 Downing	Y	N	Y	Y	Y	Y
7 Marsh	Y	N	Y	Y	Y	Y
3 Satterfield	Y	N	Y	Y	Y	Y
10 Broyhill	Y	N	Y	Y	?	Y
6 Poff	Y	N	Y	Y	Y	?
8 Scott	Y	X	Y	Y	N	Y
9 Wampler	Y	N	Y	Y	Y	Y
2 Whitehurst	Y	N	Y	N	?	Y
WASHINGTON						
7 Adams	N	N	N	N	?	N
5 Foley	Y	N	N	N	Y	N
3 Hansen	?	Y	N	N	Y	Y
6 Hicks	Y	Y	N	N	Y	Y
2 Meeds	Y	N	N	N	Y	N
4 May	Y	Y	Y	Y	Y	N
1 Pelly	Y	Y	N	X	?	N
WEST VIRGINIA						
4 Hechler	N	N	N	N	Y	N
5 Kee	Y	Y	Y	N	Y	Y
1 Mollohan	Y	N	N	N	Y	Y
3 Slack	Y	N	N	N	Y	Y
2 Staggers	Y	N	N	N	Y	N
WISCONSIN						
2 Kastenmeier	N	N	N	N	Y	N
7 Obey	Y	N	N	N	Y	N
5 Reuss	N	N	N	N	Y	X
4 Zablocki	Y	N	N	N	Y	Y
8 Byrnes	Y	Y	Y	Y	Y	N
9 Davis	Y	Y	Y	Y	N	N
10 O'Konski	Y	N	N	N	Y	Y
1 Schadeberg	Y	N	Y	Y	Y	N
6 Steiger	Y	Y	Y	N	Y	N
3 Thomson	Y	Y	Y	Y	Y	N
WYOMING						
AL Wold	Y	Y	Y	Y	Y	N

Democrats in this type; *Republicans in italics*

ATTEMPTS TO OVERRIDE VETOES DOMINATE KEY VOTES

Attempts to override Presidential vetoes in the House, curbs on military involvement in the Senate, and perennial school desegregation disputes in both chambers dominated the key Congressional votes during 1970.

Key votes spanned a wide variety of domestic and foreign issues in both the House and Senate. But four of the 28 votes—all in the House—were taken on drives to override President Nixon's vetoes of major domestic legislation.

Of the nine public bills vetoed by the President since early 1970, three involved appropriations: for the Departments of Labor and Health, Education and Welfare (HEW) for fiscal 1970, for the Office of Education for fiscal 1971, and for the Department of Housing and Urban Development (HUD) for fiscal 1971. Mr. Nixon also vetoed a hospital construction bill.

The House repassed the hospital construction and education money bills by the required two-thirds majorities; both became law when the Senate also voted to override the vetoes. House supporters of the Labor-HEW and HUD appropriation measures failed to gain the necessary two-thirds votes to override those vetoes.

Annual Issues. Many of the key votes were taken on issues which in recent years have confronted Congress annually, such as school desegregation, involvement in Vietnam, funding for the antiballistic missile system (ABM) and supersonic transport plane (SST). The appropriations bills signify a continuing dispute between President Nixon and the Democratic Congress over spending priorities.

These and several other key votes occurred on legislation almost certain to come up again in 1971. Congress went home in December without completing action on Social Security, welfare reform or trade restrictions.

Key Senate votes included efforts to limit the scope of U.S. involvement in Southeast Asia and such domestic issues as the nomination of G. Harrold Carswell to the Supreme Court, the SST, 18-year-old votes, food stamp increases and a motion to drop the trade restriction and welfare reform sections from the Social Security bill.

In the House, key votes included passage of welfare reform, voting rights, farm subsidy limitations, legislative reform and the SST.

Both chambers engaged in debates on efforts to restrict the Federal Government's school desegregation efforts. In one key vote, Senators voted 56-36 to require the Government to apply universal standards to segregation based on prior law and that based on housing patterns. This was the first crack in the coalition of northern Democrats and moderate Republicans which had engineered the Senate success of civil rights bills during the 1960s.

Other significant Senate votes centered on the "no-knock" search warrants for unannounced police investigations, electoral reform and standards for reducing pollutants from automobile engines.

The House also took other important votes on allowing amendments to the controversial bill establishing trade import controls, providing boosts in Social Security benefits when living costs rise, and refusing to concur with a Senate amendment limiting the American effort in Cambodia.

Each year, the editors of Congressional Quarterly select a series of votes as the most significant roll calls of the session. The 1970 key votes follow.

Senate Key Votes

1. NO-KNOCK SEARCH WARRANTS. One of the most controversial Administration crime control measures enacted by the 91st Congress authorized search warrants, under certain circumstances, allowing law enforcement officers to enter a place to be searched without first giving notice of their presence and intention. This "no-knock" provision was contained in the Comprehensive Drug Abuse Prevention and Control Act (PL 91-513) and, applying to arrest warrants as well, in the District of Columbia Court Reorganization and Criminal Procedure Act (PL 91-358). The key Senate vote on the provision came in January 1970 during debate on the initial Senate version of the drug bill (S 3246). Robert P. Griffin (R Mich.) proposed an amendment to add the "no-knock" provision to the bill. Sam J. Ervin Jr. (D N.C.), who opposed the provision as a violation of the constitutional guarantee against "unreasonable search and seizure," proposed an amendment to the Griffin amendment to delete the "no-knock" authorization. The Senate rejected Ervin's amendment 35-50: R 2-31; D 33-19 (ND 21-14; SD 12-15).

2. DESEGREGATION. During a two-week debate on the bill (HR 514) extending the Elementary and Secondary Education Act, the Senate considered amendments aimed at limiting the powers of the Federal Government to rectify school segregation. Debate centered chiefly on an amendment offered by John Stennis (D Miss.) requiring that school racial standards must be applied uniformly throughout the country "without regard to the origin or cause of such segregation." Stennis and other southerners said Federal desegregation efforts were designed only to deal with school districts in the South which had previously been segregated by law—*de jure* segregation—but ignored districts outside the South which were segregated because of residence patterns or other factors—*de facto* segregation. Before voting on the Stennis amendment, Senators voted 63-24 to add specific mention of both *de jure* and *de facto* segregation; this change was sponsored by Abraham A. Ribicoff (D Conn.), a leading advocate of civil rights. The series of votes, culminated by the Feb. 18 key vote on the Stennis amendment, represented the first major crack in the coalition of northern Democrats and moderate and liberal Republicans which had engineered passage of civil rights bills in the Senate during the 1960s. The Stennis amendment was adopted 56-36, with Republicans voting 27-12, and Democrats voting 29-24 (ND 11-23; SD 18-1).

3. EIGHTEEN-YEAR-OLD VOTE. In a surprise move with far-reaching implications, the Senate March 12, 1970, agreed 64-17—R 26-8; D 38-9 (ND 32-0; SD 6-9) to an amendment to the 1970 voting rights bill which lowered the voting age to 18. The House later accepted this provision, proposed by Senate Majority Leader Mike Mansfield (D Mont.), with the Senate version of the bill (HR 4249—PL 91-285). The Supreme Court in December upheld the provision lowering the voting age for Federal elections, but not for state and local elections. Approximately 11 million persons between the ages of 18 and 21 were added to the lists of potential voters in 1972 by this amendment.

4. CARSWELL REJECTION. Thirteen Republicans joined 38 Democrats April 8, 1970, to reject the nomination of G. Harrold Carswell of Florida to the Supreme Court. The Senate, by a 45-51 vote—R 28-13; D 17-38 (ND 3-33; SD 14-5)—refused for the second time in six months to confirm a man nominated by Mr. Nixon to the Court, dealing a severe blow to Administration prestige. It had already been damaged by the November 1969 rejection of the nomination of Clement F. Haynsworth Jr. of South Carolina to the Court. Carswell was opposed by civil rights groups who charged that he held segregationist views and by members of the legal profession who described him as a man of mediocre legal and judicial abilities. The defeat of his nomination marked the first time since 1894 that one President had suffered the outright rejection by the Senate of two of his Court nominations.

5. BROADCAST SPENDING. In an attempt to reduce the spiraling cost of political campaigns, the Senate April 14 adopted an amendment to limit television and radio spending by Presidential and Congressional candidates to seven cents per vote cast in the last general election. Introduced by John Pastore (D R.I.) and James B. Pearson (R Kan.), the amendment to a bill (S 3637) to amend the Communications Act of 1934, passed on almost a straight party-line vote. Republican opponents of the amendment noted that the measure did not apply to state offices where Republicans were dominant, but only to Congress which the Democrats control. Sponsors of the amendment repeatedly referred to the scope of the problem of financing Congressional campaigns. The vote breakdown was R 8-32; D 42-3 (ND 28-0; SD 14-3). The Senate Nov. 23 by four votes failed to override President Nixon's Oct. 23 veto of the broadcast spending bill.

6. CAMBODIA RESTRICTION. As a result of the U.S. entry into combat operations in Cambodia in April 1970, a move began in the Senate to limit such operations and prevent a recurrence. The leaders of this effort, mainly liberal members of the Senate Foreign Relations Committee, drafted an amendment similar to one passed in 1969 barring U.S. ground combat troops in Laos and Thailand. The amendment barring funds for U.S. Cambodian activities after July 1 without Congressional approval became known as the Cooper-Church amendment after the two main sponsors, John Sherman Cooper (R Ky.) and Frank Church (D Idaho). They chose to try

to attach their proposal to the pending Foreign Military Sales authorization (HR 15628). After seven weeks of debate, delay and attempts to water down the amendment, the Senate on June 30 accepted the Cooper-Church amendment by a 58-37 roll-call vote. The provision was amended on the floor to make it more palatable to Administration forces. It was eventually knocked out of HR 15628 but incorporated in a different form in the supplemental foreign aid authorization (HR 19911). The Cooper-Church amendment was passed by a bipartisan coalition of liberals 58-37: R 16-26; D 42-11 (ND 35-1; SD 7-10).

7. FOOD STAMPS. Pressure was strong in the Senate in 1970 to expand the food stamp program which increased the purchasing power of the poor to buy food. Sen. George McGovern (D S.D.), chairman of the Senate Select Committee on Nutrition and Human Needs, continued in 1970 as he had in 1969 to highlight the problems of hunger in the country through hearings by his Committee. The Senate in 1969 had passed a food stamp bill (S 2547) authorizing $1.25 billion for the program in fiscal 1971, but the House did not act on food stamp legislation that year. The agricultural appropriations bill (HR 17923) included funds for food stamps, which is administered by the Department of Agriculture, McGovern succeeded in amending the agriculture appropriations bill on July 8 to increase the food stamp appropriation from $1.25 billion to $1.75 billion. The vote was 43-28 in favor of the amendment, with 13 Republicans and 30 Democrats supporting the amendment and 19 Republicans, 9 Democrats opposing (ND 26-2; SD 4-7).

8. SAFEGUARD ABM. For the third year in a row, a major Senate debate revolved around the plans to construct an antiballistic missile (ABM) system. In the fiscal 1971 defense procurement authorization (HR 17123) the Administration requested $1 billion to expand the ABM system begun in 1969. Another $357 million for construction was carried in another bill. As in previous years, major opposition surfaced in the Senate. In the face of this challenge, supporters of the President's ABM plans voluntarily cut back the expansion request in order to undermine the opposition. The strategy was successful and the amendment sponsored by John Sherman Cooper (R Ky.) and Philip A. Hart (D Mich.) to block expansion was defeated Aug. 12, 1970, by a 47-52 roll-call vote: R 12-30; D 35-22 (ND 30-8; SD 5-14).

9. VOLUNTEER ARMY. An attempt was made in 1970 to move toward establishment of an all-volunteer military for the United States. This effort would have speeded up the timetable set up by the Administration for the creation of a volunteer army when the Vietnam war ends. To accomplish a speedier conversion to the volunteer military, Senators Barry Goldwater (R Ariz.) and Mark O. Hatfield (R Ore.) proposed an amendment to the fiscal 1971 defense procurement authorization. Their amendment would not have automatically created a volunteer service but would have made it possible to move toward this goal by enacting military pay raises to encourage enlistments. After debating the proposal on the floor for several weeks, the Senate Aug. 25 rejected the amendment 35-52: R 20-18; D 15-34 (ND 14-17; SD 1-17).

10. END-THE-WAR AMENDMENT. A strong Congressional and public campaign built up in 1970 around a proposal by Sen. Charles E. Goodell (R N.Y.) to limit the retention of U.S. troops in South Vietnam. Momentum on behalf of such a measure gathered as a result of the U.S. entry into Cambodia. The amendment to the defense procurement authorization was sponsored by several Senate war critics and became known as the McGovern-Hatfield amendment for Senators George McGovern (D S.D.) and Mark O. Hatfield (R Ore.). The sponsors altered the amendment a number of times to attract support. In its final form, the amendment set a ceiling of 280,000 troops in Vietnam for April 30, 1971, and set a deadline of Dec. 31, 1971, for the complete withdrawal of U.S. troops but gave the President authority to delay the pullout for 60 days if he found U.S. troops to be in danger. The amendment was rejected on a 39-55 roll-call vote Sept. 1: R 7-34; D 32-21 (ND 29-6; SD 3-15).

11. ELECTORAL REFORM. A proposed constitutional amendment to abolish the electoral college and substitute direct, popular election of the President died Sept. 17 when the Senate refused to invoke cloture (end debate) on the measure. The bill (S J Res 1) was similar to another bill that had passed the House in 1969 and which also had the endorsement of President Nixon. Sen. Birch Bayh (D Ind.) was chief sponsor of the Senate version, which would have required that the candidate receiving the largest popular vote be elected President, provided he received at least 40 percent of the votes cast. Opposed to the bill was a coalition of Senators from the South and from some states with small populations. A motion to invoke cloture was introduced Sept. 15 by Majority Leader Mike Mansfield (Mont.). When the Senate voted Sept. 17, the result was 54-36 in favor of the cloture motion, six votes short of the necessary 60. Prospect of continued and prolonged debate on electoral reform prompted the Senate to let the bill die. The vote was a victory for Senate conservatives: R 21-18; D 33-18 (ND 30-2; SD 3-16).

12. AIR POLLUTION. The Clean Air Amendments of 1970 (HR 17255), the strongest air pollution measure ever enacted by Congress, contained specific deadlines for the elimination of certain pollutants from automobile engine exhausts. In the Senate, although nearly all debate concerned these deadlines, no efforts were made to eliminate them but amendments were aimed at softening their impact. Edward J. Gurney (R Fla.) on Sept. 22 offered an amendment which would have eliminated the requirement that the manufacturer's request for extension of the deadline must be made 12 months to 24 months prior to the expiration of the five-year time limit. The Gurney amendment failed by a 22-57 vote: R 16-17; D 6-40 (ND 1-28; SD 5-12).

13. SUPERSONIC TRANSPORT (SST). One of the most controversial issues in the Senate in 1970 was the question of funding the supersonic transport (SST). The Administration had requested $290 million for the development of two prototype SSTs. The money was included in the Department of Transportation appropriation bill for fiscal 1971 (HR 17755) and approved by the House May 27. But by the time the bill got to the Senate floor on Dec. 3, intensive lobbying against the plane had been done by environmental groups. Led by Sen. William

Proxmire (D Wis.), Senate opponents of the SST argued that the plane could cause deterioration to the environment and produce an intolerable noise level. Proxmire and others also questioned the cost of the plane. Despite a strong fight by the Administration to save the funds, an amendment by Proxmire to delete the $290 million won by a 52-41 roll-call vote: R 18-21; D 34-20 (ND 25-10; SD 9-10). (Senate Dec. 31 accepted compromise to allow funds for SST to be spent through March 30, 1971, at the rate of the $210 million agreed on by conferees on the bill for fiscal 1971.)

14. SOCIAL SECURITY, TRADE, WELFARE. Senate supporters of the Trade Act of 1970 and the President's welfare reform proposals on Dec. 28, 1970, reluctantly abandoned their attempt to attach the two measures to a bill (HR 17550) increasing Social Security benefits. By a 49-21 roll-call vote the Senate approved the motion of Chairman Russell B. Long (D La.) of the Finance Committee to strip the trade and welfare provisions, as well as others creating a catastrophic health insurance program and increasing veterans' benefits, from the Social Security legislation. The action climaxed a filibuster against the trade bill which began Dec. 17. It followed a statement by Chairman Wilbur D. Mills (D Ark.) of the House Ways and Means Committee that he would not go to conference on a package bill containing all the measures the Senate had drawn together. Mills' Committee had reported the Social Security (HR 17550), trade (HR 18970) and family assistance (HR 16311) bills, and the House had passed them separately. The Finance Committee attached the various measures, including a welfare reform test program, to the popular Social Security bill in hopes of ensuring passage for all in the closing days of the 91st Congress. The maneuver backfired, and Long was obliged to move to reduce the bill to its Social Security provisions to keep the filibuster from killing even that portion of the legislation. Even this effort failed, however, when Mills refused to go to conference during the last three days of the session. Long's motion was to recommit the bill to his Committee with instructions to delete all but the Social Security provisions and report it back to the Senate immediately. Republicans voted 20-12 for Long's motion; Democrats divided 29-9 for it (ND 16-8; SD 13-1).

House Key Votes

1. LABOR-HEW VETO. On Jan. 26 President Nixon vetoed HR 13111, the fiscal 1970 appropriations bill for the Departments of Labor and Health, Education and Welfare, the Office of Economic Opportunity, and other agencies. He said that the $19.7-billion bill increased spending too much over his Budget requests and forced the Executive Branch to spend funds on programs which should be reformed. Two days later, the House failed by 52 votes to override the President's veto. A two-thirds majority of those voting—in this case 278—was needed to override, but only 226 House Members actually did so. This included 199 Democrats, including 49 southerners, and 27 Republicans. Voting to sustain the veto were 156 Republicans and 35 southern Democrats. The final breakdown was 226-191: R 27-156; D 199-35 (ND 150-0; SD 49-35).

2. FAMILY ASSISTANCE. The President listed reform of the welfare system as one of his key legislative proposals in 1970. The Family Assistance Plan which provided a Federal floor of $1,600 for poor families was the most significant legislation, Mr. Nixon said, since passage of the Social Security Act. But powerful House Ways and Means Committee Chairman Wilbur D. Mills (D Ark.) seemed cool to the proposal. The bill (HR 16311) was debated behind closed doors by the Committee from November 1969 until March 5 when it was approved by the Committee after Mills announced he wanted to send the bill to the floor. With the sudden support from Mills and a closed rule preventing any amendments on the floor, the bill was approved April 16 by a 243-155 roll-call vote: R 102-72; D 141-83 (ND 126-19; SD 15-64).

3. SOCIAL SECURITY. The President had proposed that future benefit increases in the Social Security program be made automatically when the Consumer Price Index (CPI) rose 3 percent or more in the previous year. But traditionally raising benefits has been Congressional prerogative and Wilbur D. Mills (D Ark.), chairman of the House Ways and Means Committee, consistently opposed automatic increases. Automatic increases were added to the measure, however, on the House floor May 21 in a move led by Republican Members. The vote was on a motion by Jackson E. Betts (R Ohio) to recommit the Social Security bill (HR 17550) with instructions to add provisions for automatic cost-of-living increases in Social Security benefits. The amendment was agreed to by a 233-144 roll-call vote: R 161-5; D 72-139 (ND 68-61; SD 4-78).

4. VOTING RIGHTS Liberal forces won a significant victory June 17, 1970, when the House accepted the Senate version of the voting rights bill (HR 4249—PL 91-285) extending the Voting Rights Act of 1965 for five years and lowering the voting age to 18. The Administration opposed the extension, proposing instead that the 1965 law be amended. The House late in 1969 had passed the Administration bill. In 1970 the key House vote on voting rights came when the House agreed, by a 224-183 vote, to a motion calling for a vote on the resolution (H Res 914) providing for acceptance of the Senate version of the bill. Enough Republicans voted for the motion to cancel out the votes of the Southern Democrats opposing it—R 59-117; D 165-66 (ND 138-8; SD 27-58). Had the motion or the resolution been rejected, the differing versions of the bill would have gone to conference where those opposed to the provision lowering the voting age, including House Judiciary Committee Chairman Emanuel Celler (D N.Y.), and those opposed to extension of the 1965 law, including Senate Judiciary Committee Chairman James O. Eastland (D Miss.), could have killed the provision or the entire bill.

5. HILL-BURTON VETO. By a wide 279-98 margin, the House June 25 voted to override President Nixon's June 22 veto of HR 11102, the Hill-Burton hospital construction bill. Subsequent Senate passage marked the first Presidential veto to be overridden in 10 years. The bill authorized $2.79 billion over fiscal years 1971-1973 for grants and loans to build and modernize hospitals and other health facilities. The President said the bill was too expensive. The measure also contained a program of categorical grants to hospitals that the Administration had proposed scrapping for a combination of direct loans and grants. Mr. Nixon's veto—his second since taking office—was challenged by House leaders who said the program was of such high priority that it should not be subject to expenditure reductions. Ninety-five Republicans and three Democrats voted to uphold the veto; 67 Republicans and 212 Democrats voted to override. The breakdown of the Democratic vote was ND 137-0; SD 75-3.

6. DESEGREGATION. When the House originally considered the fiscal 1971 appropriations bill (HR 16916) for the Office of Education, it adopted a series of provisions seeking to limit the Federal Government's desegregation authority. They were known as the Whitten amendments, after Jamie L. Whitten (D Miss.), which stipulated that no funds in the bill could be used to force schools already considered "desegregated" under the 1964 Civil Rights Act to bus students, abolish schools or set attendance zones either against the choice of students' parents or as a prerequisite for obtaining Federal funds; and the Jonas amendment, after Charles Raper Jonas (R N.C.), which stipulated that no funds could be used to draw up plans to prevent students from attending the schools of their parents' choice based on race or color. When the Senate considered HR 16916, it dropped all these provisions. On June 30, while the House formally agreed to send the measure to conference, Jeffery Cohelan (D Calif.) offered a motion to instruct House conferees to agree to Senate action on the Whitten and Jonas amendments. Daniel J. Flood (D Pa.), floor manager of the bill, offered a motion to table Cohelan's motion, and thus kill it. Flood's motion was adopted 191-157: R 107-35; D 84-122 (ND 18-117; SD 66-5). Conferees subsequently retained the Whitten amendments but dropped the Jonas provision.

7. CAMBODIA RESTRICTION. Debate in the House on the attempt to curb U.S. military operations in Cambodia was much more limited than in the Senate and the crucial vote came on a procedural motion rather than on the Cooper-Church amendment itself. When the Senate version of the foreign military sales bill, with the Cooper-Church amendment, was returned to the House, Donald W. Riegle Jr. (R Mich.) moved to instruct the House conferees to accept the Cooper-Church amendment. Wayne L. Hays (D Ohio) then moved to table, or kill, the Riegle motion. The Hays move was approved by the House 237-153: R 138-33; D 99-120 (ND 28-112; SD 71-8) on July 9, 1970.

8. FARM SUBSIDY LIMIT. Strong opposition to farm subsidies had developed in the House in 1968 and 1969, particularly from urban Members who cited figures showing that some individual farms received subsidies for as much as a million dollars in one year. These Members succeeded in tacking amendments onto farm legislation limiting subsidy payments to $20,000 to individual farmers, but in both 1968 and 1969 the Senate did not include ceilings, and conferees on the bills dropped the House limits. With the pressure still strong for ceilings, the Administration agreed to a $55,000 limit in the Agriculture Act of 1970 (HR 18546) which established three-year price support programs for major farm commodities. The Administration had initially recommended a $110,000 limit. The $55,000 ceiling was part of HR 18546 when it passed the House Aug. 5 by a 212-171 roll-call vote—R 86-88; D 126-85 (ND 52-78; SD 74-7).

9. EDUCATION VETO. President Nixon Aug. 11 vetoed the $4.4-billion Office of Education appropriations bill for fiscal 1971 (HR 16916) because Congress had added about $453 million to his original Budget requests. On Aug. 13, with 20 votes to spare, the House voted 289-114 to override the veto. A two-thirds majority—in this case 269—was needed to override. The final breakdown was 289-114: R 77-101; D 212-13 (ND 145-1; SD 67-12). The Senate Aug. 18 also voted to override the veto, by a 77-16 roll-call vote, and the measure was enacted into law.

10. HUD APPROPRIATIONS VETO SUS-TAINED. The President scored a victory Aug. 13 when the House failed to override his veto of the first 1971 Housing and Urban Development (HUD)-Independent Offices Appropriations bill (HR 17548). Mr. Nixon's veto of the $18,009,525,300 bill was sustained by a 204-195 roll-call vote. A two-thirds majority in both chambers is needed to override a veto. Republicans and some southern Democrats, reacting to the President's criticism of the appropriation as too costly (it was $541 million over the budget request), combined to sustain the veto. R 23-155; D 181-40 (ND 139-4; SD 42-36). A second HUD-Independent Offices Appropriations bill (HR 19830), containing $300,000,000 less than the first, was approved by the President Dec. 17.

11. CONGRESSIONAL REFORM. Congress in 1970—for the first time in 24 years—approved a comprehensive legislative reform bill. The key vote on the moderate reform measure (HR 17654—PL 91-510) came when the House, traditionally the most resistant to such efforts at reform, approved it. The Senate had passed a similar bill in 1967, but the House Rules Committee had blocked House action on the bill during the remainder of the 90th Congress. In September 1970, however, the House approved the Legislative Reorganization Act of 1970 by a vote of 326-19—R 140-6; D 186-13 (ND 127-1; SD 59-12). The 1970 Act did not deal with the seniority system, financial disclosure, lobbying regulations or the *Congressional Record,* but did make a variety of changes in the committee and floor procedures of the House and Senate and authorized expanded information resources for the Congress.

12. TRADE BILL. The House on Nov. 18, 1970, came within a few votes of opening up the controversial protectionist Trade Act of 1970 (HR 18970) to amendments from the floor. An amendment to the rule controlling House consideration of the measure, offered by Sam M. Gibbons (D Fla.), which would have opened the

bill to amendments deleting from (but not adding to) the bill, failed in a 192-201 roll-call vote. The rule change might have killed the bill in the House, since Chairman Wilbur D. Mills (D Ark.) of the Ways and Means Committee, which had reported it, said he was under strict instructions from his Committee to bring the bill to the floor under a closed rule (allowing Committee amendments only). The bill, which died in the Senate, would have imposed statutory import quotas on textiles and footwear and established procedures for imposing quotas on an estimated 200 other imports. The vote on Gibbons' amendment was the closest roll call on the trade bill. It showed that opponents did not have quite enough strength to force a change in the measure. Both the Republicans and the Democrats were split on the vote: 91 Republicans and 101 Democrats voted for Gibbons' amendment while 77 Republicans and 124 Democrats opposed it. (ND 94-52; SD 7-72)

13. SUPERSONIC TRANSPORT (SST). When the House passed the Department of Transportation appropriation bill (HR 17755) on May 27, there was strong opposition to including the $290 million recommended by the Administration for the SST program. But opponents of the SST lost by a 176-162 roll-call vote a parliamentary maneuver to send the bill back to committee with instructions to delete the funds. After the Senate Dec. 3 approved an amendment to delete the SST appropriation, another attempt was made Dec. 8 in the House to follow the Senate lead. Sidney R. Yates (D Ill.) offered a motion to instruct House conferees on the bill to agree to the Senate amendment. By a 213-175 roll-call vote, the House tabled (killed) the motion. A "yea" was a vote, in effect, for the SST. The parties split on the issue with 105 Republicans and 108 Democrats voting against the SST appropriation. The Democratic breakdown was ND45-97; SD 63-16.

14. EMERGENCY SCHOOL AID. President Nixon March 24, 1970, promised to spend $1.5 billion in fiscal 1971-1972 to improve schools in "racially impacted areas" and to aid school districts which were in the process of desegregating. The House late in December 1970 approved the Administration bill authorizing this aid, but liberals and southern conservatives blocked action on the bill in the Senate. The House approved the bill 159-77 (R 53-39; D 106-38; ND 87-2; SD 19-36). In the Senate, liberals considered the bill too vague in its standards for the desegregation effort and conservatives considered the bill a "busing bill."

SENATE VOTES ON 'NO-KNOCK', DESEGREGATION, VOTING RIGHTS, CAMPAIGN SPENDING, CAMBODIA, FOOD STAMPS

1. S 3246. Drug Control. Ervin (D N.C.) amendment to Griffin (R Mich.) amendment, striking "no-knock" provision. Rejected 35-50: R 2-31; D 33-19 (ND 21-14; SD 12-15), Jan. 27, 1970. A "nay" was a vote supporting the President's position.

2. HR 514. Elementary and Secondary Education Act Amendments. Stennis (D Miss.) amendment requiring equal enforcement throughout the country in dealing with de jure and de facto school segregation. Adopted 56-36: R 27-12; D 29-24 (ND 11-23; SD 18-1), Feb. 18, 1970. The President did not take a position on the amendment.

3. HR 4249. Voting Rights Act Amendments. Mansfield (D Mont.) amendment lowering to 18 the voting age for all Federal, state and local elections, effective Jan. 1, 1971. Adopted 64-17: R 26-8; D 38-9 (ND 32-0; SD 6-9), March 12, 1970. The President did not take a position on the amendment.

4. Nomination of G. Harrold Carswell as an Associate Justice of the Supreme Court. Rejected 45-51: R 28-13; D 17-38 (ND 3-33; SD 14-5), April 8, 1970. A "yea" was a vote supporting the President's position.

5. S 3637. Equal Time Amendment. Pastore (D R.I.)-Pearson (R Kan.) amendment imposing a seven-cent per vote (in previous statewide election) limit on TV and radio spending by Presidential and Congressional candidates. Adopted 50-35: R 8-32; D 42-3 (ND 28-0; SD 14-3), April 14, 1970. The President did not take a position on the amendment.

6. HR 15628. Foreign Military Sales. Cooper (R Ky.)-Church (D Idaho) amendment barring funds for U.S. military operations in Cambodia after July 1, 1970, unless specifically authorized by Congress, including the retention of U.S. combat forces, advisers and air activities in direct support of Cambodian forces. Adopted 58-37: R 16-26; D 42-11 (ND 35-1; SD 7-10), June 30, 1970. The President did not take a position on the amendment.

7. HR 17923. Agriculture Appropriations. McGovern (D S.D.) amendment increasing from $1.25 billion to $1.75 billion funds for the food stamp program. Adopted 43-28: R 13-19; D 30-9 (ND 26-2; SD 4-7), July 8, 1970. The President did not take a position on the amendment.

- KEY -

- Y Record vote for (yea).
- ✓ Paired for.
- ‡ Announced for or CQ poll for.
- N Record vote against (nay).
- X Paired against.
- - Announced against or CQ poll against.
- ? Absent, general pair, "present" or did not announce or answer poll.

Senator	1	2	3	4	5	6	7
ALABAMA							
Allen	Y	Y	N	Y	Y	N	N
Sparkman	Y	Y	N	Y	Y	N	X
ALASKA							
Gravel	✓	N	‡	Y	Y	‡	
Stevens	‡	Y	✓	Y	N	Y	?
ARIZONA							
Fannin	N	Y	N	Y	N	N	N
Goldwater	?	Y	✓	Y	N	N	X
ARKANSAS							
Fulbright	N	Y	Y	Y	Y	Y	Y
McClellan	N	Y	-	Y	N	N	N
CALIFORNIA							
Cranston	Y	N	Y	N	Y	Y	Y
Murphy	N	Y	N	Y	*	N	✓
COLORADO							
Allott	N	Y	N	Y	N	N	N
Dominick	X	-	✓	Y	N	N	N
CONNECTICUT							
Dodd	N	N	✓	N	‡	-	‡
Ribicoff	Y	Y	Y	N	Y	Y	✓
DELAWARE							
Boggs	N	N	Y	Y	N	N	Y
Williams	N	Y	Y	Y	Y	N	N
FLORIDA							
Holland	Y	Y	N	Y	Y	N	N
Gurney	N	Y	-	Y	N	N	N
GEORGIA							
Russell	N	Y	X	X	Y	?	-
Talmadge	Y	Y	X	X	Y	Y	N
HAWAII							
Inouye	Y	N	‡	N	Y	Y	Y
Fong	N	Y	Y	N	N	N	Y
IDAHO							
Church	N	N	Y	N	‡	Y	Y
Jordan	N	Y	Y	Y	N	N	N
ILLINOIS							
Stevenson•							
Percy	X	N	Y	N	N	Y	✓
INDIANA							
Bayh	N	-	Y	N	Y	Y	Y
Hartke	?	?	Y	N	Y	Y	?
IOWA							
Hughes	Y	N	Y	N	Y	Y	Y
Miller	N	N	N	Y	N	N	N
KANSAS							
Dole	N	Y	Y	Y	N	Y	N
Pearson	N	Y	Y	Y	Y	Y	N
KENTUCKY							
Cook	N	Y	Y	N	N	N	✓
Cooper	Y	Y	Y	Y	Y	Y	Y
LOUISIANA							
Ellender	N	Y	N	Y	Y	N	N
Long	N	Y	N	Y	Y	X	X
MAINE							
Muskie	Y	N	Y	N	Y	Y	Y
Smith	N	Y	Y	N	N	N	-
MARYLAND							
Tydings	N	N	✓	N	Y	Y	Y
Mathias	✓	N	Y	N	Y	Y	Y
MASSACHUSETTS							
Kennedy	Y	?	Y	N	Y	Y	Y
Brooke	N	N	Y	N	N	Y	Y
MICHIGAN							
Hart	Y	N	Y	N	Y	Y	Y
Griffin	N	N	X	Y	N	N	X
MINNESOTA							
McCarthy	Y	N	‡	N	-	Y	Y
Mondale	Y	N	Y	N	Y	Y	Y
MISSISSIPPI							
Eastland	Y	Y	N	Y	?	N	N
Stennis	Y	Y	N	Y	N	N	X
MISSOURI							
Eagleton	N	N	Y	N	Y	Y	Y
Symington	N	N	Y	N	Y	Y	✓
MONTANA							
Mansfield	Y	Y	✓	N	?	Y	Y
Metcalf	Y	-	Y	N	Y	Y	‡
NEBRASKA							
Curtis	N	Y	N	Y	N	N	X
Hruska	N	Y	N	Y	N	N	N
NEVADA							
Bible	N	Y	Y	Y	?	Y	N
Cannon	N	Y	Y	N	Y	Y	N
NEW HAMPSHIRE							
McIntyre	N	Y	Y	N	Y	Y	Y
Cotton	N	Y	Y	Y	N	N	N
NEW JERSEY							
Williams	Y	N	Y	N	Y	Y	Y
Case	Y	N	Y	N	Y	Y	Y
NEW MEXICO							
Anderson	N	Y	Y	?	?	Y	?
Montoya	N	Y	Y	N	Y	Y	Y
NEW YORK							
Goodell	N	N	‡	N	Y	Y	Y
Javits	‡	N	Y	N	Y	Y	✓
NORTH CAROLINA							
Ervin	Y	Y	N	Y	N	N	N
Jordan	✓	Y	N	Y	Y	Y	?
NORTH DAKOTA							
Burdick	Y	Y	N	Y	Y	Y	Y
Young	N	Y	Y	Y	N	N	N
OHIO							
Young	Y	N	Y	N	Y	Y	‡
Saxbe	N	N	Y	N	Y	Y	Y
OKLAHOMA							
Harris	Y	N	Y	N	Y	Y	‡
Bellmon	N	Y	Y	Y	N	N	N
OREGON							
Hatfield	N	-	Y	N	Y	Y	Y
Packwood	?	Y	Y	N	Y	Y	N
PENNSYLVANIA							
Schweiker	N	N	Y	N	N	Y	Y
Scott	N	N	Y	N	N	N	Y
RHODE ISLAND							
Pastore	Y	N	Y	N	Y	Y	Y
Pell	Y	N	Y	X	‡	Y	Y
SOUTH CAROLINA							
Hollings	Y	Y	Y	Y	Y	Y	Y
Thurmond	N	Y	N	Y	N	N	N
SOUTH DAKOTA							
McGovern	?	N	Y	N	Y	Y	Y
Mundt	X	?	-	‡	-	-	X
TENNESSEE							
Gore	Y	Y	N	Y	Y	Y	✓
Baker	N	Y	Y	N	N	N	‡
TEXAS							
Yarborough	✓	Y	Y	N	Y	Y	Y
Tower	X	Y	X	Y	N	N	N
UTAH							
Moss	Y	N	Y	N	Y	Y	Y
Bennett	N	Y	N	✓	-	N	N
VERMONT							
Aiken	N	Y	Y	N	Y	N	N
Prouty	?	Y	Y	N	N	N	Y
VIRGINIA							
Byrd, Jr.	Y	Y	X	Y	Y	N	N
Spong	Y	Y	Y	N	Y	Y	Y
WASHINGTON							
Jackson	N	N	Y	N	Y	Y	Y
Magnuson	N	N	Y	N	‡	Y	✓
WEST VIRGINIA							
Byrd	N	Y	Y	Y	Y	Y	Y
Randolph	Y	Y	Y	Y	‡	Y	Y
WISCONSIN							
Nelson	Y	N	Y	N	‡	✓	Y
Proxmire	Y	N	Y	N	Y	Y	Y
WYOMING							
McGee	Y	Y	Y	N	Y	N	‡
Hansen	N	Y	Y	N	N	N	N

Democrats   *Republicans*

• Not a Senator when votes were taken.
* Answered "present" to avoid possible conflict-of-interest.

HOUSE VOTES ON HEW VETO, WELFARE, SOCIAL SECURITY, VOTING RIGHTS, HOSPITAL VETO, DESEGREGATION, CAMBODIA

1. HR 13111. Fiscal 1970 appropriations bill for the Departments of Labor and Health, Education and Welfare. Reconsideration of the bill, vetoed by President Nixon Jan. 26. Veto sustained 226-191: R 27-156; D 199-35 (ND 150-0; SD 49-35), Jan. 28, 1970. A two-thirds majority (278 in this case) was required to override the President's veto. A "nay" was a vote supporting the President's position.

2. HR 16311. Family Assistance Act. Passage of the bill replacing the Aid to Families with Dependent Children program with a Family Assistance plan providing guaranteed Federal payments to poor families. Passed 243-155: R 102-72; D 141-83 (ND 126-19; SD 15-64), April 16, 1970. A "yea" was a vote supporting the President's position.

3. HR 17550. Social Security Amendments of 1970. Betts (R Ohio) motion to recommit the bill with instructions to add amendment providing for automatic cost-of-living increases in Social Security benefits. Agreed to 233-144: R 161-5; D 72-139 (ND 68-61; SD 4-78), May 21, 1970. A "yea" was a vote supporting the President's position.

4. HR 4249. Voting Rights Act Amendments. Matsunaga (D Hawaii) motion to order the previous question on the rule (H Res 914) for agreeing to the Senate amendments to HR 4249, extending the Voting Rights Act of 1965. Agreed to 224-183: R 59-117; D 165-66 (ND 138-8; SD 27-58), June 17, 1970. The President did not take a position on the motion.

5. HR 11102. Hospital Construction, Reconsideration and passage of the bill, vetoed by President Nixon June 22, extending program of Federal grants for construction and modernization of health facilities. Veto overridden 279-98: R 67-95; D 212-3 (ND 137-0; SD 75-3), June 25, 1970. A two-thirds majority (252 in this case) was required to override the President's veto. A "nay" was a vote supporting the President's position.

6. HR 16916. Office of Education appropriations bill. Flood (D Pa.) motion to table Cohelan (D Calif.) motion instructing House conferees to accept Senate amendments deleting provisions prohibiting use of funds to force busing or closing of schools and providing for freedom of choice plans. Tabling motion adopted 191-157: R 107-35; D 84-122 (ND 18-117; SD 66-5), June 30, 1970. The President did not take a position on the motion.

7. HR 15628. Foreign Military Sales. Hays (D Ohio) motion to table Riegle (R Mich.) motion instructing House conferees to concur in Senate-passed Cooper-Church amendment on Cambodia. Tabling motion adopted 237-153: R 138-33; D 99-120 (ND 28-112; SD 71-8), July 9, 1970. The President did not take a position on the motion.

	1	2	3	4	5	6	7
ALABAMA							
3 Andrews	Y	N	N	N	Y	Y	Y
7 Bevill	Y	N	N	N	Y	Y	Y
5 Flowers	N	N	N	N	✓	‡	Y
8 Jones	Y	N	N	N	Y	Y	Y
4 Nichols	Y	N	?	N	Y	Y	Y
6 *Buchanan*	N	N	Y	N	Y	Y	Y
2 *Dickinson*	N	N	Y	N	N	?	Y
1 *Edwards*	N	N	Y	N	N	Y	Y
ALASKA							
AL Pollock	Y	?	?	✓	✓	?	✓
ARIZONA							
2 Udall	Y	Y	N	Y	Y	N	N
1 *Rhodes*	N	Y	?	N	N	Y	Y
3 *Steiger*	N	N	Y	N	N	Y	Y
ARKANSAS							
1 Alexander	Y	N	N	N	?	Y	N
2 Mills	Y	Y	N	N	Y	Y	Y
4 Pryor	Y	Y	N	Y	Y	Y	?
3 *Hammerschmidt*	N	N	N	N	Y	Y	Y
CALIFORNIA							
5 Burton	Y	Y	Y	Y	Y	N	N
7 Cohelan	Y	Y	?	Y	Y	N	N
9 Edwards	Y	Y	‡	Y	Y	N	N
34 Hanna	Y	✓	N	Y	Y	N	N
2 Johnson	Y	Y	‡	Y	Y	N	N
4 Leggett	Y	Y	‡	Y	Y	-	X
15 McFall	Y	Y	N	Y	Y	N	Y
8 Miller	Y	Y	‡	Y	Y	N	Y
3 Moss	Y	Y	N	Y	Y	N	N
16 Sisk	Y	Y	N	Y	Y	N	-
38 Tunney	Y	✓	‡	Y	Y	-	N
37 Van Deerlin	Y	Y	Y	Y	Y	N	N
14 Waldie	Y	Y	Y	Y	Y	N	N
1 *Clausen*	N	Y	Y	N	Y	?	Y
10 *Gubser*	N	Y	Y	N	Y	Y	X
11 *McCloskey*	N	Y	Y	N	N	N	N
6 *Mailliard*	N	Y	Y	Y	N	N	Y
18 *Mathias*	N	N	Y	N	Y	?	Y
33 *Pettis*	Y	Y	Y	N	Y	Y	Y
35 *Schmitz* ●							
12 *Talcott*	N	Y	Y	N	Y	N	Y
13 *Teague*	?	‡	Y	N	N	Y	Y
36 *Wilson*	N	Y	Y	N	Y	Y	Y
Los Angeles Co.							
17 Anderson	Y	Y	Y	Y	Y	N	N
29 Brown	Y	Y	‡	Y	Y	N	X
22 Corman	✓	Y	N	Y	N	N	N
21 Hawkins	✓	Y	‡	Y	‡	-	N
19 Holifield	Y	Y	N	Y	Y	N	‡
26 Rees	Y	Y	N	Y	N	N	N
30 Roybal	Y	Y	N	Y	Y	N	N
31 Wilson	Y	Y	N	✓	‡	-	X
28 *Bell*	N	Y	?	Y	N	?	✓
23 *Clawson*	N	N	?	N	Y	Y	Y
27 *Goldwater*	N	N	?	N	Y	Y	Y
32 *Hosmer*	N	Y	Y	N	‡	Y	Y
24 *Rousselot* ●							Y
20 *Smith*	N	N	Y	N	Y	Y	Y
25 *Wiggins*	N	Y	Y	N	-	Y	Y
COLORADO							
4 Aspinall	Y	N	N	Y	Y	‡	X
3 Evans	Y	Y	N	Y	Y	N	N
1 Rogers	Y	Y	-	Y	Y	N	?
2 *Brotzman*	N	Y	Y	N	Y	Y	Y
CONNECTICUT							
1 Daddario	Y	Y	Y	Y	Y	?	? N
3 Giaimo	Y	Y	N	Y	?	N	N
5 Monagan	?	Y	Y	Y	Y	N	N
6 *Meskill*	N	Y	Y	Y	?	Y	?
2 *Steele* ●							
4 *Weicker*	Y	Y	Y	Y	Y	Y	N
DELAWARE							
AL Roth	N	N	Y	Y	Y	Y	Y
FLORIDA							
3 Bennett	N	N	N	Y	Y	Y	Y
4 Chappell	N	N	N	N	Y	Y	Y
12 Fascell	Y	Y	N	Y	Y	N	N
2 Fuqua	Y	N	N	N	Y	Y	Y
6 Gibbons	Y	‡	N	Y	Y	Y	N
7 Haley	N	N	N	Y	Y	Y	Y
11 Pepper	Y	Y	N	Y	✓	-	X
9 Rogers	N	N	N	Y	Y	Y	Y
1 Sikes	Y	N	‡	N	Y	‡	Y
10 Burke	X	N	N	N	Y	Y	Y
8 *Cramer*	N	N	Y	X	X	‡	✓
5 *Frey*	N	N	Y	N	?	?	Y
GEORGIA							
3 Brinkley	N	N	N	N	Y	Y	Y
7 Davis	?	N	N	N	Y	Y	Y
6 Flynt	N	N	N	N	Y	Y	Y
1 Hagan	N	N	N	N	Y	Y	Y
9 Landrum	N	N	N	N	Y	Y	Y
2 O'Neal	N	N	N	X	X	Y	Y
10 Stephens	N	N	N	N	Y	‡	Y
8 Stuckey	N	N	N	N	Y	Y	Y
4 *Blackburn*	N	N	Y	N	N	‡	Y
5 *Thompson*	N	N	Y	N	N	Y	Y
HAWAII							
AL Matsunaga	Y	Y	‡	Y	Y	N	N
AL Mink	Y	Y	Y	Y	Y	N	N
IDAHO							
2 *Hansen, O.*	N	Y	Y	Y	?	-	Y
1 *McClure*	N	N	Y	N	N	?	Y
ILLINOIS							
21 Gray	Y	Y	N	Y	Y	N	Y
24 Price	Y	Y	N	Y	Y	N	N
23 Shipley	Y	N	Y	Y	Y	Y	X
16 *Anderson*	N	Y	Y	Y	N	-	-
17 *Arends*	N	Y	Y	N	N	Y	Y
14 *Erlenborn*	N	‡	Y	X	-	Y	Y
20 *Findley*	N	Y	Y	N	Y	?	?
12 *McClory*	Y	Y	Y	Y	N	Y	Y
18 *Michel*	N	N	Y	N	N	Y	Y
19 *Railsback*	N	Y	Y	Y	‡	N	Y
15 *Reid*	N	Y	N	N	Y	Y	Y
22 *Springer*	N	Y	N	N	N	Y	Y
Chicago-Cook Co.							
7 Annunzio	Y	Y	N	Y	Y	N	N
6 Collins ●							
1 Vacancy							
5 Kluczynski	Y	Y	?	Y	Y	Y	Y
2 Mikva	Y	✓	Y	Y	Y	N	N
3 Murphy	Y	Y	N	Y	N	Y	Y
11 Pucinski	Y	Y	Y	Y	Y	N	N
8 Rostenkowski	Y	Y	N	Y	Y	N	N
9 Yates	Y	Y	Y	Y	Y	N	N
10 Collier	N	Y	Y	N	N	Y	Y
13 *Crane*	N	N	Y	N	N	Y	Y
4 *Derwinski*	N	N	Y	N	N	Y	Y
KEY							

- KEY -

Y Record vote for (yea).
✓ Paired for.
‡ Announced for or CQ poll for.
N Record vote against (nay).
X Paired against.
- Announced against or CQ poll against.
? Absent, general pair, "present" or did not announce or answer poll.

	1	2	3	4	5	6	7
INDIANA							
3 Brademas	Y	Y	Y	Y	Y	N	N
9 Hamilton	Y	Y	Y	Y	?	N	N
11 Jacobs	Y	Y	‡	Y	Y	N	N
1 Madden	Y	✓	N	Y	Y	N	N
4 *Adair*	N	N	Y	N	?	?	Y
6 *Bray*	N	N	Y	N	N	?	Y
10 *Dennis*	N	N	N	N	N	Y	Y
2 *Landgrebe*	N	N	-	N	N	Y	Y
7 *Myers*	N	N	Y	N	Y	Y	Y
5 *Roudebush*	N	N	‡	?	Y	?	Y
8 *Zion*	N	N	Y	N	N	Y	Y
IOWA							
2 Culver	Y	Y	Y	Y	Y	N	N
5 Smith	Y	Y	Y	Y	✓	?	N
3 *Gross*	N	N	Y	Y	Y	Y	Y
4 *Kyl*	N	N	?	N	✓	Y	Y
6 *Mayne*	N	Y	N	N	Y	Y	Y
7 *Scherle*	N	N	Y	Y	Y	Y	Y
1 *Schwengel*	N	Y	Y	✓	N	Y	N
KANSAS							
2 *Mize*	N	N	Y	N	Y	Y	Y
1 *Sebelius*	N	N	‡	N	Y	Y	Y
4 *Shriver*	N	N	Y	N	Y	Y	Y
5 *Skubitz*	N	Y	N	Y	N	Y	Y
3 *Winn*	N	N	‡	N	Y	Y	Y
KENTUCKY							
2 Natcher	Y	Y	N	Y	Y	N	N
7 Perkins	Y	Y	N	Y	Y	Y	Y
1 Stubblefield	Y	N	N	Y	Y	Y	Y

	1 2 3 4 5 6 7		1 2 3 4 5 6 7		1 2 3 4 5 6 7		1 2 3 4 5 6 7
6 Watts	Y N N Y Y Y Y	2 Symington	Y Y ‡ Y Y N N	11 Taylor	Y N N Y Y Y Y	1 Vacancy	
5 Carter	N Y Y N Y Y Y	7 Hall	N N Y N ‡ Y Y	10 Broyhill	N N Y N Y Y Y	2 Watson	N N Y N ? ? Y
3 Cowger	Y Y Y √ Y Y Y	MONTANA		9 Jonas	N N Y N N Y Y	SOUTH DAKOTA	
4 Snyder	N N Y Y Y Y Y	2 Melcher	Y Y N Y Y N N	5 Mizell	N N Y N N Y Y	2 Berry	N Y Y N N ? Y
LOUISIANA		1 Olsen	Y Y Y Y Y N N	8 Ruth	N N Y N Y Y Y	1 Reifel	N ‡ ‡ Y N ‡ √
2 Boggs	Y Y N Y Y N Y	NEBRASKA		NORTH DAKOTA		TENNESSEE	
3 Caffery	N N N N √ Y √	2 Cunningham	N Y Y N N Y Y	1 Andrews	N Y Y N N ‡ √	6 Anderson	Y N ‡ Y ‡ ‡ Y
7 Edwards	N N N Y Y ‡ ‡	1 Denney	N N Y N N ‡ √	2 Kleppe	N N ‡ N N Y Y	7 Blanton	Y N N Y ? ? Y
1 Hebert	X N N X Y Y Y	3 Martin	N N N N Y Y Y	OHIO		4 Evins	? N N Y Y ‡ Y
8 Long	N X N N Y Y √	NEVADA		9 Ashley	Y Y Y Y Y N N	5 Fulton	√ Y N Y Y Y N
5 Passman	N N N N Y ‡ Y	AL Baring	Y N N N Y ? Y	19 Carney ●		8 Jones	Y N N Y ‡ N Y
6 Rarick	N N N N N Y √	NEW HAMPSHIRE		20 Feighan	Y ? N Y N N Y	3 Brock	N Y Y N N ‡ Y
4 Waggonner	N N N N Y Y Y	2 Cleveland	N N Y Y Y Y Y	18 Hays	Y N ? X Y ‡ Y	2 Duncan	N N Y Y Y Y Y
MAINE		1 Wyman	N N Y N Y Y Y	21 Stokes	Y Y ‡ Y Y N N	9 Kuykendall	N Y Y N √ ‡ Y
2 Hathaway	Y Y Y Y Y N N	NEW JERSEY		22 Vanik	Y Y N Y Y N N	1 Quillen	N N Y N Y Y Y
1 Kyros	Y Y Y Y Y N N	14 Daniels	Y Y Y Y ‡ N N	17 Ashbrook	N N Y N Y Y Y	TEXAS	
MARYLAND		13 Gallagher	Y Y Y Y Y N N	14 Ayres	N Y ‡ Y ‡ ‡ Y	9 Brooks	Y N N Y Y Y Y
4 Fallon	Y Y N Y N Y Y	9 Helstoski	Y Y Y Y Y N N	8 Betts	N Y Y N N Y Y	17 Burleson	N N N N Y Y Y
7 Friedel	Y Y N Y Y N N	3 Howard	Y Y Y Y Y N N	16 Bow	N Y Y X Y Y	5 Cabell	Y ? N N Y ? Y
3 Garmatz	Y Y N Y N N N	11 Minish	Y Y Y Y Y N N	7 Brown	Y Y N Y N N Y	22 Casey	Y N N Y Y Y Y
2 Long	Y N N Y X Y N	15 Patten	Y Y Y Y Y N N	2 Clancy	N N Y N ? ? Y	15 de la Garza	Y Y N Y √ Y Y
6 Beall	N Y Y Y Y Y Y	10 Rodino	Y Y Y Y Y N N	12 Devine	N N ‡ N N Y √	2 Dowdy	N N Y N Y Y Y
8 Gude	Y Y Y Y N Y Y	8 Roe	Y Y Y Y Y N N	6 Harsha	Y N Y N Y Y Y	8 Eckhardt	Y Y Y Y Y N N
5 Hogan	Y Y Y N Y Y Y	4 Thompson	Y Y N Y N N N	5 Latta	N N Y N Y ‡ Y	21 Fisher	Y N N N Y Y Y
1 Morton	N Y Y N N ‡ √	12 Dwyer	N Y Y Y Y N N	24 Lukens	N ? Y N - Y	20 Gonzalez	Y Y N Y Y N N
MASSACHUSETTS		6 Forsythe ●		4 McCulloch	N Y Y Y Y N Y	23 Kazen	Y N N Y Y Y Y
2 Boland	Y Y Y Y Y N N	5 Frelinghuysen	X Y Y Y N N Y	10 Miller	N Y Y N Y Y Y	19 Mahon	Y N N Y Y Y Y
11 Burke	Y Y N Y Y N N	1 Hunt	N N Y N Y Y Y	23 Minshall	N N Y N Y Y Y	1 Patman	Y ? N N Y - Y
4 Donohue	Y Y Y Y Y N N	2 Sandman	N N Y N N Y Y	13 Mosher	N Y Y Y Y N N	10 Pickle	Y N N Y Y Y Y
6 Harrington	Y Y Y Y Y N N	7 Widnall	N Y Y Y N N Y	11 Stanton	N Y Y N Y Y Y	11 Poage	Y N N Y Y Y Y
7 Macdonald	Y Y Y Y Y N N	NEW MEXICO		1 Taft	N Y Y N N Y Y	13 Purcell	Y N N Y Y Y Y
9 McCormack		2 Foreman	Y N Y N N Y Y	3 Whalen	Y Y Y Y Y N N	4 Roberts	Y N - N Y Y Y
8 O'Neill	Y Y Y Y Y N N	1 Lujan	N Y Y N N ? Y	15 Wylie	N ? Y N Y Y Y	6 Teague	N N N N ? ? ?
3 Philbin	Y Y N Y Y N N	NEW YORK		OKLAHOMA		16 White	Y √ Y Y N Y Y
1 Conte	Y Y Y Y Y N N	41 Dulski	Y Y Y Y Y Y Y	3 Albert	Y Y N Y Y N N	12 Wright	Y N N Y Y Y Y
10 Heckler	Y ? Y Y N N N	34 Hanley	Y Y Y Y Y N N	2 Edmondson	Y N N N N Y Y	14 Young	Y N N Y Y Y Y
12 Keith	N Y Y Y ‡ - N	5 Lowenstein	Y Y Y Y Y N N	5 Jarman	N N N N - ‡ Y	7 Bush	N Y ? ? X √ √
5 Morse	N Y Y N N N N	39 McCarthy	Y Y ‡ Y Y N N	4 Steed	Y Y N N Y Y Y	3 Collins	N N Y N N Y Y
MICHIGAN		25 Ottinger	Y ‡ ‡ Y Y N N	1 Belcher	N N ? N N Y Y	18 Price	N N N N X ? Y
12 O'Hara	Y Y Y Y Y N N	1 Pike	Y N Y Y Y N Y	6 Camp	N N Y N N Y Y	UTAH	
18 Broomfield	N Y Y Y Y Y ‡	35 Stratton	Y Y - Y Y N Y	OREGON		1 Burton	Y Y Y Y N ‡ Y
3 Brown	N Y ‡ N Y Y Y	3 Wolff	√ Y Y Y Y N N	3 Green	Y N N N Y Y N	2 Lloyd	? Y Y Y N Y Y
10 Cederberg	N Y Y N N ‡ Y	29 Button	N Y Y N Y Y Y	2 Ullman	Y N N N Y Y N	VERMONT	
6 Chamberlain	N Y Y N Y Y Y	37 Conable	N Y Y N Y Y Y	4 Dellenback	N Y Y N N N N	AL Stafford	Y Y Y Y N N N
2 Esch	N Y Y Y ‡ - N	28 Fish	N Y Y N N N N	1 Wyatt	N ‡ Y N N Y N	VIRGINIA	
5 Ford	N Y Y N N Y Y	2 Grover	N X Y N N Y Y	PENNSYLVANIA		4 Abbitt	N N N N Y Y Y
8 Harvey	N Y Y N N N Y	38 Hastings	N Y Y Y ? ? Y	25 Clark	Y N N √ Y ? Y	5 Daniel	N N N Y Y Y Y
4 Hutchinson	N N N Y N Y Y	36 Horton	Y Y Y Y Y - N	21 Dent	Y Y N ‡ ‡ N Y	1 Downing	Y N N Y Y Y Y
19 McDonald	N Y Y Y Y Y ?	30 King	N N Y X Y Y Y	11 Flood	Y Y ‡ Y Y Y N	7 Marsh	Y N N Y Y Y Y
7 Riegle	N Y ‡ Y √ N N	31 McEwen	N N Y N Y Y √	20 Gaydos	Y Y Y √ ? N N	3 Satterfield	Y N N Y Y Y Y
11 Ruppe	Y Y Y Y N N N	27 McKneally	Y N Y N N Y Y	14 Moorhead	Y Y Y Y Y N N	10 Broyhill	N √ Y N Y Y Y
9 Vander Jagt	N Y Y N - Y	32 Pirnie	Y Y Y Y Y N N	26 Morgan	Y N Y N Y Y Y	6 Poff	N Y Y N N Y ‡
Detroit-Wayne Co.		26 Reid	Y Y Y Y Y N N	15 Rooney	Y Y N Y Y N N	8 Scott	N Y Y N Y Y Y
1 Conyers	Y Y N Y Y ? N	33 Robison	N Y ‡ Y - - N	24 Vigorito	Y Y Y Y Y N N	9 Wampler	N Y Y N Y Y Y
13 Diggs	Y ? N Y Y N N	40 Smith	N Y Y N N Y N	6 Yatron	Y N Y N Y N N	2 Whitehurst	Y Y Y Y Y Y Y
16 Dingell	Y Y N Y Y N N	4 Wydler	N Y Y Y N N Y	8 Biester	Y Y Y Y Y N N	WASHINGTON	
15 Ford	Y Y N Y Y N N	New York City		18 Corbett	N Y Y N Y - Y	7 Adams	Y Y Y Y Y N N
17 Griffiths	Y ? N Y Y N N	7 Addabbo	Y Y Y Y Y N N	13 Coughlin	N Y Y N Y ? N	5 Foley	Y Y Y Y Y N N
14 Nedzi	Y Y N √ Y N X	24 Biaggi	Y N Y Y N N N	16 Eshleman	N N Y N Y Y Y	3 Hansen	Y Y N Y Y N X
MINNESOTA		23 Bingham	Y Y ‡ Y Y N N	27 Fulton	Y ‡ Y Y N N Y	6 Hicks	Y N X Y N N Y
8 Blatnik	Y Y ‡ Y Y - N	11 Brasco	Y Y Y Y Y N N	19 Goodling	N N Y N N Y Y	2 Meeds	Y Y Y Y Y - N
5 Fraser	Y Y Y Y Y N N	15 Carey	Y Y Y Y ? ? X	23 Johnson	N N Y N N Y Y	4 May	N Y Y N Y ‡ Y
4 Karth	Y Y N Y Y N N	10 Celler	Y Y N Y Y N N	10 McDade	Y Y Y Y Y Y N	1 Pelly	N Y Y X N Y Y
7 Langen	N Y Y N N Y Y	12 Chisholm	Y N N Y Y N N	22 Saylor	N Y Y N ? ? Y	WEST VIRGINIA	
3 MacGregor	N Y ‡ N N Y Y	9 Delaney	Y N N Y Y Y Y	17 Schneebeli	N √ ? N Y N	4 Hechler	Y Y Y Y Y N N
2 Nelsen	N Y Y N N Y Y	19 Farbstein	Y Y Y Y ‡ - N	9 Ware ●		5 Kee	Y ? N Y ? ? Y
1 Quie	N Y Y Y N N Y	22 Gilbert	Y Y Y Y ‡ N N	12 Whalley	N N Y N N Y Y	1 Mollohan	Y N N Y Y N N
6 Zwach	N Y Y Y N N Y	17 Koch	Y Y Y Y Y N N	7 Williams	N N Y N N Y Y	3 Slack	Y N N Y Y Y Y
MISSISSIPPI		16 Murphy	Y Y N Y Y N N	Philadelphia City		2 Staggers	Y Y Y Y N N N
1 Abernethy	N N N N Y Y Y	13 Podell	Y Y Y Y Y N -	1 Barrett	Y Y N Y Y N N	WISCONSIN	
5 Colmer	N N ? N N Y Y	18 Powell	Y Y Y Y ? ? X	3 Byrne	Y Y ‡ Y Y ? N	2 Kastenmeier	Y Y Y Y Y N N
3 Griffin	N N N N N Y Y	14 Rooney	N Y Y N Y Y Y	4 Eilberg	Y Y N Y Y N N	7 Obey	Y Y Y Y Y N N
4 Montgomery	N N N N ‡ ‡ Y	8 Rosenthal	Y Y Y Y Y N N	5 Green	Y Y Y Y Y N N	5 Reuss	Y Y Y Y Y N N
2 Whitten	Y N N N Y Y √	20 Ryan	Y Y Y Y Y N N	2 Nix	Y N Y N Y N N	4 Zablocki	Y N Y Y Y N N
MISSOURI		21 Scheuer	Y Y Y Y Y N N	RHODE ISLAND		8 Byrnes	N Y N N Y Y Y
5 Bolling	Y Y Y Y Y N N	6 Halpern	Y Y Y Y Y N N	1 St. Germain	Y Y Y Y Y N N	9 Davis	N N Y N Y Y Y
10 Burlison	Y Y ? Y Y Y N	NORTH CAROLINA		2 Tiernan	Y Y Y Y √ N N	10 O'Konski	N Y Y Y Y N N
1 Clay	Y Y ? Y Y N N	2 Fountain	N N N N Y Y Y	SOUTH CAROLINA		1 Schadeberg	N N Y N Y Y Y
6 Hull	Y Y N Y Y Y Y	4 Galifianakis	Y Y Y Y Y Y Y	3 Dorn	N Y N N Y Y Y	6 Steiger	N N Y N Y Y Y
9 Hungate	Y Y N Y Y N Y	3 Henderson	Y N N Y Y Y Y	5 Gettys	N X N N Y Y √	3 Thomson	N Y N N Y Y Y
8 Ichord	Y N N N Y Y Y	1 Jones	N N N N Y Y Y	6 McMillan	N X N ? Y Y Y	WYOMING	
4 Randall	Y N N Y Y Y Y	7 Lennon	Y X N N Y Y Y	4 Mann	N N N N ? ‡ Y	AL Wold	N N Y N Y ‡ Y
3 Sullivan	Y N N Y Y Y N	6 Preyer	Y Y N Y Y N N				

Democrats   *Republicans*

HOUSE VOTES ON FARM SUBSIDIES, EDUCATION VETO, HUD VETO, REORGANIZATION, TRADE BILL, SST, SCHOOL FUNDS

8. HR 18546. Agriculture Act of 1970. Passage of the bill providing three-year price support programs for wool, wheat, feed grains and cotton and for a dairy program and limiting subsidy payments to $55,000 per crop. Passed 212-171: R 86-88; D 126-85 (ND 52-78; SD 74-7), Aug. 5, 1970. A "yea" was a vote supporting the President's position.

9. HR 16916. Office of Education appropriations bill, fiscal 1971. Reconsideration and passage of the bill, vetoed by President Nixon Aug. 11, appropriating $4,420,145,000 for fiscal 1971 for the Office of Education. Veto overridden 289-114: R 77-101; D 212-13 (ND 145-1; SD 67-12), Aug. 13, 1970. A two-thirds majority (269 in this case) was required to override the President's veto. A "nay" was a vote supporting the President's position.

10. HR 17548. Independent Offices-HUD Appropriations, fiscal 1971. Reconsideration of the bill, vetoed by President Nixon Aug. 11, appropriating $18 billion for Independent Offices and the Department of Housing and Urban Development. Veto sustained 204-195: R 23-155; D 181-40 (ND 139-4; SD 42-36), Aug. 13, 1970. A two-thirds majority (266 in this case) was required to override the President's veto. A "nay" was a vote supporting the President's position.

11. HR 17654. Legislative Reorganization Act of 1970. Passage of the bill improving the operation of the Congress by revising Committee procedures, making public votes taken in committee, requiring the publication of House teller votes, and making other changes in Congressional rules. Passed 326-19: R 140-6; D 186-13 (ND 127-1; SD 59-12), Sept. 17, 1970. The President did not take a position on the bill.

12. HR 18970. Trade Act of 1970. Gibbons (D Fla.) amendment to the rule under which bill was considered, permitting amendments deleting provisions from the bill. Rejected 192-201: R 91-77; D 101-124 (ND 94-52; SD 7-72), Nov. 18, 1970. The President did not take a position on the amendment.

13. HR 17755. Department of Transportation and related agencies appropriations, fiscal 1971. Boland (D Mass.) motion to table Yates (D Ill.) motion instructing House conferees to accept Senate amendment deleting $289.9 million for development of the supersonic transport (SST). Motion adopted 213-175: R 105-62; D 108-113 (ND 45-97; SD 63-16), Dec. 8, 1970. A "yea" was a vote supporting the President's position.

14. HR 19446. Emergency School Aid. Passage of the bill authorizing $1.5 billion in aid to public schools undergoing desegregation. Passed 159-77: R 53-39; D 106-38 (ND 87-2; SD 19-36), Dec. 21, 1970. A "yea" was a vote supporting the President's position.

	8	9	10	11	12	13	14
ALABAMA							
3 Andrews	Y	N	N	N	N	N	X
7 Bevill	Y	✓	✓	Y	N	N	X
5 Flowers	Y	Y	Y	Y	N	N	N
8 Jones	Y	Y	Y	N	N	Y	N
4 Nichols	Y	Y	N	Y	N	Y	X
6 Buchanan	Y	N	N	N	Y	N	Y
2 Dickinson	Y	N	N	Y	N	Y	N
1 Edwards	Y	N	N	Y	N	Y	?
ALASKA							
AL Pollock	?	✓	X	Y	✓	?	Y
ARIZONA							
2 Udall	Y	Y	Y	Y	Y	N	Y
1 Rhodes	Y	N	N	Y	X	N	✓
3 Steiger	Y	N	N	Y	Y	N	?
ARKANSAS							
1 Alexander	Y	Y	Y	?	N	N	Y
2 Mills	Y	N	N	N	N	Y	X
4 Pryor	Y	‡	✓	?	N	N	Y
3 Hammerschmidt	Y	N	N	Y	N	Y	N
CALIFORNIA							
5 Burton	Y	Y	Y	Y	N	N	Y
7 Cohelan	N	Y	Y	Y	Y	N	?
9 Edwards	N	Y	Y	Y	Y	N	✓
34 Hanna	N	Y	Y	Y	X	X	Y
2 Johnson	Y	Y	Y	Y	Y	Y	?
4 Leggett	N	Y	Y	Y	Y	N	✓
15 McFall	Y	Y	Y	?	Y	Y	Y
8 Miller	Y	Y	Y	Y	Y	Y	✓
3 Moss	N	Y	Y	Y	X	X	✓
16 Sisk	Y	Y	Y	Y	Y	Y	Y
38 Tunney	✓	Y	Y	?	Y	N	?
37 Van Deerlin	N	Y	Y	Y	Y	Y	Y
14 Waldie	N	Y	Y	Y	X	X	?
1 Clausen	N	N	Y	Y	Y	Y	?
10 Gubser	N	Y	N	Y	Y	Y	?
11 McCloskey	Y	Y	N	Y	N	Y	?
6 Mailliard	N	-	‡	Y	Y	Y	Y
18 Mathias	Y	Y	N	Y	Y	Y	?
33 Pettis	N	Y	N	‡	Y	?	?
35 Schmitz	N	N	N	N	Y	N	N
12 Talcott	N	Y	N	Y	Y	?	Y
13 Teague	N	Y	N	Y	Y	Y	?
36 Wilson	‡	N	N	Y	Y	Y	?

Los Angeles Co.	8	9	10	11	12	13	14
17 Anderson	N	Y	Y	Y	Y	Y	Y
29 Brown	N	Y	Y	Y	N	?	?
22 Corman	N	Y	Y	‡	Y	Y	Y
21 Hawkins	✓	Y	Y	Y	Y	Y	Y
19 Holifield	Y	Y	Y	Y	Y	Y	Y
26 Rees	Y	Y	Y	Y	N	Y	Y
30 Roybal	N	Y	Y	?	Y	N	Y
31 Wilson	Y	Y	Y	Y	Y	Y	✓
28 Bell	N	Y	N	Y	Y	Y	Y
23 Clawson	N	N	N	?	?	Y	?
27 Goldwater	X	N	N	Y	Y	Y	Y
32 Hosmer	N	N	N	Y	✓	Y	Y
24 Rousselot	N	N	N	Y	Y	Y	X
20 Smith	N	N	N	Y	Y	Y	?
25 Wiggins	N	N	N	Y	Y	?	N
COLORADO							
4 Aspinall	Y	Y	Y	N	?	?	?
3 Evans	Y	Y	Y	Y	Y	N	?
1 Rogers	Y	Y	Y	?	N	Y	?
2 Brotzman	N	Y	N	Y	Y	N	Y
CONNECTICUT							
1 Daddario	?	Y	Y	?	✓	✓	?
3 Giaimo	N	Y	Y	Y	Y	Y	✓
5 Monagan	N	Y	Y	Y	Y	N	✓
6 Meskill	?	Y	Y	?	Y	✓	?
2 Steele ●					Y	N	✓
4 Weicker	?	Y	Y	?	Y	?	?
DELAWARE							
AL Roth	N	Y	N	Y	Y	N	Y
FLORIDA							
3 Bennett	N	N	N	Y	N	N	N
4 Chappell	N	Y	N	Y	N	Y	N
12 Fascell	N	Y	Y	Y	Y	Y	?
2 Fuqua	Y	Y	N	Y	N	N	N
6 Gibbons	N	Y	Y	Y	N	Y	?
7 Haley	N	N	Y	N	Y	N	X
11 Pepper	Y	Y	Y	N	Y	N	Y
9 Rogers	Y	Y	N	Y	Y	N	N
1 Sikes	Y	Y	Y	N	N	Y	X
10 Burke	N	N	N	N	Y	N	?
8 Cramer	‡	X	X	Y	N	Y	?
5 Frey	N	N	N	Y	Y	Y	?

GEORGIA	8	9	10	11	12	13	14
3 Brinkley	Y	N	N	Y	N	Y	N
7 Davis	Y	Y	‡	Y	N	N	N
6 Flynt	Y	N	N	?	N	Y	X
1 Hagan	Y	Y	Y	Y	N	Y	N
9 Landrum	Y	N	N	Y	N	Y	X
2 O'Neal	Y	?	?	Y	N	Y	N
10 Stephens	Y	Y	Y	N	Y	?	X
8 Stuckey	Y	Y	?	N	Y	N	N
4 Blackburn	Y	N	N	?	N	Y	X
5 Thompson	✓	N	N	Y	N	Y	N
HAWAII							
AL Matsunaga	Y	Y	Y	Y	Y	N	Y
AL Mink	Y	Y	Y	Y	Y	N	Y
IDAHO							
2 Hansen, O.	Y	Y	N	Y	Y	✓	✓
1 McClure	Y	N	Y	?	Y	N	?
ILLINOIS							
21 Gray	?	Y	Y	Y	Y	✓	✓
24 Price	N	Y	Y	N	Y	N	Y
23 Shipley	N	Y	Y	N	Y	Y	✓
16 Anderson	Y	Y	Y	Y	Y	Y	Y
17 Arends	Y	N	N	Y	Y	Y	?
14 Erlenborn	X	N	N	Y	Y	Y	Y
20 Findley	N	N	N	Y	Y	N	?
12 McClory	Y	Y	N	Y	Y	Y	?
18 Michel	Y	N	N	N	Y	Y	?
19 Railsback	Y	Y	N	Y	Y	N	?
15 Reid	Y	N	N	Y	Y	Y	Y
22 Springer	Y	N	N	Y	?	Y	?
Chicago-Cook Co.							
7 Annunzio	Y	Y	Y	N	Y	N	✓
6 Collins ●					N	N	?
1 Vacancy							
5 Kluczynski	Y	Y	Y	?	N	Y	✓
2 Mikva	N	Y	Y	Y	N	Y	✓
3 Murphy	Y	Y	Y	N	Y	N	?
11 Pucinski	N	Y	Y	N	N	N	Y
8 Rostenkowski	?	Y	Y	N	N	N	✓
9 Yates	N	Y	Y	Y	N	Y	?
10 Collier	N	N	N	?	X	‡	Y
13 Crane	N	N	N	Y	Y	N	?
4 Derwinski	N	N	N	Y	Y	Y	Y

	8	9	10	11	12	13	14
INDIANA							
3 Brademas	N	Y	Y	Y	Y	N	?
9 Hamilton	Y	Y	Y	Y	Y	N	Y
11 Jacobs	N	Y	Y	Y	Y	N	?
1 Madden	N	Y	Y	Y	Y	N	Y
4 Adair	N	Y	N	Y	N	Y	?
6 Bray	N	-	‡	Y	N	Y	?
10 Dennis	N	N	N	N	N	N	N
2 Landgrebe	N	N	N	N	Y	Y	Y
7 Myers	Y	N	N	‡	Y	X	N
5 Roudebush	?	?	?	?	Y	?	?
8 Zion	N	N	N	Y	N	Y	?
IOWA							
2 Culver	Y	Y	Y	Y	Y	N	Y
5 Smith	Y	Y	Y	Y	Y	?	Y
3 Gross	Y	N	N	N	N	Y	N
4 Kyl	Y	N	Y	N	N	N	N
6 Mayne	Y	N	N	Y	?	N	Y
7 Scherle	Y	N	N	‡	Y	Y	X
1 Schwengel	Y	Y	Y	Y	Y	Y	Y
KANSAS							
2 Mize	Y	Y	N	Y	Y	Y	?
1 Sebelius	Y	N	N	Y	N	Y	?
4 Shriver	Y	N	Y	N	Y	Y	?
5 Skubitz	Y	Y	N	Y	?	Y	?
3 Winn	Y	N	Y	Y	Y	Y	?
KENTUCKY							
2 Natcher	Y	Y	Y	Y	Y	Y	Y
7 Perkins	Y	Y	Y	Y	Y	N	Y
1 Stubblefield	Y	Y	Y	Y	Y	Y	?

Democrats   *Republicans*

● *Not a Member when votes were taken.*

	8	9	10	11	12	13	14
6 Watts	Y	Y	Y	Y	N	Y	N
5 Carter	Y	N	N	Y	N	Y	N
3 Cowger	N	Y	Y	‡	N	Y	?
4 Snyder	Y	Y	N	Y	Y	Y	X
LOUISIANA							
2 Boggs	Y	Y	Y	Y	X	Y	Y
3 Caffery	Y	?	?	Y	N	N	X
7 Edwards	Y	‡	‡	‡	?	?	X
1 Hebert	Y	✓	✓	‡	N	Y	X
8 Long	Y	-	‡	Y	N	Y	X
5 Passman	Y	-	-	N	?	Y	X
6 Rarick	Y	-	-	N	N	Y	X
4 Waggonner	Y	N	N	Y	N	✓	X
MAINE							
2 Hathaway	Y	Y	Y	Y	N	N	Y
1 Kyros	N	Y	Y	Y	N	N	Y
MARYLAND							
4 Fallon	✓	✓	✓	?	X	Y	?
7 Friedel	Y	Y	Y	Y	N	Y	?
3 Garmatz	Y	Y	Y	Y	N	Y	✓
2 Long	N	Y	Y	Y	Y	N	Y
6 Beall	N	N	N	?	Y	Y	Y
8 Gude	N	Y	Y	Y	Y	N	Y
5 Hogan	N	Y	N	Y	N	N	Y
1 Morton	N	N	N	Y	N	Y	?
MASSACHUSETTS							
2 Boland	Y	Y	Y	Y	Y	Y	Y
11 Burke	Y	Y	Y	Y	N	N	Y
4 Donohue	N	Y	Y	Y	Y	N	Y
6 Harrington	N	Y	Y	Y	Y	N	?
7 Macdonald	N	Y	Y	Y	?	N	Y
9 McCormack							
8 O'Neill	Y	Y	Y	Y	Y	N	Y
3 Philbin	N	Y	Y	?	N	Y	Y
1 Conte	N	Y	N	Y	Y	N	Y
10 Heckler	N	Y	N	Y	Y	N	Y
12 Keith	N	Y	N	Y	Y	Y	Y
5 Morse	N	Y	N	Y	Y	N	Y
MICHIGAN							
12 O'Hara	N	Y	Y	Y	Y	N	Y
18 Broomfield	N	Y	N	Y	Y	N	?
3 Brown	N	N	N	Y	?	N	N
10 Cederberg	Y	N	N	‡	N	Y	?
6 Chamberlain	N	N	N	Y	N	Y	?
2 Esch	N	Y	N	Y	Y	N	Y
5 Ford	Y	N	N	Y	N	Y	Y
8 Harvey	N	N	N	Y	N	?	?
4 Hutchinson	N	N	N	Y	Y	N	?
19 McDonald	N	Y	N	Y	N	N	?
7 Riegle	Y	Y	Y	Y	Y	N	Y
11 Ruppe	Y	Y	N	Y	?	N	?
9 Vander Jagt	N	N	N	Y	Y	N	Y
Detroit-Wayne Co.							
1 Conyers	X	Y	Y	Y	Y	N	Y
13 Diggs	X	Y	Y	Y	Y	N	?
16 Dingell	Y	Y	Y	?	✓	N	Y
15 Ford	N	Y	Y	Y	Y	N	Y
17 Griffiths	Y	Y	?	Y	N	N	?
14 Nedzi	X	Y	Y	Y	Y	N	✓
MINNESOTA							
8 Blatnik	Y	Y	‡	‡	✓	N	Y
5 Fraser	Y	Y	Y	Y	Y	N	Y
4 Karth	X	Y	Y	Y	Y	X	Y
7 Langen	Y	N	N	Y	?	N	?
3 MacGregor	Y	Y	N	Y	N	?	?
2 Nelsen	Y	N	N	‡	Y	Y	?
1 Quie	Y	Y	N	Y	Y	N	Y
6 Zwach	Y	Y	N	Y	Y	N	?
MISSISSIPPI							
1 Abernethy	Y	N	N	N	X	Y	X
5 Colmer	Y	N	N	Y	N	Y	N
3 Griffin	Y	Y	N	Y	N	Y	X
4 Montgomery	Y	N	N	N	N	Y	X
2 Whitten	Y	Y	N	N	N	Y	N
MISSOURI							
5 Bolling	‡	Y	Y	Y	Y	?	?
10 Burlison	Y	Y	N	Y	N	N	?
1 Clay	X	?	?	Y	Y	N	?
6 Hull	Y	‡	-	‡	N	Y	X
9 Hungate	Y	Y	Y	?	Y	N	?
8 Ichord	?	Y	N	?	N	N	N
4 Randall	Y	Y	N	Y	Y	Y	N
3 Sullivan	Y	Y	Y	Y	N	N	✓

	8	9	10	11	12	13	14
2 Symington	‡	Y	Y	Y	Y	N	?
7 Hall	Y	N	N	Y	N	Y	X
MONTANA							
2 Melcher	N	Y	N	?	N	N	Y
1 Olsen	Y	Y	Y	Y	N	N	Y
NEBRASKA							
2 Cunningham	?	X	X	Y	N	Y	?
1 Denney	Y	N	N	?	N	Y	?
3 Martin	N	N	N	Y	N	Y	X
NEVADA							
AL Baring	-	Y	Y	‡	N	?	X
NEW HAMPSHIRE							
2 Cleveland	N	N	N	Y	N	N	N
1 Wyman	N	Y	N	Y	N	Y	?
NEW JERSEY							
14 Daniels	N	✓	✓	Y	Y	Y	Y
13 Gallagher	?	Y	Y	Y	✓	N	✓
9 Helstoski	N	Y	Y	Y	Y	N	Y
3 Howard	N	Y	Y	Y	N	N	Y
11 Minish	N	Y	Y	Y	Y	N	Y
15 Patten	N	Y	Y	Y	N	N	Y
10 Rodino	N	Y	Y	Y	Y	N	Y
8 Roe	N	Y	Y	Y	Y	N	?
4 Thompson	-	Y	Y	Y	Y	N	✓
12 Dwyer	N	Y	N	Y	Y	N	✓
6 Forsythe •					Y	N	Y
5 Frelinghuysen	Y	N	N	Y	Y	N	Y
1 Hunt	N	N	N	?	N	N	N
2 Sandman	N	Y	N	Y	N	Y	?
7 Widnall	N	Y	Y	?	Y	N	Y
NEW MEXICO							
2 Foreman	Y	Y	N	Y	N	Y	?
1 Lujan	✓	N	N	?	?	N	?
NEW YORK							
41 Dulski	Y	Y	Y	Y	Y	N	✓
31 Hanley	N	Y	Y	‡	N	Y	?
5 Lowenstein	N	Y	Y	Y	Y	N	Y
39 McCarthy	-	Y	Y	Y	Y	N	?
25 Ottinger	N	Y	Y	Y	?	N	?
1 Pike	N	Y	Y	Y	Y	Y	Y
35 Stratton	N	Y	Y	Y	N	Y	Y
3 Wolff	N	Y	Y	Y	Y	N	✓
29 Button	N	Y	Y	?	✓	?	?
37 Conable	N	N	N	Y	Y	N	Y
28 Fish	N	N	N	Y	Y	N	Y
2 Grover	N	N	N	Y	N	✓	Y
38 Hastings	N	N	N	Y	Y	Y	N
36 Horton	Y	Y	Y	‡	Y	N	✓
30 King	X	?	?	‡	N	X	N
31 McEwen	N	Y	N	Y	Y	Y	N
27 McKneally	Y	Y	Y	Y	N	?	?
32 Pirnie	N	Y	N	Y	N	Y	Y
26 Reid	X	Y	Y	Y	Y	N	Y
33 Robison	N	Y	N	Y	Y	N	?
40 Smith	N	N	N	Y	Y	Y	Y
4 Wydler	N	Y	N	Y	?	✓	?
New York City							
7 Addabbo	N	Y	Y	Y	Y	N	Y
24 Biaggi	N	Y	Y	Y	N	N	Y
23 Bingham	N	Y	Y	Y	Y	N	Y
11 Brasco	X	Y	Y	Y	N	N	✓
15 Carey	N	Y	Y	Y	N	N	Y
10 Celler	Y	Y	✓	?	N	N	✓
12 Chisholm	N	Y	Y	Y	Y	N	✓
9 Delaney	N	Y	Y	?	Y	Y	?
19 Farbstein	N	Y	Y	‡	Y	N	?
22 Gilbert	N	Y	Y	Y	N	N	?
17 Koch	N	Y	Y	Y	Y	N	Y
16 Murphy	Y	Y	Y	‡	N	Y	Y
13 Podell	Y	Y	Y	Y	N	N	Y
18 Powell	?	Y	Y	?	?	X	?
14 Rooney	Y	✓	✓	Y	N	Y	✓
8 Rosenthal	N	Y	Y	Y	Y	N	Y
20 Ryan	X	‡	✓	Y	Y	N	Y
21 Scheuer	N	Y	Y	Y	Y	N	?
6 Halpern	N	Y	Y	Y	N	X	✓
NORTH CAROLINA							
2 Fountain	Y	Y	N	Y	N	Y	N
4 Galifianakis	Y	Y	Y	Y	N	N	N
3 Henderson	Y	Y	N	Y	N	Y	N
1 Jones	Y	Y	N	Y	N	Y	N
7 Lennon	Y	Y	N	Y	N	Y	N
6 Preyer	Y	Y	N	Y	N	X	Y

	8	9	10	11	12	13	14
11 Taylor	Y	Y	N	Y	N	N	N
10 Broyhill	Y	N	N	Y	N	N	N
9 Jonas	Y	N	N	Y	N	Y	N
5 Mizell	Y	N	N	Y	N	Y	N
8 Ruth	Y	N	N	?	N	Y	X
NORTH DAKOTA							
1 Andrews	Y	Y	Y	Y	Y	N	✓
2 Kleppe	Y	Y	N	?	Y	Y	?
OHIO							
9 Ashley	N	Y	Y	Y	Y	N	Y
19 Carney •					Y	N	Y
20 Feighan	Y	Y	Y	Y	N	Y	?
18 Hays	Y	Y	Y	Y	N	Y	Y
21 Stokes	N	Y	Y	‡	Y	N	Y
22 Vanik	N	Y	Y	Y	Y	N	Y
17 Ashbrook	N	N	N	N	Y	Y	?
14 Ayres	Y	Y	Y	Y	N	Y	?
8 Betts	Y	N	N	Y	N	Y	N
16 Bow	Y	N	N	?	N	Y	N
7 Brown	N	Y	N	Y	?	Y	Y
2 Clancy	N	N	N	Y	Y	Y	?
12 Devine	N	N	N	‡	Y	Y	X
6 Harsha	Y	N	N	Y	Y	Y	N
5 Latta	Y	Y	N	Y	Y	N	?
24 Lukens	Y	N	N	?	N	Y	?
4 McCulloch	Y	?	?	?	Y	Y	?
10 Miller	Y	Y	N	Y	Y	Y	Y
23 Minshall	N	Y	Y	Y	N	?	?
13 Mosher	N	Y	Y	Y	Y	N	?
11 Stanton	Y	Y	N	Y	Y	N	Y
1 Taft	Y	Y	N	†	?	Y	Y
3 Whalen	N	Y	Y	Y	Y	Y	Y
15 Wylie	Y	N	N	Y	Y	N	Y
OKLAHOMA							
3 Albert	Y	Y	Y	Y	N	Y	Y
2 Edmondson	Y	Y	Y	?	X	Y	Y
5 Jarman	Y	N	N	Y	N	Y	N
4 Steed	Y	Y	N	N	N	Y	Y
1 Belcher	Y	N	N	‡	N	Y	?
6 Camp	Y	N	N	?	?	Y	?
OREGON							
3 Green	Y	Y	Y	Y	N	N	✓
2 Ullman	Y	N	Y	Y	N	Y	?
4 Dellenback	N	Y	N	Y	Y	N	Y
1 Wyatt	N	N	N	Y	Y	Y	?
PENNSYLVANIA							
25 Clark	N	Y	Y	Y	N	Y	Y
21 Dent	X	Y	Y	Y	N	X	✓
11 Flood	N	Y	Y	Y	N	Y	Y
20 Gaydos	N	Y	Y	Y	N	N	Y
14 Moorhead	N	Y	Y	Y	Y	N	Y
26 Morgan	N	Y	Y	Y	Y	N	Y
15 Rooney	N	Y	Y	Y	N	N	Y
24 Vigorito	Y	Y	Y	Y	Y	Y	Y
6 Yatron	N	Y	Y	Y	N	N	Y
8 Biester	N	Y	N	Y	Y	N	Y
18 Corbett	N	Y	Y	Y	N	Y	✓
13 Coughlin	N	N	N	Y	Y	N	Y
16 Eshleman	N	N	N	Y	N	Y	Y
27 Fulton	N	Y	Y	Y	N	Y	Y
19 Goodling	N	N	N	Y	?	Y	N
23 Johnson	N	N	N	Y	N	Y	N
10 McDade	N	Y	N	Y	N	Y	Y
22 Saylor	N	N	N	?	N	N	?
17 Schneebeli	N	N	N	‡	N	N	N
9 Ware •					N	Y	Y
12 Whalley	N	N	N	Y	N	Y	N
7 Williams	N	N	N	Y	Y	Y	N
Philadelphia City							
1 Barrett	N	Y	Y	?	Y	N	✓
3 Byrne	N	Y	Y	Y	Y	N	✓
4 Eilberg	N	Y	Y	Y	N	N	Y
5 Green	N	Y	Y	Y	Y	N	Y
2 Nix	N	Y	Y	Y	Y	N	Y
RHODE ISLAND							
1 St. Germain	N	Y	Y	Y	N	N	✓
2 Tiernan	-	Y	Y	Y	N	N	Y
SOUTH CAROLINA							
3 Dorn	Y	Y	Y	Y	N	Y	Y
5 Gettys	Y	Y	Y	‡	N	✓	N
6 McMillan	Y	Y	Y	?	N	Y	X
4 Mann	Y	Y	N	Y	N	Y	N

	8	9	10	11	12	13	14
1 Vacancy							
2 Watson	Y	Y	Y	‡	N	Y	N
SOUTH DAKOTA							
2 Berry	Y	N	N	?	?	Y	?
1 Reifel	Y	X	X	‡	Y	X	?
TENNESSEE							
6 Anderson	Y	Y	Y	Y	N	N	?
7 Blanton	✓	Y	Y	Y	N	Y	N
4 Evins	✓	Y	Y	Y	N	Y	?
5 Fulton	✓	Y	Y	Y	N	Y	?
8 Jones	Y	Y	Y	Y	N	N	N
3 Brock	Y	N	N	‡	N	Y	?
2 Duncan	Y	Y	N	N	N	N	N
9 Kuykendall	Y	N	N	Y	N	Y	?
1 Quillen	✓	Y	N	Y	N	Y	?
TEXAS							
9 Brooks	Y	Y	Y	?	N	Y	?
17 Burleson	✓	Y	N	Y	N	Y	N
5 Cabell	Y	Y	Y	N	N	Y	N
22 Casey	✓	Y	Y	?	N	Y	Y
15 de la Garza	Y	Y	N	Y	?	Y	Y
2 Dowdy	Y	Y	Y	?	X	✓	X
8 Eckhardt	Y	Y	Y	Y	Y	N	Y
21 Fisher	Y	Y	N	Y	N	Y	N
20 Gonzalez	Y	Y	Y	Y	N	Y	Y
23 Kazen	Y	Y	Y	Y	N	Y	Y
19 Mahon	Y	Y	N	Y	N	Y	N
1 Patman	Y	Y	Y	?	N	Y	?
10 Pickle	Y	Y	N	‡	N	Y	Y
11 Poage	Y	Y	Y	?	?	Y	N
13 Purcell	Y	Y	Y	?	N	?	?
4 Roberts	Y	Y	Y	Y	N	Y	N
6 Teague	Y	Y	Y	N	✓	Y	X
16 White	Y	Y	N	Y	N	Y	Y
12 Wright	✓	Y	Y	Y	N	Y	Y
14 Young	✓	Y	Y	Y	N	Y	?
7 Bush	Y	Y	N	‡	N	N	?
3 Collins	Y	N	N	Y	N	?	N
18 Price	Y	N	N	Y	X	Y	N
UTAH							
1 Burton	Y	Y	N	‡	N	Y	?
2 Lloyd	Y	N	N	Y	N	Y	?
VERMONT							
AL Stafford	X	Y	N	Y	Y	N	?
VIRGINIA							
4 Abbitt	Y	Y	N	Y	N	?	X
5 Daniel	Y	Y	N	Y	N	Y	N
1 Downing	Y	Y	N	Y	N	Y	N
7 Marsh	N	Y	N	Y	N	Y	N
3 Satterfield	N	Y	N	Y	N	Y	N
10 Broyhill	N	Y	N	Y	N	Y	N
6 Poff	Y	N	N	Y	N	?	?
8 Scott	N	N	N	Y	N	Y	N
9 Wampler	Y	N	N	Y	N	Y	N
2 Whitehurst	Y	Y	Y	‡	N	Y	?
WASHINGTON							
7 Adams	N	Y	Y	Y	Y	Y	Y
5 Foley	Y	Y	Y	Y	Y	Y	Y
3 Hansen	Y	‡	‡	Y	Y	Y	?
6 Hicks	N	Y	Y	Y	Y	Y	?
2 Meeds	Y	Y	Y	Y	Y	Y	Y
4 May	Y	N	N	Y	Y	Y	?
1 Pelly	-	N	N	‡	Y	Y	?
WEST VIRGINIA							
4 Hechler	N	Y	Y	Y	N	N	Y
5 Kee	N	Y	Y	Y	N	✓	Y
1 Mollohan	Y	Y	Y	Y	N	Y	Y
3 Slack	N	Y	Y	Y	N	Y	Y
2 Staggers	N	Y	Y	?	N	Y	Y
WISCONSIN							
2 Kastenmeier	Y	Y	Y	Y	Y	N	?
7 Obey	Y	Y	Y	Y	Y	N	Y
5 Reuss	N	Y	Y	Y	Y	N	Y
4 Zablocki	N	Y	Y	Y	Y	N	Y
8 Byrnes	Y	N	N	Y	N	N	N
9 Davis	Y	N	N	Y	N	N	N
10 O'Konski	Y	Y	Y	Y	N	?	?
1 Schadeberg	Y	N	N	Y	N	Y	X
6 Steiger	Y	Y	N	Y	N	N	Y
3 Thomson	Y	N	N	Y	N	N	?
WYOMING							
AL Wold	N	N	N	‡	?	N	?

Democrats *Republicans*

•*Not a Member when votes were taken.*

SENATE VOTES ON ABM, VOLUNTEER ARMY, TROOP LIMITS, ELECTORAL REFORM, CLEAN AIR, SST, SOCIAL SECURITY

8. HR 17123. Military Procurement Authorization. Hart (D Mich.)-Cooper (R Ky.) amendment deleting $322.2 million from the bill for deployment of the Safeguard ABM system at Whiteman Air Force Base, Mo., and Warren Air Force Base, Wyo. Rejected 47-52: R 12-30; D 35-22 (ND 30-8; SD 5-14), Aug. 12, 1970. A "nay" was a vote supporting the President's position.

9. HR 17123. Military Procurement Authorization. Hatfield (R Ore.)-Goldwater (R Ariz.) amendment increasing military salaries and recommending the creation of a volunteer army. Rejected 35-52: R 20-18; D 15-34 (ND 14-17; SD 1-17), Aug. 25, 1970. A "nay" was a vote supporting the President's position.

10. HR 17123. Military Procurement Authorization. McGovern (D S.D.)-Hatfield (R Ore.) amendment limiting to 280,-000 the maximum number of U.S. troops in Vietnam after April 30, 1971, and providing for complete withdrawal of troops by Dec. 31, 1971, but authorizing the President to delay the withdrawal for a period up to 60 days if he found the withdrawal would subject U.S. troops to clear and present danger. Rejected 39-55: R 7-34; D 32-21 (ND 29-6; SD 3-15), Sept. 1, 1970. A "nay" was a vote supporting the President's position.

11. S J Res 1. Electoral Reform. Mansfield (D Mont.) motion to invoke cloture (cut off debate) on a constitutional amendment that would abolish the electoral college and substitute direct, popular election of Presidents. Rejected 54-36: R 21-18; D 33-18 (ND 30-2; SD 3-16), Sept. 17, 1970. A two-thirds majority (60 in this case) was required to invoke cloture. The President did not take a position on the motion.

12. HR 17255. Air Quality Standards Act. Gurney (R Fla.) amendment to Dole (R Kan.) amendment, eliminating time provision from the section allowing manufacturers to seek a one-year extension of the deadline for producing 90-percent pollution-free automobiles. (The Dole amendment, later rejected by a 32-43 roll-call vote, would have permitted congressional rather than judicial review of extensions of the deadline for producing low-pollution automobiles.) Rejected 22-57: R 16-17; D 6-40 (ND 1-28; SD 5-12), Sept. 22, 1970. The President did not take a position on the amendment.

13. HR 17755. Department of Transportation and related agencies appropriations, fiscal 1971. Proxmire (D Wis.) amendment deleting the $289.9 million in development funds for the supersonic transport (SST). Adopted 52-41: R 18-21; D 34-20 (ND 25-10; SD 9-10), Dec. 3, 1970. A "nay" was a vote supporting the President's position.

14. HR 17550. Social Security Act of 1970. Long (D La.) motion to recommit the bill with instructions to delete Title III—the trade act; Title IV—catastrophic health insurance; parts of Title V—welfare provisions, and the section providing for a veterans pension increase (already enacted separately). Motion agreed to 49-21: R 20-12; D 29-9 (ND 16-8; SD 13-1), Dec. 28, 1970. The President did not take a position on the motion.

- KEY -

- Y Record vote for (yea).
- ✓ Paired for.
- ‡ Announced for or CQ poll for.
- N Record vote against (nay).
- X Paired against.
- - Announced against or CQ poll against.
- ? Absent, general pair, "present" or did not announce or answer poll.

State / Senator	8	9	10	11	12	13	14
ALABAMA							
Allen	N	N	N	N	N	Y	Y
Sparkman	N	N	N	N	-	N	Y
ALASKA							
Gravel	Y	‡	Y	Y	N	N	?
Stevens	N	✓	N	N	-	N	?
ARIZONA							
Fannin	N	Y	N	N	?	N	?
Goldwater	N	Y	N	N	?	N	?
ARKANSAS							
Fulbright	Y	X	N	Y	N	Y	Y
McClellan	N	N	N	N	N	N	?
CALIFORNIA							
Cranston	Y	Y	Y	Y	N	Y	?
Murphy	N	✓	N	?	-	N	?
COLORADO							
Allott	N	N	N	Y	N	N	Y
Dominick	N	N	N	N	N	‡	?
CONNECTICUT							
Dodd	N	N	N	Y	N	N	?
Ribicoff	Y	Y	Y	Y	N	Y	N
DELAWARE							
Boggs	N	Y	N	Y	N	N	Y
Williams	N	Y	N	N	Y	Y	Y
FLORIDA							
Holland	N	N	N	N	Y	Y	Y
Gurney	N	Y	N	N	Y	N	Y
GEORGIA							
Russell	N	N	N	N	Y	N	?
Talmadge	N	N	N	N	N	N	Y
HAWAII							
Inouye	Y	‡	Y	Y	N	N	?
Fong	N	Y	N	N	N	Y	?
IDAHO							
Church	Y	Y	Y	Y	N	‡	?
Jordan	N	Y	N	N	Y	N	Y
ILLINOIS							
Stevenson						Y	Y
Percy	Y	N	Y	N	Y	?	
INDIANA							
Bayh	Y	N	Y	Y	?	Y	N
Hartke	Y	Y	Y	Y	N	Y	N
IOWA							
Hughes	Y	✓	Y	Y	N	Y	Y
Miller	N	N	N	N	Y	Y	Y
KANSAS							
Dole	N	Y	N	N	N	N	Y
Pearson	N	Y	N	Y	Y	N	Y
KENTUCKY							
Cook	N	Y	N	Y	N	Y	N
Cooper	Y	N	N	N	N	Y	N
LOUISIANA							
Ellender	Y	N	N	N	N	N	Y
Long	N	N	X	N	N	N	Y
MAINE							
Muskie	Y	N	Y	N	Y	Y	?
Smith	Y	N	N	Y	N	Y	N
MARYLAND							
Tydings	Y	N	Y	Y	-	Y	Y
Mathias	Y	?	Y	Y	?	N	N
MASSACHUSETTS							
Kennedy	Y	N	Y	Y	?	Y	N
Brooke	Y	Y	Y	Y	N	Y	N
MICHIGAN							
Hart	Y	Y	Y	Y	Y	Y	?
Griffin	N	N	N	Y	Y	Y	N
MINNESOTA							
McCarthy	Y	N	Y	N	Y	Y	?
Mondale	Y	N	Y	Y	N	Y	N
MISSISSIPPI							
Eastland	N	N	N	N	Y	N	?
Stennis	N	N	N	N	Y	N	Y
MISSOURI							
Eagleton	Y	N	Y	N	Y	Y	?
Symington	Y	Y	Y	Y	-	Y	?
MONTANA							
Mansfield	Y	✓	Y	Y	N	Y	N
Metcalf	Y	-	Y	Y	N	✓	Y
NEBRASKA							
Curtis	N	N	N	Y	N	Y	Y
Hruska	N	N	N	N	‡	N	Y
NEVADA							
Bible	N	N	N	N	N	N	Y
Cannon	N	X	-	X	?	N	Y
NEW HAMPSHIRE							
McIntyre	N	N	Y	Y	N	Y	Y
Cotton	N	N	N	X	Y	N	?
NEW JERSEY							
Williams	Y	Y	Y	Y	N	Y	Y
Case	Y	N	Y	Y	N	Y	N
NEW MEXICO							
Anderson	N	N	?	Y	N	N	?
Montoya	Y	?	Y	✓	N	✓	?
NEW YORK							
Goodell	Y	Y	Y	Y	-	Y	N
Javits	Y	N	Y	N	Y	N	N
NORTH CAROLINA							
Ervin	N	N	N	N	N	Y	Y
Jordan	N	N	N	N	N	Y	Y
NORTH DAKOTA							
Burdick	Y	Y	Y	Y	N	Y	✓
Young	N	N	N	N	Y	N	Y
OHIO							
Young	Y	Y	Y	Y	N	Y	Y
Saxbe	Y	X	N	Y	Y	N	N
OKLAHOMA							
Harris	Y	N	Y	N	Y	N	Y
Bellmon	N	N	N	Y	?	N	Y
OREGON							
Hatfield	Y	Y	Y	Y	Y	‡	‡
Packwood	N	Y	-	Y	Y	Y	Y
PENNSYLVANIA							
Schweiker	Y	Y	Y	Y	N	Y	N
Scott	N	Y	N	Y	N	N	N
RHODE ISLAND							
Pastore	Y	Y	Y	Y	N	Y	X
Pell	Y	N	Y	Y	?	Y	N
SOUTH CAROLINA							
Hollings	N	N	N	N	N	N	?
Thurmond	N	N	N	N	Y	N	Y
SOUTH DAKOTA							
McGovern	Y	Y	Y	Y	N	Y	N
Mundt	-	X	-	-	-	X	‡
TENNESSEE							
Gore	Y	N	N	Y	?	Y	?
Baker	N	Y	N	Y	N	N	Y
TEXAS							
Yarborough	Y	Y	Y	Y	N	N	Y
Tower	N	N	N	N	-	N	‡
UTAH							
Moss	Y	Y	✓	✓	-	X	Y
Bennett	N	N	N	N	Y	N	Y
VERMONT							
Aiken	Y	N	Y	N	Y	N	Y
Prouty	N	Y	N	Y	N	Y	Y
VIRGINIA							
Byrd, Jr.	N	N	N	N	N	Y	Y
Spong	N	N	N	N	N	Y	Y
WASHINGTON							
Jackson	N	N	N	✓	N	N	Y
Magnuson	Y	N	Y	✓	-	N	Y
WEST VIRGINIA							
Byrd	N	N	N	N	N	N	Y
Randolph	Y	N	N	N	N	Y	Y
WISCONSIN							
Nelson	Y	Y	Y	Y	N	Y	N
Proxmire	Y	Y	Y	Y	N	Y	N
WYOMING							
McGee	N	N	N	?	?	Y	?
Hansen	N	N	N	N	Y	Y	Y

Democrats   *Republicans*

• *Not a Senator when votes 8-12 were taken.*

MAJOR ISSUES: SST, FOREIGN AID, INDOCHINA WITHDRAWAL

Rejection by Congress of continued development of the supersonic transport (SST) aircraft, attempts in both houses to set a withdrawal date for the return of all U.S. forces from Indochina, curtailment of the foreign aid program in the Senate and congressional approval of greater powers for the President over the economy were among the most significant issues of the 1971 session decided by record votes. Efforts to override Mr. Nixon's two major vetoes of the year—on bills creating a far-reaching child care program and providing public service jobs for the unemployed—were defeated.

Eight of the 14 key votes in the House selected by Congressional Quarterly came on recorded teller votes—authorized by the Legislative Reorganization Act of 1970. For the first time in the history of the House, members in 1971 were recorded by name on amendments involving controversial issues such as the SST, school busing, anti-war amendments, the military draft, federal aid to higher education and greater government protection for consumers. As a by-product of this reform, participation by members in votes on these and other issues increased by about 100 percent over the previous year.

Senate Key Votes

1. SUPERSONIC TRANSPORT (SST). The Senate March 24, for the second time in less than four months, rejected an amendment to continue federal financing of the SST. The vote was 46-51. Although the House failed to go along with the Senate in 1970, the fate of the commercial aircraft became apparent in 1971 when the House on March 18 also voted to kill the project. The SST funds had been included in an amendment added by the Senate Appropriations Committee to a continuing resolution (H J Res 468) providing partial funding for the Department of Transportation. *(See House key vote 1.)* Voting against further funding for the SST were 34 Democrats and 17 Republicans: R 27-17; D 19-34 (ND 11-25; SD 8-9).

2. DESEGREGATION. During consideration of an Administration-backed bill (S 1557) to provide $1.5-billion in aid to desegregating school districts, the Senate rejected an amendment requiring nationwide integration of schools. Proposed by Abraham Ribicoff (D Conn.), the amendment would have eliminated the distinction between *de jure* segregation—the result of laws and the target of most enforcement action in the 1950s and 1960s—and *de facto* segregation—the result of other factors, such as housing patterns, which had not been declared illegal or unconstitutional by the Supreme Court. This *de jure-de facto* distinction had protected non-southern areas from vigorous efforts to desegregate their schools. Ribicoff proposed that every metropolitan area be required to have integrated schools by 1985 and authorized more than $20-billion in federal aid for desegregation purposes. The Senate rejected the amendment, 35-51,

with southern Democrats splitting 7-6 in favor of the amendment which, its advocates said, for the first time would have required desegregation throughout the North. R 7-32; D 28-19 (ND 21-13; SD 7-6).

3. MILITARY DRAFT. During consideration of the military draft extension bill (HR 6531—PL 92-129) the Senate by a six-vote margin defeated an attempt to extend conscription for one year instead of the two-year proposal backed by President Nixon. An identical one-year amendment was rejected in the House by a two-vote margin. *(See House key vote 2.)* White House "arm-twisting," as it was described by freshman Sen. Richard S. Schweiker (R Pa.), was partly responsible for the Administration victory. During the Senate's two-month consideration of the draft bill, White House lobbying turned critical decisions on the draft in favor of positions taken by the President on all but two amendments voted on. The Senate June 4 rejected the one-year extension amendment by a 43-49 vote. The breakdown was R 10-29; D 33-20 (ND 28-8; SD 5-12). The Senate adopted the draft extension bill June 24 and after a drawn-out conference with the House a two-year extension was signed by the President Sept. 20.

4. WITHDRAWAL FROM INDOCHINA-I. After the Senate had taken four roll-call votes June 22 on various proposals to withdraw all U.S. troops from Indochina, Majority Leader Mike Mansfield (D Mont.) offered a substitute amendment which the Senate adopted by a 57-42 vote. Adoption of the Mansfield amendment reversed a position established two weeks earlier by the Senate in rejecting a similar withdrawal measure. The June 22 vote also marked the first time a majority in either house had supported a congressional mandate calling for the withdrawal of U.S. troops from Indochina. The Mansfield amendment set a nine-month deadline for the complete withdrawal, pending the release of all U.S. prisoners of war. The President was strongly opposed to the amendment. Twelve Republicans and a majority of Democrats supported the amendment: R 12-32; D 45-10 (ND 35-2; SD 10-8).

5. PUBLIC WORKS JOBS. On June 29 President Nixon vetoed a Democratic-sponsored bill (S 575) authorizing $5.7-billion for public works projects and regional development. The President criticized the measure because it included a $2-billion program to create public works jobs which, he said, would be the most costly and least effective method of reducing unemployment. He did not criticize other provisions of the bill which authorized $1.8-billion for general and regional economic development and a slightly smaller sum for aid to Appalachia. The Senate sustained the veto July 14 by a 57-36 vote—five short of the two-thirds majority necessary to override it. Thirty-five of 41 Republicans voted to sustain the President's position: R 6-35; D 51-1 (ND 35-0; SD 16-1).

6. LOCKHEED LOAN GUARANTEE. The Administration won a major victory in the Senate Aug. 2 when its bill to authorize a federal guarantee of bank loans for the Lockheed Aircraft Corporation was passed by a one-vote margin on a 49-48 roll call. Lockheed, the nation's largest weapons producer for the Defense Department, needed the financing to go into production with a commercial airliner and to avoid bankruptcy. To gain support for the controversial bill, Senate supporters broadened the Administration's bill (S 2308) requesting authority to guarantee financing for Lockheed into a $2-billion guarantee program for failing major businesses. Three times the Senate refused to invoke cloture and shut off debate. But the Senate also rejected efforts to recommit or drastically change the bill. On July 31, the Senate agreed to take up a related bill (HR 8432) passed by the House the previous day. *(See House key vote 6.)* It authorized only a $250-million guarantee thus providing a test of strength on the Lockheed guarantee as originally proposed. On the final vote, the Senate passed the House bill without amendment. A majority of Republicans supported the bill: R 27-17; D 22-31 (ND 13-23; SD 9-8).

7. WITHDRAWAL FROM INDOCHINA-II. In three close roll-call votes Oct. 28, the Senate defeated an amendment requiring that funds authorized for U.S. forces in Indochina be spent only to complete the withdrawal of all troops from South Vietnam. The amendment, sponsored by Frank Church (D Idaho) and John Sherman Cooper (R Ky.), had been added to a foreign aid authorization bill (HR 9910) by the Senate Foreign Relations Committee. Republicans and southern Democrats, backed by the threat of a presidential veto, were successful in the effort to delete the Cooper-Church amendment 47-44: R 30-11; D 17-33 (ND 4-30; SD 13-3).

8. FOREIGN AID. In an action throwing doubt on the future of one of the cornerstones of U.S. foreign policy, the Senate Oct. 29 defeated by a 27-41 vote a House-passed foreign aid authorization bill (HR 9910). It was the first time either house had rejected a foreign aid bill since the program was established after World War II. The 14-vote margin by which the bill was defeated resulted from the merging of many, often conflicting, positions including opposition to the Vietnam war, concern over the U.S. economy and doubts about the effectiveness of foreign aid in achieving U.S. goals. Substantial majorities opposed to the bill among northern and southern Democrats offset a narrow majority of Republican votes for passage. Foreign military aid was a principal instrument of the Nixon Doctrine: R 19-15; D 8-26 (ND 7-14; SD 1-12).

9. TAX REDUCTIONS. By a one-vote margin, the Senate Nov. 15 sustained President Nixon's tax reduction guidelines by defeating 39-40 an amendment that would have increased business taxes while granting further individual tax cuts. The breakdown was: R 1-34; D 38-6 (ND 28-1; SD 10-5). The amendment, sponsored by Birch Bayh (D Ind.), was offered during floor consideration of HR 10947, a bill reducing business and individual taxes requested by the President on Aug. 15. The bill was passed by the Senate on Nov. 22. The amendment would have increased business taxes by limiting the effect of liberalized depreciation rules established in 1971 by the Treasury Department.

10. FINANCING OF PRESIDENTIAL CAMPAIGNS. With two key Republican defections, Senate Democrats Nov. 22 succeeded in adding an amendment to the Administration's tax reduction bill (HR 10947) creating a federal fund to finance presidential election campaigns. The vote was 52-47: R 2-42; D 50-5 (ND 37-0; SD 13-5). Debate on the campaign financing amendment, introduced by John O. Pastore (D R.I.), divided along party lines. Democrats pushed the plan, which allowed taxpayers to designate $1 from their annual federal tax payments to the presidential candidate of their choice, as necessary to free candidates from dependence on wealthy contributors. Republicans, whose party treasury was well-stocked, condemned the proposal as an attempt to rescue the debt-ridden Democratic party. President Nixon had threatened to veto the bill if the Pastore proposal was adopted. Republicans Charles McC. Mathias Jr. (Md.) and Clifford P. Case (N.J.) voted for the amendment, despite strong Administration opposition, after Pastore agreed to a Mathias modification allowing each taxpayer to designate which party's candidate would receive his contribution.

11. EUROPEAN TROOP CUT. The Senate Appropriations Committee in late November added to its version of the annual defense appropriations bill (HR 11731) a section which would have limited to 250,000 men the number of U.S. troops which could be stationed in Europe after June 15, 1972—a force reduction of about 50,000 troops from the existing level. The Senate rejected the committee amendment by a 39-54 vote Nov. 23: R 5-37; D 34-17 (ND 26-7; SD 8-10). Once before during the 1st Session of the 92nd Congress the Senate had rejected a proposal to reduce U.S. troops in Europe. On the earlier vote, which took place on May 19, the troop cut proposal was rejected by a margin of 25 votes; the Nov. 23 margin was 15 votes. On both occasions, the White House exerted heavy pressure on Senators to reject any ceiling on the number of troops to be stationed in Europe.

12. ECONOMIC STABILIZATION. The Senate Dec. 1 passed a bill (S 2891) extending the President's authority to control and stabilize wages and prices. The measure passed almost without dissent by an 86-4 vote: R 41-1; D 45-3 (ND 31-1; SD 14-2). The bill extended for one year, until April 30, 1973, the authority under which Mr. Nixon imposed the wage-price freeze Aug. 15 and established Phase Two of his new economic policy in mid-November. The legislation also extended his stabilization power to cover interest rates and corporate dividends. The Senate rejected most major amendments to the bill by substantial margins. It added provisions on existing labor contracts and confirmation of the chairmen of the primary stabilization bodies the President created and appointed. It required a federal pay raise and exempted the press and other communications media from the stabilization program; the latter provision was deleted in conference. The House passed a similar bill Dec. 10. *(See House key vote 13.)* Congress cleared the bill Dec. 14.

13. REHNQUIST NOMINATION. President Nixon won confirmation of his controversial nomination of Assistant Attorney General (Office of Legal Counsel) William H. Rehnquist to the Supreme Court early in December. A small, determined opposition within the Senate, led by Birch Bayh (D Ind.), who had headed the successful opposition to earlier Nixon Court nominees Clement F. Haynsworth Jr. and G. Harrold Carswell, failed to win more than 26 votes against the nomination. They charged that Rehnquist was insensitive to the rights of minority groups and that he was not sufficiently devoted to the constitutional safeguards of individual rights. The Senate voted 68-26 to confirm the nomination, with a majority of both Democrats and Republicans voting in favor of confirmation: R 38-3; D 30-23 (ND 14-21; SD 16-2).

14. CHILD CARE VETO. Senate liberals failed Dec. 10, 1971, in an effort to override President Nixon's veto of a $6.3-billion bill (S 2007) extending the Office of Economic Opportunity (OEO) for two years, establishing a comprehensive child care program and creating a National Legal Services Corporation to provide legal assistance to the poor. President Nixon vetoed the bill Dec. 9 because of objections to the provision establishing the child care program. In his veto message, the President said the bill's child care program demonstrated "fiscal irresponsibility, administrative unworkability and family weakening implications." The vote to override the veto obtained a simple majority, 51-36, but this was seven votes short of the two-thirds majority required to override a veto: R 10-29; D 41-7 (ND 33-0; SD 8-7).

House Key Votes

1. SUPERSONIC TRANSPORT (SST). The House for the first time voted in 1971 to end federal financing of the controversial supersonic commercial aircraft effective March 30. The House rejection of the SST was a major defeat for the Nixon Administration which, together with organized labor and industry, had lobbied intensely for $134-million in fiscal 1971 appropriations to continue development of two prototypes. But the Coalition Against the SST—an alliance of citizens and environmental groups—asserted the project was a potential threat to the earth's atmosphere and an economic waste and thus should be canceled. Congress first considered legislative proposals to terminate the SST project in 1964 but until 1970, when the Senate voted to delete $290-million in fiscal 1971 appropriations, development of the plane continued. Although the House and Senate late in 1970 reached a compromise funding level ($210-million through March 30), the project was killed when the House March 18, employing the new recorded teller vote procedure for only the second time, voted 217-204 to delete the SST funds through an amendment introduced by Sidney R. Yates (D Ill.) to a continuing resolution (H Res 468) containing funds for the fourth quarter of fiscal 1971 for the Department of Transportation. The vote breakdown on the teller vote was: R 85-90; D 132-114 (ND 110-54; SD 22-60). The SST was revised temporarily May 12 when the House approved an amendment appropriating $85.3-million to continue development work. The Senate, however, refused to follow the House decision, and the SST funds were dropped in a House-Senate conference on a fiscal 1971 supplemental bill.

2. MILITARY DRAFT. During consideration of the military draft extension bill (HR 6531—PL 92-129), the House came within two votes of adopting a one-year extension instead of the two-year proposal which was backed by President Nixon. The move to cut short the President's authority to draft men into the armed forces was rejected by a 198-200 recorded teller vote with 65 Republicans voting against the Administration and 105 supporting the President's position. Democrats voted for a one-year extension by 133-95 (ND 116-35; SD 17-60) on the March 31 vote. Proponents of the one-year extension said that, if adopted, their proposal would force a discussion of the draft and the Vietnam war during the upcoming election year. Opponents said the draft and the war were two separate issues and should not be confused by either legislators or voters. The House went on to pass the two-year draft extension bill April 1 and after belated Senate action it became law Sept. 28. *(See Senate key vote 3.)* The March 31 House vote was the first heavily lobbied vote of the year relating to the military.

3. EDUCATION FUNDS. Supporters of increased federal aid to education were rebuffed in 1971 when the House refused to add almost $729-million to the education appropriations bill (HR 7016) reported by the House Appropriations Committee. The package amendment, introduced by Rep. William D. Hathaway (D Maine) and backed by the Emergency Committee for Full Funding of Education Programs, would have added funds for a variety of aid programs. The emergency committee, a coalition of all major education interest groups which was formed in 1969, had been successful in increasing education funds that year—but President Nixon had vetoed the bill as too expensive and Congress had acquiesced in the veto. In 1970, the coalition also won increased funding; the President again vetoed the bill, but Congress overrode that veto. The threat of a third presidential veto was a major factor in the House rejection by a recorded teller vote of 188-191 of the Hathaway amendment. Only 14 Republicans voted for the amendment; 149 opposed it, while 174 Democrats voted for increased funding and only 42 opposed it (ND 138-7; SD 36-35).

4. WELFARE REFORM. The highlight of two days of debate on the Administration's welfare reform bill (HR 1) came on a recorded teller vote to delete Title IV of the bill—the controversial Family Assistance Plan calling for a federally guaranteed annual income of $2,400 for a family of four without any income. HR 1 would reorganize the nation's welfare system, increase Social Security benefits by 5 percent and liberalize Medicare and Medicaid programs. The amendment to delete Title IV, offered by Rep. Al Ullman (D Ore.), was rejected 187-234: R 83-93; D 104-141 (ND 45-116; SD 59-25). HR 1 was passed later the same day by a 288-132 roll-call vote. Though a majority of Republicans and Democrats voted against the amendment, many conservatives and liberals in both parties supported the amendment because they felt the bill was either too costly or inadequate to meet the needs of the poor.

5. CBS CONTEMPT CITATION. The House July 13, by a 226-181 roll call, adopted a motion by Rep. Hastings Keith (R Mass.) rejecting a resolution (H

Res 534) proposed by the Interstate and Foreign Commerce Committee recommending that the Columbia Broadcasting System and its president, Dr. Frank Stanton, be cited for contempt of Congress. On June 24, Dr. Stanton had refused to comply with a subpoena issued by the committee's Investigations Subcommittee requesting film and sound recordings edited from the network's controversial documentary "The Selling of the Pentagon." Although contempt recommendations in the past had been approved routinely, such congressional courtesy was disregarded as the House leadership, six committee chairmen, most liberal Democrats and freshman Representatives and some conservatives backed away from the request made by Harley O. Staggers (D W.Va.), chairman of the committee. A majority of members from both parties, including the leadership, voted for the motion to reject the resolution: R 95-76; D 131-105 (ND 108-46; SD 23-59). Six of 22 committee chairman voted for the motion, while ranking minority committee members split 10-12.

6. LOCKHEED LOAN GUARANTEE. By a three-vote margin, the House July 30 passed a bill requested by the Administration (HR 8432) authorizing a federal guarantee of $250-million in bank loans for the Lockheed Aircraft Corporation. The Senate cleared the bill Aug. 2. (See Senate key vote 6.) House backers of the controversial measure broadened it in committee to provide up to $2-billion in loan guarantees for failing major businesses. The bill was scaled back to $250-million on the floor by a series of amendments agreed to by the majority and minority leadership. Attempts to amend the bill significantly were defeated, including one, rejected by a 176-205 recorded teller vote, to limit any guarantee to 90 percent of the loan involved. The House passed the bill by a 192-189 roll-call vote. As in the Senate vote, Republicans provided the margin of victory for the Administration: R 90-60; D 102-129 (ND 55-95; SD 47-34).

7. EQUAL EMPLOYMENT OPPORTUNITY. Civil rights groups suffered a slap in the face in 1971 when the House refused to approve a bill giving the Equal Employment Opportunity Commission (EEOC) the power to issue cease-and-desist orders against discriminatory employers and instead adopted a measure giving the agency the right to bring suit in federal court against such employers. The cease-and-desist powers had been sought by civil rights groups ever since the EEOC was created in 1964 without enforcement powers. In 1970, the Senate had approved a bill giving the agency these powers—rejecting the court-enforcement approach endorsed by the Nixon Administration. The House Rules Committee had blocked action by the House in the 91st Congress. When the bill granting cease-and-desist powers (HR 1746) came to the floor in September 1971 as reported by the House Judiciary Committee, John N. Erlenborn (R Ill.) proposed the court-enforcement measure as a substitute. The House adopted the substitute by a recorded teller vote of 200-195, marking a narrow victory for the conservative coalition of Republicans—who voted 131-29 for the substitute—and southern Democrats—who voted 63-16 for it—over northern Democrats (6-150).

8. CONSUMER AGENCY. The most significant consumer bill to come before the House in 1971 was HR 10835, establishing an independent consumer protection agency. As reported by the House Government Operations Committee, the bill allowed the new agency to represent consumer interests in the formal proceedings of other federal departments and agencies and to intervene on behalf of consumers in certain court suits. Although the Nixon Administration had previously opposed any legislation setting up an independent agency, it backed the committee-approved version of HR 10835. Consumer advocates favored a strengthening amendment offered by William S. Moorhead (D Pa.) which would have allowed the consumer agency to intervene in more informal proceedings of other federal agencies and given it additional authority to act when government agencies refused to investigate consumer complaints. The Moorhead amendment was rejected Oct. 14 by a 160-218 recorded teller vote. Northern Democrats supported the amendment by a 131-23 vote, but the conservative coalition of Republicans (15-138) and southern Democrats (14-57) combined successfully to defeat the amendment.

9. WITHDRAWAL FROM INDOCHINA. At the time of this Oct. 19 vote, the Senate had twice adopted an amendment sponsored by Majority Leader Mike Mansfield (D Mont.) calling for the withdrawal of all U.S. troops from Indochina pending the release of U.S. prisoner of war. (See Senate key vote 4) The version the House voted upon called for a six-month withdrawal deadline. Once before, on June 28, the House had voted on a similar proposal; it was rejected by a 44 vote margin. Although the Oct. 19 vote was not a direct up or down vote on the Mansfield amendment, adoption of a previous question motion (prohibiting House conferees to the defense bill to accept the amendment) was tantamount to its rejection. The House adopted the previous question motion by a 22-vote margin on a recorded teller vote of 215-193. Although the White House disclaimed involvement in the procedural matters concerning the vote, the President and his aides lobbied heavily to defeat the withdrawal proposal. Thirty-three Republicans voted against the President: R 139-33; D 76-160 (ND 23-138; SD 53-22).

10. SCHOOL BUSING. A solid majority opposed to the use of forced busing of children to desegregate schools showed its strength in the House late in 1971 by adding strong anti-busing amendments to the higher education-desegregation aid bill (S 659). The new majority was formed by the alliance of oldtime busing opponents from the south, with non-southern Representatives whose constituents were now facing the prospect, or dealing with the fact, of busing. The North-South coalition added amendments 1) barring the use of federal education funds for busing and forbidding any federal pressure requiring the use of state or local funds for busing, and 2) delaying, until all appeals were exhausted, the effect of any federal court order requiring busing. The strength of the anti-busing sentiment was reflected in the vote on the latter amendment, proposed by William S. Broomfield (R Mich.), which was adopted by a recorded teller vote of 235-125. The amendment was backed by 129 Republicans and 106 Democrats,

56 of whom were from outside the South. Opposing the amendment were 108 Democrats, 18 from the South, and 17 Republicans.

11. SCHOOL PRAYER. An intense lobbying battle culminated in rejection by the House in November 1971 of a proposed constitutional amendment designed to undo the effect of Supreme Court decisions outlawing officially prescribed or backed religious observances in public schools. The amendment would have added to the Constitution the statement: "Nothing contained in this Constitution shall abridge the right of persons lawfully assembled, in any public building which is supported in whole or in part through the expenditure of public funds, to participate in voluntary prayer or meditation." Introduced by Rep. Chalmers P. Wylie (R Ohio), the amendment was brought to the floor of the House through a petition, signed by a majority of the House, discharging the Judiciary Committee from consideration of the proposal. The amendment was opposed by most major organized religious groups, which feared that it would open the door for government intervention in religious matters. The amendment received the support of a majority of members, 240-163, but this was 28 short of the two-thirds majority (268) needed to adopt a constitutional amendment: R 138-26; D 102-137 (ND 48-114; SD 54-23).

12. TAX REDUCTION. House members Dec. 9 got their only chance to go on record for or against President Nixon's tax reduction proposals when they agreed to a House-Senate conference report on the bill (HR 10947—PL 92-178) by a 321-75 roll-call vote: R 158-9; D 163-66 (ND 95-57; SD 68-9). The bill, requested by President Nixon Aug. 15 as part of efforts to stimulate the economy, reduced federal taxes for calendar years 1971-73 by an estimated $15.7-billion. Key provisions included a 7-percent business investment credit, repeal of the automobile excise tax, tax incentives for exports and acceleration of a scheduled increase in the personal income tax exemption. The House Oct. 6 had passed HR 10947 by voice vote under a closed rule that prohibited floor amendments. House approval of the conference report had been in doubt until conferees agreed to delay the effective date of a controversial presidential campaign financing plan until after the 1972 election. (See Senate key vote 10)

13. ECONOMIC STABILIZATION. The House Dec. 10 deleted from a bill (HR 11309) extending and broadening the President's economic stabilization authority a provision requiring payment of wage raises including retroactive payment where appropriate— agreed to in labor contracts signed before Mr. Nixon embarked on his new economic policy Aug. 15. By a recorded teller vote of 209-151, the House accepted instead an amendment by Robert G. Stephens (D Ga.) requiring payment of such raises only if they were already financed by price or tax increases or offset by productivity increases. R 141-13; D 68-138 (ND 13-119; SD 55-19). Other raises called for in existing contracts were left subject to the guidelines of the stabilization program; the retroactive payment of raises deferred by the wage-price freeze, which the guidelines had prohibited except in limited circumstances, was not required. The House went on to pass the bill the same day by a 326-33 roll-call vote. The final bill required a federal pay raise, Senate confirmation of the chairmen and new members of the wage and price stabilization bodies and majority rule on those bodies; none of these provisions was requested by the Administration. A House-Senate conference agreement softened the effect of Stephens' amendment by requiring payment of other deferred and scheduled pay raises unless they were unreasonably inconsistent with the Administration's stabilization guidelines.

14. WITHDRAWAL FROM INDOCHINA-ADJOURNMENT. In unexpected fashion, the House Dec. 16 broke a conference deadlock on a third version of the Mansfield amendment *(See House key vote 9.)* producing agreement on a foreign aid authorization bill and clearing the way for adjournment. The foreign aid bill accepted in revised form by the Senate after the Oct. 29 defeat of HR 9910 *(See Senate key vote 8.),* had been held up in conference by the refusal of House conferees to accept the Mansfield amendment. Majority Leader Mike Mansfield (D Mont.), sponsor of the amendment setting a policy of withdrawal from Indochina within six months, had insisted that House conferees accept the provision or permit the House to vote on it separately. The issue went down to the final day of the 1st Session of the 91st Congress. Foreign Relations Committee Chairman J. W. Fulbright (D Ark.) led efforts to hold up Senate action on a resolution providing interim foreign aid funds in order to force a House vote on the amendment. On Dec. 16, Rep. William F. Ryan (D N.Y.) offered a surprise motion to instruct House conferees to the foreign aid bill to accept the Mansfield amendment. House Foreign Affairs Committee Chairman Thomas E. Morgan (D Pa.) immediately offered a motion to table (kill) the Ryan motion. Morgan's motion was adopted 130-101: R 78-12; D 52-89 (ND 18-73; SD 34-16); 201 members did not vote. Mansfield interpreted the vote as expressing the House view on his amendment, and conferees reached quick agreement on remaining differences. The Senate Dec. 17 adopted the conference report; the House delayed action until after Congress returned Jan. 18, 1972.

- KEY -

- Y Record vote for (yea).
- √ Paired for.
- ‡ Announced for or CQ poll for.
- N Record vote against (nay).
- X Paired against.
- \- Announced against or CQ poll against.
- ? Not voting, voted "present" or did not announce.

	1	2	3	4	5	6	7
ALABAMA							
Allen	N	Y	N	N	Y	Y	Y
Sparkman	Y	Y	N	N	Y	Y	Y
ALASKA							
Gravel	Y	Y	Y	Y	Y	Y	N
Stevens	Y	N	Y	N	Y	Y	Y
ARIZONA							
Fannin	Y	N	N	N	N	Y	Y
Goldwater	Y	N	?	N	N	N	Y
ARKANSAS							
Fulbright	N	Y	Y	Y	Y	N	Y
McClellan	Y	Y	X	Y	Y	N	Y
CALIFORNIA							
Cranston	N	Y	Y	Y	Y	Y	N
Tunney	N	Y	Y	Y	Y	Y	N
COLORADO							
Allott	Y	?	N	N	N	Y	Y
Dominick	Y	N	‡	N	N	N	Y
CONNECTICUT							
Ribicoff	N	Y	Y	Y	Y	Y	N
Weicker	N	N	N	N	Y	N	N
DELAWARE							
Boggs	Y	N	N	N	N	Y	Y
Roth	N	N	N	N	N	Y	Y
FLORIDA							
Chiles	N	?	Y	Y	Y	N	Y
Gurney	Y	N	N	N	Y	Y	Y
GEORGIA							
Gambrell	N	N	N	Y	Y	N	Y
Talmadge	Y	N	N	Y	Y	Y	N
HAWAII							
Inouye	Y	Y	Y	Y	Y	Y	-
Fong	Y	N	-	N	N	Y	Y
IDAHO							
Church	N	Y	Y	Y	√	N	N
Jordan	N	N	N	Y	N	N	‡
ILLINOIS							
Stevenson	N	N	Y	Y	N	N	N
Percy	N	N	√	Y	N	N	N
INDIANA							
Bayh	-	Y	Y	Y	Y	N	Y
Hartke	N	N	Y	Y	Y	N	N

	1	2	3	4	5	6	7
IOWA							
Hughes	N	Y	Y	Y	Y	N	N
Miller	N	N	N	N	N	Y	‡
KANSAS							
Dole	Y	?	N	N	N	Y	Y
Pearson	Y	N	Y	N	Y	N	Y
KENTUCKY							
Cook	Y	Y	N	N	N	Y	Y
Cooper	N	Y	N	N	N	Y	N
LOUISIANA							
Ellender	Y	Y	N	Y	N	Y	Y
Long	Y	‡	N	N	Y	Y	Y
MAINE							
Muskie	N	Y	Y	Y	Y	N	N
Smith	N	N	N	N	N	N	Y
MARYLAND							
Beall	Y	N	N	N	N	N	Y
Mathias	Y	N	Y	N	Y	N	Y
MASSACHUSETTS							
Kennedy	N	Y	Y	Y	Y	N	N
Brooke	N	Y	Y	Y	?	N	N
MICHIGAN							
Hart	N	Y	Y	Y	Y	N	N
Griffin	N	N	N	N	N	N	Y
MINNESOTA							
Humphrey	N	Y	Y	Y	Y	Y	N
Mondale	N	Y	Y	Y	Y	N	N
MISSISSIPPI							
Eastland	Y	Y	N	Y	N	Y	Y
Stennis	Y	Y	N	Y	N	Y	?
MISSOURI							
Eagleton	N	N	N	Y	N	Y	N
Symington	Y	N	Y	Y	√	N	N
MONTANA							
Mansfield	N	Y	√	Y	Y	N	N
Metcalf	N	Y	Y	Y	Y	Y	N
NEBRASKA							
Curtis	Y	N	N	N	N	N	Y
Hruska	Y	N	N	N	N	Y	Y
NEVADA							
Bible	Y	N	N	Y	Y	Y	Y
Cannon	Y	N	N	Y	Y	Y	Y

	1	2	3	4	5	6	7
NEW HAMPSHIRE							
McIntyre	N	N	N	Y	Y	Y	N
Cotton	Y	N	N	N	N	Y	Y
NEW JERSEY							
Williams	N	Y	Y	Y	Y	Y	N
Case	N	Y	Y	Y	Y	Y	N
NEW MEXICO							
Anderson	N	Y	N	Y	Y	N	N
Montoya	N	Y	Y	Y	Y	N	N
NEW YORK							
Buckley [1]	Y	N	N	N	N	N	Y
Javits	N	N	Y	N	Y	N	N
NORTH CAROLINA							
Ervin	N	X	N	N	Y	N	Y
Jordan	-	N	Y	Y	Y	N	N
NORTH DAKOTA							
Burdick	N	N	Y	Y	Y	N	N
Young	Y	N	N	Y	N	Y	Y
OHIO							
Saxbe	Y	N	N	N	Y	N	Y
Taft	Y	N	N	N	N	N	Y
OKLAHOMA							
Harris	N	√	Y	Y	‡	N	X
Bellmon	Y	Y	N	N	N	Y	Y
OREGON							
Hatfield	N	Y	Y	Y	-	N	N
Packwood	N	?	Y	N	N	Y	Y
PENNSYLVANIA							
Schweiker	N	N	Y	Y	N	N	N
Scott	Y	N	N	N	N	Y	Y
RHODE ISLAND							
Pastore	N	N	Y	Y	Y	N	N
Pell	N	N	Y	Y	Y	N	N
SOUTH CAROLINA							
Hollings	Y	‡	N	Y	Y	Y	Y
Thurmond	Y	N	N	N	X	Y	Y
SOUTH DAKOTA							
McGovern	N	Y	Y	Y	Y	N	-
Mundt	-	-	-	-	-	?	?
TENNESSEE							
Baker	Y	Y	N	N	N	Y	?
Brock	Y	‡	Y	N	N	Y	Y

	1	2	3	4	5	6	7
TEXAS							
Bentsen	N	N	N	Y	Y	?	Y
Tower	Y	-	N	N	Y	Y	
UTAH							
Moss	Y	Y	Y	Y	Y	Y	N
Bennett	Y	N	N	N	N	N	Y
VERMONT							
Aiken	N	N	Y	N	N	N	N
Stafford [2]							N
VIRGINIA							
Byrd, Jr. [3]	N	N	N	N	N	N	Y
Spong	N	N	Y	Y	Y	N	N
WASHINGTON							
Jackson	Y	Y	N	N	Y	-	√
Magnuson	Y	?	Y	Y	Y	N	N
WEST VIRGINIA							
Byrd	Y	N	N	Y	Y	Y	Y
Randolph	Y	‡	Y	Y	Y	Y	N
WISCONSIN							
Nelson	N	‡	Y	Y	Y	N	N
Proxmire	N	N	Y	Y	Y	N	N
WYOMING							
McGee	Y	N	N	N	Y	N	Y
Hansen	N	N	N	N	N	Y	Y

Democrats   *Republicans*

1. *Buckley elected as Conservative*

2. *Sen. Winston L. Prouty (R Vt.) died Sept. 10, 1971. He cast the following key votes: 1, N; 2, N; 3, X; 4, N; 5, N; 6, Y. Sen. Robert T. Stafford was sworn in Sept. 17, 1971, to replace Prouty.*

3. *Byrd elected as independent*

1. H J Res 468. Department of Transportation Appropriations, Fiscal 1971. Adoption of the committee amendment to the bill restoring $134-million deleted on the House floor for continued development of two prototype supersonic transport (SST) aircraft. Rejected 46-51: R 27-17; D 19-34 (ND 11-25; SD 8-9), March 24, 1971. A "yea" was a vote supporting the President's position.

2. S 1557. Emergency School Aid and Quality Integrated Education Act. Ribicoff (D Conn.) amendment to the committee's bill authorizing an additional $1-billion for each of fiscal years 1974 and 1975 in desegregation aid and providing federal assistance for elimination of minority-group isolation in all metropolitan area public schools. Rejected 35-51: R 7-32; D 28-19 (ND 21-13; SD 7-6), April 21, 1971. A "nay" was a vote supporting the President's position.

3. HR 6531. Military Draft. Schweiker (R Pa.) amendment to the committee's bill extending the military draft for one year (to June 30, 1972), instead of two years as provided in bill. Rejected 43-49: R 10-29; D 33-20 (ND 28-8; SD 5-12), June 4, 1971. A "nay" was a vote supporting the President's position.

4. HR 6531. Military Draft. Mansfield (D Mont.) amendment in the nature of a substitute for modified Cook (R Ky.) amendment setting a 9-month withdrawal deadline if, within 60 days of enactment, American POWs had been released by North Vietnam—Declare it U.S. policy to terminate at the earliest possible practicable date all U.S. military activities in Indochina and provide for the phased withdrawal of all troops and the accompanying phased release of American POWs not later than 9 months after enactment. Adopted 57-42: R 12-32; D 45-10 (ND 35-2; SD 10-8), June 22, 1971. A "nay" was a vote supporting the President's position.

5. S 575. Public Works Acceleration and Regional Development Extension. Reconsideration and passage of the bill, vetoed by President Nixon June 29, authorizing $5,661,500,-000 for public works projects, economic development and Appalachian Regional Commission. Veto sustained 57-36: R 6-35; D 51-1 (ND 35-0; SD 16-1), July 14, 1971. A two-thirds majority (62 in this case) is required to override a presidential veto. A "nay" was a vote supporting the President's position.

6. HR 8432. Emergency Loan Guarantees. Passage of the bill authorizing a federal guarantee of $250-million in bank loans for failing major businesses (Lockheed Aircraft Corporation). Passed 49-48: R 27-17; D 22-31 (ND 13-23; SD 9-8), Aug. 2, 1971. A "yea" was a vote supporting the President's position.

7. HR 9910. Foreign Aid Authorization. Scott (R Pa.) amendment to the committee's bill deleting Cooper-Church provision prohibiting the spending of any funds authorized for U.S. forces in Indochina for any purposes except for withdrawal or protection of troops as they withdrew. Adopted 47-44: R 30-11; D 17-33 (ND 4-30; SD 13-3), Oct. 28, 1971. A "yea" was a vote supporting the President's position.

	8	9	10	11	12	13	14
ALABAMA							
Allen	N	N	Y	N	Y	Y	N
Sparkman	√	Y	Y	N	Y	Y	Y
ALASKA							
Gravel	‡	Y	Y	Y	Y	N	?
Stevens	N	-	N	N	Y	Y	Y
ARIZONA							
Fannin	N	N	N	N	Y	Y	N
Goldwater	?	N	N	N	N	Y	?
ARKANSAS							
Fulbright	N	Y	Y	Y	N	N	Y
McClellan	N	-	N	Y	Y	Y	Y
CALIFORNIA							
Cranston	N	Y	Y	Y	Y	N	Y
Tunney	X	Y	Y	N	Y	Y	Y
COLORADO							
Allott	Y	-	N	N	Y	Y	N
Dominick	N	N	N	N	Y	Y	N
CONNECTICUT							
Ribicoff	Y	X	Y	Y	Y	N	Y
Weicker	N	N	N	N	Y	Y	?
DELAWARE							
Boggs	Y	N	N	N	Y	Y	Y
Roth	N	N	N	N	Y	Y	N
FLORIDA							
Chiles	N	Y	Y	N	‡	Y	Y
Gurney	N	N	N	N	Y	Y	N
GEORGIA							
Gambrell	X	Y	Y	Y	√	Y	-
Talmadge	N	-	Y	Y	Y	Y	N
HAWAII							
Inouye	-	Y	Y	Y	Y	N	Y
Fong	Y	N	N	N	Y	Y	Y
IDAHO							
Church	N	Y	Y	‡	Y	N	Y
Jordan	N	-	N	N	Y	Y	N
ILLINOIS							
Stevenson	Y	Y	Y	N	Y	Y	Y
Percy	Y	N	N	N	Y	√	?
INDIANA							
Bayh	N	Y	Y	Y	?	N	Y
Hartke	?	√	Y	‡	-	N	Y
IOWA							
Hughes	-	‡	Y	Y	Y	N	Y
Miller	?	N	N	N	Y	Y	N
KANSAS							
Dole	N	N	N	N	Y	Y	N
Pearson	Y	N	N	N	Y	Y	N
KENTUCKY							
Cook	N	N	N	N	Y	Y	N
Cooper	√	N	N	N	Y	Y	N
LOUISIANA							
Ellender	X	-	Y	Y	Y	Y	N
Long	?	Y	Y	Y	Y	Y	?
MAINE							
Muskie	?	Y	Y	?	?	N	√
Smith	N	N	N	N	Y	‡	-
MARYLAND							
Beall	Y	N	N	N	Y	Y	N
Mathias	Y	N	Y	N	Y	Y	Y
MASSACHUSETTS							
Kennedy	√	Y	Y	Y	Y	N	Y
Brooke	Y	-	N	N	Y	N	Y
MICHIGAN							
Hart	Y	Y	Y	Y	Y	N	Y
Griffin	Y	N	N	N	Y	Y	N
MINNESOTA							
Humphrey	√	√	Y	N	Y	N	Y
Mondale	√	Y	Y	Y	Y	N	Y
MISSISSIPPI							
Eastland	N	N	N	N	Y	Y	N
Stennis	N	Y	N	N	Y	Y	N
MISSOURI							
Eagleton	?	Y	Y	Y	Y	Y	Y
Symington	N	Y	Y	Y	Y	Y	Y
MONTANA							
Mansfield	N	Y	Y	Y	Y	X	Y
Metcalf	√	Y	Y	Y	Y	N	Y
NEBRASKA							
Curtis	-	-	N	N	Y	‡	N
Hruska	-	N	N	N	Y	Y	N
NEVADA							
Bible	N	Y	Y	Y	Y	Y	Y
Cannon	N	Y	Y	N	Y	Y	Y
NEW HAMPSHIRE							
McIntyre	Y	Y	Y	Y	Y	Y	Y
Cotton	X	N	N	?	Y	Y	N
NEW JERSEY							
Williams	?	Y	Y	Y	‡	N	Y
Case	Y	Y	Y	N	Y	N	Y
NEW MEXICO							
Anderson	Y	N	Y	Y	Y	?	?
Montoya	N	?	Y	Y	Y	Y	Y
NEW YORK							
Buckley*	‡	N	N	N	Y	Y	N
Javits	Y	?	N	N	Y	N	Y
NORTH CAROLINA							
Ervin	N	N	N	N	Y	Y	N
Jordan	N	N	N	Y	Y	Y	Y
NORTH DAKOTA							
Burdick	N	Y	Y	Y	Y	Y	Y
Young	N	N	N	Y	Y	Y	N
OHIO							
Saxbe	N	?	N	?	?	Y	N
Taft	Y	N	N	N	Y	Y	N
OKLAHOMA							
Harris	Y	Y	Y	Y	N	N	√
Bellmon	Y	N	N	N	Y	Y	N
OREGON							
Hatfield	N	N	N	Y	Y	Y	N
Packwood	Y	?	N	Y	Y	Y	N
PENNSYLVANIA							
Schweiker	Y	N	N	Y	Y	Y	Y
Scott	√	N	N	N	Y	Y	N
RHODE ISLAND							
Pastore	N	X	Y	Y	Y	Y	Y
Pell	N	Y	Y	N	Y	Y	Y
SOUTH CAROLINA							
Hollings	X	Y	Y	Y	Y	Y	Y
Thurmond	X	N	N	N	Y	Y	N
SOUTH DAKOTA							
McGovern	X	‡	Y	‡	X	N	Y
Mundt	?	-	?	?	?	?	?
TENNESSEE							
Baker	Y	N	N	N	Y	Y	N
Brock	N	N	N	N	Y	Y	N
TEXAS							
Bentsen	N	Y	Y	N	Y	Y	Y
Tower	-	-	N	N	Y	Y	N
UTAH							
Moss	Y	Y	Y	Y	Y	N	Y
Bennett	Y	N	N	N	‡	‡	‡
VERMONT							
Aiken	Y	N	N	Y	Y	Y	N
Stafford	Y	N	N	Y	Y	Y	Y
VIRGINIA							
Byrd, Jr.**	N	N	N	N	Y	Y	N
Spong	N	Y	Y	N	Y	Y	Y
WASHINGTON							
Jackson	‡	‡	Y	N	Y	N	Y
Magnuson	N	Y	Y	Y	N	Y	N
WEST VIRGINIA							
Byrd	N	Y	Y	Y	Y	Y	X
Randolph	Y	Y	Y	Y	Y	Y	Y
WISCONSIN							
Nelson	X	Y	Y	Y	N	Y	N
Proxmire	Y	Y	Y	N	Y	N	Y
WYOMING							
McGee	√	Y	Y	N	Y	Y	N
Hansen	N	N	N	N	Y	Y	N

- KEY -

Y Record vote for (yea).
√ Paired for.
‡ Announced for or CQ poll for.
N Record vote against (nay).
X Paired against.
- Announced against or CQ poll against.
? Not voting, voted "present" or did not announce.

Democrats   *Republicans*   **Buckley elected as Conservative*   ***Byrd elected as independent*

8. HR 9910. Foreign Aid Authorization. Passage of the bill authorizing appropriations of $2,929,870,000 for foreign economic and military assistance programs in fiscal 1972 under the Foreign Assistance Act of 1961 and the Foreign Military Sales Act. Rejected 27-41: R 19-15; D 8-26 (ND 7-14; SD 1-12), Oct. 29, 1971.

9. HR 10947. Revenue Act of 1971. Bayh (D Ind.) amendment to the committee's bill reducing to 5 percent from 20 percent the variance from the life of assets permitted under the Asset Depreciation Range system and providing an individual tax credit of $25 ($50 for a married couple filing a joint return) for 1971 only. Rejected 39-40: R 1-34; D 38-6 (ND 28-1; SD 10-5), Nov. 15, 1971.

10. HR 10947. Revenue Act of 1971. Pastore (D R.I.) amendment (Title X)—as modified by Allen, Buckley and Mathias amendments and other amendments adopted by voice vote—Allow each taxpayer to designate $1 of his annual tax payment for a contribution to the campaign of an eligible presidential candidate or to a public campaign fund to be shared by eligible presidential candidates. Adopted 52-47: R 2-42; D 50-5 (ND 37-0; SD 13-5), Nov. 22, 1971. A "nay" was a vote supporting the President's position.

11. HR 11731. Defense Appropriations, Fiscal 1972. Adoption of the committee amendment to the bill adding a new section prohibiting the use of funds after June 15, 1972, for the support of U.S. military personnel in Europe in excess of 250,000 men (current troop strength was 300,000 men). Rejected 39-54: R 5-37; D 34-17 (ND 26-7; SD 8-10), Nov. 23, 1971. A "nay" was a vote supporting the President's position.

12. S 2891. Economic Stabilization Act Extension. Passage of the bill extending to April 30, 1973, the President's authority to stabilize the economy and expanding the executive power provided by the Act. Passed 86-4: R 41-1; D 45-3 (ND 31-1; SD 14-2), Dec. 1, 1971.

13. Exec Rept 92-16. Rehnquist Nomination. Confirmation of the nomination of William H. Rehnquist of Arizona as an Associate Justice of the Supreme Court. Confirmed 68-26: R 38-3; D 30-23 (ND 14-21; SD 16-2), Dec. 10, 1971. A "yea" was a vote supporting the President's position.

14. S 2007. Economic Opportunity Act Amendments of 1971. Reconsideration and passage of the bill, vetoed by President Nixon Dec. 9, extending the Office of Economic Opportunity (OEO) for two years through fiscal 1974, authorizing $6.3-billion for OEO programs, establishing a comprehensive child development program and creating a National Legal Services Corporation. Veto sustained 51-36: R 10-29; D 41-7 (ND 33-0; SD 8-7), Dec. 10, 1971. A two-thirds majority vote (58 in this case) is required to override a presidential veto. A "nay" was a vote supporting the President's position.

- KEY -

Y Record vote for (yea).
√ Paired for.
‡ Announced for or CQ poll for.
N Record vote against (nay).
X Paired against.
- Announced against or CQ poll against.
? Not voting, voted "present" or did not announce.

	1	2	3	4	5	6	7
ALABAMA							
1 Edwards	N	N	N	Y	Y	Y	Y
2 Dickinson	N	N	N	Y	N	Y	Y
3 Andrews	Y	N	N	Y	N	N	Y
4 Nichols	N	N	N	Y	N	X	Y
5 Flowers	N	N	N	Y	Y	Y	Y
6 Buchanan	N	N	N	Y	Y	Y	Y
7 Bevill	Y	N	‡	Y	Y	N	Y
8 Jones	N	N	?	Y	N	N	Y
ALASKA							
AL Begich	Y	Y	Y	N	Y	N	N
ARIZONA							
1 Rhodes	Y	N	N	N	Y	Y	Y
2 Udall	Y	Y	Y	N	‡	N	N
3 Steiger	Y	Y	?	Y	Y	N	Y
ARKANSAS							
1 Alexander	Y	N	?	N	Y	Y	?
2 Mills	Y	Y	Y	N	Y	Y	N
3 Hammerschmidt	Y	Y	Y	Y	Y	Y	Y
4 Pryor	Y	Y	?	N	Y	N	?
CALIFORNIA							
1 Clausen	N	Y	N	Y	N	Y	Y
2 Johnson	N	N	Y	N	N	Y	N
3 Moss	Y	Y	Y	-	Y	N	N
4 Leggett	N	Y	Y	N	Y	Y	N
5 Burton	Y	Y	Y	N	Y	Y	N
6 Mailliard	N	N	N	N	Y	Y	Y
7 Dellums	Y	Y	Y	Y	Y	Y	N
8 Miller	N	N	Y	N	N	Y	N
9 Edwards	Y	Y	Y	Y	Y	Y	N
10 Gubser	N	N	N	N	Y	N	?
11 McCloskey	Y	Y	‡	N	Y	N	N
12 Talcott	Y	N	N	N	Y	N	Y
13 Teague	N	N	N	N	Y	Y	Y
14 Waldie	Y	Y	‡	N	Y	N	N
15 McFall	N	N	Y	N	N	Y	N
16 Sisk	Y	N	Y	N	Y	N	Y
17 Anderson	N	Y	Y	N	Y	N	Y
18 Mathias	N	N	N	Y	N	Y	Y
19 Holifield	N	N	Y	N	N	Y	N
20 Smith	Y	N	N	Y	N	Y	Y
21 Hawkins	N	Y	Y	Y	Y	Y	N
22 Corman	N	Y	Y	N	Y	Y	N
23 Clawson	N	N	N	Y	N	N	?
24 Rousselot	?	Y	N	Y	N	Y	Y
25 Wiggins	N	N	N	N	Y	Y	Y
26 Rees	Y	Y	Y	N	Y	N	N
27 Goldwater	N	Y	N	Y	Y	Y	?
28 Bell	N	N	Y	N	Y	Y	Y
29 Danielson	Y	Y	Y	N	‡	Y	N
30 Roybal	Y	Y	Y	Y	Y	Y	?
31 Wilson	N	Y	Y	N	Y	Y	N
32 Hosmer	N	N	N	N	N	N	Y
33 Pettis	N	Y	N	Y	N	Y	Y
34 Hanna	N	Y	‡	N	‡	Y	N
35 Schmitz	N	N	N	N	N	N	Y
36 Wilson	N	N	N	N	N	N	Y
37 Van Deerlin	N	Y	Y	N	√	√	N
38 Veysey	N	N	N	N	N	Y	Y
COLORADO							
1 McKevitt	Y	N	N	Y	N	Y	Y
2 Brotzman	Y	N	N	Y	N	N	Y
3 Evans	Y	Y	N	N	Y	N	?
4 Aspinall	N	N	N	N	N	N	‡
CONNECTICUT							
1 Cotter	N	Y	Y	N	Y	N	Y
2 Steele	Y	Y	‡	N	Y	Y	N
3 Giaimo	N	Y	N	N	N	Y	N

	1	2	3	4	5	6	7
4 McKinney	Y	Y	N	N	Y	Y	?
5 Monagan	Y	Y	Y	N	Y	N	N
6 Grasso	Y	Y	Y	N	Y	Y	N
DELAWARE							
AL DuPont	Y	Y	N	N	Y	N	Y
FLORIDA							
1 Sikes	N	N	N	Y	N	N	Y
2 Fuqua	Y	N	Y	Y	Y	Y	Y
3 Bennett	Y	Y	N	N	Y	N	N
4 Chappell	N	N	N	Y	N	Y	Y
5 Frey	N	Y	N	Y	N	Y	?
6 Gibbons	Y	Y	Y	N	Y	N	Y
7 Haley	N	N	?	Y	N	N	Y
8 Young	N	N	N	Y	N	N	Y
9 Rogers	Y	N	Y	Y	N	N	Y
10 Burke	Y	N	Y	Y	N	Y	Y
11 Pepper	N	N	Y	N	‡	Y	N
12 Fascell	N	Y	Y	N	Y	N	?
GEORGIA							
1 Hagan	N	N	N	Y	N	Y	Y
2 Mathis	N	Y	Y	N	Y	N	Y
3 Brinkley	N	N	N	Y	N	Y	Y
4 Blackburn	N	N	N	Y	Y	Y	Y
5 Thompson	N	N	N	Y	N	Y	Y
6 Flynt	N	Y	?	Y	N	Y	Y
7 Davis	Y	N	‡	N	N	Y	Y
8 Stuckey	?	Y	Y	N	Y	N	Y
9 Landrum	N	?	N	Y	N	Y	Y
10 Stephens	N	N	N	Y	N	Y	Y
HAWAII							
1 Matsunaga	Y	Y	‡	N	Y	N	N
2 Mink	Y	Y	Y	N	Y	Y	N
IDAHO							
1 McClure	N	?	?	Y	N	?	Y
2 Hansen	N	N	?	N	Y	N	Y
ILLINOIS							
1 Metcalfe	Y	Y	Y	N	N	-	N
2 Mikva	Y	Y	Y	N	N	N	N
3 Murphy, M.	Y	Y	?	N	N	N	?
4 Derwinski	N	N	N	Y	N	N	?
5 Kluczynski	N	N	Y	N	Y	N	√
6 Collins	Y	‡	‡	Y	Y	Y	N
7 Annunzio	N	-	Y	N	Y	N	N
8 Rostenkowski	‡	N	Y	N	Y	N	N
9 Yates	Y	Y	Y	N	Y	N	N
10 Collier	Y	N	N	N	Y	N	Y
11 Pucinski	Y	Y	Y	N	Y	N	Y
12 McClory	N	Y	N	Y	N	N	Y
13 Crane	‡	Y	N	Y	Y	Y	Y
14 Erlenborn	N	N	N	N	Y	-	Y
15 Reid	N	N	N	N	*	Y	Y
16 Anderson	N	N	-	N	Y	N	N
17 Arends	N	-	N	N	N	Y	Y
18 Michel	Y	N	N	N	N	-	Y
19 Railsback	Y	N	N	Y	N	Y	?
20 Findley	Y	N	N	Y	N	Y	Y
21 Gray	N	Y	?	N	N	Y	N
22 Springer	N	N	N	N	N	N	Y
23 Shipley	N	Y	?	Y	N	N	N
24 Price	N	N	Y	N	Y	√	N
INDIANA							
1 Madden	Y	Y	Y	N	N	N	N
2 Landgrebe	N	N	N	Y	?	Y	Y
3 Brademas	Y	Y	Y	N	N	Y	N
4 Roush	Y	‡	Y	N	Y	N	N
5 Hillis	N	N	N	Y	Y	Y	Y
6 Bray	N	N	N	‡	N	X	Y
7 Myers	Y	N	N	Y	N	Y	Y
8 Zion	N	N	N	Y	N	?	Y
9 Hamilton	Y	Y	N	Y	N	Y	N
10 Dennis	Y	N	Y	Y	Y	Y	N
11 Jacobs	Y	Y	Y	Y	Y	N	N
IOWA							
1 Schwengel	Y	Y	N	Y	N	Y	N
2 Culver	Y	Y	Y	Y	Y	Y	N
3 Gross	Y	N	N	Y	N	Y	Y
4 Kyl	-	N	N	Y	N	Y	Y
5 Smith	Y	Y	Y	N	Y	N	N
6 Mayne	Y	N	N	Y	N	Y	N
7 Scherle	Y	N	N	Y	N	N	Y

	1	2	3	4	5	6	7
KANSAS							
1 Sebelius	N	N	Y	Y	Y	Y	?
2 Roy	Y	Y	Y	N	Y	N	Y
3 Winn	N	N	N	Y	Y	Y	Y
4 Shriver	N	N	N	Y	Y	Y	Y
5 Skubitz	N	N	?	N	N	N	Y
KENTUCKY							
1 Stubblefield	N	N	Y	N	Y	N	N
2 Natcher	N	N	N	Y	N	Y	N
3 Mazzoli	Y	Y	Y	Y	Y	Y	N
4 Snyder	N	Y	N	Y	N	?	Y
5 Carter	N	N	N	N	N	√	Y
6 Watts	N	N	N	Y	N	Y	Y
7 Perkins	N	Y	Y	N	Y	N	N
LOUISIANA							
1 Hebert	N	N	?	Y	N	Y	Y
2 Boggs	N	-	Y	N	Y	N	N
3 Caffery	Y	Y	N	Y	N	Y	Y
4 Waggonner	N	N	?	Y	N	Y	Y
5 Passman	N	N	N	Y	N	Y	Y
6 Rarick	N	N	N	Y	N	N	Y
7 Edwards	-	‡	‡	-	‡	‡	?
8 Long	N	‡	?	?	?	?	?
MAINE							
1 Kyros	Y	Y	Y	N	Y	N	N
2 Hathaway	Y	Y	Y	N	Y	N	N
MARYLAND							
1 Mills[1]				Y	Y	Y	Y
2 Long	Y	Y	?	Y	N	N	Y
3 Garmatz	N	?	Y	Y	N	Y	N
4 Sarbanes	Y	Y	Y	Y	Y	N	N
5 Hogan	N	N	N	Y	-	N	N
6 Byron	N	N	Y	N	Y	Y	Y
7 Mitchell	Y	Y	Y	Y	Y	Y	N
8 Gude	Y	Y	N	N	Y	N	N
MASSACHUSETTS							
1 Conte	Y	Y	N	N	Y	N	N
2 Boland	N	Y	Y	N	Y	N	N
3 Drinan	Y	Y	N	N	Y	N	N
4 Donohue	Y	Y	Y	-	‡	-	N
5 Morse	Y	Y	N	N	Y	Y	N
6 Harrington	Y	Y	Y	N	Y	N	N
7 Macdonald	Y	N	?	N	N	N	N

	1	2	3	4	5	6	7
8 O'Neill	Y	Y	Y	N	Y	N	N
9 Hicks	Y	Y	‡	N	Y	N	N
10 Heckler	Y	Y	?	N	Y	N	N
11 Burke	Y	Y	Y	N	Y	N	N
12 Keith	N	N	N	N	Y	Y	Y
MICHIGAN							
1 Conyers	Y	Y	Y	Y	‡	N	N
2 Esch	Y	Y	‡	N	Y	X	Y
3 Brown	Y	Y	-	N	Y	Y	Y
4 Hutchinson	Y	Y	N	Y	N	Y	Y
5 Ford	N	N	N	Y	N	Y	Y
6 Chamberlain	N	N	N	N	Y	Y	Y
7 Riegle	Y	‡	Y	N	Y	N	N
8 Harvey	Y	Y	?	N	N	N	Y
9 Vander Jagt	Y	Y	N	Y	?	?	?
10 Cederberg	N	N	N	N	Y	Y	Y
11 Ruppe	Y	Y	N	N	N	√	Y
12 O'Hara	Y	Y	N	N	N	N	N
13 Diggs	Y	Y	Y	Y	Y	-	N
14 Nedzi	Y	Y	Y	N	N	N	N
15 Ford	Y	Y	Y	N	‡	X	N
16 Dingell	Y	N	N	N	Y	N	N
17 Griffiths	Y	Y	N	N	Y	X	N
18 Broomfield	Y	N	N	Y	N	Y	Y
19 McDonald	Y	Y	N	N	?	Y	N
MINNESOTA							
1 Quie	Y	Y	N	N	Y	N	Y
2 Nelsen	N	Y	N	Y	N	-	Y
3 Frenzel	Y	N	N	Y	N	X	N
4 Karth	Y	Y	N	Y	N	Y	?
5 Fraser	Y	Y	Y	Y	Y	Y	N
6 Zwach	Y	Y	N	N	Y	?	N
7 Bergland	Y	Y	N	Y	N	N	N
8 Blatnik	Y	Y	Y	-	Y	N	N
MISSISSIPPI							
1 Abernethy	N	N	N	Y	N	Y	Y
2 Whitten	N	-	N	Y	N	Y	Y
3 Griffin	N	N	N	N	Y	N	Y
4 Montgomery	N	N	N	Y	N	Y	?
5 Colmer	N	N	-	Y	N	Y	Y
MISSOURI							
1 Clay	Y	?	?	Y	Y	X	N
2 Symington	Y	Y	Y	N	Y	N	N

1. H J Res 468. Department of Transportation Appropriations, Fiscal 1971. Yates (D Ill.) amendment deleting section of the committee's bill appropriating an additional $134-million in fiscal 1972 for continued development of two prototype supersonic transport (SST) aircraft. Adopted by recorded teller vote 217-204: R 85-90; D 132-114 (ND 110-54; SD 22-60), March 18, 1971. A "nay" was a vote supporting the President's position.

2. HR 6531. Military Draft. Whalen (R Ohio) amendment extending the military draft for one year instead of two as provided by the committee's bill. Rejected by recorded teller vote 198-200: R 65-105; D 133-95 (ND 116-35; SD 17-60), March 31, 1971. A "nay" was a vote supporting the President's position.

3. HR 7016. Office of Education Appropriations, Fiscal 1972. Hathaway (D Maine) amendment to the committee's bill adding $728.6-million for education programs. Rejected by recorded teller vote 188-191: R 14-149; D 174-42 (ND 138-7; SD 36-35), April 7, 1971.

4. HR 1. Welfare-Social Security. Ullman (D Ore.) motion to delete the Family Assistance Plan provisions (Title IV) from the bill. Rejected by recorded teller vote 187-234: R 83-93; D 104-141 (ND 45-116; SD 59-25), June 22, 1971. A "nay" was a vote supporting the President's position.

Did not vote due to possible conflict-of-interest.
1. Rep. William O. Mills (R Md.) sworn in May 27, 1971, to replace Rep. Rogers C. B. Morton (R), resigned.

Democrats   Republicans

	1	2	3	4	5	6	7
3 Sullivan	Y	N	Y	Y	Y	N	?
4 Randall	N	N	Y	Y	Y	N	N
5 Bolling	Y	Y	Y	N	Y	Y	
6 Hull	N	N	N	Y	N	N	Y
7 Hall	N	-	N	Y	N	N	N
8 Ichord	N	N	Y	N	N	N	Y
9 Hungate	Y	Y	Y	Y	Y	-	N
10 Burlison	Y	N	Y	N	Y	N	N
MONTANA							
1 Shoup	Y	N	N	Y	N	N	?
2 Melcher	Y	Y	Y	N	Y	N	N
NEBRASKA							
1 Thone	Y	Y	N	N	Y	N	Y
2 McCollister	Y	N	Y	Y	Y	Y	Y
3 Martin	N	N	N	Y	N	Y	Y
NEVADA							
AL Baring	N	N	Y	Y	‡	Y	Y
NEW HAMPSHIRE							
1 Wyman	N	N	N	Y	Y	?	Y
2 Cleveland	Y	Y	N	Y	N	N	Y
NEW JERSEY							
1 Hunt	Y	N	N	Y	N	Y	Y
2 Sandman	N	Y	N	N	N	Y	Y
3 Howard	Y	Y	Y	N	Y	N	N
4 Thompson	Y	Y	‡	N	Y	N	N
5 Frelinghuysen	Y	N	N	N	Y	Y	Y
6 Forsythe	Y	Y	N	N	Y	Y	Y
7 Widnall	Y	Y	N	N	Y	Y	?
8 Roe	N	Y	‡	Y	Y	N	N
9 Helstoski	Y	Y	Y	Y	Y	N	N
10 Rodino	Y	?	Y	N	Y	N	N
11 Minish	Y	Y	Y	N	Y	N	N
12 Dwyer	Y	Y	‡	Y	Y	Y	?
13 Gallagher	Y	N	?	N	N	Y	N
14 Daniels	N	Y	Y	N	‡	Y	N
15 Patten	Y	N	Y	N	Y	Y	N
NEW MEXICO							
1 Lujan	Y	N	N	Y	N	N	Y
2 Runnels	Y	N	Y	?	N	N	Y
NEW YORK							
1 Pike	Y	Y	Y	Y	N	N	N
2 Grover	N	Y	-	Y	Y	✓	Y
3 Wolff	Y	Y	Y	N	Y	N	N

	1	2	3	4	5	6	7
4 Wydler	Y	Y	N	N	N	Y	N
5 Lent	Y	N	N	Y	Y	Y	Y
6 Halpern	Y	Y	Y	N	Y	Y	N
7 Addabbo	Y	Y	Y	Y	Y	N	N
8 Rosenthal	Y	Y	N	Y	N	Y	N
9 Delaney	N	N	?	Y	N	N	N
10 Celler	Y	Y	Y	Y	N	Y	N
11 Brasco	Y	Y	Y	N	N	Y	N
12 Chisholm	Y	N	Y	Y	Y	Y	N
13 Podell	Y	Y	Y	N	N	N	N
14 Rooney	N	N	Y	N	N	Y	N
15 Carey	Y	?	N	Y	N	Y	N
16 Murphy	N	N	Y	N	N	N	N
17 Koch	Y	‡	Y	N	Y	N	N
18 Rangel	Y	Y	Y	Y	Y	N	N
19 Abzug	Y	Y	Y	Y	Y	N	N
20 Ryan	Y	Y	Y	Y	Y	N	N
21 Badillo	Y	Y	Y	Y	Y	N	N
22 Scheuer	Y	Y	Y	Y	Y	N	N
23 Bingham	Y	Y	Y	Y	Y	N	N
24 Biaggi	Y	Y	Y	N	Y	N	N
25 Peyser	N	N	N	Y	N	N	N
26 Reid	Y	Y	Y	Y	Y	N	N
27 Dow	Y	Y	Y	Y	Y	N	N
28 Fish	Y	Y	Y	N	Y	N	N
29 Stratton	N	N	Y	?	N	N	N
30 King	Y	N	N	N	N	*	Y
31 McEwen	N	N	N	Y	N	Y	?
32 Pirnie	N	N	N	N	Y	Y	Y
33 Robison	Y	N	N	Y	N	Y	Y
34 Terry	N	N	N	Y	Y	Y	Y
35 Hanley	Y	Y	Y	N	N	Y	N
36 Horton	Y	Y	Y	N	Y	X	N
37 Conable	Y	N	N	N	Y	Y	Y
38 Hastings	Y	Y	N	Y	N	-	?
39 Kemp	N	N	N	Y	Y	Y	Y
40 Smith	Y	N	N	Y	Y	Y	Y
41 Dulski	Y	Y	Y	N	N	N	N
NORTH CAROLINA							
1 Jones	‡	N	Y	N	Y	N	N
2 Fountain	N	N	N	Y	N	N	Y
3 Henderson	N	N	N	Y	N	N	Y
4 Galifianakis	Y	Y	Y	N	Y	N	Y
5 Mizell	N	N	N	Y	N	Y	Y

	1	2	3	4	5	6	7
6 Preyer	Y	N	Y	N	Y	N	Y
7 Lennon	N	N	N	Y	N	N	Y
8 Ruth	Y	N	N	Y	N	N	Y
9 Jonas	N	N	N	Y	N	?	Y
10 Broyhill	Y	N	N	Y	N	N	Y
11 Taylor	Y	N	Y	?	Y	N	Y
NORTH DAKOTA							
1 Andrews	Y	Y	N	N	Y	N	N
2 Link	Y	Y	Y	N	Y	N	N
OHIO							
1 Keating	N	Y	N	N	Y	N	Y
2 Clancy	N	N	N	Y	N	N	Y
3 Whalen	N	Y	N	N	Y	N	N
4 McCulloch	?	?	?	?	?	?	?
5 Latta	Y	N	N	N	Y	N	Y
6 Harsha	N	?	N	N	Y	N	Y
7 Brown	N	N	N	N	Y	Y	?
8 Betts	N	N	N	N	N	Y	Y
9 Ashley	Y	Y	‡	N	Y	N	N
10 Miller	N	N	N	Y	N	N	N
11 Stanton	Y	Y	Y	N	Y	N	N
12 Devine	N	N	N	Y	N	X	Y
13 Mosher	Y	Y	N	N	Y	N	N
14 Seiberling	Y	Y	‡	N	Y	N	?
15 Wylie	Y	N	N	N	N	Y	Y
16 Bow	N	N	N	Y	Y	✓	Y
17 Ashbrook	N	N	N	‡	N	Y	Y
18 Hays	N	Y	Y	Y	N	‡	N
19 Carney	N	Y	Y	N	Y	N	N
20 Stanton	Y	Y	Y	N	Y	N	N
21 Stokes	Y	Y	Y	Y	Y	N	?
22 Vanik	Y	‡	Y	N	Y	N	N
23 Minshall	Y	N	‡	Y	N	Y	Y
24 Powell	N	N	Y	N	N	Y	N
OKLAHOMA							
1 Belcher	N	N	N	Y	N	Y	Y
2 Edmondson	N	N	N	Y	N	N	N
3 Albert	N	N	N			N	
4 Steed	N	N	Y	N	N	Y	N
5 Jarman	N	-	N	Y	N	?	
6 Camp	N	N	N	Y	N	N	Y
OREGON							
1 Wyatt	N	‡	N	N	Y	N	Y
2 Ullman	N	?	Y	Y	N	Y	N
3 Green	Y	Y	-	Y	?	N	N
4 Dellenback	Y	Y	N	N	?	X	Y
PENNSYLVANIA							
1 Barrett	?	?	Y	Y	Y	N	N
2 Nix	N	Y	Y	Y	Y	N	N
3 Byrne	N	?	Y	Y	Y	N	N
4 Eilberg	N	Y	Y	Y	Y	N	N
5 Green	?	?	?	N	Y	N	N
6 Yatron	Y	Y	‡	N	Y	-	N
7 Williams	N	N	N	Y	N	Y	Y
8 Biester	Y	Y	Y	N	Y	N	N
9 Ware	N	N	N	N	N	Y	Y
10 McDade	N	Y	N	N	Y	N	N
11 Flood	N	N	N	N	N	Y	N
12 Whalley	N	N	N	Y	N	‡	Y
13 Coughlin	Y	Y	N	N	Y	N	N
14 Moorhead	Y	Y	Y	N	Y	N	N
15 Rooney	Y	Y	Y	N	N	Y	N
16 Eshleman	Y	N	N	Y	N	Y	?
17 Schneebeli	Y	Y	N	N	N	N	Y
18 Corbett²	Y	?	N				
19 Goodling	Y	N	N	Y	N	N	Y
20 Gaydos	Y	Y	Y	N	Y	N	N
21 Dent	Y	Y	Y	-	N	✓	N
22 Saylor	Y	N	N	Y	N	-	N
23 Johnson	N	N	N	Y	Y	✓	?
24 Vigorito	N	N	N	Y	N	Y	N
25 Clark	N	?	Y	Y	N	?	?
26 Morgan	N	N	N	Y	N	N	N
27 Fulton	N	Y	Y	Y	Y	N	N
RHODE ISLAND							
1 St Germain	Y	Y	Y	N	Y	N	N
2 Tiernan	Y	Y	Y	N	Y	N	N
SOUTH CAROLINA							
1 Davis³				Y	N	Y	N
2 Spence	N	N	N	Y	N	✓	N
3 Dorn	?	N	Y	N	N	Y	Y
4 Mann	N	N	N	Y	N	N	Y

	1	2	3	4	5	6	7
5 Gettys	N	-	Y	Y	N	Y	Y
6 McMillan	N	?	N	Y	N	Y	Y
SOUTH DAKOTA							
1 Denholm	Y	Y	Y	Y	Y	N	N
2 Abourezk	Y	Y	Y	Y	Y	N	N
TENNESSEE							
1 Quillen	N	N	Y	Y	N	-	Y
2 Duncan	Y	Y	N	Y	Y	Y	Y
3 Baker	N	N	N	Y	N	Y	Y
4 Evins	Y	N	-	N	N	Y	Y
5 Fulton	Y	Y	N	Y	Y	Y	N
6 Anderson	Y	Y	N	Y	Y	Y	?
7 Blanton	N	Y	Y	N	Y	N	N
8 Jones	Y	N	‡	Y	Y	X	Y
9 Kuykendall	N	-	N	N	N	Y	Y
TEXAS							
1 Patman	Y	N	Y	N	Y	Y	Y
2 Dowdy	?	?	?	Y	N	?	Y
3 Collins	N	Y	N	Y	N	Y	Y
4 Roberts	N	N	N	Y	N	Y	Y
5 Cabell	N	N	N	Y	N	Y	Y
6 Teague	N	N	N	Y	N	Y	N
7 Archer	N	Y	N	N	N	Y	N
8 Eckhardt	Y	Y	Y	N	Y	N	N
9 Brooks	Y	N	Y	Y	Y	X	N
10 Pickle	N	N	Y	Y	N	N	Y
11 Poage	N	?	N	Y	N	?	Y
12 Wright	N	N	N	N	N	Y	Y
13 Purcell	N	N	N	‡	-	Y	Y
14 Young	N	?	N	Y	N	Y	Y
15 de la Garza	Y	N	Y	N	N	N	N
16 White	N	N	Y	N	N	Y	Y
17 Burleson	N	N	N	Y	N	Y	Y
18 Price	N	N	N	Y	N	Y	Y
19 Mahon	N	N	N	Y	N	N	N
20 Gonzalez	N	Y	Y	N	N	N	N
21 Fisher	N	N	N	Y	N	Y	Y
22 Casey	N	N	N	Y	N	Y	Y
23 Kazen	N	N	Y	N	Y	N	N
UTAH							
1 McKay	N	Y	?	N	Y	N	N
2 Lloyd	N	Y	N	Y	N	Y	Y
VERMONT							
AL Stafford	Y	Y	N	N	Y	✓	?
VIRGINIA							
1 Downing	N	N	N	Y	N	Y	Y
2 Whitehurst	N	N	Y	Y	Y	Y	Y
3 Satterfield	N	N	N	Y	N	N	Y
4 Abbitt	N	N	N	Y	N	N	Y
5 Daniel	N	N	N	Y	N	N	Y
6 Poff	Y	N	N	Y	N	Y	Y
7 Robinson	N	N	N	Y	N	Y	Y
8 Scott	N	Y	N	Y	N	N	Y
9 Wampler	Y	N	N	Y	N	Y	Y
10 Broyhill	Y	N	‡	Y	N	Y	Y
WASHINGTON							
1 Pelly	N	N	N	N	Y	N	Y
2 Meeds	N	?	Y	N	Y	N	N
3 Hansen	N	N	‡	N	‡	Y	?
4 McCormack	N	Y	N	N	Y	N	N
5 Foley	N	Y	N	Y	N	-	N
6 Hicks	N	Y	N	N	N	N	N
7 Adams	N	Y	N	Y	N	Y	N
WEST VIRGINIA							
1 Mollohan	N	N	Y	N	Y	N	?
2 Staggers	N	N	Y	?	N	Y	?
3 Slack	N	N	N	N	N	N	N
4 Hechler	Y	Y	N	N	N	Y	N
5 Kee	N	N	Y	N	N	✓	N
WISCONSIN							
1 Aspin	Y	Y	Y	N	Y	N	N
2 Kastenmeier	Y	Y	Y	N	Y	N	N
3 Thomson	Y	N	N	N	Y	N	Y
4 Zablocki	N	N	N	Y	N	Y	N
5 Reuss	Y	Y	Y	N	Y	N	N
6 Steiger	Y	Y	N	Y	N	Y	N
7 Obey	Y	Y	Y	N	Y	N	N
8 Byrnes	Y	N	N	N	N	Y	Y
9 Davis	Y	N	N	N	N	Y	Y
10 O'Konski	N	N	Y	N	*	Y	N
WYOMING							
AL Roncalio	Y	Y	Y	N	Y	N	N

5. H Res 534. CBS Contempt Resolution. Keith (R Mass.) motion to recommit (kill) a resolution, reported by the Interstate and Foreign Commerce Committee, citing the Columbia Broadcasting System (CBS) and its president, Dr. Frank Stanton, for contempt of Congress for refusing to provide certain film edited from the television program "The Selling of the Pentagon" to the committee's Investigations Subcommittee. Motion adopted 226-181: R 95-76; D 131-105 (ND 108-46; SD 23-59), July 13, 1971.

6. HR 8432. Emergency Loan Guarantees. Passage of the bill authorizing a federal guarantee of bank loans for failing major businesses (Lockheed Aircraft Corporation). Passed 192-189: R 90-60; D 102-129 (ND 55-95; SD 47-34), July 30, 1971. A "yea" was a vote supporting the President's position.

7. HR 1746. Equal Employment Opportunities Enforcement Act. Erlenborn (R Ill.) amendment in the nature of a substitute bill providing authority for the Equal Employment Opportunity Commission to bring suit against recalcitrant discriminatory employers in federal court. Adopted by recorded teller vote 200-195: R 131-29; D 69-166 (ND 6-150; SD 63-16), Sept. 16, 1971. A "yea" was a vote supporting the President's position.

* Did not vote due to possible conflict-of-interest.
2. Rep. Robert J. Corbett (R Pa.) died April 25, 1971.
3. Rep. Mendel J. Davis (D S.C.) sworn in April 29, 1971, to replace Rep. L. Mendel Rivers (D), deceased.

- KEY -

Y Record vote for (yea).
√ Paired for.
‡ Announced for or CQ poll for.
N Record vote against (nay).
X Paired against.
- Announced against or CQ poll against.
? Not voting, voted "present" or did not announce.

	8	9	10	11	12	13	14
ALABAMA							
1 Edwards	N	Y	N	Y	Y	Y	Y
2 Dickinson	N	Y	N	Y	Y	Y	Y
3 Andrews	N	Y	N	Y	Y	?	?
4 Nichols	N	Y	Y	√	Y	Y	Y
5 Flowers	N	Y	Y	Y	Y	Y	Y
6 Buchanan	N	Y	Y	Y	Y	Y	Y
7 Bevill	?	Y	Y	√	Y	N	Y
8 Jones	N	Y	Y	N	Y	Y	?
ALASKA							
AL Begich	Y	N	N	N	N	N	N
ARIZONA							
1 Rhodes	?	Y	Y	Y	Y	Y	Y
2 Udall	Y	N	‡	N	N	‡	N
3 Steiger	N	Y	Y	Y	Y	?	Y
ARKANSAS							
1 Alexander	N	N	Y	Y	Y	?	?
2 Mills	N	Y	?	N	Y	N	?
3 Hammerschmidt	N	Y	Y	Y	Y	Y	Y
4 Pryor	Y	N	Y	?	Y	?	N
CALIFORNIA							
1 Clausen	?	Y	Y	Y	Y	Y	Y
2 Johnson	N	N	‡	N	Y	N	N
3 Moss	Y	N	N	N	N	N	-
4 Leggett	N	N	N	N	Y	N	N
5 Burton	Y	N	N	N	N	N	-
6 Mailliard	?	Y	N	N	Y	Y	Y
7 Dellums	Y	N	N	N	N	N	N
8 Miller	‡	Y	N	N	Y	N	‡
9 Edwards	Y	N	N	N	N	N	N
10 Gubser	?	Y	?	?	Y	Y	?
11 McCloskey	‡	N	N	N	Y	N	N
12 Talcott	N	Y	Y	Y	Y	‡	Y
13 Teague	N	Y	Y	Y	Y	Y	Y
14 Waldie	‡	N	N	N	‡	N	N
15 McFall	N	Y	N	N	Y	N	Y
16 Sisk	N	N	?	N	Y	N	?
17 Anderson	Y	N	N	Y	N	Y	N
18 Mathias	N	Y	Y	Y	Y	Y	Y
19 Holifield	N	Y	N	N	Y	N	‡
20 Smith	N	Y	Y	Y	Y	Y	‡
21 Hawkins	‡	X	N	N	N	N	N
22 Corman	N	N	N	N	Y	-	N
23 Clawson	N	Y	Y	Y	Y	Y	Y
24 Rousselot	N	√	Y	Y	Y	Y	?
25 Wiggins	N	Y	‡	N	Y	Y	‡
26 Rees	Y	N	.	N	N	N	
27 Goldwater	N	Y	Y	Y	Y	-	‡
28 Bell	N	Y	Y	?	Y	?	?
29 Danielson	N	N	N	N	N	N	N
30 Roybal	Y	N	N	N	N	N	N
31 Wilson	N	N	Y	N	Y	-	-
32 Hosmer	N	Y	‡	Y	Y	Y	Y
33 Pettis	N	Y	Y	Y	Y	‡	-
34 Hanna	N	N	‡	N	Y	N	?
35 Schmitz	N	N	Y	N	Y	N	‡
36 Wilson	-	Y	Y	Y	√	?	Y
37 Van Deerlin	Y	N	N	N	N	N	N
38 Veysey	N	Y	Y	Y	N	‡	‡
COLORADO							
1 McKevitt	N	Y	Y	Y	Y	‡	Y
2 Brotzman	N	Y	Y	Y	Y	Y	Y
3 Evans	N	N	N	N	N	‡	N
4 Aspinall	N	Y	‡	N	Y	Y	Y
CONNECTICUT							
1 Cotter	Y	N	Y	N	Y	N	-
2 Steele	Y	N	Y	Y	Y	Y	N
3 Giaimo	Y	N	Y	Y	Y	?	N

	8	9	10	11	12	13	14
4 McKinney	N	Y	Y	Y	Y	Y	N
5 Monagan	Y	N	Y	N	Y	Y	N
6 Grasso	Y	N	Y	N	N	N	-
DELAWARE							
AL DuPont	Y	Y	Y	Y	Y	Y	‡
FLORIDA							
1 Sikes	-	Y	Y	Y	Y	Y	?
2 Fuqua	-	Y	Y	Y	Y	‡	‡
3 Bennett	Y	Y	Y	Y	Y	Y	N
4 Chappell	-	Y	Y	Y	Y	Y	N
5 Frey	N	Y	?	Y	Y	Y	Y
6 Gibbons	Y	N	Y	N	Y	Y	N
7 Haley	N	Y	Y	N	Y	N	?
8 Young	N	Y	Y	Y	Y	Y	‡
9 Rogers	N	N	Y	Y	Y	Y	N
10 Burke	N	Y	?	Y	Y	Y	Y
11 Pepper	N	N	N	N	‡	N	N
12 Fascell	Y	N	N	N	Y	Y	N
GEORGIA							
1 Hagan	N	√	N	Y	Y	Y	Y
2 Mathis	-	‡	N	Y	Y	Y	Y
3 Brinkley	N	N	N	Y	Y	Y	Y
4 Blackburn	N	N	N	Y	‡	‡	Y
5 Thompson	N	Y	Y	Y	Y	Y	Y
6 Flynt	N	X	N	Y	Y	Y	Y
7 Davis	N	Y	‡	N	Y	Y	Y
8 Stuckey	N	Y	?	Y	Y	Y	?
9 Landrum	N	N	N	Y	Y	Y	?
10 Stephens	-	‡	?	N	Y	Y	?
HAWAII							
1 Matsunaga	Y	N	Y	N	Y	N	N
2 Mink	Y	N	N	N	N	-	-
IDAHO							
1 McClure	?	Y	?	Y	Y	Y	?
2 Hansen	N	Y	?	Y	Y	Y	?
ILLINOIS							
1 Metcalfe	Y	N	-	N	‡	‡	-
2 Mikva	Y	N	-	N	‡	-	.
3 Murphy, M.	Y	N	Y	N	Y	Y	N
4 Derwinski	?	‡	‡	?	?	?	‡
5 Kluczynski	Y	N	Y	N	Y	?	?
6 Collins	Y	N	N	N	Y	N	N
7 Annunzio	Y	N	N	N	‡	-	N
8 Rostenkowski	Y	N	Y	Y	‡	?	-
9 Yates	Y	N	N	N	N	N	N
10 Collier	-	Y	Y	Y	Y	Y	‡
11 Pucinski	Y	N	Y	Y	N	N	N
12 McClory	N	Y	Y	Y	Y	Y	?
13 Crane	N	Y	Y	‡	-	Y	Y
14 Erlenborn	N	Y	Y	?	?	Y	Y
15 Vacancy							
16 Anderson	N	Y	N	Y	Y	Y	Y
17 Arends	N	Y	Y	Y	Y	Y	Y
18 Michel	N	Y	Y	Y	Y	Y	Y
19 Railsback	N	N	?	N	Y	N	Y
20 Findley	N	N	?	N	N	Y	Y
21 Gray	Y	N	Y	N	Y	Y	?
22 Springer	-	Y	Y	Y	-	-	‡
23 Shipley	Y	N	?	Y	Y	Y	?
24 Price	Y	Y	N	Y	Y	N	Y
INDIANA							
1 Madden	Y	N	N	N	N	N	?
2 Landgrebe	?	Y	Y	Y	Y	Y	Y
3 Brademas	Y	N	N	N	N	N	N
4 Roush	Y	N	Y	Y	Y	‡	N
5 Hillis	N	Y	Y	Y	Y	Y	?
6 Bray	N	Y	Y	Y	Y	Y	Y
7 Myers	N	Y	Y	Y	Y	Y	Y
8 Zion	N	Y	?	Y	Y	Y	Y
9 Hamilton	Y	N	?	N	Y	Y	N
10 Dennis	N	Y	?	N	Y	Y	N
11 Jacobs	Y	N	Y	N	N	N	N
IOWA							
1 Schwengel	-	N	Y	N	Y	N	N
2 Culver	Y	N	?	N	N	N	N
3 Gross	N	N	Y	N	Y	N	Y
4 Kyl	N	Y	Y	Y	Y	Y	?
5 Smith	Y	N	N	N	N	N	N
6 Mayne	N	Y	N	N	Y	Y	‡
7 Scherle	N	Y	Y	Y	Y	?	Y

	8	9	10	11	12	13	14
KANSAS							
1 Sebelius	N	Y	‡	Y	Y	Y	Y
2 Roy	Y	N	N	N	Y	N	N
3 Winn	N	Y	Y	Y	Y	Y	?
4 Shriver	N	Y	Y	Y	Y	Y	Y
5 Skubitz	N	Y	?	√	Y	Y	Y
KENTUCKY							
1 Stubblefield	?	N	Y	Y	Y	N	Y
2 Natcher	N	N	Y	Y	Y	N	N
3 Mazzoli	Y	N	Y	N	Y	N	N
4 Snyder	N	N	Y	Y	Y	Y	?
5 Carter	N	N	Y	Y	Y	Y	Y
6 Curlin[3]					Y	N	?
7 Perkins	Y	N	Y	N	Y	N	N
LOUISIANA							
1 Hebert	N	Y	?	Y	Y	?	?
2 Boggs	Y	N	Y	N	Y	N	N
3 Caffery	N	Y	Y	X	Y	Y	?
4 Waggonner	N	Y	Y	Y	Y	Y	?
5 Passman	N	Y	N	Y	Y	Y	N
6 Rarick	N	Y	Y	Y	N	Y	N
7 Edwards	‡	‡	‡	?	‡	‡	?
8 Long	?	?	?	?	Y	Y	?
MAINE							
1 Kyros	Y	N	N	N	Y	N	-
2 Hathaway	Y	N	N	N	Y	N	-
MARYLAND							
1 Mills	N	Y	Y	Y	?	Y	?
2 Long	Y	N	Y	N	N	N	N
3 Garmatz	N	N	Y	Y	Y	Y	N
4 Sarbanes	Y	N	?	Y	N	N	N
5 Hogan	N	Y	Y	Y	Y	Y	Y
6 Byron	N	Y	Y	Y	Y	Y	Y
7 Mitchell	Y	N	N	N	N	N	N
8 Gude	Y	N	N	Y	N	?	N
MASSACHUSETTS							
1 Conte	Y	N	N	Y	Y	Y	-
2 Boland	Y	N	Y	N	Y	Y	-
3 Drinan	Y	N	N	N	N	N	-
4 Donohue	Y	N	N	Y	Y	N	-
5 Morse	Y	N	N	N	Y	Y	N
6 Harrington	Y	N	N	N	Y	N	?
7 Macdonald	Y	N	N	N	Y	?	?
8 O'Neill	Y	N	N	Y	N	Y	?
9 Hicks	Y	N	Y	N	Y	N	N
10 Heckler	Y	N	N	Y	Y	Y	N
11 Burke	Y	N	N	Y	Y	Y	N
12 Keith	N	Y	N	N	Y	Y	?
MICHIGAN							
1 Conyers	‡	N	N	N	N	?	?
2 Esch	Y	N	Y	Y	Y	Y	-
3 Brown	N	Y	Y	Y	Y	Y	Y
4 Hutchinson	N	Y	Y	Y	Y	Y	Y
5 Ford	N	Y	Y	Y	Y	Y	‡
6 Chamberlain	N	Y	Y	Y	Y	Y	Y
7 Riegle	Y	N	N	N	N	N	N
8 Harvey	N	N	Y	?	Y	Y	N
9 Vander Jagt	N	N	Y	Y	Y	Y	Y
10 Cederberg	N	Y	Y	Y	Y	Y	‡
11 Ruppe	N	N	?	Y	Y	Y	-
12 O'Hara	Y	N	Y	N	N	N	N
13 Diggs	‡	X	?	X	?	?	?
14 Nedzi	Y	N	Y	N	N	N	?
15 Ford	Y	N	Y	N	N	N	N
16 Dingell	Y	N	Y	N	N	N	N
17 Griffiths	N	N	?	N	Y	?	?
18 Broomfield	N	Y	Y	Y	Y	Y	Y
19 McDonald	N	Y	Y	Y	Y	Y	Y
MINNESOTA							
1 Quie	N	Y	Y	Y	Y	Y	Y
2 Nelsen	N	Y	Y	Y	Y	Y	Y
3 Frenzel	N	N	Y	Y	Y	Y	Y
4 Karth	Y	N	N	N	Y	N	?
5 Fraser	Y	N	N	N	N	N	N
6 Zwach	N	N	Y	Y	Y	Y	‡
7 Bergland	Y	N	N	N	Y	Y	N
8 Blatnik	Y	N	N	N	‡	-	?
MISSISSIPPI							
1 Abernethy	N	Y	Y	Y	Y	Y	‡
2 Whitten	N	Y	Y	Y	Y	Y	‡
3 Griffin	N	Y	Y	N	Y	Y	‡
4 Montgomery	N	Y	Y	Y	‡	Y	‡
5 Colmer	N	Y	Y	Y	Y	Y	-
MISSOURI							
1 Clay	Y	N	N	N	N	?	N
2 Symington	Y	N	N	N	Y	N	N

8. HR 10835. Consumer Protection Agency. Moorhead (D Pa.) amendment to the committee's bill broadening the proposed agency's authority to intervene on behalf of consumers in the proceedings of other federal agencies and providing the agency additional authority to act when other federal agencies refused to investigate consumer complaints. Rejected by recorded teller vote 160-218: R 15-138; D 145-80 (ND 131-23; SD 14-57), Oct. 14, 1971.

9. HR 8687. Defense Procurement Authorization. Hebert (D La.) motion to order the previous question (ending further debate and blocking the possibility of amending the motion in order to instruct conferees to accept the language of the Senate-passed Mansfield troop withdrawal amendment) on the Arends (R Ill.) motion to instruct conferees not to accept any nongermane Senate-passed amendments. Motion agreed to 215-193: R 139-33; D 76-160 (ND 23-138; SD 53-22), Oct. 19, 1971. A "yea" was a vote supporting the President's position.

10. HR 7248. Higher Education Act of 1971. Broomfield (R Mich.) amendment to the committee's bill postponing effectiveness of any federal court order requiring busing for racial, sex, religious or socio-economic balance until all appeals— or the time for all appeals—had been exhausted. Adopted by recorded teller vote 235-125: R 129-17; D 106-108 (ND 56-90; SD 50-18), Nov. 4, 1971.

1. Rep. George W. Andrews (D Ala.) died Dec. 26, 1971.
2. Rep. Charlotte T. Reid (R Ill.) resigned Oct. 7, 1971.
3. Rep. John C. Watts (D Ky.) died Sept. 24, 1971. Rep. William P. Curlin (D) was sworn in Dec. 6, 1971, replacing Watts.

Democrats   *Republicans*

	8	9	10	11	12	13	14
3 Sullivan	Y	N	N	Y	-	-	-
4 Randall	N	Y	Y	Y	Y	N	?
5 Bolling	Y	Y	N	N	N	N	‡
6 Hull	N	Y	Y	✓	Y	Y	Y
7 *Hall*	N	Y	Y	Y	N	Y	‡
8 Ichord	[illegible]	?	Y	Y	Y	Y	Y
9 Hungate	N	N	Y	N	N	N	N
10 Burlison	Y	N	Y	N	Y	N	N
MONTANA							
1 *Shoup*	?	Y	Y	Y	Y	Y	Y
2 Melcher	Y	N	N	Y	Y	N	N
NEBRASKA							
1 *Thone*	N	Y	Y	Y	Y	Y	?
2 *McCollister*	N	Y	Y	Y	Y	Y	Y
3 *Martin*	N	Y	?	Y	Y	?	?
NEVADA							
AL Baring	-	Y	Y	Y	Y	Y	N
NEW HAMPSHIRE							
1 *Wyman*	N	Y	Y	Y	N	Y	Y
2 *Cleveland*	Y	Y	Y	Y	Y	Y	Y
NEW JERSEY							
1 *Hunt*	N	Y	Y	Y	Y	Y	?
2 *Sandman*	N	Y	Y	Y	Y	Y	‡
3 Howard	Y	N	N	N	N	N	N
4 Thompson	‡	X	N	N	N	N	N
5 *Frelinghuysen*	N	Y	Y	N	Y	Y	?
6 *Forsythe*	N	N	‡	Y	Y	Y	Y
7 *Widnall*	N	N	Y	Y	Y	Y	Y
8 Roe	Y	N	N	Y	Y	N	N
9 Helstoski	Y	N	N	N	N	N	-
10 Rodino	Y	N	N	N	Y	N	-
11 Minish	Y	N	N	N	Y	N	N
12 *Dwyer*	N	N	†	Y	Y	N	-
13 Gallagher	Y	N	N	N	Y	N	Y
14 Daniels	Y	N	N	N	Y	N	-
15 Patten	Y	N	N	N	Y	N	-
NEW MEXICO							
1 *Lujan*	?	Y	?	Y	?	?	?
2 Runnels	N	N	Y	Y	Y	?	?
NEW YORK							
1 Pike	Y	N	Y	Y	N	Y	N
2 *Grover*	N	Y	Y	Y	Y	Y	‡
3 Wolff	Y	N	Y	Y	Y	N	N
4 *Wydler*	N	Y	Y	Y	Y	Y	?
5 *Lent*	†	Y	Y	Y	Y	Y	‡
6 *Halpern*	‡	-	‡	‡	Y	N	N
7 Addabbo	Y	N	Y	Y	Y	N	N
8 Rosenthal	Y	N	N	N	N	N	N
9 Delaney	N	Y	Y	Y	Y	Y	?
10 Celler	Y	N	N	N	Y	?	?
11 Brasco	Y	N	Y	N	Y	N	-
12 Chisholm	Y	N	N	N	N	N	?
13 Podell	Y	N	Y	N	Y	N	-
14 Rooney	N	N	N	N	Y	N	Y
15 Carey	Y	N	N	N	Y	N	?
16 Murphy	Y	Y	N	Y	‡	?	Y
17 Koch	Y	N	-	N	Y	N	-
18 Rangel	Y	N	N	N	N	-	N
19 Abzug	Y	N	N	N	N	N	N
20 Ryan	Y	N	N	N	N	N	N
21 Badillo	Y	N	N	N	N	N	-
22 Scheuer	Y	N	Y	N	N	N	?
23 Bingham	Y	N	N	N	N	N	N
24 Biaggi	‡	N	Y	N	Y	N	-
25 *Peyser*	N	Y	Y	N	Y	N	?
26 *Reid*	Y	N	N	N	Y	N	-
27 Dow	Y	N	N	N	N	N	N
28 *Fish*	N	Y	N	Y	Y	Y	?
29 Stratton	Y	Y	Y	Y	Y	N	‡
30 *King*	N	Y	Y	Y	Y	Y	?
31 *McEwen*	N	Y	Y	Y	Y	Y	Y
32 *Pirnie*	N	Y	?	Y	Y	Y	?
33 *Robison*	N	N	Y	N	Y	Y	-
34 *Terry*	?	Y	Y	Y	Y	Y	Y
35 Hanley	Y	N	Y	Y	Y	N	?
36 *Horton*	N	Y	Y	N	Y	N	†
37 *Conable*	N	Y	Y	Y	Y	Y	‡
38 *Hastings*	N	Y	Y	Y	Y	Y	Y
39 *Kemp*	?	Y	Y	Y	Y	Y	?
40 *Smith*	N	Y	?	Y	Y	?	Y
41 Dulski	Y	N	Y	Y	Y	N	Y
NORTH CAROLINA							
1 *Jonas*	N	N	Y	Y	Y	Y	N
2 Fountain	N	Y	Y	Y	Y	Y	Y
3 Henderson	N	Y	Y	Y	Y	Y	‡
4 Galifianakis	Y	N	Y	Y	Y	?	N
5 *Mizell*	N	Y	Y	Y	Y	Y	Y
6 Preyer	Y	N	N	N	Y	Y	N
7 Lennon	N	Y	Y	Y	Y	Y	Y
8 *Ruth*	N	Y	Y	Y	Y	Y	Y
9 *Jones*	N	Y	Y	Y	Y	Y	Y
10 *Broyhill*	N	‡	Y	Y	Y	Y	Y
11 Taylor	N	N	‡	Y	Y	Y	N
NORTH DAKOTA							
1 *Andrews*	N	N	Y	Y	Y	Y	?
2 Link	Y	N	N	N	Y	N	N
OHIO							
1 *Keating*	N	Y	Y	Y	Y	Y	?
2 *Clancy*	N	Y	Y	Y	Y	Y	?
3 *Whalen*	Y	N	N	N	Y	N	N
4 *McCulloch*	?	Y	?	N	Y	Y	N
5 *Latta*	N	Y	Y	Y	Y	Y	‡
6 *Harsha*	N	Y	Y	Y	Y	N	Y
7 *Brown*	N	Y	?	Y	Y	Y	Y
8 *Betts*	N	Y	Y	Y	Y	Y	‡
9 Ashley	Y	Y	N	N	Y	Y	Y
10 *Miller*	N	N	Y	Y	Y	Y	N
11 *Stanton*	N	Y	‡	‡	Y	Y	‡
12 *Devine*	N	Y	Y	Y	Y	Y	‡
13 *Mosher*	Y	N	N	N	Y	Y	N
14 Seiberling	Y	N	N	N	N	N	N
15 *Wylie*	N	Y	?	Y	Y	Y	?
16 *Bow*	N	Y	Y	Y	Y	?	Y
17 *Ashbrook*	N	N	Y	Y	N	-	-
18 Hays	Y	Y	Y	Y	Y	N	‡
19 Carney	Y	N	?	Y	N	N	?
20 Stanton	Y	N	Y	N	N	-	N
21 Stokes	Y	-	N	N	N	-	N
22 Vanik	Y	N	N	N	N	N	N
23 *Minshall*	N	Y	Y	Y	Y	-	‡
24 *Powell*	N	Y	Y	Y	Y	?	Y
OKLAHOMA							
1 *Belcher*	?	Y	?	?	?	?	?
2 Edmondson	N	Y	Y	Y	Y	?	?
3 Albert	Y		N			N	
4 Steed		Y	Y	N	‡		Y
5 Jarman	N	Y	‡	Y	Y	Y	Y
6 *Camp*	N	Y	Y	Y	Y	Y	Y
OREGON							
1 *Wyatt*	N	Y	‡	Y	Y	Y	‡
2 Ullman	?	N	?	N	Y	Y	N
3 Green	N	N	Y	‡	Y	N	N
4 *Dellenback*	N	Y	Y	N	Y	Y	?
PENNSYLVANIA							
1 Barrett	Y	X	?	?	Y	N	?
2 Nix	Y	N	N	N	N	N	N
3 Byrne	Y	N	N	Y	Y	N	N
4 Eilberg	Y	N	Y	N	Y	?	?
5 Green	Y	N	N	N	N	N	?
6 Yatron	Y	N	Y	Y	Y	N	Y
7 *Williams*	N	Y	Y	Y	Y	Y	Y
8 *Biester*	Y	N	Y	N	Y	Y	N
9 *Ware*	N	Y	Y	Y	Y	Y	Y
10 *McDade*	Y	N	Y	Y	Y	N	?
11 Flood	Y	Y	Y	Y	Y	N	Y
12 *Whalley*	N	Y	Y	Y	Y	‡	Y
13 *Coughlin*	Y	Y	Y	Y	Y	Y	?
14 Moorhead	Y	N	N	N	Y	-	N
15 Rooney	Y	N	Y	Y	Y	N	Y
16 *Eshleman*	N	Y	Y	Y	Y	Y	‡
17 *Schneebeli*	N	Y	Y	Y	Y	Y	‡
18 *Heinz*[4]			Y	N	Y	N	-
19 *Goodling*	N	Y	Y	Y	Y	Y	Y
20 Gaydos	Y	N	Y	Y	Y	N	?
21 Dent	Y	N	N	Y	Y	N	‡
22 *Saylor*	?	Y	Y	Y	Y	Y	?
23 *Johnson*	N	Y	Y	Y	Y	Y	?
24 Vigorito	Y	N	N	‡	Y	N	N
25 Clark	Y	Y	Y	Y	Y	N	?
26 Morgan	‡	Y	N	Y	Y	N	Y
27 *Fulton*[5]							
RHODE ISLAND							
1 St Germain	Y	N	N	N	N	N	?
2 Tiernan	Y	N	Y	N	‡	-	-
SOUTH CAROLINA							
1 Davis	N	Y	N	Y	Y	Y	Y
2 *Spence*	N	Y	Y	Y	?	?	?
3 Dorn	N	✓	N	N	Y	Y	?
4 Mann	N	Y	N	Y	Y	Y	?
5 Gettys	-	Y	Y	Y	Y	Y	‡
6 McMillan	?	Y	Y	?	Y	Y	Y
SOUTH DAKOTA							
1 Denholm	Y	N	N	N	N	N	N
2 Abourezk	Y	N	N	N	N	-	?
TENNESSEE							
1 *Quillen*	N	Y	Y	Y	Y	Y	?
2 *Duncan*	N	Y	Y	Y	Y	Y	Y
3 *Baker*	N	Y	?	Y	Y	Y	?
4 Evins	N	N	Y	N	‡	?	?
5 Fulton	‡	N	Y	N	Y	N	-
6 Anderson	‡	N	N	N	Y	N	N
7 Blanton	N	N	‡	Y	‡	‡	Y
8 Jones	N	N	‡	Y	Y	Y	Y
9 *Kuykendall*	N	Y	Y	Y	Y	Y	‡
TEXAS							
1 Patman	-	✓	?	N	N	N	?
2 Dowdy	N	Y	?	✓	?	?	?
3 *Collins*	N	Y	Y	Y	Y	Y	‡
4 Roberts	N	Y	‡	Y	Y	Y	‡
5 Cabell	N	Y	‡	N	Y	Y	Y
6 Teague	N	✓	?	Y	Y	Y	Y
7 *Archer*	N	Y	Y	Y	Y	Y	?
8 Eckhardt	Y	X	N	N	N	?	N
9 Brooks	Y	Y	Y	N	Y	N	?
10 Pickle	N	Y	Y	?	Y	N	Y
11 Poage	N	Y	?	Y	Y	Y	Y
12 Wright	Y	✓	?	Y	?	?	Y
13 Purcell	N	Y	Y	Y	Y	Y	Y
14 Young	Y	Y	Y	Y	N	N	?
15 de la Garza	?	Y	N	Y	Y	N	Y
16 White	N	Y	‡	Y	Y	N	Y
17 Burleson	N	Y	Y	Y	Y	Y	Y
18 *Price*	N	Y	Y	Y	Y	Y	Y
19 Mahon	N	Y	Y	Y	N	Y	Y
20 Gonzalez	N	N	N	N	N	N	N
21 Fisher	N	Y	Y	Y	Y	Y	‡
22 Casey	N	Y	Y	Y	?	Y	?
23 Kazen	N	Y	Y	Y	Y	N	Y
UTAH							
1 McKay	Y	Y	Y	N	Y	N	Y
2 *Lloyd*	-	Y	?	?	Y	?	Y
VERMONT							
AL *Stafford*[6]							
VIRGINIA							
1 Downing	N	Y	Y	Y	Y	Y	Y
2 *Whitehurst*	N	Y	Y	Y	N	Y	?
3 Satterfield	N	Y	Y	N	Y	Y	Y
4 Abbitt	N	Y	Y	Y	Y	Y	Y
5 Daniel	N	Y	Y	Y	Y	Y	-
6 *Poff*	N	Y	Y	Y	Y	Y	‡
7 *Robinson*	N	Y	Y	Y	Y	Y	Y
8 *Scott*	N	Y	Y	Y	Y	Y	Y
9 *Wampler*	N	Y	Y	Y	N	Y	?
10 *Broyhill*	N	Y	‡	Y	Y	Y	?
WASHINGTON							
1 *Pelly*	-	Y	Y	X	Y	Y	‡
2 Meeds	Y	N	N	N	Y	N	N
3 Hansen	Y	N	Y	N	Y	N	‡
4 McCormack	Y	N	N	N	‡	N	-
5 Foley	Y	N	N	N	Y	?	N
6 Hicks	Y	N	N	Y	N	-	?
7 Adams	Y	N	N	N	Y	N	?
WEST VIRGINIA							
1 Mollohan	Y	Y	Y	Y	Y	N	?
2 Staggers	?	Y	?	Y	Y	N	?
3 Slack	?	N	Y	Y	Y	Y	?
4 Hechler	Y	N	N	Y	N	N	N
5 Kee	-	Y	?	Y	Y	N	?
WISCONSIN							
1 Aspin	Y	N	?	N	N	N	N
2 Kastenmeier	Y	N	N	N	N	N	-
3 *Thomson*	N	Y	Y	Y	Y	Y	Y
4 Zablocki	N	Y	Y	Y	Y	N	Y
5 Reuss	Y	N	N	N	N	-	N
6 *Steiger*	N	Y	Y	N	Y	Y	Y
7 Obey	Y	N	N	N	N	N	N
8 *Byrnes*	N	Y	Y	Y	Y	Y	Y
9 *Davis*	N	Y	Y	Y	Y	Y	Y
10 *O'Konski*	N	Y	Y	Y	Y	Y	Y
WYOMING							
AL Roncalio	Y	N	N	Y	‡	-	-

11. H J Res 191. School Prayer Amendment. Adoption of a proposed constitutional amendment providing that it was constitutionally permissible for persons in public buildings to participate in voluntary prayer. Rejected 240-163: R 138-26; D 102-137 (ND 48-114; SD 54-23), Nov. 8, 1971. A two-thirds majority vote (268 in this case) is required to adopt a proposed constitutional amendment.

12. HR 10947. Revenue Act of 1971. Adoption of the conference report (S Rept 92-533) on the bill reducing federal, individual and business taxes to stimulate the economy and establishing a federal presidential election campaign fund effective in 1973. Adopted 321-75: R 158-9; D 163-66 (ND 95-57; SD 68-9), Dec. 9, 1971. A "yea" was a vote supporting the President's position.

13. HR 11309. Economic Stabilization Act Extension. Stephens (D Ga.) amendment to the committee's bill limiting mandatory payment of pay raises scheduled under pre-freeze contracts and laws to those in compensation for which prices or taxes had been raised, appropriations made, funds otherwise raised or productivity increased. Adopted by recorded teller vote 209-151: R 141-13; D 68-138 (ND 13-119; SD 55-19), Dec. 10, 1971.

14. S 2819. Foreign Military Assistance Authorization. Morgan (D Pa.) motion to table Ryan (D N.Y.) motion instructing House conferees to accept the Mansfield amendment which would set a policy of withdrawal of U.S. forces from Indochina within six months upon release of all U.S. POWs. Motion adopted 130-101: R 78-12; D 52-89 (ND 18-73; SD 34-16), Dec. 16, 1971.

4. Rep. H. John Heinz III (R Pa.) sworn in Nov. 4, 1971, to replace Rep. Robert T. Corbett (R), deceased.

5. Rep. James G. Fulton (R Pa.) died Oct. 6, 1971.

6. Rep. Robert T. Stafford (R Vt.) resigned Sept. 17, 1971, to accept appointment to the Senate (see Senate chart).

C_Q **Key Votes 1972**

EQUAL RIGHTS, INDOCHINA WAR, SPENDING MAJOR ISSUES

Questions of equal rights, presidential and congressional power, federal spending, and the war in Indochina were among the key votes in 1972:

Senate Key Votes

1. EQUAL EMPLOYMENT OPPORTUNITY. A long battle to equip the Equal Employment Opportunity Commission (EEOC) with the authority to enforce findings of employment discrimination through cease-and-desist orders ended in defeat Feb. 15 when the Senate adopted, 45-39, a substitute proposal authorizing the EEOC to ask federal courts to enforce its findings. Republicans and southern Democrats provided the majority in favor of the more moderate enforcement powers: R 27-12; D 18-27 (ND 3-26; SD 15-1). Cease-and-desist powers had been the goal of civil rights advocates ever since the EEOC was created by the Civil Rights Act of 1964 without enforcement power. The Nixon administration initially proposed the court-enforcement approach as an alternative. The Senate, twice during the five-week debate on the enforcement measure (S 2515), rejected the court-enforcement approach by a two-vote margin. It reversed its position after two attempts to limit further debate on the bill had failed. The Senate passed the modified enforcement bill Feb. 22 by a 73-16 vote; and in March Congress cleared a bill similar to the Senate-approved version.

2. EDUCATION AID/BUSING RESTRICTIONS. To provide Senate conferees on the omnibus education bill (S 659) with some alternative to stringent anti-busing provisions added to that bill by the House, the Senate Feb. 29 adopted, by a 63-34 vote (R 28-16; D 35-18 (ND 33-2; SD 2-16) more moderate anti-busing language proposed by Majority Leader Mike Mansfield (D Mont.) and Minority Leader Hugh Scott (R Pa.). The language adopted by the Senate forbade use of federal funds for busing "except on the written request of local school officials," forbade such use of funds when the health of the children involved was risked by busing or when the busing impinged upon the educational process, forbade federal pressure for busing necessitating spending of state or local funds "unless constitutionally required," and postponed, until all appeals were exhausted, the effective date of any federal court order requiring busing between school districts or the consolidation of school districts. The anti-busing language contained in the final version of S 659 was similar to the Mansfield-Scott proposals *(House key vote 3)*

3. EQUAL RIGHTS. Forty-nine years after it was first introduced in the Congress, a constitutional amendment guaranteeing equal rights for men and women (H J Res 208) was approved by the Senate March 22

and sent to the states for ratification. The Senate vote was 84-8, 22 more than the two-thirds majority required: R 37-6; D 47-2 (ND 34-0; SD 13-2). The House had approved an identical constitutional amendment in October 1971 by a 354-23 roll-call vote. If approved by three-fourths (38) of the states, the amendment would be the 27th added to the Constitution. As of Oct. 19, 1972, 21 states had ratified the amendment.

4. CONGRESSIONAL IMMUNITY. Reacting to the Justice Department's contention that an aide to Sen. Mike Gravel (D Alaska) should be questioned by a federal grand jury concerning his role in Gravel's release in June 1971 of certain portions of the once-secret Pentagon Papers, the Senate March 23 voted 55-27 to approve a resolution (S Res 280) authorizing the Senate to file a friend-of-the-court brief in the case before the Supreme Court and to pay the expenses of printing Gravel's brief. At issue was the extent to which and to whom congressional immunity could be extended. In the view of the Justice Department, the constitutional protection of immunity was limited solely to members of Congress. The court June 29 held that the immunity did not shield a senator or his aide from questioning by a grand jury concerning arrangements for obtaining or publishing the papers, but only from questioning concerning legislative acts. All the votes against the resolution were cast by Republicans: R 15-27; D 40-0.

5. KLEINDIENST NOMINATION. Acting Attorney General Richard G. Kleindienst survived the longest confirmation hearing in Senate history—24 days—to win the attorney generalship June 8 by the lopsided margin of 64-19. Every Republican voting and 26 Democrats voted to confirm: R 38-0; D 26-19 (ND 12-17; SD 14-2). The President had nominated Kleindienst for attorney general Feb. 15. The Judiciary Committee, after two days of hearings, voted unanimously Feb. 29 to approve the nomination. But at Kleindienst's request, hearings were reopened March 2 after columnist Jack Anderson charged Kleindienst lied in disclaiming any role in the Justice Department's out-of-court settlement of antitrust cases against International Telephone and Telegraph Corp. (ITT). The wide-ranging hearings produced much conflicting testimony during their 22 days, but the committee voted 11-4 April 27 to reconfirm its decision.

6. MINIMUM WAGE INCREASE. By a one-vote margin, the Senate July 20 rejected a Republican-sponsored substitute proposal reducing to $2.00 and limiting the coverage of a bill (S 1861) raising the hourly minimum wage. The substitute, sponsored by Robert Taft Jr. (R Ohio) and Peter H. Dominick (R Colo.), was defeated 46-47 despite the strong support of the administration and business and agricultural lobby groups: R 30-13; D 16-34 (ND 2-33; SD 14-1). The Senate later passed a bill raising the wage floor for most manufacturing and retail employees to $2.20 and extending coverage under the Fair Labor Standards Act of 1938 to about 7 million additional workers. Earlier in the year House Republicans successfully had waged a similar effort to weaken the House version and later they blocked a move to send both versions of the bill to a House-Senate conference, killing the bill. *(House key votes 1, 10)*

7. FOREIGN MILITARY AID. For the second time in less than a year, the Senate rejected a foreign aid bill, when by a 42-48 roll call July 24, it refused to approve a bill (S 3390) authorizing appropriations of $1.72-billion in fiscal 1973 for military aid programs and $100-million for Bangladesh relief. The bill's defeat was assured earlier when the Senate, 46-49, refused to delete an amendment proposed by Edward W. Brooke (R Mass.) to cut off funds for U.S. military involvement in Indochina. With Republicans voting against final passage (14-29), supporters of President Nixon's Vietnam disengagement policies successfully united with Democratic opponents of military aid to defeat the bill: R 14-29; D 28-19 (ND 22-10; SD 6-9).

8. WITHDRAWAL FROM INDOCHINA. Reaffirming the end-the-war stance adopted two weeks earlier by its approval of the Brooke amendment to the military aid authorization bill *(vote 7 above)*, the Senate Aug. 2, by a 49-47 roll-call vote, adopted a nearly identical Brooke amendment to a military procurement bill (HR 15495). Adoption of the amendment was assured by the votes of 11 Republicans who supported the fund cut-off despite the administration's opposition to the amendment: R 11-33; D 38-14 (ND 32-5; SD 6-9). The amendment cut off funds for U.S. forces in Vietnam within four months of enactment, pending release of U.S. prisoners of war. Unlike the first Brooke amendment, which died when the Senate rejected the military aid bill to which it was attached, the second amendment was approved again when the Senate passed the military procurement bill, 92-5. As expected, House conferees refused to allow the provision to remain in the final version of the bill.

9. ABM TREATY. Giving its approval to one of two major arms control agreements signed by President Nixon May 26 during his visit to the Soviet Union, the Senate by an 88-2 roll call on Aug. 3 approved ratification of a treaty limiting defensive missiles. The treaty, negotiated at the strategic arms limitation (SALT) talks, limited both the United States and Soviet Union to two anti-ballistic missile (ABM) sites, one protecting an offensive missile site and the other the national capital. In agreeing to the treaty, each nation agreed not to protect itself against nuclear attack in the hope that mutual vulnerability would keep the other from launching its missiles.

10. NO-FAULT AUTO INSURANCE. Opponents of a national no-fault auto insurance bill (S 945) won at least a temporary victory when the Senate Aug. 8, by a 49-46 roll-call vote, sent the bill to the Judiciary Committee for further study. The vote killed the bill for the 92nd Congress. The strong bill reported from the Commerce Committee was opposed by the administration which preferred that states write their own no-fault insurance laws. Lobbying for and against the bill was intensive. Supporters included several consumer groups, the American Insurance Association, labor unions and rental car companies. Among the opponents were most governors and state insurance commissioners, the American Trial Lawyers Association and the National Associa-

tion of Independent Insurers. Twenty-eight Republicans and 21 Democrats voted to recommit the bill: R 28-13; D 21-33 (ND 7-30; SD 14-3).

11. GENERAL REVENUE SHARING. Outnumbered in the House, where representation is by population, smaller states fared relatively poorly in the formula contained in the House version of the general revenue-sharing bill (HR 14370) for distributing federal revenues among the states. In the Senate, however, where each state is equally represented, the Finance Committee, dominated by small-state senators, revised the formula to provide more money to the rural, less industrialized states of the South and West. It became clear that small states had the votes to uphold their interests and the revised formula Sept. 6, when the Senate by a 24-61 roll call rejected an amendment by Abraham Ribicoff (D Conn.) to drop the Finance Committee formula in favor of a distribution giving greater shares to larger states. All 24 votes for Ribicoff's amendment were cast by senators from states whose shares would have increased under the new formula: R 11-29; D 13-32 (ND 13-16; SD 0-16).

12. GENERAL REVENUE SHARING. Resolving a dispute between two strong-willed committee chairmen, the Senate Sept. 7, by a 34-49 vote, refused to amend the general revenue-sharing bill (HR 14370) to require annual appropriations of funds to be shared with the states. The rejected amendment was proposed by Appropriations Committee Chairman John L. McClellan (D Ark.) who objected that the Finance Committee, headed by Russell B. Long (D La.), had infringed upon his committee's jurisdiction by reporting a bill which appropriated to a trust fund funds for a five-year $29.6-billion program, bypassing the Appropriations Committee. State and local government representatives opposed subjecting revenue sharing to the annual appropriations process, arguing that they could not plan ahead for using shared revenues if the amount available each year was subject to congressional reductions through the appropriations process. Of the 34 votes cast in favor of the McClellan amendment, 21 were cast by members of the Appropriations Committee: R 11-23; D 23-26 (ND 15-17; SD 8-9).

13. SALT AGREEMENT. More than a month after approving the ABM treaty *(Senate vote 9)*, the Senate gave qualified support to a companion five-year agreement limiting deployment of offensive missiles. After a frequently acrimonious six-week debate that ended only after cloture was invoked, the Senate approved the agreement (S J Res 241) by an 88-2 roll call. In the key vote, however, the Senate, Sept. 14 before passing the resolution, by a 56-35 roll call adopted an amendment urging the United States to take a hard line in negotiations for a permanent offensive arms treaty. The amendment, proposed by Henry M. Jackson (D Wash.) and bitterly opposed by Foreign Relations Committee Chairman J. W. Fulbright (D Ark.), requested that the United States insist on equality between U.S. and Soviet offensive force levels under any future agreement and stated the position that failure to negotiate such an agreement would be grounds for abrogating the ABM treaty. With the White House endorsing Jackson's proposal, it carried with strong support among Republicans and southern Democrats: R 30-11; D 26-24 (ND 10-22; SD 16-2).

14. MASS TRANSIT. For the first time since the Highway Trust Fund was created in 1956 to finance construction of the Interstate Highway System, the Senate Sept. 19 approved an amendment to a highways bill (S 3939), by a 48-26 roll-call vote, allowing revenues from the fund to be spent on mass transit projects, including subway construction and bus purchases. Introduced by Edmund S. Muskie (D Maine) and John Sherman Cooper (R Ky.), the amendment would give states the option of using up to $800-million annually for road construction, buses, fringe parking facilities or rail transit in urban areas, instead of only highways. But the House sidestepped a vote on the issue, and the proposal later was killed in a House-Senate conference. The issue, however, would be on the agenda of the 93rd Congress, since final action was not completed on the Federal-Aid Highway Act of 1972 (S 3939). Voting for the mass transit amendment were a majority of members of both parties: R 24-8; D 24-18 (ND 19-8; SD 5-10).

15. WELFARE REFORM. Senate liberals were defeated in their effort to reform the nation's welfare system—and a death blow was dealt to all efforts at welfare reform in the 92nd Congress—when the Senate Oct. 3 agreed to kill an amendment to the Social Security-welfare reform bill (HR 1) which would create a new program of training and employment for welfare recipients and would provide a minimum guaranteed annual income of $2,600 for a family of four. President Nixon refused to support this amendment, proposed by former Secretary of Health, Education and Welfare Abraham Ribicoff (D Conn.), and said he would oppose any plan guaranteeing an annual income of more than $2,400—the figure approved by the House in 1971. Conservatives, led by Russell B. Long (D La.), chairman of the Finance Committee which had reported the bill, backed a "workfare" plan making able-bodied family heads ineligible for welfare and requiring them to take federally guaranteed jobs. In the key vote, the Senate, 52-34, accepted a motion by Long to table and thus kill the Ribicoff amendment. The motion was adopted with the support of every voting southern Democrat and of a majority of Republicans: R 24-15; D 28-19 (ND 11-19; SD 17-0). Realizing after this vote that none of the three welfare reform proposals —the Ribicoff plan, the administration plan, or the "workfare" plan—had majority support in the Senate, that body approved only tests of the three different proposals. Conferees deleted all family welfare reform provisions from the bill.

16. CONSUMER PROTECTION AGENCY. Supporters of strong consumer legislation lost their major battle in 1972 when the Senate Oct. 5 failed for a third time to invoke cloture and limit debate on a bill (S 3970) to create an independent agency to represent consumer interests before federal agencies and courts. The final vote was 52-30—three votes short of the two-thirds present and voting needed. The successful lobby campaign against the bill was waged by numerous businesses and industries, including the Grocery Manufacturers of America Inc., the National Association of Manufacturers, the U.S. Chamber of Commerce, and Procter and Gamble. The bill's sponsors laid responsibility for the bill's death on the administration. Publicly the administration supported the narrower version of the bill passed by the House in 1971, but supporters of the Senate bill charged that the administration opposed enactment of any advocacy bill and that administration acquiescence to the filibuster finally killed the bill. On the final vote, 18 Republicans and 12 Democrats opposed cloture: R 20-18; D 32-12 (ND 26-1; SD 6-11).

17. BUSING RESTRICTIONS. The strongest anti-busing bill in history died Oct. 12 when the Senate failed for the third time to invoke cloture and cut off debate on the Equal Educational Opportunities bill (HR 13915). Although the bill was supported by the President and had passed the House by a large majority, Senate Democratic and Republican liberals were able to block cloture. The key vote Oct. 12 was 49-38, nine short of the 58 needed: R 26-12; D 23-26 (ND 7-25; SD 16-1). The bill would have barred busing except to the school closest or next closest to the pupil's home and allowed the reopening of previous school desegregation cases in order that new desegregation plans could be formed in compliance with the bill's provisions restricting busing. White House aides lobbied hard for the bill and conceded to reporters that their effort to invoke cloture represented one of the few times the President chose to intervene in a procedural matter in Congress. Nixon wanted a vote on the bill and was confident the Senate would approve it if given a chance, they said. *(House key vote 8)*

18. DEBT LIMIT/SPENDING CEILING. In a sharp rebuff to President Nixon, the Senate Oct. 17 refused to yield to the President even limited authority to cut federal spending to $250-billion in fiscal 1973. Not satisfied with the compromise guidelines imposed by HR 16810, the Senate, 27-39, rejected a conference report (H Rept 92-1606) on the bill which would have exempted certain areas from spending cutbacks and limited reductions in other budget categories to 20 percent: R 15-10; D 12-29 (ND 6-24; SD 6-5). The Senate's adamant opposition to any broad grant of budget-cutting power to the President doomed Nixon's demands for the unlimited authority to hold down federal spending which had been given him by the House. Conferees later deleted the spending ceiling from the bill which increased the public debt limit to $465-billion through June 30, 1973. The issue became the major power play of 1972 between Congress and the White House, with opponents of the spending ceiling contending that it would hand over to the President Congress' chief legislative duty under the Constitution. The controversy was fueled by Nixon's threats to accuse Congress in the November elections of fiscal irresponsibility in approving increasingly high levels of spending unless members approved his spending ceiling request. *(House key vote 11)*

House Key Votes

1. MINIMUM WAGE INCREASE. The House May 11 signaled its determination to resist efforts to pass a comprehensive minimum wage bill in 1972 when it rejected, by a 217-191 recorded teller vote, a liberal version reported by the Education and Labor Committee. The conservative coalition instead adopted a substitute bill sponsored by John N. Erlenborn (R Ill.) and supported by the administration and business and agricultural interests: R 148-20; D 69-171 (ND 6-154; SD 63-17). The rejected committee provisions would have extended coverage under the Fair Labor Standards Act of 1938 to about 6 million additional workers and would have immediately boosted the minimum wage to $2.00 an hour from the existing wage floor of $1.60 an hour for most manufacturing and retail workers and $1.30 for certain farm workers, set in 1966. The substitute (HR 7130) postponed the increase until 1973 and provided no additional coverage. The Senate by a close margin later defeated a similar move to narrow the scope of its bill, and both died late in the session when the House refused to send them to a House-Senate conference committee. *(Senate key vote 6; House key vote 10)*

2. UNITED NATIONS. The UN, never a popular vote-getter in Congress, reached the nadir of esteem there May 18 when the House refused on a recorded teller vote of 156-202, to restore funding of $25,103,500 for the international body and seven affiliated agencies cut out of an appropriations bill by the Appropriations Committee. By the same vote the House refused to drop a committee provision limiting U.S. contributions to the UN and its agencies to 25 percent of the agencies' total annual assessments. The amendment to restore the funds and drop the limitation, offered by Edward J. Derwinski (R Ill.) to the fiscal 1973 State, Justice, Commerce Departments appropriations bill (HR 14989), was supported by President Nixon, but opposed by a majority of Republicans. Supporters of the amendment said it would be illegal for the United States to unilaterally reduce its contributions to 25 percent from 31.5 percent, and that the UN might go bankrupt as a result. But the conservative coalition of Republicans and southern Democrats, upset at the growing power of the communist and neutral countries in the UN, and by the admission of Red China to the body in 1971, garnered sufficient votes to defeat the amendment: R 56-99; D 100-103 (ND 92-49; SD 8-54). The Senate restored the UN funds and conferees retained them and the 25-percent limit, delaying the effective date of the limit until late 1973.

3. EDUCATION AID/BUSING RESTRICTIONS. The House June 8—by the relatively narrow margin of 38 votes (218-180)—cleared for the President's signature a landmark bill (S 659) authorizing $21-billion in federal aid to postsecondary education and desegregating school districts. Controversy over anti-busing language contained in the bill overshadowed the importance of its other provisions which authorized new programs of basic grants for every qualified needy college student, of federal cost-of-instruction allowances to colleges and universities, of expanded aid to career education and of $2-billion in aid to desegregating school districts. Late in 1971 the House had attached strict anti-busing language to the bill; early in 1972 the Senate had added more moderate restrictions. Twice—in March and in May—the House took the unusual step of voting to instruct its conferees on the bill to insist on retaining the stiff House restrictions. The votes to instruct were decisive—272-140 and 275-124—but still House conferees accepted compromise language, risking House rejection of the entire bill. The Senate killed, 44-26, an attempt to send the final version back to the conferees with instructions that they accept the House anti-busing provisions, and then adopted the conference report May 24 by a 63-15 vote. The final version managed to anger conservatives who desired more stringent restrictions and liberals who considered the compromise language unconstitutional. The division was evident in both parties on the June 8 House vote: R 89-76; D 129-104 (ND 109-44; SD 20-60).

4. GENERAL REVENUE SHARING. In a first step toward President Nixon's "great goal" of revitalizing the federal system, the House June 22, by a vote of 275-122, passed a bill sharing $29.6-billion in federal revenues with state and local governments over five years. Passage of the bill in the form reported by the Ways and Means Committee had been assured June 21 when the House agreed, 223-185, to end debate on the rule barring floor amendments to the committee bill. As passed by the House, HR 14370 favored larger, more industrialized states in distributing revenue-sharing funds and provided a bonus for states collecting income taxes. Republicans and northern Democrats gave strong support to the bill; most southern Democrats—many from rural states—voted against it: R 122-42; D 153-80 (ND 124-32; SD 29-48). *(Senate key votes 11, 12)*

5. CYCLAMATE COMPENSATION. Six House members changed their votes from nay to yea July 24, providing a seven-vote margin (177-170) to pass a bill (HR 13366) permitting food growers, manufacturers, packers and distributors to sue the federal government for losses incurred as a result of the 1969 government ban on cyclamates. Passage of the bill, said opponents, would set a bad precedent, making the federal government liable for damages every time it ordered a hazardous substance off the market. (Since the cyclamate ban, the Food and Drug Administration has put a partial ban on DES, a growth promotant for cattle, and on hexaclorophene, a substance used in many cosmetics and personal hygiene products.) The Justice Department said it would have no objection to passage of the bill. The bill died at the end of the Congress after the Senate took no action on it beyond hearings. The initial vote was 171-176 against passage—then three Democrats, Robert H. Mollohan (W.Va.), John Brademas (Ind.) and Harley O. Staggers (W.Va.) and three Republicans, William H. Harsha (Ohio), Sherman P. Lloyd (Utah) and William L. Dickinson (Ala.)—changed their nays to yeas, approving the bill: R 85-64; D 92-106 (ND 54-79; SD 38-27).

6. WITHDRAWAL FROM INDOCHINA. President Nixon's Vietnam policy in 1972 survived its most serious challenge ever in the House of Representatives, a body long dominated by members who supported U.S. participation in the Indochina war. The House Foreign Affairs Committee, in response to a request by the House Democratic Caucus, reversed its long-held position in support of U.S. involvement and voted 18-17 to add an end-the-war amendment to a military aid authorization bill (HR 16029). The committee's action for the first time sent to the House from committee a bill containing such an amendment, forcing House supporters of the President's policy to move to cut the language out of the bill. By a 229-177 recorded teller vote, the House Aug. 10 did cut from the bill the language which would have terminated U.S. involvement in the war by Oct. 1, subject to release of all U.S. prisoners of war, an accounting for men missing in action and agreement on a cease-fire to the extent necessary to protect withdrawing troops. Despite the House Democratic Caucus and Foreign Affairs Committee action in support of the end-the-war language, the House Democratic leadership—Speaker Carl Albert (D Okla.) and Majority Leader Hale Boggs (D La.)— refused to back the provision and both voted to drop it from the bill, a position supported by the conservative coalition: R 149-23; D 80-154 (ND 25-134; SD 55-20). *(Senate key vote 8)*

7. LABOR-HEW FUNDS VETO. A few hours after the President vetoed a bill (HR 15417) appropriating $30,-538,919,500 for the Department of Labor, the Department of Health, Education and Welfare (HEW) and related agencies for fiscal 1973, the House Aug. 16 failed to override the veto. The vote was 203-171—47 short of the two-thirds necessary. The President said he vetoed the bill because it was $1.8-billion more than his budget requests and because it failed to limit the amount of federal funds that could be distributed to the states for social services programs. The subsequent Labor-HEW appropriations bill (HR 16654) appropriated the same amount of money but permitted the President to impound up to $1.2-billion provided that he did not cut any one appropriation by more than 13 percent. Voting to sustain the first veto were 129 Republicans and 42 Democrats: R 22-129; D 181-42 (ND 146-8; SD 35-34).

8. SCHOOL BUSING. The depth of House opposition to the use of busing for school desegregation was demonstrated Aug. 18 when anti-busing forces rejected, by a 178-197 recorded teller vote, an amendment to the Equal Educational Opportunities bill (HR 13915) which would have declared that nothing in the bill was intended to violate the Constitution. The bill barred busing except to the school closest or next closest to a pupil's home and allowed for reopening of past school desegregation cases. The amendment, offered by Louis Stokes (D Ohio), was similar to language added by the Senate in previous years to anti-busing provisions to nullify their effect. The House—or House conferees—had often accepted this nullifying language. But opposition to busing increased in the House, particularly among non-southern representatives, as courts began requiring the transportation of students to desegregate schools in areas outside the South. More than half the members voting against the Stokes amendment represented non-southern districts: R 55-98; D 123-99 (ND 110-37; SD 13-62). The bill was then passed by a vote of 283-102, the largest showing of anti-busing strength in the House to date, but a liberal filibuster delayed Senate action and killed the bill. *(Senate key vote 17)*

9. FOREIGN TRAVEL. House conservatives, angered over statements made by antiwar actress Jane Fonda and former Attorney General Ramsey Clark while they were visiting North Vietnam, nearly succeeded Oct. 2 in passing a bill restricting travel to countries with which the United States was engaged in armed conflict. The bill, brought to the floor under suspension of the rules —requiring a two-thirds approval for passage (248 in this case)—failed to win the required votes and was defeated, 230-140. The bill was one of the few reported by the Internal Security Committee and would have applied in 1972 only to North Vietnam. Opponents of the bill claimed it was aimed at newsmen who had traveled to North Vietnam and filed stories embarrassing to the Nixon administration, particularly on the extent of U.S. bombing damage there. Existing law required government approval for travel to North Vietnam, North Korea and Cuba, but the Supreme Court ruled in 1967 that travel to a restricted area with a valid passport was not illegal. Republicans and southern Democrats voted overwhelmingly (192-39) for the bill: R 130-27; D 100-113 (ND 38-101; SD 62-12).

10. MINIMUM WAGE INCREASE. Business and agricultural lobby interests won a major victory in the House Oct. 3 when that body refused for a second time to send two different versions of a bill increasing the minimum wage to a conference committee—and thereby killed the bill for the 92nd Congress. Responding to charges that the Democratic conferees would dump the narrow House version in conference in favor of more liberal Senate-passed provisions *(Senate key vote 6)*, House members voted 188-196 to defeat the motion to send the bill to conference: R 23-137; D 165-59 (ND 147-1; SD 18-58). Working closely with Republican members of the Education and Labor Committee, business and agricultural interests pushed for promises from Democratic committee leaders to support key House-passed provisions in confe:ence. The Democratic committee members, a majority of the conferees on the bill, had staunchly supported the committee version of HR 7130 which was rejected by the House May 11. *(House key vote 1)* The ire of House members had been aroused earlier by the refusal of the committee members to follow two separate votes instructing them to fight in conference for the stringent anti-busing language added to the higher education act during House consideration in 1971. *(House key vote 3)* Last-minute talks prior to the final motion to send HR 7130 to conference deadlocked over a controversial House provision facilitating the employment of youths at wages below the applicable adult minimum which Democrats refused to accept.

11. DEBT LIMIT/SPENDING CEILING. Acceding to administration demands, the House Oct. 10 gave the President unprecedented authority to cut federal spending to $250-billion in fiscal 1973. By a 167-216 recorded teller vote, the House rejected a Democratic-backed proposal which would have merely solicited suggestions from the President on spending cutbacks for consideration when the 93rd Congress convened in January 1973: R 8-156; D 159-60 (ND 121-17; SD 38-43). As later passed by the House, HR 16810 gave the President absolute discretion to cut spending wherever he chose. Nixon had threatened to hold Congress responsible in the November elections for continued inflation and any future tax increases unless he was given broad budget-cutting power. Opponents of the measure argued that it delegated to the executive branch Congress' constitutional responsibility to allocate the tax revenues it raised. The Senate refused to go along with the President's demands and the spending ceiling and budget-cutting authority were deleted in conference from the bill raising the public debt limit to $465-billion through June 30, 1973. *(Senate key vote 18)*

12. WATER POLLUTION VETO OVERRIDE. The crucial vote overriding President Nixon's Oct. 17 veto of the Federal Water Pollution Control Act Amendments of 1972 came with the House vote to override—247-23— on Oct. 18. The Senate had voted earlier to override the veto, 52-12. The water pollution bill (S 2770), the most comprehensive and expensive environmental legislation in the nation's history, authorized $24.7-billion over three years to help clean up U.S. waters. President Nixon had proposed a $6-billion federal program, and said he vetoed S 2770 because its price tag was "staggering, budget-wrecking." The House vote to override was well over the two-thirds majority required: R 95-13; D 152-10 (ND 109-1; SD 43-9).

- KEY-

- **Y** Record vote for (yea).
- **✓** Pared for.
- **†** Announced for or CQ poll for.
- **N** Record vote against (nay).
- **X** Paired against.
- **-** Announced against or CQ Poll Against.
- **?** Not voting, voted "present" or did not announce.

	1	2	3	4	5	6		1	2	3	4	5	6		1	2	3	4	5	6
ALABAMA							**IOWA**							**NEW HAMPSHIRE**						
Allen	Y	N	Y	†	Y	Y	Hughes	N	Y	Y	†	N	N	McIntyre	N	Y	†	?	N	N
Sparkman	Y	N	Y	?	Y	Y	*Miller*	Y	Y	Y	Y	Y	Y	*Cotton*	Y	N	N	N	Y	Y
ALASKA							**KANSAS**							**NEW JERSEY**						
Gravel	N	Y	Y	•	X	N	*Dole*	Y	Y	Y	N	Y	Y	Williams	N	Y	Y	Y	X	N
Stevens	N	Y	Y	Y	Y	N	*Pearson*	N	Y	Y	N	Y	N	*Case*	N	Y	Y	Y	†	N
ARIZONA							**KENTUCKY**							**NEW MEXICO**						
Fannin	Y	N	N	N	Y	Y	*Cook*	Y	Y	Y	N	Y	Y	Anderson	?	Y	Y	Y	Y	?
Goldwater	Y	N	N	N	Y	Y	*Cooper*	Y	Y	Y	Y	Y	Y	Montoya	N	Y	Y	Y	Y	N
ARKANSAS							**LOUISIANA**							**NEW YORK**						
Fulbright	✓	Y	Y	Y	N	?	Ellender	Y	N	Y	Y	Y	✓	*Buckley**	Y	N	N	N	Y	Y
McClellan	Y	N	✓	?	?	Y	Long	Y	N	Y	Y	Y	Y	*Javits*	N	Y	Y	Y	Y	N
CALIFORNIA							**MAINE**							**NORTH CAROLINA**						
Cranston	N	Y	Y	Y	X	N	Muskie	X	Y	Y	?	N	N	Ervin	Y	N	N	Y	Y	Y
Tunney	N	Y	Y	Y	N	N	*Smith*	Y	N	Y	N	Y	N	Jordan	Y	N	Y	Y	Y	?
COLORADO							**MARYLAND**							**NORTH DAKOTA**						
Allott	Y	Y	Y	N	Y	Y	*Beall*	N	Y	Y	N	†	Y	Burdick	N	Y	Y	Y	N	X
Dominick	Y	Y	Y	N	†	Y	*Mathias*	N	Y	Y	Y	Y	Y	*Young*	Y	N	Y	N	Y	Y
CONNECTICUT							**MASSACHUSETTS**							**OHIO**						
Ribicoff	N	N	Y	Y	N	N	Kennedy	-	Y	Y	Y	N	N	*Saxbe*	Y	Y	Y	Y	Y	Y
Weicker	Y	Y	Y	N	Y	N	*Brooke*	N	Y	Y	Y	Y	N	*Taft*	X	N	Y	Y	Y	Y
DELAWARE							**MICHIGAN**							**OKLAHOMA**						
Boggs	N	Y	Y	†	Y	N	Hart	N	Y	Y	†	Y	N	Harris	N	Y	Y	?	N	N
Roth	Y	Y	Y	Y	Y	Y	*Griffin*	Y	N	Y	N	Y	Y	*Bellmon*	Y	Y	Y	N	Y	Y
FLORIDA							**MINNESOTA**							**OREGON**						
Chiles	Y	N	✓	Y	Y	Y	Humphrey	-	Y	Y	†	X	N	*Hatfield*	-	Y	Y	†	✓	✓
Gurney	Y	N	Y	Y	Y	Y	Mondale	N	Y	Y	Y	N	N	*Packwood*	?	Y	†	N	†	Y
GEORGIA							**MISSISSIPPI**							**PENNSYLVANIA**						
Gambrell	Y	N	N	Y	✓	Y	Eastland	Y	N	X	Y	Y	Y	*Schweiker*	N	Y	Y	N	Y	N
Talmadge	✓	N	Y	Y	Y	Y	Stennis	Y	N	N	Y	Y	Y	*Scott*	N	Y	Y	Y	Y	N
HAWAII							**MISSOURI**							**RHODE ISLAND**						
Inouye	N	Y	Y	?	-	N	Eagleton	N	Y	Y	Y	N	N	Pastore	N	Y	Y	Y	Y	N
Fong	-	Y	Y	Y	Y	Y	Symington	N	Y	Y	Y	Y	Y	Pell	N	Y	Y	Y	✓	N
IDAHO							**MONTANA**							**SOUTH CAROLINA**						
Church	N	Y	Y	Y	N	N	Mansfield	X	Y	Y	Y	N	N	Hollings	Y	N	Y	Y	Y	Y
Jordan	Y	Y	Y	N	Y	N	Metcalf	N	Y	Y	N	N	N	*Thurmond*	Y	N	Y	N	Y	Y
ILLINOIS							**NEBRASKA**							**SOUTH DAKOTA**						
Stevenson	N	Y	Y	Y	N	N	*Curtis*	Y	N	Y	N	Y	Y	McGovern	N	Y	†	†	N	N
Percy	N	Y	Y	Y	Y	N	*Hruska*	Y	N	Y	N	Y	Y	*Mundt*	?	?	?	?	?	?
INDIANA							**NEVADA**							**TENNESSEE**						
Bayh	N	Y	Y	†	N	N	Bible	Y	Y	Y	Y	Y	N	*Baker*	Y	N	Y	N	✓	†
Hartke	-	†	Y	†	Y	N	Cannon	Y	Y	Y	Y	✓	N	*Brock*	Y	N	Y	N	Y	Y

	1	2	3	4	5	6
TEXAS						
Bentsen	Y	N	Y	Y	Y	Y
Tower	Y	N	Y	N	Y	Y
UTAH						
Moss	N	Y	Y	Y	N	Y
Bennett	Y	Y	N	N	Y	Y
VERMONT						
Aiken	Y	Y	Y	Y	Y	N
Stafford	N	Y	Y	Y	Y	N
VIRGINIA						
Byrd, Jr.**	Y	N	Y	Y	Y	Y
Spong	Y	N	Y	Y	Y	Y
WASHINGTON						
Jackson	-	-	†	†	Y	N
Magnuson	-	Y	Y	Y	X	N
WEST VIRGINIA						
Byrd	Y	Y	Y	Y	N	N
Randolph	N	Y	Y	Y	N	N
WISCONSIN						
Nelson	N	Y	Y	Y	N	N
Proxmire	N	N	Y	Y	N	N
WYOMING						
McGee	N	Y	Y	Y	Y	N
Hansen	✓	N	N	N	Y	Y

Democrats   *Republicans*   * *Buckley elected as Conservative*   ** *Byrd elected as independent*

• *Voted present to avoid possible conflict of interest.*

1. S 2515. Equal Employment Opportunities Enforcement. Dominick (R Colo.) amendment in the nature of a substitute to provide that the EEOC general counsel would seek enforcement of equal job opportunities against recalcitrant employers by bringing suit in federal district court; should the employers be state or local governments, the United States attorney general would handle the case. Adopted 45-39: R 27-12; D 18-27 (ND 3-26; SD 15-1), Feb. 15, 1972. A "yea" was a vote supporting the President's position.

2. S 659. Omnibus Education Amendments of 1972. Mansfield (D Mont.)-Scott (R Pa.) amendment a) barring use of federal education funds for busing to overcome racial imbalance except on voluntary written request of local school officials, b) forbidding federal pressure on local school boards to use state or local funds for busing unless constitutionally required and forbidding busing which would risk the health of the children involved, impinge on the educational process or result in children attending inferior schools, and c) postponing the effective date of federal court orders requiring busing between districts or consolidation of two or more districts. Adopted 63-34: R 28-16; D 35-18 (ND 33-2; SD 2-16), Feb. 29, 1972.

3. H J Res 208. Equal Rights Amendment. Passage of the resolution containing a constitutional amendment guaranteeing equal rights for men and women. A two-thirds majority vote (62 in this case) is required for adoption of a constitutional amendment. Passed 84-8: R 37-6; D 47-2 (ND 34-0; SD 13-2), March 22, 1972. A "yea" was a vote supporting the President's position.

4. S Res 280. Congressional Immunity-Senator Gravel. Adoption of resolution authorizing the Senate to file a friend of the court brief on congressional immunity; to pay expenses contingent to preparation of the brief and expenses incurred by Gravel in printing his personal brief and supporting documents. Adopted 55-27: R 15-27; D 40-0 (ND 26-0; SD 14-0), March 23, 1972.

5. Kleindienst Nomination. Confirmation of Richard G. Kleindienst as attorney general. Confirmed 64-19: R 38-0; D 26-19 (ND 12-17; SD 14-2), June 8, 1972. A "yea" was a vote supporting the President's position.

6. S 1861. Minimum Wage Increase. Taft (R Ohio) amendment in the nature of a substitute to raise the minimum wage for non-agricultural employees covered by the Fair Labor Standards Act of 1938 prior to its amendment in 1966 to $1.80 an hour in 1972 and $2 an hour in 1973, from the existing level of $1.60; increase the hourly wage floor for workers covered by the 1966 and 1972 amendments to $1.70 in 1972, $1.80 in 1973 and $2 in 1974; raise the minimum wage for agricultural workers covered under the act to $1.50 in 1972 and $1.70 in 1973, from $1.30. Rejected 46-47: R 30-13; D 16-34 (ND 2-33; SD 14-1), July 20, 1972.

	7	8	9	10	11	12
ALABAMA						
Allen	N	?	N	Y	N	Y
Sparkman	Y	N	Y	Y	N	N
ALASKA						
Gravel	Y	Y	Y	N	Y	Y
Stevens	N	Y	Y	N	Y	Y
ARIZONA						
Fannin	N	N	Y	Y	N	N
Goldwater	N	N	X	Y	N	?
ARKANSAS						
Fulbright	N	Y	Y	Y	N	N
McClellan	N	N	Y	Y	N	Y
CALIFORNIA						
Cranston	Y	Y	Y	N	Y	N
Tunney	Y	Y	Y	N	Y	N
COLORADO						
Allott	Y	N	Y	Y	N	Y
Dominick	N	N	Y	Y	N	√
CONNECTICUT						
Ribicoff	Y	Y	Y	N	Y	N
Weicker	N	N	Y	N	Y	X
DELAWARE						
Boggs	Y	N	Y	N	Y	Y
Roth	N	N	Y	N	Y	Y
FLORIDA						
Chiles	Y	Y	Y	Y	N	Y
Gurney	N	N	Y	Y	N	Y
GEORGIA						
Gambrell	-	†	†	†	N	N
Talmadge	N	N	Y	Y	N	N
HAWAII						
Inouye	Y	Y	Y	N	Y	Y
Fong	Y	N	Y	Y	†	√
IDAHO						
Church	Y	Y	Y	Y	N	N
Jordan	N	N	Y	Y	N	N
ILLINOIS						
Stevenson	Y	Y	Y	N	Y	N
Percy	†	Y	√	N	N	N
INDIANA						
Bayh	Y	Y	Y	N	Y	Y
Hartke	N	Y	Y	N	Y	N

	7	8	9	10	11	12
IOWA						
Hughes	Y	Y	Y	N	-	-
Miller	N	N	Y	Y	N	N
KANSAS						
Dole	N	N	Y	Y	N	N
Pearson	Y	Y	Y	N	N	N
KENTUCKY						
Cook	N	Y	Y	Y	N	N
Cooper	Y	N	Y	Y	N	N
LOUISIANA						
Edwards[1]				Y	N	N
Long	N	N	Y	N	N	N
MAINE						
Muskie	?	Y	Y	N	N	N
Smith	Y	N	Y	N	N	Y
MARYLAND						
Beall	N	N	Y	N	N	N
Mathias	Y	Y	Y	Y	N	N
MASSACHUSETTS						
Kennedy	Y	Y	Y	N	Y	N
Brooke	Y	Y	Y	N	Y	Y
MICHIGAN						
Hart	Y	Y	Y	N	Y	N
Griffin	N	N	Y	X	?	N
MINNESOTA						
Humphrey	Y	Y	Y	N	Y	N
Mondale	Y	Y	Y	N	N	N
MISSISSIPPI						
Eastland	N	N	√	Y	N	Y
Stennis	N	N	Y	Y	?	Y
MISSOURI						
Eagleton	?	Y	?	Y	N	?
Symington	N	Y	Y	N	N	Y
MONTANA						
Mansfield	N	Y	X	N	N	√
Metcalf	N	Y	Y	N	-	N
NEBRASKA						
Curtis	N	N	Y	Y	N	N
Hruska	N	N	Y	Y	N	Y
NEVADA						
Bible	N	Y	Y	Y	Y	Y
Cannon	Y	N	Y	Y	-	-

	7	8	9	10	11	12
NEW HAMPSHIRE						
McIntyre	Y	N	Y	N	-	N
Cotton	N	N	Y	Y	N	Y
NEW JERSEY						
Williams	Y	Y	Y	N	Y	N
Case	Y	Y	Y	N	Y	Y
NEW MEXICO						
Anderson	?	Y	Y	Y	N	N
Montoya	N	Y	√	Y	N	Y
NEW YORK						
*Buckley**	N	N	N	Y	Y	N
Javits	Y	Y	Y	N	Y	N
NORTH CAROLINA						
Ervin	Y	N	Y	N	N	Y
Jordan	?	N	Y	Y	N	Y
NORTH DAKOTA						
Burdick	N	Y	Y	N	N	Y
Young	N	N	Y	N	Y	N
OHIO						
Saxbe	N	N	Y	Y	Y	?
Taft	Y	N	Y	N	?	-
OKLAHOMA						
Harris	Y	Y	Y	N	?	?
Bellmon	N	N	Y	Y	N	?
OREGON						
Hatfield	Y	Y	Y	Y	-	√
Packwood	N	N	Y	Y	N	N
PENNSYLVANIA						
Schweiker	Y	Y	Y	N	Y	N
Scott	N	N	Y	√	Y	N
RHODE ISLAND						
Pastore	Y	Y	Y	N	Y	N
Pell	Y	Y	Y	N	?	Y
SOUTH CAROLINA						
Hollings	Y	Y	Y	Y	N	Y
Thurmond	N	N	Y	Y	N	X
SOUTH DAKOTA						
McGovern	?	Y	Y	N	?	X
Mundt	?	?	?	?	?	?
TENNESSEE						
Baker	N	N	√	Y	N	X
Brock	N	N	Y	?	N	N

- KEY -

Y	Record vote for (yea).
√	Paired for.
†	Announced for or CQ poll for.
N	Record vote against (nay).
X	Paird against.
-	Announced against or CQ poll against.
?	Not voting, voted "present" or did not announce.

	7	8	9	10	11	12
TEXAS						
Bentsen	Y	Y	Y	Y	N	N
Tower	N	N	Y	Y	N	N
UTAH						
Moss	†	Y	Y	N	N	N
Bennett	N	N	Y	Y	N	N
VERMONT						
Aiken	N	N	Y	Y	N	N
Stafford	Y	Y	Y	Y	N	N
VIRGINIA						
Byrd, Jr.**	N	N	Y	Y	N	N
Spong	N	Y	Y	N	N	N
WASHINGTON						
Jackson	Y	N	Y	N	N	Y
Magnuson	N	Y	Y	N	-	Y
WEST VIRGINIA						
Byrd	N	N	Y	N	N	Y
Randolph	Y	Y	Y	Y	N	Y
WISCONSIN						
Nelson	Y	Y	Y	N	N	N
Proxmire	Y	Y	Y	N	N	Y
WYOMING						
McGee	N	N	Y	N	?	Y
Hansen	N	N	Y	Y	N	N

Democrats   *Republicans*   * Buckley elected as Conservative   ** Byrd elected as independent

1 Edwards appointed to fill seat left vacant by July 27 death of Ellender; Edwards took seat Aug. 7. On key vote 7, Ellender was recorded as not voting.

7. S 3390. Foreign Military Aid Authorizations. Passage of the bill authorizing appropriations of $1,820,000,000 in fiscal 1973 for foreign military aid and Bangladesh relief ($100,000,000). Rejected 42-48: R 14-29; D 28-19 (ND 22-10; SD 6-9), July 24, 1972.

8. HR 15495. Defense Procurement Authorization. Brooke (R Mass.) substitute amendment requiring a cutoff of funds for support of U.S. air, naval and ground troops in Vietnam, Laos and Cambodia within four months of enactment of the bill, pending the release of U.S. prisoners of war. Adopted 49-47: R 11-33; D 38-14 (ND 32-5; SD 6-9), Aug. 2, 1972. A "nay" was a vote supporting the President's position.

9. Exec L, 92nd Congress, Second Session. ABM Treaty. Resolution approving ratification of the treaty, signed May 26, 1972, by the United States and the Soviet Union, limiting each nation to two antiballistic missile (ABM) installations, one protecting the national capital and one protecting an offensive missile site. Ratified 88-2: R 40-1; D 48-1 (ND 34-0; SD 14-1). Aug. 3, 1972. A "yea" was a vote in support of the President's position.

10. S 945. No-Fault Auto Insurance. Hruska (R Neb.) motion to refer to the Judiciary Committee for further consideration a bill (S 945) requiring all motorists to carry insurance providing compensation for bodily injury regardless of who caused an accident in which they were involved and requiring states to pass no-fault laws containing minimum federal standards. Adopted 49-46: R 28-13; D 21-33 (ND 7-30; SD 14-3), Aug. 8, 1972.

11. HR 14370. General Revenue Sharing. Ribicoff (D Conn.) amendment revising the formula for distribution of federal revenues among the states. The revised formula gave greater shares of federal revenues to populous, highly urbanized states. Rejected 24-61: R 11-29; D 13-32 (ND 13-16; SD 0-16), Sept. 6, 1972.

12. HR 14370. General Revenue Sharing. McClellan (D Ark.) amendment appropriating $2,650,000,000 for fiscal 1972 and $5,450,000,000 for fiscal 1973 for federal revenue sharing with the states and requiring annual congressional approval of appropriations for revenue sharing in fiscal 1974-77. Rejected 34-49: R 11-23; D 23-26 (ND 15-17; SD 8-9), Sept. 7, 1972.

- KEY -

Y	Record vote for (yea).
√	Pared for.
†	Announced for or CQ poll for.
N	Record vote against (nay).
X	Paired against.
-	Announced against or CQ Poll Against.
?	Not voting, voted "present" or did not announce.

State / Senator	13	14	15	16	17	18
ALABAMA						
Allen	Y	N	Y	N	Y	Y
Sparkman	Y	-	Y	N	Y	†
ALASKA						
Gravel	N	?	X	Y	N	N
Stevens	Y	N	Y	Y	N	Y
ARIZONA						
Fannin	Y	√	Y	N	Y	Y
Goldwater	Y	?	?	N	Y	?
ARKANSAS						
Fulbright	N	N	Y	N	N	N
McClellan	Y	N	Y	N	Y	N
CALIFORNIA						
Cranston	N	Y	N	Y	N	N
Tunney	N	Y	N	Y	N	N
COLORADO						
Allott	Y	√	√	?	√	?
Dominick	Y	†	Y	N	Y	Y
CONNECTICUT						
Ribicoff	-	Y	N	Y	N	N
Weicker	N	Y	N	Y	N	-
DELAWARE						
Boggs	Y	Y	N	Y	N	†
Roth	Y	Y	Y	Y	Y	Y
FLORIDA						
Chiles	Y	Y	Y	Y	Y	N
Gurney	Y	Y	Y	N	Y	?
GEORGIA						
Gambrell	Y	Y	Y	Y	Y	Y
Talmadge	Y	N	Y	N	Y	Y
HAWAII						
Inouye	√	X	X	Y	N	N
Fong	Y	Y	Y	N	Y	†
IDAHO						
Church	N	Y	Y	√	N	N
Jordan	Y	N	Y	N	X	N
ILLINOIS						
Stevenson	N	Y	N	Y	N	N
Percy	Y	Y	N	Y	N	Y
INDIANA						
Bayh	N	N	N	Y	N	?
Hartke	N	-	N	Y	N	?
IOWA						
Hughes	N	√	N	Y	N	X
Miller	Y	Y	Y	Y	-	†
KANSAS						
Dole	Y	N	Y	N	Y	?
Pearson	Y	Y	Y	Y	N	?
KENTUCKY						
Cook	Y	N	Y	Y	†	-
Cooper	N	Y	N	N	N	Y
LOUISIANA						
Edwards	Y	N	Y	N	Y	?
Long	Y	N	Y	N	Y	Y
MAINE						
Muskie	N	Y	N	Y	N	N
Smith	N	Y	N	Y	Y	Y
MARYLAND						
Beall	Y	Y	N	Y	Y	X
Mathias	N	Y	N	Y	Y	N
MASSACHUSETTS						
Kennedy	X	Y	N	Y	N	N
Brooke	N	Y	N	Y	N	N
MICHIGAN						
Hart	N	Y	N	Y	N	N
Griffin	?	Y	Y	Y	Y	Y
MINNESOTA						
Humphrey	N	Y	N	Y	N	N
Mondale	N	Y	N	Y	N	N
MISSISSIPPI						
Eastland	Y	N	√	X	Y	√
Stennis	Y	X	Y	N	Y	Y
MISSOURI						
Eagleton	N	Y	N	†	N	Y
Symington	N	Y	Y	Y	N	N
MONTANA						
Mansfield	N	N	Y	√	N	N
Metcalf	N	†	?	√	?	?
NEBRASKA						
Curtis	†	N	Y	N	√	†
Hruska	Y	Y	Y	N	Y	Y
NEVADA						
Bible	Y	N	Y	N	Y	N
Cannon	Y	-	Y	X	Y	?
NEW HAMPSHIRE						
McIntyre	√	Y	?	†	?	Y
Cotton	Y	N	Y	N	Y	Y
NEW JERSEY						
Williams	N	Y	N	Y	N	N
Case	N	Y	N	Y	N	N
NEW MEXICO						
Anderson	Y	N	Y	Y	Y	Y
Montoya	Y	N	Y	Y	N	†
NEW YORK						
Buckley*	Y	Y	Y	N	Y	Y
Javits	N	Y	N	Y	N	N
NORTH CAROLINA						
Ervin	Y	N	Y	N	Y	N
Jordan	Y	?	Y	N	Y	N
NORTH DAKOTA						
Burdick	N	N	Y	N	N	N
Young	Y	X	Y	N	Y	Y
OHIO						
Saxbe	Y	?	Y	?	Y	?
Taft	Y	√	?	N	N	N
OKLAHOMA						
Harris	N	Y	Y	Y	?	?
Bellmon	Y	?	Y	N	Y	?
OREGON						
Hatfield	N	Y	N	†	-	?
Packwood	Y	Y	Y	Y	Y	N
PENNSYLVANIA						
Schweiker	N	Y	N	Y	N	N
Scott	Y	Y	N	Y	N	Y
RHODE ISLAND						
Pastore	Y	Y	N	Y	N	N
Pell	N	√	N	√	?	N
SOUTH CAROLINA						
Hollings	Y	N	Y	Y	Y	?
Thurmond	Y	N	Y	N	Y	√
SOUTH DAKOTA						
McGovern	X	?	?	†	-	N
Mundt	?	?	?	?	?	?
TENNESSEE						
Baker	Y	?	√	?	Y	?
Brock	Y	†	Y	N	Y	†
TEXAS						
Bentsen	Y	N	Y	Y	Y	?
Tower	†	X	†	-	Y	†
UTAH						
Moss	N	†	N	Y	N	N
Bennett	Y	Y	Y	-	Y	Y
VERMONT						
Aiken	N	Y	N	Y	Y	N
Stafford	N	X	N	Y	N	N
VIRGINIA						
Byrd, Jr.**	Y	Y	Y	N	Y	Y
Spong	Y	Y	Y	Y	Y	?
WASHINGTON						
Jackson	Y	Y	N	Y	N	Y
Magnuson	Y	Y	X	Y	Y	N
WEST VIRGINIA						
Byrd	Y	N	Y	†	Y	Y
Randolph	Y	N	Y	N	Y	Y
WISCONSIN						
Nelson	N	Y	N	Y	N	N
Proxmire	N	Y	Y	Y	Y	Y
WYOMING						
McGee	Y	?	?	?	?	?
Hansen	Y	N	Y	N	Y	Y

Democrats   *Republicans*

* *Buckley elected as Conservative*   ** *Byrd elected as independent*

13. S J Res 241. SALT Agreement. Jackson (D Wash.) amendment—as amended by voice votes to state that continued modernization of U.S. nuclear forces was required for a prudent nuclear posture but expressing the hope that such actions would become less necessary in the future—Request that any future permanent treaty on offensive nuclear arms "not limit the United States to levels of intercontinental strategic forces inferior to" those of the Soviet Union but be based rather on "the principle of equality"; endorse the maintenance of a vigorous research, development and modernization program, and provide that failure to negotiate a permanent treaty limiting offensive arms would "jeopardize the supreme national interests" of the United States and would be grounds for abrogating the U.S.-Soviet treaty limiting defensive nuclear weapons. Adopted 56-35: R 30-11; D 26-24 (ND 10-22; SD 16-2), Sept. 14, 1972. A "yea" was a vote supporting the President's position.

14. S 3939. Federal-Aid Highway Program. Adoption of the Cooper (R Ky.)-Muskie (D Maine) amendment permitting the use of up to $800-million allocated for urban system funds from the highway trust fund for rail transportation facilities. Adopted 48-26: R 24-8; D 24-18 (ND 19-8; SD 5-10), Sept. 19, 1972.

15. HR 1. Social Security. Long (D La.) motion to table, and thus kill, Ribicoff (D Conn.) amendment establishing an Opportunities for Families program to provide training and employment for welfare recipients able to work and a Family Assistance Plan guaranteeing an annual federal payment of $2,600 tied to a cost-of-living increase for a family of four headed by an unemployable adult with no outside income. Tabling motion adopted 52-34: R 24-15; D 28-19 (ND 11-19; SD 17-0), Oct. 3, 1972.

16. S 3970. Consumer Protection Agency. Ribicoff (D Conn.) motion to invoke cloture (limit further debate) on the bill creating an independent consumer protection agency to represent consumer interests before other federal agencies and courts. Motion rejected 52-30: R 20-18; D 32-12 (ND 26-1; SD 6-11), Oct. 5, 1972. A two-thirds majority of those present and voting (55 in this case) is needed to invoke cloture.

17. HR 13915. Equal Educational Opportunities. Proxmire (D Wis.) motion to invoke cloture (cut off debate) on the bill containing strong busing limits. Rejected 49-38: R 26-12; D 23-26 (ND 7-25; SD 16-1), Oct. 12, 1972. A two-thirds majority (58 in this case) was necessary to invoke cloture. A "yea" was a vote in support of the President's position.

18. HR 16810. Debt Ceiling. Adoption of the conference report (H Rept 92-1606) on the bill raising the public debt ceiling by $15-billion to $465-billion through June 30, 1973, placing a $250-billion limit on federal outlays in fiscal 1973 and authorizing the President to cut appropriations in 50 categories—excluding certain "uncontrollable" expenditures such as Social Security benefits—up to 20 percent to hold federal spending to the $250-billion limit. Rejected 27-39: R 15-10; D 12-29 (ND 6-24; SD 6-5), Oct. 17, 1972. A "yea" was a vote supporting the President's position.

- KEY -

Y Record vote for (yea).
✓ Paired for.
† Announced for or CQ poll for.
N Record vote against (nay).
X Paird against.
- Announced against or CQ poll against.
? Not voting, voted "present" or did not announce.

	1	2	3	4	5	6
ALABAMA						
1 Edwards	Y	N	N	Y	N	Y
2 Dickinson	Y	N	N	Y	Y	Y
3 Andrews, E.	Y	N	N	X	Y	Y
4 Nichols	Y	-	N	Y	N	†
5 Flowers	Y	-	N	Y	Y	Y
6 Buchanan	Y	N	N	Y	N	Y
7 Bevill	N	N	N	Y	N	Y
8 Jones	N	N	Y	N	Y	Y
ALASKA						
AL Begich	N	N	Y	Y	N	N
ARIZONA						
1 Rhodes	Y	Y	N	Y	Y	Y
2 Udall	N	Y	Y	Y	N	N
3 Steiger	Y	N	N	Y	Y	Y
ARKANSAS						
1 Alexander	Y	?	N	N	✓	N
2 Mills	N	?	N	Y	?	N
3 Hammerschmidt	Y	N	Y	Y	Y	Y
4 Pryor	N	?	✓	?	N	N
CALIFORNIA						
1 Clausen	Y	N	Y	Y	Y	Y
2 Johnson	N	Y	Y	Y	Y	Y
3 Moss	N	Y	✓	N	Y	N
4 Leggett	N	Y	Y	Y	Y	N
5 Burton	N	Y	-	N	Y	N
6 Mailliard	Y	Y	Y	•	Y	Y
7 Dellums	N	Y	N	Y	Y	N
8 Miller	N	-	✓	Y	Y	†
9 Edwards	N	Y	Y	Y	N	N
10 Gubser	Y	Y	Y	Y	•	Y
11 McCloskey	N	†	Y	Y	?	N
12 Talcott	Y	N	Y	Y	?	Y
13 Teague	Y	N	Y	Y	Y	Y
14 Waldie	N	Y	N	✓	Y	N
15 McFall	N	N	Y	N	Y	Y
16 Sisk	N	Y	N	N	Y	N
17 Anderson	N	Y	Y	Y	?	N
18 Mathias	Y	N	N	Y	Y	Y
19 Holifield	N	-	✓	N	Y	Y
20 Smith	Y	N	N	Y	Y	Y
21 Hawkins	N	Y	N	Y	N	N
22 Corman	N	Y	N	N	Y	N
23 Clawson	Y	N	?	N	Y	Y
24 Rousselot	Y	N	N	N	Y	Y
25 Wiggins	Y	-	Y	Y	Y	Y
26 Rees	N	Y	Y	N	N	N
27 Goldwater	Y	N	N	N	Y	Y
28 Bell	N	Y	Y	N	Y	Y
29 Danielson	N	N	✓	Y	Y	N
30 Roybal	N	Y	Y	N	-	N
31 Wilson	N	N	N	Y	N	Y
32 Hosmer	Y	Y	Y	Y	Y	Y
33 Pettis	Y	†	Y	†	✓	Y
34 Hanna	N	Y	Y	Y	Y	N
35 Schmitz	Y	N	N	X	Y	Y
36 Wilson	Y	N	†	X	Y	Y
37 Van Deerlin	N	Y	N	Y	N	N
38 Veysey	†	N	N	Y	Y	Y
COLORADO						
1 McKevitt	Y	N	N	Y	X	Y
2 Brotzman	Y	?	Y	Y	N	Y
3 Evans	N	Y	Y	X	N	N
4 Aspinall	N	N	Y	N	Y	?
CONNECTICUT						
1 Cotter	N	N	Y	Y	-	N
2 Steele	N	Y	Y	N	X	N
3 Giaimo	N	N	N	X	Y	N

	1	2	3	4	5	6
4 McKinney	N	Y	Y	†	X	N
5 Monagan	N	Y	Y	N	X	N
6 Grasso	N	N	Y	Y	N	N
DELAWARE						
AL DuPont	Y	Y	Y	Y	N	Y
FLORIDA						
1 Sikes	Y	N	N	N	Y	Y
2 Fuqua	Y	-	Y	X	N	Y
3 Bennett	Y	N	N	N	N	N
4 Chappell	Y	N	X	N	Y	Y
5 Frey	Y	N	N	Y	N	Y
6 Gibbons	Y	Y	N	N	Y	N
7 Haley	Y	N	N	N	N	Y
8 Young	Y	N	Y	N	Y	Y
9 Rogers	Y	N	N	N	N	Y
10 Burke	Y	?	N	?	N	Y
11 Pepper	N	Y	Y	Y	✓	-
12 Fascell	N	Y	Y	Y	N	N
GEORGIA						
1 Hagan	Y	?	N	?	?	?
2 Mathis	Y	N	N	N	N	Y
3 Brinkley	Y	N	Y	Y	N	Y
4 Blackburn	Y	-	N	N	✓	Y
5 Thompson	†	N	N	Y	Y	Y
6 Flynt	Y	N	N	N	?	?
7 Davis	Y	N	Y	?	?	?
8 Stuckey	Y	N	N	N	✓	Y
9 Landrum	?	N	N	Y	?	Y
10 Stephens	Y	N	Y	Y	Y	Y
HAWAII						
1 Matsunaga	N	Y	Y	Y	✓	N
2 Mink	N	Y	Y	Y	✓	N
IDAHO						
1 McClure	Y	N	Y	?	✓	Y
2 Hansen	N	Y	Y	N	Y	Y
ILLINOIS						
1 Metcalfe	?	?	X	✓	?	?
2 Mikva	N	Y	X	Y	X	N
3 Murphy, M.	N	Y	Y	Y	Y	N
4 Derwinski	Y	Y	X	Y	Y	Y
5 Kluczynski	N	N	Y	Y	•Y	?
6 Collins	N	Y	N	Y	N	N
7 Annunzio	N	N	N	Y	N	N
8 Rostenkowski	N	N	Y	X	N	N
9 Yates	N	Y	Y	N	N	N
10 Collier	Y	N	N	Y	†	Y
11 Pucinski	N	?	Y	Y	?	N
12 McClory	Y	Y	✓	Y	Y	Y
13 Crane	Y	N	N	Y	N	Y
14 Erlenborn	Y	Y	Y	✓	✓	Y
15 Carlson	Y	N	Y	Y	Y	Y
16 Anderson	Y	Y	Y	Y	Y	Y
17 Arends	Y	Y	Y	Y	Y	Y
18 Michel	Y	N	N	Y	Y	Y
19 Railsback	Y	Y	Y	Y	Y	Y
20 Findley	Y	Y	N	N	Y	Y
21 Gray	N	N	Y	Y	Y	N
22 Springer	Y	†	†	Y	N	Y
23 Shipley	N	N	Y	N	N	N
24 Price	N	Y	N	Y	N	Y
INDIANA						
1 Madden	N	Y	N	Y	N	N
2 Landgrebe	Y	N	N	N	?	Y
3 Brademas	N	Y	N	Y	N	N
4 Roush	N	N	Y	N	Y	N
5 Hillis	N	N	N	Y	Y	Y
6 Bray	Y	N	N	N	Y	Y
7 Myers	Y	N	Y	N	N	Y
8 Zion	Y	N	Y	Y	Y	Y
9 Hamilton	N	Y	N	Y	N	N
10 Dennis	Y	N	N	N	N	Y
11 Jacobs	N	Y	Y	N	Y	N
IOWA						
1 Schwengel	Y	Y	Y	Y	N	N
2 Culver	N	Y	Y	Y	N	N
3 Gross	Y	N	N	N	Y	Y
4 Kyl	Y	N	Y	Y	Y	Y
5 Smith	N	N	Y	Y	Y	N
6 Mayne	Y	Y	N	Y	Y	Y
7 Scherle	Y	N	Y	N	N	Y

	1	2	3	4	5	6
KANSAS						
1 Sebelius	Y	N	Y	N	Y	Y
2 Roy	N	?	Y	N	N	N
3 Winn	Y	N	Y	N	Y	Y
4 Shriver	Y	N	Y	N	Y	Y
5 Skubitz	Y	N	Y	N	Y	Y
KENTUCKY						
1 Stubblefield	?	?	N	Y	Y	Y
2 Natcher	Y	N	N	Y	N	Y
3 Mazzoli	Y	N	Y	N	Y	N
4 Snyder	Y	N	N	N	N	N
5 Carter	Y	N	Y	N	N	Y
6 Curlin	Y	N	Y	Y	N	N
7 Perkins	N	N	Y	N	N	N
LOUISIANA						
1 Hebert	Y	?	N	Y	✓	?
2 Boggs	N	?	Y	Y	✓	Y
3 Caffery	Y	N	N	Y	N	Y
4 Waggonner	Y	?	N	N	Y	Y
5 Passman	†	N	X	N	Y	†
6 Rarick	Y	N	N	N	-	†
7 Vacancy						
8 Long	N	?	N	N	?	?
MAINE						
1 Kyros	N	?	Y	Y	N	N
2 Hathaway	N	Y	Y	N	N	N
MARYLAND						
1 Mills	Y	N	N	Y	Y	Y
2 Long	N	N	Y	N	N	N
3 Garmatz	N	?	N	Y	Y	N
4 Sarbanes	N	Y	Y	N	N	N
5 Hogan	Y	N	N	Y	N	Y
6 Byron	Y	N	N	N	Y	Y
7 Mitchell	N	Y	N	✓	N	N
8 Gude	N	Y	✓	Y	N	N
MASSACHUSETTS						
1 Conte	N	Y	Y	N	N	N
2 Boland	N	N	Y	Y	N	N
3 Drinan	N	Y	N	N	N	N
4 Donohue	N	?	Y	Y	N	N
5 Vacancy						
6 Harrington	N	Y	N	Y	?	N
7 Macdonald	?	?	Y	Y	N	N

	1	2	3	4	5	6
8 O'Neill	N	Y	Y	✓	N	N
9 Hicks	N	N	Y	Y	Y	N
10 Heckler	N	Y	Y	Y	N	N
11 Burke	N	Y	Y	Y	N	N
12 Keith	?	Y	Y	Y	?	Y
MICHIGAN						
1 Conyers	N	Y	N	Y	?	N
2 Esch	Y	Y	Y	†	N	N
3 Brown	Y	Y	Y	Y	Y	Y
4 Hutchinson	Y	N	Y	N	?	Y
5 Ford	Y	Y	N	Y	Y	Y
6 Chamberlain	Y	Y	Y	✓	Y	Y
7 Riegle	N	Y	Y	Y	N	N
8 Harvey	Y	Y	Y	Y	N	N
9 Vander Jagt	Y	N	N	Y	Y	Y
10 Cederberg	Y	N	Y	Y	Y	Y
11 Ruppe	Y	Y	Y	Y	N	N
12 O'Hara	N	Y	Y	Y	N	N
13 Diggs	†	Y	X	Y	N	N
14 Nedzi	N	Y	Y	Y	?	N
15 Ford	N	?	Y	Y	N	N
16 Dingell	N	Y	Y	Y	N	N
17 Griffiths	N	Y	✓	Y	?	?
18 Broomfield	Y	?	Y	Y	-	Y
19 McDonald	Y	N	N	Y	?	?
MINNESOTA						
1 Quie	Y	Y	Y	Y	Y	Y
2 Nelsen	Y	N	Y	Y	N	Y
3 Frenzel	Y	Y	Y	Y	Y	N
4 Karth	N	Y	Y	Y	N	N
5 Fraser	N	†	N	Y	Y	N
6 Zwach	Y	N	Y	N	Y	N
7 Bergland	N	†	Y	Y	Y	N
8 Blatnik	N	Y	Y	✓	Y	N
MISSISSIPPI						
1 Abernethy	Y	N	X	X	Y	Y
2 Whitten	Y	N	N	N	†	Y
3 Griffin	Y	N	N	N	N	Y
4 Montgomery	Y	N	N	N	N	Y
5 Colmer	Y	?	N	N	Y	Y
MISSOURI						
1 Clay	N	Y	N	Y	?	N
2 Symington	N	?	Y	Y	N	N

• *Voted Present to avoid possible conflict-of-interest.*

1. HR 7130. Minimum Wage Increase. Erlenborn (R Ill.) amendment in the nature of a substitute bill—Amend the Fair Labor Standards Act of 1938 to raise the hourly wage floor for most nonagricultural workers covered under the act to $1.80 in 1972 and $2 the following year from $1.00 under existing law. Erlenborn amendment adopted by recorded teller vote 217-191: R 148-20; D 69-171 (ND 6-154; SD 63-17), May 11, 1972.

2. HR 14989. State, Justice, Commerce Appropriations, Fiscal 1973. Derwinski (R Ill.) amendment restoring $25,103,500 for the United Nations and seven affiliated agencies that was deleted by the Appropriations Committee and deleting a provision added by the committee limiting U.S. contributions to the United Nations and affiliated agencies to 25 percent of their total annual assessment. Rejected by recorded teller vote 156-202: R 56-99; D 100-103 (ND 92-49; SD 8-54), May 18, 1972. A "yea" was a vote supporting the President's position.

3. S 659. Higher Education Amendments of 1972. Adoption of the conference report (H Rept 92-1085) on the bill authorizing $19-billion for higher education programs through fiscal 1975 and $2-billion for school desegregation aid through fiscal 1974, establishing direct federal aid to needy students and postponing implementation of court desegregation orders requiring busing of school children. Adopted 218-180: R 89-76; D 129-104 (ND 109-44; SD 20-60), June 8, 1972.

Democrats   *Republicans*

	1	2	3	4	5	6
3 Sullivan	N	Y	N	Y	N	N
4 Randall	Y	N	Y	Y	N	Y
5 Bolling	-	Y	N	N	†	Y
6 Hull	†	Y	N	N	N	Y
7 Hall	†	N	N	N	N	Y
8 Ichord	N	N	Y	N	Y	N
9 Hungate	N	?	Y	Y	Y	N
10 Burlison	N	N	Y	Y	N	N
MONTANA						
1 Shoup	Y	N	Y	N	Y	Y
2 Melcher	N	N	Y	Y	?	N
NEBRASKA						
1 Thone	Y	?	Y	Y	N	Y
2 McCollister	Y	N	N	Y	N	Y
3 Martin	Y	N	X	N	Y	Y
NEVADA						
AL Baring	Y	N	N	N	N	Y
NEW HAMPSHIRE						
1 Wyman	Y	N	N	Y	N	Y
2 Cleveland	Y	Y	N	Y	-	Y
NEW JERSEY						
1 Hunt	Y	N	N	Y	Y	?
2 Sandman	Y	N	N	N	†	Y
3 Howard	N	Y	Y	Y	Y	N
4 Thompson	N	Y	Y	√	N	N
5 Frelinghuysen	Y	?	Y	Y	N	N
6 Forsythe	Y	Y	Y	Y	Y	N
7 Widnall	Y	Y	Y	Y	N	N
8 Roe	N	N	Y	Y	N	N
9 Helstoski	N	Y	Y	Y	N	N
10 Rodino	N	Y	Y	Y	N	N
11 Minish	N	Y	Y	Y	N	N
12 Dwyer	-	?	Y	Y	N	N
13 Gallagher	?	?	√	?	?	?
14 Daniels	N	?	Y	Y	Y	N
15 Patten	N	N	Y	Y	N	N
NEW MEXICO						
1 Lujan	Y	?	?	X	N	Y
2 Runnels	N	N	N	N	Y	N
NEW YORK						
1 Pike	N	Y	Y	N	N	Y
2 Grover	Y	N	N	Y	N	Y
3 Wolff	Y	Y	Y	Y	X	N

	1	2	3	4	5	6
4 Wydler	Y	N	N	Y	N	Y
5 Lent	Y	N	Y	N	Y	Y
6 Halpern	N	Y	X	Y	-	Y
7 Addabbo	N	N	Y	N	Y	N
8 Rosenthal	N	Y	N	Y	X	N
9 Delaney	N	N	N	Y	N	Y
10 Celler	N	Y	N	Y	N	N
11 Brasco	N	N	Y	Y	Y	N
12 Chisholm	N	?	N	Y	-	N
13 Podell	N	Y	Y	Y	N	N
14 Rooney	N	N	X	Y	X	?
15 Carey	N	?	Y	Y	N	N
16 Murphy	N	?	Y	Y	N	Y
17 Koch	N	Y	N	Y	N	N
18 Rangel	N	Y	N	Y	N	N
19 Abzug	N	Y	N	Y	N	N
20 Ryan	N	Y	N	X	X	N
21 Badillo	N	Y	N	Y	-	N
22 Scheuer	N	Y	Y	Y	N	N
23 Bingham	N	Y	Y	Y	N	N
24 Biaggi	N	N	Y	Y	X	N
25 Peyser	N	?	Y	Y	N	N
26 Reid	N	?	Y	Y	N	N
27 Dow	N	N	Y	N	N	N
28 Fish	Y	?	Y	Y	Y	Y
29 Stratton	N	N	Y	Y	Y	Y
30 King	Y	N	N	Y	Y	N
31 McEwen	Y	?	X	Y	?	Y
32 Pirnie	Y	Y	N	Y	•	Y
33 Robison	Y	Y	Y	Y	N	Y
34 Terry	Y	N	X	Y	?	Y
35 Hanley	Y	N	Y	X	Y	X
36 Horton	N	Y	Y	Y	N	Y
37 Conable	Y	Y	N	Y	•	Y
38 Hastings	Y	?	Y	Y	Y	Y
39 Kemp	Y	N	Y	N	Y	Y
40 Smith	Y	Y	Y	Y	Y	Y
41 Dulski	N	N	N	Y	X	N
NORTH CAROLINA						
1 Jones	Y	N	N	N	Y	N
2 Fountain	Y	N	N	Y	N	Y
3 Henderson	Y	N	N	N	N	Y
4 Galifianakis	Y	N	N	Y	N	N
5 Mizell	Y	N	N	Y	Y	Y

	1	2	3	4	5	6
6 Preyer	†	Y	Y	Y	N	N
7 Lennon	Y	N	N	N	N	†
8 Ruth	Y	N	N	Y	N	N
9 Jonas	Y	N	N	N	Y	Y
10 Broyhill	Y	N	N	Y	N	Y
11 Taylor	Y	N	N	Y	Y	Y
NORTH DAKOTA						
1 Andrews	Y	N	Y	√	N	N
2 Link	N	?	Y	Y	-	N
OHIO						
1 Keating	Y	N	Y	Y	Y	Y
2 Clancy	Y	N	N	N	Y	Y
3 Whalen	N	Y	N	N	Y	N
4 McCulloch	Y	?	N	Y	Y	?
5 Latta	Y	N	Y	Y	N	Y
6 Harsha	Y	?	Y	Y	Y	Y
7 Brown	Y	?	Y	Y	N	Y
8 Betts	Y	N	Y	Y	Y	Y
9 Ashley	N	Y	N	Y	N	N
10 Miller	Y	N	Y	Y	N	N
11 Stanton	Y	Y	Y	Y	N	Y
12 Devine	†	N	N	N	√	Y
13 Mosher	N	Y	Y	?	N	N
14 Seiberling	N	Y	Y	Y	N	N
15 Wylie	Y	N	Y	Y	N	Y
16 Bow	Y	?	N	Y	Y	Y
17 Ashbrook	Y	N	N	N	N	Y
18 Hays	-		Y	N	-	Y
19 Carney	N	Y	√	Y	N	N
20 Stanton	N	Y	Y	Y	N	N
21 Stokes	N	Y	N	Y	N	N
22 Vanik	N	Y	Y	Y	N	N
23 Minshall	Y	N	Y	Y	Y	Y
24 Powell	Y	N	N	?	N	Y
OKLAHOMA						
1 Belcher	Y	Y	N	?	Y	Y
2 Edmondson	?	N	Y	N	√	?
3 Albert	N	?				Y
4 Steed	Y	N	Y	N	Y	Y
5 Jarman	Y	N	N	N	N	Y
6 Camp	Y	N	N	N	?	Y
OREGON						
1 Wyatt	N	N	N	Y	Y	Y
2 Ullman	N	Y	N	Y	Y	N
3 Green	N	N	N	N	Y	N
4 Dellenback	Y	Y	Y	Y	Y	Y
PENNSYLVANIA						
1 Barrett	N	Y	Y	Y	N	N
2 Nix	N	N	Y	Y	N	N
3 Byrne	N	N	Y	√	?	N
4 Eilberg	N	N	Y	Y	N	N
5 Green	N	Y	Y	Y	X	N
6 Yatron	N	N	√	†	N	N
7 Williams	Y	N	Y	Y	Y	Y
8 Biester	N	Y	Y	Y	N	N
9 Ware	Y	Y	Y	Y	Y	Y
10 McDade	N	Y	N	Y	N	N
11 Flood	N	?	Y	Y	Y	N
12 Whalley	Y	Y	N	Y	?	Y
13 Coughlin	Y	Y	Y	Y	N	N
14 Moorhead	N	Y	Y		-	N
15 Rooney	N	Y	Y	Y	N	N
16 Eshleman	†	?	√	Y	Y	Y
17 Schneebeli	Y	N	Y	N	Y	Y
18 Heinz	N	Y	Y	Y	X	N
19 Goodling	Y	?	N	N	Y	Y
20 Gaydos	N	N	Y	Y	N	N
21 Dent	N	N	Y	Y	N	N
22 Saylor	N	N	N	N	N	Y
23 Johnson	Y	N	Y	Y	Y	Y
24 Vigorito	N	Y	N	Y	N	N
25 Clark	?	N	√	Y	N	Y
26 Morgan	N	Y	Y	N	N	N
27 Conover [1]		Y	Y	N	Y	
RHODE ISLAND						
1 St Germain	N	Y	Y	Y	N	N
2 Tiernan	N	?	Y	Y	N	-
SOUTH CAROLINA						
1 Davis	N	?	N	X	Y	Y
2 Spence	?	N	N	Y	N	Y
3 Dorn	Y	N	Y	Y	Y	Y
4 Mann	Y	?	N	Y	N	Y

	1	2	3	4	5	6
5 Gettys	Y	N	N	N	†	Y
6 McMillan	Y	N	?	X	Y	Y
SOUTH DAKOTA						
1 Denholm	N	?	√	N	Y	Y
2 Abourezk	N	Y	Y	N	Y	N
TENNESSEE						
1 Quillen	Y	N	Y	Y	†	Y
2 Duncan	Y	N	N	Y	Y	Y
3 Baker	Y	N	N	N	N	Y
4 Evins	Y	?	N	Y	?	N
5 Fulton	N	Y	N	Y	√	N
6 Anderson	N	N	N	Y	N	?
7 Blanton	N	?	N	?	-	N
8 Jones	Y	N	N	Y	N	N
9 Kuykendall	†	N	Y	Y	Y	Y
TEXAS						
1 Patman	Y	?	N	N	N	Y
2 Dowdy	?	?	X	X	√	?
3 Collins	Y	N	Y	N	N	Y
4 Roberts	Y	N	N	N	Y	Y
5 Cabell	Y	?	N	N	Y	Y
6 Teague	Y	N	N	N	N	Y
7 Archer	Y	N	N	N	N	Y
8 Eckhardt	N	Y	N	Y	N	N
9 Brooks	?	Y	Y	N	N	Y
10 Pickle	Y	N	N	Y	N	N
11 Poage	Y	N	N	Y	Y	Y
12 Wright	Y	?	Y	N	Y	Y
13 Purcell	N	-	N	N	Y	Y
14 Young	Y	?	Y	N	Y	Y
15 de la Garza	Y	N	N	Y	N	N
16 White	Y	N	N	Y	N	N
17 Burleson	Y	N	N	N	N	Y
18 Price	Y	N	N	N	N	Y
19 Mahon	Y	N	X	N	Y	?
20 Gonzalez	N	Y	Y	N	N	Y
21 Fisher	Y	N	N	N	N	Y
22 Casey	Y	N	N	N	Y	Y
23 Kazen	Y	?	Y	N	Y	Y
UTAH						
1 McKay	N	?	Y	N	-	Y
2 Lloyd	Y	Y	Y	Y	Y	Y
VERMONT						
AL Mallary	Y	Y	Y	N	N	Y
VIRGINIA						
1 Downing	Y	N	N	N	N	Y
2 Whitehurst	Y	N	N	N	N	Y
3 Satterfield	Y	N	N	N	N	Y
4 Abbitt	Y	N	N	Y	N	Y
5 Daniel	Y	N	N	N	N	Y
6 Poff	Y	N	N	N	N	Y
7 Robinson	Y	N	N	N	N	Y
8 Scott	Y	N	N	N	N	Y
9 Wampler	Y	N	N	Y	N	Y
10 Broyhill	Y	N	N	N	N	Y
WASHINGTON						
1 Pelly	Y	N	Y	†	Y	†
2 Meeds	N	Y	N	N	Y	N
3 Hansen	N	?	Y	Y	Y	N
4 McCormack	N	?	Y	√	Y	-
5 Foley	N	Y	Y	Y	Y	Y
6 Hicks	N	N	Y	N	Y	N
7 Adams	N	Y	Y	N	N	N
WEST VIRGINIA						
1 Mollohan	N	N	Y	Y	Y	Y
2 Staggers	N	N	Y	N	Y	N
3 Slack	N	N	N	N	Y	N
4 Hechler	N	Y	Y	N	N	N
5 Kee	N	Y	Y	Y	Y	Y
WISCONSIN						
1 Aspin	Y	Y	Y	Y	Y	N
2 Kastenmeier	N	Y	N	Y	N	N
3 Thomson	Y	Y	Y	Y	Y	Y
4 Zablocki	N	Y	Y	Y	Y	N
5 Reuss	N	Y	N	Y	N	N
6 Steiger	Y	Y	Y	Y	Y	Y
7 Obey	N	Y	Y	Y	-	N
8 Byrnes	Y	N	N	Y	N	N
9 Davis	†	N	N	N	Y	Y
10 O'Konski	Y	N	Y	Y	Y	Y
WYOMING						
AL Roncalio	N	N	Y	Y	N	N

• Voted Present to avoid possible conflict-of-interest.

1 William S. Conover (R Pa.) was sworn in May 24, 1972, to replace James G. Fulton (R), deceased (1971).

4. HR 14370. Revenue Sharing With the States. Passage of the bill providing assistance payments totaling $29.6-billion over five years to states and to local governments for high priority expenditures, encouraging states to broaden their tax systems and authorizing federal collection of state personal income taxes. Passed 275-122: R 122-42; D 153-80 (ND 124-32; SD 29-48), June 22, 1972. A "yea" was a vote supporting the President's position.

5. HR 13366. Cyclamate Compensation. Passage of the bill permitting domestic food growers, manufacturers, packers and distributors to sue the federal government for payment of losses sustained as a result of a 1969 ban on cyclamates—an artificial sweetener. Passed 177-170: R 85-64; D 92-106 (ND 54-79; SD 38-27), July 24, 1972.

6. HR 16029. Foreign Military Aid Authorizations. Bollings (D Mo.) amendment deleting provision terminating U.S. involvement in the Indochina war by Oct. 1, 1972, subject to release of U.S. prisoners of war, an accounting for men missing in action and a cease-fire to the extent required to protect U.S. withdrawal. Adopted by recorded teller vote 229-177: R 149-23; D 80-154 (ND 25-134; SD 55-20), Aug. 10, 1972. A "yea" was a vote in support of the President's position.

- KEY -

- **Y** Record vote for (yea).
- **√** Paired for.
- **†** Announced for or CQ poll for.
- **N** Record vote against (nay).
- **X** Paired against.
- **-** Announced against or CQ poll against.
- **?** Not voting, voted "present" or did not announce.

	7	8	9	10	11	12
ALABAMA						
1 Edwards	X	N	Y	N	N	†
2 Dickinson	N	N	Y	N	N	?
3 Andrews, E.	Y	N	Y	N	N	?
4 Nichols	†	N	√	X	N	†
5 Flowers	Y	N	Y	N	N	?
6 Buchanan	√	N	Y	N	N	Y
7 Bevill	Y	N	√	?	N	?
8 Jones	Y	N	Y	Y	Y	Y
ALASKA						
AL Begich	Y	Y	N	Y	Y	†
ARIZONA						
1 Rhodes	X	?	Y	N	N	N
2 Udall	Y	Y	N	Y	Y	†
3 Steiger	N	?	Y	N	N	?
ARKANSAS						
1 Alexander	Y	N	Y	N	N	Y
2 Mills	Y	N	Y	Y	N	N
3 Hammerschmidt	N	N	Y	N	N	Y
4 Pryor	√	Y	?	N	N	?
CALIFORNIA						
1 Clausen	N	Y	Y	N	N	Y
2 Johnson	Y	N	Y	Y	Y	Y
3 Moss	Y	Y	N	Y	Y	√
4 Leggett	√	?	N	Y	Y	Y
5 Burton	Y	Y	N	Y	Y	Y
6 Mailliard	Y	Y	N	√	N	Y
7 Dellums	Y	Y	N	Y	Y	Y
8 Miller	Y	-	N	Y	?	Y
9 Edwards	Y	Y	N	Y	Y	Y
10 Gubser	N	Y	Y	N	N	?
11 McCloskey	√	Y	-	Y	N	Y
12 Talcott	N	-	?	N	N	?
13 Teague	N	Y	†	†	N	Y
14 Waldie	√	†	X	Y	Y	†
15 McFall	Y	Y	N	Y	Y	Y
16 Sisk	Y	N	Y	Y	Y	Y
17 Anderson	Y	?	N	Y	Y	Y
18 Mathias	N	N	Y	N	Y	Y
19 Holifield	Y	Y	N	Y	Y	Y
20 Smith	N	N	Y	N	N	N
21 Hawkins	Y	Y	N	Y	Y	Y
22 Corman	Y	Y	N	Y	Y	Y
23 Clawson	N	N	Y	N	N	?
24 Rousselot	X	-	Y	N	N	X
25 Wiggins	N	?	N	N	N	†
26 Rees	Y	Y	X	Y	Y	†
27 Goldwater	N	N	Y	N	N	?
28 Bell	Y	Y	?	√	?	?
29 Danielson	Y	N	Y	N	Y	†
30 Roybal	Y	Y	N	Y	Y	Y
31 Wilson	Y	N	N	Y	N	Y
32 Hosmer	N	N	Y	N	N	†
33 Pettis	N	N	N	N	N	Y
34 Hanna	Y	Y	X	Y	Y	?
35 Schmitz	?	N	√	X	?	?
36 Wilson	N	-	Y	N	N	?
37 Van Deerlin	Y	?	†	Y	Y	†
38 Veysey	X	Y	Y	N	N	?
COLORADO						
1 McKevitt	N	Y	N	N	Y	N
2 Brotzman	N	Y	Y	N	N	?
3 Evans	Y	Y	?	?	?	?
4 Aspinall	Y	N	Y	†	Y	Y
CONNECTICUT						
1 Cotter	Y	Y	Y	Y	†	Y
2 Steele	Y	Y	Y	Y	N	Y
3 Giaimo	N	Y	?	√	Y	?

	7	8	9	10	11	12
4 McKinney	N	Y	N	Y	N	Y
5 Monagan	Y	Y	Y	Y	Y	†
6 Grasso	Y	Y	Y	Y	Y	?
DELAWARE						
AL DuPont	N	Y	N	Y	N	Y
FLORIDA						
1 Sikes	N	N	Y	N	Y	Y
2 Fuqua	Y	N	Y	N	Y	Y
3 Bennett	N	Y	Y	N	N	Y
4 Chappell	N	N	Y	N	N	?
5 Frey	N	N	Y	N	N	?
6 Gibbons	Y	N	N	N	Y	Y
7 Haley	N	N	Y	N	?	?
8 Young	N	Y	Y	N	N	?
9 Rogers	N	N	Y	N	N	Y
10 Burke	N	Y	N	N	Y	Y
11 Pepper	Y	Y	Y	N	Y	Y
12 Fascell	Y	Y	Y	Y	Y	Y
GEORGIA						
1 Hagan	?	N	√	X	N	?
2 Mathis	N	N	Y	N	N	Y
3 Brinkley	N	N	Y	N	Y	Y
4 Blackburn	N	N	Y	N	N	-
5 Thompson	N	?	Y	X	?	?
6 Flynt	N	N	√	N	Y	?
7 Davis	N	N	Y	N	N	Y
8 Stuckey	N	N	Y	N	Y	†
9 Landrum	N	N	√	N	N	Y
10 Stephens	N	N	Y	N	N	?
HAWAII						
1 Matsunaga	Y	Y	N	Y	†	†
2 Mink	Y	Y	-	†	Y	Y
IDAHO						
1 McClure	N	Y	√	X	?	?
2 Hansen	N	N	Y	N	N	Y
ILLINOIS						
1 Metcalfe	Y	?	X	Y	?	Y
2 Mikva	Y	Y	Y	Y	†	Y
3 Murphy, M.	Y	Y	N	Y	?	Y
4 Derwinski	N	Y	Y	N	N	†
5 Kluczynski	Y	?	Y	Y	Y	Y
6 Collins	Y	Y	X	Y	?	Y
7 Annunzio	Y	N	N	√	Y	√
8 Rostenkowski	Y	N	N	Y	?	?
9 Yates	Y	Y	N	Y	Y	Y
10 Collier	N	N	Y	N	N	Y
11 Pucinski	Y	N	?	Y	?	?
12 McClory	N	Y	N	Y	N	N
13 Crane	N	N	Y	N	N	X
14 Erlenborn	N	Y	-	N	N	-
15 Carlson	N	N	Y	N	N	?
16 Anderson	N	N	Y	N	N	Y
17 Arends	N	N	Y	N	N	†
18 Michel	X	†	Y	N	N	†
19 Railsback	√	†	Y	N	N	†
20 Findley	N	Y	N	N	N	?
21 Gray	Y	Y	N	Y	Y	Y
22 Springer	-	-	Y	N	N	N
23 Shipley	Y	N	?	Y	Y	?
24 Price	Y	Y	N	Y	Y	Y
INDIANA						
1 Madden	Y	Y	N	Y	Y	Y
2 Landgrebe	N	N	Y	N	N	N
3 Brademas	Y	Y	N	Y	Y	Y
4 Roush	Y	Y	N	Y	Y	Y
5 Hillis	√	Y	Y	?	N	Y
6 Bray	N	N	Y	N	N	Y
7 Myers	Y	N	Y	N	N	Y
8 Zion	N	N	Y	N	N	Y
9 Hamilton	Y	Y	N	Y	N	Y
10 Dennis	N	N	Y	N	N	Y
11 Jacobs	Y	Y	N	Y	Y	Y
IOWA						
1 Schwengel	Y	N	?	N	N	?
2 Culver	Y	Y	X	√	√	Y
3 Gross	N	N	?	?	?	?
4 Kyl	N	Y	√	N	N	Y
5 Smith	Y	Y	Y	Y	Y	Y
6 Mayne	N	Y	N	N	N	†
7 Scherle	N	N	Y	N	N	Y

	7	8	9	10	11	12
KANSAS						
1 Sebelius	N	N	Y	N	N	†
2 Roy	Y	Y	Y	Y	Y	Y
3 Winn	N	N	N	N	N	†
4 Shriver	Y	N	Y	N	N	Y
5 Skubitz	N	N	Y	N	N	?
KENTUCKY						
1 Stubblefield	Y	Y	Y	N	Y	Y
2 Natcher	Y	N	Y	N	Y	Y
3 Mazzoli	Y	Y	Y	Y	Y	Y
4 Snyder	N	N	Y	N	N	?
5 Carter	?	?	Y	N	N	Y
6 Curlin	Y	N	N	Y	N	?
7 Perkins	Y	Y	Y	Y	Y	Y
LOUISIANA						
1 Hebert	X	?	√	N	N	?
2 Boggs	Y	N	Y	Y	Y	?
3 Caffery	?	?	Y	N	?	?
4 Waggonner	N	N	Y	N	N	†
5 Passman	X	-	Y	N	Y	N
6 Rarick	X	N	Y	N	N	N
7 Breaux[1]						†
8 Long	?	?	Y	N	N	?
MAINE						
1 Kyros	Y	Y	N	Y	Y	Y
2 Hathaway	Y	Y	N	Y	†	Y
MARYLAND						
1 Mills	X	N	Y	N	?	?
2 Long	N	?	N	Y	Y	Y
3 Garmatz	Y	?	Y	Y	Y	Y
4 Sarbanes	Y	Y	N	Y	Y	Y
5 Hogan	N	Y	N	N	Y	Y
6 Byron	N	N	Y	X	N	N
7 Mitchell	Y	Y	N	Y	Y	Y
8 Gude	Y	†	N	Y	Y	Y
MASSACHUSETTS						
1 Conte	√	†	-	Y	N	Y
2 Boland	Y	Y	N	Y	Y	Y
3 Drinan	Y	Y	N	Y	Y	Y
4 Donohue	Y	Y	N	Y	Y	Y
5 Vacancy						
6 Harrington	√	Y	N	Y	N	Y
7 Macdonald	Y	N	N	Y	Y	Y

	7	8	9	10	11	12
8 O'Neill	√	Y	Y	Y	Y	Y
9 Hicks	Y	Y	Y	Y	Y	Y
10 Heckler	√	?	N	Y	Y	Y
11 Burke	Y	Y	Y	Y	Y	Y
12 Keith	?	?	N	N	N	?
MICHIGAN						
1 Conyers	√	Y	N	Y	Y	Y
2 Esch	Y	N	X	Y	X	Y
3 Brown	N	†	Y	N	N	Y
4 Hutchinson	N	N	Y	N	N	Y
5 Ford	N	N	Y	N	N	Y
6 Chamberlain	Y	N	Y	N	N	Y
7 Riegle	√	Y	N	Y	Y	√
8 Harvey	√	N	?	N	Y	?
9 Vander Jagt	N	†	Y	N	N	Y
10 Cederberg	N	N	Y	N	N	?
11 Ruppe	N	Y	Y	N	Y	Y
12 O'Hara	Y	Y	N	Y	?	Y
13 Diggs	Y	Y	N	Y	Y	Y
14 Nedzi	Y	N	Y	Y	Y	Y
15 Ford	Y	†	N	Y	Y	†
16 Dingell	Y	?	X	Y	Y	Y
17 Griffiths	Y	N	N	Y	N	?
18 Broomfield	N	N	Y	N	N	†
19 McDonald	?	N	Y	?	?	N
MINNESOTA						
1 Quie	N	N	Y	N	N	Y
2 Nelsen	N	N	Y	N	N	Y
3 Frenzel	N	N	Y	N	N	Y
4 Karth	Y	Y	N	Y	Y	Y
5 Fraser	Y	Y	N	Y	Y	Y
6 Zwach	Y	N	Y	N	N	Y
7 Bergland	Y	Y	N	Y	N	?
8 Blatnik	Y	Y	N	Y	Y	Y
MISSISSIPPI						
1 Abernethy	-	-	Y	N	N	X
2 Whitten	N	N	Y	N	Y	Y
3 Griffin	N	N	Y	N	N	N
4 Montgomery	N	N	Y	N	N	X
5 Colmer	N	N	Y	N	N	N
MISSOURI						
1 Clay	√	Y	X	?	?	?
2 Symington	Y	Y	N	Y	Y	Y

1 Breaux was sworn in Oct. 12 to fill seat left vacant by resignation of Edwin W. Edwards, who resigned May 9 to become governor of Louisiana.

7. HR 15417. Labor-HEW Appropriations, Fiscal 1973. Reconsideration and passage of the bill, vetoed by the President Aug. 16, appropriating $30,538,919,500 for the Department of Labor, the Department of Health, Education and Welfare and related agencies for fiscal 1973. Rejected 203-171: R 22-129; D 181-42 (ND 146-8; SD 35-34), Aug. 16, 1972. A two-thirds majority vote (250 in this case) of members present and voting is necessary to override a veto. A "nay" was a vote supporting the President's position.

8. HR 13915. School Busing. Stokes (D Ohio) amendment providing that nothing in the act was intended to be inconsistent with, or violate any provision of, the Constitution. Rejected by recorded teller vote 178-197: R 55-98; D 123-99 (ND 110-37; SD 13-62), Aug. 18, 1972.

9. HR 16742. Foreign Travel Restrictions. Ichord (D Mo.) motion to suspend rules and pass the bill authorizing the President to prohibit travel by U.S. citizens to countries engaged in armed conflict with the United States. Rejected 230-140: R 130-27; D 100-113 (ND 38-101; SD 62-12), Oct. 2, 1972. A two-thirds majority vote (248 in this case) was needed for passage under suspension of the rules.

10. HR 7130. Minimum Wage Increase. Perkins (D Ky.) motion that the House disagree with the Senate version of the bill raising the minimum wage for workers covered by the Fair

Democrats   *Republicans*

	7	8	9	10	11	12
3 Sullivan	Y	N	Y	‡	‡	
4 Randall	N	Y	Y	Y	N	‡
5 Bolling	Y	Y	-	Y	Y	‡
6 Hull	✓	-	✓	N	N	Y
7 Hall	N	N	Y	N	N	N
8 Ichord	N	N	Y	Y	N	‡
9 Hungate	Y	Y	N	Y	?	Y
10 Burlison	N	N	Y	Y	Y	?
MONTANA						
1 Shoup	N	N	Y	N	N	✓
2 Melcher	Y	?	N	Y	Y	?
NEBRASKA						
1 Thone	N	Y	Y	N	N	Y
2 McCollister	N	N	Y	N	N	Y
3 Martin	N	N	Y	N	?	X
NEVADA						
AL Baring	Y	N	✓	X	N	‡
NEW HAMPSHIRE						
1 Wyman	N	N	Y	N	N	‡
2 Cleveland	N	Y	Y	N	N	‡
NEW JERSEY						
1 Hunt	N	Y	Y	Y	N	✓
2 Sandman	N	N	Y	Y	N	Y
3 Howard	Y	Y	N	Y	Y	Y
4 Thompson	Y	Y	N	Y	Y	✓
5 Frelinghuysen	X	?	N	N	N	Y
6 Forsythe	N	N	N	?	N	✓
7 Widnall	N	Y	Y	N	N	Y
8 Roe	Y	Y	Y	Y	Y	Y
9 Helstoski	Y	Y	N	Y	Y	Y
10 Rodino	Y	Y	N	Y	N	Y
11 Minish	Y	Y	Y	Y	Y	Y
12 Dwyer	✓	‡	?	✓	?	?
13 Gallagher	✓	?	✓	?	?	?
14 Daniels	Y	N	Y	✓	Y	Y
15 Patten	Y	N	Y	Y	Y	Y
NEW MEXICO						
1 Lujan	N	?	?	X	N	Y
2 Runnels	N	N	✓	?	Y	?
NEW YORK						
1 Pike	Y	N	Y	Y	Y	Y
2 Grover	N	Y	Y	N	N	Y
3 Wolff	Y	Y	Y	Y	Y	✓

	7	8	9	10	11	12
4 Wydler	N	N	Y	Y	N	Y
5 Lent	?	N	Y	N	N	Y
6 Halpern	Y	N	?	Y	?	Y
7 Addabbo	Y	Y	N	Y	Y	Y
8 Rosenthal	Y	Y	N	Y	Y	?
9 Delaney	Y	N	Y	Y	?	Y
10 Celler	Y	Y	N	Y	Y	Y
11 Brasco	Y	Y	N	Y	‡	Y
12 Chisholm	Y	Y	X	Y	Y	Y
13 Podell	Y	Y	N	Y	Y	‡
14 Rooney	✓	?	?	✓	?	?
15 Carey	Y	Y	N	Y	N	Y
16 Murphy	Y	N	?	Y	?	Y
17 Koch	Y	Y	N	Y	Y	Y
18 Rangel	Y	Y	N	Y	Y	Y
19 Abzug	Y	Y	X	Y	Y	Y
20 Ryan[2]	✓	‡				
21 Badillo	Y	Y	N	Y	Y	‡
22 Scheuer	Y	Y	N	Y	Y	Y
23 Bingham	Y	Y	N	Y	‡	Y
24 Biaggi	Y	Y	Y	✓	N	Y
25 Peyser	Y	Y	?	Y	Y	Y
26 Reid	Y	‡	N	Y	Y	Y
27 Dow	Y	Y	X	Y	?	?
28 Fish	N	Y	N	Y	N	Y
29 Stratton	Y	N	Y	Y	N	?
30 King	N	N	Y	N	N	Y
31 McEwen	N	N	Y	N	N	Y
32 Pirnie	N	N	Y	N	N	Y
33 Robison	N	N	N	N	N	✓
34 Terry	N	-	Y	N	N	Y
35 Hanley	Y	Y	N	Y	‡	Y
36 Horton	Y	Y	Y	Y	N	Y
37 Conable	N	N	Y	N	N	Y
38 Hastings	N	N	Y	N	N	‡
39 Kemp	N	Y	N	Y	N	Y
40 Smith	N	Y	Y	N	N	Y
41 Dulski	Y	N	Y	Y	Y	Y
NORTH CAROLINA						
1 Jones	Y	N	Y	N	Y	Y
2 Fountain	N	N	Y	N	N	Y
3 Henderson	Y	N	Y	N	Y	Y
4 Galifianakis	Y	N	Y	N	N	?
5 Mizell	N	N	Y	N	N	Y

	7	8	9	10	11	12
6 Preyer	Y	Y	Y	N	N	Y
7 Lennon	-	-	Y	N	Y	N
8 Ruth	N	N	Y	N	N	Y
9 Jonas	N	N	Y	N	N	N
10 Broyhill	N	Y	Y	N	N	?
11 Taylor	Y	N	Y	N	N	Y
NORTH DAKOTA						
1 Andrews	Y	N	Y	Y	N	‡
2 Link	Y	Y	?	Y	‡	?
OHIO						
1 Keating	N	Y	Y	N	N	Y
2 Clancy	X	?	Y	N	N	Y
3 Whalen	Y	Y	N	Y	N	Y
4 McCulloch	Y	Y	N	N	N	Y
5 Latta	N	N	Y	N	N	Y
6 Harsha	N	N	Y	N	N	Y
7 Brown	N	N	Y	N	N	?
8 Betts	?	-	Y	N	N	-
9 Ashley	Y	Y	N	✓	Y	Y
10 Miller	N	Y	Y	N	N	Y
11 Stanton	N	Y	Y	N	N	Y
12 Devine	N	N	Y	N	N	Y
13 Mosher	N	N	Y	N	N	Y
14 Seiberling	Y	Y	N	Y	Y	Y
15 Wylie	N	N	Y	N	N	Y
16 Bow	N	N	Y	N	N	?
17 Ashbrook	N	N	Y	N	N	-
18 Hays	N	N	Y	N	N	Y
19 Carney	✓	?	N	Y	Y	Y
20 Stanton	Y	N	N	Y	‡	Y
21 Stokes	Y	Y	Y	Y	Y	Y
22 Vanik	Y	Y	N	Y	Y	Y
23 Minshall	N	N	‡	N	N	Y
24 Powell	N	Y	Y	N	N	Y
OKLAHOMA						
1 Belcher	N	N	Y	N	N	N
2 Edmondson	✓	?	✓	?	Y	?
3 Albert	Y			Y		
4 Steed	Y	N	Y	N	N	Y
5 Jarman	N	N	Y	N	N	Y
6 Camp	N	N	Y	N	N	Y
OREGON						
1 Wyatt	Y	N	Y	X	N	?
2 Ullman	✓	-	N	Y	N	Y
3 Green	N	N	-	✓	?	‡
4 Dellenback	N	N	Y	N	Y	Y
PENNSYLVANIA						
1 Barrett	Y	Y	N	Y	Y	Y
2 Nix	Y	Y	N	Y	Y	Y
3 Byrne	Y	N	Y	Y	?	?
4 Eilberg	Y	Y	Y	Y	Y	Y
5 Green	Y	Y	N	Y	Y	Y
6 Yatron	Y	Y	Y	Y	Y	‡
7 Williams	N	N	Y	N	N	Y
8 Biester	Y	Y	N	Y	N	Y
9 Ware	N	N	Y	N	N	Y
10 McDade	Y	Y	Y	Y	N	Y
11 Flood	Y	N	Y	Y	Y	Y
12 Whalley	N	N	Y	N	N	Y
13 Coughlin	N	Y	N	Y	N	Y
14 Moorhead	Y	Y	N	Y	Y	Y
15 Rooney	Y	N	Y	Y	Y	Y
16 Eshleman	N	N	Y	N	N	‡
17 Schneebeli	N	N	Y	N	N	N
18 Heinz	Y	Y	N	Y	N	Y
19 Goodling	N	N	Y	N	N	Y
20 Gaydos	Y	Y	Y	Y	Y	Y
21 Dent	Y	Y	Y	Y	Y	Y
22 Saylor	N	Y	Y	✓	N	Y
23 Johnson	N	N	Y	N	N	Y
24 Vigorito	Y	N	Y	N	N	Y
25 Clark	Y	Y	Y	Y	Y	Y
26 Morgan	Y	Y	Y	Y	Y	‡
27 Conover	N	Y	N	N	N	Y
RHODE ISLAND						
1 St Germain	Y	N	Y	Y	Y	?
2 Tiernan	Y	Y	N	Y	Y	Y
SOUTH CAROLINA						
1 Davis	Y	N	Y	?	?	?
2 Spence	N	N	Y	N	N	Y
3 Dorn	N	?	Y	N	Y	Y
4 Mann	N	Y	Y	N	N	Y

	7	8	9	10	11	12
5 Gettys	N	N	Y	N	N	‡
6 McMillan	✓	?	✓	N	N	?
SOUTH DAKOTA						
1 Denholm	Y	Y	N	Y	?	?
2 Abourezk	✓	‡	N	Y	?	?
TENNESSEE						
1 Quillen	N	N	Y	N	N	Y
2 Duncan	N	N	Y	N	N	Y
3 Baker	X	N	✓	N	-	‡
4 Evins	Y	N	Y	?	Y	Y
5 Fulton	Y	N	N	Y	N	Y
6 Anderson	✓	N	N	Y	N	?
7 Blanton	✓	N	Y	Y	?	?
8 Jones	N	N	Y	N	N	‡
9 Kuykendall	N	N	Y	N	N	‡
TEXAS						
1 Patman	Y	N	Y	Y	Y	?
2 Dowdy	?	?	✓	X	?	?
3 Collins	N	N	Y	N	N	?
4 Roberts	N	N	Y	N	N	?
5 Cabell	N	N	✓	N	N	?
6 Teague	X	N	Y	X	X	?
7 Archer	N	N	Y	N	N	?
8 Eckhardt	Y	?	N	Y	Y	Y
9 Brooks	Y	N	Y	Y	Y	Y
10 Pickle	N	N	N	Y	N	Y
11 Poage	N	N	Y	N	N	Y
12 Wright	Y	N	Y	✓	Y	Y
13 Purcell	N	N	✓	X	‡	‡
14 Young	Y	N	Y	Y	Y	Y
15 de la Garza	Y	Y	N	N	Y	Y
16 White	Y	N	Y	N	N	Y
17 Burleson	N	N	Y	N	N	?
18 Price	N	N	✓	N	N	Y
19 Mahon	N	N	Y	N	Y	N
20 Gonzalez	Y	Y	N	Y	Y	Y
21 Fisher	N	N	Y	N	N	?
22 Casey	Y	N	Y	Y	Y	Y
23 Kazen	Y	Y	N	Y	Y	Y
UTAH						
1 McKay	Y	Y	N	Y	Y	?
2 Lloyd	N	N	N	Y	?	?
VERMONT						
AL Mallary	N	N	N	N	N	Y
VIRGINIA						
1 Downing	N	N	Y	N	N	Y
2 Whitehurst	N	N	Y	N	N	?
3 Satterfield	N	N	Y	N	N	Y
4 Abbitt	N	N	Y	N	N	Y
5 Daniel	?	N	Y	N	Y	Y
6 Poff[3]	N	Y				
7 Robinson	N	N	Y	N	N	Y
8 Scott	N	N	✓	N	N	Y
9 Wampler	N	N	Y	X	N	Y
10 Broyhill	N	N	Y	N	N	Y
WASHINGTON						
1 Pelly	?	-	Y	N	-	N
2 Meeds	Y	Y	N	Y	Y	‡
3 Hansen	✓	‡	N	Y	?	‡
4 McCormack	Y	Y	-	?	Y	‡
5 Foley	Y	Y	N	Y	Y	Y
6 Hicks	Y	Y	N	Y	Y	Y
7 Adams	Y	Y	N	Y	Y	Y
WEST VIRGINIA						
1 Mollohan	Y	Y	✓	-	Y	‡
2 Staggers	Y	Y	Y	✓	N	Y
3 Slack	Y	N	Y	Y	Y	Y
4 Hechler	Y	Y	N	Y	Y	Y
5 Kee	Y	N	Y	Y	N	Y
WISCONSIN						
1 Aspin	Y	Y	N	Y	Y	?
2 Kastenmeier	Y	Y	Y	Y	Y	Y
3 Thomson	Y	Y	Y	N	N	✓
4 Zablocki	Y	N	Y	Y	Y	Y
5 Reuss	Y	Y	Y	Y	Y	Y
6 Steiger	N	Y	Y	N	N	‡
7 Obey	Y	Y	N	Y	Y	Y
8 Byrnes	N	N	Y	N	N	Y
9 Davis	X	-	Y	N	N	‡
10 O'Konski	Y	N	Y	?	Y	Y
WYOMING						
AL Roncalio	Y	Y	N	Y	?	‡

2 Ryan died Sept. 17, 1972.
3 Poff resigned effective Aug. 29, 1972.

Labor Standards Act of 1938 and request a conference to resolve differences between the two versions. Motion rejected 188-196: R 23-137; D 165-59 (ND 147-1; SD 18-58), Oct. 3, 1972.

11. HR 16810. Debt Ceiling Increase. Mahon (D Texas) amendment in the nature of a substitute for Title II of the bill giving the President unlimited authority to cut outlays for any program he chose to limit federal spending to $250-billion in fiscal 1973—Direct the President to submit his suggestions for spending cutbacks by Jan. 2, 1973, for consideration by the 93rd Congress. Rejected by recorded teller vote 167-216: R 8-156; D 159-60 (ND 121-17; SD 38-43), Oct. 10, 1972. A "nay" was a vote supporting the President's position.

12. S 2770. Water Pollution Control. Passage of the Federal Water Pollution Control Act Amendments of 1972, vetoed by the President Oct. 17, providing a comprehensive program to clean up the nation's waters by 1985 and authorizing $24.7-billion over three years, including $18-billion in federal grants to states for construction of waste treatment works. Passed over the President's veto 247-23: R 95-13; D 152-10 (ND 109-1; SD 43-9), Oct. 18, 1972. A two-thirds majority vote (180 in this case) was needed to override a veto. A "nay" was a vote supporting the President's position.

Congresses and Their Leaders, 80th-92nd

Committee Chairmen, 1947-1972

Congresses and Leaders - 80th to 92nd*

80th Congress
1947-1948

House: 188 Democrats
245 Republicans
1 Other
1 Vacancy

Speaker: Joseph W. Martin Jr. (R Mass.)
Majority Leader: Charles A. Halleck (R Ind.)
Minority Leader: Sam Rayburn (D Texas)

Senate: 45 Democrats
51 Republicans

Vice President: Vacant
President Pro Tempore: Arthur Vandenberg (R Mich.)
Majority Leader: Wallace H. White (R Maine)
Minority Leader: Alben W. Barkley (D Ky.)

81st Congress
1949-1950

House: 262 Democrats
171 Republicans
1 Other
1 Vacancy

Speaker: Sam Rayburn (D Texas)
Majority Leader: John W. McCormack (D Mass.)
Minority Leader: Joseph W. Martin Jr. (R Mass.)

Senate: 54 Democrats
42 Republicans

Vice President: Alben W. Barkley (D Ky.)
President Pro Tempore: Kenneth McKellar (D Tenn.)
Majority Leader: Scott W. Lucas (D Ill.)
Minority Leader: Kenneth S. Wherry (R Neb.)

82nd Congress
1951-1952

House: 235 Democrats
199 Republicans
1 Other

Speaker: Sam Rayburn (D Texas)
Majority Leader: John W. McCormack (D Mass.)
Minority Leader: Joseph W. Martin Jr. (R Mass.)

Senate: 49 Democrats
47 Republicans

Vice President: Alben W. Barkley (D Ky.)
President Pro Tempore: Kenneth McKellar (D Tenn.)
Majority Leader: Ernest W. McFarland (D Ariz.)
Minority Leader: Kenneth S. Wherry (R Neb.) (1st session-died Nov. 29, 1951)
Styles Bridges (R N.H.) (2nd session)

83rd Congress
1953-1954

House: 211 Democrats
221 Republicans
1 Other
2 Vacancies

Speaker: Joseph W. Martin Jr. (R Mass.)
Majority Leader: Charles A. Halleck (R Ind.)
Minority Leader: Sam Rayburn (D Texas)

Senate: 47 Democrats
48 Republicans
1 Other

Vice President: Richard M. Nixon (R Calif.)
President Pro Tempore: Styles Bridges (R N.H.)
Majority Leader: Robert A. Taft (R Ohio) (died July 31, 1953)
William F. Knowland (R Calif.)
Minority Leader: Lyndon B. Johnson (D Texas)

84th Congress
1955-1956

House: 232 Democrats
203 Republicans

Speaker: Sam Rayburn (D Texas)
Majority Leader: John W. McCormack (D Mass.)
Minority Leader: Joseph W. Martin Jr. (R Mass.)

Senate: 48 Democrats
47 Republicans
1 Other

Vice President: Richard M. Nixon (R Calif.)
President Pro Tempore: Walter F. George (D Ga.)
Majority Leader: Lyndon B. Johnson (D Texas)
Minority Leader: William F. Knowland (R Calif.)

85th Congress
1957-1958

House: 233 Democrats
200 Republicans
2 Vacancies

Speaker: Sam Rayburn (D Texas)
Majority Leader: John W. McCormack (D Mass.)
Minority Leader: Joseph W. Martin Jr. (R Mass.)

Senate: 49 Democrats
47 Republicans

Vice President: Richard M. Nixon (R Calif.)
President Pro Tempore: Carl Hayden (D Ariz.)
Majority Leader: Lyndon B. Johnson (D Texas)
Minority Leader: William F. Knowland (R Calif.)

* All figures apply to the day the Congress convened.

86th Congress
1959-1960

House: 283 Democrats
            153 Republicans

Speaker: Sam Rayburn (D Texas)
Majority Leader: John W. McCormack (D Mass.)
Minority Leader: Charles A. Halleck (R Ind.)

Senate: 66 Democrats
            34 Republicans

Vice President: Richard M. Nixon (R Calif.)
President Pro Tempore: Carl Hayden (D Ariz.)
Majority Leader: Lyndon B. Johnson (D Texas)
Minority Leader: Everett McKinley Dirksen (R Ill.)

87th Congress
1961-1962

House: 262 Democrats
            174 Republicans
            1 Vacancy

Speaker: Sam Rayburn (D Texas) (until his death
   Nov. 16, 1961)
   John W. McCormack (D Mass.)
Majority Leader: John W. McCormack (D Mass.)
   Carl Albert (D Okla.)
Minority Leader: Charles A. Halleck (R Ind.)

Senate: 65 Democrats
            35 Republicans

Vice President: Lyndon B. Johnson (D Texas)
President Pro Tempore: Carl Hayden (D Ariz.)
Majority Leader: Mike Mansfield (D Mont.)
Minority Leader: Everett McKinley Dirksen (R Ill.)

88th Congress
1963-1964

House: 258 Democrats
            176 Republicans
            1 Vacancy *

Speaker: John W. McCormack (D Mass.)
Majority Leader: Carl Albert (D Okla.)
Minority Leader: Charles A. Halleck (R Ind.)

Senate: 67 Democrats
            33 Republicans

Vice President: Lyndon B. Johnson (D Texas)
   (until Nov. 22, 1963)
President Pro Tempore: Carl Hayden (D Ariz.)
Majority Leader: Mike Mansfield (D Mont.)
Minority Leader: Everett McKinley Dirksen (R Ill.)

*Rep. Clem Miller was killed Oct. 7, 1962, but elected posthumously. His seat was
filled Jan. 22, 1963, by Don H. Clausen (R Calif.).

89th Congress
1965-1966

House: 295 Democrats
            140 Republicans

Speaker: John W. McCormack (D Mass.)
Majority Leader: Carl Albert (D Okla.)
Minority Leader: Gerald R. Ford (R Mich.)

Senate: 68 Democrats
            32 Republicans

Vice President: Hubert H. Humphrey (D Minn.)
President Pro Tempore: Carl Hayden (D Ariz.)
Majority Leader: Mike Mansfield (D Mont.)
Minority Leader: Everett McKinley Dirksen (R Ill.)

90th Congress
1967-1968

House: 246 Democrats
            187 Republicans
            2 Vacancies

Speaker: John W. McCormack (D Mass.)
Majority Leader: Carl Albert (D Okla.)
Minority Leader: Gerald R. Ford (R Mich.)

Senate: 64 Democrats
            36 Republicans

Vice President: Hubert H. Humphrey (D Minn.)
President Pro Tempore: Carl Hayden (D Ariz.)
Majority Leader: Mike Mansfield (D Mont.)
Minority Leader: Everett McKinley Dirksen (R Ill.)

91st Congress
1969-1970

House: 243 Democrats
            192 Republicans

Speaker: John W. McCormack (D Mass.)
Majority Leader: Carl Albert (D Okla.)
Minority Leader: Gerald R. Ford (R Mich.)

Senate: 57 Democrats
            43 Republicans

Vice President: Spiro T. Agnew (R Md.)
President Pro Tempore: Richard B. Russell (D Ga.)
Majority Leader: Mike Mansfield (D Mont.)
Minority Leader: Everett McKinley Dirksen (R Ill.)

92nd Congress
1971-1972

House: 254 Democrats
            179 Republicans
            2 Vacancies

Speaker: Carl Albert (D Okla.)
Majority Leader: Hale Boggs (D La.)
Minority Leader: Gerald R. Ford (R Mich.)

Senate: 54 Democrats
            44 Republicans
            1 Conservative Republican
            1 Independent

Vice President: Spiro T. Agnew (R Md.)
President Pro Tempore: Allen J. Ellender (D La.)
   (until his death July 27, 1972)
   James O. Eastland (D Miss.)
Majority Leader: Mike Mansfield (D Mont.)
Minority Leader: Hugh Scott (R Pa.)

CHAIRMEN OF SENATE, HOUSE, JOINT COMMITTEES, 1947-72

Following are the names and dates of terms of chairmen of standing committees of Congress from 1947 to 1972. Certain subcommittees and special committees are included because of their past importance or interest. The evolution of some committees also is indicated, such as the first one listed, the Senate Aeronautical and Space Sciences Committee, which originally was the Special Committee on Space and Astronautics.

SENATE

Special Committee on Space and Astronautics
Lyndon B. Johnson (D Texas-1957-1958)

Aeronautical and Space Sciences (renamed)
Lyndon B. Johnson (D Texas-1958-1961)
Robert S. Kerr (D Okla.-1961-1963)
Clinton P. Anderson (D N.M.-1963-)

Agriculture and Forestry
Arthur Capper (R Kan.-1947-1949)
Elmer Thomas (D Okla.-1949-1951)
Allen J. Ellender (D La.-1951-1953)
George D. Aiken (R Vt.-1953-1955)
Allen J. Ellender (D La.-1955-1971)
Herman E. Talmadge (D Ga.-1971-)

Appropriations
Styles Bridges (R N.H.-1947-1949)
Kenneth McKellar (D Tenn.-1949-1953)
Styles Bridges (R N.H.-1953-1955)
Carl Hayden (D Ariz.-1955-1969)
Richard B. Russell (D Ga.-1969-1971)
Allen J. Ellender (D Ga.-1971-1972)
John L. McClellan (D Ark.-1972-)

Armed Services
Chan Gurney (R S.D.-1947-1949)
Millard E. Tydings (D Md.-1949-1951)
Richard B. Russell (D Ga.-1951-1953)
Leverett Saltonstall (R Mass.-1953-1955)
Richard B. Russell (D Ga.-1955-1969)
John C. Stennis (D Miss.-1969-)

Preparedness Investigating Subcommittee
Lyndon B. Johnson (D Texas-1950-1953)
(Seven special subcommittees were appointed by committee chairman Leverett Saltonstall (R Mass.) to investigate specific problems, 1953-1955.)
Lyndon B. Johnson (D Texas-1955-1961)
John Stennis (D Miss.-1961-)

Banking and Currency
Charles W. Tobey (R N.H.-1947-1949)
Burnet R. Maybank (D S.C.-1949-1953)
Homer E. Capehart (R Ind.-1953-1955)
J. W. Fulbright (D Ark.-1955-1959)
A. Willis Robertson (D Va.-1959-1967)
John J. Sparkman (D Ala.-1967-)

Banking, Housing and Urban Affairs (renamed)
John J. Sparkman (D Ala.-1967-)

Interstate and Foreign Commerce
Wallace H. White (R Maine-1947-1949)
Edwin C. Johnson (D Colo.-1949-1953)
Charles W. Tobey (R N.H.-1953)
John W. Bricker (R Ohio-1953-1955)
Warren G. Magnuson (D Wash.-1955-1961)

Commerce (renamed)
Warren G. Magnuson (D Wash.-1961-)

District of Columbia
C. Douglass Buck (R Del.-1947-1949)
J. Howard McGrath (D R.I.-1949-1951)
Matthew M. Neely (D W.Va.-1951-1953)
Francis Case (R S.D.-1953-1955)
Matthew M. Neely (D W.Va.-1955-1959)
Alan Bible (D Nev.-1959-1969)
Joseph D. Tydings (D Md.-1969-1971)
Thomas F. Eagleton (D Mo.-1971-)

Finance
Eugene D. Milikin (R Colo.-1947-1949)
Walter F. George (D Ga.-1949-1953)
Eugene D. Millikin (R Colo.-1953-1955)
Harry Flood Byrd (D Va.-1955-1965)
Russell B. Long (D La.-1965-)

Foreign Relations
Arthur H. Vandenberg (R Mich.-1947-1949)
Tom Connally (D Texas-1949-1953)
Alexander Wiley (R Wis.-1953-1955)
Walter F. George (D Ga.-1955-1957)
Theodore Francis Green (D R.I.-1957-1959)
J. W. Fulbright (D Ark.-1959-)

Expenditures in the Executive Departments
George D. Aiken (R Vt.-1947-1949)
John L. McClellan (D Ark.-1949-1952)

Government Operations (renamed)
John L. McClellan (D Ark.-1952-1953)
Joseph R. McCarthy (R Wis.-1953-1955)
John L. McClellan (D Ark.-1955-1972)
Sam J. Ervin Jr. (D N.C.-1972-)

Special Committee to Investigate the National Defense Program 1947-1948
Owen Brewster (R Maine-1947-1948)

Permanent Investigations Subcommittee
Homer Ferguson (R Mich.-1948-1949)
Clyde R. Hoey (D N.C.-1949-1953)
Joseph R. McCarthy (R Wis.-1953-1955)
John L. McClellan (D Ark.-1955-)

Interior and Insular Affairs
Hugh Butler (R Neb.-1947-1949)
Joseph C. O'Mahoney (D Wyo.-1949-1953)
Hugh Butler (R Neb.-1953-1954)

Guy Cordon (R Ore.-1954-1955)
James E. Murray (D Mont.-1955-1961)
Clinton P. Anderson (D N.M.-1961-1963)
Henry M. Jackson (D Wash.-1963-)

Judiciary
Alexander Wiley (R Wis.-1947-1949)
Pat McCarran (D Nev.-1949-1953)
William Langer (R N.D.-1953-1955)
Harley M. Kilgore (D W.Va.-1955-1956)
James O. Eastland (D Miss.-1956-)

Antitrust and Monopoly Subcommittee
Herbert R. O'Conor (D Md.-1951-1953)
William Langer (R N.D.-1953-1955)
Joseph C. O'Mahoney (D Wyo.-1955-1957)
Estes Kefauver (D Tenn.-1957-1963)
Philip A. Hart (D Mich.-1963-)

Internal Security Subcommittee
Pat McCarran (D Nev.-1950-1953)
William E. Jenner (R Ind.-1953-1955)
James O. Eastland (D Miss.-1955-)

Labor and Public Welfare
Robert A. Taft (R Ohio-1947-1949)
Elbert D. Thomas (D Utah-1949-1951)
James E. Murray (D Mont.-1951-1953)
H. Alexander Smith (R N.J.-1953-1955)
Lister Hill (D Ala.-1955-1969)
Ralph W. Yarborough (D Texas-1969-1971)
Harrison A. Williams Jr. (D N.J.-1971-)

Post Office and Civil Service
William Langer (R N.D.-1947-1949)
Olin D. Johnston (D S.C.-1949-1953)
Frank Carlson (R Kan.-1953-1955)
Olin D. Johnston (D S.C.-1955-1965)
A. S. Mike Monroney (D Okla.-1965-1969)
Gale W. McGee (D Wyo.-1969-)

Public Works
Chapman Revercomb (R W.Va.-1947-1949)
Dennis Chavez (D N.M.-1949-1953)
Edward Martin (R Pa.-1953-1955)
Dennis Chavez (D N.M.-1955-1962)
Pat McNamara (D Mich.-1963-1966)
Jennings Randolph (D W.Va.-1966-)

Rules and Administration
C. Wayland Brooks (R Ill.-1947-1949)
Carl Hayden (D Ariz.-1949-1953)
William E. Jenner (R Ind.-1953-1955)
Theodore Francis Green (D R.I.-1955-1957)
Thomas C. Hennings (D Mo.-1957-1960)
Mike Mansfield (D Mont.-1961-1963)
B. Everett Jordan (D N.C.-1963-1972)

Special Committee to Study Problems of American Small Business
Kenneth S. Wherry (R Neb.-1947-1949. The special committee expired Jan. 30, 1949.)

Select Committee on Small Business
John J. Sparkman (D Ala.-1950-1953)
Edward J. Thye (R Minn.-1953-1955)

John J. Sparkman (D Ala.-1955-1967)
George A. Smathers (D Fla.-1967-1969)
Alan Bible (D Nev.-1969-)

Select Committee on Equal Educational Opportunity
Walter F. Mondale (D Minn.-1970-)

Select Committee on Nutrition and Human Needs
George McGovern (D S.D.-1969-)

Select Committee on Standards and Conduct
John C. Stennis (D Miss.-1966-)

Subcommittee on the Aged and Aging of Senate Labor and Public Welfare
Lister Hill (D Ala.-1959-1960)

Special Committee on Aging
Pat McNamara (D Mich.-1960-1963)
George A. Smathers (D Fla.-1963-1967)
Harrison A. Williams Jr. (D N.J.-1967-1971)
Frank Church (D Idaho-1971-)

Veterans' Affairs
Vance Hartke (D Ind.-1971-)

Democratic Policy and Steering Committees
Alben W. Barkley (D Ky.-1947-1949)
Scott W. Lucas (D Ill.-1949-1951)
Ernest W. McFarland (D Ariz.-1951-1953)
Lyndon B. Johnson (D Texas-1953-1961)
Mike Mansfield (D Mont.-1961-)

Democratic Senatorial Campaign Committee
Scott W. Lucas (D Ill.-1947-1949)
Clinton P. Anderson (D N.M.-1949-1951)
Earle C. Clements (D Ky.-1951-1957)
George A. Smathers (D Fla.-1957-1961)
Vance Hartke (D Ind.-1961-1963)
Warren G. Magnuson (D Wash.-1963-1967)
Edmund S. Muskie (D Maine-1967-1969)
Daniel K. Inouye (D Hawaii-1969-1970)
Ernest F. Hollings (D S.C.-1971-)

Republican Policy Committee
Robert A. Taft (R Ohio-1947-1953)
William F. Knowland (R Calif.-1953)
Homer Ferguson (R Mich.-1953-1955)
Styles Bridges (R N.H.-1955-1961)
Bourke B. Hickenlooper (R Iowa-1962-1969)
Gordon Allott (R Colo.-1969-1972)

Republican Senatorial Campaign Committee
John G. Townsend (Former Republican senator from Delaware, 1929-1941, Campaign Committee chairman, 1947-1949)
Owen Brewster (R Maine-1949-1951)
Everett McKinley Dirksen (R Ill.-1951-1955)
Barry Goldwater (R Ariz.-1955-1956)
Andrew F. Schoeppel (R Kan.-1956-1959)
Barry Goldwater (R Ariz.-1959-1963)
Thruston B. Morton (R Ky.-1963-1969)
George Murphy (R Calif.-1967-1969)
John G. Tower (R Texas-1969-1971)
Peter H. Dominick (R Colo.-1971-)

Republican Committee on Committees
Edward B. Robertson (R Wyo.-1947-1949)
Hugh A. Butler (R Neb.-1949-1954)
John W. Bricker (R Ohio-1954-1959)
Andrew F. Schoeppel (R Kan.-1959-1962)
Frank Carlson (R Kan.-1962-1969)
John J. Williams (R Del.-1969-1971)
Wallace F. Bennett (R Utah-1971-)

Republican Personnel Committee
Harlan J. Bushfield (R S.D.-1947-1949)
Styles Bridges (R N.H.-1949-1953)
Edward Martin (R Pa.-1953-1959)
Margaret Chase Smith (R Maine-1959-1963)
Norris Cotton (R N.H.-1963-1971)
Roman L. Hruska (R Neb.-1971-)

HOUSE

Agriculture
Clifford R. Hope (R Kan.-1947-1949)
Harold D. Cooley (D N.C.-1949-1953)
Clifford R. Hope (R Kan.-1953-1955)
Harold D. Cooley (D N.C.-1955-1967)
W. R. Poage (D Texas-1967-)

Appropriations
John Taber (R N.Y.-1947-1949)
Clarence Cannon (D Mo.-1949-1953)
John Taber (R N.Y.-1953-1955)
Clarence Cannon (D Mo.-1955-1964)
George H. Mahon (D Texas-1964-)

Armed Services
Walter G. Andrews (R N.Y.-1947-1949)
Carl Vinson (D Ga.-1949-1953)
Dewey Short (R Mo.-1953-1955)
Carl Vinson (D Ga.-1955-1965)
L. Mendel Rivers (D S.C.-1965-1971)
F. Edward Hebert (D La.-1971-)

Special Investigations Subcommittee
F. Edward Hebert (D La.-1951-1953)
William E. Hess (R Ohio-1953-1955)
F. Edward Hebert (D La.-1955-1963)
Porter Hardy (D Va.-1963-1969)

Armed Services Investigations (renamed)
L. Mendel Rivers (D S.C.-1969-1971)
F. Edward Hebert (D La.-1971-)

Banking and Currency
Jesse P. Wolcott (R Mich.-1947-1949)
Brent Spence (D Ky.-1949-1953)
Jesse P. Wolcott (R Mich.-1953-1955)
Brent Spence (D Ky.-1955-1963)
Wright Patman (D Texas-1963-)

District of Columbia
Everett M. Dirksen (R Ill.-1947-1949)
John L. McMillan (D S.C.-1949-1953)
Sid Simpson (R Ill.-1953-1955)
John L. McMillan (D S.C.-1955-)

Education and Labor
Fred A. Hartley (R N.J.-1947-1949)
John Lesinski (D Mich.-1949-1950)
Graham A. Barden (D N.C.-1950-1953)
Samuel K. McConnell (R Pa.-1953-1955)
Graham A. Barden (D N.C.-1955-1961)
Adam C. Powell (D N.Y.-1961-1967)
Carl D. Perkins (D Ky.-1967-)

Foreign Affairs
Charles A. Eaton (R N.J.-1947-1949)
John Kee (D W.Va.-1949-1951)
James P. Richards (D S.C.-1951-1953)
Robert B. Chiperfield (R Ill.-1953-1955)
James P. Richards (D S.C.-1955-1957)
Thomas S. Gordon (D Ill.-1957-1959)
Thomas E. Morgan (D Pa.-1959-)

Expenditures in the Executive Departments
Clare E. Hoffman (R Mich.-1947-1949)
William L. Dawson (D Ill.-1949-1952)

Government Operations (renamed)
William L. Dawson (D Ill.-1952-1953)
Clare E. Hoffman (R Mich.-1953-1955)
William L. Dawson (D Ill.-1955-1971)
Chet Holifield (D Calif.-1971-)

House Administration
Karl M. LeCompte (R Iowa-1947-1949)
Mary T. Norton (D N.J.-1949-1951)
Thomas B. Stanley (D Va.-1951-1953)
Karl M. LeCompte (R Iowa-1953-1955)
Omar Burleson (D Texas-1955-1968)
Samuel N. Friedel (D Md.-1968-1971)
Wayne L. Hays (D Ohio-1971-)

Interstate and Foreign Commerce
Charles A. Wolverton (R N.J.-1947-1949)
Robert Crosser (D Ohio-1949-1953)
Charles A. Wolverton (R N.J.-1953-1955)
J. Percy Priest (D Tenn.-1955-1957)
Oren Harris (D Ark.-1957-1966)
Harley O. Staggers (D W.Va.-1966-)

Special Subcommittee on Legislative Oversight 1957-1961
Morgan M. Moulder (D Mo.-1957-1958)
Oren Harris (D Ark.-1958-1961)

Special Subcommittee on Regulatory Agencies
Oren Harris (D Ark.-1961-1963)

Special Subcommittee on Investigations
Oren Harris (D Ark.-1963-1966)
Harley O. Staggers (D W.Va.-1966-)

Judiciary
Earl C. Michener (R Mich.-1947-1949)
Emanuel Celler (D N.Y.-1949-1953)
Chauncey W. Reed (R Ill.-1953-1955)
Emanuel Celler (D N.Y.-1955-1972)

Merchant Marine and Fisheries
Fred Bradley (R Mich.-1947)

Alvin F. Weichel (R Ohio-1947-1949)
Schuyler Otis Bland (D Va.-1949-1950)
Edward J. Hart (D N.J.-1950-1953)
Alvin F. Weichel (R Ohio-1953-1955)
Herbert C. Bonner (D N.C.-1955-1966)
Edward A. Garmatz (D Md.-1966-)

Public Lands
Richard J. Welch (R Calif.-1947-1949)
Andrew L. Somers (D N.Y.-1949)
J. Hardin Peterson (D Fla.-1949-1951)

Interior and Insular Affairs (renamed)
John R. Murdock (D Ariz.-1951-1953)
A. L. Miller (R Neb.-1953-1955)
Clair Engle (D Calif.-1955-1959)
Wayne N. Aspinall (D Colo.-1959-)

Post Office and Civil Service
Edward H. Rees (R Kan.-1947-1949)
Tom Murray (D Tenn.-1949-1953)
Edward H. Rees (R Kan.-1953-1955)
Tom Murray (D Tenn.-1955-1967)
Thaddeus J. Dulski (D N.Y.-1967-)

Public Works
George A. Dondero (R Mich.-1947-1949)
William M. Whittington (D Miss.-1949-1951)
Charles A. Buckley (D N.Y.-1951-1953)
George A. Dondero (R Mich.-1953-1955)
Charles A. Buckley (D N.Y.-1955-1965)
George H. Fallon (D Md.-1965-1971)
John A. Blatnik (D Minn.-1971-)

Rules
Leo E. Allen (R Ill.-1947-1949)
Adolph J. Sabath (D Ill.-1949-1953)
Leo E. Allen (R Ill.-1953-1955)
Howard W. Smith (D Va.-1955-1967)
William M. Colmer (D Miss.-1967-)

Select Committee on Astronautics and Space Exploration 1958
John W. McCormack (D Mass.-1958)

Select Crime Investigation
Claude Pepper (D Fla.-1969-)

Select Small Business
Walter C. Ploeser (R Mo.-1947-1949)
Wright Patman (D Texas-1949-1953)
William S. Hill (R Colo.-1953-1955)
Wright Patman (D Texas-1955-1963)
Joe L. Evins (D Tenn.-1963-)

Science and Astronautics
Overton Brooks (D La.-1959-1961)
George P. Miller (D Calif.-1961-)

Un-American Activities
J. Parnell Thomas (R N.J.-1947-1949)
John S. Wood (D Ga.-1949-1953)
Harold H. Velde (R Ill.-1953-1955)
Francis E. Walter (D Pa.-1955-1963)
Edwin E. Willis (D La.-1963-1969)

Internal Security (renamed)
Richard H. Ichord (D Mo.-1969-)

Veterans' Affairs
Edith Nourse Rogers (R Mass.-1947-1949)
John E. Rankin (D Miss.-1949-1953)
Edith Nourse Rogers (R Mass.-1953-1955)
Olin E. Teague (D Texas-1955-)

Ways and Means
(Democratic members serve as the Democratic Committee on Committees in the House)
Harold Knutson (R Minn.-1947-1949)
Robert L. Doughton (D N.C.-1949-1953)
Daniel A. Reed (R N.Y.-1953-1955)
Jere Cooper (D Tenn.-1955-1957)
Wilbur D. Mills (D Ark.-1958-)

Standards of Official Conduct
Melvin Price (D Ill.-1969-)

Democratic National Congressional Committee
Michael J. Kirwan (D Ohio-1947-)

Democratic Patronage Committee
Francis E. Walter (D Pa.-1949-1953, 1955-1963)
Harry R. Sheppard (D Calif.-1963-1965)
Joe L. Evins (D Tenn.-1965-)

Republican Policy Committee
Joseph W. Martin (R Mass.-1947-1959)
John W. Byrnes (R Wis.-1959-1965)
John J. Rhodes (R Ariz.-1965-)

Republican Committee on Committees
Joseph W. Martin (R Mass.-1947-1953)
Charles A. Halleck (R Ind.-1953-1955)
Joseph W. Martin (R Mass.-1955-1959)
Charles A. Halleck (R Ind.-1959-1965)
Gerald R. Ford (R Mich.-1965-)

National Republican Congressional Committee
Leonard W. Hall (R N.Y.-1947-1953)
Richard M. Simpson (R Pa.-1953-1960)
William E. Miller (R N.Y.-1960-1961)
Bob Wilson (R Calif.-1961-)

Republican Patronage Committee
Leo E. Allen (R Ill.-1947-1949, 1953-1955)

JOINT COMMITTEES

Atomic Energy
Sen. Bourke B. Hickenlooper (R Iowa-1947-1949)
Sen. Brien McMahon (D Conn.-1949-1953)
Rep. W. Sterling Cole (R N.Y.-1953-1955)
Sen. Clinton P. Anderson (D N.M.-1955-1957)
Rep. Carl T. Durham (D N.C.-1957-1959)
Sen. Clinton P. Anderson (D N.M.-1959-1961)
Rep. Chet Holifield (D Calif.-1961-1963)
Sen. John O. Pastore (D R.I.-1963-1965)
Rep. Chet Holifield (D Calif.-1965-1967)
Sen. John O. Pastore (D R.I.-1967-1969)
Rep. Chet Holifield (D Calif.-1969-1971)
Sen. John O. Pastore (D R.I.-1971-)

Congressional Operations
Rep. Jack Brooks (D Texas-1971-)

Defense Production
Sen. Burnet R. Maybank (D S.C.-1950-1953)
Sen. Homer E. Capehart (R Ind.-1953-1955)
Rep. Paul Brown (D Ga.-1955-1957)
Sen. A. Willis Robertson (D Va.-1957-1959)
Rep. Paul Brown (D Ga.-1959-1961)
Sen. A. Willis Robertson (D Va.-1961-1963)
Rep. Wright Patman (D Texas-1963-1965)
Sen. A. Willis Robertson (D Va.-1965-1967)
Rep. Wright Patman (D Texas-1967-1969)
Sen. John J. Sparkman (D Ala.-1969-1971)
Rep. Wright Patman (D Texas-1971-)

Economic
Sen. Robert A. Taft (R Ohio-1947-1949)
Sen. Joseph C. O'Mahoney (D Wyo.-1949-1953)
Rep. Jesse P. Wolcott (R Mich.-1953-1955)
Sen. Paul H. Douglas (D Ill.-1955-1957)
Rep. Wright Patman (D Texas-1957-1959)
Sen. Paul H. Douglas (D Ill.-1959-1961)
Rep. Wright Patman (D Texas-1961-1963)
Sen. Paul H. Douglas (D Ill.-1963-1965)
Rep. Wright Patman (D Texas-1965-1967)
Sen. William Proxmire (D Wis.-1967-1969)
Rep. Wright Patman (D Texas-1969-1971)
Sen. William Proxmire (D Wis.-1971-)

Internal Revenue Taxation
Rep. Harold Knutson (R Minn.-1947-1948)

Sen. Eugene D. Millikin (R Colo.-1948-1949)
Rep. Robert L. Doughton (D N.C.-1949-1950)
Sen. Walter F. George (D Ga.-1950-1951)
Rep. Robert L. Doughton (D N.C.-1951-1952)
Sen. Walter F. George (D Ga.-1952-1953)
Rep. Daniel A. Reed (R N.Y.-1953-1954)
Sen. Eugene D. Millikin (R Colo.-1954-1955)
Rep. Jere Cooper (D Tenn.-1955-1956)
Sen. Harry Flood Byrd (D Va.-1956-1957)
Rep. Jere Cooper (D Tenn.-1957-1958)
Sen. Harry Flood Byrd (D Va.-1958-1959)
Rep. Wilbur D. Mills (D Ark.-1959-1960)
Sen. Harry Flood Byrd (D Va.-1960-1961)
Rep. Wilbur D. Mills (D Ark.-1961-1962)
Sen. Harry Flood Byrd (D Va.-1962-1963)
Rep. Wilbur D. Mills (D Ark.-1963-1965)
Sen. Harry Flood Byrd (D Va.-1965)
Sen. Russell B. Long (D La.-1965-1967)
Rep. Wilbur D. Mills (D Ark.-1967-1969)
Sen. Russell B. Long (D La.-1969-1971)
Rep. Wilbur D. Mills (D Ark.-1971-1972)
Sen. Russell B. Long (D La.-1972-)

Library
B. Everett Jordan (D N.C.-1969-1972)

Printing
Wayne L. Hays (D Ohio-1969-)

Reduction of Nonessential Federal Expenditures
Sen. Harry Flood Byrd (D Va.-1947-1965)
Rep. George H. Mahon (D Texas-1965-)

Biographical Index of
Members of Congress, 1945-1972

BIOGRAPHICAL INDEX

(Dates of service are inclusive, starting in year of service and ending as service ends, which usually is Jan. 3 of given year.)

The names in this index include, alphabetically, all Senators and Representatives who served in Congress from Jan. 3, 1945, through Jan. 3, 1973— the 79th through 92nd Congresses. The material is organized as follows: Name, Party, State (of service), Date of birth, Date of death (if applicable), Congressional service. Other important offices held or services rendered, such as Governor, Cabinet member, etc. Where names may cause confusion, relationship is cited. Where service dates are left open, members were still serving in 1973. Where dashes appear (—) for date of birth or death, information was unavailable.

A

AANDAHL, Fred George (R N.D.), April 9, 1897-April 7, 1966; House 1951-53; Gov. 1945-50

ABBITT, Watkins Moorman (D Va.) May 21, 1908; House Feb. 17, 1948-73

ABEL, Hazel Hempell (R Neb.) July 10, 1888-July 30, 1966; Senate Nov. 8, 1954-Dec. 31, 1954

ABELE, Homer E. (R Ohio) Nov. 21, 1916; House 1963-65

ABERNETHY, Thomas Gerstle (D Miss.) May 16, 1903; House 1943-1973

ABOUREZK, James G. (D S.D.) Feb. 24, 1931; House 1971-73; Senate 1973-

ABZUG, Bella S. (D N.Y.) July 24, 1920; House 1971-

ADAIR, Edwin Ross (R Ind.) Dec. 14, 1907; House 1951-71

ADAMS, Brock (D Wash.) Jan. 13, 1927; House 1965-

ADAMS, Sherman (R N.H.) Jan. 8, 1899; House 1945-47; Governor 1949-53

ADDABBO, Joseph P. (D N.Y.) March 17, 1925; House 1961-

ADDONIZIO, Hugh Joseph (D N.J.) Jan. 31, 1914; House 1949-62

AIKEN, George David (R Vt.) Aug. 20, 1892; Senate Jan. 10, 1941-; Gov. 1937-41

ALBERT, Carl (D Okla.) May 10, 1908; House 1947-; Speaker 1971-

ALEXANDER, Hugh Quincy (D N.C.) August 7, 1911; House 1953-63

ALEXANDER, William Vollie Jr. (D Ark.) Jan. 16, 1934; House 1969-

ALFORD, Thomas Dale (D Ark.) Jan. 28, 1916; House 1959-63

ALGER, Bruce Reynolds (R Texas) June 12, 1918; House 1955-65

ALLEN, Asa Leonard (D La.) Jan. 5, 1891-Jan. 5, 1969; House 1937-53

ALLEN, James Browning (D Ala.) Dec. 28, 1912; Senate 1969-

ALLEN, John Joseph, Jr. (R Calif.) Nov. 27, 1899; House 1947-59

ALLEN, Leo Elwood (R Ill.) Oct. 5, 1898; House 1933-61

ALLOTT, Gordon Llewellyn (R Colo.) Jan. 2, 1907; Senate 1955-1973

ALMOND, James Lindsay, Jr. (D Va.) June 15, 1898; House Jan. 22, 1946-April 17, 1948; Gov. 1958-62

ANDERSEN, Herman Carl (R Minn.) Jan. 27, 1897; House 1939-63

ANDERSON, Clinton Presba (D N.M.) Oct. 23, 1895; House 1941-June 30, 1945; Senate 1949-1973; Secy. of Agriculture 1945-48

ANDERSON, Glenn M. (D Calif.) Feb. 21, 1913; House 1969-

ANDERSON, John B. (R Ill.) Feb. 15, 1922; House 1961-

ANDERSON, John Zuinglius (R Calif.) March 22, 1904; House 1939-53

ANDERSON, LeRoy Hagen (D Mont.) Feb. 2, 1906; House 1957-61

ANDERSON, William Robert (D Tenn.) June 17, 1921; House 1965-1973

ANDRESEN, August Herman (R Minn.) Oct. 11, 1890-Jan. 14, 1958; House 1925-33 and 1935-Jan. 14, 1958

ANDREWS, Charles Oscar (D Fla.) March 7, 1877-Sept. 18, 1946; Senate Nov. 4, 1936-Sept. 18, 1946

ANDREWS, George William (D Ala.) Dec. 12, 1906-Dec. 25, 1971; House March 14, 1944-Dec. 25, 1971

ANDREWS, Glenn (R Ala.) Jan. 15, 1909; House 1965-67

ANDREWS, Mark (R N.D.) May 19, 1926; House Oct. 22, 1963-

ANDREWS, Walter Gresham (R N.Y.) July 16, 1889-March 5, 1949; House 1931-49

ANFUSO, Victor L'Episcopo (D N.Y.) March 10, 1905-Dec. 28, 1966; House 1951-53 and 1955-63

ANGELL, Homer Daniel (R Ore.) Jan. 12, 1875-March 31, 1968; House 1939-55

ANNUNZIO, Frank (D Ill.) Jan. 12, 1915; House 1965-

ARCHER, William R., Jr. (R Texas) March 22, 1928; House 1971-

ARENDS, Leslie Cornelius (R Ill.) Sept. 27, 1895; House 1935-

ARMSTRONG, Orland Kay (R Mo.) Oct. 2, 1893; House 1951-53

ARNOLD, Samuel Washington (R Mo.) Sept. 21, 1879-Dec. 18, 1961; House 1943-49

ASHBROOK, John Milan (R Ohio) Sept. 21, 1928; House 1961-

ASHLEY, Thomas William Ludlow (D Ohio) Jan. 11, 1923; House 1955-

ASHMORE, Robert Thomas (D S.C.) Feb. 22, 1904; House June 2, 1953-69

ASPIN, Les (D Wis.) July 21, 1938; House 1971-

ASPINALL, Wayne Norviel (D Colo.) April 3, 1896; House 1949-1973

AUCHINCLOSS, James Coats (R N.J.) Jan. 19, 1885; House 1943-65

AUSTIN, Warren Robinson (R Vt.) Nov. 12, 1877-Dec. 25, 1962; Senate April 1, 1931-Aug. 2, 1946.

AVERY, William Henry (R Kan.) Aug. 11, 1911; House 1955-65; Gov. 1965-67

AYRES, William Hanes (R Ohio) Feb. 5, 1916; House 1951-71

B

BADILLO, Herman (D N.Y.) Aug. 21, 1929; House 1971-

BAILEY, Cleveland Monroe (D W.Va.) July 15, 1886-July 13, 1965; House 1945-47 and 1949-63

BAILEY, Josiah William (D N.C.) Sept. 14, 1873-Dec. 15, 1946; Senate 1931-Dec. 15, 1946

BAKER, Howard Henry (husband of Irene B. Baker, father of Howard Henry Baker, Jr.) (R Tenn.) Jan. 12, 1902-Jan. 7, 1964; House 1951-64

BAKER, Howard Henry, Jr. (son of Howard Henry Baker and Irene B. Baker, son-in-law of Everett McKinley Dirksen) (R Tenn.) Nov. 15, 1925; Senate 1967-

BAKER, Irene B. (widow of Howard Henry Baker and mother of Howard Henry Baker, Jr.) (R Tenn.) Nov. 17, 1901; House March 10, 1964-65

BAKER, LaMar (R Tenn.) Dec. 19, 1915; House 1971-

BAKEWELL, Claude Ignatius (R Mo.) Aug. 9, 1912; House 1947-49 and March 9, 1951-53

BALDWIN, Harry Streett (D Md.) Aug. 21, 1894-Oct. 19, 1952; House 1943-47

BALDWIN, John Finley, Jr. (R Calif.) June 28, 1915-March 9, 1966; House 1955-March 9, 1966

BALDWIN, Joseph Clark (R N.Y.) Jan. 11, 1897-Oct. 27, 1957; House March 11, 1941-47

BALDWIN, Raymond Earl (R Conn.) Aug. 31, 1893; Senate Dec. 27, 1946-Dec. 16, 1949; Gov. 1939-40; 1943-46

BALL, Joseph Hurst (R Minn.) Nov. 3, 1905; Senate Oct. 14, 1940-Nov. 17, 1942, 1943-49

BANDSTRA, Bert (D Iowa) Jan. 25, 1922; House 1965-67

BANKHEAD, John Hollis 2d (D Ala.) July 8, 1872-June 12, 1946; Senate 1931-June 12, 1946

BANTA, Parke Monroe (R Mo.) Nov. 21, 1891-May 12, 1970; House 1947-49

BARING, Walter Stephan (D Nev.) Sept. 9, 1911; House 1949-53, 1957-1973

BARKLEY, Alben William (D Ky.) Nov. 24, 1877-April 30, 1956; House 1913-27; Senate 1927-Jan. 19, 1949, 1955-April 30, 1956; Vice President 1949-53

BARR, Joseph Walker (D Ind.) January 17, 1918; House 1959-61; Secy. of the Treasury 1968-69

BARRETT, Frank A. (R Wyo.) Nov. 10, 1892-May 30, 1962; House 1943-Dec. 31, 1950; Senate 1953-59; Gov. 1951-53

BARRETT, William A. (D Pa.) Aug. 14, 1896; House 1945-47, 1949-

BARRY, Robert Raymond (R N.Y.) May 15, 1915; House 1959-65

BARRY, William Bernard (D N.Y.) July 21, 1902-Oct. 20, 1946; House Nov. 5, 1935-Oct. 20, 1946

BARTLETT, Edward Lewis (Bob) (D Alaska) April 20, 1904-Dec. 11, 1968; House (Terr. Del.) 1945-59; Senate 1959-Dec. 11, 1968

BASS, Perkins (R N.H.) Oct. 6, 1912; House 1955-63

BASS, Ross (D Tenn.) March 17, 1918; House 1955-Nov. 4, 1964; Senate Nov. 4, 1964-67

BATES, George Joseph (R Mass.) Feb. 25, 1891-Nov. 1, 1949; House 1937-Nov. 1, 1949

BATES, William Henry (R Mass.) April 26, 1917-June 22, 1969; House Feb. 14, 1950-June 22, 1969

BATES, Joseph B. (D Ky.) Oct. 29, 1893-Sept. 10, 1965; House 1938-53

BATTIN, James F. (R Mont.) Feb. 13, 1925; House 1961-Feb. 27, 1969

BATTLE, Laurie Calvin (D Ala.) May 10, 1912; House 1947-55

BAUMHART, Albert David, Jr. (R Ohio) June 15, 1908; House 1941-Sept. 2, 1942, 1955-61

BAYH, Birch E. (D Ind.) Jan. 22, 1928; Senate 1963-

BEALL, James Glenn (father of James Glenn Beall, Jr.) (R Md.) June 5, 1894-Jan. 14, 1971; House 1943-53; Senate 1953-65

BEALL, James Glenn, Jr. (R Md.) June 19, 1927; House 1969-71; Senate 1971-

BECKER, Frank John (R N.Y.) Aug. 27, 1899; House 1953-65

BECKWORTH, Lindley Gary (D Texas) June 30, 1913; House 1939-53, 1957-67

BEERMANN, Ralph F. (R Neb.) Aug. 13, 1912; House 1961-65

BEGICH, Nicholas J. (D Alaska) April 6, 1932-Oct. 16, 1972; House 1971-Oct. 16, 1972

BELCHER, Page Henry (R Okla.) April 21, 1899; House 1951-1973

BELL, Alphonzo (R Calif.) Sept. 19, 1914; House 1961-

BELL, Charles Jasper (D Mo.) Jan. 16, 1885; House 1935-49

BELL, John Junior (D Texas) May 15, 1910-Jan. 24, 1963; House 1955-57

BELLMON, Henry (R Okla.) Sept. 3, 1921; Senate 1969-; Gov. 1963-67

BENDER, George Harrison (R Ohio) Sept. 29, 1896-June 18, 1961; House 1939-49, 1951-Dec. 15, 1954; Senate Dec. 16, 1954-57

BENNET, Augustus Witschief (R N.Y.) Oct. 7, 1897; House 1945-47

BENNETT, Charles Edward (D Fla.) Dec. 2, 1910; House 1949-

BENNETT, John Bonifas (R Mich.) Jan. 10, 1904-Aug. 9, 1964; House 1943-45, 1947-Aug. 10, 1964

BENNETT, Marion Tinsley (R Mo.) June 6, 1914; House Jan. 12, 1943-49

BENNETT, Wallace Foster (R Utah) Nov. 13, 1898; Senate 1951-

BENTLEY, Alvin Morell (R Mich.) Aug. 30, 1918-April 10, 1969; House 1953-61

BENTON, William (D Conn.) April 1, 1900; Senate Dec. 17, 1949-53

BENTSEN, Lloyd Millard, Jr. (D Texas) Feb. 11, 1921; House Dec. 4, 1948-55; Senate 1971-

BERGLAND, Bob (D Minn.) July 31, 1928; House 1971-

BERRY, Ellis Yarnal (R S.D.) Oct. 6, 1902; House 1951-71

BETTS, Jackson Edward (R Ohio) May 26, 1904; House 1951-

BEVILL, Tom (D Ala.) March 27, 1921; House 1967-

BIAGGI, Mario (D N.Y.) Oct. 26, 1917; House 1969-

BIBLE, Alan Harvey (D Nev.) Nov. 20, 1909; Senate Dec. 2, 1954-

BIEMILLER, Andrew John (D Wis.) July 23, 1906; House 1945-47, 1949-51

BIESTER, Edward G., Jr. (R Pa.) Jan. 5, 1931; House 1967-

BINGHAM, Jonathan B. (D N.Y.) April 24, 1914; House 1965-

BISHOP, Cecil William (Runt) (R Ill.) June 29, 1890-Sept. 21, 1971; House 1941-55

BLACKBURN, Benjamin B. (R Ga.) Feb. 14, 1927; House 1967-

BLACKNEY, William Wallace (R Mich.) Aug. 28, 1876-March 14, 1963; House 1935-37, 1939-53

BLAKLEY, William A. (D Texas) Nov. 17, 1898; Senate Jan. 15-April 28, 1957, Jan. 3-June 14, 1961

BLAND, Schuyler Otis (D Va.) May 4, 1872-Feb. 16, 1950; House July 2, 1918-Feb. 16, 1950

BLANTON, Leonard Ray (D Tenn.) April 10, 1930; House 1967-1973

BLATNIK, John Anton (D Minn.) Aug. 17, 1911; House 1947-

BLITCH, Iris Faircloth (D Ga.) April 25, 1912; House 1955-63

BLOOM, Sol (D N.Y.) March 9, 1870-March 7, 1949; House 1923-March 7, 1949

BOGGS, James Caleb (R Del.) May 15, 1909; House 1947-53; Senate 1961-1973; Gov. 1953-60

BOGGS, Thomas Hale (D La.) Feb. 15, 1914; House 1941-43, 1947-Oct. 16, 1972

BOLAND, Edward Patrick (D Mass.) Oct. 1, 1911; House 1953-

BOLLING, Richard Walker (D Mo.) May 17, 1916; House 1949-

BOLTON, Frances Payne (mother of Oliver P. Bolton) (R Ohio) March 29, 1885; House 1940-69

BOLTON, Oliver Payne (son of Frances Payne Bolton) (R Ohio) Feb. 22, 1917-Dec. 13, 1972; House 1953-57, 1963-65

BOLTON, William P. (D Md.) July 2, 1885-Nov. 22, 1964; House 1949-51

BONIN, Edward John (R Pa.) Dec. 23, 1904; House 1953-55

BONNER, Herbert Covington (D N.C.) May 16, 1891-Nov. 7, 1965; House Nov. 5, 1940-Nov. 7, 1965

BOREN, Lyle H. (D Okla.) May 11, 1909; House 1937-47

BOSCH, Albert Henry (R N.Y.) Oct. 30, 1908; House 1953-Dec. 31, 1960

BOSONE, Reva Zilpha Beck (D Utah) —-—; House 1949-53

BOTTUM, Joe H. (R S.D.) Aug. 7, 1903; Senate July 11, 1962-63

BOW, Frank Townsend (R Ohio) Feb. 20, 1901-Nov. 13, 1972; House 1951-Nov. 13, 1972

BOWLER, James Bernard (D Ill.) Feb. 5, 1875-July 18, 1957; House July 7, 1953-July 18, 1957

BOWLES, Chester Bliss (D Conn.) April 5, 1901; House 1959-61; Gov. 1949-51

BOWRING, Eva Kelly (R Neb.) Jan. 9, 1892; Senate April 16-Nov. 7, 1954

BOYKIN, Frank William (D Ala.) Feb. 21, 1885-March 12, 1969; House July 30, 1935-63

BOYLE, Charles Augustus (D Ill.) Aug. 13, 1907-Nov. 4, 1959; House 1955-Nov. 4, 1959

BRADEMAS, John (D Ind.) March 2, 1927; House 1959-

BRADLEY, Frederick Van Ness (R Mich.) April 12, 1898-May 24, 1947; House 1939-May 24, 1947

BRADLEY, Michael Joseph (D Pa.) May 24, 1897; House 1937-47

BRADLEY, Willis Winter (R Calif.) June 28, 1884-Aug. 27, 1954; House 1947-49

BRAMBLETT, Ernest King (R Calif.) April 25, 1901-Dec. 27, 1966; House 1947-55

BRASCO, Frank J. (D N.Y.) Oct. 15, 1932; House 1967-

BRAY, William Gilmer (R Ind.) April 17, 1903; House 1951-

BREAUX, John B. (D La.) March 1, 1944; House Oct. 12, 1972-

BREEDING, James Floyd (D Kan.) Sept. 28, 1901; House 1957-63

BREEN, Edward F. (D Ohio) June 10, 1908; House 1949-Oct. 1, 1951

BREHM, Walter Ellsworth (R Ohio) May 25, 1892; House 1943-53

BREWSTER, Daniel Baugh (D Md.) Nov. 23, 1923; House 1959-63; Senate 1963-69

BRICKER, John William (R Ohio) Sept. 6, 1893; Senate 1947-59; Gov. 1939-45

BRIGGS, Frank Parks (D Mo.) Feb. 25, 1894; Senate Jan. 18, 1945-47

BRINKLEY, Jack Thomas (D Ga.) Dec. 22, 1930; House 1967-

BROCK, Lawrence (D Neb.) Aug. 16, 1906-Aug. 28, 1968; House 1959-61

BROCK, William Emerson, III (R Tenn.) Nov. 23, 1930; House 1963-71; Senate 1971-

BROMWELL, James E. (R Iowa) March 26, 1920; House 1961-65

BROOKE, Edward W. (R Mass.) Oct. 26, 1919; Senate 1967-

BROOKS, Charles Wayland (R Ill.) March 8, 1897-Jan. 14, 1957; Senate Nov. 22, 1940-49

BROOKS, Jack Bascom (D Texas) Dec. 18, 1922; House 1953-

BROOKS, Overton (D La.) Dec. 21, 1897-Sept. 16, 1961; House 1937-Sept. 16, 1961

BROOMFIELD, William S. (R Mich.) April 28, 1922; House 1957-1973

BROPHY, John Charles (R Wis.) Oct. 8, 1901; House 1947-49

BROTZMAN, Donald G. (R Colo.) June 28, 1922; House 1963-65, 1967-

BROUGHTON, Joseph Melville (D N.C.) Nov. 17, 1888-March 6, 1949; Senate Dec. 31, 1948-March 6, 1949; Gov. 1941-45

BROWN, Charles Harrison (D Mo.) Oct. 22, 1920; House 1957-61

BROWN, Clarence J. (father of Clarence J. Brown, Jr.) (R Ohio) July 14, 1893-Aug. 23, 1965; House 1939-Aug. 23, 1965

BROWN, Clarence J., Jr. (son of Clarence J. Brown) (R Ohio) June 18, 1927; House Nov. 2, 1965-

BROWN, Ernest S. (R Nev.) Sept. 25, 1903-July 23, 1965; Senate Oct. 1-Dec. 1, 1954

BROWN, Garry E. (R Mich.) Aug. 12, 1923; House 1967-

BROWN, George E., Jr. (D Calif.) March 6, 1920; House 1963-71

BROWNING, Gordon (D Tenn.) Nov. 22, 1889; House 1923-35; Gov. 1937-39, 1949-53

BROWNSON, Charles Bruce (R Ind.) Feb. 5, 1914; House 1951-59

BROYHILL, James T. (R N.C.) Aug. 19, 1927; House 1963-

BROYHILL, Joel Thomas (R Va.) Nov. 4, 1919; House 1953-

BRUCE, Donald C. (R Ind.) April 27, 1921-Aug. 31, 1969; House 1961-65

BRUMBAUGH, David Emmert (R Pa.) Oct. 8, 1894; House Nov. 2, 1943-47

BRUNSDALE, Clarence Norman (R N.D.) July 9, 1891; Senate Nov. 19, 1959-Aug. 7, 1960; Gov. 1951-57

BRYSON, Joseph Raleigh (D S.C.) January 18, 1893-March 10, 1953; House 1939-March 10, 1953

BUCHANAN, Frank (husband of Vera Daerr Buchanan) (D Pa.) Dec. 1, 1902-April 27, 1951; House May 21, 1946-April 27, 1951

BUCHANAN, John H. (R Ala.) March 19, 1928; House 1965-

BUCHANAN, Vera Daerr (wife of Frank Buchanan) (D Pa.) July 20, 1902-Nov. 26, 1955; House July 24, 1951-Nov. 26, 1955

BUCK, Ellsworth Brewer (R N.Y.) July 3, 1892-Aug. 14, 1970; House June 6, 1944-49

BUCKLEY, Charles Anthony (D N.Y.) June 23, 1890-Jan. 22, 1967; House 1935-65

BUCKLEY, James L. (Conservative-R N.Y.) March 9, 1923; Senate 1971-

BUCKLEY, James Vincent (D Ill.) May 15, 1894-July 30, 1954; House 1949-51

BUDGE, Hamer Harold (R Idaho) Nov. 21, 1910; House 1951-61

BUFFETT, Howard Homan (R Nev.) Aug. 13, 1903-April 29, 1964; House 1943-49, 1951-53

BULWINKLE, Alfred Lee (D N.C.) April 21, 1883-Aug. 31, 1950; House 1921-29, 1931-Aug. 31, 1950

BUNKER, Berkeley Lloyd (D Nev.) Aug. 12, 1906; Senate Nov. 27, 1940-Dec. 6, 1942; House 1945-47

BURCH, Thomas Granville (D Va.) July 3, 1869-March 20, 1951; House 1931-May 31, 1946; Senate May 31-Nov. 5, 1946

BURDICK, Quentin Northrop (son of Usher L. Burdick and brother-in-law of Robert W. Levering) (D N.D.) June 19, 1908; House 1959-Aug. 8, 1960; Senate Aug. 8, 1960-

BURDICK, Usher Lloyd (father of Quentin N. Burdick and father-in-law of Robert W. Levering) (R N.D.) Feb. 21, 1879-Aug. 19, 1960; House 1935-45, 1949-59

BURGIN, William Olin (D N.C.) July 28, 1877-April 11, 1946; House 1939-April 11, 1946

BURKE, Frank Welsh (D Ky.) June 1, 1920; House 1959-63

BURKE, James Anthony (D Mass.) March 30, 1910; House 1959-

BURKE, J. Herbert (R Fla.) Jan. 14, 1913; House 1967-

BURKE, Thomas A. (D Ohio) Oct. 30, 1898-Dec. 5, 1971; Senate Nov. 10, 1953-Dec. 2, 1954

BURKE, Thomas Henry (D Ohio) May 6, 1904-Sept. 12, 1959; House 1949-51

BURKHALTER, Everett G. (D Calif.) Jan. 19, 1897; House 1963-65

BURLESON, Omar Truman (D Texas) March 19, 1906; House 1947-

BURLISON, Bill D (D Mo.) March 15, 1931; House 1969-

BURNS, John Anthony (D Hawaii) March 30, 1909; House (Terr. Del.) 1957-Aug. 21, 1959; Gov. 1963-

BURNSIDE, Maurice Gwinn (D W.Va.) Aug. 23, 1902; House 1949-53, 1955-57

BURTON, Clarence Godber (D Va.) Dec. 14, 1886; House Nov. 2, 1948-53

BURTON, Harold Hitz (R Ohio) June 22, 1888-Oct. 28, 1964; Senate 1941-Sept. 30, 1945; Assoc. Justice of the Supreme Court 1945-58

BURTON, Laurence J. (R Utah) Oct. 30, 1926; House 1963-71

BURTON, Phillip (D Calif.) June 1, 1926; House Feb. 18, 1964-

BUSBEY, Fred Ernst (R Ill.) Feb. 8, 1895-Feb. 11, 1966; House 1943-45, 1947-49, 1951-55

BUSH, Alvin Ray (R Pa.) June 4, 1893-Nov. 5, 1959; House 1951-Nov. 5, 1959

BUSH, George Herbert Walker (son of Prescott S. Bush) (R Texas) June 12, 1924; House 1967-71

BUSH, Prescott Sheldon (father of George Herbert Walker Bush) (R Conn.) May 15, 1895-Oct. 8, 1972; Senate Nov. 4, 1952-63

BUSHFIELD, Harlan John (husband of Vera C. Bushfield) (R S.D.) Aug. 6, 1882-Sept. 27, 1948; Senate 1943-Sept. 27, 1948; Gov. 1939-42

BUSHFIELD, Vera Cahalan (widow of Harlan J. Bushfield) (R S.D.) Aug. 9, 1889; Senate Oct. 6-Dec. 26, 1948

BUTLER, Hugh Alfred (R Neb.) Feb. 28, 1878-July 1, 1954; Senate 1941-July 1, 1954

BUTLER, John Cornelius (R N.Y.) July 2, 1887-Aug. 13, 1953; House April 22, 1941-49, 1953-53

BUTLER, John Marshall (R Md.) July 21, 1897; Senate 1951-63

BUTTON, Daniel E. (R N.Y.) Nov. 1, 1917; House 1967-71

BYRD, Harry Flood (father of Harry F. Byrd, Jr.) (D Va.) June 10, 1887-Oct. 20, 1966; Senate 1933-Nov. 10, 1965; Gov. 1926-30

BYRD, Harry F., Jr. (son of Harry Flood Byrd) (D Va.) Dec. 20, 1914; Senate Nov. 12, 1965-1970; Senate Independent) 1970-

BYRD, Robert Carlyle (D W.Va.) Jan. 15, 1918; House 1953-59; Senate 1959-

BYRNE, Emmet Francis (R Ill.) Dec. 6, 1896; House 1957-59

BYRNE, James Aloysius (D Pa.) June 22, 1906; House 1953-73

BYRNE, William Thomas (D N.Y.) March 6, 1876-Jan. 27, 1952; House 1937-Jan. 27, 1952

BYRNES, John William (R Wis.) June 12, 1913; House 1945-73

BYRON, Goodloe E. (D Md.) June 22, 1929; House 1971-

C

CABELL, Earle (D Texas) Oct. 27, 1906; House 1965-73

CAFFERY, Patrick Thomson (D La.) July 6, 1932; House 1969-73

CAHILL, William Thomas (R N.J.) June 25, 1912; House 1959-Jan. 19, 1970; Gov. 1970-

CAIN, Harry Pulliam (R Wash.) Jan. 10, 1906; Senate Dec. 26, 1946-53

CALLAN, Clair Armstrong (D Neb.) March 20, 1920; House 1965-67

CALLAWAY, Howard H. (Bo) (R Ga.) May 2, 1927; House 1965-67

CAMERON, Ronald Brooks (D Calif.) Aug. 16, 1927; House 1963-67

CAMP, Albert Sidney (D Ga.) July 26, 1892-July 24, 1954; House Aug. 1, 1939-July 24, 1954

CAMP, John N. Happy (R Okla.) May 11, 1908; House 1969-

CAMPBELL, Courtney Warren (D Fla.) April 29, 1895-Dec. 22, 1971; House 1953-55

CAMPBELL, Howard Edmond (R Pa.) Jan. 4, 1890; House 1945-47

CANFIELD, Gordon (R N.J.) April 15, 1898-June 20, 1972; House 1941-61

CANNON, Arthur Patrick (D Fla.) May 22, 1904-Jan. 23, 1966; House 1939-47

CANNON, Clarence (D Mo.) April 11, 1879-May 12, 1964; House 1923-May 12, 1964

CANNON, Howard Walter (D Nev.) Jan. 26, 1912; Senate 1959-

CAPEHART, Homer Earl (R Ind.) June 6, 1897; Senate 1945-63

CAREY, Hugh L. (D N.Y.) April 11, 1919; House 1961-

CARLSON, Frank (R Kan.) Jan. 23, 1893; House 1935-47; Senate Nov. 29, 1950-69; Gov. 1947-50

CARLYLE, Frank Ertel (D N.C.) April 7, 1897-Oct. 2, 1960; House 1949-57

CARNAHAN, Albert Sidney Johnson (D Mo.) Jan. 9, 1897-March 24, 1968; House 1945-47, 1949-61

CARNEY, Charles J. (D Ohio) April 17, 1913; House Nov. 3, 1970-

CARRIGG, Joseph Leonard (R Pa.) Feb. 23, 1901; House Nov. 6, 1951-59

CARROLL, John Albert (D Colo.) July 30, 1901; House 1947-51; Senate 1957-63

CARSON, Henderson Haverfield (R Ohio) Oct. 25, 1893-Oct. 5, 1971; House 1943-45, 1947-49

CARTER, Steven V. (D Iowa) Oct. 8, 1915-Nov. 4, 1959; House Jan. 3-Nov. 4, 1959

CARTER, Tim Lee (R Ky.) Sept. 2, 1910; House 1965-

CARVILLE, Edward Peter (D Nev.) May 14, 1885-June 27, 1956; Senate July 25, 1945-47; Gov. 1939-45

CASE, Clifford Philip (R N.J.) April 16, 1904; House 1945-Aug. 16, 1953; Senate 1955-

CASE, Francis Higbee (R S.D.) Dec. 9, 1896-June 22, 1962; House 1937-51; Senate 1951-June 22, 1962

CASEY, Robert Randolph (Bob) (D Texas) July 27, 1915; House 1959-

CAVALCANTE, Anthony (D Pa.) Feb. 6, 1897-Oct. 29, 1966; House 1949-51

CEDERBERG, Elford Alfred (R Mich.) March 6, 1918; House 1953-

CELLER, Emanuel (D N.Y.) May 6, 1888; House 1923-73

CHADWICK, E. Wallace (R Pa.) Jan. 17, 1884-Aug. 18, 1969; House 1947-49

CHAMBERLAIN, Charles Ernest (R Mich.) July 22, 1917; House 1957-

CHANDLER, Albert Benjamin (D Ky.) July 14, 1898; Senate Oct. 10, 1939-Nov. 1, 1945; Gov. 1935-39, 1955-59

CHAPMAN, Virgil Munday (D Ky.) March 15, 1895-March 8, 1951; House 1925-29, 1931-49; Senate 1949-March 8, 1951

CHAPPELL, William V., Jr. (D Fla.) Feb. 3, 1922; House 1969-

CHASE, Jackson Burton (R Neb.) Aug. 19, 1890; House 1955-57

CHATHAM, Richard Thurmond (D N.C.) Aug. 16, 1896-Feb. 5, 1957; House 1949-57

CHAVEZ, Dennis (D N.M.) April 8, 1899-Nov. 18, 1962; House 1931-35; Senate May 11, 1935-Nov. 18, 1962

CHELF, Frank Leslie (D Ky.) Sept. 22, 1907; House 1945-67

CHENOWETH, John Edgar (R Colo.) Aug. 17, 1897; House 1941-49, 1951-65

CHESNEY, Chester Anton (D Ill.) March 9, 1916; House 1949-51

CHILES, Lawton (D Fla.) April 3, 1930; Senate 1971-

CHIPERFIELD, Robert Bruce (R Ill.) Nov. 20, 1899-April 9, 1971; House 1939-63

CHISHOLM, Shirley (D N.Y.) Nov. 30, 1924; House 1969-

CHRISTOPHER, George Henry (D Mo.) Dec. 9, 1888-Jan. 23, 1959; House 1949-51, 1955-Jan. 23, 1959

CHUDOFF, Earl (D Pa.) Nov. 16, 1907; House 1949-Jan. 5, 1958

CHURCH, Frank Forrester (D Idaho) July 25, 1924; Senate 1957-

CHURCH, Marguerite Stitt (widow of Ralph Edwin Church) (R Ill.) Sept. 13, 1892; House 1951-63

CHURCH, Ralph Edwin (husband of Marguerite Stitt Church) (R Ill.) May 5, 1883-March 21, 1950; House 1935-41; 1943-March 21, 1950

CLANCY, Donald D. (R Ohio) July 24, 1921; House 1961-

CLARDY, Kit Francis (R Mich.) June 17, 1892-Sept. 5, 1961; House 1953-55

CLARK, David Worth (D Idaho) April 2, 1902-June 19, 1955; House 1935-39; Senate 1939-45

CLARK, Frank Monroe (D Pa.) Dec. 24, 1915; House 1955-

CLARK, Jerome Bayard (D N.C.) April 5, 1882-Aug. 26, 1959; House 1929-49

CLARK, Joseph Sill (D Pa.) Oct. 21, 1901; Senate 1957-69

CLASON, Charles Russell (R Mass.) Sept. 3, 1890; House 1937-49

CLAUSEN, Don H. (R Calif.) April 27, 1923; House Jan. 22, 1963-

CLAWSON, Delwin (Del) Morgan (R Calif.) Jan. 11, 1914; House June 11, 1963-

CLAY, William (D Mo.) April 30, 1931; House 1969-

CLEMENTE, Louis Gary (D N.Y.) June 10, 1908-May 13, 1968; House 1949-53

CLEMENTS, Earle C. (D Ky.) Oct. 22, 1896; House 1945-Jan. 6, 1948; Senate Nov. 27, 1950-57; Gov. Jan. 1948-Nov., 1950

CLEVELAND, James C. (R N.H.) June 13, 1920; House 1963-

CLEVENGER, Cliff (R Ohio) Aug. 20, 1885-Dec. 13, 1960; House 1939-59

CLEVENGER, Raymond F. (D Mich.) June 6, 1926; House 1965-67

CLIPPINGER, Roy (R Ill.) Jan. 13, 1886-Dec. 24, 1962; House Nov. 6, 1945-49

COAD, Merwin (D Iowa) Sept. 28, 1924; House 1957-63

COCHRAN, John Joseph (D Mo.) Mo.) Aug. 11, 1880-March 6, 1947; House Nov. 2, 1926-47

COFFEE, John Main (D Wash.) Jan. 23, 1897; House 1937-47

COFFEY, Robert Lewis, Jr. (D Pa.) Oct. 21, 1918-April 20, 1949; House Jan. 3-April 20, 1949

COFFIN, Frank Morey (D Maine) July 11, 1919; House 1957-61

COFFIN, Howard Aldridge (R Mich.) June 11, 1877-Feb. 28, 1956; House 1947-49

COHELAN, Jeffery (D Calif.) June 24, 1914; House 1959-71

COLE, Albert McDonald (R Kan.) Oct. 13, 1901; House 1945-53

COLE, William Clay (R Mo.) Aug. 29, 1897-Sept. 23, 1965; House 1943-49, 1953-55

COLE, William Sterling (R N.Y.) April 18, 1904; House 1935-Dec. 1, 1957

COLLIER, Harold Reginald (R Ill.) Dec. 12, 1915; House 1957-

COLLINS, George W. (D Ill.) March 5, 1925-Dec. 8, 1972; House Nov. 3, 1970-Dec. 8, 1972

COLLINS, James M. (R Texas) April 29, 1916; House Aug. 24, 1968-

COLMER, William Meyers (D Miss.) Feb. 11, 1890; House 1933-73

COMBS, Jesse Martin (D Texas) July 7, 1889-Aug. 21, 1953; House 1945-53

CONABLE, Barber B., Jr. (R N.Y.), Nov. 2, 1922; House 1965-

CONDON, Robert Likens (D Calif.) Nov. 10, 1912; House 1953-55

CONNALLY, Thomas Terry (Tom) (D Texas) Aug. 19, 1877-Oct. 28, 1963; House 1917-29; Senate 1929-53

CONTE, Silvio Otto (R Mass.) Nov. 9, 1921; House 1959-

CONYERS, John, Jr. (D Mich.) May 16, 1929; House 1965-

COOK, Marlow W. (R Ky.) July 27, 1926; Senate Dec. 16, 1968-

COOK, Robert Eugene (D Ohio) May 19, 1920; House 1959-63

COOLEY, Harold Dunbar (D N.C.) July 26, 1897; House July 7, 1934-66

COON, Samuel Harrison (R Ore.) April 15, 1903; House 1953-57

COOPER, Jere (D Tenn.) July 20, 1893-Dec. 18, 1957; House 1929-Dec. 18, 1957

COOPER, John Sherman (R Ky.) Aug. 23, 1901; Senate Nov. 6, 1946-49, Nov. 5, 1952-55, Nov. 7, 1956-73

CORBETT, Robert James (R Pa.) Aug. 25, 1905-April 25, 1971; House 1939-41, 1945-April 25, 1971

CORDON, Guy (R Ore.) April 24, 1890-June 8, 1969; Senate March 4, 1944-55

CORDOVA, Jorge Luis (New Progressive P.R.) April 20, 1907; House (Res. Comm.) 1969-73

CORMAN, James C. (D Calif.) Oct. 20, 1920; House 1961-

COTTER, William R. (D Conn.) July 18, 1926; House 1971-

COTTON, Norris (R N.H.) May 11, 1900; House 1947-Nov. 7, 1954; Senate Nov. 8, 1954-

COTTRELL, James La Fayette (D Ala.) Aug. 25, 1808-Sept. 7, 1885; House Dec. 7, 1946-47

COUDERT, Frederic Rene, Jr. (R N.Y.) May 7, 1898-May 21, 1972; House 1947-59

COUGHLIN, R. Lawrence (R Pa.) April 11, 1929; House 1969-

COURTNEY, William Wirt (D Tenn.) Sept. 7, 1889-April 6, 1961; House May 11, 1939-49

COWGER, William O. (R Ky.) Jan. 1, 1922-Oct. 2, 1971; House 1967-71

COX, Edward Eugene (D Ga.) April 3, 1880-Dec. 24, 1952; House 1925-Dec. 24, 1952

CRALEY, Nathaniel Nieman, Jr. (D Pa.) Nov. 17, 1927; House 1965-67

CRAMER, William Cato (R Fla.) Aug. 4, 1922; House 1955-71

CRANE, Philip M. (R Ill.) Nov. 3, 1930; House Nov. 25, 1969-

CRANSTON, Alan (D Calif.) June 19, 1914; Senate 1969-

CRAVENS, William Fadijo (D Ark.) Feb. 15, 1889; House Sept. 12, 1939-49

CRAWFORD, Fred Lewis (R Mich.) May 5, 1888-April 13, 1957; House 1935-53

CRETELLA, Albert William (R Conn.) April 22, 1897; House 1953-59

CRIPPA, Edward David (R Wyo.) April 8, 1899-Oct. 20, 1960; Senate June 24-Nov. 28, 1954

CROOK, Thurman Charles (D Ind.) July 18, 1891; House 1949-51

CROSSER, Robert (D Ohio) June 7, 1874-June 3, 1957; House 1913-19, 1923-55

CROW, William Josiah (R Pa.) Jan. 22, 1902; House 1947-49

CRUMPACKER, Shepard J., Jr. (R Ind.) Feb. 13, 1917; House 1951-57

CULVER, John C. (D Iowa) Aug. 8, 1932; House 1965-

CUNNINGHAM, Glenn Clarence (R Neb.) Sept. 10, 1912; House 1957-71

CUNNINGHAM, Paul Harvey (R Iowa) June 15, 1890-July 16, 1961; House 1941-59

CURLIN, William P. Jr. (D Wis.) Nov. 30, 1933; House Dec. 6, 1971-73

CURTIN, Willard Sevier (R Pa.) Nov. 28, 1905; House 1957-67

CURTIS, Carl Thomas (R Neb.) March 15, 1905; House 1939-Dec. 31, 1954, Senate Jan. 1, 1955-

CURTIS, Laurence (R Mass.) Sept. 3, 1893-—; House 1953-63

CURTIS, Thomas Bradford (R Mo.) May 14, 1911; House 1951-69

D

DADDARIO, Emilio Quincy (D Conn.) Sept. 24, 1918; House 1959-71

DAGUE, Paul Bartram (R Pa.) May 19, 1898-—; House 1947-67

D'ALESANDRO, Thomas, Jr. (D Md.) Aug. 1, 1903; House 1939-May 16, 1947

DANAHER, John Anthony (R Conn.) Jan. 9, 1899-—; Senate 1939-45

DANIEL, Charles Ezra (D S.C.) Nov. 11, 1895-Sept. 13, 1964; Senate Sept. 6-Dec. 23, 1954

DANIEL, Price Marion (D Texas) Oct. 10, 1910; Senate 1953-Jan. 14, 1957; Gov. 1957-63

DANIEL, W. C. (Dan) (D Va.) May 12, 1914; House 1969-

DANIELS, Dominick V. (D N.J.) Oct. 18, 1908; House 1959-

DANIELSON, George E. (D Calif.) Feb. 20, 1915; House 1971-

DARBY, Harry (R Kan.) Jan. 23, 1895-—; Senate Dec. 2, 1949-Nov. 28, 1950

DAUGHTON, Ralph Hunter (D Va.) Sept. 23, 1885-Dec. 22, 1958; House Nov. 7, 1944-47

DAVENPORT, Harry James (D Pa.) Aug. 28, 1902; House 1949-51

DAVIDSON, Irwin Delmore (D/ Liberal N.Y.) Jan. 2, 1906; House 1955-Dec. 31, 1956

DAVIES, John Clay (D N.Y.) May 1, 1920; House 1949-51

DAVIS, Clifford (D Tenn.) Nov. 18, 1897-June 8, 1970; House Feb. 15, 1940-65

DAVIS, Glenn R. (R Wis.) Oct. 28, 1914; House April 22, 1947-57, 1965-

DAVIS, James Curran (D Ga.) May 17, 1895-—; House 1947-63

DAVIS, John William (D Ga.) Sept. 12, 1916; House 1961-

DAVIS, Mendel J. (D S.C.) Oct. 23, 1942; House April 29, 1971-

DAWSON, William Adams (R Utah) Nov. 5, 1903; House 1947-49; 1953-59

DAWSON, William Levi (D Ill.) April 26, 1886-Nov. 9, 1970; House 1943-Nov. 9, 1970

DEANE, Charles Bennett (D N.C.) Nov. 1, 1898-Nov. 24, 1969; House 1947-57

DE LACY, Emerson Hugh (D Wash.) May 9, 1910; House 1945-47

de la GARZA, Eligio (D Texas) Sept. 22, 1927; House 1965-

DELANEY, James Joseph (D N.Y.) March 19, 1901; House 1945-47, 1949-

DELANEY, John Joseph (D N.Y.) Aug. 21, 1878-Nov. 18, 1948; House March 5, 1918-19, 1931-Nov. 18, 1948

DELLAY, Vincent John (D N.J.) June 23, 1907; House 1957-59 (1957 (R), 1958 (D))

DELLENBACK, John R. (R Ore.) Nov. 6, 1918; House 1967-

DELLUMS, Ronald V. (D Calif.) Nov. 24, 1935; House 1971-

DEMPSEY, John Joseph (D N.M.) June 22, 1879-March 11, 1958; House 1935-41, 1951-March, 1958; Gov. 1943-47

DENHOLM, Frank E. (D S.C.) Nov. 29, 1923; House 1971-

DENNEY, Robert V. (R Neb.) April 11, 1916; House 1967-71

DENNIS, David W. (R Ind.) June 7, 1912; House 1969-

DENNISON, David Short (R Ohio) July 29, 1918; House 1957-59

DENNY, Harmar Denny, Jr. (R Pa.) July 2, 1886-Jan. 6, 1966; House 1951-53

DENT, John Herman (D Pa.) March 10, 1908; House Jan. 21, 1958-

DENTON, Winfield Kirkpatrick (D Ind.) Oct. 28, 1896-Nov. 2, 1971; House 1949-53, 1955-Dec. 30, 1966

DEROUNIAN, Steven Boghos (R N.Y.) April 6, 1918; House 1953-65

DERWINSKI, Edward Joseph (R Ill.) Sept. 15, 1926; House 1959-

DEVEREUX, James Patrick Sinnott (R Md.) Feb. 20, 1903; House 1951-59

DEVINE, Samuel Leeper (R Ohio) Dec. 21, 1915; House 1959-

DEVITT, Edward James (R Minn.) May 5, 1911; House 1947-49

D'WART, Wesley Abner (R Mont.) Oct. 1, 1899; House June 5, 1945-55

DICKINSON, William Louis (R Ala.) June 5, 1925; House 1965-

DICKSTEIN, Samuel (D N.Y.) Feb. 5, 1885-April 22, 1954; House 1923-Dec. 23, 1945

DIES, Martin, Jr. (D Texas) Nov. 5, 1900-Nov. 14, 1972; House 1931-45, 1953-59

DIGGS, Charles Coles, Jr. (D Mich.) Dec. 2, 1922; House 1955-

DINGELL, John David (father of John David Dingell, Jr.) (D Mich.) Feb. 2, 1894-Sept. 19, 1955; House 1933-Sept. 19, 1955

DINGELL, John David, Jr. (son of John Dingell) (D Mich.) July 8, 1926; House Dec. 13, 1955-

DIRKSEN, Everett McKinley (R Ill.) Jan. 4, 1896-Sept. 7, 1969; House 1933-49; Senate 1951-Sept. 7, 1969

DIXON, Henry Aldous (R Utah) June 29, 1890-Jan. 22, 1967; House 1955-61

DODD, Thomas Joseph (D Conn.) May 15, 1907-May 24, 1971; House 1953-57; Senate 1959-71

DOLE, Robert J. (R Kan.) July 22, 1923; House 1961-69; Senate 1969-

DOLLINGER, Isidore (D N.Y.) Nov. 13, 1903; House 1949-Dec. 31, 1959

DOLLIVER, James Isaac (R Iowa) Aug. 31, 1894-—; House 1945-57

DOMENGEAUX, James (D La.) Jan. 6, 1907; House 1941-April 15, 1944; Nov. 7, 1944-49

DOMINICK, Peter H. (R Colo.) July 7, 1915; House 1961-63; Senate 1963-

DONDERO, George Anthony (R Mich.) Dec. 16, 1883-Jan. 29, 1968; House 1933-57

DONNELL, Forrest C. (R Mo.) Aug. 20, 1884-—; Senate 1945-51; Gov. 1941-45

DONOHUE, Harold Daniel (D Mass.) June 18, 1901; House 1947-

DONOVAN, James George (D/R Liberal N.Y.) Dec. 15, 1898-—; House 1951-57

DOOLEY, Edwin Benedict (R N.Y.) April 13, 1905; House 1957-63

DORN, Francis Edwin (R N.Y.) April 18, 1911; House 1953-61

DORN, William Jennings Bryan (D S.C.) April 14, 1916; House 1947-49; 1951-

DOUGHTON, Robert Lee (D N.C.) Nov. 7, 1863-Oct. 1, 1954; House 1911-53

DOUGLAS, Emily Taft (wife of Senator Paul H. Douglas) (D Ill.) April 10, 1899; House 1945-47

DOUGLAS, Fred James (R N.Y.) Sept. 14, 1869-Jan. 1, 1949; House 1937-45.

DOUGLAS, Helen Gahagan (D Calif.) Nov. 25, 1900; House 1945-51

DOUGLAS, Paul Howard (husband of Emily Taft Douglas) (D Ill.) March 26, 1892; Senate 1949-67

DOW, John Goodchild (D N.Y.) May 6, 1905; House 1965-69; 1971-73

DOWDY, John Vernard (D Texas) Feb. 11, 1912; House Sept. 23, 1952-73

DOWNEY, Sheridan (D Calif.) March 11, 1884-Oct. 25, 1961; Senate 1939-Nov. 30, 1950

DOWNING, Thomas Nelms (D Va.) Feb. 1, 1919; House 1959-

DOYLE, Clyde Gilman (D Calif.) July 11, 1887-March 14, 1963; House 1945-47, 1949-March 14, 1963

DREWRY, Patrick Henry (D Va.) May 24, 1875-Dec. 21, 1947, House April 27, 1920-Dec. 21, 1947

DRINAN, Robert F. (D Mass.) Nov. 15, 1920; House 1971-

DUFF, James Henderson (R Pa.) Jan. 21, 1883-Dec. 20, 1969; Senate Jan. 16, 1951-57; Gov. 1947-51

DULLES, John Foster (R N.Y.) Feb. 25, 1888-May 24, 1959; Senate July 7-Nov. 8, 1949; Secy. of State 1953-59

DULSKI, Thaddeus J. (D N.Y.) Sept. 27, 1915; House 1959-

DUNCAN, John J. (R Tenn.) March 24, 1919; House 1965-

DUNCAN, Robert B. (D Ore.) Dec. 4, 1920; House 1963-67

du PONT, Pierre S., IV (R Del.) Jan. 22, 1935; House 1971-

DURNO, Edwin R. (R Ore.) Jan. 26, 1899; House 1961-63

DWORSHAK, Henry Clarence (R Idaho) Aug. 29, 1894-July 23, 1962; House 1939-Nov. 5, 1946; Senate Nov. 6, 1946-49, Oct. 14, 1949-July 23, 1962

DWYER, Florence Price (R N.J.) July 4, 1902; House 1957-1973

DYAL, Kenneth Warren (D Calif.) July 9, 1910; House 1965-67

E

EAGLETON, Thomas F. (D Mo.) Sept. 4, 1929; Senate Dec. 28, 1968-

EARTHMAN, Harold Henderson (D Tenn.) April 13, 1900; House 1945-47

EASTLAND, James Oliver (D Miss.) Nov. 28, 1904; Senate June 30-Sept. 18, 1941; 1943-

EATON, Charles Aubrey (R N.J.) March 29, 1868-Jan. 23, 1953; House 1925-53

EBERHARTER, Herman Peter (D Pa.) April 29, 1892-Sept. 9, 1958; House 1937-Sept. 9, 1958

ECKHARDT, Bob (D Texas) July 16, 1913; House 1967-

ECTON, Zales Nelson (R Mont.) April 1, 1898-March 3, 1961; Senate 1947-53

EDMONDSON, Edmond Augustus (brother of J. Howard Edmondson) (D Okla.) April 7, 1919; House 1953-73

EDMONDSON, J. Howard (brother of Edmond Augustus Edmondson) (D Okla.) Sept. 27, 1925-Nov. 17, 1971; Senate Jan. 9, 1963-Nov. 3, 1964; Gov. 1959-63

EDWARDS, Don (D Calif.) Jan. 6, 1915; House 1963-

EDWARDS, Edwin W. (D La.) Aug. 7, 1927; House Oct. 2, 1965-May 1972; Gov. May 1972-

EDWARDS, Elaine S. (D La.) March 8, 1929; Senate August 1, 1972-73

EDWARDS, Jack (R Ala.) Sept. 20, 1928; House 1965-

EILBERG, Joshua (D Pa.) Feb. 12, 1921; House 1967-

ELLENDER, Allen Joseph (D La.) Sept. 24, 1891-July 27, 1972; Senate 1937-1972; President pro tempore 1971-72

ELLIOTT, Alfred James (D Calif.) June 1, 1895-—; House May 4, 1937-49

ELLIOTT, Carl Atwood (D Ala.) Dec. 20, 1913; House 1949-65

ELLIOTT, Douglas Hemphill (R Pa.) June 3, 1921-June 19, 1960; House April 26-June 19, 1960

ELLIS, Hubert Summers (R W.Va.) July 6, 1887-Dec. 3, 1959; House 1943-49

ELLSWORTH, Matthew Harris (R Ore.) Sept. 17, 1899-—; House 1943-57

ELLSWORTH, Robert F. (R Kan.) June 11, 1926; House 1961-67

ELSAESSER, Edward Julius (R N.Y.) March 10, 1904; House 1945-49

ELSTON, Charles Henry (R Ohio) Aug. 1, 1891-—; House 1939-53

ENGEL, Albert Joseph (R Mich.) Jan. 1, 1888-Dec. 2, 1959; House 1935-51

ENGLE, Clair (D Calif.) Sept. 21, 1911-July 30, 1964; House Aug. 31, 1943-59; Senate 1959-July 30, 1964

ERLENBORN, John N. (R Ill.) Feb. 8, 1927; House 1965-

ERVIN, Joseph Wilson (brother of Samuel James Ervin, Jr.) (D N.C.) March 3, 1901-Dec. 25, 1945; House Jan. 3-Dec. 25, 1945

ERVIN, Samuel James, Jr. (brother of Joseph Wilson Ervin) (D N.C.) Sept. 27, 1896; House Jan. 22, 1946-47; Senate June 5, 1954-

ESCH, Marvin L. (R Mich.) Aug. 4, 1927; House 1967-

ESHLEMAN, Edwin D. (R Pa.) Dec. 4, 1920; House 1967-

EVANS, Frank Edwards (D Colo.) Sept. 6, 1923; House 1965-

EVERETT, Robert Ashton (D Tenn.) Feb. 24, 1915-Jan. 26, 1969; House Feb. 1, 1958-Jan. 26, 1969

EVINS, Joseph Landon (Joe) (D Tenn.) Oct. 24, 1910; House 1947-

F

FALLON, George Hyde (D Md.) July 24, 1902; House 1945-71

FANNIN, Paul Jones (R Ariz.) Jan. 29, 1907; Senate 1965- ; Gov. 1958-64

FARBSTEIN, Leonard (D N.Y.) Oct. 12, 1902; House 1957-71

FARNSLEY, Charles Rowland Peaslee (D Ky.) March 28, 1907; House 1965-67

FARNUM, Billie Sunday (D Mich.) April 11, 1916; House 1965-67

FARRINGTON, Joseph Rider (husband of Mary Elizabeth Pruett Farrington) (R Hawaii) Oct. 15, 1897-June 19, 1954; House (Terr. Del.) 1943-June 19, 1954

FARRINGTON, Mary Elizabeth Pruett (widow of Joseph Rider Farrington) (R Hawaii) May 30, 1898-—; House (Terr. Del.) July 31, 1954-57

FASCELL, Dante Bruno (D Fla.) March 9, 1917; House 1955-

FAUNTROY, Walter E. (D D.C.) Feb. 6, 1933; House Delegate, March 23, 1971-

FEAZEL, William Crosson (D La.) June 10, 1895-March 16, 1965; Senate May 18-Dec. 30, 1948

FEIGHAN, Michael Aloysius (D Ohio) Feb. 16, 1905; House 1943-71

FELLOWS, Frank (R Maine) Nov. 7, 1889-Aug. 27, 1951; House 1941-Aug. 27, 1951

FENTON, Ivor David (R Pa.) Aug. 3, 1889-—; House 1939-63

FERGUSON, Homer (R Mich.) Feb. 25, 1889-—; Senate 1943-55

FERNANDEZ, Antonio Manuel (D N.M.) Jan. 17, 1902-Nov. 7, 1956; House 1943-Nov. 7, 1956

FERNOS-ISERN, Antonio (Progressive Democrat P.R.) May 10, 1895-—; House (Res Comm.) Sept. 11, 1946-65

FINDLEY, Paul (R Ill.) June 23, 1921; House 1961-

FINE, Sidney Asher (D N.Y.) Sept. 14, 1903; House 1951-Jan. 2, 1956

FINNEGAN, Edward R. (D Ill.) June 5, 1905-Feb. 2, 1971; House 1961-Dec. 6, 1964

FINO, Paul Albert (R N.Y.) Dec. 15, 1913, House 1953-Dec. 31, 1968

FISH, Hamilton, Jr. (R N.Y.) June 3, 1926; House 1969-

FISHER, Ovie Clark (D Texas) Nov. 22, 1903; House 1943-

FJARE, Orvin Benonie (R Mont.) April 16, 1918; House 1955-57

FLANDERS, Ralph Edward (R Vt.) Sept. 28, 1880-Feb. 19, 1970; Senate Nov. 1, 1946-59

FLANNAGAN, John William, Jr. (D Va.) Feb. 20, 1885-April 27, 1955; House 1931-49

FLETCHER, Charles Kimball (R Calif.) Dec. 15, 1902; House 1947-49

FLOOD, Daniel John (D Pa.) Nov. 26, 1903; House 1945-47, 1949-53, 1955-

FLOWERS, Walter (D Ala.) April 12, 1933; House 1969-

FLYNN, Gerald Thomas (D Wis.) Oct. 7, 1910; House 1959-61

FLYNT, John James, Jr. (D Ga.) Nov. 8, 1914; House Nov. 2, 1954-

FOGARTY, John Edward (D R.I.) March 23, 1913-Jan. 10, 1967; House 1941-Dec. 7, 1944; 1945-Jan. 10, 1967

FOLEY, John Robert (D Md.) Oct. 16, 1917; House 1959-61

FOLEY, Thomas Stephen (D Wash.) March 6, 1929; House 1965-

FOLGER, John Hamlin (D N.C.) Dec. 18, 1880-July 19, 1963; House June 14, 1941-49

FONG, Hiram Leon (R Hawaii) Oct. 1, 1907; Senate Aug. 21, 1959-

FOOTE, Ellsworth Bishop (R Conn.) Jan. 12, 1898; House 1947-49

FORAND, Aime Joseph (D R.I.) May 23, 1895-Jan. 18, 1971; House 1937-39, 1941-61

FORD, Gerald R. Jr. (R Mich.) July 14, 1913; House 1949-

FORD, William D. (D Mich.) Aug. 6, 1927; House 1965-

FOREMAN, Ed (R Texas/N.M.) Dec. 22, 1933; House 1963-65 (Texas), 1969-71 (N.M.)

FORSYTHE, Edwin B. (R N.J.) Jan. 17, 1916; House Nov. 3, 1970-

FOUNTAIN, Lawrence H. (D N.C.) April 23, 1913; House 1953-

FRASER, Donald MacKay (Democrat Farmer Labor Minn.) Feb. 20, 1924; House 1963-

FRAZIER, James Beriah, Jr. (D Tenn.) June 23, 1890; House 1949-63

FREAR, Joseph Allen Jr. (D Del.) March 7, 1903; Senate 1949-61

FRELINGHUYSEN, Peter Hood Ballantine (R N.J.) Jan. 17, 1916; House 1953-

FRENZEL, William E. (R Minn.) July 31, 1928; House 1971-

FREY, Louis, Jr. (R Fla.) Jan. 11, 1934; House 1969-—

FRIEDEL, Samuel Nathaniel (D Md.) April 18, 1898; House 1953-71

FUGATE, Thomas Bacon (D Va.) April 10, 1899; House 1949-53

FULBRIGHT, James William (D Ark.) April 9, 1905; House 1943-45; Senate 1945-

FULLER, Hadwen Carlton (R N.Y.) Aug. 28, 1895; House Nov. 2, 1943-49

FULTON, James Grove (R Pa.) March 1, 1903-Oct. 6, 1971; House Feb. 2, 1945-Oct. 6, 1971

FULTON, Richard (D Tenn.) Jan. 27, 1927; House 1963-

FUQUA, Don (D Fla.) Aug. 20, 1933; House 1963-

FURCOLO, Foster (D Mass.) July 29, 1911; House 1949-Sept. 30, 1952; Gov. 1957-61

G

GALIFIANAKIS, Nick (D N.C.) July 22, 1928; House 1967-73

GALLAGHER, Cornelius Edward (D N.J.) March 2, 1921; House 1959-73

GALLAGHER, James A. (R Pa.) Jan. 16, 1869-Dec. 8, 1957; House 1943-45, 1947-49

GALLAGHER, William James (D Minn.) May 13, 1875-Aug. 13, 1946; House 1945-Aug. 13, 1946

GAMBLE, Ralph Abernethy (R N.Y.) May 6, 1885-March 4, 1959; House Nov. 2, 1937-57

GAMBRELL, David Henry (D Ga.) Dec. 20, 1929; Senate Feb. 2, 1971-73

GARDNER, Edward Joseph (D Ohio) Aug. 7, 1898-Dec. 7, 1950; House 1945-47

GARDNER, James Carson (R N.C.) April 8, 1933; House 1967-69

GARLAND, Peter Adams (R Maine) June 16, 1923; House 1961-63

GARMATZ, Edward Alexander (D Md.) Feb. 7, 1903; House July 15, 1947-73

GARY, Julian Vaughan (D Va.) Feb. 25, 1892-—; House March 6, 1945-65

GATHINGS, Ezekiel Candler (D Ark.) Nov. 10, 1903; House 1939-69

GAVIN, Leon Harry (R Pa.) Feb. 25, 1893-Sept. 15, 1963; House 1943-Sept. 15, 1963

GAYDOS, Joseph M. (D Pa.) July 3, 1926; House Nov. 5, 1968-

GEARHART, Bertrand Wesley (R Calif.) May 31, 1890-Oct. 11, 1955; House 1935-49

GEELAN, James Patrick (D Conn.) Aug. 11, 1901; House 1945-47

GENTRY, Brady Preston (D Texas) March 25, 1896-Nov. 9, 1966; House 1953-57

GEORGE, Myron Virgil (R Kan.) Jan. 6, 1900-April 11, 1972; House Nov. 7, 1950-59

GEORGE, Newell A. (D Kan.) Sept. 24, 1904; House 1959-61

GEORGE, Walter Franklin (D Ga.) Jan. 19, 1878-Aug. 4, 1957; Senate Nov. 22, 1922-57

GERLACH, Charles Lewis (R Pa.) Sept. 14, 1895-May 5, 1947; House 1939-May 5, 1947

GERRY, Peter Goelet (D R.I.) Sept. 18, 1879-Oct. 31, 1957; House 1913-15; Senate 1917-29; 1935-47

GETTYS, Thomas Smithwick (D S.C.) June 19, 1912; House Nov. 3, 1964-

GIAIMO, Robert Nicholas (D Conn.) Oct. 15, 1919; House 1959-

GIBBONS, Sam M. (D Fla.) Jan. 20, 1920; House 1963-

GIBSON, Ernest William (R Vt.) March 6, 1901-Nov. 4, 1969; Senate June 24, 1940-41; Gov. 1947-50

GIBSON, John Strickland (D Ga.) Jan. 3, 1893-Oct. 19, 1960; House 1941-47

GIFFORD, Charles Laceille (R Mass.) March 15, 1871-Aug. 23, 1947; House Nov. 7, 1922-Aug. 23, 1947

GILBERT, Jacob H. (D N.Y.) June 17, 1920; House March 8, 1960-71

GILL, Thomas P. (D Hawaii) April 21, 1922; House 1963-65

GILLESPIE, Dean Milton (R Colo.) May 3, 1884-Feb. 2, 1949; House March 7, 1944-47

GILLETTE, Guy Mark (D Iowa) Feb. 3, 1879-—; House 1933-Nov. 3, 1936; Senate Nov. 4, 1936-45; 1949-55

GILLETTE, Wilson Darwin (R Pa.) July 1, 1880-Aug. 7, 1951; House Nov. 4, 1941-Aug. 7, 1951

GILLIE, George W. (R Ind.) Aug. 15, 1880-July 3, 1963; House 1939-49

GILLIGAN, John J. (D Ohio) March 22, 1921; House 1965-67; Gov. 1971-

GILMER, William Franklin (Dixie) (D Okla.) June 7, 1901-June 9, 1954; House 1949-51

GLENN, Milton Willits (R N.J.) June 18, 1903-Dec. 14, 1967; House Nov. 5, 1957-65

GOFF, Abe McGregor (R Idaho) Dec. 21, 1899-—; House 1947-1949

GOLDEN, James Stephen (R Ky.) Sept. 10, 1891-Sept. 6, 1971; House 1949-55

GOLDWATER, Barry Morris (father of Barry M. Goldwater Jr.) (R Ariz.) Jan. 1, 1909; Senate 1953-65, 1969-

GOLDWATER, Barry M. Jr. (son of the preceding) (R Calif.) July 15, 1938; House April 29, 1969-

GONZALEZ, Henry B. (D Texas) May 3, 1916; House Nov. 4, 1961-

GOODELL, Charles Ellsworth (R N.Y.) March 16, 1926; House May 26, 1959-Sept. 10, 1968; Senate Sept. 10, 1968-71

GOODLING, George A. (R Pa.) Sept. 26, 1896; House 1961-65, 1967-

GOODWIN, Angier Louis (R Mass.) Jan. 30, 1881-—; House 1943-55

GORE, Albert Arnold (D Tenn.) Dec. 26, 1907; House 1939-Dec. 4, 1944, 1945-53; Senate 1953-71

GORSKI, Chester Charles (D N.Y.) June 22, 1906; House 1949-51

GORSKI, Martin, (D Ill.) Oct. 30, 1886-Dec. 4, 1949; House 1943-Dec. 4, 1949

GOSSETT, Charles Clinton (D Idaho) Sept. 2, 1888-—; Senate Nov. 17, 1945-1947; Gov. Jan.-Nov. 16, 1945

GRABOWSKI, Bernard F. (D Conn.) June 11, 1923; House 1963-67

GRAHAM, Frank Porter (D N.C.) Oct. 14, 1886-Feb. 16, 1972; Senate March 29, 1949-Nov. 26, 1950

GRAHAM, Louis Edward (R Pa.) Aug. 4, 1880-Nov. 9, 1965; House 1939-55

GRANAHAN, Kathryn Elizabeth (widow of William Thomas Granahan) (D Pa.) Dec. 7, 1906-—; House Nov. 6, 1956-63

GRANAHAN, William Thomas (husband of Kathryn Elizabeth Granahan) (D Pa.) July 26, 1895-May 25, 1956; House 1945-47; 1949-May 25, 1956

GRANGER, Walter Kiel (D Utah) Oct. 11, 1888-—; House 1941-53

GRANT, George McInvale (D Ala.) July 11, 1897-—; House June 14, 1938-65

GRANT, Robert Allen (R Ind.) July 31, 1905; House 1939-49

GRASSO, Ella T. (D Conn.) May 10, 1919; House 1971-

GRAVEL, Mike (D Alaska) May 13, 1930; Senate 1969-

GRAY, Kenneth James (D Ill.) Nov. 14, 1924; House 1955-

GREEN, Edith (D Ore.) Jan. 17, 1910; House 1955-

GREEN, William Joseph, Jr. (D Pa.) March 5, 1910-Dec. 21, 1963; House 1945-47; 1949-Dec. 21, 1963

GREEN, William J. III (son of the preceding) (D Pa.) June 24, 1938; House April 28, 1964-

GREENWOOD, Ernest (D N.Y.) Nov. 25, 1884-June 15, 1955 House 1951-53

GREGORY, Noble Jones (D Ky.) Aug. 30, 1897-Sept. 26, 1971; House 1937-59

GREIGG, Stanley Lloyd (D Iowa) May 7, 1931; House 1965-67

GRIDER, George William (D Tenn.) Oct. 1, 1912; House 1965-67

GRIFFIN, Charles H. (D Miss.) May 9, 1926; House March 12, 1968-1973

GRIFFIN, Robert Paul (R Mich.) Nov. 6, 1923; House 1957-May 10, 1966; Senate May 11, 1966-

GRIFFITHS, Martha Wright (D Mich.) Jan. 29, 1912; House 1955-

GRIFFITHS, Percy Wilfred (R Ohio) March 30, 1893-—; House 1943-49

GRISWOLD, Dwight Palmer (R Neb.) Nov. 27, 1893-April 12, 1954; Senate Nov. 5, 1952-April 12, 1954; Gov. 1941-46

GROSS, Chester Heilman (R Pa.) Oct. 13, 1888-—; House 1939-41; 1943-49

GROSS, Harold Royce (R Iowa) June 30, 1899-—; House 1949-

GROVER, James R. Jr. (R N.Y.) March 5, 1919; House 1963-

GRUENING, Ernest (D Alaska) Feb. 6, 1887-—; Senate 1959-69; Gov. (Terr.) 1939-53

GUBSER, Charles Samuel (R Calif.) Feb. 1, 1916; House 1953-

GUDE, Gilbert (R Md.) March 9, 1923; House 1967-

GUFFEY, Joseph F. (D Pa.) Dec. 29, 1870-March 6, 1959; Senate 1935-47

GUILL, Ben Hugh (R Texas) Sept. 8, 1909; House May 6, 1950-51

GURNEY, Chan (John Chandler) (R S.D.) May 21, 1896-—; Senate 1939-51

GURNEY, Edward John (R Fla.) Jan. 12, 1914; House 1963-69; Senate 1969-

GWINN, Ralph Waldo (R N.Y.) March 29, 1884; House 1945-59

H

HAGAN, G. Elliott (D Ga.) May 24, 1916; House 1961-1973

HAGEN, Harlan Francis (D Calif.) Oct. 8, 1914; House 1953-67

HAGEN, Harold Christian (R Minn.) Nov. 10, 1901-March 19, 1957; House 1943-45 (Farmer-Labor); 1945-55 (R)

HALE, Robert (R Maine) Nov. 29, 1889-—; House 1943-59

HALEY, James Andrew (D Fla.) Jan. 4, 1899; House 1953-

HALL, David McKee (D N.C.) May 16, 1819-Jan. 29, 1960; House 1959-Jan. 29, 1960

HALL, Durward Gorham (R Mo.) Sept. 14, 1910; House 1961-1973

HALL, Edwin Arthur (R N.Y.) Feb. 11, 1909; House Nov. 7, 1939-53

HALL, Leonard Wood (R N.Y.) Oct. 2, 1900; House 1939-Dec. 31, 1952; 1952-57

HALLECK, Charles Abraham (R Ind.) Aug. 22, 1900; House Jan. 29, 1935-69

HALPERN, Seymore (R N.Y.) Nov. 19, 1913; House 1959-73

HAMILTON, Lee Herbert (D Ind.) April 20, 1931; House 1965-

HAMMERSCHMIDT, John Paul (R Ark.) May 4, 1922; House 1967-

HANCOCK, Clarence Eugene (R N.Y.) Feb. 13, 1885-Jan. 3, 1948; House Nov. 8, 1927-47

HAND, Thomas Millet (R N.J.) July 7, 1902-Dec. 26, 1956; House 1945-Dec. 26, 1956

HANLEY, James M. (D N.Y.) July 19, 1913; House 1959-73

HANNA, Richard T. (D Calif.) June 9, 1914; House 1963-

HANSEN, Clifford Peter (R Wyo.) Oct. 16, 1912; Senate 1967-; Gov. 1963-67

HANSEN, George Vernon (R Idaho) Sept. 14, 1930; House 1965-69

HANSEN, John Robert (D Iowa) Aug. 24, 1901; House 1965-67

HANSEN, Julia Butler (D Wash.) June 14, 1907; House Nov. 8, 1960-

HANSEN, Orval (R Idaho) Aug. 3, 1926; House 1969-